McKAY'S MODERN
NORWEGIAN-ENGLISH
ENGLISH-NORWEGIAN
DICTIONARY

(*Gyldendal's*)

By H. Scavenius
and B. Berulfsen

DAVID McKAY COMPANY, INC.
New York

NORWEGIAN-ENGLISH

By H. Scavenius

FOREWORD

In the fourth edition, issued in 1945, the vocabulary and the Norwegian spelling were revised. Some obsolete material was eliminated to make room for more modern words and phrases.

In this fifth edition, only lesser corrections and up-datings of the material have been undertaken.

MARKS AND ABBREVIATIONS

Capital or small letter before - (hyphen) indicates whether the word is spelled with a capital or a small letter.

- (hyphen) indicates that the word is to be repeated as part of a compound word or before a derivational ending.

| (vertical line) indicates that only that part of the word which precedes the vertical line is to be repeated in the following word indicated by — (long dash) or - (hyphen).

— (long dash) indicates repetition of a word.

adj	adjective
adv	adverb
agr	agriculture
alm.	common
amr	American

ark	architecture
bet	sense, meaning
bl.	among
bl. a.	among other things, *inter alia*
d. s.	the same
d. s. s.	the same as
dt.	colloquial
egtl.	proper
el.	or
fig	figurative
fork.	abbreviation
gl.	old
gramm.	grammar
i alm.	generally
imperf.	imperfect tense
int	interjection
ist. f.	instead of
jur.	legal
jvf.	*cf.*
koll.	collectively
konj	conjunction
litt.	literary

m.	with	poet	poetic
mar	maritime	prep	preposition
mat	mathematics	pron	pronoun
med	medicine	sb.	somebody
merk	business	s. d.	see this
mil.	military	subst	noun
min	mineralogy	sing	singular
myt	mythology	sl.	slang
ndf.	below	sms.	compound words
ogs.	also	st.	something
o. l.	similar	tilf.	instance
osv.	and so forth	v	by
p.	on, upon	vi	intransitive verb
part	participle	vrb	verb
pts	participles	vt	transitive verb
plur	plural		

A

a. Har en sagt a, får en også si b in for a penny, in for a pound. 10 à 12 (from) 10 to 12; 5 à 6 pund 5 or 6 pounds; 4 pd. à 2 shillings 4 lbs at 2 shillings. a konto on account (of). a vista at sight. a vista veksel demand (el. sight) draft. ab (i handelsspråk) a; levertran — Oslo codliveroil a Oslo.

abandon abandonment; -ere abandon.

abbed abbot. -i (kloster, klosterkirke) abbey (Westminster Abbey el. the Abbey in London). -isse abbess. -verdighet abbacy, abbotship.

abbor se åbor.

ABC el. Abc (sj. = alfabet) abc, alphabet; (bok) abc-book, spelling-book, primer; (fig) the first rudiments.

abdikasjon abdication. abdisere abdicate.

aber: det er et — ved det there is a but in the question.

Abessin|ia (Etiopia) Abyssinia. -ier, -ierinne, -sk Abyssinian.

ablegøyer monkeytricks, larks, pose.

abnorm abnormal, abnormous. -itet abnormity. -skole school for defective children.

abonne|ment subscription. -mentsaften subscription night. -mentsbillett season-ticket, pass-ticket. abonnent subscriber; season ticket-holder. abonner|e subscribe. (på; to); jeg -er (i teater. I have a private box el. seats in a private box, I am a subscriber (to the theatre); I have a season-ticket.

abort miscarriage, abortion. -ere (föde for tidlig) abort, miscarry, have an abortion.

Abruzzene the Abruzzi.

Absalon Absalom.

abscess (materieansamling) abscess, collection of pus.

absentere seg absent oneself, (dt.) bolt.

absint (malurt) wormwood, absinthium; (likøren) absinth(e).

absol|usjon absolution. -utisme absolutism. -utist absolutist. -utistisk absolutistic.

absolutt (adj) absolute; (adv) absolutely, perforce, needs; han vil — gå he insists (up)on going; — nødvendig absolutely necessary; — ikke by no means, not at all.

absolvere absolve; — (= ta) sin eksamen pass one's examination.

absorb|ere absorb. -ering absorption.

abstinen|s abstinence. -t abstinent.

abstra|here abstract. -ksjon abstraction, abstract thought. -ksjonsevne abstractive faculty. -kt abstract; (adv) in the abstract.

absurd absurd. -itet absurdity. redusere ad absurdum reduce to an absurdity.

accelerasjon, se aks-.

accessit second prize.

accoucheur (fødselshjelper) accoucheur, obstetrician, man-midwife.

acetylén acetylene.

ad se at.

adagio (langsomt) adagio, leisurely.

Adam Adam; den gamle — (the) old Adam, the old man, unregenerate condition of man; i a-sdrakt in nature's garb. a-seple Adam's apple, pomum Adami.

addend addendum (plur. addenda). addere add; (uten objekt) do sums.

addisjon addition. -sstykke addition sum, sum in addition. -stabell table of addition. -stegn sign of addition, plus (sign), positive sign.

adel nobility; (lavadel, de fornemme: gentry); av — of noble birth; rikets — the peers of the realm. adelig noble, titled; d -e the nobles; -len (el. gods) a nobleman's estate. feoff noble. adels|brev patent of nobility. -byrd noble descent. -båren noble born. -dame, -frue lady of title, noblewoman. -frøken nobleman's daughter, unmarried lady of noble rank. -gal mad about nobility, mad after a handle to his name. -gods nobleman's estate. -herredømme power el. rule of the aristocracy. -kalender peerage. adelskap nobility. — forplikter rank imposes obligations.

adels|mann nobleman. -patent, se -brev. -preg stamp of nobility. -register (book of the) peerage. -skjold escutcheon, coat of arms. -stolthet pride of birth, aristocratic pride. -stand nobility. opphøye i adelsstanden raise to the peerage. -titel title (of nobility). -velde aristocracy.

adgang (innlatelse) admittance, admission, access; (vei til) access, approach, avenue; — forbudt el. uvedkommende forbydes — no admittance, el. trespassers will be prosecuted; få — gain admittance, be admitted; jeg fikk ikke — I was not permitted to enter; ha fri — til be free of; ha — til et bibliotek have the use of a library; vanskelig å få — til difficult of access; betaling av en shilling gir — til a fee of a shilling will pass the visitor to. adgangs|berettigelse, se -rett, -kort order el. ticket of admission. -rett right of admission, admissibility. -tegn, se kort. -tillatelse admission.

adjektiv adjective. -isk adjective, adjectival; (adv) adjectively.

adjunkt teacher (at a secondary school), who has taken the degree of cand. mag. -eksamen degree examination. Jvf. lektor, lektoreksamen.

adjunkt|stipendiat (univ.) (assistant) lecturer (a. professor). -stipendium assistant professor's stipend, fellowship.

adjutant (hos oberst eller major) adjutant; (hos en general eller kongen) aide-de-camp.

adjø good-bye.

adle ennoble; knight; **arbeidet adler** (mannen) work ennobles a man. **adling** ennoblement; knighting.

ad libitum (etter behag) ad libitum, at pleasure; to any extent.

adlyde obey, yield obedience to; **ikke** — disobey.

administr|asjon administration, management. **-asjonsutgifter** management expenses. **-ativ** administrative. **-ator** trustee, administrator. **-ere** manage, administer; **-erende direktør** managing director.

admiral admiral. **-itet** admiralty. **-itetsretten** the (Court of) Admiralty. **-sembete** admiralty. **-sflagg** admiral's flag. **-skip** admiral('s ship), flagship.

Adolf Adolph(us).

adopsjon adoption.

adopt|ere adopt; affiliate. **-ering,** se **adopsjon. -ivbarn** adopted el. adoptive child. **-ivfar** adoptive father.

adr., se **adresse.**

adress|ant addresser, sender, shipper. **-at** addressee, person addressed.

adresse address, direction; **til Deres** — for your address; — **Hr. N. N.** c/o el. (to the) care of Mr. N. N.; **besørge etter -n** forward as per address. **-avis** advertiser. **-bok** addressbook. **-brev** letter of advice, letter of conveyance. **-debatt** debate on the Address. **-kalender,** se **-bok. -kontor** advertising office. **-kort** card of address. **-re** address, direct (skip, varer) consign.

Adriaterhavet the Adriatic.

advar|e warn (**mot** against; **om** of; **om å** that), caution (**mot** against); (formane) admonish; **la deg** — take warning; **-ende** admonitory, cautionary. **-sel** warning, caution, admonition.

adverb|ial (**-iell**) adverbial; **-ielt** (adv) adverbially; **-ium** adverb.

advis (handelsuttrykk) advice; — **om** advice of; **under** — under advice, **advisere** advise.

advokat barrister, counsel, lawyer; (is. i Skottland) advocate; **-ene** (kollektivt) the counsel; (som stand) the bar. **-ur** barristership; advocacy; **ta -en** be admitted (el. called) to the bar of the Supreme Court.

aero|drom aerodrome. **-dynamikk** aerodynamics. **-litt** aerolite. **-naut** aeronaut. **-nautikk** aeronautics. **-plan** aeroplane, plane. **-stat** aerostat.

affeksj|on affection. **-onsverdi** sentimental value.

affekt excitement; emotion, (sterkere) passion; **komme i** — become excited, (sterkere) fire, fly into a passion. **-asjon** affectation. **-ere** affect. **-ert** affected, artificial.

affisere affect.

affære affair, concern, (piece of) business; **ta** — take action.

afgan|er, -isk Afghan. **A-istan** Afghanistan.

Afrika Africa, **afrika|nder** (sydafrikaner) Africander. **-ner, -nerinne, -nsk** African. **Afrikareisende** African traveller.

aften evening, night; (poetisk og om aftenen før helligdag eller tiden like før en begivenhet) eve; **jul-** Christmas-eve; **en** — one evening; **en av de første -er** one of these evenings; **god** — good evening; **det lakker mot** — evening draws nigh, it is getting dark; **i** — to-night; this evening; **imorgen** — to-morrow evening; **igår** — (**aftes**) last night, yesterday evening, over night; **i forgårs** — the night before last; **den følgende** — (on) the following evening; **-en før** overnight; **mot** — towards evening; **om -en** in the evening, of an evening, at night; **kl. 10 om -en** at ten p.m. (el. at night); **fra morgen til** — from morning to el. till night; **det er tiden til å spise (til)** —(s) it is supper time

el. time for supper; **bli og spise (til)** — (**s**) stay (to) supper; **ta seg en glad** — make a (regular) night of it; **ut på -en** late in the evening. **aften|andakt** evening prayers. **-blad** evening paper. **-bønn** evening prayer. **-dogg** evening dew. **-gudstjeneste** evening-service el. prayers. **-himmel** evening sky. **-klokke** evening bell, curfew. **-kulde** evening cold. **-kåpe** opera-cloak. **-luft** evening air. **-messe** evening service, vespers. **-post** night's mail (el. post), ogs. to-night's post **-røde, -rødme** (poet.) evening-red, evening sky. **-s,** se **aftensmat. -sang** even-song, afternoon-service.

aftensbord supper.

aften|selskap evening-party. **-skole** evening school.

aftensmat, aftensmåltid (aftens) evening meal, supper; **varm aftens** meat-tea.

aftensol evening sun, setting sun.

aftenstemning evening mood; (maleri) evening tone. **aftenstid** evening, eventide; **ved** — towards evening.

aften|stjerne evening star, Hesperus. **-stund** evening. **-svermer** hawk-moth. **-time** evening hour. **-tur** evening walk. **-underholdning** evening entertainment; **musikalsk -underholdning** musical evening.

agat agate; **sort** — jet; **islandsk** — obsidian. **-tre** agate-wood.

agave agave. **-hamp** pita.

age: holde i — discipline, keep in check.

agent agent. **-ur** agency. **-urforretning** agency-business.

agere act, play, sham; plead; (mil) operate; — **landmann** play the farmer; — **høymodig** play the magnanimous.

agglomerat (klump) agglomerate.

agglutinerende agglutinative.

aggregat aggregate.

aggressiv aggressive.

agio (oppgjeld; kursgevinst) agio. **agiotasje** (børsspill) agiotage, stockjobbing. **agioter** stock jobber.

agit|asjon agitation, propaganda, (for å verve stemmer) canvass(ing). **-ator** agitator, propagandist, canvasser. **-atorisk** agitating, stirring. **agitere** agitate, stir up the public mind, make a stir, raise a movement, canvas. — **for sine meninger** agitate one's views.

agn bait; **sette** — **på** bait.

agnat (slektning på mannssiden) agnate. **-isk** agnate, agnatic.

agne bait. **agnfisk** bait fish.

agner (pl) (på korn) chaff, husks.

agnor barb (of a fishhook).

agnostiker (en som mener vi ingen ting kan vite i religiøse spørsmål) agnostic.

agn|sild bait herring. **-skjell** mussel.

agraff agraffe, clasp, brooch.

agraman ornamental lace-work.

agrar, agrarisk agrarian.

agrement accessory.

agro|nom agriculturist. **-nomi** science of agriculture. **-nomisk** agricultural.

agurk cucumber, (mindre) gherkin. **-salat** sliced cucumber.

ah! ah! oh! **aha!** aha!

aimabel amiable.

à jour: bringe, føre — date up, bring up to date; — **med** abreast of; **holde oss** — keep us well posted; **holdt** — dated up.

akademi academy. **-ker** (filosof av Platons skole) academic; (universitetsutdannet mann) university man, college man. **-medlem** academician.

akademisk academic(al); — **borger** university man; — **borgerbrev** certificate of matriculation; **-dannelse** university education, college breeding.

akant brankursine, bear's breech; (ogs. om søyleornament osv.) acanthus.

akasie acacia.

ake slide (on a sledge), sledge, toboggan. — **ned en bakke** sled (el. sledge) down a hill (el. slope). — **seg framover** edge along, el. one's way. **–bakke** sledging hill. **–doning** trap, vehicle, dt. rig. **–føre** fit state of the roads for sledging, good sleighing (el. sledding, sledging).
akeleie columbine.
aker, se **åker.**
ake|sport sledging, tobogganing. **–tur** sledging tour.
akevitt aquavit.
akilles|hæl Achilles' heel. **–sene** Achilles' tendon.
aking, se **akesport.**
akk! ah! alas! oh! akk ja! heigh-ho!
akklamasjon acclamation; **med — by** acclamation.
akklimatiser|e acclimate, acclimatize. **–ing** acclimation, acclimatation.
akkommod|asjon accommodation; (= innstilling av øyne) adjustment of our eyes. **–asjonsveksel** accommodation bill. **–ere** accommodate, adapt, (= innstille) adjust; **–ere våre øyne for forskjellige avstander** accommodate our eyes for various distances.
akkompagn|ere accompany. **–atør** accompanist. **–ement** accompaniment.
akkord (i musikk) chord; (= overenskomst) agreement, bargain; (overenskomst om lønn beregnet etter arbeidsmengden, kvantumet av arbeid) contract; (med en kreditor om lettelse av gjeldsforhold) arrangement, composition; (= kompromiss) compromise; **få, søke — med sine kreditorer** compound el. make a composition with one's creditors; **arbeide på — work** by the job; **utby på —** offer on contract; **overta på —** contract for, undertake by contract, in the lump; (fig) **gå på — med** make terms with, compound with; **–ens ånd** the spirit of compromise. **akkordant** compounder. **akkord|arbeid** task-work, piece-work, job. **–arbeider** jobber, contract worker. **–ere** (om) agree (on), bargain (for); (med kreditorer om) compound for. **–forslag** draft of arrangement.
akkredi|tere (minister, ambassadør) accredit; **— en hos** open a credit for one with; **den –terte** the person accredited. **–tiv** letter of credit.
akkumulator accumulator, electric storage battery. **–batteri** accumulator battery, storage battery.
akkurat (adj.) exact, accurate, (om person) precise, punctual; (adv.) (nettopp) exactly, precisely, just so.
akkuratesse accuracy; punctuality.
akkusativ the accusative (case).
akkviescere (slå seg til ro) acquiesce, agree tacitly; **— ved** acquiesce in, accept.
a konto (i løpende regning) on account.
akrobat acrobat.
akromatisk (fargeløs) achromatic.
aks ear, spike; **sette —** ear, set ears; **sanke — glean. –dannet** spiciform.
akse axis.
I. aksel (skulder) shoulder; (på drakt) shoulder piece; **–blad** stipule.
II. aksel (til hjul osv.) axle, (av tre) axle-tree; (p. maskin) shaft. **— –lager** shaft-bearing, journal. **–tapp** gudgeon.
akseler|asjon (hastighetsforøkelse) acceleration. **–erende hastighet** accelerated motion.
aksent accent; **uten —,** unaccented, unstressed. **–uasjon** accentuation. **–uere** accent, accentuate. **–uering** accentuation.
aksent|for rotation.
aksept (vekselaksept) acceptance; (bekreftelse) confirmation; **forsynt med vår —** provided with our acceptance; **innfri sin —** take up one's acceptance; **nekte —** refuse acceptance. **–abel** acceptable. **–ant** (vekselbetaler) acceptor.
aksepter|e (bekrefte) confirm; (en veksel) accept, honour, protect (a bill); **–e et tilbud**

accept an offer; ikke –e dishonour, refuse; **i –t stand** duly accepted.
aksidens|er (sportler) perquisites; (for prester) surplice fees. **–arbeid** (i typografi) jobbing, piece-work. **–arbeider** piece-worker. **–setter** jobbing compositor. **–trykker** jobbing-printer. **–trykkeri** jobbing-office.
aksise (innenlandsk forbruksavgift) excise. **–avdeling** excise. **–betjent** exciseman. **–bu** excise-office. **–fri** free of excise. **–pliktig** excisable. **–skatt** excise-duty.
aksje (under L 100) share; (på L 100) stock; (pl. kollektivt) holding; (pl. fig) credit; **hans –r står lavt** he is a discredited man; **ta –r i** take stock in. **–bank** joint-stock bank. **–eier,** se **aksjonær. –foretagende** joint-stock enterprise. **–haver** shareholder. **–kapital** share capital, joint-stock. **–megler** stockbroker. **–selskap** (fork. A/S) Limited (fork. Ltd.) Liability Company, joint-stock company, company of shareholders. **–spekulasjon** stockjobbing. **–tegning** subscription (of shares). **–utbytte** dividend.
aksjonær share-holder.
aksjon action, (juridisk) criminal prosecution.
aksklipper (maskin) header.
I. akt: **erklære** (el. **sette**) **i rikets —** place (el. put) under the ban of the Empire.
II. akt (hensikt) intention, purpose, design; (oppmerksomhet) attention, care; (aktelse) esteem, estimation; **gi — på** pay attention to, attend to, take heed of, heed, mind; **gi(v) —! (** = **rett!)** attention! still! **ta i —** take care of; **ta seg i —** take care, have a care, take heed, beware (for: of); **ta deg i —!** have a care! beware! look out! (truende) have at you; **ta deg vel i —** (dt) mind your eye; **han tok seg ikke i —** he was off his guard; **holde i — og ære** hold in esteem; **holdes i — og ære** be esteemed, stand high in the estimation of.
III. akt (høytidelig handling) act, solemnity, ceremony; (i skuespill) act; **–er** papers.
IV. akt (i malerkunst) life, nude (drawn from life). **kvinnelig —** female nude.
akte (legge merke til) mind, heed, regard, attend to; (vise aktelse) respect, reverence; (holde for) regard, consider; **— høyt** think much of; **— ringe** hold light, think el. make light of, make little account of, think st. small potatoes; merk: **hvor –r De Dem hen** where are you going? **— å** intend, propose, design to; **— på** attend to, heed.
aktelse respect, regard, esteem, deference; **ha — for** have a regard for; **skaffe seg —** make oneself respected; **med (høy)— Deres** Yours respectfully, Yours most respectfully; **av — for** **lovene** in deference to the laws.
akten|for (prep) abaft. **–fra** (adv) (innabords) from abaft; (utabords) from astern. **–om** (prep) astern of.
akter (innabords) aft, after, abaft; (utabords) astern; **–st** aftermost, aftmost, (utenfor skipet) sternmost; (i flåteavdeling) rearmost; **den –ste åre** the stroke-(oar); **det går til –s for el. med ham** he is going down hill. **–dekk** after-deck. **–del** hind-part. **–ende** stern. **–feste –fortøyning** stern-fast. **–gaster** (pl) afterguard. **–hånd: i —** at the tail-end; (lig) **være i –en** be in arrear. **–inn** (adv) from astern. **–lanterne** stern light. **–last** after-hold. **–mast** aft (el. after) mast. **–plikt** stern-sheets. **–seil** after-sail. **–sete** stern-sheets. **–skarpen** after-peak, (utabords) run. **–skip** after-body. **–skott** (after el. steerage) bulk-head. **–speil** stern; (dt. = bakdel, rumpe) posteriors. **–spill** main cap 'un. **–stavn** stern, stern-post. **–stemholt** sternson. **–trapp** companion ladder. **–trosse** stern-rope. **–ut** (adv) astern; **sakke —** drop (fall, get) behind; **–utseile** leave astern, (fig) distance, leave behind.
aktiv active. **aktiv** (gram) the active (voice); **–a** assets (pl); **–a og passiva** (merk) assets and debts, debts active and passive.

aktivitet activity; **sette i** — put in activity, in action.
aktivum (merk) property, asset.
aktmessig documentary.
aktor counsel for the prosecution. **aktorat** prosecution.
akt|pågivende mindful, attentive. **-pågivenhet** attention, heedfulness. **-som** heedful, mindful, careful, attentive. **-somhet** carefulness, heedfulness, attention. **-stykke** document. **-ualitet** actuality, present interest. **-uell** actual, present. **-verdig** estimable, respectable. **-verdighet** respectability.
akust|ikk acoustics (pl). **-isk** acoustic.
akutt acute.
akva|marin aqua marina, aqua marine. **-rell** water-colours; painting el. drawing in water-colours; (konkret) water-colour drawing. **-rellmaler** water-colourist. **-rium** aquarium. **-vit** (aqua-vitæ), se **akevitt**.
akvedukt (vannledning) aqueduct.
I. **al** (i gran og furu) heart, heartwood.
II. **al** (oppfostring, avl) breeding.
alabast alabaster.
à la carte à la carte, by the bill of fare.
alarm (larm) noise, tumult, racket, uproar, hubbub, din; (anskrik) alarm; **blind** — false alarm; **rope** — (gjøre anskrik) give the alarm; **blåse, slå** — sound, beat the alarm. **-ere** alarm. **-klokke** alarm bell. **-plass** alarm-post.
albaner Alban. **A-berget** the Alban Mount.
Alban|ia Albania. **a-er; a-sk.** Albanian, Albanese; Alban.
albatross albatros.
albiño (individ med sykelig hvithet) albino.
albu|e elbow; **puffe med -en** elbow; **puffe seg fram med -ene** elbow one's way. **-støt jog with** the elbow; bruise on the elbow.
album album.
albumin (eggehvite) albumen. **-stoff** albuminous substance.
aldeles quite, entirely, totally, absolutely, altogether, utterly; — **ikke** not at all, by no (manner of) means, (dt) not a bit of it; — **som om** quite as if, for all the world as if.
alder age; **han har -en** he has the years; **for sin** — for his years; **hester av alle -er** all-aged horses; **i en** — **av** at the ago of; **døde i en** — **av to år** died aged two years; **i høy** — at a great age; **i en tidlig** — at an early age, early in life; **i en sen** — late in life; **i sin beste** — in the prime of life; **i min** — at my age, at my time of life; **i den** — da of an age in which; **han er på min** — he is (of) my age.
alderdom (old) age; **-men** old age. **alderdomssenile.** **-pensjon** old age pension. **-sløv** in one's dotage, imbecile. **-støtte** stay of one's declining years. **-svakhet** decrepitude, infirmity of (old) age.
alders|forskjell difference in years. **-følge, se ansiennitet.** **-grense** limit of age, age-limit; **falle for -grensen** retire from the service under the age-clause.
aldersstegen aged, stricken in years.
alderstillegg increase (according to length of service).
alderstrin(n) age.
alders|trygd Old-Age Pension.
aldrende elderly, oldish.
aldri never; — **mer** no more; nevermore; **nå har jeg** — **hørt så galt!** well, I never! om **han hadde** — **så mange** though he had ever so many; — **så snart ... før** no sooner ... than; **man skal** — **si** — never is a long word; **nesten** — hardly ever; **dette kan vel** — **være** Deres klær these are never your clothes?
ale opp breed.
aleine, se alene.
Aleksandria Alexandria.
aleksandrin|er, -sk Alexandrian; (vers) alexandrine.
alen: 1 alen er ca. 0,686 yard (eller ca. 0,627

meter); **ell** (i det hele gammeldags; the English ell = ca. 1, 143 meter; the Scotch ell = ca. 0,645 meter); **de er to** — **av ett stykke** they are a pair el. of a piece; **måle en annen med sin egen** — measure another by one's own standard.
alene alone, by oneself; **helt** — all alone; **være** — be alone el. private; **en ulykke kommer sjelden** — misfortune rarely comes single; (adv) only, solely; **ikke** — ... **men også** not only ... but.
alenlang an ell (el. yard) long. **-mål** ell (el. yard) -measure. **-vis** by the ell (el. yard).
alfabet alphabet. **-isk** alphabetic.
alfagras alfa.
alfons (petticoat) pensioner, pouncey, ponce, male keep.
alge alga, (pl) algæ, sea-weed.
algebra algebra. **-isk** algebraic.
Alger (byen) Algiers; **-ie** (landet) Algeria; **a-er, -sk** Algerian, Algerine.
alias (også kalt) alias.
alibi (fravær mens en forbrytelse ble begått) alibi: **bevise sitt** — prove one's (el. an) alibi.
alimentasjon(sbidrag) alimony.
alka|li alkali. **-lisk** alkaline. **-loid** alkaloid.
alke auk.
alkjemi, se alkymi.
alko|hol alcohol. **-holisere** alcoholize. **-holisk** alcoholic. **-holisme** alcoholism. **-holist** habitual drunkard. **-holometer** alcoholometer, alcoholmeter.
alkoran the Alcoran, the Koran.
alkove alcove.
alkymi alchemy. **-st** alchemist. **-stisk** alchemic(al), alchemistic(al).
all, alt (pl. alle) all; — **verden** all the world, the whole world; **hva i** — **verden skal jeg gjøre** what on earth shall I do? **han har** — **mulig grunn til å** he has every reason to; **av** — **makt with** might and main; **i** — **stillhet** (very) quietly; **til alt hell** by great good luck, as good luck would have it; **framfor alt** above all, of all things; **alt all,** everything; **alt sammen** all, everything; **alt tatt i betraktning** all things considered; **alt i ett** constantly; **hans ett og alt** his all in all, all in all with him; **i ett og alt** entirely, to all intents and purposes; **i alt** total, in the aggregate; **alt i alt** altogether, all told; **alt annet enn** anything but; **anything rather than; alt det** jeg eier my all; **alt engelsk** everything English, all matters English; **når alt kommer til alt after** all, after all is said, when all comes to all, (when) all (is) said and done, in the end; **med alt det** for all that; **med alt det at han** notwithstanding that he, for all his. **-ing;** **-e** (alle mennesker), all, everybody; **-e og enhver** everybody, each and all, (hvem som helst) anybody; **-e andre** everybody else; **vi** — **e** all of us, we all; **-e tre** all three, the whole three; **-e som en** one and all, all and sundry, (all) to a man; **-e mann** every man; **-e mann opp!** (mar) all hands ahoy! **en for -e og -e for en** jointly and separately.
Allah (Gud) Allah.
allé avenue (of trees), walk (of trees).
Alleghany-fjellene the Alleghany mountains.
allego|ri (liknelse, sinnbilledlig fremstilling) allegory. **-risere** allegorize. **-risk** allegoric(al).
allegro (muntert) allegro, lively.
allehel|gens|aften (All-)Hallow Eve; **-dag** All Saints('day).
allehånde (adj) all manner of, all kinds of, all sorts of.
allehånde (subst) all sorts of things; (krydder) allspice, pimento. **allemannsvenn** everybody's friend.
aller (skrevet i et ord for seg) of all, very, by far. — **alminneligst** the very commonest. — **best** the very best, best of all; — **best som** just as, at the very moment when, in the midst of. — **flest** by far the greatest number (of); **dem er det** — **flest av** they are by far the most

numerous. — **færrest: de -e** very few (people). — **først** first of all; **fra** — **f.** av from the very first. — **helst vil jeg** I should like best, I should greatly prefer. — **helvetes** devilish: **en** — **h. kar** a very devil of a fellow. — **høyest** highest of all; **den** — **h–e** the most High; **i** — **h–e grad** to the (very) last degree, to a degree. — **høgst** at the (very) utmost; — **kjærest** dearest (of all), most beloved; **det skulle være meg** — **k.** I should like nothing better than. — **kristeligst** most Christian. — **mest** by far the greatest part; (adv) more than ever. — **minst** least of all; the very least; **i det** — **m.** at the very least. — **nærmest: mine** — **n.** my own family. — **nødigst: det så jeg** — **n.** I should like that least of all. — **nødvendigst** most necessary (of all); **det** — **n–e.** the very necessaries (of life). — **nådigst** most gracious(ly). — **sist** last of all; **vente til** — **s.** wait to the very end. — **underdanigst** most humble; (adv) most humbly. — **øverst** the very topmost; (adv) at the very top; — **ø.** (oppe) **i el. på** at the very top of.

allerede already; (en gang tidligere) before now, ere now; — **den gang** even at that time; — **i det tolvte århundre** as early as the twelfth century; — **nå** even now; — **tidlig** quite early; — **de gamle** visste even the ancients knew; — **samme dag** the very same day; — **den omstendighet** at the very fact that el. of.

alle|sammen altogether. — **slags** of all kinds, every kind of, all kinds el. sorts of, a variety of, various. **-steds** everywhere, in all places. **-stedsnærværende** omnipresent, ubiquitous; — **vegne** everywhere.

all|fader father of all.

allfarvei high-road, high-way.

allgod all-good, all-bounteous, all-bountiful.

allgodhet supreme goodness.

allianse alliance. **-traktat** treaty of a. **alliert** allied; ally, (pl) allies.

alligator alligator.

allikevel, se likevel.

allitterasjon (bokstavrim) alliteration.

allkjærlig all-loving.

allmakt omnipotence, almightiness.

allmektig almighty, all-powerful; **den -e** the Almighty.

allonge (merk) allonge; **-parykk** full-bottom (-ed wig), full wig.

all|sidig manifold, multifarious; versatile, universal; (pt) all round. **-sidighet** versatility.

all|skaperen the Creator of all things. **-skapningen** the whole creation. **allslags** (alskens) of all kinds, every kind of, any variety of, various, miscellaneous. **allstyrende** all-governing; all-ruling.

alltid always; (i visse forbindelser) ever; **det kan jeg** — **gjøre** I can do that at any time; — **siden** ever since.

allting everything; (litt.) **hvorom** — **er** any way, however that may be.

all-tysk pan-German.

allu|dere allude. **-sjon** allusion.

allverden all the world; **hvordan i** — however, how in the name of wonders. **allvitende** omniscient, all-knowing. **allvitenhet** omniscience. **allvis** allwise. **allvisdom** supreme wisdom.

alm (tre) elm.

alm., se alminnelig.

almanakk almanac(k).

almen general, common, public, universal. **-befinnende** state of health in general. **-dannelse** general education; education of the (common). people. **-fattelig** intelligible to all, popular. **-fattelighet** simplicity, popularity. **-følelse** public spirit, philanthropy. **-gyldig** generally binding, universally received. **-gyldighet** general validity, universality. **-heten** the public. **-lesning** general reading, r. for the million. **-menneskelig** universal human. **-nytte** public good, p. utility. **-nyttig** of p. utility. **-sans, se -ånd. høyere -skole** se-

condary school. **-setning** common-place. **-vel** (det -e vel) (samfunnets tarv) common good. **-ånd** public spirit.

almenning common land(s); common.

alminnelig common, general, ordinary, (uten unntak.) universal; (mots. spesiell) general, generic; — **brøk** vulgar fraction. **-e setninger, påstander** generalizations, generalities; — **menneskeforstand** common sense; **et** — **rykte** a current belief, rumour; **den -e kirke** the universal church; **til** — **forbauselse** to the general surprise; — **stemmerett,** — **valgrett** universal suffrage; — **verneplikt** conscription, compulsion, compulsory service; (undertiden også omfattende ammunisjonstilvirkning hjemme osv.:) national service, universal service; (adv) commonly etc. **gjøre** — make general; generalize. **-gjørelse** generalization. **-het** generality, universality; **i** (sin) **-het** in general, generally; **-vis** generally, in general.

almisse alms, charity. **-utdeler** (ved kloster, hospitaler osv.) almoner.

almu(g)e the common people, the peasantry, the poor, the vulgar, the lower orders, the plebeians.

aloe (botanikk) aloe; (med) aloes (pl) **-aktig, -holdig** aloetic.

a!pakka (dyr, ull og tøy) alpaca.

Alpe|ne the Alps. **alpe-** alpine. **-fiol** cyclamen. **-horn** alphorn, alpine horn. **-rose** rhododendron. **-stokk** alpenstock.

alrune (en plante) mandrake, mandragora.

alskens, se allslags.

alt, se all.

alt (= allerede) already; — **etter** according to; — **ettersom** in proportion as; **-for** too (forsterket ved far, much, quite, altogether osv.); **-for forsiktig** cautious to a fault; **-for høflig** (ringeaktende) too civil by half; — **imens** all the while; — **mer og mer** more and more; — **som** just as, according as.

alt (musikk) alt, alto, contralto, counter- (-tenor).

altan balcony.

alter altar.

alter|bilde, se -tavle. -bok service-book. **-bord** communion table. **-duk** altar cloth.

alterert frightened, agitated; **jeg ble så** — (dt) it gave me such a turn.

alter|gang communion; **-gang holdes** the Holy Communion is celebrated. **-gjest** = (nattverdgjest) communicant. **-kar** altar vessel. **-klede** cloth. **-klær** canonicals, robes (of a priest). **-lys** altar light.

alternativ alternative.

alternere (veksle) alternate.

alter|stake altar candlestick. **-tavle** altarpiece, (med fløyer) triptych. **-trin** step. **-vin** communion wine.

altetende omnivorous.

altnøkkel alto clef.

altomfattende all-comprehending, all-embracing.

altoppofrende self-sacrificing.

altoppslukende interesse absorbing interest.

altru|isme (uegennytte) altruism. **-ist** altruist. **-istisk** altruistic.

altså consequently, accordingly, therefore, so, then.

altsanger, -inne alto singer, altist.

aluminium aluminium.

alumn, -us alumnus (plur. -ni).

alun alum. **-beis** alum-mordant. **-garve** (hvitgarve) taw. **-garver** tawer. **-garveri** tawery. **-holdig** aluminous. **-skinn** alum leather, whiteleather.

alv elf, fairy.

alve|aktig elfin-like, elfish, fairy-like. **-dans** fairy-dance. **-lett** fairy-light. **-kone, -kvinne, -møy, -pike** fairy.

alvor earnest; **med** — earnestly; **det var**

mitt — I was in earnest; gjøre — av noe set about st. seriously; bli til — become serious; ett er spøk, et annet —, se -lig talt; det er da ikke Deres —? you don't say so? for — (mots. for spøk) in earnest; (mots. midlertidig) for good; for ramme — in good, real el. sober earnest, in very e.

alvorlig earnest, serious, grave, sober, demure; holde seg — keep a grave face; (adv) earnestly etc.; — talt joking apart, raillery el. jesting aside, in earnest, seriously speaking; ta for — på take too much in earnest. -het gravity, earnestness, seriousness.

alvors|blikk grave look. -full earnest, serious, grave. -mann earnest man. -ord serious word.

alvskott elf-shot.

amalgam amalgam. -ere amalgamate.

amasone amazone. -drakt riding habit.

Amazon–elva the Amazon.

amatør amateur.

ambassa|de embassy. -dør ambassador.

amber tub. pail.

ambisjon ambition; honnett — honest ambition, proper pride.

ambolt (også i øret) anvil.

ambra ambergrease eller ambergris; (planten) boy's-love, southernwood. -busk ambertree. -duft perfume of ambergris.

ambros|ia ambrosia. -isk ambrosial.

ambulanse ambulance. -vogn ambulancewaggon.

amen amen; så sikkert som — i kjerka sure as fate.

Amerika America. a–ner, -nerinne, -nsk American. a–sk olje castor oil.

ametyst amethyst.

amfi|bium amphibious animal, amphibium. -bisk amphibious. -teater amphitheatre. -teatralsk amphitheatrical.

amme (subst) nurse. amme (vrb) (= gi bryst) nurse, suckle.

ammoniakk ammonia. -holdig ammoniacal. -vann (= salmiakkspiritus) ammoniacal water, spirit of sal ammoniac.

ammunisjon munition, ammunition. ammunisjons|kjerre munition waggon. -kasse shot box.

amne|stere grant (one) an amnesty. -sti amnesty; (-dekret) amnesty, act of oblivion.

Amor Cupid, Love. a–in Cupid.

amoralsk amoral, a-moral, non-moral.

amorti|sere (avbetale) amortise, sink. -sasjon, -sering amortisation, amortisement. -sasjonsfond sinking fund.

ampel hanging flower-pot el. lamp.

amper (irritabel) fractious, fretful.

ampère (mål for strømstyrke) ampere. -meter ammeter.

amputasjon amputation. amputere amputate.

amt, se fylke. amtmann, se fylkesmann. amts-, se fylkes-.

amulett amulet, charm.

an (adv) (f. eks. binde an), se verbene; legg an! fyr! present, fire!

an (prep. merk) to.

anabaptist (gjendøper) anabaptist.

ana|koluti anacoluthon. -kolutisk anacoluthic.

anakreontisk Anacreontic.

ana|kronisme anachronism. -log analogous. -logi analogy; i -logi med by analogy to, on the model of. -logislutning analogism. -lyse analysis; (gram) parsing. -lysere analyse; parse. -lytisk analytical; den –e metode (kjemi) the a. method, the m. of residues.

ananas pine-apple, ananas.

anarki anarchy. anarkisk anarchical. anarkist anarchist. anarkistisk anarchist.

anatema (kirkelig forbannelse, bann) anathema.

anato|m anatomist. -mere anatomize, dissect. -mering anatomizing, dissection. -mi anatomy.

—mikammer dissecting room, anatomical hall. -misk anatomical.

anbefal|e recommend, commend; -e seg take leave, retire; jeg -er meg your servant. -elsesverdig recommendable. -ende recommendatory., -ing recommendation, commendation, reference introduction.

anbefalings|brev, -skriv letter of introduction.

anbringe put, place, dispose, fix, apply, insert, introduce, (penger) invest, (varer) sell; — i handelen settle el. place in trade; — et slag hit a blow. anbrakt: vel — well applied; vel — støt home-thrust; vel — slag well planted blow; slett — misapplied, misplaced, out of place; — til rette tid seasonable, opportune, welltimed; — til urette tid unseasonable, illtimed. anbringelse placing etc., application, investment.

anbud bid, offer, tender (på for).

and duck; (historie) hoax, mare's nest, canard.

andakt devotion; forrette sin — say one's prayers. andakts|bok book of d., devotional book. -full full of d., devout. -stund, -time hour of d.

Andalusi|a Andalusia. a–er, a–erinne, a–sk Andalusian.

ande|dam duck pond. -egg duck's egg. -hagl duck-shot; -jakt duck-shooting (amr.) ducking.

andektig devout, devotional, pious. -het devoutness, devotion.

andel share, part, portion, quota; ha stor — i have a large share el. part in; kjøpe en — i buy into; kjøpe ens — buy one out; min — i utbyttet my share of the profit. andels (jvf. samvirke-) cooperative. -meieri cooperative dairy. -selskap cooperative society. -system c. system, profitsharing, (i landbruket) cooperative farming.

andemat duck-weed, duck-meat; full av — duckweedy.

Andes–fjellene (pl) the Andes.

ande|skjell (en slags småkreps) acorn-shell, barnacle. -stegg drake. -steik roast duck.

andføttes (adv) head and tail, (at) heads and points.

andlet, se ansikt.

andpusten out of breath, blown.

andra (beløpe seg til) amount to; — om apply for, request. -gende petition, motion, application; sende inn til en et -gende om noe make an application to sb. for st.

andre, se annen.

Andreas Andrew. Andreas–kors (X) St. Andrew's cross.

andrik (= andestegg) drake.

andunge duckling.

andøve lay (el. lie, rest) on the oars.

ane suspect, anticipate, guess, forebode, have a foreboding, presentiment, of; det -r jeg ikke I have no idea; (litt. jeg -r det verste my heart misgives me; intet (ondt) -nde unconscious, unsuspecting.

anekdote anecdote. -aktig anecdotal, anecdotical. -jeger anecdotist. -samling collection of anecdotes, jest-book.

anelse suspicion, foreboding, presentiment, misgiving, anticipation, presage; jeg hadde ingen — om at I had no idea that. anelsesfull full of presentiment.

anemi anaemia. anemisk anaemic.

anemone anemone, windflower.

aner (pl) (noble) ancestors, ancestry.

aner|kjenne acknowledge, own, accept, admit, recognise; ikke — not etc.; disown, disclaim; -kjennelse acknowledgment, recognition; appreciation; finne tilbørlig — receive due recognition; yte sin — pay el. bear tribute to; vinne — gain favour. -verdig creditable. -kjennende appreciative, appreciatory. -kjent (generally) recognised; (adv) så -kjent dyktig of such g. r. ability.

aneroidbarometer aneroid barometer.

ane|stolt proud of one's ancestors. **-tavle** ancestral tablet.

anfall attack, assault, charge, onset; (av sykdom) fit, access; (lidensk. utbrudd) transport, paroxysm; — av **fortvilelse** fit of despair; — av **feber** access of fever; **fikk et** — av was taken with a fit of. **anfalle** attack, assault, assail, fall upon.

anfekte (angripe, gl., brukes nå bare i nektende uttr. med betydn. **forstyrre, affisere**). **lar seg ikke** — **av** is not affected by. **-lse** vexation, anxiety; temptation.

anfordring demand. **anfordrings|bevis, -seddel** note payable on demand.

anføre (som befalende) command; (gå i spissen for) head, lead; (veilede) guide, conduct, direct; (innføre) enter, book; (angi) state, give, refer to; (berope seg på) allege, adduce, advance, urge, plead; (sitere) cite, quote; — **til sin unnskyldning** allege in one's excuse, plead; — **grunner** state reasons; — **som eksempel** quote as an instance. **anfør|er** (høvding) leader, commander, chief; (fører) guide; (leder) (f. eks. av orkester) conductor; (i et opprør) ringleader. **-ing** stating, statement; quoting, quotation; pleading. **-sel** command; direction, guidance; conductorship. **-selstegn** inverted commas (pl), (signs of) quotation, quotation-marks; **sette i** (el. **mellom**) **-selstegn** put in quotation marks, quote.

ang., se **angående.**

ange fragrance, odour, perfume.

angel (pl **angler**) (fish-)hook; **-fiske** angling; **-fisker** angler.

angel|sakser Anglo-Saxon. **-saksisk** Anglo-Saxon, Old English.

angelus (katolsk bønn) angelus. **-klokke** angelus-bell, angelus.

anger repentance, remorse, penitence, contrition, compunction, regret; **føle** — **over** repent of. **-full, -given** repentant, penitent, contrite, compunctious.

angerløs (sakesløs) guiltless, blameless, unimpeachable.

angi state, mention, report; (en) inform against, denounce (for: to); (vise) indicate, point out, assign; (til) report at, set down at, return at; (til fortolling) enter (at the custom house); — **en grunn** assign a reason; — **tonen** (musikk) give the tone el. key, (fig) take the lead; (moten) lead the fashion.

angina (halsbetennelse) inflammation of the throat.

angi|velse statement, declaration, report; information, denunciation; **med -velse av** stating. **-vende** statement. **-ver, -verske** informer, denouncer. **-veri** informing.

angjeldende (jur) the party (in question).

angle angle (etter for).

angler (folkestamme) Angles.

angli|kansk Anglican; **den -e kirke** (den engelske statskirke) the Anglican Church, the Church of England. **-isere** anglicize. **-isisme** (engelsk språkeiendommelighet) anglicism. **angli|o-amerikansk** Anglo-American. **-oman** Anglomaniac. **-omani** Anglo-mania.

angre repent, repent of, repent oneself of, rue, regret, be sorry for. **-nde** repentant, penitent.

angrep attack, assault, aggression, onset, (heftig, av tropper) charge; blaast til — sound the charge; **fornye -et** (også fig) return to the charge. **angreps|bevegelse** offensive movement. **-krig** aggressive (el. offensive) war, war of aggression. **-linje** line of approach. **-middel** means of offence, aggressive means. **-mål** object of attack. **-plan** plan of attack. **-politikk** aggressive policy. **-rekke** (fotballag) forwards. **-spiller** (i fotballag) forward. **-vis** (adv): **gå** — **til verks** act on the offensive, take up the offensive.

angrepsvåpen offensive weapon el. arms (pl).

angrip|e (i alm.) attack, assail; (fiende) engage; (heftig, som kavaleri) charge; (virke sterkt på) affect, (skadelig) injure; (tære) corrode; (ta på) exhaust, shake (the nerves, the health); (bestride) contest; (en kapital e. l.) encroach upon. **-elig** assailable; vulnerable; **-ende** (fig) trying, exhausting. **-er** assailer, aggressor.

angst (adj) anxious, apprehensive, in a state of alarm; — **for** uneasy (el. anxious) about; afraid of.

angst (subst) dread, terror, state of alarm, fear, apprehension; — **for** fear of (el. about, el. on one's account). **-full** anxious, fearful. **-rop, -skrik** cry of terror, shriek. **-svette** cold perspiration.

angå concern, regard, relate to, bear on, respect, refer to, apply to, have reference to; **hva -r det meg** what is that to me? **det -r ikke Dem** it's none of your business, it does not concern you; **hva -r** as to, as for, as regards, as respects; **hva meg -r** as to me, as for me, I for one, in my instance; **hva det -r** as to that, for that matter, on that point. **angående** (prep) respecting, regarding, concerning, touching, relative to, about, relating to, as to.

anhang (tillegg) appendix.

anhold|e apprehend, take up, seize, stop; (skip) lay embargo on; — **om** apply for, solicit. **-else** apprehension, seizure. **-elsesordre,** se **arrestordre.**

anilin aniline.

animalsk animal.

anim|ere animate, induce (til: to). **-ert** animated. **-ositet** animosity.

aning (svak luftning i ellers stille vær) cat's paw.

anis anise(-seed). **anisliker** anisette.

anke (subst) complaint, grievance, (jur.) appeal. — **over** (vrb) complain of.

ankel| ankle; **til -en** ankle-deep. **ankelledd** ankle joint.

ankelsko highlows, ankle-jacks.

anke|mål, -punkt (klagemål, klagepunkt) complaint, grievance.

ankeprotokoll protocol of grievance.

I. **anker** (hulmål) anker (c. 45,43 liter).

II. **anker** (skipsanker o. l.) anchor; (i mur) brace, iron-tie, cramp iron; (del av dynamo) armature; **-et går for a.** comes home; **kappe -et** cut the cable; **kaste** — cast el. drop a.; **kippe -et** fish the a.; **komme til -s** come to an a. **lette** (= hive) — weigh a.; **ligge til -s (for —)** ride at a. **-bedding** riding-bitts (pl.) **-bolt,** se **anker** (i mur). **-bøye** a. buoy. **-gang** a. escapement. **-gangs-ur** watch with a. e. **-kjetting** (chain-) cable. **-letting** weighing the a. **-plass** anchorage, anchoring ground. **-spill** windlass; winch. **-tau** cable.

ankestevning summons on appeal.

anklage (vrb) accuse (for: of), charge (for: with); (for retten) prosecute; arraign, indict; (for riksrett) impeach.

anklage (subst) accusation, charge; indictment; **sette en under** — **for** (jvf. **sikte en for**) accuse one of, prosecute one for. **-benk** felon's dock. **-myndighet** power of indictment. **-punkt** article of charge, item of an indictment. **anklager** accuser, complainant, (offentlig) prosecutor. **offentlig** — Counsel for the Crown (el. for the Prosecution).

anklang sympathy; **finne** — **hos** enlist sympathy with.

ankomme arrive (til Oxford: at Oxford, til London: in L., undertiden at L., til England: in E.), come (to), reach (a place). **ankomst** arrival, coming; **ved min** — at el. on my a. **ankomstperrong** arrival platform.

ankr|e anchor. **-ing** anchoring. **-ingsavgift** anchorage. **-ingsarbeid** anchor-work.

anlagt (adj), se **anlegge.**

anledning occasion, cause, reason, opportunity; **ved en** — on an occasion, at an opportunity; **ta** — **til å** take occasion to; **i** — **av** on the occasion of, in consequence of, on account of; **gi** — **til** give occasion to, give cause for, leave room for, give rise to.

anlegg (oppføring) foundation, construction; laying out (of streets, gardens); settling, planting (of colonies); (utkast) plan, design; (fabrikk) works; (gaver) talent, turn; (tilbøyelighet) bent; (v. skytning) rest; (mil) present; **vi gikk ut i** **-ene** we went into the (pleasure-) grounds. **anlegge** lay out; set out, plant; make (roads); found (schools, towns); (fabrikker) establish, erect, set up; (fig) plan; apply (a bandage); invest (money); — **sak imot** bring an action against; — **sorg** put on mourning; **når en** **-r denne målestokk** measured by this standard. **anlagt på** aimed at; **anlagt for, til** fitted for.

anleggs|arbeider navvy. **-gartner** landscape gardener. **-gartneri** l. gardening. **-kapital** funds.

anliggende affair, concern, business, matter; **viktige -r** on matters of importance.

anløp call. **-e** (mar) touch at, call at; (stål) temper; (få en viss farge) become oxidized, tarnished; **la et gevær** — bronze a gun.

anløps|plass, -sted stopping place, place el. port of call. **-tid** hour of stopping.

anmarsj advance; **være i** — be approaching, advancing, coming on.

anmasse|seg arrogate, assume, usurp. **-lse** arrogation, assumption, usurpation. **-nde** arrogant, presumptuous.

anmeld|e announce, notify, give notice of, (til en autoritet) report, (tollpliktige varer) declare; — **protest** note a p., cause a p. to be noted; — **et forslag** give notice of a motion; — **en bok** notice el. review a book. **-else** announcing etc.; announcement, notification; notice; (av bok) review, notice. **-er** announcer; reviewer, critic.

anmerk|e (merke) mark; (opptegne) note down, put down. **-ning** remark; (note) comment, note, annotation, commentary; **gi en en** — put one's name down; **gjøre -er om** comment upon. **forsyne med -ninger** annotate. **-ningsprotokoll** (på skolen) black book.

anmod|e om request, solicit; — **en om noe** ask, beg. request (st.) of one. **-ning** request, desire; **etter -ning av** at the request of; **med -ning om** requesting; **på Deres -ning** as requested; **-ning om betaling** application for payment.

Anna Anna, Ann, Anne, Annie, Nan, Nancy.

annaler (pl) annals. **annalist** annalist.

annamme (gl.), se **motta**.

anneks parish of ease, chapelry.

anneksjon annexation.

anneks|kirke chapel of ease. **-sogn**, se **anneks**. **annekter|e** annex. **-ing** annexation.

annen, intetkj. **annet**. fl. **andre** (ubest. pron.) other; (ordenstall) second; adjektiv: **en** — another, some other; **en eller** — some; **hver** — every other, every second; **som en** — apekatt like a regular monkey; **i en ganske** — **betydning** in a very different sense; — **del** the second volume; **fra ende til** — from end to end; **en** — **gang** another time; **på** — **hånd** at second hand; **den** — **januar** (on) the second of January; **det er en ganske** — **mann** he is a very different (sort of) man; **være av en** — **mening** think differently; **det er en** — **sak** that is different, that alters the case; **fra tid til** — from time to time; **i den** — **verden** in the next world, in the future life. **annet: det** — **liv** the future life; **det** — **bud** the third commandment; **ikke noe** — **sted** nowhere else; — **ekteskap** a second marriage; — **kapitel** chapter the second. **Også da** (det) **andre: den** — **bredden** the further bank; **den** — **døra** herfra the next door but one; **den** — **hansken** min the fellow to my glove. **andre** (fl.) **med** —

ord in other words; **pekuniære og** — **fordeler** pecuniary and otherwise, pecuniary and other advantages; **ta** — **klær på** change one's clothes; **komme på** — **tanker** change one's mind. **annen** **s u b s t a n t i v; en** — another person, somebody else, another; **ingen** — nobody else, no other person; **ingen** — **enn** nobody but; **en og** — some people; **en eller** — somebody (or other). **annet:** — **å bestille** other things to do; — **å tenke på** something else to think of; **fikk** — **å vite** was undeceived; **alt** — anything else; **alt** — **enn** anything but; **blant** — for one thing: inter alia, among other things; **et og** — some things; **et eller** — something (or other); **for det** — secondly, in the second place; **hva** — what else? **ikke** — nothing else; **ikke** —? is that all? **ikke** — **enn** nothing but, ogs. no other than, no more than; **det kan ikke være** — it can be nothing else, it cannot be otherwise, it cannot be helped, there is nothing else for it; **det kan ikke være enn** at it cannot be but; **jeg kan ikke** — I can do no otherwise, I cannot help it; **jeg kan ikke** — **enn tro** I cannot but think, I cannot help thinking; I cannot choose (el. help) but think, I cannot do otherwise than think, I can do nothing but think; **jeg vet ikke** — as far as I know, I know nothing to the contrary; **noe** — something else, noe som helst —) anything else; **det er noe** — that is another affair; **om ikke for** — if for no other purpose; **kan ikke være** — **enn takknemlig for** cannot be other than grateful for; **det var ikke godt** — I should be very sorry not to believe it. **andre: alle** — everybody else; **dere** — the rest of you; **ingen** — nobody else, no others; **ingen** — **enn** none but; **de to** — (el. **de** — **to**) the two others, the other two.

annendag jul Boxing-day; — **pinse** Whit-Monday; Whitsuntide Bank Holiday; — **påske** Easter-Monday.

annen|dagsbryllup second day's (wedding) festivities. **-dagsfeber** tertian fever. **-dagsmorgen** the morning of the next day, the next day in the morning. **-gradslikning** quadratic equation. **-hver** (pron., adj.) annethvert, se **hver-annen**. **-hånds** at second hand. **-lærer** assistant teacher. **-rangs** second-rate. **-steds** elsewhere, in some el. any other place. **-stedsfra** from another place. **-stedshen** somewhere else, to some other place.

annerledes otherwise, in another manner, differently; **bli** — **til sinns** change one's mind; **han er ikke** — that is his way; **ganske** — **på- litelig** far more trustworthy; **saken er ganske** — the thing is quite different; — **tenkende** such as think otherwise.

annet, se **annen**.

Anno Domini (i det Herrens år) Anno Domini, in the year of our Lord; **Anno 1713** in the year 1713.

annonse advertisement. **-byrå** advertising office. **-re** advertise. **-samler** canvasser for advertisements.

annull|ere annul, cancel, render null and void; (juridisk) defeat. **-ering** annulment.

anode (den positive elektrode) anode.

anonym anonymous; anonymous writer. **-itet** anonymousness.

anord|ne (ordne) arrange; (befale) order, ordain, decree; (medisin) prescribe. **-ning** arrangement, order, ordinance, edict, rule, regulation prescription.

anorganisk inorganic.

anpart, se **andel**.

anretning serving; (samling av retter) course; **kold** — a cold collation. **-sbord** dresser. **anret|te** (lage til) prepare, arrange; (mat) dress; (på bordet) serve (up) (forårsake) do, make, cause; **det er -tet** dinner is on the table; — **et blodbad** effect a general massacre (på: of); — **skade** do damage; — **ødeleggelse** commit ravages el. havoc.

anrop challenge.

anrop|e call to, challenge; (be) implore, invoke; — **kongen om nåde** implore the king's mercy.

ansamling accumulation.

ansats disposition; (musikk) embouchure; — **til hale** a rudiment of a tail; **hadde — til fedme** was inclined to be stout.

anse | for regard, consider, deem, judge, esteem, think, reckon, count, account, look upon as, take for; — **for å** consider to: **-else** reputation, general standing, consideration, esteem, prestige; **nyter stor** — is in high esteem; **uten persons** — without respect of persons; **gjør ikke persons** — is no respecter of persons, **-lig** (av utseende) stately, portly; (stor) good sized, (betydelig) handsome, considerable. **-lighet** portliness; greatness. **ansett** esteemed, reputable, reputed, respected, of high standing, of consideration, of note; **et vel** — **firma** a firm of good standing; **er ille** — has a bad character.

ansett|e (anslå) value, estimate, rate; (til beskatning) assess; (tilsette i embete e. l.) appoint, place; (mar) set up. **-else** valuation, estimate; assessment; appointment, engagement.

ansiennitet seniority, standing, (mil) date of commission. **etter** — by (el. in el. according to) seniority; **idet hans — først regnes fra** he only taking date from.

ansikt face; countenance, look, looks, mien, visage; **skjære -er til en** make (wry) faces, make mouths at one; **se en rett i -et** look one (full) in the face; **bli lang i -et** look blank, make el. pull a long face; **si en noe rett opp i -et** tell one st. (right) to his face; **sette opp et alvorlig** — put on a grave face; **stå — til — med** stand face to face with. **ansikts|drag** feature. **-farge** complexion. **-form** form el. make of face. **-smerter** facial neuralgia face-ache. **-trekk** features, lineaments. **-trekning** convulsion of the face. **-uttrykk** expression of countenance.

ansjos anchovy.

anskaffe procure, get, provide. **-lse** getting, procurement, provision; purchase, jvf. **ny-**.

anskrev|et (-en): er vel — hos ham is in great favour with him; **er ille — hos** stands ill with him.

anskrik outcry, halloo; **gjøre** — give the alarm, cry out, call out, halloo.

anskuelig perspicuous, plain, intelligible. **-gjøre** render plain el. intelligible, elucidate, illustrate. **-gjørelse** elucidation, illustration. **-het** perspicuity.

anskuelse (litt., filos.) intuition, perception; (synsmåte, mening) view, opinion, way of looking upon. **anskuelses|evne** intuitive power. **-metoden** the intuitive principle of instruction. **-undervisning** object teaching. **-øving** object lesson.

anslag (musikk) touch; (mekanisk) impact; (p. høvel) leader; (vurdering) estimate, valuation; (plan) scheme, plan, project, plot, design; **et — mot hans liv** a design upon el. a plot against his life. **anslå** (musikk) strike; (vurdere) estimate, rate, value, compute **(til: at);** — **for høyt,** overrate, overvalue; — **for lavt** underrate undervalue.

anspenne strain, stretch, put upon the stretch; — **alle sine krefter** strain every nerve.

anspore spur on, stimulate, incite, instigate, urge, fire; — **en til å gjøre sitt beste** put one on el. to his mettle.

anstalt preparation, arrangement, disposition; **gjøre -er til** make arrangements for; (stiftelse e.l.) establishment, institution. **-maker** schemer; meddling humbug. **-makeri** airy schemes; meddling; pose; posturings.

anstand deportment, grace. **anstandsdame** chaperon.

anstendig decent, proper; **et — parti** an eligible match; **en — pike** a decent, honest

girl. **-het** decency, decorum, propriety. **-vis** (adv) in (common) decency.

anstift|e cause, contrive, work; stir up, set on foot, raise, excite; hatch, plan. **-else** causing etc. **-er** author, instigator.

anstigende: komme — come on at speed.

anstikke (et fat) broach.

anstille institute; — **undersøkelse(r)** commence el. set on foot investigations, make el. conduct an inquiry; — **forsøk** make experiments; — **betraktninger** make reflections; anstilte seg **som om han var** pretended to be; — **seg dum** sham stupid.

anstreng|e exert, strain, tax; — **seg for** endeavour, exert oneself. **-else** effort, exertion. **-ende** laborious, fatiguing. **-ende arbeid** hard work. **anstrengt** strained; — **smil** a forced smile; —

anstrøk; (fig, utseende) appearance, aspect; (stenk) touch, tinge, dash, suspicion.

anstundende (litt.) coming, forthcoming.

anstøt (forargelse) offence, scandal, shock; **vekke** — give offence; **ta — av** take offence at. **anstøtelig** offensive, indecent. **anstøtssten** stumbling block, s. stone.

anstå be fit (el. fitting, proper); — **seg for** be suitable el. fit for, become.

ansvar responsibility, liability, accountability; **stå til** — be responsible el. answerable, answer **(for:** for; **overfor:** to); **på eget — og tilsvar** at one's own peril; **dra (trekke) til** — call to account; **dras til** — (for retten) be made amenable to justice; **fralegge seg —et for** wash one's hands of. **ansvarlig** answerable, responsible, amenable, accountable **(for:** for; **overfor:** to, before). **ansvarlighet** responsibility, accountability. **ansvars|fri** irresponsible. **-full** responsible. **-følelse** sense of responsibility. **-havende** responsible manager, man (el. person) in charge.

ansøke om (søke om) apply for, sue for, solicit. **ansøker** petitioner, applicant, supplicant. **ansøkning** petition, suit; supplication, application; — **om benådning** petition for mercy.

· **anta** (i tjeneste) engage; (en lære o. l.) embrace, espouse, adopt; (tro, sette) suppose, assume, take it; — **form** take el. assume a form; — **kongetitelen** assume the regal title; **jeg vil** — **det** I presume (el. expect) so; **bli antatt** pass. **antagelig** acceptable, admissible, eligible; **-e betingelser** acceptable terms; **en — størrelse** a fair el. goodly size; (adv) likely, probably. **antagelse** admission, acceptance, reception; engagement; adoption; assumption; supposition, theory.

antall number, multitude; **i** — in number, numerically; **overgå i** — outnumber.

Antarktis Antarctica. **antarktisk** antarctic. of south polar regions.

antaste assail, attack.

anteceden|s, pl. -ser, -tier, -tia antecedent.

antedatere antedate.

antegn|e write down, put down, note, make a note of. **-else, -ing** writing etc.; note.

antenn|e (ild osv.) kindle, light; (noe brennbart) fire, ignite, set fire to, set on fire. **-elig** inflammable, combustible.

antenne (i radio) aerial, (ofte om mottakerluftnett) antenna (flt. ae).

anticiper|e anticipate. **-ing** anticipation.

antikkirkelig Anti-Church.

antikk (adj) antique. — (subst) antique. **-en** antiquity, ancient art. — **-samling** cabinet of antiques.

Antikrist Antichrist.

antikritikk reply (to a criticism).

antik|var antiquary, antiquarian; (bokh.) second-hand bookseller. **-varisk** antiquarian; at second hand. **-vert** antiquated. **-vitet** antiquity. **-vitetshandel** old curiosity shop. **-vitetshandler** seller of antiquities, old curiosities.

antilope antelope.

antiluftskyts anti-aircraft guns, (dt.) archies.
antimakassar tidy, antimacassar.
antimon antimony, stibium.
antipati antipathy. -sk antipathetic(al).
antipode antipode.
antipyrin antipyrine (mot feber).
antisemitt anti-Semite. -isk anti-Semitic. -isme anti-Semitism.
antisept|ikk antiseptic method. -isk antiseptic. -isk middel antiseptic.
antitese antithesis.
antologi anthology.
antrasitt anthracite, blind-coal.
antrekk dress, attire.
antropolog anthropologist. -i anthropology.
antrukket (part.) attired. fint — stylish-looking.
antyd|e indicate, give a hint of; (la forstå) suggest, intimate, insinuate, hint, imply. -ning indication, intimation, insinuation, hint, suggestion; (spor) trace; en -ning av pepper a suggestion of pepper. -ningsvis by way of suggestion; (i meget liten grad) very slightly.
anven|de (bruke) employ, use (til: for); (tid) penger) spend (in), expend, bestow (upon); (gjøre nyttig) utilize; (teori, lignelse) apply (på: to), bring to bear (upon); — ille misemploy, misapply; — sin tid vel make a good use of one's time; la seg — apply. -delig practicable; — på applicable to. -delighet practicability, applicability, applicableness. -delse employment, use, application; finner — på applies to. -dt (matematikk osv.) applied, mixed.
anvis|e (påvise) show, indicate, point out (st. to one); (lære) direct; (tildele) assign, allot; (merk.) assign; — på banken give a check on the bank; — til utbetaling pass for payment; — en sum til (et bruk) appropriate a sum for. -ning (merk.) assignment, order, assignation; (bank-) check; (til å gjøre noe) direction, instruction; gi en — på refer one to. -ningsblankett blank cheque, cheque form. -ningskontor private inquiry office.
aorta (den store pulsåre) aorta.
apanasje appanage.
aparte odd, queer, out of the way; (adv) extra.
apa|ti apathy, -tisk apathetic.
ap fun, chaff; drive — med make fun of.
ape monkey, (mest fig) ape; (mar) mizenstaysail. å — etter mimic, ape. apeaktig apish, monkey-like. ape|fjes pug-face. -katt monkey; (fig) (etteraper) ape, jackanapes. -kattvesen whimsical manners.
Apenninene the Apennines.
aperitiff aperitive.
ape|spill, -streker foolery; drive — med make fun of.
aplomb self-possession, assurance.
apokryf(isk) apocryphal; de -iske bøker the Apocrypha.
apollinaris Apollinaris.
Apollo Apollo.
apoplek|si apoplexy. -tiker apoplectic. -tisk apoplectic.
apost|el apostle; A-lenes gjerninger the Acts (of the Apostles); reise med -lenes hester go on foot, trudge it, go on Shank's mare. apostolisk apostolic(al); den -e trosbekjennelse the Apostles' creed.
apostrof apostrophe. -ere apostrophize.
apotek chemist's shop, (på skip, hospital o. l.) dispensary. -er chemist, druggist, apothecary. apoteker|gutt chemist's apprentice. -krukke gallipot. -kunst (farmasi) pharmacy. -medhjelpechemist's assistant. -varer drugs. -vekt apothecary's weight, troy-weight; apothecary's scaler.
apparat apparatus.
appartement apartment, room, set of rooms.
appell (mil) (roll)-call; (juridisk) appeal; (fig) buoyancy; hunden har — the dog obeys the

call. -abel appealable. -ant apellant. -asjon appeal, appealing. -asjonsrett court of appeal. -ere appeal (til: to), lodge an appeal with.
appelsin orange. -kjerne orange-pip. -skall orange-peel. -tre orange tree.
appendicitt (blindtarmbetennelse) appendicitis.
appetitt appetite, stomach; få, gi — get, give an appetite. -lig appetizing, nice, delicate. -vekkende appetizing.
applau|dere applaud. -s applause, plaudits.
apport|ere retrieve, fetch and carry. -ør (hund som -erer) retriever.
appre|tere dress, finish. -tur dressing, finishing, finish. -turanstalt finishing-laboratory.
approb|asjon approbation, sanction. -ere approve (of), sanction. -ering, se -asjon.
aprikos apricot. -tre apricot-tree.
april April; narre en — make an April fool of one; første — All Fools' Day. aprils|narr Aprilfool. -vær April weather.
apropos by the bye, by the way, apropos; speaking of, talking of; komme — come apropos, dt. come pat.
arab|er Arabian, Arab; (hesten) Arabian horse. -erinne Arab woman. -esk arabesque. A-ia Arabia; det lykkelige — Arabia the Happy. a-isk Arabian, Arabic.
arak arrack, rack.
araméisk Aramean, Aramaic.
arbeid work; labour; (beskjeftigelse) employment; (som skal utføres) task, job; hardt — toil, drudgery, (noe utført, især åndelig) performance, production; (godt el. slett) workmanship; en forfatters -er the works of an author; de offentlige -er the public works; straff- hard labour, penal servitude; har et — fore has a work in hand; han er i — he is at (his) work; i fullt — hard at work; sette en i — set one to work; sette varer i — put goods in hand; gå på — go to work; holde en strengt til — make one work hard; det er under — it is in hand, in course of preparation; være uten — be out of work; ved sine henders — by the labour of his hands, by manual labour.
arbeide (vrb) work, labour; (strengt) toil, (som en trell) drudge; — grundig work thoroughly; — på work at, be at work on, labour at, be engaged in; — på å strive to; — seg syk fall sick from hard work; — seg fram work one's way; — seg igjennom, inn, inn i, ned osv. work one's way through, in, into, down, struggle through etc.; — seg opp (fig) work one's (own) way; — seg ut av make one's way out of.
arbeider worker, working-man, workman; (bare om legemlig) labourer; en — er sin lønn verd the labourer is worthy of his hire. -bolig labourers' dwelling, workmen's house. -forening working men's association, trades' union. -klassen labouring (or working) classes. -partiet Labour party. -saken se -spørsmålet. -samfunn, se -forening. -ske (kvinnelig —) work-woman, worker. -spørsmålet the labour question.
arbeids|anstalt workhouse. -besparende labour -saving. -dag work-day, working-day. -dyktig able to work, capable of working, able-bodied. -dyktighet working ability, faculty el. powers. -dyr working beast. -evne capacity for work. -folk labourers, workmen, operatives, workpeople. -formann foreman, overseer. -formidlingskontor employment office. -giver, -herre employer; taskmaster; (om dame) taskmistress. -giverforening employers' association. -hest work-horse, (fig) drudge. -hus (fattighus) workhouse. -innstilling strike. -klasse working-class. -klær working clothes. -kraft working power, strength to work; number of hands. -lyst love of work. -lønn wages, hire; -nen stiger wages are going up. -som work of work, wanting employment; -løse out-of-work men, unemployed; gjøre -løs throw out of work. -løshet want of employment, unemployment; -løshetsspørsmålet the question

of unemployment. **-løyse** want of employment, unemployment. **-mann** workman, labourer, working-man. **-maur** working-ant, worker-ant. **-mengd(e)** amount of work, work done. **-menneske** drudge. **-ministerium** ministry of labour. **-måte** working method. **-nedleggelse** strike.
arbeidsom industrious, hard-working, laborious. **-het** industry, laboriousness.
arbeidspose work-bag.
arbeids|priser rates of wages. **-rom** work-room, workshop; study. **-sparende** labour-saving. **-stans** stoppage of work; (fra arbeidsgivers side) lock-out. **-styrke** number of hands. **-tid** working **-hours; kort** — short hours; **etter** — en after hours; **ekstra** — overtime. **-vogn** cart, waggon. **-værelse** work-room, study.
arbitrasje (kursspekulasjon, vekselhandel) arbitrage.
arbitrær (etter skjønn) arbitrary.
areal area, stretch; (i tønner land) acreage.
arena arena.
arg wicked, bad, arrant.
arge, — **opp** (dt.) rile.
Argentin|a the Argentine, Argentina. **a–er, -sk** Argentine.
argument argument. **-asjon, -ering** argumentation, reasoning. **-ere** reason, argue.
ariadnetråd clew.
arie air, aria.
arier Aryan.
arilds tid: fra — from time immemorial.
arisk (indo-europeisk) Aryan.
aristokrat aristocrat. **-i** aristocracy. **-isk** aristocratic(al).
aritme|tikk arithmetic. **-tisk** arithmetic(al).
I. **ark** ark; **paktens** — the ark of the covenant; **Noas** — Noah's Ark.
II. **ark** (papir) sheet. **-antall** number of sheets.
arkeolog archæologist. **-i** archæology. **-isk** archæologic(al).
arkipe|lag archipelago. **A-lagus** the Archipelago.
arkitekt architect. **-onisk** architectural, architectonic. **-ur** architecture.
arkiv archives; (stedet) muniment house, record office. **-alier** archives. **-ar** archivist, keeper of the records el. archives.
arkont archon.
arktisk arctic, of the north pole.
arkvis by the sheet.
arm arm; (p. dampm.) radius; (i automobilteknikk) lever; **plass til å røre -ene** elbow-room; — **i** — arm in arm, with locked arms; **med -ene i siden** with arms akimbo; **sette -ene i siden** set (put) the arms akimbo; **kastet seg i -ene på meg** threw himself into my arms, (fig) took refuge with me; **gikk med ham under -en** walked one in arm with him; (fig) **ta en under -ene** lend one a helping hand.
armada armada; **den uovervinnelige** — the (invincible) Armada.
armatur armament.
arm|band bracelet, armlet, wristlet: **-bandsur** wrist-watch. **-bevegelse** gesture. **-bind** sling, bandage. **-brott, -brudd** fracture of an arm. **-brøst** cross-bow. **-bånd,** se **armband.**
armé army. **-befaling** general order. **-korps** army-division, army-corps.
Armen|ia Armenia. **a–er, a–erinne a–sk** Armenian.
armer|e arm. **-ing** armament.
arm|hule, -huling armpit. **-kraft** power of arm. **-ledd** brachial joint. **-lengd** length of arm.
arming (poor) wretch.
armod poverty, penury.
arm|ring bracelet, armring. **-spjeld** gusset. **-stake** branch candlestick. **-stol** arm-chair. **-stø** arm, support for the arm.
arne (poet, litt., gl. = åre, peis) hearth. **-krok** chimney corner, fireside. **-sted,** se **arne;** (fig) hot-bed, seat (**for: of**).

aroma aroma. **-tisk** aromatic.
arr scar, cicatrice, seam; (botanisk) stigma, button.
arrangement arrangement. **arrangere** arrange. **arrangør** arranger.
arrdannelse cicatrization.
arrest arrest, seizure; (på skip) embargo; (fengsel) prison, custody, confinement; **sette i** — send to prison; **belegge med** — put under an arrest, seize; **holde en i streng** — hold one a close prisoner. **arrestant** prisoner. **arrestasjon** arrest, arresting. **arrestere** arrest, apprehend, take into custody. **arrestering,** se **arrestasjon. arrest|forretning** arrest, arrestation, seizure. **-forvarer** jailer. **-hus** house of detention, lock-up. **-ordre** warrant.
arret scarred.
arrieregarde rear, rearguard.
arrig cross, ill-tempered, ill-natured; — **kvinne** ill-tempered woman, shrew, vixen, termagant. **-het, -skap** ill-temper, ill-nature.
arrivere (ankomme; hende) arrive.
arroganse arrogance, arrogancy. **arrogant** arrogant, insolent.
arsenal arsenal.
arsenikk arsenic. **-forgiftning** arsenic-poisoning. **-holdig** arsenical, arsenic.
art (vesen) nature, natural disposition; (slags) sort, kind, variety; (mots. slekt) species; (måte) fashion, way.
arte seg (slå an) grow, thrive; — **seg godt** promise well, turn out well.
arterie artery. **-blod** arterial blood.
artesisk brønn artesian well.
artianer candidate for matriculation degree.
artig courteous, polite; (komisk) funny; **vær så** —, **se vær så god. -het** civility, courtesy, politeness.
artik|kel article; (post) item, head, count; (avdelinger av et skrift) section, clause; (blad-) article, paper, (kort) paragraph. **-ulasjon** articulation. **-ulere** articulate.
artilleri artillery, ordnance; **ridende** — horse a. **-løytnant** lieutenant in the artillery, (mar) gunnery lieutenant. **-st** artillerist, artillery-man; (mar) gunner.
artisjokk, -skokk artichoke.
artist artiste. **artistisk** artistic.
artium: eksamen **artium** matriculation degree.
artiumsoppgave matriculation paper.
arts|forskjell difference in kind. **-merke** specific character. **-navn** specific name.
arv inheritance; heritage, (etter foreldre) patrimony; **tiltre en** — enter upon an inheritance; **gå fra** — og **gjeld** renounce inheritance and debts; **få i** — succeed to; **gå i** — **til** descend to; **gi til** — og **eie** bestow in full property; **ved** — by inheritance.
arve inherit, succeed to; — **en** be the heir of one; — **etter** inherit from (of).
arve (plante) chickweed; **rød** — red (el. scarlet) pimpernel.
arve|avgift legacy el. succession duty. **-berettigelse,** se **-rett. -berettiget** entitled to inheritance, capable of inheriting. **-fiende** hereditary el. born enemy. **-fiendskap** hereditary enmity. **-følge** order of inheritance, (om konge o. l.) succession, (p. gods) entail. **-følgekrig** war of succession. **-gods** inheritance, heirloom, heritage, patrimony. **-later** testator, bequeather, devisor. **-laterske** testatrix.
arvelig heritable, inheritable, hereditary; **er** — **i visse familier** runs in families. **-het** inheritability, (naturh.) heredity. **-hetsloven** the law of heredity.
arve|lodd hereditary share, share of (an) inheritance. **-lov** law of succession. **-løs** disinherited; **gjøre** — disinherit, cut off with a shilling. **-løshet** disinherison, disinheritance. **-prins** heir presumptive (to the throne). **-rett** right of inheriting el. succession, heirship. **-rettslige**

regler rules of inheritance. **-rike** hereditary monarchy. **-sete** family seat. **-skifte** partition of an inheritance. **-stykke** heirloom. **-synd** original sin; **stygg som -en** as ugly as sin.

arving heir, inheritor; (kvinnelig) heiress, inheritress, inheritrix; — **etter loven** heir-at-law; **rettmessig** — heir-apparent; **for øyeblikket nærmeste** — heir presumptive; **innsatte ham til min** — instituted him my heir.

arvtaker inheritor, heir.

A/S, se **aksjeselskap.**

asbest asbestos, asbestus.

ase toil; — **seg fram** toil onwards.

asen (gl., bib. = **esel,** men brukes som skjellsord) ass. **-inne** she-ass.

aseptisk aseptic.

asetylén (slags lysgass) acetylene.

asfalt asphalt, asphaltum. **-ere** asphalt, bitumenize.

asia (pl. **-ier**) preserved cucumber, sweet pickles.

Asia Asia. **a-t** Asiatic. **a-tisk** Asiatic, Asian; **A-tisk Tyrkia** Turkey in Asia.

asjett (dessert) plate.

I. **ask** (tre) ash; **av** — ash, ashen.

II. **ask,** se **eske.**

aske ashes (i sms. og kjemi også ash f. eks. bone-ash; også: the ash of a cigar); **legge i** — lay in (el. reduce to) ashes; **oppstod av -n** rose again from its ashes; **forvandlet til** — incinerated; **komme fra -n i ilden** fall out of the frying-pan into the fire.

aske|beger ash-cup, ash-tray. **-farget, -grå** ashy, ash-coloured, ash-gray, ash-white, ashenwhite, cinereous. **-lut** lye of ashes. **-onsdag** Ash-Wednesday. **A-pott** Cinderella. **-regn** shower of ashes.

askese asceticism.

aske|skuff (i kakkelovn) ash-pan. **-spann** ash -bucket. **-urne** cinerary urn, funeral urn.

asket, asketisk ascetic.

asketre ash; ash-wood.

asor|isk Azorian; **A-ene** the Azores, the Western Islands.

asovsk: Det a-e hav the Sea of Azov el. Azoff.

asp, se **osp.**

asparges asparagus. **-bed** bed of asparagus. **-hode** asparagus top.

aspir|ant aspirant, aspirer, candidate. **-asjon** aspiration. **-ere** aspirate; — **til, etter** aspire to.

assessor judge.

assimilasjon assimilation. **assimilere** assimilate (med: to); — **seg** assimilate.

assistanse assistance.

assist|ent assistant. **-ere** assist. **(ved:** at el. in).

associé partner.

assortere assort. **assortiment** assortment; variety.

assosiere associate.

assuranse insurance, assurance, (sjø-) underwriting, marine insurance; **besørge** — effect insurance; **tegne** — effect i., (om assurandør) underwrite the i. **-polise** insurance policy. **-premie** premium of i. **-selskap** i.-company. **-sum** sum insured. **-svik** defraudation on the underwriters. **-vesen** insurance matters. **assurandør** insurer, assurer, (især sjø-) underwriter, assu-rer|e insure, assure; **der var ikke -t** there was no insurance.

assyr|er Assyrian. **A-ia** Assyria. **-iolog** Assyriologist. **-iologi** Assyriology. **-isk** Assyrian.

asters aster.

astigmatisk astigmatic.

astigmatisme (bygningsfeil i øyet) astigmatism.

astma asthma. **-tiker, -tisk** asthmatic.

astrakan(skinn) Astrakhan fur, astrakhan.

astral|lampe astral lamp. **-legeme** astral body. **-ånder** astral spirits.

astro|log astrologer. **-logi** astrology. **-nom**

astronomer. -nomi astronomy. **-nomisk** astronomical.

asur azure. **-blå** azure.

asyl asylum, (place of) refuge. **-barn** charity child. **-skole** charity school. **-rett** the right of an asylum.

I. **at** (konj) that; **det skulle da være at** unless indeed; **jeg tviler ikke på at** I do not doubt but; **jeg vet at han er ærlig** I know that he is honest el. I know him to be honest; **det undrer meg at du kom** I wonder at your coming; **den omstendighet at han kom** the circumstance el. fact of his coming; **følgen av at han kom** the consequence of his coming; **det er ikke noe galt i at han gjør dette** there is no harm in his doing this; **nyheten er for god til at jeg kan tro den** the news is too good for me to believe it.

II. **at** (adv.) **bære seg at** do, go about it, manage; **du bærer deg galt at** you go about it the wrong way; **hjelpes at** assist (el. help) one another; **følges at** go (fig. ogs. run) together; **skilles at** part, separate, sunder.

atavisme atavism, reversion. **atavistisk** atavistic.

atel|sme atheism. **-st** atheist. **-stisk** atheistic(al).

atelier studio.

Aten Athens.

Atene Athene, Athena.

aten|er, -ienser, (iens)erinne, -(iensi)sk Athenian.

atferd (oppførsel) conduct, behaviour, demeanour, deportment: (handlemåte) proceeding(s).

atkomst (sted) access: gl. (rett) title, right, claim. **-brev, -dokument** title-deed, muniment.

Atlanterhavet the Atlantic (ocean).

atlas (samling av karter el. bilder) atlas.

atlask satin.

atlet athlete. **atletikk** athletics. **atletisk** athletic.

atmosfær|e atmosphere. **-isk** atmospheric(al:) **-iske forstyrrelser** (i radio) atmospherics, strays, X's.

atom atom. **-isk** atomic. **-teorien** the atomic theory. **-vekt** atomic weight.

atskille part, separate, divide, sever, disjoin, disunite; (kjemi) decompose; (skjelne imellom) distinguish, discriminate; — **seg** (avvike) differ; **atskillelse** separation, disjunction, disunion; (is. kirkelig) schism.

atskillig considerable, no little; — (nøytralt) several things; — (adv) considerably, rather, not a little; — **flere** several more; **-e** several, divers, various, sundry; **(-e** personer) not a few people.

atskilt separate, distinct, apart.

atsplitte scatter, disperse; (hær) rout. **-lse** scattering, dispersion.

atspre|(de) disperse, scatter, (sinnet) divert, amuse; (tankene) divert, distract; — **seg** divert, amuse, recreate oneself. **-delse** scattering etc.; dispersion; distraction; (forlystelse) diversion, recreation, relaxation; (pl) amusements. **-dt** scattered etc.; (fig) absent, abstracted. **-dthet** absence of mind.

atstadig demure, staid, steady, stable, sedate sober. **-het** demureness, staidness, steadiness.

att og fram backwards and forwards, to and fro, up and down.

attaché attaché, agent; **militær-** military agent. **attachere** attach.

atten eighteen; **-de** eighteenth.

attentat attempt; **gjøre** — **på en, mot ens liv** make an attempt on one's life, attempt one's life, try to kill one.

atter again, once more; — **andre** still others, others still; — **og** — again and again, over and over again.

attersting backstitch.

attest certificate, testimonial. **-ere** certify (med

eller uten to), attest. -ering certification, attestation.
Atti|ka Attica. a-ker Attic. attisk Attic: — salt Attic salt, Attic wit.
attityde attitude.
attmed beside, next to.
attpå in addition, into the bargain; det får du — that's thrown in; komme — come behind. -giving the giving of a premium. -sleng hangers -on.
attraksjon attraction.
attrap|p trap, take-in. -(p)ere seize, catch.
attributiv attributive. attributt attribute.
attrå (vrb) desire, covet, aspire to, yearn for.
attrå (subst) desire (etter: of), craving, yearning, longing (etter: for, etter å: to).
attråverdig desirable, covetable.
au! oh! oh dear!
au (òg) also, too.
audiens audience: få — hos get an a. of. -værelse audience room, presence chamber.
audion (radiolampe) Audion, two-electrode valve detector.
auditorium lecture room; (tilhørerne) auditory, audience, attendance.
auditør Solicitor to the Royal Army and Navy.
augiasstall Augean stables.
augur augur.
august (the month of) August; (fornavnet) A. Augustus. Augusta Augusta. augustéisk Augustan.
auke (vrb) add to, enlarge, increase; eke (out).
auke (subst) growth, increase.
auksjon (sale by) auction, (public) sale, auction sale; selle ved — sell by a.; sette til — put up to a. auksjonarius auctioneer. auksjons|bridge auction bridge. -dag day of the sale. -forvalter director of public sales (in a district), official auctioneer. -gebyr, se -omkostninger. -hammer auctioneer's hammer; komme under -en go to the hammer. -katalog sale catalogue. -kondisjoner conditions of sale. -lokale auction room, sale-room. -omkostninger auctioneer's fees. -plakat notice of sale. -pris auction-price. -regning auction-bill. -sum amount of an auction.
aur gravel.
aure trout.
au revoir au revoir, (good-bye) till we meet again.
aurikkel auricula, bear's ear.
ause (vrb) bale, dip, scoop; (av brønn og fig.) draw; — lens bale out.
ause (subst) scoop; (til suppe) ladle. -kar baler, dipper, scoop.
auspisier auspices; under hans — under his auspices.
Australi|a (fastlandet med omliggende øyer) Australasia; (Nyholland) Australia. a-er, a-erinne australsk Australian.
autentisk authentic(al).
autobiograf autobiographer. -i autobiography.
autodafé auto-da-fé, (pl. autos-da-fé).
autodidakt self-taught man.
autograf autograph. -samler, -samling collector (collection) of autographs.
autokrat autocrat. -i autocracy. -isk autocratic.
automat automaton (pl. -ta el. -tons), automatic machine, penny-in-the-slot machine. -isk automatic(al), self-acting.
automobil motor-car, (dt) car: (i Amerika brukes is. automobile) -drosje taxi. -ist motorist, automobilist. -kjører chauffeur: motorman: kvinnelig -kjører chauffeuse. -kjørsel motoring. -omnibus motor-bus.
autor author. -isasjon authorization. -isere authorize, empower. -isert authorized, licensed -itet authority. -itetstro unquestioning faith.
autotransformator (i radio) auto-jigger, auto-transformer.
av (prep): (om den handlende person i pas-

siv) by; han er aktet — enhver he is respected by every one; kjenne en — navn know one by name: snekker av profesjon a joiner by trade: ordbok av Webster dictionary by W.; bilder av italienske mestere pictures by Italian masters; f o r; gifte seg av kjærlighet marry for love; av mange grunner for many reasons; f r o m; jeg har hørt det av min søster I have heard it from my sister; blek av angst pale from anxiety; erfare av learn from (el. of); lide av suffer from; av frykt for from (el. for) fear of; av nødvendighet from necessity; i n: av størrelse, år in size, years; en av hundre one in a hundred; det er rosverdig av Dem it is praiseworthy in you; o f: en av dem som one of those who; av viktighet of importance; i kraft av by el. in virtue of; ved hjelp av by means of; bygd av tre built of wood; konge av Norge king of Norway; Deres brev av 10de your letter of the 10th; en venn av min far a friend of my father's; av seg selv of oneself, of one's own accord, spontaneously; o f f: hjelpe en av hesten help one off his horse; vask såpa av ansiktet (ditt) wash the soap off your face; o n: bli feit av fatten on; avhengig av dependent on el. of; fem av hundre (i rente) five on the hundred; av den grunn on that account; o u t o f: langt av veien far out of the way; ni av ti nine out of ten; av fortvilelse out of desperation; t o: en venn, fiende, slave av (fig) a friend, enemy, slave, to; w i t h: av hele mitt hjerte with all my heart; rød, svart av red, black with; halvdød av tretthet, latter halv dead with fatigue, laughter; — gangen = om g. at a time. -gårde se av sted; — veien se veil
av (adv.) fra først av from the first; fra barn av from a child; han vil (bli) av med he wants to be rid of; av og til now and then, occasionally, ever and anon, from time to time; av med hattene! hats off; gå av go el. get off; fargen går av the coulor rubs off.
avanse profit, advantage, advance. -ment advancement, promotion, preferment. avansere (rykke fram) advance: (forfremmes) be promoted el. preferred, rise (in the service).
avantgarde vanguard, van.
avart variety.
avbalansere balance, poise.
avbarke bark, strip.
avbe ask el. beg pardon for.
avbeite browse (upon), graze off.
avbenytte have the use of. -lse use: etter -lsen when done with.
avbestill|e annul, cancel, countermand. -ing countermand, counterorder.
avbetal|e pay off; (avgjøre) liquidate. -ing paying off; (konkret) part-payment, instalment: liquidation, discharge; ta på — take on account, by anticipation el. in part-payment.
avbikt apology; gjøre — apologize (hos en for; to one for).
avbil|de (billedh.) form, frame, model; (alm og fig) portray, delineate, draw, picture, image. -ding representation, drawing, delineation, (bare konkret) picture.
avbinde bind; (vorte) tie off; (tømmer) trim; — et hus join the timberwork of a house, put up the framework of a house.
avblek|e bleach out, fade. -et discoloured, (også fig) faded.
avblomstr|e, se blomstre av; en -et skjønnhet a faded beauty.
avblås|e blow off. -nings|apparat blow-off apparatus. -ventil escape valve.
avbrekk detriment, prejudice, injury, loss; gjøre — i injure, prejudice. avbrekke (mest i pf. part. avbrukket, -ekket.) break off.
avbren|ne, se brenne av; -t rødvin mulled (el. burnt) claret.
avbrudd interruption, intermission. avbrutt broken; (bratt) abrupt, (i bruddstykker) fragmentary; (adv) interruptedly, by fits and starts.

2 — Norsk-engelsk.

avbryt|e (en tilstand, f. eks. taushet) break; (en handling, f. eks. samtale) interrupt; (opphøre med) discontinue; (for en tid) suspend; — **bekjentskapet** cut the acquaintance; — **den elektriske strøm** cut off (el. break off) the electric current; — **ham i hans tale** interrupt him (in his speech); — **all omgang med ham** cut him dead, discontinue all intercourse with him. **-else** breaking off; interruption, intermission, break.

avbud countermessage, counterorder; **sende** — send an excuse; withdraw an invitation; **det kom** — **fra ham** he sent an excuse.

avbygd remote (el. sequestered) district.

avbøte parry, bear (el. ward) off.

avbøy|e deflect, turn off, bias. **-ning** deflection, turn.

avdal, se **avbygd.**

avdamp|e air; (få de flytende stoffer i en oppløsning til å fordampe, koke inn) evaporate. **-(n)ing** airing; evaporation.

avdanket discarded, superannuated.

avdekk|e uncover, lay open; (statue) unveil. **-ing** uncovering, exposure.

avdel|e (dele) divide, part, partition, parcel; (avsondre) partition off. **-ing** division, partition; (av forretning) branch, department; (rom) compartment; (av skrift) section; (av tropper, flåte) detachment; (av sonate) movement. **-ings-kontor** branch office, suboffice. **-ingssjef** head of department.

avdem|me dam up; — **for** dam out. **-ning** damming (up); (konkret) dam.

avdempe subdue, soften (el. tone) down; fig ogs. mitigate, qualify.

avdisputere (litt.) argue out of; **jeg lar meg ikke** — **min tro på** I am not to be argued out of my belief in.

avdra (avbetale) pay in part. **avdrag** part-payment; (fradrag, rabatt) deduction, abatement, allowance. **-svis** by instalments.

avdrift deviation, (mar) drift.

avdø die; — **fra verden** die to the world; **-d** deceased, departed, defunct; **den -de** the deceased, departed; **-de Dr. Rosen** the late Dr. Rosen; **min -de mann** my late el. poor husband.

ave—maria Ave(-Maria).

avers obverse (side).

aversjon aversion.

aver|tere advertise. **-tissement** advertisement: **rykke inn et** — advertise.

avesk|e (gl. = avkreve) **en noe** exact, demand, require (st. from one).

avfall (det som faller av i alm.) refuse, waste; (ved slaktn.) offal(s); (i husholdn.) broken victuals, leavings (pl); (av metall) refuse, dross, residue, scum, (av lær) cuttings; (mar) falling off; (mar) **støtt for** —! nothing off; keep her to! **avfalls|dynge** refuse-heap, scrap pile. **-produkt, -stoff** residual product.

avfarende bredde, lengde latitude from, longitude from; — **plass** (mar) departure.

avfarg|e decolour. **-ing** decoloration, discoloration. **-ingsmiddel** decolorant.

avfatte draw up, compose, indite, word, couch. **-lse** drawing up, composition, framing, wording.

avfeie sweep off; **-ende** careless, flippant, slighting, cavalier.

avfeldig decayed, decrepit, infirm, breaking (up). **-het** decay, infirmity, decrepitude.

avferdige dispatch, expedite, send off; put el. turn one off, dismiss, dispose of.

avfil|e touch up (with a file); file off, (glatte) burnish. **-ing** filing: (fig) brush; (filspon) filings (pl).

avfinne|seg compound, make a composition, come to an agreement, come to terms (med: with). **-lse** (litt.) composition, agreement. **avfinnelsessum** sum of acquittance.

avfolke depopulate, dispeople, unpeople.

avfolking depopulation, unpeopling.

avfyr|e fire, let off, discharge. **-ing** firing, letting off, discharge.

avfød|e (litt.) give rise to, foster.

avfør|e en noe divest (one of); — **seg** divest oneself of; pull off: purge; **-ende** aperient, evacuant, cathartic; **-ende middel** aperient etc. **-ing** motion (of the bowels), purgation (ogs. konkret) evacuation, stool.

avgang setting off, start, departure; (avsetning) sale; (forminskelse) decrease, abatement; **dødelig** — decease, (om fyrster) demise. **avgangs|bevis** discharge. **-eksamen** final examination. **-merke** starting post. **-ordre** order to leave. **-perrong** departure platform. **-signal** starting signal. **-stasjon** station of departure. **-tid** time of departure.

avgi (yte) yield, produce; (avlevere) deliver, hand, render, give up; — **en erklæring, betenkning** make a declaration, give an opinion; — **et bevis** furnish a proof; — **en kjennelse** return a verdict; — **sin stemme** vote, give one's suffrage.

avgift (leie) rent; (skatt) tax; (kommunal) rate; (toll-) duty; (for benyttelse av patent; til forfatter) royalty. **avgifts|fri** rent-free, duty-free. **-frihet** exemption from rent el. duty. **-pliktig** liable to rent el. duty; **den -pliktige tonnsdrektighet** the register tonnage.

avgjort (se avgjøre); **en** — **sak** (kjensgjerning) absolute certainty, positive fact; **anse for** — take for granted; **dermed er den sak** — and there's an end of it; **hans skjebne er** — his fate is sealed.

avgjære cease fermenting.

avgjøre (ordne, betale) settle; (fullende) finish; (bestemme) decide, ascertain, determine; **det avgjør saken** that decides (el. settles) it; **et argument som ikke avgjør spørsmålet** an argument indecisive of the question.

avgjørelse settlement, finishing: decision.

avgjørende (f. eks. om virkning, svar, slag) decisive, conclusive, final; **i en** — **tone** in a peremptory (el. decisive) tone; — **betydning** vital importance; **den** — **stemme** the casting vote el. voice; **i det** — **øyeblikk** at the critical moment; — **prøve** crucial test; — **for** conclusive of.

avglans reflection, resplendence, lustre.

avglatte smooth, polish.

avgnage gnaw off.

avgni (gni vekk) rub off; (gjøre rein) rub up, clean by rubbing.

avgrene branch off (el. out).

avgrense bound, mark the bounds of, limit.

avgrunn abyss, gulf, precipice; (fig) **forder-velsens** — the gulf of destruction.

avgrøde (gl.) (subst) crop, produce, production.

avgrøft|e ditch (off), drain. **-ning** ditching, drainage.

avgud false god, idol. **avguderi** idolatry; **drive** — **med** idolize, idolatrize. **avguderisk** idolatrous. **avguds|bilde** idol. **-dyrkelse** idolatry, worship of idols. **-dyrker** idolater, worshipper of idols. **-tjeneste** worship of idols.

avgå (dra bort) go, set off, depart, start, leave, sail; (fra embete) retire; — **til leave for;** — **ved døden** die, depart this life; **-tte skip** sailings, departures; **den -ende regjering** the outgoing ministry.

avhandl|e treat of, discuss. **-ling** discussion, (konkret) treatise, essay, dissertation, paper (om: on); (kort, gudelig) tract.

avhaspe wind off, (også fig) reel off.

avhende dispose of, make over, alienate, abalienate. **avhendelig** alienable, (ikke båndlagt) unentailed. **avhendelighet** alienability. **avhendelse** alienation, disposal.

avheng|e av depend on, hang upon. **-ig** dependent (av: on); **-ige av hverandre** (mutually) interdependent. **-ighet** dependence. **-ighetsfor-**

hold position of dependence, state of dependence.

avhente call for, go for, fetch; **la — send for; pakker -s overalt i byen** parcels collected in all parts of the town.

avhjelpe (et onde) remedy, set (to) right; (skade, klage) redress; (mangel, trang) supply, relieve, meet.

avhold abstention.

avholde en fra noe prevent, hinder, withhold, restrain one, hold el. keep one back, from st; **— forsamlinger, møter** o. l. hold assemblies, meetings etc.; (merk) **— utgiftene** defray the expenses; **— seg fra** abstain from, forbear. **-lse** holding, etc. **-n, -nde** abstemious, abstinent. **-nhet** abstemiousness, abstinence, abstention.

avholds|folk teetotalers, total abstainers. **-forening** teetotal society. **-hotell** temperance hotel. **-lokale** temperance hall. **-løfte** (total abstinence) pledge. **-mann** teetotaler, total abstainer. **-saken** the cause of (total) abstinence.

avholdt liked, popular, in favour, a favourite; **ikke —** disliked, unpopular; **meget — av a** great favourite with; **gjøre — blant** endear to.

avhøre hear; examine. **avhøring** hearing, examination.

avhøste harvest; **ha -t** have done harvesting.

avhøv|le plane (smooth); plane off, away; (fig) polish. **-ling** planing etc.; polishing.

aviasjon, se **aviatikk.**

aviatik|er aviator. **-k** aviation.

avind (nag) rancour, grudge. **-syk** envious. **-syke,** se **avind.**

I. **avis** (merk) advice.

II. **avis** newspaper, journal, public print, paper; **holde en —** take in a paper; **sette noe i —en** insert st. in the newspaper, advertise. **-and** (newspaper) hoax. **-artikkel** article, (kort) paragraph.

avis|bud newsman, newsboy. **-ekspedisjon** newspaper office.

avisere advise.

avisfeide paper war, newspaper polemics.

avislitteratur journalistic literature.

aviso|brev letter of advice. **-damper** despatch steamer. **-fartøy** despatch vessel.

avis|papir (papir av aviser) old newspapers. **-polemikk,** se **-feide. -redaktør** editor of a newspaper. **-referent** reporter. **-salg** sale of newspapers. **-skriveri** writing in the papers. **-spalte** newspaper column. **-seller** newsvender, newsvendor, newsagent, seller of newspapers.

a vista (merk) at sight.

avjaske slur over, perform carelessly, scamp; **-t** (om klær) shabby, the worse for wear.

avkall renunciation, release, quitclaim; **gi — på** give up, relinquish (one's claim to), resign, waive, (skriftlig) sign away.

avkap|pe cut (off), lop (off). **-ning** cutting off

avkaste (litt.) cast el. throw off; (innbringe) yield, produce; **— en byrde** throw el. fling off a burden; **— åket** shake off the yoke.

avkjemme comb off; **-t hår** combings.

avkjøl|e cool, refrigerate; (i is) ice; **-es** cool. **avkjøler, avkjølingsapparat** refrigerator. **avkjøling** cooling (down), refrigeration, chilling.

avkjønne desexualise.

avkjøpe buy, purchase of el. from.

avklare clear, defecate, (vin) fine, clarify; **-t smør** clarified butter.

avklarering (mar) gi (et mannskap) sluttoppgjør, se **avregning.**

avklip|pe clip, shear, cut off.

avkle(d|e) undress, strip; (om embetsdrakt) unrobe, disrobe; (fig) expose, make an exhibition of. **-ning** undressing etc.; exposure. **-ningsrom** bathing box. **-ningsværelse** dressing room.

avknappe (litt.) (knappe av) shorten, pinch off, retrench.

avkok decoction. **-e** (gl. = utkoke, innkoke) boil out, down; **-t** (flyndre) boiled (flounder).

avkom issue, offspring, progeny.

avkop|le (dmp.) disconnect. **-lingsinnretning** disconnecting gear. **-lingsmuffe** disconnecting strap.

avkort|e (korte av) abridge, abbreviate, shorten; deduct, curtail, retrench. **-et kjegle** truncated cone.

avkreft|e weaken, enfeeble, enervate; (bevis o. l.) weaken (the force of), invalidate. **-else** debility, enervation, enfeeblement, exhaustion; invalidation. **-et** weakened etc., exhausted, languishing.

avkreve demand (el. require el. request from (el. of) ask (one for st. el. st. of one) call upon one to give (show, pay) st.

avkristne dechristianize, unchristianize.

avkrok (by-)corner, by-place, recess, out-of -the-way-hole.

avkrysse check, check off.

avl (grøde, avling) crop, produce, growth (kveg-)breeding, (unger) drop, get.

avlagre (oppbevare på lager, forbedre ved lagring) store; **-t** (om varer) well seasoned.

avlagt (part), se **avlegge.**

avlang oblong.

avlat indulgence. **-sbrev** letter of indulgences. **-skremmer** seller of indulgences (el. pardons).

avle (frembringe) beget, procreate; (mest om dyr og fig) breed, generate; (mest fig) engender; (av jorda) raise, grow; **— barn** beget children; **i min hage kan det -s gode poteter** my garden will grow good potatoes. **-dyktig** procreative, able to procreate. **-dyktighet** capability of procreation, procreative power.

avled|e draw el. turn off, turn away; (tanker) divert; (vann) carry off; (lynet) conduct; (ord) derive. **— mistanken** divert suspicion; **— oppmerksomheten fra seg selv** divert attention from oneself. **-er** conductor. **-et ord** derivative, formative. **-et taktart** compound time. **-ning** deviation; (grammatikk) derivation, (avledet ord) derivative; (til jorda) earthing; (av vann) drainage. **-ningsendelse** derivational ending, formative. **-ningskanal** drain. **-ningsrør** discharge pipe. **-ningstegn** (mus), se **fortegn.**

avlegge lay down, put down, put off; (henlegge) put by, lay aside; **— (avgangs)eksamen** graduate; **— en beretning om** give (in) a report of; **— en et besøk** pay one a visit; **— ed** take an oath, take one's oath; **— et løfte** make a vow; **— (kloster)løftet** take the vows; **— det gamle menneske** put off the old man; **— en prøve på** give a proof of; **— regnskap** give an account; **— en tilståelse** make a confession; **— en vane** leave off el. unlearn a habit; **— vitnesbyrd** bear witness. (om: to); **avlagte klær** cast off el. left off clothes.

avlegger (stikling) cutting, layer.

avlegs antiquated, behind the age; obsolete, out of date; **bli — grow** out of date, out of fashion.

avleir|e deposit; **— seg** settle, form layers. **-ing** statification.

avles|e read (off); (om panteobligasjon) se avlyse. **— på termometeret** read the thermometer. **-ning** reading.

avless|e unload, discharge, unlade. **-ing** unloading.

avlever|e deliver, leave; **— et brev på posthuset** deliver, leave el. drop a letter at the post. **-ing** delivery.

avling procreation; (årsgrøden) crop.

avlire grind off.

avlive put to death, deprive of life, slay, murder. **-lse** (sj.) putting to death, slaying, murder.

avlokke coax el. wheedle out of, draw from; **— ham en tilståelse** elicit a confession from him.

avls|bruk breeding farm, (særl. om hester) stud farm. **-dyr** breeder, breeding (el. brood) stock. **-hoppe** brood-mare. **-løp** produce-stakes. **-stasjon,** se **-bruk. -valg** (natural) selection.

avluk|ke (subst) closet; (innhegning) enclosure. **avlure en noe** find out st. (by watching one), trick out of: — **en en hemmelighet** worm el. fish a secret out of one.

avluse cleanse from lice.

avlyd modification of the radical vowel.

avlys|e cancel, declare off; revoke; — **en panteobligasjon** cancel a mortgage (legally notified); — **et foredrag, et møte, et salg** cancel a lecture, a meeting, a sale. **-ning** cancelling.

avlønn|e pay. **-ing** pay, salary.

avløp discharge, issue, outfall, outlet, drain: (fig) vent, outlet; **gi — for sine følelser** give vent to one's feelings. **avløpning** (mar.) launch. **-sslede** sliding ways.

avløps|grøft, -kanal drain. **-hull** tap-hole. **-kran** escape valve. **-renne** gutter. **-rør** wastepipe: ajutage, adjutage. **-tut** spout.

avløs|e (vakt, arbeid) relieve; (om avgift) commute; (fig) (følge på) succeed, displace, follow, supersede; — **vakten** relieve the watch. **-er** reliever; successor. **-ning** relief; commutation. **-ningssum** (merk) sum paid in commutation. **-ningstid** time of relief.

avlåse lock (up).

avmag|re emaciate. **-ring** emaciation. **-ringskur** treatment for reducing weight, reducing treatment.

avmakt feebleness, debility, impotence; (besvimelse) swoon, faint; **falle i** — fall into a swoon, faint.

avmarsj marching off, march, departure. **avmarsjere** march (off), depart.

avmeie cut, reap.

avmektig (kraftløs) powerless, impotent, (svak) faint, feeble, weak; fainting, in a fainting fit, in a swoon. **-het** impotence.

avmerke mark out (cl. off), beacon.

avmønst|re discharge, pay (up el. off). **-ring** discharge, paying-up.

avmålt measured, formal; **med -e skritt** with measured steps. **-het** (litt.) formality.

avparere parry; (et spørsmål) parry.

avpass|e adapt (etter: to), suit, fit, adjust, proportion. **-ing** adaptation, suiting, jvf. **tilpasse,** etc.

avpatruljere patrol.

avpillet (mager) emaciated, thin.

avpress|e press out, squeeze out; (fig) — **en noe** extort, force, wring st. from one. **-ing** (jvf. utpressing) pressing etc.; extortion.

avprosse (mil) unlimber.

avpussing cleaning; finish; **en siste** — the finishing (el. last) touches.

avregning account, settling of account, final accounts, settlement. **gjøre — med** quit scores with.

avreise (vrb) depart, start, set out, leave **(til:** for). **avreise** (subst) departure outset.

avret|te (dressere (dyr), særl. til kunststykker) train, (hest) break in; (mur) level; (maskin) adjust; (tømmer) side. **-ting, -telse** (gl. = dressur) training.

avrigge unrig, dismantle.

avring(n)ing (telefon) ring-off.

avriss (gl.) (tegning, særl. i omriss, konturer) sketch, outline, rough-draught, (mat. og annen konturtegning) diagram. **-e** sketch, rough-draw an outline of.

avriv|e tear off, pull off; rend off; strike (a match). **-ning** tearing etc.; **kald — a** wet blanket. **-ningsblokk** block-notes, block-book. **-ningskalender** tear-off calender.

avrund|e round (off); **-et** (om stil) well rounded. **-ing** rounding.

avrust|e disarm. **-ning** disarming, disarmament.

avsats (hylle i bergveggen) ledge; (trappe—) landing (-place), resting-place; (ark) break, offset, setoff.

avsavn lack, want, deprivation.

avse afford, save, do without, spare; — **til** spare for; — **tid til å** make el. find time to; **avsett fra** without taking into consideration; independent of, apart from, aside from.

avseil|e sail; — **fra** sail from, leave. **-ing** sailing; **før -ingen** before sailing. **-ingsflagg** signal for sailing, blue peter. **-ingsordre** sailing orders. **-ingstid** time of sailing.

avsend|e forward, send (off), dispatch; (med skip) ship; (som befullmektiget) delegate. **-else, -ing** dispatch, shipment, sending. **-er** sender, dispatcher; (avskiper) shipper; (i radio) transmitter. **-ernøkkel** (i radio) manipulating key.

avsetning sale; amputation; sediment, deposit; (juridisk) sequestration; **ha, finne — sell; finner lett — sells** readily, meets with a ready sale, finds a ready market, sells well; **finner fremdeles god —** remains in favour.

avsette (fra embete) remove; dismiss, discard, discharge, deprive of office; (konge) depose, dethrone; (selle) dispose of, sell, put off, find a sale for; (merke o. l.) leave; (på kart) mark out, lay down, (mar) prick; (kjemisk) deposit; (typografisk) set up.

avset|telig removable; deposeable; saleable, vendible, marketable, merchantable. **-telighet** removability; saleableness. **-telse** removal, deprivation of office; deposition, dethronement; (foreløpig) suspension; marking etc.; amputation.

avsi countermand, -order, put off; — **dom** give judgment, pronounce el. pass sentence.

avsides remote, retired, out-of-the-way; (adv) aside, apart; — **replikk** apart, aside.

avsile strain out.

avsindig insane, mad, crazy; (rasende) frantic; distracted, cracked, deranged, out of one's senses; **en — a** maniac, lunatic; **bli — go** mad; **gjøre — drive** to madness; (adv) insanely, frantically.

avsinn madness.

avsitte work out **(en bot:** a fine).

avsjelet exanimate, lifeless.

avskaffe abolish, do away with, discontinue, abrogate. **-lse** abolishing, abolition, abrogation, extinction.

avskal|le peel el. scale off. **-ling** peeling (off); (med.) desquamation.

avskip|e ship: **fortsette å — continue** shipments. **-er** shipper. **-ning** shipping, consignment, shipment. **-ningsdokumenter** shipping documents. **-ningssted** place of shipping. **-ningstid** time of shipment.

avskjed (farvel) leave; (avskjedigelse) dismissal, dismission, discharge; (frivillig) retirement, resignation; **ta — med** el. **fra** take leave of; **ved -en** at the leave-taking; **omfavne til —** embrace at parting; **reise uten — take** French leave; **gi — discharge,** dismiss, (sl) give the sack; **ta sin — retire** (from office), resign (one's office), leave service; **forlange sin — tender** el. give in one's resignation; **han har fått sin — i unåde** he has been dismissed in disgrace; — **på grått papir** he has been turned away with scant ceremony, has got the sack.

avskjedige dismiss, discharge, (spøkende) give the sack, (amr) quit; (soldater) discharge; (regiment) disband; **-t** dismissed etc., (som har tatt avskjed) retired.

avskjeds|ansøkning, -begjæring, se **-søknad. -audiens** audience of leave. **-besøk** farewell visit, visit of leave-taking. **-beger** parting cup el. glass, grace cup. **-drikk, se -beger. -hilsen** parting salutation. **-kyss** parting kiss. **-lag** parting treat, farewell party. **-ord** parting el. valedictory word. **-pass** letter of discharge. **-preken** farewell sermon. **-sang** farewell song. **-scene** parting scene. **-stund** parting hour. **-søknad** resignation.

avskjære (skjære av) cut; (avbryte) cut; intercept; (utelukke) bar, preclude; — **en veien** intercept one; — **en tilbaketoget** cut off one's retreat; — ordet cut one short; **avskåret fra** cut off from.

avskjæring cutting off, preclusion, interception; (om dampmaskiner) cut-off, exclusion; (om parlamentsdebatt) closure; (balje) tub. **-sventil** cut-off valve.

avskoge land, (gjøre bart for skog, snauhogge) clear of woods, strip of its forests.

avskrape abrade.

avskrekke deter, frighten, scare, (mildere) discourage; **han lar seg ikke** — he is not to be daunted. **-lse** (gl.) determent, discouragement. **-lsessystemet, -lsesteorien** (jur) the deterrent system. **-nde** deterring, discouraging. (å se på) forbidding; **oppstille en som et -nde eksempel** make an example of one.

avskrift copy, transcript; **ta** — av take a copy of.

avskrive (merk): — **en sum** write off a sum, credit one for a sum.

avskriv|er copyist. **-erarbeid** copying-work. **-erfeil** error of the transcriber. **-ning** copying, etc.

avskrivning (merk) writing off; copying, transcription.

avskum (slett person) brute.

I. **avsky** (vrb) detest, abhor, abnominate, loathe.

II. **avsky** (subst) aversion (for to), abhorrence, horror (of el. for), antipathy (to), (mildere) dislike (to), disgust; **fatte, få** — take a dislike; **ha, nære** — for noe have an aversion to something, hold something in abhorrence, abhor something.

avsky(e)lig abominable, detestable, odious, hateful, disgusting, sickening. **-het** (litt.) detestableness, abominableness; (handling) atrocity.

avskygning shading; (nyanse) shade.

avskylle wash off; rinse.

avskyt|e (pf. part **avskutt**) fire (off), discharge, let off; (pil) shoot, let fly.

avskår|et part. av **avskjære; -ne blomster** cut flowers.

avslag refusal, rejection, declination, denial: — **i prisen** abatement, reduction of price, discount; **gi en** — refuse one; **få** — be refused, rejected; **bestemt** — a flat refusal.

avslip|e (slipe bort) grind off, (fig) wear off: (glatte) smooth, polish. **-(n)ing** grinding etc.

avslit|e: part. **-t** worn, torn off. **-tt av mange føtter** worn by many feet.

avslut|te (fullende) complete, bring to an end; (forhandling) close; (traktat) conclude; (lån) negotiate, contract; (bøker, regnskaper) close, balance; — **en handel** strike a bargain; — **en kontrakt** make a contract. **-ning** close, conclusion, end, winding-up, settlement; (skolers) the breaking-up of the school, the last day of school; **en trist -ning** a sad ending, a dreary finish, a dismal break-up.

avslør|e unveil. **-ing** unveiling.

avslå (en anmodning, bønn) refuse, deny; (tilbud) refuse, reject, (høfligere) decline; (angrep) repulse, repel;

avsmak (sj. = usmak) tang, disagreeable taste; (motbydelighet) distaste, disgust; dislike, disrelish; **få** — for take a dislike to; **gi en** — for give one a distaste for, disgust one with.

avsmelt|e (litt. el. geol.) melt, smelt (out, off). **-ning** melting etc.

avsnitt (av sirkel, bue) segment; (av bok) section; (tids-) period; (merk) appoint; (av festning) retrenchment.

avson|dre separate, divide; (med.) secrete, secern; (fys) isolate; — **seg** sequester oneself, (fra verden) withdraw (el. retire) from the world. **-dret** isolated, retired; **leve** — live retired, lead a retired life. **-dring** separation; secretion: isolation, sequestration, seclusion, privacy, retire-

ment, withdrawal (from the world). **avson-drings|nerver, -organer** o. fl. secretory nerves, organs etc.

avson|e (fengselsstraff) serve; (mulkt) work out. **-ing** serving; working-out.

avspeil|e (litt.) reflect, mirror; — **seg** be reflected. **-ing** reflection.

avspenning relaxation. **avspent** unbuckled, unclasped.

avsper|re bar, block up, barricade; shut out, cut off; (hamn) blockade. **-ring** blocking etc. (stang el. slå til -ring) bar. **-ringssystemet** the prohibitive system. **-ringsventil** escape-valve.

avspise en med put one off with.

avspore (få til å løpe av sporet) derail. **avsporing** derailment.

avsprettet, se sprette II.

avstamning descent, extraction.

avstand distance; (i el.) **på** — at a distance; **på lang** — in the distance, at a long distance; **på (i) en** — av at a distance of, within a distance of; **med en** — av to tommer mellom hver at intervals of two inches; **holde seg på god** — fra noe give st. a wide berth; **holde en på** — make one keep his distance; (fig) **ta** — fra keep aloof from, dissociate oneself from.

av sted away, off, along, on; — **med deg!** be off! be gone! **komme galt** — come to disaster, get into a scrape.

avstedkomme cause, occasion, bring about.

avstemme (i musikk) tune, tune up.

avstemning voting, (i parlam.) division; (hemmelig) ballot; (i radio) tuning; **sette under** — put to the vote; **komme under —, gå til** — come to the vote; **foreta** — (parl.) divide (om on); **forlange** — demand a division; **forlange skriftlig** — (ved valg) crave a poll. **avstemnings|apparat** (i radio) tuner. **-spole** turning coil.

avsteng|e (stenge ute, st. inne) shut off, cut off; (litt. og nesten bare i pf. part. = stenge (av) lock, bolt, bar. **-ning** shutting etc. **-nings-kran** stopcock.

avstigning dismounting, alighting.

avstik|ke mark out, stake off, trace; (mur) knock off; (vin) rack off. **-kende** incongruous; (om farge) glaring, gaudy; (fig) singular, excentric; **være** — imot form a contrast to. **-ker** detour, turn; (gassrør o. l.) service-pipe; (i talen) digression; **gjøre en** — til go round to.

avstive stay, (vegg) shore up, (med murverk) buttress.

avstraffe punish, chastise. **-lse** punishment, chastisement.

avstumpe curtail, dock, truncate; blunt. **-t** blunt, blunted, dull.

avstøpe cast, found. **-ning** casting etc.; (konkret) cast.

avstøve (litt., sj.) (rense for støv) dust.

avstå (overlate) resign, give up, yield up, cede, renounce, relinquish, make over; — fra (oppgi) desist from. **-else** resigning etc., resignation, renunciation, relinquishment (av land) cession. **-elsessum** consideration, compensation.

avsvale (litt.) (avkjøle) cool down.

avsverg|e abjure, forswear, renounce. **-ing** abjuration, renunciation.

avsvi singe off, scorch, parch; (om korn) blight, blast; — **(svi av) et hus** burn a house down. **-ing** singeing etc.

avsvovle (metallurg.) desulphur, desulphurate. **avsøk|e** search; (mil.) reconnoitre. **-ning** search(ing); reconnaissance.

avta (gl. = fjerne) take off, remove; (merk. = kjøpe) buy, purchase; (minske, svekkes) fall off, decay, decrease, decline, be impaired; (om sykdom, vind) abate; **ved -gende måne** when the moon is in her wane; **månen er i** — the moon is in wane. **i** — on the decline. **-ger** (kjøper) buyer, purchaser, taker. **-ing** (i kort) cut.

avtak|le (fjerne tauverk etc. fra) dismantle,

unrig; (mast) strip; **-let** (ikke i tjeneste, om krigsskip) in ordinary. **-ling** unrigging etc.

avtal|e (vrb) agree upon, appoint, concert, arrange; **-t møte** appointment, rendezvous.

avtale (subst) agreement, appointment; **det er en —** that is a bargain; **treffe — om** agree on; **treffe — om å** agree to; **treffe — med en** (om å møtes) make an appointment with one.

avtap|pet øl bottled beer. **-ning** drawing, draught.

avtekt (gl. = føderåd) annual allowance or pension reserved by one who surrenders his property to his heir.

avtjene work out; **— sin verneplikt** serve one's time as a soldier.

avtrede (subst), (privet, do) lavatory, water-closet, se **avtredelsesrom.**

avtre|(de) (fratre) resign, retire from; (trekke seg tilbake) withdraw, retire; **den -dende officer** the relieved officer. **-delse** withdrawal, resignation, cession. **-delsesrom** (på offentlige steder) lavatory, closet, water-closet (forkortet W. C.).

avtrekk (for damp etc.) outlet; proof, pull, pull-off, trigger; **hard (fig sein) i -et** hard of (el. to) pull, stiff on the trigger; **lett** (fig. **fort) i -et** quick on the trigger. **-er** trigger. **-erbøyle** trigger -guard. **-erfjær** trigger-spring.

avtrykk impression, print, copy; (særskilt) **— av** reprint from. **-ke** (trykke, gjengi, kopiere ved trykning) print, print off, strike off, take off an impression of; (segl) impress.

avtvet|te (gl. el. bib.) (vaske av, bort, v. rein) wash off; (fig) blot out. **-ning** washing (off), ablution.

avtvinge en noe (litt.) exact, extort el. wring st. from one.

avtørke, avtørre (tørke av, t. vekk) wipe up el. off el. away.

avvant med disused to, out of the habit of.

avvei wrong way; **komme på -er** go astray, go wrong, get off the right path; **føre på -er** mislead, misguide.

avveie, se **veie av** (fig) (ord o. l.) weigh; (mot hverandre) balance, poise.

avveks|lende varying, changing, alternate, various, diversified; (adv) alternately, by turns.

-ling alternation; change, variation, variety; **bringe -ling i** give variety to, relieve (the monotony el. sameness of); **til — as** (el. for) a change; **uten —** unvaried.

avvende (litt.) (vende bort, avverge) avert, prevent. **-lig** preventable. **-lighet** preventability.

avven|ne (venne av med) wean (fra, med: from); **man må få ham -t med det** he must be broken of the habit; **barnet ble -t** the child was weaned.

avvente await, wait, wait for, abide, wait to see; **— hans ankomst** wait his arrival; **— be-givenhetene** wait developments (el. events). **-nde** waiting etc., expectant.

avverge ward off, parry; (fig) (avvende) avert, (forhindre) prevent.

avvik swerving, deviation, departure, difference, disagreement; (på kompass) variation; (astronomisk) aberration.

avvik|e (vike av, skeie ut) swerve, depart, deviate, diverge; (være uoverensstemmende) differ (fra: from), disagree (with), vary. **-else** se **avvik. -ning** (mar) departure.

avvik|le unroll, unwind; **— en forretning** wind up el. settle a business. **-ling** unrolling etc.; settlement el. winding up of a business.

avvinne (tvinge fram av, avtvinge) win, compel; **— interesse** make interesting, contrive to be interested by.

avvis|e (en) refuse one admittance, turn one off, send one away, send one about his business; (bønn, forslag) reject, dismiss; (beskyldning) repudiate; (veksel) dishonour; (en påstand) overrule, (anklage) throw out (a bill), (en sak) dismiss (a cause); (barskt) rebuff, (et angrep) repel, (med forakt) pooh-pooh, scorn, spurn at, scout; **han lar seg ikke -e** he won't be rebuffed; **bli -t** (med en klage) be non-suited; **-ende** dismissing; **stille seg -ende til** decline, refuse, oppose.

avviser(stein) curbstone, corner-post. **-stolpe** direction-post. **-tavle** trespass-board.

avvisning dismissal, rejection; repudiation; rebuff. **-sdom** nonsuit. **-sgrunn** exception.

avvæp|ne disarm. **-ning** disarming, disarmament.

B

Babel Babel. **b-sk** Babylonic.

babord port; glt. larboard; **— med roret!** port the helm!

baby baby.

Baby|lon Babylon. **-lonia** Babylonia. **b-lonier** Babylonian. **b-lon(i)sk** Babylonian.

backfisch (ganske ung pike) flapper.

back (i fotball) back.

bacon (flesk) bacon.

bad bath, (i det fri) bathe; (badested) baths, watering-place, spa; (anlegg) bathing establishment; **ta et —** take a bath el. bathe; **er i —** is bathing; **reise til et —** go to a watering-place; **ligge ved —** stay (spend a season) at a watering -place.

bade bathe; (syke lemmer o. l.) foment; **— seg** bathe; **— seg i sola** bask in the sun; **— øyet i varmt vann** bathe the eye in warm water.

bade|anstalt bathing establishment. **-balje** bathing tub. **-bukser** bathing drawers. **-drakt** bathing suit, bathing dress. **-dokke** nude (china) doll. **-gjest** bather. **-hette** bathing cap. **-hotell** marine hotel. **-hus** bathing house. **-kar** bathing tub, bath. **-kone** bathwoman. **-kur** the use of mineral waters; **ta en —** take the waters. **-kåpe**

bathing cloak. **-lege** physician in (el. at el. of) a watering-place. **-mester** bath-attendant el. -man. **-reise** journey to a watering place. **-sesong** bathing-season, season at a watering-place. **-stamp,** se **-balje. -sted** (til å bade seg) bathing-place; (som man reiser til) watering-place. **-svamp** bathing sponge. **-tid** bathing-hours; se **-sesong. -tjener** bathman. **-tøfler** pair of slippers. **-ulykke** bathing fatality. **-vann** water of the bath. **-vogn** bathing-machine. **-værelse** bath-room. **bad(n)ing** bathing.

ba(d)stubad vapour bath. **ba(d)stue** bath room, bathing-room (tørkehus for korn), se **kjone.**

bagasje luggage, (amer) baggage. **-vogn** luggage-van.

bagatell trifle, bagatelle. **kaste bort tiden med -er** trifle away one's time. **-messig** frivolous, trifling.

Baiern, baiersk, bairer, se Bayern, bayersk, bayrer.

baier: en halv — (øl) a pint of Bavarian beer.

baisse decline, slump; **spekulere i -n** bear, speculate for a fall. **å baisse** bear, speculate for a fall. **baissespekulant** bear, speculator for a fall. **baissist** bear.

bajadere bayadere.
bajas buffoon, (sirkusklovn) clown. -strek buffoonery.
bajonett bayonet; med -ene på with fixed bayonets; angripe med — bayonet. -angrep bayonet-charge. -balg el. -slire bayonet scabbard.
bak (prep) behind, at the back of, in the rear of; (adv) behind; han står — det hele he is at the bottom of it.
bak (subst) back; har mange år på -en is well stricken in years; har førti år på -en is turned forty. Se også bakdel.
bakaksel (i bil) rear axle.
bak|bein hind leg; sitte på -beina sit up; reiste seg på -beina rose on his hind legs, reared; (fig) setter seg på -beina is obstinate el. unpracticable, shows fight, puts up his back. -beist ass, jack-ass, booby. -binde pinion, tie one's hands behind his back. -bord, se babord. -bygning back building. -del hind part, hinder part; (rumpe) backside, posteriors, fundament; (av bukser) the behind, the seat of one's trousers. -dør back door, pöstern.
bake bake; — brød make bread.
bakende hind part.
baken|for at the back of, in the rear of. -om behind.
bakepulver baking-powder.
baker baker; gi bakerens barn brød carry coals to Newcastle. -butikk baker's shop; gå i -butikken go to the baker's (shop); -gutt baker's apprentice.
bakeri bake-house, bakery. baker|laug baker's company. -lære: er i — is apprenticed to a baker. -mester (master) baker. -ovn (baker's) oven. -skuffe peel.
bakerst (adj) hindmost; (adv) farthest back el. behind.
bakersvenn journeyman baker.
baketter (prep) behind, in the rear of, after. baketter (adv) afterwards, too late; det tenkte han på — that was an afterthought.
bak|evje still part; creek, narrow inlet to a river. -fjøl (på en vogn) tail-board. -fot hind foot.
bakfra from behind; begynne noe — begin. st. at the wrong end.
bak fram wrong side formost, back foremost, hind before.
bak|gate backstreet, slum; -grunn (mal. og fig) background, distance; (teater) back scene; måtte tre i -en for was thrown into the shade el. eclipsed by. -grunnskulisser flat scenes, flats. -gård backyard, rear-yard; back premises; house in the backyard. -hjul hind wheel. -hode hind head. -hold ambush, ambuscade; legge seg i — for waylay; ligge i — for lie in ambush el. in wait for. -hun (outside) slab. -hånd hind hand; -hånd (kort) the younger hand; sitter (er) i — is the younger hand, the last player; ha noe i — have st. in reserve; have st. up one's sleeve.
baki (prep) in the back of; (adv) in back.
Bakindia Further (el. Farther) India.
bakk (subst) (fordekk) forecastle.
bakk (adv) (mar) aback, taken aback; brase — heave to; slå — back, reverse.
bakkanal Bacchanals. bakkant Bacchant. -inne Bacchante. -isk Bacchantic.
I. bakke (subst) hill, rising ground, rise, eminence, elevation, slope; oppover — uphill; nedover — down hill; det går nedover — med ham he is going down hill, he is sinking; (jord) ground; han ligger på -n he is lying on the ground el. on the grass.
II. bakke (brett) tray, salver; (mar) mess-kid; mess; (til å legge under) mat. bakke opp serve out el. up.
III. bakke (slags snøre) line, long-line.
bakke (vrb) (seil, maskin) back; — fyrene (benke f.) bank the fires; — av back off; — om box off.

bakke|drag range of hills. -hell declivity, slope; hill-side. -kam hill-crest. -kneik steep ascent. -land hilly country.
bakkels pastry, sweet cake.
bakkenbart whisker.
bakke|skrent, se -hell.
bakket hilly. bak|king, -ning backing.
bak|klo hind claw. -klok afterwise, afterwitted. -klokskap afterwits. -kledning back. -kropp hind-part (of the body); (p. insekt) abdomen.
Bakkus Bacchus. -dyrker Bacchanalian. -fest Bacchic feast. -stav thyrsus.
bak|lader breech-loader. -ladningsgevær, -ladningskanon breech-loading gun. -lastet backloaded. -lem hinder limb. -lengs backward(s). -lengsløp backward race. -lomme back-pocket, coattail pocket, hip-pocket. -lykt rear light, tail light. -lås: døra er gått i — the lock has slipped el. caught; dreie i — slip the lock, fix the key. -meis basket to be carried on the back. -mur back wall.
bakom behind.
bakover backwards: gå — av henrykkelse be struck all of a heap with ecstasy.
bakpart hind part; (på dyr) hind quarter.
bak|port back gate, postern. -på (adv) behind, at the back; — (prep) behind, on the back of; komme bakpå en steal upon one; så bar som — min hånd as bare as at the back of my hand. -re hind(er), rear. -rom hind compartment.
bakse (velte) tumble.
bak|sete back seat, (på motorsykkel) pillion, dicky. -side back, backside; reverse (of a coin). -slag reaction. -snakk (dial.) after talk.
bakst baking; bake, batch; (finere) pastry, pastry-work.
bak|stamn, -stavn stern.
bakste|fjøl pasteboard. -helle baxter, girdle. -kone bakeress. -ved firewood for baking.
bak|strev reaction. -strever reactionist. -stue (stue inn mot gården) back-room. -stykke back-piece, after-piece; sette nye -stykker i (bukser) reseat. -tale slander, backbite, calumniate. -talelse slander, backbiting, calumny. -ns skole the School for Scandal. -taler, -talerske slanderer, backbiter, calumniator. -talerisk, -talersk slanderous, calumnious. -tanke secret thought, underthought, mental reservation, ulterior motive, dt. little game; han kjente mine baktanker he knew my little game. -teppe back curtain, back scene.
bakterie bacterium, (pl) bacteriums el. bacteria, bacillus, (pl.) bacilli.
bakteriedyrkning cultivation of bacteria.
bakteriestamme strain of bacteria.
bakteriolog bacteriologist. -i bacteriology.
bak|trapp back stairs, b. staircase. -tropp rear, rear guard; danne -troppen bring up the rear, close the rear. -tung heavy behind, backloaded. -ut behind; slå — kick. -vaske osv. se -tale. -ved at the back of; behind. -vegg back wall. -vei secret path; gå -er use indirect practices. -vendt turned the wrong way, (fig) preposterous; (adv) the wrong way. -vendthet preposterousness.
bakverk pastry, pastry-work.
bakværelse backroom.
bal (strev) exertions, labours, toil.
balalaika (russisk sitar) balalaika.
balanse balance; holde -n keep one's balance; miste -n lose one's balance; overbalance oneself; gjøre opp — strike the b. balanseoppgjør balance -account, balance-sheet. balansere poise, (merk) balance. balanserstang balancing pole.
baldakin canopy.
balderbrå dog-gowan, May-weed.
baldyre embroider.
bale (streve) labour, strive, struggle, toil.
balg (slire) scabbard, sheath. stikke i -en sheath. dra ut av -en unsheath.
balje tub.

Balkan the Balkans. **-halvøya** the Balkan Peninsula. **-statene** the Balkan States.
balkong balcony; **-en** (teat.) the dress circle.
I. **ball** (en) ball; **slå** — play at b.; **være en kaste-** for be the sport of. **gjøre en** — (biljard) pocket (el. hole) a ball.
II. **ball** (et) ball; **på -et** at the ball; **gå på** — go to a ball.
ballade (dikt) ballade; (ståhei, halloi) row, noise; **lage** — kick up a row.
ballast ballast; **ta inn** — take in ballast; **hive -en** unballast the vessel. **legge -en til rette** trim the ballast. **-e** ballast. **-jern** kentledge. **-hiver** ballastheaver. **-hivning** unballasting. **-penger** ballastage.
ballblom globe flower.
balldame lady at a ball; partner
ball|drakt ball dress. **-dronning** queen el. belle el. reigning beauty of the ball.
balle sammen bundle up, huddle together.
I. **balle** (vare-) bale, bag; **en** — **papir** ten reams of paper.
II. **balle** (tå-, hand-)ball.
ballerina (danserinne) ballerina.
ballett ballet. **-danser** b. dancer. **-danserinne** b. dancer, b. girl. **-mester** b. master. **-personale** company of b. dancers.
ballfeber dancing fever.
ball|kavaler partner. **-kjole** ball-dress. **-kledd** dressed for a ball, in full dress, in evening dress.
ball|kort programme. **-løve** ballroom lion.
ballong balloon; (som leiketøy også) air-ball; (flaske) demijohn, carboy; (mar) balloon-jib.
ballot|ere ballot, vote by ballot. **-ering** balloting, ballot. **-erkule** ballot-ball.
ballsal ball-room.
ballsko dress shoes, pumps.
ball|spill ball playing. **-tre** bat, racket.
balsam balsam, (også fig) balm. **-duft** balsamic odour.
balsamere embalm. **balsamering** embalming, embalmment.
balsamisk balmy, balsamic, fragrant.
balstyrig ungovernable, unruly, refractory, untractable. **-het** refractoriness, unruliness.
baltisk Baltic.
balustrade balustrade.
bambus|rør bamboo. **-stokk** bamboo(-cane).
bamse he-bear: **-n** (Sir, Master) Bruin.
banal commonplace, trite, banal. **banalitet** commonplace, triteness, banality.
banan banana.
band band, tie, bord, **string;** (til pynt, ordensband) ribbon; (panne-, hår-) fillet; (anatomi) ligament; (fig.) band, bond, tie, check, restraint; **legge** — på check, restrain, lay a restraint on.
banda|sje bandage. **-sjist** bandage-maker, truss-maker.
bande band, gang.
banderole banderol(e).
bandhund bandog, bound dog.
banditt bandit, (pl) -s el. banditti, brigand.
bandjern hoopiron.
bandolær shoulder-belt, bandoleer.
bandsag band-saw, endless saw.
bandy (slags hockey) bandy.
I. **bane** (død) death, destruction; **det hogget ble hans** — that blow proved mortal to him.
II. **bane** course, path, way; (især løpebane) career; (artilleri) trajectory, track; (planets) orbit; (skøyte-) rink; (veddeløps-) course; (golf-) links; **bringe på** — start, broach, open (the subject of); **bryte en** — beat a path, open a way; **bryte seg nye -r** break new ground; **slå inn på en** — enter a course.
bane (vrb) level, smooth: **— vei over et berg** clear a way across a mountain: **-t vei** beaten el. trodden road el. track; **— seg vei** make one's way; (fig) **— veien for** pave el. prepare the way for, be the stepping-stone to.

bane|anlegg construction of railways. **-brytende** pioneering; **være** — break new ground.
banebryter pioneer.
banehogg death-blow, death-stroke.
banelegeme road-bed, (amr) rail-road track.
banemann slayer, destroyer.
banemester overseer.
banestrekning section.
banesår mortal wound.
banevokter signal-man, line-man. **-hus** signal-man's lodge.
bange (litt. =engstelig, redd) afraid, apprehensive, fearful; **gjøre en** — frighten el. intimidate one, give one a fright; **bli ikke** — don't be afraid el. alarmed; **være** — **for** (frykte) be afraid of, (for ens skyld) be uneasy, anxious on one's account el. about one, (omhyggelig) careful of; **du skal ikke være** — **for meg** never fear me; — **for hans liv** afraid for his life; — **for å** (med inf.) afraid to, (med setn.) afraid that, of -ing; **du behøver ikke å være** — **for at** you need not fear that; you need be under no apprehension that; — **anelser** apprehensions, misgivings.
banjerdekk (nederste dekk) orlop deck.
banjo (musikkinstrument) banjo. **-ist** banjoist.
I. **bank** (pryl) a thrashing, a beating.
II. **bank** (pengeinstitutt) bank; **holde** — keep the bank; **sprenge -en** break the bank. **-aksje** bank share; **-aksjer** bank stock. **-anvisning** bank-bill, check. **-assistent** clerk in a bank. **-bok** bank-book. **-bokholder** clerk in a bank. **-depositum** bank-deposit. **-direktør** bank director. **-diskonto** bank-discount.
banke (sand-, tåke-) bank; (revle) bar.
banke (= pryle) beat, thrash; (på en dør) knock, rap, tap (at a door); (om hjertet) beat, throb, palpitate; **det -r** there is a knock (at the door). **-nde tinninger** throbbing temples; — **en** thrash one, dust one's jacket; — **en spiker i** drive a nail in; — **noe inn i en** beat st. into one; — **en opp** (vekke) knock one up; — **ut** beat out.
bankekjøtt stewed beef.
bankerott (subst) bankruptcy, insolvency, failure; **spille** — become a bankrupt, fall, break. **bankerott** (adj) bankrupt, insolvent.
banketre batlet.
bankett (fest) banquet.
bankeånd rapping spirit.
bank|forretning banking business. **-funksjonær** bank-clerk. **-heftelse** mortgage (granted to the bank). **-holder** (bankør) person who keeps the bank.
bankier banker.
bankierforretning banking establishment. **-er** banking business.
banking knocking; throbbing, beating.
bank|kapital stock in bank. **-konto** bank account, banking account. **-krakk** bank smash. **-lov** bank-law. **-lån** loan in the bank. **-note** bank-note, (amr) bank bill.
bank|obligasjon bank bond.
bankobrev money letter.
bankoktroi statute of a bank.
bankopost treasure mails.
bank|provisjon banker's commission. **-revisor** bank-auditor. **-styre** governors of a bank.
bankør (bankholder) keeper of the bank.
bann ban, excommunication, interdict, anathema; **sette i** — excommunicate, anathematize. **bann|brev, -bulle** bull of excommunication.
banne swear at (one), curse; swear, use profane language; — **som en tyrk** swear like a trooper; — **på** swear to, take one's oath on.
banner banner. **-fører** standard-bearer.
banning cursing etc.
bannlyse excommunicate, anathematize; (fig) (forvise) banish. **-ning** excommunication; banishment.
bann|satt (part. av **sette**) confounded, cursed

damned; (adv) confoundedly, devilish. **–sette** excommunicate. **–settelse** excommunication. **–stråle** fulmination (of an interdict).
bantam (dverghøne) bantam. **–vekt** (nest letteste vektklasse i boksing) bantam-weight.
baptist baptist.
I. **bar** (på nåletrær) acicular leaves, pine **–needles**.
II. **bar** (utskjenkningslokale) bar.
bar (adj) bare; **med –e føtter** with his feet bare, in his bare feet; **med –e bein** bare legged; **med –t hår** bare-headed; **på –e kroppen** on the bare skin; **i –e skjorta** in his (bare) shirt; **–t lys** a naked light; **av –e medlidenhet** in pure pity; **av –e misunnelse** from mere el. sheer jealousy; **som –e fanden** confounded, devilish.
barakke hut (for soldiers), barracks.
bararmet with naked arms.
barbar barbarian. **barbari** (ukultur) barbarism; (grusomhet) barbarity, cruelty.
Barbariet Barbary.
barbarisering barbarisation.
barbar|isk barbarian, barbaric; (grusom) barbarous. **–iskhet** barbarousness, barbarity. **–isme** barbarism.
barbeint bare-legged.
barber barber (and hair-cutter).
barber|blad razor-blade.
barbere (også fig) shave; **— seg** shave.
barber|gutt barber's apprentice. **–høvl** safety razor. **–kniv** razor. **–kost** shaving brush. **–re(i)m** razor strap. **–salong** barber's and haircutter's shop. **–skilt** barber's-pole. **–skål** shaving basin, barber's plate. **–stell** shaving case. **–svenn** journey man barber, barber's man. **–såpe** shavingsoap.
I. **barde** (keltisk dikter) bard.
II. **barde** whalebone. **–hval** whale.
bardun (tau på skip) backstay.
bardus bang! like a bolt.
bare seg forbear, help, refrain from; **jeg kunne ikke — meg for å le** I could not help laughing; **jeg kunne ikke — meg** I could not help it.
bare only, mere, but; **bare han var her** if only he were here.
barett bonnet, cap.
barfrost a black frost.
barfugl moorgame, grouse.
barføtt bare-footed, bare-foot.
bar|halset bare-necked. **–hodet** bare-headed.
barhytte shelter of pine-boughs.
I. **bark** (skip) bark.
II. **bark** (på tre) bark.
barkarole (gondolførersang) barcaro(l)le.
barkasse (storbåten) launch, longboat; (sjefs-) barge.
bark|e (garve) tan; (avbarke) bark, strip, the bark from; **–t** (fig; om fargen) tanned, weather-beaten, hardened, seasoned. **–ing** tanning.
bar|lind yew-tree. **–nål** pine-needle, leaf of a coniferous tree. **–skog** pine forest. **–tre** conifer, coniferous tree.
barm bosom; (om formen) bust; **griper i sin egen —** looks into (goes home to) his own heart.
barmhjertig compassionate, merciful; **–e brødre, søstre** brothers, sisters of charity; **den –e samaritan** the good Samaritan; **–e Gud!** mercy on me! **–het** compassion, mercy, pity; **ha — med oss:** have mercy upon us! **–hets-gjerning** labour of mercy.
barn child, (spett) infant, baby, babe; **— født etter farens død** posthumous child; **han har ingen —** he has no family; **fra — av** from a child; **være med —** be with child, be in the family way; **anta i –s sted** adopt; **brent — skyr ilden** a burnt child dreads the fire, once bit twice shy; **det vet hvert — that** is familiar to every schoolboy, the merest schoolboy knows that; **av — og fulle folk får en høre sannheten** children and fools speak the truth.

barnaktig childish, puerile, infantine. **–het** childishness, puerility.
barndom childhood, (tidligste) infancy; **handelens — the** infancy of commerce; **fra –men av** from a child; **i min tidlige —** in early childhood; **går i —** is in his dotage. **barndoms|dager** days of childhood, childish days. **–liv,** se **barndom.** **–venn, –veninne** friend of one's childhood. **–år** years of childhood, childish years.
barne|alder childhood, infantile age. **–asyl** infant-asylum. **–ball** children's ball. **–barn** grandchild. **–barnsbarn** great grandchild. **–bok** children's book. **–dåp** christening, baptism. **–eventyr** nursery-tale. **–far** alleged father; **utla ham som —** fathered the child upon him. **–flokk** crowd of children, (large) family. **–fot** child's foot. **–frøken** lady nurse, nursery governess. **–fødsel** child-birth. **–fødsel i dølgsmål** concealment of pregnancy. **–født** born; **er — i N.** is a native of N. **–gudstjeneste** children's service. **–hage** kindergarten, infant school. **–hjem** infant home. **–hjelpsdag** Children's League of Pity Day. **–hospital** children's hospital. **–kammer** nursery, children's room. **–kjole** child's frock. **–kopper** small-pox. **–krybbe** day nursery. **–lammelse** poliomyelitis. **–leik** child's play. **–lue** child's cap. **–lærdom** what is learnt in childhood; catechism. **–mat** food for infants, pap. **–mor** mother (of an illegitimate child). **–mord** child-murder, infanticide. **–mordet i Betlehem** the Slaughter of the Innocents (28. desember). **–morder(ske)** infanticide. **–oppdragelse** education of children, child training. **–pike** nursery maid, nurse maid el. girl. **–pulver** composing powder. **–ran** kidnapping. **–regle, –rim** nursery rhyme. **–rov** kidnapping. **–røver** kidnapper. **–selskap** children's party. **–skje** child's spoon. **–sko** child's shoe; **har trådt sine — is** no chicken, has put off childish ways; **ikke ha trådt sine — be** in leading-strings. **–skole** school for children. **–skrik, –skrål** crying of children. **–snakk** childish nonsense. **–språk** children's language. **–stemme** voice of a child. **–strek** childish trick el. freak. **–stue** (på hospital) children's ward. **–svøp** swaddling cloth. **–sykdom** children's disease, childhood's malady. **–tro** childlike faith. **–tøy** baby linen; articles of infant wear. **–utsettelse** exposure of infants. **–utstilling** baby show. **–venn** friend to children. **–verdenen** the children's world. **–verk** child's work. **–vis: på — in** the way of children; childishly. **–vise** song for children, nursery-rhyme. **–vogn** (dyrere) perambulator; (billigere, av korgfletning) babycarriage. **–ånd** child-mind. **–år** infantile years, years of childhood.
barnlig childish, infantile, (i forhold til foreldrene) filial; **–het** childish el. childlike simplicity el. artlessness.
barn|løs childless. **–løshet** childlessness.
barnsben: fra — from childhood, from a child.
barnslig childish, infantine. **–het** se **barnlighet.**
barnsnød: være i — travail, be in labour; **hjelpe en kvinne —** lay a woman.
barokk (adj.) odd, singular, grotesque, baroque.
barokk (subst. = barokkstil) baroque.
barometer barometer. **–fall** fall of the b. **–kurve** barometric curve. **–stand** height of the barometer; **denne lave —** this low mercury.
baron (hørende til the nobility) baron; (engelsk baron kalles Lord —,** f. eks. Lord Byron, utenlandske baroner kalles Baron —). **baronesse** baroness. **baronett** (hørende til the gentry) baronet, (forkortet og anbrakt etter navnet:) **Bart.,** f. eks. **Sir Walter Scott, Bart. baroni** barony. **baronisere** make el. create a baron.
barre (av sølv, gull) bar, ingot; (mar) bar; **barriere** bærrier.
barrikade barricade. **barrikadere** barricade.
barsel lying in, confinement; (gilde) (feast in celebration of a child's) christening; **lager til — is** in the family way; **gjøre — be** confined.

-feber child-bed fever, puerperal fever. **-gilde,** se **barsel. -kone, -kvinne** lying-in woman.

barselseng childbed; **kom i** — was delivered, confined, brought el. put to bed (of); **ligge i** — lie in; **dø i** — die in child-bed, die in giving birth to a child.

barselstue lying-in room.

barsk harsh, stern, severe; (om stemme, vesen) gruff, rough; (om blikk) fierce, stern; **-t vær** inclement (el. severe) weather. **-het** harshness, sternness, gruffness, severity; inclemency.

barskog pine forest.

barsle be confined.

bart mustachio.

Bartolomæus Bartholomew. **-natten** the massacre of St. B.

bartre conifer, fir(tree), pine(tree).

baryton barytone.

bas headman, master; (notebas) master seiner.

basalt basalt.

basar bazar, bazaar, fancy-fair.

base (kjemi) base.

baseball (slags ballspill) base-ball.

Basedow: den -ske syke Graves' disease.

Basel Basel, Basle.

basere base, found, rest (**på:** on).

basilisk basilisk, cockatrice. **-blikk** basilisk glance.

basis basis, base.

basill bacillus (pl. -i), germ.

bask (lydelig slag) slap, thwack; (pryl) flogging. **baske** slap, thwack; — **med vingene** flap the wings.

basketak brush, set-to, mill.

basker, baskisk Basque.

basrelieff bas-relief, low relief.

bass (dyp stemme) bass, base.

bassanger bass-singer.

basse (tyksak) whopper, stout fellow.

basseng basin, reservoir.

bassfiol (fiolonsell) bass-viol.

bassist bass-singer.

bass|note bass-note. **-nøkkel** bass-clef. **-stemme** bass-voice. **-streng** bass-string.

bast bast, bass; **binde en med band og** — put one in irons (el. fetters).

basta (kløver ess i l'hombre) basto; (utrop) enough; **dermed** — there's an end.

bastard bastard; (bare om dyr) mongrel. **-aktig** bastard. **-art** hybrid species. **-rase** mongrel breed.

baste bind, tie (securely).

bastion bastion.

bastonade bastinado; **gi** — bastinado.

bastreip coir-rope.

basun trombone; (bibelsk) trumpet; **blåse i** — play on the trombone; (fig) **støte i** — **for** blow the trumpet for. **-blåser** trombone player. **-engel: kinner som en** — cheeks like a cherub (on a tombstone).

batalje battle, action.

bataljon battalion.

Batavi|a Batavia. **b-er, b-sk** Batavian.

bate vrb (nytte, forslå) suffice, avail; **bate** (subst) (gagn) benefit, advantage, good.

batteri battery; (mar) gun-deck; **nederste** — lower (gun-) deck. **-dekk** gun-deck. **-sjef** commanding officer.

battist battiste, cambric. **-lerret** coarse cambric.

baug (på et skip) bow. **-hals** (mar) fore-hood. **-jager** bowchaser. **-sjø** head sea. **-spryd** bow-sprit.

baule howl, bellow.

baun beacon.

baus, se **staut.**

baut (seilas mot vinden) tack.

bautastein (old Scandinavian) stone monument.

baute (krysse opp mot vinden) beat up to windward, tack.

baut skip! bout ship!

bavian (apeart) baboon; (mar) (båtvakt) boatkeeper.

Bay|ern Bavaria. **b-ersk** Bavarian. **b-rer** Bavarian.

be beg, ask, desire, solicit; (innstendig) beseech; (holde bønn) pray; — **en om noe** ask, beg st. of one; — **en om å beg** one to; **må jeg** — **Dem om saltet** I will thank you for the salt; may I trouble you for the salt; — **en fri** beg one off; — **en til middag** invite, ask, bid, one to dinner; **det -s bemerket** please to observe; **han lot seg ikke** — **to ganger** he needed no second bidding; **bad seg fritatt** begged to be excused; — **en bønn** offer (up) a prayer; — **for** intercede for; (til Gud) pray for; — **om** ask, beg for; (til Gud) pray for; — **om en almisse** ask charity; — **om ordet** ask permission to speak; **om jeg tør** — if you please; **å, jeg -r** don't mention it, no matter.

bearbeid|e work (up); (jorda) prepare; (bok) revise, remodel; (for scenen) adapt; (musikk) rescore; — **med** (kasteskyts o. l.) ply with; — **ens rygg** belabour one's back; — **en** (fig) work upon (el. practice on, manipulate) one. **-else** working; belabouring; revision; manipulation; (av skuespill) adaptation. **-er** adapter.

bebo (litt.) (sted) inhabit; (hus, leilighet) occupy, tenant. **-elig** habitable, inhabitable.

bebo|elighet habitableness. **-else** habitation, occupation. **-elseshus** dwelling house. **-elseslei-lighet** dwelling. **-er** inhabitant; occupant, occupier, inmate, dweller, resident, lodger (de tre siste med: in, de øvrige med: of).

bebreide reproach, upbraid; — **ham en forseelse** reproach him with an offence. **-lse** reproach, upbraiding. **-nde** reproachful.

bebude announce, proclaim, herald, notify, foreshadow, forebode, indicate. **-lse** announcement, notification.

bebygg|e cover with buildings; (kolonisere) settle, colonize. **-else** building; settlement, colonization.

bebyrde burden, load, encumber; **jeg vil ikke** — **Dem med** I will not trouble you with.

bed (i en hage) bed, plot.

bedage seg (stilne) lull, clear off, abate.

bedaget (gammel) aged, stricken in years.

bedding (underlag for skip) slip.

bede|dag prayer-day, fast-day, rogation day. **-dagsansikt** woeful, rueful, lackadaisical face el. countenance; **sette opp et** — pull a long face. **-hus** house of prayer, chapel. **-kammer** oratory.

bedek|ke cover, (eskortere) escort. **-ning** covering, cover; (eskorte) escort; (astronomi) occultation; (landbr.) (= parring) coverture, leap.

bede|mann undertaker. **-mannsstil** fustian.

bederv|elig perishable. **-else** decay. **-et: bli** — decay, spoil, go bad, be damaged. **varer som lett blir** — perishable goods.

bedeskammel devotional stool.

bedra deceive, beguile, impose upon, take in; (for penger o. l.) cheat, defraud, trick; — **en for cheat** el. swindle one out of; — **en i spill** cheat el. trick one at play; (svikte) play false; **skinnet -r** appearances are deceitful el. deceptive; **verden vil -s** the world will be taken in. **bedrag,** se **-eri;** (skuffelse) delusion, illusion, fallacy.

bedrager deceiver; impostor, cheat, swindler.

bedrageri deceit, deception, imposition, imposture; fraud, swindle.

bedragersk deceitful.

bedre better; **til det** — for the better; — **kvalitet** superior quality; **vet ikke** — knows no better; **forlanger ikke** — desires no better; **en** — **middag** a good (heavy) dinner; **bli** — mend; **står seg** — is better off; **De gjør** — **i å** you had better; **ingen** — (ved auksjon) going.

bedre (vrb) (forbedre) better, mend, ameliorate, improve; **Gud** — **det** ah, welladay. **-s** mend, improve; get better. **-stillet** better off.

bedrift exploit, achievement; (næringsbruk) trade, business.

bedring improvement, amendment; (etter sykdom) convalescence, recovery; **det er inntrådt en** — there is a change for the better; **er i** — is convalescent; **god** — I I hope you'll soon be better.

bedrive commit; (dt.) (bestille) do, be about; — **hor** commit adultery.

bedrøv|e afflict, distress, grieve, sadden; **bedrøvet** sorry, grieved, distressed **(over:** at). **-elig** sorrowful, melancholy, sad dismal; (ynkelig) sorry. **-elighet** sadness, sorrowfulness. **-else** sorrow, affliction, distress, grief, sadness, melancholy.

bedugget (lett berust) tipsy.

beduin Bedouin.

bedømme judge, judge of. **bedømmelse** judgment, criticism. **bedømmelseskomité** judging committee. **bedømmer** judge, critic.

bedøve (ved slag, støy og fig) stun, stupefy; (ved legemidler) anaesthetize, narcotize; (forgifte i vond hensikt) drug; **-nde midler** anaesthetics, narcotics. **-lse** stupefaction, narcotization; (tilstand) stupor; **under -lse** under an anaesthetic. **-lsesmiddel** anaesthetic, narcotic.

bedåre infatuate, beguile, befool, delude, deceive; **lot seg** — **av** was infatuated by. **-nde** infatuating, bewitching.

beedige confirm by oath, swear to; **-t forklaring** sworn deposition.

Beelzebub Beelzebub.

befal (body of) officers.

befale (byde) command, order, direct, bid, (gi i vold) commit, resign; — **over** command; **som De -r** as you please; — **sin sjel i Guds vold** commit one's soul into the hands of God; **befal|ende** commanding; commander. **-ing** command, order(s), injunction, mandate, charge; **etter** — **av** by order of; **ha** — **over** have the command of. **-ingsmann** commander; officer.

befare (ferdes på) pass, frequent; (undersøke) survey; (beseile) navigate; — **en elv** navigate a river.

befaren (sjøvant) inured (to the sea): **helsjømann** able-bodied seaman; **halv-** ordinary.

befaring passing etc.; examination; navigation.

befatning dealing, concern, avocation, something to do (with); **vil ikke ha noen** — **med det** will have no concern with it.

befatte seg med have to do with, meddle with; (bare om ting) deal in, engage in.

befengt med infested with.

beferdet frequented, crowded.

befest|e fasten, fix, secure, attach; (styrke) confirm, strengthen; (en by o. l.) fortify. **-ning** fortification.

befinne find; — **seg** be, find oneself; **hvorledes -r De Dem** how are you? how do you do? how do you feel el. find yourself? **jeg -r meg vel ved det** I find it agrees with me; **jeg -r meg ille** I feel unwell (el. sick).

befinnende health, state of health; **spørre om ens** — inquire after a person's health.

befipp|else perplexity, flurry. **-et** flurried, disconcerted, perplexed; **gjøre** — flurry, disconcert.

beflitte seg på apply oneself to; — **å strive to, try to, do one's best to.

befolk|e people, populate; (bebo) inhabit. **-ning** population. **-ningsstatistikk** population statistics.

beford|re (sende) forward; (transportere) convey, carry; (fremme) further, advance, promote; encourage; (til embete) prefer, promote; **bli -ret** (få embete) obtain an office. **befordring** forwarding; conveyance; furtherance, advancement; promotion, preferment; se **befordringsmiddel.**

befordrings|kontrakt transport contract. **-middel** (means of) conveyance. **-måte** mode of conveyance.

befrakte freight, charter. **befrakt|er** charterer. **-ning** freighting, chartering, affreightment. **-ningskontrakt** (certeparti) charter, charter -party.

befri free, set free, release, rescue, liberate; — **for** deliver el. save from, rid of, (frita for) exempt from. **-else** freeing, deliverance, delivery, release, liberation, enfranchisement; riddance; exemption. **-er** deliverer, liberator.

befrukt|e fructify, fertilize; (om planter og dyr) fecundate; (bare om dyr) impregnate; (fig) fructify. **-ende** (fig) fruitful. **-ning** fructification, fecundation, impregnation.

befullmektige empower authorize, commission; **en -t** commissioner, deputy; (i diplomatiet) a plenipotentiary.

beføl|e (fingre på, famle hen over) feel, finger, handle, paw. **-ing** feeling etc.

beføyd entitled, competent; (grunnet) well -grounded, just, legitimate, justified, sound.

begav|e med endow with, bestow (st.) on, grant (st.) to. **-else** parts, gifts, powers, talents, capacity, intelligence. **-et** gifted (med: with), talented, clever.

begeistr|et (adj) enthusiastic; (adv) enthusiastically. **-ing** enthusiasm (**for:** for, about).

beger cup, beaker, goblet, chalice; **-et fløt over** the cup was full to overflowing; **bringe -et til å flyte over** (fig) break the camel's back. **-klang** ringing of glasses.

begge both, (hver av to) either; **vi** — both of us, we both; — **to** both; — **deler** both; **som** — **of whom, who both of them; **i** — **tilfelle** in either case.

begi seg go, repair, proceed; (hende) chance, come to pass; — **seg på vei** set out: — **seg på en reise** proceed upon, el. set out (el. off) on a journey.

begivenhet event, occurrence, incident; **fattig på begivenheter** uneventful.

begjær desire, appetite, lust; (etterspørsel) demand **(etter:** for) **begjære** desire, covet; (forlange) request, solicit, ask for; — **til ekte** ask, demand in marriage; **du skal ikke** — **din nestes hustru** thou shalt not covet thy neighbour's wife.

begjæring (anmodning) request; (krav) demand.

begjærlig desirous **(etter:** of); — **etter å** eager el. anxious to. **begjærlig** (adv) greedily, eagerly, with eager eye.

begjærlighet (griskhet) cupidity, covetousness.

beglo stare at.

begonia begonia.

begrave bury, inter, entomb.

begravelse funeral, burial, interment; inhumation; (gravsted) tomb, burial place, vault. **begravelses|avgifter** burial dues. **-byrå** funeral establishment. **-omkostninger** funeral expenses. **-ritual** burial service. **-sermoni** funeral el. obsequial ceremony. **-skikker** funeral rites.

begrens|e bound, limit, circumscribe. **-et** limited; **utgave i -et opplag** limited edition. **ilden var nå -et** the fire was now within bounds. **-ning** limitation, restriction, circumscription; limits.

begrep notion, idea, conception **(om:** of) **gjøre seg** — **om** form an idea el. notion el. conception of; **det har jeg ikke** — **om** I have no idea; **står, er i** — **med å** is going to, about to, ready to, on the point of, in the act of.

begrepsforvirring confusion of ideas.

begret|e (litt. = gråte (sørge) over) deplore, mourn, lament, bewail. **-elig** deplorable, lamentable. **-else** lamentation.

begrip|e understand, comprehend, (tenke seg) conceive. **-elig** comprehensible, conceivable; **forsøkte å gjøre ham** — tried to make him understand. **-eligvis** of course.

begrodd med overgrown, overrun with.

begrunne prove, make good, make out; (utgjøre grunn) be the motive of, occasion; **er -t** i el. **på is owing to; -t** well-founded.

begrunnelse argument.

begunstige favour, countenance, encourage. **-lse** favour, preference, countenance.

begynne begin, commence (**med: with** el. **by**), enter upon, open with; **— å tale** begin to speak, commence speaking; **— å (dt)** take to el. fall to -ing; **vinteren -r tidlig** the winter sets in early; **— sin egen husholdning** set up for oneself; **— et nytt liv** turn over a new leaf; **— igjen** begin over again, start afresh; **vel begynt er halvt fullendt** well begun is half done.

begynnelse beginning, commencement, outset; **i -n** at first, in the first, in the beginning; **straks i -n** at the very beginning; **fra -n til enden** from beginning to end; **-n til enden** the beginning of the end; **begynne med -n** begin at the beginning; **ta sin — begin: gjøre -n** take the first step.

begynnelses|bokstav initial; **-bokstaver** (typograf.) capitals; **stor —** initial capital; **liten —** initial small letter. **-grunner** rudiments, beginnings, principles, elements.

begynnende incipient.

begynner beginner, novice; **skole for -e** primary school. **-arbeid: et-** the work of a beginner.

begå commit.

behag pleasure, gratification, satisfaction; **etter — at** pleasure, as you please, as you like; **finne — i** take pleasure, delight in, be taken with. **behage** please; **som De -r** as you please; **hva -r?** Sir? Madam? beg (your) pardon; dt. What? Eh? **De -t å bemerke** you were pleased to observe; **behag å ta plass** please to sit down, sit down (if you) please; **det -t ham å** he was pleased to; **det har -t Gud å** it has pleased God to.

behagelig agreeable, pleasant, pleasing, gratifying, acceptable; **jeg utber meg Deres -e meddelelser** (merk.) I request the favour of your communications. **-het** pleasantness, agreeableness; **-heter** delights, comforts: (ytringer) civilities, compliments.

behage|lyst desire of pleasing. **-syk** over-desirous to please, coquettish. **-syke** excessive desire of pleasing, coquetry.

behandle handle, manage, deal with; (vel, ille) **treat,** use; (drøfte) discuss; (handle om treat of; (patient) treat, attend; **— en ille** use one ill, illtreat one.

behandling management; treating, treatment, usage; discussion, cure. **-småte** manner of treatment, mode of dealing with.

behansket gloved.

behefte burden, encumber; **eiendommen var sterkt -t** the estate was heavily mortgaged. **-t med gjeld** encumbered with debt, involved. **beheftelse** encumbrance, involvement.

behendig handy, dexterous, deft, nimble. **-het** handiness, dexterity, nimbleness. **-hetskunst** (sj. = jonglørkunst) sleight-of-hand trick.

behenge: behengt (med sort) hung (in black).

beherske rule (over), govern, sway, master; (om beliggenhet) command; (lidenskap, stemme o. l.) be master of, control. **-else** rule, sway, dominion, mastery, command. **-er** ruler, lord, master.

behjelpelig: være en — help el. assist one, lend one a helping hand.

behjertet stout-hearted, dauntless, intrepid, resolute. **-het** courage, intrepidity.

behold: ha i — have on hand, in reserve; **er i —** remains, is left; **i god — in** safety, safe and sound, safe and well.

beholde keep, retain; **la en — noe** leave st. to one; **la en — livet** spare one's life; **— frakken på** keep on one's coat; **— noe tilbake** have st. left, remaining.

beholder reservoir, receiver, container.

beholdning stock (in hand), supply; (rest) surplus, remains (pl), remainder; (kasse) cash, balance.

behov (subst) need, requirement, necessity. **etter -et** according, to requirement; **ha — need,** stand in need of; **dekke sitt — meet** one's immediate wants.

behørig (sj. passende) due, proper; **i — form,** orden in due form, order; **i — stand** in proper condition: **på — måte** duly.

behøve need, want, require, stand in need of, have occasion for; **det -s ikke** here is no need of it, no occasion for it; **du -r ikke å komme** you need not come; **det -r neppe å sies** it need hardly be said.

behåret hairy.

beil|e til make love to, woo, court; **— til ens gunst** court one's favour. **-er** suitor, lover, wooer. **-ing** wooing etc., courtship.

bein (adj.) straight. **beint fram** straight on. **bein** (se også **ben**) (i kroppen) bone; (p. møbler o. l.) leg; **et fett — a** good prize; **spenne — for en** give legbail, pick up one's heel; **har — i nesa** has plenty of backbone, has a (little) will of his own; **ta -a på nakken** take to one's heels. **beinet, se benet.**

beinke (subst.) service, favour. **gjøre en ei —** do el. render one a service, do one a favour. **beinke, se benke.**

beis stain. **beise (tre)** stain.

beis|el, se bissel. -le, se **bisle.**

beisk, se besk.

beist, se best.

beit, se bet.

I. **beite** (agn til fisk) bait.

II. **beite** (grasgang) grazing land, pasture. (vb) graze, browse.

bek pitch. **-aktig** pitchy. **-fakkel** torch, link. **-gryte** pitch-kettle.

bekjemp|e combat, struggle with, contend with; fight down. **-else** fight against.

bekjenne (tilstå) confess, own; own up; avow; (i kortspill) follow suit; **— seg skyldig** plead guilty; **— seg til en religion** profess a religion. **-lse** (tilståelse, tros-) confession; (av religion) profession; **gå til — make** confession, make a clean breast of it. **-r** professor, follower; **Edvard B-ren** Edward the Confessor.

bekjent (well-)known, noted, familiar; **alminnelig —,** altfor vel **— notorious; det er alminnelig — at it** is common knowledge that; **så vidt meg — as** far as I know; **som — as** is (well) known, as you know, it is well known that, of course; **— for famous for; — med** acquainted with; **gjøre seg — med** noe take knowledge of; **tillat meg å gjøre Dem — med hr. N.** allow me to introduce you to el. make you acquainted with Mr. N.; **gjøre seg — ved** bring oneself into notice by; **vil ikke være det — is** ashamed to own it; **jeg kan ikke være — av å** I would not have it known el. supposed that; **du kan ikke være — av den hatten** you cannot show your face with that hat on; **du kan ikke være —** av annet you cannot in honour do otherwise. **bekjent** (subst.) acquaintance; **en god — a** friend. **-gjøre** make known, publish, notify; (i blad) advertise. **-gjørelse** publication, notification, (official) notice; advertisement.

bekjentskap acquaintance; **gjøre el. stifte — med** get acquainted with, make the acquaintance of; **gjøre nærmere — grow** more familiar, improve the acquaintance; **ved nærmere — on** more familiar acquaintance. **bekjentskapskrets** acquaintance.

bekk brook, rill, beck; **liten — brooklet.**

bekkasin snipe.

bekkaure brook trout.

bekkeblom marsh-marigold.

bekke|drag, -far course of a brook.

bekken basin (stikkbekken) bed-pan; (musikkinstrument) cymbal; (hulhet mellom hoftebenene) pelvis.

bekkesig trickling rill, trickle.

beklage lament, deplore, regret; — en be sorry for, pity; — seg over complain of; jeg -r meget at I am very sorry that; jeg -r å måtte meddele Dem I regret to inform you; han er meget å — he is much to be pitied.

beklagelig deplorable, lamentable.

beklagelse regret.

beklagelsesverdig pitiable, to be pitied.

bekle clothe, cover; — med papir paper; — med bord, planker board, plank; — med metallplater case, coat; — et embete fill el. occupy an office.

bekledning (klededrakt) clothing; (overtrekk av bord) boarding.

bekledningsgjenstand, se klesplagg.

beklemmelse faintness, sickening of the heart, uneasiness.

beklemt anxious, uneasy, faint, down-hearted.

beklemthet anxiety, uneasiness.

beklippe (hekk o. l.) trim; (fig) curtail, abridge.

beknip: være i — be at a pinch, hard up; jammed (in); komme i — get jammed.

bekomme agree with; det vil — Dem vel it will do you good; det bekom ham ille at han he fared the worse for -ing; vel —! you are welcome (to it), (ikke etter bordet); (ironisk) much good may it do you, I wish you joy of it.

bekomst: få sin — have one's fill, have enough.

bekostje pay el. defray the expenses of. -elig expensive, costly.

bekostning cost, expense, charge; sette seg i stor — incur a great deal of expense; med en — av at an expense of; på min — (også fig) at my expense el. cost; på egen — at his own expense; på — av sannheten at the sacrifice of truth.

bekranse wreath, crown with a garland.

bekrefte (stadfeste) confirm, corroborate, bear out; (utsi, vitne) affirm; (bevitne) certify, (offisielt) legalise; en -t gjenpart a certified transcript, a legalised copy; det har -t seg at it has proved true that; hvis nyhetene blir -t if the news be confirmed.

bekreftelse confirming, confirmation, corroboration; affirmation; verification; til dets — in witness el. testimony whereof.

bekreftende affirmative; in the affirmative.

beksvart pitchy, pitch black.

beksøm|sko, -støvler unpegged el. pegless shoes, boots with soles sewn on, the use of pegs being dispensed with.

bektråd wax-end.

bekvem (passende) fit, fitting, proper, suitable; (beleilig) convenient; (lett) easy; (makelig, hyggelig) commodious, comfortable; gjøre seg det -t make oneself at home; hvis det faller Dem -t if it suits your convenience; ta seg det -t take it easy. -t skotøy easy boots.

bekvemme seg til bring oneself to, persuade oneself to, submit to.

bekvemmelighet comfort, convenience, accommodation; huset er utstyrt med alle moderne -er the house is fitted up with every modern convenience. —, se leilighet (i hus). -shensyn consideration of convenience.

bekym|re grieve, trouble; — seg for be concerned about; — seg med trouble oneself with; — seg om care about, trouble oneself about. -ret (over, for) concerned, anxious (about, for).

bekymring care, concern, anxiety.

bel, se stund.

belage|seg på prepare (oneself) for, make ready for; -t på prepared for.

belagt loaded, furred, foul (tongue); veiled (voice).

belast|e load, charge; (ens konto for) debit el. charge (one el. one's account for). -et (arvelig, nervøst) tainted. -ning weight, load.

belegg coating, facing, lining; (skorpet) incrustation; (på tunga) fur; (skredders) stay,

tape and buckram; (på sykehus) number of patients, beds filled; (i hotell) number of visitors.

beleg|ge cover, coat, case, overlay; (innvendig) line; (med beviser o. l.) support; (med skorpe el. l.) incrust; (speil) silver; — med arrest place under arrest; — med sitater support with quotations; forstå å — sine ord know how to put things; belagt med toll charged with a duty.

beleilig convenient, seasonable, opportune; når det er Dem — when(ever) it is convenient to you el. suits your convenience; gripe det -e øyeblikk take time by the forelock.

beleilig (adv) opportunely, just in time.

beleir|e besiege, lay siege to, beleaguer. -er besieger. -ing siege.

beleirings|skyts heavy artillery. -tilstand state of siege; erklære en by i -tilstand declare a town in a state of siege. -tropper besieging forces.

belemre encumber, impede, burden.

beless|e load, charge, burden. -ing loading.

belest well (el. deeply el. widely) read. -het (extensive) reading.

belg (bot.) shell, pod, cod, legume; (dyreskinn) skin taken off entire, case; (vom) belly; (blåse-) bellows. **belge** (erter osv.) shell; belgetråer bellows-blower. belg|frukt pulse, podding grain. -mørk pitch dark. -mørke pitchy darkness. -vott mitten.

beleven polite, courteous. -het politeness, courtesy.

Belgi|a Belgium. b-er, b-erinne Belgian. b-sk Belgian, Belgic.

Belgrad Belgrade.

Belial (= Satan) Belial.

beliggen|de lying, situate, situated. -het situation, site; (geografisk) position; (med hensyn til vær, sol o. l.) exposure, aspect.

belive animate, quicken, vivify. -t også spirited. en — scene a stirring scene.

I. **belje** (tylle i seg) gulp, swill.
II. **belje** (brøle) squall. sette i å — begin a squall.

belladonna (medikament) belladonna.

belme, se belje I.

belte belt, girdle, band, sash, cincture, baldric; (geog) zone; Venus' — the girdle of Venus; Orions — the belt of Orion. -dyr armadillo. -spenne buckle of a belt. -sted waist.

belur|e watch (secretly). -ing watching.

belyse light, light up, illuminate; (fig) throw a light upon, illuminate, elucidate. **belysning** lighting etc., illumination, light. (fig) til — av in illustration of. belysnings|apparat illuminating apparatus. -gass illuminating gas.

belær|e instruct, teach; la seg -e be taught, take advice. -ende instructive. -ing information, instruction.

belønne reward, recompense, remunerate.

belønning reward, recompense, remuneration; (prisb.) premium, prize.

beløp amount; til et — av to an amount of, amounting to. beløpe seg til amount to, come to, make; hva kan det — what may it come to?

belåne encumber.

bemale bepaint, daub.

bemann|e (mar) man. -ing manning; (mannskap) crew.

bemektige seg seize (upon), take possession of, possess oneself of.

bemeldt said, aforesaid.

bemerke (legge merke til) perceive, notice, note; (også i bet. ytre) remark, observe; jeg tillater meg å — I beg to remark, observe, mention; — innholdet note the contents; det fortjener å -s it deserves notice; gjøre seg -t make oneself conspicuous. **bemerkning** remark, observation; gjøre -er ved remark upon.

bemidlet of means, well off, wealthy.

bemyndige authorize, empower, commission.

bemyndigelse authority, authorization etc., sanction; full power, power of attorney, warrant, authority; **etter** — by authority; **gi** — **til** authorize.

bemøye seg take the trouble (med å: to).

ben (se også **bein**) (i kroppen) bone; (lem) leg; (p. møbler o. l.) leg; **et fett** — a good prize; **spenne** — for en trip, one up; **ta -a fatt** give legbail, pick up one's heels; **har** — **i nesa** has plenty of backbone, has a (little) will of his own; **ta -a med seg** stir one's stumps; **katten kommer alltid ned på -a** a cat will always light on her own feet; **han er alltid på -a** he is always on the move; **hele huset er på -a** the whole house is astir; **komme på -a igjen** regain one's feet, recover one's legs, spring (el. leap) to one's feet; **hjelpe en på -a** (også **fig**) set el. put one on his legs; **bringe el. stille en hær på -ene** raise an army; **kan ikke stå på -a** cannot stand on his legs; **stå på svake** — totter, be in a tottering condition; **stå på egne** — stand upon one's own legs, stand alone, be self-sustaining el. selfsupporting; **gi en** — **å gå på** make one find his legs; **ta -a på nakken** take to one's heels; **er dårlig til -s** is a bad, poor, walker.

ben (adj), se **bein**.

benaktig bony, osseous.

benauelse uneasiness, nervousness.

benauet uneasy, nervous.

ben|brudd fracture. **-bygning** structure of the bones, skeleton. **-dannelse** bone-formation.

bend bend. **-e** bend. — **opp** prize open.

bendel tape. **-orm** tape-worm.

bendreier turner (in bone).

bendsel tie; (mar) seizing. **bendsle** tie; (mar) seize.

benedder caries.

benediktiner Benedictine friar, black friar.

benefise benefit. **-forestilling** benefit, bespeak (night, performance), ticket-night.

benekt|e deny, disavow. **-else** denial disavowal. **-elsesed** oath of denial. **-ende** (adj) negative; (adv) in the negative. **-ende svar** answer in the negative.

benet bony, osseous.

benev|ne name, call, designate, term, denominate. **-nelse** appellation, designation. **-ning** (mat) denomination; **gjøre om til felles** — reduce to a common denominator. **-nt:** — **tall** concrete el. applicate number; **addisjon med -e tall** compound addition.

ben|fri boneless. **-full** bony.

Bengal|en Bengal. **b-sk** Bengal; (språk) Bengalee; — **lys** Bengal lights, blue fire; **den B-ske Bukt** the Bay of Bengal.

bengel (boktr.) press-stick, rounce; (skjellsord) brute, lout. **-aktig** brutish, loutish.

benhinnebetennelse periostitis.

benhus charnelhouse.

benk bench; seat, (skole-) form; **spille for tomme -er** play to empty benches; **benke** (vrb) seat, bench.

benke (gjøre ben) straighten.

benklær trousers, pantaloons; **korte** — breeches, small-clothes.

ben|lim bone-glue. **-løs** boneless, legless. **-e fugler** beef olives. **-mel** bone-flour, ground bones.

bensin benzine, (til motor) petrol. **bensol benzene·**

ben|skinne greave, (av lær) pad; **-splint** splinter of a bone. **-stump** stump of a leg; fragment of a bone.

bent (adv) right, straight; (fig) flatly.

benytte use, make use of, employ; (som kilde) consult; — **en leilighet** take, seize el. embrace an opportunity; — **tiden** make good use of one's time, improve the time; — **sin tid på det beste** make the most of one's time; — **seg av** profit by, take advantage of, avail oneself of; — **seg av sin fordel** improve el. push one's advantage. **-lse** use, using, improvement.

benåde (en forbryter) pardon; (for dødsdom) reprieve; — **en med noe** (litt.) favour, grace, one with st., confer st. on one.

benåd|ning (ettergivelse av straff) pardon, mercy, reprieve. **-ningssøknad** petition for mercy. **-ningsrett** pardoning power.

beordre order, direct; — **en til tjeneste** order one on duty. **-t til London** under orders for L.

beplant|e plant; — **på ny** replant. **-ning** planting; (konkret) plantation.

beramme fix, appoint.

berberiss barberry. **-busk** ogs. piperidge -bush.

berede prepare; — **et måltid** prepare el. dress a meal; — **lær** dress el. curry leather; — **veien** for en pave the way for one; — **ham vanskeligheter** throw difficulties in his way; — **en til døden** prepare one for death; — **seg på** prepare for; — **seg til** get ready for. **beredt på** prepared for. **-lse** preparing, preparation.

bereden (til hest) mounted.

bered|ning (av lær) dressing. **-skap** state of preparation; **i** — in readiness; **holde i** — hold in readiness. **-villig** ready, willing. **-villighet** readiness, willingness; alacrity, promptitude.

beregne compute, calculate; (føre i regning) put el. place to account; — **seg** (i betaling) charge; — **for meget for** overcharge the goods; **jeg har -t disse varene til** I have charged these goods at; — **prisene lavt** cut prices finely; — **feil** miscalculate. **-lig** calculable. **-nde** calculating, scheming. **kasse og emballasje -s ikke** no charge for case and packing; **det -s ikke gebyr** no fees are charged.

beregnet calculated; (tilsiktet) intentional; — **på** intended for; — **på å calculated to**.

beregning computation, calculation; **ta i** — make allowance for, allow for; **ta med i -en** count with; **tok feil i sin** — was out in his calculations. **-småte** way of calculating.

bereist travelled; **en meget** — **mann** a great traveller.

beret|ning statement, account, report; **avlegge** — **om** make (draw up) a report of, make a statement of, report.

berette state, relate, report, record.

berettig|e entitle; **-et til å** entitled to, warranted el. justified in -ing; **berettiget** (adj) legitimate, lawful. **-else** right, title.

berg mountain, hill.

bergamott bergamot.

berg|arbeider miner. **-art** species of stone, mineral. **-bestigning** mountain-climbing; ascent. **-bu** mountaineer, highlander.

berge (redde) save; (ernære) support; (avling) house, gather in; — **føda** secure a livelihood, support life, keep soul and body together; — **seil** take in sail; — **seg** manage to live, make both ends meet.

berg|egn mountain district, mountainous region.

bergelønn salvage money.

Berget (polit. parti under den fr. revol.) the Mountain.

berg|full mountainous, hilly. **-gruppe** group of hills. **-gylte**, se **-sugge**. **-hall** (el. hylle) ledge.

berging saving, salvage. **bergings|damper** salvage steamer. **-kompani, -selskap** salvage association. **-forsøk** attempt to save. **-kontrakt** salvage agreement. **-omkostninger** salvage expenses.

berg|kam crest (of a mountain). **-kjede** mountain chain el. range. **-kløft** cleft, ravine, chasm. **-knaus** hill-top, knoll, rock. **-krystall** rock crystal. **-lag** layer, stratum. **-land** mountain country. **-lendt** mountainous. **-pass** mountain pass, defile. **-prekenen** the Sermon on the Mount. **-rik** mountainous, hilly. **-rygg** mountain ridge. **-sildre** saxifrage. **-skrent** precipice, brow of a mountain. **-skråning** mountain slope. **-slette** table-land.

berg|sti mountain path. **-strøm** mountain torrent. **-sugge** (fisk) wrasse. **-tatt** spirited off into the mountain. **-tind, -topp** mountain-top. **-troll** gnome. **-vegg** rocky wall. **-verk** mine. **bergverks|distrikt** mining distrikt. **-drift** working of mines. **-eier** owner of a mine el. mines. **-vitenskap** science of mining.

beriberi (sykdom) beriberi.

berider (fag., = hestedressør) riding master, rider, horse-breaker, rough-rider; (sirkusrytter) circus-rider, horse-rider, equestrian performer. **-forestilling** equestrian performance. **-selskap** horse-riding establishment, equestrian company, company of riders. **beriderske** (female) circus -rider (osv.).

berike enrich. **-lse** enriching, enrichment.

beriktige correct, rectify; (betale) settle. **-lse** rectifying, correction, rectification; **til — av** in correction of.

ɪ⸱ Berlin Berlin. **berliner** Berliner.

ɪ̈; berme dregs, lees.

› Bern Berne. **b-er** Bernese. **-eralpene** the Bernese Alps.

Bernhard Bernard. **St. Bernhardshund** Great St. Bernard dog.

bero (finnes) be; (ha sitt forblivende) stand over, rest, remain in abeyance; **-r på** is founded upon; depends on, rests with; **det -r på en** misforståelse it is due to a misunderstanding; **la det — til en annen gang** leave it for another time. **bero: stille noe i — lay** st. by for the present, let the matter rest.

berolige soothe, calm (down), quiet, tranquillize, compose, reassure, appease, set at rest el. ease. **-nde** reassuring, comforting; **— middel** sedative. **-lse** calming etc.; **det er en — å vite** it is a comfort to know.

berope seg på (en) appeal to, refer to, quote, **(noe)** plead, urge.

berserk berserk. **berserkergang** fury of a berserk.

berus|e intoxicate, inebriate; **— seg** get drunk el. tipsy. **-else** intoxication, inebriation. **-ende** intoxicating etc.; **— drikker** liquors, intoxicants. **-t** drunk, tipsy, intoxicated **(av:** with). (fig) ogs. elated; **— av seieren** elated with victory; **være -t** be in liquor.

beryktet in bad repute, notorious; **— kvinne, hus** woman, house of bad repute, of ill-fame. **-het** bad reputation.

berøm|me praise, laud, extol, commend; **-me seg av** boast of, glory in. **-melig** (rosverdig) praiseworthy, creditable; (navnkundig) glorious, illustrious. **-melighet** praiseworthiness. **-melse** (ros) praise, eulogy, commendation, credit; (navnkundighet) celebrity, renown. **berømt** celebrated, renowned, famed, famous. **berømthet** celebrity, renowned (person) celebrity.

berør|e touch; (fig) (omtale) touch on, hint at; **-te meg** smertelig made a painful impression on me; **-te meg ubehagelig** gave me a shock; **prisene — es** ikke av prices are not affected by. **-else, -ing** touching etc., contact; **komme i -ing med** come el. get into touch with; **står ikke i -ing med** has no connection with.

berøringspunkt point of contact.

berøve deprive of, bereave of, strip, divest of. **-lse** depriving etc., deprivation.

berå seg med advise (el. deliberate) with, consult.

beråd: være i — med be in (el. of) two minds. **berådd: med vel- hug** deliberately, advisedly.

besatt possessed; **— av djevelen** possessed by the devil; **— av ærgjerrighet** possessed with ambition.

bese view, inspect, look over.

besegl|e (også fig) seal. **-ing** sealing.

beseile navigate.

beseire vanquish, beat, get the better of, conquer, overcome; **— vanskeligheter** surmount difficulties. **beseirer** victor. **beseiring** victory.

besetning (bestand) stock, (av fe) live stock; (på kåpe o. l.) trimming; (mil.) garrison; (mann-

skap) crew; **hele -en omkommet, reddet** all hands lost, saved. **besetningsband** braid, lace, ribbon (for trimming).

besette (land) occupy; (plass, rolle) fill (up); (utstyre, pynte) trim; **— rollene** cast the characters el. parts; **— med** (i alm.) put st. on, set with; **— med perler** set with pearls; **— med snorer** lace; **— med frynser** fringe; **— hans plass med en annen** replace him with another; **alle hans timer er besatt** all his hours are taken up. **-lse** occupation; (av en ånd) possession; **— av et embete** appointment el. nomination to an office.

besikte inspect, survey. **besiktelse** inspection, survey. **besiktelsesforretning** survey; survey-report.

besiktige, besiktigelse osv. se **besikte** osv.

besindig considerate, discreet, sober, cool. **-dighet** discretion, coolness.

besin|ne seg change one's mind; **— seg på** recollect, call to mind, think of. **-nelse** reflection; recollection; **tape -n** lose one's senses el. one's head; **komme til — recover** one's senses; **come to sober reflection; bringe en til — bring** one to his senses.

besitte possess, be possessed of,. **besittende:** **den — klasse** the propertied class(es). **-lse** possession; occupation; enjoyment; **-lser** (land) dominions, dependencies; **ta i -lse** take possession of, possess oneself of; **vi er i -lse av** Deres brev we are in receipt of your letter.

besitter, (gl., = eier, innehaver) possessor.

besjele animate.

besk bitter, acrid.

beskadige damage, injure, hurt. **-t** også (om frukt) bruised, (om bok) mutilated. **-lse** damage, injury, hurt; defacement.

beskaffen conditioned; **annerledes — different; saken er således — the** matter stands thus; **mennesket er således -t** man is so constituted. **-het** nature; (tilstand) condition; (egenskap) quality; **sakens — the** nature of the case; **et lands naturlige — the** physical conditions of a country.

beskat|ning taxing, taxation, assessment. **-ningsrett** power of taxation. **-te** tax, assess, lay a tax upon; **de høyest -tede** the highest tax-payers.

beskik|ke (ordne) order; (ansette) appoint, commission, (i en annens sted) substitute; (juridisk) serve a notice upon; **— sitt hus** set one's house in order. **-kelse** appointment; notice.

beskitt dirty.

beskjed (svar) answer; (underretning) information; (bud) message; **legge igjen — leave** a message; **sende en — send** one word, let one know; **gi tjeneren — give** the servant his directions el. orders; **jeg sa ham ordentlig — I** told him a bit of my mind; **vite god — med** know, be up to; **jeg vet — om det** I know all about it; **jeg vet bedre — I** know better; **inntil videre — till** further notice.

beskjeden modest, unpretending, unassuming unobtrusive, mild; (måteholden) moderate. **-het** modesty, humility.

beskjeftige employ, occupy, **-t med** occupied, busied in, with, engaged in, on, upon, taken up with. **-lse** occupation, employment, pursuit.

beskjemme shame, disgrace, dishonour; (gjøre skamfull) abash; (gjøre skam på) put to shame. **-lse** shame, disgrace, dishonour. **-nde** shameful, disgraceful.

beskjenket fuddled, tipsy, in liquor.

beskjerm|e screen, shelter, shield, protect (mot: from, against). **-else** protection. **-er** protector, defender.

beskjære clip, pare, trim, (fig) curtail, reduce, pare; (bokb.) cut (the edges of); (sterkt) crop; (trær) prune, lop, trim. **beskjæring** clipping etc.

beskriv|e describe, (utførlig) detail; (geometr.) describe; **ikke til å — not** to be described;

(juridisk: beskrevet: in writing); **–ende** descriptive; **et —** dikt a descriptive poem. **–else** description, account; (juridisk) copy; **overgå** all **— pass** description; **over** all **—** beyond all expression.

besku|e gaze at, view, contemplate. **–else** viewing, inspection. **–er** viewer, beholder.

beskyld|e for accuse of, charge with, tax with, lay to one's charge. **–ning** accusation, charge, imputation (for: of).

beskylle water, wash.

beskyte fire upon el. into; **fra dette fort kan hele havnen beskytes** this fort commands the harbour.

beskytte protect, guard, defend; **— mot regnet** shelter from the rain; **–nde** protecting, protective. **–lse** protection, defence; patronage; (mots. frihandel) protection; **stille seg under ens — place** oneself under the protection of sb.; **under kanonenes —** under cover of the guns; **søke — mot** seek shelter from.

beskyttelses|farge, –likhet (protective) mimicry, protective resemblance. **–merke** trade mark. **–middel** means of protection. **–toll** protective (el. prohibition) duty, protection.

beskytter protector; patron. **–inne** protectress; patroness.

beskøyt biscuit.

beskåret: hvis det ble ham — å if it were his destiny (in his d.) to.

beslag mounting; (p. dør o. l.) iron work, butts; (i form av ring) hoop, (mindre, p. stokk o. l.) ferrule; (p. hjul) tire (mar. til blokk o. l.) strap, strapping; (jur., arrest) arrest, sequestration attachment, seizure; (p. skip) embargo; **legge — på** sequester, sequestrate, seize, place el. put under an arrest, lay an embargo on, embargo, (fig) take up, engross, engage, claim, occupy, monopolize, absorb, take hold of, trespass on; **legge fullt — på** tax to the utmost. **beslag|legge,** se **legge beslag på. –leggelse** arrest, attachment, seizure; embargo; taxing.

beslekt|et related, akin, allied (med: to), kindred; **— ord** cognate word; **–ede sjeler** kindred el. congenial souls.

beslut|te resolve, decide, determine (å: that, to med inf.; noe: st., on el. upon st.) **— seg** come to a resolution, make up one's mind; **— seg til å** make up one's mind to. **–ning** resolution, decision, (fast) determination; **fatte en —,** se **beslutte seg; det er min faste — å** I am determined to, have made up my mind to. **–ningsdyktig** in sufficient numbers to pass resolutions; **være —** be a quorum.

beslå mount, bind; (innfatte) case; (innvendig) line; (på enden) tip; (et fat) hoop; (hest) shoe; **— med spiker** stud; (mar. seil) furl; (blokk) strap. **–tt** (fig med penger) in cash; (med lærdom) well grounded el. equipped. **–ing** farriery, horse-shoeing.

besmitte infect, taint; pollute, defile, contaminate, soil. **–lse** pollution, contamination.

besmykke gloss over, colour, put a face on, palliate, extenuate. **–lse** colouring, palliation, extenuation; gloss, colour. **–nde** palliatory, extenuating.

besmøre besmear, smear.

besnakke talk over el. round.

besne get better, improve, mend.

besnær|e ensnare, inveigle; entrap. **–ende** ensnaring; fascinating. **–ing** ensnaring.

bespare|lse saving, economy. **–nde** economic.

bespis|e feed. **–ning** feeding.

bespott|e mock, scoff, deride, sneer at; **— Gud** blaspheme (God). **–elig** (blasfemisk)' blasphemous. **–else** (blasfemi) blasphemy.

best (el. beist) beast, brute. **–ialsk** bestial, beastly, brutish, brutal.

best best; **i –e fall** at best; **av –e sort** of the best quality; **jeg skal gjøre mitt –e** I shall do my best, use my best endeavours; **det –e**

jeg kan gjøre the best thing I can do; **i den –e hensikt** from the best of motives; **i den –e mening** for the best; **i sin –e alder** in the prime of life; **alt var i –e gjenge** everything went on as well as could be; **den –e** the best (of men); **den første den –e** the first comer; **det blir det –e** it will be the best plan; **det –e av det hele** var the best part of it was; **det –e du kan gjøre** er your best plan is; **han skyndte seg det –e han** kunne he made the best of his way; **på det –e** in the best manner; **til det –e** for the best, to the greatest advantage; **du gjør (gjorde) — i å gjøre det** you had better do it; **— som** just as; **allting gikk som det — kunne** everything went on at random. **beste: det almene —** the general good; **gjorde sitt —** did his best; **til — for for** the good el. benefit of, in aid of; **til — for meg** for my good; **hadde noe til —** (hadde lagt penger til side) was in easy circumstances; **hadde lagt seg noe til —** had put something by (for a rainy day); **ha en til —** (gjøre narr av en) make fun of one; **gi til —** deliver.

bestal|ling commission, patent of office.

bestand (varighet) durability; (skog-) growth; (mengde) amount; (kveg-) stock. **–del** ingredient, component part, constituent (part).

bestandig (adv) constantly, continually; always; **for —** for good, for ever. **–het** durability; constancy.

beste|borger respectable citizen. **–far** grandfather. **–foreldre** grandfather and grandmother.

bestemm|e decide, resolve, determine; (ved grenser og logikk) define; **— nærmere** define more closely, qualify; (om skjebnen) destine; (fastsette) appoint, settle, fix; **— seg** come to a determination; **loven –er** at the law provides that; **— for** el. til intend for, set apart for, design for; **— seg for** decide upon; **— forut** (om skjebnen) predestine, predetermine; **— om** el. over determine on; **— seg til** determine el. decide on, make up one's mind to; **— seg til å** determine el. decide to; **bestemt til** (om skip, reise) bound for. **begravelsen ble — til fredag** the funeral was arranged for Friday. **–ende** determining, determinative (for: of); **— for en** conclusive for one. **–else** determination; destination; (skjebne) destiny; (øyemed) purpose; definition; qualification, appointment; (politiets) regulation; **du må ta en —** you must come to a decision, make up your mind; **ta annen —** alter one's mind. **–elsessted** (place of) destination.

bestemor grandmother, (dt) granny.

bestemt (fastsatt) fixed, appointed, stated, set, certain; (nøyaktig) definite, precise; (særskilt) particular; (fast) peremptory, decided, decisive, positive; (om karakter) determined, firm; determinate; (av skjebnen) destined, fated; **den –e artikkel** the definite article; **–e timer** stated hours; **— svar** positive answer; **— avslag** a flat refusal; **i en — tone** in a peremptory tone. **bestemt** (adv) definitely; peremptorily, decidedly; positively; **jeg vet det —** I know it positively; **jeg tør ikke si det —** I won't be positive; **I don't know** for certain. **–het** precision, decision, determination.

besti|alitet bestiality, beastliness. **–alsk** beastly, bestial.

bestig|e (hest) mount; (fjell o. l., trone) ascend. **–else, –ning** ascending etc., ascent, ascension.

bestikk (etui) case (of instruments) mathematical case; (mar) (ettmålet) day's work; (i alm.) reckoning; **gjøre opp sitt —** do the day's reckoning; **gjøre galt —** miscalculate.

bestikk|e bribe, corrupt, suborn, (dt) tip; (fig) captivate. **–elig** corruptible, venal. **–elighet** corruptibility, venality. **–else** bribery, corruption (stikkpenger) bribe; **ta imot –else** take a bribe **–ende** plausible, specious, prepossessing.

bestikklugar (mar) chart-house.

bestill|e (utføre) do; (forlange, sikre seg) bespeak, order, engage; — **plasser, værelser** take el. secure places, apartments; **hva har De her å —?** what business have you here? **ha å —** med have to do with, have dealings with; **det har lite med saken å —** that is little to the purpose; **vil ikke ha noe å —** med will have nothing to say to; **han skal få med meg å —** I shall give it him. **-ing** business, occupation, employment; order, commission (**på:** for); (embete) place, office; **etter —** to order. **-ingsmann** functionary, employee.

bestjele en for noe steal st. from one, rob one of st. **den bestjålne** the robbed party.

bestorme storm, assault; (fig) assail, importune.

bestrebe seg strive, endeavour, labour, study (for å: to). **-lse** endeavour, effort, exertion.

bestride (benekte) deny; (utrede) bear, defray; **— omkostningene** defray the expense. **bestridelse** (betaling) defrayal.

bestryke coat; (mil) command, enfilade, sweep.

bestrø bestrew, strew, besprinkle, sprinkle.

bestråle irradiate.

bestyr (besvær) trouble, ado; (forretninger, kallsplikter) avocations.

bestyre manage, conduct, direct; (embete) fill, administer, perform the duties of. **-lse** management, direction, administration, se også **styre**.

bestyrelses|medlem, **-møte** etc., se **styre-**. **bestyrer** (i alm.) manager; director; (skole) head-master, principal; (av bo) trustee (to an estate). **bestyrerinne** directress, manager; schoolmistress.

bestyrke confirm, corroborate, bear out; **— en i** confirm one in. **-lse** confirmation, corroboration.

bestyrt|else consternation, amazement, dismay. **-et** amazed, disconcerted, startled, dismayed etc.).

bestøve (befrukte) pollinate.

bestøvning (befruktning) pollination.

bestå (være til) subsist, exist, be in existence; (vare) continue, endure, survive; **— av** consist of, be composed of; **— for en nøyere prøvelse** bear a close examination; **— i** consist in (el. of); **— mot** hold out against; (utholde) sustain, stand, undergo, go through; **hadde harde kamper å —** had hard battles to fight; (eksamen) pass; **— en prøve** pass el. stand el. meet a test.

bestående existing; **det —** the existing state of things; **en omstyrtelse av det —** a subversion of upstanding things.

besud|le sully, soil, befoul, defile. **-ling** sullying etc.

besvangre get with child, impregnate. **besvangring** getting with child; impregnation.

besvare answer, reply to; (ved å gjøre det samme, f. eks. en hilsen) return; (løse) solve. **-lse** answer, reply; solution; (oppgave) theme, paper.

besverg|e (ånder) conjure, (mane bort) exorcise, lay; (be) conjure, adjure, beseech. **-else** conjuring, exorcism, incantation, adjuration. **-elsesformular** formula for exorcism.

besvike for defraud (of), cheat (of, out of). **-lse** defrauding, fraud.

besvime swoon, faint, fall into a swoon, be taken faint. **-lse** swoon, fainting fit.

besvogret related (el. allied) by marriage (med: to); **jeg er — med ham** we are related by marriage.

besvær trouble, inconvenience; **falle en til —** be burdensome to one. **besvære** oppress; (uleilige) trouble, give trouble; (plage) molest, vex; (hindre, gjøre besværlig) obstruct; **— seg over** complain of.

besvær|ing complaint, grievance. **-lig** troublesome; burdensome; laborious, toilsome; (adv) with difficulty. **-lighet** trouble, inconvenience; difficulty; toil, hardship; **med —** with difficulty.

besynderlig strange, curious, singular, odd, queer; **— nok** strange to say; (adv) strangely etc. **-het** particularity, singularity, oddity.

besyv: gi sitt — med i laget put in a word or two, say also one's say; **få sitt —** be told some home truths.

besøk visit, call; (om teater o. l.) attendance; **dårlig —** a poor attendance; **avlegge en et —** pay one a visit, call on one; **et — hos, i, på** a visit to; **i el. på — hos** on a visit to; **avlegge en et uventet —** drop in upon one; **stort —** a large attendance. **besøk|e** visit, come el. go to see, call upon el. on, give a call; (et sted ofte) frequent; (offentlig sted) resort to; (forelesninger o. l.) attend. **teatret var godt -t** the theatre was well attended. **-ende** visitor; caller.

besørge do; (ha overtatt, skulle utføre) have the care (el. have charge) of; (befordre) carry, convey; (sende) forward, transmit. **— vaskingen** do the washing; **— de løpende forretninger** despatch (el. transact) routine business; **— et brev** forward a letter; **— noe gjort** see st. done.

besådd med strewed, dotted, overspread with.

bet stake lost; **bli — lose** the stake; **gjøre — cause to** lose the stake; **sette en i —** (fig) nonplus, pose, puzzle; **være i —** be at a loss.

beta seize, come over; **— en lysten til** disincline one from; **— en motet** dishearten, discourage one; **— en mælet** strike one dumb; **— en en tro** disabuse one of an impression; persuade one to the contrary; **— en hans tvil** remove one's doubts. **-tt** overwhelmed, inspired, taken, overcome (**av:** with); excited; **-tthet** rapture, transport.

betakke seg beg to be excused, decline with thanks; **jeg -r meg** I'll none of it.

betale pay; (for ting man har kjøpt) pay for; **betale for seg** pay one's way; **— en med samme mynt** pay somebody in his own coin; **-s høyt** fetch high prices; **det skal De komme til å —** you shall pay for this, I will be even with you yet; **— en like for like** pay one in his own coin; **— med gull** pay in gold; **det kan ikke -s med penger** it is invaluable, worth any money; **— seg** pay. **betal|bar** payable. **-er** payer. **-ing** (handl.) paying; (konkret) payment, fee, charge; (lønn) pay; **ta — for** charge for; **stanse sine -er** suspend payment; **innstilling av —** stoppage of payment. **betalings|dag** pay-day. **-evne** solvency. **-frist** time given for payment, respite. **-middel** circulating medium; **lovlig -middel** legal tender. **-skole** paying school. **-stans** stoppage of payment, suspension of payment. **-tid** time of payment. **-vilkår** terms el. conditions of payment.

betalt paid, (under regning) settled, (på brev) prepaid; **kjøpt og —** bought and paid for; **det skal han få —** I'll pay him out; **ta seg —** repay oneself, reimburse oneself; **ta seg godt — charge** a good price.

I. **bete** (rotfrukt) beet.

II. **bete** (lite stykke), se **bit**.

beteg|ne mark; point out, designate, indicate, characterize; (m. et navn) denominate, (bety) express, denote, signify, represent; **-nende** significant, suggestive; **— for** characteristic of. **-nelse** designation, term.

betenk|e consider, think of, reflect on, bear in mind; **— en remember one;** **— en med noe** bestow (st.) upon one; **gi en å — leave** to one's consideration, put it to one to consider; **— seg** (skifte sinn) change one's mind, think better of it; **— seg på** think (twice) of, consider, consider of, hesitate about; **— seg på å** hesitate to; **det var vel -t av ham å** he was well advised to. **betenkelig** critical, serious, problematical, unsafe, precarious, doubtful; **det gjorde ham —** it made him hesitate; **det hadde en — likhet med** it was suspiciously like; **deres tilstand er —**

they are in a serious condition el. in a precarious state.

betenkelighet (persons) scruple, hesitation, doubt, uncertainty, misgiving; (ved en sak) difficulty, seriousness, doubtfulness; **ytre –er** express one's doubts; **ha — ved å gjøre noe** hesitate before doing st.

betenk|ning hesitation, scruple; (sakkyndig erklæring) opinion; (innberetning) report; **ta i — å** hesitate, scruple to; **avgi sin — over pass** el. give one's judgment on; **jeg tar ikke i — å erklære** I have no hesitation in declaring; **uten —** unhesitatingly. **–ningstid** time for considering, for reflection; **fikk ikke lang —** was not allowed long to deliberate.

betenksom circumspect, judicious, discreet; **–het** circumspection.

betenkt: være — på intend, contemplate; **jeg må være — på å** I must be prepared to.

betennelse inflammation; **det går — i såret** the wound becomes inflamed.

betids betimes, in good time.

betimelig timely, seasonable, well-timed, opportune, pertinent; (adv) in good time, opportunely. **–het** timeliness, seasonableness.

betinge contract for, bargain for, condition, stipulate; (være en betingelse for) be the condition of; **la noe være –t av** make st. conditional upon; **er –t av** is contingent upon; **— seg** stipulate for el. that; **betingende** conditional.

betingelse condition, stipulation, qualification; terms; (fordring) requirement, requisite; **har el.** **oppfyller alle –r for** has el. fulfills all the requirements of; **på den — at han** on condition that he; **uten –r** unconditionally. **–skonjunksjon** conditional conjunction. **–ssetning** conditional clause. **–svis** conditional; (adv) conditionally.

betinget conditional (av: on), (begrenset) qualified, modified; **ha fått en — dom** be on (under) probation; **loven om betingede straffedommer** the Probation Act; **— bifall** a modified approval.

betitlet titled.

betje|ne serve; operate; **— seg av** make use of, employ. **–ning** service, working; (oppvartning) attendance.

betjent (politibetjent) policeman; (bestillingsmann) officer, functionary.

betle beg (om: for); ask alms.

betler beggar (-man, -woman, -child), mendicant. **–i** begging, beggary, mendicancy. **betlerske** beggar-woman.

betlerstav: bringe en til –en reduce one to beggary, beggar one.

beto|ne (uttale med aksent) accent, accentuate; (fremheve) emphasize, lay stress on.

betong concrete, beton; **armert — (= jern—)** ferro-concrete.

betoning accentuation, emphasis.

betrakt|e look at, gaze at, view, regard; **— som** look upon as, regard as, consider, esteem. **–er** regarder, beholder, looker-on, contemplator. **–ning** looking at etc.; (anskuelse) consideration, contemplation, reflection, meditation; (bemerkning) comment; **anstille –er over** reflect el. meditate on; **i — av** in consideration of. view of, considering; **ta i —** take into consideration; allow for, make allowance for; **sette ut av —** leave out of consideration (el. account) **komme i —** be taken into consideration, be considered, remembered, entertained; **dette kommer mindre i —** this is a secondary consideration. **–ningsmåte** view.

betre(de) tread on, set foot on, enter, enter upon.

betreffende respecting, concerning, regarding.

betrekk cover; (tapet) hangings.

betrengt (i vanskeligheter) hard pressed.

betro en noe confide st. to one, commit st. to one's charge, give st. in charge to, trust one with st., entrust st. to one; **— en at** tell one in confidence that.

betrodd (om person) trusted, confidential; — **gods** deposit, trust; **— stilling** position of trust.

betrygge secure. **–lse** securing, security. **–nde** sufficient, satisfactory. **— sikkerhet** security; **en lite — ordning** a precarious arrangement.

betrykk distress; pinch, strait.

betutt|else confusion, bewilderment, perplexity. **–et** confused, bewildered, perplexed, taken aback.

betvile doubt, question.

betving|e subdue, conquer; repress, check, curb, control; **— seg** control oneself. **–er** subduer.

bety signify, mean, import, imply, denote; (være av viktighet) matter; **det har ikke noe å —** it does not matter; **som om det hadde noe å —** as if that mattered; **har noe å —** is of great consequence; **har mye å — hos** has great interest with; **har lite å —** is of little consequence; **noe som skulle — en frokost** an apology for a breakfast; **–r ikke noe godt** is a bad omen, bodes ill. **en mann som har noe å bety** an influential man.

betyde (la forstå) give to understand, signify, intimate; imply.

betydelig (adj) considerable; (fig. også) of great note, of high mark; (adv) considerably.

betydning (av ord) meaning, signification, sense; (viktighet) significance, importance, consequence; **i dårlig — in** a bad sense; **i en viss —** in a sense; **i videre —** by extension; **i — av** in the sense of; **legge en dårlig — i** put a bad construction on; **ikke av noen —** of no consequence.

betydningsfull (viktig) important; (uttrykksfull) expressive, significant.

betydnings|løs (ubetydelig) insignificant, unimportant. **–løshet** insignificance, unimportance.

betynge make heavy; burden, load; weigh down.

beund|re admire; **–rende** admiring; (adv) admiringly. **–rer** admirer. **–ring** admiration. **–ringsverdig** admirable; (adv) admirably.

bevandret well versed, practised, skilled (i: in), conversant, familiar (with).

bevar|e keep, preserve; **Gud — kongen!** God save the king! **Vårherre — meg!** God forbid! **–es!** good gracious; **Gud –es!** (undrende) good gracious, oh dear; (innrømmende) of course, most certainly. **–t** (i behold) preserved, extant. **–ing** keeping. **–ingsmiddel** preservative.

beve tremble, shake, quake, quiver; **— av** **frykt** shake with fear; **— for** dread.

bevæg|e move, stir; (formå) induce, prompt; **han lot seg ikke —** he was not to be moved, remained unflexible; **— seg** move (om sin akse: on its axis; om sola: round the sun), (mekanisk) travel, work; (ta mosjon) take exercise. **beveget** moved, affected. **–elig** movable, (mest fig) mobile; **lett —** impressible, susceptible, excitable. **–elighet** movableness, mobility. **–else** movement, motion; (røre) stir; (mosjon) exercise; (sinns-) agitation, emotion, excitement; **sette i — put** in motion, set going; **sette himmel og jord i —** move heaven and earth, leave no stone unturned; **sette seg i —** (fig) take action; **være i bestandig —** be in constant motion el. always on the move.

bevegelses|evne power of movement, locomotion. **–lære** dynamics. **–mengde** momentum. **–nerve** motor nerve. **–organ** organ of locomotion.

beveggrunn motive, inducement.

beven (litt.) trembling, tremor.

bevendt: det er dårlig — med ham he is in a bad case; **det er ikke rart — med hans kunnskaper** his knowledge is not much to boast of, not up to much.

bever beaver. **–fanger** trapper. **–gjel** castoreum. **–hytte** beaver-hut. **–rotte** beaver-rat, nutria. **–skinn** beaver's skin.

beverte entertain, treat, regale.

bevertning (det å beverte) entertainment; (vertshus) refreshment rooms, public house.
bevertningssted refreshment room(s), tavern, public house.
bevilg|e grant, concede, vote. **-ning** (tillatelse) permission, concession; (især av penger) grant; (parlament) vote. **-srett** right to grant supplies.
bevilling (samtykke av offentlig myndighet til handel o. l.) license. **uten** — unlicensed.
bevinge wing. **-t** winged.
bevirke effect, work, bring about.
bevis proof, evidence, (på, for: of); argument; (-førelse) demonstration; (mottagelses-) receipt, acquittance; (attest) certificate; **til** — **på** in proof of; **et** — **på det motsatte** a proof of el. to the contrary; **et** — **på at** a proof that; **føre** — **for** demonstrate.
bevis|e prove, demonstrate, make good, show; — **sin påstand** establish el. make good one's case. **-førelse** (line of) argumentation, demonstration. **-grunn** argument. **-kraft** evidential force.
bevislig demonstrable, capable of being proved, evident.
bevisst: være seg noe — be conscious of st.; **være seg selv** — be sensible, be in a state of consciousness; **meg** — as far as I know; **ikke meg** — not that I know of.
bevissthet consciousness; mind; **tape -en** lose consciousness el. one's senses; **become senseless**; **bringe en til** — restore one to consciousness; **komme til** — **igjen** recover one's senses, recover consciousness, come round; **beholdt -en til det siste** was sensible to the last; **i -en om** conscious of; **det er gått over i den alminnelige** — it is popularly believed.
bevisstløs unconscious, senseless, insensible. **i** — **tilstand** in a state of insensibility.
bevisstløshet unconsciousness, insensibility.
bevitne testify, affirm, (begge med el. uten to), certify, attest, witness, bear witness to; (for retten også) depose to; (uttale) express. **-lse** attestation; expression.
bevokst covered, overgrown, overrun.
bevokt|e watch, guard. **-ning** watch, guard, custody.
bevre quiver, twitch. **-asp** aspen. **-gras, -gress** quaking-grass, lady's hair.
bevæpn|e arm. **-et** armed. **-ing** arming, armament; (rustning) armour, accoutrements.
bevågen (om fyrster: gunstigstemt) favourable; **være en** — **favour** one. **-het** (litt. velvilje, gunst) favour, good graces.
beære honour.
beånde inspire, animate.
bi: stå en — assist one; **stand by one**; (mar) **legge** — lay to, bring to; **ligge** — lie to, lie by.
bi|(e) (subst) bee. **-avl**, se **-røkt**.
bibegrep implied notion, secondary notion.
bibehold, -else retention; med — av retaining.
bibel Bible. **-fortolkning** exegesis. **-historie** biblical history, Bible story, Scripture history. **-kritikk** biblical criticism. **-lesning** Bible reading. **-ord** scriptural word. **-ordbok** dictionary of the Bible. **-oversettelse** translation of the Bible; **vår** — the authorized version. **-selskap** Bible Society. **-sk** biblical, scriptural, scripture. **-språk** text, scriptural sentence. **-sted** passage from the Bible, scripture passage. **-sterk** well versed in the Scriptures.
bibemerkning incidental remark.
bi|beskjeftigelse by-work, secondary occupation. **-betydning** connotation, by-meaning.
biblio|fil bibliophile, bibliophilist. **-graf** bibliographer. **-grafi** bibliography. **-man** bibliomaniac. **-mani** bibliomania.
biblio|tek library. **-tekar** librarian. **-teksassistent** assistant librarian.
bibringe: —en forestilling give one an idea, convey an idea to one; **— en et sår** inflict a wound upon one; **— en en mening** impress one

with an opinion; (lære) instil into, impart to, imbue with, indoctrinate with el. in. **-lse** giving etc.
bicelle cell of a honeycomb, alveolus.
bidevind close-hauled, by the wind, on a wind. **-sseiler** vessel sailing on a wind.
bidra contribute; (fig) be conducive to, instrumental in. **bidrag** contribution, addition, share, (tegnet) subscription; **levere** — **til** contribute to. **-syter** contributor; subscriber.
bidronning queen bee.
bie, se **bi(e)**.
bie (vrb) stay, wait, tarry (på, etter: for) **jeg har lært å** — I can wait.
bielv tributary, affluent.
bierverv extra source of profit el. income.
bifag subsidiary subject.
bifall approbation, approval, applause; (enighet) assent; **skjenke sitt** — approve of, give in one's adhesion to; **vinne** — meet (with) approbation. **bifalle** approve (of), assent el. subscribe to. **bifalls|klapp** plaudits (pl). **-mumling** hum el. murmur of approbation. **-rop** applause, acclamation. **-salve** round of applause. **-storm** roar of applause. **-ytring** bravo, cheer, applause.
biff beefsteak.
biflod, se **bielv**.
biform by-form.
bifortjeneste extra profit. **skaffe seg en** — **ved** add to one's income by.
bigam|i bigamy. **-ist** bigamist.
bigott bigoted; hypocritical. **-eri** bigotry; hypocrisy.
bi|hensikt by-end, by-design. **-hensyn** dary consideration.
biinntekt perquisite; **skaffe seg** — eke out one's means.
bijouterivarer bijoutry.
bikake honeycomb.
bikke tilt.
bikkje dog, tike, tyke.
bikube bee-hive.
bil, se **automobil**.
bilag voucher, appendix; (til brev) enclosure.
biland dependency, dominion.
bilbrev (skipsbygningsattest) builder's certificate; certificate of registry.
bilde, se **billede**.
bildende (kunster) plastic (arts).
bile (subst) (bredbladet øks) broad axe.
bile (vrb) (kjøre i automobil) motor, automobile.
bileg|ge (forlike) adjust, compose, make up; (vedlegge) accompany with. **-gelse** adjustment, composition, making up.
bil|ing motoring. **-ist** motorist.
biljard (spill) billiards; (bord) billiard table; **spille** — play at billiards; **et parti** — a game at billiards. „**Karoline**"- carline. **-ball** billiard -ball. **-hull** pocket. **-kule** billiard-ball. **-kø** cue. **-spill** (game of) billiards. **-spiller** billiard-player. **-værelse** billiard-room.
bil|kjører chauffeur; motorman. **-kjøring** motoring.
bille (subst) chafer, beetle.
bille inn, se **innbille**.
billed|e image, picture; portrait; (sinn-) emblem, type, symbol; (uttrykk) trope, figure, metaphor. **-bibel** pictorial Bible. **-bok** picture-book. **-dyrkelse** image worship, idolatry, iconolatry. **-dyrker** idolater, iconolater. **-galleri** picture-gallery.
billedhogger sculptor, statuary, artist. **-arbeid** sculpture, carved work, carving. **-inne** sculptress. **-kunst** sculpture, statuary.
billedlig figurative, metaphorical. — **uttrykk** figure of speech.
billed|prakt (splendid) imagery. **-rik** figurative, full of images. **-skjærer** carver. **-språk** figurative language. **-stormer** iconoclast. **-støtte** statue. **-verk** pictorial work.

billett (adgangsbillett) ticket; (brev) note; **ta — til** take a ticket for; (jernbane-) book for el. **to. kontrollere -er** examine el. check tickets. **samle —** collect tickets. **selle —** sell tickets. **-kontor** (teat.) box-office, (jernb. o. l.) booking **-office,** money-taker's office. **-kontrollør** ticket examiner. **-luke,** se **-kontor. -seller** ticket seller, ticket clerk; (teat.) box-office keeper. **billettør** money-taker, ticket-clerk, check-taker; booking **-clerk,** ticket seller. **billettutsalg** (jernbane) booking-office; (amr) ticket office.

billig (prisbillig) cheap, low-priced, inexpensive; (rimelig) equitable, fair, just; **— pris** low el. moderate el. reasonable price; **for en — pris** cheap; **et — forlangende** a reasonable demand; **det er ikke mer enn —** it is but just, only fair. **billig|e** approve of, assent to. **-else** approbation, approval. **hans — av planen** his sanction to the plan. **-het** (rimelighet) fairness.

billion billion.

bilramp (råkjører) road-hog.

bimåne paraselene, mock-moon.

binavn (sj., = tilnavn) surname; (økenavn) by-name.

bind tie, ligature; (for øynene, forbinding) bandage; (på bok) binding; (heftebind i bokbindets rygg) band; **opphøyde —** (heftebind) raised bands; (del av et verk) volume; **bære armen i —** go with one's arm in a sling; **med — for øynene** with eyes bandaged.

binde bind, tie; (garn) net; (strikke) knit; (forstoppe) bind, constipate; (forene) unite; (forpliktc) bind, commit, pledge, tie; **— buketter** make nosegays; **— nek** make sheaves; **— ens hender** tie up one's hands, (fig) tie one's hands, tie one down; **— en hest** make fast a horse; **kalken -r godt** the mortar holds well; **— koster** make brooms; **— an** engage in contest with, (ogs. om ting) close with; **— for øynene** blindfold one, bandage one's eyes; **— for en sekk** tie up a bag; **— inn** bind (a book); **— opp** tie up; **— hender og føtter** på en tie one hand and foot; **— en noe på ermet** make one believe st.; **— til** bind up; **hadde ikke annet som bandt ham til livet** had no other tie to life; **— fast til** tie on to; **— seg** bind oneself, tie one's hands. **bindende** (fig) binding (for: for, on, to), obligatory (for: on).

binde|evne (fag., om lim etc.) holding (power). **-gal** raving mad, stark mad. **-hud** (øyets) conjunctiva. **-ledd** (connecting) link; (gramm.) connective. **-middel** cement, medium; (klebende) agglutinant; excipient. **-nål** (garnnål) netting needle. **-ord** conjunction. **-r** binder; (murstein) header; (tømr.) intertie, (papir-) fastener. **-stein** binding-stone. **-strek** hyphen; (oppstrek i skrivn.) upstroke. **-tegn** hyphen. **-vev** fibrous el. connective tissue.

bindhake cramp iron, crampit.

binding (strikking) knitting; (ski-) fastening. **bindings|tre** bond-timber. **-verk** frame work, brick-and-timber; **-verks hus** frame house.

bindsel bandage, ligature.

bindsterk voluminous; **skrive -e bøker om** write large volumes on.

binge bin, hutch; (for gjødsel o. l.) bog-hole, soil-tank.

bingse, binne she-bear.

binnsåle in-sole.

binyre suprarenal gland.

bio|graf (levnetsskildrer) biographer. **-grafi** biography. **-grafisk** biographic(al).

biolog biologist. **biologi** biology. **biologisk** biological.

biomstendighet subordinate circumstance. **bi|ord** adverb. **-person** subordinate character. **-plan** biplane. **-planet** satellite. **-produkt** by **-product.** **-rett** side dish, hors d'oeuvre.

birolle subordinate part.

birøkt bee-culture, bee-keeping. **-er** bee-holder, **-keeper, -master.**

bisak matter of secondary importance.

bisam musk. **-skinn** skin of the muskrat.

bisarr bizarre, odd. **-eri** oddity.

bisetning subordinate proposition, subsidiary clause.

bisette (hensette et lik i et kapell) deposit(a corpse) in a vault. **-lse** deposition etc.; (høytidelighet forut for begravelse eller likbrenning) funeral service (preparatory to burial or cremation).

bisitter (gl., = lagdommer, meddommer) assessor, judge-lateral.

bisk (som kjæleord) doggie, **bisk** (adj) snappish.

Biskaya Biscay; **Den -iske bukt** the Bay of Biscay.

biskhet snappishness.

biskop bishop (se **bisp). biskoppelig** episcopal.

bislag porch, pent-hourse.

bisle bridle.

bismak by-taste, smack, tinge; (avsmak) tang.

bismer steel-yard. **-lodd** weight of the steelyard. **-stang** rod of the steel-yard.

bisonokse bison.

bisp bishop. **bispe|dømme** bishopric, diocese, see. **-gård** episcopal mansion. **-hue** mitre. **-stav** pastoral staff. **-stol** (bishop's) see. **-sete** episcopal residence. **-visitas** episcopal visitation. **bispinne** bishopess.

bissel (munnbitt) bit; (tøyle) bridle; **legge på** **-, ta bisselet av** bridle, unbridle (a horse). **-stang** branch (of a bit).

bissevov (barnespråk, = hund) waw, wow.

bistand assistance, aid, support; **yte en — give** el. lend one assistance, render a. to one. **rettskyndig —** legal advice, counsel.

bister (oppbrakt) exasperated, incensed; (barsk) grim, gruff, stern, glum, fierce.

bistikk bite el. sting of a bee.

bistå assist, stand by, back.

bisverm swarm of bees.

bit (en) bit, morsel.

bite bite; (om kniv o. l.) cut; (om fisk, så **— på** — en av snub one op short, cut one short; **— etter** snap at; **— fra seg** hold one s own; **— i** bite; **beit meg i fingeren** bit my finger; **— seg fast i noe** seize it. with the teeth, (fig) **seize hold of st.;** **— i seg** swallow, bite in; **— i det sure eple** swallow a bitter pill; **— i gresset** bite the dust; **— over** bite in two; **— på kroken** swallow el. take the bait, rise (to the bait); **han får ikke meg til å —** på he won't get a rise out of me; **ingenting -r på han** he is proof against anything, thick-skinned; **— tennene sammen** set one's teeth (hard), clench the teeth. **bites** bite each other; **han er ikke god å -s med** he is an ugly customer; **-s om noe** have a fight el. tussle for st.

bitende biting, cutting, (fig) caustic, sarcastic, sharp; **en — kald vind** a nipping wind; **det er en — kulde** it is bitterly cold.

biting tributary thing.

bitt bite; **få — get** a rise.

bitte very small, tiny; **en — liten mann** a little bit of a man, a diminutive man; **ikke det -ste** grann not the very least, not a bit of it.

bitter bitter; (om smak osv.) acrid; **en — stund** an hour of bitterness.

bitter (mavebitter) bitters; **en dram —** glass of bitters. **-essens** bitters. **-het** bitterness, acrimony.

bitterlig (adv) bitterly; **— kaldt** bitter(ly) cold.

bittersøt (jvf. sursøt) bitter-sweet, between sweet and sour.

bittert (adv) bitterly, poignantly.

bivoks bees' wax.

bivuakere bivouac. **bivuakk** bivouac. **-bål,** **-ild** watch-fire, camp-fire.

bivåne (overvære) be present at, attend.

biårsak subordinate cause.

bjart bright, clear, light.

bjeff yelp, bark. **-e** yelp, bark, (ringeaktende) yap; — **til** bark at.

bjelke beam, (stor) balk; (¹sær jern-) girder. **-hus** log-house. **-loft** ceiling of rafters, beam ceiling.

bjelle jingle, little bell. **-klang** jingling, jingle, sound of bells. **-ku** bell-cow.

bjolle, se bjelle.

bjørk birch.

bjørke|bark birch-bark. **-skog** birch wood. **-tre** birch-tree. **-ved** birch-wood.

bjørn bear; **den grå** — the grizzly bear; **Den store** — the Great Bear; **Den lille** — the Lesser Bear; **sell ikke huden før bjørnen er skutt** don't count your chickens before they are hatched.

bjørne|aktig bearish. **-bær** dewberry, blackberry. **-dans** bear's dance. **-far** bear's track. **-hi** bear's (winter) lair. **-jakt** bear-hunting, bear -shooting. **-jeger** bear-hunter. **-labb** bear's paw, **-mose** hairmoss. **-skinke** bear ham. **-skinn** bear's skin. **-skinnslue** muff-cap, husby. **-spor** se **-far**. **-tjeneste** awkward el. unwelcome service, disservice, ill service. **-trekker** bear-leader. **-unge** bear's cub.

bla(de) (vrb) turn over the leaves; — **etter** turn over the leaves for; — **i** turn over the leaves of; — **igjennom** run over; — **om** turn over (the leaf).

blad (av tre, bok, bord) leaf; (av kniv, saks, gras) blade; (åre-) wash, blade; (p. skrue) blade, arm; (skje-) bowl; (sag-) web, blade; (i tømring) scarf; (i vev) sley; (avis) newspaper; **disse -er** (om en bok) these pages; **et — papir** a slip of paper; **lite —** leaflet; **når bjørka har -er** when the birch is in leaf; **spille fra -et** play off, play at sight; **synge fra -et** sing off, sing at sight; **sang fra -et** sight-singing; **ta -et fra munnen** speak out, speak one's mind; **not mince the matter; -et kan vende seg** the tables may turn.

blad-, se ogs. **avis-**.

bladaktig foliaceous, resembling a leaf.

bladdannelse foliation.

bladformet formed like a leaf.

blad|grønt chlorophyl, leaf-green. **-gull** leaf gold, gold-leaf; **uekte -gull** leaf-metal. **-hjorne** axil. **-knopp** leaf-bud, gemma. **-lus** plantlouse, puceron, aphis. **-løs** leafless, aphyllous. **-melding** notice in the newspapers. **-neger** penny-a-liner. **-notis** paragraph. **-plante** foliage plant. **-prakt** leafy splendour. **-ribbe** ridge. **-rik** leafy. **-rikdom** leaviness. **-skriver** journalist. **-smører** newspaper scribbler. **-stilk** leaf-stalk, petiole. **-sølv** leaf silver; **forgylt -sølv** party gold. **-tinn** tin-foil. **-tobakk** leaf-tobacco, t. in leaves. **-utgiver** editor of a newspaper. **-veps** leaf-wasp.

blaff (svakt vindpust) cat's paw. **blaffe** (om lys) flicker; (om seil) flutter, flap. **blafre**, se **blaffe**.

blakk fallow, pale; (om hest) dun.

blakne get fallow el. pale.

blakre, se **blaffe**.

blamere disgrace, dishonour; — **seg** make oneself ridiculous, disgrace oneself.

blanchett (i snøreliv) busk.

blande mix, mingle, blend; (kort) shuffle; (metaller) alloy, amalgamate; — **seg i** andres saker meddle in the affairs of others.

blandet mixed, promiscuous; **skrifter av — innhold** miscellaneous writings; **hund av — rase** mongrel.

blanding mixing, mixture, intermixture, compound, blend; (ringeaktende) medley; (av metall) alloy, amalgamation; **-er** miscellanies; **med en — av håp og frykt** with mixed hope and terror; **den rette —** av a due proportion of.

blandings|del ingredient. **-drikk** mixed beverage. **-farge** mixed colour. **-forhold** proportion (of parts), composition. **-form** hybrid form. **-gods** unassorted goods; (dårlig) trash. **-liste** (ved valg)

split ticket. **-ministerium** composite cabinet. **-måte** manner of mixing. **-rase** cross-breed, half-breed. **-språk** mixed language.

blandkorn mangcorn, maslin, meslin.

blank shining; (især om metall) bright; (pengelens) cleaned out, tight; **med -e våpen** (fig) in fair fight; — **som et speil** smooth as a mirror; **la stå** — leave in blank; **trekke** — draw; **de -e** the white el. whites; **gjøre en** — clean one out; **et -t avslag** a flat refusal.

blanke (vrb) polish, brighten, burnish, furbish.

blankett form, blank.

blank|het brightness, polish. **-lær** sleek-leather, shine leather.

blanko blank; **in blanko** in blank.

blanko|aksept acceptance in blank. **-fullmakt** authority in blank, blank-charter. **-kreditt** blank credit. **-tratte** draft in blank.

blankpolering polishing.

blankslitt glossy, f. eks. it will turn glossy in no time.

blanksverte blacking.

blant among; from among; — **andre** amongst others, for one; — **annet** for one thing.

blasert blasé, jaded, sated.

blasfe|mi blasphemy. **-misk** blasphemous.

blass sallow(ish).

blaut (se også **bløt**) (våt) wet; (myk) soft. **-kokt** soft-boiled.

blei (kile) wedge; (vrien person) wrong-head.

bleie child's napkin, diaper, swaddling-clout.

bleik pale; (litt bleik) palish; (svært bleik) pallid; (likbleik) white, wan; **bli** — turn el. grow pale; — **av skrekk** pale with terror; **han ble både rød og** — his colour came and went, he turned all manner of colours. **bleikblå** pale blue.

bleike (subst) (fisk) whiting.

bleike (vrb) bleach. **-kalk** (klorkalk) chloride of lime. **-middel** bleaching agent. **-plass** bleach -field, bleachgreen. **-pulver** bleaching powder. **-ri** bleachery. **-tøy** bleach-clothes, bleach-linen. **-vann** bleaching liquid. **-voll**, se **-plass**.

bleik|feit flabby. **-grønn** pale-green. **-gul** straw-coloured. **-het** paleness, wanness.

bleikne grow el. turn pale, (om farge og fig) fade.

bleik|nebbet pale-looking. **-rød** pink. **-sott** green sickness, chlorosis. **-sottig** chlorotic.

blek, se **bleik**.

I. **blekk** (jern-), se **blikk**.

II. **blekk** (skrive-) ink. **-aktig** inky. **blekke** (vrb) ink. **blekk|flaske** ink-bottle. **-flekk** ink-stain, ink-blot. **-hus** inkstand.

blekke (lite blad) small leaf.

blekk|-klatt spot el. blot of ink. **-smører** scribbler, quill-driver. **-sprut** cuttle-fish, squid. **-stift** indelible pencil. **-viskelær** inkeraser.

blemme blain, blister.

blend|e dazzle; (vindu) darken; **la seg** — av be deceived by. **-ende** dazzling. **-ing** (mørklegging) black-out. **-ingsgardin** black-out blind **-lykt** dark lantern. **-verk** illusion, delusion, phantom.

blende (min) blende, mocklead.

bles, blese blaze. **bleset** blazed, with a blaze on the forehead.

bli (hjelpev. til å uttrykke passiv) be (ble elsket was loved osv.); (forbli) stay, remain; (overgang til en annen tilstand, stilling) become; (plutselig el. uvant overgang) turn; (bare ved adj.) grow, get (det siste også m. part.); (oppstå) arise, ensue, come on; (på sjøen el. valplassen, omkomme) perish, be lost; **bli her** tarry el. stay here; **hvor lenge ble du der?** how long did you stop there? **han er og -r en narr** he is a fool and ever will be (to the end of the chapter); — **stående** continue el. remain standing; — **landmann, kjøpmann, enke, tigger** osv. become a farmer, a merchant, a widow, a beggar; — **konge** become king; — **forræder** turn (a) traitor; — **protestant, kristen** turn Protestant,

Christian; — bleik (blekne) turn pale; — sur turn sour; — rik, fattig osv. grow, get, become rich, poor etc.; — sint grow, get el. be angry; — syk fall sick; det -r seint it is growing late; det -r ti daler it makes ten dollars; jeg -r 20 år i morgen I shall be twenty years to-morrow; det -r vanskelig it will be difficult; når -r det when is it to be? det ble ikke noe av det it came to nothing; hvor -r det av ham what is he about? hvor er det -tt av ham what has become of him? hva skal det bli av ham what is to become of him? hvor er det -tt av boka mi where is my book got (el. gone) to? — av med (tape) lose, (— fri for) get rid of, (avsette) dispose of; — borte (utebli) stay away, absent oneself; (tapes) be lost, disappear; for å — i lignelsen to carry out the metaphor; la det — mellom oss let us keep it between ourselves; det ble ikke med det that was not all, the matter did not stop there; dette -r mellom oss this is to go no further; — over tarry, be delayed; — til become, (komme til verden) come into existence el. life; — til is, stein osv. turn to ice, stone; — til intet come to el. end in nothing; før bergene ble til before the mountains were brought forth; — tilbake remain; be left, be behind, fall behind, hang back; — ute stay el. stop out; — (stående) ved (noe) persist in, adhere el. stick to, abide by; — ved (med) go on, proceed with; — ved å continue to; det -r ved det it is agreed el. determined; ble stadig ved å gå kept moving; lot det — med truselen confined himself to the threat; alt ble ved (med) det gamle everything went on as before. blivende lasting, permanent.

blid mild, gentle; (mild, vennlig) bland; (rolig) placid; ikke se på meg -e øyne not view kindly; han er ikke — på meg he bears me no love.

blidelig, blidt (adv) mildly, gently.

blid|gjøre soften, mitigate. -het mildness, gentleness; blandness; placidity.

I. blikk look, glance, (fig) eye; har — for has an eye for.

II. blikk (jern-) white iron, tin, tinplate; (i alm.) sheet-metal. -dåse tin (box).

blikkenslager tin-man, tinker.

blikk|instrument (metallblåseinstrument) brass instrument. -plate tinned iron plate. -smak pewtery taste. -spann tin pail.

blikk stille calm, stirless; det ble — it fell a dead calm.

blikk|tøy tin articles. -varer tin-ware.

blind blind; den -e the blind man (woman); de -e the blind; gråte seg — cry one's eyes out; — for blind to; — på det ene øye blind in (el. of) one eye; — alarm false alarm; — høne kan også finne et korn a blind man may hit the mark; — kjærlighet fond love; — lydighet blind el. implicit obedience; — lykke mere chance; — tillit, tro implicit confidence faith; blindt (adv) blindly, heedlessly. blinde: i — in the dark, blindfolded; (fig) blindly, heedlessly.

blinddør blank el. mock door.

blinde (gjøre blind) blind; (blende) dazzle.

blindebøtel (svaksynt fyr) blind beetle.

blinde|bukk blind man's buff. -hospital blind hospital, asylum for the blind. -institutt educational establishment for the blind. -mann the blind man, dummy; spille med — play dummy.

blindfødt born blind.

blindgate blind alley.

blindhet blindness, cecity. blinding (arkitektur) facing. blind|lanterne, -lykt dark lantern. -passasjer stow-away. -ramme blindframe. -skjær sunken shelf el. rock. -tarm blind gut. -tarmbetennelse appendicitis. -vindu mock el. wall-eyed window.

blink glimpse, gleam; (av lyn el. skudd) flash; (med øynene) twinkle; (på skyteskive) bull's eye, centre, white.

I. blinke gleam, twinkle, glimmer; (med øynene) blink, twinkle; — til wink at el. to.
II. blinke (trær til felling) score, spot. blink|fyr revolving el. intermitting light. -hinne nictitating membrane.

blinkskudd hit in the centre, hit in the bull's eye.

blod blood; (utgytt, størknet) gore; utgyte — shed blood; rød som — scarlet; sette vondt — make bad blood, breed ill-blood; — er tykkere enn vann blood is always thicker than water; close sits my shirt, but closer my skin; -ets bånd the ties of blood; en prins av -et a prince of the blood (royal); slå kaldt vann i -et be cool; svømme i — swim, welter in blood; det ligger i -et it is bred in the bone; er gått dem i -et has become their second nature; sette en skrekk i -et give one a fright; hans — kom i kok his blood was up; med kaldt — in cold blood; han har fått — på tann he has tasted blood; slå en til -s draw blood of one; mitt — ble til is my blood ran cold.

blod|appelsin blood-orange. -bad carnage slaughter, massacre. -bestenkt covered with blood, blood-stained. -brekning vomiting of blood. -brokk hematocele. -byll anthrax. -bøk bloody beech. -dannelse sanguification. -dannende blood-making, sanguigenous. -dråpe drop of blood. -dryppende dripping with blood. -dåd deed (work) of blood. -dåp blood baptism. -eik scarlet oak. -farget blood-stained, ensanguined. -fattig bloodless, anæmic. -fattigdom bloodlessness, anæmia, exanguinity. -fersken nectarine. -flekk stain of blood. -flekket blood -stained. -flod hemorrhage. -forgiftning blood-poisoning, pyæmia. -gang dysentery, blood-flux. -hevn revenge for blood-shed. -hevner avenger of blood. -hund blood-hound; (fig) bloody tyrant.

blodig (blodbestenkt) blood-stained, gory; (som koster blod) sanguinary, bloody; (ublu) exorbitant; (grusom) cruel; en — kamp a sanguinary struggle; en — urett a grievous injustice. Maria den -e Bloody Mary. (adv) hevne seg — take a bloody revenge.

blod|igle leech. -jaspis bloodstone. -kar blood -vessel. -klump clot of blod. -legeme blood corpuscle. -løs bloodless. -løshet bloodlessness, exsanguinity. -mangel anæmia, bloodlessness. -omløp circulation of the blood. -oppkastning vomiting of blood. -overfylling hyperæmia. -overføring transfusion. -penger blood-money, price of blood. -propp blood-clot, embolism, thrombus. -pudding black pudding. -pøl pool of blood. -pølse black pudding. -rensende blood-purifying. -rensende middel abluent, detergent. -rik plethoric. -rikhet plethora, plethory, fullness of blood. -rød blood-red, scarlet.

blods|dråpe drop of blood; til siste — to the last drop of my blood. Kristi — (blomst) fuchsia. -hest, -hoppe bloodhorse, blood-mare. blod|skam incest; i — incestuously. -skutt (om øyne) bloodshot. -spor track of blood. -sprengt blood-shot. -spytning spitting of blood, hemoptysis. -stigning congestion; determination of blood to the head. -stillende blood-stopping, hemastatic, styptic; -stillende middel, kraft styptic, stypticity. -stråle jet of blood. -styrtning violent hemorrhage; (fra livmora) flooding. -suger blood-sucker vampire; (fig ogs.) extortioner. -sugeri vampirism.

blodsutgytelse bloodshed, effusion of blood. blod|svette bloody sweat. -system circulation. -tap loss of blood, hemorrhage. -tørst blood -thirstiness. -tørstig bloodthirsty, sanguinary, bloody-minded. -underlepen livid. -uttredelse, extravasation of blood. -uttømmelse effusion of blood. -vann serum. -varme bloodheat. -vitne martyr. -væske plasma. -åre vein. -årebetennelse phlebitis.

blokade blockade; bryte -n run el. break the b. -brudd breach of blockade. -bryter blockade-

runner. **-skip** blockading vessel. **-tilstand** a state of blockade.
blokere blockade, block up; (typograf.) turn.
blokering blockade.
blokk block; (trekloss, tømmer) log; (skomakers) boot-tree; **sette på** — tree.
blokke opp put on the block, stretch.
blokkebær bog (el. marsh) whortleberry.
blokk|hus log-house; (mil) block-house; (mar) shell. **-is** block ice. **-maker** blockmaker.
Blokksberg the Brocken; **dra til** —! I wish you (were) at Jericho.
blokkskip (armed) hulk, block-ship.
blokksystem (til forhindring av togsammenstøt) block-system.
blokkvogn (lav transportvogn) truck car.
blomkarse Indian cresses.
blomkål cauliflower.
blomst (plante) flower; (plantedel som bærer frukten fram) blossom; (blomstring) bloom; **frukttrærne står i** — the fruit-trees are in blossom el. bloom; **lindetrærne står i** — the limetrees are in flower; **i ungdommens (fagreste)** — in the bloom of youth; **retoriske -er** flowers of rhetoric; **stå i** — be in flower, be in blossom; (især om frukttrær), be in bloom; **sette -er** flower, blossom.
blomster|anlegg parterre of flowers. **-bed** flower-bed. **-beger** calyx. **-blad** (kron-) petal; (blad) ved el. mellom blomster) floral leaf. **-bord** flower-stand. **-bukett** nosegay, bouquet. **-bunn**, se **fruktbunn**. **-dannelse** florification. **-duft** fragrance el. scent of flowers. **-dyrkning** culture of flowers, floriculture. **-eng** flowery mead. **-fest** floral fete. **-flor** show of flowers. **-frø** flower-seed. **-gartner** florist. **-glass** flower-vase. **-hage** flower-garden. **-handler**, **-handlerske** dealer in flowers, florist. **-knopp** flower-bud. **-krans** garland, wreath el. (om hodet) chaplet of flowers **-krone** (blomstens kronblader) corolla. **-kurv** basket of flowers. **-løk** flower bulb el. root. **-maler** flower-painter. **-maleri** flower-painting. **-pike** flower-girl. **-pinne** prop. **-plante** flowering plant. **-potte** flower-pot. **-rik** flowery. **-rike** floral kingdom. **-språk** language of flowers, floral language. **-stengel** stem. **-stilk** flower-stalk, peduncle. **-støv** pollen. **-torg** flower-market. **-utstilling** flower-show. **-vase** flower-vase. **-vrimmel** profusion of flowers.
blomst|re flower, blossom, bloom, blow, (fig) flourish; **— av** go out of flower, shed the blossoms; (falme) fade, decay; **den har blomstret av** it is out of flower, it has done flowering. **-rende** flowering, (fig især) prosperous; (om stil) florid, flamboyant; (om utseende) florid; **en ung** — pike a young blooming girl; **i den** — alder in the flower of age. **-ring** flowering etc. **-ringstid** flowering season; (fig) flourishing age; (velmaktsdager) heyday, f. eks. in the heyday of youth.
blond fair, fair-haired, fair-complexioned, blonde.
blonde(r) lace; (silke-) blond-lace; (ekte, av tråd) thread edging-lace; (uekte) cotton edging-lace.
blondine fair girl, blonde.
blot sacrifice. **blote** sacrifice.
blott (gl.) (adj) (naken, bar) bare, naked; mere, pure, sheer; **se med det -e øye** see with the naked eye; **tro en på hans -e ord** believe one's bare word.
blott (glt., adv., = bare) only, merely, but; (med nød) barely; (ene og alene) solely.
blott|e bare, denude, lay bare; **— hodet** uncover (one's head); **med -et hode** uncovered; **-et** (stilling o.l.) exposed; **-et for** destitute el. devoid of; **-et for all pliktfølelse** lost to all sense of duty; **— seg for penger** come short of money, leave oneself without money; **— sin uvitenhet** betray one's ignorance; **— ens uvitenhet** expose one's ignorance; **— seg** expose oneself. **-else** baring etc.; destitution; betrayal; exposure.

blott|legge expose, lay bare. **-stille** commit el. expose, lay open.
blu|ferdig bashful, modest, coy. **-ferdighet** bashfulness, modesty, coyness.
bluff (skinnmanøvre) bluff, **bluffe** bluff.
blund wink, snatch of sleep, nap; **få seg en** — take a nap; **det kom ikke** — på mine øyne I couldn't get a wink of sleep. **blunde** nap, doze slumber.
blunk twinkle; **på et** — in the twinkle of an eye.
blunke blink, twinkle; **— til** wink at el. to.
bluse (dame- el. arbeidsbluse) blouse; (for gutter) tunic; (kittel) smock-frock. **-kledd** bloused.
blusel, se **blyghet**.
bluss (fakkel) torch, flambeau, link; (ild) blaze, flash, flame; (mar) flash; (gassbluss) jet, (jet of) light; **lystre ål ved** — spear eels by torchlight.
blusse blaze, flame; (bruke blussignaler) burn a flare (i ansiktet) glow, burn, flush; **— opp** flare up, leap up, kindle with, (fig) fire (up). **-nde** blazing, aflame; **-nde rød** blushing deeply; **hun ble -nde rød** she blushed to the roots of her hair. **med -nde kinn** with rosy el. glowing cheeks.
bly (subst) lead; **av** — leaden; **tekke med** — lead.
blyaktig resembling lead, plumbeous.
blyant (mineral) black-lead, graphite; (til å skrive med) pencil, lead-pencil. **-holder** portcrayon. **-skisse** pencilled sketch. **-spisser** pencil -pointer.
blyant|strek pencil-stroke, pencil-mark. **-stump** stump of a pencil. **-(s)tegning** pencildrawing.
blyerts lead ore.
blyg (adj) bashful, coy, retiring. **-es** blush, be ashamed (ved: at).
blyghet, **blygsel** bashfulness.
blygrå leaden (grey), livid.
bly|holdig leaded. **-hvitt** white-lead, ceruse. **-klump** lump of lead. **-kule** bullet. **-lodd** plump, plummet.
bly|tekker plumber. **-vann** Goulard's extract, lead-wash.
blære (luft-) bubble; (vable) blister, vesicle; (urin-) bladder; (i jern) flaw, blister; (i glass) bleb; (person) bragger, boaster, strutter. **blære** seg swagger, vaunt; talk big. **-aktig** vesicular **-betennelse** inflammation of the bladder, cystitis. **-katarr** catarrh of the bladder, vesical c., cystirrhæa. **blæreti** (blæret opptreden, viktigmakeri) braggardism, rodomontade. **blæret** (adj) (full av blære) bladdery, vesicular; (dt. oppblåst, viktig) gassy, swaggering.
blo(de) (miste blod) bleed; **— seg ihjel** bleed to death.
blødersykdom hemophilia.
blødme (vittighet) quibble, pun.
blødning bleeding, hemorrhage.
bløt soft; (om toner, språk) sweet; **-t skinn** soft, smooth, delicate skin; **-e farger** soft, mellow, delicate colours; **-t gemytt** gentle disposition; **-t hjerte** tender heart; **bli** — om hjertet feel one's heart touched. Se også **blaut**.
bløt|aktig effeminate, enervated. **gjøre** — effeminate, enervate. **-aktighet** effeminacy. **-dyr** pulpy animal, mollusk.
bløt|gjøre soften, mollify. **-het** softness. **-het i hjernen** softening of the brain. **-hjernet** soft-headed, soft-witted. **-hjertet** soft el. tender-hearted. **-kokt** soft-boiled.
bløyt: legge i — soak, steep; **legge sitt hode** i — cudgel el. rack one's brains.
bløyte (gjennombløyte) soak, steep; (bløyte ut) macerate; (fukte) wet.
blå (adj) blue; **-t øye** (av slag) black eye; — ringer under øynene eyes surrounded by a blue circle; **slå en gul og** — beat one black and blue; **i det** — airy, airily, at random, in nubibus.

himmelens blå (subst) heaven's azure. blåaktig bluish.

blå|bær bilberry, whortleberry, blue-berry. -farget blue; dyed blue. -frossen blue with cold. -grønn bluish green, glacous. -grå bluish grey, blue-gray.

blå|klokke (plante) bluebell, harebell. -leire potter's clay. blålig bluish.

blå|lys blue light. -malt painted blue. -mandag blue Monday, Saint Monday. -meise blue titmouse. Blåmyra (om sjøen) the Blue.

blåne (bli blå) become el. look blue; (gjøre blå) blue.

blåne (subst) blue (hazy) distance; purple hill el. mountain.

blåpapir blue paper, carbonic paper; kopi på — ogs. carbon copy.

blårev blue fox, arctic fox.

blårutet blue-chequered el. b.-checkered.

blåse blow; — sterkt blow hard; jeg -r i ham a fig for him, I don't care a pin for him; det var som blåst bort there was no trace of it to be seen; -r vinden fra den kant! oho! that's what you want; — på trompet sound the trumpet; — i fingrene blow one's nails; — over ende blow down, blow in, overturn; det blåste opp it came on to blow; — (på) fløyte play on the flute; — på ilden blow the fire; det er som blåst it is as clean as a new penny. -belg (pair of) bellows. -instrument wind-instrument. blåser(e) (musikk) brass(es), wind-players.

blåse|rør blowpipe. -vær windy weather.

blåsing blowing.

Blåskjegg Bluebeard.

blå|skjell muscle, mussel. -spraglet speckled with blue. -stivelse blue, blue starch. -stivet blue-starched. -stripet with blue stripes. -strømpe blue stocking. -sur melk milk become sour without curding. -svart bluish black. -symre blue anemone. -syre prussic acid.

blåst wind, blast, blowing weather; gjøre — (av) brag, boast (of), make a fuss (about).

blåveis, se -symre.

bo (vrb) live, dwell, reside; — til leie live in lodgings; — til leie hos en lodge with one; — sammen (som mann og kone) cohabit, (om kamerater) chum together; du -r pent her you are nicely lodged here; jeg -r svært billig the rent is cheap; jeg vet ikke hva som -r i ham I don't know what is in him.

bo (subst) (bolig) abode; sette, feste — settle, establish oneself; (etterlatenskap) estate; (konkursbo) insolvent estate; hans — er forseglet his effects are sealed up; sitte i uskiftet — retain undivided possession of the estate of a person deceased; oppgi sitt — make an assignment of one's affairs.

boa (kvelerslange; pelskrage) boa.

bobestyrer liquidator, trustee.

boble (subst) bubble. boble (vrb) bubble.

bod, se bu.

bodmeri (slags pantsettelse av skip) bottomry. -attest certificate of b. -brev bill of b. -lån b. loan. -premie b. premium.

boer (hollandsk kolonist i Syd-Afrika) Boer. -venn pro-Boer. -vennlig pro-Boer.

bog (på dyr) shoulder.

boge, se bue.

boggivogn (slags jernbanevogn) bogie.

bogne se bugne.

bog|lam chest-foundered. -ledd shoulder-joint.

bohave furniture; (nagelfast) fixtures.

bohem Bohemian. -vesen bohemianism.

boi (slags tøy) baize.

boikotte boycott, ostracise. boikotting boycott, ostracism.

bok book; en — papir a quire of paper; bøkenes — the book of books; tale som en — talk like a book, talk like print; jeg har Dem ikke i mine bøker your name is not on my books; holde — over keep an account of; føre

til -s book, enter in a book el. on the books, make an entry of; -anmeldelse book-review. -auksjon book-sale. -avl literature. -bind book-cover.

bokbinder bookbinder. -i book bindery. -profesjon book-binding, trade of a bookbinder. -svenn journeyman bookbinder.

bokeiermerke (ex libris) book-plate.

bokelsker bibliophile, book-lover.

bokfink chaffinch.

bok|forlag book-publishing business. i -form in book-form, in volume. -fortegnelse catalogue of books. -føre enter, book. -føring, -førsel book-keeping. -gull leaf gold. -handel book-trade, bookselling trade; (butikk) book-(seller's) shop; er ikke lenger i -handelen is out of print, O. P.

bokhandler bookseller. -forening booksellers' union. -medhjelper bookseller's clerk.

bok|holder book-keeper, accountant. -holderi book-keeping; enkelt og dobbelt — single and double entry book-keeping.

bokhvete buckwheat. -gryn buckwheat groats.

bokhylle book-shelf.

bok|lade bookseller's shop; (amr) bookstore -ladepris publication price, published el. selling p.; -ladepris en shilling published at a shilling. boklig literary; -e kunster letters.

boklærd book-learned. bok|lærdom book learning, -lore. -marked book-market. -merke book-mark, (book-)marker, register. -orm bookworm, book-hunter. -pakke book-parcel. -reol bookcase.

boks (blikk-) tin; (rom i bank) box; anbringe i sin — put in one's box.

bok|samler collector of boks. -samling collection of books.

bokse (vrb) box. -hanske boxing-gløve. -ing boxing; -ekamp, -ematch boxing-match, prize-fight. -er boxer; prize-fighter.

bok|skap bookcase, bookpress. -språk book el. literary el. written language. engelsk — book English.

bokstav letter, character; en stum — a mute; store -er capital letters; etter -en literally; med latinske -er in Roman letter(s); forsyne (merke) med -er letter.

bokstavelig literal; (adv) literally, in a literal sense; (fullstendig, ogs.) positively, in literal earnest; — sant strictly true.

bokstavere spell; — feil misspell. bokstavering spelling.

bokstav|feil literal error. -gåte puzzle el. riddle in letters. -regning algebra. -rekke alphabet. -rett, -riktig literal. -rim alliteration. -skrift (writing in) letters, alphabetic writing.

boktrykker (master) printer, typographer. -farge printer's ink, printing ink. -gutt printer's apprentice. -i (stedet) printing office, printing house; (det som hører til å trykke) printing materials. -kunsten the art of printing, typography. -lære prenticeship to printing. -presse printing press. -svenn journeyman printer. -sverte printer's ink, printing ink.

I. bol (kropp uten lemmer) trunk.

II. bol (vepse— o. l.) nest.

bole (bib., arkais.) have illicit intercourse. -r fornicator; paramour. -rske fornicatress; paramour.

bolig house, dwelling, habitation, abode, residence; (leilighet) lodgings, rooms. -forholdene the housing problem. -lov housing bill, housing act. -nød housing famine. -spørsmålet the housing question.

boline (tau som sideliket på et råseil bringes framover med) bow-line.

bolk (mell. båser) stallbars; (tidsrom) period, spell.

I. bolle (til drikkevarer) bowl, basin.

II. bolle (hvete-) bun, muffin; (kjøtt-) dumpling.

bolne swell, fester. bolning swelling.

bolsjevik Bolshevik, Bolshevist. **bolsjevisme** Bolshevism.

bolster (pute, dyne) bolster.

bolt (jernnagle) bolt, iron pin; (i seil) band. **bolte seg** roll, gambol, frolic, tumble about.

bolverk pier, quay, breakwater, wharf; (vern) bulwark.

I. **bom** bar; (på vei) turnpike, toll-bar; (til gymnastikk) horizontal bar; **sette** — **for** put a stop to.

II. **bom** (feilskudd) miss. **skyte** — make a miss, miss the mark.

bombard|ement -bombardment. **-ere** bombard, shell; (med stein, skjellsord o. l.) pelt.

bombast bombast, rant, fustian. **-isk** bombastic, high-sounding.

bombe shell, bomb. **-attentat** bomb outrage. **-fast** shell-proof.

bombåt (båt som bringer varer til et skip) bumboat.

bomerang, se **boomerang**.

bommann toll-keeper.

bomme make a miss, blunder; (dt. tigge, «slå» en for penger) bum.

bomme (niste-) large wooden box, provision box.

bommert blunder; **begå en** — make a blunder.

bommesi (tykt bomullsstoff) fustian.

bomolje olive oil.

bompenger turnpike money.

bomsterk exceedingly strong, herculean.

bomstille stone-still, stock-still.

bomull cotton wool.

bomulls|dyrking cotton cultivation. **-fabrikk** cotton factory, cotton mill(s). **-flanell** flannelette. **-fløyel** c. velvet, Manchester velvet. **-frø** cottonseed. **-frøkaker** cotton-cakes, cotton-seedcakes. **-frøolje** cotton-oil, cotton-seed oil. **-garn** cotton (yarn). **-spinneri** cotton factory, c. mill. **-tråd** c. thread. **-tøy** cottonlinen el. -cloth, long cloth, calico. **-varer** cottons, **-veveri** cotton mill.

bon ticket, pay-ticket.

bonbon sugar-plum, bonbon. **bonboneske, bonbonniere** bonbonniere, comfit-box.

bonde peasant, countryman, rustic, farmer; (med ringeakt) boor, clown; (i sjakk) pawn; det ville bli en — **på en herremann** that would be rather a downfall; **det kan du innbille bønder** go and tell the marines!

bonde|aktig boorish, clownish, rustic. **-arbeid** farm work. **-bryllup** rustic wedding. **-dans** rustic dance. **-drakt** rustic garb, dress of a peasant. **-fanger** confidence-man, fool-farmer. **-født** born of peasants. **-gutt** peasant boy. **-gård** farm. **-jente** country lass el. wench. **-kone** country woman, farmeress. **-kost** rustic fare. **-mann** peasant, countryman. **-mål** country dialect. **-pike** peasant girl, country lass. **-rose** (peon) peony. **-skikk** country fashion. **-stand** peasantry, yeomanry. **-stolthet** rustic pride. **-tamp** country clown el. lout. **-venn** friend of the peasantry. **-vis: på** — in a country -like way, after the fashion of peasants. **bondsk** boorish, clownish.

bone polish, (bee's)wax.

bonitere value. **bonitering** valuation.

bonitet value, quality.

bonmot joke, witticism, bonmot.

bonne (barnefrøken) nursery governess.

bonus (til forsikrede) bonus.

bonvivant good-liver, free-liver.

boomerang (australsk kastevåpen) boomerang.

bopel (place of) residence; **forandring av** — removal.

I. **bor** (grunnstoff) boron.

II. **bor** (redskap) bore; (til metall ogs.) drill; **lite vri-** gimlet; **stort** — auger.

boraks borax.

I. **bord** (kant) border, edge, trimming; (i bok-binddekorasjon) margin border.

II. **bord** table; **dekke -et** lay the table; **lay**

the cloth; **kaldt** — a cold luncheon el. dinner; **gjøre reint** — make clear work, make a clean field; **ta av -et** take away, clear the table, remove the cloth; **etter -et** after dinner; **stå opp fra -et** rise from table; **skilles fra** — **og seng** be separated from bed and board; **før -et** before dinner; **maten er på -et** dinner is served; **gå til Guds, Herrens** — partake of the Lord's supper; **sette seg til -s** sit down to dinner el. supper, sit down to the table; **sitte til -s** sit at table; **føre en dame til -s** bring (take) a lady down to dinner, hand a lady to dinner; **lese til -s** say grace; **sette foten under eget** — establish oneself in life **drikke en under -et** drink one under the table; **ved -et** at table. during dinner el. supper; **varte opp ved -et** ·wait at table; **ved sluttet** — in private.

III. **bord** (skipsside) board; **fra -e** from alongside; **legge roret i -e** put the helm hard over. Se ogs. **ombord** og **overbord**.

IV. **bord** (fjøl, planke) board.

bord|bein leg of a table. **-bønn** grace. **-dame** dinner partner. **-dans** (få et bord til å danse) tableturning. **-dekning** laying a table. **-duk** table-cloth.

borde (entre eller: legge til på siden av et skip) board, lay alongside.

bordell bordel.

bord|ende head el. foot of the table.

bordereau (ordre fra en speditør til en annen) way bill.

bord|herre dinner partner. **-kant** edge of table. **-kavaler** dinner partner. **-klaff** flap of the table. **-klokke** handbell; dinner-bell, table-bell. **-kniv** table-knife. **-konversasjon** table-talk. **-løper** table-runner. **-oppsats** centre-piece, centre-ornament; cruetstand. **-plate** table slab, table top. **-setning** relay, party of diners. **-skikk** manners at table, behaviour at t.; **holde** — behave oneself at table. **-skive** leaf of a table. **-skuff** table -drawer. **-tale** dinner-speech. **-teppe** table-cover, table-cloth. **-vegg** board-partition.

bore bore, pierce; (i metall) drill; (hjerneskalle) trepan; (tønne) broach; (skip) scuttle; — **en brønn** sink a well; — **i senk** (ved påseiling) run down; **borte kniven i hans hjerte** plunged the knife into his heart. **-bille** boring beetle. **-maskin** drilling-machine.

I. **borg** (brok, kjetting som en rå el. gaffel henger i) sling.

II. **borg** (slott) castle.

III. **borg** (kreditt) credit, trust; dt. tick; **ta på** — take on credit, borrow. **borge** (ta på b.) borrow; (kreditere) credit, trust; — **for** vouch for, answer for.

borgen; se **kausjon; gå i** — **for** be surety for, bail one.

borger citizen. **-brev** burgess ticket; akademisk — certificate of matriculation. **-dyd** civic virtue. **-konge** citizen king. **-krig** civil war.

borgerlig civil, civic; (som vedk. borgere i en by) municipal; (jevn) homely, plain; — **frihet** civil liberty, l. of the subject; — **erverv** trade; — **stilling** position; **stå opp, gå til sengs i** — **tid** keep good hours; — **ekteskap** civil marriage; — **drama** domestic drama; **en** — a commoner; (adv) — **død** civilly dead; — **vidd** married before the registrar. **-het** homeliness.

borgermester mayor. **-dyd** mayoral virtue; **forsiktighet er en -dyd** discretion is the better part of valour. **-embete** mayoralty. **-mave pot** -belly. **-mine** air of great importance.

borger|plikt duty of a citizen. **-rett** citizenship; (borgerskap) freedom of a city; **har -rett i** has got the freedom of, is free of; **ordet har fått** · **rett** the word has been naturalized. **-skap, se** -**rett;** (samtlige borgere) citizens, citizenry, orporation, community, commonalty; **ta** — take out one's freedom; **få** — **i en by** obtain the freedom of a town, be made free of a city. **-skole** middle-class school. **-stand** middle-class (of towns), commonalty. **-væpning** town-militia, civic guard, trainband. **-ånd** civism, public spirit, good citizenship.

borg|fengsel dungeon. **-frue** lady of the castle, chatelaine. **-gård** (castle) court. **-herre** lord of the castle, chatelain.

borgis (en skriftstørrelse) bourgeois.

borgstue servant's hall.

boring boring, sinking; (kaliber, løp) bore.

borket of a palish yellow tinged with red.

bornert narrow-minded, strait-laced. **bornerthet** narrow-mindedness.

borre burdock; (frukten) bur.

borsyre boric-acis, boracic acid, hydric borate.

bort away, off; **han må** — he must go; **bort!** away! be gone! — **med fingrene!** hands off! **gifte** — marry off; **jage** — drive away, expel; **kalle** — call away; **bli kalt** — (ved døden) pass away, be taken; **Gud har kalt ham** — God has taken him to himself; **klatte** — fritter away, waste; **lodde** — dispose of by lottery; **rive** — carry el. snatch el. tear away; **rydde** — clear away; (fig) remove, smooth away; **se** — fra set aside, waive, look at it apart from, discount; **sende** — dismiss, send away; **skjemme** — indulge, spoil; **skjøte** — convey; **skusle** —, se **klatte** —; **ta** — remove, take away; **tinge** — hire el. let out; bargain away; **vende** — avert, divert, turn away; **vise** — dismiss, refuse admittance, turn away, expel; **ødsle** — dissipate, squander, waste.

borte away; absent; **være** — be lost el. gone; **bli** — (utebli) stay el. remain away, (gå tapt) be lost; **langt** — far away, far off; **dobbelt så langt** — at twice the distance; **jeg blir ikke lenge** — I shall not be long; **død og** — dead, dead and gone.

bortenfor (prep) off, beyond; (adv) beyond.

borteskamotere spirit away.

bortest (adj) furthermost; **den -e siden** the off hand side.

bort|fall falling away; omission; being dropped. **-e drop**, be omitted, fall away; be discontinued.

bortforklare explain away.

bort|forpakte farm, rent, let, lease out. **-forpaktning** farming etc., location.

bortfortolke interpret el. explain away.

bort|føre carry off; (flykte med) run away el. elope with; **la seg** — av run away with. **-førelse** carrying off; (ulovlig) abduction; (kvinnes) elopement (with).

bortgang (død) death, decease, passing (away). **bort|kommet** lost, gone. **-komne saker** lost property.

bortlede (vann) drain off; (en elv, tanker) divert; (mistanke) ward off.

bortlisitere contract (til: with).

bortlodning lottery.

bortre further, off.

bortreise (subst) departure. **-reist** gone away.

bortsett fra setting aside, waiving, apart from, aside from, independent(ly) of. **— fra følgende** consequences apart.

bortvendt (adj) averted, diverted.

bortvisning dismissal, expulsion.

bortvære blow away, scatter.

bosatt, bosittende resident, settled, established; **være** — i reside in.

boset|te seg establish oneself, settle, take up one's abode. **-telse** establishment, settlement, domiciliation.

Bosnia Bosnia. **bosnisk** Bosnian.

bosnjak (innbygger i Bosnia) Bosnian.

Bosporus the Bosporus el. the Bosphorus.

boss dust, sweepings; **-kasse** dustbin.

bosted, se **bopel**.

bot (lapp) patch; (forbedring) amendment, correction; (botshandling) penance; (mulkt) fine, penalty; **råde** — på remedy; correct, amend; **gjøre** — do penance, make atonement; **love** —

og bedring promise reform, promise to turn over a new leaf.

bota|niker botanist. **-nikk** botany. **-nisere** botanize, herborize. **-niserkasse** botanical case, botanising box. **-nisk** botanical.

bote|middel remedy (**for:** of) **-von** chance of repair.

botferdig penitent, repentant, contrite. **-het** penitence, repentance, contrition.

botn, se **bunn**.

botne reach the bottom.

Botniske Bukt the Gulf of Bothnia.

bots|dag penitential day. **-fengsel** penitentiary. **-predikant** preacher of repentance. **-preken** penitential sermon, sermon on repentance. **-øvelse** penance, penitential exercise.

bourgeois (bursjoa) (en skriftstørrelse) bourgeois. **-ie** (borgerskap) bourgeoisie.

bovenbram royal. **-bardun** r. backstay. **-rå** r. yard. **-seil** royal. **-skjøt** r. sheet.

bovenkryss mizen top-gallant.

bovenvekt top-weight.

bra (adj) honest, worthy; (adv) well; **en** — kar a decent fellow; **en** — pike a good girl; **bli** — get right, get well; **nå hadde hun det** — she was doing well now; **det er** —, **gutten min** well done my boy; **med meg er det** — I am all right; **det er** — **nok** that is all very well.

brahet honesty, worthiness.

brak crash, crack. **brake** crash.

I. **brakk** (om vann) brackish.

II. **brakk** (om jord) fallow; **ligge** — lie fallow. **-land** fallow-land. **-mark** fallow-field.

brakk|nese flat nose. **-neset** flat-nosed.

brakkvann brackish water.

bram ostentatious display, show; **med brask og** — ostentatiously.

bramfri unostentatious.

bramin brahmin.

bramme med boast of, make a show of, display. **-nde** ostentatious.

bramrå topgallant yard.

brann fire, conflagration; (brennende stykke tre) brand, firebrand; (i korn) blight, blast; **sette, stikke i** — set on fire, set fire to, (også fig) fire; **komme i** — catch fire, take fire; **stå i** — be on fire; **-alarm** f. alarm. **-alarmapparat** fire alarm (box), signalbox; **-assuranse**, se **brannforsikring**. **-bil** fire-engine; **-byll** carbuncle. **brannet** dark-striped, brindled, tabby. **brann|fakkel** incendiary torch, (fig) firebrand. **-fare** danger of fire. **-farlig** inflammable, liable to catch fire. **-folk** firemen, fire brigade. **-forhor** examination in a case of fire. **-forsikring** fire insurance. **-forsikringsselskap** fire insurance company. **-gavl** brick gable-wall. **-gul** flaming yellow, orange-coloured. **-hake** fire-hook. **-inspektør** fire-warden. **-kasse** (brannforsikringskasse) f. insurance fund. **-klokke** fire-bell, alarm bell. **-konstabel**, se **-mann**, **-korps** fire-brigade. **-kran** fire-plug, f. cock. **-lidt** fire sufferer. **-lukt** burning smell. **-lykt** signal lantern in cases of fire. **-mann** fireman. **-mur** fire-proof wall, party-wall. **-pil** fire-arrow. **-polise** fire insurance policy. **-redskaper** fire implements. **-rop** cry of fire, alarm of fire. **-ror** fuze, fuzee. **-seil** jumping sheet. **-sikker** fire-proof; **gjøre** — fireproof. **-sjef** fire-chief. **-skade** damage by fire. **-skatte** levy a contribution on requisition. **-skjær** gleam of (the) fire. **-slange** fire-hose, water-hose. **-slokningsapparat** fire-extinguisher. **-sprøyte** fire-engine. **-stasjon** fire-station. **-sted** place of a fire. **-stifter** fireraiser, incendiary. **-stiftelse** incendiarism, arson. **-stige** fire-ladder, fire-escape. **-sår** burn. **-takst** valuation for insurance. **-trygd** fire insurance. **-vakt** watch el. guard of firemen. **-ventil** fire plug, F.P. **-vesen** fire-office, fire-service; (brannfolka) the firebrigade. **-øvelse** fire-drill.

bras (tau ved begge ender av en rå) brace; **le** — lee brace; **lo** (luv) — weather brace.

I. **brase** (styrte) crash; — **imot** knock against; — **ned** come down with a crash; — **sammen** collapse.
II. **brase** (dreie ved hjelp~av brasene) brace; — **an** b. to; — **bakk** b. aback.
III. **brase** (steike) fry, roast, cook.
Brasil Brazil, the Brazils. **b–er, b–sk** Brazilian.
brask: med — og bram ostentatiously.
brasme (fisk) bream.
brast: stå last og — med share good or bad luck with.
bratsj viola, tenor violin. **-ist** violist.
bratt (steil) steep, precipitous; (plutselig) abrupt, sudden; **få en — ende** be brought (el. come) to an abrupt termination, end abruptly.
brattlende steep ground. **-lendt** bluffy, cliffy.
braute brag, vapour, make a boast (av: of), vaunt.
bravade (pral) boast, piece of bluff. **-r** bravado, bluff.
bravo! bravo! **-rop** cry of bravo. **bravissimo!** bravissimo!
bravur (glimrende sikkerhet) bravura. **-arie** bravura. **-nummer** bravura.
bre (subst) glacier; (snø-) snow-field, field of eternal snow.
bre(de) (vrb) spread. — **seg** (bli bredere) broaden; (om smitte el. ild) spread; (om person) spread oneself.
bred (vid) broad, wide; (om stilen) diffuse; **seks fot lang og fire** — six feet by four; **gjør seg** — looks big, gives himself airs; **fører en — pensel** is lavish of his colours. **-t** (adv) broadly etc.; **vidt og -t** far and wide. **-bladet** broad-leaved; (kniv) broad-bladed. **-brystet** broad-chested. **-buket** broad-bellied.
bredd border, edge, margin (av elv) bank; (av innsjø el. hav) shore; (i kjøle) breadth, gore **ved havets — on** the seashore; **gikk over sine -er** overflowed its banks.
bredde (tverrlengde) breadth, width; (stilens) diffuseness; (geografisk) latitude; **i -n** across; **under nordlig** — in north latitudes; **på 33 grader sydlig** — **,n** l. 33' south. **-grad** degree of latitude: under våre **-er** in our latitudes. **-sirkel** circle of latitude.
breddfull brimful.
bred|flabbe broad-jawed. **-fotet** broad-footed.
bred|side broadside. **-skuldret** broad-shouldered. **-skygget** broad-brimmed. **-snutet** (sko) squaretoed. **-sporet** broadgauge.
bregne fern. brake.
brei, se **bred**.
breie, se **bre(de)**.
breidd, se **bredde**.
breke bleat, baa. **breking** bleating, baaing.
brekk (brudd) break, rupture, breach, crack, rent; (beskadigelse) breakage.
brekkasje breakage.
brekke (subst) a steep ascent.
brekke (vrb.) break, fracture; — **nakken** break one's neck; — **lasta** break bulk; — **opp** break open; — **seg** vomit, puke. **brekk|jern** jemmy, crowbar. **-middel** emetic. **-pulver** emetic powder. **-stang** iron crow, lever. **-vogn** brake(s)van.
brekning vomiting.
brem border, edging, trimming; (frynse) fringe.
bremme (vrb) border, edge, trim.
brems (insekt) gadfly, horsefly.
bremse (stanseapparat) brake. **bremse** (vrb) brake; (fig) check, restrain. **bremse|apparat** braking apparatus. **-mann** brake(s)man. **-sko** brakeshoe. **-stang** brake lever. **bremsing** braking.
brenn|bar combustible, inflammable. **-barhet** combustibility, inflammability.
bren|ne (vt) burn; scorch, sear; commit to the flames; (lik) cremate; (etse) cauterize; (om nesle) sting; (vi) burn, be on fire. — **potter, teglstein** bake pots, tiles; — **brennevin** distil spirits; — **kaffe** roast coffee; — **av begjærlighet, vrede**

burn with desire, anger; **det -er i ovnen** there is a fire in the stove; **det har -t i natt på to steder** there was a fire last night in two places; **huset brant ned** the house was burnt down; — **av** burn, burn down; (kanon) fire, discharge; (krutt) flash; (fyrv.) let off fireworks; — **etter å** burn with desire to; **han(s hjerte) -er for henne** he dotes upon her; **det har -t for ham** there has been a fire at his house; — **inne** (en annen) burn one (to death) in his house; (selv) perish in the flames; — **inne med** be left with . . . on one's hands; — **ned** burn out; — **opp** burn, be burnt, be destroyed by fire; — **seg** (fig) burn one's fingers.
brenne (subst), se **ved**.
brenne|merke (subst) brand, stigma. **-merke** (vrb) brand, stigmatize. **-merking** branding, stigmatizing.
brennende scorching, burning; — **spørsmål** burning question.
brennenesle nettle. **brenner** (i lamper) burner.
brenneri, se **brennevins-**.
brennevin spirits, ardent spirits, liquor; (whisky) whisky; (genever) gin; (konjakk) brandy; **gjennomtrukket med** — brandied. **brennevins|-brenner** distiller of spirits. **-brenneri** distillery. **-brenning** distilling, distillation. **-glass** dramglass. **-utsalg** spirit shop.
brennglass burning-glass, sun-glass.
brenning burning etc.; (i tre) poker-painting, poker-drawing; (i sjøen) surf, breakers.
brenn|offer burnt sacrifice. **-punkt** focus.
brensel fuel, firing. **-besparende** fuel-saving. **-forbruk** consumption of fuel. **-(s)verdi** value as fuel.
brent (av brenne) burned, burnt; — **barn skyr ilden** the burned child dreads the fire; — **mandel** burned almond, praline.
bresje breach; **gjøre, skyte** — make a breach; **stille seg** (eller **gå) i -n** step into the breach; **ha stilt seg i -n** stand in the breach.
brest, breste, se **brist, briste**.
I. **brett** board; (bakke) tray; **på ett** — at once, off-hand; **på det svarte** — in bad odour, on the black list.
II. **brett** turned-down el. turned-up edge; (i bok) dog's ear, (fold)crease; **legge en — på** double (down), turn down; **legge en — i en bok** dog's ear a page; **legge — på** (fig) lay stress on, attach importance to.
brette: — **opp** turn, el. double up; — **ned** turn down; undouble.
brettspill boardgame.
brev letter, epistle, missive, (mindre) note; **veksle — med en** correspond with one; **gi — på** give in writing; **et — knappenåler** a paper of pins. **brev|ark** note sheet. **-bok** (kopibok) letter-book; (samling av mønsterbrev) letter-writer. **-due** carrier (pigeon), homing pigeon. **-form** epistolary style; **i —** in the form of a letter. **-hemmeligheten** the inviolability of letters, the privacy of correspondence. **-kasse** letter-box; **-kort** post-card, postal card; **-kort til utlandet** foreign post-card, lukket **-kort** letter-card. **-mappe** letter-book, letter-case. **-ombæring** delivery. **-papir** letter-paper, note-paper (luksuspapir): fancy-paper. **-porto** postage, postage-rate. **-post** letter-post. **-presser** paper-weight. **-skriver** letter-writer. **-skriving** letter-writing. **-stil** epistolary style of writing. **-veksle** (vrb) (litt., sj.) correspond. **-veksling** correspondence; **stå i -veksling** correspond, cultivate a correspondence. **-vekt** letter-balance, letter-weigher.
bridge, el. **bridsj** (kortspill) bridge.
brigade brigade. **-general** brigadier, brigadier-general. **-øvelse** brigade drill.
brigg (tomastet skip) brig; **rigget som —** brigrigged.
brikett briquet; **-er** (også) patent-fuel.
brikke (treplate) wooden plate; (i spill) man, piece.

briljant (adj) brilliant. **briljant** (slepen diamant) brilliant.
briljantine (et hårmiddel) brilliantine.
briljere (glimre) shine.
brille|futteral spectacle-case. **-glass** spectacleglass el. -lens. **-innfatning** spectacle-frame.
briller (pl) spectacles, glasses.
brille|slange hooded snake, cobra (de capella). **-stenger** (pl) spectacle-frame.
brim, se **brenning.**
bringe (til den talende) bring; (ellers) take, carry, convey; **bring meg den boka** bring me that book; **bring dette brevet på posthuset** take (el. carry) this letter to the post-office; **— et offer** make a sacrifice; **— det vidt** be very successful, achieve great things, go far; **— for dagen** bring to light; **— en fra den tanke** make one change his mind; **— fram** bring forward; **— lys i** clear up; **— i erfaring** learn, ascertain; **— ham inn på** (emne) draw him on to talking of. **— ulykke over** bring calamity on; **— noe over sitt hjerte** bring oneself to, find in one's heart; **— på bane** broach; **— — en på fote igjen** retrieve one's affairs, bring his affairs round again; **— en til seg selv** restore one to consciousness; **— til taushet** silence; **— en til å . . . make one . . .; — det dertil at** bring matters to such a pass that; **— ut blant folk** spread abroad; **— en ut av det** put one out; **— ham ut av seg selv** drive him beside himself.
bringe (bryst) chest.
bringebær raspberry. **-busk** raspberry-bush. **-saft** r. syrup. **-syltetøy** r. jam.
bris breeze.
I. **brisk** (einer) juniper. **-elåg** decoction of juniper.
II. **brisk** (fast seng) pallet, couch of boards.
briske seg swell, show off. **— av noe** plume oneself on.
brisling (fisk) sprat.
brissel (en kjertel) sweetbread, pancreas.
brist (skavank) defect; (mangel) lack.
briste burst, crack, break (også fig om hjertet); (slå feil) fail; **øynene -r** the eyes grow dim; **det får — eller bære** it must break or bend; **da brast min tålmodighet** I got out of all patience; **— i latter** burst out laughing; **— i gråt** burst out crying, burst into tears. **-ferdig** ready to burst.
Brit|annia Britain. **b-isk** British. **-(t)e** Briton. **bro,** se **bru.**
I. **brodd** sting; **stampe mot -en** kick against the pricks; **uten — stingless.**
II. **brodd** (is-) icecalk, icespar; (på hest) frostnail.
broder (gammeldags form for bror), se **bror** etc.
brodere embroider; (utsmykke) adorn. **broder|garn** embroidering thread. **-mønster** pattern for embroidering. **-ramme** embroidering-frame.
broderi embroidery. **-forretning, -handel** fancy shop. **brodering** embroidering.
broderlig brotherly, fraternal. **-het** fraternal spirit.
broder|lag fraternity. **-mord** fratricide. **-morder** fratricide. **-ånd** brotherly spirit.
brodne kar i alle land every country has its drawbacks; there are black sheep in every flock; **brodne panner** broken heads.
brok, se **bukse.**
brokade brocade.
broket pied, party-coloured, motley, variegated, chequered; **-e farger** gay colours; **— hest** piebald (horse); **det ser — ut** it has an awkward look; **her går det — for seg** these are strange goings-on; **han gjorde det — for meg** he was rather too bad.
brokk (sykdom) rupture, hernia.
brokk|belte hernial belt. **-bind, -bånd** truss, suspensory, hernial bandage.
brokker (subst pl) fragments, scraps, bits.

brokkfugl plover.
brokk|pasient sufferer from hernia. **-tilfelle** rupture, case of hernia.
brom brome, bromine.
brom|kalium bromide of potassium, potassic bromide. **-syre** bromic acid.
bronkial bronchial.
bronk|ier (pl) bronchiæ. **-itt** bronchitis.
bronse bronze, (hard) brass. **-alder** bronze age el. period. **-farge** b. colour. **-farget** b.-coloured. **-medalje** b. medal. **-re** bronze. **-saker** bronzes.
bror (den gamle form **broder** brukes i litt. smnsetn.) brother; (frimurer) brother mason; (munk) brother, friar; (pl) i religiøs stil: brethren; **omgåes som brødre** fraternize; **10 daler verdt mellom brødre** 10 dollars and cheap at that (price); **brødrene R.** (firma) R. Brothers. **-datter** niece.
bror|folk sister nation. **-forbund** fraternity. **-hat** fraternal hatred. **-hilsen** brotherly greeting. **-hånd** fraternal hand.
bror|kjærlighet fraternal el. brotherly love. **-kyss** fraternal kiss. **-part** brother's share; **ta -parten** take the lion's share. **-plikt** brother's duty, duty as a brother. **-skap** brotherhood, fraternity; **ikke — i kortspill** I would cheat my own father at cards. **-strid** dissension between brothers. **-sønn** nephew.
brosje brooch.
brosjyre booklet, pamphlet, brochure.
brott (se også **brudd**) fragment, shard; (i sjøen) breakers, surf. **-sjø** breaker, heave sea.
brr! (gysning o. l.) ugh! se **prr!**
bru bridge; (havnebru) pier, jetty; **slå — over** throw a bridge over, bridge over. **-bue** arch (of a bridge).
brud bride; **stå — be** el. get married.
brudd (revne) breach, rupture, fracture; **fri for — (merk.) free from breakage; **det er kommet til et — mellom dem** they have fallen out, quarrelled.
brudd|flate surface of fracture. **-stykke** fragment. **-aktig** fragmentary.
brude|drakt bridal dress. **-ferd** wedding (festival); wedding procession. **-folk** bridal couple. **-følge** wedding procession. **-fører** (den som fører bruden til alteret) bestman to the bride, bridesman. **-gave** nuptial present. **-kammer** nuptial chamber. **-kjole** bridal el. wedding gown. **-krans** nuptial wreath. **-par** bridal pair, new-married couple. **-pike** bride's maid. **-seng** bride-bed, nuptial bed. **-skammel:** **føre til -skammelen** lead to the altar. **-slør** bridal veil. **-utstyr** wedding outfit, trousseau.
brudgom bridegroom.
brudulje falling-out, shindy, row.
brugde basking shark.
bru|hode bridge-head.
I. **bruk** use, employment; (skikk) practice, custom, usage; **gjøre — av** make use of; **til — for** for the use of; **ingen — for** no use el. occasion for; **det er skikk og — her** it is the custom here; **gå av — go** out of use, fall into disuse, fall into abeyance; **komme i — get** el. come into use; **ta i — take** into use.
II. **bruk** (gårds-) farm; (sag-) saw el. timber mills (amer.: lumber m.).
brukar (bridge)pier.
bruk|bar fit for use, usable, serviceable, efficient; **i -bar stand** serviceable. **-barhet** fitness for use, usefulness.
bruke use, employ; (forbruke) consume; (penger) spend; (pleie) be in the habit of; **— sin tid godt** make a good use of one's time; **— noe mot en sykdom** take something for a complaint; **— munn** use bad (impertinent, abusive) language; **— bena** make use of one's legs; **det kan han — that** is in his way; **vi brukte to dager til å** it took us two days to el.

we took two days to; — **lang tid til å** be slow of -ing; — **opp** consume, expend, use the whole; — **seg** (bruke munn) use language, abuse; det **-s ikke her til lands** it is not the custom in this country. **brukte klær** second hand clothes.
brukelig, se **brukbar;** (vanlig) customary, usual.
bruker user; holder, tenant; (jur.) usufructuary.
bruks|anvisning directions for use. **-forening** supply association. **-gjenstand** article for use. **-rett** right of using, usufruct.
bruleg|ge pave. **-ger** paver, pavior. **-gerjomfru** paving-beetle. **-ning** paving; pavement.
brum growl. **-basse** growler; **brumle** hum, buzz. **brumme** growl; (fig) grumble.
brun brown; **det -e på steika** the crust. **brune** brown, embrown; (huden) bronze; (kjøtt) brown, fry; **-t smør** browned el. burnt butter.
brunett dark-complexioned. **brunhåret** brown -haired.
brunkol, brunkull brown-coal.
brunst (hundyrs) heat; (handyrs) rut, rutting. **brun|stekt** done brown. **-stein** manganese.
brunstig in heat; rutting.
brunsttid time of heat; rutting time.
brus (brusende lyd) rushing sound, roar; (oppbrusing) effervescence, fiz; (limonade) effervescing lemonade.
bruse (vrb) effervesce, froth, foam; (havet) roar, rush; **han -r lett opp** he is apt to fly out, fire up.
bruse (bot.), se **brisk.**
brus|hane (fugl) ruff. **-hode** hot-headed person.
brusk gristle, cartilage. **-aktig** gristly, cartilaginous.
bruspulver effervescent powder, soda powder.
brustein paving-stone, pavement-stone.
brusten (av **briste)** (revnet) broken, cracked; (om øyne) dimmed, grown dim, filmed in death, glazed.
brutal brutal, churlish, bullying; **en — person** a bully. **-itet** brutality.
brutto|beløp gross-amount. **-inntekt** gross amount of receipts, gross earnings. **-vekt** gross-weight.
bry (vt) trouble, put to trouble; **bry seg med** bother (oneself), trouble (oneself) about el. with; **— seg om** care about el. for, concern (oneself) about, mind; **å, bry Dem ikke om det!** don't trouble yourself, never you mind; **bry deg ikke om meg** never mind me; **jeg -r meg ikke om det** I don't care about it el. for it; **jeg -r meg ikke om å gå** I don't care to go el. about going.
bry (subst.) trouble, pother; bother.
brydd embarrassed, self-conscious.
brydde, se **spire.**
brygg brewing.
Brügge Bruges.
brygge (kai) wharf, quay.
brygge (vrb) brew.
brygge|kar brewing vat. **-kjele** brewing copper.
brygger brewer. **-hest** brewer's dray horse. **-hus** laundry, wash-house. **bryggeri** brewery, brewing house. **-arbeider** brewer's man, drayman. **-mester** master brewer. **-vogn** draycart.
bryggesjauer lumper, quay porter.
brygning brewing.
bryllup wedding, nuptials, bridal, marriage; **ha, holde** — celebrate a wedding, be married; **være i** — be at a wedding. **bryllups|dag** wedding day. **-ferd** wedding festival, bridal. **-fest** nuptial festival. **-gave** wedding present. **-gilde** wedding (-feast). **-kjole** wedding gown. **-klær** nuptial el. wedding garments. **-reise** wedding-trip.
bryn eyebrow.
brynde heat, passion, lust.
bryne (subst) sharpening stone, whetstone; (vrb) sharpen, whet.
brynje coat of mail, cuirass. **-kledd** mailclad.

brysk blunt, churlish.
brysom troublesome, trying.
Bryssel Brussels. **brysseler|kniplinger, -tepper** Brussels lace, carpets.
bryst (mest om det utvendige) breast; (om det innvendige og det hele) chest; (insekts) thorax; (på bolt, skrue o. l.) shoulder; **gi — give suck; legge til -et** suckle; **slå seg for -et** strike (smite) one's breast; **ha svakt, sterkt — have a weak, strong chest; ha vondt i -et** have a pain in one's chest; **— mot — breast to breast. -bilde** half-length picture. **-drå-per** pectoral essence. **bryste seg** draw oneself up, bridle up, (av noe) boast of st. **bryst|finne** pectoral fin. **-harnisk** breastplate, corselet. **-kasse** chest. **-kjertel** mammary gland. **-krampe** spasm in the chest. **-lomme** breast-pocket. **-nål** breastpin, shirt-pin, brooch. **-panel** dado. **-saft** pectoral syrup. **-sløyfe** breastknot. **-smekke** (gammeldags) stomacher; (siklesmekke) bib. **-stem-me** natural voice, chest voice. **-sukker** jujube, lozenge, barley-sugar. **-svak** weak-chested. **-syk** having a complaint in the chest. **-syke** disease of the chest, chest-complaint. **-tone** chest note. **-vern** breast-work, parapet. **-vorte** nipple.
bryte (brekke) break; (om lyset) refract; (om sjøen) break; **— sitt hode** puzzle, rack, cudgel one's brain; **— sitt løfte** break one's promise; **— laget part company; — isen break** the ice; **— tausheten** break silence; **— av break** off; (i talen) stop; **— fram break** (el. burst) forth, emerge; **dagen brøt fram** day broke, dawned; **— inn i et hus** break into a house; **— løs** break loose; **— med en** break with one; **— med en** vane break (oneself of) a habit; **— opp break** el. force open; (avmarsjere) march; (om sår) burst; **selskapet brøt opp** the party broke up; **— sta-ven over** condemn; **på det tyske** have a German accent; **— ut** (av fengsel) break (out of) prison; **ilden brøt ut** the fire broke out **brytekamp** wrestling-match. **-kunst** the art of wrestling, wrestling.
bryter (atlet) wrestler; (elektr.) switch. **-matte** wrestling-ground. **-tak** (grasp in) wrestling. **brytes** be broken etc.; (kamp) wrestle.
brytning breaking etc.; wrestling; (fig) conflict; **lysstrålenes** — refraction of light. **bryt|ningsfeil** (i øyet) error of refraction. **-ningsvinkel** angle of refraction.
bræ melt; pay over (with tar or pitch).
bræke, se **breke.**
brød bread; **et brød** a loaf (of bread); **ristet — toast; det gikk som varmt hvete—** it sold like wildfire; **tjene sitt —** earn el. make one's bread; **earn one's living; være i ens — eat one's bread; ta -et av munnen på en** take away one's bread; **den enes død, den annens brød** one man's breath another man's death. **brødbakke** bread-basket. **-brøde** (overtredelse) fault, blame, guilt. **-betynget,** conscious (of one's guilt), guilty. **-full** faulty, guilty, culpable.
brød|emne bread stuff. **-frukt** bread-fruit. **-fø** supply with bread-stuffs; maintain, support. **-kniv** bread-knife. **-korn** bread-corn. **-kurv** bread basket, pannier. **-leiv** flap of bread. **-løs** bread-less, without bread. **-løse** kunster unprofitable pursuits. **-mangel** scarcity of bread. **-nid** (professional) jealousy. **-pose** bread-bag; (soldats) haversack, carry-all.
brødremenigheten the United Brethren.
brød|skorpe crust of bread. **-skrift** (typ.) body type. **-smule** crumb of bread. **-spade** peel. **-studium** professional study. **-suppe** panade. **-terning** sippet.
brøk fraction; uekte **— improper fraction. -del** fractional part, fraction. **-regning** fractions. **-strek** line of fraction.
brøl roar, bellow. **brøle** roar, bellow.
brøl(e)ape (amerikansk apeslekt) howler; (skrålhals) bawler; (høyrøstet taler) ranter.

brønn well; det er for seint å lukke -en når barnet er druknet lock the stable-door, before the steed is stolen; after death the doctor. –borer well-borer. –graver well-digger. –karse water-cress. –kur: ta –kur take el. drink the waters. –vann well-water.

brøst (mangel, feil) fault, defect, flaw, imperfection. –feldig decayed, ruinous, dilapidated, out of repair. –feldighet decay, ruin, dilapidation.

brøstholden (forurettet) aggrieved.

brøyte break, turn; (gjøre vei) clear a road. brå abrupt, sudden. –dyp deep close-to, steep -to. –død sudden death. –hast hot (el. violent) hurry. få en — ende come to an untimely end. bråk (subst) fuss, boisterousness, noise. –e (vrb) to fuss, to bluster, to make a noise. –ende fussy, boisterous, noisy.

brå|kulde a sudden spell of cold.

bråne, se smelte.

brå|sinne a sudden passion. –stanse to stop short.

bråte abat(t)is, obstruction of felled (el. a tangle of) trees; (rydning, avbrent stykke i skogen) burnt land, burns, clearing; (dt = mengde) heap(s), swad. (med: of). en (hel) — med brever a (complete) swad of el. (heaps of) letters. –brenning (clearing land by) burning, burning of rubbish from gardens etc. –land (land. jord ryddet ved -brenning) burnt land, burns.

brått (adv) abruptly, suddenly.

bråvakker pretty at first sight. –vende to turn short. –vending a short turn.

bu! (interj.) bo!

bu (subst) booth, stall; (butikk) shop.

bu (vrb), se bo.

bud (befaling) command, commandment, order; (ærend) message; (sendebud) messenger; (tilbud) offer; (ved auksjon) bid, bidding; de ti — the ten commandments, the decalogue; –et venter bearer waits; sende — etter send for; sende — til en send to one, send one word; la det gå — etter ham let him be sent for. –bringer bearer of a message, messenger.

Buddh|a Buddha. b–ismen Buddhism. –ist Buddhist. b–istisk Buddhist(ic).

budeie dairy (el. milk) maid, dairy woman. budsjett budget, supply, ways and means, estimates: bevilge –et vote supplies. budsjettere budget, estimate for.

budskap tidings.

bue bow (fiolin) bow, dt. fiddlestick; (hvelving) arch; (sirkel-) arc; (linje) curve; (musikk) tie; spenne –n for høyt aim too high, make too great pretensions. –formet bowed, curved, arched. –føring bowing. –gang arcade, archway. –lampe arc-lamp. –skytning archery. –skytter archer, bowman. –streng bowstring. –strøk stroke of the bow.

buffer (fjærende støtapparat) buffer.

buffet (spisestuemøbel) sideboard; (disk i restaurant) refreshment bar; (aftenanretning) ball supper. –jomfru bar-maid.

bugne bulge, bend; de –nde sail the bellying sails el. canvass; greina –r av frukt the branch bends under the weight of the fruit; bordet –r av retter the table groans under the weight of the dishes.

buk belly, abdomen, paunch; –finne abdominal fin. –hinnebetennelse peritonitis.

bukett bouquet, nosegay.

I. bukk (geiteb.) he-goat, ram-goat; (råb.) buck; (trebukk til bord) horse, trestle; (maste-bukk på skip) sheer-legs, sheers; (kuske-) box; (tjenersete) dickey; hoppe — play at leap-frog; stå — make, give, proffer a back; stå — for en give one a leg up; skiller fårene fra –ene (bib.) divideth the sheep from the goats.

II. bukk (hilsen) bow; gjøre et — make a bow.

bukke bow, bend; (bøye seg) bow, bend the

head, incline (the head); — dypt bow low, bow profoundly; — for en bow to one; — seg (ned) stoop; — under succumb; — under for succumb to, sink beneath, be overcome by. bukkel (kroll i håret) ringlet.

bukke|skinn buckskin. –skjegg goat's beard. –sprang caper, capriole.

bukking bowing etc.; — og skraping bowing and scraping.

buksbom box. –hekk box-hedge.

bukse, se bukser.

bukse|bak seat of trousers. –bein leg of trousers. –bjørn (hel, lukket nattdrakt for småbarn) combination garment. –knapp trouser button. –linning waistband. –lomme trouser pocket. –laus breechless.

bukse|r trousers; (ride-) breeches; (løstsittende, samlet ved kneet) knicker-bockers; (korte dameeller barnebukser) pantalettes; (underbukser) drawers; et par — a pair of trousers; jeg har revet -ne mine i stykker I have torn my trousers: han skalv i –ne his heart was in his hose (el. went down to his heels, shoes).

buksere tow, tug. bukser|båt tow-boat, tug- (-boat). –ing towing. –line towline. –penger towage. –trosse tow-rope, hawser.

bukse|sele brace, suspender. –tøy trousering.

bukspytt pancreatic juice. –kjertel pancreas.

bukt bend, turn, curve, sweep, winding; (hav-) gulf, bay; (i tømmer) round; (av tau) (mar) bight; (oppkveilet) fake; slå — make turns; få — med manage, master, get the better of. buk|taler ventriloquist. –taleraktig ventriloquial. –taleri ventriloquism, ventrilocution.

bukte bend, wind, meander. buktet curved, winding, sinuous, tortuous. buktning winding etc., sinuosity.

bulder noise, crash, uproar; (av vogner o. l.) rumble, rumbling.

buldre (larme, rumle) roar, rattle; (skjenne) bluster; –basse blusterer.

bule (knopp på metallarbeid) boss, embossment; (opphøyning på et legemes overflate) bump, lump, protuberance; (i hatt) knock; (kneipe) low place of amusement. –hatt knockabout hat, billycock hat. –t bossed, embossed; dented.

bulevard boulevard.

Bulgar|ia Bulgaria. b–, b–sk Bulgarian.

buljong broth, clear soup. –terning meat lozenge, cake of soup, beef-tea.

bulk dent, dint, knock. bulket dented, dinted. bulldogg bulldog.

bulle (pavelig) bull.

bulletin bulletin.

bulme(urt) henbane.

bum! (int) bang!

bu|mann resident, farmer. –merke signation, totem.

bums bang! dash! slap! et bums a thump. bunad national costume el. dress.

bundet av binde: — varme latent heat. bunding, se strikketøy.

bundsforvandt (forbundsfelle) ally.

I. bunke heap, pile; samle i — hoard (up money). bunke (vt) sammen heap up; — seg opp accumulate.

bunker (kolrom i dampskip) bunker. –kol –kull coal for bunkers.

bunn bottom; (i tøy) ground, groundwork; nå — (red føttene) feel the ground; ikke nå — be out of one's depth; slå –en inn el. ut på break the bottom of, stave in; til –s, til –en to the bottom; (fig) thoroughly; komme til –s get at (el. to) the bottom of; i — og grunn utterly, radically.

bunne (stå bunn) feel el. touch bottom; — (fig) be bottomed on, rest on.

bunn|fall sediment, deposit, precipitate, grounds. –fattig utterly destitute. –felle precipitate, throw down. **-felle seg, -felles** be precipitated. **-felling** precipitation. **-fordervet** utterly depraved. **-fryse** freeze to the bottom. **-garn** seine. **-løs** bottomless, unfathomable; **være i -løs gjeld** be over head and ears in debt; **-løs uvitenhet** boundless ignorance. **-råtten** completely rotten.

bunn|skrape(r) dredge. **-slepevad** trawl-net. **-stykke** bottom piece; (i kanon) breech.

bunt bundle, bunch; **en — høy** a truss el. bootle of hay.

bunte bundle, make up in bundles.

buntmaker furrier, skinner. **-varer** furs and skins.

bur cage; **sette i — cage.**

burde, se bør.

bure (brøle) low.

Burgund Burgundy. **b-er** Burgundian; (vin) Burgundy. **b-isk** Burgundian.

burlesk burlesque. **burleske** burlesque.

burnus (arabisk kappe) burnoose.

bus (hodekulls) slap, bang; **løpe — på** bounce against.

buse på be precipitate, go in head foremost; **buse ut med** blurt out.

busemann (skremmebilde) bugbear, bugaboo, bogey, bogy, bogie, bloody-bones; (i nesen) dirt formed in the nostrils.

busk bush, shrub.

buskaktig bushy, shrubby, arbuscular.

buskap cattle, live stock; (småfe) flock; (storfe) herd.

buskas thicket, shrubbery.

busket bushy, shrubby; (om pels) shaggy.

busk|mann bushman. **-plante** shrubby plant.

I. **buss** (omnibus) bus.

II. **buss** (skrå, lite stykke skråtobakk) quid of tobacco, (amr.) chaw.

busserull smock frock, jumper.

bust bristle; **reise — (fig) bristle up.**

bustet dishevelled; **hun er — på håret** her hair is dishevelled.

butikk (shop); (amr) store; **drive — keep** a shop; (amr) run a store. **butikk(s)gutt** shop-boy. **-jomfru** shop-woman.

I. **butt** (mutt) sulky, surly, snappish.

II. **butt** (ikke spiss) blunt, thick.

butt (subst) tub.

butter-deig puff-paste.

buttet chubby, dumpy.

by town; (domkirkeby, større by, utenlandsk by) city; **bo i -en** live in town; **han er i -en** he is out; **reise fra -en** leave town; **piken er i -en** the maid is gone an errand; **gå i -en** go on errands; **gå omkring i -en** walk about the town.

by|befolkning, townspeople, town population. **-bud** (ticket-)porter, commissionaire.

by(de) (befale) command, order, bid, charge, enjoin; (innby) ask, invite; (tilby) offer, proffer, tender; (gjøre bud) bid, offer; **får jeg — Dem en kopp te?** will you take a cup of tea?; **og det tør De — meg** dare you take such liberty with me? **dare you say that to my face? han lar seg — allting** he puts up with anything; **— opp** raise the price of; **— en opp til dans** ask one to dance; **— over et kongerike** rule, sway a kingdom; **— over** (overby) outbid; **— på bid** for, make a bid for; **— seg til** offer oneself.

bydemåte (gram.) (imperativ) the imperative mode.

bydende commanding, imperious; **— plikt, nødvendighet** imperative duty, necessity; **det ble en — nødvendighet for han** it became imperative for him.

bye shower; (vind-) squall; (torden-) thunderstorm; **det trekker opp til en —** a squall is brewing; **fikk en — over seg** was caught in a squall. **-vær** showery el. squally weather.

byfoged town judge.

byfolk towns-people, -folk; town-bred p.

bygd country, (rural) district, parish. **komme på -a** come upon the parish.

bygde|folk parishioners. **-interesser** local interests. **-sagn** local tradition.

I. **bygg** barley.

II. **bygg** building operations; building. **bygg|aks** ear of barley. **-brød** barley bread.

bygge build, construct; **— og bo** take up one's abode; **bygd av eik, jern** (mar) oak-built, iron-built (o. fl.); **bygd i utlandet** foreign-built; **velbygd** (om person) well-built, well-knit; **— opp igjen** rebuild; **— på** (fig) rely on, trust to, rest upon; **— til** make additions to a building. **-arbeid** building work; building enterprise. **-fag** building trade. **-fond** building fund. **-forening** building society. **-grunn** building site. **-lov** building by-laws. **-lyst** passion for building. **-lån** building advances. **-materialer** building materials. **-måte** architecture, style of building. **-overslag** builder's estimate. **-plass** building ground (plot el. lot), site. **-skikk** style of building. **-spekulant** building speculator, jerrybuilder.

byggherre owner of a house (in construction), builder's employer.

byggkorn barley corn.

byggmester builder, master builder, architect.

byggraut barley -meal porridge.

byggryn barley groats.

bygning building, structure, edifice, pile, fabric; (bygningsmåte) build, frame, construction; **huset er under — the** house is building, is being built; **han er svak, sterk av —** he is of a delicate, robust frame (ogs. make). **bygnings|avgift** tax on buildings. **-blokk** block of buildings. **-del** structure. **-entreprenør** master-builder. **-kommisjon** board of works. **-kompleks** pile of buildings. **-konduktør** overseer. **-kunst** architecture. **-lov** building-regulations; **-måte** style of building, architecture. **-regler** rules laid down for construction. **-snekker** joiner. **-tegning** draught, working-drawing. **-utvalg** building committee. **-vesen** (matters relative to) public works.

bygsel lease, leasehold. **-brev** lease.

bygsle lease, take on (a) lease of.

by|gutt, se bymenneske.

byks bound, jump. **bykse** bound, jump.

by|liv town life. **-lov** municipal law.

byll boil, blain. **byllepest** bubonic plague.

bylt bundle, parcel. **-e** bundle, tie up in a bundle.

by|mann, -menneske townsman, town-dweller, town-bred man; cockney.

by|nytt town news, news from town. **-post** town-post, town delivery.

byrd birth, descent.

byrde burden, load, charge, fardel; **livet er ham en —** life is a burden to him; **falle til —** be a burden to. **-full** burdensome, onerous, grievous.

by|regulering town-planning. **-rett** town court of law.

byrg proud, uppish.

byrå office; **Reuters — R.**s Agency. **-sjef** chief clerk.

byrå|krat bureaucrat. **-krati** bureaucracy; (-kratiet) officialdom. **-kratisk** bureaucratic.

Bysans Byzantium. **bysantiner** Byzantine. **bysantinsk** Byzantine.

bys|barn native of a town; **vi er -barn** we are fellow-townsmen.

by|seller local agent. **-skriver** town clerk.

bysse, se kabyss.

bysse (vt) lull (asleep, to sleep).

byste bust.

bystyre (= kommunestyre i by), city (town) council, (amr.) townsmen. **-medlem** city councillor, (amr) townsman; jvf. kommunestyre, ordfører, formannskap.

bytning (ex)changing.

bytte (ombytning) exchange; (krigs-) booty

spoil, prey; **i** — mot in exchange for; **gjøre** — make booty; **gjøre et dårlig** — change for the worse; **være et** — for (fig) be a prey to.

bytte (vrb) change, exchange, barter; — **seg til noe** get in exchange; — **hatt med en** (ex)change hats with one; **jeg vil ikke** — **med ham** I would not change places with him, I would not be in his shoes; **-handel** exchange (trade). I. **bytting** (i folketro) changed child, changeling. II. **bytting,** se **bytning.**

bæl (breking) baa! (hånlig) ugh.

bær berry.

bære carry; (is. fig i faste forb.) bear; (holde oppe) support; (utholde) sustain; (tåle) endure, suffer; (være iført, gå med, slite) wear (f. eks. trousers, a crown, a moustache, a smile, a sword, mourning, glasses); — **nag til ham** bear him malice; — **vitnesbyrd om** bear witness el. testimony to; **det -s meg for** I have a presentiment, somethings tells me; **hvor -r det hen?** where are we going? — over med bear with; **-r på en sykdom** has a desease latent in him; — **på en hemmelighet** have a secret; — **seg** (om et foretagende) pay, succeed; (jamre, klage, ta på vei) moan, wail, carry on, rave. — **seg at** behave, act, go about it; **slik -r han seg alltid** at that is the way he always does; — **seg at** med (behandle) serve.

bære|bør hand-barrow. **-evne** bearing strength; (et skips) carrying capacity, dead weight capacity. **-kraft** strength to bear; (et skips) buoyancy. **-r** carrier, porter; bearer. **-stol** sedan-chair.

bø (egtl. gård) farm; (innmark) home fields. **bøddel** hangman, executioner; (plageånd) tormentor. **-aktig** hangman-like; barbarous. **-sverd (-øks)** executioner's sword (axe). **bøffel** buffalo; (grov person) boor. **-aktig** boorish. **-hud** buffalo's hide. **-lær** buff (skinn). **Bøhm|en** Bohemia. **b-er,** **b-erinne, -isk** Bohemian.

bøk beech. **bøkaske** buck-ashes. **bøke** (koke i ut) buck. **-kar** buckingtub. **-lund** beech-grove. **-nøtt** beech-nut. **-skog** forest of beech-trees. **-tre, (-ved)** beech-wood.

bøkker cooper. **-mester** master cooper. **-svenn** journeyman-cooper. **-verksted** cooper's shop. **-verktøy** cooper's tools.

bøle (kiste) bin, hutch, (oppholdssted) haunt, dwelling.

bølge, bølgje wave, billow; (større) sea; **en** — **slo over skipet** a sea broke over the ship. **bølge, bølgje** (vrb) wave, undulate; **-nde** bl. a. billowy; wavy; rolling, undulating. **-nde lokker** flowing locks; **-nde barm** heaving bosom. **bølge|bevegelse** undulation, wave-motion. **-blikk** corrugated iron. **-bryter** breakwater. **-dal** trough of the sea. **-damper** wave-subduer. **-gang** swell, sea. **-lengde** wavelength. **-linje** wave-line, undulating line. **-måler** wavemeter. **-slag** beating el. dashing of the waves, (svakt) ripple. **-topp** wave-crest.

bøling cattle, livestock; (av småfe) flock, (av storfe) herd.

bølle (ramp, rå person) rough.

bønn (i alm. el. til Gud) prayer; (bønnfallelse) entreaty, appeal; (påkallelse) supplication; (innstendig) solicitation; (forlangende) request; (skriftlig) suit, petition; **den første** — **i Fader vår** the first petition.

bønne bean; (kaffe-) berry, coffee-berry. **bønnebok** prayer-book, book of prayers. **bønnemøte** prayer-meeting. **bønne|stake, -stang** bean-pole, bean-stalk. **bønnfalle** entreat, beseech, implore. **bønn|høre** grant (a prayer el. petition), hear, listen to (one); **bli -hørt** gain a hearing, find favour, be successful (in one's suit). **-hørelse** granting etc. **bønnlig** suppliant, imploring, pleading, appealing. **bønnskrift** petition.

bør (pres. av **burde**) ought; **du** — **gjøre det** you ought to do it; **det** — **gjøres** it ought to be done; **som seg hør og** — as is meet and proper. I. **bør** (byrde) burden, charge, load. II. **bør,** se **bæreber.** III. **bør** (medvind) fair wind. **børnskap** fisherman's gear. **børs** exchange, 'change; (utenlandsk) bourse; **på -en** on 'change; (i -bygningen) in the exchange. **-dag** exchange-day, 'change-day. **børse** gun. **-kolbe** butt-end of a gun. **-kule** musket ball, musket bullet. **-ladning** charge of a gun. **-løp** gun-barrel. **-lås** gunlock. **-maker** gun-maker. **-pipe** gun-barrel. **-skott, -skudd** gun-shot. **børs|forretninger** exchange-business. **-jobberi** stock-jobbing. **-kurs** exchange. **-mann** exchange man. **-matador** swell on 'change. **-megler** stock-broker. **-pris** exchange. **børs|rykte** report on 'change. **-spekulant** speculator in the stocks, stock-jobber. **-spekulasjon, -spill** stock-jobbing. **børste** (subst) (til klær) brush; (om person) boor, caitiff; **børste** (vrb) brush; — **støvler** clean el. polish boots. **-maker** brushmaker. **-maskin** brushing-mill. **børstid** 'change time. **børt,** (dial., = rekkefølge, **«tur»**) turn, due chance. **bøs** (bister) grim, fierce, gruff. **bøss** dust, sweepings; **ikke det** — not a particle. I. **bøsse** box; **spytte i -a** be bled (freely), shell out. II. **bøsse,** se **børse.** **bøte** (sette i stand) mend, patch, botch; (betale bøter) pay (a fine); — **for** pay el. suffer for, make up for; — **med livet** pay with one's life, suffer death; — **på en mangel** supply a want, remedy a defect, atone (el. make amends) for deficiency. **bøtte** tub, coop; bucket; **-papir** hand paper. **bøy, bøye,** se **bye;** (= bøyning) bend, curve. **bøye** (til fortøyning, sjømerke) buoy; (rednings-bøye) life-buoy; **forsyne** (farvann) **med -r** buoy. **-penger** buoyage. **bøye** (vrb) bend, bow; (gram) inflect, decline; — **sitt sinn** yield; — **ens stolthet** bring down el. tower one's pride. — **av** turn, deflect, trend (off); — **seg** (om person) bow, submit, defer (for: to); (om ting) bend; (om elv o. l.) turn. **bøyelig** flexible, pliable, pliant. **bøyelighet** flexibility, pliability, pliancy. **bøyg** (i folketroen) bugbear, ogre; **den store -en** the strangling meshes of the past. **bøyle** hoop, ring, bow; (på kjetting) shackle; (til leseil) boom-iron. **bøyning** bending etc.; (gram) inflection. **bøynings|endelse** termination, case-ending. **-form** case. **-lære** accidence. **-mønster** paradigm. **-måte** (deklinasjon) declension; (konjugasjon) conjugation. **både ... og** both ... and; **han er større enn** — **du og jeg** he is taller than either you or I. **båe** sunken rock, shelf. **båke** (mar.) beacon (moored in shoal water). **bål** fire, (likbål) pyre, (funeral) pile; **døde på -et** was (tied to a stake and) burned to death, suffered death by fire el. at the stake; **dømtes til** — **og brann** was condemned to the stake el. to the flames. **bålferd** (likbrenning) cremation. **bånd** band, tie, bond, string; (til pynt, ordensbånd) ribbon; (panne-, hår-) fillet; (anatomi) ligament; (fig) band, bond, tie, check, restraint; **vennskaps-** ties of friendship; **legge** — **på** check, restrain; lay a restraint on; **leie** **(hund) i** — lead in a leash. **-besetning: med** — trimmed with ribbon. **bånd|fabrikk, -fabrikasjon**

ribbon-manufacture. **–formig** ribbon shaped. **–kjede** (mekanikk) bandchain. **–sløyfe** bow (of ribbon), favour. **–vev** ribbon **–weaver's** loom. **–vever** ribbon-weaver.
  I. **båre** (lik-) bier; (til syke) stretcher; handbarrow.
  II. **båre, se bølge.**
  båren: født og — born and bred.
  bås stall, (lukket på alle sider) pen; **sette på –en stall; er ikke god å stå i** — med hard to get along with.
  båt boat, (liten, flatbunnet) skiff, (liten, lett) punt.
  båt|bru (pongtongbru) bridge of boats. **–brygge** causeway. **–bygger** boat-builder. **–byggeri** boat-

–builder's yard. –bygging boat-building. **–fart** boating. **–folk** boat's crew.
  båt|formet, –formig boat-shaped. **–fører** boatman.
  båthavn harbour for boats. **–kvelv** upturned boat. **–ladning** boatload. **–lag** boat's crew; party of boats. **–lengde** boat's length. **–mannskap** boat's crew. **–naust** boathouse el. -shed. **–rip** boat's gunnel.
  båts|hake boat-hook.
  båtsmann boatswain. **–smatt** b.'s mate. **–spipe** b.'s whistle el. call; **blåse i –a** wind the call.
  båt|skur, se –naust.
  båt|stø place for landing. **–transport** conveyance by boat. **–tur** boating excursion el. party.

C

C, c (bokst. og musikk) C, c.
  ca. ab., say.
  cancer (med., = kreft) cancer.
  carte blanche (uinnskrenket fullmakt, frie hender) carte blanche.
  celeber celebrated, renowned.
  celle cell. **–dannelse** cell-development, cell-formation. **–dannet, –formet** cellular. **–fengsel** Pennsylvanian jail **–kjerne** cellular nucleus. **–system** cellular system, solitary confinement system, Pennsylvania system. **–vev** cellular tissue.
  cellist (violon)cellist. **cello** cello. **–spiller =** **cellist.**
  celluloid celluloid. **cellulose** cellulose.
  celsius–termometer centrigrade thermometer.
  cendré (askefarget) ash-coloured, sandy.
  census census, amount of taxes paid.
  centi|gram centigramme. **–liter** centiliter. **–meter** centimeter.
  centner hundredweight, Cwt. **–tung** heavy as lead. **–tyngde, –vekt** leaden weight.
  cernere (mil.) surround, invest.
  certeparti (merk.) (ɔ: befraktningsdokument) charter (party); **ifølge** — as per charter; **ligger under** — is under charter.
  cesjon (jur.: overdragelse av fordring) cession.
  cess (musikk) c flat.
  cesur cesura, cesural, pause, rest.
  champagne champagne. **–glass** champagneglass.
  champion (mester i idrett) champion.
  chang|eant, –erende shot(-coloured). **–ere** change; (ridn.) change hand, change the horse.
  chanse, se sjanse.
  chapeau|bas opera-hat. **–claque** opera-hat.
  ʇ**harabanc** break, sociable, waggonette.
  charge (mil., = kavaleriangrep) charge. **chargé d'affaires** chargé d'affaires, person in charge.
  chargere (mil., merk.) charge.
  charmant charming. **charme** charm. **charmere** charm. **charmør** charmer.

charpi lint; **plukke** — ravel lint.
  chartre (vrb) (mar., merk.) (= befrakte i timecharter) charter.
  chassis (understell på bil) chassis.
  chaussé, se sjåsé.
  chemise (damelinnet) jvf. **serk** chemise.
  chesterfield(møbler) Chesterfield.
  chevaleresk (ridderlig) chivalrous.
  chic (fiks, flott) chic.
  City (Londons City) the City (of London).
  chiffoniere chest of drawers, cheffonier.
  Chile (opr. inka-f. ant. **Chili**) Chili. **chilisalpeter** nitrate of soda.
  cicerone cicerone, guide.
  ciceroniansk (filol., litt. om uttrykksmåte og stil) ciceronian.
  cif (merk) c. i. f. (cost, insurance, freight).
  cikade (zool. betegn. for en mengde insektarter) cicada.
  ciss (musikk) C sharp.
  cistercienser (medlem av -ordenen) Cistercian.
  cisterne cistern, tank.
  citadell citadel.
  citant (saksøker) plaintiff.
  clairvoyance second-sight, clairvoyance.
  clairvoyant clairvoyant.
  clou: dagens — the great hit of the day.
  cocktail cocktail.
  combination(s) combinations, (chemise and drawers in one).
  contumaciam: in — by default.
  crème: la — **de la** — the pick of the bunch. Se ellers **krem.**
  crescendo crescendo.
  cricket cricket. **–bane, –plass** cricket-ground. **–spiller** ogs. cricketer, bowler.
  croupier croupier, groom.
  cul-de-sac blind alley, cul-de-sac.
  cyankalium cyanide of potassium.
  Cypern Cyprus. **cypervin** Cyprus wine.
  cæsa|risk cesarean. **–rismen** cesarism.

D

D, d. D, d; forkortelser: d. fork. f. **dag** day, **dato** date; d. fork. f. **den** the; d. å. fork. f. **dette år** this year.
  da (adv.: så, den gang) then; (tidsbindeord: den gang da) when; (årsaksbindeord: ettersom) as; (= i hvert fall) at least; (= altså) then; (= i så fall) then; **nå da** now that; **nå og da** now and then; — **jeg var fraværende, kunne jeg** being absent I could; **det tror jeg** — at least

I believe so. Andre eksempler: I was then too much occupied; — things will be different then; — when he saw me he called out; — as he refuses, we can do nothing; — take it then; — have it your own way then; — then you mean to say that I am a liar.
  I. **daddel** (frukt) date. **–palme, –tre** date palm, date tree.
  II. **daddel** blame, censure; **uten frykt og** —

without fear and (without) reproach. **-fri** blameless, irreproachable. **-verdig** blamable, reprehensible.

dadle blame, censure, reprehend, find fault with. **-syk** censorious, fault-finding. **-syke** censoriousness.

dag day; **hele -en lang** (el. **igjennom**) the livelong day; **hele -en** all day, the whole day, the whole of the day, all day long; **i hele —** all day) today; all this day; **en vakker —** one fine day; **avisen for i —** to-day's number; **jeg gir en god — i ham** I don't care a fig for him; **gjøre seg en glad —** make a day of it; **annenhver —** every other day; **ha gode -er** live at ease, have a good time (el. **happy** days) of it; **i gode og vonde -er** through good and evil report; **ende sine -er** finish one's days; **klart som -en** clear as noonday; **det er som — og natt** it is light to dark; **sett bedre -er** seen better things; **det gryr av —** the day dawns (breaks), it dawns, it is dawning; **dette barnet er faren opp av -e** this child is the picture of his father, his f. all over; **en av -ene** one of these days; **på denne tid av -en** this time of day; **ta av -e** put el. do to death; **ta en av -e** (fig) put el. take one down, cut one's comb; **komme av -e** come by one's death el. end; **— etter —** day by day, day after day; **-en etter** on the morrow, the next day; **andre -en etter** on the second day; **— for —** from day to day; **komme for -en, for en —** come to light, transpire, turn up; **bringe for -en** bring to light, lay bare; **hemmeligheten er nå kommet for -en** the secret is out now, the murder is out; **legge for -en** display, manifest, show off, exhibit; **forleden — the other day; fra — til — se: — etter —; i disse -er** lately, latterly, in these days; **i mange -er** for many a day, these many days; **i gamle -er** in days of yore; **aldri i mine -er** never in my life; **i våre -er** in our day, at the present day, at this day; **om -en** by day, during the day, in the daytime; **2 shill. om -en** 2 s. a day el. per diem; **i — (om) åtte -er** this day week; **i — (om) fjorten -er** this day fortnight; **om noen -er** in a few days; **på -en to a day; det var langt ut på -en** the day was far advanced; **til langt på -(en)** til late in the day; **hva tid er det på -en?** what time of day is it? **nå til -s** now-a-days; **til -enes ende** to the end of time; **— ut og — inn** day after day; **ved høylys —** in broad day-light; **ved -ens frembrudd** at dawn of day.

dagsarbeid day work, day labour. **-arbeider** day labourer, journey-man. **-blad** daily (paper), d. print. **-bok** diary, journal. **-brekning** break of day, day-break. **-driver** idler, lounger, saunterer. **-driveri** lounging, sauntering, idling, dawdling. **-driverliv** life of idleness. **-drøm** daydream.

dages (vrb) dawn.

dagevis: i — for days (together). **daggammel** day-old; **— fisk** over-days.

daggert dagger, dirk, poniard.

daggry dawn, daybreak; **ved —** (i grålysningen) at dawn, at break of day. **-leier,** se **-arbeider.**

dagjeldende then in force; prevalent at the time.

daglig daily, quotidian, diurnal; (alminnelig) ordinary, common; **til —** every day; for e. d. use; **-antrekk** everyday clothes; **tre ganger —** three times a day. **-dags** daily, every days; commonplace. **-stue** parlour, sitting-room, living-room. **-tale** familiar language.

daglinnet chemise. **-lysning** daylight. **-lønn** daily pay, daily wages. **-ning** dawn. **-penger** daily pay, day's pay. **-renning** dawn.

dagsarbeid day's work. **-befaling** (mil.) order of the day.

dagsinntekt daily receipts. **dagskole** dayschool.

dagskurs exchange of the day, current rate.

dagslys daylight. **-mars** march. **-orden** order of the day; **the** notice paper, the business p. (for the day) (på kartet) the docket, the agenda; (fig) **stå på -en** be the order of the d. **-presse** daily press. **-reise** day's journey. **dagstøtt** (adv) regularly every day. **dags|verk** day's work. **dagltjeneste** (mots. natt-tj.) day duty.

daguerreotypi daguerreotype.

daglvakt (vakt om dagen) daywatch; (morgenvakt på skip, fra kl. 4 til 8) morning-watch. **-viss** unfailing, regular.

dakapo! encore! forlange — encore.

daktyl dactyl. **daktylisk** dactylic.

dal valley, vale, dale. **-botn** bottom of a valley. **-bu** dalesman.

dale sink, go down; **— ned på** descend upon; **hans lykke begynner å —** his fortune is on the wane. **daling** sinking, descent.

daler dollar.

dalevende then living, contemporary. **dalføre** extended valley.

Dalila Delilah.

dall (dial., = amber) (covered) tub, pail. **dallrype** Norwegian ptarmigan, white grouse. **-søkk** dell, dingle.

I. **dam** (spill) draughts; (amr) chequers; (brikke gjort til dam) dam, king; **spille —** play at draughts; **bli —** go to king; **gjøre til —** crown.

II. **dam** (vannansamling) pond; (mindre) pool; (pytt) puddle. **dam** ogs. **demning.**

damask damask. **-es** damask-. **-vever** damask-weaver.

dambrett draught-board; (amr) chequer-board. **dambrikke** draught-man; (amr) chequer.

dame lady; (i kort) queen; **mine -r** Ladies; **en -s vesen, et v. som en —** ladylike manners; **min —** (i dans, ved bordet) my partner; **spille — affect** the airs of a (fine) lady. **-aktig, -messig.** **-drakt** lady's dress. **-garderobe** ladies' cloakroom. **-hanske** lady's glove. **-hatt** bonnet. **-kahytt** ladies' cabin. **-kjole** lady's dress. **-kupé** ladies' compartment. **-kåpe** lady's cloak. **-linnet** chemise. **-messig** ladylike. **-portrett** lady's portrait. **-pynt** finery. **-roman** lady's novel. **-sal** sidesaddle. **-salong** ladies' saloon. **-selskap** ladies' party, ladies' company. **-sko** lady's shoe. **-skredder** ladies' tailor. **-tekke: han har —** he is a favourite with ladies. **-venn** ladies' man. **-verdenen** the fair sex. **-veske** lady's bag. **-værelse** ladies' room.

dammusling freshwater mussel.

damoklessverd Damocles' sword.

damp (vann-) vapour; (av kokende vann) steam; (røyk, dunst) smoke, fume, exhalation; **for full —** full speed; **slippe -en** blow off the steam; **slippe -en på** turn on the steam; **åpne for -en** open to steam. **-aktig** vaporous. **-bad** steam-bath, vapour-bath. **-barkasse** steam-launch. **-beholder** steam chest. **-bukserbåt** steam tow-boat, steam-tug. **-båt** steamboat, steamer. **-dannelse** generation of steam. **dampe** steam; (gå med damp) steam; (røyke) blow clouds, smoke.

damper steamer. **-fart** steam navigation. **-fartøy** steamer, steam vessel. **-ferje** ferry-steamer. **-fløyte** steam whistle. **-form: i —** in the form of steam. **-hammer** steam hammer. **-ing** steaming, smoking. **-kjel** boiler. **-kjøkken** steam kitchen. **-koking** steaming. **-kraft** steam-power. **-maskin** steam-engine. **-maskinlære** steamengineering. **-mølle** steam mill. **-måler** steam-gauge, manometer. **-pipe** steam-whistle. **-plog** steam plough. **-presse** steam-press. **-pumpe** steam pump, donkey. **-rør** steam-pipe, steam-tube. **-sag** saw-mill.

dampskip steamer, steamship, ofte forkortet: s. s., især ved navn, f. eks. the s. s. «Bergensfjord»; **reise med —** go by steamer. **dampskips|anløpssted** port of call for steamers. **-ekspedisjon** steam-boat office. **-flåte** steam fleet, steam navy. **-forbindelse** steam communication. –fører captain of a steamship. –leilighet conveyance by steam, passage in a steamer; med første — by first steamer. –linje steam-line. –seilas steam-navigation. –selskap steam-navigation company. Det forenede –selskap the General Steam Navigation Company. –skrue steam propeller, screw propeller. –trafikk steam traffic. damp|skorstein funnel, waste-steam funnel. –sky vaporous cloud. –sprøyte steam fire-engine. –sylinder steam-cylinder. –treskemaskin steamthrashing machine. –tørret steam-dried. –utvikling generation of steam. –vask steamboiling. –vaskeri steam-laundry. –ventil steamvalve. damspill draught-board (and men). dandere fashion, shape. Danelagen Danelagh, Danelaw. dane, se danske. dank: drive — idle about, loaf. Danmark Denmark. danne (forme) form, shape, mould, fashion; (bibringe kultur) educate, cultivate, polish, refine; –r futurum på makes el. forms the future in; — seg (oppstå) form; — seg et begrep om form a notion of. dannelse (kultur) culture, education, refinement; (oppståing) rise, growth; (formasjon) formation. dannelses|anstalt educational establishment. –middel means of refinement. –prosess process of formation el. development. –trin grade of civilisation. dannet (veloppdragen) well-bred; (beleven) refined, polite; (opplyst) enlightened, well-informed; (av fin opptreden) gentlemanlike, ladylike; en — dame a lady; en — mann a gentleman, a man of education; — selskap polite society. dans dance; (handlingen) dancing; føre opp en — lead a dance; gå ut av –en go to the wall. dance dance; (om hest) prance; — etter ens pipe dance as one pipes. –gal madly fond of dancing. –golv dancing floor. –lyst passion for dancing. –lærer dancing-master. –moro dancing party. –musikk dance music. –nde dancing; de –nde those dancing, the dancers. danseplass dancing-place; room for dancing. danser, danserinne dancer. danse|sal dancing-room. –sko pump. –skole dancing-school. –trin (dancing) step. –tur figure. –øvelse dancing-exercise. dansing dancing. dansk Danish; en –e a Dane. danskhet Danishness; (= danisme) danism. dansk–norsk Dano-Norwegian. dask slap, cuff. daske slap, cuff. data (kjensgjerninger, plur. av datum) data, facts, items of information. dater|e date; — seg date. –ing dating, date. datid (den daværende tid) that age. dativ the dative (case); står i — is in the dative. dato (tidsangivelse) date; (dag i måneden) day of the month; dags — this day; til — up to the present date; fra — after date, from date; av gammel — of old standing; av ny — recent; under gårs — under yesterday's date. datter daughter. –barn daughter's child. –datter granddaughter (by a daughter). –sønn grandson, (daughter's son). datum date. dau (om dyr) dead; (dorsk) dull. dauing dead man (woman), ghost, spectre. davit (på et skip) davit. daværende of that time, at that time, then; for the time being; den — eier the then owner. d. e. fork. f. det er that is. de (personlig pron) they; (demonstrativt pron) those; (adjektivets bestemte artikkel the. De you. De der! I say! debatt debate. –ere debate. debet debit; til — for Dem to the debit of your account –side debit- el. debtor-side. debitere debit, (en for noe) carry el. place to one's debit; (fig) allege, pretend, trump up. debitor debtor.

debut debut, first appearance. debutant debutant. debutantinne debutante. debutere make one's debut (on the stage), come out. decharge discharge. dechiffrer|e decipher. –ing deciphering. dedikasjon dedication. dedisere dedicate. deduksjon (slutning fra det alm.) deduction. defekt defective; — tilstand defectiveness. defen|sjon defence. –siv defensive. –sor counsel for the defence. deficit deficit, deficiency. definere define. definisjon definition. deg you, (når subjekt og objekt er samme person) yourself; (i høytidelig tale, i Bibelen, bl. kvekere) thee; vask —! wash yourself. degenerasjon degeneration. degenerere degenerate. degge for coddle. degrad|ere degrade; — til menig reduce to the ranks. –ering degradation. deig dough; sette — prepare the dough. –eltemaskin kneading-machine, dough-kneader, -mixer. –trau kneading-trough. deilig (vakker) beautiful, beauteous, charming; (ironisk) nice; fine; (lekker) delicious. –het beauty, beauteousness. deise tumble, topple, pitch. de|isme deism. –ist deist. –istisk deistic(al). dekadanse decadence, decay, decline. dekade decade. dekadent decadent. dekan(us) (forstander for et fakultet) dean, president of a faculty. dekk (skipsdekk) deck; forsynt med — decked; uten — undecked. –blad (i sigar) wrapper, outside. dekke (vrb) cover; (utgifter) meet, cover; (sjakk) protect; — bordet lay the table; — middagsbordet lay the dinner; — frokostbordet lay the breakfast; det er dekket til 20 personer the table is laid for 20; –t av under cover of; –t i ryggen av backed against; — seg (merk.) reimburse oneself; — seg for tap secure oneself against loss; — opp for en treat, regale one; — over veil; (unnskylde) palliate. dekke (subst) cover, covering; (lag) layer, coat; spille under — collude; spilling under — collusion; spille under — med hverandre play into each other's hands. –kurv table basket. dekken horsecloth. dekketøy table linen. dekks|båt decked boat. –last deck-cargo. –passasjer deck passenger. dekkstilling covered position; i — under-cover. deklam|asjon declamation, recitation. –asjonsnummer recitation. –ator declaimer, reciter. deklam|atorisk declamatory. –ere declaim, recite, (ringeaktende) spout, rant. deklar|asjon declaration. –ere declare; publish, make public. deklassere unclass. deklin|abel declinable. –asjon (gram) declension; (kompassnålens misvisning) declination; (stjernes avstand fra ekvator) declination. –ere decline. dek|ning covering; — av gjeld payment of a debt; søke — seek cover, (merk) reimburse oneself. dekokt decoction. dekolletert low (-necked), low-bosomed, décolleté. dekor|asjon decoration. –asjoner scenery –asjonsforandring change of scenery. –asjonsmaler ornamental painter. –ativ ornamental. –atør decorator, ornamentist. –ere decorate. dekort (merk.) deduction, discount. –ere deduct. dekorum propriety, decorum. dekret decree. dekretere decree.

deksel cover, lid.

dekstrin dextrin.

del part, portion; (av bok) volume; (andel) share; **en** — some few; **en** — av det part of it; **en hel** — a great deal, a good deal; **en av -ene** one or the other, (hvilken som helst) either; **ingen av -ene** neither; **begge -er** both; **ha** — **i** have a share in, ta — **i** take part in, partake of, be a party to, share in, participate in, join in; (vise deltagelse for) interest oneself for, sympathize with; **jeg for min** — personally el. for my part, I; I for one; **for en** — partly, in part; **for en stor** — in a great measure, in great part; **for største -en** for the most part, mostly; **til** **-s** partly. **-aktig i** partaking of, sharing in. **-aktig-gjøre** give a part in. **-aktighet** participation; (i forbrytelse) complicity. **-bar** divisible.

dele divide, part (ha del i) partake of; (med el. imellom) share; — **byttet** divide the prey, divide the spoils; — **hans anskuelse (følelser)** share his view (feelings); — **i to like deler** divide into two equal portions, halve; — **i fire like** **deler** divide in four equal parts, quarter; — **imellom** divide el. share between; — **halvt med** go halves with; — **seg** divide; (i grener o. l.) branch, ramify.

deleg|asjon delegation. **-ere** delegate. **-ert** delegate. **-ertmøte** assembly of delegates.

delelig divisible.

delfin dolphin.

delikat (lekker) delicious, dainty, choice, nice, savoury; (fintfølende) delicate; (*kilden*) delicate; **en** — **sak** a delicate subject. **delikatere seg med** feast on.

delikatesse (rett) delicacy, dainty; (finfølelse) delicacy. **delikatesse|handel** Italian ware-house, a provision dealer's. **-handler** Italian ware-house-man; provision dealer.

deling division, partition; (¼ kompani soldater) platoon; **Polens** — the partition of Poland; **spille på** — go halves.

delinkvent criminal, culprit.

delirium delirium; **delirium tremens** delirium tremens, the d. t.

delkredere (merk.) delcredere.

dels in part, partly; **dels ... dels** partly-partly, what ... what; what with ... what with; — **med** **makt**, — **med list** what by force, what by policy; — **ved hjelp av frisk luft**, — **ved hjelp av mosjon** what with fresh air, what with exercise.

delta (subst.) delta.

delta i take part el. share in, partake of, participate in; **-gende** sympathising, sympathetic. **-gelse, -kelse, -king, -ing** participation; (medfølelse) sympathy.

deltager, deltaker sharer, partaker.

dem them.

Dem you; (når subjekt og objekt er samme person) i entall; yourself, i flertall: yourselves **dema|gog** demagogue. **-gogisk** demagogical.

demarkasjonslinje line of demarcation.

demaskere unmask.

demen|tere disclaim, disavow. **-ti** disavowal, dementi.

demisjon: inngi sin — give in one's resignation. **demisjonere** resign.

dem|me dam; — **opp for** dam in el. up, pen. **-ning** dam, embankment.

demobilisere demobilize.

demokrat democrat. **-i** democracy. **demokratisere** democratize. **demokratisering** democratization. **demokratisk** democratic(al).

demole|re (mil.) demolish. **-ring** demolition.

demon demon. **demonisk** demoniac, demo-niacal.

demonstrant demonstrator.

demonst|rasjon demonstration. **-rativ** demon-strative, ostentatious. **-rere** demonstrate.

demoralise|re demoralize, corrupt. **-ring** de-moralization, corruption.

dempe quench, suffocate, smother, quell,

muffle, deaden; (et instr.) mute; — **ilden subdue** the fire; — **et opprør** quell an insurrection, suppress (put down) a riot; — **fargen** soften the colour; — **sin stemme** lower one's voice; — **sine** lidenskaper subdue (el. temper) one's passions; **med -t røst** in a subdued tone, in an undertone. demper quencher etc., (i radio) damper; **legge en — på** check.

dempepedal soft pedal.

dempespole (i autoteknikk) dimmer resistance.

demre grow dark, darken; dawn; **den -r gjen-nom tåken** it looms through the mist; — **for en dawn** upon somebody. **-nde** dim.

demring (morning) twilight, dawn.

den (personlig pron) it (om dyr ofte he eller she); (demonstrativt pron) that; (adjektivenes best. artikkel) the; **den ... selv** it ... itself; **den som** he el. she that; he el. she who; **den mann** som the man who; **den tosken!** fool that he is; **den og den** so and so; (dt.) **den går ikke** it's no go; (dt) **den var verre!** that beats all. denaturer|e denature, methylate. **-t spiritus** methylated spirit, denatured alcohol.

denatureringsmiddel denaturant.

dengang then, at the time; that time; **det var** **dengang** times alter, you see; **den gang da** when.

denge bang, lash, thrash, thwack.

denne (pron) this; (= den sistnevnte) the latter; **den 6te -s** the 6th instant (inst.).

departement department. **-al** departmental. **-skontor** public office. **-ssjef** head of department, undersecretary.

depesje dispatch; (telegr.) message, tele-gram.

deplasement (skips) displacement.

depo|nere deposit, lodge. **-nering** depositing. **deport|asjon** transportation. **-ere** transport. **depositum** deposit. depot depot.

deput|asjon deputation. **-ert** deputy. **-ert-kammer** legislative chamber.

der (pron) who, which, that, se som.

der (adv) there; — **i landet** in that country; **hvem** —! who is there, who goes there! — **er** han there he is.

derav of it, of this, of that, thereof; — **følger** thence (it) follows. **der bort** there. **der borte** over there, round there.

dere you.

deretter after that, afterwards, subsequently, thereafter; **året** — the next el. following year; **kort** — shortly (afterwards); **det ble også** — **the** result was as might be expected.

deres (som adj) their; (som subst) theirs; **Deres** (som adj) your; (som subst) yours.

der|for for it, for that, therefore; on that ac-count, for that purpose; **· + er -for at** this is why. **-fra** thence, from thence, therefrom; **reise** — leave there. **-hen**, se **-bort**. **-henne**, se **-borte**. **-hos** besides, withal. **-i** in it, in that, therein. **-iblant** among them, including. **-imellom** amongst el. between them. **-imot** on the other hand, on the contrary. — **inn** in there, therein, into it. — **inne** in there, in that place. **-innefra** from within there.

der|med with it, with that, with this; there-with; (med disse ord) so saying, at this; — **ned** down there. — **nede** down el. below there. **-nest** next, in the next place, then. **-om** about it, about that, on the subject; of that fact. — **omkring** there about. — **opp** up there. — **oppe** up there, above there.

deroute (sammenbrudd) break-down.

der|over over there, across there; **hundre og** **-over** a hundred and upwards; **det som er -over** what there is more than that; **-på** on it, on that, thereupon; after this, after that, then, next; **dagen -på** the next day.

dersom if, in case.

dersteds there.

dertil to it, to that, to that place; for that

purpose; besides; — **kommer at** moreover, add to this that. **der|ut** out there. — **ute** without there, out there. — **utefra** from out there. **-under** under it, below there; less. **derved by it,** thereby; by that means. **dervisj** dervish. **derværende** there (present). **desarmere** disarm, dismantle. **desarmering** disarmament. **desavue|re** disavow, repudiate. **-ring** disavowal. **descendent** descendant. **desember** December. **deser|sjon** desertion. **-tere** desert. **-tør** deserter, runaway. **desider|e** decide. **-t** decided. **design|asjon** list, specification. **-ert** designated (til: for el. to). **desigram** decigram(me). **desiliter** decilitre. **desillusjonere** disillusion, disillusionize. **desillusjonering** disillusionment. **desimal** decimal. **-brøk** d. fraction. **-komma** decimal dot. **-regning** d. arithmetic. **-vekt** d. balance. **desimere** decimate. **desimering** decimation. **desinfeksjon** disinfection. **-smiddel** disinfectant. **desinfise|re** disinfect. **-rende midler** disinfectants. **-ring** disinfection. **desmer** civet. **-katt** civet cat. **desorgani|sere** disorganize. **-sasjon, -sering,** disorganization. **desorientere** put out, confuse. **despekt** disrespect. **desperasjon** desperation. **desperat** desperate. furious. **despot** despot. **-i** despotism. **-isk** despotic(al). **-isme** despotism. **dess D** flat. **dess, se desto.** **dessert** dessert. **-kniv** d. knife. **-skje, -skei** d. spoon. **-tallerken** d. plate. **dessforuten** besides that, moreover, withal, over and above. **dess|uaktet** notwithstanding this el. that. **-uten** besides, in addition. **-verre** unfortunately, I am sorry to say, alas! more's the pity, (sl) worse luck. **destillasjon** distillation. **destillat** distillate. **-ør** spirit-dealer. **destiller|e** distil. **-kar, -kjel** still. **-kolbe** alembic, retort. **-ovn** distilling furnace. **desto** the; — **bedre** the better, so much the better; — **heller** the rather; **ikke** — **mindre** nevertheless, notwithstanding that. **destruksjonsovn** destructor. **det** (personlig pron) it, (i visse tilfelle) he, she, they; (demonstrativt pron) that; (adjektivets bestemte artikkel) the; (gående på en hel setning) so; (som subj. ant.) there; **det** **regner** it rains; **hvorfor det?** why so? **hvorfor gjorde du det?** why did you do that? **det var hans ord** such were his words; **var det hans siste ord?** were those his last words? **det tenkte jeg nok** I thought as much; **og hvem har ikke det?** as (el. and) who has not? **det er** (siktende til et foregående personl. subjekt el. objekt) he is, she is, they are; **det er en dårlig kar** he is a bad fellow, etc.; **det er meg** it is I; **det er** (vil si) that is; **det er det som jeg vil vite** that is what I want to know; **ja, det er det** yes, it is; **det er det også** so it is (indeed); **De sier ikke det?** (uttrykk for forbauselse) you don't say so; **hvorfor det?** why so? **ikke det jeg vet** not that I know of; **og det en dame** and a lady too; **ja, jeg vet det** yes, I know; **gjør det!** do! **det å** reise travelling; **det at han har reist** the fact of his having travelled; **det at du vant veddemålet, har kostet meg** your winning the

bet has cost me; **det var noen barn i hagen** there were some children in the garden. **detasjement** detachment. **detalj** detail, retail, particular; **selle i** — retail; **handle en gros og en detalj** deal whole -sale and retail; **gå i -er** enter into details el. particulars. **detaljert** minute, explicit. **-handel** retail trade. **-handler** retailer. **detaljist** retailer, retail dealer, shopkeeper. **detektiv** detective. **-korps** secret service. **determin|ert** resolute. **-isme** determinism. **detonasjon** (eksplosjon, knall) detonation. **detoniser|e** dethrone. **-ing** dethronement. **dette** (pron) this. **dette** (vrb) se **falle.** **devise** device, posy. **diadem** diadem. **diagnose** diagnosis; **stille en** — diagnose, make a diagnosis (of), diagnosticate. **diagonal** diagonal. **diakon** deacon; (male, man) nurse. **diakonisse** deaconess; nursing sister. **-anstalt** nursing sisters' institution. **dialekt** dialect. **dialek|tiker** dialectician. **-tikk** dialectics. **-tisk** dialectical. **dialog** dialogue. **diamant** diamond. **-ring** d. ring. **-sliper** diamond-cutter. **-slipning** grinding of diamonds. **-smykke** set of diamonds. **diame|ter** diameter. **-tral** diametrical. **-tralt** motsatt diametrically opposed to. **diaré** diarrhoea. **die** (subst.) mother's milk; **gi** — suckle, give suck, **die** (vrb) suck. I. **diét** (om kosten) diet; regimen; **streng** — low, strict diet el. regimen; **sette en på bestemt diét** restrict to a certain diet; **holde** — be under diet, diet, (streng) be on low diet. II. **diet** (pl. **-er**), **-godtgjørelse** (dagpenger) subsistence money, allowance. **differens** difference, (merk) balance. **differensiere** differentiate. **differensiering** differentiation. **differensrekke** arithmetical progression. **difteri** diphtheria. **digel** crucible, melting-pot. **diger** big, bulky, burly. **digresjon** digression. **dike** (oppkastet voll) dike, dam. **dikke** (under haken) ketcher. **dikkedarer** antics, capers; **gjøre** — mince the matter. **diksjon** diction. **dikt** poem; (noe oppdiktet) fiction. **-art** species of poetry. **diktat** dictation; **skrive etter** — write to el. from d. **diktator** dictator. **diktatorisk** dictatorial. **diktatur** dictature, dictatorship. **dikte** (oppdikte) invent; (skrive poesi) make poetry el. verses, compose verse. **-kunst** (art of) poetry. **dikter** poet. **-evne** poetical talent. **-gasje** poet's pension. **-hjørne** (i Westminster Abbey) Poets' Corner. **-inne** poetess. **dikterisk** poetical. **dikter|kall** poetical vocation. **-liv** poet's life, life poetic. **-natur** poetical nature. **-språk** poetical language. **-talent** poetic talent. **-verk** poem, poetical el. imaginative work. **på -vis** after the manner of poets. **-ånd** poetical genius. **-åre** poetical vein. **diktere** dictate. **diktning** poetical composition, poetry. **dilemma** dilemma. **dilettant** amateur, dilettante. **-forestilling** private theatricals, amateur performance. **-messig** amateurish, dilettantish. **diligence** stage-coach. **-fører** guard. **-hest** stager. **-kontor** coach-office. **-kusk** stage-coach-man. I. **dill** (plante) dill, dillseed.

II. **dill** (tull og tøv) rot, twaddle.
dilla (pop. for delirium) the horrors, the jims, the jumps.
dille (tøve) talk rot, twaddle.
dilt jog-trot. **dilte** jog along.
dim hazy, dim.
dimensjon dimension, size; (av tømmer el. jern) scantling. **-stabell** scale of scantlings.
diminutiv diminutive. **-endelse** d. termination.
dimisjon discharge, release; sending up for the matriculation examination.
dimisspreken probational sermon.
dimittend pupil who is sent up for the matriculation examination.
dimittere dismiss; (til en eksamen) send up for an examination; (til univ.) certificate for the university.
dimme dimness, haze, blur.
din (som adj) your, (som substantiv) yours; i høytidelig tale og i Bibelen, som adj. thy; som subst. thine; — **hatt** your hat; **hatten er** — the hat is yours; — **tosk** you fool.
dine your, yours, se **din**.
dingeldangel (dangling) gewgaws, bobs.
dingeling dingdong.
dingle dangle, bob, swing to and fro; (i galgen) swing.
diplom diploma. **-at** diplomatist. **-atfrakk** frock-coat. **-ati** diplomacy. **-atisk** diplomatic(al); **et** — **fiff** a stroke of policy.
direk|te direct; (adv), directly. **-sjon** direction; (styre) board of directors, directorate, governing body, committee. **-sjonsmedlem** director. **-torat** directorate. **-trise** directress, directrix. **-tør** director, manager, managing director.
dirigent (i alm.) director; (av møte) chairman; (musikk) conductor, bandmaster.
dirigere conduct; (om musikk, også) lead; (lede et møte) hold the chair, be in the chair.
dirk picklock. **dirke** (en lås) pick. **dirkefri** not to be picked, thief-proof.
dirre quiver, vibrate. **dirring** quivering, vibration.
I. **dis** (gudinne) goddess.
II. **dis** (tåke) haze.
disharmo|nere be discordant. **-ni** discord, disharmony. **-nisk** discordant.
dishonorere (veksel) dishonour.
disig hazy. **-het** haziness.
disip|lin (tukt) discipline; (fag) branch of knowledge. **-linere** discipline. **-linering** discipline. **-linærforseelse** breach of discipline. **-linærstraff** discretionary punishment. **-pel** (elev) pupil, scholar, disciple, (bibel) disciple.
disk counter, (i utskjenkningslokale) bar.
diskant treble, soprano. **-nøkkel** soprano clef.
diske opp dish el. serve up; — **for en treat** one with dainties.
diskenspringer counter-jumper.
diskon|tere discount. **-tering** discounting.
diskonto discount. **-bank** bank of discount. **-fot** rate of discount. **-forretninger** discounts, discounting. **-lån** loan on discount. **diskontør** discounter; (om privat pengeutlåner) moneylender.
diskos discus. **-kaster** discus-thrower. **-kasting** discus-throwing.
diskresjon discretion; (taushet) reticence.
diskret discreet.
diskurs discourse.
disku|sjon discussion. **-tere** discuss.
diskvalifisere disqualify.
dispasj (merk.) statement of average.
dispasjør average stater, average adjuster, arbitrator of averages.
dispen|sasjon dispensation. **-sere** dispense, exempt, grant dispensation (fra: from).
dispo|nere dispose (over: of; til: to); **-nent** (acting) manager. **-nibel** available. **-sisjon** (ordning) disposition; (utkast) outline, skeleton; (rådigh.) disposal; **til Deres** — at your disposal.

disput|as disputation; (avhandl.) dissertation, act, thesis. **-ator** disputant. **-ere** dispute, reason, argue (the point). **-t** dispute, argument.
diss (i musikk) D sharp.
disse these; (= de sistnevnte) the latter.
dissek|ere dissect. **-sjon** dissection. **-sjonskniv** scalpel. **-sjonsrom** dissecting room. **-tor** dissector.
dissens difference of opinion.
·issenter dissenter, non-conformist.
dissentere dissent.
dissenter|kirke chapel. **-prest** minister.
dissonans dissonance, discord.
distance distance. **-måler** distance-meter.
distansere distance; **bli distansert** fall behind.
distanseritt ride against time.
distingvert distinguished.
distinksjon distinction; mark of distinction.
distinkt distinct.
distr|ahere distract, draw away, disturb. **-aksjon** absence of mind, absent-mindedness. **distré** absent (-minded).
distrikt district; (retts-) circuit; (politibetjents) beat; (postbuds) round, walk. **distriktslege** local medical officer.
dit thither, there; **hit og** — to and fro. **dit bort** thither.
ditt your, yours, se **din**.
ditt og datt one thing and the other, sundries; odds and ends, odd snatches.
ditto ditto, the same, likewise.
diva (primadonna) diva.
divan couch. **-bord** sofa-table.
diverg|ere diverge. **-ens** divergence.
diverse (flere forskjellige) divers, sundry.
divi|dend (tall som skal deles) dividend. **-dende** (utbytte av aksjer o. l.) dividend.
dividere divide; — **16 med 2** divide 16 by 2. **divi|sjon** (regningsart, hæravdeling) division. **-sjonsstykke** sum in division. **-sjonstegn** sign of division. **-sor** divisor.
djerv bold, (-talende) outspoken; (likefram) rough. **-het** boldness.
djevel devil, fiend.
djevelsk demoniac, fiendish, devilish, diabolical; **le** — laugh a fiendish laugh.
djevelskap devilry; infernal stuff, abomination. **djevelunge** imp.
djevle|besettelse demoniacal possession. **-besvergelse** exorcism. **-besverger** exorcist. **-spill** diabolo, devil on two sticks.
djunke (kinesisk skip) junk.
djup se **dyp**.
d. m. fork. f. denne måned this month.
do. fork. f. **ditto** ditto, do.
do (privét) convenience, privy.
dobbelt double, twofold; — **bunn** a false bottom; — **spill** double-dealing; — **bokholderi** bookkeeping by double entry. **dobbelt** (adv) double, doubly; twice; **se** — see double; — **så mange** twice as many, double the number; — **så mye** twice as much, as much again. **dobbeltgjenger** alter ego, double, fetch. **-hake** double chin. **-het** doubleness, (bare fig) duplicity. **dobbeltløpet børse** double-barrelled gun.
dog however, yet, still; (i daglig tale; alltid sist i setn.) though; **det er** — **farlig!** it is dangerous, though; **og** — (and) yet; **det er** — for **galt** it really is too bad; **det skal jo** — **gjøres** after all, it must be done sooner or later.
doge doge (i Venedig og Genua).
dogg dew. **-dråpe** dewdrop.
dogge (stor, kraftig, især eng. hund) mastiff.
doggie (vt) bedew (vt); **det -er** the dew is falling. **-et** dewy. **-fall** dew(-fall). **-perle** dew-spangle.
dogma|tiker teacher of doctrinal theology. **-tikk** dogmatics. **-tisere** dogmatize. **-tisk** dogmatic(al). **dogme** dogma.
I. **dokk** (for skip) dock; (tørr- dry-dock, graving -dock; „våt"- (havnebasseng) wet dock; **skipet trenger til å komme i** — the ship requires

docking; **gå i** — dock, go into dock. **-avgifter** dock dues.

II. **dokk** (fordypning) depression, cavity (liten, f. eks. i kinnet) dimple.

dokke (til leik) doll; (menneskefigur) dummy; (marionett-) puppet; (garn-) skein. **-aktig** doll-like. **-barn** doll. **-hus** baby house, doll's house. **-spill** puppet-show. **-stas, -tøy** doll-finery (leketøy) toys, baubles. **-stue,** se **-hus. -vogn** doll's perambulator.

dokk|sette dock. **-setting** docking.

doktor doctor, (lege ogs.) physician **(doctor** theologiæ doctor of divinity, D. D.); **bli** — become a doctor. **-diplom** doctor's diploma. **-disputas** thesis for a doctor's degree. **-grad** doctor's degree, doctorate.

doktrin doctrine. **-ær** doctrinaire, viewy; doctrinarian.

dokument document, deed, paper, instrument **dokumentere** substantiate, verify; — **seg** prove oneself, prove one's identity. **dokumentering** substantiation. **dokumentfalsk** forgery (of documents).

dolk dagger, poniard. **dolke** dagger, stab. **dolkestøt** stab with a dagger.

I. **dom** (kuppel) dome.

II. **dom,** se **domkirke.**

III. **dom** sentence; judgment, decree, doom; (kjennelse) award, verdict, decision; (mening) opinion; (filosofi) proposition, judgment; **få sin** — receive sentence; **felle, avsi** — pronounce, pass sentence; **vente sin** — await trial; **i dyre -mer** at an exorbitant rate, at extortionate prices; **på -mens dag** in the day of judgment. **dombjelle, dombjølle** harnessbell.

domene (public) domain, crown-land. **dom|felle** condemn, convict; **den -felte** the condemned party, the convict. **-fellelse** condemnation, conviction.

domin|ere overlook, command, domineer, lord it over, bully. **-erende** commanding; — **person** bully. **-ering** domineering.

dominikaner Dominican (friar).

domino domino; (spill) dominos el. dominoes. **-brikke** domino.

domisil address, domicile. **-iere** domiciliate, make payable. **-iert veksel** addressed bill.

domkirke cathedral; minster.

dommedag the day of judgment (doom). **dommedagsvær** judgment weather.

dommer judge, justice; (freds-) magistrate; (voldgiftsdommer) arbitrator, arbiter; (i fotball) referee; (ellers i sport) umpire; **dommerne og advokatene** the bench and the bar; **gå inn til sin** — go to one's account; **hvem har satt ham til** — **over andre?** who has made him a judge of others? **-mine** judicial air. **-standen** the Bench. **-sete** judgment seat. **-verv** judicature seat.

dompap bullfinch, flat, gull.

domprost dean.

doms|akt copy of a sentence, judgment paper. **-mann** (meddomsm.) lay associate (judge).

domstol court of justice; lawcourt, (utenlandsk) tribunal; **bringe en sak for -en** go into court.

Donau the Danube.

done snare, gin. **-fangst** ginning, snaring.

doning implements, tools.

donkeymaskin donkey-engine.

donkraft jack-screw.

donquijotisk quizotic.

dont task, business, work; **passe sin** — mind one's business.

doppsko ferrule.

dorg trailing line; **-e** hook.

Dorotea Dorothy.

dorsk indolent, sluggish, slothful, dull, torpid. **-het** indolence, dullness, sloth.

dose, se **dosis.**

dosent lecturer. **-ur** lectureship.

dosere lecture on, teach. **doserende** dogmatic, argumentative.

dosis dose.

dosmer blockhead, dunce, dolt.

dotere endow.

dott lump, plugg; (om person) muff, doughface; **en** — **høy** a handful of hay; **en** — **bomull** a dab of cotton-wool.

doven lazy, idle, slothful, sluggish; (øl osv.) flat, stale, vapid.

dovendyr (slags pattedyr) sloth; (doven person) lazy dog.

dovenkropp, dovenlars lazy dog.

dovenskap sloth, laziness; **lide av** — be ill of the Lombard fever. **dovne** (om lem) get numb. — **seg** idle, lounge.

dovning (samling til arbeid) (amr) bee.

dr. fork. f. **doktor** doctor, Dr., f. eks. Dr. Johnson.

drabant halberdier, yeoman of the guard; (ironisk) myrmidon; (astronomi) satellite.

drabelig doughty, tremendous, stalwart.

dra(ge) (trekke) draw, pull, drag; (bevege seg) go, pass, march, move; **en -n sabel** a drawn sword; — **et sukk** draw el. fetch a sigh; — **en slutning** draw a conclusion; — **fordel av** derive advantage from; — **av sted** set out; — **bort** go away, leave; — **fram** draw forth, bring to light; — **i tvil** question, call in question; — **hjemover** make towards home; — **til regnskap** call to account; — **til seg** attract; — **ut** march out, sally forth; — **utenlands** go abroad; — **ånde** draw one's breath; **drages med** be afflicted with; — **med døden** be in the last agonies, in the agony of death.

drag (trekk) pull, tug; (av nett) draught, haul; (slag) blow, stroke; (av sigar) whiff, puff; (på vogn) shaft; **tømme i ett** — drink at a draught; **i fulle** — to the full.

drage, se **drake.**

dragelse (tiltrekn.) attraction (tilbøyligh.) bent, bias, leaning.

dragende attractive, irresistible.

drag|kiste chest of drawers. **-kjerre** hand-cart. **-not** drag-net, sweep-net. **-spell** accordion. **-sug** (back-)surf, undertow.

dragon dragoon.

drake (fabeldyr) dragon; (leketøy) kite; (sint kvinnfolk) termagant, vixen. **-skip** drake, war -dragon.

drakonisk Draconian.

drakt (kledning) dress, garb, costume, attire, apparel, suit of clothes; (ride-) habit. **-skjørt** tailor-made frock. **-stoff** suiting.

dram (brennevin) dram.

drama drama. **-tiker** dramatic author. **-tisere** dramatize. **-tisk** dramatic(al). **-turgi** dramaturgy. **-turgisk** dramaturgic.

drammeglass brandyglass.

dranker drunkard, sot, drinker.

drap manslaughter, homicide.

drap|ere drape, deck, hang (with drapery). **-eri** drapery.

draps|mann homicide, manslayer. **-sak** homicide case.

drasse (dra på) drag (along).

drastisk drastic.

dratte drop.

draug banshee, bogie, (water-) sprite.

dravat (plutselig storm) thunder-gust, sudden gale and hard work.

dravle curds of milk, curds and whey mixed with sweet cream.

drege drawl. **-nde** drawling.

dregg grapnel, creepers, drag. **-e** (vrb) drag.

dreibar revolving.

drei|e turn; (på dreierbenk) turn, cut in the lathe; **vinden har -dd seg** the wind has shifted (veered); **jorda -er seg om sin akse** the earth revolves on its axis; — **av** turn aside el. off; (mar) bear away; — **bi** (mar) bring to; heave

to; — talen hen på turn the conversation upon; — om hjørnet turn the corner; — opp mot vinden (mar) haul the wind, come to; — seg om turn upon; — seg om på hælen turn round on one's heel; samtalen -r seg om ... the conversation turns upon ...; det -r seg om hvorvidt the question is whether.
dreiebenk (turning) lathe.
dreier turner.
dreiel diaper, huckaback.
dreierlære: sette i — apprentice to a turner.
dreie|skive (på jernbanen) turn-plate, -table, turning-platform; (pottem.) pallet.
dreining turn, turning; rotation.
drektig heavy, teeming, with young; (som laster godt) burdensome; 100 tonns — of 100 tons burden. -het state of being with young; tonnage, burden.
drenere drain. -ing draining. -srør drain-(ing)-tile el. -pipe.
dreng (tjenestegutt p. landet) (servant-)man. -estue servants' hall. -kall (ungkar) oldish bachelor.
drepe kill, slay, put to death. -nde mortal; (kjedelig) tiresome.
dresin trolly.
dress suit of clothes.
dress|ere train; (om hester og hunder ogs.) break, break in. -ert selhund performing seal.
dressur training, drill, breaking in.
dressor trainer, (horse) breaker.
drett (fiske-) draught, haul, take.
drev (hjul) pinion; (opplukket hamp) (tjæret, utjæret) (black, white) oakum.
dreven expert, versed, experienced, practised, skilled.
drevet arbeid chasing, embossed work.
drev|sand, -snø drifting sand, snow.
drift instinct, impulse, bent, inclination (driving) working, conduct, management, control, economy; (fe) drove; (avdrift) lee-way; av egen — of one's own accord el. free will, unbidden, spontaneously; gå i — (mar) go adrift; komme i — (i gang) get into working order; innføre elektrisk — introduce electric drive; sette i — set going; i full — in full work. drifte|bonde grazier. -fe, -kveg grazier's cattle. -kar, se -bonde.
driftig active, stirring, driving, pushing, enterprising. -het activity.
drifts|anlegg working plant. -bestyrer manager; traffic manager. -kapital trading capital, floating capital, working capital. -materiell rolling stock. -omkostninger, -utgifter working expenses, expenses of running. -år business year.
drikk drink, draught, beverage; (det å drikke) drinking; sterke -ker (ardent) spirits, spirituous liquors; bli forfallen til — take to (addict oneself to) drinking; slå seg på — take to drinking.
drikke drink; — te take tea; hva vil De —? what will you take? — et glass vin take a glass of wine; — som en svamp drink like a fish; han -r he is addicted to drinking; — ens skål drink (to) one's health; — tett drink hard el. deep; — seg full get drunk, drink oneself drunk; — en full make one drunk; — av flaska drink from el. out of the bottle; — seg ihjel kill oneself with drinking; — et glass med en take wine with one; — opp spend in drinking; drink out; — en tår over tørsten take a drop too much; — på ens velgående drink to one's health; — ut drink off.
drikk|feldig given to drink, addicted to drinking. -feldighet drunkenness, addictedness to drinking, intemperance.
drikke|bror pot-companion, toper. -gilde drinking-bout, carouse, bout. -kar drinking vessel. -lag drinking-bout. drikkelig drinkable. drikke|ondet the drink(ing) evil. -pe· ger tip, gratuity, consideration. -vann drinking water.

-varer drinkables. -vise drinking song. drikking drinking. drikkoffer drink offering, libation.
drillbor drill. drille (bore) drill.
driste seg til presume, dare, venture.
dristig bold, hardy, daring, audacious; de -ste forventninger the most sanguine expectations. dristighet boldness, hardiness, hardihood, assurance, daring(ness), audacity, temerity, presumption.
driv|anker drog, drogue. -benk (gartn.) forcing frame, hotbed.
drive drive; (tvinge) force; impel; (fig) urge, prompt; (metall) chase; (maskin) operate, run, work; (gå og drive) lounge, saunter; (mar) drive, drift, be adrift; drag the anchor; det er drevet et vrak inn på stranda a wreck has drifted el. has been driven ashore; — et hjul o. l. move; — en gård manage a farm; — en beskjeftigelse, studier pursue, follow, carry on an occupation, studies; — et teater run a theatre; — en næringsvei carry on a trade, business; -r betydelig handel og fabrikkvirksomhet is largely engaged in trade and manufactures; — vekster force plants; — det vidt i noe make a great proficiency in something; — av (mar) drift off; svetten -r av ham he drips with perspiration; hans klær drev av vann his clothes were dripping wet; drivende av svette (om en hest) all in a lather; — tiden bort while away the time; idle away time; skyene -r fra S. V. the clouds are drifting from the S. W.; — fram propel, work; (blomster) force; (fig) impel, urge on; — igjennom force through; det -s med dampkraft it is worked by steam power; — noe med lyst prosecute a thing with ardour; — gjøn med make sport, fun of; — om go idling about; — frakten opp raise the freights; uværet -r over the storm will pass over; — på flukt put to flight; — det til skole-lærer attain the rank of a schoolmaster; — det til å stå opp manage to get out of bed; — tilbake drive back, repel, repulse; — ut djevler cast out devils, exorcise; -ende hvit white as the driven snow. -nde våt dripping wet.
drive (subst) drift (of sand, snow etc.).
driver lounger, idler.
driveri lounging, sauntering.
driv|fiske drift-net fishing. -fjær spring; (motiv) spring of action, motive. -garn drift-net. -hjul driving-wheel; (fig) motive power. -hus hothouse, conservatory; (uten kunstig varme) glass-house. -husplante hot-house plant. -is drift-ice, floating ice. -kraft moving power, motive power. -reim driving belt, belt, wheel-band. -tømmer drift timber, floating timber. -våt dripping wet.
drog|er drugs. -ist druggist, dry-salter.
dromedar dromedary.
drone (hanbie; unyttig menneske) drone.
dronning queen; spille — queen it; ballets — the belle of the ball.
dronningaktig queenly.
dronningbonde (i sjakk) queen's pawn.
droplet dapple, piebald.
drops sugarplum.
drosje cab, fly; (firhjulet) fourwheeler; (dt) growler. -bil taxi. -holdeplass cab-stand. -kusk cabman, fly-driver. -takst cab fare(s); (trykt) book of fares.
drott (poetisk for konge) king.
drue grape. -formet grapelike. -høst vintage. -klase cluster of grapes. -saft juice of the grape. -sukker grape-sugar, glucose.
drukken intoxicated, drunk, tipsy, in liquor, the worse for liquor; (foran navnord) drunken; — av glede intoxicated with joy. drukken|bolt drunkard.
drukkenskap drunkenness, intoxication.
drukne (vt) drown; (vi) be drowned; han -t katten he drowned the cat; han -t he was drowned; han er nær ved å — he is drowning;

den -r el som henges skal he who is born to be hanged will never be drowned. **drukning** drowning.

drunt (somlekopp) drone, sluggard. **-e lag,** loiter.

dryade Dryad.

dryg, se **drøy.**

drygd heaviness, capaciousness, bulk stoutness; **han har det i -a** he makes up in breadth for what he lacks in height.

dryge, se **drøye.**

drypp drop, drip. **-ing** dripping.

dryppe drip; (om rennende lys) gutter; **— el steik** baste a roast; **det -r fra takene** the eaves drop.

dryppstein stalactite. **-shule** stalactic cave.

dryss drizzle, sprinkling, dusting.

drysse (vt) sprinkle; (vi) drop el. fall (in small particles), crumble.

drøfte inquire into, discuss, sift, canvass, talk over, compare notes on; **— saken** argue the case (point). **drøftelse** discussion.

drøm dream; **i -me** in a dream, in my dreams.

drømme dream, be in a dream; **drøm behagelig!** pleasant dreams to you.

drømme|aktig dream-like. **-bilde** vision, phantasm. **-liv** dream-life. **-løs** dreamless. **-nde** dreamy. **-r, -rske** dreamer. **drømmerisk** dreamy.

drømme|syn vision. **-tyder** interpreter of dreams. **-tydning** interpretation of dreams **-verden** dream-land. **drømming** reverie, day-dream.

drønn boom. **drønne** boom.

drøpel uvula.

drøv cud; **tygge — chew** the cud, ruminate; (fig) harp (**på**: on).

drøv|tygge ruminate; (fig) harp on. **-tygger** ruminant, cud-chewing animal. **-tygging** (fig) harping.

drøy substantial, large, heavy, bulky, stout; (som rekker langt) that goes a long way; hard; smart; **si en -e ord** use strong language to one; **et -t arbeid** a tough piece of work.

drøye (vrb) make someth. go far, last as long as possible.

dråk good for nothing.

dråpe drop; **de ligner hverandre som to -r vann** they are as like as two peas; they are like two peas in a pod; **en — i havet** a drop in the bucket. **-formet** droplike. **-teller** dropping -tube el. -glass. **-vis** in drops.

ds. fork. f. **dennes** inst.

d. s. fork. f. **det samme** the same.

d. s. s. fork. f. **det samme som** the same as.

du you; (i høytidelig tale, i Bibelen, av kvekerne og provinsielt) thou; **du ... selv** you ... yourself; **du gode Gud!** great heavens!

dubbe bob up and down; (i halvsøvne) nod.

dublere double; (en rolle) understudy.

dublett duplicate.

due pigeon; (især fig) dove. **-egg** pigeon's egg. **-hauk** goshawk, merlin. **-hus** pigeon-house, dove-cot.

duell duel (**på**: with).

duel|lant duellist. **-lere** duel, fight a duel el. duels. **-lering** duelling.

due|lignende dove-like. **-post: med — by** carrier-pigeons. **-slag,** se **-hus.**

duett duet; duo.

due|unge young pigeon. **-urt** willow-herb.

duft fragrance, odour, perfume.

dufte exhale odour el. fragrance; **det -t av roser der** there was an odour of roses. **duftende** fragrant, odoriferous, balmy, odorous.

duge be good, be fit; **det duger ikke til noe** it is good for nothing, it is no good; **det duger ikke å** it doesn't answer, it won't do to; **som slett ikke duger** worthless; **så det duger** to some purpose; **alt det som dugde** all that was worth anything; everybody that was anybody; **jeg**

duger ikke til I'm no good at ...; **duge til sjømann** be fit for a sailor.

dugelig fit, apt, able, capable; **— til** fit for, capable of. **-het** fitness, aptness, ability, capability.

dugg, se **dogg.**

dugurd second breakfast, lunch. **-søkt** spell of working between first and second breakfast.

duk (bordduk) cloth; (seilduk) canvas. **duke** lay (a table) spread.

dukat ducat.

dukke duck, plunge, dip, souse, immerse; dive; **— fram** pop out; **— opp** rise to the surface, emerge, turn up; **— med hodet** stoop, **det -r opp i meg** it dawns upon me.

dukke (subst), se **dokke.**

dukkert plunge; (på hodet) header; **gi en — duck** one; **ta seg en — take** a header.

dukknakket stooping, poke-neck.

duks head(-boy), captain, senior.

dulm|e assuage, allay, soothe. **-ende** soothing. **-ing** abatement, alleviation.

dult (av dølge) reserved.

dult (subst) punch. **dulte** punch.

dum stupid, stolid; foolish; **— strek** folly, foolish prank; **-t snakk** stuff, nonsense; **— nok til å** fool enough to; **det var -t av meg å** I was foolish to; **ikke så -t** not half bad; **ikke så — som han ser ut til** not such a fool as he looks.

dum|dristig fool-hardy, rash. **-dristighet** fool -hardiness, rashness.

dumdum (slags eksploderende geværkule) dumdum, dumdum bullet.

dumhet stupidity; (dum strek) folly, foolish thing, blunder.

dummepeter (bajas) buffoon, merry andrew.

dump (adj) dull; (bare om lyd) low, hollow, muffled.

dump (subst) (fordypning) depression; (i landsk.) dell, dingle; (i slede, vogn) bottom, lower portion; (fall) plump, tumble; (lyden v. fallet) thud.

dumpe tumble, plump; dt. (til eksam.) be floored, be plucked el. ploughed; **— ned** (som fra himmelen) drop in.

dumphet dullness.

dumping (oversvømmelse av utenlandske varer til lav pris) dump, dumping.

dum|rian fool, blockhead, loggerhead. **-stolt** bumptious. **-stolthet** bumptiousness.

dun down. **med — på haken** having down on the chin, downy-chinned. **-bløt** downy.

dunder banging, rattle, roar, thunder.

dundre thunder, rattle, bang, roar; **en -nde løgn** a swinging lie; **en -nde hodepine** a splitting headache; **gi en en -nde skjennepreken** blow one up, read one a lesson. **dundring** rumbling sound, roar.

dundyne downbed.

dunet downy.

I. **dunk** (en) stone bottle el. jar; (av tre) keg; (av blikk) tin.

II. **dunk** (et) thump, knock.

dunke (vrb) bump, knock, tap, thump.

dunkel dark, dim, obscure; **en — erindring** a dim, faint el. vague recollection.

dunkjevle (plante) reed-mace.

dunst vapour, exhalation.

dunste evaporate, exhale, reek.

dun|teppe down quilt. **-vær** downery, place where eider-down is gathered.

dupere dupe, impose on, bluff, hoodwink.

duplikat duplicate.

duplikk rejoinder.

duppe (saus) sauce.

dur major; **C dur** C major.

dur (varig lyd) drone, murmur; (sterkere) boom, roar, rush.

durabel substantial, tremendous.

durchlauchtig serene. **durchlauchtighet** Serene Highness.

dure drone, murmur (sterkere) roar, rush.
durk|dreven cunning, crafty. -drevenhet cunning.
dus: leve i sus og — lead a life of riot, of revelry.
dus: drikke dus drink (propose) a brotherhood.
dusin dozen. dusin|kram catchpenny wares. -menneske commonplace person. dusinvis by the dozen.
dusj showerbath, douche; en kold — a douche of cold water.
dusk tuft; (til stas) tassel. -elue tasselled (el. tufted) cap.
duskregn drizzling rain. -e drizzle.
dust: ikke det — not a particle. jeg bryr meg kke det — om det I don't care a fig (a straw).
duste (pudre) dust, powder.
dusting, se tomsing.
dusør gratuity, reward.
dutte noe på en father something on one, saddle one with.
duv|e (mar) pitch. -ing pitching.
dvale lethargy, torpor; (magnetisk, henrykkelse o. l.) trance; ligge i — lie dormant, be torpid. -drikk soporific. -lignende lethargic. -liv dormant life.
dvask dull, indolent.
dvaskhet dullness, indolence.
dvele tarry, linger (fig) — ved dwell (up)on.
dverg dwarf. -aktig dwarfish. -bjørk dwarf -birch. -folk pygmy race. -mål, se ekko.
dvs. fork. f. det vil si that is.
dy seg be quiet, restrain oneself, forbear; han kunne ikke — seg he could not help himself.
dybde depth; profundity. -forholdene (mar) the soundings.
dyd virtue; gjøre en — av nødvendighet make a merit (virtue) of necessity. dydig virtuous. dydighet virtuousness. dydsiret demure, smug.
dyds|mønster paragon of virtue. -predikant moralizer. -preken moralizing sermon.
dyffel (ullstoff) duffel, duffle.
dykker diver; (fugl) diver. -apparat diving apparatus. -drakt diving dress. -klokke diving-bell.
dykning diving.
dyktig clever, able, capable, efficient; (anselig) goodly; — i matematikk clever at mathematics; en — porsjon a goodly portion; han fikk — bank he got a sound drubbing; (adv) very remarkably; sufficiently; — med plenty of; han ble — våt he got a complete soaking. -het fitness, aptness, ability, efficiency, capacity, proficiency.
dynam|ikk dynamics. -itt dynamite. -ittattentat dynamite outrage. -ittmann dynamiter, dynamitard.
dynamo dynamo, dynamo-electric machine, generator. -meter dynamometer.
dynast|i dynasty. -isk dynastic.
I. dyne (klitt) dune, down.
II. dyne (sengklær) feather-bed, down-bed, eiderdown; komme fra -a i halmen fall out of the frying-pan into the fire. -trekk, -var bed -tick, bedsacking, case of a feather-bed.
dynge (subst) heap, mass, pile. dynge opp (vrb) heap, amass, accumulate; — seg opp accumulate. -vis in heaps.
dyngvåt wringing wet, drenched.
dynke sprinkle.
dynn mire, mud. -aktig, dynnet miry, muddy.
dyp dep, profound; bli -ere deepen; en — hemmelighet a profound secret; — taushet deep el. profound silence; — søvn deep el. fast sleep; — sorg (i klededrakt) deep mourning; — elendighet extreme misery; et -t åndedrag a long-drawn breath; et -t bukk a low el. profound bow.
dyp (subst) deep, depth; -et the deep; komme

ut på -et (om badende) get out of his depth; be carried into deep water.
dypp dip, dipping.
dyppe dip; plunge, immerse.
dypsindig profound. -het depth of understanding.
dy t (adv) deeply, deep; — inn i skogen far into the wood; skipet stikker for — the ship bears; han stikker ikke — he is no conjurer, he will never set the Thames on fire; sukke — heave a deep sigh; bøye seg — bend low; synke — i ens aktelse sink low in one's esteem. -følt deeply felt, heartfelt. -gående (om røtter) striking deep, (mar) deep-drawing, deep. -lastet deep el. heavily loaded. -liggende øyne deep-set, deeply recessed. -seende penetrating.
dyr (adi) dear, expensive, high-priced; her er -t it is dear living here; det er -e tider vi lever i it is dear living now-a-days; dyrt (adv): det fikk han betale — for it cost him dear, he had to pay dear for it; sverge høyt og — take a solemn oath.
dyr (subst) animal; (mest om større pattedyr) beast; (av hjorteslekten) deer; (ringeaktende) brute, beast; gjøre til — bestialize, brutalize. dyre|aktig brute-like, animal-like. -art species of animals.
dyrebar dear, dearest.
dyre|beskyttelsesforening Society for prevention of cruelty to animals. -hagl buck-shot. -hage zoological gardens. -hud (hjortelær) deer skin. -kjøpt dearly bought el. purchased. -kjøtt (dådyr) venison, (reinsdyr) reindeer-flesh el. meat. -krets (astronomi) zodiac. -livet animal life. -lår haunch of venison. -maler animal painter. dyre|riket animal kingdom. -rygg saddle of venison. -steik roast venison (særl. om reinsdyrkjøtt) roast reindeer-flesh el. -meat. -temmer tamer of wild beasts. -verden (alle dyr innenfor et område) fauna; (dyreriket) the animal kingdom.
dyrisk animal; brutish, bestial. -het brutishness.
dyrkbar cultivable, arable.
dyrk|e (jorda) cultivate, till; (korn, osv.) grow, raise; (kunster osv.) study, cultivate; (Gud) worship. -else cultivation, culture, tillage; study, pursuit; worship. -er cultivator; tiller; votary; worshipper, devotee. -ning cultivation; bringe under — bring into (under) cultivation. -ningsmåte mode of cultivation.
dyr|lege veterinary surgeon, farrier. -legekunst veterinary art. -legeskole veterinary school. dyr|plager tormentor of animals. -plageri cruelty to animals. -skue cattle-show.
dyrtid dearth, scarcity, high prices; dyrtidstillegg supplement of pay, (cost of living) bonus.
dysenteri (blodgang) dysentery.
dysse (steinaldergrav) barrow, cairn.
dysse (lulle i søvn) lull, hush; — i søvn hush el. lull asleep; (fig) send to sleep; — ned et rykte hush up a report.
dyst combat, fight, tilt, joust; brush, bout; set-to, shock, brunt; (fig) battle; våge en — med en venture a bout with one, run a tilt with one; våge en — for en take up the cudgels for.
dyster sombre, gloomy.
dyst|løp, -ritt tournament, tilting, jousting.
dytt nudge, prod, touch. dytte (vt) plug up, stop; (mar) caulk; (vegg) chink; (vi) — til nudge, prod, touch (with the elbow).
dyvelsdrek asafetida.
dyvåt, se dyngvåt.
dø die; — av feber die of a fever; — av kolera die of cholera; — av sult die from starvation, die by famine; — av sorg die of grief, die through sorrow; — av latter die with (of, from) laughter; vi må alle — we all owe Heaven a death; — for egen hånd die by (eller at) one's own hand; — for morderhånd die by (eller at) the hand of a murderer; — for fedre-

landet die in defence of one's country; — bort die el. drop off; — hen die, die away, expire. — ut, se utdø; han skal ikke — i synden he will catch it; jeg vil — på at det er sant let me die, if it be not true; han er død (o: avgått ved døden) he has died; en døende a dying man (woman).

død (subst) death, decease, demise, end; han tok sin — av det it was the death of him; finne sin — meet one's d., perish; den visse — certain death; — og pine! zounds! the deuce! by Jove! du er -sens you are a dead man; ligge for -ens (by) on the point of death, at death's door; gå i -en meet death; tro inntil -en faithful unto death; mot -en gror ingen urt there is no medicine against death; gremme seg til -e grieve oneself to death, die of a broken heart; kjede en til -e bore one to extinction (death); avgå ved -en die.

død (adj) dead, inanimate; en — a dead body, a corpse; de -e the dead; den -e the dead man (woman), the deceased; ligge som — lie as one dead; han var — lenge før den tid he had died long before that time; han er nå død (og borte) now he is dead (and gone).

død|blek deadly pale, with blanched cheeks. -bringende fatal, lethal. -drukken dead drunk, blind-drunk.

dødelig deadly, mortal; — angst mortal dread (el. fear); — sykdom mortal illness; — sår mortal wound; for alminnelig -e to ordinary mortals; — forelskelse love to distraction; — fiende deadly el. mortal enemy; en — a mortal; — såret mortally wounded; — forelsket over head and ears in love. døde|lighet mortality, death-rate(s). -lighetsforholdene the death-rate. -lighetstabell bill of mortality, actuarial table.

død|fødsel still birth. -født still-born, dead-born. -kjøtt proud flesh. -lignende death-like.

dødning dead man (woman), ghost, spectre. -aktig ghostlike, spectral, cadaverous. -ansikt cadaverous face. -bein dead men's bones; kors-lagte — cross-bones. -hode death's head.

døds|angst (angst for døden) horror el. dread of death. -attest certificate of death. -bo estate of a person deceased. -budskap tidings of (one's) death. -dag day of death, dying day. -dom sentence of death; (dokument) death-warrant; (overført bet.) doom. -dømt sentenced to death, (overført bet.) doomed. -ens a dead man. -fall death; på grunn av -fall i familien owing to bereavement. -fare danger of death, mortal peril. -fiende mortal enemy. -forakt contempt for (of) death. -kamp agonies (of d.). -kulde chill of death. -kval pangs of death. -leie death-bed, dying bed. -liste obituary, death-roll, list of the dead. -maske death-mask. -merket doomed. -måte manner of death. -seiler (spøkelsesaktig skip) phantom ship. -skrik death-shriek. -stille silent as the grave. -stillhet dead silence. -stivhet cadaveric rigidity. -straff capital punishment; under -straff on pain of death. -stund hour of death. -støt death-blow, -stroke. -sukk dying groan. -svette sweat of death, death damp. -syk mortally ill. -synd mortal sin, deadly sin. -søvn sleep of death. -tanker thoughts of d. -tegn signs of d. -trett dog-tired. -år year of death; hans — the date of his death. -årsak cause of death.

dødvanne dead-water, doldrums.

døende dying.

døgenikt good-for-nothing (fellow), ne'er-do-well.

døgn day and night, 24 hours; fire timer i -et four hours in the twenty four; -ets smak the fashion of the moment, of the day. -flue ephemera. -litteraturen current literature. -liv ephemeral life. -vesen ephemeral being.

døl dalesman, glensman. -ekone daleswoman.

dølge conceal, hide.

dølgsmål concealment; ikke legge — på make

no concealment of; fødsel i — concealment of birth, concealing birth.

dømme judge, form a judgment of; (om domstol) pronounce judgment, pass sentence, sentence, judge; condemn; (bøter) fine; når vi -r ham etter vår målestokk if we judge him by our standard; så vidt man kan dømme av el. etter skinnet to judge from appearances; — en fra livet, — en til døden pass sentence of death on one; fangen ble dømt til et halvt års straff-arbeid the prisoner was sentenced to 6 months imprisonment with hard labour; se idømme! etter alt å — apparently; — om judge of. -kraft judgment, discernment. -syk censorious. -syke censoriousness.

dønn rumble, boom. dønne rumble, boom.

dønning swell.

døpe baptize, christen. -font (baptismal) font. -navn Christian name.

døper baptizer, baptist; Johannes Døperen John the Baptist.

dør door; der er -a you know where the door lies; vise en -a show one (to) the door; stå for -en (være forestående) be at hand, be near, draw near; lukke -a for nesa på en shut the door upon one; feie for sin egen — sweep before one's own door; for åpne, lukkede -er with open, closed doors; gå ens — forbi (unnlate å besøke en) give one the go-by; innen -s within doors; sitte lunt innen -s be in easy circumstances; sett aldri din fot innenfor min dør mer never darken my door again; bo — i — med en live next door to one, be one's next door neighbour; jage på — turn one out of doors; banke på -a knock at the door; renne på -ene hos en pester, bore one with visits; følge en til -a see one out; stå i -a stand in the door-way.

dør|fylling panel of a d.

dørgende — full chock-full; — stille stock still.

dør|gløtt: i -en in the half-opened door. -hank door handle.

dørk deck, floor, flooring.

dør|karm door-case, frame of a door. -klokke door bell. -plate door-plate.

dørslag sieve, colander.

dør|stolpe door-post. -terskel threshold. -trin threshold. -vokter door-keeper, porter, janitor. -åpning door-way.

døs (state of) drowsiness, doze; lethargy.

døse doze; — hen (gli over i blund) doze off; — sin tid bort doze away one's time. døsig drowsy; — varme smouldering fire.

døsighet drowsiness.

døtre pluralis av datter.

døv deaf; — for deaf to; — på begge ører deaf of (in) both ears; vende det -e øre til turn a deaf ear upon.

døve deafen; (dempe, lindre) deaden; (sløve) blunt; — smerten deaden the pain.

døveskole deaf school.

døv|het deafness, surdity. -stum deaf and dumb, deaf-mute. -stummeanstalt deaf and dumb institution.

døye put up with; endure, suffer, stand; brook, digest; — vondt rough it.

døyt: jeg bryr meg ikke en — om det I don't care a bit for it; I don't care a hang for it.

døyve (vise seg overlegen over) despatch, dispose of. Se døve.

dåd deed, achievement, exploit, act; i råd og — in word and deed. -løs inactive. -løshet inactivity. -rik active, deedful. dåds|kraft energy, enterprise. -kraftig energetic. -trang impulse of activity.

dådyr deer, fallow deer. -skinn buckskin.

då|hjort buck. -kalv fawn. -kolle doe.

dåne swoon, faint. -ferdig ready to faint.

dåning swoon, fainting fit.

dåp baptism, christening; holde over -en hold

(el. present) at the font. **dåps|attest** certificate of baptism. **-kjole** christening gown. **-pakt** baptismal covenant. **-ritualet** the Baptismal Service.
dåre fool; **Vårherre er alle -rs formynder** fools have fortune. **dåre, se bedåre.**
dårlig (slett) bad, poor, sorry, worthless, useless, indifferent; (f. eks. om materialer) un-

sound; (syk) ill, unwell, poorly, bad; — **vær** bad weather; **en — unnskyldning** a lame apology; — **hode** a poor head; **det er — med ham i dag** he is but poorly to-day. **-het** (elendighet) misery. **dårskap** folly; piece of folly.
dåse tin, box. **-kjøtt** potted meat. **-mikkel** nincompoop, soft fellow, muff.
dåvilt venison.

E

E, e, E, e.
eau de Cologne Eau-de-Cologne.
ebbe (subst) ebb, ebb-tide, low water; — **og flo** flux and reflux (of the tide), tide, high and low water; **det er** — the tide goes out; **det er — i kassa** I am low in funds. **ebbe** (vrb) ebb. **ebbetid** ebbtide; **det er** — the tide is ebbing.
ebonitt ebonite.
ed oath; **falsk** — perjury; **avlegge** — take one's oath, swear, be sworn; **jeg vil avlegge — på det** I'll take my oath of that, I'll be sworn to that; **bekrefte med** — affirm by (on one's) oath; **ta en i** — take one's oath, put one to his oath, swear one in; **under -s tilbud** upon oath; **sverge falsk** — perjure oneself.
edda Edda. **-dikt** Eddaic poem.
edder venom; **spy** — **og galle** vent one's venom. **full av** — venomous.
edder|kopp spider.
eddik vinegar. **-fabrikant** vinegar manufacturer. **-fabrikk** vinegar manufactory. **-sur** sour as vinegar; (kjemi) acetic; (fig) vinegary. **-syre** acetic acid.
edel noble; — **hest** blood horse; **edle metaller** precious (el. noble) metals; **de edlere deler** the vital parts el. organs.
edel|gran silver-fir. **-het** nobleness.
edelig on oath; — **forklaring** deposition, affidavit; — **utsagn** affidavit.
edelmodig nobleminded, magnanimous, generous. **edelmodighet** magnanimity, generosity.
edelstein precious stone, gem; **uekte** — paste.
Eden Eden.
eder|dun eider down. **-fugl, se ærfugl.**
edfeste swear, swear in; **være -t** be upon one's oath. **edfestelse** swearing-in.
edikt edict.
edru sober.
edruelig sober. **edruelighet** sobriety.
eds|avleggelse taking an oath. **-brudd** oath-breaking. **-bryter** oath-breaker. **-forbund** confederation. **-formular** form of an oath.
edsvor|en sworn; juror, juryman; **-nes kjennelse** verdict. **-nerett** jury.
Edvard Edward.
effekt effect, sensation; **gjorde formelig** — produced quite an effect; **for -ens skyld** for effect; **jage etter** — hunt (strain) for effect. **-er** effects, chattels; (oblig.) stocks. **-full** full of effect, impressive, sensational, telling. **-iv** effective, efficient. **-uere** effect, execute. **-uering** execution.
effen even (se ogs. **ueffen**).
eftasverd afternoon meal.
efoy ivy. **-kledd** ivy-mantled.
egen own, proper; (eiendommelig) characteristic, peculiar (**for:** to); (særegen) particular; (underlig) odd, strange, singular; (særskilt) distinct, separate; **han har sitt eget hus** he has a house of his own; — **inngang** a private entrance; **med en dristighet som er** — **for ham** with his characteristic boldness.
egenartet peculiar. **-het** peculiarity, oddness, singularity, idiosyncrasy.

egen|hendig done (written) with one's own hand, in (one's) own writing, autograph; — **skrivelse** autograph (letter); **må inngi — søknad** must apply in their own hand el. writing. **-kjærlig** selfish, egotistical. **-kjærlighet** selfishness, egotism.
egen|mektig arbitrary, absolute, despot'c, highhanded; (adv) arbitrarily; — **å skaffe seg rett** to take the law in one's own hand. **-mektighet** arbitrariness, arbitrary el. high-handed proceeding. **-navn** proper name. **-nytte** self-interest, selfishness, self-seeking. **-nyttig** selfish, interested, self-seeking. **-rådig** wilful, self-willed, arbitrary. **-rådighet** wilfulness, arbitrariness. **-sindig** wilful, self-willed, obstinate, **-sindighet** wilfulness, self-will, obstinacy.
egenskap quality, property, point; qualification; **i** — **av** in the capacity of.
egentlig proper, real, precise; **det -e England** England proper; **i ordets -e betydning** emphatically, in the true(st) sense of the word, literally; (adv) properly, really, by rights, after all; — **talt** properly el. strictly speaking; **ikke** — not precisely, not exactly, not quite, scarcely.
egenvilje wilfulness.
I. **egg** (på kniv) edge.
II. **egg** (et) egg; **legge** — lay; **ligge på** — cover eggs, sit.
egge stir, goad; **-nde** stimulating, inciting.
egge|dosis yolks of eggs with sugar (beaten together). **-glass** egg-cup. **-hvite** white of an egg, ovalbumen, glair.
eggehvite|holdig albuminous. **-stoff** albumen.
egge|kake omelet. **-plomme** yolk of an egg. **-rore** battered eggs. **-skall** egg-shell. **-toddy** egg-flip, egg-nog.
egg|formet egg-shaped, oval, ovoid. **-legging** laying. **-stokk** ovary. **-syk** anxious to lay. **-vær** eggery, place where eggs of sea-birds are gathered.
egle pick a quarrel, quarrel; — **seg inn på** pick a quarrel with.
egn country, region, parts, neighbourhood; **her i -en** in these parts.
egne seg (for, til) be fit for, adapted to, lend itself to. **egnet** fitted, proper, suitable; likely; — **til å** calculated to.
egne (sette agn på) bait (a fishhook).
ego|isme selfishness, egotism, egoism. **-ist** egotist, selfseeker. **-istisk** selfish, egotistic(al).
Egypt Egypt. **e-er, e-isk** Egyptian.
ei (i poesi og gml. stil) not.
ei! ah! oh! aha! why! eigh! **ei ei!** indeed! bless me!
eid isthmus, neck of land.
eie (besittelse) possession; **få det til** — have it for one's own.
eie (vb) own, possess; **alt det jeg -r og har** all my worldly possessions.
eieform the possessive case, the genitive.
eiegod sweet-natured, tender-hearted. **-het** tender-heartedness, mildness.
eiendel property (uten pl); possession.
eien|dom possession, property; (jordeiendom)

estate; (hus, især større) premises; **fast –dom** real estate.
eiendommelig peculiar, characteristic(al), individual. **eiendommelighet** peculiarity (peculiar) feature, characteristic, distinction. **eiendoms|besitter** proprietor, lord of the manor. **–fellesskap** community of goods. **–kommisjonær, –megler** estate-agent, land-agent. **–overdragelse**, se **–salg –pronomen** possessive pronoun.
eiendoms|rett right of possession, owner-ship; **loven om den litterære –rett** the Copyright Act; **–retten til tingen** the property in the thing. **–salg** estate sale. **–skjøte** deed of conveyance.
eier owner, proprietor; **være — av** be the owner of, possessor of; **skifte —** change hands. **–inne** owner, proprietress.
eiermann owner; **den rette —** the real owner. **eik** oak.
I. **eike** (båt) canoe, dory, punt.
II. **eike** (i hjul) spoke.
eike|bark oak-bark. **–blad** oak-leaf. **–lauv** oak **-leaves. –malt** oak-painted, wainscoted.
eikenøtt acorn. **–kaffe** acorn coffee.
eike|skog oak wood, oak forest. **–tre** (eik) oak tree; (ved) oak wood. **–tømmer** oak timber.
eim (damp, duft) vapour, exhalation, odour.
einebær juniper berry. **–brennevin** gin.
einer juniper. **–låg** decoction of juniper. **–ris** juniper twigs.
einstape bracken, brake.
einstøing lone Jack.
eir, eire, se **irr, irre.**
eiter, se **edder.**
eiter|orm, –pose, –tann, se **giftorm** etc.
ekkel disgusting, loathsome, fulsome.
ekkelhet disgust, loathsomeness.
ekko echo; **gi —** echo.
eklatant striking, startling, conspicuous; **— nederlag, seier** signal defeat, victory.
eklipse (formørkelse) eclipse.
ekliptik ecliptic.
ekorn squirrel.
eks– (forhenværende) ex-, late.
eksakt exact; **— vitenskap** exact science.
eksaltasjon over-excitement.
eksaltert over-excited; wild, fantastical.
eksamen examination, (dt) exam; **ta —** pass an examination; **ta medisinsk —** graduate in medicine; **tok ingen —** left the university without a degree. **komme like fra –bordet** be fresh from the schools. **–karakter** mark, class. **–kommisjon** Examination el. Examining Board, B. of examiners. **–oppgave** examination paper. **–spørsmål** examination question. **–vitnesbyrd** passing certificate.
eksamin|and examinee, candidate. **–asjon** examination. **–ator** examiner. **–ere** examine, catechize, try; question.
eksegese exegesis. **ekseget** exegete. **eksegetisk** exegetic.
eksek|usjon execution, distress, attachment, seizure; **gjøre —** put in an execution, a distress; **gjøre —** i distrain. **–usjonsforretning** distress. **–utiv** executive. **–utivmakten** the executive (power). **–utor** executor. **–vere** execute.
eksellense excellency; **Deres —** Your Excellency.
eksellent excellent. **eksellere** excel.
eksem eczema.
eksempel example, instance; (tidligere) precedent; (opplysende) illustration; **for — for** instance, for example, say; **et — på det motsatte** an instance to the contrary; **anføre som —** instance, exemplify; **gi — give** (set) an example; **ta — av** take e. by el. from; **statuere et — på en** make an example of one; **for –ets skyld** for the sake of argument; **følge –let** follow suit; **opplyse ved eksempler** exemplify, illustrate.
eksempelløs unparalleled, unexampled, un precedented. **eksempelvis** as an expamle.

eksemplar (av bok) copy; (f. eks. av plante) specimen.
eksemplarisk exemplary. **eksemplariskhet** exemplariness.
eksentrisk eccentric.
eksepsjonell exceptional, forming an exception.
ekserpere extract. **ekserpt** extract.
ekserser|e exercise, drill. **–plass** drillground. parade-ground. **–reglement** drill-book. **eksersis** exercise, drill.
eksesser outrages.
ekshaust (el. **eksos**) exhaust.
iksil exile.
eksistens existence; (om en person) being, character; **tvilsomme –er** questionable characters. **dokumentere sin –berettigelse** justify our existence. **–middel** means of subsistence.
eksistere exist.
eksklu|dere expel. **–sjon** exclusion. **–siv** exclusive. **eksklusive** exclusively of, exclusive.
ekskommunikasjon excommunication. **ekskommunisere** excommunicate.
ekskrementer excrements, fæces, excreta.
ekskursjon excursion.
ekslibris book-plate, ex libris.
eksotisk exotic.
ekspedere (sende) despatch, forward; (utføre) despatch, transact; (gjøre av med) despatch, dismiss, dispose of, settle; (en kunde) attend, serve. **–isjon** expedition; forwarding, sending; (kontor) office. **–isjonslokale** office-(room) **–isjonstid** office hours, hours of business. **–itrise** shopgirl, shop-woman. **–itt** expeditious, prompt, businesslike. **–itør** shop-assistant; agent.
ekspektanse expectancy. **stå på –lista** be on the docket.
eksperiment experiment (med: on). **–al** experimental. **–ere** experiment. **–ering** experimentation.
ekspert expert.
eksploatere make capital out of; (mine) work. **eksploder|e** explode. **–ende** explosive. **–ende saker** explosives.
eksplosivstoff explosive.
eksplo|sjon explosion. **–sjonsfri** unexplosive.
eksponent index, exponent.
eksport exportation, export. **–ere** export. **–firma** exporting-house. **–forbud** prohibition of export (på: of). **–forening** export association. **–forretning** export-house. **–hus** exporting-house. **–ør** exporter.
ekspress express; **med— by** e.; (adv) expressly, **–tog** express train.
ekspropri|asjon dispossession. **–ere** (person) dispossess; (grunn) appropriate to public uses.
ekstase ecstasy.
ekstempore extempore, extemporary; (adv) extempore, off-hand, on the spur of the moment. **–re** extemporize, speak extempore. **–ring** extemporization.
ekstra extra. **– fin** superfine. **–arbeid** overtime work; (som straff i skolen) extra task. **–avgift** additional dues. **–betaling** extra pay.
ekstraksjon extraction. **ekstrakt** extract; (uttog) abstract.
ekstranummer (blad) special issue (edition); (dacapo) encore, f. eks. he added two encores.
ekstraomkostninger extra charges.
ekstraordinær extraordinary, exceptional. **— generalforsamling** special general meeting.
ekstra|skatt extra surtax, surtax. **–tog** special train. **–utgifter** extraordinary expenses.
ekstravaganse extravagance.
ekstravagant extravagant.
ekstrem extreme. **–itet** (om armer og bein) extremity.
ekte (ektefødt) legitimate, lawfully begotten; (uforfalsket) genuine, true; **— farge** lasting colour; **— fødsel** legitimacy; **— barn** lawfully begotten child; **— steiner** precious stones; **—**

sølv real silver; — **havana** a real Havana; **en** — **engelskmann** a true(-born) Englishman. **ekte: ta til** — marry. **ekte** (vrb) marry. **ekte|felle** spouse, consort. **-folk** man and wife. **-halvdel** better half. **-herre** spouse, lord. **-hustru** wedded wife. **-make, se -felle. -mann** married man, husband. **-pakt** marriage contract. **-par** married couple. **-seng** marriage bed.

ekteskap matrimony, marriage, wedlock; (liv) married life; **i sitt første** — **hadde han en datter** by his first marriage he had a daughter. **ekteskaps|brudd** adultery. **-bryter** adulterer. **-brytterske** adulteress. **-byrå** matrimonial agency. **-kontrakt** marriage-contract. **-løfte** promise of marriage.

ekteskapelig matrimonial, conjugal, connubial. **ektestand** matrimony, marriage, wedlock, married state. **ektevie** marry.

ekteviv (nå bare spøkefullt) wedded wife. **ekthet** genuineness.

ekvator the equator, the line; **under** — on the equator. **ekvatorial** equatorial.

ekvilibrist equilibrist.

ekvivalent equivalent.

ekvipasje equipage, carriage.

ekvipere equip, fit out.

ekvipering equipment, fitting out.

ekviperingsforretning outfitting establishment.

ekvivokk equivocal; indelicate.

elastikk elastic, elastic string (el. band). **elastisitet** elasticity, springiness. **elastisk** elastic, springy.

eld, se ild.

elde, se ilde.

elde old age, age; antiquity. **eldes** grow old, age. **eldgammel** very ancient, very old.

eldhug ardour, zeal.

eldre older, (nesten bare attributivt, om personer, især søsken) elder; **en** — **dame** an elderly lady.

eldst oldest, eldest; **fra de -e tider** from the earliest times. **eldste** (i religionssamfunn) elders.

elefant elephant; **gjøre en mygg til en** — make a mountain of a mole-hill.

eleganse elegance. **elegant** elegant, fashionable. **elegi** elegy. **elegisk** elegiac.

elektri|ker electrician. **-sere** electrify. **-sering** electrification. **-sermaskine** electric(al) machine. **elektrisitet** electricity; **henrette ved** — electrocute. **-sleder** conductor. **-slære** the science of electricity. **-småler** electrometer.

elektrisk electric; — **lys** electric lighting; — **lysekrone** electric chandelier; — **pære** electric bulb; — **strøm** circuit, current.

elektro|magnet electro-magnet. **-magnetisk** electro-magnetic. **-magnetisme** electromagnetism.

elektrometer (måler) electrometer.

elektromotor electromotor.

elektron electron.

elektroplett electroplate.

elektroskop electroscope.

elektrotekni|ker electro-technician. **-kk** electro-technics..

element element. **-arbok** primer. **-arskole** primary school. **-ær** elementary, primary.

elendig (adj) wretched, miserable, piteous. **-het** wretchedness, misery.

elev pupil, scholar. **-arbeid** pupil's work.

elevasjon elevation; **med stor** — at high elevations.

elevator lift; (især varc-) elevator, hoist.

elevere elevato.

elfenbein ivory. **-s-** ivory. **Elfenbeinskysten** the coast of Ivory.

elg (elgsdyr) elk (amr.) moose. **-ku** female elk; cow, moose. **-okse** male elk, bull moose.

elgsblakk grey.

Elias Elias; (i Bibelen) Elijah.

eliksir elixir.

eliminasjon elimination, extermination. **eliminere** eliminate, exterminate.

Elisa Eliza; (i Bibelen) Elisha.

elite pick, elite. **-mannskap** picked crew, picked men.

eller or; — **også** or else; **enten han** — **jeg** either he or I; **hverken han** — **jeg** neither he nor I.

ellers else, otherwise; (til andre tider) ordinarily, generally; (i motsatt fall) or; — **takk** thank you all the same; — **ingen** nobody else; — **intet** nothing else; **er der** — **noe** anything else?

elleve eleven. **-årig, -års** eleven years old.

ellevill crack-brained, wild; — **av glede** mad with joy.

ellevte eleventh; **den** — **august** the eleventh of August, August 11th.

ellevtedel eleventh (part).

ellipse ellipsis; (geometrisk) ellipse.

elliptisk elliptical.

Elsass Alsace.

elsk fancy; **legge sin** — **på** take a fancy to, form an attachment to.

elske love; **høyt -t** dearly beloved; **gjøre seg -t av** win the love of, endear oneself to, ingratiate oneself with; **min -de** my darling; **de -nde** the lovers; **et -nde par** couple of lovers.

elskelig lovable. **elskelighet** lovableness, lovability.

elsker lover, (av noe) admirer. **-faget** lover's parts. **elskerinne** sweetheart, mistress.

elskerrolle lover's part.

elskov love.

elskovs|barn love-child. **-bånd** tie el. band of love. **-dikt** love poem. **-drikk** philter, love-potion. **-full** amourous. **-gud** god of love, Cupid. **-middel** love charm. **-ord** words of love. **-pant** pledge el. token of love. **-rus** love raptures. **-sukk** lovesigh.

elskverdig amiable. **-het** amiability; **si -heter** pay compliments.

elte knead. **elting** kneading.

elv stream, river.

elveblest (hudsykd.) hives, nettlerash.

elve|bredd bank of a river. **-drag** (el. -far) course of a r., watercourse. **-dur** roar of a r. **-leie** river-bed. **-mel** river steep. **-munning, -os** estuary, mouth of a r.

elys|ium Elysium. **-eisk** Elysian.

emalje enamel. **-farge** enamel-colour. **-re** enamel.

emanasjon emanation.

emansip|asjon emancipation. **-ere** emancipate.

emball|asje packing. **-ere** pack (up), bale.

embargo embargo; **legge** — **på** lay an embargo on.

embete office, place, post; **bekle(de) et** — hold, fill an office; **søke et** — apply for an office; **forestå et** — discharge el. fill an office; **bli ansatt i et** — be appointed to an office; **bli avsatt fra et** — be dismissed from office; **ute av** — out of office; **på embets vegne** in virtue of one's office, officially.

embets|bolig official residence. **-bror** colleague. **-drakt** official costume. **-ed** oath of office, official oath. **-eksamen** degree examination. **-forretning** function, official business. **-førsel** discharge of office. **-jeger** place-hunter. **-mann** official, functionary, (public, government-)officer, placeman; (civil el. public) servant, office-bearer; **en høy -mann** one high in office. **-messig** official. **-misbruk** abuse of official power. **-myndighet** official authority. **-plikt** official duty. **-reise** official tour. **-skriv** official letter. **-standen** the Civil Service; the public functionaries. **-stil** official style of writing.

embetstid period of office; **i sin** — while in office.

embetstiltredelse entering into office.

embetsvirksomhet official labours.

emblem emblem.

embonpoint stoutness.

emeritus emeritus; **professor** — Emeritus professor.

emigrant emigrant. **emigrasjon** emigration.

emigrere emigrate.

Emil Emilius. **-ie** Emily.

emisjon emittere issue.

emmen luscious.

emne (gjenstand for behandling) subject, theme, topic; (stoff, materiale) material; (stykke jern eller stål) billett.

emne (bestemme til) intend (for).

emolumenter (fordeler, inntekter) emoluments.

emploi employment. **-ere** employ.

en (fransk): — **bloc** in the lump; — **face** full face; — **famille** in a family way; **leve** — **garçon** live in lodgings; — **gros** wholesale; — **passant** in passing, by the way.

en, et (artikkel) a, an; **for en tjue år siden** some twenty years ago.

en, ett (tallord og ubest. pron) one; — **gang** once; — **gang** — **er** — once one is one; — **gang to er to** once 2 are 2; — **eller annen** some one, some one or other; — **og samme** one and the same; — **for** — one by one; — **og tjue** twenty one; **en underlig** — an odd fish; — **på øret** a box on the ear; **det kommer ut på ett** it is all one, it comes to the same thing; **ett er det å ... et annet** it is one thing to ... another to; **ett av to** take your choice; **under ett** together; **de selles under ett** they are sold in a lot; **det ene beinet mitt** one of my legs; **den ene med den andre** one with another, on an average; **det ene med det andre** one way and another; **og det ene og det andre** and what not. **-aktsone** act. **-armet** one-armed. **-benet** one-legged.

encyklopedi (en)cyclopedia.

enda even still, even then; **ikke** — not even then, not, yet; **enden er ikke** — the end is not yet; **ikke så gal** — not so bad after all; **hvis han** — if he only.

ende (subst) end, termination; (ytterste) extremity; (øverste) top; (bakdel) fundament; (tauende) rope, rope's end; **spinne en** — spin a yarn; **ta en sørgelig** — come to a sad end; **når -n er god er alting godt** all's well that ends well; **hva skal -en bli** where will it all end, what's the end to be? **gjøre** — **på** put an end to, make an end of; **få** — **på en kjedsommelig dag** get through a tedious day; **ta en** — **med forskrekkelse** end in disaster; **fra** — **til annen** from end to end, from one end to the other; **på** — on end; **være til** — be at an end; **komme til** — **med** finish, terminate, conclude, bring to an end.

ende (vrb) end, finish, close, terminate, conclude; — **med result in**; — **med å si** finish by saying; — **på** end in.

endefram straightforward (undert. bluff).

ende fram straight ahead el. forward.

endekker (flygemaskin) monoplane.

endelig (adj) (begrenset) finite, limited; (til slutning) final, ultimate, definitive; (adv) at last, at length, finally, in fine, ultimately; **det må De** — **ikke glemme** be sure not to forget.

endelighet finiteness.

endelikt end, death.

ende|else, -ing ending termination.

ende|løs endless, interminable. **-mål** final, ultimate object.

ende|punkt extreme point, terminus. **-resultat** final result. **-tarm** rectum. **-til** direct, blunt, straightforward. **-vende** turn upside down, capsize; put the back part foremost.

endog even.

endosse|re endorse, back. **-ment, -ring** endorsement. **-nt** endorser.

endre alter, amend.

endrektig harmonious. **-het** harmony, concord.

endring alteration.

endringsforslag amendment; **stille et** — move amendment.

ene: — **og alene** solely; — **og alene for å** for the sole purpose of; **det** — **brev** that one letter; **-berettiget: være** — **til** have the monopoly el. exclusive privilege of.

eneboer anchorite, hermit, recluse. **-liv** solitary life, hermit's life. **-ske** hermitess, anchoress.

enebolig private residence.

ene|forhandler sole seller, sole selling agent. **-forhandling** sole agency. **-forhandlingsrett** sole (selling) right. **-handel** monopoly. **-herre** sole master, autocrat. **-herredømme** sole sway, autocracy. **-hersker, -herskerinne** absolute monarch; sovereign. **-konge** sole king.

enemerker precincts, domain; **gå inn på en annen manns** — trespass.

enepike general servant.

ener one, unit.

enerett monopoly, exclusive right el. privilege.

energi energy. **-forbruk** consumption of energy. **-mengde** quantity of energy. **energisk** energetic, earnest; (adv) energetically.

enerver|e enervate. **-ing** enervation.

enerådende uncontrolled (master).

enerådig absolute, uncontrolled. **enerådighet** independent power.

enes agree, come to an understanding.

eneste, one, only, sole, single; — **arving** sole heir; **ikke en** — not one; **en** — **gang** only once; **den** — the only (one), the one; **de** — the only (ones); — **i sitt slags** unique; **hver** — every (single); **hver** — **en** every one; **det** — the only thing; **det** — **merkelige ved** the only remarkable thing about; **han var** -- **barn** he was an only child; **hver** — **en** every one, to a man.

enestående unique, exceptional, phenomenal, isolated; **noe** — a record.

ene|tale soliloquy, monologue. **-utsalg** sole vendors. **-velde** absolute power. **-veldig** absolute, uncontrolled, autocratic. **-voldsherre** absolute ruler, autocrat. **-voldskonge** absolute king. **-voldsmakt** absolute power. **-voldsregjering** absolute government.

enetasjes one-storied.

enfold simplicity.

enfoldig simple, silly; **en** — **stakkar** a simpleton. **enfoldighet** simplicity, silliness.

eng meadow.

en gang, engang (en enkelt gang), once, on one occasion; (i fortiden) once, one day; (den tid) at one time; (i framtida) some day, one day (or other); **det var** — once upon a time there was, el. there was once; **tenk Dem** — well! imagine; **ikke** — not even; **kommer De endelig** — here you are at last; — **imellom** now and then, sometimes, occasionally; — **til så mye** as much again; — **til så stor** as big again.

engasje|ment engagement; (forpliktelse) liabilities. **-mentskontor** general agency, employment office. **-re** engage; (til dans) ask (to dance); take a partner.

engel angel; (overført bet.) angelic being; cherub; **det går en** — **gjennom stua** an angel passes through the room.

engelsk English; **på** — in English; **den -e kirke** the Anglican Church, the Church of England; — **plaster** court-plaster, sticking p.; — **salt** (epsom) salts; — **syke** rickets; **som lider av** — **syke** rickety; — **norsk** Anglo-Norwegian; — **-norsk ordbok** English and Norwegian dictionary.

engelsk|mann Englishman; (amr) Britisher. **-vennlig** Pro-English.

engifte monogamy; **som lever i** — monogamous.

eng|kall yellow rattle. **-karse** cuckoo-pint. **-kløver** meadow trefoil. **-land** meadow land el. bottom.

England England.

engle|aktig angelic. **-barn** little angel. **-hode** cherub's head. **-kor** chorus of angels. **-makerske** baby-farmer(ess). **-mild** angelically mild.

englender, -inne Englishman, Englishwoman.

englerke skylark.
engle|røst angel's voice. **–skare** host of angels. **–vinge** angel's wing.
engpiplerke titlark.
engros|forretning wholesale business. **–handlende** wholesale dealer. **–pris** wholesale price, trade-price.
eng|smelle spattling poppy. **–soleie** bachelor's-button. **–sprette** grasshopper, locust. **–syre** common sorrel.
engste alarm, frighten; — **seg** be alarmed.
engstelig uneasy, apprehensive; (bekymret) anxious; (omhyggelig) scrupulous, solicitous; — **for** uneasy etc. about. **engstelighet** apprehension; anxiousness; diffidence.
engstelse uneasiness; anxiety.
enhendt one-handed.
enhests one horse.
enhet unity; (ener) unit; **tidens og stedets** — the unities of time and place; **gå opp i en høyere** — be fused in a higher unity.
enhjørning (ogs. enhyrning) unicorn.
enhovet whole-hoofed. — **dyr** soliped.
enhver any, every; (enhver især) each; (bare substantivisk) every one, everybody, any one, anybody; **alle og** — everybody.
enig unanimous; **jeg er** — **med ham** I agree with him, I am at one with him; **være** — (**om, om at**) be agreed (about, that); **bli** — come to an agreement el. to terms; **bli –e om** agree el. contract for; **være** — **med seg selv** have made up one's mind.
enighet concord, harmony, union, agreement. — **gjør sterk** Union is Strength. **–serklæring** endorsement.
enke widow; (rik, fornem) dowager; **ble tidlig** — was left an early widow; **sitte som** — live in widowhood. **–drakt** widow's weeds. **–dronning** queen dowager; (kongens mor) queen mother. **–frue** widow-lady. **–kasse** widow's fund.
enkel simple, plain. **–het** plainness, singleness, simpleness.
enkelt single; (ikke sammensatt) simple; (særegen, personlig) individual; (ensom) solitary; **et** — **bind** (av en rekke) an odd volume; **en** — **gang** once in a way; **hver** — every single el. individual; **–e** some, a few; **–e bemerkninger** a few (stray) remarks; **noen –e ganger** occasionally; **den –e** the individual; **i hvert** — **tilfelle** in each individual case; **i dette –e tilfelle** in this particular case; **–het** detail, particular. **gå inn på –er** go into details. **–knappet** single-breasted. **–løpet** (gevær) single-gun. **–mann** the individual. **–vis** singly.
enke|mann widower. **–pensjon** widow's pension. **–sete** dowager seat el. mansion. **–stand** widowhood.
enlig, se **enslig**; **den –e stand** the single state, celibacy.
enmastet single-masted.
enn (etter komparativ) than; (foran komp.) still, even; **andre** — others than el. besides; **ikke annet** — nothing but; **hva annet** — what else but; **ingen annen, ingen andre** — none but; **hva som** — **skal hende** happen what may, whatever may happen; **hvor mye jeg** — **leser** however much I read; **hvor morsomt et besøk i Windsor** — **kunne være** however nice a visit to Windsor might be; **om han** — **bød meg aldri så mye** even if he offered me ever so much; — **ikke noen** even.
ennogså, se **endog**.
enn si let alone, still less.
enn videre further, again, still further, still more.
ennå yet, as yet, still, even now; — **en ting** one thing more; — **en gang** once more, once again, over again; — **i ettermiddag** (ikke lenger siden) only this afternoon, (allerede) this very a.; — **i forrige årh.** as late as the last century; — **mindre** still less, even less.

enorm enormous.
enquete (i avis) enquete, newspaper enquiry.
enrom: i — in private, privately.
ens identical, the same; **alle barna går** — **kledd** the children are all dressed alike. **–artet** homogeneous, uniform. **–artethet** homogenousness, uniformity.
ensbetydende med tantamount to.
ense regard, heed, notice, pay heed to.
ensemble ensemble, whole, general effect.
ens|farget (likt farget) of one colour (med én farge) one-coloured. **–formig** uniform, monotonous, same, undiversified. **–formighet** monotony, sameness.
en|sidet one-sided. **–sidig** partial, one-sided, of one idea. **–sidighet** partiality, one-sidedness.
enskjønt though, although, notwithstanding, albeit.
enslig solitary, single. **to –e** (folk) a married couple without children.
enslydende of a similar sound, consonous.
ensom lonely, lonesome, solitary. **ensomhet** solitude, loneliness.
enspenner one-horse carriage.
ensporet single-rail.
enstavelses– monosyllabic.
enstavelses|ord monosyllable. **–tonelag** monosyllabic stress.
ensteds somewhere.
enstemmig (felles for alle) unanimous; (motsatt flerstemmig) unison; (adv) unanimously; in unison. **enstemmighet** unanimity.
enstonig monotonous. **–het** monotony.
enstydig synonymous. **–het** synonymy.
entall the singular (number).
enten either; — ... **eller** either ... or; — **det er riktig eller galt** whether (it be) right or wrong.
ententen the Entente.
entledige, se **avskjedige**.
entomo|log entomologist. **–logi** entomology. **–logisk** entomological.
entoms one-inch; — **planker** inch stuff.
entre (gå til værs i vantene) ascend, climb; (gå om bord i) board.
entré (forstue) (entrance-)hall; (adgang) admission; (avgift for adgang) admission-money; **ta** — make a charge for admission. **–nøkkel** latch-key.
entre|prenør enterpriser, undertaker; (av arbeid) contractor.
entring boarding. **–sforsøk** attempt at boarding.
entusias|me enthusiasm. **–t** enthusiast. **–tisk** enthusiastic.
envis obstinate. **–het** obstinacy.
enøyd one-eyed; **blant de blinde er den enøyde konge** among the blind a squint is king.
eolsharpe Eolian harp.
epide|mi epidemic. **–mihospital** isolation hospital. **–misk** epidemic.
epigon epigone.
epigram epigram. **–dikter** epigrammatist. **–matisk** epigrammatic(al).
epiker epic poet.
epikure|er Epicurean. **–isk** Epicurean.
epilep|si epilepsy, falling sickness. **–tiker** epileptic. **–tisk** epileptic(al).
epilog epilogue.
episk epic; — **dikt** epic (poem).
episod|e episode. **–isk** episodical.
epistel epistle.
eple apple; **bite i det sure** — make a virtue of necessity. **eple|blomst** apple-blossom. **–grøt** stewed apples. **–kart** hard (unripe) apple. **–kjerne** apple-pip. **–mos** applesauce. **–most** cider. **–sjel** apple-jelly. **–skive** apple fritter. **–skrelling** paring of an apple. **–tre** apple-tree.
epoke epoch; **gjøre** — form an era. **–gjørende** epoch-making.
epos epic, epos.

epålett epaulet, shoulder-strap, shoulder-knot.
eremitt hermit. -bolig hermitage.
eremittkreps hermit-crab.
erfare experience, learn, ascertain, understand. -n experienced.
erfaring experience, practice; bringe i — get information of, come to the knowledge of, learn; tale av — speak from experience.
ergerlig vexatious, provoking, annoying, aggravating; bli — over be vexed el. annoyed at something; være — på be vexed with.
ergre vex, annoy, provoke, fret; — seg be vexed, annoyed; — seg over be vexed at, fret at, be annoyed by, (over at) that.
ergrelse vexation, annoyance, chagrin.
erholde obtain, get; receive; som lar seg — obtainable; (om fordringer) recoverable.
erind|re remember, recollect, call to mind; (om) remind, put in mind (of); så vidt jeg kan — to the best of my recollection; man må — let it be remembered. -ring remembrance; recollection, reminiscence; (påminnelse) admonition (om: of); (gave) keepsake; memento, souvenir; til — om in memory of; ha i — bear in mind; bringe i — remind of, bring to memory.
erke- arrant, the veriest; arch. -biskop arch -bishop. -dum amazingly stupid. -engel archangel. -fe arrant fool. -hertug archduke. -kujon arrant coward. -løgner arch-liar. -slyngel arrant knave.
erkjen|ne acknowledge, own, admit, recognise; (for seg selv) feel; (fatte) apprehend, comprehend; — seg skyldig plead guilty. -else acknowledgement, admittance, cognition, recognition; apprehension, comprehension, understanding; komme til sannhets — be brought to see the truth. -tlig thankful, grateful. -tlighet gratefulness, thankfulness, acknowledgements.
erklær|e declare; — seg skyldig plead guilty; — krig declare war; en -t hater av an avowed enemy to. -ing declaration; opinion; certificate.
erkyndige seg om inquire about el. into, make inquiry after.
erle wagtail.
erlegge pay down, disburse.
erme sleeve; -beskyttere dress preservers. -forkle pinafore. -gap hole for the sleeve. -knapp sleevebutton.
ernær|e maintain, support; (fysisk) nourish; cater for; — seg som earn a livelihood as. -er supporter, maintainer, bread-winner. -ing maintenance, support; nourishment, nutrition.
erobre conquer. erobrer conqueror. erobring conquering, conquest.
erotikk love, love-making.
erotisk erotic(al).
erstatning compensation, indemnification, damages; forlange 500 L i — lay one's damages at 500 L; til — by way of compensation.
erstatnings|krav claim for compensation; gjøre -krav gjeldende sue for compensation, claim damages. -plikt liability. -pliktig liable (to make compensation.
erstatte replace; (gi erstatning) compensate, indemnify (one for), make good, make up for.
I. ert pea.
II. ert: gjøre noe på — do st. on purpose.
erte tease (med: about) irritate, vex; (spøke) joke; det var noe man stadig ertet ham med it was a standing joke against him.
erte|belg peasecod, pea-shell, pea-pod. -blomst papilionaceous flower; (blomsterert) sweetpea. -blomstrede papilionaceous plant. -hesje peasestack.
ertekrok teaser.
erteris pea-straw; de henger sammen som — they are thick as inkle-weavers.
ertevoren given to teasing.
erting teasing, irritation, banter, joke.
erts ore. -holdig metalline, ore-bearing.

erverv trade, livelihood, calling. erverv|e acquire, earn, gain. -e seg acquire. -else acquiring, acquisition, acquirement. ervervs|gren branch of industry. -kilde source of gain, means of livelihood el. subsistence, support, dependence. -løs unemployed. -messig professional.
Esaias Isaiah.
esdragon eddik tarragon vinegar.
ese (gjære) ferment; (heve seg) rise.
esel donkey; (mest fig) ass, jackass.
eselaktig ass-like, asinine.
eselspark (fig) kicking the dead lion.
eseløre ass's ear; (i bok) dog's ear.
I. esing (gjæring) fermentation, work.
II. esing (på båt) gunnel, gunwale.
eskadre squadron. -sjef commodore. eskadron squadron. eskadronsjef major.
eske (foreldet, = kreve); — lyd (= slå til lyd) demand silence; (utfordre) challenge.
eske (subst) box, casket. -lokk box-lid. -maker band-box-maker.
eskimo Eskimo, Esquimau; (pl) -aux. -hytte igloo.
eskorte escort. -re escort.
esle (bestemme til et øyemed) earmark, intend; (akte) intend; (tiltenke) intend, mean; (levne, forbeholde) leave, reserve. det var eslet (til) deg it was meant for you.
espalier espalier, trellis, trellis-work; danne — ke a lane, line the route (street).
esp...anto Esperanto.
esplanade esplanade.
esprit esprit, wit.
I. ess: være i sitt — be in high spirits, feel fit; ikke i sitt — out of sorts, not himself; jeg er ikke riktig i mitt — I don't feel quite myself, I'm not quite the thing.
II. ess (eneren i kortspill) ace.
III. ess (i musikk) E flat.
essay essay. -ist essayist.
esse forge, furnace.
essens essence.
estetiker æsthetic. est|etikk esthetics el. æsthetics (pl). estetisk esthetic(al) el. æsthetic(al).
Estland Esthonia. est|lender, -isk, -nisk Esthonian.
estrade estrade, stand.
et (ubest. art. for intetkj.), se en.
etabl|lere establish; — seg settle, establish oneself in business, open (start) a shop. -lering, -lissement establishment.
etappe station, halting-place.
etarsekk (storeter) eater, feeder, gormandizer.
etasje story, floor, flat; i første — on the ground-floor; annen — the first floor; tredje — second floor; øverste — top floor; (spøkende; hodet) the upper story. -re canterbury, whatnot, (til noter) music-stand. etasjes floored, storeyed; en -t — bygning a four-floored building.
etat department, service.
etcetera et cetera.
ete eat; (fortære, om skarpe væsker) corrode; gi å — feed. -r seg igjennom eats its way through.
etegilde feed.
eter ether. eterisk ethereal.
etikette etiquette; (seddel) label.
etikk ethics. etisk ethic.
eting gormandizing.
etno|grafi ethnography. -grafisk ethnographic.
ets corrode; (med.) cauterize; (tegn.) etch; en -t tegning an etching; -nde caustic, corroding; -nde substanser caustics, corrodents.
et|steds somewhere.
ett, se en (tallord).
I. etter (prep) after; (bak) behind; (nest etter) next to; (som etterfølger) after, in succession to; (i følge) according to; den ene — den andre in succession; innfinne seg — et avertissement call in answer to an advertisement; — befaling by command; begjærlig — desirous of; — behag

as you please; at pleasure; — **diktat** to dictation; **dømme** — **det utvortes** judge by el. from appearances; — **forgodtbefinnende** at discretion; **gripe** — catch at; **handle** — **et prinsipp** act up to a principle; **hette John** — **sin far** was called J. after his father; **8 dager** — hverandre 8 days running el. in succession; — **hukommelsen** from memory; — **det jeg har hørt** by el. from what I have heard; **år** — **Kristi fødsel** in the year of our Lord; — **leilighet** as suits your convenience; **litt** — **litt** by little and little, by degrees; — **min mening** in my opinion; — **naturen** from nature; **synge** — **noter** sing by note; **gå** — **nesen** follow one's nose; **jeg gikk tilbake** — **et lys** I returned for a light; — **dette prinsipp** upon this principle; — **denne regel** by this rule; **slå** — aim a blow at; **smelle døra igjen** — **en** slam the door on one; — **min smak** to (el. in) my taste; **tale** — speak in imitation el, mimic one's speech; — **tur** by turns; — **mitt ur** by my watch; — **vekt** by weight; **han var** — **ham** he gave it him; **politiet var** — **ham** was on his tracks; **være** — **ønske** answer one's wishes; — **å ha** after having. II. **etter** (adv) after; (bak) behind; **året** — next year; **gjøre noe** —, se **ettergjøre**; **si noe** — repeat; **kort** — shortly el. soon after.
etterape ape, mimic.
etterat after, when.
etterbetaling after-payment.
etterbyrd after-birth.
etterdater|e postdate. **-ing** postdating.
etterdi (i juridisk språk) whereas.
etterdikte imitate, copy (poetry).
etterdiktning imitation.
etterdønning after-swell.
etterforsk|e inquire into, investigate, explore, scrutinize, search. **-ning** inquiry into, investigation, exploration.
etterføl|ge follow, succeed. **-gelse** succession; following, imitation; **Kristi etterfølgelse** imitation of Christ. **-gelsesverdig** worthy of imitation. **-gende** subsequent. **-ger**, **-gerske** follower, successor.
etter|gi remit, pardon, excuse. **-givelse** remission. **-givende** indulgent, yielding, pliable, compliant. **-givenhet** compliance, indulgence, facility.
etter|gjøre counterfeit, forge; imitate, ape. **-gjorte varer** counterfeit articles.
etterglemt left behind. **kontor for** — **reisegods** left luggage office.
ettergå inspect, examine; (bilde etc.) retouch; (linjer, omriss) retrace.
etterherme, se **-ape**.
etterhøst after-crop.
etterhånden gradually, by degrees; — **som** (in proportion) as.
etterklang resonance; (fig) re-echo.
etterkomme comply with, perform, observe; — **innbydelsen** comply with the invitation; **ikke** — disobey.
etterkommer descendant; **-e** posterity.
etterkrav claim; beregne **omkostningene som** —, ta — take charges forward.
etterkur after treatment.
etterla|te leave, leave behind, remit; (testamentere) leave (by will); — **seg** leave behind; **-te skrifter** posthumous works; **de -tte** the survivors.
etterla|tende negligent, remiss. **-tenhet** negligence, remissness. **-tenskap** property left, effects.
etterleve, se **etterkomme**. **-lse** compliance, observance. **-nde** surviving; **de** — the survivors.
etterlign|e imitate, copy. **-else** imitation, copy. **-elsesevne** imitative power. **-elsesverdig** worthy of imitation. **-er** imitator, copier. **-ing**, se **-else**.
etterlyse advertise for, ask for by public notice; (ved politiet) make a hue-and-cry after.
etterlysning advertisement, hue-and-cry.
etterlyst (av politiet) wanted.
ettermann follower, successor.

ettermat second dish; meat.
ettermid|dag afternoon (d. e. tiden etter kl. 2 eller mellom lunsj og middag); **det skjedde kl. 3** — it happened at three o'clock P. M. **-dags** afternoon; post-meridian, after-dinner. **-dagskjole** afternoon dress.
ettermæle posthumous fame, renown, name.
etternavn surname, family name.
etternevnte the following named.
etternøler laggard, straggler; (som er sent ute) a late-comer.
etterplapre echo, parrot, repeat.
etterretning intelligence, accounts, advice, notice, information, news; **en** — a piece of intelligence: **de siste -er** the latest news.
etterretningsvesen intelligence service.
etterrett dessert.
etterrettelig: holde seg en befaling — observe an injunction, attend to an order.
etterse inspect, examine, see to.
ettersende forward, send on.
ettersetning consequent clause.
ettersiktveksel bill payable after sight.
etter|skrift postscript. **-skrive** imitate (a handwriting); forge, counterfeit. **-skudd** after instalment el. payment.
etter|slekt posterity. **-slett** after-math. **-smak** after taste; tang. **-smekk** after-clap.
ettersnakk after-talk. **-e** echo, copy, parrot. **-er** repeater, copyer, parrot. **-ing** echoing, parrotry.
ettersom as, since, seeing that; **alt** — according as.
ettersommer end of the summer; after-summer, Indian summer.
etterspill after-piece, after-play, conclusion; (musikk) postlude.
etterspor|e track, (fig) trace out. **-ing** tracking.
etterspurt: disse varene er meget — these goods are in great demand, request, favour, are much run after.
etterspørsel inquiry; demand; **det er liten** — **etter** there is small demand for.
etterstrebe aim at, aspire to, affect; persecute; — **ens liv** plot against, attempt one's life, **-lse** aspiration, plot, attempt; persecution.
ettersyn inspection; **til** — for inspection, on view, to be viewed; **ved nærmere** — on a closer inspection.
ettersøk|e search after. **-ning** search.
ettertanke reflection, meditation; **ved nærmere** — on reflection.
ettertid after times, after ages; **for -en** in future.
ettertrakt|e, **-ning**, se **etterstrebe**
ettertrykk emphasis, stress; (av bok) piracy; — forbudt Copyright, copyrighted, all rights reserved; **legge** — på lay stress upon, emphasize, accentuate. **-elig** emphatic(al), forcible.
etterveer after-pains; (fig) after-cost; **føle** — **etter** suffer from the effects of.
etterverdenen posterity, after-ages.
ettervirkning after-effect, secondary effect.
ettmål 24 hours.
ett-tall (number) one, unit.
ettårig of one year. **ettårs** one year old.
etui case.
etyde study, exercise.
etymolog etymologist.
etymo|logi etymology. **-logisk** etymological.
Eugen Eugene.
Europ|a Europe. **e-eer** European.
europeisk European; **er** — **berømt** has a European reputation; — **Russland** Russia in Europe.
Eva Eve. **e-datter** daughter of Eve.
evakuere evacuate.
evange|lisk evangelic(al). **-list** evangelist. **-lium** gospel; **Matteus** — the gospel according to St. Matthew.
eventualitet eventuality, contingency.
eventuell possible, contingent. **eventuelt** (adv)

possibly, if possible, perhaps if necessary, if desired.

eventyr (opplevelse) adventure; (fortelling) fairy-tale, nursery-tale, (fire-side) story; **gå ut på** — go in search of adventures, seek adventures. **-aktig** fanciful, unreal. **-er** adventurer. **-erske** adventuress. **eventyrlig** fairy-like, fictional; romantic, marvellous. **eventyrlighet** marvellousness.

evfemisme euphemism.

evidens evidence. **evident** evident.

evig eternal, perpetual, everlasting; **det -e liv** life eternal el. everlasting; **den -e fordømmelse** perdition; **den -e ild** everlasting fire; — **snø** perpetual el. perennial snow; **den -e stad** the eternal city; **den -e jøde** the wandering Jew; **til** — **tid** to all eternity; **gått til den -e hvile** gone to his long home; **for** — **for ever** (and ever), eternally; **hver -e en** every mother's son (of them); every blessed one; **hver -e natt** every mortal night; (adv) eternally, for ever. **-grønn** ever green.

evighet eternity; **en hel** — an age; (untold) ages; **aldri i** — never; **fra** — **til** — world without end; **hvor i all** — how in the name of wonder. **-sblomst** cudweed; goldy locks. **evinnelig** continual, perpetual; (adv) eternally, to all eternity. **-het, se evighet: i en** — for ever. **evje** still part, creek.

evne ability, power, faculty; (råd) means; **har** — **til å** has the faculty of -ing, has it in him to; **gode -r** good parts; **etter** — according to one's means; to the best of one's ability. **evne** (vrb) be able, have the ability. **evne|løs** incapable. **-rik** gifted, of great powers. **evnukk** eunuch.

evolusjon (utvikling, også manøvre med tropper el. skip) evolution. **-steori** theory of evolution.

exlibris, se ekslibris.

extenso: in — in detail; at length, at large.

F

F, f F, f.

fabel fable; story, tale. **-aktig** fabulous; **til en -aktig pris** at fancy prices. **-aktighet** fabulousness. **fable** fable.

fabrikant manufacturer, maker.

fabrikasjon manufacture, manufacturing.

fabrikat manufacture, make, product.

fabrikere manufacture; (oppdikte, forfalske) fabricate.

fabrikk manufactory, factory, mill; (bygning) factory-buildings, works. **fabrikkarbeid** factory-work; mill-labour; (litterært) hackwork. **-arbeider** factory hand. **-arbeiderske** factory girl.

fabrikk|bestyrer manager of a factory. **-by** manufacturing town. **-drift** manufacturing industry.

fabrikkmessig wholesale, in a manufactory way.

fabrikk|pike factory girl. **-skorstein** factory chimney. **-stempel** trade mark. **-tilsyn** factory inspection.

face: en — full face.

fadder god-father, god-mother, sponsor; **stå, være** — **til** stand el. be god-father, god-mother to. **-gave** christening present. **-sladder**, gossip, gossiping.

fader foreldet form for **far**, brukes enda i sm.setn.: **fader|bryst** paternal breast. **-glede** paternal delight, father's joy. **-hånd** fatherly hand. **-kjærlighet** paternal love. **faderlig** fatherly, paternal, parental. **faderlighet** fatherliness.

fader|mord parricide. **-morder, -morderske** parricide. **-mordere** (snipper) side-boards. **-vår** the Lord's prayer; **kunne noe som sitt** — have st. at one's fingers' ends; **kan mere enn sitt** — is up to snuff, up to a thing or two.

fadese blunder, solecism.

fag (i bygning) bay, window; (i reol o. l.) pigeon-hole; (i skole) subject; (område) department, line, subject, province, profession; **et** — **gardiner** a set of curtains for a window; **av** — by profession.

fag|arbeider skilled workman. **-blad** professional paper.

fager (skjønn) fair, beautiful. **-het** beauty.

fag|forening trade union. **-kunnskap** professional el. special knowledge. **-kyndig** expert. **-lig** technical, skilled. **-litteratur** (praktisk) trade literature, (vitenskapelig) professional literature **-lærer** special teacher, professional teacher. **-lært** skilled. **-mann** professional (man). **-messig** skilled.

fagna worthy, excellent.

fagnad joy, delight, pleasure.

fagott (treblåseinstrument) bassoon.

fagstudium professional study.

fagutdannelse professional training.

fajanse faience, crockery, Delft-ware, delft.

fakir fakir, fakeer.

fakke catch, nab, take up.

fakkel torch, flambeau, link. **-bærer** link-man, torchbearer. **-tog** torch-light procession.

faks mane.

faksimile facsimile.

fakta plur. av **faktum**.

fakter grimaces, antics.

faktisk (adj) founded on fact, actual; **de -e forhold** the facts; **det er** — it is a fact; **den -e eier** the virtual possessor.

faktisk (adv) as a matter of fact, actually, in fact, in point of fact; **de holdt** — **på å drikke seg ihjel** they were actually drinking themselves to death.

faktor factor; (boktr.) overseer.

faktotum all in all, factotum, man-of-all-work.

faktum fact.

faktura invoice. **-beløp** amount as per invoice. **-skriver** invoice-clerk. **fakturere** invoice.

fakul|tativ optional. **-tet** faculty.

I **fal**, se **aske**.

II. **fal** (rør, holk) socket, hose.

fal (adj) (til salgs) for sale.

falanks phalanx.

falby offer for sale, expose to sale.

fald (kant, søm) hem.

falde (vrb) hem.

falk falcon, hawk; **falkejakt** hawking.

falkoner falconer.

fall fall, downfall, tumble; **i** — in case, in the event; **i så** — in that case; **i all** —, **i alle** —, **i hvert** — at any rate, at all events, in any case, anyhow, any way; **i motsatt** — on a contrary supposition, if not, on the other hand. **det var sterkt snø-** there was a heavy fall of snow. **-bom** portcullis. **-dør** trap-door; (ved hengning) drop.

falle fall, drop, tumble; (i krig) fall, be killed; **barometeret -r** the mercury is falling; **teppet -r** the curtain descends, drops; (som anvisning i skuespill) Curtain! **det falt noen ord** some words passed; **det er falt dom i saken** the cause is adjudged; **ta det som det -r take** it as it comes; **verset -r tungt** the line is heavy;

det -r meg lett I find it easy; la en sak — drop an affair; jeg lot noen ord — om det I let fall el. drop a few words about it, (mar) la —! keep her off! — av fall off; (om hår o. l.) come off; (avmagres) fall away; det som -r av leavings, shavings, remnants, (inntekter) extras; det -r av seg selv it is a matter of course, that goes without (the) saying; — bort cease, drop; det -r bort med årene it wears off with age; — for fiendens sverd fall by the sword of the enemy; — for fristelsen fall to the temptation; når Deres vei -r forbi when you come my way; — fra fall off; (dø) die, drop off; — i (på is) fall through; — i hendene på en fall into one's hands; det -r i min smak it suits my taste; — i øynene strike el. catch the eye, be conspicuous; — i tanker fall into a revery; — for undring, i staver be struck with astonishment; — i ens smak be (suited) to one's taste, strike one's fancy; — igjennom be rejected; (forslag) be lost, defeated; (ved valg) be thrown out; (ved ballotering) be blackballed; (ved eksamen) be refused, rejected, plucked, ploughed, fail; — inn happen, occur, fall; come in, strike in, fall in; det -r meg inn it strikes me, it occurs to me; det kunne aldri ha falt meg inn it could never have come into my head; — inn i et land invade a country; — inn under fall under; — ned come down; — om fall down; (om ting) tumble over; falt meg om halsen threw himself about my neck; — over fall upon; — på hit upon, think of, bethink oneself of; han falt på å gifte seg he took it into his head to marry; hvordan -r du på det what makes you think of that? da falt en redsel på ham then a dread came over him; natta -r på night is coming on, closing in; skylden vil — på Dem the blame will be laid on you; — sammen collapse; — sammen med coincide with; be identical with; — en til besvær be troublesome to one; — tilbake fall back; (om sykdom) relapse; — tilbake på (fig) recoil upon; — til ro acquiesce; — ut fall out, come out; (fig) turn out, fall out; — ut i fall into; — seg fall, come, chance, happen; når det -r seg så in good time, when occasion offers.

falleferdig falling to pieces, tumbledown, in a state of decay, ruinous.

fallen fallen; **fallen engel** fallen angel; — **pike** fallen (el. lapsed el. ruined) girl, **falne og sårede** killed and wounded.

fallende falling; **fallende tendens** (for priser) downward tendency.

fallent bankrupt. **fallere** fail (in business), become bankrupt, break.

fall|gitter portcullis. **-gruve** pitfall. **-hastighet** falling velocity.

fallitt bankruptcy, failure, insolvency; **gå** —, se **fallere**.

fallitt (adj) bankrupt; **erklære seg** — file a declaration of bankruptcy, go into bankruptcy, give it up; **erklære en** — (om retten) adjudge one (a) bankrupt; **forlange en erklært** — present a bankruptcy petition against one.

fallittbehandling bankruptcy-inquiry; **hans bo, som er under** — his insolvent estate.

fallittbo bankrupt's estate; **kreditorene i hans** — the creditors under his bankruptcy; **bestyrer av** — liquidator.

fallitt|erklæring declaration of bankruptcy; admission (el. confession) of failure.

fall|lem hatch on hinges. **-nett** (mar) (overhead-) netting. **-port** large trapdoor, (mar) hanging port-lid.

fallreip (inngangsåpning i skipssida) gangway; (utenbords skipstrapp derfra) accommodation ladder (reip til å holde fast i ved den) manrope; **glass på -et** parting cup, stirrup cup.

fallskjerm parachute. **-hopper** parachutist.

fallsmål (jur) (bøte for uteblivelsen som vitne) fine for contempt of court.

fall|syke epilepsy. **-øks** guillotine.

falme fade.

fals (fold i bok) fold, guard; (tømmerarb.) groove, channel, notch. **-ben** folding-stick.

false fold; groove, notch.

falsemaskin folding machine.

falsett falsetto, head-voice.

falsjern folding-tool.

falsk (adj) false, spurious; (bare om personer) false-hearted; (ettergjort) counterfeit, forged, (amr) bogus; (uriktig) false, wrong, unsound; **-e sedler** forged notes; **-e diamanter** mock diamonds, paste; — **spill** card-sharping .— **spiller** card-sharper. **-e toner** discordant notes; — **angivelse, uttydning** misstatement, misinterpretation.

falsk (adv) falsely; **spille** — cheat at play; **sverge** — perjure oneself, swear falsely; **synge** — sing out of tune.

falsk (subst) (dokumentfalsk) forgery, falsification; (falskhet) falseness, duplicity. **-het** falseness, duplicity; falsity, fallacy. **-myntner** (counterfeit) coiner, (sl) smasher. **-myntneri** coining. **-ner** forger, falsifier. **-neri** forgery, falsification.

falsum (falskneri) forgery.

familie family; **i** — **med** related to, a relation of; **av god** — well connected. **-forhold** family relations. **-hemmelighet** (av ubehagelig art) skeleton in the cupboard. **-krets** domestic circle. **-likhet** family likeness. **-liv** domestic life, home life. **-navn** family-name, surname. **-tvist** family discord.

familiær familiar, free and easy.

famle grope, fumble (etter: for); — **seg fram** grope one's way; — **ved** fumble at, finger, handle. **famling** groping.

famn, se **favn**.

fanati|ker fanatic. **-sk** fanatic(al). **-sme** fanaticism.

fanden the devil, the fiend, the deuce, old Harry; **for** —! confound it! — **og hans oldemor** the devil and his dam; — **til fyr** the devil of a fellow; **det var som** —! the deuce; **fy for** —! fie! shocking! **gå** — **i vold!** go to Jericho! go to the devil; you be hanged! be hanged to you; — **osså** devil a bit; **som bare** — like hell. — **ta** el. **gale meg, om jeg gjør** I will be hanged if I do, I will see you hanged first; — **er los** the devil to pay; **male** — **på veggen** raise bugbears, conjure up ghosts; **jeg tror** — **plager deg!** are you stark raving mad? **det bryr jeg meg** — **om** (I don't care) a fig for it! **for** — **får sko på** at an unearthly hour in the morning, at some unholy hour; — **hjelper sine** the old gentleman helps his own; **når man gir** — **en lillefinger** osv. give the devil an inch and he will take an ell. **fandens** devilish, diabolical; **en** — **kar** a devil of a fellow; **fanden|ivoldsk** dare-devil. **-skap** devilment, devilry.

fane banner, standard, colour, colours; **med flyvende** — **og klingende spill** with colours flying and drums beating. **-bærer** standard-bearer. **-ed** oath on the colour. **-flukt** desertion of his colours. **-innvielse** consecration of colours. **-marsj** march played while trooping the colours. **-tog** procession with flags. **-vakt** colour-sergeants, (amr) color-guard.

fanfare fanfare, flourish.

fang grasp, hold, (skjøt) knee, knees, lap; **tok barnet på -et** took the child on his knee el. lap.

fangarm tentacle.

fange (vrb) catch, capture.

I. **fange** (et) armful, armload.

II. **fange** (en) prisoner, captive; **ta en til** — make one prisoner.

fange|bur dungeon. **-drakt** prison dress. **-gård** exercising yard. **-kost** prison diet, prison fare. **-leir** prisoner's camp, prison camp.

fangenskap captivity, confinement, imprisonment.

fanger (selfanger) sealer; (hvalfanger) whaler.

fange|skip convicts hulk. **-tårn** dungeon, keep. **-vogn** prison van; (sl.) Black Maria. **-vokter** jailer.

fangline painter.

fangskinn leathern apron, leather apron.

fangst catching, taking; (bytte) capture; (av fisk) catch, draught, haul, take.

fant (landstryker) tramp, gipsy.

fantaktig rascally, scampish.

fantasere (musikk) play voluntaries; rave, extemporize; (i villelse) rave, be delirious el. incoherent.

fantasi fancy, fantasy, imagination; (musikk) fantasia, voluntary. **-bilde** chimera. **-full** imaginative. **-løs** unimaginative. **fantast** visionary, fancy-monger. **fantasteri** fantasticalness, fancies. **fantastisk** fantastic(al), whimsical.

fante|følge gipsy gang. **-gå** run away from one's master. **-ri, -skap** foolings; trumpery. **-språk** flash, Romany. **-strek** rascally trick, piece of knavery. **-vane** bad el. nasty habit.

fantom phantom.

I. **far** (spor) track, trail.

II. **far** father, parent; (poet. og om hester) sire; **fedre** fathers, ancestors; **far til the father of; er gått til sine fedre** has been gathered to his fathers; **fedrene** our fathers.

Farao Pharaoh.

farang, se **smittsom sykdom.**

farbar passable, practicable; navigable.

farbror father's brother, paternal uncle.

fare (vrb) (reise) go, travel; (om skip) sail; (styrte, ile) rush, dart, dash, bolt, bounce; **komme -nde inn** rush in; **ordet for ut av munnen på ham** the word slipped out of his mouth; — **med korn** be engaged in the corn trade; — **med et skip** sail in a ship; — **med løgn,** sannhet tell lies, truth; **hun for om halsen på ham** she threw herself about his neck; — **opp** start up, spring to one's legs, jump, (i vrede) fire up; — **på Østersjøen** trade to the Baltic; — **løs på en** rush el. fly at one; — **sammen** start, get a start; — **til sjøs** be a sailor, be at el. to sea; — **til himmels** ascend into heaven; — **til helvete** go to hell; — **vill** go astray, lose one's way, stray.

fare (subst) danger, peril, jeopardy, hazard, risk; **stå i — for** be in danger of; **løpe — for** run el. incur the risk of; **bringe i — endanger,** peril, hazard, place in jeopardy, jeopardize; **det har ingen —** there is no danger, no fear; **med — for** at the risk; **uten —** without danger, with impunity; out of danger.

faredag hiring day.

farefri free from danger, safe.

farefull dangerous, pregnant with peril.

fareklasse risk class.

faren: ille — badly off; **vel —** well off.

faresone danger zone.

faretruende perilous.

farfar grandfather, father's father.

farge (subs) colour, hue; (fargestoff) dye; (maling) paint; (i kortsp.) suit; **skifte — change** colour.

farge (vrb) dye, colour, stain; — **av** rub off, lose colour, be discoloured.

farge|blanding mixture of colours. **-blind** colour-blind. **-blindhet** colour-blindness, daltonism. **-brytning** refraction of colours. **-givning** colouring. **-glød** glow of colours. **-handel** colour shop. **-handler** colourman; (som fører artikler for kunstnere) artist's colourman. **-kjel** dyer's vat. **farge|lagt** coloured. **-legge** colour. **-legging** laying on colour, colouring. **farge|lære** science of colours. **-løs** colourless; (fig) neutral. **-løshet** colourlessness; neutrality. **-prakt** brilliancy of colour(s).

farger dyer.

farge|ri dye-house. **-rikdom** richness of colour. **-rivning** c.-grinding. **-sans** sense of colour. **-skrin** colour-box. **-spill** play of colours. **-stoff**

dye, dyestuff; pigment, colouring matter. **-symfoni** symphony in colour. **-tone** colour-tone. note of colour. **-trykk** lithochromy, colour-printing. **-virkning** effect of colour. **farging** dyeing.

farise|er pharisee. **-isk** pharisaical. **-isme** pharisaism.

fark rogue, tramp.

farkost (water)craft.

farlei direction, track (mar. især) fairway.

farlig dangerous, perilous, hazardous; dt. **en — mengde penger** an awful lot of money; **et — bryderi** a lot of trouble; (adv) dangerously; (sl) immensely, excessively. **-het** dangerousness, perilousness.

farm (skipslast) cargo, freight, load; (gård) farm.

farmann traveller.

farma|kopö pharmacopoeia. **-si** pharmaces. **-søyt** pharmaceutist, chemist's assistant. **-søytisk** pharmaceutic(al).

farmer farmer.

farmor (paternal) grandmother.

I. **fars|e** forced meat. **-ere** force, farce.

II. **farse** (sl. komedie) farce. **-aktig** farcical.

farskap fatherhood, fathership, paternity.

farsnavn patronymic.

farsott epidemic.

farsside: på -n paternal.

fart (skips) headway, way; (hastighet) hurry, rate, speed; impetus, momentum; (reise) voyage; **i en —** in a hurry el. trice; **med en — av** at the rate of; **han kom inn med en slik — at** with so much way upon him that; **i full —** (at) full speed; **komme i —** put on the pace, gather way, fetch headway; **gjør god —** has good way on her; **strømmen løp med sju mils —** the tide went at the rate of seven miles; **være på -en** be on the move.

farte omkring gad about.

fartøy vessel, craft, boat.

farvann waters, sea, seas, seaway; **-et er fritt** (fig) the coast is clear.

farvel good-bye, adieu, good-day; (høytid.) farewell; — **så lenge** good-bye for the present el. till we meet again; **si — til** bid good-bye to.

fasade front, frontage.

fasan pheasant. **-gård** pheasantry.

fascisme Fascism, the Fascist movement. **fascist** Fascist. **fascistisk** Fascist.

fase phase.

fasett facet, bevel. **fasettere** bevel.

fasit answer. **-bok** answers key. **-liste** key

fasjonabel fashionable.

faskin (bunt av greiner) fascine.

fasong shape, make, cut.

fast firm; (motsatt flytende) solid; (tett) compact; (standhaftig) fast, steadfast; (om stemme) fast, steadfast; (om markedet) firm, (bestemt) fixed; **en — ansettelse** a permanent situation. **a regular** employment; — **arbeid** regular el. permanent work; **-e arbeidere** regular el. established labourers el. hands; **de -e deler** the solid parts; — **eiendom** real property; — **fot** a firm footing; **et — forsett** a firm el. fixed purpose; **en — liten fyr** a tight little fellow; — **føde** solid food; **en — kunde** a regular customer; **det -e land** the main land; **-e lege-mer** solids; — **lønn** a fixed salary; **-e priser** fixed prices; **-e regler** established rules; — **rygg** (i bokbinding) tight back; **bli — ved** persist in; **gjøre — fasten,** make fast; (mar) make fast, belay; **holde — ved** el. på hold on by, (fig) adhere, stick to; **sitte — stick** (fast); **sitte i salen** have a firm seat; **slå — se fastslå: stå — (fig) be at a dead lock; det står — it is an established fact. fast (adv) firmly.

faste (vrb) fast. **faste** (subst) fast; (fastetiden) Lent. **-dag** fast-day. **-gudstjeneste** Lent service. **-kost** lenten food.

fastelavn Shrovetide. **fastelavns|bolle** cross

bun. –løyer Shrovetide sports (el. fun). **–mandag** Shrove-Monday, Collop-Monday. **–narr** merry Andrew. **–søndag** Quinquagesima, Shrove-Sunday.

fastende: jeg er — I have not yet eaten anything, I have not broken my fast; **på — hjerte** on an empty stomach, the first thing in the morning. **fastepreken** lent-sermon.

faster father's sister, paternal aunt.

fastetid time of fasting. Lent.

fasthet firmness; solidity; compactness; fastness; fixedness.

fast|holde se holde fast; (påstand) stick to, insist on; **— at** insist that. **–land** main, mainland; continent; **det europeiske –land** the Continent, continental Europe. **–lands–** continental. **–lønt** salaried. **–sette** (en tid) appoint, fix; (en pris) fix, settle; (betingelser) stipulate; (regler) establish, lay down; **–sette lønna til fix** the wages at. **–settelse** appointing etc.; appointment, fixation; settlement; stipulation; establishment. **–slå** (fastsette) fix; (bevise) establish; (bevitne) record; (anta) adopt; (få visshet for) ascertain. **–slått** (også) conventional, stereotyped.

fat dish; (tønne) cask, butt, hogshead, puncheon; **øl fra —** beer from the wood, draught beer.

fatal unlucky, unfortunate, calamitous; (ubehagelig) odious. **–isme** fatalism. **–ist** fatalist. **–itet** calamity, adversity.

fatamorgana fata morgana, mirage.

fate, se **fenge.**

fating body (of a carriage).

fatle arm-rest, sling.

fatning composure, self-possession; **bringe ut av —** disconcert, discompose, put out of countenance; (ved blikk) stare out of countenance; **outface; uten å tape –en** with composure, composedly, coolly.

fatt: det er ikke slik — that's not the way of it; **det er galt — med ham** all's not right with him; **ta — på** catch hold of, (om arbeid) turn to, set to work with; **få — i** get hold of; **jeg vet ikke hvor jeg skal få — på ham** I don't know where to find him.

fatte (gripe) catch; (begripe) comprehend, understand, conceive, imagine; **— lett** be quick of apprehension; **— seg** compose oneself, be composed; **— mot** take courage; **— tilbøyelighet for** form an attachment for (el. to); **— kjærlighet, uvilje** take a fancy, a dislike (to); **— en beslutning** come to a resolution; **— seg i korthet** be brief. **–evne** apprehension? capacity. **fattelig** comprehensible, intelligible. **fattelighet** comprehensibility, intelligibility.

fatter paterfamilias, the governor, the old man.

fattet composed, collected; **være — på alt** be prepared for whatever may happen.

fattig poor, needy, indigent, portionless; **den –e** the poor man, person; **de –e** the poor; **de –e i ånden** the poor in spirit; **— på** deficient in, destitute of; **etter — leilighet** to the best of my poor ability. **–bøsse** poor-box, alms-box. **–dom** poverty, penury, indigence.

fattig|folk the poor, the indigent. **–fornem** shabby-genteel. **–forstander** overseer of the poor, relieving officer, poor-law inspector. **–forsørgelse** provision for the poor. **–gutt** beggarboy. **–hjelp** parish relief; (i hjemmet) out-relief, out-door relief. **–kasse** fund for the relief of the poor. **–kone** beggar woman. **–kvarter** poor quarter. **–lem** pauper. **–lovgivningen** the Poor Laws. **–mann** poor man. **–mannsbakkels** flead cake. **–ondet** pauper-dom, pauperism. **–pleie** relief of the poor. **–slig** beggarly, poor, mean. **–vesen** institution for the relief of the poor, the charities.

faun faun.

fauna fauna.

favn embrace; (mål) fathom (pl. fathoms og fathom); **på 9 –er vann** in nine fathoms (of)

water; styrte seg i ens — rush into one's arms; **tok ham i — took** him into his arms; **en — ved** a cord of wood. **–sette** cord. **–setter** wood-measurer, corder.

favne embrace, clasp, hug; **— opp** (måle ut favner) fathom.

favneved cord-wood.

favntak embrace, hug.

favor|isere favour. **–itt** favourite, minion.

favør favour; **i min — in** my favour; **i — av de fattige** in favour of the poor.

I. fe fairy. **–aktig** fairy-like.

II. fe (dyr) cattle, beast; (fig) ass, block-head. **–avl** cattlebreeding el. raising.

feber fever; **få — have** a fever. **–aktig** feverish; **i –aktig spenning** in a fever of expectation. **–diét** fever diet. **–drøm** feverish dream, delirium. **–døs** feverish sleep. **–fantasi** feverish hallucination. **–fri** apyretic, without fever. **–het** feverish. **–stillende** febrifuge, antifebrile. **–tilstand** febrile state. **–villelse** delirium.

febril febrile.

febrilsk fidgety, in a fidget.

februar February.

fedd (garnmål) skein. **fedde** (verb) skein.

fedme fatness.

fedre av far; –dyrkelse ancestor el. ancestral worship. **–land**(native) country. **–landshistorie** national history. **–landsk** national, patriotic. **–landskjærlighet** patriotism. **–landssang** patriotic song, national anthem. **–landssinnet** patriotic, public spirited.

fedrene (adj) paternal, ancestral.

fe|drift grazing, pastoral industry.

fedronning fairy-queen, Queen Mab.

fe|fot: ligge for — lie in pasture, (fig) lie common. **–hage** pasture, cattle run. **–hode** blockhead, dunce. **–hund** collie shepherd's dog.

fei: i en — with a whisk, in a jiffy.

feide (subst) quarrel; (mellom familier) feud; (krig) war; (litterær) controversy. **feide** (vrb) make war.

feie sweep; **— av dt.** send (one) about his business; slur over. **–kost** broom, besom. **–nde** (av utseende) dashing; **det gikk — it** went on swimmingly.

feig cowardly, dastardly, recreant, craven. (døden nær) on the verge of death. **–het** cowardice, poltroonery; **vise — dt.** show the white feather.

feil (feiltagelse) error, mistake; (mangel) defect. **feil** (adj) wrong, erroneous, incorrect; **en — hatt** somebody else's hat. **gå inn i et — værelse** enter the wrong room.

feil (adv) amiss, wrong, erroneously; **avlevere — misdeliver; avskrive — miscopy; ta — mistake, be mistaken, be wrong; ta — av tiden** mistake the time; **ta — av en** be mistaken el. deceived in one, mistake one; **jeg tar — I** am mistaken; **han tok ikke mye — he** was not far out; **det vil ikke slå — at han kommer** he will be sure to come; **— datert** misdated; **gå, kjøre, ri — go** the wrong way, miss the way; **se — be mistaken; skrive — make** a slip of the pen; **skyte — miss** (the mark); **slå — fail; tre — make** a false step, slip.

feil|aktig faulty, erroneous, mistaken, wrong; **–aktig oppgivende** misstatement; **fremstille, oppfatte –aktig** misrepresent, misconceive (o. fl.). **–aktighet** error, incorrectness. **–bar** (utsatt for å ta —) fallible.

feile (forsé seg) err, do amiss; (skyte feil, forfeile et mål) miss; (mangle) be wanting; (lide av) ail; **det feilte mye på at han var ... he** was far from being ...; **det feilten ham ikke på** he was not wanting in; **hva –r Dem?** what ails you, what is the matter with you?

feil|fri faultless, without a fault. **–frihet** faultlesness. **–full** faulty, full of faults. **–grep** error, mistake, slip. **–lesning** misreading. **–regning** miscalculation. **–skrift, –skrivning** slip of the pen, misscript. **-skudd** miss. **-slagen** disappointed, baulked; **-slagen forhåpning** disappointment. **-slutning** erroneous inference. **-slått, se -slagen. -syn** error of the eye; (fig) misunderstanding, error in judgment. **-tagelse** mistake; **ved en — by** mistake. **-tenning** misfiring. **-trekk** wrong move. **-trin** false step, slip. **feire** celebrate, solemnize, keep. **-t** popular, much admired. **feit** fat, se ogs. **fet. tjukk og — stout; — kost** rich diet; high living; **den retten er for — for meg** that dish is too rich for me; **— jord** rich soil; **bli — fatten (av: on). feit|ost** cream el. rich cheese. **-sild** matie, matty. **fekar** drover. **fekte** fence; (kjempe) fight, combat; **— i lufta** battle with air; **-hanske** fencing-glove. **-kunst** art of fencing. **-mester** fencing-master. **fekter** fencer; fighter. **fektesal** fencing-room. **fektning** fencing; (trefning) fight, engagement, combat. **fele** fiddle. **-spiller** fiddler. **feleger** cattle camp, drover's camp. **felg** (på hjul) felly. **fell** pelt; skin-rug; fur (el. skin) bedcover **-bereder** (hvitgarver) currier, leather-dresser. I. **felle** (kamerat) fellow, companion, associate. II. **fell|e** trap; (fig) pitfall; **gå i -a** be caught in the trap, fall into the trap; **sette opp en — for** lay a trap for. **felle** (vrb) fell, cut, cut down; (drepe) strike down, slay; **— tårer** shed tears; **— dom** pass sentence; **— blader, tenner, takker** shed leaves, teeth, horns; **— fjær, hår** moult. **-nde** condemnatory; **— bevis** damning proof. **-tid** moulting season. **felles** common, joint; **ved — hjelp** between them (us etc.); **— mål** common measure; **for — regning** on joint account; **— interesse** community of interest; **gjøre — sak med** cast one's lot with; join hands; **vår — venn** our mutual friend; **være — om noe** have something in common; be partners in st. **felles|anliggende** joint concern. **-bakeri** co-operative bakery. **-bo** joint estate. **-kjønn** common gender. **-måltid** public dinner. **-navn** common name. **-nevner** common denominator el. divisor. **-preg** common stamp. **-skap** fellowship, community; **opptre i — act** in concert el. together. **-skole** co-educational school. **-titel** general title. **-undervisning** system of mixed schools, co-education. I. **felt** (et) field; compartment; (i brettspill) square; (område) department, province, sphere. II. **felt** (en) field; **dra i -en** take the field. **felt|artilleri** field-artillery. **-flaske** canteen. **-fot:** være, stå på **-fot** be on the war establishment; **leve på -fot** live as in a camp. **-herre** commander, general. **-herredyktighet** generalship. **-herrekunst** strategic art. **-kjøkken** field-kitchen. **-lasarett** field-hospital. **-liv** camp life. **-manøvre** sham battle. **-marskalk** field marshal. **-messig** fit for the field; **-messig påkledning** campaign attire. **-prest** army-chaplain. **-rop** watch-word, password, parole, (mest fig) (rallying-)cry. **-seng** campbedstead. **-slag** pitched battle. **feltspat** felspar. **felt|stol** camp-stool. **-tjeneste** active service in the field, field-duty. **-tog** campaign. **-vakt** outpost. **fem** five; **han kan ikke telle til — he** does not know B from a battledoor el. a hawk from a handsaw; **la — være like** care about nothing; **gå fra sine fulle — stray** from one's five wits; **han er ikke ved sine fulle — he** is not in his right senses el. mind. **-akts** fiveact. **-børing** ten-oar(ed boat). **-dobbelt** quintuple. **-fingret** quinate. **-foll -follig** fivefold, quintuple. **-fotet vers** pentameter. **-grenet** five-pronged.

feminin feminine. **femininum** the feminine gender; feminine noun. **feminisme** feminism. **feminist** feminist. **femkamp** pentathlon. **fem|kant** pentagon. **-kantet** pentagonal. **fem|mer** five. **-punding** (kanon) five-pounder. **-sidet** pentahedral. **-tall** the number five. **femte** fifth; **det — bud** the sixth commandment; **for det — fifthly,** in the fifth place; **som det — hjul** på en vogn one too many. **femtedel** fifth part, a fifth. **femten** fifteen. **femtende** the fifteenth. **femtepart,** se **-del. fem|ti** fifty. **-årig, -års** five years old. **fenaknok(e)** knuckle-end of mutton-ham. **fender** fender. **-pute** skid. **feng|e** catch fire, take fire, ignite, kindle. **-elig** inflammable. **feng|hette** (percussion) cap. **-hull** touch hole, vent. **-krutt** priming. **-rør** tube. **-sats** primer. **fengsel** prison, jail; (fangenskap) imprisonment, confinement. **fengsels|gård** prison-yard. **-straff** penalty of imprisonment. **-tid** time of i. **-vesenet** prison matters, the prisons. **fengsle** imprison, commit to prison, incarcerate; **— oppmerksomheten** fix, engross, absorb, rivet the attention; **hennes skjønnhet -t ham** her beauty captivated him. **fengslende** engrossing etc., enthralling. **fengsling** imprisonment incarceration. **fenomen** phenomenon. **-al** phenomenal. **fenrik** ensign. **fente** (kv. fant) woman tramp, gipsy woman **ferd** expedition; (oppførsel) conduct,behaviour; (framgangsmåte) proceeding; **fra første — from** the beginning, from the very outset; **være i — med** be about; **gi seg i — med** set about, embark on, address oneself to; **på -e:** hva er det på -e? what's the matter? det er **noe galt på -e** there is something amiss el. wrong; **der er fare på -e** there is danger afoot, mischief is brewing. **ferdes** journey, travel; (være i bevegelse) be in motion, be on the move. **-lass** carrier's load. **-mann** traveller, carrier, teamster. **-vogn** teamster's, carrier's waggon. **ferdig** (rede) ready, prepared, in readiness; (fullendt) finished, done; **være — med** have el. **be done** with; **gjøre — get** a thing ready; (fullende) finish; (dt) **han er — he** is finished, done for. **ferdighet** dexterity, skill, adroitness, expertness, address. **ferdig|laget, -sydd** ready-made. **ferdsel** road-traffic. **ferdselsmidler** means of conveyance. **ferdsels|vei, -åre** thoroughfare. **ferie** vacation, holidays, holiday; (parlamentsferie) adjournment, recess; **reise hjem i -n** go home for the holidays. **-dag** holiday. **-kursus** holiday course. **-lesning** holiday reading. **-opphold** holiday visit. **feriere** holiday. **feriereise** holiday trip. **feriereisende** holiday tripper. **ferietur** holiday trip. **ferje** (vrb) ferry. **ferje-båt** ferry-boat, wherry, ferry. **ferje|folk** ferrymen. **-lønn** ferriage. **—mann** ferryman, waterman. **-sted** ferry. **ferm** smart, clever (i, til: at). **ferment** ferment. **fermhet** cleverness. **ferniss** varnish. **-ere** va. |sh. **fernissering** varnishing. **.ernisseringsdag** varnishing-day. **fersk** fresh, sweet; (fig) green, verdant; **gripe på — gjerning** take, seize in the very act, catch red-handed.

fersken peach.
ferski|het freshness, sweetness. **-mat** fresh provisions. **-vann** fresh water. **-vanns-** fresh -water.
fert scent; **få -en av scent**, get scent of.
fe-råk cattle-track, **-sjå**, se **dyrskue**.
feslott fairy palace, enchanted castle.
fess F flat. **-ess** F double flat.
fest feast, festival, fête, celebration. **-aften** festive night. **-arrangør** master of the ceremonies. **-dag** festival-day, holiday. **-forestilling** special performance.
feste (noe å feste med) fastening; (for hendene, føttene) hold; (på sabel) hilt, handle; (forpaktning) lease.
I. **feste** (vrb) fasten, fix, secure; — **rot** take root; — **tjenestefolk** engage servants; — **en gård bort** lease a farm; — **på papiret** commit to writing, commit to paper; **holde oppmerksomheten -t ved noe** keep one's attention on; — **sitt håp på fix** one's hope upon; — **seg bort** hire oneself; — **seg i erindringen** take hold of the memory.
II. **feste** feast, banquet.
feste|bonde tenant, leaseholder; **-brev** lease-contract. **-folk** betrothed couple. **-kontor** registry -office, registry for servants. **hennes -mann** (forlovede) her affianced one **-møy** (poet) affianced bride. **-mål** (høytidelig forlovelse) betrothal. **-penger** earnest-money.
festivitas festivity.
festivitet festivity, entertainment. **-s-lokale** assembly-rooms.
fest|kantate festival cantata. **-komité fête** committee.
festlig festive, festal, solemn; — **smykket** festively decorated. **festlighet** festivity. **festligholde** celebrate. **festmåltid** feast, banquet, festive entertainment.
festne fasten, solidify; (fig) consolidate.
festning fortress, fort. **festnings|anlegg** fortification. **-arbeid** fortification; **dømmes til** — be sentenced to hard labour. **-artilleri** garrison artillery, position guns. **-grav** ditch, moat. **-verk** fortification. **-voll** rampart.
festong (girlandebue) festoon.
fest|sal banqueting hall, festival hall. **-skrift** commemorative writing. **-skrud** holiday attire. **-stemning** festivity, holiday mood. **-stemt** in a holiday mood, light-hearted. **-tale** principal speech. **-tog** procession.
fet, se ogs. **feit** fat; **-e typer** large type, heavy t., fat faced t., blacker t.; **et -tt embete** a lucrative office; **ett -tt** dt. all one.
fetere make much of, fête.
fetevarehandler butterman, cheesemonger, provision dealer.
fetevarer fat goods, provisions, chandler's wares.
fetisj fetish el. fetich.
fetisjdyrkelse fetichism, fetish worship.
fetladen fattish.
fetning fattening.
fett (subst) fat, grease; **-aktig** fatty. **-dannelse** formation of fat.
fette grease, besmear with grease.
fetter cousin; male cousin. **-skap** cousinship.
fettet greasy.
fett|flekk spot of grease. **-kjertel** sebaceous gland; oil-bag. **-klump** lump of fat. **-kuler** oil-globules. **-lær** greased leather. **-stoff** fatty substance el. principle. **-svulst** steatoma, lipoma. **-syke** obesity, corpulence. **-syre** sebacic el. fatty acid. **-vev** adispose tissue.
f. f. (av fineste sort) A 1, first-class, first-rate, capital.
fiasko failure, fiasco; **gjøre** — fail (utterly).
fiber fibre, filament, funicle.
fichu neckerchief.
fideikommiss entail, feoffment in trust. **-besitter** feoffee in trust.

fidibus paper-match, spill, (candle-) lighter; pipe-light.
fidus (tillit) confidence (til: in).
fiende enemy, (gammelt og poet) foe; **være en** — av be an enemy to; **skaffe seg -r** make enemies; **gjøre en til sin** — make an enemy of one; **falle i -vold** fall into the hands of an enemy. **fiendsk** inimical.
fiendskap enmity; **l** — **med** i **t e** imity with. **fiendtlig** hostile; inimical. **fiendtlighet** hostility.
fiff contrivance, trick. **fiffdame** elegant, stylish lady. **fiffe** (opp) make smart, smarten up. **fiffig** sly, crafty, cunning. **fiffikus** cunning dog.
figur figure, shape; (linjetegning) diagram, figure; **portrett i hel** — full-length portrait.
figurere figure, f. eks. figure as a philanth opist.
figurlig figurative.
fik box on the ear.
fike box el. slap one's ears.
fiken fig. **-blad** fig-leaf. **-tre** fig-tree.
fikle fumble. — **med** tamper with.
fiks fixed; dt. smart; — **idé** fixed idea, monomania, crotchet; **en mann med -e idéer** monomaniac, dt. crotcheteer; — **og ferdig** quite ready, trim and tight. **fikse opp** dress up, make smart.
fiksér|bad fixing-bath. **-bilde** photographic puzzle, puzzle picture.
fiksere (fastsette) fix, determine, settle; (se stivt på) fix, fix with one's eyes, look fixedly at. **fiksfakserier** tricks, dodges, hanky-panky, hanky.
fiksjon fiction.
fiksstjerne fixed star.
fil (verktøy) file. **-benk** vice-holder.
filantrop philanthropist. **-i** philanthropy. **-isk** philanthropic(al).
filateli philately, stamp-collecting.
filatelist philatelist.
file (bearbeide med fil) file; (polere) polish.
filer|e net. **-ing** netting.
filet (stykke kjøtt el. fisk) fillet.
filharmonisk philharmonic.
fil|hogg file-cut. **-hogger** file-cutter.
filial branch, subordinate institution el. establishment.
filigransarbeid filigree, filigrane.
filipens pimple; **full av -er** pimpled.
filipine philippine.
Filippinene the Philippines.
filister Philistine; (spissborger) philistine, philister, gigman, narrow-minded person. **-aktig** narrow-minded, matter-of-fact. **-i** philistinism. **filistrøs** philistine, matter of fact.
fille rag, tatter; **rive i -r** tear to pieces. **-dokke** rag doll. **-gamp** jade, nag. **-handler** dolly (el. rag) man. **-rye** patchwork (el. piece-) rug. **-teppe**, se **-rye**.
fillet(e) ragged, tattered.
film film. **filmatisere** film.
filmdrama film-drama.
filme (oppta i levende bilder) film, take a film, make a film, film for the cinematograph; (kokettere) flirt.
filmskuespiller film-actor, film-artist. **-inne** film-actress.
filmstjerne film-star.
filolog philologist. **-i** philology. **-isk** philologic(al).
filosof philosopher. **-ere** philosophize. **-i** philosophy. **-isk** philosophic(al).
fil|skrue hand-vice. **-sponer** filings.
filt felt. **filte** felt; **filte seg sammen** become matted, mat.
filter filter, strainer.
filthatt felt hat.
filtrerapparat filtering machine. **filtrere** filter, strain, percolate. **filtrering** filtration, percolation.
filtrerpapir filter-paper.

filt|sko felt-shoe. **-såle** felt-sole.
filur sly dog. **-eri** trick(s), dodge(s).
fimre vibrate, quiver. **-hår** cilia.
fin fine, delicate; **den -e verden** the fashionable, polite world; society; **-t vesen** elegant address, genteel manners; **en — diplomat** a subtle diplomatist; **-t gull** pure gold; **en — hentydning** a sly allusion, hint; **et -t håndkle** a smooth towel; **— hørsel** a quick ear; **en — iakttager** a shrewd observer. **-t papir** first-rate paper.
finale finale.
finans|er finance, finances. **-iell** financial. **-iere** finance. **-mann** financier. **-minister** minister of finance, finance-minister; (i England) Chancellor of the Exchequer. **-ministerium** ministry of finance, treasury. **-vesen** finance, financial concerns. **-år** fiscal el. financial year, revenue year.
fin|brenne refine. **-bygd** delicate, delicately built.
fin|er veneer. **-ere** veneer. **-erer** inlayer. **-ering** veneering.
finesse subtlety; nicety.
finfin of the finest fine, ultra swagger.
finfølelse delicacy of feeling, sensitiveness.
finger finger; **ha lange fingrer** be light-fingered; **vil ikke røre en — for å** will not lift a finger to; **gi ham en — og han tar hele hånden** give him an inch and he will take an ell; **peke fingrer av** point at; **fingrene av fatet!** hands off! paws off! **han klør i fingrene etter å** he is dying to; **få fingrer i** lay hands on; **ha en — med i spillet** have a finger in the pie, in it; **se gjennom fingrer med** connive at, wink at; **ikke legge fingrene imellom** handle (one, something) without mittens, not spare one; **få over fingrene** get a rap on the knuckles; **telle på fingrene** count on the fingers; **han kan det på fingrene** he has it at his fingers' ends; **se en på fingrene** watch one closely, have an eye upon one; **har et øye på hver — ** has all his eyes about him; **slå en på fingrene** rap one on the knuckles.
fingeravtrykk fingerprint.
fingerbredd finger's breadth.
fingerbøl thimble; (plante) se **revebjelle.**
fingere feign.
finger|ferdighet dexterity; (musikk) skill of execution. **-kløe** itching fingers. **-kyss** blown kiss. **-nem** handy. **-nemhet** handiness. **-pek** hint.
finger|setning (på piano) fingering. **-spiss** finger's end, finger tip. **-språk** finger language, dactylology, manual alphabet. **-tupp,** se **-spiss. -øvelser** (pl) finger exercises. **fingre** finger.
finhet fineness, delicacy.
finkam small-toothed comb.
finkjensle, se **-følelse.**
finke (fugl) finch.
finkel (simpelt brennevin) bad liquor.
finkenett (mar) netting.
finkornet fine-grained.
fin|male grind small, powder. **-masket** fine-mesh, fine-meshed.
finn Laplander, Lapp.
I. **finne** (finnlender) Fin, Finn, Finlander.
II. **finne** (på fisk) fin.
III. **finne** (i huden) blackhead, pimple.
finne (vrb) find; **— hurtig avsetning** meet a ready sale; **— døden** meet one's death; **— kjøpere** meet buyers; **— leilighet** meet with an opportunity; **— sted** take place; **— tid til** make time to; **— tilslutning** meet with encouragement; **dersom De -r for godt** if you think proper, if you choose, see good; **— fram** fetch out, bring to light; **— igjen** recover; **— på** think of, hit upon, bethink oneself of; **— tilbake, ut** find one's way back, out; **— ut** (utfinne) make out; **— ut av** make out, unravel; **kan hverken — ut eller inn** can make nothing of it; **— seg i** put up with, stand, submit to. **finnes** (passiv av finne) be found; (være til) be found, exist (forekomme) occur.

finne|lønn finder's fee. **-r** finder. **-sted** finding-place; habitat, station.
finnet (i ansiktet) pimpled.
finn|gras wire grass. **-hval** finback, rorqual.
Finn|land Finland. **-landsk** Finland. **-lender** Finlander. **-mark** Finmark.
finnmudd (el. -mutt) Lapp furcoat.
finnsko Laplander's brogue, moccasin, shoepack.
fin|pusse finish, polish up, give the finishing touch. **-sikte** (mel) flour-bolt. (fig) sift.
finsk Finnish; (the) Finnish (language); **den Finske Bukt** the Gulf of Finland.
finstilt in small print.
finstøtt finely powdered.
finte (i fektekunst) feint; (list) trick, fetch; (spydighet) wipe, sneer, skit; **gi en -r** sneer at.
fintfølende sensitive.
fiol violet. **-blå** violet.
fiolett violet purple.
fiolin violin, fiddle. **-bue** violin-bow, fiddle-stick. **fiolinist** violinist, violin-player.
fiolin|kasse violin-case. **-maker** violin-maker. **-nøkkel** treble clef. **-spill** violin playing. **-stol** bridge of a violin. **-streng** string of a violin, fiddle-string.
fiolon|sell violoncello. **-sellist** violoncellist.
fiolrot orris-root.
fipp tip. **-skjegg** chintuft.
firbein, se **firfisle.**
firdobbelt quadruple, fourfold.
fire (tallord) four; **på alle — ** on all fours. **-knapps hansker** four-button gloves. **-manns whist** four-handed whist. **-mannslag** team of four; **— og tjue** four-and-twenty, twenty-four.
fire (vrb) ease off, lower, veer, veer away; (fig) yield, give way, give up (to).
fire|tall number four.
fir|fisle lizard. **-føtt** fourfooted; **et — dyr** a quadruped. **-grenet** four-branched. **-hendig** (musikk) for four hands; **spille -hendig** play duets. **-hendt** four-handed. **-hjulet** four-wheeled. **-kant** square, quadrangle. **-kantet** quadrangular, square. **-klang** chord of the seventh. **-kløver** four-leaved clover; (gruppe av fire) quartet. **-kort** all-fours. **firlinger** four at a birth.
firma firm, house; **under —** under the firm of.
firmament firmament.
firmenning third cousin.
firskåren square-built, squarely built, thickset.
fir|spann team of four; **kjøre med — ** drive four-in-hand. **-spenner** four-horse(d) carriage. **-sprang: i —** at a gallop, at full speed. **-stemmig** in four parts, four-part. **-strøken C** C with four strokes.
firtoms four inch.
firårig four years (old).
fisk fish; (typograf.) pi(e); **så frisk som en — ** as sound as a roach el. trout; **hverken fugl eller — ** neither fish nor flesh (nor good red herring); **falle i —** go to pi(e).
fiskaktig, fishy, fishlike.
fiske (vrb) fish, angle (for fish); **— i rørt vann** fish in troubled waters.
fiske (subst) fishery, fishing.
fiske|agn bait. **-avl** fish-culture, pisciculture. **-bein** fishbone; (tilberedt hvalbarde) whalebone. **-bolle** fish-ball. **-brygge** fishing wharf el. dock. **-fangst** fishing, fishery. **-farse** minced fish. **-garn** fishing-net. **-gjelle** gill. **-greier** fishing tackle; **-handler** fishmonger; (hunkjønn) fishmongeress; **-kort** (som gir adgang til å fiske) fishing-ticket; **-kjerring** fish-wife; **-krok** fish(ing. hook. **-kvasse** well-boat. **-kyndig** ichthyologist **-lek** (rogn) spawn. **-lim** fish-glue, isinglass. **-melke, -mjølke** milt, soft roe.
fisker fisherman; angler. **-båt** fishing boat, coble.
fiske|redskap, se **-greier. -rett** dish of fish; (rettighet) right of (free) fishing, privilege of fishing.

fiskeri fishing, fishery; angling. **-inspektør** (el. **-direktør**) inspector of fisheries. **-oppsyn** fishery protection. **-produkter** produce of fisheries.
fiskerjente fisherman's daughter, fisher-girl.
fiskerkjelke fisherman's sleigh.
fisker|kone fisher's wife; (k., som seller fisk) fish-woman.
fiskerogn roe, hard roe; (især gytt) spawn.
fiske|ruse, se **ruse**. **-skjell** scale of a fish. **-snøre** fishing-line. **-stang** angling-rod. **-stim** shoal of fish. **-torg** fishmarket. **-utklekning** fish -hatching. **-vær** fishing station el. village; **-yngel** fry, young fish.
fiss F sharp. **-iss** F double-sharp.
I. **fistel** (med.) fistula.
II. **fistel** (stemme) falsetto.
fjas foolery, nonsense. **fjase** trifle, toy.
fjed step; **rettet mine — bent my steps.**
fjel (brett) board.
fjell mountain, hill; (om grunnen) rock. **-bekk** (rivende) mountain torrent. **-bestiger** Alpine climber. **-bu** mountainer, highlander. **-bygd** mountain district. **-folk** mountaineers, highlanders, mountain people. **-frass**, se **jerv**. **-gård** hill-farm. **-hammer** crag. **-kam** crest of a m. **-kjede** chain el. range of mountains. **-kløft** ravine, mountain cleft el. fissure. **-land** mountainous country. **-rygg** ridge of a m. **-rype** ptarmigan. **-sko** alpine boot. **-skred** mountain slide. **-skrent** cliff, precipice. **-stav** alpenstock. **-sti** mountain-path. **-stue** m. station. **-tind** m. peak. **-topp** m. top, hill-top. **-vann** mountain lake el. tarn. **-vidde** mountain-wilds.
fjerde (tallord) fourth; **det — bud** the fifth commandment; **for det — in** the fourth place, fourthly. **-del** fourth part, fourth, quarter; **-dels** note crotchet; **-dels** pause crotchet rest; tre **-dels takt** three crotchets time. **-mann:** være **— make** a fourth. **-part,** se **-del.**
fjerding quarter; (veilengde) quarter of a Norwegian mile; **en — smør** a firkin of butter. **-kar** half a peck. **-spund** quarter of a pound. **-svei** quartermile. **-år** quarter of a year, three months; **fem -år** fifteen months. **hvert -år** quarterly; every three months.
fjern far, far-off, distant, remote; **i det -e** in the distance; **fra — og nær** from far and near; **det være -t fra meg å** far be it from me to; **ikke -este idé om** not the remotest idea of; **ikke i -este måte** not in the least; **ikke -este grunn** not the shadow of a reason.
fjerne remove, retire, withdraw; **— seg** retire, withdraw.
fjernelse removal, withdrawal.
fjernhet remoteness, distance.
fjernt (adv) far, far off, remotely, distantly.
fjes mug, phiz.
fjesk great fuss; compliments paid, courting.
fjeske pay court to (for).
fjetre fetter, hamper, trammel. (fig) spell-bind, fascinate, lay under a spell. **-t** charmed to the spot.
fjolle behave like an idiot. **fjollet** idiotic(al), silly, sottish. **fjollethet** imbecility. **fjolling** fool.
fjong stylish, smart.
fjord bay, firth, fjord, estuary, inlet; (i nordiske land) fjord. **-botn** head of a fjord. **-gap** mouth of a firth. **-hest** pony of the sea-side breed.
fjor|gammel, se **årsgammel**. **-kalv** yearling calf.
fjorten fourteen; **— dager** a fortnight. **-daglig** fortnightly. **-de** fourteenth. **-dedel** fourteenth. **-årig**, **-års** fourteen years old.
fjær feather, plume; (på lås osv.) spring; (i vogn: ofte) cee, C-spring; (fugls) plumage; **komme ut av fjærene** turn out; **pynte seg med lånte fjær** strut in borrowed feathers. **-aktig** feathery. **-ball** shuttle-cock; **spille -ball** play at battle-door and shuttle-cock. **-busk** tuft of

feathers, plumage. **-dannet** penniform. **-dyne** feather-bed.
fjære (mots. flo) ebb, ebb-tide, low water; (strand) beach, sands.
fjære (vrb) spring; **fjærende** elastic, springy. **fjær|fe** poultry. **-feavl** poultry-breeding. **-felling** moulting. **-kledning** plumage. **-kost** feather-brush. **-kre**, se **-fe**. **-lett** featherly, light as a feather. **-penn** quill(pen), Dutch pen. **-sky** cirrus. **-topp** tuft of feathers, crest. **-vekt** (sport) featherweight. **-vilt** wild fowl. **-vogn** spring-cart.
fjol, se **fjel**.
fjor, se **fjær**.
fjos cow-stable, byre. **-drift** dairying. **-stell** dairy management.
fjåset foolish.
flabb (munn, gap) jaw; (en hunds) flews; (nesevis fyr) impudent fellow. **flabbet** jawy, flippant.
flaberg ledge of naked rock.
flabrød (flatbrød) flap of bread, bannock.
flage (vind-) flaw el. gust of wind; (anfall) fit.
flageolett flageolet.
flagg flag; ensign; (nasjonsfl.) colours; **heise — hoist,** heave out the flag el. colours; **stryke — strike,** lower the flag el. colours; **føre falsk — wear** false colours. **-duk** bunting.
flagge hang el. put out a flag el. flags, (mar) display colours; **det -r i byen** the town is decorated with flags, is flagged.
flaggermus bat.
flagging display of bunting, flag-flying.
flaggline colour line.
flaggskip (med admiralen) flag-ship.
flagg|smykt beflagged. **-spette** woodpecker. **-stang** flag-staff.
flagrant flagrant. **in flagranti** in the very act.
flagre flicker, (også fig) flutter; (med vingene) flap. **-nde lokker** flowing, dishevelled locks.
flak flake; (av is) floe; (p. klesplagg) flap.
flakke roam, rove, ramble; (om lue, lysning) flicker, waver.
flakong scent-bottle, smelling-bottle.
flaks (med vingene) flap, flutter; (hell): **ha — be** in luck.
flaks|e flap. **fuglen -te med vingene** the bird flapped its wings.
flamingo flamingo.
flamlender Fleming.
flamme (subst) flame, blaze; (den elskede) fancy, love; (i tøy) wave; (i tre, stein) vein, streak, wave; **står i -r** is in flames; **sette i -r** inflame.
flamme (vrb) flame, blaze; (ustadig, blafre) flare. **en -nde ild** a roaring, blazing fire; **— i været** flare up. **-hav** ocean of fire. **-skrift** indelible characters. **-t** veined, waved, streaked, curled.
flamsk Flemish.
Flander|n Flanders. **f-sk** Flemish.
flane giddy girl, flirt, coquette. **flane** (vrb) flirt.
flanell flannel.
flanke flank; **falle i -n** take in flank. **-angrep** attack in flank. **-marsj** flank march. **flankere** flank.
flanør loafer, man about town, idler.
flaske bottle, flask; (apotekerf.) phial; **helle på -r** bottle. **øl på -r** bottled beer.
flaske: — opp bring up by hand, drynurse; **— seg** succeed; **det vil ikke — seg** it's no go.
flaske|bakke bottle-tray. **-brott** piece of broken bottle. **-eple** melonapple. **-etikett** label. **-for** bottle-case, cellaret. **-grønn** bottle-green. **-hals** neck of a b. **-korg** bottle basket. **-kork** cork, stopper. **-skylling** bottlewashing. **-skår** (pl) broken bottles, bottle-ends. **-stativ** bottlestand.
flass dandriff, dandruff.
flasse be subject to dandruff.
flat flat; dt. (flau) blank, nonplussed, sheep-

ish; **føle seg** — feel sat-upon; **den –e hånd** the palm of the hand; **–t land** level land; **slå** — flatten. **–brystet** flat-breasted. **–brød,** se **flabrød.** **–bunnet** flatbottomed.

flate flat, plane figure. **–innhold** superficial content, area. **–lyn** (gjenskinnslyn) sheet-lighting. **–mål** surface measure.

flat|het flatness. **–lus** crab-louse. **–trykt** flattened; (mat) oblate.

flattere flatter.

flau flat, vapid, insipid; (merk) dull, flat; — **vind** light wind; — **vittighet** bad joke; **gjøre** — embarrass; **bli** — be ashamed, feel sheepish; **se** — **ut** look sheepish, blank, small, foolish, sold; **jeg er ganske** — I feel quite faint. **–het** flatness, vapidness, insipidity; dullness; faintness, faintishness. **–se** impertinence, insipid joke.

flegma phlegm, dullness, indifference. **–tiker** phlegmatic person. **–tisk** phlegmatic.

fleinskallet bald-pated, bald at the crown.

fleip flippant person; buffoon.

flekk speck; (smussflekk) smudge, blur; (fig) spot, stain; **kom ikke av –ken** made no progress at all; **var ikke til å få av –ken** could not be induced to move.

flekke (ganske liten by) non-corporate town, borough.

flekke (vrb) speck, stain, spot; (dra av skinn o. l.) rip, slit; (bark etc.) peel; slit, cleave; — **tenner** bare the teeth.

flekket speckly, spotted, stained.

flekk|tyfus spotted typhus. **–vann** abstergent, scouring drops.

fleng: i — indiscriminately, promiscuously.

flenge (rift) slash, gash. **flenge** (vrb) slash.

flens|e flense. **–ing** flensing.

flepe blubber, snivel, pule. **fleping** blubbering.

flere more; (atskillige) several; (forskjellige) various; — **ganger** several times; **hvem** —? who else? **ikke** — no more, nobody besides; — **hundre** many hundred: **etter** — **måneders** **fravær** after months of absence.

fler|guderi polytheism. **–het** plurality, majority. **–koneri** polygami. **–sidig** manysided, versatile. **–sidighet** versatility. **–stavelsesord** polysyllable. **–stemmig sang** part-singing.

flerre tear.

flertall (pluralis) the plural (number); (de fleste) majority, plurality, generality.

flertallsvelde the rule of majority.

fler|tydig ambiguous. **–tydighet** ambiguity.

fler|årig of several years, several years old.

fles (lavt skjær) low-lying islet.

flesk pork, bacon. **fleske|fett** fat of pork. **–pannekake** omelet with bacon. **–pølse** pork sausage. **–side** side of bacon. **–svor** bacon-rind. **–t** obese, overfed.

flest most, **som folk er** — like the common run, like the generality of people; **de –e** most people; **de –e bøkene mine** most of my books; **i de –e tilfelle** in most (el. in the majority of) cases.

fletning (det flettede, f. eks. hår) plait, braid (det å flette) plaiting, braiding.

flette (vrb) plait, braid; — **en korg** make a basket; — **en krans** wreathe a garland.

flette (subst) braid, plait. **–band** braid ribbon.

fli (rydde, pynte) tidy, trim; (levere) hand.

flid diligence; (arbeidsomhet) industry; (åndsanstrengelse) application; **gjøre seg stor** — take great pains.

flidspremie prize for diligence.

flik lap, flap; corner (bot) lobe. **fliket** lobate, lobated.

flikk (lapp) patch.

flikk|e patch, piece, botch, vamp up; (sko) cobble. **–verk** patching, patchwork.

flimre glimmer.

flingre (snø–, etc.) thin flake el. slice, chip, scale.

flink smart, quick, brisk, active; clever, able; — **i historie** clever (eller: good) at history.

flint (steinart) flint; **fly i** — be bursting with rage, fly (el. get) into a rage. **flinte|børse** (gevær) gun, musket, fowling-piece. **–lås** flint-lock.

flintestein flint; gun-flint.

flir giggle, (hånlig) sneer.

flire giggle, sneer.

flis chip, splinter, flinders (pl).

flise (flat stein) tile; (i brulegning) flag(stone).

flise (vrb) chip, splinter.

flise|lagt flagged. **–spikkeri** trifling, standing upon trifles. **–t** chippy, splintery.

flitter tinsel. **–gull** leaf-brass. **–stas** tinsel.

flittig diligent; studious, industrious, sedulous; — **besøker** frequent visitor; **gjøre** — **bruk av** make diligent use of; **studere** — study hard.

I. **flo** (lag) layer; (rad) row.

II. **flo** (mots. ebbe) flood-tide, flood.

flod, se **elv. –arm** branch (of a river). **–bekken** river basin, area drained by a river, watershed. **–bredd** river-bank, river-side. **–bølge** tide wave. **–gud** river god. **–hest** river-horse, hippopotamus.

floke (subst) ravel, tangle; (vrb) ravel, (en-) tangle; **en –t hespel** a tangled skein.

flokk (skare mennesker) troop, party, band, body; (fe) herd; (sauer) flock; (hunder, ulver) pack; (fugler) flight, flock; **ferdes i** — be gregarious; **løfte i** — combine their efforts; **i** — **og** **følge** in a body.

flokke (samle i flokk) gather, collect; — **seg** flock, crowd, throng.

flokkes flock, crowd, gather; — **om** crowd round.

flokketall: i — in crowds.

flokkevis in crowds, in flocks; (om hordedyr) gregariously.

flokk|silke floss-silk, **–ull** flock-wool.

flokse giddy girl, flirt, coquette.

flolegge pack (up) in rows.

flom flood, heavy water, swelling (oversvømmelse) inundation, overflow.

flomme swell, be in flood, (i vinden) flow, stream.

flom|skade flood damage. **–vann** floods, flowage.

flomål (el. **–merke**) flood-mark, highwatermark.

I. **flor** (sørgeflor) crape, gauze.

II. **flor** (blomstring) bloom, flowering, blossom; **stå i** — bloom, be in full blow. **flora** (botanikk) flora.

Floren|s Florence. **f–tiner, f–tinerinne** Florentine. **f–tinsk** Florentine.

florere (ha framgang) flourish, thrive greatly.

florett foil. **–fektning** foil-fencing.

flormel fine flour, whites.

floskel mere phrase, set phrase. **–maker** ranter.

floss floss; (lo) nap, shag.

floss(–hatt) tall silk-hat.

flosse fray. **flosset** (slitt) frayed.

flo–tid flood-tide.

flotilje flotilla.

flott (flytende) afloat; (fri og ugenert) free, free and easy; (fin, pyntet) spruce, smart, stylish; (rundhåndet) liberal; (altfor rundhåndet) too liberal, extravagant; — **fyr** swell, dasher; — **påstand** off-hand (el. sweeping) assertion; **bringe** — set afloat, float; **komme** — be floated; **leve** — live luxuriously. **–het** nonchalance, jauntiness, extravagance.

flotte seg s 'read oneself; — **seg med** sport.

flottenheimer swell, extravagant.

flottør float floater, float-gauge.

flu (skjær) half-tide rock.

flue fly; **slå to –r med ett smekk** kill two birds with one stone, kill two flies with one flap; **ha –r i hodet** have a bee in one's bonnet, have one's head full of wasps; **sette en –r i** **hodet** turn one's head; **døde som –r** died like flies.

flue|deksel meat-safe, meat-screen. **-egg** fly
-blow. **-flekket** fly-blown. **-gift** fly-poison. **-papir**
fly-paper. **-skitt** fly-specks. **-smekker** fly-flap.
-snapper (fugl) fly-catcher. **-sopp** toadstool.
fluidum fluid, liquid.
fluks (= straks) at once, immediately, forthwith.
flukt escape; (flyging) flight; (høy f.) soaring;
(fig) spirit, vigour; **slå på** — put to flight;
gripe i -en (fig) catch by the forelock; **i** — **med**
flush, level, even, in a line with.
fluktstol lady's chair, low reclining-chair.
fluktu|asjon fluctuation. **-ere** fluctuate.
flunke, flunkende: — **ny** fire-new.
I. **fly, se flyge, flyve;** (flykte) flee; (flykte for)
flee before, shun.
II. **fly** (strø ut agn) ground-bait, bait up the
ground.
I. **fly** (subst) (fjellvidde) mountain plateau.
II. **fly** (småinsekter) flying insects, gnats etc.
III. **fly, se flygemaskin.**
fly(ge) fly; (i aeroplan) aviate, travel in aircraft, manage aircraft, plane; — **høyt** soar;
døra fløy opp the door flew open; **han fløy opp he**
started to his feet; — **løs på en** fly at one.
flyge|båt flying-boat. **-blad** pamphlet. **-evne**
faculty of flight. **-fisk** flying fish.
flyge|ferdig fledged (om fugleunger). **-hud**
wing-membrane. **-idé** fancy, whim, caprice.
-kunst art of flying, aviation. **-maskin** aeroplane, airplane.
fly(g)ende flying; **i** — **fart in** a great hurry,
post haste; — **sint in** a towering passion; —
hund, rev (flaggermus) fox-bat.
flyge|oppvisning flying display. **-plass** aviation
ground, aerodrome. **-post** air post, air mail.
flyger airman, aviator, pilot. **-tokt** air-raid.
flyge|redskap organ of flight. **-rute** flying
route, air route. **-sand** quick-sand. **-skole** flying
school. **-skrift** pamphlet. **-sport** aviation. **-tanke**
passing thought. **-teknikk** technique of aviation.
-tur fly, flight. **-vesen** air service. **-øvelse** flying
exercise.
flyging flying; (flygers virksomhet) flying,
aviation; (en enkelt) flight.
I. **flygel** grand (piano).
II. **flygel** (treskeredskap) flail.
flying (farting) gadding about.
flykte fly, run away (for: from).
flyktig (som lett fordamper) volatile; (ustadig) inconstant, fleeting, transitory; (om karakter) giddy; (hastig) hasty, cursory; **et** — **besøk** a flying visit; **et** — **utkast** a rough sketch;
(adv) cursorily, hastily, in passing; **betrakte** —
take a cursory view of. **-het** volatility, giddiness. **flyktning** fugitive; (især av politiske el.
religiøse grunner) refugee.
flyndre (fisk) flounder; (treplate som hører til
en logg) log-chip.
flyte (renne) flow, run; (på vannet) float;
det vil — **blod** blood will be shed; — **over** run
over, overflow. **-bru** (pontongbru) floating bridge.
-dokk floating dock. **-evne** buoyancy. **flyting**
flowing.
flytende fluid, liquid; (tale) fluent; — **foredrag**
fluency of speech; **tale** — **engelsk** speak English
fluently, speak fluent English; **i** — **tilstand in**
a liquid state.
flytning moving, removal, transfer, move,
flitting.
flytt|bar transportable, moveable. — **blokk**
boulder, erratic block.
flytte move; remove, shift; — **inn** take possession, move in; — **ned** (i subtraksjon) carry;
— **seg** move, make room. **-bil** furniture van,
pantechnicon van. **-dag** removing day. **-folk**
porters. **-lass** vanful of furniture.
flyttlapp nomadic Lapp, Lapp nomad.
fly(ve) og sammensetninger, se **flyge.**
flære, se flerre.
flø (om sjø): **det -r** the tide is on the flow.

flømme be flooded.
flørt (kurmakeri) flirtation; (person som
flørter) flirt. **flørte** flirt.
fløte (vrb) (tømmer) float, raft.
fløte cream; **sette** — cream; **skumme -n av**
(også fig) cream off. **-fjes** effeminate el. milksop
face. **-graut** cream porridge. **-kake** cream-cake.
-krukke cream-pot. **-mugge** cream jug. **-ost**
cream cheese.
fløter raftsman, (amr ogs.) lumberjack. **-hake**
picaroon, pike-pole.
fløte|skje cream-ladle. **-skjegg** milk-sop. **-skum**
whipped cream, whip. **-snerk** skin of boiled
cream. **-saus** bechamel.
fløting flotage, floatage.
fløttmann, se ferjemann.
fløy (vind-) vane; (av flåte, hær, bygning)
wing; (av bord, dør osv.) leaf; (ved bru) water-
wing. **-adjutant** aide-de-camp. **-dør** folding door.
fløyel velvet. **fløyels|aktig** velvetlike. **-beset-
ning** velvet-trimming. **-bløt** soft as velvet. **-bånd**
velvet ribbon. **-drakt** v. dress. **-hanske** velvet
glove; **ta med -hansker på** handle very leniently.
-kjole velvet dress. **-stoffer, -varer** velvet
goods, velvetings.
fløymann flank file, pivot-man.
I. **fløyt** (subst) whistle; (fugls) warble, call.
II. **fløyt** (noe som flyter) floatage; (tømmer
som fløtes) floating logs.
fløyte (subst) flute; (pipe) whistle, pipe.
fløyte (vrb) whistle, pipe; — **på en hund**
whistle for a dog; — **sin hund tilbake** whistle
one's dog back; (tømmer), se **fløte.**
fløyteklaff flute-key.
fløyten dt. gone off; **gå** — be lost.
fløyte|spill playing, performance on the flute.
-spiller player on the flute, flutist, flautist.
-stemme flute part. **-tone** tone of a flute, flute-
like note.
fløyting whistling.
flå (fjellavsats) ledge, (vasspytt) puddle.
flå (vrb) flay, skin; (fig) fleece; — **av** strip off.
-er flayer; (sakfører) fleecer, extortioner. **-eri**
fleecing, extortion(s).
flåing flaying, excoriation.
flåkjeft loose talker. **-et** flippant, leaky.
flåseri loose talk, flippancy.
flåset = flåkjeftet.
flåte fleet, squadron; (en stats) navy; (kof-
fardif.) fleet of merchantmen; (liten fl.) flotilla; (tømmerfl.) float, raft.
flåte|basis naval base. **-demonstrasjon** naval
demonstration. **-manøvrer** naval manoeuvre.
-mønstring. -revy naval review. **-stasjon** naval
base, naval station.
fnatt itch, scabies. **-et** itchy. **-midd** itch mite.
fnise titter, giggle. **fnising** giggle, titter.
fnokk flue, mote; (bot) pappus. **-et** fluffy;
pappous.
fnugg mote, fluff, (snø-) flake.
fnyse snort, snuff; (fig) fret and fume, chafe.
-nde sint over det in a fume of anger about it.
fnysing snorting etc.
fob el. **f. o. b.** (fritt ombord) fob, f. o. b. (fork.
f. free on board).
foged bailiff; sheriff; **-embete** sheriffship.
I. **fokk** (fyking) spray, shower, drift, storm.
II. **fokk** (seil) foresail.
fokke|bras fore-brace. **-mast** foremast. **-rå**
f. yard. **-skjøt** f.-sheet. **-vant** f. shrouds.
foksterrier fox-terrier.
fokus (brennpunkt) focus, (pl) foci and focuses.
I. **fold** fold; (legg) plait, double; (merke etter
fold) crease; **legge i -er** plait; **legge sitt ansikt i alvorlige -er** put on a grave face; **komme
i sine gamle -er igjen** settle down (once more)
in one's old way.
fold (grødeutbytte), se **foll.**
folde (på tøy) fold plait; — **hendene** fold,
clasp one's hands; **med -de hender** with clasped
hands; — **ut** unfold. **folde|kast** folding of drapery.

–rik richly folded. **folding** folding.
fole (ung hest) colt. **fole** (føde føll) foal.
foliant folio.
I. **folio** (bakgrunn) foil; **tjene som — for** (fig) serve as a foil to.
II. **folio** folio; (i banken) account; **på — at** (el. on) call. **–ark** folio, foolscap.
folk (nasjon) people (pl peoples); (mennesker) people; (besetning) crew, hands; (arbeidere) hands; **–a** (tjenerskapet) the servants; **jeg kjenner mine — I** know whom I have to deal with, I know my company; **hva vil — si** what will people say, what will Mrs. Grundy say; **når slikt rykte kommer ut blant — if** such a report should get abroad.
folke|avstemning plebiscite, referendum, vote of the people. **–beslutning** popular decree.
folke|bibliotek public library, people's library. **–blad** popular paper. **–bok** popular book, people's book. **–diktning** popular poetry. **–etymologi** popular philology. **–ferd** tribe. **–fest** national festival, public rejoicing. **–fiende** enemy of the people.
Folkeforbund|et the League of Nations. **–spakten** the Covenant of the League of Nations. **–srådet** the Council of the League of Nations.
folke|forlystelse popular amusement el. sport. **–forsamling** public meeting, assembly of the people. **–frihet** national liberty. **–gave** gift of the people. **–gunst** popularity, popular favour. **–hop** crowd of people, mob. **–høgskole** popular high school. **–karakter** national character. **–kirke** national el. established church. **–kjøkken** public kitchen. **–komedie** popular comedy. **–leder** leader of the people, popular leader, demagogue. **–lesning** popular reading.
folkelig popular.
folke|liv manners, customs of a people. **–masse** crowd. **–mengde** population. **–minne** popular tradition; **–minner, minneforskning** folklore. **–munne:** være, komme i — be, become the common talk. **–møte** popular meeting.
Folkenes forbund the League of Nations.
folkeopplysning enlightenment of the people, general education; **–en står høyt** the standard of general education is high.
folke|parti popular el. democratic party. **–rase** race. **–reisning** rise of the people. **–representant** deputy, representative of the people, member (of parliament). **–representasjon** legislature. **–rett** international law. **–rik** populous. **–sak** national affair el. question; national cause. **–sagn** popular tradition, legend. **–sang** folk-song. **–sanger** popular bard. **–skare** crowd of people. **–skikk** national custom. **–skole** board (el. parish) school; (i Amerika) public school. **–skolelov** elementary education act. **–skolelærer** elementary school teacher. **–skrift** popular book. **–slag** people, nation, tribe. **–snakk** idle report(s), (town)talk, scandal. **–språk** popular language. **–stamme** tribe.
folke|stemning public sentiment. **–stue** servants' room. **–taler** popular speaker. **–teater** people's theatre. **–telling** census. **–tellingsliste** census paper. **–tog** public procession. **–tom** depopulated, deserted. **–tribun** tribune of the people.
Folkets Hus the People's Hall.
folke|utgave people's edition. **–vandring** migration (of nations, tribes). **–venn** friend of the people. **–vilje** national will. **–vise** (ancient) ballad; popular ditty. **–væpning** arming of the people. **–yndest** popularity. **–ånd** national spirit.
folklore (folkeminneforskning) folklore. **folklorist** folklorist.
folksom much frequented, crowded, populous.
foll (om grøde) fold.
follekniv clasp-knife; (stor) jack-knife.
folunge, se **føll.**
fomle fumble.
fommel buttercup-fingers.
fond fund, (kapital) funds; (rentebærende verdipapirer) stock, stocks.

fonds|børs, –marked stock exchange.
fone|tiker phonetician, phonologist. **–tikk** phonetics. **–tisk** phonetic.
fonn field of eternal snows; drift of snow.
fonograf phonograph. **–valse** phonographic record.
font font, baptismal font.
fontene fountain, jet, jet d'eau.
for (prep) for, before, to, at, of, in, by, from, on, as; **f o r: en gang — alle** once for all; **— alltid** for ever; **ikke — alt i verden** not for the world; **hvor mye skal De ha — det** what do you charge for it? **— mitt vedkommende** as for me, for my part; **b e f o r e: møte — en dommer** appear before a judge; **forsvinne — vanish** before; to: **like (over) — right** opposite to, over against, facing; **fremmed — a** stranger to; **av viktighet — of** importance to; **tok hatten av — took** off my hat to; **a t: — nærværende** at present; **— mine føtter** at my feet; **— en pris av** at the rate of; **o f: — redd — afraid** of; **gjenstand — subject** of; **til gunst — in** favour of; **bli fri — get** rid of; **i n: — så vidt** in so far as; **— det første, andre** in the first, second place; **— en del** in part; **han talte — ham** he spoke in his behalf; **finne nåde — ens øyne** find favour in one's sight; **— alvor** in earnest; **b y: han bor — seg selv** he lives by himself; **— seg selv** by oneself; **dag for dag** day by day; **f r o m: bevare — save** from; **skjule — conceal** from; **o n: lukke døra — nesa på en** shut the door on one, in one's face; **a s: anse — avgjort** consider as settled; **hva er dette — noe** what is this? **hva er dette — en person** what sort of person is that? **jeg holder det ikke — rådelig** I don't think it advisable; **gjerne — meg** with all my heart; **noe — noe** give and take; **jeg er ikke mye — det** I don't much like it; **— lenge siden** long ago.
for (adv) (foran) before; (med infinitiv) to, in order to; **— ikke å** not to; (motsatt akter) fore; (altfor) too; **— mye** too much; **med gardinene — with** the curtains drawn; **jeg kan ikke gjøre — I** cannot help, it is not my fault; **jeg er ikke mye — at I** do not much like to.
for (konj) for, because.
I. **for** (i klær) lining.
II. **for** (mat til dyr) fodder, provender, forage, feeding; (porsjon f.) feed; **sette, holde en hest på — put** out, keep a horse at livery; **stanse for å gi hestene — stop** to bait; **vil ikke ta –et** is off his feed.
forakt contempt (**for:** for, of), disdain, scorn; **nære — for en** hold one in contempt; **med — for** in contempt of. **forakte** despise, contemn, disdain, scorn, hold in contempt; **ikke å — not** to be despised. **foraktelig** (som fortjener forakt) contemptible, despicable; (som viser forakt) contemptuous. **foraktelighet** contemptibleness.
foran (prep) before, in front of, in advance of; (adv) before, in front, in advance; **— i boka** somewhere in the earlier part of the book; **være — lead; gå — take** the lead; **komme — get** the lead; **holde seg — keep** the lead.
foran|derlig changeable, variable; fickle, inconstant. **–derlighet** changeableness, variableness, mutability.
forandre change, alter, convert, shift; **det –r saken** it alters the case, it changes things. **— seg** change, alter.
forandring alteration; (omveksling) change; (avvikelse) variety; (ny innretning) innovation; **gjøre –er i** innovate on; **til en — by** way of a change el. variation, for a change; **— fryder** variety is charming.
forankre anchor, bring up; moor.
foranled|ige bring on, bring about, occasion, give rise to. **–ning** occasion, cause; **ved minste — on** the slightest provocation.
foranstalt|e cause to be done, see done, ar-

range, direct. **-ning** provision, measure, arrangement, plan, preparation; agency, direction; **på min** — by my directions; **treffe** — take el. adopt measures, take action.
foranstående above; the foregoing.
forarbeid (subst) preliminary work.
forarbeide (vrb) work, manufacture, make.
forarbeidelse working; make, manufacture.
for|arge scandalize, give offence el. scandal to (bibelsk) offend; **-argelig** scandalous, offensive. **-argelse** scandal, offence; **vekke** — give scandal; **ta** — av take offence at, be scandalized at. **-arges over** be scandalized at.
forarme impoverish. **-lse** impoverishment. **-t** impoverished.
forat (konj) that, in order that; — **ikke** lest.
forband (mur-forband) bond.
forbanne curse, execrate; — **seg på** swear to el. that. **-lse** curse; imprecation; execration; **mitt livs** — the bane of my existence. **forbannet** accursed, cursed; (adv) cursedly, devilish.
forbarme: — **seg over** pity, commiserate, compassionate, take pity on; have mercy on; **Gud** — **seg!** God bless me! (God) bless my soul! **-lse** compassion, commiseration, pity.
forbau|se amaze, astonish; (sterkere) astound. **-selse** amazement, astonishment; (målløs) stupefaction. **-sende** amazing etc.; (adv) amazingly, wonderfully. **-set** amazed, in astonishment, astonished.
forbe|dre better, improve, amend; — **seg** improve, reform. **-drer** improver, reformer. **-dring** improvement, amelioration, amendment; reformation; (av tekst) emendation. **-dringsanstalt** reformatory. **-dringshus** house of correction.
forbe|hold reservation, salvo, clause, proviso, restriction; **hemmelig** — mental reservation; **jeg sier det med alt** — I speak under correction; **ta** — imot take exception to. **-holde seg** reserve, keep (to oneself); — **seg** at make it a condition that. **-holden** reserved, close, reticent. **-holdenhet** reserve.
forbemerkning prefatory remark.
forbe(i)n fore leg.
forbe(i)|nes ossify. **-ning** ossification.
forberede prepare, arrange; — **en på noe** prepare one for st.; — **seg til** prepare (oneself) for; — **seg på en lekse** prepare (el. get up) a lesson. **-lse** preparation, preparative arrangement; **treffe -lser til** make preparations for.
forberedelses|klasse elementary form el. class. **-skole** preparatory school. **forberedende** preparatory, initiatory.
forberg promontory, headland, foreland.
forbi (prep) by, past; beyond; (adv) (om sted) by, past; (om tid) at an end, gone, over, past; **komme** — pass; **la en leilighet gå** — let slip el. neglect an opportunity; **gå** — pass; (ved avansement) pass over (for promotion), step over the head of; **det er** — **med ham** it is all over with him, he is a dead el. gone man; **gjøre det** — (om forlovelse) break it off; **skyte** — miss.
forbigang passing by. **forbi|gangen** past, be-gone; **la oss ikke tale mer om det -gangne** let bygones be bygones.
forbi|gå pass by (el. over); (utelate) omit, leave out; (ved avansement) pass over (for promotion); — **noe i taushet** pass by st. in silence **-gåelse** neglect, omission. **-gående** temporary, transitory, transient; **i** — in passing, as I pass, by the way, incidentally.
forbilde type, prototype; (mønster) model, pattern; **ta til** — take for a model.
forbind|e connect, combine; (et sår, en såret) dress, bandage (a wound); **jeg -er ingen bestemt forestilling med det** it conveys to me no definite idea; **forbundet med** (f. eks. fare) attended with; **den fare som er forbundet med det** the danger involved in it, incident to it; **jeg er Dem meget forbunden** I am very much obliged to you.

forbindelse (forening) connection, combination; (forbund) league, association; (samferdsel) communication, intercourse; (samkvem) intercourse; (forlovelse) engagement; (ekteskap) alliance; (i kjemi) compound; **i denne** — in this connection; **i** — **med** together with, coupled with; **sette i** — connect; **sette ut av** — disconnect; **sette seg i** — med communicate with, establish a connection el. communication with; **mine finske -r** my Finnish connections.
forbindelses|ledd link of connection. **-punkt** point of union, junction.
forbinding dressing, bandaging.
forbindings|saker (pl) dressing-apparatus. **-stoffer** dressings. **-veske** dressing-case.
forbindtlig obliging, complaisant; **-st** (underskr.) Yours truly. **-het** (forpliktelse) obligation; (høflighet) obligingness, complaisance; **uten -het** (merk) without prejudice.
forbistret confounded, dashed; (adv) confoundedly, desperately.
forbit|re embitter. **-relse** exasperation. **-ret** exasperated (**på:** against, over: at), enraged, furious.
forblend|e (belegge, dekke) face. **-ingsstein** (naturlig) facing-stone; (kunstig) facing-brick.
forbli remain, stay, abide; **det må** — **ved det** there the matter must rest.
forblind|e blind, hoodwink, delude, infatuate. **-else** blindness, infatuation.
forblivende: det må ha sitt — **med det** there the matter must end el. rest.
forblommet covert, ambiguous; **gi å forstå på en** — måte hint darkly.
forblø seg bleed to death. **forblødning** hemorrhage.
forbløffe take aback, disconcert, bewilder; **uten å la seg** — nothing daunted. **det -t ham** it staggered him.
forbløffelse bewilderment.
forbløffende disconcerting, startling; (i høy grad) stupendous.
forbløffet bewildered, taken aback, disconcerted.
forbokstav initial.
forborgen cryptic, hidden, occult.
forbrenn|e burn, scorch. **-ing** burning; (oppbrenning) combustion. **-ingsprodukt** product of combustion. **forbrent** burnt, (av sola) parched.
forbruk consumption. **forbruk|e** consume, use up. **-er** consumer.
forbruks|artikler articles of consumption. **-avgift** consumption duty.
forbruk|sforening co-operative society. **-spriser** co-operative prices. **-sutsalg** co-operative store.
forbryte (fortape) forfeit; **hva har jeg forbrutt?** what is my offence el. crime?; **ha sitt liv forbrutt** forfeit life; — **seg** offend, trespass.
forbrytelse crime; (svær f.) felony, (forseelse) misdemeanour.
forbryter criminal; (politisk) offender.
forbryter|ansikt hangdog face. **-bane** a career of crime. **-benk** (felon's) dock. **-koloni** convict colony. **-sk** criminal, guilty.
forbryterspire imp of depravity, embryo felon.
I. **forbud** (det å forby) prohibition, interdiction; inhibition; **nedlegge** — mot place an interdict against, put a veto on.
II. **forbud** (bebuder, forløper) forerunner, precursor, (poet) harbinger (**på, for:** of).
forbuden forbidden; — **frukt smaker best** forbidden fruit is sweet; **forbudne varer** prohibited goods, contraband.
forbudsavstemning prohibition plebiscite.
forbudslov prohibition law.
forbudsmann, forbudstilhenger prohibitionist.
forbudsvennlig prohibitionist.
forbund alliance, league, confederacy, confederation; (pakt) covenant; **inngå, slutte, bryte, oppheve et** — enter into, form, break, dissolve a league.

forbundet combined, connected; (om sår) bandaged; (alliert) allied, confederate; (forbindtlig) obliged.

forbunds|felle ally. -stat federal state.

forby forbid, prohibit, interdict, inhibit; det — Gud heaven forbid; — ham å gjøre det forbid him to do so; det -r seg selv it is a moral impossibility.

forbygge seg overbuild.

forbygning front-building.

forbyt|ning change. -te change.

forbønn intercession; gå i — for meg hos intercede for me with.

fordamp|e evaporate. -ning evaporation.

fordanser leader of a dance.

fordekk fore part of the deck.

fordekt covertly.

fordektig (adj) suspicious (adv) suspiciously.

fordel advantage, profit; (vinning) også gain, gains; -er og mangler advantages and disadvantages; med — profitably, to advantage; til — for for the benefit of; vise seg til sin — appear to advantage; høste — av derive advantage el. benefit from, profit by; jeg ser min — i å I see it to my interest to; forandre seg til sin — change for the better.

fordelaktig advantageous, profitable, lucrative; vise seg fra den -ste side appear to the best advantage; show off to advantage; -e betingelser liberal terms; et — ytre a prepossessing appearance; — kjent favourably known.

fordel|e distribute, apportion, divide; (spre) disperse; — rollene assign the parts; — seg disperse. -ende (middel) discussive, discutient. -ing distribution, division, apportionment; dispersion; discussion.

forderve spoil, damage, (moralsk) corrupt, deprave; (blodet) vitiate; (magen) disorder, derange.

fordervelig pernicious, ruinous, fatal; lett -e varer perishable goods, goods easily spoiled el. damaged.

fordervelse corruption, depravation, depravity; (besmittelse) vitiation; styrte en i — ruin one.

fordervet depraved, corrupted, demoralized; slå — hurt severely (by beating), maul; le seg — be ready to die with laughing; arbeide seg — work oneself to death.

fordi because.

fordob|le double, redouble. -ling doubling, duplication.

fordom prejudice, prepossession. fordoms|fri unprejudiced; unconventional. -frihet unprejudicedness. -full prejudiced.

for|dra bear, endure; jeg kan ikke — vin I hate wine. -dragelig tolerant. -dragelighet toleration.

fordre claim, demand, require; exact.

fordreie distort, twist; (bare fig) pervert, misrepresent, put a false construction on; — hodet på en turn one's head. -lse distortion, contortion; (fig) perversion.

fordring claim, demand; tidens -er the exigencies of the times; gjøre — på lay claim to, pretend to; gjøre — på å være claim to be; stille altfor store -er til exact too much from el. of; gjøre sine -er gjeldende prefer el. put in a claim.

fordrings|fri unpretending, unassuming. -full full of pretensions, pretentious, assuming; exacting, exigent; ambitious. -fullhet pretentiousness, exactingness. -haver creditor. -løs unpretending, unostentatious, unambitious, quiet -løshet unpretendingness.

fordriste seg make bold, venture, presume.

fordrive drive away, expel, oust; dispel; — tiden while away, pass (away) time. -lse driving etc.; expulsion.

fordrukken drunken, sottish. -het drunkenness, addiction to drink.

fordufte evaporate; (spøkende) vanish (into thin air), make oneself scarce.

fordum anciently, formerly, of yore.

fordumme|lse (intellectual) weakening; stupidity. -s become stupid.

fordums former, quondam.

fordunk|le darken, obscure; (overstråle) eclipse, outshine, throw into shade. -ling darkening. fordunst|e evaporate. -ning evaporation.

fordype deepen; — seg i lose oneself in, be absorbed in, absorb oneself in, dive into; — seg i seg selv be wrapped up in one's own thoughts; -t sunk, dished; (fig) -t i deep in, buried in; -t i betraktninger lost in meditation; -t i en bok intent upon a book.

fordypning deepening; (liten f.) dimple; (får) groove; (merke etter trykk) depression; (hakk) indentation, dent; (indre vindus- el. dørfordypn.) embrasure; (nisje) niche; (f. i vegg, f. eks. alkove) recess.

fordyre enhance the price of. -lse (av) enhancement in the price (of).

fordølg|e conceal (for: from). -else concealment.

fordøm|me denounce, condemn, doom. -melig condemnable, culpable. -melighet wickedness. -melse denunciation, condemnation; (bibelsk) damnation. fordømt (dømt) condemned; (forbannet) confounded, damned; fordømt! damn it! confound it! de fordømte the damned.

fordøy|e digest. -elig digestible. -elighet digestibility. -else digestion; dårlig -else indigestion, dyspepsia.

I. fore (gi dyr for) fodder, feed.

II. fore (sette for i) line; (med pelsverk) fur; (med vatt) wad.

fore, se føre. saken var — (i retten) the case was heard. legge seg — settle down, make a lengthened stay; gjøre seg — lay oneself out for admiration.

forebringe advance, state.

forebygge prevent; -nde middel preventive.

foredle refine, improve, ennoble, elevate. foredling refinement, improvement.

fore|dra deliver; execute. -drag (tale) address; (foreslesning) lecture, paper (to be read); (fremsigelse) delivery; (språkbehandling) elocution, diction; (spill el. sang) execution; holde — om deliver a discourse, lecture upon. -dragsholder lecturer. -dragslokaler lecture rooms.

forefalle happen, occur, take place, pass; villig til å gjøre hva som -r willing to make oneself generally useful.

foregangsmann initiator, leader, pioneer.

fore|gi pretend, allege, give out; -given pretended, sham, supposed. -givende pretence. -gripe anticipate.

foregå take place, go on, be in progress; — andre med et godt eksempel set a good example to others. -ende preceding, previous; den -ende dag the day before.

fore|havende intention, purpose, project. -holde en noe remonstrate with sb. on st., expostulate with sb. for st.

fore|komme (inntreffe) occur, be met with, be found; (synes) seem, appear; -kommer svært ofte is of very frequent occurrence. -kommende obliging, complaisant. -kommenhet obligingness, courtesy, kind attentions.

forekomst occurrence, existence; alminnelig -lig til å gjøre hva som prevalence; f. eks. the prevalence of globetrotting.

foreldet antiquated, obsolete, out of date.

foreldre parents.

foreldreløs orphan; et -t barn an orphan.

forelegg (framlagt dokument) exhibit; (overslag) estimate; (jur) fine (imposed by a magistrate).

forelegge bring, place el. put before, submit to; — en et spørsmål put a question to one.

fore|lese read, recite (to). **-leser** reader, lecturer.

forelesning lecture; **holde -er over** give lectures on, lecture on; **gå på -er** attend lectures. **forelesnings|katalog** list of lectures. **-rekke** course of lectures.

forelIgge lie (el. be, be placed) before; (til drøftelse) be at issue, be under consideration.

forelske seg i fall in love with. **forelskelse** love, falling in love. **forelsket** in love (**i**: with), enamoured (**i**: of, with).

foreløpig (adj) preliminary, provisional; (adv) temporarily, provisionally, for the present.

forende front part; (mar) head, bows.

forene unite, join, combine, connect; **— seg** unite; **— seg med** join; **la seg — med** be consistent with, stand together with; **det lar seg ikke — med it is** inconsistent (el. incompatible) with. **De forente stater** the (United) States. **-lig** reconcilable, consistent, compatible (with).

forening union, combination, junction; association; **selskapelig — society, club; i —** combined, jointly, in concert, between them; **i — med** coupled with.

fore|satt superior; superior officer. **-sette seg** propose (to oneself), determine. **-si** dictate to. **-skrevet** prescribed. **-skrive** prescribe (st. to one), order; **loven -skriver** the law provides. **-slå** propose, move. **-snakke** din one's ears with; talk one into the belief that. **-speile** hold out (the prospect of st.) to one. **-spelling** illusion, vision. **-spørre hos en om noe** inquire of one about st. **-spørsel** inquiry.

forestille present (to), introduce (to); (foreholde) represent; **hva skal det — ?** what does it (all) mean? **— seg** conceive, imagine, picture el. figure to oneself, realize; **De kan nok — Dem** you may easily imagine.

forestilling presentation, introduction; exhibition; representation; (innsigelse) remonstrance, (skriftlig) memorial; (skuespill) performance, play; (begrep) apprehension, conception, idea; **uriktig — misrepresentation, misconception; gjøre seg en — om** form a conception of; **gjøre en -er** remonstrate with one.

fore|stå (lede) manage, conduct, be at the head of, in charge of; **-stå et embete,** se **bekle(de);** (kunne ventes) draw nigh, be at hand, approach; be imminent; **hva som -står meg** what awaits me, is before me, in store el. reserve for me. **-stående** ensuing, approaching, forthcoming, (truende) imminent.

fore|sveve flit el. be before one's eyes, wander before el. be present to one's mind; **det -svever meg dunkelt at** I have a dim notion that.

fore|ta undertake, institute, make, go through, take in hand. **-tagende, foretak** undertaking, enterprise, venture. **-taksom** enterprising. **-taksomhet** enterprise. **-taksomhetsånd** (spirit of) enterprise.

forete seg overeat, surfeit.

foreteelse phenomenon, appearance.

foretrede audience. **få — hos** have an audience with.

foretrekke prefer (**for:** to).

forett over-fed, over-gorged, pampered.

forevige eternize, immortalize, perpetuate. **-lse** perpetuation, immortalization.

forevis|e show, exhibit. **-er** exhibiter, showman. **-ning** exhibition, showing.

I. **forfall** (jur): **lovlig — sufficient excuse; ha — be** prevented.

II. **forfall** (det at noe forfaller) decay, disrepair, dilapidation, ruinous state; (fig) decline, decadence; **— av en veksel** expiration, maturity (of a bill); **i — in** a state of decay, on the decline. **forfall|e** decay; (hjemfalle) be forfeit; (veksel etc.) become due, fall due, expire, come to maturity; **— til** take to, addict oneself to, give oneself up to. **-en** ruinous, decayed, dilapidated, out of repair; payable, due, matured, (over tiden)

overdue; addicted, given (til drikk: to drink) **-enhet** addiction to drink, se ogs. **forfall.**

forfalls|dag (merk) day of payment. **-periode** period of decadence. **-tid** maturity, time of payment.

forfalsk|e falsify, forge, adulterate, sophisticate. **-ning** falsification, forgery, adulteration, sophistication.

forfatning (tilstand) state, condition, plight; (stats-) constitution. **forfatnings|brudd** infringement of the constitution. **-kamp** constitutional struggle. **-stridig** unconstitutional.

forfatte compose, write, pen, indite.

forfatter author, composer, writer. **forfatter|honorar** author's fee, copy-money. **-inne** (lady) author, woman writer, authoress. **-navn** name of an author; (psevdonym) penname. **-ry** literary reputation. **-skap** authorship; literary work. **-talent** literary powers. **-virksomhet** literary efforts, authorship.

forfedre (pl) forefathers, ancestors.

forfeile miss, fall in, fall short of. **-t** mistaken; a failure.

forfekte defend, assert, maintain, vindicate, advocate, champion. **-r** defender, vindicator, advocate (of), stickler (for).

forfengelig vain; **ta — take** in vain. **-het** vanity.

forferde terrify, appal, affright, dismay; **-s** be terrified etc.; **stå ganske -t** stand aghast, be struck aghast (**over:** at). **-lig** terrific, appalling, frightful, horrific, dreadful; monstrous, tremendous. **-lse** terror, horror, fright, consternation, dismay; **det tok en ende med -lse** the end was terrific.

forferdige make, manufacture. **-lse** making, manufacturing.

forfine refine. **-lse** refinement.

forfjamselse confusion, bewilderment.

forfjamset confused, bewildered.

forfjor: i — the year before last.

forflate flatten.

forflere multiply.

forflyktige volatilize. **-lse** volatilization.

forflytte remove, transfer, move. **-lse** removal, transfer; move.

forfløyen giddy, heedless; volatile, harum-scarum; **en — idé** a whimsical idea.

forfordel|e prejudice. **-ing** prejudice.

for fote indiscriminately.

forfra from before, in front; (om igjen) over again, from the beginning; (mar) from forward, from ahead; **begynne livet — begin** the world anew.

forfransk|e gallicize, frenchify. **-ning** gallicizing, frenchifying, frenchification.

forfremme advance, prefer, promote. **-lse** promotion, advancement, preferment.

forfrisk|e refresh, recreate. **-ende** refreshing. **-ning** refreshment.

forfrossen frozen, benumbed with cold, chilly, shivery.

forfrys|e freeze, frost. **-ning** frost-bite.

forfusk|e bungle, botch.

forfølge pursue; (til retten) prosecute; (en i alm.) persecute; (spor) trace; (drive igjennom) follow up. **-lse** pursuit; prosecution; persecution. **-lsesvanvidd** mania of persecution. **forfølger** pursuer, persecutor.

forføre seduce, debauch. **-lse** seduction. **-nde** seductive. **-r, -rske** seducer, debaucher. **-risk** seductive.

forføtte (skomakeruttr.) foot, new-front, new -foot.

forføye over command, have at one's disposal; **— seg** repair betake oneself (to a place). **forføyning** measure, step; rettslig **— legal** proceedings; **stille til ens — place** at one's disposal.

forgang (i fjøs og stall) passage in front of the manger.

forgangen foregone, gone by.

for|gape seg I dote on; **–gapt** I doting upon, taken with.

forgasser (karburator) carburettor.

forgi poison, destroy by poison.

forgift|e poison, envenom. **–et** poisoned. **–ning** poisoning.

forgjeldet in debt, involved in debt.

forgjengelig perishable, transient, transitory, passing. **–het** perishableness, transitoriness.

forgjenger, **–ske** predecessor.

forgjeves (adj) vain; (adv) in vain, vainly.

forgjøre (forhekse) bewitch.

forgnagd commonplace, hackneyed, trite, well-worn.

forglem|me forget; **ikke å —** not forgetting; last not least. **–melse** oblivion, forgetfulness; **ved en –melse** inadvertently.

forglemmegei forget-me-not.

forgodtbefinnende: etter — at pleasure; **handle etter eget —** use one's pleasure.

forgremmet careworn, pining, grief-worn.

forgrene|seg ramify, branch (off). **–t** ramified; **vidt –t** far branching.

forgripe seg (på fremmedes penger) make free (with the money of others); (på en) lay hands on, outrage, use violence against.

forgrodd overrun.

forgrove coarsen, vulgarize.

forgrunn foreground; (av scenen) front of the stage. **forgrunnsfigur** conspicuous character.

forgrått red with weeping, exhausted w. w.

forgude idolize. **–lse** idolatry.

for|gylle gild; **— opp** regild; **–gylt** gilt; **sølv –gylt** silver gilt. **forgyller** gilder.

forgylling gilding.

forgå perish; **holder på å — av nysgjerrighet etter å få vite** is dying to know.

forgård fore-court.

forgårs: i — the day before yesterday; **i — morgen** the day before yesterday in the morning.

forhal|e delay, retard; (mar) haul, shift, move, warp away. **–ing** delay; (mar) shifting.

forhall entrance hall, vestibule, lobby.

forhand|le transact, treat, negotiate; (selge) sell, dispose of. **–ler** dealer, vender. **–ling** transaction, negotiation; sale; (drøftelse) discussion; **–linger** (f. eks. parlamentets) proceedings; **ha varer til –ling** have goods on commission.

forhandlings|emne subject of discussion. **–grunnlag** basis for negotiation. **–protokoll** minutes, journal of proceedings.

forhaste| seg be in too great a hurry, overhurry oneself. **–lse** precipitation, overhastiness.

forhaste|t hurried, hasty, premature; **trekke –de slutninger** jump at el. to conclusions.

forhatt hated, detested; abhorred; (ubehagelig) odious; **gjøre seg — hos (av)** make oneself odious to.

forheks|e bewitch, enchant. **–else** bewitching, enchantment.

forheng curtain.

forhenværende former, past, sometime, late, ex-, f. eks. ex-schoolmaster.

for|herde harden, indurate; **–herdet** hardened etc., obdurate, callous. **–herdelse** induration; (fig) obduracy.

forherlige glorify. **–lse** glorification.

forhindre hinder, prevent (i: from).

forhindring prevention, hindrance, impediment, obstacle. **–sløp** hurdle-race.

forhippen på eager for, bent on, intent on; **— — å** eager to.

for|historie previous history; **–historisk** pre -historic.

forhjul fore-wheel.

forhog|ge cut up. **–ning** barricade.

forhold (oppførsel) conduct; (målestokk) scale; (forbindelse) connection (with), bearing (upon); (størrelse) proportion; (slektsforhold) relation; (omstendighet) fact, circumstances; (mat) rate,

ratio; **–ene på fastlandet** (the) continental affairs; **i — til** in proportion to, proportionate to; **stå i — til** be proportionate to el. commonsurate with; (en kvinne) have a love intrigue with; **stå i et godt — til** be on good el. friendly terms with; **og... i — til det (i samme —) and... to match**, corresponding; **etter våre små — in our little way.**

forholde (unndra) withhold from, keep out of, deprive of.

forholde seg behave el. conduct oneself; **saken –r seg slik** the matter stands thus; **når det –r seg slik** when that el. such is the case; **— seg rolig** keep quiet; **10 –r seg til 5 som 16 til 8** 10 is to 5, as 16 to 8.

forholdsmessig proportionate, proportional, comparative; **— andel** quota.

forholds|ord preposition. **–regel** measure. **–tall** proportional. **–tallsvalg** proportional representation. **–vis** (sammenligningsvis) comparatively; (forholdsmessig) proportionally; **–vis få** comparatively few.

forhud|e sheathe, metal (a ship). **–ning** sheathing.

forhugge, se **forhogge**.

forhus front building.

forhutle spoil, bungle.

forhyr|e hire, engage, ship. **–ingskontor** shipping office.

for|høye heighten, raise; (virkninger) improve; (lønn) increase; (priser) enhance. **–høyelse** heightening etc; enhancement. **–høyning** (høyt sted) rising ground, eminence; (i værelse osv.) platform.

forhør examination; **ta i —** examine. **–e** examine, interrogate; ask, inquire, make inquiry. **–sdommer** examining judge, examining magistrate, examiner. **–sprotokoll** proces-verbal, record of evidence. **–srett** court of interrogatory.

forhånd (i kort) lead, elder hand; **være i —** have the lead; **på —** beforehand, in advance, by anticipation, at the outset.

forhånden (adv) at hand; (nær forestående) approaching. **–værende** at hand, present, existing, actual.

forhånds|avgjørelse prejudgement. **–inntrykk** anticipation. **–slutning** foregone conclusion.

forhåne outrage, scoff, mock, insult.

forhånelse outrage, insult.

forhåp|entlig it is to be hoped. **–ning** hope, expectation; **gjøre seg –ning om** expect. **–nings-full** hopeful.

forhår front hair.

Forindia India.

I. **foring** (av klær) lining; (mar) ceiling, foot -waling.

II. **foring** feeding. **foringsforsøk** feeding experiment.

forivre|seg grow too warm, fire up. **–lse** heat, fit of anger; hot-headed blunder.

forjag|le dispel, turn out. **–d** driven, harassed, hurried. **–ethet** harassment; hurry, scurry.

forjette (foreldet = love) promise. **det –de land** the Promised Land. **–lse** promise.

fork (høygaffel) pitchfork.

forkammer: (hjertets) **forkamre** the auricles of the heart.

forkalk|e calcine. **–ning** calcination, (se åre-).

forkaste reject; **forslaget ble –t** (også) the motion was lost. **–lig** objectionable, improper. **–lighet** impropriety. **–lse** rejection.

forkavet in a bother, bustling, flurried, flustered.

forkjemper champion, advocate.

forkjetre stigmatize as heretical; (nedsette) disparage, denounce. **forkjetring** accusation of heresy; denunciation.

forkjæle spoil, pet, coddle. **–lse** petting, indulgence.

forkjærlighet predilection (for), partiality (to), prejudice in favour of.

6 — Norsk-engelsk.

forkjært wrong, preposterous, absurd; (adv) wrong, the w. way. **-het** absurdity.

forkjøl|e seg catch el. take (a) cold; **bli -t** catch el. take cold, get a cold; **jeg er -t** I have (got) a (bad) cold. **-else** cold, chill.

forkjøp: komme en i -et forestall one, be beforehand with, gain a march on.

forkjøpe seg buy too dear.

forkjøpsrett (right of) pre-emption, refusal.

forkla|re explain, expound; (for retten) depose, give evidence; (herliggjøre) glorify, transfigure; **-rende** explanatory, illustrative; **-ret** beatified.

forklarelse transfiguration, glorification.

forklaring explanation; (sjøforklaring) declaration; (vitne-) evidence, deposition.

forklarlig explicable.

forkle apron; (barneforkl.) pinafore.

forkle (vrb) disguise. **-dd** (ogs.) in disguise. **-dd som** disguised as, in the disguise of. **-dning** disguise.

forkleine belittle, disparage. **-lse** disparagement.

forklud|re bungle. **-ring** bungling.

forknytt dispirited, cowed, faint-hearted. **gjøre — dishearten**, dispirit. **-het** faint-heartedness.

forkommen exhausted, starving, overcome (av: with); (av kulde) benumbed (with cold); (av sult) famished.

forkommenhet exhaustion, decay.

forkopre copper.

forkort|e shorten, abridge; (brøk, ord) abbreviate; (i tegning) foreshorten; (sammentrekke) contract. **-else, -ning** shortening, abridgment, abbreviation; (om brøk) cancellation; contraction.

forkrenkelig corruptible, perishable. **-het** corruption.

forkropp fore part of the body.

forkrøplet stunted, scrubby.

forkuet cowed, subdued.

forkull|et charred. **-ing** carbonization.

forkunnskap(er) previous knowledge.

forkvakle mismanage, bungle, spoil.

forkynne announce, proclaim; (juridisk) serve (on one); (ordet) preach, declare. **-lse** announcement, proclamation, service, preaching.

forlabb forepaw.

forladnings|gevær, -kanon, -rifle, -våpen muzzle-loader.

forlag (bokforl.) publishing business; **utgi på eget — publish** at one's own expense; **på forfatterens — printed** for el. published by the author; **denne boka er utkommet på hans — he** is the publisher of this book.

forlags|artikkel publication, publisher's work. **-bokhandel** publishing-firm. **-bokhandler** publisher. **-rett** copyright.

forlang|e ask, demand, ask for, call for, desire; **han -te 2 pund av meg for det** he charged me 2 pounds for it.

forlangende request, demand; **på — when** required, if demanded.

forlanterne headlight.

forlate (fjerne seg fra) leave, quit; (svikte) forsake, abandon, desert; (tilgi) pardon, forgive; **— dette sted** leave here; **hermed -r vi ... (et emne) so much for ...; alt forlatt!** all right! **forlat oss vår skyld** forgive us our trespasses.

forlate seg på rely on, depend on, trust to.

forlatelse pardon, forgiveness; **jeg ber om — I** ask el. beg your pardon.

forlatt forsaken, abandoned; **— skip** derelict. **-het** desertion.

forlede beguile, mislead, seduce.

forleden: — dag the other day, one day recently.

forlegen embarrassed, at a loss, puzzled, perplexed, put out; (av vesen) shame-faced; (begjærlig) anxious, eager (etter å: to); **aldri — for svar** never at a loss for an answer.

forlegenhet embarrassment, perplexity; dilemma; (trang) want; **være i — be** at a loss; (for penger) in want of money; **sette i — perplex**, puzzle, embarrass.

forlegge mislay, (et skrift) publish. **-lse** removal; mislaying. **forlegger** publisher. (Se ogs. senge-).

forlene (hist) enfeoff (med: in); (fig) grant, invest (with), lend (to).

forlenge lengthen, elongate, prolong.

forlengelse lengthening, prolongation.

forlengs forwards.

forlengst long ago.

forles|e seg overread oneself, read too hard. **-t** knocked up with reading.

for|libe seg i take a fancy. **-libelse** fancy. **-libt** smitten (with), spooney (on).

forlik agreement, adjustment, reconciliation, accommodation; **slutte — med** come to an agreement with, make up the (el. a) difference with, make terms with; **det kom til — matters** were accommodated; **et magert — er bedre enn en feit prosess** a lean agreement is better than a fat judgment.

forlike reconcile; **— seg med** be reconciled to.

forlikes agree.

forliks|kommisjon Court of Conciliation. **-kommissær** commissioner of a Court of Conciliation. **-mann, -megler** mediator, conciliator. **-nemnd, se -kommisjon. -vilkår** terms.

forlis shipwreck. **forlise** be lost, be wrecked, be cast away, come to grief.

forlodds in advance, beforehand.

forlokke entice, seduce.

forlo|ren (uekte) false, mock, sham; **den -rne sønn** the prodigal son; **-rent hår** false hair; **-ren skilpadde** mock-turtle.

forlove engage (to); **-t med** engaged to (marry); **han -de** his promised bride, his fiancée, his intended.

forlovelse engagement (med: to). **forlovelses-ring** engagement ring.

forlover sponsor; he that gives the bride away; (brudgommens) best man, bridegroom's man.

forluke fore-hatch.

forlyd initial sound.

forlyde: det -r it is reported, understood; **la seg — med** hint, intimate, give to understand. **etter -nde** according to report.

forlyste delight; **— seg** amuse oneself.

forlystelse delight, amusement, recreation.

forlystelses|skatt entertainment tax. **-sted** place of amusement, (p. of public) resort. **-syk** pleasure-seeking; **-sykt menneske** pleasure-hunter. **-syke** pleasure-hunting.

forløfte seg overstrain oneself by lifting; (fig) **— seg på** break down in. **-lse** strain; (fig) breakdown, failure.

forløyet lying. **-het** lying, mendacity.

forløp expiration, lapse; (gang, f. eks. sykdoms) course, progress; **etter ett års — after** (el. at the end of) a year. **forløpe** pass away, elapse, expire; **— seg** put one's foot in it, commit oneself, blunder; **— seg mot sin overordnede** happen to offend a superior (by presumptuous manners el. language).

forløpelse blunder, indiscretion.

forløper forerunner.

forløs|le (om fødsel) deliver; (religiøst) redeem. **-er** redeemer, deliverer. **-ning** redemption, deliverance; (nedkomst) delivery.

form form, make, shape; (støpef., også fig) mould; (typograf) form, chase; **for -ens skyld** for form's sake, as a matter of form.

formal|e grind. **-ing** grinding.

formalitet formality, (matter of) form.

formane exhort, admonish, warn.

formangel scarcity of fodder.

formaning exhortation, admonition, warning.

formann (i geled) front-rank man; (forgjen-

ger) predecessor; (ved håndverk) foreman, head man; (i forsamling) chairman, president; (i underhuset) speaker. -skap presidency, (i bystyret) town or parish council (as distinct from the Representative Body). -skapsmedlem councillor. formannsverdighet chairmanship, speakership, presidency.
formasjon formation.
formaste| seg presume. -lig presumptuous.
formastelighet presumption.
format format, size (of a book).
forme form, fashion, shape; (støpe etter modell el. i form) mould.
formedelst on account of, owing to.
formel formula form.
formelig actual, positive, regular; (adv) actually, absolutely, fairly, positively; in form.
formel|l (adj) formal. -t (adv) formally.
formene forbid, prohibit.
formening opinion, judgment.
formentlig supposed; (adv) I think, I believe.
former moulder.
formere (militært) form; (forøke antallet) increase, multiply; — seg multiply.
formering (formerelse) multiplication, propagation; (formasjon av tropper) formation.
form|feil informality. -full courteous. -fullendt formally perfect, finished, elegant. -fullendthet elegance.
formiddag forenoon, morning, A. M.; i — this morning; kl. ti om -en at ten (o'clock) in the morning, 10 A. M. formiddags|gudstjeneste morning service. -mat luncheon.
formidl|e effect, be instrumental in. -er instrument, medium. -ing effectuation, bringing about.
formilde (lindre) alleviate, assuage, soothe; (bløtgjøre) mollify, soften; (v. tilsetning) temper mitigate. -nde omstendighet extenuating circumstance.
forminske decrease, diminish, lessen, extenuate, take from, detract from; -s decrease, diminish etc.; i -t målestokk on a small scale. -lse decrease, diminution, reduction, retrenchment, abatement.
form|lære accidence. -løs formless, shapeless, irregular, immethodical. -løshet formlessness; informality.
formod|e suppose, surmise, conjecture, presume. -entlig probably, presumably, most likely, in all likelihood, I suppose.
formodning supposition, surmise, impression, guess, conjecture, theory.
form|sak matter of form; som en ren — in a perfunctory manner. -sans sense for beauty of form. -spørsmål question of form, formality.
formue fortune, property; (evne) ability, power; ha en — på 10,000 pund be worth 10,000 pounds. formuende wealthy, opulent.
formuerett real law. formues|fellesskap community of goods. -forhold fortune. -skatt property tax. -omstendigheter circumstances.
formular formula, form.
formuler|e formulate. -ing formulation.
formumme muffle; disguise, mask.
formynder guardian. -i, se overformynderi. -skap guardianship. formynderske (female) guardian.
formæl|e espouse. -ing nuptials.
formørke darken, obscure, eclipse.
formørkelse darkening; eclipse.
formå (vi.) be able (to), capable (of); (vt.) prevail on, persuade, induce, bring; — mye hos en have great influence el. interest with one; alt hva man -r all in one's power; ikke — å be unable to; du må ta til takke med det huset -r you must take pot-luck. -ende influential.
formål intent, aim, end, purpose.
formålstjenlig (suitable) to the purpose, appropriate, expedient.

fornagle nail up; — en kanon spike el. nail a gun.
fornavn Christian name, first name.
fornedre debase, abase, degrade, humble. -nde degrading. -lse abasement, debasement, degradation. -lsestilstand state of degradation.
fornekte (ikke vedkjenne seg) renounce, disown; ikke — sin karakter be true to one's character.
fornektelse denial, disavowal, renunciation.
fornem distinguished, of quality, of distinction, of position, of rank; en — mann a man of rank el. quality; — mine an air of superiority, a stately el. superior air; den -me verden the fashionable world, (high) society, high life.
fornemhet distinction, gentility.
fornemme feel, be sensible of, perceive, notice.
fornemmelse feeling, perception; fine -r high notions.
fornik|le nickel-plate. -ling nickel-plating.
fornlevninger relics of antiquity, antiquities.
fornorsk|e translate el. do into Norwegian (gjøre norsk) norwegianize. -ning translating etc.; (konkret) Norwegian translation el. version.
fornuft reason; den sunne — common sense; tale — talk sense; bringe en til — bring one to reason el. to his senses, restore one to sanity; ta imot — listen to reason; være ved sin fulle — be in one's right senses. -giftermål marriage of convenience.
fornuftig rational, reasonable, sane, sensible; discreet, judicious; et — vesen a rational being; intet — menneske no one in his senses; være så — å have the sense to.
fornuft|igvis reasonably, in reason. -messig rational. -messighet rationality. -stridig contrary to reason, absurd. -vesen rational being.
forny|e renew, renovate; (veksel) prolong; ta under -et overveielse reconsider, think better of. -else renewal, renovation; prolongation.
fornærme offend, insult, affront. -lig insulting, offensive. -lse insult, affront. ingen —! no offence! -t offended (på: with, over: at); bli -t over take offence at.
fornøden requisite, needful, necessary; nekte seg det fornødne deny oneself the necessaries of life. -het necessity, requirement.
fornøgd, fornøyd(d) delighted, pleased, happy (at), glad (of); content, contented.
fornøye content, please, delight, gratify. -lig delightful, pleasant. -lighet delightfulness; contentment.
fornøyelse pleasure, gratification; delight; diversion, amusement; finne — i take pleasure in, delight in; ha — av derive satisfaction from; det er meg en stor — it gives me great pleasure to; jeg har ikke den — å kjenne ham I have not the privilege of knowing him; ja med — with all my heart, by all means; god —! I wish you may enjoy yourself.
forord preface, prefatory note; — bryter trette contract makes the law void.
forord|ne ordain, order (om legen) prescribe. -ning ordinance, decree.
forover forward. -bøyd stooping.
forpakt|e farm, rent, take a lease of. -er tenant, (tenant) farmer, lessee. -ergård farm, holding. -ning farming; ha, ta en gård i — rent a farm. -ningsavgift (farm-) rent.
forpest|e poison, infect. -ing infection.
forpint tortured, racked.
forpjusket tumbled, rumpled.
forplant|e propagate; (overføre) transmit; — (om dyr) breed, propagate (om ting) be transmitted, spread. -ning transplantation; propagation; transmission. -ningsevne power of reproduction. -ningsredskap organ of r., generative organ.
forplei|e board, feed, maintain. -ning nursing, attendance, maintenance.

forpleiningsvesen commissariat.
forplikte bind, engage, oblige; — seg pledge oneself, engage, covenant; -t (in duty) bound. -lse obligation (overfor: to), engagement, liability; oppfylle sine -lser act up to one's engagements. -nde obligatory, binding.
forplum|re confuse, make a mess of; — seg get confused. -ret perplexed.
forplumring confusion, perplexity.
forpost outpost, advanced guard.
forpote forepaw.
forpupning pupation.
forpuppe seg pass into the chrysalis state.
forpurr|e frustrate, foil. -ing frustration.
forpustet breathless, out of breath, blown.
forrang precedence, primacy (fremfor: to).
forranglet debauched.
forregne seg miscalculate, misreckon; du har -t deg you are out in your calculations.
forrente pay interest on; — med 6 prosent pay 6 percent on; — seg yield interest; — seg godt yield good interest el a good return.
forrest foremost, front; (adv) foremost.
forresten however, be it said, by the bye, by the way.
forretning business; (næringsvei) trade; (kall) vocation; (affære) affair; (embets-) function, duty; en stor — a large concern; gjøre -er do business; ha mange -er have a great deal of business; har to -er has two businesses; i -er on business.
forretnings|anliggende affair. -brev business letter. -dame business woman. -drift trade -forbindelser business connections. -foretagende business concern. -fører manager (of a b.). -gang course of business. -liv business-life, trade. -lokale business premises. -mann man of business. -messig businesslike. -ministerium working government. -moral business morality. -orden (i riksdag) parliamentary procedure. -reise commercial trip. -sak business affair. -språk commercial language.
I. forret (forrettighet) prerogative, privilege.
II. forrett (mat) first dish, entrée.
forrette perform, discharge, execute; (som prest) officiate; — v. en begravelse perform a funeral. han kom hjem med vel -t sak he returned home after having fully accomplished his purpose.
forrettighet prerogative, privilege.
forrevet torn, scratched; (om kystlinje, fjelltinder) ragged; (om skyer) riven, tattered.
forrige former, previous; — uke last week; den 4de i — måned the 4th ult.
forrigg fore-rigging.
forringe disparage; detract from, derogate from. -lse debasement; disparagement derogation.
forrom (på skip) forehold.
forrykende furious, tremendous.
forrykke displace; (fig) disturb.
forrykt (avsindig) crazy, cracked, crackbrained. -het craziness, folly.
forræd|er traitor (mot: to) betrayer (of). -eri treason, treachery. -ersk treacherous, traitorous, treasonable; (adv) treacherously etc. -erske traitress.
forrær fore-yards el. headyards.
forråd supply, store, provision; ha — av have a store of, have in hand.
forråde betray.
forrådskammer store-room.
forråe brutalize, coarsen.
forråtne rot, putrefy, decay. -lse putrefaction, corruption; som forhindrer — antiseptic; gå i — putrefy.
forsage (svikte) fail, (fig) lose heart; (si seg løs fra) renounce. -lse renunciation.
forsagt despondent, disheartened, dispirited.
forsagthet despondency.
forsal hall, vestibule, lobby.
forsalg advance sale.

forsamle assemble, congregate, gather together; — seg meet, assemble.
forsamling assembly, assemblage, meeting, convention, gathering.
forsamlings|frihet right of public meeting. -hus house of assembly, meeting-house. -sal meeting hall.
forsanger leader (of a choir).
forsats|blad fly-leaf, blank leaf. -papir end paper.
forse (styrke) force; (fig) forte, strong point.
forse seg do amiss, do wrong, make a mistake; — seg på fall in love with; (under svangersk.) get a shock from. -else mistake, oversight, fault, error, slip.
forseg|le seal, seal up. -ling sealing; under -ling under seal, sealed.
forseil headsail, pl. også head canvas.
forselge deal in, sell. -r dealer, vender, vendor.
forsende send off, dispatch, forward, transmit. -lse sending etc., transmission.
forser|e force. -t forced, strained.
forsete front seat; presidency, chairmanship; ha -t preside, take the chair.
forsetning antecedent, preceding sentence.
forsett purpose; med — on purpose, purposely. of set purpose; gode forsetter good intentions.
forsette (forflytte) remove, transfer.
forsettlig intentional, wilful, studied.
forside front, foreside.
forsik|re assure, protest; (assurere) insure; — høyt og dyrt vow; — en om assure one of; — et hus, skip insure a house, ship; den -rede the insured, the insurant. -ret insured.
forsikring assurance, protestation; (mot brann osv.) insurance, assurance.
forsikrings|agent insurance agent, agent of an insurance-company. -anstalt insurance-office. -betingelse condition of insurance. -klausul insurance-clause. -polise insurance-policy, policy of insurance. -premie premium of insurance. -selskap insurance company. -tager, -taker insuree, policy-holder.
forsiktig cautious, circumspect, prudent, wary, guarded; — med hva ... cautious in what ...; det er best å være — it's as well to be on the safe side; —I (påskrift) with care.
forsiktighet caution, circumspection, prudence, wariness. -sregel (measure of) precaution, precautionary measure (treffe: take).
forsimple coarsen. forsimpling coarsening.
forsinke delay. forsinkelse delay.
forsinket (om skip, post) late, belated, behind (its) time, after its time, overdue.
forsire decorate, adorn.
forsiring decoration, ornament.
forskall|e (bordkle) board. -ing boarding, lathing, laths.
forskanse intrench, ensconce, barricade.
forskansning intrenchment, barricade.
forske: -i inquire into, investigate, explore; — etter search for; -nde searching (look), inquiring (spirit).
forsker inquirer, searcher, investigator.
forsker|blikk searching glance. -øye searching eye. -ånd spirit of inquiry.
forskip forepart of a vessel.
forskinn (skomakers forkle) apron.
forskjell difference; distinction; — i alder difference of age; — i år difference in years; gjøre — på (eller mellom) distinguish, make a distinction between; uten — indiscriminately.
forskjellig different (from el. to); (tydelig atskilt) distinct; (atskillige) various, miscellaneous; være — differ; på — måte differently.
forskjellig|artet varied, heterogeneous, heterogeneal, diversified. -het diversity.
forskjerm dashboard, splashboard.
forskjertse forfeit.
forskjære spoil in cutting, miscut.

forskjær|gaffel carving fork. **-kniv** carving knife, carver.
forskjønne embellish, grace, beautify. **-lse** embellishment, beautification. **-lsesmiddel** cosmetic.
forskning inquiry, investigation, research.
forskole preparatory school; preparation.
I. **forskott**, se **forskudd**.
II. **forskott** (i skip) fore bulkhead.
forskrekke frighten, terrify. **-lig** awful, frightful, terrible, dreadful, horrid, grievous.
forskrekkelse fright, terror.
forskremt scared, frightened.
forskrift (i skolen) writing copy, copy-slip, copy-head; (befaling) directions, instructions (pl), precept; (leges) prescription.
forskriv|e (varer) bespeak, order, write for; (overdra som pant) mortgage, pledge, pawn; — **seg til djevelen** make a bargain with the devil; — **seg til noe** bind oneself by bond, enter into a bond. **-(n)ing** order; bond; (feil) slip of the pen.
forskru|e hodet på en turn one's head. **-dd** excentric, extravagant, high-flown. **-ddhet** extravagance; excentricity.
forskudd advance (of money); **gi** — advance (money); **stå i** — come el. be under advance.
forskudds|betaling prepayment. **-vis** in advance; **betale** — advance.
forskusle fritter away, waste.
forskyldt well deserved, richly deserved; **få lønn som** — get one's deserts; **lønn som** —! serve him right!
forskyt|e cast off, disown, repudiate, put away.
forskyv|e displace, shift; dislocate; — **seg** get displaced. **-(n)ing** shifting.
forskåne spare. **-lse** sparing.
I. **forslag** proposal, (**om, til**: for, of), proposition; motion; (lov-) bill; (musikk) appoggiatura, grace-note; **anta et** — accept a proposal. **gjøre en et** — make a p. to one; **stille et** — make a motion.
II. **forslag** (til forslå = være tilstrekkelig): **det er ikke** — **i pengene** the money goes but a little way.
forslagen artful, crafty. **-het** artfulness, craft.
forslagsstiller proposer.
forslitt worn out; (fig) hackneyed, stale, trite, well-worn, fatigued.
forsluke| seg gorge oneself. **-n** greedy (**på**: of), voracious. **forslukenhet** greediness, voracity.
I. **forslå** (strekke til) suffice, be sufficient, avail.
II. **forslå** (skade) batter, bruise, hurt.
forsmak foretaste, earnest (**på**: of).
forsmedelig disgraceful, ignominious.
forsmekte languish, pine away, starve, die (av: with).
forsmå slight, disdain, refuse.
forsnakke seg make a slip of the tongue; (si noe man ikke skulle) babble out el. let out a secret, let the cat out of the bag. **-lse** slip of the tongue.
forsnevr|e narrow, contract. **-ing** contraction (anat.) stricture.
forsommer early (part of) summer.
forsone reconcile; (formilde) propitiate, conciliate, appease; — **seg med en** be reconciled to one; — **seg med noe** reconcile oneself to. **-nde trekk** redeeming feature. **-r** atoner, expiator. **forsoning** reconciliation, propitiation; atonement, expiation. **forsonlig** placable, conciliatory. **forsonlighet** placability.
forsoren rakish, dare-devil, swaggering.
forsorenhet swagger.
forsorg (provident) care; (understøttelse) poor relief. **forsorgs|forstander** overseer, relief officer. **-vesen** pauper administration.
forsove seg over-sleep oneself.
forspann team; relay.
forspent put to; **det er** — the horses are put to; **en vogn** — **med fire hester** a carriage and four.

forspill prelude; (på teateret) introductory piece.
forspil|le forfeit, lose; (for andre) spoil, mar; **et -t liv** a life run to waste.
forspise seg overeat oneself.
forsprang start, lead; **ha** — for have the start of; **få et kvarters** — for en get the start of one by a quarter of an hour; **beholde -et** keep the lead.
forstad suburb. **forstads-** suburban.
forstamn, se **forstavn**.
forstand understanding, intellect, sense; (mening) meaning, sense; **min** — **står stille** I give it up; **sunn** — good sense, common sense; **god til å få** — av full of meaning; **gå fra -en** lose one's senses, wits. go out of one's mind, run el. go mad; **være fra -en** be deranged; **i egentlig** — in the proper sense of the word; **i en viss** — in one sense; **miste sin** — lose one's reason; **det overgår all** — it passes all understanding; **det går over min** — it is above my comprehension, is beyond me; **ha** — **på** be a judge of; **ta skade på sin** — take leave of one's senses; **du taler som du har** — til you speak according to your lights; **etter min ringe** — to the best of my poor understanding.
forstander principal, manager, director, superintendent. **-inne** directress, superior.
forstandig sensible, intelligent. **-het** sensibleness, good sense.
forstands|menneske matter-of-fact person. **-messig** rational.
forst|assistent **-betjent** forester, ranger.
forstavelse prefix.
forstavn stem, bow, prow.
for|stemme mistune, put out of tune; (fig) cast a gloom on. **-stemt** out of tune; (fig) **være** — be low, out of tune, out of spirits, in low spirits. **-stemthet** low spirits, dejection of spirits.
forsteine petrify, turn to stone; (fig) **-t** (av skrekk) petrified; (om anskuelser o. l.) fossilized; **som forsteinet** like one stricken to stone. **forsteining** fossil, petrifaction, fossilization.
forsterk|e strengthen, fortify; reinforce. **-er** (i radio) amplifier. **-ning** reinforcement.
forstille (sin stemme o. l.) disguise, dissimulate. — **seg** dissemble, feign, simulate, sham; **-lse** dissimulation, sham, disguise. **-lseskunst** dissimulation.
forstilt feigned, sham.
forstmann forester, forest-engineer.
forstikke seg hide.
forstokkelse obduracy.
forstokket hardened, obdurate, callous.
forstoppe choke up, obstruct, stuff; **være -t** be costive. **-lse** obstruction, constipation, costiveness.
forstrek|ke (en arm osv.) strain, sprain; (en med) advance (to one), help one out in; — **en med kontanter** supply. **-ning** strain, sprain, elongation; advance.
forstudier preliminary studies.
forstue (subst) entry, (entrance-) hall, lobby.
I. **forstue** (vrb) strain, sprain. **forstuing** sprain.
II. **forstue**: (om last) — **seg** shift; **lasten -r seg** the cargo shifts.
forstumme be mute, be struck dumb; (om lyd) die out.
forst|vesen forest matters, woodcraft, forestry. **-vitenskap** forest science.
forstykke front-piece; (i skjorte) front.
forstyrre disturb, interrupt, interfere with; (bringe i uorden) disarrange, unsettle; (bry) trouble; (forvirre) disorder, derange, discompose, ruffle, distract; (komme til uleilighet) intrude; **jeg håper jeg ikke -r** I hope I don't intrude. **forstyrrelse** disturbance, interruption; disorder, derangement, distraction, trouble, intrusion., **forstyrret** confused; (i hodet) distracted, deranged, light-headed, crazy.

forstøkt, se **forskrekket, forskremt.**
forstørre enlarge; magnify. **-lse** enlargement. **-lsesglass** magnifying-glass, magnifier, microscope.
forstøte cast off, disown.
forstå understand; (innse) see; — **sitt fag** know one's business; **-r De det?** do you understand? **han -r å** he knows how to; **hva -r man ved** what is meant by; **det -r seg!** of course! **det -r seg av seg selv** that's a matter of course, that goes without (the) saying; — **seg på** understand about, be a judge of, have a knowledge of, be skilled in; **la** — hint, intimate, imply. **forstå(e)lig** intelligible; **gjøre seg** — make oneself understood. **forstå(e)lighet** intelligibility.
forståelse understanding, intelligence; (klar oppfattelse av noe) realization; **komme til** — come to an understanding; **leve i god** — **med** live on good terms with.
forsulten starved, famished, hungered, ravenous, sharp-set.
forsumpe stagnate.
forsure embitter.
forsvar defence; **si til** — **for** say in defence of; **til sitt** — in el. for his defence.
forsvare defend; justify, advocate; **jeg kan ikke** — **å** I am not justified in -ing; — **seg** make a defence.
forsvarer defender; advocate; **møte som** — appear for (on) the defence.
forsvarlig defensible, warrantable, justifiable; creditable; (sikker) secure, sure; (kraftig, stor) huge, big; — **arbeid** warrantable work; **i** — **stand** in proper condition; **holde i** — **stand** keep in proper repair; (adv) properly, warrantably, unexceptionably.
forsvars|departement war office. **-evne** defensive power. **-forbund** defensive alliance el. league. **-krig** defensive war. **-linje** line of defence. **-lov** defence of the realm act. **-løs** defenceless. **-middel** means of defence. **-minister** minister of defence, secretary of state for war. **-plan** plan of defence. **-saken** the cause of the national defence. **-skrift** written defence. **-stand: sette i** — put into a state of defence. **-tale** apologetical discourse, speech of defence. **-venn** supporter of the national defence. **-vennlig** in favour of a strong national defence. **-vesen** system of the national defence, defensive system, army and navy. **-vilje** will(ingness) to defend the nation. **-våpen** defensive weapon, weapon of defence.
forsverge forswear; **jeg ville ha forsvoret at det var den mannen** I could have sworn it was not that man; **man skal ingenting** — let us swear no oaths about it.
forsvinn|e disappear, be lost to sight, vanish; **forsvinn!** make yourself scarce! **-ende** vanishing; (fig) infinitesimal, evanescent, minimal. **-ing** disappearance. **-ingspunkt** vanishing point.
forsvunnet gone, lost, missing.
forsyn providence. **-et** Providence.
forsynde seg sin, offend. **-lse** sin, offence.
forsyn|e supply, furnish, provide; (med levnetsmidler) victual, provision; (ved bordet) help (med: to); **forsyn Dem!** help yourself; **vel -t** (med varer) well assorted. **-ing** supply, provision. **-lig** provident, prudent, cautious, careful. **-lighet** providential care; circumspection.
forsøk trial, experiment (med: on, of), attempt (på: at), essay; **det er et** — **verdt** the attempt is worth making; **hans første litterære** — his first literary effort; **et mislykt** — a failure.
forsøke try, essay, attempt; — **seg i** try one's hand at.
forsøks- trial. **-dyr** experimental animal. **-leder** experimenter, experimentalist. **-vis** experimentally, by way of experiment.
forsølv|e plate, silver. **-ing** plating.
forsømme neglect, omit; — **den beleilige tid** let the opportunity pass el. slip; — **en time** miss a lesson. **-lig** negligent, neglectful, remiss. **-lighet** neglectfulness, remissness.
forsømmelse neglect, negligence, omission.
forsømt neglected; **innhente det -e** make up for the lost time.
forsørge provide for, take care of, maintain, support. **-lse** provision, support, maintenance.
forsørgelses|anstalt asylum. **-berettiget** entitled to parish relief, settled. **-rett** settlement.
forsørger provider, supporter, maintainer.
forsøte make sweet, sweeten. **-lse** sweetening.
for så vidt (konj) in so far as; provided that; (adv) so far, to that extent.
fort (subst) fort.
fort (adv) fast, quickly.
forta seg pass away, vanish, wear off; (overanstrenge seg) overexert el. overstrain oneself.
fortale preface.
fortann front tooth, fore tooth.
fortape lose; — **seg i** be lost in.
fortapelse (av rettighet) forfeiture; (fordømmelse) perdition.
fortapt lost; (motløs) disheartened, dejected.
fortau footway, footpath, (foot-)pavement; (amr) side-walk.
fortegn (mat) sign; (i musikk) signature.
fortegne catalogue; inventory, list.
fortegnet incorrectly drawn, out of drawing.
fortegning (mønstertegning) drawing copy; (feiltegning) misdrawing, incorrect drawing.
fortelle tell, relate, narrate, recount; — **igjen** repeat. **forteller** teller, narrator, relater. **fortelling** tale, narrative, narration, relation, story.
fortenke en i blame one, find fault with one.
fortenkt absorbed, lost in thought, pensive, preoccupied.
forteppe curtain, act drop.
forterpet commonplace, trite.
fortersket hackneyed, trite, well-worn.
fortet|ning condensation, compression. **-ningspumpe** air-compressor.
fortette compress, condense.
fortid past, the past, olden time(s); **la -en være glemt** let bygones be bygones; **hans** — his past life, his former life; **tilhører -en** is of the past. **fortidslevninger** antiquities.
fortie conceal (for: from), keep secret, suppress, be silent on.
fortielse concealment, suppression.
fortil before, in front.
fortin|ne tin. **-ning** tinning.
fortjene deserve, merit; **det -r å merkes** it is worth notice.
fortjeneste earnings, gain, profit; (fortjenthet) merit, desert; (ytt tjeneste) service; **ha god** — av make a good deal by; **har store -r av** has rendered great services to; **dette var hele min** — that was all I made by it; **dersom det gikk oss etter** — if we had our just deserts; **over** — beyond his desert.
fortjenstfull deserving, meritorious.
fortjenstmedalje medal for merit.
fortjent: gjøre seg — **av** deserve well of. **gjøre seg** — **av staten** ogs. do the state service; — **til** deserving (of), worthy of; (om straff) condign.
fortløpende progressive, continuous.
fortne accelerate, quicken.
fortolk|e interpret, expound; (uttyde) construe. **-er** interpreter, expounder. **-ning** interpretation, exposition; construction. **-ningskunst.** science of interpretation; (teologi) hermeneutics.
fortoll|e pay duty (for), pay the customs el. duties on. **-et** duty paid. **-ing** payment of duty.
fortom (på snøre) snell.
fortomset bewildered, confused.
forto|ne loom, appear, stand out. **-ning** looming, appearance.
fortopp (mar) fore masthead, fore rigging.
fortred harm, mischief, hurt; trouble, annoyance, vexation; **gjøre** — do harm; **volde** — annoy, cause annoyance.

fortred|elig cross, out of humour; (ubehagelig) troublesome, annoying. **-elighet** ill-humour; trouble, annoyance.

fortreffelig excellent, capital. **-het** excellence.

fortrekke (fjerne seg) decamp, depart, retire; (om ansiktsuttrykk) distort, twist; **— ansiktet** make a wry face; **uten å — en mine** without wincing, without moving a muscle of his face; **han måtte —** he was obliged to withdraw, to take himself off.

fortreng|e expel, dislodge, displace, supplant, supersede. **-sel: til — for** to the displacement of.

fortrin preference; superiority, advantage, preeminence; privilege; (første plassen) precedence; (fordel) advantage, excellency, merit.

fortrinlig superior, excellent, capital; (adv) eminently, preeminently; capitally, excellently. **fortrinlighet** superiority, excellence.

fortrinsrett preference, priority.

fortrinsvis by preference, for all others.

fortro (seg) confide (**til:** in). **-lig** confidential; **en — venn** an intimate el. familiar friend; **komme, stå på en — fot med** become familiar with, be on intimate terms with; **gjøre seg — med** make oneself familiar with; familiarize oneself with el. to; **jeg gjorde ham til min -e** I made him my confidant.

fortrolighet confidence; familiarity, intimacy; **ha — til** have confidence in; **i — in** confidence, confidentially.

fortropp vanguard, van (of an army).

fortrukket distorted, drawn.

fortrykt depressed, bowed down; **i -e kår** in straitened circumstances.

fortrylle charm, enchant, fascinate.

fortryllelse charm, enchantment, fascination, spell; **heve -n** disenchant one. **fortryllende** charming, enchanting; **fortryllet** charmed, enchanted.

fortryte rue, repent, regret, be sorry for. **-lig** offended (**på:** with), vexed, hurt, piqued; **ta — opp** take ill, in bad part. **-lse** regret, repentance; (misfornøyelse) displeasure, resentment; **uten —** without offending, by your favour.

fortrøst|e seg trust, put confidence (**til:** in). **-ning** confidence, trust, reliance (in); **i — til** trusting to. **-ningsfull** confident.

fortsette (vi) continue, go on; (vt) pursue, carry on, proceed with, take up.

fortsettelse continuation, prosecution, pursuance; **— følger** to be continued.

fortsettelsesskole continuation school.

fortumlet confused, perplexed; **være — i hodet** be out of one's mind, wits.

Fortuna Fortune; **fru — Dame Fortune.**

forturet dissipated, debauched, knocked up by revelry.

forturner flugelman, fugleman. **være — fugle.**

fort vekk incessantly; very commonly.

fortvile despair; **man skal aldri — never** say die; **det er til å — over** it is enough to drive one to despair.

fortvilelse despair, desperation; **bringe til — drive** (reduce) to despair.

fortvilet desperate; (noe svakere, om person) in despair, disconsolate; (adv) desperately.

fortykke thicken. **-lse** thickening.

fortynne dilute, thin. **-t** dilute, diluted.

fortynning dilution, attenuation, rarefaction.

fortysk|e Germanize. **-ning** Germanization.

fortære consume; devour; **-s** (om metall o. l.) waste, be eaten away.

fortæring consumption; expenses.

fortørke dry up, parch; (fig) sear.

fortørne offend, provoke, anger, exasperate; **bli -t** be offended, take offence (**på:** with, **over:** at); **-t** exasperated, irate.

fortørnelse displeasure, resentment.

fortøye moor; (båt) make fast.

fortøyning mooring.

forulemp|e (tilføye overlast) molest; (plage, genere) annoy. **-(n)ing, -else** molestation; annoyance.

forulyk|ke fail, miscarry, be lost, perish; **skipet -ket** the ship was lost, wrecked. **-ket** gone to wreck, decayed.

forunderlig wonderful, marvellous, strange, surprising; (underlig) singular, odd; (adv) strangely, singularly; **— nok** strange to say.

forundersøkelse preliminary inquiry.

forun|dre surprise; **— seg over** wonder, marvel, be surprised at. **-dring** wonder, surprise; **falle i — be** struck with astonishment.

forunne grant.

foruren|se (gjøre urein) contaminate, pollute, foul. **-sning** contamination, pollution, fouling.

forurette injure, wrong; **den -de** the injured party. **-lse** injury, wrong.

forurolige disquiet, alarm; **— fienden** harass the enemy. **-nde** alarming.

forut in advance, ahead, before, beforehand; (i skip) forward; **— for** ahead of; in advance of; **en seiler —! a** sail ahead! **— for sin tid** in advance of one's age; **en ting hadde han — for meg** one thing he had before me. **-anelse** presentiment. **-bestemme** predestine, predetermine. **-bestemmelse** predetermination, predestination. **-bestemt** predeterminate.

foruten (prep) besides, in addition to.

forut|fattet preconceived; **— mening** prejudice. **-gående** foregoing, preceding, antecedent. **-inntatt** prepossessed, prejudiced (in favour of, against). **-satt at** provided el. supposing that, if, if so be that.

forutse foresee. **forutseende** (framsynt) foresighted; (forsynlig) provident. **forutseenhet** foresight.

forutsetning supposition, assumption presupposition, hypothesis, theory; (egenskap) capacity, qualification.

forutsette (gå ut fra) suppose, presuppose assume; **jeg -r som gitt** I take it for granted.

forut|si foretell, predict, prognosticate. **-sigelse** prediction.

forutskikke (meddele i forveien) premise.

forvalte administer, manage; **— dårlig** mismanage.

forvalt|er steward, manager, agent; (mar) paymaster (and purser). **-ning** administration, management.

forvand|le transform, change, convert, transmute, metamorphose; **— til gull** turn to (el. into) gold. **-ling** transformation, transmutation, metamorphosis, conversion.

forvansk|e distort, disfigure, misrepresent; corrupt, pervert. **-ning** distortion, misrepresentation, corruption, perversion.

forvar|e keep. **-ing** keeping, (safe-)custody, safe keeping; charge; preservation; **sette i — take** into custody; **ha i — have** charge of.

forvarsel (varsel) omen, presage.

forvei|en: i — before; (tid) beforehand; (tidligere) previously; **gå i — go** ahead; lead the way.

forveksle mistake (**med:** for), confound.

forveksling confusion, mistake; **det foreligger en — it** is a case of mistaken identity.

forvende (forvrenge) distort, pervert, wrest.

forven|ne spoil, coddle. **-t** spoiled (smak) pampered, dainty.

forvente expect.

forventhet pampered taste.

forventning expectation, anticipation; **det svarte ikke til min — it** fell short of my expectation; **mot min — contrary** to my expectation(s); **over — more** (better) than could be expected; **i — om** looking forward to, awaiting, in expectation of. **forventningsfull** expectant, full of expectation.

forverden former age(s), former world, antediluvian world.

forver|re make worse, worsen, deteriorate; (en sak) aggravate. **-ring** worsening, aggravation.

forvik|le entangle, complicate. **-ling** complication, intricacy, entanglement.

forville lead astray, mislead, bewilder, perplex; — **seg** lose one's way, stray, go astray.

forvillelse bewilderment, perplexity; **ungdommens -r** aberrations of youth.

forvinne recover, overcome; (sorg) get the better of, live down; — **et tap** recover a loss; — **en sykdom** recover from an illness.

forvir|re confuse, derange, confound. **-ret** confused; — **snakk** nonsense. **-ring** confusion, bewilderment; derangement; **bringe** — **i noe** throw st. into confusion.

forvise banish, exile.

forvisning (landsforvisning) banishment.

forvisse seg om assure oneself of; ascertain, make sure of; **være -t om** be sure of; **De kan være -t om at** you may rest assured that, be convinced that.

forvissning assurance, ascertainment.

forvitre decompose, disintegrate, weather away. **forvitring** disintegration.

forvokst: et — **barn** a deformed child.

forvolde cause.

forvorpen depraved, reprobate.

forvorpenhet depravity.

forvreng|e distort, twist. **-ning** distortion.

forvri twist, dislocate, sprain; (fig) warp, pervert.

forvridd distorted, twisted out of shape.

forvridning twisting etc.; dislocation, luxation.

forvrøvle throw into a hopeless jumble, make an absurd mess of.

forværelse anteroom, antechamber.

forvågen adventurous, venturesome, daring, rash, audacious.

forvåket exhausted with watching.

foryng|e make young, rejuvenate, renew. **-s** grow young again. **-ise** renewal of youth, rejuvenescence.

forære| en noe make one a present of st., present one with st., present st. to one. **få den -nde** be presented with it.

foræring present, gift.

forøde dissipate, misspend.

forødelse dissipation, waste.

forøk|e increase, augment, add to, enhance. **-else** increase, augmentation, accession. **-t** (om utgave) enlarged, enl.

forønsket wished-for, desired.

forøve perpetrate. **forøver** perpetrator.

for øvrig, se **øvrig**.

forår, se **vår**.

forårsake cause, occasion.

fosfat phosphate.

fosfor phosphorus. **-esere** phosphoresce. **-nde** phosphorescent.

fosforsur phosphorated; **-t salt** phosphate.

fosforsyre phosphoric acid.

foss waterfall, cataract.

fosse (styrte ned) gush.

fosse|dur roar of a cataract. **-grim** (slags nøkk) nick, nicker. **-kall** (fugl) water-ousel, dipper. **-stryk** cascade, rapid.

fossil (forsteining) fossil.

fossil (adj) fossil.

fostbror (som har blandet blod med en annen) brother-in-blood. **-skap** brotherhood-in-blood.

foster fetus; (umodent) embryo; (fig) production; **et** — **av hans innbilningskraft** a phantom of his imagination. **-barn** (pleiebarn) fosterchild. **-bror** foster-brother. **-datter** foster -daughter. **-far** foster-father.

fosterfordrivelse feticide, criminal abortion, aborticide. **fosterfordrivende** abortive.

foster|foreldre foster-parents. **-land** native land. **-mor** foster-mother. **-sønn** foster-son.

fostre (subst) foster-child (Adalsteins-)

fostre rear; (fig) breed.

fot foot; (bord) leg; (glass) stem; (mast) heel; (spor, fert) scent; **få** — (jaktuttr.) find a scent; **ta -en på nakken** quicken one's pace, take foot in hand; **sette sin** — **i** set foot in; — **for** — slowly, step by step, at a foot's pace, foot by foot; **jeg kastet meg for hans føtter** I threw myself at his feet; **gå på sin** — go on foot; **komme på -e** recover, retrieve oneself; **hjelpe en på -e** help one on his legs, set one up; **på stående** — off-hand, out of hand, extempore; **stå på en god, dårlig** — **med en** be on good, bad terms with one; **på en fortrolig** — on terms of intimacy; **stå på svake føtter** be shaky; **komme på fri** — be set at liberty, be released; **være på fri** — be at large; **leve på en stor** — live in high style, in a magnificent style; **være på like** — **med** be on an equal footing, on a footing of equality (with); **stille på like** — **med** place on an equality with; **falle til -e** submit, yield, humble oneself; **til -s** on foot, afoot; **tre under føtter** trample under foot.

fot|angel man-trap, caltrop. **-bad** foot-bath.

fotball football. **-kamp** football match. **-lag** football team. **-spiller** footballer. **-uttrykk** football term.

fotballe ball of the foot.

fotefar footmark, footprint.

fotende (av seng) footboard.

fot|fall prostration; **gjøre** — **for** prostrate oneself before. **-feste** footing, foothold. **-folk** (pl) foot, infantry, foot-soldiers. **-gjenger** pedestrian, (foot-)passenger; **rask -gjenger** fast walker. **-jern** iron anklet. **-lag** step. **-lenke** fetters. **-note** foot-note.

fotograf photographer.

fotografatelier photographic studio.

fotografere photograph.

fotografering photography.

fotografi (framgangsmåten) photography; (bilde) photograph, photo. **-album** photograph-book. **-apparat** camera, photographic apparatus. **-ramme** photo-frame.

fotografisk photographic.

foto|gravyr photo-engraving. **-litografi** photolithography. **-typi** phototype.

fot|pleie pedicure. **-pose** foot-lag, foot-muff. **-pute** foot-cushion. **-rapp** swift-footed, fleet.

fotsbredd foot-breadth.

fot|sid reaching the foot, long to the ground. **-skade** a bad foot. **-skammel** foot-stool. **-skifte** pace. **-slag** foot-fall. **-soldat** foot-soldier. **-spark** kick.

fotspor foot-step, foot-print; **tre el. gå i ens** — walk in el. follow (in) one's footsteps.

fot|svette sweating of the feet. **-såle** sole of the foot. **-trin** footstep, footfall, tread. **-tur** journey on foot, walking tour. **-tøy** footwear, boots, shoes. **-vask** washing of the feet.

foyer (skuespillernes) greenroom; (publikums) foyer, lobby.

fra (prep) from; **han er** — **Oslo** his is from Oslo, a native of O.; — **tid til annen** from time to time; — **i dag** av from this day; — **den tid av** since (that); — **nå av** henceforth; **høyst 12 fot** — **vinduet** within 12 feet of the window; — **min ungdom av** from my youth up; **være** — **seg selv** be beside oneself; — **hverandre** asunder, in two; **skilles** — **hverandre** separate, part; (adv): **det gjør hverken** — **eller til** that is neither here nor there; **trekke** — deduct; (konj): — **jeg var 4 år gammel** since I was four years old; — **jeg var barn** from a child.

frabe seg deprecate, prohibit; decline; **ha seg noe frabedt** deprecate st.

fradrag deduction, abatement; **etter** — **av omkostninger** deducting expenses.

fradømme sentence to lose, deprive (of).

fra|fall falling off, defection; (fra religion) apostasy. **-falle** give up, abandon, relinquish waive (a claim). **-fallen** apostate, renegade.

fraflytte leave, remove from.

fragment fragment, scrap.

fragmentarisk fragmentary, scrappy.

fragå (benekte riktigheten av) deny; gå fra) disavow, recede from.

frakjenne en noe pronounce one destitute of; **man kan ikke — ham dyktighet** his ability is unquestionable, undisputable.

frakk coat; (diplomatfrakk) frock-coat. **frakke| krage** coat-collar. **-skjøt** coat-lap.

fraksjon (del av et politisk parti) section.

frakt freight; (til lands) carriage; (ladning) cargo, freight; **til høy —** at a high rate of freight. **-brev** bill of carriage, carriage-note; (mar) bill of lading. **-damper** cargo-steamer.

frakte (føre) carry, convey; (leie) freight, charter. **frakt|fart** carrying trade. **-fri** carriage **-free; -fritt** (adv) carriage-paid. **-gods** goods (on freight). **stykke -gods** package. **-kusk** el. **-mann** carrier, waggoner. **-vogn** (carrier's) waggon.

fraktur Gothic letter, black letter; (med) fracture.

fralands offshore, from landwards; **— vind** land-breeze.

fralegge seg disavow, disclaim, clear el. exculpate oneself (from), deny.

fraliste trick (one) out of.

fralokke coax out of; **— en noe** wheedle one out of st.

fram forth, forward, on; **lenger —** further on; **— med dere!** get out; **— og tilbake** backwards and forwards, to and fro, up and down; **det er langt —** we have a long way before us; **si —!** say on! **fram —** se ogs. **frem-**.

frambrott, se **frembrudd.**

frametter, se **framover.**

framferd conduct, proceeding; **det er ingen — i ham** he has no energy (enterprise, go).

framfor before, above, beyond, in preference to, preferably to, rather than; **— alt** above all.

framfusen|de headlong, precipitate, impetuous. **-het** precipitancy, impetuosity.

framgang advance, progress, proficiency, advancement, prosperity, success; **gjøre —** make progress. **-småte** mode el. manner of proceeding, plan, method, line of action; course.

framhaldsskole, se **fortsettelsesskole.**

framifrå excellent, high-class.

framkommelig passable, practicable.

framkomst progress; (ankomst) arrival; (tilsynekomst) appearance; (opprinnelse) origin. **-middel** conveyance, (means of) locomotion.

framlegg motion, proposal.

framlyd initial sound.

framlån loan at second hand.

framme (adv) in, out, there, on the spot; **la noe ligge —** leave st. about; **langt —** far forward.

fram|møte (subst) appearance, attendance. **-møtt** in attendance.

framom past.

framover forward; (avsted) along; (i framtida) in future, hereafter; **i lange tider —** for a long time forward el. to come; (liggende **—)** procumbent.

frampå (adv) in front; (prep) in front of. **snakke —** (dt) hint, throw out a hint.

framslenge bread-and-butter miss, growing girl, flapper.

framsteg progress, proficiency. **gjøre —** make progress, go on.

framstegs|kvinne advanced woman. **-mann** progressionist, progressist. **-parti** progressive party.

framstøyt (plutselig frontangrep) dash, onset, onrush.

framsyn foresight. **-t** foresighted, far-seeing, far-sighted, prospective; (synsk) second-sighted.

framtanke timely care, forethought, providence.

framtid future, futurity; **i -a** in future, for the future; **i en ikke fjern —** at some not very distant day. **-ig** future, coming, prospective.

framtids|bilde vision of the future. **-dager** coming days. **-musikk** music of the future. **-stat** state of the future. **-utsikter** future prospects.

franarre en noe trick one out of st.

frank (mynt) franc.

frank og fri free and unrestrained.

franke|re frank, pre-pay. **-ring** prepayment (of postage).

Frankfurt am Main Frankfurt on the Main.

franko (om brev) (post-)paid, prepaid; (om pakker) carriage-paid. **— omkostninger** net of charges.

Frankrike France.

fransk French.

fransk (det franske språk) French; **på —** in French; **oversette til —** translate into French.

franskbind calf-binding; **innbundet i —** bound in calf.

fransk|brød French roll. **-engelsk** Franco-English. **-mann** Frenchman; **-mennene** the French. **-sinnet** pro-French.

frarane despoil el. rob of.

fraregne deduct. **-t** apart from, exclusive of.

frarive tear, wrench from.

fraråde advise against, dissuade from.

frasagn legend. **det går — om ham ennå** many tales are told of him even yet.

frase empty phrase, set phrase, fine phrase; **-r** cant. **-aktig** hollow, mouthy. **-flom** torrent of empty phrases. **-helt, -maker** phrasemonger, ranter, maker of fine phrases. **-makeri** rant.

frasi| seg renounce, resign; **— seg tronen** abdicate. **-gelse** renunciation, resignation, abdication.

fraskilt divorced.

fraskrive seg sign away, renounce.

frastand distance; **på —** at a distance.

frastjele rob of, steal from; **han ble frastjålet pungen sin** he had his pocket picked of a purse.

frastøtende repulsive, forbidding.

frata take away, deprive of.

fraternisere fraternize.

fratre retire from, withdraw from, leave, relinquish, resign; **en -dende embetsmann** a retiring officer. **-lse** retirement, withdrawment, resignment.

fratrekk, se **fradrag.**

fravende en noe defraud one of st.

fravike (avvike fra) depart from, deviate from. **-lse** departure, deviation.

fravriste en noe wrest, wring st. from one.

fravær absence; non-attendance; **glimre ved sitt —** be conspicuous by one's absence, be conspicuously absent.

fraværende absent; **de —** the absent, those absent; **de — har alltid urett** the absent are always at fault; **med et — blikk** ogs. vacantly.

fred peace; **være i —** be at peace; **la en være i —** leave one in peace; **holde —** keep the peace; **slutte —** make peace, conclude a peace, make one's peace with; **lyse — over** proclaim inviolate, preserve; **man har ikke — lenger enn naboen vil** nobody can live in peace longer than his neighbour pleases; **trodde det var — og ingen fare** thought all safe; **ved -en i Kiel** at (by) the peace of K.

fredag Friday; **i -s** (forrige **—)** last Friday; **på —** on F., next F.; **om -en** on Fridays.

frede (beskytte) preserve, protect; **et -t sted** a sanctuary.

fredelig (fredfylt) peaceful; (fredselskende) peaceable; f. eks. peaceful times; a peaceable. temper; a peaceable citizen. **fredelighet** peacefulness; peaceableness.

Frederik Frederic, Fred. **-ke** Frederica.

fredhellig sacred, inviolate.

fredlys|e (frede) protect. **-ning** prohibition.

fredløs outlaw. **fredløshet** outlawry.

fredning protection. **frednings|lov** protection act. **-tid** close time.

fredsartikkel article of peace.
freds|betingelse condition of peace. **-brott** -brudd breach of p. **-dommer** justice of the p. **-forstyrrer** disturber of the peace.
freds|konferanse peace conference. **-kongress** congress of peace.
freds|megler mediator of peace. **-megling** mediation of peace.
fredsommelig peaceable.
fredsommelighet peaceableness.
freds|pipe pipe of peace. **-prisen** (Nobels) the (Nobel) Peace Prize. **-saken** the cause of peace, the peace movement. **-slutning** peace, conclusion of peace. **-stifter** peacemaker. **-tider** times of p. **-tilstand** state of p. **-traktat** treaty of p. **-underhandling** peace negotiation. **-venn** peace-lover, (en som vil ha krig avskaffet) pacificist, pacifist. **fredsvennlig** peaceable, peace -loving; pacifist.
fredsæl (fredselskende) peace-loving.
fregatt frigate; **-en Ørnen** the Eagle frigate.
fregne freckle. **fregnet** freckled.
freidig buoyant, cheerful; **med — mot** nothing daunted. **-het** assurance, confidence, buoyancy.
frekk audacious, impudent, forward; shameless. **-het** audacity, impudence; (dt) front, cheek.
frekvens frequency; **høy —** high frequency; **lav —** low frequency. **-måler** frequency meter.
frekventere frequent, attend.
frelse (subst) rescue, preservation; liberation; (saliggjørelse) salvation; (sikkerhet) safety; (det å komme unna) escape. **-ns hær** the Salvation Army.
frelse (vrb) save, preserve; free, rescue. **-nde** saving.
frelser saver, preserver, rescuer; **vår Frelser** Our Saviour.
Frelsesarmeen the Salvation Army.
fremad forward, onward, ahead. **-skridende** advancing, forward. **-strebende** go-ahead.
fremblom|stre (fig) rise, spring up. **-string** rise, growth.
frembringe produce, yield, generate; (bringe fram) forward. **-lse** producing, production; (konkret) produce, product.
frembrudd outbreak; **dagens —** peep of day, day-break; **ved mørkets —** at nightfall.
fremby offer, present.
fremdeles still; moreover, furthermore; further, again.
fremdra, se dra fram.
fremdrive, se drive fram.
fremføre adduce, advance; **— en bønn** prefer a petition.
fremgå: det -r av det han sier it is evident, it appears, from what he says. **betydningen -r av sammenhengen** the context brings out the meaning.
fremherskende predominant, prevalent, prevailing, paramount; **være —** prevail.
fremheve set off, show, bring into relief, give prominence to; lay stress (emphasis) upon, emphasize.
fremhjelpe, se hjelpe fram.
fremholde hold out, hold up.
fremkalle call forth; (i teatret) call out el. for, call before the curtain; (foranledige) occasion, produce, elicit, call forth; (fotogr.) develop. **-lse** calling forth; call; development.
fremkomme med bring forward, produce, broach; f. eks. she waited for him to broach his business.
fremlegge produce; lay on the table; (til bedømmelse, til vedtaking) submit.
fremleggelse production.
fremleie (subst) under-letting, sub-letting.
fremlokke, se lokke fram.
fremme (vrb) forward, further, promote, advance; take in hand.

fremme (subst) furtherance, promotion, encouragement, advancement.
fremmed strange; (utenlandsk) foreign, alien; **under et — navn** under an assumed name; **kald og —** cold and distant; **en —** a stranger, foreigner, (besøkende) visitor; **vilt -e** entire strangers; **be -e** invite company; **han har aldri -e** he sees no company; **han har mange -e i aften** he has a numerous party this evening; **jeg er — her** I am a stranger here; **det er meg — it** is foreign el. alien to my nature.
fremmedartet heterogeneous.
fremmed|bok visitor's book. **-herredømme** foreign dominion. **-ord** foreign word. **-ordbok** dictionary of foreign words.
fremmelig advanced, forward.
fremragende (utmerket) prominent, eminent, leading.
fremre (komp. til fram) anterior, front.
fremrykket advanced.
fremrykning advance, onward march.
fremsende forward, transmit.
fremsette advance (f. eks. an opinion, a theory); **— et forslag** make a proposal; **— et krav** prefer a claim; **— et lovforslag** bring in a bill.
fremsi, se si fram.
fremsigelse recital, recitation, delivery.
fremskaffe procure.
frem|skreden advanced, forward; **da tiden var så langt —** it being so late. **-skridende** advancing.
fremskritt, se også **framsteg** progress, proficiency; **gjøre —** make progress, go on.
fremskritts|kvinne advanced woman. **-mann** progressionist, progressist; **-parti** progressive party.
fremskutt advanced.
fremskynde hasten, accelerate, expedite, quicken; help on, hurry on, precipitate.
fremspirende budding.
fremspring projection, overhang.
fremspringende projecting, salient.
fremst (adj) anterior, front; foremost, leading.
fremst (adv) in front, in the forefront; **først og —** primarily, before all, in the first instance.
fremstamme stammer forth, falter out.
fremstille bring forward, present, produce; (avbilde) represent; (rolle) personate; embody; (skildre) state, give an account of; (kjemi) exhibit; **— seg** appear, present oneself; represent oneself.
fremstiller exponent, impersonator, interpreter.
fremstilling representation; impersonation, personation, embodiment, presentment; view, picture, sketch, account, statement; (fabrikasjon) making, manufacture; (stil) style of writing, diction.
fremstillings|evne descriptive power. **-måte** style. **-omkostninger** expenses of production.
fremstå, se stå fram.
fremstående projecting, jutting (out), prominent, outstanding; **— underkjeve** underhung jaw.
fremtid, se framtid.
fremtoning phenomenon, appearance.
fremtre(de) appear, make one's appearance; se ogs. tre(de) fram.
fremtreden appearance, advance.
fremtredende prominent, conspicuous, pronounced, marked, distinctive; **være sterkt —** come out strongly; **spille en — rolle** play a prominent part.
fremtrylle, se trylle fram.
fremture i persist in, persevere in.
fremtvinge, se tvinge fram.
fremvise, se vise fram.
fremvisning exhibition, display.
frende kinsman, relative, relation; **— er — verst** it is always our best friend who betrays us, **-løs** without kinsmen etc.
frendskap kindred, kinship.
frenke (poet.: kv. slektning) kinswoman.
frese fiz, fizzle; (sprake) crackle; (sprute) sputter; (visle) hiss.

fresko fresco. **–maleri** fresco-painting.

fri (adj) free; (av vesen) free and easy, bold, fast, emancipated; (ledig) disengaged; (at liberty; — **adgang til** free access to; — **kjærlighet** free love; — **luft** the open air; **gi –tt løp** give full play, free scope to; — **utsikt** a free el. open prospect el. view; **i det** — in the open air; **en dag i det** — a day out; **og alltng –tt** and all found; **på** — **fot** at large; **gå** — come off el. pass scot-free; **vi har** — we have a holiday; **vi har** — i ettermiddag we have a half-holiday; **når vi hadde et øyeblikk** — whenever we had a moment of leisure; **den hånd jeg hadde** — my disengaged hand; **be seg** — ask leave of absence; **la meg være** — I beg to be excused; **må jeg være så** —? may I take the liberty? — **av** (mar) clear of; — **for** free from (el. of); — **for skatter** exempt from duties el. taxes; **det er ikke –tt for at han drikker** he is not free from drinking; **det står Dem –tt for å gjøre det** you are free, welcome, at liberty to do it; **være for** — **mot** en make too free with one; **ta seg** — take (make) a holiday; **ordet ble gitt –tt** the meeting was declared open for remarks; **ha –e** hender be free to act. have a free hand.
I. **fri** (beile) propose, make an offer (til: to).
II. **fri** (redde) deliver; **Gud** — **og bevare oss! Lord** deliver us! — **oss fra det vonde!** deliver us from evil! — **seg ved ed** clear oneself by oath.
friaften off night.
fri|billett free ticket, free admission, order; **der er ingen –er** there is no free list; **free list** suspended; (p. jernbane) free pass. **–bolig** free -lodging. **–brev: gi dem** — **på** patent them to. **–bytter** freebooter. **–bytteri** freebooting. **–båren** free-born.
fridag holiday, liberty day; (tjeneres) day out.
frieksemplar free copy, presentation copy.
frier suitor, wooer. **–brev** proposing letter. **–føtter: gå på** — go a-wooing; be looking out for a wife.
frieri courtship, wooing; proposal, demand in marriage.
frifinne acquit, discharge, absolve.
frifinnelse acquittal, discharge.
frigi free, release.
frigivelse release, emancipation.
frigjøre set free; — **seg for** emancipate oneself from. **frigjørelse** emancipation.
frihandel free trade. **–smann** freetrader.
frihavn freeport.
frihet freedom, liberty: **dikterisk** — poetical license; **ta seg den** — å take the liberty, make free el. bold to; **jeg tar meg den** — å I beg leave to; **sette i** — set free, at liberty, at large, release; **ta seg –er** take liberties.
frihets|berøvelse arrest, imprisonment. **–brev** charter. **–dag** independence day. **–krig** war of independence. **–mann** liberal, democrat. **–trang** thirst for liberty.
frihjul (på sykkel) free wheel.
fri|hånd: på — off hand. **–håndstegning** free -hand drawing.
frikar: han er — he has it all his own way.
frikassé fricassee, stew.
frikirke congregational church, free church.
frikirkelig congregational el. free church.
frikjenne acquit (for: of); f. eks. he was acquitted of the charge. **frikjennelse** acquittal.
friksjon friction.
frikvarter play-time, break, recess.
frilager bonded warehouse.
friland open ground.
frilands outdoor.
frille concubine, mistress.
frilufts|idrett out-of-door exercise. **–liv** open-air existence. **–menneske** open-air liver. **–teater** open-air theatre.
frilyndt broad-minded, liberal (-minded).
frimenighet independent congregation.

fri|merke stamp, post-stamp. **–merkesamler** stamp-collector. **–merkesamling** collection of stamps. **–minutt, se –kvarter.**
frimodig frank, open, free-hearted, cheerful, fearless. **–het** frankness etc.
frimurer freemason, mason. **–i** freemasonry, masonry. **–losje** freemason's lodge; (lokalet) masonic hall. **–tegn** masonic sign.
friplass (i teater) free admission; (p. skole) free scholarship.
fripostig impudent, bold-faced. **–het** effrontery.
frise frieze.
friser Frisian, Frieslander.
frisere dress (the hair). **frisérkåpe** dressing -gown. **frisértrøye** dressing-jacket.
frisinn liberality, liberal views. **frisinnet, se –lyndt.**
frisisk Frisian.
frisk fresh; (sunn) healthy, in good health, well, hearty; (ufordervet) sound, sweet; — **mot!** courage! **være ved -t mot** be of good cheer (heart); **trekke** — **luft** take the air el. an airing; — **som en fisk** as fit as a fiddle; **begynne på en ny** — start afresh el. in fresh.
friskare free-corps.
friske freshen; — **opp** refresh, revive.
friskfyr coxcomb, swell. **–vesen** coxcombry, flippancy, free and easy proceeding.
friskhet freshness.
friskne: — **til** rally, recover; (om vind) brisken up, get up, freshen.
friskole free school, national school.
friskyss free conveyance.
frispark (i fotball) free kick.
frispråk: han har — he may speak freely, he has a licensed tongue.
frist respite, grace, delay.
fristat republic, commonwealth.
friste (lide) experience; (føre i fristelse) tempt; — **livet** support life; — **lykken** try one's luck; **føle seg -t til** be under a temptation to. **fristed** (place of) refuge, resort, asylum.
frist|else temptation. **–er** tempter. **–erinne** temptress.
frisyre style el. mode of dressing the hair; head of hair.
frisør (også kvinnelig) hair-dresser.
frita exempt (from), excuse (from). **–kelse** exemption dispensation, immunity.
fritalende frank of speech, plainspoken.
fritenker freethinker. **fritenkeri** freethinking. **fritenkersk** freethinking.
fri|tid leisure time, off-time. **–time** leisure hour, spare h., interval of leisure.
fritt (adv) freely; (gratis) gratis, free of charge; **jeg tilstår** — at I am free to own that; — **ombord** free on board; — **fra borde** free ex ship; **stå** — (om hus) stand isolated, detached, be exposed to view; **det står Dem** — å . . . you are free to . . .
fritt|e (utspørre) question, interrogate. **–ing** questioning, (pågående) inquisitiveness.
fritt|liggende, –stående detached, isolated.
frivakt (frihet for vakt) off-watch, watch below; **ha** — be off duty.
frivillig voluntary, spontaneous, free-will; volunteer. **–het** voluntariness, spontaneousness.
frivol frivolous; (lettferdig) loose, immoral.
frivolitet looseness, immorality.
frk. (foran ugift kvinnes navn) Miss. **frk.** Johnson Miss Johnson.
frodig vigorous, luxuriant, rank.
frodighet luxuriance.
frokost (morgenmat) breakfast; (formiddagsmat) luncheon, lunch; **spise** — breakfast, lunch; **hva har du spist til** — what have you had for breakfast, luncheon. **–pause** luncheon adjournment.
from (gudfryktig) pious; (kjærlig og blid) gentle, mild; **et -t ønske** a vain wish; **et -t bedrag** a pious fraud.

fromasj cream.
fromesse matins.
from|het piety; gentleness, mildness.
fromme: på lykke og — at random, at a venture, at hap-hazard.
front front; **gjøre** — imot turn head against, face. **-forandring** changing front, change of front.
fropreken matins; early prayers.
frosk frog. **-e-egg** frog's spawn. **-ekvekk** croaking of frogs. **-unge** tadpole.
frossen frozen, frostbitten.
frost frost; **ha** — i **hendene** have chilblains on the hands. **-middel** remedy for chilblains. **-skadd** injured by frost. **-vær** frosty weather.
frotterbørste flesh-brush.
frottere rub.
frotter|hanske flesh-glove, loofa bath-glove. **-håndkle** rubber. **-ing** rubbing. **-svamp** loofa, luffa.
fru (foran gift kvinnes navn) Mrs. **fru Johnson** Mrs. Johnson. **fru Fortuna** Dame Fortune.
frue (husfrue) mistress; (i tiltale, uten navn) madam; **vår** — (Jomfru Maria) Our Lady; **husets** — the lady of the house; **er -n hjemme?** is Mrs. N. el. (til tjener) your mistress at home? **min** —! madam; **nådige** — your ladyship. **fruenavn** married name.
fruentimmer woman. (foraktelig) female creature.
frukt fruit; (fig) product, benefit, profit; **forbuden** — smaker best forbidden fruit is sweet, stolen things are sweet; **-en av ekteskapet** the issue of the marriage.
frukt|avl fruitfarming, fruitgrowing. **-bar** fruitful, fertile; (om vekster, dyr) prolific; **gjøre** — fertilize.
fruktbarhet fruitfulness, fertility, fecundity.
frukt|blomst blossom; **-bringende** productive, profitable; **-bunn** (bot) receptacle, thalamus. **-bærende** fructiferous.
frukt|e avail, profit. **-esløs** fruitless, bootless, unavailing. **-esløshet** fruitlessness.
frukt|hage orchard. **-handel** fruit-trade, trade in fruit.**-handler** fruiterer. **-handlerske** fruiteress. **-knute** (bot) germ, ovary. **-rikdom** abundance of fruit.
fruktsommelig pregnant, with child, in the family way; enceinte; **bli** — get with child; (fig) **gå** — med be big with, brood on.
fruktsommelighet pregnancy.
frukt|tre fruit-tree. **-utsalg** fruiterer's shop. **-vin** fruitwine, domestic wine.
fryd joy, delight.
fryde rejoice, gladden, cheer; — **seg ved** rejoice at. **frydefull** joyful, joyous.
frykt fear, dread, fright, alarm, apprehension (for: of, for ens skyld: for); **av** — for at lest, for fear that; **uten** — for følgene fearless of consequences; **jeg nærer ingen** — for at I am under no apprehensions that.
frykte (noe) be apprehensive of, (for ens skyld) be anxious about; fear, dread, apprehend; — **for** fear.
fryktelig fearful, frightful, dreadful, formidable, redoubtable.
fryktinngytende fear-inspiring.
fryktløs fearless. **-het** fearlessness.
fryktsom timid. **fryktsomhet** timidity.
frynse fringe; **besette med -r** fringe.
fryse freeze, congeal; (om person) be cold, feel cold, be chilled, feel chilly; **det frøs sterkt** it froze hard; — **ihjel** be frozen to death. **-inne** be frozen up, ice-bound; **skipet frøs i ne** the ship was frozen in; **han frøs på hendene** his hands were cold; — **til** be frozen up, covered with ice. **-maskin** freezingmachine, freezer, refrigerator.
frysepinne chilly body, shivery body.
frysepunkt freezing point; congealing point.
fryseri cold storage plant, freezing works.

fræg famous: excellent, splendid.
frø (subst) seed; **gå i** — run to seed.
frø seg seed; shed the seed.
frø|handel seed-trade; seed-shop. **-handler** seedsman, seed-merchant.
frøken (om ugift kvinne) (unmarried) lady; (foran ugift kvinnes navn) Miss; (i tiltale uten navn) madam; **en adelig** — a nobleman's daughter; — **Johnsen** Miss Johnson; **Deres** — **datter** your daughter; **min** —! madam! **-ene Johnson** the Miss Johnsons.
frø|korn grain of seed. **-olje** seed-oil.
frå, se fra.
fråde (subst) froth, foam; **-n stod om munnen på ham** he foamed at the mouth. **fråde** (vrb) froth, foam.
fråsse, fråtse gormandize, gorge oneself; (fig) — i revel in. **-r** gormandizer, glutton, huge feeder.
fråsseri, fråtseri gormandizing, gluttony.
fuga fugue.
fuge (subst) groove, joint; **komme ut av sine** -r get out of joint. **fuge** (vrb) groove, joint.
fugl bird, fowl; (fjørfe) fowl, poultry; (skyteskive) popinjay; **en** — i **hånden er bedre enn ti på taket** one bird in hand is worth two in the bush; **jeg har hørt en** — **synge om** I have heard it slily hinted; **hverken** — **eller fisk** neither bird nor fish; neither head nor tail; **la den -en fly** think no more of that.
fugleaktig birdlike.
fugle|berg bird rock, fowling cliff. **-bur** birdcage. **-børse** fowling-piece. **-fanger** bird-catcher, fowler. **-fangst** bird-catching, birding. **i -fluktslinje** as the crow flies. **-frø** bird-seed. **-handel** dealing in birds. bird-seller's shop. **-handler** dealer in birds, bird-fancier, bird-seller; **-konge** wren. **-kvitter** chirping of birds. **-lim** bird-lime. **-nebb** beak (of a bird). **-nett** fowler's net. **-per spektiv** bird's-eye-view. **-rede, -reir** bird's nest. **-sang** song of birds, singing, warbling of birds. **-skitt** bird's dung. **-skremme** scare-crow. **-trekk** passage (of birds). **-unge** young bird, nestling. **-vilt** wild fowl, game birds. **-vær** (bird) rockery, rock or small island where numbers of seabirds breed.
fuks (hest) sorrel horse, chestnut; (på skolen) dunce.
fuksia fuchsia.
fukte moisten, wet.
fuktig moist, damp, humid, dank. **-het** dampness, humidity, (konkret) moisture. **med flekker etter** — (om bok) dampspotted, waterstained. **-hetsmåler** hygrometer.
ful witty, shrewd, sly.
full full (av: of), replete (with); (fullstendig) complete; (beruset) drunk; (om månen) full. **at full; drikke seg** — get drunk; **ha -t opp av** have plenty of, abundance of; **i ordets -e betydning** in every sense; **skrike av** — hals roar; **spille for -t hus** play to crowded houses; **med -e hender** freely; **i -t mål** to the full; **-e navn** name in full; **den -e sannhet** the whole truth; **-e seil** (mar) full sails; **for -e seil** with all sails set; **ta skrittet -t ut** go the whole length; **slå -t slag** (om klokka) strike the hour. **fullt** (adv) fully, quite; — **bemannet** full-manned; — **ferdig** complete; **utsprungen** full-blown; **ikke** — not quite; — **ut** fully, every bit in full; — **og fast** firmly, fully, quite.
full|befaren able (-bodied). **-blodig** full-blooded, plethoric. **-blodighet** plethory, plethora. **-blods** thorough-bred; (fig) **en** — yankee a Yankee of the Yankees. **-blodshest** thorough-bred (horse), blood-horse.
full|byrde accomplish, perform. **-byrdelse** enforcement, performance, accomplishment. **-båren** full-grown.
full|ende complete, finish; **vel begynt er halvt -endt** the beginning is half the battle; well begun is half done. **-ending** completion,

consummation. **-endt** accomplished, consummate, perfect. **-føre** carry through.

full|kommen perfect, complete; (adv) perfectly, to the full, fully. **-kommenhet** perfection.

fullmakt full powers, power of attorney, authority, warrant, proxy.

full|mektig (på kontor) head clerk, first el. leading c.; (befullmektiget) attorney, agent. **-moden** fully ripe. **-myndig** of age. **-måne** full moon. **-proppet** crammed, full-stuffed. **-rigger** full-rigged ship. **-skap** drunkenness, inebriety.

full|stendig complete, full. entire, thorough, utter, out and out; (adv) completely etc. **-stendiggjøre** complete, make complete. **-stendiggjørelse** completeness, fulness. **-takke** thank enough. **-tallig** complete in number; **et — møte** a quorum.

full|tonende full-toned, sonorous. **-tro** trusty. **full|vektig** of the full weight. **-vektighet** full weight. **-voksen** full-grown, of full growth.

fundament foundation, basis.

fundamental fundamental.

fundas charter of foundation.

fund|ere found; (om penger) fund; (gruble) cogitate, muse. **-ering** foundation; (grubling). musing(s), reflection; (fig) **vel -ert** well grounded

fungere act, officiate, hold office, functionate, function.

funke (elektr.) spark.

funk|le sparkle, glitter. **-ling** sparkling.

funksjon duty, function; **i — in** charge.

funksjonær employee, functionary, officer, office-holder, office-bearer. **-er** (personale) staff.

funn finding, discovery; thing found, find.

furasje provender, forage. **furasjere** forage.

fure (vrb) furrow; (i hud) line.

fure (subst) se **får**; (rynke) wrinkle.

furér quartermaster-sergeant.

furet (rynket) wrinkled.

furie fury. **-aktig** fury-like.

furore sensation; **gjøre — be** all the rage.

furt|e sulk, be in the sulks. **-en** sulky. **-ekrok** sulking corner; (om person) sulky person. **-ing** sulking, sulks.

furu fir, Scotch fir; (tresort) pine (-wood), red deal.

furu|bord deal-table; deal-board. **-kongle** pine **-cone. -mo** pine-barren. **-nål** fir-leaf. **-planke** deal-plank. **-skog** forest of firs. **-tre** fir-tree. **-ved** fir-wood.

fus (ivrig) eager, keen.

fusel fusel. **-fri** free from fusel.

fusentast hare-brained fellow, harum-scarum fellow, mad-cap. **-eri** giddiness.

fusk cheating; **fare med — cheat; gjøre —** med tamper with.

fuske cheat; **— i spill** cheat at play; **— med, i** dabble in, bungle at; **— en i handverket** spoil one's trade.

fusker dabbler, bungler, smatterer. **-aktig** bungling, unworkmanlike. **-arbeid** scamped work. **fusk|eri, -ing** se **fusk.**

fustasje cask, barrel.

fut bailiff, sheriff.

futt puff; (fig) spunk; **som det er — i grilly,** spunky.

futte burn el. flash with a puff.

futteral case, cover.

futurisme (moderne kunstretning) futurism.

futurist futurist. **futuristisk** futurist.

futur|um the future (tense). **-isk** future.

fy! fie! **— skam deg!** shame! fie upon you! fie for shame!

fyk drift, flurry, storm.

fyke drift. **-vær** a drift wind.

fylde plenty, abundance; **tidens — the** fullness of time.

fyldest: gjøre — give satisfaction, be satisfactory, up to the mark; **gjøre god — for seg** acquit oneself well; **gjøre — for** serve instead of, replace; **han gjør — for** to he is worth two;

gjøre — for sin lønn earn one's wages. **-gjøre** satisfy, compensate. **-gjørende** satisfactory.

fyldig full, plump; complete, copious; (om vin) of a good body, rich. **-het** plumpness etc.

fylke array, draw up; **— seg om** flock round.

fylke (subst) county, shire; prefecture.

fylkes|mann county sheriff, governor, prefect. **-ting** county parliament.

fylking (battle) array.

I. **fyll** (i mat) stuffing; (til veier) ballast; (stopp) padding; (i mur) packing.

II. **fyll** (drukkenskap) drunkenness; swilling, guzzing; **i -a** in drink, under the influence of drink.

fylle (vrb) fill, replenish; **— en gås** stuff a goose; **fyll deres glass!** charge your glasses; **barnet -r to år i dag** the child completes its second year to-day; **har nylig fylt sitt syttende år** is just entering on her eighteenth year; **— på fat, tønner** put into casks, barrels; **— kull** coal; **skipet måtte — vann der** the ship was obliged to water there; **-r ikke mye** does not take up much room.

fylle (subst), se **fylde.**

fylle|bøtte guzzler, swiller. **-kalk** makeweight; (litt.) padding. **-penn** fountain-pen. **-ri,** se **fyll** II.

fyllest, se **fyldest.**

fyllig, se **fyldig.**

fylling (i dør el. panel) panel.

fynd emphasis, pith; **med — pithily. med —** og **klem** to good purpose, with a will.

fyndig pithy, emphatic. **-het** pithiness. **fynd-ord** laconism, pithy saying.

I. **fyr** (om person) fellow, chap; **en snurrig —** a queer chap, an odd fish.

II. **fyr** (ild) fire; **gi — fire; han er — og flamme** he is all fire and flame; **det tok — i kjolen** the gown caught fire; **sette — på** set on fire.

III. **fyr** (lys for sjøfarende) light.

fyraben time for leaving off working; **holde — leave** off working.

fyrbøter stoker.

fyre fire, heat; (passe en ovn) stoke; (skyte) fire; **fyr! fire!** give fire! **— i ovnen** light the fire, heat the stove; **— opp** fire up.

fyrig fiery, high-spirited, ardent, fervid; (hest) fiery, high-mettled.

fyrighet fire, ardour, fervour.

fyring firing, stoking.

fyrrom stoke-hole, stoke-hold.

fyrskip light-ship, light-vessel.

fyrste prince. **-hus** princely el. royal house. **-lig** princely; (adv) in a princely manner. **-(n)dømme** principality. **-slekt** race of princes.

fyrstikk match. **-eske** match-box. **-fabrikk** match-factory.

fyrstinne princess.

fyr|stål fire-steel. **-tøy** tinder-box. **-tårn** light-house.

fyrverker pyrotechnist, fire-worker. **-i** (display of) fireworks.

fyr|vesen lighthouse system. **-vokter** light -keeper.

fysiker natural el. physical philosopher. physicist.

fysikk physics, natural philosophy.

fysikus head physician.

fysiognomi physiognomy, countenance.

fysio|log physiologist. **-logi,** physiology. **-logisk** physiological.

fysisk physical; **i — henseende** physically.

fæl disgusting, hideous, ghastly, grim, horrid, forbidding. **fælt** (adv) disgustingly etc.

fælen apprehensive, frightened, afraid.

færing (båt) four-oar boat, four-oar.

færre, færrest, se **få.**

Færøy|ene the Faroe Islands. **-ing** Faroe Islander, Faroese.

fø (nære) feed.

føde (næring) food, aliment; (dyrs) feed; **ta — til seg** take food.

føde (vrb) (bringe til verden) bear, bring forth, give birth to. **født** born; **han er — englender** he is a native of England, he is an Englishman born el. by birth; **en — taler** a born orator, an orator born; **han er — i London** he was born in London; **fru A. — B.** Mrs. A. late Miss B. **føde|by** native town. **-bygd** native parish. **-land** native country, birth-country. **-middel** article of food.

føderåd allowance, pension, paid to a peasant by his heirs after the cession of his estate. **ta —** become a pensioner. **-s|kone, -mann** pensioner upon one's own estate. **-stue** room el. house where the pensioner lives.

føde|sted native place, birthplace. **-varer** provisions, victuals.

fødsel (nedkomst) delivery; (byrd) birth, nativity; **ved, etter -en** at, after birth; **av —** by birth; **norsk av —** a native of Norway. **fødsels|attest** certificate of birth. **-dag** birthday, natal day. **-dagsbarnet** the hero of the day **-dagsgave** birthday present. **-hjelp** obstetric aid; se **-vitenskap. -hjelp** midwifery, obstetric aid. **-smerter** pains, throes of childbirth, birth-throes. **-stiftelse** lying-in hospital el. institution. **-tang** forceps, extractor. **-tid** time of birth, of delivery. **-veer,** se **-smerter. -vitenskap** midwifery, obstetrics, obstetric medicine. **-år** year of (one's) birth.

født se under **føde.**

føflekk mole, mother-spot, birth mark.

følbar tangible, perceptible.

føle feel; **— dypt** be keenly alive to; **han vil nok komme til å —** det he will smart for it; **jeg har fått — I** know to my cost; **den som ikke vil høre, må —** he who will not hear advice must suffer; **det er hardt å — på** it feels hard; **til å ta og — på** palpable; **— en på tennene** sound one; **— seg** have a high opinion of oneself; **— seg fornærmet** feel injured; **— seg forpliktet** feel bound; **— seg som et ganske annet menneske** feel quite another person; **— seg for** el. fram feel one's way el. ground. **føle|horn** feelers, antennæ. **-hår** feelers, tentacles.

følelig (især: ikke ubetydelig) perceptible, severe (f. eks. blow, loss).

følelse feeling, sensibility; (fornemmelse) sensation; (sinnsbevegelse) emotion; (i uttrykket) expression, pathos; (bare om sansen) touch; **fin — sensibility; uvilkårlig — instinct; med —** ogs.: feelingly; **det har en på —** that is a matter of instinct; **jeg har en — som om I** feel as if; **jeg hadde en sterk — av** at the feeling was strong upon me that. **følelses|liv** emotional nature. **-løs** unfeeling, insensible, apathetic, callous. **-løshet** insensibility, apathy. **-menneske** susceptible, impulsive man (el. woman), emotional man (woman). **-sak** matter of sentiment. **-utbrudd** outburst of feeling.

føle|nerve sensory nerve. **-ri** sentimentality. **-sans** sense of touch. **-tråd** feeler, tentacle.

følge follow, succeed, ensue; (ledsage) attend, accompany; (med øynene) watch; (etterspore) trace; **— en politikk** pursue a policy; **— sine tilbøyeligheter** indulge one's inclination; **— en til døren** see one out; **— sitt eget hode** have one's own way; **— en hjem** see, bring el. attend one home; **— lik** attend a funeral; **følg mitt råd!** take my advice! **han svarte som -r** he answered as follows, to the following effect; **det -r av seg selv** that's a matter of course, that goes without the saying; **herav -r** hence it follows; **— etter** (som etterfølger) succeed; **— med** (fig) follow, keep pace (with); **— med tiden** keep abreast of the times, move el. go with the times; **du må ta hva som -r med** you must take the consequences; **-s at** go together, (fig) run el. go tog·ther; **-s med** go along with.

I. **følge** (subst) (rekkefølge) succession; (resul-

tat) result, consequence; **har til — at** leads to the consequence that, results in; **det kan ha viktige -r** it may be attended with important consequences; **som — av** consequent to; **som — herav** in consequence, consequently.

II. **følge** (selskap) company; (de ledsagende) retinue, suite, train, attendance, followers; **i — med** in the company of; **slå — join** company. **-blad** accompanying paper. **-brev** accompanying el. covering letter; (i postv.) despatch note.

følgelig consequently, in consequence.

følgende the following; **— ord** the following words; **— er en fortegnelse over** the following is a list of; **i det —** in the sequel; **på hverandre — successive; det derav —** tap the loss made in consequence.

følge|rekke succession. **-riktig** consistent. **-riktighet** consistency; **mangel på —** inconsistency. **følge|seddel** accompanying note; (tollv.) shipping note. **-setning** consequent. **-skap,** se **følge. -svenn** follower, attendant, companion. **-verdig** worthy of imitation el. of being followed up.

følgje (subst og vrb) se **følge.**

føling touch; **ha — med** be in touch with.

føljetong (roman som kommer i bruddstykker) serial, feuilleton.

føll foal; (især hingst-) colt; (hoppe-) filly.

følle foal.

føllhoppe brood mare.

følsom (med fin følelse) feeling, emotional, sensitive; (meget —) sentimental. **-het** feeling, sensibility, sensitiveness; sentimentality.

føn, -vind fœhn, very dry thaw-wind.

før (korpulent) stout.

før (prep) before, prior to, previous to; (adv) before, previously, formerly; (konj) before, ere; (hellere) rather; **— vil jeg sulte I** will rather starve el. I will starve first; **jo — jo heller** the sooner the better; **— eller senere** sooner or later; **han bodde her —** he used to live here; **ikke — no** sooner; not until then; **ikke — så no** sooner . . . . than; **forskjellige fra —** different from what they used to be.

føre (adv) before. **bedre — var enn etter snar** fast bind fast find.

føre (vrb) carry, convey; (lede) guide, conduct, lead; (anføre) command, lead; (en vare) keep; (bøker) keep; **kjøreturen førte oss gjennom en skog** our drive took us through a wood; **— et fartøy** command a vessel; **— kården** wield the sword; **— korrespondansen** carry on the correspondence; **— krig** make war, wage war; **— et gudfryktig liv** lead a pious life; **— et navn** bear a name; **— ordet** speak, be the spokesman; **— det store ord** lay down the law; **— pennen** wield the pen; **— prosess** carry on a lawsuit; **— regnskap** keep accounts; **— en sak** conduct a case; **det spiller han -r** the language he uses; **— et skip** command el. sail a ship; **— usømmelig tale** use indecent language; **— talen hen på** turn the talk upon; **— en vare** deal in an article, keep an a. on sale; **— vitner** produce el. call witnesses; **— våpen** carry arms; **— an** lead the way; **— fram for** en usher into one's presence; **-r bort til** leads to, takes you to; **— i pennen** pen; **hva han -r i sitt skjold** what his intentions are; **— inn** introduce; (i regnskap) enter; **— med seg** bring along with one, (være ledsaget av) be attended with; (fig) render it necessary; **førte oss omkring på eiendommen** walked us over the estate; **førte oss omkring i kirken** took us through the church; **— opp** (i dans) lead the dance; **— opp som inntekt, utgift** place to the account of income, expenditure; **— sammen** bring together; **— til** lead to, result in; **— ut i livet** realize, bring into concrete existence; **— vill** lead astray; **— seg** carry oneself, bear oneself; **måte å — seg på** carriage, deportment.

føre (subst) (state of) the roads, wheeling; **i godt — when** the roads are in good condition; **det er dårlig — it** is bad walking, the roads are

in a bad state; the roads are heavy; **det er vått, sølet** — it is wet, dirty under foot. **-forhold** conditions under foot and wheel.
førelse guidance, conduct, direction, management; (Guds) dispensation.
førende leading.
førenn (konj) before, ere.
fører (veiviser) guide; (av skip) master, commander; (partifører) leader.
førerskap command, leadership.
førhet stoutness, corpulence.
forhistorisk pre-historic.
føring (abstr), se **førsel**; (lass, last) cargo, freight, load. **førings|båt** barge, cargo-boat. **-mann** barge-man.
forlaten stoutish, stout. **-het** stoutness. **førlig** stoutish; (rask) able-bodied, sound. **førlighet** health, vigour.
før-norsk pre-Norse.
før|nåtid (gram) the perfect (tense). **-omtalt** before mentioned.
førr, se **førti**.
førsel transport, conveyance, carriage.
først (adv) first; (i førstningen) at first; **gå** — lead the way; — **på vinteren** at the commencement of winter; — **i mai** early in May; (ikke før) not before May; **han kom** — **for en halv time siden** he came only el. but half an hour ago; — **nå** but now; — **da** (adv) not till then, (konj) only when; **når** — (when) once; — **nylig** but recently; **de skal** — **ha bryllup om et halvt år** they are not to be married for six months yet; **fra** — **av** from the first, at first, in the first case el. instance, originally, from the beginning, at (el. from) the outset; **fra** — **til sist** from first to last.
først (ordenstall, nummer) first; **-e mosebok** Genesis; **den — e den beste** the first that offers, any one; **for det -e** in the first place, first, firstly, to begin with, for one thing; **ikke for det -e** not yet awhile; **med det -e** as soon as possible, at an early day, shortly; **noe av det -e han sa** one of the first things he said; **noe av det -e de gjorde** one of their earliest acts; **av -e sort** first-rate; dt. tiptop; **en -e klasses passasjer** a first-class (passenger); **ved -e leilighet** at the first opportunity; **ett av de -e nummer** an early number; **en av de -e dager** at an early day; **i de -e dager av august** in the early days of August; **-e juledag** Christmas day; **-e påskedag** Easter Sunday; **-e pinsedag** Whitsunday; **-e, andre, tredje gang** (ved auksjon) going, going, gone.
første|forestilling first performance (of a play), first night. **-fødselsrett** (right of) primogeniture. **-født** first-born. **-grøde** first fruits. **-hjelp** first aid. **-hånds** first-hand, original. **-kammer** upper house. **-lærer** head teacher. **-mann** the first man. **-rangs** first class. **-styrmann** first mate, chief officer.
førstkommende next, ensuing; **den 3dje** — on the 3rd prox(imo). **førstning: i -en** at first, **først-nevnte** the first mentioned el. named, (av to) the former.
førti forty; **i -ene** in the forties.
førti|ende fortieth. **-årig** forty years old. **-årsalderen** the age of forty.
føy!, se **fy!**

føye: falle til — yield, submit; **med full** — with reason.
føye (rette seg etter) indulge, please, humour; (passe) adapt, fit, suit; (ordne) ordain, dispose; — **sammen** join, connect, unite, put together; — **sine ord** turn one's words; — **til** add; — **seg etter** conform to, accommodate oneself to, humour, comply with.
føyelig indulgent, compliant, complying, accommodating. **føyelighet** pliancy, complaisance.
føyke drift, shower.
føyse (vrb) (feie, jage vekk) brush, hurry. — **på dør** turn out, kick downstairs.
få (vrb) get; receive; obtain, gain; acquire, have; **få en sykdom** catch an illness; **fåes hos alle bokhandlere og i utsalgene på jernbanen** to be had (el. obtained) of all booksellers and at the railway' bookstalls; **du skal aldri** — **fatt på mine nøkler** you shall never get at my keys; **la oss** — **litt frokost** let us have some breakfast; **jeg fikk et brev** I had a letter; — **unger** bring forth, produce young; — **lønn som forskyldt** be rightly served; — **godhet, avsky for** take a liking, an aversion to; — **lyst til** take a fancy to; **jeg har -tt frakken min reparert** I have had my coat mended; **når jeg -r lest boka** when I shall have read the book; **jeg -r vel gjøre det** I suppose I shall have to do it; **det -r være som det vil** be that as it may; **vi -r se** we shall see; **du -r bli hjemme** you must stay at home; — **vite el. høre noe** hear, learn st., be informed of st.; **han kunne slett ikke** — **den tanken ut av hodet** he never could get it out of his head; — **en fra noe** turn one's mind from st.; — **fram et ord** utter a word, get in a word; — **igjen** recover, regain; (småpenger) receive (in) change; **fikk ham med** made him come, brought him; — **en til å gjøre noe** make one do st., get one to do st.; — **til å le** set one laughing, make one laugh; **så vidt jeg kunne** — **ut av ham** as far as I could obtain it from him; **jeg kan ikke** — **noe ut av det** I can make nothing of it; — **hverandre** marry; **du skal** — **!** won't you catch it! — **imot en** conceive a dislike to, take a prejudice against; — **på** (om tøy) get on.
få (motsatt: mange) few; **færre** fewer; **færrest** fewest; **noen** — (motsatt ingen) a few; **ikke** — not a few; **bare** — few, only a few; **noen** — **trofaste** a faithful few; **noen** — **utvalgte** a select el. chosen few; **noen ganske** — a very few; — **eller ingen** few, if any; **med** — **ord** in a few words, briefly.
fåfengt futile, ineffectual, vein.
fåmannsvelde oligarchy.
fåmælt of few words, reticent, silent. **-het** reticence, natural silentness, taciturnity.
få|nytte futility, uselessness. **til** — **-s** to small purpose. **-nyttig** futile, useless.
får, se **sau**; sheep; **fåre|hue** (skjellsord) blockhead, ninny. **-hund** collie, shepherd's dog. **-kjøtt** mutton. **-klær:** ulv i **-klær** wolf in sheep's clothing. **-kotelett** mutton chop. **-lår** leg of mutton. **-skinn** sheepskin; (til bokbind) roan. **-stek** roast mutton. **-syke** rot.
fåtall minority, few. **fåtallig** few in numbers.
fåtallighet fewness.
fåvett folly, unwisdom. **-ig** foolish, unwise.

G

G, g G, g.
gaffel fork; (mar) (til seil) gaff; (ellers) crotch. **-bit** snack. **-deling** bifurcation. **-delt** crotched, forked. **-fokk** fore-trysail. **-formet** forked, furcate(d). **-seil** gaff-sail; trysail.
gafle fork. — **i seg** fork up.

gagn benefit, good, gain, advantage, profit; **være til** — **for** en benefit one, be of b. to one; **ha** — **av** benefit el. be benefited by; **gjøre** — work, make oneself useful; **gjør** — **for** to is worth two.
gagne benefit, advantage, be of advantage to.

gagnlig beneficial, advantageous, serviceable, useful; **inngyte dem en — skrekk** strike a wholesome terror into them. **gagnlighet** serviceableness, profitableness, usefulness, advantage. **gagn|tre, –tømmer** timber.

gal mad, rabid; (sint) mad, wild, frantic; (feil) wrong, improper; **en — mann** a lunatic; **en — hund** a mad el. rabid dog; **så –t har man sett for** such things have been; **bli — go** mad; (sint) fly into a passion; **ingenting er så –t at det ikke er godt for noe** it is an ill wind that blows nobody good; **når –t skal være** if the worst happens; **være — etter** be foolishly fond of, be mad after el. about; **hva –t er det i det** where is the harm; **det er til å bli — over** it's enough to drive one mad; **— på en** angry with one. **galt** (adv) wrong; **komme –t avsted** get into a scrape; **om all ting gikk –t** even if the worst came to the worst; **det hadde nær gått ham —** he had a narrow escape.

galant polite, complimentary; (bare mot damer) gallant. **–eri** politeness, gallantry.

galanteri|handel fancy-shop. **–handler** fancystationer, dealer in fancy articles. **–varer** fancy articles, trinkets.

I. **galder** (hestesykdom) wind-gall.

II. **galder** (trolldom) enchantments, incantations, spells.

galdre practise enchantments etc.

gale crow.

galeas schooner.

galehus lunatic asylum.

galei galley; **hva ville han på den —** what was he doing in that galley? **gå på –en** lead a wild life, go on the spree. **–slave** galley slave.

galen, se **gal. galenskap,** se **galskap.**

galfrans madcap, jackanapes.

galge gallows, gibbet. **galgen|–frist** a short respite. **–fugl** gallows-bird, hangdog, Newgatebird. **–humor** scaffold mirth.

galimatias gibberish, nonsense.

galing crowing.

Galisi|a Galicia. **g–er, g–sk** Galician.

galla state. **–drakt** court dress; full dress, evening dress. **–forestilling** gala-representation. **–kårde** dress-sword. **–uniform** dress uniform. **–vogn** state-carriage.

galle gall, bile; (fig) **få ens — til å løpe over** stir one's bile; **utløse sin — vent** one's spleen, pour out one's bile. **galle|blære** gall-bladder. **–feber** bilious fever. **galleple** gall (-nut).

galler Gaul.

galleri (plass i teater; malerisamling) gallery; **spille for –et** play to the gallery.

galle|stein gallstone. **–syk** bilious. **–syke** bilious complaint, biliousness.

Gallia Gaul.

gallion head of a ship. **gallionsfigur** figure head, figure on the head.

gallisisme gallicism.

gallisk Gallic.

gallveps gall-fly, gall-insect.

galmanns|snakk galimatias, nonsense. **–verk** act of a madman.

galneheie tomboy, hoyden.

galning madman, madcap.

galon lace. **–ert** laced.

galopp (kort g) canter; (full —; også dans) gallop; **i —** at el. in a canter; **i full —** at full gallop; **ride i kort —** canter.

galoppade gallopade.

galoppere gallop. **–nde tæring** galloping consumption; acute phthisis.

galskap madness, frenzy; (gal strek) mad prank.

galt (foreldet og poet. om råne) boar; (gjeldt råne) hog.

galva|nisere galvanize. **–nisering** galvanization. **–nisk** galvanic. **–nisme** galvanism. **–nometer**

galvanometer. **–noplastikk** galvanoplastics. **–noplastisk** galvanoplastic.

gamasjer gaiters; (lange) leggings.

gamla (fam. tiltale) gammer, old woman, (omtale) the old woman.

gamleheim old age home, old people's home. **gamlen** (fam. tiltale) old man, (omtale) the old man.

gamling old man, old fellow.

gammal, se **gammel.**

gamme (finne-) (Lapp) dug-out, turf-hut.

gammel old; (fra gamle tider) ancient; (fra oldtiden, gammeldags) antique; (som har bestått lenge) long established, of long standing; (av alder) aged; (motsatt frisk, om brød, øl o. l.) stale; **— tobakksrøyk** stale tobacco smoke; **–t bly,** etc. broken lead etc.; **40 år — forty** years of age, aged forty; **fra — tid** from time immemorial; **de gamle** the old ones, (om oldtidens folk) the ancients; **hvor — er han?** what age is he? **la alt bli ved det gamle** let all be as it was; **henge ved det gamle** cleave to the old (the old order of things); **ved det gamle** as usual; **han ble den gamle** he remained just the man he was; **på sine gamle dager** in his old age; **i gamle dager** in olden time, of old, in old times; **— jomfru** old maid, spinster.

gammel|aktig elderly, oldish. **–dags** old-fashioned, antiquated, old-world; (adv) in an old-fashioned manner el. style.

gammel|kjent old familiar. **–klok** precocious, **–manns** of old age, senile. **–norsk** old Norwegian, (old) Norse. **–ost** old-milk cheese.

gammen (gmlt. og poet.) mirth, merriment; **leve i fryd og —** have a merry life of it.

gamp (work-) horse.

gan (p. fisk) throat and gills; ogs. offal of fish.

gand (finnetrolld.) Lapp enchantments, spells. **legge — for** lay under a spell. **–finn** Lapp enchanter.

gane (vrb) (fisk), gut, (amr) gib. **–jente** girl employed in gutting. **–kniv** knife used for gutting.

gane (subst) palate, roof of the mouth.

gane|lyd palatal sound. **–seilet** the soft palate.

gang walk; (måte å gå på) gait; (tidens g.) course; (kronometers) rate; (sykdommens) process; (i park eller hage) alley; walk; (i hus) corridor, passage; (større) hall; (gjentagelse) time; **i — in** motion, in operation, going; **sette i — set** a going, set on foot, put in train, (dmp) start; **sett maskinen i —! set** on! **holde noe i — keep** st. going; **jeg kjenner ham på –en** I know him by his step; **er godt i — med å** is in a fair way to; **i full — in** full activity; **komme riktig i — get** into working order; **ha sin — i et hus** have the run of a house; **tiden gikk sin — time** rolled on; **la det gå sin — let** the matter take its course, let things take their own course; **gå all kjødets — go** the way of all flesh; **så er verdens — that** is the way of the world; **en — once; en — ingen — once** does not make a habit, once is no custom; **en av –en twice** el. twice; **jeg lot meg det ikke si to –er** I needed no second invitation el. bidding; **tre –er three** times, thrice; **3 –er 2 er 6** three times two are six; **en — for alle** for good and all, once for all, definitely; **en annen — another** time; (i framtida) some other time; **en og annen — occasionally,** once in a time; **på en — at** once; together; **for en –s skyld** for once (and away); **en — til** once more; **— på — over** and over again; **denne ene — this** once; **den ene — that** once; for **denne — for** this once; **ikke en eneste — never** once.

gang|art pace. **–bar** current, marketable. **–barhet** currency. **–brett** plank (across a ditch).

ganger (gmlt. og poet.) steed.

Ganges the Ganges.

gang|før able to walk. **-klær** wearing apparel, clothing. **-kone** charwoman, laundress. **-kurv** go-cart.

ganglie ganglion.

gangspill (mar) capstan.

gang|sti foot-path, walking-path. **-syn** eyesight enough to walk by oneself.

ganske (adv = aldeles) quite, entirely, wholly; (temmelig) fairly, pretty; **jeg er — enig med ham** I quite agree with him; **— annerledes** far otherwise; **noe — annet** something quite different; **— visst** certainly, to be sure.

I. **gap** mouth, throat (of an animal); (åpning) gap, opening, chasm; **døra står på vidt —** the door is wide open.

II. **gap** (om person) fool; flippant person, chatterbox.

gape gape; (gjespe) yawn. **-nde sår** yawning wound.

gapestokk pillory; **sette i -en** pillory.

gap|et chatty, babbling. **-ing** gaping, yawning. **-ord** flippancy. **-skratte** laugh uproariously, roar with laughter.

garant guarantor, security.

garantere guarantee, warrant.

garanti guarantee, guaranty, security. **-fond** guarantee fund.

garasje garage, automobile stable.

gard, se **gjerde** og **gård.**

garde guards, guard. **-husar** hussar in the horse-guards. **-kaserne** barracks of the guards. **-officer, -offiser** officer of the guards, guardsman.

gardere guard, protect.

garderobe wardrobe; (værelse) cloak-room, crush-room, wardrobe.

gardgutt heir to a farm.

gardin curtain. **-holder** curtain-rest. **-kappe** valance. **-preken** curtain-lecture. **-snor** curtain-string. **-stang** curtain-rod. **-stokk** roller.

gardist guardsman.

gardjente heiress to a farm.

gardstaur fence-picket, hedge-stake.

garn yarn, thread, cotton;. (fiskeg.) net; **fange en i sitt —** entangle one in one's toils, meshes; **han er blitt fanget i sitt eget —** the biter has been bit; **legge sine — ut etter** lay one's toils for, be angling for. **-binding** netting. **-bruk** se **-fiske.**

garner|e trim. **-ing** trimming; flounce, ruffle.

garn|fiske (gill-) net fishing.

garn|handel trade in yarn, twist etc. **-handler** haberdasher. **-hespel** hasp, hank, skein.

garnison garrison. **-ere** be garrisoned, be quartered (in, at).

garn|lenke, se **-setning.**

garn|nøste ball of yarn. **-setning** shooting of nets; (konkr.) shot. **-sild** net herring. **-vase** tangle of nets. **-vinde** reel.

garp (skrytende person) boaster, braggart; (hist) Hanseatic merchant at Bergen in Norway.

gartner gardener, nursery-man. **-gutt** gardener's prentice. **-i** gardening; (konkr) garden(s), nursery garden el. grounds.

garve (huder) tan; (skinn) dress; (stål) tilt; **— bark tan**

garver tanner. **-gård** tan-yard.

garver|håndverk tanner's trade. **-i** tannery.

garve|stoff tannin. **-syre** tannic acid. **garving** tanning.

gas (slags stoff) gauze.

gaselle gazelle.

gasje salary, pay, wages, stipend. **-liste** pay-bill, pay-roll. **gasjere** pay.

gasometer, se **gassmåler.**

gass gas; **-en var tent** the gases were lit. **-angrep** gas attack. **-apparat** gas-cooking-apparatus. **-arbeider** gas-fitter. **-arm** bracket. **-artet** gaseous. **-beholder** gas-holder. **-belysning** gas-light, lighting with gas. **-besparende** gas-saving. **-bluss** gaslight, gas-jet. **-brenner** (gas)burner.

gasse gander.

gasse seg feast, regale (on).

gass|flamme, se **-bluss. -forbruk** consumption of gas. **-innlegg** fitting of gas. **-ledning** gas-delivering pipe, main-pipe. **-lukt** smell of gas. **-lykt, -løkt** gas-lamp. **-lys** gaslight. **-maske** gas mask. **-måler** gas-meter, gasometer. **-olje** gas-oil. **-ovn** gas-furnace, gas-stove. **-regulering** (i bil) throttle. **-rør** gas-pipe. **-spill** waste of g. **-verk** gas-works.

gast (mar) man, hand, jack.

gastrisk gastric; **-feber** enteric fever.

gastro|nom gastronome, gastronomer, gastronomist. **-nomi** gastronomy. **-nomisk** gastronomic(al).

gat|e street; **på -a** in the street; **gå omkring i -ene** walk about the streets; **(fig) gå over i en annen -e** alter one's tactics; **fortsette i samme -e** hold on; **vindu til -a** front window, **værelse til -a** front-parlour, front-room.

gate|dør street-door. **-dørsnøkkel** latch-key. **-feier** street-sweeper, scavenger. **-feining** sweeping of the streets. **-gutt** street-boy, (street) Arab; (amr) guttersnipe. **-guttstrek** blackguardism. **-legeme** roadway. **-lykt, -løkt** street lamp. **-opptøyer** street-riot. **-pike** street wench. **-predikant** street-preacher, ranter. **-renovasjon** street cleaning, scavenging. **-sanger** street-singer, ballad-singer. **-selger, -sellerske** coster-monger, coster, street-seller. **-slusk** street lounger, gentleman of the pavement. **-språk** street slang, street parlance. **-stein** paving stone. **-vise** street ballad.

gatt (zool) anus; (mar) hole. **-finne** anal fin.

gauk cuckoo; (som driver ulovlig brennevinshandel) unlicensed liquor dealer, whistler; (amr) dive-keeper.

gauk|e sell liquor on the sly, whistle. **-esjapp** speak-easy. **-esyre** cuckoo's meat. **-ing** sly-grog selling, whistling.

gaul howl. **gaule** howl, caterwaul.

gaupe lynx.

gautjuv knave, sharper.

gave gift, donation, endowment; (foræring) present; (naturg.) endowment, turn, talent. genius, gift, parts. **-brev** deed of gift.

gavl gable(-end).

gavmild liberal, munificent, bounteous, bountiful, free-handed, open-handed. **-het** munificence, bountifulness, bounteousness.

gavott gavot.

geberde gesture; **geberde seg** behave, carry on.

gebet territory; (fig) domain.

gebiss set of (artificial) teeth.

gebrokken broken; **på -t norsk** in broken Norwegian; **tale -t norsk** speak in broken Norwegian.

geburtsdag, se **fødselsdag.**

gebyr fee.

gedigen (sølv osv.) native; (fig) genuine, pure, sterling.

gehalt content; alloy; (fig) worth, value.

geheimeråd privy council, privy councillor.

geheng sword-belt.

gehør ear; **spille etter —** play by (the) ear. **finne — hos** gain one's ear; **skaffe seg —** make one's voice heard.

geil (subst), se **gjel.**

geil ruttish; (om mennesker) lascivious.

geip grimace, mouth; pout, pouting lips. **-e make** a face, pull a face. **— stygt** pull a horrible grimace.

geistlig clerical, ecclesiastical; **den -e stand** the clerical order; **en — a** clergyman, divine. **geistlighet** clergy.

geit goat; (she-)goat, nanny-goat.

geitebukk he-goat, billy-goat.

geitehams wasp, hornet.

geite|melk — mjølk goat's milk. **-ragg** goat's hair. **-rams** (bot.) willow-herb.

geitost cheese made of goat's milk.

gelati elatine.

gelé jelly, glaze; **1** — jellied. **-aktig** jellied; **bli** — jelly.

geled rank; (i dybden) file.

gelender balusters, banisters, railing; (trappe-gelender) balustrade of a staircase, stair rail.

gemakk apartment.

gemal, -inne consort, spouse.

gemen low, mean, vile; gross, dirty; **-het** vulgarity, meanness; **-heter** dirty language.

gemme (edelsten) (cut) gem; (opphøydd) cameo.

gemse chamois. **-jakt** chamois-hunting. **-jeger** chamois-hunter.

gemytt temper, disposition, mind. **gemyttlig** (hyggelig) snug, pleasant; comfortable; (hjertelig) hearty, genial, open-hearted. **gemyttlighet** geniality, pleasantness; jollity.

gendarm gendarme, armed policeman, constable.

gene restraint, inconvenience, nuisance.

genea|log genealogist. **-logi** genealogy. **-logisk** genealogical.

general general. **-adjutant** adjutant-general. **-agent** chief agent. **-agentur** general agency. **-auditør** auditor-general. **-bass** thorough-bass. **-feltmarskalk** field-marshal general. **-felttøymester** master general of ordnance. **-forsamling** general assembly, general meeting. **-fullmakt** general power of attorney. **-guvernør** governor-general. **-inne** general's lady; **fru -inne** N. Mrs. General N. **-intendant** commissary-general. **generalisere** generalize.

generalisering generalization.

general|issimus generalissimo, commander in chief. **-konsul** consul general. **-løytnant** lieutenant general. **-major** major general. **-prøve** dress rehearsal. **-sekretær** secretary-general. **-stab** the (general, general's) staff. **-stabskart** ordnance map. **-statene** (i Holland) the States General.

generasjon generation.

generator generator.

generell general.

generisk generic.

Genf Geneva; **konferansen i** — the conference of Genéva. **genfer** Genevan. **-sjøen** the Lake of Geneva, Lake Leman.

geni genius.

genial ingenious.

genialitet genius, ingeniousness, ingenuity.

genistrek stroke of genius.

genitiv the genitive (case).

genius genius (flertall: genii), guardian angel.

genre style, manner. **-maler** painter of genre. **-maleri** genre (picture), painting of incident.

genser Guernsey shirt, Guernsey.

gentil genteel.

gentleman (fin mann) gentleman.

Genu|a Genoa. **g-eser, g-esisk** Genoese.

geo|graf geographer. **-grafi** geography. **-grafisk** geographical.

geo|log geologist. **-logi** geology. **-logisk** geological.

geo|metri geometry. **-metrisk** geometrical.

Georg George.

georgine dahlia.

geranium geranium.

geriljakorps guerilla band, guerilla party.

geriljakrig guerilla.

german|er Teuton, (ancient) German. **-isere** Germanize. **-isme** Germanism. **-ist** Germanist.

germansk Teutonic, Germanic.

gesandt ambassador, minister, envoy.

gesandtskap embassy, legation.

gesims cornice.

geskjeftig meddlesome, meddling; **en — person** a busy-body. **-het** meddlesomeness.

gestikuler|e gesticulate. **-ing** gesticulation.

gestus gesture.

getto (jødekvarter) ghetto.

gevant raiment, drapery.

gevekst excrescence.

gevinst profit, gains; (i lotteri) prize; (i spill) winnings; — **og tap** profit and loss; **komme ut med** — come up a prize.

gevir horns, head (of a deer).

gevær musket, gun; **vakt i** —! turn out the guard! **rope i** — call to arms; **strekke** — lay down one's arms. **-fabrikk** small-arms factory. **-ild** musketry. **-kolbe** butt-end of a musket el. gun. **-kule** bullet. **-løp** gun- el. musket-barrel. **-salve** volley of musketry.

ghetto, se getto.

gi give; (yte) yield, produce; (betale) pay;(kort) deal (cards); — **galt** make a misdeal; **det er Dem som skal** — it is your deal; **Gud** — God grant, would to God; **jeg skal** — **ham** (truende) I'll give it him, have it out of him el. with him; — **et eksempel** set an example; — **en hånden** shake hands with one; **-en forestilling** act a play; **jeg -r Dem rett** I grant you are right; — **av seg** yield,produce; — **etter** give way, yield; **han -r ingen etter i lærdom** he is inferior to none in learning; — **en et arbeid** set one a task; — **en lekse** give one a lesson; **jeg -r ikke meget for den slags** I don't much value that kind of thing; — **fra seg** give up, surrender; — **igjen** give back, return; — **penger igjen** give one change; **jeg kan ikke** — **igjen** I have no change; — **en noe inn** give one physic; — **en noe med** give one something to take along with him el. on departure; — **om** (kort) deal over again; **der ble -tt om** there was a fresh deal; — **ballen opp** (i fotball) kick off; — **til kjenne** make known; — **tilbake, se igjen**; — **ut** lay out, expend, utter; — **ut for** give out el. pass off for; **det -r seg av seg selv** that is a matter of course; — **seg give up el. in**; (få en revir) give way; (gå over) wear off; — **seg av med** meddle with, have to do with; — **seg tid** take time; — **seg av smerte** groan with pain; — **seg Gud i vold** commend oneself to God; — **seg til** take to, betake oneself to, give oneself up to; — **seg til å gråte** fall a-crying; — **seg ut for** pass oneself off for, give oneself out for, personate; **det gis** there is, there are.

gibbe (bomme, skifte bommen fra den ene side til den andre) gybe.

gid (interjeksjon) would; I wish; o, that; — **han var her would el. o**, that he were here! — **pokker tok ham!** confound him!

gide have a mind to, feel inclined to; **jeg -r ikke** I will not, won't, I do not choose to, cannot be bothered to; **jeg gad vite** I should like to know, I wonder.

gift (adj) married (med: to).

gift (subst) poison, venom; **spy** — (fig) vent one's venom el. rage; (sl) **det kan du ta** — **på** I promise you, you may take your oath on it; (amr) you bet. **-blander, -blanderske** poisoner. **-blanderi** po!soning.

gifte marry, wed; — **bort** give away in marriage; **bli gift** marry, be married (med: to); — **seg med en** marry one; — **seg igjen** remarry; — **seg til penger** get money by one's marriage, marry a fortune.

gifteferdig marriageable.

giftekniv match-maker, marriage-maker.

giftermål marriage.

gifte|syk anxious to be married. **-tanker: gå i** — be absent, be in the clouds.

gift|fri non-venomous. **-gass** poison-gas.

giftig (inneholdende gift) poisonous, venomous; (fig) venomous, virulent. **-het** poisonousness, venomousness, virulence.

giftkjertel poison-gland. **-tann** falx (pl. falces), poison-fang.

gigant giant. **-isk** gigantic.

gigg (både om kjøretøy og båt) gig.

gikt rheumatism; gout. **-anfall** attack of (the) gout. **-brudden** gouty. **-feber** rheumatic fever. **-smørelse** rheumatic liniment.

giktsvak affected with rheumatism.

gild bully, capital, excellent, prime, rattling, topping; (om farger) gaudy; **det skulle være -t** would be a topping thing.

gilde feast, banquet, merry-making; (laug) guild; **han kommer til å betale -t** he will have to pay the piper. **-sal** banquet hall. **-skrå** (hist) guild statutes.

gildre (subst) trap (for beasts).

gildre (vrb) set a trap.

giljotin guillotine. **-ere** guillotine.

gips gypsum; (brent) plaster. **-avstøpning** plaster-cast, gypsoplast.

gipse overlay with plaster, plaster.

gips|er plasterer. **-figur** plaster-figure. **-maske** plaster-cast. **-mel** powdered gypsum.

gir (på sykkel og bil) gear; **høyt — high** gear; **lavt — low gear.

giraff, se **sjiraff.**

girant (bankspr.) endorser.

gire (gi et visst gir) gear.

girere endorse.

girkasse gear-box, også: transmission mechanism.

girlander garland, festoon.

giro (bankspr.) endorsement. **girobank** circulation-bank, bank of deposit.

gisp gasp. **gispe** gasp. **gisping** gasping.

gis|se (gjette) guess; (bedømme avstand fra land) reckon. **-t bredde** latitude by account. **-ning** guessing; (konkret) guess, conjecture.

gissel hostage.

gissen, gisten opened, broken out into chinks. (om båt, balje o. l.) leaky; (om skog) sparse, thin.

gitar guitar.

gitter railing; grate; trellis, lattice; (i radio) grid. **-dør** grated door. **-port** trellised gate, iron gate. **-verk** lattice el. trellis work. **-vindu** lattice window.

gi(v)akt! attention!

given, givet, gitt: under de givne omstendigheter under the particular circumstances; **en given sak** a matter of course, a foregone conclusion; **det er ikke enhver gitt** it is not given to everybody; **anta for givet** take for granted.

giv|er, -erinne giver, donor; **en glad -er** a cheerful giver.

gjalle ring, resound, echo.

gjedde pike.

gjel gully, ravine, mountain pass.

gjeld (gold) barren, dry, (om handyr) castrated.
I. **gjeld** debt; **komme i — get** el. run into debt; **stå i —** il be in one's debt, stand indebted to one; **sitte i bunnløs —** be deeply in debt; **gjøre —** contract debts, run into debt. **-bunden** involved in debt, encumbered with debt.
II. **gjeld,** se **prestegjeld.**
I. **gjelde** (være verd) be worth; (være i kraft) apply, be in force; (angå) refer to, apply to, concern; **— for** pass for, be looked upon as; **det -r ikke** that goes for nothing; **det kan ikke — for noe bevis** that cannot be taken as a proof; **billetten -r 45 dager** the ticket is available for 45 days; **denne lov -r ikke mere** this law is no longer in force; **når det -r, skal man finne meg** when wanted I shall be found; **her -r det å ha mot** here all depends on courage; **det -r om hvem ...** the point is who ...; **for ham gjaldt det** the question with him was; **det -r også om dette** it holds good of this too, it is applicable to this too; **nå -r det** now for it; **det -r hans ære** his honour is concerned; **som om det gjaldt hans liv** for dear life, as if his life depended on it; **om det -r mitt liv** to save my life; **det -r meg** it is aimed at me, (angår meg) it concerns me.
II. **gjelde** (kastrere) geld, castrate.

gjeldende (billett) available; (lov) in force; **gjøre —** (f. eks. påstander) maintain, urge; (en fordring) advance (a claim); (kunnskaper, skjønnhet) set off; (grunner osv.) enforce, urge;

(innflytelse) bring to bear; (som unnskyldning) plead; **gjøre seg — assert** oneself, put oneself forward.

gjeldfri free from debt, out of debt; **— eiendom** unencumbered property.

gjelding (kastrat) eunuch. (abstr.) gelding, castration. **gjeldokse** bullock, gelt bull.

gjelds|bevis bond. **-brev** bond. **-fengsel** debtor's (debtors') prison; **komme i — become** a prisoner for debt. **-fordring** claim. **-forskrivning**, se **-bevis.** **-post** item (of a debt).

gjelle gill. **-blad** gill-fibre. **-åpning** gill-opening.

gjemme keep, lay by, hide, treasure, save; **— seg** hide (away).

gjemme (et) keeping, custody; (-sted) depository, repository receptacle.

gjemmested hiding place; depository, receptacle.

gjemsel, se **gjemmested; leke — play** least in sight, play hide-and-seek.

gjen|besøk return visit. **-bo, -boerske** opposite, neighbour. **-dikte** recompose, re-create. **-drive** confute, refute. **-drivelse** refutation. **-døpe** rebaptize. **-døper** anabaptist. **-døperi** anabaptism.

gjen|ferd apparition, spectre, ghost; **hans —** his ghost, spirit. **-forening** reunion. **-forsikre** re-insure. **-forsikring** re-insurance. **-fortelle** re-narrate, re-tell, repeat. **-fortelling** re-narration, reproduction. **-fødelse** regeneration. **-født** regenerate.

gjeng (arbeids-, bande) gang; party; squad. **hele -en** the whole lot of them.

gjenganger, se **gjenferd. -aktig** spectral.

gjenge (på skrue) thread, groove; (låsgjenge) ward; (på vogge) rocker; (gang) course, progress; **alt er kommet i — igjen** everything has resumed its regular course; **tingene kom i sin gamle —** things fell back into their old grove; **saka er i god —** the matter is in good train.

gjengi (uttrykke) express; (oversette) render, translate; **— friheten** restore to liberty. **-velse** (fremstilling) representation; (av ytring o. l.) account, repetition; (oversettelse) version, rendering.

gjengjeld requital, return, retribution; **gjøre —** make a return, retaliate; **til — in** return, as a set off.

gjengjelde requite, return, repay; (om følelser) o. l.) reciprocate; **— vondt med godt** return good for evil.

gjengs (gangbar) current; (alminnelig forekommende) prevalent, prevailing.

gjeninnsette (tilbakekalle) replace; restore, reinstate. **-lse** restoration, reinstatement.

gjenkalle seg (i erindringen) call to mind, call back to memory, recall.

gjen|kjenne recognize, identify. **-kjennelig** recognizable. **-kjennelse** recognition, identification.

gjenklang echo, resonance; (fig) sympathy.

gjenlevende surviving, survivor.

gjen|lyd echo, resonance. **-lyde** echo, resound, ring, reverberate, (av: with).

gjenløse redeem. **-løser** redeemer. **-løsning** redemption.

gjenmæle reply; **ta til — reply.

gjennom (prep) through; (adv) thoroughly. **— ærlig** thoroughly honest. **— dannet** (highly) accomplished.

gjennomarbeide go el. work through.

gjennombake bake through, bake thoroughly.

gjennombla turn over the leaves of (a book), peruse.

gjennomblaut wet through, drenched.

gjennombløyte drench; soak.

gjennombore pierce through, perforate; **— en** stab one, run one through (the body, with a sword). **-nde blikk** piercing look el. glance.

gjennombrott, -brudd breaking through; (åndelig) awakening, revival, transformation;

komme til — (fig) break forth, break out ,orci its way, prevail.

gjennombrutt (om mønster) transparent, open-work.

gjennombryte break through.

gjennomfart passage, thoroughfare.

gjennomfrossen thoroughly frozen.

gjennomføre carry through; carry out, work out, accomplish, go through with, effect.

gjennomføring carrying out, accomplishment.

gjennomført congruous, consistent, elaborate, thorough.

gjennomgang passage, thoroughfare.

gjennomgangsbillett through ticket. **seller De —er til London?** do you book through to L. **-gods** transit goods. **-reisende** passer through, passing traveller, (amr) transient.

gjennomgangsstadium transition stage.

gjennomgangs|tog through train. **-toll** transit -duty. **-vei** thoroughfare. **-vogn** (motsatt kupé-vogn) corridor car.

gjennomgløde heat through; (fig) inflame, kindle.

gjennomgripende thorough, radical, sweeping.

gjennomgå (lide) go through, suffer undergo; (gjennomse) examine, go over, look over, go through; (f. eks. et kursus) pass through (a course of study); **— en lekse med en** go over a lesson with one. **De har -tt mye** you have had great trials.

gjennomgående (adj) through; (fig) pervading, universal.

gjennomgående (adv) (i alm.) generally, universally; (helt igjennom) from the beginning to the end, throughout, altogether; (dt.) all round.

gjennomhegle (skjelle ut) give a good rating, scold well.

gjennomhullet perforated, riddled.

gjennomisne chill.

gjennomkjørsel passage for carriages; **— for-budt** no thoroughfare.

gjennomkokt done enough.

gjennomkrysse cross, traverse.

gjennomlese read through, peruse.

gjennomlesning reading, perusal.

gjennom|lyse (f. eks. m. røntgenstråler) trans-luminate. **-lysing** translumination.

gjennom|løpe (m. øynene) glance el. look over; **han -løp brevet** he ran his eyes over the letter.

gjennommarsj march (through).

gjennompløye toil el. wade through.

gjennompryle drub soundly.

gjennomreise (subst) journey through, passage through; **han var her på** — he was passing through here. **-visum** visa valid for passing through.

gjennomreise (vrb) pass through, traverse.

gjennomrote rummage.

gjennomse see through, look over, inspect, revise; **-tt utgave** revised edition.

gjennomsiktig transparent; (fig) lucid.

gjennomsiktighet transparency.

gjennomskjære cut (through), intersect, traverse, permeate.

gjennomskjæring cut, cutting.

gjennomskue see through, see into.

gjennomskuelig: **lett — easily** seen through.

gjennomskutt (med hvite blad, om en bok) interleaved.

gjennomsnitt diameter; (i tegning) profile; (middeltall) average; **i — on** an average, at the average; **ha i — average.**

gjennomsnittlig average, medium; (adv) on an average.

gjennomstekt done enough.

gjennomstikke pierce, run through.

gjennomstreife range, wander through.

gjennomstrømme flow through, run through; (om følelse) thrill.

gjennomsyn inspection, examination; **ved — av bøkene** on going through the books.

gjennomsøke search (through), scour.

gjennomtenke think through, consider thoroughly.

gjennomtrekk (thorough) draught.

gjennomtrenge penetrate, pierce, permeate; (om væske) soak, saturate.

gjennomtrengende piercing; **— blikk** piercing glance; **— kulde** piercing cold; **— skrik** piercing shriek.

gjennomtørr quite dry.

gjennomveve interweave.

gjennomvæte drench, soak.

gjennomvåk|e watch through; **-te netter** wakeful nights.

gjennomvåt drenched, wet through.

gjenoppblussing fresh outbreak.

gjenoppbygge rebuild.

gjenoppføre rebuild, re-erect.

gjenoppleve relive. **-lse** reliving.

gjenopplive revive, resuscitate. **-nde middel** restorative.

gjenopplivelse revival, resuscitation.

gjenopprette re-establish, restore, redress.

gjenopprettelse re-establishment, restoration.

gjenoppstå rise again; be resurrected.

gjenoppta take up again, resume; (et stykke) revive. **-gelse** resumption; revival.

gjenopptreden re-appearance.

gjenpart copy, transcript, duplicate; **ta en — av** draw up a copy of, copy out.

gjensidig mutual, reciprocal, on both sides; (adv) mutually, reciprocally. **-het** reciprocity.

gjensitter pupil not moved.

gjenskape re-create.

gjen|skinn reflection **-skjær** (faint) reflection.

gjenspeil|e reflect, mirror. **-ing** reflection.

gjenstand (for handling el. følelse) object; (emne) subject; (rørlig ting) object, thing. Eks. the Bible had been the object of his study; object of (el. for) charity, respect; subject of the conversation, the debate, the experiment.

gjenstridig refractory, obstinate, restive, stubborn. **-het** refractoriness, obstinacy.

gjensvar rejoinder.

gjensyn meeting (again); **på —! till** we meet again! so long!

gjenta repeat, reiterate; **— seg** recur; **gjentagne ganger** repeatedly, again and again.

gjen|tagelse, -takelse repetition, reiteration; recurrence.

gjentagende (adv) repeatedly.

gjentjeneste return el. requital of service; **jeg skylder ham en** — I owe him a good turn; **det skal glede oss meget å være til** — we shall be most happy to serve you in return.

gjenvalg re-election; **være på** — stand for r.

gjen|veg, -vei short cut; **gå en** — make el. take a short cut.

gjenvelge re-elect.

gjenvinne regain, recover, retrieve; **— sin helbred** be restored to health.

gjenvisitt return visit.

gjenvordighet adversity, hardship.

gjerde fence; (levende) hedge; (av stein) wall. **gjerde inn** (vrb) fence in.

gjerde|fang fencing material. **-hold** the maintenance of fencing. **-stav,** se **gardstaur.**

gjerde|smutt wren, kitty-wren. **-tråd** fencing wire.

gjerne (villig, med glede) willingly, readily; (som oftest) commonly, generally, mostly; **jeg vil(le) — ha en kopp te** I want a cup of tea; give me a cup of tea, please; **mer enn — mo t** willingly; **det tror jeg** — I dare say; **det kan du — gjøre** you may do that if you like; **— for meg** I have no objection; with all my heart; **slik går det** — that is commonly the way; **jeg ville — vite** I should like to know; **å ville — like** to, love to; **så — jeg ville** however much I might wish it; **likeså — as** soon, (just) as well; **det kan — være** it may be, it is quite possible; **han kom — om aftenen** he would come in the evening.

gjerning deed, act, action, doing, work; (forretning, kall) business, calling; **-er** works; **tegn og underlige -er** signs and wonders; **på fersk —** in the very act; **i ord og —** by word and deed; **en god —** a good action; **gjort —** står ikke til å endre what is done cannot be undone; it is no use talking of spilt milk; **han ligger på sine -er** he has got his deserts.

gjernings|mann doer, perpetrator. **-ord** verb. **-sted** place of perpetration.

gjerrig avaricious, niggard. **-het** avarice. **-knark** miser.

gjesp yawn. **-e** yawn.

I. **gjest**, se **gjær.**

II. **gjest** guest; (besøkende) visitor, visitant; (fremmed) stranger; (i vertshus) visitor,customer; **by en til —** invite one to dinner (lunch etc.); **ubuden —** intruder. **gjeste** visit.

gjeste|bud banquet, feast. **-opptreden** special performance (av: by), star appearance. **-rett** right of hospitality; (jur) Court of Passage. **-rolle** part performed by a stranger, starring part; **gi -roller** star it. **-rom** (for reisende) parlour, common room (at an inn). **-spill** special performance.

gjeste|venn guest. **-vennlig** hospitable. **-vennskap** hospitality. **-værelse** visitor's room, spare bed-room.

gjestfri hospitable. **gjestfrihet** hospitality.

gjestgiver innkeeper, landlord. **-gård, -i** inn. **-ske** innkeeper; landlady.

gjete, se **gjæte.**

gjetning guessing; guess, conjecture.

gjetord report, rumour.

gjette guess, divine; **— en gåte** solve a riddle; **jeg -r på ham** I guess it is he. **-evne** power of divination. **-verk** guesswork.

gjord (reim om hestens kropp) girth; (av tre, metall) hoop. **slå —** play at trundle-hoop.

gjorde (en hest) girth; (hist.: spenne belte om) gird. **han -t seg med sverdet** he girt on his sword.

gjure (surre, spenne fast) fasten on.

gjær yeast, barm, ferment.

gjære: i — going on, brewing, in the wind.

gjære (vrb) ferment, work.

gjæring fermentation. **gjærings|middel** ferment. **-prosess** fermentative process.

gjæte herd, guard, tend.

gjæter herdsman, shepherd. **-gutt** shepherd boy. **-hund** sheep dog, shepherd's dog. **-jente** shepherdess, shepherd girl. **-stav** crook. **gjæting** herding.

gjæv excellent; gallant. **-het** excellence; gallantry.

gjø bark, bay (av: at); **den hund som -r, biter ikke** barking dogs seldom bite.

gjø(de) fatten (up).

gjødning manuring; manure, dung.

gjødnings|middel, -stoff manure, fertilizer. **-verdi** manurial value.

gjødsel manure, dung. **-greip** dung fork. **-haug** dung-hill, manure heap. **-kjerre** dungcart.

gjødselvann liquid manure. **gjødselvanns|beholder** receptacle of liquid manure, manure water cart.

gjødsle manure, dung; (med gjødselvann) fertilize with liquid manure, apply liquid manure.

gjøgl humbug, buffoonery.

gjøgle juggle; (drive narrestreker) play the buffoon. **-r** juggler; buffoon, merry Andrew. **-rske** juggleress.

gjøglerstreker juggling tricks.

gjøgris fatting pig.

gjøing barking, bark.

gjøkalv fatted el. fattening calf.

gjemme, se **gjemme.**

gjøn fun, chaff, chaffing. **drive — måke** fun (med: of).

gjøne chaff, make fun.

gjøre do; (om et spesielt virke og særl. om konkrete gjenstander) make; **— opp ild** light a fire; **dette har gjort hans lykke** this has been the making of him; **— plass** make room; **han gjør sine saker godt** he plays his part well, does very well; **— et skritt** take a step; **— en et spørsmål** put a question to one, ask one a question; **— en uleilighet** give one trouble; **— løs** make loose; **— fast** make fast; **— en lykkelig, rik** make (også om varigere virkning: render) one happy, rich; **ikke så rik som man gjør ham til** not so rich as people make him out to be; **— en gal** drive one mad; **han gjør deg ikke noe** he will do you no harm; **det gjør vondt** it hurts; **det gjør meg vondt** I am sorry; **det gjør meg godt** it does me good; **det gjør ingenting** it is no matter; **det gjør ikke noe til saken** that is nothing to the purpose; it is no odds at all; **hva gjør det** what of that? what's the odds? **det gjør hverken fra eller til** that's neither here nor there; **han visste hva han gjorde** he knew what he was about; **kan ikke mindre — det** won't less content you? **can't** less do the turn? **han gjør det ikke lenge** he won't last long, he is going fast; **jeg gjør det ikke** (avslag) I shall do no such thing, I shall do nothing of the kind; **bedra gjør han** he does cheat; **og det gjorde vi** and so we did; **dette gjorde** at this had the effect that, **did** so much that; **det må -s** it must be done; **— seg elsket, fryktet** make oneself beloved, feared; **— seg gal, syk** pretend to be mad, ill; **— seg begrep om** form an idea of; **— seg den uleilighet** take the trouble; **— seg til av** take pride in, pride el. plume oneself on; **det lar seg ikke —** it cannot be (done), is not to be done; **så vidt det lar seg —** as far as practicable; **— mye av en** (holde av en) like one, make much of one; **hvor har du gjort av ...?** what have you done with ...? where have you put, left ...? **— det av med** make away with, dispose of; **— etter, se ettergjøre; jeg kan ikke — for det** I cannot help it, it is not my fault; **— forretninger i trade in, deal in; — i penger** turn into money; **gjorde vel i å** did well to; **gjorde ikke klokt i** was not doing a prudent thing in; **— en imot** offend one; **ha å — med** have to do with, be concerned with; **de gjorde med ham hva de ville** they had their will of him; **det er ikke gjort med å snakke** talking will not do it; **gjør mot andre som du vil de skal — mot deg** do unto (el. by) others as you would be done unto; **— om alter; det er meg om å — it is an object with me, I am anxious about it; det som er skjedd, kan ikke -s om** what's done can't be undone; **— opp** make up, settle; **— en til sin venn, fiende** make a friend, enemy of one; **han har gjort henne til sin kone** he has made her his wife; **det kan ingen — noe ved** nobody can help it; **det kan jeg ikke — ved** I can do nothing to that, I cannot help that; **det er ingenting å — ved** det it cannot be helped.

gjøremål business, duties.

gjørlig practicable, feasible.

gjørme mire, mud, dregs. **-t** turbid, muddy, miry, dreggish.

gjørs på (dt) do it on purpose, make a point of.

gjørtler brazier.

gjøs (lite flagg) (union) jack.

glacéhansker kid gloves; (dt) kids.

glacialtid (istid) glacial epoch.

glacis glacis.

glad glad, joyful, joyous, cheerful; **— over å høre om** det glad to hear of it; **være — rejoice; være — over** be glad of el. at, be delighted with, at; **jeg er like —** I don't care; **gjøre seg en — dag** make a day of it; **levde i den -e tro** fondly imagined. **-elig** gladly etc.

gladiator gladiator.
gladlyndt merry-dispositioned, jovial, genial.
glam (særl. hunde-) baying.
glamme bay, bark.
glane stare, gape (på: at).
glans splendour; (stråleglans) lustre; (av tøy) gloss; (politur) polish; **sette — på** give a gloss to; **ta -en av** take the gloss off; **viste seg i all sin —** appeared in all his glory; **gjøre noe med — do st.** in grand style; **komme fra noe med — come out of st.**, come off, with flying colours.
glansbilde glazed el. glossy picture.
glansfull effulgent, resplendent; (utmerket, berømmelig) splendid, illustrious.
glans|lerret glazed linen. **-løs** lustreless, lacklustre; dull, dead; (fig) without splendour. **-løshet** deadness. **-papir** glazed paper. **-periode** days of glory, palmy days. **-punkt** crowning effort, crowning hit, noblest feature, acme. **-rolle** crowning performance, favourite part. **-stivelse** glazed starch. **-tid,** se **-periode.**
glaser|e glaze; (overtrekke med sukker) ice. **-ing** glazing; ice.
glass glass; (ølglass) tumbler; (mar) bell; **slå seks —** strike six bells; **sette i — og ramme** frame and glaze; **et — vann** a glass of water; **drikke et — med en** take (a glass of) wine with one.
glass|dråper glass-tears. **-fabrikasjon** glass -making.
glasshus: en skal ikke kaste stein når en selv sitter i — those who live in glass-houses should not throw stones.
glass|kitt glass-cement. **-klokke** bell glass, glass shade. **-kolbe** balloon. **-kork** glass stopper. **-kule** glass-globe el. -ball. **-kuppel** (til ur) glass-shade; (til lampe) lamp globe.
glasslegeme (i øyet) vitreous body, corpus vitreum.
glassmagasin glass shop.
glassmaleri stained glass.
glass|masse glass-metal, frit. **-mester** glazier. **-mesterdiamant** glazier's diamond. **-mesterkitt** glazier's putty.
glassperle glass-bead.
glass|puster glass blower. **-pusteri** glass-blowing, glass-works. **-rute** pane (of glass). **-saker** glass-ware. **-skap** glass press, g. cabinet, g. case. **-skår** fragment of glass. **-sliper** glass-grinder. **-sliperi, -slip(n)ing** glass-grinding, glass-cutting. **-splint** splinter of glass. **-tak** glass-roof.
glassverk glass-works.
glassøye glass-eye.
glasur glazing, glaze; (på tennene) enamel.
glatt smooth; (motsatt krøllet) plain; (så at man glir) slippery; (glatthåret) sleek; (slesk) oily; **— lag broadside; — ring, silketøy** plain ring, silk; **— is** slippery ice; **— tunge** smooth tongue; **— som en ål** slippery as an eel; **— å gå** slippery walking. **glatt** (adv) smoothly; **det gikk ikke så —** it was not all plain sailing.
glattbarbert clean-shaved.
glatte smooth.
glatt|haket smooth chinned, smooth-faced, beardless. **-het** smoothness. **-høvel** smoothing-plane. **-høvle** plane smooth. **-håret** smooth -haired, sleek-haired. **-is** glazed frost; **bringe på -is** tempt, put to the test, lead into a scrape. **-løpet gevær, kanon** smooth bore. **-raket** clean shaven, smooth-shaven, clean shorn. **-slepen** polished. **-slip(n)ing** polishing.
glatt|tunget smooth-tongued. **-tungethet** smoothness of tongue.
glaubersalt Glauber's salt.
glede joy, delight, pleasure; **bordets -r** the luxuries of the table; **det er meg en — å** I am happy to, it gives me great pleasure to; **ute av seg selv av —** beside oneself with joy; **gråte av —** weep for joy; **finne — i** delight in, take delight in; **jeg har ingen — av det** it gives

me no satisfaction; **med — gladly; til stor — for** for the great delight of.
glede (vrb) gladden, cheer; **det -r meg** I am glad of it; **det -r meg at** I am glad to el. that **— seg** rejoice; **— seg ved** el. over rejoice at; **— seg ved** (å besitte) rejoice in, enjoy; **— seg til** look forward (with pleasure) to.
gledelig joyful, joyous, glad, gratifying, pleasant; **— jul** a merry Christmas. **-vis** happily.
gledeløs joyless, cheerless, dreary.
gledes|bluss bonfire. **-budskap** glad tidings. **-dag** day of rejoicing. **-pike** prostitute. **-rus** transport of joy. **-skrik** shout of joy. **-tegn** token of joy. **-tid** time of rejoicing. **-tårer** tears of joy.
glefs snap, bark. **-e** snap (etter: at), bark. **— i seg** bolt.
glemme (subst): **gå i —** pass into oblivion, lapse out of memory.
glemme (vrb) forget; (det man har lært) unlearn; **gjemt er ikke glemt** omittance (forbearance) is no acquittance el. all's not lost that's delayed; **jeg har glemt hans navn** I forget his name; **det hadde jeg rent glemt** I quite forgot that. **— etter seg** leave.
glemmeboka: skrive **i —** forget, consign to oblivion; **det er kommet i —** I have forgotten it, it has escaped my memory.
glemsel oblivion, forgetfulness.
glemsom forgetful, oblivious.
glemsomhet forgetfulness, obliviousness.
glente kite.
gletsjer glacier.
glette (gløtt i skyene) clear interval (in the sky), bit of blue sky.
gli(d): på **— going; få på —** set going.
gli(de) slip; (gli på is, gå sakte, snike seg) slide; (bevege seg lett) glide; **— ut** slip; **— lett henover** touch lightly upon, slide over.
glideflukt volplane; **gå ned i —** volplane; **redde seg ved —** save oneself by volplaning.
glide|lyd glide. **-lås, -spenne** zip.
glider (mekan) slide.
glidning gliding, slide; (skruens) slip.
gliedermann lay-figure.
glimmer glimmer, glitter; (falsk) false lustre, tinsel; (mineral) mica, glimmer. **-gull** yellow glimmer. **-stas** tawdry finery. **-stein** glimmer, mica. **-sølv** argentine mica.
glimre glitter, glisten, glister; (fig) shine.
glimrelyst love of show (el. display).
glimrende brilliant, splendid.
glimt gleam; (flyktig blikk) glimpse; (av lyn) el. fyr) flash; **få et — av** catch a glimpse of.
glimte gleam, flash.
glimtfyr flashing light. **glimtvis** by glimpses.
glinse glisten, shine.
glipe (smal åpning) opening, crack.
glipe (vrb) be on the crack, be a little apart.
glipp: gå — av miss, fail of, lose.
I. glippe fail; **det -t for ham** he failed, he was disappointed.
II. glippe (med øynene) blink, twinkle, wink (one's eyes).
glir|e (blinke) twinkle, blink (m. øynene: one's eyes). **-øyd** blinking.
glis grin, sneer, snicker.
glise grin, sneer, snicker.
glis(s)en, se **grissen.**
glitre glitter. **glitring** glitter, glittering.
glitte (polere tøy el. papir) calender, glaze.
glo (subst) hot el. live coal fl. **glør også:** embers.
glo (vrb) stare, gaze, gape (på: at).
globus globe.
gloende (glødende) red-hot; (om farge) gaudy; **sanke — kull på hans hode** heap coals of fire upon his head. **— rød** flaming red.
glo|het burning hot. **-hete** red heat.
gloret (gild) flaring, gaudy, glaring, tawdry.
glorie glory, halo, nimbus; (om hele legemet) aureola. **glorverdig** glorious.

glorød fiery red.
glose vocable; **-bok** wordbook, glossary. **-forråd** vocabulary.
glossar(ium) glossary.
glugg(e) hole, aperture; **-r** (øyne) goggles.
glunt (gutt) boy.
glup firstrate, prime, slashing.
glupende ravenous, ferocious.
glupsk ravenous, rabid, voracious, ferocious.
glupskhet ravenousness, ferocity.
glyptotek glyptotheca.
glyserin glycerine.
glød (subst), se **glo**, (fig) glow.
glø(de) (bringe i glød) make white hot; (være i glød) glow; (fig) burn (av: with).
glødelampe incandescent lamp.
glødende red hot; burning.
gløde|nett (til gassbluss) incandescent mantle. **-ovn** heating-furnace. **-tråd** (tråden i glødelampe) filament.
glødning ignition, heating.
gløgg quick to see; smart.
glømme, se **glemme**.
gløse, se **gløde**.
gløtt aperture, small opening. **døra stod på —** the door was left ajar, stood ajar; (glimt) snatch. **et — av sol** snatch of sunshine. **i daggløtten** at peep of day, at the first glimmer of day.
glåme, glåpe, se **glo** (vrb).
gnage gnaw; (ved gnidning) fret, chafe, gall.
gnager rodent, gnawing animal.
gnaske crunch. **gnasking** crunching.
gneis gneiss.
gneldre shriek, shrill; (bjeffe) yelp; (gjø) bark. **-bikkje** yelping tike.
gni(de) rub; (for å varme) chafe; **— løs på fiolinen** scrape away at the violin; **— seg i hendene** rub one's hands.
gnidder small, cramped writing, niggle.
gnidning rubbing, friction.
gnidningselektrisitet frictional electricity.
gnidningsmotstand friction.
gnidre write a close and crabbed hand. **-t** close and crabbed (hand-writing).
gnidsel: gråt og tenner — weeping and gnashing of teeth.
gnier miser, niggard, hunks, curmudgeon, screw. **gnieraktig** niggardly, stingy, sordid.
gnieraktighet, gnieri niggardliness, stinginess, sordidness.
gnikke, se **gni(de)**.
gnisle creak, grate, saw, grit; **— m. tennene** gnash one's teeth.
gnisse, se **gnisle**. **— mot noe** be rubbed against st.
gnist spark, scintilla; (fig) vestige, remnant; **— av håp** spark of hope, ray of hope.
gniste (om hund) whine.
gnistfanger spark-arrester, -catcher.
gnistre sparkle; **hans øyne -t av vrede** his eyes flashed with anger.
gnisttelegraf wireless (telegraph).
gnisttelegrafi radio-telegraphy.
gnu (slags antilope) gnu.
gnu (vrb) rub, chafe.
gny din, clamour.
gnål incessant humming, singsong; (mas) importunities.
gnåle hum incessantly; keep begging, keep importuning one; always harp on one string.
gobelinstapeter gobelins, tapestry hangings.
god good; (snill) kind; **den -e** the good man; **de -e** the good; **mannen er — nok** the man is safe enough; **han blir snart — igjen** he is easily reconciled, he soon comes round again; **han er ikke — å komme nær** he is a rough customer; **de er begge like -e** they are a pair cl. of a piece; **dt. den er — that is a good one! vær så — be so kind as to . . .**, please, if you please; (tilbydende) there it is (dt) there you are; help yourself; **ja, vær så — (tillatende)** by all

means, you are quite welcome; **vær så — å la meg vite** kindly let me know; **så, det er -t** there, that will do; **det er meget -t!** I like that (now)! **det er -t nok** that is all very well, so far so good; **det er likeså -t å** it is as well to; **la det være -t** let that pass, never mind that, say no more about it; **det var ikke -t om** it would not be well, it would be a bad thing if; **det er ikke -t å vite** it is hard to tell; **han gjør mye -t** he does a great deal of good; **gjøre -t igjen** make amends for; **det vil gjøre alt -t igjen** that will set all to rights again; **ha -t av** derive benefit from, profit by; **det har De -t av** it will do you good; **mer enn han har -t av** more than is good for him, agrees with him; **nyte -t av** have the benefit of; **det har han -t av** it serves him right; **hva sa han til -t?** had he any good news? **det -e good**, what is good; **for mye av det -e** too much of a good thing; **det er ikke for det -e** it is for no good purpose; **med det -e** by fair means, amicably; **med det -e eller vonde** by fair or foul means; **jeg gir ham en — dag** I don't care a rush el. straw about him; **når enden er — er alltid -t** all's well that ends well; **noe -t juks** precious trash; **-t kort** winning card, king card; **en — mil** a good el. full mile, a good long mile; **vær ved -t mot** be of good cheer; **ens -e navn og rykte** one's fair name, fair fame, character; **for et -t ord** for a trifle, for an old song, for the asking; **for -e ord og betaling** for love and money; **jeg var en — tosk** a precious fool I was; **et -t utfall** a happy issue; **-t utkomme** easy competency; **han har — -t utkomme** he is well off, well to do; **-t vær** fine weather; **dt. be om -t vær** cry mercy; **svært -e venner** great friends; **— vind** fair wind; **ikke med min -e vilje** not willingly, not if I can help it, not if I know it; **være — for** (så og så mye) be worth . . .; **gå — for** stand bail for; **enhver er — for seg** every one is good for something; **være — imot** be kind to; **de er like -e om det** dt. they are in the same boat; **jeg holder meg for — til å** I am above -ing.
god aften good evening.
godartet mitigated, benign, mild.
godbit dainty bit el. morsel, titbit.
god dag how do you do? (besvares med: how do you do?); good day! good morning! good afternoon!
gode (subst) good, benefit, blessing; **det høyeste — the** supreme good; **til — due; han har et års hyre — he** has one year's pay due; **holde til — overlook**, bear with, make allowance for; **gjøre seg til — indulge el. regale oneself; det kom meg til — at** it was for my advantage that.
gode (utt. gåde) (på Island) priest, parish chieftain.
godeste: du -e (Gud)! good gracious!
godfjott, -et silly-soft.
godgjørende beneficent, charitable.
godgjørenhet beneficence, charitableness.
godhet goodness; kindness; **fatte — for** take a liking to; **ha den — å** be so kind as to, have the goodness to; **en vares — the** quality of an article.
god|hetsfullt kindly. **-hjertet** good-hearted, kind-hearted. **-hjertethet** goodness of heart, good-heartedness, kind-heartedness. **-kjenne** sanction, approve (of), endorse; **ikke -kjenne** disapprove of. **-kjennelse** sanction, approval. **-kyndt** good-natured. **-lag: være i — be** in high spirits. **-lidende** pleasant, likeable. **-lyndt**, se **-kyndt**. **-modig** good-natured, sweet-tempered. **-modighet** good-nature. **— morgen** good morning. **-natt** good night.
godord (utt. gåd-, på Island) the office of parish chieftain and priest.
1. **gods** (varer) goods (pl); (mar) stores; (til fartøy, seil osv.) gear; **det bergede — the** property saved.

II. **gods** (jordegods) estate, landed property. **gods|eier** landed proprietor, estate owner. **-eierske** proprietress (of an estate). **-ekspedisjon** (jernb.) goods service. **-ekspeditør** goods manager. **-forvalter** land steward, agent, estate manager. **-innlevering** goods entrance. **godskrive** credit, give credit for. **godslig,** se godmodig. **godsnakke** speak gently, coax. **gods|tog** goods-train, luggage-train; (amr) freight-train, baggage-train. **-trafikk** goods traffic, carrying-traffic. **-vogn** (åpen) truck; (lukket) luggage-van, goods-van; i Amerika: (åpen) freight-car; (lukket) baggage-car.

godt (adv) well; **ha det —** be well off, be comfortable; **—! good! kort og —** in short; **— og vel** something more than; **så — som** as good as, all but, practically; **så — som ingen** scarcely any; **for så — som ingenting** for half nothing; **sove —** sleep soundly; **mene det — med en** mean well by one.

godta pass, pass fit.
godtatt (slang) O. K.
godtfolk (good) people; **hvor — er kommer —** til birds of a feather flock together.
godtgjøre make good; **— en noe** indemnify one for st.; (bevise) prove, substantiate, make out, establish.
godtgjørelse compensation, amends (pl), allowance.
godt|kjøps cheap, low-priced. **-kjøpsroman** shilling dreadful. **-kjøpsutgave** penny edition, cheap edition.
godtroende confiding, simple-hearted.
godtroenhet confidingness, simplicity.
godtykke discretion, pleasure (etter g.: at p.).
god|vilje (hearty) good will. **-villig** (adv) voluntarily, willingly.
godvær fine weather. **i —** ogs.: on fine days.
godværsdag fine day.
gold barren, sterile; (om kyr) dry.
goldhet sterility, barrenness.
I. **golf** gulf.
II. **golf** (spill) golf, golfing. **-bane** golflinks.
Golfstrømmen the Gulf-stream.
Golgata (Mount) Calvary, Golgatha.
golv floor; **legge — i** floor. **-klut** rubbing cloth. **-lagt** floored. **-legging** floor-laying, flooring. **-matte** mat. **-planke** floring board. **-skrubb** scrubbing brush. **-teppe** carpet.
gom, gomme gum.
gomle mumble, munch. **gomlere** edentates.
gondol gondola; (til ballong) car. **-fart** row el. excursion in a gondola. **-fører** gondolier.
gongong gong, tam-tam.
gople (manet) jelly-fish.
gording (på skip) buntline.
gordisk Gordian.
gorilla gorilla.
goro wafer. **-jern** wafer irons.
goter Goth.
gotikk Gothicism. **gotisk** Gothic; **gotiske bokstaver** black letters.
gotte: — seg regale oneself; (fig) hug oneself; **— seg over** feel amused at, enjoy.
gotter (slikkerier) goodies, sweetmeat.
gourmand gastronomist, epicure.
grad degree; (rang) rank, grade; (om slektskap) remove; **termometeret viser 8 -ers kulde** the thermometer marks 8 degrees of cold; **i den —** to such a degree; **til en viss —** in measure, in degree, to some extent, to a certain extent; **i høy —** highly, eminently; **i hvor høy —** to what extent; **i høyeste —** in the highest el. last degree, to a degree, excessively; **en — større** a size larger. **-asjon** gradation, climax.
grad|bue graduated sector of a circle; arc. **-bøyning** comparison. **-e** gauge; apply the thermometer. **-ere** graduate. **-ering** graduation. **-estokk** water-poise.
grad|ing gauging. **-inndeling** graduation. **-mål**

scale. **-måling** measurement of degrees. **-forskjell** difference in degree. **-vis** gradual; (adv) gradually, by degrees.
grafisk graphic(al).
grafitt graphite, black-lead.
grafolog graphologist. **-i** graphology.
Gral: den hellige — the Holy Grail.
gram gram, gramme.
grammatikalsk grammatical; **— bommert** error in grammar, bad grammar **grammatiker** grammarian. **grammatikk** grammar. **grammatisk** grammatical.
grammofon gramophone. **-plate** gramophone record. **-stift** gramophone needle.
grams: kaste penger i — throw money for scrambling, (fig) play at ducks and drakes with money. **gramse** snatch, snap, grab.
gran (tre) spruce, spruce-fir, Norway spruce.
granat (edelsten) garnet; (frukt) pomegranate; (mil) shell. **-eple** pomegranate. **-kardeske** shrapnel. **-splint** splinter of a shell. **-stump** fragment of a shell. **-tre** pomegranate.
granbar pine needles.
grangivelig (adv) accurately.
grandios grand, grandiose.
grand|onkel, -tante grand- el. great-uncle, -aunt.
granholt fir-grove, grove of spruce-firs.
granitt granite. **-brott, -brudd** granite-quarry. **-fjell** granitic rock.
gran|kongle fir-cone, cone of the spruce. **-legg** bole el. trunk of a spruce-fir. **-li** fir-covered el. piny slope, firry hillside.
granplanke deal board.
grann (liten smule) atom, smallest particle.
grann (adj) slender; (sj) distinct, plain, vivid.
granne neighbour, se for øvrig nabo og naboskap.
granske inquire into, search into; **— etter** search for. **gransker** inquirer, student.
gransker|blikk, -øye searching glance; investigating eye. **-ånd** inquiring spirit.
gransk(n)ing inquiry, research.
granskog spruce-forest.
grant (adv) plainly, distinctly.
grantre, se gran.
grapefrukt grape-fruit.
gras grass, herbage; **slå —** mow grass, cut grass; **ha penger som —** roll in money; **tjene penger som —** make heaps of money; **mens -et gror, dør kua** while the grass grows, the steed starves.
gras|benk grass-seat. **-etende** graminivorous, herbivorous. **-frø** grass-seed. **-grodd** grass-grown. **-grønn** gras-green, prasinous. **-hoppe** grasshopper; locust.
grasiøs graceful.
gras|lauk, -løk chives, chive garlic. **-plen** lawn. **-rik** grassy.
gras|sat: gå el. løpe — run riot, run amuck. **-sere** rage, be prevalent, prevail; (foraktelig) be rampant, run rampant.
gras|strå stalk of grass; blade of grass. **-teppe** carpet of turf, velvet lawn. **-torv** green turf, sod. **-vekst** growth of grass.
gratiale gratuity.
grat|ie grace. **-ier** (pl) the Graces.
gratifikasjon gratuity.
gratis for nothing, free of charge, gratis, gratuitously. **-passasjer** free passenger, (amr) deadhead.
gratist free scholar, foundationer. **-eri** free system.
gratul|ant congratulator. **-asjon** congratulation. **-ere** congratulate (med: on), give one joy (of).
graut porridge, boiled groats, stirabout, hasty pudding; (av frukt) marmalade, jelly.
graut|omslag poultice.
grav pit, ditch, trench; (for døde) grave, tomb; (festnings-) moat, fosse; **den hellige —** the

Holy Sepulchre; **jeg trodde den hellige** — **var vel forvart** I thought all danger was past; **taus som —en** as silent as death; **følge til —en** attend at a funeral; **være på —ens rand** be on the brink of the grave; **stå med det ene ben i —en** have one foot in the grave; **(fig) legge en i —en** bring one to his grave; **se ut som en som har ligget i —en** look like one risen from the dead; **den som graver en** — **for andre, faller selv i den** harm watch, harm catch; he sets a trap to catch his own feet.

grav|alvor funereal gravity. **-alvorlig** intensly earnest.

grave dig; — **ut, opp dig** out, up; disinter, unearth. **-ned** bury; **-r seg inn i, igjennom** o. fl. digs his way into, through etc.

gravemaskin excavator.

graver (og kirketjener) sexton.

gravere engrave.

graverende aggravating, aggravated, grave, grievous.

grav|fred security of cemeteries, peace of the grave. **-funn** grave-find. **-haug** grave-mound; barrow. **-hvelving** burial vault, family vault.

gravid gravid, pregnant.

graving digging, excavation.

gravit|asjon gravitation. **-ere** gravitate. **-etisk** grave, solemn; (adv) gravely, solemnly.

grav|kapell mortuary chapel. **-kors** monumental cross. **-legge** entomb. **-luft** sepulchral air. **-lund** mortuary grove. **-monument, -mæle** (sepulchral) monument.

gravrust corrosion.

gravrøst sepulchral voice; **med** — in a s. v.

grav|røver violator of tombs. **-skrift** epitaph. **-sted** burial place. **-stein** tomb-stone. head-stone. **-støtte** sepulchral column. **-urne** sepulchral urn. **-øl** funeral feast, wake.

gravør engraver.

grei clear, disentangled, straight; (tydelig) plain; (reell) straight; (rask) expeditious. **et -tt svar** a plain answer; **det var -tt han visste det** it was plain to see he knew it; **det er ikke -tt** it is no easy matter.

greie (vrb) (ut) clear, disentangle, ravel, straighten (out); (kjemme) comb; (ordne) arrange, make all right, put straight; (rå med) manage. **jeg tenker De -r det** I dare say you'll carry through. — **det fint** come off clean, do capitally, get along very well, manage nicely. — **å** contrive to, manage to. — **seg** do, manage, come right, pull along. — **seg med sine inntekter** make ends meet; **det** — **seg nok** it'll be all right; **la ham** — **seg selv** leave him to his own devices; **det -r seg så vidt** it is going to be a close thing. — **med en sak** arrange about a matter. — **opp i en sak** set matters straight. — **med ham** settle with him.

greie (subst) arrangement, order; business, matter, thing. **-r** (pl) gear, contrivance(s), paraphernalia, tackle, things. (jvf. fiske- fishing -tackle, kjøre- harness). **han hadde aldri fått helt** — **på det** he never quite got it straight. **det er ingen** — **å få på ham** there is no making him out. **ha** — **på** be up to. **dette er fine -r!** nice business this!

greiekam, se **kam.**

greihet readiness, expedition.

grein, se **gren.**

greip dungfork.

greitt (adv) clearly; — **og klart** fairly and squarely.

Grekenland Greece.

greker Greek. **-inne** Greek woman.

grell glaring, loud; (mal.) crude; **skildre med -e farger** overdraw; **stikke grelt av imot** contrast (strongly) with.

gremme grieve, vex; — **seg** grieve, repine (over: at); — **seg ihjel** die of a broken heart.

gremmelse fret, grief, vexation.

gren branch; (bare på tre) bough (fig) branch.

grenader grenadier.

grend cluster of houses or farms, neighbourhood, hamlet.

grene seg branch, fork.

grense (subst) frontier, confine, limit, bound, boundary, border; **over alle -r** out of all bounds; **holde seg innenfor en viss** — keep within (certain) bounds; **sette** — **for** set bounds to.

grense (vrb) til be bounded by, border on; **det -r til det vidunderlige** it is little short of a miracle; — **sterkt til** go to the verge of; **mistanke som -r til visshet** suspicion almost amounting to certainty.

grense|befaring survey of boundaries. **-by** frontier town. **-krig** border war. **-land** border-land. **-linje** boundary. line, line of demarcation. **-løs** boundless; inordinate, excessive. **-løshet** boundlessness. **-regulering** settling the boundaries. **-røys** boundary cairn. **-skjell** bound, limit. **grense|stasjon** frontier station. **-stat** border state. **-stokk** boundary post. **-stridigheter** boundary controversies. **-tilfelle** border-line case. **-toll** frontier toll. **-vakt** frontier guard.

grep (etter noe) grasp, gripe; (på sverd) hilt; (på dør) handle; (på saks) branch; **ha det rette** — **på** have, know the knack of, have a knack at (-ing); **gjøre et falsk** — take a wrong note; **et heldig** — a happy hit; **med sikkert** — with an unfailing grasp.

grepa (prektig) prime, splendid, rattling good.

grepethet rapture, ecstacy.

gresk Greek, Grecian.

gress, se **gras.**

gresse, se **beite.**

gresselig awful, horrible, shocking; (adv) awfully etc.— **morsomt** awfully jolly.

gress|enke grass-widow. **-enkemann** grass -widower.

gressgang, se **beite.**

gresskar gourd, pumpkin.

gretten cross, fretful, peevish, querulous; sulky; **være** — be cross, sulk.

grettenhet fretfulness, peevishness.

grev grubaxe, mattock, pick.

greve count; (engelsk) earl. **-krone** coronet.

grevinne countess.

grevling badger.

grevlinghund badger-dog, dachs-hound.

grevskap (gods) count's estate; (provins), county, shire. **grevskaps|rett** county court. **-råd** county council.

gribb vulture. **gribbenille** termagant, vixen.

grid (hist) security, peace; mercy, quarter.

griff (heraldisk dyr) griffin, griffon.

griffel slate pencil; (bot) style. **-holder** port -crayon.

griljere grill.

grille (alm.: innfall) whim, vagary, crotchet, fancy, crack; **sette en -r i hodet** turn one's head.

grim ugly, hideous; (i mindre grad) plain (-featured), homely.

grimase grimace, **gjøre -r** grimace, make faces.

grime halter; **legge** — **på** halter.

grimet (m. striper av smuss) streaked, striped; grimy, begrimed.

grimhet ugliness, hideousness; plainness.

grin grin; crossness.

grind gate, wicket, hatch.

grindhval ca'ing whale.

grine (være gretten) be cross, fret; (skjenne) nag; (gråte) blubber.

grinebiter grumbler.

grinet cross-grained, peevish, naggy.

gripe catch, seize, pounce upon, grip; (med et fast tak) grasp, gripe; (pågripe) apprehend; (om anker) take hold, bite; (fig) affect; — **en leilighet** seize an opportunity, avail oneself of an opportunity; — **en tanke** take up an idea; — **an go** about, attack; — **saken an på den rette måte** go the right way to work; — **etter**

catch at; — **fatt på** take el. lay hold of; **grep for seg** held his hand before him; — **i lomma** thrust one's hand into one's pocket; — **i sin egen barm** search one's own bosom; — **en i løgn** catch one lying el. in a lie; — **inn i enter** into, bear on; (utilbørlig) encroach upon, intrench upon; — **inn i hverandre** work into each other, catch; — **inn** interfere; — **om seg** spread; — **til et middel** resort to, have recourse to an expedient; — **til våpen** take (up) arms; — **flukten** take to flight; **grepet ut av lufta** (utterly) gratuitous; **grepet ut av livet** true to life.

gripende affecting, impressive, thrilling.

griperedskap prehensile organ.

gris pig; (om person) beast; **grise** (få grisunger) farrow, litter down, pig; (søle) make a mess; — **seg til** dirty oneself.

grise|binge pig-pen, pig-sty. **-bust** hog's bristle, bristles. **-bøle** litter of pigs. **-hus** hog -cote, piggery. **-labber** pig's pettitoes. **-purke** sow with pigs. **-ri** nastiness. **-steik** roast pig. **-sylte** soused pig.

griset dirty.

grisetro hog's trough.

grisk greedy (etter: of). **-het** greediness.

grisle egtl. spread thinly; give a glossy surface to loaves of bread.

grissen far apart, scattered, sparse.

grisunge porket, porkling.

gro grow; — **fast** become fixed, strike root.

grobian churl, brute.

groe (i potet) chit, sprout.

gro|bunn el. **-botn** soil, genial soil.

grokjøtt: ha godt — a good healing flesh.

grom excellent.

grop cavity, hollow.

gros: en — wholesale. — **handel** wholesale-business.

gross gross; **bærens** — the bulk of the army.

grosserer, grossist wholesale dealer, (wholesale) merchant.

grotesk grotesque.

grotid season of vegetation el. growth.

grotte grotto, grot.

grov coarse; (uanstendig; utillatelig stor) gross; (uhøflig) rude; (svær) large, big; **-t arbeid** drudgery; **-t bedrageri** palpable cheat; — **feil** grave mistake; — **forbrytelse** high misdemeanour; **-t lerret** coarse linen; — **løgn** gross lie; — **løgner** impudent liar; **en** — **spøk** a rude joke; — **tone, stemme** rough tone, voice; **-e trekk** coarse features; — **villfarelse** gross el. grave error: **det er for -t** that's too bad. **-brød** coarse, brown bread.

grov|elig grossly. **-fil** bastard file, rough file.

grovhet coarseness; grossness; rudeness; roughness; (pl) rude behaviour, language; **si en -er** be rude, say rude things to one.

grov|høvel rough plane. **-kornet** coarse-grained. **-skåren** coarsely cut. **-smed** blacksmith. **-smed-arbeid** black-work.

gru horror, terror; **det er en** — **å se** it is horrible (shocking) to behold.

grub|le muse, ponder, brood, ruminate (on). **-lende** brooding. **-ler** muser. **-leri** musing, revery. **-lisere, se gruble.**

grue for dread, tremble at, shudder at; **jeg -r ved å tenke på** ... it makes me shudder to think of.

grue (ildsted) hearth, hearth-stone, fire-place. **gru|elig** horrid, horrible, shocking. **-full** horrid.

grum sj. se **grusom.**

grums sediment, grounds.

grumset muddy, thick, turbid.

grunde (tenke) muse, ponder (på: on, over).

grundig (adj) profound, solid, thorough-going; **en** — **helbredelse** a radical cure.

grundig (adv) thoroughly; **jeg hater ham** — I hate him from the bottom of my heart, most cordially; **kjede seg** — be bothered to extinction; — **forhatt** wellhated.

grundighet solidity, thoroughness.

grunker hoards of money, tin (sl).

grunn (adj) shallow, shoal.

grunn (subst) ground; (jord) soil; (bygnings o. l.) ground; plot, site; (amr) lot; (fornuftgrunn) reason (til: for); (bevirkende årsak) cause (til: of); (grunnlag) foundation, groundwork; (-lag i maling) priming, ground; **det stille vann har den dype** — still waters run deep; **De spør om mine -er** you ask my reasons; **av hjertens** — from the bottom of my heart; **av hvilken** —? for what reason? **fra -en av,** radically; **forstå noe fra -en av** understand thoroughly, perfectly; **i -en** at bottom, in the main, after all, considering all things; **i bunn og** — utterly, totally; **med** — reasonably; **med god** — very reasonably, with good reason; **med en viss** — plausibly; **på min** — on my premises; **på norsk** — on Norwegian soil; **komme på** — run aground, strike; **stå på** — be aground, on shore; **sette på** — ground, run aground; **på** — **av** on account of, owing to, due to, by reason of, (at) on the ground that; **gå til -e** (fig) be ruined; **legge til** — follow, take for one's base, make ... the base (for: of), use as a text-book; take as a text; **legge -en til** lay the foundation of; **ligge til** — for underlie; **-en til** at the reason why; **det er ingen** — **til å** there is no reason why; **jeg har ingen** — **til å** I have no reason el. occasion to.

grunn|areal area. **-avgift** groundrent. **-begrep** fundamental notion. **-betydning** primary signification.

grunne (subst) (i sjøen) bank, shoal. **få av -n** get afloat, get off.

grunne (vrb) ground, found, establish, lay the foundation of; (i maling) prime, ground; (fig) — **på** found on; **en -t mistanke** a well founded suspicion; **-t på** in consequence of.

grunn|eiendom landed property. **-eier** house-owner; (eier av jord) landed proprietor, (ground) landlord. **-falsk** radically false. **-farger** primitive el. primary colour: (fremherskende f.) predominating colour. **-feste** build on a solid foundation; — **seg** consolidate. **-festelse, -festing** establishment (on a solid foundation). **-festet** fixed. **-fjell** bedrock. **-flate** basis, base. **-fond, se -kapital. -form** primitive form. **-forskjell** fundamental (el. essential el. deeply-rooted) difference. **-forskjellig** essentially el. intrinsically different.

grunning priming.

grunn|kapital stock, funds, paid up capital. **-komisk** highly comical.

grunnlag base, basis, foundation; **danne -et for** form the basis of; **på** — **av** on the basis of.

grunn|legge found, lay the foundation of. **-leggelse** foundation. **-legger** founder.

grunnlinje base.

grunnlov fundamental law, constitution. **grunnlovgivende forsamling** Constituent Assembly.

grunnlovs|bestemmelse provision of the fundamental law. **-brudd** violation of the f. l. **-dag** Constitution Day, the anniversary of the Constitution. **-fiendtlig** anticonstitutional. **-forandring** amendment of the fundamental law. **-messig** constitutional. **-stridig** anticonstitutional. **-tro** constitutionalist.

grunn|lærd profoundly learned, erudite. **-lære** fundamental doctrine.

grunnlønn basis salary, basis wage, commencing salary.

grunn|løs groundless, baseless. **-løshet** groundlessness. **-mangel** fundamental want el. defect. **-mur** brick wall. **-murt** brick-built; (fig) firm, deep-rooted, unconquerable.

grunn|ord primitive word; **-pille** main pillar, m. prop. **-plan** ground-plan. **-preg** essential stamp el. feature. **-prinsipp** fundamental principle.

grunn|pris basis price. **–regel** fundamental rule. **–rik** very-rich. **–riss** ground plan. draught, outline. **–setning** principle, maxim; (mat) axiom; **en mann uten –er** an unprincipled man. **–sette** run aground. **–skatt** land-tax.

grunnskole (som gir den elementære undervisning) elementary school.

grunn|skudd shot between wind and water. **–språk** (det språk en bok er skrevet i) original language. **–stamme** stock. **–stein** foundation stone, first stone. **–stoff** element. **–stykke** piece of land. **–støte** strike, strand. **–støt(n)ing** striking the ground. **–syn** fundamental view.

grunn|takst assessment of ground rent. **–taljer** relieving tackles. **–tall** cardinal number. **–tanke** fundamental idea el. notion. **–tone** keynote. **–trekk** outline, sketch; characteristic, essential feature. **–vann** (under)ground water; (mar) bilgewater.

grunnverdi ground value.

grunn|voll foundation, basis, base, groundwork. **grunnærlig** perfectly honest.

gruoppvekkende shocking, horrible, horrid.

gruppe group. **–re** group. **–ring** grouping.

grus gravel; (mur-) rubbish; **synke i — fall to ruins; styrte i — lay in ruins. –gang** gravel walk. **–lagt** gravelled. **–legging** gravelling, (jernb.) ballasting. **grus(n)ing** gravelling.

grusom cruel. **–het** cruelty.

grus|tak gravel-pit. **–vei** gravelled road.

grut (i kaffe) grounds, grouts. **–et** grouty, muddy.

gruve (subst) pit; (bergverks-) mine; (fordypning i alm.) hollow. **–arbeid** mining (work). **–arbeider** miner, pitman. **–drift** working mines, mining.

gru(v)e (nesegrus) stoopingly. pronely; **kaste seg —** ned fall prone el. prostrate.

gry (vrb) dawn, break, peep; **dagen –r** the day dawns, the day is breaking, it dawns. **gry** (subst) dawn, day-dawn, peep of day.

gryn groat, grit; peeled grain. **–et** gritty. **–mel, –mjøl** pollard. **–sodd** mutton broth.

grynt grunt. **gryntе** grunt. **grynting** grunting. **gryte** pot; (t. fisk) kettle; **små –r har også ører** little pitchers have large ears. **gryte|klut, –lapp** kettle-holder. **–lokk** potcover, pot-lid. **–sleiv** ladle.

grø(d)e crop, produce, product, production; **–rik** fruitful. **–tid** season of vegetation. **–vær** genial weather. **–år:** godt, dårlig — productive, unproductive year.

grøft ditch, trench. **grøfte** ditch, trench. **grøfte|graver** ditcher. **–kant** edge of a ditch. **–vann** ditchwater.

Grønland Greenland. **grønlandsfarer** Greenland man, whaler. **grønlandsk** Greenland.

grøn|lender, –lenderinne Greenlander.

grøn(n) green; (bare om gras og fig) verdant; (ungdommelig) raw; **dra ut i det –e** take a trip into the country; **sove på sitt –e øre** be fast asleep; (spøkende) **ved min –e side** beside me; **Det –e forberg** Cape Verd; **i hans –e ungdom** in his salad days. **–e erter** green peas.

grønn|farget dyed green; green-coloured. **–før** green crops; green food el. fodder. **–fore** feed on green food. **–foring** soiling. **–gul** greenish yellow. **–het** greenness, viridity. **–ing** green. **–kledd** dressed in green. **–kål** kail, kale, borecole.

grønnlig greenish.

grønn|saker greens, vegetables. **–saktorg** vegetable market. **–saltet** corned. **–skolling** greenhorn, puppy.

grønn|svær green-sward, sod. **–såpe** soft soap.

grønske verdancy, green stain; green el. pond scum.

grønt (som subst) green; greenery; (grønnsaker) vegetables. **–handler, –handlerske** greengrocer.

grøpp (grovmalt korn) bruised grain.

grøppe (grovmale korn) grind coarsely.

gross, se **gys. grøsse,** se **gyse; det –r i meg bare jeg tenker på det** I shudder to think of it.

grøt, se **graut.**

grøtstein (kleber) potstone.

grå gray, grey, grizzled; **–tt vær** dark el. cloudy weather; **den — oldtid** remote antiquity; **det setter ham — hår i hodet** it troubles him sorely; (fig); **male –tt i –tt** paint in dark colours. **–aktig** grayish, grizzly. **–blå** bluish grey.

gråbein, se **ulv.**

gråbror (fransiskaner) Grey Friar.

grådig greedy, voracious.

grådighet greediness, voracity, avidity.

grå|dyr reindeer. **–gås** wildgoose.

grå|herdet hoary, gray-headed. **–het** grayness. **–håret** gray-haired, hoary. **–kledd** dressed in gray.

grå|melert mixed grey. **–ne** turn gray. **–pære** Lammas pear. **–skjegg** gray-beard. **–skjegget** gray-bearded. **–sprengt** grizzled.

grå|spurv sparrow. **–stein** rubble.

gråt weeping; **briste i — burst into tears. –blandet** mingled with tears. **–full** tearful.

gråte cry, weep (over: for; **av glede:** for el. with joy); **— ut** weep one's fill; **— seg blind** cry one's eyes out; **gråtende: med — tårer** weeping, dissolved in tears.

gråteferdig ready to cry.

gråte|kone hired mourner. **–pil** weeping willow.

gråt|kvalt stifled by sobs. **–løs** tearless.

gråt|mild lachrymose, tearful. **–mildhet** lachrymosity, tearfulness.

grå|verk squirrel skin. **–vær** grey el. cloudy weather. **–værsdag** grey day.

guano guano.

gubbe old man, veteran, greybeard.

Gud God; **— skje lov! — være lovet!** thank God. God be praised! **— bevare meg!** bless me! **dear me! ja, — bevares by all means, most certainly; det forbyde —!** Heaven forbid! **ved — by God! så sant — hjelpe meg!** so help me God! **— forbarme seg!** Good gracious; mercy on us! **å, du godeste — dt.** my goodness me! **jeg takker min —** I thank my stars; **—! (dt) my stars! dear me! — skal vite** (ɔ: det er sikkert) Heaven knows; **— vet, — må vite** (ɔ: jeg gad vite) Heaven knows; **ja det vet — jeg vil** I will. most certainly, most decidedly; **han har, — vet av hva grunn . . . he has, for some reason best known to himself; om — vil** please God, please Heaven, God willing; **— gi** would to God, God grant, would to Heaven, wish to Heaven; **gi seg — i** vold commend oneself to God; **— fader** God the Father; **— Herren** the Lord God; **— Sønn** God the Son; **I guder!** ye powers (above); **et syn for –er** a sight to see; **et –s barn** a child of God, **–s bord** the Lord's supper el. table med **–s hjelp,** se: **om — vil; –s død! 's death! en –s lykke** a most fortunate thing; **denne –s mann** this godly man; **–s mor** the Mother of Our Lord; **hva i –s navn . . . what on earth . . .; for –s skyld** for God's sake, for the love of God; **–s tilskikkelse** divine dispensation; **–s under** miracle; **det var et –s under,** at han unnslapp he had a miraculous el. providential escape; **her er en –s velsignelse av stoler** here is plenty of chairs, here are chairs galore.

gud|barn godchild. **–datter** goddaughter. **–dom** godhead, deity, divinity. **–dommelig** divine. **–dommelighet** divinity, deity.

gude|bilde idol. **–drikk** nectar; delicious drink. **gudelig** godly, pious; (andektig, oppbyggelig) devotional. **gudelighet** godliness, piety.

gudelære mythology.

gude|sagn myth. **–verden** world of gods mythic world, mythology.

gud|far godfather. **–fryktig** godly, pious, god-fearing. **–fryktighet** godliness, piety. **–hengiven** resigned (to the will of God). **–hengivenhet** resignation. **–inne** goddess.

gud|lignende god-like. **–løs** godless, implous. **–løshet** godlessness, impiety. **–menneske** God-man, God and man. **–mor** godmother.

guds|barn child of God. **–begrep** notion of God. **–bespottelig** blasphemous. **–bespottelse** blasphemy. **–bespotter** blasphemer. **–dom** (Guds straff) judgment of God; (gammel rettsprøve) ordeal. **–dyrkelse** divine worship. **–dyrker** worshipper. **guds|engel** angel of God. **–forakter** despiser of God. **–forgåen** graceless, abandoned. **–forgåenhet** gracelessness, depravity. **–forhold** religious position. **–forlatt** God-forsaken. **–fornektelse** atheism. **–fornekter** atheist. **–fred** truce of God. **–frykt** fear of God. **–hus** temple. **–jammerlig** pitiful, miserable.

gudsord word of God; **— fra landet** innocent.

gudstjeneste (divine) service; **etter –n** after church; **–n begynner** divine service begins.

gudsønn godson.

gufs air, breath, gust, puff (of wind) sudden rush of air.

Guinea Guinea. **–bukta** the Gulf of Guinea. **–kysten** the coast of Guinea.

gul yellow; **slå en — og blå, — og grønn** beat one black and blue; **han ergret seg — og grønn** it irritated him beyond endurance; **den –e feber** the yellow fever, Yellow Jack; **det –e** yellow, the yellow colour. **–aktig** yellowish.

gulasj (egtl. ungarsk ragout m. salt og pepper **— gulyas**, men brukt fig. om egennyttig utnyttelse av vanskelighetene under krigen) profiteering practice. **–baron** (krigsjobber) profiteer.

gul|blakk fallow. **–brun** tawny.

gul|erot carrot. **–grå** yellowish grey. **–håret** yellow-haired. **–hvit** creamcoloured, creamy white.

gull gold; **det er ikke — alt som glimrer** all is not gold that glitters; **love — og grønne skoger** promise wonders, promise mountains of gold; **tro som — true** as steel; **det er — verdt** it is worth its weight in gold.

gull|aktig gold-like. **–alder** golden age. **–barre** ingot, bar of gold. **–beslått** gold-mounted. **–bille** golden beetle. **–blad** gold-leaf. **–blekk, –blikk** plate of gold. **–brand** ring-finger. **–briller** gold-rimmed spectacles. **–brodert** embroidered with gold. **–bryllup** golden wedding. **–fisk** goldfish.

gull|fot gold standard. **–frynse** gold-fringe. **–førende** auriferous, gold-bearing. **–glans** golden lustre. **–glinsende** glittering as gold. **–graver** (gold-)digger. **–grav(n)ing** gold-digging. **–grunn** goldground; gold size. **–gruve** gold mine; (amr) placer. **–gul** golden (yellow). **–holdig** containing gold. **–håret** golden-haired.

gullig yellowish.

gull|innfatning golden setting. **–kalv** golden calf. **–kant** gilt edge. **–kjede** gold chain. **–klump** (gold-)nugget. **–knapp** gold button. **–knappet stokk** gold-headed cane. **–korn** grain of gold. **–leie** gold-diggings.

gull|lokket with golden locks, golden-haired. **–maker** alchymist. **–makeri** alchymy.

gullmark gold mark.

gullmedalje gold medal; **drikker til den store — drinks** as for a wager.

gull|mine gold mine. **–mynt** gold coin.

gull|oppløsning solution of gold. **–papir** gold paper. **–penger** gold-money. **–randet: — sky** gold-tipped cloud. **–regn** golden shower; (bot) laburnum. **–rik** rich in gold. **–sand** gold-sand; yellow shining sand. **–sko** golden shoe. **–smed** jeweller, goldsmith; (insekt) dragon-fly.

gullsnitt gilt edges; **— øverst** gilt head; **med — gilt-edged**.

gull|snor gold-braid. **–stas** gold-jewelry. **–stol** golden chair; **bære en på — carry** one in a king's cushion, chair one **–stykke** gold piece. **–støv** gold dust. **–tresse** gold-lace. **–trykk** gold-printing. **–tråd** gold wire; gold-thread. **–tørst** thirst of gold. **–ur** gold watch. **–vasker** gold washer. **–vasking** gold-washing. **–vekt** assay

balance, gold weight; **veie sine ord på — weigh** every word. **–virket** wrought with gold.

gullåre vein of gold.

gulne turn yellow.

gulpe opp gulp up.

gul|sott jaundice. **–sottig** jaundiced. **–spurv** yellow-hammer. **–stripet** yellow-striped.

gulv, se golv.

gumiere (zoologi), se **gomiere.**

gummi gum; (arabisk) gum-arabic; (oppløst) gum-paste, liquid-gum. **–aktig** gummy, gummous. **gummidekk** (på sykkel) rubber tire.

gummiere gum; **gummiert konvolutt** adhesive envelope.

gummi|hjul rubber-tyred wheel. **–kalosje** rubber shoe. **–lerret** caoutchouc-linen. **–plante** India-rubber tree. **–ring** rubber-tyre. **–støvler** gum-boots. **–tre** gum-tree. **–tøy** caoutchouc-tissue.

gump (på fugl) rump.

gungre resound. **gungring** resounding.

gunst favour; **til — for** in favour of; **til — for meg** in my favour; **stå i — hos** be in favour with; **komme i — hos** obtain favour with.

gunstbevisning favour.

gunstig favourable, propitious.

gurgle (seg) gargle; (om lyden) gurgle. **–vann** gargle. **gurgling** gargling.

gusten sallow, wan. **–het** sallowness.

gutere relish, enjoy.

gutt boy, lad; (læregutt) apprentice; **da jeg var — when** (I was) a boy; **fra — av** from a boy. **–aktig** boyish, puerile. **–aktighet** boyishness, puerility.

guttaperka gutta-percha. **–varer** rubber-goods.

gutte|alderen boyhood. **–barn** male child. **–klær** boy's clothes. **–skole** boy's school, school for boys. **–strek** boyish trick el. prank. **–år** boyish years, years of boyhood.

guttural (adj og subst) guttural.

guvern|ante governess. **–ement** government.

guvernør governor.

gyger (trollkjerring) giantess.

gylden florin, guilder.

gyldig valid. **–het** validity.

gyl|len golden, gold; **den –ne åre** the piles, hæmorrhoids, (pl); **det –ne skinn** the golden fleece; **–ne dager** palmy days, dt. piping times; **–ne ord** words of gold; **den –ne middelvei** the golden mean.

gyllenlakk wallflower, gillyflower.

gyllenlær gilt and figured leather.

gymnasiast collegian.

gymnast gymnast; **–iker** gymnast, gymnastic, **gymnastikk** athletics, gymnastics. **–lokale** gymnasium. **–lærer** teacher of gymnastics, drill-master. **–oppvisning** gymnastic display.

gymnastikk|sal gymnasium. **–sko** athletic shoes.

gymnastisere practise athletic excercises.

gymnastisk gymnastic.

gynekolog gynecologist.

gynge (vrb) swing, rock; **–nde grunn** unsafe ground, a quagmire.

gynge (subst alm. huske) swing. **–hest** rocking horse. **–stol** rocking-chair. **gynging** swinging.

gys shudder.

gyse shudder; **det –r i meg** I shudder; **— tilbake for** shrink from.

gys|elig horrible. **–elighet** horror. **–ing** shuddering, shudder.

gyte pour, shed; (om fisk o. l.) spawn.

gytje bathing-mud. **–bad** mud-bath.

gyve fly, fuz.

gyvel broom.

gå go; (spasere) walk; (sin vei) come away, leave, go; (passere) pass; (strekke seg) run; (om maskiner o. l.) move, work; **la oss — let** us be going; **jeg bad ham — I** told him to be gone; **det gikk ganske annerledes** it fell out quite differently; **det får — som det vil** happen what may; **det gikk dårlig med det fore-**

tagendet that enterprise did not succeed; det
gikk som jɛg tenkte it fell out as I expected;
slik -r det i verden that is the way of the
world; hvordan -r det deg (i verden)? how
goes the world with you? det -r ikke it's no go,
it won't do; det gikk ikke it didn't answer; det
-r nok it will be all right; det gikk i døra the
door was opened, shut; tiden -r time flies (fast);
få tiden til å — while away time; dampskipet
-r klokka 1 the steamer sails el. leaves at one
(o'clock); denne mynten -r ikke her i landet
this coin is not current in this country; B. -r
(teat) Exit B.; E. og B. -r Exeunt A. and B.;
dette stykket gikk tjue ganger i trekk this play
ran for twenty nights; forestillingen gikk ganske
godt the performance went off pretty well;
uret -r ganske godt the watch keeps time well
enough; -r vel fort is rather fast; sjøen -r
høyt the sea runs high; disse varene -r fort
these goods sell, go off rapidly; -r langsomt
find a slow sale. — ledig be idle; la — (mar)
let go! (fig) la —! here goes! — sin vei go one's
way, come away; — seg en tur take a walk;
— seg trett tire oneself with walking. -ende:
holde det -ende keep the pot boiling, the game
alive; hun hadde spillet -ende she had the
game in her own hands.

gå| an: det -r an it will do, it answers well
enough, it is pretty fair; det -r aldri an that
will never do.

gå| av: hva -r det av ham? what's the matter
with him? what possesses him? — av (av gå)
retire; børsa gikk av the gun went off; fargen
-r av the colour comes off, rubs off. — av med
seieren carry the day; — av møte go out of
fashion; -r av seg selv is mere child's play.

gå bort go away, leave.

gå| etter (hente) go for, (rette seg etter) go
by; (undersøke) look into; der er -tt bud etter
ham he has been sent for; (fig) ha noe å — etter
have something to go upon; alt er -tt etter
ønske for ham everything has succeeded to his
wishes; — etter lyden follow the sound, go
after the sound.

gå| for (om mynt) be worth, be current at
(på auksjon) be knocked down at; — for pass
for; han -r for en rik mann he is looked upon
as a wealthy man; — for en go for one, go
in another's place; hva -r for seg her? what
is going on el. forward here? når skal det —
for seg when is it to come off?

gå foran (prep) go before. precede; (fig) be
paramount to; (adv) lead the way.

gå| forbi go el. pass by; la ... eilgheten —
forbi let the opportunity slip.

gå forut for precede.

gå| fra leave, leave behind; (fraregnes) be de-
ducted; — fra kone og barn desert wife and
children; — fra et kjøp recede from a bargain,
retract a bargain; — fra sitt ord disavow,
deny el. go back from one's word; han gikk
fra gård og grunn his estate went to the hammer; — fra arv og gjeld renounce inheritance
and liabilities; — fra forstanden run el. go mad.

gå| fram go on, get on, advance; (bære seg
at) go about it, work, act, behave; — framover
progress, make progress.

gå| hen: — ubemerket hen pass unnoticed; —
ustraffet hen go unpunished; — lett henover
touch lightly upon.

gå| i: — hundene go to the dogs; hun -r
i sitt 18de år she is in her 18th year; døra
er -tt i baklås the lock (of the door) has slipped
el. caught; — i drift (mar) go adrift; — i sorg
be in mourning; — i femte klasse be in the fifth
class; — i kloster take the veil; turn monk;
— i været go up, rise; det gikk mark i det
it became worm-eaten; det gikk koldbrand i
mortifikation set in; — i seg selv think better of
it, repent.

gå igjen reappear, haunt the house.

gå| igjennom go through, get through, pass
through, (lide), undergo; forslaget, søknaden
gikk igjennom the motion was carried, the
petition was granted.

gå imellom go between, interfere. intervene.

gå imot: skjebnen gikk ham imot things went
against him.

gå| inn (tre inn) go in, enter; — inn (i hær
e. l.) enter; join; (om en avis) cease to appear,
come to an end; (om et selskap, forretning)
expire; — inn i go into, enter; — inn på (en)
fall el. set upon, (noe) agree to, fall into, submit
to; (en spøk o. l.) fall into, humour, enter into
the spirit of; (behandle) go into; jeg -r nødig
inn på å it goes hard with me to; — inn i en
havn put into a harbour; han er nylig -tt inn
i sitt 18de år he has entered his 18th year;
denne planen gikk inn igjen that plan was
abandoned; la oss — inn til damene! let us join
the ladies.

gå i stykker, sund break.

gå| med (en person) go along with,
(klær osv.) wear; (paraply o. l.) carry; — med
tæring i kroppen have a disposition to consumption; hvorledes -r det med helbreden?
how is your health? hvordan -r det med pro-
sessen? how do you get on with your lawsuit?
slik -r det med de fleste that is the way
with most people; hele sommeren -r med it
takes all summer; det -r med (på kjøpet) that's
thrown in; det -r mye med much is consumed.

gå ned (om sola) go down, set; (om urverk)
run (itself) out.

gå nedover descend. han gikk — trappa
descended the stairs.

gå| om: — om igjen go back again, be reversed;
la handelen — om igjen relinquish the bargain;
— om(kring) go about; go round; jeg -r omkring med en plan I have a scheme in my
head.

gå| opp (om vinduer dører) open, fly
open; (om sol teppe, pris) rise; (om knute)
come untied; (i knappingen) come unbuttoned; (om regnstykke) come right, work
out; (om kabal) come out, come right; døra
gikk opp og igjen the door opened and shut;
7 -r opp i 49 7 measures 49; — opp i røyk end in
smoke; opp til (eksamen) go in for, up for;
det gikk opp for meg it dawned upon me, I became conscious (of el. that), I began to realize;
det gikk plutselig opp for meg it flashed upon
me that; — helt opp balance; (fig.) det -r opp
i opp it is an even balance.

gå oppover ascend; han gikk — trappa
ascended the stairs.

gå over cross; (overskride) exceed, surpass;
(smerte) cease, go off; (vrede) vanish, pass
away; (uvær) cease, subside; (til en mening)
come round (to an opinion); (til noe annet)
turn, go on, proceed (to); det er -tt over i vårt
språk it has passed into our language; — over
i reserven pass into the reserve; — over til
kristendommen become a Christian; — over til
den katolske kirke join the Church of Rome.

gå| på (framover) go ahead, go on, make play;
(om en hanske o. l.) go on; (fortere) quicken
one's pace; — på ball go to a ball; — på kaféer
frequent cafés; — løs på go for; det -r på livet
løs it is a matter of life and death; han -r like
løs på saken he does not beat about the bush;
— tilbake på (et visst ord) refer to; det -r på hans
regning it is placed to his account; munnen -r på
ham he rattles away; dette er hardt å — på this
is hard lines; det -r for ofte på it happens too
frequently; det -r 20 shilling på et pund 20
shillings make a pound, go to a pound; visen
-r på melodien... is sung to the tune
of ...

gå| til: vannet gikk ham til halsen the water
reached up to his neck; det -r mange penger til
it takes a good deal of money; hvor mye tøy

-r det til kjolen? how much cloth is required for the dress? **hvordan -r det til?** how is it done? **slik gikk det til** at thus it happened el. came to pass that; **slik -r det til i verden** that's the way of the world; **det gikk muntert til** it was a jolly affair; **det gikk underlig til med den saken** it was a queer business; **klokka -r til 12** it is past eleven (o'clock), it is getting on for twelve; — **til scenen** go on the stage; — **til lovart av** (mar) weather.

gå | tilbake (om handel etc.) go back, be broken off, go off; (om vannet) recede; **det er -tt tilbake med ham** his affairs are in a reduced state, he has gone down in the world.

gå | under: byen gikk under the town was destroyed; **skipet gikk under** the ship went down, the ship foundered; **han -r navn av** he is known el. goes by the name of;

gå ut: plantene gikk ut the plants died; **ilden, lyset gikk ut** the fire, candle went out; — **ut og inn** run in and out; (i et hus) have the run of a house; — **ut av** go out of, leave; **jeg -r ut fra** my starting-point is, I start by understanding, I take it for granted (at the outset); I write upon the footing that; **hans ondskap gikk ut over ham selv** his malice recoiled on himself; **det vil — ut over ham** he will have to suffer; **la det — ut over en** fall upon one; **la sitt raseri — ut over** vent el. visit one's rage upon; — **ut på** tend to, terminate in; **hans streben -r ut på** his object, aim is; **svaret gikk ut på at** the answer was to the effect that . . . **på å bevise** was directed to the purpose of showing; **jeg så hva alt dette gikk ut på** I perceived the drift of all this; **anklagen -r ut på** at the charge is that; **døra -r ut til galleriet** the door opens into el. on

the gallery; — **ute** be out. **gå videre:** go on; **la — videre** pass on.

går: i går yesterday; **i går aftes** last night, yesterday evening. **i går morges** yesterday morning.

gård yard, court, court yard; (forpakter-) farm, farmstead; (større) estate; **værelse til -en** back-room. **-bruker** farmer. **-eier** owner of a house, farm.

gård|mann freeholder. **-mannskone** freeholderwife.

gårds|gutt man-servant, outdoor-servant; (på skyss-skifte) hostler. **-hund** watch-dog.

gårdsplass court-yard.

gårs|dagen yesterday. **-dato: av — dated** yesterday.

gås goose; (fig) goose, simpleton, ninny; **det er som å slå vann på -a** it's like pouring water on a duck's back.

gåse|dun goose-down. **-fett** goosefat. **-fjær** goose-feather; (til penn) goose-quill. **-gang** single file, Indian file, goose-step, follow-my-leader **gå i** — walk in single file, walk in a line, one after the other. **-hud** goose-skin, goose-flesh. **-kjøtt** goose (-flesh). **-kråser** (goose) giblets. **-leverpostei** g-liver pie, Strassburg pie. **-steik** roast goose.

gåsevin Adam's ale, water.

gåsevokter goose-herd.

gåseøyne (anførselstegn) inverted commas, signs of quotation.

gåsunge gosling; (bot) March-brown, palm.

gåte riddle, enigma; **gjette** el. **løse en** — guess, solve, find out a riddle; **det er en fullstendig — for meg** it is a wonder of wonders to me, it is a perpetual mystery to me; **tale i -r** talk puzzles.

gåtefull enigmatical; puzzling.

H

H, h H, h; (musikk) B.

ha! (int) ha! aha!

ha have; **brevet har den dato** the letter bears that date; **han har ingenting** he does not possess anything, he is worth nothing; **han har ingen penger** he has (got) no money; **har du en kniv? penger?** have you got a knife? any money? — **omgang med** associate with, keep company with; **hva vil De** — what do you want? (om mat eller drikke) what will you take? **hva skal De** —? (betaling) what is your charge? **å, den som hadde en stol!** O for a chair! **han vil — dem til å gjøre det** he wants them to do it, he will have them do it; **han har det bra,** (om helbred) he is well **han har det godt,** smått (om kår) he is well off, ill off; **hvordan har De det?** how are you? **nå har jeg det** I have it; **der har vi det** that's it; **det har han etter sin far** in that he takes after his father; **vi har ennå langt hjem** we are still far from home; **jeg har ikke mye igjen** I have not much left; **jeg har ingenting imot** I have no objection to; **jeg har mye imot** I object strongly to; **har du boka med?** have you brought the book? **han hadde svart hatt på** he wore a black hat; **han hadde hatten på** he had his hat on; **har De en kniv på Dem?** have you a knife about you? **det har ikke stort på seg** it is no great matter, of small consequence, comes to very little; **jeg har bare to igjen** I have only two left; **alt det jeg har igjen** all that remains to me; **vi har ingen penger til overs** we have no money to spare; **han har mye til overs for meg** he is very fond of me, he has a great regard for me; **han har ikke noe til overs for meg** he does not care for me; **han har vanskelig for å** he has some

difficulty in; **han har lett for å** it is easy for him; **han har noe hemmelighetsfullt ved seg** there is some mystery about him.

habengut goods and chattels.

habil able. **habilitere** qualify.

habitt habit. **habitus** habit.

hafelle, se gjerde.

hage garden, (hest-) enclosure, paddock, (frukt-) orchard. **-bruk** gardening, horticulture. **-bruksselskap** horticultural society. **-bruksutstilling** horticultural exhibition. **-kniv** pruning knife. **-port** garden gate. **-redskap** garden-implement. **-saks** gardener's shears. **-selskap** garden party. **-stue** garden-room.

hagl (ishagl) hail; (et enkelt) hailstone; (til å skyte med) (small) shot; (et enkelt blyhagl) a shot (plur: shot).

haglbye hail shower, hail storm.

haglbørse fowling-piece, shot-gun.

hagle hail; (om kuler) fall like hail, like a shower, patter; **svetten -t av ham** perspiration streamed down his face.

hagl|korn hail-stone. **-pung** shotbag, shot-pouch. **-skade** damage done by hail. **-vær** hailstorm, haily weather.

hagtorn hawthorn, white thorn.

hai shark.

I. **hake** hook; (fig) drawback (**ved:** to, upon). **hake** (vrb) hook; — **seg fast i** hook on to.

II. **hake** (ansiktsdel) chin. **-kløft** dimple in the chin. **-kors** fylfot, swastika. **-reim** chinstrap. **-skjegg** chinbeard. **-smekke** bib, feeder.

hakk hack, notch, indentation.

hakke (subst) pick, pickaxe, mattock.

hakke (vrb) hack, hoe, grub; (om fugler) peck (**på:** at); (kjøtt) chop, mince; (i talen) stutter;

jeg -r tenner av kulde my teeth are chattering with cold; — **på** (fig) carp at.
hakke|blokk chopping-block. **-brett** chopping-board; (mar) taffrail. **-kniv** chopping-knife, meat-chopper.
hakkels(e) chaff; **skjære** — chop straw. **-kiste** bin for chaff. **-maskin** chaff-cutter.
hakke|mat minced meat, mince-meat; (fig) gallimaufry. **-pølse** white pudding, chitlings **-spett** nicker, wood-pecker. **hakking** (i talen) stuttering, hemming and hawing.
hal (et) pull, tug, haul.
hale haul, pull; — **i buksene** hitch up one's trousers; — **inn** haul in; — **inn på et skip** gain upon a ship; — **ned** haul down; — **ut** (fig.) delay, put off.
hale (subst) tail. **-finne** tail-fin. **-fjær** tail-feather.
I. **hall** (en) large saloon, hall.
II. **hall** (skråning) dip, inclination, incline, slant, slope.
halleluja hallelujah!
halling (dans) fling.
hallo halloa! hallo! (ansporende rop til jakt-hunder) tally-ho!
hallomann (i radio) speaker, announcer.
hallusinasjon hallucination.
hallusinere hallucinate.
halm straw.
halma (et brettspill) halma.
halm|lass cart- el. waggon load of straw. **-sekk** straw-bag; (som madrass) strawbed. **-strå** straw; **den som holder på å drukne griper etter et** — a drowning man will catch at a straw (el. clutch at straws). **-tak** thatched roof. **-visk** wisp of straw.
halo! halloo, hollo, holloa! **halol** (subst) uproar, hubbub, row; **lage** — kick up a row.
hals (særlig den ytre og bakerste del av halsen) neck; (strupen, den forreste del av halsen) throat; (på note) stem; (til seil) tack; (på gaffel, anker) throat; (på fat) quarter; **brekke -en** break one's neck; **gi** — give tongue, challenge; **strekke** — stretch out one's neck; **knekke -en på en flaske** crack a bottle; **rope av full** — cry out at the top of one's voice; **le av full** — roar with laughter; **ha vondt i -en** have a sore throat; **helle i -en på en** pour down one's throat; **med hjertet i -en** with my heart in my mouth; **falle om -en på en** fall upon one's neck; throw oneself about (upon) one's neck; **dreie -en om på en** wring the neck of; **over** — **og hode** in hot haste, precipitately, in a great hurry, with the utmost speed, (om løp) head over heels; **ha (fått) på -en** be encumbered with, have got upon one's hands; **få en feber på -en** get a fever; **skaffe en noe på -en** saddle one with, plague one with; **han er en spesialist, en tory på sin** — he is a specialist of the specialists, a Tory of the Tories, etc.; **han er engelskmann på sin** — he knows English thoroughly.
hals|betennelse inflammation of the throat, angina, sore throat. **-bind** cravat; (gmlt. og mil.) stock.
hals|brann heartburn, water-brash. **-brekkende** breakneck.
hals|byll boil in the throat. **-bånd** necklace, necklet; (til hunder) collar.
halse (gjø) give tongue, bay; (kuvende) wear.
halsesyke, se **halsbetennelse**.
halshogge behead, decapitate.
halshogging decapitation.
hals|hvirvel vertebra of the neck. **-jern** iron collar.
halskar man at the tack.
hals|kjede neck-chain. **-linning** band (of a shirt).
halsløs neckless; — **gjerning** capital offence, hanging matter, hanging affair.
hals|onde complaint in the throat. **-(og hånds)-rett** (hist) power of life and limb, of life and

death. **-sløyfe** neck-knot. **-smykke** ornament for the neck.
halsstarrig stubborn, obstinate, stiff-necked.
halsstarrighet stubbornness, obstinacy.
hals|stemme falsetto, head-voice. **-stykke** (av slaktet dyr) neck. **-sykdom** complaint in the throat. **-tilfelle** complaint el. disease in the throat. **-tone** falsetto note. **-tørkle** neck-cloth, neck-handkerchief, neck-tie; (manns) cravat; (dames) fichu, (strikket) comforter, muffler.
halt lame (of a leg), lamed, halting; — **på det ene benet** lame of one leg.
halte halt, limp, hobble, walk lame, go halt; **-nde lignelse** halting comparison; **enhver lignelse -r** every comparison halts. **halte|fanden** the Devil on two sticks. **-pink** hopins. **halthet** lameness. **halting** halting etc., limp.
halunk villain, scoundrel.
halv half; **en** — **alen** half an ell; — **sorg** half (el. second) mourning; — **pris** halfprice; **for** — **pris for half price**; — **pause** minim rest; **-e forholdsregler** halfmeasures; **-e kloden** half the globe; **-e Norge** half Norway; **et -t år** half a year, six months; **to og en** — **mil** two miles and a half, two and a half miles; **to og en** — **penny** twopence half-penny; **en** — **gang til så lang** half as long again; **klokka er** — **tolv** it is half past eleven (o'clock); **det -e** half (of it); **barn det -e children** half-price; (adv) **halvt** half; **-t om -t** nearly, well night; **dele -t, være -t om** go halves, dt. go snacks (with); **han gjør ingenting -t** he does nothing by halves.
halv|annen one and a half; **halvannen penny** three halfpence, penny half-penny, a penny halfpenny. **-ark** half sheet. **-befaren** (matros) ordinary seaman. **-bemannet** half-manned. **-bevisst** half conscious, semi-conscious.
halvbind (bokbind med rygg av annet materiale enn sidene) half binding.
halv|blind purblind, parcel-blind. **-blods** half-blood, half-breed. **-bror** half brother. **-brukt** half-worn. **-dannelse** superficial education, semi-civilization. **-dannet** half-bred, half-educated, under-bred. **-del** half; **-delen** one half; **-delen av dem som** half those who. **-død** half-dead. **-dør** half-door, latch (of a door). **-edelsten** semiprecious stone. **halvere** halve, bisect. **-erme** half-sleeve. **-femte** four and a half. **-ferdig** half done, half -finished; **jeg er ikke -ferdig med å spise** I have not half done eating. **-fetter** second cousin. **-fjerde** three and a half. **-flaske** half-bottle. **-full** half full; (om et menneske) half drunk, half-gone, half seas over. **-gal** half mad, half gone; dt. **han er jo -gal** (ubesindig) he is so senseless. **-gammel** oldish. **-gjort** half done. **-gras** sedge plant. **-gud** demi-god. **-hanske** mitten, half-mitten. **-het** incompleteness; (fig) indecision, vacillation; half-measures. **-hundre** fifty. **-hundreårig** **-hundreårs** of fifty years, fifty years old. **-hundreårsdagen** the fiftieth anniversary. **-høyt** in a half-whisper. **-kaste** half-caste. **-klar** dim. **-klode** hemisphere. **-krets** semi-circle. **-kule** hemisphere. **-kuleformet** hemispherical, semi-globular. **-kusine** second cousin. **-kvalt** half-smothered. **-kvedet: han forstår en** — **vise** he can take a hint.
halvleik (i fotball) halftime, time.
halvmillionær semi-millionaire.
halv|mett half-satisfied; **jeg er ikke -mett** I have not half done eating. **-moden** half ripe. **-mørke** twilight. **-måne** half-moon, crescent. **-månedannet** crescent-shaped, semilunar, crescentic. **-månedlig** half-monthly, semimonthly. **-onkel** half-uncle. **-silke** silk-cotton. **-sirkel** semi-circle. **-sirkelformig** semi-circular. **-slitt** half -worn. **-sløv** half-idiotic. **-sove** doze, drowse. **-spenn** (om skytevåben) half-coke(i — on, at). **-stekt** half-done. **-stikk** half-hitch. **-strømpe** sock; (for barn) half-hose. **-studert** half-learned; **-studert røver** smatterer, sciolist. **-søsken** half -sisters and half-brothers. **-søster** half-sister.

-søvn slumber, doze. **-såle** (vrb og subst) half-sole. **-tak** pent-roof. **-tone** semi-tone. **-tredje** two and a half; **-tullet** dt. du er nok — you are not in your right mind! you are not quite right! **-tulling** simpleton, half-witted person. **-ull** half-wool. **-ullen** half-woollen.

halvvei: på -en half-way, midway.

halvveis half-way, midway; (nesten) almost, in some degree, in a manner; **jeg har — lyst til å** I have half a mind to.

halv|vill semi-savage. **-voksen** half-grown **-våken** half awake.

halv|øy peninsula. **-åpen** half-open. **-år** half-year, six months. **-årig** half a year old. **-årlig** half-yearly, semi-annual; (adv) half-yearly. **-års** of six months. **-årsvis** half-yearly.

ham him; **det er** — it is he; dt. it's him.

ham (subst) slough; **skyte** — cast the s. el. skin. **hamle, se skåte; kunne — opp med** be able to cope with, be a match for, be even with.

hamleband oar-grummet.

hammer hammer; (trehammer) mallet; (på dør) knocker; (i øret) malleus, hammer; **komme under -en** come under the hammer, go to the hammer, be brought to the hammer. **-hai** hammer-head. **-hode** hammer-head. **-slag** stroke of a hammer. **-tegn** sign of the hammer.

hamn, se havn; (beitemark) grazing ground, pasture, pasture-field, cattle range. **-ehage** enclosed pasture-field.

hamp hemp; **av** — hempen.

hampe|frø hempseed. **-garn** hemp yarn. **-olje** hemp seed oil. **-reip** hempen cord. **-tau** hemp rope.

hamre hammer. **hamring** hammering.

hams (nøtte-) hull.

hamskifte moult, moulting, mewing.

hamstre (hemmelig samle sammen) hoard.

han he; **han . . . selv** he . . . himself.

han|bie drone. **-blomst** male flower.

hand, se hånd. -bak back of the hand.

handel trade, commerce, traffic; (en handel eller avtale) bargain; **slutte en** — strike a bargain; **gjøre en god** — (om kjøper) buy a bargain; (om selger) make a good market; **være ved -en** be employed in trade; **drive** — carry on trade; **drive — med** (f. eks. ost) carry on the trade el. business of (a cheese-monger); **komme i -en** come into the market; **er ikke i -en** is not in the market; **— og vandel** conduct, habits; **i — og vandel** in trade, in business, in common intercourse.

handels|affære commercial affair, matter of trade. **-akademi** mercantile academy. **-artikkel** article of trade, commodity.

handelsattaché commercial attaché.

handels|beretning trade-report, commercial advice el. report. **-berettiget** licensed trader. **-betjent** merchant's clerk, shopman. **-brev** commercial letter. **-by** commercial city el. town. **-departement** the board of trade. **-fag** mercantile line. **-flåte** fleet of merchantmen; mercantile marine. **-folk** commercial nation; tradesmen. **-forbindelse** commercial connection. **-foretagende** commercial enterprise. **-fullmektig** head-clerk. **-gartner** florist and nursery-man, market-gardener. **-gartneri** market gardens. **-gymnasium** mercantile gymnasium. **-hus** commercial house, firm, mercantile establishment. **-kammer** chamber of commerce. **-kompani** trading company. **-korrespondanse** commercial correspondence, mercantile correspondence. **-kutyme** custom in trade, trade usage. **-kyndig** commercial. **-kyndighet** commercial knowledge. **sette i -lære** bind (one) apprentice to a shopkeeper; **han er i -lære** is in apprenticeship with a shopkeeper. **-mann** merchant, trader; (gateselger) hawker, street hawker. **-marine** mercantile marine. **-minister** president of the board of trade; minister of commerce. **-monopol** commercial monopoly. **-moral** commercial morality. **-om-**

setning commercial transaction(s). business,trade. **-ordbok** commercial dictionary, trade-dictionary, dictionary of commerce. **-plass** emporium, place of trade. **-regning** commercial arithmetic. **handels|reisende** commercial traveller. **-rett** (lover) commercial law; (rettighet) license for trading. **-ship** merchantman. **-skole** commercial school. **-stand** mercantile class. **-traktat** commercial treaty. **handelsuttrykk** trade-term, commercial term. **handels|vare** merchandise. **-vei** route of commerce. **-verden** commercial world. **-vesen** trade, commerce, commercial matters. **-virksomhet** commercial transactions el. operations. **-vitenskap** science of commerce. **-øyemed: i** — for purpose of trade. **-ånd** commercial spirit.

hand|fallen embarrassed, puzzled. **-fare** finger, handle, manipulate. **-faring** fingering, handling, manipulation. **-fast** strong, stout.

handikap handicap. **handikappe** handicap.

handlag handiness, the proper knack manual adroitness.

handle act; (omgås med) treat, use, deal with; (drive handel) trade, deal, traffic; **— etter** act on; **— etter eget tykke** use one's own discretion; **— med noe** deal in st.; **— med en** do business with one; **— om** be about, treat of.

handledyktig vigorous, energetic.

handledyktighet activity, energy.

handle|form (gram) the active (voice). **-frihet** freedom of action. **-måte** proceeding, way of proceeding.

handlende, handler tradesman, merchant.

handling action, act; (i skuespill) plot; (akt i skuespill) act; (høytidelig) ceremony, function; **-en foregår på** the scene of action is laid at; **det er mangel på — i stykket** there is a deficiency of action in the play.

han|due cock-pigeon. **-dyr** male.

hane cock; (på kran) (stop-)cock; screwtap, faucet; **eneste — i kurven** the cock of the walk, the captain of the show, the head of the drum; **den røde** — the red cock (ogs. om ild). **-ben: gjøre — til** pay one's addresses to, make sheep's eyes to. **-bjelke** collar-beam.

han|esel jack-ass. **-fasan** cock-pheasant. **-fisk** milter. **-fugl** male (bird), cock. **-føll** colt.

hane|kam cock's comb. **-kamp** cock-fight.

hanekylling cockerel.

hang bent, bias, inclination, propensity.

hangar (flygemaskinskur) hangar, aeroplane shed.

hangle be ailing el. sickly. **— igjennom** get through by the skin of one's teeth.

hanhare buck-hare, male hare.

hank handle, ear; **ha hånd i -e med en** have a hold of one, have a person under one's thumb.

han|kanin buck-rabbit. **-katt** tom-cat.

hankeløs without a handle.

hankjønn male sex, male gender; (gram) the masculine gender.

hann he, male; (om visse fugler) cock. (Sammensetninger med **hann-, se han-**).

Hannover Hanover. **h-aner, h-ansk** Hanoverian.

hanoter dog-otter.

hanplante male plant.

hanrei cuckold; **gjøre til** — cuckold.

hanrev he-fox, dog-fox.

hans his; **brorens og — brev** his brother's letters and his own.

Hans John, Jack, Hans.

hans|a (hist) Hanse. **-eat** native, inhabitant of one of the Hanse towns. **-eatisk** Hanseatic. **-aforbundet** the Hanseatic League.

hansel handsel, earnest.

hansestad Hanse town, Hanseatic town

hanske glove. **-fabrikk** glove-manufactory. **-finger** stall. **-knapper** button-hook. **-maker** glover. **-skinn** glove leather.

hanspurv cock-sparrow.

Harald Harold.
hard hard; (streng) harsh, severe; — mot hard upon, harsh to; **ha — mage** be costive; **det vilde være -t om** it would be hard lines if; **-t mot -t** measure for measure; **sette -t imot -t** repel force by force; **hardt** (adv) hard, hardly etc.; **det gikk — til, holdt** — it was with difficulty, with much ado; **jeg savnet** — I sorely missed; **han sov** — he slept heavily. — **babord! hard a-port!** — **i le! hard a-lee!**
hardfrossen hard-frozen, congealed.
hard|før hardy. **-førhet** hardiness.
hardhaus hardy el. sturdy fellow; a diehard.
hardhendt hardhanded, rough. **-het** handedness, roughness.
hardhet hardness; (strenghet) harshness, roughness.
hard|hjertet hard-hearted. **-hjertethet** hard-heartedness. **-hudet** hard-skinned, callous. **-hudethet** callosity. **-koke** boil hard. **-kokt** hard boiled.
hardnakket stiff-necked, obstinate, persistent; (adv) obstinately; **holder — fast på den tro at** persists in believing that. **hardnakkethet** obstinacy, stubbornness, persistency.
hare hare; **ha et -hjerte** be chicken-hearted, hare-hearted. **-jakt** hare-hunting, hare-shooting. **-labb** hare's foot; **fare over noe med en —** do a thing carelessly.
harem harem, seraglio.
hare|skår lagostoma, harelip; **ha — be** harelipped. **-stek** roast hare. **-unge** young hare, leveret.
harke hawk. **harking** hawking.
harlekin harlequin. **harlekinsløyer** buffoonery.
harm (adj) indignant (på: against, with); **bli — feel** indignant, be vexed.
harme (subst) wrath, ire, resentment. **harme** (vrb) anger, exasperate. **-lig** (som volder harme) vexatious.
harmfull ireful, wrathful, resentful, indignant.
harmløs harmless, inoffensive.
harmonere harmonize; (fig) be in harmony, character el. keeping with; **ikke — med** be out of keeping with; **— med en** sympathize with one.
harmoni harmony, concord, unison.
harmonika concertina, harmonica; (glass-) musical glasses el. accordion.
harmoni|lære harmonics (pl).
harmo|nisere harmonize. **-nisk** harmonious.
harmonium harmonium.
harnisk armour; **komme i — fire up; sette i — provoke, enrage.**
harpe (musikkinstrument) harp; (redskap til rensing el. sortering) screen; **spille på — play** on the harp, harp.
harpe (vrb) (rense, sortere) screen.
harpe|spill playing on the harp. **-spiller, -spillerske** harpist, harper.
harpiks resin. **-aktig** resinous.
harpun harpoon. **-er** harpooner. **-ere** harpoon. **-jern** harpoon-head.
harselas teasing, worrying.
harselere tease, worry.
harsk rancid. **-het** rancidness, rancidity.
harv (subst) harrow.
harve (vrb) harrow.
has: få — på lay to hee .
hasard hazard, chance, risk. **-spill** game of chance; gambling. **-spiller** gambler.
hase (sene i benet) hamstring; (ledd) hough, ham; **skjære -ne over på** hamstring.
hasp(e) (subst) hasp.
hassel hazel. **-busk** hazel bush. **-kjepp** hazelstick. **-nott** hazel nut.
hast hurry, speed; **det har ingen — there is** no hurry; **i — in a hurry; i rivende — in hot** haste; **han har ikke noen — med å** he is in no hurry to.
haste hasten, hurry, speed, haste; **-r! (på** brev) immediate, urgent; **det -r ikke** there is no

hurry; det -r med denne saken this business requires dispatch.
hastemt bombastic, high-falutin.
hastig hurried, quick; (overilet) hasty; hastily.
hastighet rate of motion, rate of speed, rate, velocity, speed.
hastverk hurry, haste; **ha — be in a hurry; hvorfor har De slikt — why are you in such** a hurry? **— er lastverk** haste makes waste, good and quickly seldom meet.
hastverksarbeid hurried work.
hat hatred (til: for, of, against, to) hate, spite (against); **bli lagt for — incur odium, be** subject to hatred; **nære — til** hate, bear hatred towards. **hate** hate. **hatefull** spiteful. **hater** hater (of), enemy (to).
hatsk rancorous. **-het** rancorousness.
hatt hat; (damehatt) bonnet; (når den mer ligner en herrehatt) hat; (hette, av forsk.slags) hood, cap, top; **stiv — bowler, round hat; ta -en av** lift el. take off one's hat (for: to); **ta til -en** touch one's hat; **sette -en på** put on one's hat; **trykke -en ned i øynene** slouch one's hat; **slå -en ned over øynene på en** bonnet one; **være på — med** have a nodding acquaintance with; **være kar for sin — hold** one's own; **gi en noe å henge -en på** give one a handle.
hatt|børste hat-brush. **-efabrikk** hat-manufactory. **-efor** lining of a hat. **-eform** block. **-efutteral** hat box. **-emaker** hatter. **-emakersvenn** journeyman hatter. **-enål** bonnet-pin **-epynt** trimming of a bonnet. **-eske** hat-case; (til damehatt) bandbox. **-eskygge** brim of a hat; (på damehatt) front. **-estativ** hat-stand.
haubits howitzer.
haug hill (dim.) hillock; heap, pile; (jord-, grav-) mound.
haugbonde (i folketru) inhabitant of a barrow.
haugevis in heaps, by heaps.
haugfolk hillfolk, elves, fairies.
hauglegge bury, lay in a barrow.
haugtusse, se **hulder.**
hauk hawk; **— over — diamond cut diamond;** the biter bit.
hauk|e call, cooey, shout. **-ing** call, cattle-call. **hauke|nebb** hawk's bill. **-nese** hawk-like nose, hook (el. hooked) nose.
haus pate, noddle.
hausse rise, expansion of prices; **spekulere i —** speculate for the rise, be bullish. **-spekulant** bull.
hautrelieff alto-relievo, high relief.
hav sea; (verdenshav) ocean; **1000 fot over -et** 1000 feet above the level of the sea.
Havana (the) Havana. **h-brun** cigar-coloured.
h-sigar Havana. **havaneser** Havanese; Havana.
havarere be wrecked.
havarert damaged; (om varer) sea-damaged; **i — tilstand** in a damaged state.
havari damage, break-down, average; **— grosse** (merk) general average, gross average; **— particulière** particular average; **— ordinaire** petty average; **under — under average.**
havariattest average certificate.
havarisak case of average.
havarist wrecked sailor, wrecked ship; cast away.
hav|blikk (dead) calm; **det ble — it fell a** dead calm. **-bryn** sea-margin. **-bukt** bay, gulf. **-bunn** bottom of the ocean, sea-bed.
hav|dyp the deep, depths of the ocean; **undersøkelser av -dypet** deep-sea explorations. **-dyr** marine animal. **-dønning** ocean swell.
havesyk covetous. **havesyke** covetousness.
hav|fisk sea-fish. **-frue** mermaid. **-gud** sea-god. **-gudinne** sea-goddess. **-gul(e)** sea-breeze. **-katt** catfish. **-klima** maritime climate. **-mann** merman. **-måke** black-backed gull.
havn harbour, port; (fig) haven; **ligge i — be** in port.
havne put into a harbour, enter a port; (fig) find el. get rest; **— i** end in.

havne|anlegg (pl) harbour-works. **-arbeider** docker. **-avgifter** harbour dues, port charges. **-bane** dock-sidings. **-betjent** harbour officer. **-by** seaport town. **-foged** harbour master, captain of the port.

havne|kontor harbour-master's office. **-myndigheter** port authorities. **-plass** harbour accommodation. **-vesenet** the administration of harbours; the harbour authorities.

havre oats (pl). **-brød** oaten bread. **-dyrking** growing el. cultivation of oats. **-graut** (oatmeal) porridge. **-gryn** (oaten) groats, grits. **-høst** oatcrop, oatharvest. **-mel** oatmeal. **-velling** (water) gruel. **-åker** oat-field.

havskilpadde turtle.

havsnød distress (at sea).

hav|strand beach, sea-margin. **-tåke** sea-fog. **-ørn** sea-eagle. **-ål** conger (-eel), sea-eel.

hebraisk Hebrew; **det er — for meg** it is all Greek to me. **hebreer** Hebrew.

Hebridene the Hebrides.

hede (lyngkledd landstrekning) heath.

hedendom heathendom.

heden|faren, -gangen departed, dead-and-gone. **heden|old** heathen ages (pl) **-sk** heathen, pagan, heathenish, gentile. **-skap** paganism, heathenism.

heder honour, glory. **-full** glorious, honourable. **-kront** covered el. crowned with glory.

hederlig honourable; (redelig) honest; (berømmelig) glorious. **-het** honourableness.

heders|bevisning mark of respect, honour. **-dag** day of glory. **-gave** gift el. present of honour. **-gjest** guest of honour, guest of the occasion. **-mann** honourable man, worthy (man). **-plass** place of honour. **-post** post of honour. **-tegn** badge of honour. **-titel** title of honour.

hedning heathen, pagan, gentile.

hedre honour.

hefte (del av bok) part, number; (bok) pamphlet, brochure, booklet; (stitched) manuscript; (på sverd) hilt, handle.

I. **hefte** (oppholde) delay, detain, keep; (jur) apprehend.

II. **hefte** (vrb) fix, attach, fasten; (med tråd) baste; (klebe) stick; (bok) stitch, sew; **— med knappenåler** pin; **— opp** tuck up; **det -r stor gjeld på denne eiendommen** this estate is greatly encumbered. **-lse** (gjeld) lien, encumbrance, charge; (pante-) mortgage.

heftevis in parts.

heftig vehement, violent, impetuous; (smerte o. l.) acute, intense, severe; **bli — get** into a passion. **-het** vehemence, violence, impetuosity; intensity.

heftplaster sticking-plaster, adhesive plaster.

hegg, heggebær bird-cherry.

hegn fence, enclosure; (levende) hedge.

hegne om screen.

hegre heron. **-fjær** heron's feather, egret.

hegring mirage.

hei (subst) heath, (heathery) moor; woodless plateau, upland.

hei! heida! ho! halloh!

heil, se **hel.**

heilo golden plover.

heim, se **hjem** (subst) home, (adv) home **-bygd** native parish.

heime, se **hjemme.**

heime|brenner unlicensed distiller. **-brenning** unlicensed distillery.

heimføing provincial, home-bred person.

heis hoist, lift.

heise hoist; (om flagg og lette ting) run up. **heise|apparat** (el. **-innretning** el. **-verk**) hoisting apparatus, hoist. **-kran** crane.

heit, se **het.**

I. **hekk** (rekke av busker til hegn) hedge; (i stall) rack; (sportsuttrykk) hurdle.

II. **hekk** (del av skip) stern frame. **-jolle** sternboat.

hekke (yngle, ruge) hatch, breed, nidificate. **hekkeløp** hurdle-race.

hekle (subst) (til lin og hamp) hatchel, hackle; (til fiskefangst) rake, rake-hook.

hekle (vrb) crochet; (lin og hamp) hatchel, hackle. **-arbeid** crochet-work. **-nål** crochet-hook; **-tøy,** se **-arbeid. hekling** crocheting.

heks witch, hag, sorceress; **din lille —! you** little rogue, minx, el. gipsy! **en gammel — an** old hag.

hekse practise witchcraft; call up (produce convey, change) by magic; **han kan — he is a** sorcerer.

hekse|kunst witchcraft. **-kunster** (pl) spells, charms, (pl) **-mel** vegetable sulphur, witch-meal. **-mester** wizard, sorcerer, necromancer, conjurer; **han er ingen -mester** he is no conjurer.

hekseri witchcraft, witchery, sorcery, necromancy, art-magic; **det er ikke noe — it is** easily done, there is no sorcery el. witchcraft in it.

hekse|skudd a crick in the back, (a touch of) lumbago.

hektar hectare (1 hektar = 2,4711 acres).

hekte (subst) clasp, hook; **-r og kroker** hooks and eyes.

hekte (vrb) clasp, hook; **— opp** unclasp, unhook.

hektisk hectic.

hektograf hectograph, manifold-writer.

hektografere hectograph, copy with a manifold.

hektogram = 0,22046 lb. (eng. pund). **hektoliter** = 175,98 pints (halvpotter).

Hel (dødsgudinnen) Hel, Hela.

hel, whole, entire; **— note** whole note, semibreve; **— pause** bar-rest, semibreve rest; **-t tall** whole el. integral number; integer; **-e verden** all the world, the whole world; **-e den tid** (for) the whole of that time; **-e tiden** all along; **-e Norge** the whole of Norway; **i -e Norge** in all Norway; **fire -e dager** four clear days; **-e tjue** as many as twenty; **-e uker,** **måneder** for weeks, months; **-e året igjennom** throughout the year; **en — del** (om entall) a great deal; (om flertall helst) a great number (of), a great many; **en — del lengre** ever so much longer; **en — mengde** quite a number; **det -e** the whole (thing); **i det -e** (i alt) altogether, in all, on el. in the whole; (i det -e tatt) upon el. on the whole; (i betingelsessetn. og etter superl.) at all; **hans utseende i det -e** his general appearance; **samfunnet, verden i det -e** society, the world at large; **det er det -e** that is all (about it); **— og holden** safe and sound; (adv) entirely. **helt** (adv) quite, totally, entirely; **— igjennom** right through; (fullstendig) all through, throughout; **— eller delvis** in whole or in part.

helaftenstykke whole-evening play.

helbefaren (mar) able.

helbind full binding.

helbred health. **-e** heal; (kurere) cure. **-elig** curable. **-else** cure, healing; (det å komme seg) recovery.

**helbreds|hensyn: av — from motives of health. -tilstand: hans — the state of his health.

helde (subst) (til hest) hobble.

helde (vrb) hobble.

heldekker flush-decked boat.

heldig lucky, fortunate; successful; prosperous; (om uttrykk) felicitous; (skikket) eligible; (gagnlig) beneficial; (tilrådelig) advisable; **et — ytre** a winning presence; **det gikk — it turned out** well; **hvis det går — if** fortune favours.

heldigvis luckily, fortunately, as good luck would have it.

hele (subst): **et sammenhengende—a connected** whole; **et ordnet — an ordered** whole.

I. **hele** (vrb) heal; **-s** be healed, heal up.

II. **hele** (hjelpe tyv) receive stolen goods.

heler, –ske receiver of stolen goods; **–en er ikke bedre enn stjeleren** the receiver is as bad as the thief.
heleri receiving (of stolen goods).
helferd descent into the realm of Hela; death.
helflaske large bottle.
helg holiday(s), Sunday.
helgeklær one's Sunday best.
helgen saint. **–bilde** image of a saint. **–glorie** halo of glory. **–inne** saint. **–legende** legend. **–levninger** relics. **–sagn** legend. **–skrin** shrine for relics.
Helgoland Heligoland, Helgoland.
helgryn peeled barley.
Helheim the realm of Hela, of death.
helhet totality, entireness; entirety; **i sin —** in its entirety, in whole.
helhetsinntrykk general impression.
I. **hell** (bakke-) inclination, slope; **fatet står på —** the cask is a-tilt.
II. **hell** (lykke) good luck, success; **for et hell!** what a stroke of luck! **sitte i —** be in luck; **ha — med** succeed in; **hadde det — å** had the good fortune to; **til alt —** as good luck would have it, fortunately.
Hellas Greece.
helle (subst) flag, flagstone, slab, slabstone.
helle (vi) slant, slope, incline, lean; **dagen –r** the day declines; **— til et parti** lean to el. towards a party; **— seg** lean; **— seg opp til** lean up against; (vt) (skjenke) pour, run; **— over** (på en karaffel el. l.) decant.
helleflyndre halibut, holibut.
hellelagt flagged, paved with slabs.
hellen|er Greek, Grecian; **–erne** the Hellenes. **–sk** Hellenic, Hellenian.
heller rather, sooner; **— enn gjerne** most willingly; **jo før jo —** the sooner, the better;
heller| ikke nor, no more; not... either; **— ikke var de vakre** they were not good-looking either; **ikke jeg —** nor I (either); **jeg sa — ikke et ord** and I too said no word; **hverken ... eller ... og —** like neither ... nor ... nor yet; **det har — aldri vært påstått** nor has it ever been asserted; **det har jeg — ikke sagt indeed,** I have said no such thing.
helleristning (abstrakt) petroglyphy; (konkr.) rockcarving.
hellig holy, sacred; **ikke noe er — for ham** nothing is sacred to him; **ved alt som er —** by everything sacred, by all that is sacred; **den –e ånd** the Holy Ghost; **den –e allianse** the Holy Alliance; **den –e jomfru** the blessed Virgin, the Holy Virgin; **— krig** holy el. sacred war; **Det –e land** (the) Holy Land; **den — skrift** holy writ; **den –e stad** the holy el. sacred City; **den –e ektestand** the holy state of matrimony; **Ludvig den –e** Louis the Saint; **de –e** the saints (skinnhellige) devotionists, religionists; **de siste dagers –e** the Latter-day-saints; **det –e** the Sanctuary; **det –ste** the most Holy; **— trekongersdag** Twelfth Day, Epiphany; **hellig** (adv): love høyt og **— promise** solemnly.
hellig|aften eve of a holiday. **–brøde** sacrilege. **–dag** holy day, holiday; **stor –dag** festival. **–dom** sanctuary; (ting) sacred thing.
hellige hallow, consecrate, sanctify; (holde hellig) keep holy, observe; (innvie) devote, dedicate (to); **–t vorde ditt navn!** Hallowed be thy name! **hensikten –r midlet** the end justifies the means.
helliggjøre hallow, sanctify.
helliggjørelse hallowing, sanctification.
hellighet holiness, sacredness. **Hans H.–** His Holiness.
hellig|holde keep holy, observe; celebrate. **–holdelse** keeping holy, observance; celebration. **H.–ånd** the Holy Ghost.
helling (skråning) slope, declivity; (fig) inclination (til: to), bias, leaning (towards); **være**

på –a be on the decline; **dagens —** the decline of day. **–svinkel** angle of inclination.
helnote semibreve.
helrandet (bot) entire.
helse (vrb), se **hilse.**
helse (subst) health; **ha god —** be in health; **få helsa igjen** recover. **–bot** a benefit to health, a cure, a remedy. **–løs** broken in health, invalid. **slå ham —** cripple him for life.
helsidesbilde full-page illustration el. picture.
helsilke all-silk, pure silk.
helskinnet with a whole skin.
helskjegg a full beard.
helsott mortal disease.
helst preferably; (etterstilt) for preference (især) especially, more particularly; **jeg ville — I** should prefer; **du bør — gå** you had better (best) go.
hel|stat whole-state. **–støpt** (all) of one piece; (fig) foursquare. **–støphet** wholeness, fusion.
I. **helt** (fisk) gwiniad, freshwater herring.
II. **helt** (tapper person) hero.
helte|dikt epic. **komisk –dikt** mock-heroic poem. **–diktning** heroic poetry. **–død** heroic death. **–dåd** heroic deed, exploit. **–gjerning** heroic deed. **–kamp** heroic combat. **–modig** heroical. **–mot** heroic courage, heroism. **–rolle** heroic part. **–ry** heroic fame. **–sjel** heroic soul. **–skikkelse** heroic figure. **–vis: på — heroically. –ånd** heroic spirit, heroism.
heltinne heroine.
hel|ull, –ullen allwool.
helvete hell; **reis til —! go** to the devil! you be hanged! **gjøre en — hett** lead one a life. **–s** devilish; **en –s kar** a devil of a fellow.
helvetesild (hudsykdom) shingles.
helveteskval infernal torment.
helvetes|maskin infernal machine. **–pine** infernal torment.
helvetessten (lapis infernalis) lunar caustic.
helvt, se **halvdel.**
hemme check, repress, restraint, hamper.
hemmelig secret; (i smug) clandestine; (mots. offentlig) private; **— ekteskap** private marriage; **— skriftemål** auricular confession; **en — mistanke** a lurking suspicion; (adv) secretly etc.; (under fire øyne) in private.
hemmelighet secret; (hemmeligholdelse, taushet) secrecy; (mysterium) mystery; **gjøre en gen — av det** made no secret about it; **gjøre en stor — av noe** keep something a close secret; **i all — secretly,** by stealth; **ha en — for en** have a secret from one; **valgets — the** secrecy of the ballot.
hemmelighetsfull mysterious; secretive; **en — mine** an air of mystery. **–het** mysteriousness; secretiveness.
hemmelig|hetskremmer secretive person. **–hetskremmeri** secretiveness.
hemmende restrictive.
hemoroider piles, hemorrhoids.
hempe loop.
hemsedal (halvloft over sperreloftsstue) bed-loft.
hemsko drag, clog.
hen = bort away. **hvor skal De —?** where are you going? where are you bound? **stirre — for seg** stare at vacancy, at mid-air.
henblikk look, regard (to), consideration (of); **med — på** taking into consideration, with a view to.
hende: i —, se **hånd.**
hende, happen, chance, occur, befall, come to pass; **det kunne nok — may** be; **det har hendt ham en ulykke** he has met with a misfortune; **slikt kan — den beste** accidents will occur.
hendelse (treff) chance; (i en historie el. i et skuesp.) incident; (begivenhet) occurrence; (tildragelse) adventure; (ulykkelig h.) accident.
hendig deft, dexterous; (om ting) handy.
hendighet deftness, dexterity; handiness.

hendø (om lyd) die away el. down.
henfalle fall, lapse. **-n til drikk** much given to drinking.
henføre (fig) (henrykke) entrance, transport; — til refer to, ascribe to. **henført** (fig) ecstasied, entranced, wrapped.
heng (svak vind) a light airing, an air of wind.
I henge (vi): (være hengt opp) hang, be suspended (by); **stå og** — stand idle; lounge; — **fast** stick; — **etter** en dangle after one, be at one's heels; **han -r i klubben bestandig** he haunts the club perpetually; **han hang fast med foten** his foot caught; **treet -r fullt av frukt** the tree is loaded with fruit; — **i keep at it, work hard;** — **med** (f. eks. hodet) droop; hang (one's head); — **over bøkene** be poring over the books; — **på veggen** hang on the wall; — **sammen** stick el. hold together, cohere; **hvordan -r det sammen med denne saken?** how does that matter stand? **det -r ikke riktig sammen** there is something wrong; — **ved** adhere to; — **ved noen** (av hengivenhet) be attached, cleave, cling to one.
II henge (vt) hang (bøyes: hung, hung), suspend· (drepe ved hengning) hang (bøyes: hanged hanged); **henges, bli hengt** be hanged; (sl) swing, hang; — **seg** hang oneself; — **seg i** (fig.) catch hold of, carp at. Se også **hengende.**
henge|ask weeping ash. **-bjørk** weeping birch. **-bru** suspension bridge. **-hode** a crestfallen, chap-fallen person; (hykler) hypocrite, canter. **-krøller** hanging curls. **-køye** hammock. **-lampe** hanging lamp, ceiling-lamp, suspension-lamp. **-lås** padlock. **-myr** quaking bog, quagmire.
hengende hanging, pendent; **bli** — **catch,** stick; **remain** hanging; **bli** — **ved be caught by.**
henge|pil weeping willow.
hengi seg abandon oneself (to) indulge (in), give oneself up (to); (for andre) sacrifice oneself. **-velse** abandonment; acquiescence; resignation. **-ven** (en —) attached, devoted, well-affected (to); **Deres hengivne E. Smith** Yours affectionately E. Smith (andre uttrykk til unde skrift på brev: Believe me, yours respectfully; Yours truly; I am, dear Sir, yours truly; Yo·· faithfully; Yours sincerely); **din hengivne sønn** Your loving son; Your affectionate son; **din hengivne tante** Your affectionate aunt.
hengivenhet (vennskap) affection, attachment, devotion, devotedness; **jeg vant hans** — **I** attached him to me.
hengsel hinge.
hengsle (tømmer-) (timber-) boom.
hengslet(e) loose-jointed, loosely-limbed.
henhold: i — **til** with reference to, pursuant to, according to, as per, in conformity with; **i** — **til innlagte liste** as per list inclosed; **i** — **til Deres forlangende** in compliance with your request.
henholde seg til refer to, appeal to; **jeg -r meg til mitt brev av** I beg reference to my letter of.
henholdsvis respectively.
henimot towards. — **aften** towards evening.
henkaste let fall, throw out, drop; (på papiret) write down hastily; **en løst -t tegning** a sketch; **-t ytring** casual remark; **-t ord** chance-word; **i en lett -t tone** carelessly, in an off-hand way.
henlede direct; — **oppmerksomheten på** direct, draw el. invite (the) attention to.
henlegge en sak (jur) lay aside, shelve. — **scenen til** lay the scene at el. in.
henne (adv); **jeg vet ikke hvor han er** — I don't know where(about) he is; **hvor har du vært** —? where(ever) have you been?
henne (pron) her, hennes her; hers.
henrette execute. **-lse** execution.
Henrik Henry, Harry.
henrive carry away, transport; (henrykke) fascinate, enrapture, charm. **la seg** — **til skarpe ord** be provoked to sharp words.

henrivende fascinating, charming, ravishing.
henrykke (fig) charm, fascinate, enchant enrapture; **være aldeles henrykt over** go into ecstasies over.
henrykkelse transport, rapture, ecstasy.
henseende respect, regard; **i den** —, in that respect el. particular; **i alle -r** in all respects; **i mange -r** on many accounts; **i enhver** — (in) every way; **i visse -r er det nyttig** for certain purposes it is useful.
hensette (i tanken) — **seg til** transport oneself in imagination to, imagine oneself in.
hensikt intention, design, purpose, intent, view; **med** — on purpose, intentionally; **uten** — unintentionally; **i den** — å with the intention el. for the purpose of -ing; **ha til** — å intend to, el. -ing; **jeg gjorde det i den beste** — I acted for the best; **reelle -er** honourable intentions. **mot -en** contrary to the purpose, inappropriate.
hensikts|løs without purpose, aimless, purposeless.
hensiktsmessig suitable to the purpose, adequate, appropriate, effective, serviceable, convenient; (framgangsmåte o. l.) expedient; **være** — answer; **det ville være** — å it would be a good plan to; **hensynet til det som er** — the consideration of expediency. **-het** suitability, adequacy, appropriateness, policy, expediency.
henstand respite, prolongation.
henstille (beskjedent foreslå) suggest.
henstilling (antydet forslag, fingerpek) suggestion.
hensykne droop, languish, decay.
hensyn respect, regard, consideration; **av** — **til** out of regard to, on the score of, in view of; (skyldig hens.) in deference to; **med** — **til** as to, with r. to, in r. to, relative to; **uten** — **til** without r. to, regardless of, irrespective of; **uten** — **til om** no matter whether . . . or not; **ta** — **til** take into consideration el. account; pay el. have regard to; pay attention to; provide for; make allowance for; **det blir ikke tatt noe** — **til** no account is taken of; **det blir ikke tatt noe** — **til klagen** the complaint will not be entertained; **når vi tar** — **til** respect being had to, when we consider; **-et til våre egne interesser** a regard for our own interests.
hensyns|betegnelse, se **-ledd. -form** dative (case).
hensynsfull considerate, thoughtful, kind.
hensynsfullhet consideration, deference.
hensynsledd indirect object.
hensynsløs inconsiderate, regardless, heedless. **reckless,** indiscriminate, uncompromising, rough. **hensynsløshet** regardlessness, heedlessness, recklessness.
hensunket i lost in, absorbed in, wrapped in.
hente fetch, go for, come for; — **en bil** call a taxi; — **næring fra** draw nutriment from; **hentyde** (sikte til) allude, advert (til: to) hint (til: at).
hentydning allusion, hint.
henved about, near, nearly, towards.
henvende turn direct (til: to); **henvendt til** publikum addressing the audience; — **seg til** address oneself to, apply to; — **seg om** apply for.
henvendelse address, application; **ved** — **til** upon application to.
henvise direct; (til hjemmelsmann o. l.) refer (to); **være henvist til** be reduced to, cast upon, beholden to, (til å) under the necessity (of -ing) of.
henvisning direction; reference; (til annet ord i register, ordbok) cross-reference; **under** — **til** referring to.
her here; — **i byen, landet** in this town, country; — **fra byen** from this town; — **og der** here and there; — **og hisset** here and hereafter, in this world and the world to come.
herald|iker one skilled in heraldry, herald. **-ikk** heraldry. **-isk** heraldic.

herbarium herbarium, hortus siccus.
herberge (vertshus) inn; (kvarter) lodgings, quarters. **herberge** (vrb) harbour, lodge.
herde harden, indurate; — stål temper steel; — seg harden oneself, make oneself hardy.
herdebrei broad of shoulder.
herdning hardening etc.; (av metall) tempering.
her|etter hereafter, henceforth, after this, in future, from now on. -fra from hence, from here, from this; når reiser De -fra? when do your leave here, el. l. this?
   her hjemme at home. — inn herein, in here. — inne within, in here. — innefra from within here.
herje ravage, lay waste, devastate, harry.
herjing ravaging; (konkret) ravage, devastation.
herk (skrap) bad stuff, trash.
herkomst descent, parentage, extraction, origin.
Herkules Hercules. **herkulisk** Herculean.
herlig excellent, glorious, grand, magnificent; (adv) gloriously.
herlig|gjøre glorify. -gjørelse glorification.
herlighet excellence, glory, magnificence, grandeur; det er hele -en that's the whole concern; der ligger hele -en there it lies (all smashed)!
hermafroditt hermaphrodite.
herme mimic. — etter mimic.
hermed herewith, with this; so.
hermelin ermine.
hermelins|kåpe robe el. cloak lined with ermine.
hermetikk canned goods, tinned meats. -boks tin-can. -fabrikant canner. -fabrikk canning company. -åpner tin-opener.
hermetisk hermetic(al); — nedlagt kjøtt preserved meat; — lukket hermetically sealed. -e fødemidler preserves.
herming mimicry.
her ned down here. — nede down here. — nedenfra from here below. — nedenunder here below.
Herodes Herod; sende fra — til Pilatus send from pillar to post, send hither and thither.
hero|isme heroism. -isk heroic(al).
herold herald.
her omkring hereabouts.
her opp, oppe up here.
heros hero.
her|over over here, on this side; hereat, hereon. — overfor opposite, on the other side.
herre (overherre) lord; (mots. tjener, folk) master; (mots. dame, ogs. «fin herre» mots. «simpel mann») gentleman; H-n the Lord: H-ns bord the Lord's Supper; H-ns bønn the Lord's Prayer; H-ns salvede the Lord's anointed; i mange -ns år for many a long year; i det -ns år ... in the year of Our Lord; H-ns vilje skje! the Lord's will be done! nådige —! my Lord! min —! Sir! mine -r! Gentlemen; mine damer og -r Ladies and Gentlemen! hr. Mr. (brukt foran egennavn, f. eks. Mr. Smith), Esq. el. Esqr. (i utenpåskrift på brev, f. eks. T. Smith, Esq.). hr. general N. General N.; hr. general! (borgermester osv.) Sir! Deres hr. far (Mr. N.) your father; -ne A. og B. Messrs. A. and B.; — og frue master and mistress; være sin egen — be one's own master; (om kvinner: mistress); be a free agent; være — over (fig) be master of, master; bli — over get the better of; av grunner som jeg ikke er — over for reasons beyond my control; bli — over ilden get the fire under; spille — lord it (over), carry it high; enhver er — i sitt hus every man's house is his castle; konen er — i huset the wife rules the roast; som -n er, så følger ham hans svenner like master, like man.
herrebad gentlemen's baths.
herred canton, circuit, district, hundred.
herredrakt gentleman's costume, man's dress.

herredømme sway, rule, dominion; mastery, command, grasp; — over språket command of language; — over seg selv self-possession, self-command, self-control; har stort — over ham has el. exercises a great ascendency over him.
herre|ekvipering gentlemen's furnishing goods. -gård manor, manorial estate, gentleman's seat, manor-seat, manor-house. -gud! dear me! well! **herre|kort** (billedkort i kortspill) court-card -liv lordly life, easy, luxurious life; føre et -liv live like a lord. -løs ownerless, unowned, masterless; en -løs hund a stray el. ownerless dog. -mann lord of a manor, landed proprietor, squire. -middag gentleman's dinner. -måltid lordly repast. -portrett gentleman's portrait. -rett delicious dish, feast. -selskap gentlemen's party; gentlemen's company. -sete manor-house, manor-seat, lordly seat. -skredder (gentlemen's) tailor. -støvel gentleman's boot. -vis: på — in a lordly manner.
herrnhuter Moravian.
herskap master and mistress, my lord and my lady; -et er ute masters are out.
herskapelig (som tilhører et adelig herskap) seigneurial, manorial. **herskaps|bolig** gentleman's residence, aristocratical mansion. -kusk gentleman's coachman.
herske sway, rule; (ta, få overhånd) reign, prevail, predominate. -nde reigning etc., prevalent; den -nde religion the established el. prevailing religion; ett av de -nde folk i Orienten one of the imperial nations of the East.
hersker sovereign, master, ruler, despot, -blikk commanding look. -inne mistress. -makt supreme authority, sovereignty. -mine look of a ruler, commanding air. -ånd ruler's spirit.
herske|syk imperious, domineering. -syke appetite for rule, ambition, imperiousness.
her|steds here, in this place. -til to this.
hertug duke. -dømme duchy, dukedom. **hertugelig** ducal. **hertuginne** duchess.
her|under under here, below here; -under hviler here lies; -ut, -ute out here -ved hereby, by this; (i dokumenter) by these presents; (i denne henseende). on this subject, point, head, concerning this, here; -værende in el. of this place, here, here present, residing here, resident.
hes hoarse, husky. -(e)blesende out of breath, (fig) breathless, flurried, bustling.
hesje (subst) haydrying frames, drying stand.
hesje (vrb) frame, stand.
heslig ugly, hideous.
heslighet ugliness, hideousness.
hespe (garn-) hank. **hespe** (vrb) form into hanks.
hesp|el reel, hasp. -le reel.
hespetre reel for winding yarn.
Hessen Hesse; — Kassel Hesse Cassel. **hesser,** hessisk Hessian.
hest horse, (øyk) nag; (liten) pony; (ridehest) mount; (i gymnastikksal) vaulting horse; til — on horseback, mounted; stige til — mount (a horse), take horse; stige av -en dismount, alight from a horse; sette seg på den høye — give oneself airs, ascend the high ropes, ride the high horse.
heste|brems horse-fly. -dekken horsecloth. -dressur horse-breaking. -dressør horse-breaker. -elsker horse-fancier. -flue forest-fly. -for horse -meat. -fot horse-foot; stikke -foten fram betray the cloven foot (hoof). -handel dealing in horses. -handler horse-dealer. -hode horse's head. -holder job-master. -hov horse's hoof; (plante) coltsfoot. -hud horse's hide. -igle horse-leech. -kastanje horse-chestnut. -kjenner judge of horses, judge of horse flesh. -kjøtt horse flesh, horse-beef. -kraft; et dampskip på 50 -krefter a steamer of 50 horse power. -kur rough remedy. -man, -manke horse's mane. -marked horse-fair. -møkk horse-dung. -passer horse-minder, horse

-man. **-pære** horse-turd. **-sko** horse-shoe. **-sko-søm** hobnail, horse(-shoe-)nail. **-tramping** stamping of horse. **-trav** trotting of a horse. **-tyv** horse stealer. **-tyveri** horse-stealing. **-utstilling** horse-show. **-veddeløp** horse-race.

hestfolk horse, cavalry.

het hot; **-e viner** heady wines; **den -e sone** the torrid zone; — **om ørene** uneasy, nervous; **det er svært -tt mellom dem** they are very thick; **det gikk -tt til** it was hot work.

hete (subst) heat; **i den første** — in the first transport.

hete (vrb) be called, be named; **hva -r det på norsk?** how do you call that in Norwegian? **what is the Norwegian for that?** **som det -r i visa** as the song has it, as the old song goes; **det er noe som -r å være** . . . there is such a thing as being . . .

hete|blemmer rash, prickly heat. **-slag** heat -stroke, heat-apoplexy.

hette hood, cowl, cap.

hetære courtesan, hetæra.

I. **hevd** prescription, prescriptive right; (besittelse) possession; (sedvane) custom; **holde i** — keep in preservation; **få** — **på noe** acquire right of prescription to a thing.

II. **hevd se gjødsel. hevde se gjødsle.**

hevde maintain, assert, uphold; — **sin plass,** — **seg** hold one's own.

hevdelse maintenance, assertion.

hevdvunnen prescriptive, vested; (fig) timehonoured, old established.

heve raise; (fjerne) remove; (kontrakt) cancel, break off; (strid) settle; (møte) dissolve, adjourn; (stemmen) raise, elevate; — **forlovelsen** break off the match; — **penger** receive el. draw money; — **penger på en anvisning** osv. cash a check; — **til skyene** laud to the skies, extol to the clouds; **da retten ble -t** when the court rose; — **seg** rise, swell; (om fjell) tower, rear themselves; (om deig) rise; — **seg over noe** rise superior to; **være -t over** (fig) be above, superior to; **-t over all ros, tvil** beyond all praise, doubt.

hevelse rising, swelling; tumor.

hevert siphon.

hevn revenge, vengeance; — **over** revenge upon; **ta en grusom** — **over** wreak a cruel vengeance upon.

hevne revenge, avenge; — **seg på** be revenged on, avenge oneself of el. on, take vengeance on, wreak one's vengeance upon; **det -r seg** it brings its own punishment.

hevner avenger, revenger.

hevngjerrig revengeful, vindictive.

hevngjerrighet vindictiveness, revengefulness.

hi winter lair; **ligge i** — lie dormant.

hieroglyff hieroglyph. **-isk** hieroglyphic.

hike aspire (etter; after, to).

hikk hiccough, hiccup.

hikke (vrb) hiccough, hiccup. **hikke** (subst) hiccough.

hikst catch (of breath), pant. **hikste** catch one's breath, pant. — **etter** gasp for.

hildre fascinate, weave a spell round.

hildring looming; (meteorologisk) mirage.

hill! hill deg! hail! all hail!

hilse greet, salute, bow to; (motta på en eller annen måte) hail, receive, welcome; — **på en** (besøke) give one a call, pay one's respects to; — **med flagget** dip the colours; — **med hurrarop** cheer; **han hilste igjen** he acknowledged me; **han bad å** — he left his respects; **han bad meg** — **alle venner** he desired to be remembered to all his friends; **hils ham fra meg** remember me to him, give him my compliments; **jeg skulle** — **fra professoren og si** with the professor's compliments I was to say; **hils henne kjærlig** give my love to her; **hils hjemme** compliments at home; **jeg kan** — **fra** I have just seen.

hilsen (personlig) salutation, greeting; (sendt) compliments, message, words, remembrances; **sende sin** — present one's compliments; **de sender alle en vennlig** — all unite in kindest regards. **kjærlig** — fra love from; **ærbødig** — respects; **som en** — in greeting.

Himalaja the Himalayas.

himle (med øynene) roll el. turn up one's eyes. **himling** coved ceiling.

himmel (himmerike) heaven; (himmelhvelving) sky, skies; (senge-) tester; (tron-) canopy; **-en er overskyet** the sky is overcast; **sola stod høyt på -en** the sun was high; **sette** — **og jord i bevegelse** move heaven and earth; **et lyn fra klar** — a bolt out of the blue; **å** — oh heavens! **for -ens skyld** for heaven's sake; **fare til -s** ascend to heaven; **komme i -en** go to heaven; **i den syvende** — in ecstasies, supremely happy, in the seventh heaven.

himmel|blå skyblue, azure. **-egn** zone, climate. **-fallen** fallen from the skies; **han stod som -fallen** he was struck with amazement, (dt.) you could have knocked him down with a feather.

himmel|fart ascension; **Kristi -fartsdag** Ascension-day, Holy Thursday. **-flukt** heavenward flight. **-hvelving** vault of heaven. **-høy** high as heaven, towering; **rope -høyt** cry with all one's might, bellow. **-legeme** heavenly body, celestial body, orb. **-port** gate of heaven. **-rommet** the heavens. **-seng** tester bed, four-poster.

himmelsk heavenly, celestial; **det -e rike** the heavenly kingdom; (China) the Celestial Empire.

himmelsprett tossing in a blanket; **leke** — **med blanket,** toss in a blanket.

himmel|stige Jacob's ladder. **-stormende** heaven-storming. **-stormer** heaven-stormer. **-strebende** heaven-aspiring, heaven-directed. **-strøk,** se **-egn. -tegn** sign of the zodiac. **-vendt** upturned.

himmelvid very wide, very distant; — **forskjell** very wide difference.

himmelvidt (adv) widely; — **forskjellig** different as heaven and earth, day and night.

himmerik heaven, the kingdom of heaven; **-es rike** the kingdom of heaven.

hin (sj.) that, hint that, **hine** those; **dette og hint** this and that.

hinannen, se **hverandre.**

hind hind.

hinder hindrance, impediment, obstacle; (ved ritt) jump, fence; **være til** — **for** be a hindrance to; obstruct; **det er ingenting til** — **for** there is nothing to prevent. **-ritt** steeple-chase.

Hindostan Hindostan. **-sk** Hindostanee.

hindre prevent, hinder, obstruct, impede; — **en i** prevent one from.

hindring hindrance, obstacle, impediment, obstruction; **legge -er i veien for** put obstacles in the way of; **støte på -er** meet with obstacles.

hindu Hindoo, Hindu.

hingst stallion, stone-horse. **hingsteskue** stallion-show. **hingstføll** horse-colt.

hinke limp, hobble. **hinking** limping, hobbling. **hinne** membrane, pellicle; (svært tynn) film. **-aktig** membranous, membranaceous.

hinsides beyond, on the other side (of); **et** — a hereafter, the beyond.

hinsidig; det -e the beyond, the hereafter.

hipp fling, shy; **gi et** — **til** have a fling at. **hipp!:** — **hurra** hip hip hurrah!

hipp som happ as broad as long, six of one and half a dozen of the other.

hird (king's) body-guard, (king's)men. **-mann** body-guardsman, king's man. **-prest** king's chaplain.

hirse (bot) millet. **-frø** millet-seed.

hisse heat; incite; (egge) set on, hound on; — **på hverandre** set together by the ears; **-nde** heating; — **seg opp** work oneself up.

hissig hot, hot-headed, quick-tempered, passionate; (fyrig, heftig) fiery, ardent; (begjærlig) eager; (om sykdom) acute; **bli** — fly into a passion; **ikke så** — soft! softly! gently! — **etter** el. **på eager** for, after. **-het** passion, heat.

hissigpropp hotspur.

hist (sj.) yonder; — **og her** here and there.

historie (historisk beretning, historie som vitenskap) history; (fortelling) story; **-n** history; **den nyere** — modern history; **en sørgelig** — a sad affair, sad business; **det er en fin** — a pretty piece of business this! this is a nice go! **hva er dette for -r?** what is all this business about? **hele -n** the whole concern; **derom tier -n** that is not on record; **den største general -n kjenner** the greatest general on record; **det vil gå over i -n** it will go down to history.

historie-forsker historian. **-forskning** historical research. **-maler** historical painter. **-maleri** historical painting. **-skriver** historical writer, historiographer. **-skrivning** historical writing.

historiker historian.

historisk historical; **det er** — it is a matter of history; — **kjent** of historic note.

hit hither, this way, here; — **og dit** hither and thither, here and there; — **med boka** give me the book (directly)! **-bort** hither.

hitte|barn foundling. **-barnshospital** foundling hospital. **-gods** goods found; (jur) waif.

hittil hitherto, till now, so far, thus far.

I. **hive** (trekke, hale) heave; (kaste) throw, heave; **hiv oho!** heave ho!

II. **hive** (etter pusten) pant, gasp.

hjalt hilt.

hjell loft (of loose boards); (til å tørke fisk på) drying stage, flakes for drying fish, fish -flakes. **-tørket** flake-dried.

hjelm helmet, helm.

hjelmbusk plume (crest) of a helmet.

hjelm|gitter visor, beaver. **-kam** crest-holder.

hjelp help; (bistand) assistance, aid, succour; (understøttelse) support, relief; (legemiddel) remedy (against); **hjelp!** help! (mot mordere) murder! **yte** — render aid; **søke** — hos en apply to one for help; **med Guds** — God (Heaven) willing; **rope om** — scream, cry out for help; **komme en til** — come to one's assistance; **være til** — for en be of good help to one; **være til god** — for en stand one in good stead; **ta til** — have recourse to; **ta fantasien til** — draw upon imagination; **ta natta til** — sit up all night; **uten** — unaided; **ved** — av by means of; **ved Guds** — thanks to God; **yte den første** — render first aid.

hjelpe help, aid; (understøtte) assist, succour, support, relieve; (gagne) be of avail el. use; (om legemidler) be good (mot; for); **det hjalp** it had a good effect; **med det er han hjulpet** that will serve his turn, that will do for him **det har ikke hjulpet meg** I am none the better for it; **hva -r det?** what avails it? **hva -r det å** what is the good of -ing; **det -r ikke** it avails nothing, is no good; **det skal** — **godt** much good it will do; **det får ikke** — there is no help for it; **så sant** — **meg Gud** so help me God! **hva vil det** — **meg?** what shall I be the better for it? **han hjalp meg å flykte** he aided my escape; **svømte ut for å** — **meg** swam to my aid; — **en av med** rid one of; — **fram** advance, encourage, forward; — **en fram i verden** help one up in the world; — **en i, ut av en båt, vogn** hand one into, out of a boat, carriage; — **ham å få frakken på** help him on with his coat, help him into his coat; **det -r mot hodepine** it is good for the headache; — **en med å** assist one in -ing; **for å** — **på inntektene** by way of eking out one's income; — **på ens hukommelse** assist one's memory; — **til** lend a (helping) hand; — **en til rette** put one in the right way, set one right; **vi må -s** at we must assist one another; — **seg** make (a) shift, manage,

get on; — **seg så godt han kan** manage for himself.

hjelpe- auxiliary.

hjelpeaksjon relief action.

hjelpeekspedisjon relief expedition.

hjelpekilde resource; **rik på -r** full of resources.

hjelpe|lærer assistant teacher, usher. **-løs** helpless, shiftless. **-løshet** helplessness. **-middel** remedy, expedient, aid, help. **-ord** auxiliary word. **-r** helper, aider, assistant. **-tropper** auxiliaries, auxiliary troops. **-verbum** auxiliary (verb).

hjelpsom ready to help, willing to help.

hjelpsomhet readiness to help.

hjem (subst) home; **i -met** at home.

hjem (adv) home.

hjemfalle (til) revert, fall, devolve (upon); **han er -n til straff** he has incurred penalty.

hjem|faren; gift og — married and settled. **-fart** journey home; (til sjøs) passage home. **-føre** lead home; import.

hjem|kalle summon home, recall; (om døden) summon one away. **-kommet** returned (home), arrived.

hjemkomst return home, arrival, homecoming.

hjemland native land, native country.

hjemle make out a title to; (bevise lovlighet) justify, warrant; (berettige) authorize, bear out; **-t** authenticated.

hjem|lig domestic, home-like, cosy, snug, comfortable. **-liv** home life. **-lov** furlough, leave of absence.

hjemløs homeless. **-het** homelessness.

hjemme at home; **her** — (at) home here; **være** — **fra skolen** be home from school; **er B. —?** is B. in? **han var ikke** — he was from home; **lat som om du var** — make yourself at home; **jeg er ikke** — **for noen** I will see nobody; **han nektet seg** — he pretended to be out; **høre** — **i** be a native of, hail from; (et land, en by) be domiciliated in; **skipet hører** — **her** the ship belongs here; **det har ingen steder** — it is neither here nor there; **arbeide** — (om håndverker) take in work, work in one's own room; **være** — **i** be at home in, conversant with.

hjemme|arbeid home-work. **-avlet** home-grown, home-bred. **-bakt** home-baked. **-døpe** baptize privately, half-baptize. **-dåp** private baptism, home christening.

hjemmeforbruk home consumption.

hjemmefra from home; **da jeg reiste** — when I left home.

hjemme|gjort home-made. **-hørende** native (of), indigenous, belonging to, owned; (bosatt) domiciliated.

hjemmel warrant, authority; (bevis) proof of lawful acquisition; (fullmakt) full power.

hjemmelaget home-made.

hjemmelsmann authority, informer.

hjemmemenneske stay-at-home man (el. woman).

hjemmesitting sitting at home, sedentary life.

hjemmevant at home; domesticated.

hjem|over homeward. **-reise** homeward route el. journey. **-sendelse** forwarding el. sending home.

hjemstavn native soil, native land.

hjemstavns|lære regional study. **-rett** a settlement; **hindre en fra å få** — **i kommunen** keep one from being chargeable to the parish.

hjemsøke visit (på: upon); (forurolige, plage) infest; — **fedrenes synder på barna** visit the iniquity of the fathers upon the children; **hjemsøkt av sykdom** afflicted with sickness.

hjemve homesickness; **ha** — be homesick.

hjemvei way home, return home, walk home, ride home; **være på -en** be homeward bound.

hjemvendt returned.

hjerne brain; (forstand) brains; **den store** — the brain proper, the cerebrum; **den lille** — the little brain, the cerebellum; **bry (bryte) sin** —

med **noe** puzzle (rack) one's brain(s) about something; **legge sin — i bløyt** rack one's brains.
hjerne- cerebral, of the brain.
hjerne|betennelse inflammation of the brain, brain fever. **–bløthet** softening of the brain. **–boring** trepanning. **–hinne** membrane of the brain; **betennelse i –hinnene** meningitis. **–masse** cerebral matter. **–rystelse** concussion of the brain. **–skalle** skull, cranium, brainpan. **–slag** apoplexy. **–spinn** chimera. **–sykdom** disease of the brain. **–virksomhet** cerebration, action of the brain.

hjerte heart; **–t mitt banker** my heart beats; **–t mitt banker sterkt** my heart throbs; **åpne, lette sitt —** unbosom oneself, disburden one's mind **(for: to); det som –t er fullt av, løper munnen over med** out of the full heart the mouth speaks; **mitt — er fritt** I am fancy-free; **tape sitt —** lose one's heart; **av et oppriktig —** sincerely; **–ns gjerne** by all means, with all my heart; **–ns glad** heartily glad; **–ns glede** heart-felt joy; **–ns god** exceedingly kind el. good-natured; **–ns mening** real opinion; **–ns venn** bosom friend, chosen friend; **av hele mitt —** with all my heart; **av –ns lyst** to my (his etc.) heart's content el. delight; **ha — for** have some feeling for; **det kommer fra –t** it proceeds from my heart, I am in earnest; **det skjærer meg i –t** it cuts me to the heart, gives me a bitter pang; **i sitt innerste —** in his heart of hearts; **lett om –t** light of heart; **jeg er tung om –t** my heart is heavy; **jeg kan ikke bringe det over mitt —, jeg har ikke — til å** I cannot find it in my heart to, have not the heart to; **ha noe på —** have something on one's mind; **det som ligger meg mest på —** what I have most at heart; **legge en noe på —** urge something upon one; **hånden på –t** honour bright! **han har –t på rette sted** his heart is in the right place; **legge seg på —** take, lay to heart; **bærer under sitt —** carries under her belt.

hjerte|angst agony of fear. **–banking** palpitation of the heart. **–blod** heart's blood. **–feil** organic disease of the heart. **–fred** heart's ease, heart-ease, peace of mind. **–kammer** ventricle of the heart. **–knuser** lady-killer; (sl.) masher. **–lag** disposition.
hjertelig hearty, cordial; (adv) heartily, cordially; **le —** laugh heartily; **takke en —** thank one cordially; **— gjerne** with all my heart.
hjertelighet cordiality, heartiness.
hjerte|løs heartless. **–løshet** heartlessness. **–menneske** generous heart, kindly heart.
hjertens|kjær (subst) sweetheart. **–venn** chosen friend.
hjerteonde disease of the heart.
hjerter (i kortspill) hearts; **— ess, konge, dame, knekt, to, tre osv.** ace, king, queen, knave, deuce, three etc. of hearts; **en —** a heart.
hjerterom; hvor det er — er det også husrom heart-room makes house-room, where there is a will, there is a way.
hjerteskjærende heart-rending, heart-piercing, heart-breaking.
hjerteslag pulsation of the heart, heartbeat; (sykdom) an apoplexy of the heart.
hjertestyrkende cordial.
hjerte|styrkning cordial. **–sukk** deep-drawn sigh; ejaculatory prayer. **–syk** sick at heart. **–sykdom** disease of the heart, heart disease. **–sår** wound in the heart. **–tyv** charmer.
hjord herd, flock. **–vis** in herds, gregariously.
hjort deer, red-deer, hart, stag.
hjorte|kalv red-deer calf. **–skinn** buckskin, deer-skin. **–skinnshansker** buckskin gloves. **–takk** hartshorn. **–takker** antlers of a stag. **–takksalt** (volatile) salt of hartshorn. **–takksdråper** spirit of hartshorn.
hjul wheel; (til trillebår o. l.) trundle; (på dampskip) paddle-wheel; (under stol) caster; **han er femte — på vognen** he is a fifth wheel to the coach.

hjul|aksel axle-tree. **–beint** bandy-legged, bow-legged, outkneed. **–båt** wheel-boat; paddle-boat. **–damper** paddle-steamer, side-wheel steamer. **–kasse** paddle-box. **–maker** wheel-wright. **–spor** rut, track. **–verk** wheel work.
hjuring, se **gjætergutt.**
hjørne corner; (humør, sinn) humour, mood. **om –t** round the corner; **svinge om –t** turn the corner; **han bor på –t av** he lives at the corner of.
hjørne|butikk corner-shop. **–skap** corner-cupboard. **–stein** corner-stone. **–tann** corner-tooth. **–værelse** corner-room.

hk., h. k., HK. fork. f. **hestekraft** horse power, H. P.
H. K. H. fork. f. **hans kongelige høihet** His Royal Highness.
hm hem! ahem!
H. M., fork. f. **Hans Majestet** His Majesty, og for **Hennes Majestet** Her Majesty.
hoho aha!
hockey hockey.
hode head; (på pipe) bowl; **urolige –r** turbulent spirits; **ha et godt —** have good abilities, be clever, **tape –t** lose one's head; **holdt på å bite –t av meg** nearly bit my head off; **følge sitt eget —** follow one's own humour, have one's own way; **det er ikke etter mitt —** it is not to my fancy, I do not approve of it; **kort for –t** snappish, gruff, short-spoken; **sette seg noe i –t** take a thing into one's head; **regne i –t** reckon in one's head el. by the mental process; **jeg kan ikke få det inn i –t mitt** I cannot understand it, it will not go down with me; **han er ikke riktig i –t** he is not in his right senses; **ha vondt i –t** have a (bad) headache; **ha litt i –t** be tipsy; **legge sitt — i bløyt** rack one's brains; **henge med –t** hang down one's head; **treffe spikeren på –t** head the nail, hit the nail on the head; **vokse en over –t** get beyond one's control; **se over –t** look down upon; **rage et helt — over** stand head and shoulders above; **med hatt på –t** with a hat on his head; **stupe på —** (ved dukking) take a header; **sette saken på –t** turn things upside down; **om jeg så står på –t eller bena** I am as one in a dream; **stikke –ne sammen** lay heads together, compare notes; **kan ikke få det ut av –t** cannot get it out of my head; **uten —** headless; **som stiger til –t** heady.
hode|arbeid brain work. **–bevegelse** movement of the head. **–brudd** el. **–bry** racking of the brain. **–bunn** scalp, skin of the head. **–gjerde** bed's head. **–hud** el. **bunn.** **–kulls** headlong, head foremost. **–løs** headless. **–pine** headache; **jeg har —** I have a headache. **–plagg** (head) covering. **–pute** pillow. **–pynt** head-dress. **–regning** mental calculation el. computation, mental arithmetic. **–telefon** (til radio) (a pair of) head telephones, head-phones, head-piece. **–vask** washing of the head, shampooing.
hoff court; **ved –et** at court.
hoff|ball court-ball. **–dame** court lady, lady in attendance; lady in waiting. **–drakt** court dress. **–embetsmann** court functionary.
hofferdig proud, haughty, supercilious. **–het** haughiness, superciliousness.
hoff|etat civil list. **–folk** courtiers. **–fähig** presentable at court. **–gunst** court favour. **–intriger** court intrigues. **–jegermester** master of the hounds. **–kavaler** gentleman of the court. **–leverandør** purveyor to the court. **–mann** courtier. **–marskalk** Lord Steward. **–narr** court jester, c.fool. **–personale** members of the royal household. **–prest** king's chaplain, court-c. **–sjef** Lord Chamberlain. **–sorg** court mourning.
hoff|tjeneste employment at court. **–vant** accustomed to courts.
hofte hip, haunch. **–betennelse** coxitis. **–ledd** hip joint. **–skade** affection of the hip, dislocation of the hip. **–skål** socket of the hip joint.
hogg cut, slash, blow, stroke; **få — get** a drubbing.

hogge cut, hew; (smått) chop; (flenge) slash; (med nebbet) pick; peck; (dt.) (gripe) snatch, clutch; — **ved** chop wood; **skipet -r** the ship thumps, bumps; — **av** cut off; — **ned for fote** cut down indiscriminately; — **opp** (skip) break up; — **over** cut (in two); — **løs på hverandre** fall upon one another; — **sønder og sammen** cut to pieces; — **til** strike; (tilhogge) hew; — **ut i stein** carve in stone; **har hogd seg i handa** has cut his hand; — **seg igjennom** cut (one's way) through; make el. force one's way through.

hogge|stabbe chopping-block. **-r** hewer.

hogging cutting etc.

hoggjern chisel.

hoggorm viper, adder.

hoggtann fang (større hjørnetann f. eks. hos villsvin, framstående tann) tusk.

hogst cutting, felling.

hoi hoy! ahoy!

hokuspokus hocus-pocus.

hol, (adj) se **hul.**

hol, (subst) se **hull.**

I. **hold** flesh; condition; **i godt** — in good case el. condition, stout.

II. **hold** (tak) hold, holding, holdfast. (sting) pain, stitch. (avstand) range (of gunshot), distance. (kant, side) quarter; **fra alle** — from all quarters, on all hands. **det er ikke noe** — **i ham** he has no firmness of character. **på nært** — near at hand.

holdbar tenable; (om grunn) valid; (varig) durable; (om farge) fast; (om klær) good wear.

holdbarhet durability; keeping qualities.

holde (vt) hold; (beholde vedlikeholde, oppholde) keep; (feire) keep, observe; (underholde) maintain; (vedde) bet; (et blad) take in; (et mål) measure; (romme) hold; — **hest** keep a horse; — **møte** sit; — **sitt ord** keep one's word; — **pusten** hold (in) one's breath; **må** — **senga** is confined to his bed; — **stikk** hold good; — **en tale** make a speech, deliver an address; — **en tone** hold on el. sustain a note; — **vann** hold water; — **en med klær** (osv.) find one in clothes, keep one in c.; — **lag** med associate with, keep company with; — **en med selskap** keep one company; — **tilbake** hold back, detain;— **tårene tilbake** refrain from tears el. from weeping.

holde (vi.: stanse) stop; stand; (ikke briste) hold; (vare) last; **det vil** — **hardt** it will be hard work; **vogna -r for døra** the carriage is (waiting) at the door; — **seg** hold out; (om matvarer) keep; (godt, om tøy, ogs. fig) wear well; (skikk o. l.) continue, be still prevalent; — **seg tapper** behave gallantly; — **seg rolig** keep quiet; — **seg borte** keep away; **dette tøyet -r seg ikke i vasken** this stuff won't bear washing; **prisene -r seg høye, faste** osv. prices rule high, firm etc.; **hvis det gode været -r seg** if the weather remains fine; — **an** hold on; (hest) pull up, rein up; — **av** (man) bear away, keep off; — **fast** hold firmly, keep hold of; — **fast på** (fordring) stand out for; — **fast ved** stick to, adhere to; — **for** hold to be, consider to be, look upon as; — **for riktig** take to be right; — **fra** keep off; — **fra hverandre** keep separate; — **seg fra** abstain from, shun; — **fram** hold out (one's hand, a child); — **igjen** resist, retard the motion; — **øynene igjen** keep the eyes shut; — **seg inne** keep within doors, keep (to) one's home; — **med side with, agree with; — **opp** hold up; — **opp med** leave off, cease, stop; — **opp med skytingen** cease fire; — **seg oppe** keep afloat; — **på** keep, detain; (en mening o. l.) stick to, adhere to, stand upon, stand out for; (foretrekke) be for; — **på med** be engaged in, be busy with; — **på å ...** be -ing, be in the act of -ing; — **seg på bena** keep one's feet; — **sammen** keep el. hold together; — **en til arbeid** keep one to his work; — **seg til** abide by, stick to; — **ut** endure, stand; — **ut fra hverandre** distinct; — **ut**

med en bear with one; — **vedlike** keep up, keep in repair.

holden: hel og — (i god behold) safe and sound; (fullstendig) (adv) entirely, every inch; **en** — **mann** a man well to do in the world.

holde|plass halting place; (plass hvor biler kan anbringes) park, parking place; (for drosjer) (cab-)stand, (cab-)rank, standing. **-punkt** hold, (fig) fact; **ikke noe** — **for klagene** no fact in support of the complaints.

holdning bearing, carriage; (oppførsel) deportment, behaviour, attitude; firmness, balance.

holdningsløs weak, half-hearted, vacillating.

holdningsløshet weakness; (moralsk) lack of moral balance.

holdt halt! **gjøre** — halt.

hole (subst), se **hule.**

hole catch, get; **der er ingenting å** — there is nothing to be got.

I. **holk** (beslag, ring) ferrule. (dunk, kar) tub.

II. **holk** (gmlt. skip) hulk.

Holland (Nederland) Holland.

hollandsk (nederlandsk) Dutch.

hollender (nederlender) Dutchman. **-inne** Dutchwoman. **-ne** the Dutch.

holme holm, islet.

holmgang (gml. form for tvekamp) camp-fight, trial by battle.

holt (skog-) clump of trees, grove.

Homer Homer. **h-isk** Homeric.

homogen (ensartet) homogenious.

homøo|pat homœopathist. **-pati** homœopathy. **-patisk** homœopathic.

honnett honourable, fair-dealing.

honning honey. **-kake** ginger-bread. **-søt** sweet as honey, honeyed. **-såpe** honey soap.

honnør honour; **gjøre** — do the honours; act as host (hostess); **gjøre** — **for flagget** salute the colours; **med full** — with full honours; **fire -er** (i kortspill) four by honours.

honorar fee, honorary, honorarium; **jeg tar ikke noe** — I charge no fee(s).

honoratiores the quality, the gentility.

honorer|e fee, pay; (veksel) honour, protect, answer; **ikke** — dishonour, leave in sufferance. **-ing** protection; **vekselen vil bli -t prompte** the bill will meet with due protection.

hop multitude, crowd, shoal; **-en, den store** — the multitude, the common herd, the vulgar.

hope opp heap up, accumulate; congest. **hopetall: i** — in heaps, in crowds.

hopp jump, skip, hop.

hoppe (subst) mare. **-føll** filly.

hoppe (vrb) jump; skip; hop; — **over et gjerde** leap a fence; **hjertet -t i ham** his heart leaped within him. — **tau** skip. **hopper** leaper, jumper. **hoppetau** skipping-rope.

hopprenn ski-race with jump.

hor adultery; **du skal ikke bedrive** — thou shalt not commit adultery.

Horats Horace.

horde horde.

hordevis in hordes. **dyr som lever** — gregarious animals.

horisont horizon; **i -en** on the horizon; **over min** — above my reach, (dt.) above my hook, a cut beyond me.

horisontal horizontal.

hormon (indre sekresjon) hormone.

horn horn; **ha et** — **i siden til en** bear el. owe one a grudge; **blåse på** — blow a horn; **løpe -ene av seg** sow one's wild oats.

hornaktig horny, corneus.

horn|blåser hornblower, player. **-briller** horn-rimmed spectacles. **-et** horned, cornute(d). **-formet** horn-shaped, corniform. **-gjel** garfish.

hornhinne cornea. **-betennelse** inflammation of the cornea.

horn|hud horny skin, callosity. **-kveg** horned cattle. **-musikk** horn-music. **-signal** horn-blast. **-skei, -skje** horn-spoon.

horoskop horoscope; **stille ens** — cast one's horoscope el. nativity.

hortensia (plante) hydrangea.

hos with; (med genitiv etter på engelsk) at; (ved siden av) by; **han har vært** — **meg** he has been with me; — **min onkel** at my uncle's; **sitte** — **en** sit by one; — **romerne** among the Romans; **gesandt, doktor** — ambassador, physician to; **i gunst** — in favour with; **en svakhet** — a weakness in; **en vane** — a habit with; **spise middag** — dine with; **ta tjeneste** — enter (into) one's service; **se folk** — **seg** see company; **jeg var** — **hr.** Smith I was at Mr. Smith's; **som det heter** — **Byron** as Byron has it; **utgi en bok** — **en bokhandler** publish a book with a book-seller.

hose hose, stocking; **gjøre sine -r grønne** curry favour; **så lett som fot i** — as easy as kiss hand. **-bånd** garter. **-båndsorden** order of the garter. **-båndsridder** knight of the garter. **-lest** stocking-foot; **på -en** in one's stockings. **-skaft** footless stocking, leg of a stocking.

hosianna hosanna.

hos|lagt enclosed; accompanying; **-lagte skrivelse** the enclosed letter.

hospital hospital, infirmary; almshouse; **på -et** in the hospital; **bli innlagt på et** — be put in hospital; **bli utskrevet fra -et** be dismissed from h.

hospitalsskip floating hospital.

hospit|ant temporary student. **-ere** attend as a temporary student.

hospits hospice.

hosstående present.

hoste (subst) cough.

hoste (vrb) cough.

hoste|anfall fit of coughing, coughing fit. **-pastiller** cough-lozenges.

hostie (nattverbrød) host.

hotell hotel, inn. **-eier** hotel proprietor. **-gutt** hotel servant, boots (med verbet i sing.). **-vert** master of a hotel, innkeeper.

hottentott Hottentot.

I. **hov** (gude-; utt. håv) sacrificial temple.

II. **hov** (på hest) hoof.

hovdyr hoofed el. ungulate quadruped.

hoved|agentur head agency. **-angrep** principal attack. **-anke** principal grievance. **-anklage** main charge. **-arbeid** main work. **-arving** principal heir (heiress). **-avdeling** grand el. great division. **-bane** trunk line. **-beskjeftigelse** chief employment. **-bestanddel** main ingredient el. constituent. **-bok** ledger. **-bygning** main building. **-bøle** manor. **-ekspedisjon** Chief Office. **-fag** principal (subject of) study. **-feil** principal fault. **-fløy** main wing. **-formål** main end, chief aim. **-forretning** main business. **-forskjell** main difference. **-gate** main street, leading street, thoroughfare. **-grunn** principal reason. **-gård** manor. **-hjørnesten** headstone of the corner. **-hær** main body of an army. **-inngang** main entrance. **-innhold** substance, main purport; chief contents; a summary. **-inntekt** chief revenue. **-jernbane** trunk line. **-kilde** main source. **-kontor** chief (el. head) office. **-kreditor** principal (el. main) creditor. **-kvarter** head-quarters. **-landevei, se -vei. -ledning** main; main conductor. **-linje** principal line; se **-bane, -rute. -løp** main channel. **-mangel** main defect. **-mann** principal; (opphavsmann) author; (i opprør) ringleader. **-masse** bulk. **-motiv** chief motive; (i musikk) leading motive. **-næring** chief food. **-nøkkel** master key, pass-key, skeleton key, passe-partout. **-oppgave** main task. **-opplagssted** chief emporium. **-person** principal person; (teater) leading character. **-post** principal item. **-postkontor** central post-office; general post-office; G. P. O. **-prinsipp** fundamental (el. leading) principle. **-produkt** staple (product). **-punkt** main point. **-redaktør** editor in chief. **-regel** principal rule. **-register** general index. **-rengjøring** thorough cleaning, cleaning-out. **-rolle** principal part, leading (principal, chief el. central) character. **-rute** main route. **-sak** main point, great thing; **han har rett i -en** he is right in the main. **-sakelig** main; (adv) mainly, principally. **-sete** principal seat el. residence. **-setning** (gram) principal proposition. **-skip** (i kirke) nave. **-stad** capital, metropolis. **-stadsmetropolitan. -stamme** (tre) main trunk; (folk) chief tribe; (fig) main stock. **-stasjon** (jernb.) terminus; (for flåten) principal naval station. **-styre** directors. **-styrke: hans** — (mil) the bulk of his forces; (fig) his forte, his strong point. **-sum** sum-total. **-tanke** leading idea. **-trapp** principal stairs el. staircase. **-vakt** main guard (-house). **-vei** trunk road, principal road. **-vekt: legge -en på** lay particular stress on. **-vitne** principal witness.

hoven swelled, swollen, swoln; (fig) puffed up, arrogant.

hovenhet swelling; (fig) arrogance.

hovere exult, crow.

hoveri (gmlt.; pliktarbeid) soccage, villenage; (fig) drudgery.

hovering exultation.

hovmester (huslærer) private tutor; (mar) steward; (overkelner) butler.

hovmod haughtiness, arrogance; pride; — **står for fall** pride will have a fall; pride goes before destruction. **hovmodig** haughty, arrogant; overbearing, proud.

hovne, — opp swell.

hov|skjegg fetlock. **-slag** clattering of horses' hoofs. **-smed** farrier, shoeing smith. **-spor** hoofprint. **-tang** claw-wrench, farrier's pincers.

hr. Mr. (brukt foran egennavn og noen titler, f. eks. Mr. Smith; Mr. President); Esq., Esqr. (i utenpåskrift på brev, f. eks. T. Smith, Esq.). Militære og akademiske titler med eller uten navn etter brukes i alm. uten noen tilføyelse: **hr. korporal** Corporal; **hr. kaptein** Captain; **hr. doktor** Doctor; **hr. professor** Professor.

hu! oh!

hubro eagle- (el. great horned) owl.

hud skin; (sedv. om tykt, håret skinn) hide; **skjelle en -en full** abuse one grossly; **med — og hår** entirely.

hud|avskrapning abrasion (of skin). **-farge** colour of the skin; (ansiktets) complexion. **-fille** flap of the skin. **-fletning** flagellation, scourging, flogging. **-flette** scourge, lash, flog; (fig ogs.) cut up. **-fold** fold of the skin. **-løs** galled, raw. **-løshet** excoriation, raw. **-pleie** culture of the skin.

Hudson-bukten Hudson Bay.

hudstryke scourge. **hudstrykning** scourging.

hudsykdom cutaneous disease, skin disease.

hue (lue) cap, bonnet.

huff! oh, ugh.

hug mind, mood. **det rant meg i -en** I called to mind. **hans — står til det** his mind is bent upon it. **kom i — at du helligholder hviledagen** remember the sabbath day, to keep it holy.

huge please.

hugenott Huguenot.

hugg, hugge, se hogg, hogge.

huglegge fix (el. set) one's heart on, set one's mind on.

Hugo Hugh.

hugse, se huske.

hugstor large (el. wide) -minded.

hui: i — og hast hurriedly.

huie shout, halloo; (truende) hoot.

huk: sitte på — squat on the ground.

huke seg ned crouch, squat; (av frykt ogs.) cower.

hukommelse memory; **en god** — a strong memory; **etter -n** from memory; **-n min svikter** my memory fails me.

hukommelses|feil slip of the memory, misrecollection. **-kunst** art of memory; mnemonics. **-sak** act of the memory, learning by rote.

hul hollow; (konkav) concave; **den -e hånd** the hollow of the hand. **-brystet** hollow-chested.

hulder hill-lady, wood-nymph; (Norwegian) fairy. **-folk** fairies. **-lokk**, **-slått** fairy's music.

hule (vrb) hollow; — **ut** hollow (out).

hule (subst) cave, cavern, grotto; (vilt dyrs hule) den. **-boer** cave-dweller, troglodyte.

hul|het hollowness. **-ing** hollowing; (konkret) hollow.

hulke sob.

hulkinnet hollow-cheeked.

hull (bare i poesi og gmld. stil) (trofast) faithful, loyal; (gunstig stemt) kind; (yndig) lovely.

hull hole; (bort) perforation; (stukket) puncture; (åpning) aperture; (gap) gap; (lakune) blank, gap, void, deficiency, lacuna, chasm; **slå — i hodet** break one's head; **skjære, slå, brenne — på** cut, knock, burn a hole in; **det går — på byllen** the abscess breaks; **få — på luftringen** have one's machine punctured; **med -er på albuene (hælene)** out at the elbows (heels); **ta — på** (en tønne) broach (a barrel); **hullet** full of holes.

hullfald hemstitch, open-work hem. **sy —** hemstitch.

hullsalig (passing) graceful el. gracious.

hullskap (foreldet, bare i uttr.:) **sverge — og troskap** take the oath of allegiance; **oppsi — og troskap** withdraw one's allegiance from.

hullsøm, se **hullfald**.

hulmål measure of capacity.

hulning hollow, depression.

hulrom cavity.

hul|slipe grind hollow. **-speil** concave mirror.

hulter til bulter pell-mell, helter-skelter, at sixes and sevens.

hulvei gorge, ravine, defile.

huløyd hollow-eyed, with eyes deep sunk.

human humane. **-isme** humanism. **-ist** humanist. **-istisk** humanistic. **-itet** humaneness, humanity.

humbug humbug. **-maker** humbugger; sham.

I. **humle** (insekt) humble-bee. **-blomst** avens. **-bol** humble-bee's nest.

II. **humle** (plante) hop (blomstene, varen) hops; **-ranke** hop-bind, hopvine. **-stang** hop-pole.

hummer lobster. **-fangst** lobster -fishery. **-klo**, **-saks** lobsters' claw. **-teine** lobster -pot.

humor humour. **-eske** humorous story. **-ist** humorist. **-istisk** humorous.

hump hummock; (i vei) lump, protuberance.

humpe limp, hobble.

humpet hummocky, lumpy, rough.

humre (om hest) nicker low, whinny.

humør (godt el. dårlig) spirits; **i godt —** in good spirits, in high spirits; **i dårlig —** in low spirits, out of sorts; (oppførende) in a temper; **få i godt —** bring round; **når han var i det —** when in the humour. **-syke** spleen, mumps, blue devils.

hun (pron) she.

I. **hun** (subst) se **hunn**.

II. **hun** (ved), se **bakhun**.

hun|ape she-monkey. **-bjørn** she-bear. **-blomst** female flower.

hund dog; (om jakthunder også) hound; (om et koppel i jakt) the pack; **mange -er om ett bein** there are always more round pegs than round holes; **røde -er** the rose-rash, the false measles; **gå i -ene** go to the dogs, go to the bad; **som en våt —** quite abashed; **skamme seg som en —** be thoroughly ashamed; **en skal ikke skue -en på hårene** appearances are deceitful; **leve som — og katt** agree like cats and dogs; lead (live) a cat-and-dog life.

hundeaktig canine, doggish.

hunde|dager dogdays. **-galskap** hydrophobia. **-gjøing** baying of dogs. **-halsband** dog's collar. **-hus** kennel, dog-house. **-hvalp** pup, puppy.

-kaldt villainously cold. **-kjeks** biscuits, dog-cakes; (plante) wild chervil, pig's parsley. **-koppel** leash of dogs el. hounds; pack of hounds. **hunde|lenke** dog-chain. **-liv** dog's life. **-mat** dog's meat. **-pisk** dog-whip. **-skatt** dog-tax, tax on dogs. **-skinn** dog's skin. **-slekten** the dog-kind. **-stjerne** dog-star, canicula. **-syke** distemper in dogs. **-vakt** (mar) middle watch. **-vis: på —** dog-fashion. **-vær** villainous weather.

hundre a hundred; **ett —** one hundred; **to — egg** two hundred eggs; **om — år er allting glemt** it's all one a hundred years hence; **hundrede** (ordenstall) hundredth.

hundre|del hundredth, centesimal (part). **-fold** centuple. **-fold** a hundred fold. **-vis: i —** by hundreds, by the hundred. **-år** century. **-årig** a hundred years old; (som inntreffer hvert 100 år) centennial, centenary; **en -åring** a centenarian. **-årsdag** hundredth anniversary, centennial day. **-årsjubileum** centenary, centennial jubilee.

hundse treat like a dog, ride rough-shod over, sit upon. **hundsk** dog-like; contemptuous.

hundsvott driver's seat; dickey; (om person) scamp, vile wretch.

hun|due hen pigeon. **-elefant** female elephant. **-esel** she-ass, jenny ass. **-fisk** female fish, spawner. **-fugl** female bird, hen-bird.

hunger hunger; (hungersnød) famine; **dø av — perish with hunger el. by famine; — er den beste kokk** hunger is the best sauce. **hungers|død** death by starvation; **dø -en** perish of starvation. **-nød** famine.

hungre, se **sulte, være sulten; — etter** hunger for.

hun|hare doe-hare. **-hund** bitch. **-kanin** doe-rabbit. **-katt** she-cat, tabby-cat, tib-cat. **-kjønn** (gram) the feminine gender; (kvinnek.) female sex. **-kjønnsendelse** feminine termination. **-løve** lioness.

hunn (subst) (i alm. om firb. dyr) she, female; (i alm. om fugler) hen-bird.

hun|rakle fertile catkin. **-rev** vixen, bitch -fox. **-rotte** doe-rat. **-spurv** hen-sparrow. **-tiger** tigress. **-ørn** hen-eagle, eagless.

huri houri.

hurlumhei hurry-scurry, hurly-burly.

hurpe (dt.) old dowdy.

hurra! huzza! hurrah, hurra! **rope — cheer**, hurrah, huzza; **rope — for** cheer.

hurrarop cheer, cheering.

hurtig (adj) quick, fast; (rask) prompt, expeditious; (ikke om person) speedy, rapid; **— til beins** swift, swift-footed, fleet.

hurtig (adv) (i løpet av kort tid) quickly; (snart etter) soon; (med fortsatt sterk fart) fast.

hurtighet rate, quickness, speed, rapidity, celerity, promptitude, despatch.

hurtig|løp foot-race. **-løper** (fast) runner, racer. **-rute** fast service, rapid transit. **-seiler** fast sailer. **-skyting** rapid firing.

hurtigtog fast train, quick train, express-train, express.

hus house; (lite) cottage; (snegle-) house, shell; (handels-) house, firm; **her i -et** in this house; **der i -et** in that house; **herren og fruen i -et** the master and mistress of the house; **verten i -et** (som eier det) the landlord; **vertinnen i -et** the landlady; **fullt — a** crowded house; **i -et** (på stedet) on the premises; **foran -et** in front of the house; **bringe i — garner**, get in; **bo i — sammen** live in the same house; **jage en ut av -et** turn one out of doors; **føre stort — live** in great style; **holde — keep** house, (spare) economize; (ta på vei) go on, rage, storm; **holde — for en** keep one's house, be one's house-keeper; **holde godt — med** husband, be careful of; **holde dårlig — med** waste; **ta til takke med det -et formår** take pot-luck.

husapotek family medicine-chest.

husar hussar.

husarbeid house work, domestic industry.

husbehov: til — for household use; (såvidt) just the needful, no more than is required; moderately.

husbestyrerinne housekeeper, manager.

husbond (herre) master; (amr) boss; (ektemann) husband. **husbonds|dreng** head servant. **–folk** masters. **–kar,** se **–dreng. –rett** the right to be master in one's own house.

husbruk: til — for home purposes; for home consumption; for home wear.

husdyr domestic animal.

huse house, harbour.

huseier house-owner.

husere go on; make havoc; **— med** bully.

hus|fang building materials. **–far** head of a family, householder, master; (mest spøkende) paterfamilias; **en god —** a good family-man. **–felle** fellow lodger, housemate.

husflid domestic industry.

husfred domestic peace; **hva gjør man ikke for –ens skyld** anything for a quiet life.

husfritt rentfree.

hus|frue mistress (of the house). **–geråd** household furniture, chattels. **–hjelp** (tjenestepike) maid, maid-servant, domestic servant. **–holder** householder; **en god, dårlig —** a good, bad economist. **–holderske** housekeeper; manager. **–holdning** housekeeping, management of a house.

husholdnings– household. –bok book of household accounts. **–elev** housekeeping pupil. **–penger** money for household expenses, house-money, **–saker** household affairs. **–skole** (training) school of cookery.

hus|hovmester master of the household, steward. **–jomfru** housekeeper.

huskapellan domestic chaplain.

I. **huske** (vrb) remember, recollect, call to mind; **jeg –r godt** I well remember, I perfectly recollect **jeg –r ikke navnet hans** I forget his name; **hvis jeg ikke –r feil** if my memory serves me; **— på** remember, mind, bear in mind; **— en på noe** (dt) put one in mind of something; **— en noe** remember one for something.

II. **huske** (vrb) (gynge) seesaw, swing.

huske (subst) swing.

huskeseddel reminder.

huskestue: det vil bli en ordentlig — there will be the devil of a row.

huskjent well acquainted with the house.

huskors domestic nuisance.

husleie (house) rent. **–lov** rents restriction act, rent act. **–nemnd** committee for the control of rents, rent control.

huslig domestic, domesticated; (flink i huset) thrifty.

huslighet thrift, domesticity.

hus|ly shelter. **–lege** family physician el. doctor. **–lærer** family tutor, house tutor, private t., domestic t. **–lærerpost** situation as a family t. etc.

hus|mann cottager, cotter, cottar. **–mannskone** cottager's wife. **–mannskost** homely fare. **–mannsplass** cottage allotment. **–stue** cot house; (uten jord) cottage.

hus|mor mistress, housewife, housekeeper. **–nummer** number. **–orden** house-rule. **–postill** family book of sermons. **–rom** house, housing, accommodation. **–råd** household remedy. **–skikk** custom of a house. **–sopp** dryrot. **–stand** household, family. **–stell** domestic management, housewifery. **–tak** roof of a house. **–tomt** house-lot, site.

hustre, se **hutre.**

hustru wife.

hus|tukt domestic discipline. **–tyrann** domestic tyrant. **–undersøkelse** search of the house.

husvale (gmlt.) soothe, solace, comfort. **–lse** solace, comfort.

husvant accustomed to the house, domesticated.

husvarme house-warmth; (fortrolighet og tilnærmelse mellom medlemmer av samme husstand) propinquity.

husvenn friend of the family.

husvert landlord; (kvinnelig) landlady.

husvesen domestic economy, household affairs.

hus|vill homeless, houseless. **–vær** houseroom, lodgings, a house. **–vøling** mending, repairing of a house.

hutle botch, bungle; **— seg igjennom** (hangle igjennom) live poorly, live miserably, keep the wolf from the door.

hutre (av kulde) shiver, shrink.

hva what; **hva!** (utrop) what! how! eh? **— som** what; **— du så gjør** whatever you do; **vet du —** I tell you what; do you know; **— for** (en, et, noen) what; **— for en mann er det?** what man is that; **— var det for en støy?** what noise was that? **— behager?** (I) beg your pardon? el. (til en herre) Sir? (til en dame) Madam? (dt.) What? Eh? **— urimelig er det i** where is the absurdity of; **— så** what then? what of that; what next? **— som helst** whatever, whatsoever.

hval whale. **–barde** whale-bone, baleen. **–båt** whaleboat. **–fanger** (mann) whale fisher, whaleman; (skip) whaler. **–fangerselskap** whaling company. **–fangst** whale-fishery, whaling. **–kjøtt** crang, creng. **–kokeri** boilery; **flytende —** floating boilery. **–olje** whale-oil.

hvalp puppy, whelp; **få –er** whelp, pup.

hvalpesyke the distemper.

hvalpet puppyish.

hval|rav spermaceti. **–ross** walrus, morse, seahorse. **–spekk** whale blubber. **–unge** whale-cub. **–åt** whale's food.

hvass se **kvass.**

I. **hvelv** arch, vault.

II. **hvelv** (båt–) se **kvelv.**

hvelve arch, vault. **hvelvet** arched, vaulted.

hvelving arch, vault.

hvem who; **— av dem?** which of them? **— der** who is that? who goes there? **— som helst** anybody.

hver every; (av to eller flere) each; everybody; se **enhver; — (den) som** whoever; **— annen** every second, every two; **— annen time** every two hours; **— især** each; **i –t** fall in any case; **de gikk — sin vei** each went his own way, they went their several ways; **gi — sitt** give every man his due; pay one's way; **— for seg** separately, individually, severally; **han kan være her –t øyeblikk** he may be here any minute; **trekke — sin vei** pull different ways; **gud og — mann** vet all the world knows; **— beholder sin mening** we each keep our opinion.

hverandre each other, one another; **tett på —** in rapid succession.

hverdag week day. **hverdags–** every-day, commonplace; trite, trivial; **til hverdags** on week days; usually.

hverdags|ansikt every-day face. **–arbeid** daily work, every-day work. **–bruk** everyday use el. wear. **–klær** everyday clothes. **–kost** daily fare, homely fare.

hverdags|lig commonplace, every-day. **–livet** every day life, common life, this work-a-day world el. life. **–menneske** every-day person.

hver gang every time, whenever.

hverken (konj) neither; **— han eller jeg** neither he nor I.

hvermann every man, everybody.

hvese hiss. **hvesing** hissing.

hvete wheat; (i Engl., ikke i Skottl. el Amerika) corn.

hvete|bolle muffin. **–brød** wheaten bread, wheaten loaf.

hvetebrødsdager honeymoon; **par som feirer —** honeymooners.

hvete|høst wheat-harvest. **–korn** wheat-grain. **–mel** wheat-flour; **fint —** semoule.

hvil breathing spell, rest. **holde** — make a halt.
hvile (subst) rest, repose; **gå inn til den evige** — go to one's eternal home.
hvile (vrb) rest, repose; (i gamle gravskrifter) **herunder -r** here lies; **det -r en gjeld på godset** the estate is encumbered with a debt; — **tungt på weigh** el. sit heavy on; — **seg** take rest. **hviledag** rest day day of rest.
hvile|løs restless. **-løshet** restlessness. **-punkt** (tyngdep.) centre of gravity; (mekanikk) point of support.
hvilested place of rest, resting place.
hviletid time of rest.
hvilken (uttetkjønn: hviiket, pluralis: hvilke). 1: (spørrende pronomen i begrenset spørsmål) which. 2: (spørrende pronomen i ubegrenset spørsmål) what. 3: (relativt pronomen, som henviser til en foregående setning, stivt språk, ikke dagligtale) which. Eksempler: 1: which is which? which song do you prefer? which chapter do you prefer? which of these books do you like best? **hvilken av dem?** which of them? 2. **hvilke** (c: hva for noen) **bøker liker du?** what books du you like? **hvilken lege kan hjelpe meg?** what doctor can help me? 3. **de sa at jeg hadde gjort det, hvilket var løgn** they said I had done it, which was a lie.
hvilken enn whichever; **hvilken vei jeg enn vendte meg** whichever way I turned.
hvilken som helst any, any whatever; **hvilket som helst tall** any number whatever.
hvin, hvine se **kvin, kvine.**
hvirvel whirl; (i vannet) whirlpool, eddy; (knokkel) vertebra (pl. -bræ). **en** — **av fornøyelser** a whirl of entertainments. **slå en** — beat a roll (on a drum). **-dyr** vertebral el vertebrate (animal) backboned animal. **-løs** invertebrate, invertebral; **-øse dyr** invertebrates. **-sentrum** centre of depression. **-storm** hurricane, cyclone typhoon. **-søyle** vertebral column, spinal column. **-vind** whirlwind. **hvirvle** whirl; (om vann) eddy.
hvis (dersom) if, in case; — **ikke** unless. if . . . not; (i motsatt fall) if not; — **det er så** if so; supposing that to be the case; — **han ikke hadde vært** but for him, were it not for him; — **man skal tro ham . . .** to believe him . . .
hvis (genitiv) whose; (bare om dyr og ting) of which; **til** — **ære** n honour of whom.
hviske whisper; — **til en** whisper (to) one. — **noe i øret på en** whisper something in one's ear. **-nde** whispering; (adv) in a whisper, in whispers.
hvisking whispering.
hvit white; **det -e i øyet** the white; **de -e** the Whites; **hvitbjørn** white bear, polar bear.
hvite (eggehvite) white.
hvitetirsdag Shrove Tuesday.
hvite|vareforretning linen-draper's shop.**-varehandler** linen-draper. **-varer** linen drapery.
hvit|glødende heated to whiteness, white-hot, incandescent. **-het** whiteness. **-håret** white-haired, hoary.
hvitkalket whitewashed, white-limed.
hvitkledd clad in white.
hvitkløver white clover; (Irlands nasjonalblomst) shamrock.
hvitkål white cabbage.
hvitlett fair-complexioned.
hvitløk garlic. **-lyng** white heath(er).
hvitmalt painted white.
hvitne whiten.
hvitning whitewashing.
hvitsymre white anemone, wood a., wind-flower.
hvitte white-wash.
hvitting (fisk) whiting.
hvitveis, se **-symre.**
hvor (sted) where; (grad) how; — **er du?** where are you? — **stor var ikke min forundring** what was my surprise; — **vakker hun er** how beautiful she is!

hvorav whereof, of which, of whom.
hvordan how; of what kind; — **har De det?** how are you? **fortell meg** — **han er** tell me what he is like; — **været så er** no matter what the weather might be.
hvorfor (adv og konj.) wherefore, why, what for; for which; — **det?** why so?
hvorfra from which; wherefrom, whence.
hvorhen where, whither, whereto.
hvorhenne where.
hvori wherein, in which; into which. **-blant** among which. **-gjennom** through which. **-mot** (adv) whereas.
hvorledes, se **hvordan.**
hvor lenge how long. — **mange** how many. — **mye** how much; — **mye enn** however much.
hvor|om about which, whereof; — **allting er** any way, however that may be. **-på** on which; (om tid) whereupon, after which, when.
hvor som helst anywhere; (rel) wherever.
hvor|under under which. **-ved** (ved hvilket) whereat, at which; (ved hvilket middel) by which means.
hvorvidt (om) whether.
hyasint hyacinth.
hybel den, cabin.
hydrat hydrate.
hydraulisk hydraulic.
hydroaeroplan hydroaeroplane, sea plane.
hye (rise, slå) hide, lash.
hyene hyena.
hygge (subst) comfort, ease; snugness, cosiness.
hygge (for en) (vrb) make (one) comfortable, study el. promote one's comfort; — **seg** feel at home.
hyggelig comfortable, snug, cosy, home-like.
hygiene hygiene, sanitation.
hygienisk hygienic.
hykkelsk hypocritical.
hykle feign, simulate, dissemble; (for en) play the hypocrite (to one).
hykler hypocrite, dissembler. **-i** hypocrisy, cant. **-sk** hypocritical. **-ske,** se **hykler.**
hyl howl, yell.
hyl|e yell, howl; cry, whine. **-er** howler. **-ing** yelling.
hyll elder.
I. hylle (subst) shelf; (eller nett i kupéer) rack; (i fjellet) ledge. **anbringe i -r** shelve; **være kommet på sin rette** — be in one's right place; **legge på -a** lay on the shelf.
II. hylle (dekke, hylster) shroud.
I. hylle (inn) (vrb.) wrap, cover, shroud.
II. hylle (gi hyllest) pay el. do homage to, swear allegiance; **la seg** — **av** receive the homage of. — **en mening** hold (to) an opinion.
hyllemargskule pith ball.
hyllest favour; homage.
hylle|te elder tea. **-tre** elder tree.
hylling homage. **-sed** oath of allegiance.
hylse case, casing; (patron-) catridge case.
hylster covering case; (pistolh.) holster; **det jordiske** — the mortal frame.
hymen hymen.
hymne hymn.
hynne cushion; **belagt med -r** cushioned.
hyper|bel hyperbola. **-bol** hyperbole.
hyperkritisk hypercritical.
hypnose hypnosis.
hypno|tisere hypnotize. **-tisk** hypnotic. **-tisme** hypnotism.
hypokon|der hypocondriac. **-dersk** hypochondriac, splenetic, (dt.) hyppish. **-dri** hypochondria, hypochondriasis; (dt.) hyp, spleen.
hypo|tek mortgage, pledge. **-tese** hypothesis. **-tetisk** hypothetic(al).
hypp! hop!
hyppe (poteter) hill, earth.
hyppe|jern hoe. **-plog** earthing-plough.
hyppig frequent; (adv) frequently. **-het** frequency.

hyrde (nu bare i bibelsk og geist. betydn. og i forb. som hyrdediktn. o. l. Se ellers **gjæter**) shepherd. **den gode** — the good shepherd. **-brev** pastoral (letter). **-dikt** pastoral (poem), bucolic, idyl. **-dikter** bucolic poet. **-diktning** pastoral el. bucolic poetry.

hyrde|stav pastoral staff, crook, (fig) crosier. **-time** hour of billing and cooing, an hour's courting. **-tone** (fig) dulcet note. **hyrdinne** shepherdess.

hyre (subst) hire; (lønn) wages; (til sjøs) pay; ta — med . . . ship el. sign articles onboard the . . .; **få** — be engaged, obtain a berth; ha sin fulle — med have enough to do with.

hyre (vrb) hire, engage; se **forhyre**.

hyre (sett klær) kit, outfit.

hyre (utruste med klær) fit out with clothing. **hyre|bas** shipping master; (amr) boarding-master; (verver) crimp. **-kontrakt** articles (of agreement).

hyse haddock.

hysj! hush! (i en forsaml.) order! order!

hysje hush; (gi mishag til kjenne) hiss; — på en hiss (at) one.

hyssing housing, houseline; pack-thread, twine. **hyste|ri** hysterics. **-risk** hysterical; **bli** —, få et — **anfall** go into hysterics.

hytt: i — **og vær** heedlessly at random.

hytte — **seg for** guard against.

hytte (subst) hut, cottage, cabin; (elendig hytte) hovel; (hos eskimoene) igloo; (mar) poop; **en** — **og hans hjerte** love in a cottage.

hyv: ta **-en** fatt scoot, pick up one's heels, show the heels.

hæl heel; **sette nye -er** på re-heel; **følge en i -ene** dog one; **følge like i -ene** tread closely on the heels of; **like i -ene** på hot-foot upon. **hæl|flekk** (el. **-flikk**) heel-piece, heel-tap. **-flekke** (el. **-flikke**) heel (-piece, -tap). **-flekking** (el. **-flikking**) heeling. **-jern** (på støvler) heel-tip.

hær army; (hærskare) host. **-avdeling** division (of an army).

hær|fang, se **krigsbytte. -ferd** warfare.

hærforordning Army Act.

hærfører commander of an army.

hær|makt forces. **-pil** (gmlt.) war message arrow. **-skare** host. **-skjold** (gmlt.): **føre** —imot levy (el. wage) war upon. **-skrik** battle cry. **-styrke** (military) force. **-tatt** conquered, won (and held) by the sword. **-verk** assault, violence; ravage, havoc.

hæv, se **gjev.**

hø, se **fjelltopp.**

høflig civil; (utpreget høflig) polite.

høflighet politeness, courtesy, civility; — **koster ingen penger** soft words hurt not the mouth, good words cost nought.

høg, se **høy.**

høgd, se **høyde** (i lende) hill, height, eminence.

høgdedrag ridge of elevation, of hills.

høg|fjell lofty mountain, alp; (is. koll.:) mountain region, high plateaus. **i,** på **-et** on the mountains. **-fjells-** Alpine. **-fjellsluft** mountain air. **-fjellssanatorium** mountain health -resort.

høgre, se **høyre.**

høgre skole secondary school, advanced school.

høgsete throne, high el. elevated seat.

høgskole university; academy; (folke-) popular academy, school for young peasants.

høgslette high level, table land.

høgst dags in the middle of the day, at noon. **høgst nattes** at dead of night, in the middle of the night, at midnight.

høgtid, se **høytid.**

høgsterett supreme court, final court of appeal; (i England) court of the king in parliament.

høker (gmlt. for kjøpmann) (tallow-)chandler, provision-dealer. **-aktig** hucksterlike. **-butikk** chandler's shop, provision-shop.

høkervarer chandlery.

høkre huckster; sell by retail; hawk.

høl (i elv) deep pool.

hølje pour (with rain). **det -r ned** it pours with rain, the rain comes down in torrents.

høne hen, fowl; **jeg har en** — **å plukke med Dem** I have a crow to pluck (el. a bone to pick) with you.

høne|blund cat's nap. **-kylling** hen chicken.

høns fowls, poultry.

hønse|fugl gallinaceous bird. **-gård** poultry yard, hennery, fowl-run. **-hauk** chicken-hawk, goshawk. **-hold** chicken raising. **-hus** poultry-house, fowl-house, hen-coop. **-ri** hennery. **-stige** hen-roost.

hørbar audible.

høre (oppfatte med høresansen) hear; (høre etter) listen; (oppfatte) catch; (skjelne) distinguish; (komme til å høre tilfeldig) overhear; (eksaminere) catechise; **hør!** (for å vekke en annens oppmerksomhet) I say! look here! (som bifallsrop) hear! (som oppfordring til å høre etter) listen! just listen! only listen! **hør her!** listen! look here! **bli hørt** (på skolen) be called up, be on; **ikke så han hørte det** not in his hearing; **de har ingenting å la hverandre** — the one is just as good as the other; **det lar seg** — there is some reason in that; **få** — learn; **få** — **for noe** be blamed for something; **jeg har hørt si** I have heard it said, I have heard tell, I have been told; **nå har jeg hørt det med!** el. **en skal** — **mye!** come! come! that beats all! that's rather too bad; **hva er det jeg -r?** what is this I hear? **som det seg hør og bør** as is meet and fitting; duly and dutifully; **jeg har hørt det av min søster** I have heard it from my sister; — **etter** listen to, attend to, give ear to. — **guttene i leksene** hear (the boys repeat) their lessons; — **innom** en call on one; — **inn under** fall under; — **med** be one of . . .; (fig) **han -r bare etter med det ene øre** he is only half listening; — **om** hear of; **ville ikke** — **noe om det** would not hear of it; — **på** listen to; **han -r ikke på det øre** he hears nothing with that ear, (fig) he turns a deaf ear to it; — **sammen med** be of a piece, belong to the same class el. series; — **til** I belong in; — **til, hjemme på** et sted be a native, a resident of a place; **det -r til** it is fit and proper, it is the right thing; **jeg har ikke hørt noe til ham** I have heard nothing of him; I have had no news of him; **man har aldri hørt noe til ham** he has never been heard of; — **til slutt,** — **til ende** hear out.

høreapparat hearing-apparatus.

høreredskap organ of hearing.

høre|rør ear-trumpet, hearing-trumpet; (på telefon) receiver. **-sans** sense of hearing.

hørevidde! innenfor, utenfor — within, out of el. beyond earshot (hearing).

hørlig audible.

hørsel hearing.

høst (innhøstning) harvest; (avling) crop; (årstiden) autumn; (amr.) fall (of the year); **i** — this autumn; **om -en** in (the) autumn; **til -en** in the autumn.

høst|aktig autumnal. **-dag** autumn day.

høste harvest, reap; **som en sår, så -r en** as you sow you must reap.

høst|fest harvest festival. **-folk** harvesters, reapers. **-gilde** harvest supper, harvest home. **-jevndøgn** autumnal equinox. **-sæd** autumn -sown corn. **-takkefest** thanksgiving sermon of harvest-home.

høsttid harvest time.

høstutsikter prospect for the harvest.

høvding chief, chieftain.

høve (subst) occasion; opportunity. **nytte -t** avail oneself of the opportunity, improve the opportunity el. occasion.

høve (vrb) fit, suit, be convenient el. suitable.

høvedsmann leader, captain.

høvel plane; (bokb.) plough(-knife).

høvel|benk joiner's bench, planing-table. **-flis** wood shaving(s).
hovelig convenient, appropriate, suitable. **opptre** — behave properly.
høvel|jern plane-iron. **-spon** shaving, (kollekt.) shavings.
hovisk (beleven) courteous, courtly, polite; (ærbar) modest, decent.
høvle plane. **-maskin** planer. **-ri** planing mills el. works.
høvling planing.
høy (subst) hay.
høy (adj) high, lofty; (person, tre o. l.) tall; (lydelig) loud; **for** — (falsk) too sharp; **det er for -t for meg** it is above my comprehension, it is beyond me, it is over my head; — **alder** advanced age; **i en** — **alder at a good old age**, at a great age; **han er fire fot** — he is four feet high; **snøen ligger tre fot** — the snow is three feet deep; **på sin -e hest** on the high horse, on the high rope; **-e herrer** great men; **-t til loftet** lofty; **en** — **mann** a tall man; **to, tre, fire mann** — two, three, four deep; — **panne** a lofty forehead; **i egen -e person** in person; **den -e port** the Sublime Porte; **en** — **pris** a high price; **en** — **stemme** (en kraftig s.) a loud voice; (en s. som ligger høyt) a high voice; **ha en** — **stjerne hos en** be in high favour with one; — **sjø** heavy sea, high sea; **det er på -e tid** it is high time, it is quite time; **-ere** higher, taller, louder etc.; **-ere klasse** higher class; (på skolen) upper, senior el. advanced form el. class; **-ere officerer** superior officers; **-ere bud** an advance; **etter -ere befaling** by order; **i -ere forstand** in a higher sense; **høy|est** highest, top etc.; **det -este gode** the supreme good; **den -este nytelse** the height of enjoyment; **-este pris** top price; **den -este nød, fare** the utmost distress, danger; **den Høyeste** the Most High; **i -este grad** in the highest degree; **på -este sted** in the highest quarter; **høyt** (adv) highly, high; (om stemmen) loud; **-t aktet** highly respected; **spille -t** play high; **-t regnet** at the outside, on an extreme estimate; **elske en -t** love one well el. dearly; **sverge -t** og **dyrt** swear most positively; **lese -t** read out el. aloud; **høyere!** speak up! **høyst** (adv) in the highest el. last degree; most, highly, extremely; **det er høyst viktig** it is of the utmost consequence.
høyadel peerage.
høy|akte esteem highly. **-aktelse** high esteem; (i brev) **med** — Yours most respectfully. **-alter** high altar. **-barmet** high-bosomed.
høybrystet high chested. **-båren** high-born.
høyde height; elevation; (nivå) level; (vekst) stature, tallness; (lydens) loudness; (musikk) pitch; (geogr. og astron.) altitude; **på -n av Cadix** off Cadix; **i** — **med**, (fig) **på** — **med** equal to, (on a) level with, abreast of; **holde seg på** — **med hverandre** keep level; **da jeg var på Deres** — when I was your height.
høyde|måler altimeter, quadrant. **-måling** measuring of heights, (astron.) taking altitudes, altimetry. **-punkt** height, climax, summit, zenith. **-sprang** high jump; high jumping.
høydevekst growth in height.
høyenloft (foreldet) upper story.
høyesterett, se **høgsterett**.
høyfjell, se **høgfjell**.
høy|forræder one guilty of high treason, traitor. **-forræderi** high treason. **-forrædersk** treasonable.
høyfrekvens (i radio) high frequency.
høy|gaffel pitch-fork. **-halset** high(-necked).
høyhet highness, elevation, loftiness, sublimity; (titel) Highness; **Deres kongelige** — Your Royal Highness.
høy|hjertet high-minded, magnanimous. **-hælet** high-heeled.
høying haying, hay-making.
høy|kant: på — on edge, edgewise, on its narrow end. **-land** highland, upland.

høylass load of hay.
høy|lender, -lending (skotte) Highlander.
høylig highly, greatly.
høyloft hay-loft, mow.
høylys: ved — **dag** in broad daylight.
høylytt loud, clamant; (adv) aloud, loudly, clamantly.
høy|låve hay-barn, hay-shed. **-madrass** hay-mattress.
høy|messe morning service; high mass. **-modig** high-minded, magnanimous. **-modighet** high -mindedness, magnanimity. **-mælt** loud, loud-mouthed, loudtongued. **høyne** raise elevate.
høyning raising, elevation.
høyonn hay-making.
høypullet high-crowned.
høyre right; (parti) the Right; **på** — **hånd** on the right hand; **han er min** — **hånd** he is my factotum el. right-hand man; **til** — to el. on the right; — **om!** right about face! **se til** —! eyes right!
høyreblad (avis) conservative paper.
høyremann conservative.
høyrygget high-backed.
høy|rød high-red. **-røstet** loud, vociferous. **-røstethet** loudness. **-sinnet**, se **-modig**. **-sinn**, se **-modighet**.
høyskole, se **høgskole**.
høyspenning high tension.
høyspent highly tensioned, at high tension.
høyst, se **høy**.
høystakk hay-stack; hay-rick.
høystbefalende commander-in-chief.
høystbeskattet highest tax-payer.
høystbydende the highest bidder.
høystemt high-pitched.
høyst fruktsommelig in an advanced state of pregnancy, near her time.
høystrå hay-stalk.
høystærede! (much respected) Sir!
høysåte cock of hay.
høyt|begavet highly gifted. **-betrodd** highly trusted, trusty; invested with high authority. **-elsket** dearly beloved. **-flyvende** high-flown, (high-)soaring. **-fortjent** highly deserving.
høytid festival, feast.
høytidelig solemn, ceremonious. **-het** solemnity, pomp, state, ceremony, formality. **-holde** celebrate. **-holdelse** celebration, commemoration.
høytidsdag festival day, holiday.
høytidsfull solemn.
høytidsstund festive el. festal hour.
høytklingende (high-)sounding.
høytorg hay-market.
høytrykk high (full) pressure.
høytstående high-placed.
høyttaler (i radio) loud-speaker. Eks.: the order was broadcast by loud-speakers.
høyttravende high-flown, grandiloquent; sounding, specious; — **tale** tall talk, fustian.
høy|tysk High-German. **-vann** high water. **-velbåren** Right Honourable.
høy|vogn hay cart. **-vær** high(making) weather.
høyærverdig Right Reverend. **Deres høy-ærverdighet** Right Reverend Sir. **-ættet** high -descended, of high descent.
I. **hå** (slags hai) shark, dog-fish, hoe.
II. **hå** (etterslått) after-growth of grass, after -math, second crop el. cut.
håball (dial.: midtsommer) midsummer.
Haag the Hague.
hå|kall, -kjerring Greenland shark.
hål (glatt) slippery, frosty.
hålke frostiness, slipperiness. **-føre** glazed el. slippery roads.
hån scorn, disdain.
hånd hand; **den flate** — the palm; **den hule** — the hollow of the hand; **gi en -en** shake hands with one; **gi hverandre -en** shake hands; **rekke en en hjelpende** — stretch out a helping

hand to one; **slå –en av en** forsake, abandon one, cast one off, throw one over; **de for ens —** die by (el. at) one's hands; **de for egen —** die by (el. at) one's own hand; **det første som falt ham i –en, i hendene** the first that came to hand, came handy; **jeg kunne ikke se en — for meg** I could not see my hand before me; **fra — til munn** from hand to mouth; **få fra –en** get out of hand; **arbeidet går fort fra –en for ham** he is getting on well with the work; **den gikk fra — til —** it was handed about; fra første — from the best authority el. source; **med kraftig —** with a vigorous hand; **han lovte med — og munn** he pledged his word; **med egen —** with my own hand; **skrevet med hans —** written in his hand; **holde sin —** over hold out a protecting hand over; **på egen —** of one's own accord; for oneself; at one's own risk; (alene) single-handed; **på høyre —** on the right hand; **på rede —** at hand, handy; **på fri —** by hand, only with the hands; **tegne på fri —** draw without the aid of rule el. compass; **skyte på fri —** shoot without rest; **på annen —** at second hand; **gi penger på –en** give money in hand; **legge — på en** lay (violent) hands on one; **legge –en på verket** put one's shoulder to the wheel; **legge siste — på** put the finishing stroke to; **–en på hjertet!** honour bright! **under hans — og segl** under his hand and seal; **for –en** at hand, handy; **gå en til hånde** assist one; **ha frie hender** be one's own master, have free play; **gi en frie hender til å** leave it optional with one to; **lever av sine henders arbeid** lives by the labour of his hands; **har hendene fulle** has his hands full; **klappe i hendene** clap one's hands; **falle i hendene på en** fall into one's hands; **legge hendene i fanget** sit idle; **ha penger mellom hendene** have money in hand; **ble borte mellom hendene på meg** slipped through my fingers; **ta imot et tilbud med begge hender** jump at an offer; **bundet på hender og føtter** tied hand and foot; **bære på hendene** (fig) dote upon; **slå hendene sammen av forferdelse** hold up one's hands in horror.

håndarbeid needlework; (motsatt maskinarbeid) work done with the hands.

håndbagasje small luggage.

hånd|bak back of the hand. **-balle** ball of the hand. **-bevegelse** movement of the hand, gesticulation. **-bibliotek** reference library. **-bok** manual, hand-book, handy book, text book.

håndfesting (hist.) charter. **-flate** palm of the hand. **-full** handful. **-gangen mann** (hist.) liege vassal.

hånd|gemeng fisticuffs, fray, scuffle; close combat el. fight, hand-to-hand; **komme i –gemeng** come to close quarters. **-gjerning** manual work el. labour. **-gjort** hand made. **-granat** hand grenade, grenade. **-grep** handle; (på sverd) hilt; (grep med h.) grasp; (riktig bruk av hånden) manipulation (fig) knack, dexterity.

håndgripelig palpable; — **spøk** practical joke. **håndgripelighet** palpableness, obviousness; **det kom til –er** they fell to loggerheads; **ingen –er** no fighting.

håndheve maintain.

håndhever maintainer, vindicator, asserter; **ordenens —** the custodian of order.

hånd|jern manacle, handcuff, hand-fetter; **legge –jern på** manacle, handcuff. **-kjøp** retail; **selle i —** ogs. sell over the counter. **-klapp** clapping of hands, handclapping. **-kle** towel; (uten ende) jacktowel, roller-towel. **-kleholder** towel-horse. **-klelerret** towelling. **-koffert** handbag, portmanteau, Gladstone bag; (amr.) gripsack.

håndkort: gode — a good hand.

håndkraft (mots. damp-, maskin-) hand -power; **med —** by hand.

hånd|kyss kiss on the hand. **-lag** handiness, the proper knack, manual adroitness. **-langer**

helper, assistant, tender; (murh.) hodman. **-ledd** wrist. **-linning** wristband. **-lykt** hand-lantern. **-ordbok** compendious dictionary. **-pant** pawn, pledge. **-penger** earnest (money), arle(s)penny. **hand-money**; (til soldater) press money, bounty. **-pleie** manicure. **-presse** handpress. **-rot** carpus, wrist. **-sag** handsaw.

håndsbredd handbreadth.

håndskrevet handwritten, manuscript. M. S.

håndskrift manuscript; handwriting, hand; (forskrivning) note of hand. **-samler** autograph -collector.

håndskrivelse (egenhendig skr.) autograph.

håndskytevåpen handgun; (plur ogs.) small -arms.

håndslag (slag) hand-blow; (håndtrykk) squeeze el. shake of the hand; (løfte) solemn promise. **håndsopprekning** show of hands.

håndspåleggelse imposition (of hands).

håndsrekning a hand's turn, a hand.

hånd|sydd hand-sewn el. -made. **-tak** (skaft) handle; (knapp) button, knob. **-tegning** design, sketch; (frihåndstegning) free-hand drawing, drawing.

håndtere handle, manage, wield. **håndtering** handling etc.; (håndverk) trade, craft, handicraft. **håndterlig** manageable.

håndtrykk squeeze, pressure of the hand, handshake, hand-grip.

håndvending: i en — in no time, in the twinkling of an eye.

håndverk trade, handicraft, craft.

håndverker tradesman, mechanic, artisan, craftsman, handicraftsman. **-forening** mechanics' association. **-lære: være i —** serve one's apprenticeship.

håndverks|folk mechanics, craftsmen. **-laug** trade's corporation, craft-guild. **-mester** master mechanic. **-messig** mechanical. **-stand** industrial class. **-svenn** journeyman.

håndvevd woven by hand.

håne scorn, scoff at.

hånlatter scornful laugh(ter), sneer.

hånle laugh a scornful laugh.

hånlig (adj) contemptuous, scornful, disdainful. **hånlig** (adv) scornfully; **omtale —** belittle.

hånsmil disdainful smile, sneer.

hånsord scornful words, taunts (pl).

håp hope; (fremtidshåp, utsikt: også) expectation; **gjøre seg — om** hope to obtain, have hopes of; **i — om at** in the hope that, in hopes that; **jeg har —** I have some hope; **nære —** be in hopes; **nære godt —** be in good hope; **nære godt — om** be sanguine of el. as to; **oppgi —** el lose hope; **sette sitt — til** hope in, set one's hope in; **Det gode –s forberg** the Cape of Good Hope.

håpe hope; (sterkere) trust; (med objekt) hope for; **det vil jeg —** I hope so; **det vil jeg da ikke —** I (should) hope not; **en får — it** is to be hoped.

håpefull hopeful, promising. **en — ung mann** ogs.: a youth of great hope.

håpløs hopeless, (om personer) past hope. **det er ganske –t** it is a hopeless case. **håpløshet** hopelessness.

hår hair; **sette opp –et** dress one's hair; **rive seg i –et** tear one's hair; **på et hengende —** within a hair's breadth, within an ace; **han er ikke et — bedre** he is no whit better, there is not a pin to choose between them; (fig) **være i –ene på hverandre** be at loggerheads el. by the ears; **sette hatten på tre —** cock one's hat (on three hairs); **–ene reiste seg på hodet mitt** my hair stood on end; **med hud og — skin** and all.

hår|avfall (med) alopecy. **-band** head-band. **-bevokst** hairy. **-bunn** scalp. **-børste** hairbrush.

håret hairy.

hår|farge colour of the hair. **-fargingsmiddel** hair-dye. **-fasong** manner of doing el. way of

wearing one's hair. **-felling** shedding the hair; (om dyr) moulting. **-fin** fine as a hair, capillary; (fig) extremely nice. **-fletning** braid of hair. **-formet** capillary. **-fylle** profusion of hair. **-kar** capillary (vessel). **-kledning** hairy coat. **-klipning** hair-cutting. **-kløver** hair-splitter. **-kløveri** hair-splitting.
hår|lokk lock of hair. **-løs** hairless. **-nett** net for the hair, hair-net. **-nål** hairpin, black-pin. **-olje** oil for the hair. **-pisk** pigtail, queue. **-pleie** care of the hair. **-pynt** dressing of the hair, hair-dress. **-reisende** hair-raising, horrific. **-rik**

hairy. **-rikdom** hairiness. **-rot** root of a hair. **-rør** capillary tube.
hårsbredd hair-breadth; (fig) shade, degree. **hår|skill** parting of the hair (on the head). **-sløyfe** bow of ribbon (on the hair), top-knot. **-spenne** hair grip. **-sår** (fig.) sensitive, tenderly susceptible, thin-skinned.
hår|tjafs tuft of hair. **-tufse** knot of hair. **-ull** hair-wool. **-valk** roller, pad of hair. **-vann** hair-wash. **-vask** washing of the head. **-vekst** growth of hair, head of hair.
hås hoarse, husky.
håv bag, landing-net, (insekt-) sweep-net.

I

I, i I. i.
i in; (inne i) in, within; (foran byers navn) at el. in (det siste især ved større byer); (inn i) into; (om tidens lengde) for; **i (inn i) huset, i vannet** into the house, into the water; **i London** in London; **på besøk i London** on a visit to London; **her i byen** in this town; **i Gravesend** at Gravesend; **en by i Italia** a city of el. in Italy; **b i a** (a : b) a by b., el. b. in a.; **a i fjerde** a to the fourth (power); **i og for seg** in itself, per se; **god nok i seg selv** good enough of itself; **god i sitt slags** good of its kind; **flink i** clever at, good at; **fordypet i en avis** buried in a newspaper; **i ett drag** at a draught; **i ethvert tilfelle** at any rate, at all events; **i dype tanker** in deep thought; **gå i operaen** go to the opera; **han har vært borte i 4 måneder** he has been 4 months absent; **i flere minutter** for several minutes; **i de siste ti år** during the last ten years, for ten years past; **i forrige uke** last week; **ta, holde en i hånden** take, hold one by the hand; **skjære seg i hånden** cut one's hand; **falle i søvn** fall asleep; **falle i dyp søvn** fall fast asleep, fall into a sound (el. deep) sleep; **to fugler satt i et tre** two birds were sitting on a tree; **skåret i tre** cut on wood; **han er i direksjonen** he is on the committee; **i like måte** the same to you.
I (personlig pronomen) (foreldet) you.
i aften, i aftes, i akt, i år, se **aften, akt, år.**
iaktta observe, notice, watch; (etterleve) observe.
iakttagelse observation.
iakttagelsesevne faculty of observation.
iakttager observer.
iallfall any way, at any rate, at all events, in any case; (dt.) anyhow.
i alt, se **alt.**
ibenholt ebony.
iberegne include (in an account), count.
iberegnet inclusive of, including; **dikteren selv** — including the poet himself, the poet included.
iblandet intermixed.
iblant among, amongst.
iboende immanent, inherent (in).
i dag today, to-day; — **åtte dager** this day week; **ennå den dag** — (to) this day, at this day; at the present day; **fra** — **av** from this day; **«Times» for** — today's Times. — **morges** this morning.
idé idea; **jeg får en** — an idea strikes me, I have a plan; **han har den dumme** — **at** he has a stupid notion that; **gjøre seg en** — **om** form an idea of; **gi** — **en til** suggest.
ideal (forbilde) ideal.
idealisere idealize.
ideal|isering idealizing. **-isme** idealism. **-ist** idealist. **-istisk** idealistic. **-itet** ideality.
idéassosiasjon association of ideas.
ideell ideal.

idelig continual, perpetual; (adv) continually perpetually.
idéløs idealess. **-déløshet** flatness.
identifisere identify.
identifikasjon identification.
identisk identical.
identitet identity.
idérik rich in ideas. **idérikdom** wealth of ideas.
idet (konj) as, when; — **han kom inn, så han ...** on entering he saw ...
i det hele tatt altogether, on the whole.
i det minste at least.
i det samme at the same moment; (konj) the moment.
idéverden ideal world, imaginary world.
idiom idiom. **-atisk** idiomatic(al).
idiosynkrasi idiosyncrasy.
idiot idiot, natural, natural fool.
idiotanstalt lunatic asylum.
idiotisk idiotic.
idiotisme (egenhet) idiotism; (dumhet) idiocy.
idrett manly exercise; sport, pursuit; (dåd) achievement.
idretts|lag (forening) sports club; (landslag etc.) team. **-mann** sportsman. **-merke** athletic badge. **-plass** sports ground. **-stevne** sports meeting.
idyll idyl. **idyllisk** idyllic, pastoral.
idømme sentence (to); (bøter) impose; **han ble idømt en bot på ti pund** he was fined ten pounds.
ifall if, in case.
i fjor last year.
i fleng indiscriminately, promiscuously.
i forfjor the year before last.
iforgårs (ogs. **i forg.**) the day before yesterday.
i forveien, se **forveien.**
ifra, se **fra.**
ifølge (prep) pursuant to, agreeably to, according to, in consequence of; (om lov o. l.) by the operation of, under; — **faktura** as per invoice; — **innbydelse** in response to invitations; — **teksten** according to the text; **jeg er kommet** — **avertissement** I have come in answer to an advertisement; (merk.) — **Deres brev av 16. ds.** in pursuance of (el. to) your favour of 16th inst.
iføre array in, attire in; — **seg** put on; **iført grønn frakk** dressed in a green coat.
igjen again; **slå** — return a blow; **gi** — give back, restore; (vekslepenger) change (på: to); **ta** — take back; **det er ikke mye** — there is not much left; **ikke mine ord** — I that's between you and me, mum's the word; **De har gitt meg galt** — my change is not right; **hvor er de pengene du fikk** —? where is the change?
igjengrodd overgrown, overrun.
igjennom through; **slå seg** — make both ends meet; **helt** — thoroughly; uniformly; out-and-out; **hele dagen** — all day long; **hele**

året — all the year round; **hele boka** — troughout the book; **hele mitt liv** — troughout the whole course of my life.

i **gjerde** el. i **gjære** astir, brewing, on foot, in the wind.

igle leech. **sette –r** apply leeches.

i **glemme: gå** — pass into oblivion, lapse out of memory, be forgotten.

ignorant ignorant person, ignoramus.

ignorere take no notice of, ignore, disregard; (en person) give (one) the cut, cut (one).

i **går** yesterday; — **morges** yesterday morning; — **aftes** last night.

i **hel,** se i **hjel.**

i **hende** in hand, in one's hands.

ihendehaver holder, bearer; depositary; **obligasjonen lyder på –en** the bond is payable to the holder.

ihendehaversjekk bearer cheque.

ihendehaverobligasjon bond payable to bearer.

iherdig persevering, persisting. **–het** perseverance, tenacity of purpose.

i **hjel** dead, to death; **bite, slå, skyte en** — bite, strike, shoot one dead; **stikke** — stab (to death); **sulte** — die of starvation; **drikke, arbeide seg** — drink, work oneself to death el. into one's grave; **slå tiden** — kill the time.

i **hvert fall** at any rate, at all events, anyway.

ikke not; — **mer** no more; — **mindre** no less; — **videre** no further; **jeg ser** — I do not see; — **desto mindre** not the less, none the less for that; **og det er** — **lite** and that is no little; **i** — **liten grad** in no slight degree; — **jeg heller** nor I (neither); — **noen,** noe (adj) no; — **noen** (subst) nobody; — **noe** (subst) nothing; — **det?** indeed? no? really not? **hvor forskjellige er** — . . . how different are . . .; **hvem må** — . . .? who but must . . .; **om** . . . **eller** — whether . . . or not.

ikle, se **iføre;** (fig) clothe (in words).

i **koll,** se **omkull.**

ikrafttreden coming into force.

i **kring,** se **omkring.**

i **kveld,** se **kveld.**

il **haste,** hurry.

i **land,** se **land.**

i **lage** in order.

ilbud express; **pr.** — per express.

ild fire; (brann) fire, conflagration; (fig) fire, ardour; **øyets** — the brilliancy of the eye; **gjøre opp** — make a fire; **gi** — fire; **man skal ikke leke med –en** let sleeping dogs lie; **brent barn skyr –en** a burnt child dreads the fire; **sette** — **på** set on fire, set fire to, fire; **tenne, slokke –en** light, put out the fire; **utholde en** stand the fire; **gå i –en** go into fire; **gå gjennom** — **og vann for en** go through fire and water for one; **være i –en** be under fire; be engaged; **ved –en** at the fire.

ilddåp baptism of fire.

ilde (vrb) fire, light up; heat. **det blir ikke –t i det værelset** that room is not heated.

ildebrann fire, conflagration.

ilder pole-cat.

ild|fast fire-proof, fire-resisting, incombustible; **–fast stein** fire-brick. **–flue** fire-fly. **–full** full of fire, fiery. **–fullhet** ardour, fire.

ild|kule fire-ball. **Ildlandet** Tierra del Fuego. **ildmørje** live embers.

ildne animate; fire, inspirit.

ildprøve fiery ordeal.

ildraker poker.

ildregn shower of fire.

ildrød fiery red, flame-coloured.

ilds|fare danger of fire. **–farlig** combustible, inflammable.

ilds|ikker safe from fire.

ildskjær gleam of the fire.

ildskuffe fire-shovel.

ildslue flame of fire.

ildsprutende ignivomous; — **berg** volcano.

ildspåsettelse incendiarism, incendiary fire.

ildsted fire-place, hearth.

ildstrøm torrent of fire.

ildsvåde fire.

ild|tang tongs. **–tilbedelse** worship of fire. **–tilbeder** fire-worshipper.

ildvåpen fire-arm.

ile (vrb) hasten, hurry, run, make haste; — **til** hurry off to; — **en til hjelp** hurry to one's aid.

I. **ile** (subst) (oppkomme) spring, well.

II. **ile** (subst) (dregg) stone sinker, wooden graplin.

ilegg (på ovn) opening of a stove.

ilegge, se **idømme.**

ilgods express-goods, dispatch-goods; fast freight. **–ekspedisjon** grande vitesse service.

iligne (skatt) assess, rate.

i **like måte** likewise, in like manner; (svar) the same to you, (Sir)!

iling (regn) shower, (vind) squall.

ilk(e) callosity.

ille ill, badly; **det vil gå deg** — you will fare badly, it will go hard with you; **det er** — it is a bad thing, a bad job; **hun er ikke** — she is rather pretty, not amiss; **ta** — **opp** take amiss, take in bad part.

illebefinnende indisposition; **lide av et lett** — be slightly indisposed.

illegal illegal. **–itet** illegality.

illegitim illegitimate. **–itet** illegitimacy.

ille|luktende unsavoury, evil-smelling; **–lydende** ill-sounding, harsh.

ille|sinnet ill-natured, evil-minded, ill-intentioned, evil-disposed. **–varslende** ill-boding, ill -omened, sinister.

illgjerning (gmlt.) evil doing, iniquity. **–smann** evil-doer, malefactor.

illiberal illiberal. **–itet** illiberality.

illojal unfair, disloyal; — **konkurranse** unfair competition.

illojalitet disloyalty.

illskrike squall, shriek viciously.

illudere illude.

illumi|nasjon illumination. **–nere** illuminate; (en tegning) colour. **–nering** colouring.

illusjon illusion; **jeg gjør meg ingen –er om** I cherish no illusions el. vain hopes about; **rive ut av –en** disillusion.

illusorisk illusory, delusive.

illustrasjon illustration.

illustrere illustrate. **illustrert** illustrated, pictorial.

ilmarsj forced march.

ilsk, se **ilter.**

ilsom hurried, precipitate.

iltelegram express telegram.

ilter hasty, testy, petulant; irritable.

ilterhet hastiness, petulance, irritability.

iltog fast train.

imaginær imaginary.

imellom between, betwixt; **tittet fram** — . . . peeped forth from among . . .; (adv) between; **legge seg** — intervene, interpose; **engang** — once in a while, now and then. Se også **mellom.**

imens (konj.) while, whilst; (adv) (in the) meantime (in the) meanwhile.

i **middags** at noon.

imidlertid (i mellomtiden) meanwhile, meantime, in the meanwhile; (dog) however, still, at the same time.

imitasjon imitation. **imitativ** imitative. **imitere** imitate.

immateriell immaterial, incorporeal.

immatrikulere (v. univ.) enter, matriculate.

immoralitet immorality.

immun immune (**mot smitte:** from infection).

immunitet immunity.

i **morgen, i morges,** se **morgen.**

imot (for å uttrykke motstand; eller = støttet imot, støtende imot; eller = sett på bakgrunn av) against; (uoverensstemmelse, mot-

setning) contrary to; (henimot) towards; (forhold) to, towards; (sammenligning) compared to. to, as against; — **after** towards evening; **bort** — **huset** towards the house; — **sin vilje** against his will, in spite of himself; **handle** — **ens ønsker** act in opposition to one's desires; **være** — **partiet** be opposed to the match; **jeg har ikke noe** — **ham** I have no particular dislike to him; **det er meg** — **at han kommer** I object to his coming; **jeg har ikke noe** — **at han kommer** I have no objection to, do not object to, do not mind his coming; **hvis De ikke har noe** — **det** if you have no objection; **jeg har ikke noe** — **å** (med inf.) I have no objection to, do not mind to; **gjøre en** — act contrary to one's will, cross one; **si** —, **se motsi; vedde ti** — **en bet** ten to one. imot (adv): **vinden er** — it is a contrary wind, an adverse wind; **lykken var ham** — fortune did not favour him.

imperativ the imperative mood.
imperfektum the imperfect el. past tense.
impertinent impertinent, rude pert.
implisere implicate, involve.
imponere impress, awe, overawe. **-nde** imposing, commanding. **lite -nde** un-imposing, un-impressive.
import importation. **-ere** import. **-firma** importing-house. **-handel** import-trade. **importør** importer.
impotens impotence. **impotent** impotent.
impregnere imbue, saturate (with).
impresario manager, impresario.
improvisasjon improvisation.
improvisator improvisator, improviser.
improvisere improvise, extemporize; **improvisert** impromptu; rough-and-ready.
improvisering improvisation.
impuls impulse. **impulsiv** impulsive.
i møte, se **møte.**
imøtegå oppose (one), meet, refute, disprove (an argument etc.).
imøtekomme meet, accomodate. humour, hold out a hand to. **-nde** friendly, obliging.
imøtekommenhet friendliness, obligingness.
imøtese look forward to, anticipate, expect, await.
inappellabel final, inappealable.
i natt, se **natt.**
incitere stimulate.
indeks index. **sette på** — index.
inder East Indian, Hindoo.
inderlig heartfelt; **det gjør meg** — **vondt** I am intensely sorry; **jeg ønsker** — I heartily wish; **elske** — love deeply el. dearly; **ble** — **flau** felt desperately sheepish; — **gjerne** with all my heart. **inderlighet** cordiality, heartiness.
India (Forindia) India.
indianer Indian. **-hytte** wigwam. **-høvding** Indian chief. **-kone, -kvinne** squaw.
indiansk Indian.
indignasjon indignation.
indignert indignant **(over:** at).
indigo indigo. **-blått** indigo blue.
indikativ the indicative (mood).
indirekte indirect; (forutsatt) implied; — **tale** oblique speech; (adv) indirectly, by implication.
indisk Indian.
indisiebevis presumptive el. circumstantial evidence.
indisium indication; (jur) presumptive ground.
indiskresjon indiscretion. **indiskret** indiscreet.
indisponert (uopplagt) indisposed, not in humour.
indisposisjon (upasselighet) indisposition.
individ individual. **-ualisere** individualize. **-ualisering** individualization. **-ualitet** individuality. **-uell** individual.
indolens indolence. **indolent** indolent.
indre (adj) inner, interior, inward, inside; **det** — **Afrika** the interior of Africa, Central

Africa; — **uroligheter** domestic disturbances; — **verd** intrinsic value; **det** — the interior. **det** — **av jorda** — the bowels of the earth.
indre (subst) interior; **menneskets** — the heart of man, the inner man; **i mitt** — inwardly, mentally.
indre|misjon home mission. **-politisk** of domestic politics, domestic political.
induksjon induction.
induksjonselektrisitet induced electricity.
induksjonsmaskin induction machine.
industri industry, industrial arts, trade. **-alisme** industrialism. **-drivende** industrial; manufacturer. **-ell** industrial. **-forbund** industrial society. **-foretagende** industrial undertaking. **-sentrum** industrial centre. **-utstilling** industrial exhibition.
infam infamous. **infami** infamy.
infanteri infantry, foot (soldiers). **-regiment** foot regiment. **-st** foot soldier.
infeksjon infection.
infeksjonssykdom infectious disease.
infernalsk infernal, ogs. unearthly.
infinitiv the infinitive (mood). **-isk** infinitive, infinitival.
infisere infect. **infisering** infection.
inflam|masjon inflammation. **-mere** inflame.
inflasjon inflation. **inflatere** inflate.
influensa the influenza.
influere (på) affect, influence.
inform|asjon lessons (pl.). **-ere** give lessons.
infusjonsdyr, infusorier infusory, (pl.) infusories el. infusoria.
ingefær ginger; **syltet** — preserved ginger.
ingen (adjektiv) no; (især foran et, el. etter nylig nevnt substantiv) none; (om to) neither; (substantiv; om flere) no one, nobody; (subst. om to) neither; **jeg har** — **penger, og du har heller** — I have no money, and you have none either; — **kan hjelpe meg** nobody can help me; — **lege kan hjelpe meg** no doctor can help me; — **annen enn du** no one but you; — **andre enn dumme folk tror** . . . none but fools think . . .; — **av dem** none of them, (om to) neither of them; **penger hadde han** — **av** money he had none.
ingeniør engineer. **-officer** officer of the engineers. **-vitenskap** engineering.
ingenlunde (sj.) by no means, not at all.
ingenmannsland No Man's Land.
ingen som helst no . . . whatever; none whatever; no one whatever.
ingensteds nowhere; **det hører** — **hjemme** it is neither here nor there.
ingenting nothing; **late som** — look innocent, look as if nothing were the matter.
ingrediens ingredient.
inhabil disqualified; **gjøre** — disqualify. **-itet** disqualification.
inhalasjon inhalation. **-sapparat** inhaler.
inhuman unfeeling, unkind, harsh.
inhumanitet harshness.
initialer initials.
initiativ initiation, initiative; **ta -et til** take the initiative in; **på** — **av** on the initiative of.
injuriant libeller.
injurie insult, defamation; (skriftlig) libel. **-prosess** action for insult, action for libel.
injuriere libel, insult.
inkarn|asjon incarnation. **-ert** incarnate.
inkassasjon collection, recovery.
inkassator collector (of debts), receiver.
inkasso collection, recovery; **besørge** — procure payment. **til** — for collection.
inkasso|forretning collection-business. **-omkostninger** expenses of collection.
inklinasjon love, fancy; (magnetn.) inclination, dip. **-sparti** love-match, marriage of sentiment.
inklusive inclusive (etterstilt); inclusive of, including (foranstilt).
inkognito (adv) incognito; **reise** — travel incognito el. under an incognito.

inkompetens incompetency, incompetence.
inkompetent incompetent.
inkonsekvens inconsistency.
inkonsekvent inconsistent.
inkubasjonstid period of incubation.
inkurabel incurable.
inkurie oversight; **ved en — by an oversight,** inadvertently.
inkvisisjon inquisition.
inkvisitorisk inquisitorial.
inkvirere examine.
inn in; **— av in at, in by; — i into; slå rutene — break the windows; — til London** up to London; **— under jul** near Christmas, just before Christmas.
inna-: For sammensetninger med **inna-,** se også **innen-.**
innabords on board, in board, inside.
innad in, inward, inwards. **-vendt** turned inwards; **(fig)** introspective, contemplative. **-vendthet** contemplativeness.
innafor within, inside.
innanke appeal. **innanking** appealing, appeal.
innarbeid|e work in; **en godt -d forretning** a well established business.
innaskjærs in sheltered waters.
innbefatte include, comprise, comprehend, embrace; **heri -t** including.
innbegrep comprehension.
innberetning report, return.
innberette report.
innbetale pay in, pay up.
innbetaling payment.
innbil|le make (one) believe; **det skal du ikke få -t meg!** don't tell me! **— seg** imagine, fancy.
innbilning imagination, fancy; **(om seg selv)** conceit; **en filosof i egen — a would-be philosopher.**
innbilningskraft imagination, fancy.
innbilsk conceited.
innbilskhet conceit, conceitedness.
innbilt imaginary, fanciful.
innbinde bind. **innbinding** binding.
innbitt (fig) sullen.
innblande intermingle, intersperse; **bli -t i** be mixed up in el. with.
innblanding meddling, intervention, interference.
innblikk insight, glimpse, peep (into).
innbo furniture, moveables.
innbrenne brand, mark with a hot iron; **(farger)** burn (into).
innbringe (om pris) make, fetch, realize.
innbringende lucrative, profitable, remunerative.
innbrott, innbrudd housebreaking, burglary; **gjøre — i et hus** break into a house; **det er gjort — i huset** the house has been broken into.
innbruddsforsikring burglary insurance.
innbruddstyv burglar, house-breaker.
innbruddstyveri burglary.
innby invite.
innbydelse invitation. **innbydelses|skrift** program. **-skrivelse** letter of invitation.
innbydende inviting; appetizing; **lite — un**-inviting.
innbyder promotor.
innbygger inhabitant.
innbyrdes mutual, reciprocal; (adv) mutually.
inndele divide; classify.
inndeling division; classification.
inndra draw in el. into; (mynt) call in; (blad) suppress; (sette ut av kurs) withdraw; **— en post** draw off a post; **— en tillatelse** cancel a permission; **— ens pensjon** stop one's pension; **— en eiendom** confiscate, seize an estate. **-gelse** drawing etc.; confiscation.
inndriv|e drive in, (fordringer) call in, recover; (skatter) collect, levy, (taxes). **-ning** driving etc.; (av skatter) collection, levying.

inne in, within; **der — in** there; **langt inne i landet** far up in the interior, in the heart of the country; **en by — i landet** an inland town; **være — i noe** have mastered something; **holde seg — keep** indoors.
innebrenne, se **brenne inne.**
innebære convey, import, involve, imply.
inneforing stall-feeding.
innefrossen frozen up, ice-bound.
inne|ha hold. **-haver** possessor, proprietor, occupant; (av kall, embete) incumbent; se **ihendehaver.**
inneholde hold, contain.
innelukke (vrb) shut in, shut up.
innelukke (subst) enclosure.
innen within, inside; (tid, før) before, within; **— jeg reiser** before leaving. **-at: lese — read** by book.
innenbys within the town; **— folk** townsfolk, towns-people; **— medlemmer** town members; **— veksel** promissory note.
innen|dørs within doors. **-fra** from within, from the inside. **-lands** in the country, at home.
innenlandsk domestic, home, native; **— handel** country trade, internal commerce; **-e brever** inland letters; **-e nyheter** home-news; **-e planter** native plants.
innenriksdepartement home department.
innenrikshandel inland trade.
innenriksminister minister of the interior; (i Engl.) home secretary.
inner|del inner part, interior. **-flate** inner surface. **-kant** inner edge; inside. **-lomme** inside pocket.
innerst inmost, innermost; **i mitt -e hjerte** in my heart of hearts; (adv) farthest in; **— i værelset** at the farther end, in the inmost part of the room.
innesitting keeping the house, staying at home.
inneslutte inclose; (lukke inne) confine, lock up; (omringe) invest, surround, hem in; (innbefatte) include, comprise. **-t** (i seg selv) reserved. **-thet** reserve.
innesperre shut up, lock up, imprison. **innesperring** confinement, imprisonment, detention.
innestengt shut up, confined.
innestå (om en kapital) be lodged, deposited; (være ansvarlig for) answer for, vouch for; **— for at** go bail that.
innett suppressed; **— raseri** suppressed rage; (adv): **— rasende** mad with suppressed rage.
innetter inwards; (in mot land) inshore.
inneværende (år osv.) present, current.
innfall (fiendtlig) raid, incursion, invasion, inraid; (tanke) conceit, fancy; (plutselig) whim, freak; **jeg fikk et — a thought struck me.**
innfallen emaciate, gaunt; (øyne, ansikt) sunk, sunken; **innfalne kinn** hollow cheeks.
innfalls|lodd axis of incidence; **-vinkel** angle of incidence.
innfange capture, catch.
innfatning mounting; (av edelsten) setting; (brille-) rim; (ramme) frame, border; (helt omsluttende) case, casing.
innfatte border, edge, mount; (i ramme) frame; (juveler) set. **innfatting** bordering, setting osv.
innfelle fay, let, trim in. **innfelling** (abstr.) faying etc.; (konkr.) inlet, inset, inlay; (i tøy) insertion; (i skjorte) shirt-front, bosom.
innfinne seg appear, attend, make one's appearance, present oneself.
innflytelse influence; **ha — på** influence; **ha — hos** have interest with.
innflytelsesrik influential, potent.
innflytningsgilde house-warming.
innflytter immigrant.
innfor|live incorporate (i: in, into, with). **-livelse** incorporation; identification.
innfri meet, redeem; **— en veksel** pay a bill.

innfrielse redemption; **-n av vekselen** the payment of the bill.
innful (forsterkn. til ful) crafty, deep, wily.
innfødsrett right of a native el. naturalized person; **gi en — naturalize** one; **berøve en — disnaturalize** one; **få — get certificate of naturalization**.
innfødt native; **en — nordmann** a native of Norway.
innfør|e import; (i selskap, noe nytt) introduce; **— i regnskap, bok** enter in an account, a book. **-sel** introduction; (av varer etc.) importation, imports.
innførselsartikkel import.
innførsels|forbud prohibition. **-toll** import duty.
inngang entry, entrance; **ved -en** at the door; **inngangs|billett** admission ticket. **-penger** entrance, entrance fee, initiation fee. **-salme** entrance hymn.
inngi give in, present; (innskyte) inspire one with, instil into one, suggest to one; **— søknad om avskjed** send in el. tender one's resignation.
inngifte (subst) intermarriage.
inngifte (vrb) marry into.
inngivelse suggestion, inspiration.
inngni rub in; (en syk fot o. l.) embrocate.
inngnidning rubbing in, embrocation.
inngravere engrave.
inngrep encroachment; (med.) surgical operation; **gjøre — i** encroach, (in)trench upon, trespass on.
inngripende radical, thorough.
inngrodd deeply rooted, inrooted, ingrained, inveterate.
inngyte (fig) inspire with, instill.
inngå enter, go in; **— et ekteskap** enter into el. contract a marriage; **— et veddemål** make a wager; **start a bet; — et forlik** make a compromise.
inngående thorough.
innhegne fence in, enclose.
innhegning fence, enclosure.
innhente overtake, come up with, catch (up with), run down; (mening, samtykke osv.) procure; (det forsømte) make up for, recover.
innhogg charge; **gjøre — i maten** fall to.
innhol concave, hollow.
innhold contents, substance; subject-matter, argument; (Deres . . . mottatt) **og -et bemerket** (merk.) and contents noted.
innholdsangivelse declaration of contents.
innholds|fortegnelse, -liste index, contents, table of contents.
innholdsløs of no el. trifling contents, meagre, empty.
innholdsrik full of matter; full of import.
innhylle envelop, wrap up, fold up, muffle up, shroud.
innhøst|e house, gather in, harvest, get in. **-ning** housing etc.
inni inside, within.
innimellom, se **imellom**.
innjage: — en skrekk strike terror into one, strike one with terror.
innkall|e call in; summon, cite. **-else, -ing** calling in; summons.
innkasse|re cash, receive, recover, collect **-ring** cashing, collection, recovery.
innkast (i fotball) throw-in.
innkjøp purchase. **innkjøpe** purchase.
innkjøpspris original cost, prime cost, trade price; **under — under** cost, at a sacrifice.
innkjøre (et dyr) break, break to harness. Se ogs. **kjøre inn**.
innkjørsel (kjørevei til et hus) drive.
innklamre inclose in brackets.
innklare|re enter inwards, clear in. **-ring** entry, clearance inwards.
innkle (med bord) board over.

innknepet contracted, narrow, squeezed in.
innkomme: -nde fartøyer incoming vessels.
innkomst income, revenue.
innkrev|e collect, demand payment of. **-(n)ing** collection, recovery.
innkvartere quarter, billet; **— hos** billet upon.
innkvartering quartering. **-sseddel** billet.
innland home-country; inland.
innlasting shipping, shipment.
innlate (refl. vrb.): **— seg i samtale** enter into conversation; **— seg på** engage in, enter into el. on; (foretagende) embark in; **— seg på å** undertake to.
innlatende communicative, familiar.
innlede introduce; preface; open; usher in; (undersøkelse) set on foot; (planer osv.) initiate; **— underhandlinger** enter into negotiations.
innledende preliminary, introductory, preparatory, prefatory.
innleder introducer, initiator.
innledning introduction, opening, preface.
innledningstale introductory speech.
innlegg (i brev) enclosure; (skredd.) tuck; (jur) plea.
innlegge (med gull osv.) inlay; **— på hospital** admit, remove to the hospital; **innlagt** (i brev) enclosed, under this cover; **innlagt arbeid** inlaid work; **— seg ære** gain honour.
innleg|ging, -ning inlaying, inlay.
innleie, innleiing, se **innlede, innledning**.
innlemm|e incorporate, annex. **-else** incorporation, annexation.
innleve seg i, se **leve seg inn i**.
innlevere deliver; (til posten) post.
innlevering delivery, posting.
innlosjere lodge, quarter, berth; **— seg** take lodgings.
**innlyd: i — medially.
innlysende evident, obvious, manifest.
innløp (til havn) entrance, inlet, mouth (of a harbour).
innløpe (i havn) enter; (ankomme) arrive, come to hand, be received.
innløse redeem, release, take up.
innløs(n)ing redemption.
innlån borrowing. **-srente** interest on deposits.
innmari, se **innful**.
innmark home fields.
innmarsj entry.
innmat pluck; (fig., spøkende) contents.
innmelde enter; (i et selskap osv.) propose for admission; **— seg,** se **melde seg inn. -lse** entry.
innmur|e wall in, immure. **-ing** walling etc.
innom: kom —! look round here.
innord|ne dispose in the proper order. **-seg** fall into line. **-ning** disposing etc.
innover (adv) inwards; -(prep) along.
innpakke pack up; (merk.) pack, bale up; (om person) wrap up. **han var så -t at** he was so muffled up that.
innpass access, admittance, entrance. **innpasse** fay el. fit in.
innpisker (i parlamentet) whip.
innplante plant; implant.
innplant(n)ing planting; implantation.
innpod|e ingraft, graft; **— en noe** inoculate one with st. **-(n)ing** grafting.
innprege stamp (i: on); (innskjerpe) inculcate; se **innprente**.
innprent|e imprint on, impress on, inculcate on; **— seg** impress el. imprint on one's mind. **-ing** imprinting etc.
innpå (prep) close upon; **gå — en** worry one; (adv) close.
innramme frame.
innrange|re range. **-ring** ranging.
innrede fit up. **innredning** fitting up.
innregistrere register, record, book.
innretning arrangement; (større anordning) constitution; (redskap) contrivance, device.

innrette arrange; institute; accommodate, adjust, adapt; — **det så at** contrive that; **et vel -t hus** a well regulated house; — **seg** arrange; make one's arrangements; — **seg etter de nye forhold** adapt oneself to the new conditions; — **seg på å be** prepared to.
innrisse scratch (on).
innrullere enrol; **la seg** — enlist.
innrullering enrolment.
innrykk run of visitors.
innryk|ke insert (in a paper). **-ning** insertion, (om hær) entry.
innrømme allow, grant, concede; (ikke nekte) admit, own; (avstå) cede, give up **(en noe:** st. to one); **jeg -r Dem 2 % provisjon** I allow you 2 % commission.
innrømmelse admission, concession.
innsamle collect, gather. **innsamling** collection, gathering; (av penger) subscription.
innsats stake, stakes.
innse see, perceive, comprehend.
innseiling entrance, approach; **under —en on** entering.
innsende send in; remit, transmit; (til blad) contribute. **-lse** sending in; forwarding, transmission.
innsender sender, remitter, transmitter; (av bidrag, penger osv.) contributor; (i et blad) correspondent.
innsenkning dent, indent, hollow.
innsette install, instate; — **igjen** reinstate; **han innsatte ham til sin arving** he made him his heir; — **i sitt sted** substitute. **-lse** instalment; inauguration; reinstatement.
innside inside; **på -n av** inside.
innsig gradual approach; (fig) infiltration, influx.
innsigelse objection, exception, protest.
innsikt insight **(i:** in, into), information.
innsiktsfull competent, understanding.
innsjø lake.
innskipe ship, embark; — **(seg) på ny re-embark. innskiping** shipment; embarkation.
innskjerpe enforce, enjoin **(en noe:** st. on one).
innskjerpelse enforcement.
innskott, se **innskudd.**
innskrenke restrict; limit, confine; — **seg** retrench; **det -r seg til** it is confined to; — **seg til** confine oneself to. **-t** restricted, etc.; (monarki) limited; (i åndelig hens.) weak, of a confined intellect, shallow; **i -t forstand** in a limited sense; **bo svært -t** be rather confined for room.
innskrenk|ethet shallowness. **-ning** limiting, etc., limitation, restriction; retrenchment; modification, qualification.
innskriden interference, intervention.
innskrift inscription, legend; — **på** inscription on; — **over** (en grav) inscription over; (en person) inscription to.
innskriv|e inscribe; **la seg** — enter one's name, be entered. **-ning** entering, booking. **-ningspenger** booking fee.
innskrumpet shrunken.
innskudd contribution, quota; (ved inntredelse) entrance fee; (i bank) deposit.
innskyte insert, put in; (om penger) pay in **innskytelse** intuition, inspiration.
innskyter depositor.
innsmigre seg hos en ingratiate oneself with one (by flattery), insinuate oneself into one's favour.
innsmigrende ingratiating, ingratiatory, insinuating.
innsmuglet smuggled in; (fig) surreptitious.
innsmurt rubbed el. smeared (with an ointment); — **med fett** greased.
innsnevring narrow pass, pass, defile; (av havet) strait, straits, channel, sound.
innsnike seg slip in, creep in (into).
innsnitt incision, cut, notch.

innsnøre lace in, lace tightly, constrict.
innsprøyte squirt in(to), inject, syringe.
innsprøytning injection.
innstendig urgent, pressing, earnest; (adv) urgently, earnestly; **be** — (most) earnestly entreat, particularly request, beseech.
innstevn|e summon, cite; **-te** the defendant. **-ing** summons, citation.
innstifte institute. **-lse** institution.
innstil|le propose; (til embete) nominate, present; (maskin o. l.) adjust; (om instrument) set right; (om kikkert) focus; (stanse) stop, suspend; (avlyse) cancel; — **sine betalinger** suspend el. stop payment; **den -te** the nominee.
innstilling proposition; nomination; presentation; adjustment; (komités) report.
innstillingsrett right of nomination.
innstudere study, con, get (by heart); (musikk) practise; (om et stykke på teateret:) la — put into rehearsal. **innstudering** studying etc.; **være under** — be in rehearsal.
innstyrtning caving in, collapse, falling (in).
innsuge suck in, absorb; imbibe.
innsunken sunken.
innsvøpe envelop, wrap up, muffle up.
innsåpe soap; (ved barbering) lather.
innta (måltid) partake of; (ved elskverdighet) captivate, charm, fascinate; — **en by, festning** carry a town, fortress; — **sin plass** take one's seat; **være -tt i** be taken, smitten, captivated with; **være -tt imot** be prejudiced against. **-gelse** (av by etc.) taking, carrying; (av ballast) taking-in (of ballast), ballasting. **-gende** captivating, fascinating, engaging, charming, prepossessing, winning; **lite** — unprepossessing; **det — i hennes vesen** the fascination el. charm of her manner.
inntak inntake, offtake. **inntaksdam** catchwater drain el. réservoir.
inntegn|e note down, write, enter (in a book), book. **-ing** noting etc. **-ingskontor** booking-office.
inntekt income; (is. statens) revenue; (av skuespill, konsert osv.) receipts, takings, proceeds (pl); **ta til** — appropriate.
inntekts|kilde source of revenue; (om statens) ways and means. **-skatt** income tax.
inntil (tid og sted) to, as far as; up to; (bare tid) till, until; — **året 1400** down to the year 1400; **en mulkt av** — a fine not exceeding; **så lenge** — until.
inntilbeins: gå — toe in (in walking), turn in one's legs.
inntog entry, entrance; **holde sitt** — make one's entry.
inntre happen, occur, come to pass, set in, supervene; **ved -dende leilighet** as oppurtunity offers. **-delse** entrance; commencement; occurrence. **-delsesgebyr** entrance fee.
inntrengende impressive, forcible, earnest.
inntrenging intrusion, entrance.
inntrykk impression; **gjøre et gunstig** — **på** impress one favourably; **gjør et sterkt** — is very impressive; **gi** — **av** at convey the impression that; **mottagelig for** — impressionable.
innunder below, under; — **jul** near el. just before Christmas.
innvandre immigrate. **innvandrer** immigrant.
innvandring immigration.
innvars|le summon; (beramme) appoint, announce; (fig) inaugurate. **-ling** summons.
innved against, close by el. to.
innvende (imot) object (to), **jeg har ingenting å** — **imot det** I have no objection.
innvendig internal, inward, inside; **det -e** the inside; (the interior); (adv) internally, inwardly; **le** — laugh inside.
innvending objection **(imot:** to el. against); **gjøre -er** urge, raise el. make objections; **demur; ikke gjøre noen** — offer no objection.

innvidd: de -e the initiated, those who know.
innvie consecrate, (til noe) dedicate; (høytidelig åpne) inaugurate; **— i** (en hemmelighet) initiate in, take into (a secret).
innvielse consecration; dedication; inauguration; initiation.
innvik|le fold up, wrap up; (bringe i ulage) entangle; involve, implicate; (i strid) embroil; **— seg i** get entangled in. **-let** intricate, complex; **gjøre -let** complicate. **det -lede ved en sak** complexity, intricacy.
innvilge (i) consent (to), grant, comply (with). **-lse** granting etc.; consent.
innvinn|e earn, gain; (få tilbake) recover; (land) reclaim. **-ing** gain, recovery, reclamation.
innvirk|e på exert influence on, act on, reaction, operate on, influence,affect. **-ning** influence, action.
innvoller entrails, bowels; **som hører til -ne** intestinal.
innvollsorm helminth, intestinal worm.
innvortes inward, internal, inner; (adv) inwardly, internally.
innvortes (subst) inside.
innvotere admit (by ballot), vote (i: into).
innvåner inhabitant.
innynde seg ingratiate oneself (hos: with).
innøve practise, exercise; (soldater) train, discipline; (rekrutter) drill; (hest) break. **-lse** practising, training; drilling; breaking.
innånd|e inhale, breathe, respire; **-ing** respiration, inhalation.
inokulere bud, inoculate.
insekt insect. **-etende** entomophagous. **-pulver** insect(-destroying) powder. **-samling** collection of insects.
inserat advertisement, notice, article.
insignier insignia (pl.)
insinuasjon insinuation, innuendo.
insinuere insinuate, hint.
insistere insist (på: upon).
insolv|ens insolvency. **-ent** insolvent.
inspek|sjon inspection. **-sjonshavende** superintendent.
inspektrise lady inspector.
inspektør inspector.
inspir|asjon inspiration. **-ere** inspire.
inspise|re inspect, examine. **-ring** inspection.
install|asjon installation. **-ere** install.
instans: første — court of the first instance; **i første — in** the first instance; **i siste — in** the last resort, finally; **de lavere -er** the courts below.
instinkt instinct. **-messig** instinctive, intuitive; (adv) instinctively, by instinct.
institusjon institution.
institutt institute, institution. **-bestyrer** principal of an institue. **-bestyrerinne** lady principal.
instruere instruct, give directions.
instruks instructions (pl).
instruksjon instruction, direction.
instruktiv instructive.
instruktør instructor; (scene-) stage manager.
instrument instrument. **-al** instrumental. **-ere** adapt for the orchestra. **-ering** instrumentation. **-maker** instrument-maker.
insurbordinasjon insurbordination.
insurgent insurgent.
intakt intact.
inte|gral integral. **-gralregning** integral calculus. **-grerende** integral. **-gritet** integrity.
intellektuell intellectual.
intelligens intelligence.
intelligent intelligent, intellectual.
intendant intendant: (intendanturofficer) commissary. **-ur** intendancy; (forpleiningskorpset) army service corps, A. S. C.: (litt gammeldags) commissariat.
intens intense.
inten|sitet intensity. **-siv** intense.
interessant interesting, of interest; (tankevekkende) suggestive.

interesse interest; **ha el. vise — for** interest oneself for; **ha — av** have an interest in; **finne — i** take (an) interest in; **det ligger ikke i min —** it is not to my interest; **vareta ens —** look after one's interests; **nyhetens —** the charm of novelty.
interesseløs uninteresting; uninterested.
interessent shareholder.
interessentskap company, association.
interessere interest; concern; **— seg for** interest oneself for, take an interest in.
interessert interested; (egennyttig) self-interested, covetous; **være — i** have an interest in, be concerned in.
interessesfære sphere of interest.
interimistisk interimistic, temporary.
interimsaksje (el. **-bevis)** scrip; **innehaver av interimsbevis** scrip-holder.
interimsregjering provisional government.
interiør interior.
interjeksjon interjection.
intermesso interlude, intermezzo.
internasjonal international.
internasjonale (det internasjonale arbeiderforbund) International, Internationale, International Working Men's Association. **tredje —** (stiftet av bolsjevikene i 1918) 3rd Internationale.
Internasjonalen (sosialistisk sang) the Internationale.
internat (pensjonsskole) boarding-school.
internere (holde på et bestemt sted) intern. **internering** internment.
interpell|ant questioner, interpellant. **-asjon** question. **-ere** put a question to (one), interpel(late).
interpolere interpolate.
interpunksjon punctuation. **-stegn** punctuation -mark.
interregnum (tronledighet) interregnum.
interrogativ (spørrende) interrogative.
intervall interval.
interven|ere intervene. **-sjon** intervention.
intervju interview.
intervjue interview.
intervjuer interviewer.
intet (erstattes helst av ingenting el. ikke noe) (adjektiv:) no; (især foran of eller etter nylig nevnt substantiv) none; (om to) neither; (substantivisk om ting) nothing; **— middel kan** hjelpe oss no remedy can help us; **det er — nytt under sola** there is nothing new under the sun; **den som — våger — vinner** nothing venture, nothing have; **hvor — er, har** keiseren tapt sin rett where nothing is to be had, the king must lose his right; **et — (a** mere) nothing, nought.
intet|kjønn the neuter gender. **-kjønns-** neuter.
intetsigende insignificant, unmeaning, fatuous.
intim intimate.
intimidere (skremme) intimidate.
intimitet intimacy.
intole|rans intolerance. **-rant** intolerant.
inton|ere intone. **-ering** intonation.
intransitiv intransitive, neuter.
intri|gant (adj) intriguing, scheming. **-ge** intrigue, plot, machination. **-ge-maker** schemer, intriguer. **-gere** intrigue.
introdu|ksjon introduction. **-sere** introduce.
intuisjcn (umiddelbar oppfattelse) intuition.
intuitiv intuitive.
invalid (adj) disabled; (subst) invalid; (fra krig) disabled soldier.
invalideforsørgelse disablement pay.
invalidehospital hospital for invalids.
invaliditet disablement.
invasjon invasion.
invektiv (skjellsord) invective.
inventar inventory; stores; (bohave) furniture; (til bedrift) trade fixtures; (om uunnværlig el. uunngåelig person) fixture. **-liste** inventory.
inversjon inversion.
invertere invert.

invitasjon invitation.
invitere invite; (i kortspill) lead; —i **en farge** lead el. open a suit.
invitt invitation; (i kortspill) (first) lead.
involvere imply, involve.
ion (slags atom) ion.
i overmorgen the day after to-morrow.
irer Irishman; **-ne** the Irish.
irettesette reprove, rebuke, reprimand, lecture.
irettesettelse reprimand, reproof, rebuke.
iris (sverdlilje) iris; **blå** — blue flag.
Irland Ireland, Eire.
irlender Irishman; **-inne** Irishwoman; **-ne** the Irish.
ironi irony. **ironiker** ironist.
ironisere speak ironically.
ironisk ironical; (adv) ironically, by way of irony.
irr ærugo, rust of copper, verdigris.
irrasjonal irrational; — **størrelse** surd.
irre rust. **-t** æruginous, rusty.
irregulær irregular.
irrelevant (saken uvedkommende) irrelevant.
irreligiøs irreligious. **-itet** irreligiousness, irreligion.
irri|tabel irritable. **-tasjon** irritation.
irritere get on one's nerves, irritate.
irsk Irish.
is ice; (spisel.) ice-cream; **bringe en på glatt-get** one into a scrape; **bryte -en** break the ice; **mitt blod ble til** — my blood froze.
is|aktig icy. **-avkjølt** iced.
is|berg iceberg. **-bjørn** polar bear. **-blokk** block of ice. **-blomst** (på ruten) ice-fern. **-brann** injury (to grass) from ice. **-bre** glacier. **-brodd** iceccalk, (p. hest) frost-nail. **-bryter** ice-breaker; ice boat.
iscenesett|e get up, mount. **-else** getting-up, get-up.
is|dekke sheet of ice. **-drift** drifting of ice.
ise ice. **det -r i tennene** my teeth are on edge.
ise (delfin), se **nise**.
iseddik glacial acetic vinegar.
isenkram hardware, ironmongery. **-handel** hardware business.
isenkremmer hardwareman, tin and iron man.
i senn (på en gang, av gangen), se **gang**.
is|flate sheet of ice. **-flak** flake of ice; (lite) patch of ice; (stort) floe.
isfri free from ice, open.
is|fugl kingfisher. **-gang** drifting el. running of the ice; **det var** — i elva the river was drifting ice. **-hav** icy sea, frozen sea; Arctic sea (det nordlige); Antarctic sea (det sydlige). **-kake** ice-cake, icc. **-kald** cold as ice, icy, ice-cold. **-kasse** ice-box, icechest, refrigerator.
iskjeller ice-cellar.
is|krem ice-cream. **-lag** sheet of ice.
islagt ice-bound, frozen up.
islam Islam. **-ismen** Islamism. **-itt** Islamite.
Island Iceland.
islandsk Icelandic, Iceland; — **mose** Iceland moss.
islender (islandsk trøye) Iceland jacket el. sweater, vest.

islending Icelander; (hest) Iceland pony.
islett woof. **-tråd** shoot.
ismaskin freezer, ice-cream machine.
isne chill, run cold; **fikk mitt blod til å** — made my blood freeze; **-nde** freezing, chilling.
isolasjon insulation, isolation.
isolator insulator.
isolere isolate, insulate.
isolerskammel insulating stool.
isplog ice-plough.
ispose ice-bag.
isprengt sprinkled, speckled, spotted.
ispudding iced cream.
israelitt Israelite, Jew. **-isk** Israelitic.
isranunkel, se **reinblom**.
isse crown (of the head), top.
is|skap ice-safe. **-slag** glazed frost. **-svull** rough sheet of ice.
i sta, **i stad** a while ago.
issørpe brash.
i stand, se **stand**.
istandbringe bring about.
istandsette repair, mend, refit, restore.
istandsettelse repair, restoration.
istapp icicle.
istedenfor (prep) instead of, in lieu of.
istemme join (in singing), chime in; (begynne å synge) commence singing, strike up; (fig) agree to, assent to, echo, re-echo.
ister (fett) inside fat. **-sild** matie. **-vom** paunch.
istiden the glacial period el. age.
istme isthmus.
i stykker (ogs. i sund) asunder, to pieces, in two; broken, torn; **gå** — go to pieces; **vinduet er** — the window is broken; **revet** — torn (asunder) **slått** — smashed, broken.
i stå: **gå** — come to a standstill; **er gått** — is at a stand-still.
isvann iced water.
især in particular, particularly, especially; **hver** — each; severally.
Itali|a Italy. **-ener**, **-enerinne** Italian.
italiensk Italian.
itel (blæreorm) bladderworm.
itu, se **i stykker**.
i vente in expectation, in prospect.
iver zeal, ardour, eagerness; **med** — eagerly; **hans** — for saken his ardour in the cause.
ivre declaim; (preke mot) preach down; (for) be warm for.
iverksette bring about, carry into effect, execute, give effect to.
iverksettelse execution.
ivrer zealot.
ivrig zealous, ardent, eager; — samtale animated conversation; — etter eager for, after, on; — etter å eager el. anxious to.
i været up, aloft.
iørefallende ear-catching.
i øvrig besides, for the rest.
iøynefallende easily perceptible, conspicuous, obvious, marked, glaring.
i år, se **år**.

J

J, j J, j.
ja (bekreftende) yes; (som innledning: ja, ser De) well; (= ja, endog, hva mer er) nay, indeed, in fact, (or) even, moreover; besvare med **ja** answer in the affirmative; **det var seks jaer og syv neier** there were six ayes and seven noes; (i overhuset: contents og non contents); **ja men** well, but; **ja, hva er det å gjøre ved**

det? well, what is to be done? **han fikk ja** (om en frier) he was accepted; **ja vel!** oh yes! (yes) certainly; **han øver seg hver morgen i flere timer, ja**, i flere timer enn jeg bryr meg om å høre på hans musikk he practises every morning for several hours, indeed for more hours than I care to listen to his music.
jafs gob, gobbet, mouthful.

jag hurry, hubbub.
jage (vt) chase; hunt; (fordrive) drive (away, off, out etc.); (mar) chase; (vi) (— avsted) speed, tear, race it; (på) urge on, hurry; — **livet av en** kill one (with fatigue); — **bort, vekk** turn el. send away; — **etter hunt** for; **han ble jagd fra gården** he was turned out of his farm; — **på dør** turn out, send about his business; — **på flukt** put to flight.
jager (krigsskip) chaser; (seil) flying-jib; (torpedo-) destroyer.
jaging chasing, hunting.
jaguar jaguar, ounce.
jakett cut-away coat, cut-away, morning coat.
jakke jacket, coat. **-dress** (hverdagsdress) business suit.
Jakob James; (bibelsk) Jacob. **-iner** Jacobin. **-it** Jacobite. **-itisk** Jacobitical.
jakobsstige Jacob's ladder.
I. **jakt** (fartøy) sloop; (lyst-) yacht.
II. **jakt** chase, sporting, sport, hunting, shooting; (-rett) right of killing game; (kunst) huntsmanship, sportsmanship, sporting; **den ville** — the wild hunt, Arthur's chase; **gå på** — go (out) shooting; **være på** — **etter** be in pursuit of; **gjøre** — **på** pursue; (skip) chase, give chase to.
jakt|bytte bag(s). **-børse** fowling-piece. **-distrikt** hunting el. shooting ground(s). **-falk** gerfalcon. **-hund** hound; sporting dog. **-hytte** hunting el. shooting lodge, seat.
jakt|kniv hunting-knife. **-lov** game-act. **-parti** hunting party, shooting party. **-rett** right of killing game. **-revier** hunting-ground(s); (fredet) preserve. **-rifle** sportsman's rifle. **-tid** hunting el. shooting season. **-vogn** shooting-gig, dog-cart.
jam- i sm. setninger, se ogs. **jevn**.
jam|be iambus. **-bisk** iambic.
jamen certainly, indeed.
jammer lamentation, wailing; (elendighet) misery; **en** — **å se** a miserable sight. **-dal** vale of sorrow el. tears.
jammerlig miserable, wretched, pitiable.
jammerlighet wretchedness, pitiableness.
jammerskrik doleful cry, wail.
jamn, se **jevn**.
jamre wail; — **over** bewail. **jamring** wailing.
jamsides side by side, abreast.
jamstilling equal position.
jamt og samt constantly, continually; frequently.
jamvekt equilibrium, equipoise, balance; se også **likevekt**.
janitsjar Janizary. **-musikk** Janizary el. Turkish music.
januar January.
Japan Japan. **j–er, j–erinne, j–eser, j–eserinne** Japanese.
japanesisk, japansk Japanese, Japan.
jar el. **jare** selvage.
jarl earl. (norsk) ogs. **jarl** el. **yarl**. **-edømme** earldom.
jask hasty work.
jaske work hastily el. carelessly; — **av slur** (over), scamp.
jaspis jasper.
Java Java. **j– kaffe** Javan coffee, Java. **j–neser, j–nesisk** Javanese.
jazz (slags musikk) jazz.
Jeanne D'Arc Joan of Arc.
jeg I; — **selv** I myself; — **ulykkelige!** unhappy me! wretch that I am! — **gjør det ikke** I don't (myself). **jeg** (subst) ego, self; **-et** the ego; **mitt annet** — my second self, my alter ego; **han tenker bare på sitt eget** — he thinks only of number one; **hans eget kjære** — his own dear self.
jeger sportsman, hunter; (kv. —) huntress; (soldat) light-infantry man; rifle-man (på et gods) game-keeper. **-kor** hunting chorus. **-korps** light cavalry corps. **-liv** sportsman's life. **-mester** Master of the buck-hounds.

jeksel back-tooth, jaw-tooth, grinder.
jenke accomodate, fit.
jente girl, lass, lassie.
jentunge little girl, slip of a girl; (foraktelig) chit of a girl.
Jeremi|as Jeremiah. **j–ade** jeremiad.
jern iron; **gammelt** — scrap iron; **smi mens -et er varmt** strike while the iron is hot; **ha mange** — **i ilden** have irons in many fires, have many irons in the fire; **han er et** — he is a regular steam-engine.
jernalder iron age el. era.
jernbane railway; (især amr) railroad; **reise på** — go by rail(way).
jernbane|administrasjon administration of railways. **-anlegg** construction of railways. **-arbeider** navvy.
jernbanebru viaduct, railway bridge.
jernbanedrift operation of railways.
jernbane|fart railway speed. **-forbindelse** communication by rail. **-hotell** terminus hotel. **-kjørsel** railway traffic. **-konduktør** guard; (amr) conductor. **-kupé** compartment. **-linje** (railway) line.
jernbanenett railway system.
jernbane|skinne rail. **-stasjon** railway-station; (amr) railway depot.
jernbanestyre railway administration.
jernbanesville (railway-)sleeper.
jernbanetakst tariff.
jernbane|tog train, railway-train. **-transport** carriage by rail. **-tur** ride, run, trip on the railway. **-ulykke** railway accident. **-vogn** railway-carriage; (amr) railroad car.
jernbeslag iron-binding, ironband.
jernbeslått iron-bound, iron-studded.
jern|blekk, -blikk sheet-iron, iron-plate. **-byrd** ordeal by fire. **-filspon** iron filings (pl.). **-flid** unwearied application. **-forhudet** iron sheathed. **-gitter** iron-grate, iron-railing. **-gruve** iron-mine. **-handel** iron-trade. **-handler** dealer in iron, ironmonger. **-helbred** iron constitution.
jern|hard hard as iron. **-holdig** ferruginous; (om vann) chalybeate.
jern|kledning (mar) external plating. **-kledd** iron-clad; steel-clad. **-kur** iron-cure, chalybeate course. **-netter** frosty August nights. **-oppløsning** solution of iron. **-piller** iron pills. **-seng** iron bed. **-skinne** iron band; (f. eks. på jernbanen) iron rail. **-sponer** iron filings. **-stang** iron bar; (kubein) iron-crow. **-støper** iron-founder. **-støperi** iron-foundry. **-varer**, se **isenkram**. **-(og stål)vareforretning**, se **isenkramhandel**. **-verk** iron work(s). **-vilje** iron will. **-vin** ferruginous wine.
jerpe (hønsefugl) hazel-grouse.
jersey|drakt jersey suit. **-trøye** jersey (jacket).
Jerusalem Jerusalem; **-s skomaker** the wandering Jew.
jerv glutton; (amr) wolverene.
jesuitt Jesuit. **jesuitterorden** order of Jesuits.
jesuittisk jesuitical.
jesuittisme Jesuitism, Jesuity.
Jesus Jesus; — **Kristus** Jesus Christ; **Jesu Siraks bok** Ecclesiasticus. **-barnet** the child Jesus, the infant Saviour.
jette, se **jotun**. **-gryte** kettle-hole, pot, pot-hole.
jevn even, level, plain, smooth; uniform, equal, steady, constant; (simpel) plain, simple, natural, artless; — **gang** even pace; **et -t humør** an even temper; — **mann** plain man.
jevnaldrende of the same age.
jevnbyrdig of equal birth; co-equal.
jevndøgn equinox.
jevndøgnsstorm equinoctial gale.
jevne level, even; (fig) smooth (down). adjust, set right; — **suppe med mel** thicken soup with flour.
jevn|føre confer, compare, collate. **-føring** collation, comparison. **-god** equal, equivalent. **-het** evenness, plainness.

jevning levelling; (likemann) compeer; (til suppe) thickening.
jevnlig frequent; (adv) frequently.
jevnsides, se **jamsides**.
jevnstille place side by side, put on a level.
jevnt levelly, evenly; — **dyktig** of average ability, all-round; — **god** level, average, fair.
jo yes; **har han ingen barn?** — han har mange has he no children? yes, to be sure, he has a great many; **du har** — **vært der?** you have been there, have you not? **der er han** — why, there he is; **det er** — **noe snakk** that is nonsense, you know el. see; —, **han er den rette** ay, he is the right sort of fellow, indeed; — **mer**, — **bedre** the more, the better; —, —! yes, I dare say; — **visst** to be sure; (hånl.) I dare say.
jobb job.
jobbe job. **-r stock-jobber. -tid** boom times.
jobbing stock-jobbing.
jobspost evil tidings.
jockey, jockey. **-klubb** jockey club.
I. jod iodine.
II. jodd (bokstaven) (the letter) jay.
jod|forbindelse iodide. **-holdig** iodic. **-kalium** iodide of potassium, potassic iodide.
jodle jodel. **jodling** jodeling.
jodoform iodoform.
Johan John. **-ne** Joan, Jane.
Johannes John. **j-brød** carob-bean.
johanitter|orden Order of St. John, Order of Malta. **-ridder** Knight of St. John.
jolle yawl, jolly-boat. **-bom** davit.
jomfru young lady, girl, maid; (møy) virgin, maiden; (titel) Miss; (hus-) house-keeper; (butikk-) shop-woman, young lady; (brulegger-) rammer, beetle; (stjernebilde) virgo; **gammel** — old maid; — **Maria** the Virgin Mary; **den hellige** — the (holy) Virgin.
jomfrubur lady's bower.
jomfrudom virginity, maidenhead, maidenhood.
jomfruelig virgin, virginal; (som egner seg for en j.) maidenly, maiden. **-het** maidenliness.
jomfru|krans bridal wreath. **-nalsk** maidenlike. **-stand** maidenhood. **-tale** maiden speech. **-ære** maiden honour.
jonsok Johnsmass, Midsummer day, St. John's day. **-bål** fire of Midsummer eve, St. John's fire. **-kveld** Midsummer eve. **-leite:** ved — about Midsummer time.
jord earth; (overflaten på jorda) ground; (jordbunn, land) soil, land; (jordegods) land. **-ens produkter** the productions of the soil; **falle i god** — fall into good ground; **her på -a** here on earth; **falle til -en** fall to the ground; **følge en til -en** follow one to his grave; **synke til -en** sink to the ground; **kaste, slå til -en** throw, knock down; **under -a** under ground.
jordaktig earthy.
jord|arbeider field-labourer; (gravemaskin) navvy, excavator. **-bruk** agriculture, husbandry, farming. **-bruker** agriculturist, husbandman, farmer.
jordbunden earth-bound.
jordbunn soil.
jordbær strawberry. **-bed** strawberry-bed. **-plante** strawberry plant. **-saft** strawberry sirup. **-syltetøy** strawberry jam.
jord|dannelseslære geology. **-drott** landlord. **-dyrk(n)ing** agriculture. **-dyrk(n)ingslære** science of agriculture.
jorde (verb) bury, inter.
jorde (subst) (arable) field. fl. **-er** ogs. grounds, land.
jorde|bok rental, rentroll. **-ferd** funeral. **-gods** landed property, estate.
jordeiendom landed property, estate.
jordeier landed proprietor, landowner.
jord(e)liv earthly existence.
jordeple, se **potet**.

jorderike the earth.
jord|fall fall of earth, sinking of the ground. **-farge** earthen hue. **-farget** earth-coloured.
jord|fellesskap community of land. **-feste** inter. **-festelse** burial, interment. **-forbindelse** (i radio) earth connection. **-hytte** mud cabin.
jordisk earthly, terrestrial, sublunary.
jord|klode globe. **-klump** clod of earth. **-kreps** mole-cricket. **-lag** layer el. stratum of earth. **-ledning** (for lynavl., radio etc.) earth connection. **-lodd** lot of ground. **-loppe** turnip-fly. **-magnetisme** terrestrial magnetism. **-nøtt** peanut, earth-nut. **-mor** midwife. **-olje** petroleum, rock oil. **-omseiler** circumnavigator (of the globe). **-omseiling** circumnavigation (of the globe). **-omveltning** convulsion of the earth. **-overflate** surface of the earth. **-periode** geological period el. epoch. **-påkastelse** ceremony of casting earth upon the coffin at a burial. **-rystelse, -skjelv** earth-quake. **-skokk** Jerusalem artichoke. **-skorpa** the crust of the earth. **-skred** land-slide, earth-slide, land-slip. **-skyld** ground rent. **-slag** mildew. **-slått** mildewed; (om papir) foxed, foxmarked. **-smak** earthy taste.
jordsmonn soil, ground.
jord|strøk region, climate, zone. **-tange** isthmus, neck of land. **-utstykning** parcelling. **-vei** arable land; farm, holding. **-vendt** bent on earthly things. **-voll** earthen mound el. rampart.
jort (drøv) cud.
jorte chew the cud.
Josef Joseph, (dt.) Joe. **-ine** Josephine.
jotun (fl. jotner) (myt.) giant. **-heimen** the land (world) of the giants, giant-land. **-kvinne** giantess.
jour: à **jour** up to date, posted up; à **jour med** posted up in, abreast of, level with, au courant of. **føre á jour** bring up to date.
jourhavende on duty, in charge.
journal (merc) journal, day-book, memorandum book; (mar) journal, log-book; **føre** — keep a journal; **innføre i -en** enter in the j.; journalize.
journal|ist journalist, gentleman of the press, press-man. **-istikk** journalism. **-stisk** journalistic.
jovial jovial. **-itet** joviality, jovialness.
jo visst, se **jo**.
jubel exultation, jubilation; (glede) rejoicing(s). **-rop** shout (of joy, of triumph). **-sang** jubilant hymn, pæan; (rel.) carol. **-år** (year of) jubilee.
jubilere celebrate a jubilee.
jubileum jubilee; jubilee meeting.
jubileumsdag jubilee edition.
jubileumsutstilling jubilee exhibition.
juble shout (with joy), exult, be jubilant; **-nde** jubilant, exultant.
jubling exultation, jubilation.
Judas Judas. **J-kyss** Judas kiss, treacherous kiss. **j-penger** Judas gold, a traitor's wages.
judisiell judicial. **-ium** judgment.
Jugoslavia Jugo-Slavia.
jugoslavisk Jugo-Slav.
jugl gauds, gaudy finery.
jugle: — **til**, — **ut** bedizen, rig out. **-t** gaudy.
juks rubbish, trumpery.
jukse cheat. **-maker** cheater.
jul Christmas; **feire** — spend el. celebrate Christmas; **i -a** at Christmas; **ønske en gledelig** — wish one a merry Christmas.
julaften Christmas eve.
jule, se **pryle**.
jule|bukk bugbear. **-dag** Christmas-day; **annen -dag** Boxing-day, St. Stephen (ikke helligdag). **-ferie** C. holidays (pl), C. vacation. **-fest** festival of Christmas. **-gave** (til familie og venner) Christmas present; (slags drikkepenger) Christmas-box.
jule|glede C. merrymaking; (bot) perennial begonia. **-helg** C. holidays. **-kake** C. cake.

-kort C. card. -kut (kappkjøring, gml. skikk) C. race. -kveld, se -aften.
jule|lys Christmas candle. -merker (forvarsler) prognostics. -morgen C. morning. -natt C. night.
jule|rose C. rose. -salme C. hymn. -sang C. song, C. carol. -selskap C. party. -tid Christmas (time). -tre C. tree. -uke C. week. -utstilling C. show.
juli July.
juliansk Julian; den -e kalender the Julian Calendar.
Julie Julia; Romeo og — Romeo and Juliet.
juling, se pryl.
jumpe jump.
jumper jumper.
jungle jungle.
jungmann ordinary (seaman), boy.
juni June.
junior junior.
junker young gentleman el. nobleman; squire; (ring akt.) lordling. -herredømme rule el. ascendency of the petty nobility. -vesen arrogance of lordlings.
Juno Juno.
junonisk Juno-like.
Jupiter Jove, Jupiter.
jur udder, bag.
juradannelse Jura el. Jurrassic formation.
juridisk juridical; det -e fakultet the faculty of law; — bok law book; -e forelesninger lectures on jurisprudence; — kandidat young lawyer (called to the bar); — konsulent law adviser; — student law student.
jurisdiksjon jurisdiction.
jurisprudens jurisprudence.
jurist (rettslærd) lawyer, jurist; (student) law student. juristeri legal chicane, lawyer's tricks. juristkollegium inn of court.
jury jury; være medlem av en — s.t el. be on a jury.
juryliste list of jury, panel.
jurymann juror, juryman.
jus (rettsvesen) law.

just just, precisely. exactly; ikke — el. — ikke not exactly.
justere ad'ust, size, gauge.
justerer adjuster of weights and measures, gauger; type-justifyer.
juster|ing adjusting, sizing. -kammer office of standard weights and measures. -mester inspector of weights and measures.
justis administration of justice; holder streng — rules with a rod of iron. -departement ministry of justice. -minister minister of justice; (i England) Lord High Chancellor. -mord judicial murder.
justit|arius lord chief justice. -ell judicial.
jute jute(-hemp). -plante jute-plant.
jutul, se jotun.
juv abyss, gorge, ravine.
juvél jewel, gem. -besatt jewelled.
juveler jeweller. -arbeid jeweller's work. -butikk jeweller's shop.
juvél|skrin jewel-box, casket. -smykke set of jewels.
jyde Jute, Jutlander.
Jylland Jutland.
jypling (nedsettende) very raw youngster, impudent young fellow.
jysk Jutlandish.
jærtegn sign, prodigy, miracle.
jøde Jew; den evige — the wandering Jew. -aktig Jewish. -fiendtlig antisemitic. -folk Jewish people. -forfølgelse persecution of the Jews. -gutt Jewish boy. -hat hatred of the Jews. -kone Jewish woman, Jew's wife. -kvarter Jew's ward, Jewry, ghetto. -pike Jewish girl. -vis: på — in Jewish fashion.
jødinne Jewess. jødisk Jewish.
jøkel glacier. -elv glacier torrent. -gjerde se morene.
jøss(es) Lord! Lor! Lawks
jål fun, chaff
jåle (vrb)' — med loot, make fun of.
jåle (subst) nonsensical woman.
jålet foolish, nonsensical.

K

Ord som ikke fins under K, kan søkes under C og Ch.
K, k K, k.
kabal cabal; (med kort) patience; legge -r play patience.
kabaret cabaret.
kabb (planke-), se kabbe.
kabbalist (kjenner av den hemmelighetsfulle jødiske overlevering) cabalist. kabbalistisk cabalistic.
kabbe piece chopped off a felled tree.
kabel cable. -feil fault in the cable. -hylster external covering of the cable. -legging (of) cables. -lengde cable's length. -prøve test of the cable. -skip cable-ship. -telegram cablegram.
kabinett cabinet; (lite kammer) closet. kabinetts|befaling government-order. -bilde cabinet picture. -sekretær private secretary. -spørsmål cabinet question.
kabriolett cabriolet, cab.
kabyler Kabyles.
kabyss (skipskjøkken) galley.
kadaver carcass.
kadens cadence.
kadett (military, naval) cadet, midshipman. -messe gun-room, the midshipmen's mess. -skip training ship for naval cadets.
kadrer (pl) skeleton (of a regiment).
kafé café coffee-house, refreshment-rooms (pl); (i hotell) coffee-room. -vert café proprietor.

kaffe coffee; brenne — roast coffee. -brun coffee coloured. -bønne (coffee) berry. -doktor coffee and brandy. -ekstrakt essence of coffee. -grut coffee-grounds.
kaffein caffein(e), coffein(e).
kaffe|kanne coffee-pot. -kopp coffee-cup. -kvern coffee-mill, coffee-grinder. -pose (til trakting) coffee-strainer, coffee-filtering bag.
kaffer Kaffir.
kaffe|slaberas gossip. -surrogat coffee-substitute. -søster coffee-drinker. -tre coffee-tree.
kaftan caftan.
kagge keg.
kahytt cabin; (på lystbåter) cuddy; (f. enkelte passasjerer) state-room.
kahytts|gutt cabin boy. -plass cabin (passage). -trapp cabin stairs, companion-way.
ka quay, wharf, embankment; ved — alongside wharf.
kaie jackdaw.
Kain Cain. kainsmerke brand of Cain.
kajakk caiac, kayak.
kajennepepper Cayenne pepper.
kakadu(e) cockatoo.
kakao cocoa. -bønne cocoa(-bean). -pulver powdered cocoa-bean.
kake cake; (konditorkake, butterdeigskake) pastry; (terte) tart. -baking cake-making. -form cake-form. -linne (mildvær like før jul) a short spell of soft weather (in December).

kake(r)lakk cockroach.
kakespade cake-slice.
kaki khaki. **–kledd** dressed in khaki
kakke (banke) tap, knock.
kakkel|omn, –ovn stove.
kakkelovnskrok chimney corner.
kakle cackle. **kakling** cackling.
kakse (storbonde) farmer in a large way, yeoman; (som slår stort på) bigwig, nob.
kakstryke scourge, whip (at the post).
kaktus cactus.
kala (plante) calla.
kalamitet calamity.
kalas carousal, feast, treat.
kald cold, frigid; **jeg ble — I** got a chill.
kaldblodig cold-blooded; (rolig) cool; (adv) in cold blood; coolly.
kaldblodighet coolness.
kald|flir frigid sneer. **–flire** sneer frigidly. **–krem** cold-cream. **–meisel** cold-chisel. **–røyke** smoke dry, smoke an unlighted cigar, suck an empty pipe.
kaldsindig cool, calm.
kaldsindighet coolness, calmness.
kaldsvette sweat cold, be in a cold perspiration.
kaldtvannskur cold-water cure.
kalebass (tropisk frukt) calabash.
kaleidoskop kaleidoscope.
kalender calendar.
kalesje hood, carriage-hood, calash; **slå –n opp** put up the hood; **slå –n ned** put down the hood.
kalesjevogn hooded carriage, calash.
kalfatre caulk. **–r** caulker.
kali potash.
kaliber caliber, bore; (fig) kind, stamp. **–mål** cylinder gauge.
kalifat caliphate. **kaliff** caliph.
Kaliforni|a California. **k–sk** Californian.
kali|hydrat hydrate of potash. **–lut** potash-lye. **–salpeter** nitrate of potash.
kalium potassium.
I. **kalk** (beger) chalice; (bot) calyx; (fig) cup.
II. **kalk** (jordart) lime; (blandet med sand) mortar; (til hvitning) whitewash; (pussekalk) plaster; **brent — quick-lime. –brenner** lime-burner. **–brenneri** lime-kiln. **–brott, –brudd** lime-quarry.
kalke lime, mortar, limewash, plaster; **–de graver** whited sepulchres.
kalker|e calk, calque, counterdraw, trace. **–ing** calking etc. **–papir** tracing-paper.
kalk|gruve lime-pit. **–holdig** lime-charged. **–jord** calcareous earth. **–lag** layer of lime. **–omn** lime-kiln. **–puss** plastering, stucco. **–steinsbrott** limestone quarry.
kalkulasjon calculation.
kalkulere calculate.
kalkun turkey. **–hane** turkey cock. **–høne** turkey hen.
kalkunsk (fig) stuck up.
kalkvann lime-water.
kalkyle calculation.
I. **kall** (gml. mann) old man.
II. **kall** inclination (to, for), turn (for); call; (stand, håndtering) calling, profession, vocation; (prestekall) living.
kalle call; (til geistlig embete) present (to a living); **la en — send** for one, call one in; **kom som han var kalt** came most opportunely, in the nick of time; **— fram,** se **fremkalle; — opp etter call** after; **— på call; være kalt til, føle seg kalt til noe** be fit for, feel inclined for a thing; **— til live call** into life el. being; **— tilbake** recall.
kallelse call, inclination, turn.
kalli|graf calligrapher. **–grafi** calligraphy. **–grafisk** calligraphic(al).
kalling bad names (called).
kalls|brev letter of presentation (to a living). **–kapellan** capellanus pro loco; perpetual curate. **–plikt** professional duty.
kalmus (plante) sweet flag. **–rot** sweet flag.

kalori (varmeenhet) calorie.
kalorimeter calorimeter.
kalosje galoche, galosh, golosh.
kalott scull-cap; (katolsk prests) calotte.
kalun tripe, chawdron.
kalv calf; **med — in calf.**
kalvbeint baker-legged, knock-kneed.
kalve (ogs. om bre) calve.
kalve|binge calf-pen. **–dans** capers; (rett av råmelk) cheese of biestings. **–frikassé** stewed veal. **–hage** calves' enclosure. **–kjøtt** veal. **–kryss** (gmlt.) shirt-frill. **–skinn** calf-skin; (pergament) vellum. **–steik** roast veal, joint of veal. **–tid** calving time el. season.
kalving calving.
Kalvin Calvin. **k–isme** Calvinism. **k–ist** Calvinist. **k–istisk** Calvinistic. **k–sk** Calvinistic.
kalvkasting premature birth of calf.
kam comb; (på berg, bølge) crest; (på slakt) neck; **skjære alle over en — treat** all alike; **har fått — til sitt hår** has found his master, is henpecked; **rød i –men** flushed.
Kam (bibl) Ham.
kamarilja cabal, clique, junto, camarilla.
kamé cameo.
kamel camel. **–driver** camel-driver.
kameleon chameleon.
kamelhår camel's hair.
kamelia (plante) camellia.
kamera (fotografiapparat) camera.
kamerat companion, friend; (dt.) chum, comrade; (til sjøs) shipmate; (i tiltale) old fellow; (officer) brother officer; (soldat) brother soldier; (skole-) school-fellow; (universitets-) fellow-student, college-friend.
kameratekteskap companionate marriage.
kameratskap fellowship, companionship.
kameratslig companionable, comradely, (dt.) chumly.
kamfer camphor. **–dråper** camphor-essence. **–olje** camphor-oil. **–spiritus** spirits of camphor.
kamgarn worsted.
kamille wild camomile. **–te** camomile tea.
kamin fire-place, chimney. **–gesims** mantlepiece. **–gitter** fender, fire-guard. **–plate** hob. **–rist** fire-grate.
kammer chamber; room.
kammerduk cambric.
kammer|frue lady of honour. **–frøken** maid of honour. **–herre** chamberlain. **–musikk** chamber music. **–musikus** court musician. **–pike** lady's maid; (i hoteller) chambermaid. **–sanger(inne)** private singer to the king.
kammertjener valet.
kammertone concert-pitch.
kammusling scallop(-shell).
I. **kamp** (fjelltopp) (broadish, roundish) hilltop.
II. **kamp** fight, combat, struggle, contest, conflict; engagement; **— på liv og død** mortal strife.
kampaeroplan fighting aeroplane.
kampanje campaign.
kampberedt ready for action, in fighting trim.
kampdommer (gmlt., i turnering) judge of the field el. lists; (i moderne sport) umpire.
kampdyktig able to fight, in fighting condition; (mil) effective. **–het** efficiency, fighting power.
kampere camp, be encamped.
kampestein boulder.
kamp|felle fellow-combatant, companion in arms. **–hane** game-cock.
kamp|iver, –lyst eagerness to fight, love of fighting; (dt.) fight. **–lysten** eager for the fight, eager for battle; (dt.) full of fight. **–plass** field of battle, battleground, scene of action; arena, lists. **–udyktig** not in a fighting state, disabled; **gjøre –udyktig** disable.
kamuflasj camouflage.
kamuflere camouflage.
Kanada Canada. **kanadi|er, –isk** Canadian.

katastrof|e catastrophe, crash. **-al** catastrophic.
katedral cathedral (church). **-skole** cathedral school.
katego|ri category. **-risk** categorical.
kate|ket junior curate. **-kisere** catechise.
katekisme catechism.
katet (side i rettvinklet trekant) side.
I. **kateter** chair, cathedra, desk.
II. **kateter** (kirurgisk instrument) catheter.
kato|likk Catholic, Roman Catholic. **-lisisme** Catholicism. **katolsk** Catholic.
Katrine Kate. **k-plomme** French plum.
katt cat; (tamp) cat o'nine tails; **vill — cata-mountain, catamount; han gjør ikke en — fortred** he wouldn't hurt a fly; **i mørke er alle -er grå** all cats are grey in the dark, when candles are out all cats are grey, Joan's as good as my Lady in the dark; **en — har lov til å se på en konge** a cat may look at a king; **kjøpe -en i sekken** buy a pig in a poke; **leve som hund og — live** like cat and dog; **når -en er borte danser musene på bordet** when the cat is away the mice will play; **som -en om den varme grauten** like a cat about hot milk.
kattaktig catlike, cattish.
katte|fjed catlike step el. tread; **på — stea:thily. -gaul** caterwauling.
kattehale (planten) willow-weed.
katte|klo cat's claw. **-musikk** (av katter), se **-gaul. -pine** scrape, strait, hopple. **-pus** pussy.
katte|slekten (the) catkind, the feline race. **-vask** an apology for washing.
kattost (bot.) mallow.
katt|ugle brown owl, wood owl. **-unge** kitten, kit.
kaudervelsk gibberish, jargon.
kaue, se **hauke.**
kausjon security, surety, bail, caution; **stille — give** security, put in bail; **bli løslatt mot — be bailed** out; **-ere** be surety, stand surety, bail. **-ist** surety.
kaut proud.
kautél precaution, safeguard.
kautsjuk India rubber, caoutchouc.
kav (adv) utterly. **— bergensk** broad, intensely, ultra Bergense.
I. **kav** (subst) struggling; (travelhet) bustle; (oppkavethet) fluster.
II. **kav** (havdyp) deep, depths of the ocean.
III. **kav** (tett snøfall) snow-flurry, **-storm.** (tett drev, sjørøyk) drifting sleet, seasmoke.
kavalér cavalier; (ved hoffet) gentleman in waiting; (i dans) partner; (spottende) beau.
kavaleri cavalry, horse.
kavalerist trooper, horseman, horse-soldier.
kavalérmessig gentlemanlike, gentlemanly; (flott, avfeiende) cavalier.
kavalkade cavalcade.
kave (vrb) struggle; flounder, sprawl, scramble; (ha det travelt) bustle about; (streve) toil.
kavere, se **kausjonere.**
kaveringsmann (ved bryllup) best man el. bridegroom's man.
kaviar caviar, caviare; **— for den store hop** caviar to the general.
kavl small buoy, float.
kavle roller. **-sjø** choppers, chopping sea.
kavring wheat biscuit; (amr.) cracker.
kediv khedive.
kei, se **kjed.**
keip rowlock.
keiser emperor; **hvor intet er, har -en tapt sin rett** where nothing is, the king must lose his right.
keiser|dømme empire. **-hoff** imperial court.
keiserinne empress. **-pære** white butter-pear.
keiser|lig imperial. **-prins** Prince Imperial. **-snitt** cesarean section el. operation.
keitet awkward, clumsy; (adv) awkwardly; **-het** awkwardness.

keiv|e the left hand. **-hendt** left-handed.
kelner waiter.
kelt|er Celt. **-isk** Celtic.
kemner (chief) rate collector, city chamberlain.
kenguru kangaroo.
kentaur centaur.
keramikk the ceramic art, the art of pottery; (konkr.) ceramics.
Kerberus Cerberus; (fig) dragon.
K. F. U. M. fork. av kristelig forening for unge menn: Y. M. C. A., Young Men's Christian Association. **K. F. U. K.** fork. av kristelig forening for unge kvinner. Y. W. C. A., Young Women's Christian Association.
kg. fork. av **kilogram** kilogram.
kgl. fork. av **kongelig** royal.
kik: få — på set eyes upon, catch sight of.
I. **kike** peep, peer; (se nøye, speide) pry; **— fram** peep (out).
II. **kike** (under kikhoste) whoop, hoop.
kikhoste hooping cough, chincough.
kikhull peep-hole.
kikke, se **kike** I.
kikkert (større) telescope; (mindre) spy-glass, field-glass; (teater-) opera-glass, lorg-nette; **ha i -en** have one's eyes upon, be on the look-out for, have st. in the wind.
kilde, i egt. bet. se **kjelde.** (Fig.) source; fountain-head; (skriftl.) source. **fra pålitelig — from** good authority.
kilden (adj) (sak) delicate, awkward.
kilde|skrift original (text); primary source. **-sted** source. **-studium** study of the sources.
kildre (fig) tickle, titillate. **det -t hans humoristiske sans** it tickled his sense of humour.
I. **kile** (vrb) tickle.
II. **kile** (vrb) wedge; **— seg fast** jam; **— på** bestir oneself.
I. **kile** (subst) wedge, slice; (i tøy) gore.
II. **kile** (spill) ninepin, skittle; **spille -r** play at ninepins.
kilebane ninepin-alley.
kileformet cuneiform, wedge-like el. **-shaped.**
kilegutt marker at ninepins.
kileinnskrift cuneiform el. arrowheaded inscription.
kilekule bowl.
kilen (lett å kile) ticklish, ticklesome. **-het** ticklishness.
kileskrift cuneiform el. arrow-headed characters el. letters (pl), wedge-writing.
kilespill game of ninepins; (et antall kiler) set of ninepins.
kilevink (ørefik) tingler.
kiling, se **kje.**
kilo (kilogram) kilo. **kilogram** kilogram.
kilometer kilometer.
kiltre tuck.
kim|e (subst) germ. corcle; (fig) germ, seed. **-blad** cotyledon, seed-lobe. **-dannelse** embryogony.
kime (vrb) (ringe) ring, chime; **det -r** the bells are ringing. **kiming** ringing, chiming.
kimming (sea) horizon; (på skip) bilge.
kimse toss the head; **— av noe** turn up one's nose at a thing; **ikke til å — av også:** not to be sneezed at.
kimæ|re chimera. **-risk** chimerical.
Kina, (nå China) China. **k-bark** (Jesuit's) bark, Peruvean bark, quinquina, cinchona. **k-farer** Chinaman.
kinematograf cinema, cinematograph.
kineser Chinaman (plur: Chinamen), Chinese (uforandret i plur).
kineserinne Chinese.
kinesisk Chinese.
kingel spider. **-vev** spider's web, cobweb.
kinin quinine. **-pille** quinine pill.
kink (bukt på tau) kink; **slå -er** kink.
kinkig (vanskelig, lei) awkward, invidious.
kinn cheek. **-bakke** mandible. **-bein** cheekbone.

kinne (subst) churn; (vrb) churn. **-melk, -mjølk** butter-milk.

kinn|skjegg whiskers. **-tann** grinder, jawtooth.

kino, se **kinematograf.**

kiosk kiosk.

kipen frisky, coltish.

kippe jerk, fling; (ankeret) fish; (om sko) slip off at the heels.

kirke church; (dissenter-)chapel; **gå i -n** go to church; **han er i -n** he is at church; **jeg har vært i -n** I have been to church. **kirke|bakke** meeting place at the entrance of a church. **-bok** church el. parochial register. **-bygning** church, church edifice. **-bønn** church prayer; (i England) common prayer. **-bøsse** poor-box. **-departement:** Kirke- og undervisningsdepartementet Church and School department. **-far** father of the church. **-fest** church festival. **-fyrste** ecclesiastical prince. **-gang** church-going. **-gjenger** church-goer. **-golv: på -golvet** in (the) church. **-gård** graveyard, cemetery; (ved kirken) church-yard. **-historie** church history, ecclesiastical h. **-klokke** church bell. **-konsert** sacred concert.

kirkelig ecclesiastical; church-.

kirke|lov canon law. **-musikk** church music, service music; sacred music. **-møte** synod, church conference. **-rett** canon law. **-ritual** church ritual. **-rotte: så fattig som en —** as poor as a church mouse. **-samfunn** religious community. **-sang** church singing. **-sanger** parish-clerk, precentor. **-skip** nave (of the church). **-skjenner** sacrilegist. **-sogn** parish. **-spir** church spire. K-staten the Ecclesiastical States, the States of the Church, the Roman States, the Papal States. **-statsråd** secretary of state for ecclesiastical affairs. **-tid** church time; **etter -tid** after church. **-tjener** church official. **-tukt** church discipline. **-tårn** church steeple. **-ur** church clock. **-verge** church-warden. **-vesen** church-matters el. affairs. **-år** Christian year.

kirsebær cherry. **-likør** cherry brandy, cherry-cordial. **-rød** cherry. **-saft** cherry-juice. **-stein** cherry-stone. **-stilk** cherry-stalk. **-suppe** cherry-soup. **-tre** cherry (tree). **-vin** cherry-wine.

kirurg surgeon. **-i** surgery. **-isk** surgical.

kis (mineral) pyrites.

kisel (ren) silica; (i uren, naturlig tilstand) silex; (elementet) silicium, silicon. **-aktig** silicious. **-jord** silicious earth. **-stein** pebble (stone).

kisle (få kattunger) kitten.

kiste chest; (mar) locker; (lik-) coffin. **-botn, -bunn** bottom of a chest; **han har noe på -bunnen** he is well-to-do, warm. **-glad** awfully glad. **-klær** holiday clothes, Sunday best.

kitt putty. **kitte** putty.

kittel smock-frock, blouse.

kiv quarrel, dispute, wrangling. **-aktig** quarrelsome, contentious. **-aktighet** quarrelsomeness, contentiousness.

kives quarrel, dispute, wrangle.

kjake, se **kinn.**

kjapp quick (mund-) glib.

kjas, se **strev** el. **kav.**

kje goatling, kid, kidling.

kjed weary (av: of), tired (av: of); (bedrøvet) sorry; **bli — av** tire of.

kjede (vrb) tire, weary, bore; **— seg** be bored; **— seg ihjel** be bored to extinction.

kjede (subst) chain; (mil) line, cordon; (i dans) (the) right and left (figure); (fig) series, chain, train; **danne —** form the chain.

kjedelig tiresome, tedious, prosy, wearysome, irksome, slow; (ergerlig) annoying, unpleasant; **— person** bore. **-het** (nt. leit) annoyance.

kjedesting chain stitch.

kjedsommelig, se **kjedelig. -het** tediousness wearisomeness, boredom, tedium.

kjee (få kje) kid.

kjeft jaw, muzzle, chops; **hold —** hold your tongue, (spøkende) hold your noise; **ikke en —** not a living soul. **-es** squabble, bicker. **-ing** jawing.

kjegle (mat) cone; (typograf.) shank, body. avskåret **—** truncated cone.

kjegle|dannet conical. **-snitt** conic sections, conics (pl).

kjekk brave, bold; (dt.) game; (amr)⁻stout.

kjekl wrangling.

kjekle wrangle, squabble.

kjeks biscuit.

kjelde spring, fountain; i fig. bet. se **kilde. kjeldevann** spring water.

kjeldevell fountain (-head), spring.

kjel(e) kettle; (vaske- el. brygger-, kopper-) copper; (stor) caldron; (damp-) boiler. **-flikker** tinker. **-formet** kettle-shaped.

kjelesmed boilersmith, boiler-maker.

kjelestein fur(-stone), (boiler) scale, incrustation.

kjelke little sledge, hand-sledge, hand-sleigh. **-bakke, -føre,** se **akebakke, -føre.**

kjeller cellar; (hvelvet) vault.

kjeller|etasje basement. **-hals** descent into a cellar. **-lem, -luke** trap-door of a cellar, cellar-flap. **-mester** butler; cellarman. **-rom** cellarage. **-trapp** cellar-stairs.

kjeltring scoundrel, villain. **-aktig** villainous, scoundrelly. **-pakk** a set of scoundrels. **-strek** villainy.

kjemi chemistry. **kjemikalier** chemicals, drysalteries, drugs.

kjemiker chemist.

kjemisk chemical.

kjemme comb.

kjempe (stort menneske) giant; (plante) waybread.

kjempe (vrb) fight, combat, contend, struggle; **— om prisen** contend for the prize; **— med seg selv** struggle with oneself; **— ut,** se **utkjempe; — seg fram** fight one's way; **de -nde** the combatants, the contending parties.

kjempe|arbeid gigantic el. Herculean work. **-bilde** colossal figure. **-kar** gigantic fellow. **-messig** gigantic, giantlike.

kjempe|skip monster ship. **-skikkelse** gigantic figure. **-slange** boa. **-slekt** race of giants. **-sterk** of gigantic strength. **-stor** gigantic. **-størrelse** gigantic size. **-vekst** gigantic stature. **-vise** ancient (Northern) ballad.

kjennbar knowable.

kjenne know; (dømme) judge, pass sentence; **lære en å —** make one's acquaintance; **— skyldig** find guilty; **— en av utseende, navn** know one by sight, name; **— en på røsten, gangen** know one by his voice, gait; **— til** know of el. about; **kjennes ved** acknowledge, own.

kjenne: gi seg til — make oneself known.

kjennelig recognizable (på: by); (merkbar) perceivable, perceptible, discernible.

kjennelse judgment, decision, award, finding, ruling; (jurys) verdict.

kjennemerke mark, sign, criterion.

kjenneord (gram) article.

kjenner judge, connoisseur. **-blikk, -mine** look, air of a connoisseur.

kjennetegn distinguishing mark, characteristic(s).

kjenning (mar) sight (of land); (bekjent) acquaintance.

kjennskap knowledge (til: of); acquaintance (til: with).

kjensel: dra — på know (again), recognize.

kjensfolk acquaintances, friends.

kjensgjerning fact.

kjensle feeling; sensibility.

kjent known, familiar; acquainted; **et — ansikt** a familiar face; **jeg er ikke — her i** don't know my way about here; **han er godt — i byen** he knows the town well. **-mann** man acquainted with the locality; (mar.) private pilot.

kjepp stick, cudgel; **som -er i hjul** like a house on fire. **-hest** hobby-horse, hobby.

kjepphøy arrogant, overbearing, big.

kjerke, se kirke.

kjerne (vrb) churn.

I. kjerne (smør-) churn.

II. kjerne (nøtt) kernel; (appelsin, eple) seed. pip; (celle; fig. første begynnelse) nucleus; (i en sak) substance, essence, pith, heart; (i en hær) flower, picked men; (det beste av noe) flower, pick.

kjernehus core.

kjernekar sturdy fellow.

kjernemelk butter-milk.

kjerne|ord pithy word. **-punkt** heart, essence. **-sunn** healthy. **-tropper** choice el. picked troops.

kjerning butter-making, churning.

kjerr (kratt) bush, shrubbery, brake.

kjerre small car; cart.

kjerring old woman, crone. **-ris,** se **dvergbjørk. -rokk** (bot.) horsetail.

kjerring|sladder, -snakk old woman's twaddle.

kjerte candle, taper.

kjertel gland. **-hevelse** glandular swelling. **-knute** indurated gland. **-svak, -syk** scrofulous. **-svulst** struma. **-syke** glandular disease, scrofula, king's-evil.

kjertesvein (gmlt) taper-bearer.

kjerub cherub.

kjerv(e) (subst) bundle, sheaf.

kjese (til ysting) cheese-lep, keslop.

kjette she-cat, tabby-cat.

kjetter heretic. **-bål** pile for burning heretics. **kjetteri** heresy. **kjettersk** heretical.

kjetting chain; (anker-) (chain-)cable.

kjeve jaw. **-bein** jaw-bone.

kjevle (subst) paste-roller, rolling-pin.

kjevle (vrb) roll (paste etc.).

kjole (damekjole) dress, frock, gown; (prestek.) gown; (herrek.) dress-coat; (til småbarn) frock; (til spebarn) long-clothes. **-liv** bodice.

kjolesøm dressmaking.

kjoletøy stuffs, dressfabric, dressmaterial.

kjone (tørkehus for korn) kiln, oast-house.

kjortel coat.

kjæle fondle, caress, pet.

kjælebarn, kjæledegge fondling, pet, darling.

kjælen fond, loving, affectionate.

kjælenavn pet name. **kjæling** caressing.

kjær dear; **-e!** (forundr.) dear me! (bønn) pray; **-e!** my dear **mine -e** my dear ones, those dear to me; **mitt -este** what is dearest to me; **inderlig — dearly beloved.**

kjæremål complaint, grievance; (anke) appeal. **forkaste -et** dismiss the appeal. **godkjenne -et** allow the appeal. **kjæremålsutvalg** judicial committee on appeals.

kjæreste fiancé(e), intended, lady-love; (i mer folkelig språk) sweetheart, young man; **de to -r** the two lovers. **-brev** love-letter. **-folk** lovers. **-sorg** love trouble.

kjærkommen welcome, acceptable.

kjærlig kind, affectionate; (adv) kindly.

kjærlighet love, affection; (sterk) passion; (menneske-) charity; (is. rel.) loving kindness, **tro, håp og — faith, hope and charity; kaste sin — på** bestow one's love upon; **ulykkelig i — crossed in love; gammel — ruster ikke** old love lies deep.

kjærlighets|brev love-letter. **-dikt** love-poem. **-erklæring** declaration of love. **-eventyr, -forhold** love-affair. **-forsikring** protestation of love. **-gjerning** act of charity. **-gud** God of Love. **-historie** love-affair; (fortelling) love-tale. **-pant** pledge of love.

kjærtegn caress, endearment. **-tegne** caress.

kjæte (subst) wantonness, wildness.

kjæte (vrb): **— seg** frolic.

Kjøbenhavn Copenhagen. **k-er** native of C.

kjød (i bibelske uttr.) flesh. Eks.: **Så lenge vi er i kjødet — so long as we soujourn in the flesh. Gå all kjødets gang — go the way of all flesh.**

kjødelig carnal, fleshly; **-e søsken** full brothers and sisters; **— bror til** own brother to; **— fetter** cousin-german; **— slektning** blood relation.

kjødelighet fleshliness, carnality.

kjødslyst (bibl.) carnal lust.

kjøe, se **aure.**

kjøkemester (i bondebryllup) master of the revels.

kjøkken kitchen; (mar) galley; (matens tillaging) cookery.

kjøkken|be-k dresser. **-forkle** kitchen apron. **-hage** kitchen el. vegetable garden. **-salt** common salt; kitchen-salt. **-sjef** (overkokk) chef. **-skriver** kitchen-hunter, mollycoddle. **-trapp** kitchen-stairs, back-stairs. **-tøy** kitchen utensils el. furniture.

kjøl keel; **på rett — on an even keel, righted; få på rett — right; komme på rett — right** itself; **med -en i været** bottom up-wards.

kjøle cool; **— sitt mot på vent** one's rage on; **-nde** cooling, refrigerant.

kjøledrikk cooler, cooling draught.

kjøler cooler, refrigerator; (i bil) radiator.

kjøle|rom refrigerator chamber. **-skap** refrigerator. **-vogn** refrigerator carriage el. car.

kjøl|hale (et skip) careen; (en mann) keelhaul. **-haling** careening; keelhauling.

kjølig cool; (svalende) cooling. **-het** coolness.

kjølmark wireworm.

kjølne cool, become cool.

kjøl|svin keelson. **-vann** wake. **-vannslinje** line ahead.

kjønn sex; (gram) gender; **det smukke —** the fair sex; **det sterke — the sterner (stronger) sex.**

kjønns|bøyning inflection denoting the gender of a word. **-drift** sexual desire el. impulse. **-endelse** termination of gender. **-forhold** sexuality. **-forskjell** difference of sex. **-lem** genital member. **-lig** sexual; (adv) sexually. **-liv** sexual functions. **-løs** sexless, asexual, neuter. **-løshet** absence of sexual characteristics. **-nytelse** sexual gratification. **-organer** sexual organs.

kjønrøk lampblack, pine-soot.

kjøp purchase; buying; (handel) det kjøpte eller solte) bargain; **slutte et — conclude a bargain; billig — a bargain; for godt — at** a cheap, reasonable rate; **det går med på -et** that is thrown in.

kjøpe buy, purchase (av: from, of) **— inn** buy el. lay in; **— opp** buy in; buy up; (en gros) engross; (forut) forestall, regrate; **— seg fri** buy oneself off.

kjøpe|kontrakt contract of purchase, purchase deed. **-lyst** inclination to buy; demand.

kjøper buyer, purchaser; **være — til** be in the market for.

kjøpesum purchase money.

kjøpetvang: uten — without any buying obligation.

kjøpmann merchant, trader; (detaljist) tradesman, shopkeeper.

kjøpmanns|stand mercantile class, the trade. **-ånd** mercantile spirit.

kjøpskål cup el. drink clinching a bargain.

kjøpslå bargain, make a bargain.

kjøpstad (market-) town; country-town, provincial town.

kjøpstads|privilegium, -rettighet(er) chartered privileges of a market-town.

kjør: i ett — at a stretch.

kjørbar available, practicable (for vehicles).

kjøre drive; (med tog el. l.) ride; **— en tur** take a ride in a carriage, a drive; **— en rundt** (fig) bewilder one; **— inn hester** break horses. **— inn en forsinkelse** make up for a delay. **—**

med fire hester drive four in hand; **— opp med** (fig) bring forward; **vil De kjøre med til . . .** may I offer you a lift to . . .; **— på** (dt.) go ahead; **— fortere** drive faster; **kjør på!** drive on!
kjøre|doning rig, trap, vehicle. **-kar** driver; carter. **-kort** driving licence, driver's licence; **kjørel** plate el. dish, vessel; (plur. kjørler) plates and dishes, pots and pans.
kjøreplan time-table.
kjører carman, carrier, carter, drayman, teamster, waggoner; coachman, driver.
kjøre|tur drive, ride. **-vei** carriage road; cart road.
kjørsel driving.
kjøter cur. **-aktig** currish.
kjøtt flesh; (som føde) meat; (på frukt) flesh, pulp.
kjøtt|bein bone with some meat on it. **-berg** mountain of flesh. **-bolle** force(d-)meat ball, resole. **-deig** forcemeat, mince-meat. **-ekstrakt** extract of meat. **-etende** carnivorous.
kjøtt|farse forced meat. **-full** fleshy; (slakt) meaty; (om frukt) pulpy. **-gryte** flesh-pot. **-hue** blockhead, numskull. **-kake** hashed-meat cake. **-kniv** cleaver. **-kvern** meat-cutter; sausage mill. **-mat** (flesh-)meat. **-meis** titmouse, tomtit. **-rett** dish of meat. **-suppe** soup. **-trevl** muscular fibre.
kjøve stifle, smother.
kl. fork. av **klokka**: o'clock; el. **klasse**: class, form.
klabbe (slå) beat, knock; **(— seg sammen)** cake solid, clog, clog together. **-føre** roads of balling, cloggy el. sticky snow.
kladas blotch, blur.
kladd rough-draught, foul copy. **-ebok** rough -book.
kladdeføre, se **klabbeføre**.
klaff leaf, flap; (på blåseinstrumenter) key; (ventil) valve.
klaffe (stemme) tally; **få alt til å — make** it all come right.
klaffebord folding table.
klage (vrb) complain (**over**: of, **til**: to); **-t sin nød for meg** disclosed his troubles to me.
klage (subst) complaint; (-skrik) lamentation; (jamring) wailing; **føre — over** complain of; **inngi en — mot en** lodge a complaint against one.
klage|brev criminatory letter. **-dikt** elegy. **-mål** complaint.
klagende dolorous, mournful, plaintive.
klagepunkt count, charge.
klager, **-ske** plaintiff, prosecutrix.
klage|sang elegy. **-skrift** written complaint.
klake (subst) lump of ice, frozen earth.
klaket frosted el. frozen.
klakk, **klakører** (pl) claque, claquers, hired applauders.
klam clammy, damp. **-het** dampness.
klamme(r) (typograf.) brackets.
klammeri altercation, quarrel.
klamp (kloss) block; clamp; (om foten) clog.
klampe (gå tungt) clamp, clump.
klamre seg til grasp, gripe, cling to.
klander fault-finding; reprimand rebuke.
klandre find fault with, rebuke.
klang sound, clang, ring, clink, chink; **navnet har en god — the name is very popular. -bunn** sound-board, sounding-board. **-farge** timbre, tone colour. **-figurer** sonorous figures. **-full** sonorous. **-fullhet** sonorousness. **-løs** soundless, dull-toned, husky. **-løshet** huskiness.
klapp tap; (bifallskl.) applause, clapping of hands; (i hjertet) valve.
klappe (i hendene) clap (one's hands), applaud; (som kjærtegn) pat, caress; **-t og klart** all ready, all right.
klapperslange rattlesnake.
klapp|jakt battue. **-myss** hooded seal, hoodcap.
klapp|salve round of applause. **-sete** flap-up seat. **-stol** folding camp-stool.

klapre clatter, rattle; (om tenner) chatter; **klapring** clattering etc.
klaps slap; (pl) a drubbing.
klapse slap, box one's ears.
klar clear; (lys, strålende) bright; (om vann) limpid; (vær, himmel) serene, bright; (tydelig) plain, evident; (mar) clear, ready; **en — kjole** a clear muslin; **han er — nå** he is ready now; **— til å vende** (mar) ready about; **gjøre -t skip** clear (a ship) for action: **være — over** have a clear understanding of el. that; **stod -t for meg** was clear before me.
klare (i skog) clearance, glade; (i is) clearing, lane.
klare (vrb) clear; (avklare) clarify; (kaffe) set; (grele) manage; **— seg**, **— biffen** hold one's own, pull through, find a way out of something, come right, manage.
klarere (vrb) clear; **— en gjeld** clear el. discharge a debt; **— en regning** settle an account.
klarering (merk) clearance.
klareskinn settling skin, fish-skin for settling coffee.
klarhet clearness; limpidity; plainness; (gjennomsiktighet) transparency.
klarhodet clear headed.
klarinett clarinet. **-blåser** performer on the clarinet.
klaring clearing, clearance.
klarsynthet clear-sightedness.
klarøyd bright-eyed.
klase cluster, bunch.
klask smack. **klaske** smack.
klasse class; (på skolen) form, class, (amr.: grade); **første -s** first-rate; **en første -s billett** a first class ticket; **sette i — med** class with. **klasse|hat** class-hatred. **-inndeling** classification. **-kamerat** class-mate, class-fellow. **-kamp** class-war. **-lotteri** lottery conducted on the class principle. **-lærer** form master, tutor. **-værelse** class room.
klassifisere classify, class.
klassifisering classification.
klassiker classic. **klassisisme** classicism. **klassisk** classic(al).
klatre climb; **— i trær** climb trees. **-fot** climbing foot. **-fugl** climbing bird. **-stang** climbing pole.
klatt (blekk-) blot; (smør-) pat; (klump) lump. **klatt|gjeld** petty debts, driblets. **-maling** daubery.
klausel clause.
klauv hoof. **-dyr** cloven-footed animal.
klauvsyke root-rot. **munn- og klauvsyke** the foot-and-mouth disease.
klave (cow's) collar.
klavér piano, forte-piano, piano-forte. **-skole** piano-forte primer. **-uttog** piano-forte arrangement.
klaviatur clavier, key-board.
kle(de) (vrb) clothe, dress; (passe) become, be becoming, sit well on; **det -r ikke** it is unbecoming, looks badly; **— seg** dress; **— av seg** undress, take off one's clothes; (helt) strip; **— av en til skjorta** strip one to the skin; **være kledd i** wear; **— seg om** change one's dress; **— på seg** dress, put on one's clothes; **— seg ut** disguise oneself, dress up.
klebe (vi) stick, cleave, adhere (**ved**: to); (vt) stick, paste; **— opp** paste.
kleberstein steatite, massive talc.
klebrig sticky, adhesive, viscous. **-het** stickiness, adhesiveness.
klede (stykke tøy til å dekke noe med) cloth; (stoffet) cloth, woollen cloth, broadcloth.
klede|bon garment, raiment. **-drakt** dress, apparel.
klede|handel cloth trade. **-handler** cloth trader.
klede|lig becoming, graceful. **-varer** cloths.
klegg breeze, cleg, gadfly, horsefly.
kleinsmed locksmith.

kleise, se **lespe**.

kleiv steep rocky ascent, rock passage, steep pass.

klekk yielding, weak.

klekke hatch. **-lig** considerable, sufficient, round. **-sted** hatching haunt el. place. **-tid** hatching season.

klem pinch; crush; squeeze; **på** — ajar; **med fynd og** — forcibly.

klematis clematis, virgin's bower.

klemme (subst) clip, pin; (klype) pinch, strait; (fig.) grip, hold; **sette i** — drive to bay, corner; **komme i** — get jammed; (fig.) get into a scrape.

klemme (vrb) squeeze, jam, pinch; — **på** press on, bestir oneself.

klemt toll. **-e** toll. **-ing** tolling.

klenge cling, stick. — **seg inn på** cling to, tag after. **-navn** nickname, sobriquet.

klenodie jewel, gem, treasure.

I. **klepp** (hake) gaff.

II. **klepp** (melklump) lump of flour.

kleppet lumpy.

kleptoman kleptomaniac. **-i** kleptomania.

kleresi clergy, priesthood.

klerikal clerical.

klerk priest.

kles|børste clothes-brush. **-kammer(s)** clothes closet. **-klype** clothesclip. **-kott**, se **-kammer(s)**. **-kurv** clothes-basket, laundry hamper. **-plagg** garment, article of dress el. clothing. **kles|skap** clothes-press, wardrobe. **-snor** clothes -line, clothes drying cord.

klett bluff, cliff.

kleve closet; (gmlt. soverom) cubicle.

kli bran. **-aktig** bran-like.

klient client. **klientel** clientage.

I. **klikk: slå** — miss fire, snap; (fig) fail.

I. **klikk** set, gang, clique.

klikke (vrb) miss fire, fail.

klikkvesen cliquism.

klima climate.

klimatfeber climate fever.

klimatisk climatic.

klimpre thrum, strum, twang.

klin (søl) dirt, slop, smear; (klissete kjærtegn) clinging caresses.

kline paste, smear; (kitte til) lute. — **til** dirty; — **seg inn til** stick close to, cling to.

kling (lefse-) buttered damper el. flap of bread.

klinge (subst) blade of a sword el. dirk; **den flate** — the flat of the blade.

kling|e (vrb) sound, jingle; **-ende** (fig) resounding, sonorous; **en -ende frost** a hard frost. med **-ende spill** with drums beating and trumpets sounding. **-ende mynt** hard cash, specie. **-k ang** dingdong; (ordklang) jingle of words, tuneful nonsense. **-re** jingle, tinkle, clink, chink.

klinikk clinic el. clinical hospital; (undervisning) clinic el. clinique.

klining (det å kline), se **klin**.

klining (lefse-), se **kling**.

kliniak clinic(al).

klinke (på dør) latch; (til porselen) rivet.

I. **klinke** (lodde) rivet.

II. **klinke** (med glassene) touch glasses (**med**: with).

III. **klinke** (spill) play at chuckfarthing. **-kule** alley-taw, marble.

klinte cockle.

klipe, se **klype**.

klipp clip, cut, snip.

klippe (subst) rock. full av **-r** rocky.

klippe (vrb) clip cut: — **håret** cut the hair; — **sauer** shear sheep; — **håret kort** crop the hair; — **en** cut one's hair.

klippe|blokk (block of) rock. **-fast** firm as a rock.

klippe|grunn rocky ground. **-kyst** rocky coast. **-maskin** clipper; shearing machine. **-spiss** pinnacle of rock. **-stykke** fragment of rock. **-vegg** wall of rock. **-øy** rocky island.

klippfisk split cod, klip-fish.

klipping cutting, clipping, crop.

klirr clash, clink, jingle, clank.

klirre clash, clink, jingle, clank.

kliss sticky mass, viscosity, sticky things.

klisse stick; (ikke snakke rent) lisp. **-t** greasy, smeary, sticky.

kliss|klass plashy, plish-plashy. **-våt** dabby, drenched.

klister paste. **-potte** paste bowl, paste pot.

klistre paste.

klitt (i Danmark) down.

klo claw; (en rovfugls) talon; (skrift) scrawl, fist; (mar) jaw, throat; **få klørne i** get into one's clutches; **slå -a i** clutch, grab, punch upon.

kloakk common sewer. **-innhold** sewage. **-rør** pipe-drain. **-anlegg** sewerage.

klode globe, sphere.

klok wise, prudent, judicious, clever, sagacious; **han er ikke riktig** — he is not quite in his senses; **jeg kan ikke bli** — **på det** I cannot make it out. I can make nothing of it; — **mann** cunning man; — **kone** cunning el. wise woman; **han var** — **hvis han . . .** he exercised sound judgment in -ing, was wise to.

klokk|e bell; (ur) clock, watch; (slagur) clock; **hva er -a?** what's the time? what time is it? what o'clock is it? **-a er tolv** it is twelve (o'clock); **-a er halv ett** it is half past twelve (o'clock); **-a er mange** it is late; **si hva -a er** tell the hour; **-a mangler fem minutter på fem** it is five minutes to five (o'clock); **-a er ikke mye over sju** it is not long gone seven; **-a fire at four o'clock; når -a er sju** by seven.

klokke|blomst bell-flower. **-bøye** bell-buoy. **-formet** bell-shaped. **-klang** sound of bells. **-kolv** tongue el. clapper of a bell. **-lyng** bellheather.

klokker sexton, bell-ringer, parish clerk.

klokke|reip bell-rope. **-ren** clear as a bell. **-ringing** chime, peal of bells.

klokke|slag stroke of a clock. **-slett** hour. **-spill** chime of bells. **-streng** bellrope. henge **i -strengen** be a slave to the hour. **-støper** bell-founder. **-støperi** bell-foundry. **-time** hour by the clock. **-tårn** steeple, bell-tower, campanile.

klokskap wisdom, prudence, cleverness, sagacity. **-shensyn** prudential motives.

klopp (rustic) footbridge; (is. av én planke) ligger.

I. **klor** chlorine.

I. **klor** (merke etter kloring) scratch; (amr.) claw.

kloral chloral.

klore scratch; (om skrift) scrawl.

klorkalk chloride of lime.

kloroform chloroform. **-ere** chloroform.

klorvann chlorine-water.

klosett water-closet, W. C.

kloss (subst) log, block, stock, stub, stump; (fig) bungler, simpleton, muff.

kloss (adv) close; — **opptil** quite close to; — **opp i vinden** jammed on the wind; closehauled.

klosset clumsy, awkward, left-handed.

klossrevet (med alle rev tatt in) close reefed.

kloster cloister, monastery, convent. abbey; (nonnekloster) nunnery; **gå i** — turn monk; take the veil.

kloster|bror friar. **-bygning** monastic building. **-gård** conventual yard. **-kirke** conventual church. **-liv** monastic el. conventual life. **-løfte** conventual el. monastic vows. **-regel** monastic rule.

klov, se **klauv**.

klovn clown, buffoon.

I. **klubb** (blod-) black pudding.

II. **klubb** (sluttet selskap) club.

klubbe (subst) mallet; (wooden) mall; pounder; **club**.

klubbe (slå med k.) club.
klubb|lokale club-house. **-vert** club-steward.
kludder bungling.
kludre bungle.
klukk cluck el. clucking of a hen. **klukke** cluck. **klukklatter** chuckle. **klukkle** chuckle.
klump lump, clump; (jord-) clod; **l — in a** cluster, clustered. **klumpe seg** clot.
klumpet lumpy, clotted.
klump|fot club-foot. **-sukker** crushed loaf-sugar, lumps, crushed.
klumse strike mute, spell-bind, fascinate.
klunger bramble, brier; **-kjerr** bramble-bush; **-rose** dog-rose.
klunk (av noe flytende) guggle, gurgle, clunk; (tiur-) call; (på instrument) strum, strumming.
klunke gurgle, guggle, cluck; call; strum.
kluss trouble, ado; fuss; blur.
klusse blur; **— med** tamper with, meddle with; fuss about.
klut rag, clout; **hver eneste — (mar)** every stitch of canvas, every rag.
klutepapir ragmade paper.
klynge (subst) cluster, group, knot. **klynge** (vrb): **— seg til** cling to.
klynk whimper, whine.
klynke whimper, whine. **klynking** whimpering etc.
klyp nip, pinch.
klype (subst) clip; (f. eks. av snus) pinch.
klype (vrb) nip, pinch.
klyse clot.
klyss (hull til ankerkjettingen) hawse, hawse-hole. **-tre** hawse-plug.
klystér clyster, injection, enema.
klystérsprøyte syringe.
klyve clamber, climb.
klyveled stile.
klyver (standing) jib. **-bardun** jib-guy.
klær clothes, garments, wearables; dt. clothing; **— skaper folk** fine feathers make fine birds, the tailor makes the man; **med -ne på** with his clothes on, in his clothes; **i fulle —** fully dressed; **jeg har ikke vært av -ne på . . .** I have not had my clothes off for . . .
klø (vt) scratch, claw; (vi) itch; **— seg i hodet** scratch one's head; **— seg bak øret** scratch one's ears; **jeg -r i fingrene etter å** my fingers itch to; I have an itching desire to.
kløing itch, itching.
kløft cleft, chink, crack, crevice, rift, canny, fissure; (i haken) dimple. **-et** cleft, cloven.
klokk, se **klekk.**
kløkt shrewdness, sagacity, cleverness. **-tig** shrewd, clever, sagacious.
kløne blockhead, blunderer; **klønet** awkward, clumsy.
klør fl. av **klo.**
kløv pack, pack for a horse, pack-load.
kløve pack on horseback, pack.
I. **kløver** (i kortspill) clubs; **en — a club; — ess, to, tre** osv. the ace, deuce, three etc. of clubs; **— konge, dame, knekt** the king, queen, knave of clubs.
II. **kløver** (plante) clover, trefoil. **-blad** clover leaf. **-eng** clover field.
kløv|hest pack-horse. **-meis** pannier. **-sal** pack-saddle, pair of panniers.
kløyve cleave, split.
klå, se **klø;** (fig) pitch into, give it (one).
klåfinger fingerer; (fig) meddler.
kna knead, work.
knabb knoll.
knabbe (ta uten lov) grab, snatch.
knagg peg. **-rekke** rack.
knake creak, groan. **knaking** creaking.
knakke (banke) beat, knock.
knakkpølse smoked sausage.
knall report, explosion, crack.
knallbongbong cracker.
knalleffekt clap-trap; grand effect.

knallhette percussion-cap, copper-cap, detonating cap.
knallperle detonating bomb; percussion cap.
knapp (adj) scant, scanty, short; **det er knapt med penger, egg** osv. money is scarce, eggs are scarce, there is a scarcity of money etc.
knapp (subst) (i klær) button, (løs til snipp etc.) stud; (på sal) pommel; (mar) truck; **telle på -ene** count the buttons.
I. **knappe** button; **— igjen** button up; **— opp** un-button.
II. **knappe: — av l, av på** stint, curtail.
knappenål pin; **en kunne nesten høre en — falle** one might almost hear the falling of a pin. **knappenåls|brev** a paper of pins. **-hode** head of a pin. **-stikk** the prick of a pin.
knapphet scantiness, straitness; stinginess, closeness.
knapphull button-hole.
knapt (adv) barely, scantily.
knark crabbed fellow, fogey.
knart (fjell-), se **knatt.**
knas: gå l — go to shivers.
knase crackle, scrunch. **knaske** scrunch.
knastørr dry as a bone.
knatt (fjell-) crag.
knaus crag, rock.
kne knee; (ledd) joint; (mar) knee; **falle på — fall,** go el. drop (down) on one's knees; **komme på knærne** be reduced in one's circumstances; **på —!** down on your knees! **bøye — for** bow the knee to el. before.
knebel gag.
knebelsbart mustachio.
kneble gag.
knebukser breeches, knee-shorts; (moderne, vide og side) knicker-bockers.
knebøyning bending of the knee, genuflection.
kne|dyp knee-deep. **-fall** kneeling, genuflection; (plass foran alter) communion-rails.
knegge neigh, whinny; (le) cackle.
kne|gå knuckle one's knees along another's ribs. **-høy** knee-high, up to the knee-joint. **-høne** (feiging) weak-kneed person, jellyfish, weakling.
kneik small slope (in a road).
kneipe public-house, tavern. **-vert** keeper of a tavern.
kneise strut, carry the head high.
kneken close, close-fisted, mean.
I. **knekk** crack, snap; (brudd) break, crack, snap; (ledd, bøyning) abrupt bend, elbow, joint; (fig) injury, shock. **han har fått et — for livet** his health has received a shock, is broken.
II. **knekk** (kokt sirup og sukker) lollipop, lolly.
knekke crack, snap, spring, break; **— en nøtt** crack a nut; **— nakken** break the neck.
knekkebrød clap-bread, frame food-bread.
knekt fellow, chap; (i kort) knave; (skjells-ord) rogue.
knele kneel.
kneledd knee-joint.
knep (fiff) trick, artifice.
knepen, se **knapp: en — majoritet** a narrow majority.
knepp click.
kneppe click; (om tiur) click; **— på en fele-streng** strum a fiddle-string; **— av** (om fotograf) snap.
knepping clicking.
I. **knert: en liten —** nipper, little shaver.
II. **knert** (lett slag) slight knock.
knerte (slå lett) flick; (hogge) chop; (skyte) pop.
kne|sette adopt. **-skade** a bad knee. **-skjel** knee-pan, knee-cap. **-varmer** knee-cap.
kniks courtesy; **— e** drop a courtesy.
knip pinch, squeeze; **— i magen** gripes (pl); griping pains.
knipe (subst) pinch, dilemma, hobble, scrape; **komme i —** get into a scrape.

knipe (vrb) pinch, nip; (spare) spare, pinch; (stjele) purloin; **nå -r det!** now for a push! now comes the tug of war! **når det -r** at a pinch; **det knep!** that was a hard rub, a close shave; **det -r for ham** he is out, hard up; — **seg igjennom** slink through; — **på** be sparing of.
knipen med sparing of.
kniperi stinginess.
knipe|tak pinch, scrape. **-tang** tweezers, pliers.
kniple make lace. **-pinne** bobbin, bone. **-pute** lace-maker's cushion.
knipling (det å kniple) lace-making. **-er** lace.
kniplingsbesetning lace trimming.
kniplingskrage lace collar.
knippe bunch; bundle.
knips snap, crack; (med fingrene) (finger-) fillip; **gi en et** — **på nesa** give one a fillip on the nose.
knipse snap one's fingers (**til:** at).
knipsk prudish, pert. **-het** prudery, pertness.
knirke creak; (skurre, irritere) jar. **knirking** creaking creak; (fig) jar, hitch.
knis giggling, giggle, snicker, titter.
knise giggle, snicker, titter.
knistre (om hund) whine.
knitre crackle. **knitring** crackling.
kniv knife; **ha -en på strupen** have the halter round one's neck; **krig på -en** war to the knife.
knivsblad blade of a knife.
kniv|skaft handle of a knife. **-smed** cutler. **-spiss** point of a knife. **-stikk** knife-thrust.
knok(e) knuckle; (ben) bone.
knokkel bone. **-mannen** the king of terrors.
knoklet bony.
knoll knoll; (jord) clod; (botanikk) tuber; **knollet** tuberous.
knop (på logglina) knot; **vi gjør 7** — she makes seven knots; **et dampskip som gjør 7** — a steamer, speed 7 knots. **-e** knot; make knots.
knopp (lauv- el. blomster-) bud; **skyte -er** be in bud, put forth buds. **-e seg** bud. **-et** budding.
knopp|skjell raments. **-skyting** budding; (formering ved —) gemmation. **-urt** bull-weed, centaury.
knort knot, gnarl, knag.
knortekjepp knotty el. ragged stick.
knortet knotty.
knot affectation in speaking, fine speaking.
knote affect fine speaking, speak finely or mincingly, mince.
I. **knott** button, knob.
II. **knott** (insekt) sandfly, midge.
knubb (kubbe) log, block; **knubbet** knotty. **knubb|ord** hard el. sharp words. **-ved** log-ends.
knudret rugged; (stil) ungraceful.
knuge press, squeeze; **bli -t av** be oppressed with; — **hjertet sammen på en** wring one's heart.
knugende oppressive; distressing, heart-sickening.
knurr growl, snarl.; (fig) murmur, grumbling; (fisk) gurnard.
knurre growl, snarl.; (fig) murmur, grumble.
knurrhår whiskers (pl).
knurring growling, snarl, murmuring, grumble.
knuse crush, smash; break; (smått) bruise; **det -r mitt hjerte** it breaks my heart; **med knust hjerte** with a broken heart.
knusemaskin crusher, crushing mill.
knusende crushing. **et** — **slag** a crushing blow, a knock-out blow. **det var ham** — **likegyldig** he was profoundly (el. serenely) indifferent.
knuseverk crushing mill.
knusk amadou, black match, tinder, spunk. **-tørr** ash dry, bone dry.
knusle play the niggard. **-ri** niggardliness, meanness. **-t** niggardly, mean.
knuspe (knase mellom tennene) craunch, crunch.
knussel, se knusleri.

Knut Canute.
knute knot; (utvekst) bump, protuberance; **slå en** — tie a knot; **hogge -n over** cut the (Gordian) knot; **det kom en** — **på tråden** quarrelled; **det er -n** there is the rub, there lies the issue.
knutepunkt (på jernbane) junction.
knutt knout. **-e** knout.
kny (subst) slightest sound; **han gav ikke et** — not the slightest sound escaped him.
kny (vrb) breathe a word; **uten å** — without a murmur.
knyst bunion.
knyte tie. — **opp** untie, undo.
knytte, se knyte (binde, filere) knot, net; (fig) attach, bind, tie; — **en forbindelse** establish a connection; — **neven** clench the fist; — **neven til en** shake one's fist at one; — **forventninger til** form expectations of; — **en samtale med** begin a conversation with; — **seg til** attach oneself to, associate with; **der -r seg en viss interesse til** some interest attaches to; **hans navn er -t til** his name is identified el. associated with; **det -r seg en historie til dette** hereby hangs a tale.
knytte (subst) bundle.
knytteneve clenched fist, doubled-up hand.
knær fl. av **kne.**
knø, se kna.
koagulere coagulate.
koalisjon coalition.
kobbe seal.
kobbel collar, couplings; (dyr) leash; **et** — **hunder** a leash (tre) el. couple (to) of hounds.
kobber, se kopper.
kobbung(e) bottle-whelk.
koble, se kople. -t (bot) digitate.
kobler pander. **-i** (rufferi) pandering. **-ske** panderess.
kobolt cobalt.
I. **kode** (i telegrafering) code, cable-code.
II. **kode** (ankelbein på hest) pastern.
kodeks codex.
kodetelegram code-telegram.
kodi|fikasjon codification. **-fisere** codify.
kodilje: hele -n the whole lot.
kodisill codicil.
koeffisient co-efficient.
koff (mar.) koff; (i biljard) massé, massé-shot.
koffardi|fart merchant service; navigation. **fare i** — be in the merchant service. **-kaptein** captain el. master of a merchantman, merchant-captain. **-skip** merchantman, trader.
koffert trunk, box; (mindre) portmanteau. bag.
kofte, se kufte.
kogger (til piler) quiver.
kogle (trylle) juggle, charm.
kogleri jugglery, hocus-pocus.
kohe|rens coherence. **-sjon** cohesion.
koie shanty, sheeling.
kok boiling, boiling state; **være i** — be boiling ; **gå av** — cease el. have done boiling, be off the boil; **i** — boiling, on the boil.
kokain cocaine.
kokarde cockade.
koke boil; (syde) seethe; (lage mat i alm.) cook; — **for mye** overdo; — **for lite** underdo; **det kokte i meg** my blood boiled (within me); — **opp igjen** reboil; — **over** boil over.
koke|apparat cooking apparatus. **-bok** cookery book; **det var ikke etter min** — I did not very much relish it. **-kar** cooking vessel. **-kone** (female) cook, professional cook. **-kunst** (art of) cookery, culinary art. **-kunstner** master of the culinary art. **-plate** hot-plate. **-punkt** boiling point. **-ri** boilery. **-stell** cooking things.
kokett coquettish.
kokette coquette, flirt; f. eks. she was not a flirt, not even a coquette, but she was dangerous.

kokettere coquet, flirt.
koketteri coquetry, flirtation.
kokhet boiling hot; (dt.) piping hot.
kokk cook, man-cook; (overkokk) chef; **hunger er den beste** — hunger is the best sauce.
kokke, se **kokkejente.**
kokkegutt cook's boy, scullion.
kokkejente cook, cook-maid. **-kone** hired cook. **-pike,** se **-jente.**
kok|ning boiling; cooking. **nok kaffe til to -er** coffee enough for two kettle uls.
kokong cocoon.
kokos|kjerner (tørrede) cobra, copra. **-nøtt** cocoa-nut. **-nøttolje** cocoa-nut oil. **-palme, -tre** cocoa (-tree).
koksalt common salt, kitchen salt.
kol, se **kull.**
kolbe (på gevær) butt-end; (artilleri) head; (kjemi) cucurbit, retort; (botan.) spadix.
kolbrenner charcoal burner.
koldbrann gangrene, mortification, sphacelus; **det går — i såret** the wound gangrenes.
koldfeber ague.
koldkrem cold cream.
koldsindig cool, calm.
koldsindighet coolness, calmness.
kole (tranlampe) train-oil lamp.
kolera (the) cholera. **-artet** choleriform, choleraic. **-basil** cholera bacillus. **-epidemi** c. epidemic. **-flue** thrips. **-smittet** infected by cholera. **-tilfelle** case of cholera.
koleriker choleric man.
kolerine cholerine, British cholera.
kolerisk choleric.
kolibri colibri, humming-bird.
kolikk colic, gripes.
kolje (fisk) haddock.
koll knoll, rounded mountain top.
kollasjon collation. **-ere** collate. **-ering** collation.
kollbøtte somerset; **slå -r** cut somersets; tumble (head-over-heels).
I. **kolle** (trekar) wooden (milk)pan.
II. **kolle** female animal without horns; (om ku) humble-cow.
kolle|ga colleague, brother official. **-gial** brotherly.
kollegiemedlem collegian, collegiate.
kollegium college; (samfunn av embetsmenn) council, board, (akademisk k.) senate of a university.
kolleksjon (samling) collection.
kollekt (bønn) collect; (innsamling) congregational collection.
kollektiv (adj) collective. **kollektiv** (subst) collective noun.
kollektør collector.
koller (hestesykdom) the staggers.
kollet(e) hornless; (amr) muly.
kolli (pl. av **kollo**) packages, parcels, pieces (of luggage).
kollidere collide, clash, interfere.
kollisjon collision, clashing; **komme i — med** come in collision with.
kollodium collodion.
koll|segle, -seile capsize, be upset.
kolmile charcoal kiln.
kolon colon.
koloni colony, settlement. **handel m. -ene** colonial trade. **minister for -ene** colonial secretary. **-al** colonial.
kolonial|forretning business in colonial goods. **-handel** grocery trade. **-handler** grocer. **-varer** (articles of) colonial produce, grocery (goods); (amr) groceries.
kolonihage allotment.
koloniregjering colonial government.
koloni|sasjon colonization. **-sere** colonize, settle. **-st** colonist, settler.
kolonnade colonnade.
kolonne column.

koloratur colorature. **-sang** passage singing. **-sanger(inne)** passage singer.
kolorere colour.
kolorist colourist.
koloritt colouring.
koloss colossus. **-al** colossal.
kolport|asje colportage. **-ere** distribute by colporteurs. **colpor. -or** colporter, colporteur.
kolsvart coal black, jet black.
kolumne column. **-titel** running title, heading, head line, catch-title.
kolv clapper, tongue.
kombattanter combatants.
kombin|asjon combination. **-asjonsevne** synthetical faculty. **-asjonslås** combination lock. **-ere** combine. **-ering** combining, combination.
komed, ant actor, player.
komedie comedy, play; **spille** — act, play, perform; **det er bare en** — (om en skikk el. l.) it is a conventional humbug; **det er en ren** — it is a farce, it is as good as a play. **-spill** acting.
komet comet. **-bane** comet's orbit. **-hale** comet's tail. **-kjerne** comet's nucleus.
komfort comfort. **-abel** comfortable.
komfyr kitchen-range, kitchener.
komiker comic actor; (i operaen) buffo; (i sirkus o. l.) funnyman.
komikk comic art.
komisk comic, comical.
komité committee; **sitte i -en** be on the c. **-behandling** consideration in committee (av: on). **-formann** chairman of c.
komma comma. **-feil** error in punctuation.
kommag, se **finnsko.**
komman|dant commandant, governor. **-dantskap** governorship; governor. **-dere** order; (-over) command, be in charge of; **den -derende officer** the commanding officer, the o. in charge; **-derende admiral** commander-in-chief, the admiral in command. **-dersersjant** sergeant major.
kommandittselskap limited liability company.
kommando (en) command; (kommandoord) word of command; **ha -en, føre** — be in command; **heise -en på** (et skip) put (a ship) in commission; **stryke -en** put (a ship) out of commission.
kommando|bru captain's bridge. **-ord** word of command, command. **-stav** baton.
kommandør captain; (amr) commodore (dette er i England en midlertidig titel som overgang til rear-admiral); (av ridderorden) commander (of an order).
kommatere punctuate with commas.
komme come; **nå -r turen til meg** now is my turn; **nå -r det an på hva han vil gjøre** now it depends on what he will do; **det -r an på deg** it rests with you; **det -r an på** it depends, that depends; **kom an!** come on! — av (grunnen) come off; **det -r av it** comes of, is from; **hva -r dette av?** why is this? — av sted get away; — bort fra saken wander, digress, travel out of the record; — bort til come up to; -etter (for å hente) noe — come for st.; — etter sannheten get to the truth of the affair; — etter (adv) med neste tog come on by the next train; la saken — for dommeren bring the case before the magistrate; — forbi come el. pass by; — fore (om en sak) come on; — fra hverandre part company; — vel, dårlig fra det get off well, ill; 8 fra 13 -r 5 8 from 13 leaves 5; — fram get on; (i verden) rise (in the world), make one's way; — fram av, fra emerge from; — fram med produce, bring forward, advance; — i fare, dårlig selskap osv. get into danger, into bad company etc.; — i et hus visit at a house; — i forbindelse med form a connection with, get associated with; — i slagsmål fall a fighting, come to blows; — i veien for en cross one; — igjen come back, return; jeg skal — igjen an annen gang I shall call again; det -r igjen it'll pay in good time; — inn på et spørsmål trench on a

question; — **inn under en lov** come within the danger of a statute; — **med** come along (with me, us, them etc.); **med det –r du ikke langt** you'll make no great way with that; — **opp mot** compare, bear comparison with; — **på** happen, come to pass; (pris) come to; **natta kom på** night came on; **jeg kan ikke — på navnet** I cannot hit upon the name; **hvordan kom De på det innfallet?** what put that into your head? — **på tale** be mentioned; — **til noe** get at el. reach a thing, (få) come by a thing; — **til krefter** recover strength; — **til en slutning** arrive at a conclusion; **det var nå –t til det at** matters had now arrived at such a pass that; **hertil –r** at besides, moreover, add to this that; — **til å** (tilfeldig) happen to; **hvis jeg skulle — til noe** if anything should happen to me; **la det — til prosess** go to law; **det –r til å koste, beløpe seg til** osv. it will cost, amount to etc.; **jeg –r til å gjøre det** I shall have to do it; **han vil — til å angre det** he will repent of it; — **til seg selv** come to oneself, recover one's senses, come to; — **ut** (om bok) be published; — **ut av** get out of, (fig) find out of, make anything of, get over, get on with; — **ut av det** (m. inntekter) make both ends meet; **det kom ingenting ut av det** nothing came of it; — **ut av det med en** get on with one; **det er –t ut blant folk** it has got abroad, got wind; — **mye ut blant folk** go much into company, mix much with the world; **det –r ut på ett** it is all one, it comes to the same (thing); — **ved** concern, regard; **det –r ikke saken ved** that is nothing to the purpose; **det –r ikke meg ved** it is no business of mine; **hva –r det meg ved?** what is that to me? what has this to do with me? — **seg** improve, be improving; (trives) thrive; — **seg av sine sår** recover of one's wounds; **han –r seg godt** he is improving (in health el. circumstances); — **seg av en sykdom** recover from an illness.

komme (subst) coming, advent.
kommende coming, next; **i — dager** in the days to come; — **slekter** after ages; **de — og gående** comers and goers.
kommensurabel commensurable.
kommentar commentary, comment.
kommentere comment on.
kommers a row, a lark; være på — be on the spree.
kommersiell commercial.
kommis (medhjelper) assistant, clerk.
kommisariat commissariat.
kommisjon commission; (nevnd) board; **i —** in commission; **gi en i — charge** one with, order one to; **jeg har i — å** I am ordered to; **sende i —** consign; **pr. —** on commission.
kommisjons|gebyr commission. **-handel** (general) commission business. **-lager, -varer** goods in commission.
kommisjonær commissioner, (commission-)agent, factor.
komissær commissary, commissioner.
kommittent committer.
kommode chest of drawers; (amr) bureau.
kommunal civic, local, parochial; (i by) municipal. **– skole** board school, communal school. **-e skatter** local taxation, town el. parish rates, local burdens.
kommunal|forvaltning local government. **-vesen** municipal institutions.
kommune community, corporation, local body, municipal body el. corporation, municipality; (amr.) township; (i Frankrike) commune.
kommune|hospital municipal hospital. **-lokale** municipal hall, town hall. **-lege** city medical officer. **-skatt** local (municipal, parish, town) rate el. tax. **-styre** city el. town council. **-styremedlem** city councillor.
kommunikant communicant.
kommunikasjon communication.
kommunikasjonsmidler means of transit el. intercourse.

kommuniké communiqué, official intimation.
kommunion, se altergang.
kommunisere communicate, impart; (gå til alters) go to communion, partake of the Lord's supper.
kommunisme communism.
kommunist communist.
kommunistisk communistic.
kompakt compact, solid, dense.
kompan fellow, customer.
kompani (avdeling soldater) company; (handels-) company, partnership, copartnership; **være i — med** be partners with; **gå i — med** enter into partnership with, go partners with.
kompanisjef chief of company, captain.
kompaniskap partnership.
kompanjong partner; **oppta som — i forretningen** admit as a partner in the business, take into partnership; **passiv —** sleeping partner.
kompar|asjon comparison. **-ativ** (adj) comparative. **-ativ** (subst) the comparative (degree).
komparere compare.
kompass compass, mariner's compass. **-nål** needle. **-rose** compass-card. **-strek** point of the compass.
kompensasjon compensation.
kompet|anse competence. **-ent** competent.
kompil|asjon compilation. **-ator** compiler. **-ere** compile.
kompleks (subst) collection, mass; (av bygninger) block; (psykologisk) complex. **kompleks** (adj) complex.
komplement complement.
komplett complete; **i — stand** (when) complete. **-ere** fill up, complete. **-ering** completion.
kompliment compliment; **jeg gjør ingen –er** I do not make much ceremony, do not stand upon ceremony; **uten –er** unceremoniously. **-ere** pay one's respects to.
kompli|kasjon complication. **-sere** complicate. **-sert** complex, complicated.
komplott plot, conspiracy, combination.
kompo|nere compose. **-nist** composer. **-sisjon** composition.
komposisjons|lære (art of) composition. **-talent** talent for composition; (om forfatter) constructive skill el. power. **kompositum** compound (word).
kompost compost.
kompott compote, stewed fruit.
kompress compress, bolster.
komprim|ere compress. **-ert luft** compressed air.
kompromiss compromise. **-forslag** suggestion for a compromise.
komse Lapp cradle.
komtesse earl's daughter. — **N. N.** Lady N. N.
kondensator condenser.
kondens|ere condense. **-ering** condensation.
kondisjon (vilkår) condition, term; (tilstand) condition; (tjeneste) place, service.
konditor confectioner. **-i** confectioner's shop **-varer** confectionery.
kondol|anse condolence. **-ere** condole with.
kondor (slags gribb) condor.
konduite management, judgment, wisdom. **-messig** judicious, prudent, skilful. **-sak** matte left to individual judgement.
konduktor (elektrisk leder) conductor.
konduktør guard; (amr) conductor.
kone (hustru) wife; (kvinne) woman; **en gift — a** married woman; — **i huset** mistress of the house; **ta seg en —** take a wife; **ta til —** take for one's wife.
konebåt boat pulled by women.
konfeksjon ready-made dresses. **konfeksjons|forretning** ready-made clothes shop. **-handler** merchant tailor.
konfekt comfit, confect, confectionery; dry, hard) sweet-meats; (amr) candy; **grov — (**fig) rough treatment.

konfer|anse conference, parley. **–ere** confer; (sammenligne) compare, check.

konfesjon confession, creed. **konfesjonsløs** nonsectarian.

konfidensiel|l confidential; **må behandles strengt –t** must be treated in absolute confidence.

konfirm|ant candidate for confirmation. **–a-sjon** confirmation; (bekreftelse) ratification. **–asjonsattest** certificate of confirmation.

konfirmere confirm; (bekrefte) ratify.

konfisk|asjon confiscation, seizure, forfeiture, arrest. **–ere** confiscate, seize, arrest.

konflikt conflict, collision.

konform conform.

konfront|asjon confrontation. **–ere** confront.

kon|fus confused. **–fusjon** confusion.

konføder|asjon confederation, confederacy. **–ert** confederate.

kong (byll) furnucle.

kong, (foran navn), se **konge.**

konge king. **–brev** letters patent; (til ekteskap) marriage license. **–dømme** royalty, monarchy; (rike) kingdom; **–dømme av Guds nåde** divine right. **–flagg** royal standard. **–krone** royal crown. **–kroning** coronation of a king. **–kåpe** royal mantle.

kongelig royal, regal, kingly; **det –e hus, de –e** the Royal Family; **i –e personers nærvær** in the presence of royalty. **–sinnet** royalist.

konge|losje royal box. **–lys** (bot.) high taper, Aaron's rod. **–makt** royal el. regal power. **–makten** (ogs.) the prerogative of the Crown. **–mord** regicide. **–morder** regicide.

konge|par royal couple. **–rekke** line of kings, list of kings. **–rike** kingdom, realm; **–t Norge** the kingdom of Norway.

konge|røkelse incense. **–stamme** royal race el. lineage. **–stol** royal seat. **–tiger** royal tiger. **–titel** royal title. **–vei** (king's) highway. **–venn** royalist.

kongeverdighet royal dignity, royalty.

kongeørn golden eagle, imperial eagle.

kongle (på nåletrær) cone, strobile.

konglomerat conglomerate.

kongress congress.

kongru|ens congruity. **–ent** congruent.

kongs|emne heir to the crown; (som gjør fordring på kronen) pretender, claimant. **Kongsemnerne** (Ibsen) The Pretenders. **–gård** King's court, royal castle el. palace.

konisk conical.

konjakk cognac, French brandy, brandy.

konjektur conjecture.

konjugasjon conjugation. **konjugere** conjugate.

konjunksjon conjunction.

konjunktiv the subjunctive mood.

konjunktur conjuncture; state of affairs at particular moment, state of the market.

konk (jargon for **konkurs**).

konkav (buet innover) concave.

konkludere conclude, wind up.

konklusjon conclusion.

konkret concrete.

konkubi|nat concubinage. **–ne** concubine.

konkur|ranse competition. **–rent** competitor.

konkurrere compete (med: with, om: for). **–nde** competitive. **–nde foretagende** opposition enterprise.

konkurs failure; **gå –** fail, file one's balance-sheet; go into bankruptcy; **–behandling** bankruptcy-proceedings. **være under –** be in bankruptcy. **–bo** insolvent estate. **–lov** Insolvent Act, act of bankruptcy.

konkylie shell.

konossement bill of lading (forkortet: B|L); **– over, på** B|L for; **gjennomgående –** through B|L.

konsekvens consistency; consequence.

konsekvent consistent.

konsentrasjon concentration.

konsentrere concentrate; **– seg** concentrate oneself, limit oneself; **– seg om** centre in, be centred in. **konsentrering** concentration.

konsept rough draught, foul copy; **bringe ut av –ene** confound, disconcert, nonplus; **gå fra –ene** be disconcerted, put out, lose one's head.

konseptpapir copy(-paper).

konsert concert; (musikkstykke) concerto; **jeg skal på –** I am going to a concert. **–flygel** concert grand. **–sal** concert-hall.

konservatisme conservatism.

konservativ conservative.

konservator keeper.

konservatorium conservatory.

konserver conserves.

konservere keep, preserve.

konservering preservation.

konsesjon concession, contract, franchise. **konsesjonshaver** concessionaire, contractor.

konsignant consignor.

konsignasjon consignment; **varer i –** consignment(s); **motta varer i –** receive goods by c. **–sforretning** business on consignment.

konsignatar consignee.

konsignere consign.

konsil council.

konsipere draw up, draft, pen.

konsipist penner, writer, draftsman.

konsis concise.

konsistens consistency.

konsolide|re consolidate. **–ring** consolidation.

konsoll console, bracket.

konsonant consonant. **–fordobling** consonant doubling. **–isk** consonantal.

konsort|er compeers. **–ium** partnership.

konspirere conspire.

konstabel policeman; (gmlt. og mar.) gunner.

konstant invariable, constant.

Konstantinopel Constantinople.

konstatere ascertain; state; record.

konstellasjon constellation.

konstern|asjon consternation. **–ert** dismayed, stupefied.

konstitu|ere depute. **–ert** deputy, acting. **–sjon** constitution. **–sjonell** constitutional.

konstru|ere construct; (gram) construe. **–ksjon** construction; structure. **–ktør** constructor.

konsul consul. **konsularagent** consular agent.

konsulat consulate, consulship. **–avgift** consulage. **–gebyrer** consular fees. **–sertifikat** consular certificate. **–vesen** consular service el. system.

konsulent counsellor, adviser, referee; **juridisk –** legal adviser.

konsulere consult.

konsultasjon consultation. **–stid** office hours.

konsum consumption. **–ent** consumer.

konsumere consume.

kont (never-) tall bark bag or basket.

kontakt contact, touch; (elektr.) switch.

kontant in (ready) money, in cash, money down; (dt.) in pocket; **pr. –** for cash; in ready money; **–er** ready money, cash; **han betalte alt –** he paid for everything in cash down. **–beholdning** cash in hand; (statskassens) balance(s) in Exchequer, Exchequer balance. **– betaling** immediate cash; **– utlegg** money disbursed, out-of-pocket.

kontenanse, se **fatning.**

kontinent continent. **–al** continental.

kontingent contingent; subscription.

konto account; **åpne en – i en bank** open an account with a bank; **skrive på ens –** put down to one's account; **à –** on account.

kontokurant account current.

kontor office; (handels-) counting-house; (amr) bureau.

kontordame girl, lady el. woman clerk.

kontorist clerk.

kontormann business man.

kontor|personale office clerks. **–post** a situation as a clerk; clerkship. **–sjef** head el. chief of an office, chief el. secretary of a department, managing clerk. **–stol** office-stool. **–tid** office

hours, hours of attendance. **-utgifter** office expenses.
kontra versus; **pro og** — pro and con. **-alt** contralto. **-bande** contraband. **-bass** double-bass. **-bok** pass-book.
kontrahent contractor.
kontrahere contract.
kontrainnlegg counter plea, replication.
kontraklage counter-charge.
kontrakt contract; **bestride en** — dispute a contract; **slutte** — make a contract, enter into a contract.
kontraktbrudd breach el. violation of contract.
kontraktmessig stipulated by contract.
kontraktsvilkår terms of the contract.
kontra|ordre counter-order. **-part** adversary, opponent. **-prøve** counter-verification. **-punkt** counter-point. **-signere** countersign.
kontrast contrast. **-ere** contrast.
kontrasøksmål cross-action, counter suit.
kontravisitt return call.
kontre–admiral Rear-Admiral.
kontroll supervision, control. **-ere** check, verify, test. **-ering** checking etc. **-komité** inspecting committee.
kontrollur time recorder.
kontrollør controller, check-clerk; (i teatret) box-keeper, stall-keeper.
kontrovers controversy.
kontubernal room mate, chum.
kontur outline, contour.
kontusjon contusion, bruise.
konvall lily of the valley.
konveks (hvelvet utover) convex.
konven|ere suit, be convenient to, suit one's convenience. **-iens** convenience, propriety. **-iensgiftermål** marriage of convenience.
konvensjon (overenskomst; skikk og bruk) convention.
konvensjonell (hevdvunnen) conventional.
konvent (parlamentsmøte) convention.
konvers|abel conversational. **-asjon** conversation. **-asjonsleksikon** encyclopædia. **-asjonstalent** conversational powers. **-ere** converse.
konvertere convert. **konvertitt** convert.
konvoi convoy. **-ere** convoy.
konvolutt envelope, wrapper.
konvul|sivisk convulsive. **-sjon** convulsion.
kooperativ co-operative. **kooperere** co-operate.
koordinasjon co-ordination.
kop gaper, gaping simpleton.
kope gape, stare.
kopi copy, transcript. **-blekk** copying ink. **-bok** copy-book, letter-book. **-ere** copy, transcribe.
koping staring.
kopipapir copying-paper.
kopipresse copying-press.
kopist copying-clerk, copyist, transcriber.
kople couple.
kopler pander. **-i** (rufferi) pandering. **-ske** panderess.
kopling coupling; clutch.
koplingspedal clutch pedal.
kopp cup; — **og skål** a cup and saucer; **en** — **te** a cup of tea.
kopparr pock-mark.
kopparret pitted by the small-pox.
koppe (sette kopper) cup.
koppe|attest vaccination certificate. **-epidemi** small-pox epidemic. **-innpodning** inoculation of the small-pox.
kopper (sykdom) small-pox.
kopper (metall) copper; **beslå med** — copper. **kopper|aktig** coppery. **-dank** copper. **-erts** copper ore. **-forhudet** coppered, sheathed with c., copperbottomed. **-forhudning** c. sheathing, coppering. **-gruve** c. mine. **-holdig** containing c., coppery, cupriferous. **-hytte** c. smelting house. **-kjel** copper, wash-house copper. **-mynt** c. coin, copper. **-rød** copper-coloured. **-skilling** copper. **-smed** copper-smith. **-stikk** copper-plate engrav-

ing, print. **-stikker** engraver, chalcographer. **-tråd** c. wire. **-verk** c. mine. **-vitriol** blue vitriol. **-åre** copper vein.
kopra (tørkede kjerner av kokosnøtt) copra.
kopre copper. **-t** coppery.
kopul|a copula. **-ere** marry.
kor chorus; (sangerne) choir; (kirke) chancel, choir.
koral (salmemelodi) choral.
korall (koralldyrs bolig) coral. **-dyr** coralpolyp. **-fisker** coral diver el. fisher.
koralløy coral island; atoll.
koranen the Koran.
korde chord.
kordong cordon.
korg basket; (pakkorg) hamper, (til glass o. l.) crate. Se ellers **kurv**.
korgutt chorister(-boy).
korint currant, currant grape.
kork cork. **-aktig** corky. **-avfall** cork-shavings el. cuttings. **-belte** cork life-belt. **-bøye** cork -buoy. **-etrekker** cork screw. **-skjærer** cork -cutter. **-sponer**, se **-avfall**. **-såle** cork-sole.
korn corn, (ikke om sæd på marka) grain; (sikte-) aim, sight; **et lite** — (dt) a bit; **ta på -et** take one's aim at, cover. **-aks** ear el. spike of c. **-avl** raising of c. **-band** sheaf, sheaf of corn. **-blomst** c. flower, corn bluebottle. **-blå** azure light blue. **-brennevin** corn brandy, whisky.
kornet granulary, granulous.
kornett (blåseinstrument) cornet.
korn|handler corn-merchant. **-høst** corn harvest.
korn|land corn-growing country. **-lass** cartload of c. **-låve** barn. **-magasin** c. magazine. **-mangel** scarcity el. dearth of c. **-mo** sheet -lightning. **-mål** c. measure. **-måler** c. meter. **-nek** sheaf of c. **-opplag** magazine of grain. **-rensing** winnowing. **-rik** abounding in c. **-stakk** stack of c. **-staur** pole for drying corn. **-toll** corn duty. **-åker** corn field.
korp, se **ramn**.
korporal corporal.
korporasjon corporation.
korporlig corporal, bodily.
korps corps, body.
korpslege regimental surgeon.
korpsånd corporate spirit, esprit-de-corps, brotherly spirit, class feeling.
korpulense stoutness, portliness, corpulency.
korpulent corpulent, stout, portly.
korpus body.
korrekt correct; **skrive** — write grammar. **-het** correctness.
korrektiv corrective.
korrektur proof(-sheet); **annen** — revise, second proof; **lese** — read the proof-sheets, correct the press. **-ark** proof-sheet. **-leser** (press-, proof-) reader, corrector of the press. **-lesning** proof-reading.
korrespondanse correspondence.
korrespondent correspondent; (på kontor) corresponding clerk.
korrespondere correspond; **-nde medlem** foreign associate member. **-nde reder** managing owner, ship's manager.
korridor corridor.
korrigere correct.
korrupsjon corruption.
korrupt corrupt.
kors cross; (lidelser) affliction, tribulation; (for tanken) crux; **gjøre -ets tegn** make the sign of the cross; **legge armene, bena over** — cross the arms, legs; **med bena over** — cross-legged; **krype til -et** humble oneself; **enhver har sitt** — to each his suffering; **slå** — **for seg** cross oneself. **—!** (int) Lord! Bless me!
kor|sang choral song, chorus. **-sanger** chorister, chorus singer; (kvinnelig) chorus girl.
korsar corsair.

kors|blomstret crusiferous plant. **-bærer** cross-bearer. **-bånd** postal band; wrapper; cross-band. **under** — cover in bands, by book post. **-bånds-forsendelse** book-packet.

korse seg cross oneself, make the sign of the cross; **korse seg over** be awfully shocked el. scandalized at.

korsedderkopp cross-spider.

korsett corset, stays.

kors|fane banner of the cross. **-farer** crusader. **-feste** crucify. **-festelse** crucifixion. **-formet** cruciform. **-gang** cross-walk, cloister(s) (fig) via crucis, via dolorosa.

Korsika Corsica. **k-ner, k-nsk** Corsican.

kors|lagt crossed, folded. **-nebb** cross-bill, redback. **-rygg** loins, lumbar regions. **-sting** cross-stitch. **-tog** crusade. **-vei** cross-road. **-vis** crosswise, across, crossways.

kort (spillek.) card; (visittk.) card; (billett) ticket; **gi** — deal; **gode** — a good hand; **spå i** — tell fortunes by cards; **legge -ene på bordet** (fig) put one's cards on the table; **ha alle** — **på hånden** have the game in one's own hand.

kort (adj) short; (kortfattet) brief; **om** — **tid** in a short time, shortly, within short, before long; **for** — **tid siden** a short time ago; — **etter** shortly after; **en -ere vei** a nearer way; — **sikt** (merc) short sight; **-siktig veksel** short bill; **fatte seg** — be brief; — **sagt** in short, to cut the matter short; — **og godt** in so many words; — **og godt, jeg vil ikke** the long and the short of it is, I will not; **gi en** — **beskjed** cut one short; send one about his business; **komme til** — come off a loser; — **for hodet** hasty, short-spoken; **gjøre** — **prosess** make short work of it.

kort|beint short-legged. **-brev** letter-card.

kortevarer hardware; haberdashery.

kortfattet concise, brief.

korthalset short-necked.

korthet shortness; (bare om tid og tale) brevity, briefness; (kortfatteth.) conciseness; **i** — briefly, put in short, in a few words.

korthåret short-haired.

kortklipt closely-cropped, short-cut.

kortkunst trick with cards, card trick.

kortleik pack of cards.

kortsiktig short, short-dated; — **lån** loan of short notice.

kortslutning short circuit; **fremkalle** — short-circuit.

kortspill card-playing; card-game; **i** — at cards. **kort|spiller** card-player. **-stokk** pack of cards; undealt surplus of a pack.

kortsynt (fig) short-sighted. **-het** (fig) short-sightedness.

kortvarig of short duration, short-lived, transitory. **-het** short duration.

korvett corvet, sloop of war.

koryféer leaders.

kos, se **kurs; stryke sin** — clear, cut away, make off.

kosakk Cossac.

kose (seg) cose, snug, be snug. **-lig** cosy, snug.

kosinus (mat.) co-sine.

kosmetikk cosmetic. **kosmetisk** cosmetic.

kosmopolitt cosmopolite, cosmopolitan.

kosmopolittisk cosmopolitan.

koss heap, pile; se **iskoss.**

kost (mat) board, boarding, food, victuals, fare, living; (dt.) grub; — **og lønn** board and wages; **mager** — slender fare; **ha fri** — have free board; **sette en i** — put one out to board, board one; **være i** — hos board with; **ha en i -en** board one; **holde seg selv med -en** find oneself.

kost (feiekost) broom, besom; (malerkost) brush; **nye -er feier best** new brooms sweep clean.

kostbar precious, valuable; (dyr) expensive, costly, sumptuous; **gjøre seg** — make oneself precious. **-het** costliness, expensiveness.

koste, se **feie; så det kost** at a rattling speed, at a good pace.

koste cost; **hva -r det?** what is the price el. figure? how much is it? **det -r ikke noe** there's nothing to pay; **hva -r det Dem?** what does it stand you in? **hva -r denne stolen?** how much for this chair? **det får** — **hva det vil** at any price, at all costs; **det vil** — **hans liv** he will pay with his life for it, it is as much as his life is worth; — **mye på** spend a good deal of money on.

kostebinder broom-maker, broom-man.

kostelig costly, precious; (morsom) delightful.

kostende cost, price, expense.

kosteskaft broom-stick, broom-staff.

kostforakter dainty feeder; **han er ingen** — he is not over-nice, not very fastidious.

kost|gjenger boarder. **-hold** boarding. **-penger** board; (til tjener) board-wages. **-skole** boarding-school.

kostyme costume; **i** — in character. **-ball** fancy(-dress) ball, costume-ball. **-prøve** dress rehearsal.

kotelett cutlet, chop.

koteri coterie, clique, fraternity, ring. **-vesen** cliquism.

kotiljong cotillon.

kott small closet.

koturne cothurn, buskin.

kove closet.

kovne be suffocating; be dying with heat.

kooye, se **kuoye.**

kr. fork. av **krone,** ca. 1 s. 1½ d.

krabask whip, scourge.

krabat (fyr) chap, fellow.

krabbas-tømmer unmarked timber afloat, unidentified timber.

krabbe crab, (dregg av tre) rough graplin.

krabbe (vrb) crawl, scrabble, scramble.

krabbe|fangst crabbing. **-skall** crab's shell.

kraft strength; (evne, legemlig og åndelig) power; (makt) force; (kraftighet) vigour; (energi) energy; (maskins) power; (spenning) strain, stress, **av alle krefter** with might and main, with all one's might; **anspenne alle krefter** strain every nerve; **legge** — **i** throw one's strength into; **går med full** — is going (at) full speed; **prøve krefter med** try one's strength against; **komme til krefter** gain el. recover strength; **i sin ungdoms fulle** — in the full vigour of youth; **teatrets beste krefter** the best actors of the theatre; **i** — **av** (en lov o. l.) in el. by virtue of; **sette i** — put in force, enforce, execute; **sette ut av** — annul, abrogate; **tre i** — come into force el. operation, take effect, operate; become available.

kraft|anstrengelse exertion of strength, (vigorous) effort. **-for** strong food.

kraftfull vigorous; powerful; strong, forcible; energetic.

kraft|gjødning powerful manure. **-idiot** utter idiot.

kraftig strong, vigorous, powerful, energetic, forcible.

kraft|kar muscular fellow. **-løs** impotent; (avmektig) powerless; (svak) nerveless; invalid, **-løshet** lack of strength, impotence; (svakelighet) invalidity, feebleness.

kraft|måler dynamometer. **-ord** powerful, energetic word. **-prestasjon** feats of strength. **-prøve** trial of strength. **-spill** waste of energy. **-språk** energetic language.

kraft|stasjon electric power station. **-tap** loss of power el. purchase. **-tak** vigorous pull, push el. burst. **-uttrykk** powerful, energetical expression. **-utvikling** development of power; (mekanisk) purchase.

krage collar; (pels- o. l.) tippet; **ta en i -n** collar one, take one by the collar. **-bein** collar bone. **-støvel** top-boot, tops.

krake (kroket tre) stunted tree; (svekling) dwarf, weakling; (sjøuhyre) kraken.
krakilsk contentious, cantankerous, quarrelsome.
I. **krakk** (handelskrise) crash, collapse.
II. **krakk** (til å sitte på) stool.
krakkmandel shell-almond; thin-shelled almond.
kram ware, wares; (skrap) trash, trumpery; **gammelt — frippery; noe kjedelig — a bore, a flat (or heavy) affair.
kram (adj, om snø) clogging, wettish.
kram|bu shop. **-handel** retail trade. **-kar** pedlar.
kramme (klemme) crumple, crush.
krampaktig convulsive.
I. **krampe** (jernkrok) cramp, clasp; (liten) staple.
II. **krampe** (ufrivillig muskelsammentrekning) spasm; fit, convulsions; cramp; (stivhet) crick; **ligge i — be in a fit; jeg fikk — I was taken with a cramp.
krampe|anfall fit. **-gråt** convulsive el. hysteric crying. **-latter** hysteric laughter. **-stillende** antispasmodic; **— middel** spasmodic, antispasmodic. **-tilfelle** spasmodic affection. **-trekning** convulsions.
kramse feel, touch; paw.
kramsfugl fieldfare.
kramvarer small wares.
kran crane. **-avgift** cranage.
krangel quarrel, quarrels.
krangle pick a quarrel (quarrels). **-fant** quarreller, quarrelsome fellow. **-syk** brawling, quarrelsome. **-t**, se **-syk.**
kranium cranium.
krank (især i dial.:) **uta blank, inna — fair without and foul within. Se ellers **skrøpelig, svak.**
krans wreath, garland, chaplet.
kranse crown with flowers.
kranse|kake tall macaroon cake. **-lag, -skål** house-raising, roofing-supper.
krapp (kort) short; (trang) narrow; (brå) sudden; (hardt strammet) tight, taut; **— sjø** a short sea; **en — sving** a sharp turn, a sudden bend.
krapyl rabble.
krasle crackle, crash, crisp.
krass gross, crass.
krasse, se **klore** og **skrape.**
krater crater.
kratt thicket, brushwood, scrub, copse.
krattbevokst covered with scrub.
krattskog copse wood.
I. **krav** (fordring) claim, call; (hiken) craving; **gjøre — på** lay claim to.
II. **krav** (tynn isskorpe) crizzle, new ice.
kravbrev dunning letter.
krave (om isdannelse) crizzle, freeze; **— seg** freeze.
krave (subst), se **krage.**
kravle crawl, creep.
kravløs free from claims.
kre (sj.) creature, animal, (is.:) **et lite — little animal, mite.
kreatur animal; (kveg) cattle, live stock; (hånsord) creature; (fig) tool. **-sykdom** disease of cattle. **-vogn** cattle-box el. -car, box-car.
kredense present after tasting it.
kreditere sell on credit; **— en noe** trust one for something; **— en for noe** credit something to one, credit one with something.
kreditiv letter of credit; credentials.
kreditor creditor.
kreditside credit-side.
kreditt credit, trust, (dt.) tick; **på — on** credit el. trust; **ta på — take upon trust, take up upon credit; **gi — give credit, trust (one); **åpne en — hos** lodge el. open a c. with. **-brev** letter of credit.

kreere create.
kreft cancer; (i tre) canker. **-aktig** cancerous; cankerous. **-byll** cancerous ulcer.
kreft|knute cancerous induration, schirrus. **-middel** remedy against cancer. **-svulst** cancerous tumour. **-sår** cancerous sore.
kregda the measles.
krek poor creature, poor thing; creeping thing el. creature.
kreke crawl, creep.
krekling crakeberry, black crawberry, heathberry.
krem whipped cream; (hud-) cream; (egge-, vanilje-) custard.
kremasjon cremation.
krematorium crematory, crematorium.
kremere cremate.
krem|farget, -gul cream-coloured, creamy.
kremmer (gmlt.) shopkeeper, retailer. Se ogs. **kramkar. -folk** nation of shopkeepers. **-hus** cornet, coffin. **-sjel** mercenary soul.
kremt slight cough, throat-clearing.
kremte clear one's throat cough.
krenge lie along, careen, heel; (vrenge, sj.) turn inside out. **krenging** turning etc.; (mar) heel, heeling over.
krenk|e violate; (en) hurt, injure, offend, vex, mortify. **-else** violation, injury, vexation, mortification, indignity. **-ende** insulting, offensive.
kreol, -erinne Creole.
kreosot creosote.
krepere give up the ghost.
krepp crape.
kreppe crape. **-t** curled.
kreps crawfish, crayfish; **K-ens vendekrets** the tropic of Cancer. **krepse** catch crawfish.
krepsegang retrograde movement; **gå — go** backward.
kresen dainty, nice, particular, fastidious.
kresenhet daintiness.
kreti og pleti the common herd.
kretin|er Cretin. **-isme** cretinism.
krets circle; (av personer) ring; (forretningsk.) sphere (of activity); (omgangsk. o. l.) circle; (familiek.) family circle; (distrikt) district, precinct; **slå el. slutte — form a circle. **i vide —er** widely. **-bevegelse** circular motion, gyration. **kretse** circle.
krets|fengsel county jail. **-forstander** (i forsorgsvesenet) district visitor. **-gang** circular course. **-løp** circulation, circular motion; gyration.
kreve crave, demand; (fordre) claim; (som rett) exact; (utkreve) require; **— en for gjeld** call for payment of one's debt; (påtrengende) dun; **— inn skatter** gather el. collect taxes; **— inn penger** collect money; **— til regnskap** call to account.
krible og krable creep, have a creeping, prickling, tickling sensation. **kribling** creeping, creeps.
krig war; **føre — wage war, make war, carry on war; war; (med: against, on); **ligge i — med** be at war with; **erklære — declare, proclaim war against; **gå i -en** go to the wars; **tjene i -en** serve in the wars; **slik er -ens gang** wars bring scars.
kriger warrior. **-sk** martial, warlike. **-ånd** warlike spirit.
krigførende belligerent.
krigsaeroplan warplane.
krigs|bruk: til — for war-purposes. **-dans war-dance. **-erklæring** declaration of war. **-fange** prisoner of war. **-fangenskap** captivity. **-fare** dangers el. risks of war.
krigs|fot: sette på — put upon the war-establishment, on a war-footing; (fig) **stå på — med be at enmity with. **-folk** soldiers. **-forhør** trial by court martial.
krigs|fortjeneste war-time profits. **-førsel** warfare. **-gal** (madly) bent upon war, bellicose. **-galskap** mania for war, warlike ardour. **-gud**

god of war. **-historie** history of war, military history. **forfatter av -historie** military historian. **-kamerat** fellow-soldier el. officer, companion in arms, war-comrade. **-kasse** army-chest, military chest. **-korrespondent** war correspondent. **-kunst** art of war, military art. **-kyndig** skilled in the art of war. **-list** stratagem. **-lov** martial law. **-makt** armament, military force; (til vanns) naval force.

krigs|maling (også om selskapsantrekk) warpaint. **-mann** warrior. **-maskin** engine of war. **-materiell** munition; (særlig om krutt og projektiler) ammunition; war material. **-minister** minister of (for) war; (i England) secretary for war. **-ministerium** war-office, war-department. **-musikk** martial music. **-omkostninger** expenses of war. **-rett** court martial; **stilles for — be** tried by a court martial. **-rop** war cry. **-rustning** armament. **-råd** council of war. **-sang** war-song. **-skadeserstatning** war indemnity. **-skatt** war-tax, contribution. **-skip** man of war, warship. **-skueplass** theatre el. seat of war. **-spillet** the game of war. **-stien** the war trail el. path. **-styrke,** se **makt.** **-tid** time of war. **-tidspriser** war prices. **-tilstand** warlike situation. **-tjeneste** military service, war service; **gjøre — do** military duty. **-tog** military expedition. **-tukt** military discipline. **-tummel** turmoil of war. **-utsikter** warlike prospects. **-vesen** military matters. **-vitenskap** military science.

krik corner; (liten vik) creek; (øye-) corner of the eye. **gå i -er og kroker** follow a zigzag course. **i alle kroker og -er** in nooks and corners.

krikkand teal.

krilla the measles.

Krim the Crimea.

Krim-krigen the Crimean war.

krim, se **snue.** **-full,** se **forkjølt.**

kriminal criminal. **-dommer** judge of a crown-court. **-domstol** criminal court. **-ist** criminalist. **-lovbok** penal code. **-prosess** criminal proceedings. **-rett** criminal law. **-sak** criminal case.

kriminell criminal; **— forbrytelse** c. offence;

krimskrams trumpery, rubbish.

kring (prep), se **omkring.**

kring (adj) agile, quick; (hendig) deft.

kringkaste broadcast.

kringkasting broadcasting.

kringle ring-twisted cake el. bun, twist.

kring|om, se **omkring; -sette** beset, hem about, surround. **-sjå** (subst) circular panorama, wide view.

krinkelkroker odd nooks and corners.

krinoline crinoline.

krins, krinsel, se **krets.**

krise crisis, pl. crises. **-tid** period of economic crisis, period of depression.

krisis, se **krise.**

krisle tickle. **-hoste** tickling cough.

kristelig Christian, Christianlike.

kristen Christian; **en — a** Christian. **-dom** Christianity. **-het** Christendom. **-kjærlighet** charity. **-liv** Christian life. **-tro** Christian faith.

Kristian Christian.

Kristi blodsdråpe fuchsia.

Kristi himmelfart the ascension of Christ;

Krist himmelfartsdag Ascension day.

Kristine Christina.

kristne christen.

Kristoffer Christopher, Kit.

kristtorn holly.

Kristus Christ; **før — B. C.,** before Christ. **-bilde** image of Christ.

kriterium criterion.

kritiker critic; (anmelder) reviewer.

kritikk criticism, critique; (anmeldelse) review; **under all — contemptible,** below notice.

krit|ikkløs uncritical. **-isere** criticise.

kritisering criticising, criticism.

kritisk critical.

kritt chalk; **ta på — (dt.)** (egtl. kreditt) buy

upon tick. **-aktig** chalky. **-brott** chalk pit. **-dannelse** chalkformation. **kritte** chalk. **komme i kritthuset** get into high favour; **være i kritthuset hos en** be in one's good graces, in one's books.

kritthvit white as chalk.

kritt|lag layer of chalk. **-pipe** clay pipe, earthen pipe. **-strek** chalk line. **-tegning** crayon-painting; crayon.

I. **kro** (vertshus) inn, public-house.

II. **kro** (hos fugler) craw, crop.

kro seg (egtl. om fugler) swell the craw; (fig) plume oneself, look big.

krok corner, nook; (jern-) hook, crook; (fiske-) hook; (bøyning) bend; (omvei) détour. **sette -en på døra** hook the door; **få på -en** hook; **bite på -en** catch el. swallow the bait, rise to the bait, bite at the hook. **trekke — pull fingers. en stakkars — a** poor creature. **den gamle -en** the poor old body.

krokan croquant.

krokere croque, croquet.

kroket crooked.

kroki (rough) sketch.

krokket croquet. **-bøyle** croquet-hoop.

krokne crook, crouch, double oneself up.

krokodille crocodile. **-tårer** crocodile tears.

krokrygg stoop-shouldered person, stooper. **-et** stoop-shouldered.

krokus crocus.

krokvei circuitous el. round-about way; (fig) **gå -er** use indirect el. underhand means.

krom chrome, chromium.

kromatisk chromatic.

kromsyre chromic acid el. anhydride.

kronblad petal.

krone crown; (pave-) tiara; (adelskr., grevekr.) coronet; (av et tre) top, crown; (blomsterkr.) corol, corolla, (på jeksel) corona; **sette -n på** (fig) crown, put the coping-stone on.

krone (vrb) crown; **— ham til konge** crown him king.

kronglebjørk crooked el. twisted birch-tree.

kronglet(e) crabbed, intricate; (knudret) rugged.

kron|gods crown-land. **-hjort** (royal) stag.

kronikk chronicle.

kroning coronation.

kronisk chronic.

krono|log chronologer. **-logi** chronology. **-logisk** chronological. **-meter** chronometer.

kronprins (i England) Prince of Wales; (i andre land) Crown Prince.

kronprinsesse (prinsen av Wales' gemalinne) Princess of Wales; (annen kronprins's gemalinne) Crown Princess.

kron|rake shave the crown of. **-raket** tonsured, shaven-headed. **-raking** tonsure.

kropp (legeme) body; (uten hode, armer og bein) trunk, barrel; (slaktet) carcase; **doven — lazybones; skjelve over hele -en** shake all over; **han har ikke skjorte på -en** he has no shirt to his back.

kropps|arbeid manual labour. **-føring** carriage **-lyte** bodily defect.

krot (utskjæring, utsying) scroll-work, scrolls; flourishes. **krote** scroll, deck with scrolls; (rable) scratch, scrawl.

kruggrygget bent, bowed, a little hunchbacked.

krukk|e pitcher, jar; (apoteker-) gallipot; **-a går så lenge til vanns, at den kommer hankeløs hjem** the pitcher goes to the well till it comes home broken at last.

krull scroll, flourish; cluster, curl.

krum curved, crooked. **-bøyd** bowed, curved. **-het** crookedness, curvation. **-kake** rolled wafer.

krumme (gjøre krum) bend, bow; **jeg vil ikke — et hår på hans hode** I will not hurt a hair of his head.

krumning bending, bend, curve, curvature.

krum|rygget crook-backed. **-sabel** scimitar.

krumsprang capers, gambols, antics; **gjøre — cut capers;** (fig) shuffle, prevaricate.

krumtapp crank.
I. **krus** jug, mug.
II. **krus** (f. eks. på vann) ripple; (kruset hår) friz; (stas) fuss; **gjøre — av** make a great fuss about. **-bladet** curly-leaved. **kruse** (vann etc.) curl, ripple; (sterkere) ruffle; (hår) crimp, crisp, curl, friz.
kruse|dull flourish, scroll. **-mynte** balm-mint. **-t** curly.
krusfat earthen dish.
krusifiks crucifix.
krus(n)ing curling; (på vann o. l.) ripple.
krus|persille curled parsley. **-tøy,** se **steintøy.**
krutt powder, gun-powder; **skyte med løst —** fire blank; **han har ikke oppfunnet -et** he is no conjurer, no great luminary, he will never set the Thames on fire; **ikke et skudd — verd** not worth powder and shot; **ha luktet —** have smelt powder.
krutt|fabrikasjon manufacture of gunpowder. **-forråd** supply of gunpowder. **-horn** powder-horn, powder-flask. **-kammer** powder-room. **-kjerre** powder cart. **-kjerring** devil, wildfire. **-ladning** charge of powder. **-ledning** train of gunpowder. **-lukt** smell of gunpowder. **-magasin** powder-magazine. **-mine** (powder-)mine. **-røyk** smoke (of gunpowder). **-sammensvergelsen** the gunpowder plot. **-tønne** powder-barrel. **-tårn** powder magazine. **-verk** powder mill. **-vogn** powder-waggon.
kry (adj) proud, conceited; spry, brisk.
kry (vrb) swarm.
krybbe manger, crib; **når -a er tom, bites hestene** when poverty comes in at the door, love leaps out of the window. **-biter** crib-biter.
krydder, -i, spice, seasoning. **krydder|nellik** clove. **-pose** sweet-bag. **krydre** spice, season; (fig) interlard, point. **krydret** spiced, seasoned.
krykje (måke) kittywake.
krykke crutch; **gå på -r** walk with crutches.
kryl, se **pukkel.**
krympe shrink, sponge; **— seg sammen** shrink; (fig) **— seg** (som en orm) writhe; **— seg ved** el. **for** be loath el. reluctant to, shrink from, hang back from.
kryp vermin, creeping things.
krypdyr reptile.
krype creep; (kravle) crawl; (om tøy) shrink; **en må lære å — før en kan gå** you must learn to creep before you go; (fig) **— for en** fawn upon, cringe to; **en kan likeså gjerne hoppe i det som — i det** it is no use beating about the bush; **— sammen** crouch; **krypende** crawling; (fig) servile, cringing, grovelling.
kryperi cringing.
kryp|skytter poacher. **-skytteri** poaching.
krypsoleie creeping crowfoot.
kryptkirke crypt.
kryptogam cryptogamous, cryptogamic.
kryptogamer cryptogams.
krysantemum chrysanthemum.
krysning crossing; cross- el. half-breeding; (konkret) cross-, half-breed.
krysolitt chrysolite.
kryss cross; (for en note) sharp.
krysse cross, cut across; (om dyr) cross; **— hverandre** cross each other, intercross; (seile att og fram) cruise.
krysser cruiser.
kryss|forhør cross-questioning, cross-examination. **-forhøre** cross-question, cross-examine.
kryssild cross-fire.
kryssing crossing.
kryssordoppgave crossword puzzle.
krysstokt cruise.
krystall crystal.
krystallaktig crystalline.
krystall|form form of a crystal, crystalline form. **-klar** (clear as) crystal, crystalline.
krystallisere seg crystallise, be crystallized.
krystallisering crystallization.

kryste squeeze, press; **— en i sine armer** hug one.
kryster coward. **-aktig** cowardly.
krøke bend, crook; **den må tidlig -s som krok skal bli** soon crooks the treee that good gambrel would be. **— seg sammen** double oneself up. **krøkne** curve, grow crooked.
krøll curl, frizzle. **katten skjøt — på ryggen** arched his back. **slå — på seg** bend, curve.
krølle (subst) se **krøll.**
krølle (vrb) curl; (om papir, klær) crease, crumple, rumple; **— seg** curl; crumple.
krøllet curly; crumpled, creasy.
krøll|hår (prepared, curled) horsehair. **-håret** curly-haired. **-hårsmadrass** horsehair mattress.
krølltang curling iron, crimping iron.
krølltopp curly-pate.
krønike chronicle, annals; (dt.) fable. **-skriver** chronicler, annalist.
krøpling cripple.
krøtter, se **kreatur.**
krå, se **krok.**
kråke crow. **-fot** club-moss. **-mål** gibberish. **-sølv** mica. **-ting** egtl. parliament of crows. **-tær** (dårlig skrift) pot-hooks, scrawl.
krås (på fugl) crop, craw.
ku cow; **glo som ei — på en rødmalt vegg** stare like a stuck pig. **ha det som ei — i ei grønn eng** be el. live in clover, **mens gresset gror, dør -a** while the grass grows the steed starves.
Kuba (nu Cuba) Cuba. **k-ner, k-nsk** Cuban.
kubb log-ends.
kubbe log, stump. **-stol** log-chair.
kube hive.
kubein (brekkjern) jemmy, crowbar.
kubikk|fot cubic foot, foot cube. **-innhold** cubic content(s), cubage, volume. **-rot** cube root. **utdragning av -a** extraction of the cube root. **-tall** cubic number. **kubisk** cubic(al).
kubisme (en kunststil) cubism.
kubist cubist. **kubistisk** cubistic.
kubus cube.
kue cow, subdue.
kufte jacket, mantlet; coat.
kuguar cougar.
ku|hale cow's tail. **-hud** cow's hide.
kujon coward, poltroon, dastard, craven. **-ere** cow. **-eri** cowardice.
kujur cow's udder.
kukake cow-turd.
kukelure mope, sit moping.
kukopper cow pox, the vaccine disease.
kul boss, bulge, knob, protuberance; (etter slag) bump.
kulant easy, expeditious.
kulde cold, frost; (egenskap) coldness; (mest fig) frigidity, frigidness; **gyse av —** shiver, shake with cold.
kuldegrad degree of frost.
kuldegysning cold shiver, shivering fit.
ku'd|skjær susceptible of cold. **-skjærhet** susceptibility of cold. **-slå** take off the chill.
kule (blåse) blow, breeze; **— opp** freshen.
I. **kule** (hule) pit, hollow.
II. **kule** globe, sphere, orb; (mat) sphere; (kanon-, gevær-) ball, shot; cannon-ball, musketball, pistol-ball; (bare om gevær-) bullet; (biljard) ball; (til valg) ballot; (til kiler) bowl; **svart —** (ved votering) black-ball; **skyte en — gjennom hodet** på ei blow one's brains out.
kuleform (f. som en k.) globular form; (til støyping) bullet-mould.
kulelager (i maskin) ball-bearing.
kule|regn shower, storm of balls el. bullets. **-sprøyte** machine gun. **-støper** founder of balls. **-støping** founding of balls.
kuli coolie.
kulinarisk culinary.
kuling breeze; **frisk —** fresh breeze.
kulisse scene, wing, slip; **bak -ne** behind the scenes; **de som har vært bak -ne** (dt.) those in the know.

I. **kull** (unger) brood, hatch; (av pattedyr) litter; **to — barn** children of two (marriage-) beds; **lyse i — og kjønn** legitimate.

II. **kull** (tre-) charcoal; (stein-) coal; (i kjemi) carbon; **gloende —** living coal; **sanke gloende — på ens hode** heap coals of fire on one's head; **utbrente —** dead coal; **ta inn —** coal, take in coal, bunker; **forsyne med —** coal. **kullaktig** coaly; (i kjemi) carbonic.

kull|boks coal-hod, coal-scuttle. **–damper** steam collier.

kulle (ta inn kull) coal, bunker; **for å —** ogs. for bunkers.

kull|forbruk consumption of coal. **–gass** coalgas. **–gruve** coal mine, c. pit. **–handler** coalmerchant, collier.

kullild coal fire.

kullkaste overthrow; (planer) defeat, overturn (plans); (beregninger) upset (calculations); (et testamente) set aside (a will).

kull|kjeller coal-cellar, coal-hole. **kull|lemper** (på dampskip) coal-trimmer. **kull|losser** coal-whipper. **kull|opplag** coal-depot. **–os** coal vapour. **kull|sjauer** coal-whipper. **–skip** collier. **–skuffe** coal-scoop.

kullsvart coal black, jet black.

kull|stoff carbon. **–stoffholdig** carbonaceous. **kullsur** carbonic; **–t** salt carbonate; **— 'all** carbonate of potash, potassic carbonate.

kull|sviertro blind belief, unreasoning faith. **–syre** carbonic acid.

kulltegning charcoal drawing.

kulminasjon culmination.

kulminere culminate.

kulp, se **høl.**

kulse shiver, feel somewhat cold.

kult (kloss) block; (liten stang); se **rorkult** (trestubb) stub, stump; (kraftig vokst dyr el. menneske, f. eks. unggutt) lump of a lad, stout lad. **kulten** (adj) stoutly built, thickset; se ogs. **muggen.**

kultivator (åkerbruksredskap) cultivator.

kultivere cultivate.

kultur culture, civilization. **–folk** civilized nation. **–historie** history of civilization. **–tilstand** (state of) culture. **–utvikling** progress of civilization.

kultus cult.

kulør colour. **kulørt** coloured; **–e lykter** variegated lamps.

kum bowl, basin; (stor beholder) tank; (til fisk) well; (bade-) bathing-box.

kumle, se **bolle.**

kummer grief, distress, affliction. **–full** sorrowful. **kummerlig** miserable, wretched.

kumulere cumulate.

kun, se **bare.**

kunde customer, patron, client; **mange –r** a good run of custom.

kunne be able; **jeg kan** I can, I am able; (muligens) I may; **jeg kunne** I could, I was able; (muligens) I might; **jeg har kunnet** I have been able; **jeg har –t gjøre det, da jeg var yngre** I could do it when I was younger; **han begynner å — lese** he is beginning to read; **forat de kunne . . .** that they might; **slik kunne han sitte i timevis** thus he would sit for hours; **å ville er ett, å — et annet** willing is one thing, being able is another; **det går som det best kan** it goes on anyhow; **nå kan det være nok** that will do; **jeg kan ikke mer** I am exhausted; **det kan gjerne være** that may be; **— gresk, latin** know Greek, Latin; **gutten kunne sin lekse** the boy knew his lesson; **det kan jeg ikke** I cannot (do it); **det kan jeg ikke gjøre for** it is not my fault; **hva kan jeg for at is** it my fault that, how can I help that . . . ; **den kan vel veie en ti pund** it will weigh some ten pounds.

kunngjør|e make known, publish, notify. **–else, –ing,** publication, notification.

kunnskap knowledge, information; (underretn.) intelligence; **få — om** receive information or intelligence of; **han har mange –er** he is a man of great learning, acquirements el. information; **gode –er i matematikk** a good knowledge of mathematics; **han har overflatiske –er i engelsk** he has a smattering of English.

kunnskapsrik rich in knowledge, well-informed.

kunst art; (behendig) trick; **–en å herske** the art of ruling, the art how to rule; **det er nettopp –en** there's the art of it; **det er ingen —** that's easy enough; **gjøre –er** perform el. play tricks; **de skjønne –er** the fine arts; **— og håndverk** liberal and industrial arts; art and craft; **det ble en ren —** it became a science; **det er hele –en** that is where all the art lies; **ved — by** art, artificially; **tidsskrift om —** art periodical; **være ekspert i en —** be skilled in an art, be expert; **den svarte —** the black art, necromancy.

kunst|akademi academy of arts. **–anmelder** art-critic. **–art** branch of art. **–begeistring** enthusiasm for the arts. **–berider(ske)** equestrian performer, circus-rider. **–dommer** (art)-critic. **–elsker** amateur, lover of art. **–ferdig** expert, skilful; (om ting) elaborate, ingenious. **–ferdighet** skill, dexterity (in an art), art-skill. **–flid** (mechanical) industry. **–forstand** knowledge of art. **–gjødning** artificial manure. **–grep** knack; (knep) device, artifice, trick.

kunst|handel printseller's shop; fancy-stationer's h . **–handler** print-seller, fancy-stationer. **–historie** history of the fine arts, art history. **–håndverk** art handicraft.

kunstig artificial, imitative, elaborate; (kunstferdig utført) curious; (original) quaint; (listig) ingenious; (uekte) imitation. **–het** artificialness, artificiality.

kunst|industri art industry. **–kjenner** judge of the fine arts, connoisseur. **–kritiker** art-critic. **–kritikk** art-criticism.

kunstle over-refine. **–ri** over-refinement, subtlety. **–t** elaborate, affected.

kunst|løs artless, simple, inartificial. **–maler** artist painter.

kunstner artist. **–bane** career (of an artist). **–hjem** artist's home.

kunstnerinne (female) artist, lady artist. **kunstnerisk** artistic. **— dyktighet** artistic skill. **kunstner|liv** artist's life. **–sjargon** art-cant. **–stand** profession of artists. **–stolthet** artist's pride, professional pride. **–verd** worth as an artist, artistic merits.

kunst|nytelse artistic enjoyment. **–produkt** production of art. **–retning** style of art, school (of artists). **–samling** collection of works of art. **–sans** taste for the fine arts. **–skatt** art -treasure. **–skole** school of arts. **–smør** (margarin) artificial butter, butterine, oleo-margarine. **–snekker** cabinet-maker. **–stykke** feat, trick. **–utstilling** fine-arts exhibition, art-show, art exhibition. **–uttrykk** technical term, technicality, term of art. **–verdi** art value. **–verk** work of art.

kup hit, stroke.

kupé compartment.

kupert rough, rugged. **— terreng** broken el. uneven ground.

Kupido Cupid.

kuplett couplet; verse.

kupong coupon; ogs. dividend warrant.

kuppel cupola, dome; (lampe-) globe, shade. **–formig** domical, domed.

I. **kur** (ved hoff) levee, drawing-room; **gjøre — til** make love to, pay (one's) court to; **gi —** hold a court, hold a drawing-room.

II. **kur** (helbredelsesmetode) cure, course of treatment; **gjennomgå en —** undergo a treatment, be under medical treatment; **forebyggelse er bedre enn —** prevention is better than cure.

kuranstalt sanatory.

kurant current.

kurator guardian; (for offentl. stiftelsers midler) trustee.

kure lie or sit quiet; brood, sit brooding **ligge -nde stille** lie as mum as mice.

kurér courier, express. **-tog** express train.

kurgjest visitor (at a watering-place).

kurere cure, heal.

kurfyrst|e elector, electoral prince. **-endømme** electorate. **-inne** electress.

kuri|ositet, -osum (object of) curiosity.

kuriøs curious, singular.

kurmaker admirer, lover, beau.

kurmakeri court, love-making.

kur|metode medical treatment, curative method. **-penger** fee (for medical treatment).

kurre knot, twist, tangle (of thread); **det er kommet en — på tråden** they have quarrelled; (dt.) they have had a miff.

kurre (om due o. l.) coo. **kurring** cooing.

I. **kurs**, se **kursus**.

II. **kurs** course; (merk) quotation, (rate el. course of) exchange, (mest fig) currency; **fortsette sin — go** on one's course, keep on; **sette -en mot make** for, shape a course for. **-en er falt, steget** there is a general fall, rise; **-en på statsobligasjoner er** stocks are at; **faller, stiger i —** are falling, rising; **sette ut av —** demonetise; **etter el. til en — av** at the exchange of; **stå lavt i —** be at a discount; **høyt i —** at a premium; **til den sist noterte —** at the last quoted exchange.

kursal pump-room, kursaal.

kurs|beregning quotation. **-fall** fall.

kursforandring change of course.

kursiv italics. **-skrift** italics.

kursliste exhange-list, list of exhange.

kursnotering quotation.

kursorisk cursory.

kurs|svingning fluctuation in exchange. **-tap** loss in rate of exchange.

kursted health resort.

kursus course, curriculum.

kurtasje (meglerlønn) brokerage.

kurtisane courtesan.

kurti|sere flirt with. **-sør** (male) flirt.

kurv basket; (pakkekurv) hamper, (til glas o. l.) crate; **hun gav ham -en** she rejected him, (dt.) gave him the mitten.

kurv|arbeid basketware, basket work. **-blomstret** composite.

kurve curve.

kurv|flaske wicker bottle; (svært stor) demijohn. **-fletning** wicker-basket work. **-maker** basket-maker. **-makerarbeid** wicker work. **-stol** basket chair, wicker chair.

kusine cousin.

kusk coachman, driver.

kuske keep down, subdue, (ogs. kjøre) drive.

kuskebukk (coach-)box, driver's seat.

kuslag breed of cows.

kusma mumps.

kust: holde — på, over = kuste keep in discipline, keep in order.

kustode custos, custodian; (et ord som er trykt nederst på en bokside, og som den følgende side begynner med) catch-word.

kustus, se **kust**.

kut (løp) run, **kute** (vrb) cut and run.

kutte (monk's) cowl.

kutte (vrb, hogge av) cut.

kutter cutter.

kutyme usage, custom; **det er — at** it is customary that.

kuv roundish tap, hump.

kuvende veer, wear. **kuvending** veering.

kuvert cover.

kuvung, se **kobbung**.

kuøye (mar.) bull's eye.

kvad lay, song.

kvaderstein square stone, freestone.

kvadrant quadrant.

kvadrat square; **to fot i —** two feet square. **-fot** square foot. **-innhold** square contents.

kvadratisk quadratic, square. **kvadrat|mil** square mile. **-rot** square root. **-tomme** square inch.

kvadr|atur quadrature, squaring. **-ere** square. **-ilje** quadrille.

kvae resin.

kvakl bother, trouble, worry.

kvak|le bungle at, dabble in a thing, tamper with. **-leri** (fusk) bungling; (i legekunsten) quackery. **-salver, -salverske** quack(doctor), empiric. **-salveri** quackery.

I. **kval** pang, agony, anguish, torment.

II. **kval**, se **hval**.

kvalfull agonizing.

kvalifikasjon qualification, pretension.

kvalifi|sere qualify; **-sert** (jur.) aggravated.

kvalitativ qualitative.

kvalitet quality; **prima —** first quality.

kvalm (adj) close, oppressive, stuffy; sick. **kvalm** (subst) (støy) row; **gjøre — for ingenting** kick up a dust about nothing.

kvalme (subst) nausea, sickness, qualm.

kvalmende nauseating.

kvamne be choking.

kvanti|tativ quantitative. **-tet** quantity.

kvantum quantity.

kvapset squabby.

kvar (adj.) still, noiseless, soundless; **ligge —** lie up; **legge seg —** settle down.

kvare seg (om høns) go to roost; (om mennesker) shake oneself down for the night.

kvart quarter, fourth; (format) quarto.

kvartal quarter (of a year). **kvartals|beretning** quarterly report. **-vis** quarterly.

kvartark quarter of a sheet.

kvartbind (volume in) quarto.

kvarte (stjele) hook, nab, purloin.

kvartel (fjerding) firkin.

kvarter quarter; (av tiden) quarter (of an hour); (oppholdssted) quarters; **klokka er et — over elleve** it is a quarter past eleven; **et — på tolv** a quarter to twelve, three quarters past eleven; **vi ventet tre —** we waited for three quarters of an hour; **i det siste -s tid** this quarter of an hour; **gå i —** go into quarters; **ta sitt —** take up one's quarters. **-mester** quartermaster.

kvarteron (barn av hvit og mulatt) quadroon.

kvarterslag quarter-stroke; **slå —** strike the quarters.

kvartett quartet, quartette.

kvartformat quarto.

kvarts quartz. **-åre** vein of quartz.

kvart|side quarto page. **-utgave** quarto.

kvarv round of logs in a timber-house.

kvas (kvist og —) brushwood, faggots.

kvase (floke), se **vase**.

kvass sharp, keen, acute; **— tunge** caustic tongue. **-då(e)** (plante) hempnettle. **-mælt** caustic, sharp-tongued. **-het** keenness, sharpness, acuteness.

kvast tassel, tuft, frog.

kve (cattle-)pen, fold, sheepcot(e).

kvede (frukt) quince.

kvede (synge) sing, chaunt.

kvede (subst) lay, song.

kvee (sette i kve) fold.

kvefs wasp. **-ebol** wasp's nest, (fig) nest of hornets; **stikke handa i et —** poke one's hand into a hornet's nest; put one's hand into a beehive. **-estikk** wasp's sting.

kveg cattle. **-avl** breeding el. rearing of cattle. **-bestand, -besetning** stock of cattle. **-drift** herd of cattle, drove of cattle; se ogs. **-avl. -driver** (driftekar) drover.

kvege, refresh, recreate.

kveg|handel trade in cattle. **-handler** dealer in cattle. **-hjord** herd of cattle. **-marked** cattle-fair, cattle-market. **-oppdretter** cattle raiser. **-pest** murrain, cattle plague.

kveike, se **tenne**.

kveil coil (of rope), fake. **kveile** coil (down, up); fake (down).
kveise blotch.
kveite (fisk) halibut, turbot.
kveker quaker; (kvinnelig) quakeress, quaker woman.
kvekk (om frosk) croak, croaking; **han gav ikke et — fra seg** he did not utter a sound; (dt.) **jeg forstår ikke et —** I am quite at sea.
kvekke croak. **kvekking** croaking.
kveld evening, eve; **se aften; i —** in the evening, this evening, to-night.
kvelde grow towards night; (om personer) knock off work at nightfall, go to rest.
kvelding evening twilight.
kveldknarr eve-chur, goatsucker, night-jar.
kvelds|verd, se **aftensmat**, **-økt** spell of work between dinner and supper.
kvele strangle; (med røyk el. l.) stifle, suffocate; (ved at strupen fylles med ett eller annet) choke; (ved å berøve luft, f. eks. ved tett tildekning) smother; (fig) quell; (dempe, undertrykke) stifle, smother; (stanse, undertrykke, liksom ved kvelning, f. eks. planter i veksten) choke; **jeg holder på å bli kvalt** I am nearly choking; (fig) **— i fødselen** nip in the bud; **halvkvalt stemme** stifled voice.
kvelerslange boa constrictor.
kvelning strangling, suffocation.
kvelstoff nitrogen. **-holdig** nitrogenous.
kvelv (båt-) bottom; upturned boat; **ride på -et** sit astride on the upturned boat, se ellers **hvelv**.
kven Quain. **-sk** Quainish.
kveppe give a start; **det kvapp i ham** he gave a start. **kveppen** easily frightened, timorous.
kverk throttle, throat.
kverke throttle. **-tak** a hold of one's throat.
kvern quern, hand-mill. **-bruk** grain-mills. **-kall** tub-wheel. **-knurr**, se **fossegrim**. **-renne** millrace.
kverrsette sequestrate, seize, place el. put under an arrest, lay an embargo on, embargo.
kversill (hestesykdom) strangles.
kverve, se **dreie, svinge**. **— bort**, se **forsvinne**; **— ens syn** bias (el. glamour) one's sight, cast a glamour over one. Se **synkverve**.
kvese, se **hvese**.
kvesse whet, sharpen. **-stein** whetstone, sharpener.
kveste wound, hurt.
kvestelse bruise, contusion, hurt.
kvestor treasurer, bursar.
kvestur bursary, bursarship.
kvide pain, agony.
kvige heifer. **-kalv** cow-calf.
kvie seg feel reluctant, hang back.
kvikk lively, quick; clever, smart, witty. **-het** liveliness etc. **-e opp** enliven, rouse, cheer up; **-sand** quicksand.
kvikksølv quicksilver, mercury; **han har — i bena** he is ever on the wing, very restless. **-barometer** mercurial barometer. **-belegg** quicksilvering. **-kur** mercurial cure. **-søylen** the mercurial column. **-termometer** mercurial thermometer.
kvikne (til) brisk up, mend, rally, recover.
kvil, se **hvil**.
kvin piercing shriek; (om vinden) whistling.
kvin|e shriek. **-ende** strident, piercing.
kvink chirp, piping; whimpering, whine.
kvinke, kvinkelere pipe.
kvinne woman, female; **-n** (i alm.) woman.
kvinneaktig effeminate, womanish.
kvinneaktighet effeminacy.
kvinnebevegelse woman's movement.
kvinne|drakt female dress, woman's dress. **-forening** women's association. **-født** born of woman, womanborn. **-gunst** woman's favour. **-hater** womanhater, misogyinst. **-jeger** woman hunter. **-kjær** fond of the sex. **-kjønn** female sex, womankind. **-klær** female dress, woman's attire.

kvinnelig female; (mots. mannlig) feminine; (passende for kvinner) womanly, ladylike.
kvinnelighet womanliness, womanhood.
kvinne|list female cunning, woman's wiles. **-lege** gynecologist. **-menneske** (ringeaktende) woman. **-saken** the woman question, the woman's cause. **-sakskvinne** feminist, a women's leader. **-skikkelse** female form; (kvinne) woman **-snakk** women's el. female gossip. **-spørsmålet** the woman question. **-stemmeret** woman suffrage, votes for women. **-sykdom** disease of women. **-venn** lover of the sex. **-verk** woman's work. **-vis** the manner el. way of women. **kvinnfolk** womankind; woman.
kvint (i fektn.) quint; (på fiolin) first string, treble string; (vekt) five grams.
kvintessens quintessence, elixir.
kvintett quintet.
kviskre, se **hviske**.
I. **kvist** (grein) twig, sprig, spray.
II. **kvist** (i et hus) garret, attic.
kviste lop off the twigs, strip.
kvist|et twiggy. **-fri** (stamme) clear-boled; (bord etc.) knotless, free from knots; **-hull** knot-hole.
kvist|kammer garret. **-leilighet** dwelling in the garret, garret rooms.
kvit, se **hvit**.
kvitre chirp, twitter. **kvitring** chirping etc.
kvitt rid, quit (of), done for; **bli — noe** get rid of, be quit of; **nå er vi —** now we are quits.
kvitte balance accounts.
kvittel, se **ullteppe**.
kvitter chirping.
kvittere receipt, give a receipt el. acquittance for, discharge; **betalt, hvorfor -s** (merk.) settled.
kvittering receipt, acquittance (for: for).
kvota, -del quota.
kvotient quotient.
kvotientrekke geometrical progression.
kykeliky! cock-a-doodle-doo!
kyklop cyclops. **kyklopisk** cyclopean.
kyle fling, toss (with violence).
kylling chicken. **-høne** mother hen.
kyndig well-informed; **— i** conversant with.
kyndighet knowledge, skill.
kyn|iker cynic. **-isk** cynic(al). **-isme** cynicism.
kyr pl. av **ku**.
kyrasér cuirassier.
kyrass cuirass, breastplate.
kyse hood, calash.
kyse (skremme) scare, frighten.
kysk chaste. **-het** chastity, chasteness.
kyss kiss; **sende et —** blow a kiss.
kysse kiss; **— på fingeren til en** kiss one's hands to one.
kyst coast shore; **langs -en** along shore, coastwise.
kyst|båt coaster, coasting boat. **-beboer** inhabitant of the coast. **-by** seaside town. **-damper** coasting-steamer. **-farer** coaster. **-fart** coasting, coastal navigation. **-fartøy** coasting vessel. **-fiske** coast fishing. **-forsvar: til —** for shoredefence. **-fyr** coast-light. **-land** coast. **-linje** coastline. **-strekning** (tract of) coast. **-vakt** coast guard.
kyt, se **skryt. kyte**, se **skryte**.
I. **kø** (biljard) cue.
II. **kø** (rekke) file, single file.
kølle club, mace.
køllert buff jacket.
Køln Cologne.
køy(e) bett; (hengekøye) hammock; cot; fast — bunk; køye (vrb); **gå til køys** go to bed, turn in, nestle in.
køye|klær bedding. **-plass** berth; anvise — berth.
kål cabbage; (suppe) cabbage-soup; **gjøre — på** put an end to, put down, make havoc of. **-hode** head of cabbage. **-mark** caterpillar. **-plante** plant of the cabbage kind. **-rabi, -rot**

kohlrabi, Swedish turnips. **-stokk** cabbage-stalk. **-suppe** cabbage-soup.
kåpe cloak; **dekke med kjærlighetens —** cover with the cloak of charity.
I. **kår** condition, circumstances (pl); **han sitter i gode, dårlige, små, trange —** he is well off, badly off, in easy, poor circumstances.
II. **kår**, se **føderåd**.

kårde (straight) sword, rapier. **-feste** sword-hilt. **-stikk** stab.
kårje choose. **folkets -ne** the chosen of the people.
kåsjeri causerie, chat, gossip. **-ør** talker.
kåt wild, wanton; frolicsome; **— munn** a flippant tongue. **-het** wantonness; (villskap) wildness. **-munnet** flippant. **-munnethet** flippancy.

L

L, 1 L, l.
la el. **lade** (skytevåpen) load, charge.
la el. **late** (etterlate i en viss tilstand) leave; (tillate) allow, permit, let, suffer; (bringe til å) cause to, let, make; **— en, noe være (i fred)** let one, something alone; **— være å** desist el. refrain from, forbear; **kunne ikke — være å smile** could not help smiling; **la være!** have done; don't! **la det være** drop that! **la så være!** well and good! **la oss gå** let us go; **— en være alene** leave one alone; **— noe stå, ligge** (f. eks. på bordet) leave a thing (on the table); **— døra stå åpen** leave the door open; **— fare** leave off; **— en hente** send for one; **la ankeret gå!** let fall the anchor! **— en frakk sy** have a coat made; **— bordet reparere** have the table mended; **— ham drepe** order him to be killed; **det -r seg ikke gjøre** it can't be done; **det -r seg høre** that is something like; **— seg se** make one's appearance; **det -r ingenting tilbake å ønske** it leaves nothing to be desired. Se ellers **late II.**
laban lout; **doven —** young lazybones; **lang — overgrown** stripling.
labank bar, batten, crossbar.
labb paw; **suge på -en** suck one's paws.
labbe pad, trudge.
laber light; **— kuling** mackerel-breeze.
laborant chemist; assistant in a laboratory.
laboratorium laboratory.
laborere experimentalize.
labyrint labyrinth, maze.
labyrintisk labyrinthic, mazy.
ladd (sokk) worsted overshoe, oversock.
ladested port of loading; small seaport town.
ladning (handlingen) loading; (last) cargo, consignment; (krutt) charge; (skarpt) load.
laft block, bond. **lafte** bond. **-bygning** log -house. **laftverk** logs notched and joined at the ends.
lag layer, stratum; (selskap) party, company; (maling o. l.) coat, coating; **gi fienden det glatte —** give the enemy a broadside; **gi sitt ord med i -et** put in one's oars; **gi seg i — med en** associate with, (noe) set about; **ha godt — med** have a knack; **her på — somewhere** here. **about here.**
lag|deling stratification. **-delt** stratified.
lage: i — in order; **av —** out of order, out of gear; **bringe ut av —** (fig) unhinge; **bringe el. få i —** put to rights; **han er rent av —** he is quite out of his senses: **verden er av —** the world is out of joint.
lage (vrb) make, prepare, concoct; (ord) coin; (oppdikte) concoct; fake, fake up; **— mat** dress victuals, cook; **— til** prepare; **— seg til** make (oneself) ready, make arrangements, prepare; **— til barsel** be in the family way.
lagelig, se **passelig, bekvem.**
lager stock, store; (lokale) store-room(s), store-house, ware-house; **på —** in stock, on hand; **ikke på —** out of stock.
lagermann warehouse assistant.
lagerparti stock lot.
lagerrom store-room.
lagerøl lager-beer.

lagkake layer-cake, jam cake made in layers.
lagmann judge, presiding magistrate. **-srett** court of assize; **kreve saken innbrakt for —** desire the case to be dealt with by judge and jury.
lagnad fate, destiny, fortune.
lagre store, warehouse.
lagrette (hist.) advisory jury; witnesses appointed by authority; (i ny tid) jurors, jury. **-smann** advisory juryman; juror.
lagsmann member; (i idrett) member of a team.
lagsogn circuit, jurisdiction.
lagtinget smaller division of the Norwegian parliament.
lagune lagoon.
lagverje guardian (to a widow).
lagvis in layers.
I. **lake** brine, pickle.
II. **lake** (fisk) burbot.
lakei lackey. flunkey. **-vesen** flunkeyism.
laken sheet. **-lerret** sheeting.
lakk (sealing-) wax; (til ferniss) lac; **en stang — a** stick of sealing-wax.
I. **lakke** (forsegle) seal.
II. **lakke** (nærme seg, gå) draw nigh, approach; **det -r mot enden** it is drawing to an end.
lakkerje lacker, japan. **-ing** lackering; japanning.
lakk|farge lake, drop-colour. **-ferniss** lac varnish. **-sko** patent leather shoes; (lette, til dans) pumps.
lakmus litmus. **-papir** litmus paper.
lakon|isk laconic. **-isme** laconism.
lakris liquorice. **-rot** l. root, sweet-root.
laks salmon.
laksefarget salmon-coloured.
laksere purge.
laksermiddel purgative, cathartic, aperient.
lakse|trapp fish- (el. salmon-)pass. **-varp** weel.
laksyngel salmon fry.
lakune blank, gap, lacuna.
lalle babble.
lam (subst) lamb.
lam (adj) palsied, paralysed, paralytic.
lama (dyr) llama, lama; (prest) Lama.
lamell (elektrisk) lamel, lamella (pl. -læ).
lamhet palsy; (også fig) lameness.
I. **lamme** (gjøre lam) palsy; (også fig) paralyse.
II. **lamme** (få lam) lamb (down).
lammekjøtt lamb; mutton.
lammelse, se **lamhet.**
lammestek roast-lamb; roast mutton.
lammeull lamb's wool el. fleece.
lampe lamp.
lampe|feber stage-fright. **-glass** lamp-glass, chimney. **-kuppel** lamp-globe. **-lys** lamp-light. **-pusser** lamp-lighter, lamp trimmer. **-skjerm** lamp shade.
lampett sconce, bracket lamp.
lampe|veke, -veike lamp-wick.
lamprett (fiskeslekt) lamprey.
lamslå paralyze.
land land; (egn; landet; motsatt byen) country; (eiendom) land, lands; **fast —** main land, continent; **brakk —** fallow ground; **flatt —**

low land, flat land; **høyt** — high land; **et stykke** — a piece of ground el. land; — **i sikte** land ho! i — on shore; **gå i** — go on shore, disembark; **sette i** — set, put on shore, land; **her i -et** in this country; **inn(e) i -et** inland; **en by inne i -et** an inland town; **vite hvor -et ligger** know the lie of the land; **vinden stod fra** — the wind was offshore; **omgitt av** — landlocked; **få på** — **(en fisk)** land; **reise over** — go by el. over land; **på -et** in the country; **dra ut på -et** go into the country; **bo på -et** live in the country; **sette på** — beach; **til -s** by land; **reise ut av -et** go abroad.

landarbeider farm labourer.
landauer landau. **-lett** landaulet, brougham.
landavståelse cession of territory.
landbefolkning rural population.
landboer countryman, farmer, country dweller.
landbruk agriculture.
landbruker agriculturist, farmer.
landbruksdepartement board of agriculture.
landbruks|forhold rural matters. **-høgskole** (veterinary and) agricultural college, college of agriculture. **-konsulent** consulting agriculturist.
landbruksprodukter agricultural products.
landbruksskole agricultural school.
landdag diet.
lande land.
landefred the King's peace.
landeiendom landed property. **eier av** — landed proprietor.
landemerke boundary line.
lande|plage general plague el. scourge; (fig) public nuisance. **-sorg** general sorrow el. mourning.
landetat army list.
landevei (high)road, highway; **den slagne** — (fig) the beaten track.
landeveisrøver highwayman.
landfast med contiguous to, connected with.
landfeste land-tie.
landflyktig exiled, banished.
landflyktighet exile, banishment; **jage i** — exile.
landgang landing; (fiendtl.) descent; **gjøre** — **på** make a descent on; (konkr.) gangway, gangway plank, gangboard.
landgangs|brygge landing-pier, landing-stage. **-båt** surf-boat.
land|grense frontier; (motsatt sjøgrense) land frontier. **-handel** country trade. **-handler** country tradesman, country dealer. **-handleri** local store.
landhusholdning farming el. rural economy.
landhusholdningsselskap agricultural society.
landhær land army el. force(s).
landing landing. **-splass** landingplace.
landinnvinning reclaiming of land, reclaimed land.
land|jorda (dry) land. **-kart** map. **-kjenning** (mar) land-fall; (peilinger) bearings; **få -kjenning** sight the land. **-krabbe** (skjellsord) landsman, (land-)lubber.
landlig rural, rustical.
land|ligge day el. time ashore, no fishery, dead day. **-ligger** resident in the country, ruralist, summer resident.
land|liv country life el. rural life. **-lov** liberty (ashore), land-leave. **-lovsdag** liberty day. **-luft** country air. **-mann** countryman, farmer. **-manns-** farmer's, agricultural. **-måler** surveyor. **-målerstang** surveyor's rod. **-måling** surveying. **-officer** officer in the army. **-område** territory. **-peiling** (taking the) bearing of a point on land. **-postbud** rural postman. **-reise** overland-journey.
landsby village.
landsbygd rural district. **på -a** in country places, in rural parts.
landsdel part of the country.
landsens (gml. gen) of the country, rural, provincial; innocent.

landsete country-seat, country-residence.
landsetning landing, disembarkation.
landsette (sette i l.) land, disembark; (et skip) run ashore, beach.
lands|faderlig kingly, paternal. **-far** sovereign, father of a people. **-forræder** traitor. **-forræderi** treason. **-forræder(i)sk** treacherous, treasonable. **-forvise, -forvisning,** se **forvise. -herre** regent, ruler, sovereign. **-kall** country living.
landskap landscape; (provins) province.
landskaps|bilde landscape, prospect. **-maler** landscape painter. **-maleri** (painting of a) landscape. **-maling** landscape painting.
landskilpadde tortoise.
landskirke country church.
landskjent noted throughout the country; **menn med -e navn** men whose names are household words.
landsknekt lansquenet.
land|skyld land-rent. **-skyss** overland conveyance.
lands|lov law of the land. **-mann** countryman, compatriot. **-manninne** countrywoman. **-mål** New-Norwegian.
land|snegl land snail. **-sogn** country-parish.
lands|prest country parson. **-sak** national issue. **-skikk** custom of the country.
land|sted country house el. cottage, summer resort. **-strekning** extent el. tract of land. **-strimmel** strip of land. **-stryker, -strykerske** tramp, tramper, vagrant.
landsulykke national calamity.
landsøl (amr.) bevo, nearbeer.
land|tunge isthmus, neck of land, land-strait. **-toning** view, landmark. **-tunge** tongue of land, spit. **-tur** excursion into the country, picnic.
landvern (i England) militia; (i Norge) second levy, reserve. **-smann** militiaman, reservist.
landverts overland.
landvin home-grown wine.
landvinning accession of territory.
landøkonomi farming economy.
lang long; (om vei) far, (fjern) distant; **tiden faller meg** — I find the time long; **i (på)** — tid for a long time, this long time; **tar** — tid takes long; **8 tommer** — **og 4 tommer bred** 8 inches long by 4 broad, 8 inches by 4; **så** — **han var** at full length; **falt så** — han var measured his length (on the ground), fell his length on the ground; **temmelig** — lengthy; **han ble** — **i ansiktet** his face fell; **var svært** — **i ansiktet** wore a very long face; **i lengre tid** for a length of time; **et lengre besøk** a protracted el. lengthened visit; **i det lengste at** the longest; **du har vært her din lengste tid** your time here is soon at an end; **så** — **dagen er** the livelong day; **han er så snill som dagen er** — he is as good as good; **tiden faller** — **for ham** time hangs heavily (on his hands); **hvor -t er det til B.?** how far is it to B.? how far do you call it from this to B.? **langt** (avstand) far; **halvparten så** — half that distance; **vi har** — **hjem** we have a long way home; — **borte fra** far off; —, **lenger, lengst borte** far, farther, farthest off el. away; — **fra** (i avstand) from a distance; (motsatt nær ved og fig) far from; (langveis fra) from afar; — **fra lykkelig** far from happy; **det er** — **fra så vakkert som** . . . it is not nearly (el. not anything like, nothing like) so fine as . . .; **det er** — **fra å dårlig** it is far from being so bad; — **fra! far** from it; **det være** — **fra meg** far be it from me; — **fram** far; **han så** — **fram i tiden** he looked far into futurity; — **framme** far on; — **inn, — inne** far in; — **inn i** far into; — **om lenge** at last, at length, after a long time; — **ut på dagen** late in the day el. morning; — **tilbake** far back; — **ut på natta** at el. till a late hour of the night, far into the night; **til** — **ut på sommeren** far into the summer.
lang|aktig rather long, lengthy, longish. **-beint** long-legged.

langdrag: trekke i — protract, spin out; (intrans) hang fire, make slow progress.
lange hand, pass; — til en fetch one a blow; **— etter** reach after (at).
lange (fisk) ling.
lang(e)leik Norwegian dulcimer.
langelig slowly; wistfully.
langemann (finger) long-man.
langfart distant el. long voyage.
lang|finger middle-finger. **-fingret** long-fingered; (fig) light-fingered.
langfredag Good Friday.
langgrunn shelving (and shallow). **det er langgrunt her** it shoals for some distance here.
langhalset long-necked.
langhornet krøtter long-horns.
langhåret long-haired.
langlivet long-waisted; (som lever lenge) long-lived.
langmodig longsuffering.
langmodighet longanimity.
langneset long-nosed.
langrenn long-distance run (on ski).
langs: på — lengthwise, lengthways, longitudinally; (prep) (i strekning med) along; **— etter, — med** along, lengthways of; **gå — med** (kanten av) skirt; **— landet** along the shore; **— siden** (av et skip) alongside.
langsiden the length.
langsiktig of long date, long. **— politikk** far-seeing policy.
langsiktsveksel bill of long date.
langsint bearing a grudge long, implacable.
langskips fore-and-aft.
langsom slow, tardy.
langsomhet slowness, tardiness.
langstrakt lengthened, stretched in length.
langsynt long-sighted.
langsynthet long-sightedness.
langt, se **lang.**
langtekkelig dull, tedious, heavy.
langtrekkende far-reaching; (om våpen) long -range.
langtrukken lengthy, prolix, long-winded.
langtrukkenhet longwindedness.
langtur distant el. long journey.
lang|varig Long, of long duration, protracted, long-lasting, tedious. **-varighet** slowness, protraction. **-veisfarende** far-faring; distant traveller. **-veis fra** from afar; (langt bort) far off.
lanse lance, spear, pike.
lansere start, set up.
lansett lancet.
lanterne lantern. **signaler med — signal**lights.
lapidarstil lapirady style.
I. **lapp** (tøy) patch; (papir) scrap.
II. **lapp** Laplander, Lapp.
lappe patch, piece.
lappeskomaker cobbler.
lappeskredder mender of old clothes, patcher.
lappeteppe piece-rug, rag-carpet, patchwork counterpane.
lapping patching, piecing.
lappisk Lapp, Lappish.
Lappland Lapland. **l-sk** Lapland, Lappish.
lapplending (i Sverige) Laplander.
lappverk patchwork.
laps beau, dandy, swell; (spradebasse) coxcomb.
lapse seg strut, swagger; **— med sport,** air.
lapse|ri coxcombry; foppish el. frivolous conduct. **-t** foppish, frivolous.
lapskaus lobscouse, hash.
lapsus slip, lapse; **— calami** slip of the pen; **— linguæ** slip of the tongue.
larm noise, alarm. **larme** make a noise.
larmende noisy.
larv contemptible fellow.
larve caterpillar, grub, larva, maggot.
lasarett lazaret, lazaretto; (ombord) cock-pit.

lasaron lazzarone, tramp.
lasket fleshy, sleek, obese.
lass load; (fig) **trekke -et** bear the burden of the day, bear the brunt; **liten tue velter stort —** little strokes fell great oaks.
lassevis by the load, in loads.
lasso lasso, lariat.
I. **last** (vanesynd) vice.
II. **last** (bør) burden, charge; (ladning) cargo; (lasterom) hold; (trelast) timber, (amr) lumber; **legge en noe til —** lay something to one's charge; **brekke -en** (mar) break bulk; **stue -en** stow the cargo, trim the hold.
lastdyr beast of burden.
I. **laste** load; **-t laden; -t med kull** coal-laden.
II. **laste** (klandre) blame, censure.
laste|automobil, lastebil (åpen) motor-lorry; (lukket) motor-van. **-avgift** lastage money. **-båt** cargo boat, tramp-ship, tramp. **-damper** cargo el. tramp steamer.
lasteevne carrying capacity.
lastefull vicious, depraved. **-het** depravity.
lasteklar ready. **laste|penger** tonnage (dues). **-pram** lighter. **-rom** hold.
lasting (tøy) lasting, prunelle.
last(n)ing loading.
lastningsomkostninger loading expenses.
lastokk ram-rod.
lastverdig blameable, reprehensible.
lastverk: hastverk er — haste makes waste.
lasur transparent coating.
lasurfarge glazing-colour.
lat lazy, indolent, slothful.
I. **late** (vi) seem, appear; (gi seg utseende av) feign, pretend, affect; **— til å** appear to, look as if; **det -r til det** it appears so; **— som om** pretend to el. that; **— som ingenting** look innocent, unconscious, appear as if nothing were the matter.
II. **late** (vt.) se **la; — sitt liv** lay down one's life. **— vannet** make water.
III. **late seg,** se **dovne seg.**
latent latent.
laterna magica magic lantern.
lathet laziness, indolence, sloth.
latin Latin. **-er** (nasjon) Latin; (studium) Latin scholar, Latinist.
latinerseil lateen-sail.
latinsk Latin; **— stil** Latin; **-e bokstaver** Roman letters.
latinskole grammar school, classical school.
latmanns|bør lazyman's load. **-liv** life of idleness.
latrin privy.
latside: ligge på -n be idle, do nothing.
latskap laziness, indolence, sloth.
latter laughter, laugh; (tilbaketrengt latter) chuckle; **briste i —** burst out laughing; **sette i en —** set up a loud laugh; **få seg en god —** enjoy a hearty laugh; **slå det bort med —** turn it off with a laugh, laugh it off; **gjøre til —** ridicule, turn into ridicule; **sitte i en ustanselig —** be in a constant roar of laughter; **gjøre seg til —** make oneself ridiculous; **vende -en mot noe annet** turn the laugh against st. else; **være, bli til —** for folk be, become a common laughing-stock.
latterhjørnet the laughing humour; **være i —** be laughy.
latterkor chorus of laughter.
latterkrampe convulsive laughter.
latterlig laughable, ridiculous, ludicrous, droll. **-gjøre** ridicule, turn into ridicule, cast ridicule upon. **-het** ridiculousness.
latter|mild laughy. **-mildhet** laughiness. **-salve** burst of laughter. **-vekkende** laughable.
I. **laug** (sammenslutning av handverkere) corporation, guild; (fig) craft, fraternity; **oppta i et —** make (one) free of a corporation.
II. **laug,** se **bad. lauge,** se **bade.**
laugs|artikler statutes of a guild. **-oldermann**

bencher. **–rettighet** corporate freedom. **–vesen** corporation. **–ånd** corporate spirit.

lauk, se løk.

lauparsko ski-runner's shoe (with soft soles and the seam at the top).

laurbær bay-berry; (fig) bays, laurels. **–blad** laurel el. bay leaf. **–krans** laurel wreath, laurels. **–tre** laurel el. bay (tree).

lauv leaf; leaves, foliage, leafage.

lauv|fall, –fallstid fall (of the leaf). **–hytte** bower, arbour.

lauv|jord leafmould, el. -soil. **–rik** leafy. **–sprett** shooting of the leaf, leafing. **–stakk** stack of fodder leafage. **–tre** leaftree, hardwood tree. **–verk** foliage, leafage.

lav low; (om vann) low, shallow; (uedel) low, mean, base; **lavt** low; **sette prisene lavt** put prices low.

lav (planteart) lichen.

lava lava.

lavadel gentry.

lavalder responsible age, minimum age.

lavastrøm torrent of lava.

lave (henge i mengde) dangle, hang down (in abundance, in clusters). **hagene –r av frukt** the orchards hang thick with fruit.

lavendel lavender.

lavere (mar.) (vrb) tack, beat.

lavere|liggende lower, lower-lying. **–stående** inferior, lower.

lavering tacking, beating.

lavett (gun-)carriage.

lavfrekvens low frequency.

lavine avalanche.

lav|kirkelig Low Church. **–komisk** burlesque, farcical.

lavland lowland.

lav|loftet low-ceilinged. **–mælt** low-voiced. **–mål** minimum; low level.

lav|pannet (fig) base-minded. **–pullet** low-crowned. **–sinnet** low-minded.

lavslette bottom.

lavspent low-tension(ed), at low tension.

lavstammet low-stemmed; (fig) undersized.

lavtliggende low-lying, low.

lavtrykk low pressure.

lavtrykksmaskin low-pressure engine.

lavtstående low, inferior.

lavttenkende low-minded, low-thoughted.

lavvanne low water, (lowest) ebb.

lavvannsmerke low-water mark.

le (subst.) shelter; (mar) leeward, lee; **en seiler —! a** sail to leeward! **ror i —! helm** a-lee!

le (vrb.) laugh; **— hjertelig, inderlig godt** chuckle; **— høyt** laugh aloud, out; **— en rett opp i øynene** el. **ansiktet** laugh in one's face; **— av** laugh at; **— til en** laugh on one; **jeg må —** it makes me laugh; **— over hele ansiktet** be on the broad grin; **— en ut** laugh at one; (bespotte) laugh one to scorn; **— seg ihjel** el. **fordervet** die el. split one's sides with laughing; **— i skjegget** laugh in one's sleeve; **det er ikke noe å — av** this is no laughing matter; **den som –r sist, –r best** he laughs best who laughs last, those laugh best who laugh last, he who wins may laugh.

lealaus limp, loose of joint, ramshackle, rickety, (ogs. fig) limp, weak-kneed.

lebelte (forstuttr.) protecting belt.

I. led (grind) wicket, gate; (med stenger til å dra ut) barway.

II. led, se lei.

ledd (el. **led**) joint; (av kjede) link; (slektskaps-grad) degree (of kindred), remove, generation; **av —** out of joint; **sette i —** set.

ledd|dannelse articulation. **–deling** division in joints; articulation. **–delt** articulate(d). **–et** jointed. **–dukke** jointed puppet, mannikin. **–dyr** articulate, articulate (el. jointed) animal.

ledd|vann dropsy in the joints. **–verk** gout.

leddvis joint by joint.

lede (føre) lead; (veilede, styre) guide; (ved rør) conduct; (styre) direct; (anføre) conduct; (fig) lead, conduct, guide; **— forhandlingene** be in the chair, preside; **— bort** (vann) carry off; **— samtalen hen på** lead up to; **la seg — av** be governed (el. guided) by; **–t av** (et hensyn o. l.) guided by.

ledebånd leading-strings; **gå i ens —** be led (entirely) by one.

ledelse direction, guidance, management; **under — av** under the charge of; **overta –n av** take charge of.

ledemotiv representative theme.

ledende leading; (fysikk) conductive; **— artikkel** leader; (amr) editorial; **— tanke** leading el. dominant idea; **— grunnsetning** guiding principle.

leder guide; (fys) conductor; (i avis) leader.

ledere hurt, injure.

ledestjerne load-star, guiding-star.

lede|tone leading note el. tone, sensible note. **–tråd** (nøkkel) clew, clue; (veiledning) gulde.

ledig (om plass) vacant, unoccupied, disengaged; (tilovers) spare; (ubeskjeftiget) unemployed, idle, disengaged; (uten arbeid) out of work el. place; **les og — (ugift) single; — plass** vacancy; **— time** leisure hour, spare hour.

lediggang idleness; **— er rota til alt vondt** idleness is the root of all evil, an idle brain is the devil's workshop.

ledig|gjenger idler, vagrant. **–het** vacancy; want of employment.

leding war; **gå i —** (fig) enter the lists; go on the war-path. **lednings|ferd** warlike expedition. **–utbud** summons to arms.

ledning (vann- osv.) main; (telegraf-) wire, line; (fys) conduction.

lednings|evne conductive power. **–rør** conduct-pipe. **–tråd** conducting wire.

ledsage (følge i alminnelighet) accompany; (ledsage for å passe, yte tjeneste etc.) attend; (med musikk) accompany.

ledsagelse accompaniment; attendance; (til forsvar) escort.

ledsager companion.

ledtog: være i — med en be one's accomplice, be in league with.

lee (røre på) move slightly, just move. **— på hodet** wriggle one's head. **— på låsen** try the lock.

lefle coquet, flirt, (fig) dally. **lefling** flirtation

lefse flat bannock. **–kling** el. **–klining, se kling.**

legal legal.

legali|sere authenticate, legalize. **–sasjon** authentication, legalisation.

legasjon legation.

legasjonssekretær secretary of legation el. embassy.

legat legacy, bequest.

legator testator, legator.

legd (fattigdistrikt) union. **være på —** be lodged as a parish pauper.

legde|gutt, –jente pauper boy (girl) (quartered on a farmer or farmers). **–kall** old parish pauper.

legdslem parish pauper.

lege (i alm. ogs. huslege) doctor, medical man; (spesialist, som ikke opererer) physician; (kirurg, militærlege, skipslege) surgeon; (alm. praktiserende lege) general practitioner, practitioner.

lege (vrb) heal, cure; **leges** heal (up); **legende** healing, curative, therapeutic.

lege|attest medical certificate. **–behandling** medical treatment. **–besøk** professional el. medical visit. **–bok** medical book. **–drikk** potion. **–hjelp** medical aid el. advice, medical relief. **søke –hjelp** apply to a physician, call a ph. **–honorar** physician's fee. **–kraft** healing power. **–kunnskap** medical knowledge. **–kunst** art of healing, medical art. **–kyndig** skilled in medicine, therapeutic.

legeme body; (mest om mennesket) (bodily) frame.

legemiddel medicine, drug, medicament.

legemlig bodily, corporal, (materiell) corporeal. — **beskaffenhet** constitution, habit (of body). **-gjøre** embody, incarnate. **-gjørelse** embodiment, incarnation. — **svakhet** bodily infirmity.

legems|beskadigelse hurt, injury. **-bygning** frame (of body), (bodily) structure. **-del** part of the body. **-feil** bodily defect. **-fornærmelse** assault, crime against the person. **-stor** full-size. **-straff** corporal punishment. **-størrelse** size; i **full** — (in) full size, as large as life; **et portrett i full** — a life-size portrait. full-life portrait. **-øvelse** bodily exercise.

legende legend. **legendarisk** legendary.

I. **legere** (testamentere) bequeath.

II. **legere** (i kjemi) alloy. **legering** alloy.

legervall (mar.) lee shore.

lege|råd medical advice. **-skjønn** medical inspection. **-standen** the medical profession. **-tilsyn** medical attendance. **-urt** medicinal plant, simple. **-vakt** ambulance depot. **-vaktstasjon** ambulance, first aid station. **-vitenskap** medical science, science of medicine. **-vitenskapelig** medical; professional. **-visitasjon** medical examination.

I. **legg** (et) fold, plait; (på klesplagg) tuck; (på tau) lay; (av papir) lift; **legge i** — fold, plait, lay in folds.

II. **legg** (på bein) calf.

legge put, lay; — **egg** lay (eggs); — **en plan** draw up a plan; **legg roret styrbord, babord!** starboard the helm, port the helm; — **seg lie down**; (til sengs) go to bed; (fig) **gå hjem og** — **seg** shut up, go home to one's mother; **vinden har lagt seg** the wind has subsided; **sundet har lagt seg** the sound is frozen (over); — **an level**, take aim; — **an på** (noe) affect, study; (en herre) set one's cap at el. for, make a set at; — **bi** lay to, bring to; — **seg etter** apply oneself to, cultivate; lay oneself out for; — **seg for anker** anchor; — **fra land** put off; — **hen** (en sak) lay aside; — **i ovnen** light a fire in the stove; — **seg imellom** interpose, interfere; — **inn** (vann, gass) lay on; — **inn en kjole** take in a dress; — **inn et godt ord for en** put in a good word, say a kind word for one; — **ned grønnsaker, frukt** preserve vegetables, fruit; — **ned smør, sild** pack butter, herrings; — **opp kortene sine** face one's cards on the table; — **seg opp penger** lay up, lay by el. save money; — **opp melk** make curd; — **opp råd** lay plans; — **på prisen** raise the price; — **sammen** put together; fold up; (addere) add up, sum (up); (tøy) fold; — **til** add; (et skip) come alongside; — **seg til** (noe nytt) invest in, set up, start; (penger) accumulate, (kunnskap) pick up; — **seg til vaner** contract el. assume habits; — **ut en kjole** let out a dress; — **ut penger** lay out money; — **en ut som barnefar** father a child upon one; — **seg ut** grow stout, fill out, put on weight; — **seg ut med** quarrel, fall out with.

legge|bein fibula. **-beskytter** pad, shin-guard. **-brodd** (hos insekter) ovipositor. **-høne** laying hen.

leggetid period of laying eggs.

legging (lang gamasje) legging.

legion legion. **legionær** legionary.

legitim legitimate. **-asjon** legitimation. **-asjonsbevis** certificate of identity. **-ere** legitimate; — **seg** get oneself recognized, justified, prove one's identity. **-ering** legitimation.

legre, — **seg** (agr.) encamp.

lei direction, track; **på lang** — far and wide, for miles and miles; (seilløp) approach, channel, fairway, track; **den indre** — the inshore channel.

lei (adj) (slem) wicked; (ubehagelig) awkward, invidious; (vanskelig) awkward, hard; (bedrøvet) sorry; **hun ble aldri** — **av dem** she never tired of them; **bli** — **av det** ogs. have enough of it, get to hate it.

leide safe conduct. **-brev** letter of safe conduct.

leider (mar) ladder.

leidnerflaske Leyden jar.

I. **leie** (et) couch; (mineralogi) stratum; (elve-) bed; **skyve ut av** — displace.

II. **leie** hire, rent; **huset er til** — the house is to let; **bo til** — be a tenant el. lodger; live in lodgings, live in chambers; **ha til** — rent; **betale i** — pay for rent.

I. **leie** (vrb) hire; (hus, jord) rent; — **bort** hire out, rent; — **ut** lend on hire, let (out).

II. **leie** (føre v. hånden) lead (by the hand).

leie|bibliotek circulating library. **-boer** lodger. **-gård** flat-house; (amr.) apartment-house.

leiekontrakt contract, lease of house.

leiemål time of lease el. renting.

leier hirer, renter, lodger.

leie|svenn hireling. **-tid** term of lease. **-tjener** hired waiter. **-tropper** mercenaries.

leik, leike, se **lek, leke.**

leiken frolicsome, gamesome, playful.

leilending lease-holder; tenant farmer.

I. **leilighet** (beleilig tid el. øyeblikk) opportunity, chance; (anledning) occasion; (bekvem tid) convenience; **benytte en** — take an opportunity; **gripe en** — seize el. embrace an opportunity; — **gjør tyver** opportunity makes the thief; **etter fattig** — in my little way; **når De har** — **til det** at your convenience; **finne, gi** — **til å** find, give, an opportunity of -ing; **ved** — on occasion; at your convenience, when opportunity offers; **ved den -en** upon that occasion, at the time.

II. **leilighet** (bolig) rooms, flat, suite of rooms, apartments, house, dwelling, accomodations.

leilighets|arbeid occasional work. **-dikt** poem on some particular occasion, topical poem. **-kjøp** chance bargain. **-tilbud** chance offer.

leilighetsvis occasionally, on an occasion, incidentally.

I. **leir** (el. leire) clay, loam. **-aktig** clayey.

II. **leir** camp; **ligge i** — be encamped; **slå** — pitch a camp. **-bål** camp-fire.

leire el. **encamp**; (fig) settle.

leiret clayey, loamy.

leir|fat earthen dish. **-grav** clay pit. **-grunn** clay soil. **-gryte** earthen pot. **-holdig** argillaceous. **-jord** clay, clayey soil; (kjemi) alumina, aluminic oxide. **-krukke** earthen pot. **-lag** stratum of clay.

leir|plass camping-ground, camping place. **-slagning** encampment.

leir|varefabrikant potter. **-varer** earthen-ware, fictile ware.

leite på tell upon, try.

leite, se **lete.**

leite (omtrentlig tid) approximate time; **ved dette** — about this time; **ved jonsok** — about midsummer.

leiv (brød-) flap of bread, bannock.

lek game, play; **det ble enden på -en** that was the end of it; **holde opp mens -en er god** let well alone. (fugle-) call, pairing note and antics.

lek (adj) lay. **-bror** lay brother. **-dommer** non-professional judge.

leke (vrb.) play; — (f. eks. blindebukk) play at (blindman's buff).

leke (subst) (child's, infant's) toy, plaything.

lekekamerat playfellow, playmate.

lekeplass play ground.

leke|stue play-room. **-søster** playfellow. **-tøy** toy. **-tøysbutikk** toy-shop.

lekfolk the laity.

lekk (subst) leak. **lekk** (adj) leaky; **bli, springe** — spring a leak. **lekkasje** leakage.

lekke leak; (om fartøy) make water.

lekker dainty, nice, delicate; **gjøre seg** — for curry favour with. **-bisken** dainty, delicacy. **-munn** sweet tooth. **-sulten** lickerish, dainty.

lekmann layman, one of the laity.
lekmanns|preken lay sermon. **-skjønn** lay opinion.
lekpredikant lay preacher.
lekse lesson, task; **gi en en** — set one a task; **lese på -a si** — con over one's lesson, **kunne -a si** know one's lesson; **lære en** — learn a lesson, get up a task.
lekse opp for en ring a peal in one's ear.
lekselesing preparation.
leksikalsk lexical.
leksik|ograf lexicographer. **-on** dictionary.
leksjon (fig): **gi en en** — read one a lecture.
lekte (subst) lath. **lekte** (vrb) cover with laths.
lektekapp lath-cuttings.
lekter (flatbunnet pram) lighter. **-mann** lighter-man. **-penger** lighterage.
lektor (ved gymnasium) master; (slags docent) lecturer (i: in).
lektorat mastership; lectureship.
lektyre reading.
lell (adv) (dt.) all the same; whether or no. **nei** — not really?
I. **lem** (en) trapdoor; (luke) shutter.
II. **lem** (et) member; (bare om armer og bein) limb.
lemen Lapland marmot, (Norwegian) lemming.
lemfeldig lenient, mild, indulgent. **-het** lenity, mildness, softness, tenderness.
lemleste mutilate; maim, disable, cripple. **-lse** mutilation, maiming.
lempe (etter: to) adapt, suit, accommodate; (ballast) shift; (kull) trim; — **seg** be accommodating, accommodate oneself (etter: to). — **på** modify, soften down.
lempe gentleness, softness; **med** — gently.
lempelig gentle, soft, mild, lenient; (adv) gently.
lempelse modification.
lemster stiff, stiffened (with fatigue, with the exertion).
len feoff, fief, fee, feud.
lend loin. **lende-** lumbar.
lende (terreng) ground, land, soil.
lende|gikt, -verk lumbago.
lend(er)mann (hist.) feudatory.
lene lean, incline; — **seg til** lean against; — **seg på** lean on.
lenestol armchair, easy-chair.
lengd, lengde length; (geografisk) longitude; **i -n** in length; (fig) in the long run, permanently; **i sin fulle** — at length.
lengde|grad degree of longitude. **-mål** measure of length. **-retning** longitudinal direction. **-sirkel** circle of longitude. **-sprang** long jump.
lenge long; **det varer** — **før han kommer** he is long in coming; **sitt ned så** — sit down the while; **farvel så** —! so long! **han gjør det ikke** — he is drawing fast to an end; **for** — **siden** long ago; **lenger** longer; **ikke -r** no longer no more; **det er ikke -r siden enn igår** at only yesterday; **lengst** longest; **den lengstlevende** the survivor, the longest liver.
I. **lenges** (lengte) long (etter: for, after); — **etter å** long to.
II. **lenges** (bli lenger) become longer, lengthen.
lengsel longing, yearning.
lengselsfull longing.
**lengt, se lengsel.
**lengte, se lenges.
lenke chain; (til bena, fotjern) fetter; **legge i -r** put in irons, fetter; **ta -ne av** unchain.
lenke (vrb) chain, fetter; (sammenlenke) link.
lenkebinde chain, fetter.
lenkehund chain-dog.
lens (tom) cleared, empty; (mar.) free (from water); (fig) devoid (of); — **for penger** out of cash; — **for kull** run out of coal; **pungen er** — the purse is empty; **øse** — bale out; **slå** — free.
lens (fordevindsseilas) run before the wind.

lens|adel feudal nobility. **-besitter** feoffee.
I. **lense** run before the wind; (i storm) scud, spoom.
II. **lense** (tømme) clear, empty, free; (øse lens) bale.
lense (tømmer-) boom-channel, timber-boom.
lens|ed oath of fealty. **-greve** feudal count. **-herre** feudal lord, liege lord.
lensing (tømming) clearing; (i storm) scudding.
lensmann (vasall) vassal, liege, feoffee; (i moderne betydn.) bailiff, rural mayor.
lensmanns|arrest cage, lock-up house. **-bestilling** rural mayoralty. **-kar** bailiff's man. **-søvn** dog el. fox sleep.
lens|tid feudal ages. **-vesen** feudalism.
leopard leopard.
lepe lip; **det skal ikke komme over mine -r** it shall not pass my lips; **på alles -r** in everybody's mouth.
lepe|blomst labiate flower. **-blomstret** labiate. **-lyd** labial sound.
lepe|pomade lip-salve. **-stift** lip-stick.
lepje lap. **lepjing** lapping.
**leppe, se lepe.
lerke lark; (dt.) (lomme-) pocket-flask, pocket-pistol.
lerketre larch, larch-tree.
lerret linen, linen cloth; (malers) canvass.
lerrets|bluse smock-frock. **-handel** linen trade. **-handler** linen-draper. **-skjorte** linen shirt. **-vever** linen-weaver.
lese read; (gjennomlese) peruse; (ha time) be in class, teach a class; — **korrektur** read for the press; — **feil** misread; — **noe etter** read over; — **for en** read to one; — **i en bok** read a book; — **med en** give one lessons; — **opp av en bok** read from a book; — **over** study, read up; — **til eksamen** read for one's examination; — **ut** finish.
lese|bok reading-book, reader. **-drama** reading drama. **-forening** reading society. **-ferdighet** knowledge of reading. **-hest** hard reader, plodder.
leseil studdingsail.
lesekrets circle of readers, reading circle.
leselig legible, readable.
lese|lyst love of reading. **-måte** manner of reading; (i håndskrift) reading. **-plan** course of study. **-prøve** (på et skuespill) reading (-rehearsal). **-pult** reading-desk.
leser reader. **-inne** reader, fair reader.
lese|sal reading-room. **-selskap** reading society. **-stykke** reading piece, selection. **-verdig** worth reading. **-værelse** reading-room. **-øvelse** reading-exercise.
lesiden (mar) the lee side.
lesjon injury, lesion.
leske slake, quench; — **kalk** slake lime; **-drikk** refreshing beverage. **leskende** refreshing.
lesning reading.
lespe lisp. **lesping** lisping.
lesse load; — **på** load; — **av** unload.
I. **lest** (merk.) (mål på varer) last.
II. **lest** (skomakerl.) last; **skomaker bli ved din** — the cobbler is not to go beyond his last.
letargi lethargy. **-gisk** lethargic(al).
lete (søke) seek, search, look (etter: for, after); — **opp** seek, seek out.
leting seeking, search.
letne lighten; (om tåke) ease; (om regn) begin to let up el. hold off.
letning (mar) getting under way; (av ankeret) weighing.
lett (mots. tung) light; (mots. vanskelig) easy, facile; (ubetydelig, svak) slight; (hurtig, behendig) nimble; (om tobakk) mild; — **til beins** light-footed; **et** — **sinn** a buoyant disposition; **han ble** — **om hjertet** his heart grew light; **det ville gjøre saken -ere for oss** it would facilitate matters.
lett (adv) lightly; easily, readily; slightly; **blir** — ... is apt to be ...; — **såret** slightly

wounded; **ta — på** handle leniently; **han har — for historie** he is quick at history; **han tar verden —** he takes the world easy.
lett (farge) hue, complexion.
lett|bevegelig easily moved, impulsive. **-brukt** easy to work.
lette (gjøre mindre tung) lighten, ease; (gjøre mindre vanskelig) facilitate; (løfte) lift; (sitt sinn) disburden; (hjertet) ease, relieve; (om skip) get under way; (om tåke) clear, lift; **— ankeret** weigh anchor; **med -t hjerte** with a feeling of relief.
lettelse lightening; facilitation; (hjelp) relief; (trøst) comfort; (lindring) alleviation.
letter (innbygger i Lettland) Lett.
lett|fattelig intelligible, facile. **-fengelig** inflammable. **-ferdig** frivolous; (om seder) wanton, loose. **-ferdighet** frivolity, frivolousness, levity, looseness. **-fordøyelig** easy of digestion. **-fordøyelighet** digestibility. **-fotet** light-footed.
letthet lightness; (mots. vanskelighet) ease, facility; (utvungenhet) ease; (sinnets) bouyancy.
lettisk Latvian.
lett|kjøpt cheap. **-kledd** lightly clad el. dressed.
Lettland Latvia.
lett|lest easily read. **-livet** easygoing, buoyant, light-souled.
lettmatros ordinary seaman, light hand.
lettsindig lightminded, light, frivolous; (sterkere) extravagant, reckless.
lettsindighet, lettsinn thoughtlessness, flightiness, giddiness, levity; folly, extravagance, recklessness.
lett|troende credulous. **-troenhet** credulity. **-vakt** easily aroused. **-vekt** lightweight. **-vint** handy, practical; (om metode) ready; (om person) rash, superficial. **-væpnet** light-armed.
levant|en the Levant. **-iner** Levantine.
leve live, be alive; **hr. S. —! Mr. S.** for ever; **lenge — kongen!** long live the king! **hvordan -r De?** how are you? **— et sørgelig liv** lead a miserable life; **— av** live el. subsist (bare om dyr: feed) on; **— av sine penger** live on one's fortune; **ingenting å — av** no means of livelihood; **hverken til å — eller dø av** merely to starve upon; **la oss få noe å —** let us have some food; **— for** live for; **— for seg selv** live a retired life; **— seg inn i** familiarize oneself with, live into, identify oneself with; **— opp igjen** revive; **— over evne** outrun one's income; **han -r på en stor fot** he lives in great style; **lev vel!** farewell, good bye! **leve!** utbringe et **— for** drink long life to.
leve|alder age, length of life; generation. **-attest** certificate of existence. **-brød** (utkomme) livelihood; (bestilling) place, situation, employment. **-brødspolitiker** one who makes politics a means of livelihood, place-hunter, officeseeker; (amr) carpet-bagger. **-dager** life, born days. **-dyktig** capable of living, viable. **-dyktighet** vitality.
leve|lyst enjoyment of life. **-mann** man about town, fast liver. **-måte** (m. å leve på) mode of living, habits; (vesen) manners, breeding; (kost) food, fare, provisions.
leven (støy, moro) a noise, uproar. **holde —** kick up a row, have a lot of fun.
levende living; (i live) alive; (især foran dyrenavn) live; (fig) lively; **de —** the living; **— bilder** moving pictures; **dyr som føder — unger** viviparous animal; **— hat** intense hatred; **ikke et — ord** not a syllable; **— følelse** lively feeling; **— ønske** strong desire; **— hegn** (quickset) hedge; **— innbilningskraft** vivid imagination; **— språk** living el. modern language; **minner meg — om** reminds me forcibly of.
levendegjøre animate; (legemliggjøre) embody.
lever liver; **snakke fra levra** speak freely, plainly, out.
leverandør furnisher, provider; (særl- av

levnetsmidler) purveyor; **(til hær og flåte)** contractor.
leveranse delivery; supply, contract; requisition; **på —** on delivery.
levere hand; (avlevere) deliver; (fornødenheter) furnish, supply, provide; (producere) produce; (til et blad o. l.) contribute; **fritt levert** delivered free.
leveregel rule of life.
levering delivery; supply; (av bok osv.) part, number; **prompte —** prompt delivery; **senere —** forward (delivery).
leveringsbetingelser terms of delivery.
leveringsdag day of delivery.
leverings|frist, -tid time of delivery.
lever|postei (goose-)liver pie. **-pølse** liver sausage. **-sykdom** liver complaint. **-tran** (cod-) liver oil.
leve|sett mode of living, habits. **-standard** standard of living.
leve|tid life-time; (historisk) date; **lang -tid** long life, longevity. **-vei** business; career. **-vis** mode of living, habits. **-år** years of (one's) life.
levitt Levite.
levkøy stock.
I. **levne** leave; **han -t ingenting til meg** he left nothing for me.
II. **levne opp** revive.
levnet life. **levnets|beskrivelse** life, biography. **-løp** career. **-midler** victuals, provisions.
levning remnant; (også avfall) leavings; (av mat) broken victuals; **jordiske -er** mortal remains; **-er fra oldtiden** ancient remains, relics of antiquity.
levre coagulate. **levret** clotted; **— blod** (også) gore.
lev vel farewell, good-bye.
l'hombre ombre.
li (wooded, grassy) mountain side.
I. **li** (om tid) glide on, wear on, advance.
II. **li: li vondt** suffer hardships.
liaison connection.
lian liane, liana.
liberal liberal; (i anskuelser, ogs.) catholic; **de -e** the liberals. **-isme** liberalism. **-itet** liberality; catholicity, breadth.
libertiner libertine.
libhaber fancier; (intending) buyer.
libhaberi fancy, amateurship.
licentiat licenciate.
lide (gjennomgå) suffer, endure; **— mangel på** suffer from want of; **— et tap** suffer el. sustain a loss; **— av** suffer from; **er meget lidende** suffers greatly, is in great pain.
lideform (gram) the passive (voice).
lidelse suffering. **lidelsesfelle** fellow-sufferer.
lidelseshistorie history of one's sufferings; (Kristi —) the history of the passion of Christ.
liden|skap passion. **mangel på —** apathy, dispassion. **-skapelig** passionate, impassioned; enthusiastic. **-skapelighet** passionateness. **-skapsløs** dispassionate, passionless, unimpassioned.
liderlig lewd, lecherous, bawdy, dissolute, debauched. **-het** lewdness, lechery.
liert med intimate with.
liflig delicious. **-het** deliciousness.
liga league.
ligge lie; (om høne) sit; (om skip, i en viss retning) stand; **-r i Frankrike, ved Nilen** is in France, on the Nile; **— i senga** be in bed; **— til sengs** (syk, holde senga) be ill in bed, keep one's bed, be bedridden (bedrid); **la det —! let** that alone! **— bi** for tackel og tau lie a-hull; **— for motvind** be wind-bound; **— for døden** be on the point of death; **det -r ikke for meg** it is not in my line; **— hos** lie with; **— i barselseng** lie in; **deri -r that** implies; **det -r i ordene** it is implied el. conveyed in the words; **det -r i . . .** it is a consequence of . . .; **— i hjel** overlay; **— over et par dager** make a stay of

a couple of days; — **over** (på et sted) **om vinteren** winter; — **på landet** stay in the country; — **på sitt ytterste** be at the last extremity; — **på sine gjerninger** be slain in the act (of committing crime el. violence); — **under** succumb; (**for:** to); get the worst of it, of the battle; **byen -r ved en elv** the city stands el. **is** situated on a river; **huset -r ved stranda** the house stands on the seashore; **liggende** lying etc.; situated. **ligge|dag** (om skip) day of demurrage, layday. **-dagspenger** demurrage. **-høne** broodhen sitter.

ligne resemble, be like; (sammenl.) liken, compare (**med:** to); (om skatter) apportion, assess; **portrettet -r ikke** the portrait is not like; **det kunne — ham å** he is very likely to; **det -r ingenting** it is too bad, it is absurd; **ikke det som -r** no such thing (as).

lignelse (parabel) parable.

lignende similar, the like; **noe —** anything of this sort; **noe — som** something like; **og —** and the like.

ligning (av skatt) apportioning, assessment; (i mat. og astronomi) equation.

ligningsmann (som gjennomgår selvangivelsene) assessor.

ligningsnemnd commission for the assessment of taxes, board of assessors.

liguster privet. **-svermer** privet moth.

I. **lik** (subst) corpse, dead body; **ligge —** lie dead; **blek som et —** pale as death; **— et i lasten** a skeleton in the cupboard; **pynte et —** lay out a corpse; **følge —** attend a funeral.

II. **lik** (mar) roping, bolt-rope.

lik (adj) like; (lignende) similar; (om størrelser) equal (to).

lik|blek pale as death, ghostly. **-brenning** cremation. **-bærer** coffin-bearer, under-bearer. **-båre** bier. **-drakt** grave-clothes, shroud.

like (adj): like tall even numbers.

like (adv) straight; equally, alike; (nøyaktig) exactly; — **stor** equal; — **lite** as little, none the more; **jeg er -glad** I don't care; — **etter** immediately after; — **for nesen på ham** under his very nose; — **foran, for** immediately before; — **fra** (om stedet) straight from; **når han kommer — fra universitetet** when fresh from college; **gikk — bort til ham** went straight up to him; **— i syd** due South; **se en — i ansiktet** look one full in the face; — **ned** straight down, — **opp** straight up; — **overfor** right opposite (to), over against, facing; (fig.) in the presence of, in the face of, in view of; (om motsetning) as against; **stå — overfor hverandre** face each other; — **på nippen** on the very point, (of); — **siden** ever since; — **til London** as far as L.; — **under** right under; — **ved** close by.

like (subst) (make) match; se **-mann: uten** unparalleled, unique; **det fins ikke hans —** he has not his match, is unrivalled; **gi en — for —** return like for like, give one as good as he brings; (dt.) give one tit for tat.

like|artet homogeneous. **-artethet** homogeneousness, homogeneity.

like|bent isosceles. **-berettigelse** equal right, equality of r. el. rights, reciprocity. **-berettiget: være —** have an equal right el. e. rights. **-dan** equal, alike; (av samme form) of the same form, equiform. **-dan** (adv) in the same manner; the same. **-dannet** uniform, similarly shaped; (geometri) similar. **-dannethet** uniformity, similarity.

likefram (adj) plain; (bare om pers.) off-hand, straight- forward, blunt; (fullstendig) downright, flat; (adv) (fig) bluntly, roundly, plainly; in a straight-forward manner, pointblank; (absolutt) simply, downright.

likeframhet plainness, simplicity, bluntness.

like fullt all the same, still.

likeglad happy-go-lucky, devil-may-care, reckless.

likegyldig indifferent; unconcerned; careless; regardless; thougtless (**for:** of); of no consequence; **han er meg — he is** nothing to me.

likegyldighet indifference, unconcern; disregard, recklessness (**for:** of).

likeledes (adv) likewise; (også, tillike) also, too.

likelig proportionate, in equal proportion; (adv) proportionally, in equal proportions, equally.

like|lydende (som lyder ens) similar in sound; (som stemmer ordrett) exactly corresponding, of the same tenor. **-løpende** parallel. **-mann** equal, peer.

likere, likest, se **bedre, best.**

likeretter (i radio) rectifier.

like|sidet of equal sides, equal on all sides, equilateral. **-sidethet** equilateralness.

likesinnet of the same mind, of one mind, similarly disposed, like-minded.

like|stilt equally situated. **-stilling** equal position.

likestrøm (elektrisk) direct current.

likesæl, se **likeglad.**

like|så (adv) likewise, the same, as well; (ved adj) as, equally; **-så . . . som** as . . . as; **— så vel**, se **såvel; -så lite** as little; **jeg kunne -så lite se det som . . .** I couldn't see it any more than . . .; **-så gjerne** just as well.

liketil off-hand.

likevekt equilibrium, equipoise, balance; **i — equilibrious; ute av —** unpoised; **bringe en ut av —** take one off his legs, throw one off his balance; **bringe el. holde i —** equilibrate, keep in equipoise el. in an equilibrium, balance; **holde -en** poise; **miste -en** lose one's equilibrium el. balance.

likevektslære statics.

likevektspunkt point of equilibrium.

likevel still, yet, notwithstanding, nevertheless, for all that, all the same.

likevinklet equiangular.

lik|ferd funeral. **-flekk** livid spot. **-følge** funeral procession.

likgift ptomaine.

likhet likeness, resemblance, similarity, similitude; (i rettigheter) equality; (overensstemmelse) conformity; **i — med** like, in conformity with, in common with, after the fashion of, on the lines of.

likhets|punkt point of resemblance. **-tegn** sign of equation.

lik|kapell mortuary, dead-house. **-kiste** coffin. **-kjeller** (p. hospital) mortuary. **-klede** pall. **-klær** grave-clothes. **-laken** winding sheet. **-lukt** death-scent.

likne, liknende, likning osv., se **ligne, lignende, ligning.**

lik|røver despoiler of dead bodies, graverobber. **-salme** funeral hymn. **-skjorte** shroud.

lik|som (lik) like, in common with; in imitation of; (som om) as if; (så å si) as it were; **-som . . . således** as . . . so also; **-som litt forandret** altered some way; a little bit a; **-som det også er unødvendig** it being, besides, unnecessary.

lik|strå lying in state. **-stue** room in which a corpse is laid. **-svøp** shroud. **-syn** inspection of a dead body, post-mortem examination; (i England) coroner's inquest. **-synsmann** coroner. **-tale** funeral oration.

likså, se **likeså.**

lik|tog funeral procession. **-torn** corn. **-tornoperatør** chiropodist, corn-cutter. **-tyv** bodysnatcher, resurrection-man.

likvogn hearse.

likvid (adj) clear.

likvid (subst) (lyd) liquid.

likvidasjon liquidation.

likvidator liquidator.

likvidere wind up, liquidate.

likvidering liquidation.

likør liqueur, cordial. **-fabrikant** dealer in cordials.

lilje lily.
liljehvit lily-white.
liljekonvall lily of the valley.
lilla lilac, mauve.
lille, se liten: den — (om barn) the baby; **L- bjørn** the Lesser Bear; **hør her, min — venn** I say, little one.
Lille|asia Asia Minor.
lillefinger little finger; **snor ham om -en sin** turns him round her little finger.
Lilleput Lilliput.
lilleslem all the tricks bare one, little slam.
lilleviser short hand.
lim glue; (fugle-) lime.
lime (vrb) glue.
lime (subst) (kost) besom, broom.
limfarge size paint, distemper.
liming gluing; (bokb.) backing; **gå opp i -en** become unglued.
limitere limit.
limitum (den høyeste eller laveste pris en agent må kjøpe eller selge til) limit.
limkoking glue-making.
limonade lemonade.
lim|pinne lime-twig. **-potte** glue pot.
lin flax. **lin-** flaxen. **-aktig** flaxy.
lind linden(-tree), lime.
linde|blomst linden-blossom. **-tre** linden-tree, lime-tree; lime-wood.
lindre relieve, alleviate, ease, assuage.
lindring relief, alleviation.
linerle wagtail.
lin|e line, rope; (til fiske) long-line, bulter, night-line, trimmer; **la ham løpe -a ut** give him rope enough, play him to the end of the line; **på slapp —** on the slack rope.
lineamenter lineaments, features.
line|dans rope-dancing. **-danser** rope-dancer.
linefiske longlining.
lin|farget flaxen. **-frø** flax-seed. **-garn** flax-yarn.
lingeri linen-drapery. **-handler** linen-draper.
linhekle flax-comb.
linjal rule, ruler.
linje line; **passere -n** cross the line; **på — med** (fig) on a level with; **over hele -n** all along the line, all round.
linje|betaling lineage. **-formig** (bot.) linear. **-kompani** company of the line. **-mann** (i fotball) linesman. **-papir** (ruled) lines.
linjere rule. **— en strek** rule a line.
linjering ruling.
linje|skip line-of-battle ship. **-tropper** troops of the line, regulars.
linklede linen-cloth.
linn (adj) soft, mild.
linne, se linnvær.
linnea linnæa, twinflower.
linnet linen; shirt. **-skap** press for linen.
linnhet softness, mildness.
linning band.
linn|saltet mild-cured, slightly salted; **-vær** soft el. mild weather.
linoleum linoleum.
linolje linseed oil.
linon lawn.
linse (slags belgfrukt) lentil; (glass og i øyet) lens.
lin|søm plain needle-work, white sewing. **-torskemunn** butter-and-eggs, flaxweed. **-tråd** linen thread. **-tøy** linen.
lire (italiensk mynt) lira (plur: lire).
lirekasse barrel-organ, street-organ.
lirekassemann organ-grinder.
lirke wriggle, worm, tamper; **— seg ut av** wriggle out of; **— seg inn i** worm oneself into; **— med** cajole, coax, try to bring round.
lirumlarum jingle, ding-dong.
lise (lindring) solace, relief.
lisens licence, license.
lisitasjon contracting, public offer for contract, reception of tenders for contract.

lisitere offer on contract; **i morgen -s leveransen av** to-morrow tenders will be received for.
Lissabon Lisbon.
lisse lace, string.
I. **list** (lurhet) cunning, wile, statagem, artifice; **sette — mot —** oppose art to art.
II. **list** (kant) list; (forgylt) fillet.
liste (fortegnelse) list, inventory catalogue.
liste (vrb) move gently, steal; (noe fra en) shuffle (one out of a thing); **— noe inn** insert by stealth; **— ut** elicit, worm out; **— seg** sneak, slink; **— seg bort** slip el. steal away.
listig cunning, artful, sly, wily.
listighet cunning, slyness.
I. **lit** trust, confidence; **feste — til** credit, give credence to; **sette sin — til** put confidence in; **pin** one's faith to.
II. **lit: i lengste -en** as long as possible; **i siste -en** at the last moment, at the eleventh hour; **vente til siste -en** wait el. put it off till the last moment.
litani litany, anthem.
Litau|en Lithuania. **l-er, l-isk** Lithuanian.
lit-de-parade: ligge på — lie in state.
I. **lite på** (stole på) confide in, trust, depend el. rely on.
II. **lite** (seg med), se **nøye.**
liten, lite little, small, diminutive; **litt a** little, some; **— for min alder** undersized for my years; **fra — av** from a child; **lite eller ingenting** little or nothing, next to nothing; **— glede** small joy; **en penny for lite** a penny short; **om litt** shortly, presently; **og litt til** and something more; **lite** (adv) little; **litt a bit**, slightly, a little; **det er litt lite** it is rather little; **litt etter litt** by (slow) degress, by little and little, little by little; **likeså lite som** no more than.
litenhet littleness, smallness, diminutiveness.
liter liter.
lito|graf lithographer. **-grafere** lithograph. **-grafi** lithograph. **-grafisk** lithographic(al).
litt, se liten.
litterat literary man.
litteratur literature, letters. **-anmelder** literary critic. **-historie** literary history. **-historiker** literary historian. **-historisk** of the history of literature.
litterær literary. **-t tidsskrift** critical review.
liturgi liturgy. **-sk** liturgic.
liv life; (om klær) body; (kjoleliv) bodice; (midje) waist; (livlighet) gaiety, spirit, animation, go, activity, stir; **sette — i** stir up; **om det gjaldt mitt —** for my life; **med — og sjel** heart and soul; **kamp på — og død** a mortal combat; **så lenge det er —, er det håp** while life remains, there is hope; **han svever mellom — og død** his life hangs by a thread; **sette til livs** dispatch; **ville en til livs** want to pick a quarrel with one; **av alle livsens krefter** for dear life, desperately; **i live** alive, above ground; **i levende -e** in his (etc.) lifetime, in the body; **komme til -e igjen** come to life again, revive; **kalle til -e** call into existence; **livet til;** ta **-et av seg** lay violent hand upon oneself, make away with oneself; (spøkende) **du tar -et av meg** you will be the death of me; **hold deg tre skritt fra -et!** keep your distance! stand off! **holde seg en fra -et** keep one at a distance; **sette -et inn på** stake one's life upon; **tok henne om -et** threw my arm around her.
livaktig (om likhet) lifelike, lively, as like as life; (f. eks. om drøm) vivid; (adv) exactly.
liv|aktighet lifelikeness. **-belte** (waist) belt, girdle, cincture, baldric. **-berge** (seg) keep body and soul together, manage to eke out an existence. **-bøye** life-buoy. **-bånd** sash. **-båt** life-boat.
I. **live en opp** rouse one, cheer one up.
II. **live, se verne.**
liv|egen serf. **-egenskap** bond-service, serfdom.
livende: — redd in mortal fear, in a panic of fear.

liv|full lively. -garde body-guard, life-guard. -gardist life-guardsman. -gjord girth.
liv|jeger chasseur. -kjole body-coat. -kusk state-coachman.
livlege physician in ordinary.
livlig lively, vivacious, animated, brisk, mercurial, spirited, sprightly, gay.
livlighet liveliness, vivacity, gaiety.
liv|løs lifeless, inanimate. -løshet lifelessness, inanimation.
livmor womb, uterus.
livne (opp, til), se levne.
livnære keep, maintain, support; — seg ogs. subsist.
Livorno Leghorn.
livré livery.
livredd in bodily fear, in a funk.
liv|reim, -rem girth.
livrente annuity.
livrett favourite dish.
livsalig blessed, blissful, genial.
livs|anskuelse view of life, moral view. -arving heir (of the body), child. -arvinger issue. -betingelse essential condition, condition of life; en -betingelse for of vital importance el. vital to. -bilde picture from life. -eliksir elixir of life. -erfaring experience in el. of life, life experience. -fange prisoner for life. -fare danger of life. -farlig perilous; mortal. -fornødenhet necessary el. requisite of life.
livsforsikring life-insurance.
livsforsikrings|anstalt life-insurance office, Life Office. -polise life-insurance policy. -premie life-insurance premium. -selskap life-insurance company.
livs|førelse life, career, conduct through life. -gjerning lifework. -glad light-hearted, buoyant. -glede joy of life. -historie history of one's life, life history. -kilde source of life. -kraft vital power. -kraftig vigorous. -lede disgust of life, life-weariness. -ledsager, -ledsagerinne partner for life; partner of one's existence. -lyst joy of life, happiness. -løgn sham. -løp career, course of life.
livsoppgave: hans — the task el. aim of his life, his one purpose, aim, business el. mission in life.
livs|opphold (means of) sustenance, subsistence, maintenance of life. en -sak for of vital importance to. -slave, se -fange. -spørsmål matter of life and death, of vital importance. -stilling position in life, profession, walk of el. in life. -straff capital punishment; under -straff on pain of death. -tegn sign of life. -tid lifetime, time of life; på -tid for life; (om fengsel) during royal pleasure. -tre tree of life. -trett life-weary, world-weary. -tretthet, se -lede. -tråd thread of life.
livstykke bodice.
livsvandel conduct (of one's life).
livsvarig for life; -e medlemmer life members. — fengsel life imprisonment, imprisonment for life.
livsytring manifestation of life.
livsånder animal spirits.
livtak wrestling; ta — wrestle.
livtjener body servant.
livvakt body-guard.
livøre, se føderåd.
ljom booming, boom; echo. ljome boom, re-echo, resound.
ljore luffer, smoke-hole.
ljuge, se lyge.
ljå scythe. mannen med -en the old man with the scythe, the Old Reaper.
I. lo (på tøy osv.) nap, shag, pile.
II. lo (utresket korn) (unthreshed) grain, grain in the straw.
III. lo (vindsiden av skip) weather; på -baug on the weather bow. Se ogs. luv og luvart.
lockout lockout.

lockoute lock out.
loco (merk) on the spot, spot.
I. lodd (til lodding av metall) solder.
II. lodd (del, skjebne) lot, share, portion; (i lotteri) share; kaste, trekke — om cast, draw lots el. cuts for; falle i ens — fall to one's lot.
III. lodd (på vekt, ur) weight; (håndverkers) plummet, plumb; hive -et (mar) throw the lead.
I. lodde (måle havdybde) sound; (fig) plumb.
II. lodde (om metall) solder.
III. lodde ut lot; dispose of by lot.
lodde (fisk) capelan, capelin, lodde.
loddelampe soldering lamp.
lodden shaggy; (dunet) downy; (ullen) woolly; (håret) hairy. -het shagginess, hairiness.
loddhiver (mar) leadsman.
lodding (av metall) soldering; (peiling) sounding.
lodd|kast cast el. heave of the lead. -kasting casting of lots.
lodd|line (mar) lead-line. -linje plumb-line.
loddrett perpendicular, vertical. -het perpendicularity, verticalness.
loddseddel lottery ticket.
loddskudd cast of the lead, sounding.
loddtrekning drawing of lots; ballot.
loet (om tøy) nappy, pil(e)ous, pilose.
loff (sl. brød) longish wheaten loaf.
loffe (mar) luff.
loft loft.
loftsbu store-room in a loft.
lofts|kammer room in a loft. -luke loftshutter. -vindu dormer window.
logaritme logarithm. -tabell table of logarithms.
logarv|e (garve med bark) tan. -er tanner. -ing tanning.
loge, se lue.
logg (til å måle et skips fart) log.
logg|bok log-book. -brett log-board.
logge heave the log.
loggemaskin patent log.
loggia loggia.
logg|line (mar) log-line. -rull log-reel.
logiker logician. logikk logic. logisk logical.
logn, se lun.
logogriff logogriph, word-riddle.
logre wag the tail; — for en fawn upon one.
lojal loyal. -itet loyalty.
lokal local. de -e forhold local peculiarities.
lokale premises, room(s), set el. suite of rooms, office, shop. lokalisere localize. lokalisert well acquainted with the place. lokalitet locality; (amr) location. lokal|kunnskap local knowledge. -patriotisme sectionalism.
I. lokk (på gryte, eske etc.) cover, lid.
II. lokk (hår) lock, curl, tress, ringlet.
III. lokk (ku-) call, cattle-call, decoy-song; (om fugl) call, call-note.
I. lokke call (om hår) curl.
II. lokke allure, lure, entice, decoy; tempt, seduce; (om fugl) call; (på ku) call (the flock), sing the decoy song; — fram lure out, lure forth, elicit; — på call; — noe fra en coax one out of a thing; jeg fikk -t ut av ham at I fished out of him that.
III. lokke (bore hull) punch.
lokke|due stool-pigeon. -fugl decoy (bird).
lokke|hode curly head.
lokke|mat bait. -middel means of enticement, lure.
lokket curly, curled.
lokking call, calling.
lokomobil locomobile.
lokomotiv locomotive (engine), engine. -fører (engine-)driver; (amr) engineer.
lom (fugl) loom, loom.
lombard Lombard. Lombardi Lombardy.
lomme pocket; (spøkende) pouch; putte i -n pocket; ha penger i -n be flush (of money).

-bok pocket-book, wallet. **-format** pocket-size.
-kam pocket-comb. **-kniv** pocket-knife.
lommelykt electric torch lamp, electric torch.
lomme|ordbok pocket dictionary. **-penger** pocket-money, spending-money. **-speil** pocket -(looking-)glass. **-tyv** pickpocket. **-tyveri** pocket -picking; **begå -tyveri** pick pockets. **-tørkle** pocket-handkerchief. **-ur** watch.
London London; **i** — in London, in town; **toget fra** — the down train. **l-er** Londoner. **l-er-toget** (til L.) the up train. **l-sk** London.
loppe flea. **loppe seg** catch fleas. **-bitt** flea-bite. **-jakt** flea-hunting. **-stikk** flea-bite.
lorgnett eye-glass, (pair of) eye-glasses, glasses, lorgnette. **-ere** eye-glass.
lorje barge, lump, punt.
lort turd; (smuss) dirt, filth, (søle) mud. **-et** dirty, filthy, foul.
I. **los** (jaktuttr.) bay, challenge, cry; **hundene får** — the hounds open in full cry (**på**: against).
II. **los** pilot. **-avgift** pilotage. **-båt** pilotboat.
lose pilot, (fig. ogs.) pioneer.
los|fisk pilot-fish. **-flagg** pilotflag; **heise** — hoist a signal for a pilot. **-formann** deputy pilot-master. **-gutt** pilot's apprentice.
losing piloting, pilotage.
losje (i teater) box; (frimurer-) lodge. **-plass** seat in a box. **-rad** tier of boxes; **første** — dress circle; **annen** — family circle.
losjere lodge; live in lodgings. **-nde** lodger.
losji lodging, lodgings. **-hus** lodging-house.
loslitt threadbare.
los|oldermann master-pilot. **-patent** pilot's licence. **-penger** pilotage.
loss (mar) loose; **—! go amain! let go! kaste — let go; kaste et tau** — cast off a rope; **gjøre et seil** — loose a sail.
losse discharge, unload, land. **-bom** derrick. **-dager** discharging days. **-greier** cargo el. discharging gear.
losse|penger fees for unloading. **-plass** place of discharge; (brygge) wharf. **-pram** lighter.
lossing discharging, unloading.
los|stasjon pilot station. **-takst** pilotage rate. **-tjeneste** pilot service.
lostvang compulsory pilotage.
losvesen pilotage; pilotage authorities; pilot establishment.
Lotringen Lorraine.
lott share; (på fiske) lay, dolefish; (min) claim.
lottekar sharehand.
lotteri lottery. **-gevinst** prize (in the lottery). **-kolleksjon** lottery-office. **-kollektør** lottery -office keeper. **-seddel** lottery-ticket. **-spill** playing in the lottery.
I. **lov** (tillatelse) leave, permission; **få — til å** be permitted to; **får jeg —?** may I? do you mind? **dog skal jeg få — til å si at . . .** however, I beg to say that . . .; **gi** — permit, give one's permission; **jeg gir Dem fritt — til å** I leave you free to.
II. **lov** (ros) praise, commendation; (skussmål) rykte) character, reputation; **gudskjelov!** God be praised! thank God!
III. **lov** (i alm.) law; (enkelt) statute, act (of parliament); — **og rett** law and justice; (ifølge **-en** according to law; **mot -en** contrary to law; **ved** — by statute; **gi -er** give, enact, make laws; **bli** — become a law, pass into a law; **oppheve en** — repeal a law; **uten** — **og dom** setting aside the forms of law; **forvrenge -en** put a false construction on the law; **foreskrive en -er** dictate to one, give laws to.
lovart, se **luvart**.
lov|bestemmelse legal el. statutory provision. **-bok** code of laws. **-brott, -brudd** violation of the law. **-bud** ordinance, statute.
I. **love**: **på tro og** — on one's honour.
II. **love** (håndflate) palm of the hand.
I. **love** (prise) praise, laud, extol; **Gud være -t** God be praised.

II. **lov|e** (gi et løfte) promise; **jeg skal — for at** I will warrant that, you may be sure that, I promise you that; — **seg mye av** expect much from; **jeg har -t meg bort** I am engaged; **å — er ærlig, å holde besværlig** to promise is one thing, to perform another; saying and doing are two things.
lovende promising, of promise; (ikke om person) auspicious; **lite** — unpromising.
lovere (seile att og fram) cruise, hold off and on.
lov|fast legal, regular. **-feste** establish by the law.
lovformelig legal, conformable to law; — **kontrakt** specialty.
lovforslag bill.
lovfortolker interpreter of the law.
lov|givende legislative. **-giver** lawgiver, legislator. **-givning** legislation; laws, statutes. **-givningsmakt** legislature. **-grunnet** founded in law. **-gyldig** valid in law.
lov|gyldighet validity in law. **-hjemmel** legal authority. **-kjennskap** knowledge of the law, legal knowledge.
lovkyndig learned in the law.
lovkyndighet (kjennskap) legal knowledge; (vitenskapen) law, jurisprudence.
I. **lovlig** (temmelig) rather.
II. **lovlig** lawful, legal; **gå i sitt -e ærend** be about one's lawful business. — **betalingsmiddel** circulating medium, currency. **-het** lawfulness, legality.
lov|lydig law-abiding. **-lydighet** loyalty, law-abidingness. **-løs** lawless. **-løshet** lawlessness; anarchy. **-medholdig** legal. **-messig** (adj) according to law, legal. **-messig** (adv) conformably to law. **-messighet** conformity to law, lawfulness, legality.
lovord praise, commendation.
lovott Canadian glove, mitten, mufflers.
lovover|tredelse misdemeanour, offence. **-treder** law-breaker, offender.
lovprise praise, laud, extol. **-r** praiser, lauder. **lovprisning** praising; praise.
lovsamling body of laws.
lovsang anthem of praise, hymn, pæan.
lovsigemann (hist.) lagman, lawman, law -speaker.
lovskraft legal validity.
lov|sted passage in the law. **-stridig** illegal. **-stridighet** illegality.
lov|synge chant the praises, hymn, sing praises to. **-tale** eulogy, eulogium, panegyric, encomium.
lov|tidende Law Gazette. **-trekker** chicaner, pettifogger. **-trekkeri** chicanery, legal chicane. **-utkast** draft bill. **-uttrykk** law-term.
lubben plump; (dt.) podgy; (især om barn) chubby.
Ludvig Lewis.
lue (flamme; subst) blaze, flame; **huset står i -r** the house is in flames; **i lys** — all in a blaze el. in flames.
lue (vrb) blaze, flame. — **opp** spring into flame.
lue (hodeplagg) cap.
luffe (på hval) swimmer, pectoral; (på skilpadde) flipper.
luft air; **i fri** — in the open air; **trekke** — draw breath; **jeg kan ikke få** — he cannot draw his breath; **trekke frisk** — take (the) air; **gi sin harme** — give vent to one's indignation; **skaffe seg** — i find vent in; **et slag i -a** beating the air; **sprenge i -a** blow up; **skipet fløy i -a** the ship blew up; **det ligger i -a** it is in the air; **grepet ut av -a** utterly unfounded; **leve av** — live upon air.
luftavkjølt air-cooled.
luftbad air bath.
luft|ballong (leketøy) air-ball; (stor ballong) balloon, air-balloon; **reise i -ballong** balloon. **-blære, -boble** air-bubble. **-bremse** pneumatic brake. **-børse** air-gun.

lufte (vi.) blow gently; (vt.) air; — **opp i** let fresh air into; — **seg** take an airing, take the air; — **ut** air.
luftfart aeronautic excursion; acronautics.
luft|flåte air fleet; aerial navy. **-fornyelse** ventilation.
luft|hamn, -havn air port, aerodrome.
lufthull air-hole, vent(-hole); (åndehull) breathing-hole, spiracle.
luftig airy, breezy. **luftighet** airiness.
lufting airing.
luftkastell castle in the air, airy castle.
luftkrig air war.
luft|lag stratum of air. **-ledning** overhead wires. **-linje** air-line. **-motstand** resistance of air.
luftnett (i radio) aerial.
luftning breeze.
luft|pute air-cushion. **-pumpe** air-pump, pneumatic pump. **-pust** breath of air. **-reise** air voyage. **-ring** pneumatic tire. **-rør** air-pipe, ventiduct; (i halsen) windpipe, trachea. **-rør-snitt** laryngotomy. **-røtter** aerial roots. **-seilas** aerial navigation, ballooning. **-seiler** aeronaut.
luftskip air ship.
luftskipper balloonist, aeronaut.
luftslange pneumatic tire.
luft|slott airy castle. **-speiling** mirage, fata morgana. **-sprang** caper, gambol, capriole. **-strøk** clime. **-strøm** current of air. **-tett** air-tight. **-tetthet** density of the air. **-tom** void of air; **-tomt rom** vacuum, void. **-tomhet** vacuity.
lufttrafikk air traffic, air service.
luft|trykk pressure (of the air), atmospherical pressure. **-trykksmåler** baroscope. **-tørket** air-dried. **-ventil** vacuum valve.
luftånd aerial spirit.
lugar (mar) berth; forecastle.
lugg hair of the head.
lugge pull by the hair.
lugger lugger. **-seil** lug-sail.
Lukas Luke.
luke trap-door; (til å legge over) shutter, (mar) hatch; (åpningen) hatch-way.
luke (vrb) weed. **-hakke** weeding-hook. **-kone** weeder. **-maskin** weeder.
lukke (subst) fastening, lock.
lukke (vrb) shut (up), close; — **seg** shut, close; — **døra for** en shut the door on el. against one; — **en inn** let one in; — **en inne** lock one up; — **opp** (åpne) open; (når det ringer) answer the door el. the bell; — **seg over** close on; — **en ut** let one out; — **en ute** shut one out; exclude.
lukkemuskel constrictor.
lukket closed; **en** — **vogn** a close carriage; **en** — **bok** (fig) a sealed book; **for lukte dører** with closed doors, in private. **lukketid** closing hour. **lukning** closure, shutting. **luknings-bestemmelse** (early) closing orders.
luk|rativ lucrative. **-rere** make profit.
luksuriøs luxurious.
luksus extravagance, magnificence, splendour; luxury. **-artikler** articles of luxury, luxuries. **-varer** articles of luxury, fancy goods.
lukt (adv. like) straight.
lukt smell; (bare om sansen) smelling; (både om evnen og om det som luktes) scent; (behagelig el. ubehagelig) odour; **brent** — burnt smell.
lukte smell; — **lunta** smell a rat; — **godt** have a good smell; **det -er av kamfer** it smells (like) camphor; — **på noe** smell (at) a thing. **-flaske** smelling-bottle, scent-bottle. **-organer** organs of smell, olfactory organs. **-sans** sense of smell.
lukt|fri inodorous. **-løs** odourless.
lukullisk Lucullian.
lulle lull.
lummer sultry, sweltering, close.
lummer|het (adj) sultry. **-hete** sultriness.
lumpe do, trick; **jeg lar meg ikke** — I am not going to be done; I will hold my own.

lumpe (potetkake) potato damper.
lumpen paltry; (sterkere) scurvy, shabby, mean.
lumpenhet paltriness; shabbiness, scurviness, meanness.
lumre render hot and close; **det -r en om ørene** the heat is suffocating.
lumsk cunning, sly, deceitful; (f. eks. om sykd.) insidious; (adv) slyly etc. **lumskelig** slyly.
lumskeri, lumskhet cunning, deceitfulness.
lun sheltered, warm, snug.
lund grove.
lunde (fugl) masked diver, puffin.
lune (vrb) shelter; make warm.
lune (subst) humour, mood, spirits; (innfall) whim, caprice; **være i godt, dårlig** — be in good, bad spirits; **skrive, tale med** — write, speak with humour.
lunefull, lunet capricious, whimsical.
lunge lung; (bare om dyr) lights (pl).
lunge|betennelse inflammation of the lungs, pulmonary inflammation, pneumonia, pneumonitis. **-mos** chitterlings. **-slag** apoplexy of the lungs. **-tuberkulose, -tæring** consumption (of the lungs), tuberculosis of the lungs, phthisis.
lunhet warmth, genial temperature.
I. **lunk** (dt.) (moderat oppvarming) warm.
II. **lunk** (langsomt trav) jog, jog-trot.
I. **lunke** make lukewarm, tepefy.
II. **lunke** av sted jog along.
lunken tepid, lukewarm. **-het** tepidness, lukewarmness.
lunne (subst) pile, stack (of timber).
lunn|e (vrb) pile, stack. **-ing** piling, stacking.
lunsj lunch, luncheon.
lunte (gå langsomt) lag, loiter.
lunt|e match; **lukte -a** smell a rat. **-ebørse** match-lock.
luntetrav jogtrot.
lupe magnifying-glass, lens.
lupin lupine.
lupus (hudsykdom) lupus.
I. **lur: stå, ligge, være på** — stand el. be on the watch, lie in wait (etter: for).
II. **lur** (kort søvn) doze, snooze.
III. **lur** (blåseinstrument) lure.
lur (adj) cunning, sly; trickish, tricky.
I. **lure** (blunde) nap, doze.
II. **lure** listen, eavesdrop; (på en; på leilighet) lurk, spy, lie in wait (for), waylay (one); (bedra) best, draw, fool, gull; (i kort) finesse; **han er ikke lett å —!** you won't catch him napping! — **seg, se liste seg.**
lurendreier rogue. **lurendreieri** roguery.
lurer listener, eavesdropper; lurker. **lu*reri** listening; trick, tricking.
lureteppe couvre-pied, rug.
lurifas, luring rogue, slyboots.
lur|leik, -lokk, -låt ranz-des-vaches.
lurv shock (of hair), a shock head.
lurvehår crisp, curly hair.
lurveleven hubbub, hullabaloo, uproar.
lurvet shabby. **-het** shabbiness.
lus louse, pl. lice; (plante-) aphis, pl. aphides; (om person) shinflint. **luse** louse. **luse|biter** skinflint, luset lousy.
lushatt (bot) aconite, helmet-flower, monk's-hood.
lusing box on the ear.
luske sneak, skulk about; — **av sted** slink away, sneak off; — **seg fra** sneak away from, evade; — **unna** shirk duty or work, play the shirk.
lut (subst) lye, lixivium; **gå for** — **og kaldt vann** be left to take care of oneself.
lut (krumbøyd) bent, stooping.
lutaske buck-ashes.
lutdoven awfully lazy.
I. **lute** (legge i lut) steep el. soak in lye.
II. **lute** (bøye seg) stoop, bend, lean forward.

lutefisk codfish steeped in a lye of potash.
lutende stooping; stoop-shouldered.
luther|aner Lutheran. **–dom** Lutheranism, Lutherism. **luthersk** Lutheran.
lut|ing steeping in lye. **–pose** leach, letch.
lutre purify; chasten, sanctify. **lutring** purification, chastening.
lut|salt lixivial salt. **–vask** bucking.
lutt lute.
lutter (gmlt., sj., nå nærmest spøkefullt) pure, sheer, mere, nothing but. **jeg er — øre** I am all attention el. ears.
luttstreng lute-string.
luv: (fig) **ta –en fra en** beat, outdo, outship one.
luvart (mar); **til — to** windward. **holde seg til — av** keep the weather of.
ly shelter, cover; **være i — be** sheltered; **søke — seek** (el take) shelter; **i — av** under shelter of.
lyd sound; **han gav ikke en — fra seg** he did not say a word; he did not stir; **slå til —** order silence.
lydbetegnelse phonetic system.
lydbølge acoustic wave.
lyddemper silencer, muffler, sound-deadener.
I. **lyde** sound; **slik lød ordene** these were the words, he spoke to this effect; **brevet –r slik:** the letter reads as follows; **det –r ennå for ørene mine** it still rings in my ears; **passet –r på hans navn** the passport is made out in his name; **anvisningen lød på 5 pund** the cheque was for 5 pounds; **obligasjonen –r på ihendehaveren** the bond is payable to the bearer.
II. **lyde** (adlyde) obey; **— et navn** answer to a name.
lydelig audible, loud; (adv) audibly, loudly, aloud.
lydfolk subject nation.
lyd|forhold acoustics; phonetic peculiarity. **–hør** quick of hearing.
lydig obedient, dutiful, obsequious.
lydighet obedience, dutifulness.
lydlengde quantity.
lydlig phonetic.
lydlikhet similarity of sounds.
lydlære acoustics (pl); phonology, phonetics.
lydløs (uten lyd) soundless; (om maskin) noiseless, silent. **— stillhet** dead silence.
lydløshet silence; soundlessness.
lydrike dependency, subkingdom.
lydskrift phonetic writing, sound-writing.
lydtegn phonetic character.
lye, se lytte.
lyge, se lyve.
lykke (skjebne) fortune, luck, chance; (hell) good fortune, good luck, prosperity, success; (i høyere bet.) happiness; **— på reisen** a pleasant journey el. voyage to you; **–n var bedre enn forstanden** he was more lucky than wise; **prøve –n** try one's luck el. fortunes; **gjøre — be** successful, succeed, take el. make a hit; **gjøre sin — make** one's fortune; **ha –n med seg** be fortunate; **til all — fortunately,** luckily, as good luck would have it; **til — med** I give you joy of; **ønske en til —,** se lykkønske.
lykke|hjul wheel of fortune. **–jeger** fortune-hunter.
lykkelig happy, fortunate, lucky, prosperous, successful; **— over** happy about. **–vis** fortunately, luckily, happily.
lykkeridder adventurer.
lykkes succeed; prosper; **det lyktes ham å** he succeeded in; **forsøket lyktes for ham** he succeeded in the attempt.
lykke|skilling lucky penny, purse-penny. **–stjerne** lucky star. **–treff** lucky hit.
lykksalig happy, blissful. **–gjøre** bless, beatify. **–het** happiness, bliss, felicity, beatitude.
lykkønsk|e congratulate (**med:** on), felicitate (**med:** on). **–ning** congratulation.

lykt lantern; (til gatebelysning) street-lamp; **–emann** Jack-o'-lantern, Will-o-the-wisp, marsh -fire. **–eskinn** lamp-light. **–estolpe** lamp-post. **–etenner** lamp-lighter.
lymfe lymph. **–kjertel** lymphatic gland.
lyn lightning; (lynstråle) flash of lightning; (fig) flash; **–et slo ned i huset** the house was struck by lightning; **med –ets fart** quick as lightning.
lynavleder lightning conductor, conductor.
lynche lynch.
lynde disposition, temper.
lyne lighten, flash; **i –nde fart** at a furious rate; **–nde sint** furiuos, in a great passion.
lyng heather. **–bakke** heathery hill. **–brann** heather on fire, heath-fire.
lynglimt flash of lightning.
lyngmo heath, heathery moor.
lyn|ild lightning. **–nedslag** stroke el. flash of lightning.
lynsje lynch.
lyn|slått thunderstruck. **–snar** lightning-swift. **–stråle** flash of lightning.
lyr (fisk) pollack.
lyre lyre. **–formig** lyrate.
lyriker lyric poet, lyrist. **lyrikk** lyric poetry. **lyrisk** lyrical; **— dikt** lyric.
I. **lys** light; (skarpt, skjærende) glare, (flamme bluss) flare; **det gikk et — opp for meg** a light flashed el. dawned upon me; **bringe — i** clear up; **gå ut av –et!** get out of my light; **stå i –et for seg selv** stand in one's own light; **kaste — over en ting** throw (el. let in) light on a subject; **se i et annet — take** a different view of; **føre en bak –et** impose on one, humbug one.
II. **lys** (legeme som lyser) light, luminary; (av talg osv.) candle; **ved — by** candle light, by lamp-light; **pusse, slokke –et** trim, put out the candle; **–et sloknet** the candle went out; **–et brenner klart, matt, renner, blafrer** the candle burns brightly, dimly, runs, flames, flares; **sette sitt — under en skjeppe** put one's candle under a bushel.
lys (adj) light, luminous, lucid; **ved høylys dag** in broad daylight; **–t hår** light el. fair hair; **— hud** fair skin; **et –t hode** a clear head, intellect; **–t øyeblikk** lucid interval; **et –t værelse** a light room.
lysalv light elf, elf of light.
lysbehandling light cure.
lys|bilde lantern view, lantern slide. **–foredrag med –bilder** lantern-lecture. **–brytning** refraction. **–bølge** light-wave. **–bøye** lighted buoy.
lyse light, shine; **lampen –r godt** the lamp lights well; **— til ekteskap** publish the banns of marriage; **— velsignelsen** give the benediction. **gleden lyste ut av øynene på ham** his eyes beamed with delight; **— en ut, nedover trappene** light one out, downstairs.
lyse: i — by daylight, with daylight.
lysende luminous, shining, bright.
lyse|blå light blue. **–brun** light brown. **–grønn** light green. **–grå** light grey. **–gul** buff, light yellow.
lysekrone chandelier, lustre.
lyse|rød light red, pink. **–saks** snuffers (pl). **–skjerm** screen, shade. **–slokker** (candle-)extinguisher. **–stake** candlestick. **–stump** candle-end. **–støper** tallow-chandler. **–støpning** candle-making. **–tande** snuff of a candle.
lysevne illuminative power.
lys|gass illuminating gas. **–glimt** glimpse of light.
lyshåret light- el. fair-haired.
lysing (til ekteskap) banns.
lyskasse light-room, area-opening.
lyskaster search-light; (undervanns-) hydroscope.
lyske (vrb) louse.
lyske (subst) groin; inguen.
lyslett blonde, fair (el. light-) complexioned

lys levende all alive; one's own living self, bodily.

lys|lære optics, photology. **–mansjetter** candlestick-ornaments. **–maskin** electric dynamo. **–måler** photometer.

lys|ne lighten; (dages) grow light, dawn. **–ning** lightening etc.; (i skog) glade.

lys|punkt luminous el. bright point el. spot. **–side** (opplyst s.) light el. luminous side; (fig. motsatt skyggeside) bright el. favourable side. **–signal** lights signal. **–skjær** gleam of light. **–sky** afraid of light. **–skyhet** dread of light; obscurantism. **–stripe** streak of light. **–stråle** ray of light.

lysstyrke candle power; eks.: a 300 candle-power lamp.

lyst (fornøyelse) delight, pleasure; (tilbøyelighet) inclination, liking; **kjødets** — the lust of the flesh; **få — til å** take a fancy to, take it into one's head to; **ha — til å** feel inclined to, have a (great) mind to, be desirous of; **gi en — til** give one a liking to; **beta en –en til** put one out of conceit with; **hver sin** — every one to his liking; **–en driver verket** nothing seems hard to a willing mind; **så det er en** — in good earnest; **få styrt sin** — get one's fill **(til:** of); **med liv og** — with pleasure, with a will, with spirit; **el blott til** — not for amusement only.

lyst|båt pleasure-boat. **–damper** pleasure steamer.

lyste desire. **lystelig** pleasant; **lite lystelig** far from pleasant. **lysten** desirous, covetous **(på:** of), (i seksuell bet.) lascivious. **lystenhet** longing, craving; lasciviousness.

lyster (fiskeredskap) fish-spear.

lyst|fartøy pleasure-vessel, yacht. **–fiske** fishing for amusement. **–følelse** pleasurable feeling. **–hus** summer-house, pleasure-house; (lauvhytte) arbour, bower.

lystig merry, gay, jolly, jovial, blithe, jocund; **gjøre seg** — over make merry with, ridicule; (bare om person) quiz; **hun gjorde seg** — over **hans lettroenhet** she was very happy at the expense of his credulity; **en — fyr** a jolly fellow.

lystighet mirth, merriment, gaiety, jollity, hilarity.

lyst|jakt (fartøy) yacht. **–kutter** yacht.

I. **lystre** obey, (roret) answer (the helm).

II. **lystre** (fiske m. lyster) spear, strike.

lyst|reise pleasure trip, excursion. **–reisende** excursionist, holiday-maker.

lystrykk photolithography.

lyst|seilas yachting. **–slott** pleasure palace. **–spill** comedy. **–spillforfatter** writer of comedies. **–tur** pleasure trip.

lyståke luminous haze.

lysvirkning effect of light.

lys våken wide awake, broad awake.

lyte (feil) blemish, fault, defect, vice.

lytefri faultless, without blemish.

lytt (tydelig) distinctly; **høyt og** — loudly; (fulltonende) sonorously; (stille) softly; **det er så** — her they hear so well, the walls are so thin; **i kveld er det — i været** to-night sound travels easily.

lytte listen, hearken, give ear **(til:** to); play the eavesdropper; **— etter** listen for; **lytt!** hark!

lyttepost (militær) listening-post.

lytting listening etc.; eavesdropping.

lyve lie, tell a lie el. falsehood, tell a fib; **— for en** tell one a lie; **— på en** belie one, tell lies of one; **— noe på en** impute st. to one falsely; **for ikke å — to** tell the truth, with no nonsense.

læge osv., se **lege.**

læger, se **felæger.**

læke, se **lege.**

lær leather; se ogs. **skinn; av — leathern;** **–aktig** leathery, coriaceous. **–artikler** leather articles. **–belte** leather belt.

lærd learned, erudite; **en — skole** a grammar-school.

lærd (subst) scholar, man of letters.

lærdom learning, erudition, scholarship; (undervisning) instruction.

lære (andre) teach; (selv) learn; **— utenat** learn by heart el. by rote; **man –r så lenge man lever** we live and learn, it is never too late to learn; **— av** learn of (mest om pers.) el. from (mest om ting); **— fra seg** teach; **— en å** teach one (how) to.

lære (subst) (læresetning) doctrine, dogma; (undervisning) lesson, instruction; (advarsel) lesson; (håndverks-) apprenticeship; **sette i — hos** bind apprentice to.

lære|anstalt academy, college, school. **–bok** class-book, text-book. **–brev** articles, indentures (of apprenticeship). **lære|frihet** liberty of instruction. **–gutt** apprentice. **–kontrakt** indentures, articles. **–lyst** eager desire for acquiring knowledge. **–mester** master (of an apprentice); teacher. **–måte** method of instruction, mode el. method of teaching, tutorial method. **–nem** quick (at learning), quick to learn. **–nemhet** quickness (of intellect).

lærepenger (ubehageligheter på grunn av manglende erfaring): **det var dyre — for ham** the lesson cost him dear; **jeg har måttet betale —** I learned it to my cost, I have had my lesson. **det vil være en lærepenge for deg** it will be a lesson to you.

lærer teacher, master, instructor, tutor. **–eksamen** teacher's certificate examination. **–embete** office of a teacher; appointment el. situation as a teacher. **–gasje** teacher's salary. **–gjerning** teaching.

lærerik instructive, informing, suggestive.

lærerinne (female) teacher, instructress, preceptress, tutoress, schoolmistress, governess. **–eksamen** lady teacher's certificate examination. **–værelse** mistresses' room.

lærer|kollegium teaching staff. **–møte** teachers' meeting. **–personale** teaching staff. **–post** teachership. **–seminarium** teachers' training college. **–stand** teaching profession. **–utdannelse** teacher training. **–værelse** (teachers') common room.

læresetning axiom, maxim, thesis, theorem, tenet.

lære|tid apprenticeship; **gjennomgå sin —** finish one's apprenticeship. **–år** years of apprenticeship.

lær|handel leather trade. **–handler** dealer in leather, leather-seller. **reim, –rem** leather strap. **–sekk** leather bag. **–varer** leather goods. **–veske** leathern wallet.

lærvillig docile, teachable, apt. **–het** docility, teachableness, teachability.

læse, se **låse.**

lø pile up, stack.

lød (farge) hue, colour.

lødig fine, genuine, pure; **16– sølv** pure silver; **13¹/₄– sølv** standard silver. **lødighet** fineness.

løe (subst) barn.

løft lift; (fig) big effort, dead lift.

løfte (vrb) lift, raise; (åndelig) elevate; **— på lift at; — på hatten** lift one's hat. **i -t stemning** (ironisk) elevated, high.

løfte (subst) promise, **høytidelig — vow; gjøre et — vow** el. take a vow; **holde, bryte et — keep, break a promise; ta det — av en** at make one promise that.

løfte|brudd breach of promise. **–kran** (derrick) crane. **–muskel** levator. **–rik** promising, full of promise.

løfte|stang lever. **–ventil** lifting valve.

I. **løfting** (på vikingskip og nordlandsbåt) high poop.

II. **løft(n)ing** lifting, lift; elevation.

løgn lie, falsehood; **liten — fib; uskyldig — white lie; åpenbar — palpable lie; det er —**

it is a lie; **si en** — tell a lie; **beskylde en for**
— give one the lie; **gripe en i** — catch one in
a lie; **det er** — i din hals you lie in your throat.
-aktig lying, mendacious. **-aktighet** lying, mendacity. **løgner, løgnerske, løgnhals** liar; **gjøre
en til løgner** give one the lie.
løgste, se **gjøre til løgner.**
løk onion; **blomster-** bulb.
I. **løkke** (engstykke) inclose, close; paddock.
II. **løkke** (renne-) loop, noose.
løkt, se **lykt.**
lømmel lubber, lout; (slyngel) scamp. **-aktig**
lubberly, loutish; rude. **-alderen** the hobbledehoy
age.
lønn (for viss tid, arbeids-) wages, wage;
(gasje) pay; (honorar) salary; (belønning)
reward; **med en** — av at a salary of; **det var**
— **som forskyldt** serve him right.
I. **lønn:** i — (hemmelig) privately, secretly,
clandestinely, in private.
II. **lønn** (tre) maple.
lønndom: i — secretly, in private.
lønndør concealed door, private door.
lønne (betale) pay; (gjengjelde) repay; (belønne) reward; **det -r seg ikke** it is not worth
the trouble el. while; **en godt -t embetsmann**
a well-paid functionary; — **seg** pay.
lønnende paying, remunerative; **lite** — unremunerative, ill-paid, unprofitable.
lønngang secret passage.
lønning (lønn, gasje, sold) wages; salary,
stipend, pay.
lønnings|dag pay day. **-klasse** scale of pay.
-skala scale of pay.
lønnkammer private closet.
lønnlig secret, private.
lønns|avtale wages agreement. **-forhøyelse**
increase of wages. **-kamp** wages dispute. **-kon-
flikt** wages dispute. **-krav** (krav om høyere lønn)
demand for higher wages; (det som forlanges i
lønn) wages required. **-regulativ** scale of pay.
lønnsom, se **lønnende.**
lønns|pålegg, se **-forhøyelse. -regulering**
adjustment of wages. **-spørsmål** wages question.
-tillegg, se **-forhøyelse.**
lønnvei secret way.
lønsk clandestine, secret, furtive.
lønt, se **lønnende.**
løp run, course; (om en elv) course; (om
en del av en elvs løp) reach; (i børse, pistol)
barrel; (i kanon) bore; (om tiden) course;
(musikk) run; (vedde-) race; **gi sorgen fritt**
— give a loose to sorrow; **i tidens** — in the
process of time; **i** — running; **i -et av** in, in
the course of, within, during.
løpe (oste-), se **løype.**
løp|e run; (gå i en viss retning) range, trend;
(om vei) lead; (om dyr i paringstid) rut; **la
munnen** — run on, jabber away, rattle away;
— **sin vei** run away, make off, decamp; —
seg trett fatigue el. tire oneself with running;
hissigheten løp av med ham his temper got
the better of him; — **hornene av seg** sow one's
wild oats; — **av stabelen** be launched; **lot
øynene** — **nedover siden** passed el. ran his
eyes over the page; **det fikk tennene til å** —
i vann på meg it made my mouth water; —
inn i en havn put into a port; — **med sladder**
go about gossiping; **det løp kaldt nedover
ryggen på meg** a cold shivering ran down my
back; — **på døra hos en** importune one; **noe
å** — **på** a margin; **ha noe å** — **på** have something
to come and go upon; (om penger) something
in hand; **melken er -t sammen** the milk is
curdled; **her -er trådene sammen** here the clues
converge; **terminen er utløpet** the term is
expired; **timeglasset er -t ut** the hourglass
has run down; — **ut i en spiss** taper into a
point; **hesten løp ut** the horse ran away, bolted;
løpende running; — **konto** current account;
— **år** current year.

løpe|bane (et menneskes) career. **-bille** ground
-beetle. **-dag** (om veksler) day of grace. **-fot**
cursorial foot. **-fugl** courser. **-grav** trench.
-gutt errand-boy. **-ild** train (of gunpowder);
ryktet gikk som en -ild the report spread like
wild-fire. **-kran** travelling crane.
løpenummer running number, progressive el.
continuous number.
løpepass: få — get one's travelling ticket,
be sacked; **gi en** — sack one, turn one off,
dismiss one.
løper (slags teppe) runner; (tjener) running
footman; (i sjakk) bishop.
løpe|seddel circular, handbill. **-tid** (dyrs)
rutting time; (merk) date. **-tur** run.
løpsk apt to run away; **hesten løp** — the
horse ran away, bolted; **en** — **hest** a runaway
horse.
lørdag Saturday.
løs loose; (slapp) slack; (ubundet) lax; **nå er
fanden** — there's the devil to pay now; **-t krutt**
blank cartridges; — **mave** a relaxed stomach;
gjøre et -t overslag over estimate roughly; **-e
rykter** vague reports el. rumours; **-t skudd**
blank shot; **-t snakk** idle talk; **nå går det —!**
now for it! **de gikk** — **på hverandre med nevene** they set to with their fists; **slippe** —
(andre) let el. turn loose; (selv) escape; **slå** —
på let drive at; **slå seg** — enjoy oneself in good
earnest; — **og ledig** free, unfettered; idle,
unemployed, (ugift) single; **-t og fast** all sorts
of things; **løst** (adv) loosely.
løsaktig loose, light.
løsaktighet looseness, lightness.
løsarbeid casual employment el. labour. **-er**
casual labourer, day-labourer.
løse loosen, unfasten; (løslate) let loose; (løse
op) untie; (befri) release; (løse fra, frita) absolve; — **en knute** untie a knot; — **billett** buy
a ticket; — **kongebrev** get a marriage-license;
— **et pant** redeem a pledge; — **en gåte** solve
a riddle; — **en oppgave** solve el. work out a
problem; — **en tvil** solve a doubt; — **en vanskelighet** settle a difficulty; — **fra** absolve el.
relieve from; — **inn** (noget pantsatt) get out of
pledge; **i dag ble det løst opp for henne** to-day
she was released.
I. **løselig** cursory, vague; (overflatisk) desultory, perfunctory, superficial; — **blikk på**
cursory view of; **etter** — **skjønn** by free estimate;
(adv) slightly, vaguely; (ikke grundig) desulto-
rily; (overflatisk) superficially; **se** — **igjennom**
run over.
II. **løselig** (til å løse) solvable.
løsen word, watchword, countersign.
løse|penger, -sum ransom.
løs|gi release, set free. **-givelse** release. **-gjen-
ger** vagrant, vagabond, tramp; (politisk) free-
lance in parliament, wild man; (amr) mugwump. **-gjengeri** vagrancy; freelancing; (amr)
mug-wumpery.
løskjøpe ransom.
løslate let loose, release.
løslatelse release, liberation.
løsmunnet (om hest) light in hand; (om person)
flippant, glib, tattling.
løsne loosen, relax; — **et skudd** discharge a
gun.
løsning loosening, relaxation; (av oppgave;
syre) solution.
løs|revet disconnected. **-rive seg** break away.
-rivelse break, emancipation. **-sloppen** (fig)
licentious, loose.
løsøre moveables, chattels (pl).
løsøreauksjon furniture sale.
løve lion (laps) dandy.
løve|brøl lion's roar. **-hjerte** lion-heart. **-hud**
lion's skin. **-hule** lion's den. **-jakt** lion-hunting.
-jeger lion-hunter. **-munn** (plante) dragon's
mouth, lion's snap.
løve|skinn lion's skin. **-tann** (en løves tann)

lion's tooth; (botan.) dandelion. **-unge** lion's whelp el. cub, lionel.
løy (adj) laxy, sluggish, slothful, desultory; **en — kuling** a slack wind.
løybenk couch.
løye (mar) abate, moderate; **— av** become el. fall light.
I. **løye** (opphold i stormvær) lull (in the wind).
II. **løye** (fisk) bleak.
løyen, se **løyerlig**.
løyer (morskap) fun, sport; **drive — med** make fun of.
løyerlig funny, droll, ludicrous; (underlig) queer, odd.
løyert (barnesvøp) swaddling cloth; (ring i kanten av et seil) cringle.
I. **løype** (oste-) cheese-lep; rennet, runnet.
II. **løype** timber slide; ski-ing course (el. slide), ski-track. **-streng** aerial transport wire.
løyse, se **løse**.
løytnant lieutenant; **i marinen** l. in the (Royal) Navy.
løyve (subst), se **tillatelse**.
løyve (vrb), se **bevilge**.
løvinne lioness.
I. **låg** (væske) (egtl.) water, liquid; (alm.) decoction.
II. **låg** (tre som er falt) fallen tree, windfall(en) tree.
låg (adj), se **lav**.
låghalt lame, limping (from having legs of unequal length).

låk, se **dårlig**.
lån loan; **få ordnet et —** negotiate a loan; **oppta et —** raise a loan; **til -s, som —** on loan; **få til -s** have the loan of; **han har den til -s** he has borrowed it; **leve på —** live of loans.
låne borrow (of, from); (låne ut) lend; (amr.) loan.
låne|kontor pawn-shop, loan-office. **-seddel** pawn ticket.
lån|giver lender. **-ord** loan-word. **-søker** applicant for a loan. **-tager** borrower.
lår thigh; (av slaktet dyr) leg.
lårbein thigh-bone.
låring quarter.
lårstykke (av okse) rump-piece, round; (av mindre dyr) leg.
lås lock; (liten l. på halsband el. l.) locket; (henge-) padlock; (til gevær osv.) lock; **sette — for** padlock; **gå i —** lock; (fig) come right; **under — og lukke** under lock and key.
låse lock; (sette hengelås for) padlock; **— av** lock; **— ned** lock up, lock away; **— opp** unlock; **låst og lukket** locked and bolted.
låsesmed locksmith.
låsferdig lockable, provided with a lock.
låt sound, ring; (melodi) air, strain, song; (støy, ulyd) din, noise; (fugle-) call, call-note.
låte sound, resound, din; **de syntes dette låt godt** they thought this had a pleasant ring, sounded all right.
låve barn. **-bru** barn bridge. **-dør** barn door. **-golv** threshing floor.

M

M, m M, m.
m fork. f. **meter**, meter.
madam (med etterfølgende etternavn, i tiltale til gift kvinne av lavere stand, nå foreldet) Mrs.
maddik maggot, worm.
Madeira Madeira.
madeira (vin) Madeira.
madjar Magyar. **-isk** Magyar.
madonna Madonna. **-bilde** image of the Virgin.
madrass mattress.
magasin storehouse, warehouse; (blad) magazine.
magasinere store, warehouse.
magasinering storing, warehousing.
magasingevær magazine-gun.
mage, se **mave**.
mager (motsatt: feit) lean, meagre; spare; thin; (uttært) gaunt; (tarvelig) poor; **— kost** scanty fare; **det magre** (om kjøtt) the lean. **-het** leanness, meagreness.
magi magic. **magiker** magician.
magisk magic(al).
magister master of arts, M. A.; **-grad** M. A. degree.
magistrat magistracy. **magistratsperson** magistrate, town clerk.
magnat (fornem adelig) magnate.
magnesia (avførende pulver) magnesia.
magnesium (mineral) magnesium.
magnet magnet, loadstone; **kunstig —** (artificial) magnet. **-isere** magnetize; mesmerize. **-isering** magnetisation. **-isk** magnetic, magnetical. **-isme** magnetism; dyrisk **—** animal magnetism, mesmerism. **-isør** magnetizer, mesmerizer. **-nål** (magnetic) needle.
magnium magnesium.
magnolia (plante) magnolia.
mahogni mahogany. **-tre** mahogany

mai May. **-blomst** May-flower. **en -dag** a day in May.
maie ut, se **utmaie**.
maigull (bot.) golden saxifrage.
Mainz Mayence, Mainz.
mais maize, Indian corn. **-brød** corn-bread. **-kolbe** corncob. **-mel** Indian meal.
majestet majesty; **Deres M.!** Sire! Your Majesty! **majestetisk** majestic.
majestetsforbrytelse lese-majesty.
majolika majolica.
majones mayonnaise.
major major.
majorat majorat.
majoritet majority; **være i —** be in a el. the majority.
mak ease, quiet, leisure; **i ro og —** leisurely, at one's ease; **fare i —** take one's ease.
makadamiser|e macadamize; **-t vei** macadamroad. **makadamisering** macadamization.
makaroni mac(c)aroni.
make match, equal; (om ting som utgjør et par) fellow; (han el. hun; ektefelle) mate; **jeg har aldri sett -n** I never saw the like of it el. anything like it.
make (tilsvarende) corresponding, like; (etterstilt) to match.
mak|e (innrette) manage, contrive; **han -te det så at han slapp** he managed (el. contrived) to escape; **make seg** shape itself; (om vær) abate, moderate.
makelig (om stol etc.) easy, comfortable, commodious; (om person) indolent, ease-loving, easy-going person; **gjøre seg det —** take one's ease; (adv) at one's ease, comfortably; (med letthet) quite easily. **-het** ease, comfort, (om person) indolence.
makeløs matchless, peerless, unparalleled, incomparable; (uten like, enestående) unexampled; (adv wonderfully, exceptionally.

makeskifte (subst) exchange. (vrb) exchange. -brev deed of exchange.
makk, se mark.
makkabeerne the Maccabees.
makke sammen bungle, huddle (up).
makker partner. -skap partnership.
makkverk bungling work, botch.
makrell mackerel. -fangst mackerel fishery. -størje tunny-fish.
makron macaroon.
maksimalpris maximum price.
maksime maxim.
maksimum maximum. maksimums- maximum. -termometer maximum thermometer.
maksvær easy el. moderate weather.
makt might, potency; (især styrke, kraft) power, strength; (herredømme) sway; power; de krigførende -er the belligerent powers; den utøvende — the executive power; av all sin — with all one's might, with might and main; det står ikke i min — it is out of my power; ha ordet i sin — speak fluently, have words at command; med — by (main) force, forcibly; komme til -en come into power; det står ved — it is in force, is valid; ha -en be in power.
maktbegjær lust of power.
makte manage, master, grasp, get the better of; — å be able to; ikke — en oppgave be unequal to a task.
maktesløs powerless, impotent; (ugyldig) null and void.
maktesløshet powerlessness, impotency.
maktfullkommenhet sovereign el. absolute power. -følelse sense of power. -haver ruler. -lysten greedy of power. -middel instrument of power. -område dominion, domain.
maktpåliggende important, momentous, of great consequence; det var dem — å they were anxious to, took pains to, made a point of.
maktspråk dictatorial command. -stilling vantage ground. -stjele strike powerless, unnerve. -syk ambitious, imperious. -utfoldelse display of power.
makulatur waste-paper; (-ark) waste-sheet; gjøre til — put to the waste paper. -ere maculate, deface.
malaj|er Malay. -isk Malay, Malayan.
I. male paint; — med olje paint in oil; — med vannfarger paint in water-colours; — etter naturen paint from nature; la seg — sit for one's portrait, have one's portrait taken; han -r på et landskap he is (engaged in) painting a landscape; malende pictorial, graphical.
II. male (på kvern) grind, crush.
malemåte manner of painting, brushwork.
maler painter; (kunstmaler) artist; (håndverker) house-painter. -arbeid painter's work, brushwork. -farge paint, painter's colours.
maleri painting, picture. -handler picture-dealer. -kjenner judge of pictures.
malerinne lady painter.
maleri|ramme picture-frame. -samling collection of paintings, picture-gallery. malerisk picturesque. maleriutstilling picture exhibition.
maler|kasse painter's box. -kost painter's brush, paint-brush. -kunst art of painting. -lære: sette i -lære bind apprentice to a house-painter; være i -lære be in apprenticeship with a house-painter. -mester master house-painter. -pensel painting brush, hair-pencil. -pøs colour-pot. -sal (teater) scene-room. -skole school of painting; (kunstnerling) school of painters. -stokk mostick, maulstick. -svenn journeyman painter. -verksted house-painter's workshop.
I. maling brushwork, painting, (med pensel) painting; (farge) paint.
II. maling (på kvern) grinding.
malise archness, wickedness.
malje (til hekte) eye.
malkontent discontented, malcontent.
malm ore; (metall) metal; (metall med en blanding av kopper) brass.

malm|art species of ore. -fjell ore-containing rock. -full (klangfull) sonorous. -furu red deal free from sap. -gruve metal mine. -holdig metalliferous, metalline. -klang metallic sound. -leie stratum of ore. -rik abounding in ore. -røst powerful voice. -åre metallic vein.
malplasert misplaced.
malproper dirty.
malstrøm eddy, whirlpool.
malt malt; gjøre — malt, make malt.
malte malt.
maltekstrakt extract of malt.
malt|er maltster, malt-man. -eri malt-house. -maltgro malt-dust. -ing malting. -karameller malt lozenges. -kvern malt-mill.
malteser|ordenen the Order of Malta. -ridder knight of Malta. maltesisk Maltese.
maltraktere maltreat, damage.
malurt wormwood. -beger cup of bitterness.
malva (kattost) mallow.
malvasier (gresk vin) malmsey.
mamelukker (bukser) pantalets.
mamma mamma, mammy. -dalt mammy's darling.
mammon mammon; den urette — the mammon of unrighteousness, the ill-gotten gains.
mammon|dyrkelse mammon-worship. -dyrker, -trell worshipper of mammon.
mammut mammoth.
man (når den talende medregnes) one, a man, a fellow, a girl, we; (når den tiltalte medregnes) you; (når hverken den talende eller den tiltalte medregnes) they; ofte kan, «man» gjengis ved omskrivning med passiv; når — er trett, vil — gjerne hvile when one is tired, one likes to repose; godt, men — må derfor ikke tro . . . well, but therefore you must not think; vi har riktignok ikke vært der, men — er da ikke hans slaver indeed, we have not been there, but then we are not his slaves, you see; — sier people say; it is said; — fant ham they found him, he was found; — har sagt meg I have been told; — kan ikke vite det there is no knowing; — må henvende seg til apply to.
man (manke) mane.
mandag Monday; forrige — last Monday; om -en every M., on Mondays.
mandant principal; (velger) constituent.
mandarin mandarin.
mandat (verv) charge, task, commission; mandate; nedlegge sitt — resign one's seat. -ar(ius) mandatary, agent, proxy.
mandel almond; (halskjertler) almond, tonsil. -pudding almond-pudding. -formet almond-shaped.
mandel|kli almond-powder. -melk almond-milk, orgeat. -olje almond-oil. -tre almond-tree.
mandig manful. -het manfulness.
mandolin mandolin.
mandrill (bavianart) mandrill, drill.
mane (ånder) conjure, raise ghosts; — fram conjure up, raise; — bort, ned exorcise, lay.
manér manner; (maniererthet) mannerism. -lig mannerly, decorous. -lighet mannerliness.
manesje manege.
manet blubber, jellyfish.
mangan manganese.
mange many; svært — very many, a great many; — penger much money; — takk many thanks, thank you very much; hvor — er klokka? what is the time? klokka er — it is late.
mange|armet many-armed. -artet multifarious. -dobbelt manifold, multiplied; (adv) many times. -farget many-coloured, variegated. -fold manifold. -gifte polygamy. -hodet many-headed. -kant polygon.
mangel want, lack, absence; (nød, trang) need; (knapphet) scarcity; (feil) defect, deficiency, shortcoming, drawback; demerit; lide — suffer

want; **ha — på** be in want of, be short of; **av — på** for want of; **i — av** in default of; for lack el. want of, in the absence of; **i — av det** failing that, that failing.

mangeleddet with many joints; (matem.) multinomial.

mangelfull defective, deficient. **–het** defectiveness, deficiency.

mangemillionær multimillionaire.

mang|en, mangt many; **— en** many a one; **— en gang** many a time, often; in many cases; **mangt og mye** (a great) many things.

mange|sidet many-sided, versatile. **–sidethet** versatility, many-sidedness. **–steds** in many places. **–stemmig** for many voices. **–årig** of many years, of many years' standing.

mangfoldig multifarious, manifold, multitudinous; **-e** ever so many, numbers (of). **-gjøre** multiply. **–gjørelse** multiplication. **–het** multiplicity, multitude, variety.

I. **mangle** (ikke ha) want, lack, be destitute of; (ikke finnes) be wanting, be missing; **det –t bare!** that only was wanting! what next! **den –r ti minutter på 5** it's ten minutes to five, wants ten minutes to el. of five (o'clock); **det –t ikke på** there was no want of; **intet syntes å — i hans storhet** nothing seemed wanting to his grandeur; **det –nde** what is wanting; the deficiency, the defect(s).

II. **mangle** (rulle) mangle, calender.

mangle|stokk, –tre roller.

mani mania, craze.

manierert, maniert mannered. **–het** mannerism.

manifest manifest, manifesto. **–asjon** manifestation. **–ere** manifest.

manikyre manicure.

manipulasjon manipulation.

manipulere manipulate.

manke withers, mane. **–brott, –brudd** wrung withers. **–brutt** wither-wrung.

mankere fail, be wanting; miss.

manko (merk.) deficiency, wantage.

mann man; (ektem.) husband; (til å utføre arbeid) hand; **— og kone** man and wife; **3000 — 3000 men; alle —** all hands; **alle som en —** one and all, to a man, with one consent, all unanimously; **— for —** man by man; **være — for noe** be equal to; (svare for) warrant, be responsible for; **— og — imellom** between man and man; **— imot —** man to man; **skipet gikk under med — og mus** the ship went down with every mother's soul, with all hands onboard; **en — på en million** a man worth a million; **pr. — a** head, a man; **1000 — til fots og 200 — til hest** 1000 foot and 200 horse; **til siste — to** the last man.

manna manna. **–saft** manna-emulsion.

mann|bar marriageable, nubile. **–barhet** marriageable age, marriageableness.

manndom manhood, virility.

manndoms|alder years el. age of manhood. **–kraft** strength of manhood. **–år, se alder.**

mann|drap homicide; (ikke overlagt) manslaughter. **–draper** homicide, manslayer.

manne man; **— rær** man ship; **— seg opp** man oneself, muster pluck.

mønne|bot blood fine; **–fall** slaughter, loss of life.

mannequin mannequin.

mannevett human wisdom.

mannfolk male, man; (plur.) men. **–hater** man-hater.

manngard ring of men (or women; **gjøre —** raise a posse.

mannhaftig stout-hearted, doughty, stalwart; (om kvinne) mannish. **–het** doughtiness.

mannhull (i dampkjele) manhole.

mann|jamning comparison, parallel of man with man. **–jamt** (adv) in a body, solidly.

mannkjønn male sex.

mannlig male, masculine, virile; **— rim** male el. single rhyme.

manns|arbeid man's labour. **–avdeling** men's division. **–drakt** male apparel el. attire. **–emne** boy, lad, youth; **et godt —** a lad of promise.

mannshjerte manly fortitude, intrepidity; **har du mot og —** if you are not a coward, if you are a man.

mannshøy of a man's height.

mannshøyde a man's height.

mannskap (tropper) troops, men; (skipsbesetning) crew, ship's company.

manns|klær men's clothes, male apparel. **–kor** male choir.

mannsling bit of a man, manikin.

mannsløft man's charge el. load.

mannsmot manhood, manly courage.

mannsperson male.

mannsside male line.

mannsstemme man's voice, male voice.

mannsterk strong in numbers, in great force; **møte —** muster strong.

mannstukt discipline.

manntall register, census; **holde — take a** census, make up a return of population. **manntalls|fører** censual registrar. **–liste** return of population; census-paper.

mannvond dangerous, vicious, likely to attack people.

manometer manometer; steam-gauge.

mansjett cuff, ruffle; (fast) wristband; **støtt på –ene** (dt.) piqued. **–knapper** cuff-buttons, studs, sleeve-links. **–skjorte** gentleman's (full) shirt.

mantilje mantilla.

mantisse mantissa.

manudu|ksjon coaching. **–ktør** (special) tutor, coach. **–send** pupil. **–sere** prepare (a student) for an examination, coach.

manuell manual.

manufaktur (manufakturvarer) drapery goods.

manufaktur|handel drapery; (amr) business in dry goods; (butikk) draper's shop, dry-goods store. **–handler** draper, dry goods merchant. **–varer** drapery goods.

manuskript manuscript (skrives i regelen MS); (til setteren) copy, matter; **trykt som —** printed for private circulation.

manuskriptsamling collection of MSS.

manøvre manoeuvre.

manøvrere manoeuvre.

manøvrering manoeuvres.

mappe portfolio, paper-case; (skrive-) blottingbook.

marabu (indisk stork) adjutant, marabout.

marbakke steep bottom.

mare nightmare, incubus.

marekatt (long-tailed) monkey.

mare|kvist crow's nest, witches' broom. **–lokk** elf-lock, plica.

mareritt attack of the nightmare.

I. **marg** (i bok) margin; **i –en** on el. in the margin.

II. **marg** (i bein) marrow; (i tre) pith; (fig) vigour; **gjennom — og bein** through nerve and bone.

margarin margarine.

margbein marrow-bone.

marg|full marrowy, pithy. **–løs** marrowless, pithless. **–stjele** enervate, unnerve.

margpudding marrow-pudding.

Marg(a)rete Margaret.

Maria Mary, Maria; **jomfru —** the (Holy) Virgin, the Virgin Mary. **Maria|bilde** image of the Virgin. **–dyrkelse** mariolatry.

Marianne Mary Ann.

mari|hand cullion, (palmate) orchis. **–høne** lady-bird. **–kåpe** dewcup, lady's mantle.

marine navy. **–bilde** marine picture. **–blå** navy blue. **–budsjettet** the Naval Estimates. **–kikkert** binocular telescope. **–maler** marine painter. **–maleri** seapiece. **–opplag** naval stores.

marinere marinate, pickle.

marine|soldat marine. **-årbok** naval list.
marinøkkelband cowslip.
marionett puppet. **-spill**, **-teater** puppet-show
el. play.
maritim maritime.
I. **mark** (mynt) mark; **-en faller** the mark
falls; **-en stiger** the mark is rising; (vekt) half
a pound, eight ounces.
II. **mark** el. **makk** maggot, worm; **det gikk —
i det** it became worm-eaten; **full av —** maggoty.
III. **mark** field; ground, land; **åpen —** open
field; **en vid — for** a wide field for; **rykke i -en**
take the field; **slå av -en** beat out of the field,
beat off the field; **i -en** in the fields.
mark|arbeid field work. **-arbeider** field la-
bourer. **-blomst** field flower, wild flower.
marked fair; (avsetningssted) avsetning av
varer) market; **gå på -et** go to the fair; **det
hadde vært —** there had been a fair; **det er
et godt — for kaffe** it is a good market for
coffee; **-et går ned** the market comes down.
kaste inn på -et throw on the market.
markeds|dag fairday. **-gave** fairing. **-plass**
fair-ground. **-pris** market-price.
marke|gård hillfarm. **-høy** mountain hay.
marken, se **marked**.
markere mark.
marke|skjell boundary between farms. **-slått**
outfield.
marketenter sutler. **-i** sutler's trade; (bua)
canteen. **-ske** sutler-woman.
markfiol dog-violet.
mark|greve margrave. **-grevinne** margravine.
-grevskap margraviate.
marki marquis. **markise** marchioness.
markise (solseil) awning.
markjordbær wild strawberry.
markkurs rate of the mark exchange.
markmus field-mouse, field vole.
markskriker quack, mountebank. **-i** quackery,
mountebankery. **-sk** quackish, puffing.
markstukken pricked by worms, worm-eaten.
Markus Mark.
markør marker, waiter.
marmelade marmalade.
marmor marble; **bryte — quarry** marble.
marmor|blokk marble block. **-bord** marble
-top table.
marmor|brott, **-brudd** marble-quarry.
marmorere marble.
marmor|golv marble floor. **-kiste** m. coffin.
-plate m. slab; **servant med -plate** washstand
with marble top. **-slott** marble-palace. **-stukk**
marble stucco. **-støtte** marble column; marble
statue. **-åre** vein of marble.
marodere maraud. **marodør** marauder.
marokin morocco.
marokkansk, **Marokko** Morocco.
mars March. **-fiol** March violet, sweet violet.
marsipan marchpane.
marsj march; **på -en** on the march; **blåse en
— strike up a march; gjøre på stedet —** mark
time.
marsjal (field) marshal; (festmarsjal) usher.
-stav marshal's baton. **-verdighet** marshalship.
marsjandise|r fripper, fripperer, dealer in
second-hand goods, broker, old-furniture seller.
-bu, **-handel** frippery.
marsjere march; **ia —** march.
marsj|ferdig ready to march. **-orden** march-
ing order. **-ordre** marching order.
marsk (lavt kystland) marsh.
marskland marshland, marshy country.
marsvin (liten gnager) guinea-pig.
marter torture, agony. **-kammer** torture-
chamber. **-redskap** instrument of torture.
martialsk martial, fierce.
martre torture, agonize. **-nde** excruciating.
martyr martyr; **gjøre til — martyr; en —
for den gode sak** a martyr in the good cause.
-dom martyrdom. **martyrium** martyrdom.

I. **mas** (besvær, møye) trouble, bother.
II. **mas: knuse i — grind** to atoms; **koke i —**
boil to pieces, mash (by boiling).
I. **mase** (i stykker) mash.
II. **mase** (gnåle) be persistent, ring the changes
on; (streve, gjøre bråk) fuss (about), bother.
— med have no end of trouble with.
masekopp persistent person. **maset** bother-
some, fussy.
mask (resten av maltet etter kokingen) grains.
I. **maske** (i nett) mesh; (i strømpe o. l.) stitch;
slippe ned en — drop a stitch; **ta opp en —**
pick up a stitch.
II. **maske** (for ansiktet) mask; (fig) disguise;
(skuespillers) make-up; **ta** (el. **rive**) **-n av** unmask.
maskeball masked ball, fancy ball.
maskekar grain vat.
maskepi fellowship; **ha — med** have much
to do with.
maskerade masquerade, mask, mummery.
maskere mask; **— seg** mask, put on a mask.
maskering masking.
maskespill masque, mask.
maskin machine; (særlig større m., dampm.)
engine; (te-) (tea-)urn.
maskin|arbeid machine work. **-arbeider**, se
-smed.
maskindeler machine parts, engine parts,
fittings.
maskineri machinery, enginery.
maskin|fabrikant machinist; engine-builder.
-fabrikk engine el. machine factory. **-folk** engineers; (på teater) scene-shifters. **-garn** machine (-spun) cotton.
maskingevær machine gun.
maskinhall (på utstilling) machine hall.
maskiningeniør mechanical engineer.
maskininspektør superintending engineer.
maskinist engineer; engine man, engine
-minder.
maskinkanon machine gun.
maskinklipt (om håret) cut by machine.
maskin|kraft engine-power. **-kjeller** (teater)
(machinery) dock. **-lære** (applied) mechanics
(pl). **-messig** like a machine, mechanical. **-mester**
engineer; (på teatret) master of the scenery.
-olje engine oil, lubricating oil. **-rom** engine-
room. **-skade** engine trouble, machine trouble,
damage to the engine, breakdown.
maskinskrive type, typewrite.
maskinskriver typist.
maskinskriverske lady typist.
maskinskrivning typing.
maskin|smed blacksmith for machinery. **-sydd**
machine-made, machine stitched. **-søm** machine
work, machining. **-tegning** engineering drawing.
-verksted machine-works; machine-factory,
machine-shop. **-vesen** machinery, engineering.
maskot mascot.
maskulin masculine. **maskulinum** the masculine gender; masculine noun.
mas|omn, **-ovn** blast el. smelting furnace.
massakre massacre.
massakrere massacre, mangle, mutilate, cut
to pieces.
massasje massage; (hos frisør) shampooing.
-behandling massage.
masse mass, bulk; (boets) assets, estate; (pa-
pir-) pulp; **en — mennesker** a crowd; (fig) **en
— el. -r av** lots of; **-n** the great body of the
people, the million, the masses. **-herredømme**
mobocracy. **-mord** wholesale murder. **-morder**
wholesale murderer. **-møte** mass meeting. **-ned-
slaktning** wholesale killing. **-oppbud** levy in
mass.
masseproduksjon mass production.
massere massage; (hos frisør) shampoo.
masse|utnevnelse wholesale appointment. **-vis:
i —** in masses, in great quantities, in multi-
tudes, wholesale.

massing, se **messing.**
massiv massive, massy; (ikke hul) solid.
massør masseur.
massøse masseuse, bathwoman.
mast mast; **kappe –a** cut away the mast; **et skip uten –er** a dismasted ship. **maste|kurv** top. **–topp** mast-head. **–tre** mast(-tree).
mastiks (plante og stoff) mastic.
masurka mazurka.
I. **mat** (føde, næring) food, provisions; (tillaget mat) viands, eatables (pl); **lage — cook; to retter —** two dishes; **er utmerket —** is excellent eating; **–en** (middags-, aftens-) **er servert** dinner, supper is on the table, is ready; **det er — for Mons** that is meat and drink to him.
II. **mat** (mar.) mate; (især sammensetn.; se båtsmanns-).
matador matadore; mighty man, swell.
mate feed.
matema|tiker mathematician. **–tikk** mathematics (pl). **–tiklærer** mathematical teacher. **–tisk** mathematical.
mateple cooking-apple.
materiale material, materials.
materialforvalter store-keeper.
materia|lisme materialism. **–list** materialist. **–listisk** materialistic(al).
materie matter, stuff; (f. eks. i et sår) matter, pus; (emne glt., sj.) subject; **en bok i —** a book in sheets, in quires.
materiell (adj) material, corporeal, sensual, substantial; **–e nytelser** material comfort.
materiell (subst) materiel; (drifts-) plant; **rullende —** rolling-stock.
mat|fat (fat med mat) dish of meat. **–fett** dripping. **–frier** parasite, sponger. **–frieri** cupboard-love.
Mat(h)ilde Matilda, Maud.
mat|hug, se **–lyst. –hus: et godt —** a house where a liberal table is kept.
matiné morning concert.
mating feeding.
mat|jord mould. **–kjele** (mar.) mess-kettle. **–klokke** dinner bell, dinner-gong. **–krok** hearty eater. **–kurv** provision basket. **–lagning** cooking, cookery. **–lei** off one's feed el. victuals. **–lens** out of provisions. **–levninger** broken victuals. **–lukt** smell of dinner; dinnery atmosphere. **–lyst** appetite; **gav meg —** gave me an appetite. **–mor** mistress of a house. **–nyttig** useful for food. **–olje** olive oil.
matpapir sandwichpaper.
matrester broken food.
matrikkel register, roll. **matrikulere** register.
matrikulering registration.
matrise matrix.
matro peace for eating.
matrone matron. **–aktig** matronly.
matros sailor, seaman, mariner; (dt.) tar. **–drakt** sailor's dress. **–gutt** (dekksgutt) sailor-boy, deck boy. **–trøye** grego, pea-jacket.
mat|skap (provision) cupboard. **–skreppe** provision bag. **–spann** dinner pail, meat-carrier. **–strev** toil for the material wants and comforts.
matt faint, languid; (svak) faint; (ikke skinnende) dim, dull, dead, not glossy; (dikt o. l.) dull, flat; (i sjakk) mate; **— forgylling** dead gilding.
matte enfeeble, exhaust.
matte (subst) mat, rug; **–r** ogs. matting. **–binder** mat-maker.
mattere (gjøre overflaten av glass matt) frost.
matthet faintness, languor, debility; dullness, dimness; flatness, vapidity.
mattslipt frosted, ground.
mat|varer eatables, provisions. **–vin** ordinary wine.
maule mumble, munch.
maur ant.
maure (bot.) maiden-heads, petty mugget.
maur|er Moor. **–isk** Moorish.

maursluker ant-bear, ant-eater. **–tue** ant-hill.
mausergevær Mauser, Mauser rifle.
mausoleum mausoleum.
mave stomach, belly; **ha en dårlig —** have a weak stomach; **ha vondt i –n** have a pain in one's stomach; **ligge på –n for** cringe to; **legge seg til —** be getting stout.
mave|belte flannel waist. **–betennelse** inflammation of the stomach, gastritis. **–katarr** stomachic catarrh. **–knip** belly-ache, gripes (plur.). **–pumpe** stomach-pump. **–saft** gastric juice. **–sekk** stomach. **–smerter** stomach-ache, belly-ache. **–styrkende** stomachic; **— middel** stomachic cordial. **–sykdom** disease of the stomach. **–syke** diarrhea.
med (landmerke) landmark, fairway mark.
med with; (om befordringsmiddel) by; (i selskap med, tillike med) along with, together with; **hva er det i veien — ham?** what is the matter with him? **— dampskip** by steamer; **— tog** by train; **— det gode eller vonde** by fair or foul means; **multiplisere, dividere —** multiply, divide by; **— tiden** in time; **— andre ord** in other words; **— ett ord** in a word; **handle — deal** in; **— forsett** on purpose; **holde våkent øye —** keep a watchful eye on; **ha medlidenhet — have** compassion on; **— ett sprang** at one bound; **den historien — . . .** that affair el. story about . . .; **bære seg galt at — noe** set about a thing in a wrong way; **rikelig — penger** plenty of money; **det blir bedre — ham** he is getting better; **det går langsomt — arbeidet** the work gets on slowly; (adv) **han var — i følget** he was one of the suite; **vil De være —?** will you make one of the party? **jeg var ikke —** I was not present; (fig) **er De —?** do you follow me? **han gikk —** he went along with us (them etc.); **og jeg — and** I too; **være — på** join in; **en mann som er — i verden** a man about town; **en mann som har vært —** a man who has seen life.
medalje medal.
medaljong locket.
medaljør medal-engraver.
medansvar co-responsibility.
medansvarlig co-responsible.
medansøker fellow applicant.
medarbeider fellow-labourer, co-labourer, collaborator, cooperator; (i en avis) contributor (to); **de faste –e** (i avis) the staff. **–skap** collaboration.
medarrestant fellow-prisoner.
medbeiler, –ske rival.
medbestyrer assistant principal.
medborger fellow citizen, (fellow-)townsman.
medbringe bring (along with one).
medbringer (i maskin) driver.
medbroder colleague, brother.
medbør fair wind.
meddele state, report; communicate (to), impart (to); (underrette) inform; (merk: varsle, advisere) advise; (gi et inntrykk) convey (an impression); (sakramentet) administer (the sacrament).
meddelelse advice, communication; (opplysning) information; **gi — om** advise; **nærmere –r** further particulars; **— angående trassering** drawing instructions.
meddelsom communicative.
meddelsomhet communicativeness.
meddirektør fellow-director, co-director.
med|dommer associate (judge). **–domsmann** lay associate (judge). **–domsrett** court of a professional judge sitting with laymen.
medeier joint el. part proprietor el. owner.
medfart treatment, usage. **boka fikk en hård — av kritikken** the book was roughly handled by the critics.
medfødt congenital, innate; **være en —** be born el. inbred in one.
medfølelse sympathy, fellow-feeling.

medfør pursuance, consequence; **i embets —** in virtue of one's office. **i sakens —** in accordance with the nature of the case.

medføre (fig) involve, entail.

medgang prosperity, success.

medgi (innrømme) admit.

medgift dower, dowry, (marriage-)portion.

medgjørlig manageable, pliable, facile, amenable, complying. **-het** pliancy, facility.

medhjelper assistant, coadjutor.

medhold approbation; countenance, support; **hans meninger fant — hos mange** many assented to, approved of, embraced his opinions; **hun gir ham — i alt han gjør** she applauds anything he does; **i — av** (i overensstemmelse med) conformably to.

medhustru fellow-wife.

medikament remedy, medicine, drug.

medikus medical man.

medinnbefattet (equally) included.

medinnehaver joint possessor, partner.

medio in the middle of.

medisin medicine, physic.

medisiner medical student.

medisin|flaske, –glass vial, phial.

medisinsk medical, medicinal, medicated.

medisinskrin medicine-chest.

medister chopped fat and lean of pork; **–pølse** pork sausage.

medium medium.

medkjensle, se **medfølelse.**

medkontrahent joint-contractor.

medkristen fellow Christian.

medlem member; (av et selskap, en stiftelse osv.) fellow. **medlems|bidrag** subscription of members. **–kort** membership card. **–liste** list of members. **–tall** number of members, membership.

medlidende compassionate, sympathizing.

medlidenhet pity, compassion, sympathy; **ha — med** have pity on, pity, compassionate.

medlyd consonant.

medlærer, –inne fellow-teacher.

medmenneske fellow-man, fellow-being.

medmindre unless.

medregent co-regent.

medregne count (in).

medreisende fellow-traveller.

medsammensvoren co-conspirator.

medskapning fellow-creature.

medskyld complicity.

medskyldig (adj.) accessory (**i:** to). **medskyldig** (subst) accomplice (**i:** in).

medspiller fellow-player.

medstifter joint founder.

medtatt (av støt) battered; (skadd) damaged; (slitt) the worse for wear; (skrøpelig) crazy, shattered; (av sykdom) fallen off, reduced; (trett) fagged, jaded, exhausted; **han er blitt svært — av denne sykdommen** he has fallen off very much in this illness.

medtjener fellow-servant.

medunderskrift countersignature.

medunderskrive countersign.

medunder|skriver joint signer. **–tegne** countersign.

Medusa Medusa, Gorgon. **m–hode** Gorgon face, Gorgon head, Medusa's head.

medutgiver joint editor.

medvind fair wind.

medvirk|e co-operate, concur, contribute, be conducive (**til:** to, towards). **–ning** co-operation, concurrence, agency; intervention.

medviter, –ske (one) privy to el. cognizant of, a party to.

medynk pity, compassion, commiseration; **ha — med** have pity on; feel compassion for.

medynksfull compassionate, full of pity.

meg me; (som object, når subjektet er: jeg) myself; **det er — it is I; en venn av —** a friend of mine; **han vasker —** he washes me; **jeg vasker — I** wash myself.

megafon megaphone.

megen, se mye. med — møye with great pains.

meget (foran adj. og adv. i positiv) very; (foran adj. og adv. i komparativ, ved substantiver og verber) much; **han er — vennlig, — vennligere enn du tror** he is very kind, much kinder than you think; **jeg er — glad i ham** I like him much; **det gleder meg — I** am very glad; **jeg omgås ham — I** see him very often; **jeg ber — om forlatelse I** beg a thousand pardons; **så — mer som** (so much) the more because.

megetsigende meaning, suggestive.

megle mediate, negotiate (peace).

megler mediator, intercessor; (merk) broker. **–eksamen** examination required for carrying on a broker's business. **–forretning** broker's business. **–gebyr, –lønn** brokerage. **–rolle** the part of a mediator. **meglerske** mediatress.

megling mediation, intercession.

meglingsforslag mediatory suggestion.

meglingsforsøk attempt at mediation.

mehe (karaktersvak, uselvstendig person) yea-brother, yay-nay.

mei (sleigh)runner.

meie (slå) reap, mow (down).

meieri dairy, dairy farm. **–bestyrer** manager of the dairy. **–drift** dairy-farming, dairying. **–produkter** dairy produce. **–smør** dairy butter.

meierist dairy-man.

meierske dairy-woman.

mein (skade), se **men.**

meine, meining, se **mene, mening.**

meis (bak-) basket to be carried on the back, dosser. Se ogs. **kløvmeis.**

meis(e) (fugl) tomtit, titmouse.

meisel chisel.

meisle chisel, carve, chip.

meite (fiske m. stang) angle. **–mark** angleworm.

mekaniker mechanician, mechanical engineer.

mekanikk mechanics; (mekanisme) mechanism, action.

mekanisk mechanical, automatic; (adv) mechanically.

mekanisme mechanism, action, gear, gearing.

mekle, mekler, se **megle, megler.**

mekre baa, bleat.

meksikaner, –inne, meksikansk Mexican.

mektig mighty, powerful, potent; **være noe — be** master of, have the full command of. **mektig** (adv) (dt) mighty.

I. **mel** meal; (fint mel, siktemel) flour.

II. **mel** (sand-) sandy bluff el. steep.

melaktig mealy, farinaceous.

melan|koli melancholy. **–koliker** melancholic.

melankolsk melancholy.

melasse molasses, melasses.

melbøle meal-tub.

melde report, notify; (forkynne) announce; (bebude) intimate; (omtale, fortelle) mention, make mention of, state; (gi underretn. om) give information of; (i kortspill) declare; **la seg — send** in one's name el. card; **— seg** (hos en) announce oneself, (mil) report oneself (to one); (som ansøker) apply, become a candidate, stand; **det har meldt seg mange til denne posten** there have been numerous applications for this office; **— seg inn** enter one's name (on the books) **— seg syk** put oneself on the sick list; **— seg ut av en forening** withdraw one's name from a society.

melde|plikt obligation to report oneself. **–seddel** written notification el. warning.

melding announcement; statement; (innberetning) report; (i kortspill) declaration.

meldrøye (bot.) ergot.

meldugg mildew.

mele meal, flour, mix with flour; **— sin egen kake** feather one's nest, line one's own purse.

melen (ogs. om potet) mealy, floury.

melere mix.

melet mealy.
mel|handel meal-man's trade. **-handler** meal-man.
melis single refined (loaf-sugar).
melk milk. **melkaktig** milky, lacteous.
melke (hos fisk) milt.
melke (vt.) milk; (vi.) give el. yield milk.
melke|bu dairy. **-butikk** milkman's shop, dairy; (amr) creamery. **-bøtte** milkpail. **-feber** milk fever. **-fisk** milter. **-handler** dairyman. **-kjertel** lacteal gland. **-kolle** milk-pan. **-krakk** milking-stool. **-ku** milch-cow, milk-cow. **-mat** milk-food, milk-meat. **-mann** milk-man. **-maskin** milker. **-mugge** milk-pitcher, milk-jug. **-papp** milk thickened with flour. **-prøver** lactometer. **-syre** lactic acid. **-tann** milk-tooth, temporary tooth.
melke|utsalg dairy, milk-shop. **-vei** milky way, galaxy. **-velling** milk-soup. **-vogn** milk-waggon.
melking milking.
melklister paste (made of flour).
mellom between, betwixt; (iblant) among; **— kl. fire og fem** (at) between four and five; **— oss sagt** between ourselves, between you and me.
Mellom-Afrika Central Africa.
mellomakt interval between the acts, wait, entr'acte. **mellomaktsteppe** act-drop.
Mellom-Amerika Central America.
mellombygning middle building.
mellom|dekk between-deck; (tredje plass) steerage. **-dekkspassasjer** steerage passenger. **-dekksplass** steerage.
mellomdør door of communication.
Mellom-Europa Central Europe.
mellomfin middling fine.
mellomfolkelig international; **— samkvem med jernbanen** interchange of international traffic by rail.
mellomfornøyd not overjoyed.
mellomgrad intermediate degree.
mellomgrunn (på et maleri) middle (distance).
mellomgulv midriff, diaphragm.
mellomhandel carrying trade, transit trade.
mellomhandler negotiator; (megler) mediator.
mellomhand (i kortspill) middle hand, third hand.
mellomklasse middle class; (på skolen) middle form.
mellomkomst intervention, interference.
mellomlag intermediate layer.
mellomlanding (flyvers) intermediate landing.
mellomledd intermediate link; (av finger el. tær) middle phalanx.
mellomlegg (v. bytte) balance.
mellomliggende internacent, lying between; **— tid** intermediate time, interval.
mellommann middleman, intermediary, go-between; deputy.
mellommat luncheon, snack.
mellommåltid collation, lunch, tiffin.
mellompris medium price.
mellomproporsjonal mean proportional.
mellomregning accounts.
mellomrett side-dish, entremets.
mellomriks- international, interstate.
mellomrom interval; (lite m.) interstice; (rom mellom to ting) intermediate space, space between; (typograf. og musikk) space; **med — at intervals**, intermittingly, between whiles; **med lange — at long intervals; døde med få dagers —** died within a few days of each other; **med — (som har åpninger)** having intervals, interstitial; (adv) intermittently.
mellomspill interlude; by-play.
mellomst: den -e the middlemost, the midmost.
mellomstasjon intermediate station.
mellomstilling intermediate position.
mellomstor middle-sized.

mellomstykke middle piece.
mellomstørrelse middle el. medium size.
mellomtid interval, interim; **i -en** in the interval, in the meantime, meanwhile.
mellomtilstand middle state.
mellomtime leisure hour.
mellomting something between.
mellomtoner middle tones.
mellomvegg partition wall.
mellomvekt (i brytning) middleweight.
mellomverk insertions, inserted lace.
mellomværende (regning) account; (strid) difference; **avgjøre et — (regning)** settle accounts; (strid) **make up a difference.**
melodi melody; (til en sang) tune, air. **-rikdom** melodiousness, richness in melody.
melodisk, melodiøs melodious, tuneful.
melodrama melodrame, melodrama.
melodramatisk melodramatic.
melon melon. **-bed** melon-bed. **-benk** (drivbenk) melon-frame. **-gresskar** bush-gourd. **-kaktus** melon-thistle. **-kjerne** melon-seed.
melrakke (hvitrev) arctic el. polar fox.
melskrubb (larve av melbillen) meal-worm.
melte, se malte.
membran membrane.
membranøs membranaceous.
memoarer memoirs.
memorandum memorandum.
memorere commit to memory, memorize, study.
men but; **— likevel** but yet; **det er dog et „men" ved det** there is a but in the question; **ikke noe „men"** no buts.
men (skade) harm, hurt, damage, injury.
menade mænad.
menasje housekeeping; **føre egen —** keep house.
menasjeri menagerie, (wild-beast) show. **-eier** showman.
mene (være av den mening) be of opinion; (ha i sinne, tenke på, sikte til, ville si) mean; (tenke, tro, holde for) think; **hva -r De** what do you think? **man -r at** it is thought that; **— det godt med en** mean well by one, be well intentioned towards one; **jeg mente ikke noe vondt med det** I meant no harm; **det var ikke slik ment** I didn't mean that; **det skulle jeg — I** should think so, I believe you, rather; **— det alvorlig** be in earnest; **han -r det samme som jeg** he thinks of it the same as I do.
mened perjury; **begå —** commit perjury.
meneder perjurer. **menedersk** perjured.
mengd(e) multitude, number, numbers; (overflod) abundance; (av mennesker) crowd; **det er -n som skal gjøre det** it is the quantity does it; **en hel —** a lot of, a great many; **den store — the million**; the vulgar, the general; **en — forskjellige** a variety of. **i mengdevis** in quantities.
menge mix, mingle.
menig: — soldat common soldier, private.
menighet (i kirken) congregation; (sognefolk) parishioners; (sogn) parish. **menighets|diakonisse** parish nurse. **-pleie** congregational charity. **-råd** congregational council. **-søster** parish sister.
menigmann the common people; the commons.
mening (anskuelse) opinion; (betydning, logisk sammenheng) meaning, sense; (hensikt) intention; **si sin — rett ut** speak one's mind plainly; **det er delte -er** opinions differ; **det er det ingen — i** that is nonsense, there is no sense in that; **hva er -en med** what is the meaning of; **oppta i en god —** put a good construction on; **etter min —** in my opinion; **være av den —** at be of opinion that; **den offentlige —** public opinion; **få — i** make sense of; **det kan ikke være to -er om . . .** there can be no two opinions as to. **noe som ødelegger -en** fatal to the sense.
menings|felle one being of the same opinion

with another; **vi er –feller** we are of the same
opinion. **–forskjell** difference of opinion. **–frihet**
freedom of opinion. **–løs** meaningless, unmeaning,
nonsensical. **noe –løst** an absurdity, unmeaning-
ness.
meningsutveksling exchange of views.
menneske man, human being, man and (el.
or) woman, person; **det nye, gamle, indre —**
the new, old, inner man; **intet —, ikke et —**
nobody, no one; **alle –r** all men, everybody;
unge –r young people; **vi er alle –r** we are all
weak mortals; **–t spår, Gud rår** man proposes,
God disposes; **en mengde –r** a crowd of people;
hva er det for et — what kind of a person is
he? **la oss nå være –r** let us have no nonsense.
menneske|alder age of man; (slektledd)
generation, age. **–barn** man. **–bryst** human
breast. **–eter** man-eater, cannibal. **–eteri** cannibal-
ism, anthropophagy. **–fiende,** se **–hater, –fiendsk.**
–fiendtlig hostile to man, misanthropical.
–forstand human understanding; **han har ikke**
engang alminnelig –forstand he wants even
common sense. **–frykt** fear of man. **–føde** human
food. **–handel** traffic in human flesh. **–hat** misanthropy. **–hater** misanthrope, man-hater.
menneskeheten mankind, humankind.
menneske|kjenner judge of character, human-
ist. **–kjærlig** humane, charitable, philanthropic.
–kjærlighet philanthropy, charity, love of mankind. **–kjøtt** human flesh. **–kunnskap** knowledge
of men el. human nature.
menneskelig human; (menneskekjærlig) humane; **det er —** it is human nature; (adv)
humanly; humanely; **— talt** humanly.
menneskelighet humanity.
menneske|liv human life; **tap av –liv** loss of
life. **–mengde** crowd. **–mylder** swarm of people.
–natur human nature. **–offer, –ofring** human
sacrifice. **–par** pair el. couple of human beings.
–rase race of men, race of mankind. **–rettighet**
right of man. **–røst** human voice. **–sjel** human
soul. **–skikkelse** human shape.
menneskesky shy (of man); **være —** shun the
society of men.
menneske|skyhet shyness. **–slakteri** butchery.
–slekt mankind, human species. **–tilværelse**
existence of man.
mennesketom deserted; (ubebodd) desolate.
menneske|venn altruist, philanthropist. **–venn-**
lig altruistic, philanthropic, benevolent. **–verd**
worth (of man). **–verdig** human, worthy of (a)
man. **–verdighet** dignity of man.
menneske|verk work of man. **–vett** human
sagacity. **–vrimmel** crowd, throng of people
–ånd human spirit.
mens while; **(— derimot)** whereas.
menstruasjon menstruation.
menstruere menstruate.
mensur mensuration, measurement.
mensvoren forsworn, perjured.
mental mental. **— undersøkelse** examination
of one's mental condition, psychiatric test.
mente: en i — carry one.
mentor mentor, monitor.
menuett minuet.
meny bill of fare.
mer more; **ikke — enn** no more (el. not
more) than, as little as; **ikke et ord —!** not
another word; **hva —?** what else? **hva — er**
more than that, moreover; **jeg ser ham aldri —**
I shall never see him again, I shall see him no
more; **jeg kan ikke —** I give it up, I am knocked
up; **en grunn —** an additional reason; **du får**
aldri — en lykkelig stund you'll never have
another happy hour; **jo —, desto bedre** the
more . . . the better; **så mye — som** especially
(el. all the more) as; **så mye — verdifull som**
the more valuable that.
mergel marl. **–gjødning** marling. **–grav** marl
pit. **–grus** marly gravel. **–jord** marly soil. **–lag**
ay er of marl. **–stein** marlstone.

mergle marl. **mergling** marling.
merian marjoram.
meridian meridian; **gå igjennom –en** pass el.
cross the m. **–bue** meridional arc.
merinntekt surplus receipts.
merino merino. **–sau** merino.
meritter achievements.
merkantil mercantile.
merkbar discernible, perceptible, observable,
appreciable, noticeable, sensible, marked. **–t**
(adv) discernibly etc.
merke (subst) mark, token, sign, note; (sjømerke) beacon; **bite — i** (dt.) note, take note
of, single out; **legge — til** take notice of, notice,
attend to; **verd å legge — til** noteworthy.
merke (vrb) mark; (med bokstaver) letter;
(med tall) number; (legge m. til) heed, note,
notice; (kjenne) find, perceive; **(— tømmer)**
score. **vel å — mind well, observe, remember;**
— seg mark; **merk deg, du må ikke** mind, you
must not; **la seg — med** give to understand.
— opp (farvann) mark, buoy; (sti) mark (out).
merke|blekk marking-ink. **–dag** red-letter day.
–hammer (til tømmer) scorer, timber-scribe.
–jern marking-iron. **–lapp** label.
merkelig remarkable, notable; (underlig,
interessant) curious; (adv) remarkably etc.;
— nok strange to tell, strangely, for a wonder.
merker, se **tømmer-.**
merke|seddel label. **–smann** (hist.) standard
-bearer. **–stein** boundary stone. **–år** memorable
year.
merknad remark, observation.
Merkur Mercury. **merkurial|isme** mercurial
rash. **–salve** mercurial ointment.
merkverdig remarkable, notable; (underlig)
curious; (minneverdig) memorable.
merkverdighet remarkableness; remarkable
thing, curious feature el. fact.
merle (subst) (mar) eyelet-grummet.
merlespiker marline-spike.
merr mare; (skjellsord) jade.
mers topp.
merse|fall topsail-halyard. **–rå** topsail-yard.
–skjøt topsail-sheet.
merskum meerschaum.
mers|seil topsail. **–seilskuling** topsail breeze.
merutbytte extra profit.
merutgift excess of expenditure.
mesallianse misalliance.
mesan spanker. **–mast** mizen mast.
mesanin mezzanine.
mesén Maecenas, patron.
meséneksemplar complimentary copy.
mesk mash.
meske (ved brygging) mash. **— seg** batten,
fatten, pamper. Se ogs. **gjø(de).**
meskekar mash-tub.
mesking (ved brygging) mashing.
meslinger the measles.
mesmerisme mesmerism.
Mesopotámia Mesopotamia.
I. messe (kjøpestevne) fair.
II. messe (høymesse, sjelemesse) mass. **høre —**
attend mass; **holde —** celebrate mass; **lese —**
say mass, mass.
III. messe (felles bord) mess; (om rommet)
mess-room; (officersmesse) wardroom, gun-room.
høre til samme — mess together.
messe (vrb) (protestantisk) chant, intone,
intonate; (katolsk) say mass.
messe|fall no service. **–forstander** caterer.
–hakel casula, chasuble. **–kamerat** mess-mate.
–serk, –skjorte surplice.
Messias the Messiah.
Messina: Messinastredet The Straits of Messina.
messing brass. **–beslått** brass-mounted. **–blikk**
latten-brass, brass-plate. **–skilt** brass-plate. **–tråd**
brass-wire. **–varer** brass-ware.
mest most; **for det –e** generally; **det — mulige**

as much as possible; **han er — ærgjerrig** he is the most ambitious.
mest, se **nesten.**
mestbegunstiget most-favoured.
mestendels for the most part.
mesteparten the bulk, the best (el. **better, greater, major)** part.
mester master; **(frimurer-) master-mason; (håndverks-) master-workman; være — i (en kunst)** be master of, be an adept (el. a proficient) in; **ingen — no** good hand (at); **jeg er ingen — i dette** I am no good hand at this.
mester|brev master-tradesman's certificate. **-hånd** the hand of a master, a masterly hand.
mesterkokk master-cook.
mesterlig masterly.
mesterlighet masterliness.
mester|mann (gmlt. og i eventyrene) executioner, hangman. **-prøve** master-tradesman's test. **-sanger** master-minstrel.
mesterskap mastery, mastership; (i sport) championship.
mester|skudd masterly shot. **-skytter** crack shot. **-spiller** masterly player el. performer. **-stykke** master-piece; master-stroke. **-svenn** foreman of a workshop, head-journeyman. **-svømmer** champion swimmer. **-trekk** masterly move; (fig) master-stroke. **-verk** masterly work el. performance.
mestis (blanding av hvit og indianer) mestizo.
mestre (være overlegen) overmatch; (være herre over) master, manage.
meta|fysiker metaphysician. **-fysikk** metaphysics. **-fysisk** metaphysical.
metall metal. **-aktig** metallic. **-blanding** metallic composition. **-glans** metallic lustre.
metallisk metallic.
metall|støper metal-founder. **-tråd** wire. **-varer** hardware, metallic goods.
metallverdi metal value.
metallåre vein of metal.
metamorfose metamorphosis.
meteor meteor. **-fall** fall of aerolites. **-jern** meteoric iron, aerolitic iron.
meteorolog meteorologist.
meteorologi meteorology.
meteorologisk meteorologic(al).
meteorstein aerolite, meteoric stone.
meter metre. **-systemet** the metric system.
metier trade, calling.
meto|de method; system; **bringe — i** methodize, reduce to method. **-disk** methodical.
metodisme methodism.
metodist Methodist.
metresse mistress.
metrikk metrical art, metrics. **metrisk** metrical. **metrum** metre.
mett satisfied, satiated, sated, full-fed; **spise, drikke seg — eat,** drink to the full, one's fill; (fig) **— av noe** tired, sick of (a thing); **— av dager** full of days.
mette satiate, sate, satisfy; (kjemi) saturate.
mette (subst) **ete -n sin** eat el. have one's fill.
mettelse satiety; (kjemi) saturation.
Metusalem Methuselah.
Mexico Mexico.
mezzosopran low soprano, second-treble voice, mezzo soprano.
midasøre Midas' ear.
midd mite.
middag noon, midday, noon-day; (måltid) dinner; **igår —** yesterday at noon; **spise — dine; spise oksestek til —** dine off el. on roast beef; **bli til —** stay (for) dinner; **be en til —** invite one to dinner; **hva skal vi ha til —?** what shall we have for dinner? **sove —** take a nap after dinner.
middags|bord dinner, dinner-table; **ved -bordet** at dinner. **-hvil** rest at noon, siesta. **-høyde** meridian attitude. **-lur** after dinner nap. **-mat**

dinner. **-måltid** midday-meal. **-selskap** dinner party. **-sol** meridian sun, noonday sun. **-stund** noon-tide, hour of noon. **-søvn** nap after dinner, after-dinner nap. **-tid** noon-tide. **ved -tid** at el. about noon.
middel means; (forholdsregel) means, measure; (i en knipe) expedient; (hjelpemiddel) remedy; (hjelpekilde) resource; (legemiddel) remedy; **leve av sine midler** live upon one's means; **offentlige midler** public money.
middel|alder middle age. **-alderen** the middle ages. **-alderlig** mediæval, middle-age.
middelaldrende (halvgammel) middle-aged.
middelbar indirect, mediate.
middelhastighet average speed.
Middelhavet the Mediterranean.
middelhøyde middle height, medium height; **under — under** the average height; **en mann under —** an undersized man.
middelmådig middling, indifferent, mediocre. **middelmådighet** mediocrity.
middelpris average price.
middelpunkt centre.
middels (adj) middling, average.
middelshøy of middle height el. stature.
middelskole middle school, intermediate school. **-eksamen** intermediate examination. **-undervisning** intermediate education.
middelstand the middle classes.
middelstor average-sized, middle-sized.
middelstørrelse average el. medium size. **under — below** the middle size.
middelsår average year.
middeltall mean; **ta -et av** strike an average of.
middeltemperatur mean temperature.
middeltid mean time.
middelvei middle course, mean; **den gylne —** the golden mean, the happy medium.
midje middle, waist.
midler mediator.
midlertidig provisional, temporary, interim; (adv) provisionally, ad interim, temporarily.
midnatt midnight; **ved — about,** at midnight.
midnatts|sola the midnight sun, the unsetting sun. **-tid** midnight, dead of the night. **-time** midnight hour.
midt centre, middle; **— at, — etter** after el. along the middle (of); **— for, — foran** before the middle el. centre of, straight before; **— i** in the middle of, (fig) amidst, amid, in the midst of; **— iblant** in the midst of; **— igjennom** through the middle of, straight through; **— imellom** midway el. half way between; **— på dagen** in the middle of the day; **— på natta** in the dead of night; **gå — over** break in two; **— på** in the middle of; **til — på beinet** mid-leg; **— under** in the midst of.
midte middle; **i vår — in** the midst of us, among us; **en av vår —** one from among us.
midterst midmost, middlemost, middle.
midtfjords in the middle of the fiord.
midt|linje centre-line, median line. **-parti** central part. **-punkt** centre, central point
midtre komp. av **midt,** se **midterst.**
midtskips midship, in (the) midships.
midtsommer midsummer. **-s** in the middle of summer, at midsummer. **-tid** midsummer-tide.
midtstykke centre-piece, central piece.
midtveis half-way, mid-way.
midtvinters in mid-winter.
migrene megrim, migraine.
mikado (Japans keiser) Mikado.
Mikal, Mikkel Michael; (navn på reven) Renard, Charley. **mikkelsmess** Michaelmas-day
mikrobe microbe.
mikro|fon microphone. **-kosmos** microcosm. **-skop** microscope. **-skopisk** microscopic(al).
mikstur mixture, draught, potion.
mil: dansk **—** (4¹/₇ engelske) Danish mile; **engelsk —** mile; **fransk —** league; **norsk —**

(6¹/₄ engelske) Norwegian mile; **tysk** el. **geografisk —** German mile.

Mila|no Milan. **m—neser, m—nesisk** Milanese.

mild mild; (lempelig) lenient; (blid, from) gentle; **-e gaver** charities, benefactions; **mildt** (adv) mildly; leniently etc.; **-est talt** to say least (of it), to say no worse.

mildhet mildness, gentleness; lenity.

mildne mitigate, alleviate, temper; (berolige) soothe, appease.

mildvær mild el. soft weather. **en –sdag** a mild day.

mile (kolmile) charcoal-kiln.

mile|lang miles el. a mile long. **–pel, –stolpe** milestone. **–vidt** miles, for miles.

militarisme militarism.

militarist. -isk militarist.

mili(t)s militia.

militær (adj) military, army. **militær** (subst) (soldat) military man, soldier.

militæretat army (list).

militærflyger army pilot, military pilot.

militær|lege army surgeon. **-lue** soldier's cap. **-makt** military force. **-musikk** military music. **-nekter** objector to military service. **-orkester** military band. **-tjeneste** military service.

miljø milieu, surroundings.

milliard milliard.

million million. **milliontedel** millionth (part).

millionvis (adv) by millions. **millionær** millionaire.

milt milt, spleen. **-brann** anthrax, splenic fever. **-syk** splenetic. **-syke** spleen, hypochondria.

mimiker mimic. **mimikk** mimics (plur.), mimic art; play of feature. **mimisk** mimic(al).

mimose mimosa, sensitive plant.

mimre quiver, twitch.

min, mi, mitt, mine (adjektivisk) my; (substantivisk) mine, my own; **barnet mitt** my child; **barnet er mitt** the child is mine; **jeg skal gjøre mitt til det** I'll do my best.

minaret minaret.

mindre smaller, less, minor, lesser; **—** **diktere** minor poets; **— leiligheter** (rather) small houses; (adv) less, **enda —** still less; **ikke —** no less; **en tomme — enn 6 fot** an inch short of six feet; **så mye —, desto —** so much the less; **hvor mye —** how much less; **med —** unless; **ikke — . . . fordi** not the less . . . because; **— god** not quite good.

mindre|tall minority. **-verdig** inferior. **-verdighet** inferiority. **-verdighetsfølelse** a feeling of inferiority.

mindreårig under age; **etterlatende en — sønn** leaving a son in his minority; **være —** be a minor, be under age.

mindreårighet minority, nonage.

I. **mine** (uttrykk) air, look, mien; **en barsk —** a stern look, a frown; **gi seg — av** pretend to be, set up for; **gjøre — til å** make as if he would; **uten å fortrekke en —** without changing a feature, without a wince; **holde gode -r over-for en** keep up appearances with one; **gjøre gode -r til slett spill** put a good face on matters, put the best face on it.

II. **mine** (gruve, sjømine) mine; **la en — springe** spring a mine. **-arbeider** miner. **-bor** blasting rod. **-bygger** miner. **-bygging** mining, construction of mines.

mine|båt torpedo-boat. **-fare** mine danger. **-felt** mine-field. **-gang** gallery (of a mine). **-graver** miner. **-graving** mining.

mineral mineral; **mineralog** mineralogist; **mineralogi** mineralogy; **mineralogisk** mineralogical.

mineral|rike mineral kingdom. **-samling** collection of minerals.

mineralsk mineral.

mineralvann mineral water. **-fabrikant** mineral water manufacturer.

minere mine, blast.

mine|skudd blast, blasting shot. **-sperring** mine barrier el. block.

minespill play of features.

minesprengning explosion.

minespråk pantomime.

mineutlegger (skip) mine-layer.

miniatyr miniature; **i —** in miniature, in little; **diminutive; tegne i —** draw in little. **-maler** miniature-painter. **-maleri** miniature-painting. **-utgave** miniature edition, diamond (el. pearl) edition.

minimal (adj) minimal, minimum.

minimalfrakt bottom freight.

minimum minimum; **redusere til et —** minimize; **-s-avstand** minimum distance.

minister minister, secretary of state; (gesandt) envoy, minister. **-ansvar** a minister's responsibility, ministerial responsibility.

ministeriell ministerial.

ministerium ministry, cabinet; **tre, komme inn i ministeriet** enter the ministry, come into office; **tre ut av ministeriet** go out; **være i ministeriet** be in office.

minister|krise ministerial crisis. **-president** premier. **-skifte** change of ministers, change of ministry. **-taburett** seat in the cabinet.

I. **mink** (zool.:) mink.

II. **mink** (svinn:) decrease, diminution, lessening.

minke decrease; dwindle, shrink.

I. **minne** (samtykke) consent.

II. **minne** (erindring) reminiscence, remembrance; (hukommelse) remembrance, memory, commemoration; (erindringstegn, minnetegn) memento, souvenir, remembrance; (levning) relic, reminder; (minnesmerke) memorial, monument; **være i friskt —** be fresh in remembrance; **til — om** in commemoration of, commemorative of; **i manns —** within el. in the memory of man, within living memory; **gå meg av —** pass from my mind.

minne (vrb) remind, put in mind (**om:** of), call to one's remembrance, be suggestive of; (advarende) warn.

minne|beger commemorative toast. **-fest** commemorative festival, commemoration. **-gave** remembrance, souvenir, keepsake, memorial. **-krans** memorial wreath.

minnelig amicable; **— avgjørelse** compromise. **minnelighet: i —** by agreement of both parties.

minnelse (påminnelse) admonition, reminder; (av sykdom osv.) slight touch, return, reminiscence.

minnerik rich in recollections.

minnes (erindre) remember, recollect; **jeg —** at jeg har truffet ham I remember meeting him; **om jeg — rett** if my memory serves me.

minnesanger minnesinger, (German) troubadour.

minneskrift memorial.

minnesmerke monument, tomb; memorial.

minne|stein monumental stone. **-støtte** monumental column. **-tale** commemorative oration, memorial address. **-tavle** memorial tablet el. plate. **-tegn**, se **minne.**

minneutstilling commemorative exhibition.

minneverdig memorable.

minning, se **minnelse.**

minoritet minority; **være i —** be in a (el. the) minority.

min santen really, on my word.

minske dimish; **— seil** shorten sail, **— et skips fart** lessen, slacken, deaden a ship's way.

minsk(n)ing diminution.

minst least, smallest; **ikke det —e** not a bit; **i det -e** at least; **ikke i -e måte** not in the least; (når talen er om to, brukes gjerne komparativ): **gi meg det -e stykket, og behold du det andre** give me the smaller piece, and keep you the other; **det — mulige** a minimum; **det -e av**

barna the youngest of the children; (adv) least; (i det minste) at least, at the least.
minstelønn minimum el. standard wages.
minus minus; (adv) less, minus.
minutiøs minute.
minutt minute; **for et — siden** this minute; **på -et** to a minute, to the minute; **jeg skal være her på -et** I shall be here in a minute.
minutt|skudd minute gun. **-viser** minute-hand.
minør miner.
mirakel miracle; **gjøre mirakler** do el. work miracles.
mirakel|kur miraculous cure. **-maker** miracle-worker, -monger. **-mann** wonderful man. **-tro** belief in miracles.
mirakuløs miraculous.
misantrop misanthrope.
misantropisk misanthropic(al).
misbillige disapprove (of); **-nde mine** frown.
misbilligelse disapprobation, disapproval.
misbruk abuse, misuse, misusage, misemployment; malpractice.
misbruke abuse, misuse, misemploy.
misdanne deform, misfashion, misshape.
misdannelse deformity, mal(con)formation.
misdeder, -ske malefactor, misdoer.
misére pitiableness, pitiable affair.
misforhold disproportion, incongruity.
misfornøyd displeased, discontented, dissatisfied.
misfornøyelse discontent, dissatisfaction.
misforstå misunderstand, misconceive, misapprehend, mistake.
misforståelse misunderstanding; (det å forstå uriktig) misapprehension, misconception; **ved en —** in error, under a wrong impression.
misfoster monster, abortion.
misgjerning misdeed, crime, offence.
misgrep mistake, error, blunder, fault, wrong move; **begå —** commit blunders.
mishag displeasure, dislike, disapprobation.
mishage displease. **mishagsytring** expression of disapproval el. displeasure.
mishandle ill-treat, maltreat, ill-use.
mishandling ill-treatment, ill-usage.
misjon mission. **misjons|arbeid** mission work. **-vesen** missionary concerns.
misjonær missionary.
miskjenne misjudge, misvalue, fail to appreciate; **miskjent** unappreciated, misappreciated.
miskjennelse misjudgment.
misklang dissonance, discord, jar.
miskle be unbecoming to, misbecome.
miskmask hodge-podge, medley, mishmash.
miskreditt discredit; **bringe i —** bring into discredit el. disesteem, discredit.
miskunn mercy, mercifullness. **-e seg** show mercy, be merciful; (bibl.) have mercy (over: on). **-elig** (bibl.) merciful.
mislig doubtful, precarious, hazardous; questionable, irregular; **— styrelse** mismanagement.
mislighet precariousness; irregularity.
misligholde break, fail to fulfil.
misligholdelse (av kontrakt) breach of a contract; (av obligasjon) non-payment.
mislike dislike.
mislyd dissonance, discord, jar.
mislykkes fail, not succeed; **det mislyktes for ham** he failed, did not succeed; **et mislykt forsøk** an unsuccessful attempt, a failure.
mismodig desponding, despondent, dispirited.
mismot despondency.
misnøyd, se -fornøyd.
misstemning ill-humour; (misfornøyelse) dissatisfaction.
mista seg err, be in error, mistake, be mistaken.
mistak error, mistake.
mistanke suspicion; misgivings; **fatte — til en** conceive suspicion against one; **ha — til en** suspect one; **ha — om noe** entertain a

suspicion of a thing; **-n falt på ham** he was suspected.
mistbenk hotbed, forcing frame.
miste lose, be deprived of; forfeit.
misteltein mistletoe.
mis|tenke suspect **(for:** of); **han er -tenkt for å stjele** he is suspected of stealing; **bli -tenkt** fall into suspicion.
mistenkelig suspicious, suspicious-looking.
mistenkeliggjøre render suspect, throw suspicion on.
mistenkelighet suspiciousness.
mistenksom suspicious; **se med -me øyne på** view with an eye of suspicion.
mistenksomhet suspiciousness, suspicion.
mistillit distrust, diffidence; **ha — til** distrust.
mistillitsvotum want-of-confidence vote, vote of no confidence, vote of censure.
mistro (subst) distrust; **vekke — til** discredit.
mistro (vrb) distrust.
mistroisk distrustful, mistrustful, suspicious.
mistroiskhet suspiciousness.
mistrøstig desponding, disconsolate, disheartened. **gjøre — dishearten.**
mistrøstighet despondency.
mistvil despair; misgiving(s).
mistvile despair, despond **(om:** of).
mistyde misinterpret, misconstrue.
mistydning misinterpretation, misconstruction.
misunne envy, grudge.
misunnelig envious **(over:** of, at); **være — på en for noe** envy one st.
misunnelse envy.
misunnelsesverdig enviable; **lite — unenviable.**
misunner envier.
misvekst failure of crops, bad harvest.
misvisende misleading, fallacious, deceptive; **det — i å** the fallacy of; **— kurs** course by compass, magnetic course.
misvisning error of the compass, variation; mistake, delusion.
mitraljøse mitrailleuse; Gatling gun.
mitt, se min.
mjuk, se myk. -ne, se mykne.
mjau mew. **-e** mew.
mjød mead. **-urt** meadow-sweet, queen of the meadows.
mjøl, se mel.
mjølk, se melk.
mjøll mote, flake; dust; **-snø** loose, powdery snow.
mjå, se smal, slank.
mnemonevtikk mnemonics.
mo (sandy) plain; (lyngmo) heath, (heathery) moor; (ekserserplass) country drill-ground.
mo (adj) weak; **— i knærne** weak about the knees.
mo: — alene all alone by oneself.
mobb mob.
mobilisere mobilize.
mobilisering mobilization.
modal modal; **-e hjelpeverber** defective auxiliary verbs.
modell model; (levende) model, sitter.
modellere model, frame, mould.
modellering modelling, framing, moulding.
modellerskammel posture-frame.
modell|skole school for drawing after living models. **-tegning** model drawing.
modellør modeller.
moden ripe, mature; **— til** ripe for; **en — mann** a staid man; **i den modnere alder** in maturity; **etter -t overlegg** upon mature consideration.
modenhet ripeness, maturity; **komme til — ripen,** mature. **modenhets|alderen** maturity. **-bevis** testimonial of capacity.
moder (eldre form for mor, brukes i enkelte sammensetninger).

moderasjon moderation; (avslag) abatement reduction.
moderat moderate, reasonable.
moderere moderate.
moderkirke mother church.
moder|kjærlighet maternal love, a mother's love, mother love. **–land** mother-country, parent country, home country, old country.
moderlig maternal, motherly.
moderlighet motherliness.
moder|mord matricide. **–morder, –morderske** matricide.
moderne fashionable; (nåværende) modern.
modernisere modernize.
moderskap maternity, motherhood. **–sforsikring** maternity insurance.
moder|skip mother-ship, depot-ship. **–stat** parent state.
modifikasjon modification; qualification; **sannhet med –er** truth with a difference.
modifisere modify; (ved innskrenkning) qualify. **modifisering,** se **modifikasjon.**
modig courageous, plucky; **gjøre — embolden; gråte sine –e tårer** weep bitterly.
modist milliner.
mod|ne ripen. **–nes** ripen. **–ning** ripening. **–ningstid** season el. time of ripening.
modulasjon modulation. **modulere** modulate.
modus mood.
moiré watered silk, tabby.
mokant sarcastic.
mokasin moccasin.
Mokka Mocha. **m–kaffe** Mocha (coffee).
molbakke steep bottom.
molboaktig Gothamite, silly.
molboene the wise men of Gotham.
mold mould. **–et** earthy. **–jord** mould.
moldvarp mole. **–arbeid** mole's work, subterraneous working. **–grå** mole coloured. **–skudd** mole-hill, mole-cast.
molefonken sulky.
molekyl molecule.
molekylær molecular.
molest molestation. **molestere** molest.
I. **moll** (lett bomullstøy) mull.
II. **moll** (musikk) minor, the minor key. **moll|akkord** minor chord. **–skala** minor scale. **–toneart** minor key.
mollusk mullusk.
molo mole, pier.
molok Moloch.
molskinn (tykt tøy til arbeidsklær, særl. for murere) moleskin.
molte cloud-berry.
molukkerne the Moluccas.
molybden molybdenum.
moment moment; (i mekanikk) momentum, impetus; (faktor) element, factor; (-er, f. eks. i en tale) heads.
momentan momentary.
momentlukker instantaneous shutter.
mon I wonder (whether el. if), I should like to know (whether el. if); **— det er mulig** is that really the case?
monade monad.
monark monarch. **–i** monarchy. **–isk** monarchical.
mondén fashionable.
moneter (penger) tin.
mongol Mongol. **M–iet** Mongolia.
mongolsk Mongol, Mongolian.
monisme monism.
monitor monitor. **–kanon** turret gun.
monn degree; (forskjell) difference; (virkning) avail, effect; (framgang) advance, progress; **–er drar** all ekes, all's fish that comes to net; **ta sin — igjen** indemnify oneself, even up things.
monne avail, eke, suffice; **det –t lite** it was of little avail.
monogam monogamous.

monogami monogamy.
monokkel monocle, single eye-glass.
mono|log monologue, soliloquy. **–man** monomaniac. **–mani** monomania.
monoplan monoplane.
monopol monopoly (**på:** of).
monopolisere monopolize.
monoton monotonous, monotonical.
monotoni monotony.
monstrans monstrance.
monstrum monster. **monstrøs** monstrous.
monsun monsoon.
montere mount; (utruste) equip; (møblere) fit up, fit out, furnish.
montering installation, mounting, equipment, furnishing.
montre show-case.
montro, se **mon.**
montør fitter; (ved flygemaskiner) mechanic; (elektrisk) electrician.
monument monument, memorial; **— over** monument to (of).
monumental monumental.
mops pug, pug-dog. **–enese** pug-nose.
mor mother, maternal parent; (bare om dyr) dam; **Guds — Our Lady, the Virgin Mary; bli — become a mother; ingen –s sjel** no living soul.
moral morality, morals; (hærs moral) morale, moral; (av fabel el. dikt) moral, moralization; (sedelære) moral philosophy, ethics.
moralisere moralize.
moralisering moralizing, moralization.
moralist moralist; moralizer.
moralitet morality, morals.
moral|lov moral law. **–predikant** moralist. **–preken** moral sermon. **–prinsipp** moral principle.
moralsk moral; (adv) morally, in respect of morals.
morass morass.
moratorium letters of respite.
morbror mother's brother, maternal uncle.
morbær mulberry. **–saft** mulberry-syrup. **–tre** mulberry-tree.
mord murder (**på:** of); **begå et — commit** (a) murder.
mord|anslag murderous design, attempt on life. **–attentat** assault on life, attempted murder. **–brann** arson, incendiarism. **–brenner** incendiary.
morder murderer. **–hule** murderer's den. **–hånd** hand of an assassin.
morderisk murderous, bloody.
morderske murderess.
mord|forsøk attempt on life. **–våpen** murderous weapon.
more amuse, divert, entertain; (få til å le) tickle; **— seg** enjoy oneself, amuse oneself; **— seg med** amuse oneself with; **— seg over, med** be amused by, with; **mor deg godt!** I wish you may enjoy yourself; **de –t seg godt over stykket** they greatly enjoyed the play.
moreld, se **morild.**
morell morel (cherry), morello.
moréne moraine.
morfar mother's father, maternal grandfather.
Morfeus Morpheus.
morfin morphia, morphine. **–innsprøytning** injection of morphia.
morfinist person addicted to the use of morphia, morphi(n)omaniac.
morfinsprøyte morphia syringe.
morfolo|gi morphology. **–gisk** morpholigic(al).
morganatisk morganatic.
morgen morning; (morgendag) morrow; **god — good morning; sove til den lyse — sleep till broad daylight; — og aften** (every) morning and evening; **fra — til aften** from morning till night; **i — to-morrow; i — aften** to-morrow night; **i — tidlig** (early) to-morrow morning;

til i — på denne tid till this time to-morrow; om **-en** in the morning, of a morning; **i morges** this morning; **igår morges** yesterday morning. **morgenandakt** morning prayers.
morgen|belysning morning light. **-blad** morning paper. **-blund** morning slumber. **-bønn** morning prayers. **-dag** morrow.
morgen|demring morning twilight, early dawn. **-fugl** early riser. **-gave** «morning gift» (bridegroom's gift to the bride on the morning after the wedding). **-gretten** who has got out of bed the wrong side. **-gry** dawn of morning. **-kaffe** morning's coffee. **-kjole** morning-gown. **-kvist:** på **-en** at early morning, in the small hours. **morgen|mat, -måltid** breakfast. **-post** morning's mail. **-røde** dawn, aurora. **-salme** morning-hymn. **-sang** morning song. **-side:** på **-en** early in the morning. **-skjær** peep of day. **-sko** slippers. **-sol** morning sun. **-stjerne** morning star. **-stråle** morning ray. **-stund** morning-time. **-stund har gull i munn** early to bed, and early to rise, makes a man healthy, wealthy, and wise; the early bird catches the worm. **-søvn** morning sleep. **-tog** morning-train. **-tur** morning-walk, morning's walk.
morges, se **morgen.**
morgne seg shake off sleep, get fairly awake.
morian Moor, blackamoor.
morild phosphorescence (of the sea).
morken decayed, decaying, rotten; (skjør) brittle.
morkne decay.
morløs motherless, bereaved.
mormon Mormon. **-isme** Mormonism.
mormor mother's mother, maternal grandmother.
moro amusement, fun, a lark, a spree. **jeg skulle ha — av å se** I should like to see. **for — skyld** for the fun of the thing.
morosam, se **morsom.**
morsarv maternal inheritance el. succession.
morsk fierce-looking, glum, grim.
morskap amusement, diversion, pastime; **finne —** i take delight in; **til —** for amusement. **morskaps|bok** book of entertainment. **-lesning** light reading.
morske seg be fierce el. angry.
mors|liv (mother's) womb. **-melk** mother's milk. **-merke** mole. **-mål** mother-tongue, native language, vernacular.
morsom amusing, diverting, entertaining; funny, droll. **det -me ved noe** amusing el. entertaining quality.
morsomhet (morsomt innfall) joke, jest; **si -er** be witty, say witty things, crack jokes.
morssiden: på — on the mother's side. **onkel på —** maternal uncle.
mors|sjel: hver — every mother's son, every man Jack. **-stykke** good turn, kindness. **-ætt** maternal race.
mort (fisk) roach.
mortalitet mortality.
mortalitetsliste table of mortality.
Morten Martin.
mortens|aften Martinmas-eve. **-dag** Martinmas. **-gås** Martinmas goose.
morter (til støtning) mortar.
mortér (slags kanon) mortar.
mortifikasjon annulment, cancellation. **mortifisere** declare null and void, nullify, annul.
mos (lunge- etc.) pulp, mash.
mosaikk mosaic. **-arbeid** mosaic (work), tessellation. **-arbeider** inlayer, mosaicist. **-golv** mosaic pavement.
mosaisk Mosaic(al).
mose (plante) moss. **-aktig** mossy, moss-like.
mosebok book of Moses; **de fem mosebøker** the Pentateuch.
mose|dott lump el. plug of moss. **-fly** mossy plateau. **-grodd** moss-grown. **-kledd** moss-clad, mossy. **-lag** moss-cover.

moseloven the Mosaic law, the Levitical law.
moselvin moselle.
mose|rose moss-rose. **-teppe** carpet of moss. **-tue** tuft of moss.
mosjon exercise; **ta —, -ere** take exercise; be out for a constitutional, walk constitutionally, take exercise, take the air.
moské mosque.
moskito mosquito.
moskitonett mosquito-net (el. curtain).
moskovitt, -isk Muscovite.
moskus musk. **-dyr** musk(-deer). **-okse** musk-ox. **-rotte** musk-rat.
Moskva Moscow.
most (eple-); cider; (drue-) must.
moster mother's sister, maternal aunt.
mot (prep.) against; (henimot) towards; (jur.) versus; (om vederlag) on, on condition of, against, at; (i sm. ligning m.) to. **et lån — sikkerhet** a loan against security. **huset ligger — syd** the house stands to the south. **snill — kind to. — aften** towards evening. Se ogs. **imot, mot** (adv.), se **imot.**
I. **mot** (subst) courage, spirit, mettle, pluck, heart; **friskt —!** cheer up! never say die! **sette — i** encourage, reassure, put heart into; **være ved godt —** be of good cheer el. heart; **være til -e** feel; **være vel, ille til -e** feel at ease, be uneasy el. uncomfortable; **bli underlig til -e** feel awkward el. strange; **hadde ikke — til å** had not the heart to; **fatte —** take courage el. heart, cheer up; **tape -et** lose courage el. heart; **holde -et oppe, ikke tape -et** keep heart; **ta -et fra** discourage, dishearten.
II. **mot,** se **møte. godt —!** well met!
motarbeide counterwork, countermine, counteract, counterplot, withstand. **-lse** countermining etc.
motbakke acclivity, ascent.
motbefaling counterorder.
motbeskyldning counter-charge.
motbevegelse countermovement, contrary motion.
motbevis disproof, refutation.
motbevise disprove, refute.
motbydelig disgusting, loathsome, distasteful.
motbydelighet loathsomeness, disgust; **ha — mot** feel disgust at, feel aversion to, loathe.
motbør contrary wind(s); (fig.) a check, opposition; **møte —** be opposed.
mote fashion, mode; **leve etter -n** live fashionably, live in a fashionable style; **bringe på — bring into fashion; gå av —** go out of fashion; **det er blitt —** it is fashionable, it is the fashion, it is in vogue; **siste —** newest style; **angi -n** set the fashion; **etter nyeste —** to the latest fashion; **komme på —** come in, come into fashion; become the fashion.
mote|artikkel fancy-article. **-blad** fashion paper. **-dame** fashionable lady, lady of fashion.
mote|dukke dress doll. **-handel** milliner's trade; milliner's shop. **-handler** man-milliner. **-handlerinne** milliner. **-herre** fashionable gentleman, dandy, exquisite, beau. **-journal** fashion-book, fashion-sheet.
mote|laps, -narr dandy, fop.
moteprest fashionable preacher.
motepynt millinery.
mote|sak quite a fashion. **-skjønnhet** fashionable beauty. **-varer** articles of fashion, fancy goods, fancy articles.
motfallen disheartened, dispirited, despondent, crest-fallen.
motfallenhet despondency, dismay dejection.
motforestilling remonstrances.
motforslag counter-motion, c.-proposal.
motgang adversity.
motgift antidote, counter-poison.
mothake barb; **forsynt med -r** barbed.
motig, se **modig.**
motiv motive; (musikk) motive, motif, motivo.

theme; (malerk.) incident; **-er** (til lov o. l.) grounds.

motiver|e motive; justify, warrant; (anføre grunnene for) explain the motives of, state reasons for; (i et drama) lead up to; **en -t fremstilling** a reasoned statement.

motivering explanation (of the reasons), vindication.

motkandidat competitor, rival candidate.

motklage recrimination, counter-charge.

motløs faint-hearted, out of heart, spiritless, dispirited, desponding. **-het** faint-heartedness.

motmanøvre counter-manœuvre.

motmæle contradiction. **ta til —** reply.

motor motor. **-briller** motor-goggles. **-båt** motor-boat. **-drift** motor-power. **-fartøy** motorvessel.

motorisk motory.

motor|skade motor-trouble. **-sykkel** motorcycle. **-syklist** motor-cyclist. **-vogn** motor-car, autocar, motor-vehicle.

motpart adversary, opponent, opposite party.

motparti adverse el. opposite party, opposing side; **holde med -et** side with the opposite party.

motregning opposite account, counter-balance, contra-account.

motsatt opposite, contrary; (omvendt) reverse, converse; **i — fall** on a contrary supposition, if not, otherwise; **nettopp det -e** the exact reverse; **uttale seg i — retning** express oneself to the contrary; **gjøre det stikk -e av** av do quite the contrary of.

motsetning opposition, contrast; **i — til** as contradistinguished from, as distinct from; **danne en — til** stand opposed to.

motsette seg set oneself against, oppose.

motsi contradict, gainsay; (bestride) challenge; **— seg selv** give oneself the lie; give oneself away.

motsigelse contradiction; **stå i — til** be in contradiction to. **-lyst** spirit of contradiction.

motsigende contradictory.

motsjø headsea.

motskrift refutation, rejoinder.

motspill defence. **-er** adversary.

motstand resistance, opposition; (indre) reluctance, repugnance. **gjøre — mot** oppose resistance to, hold out against; **ikke gjøre — offer** no resistance.

mot|stander, **-standerske** opponent, antagonist.

motstandsdyktig capable of resistance.

motstands|evne, **-kraft** power of resistance.

motstrebende reluctant; (adv) reluctantly, grudgingly.

motstrid opposition; **dette er ikke i noen — med** this is not at all at variance with.

motstridende incompatible, contradictory, conflicting.

motstrøm counter-current; cross current.

motstøt counter-shock.

motstå resist, withstand; **-ende** opposite.

motsvare correspond to, be equivalent to.

motta (få) receive; (ikke avslå, anta) accept; **jeg kan ikke — hans tilbud** I cannot accept his offer; **jeg har -tt** (fått) **et brev** I have received a letter; **vi har -tt Deres ærede** we are in receipt of your favour, your favour has come to hand.

mottagelig: — for (dannelse, følelse, inntrykk osv.) susceptible of; (sykdom o. l.) liable to; **— for grunner** amenable to reason; **gjøre — for** predispose to.

mottagelighet receivableness, receptibility; susceptibility (of), receptiveness; (mottagelsesevne) receptivity; (for sykdommer o. l.) liability (to), predisposition (for).

mottagelse reception; (av ting) receipt; (opptagelse, antagelse) acceptation; **etter -n av Deres brev** on receipt of your letter.

mottagelsesbevis certificate of receipt, receipt, acquittance.

mottagelsestid hours of admission.

mottagelsesværelse receiving room; (i selskapslivet) reception room, drawingroom.

mottager receiver, recipient.

mottagerstasjon (i radio) receiving station.

mottakelig, mottakelse, motta(k)ing osv., se **mottagelig, mottagelse** osv.

motto motto.

mottrekk countermove.

mottrykk counter-pressure.

motvarme (v. skogbrann o. l.) a brack fire, subsidiary fire.

motveksel counter-bill of exchange.

motvekt counter-weight, counter-balance; (mest fig) counterpoise.

motverge defence; **sette seg til — put** oneself in a posture of defence, turn to bay.

motvilje reluctance, repugnance, refractoriness. **motvillig** reluctant, refractory.

motvind contrary wind, head wind.

motvirk|e counteract, counterinfluence; discountenance. **-ning** counteracting; counteraction; reaction.

movere move.

mudd, se **finnmudd**.

mudder mud, mire; (støy, kvalm) noise, uproar, disturbance; **gjøre — kick** up a row (el. dust), make a fuss (**om**: about). **-aktig** muddy.

mudder|maskin dredging machine, dredger, mud dredge. **-pram** mud-barge, mud-flat, mud -lighter; se **-maskin. -pøl** slough. **-vann** muddy water.

mudre dredge. **mudret** muddy.

muffe muff; (på ledninger, rør o. l.) socket.

muffedise muffetee, wristlet, cuff.

mug(e) (subst) (flokk, stor forsamling) crowd, multitude; the common people.

I. **mugg** (sopp) mould.

II. **mugg** (slags tøy) twill.

mugge (vrb) (være sur) be morose el. fretful; grumble, fret.

mugge (subst) ewer, jug, pitcher.

muggen musty, mouldy, fusty; (mutt) sulky, crusty; **-t** (adv): **lukter — has** a mouldy smell. **-het** mustiness etc.

mugne mould, get el. grow mouldy.

Muhammed Mohammed. **muham(m)edan|er**, **-sk** Mohammedan, Mohametan.

mukk (kny) mutter, grumbling; **han sa ikke et — he** did not open his mouth; **forstod ikke et levende — was** quite at sea.

mukke mutter, grumble.

mukker (treavfall) chippage, chips of wood.

mukking grumbling.

mulatt mulatto. **-inne** mulatto woman.

muld, se **mold.**

muldyr mule. **-driver** muleteer, mule-driver.

mule (munn) muzzle, snout.

mule|band muzzle. **-pose** nose-bag.

mulesel hinny.

mulig possible; eventual; practicable; **det er meget — at han trodde det** he very likely believed it; **meget — I** dare say; **den høyest -e lønn for det minst -e arbeid** the maximum of wage for the minimum of work; **på alle -e måter** in all manner of ways; **den -e fare** the danger, if any; **så kortfattet som — as** brief as possible; **gjøre seg mest — umak** take every pains, use one's best endeavours; **så godt som — as** good as possible.

muligens (adv) possibly.

muliggjøre make el. render possible.

mulighet possibility, chance (**for**: of); potentiality; (eventualitet) contingency; **det er en — for** it is just possible that; **en fjern — for** the off-chance of.

muligvis, se **muligens.**

muljere (i fonetikk) liquefy, soften.

mulkt fine, mulct, amercement; **ble ilagt en stor — was** heavily fined; **idømt en — på 14 sh.**

fined 14 sh.; **det er satt — for** det a penalty attaches to it; **under en høy** — under penalty of a heavy fine.

mulkter|e fine, amerce. **-ing** fining.

mulle, se **mumle.**

mulm darkness, gloom; **i — og mørke** in the dead of night.

multipli|kand multiplicand. **-kasjon** multiplication. **-kator** multiplier, multiplicator.

multiplisere multiply.

multiplum multiple.

mumie mummy. **-aktig** mummylike.

mumle mutter, mumble; **— i skjegget** mutter to oneself. **mumling** mutter, muttering.

mumse, se **gumle.**

München, Munich.

mundering, mundur uniform, accoutrement, equipment.

munisipal municipal.

munisjon amunition, munition.

munk monk, friar, conventual.

munke (slags kake) doughnut.

munkebind (gamle hellærbind) monastery binding.

munke|drakt monastic dress. **-hette** monk's hood. **-kappe** cowl. **-kloster** monastery. **-kutte** cowl. **-latin** monkish Latin. **-løfte** monastic vow; avlegge **-løftet** take the monastic vow. **-orden** monastic order. **-vesen** monachism, monasticism.

munn mouth; **bruke — use** (impertinent) language; jaw, lip, mouth; **holde — (tie stille med noe) keep** a secret, keep one's own counsel, be discreet; **hold —! hold** your tongue! shut up! **ta -en full** (være fordringsfull) open one's mouth wide, be exorbitant in one's demands; (overdrive) exaggerate, draw a long bow; **snakke en etter -en** coax one, wheedle one; **ta bladet fra -en** speak one's mind, tell a piece of one's mind; **være grov i -en** have a foul tongue; **legge ordene i -en på en** put words in another's mouth; **snakke i -en på hverandre** speak all at once; **slikke seg om -en etter** cast a sheep's eye on; **slå seg selv på -en** give oneself the lie; **-en står ikke på ham** he talks incessantly; **stoppe -en på** put one to silence; **få -en på glid** set one's tongue a-going.

munn|bitt (på tømme) bit. **-dask** slap on the mouth.

munn|full mouthful. **-harmonika** child's harmonica, mouth-organ, jew's harp. **-hell** by-word, familiar saying, adage. **-høggeri** wrangling, altercation, bickering. **-hogges** bandy words, wrangle, bicker. **-hule** cavity of the mouth.

munning mouth, outlet; (større, ved havet) estuary; (på skytevåpen) muzzle.

munn|kjapp glib, voluble. **-klemme** lock -jaw.

munnkurv (dog's) muzzle; **sette — på** muzzle; **med —** muzzled. **munnkurvlov** (fig) gag-law.

munnkåt flippant, impertinent, pert. **-het** flippancy, pertness.

munniær glibness of tongue, volubility; **ha et godt — have** the gift of the gab.

munn- og klausyke foot-and-mouth disease. **munn|skjenk** cup-bearer. **-smak** taste. **-spill,** se **-harmonika. -stykke** (til sigar og sigarett) holder; (på blåseinstrumenter) mouth-piece.

munnsvær mere words, idle promises, breath. **munn|vann** gargle. **-vik** corner of the mouth.

munter lively, cheerful, sprightly, merry, gay. **munterhet** cheerfulness, liveliness, gaiety.

muntlig verbal, oral; (adv) verbally, orally, by word of mouth; **— eksamen** viva-voce examination, oral examination. **muntlighet** oral proceedings.

muntrasjon frolic, jollification. **-sråd** fun -provider, master of the revels.

muntre cheer, enliven.

mur wall; **tie som en — be mute as a fish. murbrekker** battering ram.

mure build with brick el. stone, do mason's work; **— en vegg** build up a wall; **— til** wall up, brick up, build up; **-t** brick(-built).

murer bricklayer, waller, mason. **-gutt** (læregutt) bricklayer's apprentice. **-håndlanger** hodman, mason's tender. **-håndverk** masonry.

murerlære: sette i — apprentice (one) to a bricklayer; **være i — be** in apprenticeship with a bricklayer.

murersvenn journeyman bricklayer.

murhus brickbuilt house.

muring walling, brick-laying.

mur|kalk mortar. **-kitt** cement. **-krans** battlement. **-krone** mural crown.

murmeldyr marmot; (sl) surly, crabbed person.

mur|mester master-bricklayer. **-pille** pier. **-puss** plastering.

murre mutter, grumble.

mur|skei, -skje trowel. **-stein** brick. **stykke — brickbat. -tind(e)** battlement. **-tvang** the compulsory use of stone or brick in building a house.

murverk brickwork, masonry.

mus mouse; **når katten er borte, danser -ene på bordet** when the cat is away, the mice will play; **det gikk under med mann og — it** went down with every mother's soul.

muse Muse; **de ni -r** the nine Muses.

muse|felle mouse-trap. **-hol, -hull** mouse-hole; **jage en i et -hull** frighten one out of his wits.

muselmann (muhamedaner) Mussulman pl. Mussulmans, Moslem.

musereir mouse's nest.

musetenner (små tenner) small teeth.

museum museum. **museumsgjenstand** museum specimen.

musikalier music, music-books.

musikalsk (ikke om person) musical; **han er — he** is fond of music, is a musician.

musikant player, musician.

musiker musician.

musikk music; **sette — til** set to music.

musikkanmelder musical critic.

musikk|forening (phil)harmonic society. **-handel** (butikk) music-shop. **-handler** music-seller. **-korps** band of musicians. **-lærer** music-master, professor of music. **-lærerinne** music-mistress. **-stykke** piece of music. **-time** music-lesson. **-undervisning** instruction in music.

musikus musician.

musisere make music.

muskat nutmeg. **-blomme** mace. **muskateller** (vin) muscatel. **muskatnøtt,** se **muskat.**

muskedunder (børse) blunderbuss.

muskel muscle. **-bunt** muscular bundle. **-kraft** muscular strength el. power. **-spill** play el. swelling of the muscles. **-sprengning** rupture of the muscles. **-sterk** brawny, muscular. **-stramning** tension of the muscles. **-trekning** spasm, cramp. **-vev** muscular tissue.

musketer musketeer.

muskett musket.

muskulatur muscles, muscling.

muskuløs muscular.

musling shell, bivalve; (blåskjell) mussel, muscle.

muslingskall (mussel-) shell.

musselin muslin.

mussere effervesce; (om vin) froth, foam. **-nde vann** aerated waters.

mustang (vill preriehest) mustang.

musvåk buzzard, mouse-hawk.

mut, se **finnmudd** (el. **-mut).**

mutbar (min.) licenseable.

mute (min.) apply for a license to work a claim.

mutt sulky. **-het** sulkiness.

mutter, se **møtrik.**

mye much; **han kan — he** knows a good deal; **det var — indeed!** you don't say so! **han har fått litt for — (han er beruset)** he is rather tipsy;

det var — at han kom seg it was a wonder that he recovered.

mygg gnat; gjøre en — til en elefant make mountains of molehills.

myggestikk sting of a gnat.

myggesverm swarm of gnats.

mygle, se mugne.

myk limber, lithe; (ogs. fig) pliable, supple; gjøre en — bend one, render one submissive.

myke limber, make pliable.

mykne limber, supple, become pliable.

mylder throng, crowd, shoal.

myldre swarm, shoal; gatene -r av mennesker the streets are swarming with people.

mynde grey-hound.

myndig powerful; (bydende) imperious, haughty, authoritative; (jur) of age; være — be of age; erklære for — emancipate; bli — come of age.

myndighet authority; authoritativeness; (myndig alder) majority; rådgivende — advisory powers; -ene those in authority; powers that be.

myndighets|alder (full) age. -bevilling letter of majority. -erklæring coming of age.

myndling ward.

mynt coin; (stedet) mint; slå — coin money; gangbar — current coin; et lands — the coinage of a country; med klingende — in cash (down); betale en med samme — pay one back in his own coin el. in kind; kaste — og krone play at cross and pile.

mynte (vrb) coin, stamp, mint; det var -t på Dem that was meant for you, aimed at you, you were aimed at.

mynte (plante) mint.

mynt|enhet unit of coinage; uniformity of currency. -fot standard (of coinage). -guardein assayer of the mint. -kabinett cabinet of medals and coins. -kyndig skilled in numismatics.

myntlov monetary law.

myntmester mint-master; (over-) master of the mint.

mynting coining.

mynt|samler collector of coins. -samling collection of coins and medals. -sort species of coin. -stempel die, coin. -system monetary system. -vitenskap numismatics.

myr marsh, morass, bog, moor. -aktig boggy. -bunn boggy land, boggy ground.

myrde murder. myrderi murdering, massacre, butchery.

myr|drag stretch of boggy land. -dyrking cultivation el. reclaiming of bogs. -hol, -hull mudhole.

myriade myriad.

myr|jern bog-iron. -jord, -lende boggy soil. -lendt boggy, fennish, marshy, swampy. -malm, se -jern.

myrra myrrh. -essens tincture of myrrh.

myrsnipe snipe.

myrt myrtle; (bruder pyntes i England med orange-blossoms, som hos oss med myrt).

myrtekrans myrtle-wreath.

myrull bog cotton, cotton-grass.

myse (med øynene) blink, wink, twinkle.

myse (subst) whey, serum of milk.

mys|ost whey-cheese. -smør soft cheese made of whey.

myst|erium mystery. -erløs mysterious. -ifikasjon mystification, hoax. -ifisere mystify, hoax, play on.

mystiker mystic.

mystikk mysticism, occultism.

mystisisme mysticism.

mystisk mystic(al).

myte (vrb., felle hår el. fjær) moult.

myte (subst) myth.

mytisk mythic(al).

mytolog mythologist. -i mythology. -isk mythological.

mytteri mutiny; gjøre — mutiny, turn mutinous; få i stand — raise a mutiny; deltagerne i -et the mutineers. anstifteren av et — ringleader of a mutiny.

Mähren Moravia.

mæle (subst) (røst) voice; miste -t lose the power of speech.

mæle (vrb) utter, articulate; speak.

møbel piece of furniture; møbler furniture.

møbel|handler upholsterer, furnituredealer. -magasin upholstery el. furniture establishment. -snekker cabinet-maker. -stoff furniture stuff(s), upholstery stuff. -trekk, se stoff.

møblement furniture, suite (of furniture).

møblere furnish (a room el. a house).

møde pains, trouble.

mødrene maternal, on the mother's side. -arv, se morsarv.

møkk dung, muck. -haug dung-heap. -greip dung-fork. -kjerre dung-cart. -lass cart-load of dung. -spreiing spreading the manure. -vogn dung-waggon.

mølje jumble, mix; litter; (rett mat) flap of bread with liver-fat or lard.

møll moth; det er gått — i frakken the moths have been at the coat.

møll|e mill; det er vann på -a hans that draws water to his mill; den som kommer først til -a, får først malt first come, first served. Se ogs. kvern.

møllebruk (flour-, flouring, grain, grinding, grist) mills.

mølle|bygger mill-wright. -dam mill-pond. -demning mill-dam. -hjul mill-wheel.

møller miller.

møllestein mill stone.

møllett moth-eaten.

mølle|verk mill-work. -vinge wing of a mill.

møne comb el. ridge of a roof.

mønje red-lead, minium.

mønsås ridge-piece, ridge-tree, roof-tree.

mønster model, pattern, paragon; (til en kjole osv., i tøy) pattern; (gram) paradigm; etter — to pattern; være et — for en set one a pattern; ta en til — take pattern from.

mønster|bok pattern-book. -bruk model farm.

mønstergyldig model, worthy of being taken for a model.

mønster|skole model school, normal school. -verdig exemplary. -verdighet exemplariness. -verk classical work.

mønstre muster, review, inspect; (fig) eye (over), scan; examine critically, review.

mønstret figured; — tøy fancy-cloth.

mønstring mustering, review, survey; (opprop) roll-call. (mar.) muster. mønstrings|kontor (mar.) local marine board. -liste (mar.) muster-roll, crew's list.

mør mouldering, crumbling; (om kjøtt og annet spiselig) tender. -banke drub soundly. -banking sound drubbing.

mørbrad (tender-) loin; (av okse) sirloin; (den egentlige) underside.

mørje (ild-) live embers.

mørk dark, gloomy; før det ble -t before dark.

mørke dark, darkness, gloom, obscurity; i — in the dark; i nattens — in the dead of night. mørke|blå dark blue. -brun dark brown.

mørkekammer dark room.

mørke|rød deep-red. -tid season of obscuration.

mørk|hudet dark-hued, dark-complexioned. -håret dark-haired. -laden of a dusky hue.

mørkne darken.

mørkning night-fall; (evening) twilight; i -en after dark, at nightfall.

mørkredd afraid in the dark.

mørser mortar.

mørtel mortar.

møte (vrb) meet, meet with, fall in with, encounter; (motstå) face, front, confront;

(innfinne seg) appear, attend, make one's appearance; — opp muster; — opp med put forward.

møte (subst) meeting, rendez-vous, encounter; (parlaments-, retts- osv.) sitting; holde — sit; gi — i retten appear in court; gå en i — go to meet one; gå faren, døden rolig i — meet el. face danger, death with composure.

møtes meet; — med en meet one.

møtested place of meeting, place of appointment, rendezvous; (under jakt) meet.

møtetid time of meeting.

møtrik nut.

møy maid, maiden, virgin.

møydom maidenhood, virginity.

møye pains, trouble.

møysommelig troublesome, laborious.

møysommelighet troublesomeness, laboriousness.

må, se måtte.

måfå: på — at haphazard.

måg, se svigersønn.

måke (subst.) gull, mew.

måke (vrb) clear away, shovel; — vei clear a road.

I. mål (språk) tongue, language, idiom; (mæle) voice, speech.

II. mål measure; (omfang) dimension; (hensikt) goal, end, object; (i fotball) goal; (i leik, fristed) home, house; (å skyte på) butt, mark; (ved veddeløp) winning-post; ta — av en til klær take one's measure; measure one for garments; holde — be up to the standard; i fullt — amply, in ample measure; skyte til -s fire el. shoot at mark el. target; føre til -et answer the purpose; han nådde sitt — he gained his end el. point, attained his end el. object.

målbevisst purposeful. målbevissthet earnestness of purpose.

målbinde nonplus, silence.

måle measure; (innhold av fat osv.) gauge; — om igjen, etter re-measure; — opp (land) survey; — seg med en compete with one; han kan — seg med ham he is equal to him, a match for him; kan ikke — seg med cannot be compared with.

måle|brev (mar) bill of measurement; bill of a ship's tonnage. -bånd tape-measure. -enhet unit el. standard of measurement. -kjede measuring chain, landchain.

målemne (hist.) matter in question, object, business; bære fram sitt — state one's business måler meter, measurer; (insekt) looper, geometer.

målestokk standard, rule; (ved landkart, tegninger osv.) scale; (fig) i stor, liten — on a large, small scale; i forminsket, forstørret — on a reduced, enlarged scale.

målforhold (pl.) proportions.

målføre dialect, idiom.

måling measuring, measurement.

mållag association of adherents of the New Norwegian linguistic movement.

mållinje (i fotball) goal line.

målløs speechless.

I. mål|mann (i fotball) goal-keeper.

II. mål|mann adherent of the New Norwegian linguistic movement. -sak language cause; se målstrev.

mål|skyting target-practice. -spark goal-kick. -stang (i fotball) goalpost.

mål|strev struggle for a language; struggle for the New Norwegian linguistic movement. -strever struggler for a language; se ogs. målmann II. -strid conflict about a language; conflict between adherents and non-adherents of New Norwegian.

måltid meal.

måltrost song-thrush, (poet.) mavis.

målvokter (i fotball) goal-keeper.

måne moon; (på hodet) bald spot. -ns bane the orbit of the moon; -n er i avtagende the moon is in her wane; den tiltagende og avtagende — the waxing and the waning moon; belyst av -n moonlit.

måned month; om en — in a m.; i denne — this m.; den første i denne — on the first of this m.; en -s tid a month's time; en tre -ers tid etter in about three months; pr. 3 m. d. at three months' date.

månedlig monthly.

måneds|betaling monthly allowance. -blad monthly paper. -dagen deretter that day month. -lov a monthly holiday. -lønn monthly wages. -penger monthly allowance of money. -pike daily servant. -rose monthly el. Damask rose. -skrift monthly (journal, magazine, review). -vis by the month, monthly; i -vis for months.

måne|fase phase of the moon. -formørkelse eclipse of the moon. -kart chart of the moon. -klar moonlight. -krater lunar crater. -kvarter quarter of the moon. -lys (subst) moon-light. -lys (adj), se -klar. -observasjon lunar observation. -omløp lunation. -regnbue lunar rainbow. -skifte change of the moon. -skinn moonlight, moonshine; i -skinn by moonlight. -skinnsaktig moon-shiny. -skinnsnatt moonlight el. moonshiny night. -stråle moon-beam, moon-ray. -syk lunatic, moonstruck. -syke lunacy, moon-madness. -år lunar year.

måpe mope. måping moping.

mår marten. -skinn marten-skin.

måse, se måke.

måskje, se kanskje.

måte manner, way, fashion; (måtehold) moderation; holde — be moderate, keep within compass, observe moderation; i like —, på samme — in like manner; (etter lykkønskning) the same to you, I wish you the same; i minste — in the least, at all, ever so little; med — moderately, with el. in moderation; allting med — there is reason (el. a mean) in all things; det er — med not excessively; over all — excessively, beyond measure; på en viss — in some way, after a fashion; in a certain measure, to some extent; på en eller annen — by some means or other; på ingen — by no means, on no account; det gjør jeg på ingen — I shall do no such thing, I shall do nothing of the kind; på ingen mulig — by no manner of means; not on any consideration; på annen — otherwise.

måte|hold moderation; (i nytelser) temperance. -holden, -holdende moderate, temperate. -holdsforening temperance-society.

måtelig middling, mediocre, indifferent; (adv) indifferently. -het mediocrity.

måtte (tillatelse, nåtid) may; (fortid) might; (nødvendighet, nåtid) must, am obliged; (fortid) must, had to, was obliged; (forbud) må ikke must not; må jeg spørre? may I ask? De må så si! you may wel say that! må jeg spørre ... would you permit me to ask? jeg må nødvendigvis gå I must be off; jeg må svært ofte sende ham til byen I am obliged to send him to town very often; jeg må bemerke I am bound to remark; han måtte gå he was obliged (el. he had) to walk; jeg måtte tro at ... I was led to believe that ...; når det må så være when needs must be; han merket han måtte til he found there was no escape, that he was in for it; jeg må komme meg av gårde I must be off; jeg må hjem I must go home; det må mange penger til much money is needed; han må ut på jordet he must go into the field. må vite of course, you know, don't you know.

N

N, n N, n. br. N. N. Mr. *******, Mr. such a one.
nabo neighbour; **nærmeste — next door** neighbour. **nabo-** neighbouring, next.
nabob nabob.
naboerske (female, fair) neighbour.
nabofolk neighbouring nation; neighbours.
nabohus neighbouring house, next (-door) house.
nabolag (et steds nærmeste omegn) vicinity, neighbourhood.
naborike neighbouring kingdom el. country.
naboskap neighbourhood, neighbourship; **holde godt — med en** live upon terms of good neighbourship with one, be a good neighbour to one.
nabovinkel adjacent angle.
nadir (laveste punkt, motsatt senit) nadir.
nafs snatch.
nafse snatch at, nibble, munch, chew.
nafta naphtha. **-lin** naphthaline.
nag (samvittighetsnag) remorse, compunction; (hat) rancour, spite; **bære — til en** bear malice to one, bear one a grudge, owe one a spite; **få — til en** conceive a grudge against one.
nage gnaw; **-nde bekymring** corroding care, carking care, rankling care.
nagle (subst.) nail; (av tre) pin, treenail; (klink-) rivet.
nagle (vrb) nail; (fig) **-t til stedet** riveted to the spot; **han satt som -t til stolen** he sat as if he were nailed to the chair.
naglefabrikk nailery.
nagle|fare inspect el. overhaul the nails of an implement; (fig) go over (very critically), minutely examine. **-faring** thorough overhaul, narrow examination.
naglefast nailed down, immovable; **-e gjenstander** fixtures.
naglegap: -ene i hans hender the print of the nails in his hands.
naglesmed nail-smith, nailer.
nagling nailing.
naiv artless, childish, naive.
naivitet naiveté, artlessness, naivety.
najade (kjeldenymfe) Naiad.
naken naked, nude, bare; **nakne kjennsgjerninger** hard facts. **-het** nakedness. **-kultur** nudism. **tilhenger av -kulturen** nudist.
nakke back of the head, nape of the neck; **nakke-** cervical, occipital; **ta en i -n** seize one by the neck el. by the collar, collar one; **ta på -n** shoulder; **satte foten på -n av sin konge** set the foot on the neck of his king; **kaste på -n** give one's head a toss, turn up one's nose (av: at); **ta bena på -n** take to one's heels; **være på -n av en** be hard upon one; come down upon one; **har øyne i -n** has eyes at the back of his head.
nakkedrag back-of-the-head blow.
nakkegrop hollow of the neck.
nakkespeil hand-glass.
nam (jur.) distress, seizure.
nankin (sl. tøy) nankeen. **-sbukser** nankeens.
napp snatching, snatch, snap; (av fisk) bite.
nappe snatch; (fange) nab; (rapse, stjele) filch, nap; **— etter** snatch at, snap at.
nappetak bit of a dust, scramble.
nar|hval el. **-kval** narwhale.
narkose narcosis.
narkotisk narcotic; **— middel** narcotic.
narr fool; (f. eks. hoffnarr) buffoon, jester; (narraktig i påkledning og vesen) coxcomb; **holde en for — make** a fool of one, humbug, fool el. hoax one; **gjøre — av en** make game el. a jest of one, deride, mock, ridicule one; **gjøre**

seg til — make a fool of oneself; make oneself a laughing-stock; **en innbilsk — a** conceited fool el. puppy.
narraktig foolish. **-het** foolishness.
narre dupe, trick, hoax, fool; **— en for** disappoint one of; **— noe fra en** trick el. cajole one out of a thing; **— noe på en** humbug one into taking something; palm st. off upon one; **— en til å gjøre noe** lure one into doing something; **— en til å tro** make one believe; cheat one into the belief that.
narre|bjelle fool's bell. **-fakter** foolish antics. **-ferd** foolish behaviour, fool's errand. **-hette** fool's cap. **-kappe** fool's cloak.
narrer foolery, nonsense.
narre|stav fool's bauble, stick of bells. **-strek** foolish trick, foolery, nonsense. **-verk** folly.
narrifas coxcomb.
narsiss (plante) narcissus, daffodil.
narv (hårsiden av lær) grain. **narve** grain.
nasal nasal. **nasalere** nasalize.
nasjon nation.
nasjonal national.
nasjonal|bank bank of the state. **-drakt** national costume el. dress. **-eiendom** national property. **-eiendommelighet** nationalism. **-farger** national colours. **-formue** public wealth.
nasjonalisere nationalize.
nasjonalisering nationalization.
nasjonalisme nationalism.
nasjonalist nationalist.
nasjonalistisk nationalistic.
nasjonalitet nationality.
nasjonal|råd: kvinnenes — National Council of Women. **-sak,** se **landssak. -sang** national song. **-sangen** the national anthem. **-økonom, -økonomi,** se **statsøkonom.**
Nasjonenes Forbund the League of Nations; **-sråd** the council of the League of Nations.
naske filch, pilfer. **-ri** filching etc.
nativitet nativity; **stille ens — cast** one's nativity.
natrium sodium.
natron soda; **dobbeltkullsurt — bicarbonate** of soda, sodic hydric carbonate.
natt night; **hele -a** all night; **holde ut hele -a** make a night of it; **ønske en god — wish** one a good night, bid one good night; **i — (fore-gående —)** last night; (denne — eller kommende —) to-night; **i går — the** night before yesterday; **i -ens stillhet** at dead of night, in the dead of the night; **hele -a igjennom** all night, throughout the night; **om -a in** the night, at night, by night, in the night-time; **-a mellom den 6. og 7. i denne måned** on the night of the 6th to the 7th of the present month; **sitte oppe om nettene** sit up nights; **-a over** all night; **bli -a over i** pass the night in; **langt ut på -a late** in the night; **gjøre — til dag** turn night into day.
natt|arbeid night-work. **-bord** bedroom table, table. **-drakt** night-dress.
natte|dogg night-dew. **-frieri** bundling. **-frost** night-frost.
nattegjest night-guest.
natte|hvile night's rest, night-rest. **-kommers** revelry at night, nocturnal revel. **-kulde** night-cold. **-kvarter** night-quarters. **-leie** bed (for the night). **-leir** night-camp el. encampment. **-leite** by night. **-losji** night-lodging, accommodation for the night. **-luft** night air. **-ly** shelter for the night, a night's shelter. **-løperi,** se **-frieri. -rangel** night revel. **-rangler** night reveller. **-regn** rain in the night. **-reise** night-journey, travelling in the night.

nattergal nightingale.

nattero night's rest, night-rest.

natte-søvn night's sleep, sleep at night. **–tid** night-time; **ved –tid** at night. **–time** nocturnal hour; hour of the night. **–vakt** night-watch; night service. **–vandrer** night-farer, night-traveller. **–vandring** night-wandering. **–vind** night-wind, night-breeze. **–våk(ing)** night-watching, late hours.

natt|fiol night-smelling rocket. **–hus** (mar) binnacle **–kafé** night-house. **–kappe** night-cap. **–kikkert** night-glass. **–kjole** night-gown. **–klokke** night-bell. **–lampe** night-lamp.

nattlig nightly, nocturnal.

natt|lys night-candle, rushlight; (bot) evening primrose. **–potte** chamber-pot. **–ramn**, se **kveldknarr**.

natt|side dark side. **–signal** night-signal. **–skjorte** night-shirt. **–stol** close-stool. **–svermer** (sommerfugl) night-butterfly. **–syn** night-sight. **–tjeneste** night service. **–tog** (på jernbanen) night-train. **–trøye** night-jacket. **–tøy** night-dress; (pyjamas) night suit. **–vekter** (night) watchman. **–verd** supper; **den hellige** — the Lord's supper. **–verdbord** communion table. **–verdbrød** (oblat) communion bread, consecrated wafer. **–gjest** communicant.

natur nature; (om mennesker) nature, constitution; (sinn) temper, disposition. **–en** nature; **den vakre** — the beautiful scenery; **av** — **by** n., naturally; **heftig** — vehement el. impetuous disposition; violent temper; **–en går over opptukelsen** nature passes nurture; **–ens gang** the course of nature; **–ens orden** the nature el. natural order of things; **etter –ens orden** in the order of nature; **det ligger i sakens** — it is natural, a matter of course; **ifølge sin** — of its very nature; **det lå ikke for hans** — it was not in his nature; **tegne, male etter –en** draw, paint from life el. nature.

natura: betale in — pay in kind.

naturalier natural objects el. products; natural curiosities.

naturalisere naturalize.

naturalisering naturalizing, naturalization.

naturalisme naturalism.

naturalistisk naturalistic.

natur|anlegg natural talent el. turn. **–barn** child of nature. **–begivenhet** phenomenon, natural event. **–drift** natural instinct, natural impulse. **natur|fag** natural science subject. **–feil** natural defect. **–filosof** naturalist. **–forhold** nature. **–forsker** naturalist. **–forskning** study of nature.

naturfredning protection of natural beauty (el. scenery).

natur|frembringelse production of nature, natural product. **–gave** natural endowment el. gift. **–historie** natural history, nature study. **–historiker** naturalist. **–historisk** belonging to natural history, of natural history. **–kraft** power of nature el. of elements. **–kunnskap** knowledge of nature; k. of natural objects.

naturlig natural; (ikke affektert) artless; (uvilkårlig) spontaneous; (medfødt) constitutional, native; **en** — **sønn** a natural son, a bastard; — **ynde** native grace; **en** — **død** a natural death; — **vesen,** — **stil** natural, unaffected manners, style (of writing); **det faller ikke** — **for meg** it does not come natural to me. **naturlig** (adv) naturally; **det går ikke** — **til** there is something supernatural in this; **det går ganske** — **til** there is nothing extraordinary in it; **i mere enn** — **størrelse** larger than life, above its natural size.

naturlighet naturalness.

naturligvis of course, naturally.

natur|lege natural healer. **–lov** law of nature. **i overensstemmelse med –ene** conformable to the laws of nature. **–lyd** natural sound. **–lære** physics. **–menneske** child of nature. **–merkverdighet** natural phenomenon el. curiosity. **–nød-**

vendighet physical necessity. **–opfattelse** view of nature. **–sans** feeling for nature. **–skjønnhet** beauty of scenery. **–smør** natural butter. **–spill** freak el. sport of nature. **–språk** natural language. **–stridig** contrary to nature. **–tilstand** natural state. **–trekk** natural trait. **–tro** true to nature el. life, natural. **–troskap** naturalness, fidelity to nature. **–vitenskap** science of nature, physics. **–vitenskapelig** physical.

natyrell nature, natural disposition.

nau, se **nød.**

naue: det –r ikke there is no harm in it, it is no matter.

naust boat-house, boat-shed.

naut neat, neat cattle; (fig) ass, fool.

nautet foolish.

nautikk nautical science.

nautil nautilus.

nautisk nautic(al).

nav (hjulnav) nave, hob, hub; (dmp.) boss.

navar auger.

navigasjon navigation.

navigasjons|bok book of navigation. **–skole** nautical academy, navigation school. **–tabeller** navigation tables.

navigatør navigator.

navigere navigate.

navle navel. **–bind** umbilical bandage. **–brokk** umbilical hernia, omphalocele. **–formig** navel-shaped, umbilicate. **–streng** navel string, umbilical cord.

navling cutting of the navel-string at birth.

navn name; (benevnelse) appellation; **hva er Deres** —? what is your name? **hva er barnets** — name this child; **godt** — **og rykte** good repute el. reputation; **vinne et** — make one's mark, win a reputation; **kjenne en av** — know one by name; **har fått sitt** — **av** derives its name from; **fortjener** — **av** deserves the name of; **i Guds** — in God's name; **kjært barn har mange** — a pet child has many names; **pengene står på hans** — the money is banked under his name; **under** — **av** under the name of; **går under** — **av** goes by the name of, is known as; **sette sitt** — **under** put one's name to; **en mann ved** — **N.**, a person by the name of N.; **kalle en ting ved sitt rette** — call a spade a spade.

navne (subst) namesake.

navne (vrb) mark.

navne|blekk marking-ink. **–brett** name board. **–bytte** interchange of names. **–dag** name-day, day el. anniversary of one's name, Saint's day. **–duk** sampler. **–fetter** name-sake. **–forandring** change of name. **–liste** list of names, nominal list, name-roll, nomenclature, poll. **–opprop** call, calling over; (opprop av soldatenes navn) rollcall. **–plate** name-plate. **–siffer** cipher. **–skilt** signboard. **–trekk** monogram, cipher.

navn|gi name, mention by name. **–gjeten, –kundig** celebrated, renowned, famous. **–kundighet** renown, celebrity, fame.

navnlig particularly, specially, notably.

navnløs nameless. **navnløshet** namelessness.

navnord noun.

ne wane (of the moon).

Neap|el Naples. **n–olitaner, n–olitanerinne, n–olitansk** Neapolitan.

nebb beak, bill; dt. **henge med –et** be down in the mouth; hang one's ears; **være blek om –et** (bleknebbet) be pale in the face, look ill; **med** — **og klør** tooth and nail.

nebbdyr ornithorhynchus, duckbill, water-mole.

nebbe (small) jug.

nebbes bill.

nebbet beaked; (fig) cheeky, pert, saucy.

nebbetang (a pair of) pliers, tweezers.

ned down; — **med . . .** down with . . .; (mar) — **med roret** helm's-a-lee!

nedad, se **nedover. –gående** downhill. **–vendt** turned downwards.

nedarv|es be transmitted. **-et** inherited, handed down, transmitted.

nedbe invoke, pray for.

nedblåst blown down, windfallen; — **frukt** windfall.

nedbrent burnt down, burnt to the ground.

ned|brett turned-down edge el. brim. **-brettet snipp** turn-down collar.

ned|bryte break down, demolish. **-brutt på sjel og legeme** broken in body and mind.

nedbryting breaking down, demolition.

nedbøyd: — **av sorg** weighed down by sorrow, downcast, dejected.

nedbør downpour, (rain-)fall.

neddysse hush (up), quell, stifle.

nede down; **der** — down there.

neden|for (prep og adv) below; (i et skrift) hereafter; (nederst på siden) at foot; — **anført** undermentioned, undernoted; **som** — **anført** as under, **-fra** from below, from beneath. **-om** round the foot el. base, round below; (spøkende) **gå -om og hjem** go to the bottom.

nedenstående at foot, below, undernamed; — **underskrift** the signature at foot; — **referanser** the references mentioned at foot.

nedentil below, in the lower parts, inferiorly.

nedenunder beneath, underneath; (i huset) downstairs, down below.

nederdrektig vile, base, mean.

nederdrektighet vileness, baseness, meanness.

nederlag defeat, overthrow; carnage, slaughter; (bare fig) discomfiture; **lide** — be defeated; **tilføye** — inflict a defeat upon, defeat.

Neder|land Holland. **n-landsk** Dutch, Flemish. **-lender** Netherlander, Dutchman.

nederside lower side.

nederst lowest, nethermost; **sitte** — **ved bordet** sit at the bottom of the table.

nedertysk Low German.

nedetter downwards.

nedfall downfall.

nedfart descent.

nedfor down; (om helbred) low; (nedbøyd) broken-hearted.

nedgang going down; (nedstigning) descent; (til et sted) passage down (to a place); (fig) falling off; (om sola) setting; **ved sol-** at sunset; — **i verdi** depreciation.

nedgravning burying.

nedgående descending, going down; (om sola) setting.

nedhengende hanging (down).

ned|ising glaciation. **-ist** glaciated.

nedkalle call down.

nedkjørsel carting el. driving down; (stedet) carriage road down.

nedkomme (om barselkvinner) be delivered (med: of), give birth to.

nedkomst delivery.

nedlate seg til condescend, stoop (to). **-nde** condescending; **behandle -nde** patronize.

nedlatenhet condescension.

nedlegge (penger osv.) deposit; sink; (fig) (om innsigelser osv.) lodge, place, enter; (om bestilling, embete) give up, resign, lay down, throw up, vacate; (kronen) abdicate; (en forretning) give up; (drepe) slay; (om universitet, skole osv.) abolish, discontinue; (nedsylte) preserve, pickle; (instinkt) implant; — **arbeidet** strike work; **hermetisk nedlagt** tinned, canned.

nedleggelse laying down etc., deposition; abdication; abolition.

nedlegning (av agurker osv.) pickling; tinning.

nedover (adv) downwards, down; (prep) down. **seile** — **en elv** drop down a river. — **bakke(n)** down-hill, down the hill. **gå** — **trappa** go downstairs.

nedpå down.

nedrakke run down, abuse.

nedrakning running down, abuse.

nedre lower; — **Donau** the Lower Danube; — **Egypt** Lower Egypt.

nedrig base, mean, vile, abject.

nedrighet baseness, meanness.

ned|ringe cut low (the body of a dress). **-ringet** low(-necked), low-bosomed (dress).

nedrivning pulling down etc.; **kjøpt til** — bought to pull down.

nedrustning reduction of warlike establishment.

nedsab|le sabre, cut down, put to the sword, massacre. **-ling** sabring etc.

nedsalt(n)ing salting, curing, pickling.

nedsenk(n)ing sinking, lowering, immersion, submersion.

nedsette set down, put down; (priser, skatter osv.) abate, reduce, lower; (i verdi) depreciate; (i omdømme) disparage; (svekke) impair; — **en kommisjon** appoint a commission; — **ens fortjenester** depreciate one's merits, detract el. derogate from one's merits; — **en** (i folks aktelse) disparage one; — **seg** settle, establish oneself; **til nedsatte priser** at reduced prices el. fares.

nedsettelse setting down etc., abating etc., abatement, diminution; reduction; appointment depreciation, disparagement; settlement; establishment.

nedsettende disparaging, depreciatory.

nedskrive pen, put down (in writing), commit to writing; (redusere) reduce, write down; **mens dette -s** at the time of this writing.

nedskrivning committal to paper el. writing; (av kapital) reduction, writing down.

nedslag (nedgående slag) down-stroke; (om lyn) stroke; (fugls.) pounce, swoop; (kjemi) precipitate.

nedslagen: med nedslagne øyne with his (or her) eyes cast down.

nedslagsdistrikt fluvial basin.

nedslakte, se **slakte.**

nedslakting killing, butchering, butchery.

nedslå (motet) damp, chill; (håpet) destroy.

nedslående disheartening, discouraging.

nedslått dejected, desponding, downcast.

nedslåtthet dejection, low spirits.

nedsnødd snowed up, snow-smothered.

nedst, se **nederst.**

nedstamme descend, be descended; (fig) be derived (f. eks. fra latin — from Latin).

nedstamning descent.

nedstemme (fig) (begeistring osv.) abate, moderate, tone down; — **sine fordringer** lower one's pretensions.

nedstemt dejected, cast down.

nedstemthet low spirits, dejection.

nedstigende: — **linje** the descending line.

nedstigning descending, descent.

nedstyrtning rush, precipitation.

nedsunket: — **i fattigdom** sunk into poverty; — **i grublerier** deep in meditation.

nedtagelse: Kristi — **av korset** the deposition of Christ.

nedtegne, se **nedskrive.**

nedtrykt depressed. **nedtrykthet** depression.

nedtrådt trampled, trodden down. **-e sko** shoes (trod) down at (the) heel(s), slipshoes.

nedtur down passage el. trip.

nedverdige degrade, disgrace, debase, demean, abase. **-lse** degradation, debasement.

nefritt nephrite, jade.

negasjon negation.

negativ (adj) negative.

negativ (subst) negative.

negativbilde negative.

negativisme negativism.

negativist negativist, negationist.

neger negro; (ringeakt.) nigger. **-befolkning** negro-population.

neger|handel negro slave-trade. **-kvinne** negress, negro-woman. **N-kysten** the Slave Coast.

-marked slave-market. **-pike** negro-girl. **-slave** negro-slave.

negerslaveri negro-slavery; **motstander av -et** abolitionist.

negl nail; **bite -er** bite one's nails; **så mye som det kunne ligge på en** — as much as would fill a filbert.

negle|børste nail-brush. **-merke** nail-mark.

neglerot (neglens bakerste del) root of finger-nail; (løsrevet stykke av huden om neglerota) agnail, hangnail.

neglesaks nail-scissors.

neglisjé undress.

neglisjere neglect.

nei no; (som svar til herre) no, sir! (som svar til dame) no, madam! —, **slett ikke!** no, not at all, by no means; —, **sannelig ikke!** no, certainly not! **jeg mener** — I think not; —, **bare se!** only see! do but look! —, **nå har jeg aldri hørt maken** well, I never heard the like of it; **gi en et** — give one a refusal; **få — av en pike** (som frier) be rejected el. refused, (sl) get the sack; **mitt — er så godt som ditt ja** my nay is just as good as your aye.

neie courtesy, make el. drop a courtesy. **neiing** courtesying.

neimen (adv) indeed no; — **om jeg gjør** blest if I do!

nek sheaf; **binde** — bind el. make sheaves, sheaf.

nekrolog (minneord) obituary, necrology. **-forfatter** obituarist, necrologist. **nekrologi** necrology. **nekrologisk** necrologic.

nekromant (åndebesverger) necromancer. **nekromanti** (åndebesvergelse) necromancy.

nektar nectar.

nekte deny; (en noe) refuse; **jeg -r ikke I** own; — **seg hjemme** deny oneself **(for:** to). **nektelse** denial; negative; (gram) negative. **nektende** negative; **gi et** — **svar** answer in the negative.

nellik gilliflower; (alm. slektsnavn) pink; (kjøttfarget) carnation (-pink), clove-gilliflower; (krydder-) clove. **-olje** oil of cloves.

Nemesis Nemesis.

nemlig (foran oppregning eller ‹at›) namely; (i forretningsstil) viz, (som leses: namely eller to wit); (mindre betonet) because, for, the fact is that.

nemme (vrb) apprehend, learn.

nemme (subst) apprehension.

nemnd committee; (domsnemnd) jury.

nennsom lenient, indulgent.

nennsomhet lenity, indulgence.

nepe turnip. **-formig** napiform. **-gras** tops of turnips. **-stappe** mashed turnips.

nepotisk nepotic. **nepotisme** nepotism.

neppe hardly, scarcely, scarce; — **nok** barely; — ... **førenn** no sooner ... than, as soon as ever, hardly ... when.

Neptun Neptune.

nereide (havnymfe) Nereid.

nerium nerium.

nerts mink.

nerve nerve; **hun går meg på -ne** (gjør meg nervøs) she gets on my nerves; **han vet ikke hva -r er** he does not know what nerves are; **-r av stål** nerves of steal; **anspenne alle -r** strain every nerve.

nerve|anfall nervous attack. **-feber** nervous fever. **-fiber** nervous fibre. **-gikt** atonic gout. **-knute** ganglion. **-lidelse** nerve pains. **-lære** neurology. **-onde** nervous complaint. **-pirrende** stimulating the nerves. **-pirring** stimulation of the nerves. **-rystelse** nervous shock. **-rystende** nerve-shaking. **-sentrum** nervous centre. **-slag** nervous apoplexy. **-smerter** neuralgia. **-styrkende** nervine, tonic, neurotic, bracing. **-svakhet, -svekkelse** nervousness, nervous debility. **-sykdom** nervous complaint. **-system** nervous system. **-tråd** nervous fibre.

nervøs nervous; (dt) fidgety; (pirrelig) excitable.

nervøsitet nervousness.

nes point, headland.

nese nose; **pusse -n** blow one's nose; **rynke på -n** turn up one's nose; **sette -n høyt** give oneself airs, carry it high; **ilke for -n på en** under one's (very) nose; **slå døra igjen for -n på en** slam the door in one's face; **kaste en noe i -n** cast el. throw st. in one's teeth; **ligge med -n i været** be dead and gone; **få lang** — be disappointed, have one's trouble for one's pains; **peke** — cock a snook; **stikke -n sin i alt mulig** poke one's nose into every corner; **holde -n sin vekk fra** keep one's nose out of; **holde på å miste både** — **og munn** look blank; **det kan du bite deg i -n etter** you may whistle for it; **ta en ved -n** take one in.

nese|bein nasal bone. **-blod** bleeding at the nose. **-bor** nostril. **-brusk** cartilage of the nose. **nesegrus** flat on the face, prostrate. **nese|klemme** double eyeglass, barnacle. **-lyd** nasal sound. **-løs** noseless. **-rot** root of the nose. **-rygg** bridge of the nose. **-sjø** head-sea. **-styver** rap over the nose. **-tipp** tip el. point of the nose.

nesevis pert, saucy, impertinent; **hr.** — Mr. Impudence; **frøken** — Madam Pert; Miss. **-het** sauciness, pertness, impertinence; cheek.

neshorn rhinoceros.

nesle nettle.

neslefeber nettlerash.

nest (subst) tack, (temporary) stitch.

nest (adj og adv) next; (prep) next to; **-e dag** (the) next day; **den 4de i -e måned** on the 4th proximo; — **etter** immediately after.

nest best second best, next best.

neste (subst) neighbour; **du skal elske din** — thou shalt love thy neighbour; **-n** our neighbour.

neste (vrb) baste, tack.

nest eldst oldest but one; — **-e sønn, datter** second son, daughter; — **-e officer** next senior officer.

nesten (adv) almost, nearly, all but, well nigh; — **ikke** hardly; scarcely; — **aldri** scarcely el. hardly ever; — **ingen** scarcely any; — **umulig** hardly (el. scarcely) possible. **jeg hadde** — **glemt** I had almost forgotten; **jeg hadde** — **falt** I had nearly fallen.

nest|formann vice-president. **-følgende** the following; the next but one. **-kommanderende** second in command; (på et skip) first-lieutenant, second officer.

nest nederste the second from the bottom.

nest sist last but one.

nestsøskenbarn second cousin.

nest yngst youngest but one.

nest øverste the second from the top.

nett (pen) neat, nice; **du er en** — **en** you are a nice el. precious fellow, you are.

nett (subst) net; (mar) netting; (fig) (nerve-, åre- o. l.) plexus; (tarm-) caul, amentum.

nettformig reticular.

netthendt deftfingered, handy, neat-handed.

netthet neatness.

netthinne (i øyet) retina.

netting netting, netted wire.

nettmelon netted melon.

netto net, neat; **innbringe** — net. **-beløp** net amount. **-fortjeneste** net profit, margin (of profit). **-inntekt** net revenue.

nettopp just; — **denne** this particular; — **denne natta** this night of all others; — **her!** here, of all places (in the world).

nettopris net price, real price, short price.

netto|saldo net balance. **-utbytte** net proceeds. **-vekt** net weight.

nettverk net-work; (av nerver, årer) plexus.

neve fist; **knytte -n** clench one's fist; **det passer som en knyttet** — **til et blått øye** it's

neither here nor there; **en — penger** a fistful of money.
neve|drag blow with one's fist. **–hilse** shake hands with; **–kamp** boxing match, fist-fight.
nevenyttig handy. **nevenyttighet** handiness.
never birch-bark.
neverett club-law.
never|kont tall bark bag el. basket. **–skrukke** bark bag el. scrip. **–tak** bark roof. **–tekt** bark -thatched.
neve|slag, se **–drag. –tak** grip el. hold of one's fist. **–tas** shake hands.
nevnd, se **nemnd.**
nevne name; (omtale) mention; (særskilt) articularise.
nevneform nominative. **nevnelse: med navns — mentioning the name el. names.
nevner denominator.
nevneverdig worth mentioning.
nevralgi neuralgia. **nevralgisk** neuralgic.
nevø nephew.
New Zealand New Zealand.
ni nine; (i kilespill) **alle — all nine.
ni–: niarbeide work hard, slave, toil.
nid envy, spite, malice.
niding villain. **nidingsverk** piece of villainy; cowardly deed.
nidkjær (meget ivrig) zealous; **jeg Herren din Gud er en — Gud** I the Lord thy God am a zealous God.
nidkjærhet zeal.
nidobbelt nine-fold.
nidsk envious; (gjerrig) niggard, sordid. **–het** envy, niggardliness.
nidvise verse lampoon, libellous ditty el. song.
niende ninth; **for det — in the ninth place, ninthly; — (og tiende) bud** tenth commandment.
niendedel ninth.
nier nine.
niese niece.
nifold(ig) nine-fold.
nifs (adj) creepy.
niglane stare hard and long, stare intently.
nihale|t: den –de katt the cat o'nine tails.
nihil|isme nihilism. **–ist** nihilist. **–istisk** nihilistic.
nikant enneagon. **–et** enneagonal.
nikk nod, beck.
nikke nod.
nikkedokke (kinesisk ledd-dokke) nodding Chinese mandarin.
nikkel nickel.
nikkers plus-fours.
Nikolai, Nikolaus Nicolas.
nikotin nicotine. **–forgiftning** nicotine poisoning.
Nilen the (river) Nile.
Nil|dalen the valley of the Nile. **–deltaet** the delta of the Nile. **–landene** the Nile countries.
Nils Neil.
nimbus nimbus, halo, glory.
nipp (liten slurk) sip; **på –pet** on the point of.
nippe (ta små slurker) sip; **— til vinen** sip the wine.
nippedrikk sipping. **nippedrikker** sipper.
nippflo neap tide.
nipssaker trinkets, knick-knacks.
nise porpoise, snuffer.
nisidet enneahedral.
nisje niche.
niss (barnespr) water made, wet. **nisse** piddle, make water.
nisse hobgoblin, puck, Robin good boy.
nistavelse= enneasyllabic, of nine syllables.
niste (subst) travelling provisions. **niste ut** (vrb) provision, victual. **–bomme** provision box. **–skreppe** provision bag el. wallet.
nistirre, se **niglane.**
nitall (figure of) nine.
nite (i lotteri) blank.
nitid neat, tidy.

nitrat nitrate.
nitroglyserin nitro-glycerine.
nitte (klinke jernplater) clinch, rivet.
nitten nineteen. **–de** nineteenth. **–dedel** nineteenth part. **–årig** nineteen years old.
nitti ninety. **–ende** ninetieth. **–årig** nonagenarian. **–åring** nonagenarian.
nivellere level. **nivellering** levelling.
nivellerinstrument levelling instrument.
nivå level; **være på — med** be on a level with.
Nizza Nice.
niårig nine years old.
Noas ark Noah's ark.
nobel noble.
Nobel–pris Nobel Prize. **n–tager** recipient of the Nobel Prize.
noblesse (om stand, vesen) nobility.
nocturne, se **nokturne.**
noe (adj: litt) some; (adj: noe som helst) any; (subst: et eller annet) something; (subst: noe som helst) anything; (adv: i noen grad) somewhat, a little; **jeg har — øl** I have some beer; **jeg har, — av det her** I have some of it here; **jeg har ikke — øl** I have not any beer; **— usedvanlig var hendt** something unusual had happened; **kan jeg gjøre — for Dem?** can I do anything for you? **— døv** somewhat deaf; **ikke — not** anything, nothing; **hva for —?** what? **hva er det for —?** what is that? **De sier —! a good idea! det er — for meg** that is just the thing for me; **slikt — som** something like; **eller slikt — or** the like; **det blir nok — av ham** he will do well enough, he will get on; **— nær** all but, almost.
noen (adj: en viss mengde) some; (adj; noen som helst) any; (subst om person: en eller annen) somebody; (subst om person: noen som helst) anybody; **de ytte oss — hjelp** they gave us some help; **de kunne ikke yte oss — hjelp** they could not give us any help; **han har penger, har du —?** he has money, have you any? **— må ha sagt noe** somebody must have said something; **er det ikke — som vil hjelpe meg?** isn't there anybody who will help me? **— gang** at any time, ever; **— som helst** (adj) any; (subst) anybody, any one.
noen (pl) (adj) some; (subst) some; **— bøker** some books; **ønsker De bøker?** her er **— do** you want books? here are some; **— tror** some people think; **— og tjue** twenty odd.
noenlunde tolerably, fairly, passably.
noensinne ever.
noensteds anywhere; **— fra** from anywhere.
noenting (noe) something; anything.
noe som helst (adj) any; (subst) anything.
I. nok (adj) enough, sufficient, plenty; **en er — one** will do; **vi har — og mer enn — we have got enough and to spare; **han får aldri — he** is never satisfied; **det vil være — med noen ganske få** a very few will answer; **seg selv — self-contained, self-centred; **— sagt** enough; **av det** suffice it to say; **ikke — med det** that is not all; **la det så være — enough of that; **det er — av dem som** there are not wanting those who; **nei, nå har jeg — av det** well, that beats all; **ha — å leve av** have sufficient to live upon; **han hadde — å gjøre med å** he had as much as he could do to ...; **det er — that** will do.
II. nok (adv) enough, sufficiently; **stor — large** enough; **dum — til å fool** enough to; **du forstår meg — I** am sure you understand me; **du kan — le av det** you may well laugh (at that); **det kan du — si** you may well say that; **jeg gad — vite** I should (very much) like to know; **han kommer — he** is sure to come, he will come sure enough; **du kan — tenke** you may easily imagine; **det tror jeg — I** rather think so, I dare say; **jeg tenkte meg — det** I thought as much.
nokk (rånokk) yard-arm.
noksagt: han er en — a something else.

noksom (tilstrekkelig) enough, sufficiently. **nokså** fairly; — **søt** fairly nice.

nokturne nocturne, notturno.

nomade nomad, nomade. **-folk** nomadic people, nomadic tribe. **-liv** nomadism.

nominativ nominative; **i** — in the n. (case). **nominell** nominal. **nominere** nominate.

non (tidspunkt) the hour of the afternoon meal. **non** (eksamenskarakter): **få** — take a fourth class.

nonchalanse carelessness, nonchalance.

nonchalant careless, nonchalant.

nonne nun.

nonne|drakt habit el. garb of a nun. **-kloster** nunnery. **-liv** life of a nun. **-løfte** conventual vow.

nonsbel the hour of 3 or 4 p. m. Se **non**. **nonsens** nonsense.

I. **nor** (lite barn) baby.

II. **nor** (vik) frith (with a narrow inlet).

nord north; **rett** — due north. **N. t. V. N.** by W., **N. t. Ø. N.** by E., **N. N. V. N. N. W.** osv.; — **for** north of; **i** — (in the) north; **fra** — from the north; **mot** — (to the) north, northward.

norda|fjells north of the Dovre. **-for**, se **nordenfor**.

Nord-Afrika North Africa.

Nord-Amerika North America; **-s Forente Stater** the United States of North America.

nordamerikansk North American.

norda|storm northerly gale. **-vind** north wind, norther.

nord|bagge (glt.) Norwegian pony; (fig, ringeaktende) Norwegian. **-bu** Northman, Hyperborean. **-etter** northward.

Norden the North; the Scandinavian North, Scandinavia.

norden|for (to the) north of; (adv) in the north. **-fra** from the north(ward). **-om** (to the) northward of.

nordfjording horse of the Nordfjord-breed.

nordgrense northern limit.

nordgående (strøm) northerly; (skip) going north, northward bound; **for** — on her way north.

Nordhavet the Northern Sea.

nordisk northern, Scandinavian.

nord|kant north side, northern parts. **N-kapp** (the) North cape. **-kyst** northern coast el. shore. **N-land** northern country; Norland (in Norway). **-lending** native of Norland.

nordlig northern; (retning) northerly; to the north; — **bredde** north latitude; **den -e polarsirkel** the Arctic Polar circle; **nordligst** northernmost.

nord|lys northern lights, aurora borealis. **-mann** Norwegian. **-ost** northeast. **-ostlig** north-easterly; to the north-east. **-ostvind** northeast wind. **-over** (to the) northward.

nordpol north el. arctic pole. **-aregnene** the arctic regions. **N-arhavet** the Arctic Ocean.

nordpols|ekspedisjon arctic expedition, expedition to the north pole. **-farer** arctic navigator.

nordpunktet the north.

nordpå in the North; (retning) northward.

nordre northern.

nord|side north side. **-spiss** north point. **N-statene** the Northern States. **-stjerne** north star, polar star. **N-sjøen** the North Sea. **-tysk** North German. **N-Tyskland** Northern Germany. **-vestlig** northwesterly. **-vestpassasje** north-west passage. **-vestvind** northwestwind, north-wester. **-ostlig** north-eastern.

Norge Norway.

norm norm, rule, standard.

normal normal.

normalarbeidsdag normal working-day.

normalisere normalize, standardize.

normalvekt standard-weight.

Normandiet Normandy.

normanner, normannisk Norman.

normere regulate.

norne norn, norna.

norsk Norwegian; (gammel-) Norse. **et — -engelsk leksikon** a Norwegian and English dictionary.

norsk|het norwegianness. **-sinnet** pro-Norwegian.

norvagisere norwegianize.

norvagisme norwegianism.

I. **not** (fiske-) seine, sweep-net; (skotsk) trawl.

II. **not** (fure) groove.

nota (merk) bill of parcels; **ta seg ad notam** take a note of.

notabel notable. **-forsamling** assembly of notables.

notabene observe, mind (well).

notabilitet distinguished person, notability.

notar notary.

notarius publicus notary public.

notat note.

not|bas master seiner. **-bruk** seine (and seinegang). **-båt** seining barge el. boat.

I. **note** note, annotation; (under teksten) footnote; **diplomatisk** — diplomatic paper el. note, memorandum.

II. **note** (musical) note; **-r** (musikalier) music; **spille etter -r** play by (the) note; **være med på -ene** be in the secret, be in the swim; **skjelle ham ut etter -r** rate him at score.

note|blad sheet of music. **-bok** music-book, singing-book. **-hefte**, se **-bok**. **-lesning** reading of music. **-linje** music-line. **-mappe** music-portfolio. **-papir** music-paper. **-pult** music-desk.

notere note, record; (om priskurant) quote.

notering noting; quotation.

noteringsbok notebook, memorandum-book.

note|skrift notation. **-skriver** copier of music, music-copyist. **-stikker** engraver of music. **-stol** music-desk. **-system** staff.

notifikasjon notification. **notifisere** notify.

notis note, remark; (i blad) paragraph; **ta — av** take notice of. **-bok**, se **noteringsbok**.

notorisk notorious, well-known.

notsteng seine-full.

nov corner (of a log-house).

novelle short story. **-forfatter(inne)** writer of short novels.

novellistisk in the form of a short novel.

november November.

novi|se novice. **-siat** noviciate.

nu (adv), se **nå**.

Nubi|a Nubia. **-er, n-erinne, n-sk** Nubian.

nudd brad, sprigg.

nudel noodle.

nugg friction, rubbing; chafe.

nugge rub, chafe.

null zero, cipher, nonentity; (ingenting) nought; (i spill og sport undertiden) love; **stå på** — be at zero; **er nesten lik** — is almost nil.

nullitet nullity; (person) cipher.

nullpunkt (på termom.) zero; (nivell.) datum.

numérisk numerical.

numismatik|er numismatist. **-k** numismatics.

numismatisk numismatic.

nummer number; (av blad) impression, issue; (av en forestilling) performance; (ved veddekamp) event; (på auksjon) lot, entry; — **1 og 4 Nos.** 1 and 4; **mitt** — **er 7³/₄** (om hansker) my size is seven and three quarters; **et** — **for lite** a size too small; **gjøre et stort** — **av** make the most of.

nummerere number; **nummerert plass** (i teateret) reserved seat.

nummer|ering numeration. **-følge** serial succession, consecutiveness. **-taing** the taking of chances.

nunatak (fjellkam i arktisk egn) nunatak.

nuntius nuncio.
nupp pustule.
nuppe pluck.
nuppereller tattings.
nupret (om tøy) burled.
nurk: dt. **liten** — dapperling, mannikin.
nuss: dt. **lite** — a little chit.
nut mountain top, peak.
nutid, se **nåtid**.
nuværende, se **nåværende**.
ny new; (og usedvanlig) novel; (frisk, av året, annen) fresh; — **i tjenesten** a new hand; **-e koster feier best** new brooms sweep clean; **den -ere historie** modern history; **de -ere språk** the modern languages; **i den -ere tid** in recent times; **-este etterretninger** late el. recent accounts; **fra -tt av** anew; **på -tt** anew, afresh;
ny (månefase) change (of the moon), new moon; **i — og ne** rarely, at long intervals.
nyankommen new arrival, newcomer, lately arrived.
nyanse shade. **nyansere** shade off, vary.
nybakt newly baked; (fig) new-fangled; (om person) new-fledged, upstart.
nybegynner novice, young el. green hand.
nybrent recently burnt; — **kaffe** freshly roasted coffee.
nybrott clearing, new-broken ground; **nybrottsmann** backwoodsman.
nybrygget newly brewed.
nybygd colony, settlement.
nybygg house in course of erection, new construction. **-e** colony, settlement.
nybygger colonist, settler.
nybær (om ku) fresh-calved.
nydelig nice, charming, lovely.
nyere (komparativ) newer; (moderne) modern, late, recent.
nyervervet just acquired.
nyest (superlativ) newest; **-e nytt** the latest news.
nyfallen: **hvit som** — **snø** white as the driven snow.
nyfiken curious, inquisitive. **-het** curiosity.
nyforlovet recently engaged; **de nyforlovede** the couple recently engaged.
Nyfundland Newfoundland.
nyfundlender (hund) Newfoundland dog.
nyfødt newborn.
nygift newly married; **et — par** a newly married pair el. couple.
nygreker modern Greek, Romaic.
nygresk modern Greek, Romaic.
nygrodd newly grown.
nyhet (beskaffenheten) newness, novelty, recentness; (noe nytt) news, novelty; **en** — a piece of news. **nyhetskremmer** newsmonger.
Nyholland New-Holland, Australia.
nying fire (lit in the open).
nykjernet fresh (churned).
nykk jerk, pull.
nykke (vrb) jerk, pull.
nykke (subst) se **innfall, lune**.
nyklekt fresh hatched.
ny|kokt new-boiled. **-komling** newcomer. **-laget** fresh (made). **-lagt** fresh-laid. **-lende** new land.
nylig lately, of late, newly, recently; **nå** — of late, lately; **hennes** — **avdøde mann** her late husband.
nymalt freshly painted. — **kaffe** freshly ground coffee.
nymfe nymph.
nymotens newfangled, new-fashioned.
nymåne new moon; **det var** — **igår** there was a new moon yesterday.
nynne hum, croon.
ny|omvendt newly converted; new convert, neophyte. **-oppdaget** recently discovered. **-oppført** newly erected.
I. nype hip. **-busk**, se **-torn**. **-hekk** dog-briar hedge. **-rose** dog-rose. **-torn** hip-tree, dog-rose, dog-briar, wildbriar.

II. nype (finger-) pinch. **en** — **salt** a pinch of salt.
nype (vrb) nip, pinch, tweak.
nypløyd freshly ploughed.
nyre kidney. **-betennelse** inflammation of the kidneys, nephritis. **-fett** suet, kidney-fat. **-grus** gravel (in the kidneys). **-kolikk** pain in the kidneys, nephralgy. **-stein** nephrite. **-stykke** loin. **-sykdom** kidney disease. **-talg** suet. **-tilfelle** nephritic complaint.
nys (nysing) sneeze. **nyse** sneeze.
nysgjerrig curious, inquisitive, prying.
nysgjerrighet curiosity, inquisitiveness.
nysilt new, fresh from the cow.
nysing sneezing, sternutation, sneeze.
nyslipt new-sharpened.
nyslått (om gras) new-mown; (om mynt) fresh stamped; **blank som en** — **toskilling** bright as a new sixpence.
nysnø fresh el. new-fallen snow.
nyss (subst) (vink, antydning) hint, intimation, inkling.
nyss (adv), se **nylig**.
nysølv German silver, white copper.
nyte enjoy; (like godt) relish; (spise, drikke) have, partake of; **jeg har ikke nytt noe i dag** I have tasted no food to-day; — **godt av** have the benefit el. privilege of; — **samme beskyttelse** meet with the same protection; **alt det gode jeg har nytt i hans hus** all the kindness I met with at his house; **etter å ha nytt en solid frokost** after partaking of a substantial breakfast.
nytelse enjoyment, fruition; **-r** enjoyments; sensual enjoyment el. pleasure; **en ren** — quite a treat, relish; **avholde seg fra -n av** abstain from the use of.
nytelsessyk self-indulgent, pleasure-seeking.
nytelsessyke self-indulgence.
nyting, se **nytelse**.
nytt (nyheter) news; **hva** —? what news? what's the news? **intet** — **er godt** — no news is good news; **gammelt og** — things old and new.
nytte (vrb) be of use (to one), serve, avail; (utnytte) turn to account; **det -r ikke** it is (of) no use, it is no good; **hva kan det** — ? what is the use (of that)? **hva kan det** — **å** what is the use of -ing; — **høvet** improve the opportunity, avail oneself of the opportunity; — **tiden** improve the time.
nytte (subst) utility, use, benefit, advantage; **gjøre** — be of use, be helpful; **dra** — **av** be benefited by; **være en til** — be of use to one; **det er til ingen** — it is (of) no use, of no avail, to no purpose; **det gjorde samme -n** it did just as well, served the same purpose.
nytte|dyr useful animal. **-løs** useless. **-vekst** profitable plant. **-verdi** utilitarian value.
nyttig useful, serviceable, profitable. **-gjøre seg** make use of, take advantage of.
nyttighet usefulness, serviceableness.
nyttår new-year; **godt —!** a happy new year. **nyttårs|aften** new-year's eve. **-dag** new-year's day. **-gave** new-year's gift. **-gratiale** new-year's gratuity. **-lykkønskning** congratulation on the new year. **-morgen** the first morning of the new year. **-natt** new-year's night. **-visitt** new-year visit. **-ønsker** wishes for the new year.
nyår, se **nyttår**.
nær (se også **nærmere, nærmest, nest**) (adj) near, close; **en** — **slektning** a near relation; **en** — **forbindelse** a close connection; **stå i** — **forbindelse med** be closely connected with; (prep) near; (forestående) at hand; — **ved** close upon, hard on, near; (adv) hard by; **jeg er like** — I am just where I was; **det ligger** — **å anta** it is an obvious conclusion; — **forestående** approaching; **være** — **ved å** be on the point of, ready to; **ikke på langt** — not nearly; **ikke på langt** — **så god** not so good by far; **det gikk** — **innpå ham** it hit him hard; **komme**

— approach; **gå (en) for** — treat unfairly; take too great liberties with; **ta seg** — **av noe** take a thing to heart; **grunnen ligger** — the cause is not far to seek; **stå en svært** — be closely connected with one; **på én** — except el. wanting one; **på det** — at with the exception that, except that.

nærbeslektet nearly related.

nære nourish, feed; (**ernære**) support, maintain; (en følelse) entertain, nourish, cherish; — **seg** live; (dyr) feed (av: on); (ernære seg) get a living, earn a livelihood; — **hat** nourish el. bear hatred (towards); — **håp** entertain hope; — **avsky for** hold in aversion; **jeg -r ingen tvil om** at I have no doubt but that. **-nde** nutritious, nutritive.

nær|gående offensive, indiscreet, forward. **-gåenhet** indiscretion, forwardness.

nærhet neighbourhood; **i -en** near, neighbouring, in the neighbourhood; **gatene i -en** the neighbouring streets; **i -en av** near to, close to.

nærig sordid, stingy, near. **-het** sordidness, nearness.

næring (føde) nourishment, food; (underhold) support, maintenance, sustenance; livelihood; (levevei) trade, business, custom; **gi** — (fig) foment, cherish; **gå en i -en** spoil (one's) trade; **ta** — **til seg** take nourishment; **sette tæring etter** — live within one's income.

nærings|brev license. **-drift** trade, business. **-frihet** liberty of industry. **-kilde** means of subsistence. **-middel** article of food, food resource. **-sorger** cares for the necessaries of life, uneasiness about the means of living. **-vei** trade business, livelihood. **-verdi** food value. **-vett** a sense of economy, a good business head. **ha** — know on which side one's bread is buttered.

nærkamp close action, struggle hand to hand.

nærliggende adjacent, neighbouring; **av** — **grunner** for obvious reasons.

nærme bring el. draw near; — **seg** draw near, near, approach, be approaching.

nærmere (komparativ av **nær**) nearer; (ytterligere) further; — **opplysninger** further particulars, particulars; **tenke** — **over saken** consider, go into the matter; — **Gud, til deg** nearer, my God, to thee.

nærmest (superlativ av **nær**) nearest, (om nabo) next-door; (adv: nesten) rather; (adv: særlig) more particularly; **ens -e** those nearest to one; **mine -e naboer** my next-door neighbours; **jeg har medlidenhet med henne, mens jeg** — misunner **ham** I pity her, while I rather envy him; **enhver er seg selv** — charity begins at home; **den -e omegn** the immediate neighbourhood; **de -e dager** the next few days.

nær|på (adv) nearly. **-skyldt** nearly allied, near of kin. **-stående** near. **-synt** short-sighted. **-synthet** short-sightedness.

nærtagende (too) sensitive. **-het** sensitiveness.

nær ved close by.

nærvær presence; **i fremmedes** — before company.

nærværende present; this; — **bok** this book; **ved** — **skal jeg underrette Dem om** (merk.) this is to inform you.

nø, se node.

nø el. **nød** (trang) need, want, necessity, distress; perplexity; **lide** — suffer want; — **bryter alle lover** necessity has no law; **det har ingen** — no fear of that; **av** — from want; **-ens time** in the hour of need; **med** — **og neppe slapp han derfra** he had a narrow escape.

nødanker sheet-anchor.

nødbrems emergency brake.

nøde oblige, constrain, force, compel; (overtale) urge, press.

nødflagg flag of distress.

nødhavn harbour of refuge.

nødhjelp make-shift, shift.

I. **nødig** (nødvendig) needful, necessary, requisite; **ha** — (sj), se **behøve**.

II. **nødig** (ugjerne) reluctantly; **jeg vil** — I do not like, I object to; **jeg gjør det** — I do not like to do it.

nøding pressing, urging.

nødlanding (flyvers) forced landing; **foreta en** — make a forced landing.

nød|lidende needy, necessitous, indigent, distressed. **-løgn** white lie. **-mast** jury-mast. **-rop** cry of distress. **-ror** jury el. makeshift rudder. **-sage** necessitate, constrain, oblige, force.

nødsarbeid relief work.

nødsfall: i — in case of need, at a pinch, in (on, at) an emergency.

nød|signal (mar) signal of distress, distress signal. **-skilling** sparemoney. **-skrik**, se **-rop**. **-skudd** distress gun.

nødstid time of need.

nødstilfelle emergency; **i** — in case of need.

nød|tvunget necessitated, forced, compelled by necessity.

nødtørft necessities of life; **forrette sin** — do one's business.

nødtørftig strictly necessary.

nødtørftighet need, necessity.

nødvendig necessary, needful, requisite; **mangle det -e** want the necessaries of life.

nødvendiggjøre necessitate, compel.

nødvendighet necessity, needfulness, matter of necessity; **av** — from necessity; **gjøre en dyd av** — make a virtue of necessity.

nødvendighetsartikkel necessary.

nødvendigvis necessarily, of necessity.

nødverge self-defence; **i** — in one's own defence.

nøgd, se **fornøyd**.

nøkk river sprite, Nixie.

nøkkel key; (musikk) clef, key; (til gåte) clue.

nøkkelost Dutch clove cheese.

nøkle|bein collar-bone, clavicle. **-blomst** cowslip. **-brett** keyboard. **-hull** key-hole. **-knippe** bunch of keys. **-kurv** key-basket. **-ring** key-ring. **-skjegg** bit el. web of a key, key-bit.

nøktern sober. **-het** sobriety.

nøle linger, dawdle, delay, hesitate, loiter. **-nde** hesitating.

nøre opp feed a fire, light a fire.

nøste (vrb) wind up (thread) into balls.

nøste (subst) ball (of thread, of cotton). **-kopp** cotton box.

nøtt nut; **en hård** — a hard nut to crack, a tough nut, poser, puzzler. **plukke -er** nut.

nøttebrun nut-brown.

nøtte|busk hazel (shrub). **-hekk** hazel hedge. **-kjerne** kernel of a nut. **-klase** cluster of nuts. **-knekker** (pair of) nutcrackers. **-olje** nut-oil. **-plukking** nutting. **-skall** nut-shell; (båt) cockle-shell. **-skrike** jaybird, jay.

nøyaktig (adj) exact, accurate; punctual; (adv) exactly, to a nicety.

nøyaktighet exactness, accuracy, punctuality.

nøyd, se **fornøyd**.

nøye (vrb): **la seg** — be content, content oneself, rest satisfied (**med**: with); — **seg**, **nøyes med å** be content to.

nøye (nøyaktig) accurate, exact, precise; (adv) accurately, exactly, minutely; **man må ikke regne det så** — med ham one must not be over particular with him; **tok det ikke så** — med was not scrupulous about; **jeg vet det ikke så** — I don't know exactly; **se** — **etter, til** look narrowly (into); **passe** — **på** keep a sharp look-out, watch closely; **iaktta** — observe minutely.

nøye|regnende, -seende particular, nice (**med**: about); economical.

nøysom easily contented, contented with little.

nøysomhet contentment.

nøyte seg, se **skynde seg.**
nøytral neuter; (gram) neuter; **holde seg —** keep (remain) neutral, stand neuter, observe neutrality.
nøytralisasjon neutralization.
nøytralisere neutralize.
nøytralitet neutrality.
nøytralitets|erklæring declaration of neutrality. **-forsvar** defence of neutrality. **-krenkelse** violation of neutrality. **-politikk** policy of neutrality.
nøytrum the neuter gender; (ord) neuter noun, pronoun etc.
nå (tid) now, at present; (under de givne forhold) as it is el. was; (tonløs part.) well, really, you see; (når beskjed mottas) well; (spørrende) well? (oppmuntrende) come, come; (beroligende) irettesettende) there, there! **— da!** hollo! what next! **nå og da** now and again; **nå, da** now that; **fra nå av** henceforth, henceforward, from now; **nå må han være der he** must be there by now.
nå (subst) the present; **i et —** in a moment, in a twinkling, in a trice, in no time.
nå (vrb) reach, get at; gain; (oppnå) attain (to); (innhente) get up with; (til) reach, extend (to).
nåbleik (likbleik) ghastly.
nåda, se **nå!**
nåde grace, favour; (mildhet) clemency; (barmhjertighet, medlidenhet) mercy; (titel for adelige damer) ladyship; (titel for høytst. pers.) grace; **Deres —!** your ladyship! your grace! Mylord! Mylady! **nåde! nåde!** mercy! mercy on me! **uten — og barmhjertighet** pitilessly; **av Guds —** by the grace of God; **leve på ens —** live upon one's charity; **av — og barmhjertighet** on sufferance; **finne — for ens øyne** find favour in one's sight el. eyes; **la — gå for rett** temper justice with mercy, extend mercy; **be om —** cry mercy, appeal for mercy, sue for pardon, beg for one's life; **få sin avskjed i —** be honourably discharged; **ta til —** accept el. restore to favour; **overgi seg på — og unåde** surrender at discretion, unconditionally; **uten —** without mercy.
nåde: Gud — dem God have mercy upon

them! **Gud — deg, hvis . . .** you had better not . . ., I wouldn't advise you to . . .; woe betide you, if . . .
nådegave (i teologi) gift of grace.
nådemiddel means of grace.
nåderik merciful.
nådesbevis favour.
nådestøt death blow, coup de grace.
nådig gracious; **Gud være oss —!** God have mercy upon us! **Gud være meg synder —!** God be merciful to me, a sinner! **vår -ste konge** our gracious sovereign; **behaget aller nådigst å** was graciously pleased to.
nådsens|brød bread of charity, charitable maintenance. **-år** year of grace.
nål (synål, magnetnål) needle; (knappe-) pin; (bot.) needle; **stå som på -er** be upon thorns; **træ i en —** thread a needle.
nåle|bok needle-book. **-brev** paper of needles el. pins. **-fabrikk** needle manufactory. **-formet** in the shape of a needle. **-hus** needle-case. **-maker** needle-maker; pin-maker, pinner. **-penger** pin-money. **-pute** pin-cushion. **-skog** pine-forest, forest of firs. **-spiss** point of a needle. **-stikk** prick with a needle, pin-prick. **-tre** fir (tree), pine, conifer.
nålevende now living, now alive.
nåløye eye of a needle.
når when, at what time; (hvis) if; **— jeg skal si Dem sannheten** to tell you the truth; **— så er** if so, if that is the case, that being so; **— bare** if only; (forutsatt) so that; **— det skal være** at any time; **— han taler, taler han** godt when he does speak, he speaks well.
når som helst whenever, whensoever, at whatever time, at what time soever! (adv) (at) any time (whatever).
nåtid the present times, the present day; (gram) the present (tense). **-ens historie** modern history.
nåtidsmenneske man of the present age.
nåtildags now-a-days.
nåt|le sew. **-lerske** shoe-binder. **-ling** shoe-binding.
nåvel well (then).
nåværende present, now prevailing.

O

O, o O, o.
o (interj., foreld., poet.) O! Oh!
oase oasis.
obdu|ksjon dissection. **-sent** dissector. **-sere** dissect.
obelisk obelisk.
oberst colonel. **-inne** colonel's lady; **fru — A.** Mrs. Colonel A. **-løytnant** lieutenant-colonel.
objekt object.
objektiv (adj) objective.
objektiv (subst) objectglass, objective. **objektivere** objectify. **objektivering** objectification.
objektivitet objectiveness, objectivity.
oblat wafer.
obligasjon bond; (stats-) government bond; (stats-) **-er** stock; (flere slags) stocks (pl.).
obligasjonsinnehaver bond holder.
obligat obliged, inevitable; (i musikk) obligato.
obligatorisk compulsory, obligatory, binding.
obo oboe. **-ist** oboist.
observ|asjon observation, sight. **-ator** observator, observer; assistant astronomer. **-atorium** observatory. **-ere** observe.
obskur obscure.
obskurant obscurant, obscurantist. **-isme** obscurantism.

obsternasig recalcitrant, refractory.
obstruksjon obstruction.
odd (spiss) point.
odde (pynt) point, head, tongue of land.
odde (ulike) unmatched; **-tall** uneven numbers.
ode ode.
odel allodial possession. **odels|bonde** proprietor of an allodial farm. **-brev** patent of allodial privileges. **-gård** allodium. **-rett** allodial law; allodial privilege. **-sak** lawsuit in the matter of allodials.
Odelstinget the larger division of the Norwegian parliament.
odiøs invidious.
odle (drive, dyrke) farm, improve, till.
offensiv offensive; **ta -en** take he offensive.
offentlig public; **et — fruentimmer** a woman of the town; **på — bekostning** at the public expense; **den -e mening** public opinion; **det -e** Government, the State.
offentliggjøre publish, give publicity to, make public. **offentliggjørelse** publication.
offentlighet publicity.
offer (til prest) offering, oblation; (som bringes en) sacrifice; (person) victim; **— for** victim to, the victim of.

offerere offer.
offerlam sacrificial lamb, victim.
offerte offer, tender, proposal.
offervilje charity; generosity; self-sacrifice.
offervillig self sacrificing, willing to make sacrifices. **offervillighet** self-sacrifice.
officer (military) officer, commissioned officer.
officers|aspirant applicant for a lieutenant's commission. **-besetning** staff of officers. **-eksamen: han har tatt** — he has passed (his examination) as a lieutenant. **-messe** mess. **-rang** the rank of an officer. **-standen** military and naval officers.
offiser osv., se **officer.**
offisiell official.
offisin (trykkeri) printing office.
offisiøs half-official.
offside (i fotball) offside.
ofre sacrifice; — **livet** lay down one's life; — **sin tid, sitt liv på** devote one's time, life, to; — **det en tanke** give it a thought; — **seg** sacrifice oneself, devote oneself (**til:** to).
ofring sacrifice, immolation.
ofte often, frequently; **ikke -re** never again; **han kommer** — **hit** he frequents this place; **som -st** most frequently, far oftener than not.
og and.
òg el. **også** also, too, as well; **ikke alene ... men** — not only ... but (also); **eller** — or else ; — **virkelig, da** — indeed, in fact; **og han kom** — (virkelig) and he did come, and come he did.
ohm ohm.
oker ochre. **-aktig, -gul** ochreous.
okkult occult. **okkultisme** occultism.
okkup|asjon occupation. **-ere** occupy.
okse ox (pl oxen); bull, bullock. **okse|blod** blood of oxen. **-bryst** breast of beef **-driver** drover.
oksefilet fillet of beef.
okse|halesuppe ox-tail soup. **-hode** (vinfat) hogshead. **-hud** ox-hide. **-kjøtt** beef.
okse|marg ox-marrow. **-stek** roast-beef. **-tunge** neat's tongue, ox-tongue.
okseøye (plante) oxeye.
Oksidenten Occident.
oksyd oxide. **-ere** oxidize. **-ering** oxidation.
oktant (figur) octant; (instrum.) quadrant.
oktav (format og bok) octavo; (musikk) octave. **-ark** octavo sheet. **-format** octavo.
oktober October.
oktroa octroi, concession. **-jere** grant.
okular, -glass eye-piece, ocular.
okule|re inoculate. **-ring** budding, inoculation, grafting.
oldefar great grandfather.
oldemor great grandmother.
oldenborre May-bug, cockchafer.
oldermann master of a corporation.
old|frue state housekeeper; head laundress. **-funn** find of antiquities. **-gransker** antiquary, antiquarian. **-granskning** antiquarian research.
olding old man.
oldingaktig senile. **oldingalder** old age.
old|kirke early church. **-kvad** ancient lay el. poem.
oldnordisk Old Northern.
old|norsk Old Norwegian, Old Norse. **-saker** antiquities, objects of antiquity. **-tid** antiquity, olden time. **-tidsminne** monument of antiquity. **-tidsvitenskap** archæology.
Ole Auley.
oleander oleander.
oligarki oligarchy. **oligarkisk** oligarchic(al).
oliven olive. **olivenfarget** olive-coloured.
olivenolje olive-oil.
olje oil; **helle** — **på ilden** add fuel to the fire; **den siste** — extreme unction; **smøre med** — oil.
olje (vrb) oil.
oljeaktig oily.
Oljeberget the Mount of Olives.

oljeblad olive leaf.
oljefarge oil-colour; **male med -r** paint in oil.
olje|grein olive branch. **-hyre** kit el. suit of oilskin. **-kake** oil-cake. **-klær** oilskins. **-krukke** oil-jug. **-lampe** oil-lamp. **-lerret** oilskin. **-maleri** oil-painting. **-maling** oil-paint. **-mølle** oil-mill. **-tre** olive; oil-tree. **-trykk** chromo-lithography.
olle issue of water, spring, well.
olm furious, mad.
olsok St. Olave's day, July 29.
Olymp(en) Olympus.
olympiade olympiad.
olympisk (guddommelig) Olympian; (som hører til Olympia) Olympic; **de -e leker** the Olympic games.
om (konj) whether, if; (dersom) if; (om enn, om så) even if, even though; **hvem vet** — **ikke?** who knows but? — **Gud vil** God willing; — **enn,** — **så** though; — **nå så var** what though? — **det så var kyrne, så ... the** very cows ... ; — **jeg vil** won't I.
om (prep) about; **forestilling, tanke, håp** osv. — idea, thought, hope, etc. of; **en avhandling** — a treatise on; **overbevist** — **at** convinced that; **spille** — **penger** play for money; **kastet seg** — **halsen på ham** threw herself on el. about his neck; **være tre** — **en** be three to one; **være sen** — be long in; **jeg er lett, tung** — **hjertet** my heart is light, heavy (within me); **det er meg** — **å gjøre** it is an object with me; **side** — **side** side by side; **posten kommer** — **mandagen og fredagen** the mail arrives on Mondays and Fridays; — **morgenen, eftermiddagen** in the morning, afternoon; — **sommeren, vinteren** in summer, winter; — **en** time in an hour, in another hour; — **en måned** in a month, in another month; — **litt** shortly, presently; **en gang** — **året** once a year; **10 dollar** — måneden 10 Dollars a month; **være** — **seg** be active, sharp; (adv) **falle** — fall down; **gjøre noe** — **igjen** do a thing over again.
omadressere redirect.
omarbeide remodel, remake, reconstruct, recast, new-model, rewrite, re-edit; (for scenen) adapt.
omarbeidelse remodelling etc.; (omarbeidd verk) remodelled work; adaptation.
omatt over again.
ombeilet courted.
ombestemme seg change one's mind el. purpose. **-lse** change of purpose.
ombinde tie el. bind round, gird.
omboende neighbouring; (sub.) neighbours.
ombord onboard, aboard, on shipboard, onboard ship; — **i** onboard (of); **ta (noe)** — ship.
ombordbringelse shipment.
ombordværende onboard.
ombrekke (typogr.) overrun, make up, impose.
ombrekker maker-up, impositor.
ombrekning overrunning.
ombringe distribute; (om post) deliver; (drepe) destroy, kill. **-lse** distribution.
ombud commission, charge, office; (fullmektig) agent, deputy. **-smann** commissioner, official.
ombygging rebuilding, alteration.
ombytte (subst) change of clothes.
ombytting exchanging.
ombæring carrying about; (av brever osv.) delivery.
ombølge wave round.
ombøyning bending.
omdanne transform, convert, remodel, reshape. **-lse** transformation, conversion.
omdebattert under discussion **et meget** — spørsmål a vexed question.
omdeling distribution.
omdiktning remodelling.
omdisputert disputed.
omdreiende revolving, rotatory. **-bevegelse** rotatory motion.

omdreining turning, revolution, rotation.
omdreiningshastighet velocity of rotation.
omdømme judgment, opinion reputation.
omegn neighbourhood, surrounding country,
environs (pl).
omelett omelet.
omen omen et — om an omen that.
omenskjønt although.
omfang circumference; (utstrekning) extent;
en stemme av stort — a voice of great compass.
omfangsrik extensive, bulky.
omfatte encompass; (innbefatte) comprise,
comprehend, embrace, cover. omfattende comprehensive, extensive, wide-ranging, sweeping.
omfavne embrace, hug.
omfavnelse embracing, embrace, hug.
omflakkende roving, strolling, wandering,
erratic. -flakking roaming, rambling.
omflytning translocation; moving.
omflytt (av hav) surrounded (by the sea).
omforme modify, reform.
omfram(t) (adv.) in addition, into the bargain.
— flink eminently qualified.
omgang (omdreining) revolution, rotation,
turn; (samkvem) intercourse, commerce, communion. company; (krets) acquaintance; (behandling) treatment, management; (i kortspill,
strikning) round; (i cricket) innings; fortrolig
— familiar intercourse; ha — med associate
with, keep company with; det går på — it is
done by turns; lettsindig — med sannheten
disregard of truth; en — juling a sound thrashing el. whipping.
omgangs|krets circle of one's acquaintance.
-lærer visitant teacher. -skole ambulatory
school. -språk conversational language, colloquial language. -syke, se epidemi. -tone tone
of conversation. -venn associate.
omgi encompass, surround, environ, encircle;
— seg med surround oneself with; (om personer)
associate with.
omgivelse encompassing etc.; (ens omgang)
associates, circle of friends, those around one;
(det som omgir en) surroundings, environ-
ments; (bare om landskap) scenes (pl).
omgjengelig companionable, sociable.
omgjengelighet sociability.
omgjengelse intercourse.
omgjerde fence round, hedge round.
omgjorde gird round.
omgå (mil) turn, outflank; (en befaling osv.)
elude, evade; (spørsmål) fence. -else evasion.
-ende bevegelse turning movement. -ende, pr.
-ende (post) by return of post.
omgås have intercourse with, converse with;
(behandle) manage, treat, deal with; — med
tanker om meditate, have in one's head; si
meg hvem du —, og jeg skal si deg hvem du
er tell me the company you keep, and I'll tell
you what you are.
omhandle treat of.
omheng bed curtains (pl). -sseng four-poster.
omhu care, concern, solicitude; ha — for
take care of.
omhyggelig careful (of). -het carefulness,
pains.
omigjen again, over again; — og — over
and over again; tenke — think again; unthink
a thought.
ominøs ominous.
omkalfatre re-caulk; (lage helt om på) re-mo-
del, transform.
omkalfatring transformation.
om kapp, se kapp.
omkast sudden turn.
omklamre clasp, cling to.
omkledd having changed one's dress el.
clothes.
omkledning change of dress.
omkomme perish.
omkontrahert agreed upon.

omkostning cost, expense, charge; betale -ene
defray the expenses; diverse -er sundry expenses; idømme saksomkostninger condemn to
costs.
omkostningsfritt clear of expenses.
omkostningskonto expenses-account.
omkranse wreathe, encircle.
omkrets circumference, circuit, compass;
(geom) circumference; i -en on the circumference; i ti mils — (for) ten miles round; within
ten miles.
omkring round, around, about; spasere —
walk about; gå — byen walk round the town;
gå — i byen, gatene walk about the town,
about the streets.
omkring|boende residing around; neighbours.
-liggende circumjacent. -stående bystanders.
omkull down; rive — upset.
omkvarv round.
omkved burden, refrain.
om lag about; — som much as; — det samme
much the same; så — thereabouts.
omland surrounding country.
omlaste (varer til annet skip) tran(s)ship.
omlastning tran(s)shipment. omlastningssom-
kostninger tran(s)shipment expenses.
omlegge (annerledes) change the position el.
direction of, lay, place differently.
omlegning relaying, alteration, reconstruction;
— av arbeidstiden rearrangement of hours.
omlessing reloading.
omlyd (vowel-)mutation.
omløp circulation, course, rotation; sette i
— (veksler osv.) issue; (et rykte) circulate, set
afloat; (penger) circulate; — i hodet brains,
readiness, management.
 omme (til ende) over, at an end, out; tiden
er — time is up; døde innen året var — died
within the year.
omn, se ovn.
omnibus omnibus; (automobil) motor-bus.
-konduktør omnibus-conductor, motor-bus c.
-kusk omnibus driver. -rute o. el. m. line.
omordjne re-arrange. -ning re-arrangement.
omorganisasjon reorganization.
omorganisere reorganize.
omplanting transplanting, replanting.
omposterje transpose. -ing transposition.
om|redaksjon re-drafting; re-wording; re-writ-
ing. -redigere re-draft etc.
omreisende itinerant, travelling, touring.
omringe surround, beset.
omriss outline, contour.
omrøring stirring.
områ seg cast about, consider.
område territory, domain, pale.
omseggripende spreading, growing, rampant.
omseille circumnavigate, sail round. -ing
circumnavigation.
omsetning (merk.) turn-over, sale, trade;
(penge-) — a money transaction. det er liten —
there is but little business doing. omsetnings-
beløp amount turned over; (i butikk) drawings.
omsette (avhende) turn over, dispose of, sell;
(gjøre i penger) realize.
omsettelig negotiable.
omsetting (typ.) reset.
omsider at length, eventually.
omsikt circumspection, forethought, discretion. omsiktsfull circumspect.
omskape new-model, remodel, transform.
-else, -ing remodelling.
omskifte (subst) change, alternation.
omskiftelig changeable.
omskiftelighet changeableness.
omskiftelse change, turn, vicissitude (of
fortune).
omskiftning change.
omskiple tran(s)ship. -ning tran(s)shipment.
omskjære circumcise. -lse circumcision.

omskrift transcript; (konkret) rewriting, copy; (på mynt) legend.

omskrive (uttrykke indirekte) express by a circumlocution; describe in a roundabout way, paraphrase; (geom) circumscribe; **de omskrevne varer** the goods mentioned.

omskrivning re-writing; circumlocution, paraphrase.

omslag (på brev) envelope, cover, wrapper; (helbredende) poultice, fomentation, cataplasm, compress; (i været) change; (i stemning) revulsion (of feeling), reaction, turn; (i livsforhold) turn of fortune; (til det verre) reverse; **legge — på** apply a cataplasm to, poultice, foment.

omslutte enclose, include, encompass.

omslynge twist round, twine round, encircle; (omfavne) embrace.

omsmelting remelting.

omsorg care; **dra — for** take care of (el. that), see that. **omsorgsfull** careful.

omspenne span round; (omringe) hem in; **omspent av luer** beset with flames.

omspurt in question, inquired about.

omstemme en make one change his opinion, bring one round; **bli omstemt** come round.

omsten|delig circumstantial, detailed, particular; (adv) circumstantially, in detail. **-delighet** circumstantiality, particularity.

omstendighet circumstance, fact; (ledsagende) incident; (det særegne ved en begivenhet) particular, detail; **-er** (overdreven høflighet) ceremonies, formalities; **det kommer an på -ene** that depends; **etter -ene** as the case might be; **han er nokså bra etter -ene** he is very well considering; **under alle -er** at all events, at the best; **være i -er** be in the family way el. in an interesting situation; **gjør ingen -er** don't stand upon ceremony; **uten (videre) -er** without (further) ceremony; **han gjorde så mange -er** he started so many objections.

omstigning change.

omstille set el. dispose differently, transpose.

omstilling transposition, inversion.

omstreifende erratic, roaming, roving, vagrant.

omstreifer vagrant, tramp.

omstreifing roaming, vagrancy.

omstridt at issue, in dispute, disputed.

omstrålt av irradiated with.

omstuing restowing.

omstyrt|e overthrow, overturn, subvert. **-else, -ing** overthrowing, overthrow, subversion.

omstøping recasting.

omstøte (fig) subvert; (oppheve) set aside, abrogate, reverse; (gjendrive) refute.

omstøtning subversion.

omstående standing round; **de — the** bystanders; **— vil De finne en fortegnelse** overleaf (el. on the next page) you will find a list; **se — side** see over!

omsut, se **omsorg.**

omsverme swarm round el. about.

omsving (omslag) sudden change, revolution.

omsvøp (departementsmessige) redtape; (i alm.) circumlocution; **gjøre — beat** el. go about the bush, make digression.

omsydd altered, made over again.

omtale (subst) mention, mentioning; (common) talk, report; **kjenner ham av — know** him by repute.

omtale (vrb) mention, make mention of, notice, speak of; refer to; **den omtalte bok** the book in question (el. before mentioned).

omtanke forethought, thoughtfulness, thought.

omtelling recount.

omtenksom thougtful. **-het,** se **omtanke.**

omtrent about; **— som** much as; **— det samme** much the same; **så — thereabouts. -lig** approximate, rough; (adv) about.

omtrykning reprinting.

omtumle toss about, knock about; **-t av storm** tempest-tossed. **omtumlet** tossing about.

omtvistelig contestable; debatable, disputable.

omtvistet disputed.

om|tyde give a new-reading of . . ., assign a different sense to . . .; **-tydning** new reading, assignment of a different sense.

omtåket (uklar) dim, hazy; (drukken) hazy, fuddled; obfuscated, disguised in liquor. **— tilstand** muddiness, fuddled condition.

omvalg re-election.

omvandrende itinerant.

omvandring wandering, perambulation.

omvei circuitous way, roundabout way, détour; **gjøre en — make** a circuit; **på (ad) -er** by devious ways, by a roundabout method.

omveksling alternation, vicissitude; (til det verre) reverse (of fortune).

omveltning overturning, upsetting; revolution; **bevirke en — i** revolutionize.

omvende convert; **— seg** reform, be converted; **en omvendt** a convert.

omvendelse conversion.

omvendelses|forsøk attempt at conversion. **-iver** proselytizing zeal. **omvending** turning round.

omvendt inverted; (fig) converse; **— forhold** inverse ratio el. proportion; (adv) conversely; **og — and** conversely, and vice versa.

omverden world around, surrounding world, surroundings.

omviser guide, cicerone.

omvisning showing about.

omvurder|e revalue. **-ing** revaluation.

ond bad, evil, wicked, se ogs. **vond; -e tider** hard times; **-e tunger** wicked tongues; **-e øyne** evil eyes; **en — ånd** an evil spirit; **den -e** the evil one, the devil; **med det -e eller med det 'gode** by foul or fair means.

ondartet ill-natured, ill-tempered; (om sykdom) dangerous, malignant.

onde (et) evil, ill; malady, complaint; nuisance; **det er et —, men et nødvendig — it is** a nuisance, but a necessary nuisance; **av to -r velger man det minste** of two evils choose the less.

ondsinnet evil-tempered.

ondsinnethet evil temper.

ondskap malice, wickedness, malignity.

ondskapsfull malicious, malignant, spiteful.

ondulere wave.

onestep one-step.

onkel uncle; (om lånekontor) my uncle, uncle Tom. **onkel-** avuncular.

onn (høy-, vår-) season, time for some farm-work. **-efolk** farm hands working during the «onn».

onsdag Wednesday.

onyks onyx.

opal opal.

opera (spill, bygning) opera; (bygning) opera-house. **-bygning** opera-house. **-sanger, -sangerinne** opera-singer. **-selskap** company of opera-singers.

operasjon operation.

operasjonsbord operating table.

operasjonsstue operating chamber, surgery.

operatekst text of an opera.

operatør operator.

operere perform an operation, operate; **— en pasient** operate upon a patient; **-s, la seg — undergo** an operation, be operated on.

operette operetta.

opiat opiate.

opinion public opinion (el. feeling). **opinions-ytring** expression el. manifestation of public opinion el. feeling.

opium opium. **-sdråper** laudanum.

opp up; (opp i en høyere etasje) up-stairs; **lukk — døra** open the door; **vinduet fløy — the** window flew open; **stå — mot** (f. eks. en vegg) stand against; **— og ned** up and down; to and fro; **vende — ned** turn upside down; **— av**

vannet, — **av senga** out of the water, out of (the) bed; **opp (med deg)!** get up!
oppad|strebende aspiring. **-vendt** upturned.
oppagitert worked-up.
oppamme nurse, suckle.
oppankret anchored. **oppankring** anchoring.
opparbeide cultivate, improve, work up. **-lse** cultivation, improvement, working.
oppbevar|e save, keep, preserve. **-ing** saving, preservation, safe-custody. **-ingssted** depository, place of deposit.
oppblande mix, qualify; (spe) dilute.
oppblomstrende flourishing, rising.
oppblomstring flourishing, rise.
oppblussing blaze, flash.
oppblø(y)tt softened, soaked; **veiene var** — the roads were saturated el. sodden.
oppblåst inflated; (self-)conceited, elate, self sufficient; — **av stolthet** puffed up, inflated with pride.
oppblåsthet elation, conceit, conceitedness.
oppbrakt (sint) enraged, exasperated; (se også **oppbringe**). **oppbrakthet** exasperation.
opp|brett turn up. **-brettet** rolled up, tucked up, turned over.
oppbringe (et skip) seize, capture (a ship).
oppbringelse capturing, capture, seizure.
oppbrudd departing, departure; (fra bordet) rising.
oppbrukt consumed, exhausted; (om penger) spent.
oppbrus|ende effervescent, ebullient. **-ing** effervescence, ebullition; (bare fig) huff, emotion, fume.
oppbud (styrke) posse; (utskrevet) levy.
oppby summon, levy, muster; (fig) exert, put forth. **han oppbød alle sine krefter** he put forth el. exerted all his strength. **med oppbydelse av** mustering.
oppbygge (virke moralsk oppbyggelig på) edify.
oppbyggelig edifying.
oppbyggelse (moralsk) edification.
oppbyggelsesskrift book of devotion, religious book; (religious) tract.
oppbæring carrying up.
oppdage (i alm.) discover; (oppspore, komme på spor etter, f. eks. en forbrytelse) detect; (øyne) descry; (komme etter, bli klar over) find out, find; (gjennomskue) find out.
oppdagelse discovery; detection.
oppdagelses|betjent detective. **-politi** detectives, detective police, detective service. **-reise** voyage of discovery. **-reisende** explorer.
oppdager discoverer; (oppdagelsesbetjent) detective.
oppdekning laying; **det var en praktfull** — the table was laid in a splendid way.
oppdemme dam up.
oppdemming damming up.
oppdikte fabricate, trump up.
oppdiktelse, oppdiktning fabrication.
oppdiktet fictitious.
oppdra educate, bring up, breed.
oppdrag task, commission; **ha i** — **å** be charged with the task of el. to.
oppdragelse education, breeding, upbringing.
oppdragelsesanstalt educational establishment; (for vanskelige barn) reformatory.
oppdragelsesmåte system of education.
oppdragende educative.
oppdrager educator; (hovmester) tutor.
oppdragerinne tutoress, governess.
oppdrett breeding, rearing, raising (of cattle); young cattle.
oppdrette breed, raise.
oppdretter breeder.
oppdrift buoyancy, power of flotation.
oppdrive procure, raise; — **penger** raise money; **det er ikke til å** — it is not to be had. **en godt oppdrevet gård** a farm carefully improved, in a high state of cultivation.

oppdynging heaping up, accumulation.
oppdyrke reclaim, bring under cultivation.
oppdyrking cultivation, culture.
oppe (adv) up, above; (ovenpå i huset) upstairs; **der** — up there, there above; **her** — up here; — **fra** from above; **han er ikke** — **ennå** he is not out of bed yet; **han er tidlig** — **om morgenen** he is an early riser.
oppe seg improve, bestir oneself.
oppebie await, wait for.
oppebære receive; (om offentl. penger) collect.
oppebørsel receiving, collecting.
oppegge egg on, instigate.
oppeiske raise, nurse; (fig) foster, nurse, encourage.
oppett eaten out, eaten up.
oppetter up; upwards.
oppfange catch, pick up; (oppsnappe) intercept.
oppfarende . passionate, choleric, fiery, hot -tempered, irascible.
oppfarenhet vehemence, irascibility.
oppfart ascension.
oppfatning apprehension; interpretation, construction, reading, view; **etter min** — in my opinion, as I understand it.
oppfatningsevne (power of) apprehension.
oppfatte apprehend, perceive; (fortolke) interpret, construe, read; — **fort** be quick of apprehension.
oppfinn|e invent. **-else** invention. **-er** inventor. **-som** inventive. **-somhet** ingenuity, power of invention, inventive power, inventiveness.
oppflamme inflame, kindle.
oppflaske bring up on the bottle, handfeed.
oppflytning remove, promotion.
oppflytte en elev (på skolen) remove a disciple.
oppfor up; — **bakke** up-hill.
oppfordre require, call upon, invite, exhort.
oppfordring summons, challenge, invitation, appeal; **på** — upon application, on demand.
oppforing feeding.
oppfostre rear, bring up; (fig) foster.
oppfostring rearing, bringing up, nurture.
oppfostrings|bidrag maintenance, aliment. **-hus** charity-house, charity-school.
oppfriske refresh, rub up; (fig) revive.
oppfylle (fig:) fulfil, grant, act up to; — **et løfte** fulfil a promise; — **et ønske** fulfil a wish, meet a wish; — **en bønn** grant a request; — **sine plikter** fulfil (el. discharge) one's duties; — **ens forlangende** comply with one's request; **oppfylt av beundring** filled with admiration.
oppfyllelse fulfilment; **gå i** — be fulfilled, come true.
oppfylling filling up, filling in.
oppfyring lighting a fire el. fires.
oppfødd (adj) brought up, reared, bred, nourished.
oppføre (bygge) construct, erect, raise; (om skuespill) perform, act, enact, bring out; (produce; (dans) lead off; (i et regnskap) put down, enter, specify; — **seg** behave (oneself), conduct oneself; — **seg dårlig** misconduct oneself; **oppfør deg ordentlig!** behave yourself! behave yourself properly!
oppførelse (av bygning) erection; (av skuespill) performance; **under** — in course of erection; **bringe til** — bring out; **kom ikke til** — was not placed upon the stage. **første gangs** — the first night's performance. **oppførelsesrett** stage right, acting rights.
oppførsel behaviour, conduct, comportment, demeanour. **oppførselskarakter** conduct-mark.
oppgang ascent, rise, rising; (i et hus) stairs; (forbedring) rise, improvement.
oppgangstid time of rising; (om forretninger) improving conjuncture.
oppgave (oppgivende) statement; (i detaljer) specification; (til løsning) problem, task; (still-) subject; (eksamens-) paper; (verv) business

study, task; **det er vår — å** it is ours to; **jeg har gjort det til min — å** . . . I have made a point of; (merk.) **ifølge —** as advised; **med —** with advice.

oppgi give up, forego; (plan, tanke) dismiss, abandon, relinquish; (en syk) give over; — **forretningene** relinquish, throw up el. decline business; — **ånden** give up the ghost; — **en gåte** propose a riddle; **han oppgav meg sin adresse** he gave me his adress; — **nøye** specify; — **for lavt** understate; — **sitt bo til rettens behandling** surrender one's estate to the creditors, to a commission of bankruptcy.

opp|givelse, -givende giving up, abandonment; (f. eks. av sin gjeld) statement; **etter —** according to statement; **i henhold til —** as per instruction.

oppgjeld agio.

oppgjør settlement, clearing, adjustment.

oppgjøre make up, settle.

oppglødd heated, made redhot; enthusiastic.

oppgraving digging up, disinterment.

oppgulp disgorgement.

oppgående rising; **for —** upward-bound.

opphalerbedding (repairing) slip.

opphav origin, source; authorship.

opphavsmann originator, author.

oppheng(n)ing hanging, suspension.

oppheng(n)ingspunkt point of suspension.

opphengt hung, slung, suspended **(i, etter:** by; **i, fra:** from).

opphete heat, make hot; — **for sterkt** overheat. **opphetning** heating.

oppheve break off, do away with, abolish, abrogate, repeal; (en virkning) neutralize; (en kontrakt, forsikring) cancel; — **hverandre** neutralize each other.

opphevelse abolition, abrogation, repeal; **gjøre mange -r over noe** make a great ado el. fuss about a thing; **uten -r** without (further) ceremony.

opphisse excite, stir up, set on, provoke, inflame. **opphisselse** irritation.

opphjelp advancement, promotion.

opphjelpe promote, encourage, restore.

opphogging breaking open, cutting up, (et skip) breaking up.

opphold stay, sojourn; (underhold) subsistence, maintenance, sustenance, support; (utsettelse) delay; (stans) intermission; (pause) pause, hold.

oppholde (underholde) uphold, support, sustain; (stanse) delay, detain; — **seg** (bo) stay, reside, live, sojourn; — **seg ved noe** dwell on a matter; — **seg over noe** animadvert upon, censure.

oppholds|bok permit of residence. **-sted** place of residence.

oppholdsvær interval of fine weather.

opphope heap up, accumulate; congest.

opphoping accumulation, congestion.

opphovnet swollen. **opphovning** swelling.

opphør cessation, intermission, discontinuance. **selges ut på grunn av forretningens —** will be sold at a great reduction on account of giving up business.

opphøre cease, discontinue, leave off; — **med forretningen** decline business, give up business.

opphøye raise, elevate, exalt; — **i tredje potens** involve to the third power; — **en til ære og verdighet** raise one to honour and dignity. **opphøyd|arbeid** relief, raised el. embossed work; **halvt —** demi-relief; **helt —** high-relief; **opphøyde bokstaver** (for blinde) embossed letters el. type.

opphøyelse raising, elevation, exaltation; (forfremmelse) preferment; (mat) involution.

opphøyet (høy) elevated; (fremstående) raised; (edel) elevated, lofty, sublime; **en — tanke** a sublime thought; — **forakt** supreme contempt **(for:** for).

oppildne inflame, fire.

oppimot against.

oppirre irritate, exasperate, provoke.

oppirring provocation, irritation.

oppkalle etter call el. name after.

oppkast vomit.

oppkaste throw up; (grave) dig; — **seg til dommer** assume the authority of a judge.

oppkast(n)ing vomiting, vomition.

oppkavet bustling, flurried.

oppkjøp buying up, engrossing, engrossment; forestalling.

oppkjøpe, se kjøpe opp.

oppkjøper buyer up, engrosser; forestaller.

oppkjørsel driving up; approach, carriage way.

oppkjørt (om vei) cut-up, rutty.

oppklar|e clear up, elucidate; (opplyse) illumine; **mysteriet ble -t** the mystery was cleared up; **-e et omtvistet punkt** elucidate a disputed point. **-ing** clearing (up), elucidation.

oppkle clothe. **oppkledning** clothing.

oppklebe paste **(på:** upon); **-t på lerret** mounted on linen.

oppklebning pasting, mounting; — **av plakater er forbudt!** stick no bills!

oppklort full of scratches.

oppknappet unbuttoned.

oppkok slight boiling, boil (up); (gjentatt koking) second boiling, cooking up; (fig) reiteration, rehash, reproduction, rehearsal; **gi et —** boil up; **disse artiklene er bare et — av andre blader** these are only second-hand articles.

oppkomling parvenu, upstart.

oppkomme (subst) issue of water; spring, well.

oppkomst origin, rise; (framgang) advancement, development; **i —** rising, improving.

opp|krav collection, levy. **-kreve** collect, levy; **-krever** collector, levier.

oppkrev(n)ing (av skatter) collection.

oppkveilt coiled down el. up.

oppkvikke brisken, liven up; recreate. **oppkvikking** livening up; recreation.

opplag (av varer) stock, store; (av en bok) impression, issue, edition; **nytt —** reissue; **i —** (på tollbod) in bond; **skip i —** laid up ships.

opplagret stored (up); warehoused.

opplags|avgift storage, warehouse rent. **-plass** storage, warehouse accommodation. **-sted** depot, store.

opplagt (i humør) in the humour, in a humour, in spirits **(til:** for, **til å:** to); (sikkert) assured, safe; (selvfølgelig) evident, obvious; **ikke —** out of humour; **ikke — til spøk** in no joking humour; **jeg føler meg ikke — til det i aften** I don't feel up to it to-night; **jeg har — spill** I have the game in my hand.

opplagthet humour, spirits.

oppland surrounding el. tributary country, trade district, the country behind a town.

opplate: — sin røst raise one's voice.

oppleser reader.

opplesning reading (aloud); (offentlig) recital.

opplemme cut up, limb.

opplett (om vær) dry el. fine. **-(s)dag** dry el. fine day.

opplev|e live to see, survive to see; (hendelse) meet with; **har -d mye** has had many experiences.

opplevelse experience, adventure.

oppliv|e revive, reanimate; (oppmuntre) enliven, cheer, exhilarate. **-else** revival, reanimation; enlivening, exhilaration. **-ende** exhilarating, lively. **-ningsmiddel** resuscitant.

opplosset landed, unshipped.

opplossing landing, discharging.

opplyse light up, illuminate, illumine; (med eksempler) elucidate, throw light upon, illustrate; (meddele) show, point out, give information of; (underrette) inform; **en opplyst tidsalder** an enlightened age.

opplysende elucidatory, lightgiving; — **eksempel** illustration; — **med hensyn til** illustrative of.

opplysning lighting; (åndelig) enlightenment; education; information, intelligence, evidence, (pl) details; **innhente -er** gather el. procure information; **nærmere -er** particulars.

opplysnings|arbeid educational work. **-byrå, -kontor** inquiry-office, information bureau.

opplæring teaching, training.

opplært taught, trained (up), schooled.

oppløfte (bare fig) raise, elevate; **et -nde syn** an exalting sight.

oppløftelse elevation; exaltation.

oppløp disorderly mob; (i opprørsk hensikt) riot, tumult; **i -et** (veddel.) at the finish.

oppløpen overgrown.

opp|løse loose, untie, undo; (hær) disband, disembody; (forsamling, ekteskap, vennskap) dissolve; (desorganisere) disorganize; (kjemi) resolve, decompose; (mekanisk, tilintetgjøre sammenhengen) disintegrate; **-løsende** dissolving, disintegrating; (for hoste) expectorant; **-løsende middel** (for hoste) expectorant; **-løst i tårer** dissolved in tears; **med -løst hår** with dishevelled hair; **-løse seg** dissolve, melt, resolve, be dissolved **(i:** into); (om skyer) disperse; **forsamlingen -løste seg** the assembly broke up.

oppløsning loosening; breaking up; dissolution; disorganization; (på gåter) solution; (kjemi) resolution, dissolution, decomposition; (konkret) solution; disintegration; (død) dissolution.

oppløsningstilstand state of decomposition; (fig) state of disintegration.

oppmagasinere store, store up, warehouse.

oppmann umpire, arbitrator, referee.

oppmarsj march up, marching up.

oppmarsjere march up.

oppmerksom attentive **(mot:** to), observant **(på:** of); **gjøre — på** point out, call attention to; **bli — på** perceive, remark, notice.

oppmerksomhet attention; (høflighet) attention, act of attention, compliment **(mot:** to); **henlede ens — på** call one's attention to; **skjenke en sak — på** pay attention to (el. on) a matter; **vise ham —** show (el. pay) him attention; **vekke —** attract attention.

oppmudring dredging.

oppmunt|re cheer, enliven, animate; (gi mot) encourage; (formane) exhort; (fremme) encourage, promote. **-rende** encouraging; **lite -rende** discouraging.

oppmuntring enlivening; encouragement exhortation, incentive; (atspredelse) diversion, recreation; **mangel på —** discouragement.

oppmåling surveying.

oppmålingsfartøy surveying vessel.

oppnavn nickname, sobriquet.

oppnevne appoint, name; (oppstille) nominate.

oppnå attain, gain; **— å** manage to.

oppnå|else attainment. **-lig** attainable.

oppofre sacrifice, immolate; (hengi) devote.

oppofrelse sacrifice; (egenskap) devotedness.

oppofrende devoted.

oppom egtl. up past, up over; **se — call** up, look in upon.

opponent opponent.

opponere make opposition; **— mot** oppose.

opportun expedient, opportune.

opportunist, opportunistisk opportunist.

opportunitet expediency.

opposisjon opposition. **-ell** given to contradiction; (subst.) oppositionist. **opposisjons|blad** opposition paper. **-mann** oppositionist. **-parti** opposition (party).

oppover up, upward **(— bakke)** up-hill.

opp-pakning (til soldat) equipment; **med full — in** full marching order.

opp-passer attendant, man, servant.

opp-plantet (adj) (kanon) planted; (bajonett) fixed.

opp-pløyd ploughed up.

opp-pusset touched up, smartened; (m. kalkpuss) replastered; (om leilighet) renovated.

opp-pussing touching up etc., renovation, decoration.

opp-pustet puffed out, inflated.

opprakt uplifted. **-e hender** uplifted hands.

oppramsing repeating, repetition.

oppredd (seng) ready made.

oppregning enumeration.

oppreisning reparation, redress; (æresopp.) satisfaction.

oppreist erect, upright.

oppreklamert boomed, puffed.

opprett upright, erect.

opprette institute, found, establish; (om skade) repair; (tap) retrieve; (forsømmelse) make up for; **— et testamente, en kontrakt** make a will, a contract.

opprettelse founding, foundation, institution, reparation.

opprett|holde support, uphold; maintain. **-holdelse** maintenance.

opprettstående upright; **— piano** upright piano, cabinet-piano.

opprevet (fig) harrowed; (om nerver) shattered, torn. Eks.: my nerves are on edge, in rags.

opprktig sincere, candid; **— talt** candidly, to tell the truth. **oppriktighet** sincerity, candour.

opprinne spring, dawn, open, arise; **den dag -r aldri** that day will never come.

opprinnelig original, pristine, primitive, primeval, primary; (adv) originally.

opprinnelighet primariness, primitiveness.

opprinnelse origin.

opprinnelsessertifikat certificate of origin.

oppring(n)ing (i telefon) call.

opprivende disrupting, tearing, harrowing.

opprop call; (fig) appeal.

opproper (ogs. v. auksjon) caller.

opprulle, se rulle opp.

opprydding clearing, clearance.

opprykking plucking out, pulling up; rooting out.

opprykning promotion.

opprømt cheerful, gay, in good humour el. spirits. **opprømthet** cheerfulness.

opprør (uro) uproar; (oppstand) rebellion, sedition, insurrection; (tumult) riot; (mytteri) mutiny, revolt; (i sinnet) agitation, excitement, tumult; **gjøre — revolt,** rebel; **få i stand et — stir** up a revolt.

opprør|e excite, rouse, stir up, agitate; (forarge) offend, shock; **-ende** shocking, revolting, outrageous.

opprører rebel, insurgent.

opprørsk rebellious, seditious, mutinous.

opprørskhet rebelliousness, seditiousness.

opprørslov riot act.

opprørt (om havet) rough, agitated; (fig) shocked, revolted.

opprådd at a loss, perplexed.

oppsalt ready saddled. **oppsaling** saddling.

oppsamling collection, accumulation, storage.

oppsang song, singing out, chorus-cry.

oppsats stand; (skriftl.) se **oppsett.**

oppsatt på bent upon, intent on.

oppseiling sailing up; **under — sailing** up.

oppsende, se sende opp; (bønn) offer up.

oppsetsig refractory, stubborn.

oppsetsighet refractoriness, insubordination.

oppsett (i avis o. l.) paper, article.

oppsette (skriftl.) put down, write, pen, compose, draw (out); (utsette) put off, defer, postpone, procrastinate; **— et bønnskrift** draw up a petition; **oppsatt hår** hair done up high.

oppsettelse postponement, delay, procrastination.

oppsi (leier, leilighet) give notice to quit; (frasi seg) renounce, throw off; (traktat) denounce (the end of); **— en kapital** recall a capital; **— sin tjeneste** give notice (of leaving); **bli oppsagt** get notice to quit.

oppsigelig terminable; (obligasjon) redeemable; (om funksjonær) removable.

oppsigelse warning, notice to quit; denunciation; **en måneds** — a month's notice; **uten** — without giving notice.
oppsigelsestid length of notice.
oppsikt sensation, noise, stir; **gjøre, vekke** — make a sensation, a noise. Se **oppsyn.**
oppsiktsvekkende sensational.
oppsitter freeholder, owner.
oppskak|ende flurrying, perturbing. **-et** flurried, perturbed.
oppskjær meat in slices.
oppskjæring cutting, shredding, slicing.
oppskjørtet with skirts kilted up; (fig) very busy, in a bustle.
oppskremt roused, started, alarmed, startled.
oppskrift recipe, receipt; copy; — **på en omelett** recipe for an omelette.
oppskrubbet grazed, abraded.
oppskrudd: — **pris** exorbitant el. extortionate price.
oppskrytt overpraised, puffed.
oppskylling washing up.
oppskylt washed up; washed ashore; — **land** alluvial soil.
oppslag (på klesplagg) cuff, facing(s), lapel; (plakat) bill, placard; (av forlovelse) rupture, breaking off.
oppslagsbok book of reference.
oppslagstavle notice board.
oppsluke swallow up, engulf.
oppslå, se slå opp. — **sin bolig fix** one's residence; **-tt krage** turned up collar; **med -tt paraply** with his umbrella spread.
oppsnappe snatch, pick up; (fig) catch; (brev) intercept.
oppspart: -e penger savings.
oppspedd diluted, thinned; (m. vann) watered.
oppspilt distended; (fig) in high spirits. **med —gap** with jaws distended. **med -e øyne** wide -eyed.
oppspinn invention, device, fabrication.
oppspore track out, trace out, scent out.
oppspurt spurt at the finish.
oppspytt phlegm, expectorations.
oppspørre find out, inquire out.
oppstalle stable, stall, keep.
oppstand insurrection, rising; **gjøre — rise** (in rebellion), rebel, revolt; **deltager i** — insurgent.
oppstandelse (fra de døde) resurrection; (røre) excitement, hubbub, stir.
oppstander scaffolding pole, upright.
oppstaset dressed up.
oppstemt (i godt humør) in high spirits.
oppstigende ascending.
oppstigning ascension, ascent, rise.
oppstille set up, put up; arrange, form; se ogs. **stille opp:** — **i regel** lay down a rule; — **som et eksempel** instance as an example.
oppstilling setting up, putting up; arrangement, disposition; fitting; setting; drawing up; stationing; (om soldater) falling in.
oppstiver, se oppstrammer.
oppstoppernese pug-nose, upturned nose.
oppstrammer nerver, tonic, pick(-me)-up; (skarp tiltale) rating, talking-to.
oppstrøk up-stroke; (musikk) up-bow.
oppstuss hubbub.
oppstyltet stilted, on stilts.
oppstyr disturbance, pother.
oppstøt eructation (from the stomach).
oppstøve ferret out, hunt up el. out.
oppstå rise, come up, come into existence; **sekter -r** sects spring up; **det oppstod en trette** a quarrel arose; — **fra de døde** arise.
oppstående rising, prominent. — **snipper** stick-up, stand up el. standing collars.
oppsuge suck up, absorb.
oppsummere sum up.
oppsummering summary.
oppsving rise; increase; improvement.
oppsvulm|et swelled, swoln. **-ing** swelling.

oppsydd sewn up; **-e klær** ready made clothes.
oppsyn inspection, superintendence, charge; supervision. **ha** — **med** look after, superintend, have charge of; (dt. ansikt) phiz. **jeg liker ikke -et på ham** I don't like the cut of him.
oppsyns|fartøy vessel in charge; fishery protection vessel. **-havende** superintending, in charge. **-mann** inspector, superintendent, overseer, supervisor.
oppsøke seek out, find out, look out, search out.
oppta (tid, oppmerksomhet) take up, engross, occupy; (f. eks. i en bok) embody; (i seg) admit, receive; (forslag) advocate; — **forhør over en** examine a person; — **et lån** make el. raise a loan; — **et fremmed ord, en ny mote** adopt a foreign word, a new fashion; — **som en fornærmelse** take (el. look upon) as an insult; — **som medlem** admit as a member; **opptatt: plassen er** — the seat is occupied, engaged; **få** — (i tidsskrift etc.) obtain publication for; **bli** — (i avis) appear; **jeg er svært** — I am very busy; **min sterkt opptatte tid** press of business; **svært** — **av** full of; **saken er** — **til doms** the record is closed.
opptagelse taking up, recovery; admission, reception; adoption.
opptagelsesprøve examination for admission, entrance examination.
opptakt rise, arsis.
opptegne note down, set down, record.
opptegnelse note, memorandum, jotting, record.
opptelling adding up; enumeration.
opptenkelig imaginable, conceivable.
opptog procession, pageant, show.
opptre(de) appear, come forward, come upon the scene, make one's appearance; act; — **for** appear el. act in behalf of, take one's part; — **i en rolle** play el. bear a part; — **for første gang** (på scenen) make one's first appearance.
opptreden appearance; (vesen) deportment, demeanour; (handlemåte) course of action, manner of proceeding.
opptrekkende: et — **uvær** a storm that is brewing.
opptrek|ker swindler, cheat, sharper. **-keri** swindling, swindle, cheating, extortion.
opptrevlet unravelled. **opptrevling** unravelling.
opptrin scene, spectacle, episode.
opptrykk impression, reprint. **-e** reprint.
opptråkket well-trodden.
opptukt|else, -ing disciplining, discipline, tutoring, training.
opptur journey up; (til sjøs) passage up; (dt.) uptrip.
opptøyer disorders, row, riot.
opptårne pile up, heap.
oppunder up under.
oppvakt intelligent, quick-witted, clever.
oppvakthet intelligence, smartness.
oppvarde cairn out el. up.
oppvarme warm, heat; (om mat) warm up, re-cook. **oppvarming** warming etc.
oppvarte wait upon el. on, attend; (besøke) wait upon el. on; — **ved bordet** wait el. attend at table; — **en med** regale one with; treat one to; **en -nde kammerherre** a chamberlain in waiting.
oppvarter waiter.
oppvartning waiting, attendance; **gjøre sin** — **hos en** wait on one, pay one's respects to one, do homage to one.
oppvartningspike waitress, waiting woman.
oppvask washing up.
oppvask|balj(e) dish tub. **-pike** scullery maid. **-klut** dish-cloth.
oppveie balance, counter-balance, out-balance, outweigh, compensate for; — **noe med gull** pay st. with its weight in gold.
oppvekke, se vekke. — **fra de døde** raise from death.
oppvekkelse: — **fra de døde** resuscitation.

oppvekst growth; **i min** — in my youth.
oppvigl|e stir el. work up. **— til voldshandlinger** instigate acts of violence. **-er** mischief-maker, demagogue, instigator. **-eri** instigation, mischief -making. **-ersk** incendiary, instigating.
oppvise show, exhibit.
oppvisning display.
oppvoksende: den — **slekt, ungdom** the growing el. rising generation.
oppvåkning awakening, wakening up.
opp|øve exercise, train, drill. **-øvelse** exercise, training.
oppå on, upon.
optiker optician. **optikk** optics (pl).
optikus, se **optiker.**
optim|isme optimism. **-ist** optimist. **-istisk** optimist, optimistic.
optisk optical; — **bedrag** optical delusion. **or** (tre) alder.
orakel oracle. **-messig** oracular.
orakelspråk oracle, oracular saying.
orangutang orangoutang.
Orania Orange.
oransje orange. **-gul** orange, orange-coloured. **-lund** orange-grove. **-ri** orangery. **-skog** orangewood. **-tre** orange (-tree).
oratorisk oratorical.
oratorium (musikk) oratorio.
ord word, term, expression; (glose) vocable; **-et** (bibelsk) the Word; **et** — **er et** — **og en mann er en mann** man's word, man's honour; **det ene** — **tok det andre** one word brought on the other; **gi en gode** — speak one fair; **et godt** — **finner et godt sted** a good word always tells; **tomme** — vain words; **for gode** — **og betaling** for love or money; **med ett** — in a word; **med andre** — in other words; **med rene** — roundly, in so many words; — **til annet,** — **for** — word for word, verbatim; **be om -et, forlange -et** request leave to speak; **-et er fritt** the meeting is open for remarks; **føre -et** be the spokesman; **gå fra sitt** — not to stand to one's word; **jeg har gitt ham mitt** — **på det** I have given him my word on it; **gi -et til en** allow to speak; **ha, få** — **for** have, get the reputation of; **ha -et** have the right to speak; **holde sitt** — be as good as one's word, keep one's word; **legge et** (godt) — **inn for en** speak a word in one's favour, say a word for one; **ta -et** rise and speak; **ta til** — **e** commence speaking; **ta en på -et** take one at his word; **De kan tro meg på mitt** — you may take my word for it.
ord|betydning literal signification. **-bok** dictionary. **-boksforfatter** dictionary-maker, lexicographer. **-bøyning** inflection. **-dannelse** formation of words.
orde (vrb) introduce (the subject of), divert to. — **om** mention.
I. **orden** order; **etter** — in order, one after another; **for -s skyld** for regularity's sake; **i** — in order, right; **ikke i** — not in order, not right; **få** — **på, bringe i** — put in order, set right, put to rights, adjust, arrange; **er gått i** — is settled, arranged, all right; **i en** — right, fitting; **kalle til** — call to order; **hører til dagens** — is of every day occurrence; **utenfor -en** out of the ordinary course.
II. **orden** (ridderorden osv) order; **bli opptatt i en** — be admitted el. received into an order. **dele ut -er** confer honours.
ordens|bror brother of a religious order. **-bånd** ribbon. **-drakt** habit of an order. **-insignier** insignia el. badges of an order. **-kapitel** chapter of an order. **-kjede** collar el. chain of an order. **-løfte** vows of an order. **-mann** monitor. **-marsjal** steward; sergeant-at-arms. **-menneske** person of orderly el. regular habits. **-politi** constabulary, police force on beat. **-regel** rule el. statute of an order. **-sans** sense of order. **-tall** ordinal number. **-tegn** badge. **-vesen** honours system; system of religious orders.

ordentlig orderly, proper, regular, regulated; (adv) properly, regularly; — **behandling** honest treatment; **det brenner ikke** — it does not burn properly; **være** — **kledd** be decently dressed.
ordflom torrent of words.
ordforklaring verbal explanation.
ord|forråd vocabulary. **-føyningslære** syntax.
ordfører spokesman; chairman; exponent.
ordgyter great talker el. chatterer.
ordgyteri wordiness, verbosity, verbiage.
ordholden true to one's word, as good as one's word.
ordholdenhet adherence to one's word, trustworthiness.
ordinand candidate for orders.
ordinasjon ordaining, ordination.
ordiner|e ordain; (om lege) prescribe; **la seg** —, **bli -t** take orders, enter into orders; **-t** in (holy) orders.
ordinær (normal) ordinary; (simpel) common, inferior, vulgar. **-t medlem av en forening** ordinary member of a society. — **professor** professor in ordinary.
ordklasse part of speech.
ord|kløver hair-splitter. **-kløveri** hair-splitting.
ordknapp chary of words, taciturn.
ordknapphet chariness of words, taciturnity.
ordlyd verbal sound; (uttrykksmåte) wording; **etter –en** literally.
ordlydende literal; (adv) literally, verbatim.
ordne order, regulate, adjust, arrange, sort, put in order; (i militærspråket) draw up, array; (i klasser) class, distribute.
ordning ordering, arrangement, adjustment.
ordonnans orderly.
ordre order, orders; **etter** — by order; — **på** order for; **til** — **av N.** to the order of N., order N.; **til N. eller** — to N. or his order.
ordreblankett order-form, order-sheet.
ordrebok order-book.
ordrekke series of words.
ord|rett literal, verbatim. **-rik** rich, copious of language; (vidløftig) verbose, wordy. **-rikdom** richness of language.
ord|samling vocabulary. **-skifte** exchange of words, argument, debate. **-skvalder** blustering talk, verbiage. **-spill** pun, quibble, play on words. **-språk** proverb, adage. **-språksle(i)k** acting charades.
ord|stilling position of (the) words, phraseology. **-strid** altercation, dispute, argument. **-strøm** torrent of words. **-styrer** chairman. **-tak, -tøke** phrase, turn of phrase; adage. **-valg** choice of words. **-veksel** altercation.
ore|kratt alder-clump. **-tre** alder tree.
organ (del av legemet, stemme, avis) organ; (taleorgan) organ of speech; **han har et vakkert** — he has a fine organ.
organisasjon organization.
organisasjons|omkostninger expenses for organization. **-talent** organizing powers.
organisator organizer.
organisatorisk organizing (evne: capacity).
organisere organize.
organisk organic; — **kjemi** organic chemistry.
organisme organism.
organist organist.
orgel organ. **-pipe** organ-pipe.
orgelpulpitur organ-loft.
orgel|punkt organ-point. **-spill** playing on the organ. **-spiller** organ-player. **-verk** organ.
orgie orgy.
orient|aler, -alerinne Oriental. **-alist** orientalist, Oriental scholar. **-alsk** Oriental, Eastern.
Orienten the East, the Orient.
orientere set right, orient, orientate; — **seg** take the bearings, find one's bearings; **han kunne ikke** — **seg** he could not make out where he was, he had lost the bearings.
orientering orientation. **-sevne** power of o.

original original; novel; (egen) eccentric; **en original** (person) an original, a character, an eccentric.
originalitet originality.
Orions belte the belt of Orion.
orkan hurricane. **orkanaktig** hurricane-like.
orke (vrb) be able to, be capable of, be good for; **hun spiste til hun ikke -t mere** she ate till she could eat no more.
orke (subst) labours, work; **det er et helt —** it's a great business.
orkester orchestra, orchester, band. **–dirigent** conductor of an orchestra; (militær) band -master.
orkestermusikk orchestral music.
orkidé orchid.
Orknøy|ene the Orkneys, the Orkney Islands. **o–ing** Orkneyman.
orlog (gmlt.) war, warfare; (sjøkrigstjeneste) sea-service.
orlogs|flagg naval flag. **–kaptein** Captain in the Royal Navy. **–mann** man-of-war. **–tjeneste** seaservice, naval service, service in the navy. Se ogs. **marine.**
orlov furlough, leave of absence; **han har —** he is absent on leave.
orm worm, (slange) snake.
orme|bol snake's nest, nest of vipers. **–gras** fern. **–ham** slough, cast-off skin of a snake. **–pulver** worm-powder. **–topper** worm-lozenges.
ormunge young snake.
orna|ment ornament. **–mentere** ornament.
ornamentering ornamentation.
ornamentikk ornamentics, ornamenting art.
ornat robe; (fullt geistlig) canonicals(pl);(katolsk messedrakt) vestment; (prestekjole) cassock, gown.
ornito|log ornithologist. **–logi** ornithology.
ornitologisk ornithologic(al).
orr|e black cock, heath cock. **–fugl** black grouse; (koll.) black game. **–hane, se orre. –høne** grey hen, heath hen.
ortodoks orthodox. **ortodoksi** orthodoxy.
ortografi orthography.
ortografisk orthographic, orthographical.
ortopedi orthopedy, orthopraxy.
ortopedisk orthopedic.
I. **os** (røyk, damp) smoke (of lamps, candles).
II. **os** (elveos) mouth of a river, outlet.
ose smoke; (om lampe) burn black.
osean ocean. **–damper** ocean-going steamer.
oske, se aske.
Oskoreia Arthur's chase.
Oslo Oslo.
oson ozone. **–holdig** ozonic. **–holdighet** amount of ozone.
osp asp, aspen, asp-tree.
oss us; (refleksivt) ourselves; **han forsvarer —** he defends us; **vi forsvarer —** we defend ourselves; **en venn av —** a friend of ours.
ost (øst) East; **O. til N. E. by N.**
ost cheese; **lage —** make cheese.
ostaktig caseous, cheese-like, cheesy.
oste seg coagulate, curdle.
oste|butikk cheese-shop. **–form** cheese hoop el. mould. **–handel** cheese-trade; (butikk) cheese -shop. **–handler** cheese-monger. **–klokke** cheese -cover. **–løype, se løype.**
ostentasjon ostentation, parade.
osteprøver searcher, pale, cheese-scoop.
oste|skorpe cheese-paring, rind of cheese. **–snei** cheese-paring. **–stoff** caseine.
Ost|india India, the East Indies. **ostindia- farer** (East-) Indiaman. **–indier** East-Indian. **ostindisk** East-Indian. **Det -e kompani** the East India company.
ost|nordost East North East. **–sydost** East South East.
ostrakisme ostracism.
osv. (fork. f. og så videre), and so forth, etc.
oter otter; (fiskeredskap) (fishing) otter, beam (el. otter) trawl. **–skinn** otter-skin.

otium leisure.
I. **otte** (tidlig morgen) early morning.
II. **otte** (frykt) fear.
ottesang matins, matinsong.
ottoman Ottoman. **–sk** Ottoman.
outrere exaggerate, overdo.
outrigger outrigger.
outsider outsider.
ouverture overture.
ova–, se oven–.
oval (adj) oval. **oval** (subst) oval.
ovarium ovary.
ovasjon ovation.
oven (el. ova) above; (adv) **— i kjøpet** into the bargain, to boot, too; (prep); **— vanne** above water; **— senge** out of bed.
oven|anført above mentioned. **–bords: —** skade damage to the topsides el. upper works. **-for** (adv) above, higher up, farther up; (prep) above. **–fra** from above, from the top; from on high.
oven|nevnt above-mentioned. **–om** round about. **–på** (prep) on, upon; (adv) on the top; **–på omnibussen** on the top of the omnibus; **han er ovenpå** (i en høyere etasje) he is upstairs; (fig) he has the best of it; he is all right.
oven|stående the above, the foregoing; the premises; (adv) above. **–til** above, at the top.
I. **over** (prep) over; **— hele byen** all over the town, all the town over; **han skalv — hele legemet** he trembled all over; (høyere enn, mer enn) above; **han er — 70** he is above 70 el. upwards of 70; (på den andre siden av noe) across; **jeg så ham gå — gata** I saw him cross the street el. go across the street; **— all måte** beyond measure; **det går — min forstand** that's beyond my reach; **han reiste — A. til B.** he went by the way of A. to B.; **han reiste — London** he went via London, by way of London; **reise — land** go (el. travel) by land; **— middag** past noon; **klokka er — to** it is past two (o'clock); **et kart — Norge** a map of Norway; **få hevn — en** be revenged on one; **ønske godt, vondt — en** wish blessing, curses upon one; **henrykt — delighted at; anger — remorse for; arbeide — tiden** work over-time; **snakke — seg** rave; **naturen går — opptuktelsen** nature passes nurture; **what is bred in the bone won't go out of the flesh; vinteren — throughout the winter; det går ut — ham** he is in for it.
II. **over** (adv); **gå — til** go across to; **se snart — til oss** you'll soon come (round) and see us; **brekke — break in two; skjære, klippe — cut through; springe — et ord** skip a word; **uværet drev — the storm blew over.
overall (arbeidstøy) overall.
overalt everywhere, in every place; **— i verden** in all parts of the world, all over the world.
overanfører commander in chief.
overan|strenge overwork, over-exert, over-strain. **–strengelse** overworking; overwork, over -exertion. **–strengt** overwork, overworked.
overarm upper part of the arm.
overbalanse: ta — overbalance oneself; en — av a balance to the good of.
overbefaling chief command.
overbefolket over-populated.
overbefolkning excess of population.
overbestyrer head manager.
overbevise (få til å tro) convince (om: of); (felle for retten) convict. Eksempler: The prisoner convinced the court of his innocence; the prisoner was convicted of murder; **— en om det motsatte** convince one to the contrary **-nde** convincing, cogent.
overbevisning conviction; persuasion.
overbibliotekar principal librarian.
overbitt protrusion of the upper jaw.
overblikk view, prospect, general oversight.

over bord overboard; **gå —** go òverboard.
overbredsel (upper) bedclothes, blanket.
overbringe bring. **overbringer** bearer.
overbud outbidding, higher bid.
overby outbid, overbid.
overbygge cover (in).
overbygning covering(-in).
overbærende indulgent, lenient (**med:** to).
overbærenhet indulgence, forbearance.
overdekk upper deck.
overdel upper part.
overdenge load, heap upon.
overdommer chief justice.
overdomstol superior tribunal.
overdra make over, transfer; (myndighet) delegate; (fast eiendom) convey; (gi som verv) charge with, commission, entrust to el. with.
overdragelse making over, transfer, transference, delegation, conveyance, charging etc.
overdragelsesdokument (deed of) conveyance.
overdreven exaggerated, carried to excess; **-t forlangende** exorbitant claim; **— pris** exorbitant price; **— beskjedenhet** excessive el. extreme modesty; **— samvittighetsfullhet** over-conscientiousness; **det er visst overdrevet** that, surely, is exaggerated; **-t engstelig** overanxious.
overdrive exaggerate, overdo; overstate.
overdrivelse exaggeration, overdoing; overstatement; **forsiktig inntil —** cautious to a fault.
overdyne feather bed.
overdøve drown, stifle, overnoise; **— sin samvittighet** stifle the voice of one's conscience.
overdådig luxurious. **overdådighet** luxury.
overeksponert (om bilde) over-exposed.
over ende topsy-turvy; **falle —** fall el. drop down; **kaste en —** throw one down, floor one.
overens: stemme — agree, accord, harmonize; **ikke stemme —** disagree; **komme — om** agree on, come to an agreement upon.
overenskomst agreement, accord, compromise, concert; (med kreditorer) composition; **slutte el. treffe en —** make an agreement; **etter felles —** by mutual consent el. accord.
overensstemmelse accord, accordance, conformity; **i — med** in accordance with.
overensstemmende med in accordance with, consistent with, consonant to; (adv) agreeably to, conformably to.
overerme half-sleeve.
overernære over-feed.
overfall assault.
overfalle fall upon, assault, assail, attack.
overfallsmann assailant, assaulter.
overfart passage, run; crossing.
overfladisk superficial, shallow. **-het** superficiality, shallowness.
overflate surface.
overflod abundance, plenty.
overflytte transfer.
overflødig superfluous, abundant, superabundant, plentiful, copious; (adv) superfluously etc.
overflødighet abundance, superabundance, plenty, profusion, surplus.
overflødighetshorn cornucopia, horn of plenty.
overfløye leave behind, distance, outstrip.
overfor (prep) opposite, over against; (fig) in the face of; in the case of; **— hverandre** face to face, facing each other, **overfor** (adv) opposite.
overforfinelse over-refinement.
overforfinet over-refined.
overformynder public trustee.
overformynderi public trustee office.
overfrakk great-coat, over-coat.
overfuse abuse, load with abuse.
overfylle overcrowd, overfill.
overfylt overfilled, overfull, overcrowded; **markedet er —** the market is glutted.
overfølsom over-sensitive.
over|føre carry over, convey over, bring over, transport, transfer; **-ført** metaphorical, figurative, (regnsk.) brought forward.

overføring transport, carriage, conveyance.
overgang going el. passing over, crossing; (stedet) passage, crossing, stepping-stone; (til fiende) desertion; (fra en toneart, tilstand til en annen) transition; (stemmens), se **stemmeskifte.**
overgangs- transition, connecting.
overgangsalderen the age of puberty.
overgangsbillett transfer-ticket; (dt.) transfer.
overgangstilstand transitional state.
overgeneral commander in chief.
overgi deliver (over), hand over, consign; (en by) surrender; **— seg** surrender.
overgivelse (av en by) surrender; (overlevering) delivery.
overgiven frolicsome, merry (to excess), in uncontrollable spirits.
overgivenhet exuberant mirth, frolicsomeness.
overgjær surface-yeast.
overgjæring surface fermentation.
overgrep encroachment.
overgrodd overgrown, overrun.
overgyte pour upon, infuse.
overgå exceed, be in excess of, excel, out-do, outgo, outstrip, surpass, transcend.
overhaling overhauling; (fig) blow-up.
overhendig excessive; tremendous, violent; **— sjø** an overgrown sea; **— vær** tremendous weather.
over|heng importunity. **-henge** importune.
overhengende projecting; (truende) impending, imminent.
overherre lord paramount, liege lord.
overherredømme supremacy, sway.
overhode (supreme) head, chief.
overhodet (adv) upon the whole, after all, generally, altogether.
overhoffmarskalk Chief Marshal of the Household. **-embetet** office of the Chief Marshal of the Household.
overhoffmester Steward of the Household.
overhoffmesterinne first Lady of Honour.
overholde keep. **overholdelse** keeping.
overhud cuticle, epidermis.
Overhuset (i det engelske parlament) the Upper House, the House of Lords, the Lords.
overhølje deluge, overwhelm.
overhøre (eksaminere) examine, catechize; (ikke høre) miss, not hear; (late uenset) ignore; **jeg har overhørt det ordet** I did not hear that word, that word escaped me.
overhørig (jur.) contumacious. **sitte —** not to comply with.
overhørighet (jur.) contumacy.
overhøring (eksaminasjon) catechising, examination.
overhøvle plain (over); (fig) dress down.
overhøyhet, se **overherredømme.**
overhånd upper hand, ascendancy, prevalence, predominance; **få — over** prevail over, get the better of. **ta — (om noe vondt)** gain head, be rampant.
overhåndtagende growing, spreading, prevailing, rampant.
overilelse precipitation, precipitance, precipitancy, overhastiness.
overilt rash, precipitate, overhasty; (adv) precipitately.
overingeniør chief engineer.
overjordisk unearthly, superhuman.
overkammerherre Lord Chamberlain of the Household.
overkanonér chief gunner.
overkant upper side, top; upper edge.
overkelner head-waiter.
overkirurg head-surgeon.
overkjeve upper jaw.
overkjørsel passage for carriages; (ulykke) case of running over.
overkjørt run over.
overklasse governing class, upper classes.

overkokk chef, head-cook, master-cook.
overkommando chief command.
overkomme (be able to) manage, be equal to; (en pris) afford. **vi hadde mer å gjøre enn vi kunne** — we had more on our hands than we could attend to.
overkommelig practicable, surmountable, bearable.
overkomplett supernumerary.
overkonstabel (i politiet) police sergeant.
over kors crossly, crosswise; **med armene** — with arms crossed, cross-armed; **med bena** — cross-legged.
overkropp upper part of the body, bust.
overladning (elektrisk) overcharging.
overlag (subst) overlay; coat, lining; (tynt) wash.
overlag (adv) exceedingly, excessively.
overlagt (adj) deliberate, studied; intentional; wilful; — **mord** wilful murder.
overlast molestation, injury.
overlate leave, deliver up; (avse) spare; (selge) sell.
overledelse chief direction; (hovedkvarter) headquarters.
overlege chief physician, head doctor; (på skip) master-surgeon; **-n ved hospitalet** the Senior Physician of (el. to) the hospital.
overlegen superior; masterful; (i vesen) supercilious, patronizing; **være en** — be superior to one.
overlegenhet superiority.
overlegg premeditation, reflection; **med** — deliberately el. with premeditation.
overlegning deliberation, conference, discussion.
over|lepe (-leppe, -lippe) upper lip.
over|lesse overburden, overload; (fig) overcharge. **-lessing** overloading, overburdening; (på skolen) over-pressure.
over|leve survive, outlive. **-levende** surviving.
overlevelsesrente reversion, reversionary annuity.
overlevere deliver, hand, present, surrender; **det overleverte** the traditions. **overlevering** delivering, delivery, surrender; transmission, tradition.
overligge (mar) stay. **-dag** day on demurrage, extra lay-day. **-dagspenger** demurrage.
overliste over-reach, dupe, outwit.
overlos head-pilot.
overlys top light.
overlytt loudly, with (el. in) a loud voice.
overlær upper leather, vamp.
overlærer principal teacher, head-master.
overløper deserter, runaway.
overløping (til fienden) desertion.
overmakt superior force; superiority; upper hand, mastery.
overmann superior; **han fant sin** — he found his match; **mine overmenn** my superiors, my betters.
overmanne overpower, bear down.
overmektig predominant.
overmenneske superman.
overmenneskelig superhuman.
over|mett surfeited, glutted, cloyed; **spise seg** — surfeit, overcloy, overgorge oneself. **-metthet, -mettelse** surfeit.
overmoden over-ripe, too ripe.
overmodenhet overripeness.
overmodig presumptuous, arrogant, insolent, overweening. **-het, se overmot.**
overmorgen: i — the day after to-morrow.
overmot presumption, arrogance, insolence, overweening pride.
overmunn upper jaw.
overmål superabundance, excess. **til** — to (in) excess.
overmåte exceedingly, extremely.
overnatt|e put up for the night. **-ing** stoppage for the night.

overnaturlig preternatural, supernatural.
overoppsyn superintendence, chief direction, control; **føre** — med superintend.
overordentlig (adj.) extraordinary; (adv) extraordinarily, remarkably, exceedingly.
overordnet superior.
overpleierske head nurse.
overproduksjon over-production.
overrabbiner chief rabbi.
overraske surprise, take by surprise; **-t over** surprised at.
overraskelse surprise.
overreise passage.
overrekke hand (over), present, deliver.
overrekkelse handing (over), delivery.
I. **overrenn** (i skibakke) upper run, track before the big jump.
II. **overrenn** (av folk) a perpetual run.
overrenne (renne på dørene) pester with visits.
overrett superior court (of justice).
overretts|assessor judge of a superior court. **-sakfører** barrister of a superior court.
overrisle irrigate. **overrisling** irrigation.
overrumple take by surprise, take one off his guard.
overrumpling surprise.
oversanselig supersensual, supersensible, metaphysical, transcendent, transcendental; **læren om det -e** metaphysics (pl). **-het** transcendentalism, transcendentality.
overse survey, view, have a (full) view of; (ikke se) not notice, pass over, overlook, miss, fail to see el. detect; (se gjennom fingrer med) connive at, wink at; (ringeakte) look down upon, treat superciliously.
oversende despatch over, transmit.
oversendelse despatch, transmission.
oversetig (bot.) superior, epigynous.
oversette translate, turn, render, do (til norsk: into Norwegian); — **med** render by; — **galt** mistranslate.
oversettelse translation, version.
oversetter translator.
overside top.
oversikt survey, general view, account (over: of); **kort** — summary, synopsis, conspectus. **-lig** surveyable; lucid, perspicuous; (kortfattet) summary.
oversitte delay compliance (with); — **fristen** exceed the delay el. time.
oversivilisert over-educated.
oversjøisk oversea, beyond sea.
overskjegg mustache, moustache.
overskjæring cutting, dividing.
overskjønn re-estimation, resurvey.
overskott, se overskudd.
over skrevs astride, strideways.
overskride overstep, surpass, exceed, go el. pass beyond; (om befalinger) transgress. **-lse** overstepping; (av sum) excess.
overskrift heading.
overskudd surplus, excess, balance; profit, margin (of profit), lay-by.
overskue survey, overlook, command, take in at one view. **overskuelig** that may be surveyed; (fig) clear, perspicuous. **i en** — **framtid** within a measurable distance of seeing.
overskuelighet clearness, perspicuity.
overskyet cloudy, overcast.
overskygge over-shade.
overskylle flood, overflow.
overskytende surplus, additional; — **saldo i vår favør** balance remaining due to us.
overslag estimate; **gjøre et** — form an estimate (of).
oversmurt (be)smeared, bedaubed.
over|spent extravagant, eccentric, high-flown, romantic.
overspenthet extravagance, eccentricity.
oversprøyte squirt over; (tilsøle) bespatter.
overstadig jubilant, elated; — **beruset** excessively drunk; — **glad in** extravagant spirits.

overstadighet exuberant spirits.
overstell top, tops.
overstemme (vrb) out-vote; (fig) overrule.
overstemme (subst) upper voice part.
overstemple stamp over; (frimerke) cancel; surcharge.
overstige exceed, surpass, be in excess of.
overstrykning coating, overscoring, scratching.
overstrødd strewn, sprinkled (over). **et bord — med papirer og bøker** a table scattered with papers and books.
overstrøket se under **stryke over, — ut.**
overstrømmende exuberant, profuse.
overstråle outshine, eclipse, outblaze.
overstykke upper piece el. part.
over styr: gå — miscarry, fail, come to nought; sette — waste, spend, squander (away), run through.
overstyre chief management.
overstå overcome, go through, get over el. through.
oversvømme inundate, overflow, flood, deluge; (bare fig) overrun.
oversvømmelse inundation, deluge, overflow.
oversyn surveying; (juridisk) resurvey.
oversøster head nurse.
oversådd strown, sprinkled over (med: with).
overta accept; (et embete) enter upon; (kommandoen) take; (arbeid) undertake, take upon oneself, take charge of.
overtagelse taking possession of; undertaking.
overtak grasp over the arms (in wrestling); fig) upper hand, overhand, advantage.
over|takelse, -ta(k)ing, se **overtagelse.**
overtale persuade, prevail upon el. on.
overtalelse persuasion.
overtalelsesevne persuasiveness.
overtalende persuasive.
overtallig supernumerary, in excess; **en — a supernumerary.**
overtann upper tooth.
overtegne (lån) more than cover, over-subscribe.
overtegning over-subscription; **i tilfelle av — if more shares are subscribed for than can be supplied.**
overtid over-hours, over-time; **arbeide på — work overtime. overtidsarbeid** overtime work, extra-work, work after hours.
overtilsyn superintendence.
overtollinspektør inspector general of the customs.
overtre(de) transgress, trespass against, contravene, break (through). **overtredelse** transgression; **— av** infringement of.

overtreffe excel.
overtrekk cover, case. **overtrekkserme** half -sleeve.
overtro superstition. **-isk** superstitious.
overtrukket covered, coated; (himmel) overcast.
overtrumfe outdo, cap, distance.
over tvert: bryte — cut the matter short.
overtyde convince (om: of).
overtydning conviction, persuasion.
overtøy overclothing, overwear.
overvann surface water.
overveie weigh, ponder, reflect (upon); **vel -d** well-weighed, judicious; **alt vel -d** all things considered. **dette skritt var ikke vel -d** this was an inconsiderate step.
overveielse weighing, deliberation, reflection; **ta under —** take into consideration, think about, entertain; **ta under fornyet —** reconsider, think better of, review; **etter nærmere — on** consideration, on second thoughts.
overveiende predominant, paramount; **den — del** the great majority; (adv) mainly, chiefly.
overvekt over-weight; (om reisegods) excess baggage; (fig) preponderance; predominance; **ha — over** outweigh; (fig) **få -en** prevail.
overvelde overwhelm, overpower, overcome.
overveldende overwhelming.
oververdenen ideal world, supernal world.
overvettes excessive; (adv) excessively.
overvinne vanquish, conquer, beat, overcome, worst; **— seg til å** prevail on oneself to.
overvinnelse conquest, vanquishment; **med — with** an effort.
overvint|re winter. **-ring** wintering.
overvurdere overrate, overvalue.
overvurdering overvaluation, overestimate.
overvær presence, attendance; **i — av** in the presence of.
overvære be present at, attend, witness.
overvåke superintend, watch over.
overøse med pour upon, pour over; (fig) heap upon, overwhelm with, shower upon.
overøvrighet superior magistracy.
over|årig overaged; superannuated. **-åring** overaged person.
ovn oven; (smelte-) furnace; (kakkelovn) stove; (tørke-, brenne-) kiln. **legge i -en** light el. make a fire (in the stove); **se til -en** mend the fire.
ovnskjerm firescreen.
ovns|krok chimney corner; fireside. **-rør** stove pipe. **-tørket** oven-dried, kiln-dried. **-varme** stove heat.

P

P, p P, p.
p. fork. f. **pagina** page; **pund** lb; pound, **på** on.
pst. fork. f. **prosent** percent.
p. t. fork. f. **pro tempore** pro tem.
pace pace.
pacer pacer.
padde toad.
padle paddle.
paff! bang! puff!
pagai paddle.
pagaie (vrb) paddle.
pagi|na page. **-nere** page. **-nering** paging.
pagode (indisk tempel) pagoda.
pakettbåt packet, packet-boat, liner.
pakk (pøbel) mob; low set (of people).
pakk|bu warehouse. **-duk** (strie) packcloth, packing-canvas.
I. pakke (vrb) pack. **— opp, ut** unpack; **— inn** pack up. **— seg inn** muffle el. wrap oneself up.

II. pakke: — seg take oneself off, make off, decamp, pack (off), go packing; **pakk deg!** get you gone, be gone, go about your business.
pakke (subst) packet, parcel, package.
pakkenelliker traps.
pakkepost parcel post, heavy mail.
pakkesel pack-ass, sumpter.
pakk|gods packed goods. **-hus** warehouse, storehouse; **lagre i —** warehouse. **-husmann** warehouse-man, storehouse-keeper. **-husleie** warehousing charges.
pakkis pack (of) ice, (polar) pack.
pakk|kurv hamper. **-mester** pack-master.
pakk|papir packing-paper, brown paper. **-vogn** luggage-waggon; van.
pakning packing, stuffing.
pakt covenant, confederacy, confederation, alliance; **inngå, opprette en — med** make a covenant el. an alliance with one, enter into a

confederation with one; **P-ens ark** the arc of the covenant.
pal (mar) pawl; hive — heave pawl; (fig) **sitte** — be at a deadlock.
palankin (indisk bærestol) palanquin.
palass palace. **palassaktig** palatial.
palatal palatal.
palaver (snakk) palaver.
pale (småsei) billard, young coalfish.
palé palace.
paleografi (studium av gamle håndskrifter) palaeography.
paleontologi (forsteiningslære) palaeontology.
Palestina Palestine.
palett palette, pallet.
palisade palisade.
palisander (black) rosewood.
paljetter spangles.
pall (benk) settle; (forhøyet golv) raised floor; (peishylle) chimney-shelf.
pallask (ryttersverd) broadsword.
palliativ palliative.
palltosk, se **krabbe.**
palme palm, palm-tree; **stå med -r i hendene** come off with flying colours.
palmesøndag Palm Sunday.
Pamfilius: en lykkens — a spoiled child of fortune.
pamflett (smedeskrift) libel; (flyveskrift) pamphlet.
Pan Pan.
panegy|riker panegyrist. **-rikk** panegyric. **-risk** panegyric(al).
panel wainscot. **panele** wainscot.
pangermanis|me pan-Germanism. **-t** pan-Germanist.
panhellenis|me pan-Hellenism. **-t** pan-Hellenist.
panikk panic, scare; **det oppstod** — a panic set in. **panisk** panic; — **skrekk** panic.
I. **panne** (stekepanne) pan.
II. **panne** (ansiktsdel) forehead; (mest poet. og fig) brow, front; **rynke -n** knit the brows, frown.
pannehår (kort forhår, som henger ut over pannen) fringe; (lokk like over pannen) forelock.
pannekake pancake.
panne|lugg, se **-hår.**
pannerynking frown.
panoptikon (vokskabinett) waxwork show, display of ceroplastic art, (det mest kjente i England er «Madame Tussaud's Exhibition»).
panorama panorama; panoramic view.
panser mail, coat of mail; armour(-planting).
panserautomobil armoured car.
panserbåt armoured vessel.
panser|plate plate of mail. **-skip** ironclad.
pansre mail; **den -de neve** the mailed fist.
pant pawn, pledge; (i faste eiendommer) mortgage; (i pantelek) forfeit; **sette i** — pledge, pawn; **håndfått** — pledge, pawn, gage (given in hand); **låne mot** — (låne ut) lend on pledge, (selv låne) borrow on pledge; **sette, gi i** — give in pledge, pledge, pawn; (faste eiendommer) mortgage; **løse et** — redeem a pledge.
pante distrain, seize; **han ble -t for skatt** his goods were distrained for taxes.
pante|bok register of mortgages. **-brev** letter of hypothecation, mortgage, deed of mortgage. **-heftelse** mortgage.
panteisme pantheism. **panteist** pantheist.
panteistisk pantheistic.
pantele(i)k game of forfeits.
pante|låner pawnbroker. **-lånerforretning** pawnbroker's office. **-låneseddel** pawn ticket. **-mann** levier.
panter (dyr) panther.
pante|rett right of the pawnee, right of seizure. **-sikkerhet** mortage-security.
panthaver pledgee, pawnee; mortgagee.
panting distraining, distress, seizing.
pantobligasjon mortgage-bond.

pantomime pantomime, dumb show.
pantsette pawn, pledge, mortgage.
papegøye parrot; **skyte -n** make a lucky hit, strike oil. **-aktig** parrotlike, parrot.
papiljott (curl-)paper, papillote.
papir paper. **-drake** paper-kite. **-fabrikk** paper-manufactory, paper-mill. **-fabrikant** paper -maker. **-fabrikasjon** manufacture of paper. **-forretning** stationery. **-handel** stationery business. **-handler** stationer. **-kniv** paper-knife, paper-cutter. **-korg, -kurv** waste-paper basket. **-masse** paper-pulp. **-penger** paper money. **-pose** paperbag. **-saks** paper-shears.
papisme popery, papistry. **papist** papist.
papistisk papistic(al), popish.
papp pasteboard; (takpapp) tarboard; (kartong) cardboard.
pappa papa, pa.
papp|arbeid pasteboard work. **-bind** boards, boarding. **-eske** pasteboard box. **-kartonnasje** boards. **-masjé** papier maché.
papyrus papyrus (fl. -ri).
par (nødvendig sammenhørende) pair; couple; (i enkelte tilfelle) brace; (noen få) couple, a few, some; **et** — **hansker** a pair of gloves; **et** — **hester** a pair of horses; **et lykkelig** — a happy pair el. couple; **et** — **dråper** a couple of drops; **et elskende** — a loving couple; **et** — **dager** a couple of days, a few days, a day or two; **et** — **bøker** a couple of books, some books; **der var bare et** — **mennesker** there were only very few people; **et** — **ender** a brace of ducks; **et** — **mynder** a brace of greyhounds; **et** — **pistoler** a brace of pistols; **et** — **kopper** a cup and saucer.
parabel parable.
parade parade; (i fektning) parry; (æresbevisning, med sabel) lowering one's sword (to the salute). **-antrekk** full dress. **-marsj** march -past. **-re** parade. **-seng** bed of state. **-uniform** full uniform.
paradis paradise. **hoppe** — play at hopscotch. **-eple** paradise-apple. **-fugl** bird of paradise. **-hopping** hop-scotch.
paradisisk paradisiacal, paradisiac.
paradoks paradox.
paradoksal paradoxical.
paradoksmaker paradox-monger.
parafin paraffine.
parafrase paraphrase.
paragraf paragraph, section.
parallakse parallax.
parallell parallel (med: to).
parallellisere compare, place side by side.
parallellogram parallelogram.
paralyse paralysis. **paralytisk** paralytic.
paranøtt Brazil nut, Paranut.
paraply umbrella; **slå opp en** — put up an umbrella; **slå ned en** — take down an umbrella. **paraply|maker** umbrella-maker. **-stang** umbrella-stick. **-stativ** umbrella-stand.
parasitt parasite. **parasittisk** parasitic(al).
parasoll parasol, sun-shade.
parat ready, in readiness, at hand.
paravane paravane.
parcene the Fates, Destinies, Parcae.
pardong quarter; **gi** — give quarter.
pare pair, match; — **seg, -s** pair, copulate.
parentes parenthesis, round brackets (pl.) **i** — parenthetically; **i** — **bemerket** by the way. **-tegn** sign of a parenthesis. **parentetisk** parenthetic(al).
parere parry, ward off; (adlyde) obey; (vedde) bet, lay a wager.
parerplate guard.
parforse|jakt hunting with hounds; hunt. **-jeger** fox-hunter. **-ritt** ride against time.
parfyme perfume.
parfyme|butikk perfumery. **-handler** perfumer. **parfymere** perfume. **parfymering** perfuming.
parhest horse to match. **-er** match(ed) horses.
pari par; **til** — at par; **i** — at par; **under** —

below par, at a discount; **over** — at a premium, above par.
paria Pariah.
paring copulation. **parings|tid** pairing time.
-valg sexual selection.
Paris Paris; **fra** — Parisian, of Paris.
pariser Parisian. **pariserinne** Parisian lady.
parisisk Parisian.
parisk marmor Parian marble.
park (anlegg) park; (dyre-) deer-park, preserves; (fiske-) pond.
parkering (anbringelse av biler) parking, park.
parkett stalls; (amr) parquet.
parkettgolv parquetry, parquet flooring.
parklegge lay out as an ornamental park.
parla|ment parliament; the house. **-mentarisk** parliamentary. **-mentarisme** parliamentary system. **-mentere** parley, negotiate. **-mentering** parley, negotiaion.
parlaments|beslutning vote of parliament.
-medlem member of parliament, M. P. **-møte** sitting of parliament. **-samling** session. **-valg** parliamentary election.
parlamentær parlementaire.
parlamentærflagg flag of truce.
parlor phrase-book.
parmesan(ost) Parmesan(cheese).
parnass Parnassus.
parodi parody, burlesque. **parodiere** parody.
parodisk parodic(al).
paroksysme paroxysm.
parole parole, pass-word.
parre, se **pare.**
parsell lot (of ground). **parsellere** parcel out.
part part, portion, share; (jur) party; **jeg for min** — for my part I, I for one; **få** — **i** get a share in; **hver av -ene** each party.
partere quarter. **partering** quartering.
parterr pit.
parthaver part-owner.
parti parcel, lot; (konsignert) consignment; (del, stykke) part; (politisk) party, faction; (elever) class; (giftermål) match; (musikk) part; **ta** — join a party, take sides; **ta sitt** — make one's choice; **et** — **sjakk** a game of chess; **et godt** — a good match; **gjøre et dårlig** — throw oneself away.
partiell partial.
partifelle member of the same party.
partigjenger partisan.
partihensyn party consideration.
partikkel particle.
partikulær particular, private.
parti|løs neutral. **-mann** party-man. **-messig** partisan. **-politikk** party politics. **-politisk** party; **med** — **formål** for the purpose of party politics. **-sak** party question.
partisan partisan.
partisipant partner.
partisipp participle.
partisk partial. **partiskhet** partiality.
partispørsmål party question.
parti|stilling position of parties. **-strid** party dispute. **-taing** taking of sides, siding.
partitur score, partition.
partivesen factions. **partivis** in large lots.
partiånd party-spirit.
partout by all means. **-billett** pass.
partsinnlegg (jur) plea made by one of the parties.
parveny upstart, parvenu.
parvis in pairs, in couples.
parykk peruke, wig, periwig. **-blokk** wig-block. **-maker** peruke-maker, periwig- el. wig-maker. **-stil** periwig style, rococo. **-tiden** the rococo age.
pasient patient, sick person, sufferer; **han er** — he is ill.
pasifisere pacify.
pasja pasha, pacha.
pasje page.
pasje|frisyre, -hår bobbed hair.

pasjon passion.
pasjonert impassioned, passionate.
pasjonsblomst passion-flower.
pasjonsskuespill passion-play.
paskvill pasquinade, lampoon.
pasning (prøving av klær) fitting el. trying on.
I. **pass** (reisepass) passport.
II. **pass** (i kortspill): **si** — pass; **jeg sier** — I beg to be excused, I will have none of it.
III. **pass** (fjellpass) pass, passage, defile.
IV. **pass** (tilsyn, pleie) attention, care, looking to; nursing.
V. **pass: til** — apropos, patly; **vel til** — comfortable, (dt.) as fit as a fiddle; **komme til** — come in handy el. pat, come in the very nick.
passabel passable.
passasje passage; (ferdsel) circulation, traffic; **ingen** —! no thoroughfare!
passasjer passenger. **første klasses** — (ombord) cabin-passenger. **annen, tredje klasses** — steerage-passenger. **-båt** passage-boat; passenger steamer. **-frakt** passage-money, fare. **-gods** (passengers') luggage. **-liste** list of p. **-skip** p. ship. **-trafikk** passenger-traffic.
passat trade-wind.
I. **passe** (i kortspill) pass.
II. **passe** fit, adapt; (pleie, vokte) tend; (være passende) be appropriate, be to the purpose; (stemme overens) agree, correspond (with); — **sine forretninger** mind one's business; — **det beleilige øyeblikk** watch the favourable opportunity; — **tiden** be in time; **hatten -r Dem ikke** the hat does not fit you; **det -r meg ikke** it does not suit me; **det -r utmerket** that happens very well; — **for** suit (the case of); — **inn** let in; — **inn i** fit in with; — **med** agree el. tally with; **få noe til å** — **med** square st. with; — **på** take care of, look after; **pass på!** take care! beware! look out! — **sammen** go (well) together; **dette tøyet -r ikke til en kjole** this stuff is not fit for a coat; **nøkkelen -r til låsen** the key fits the lock; **-r til rollen** becomes the character; — **seg** be fit, be fitting, become, be proper, be suitable; — **seg selv** take care of oneself, mind one's own busines; **pass Dem selv!** mind your own business! **passende** becoming, befitting, proper; suitable, convenient; (adv) becomingly, suitably, conveniently.
passelig suitable, convenient, moderate. (adv) suitably etc.; **å, så** —! Well, tolerably so!
passende, se **passe.**
passer (pair of) compasses; dividers. **-bein** branch el. leg of a compass.
passere pass, pass by, pass through; (hende) occur, happen; — **linjen** cross the line el. equator; **passer gata!** go on! **det har aldri passert meg før** it never happened to me before; **det kan til nød** — it will do (for want of better), let it pass; **la** — pass; **passer!** proceed.
passérseddel permit.
pass|gang pace, amble, ambling; **gå** — amble, pace. **-gjenger** pacer, ambler.
passiar (small) talk, gossip, chat; **slå av en** — have a chat.
passiare gossip, talk, chat.
passinnehaver passport-holder.
passiv (adj) passive; unresisting; — **kompanjong** (i firma) silent el. dormant partner.
passiv (lideform) the passive (voice).
passiva (pl. av passivum, gjeldsposter) debts, liabilities.
passivitet passiveness, passivity.
passkontor passport-office.
passpåtegning visa el. visé of passport.
passtvang passport restrictions; **oppheve -en** remove the passport restrictions.
passus passage.
pass|vesen passport-establishment. **-visering** visa of passport, visa-ing, viséing. **-visum** visa, visé.
pasta paste.

pastell pastil, crayon. **-farger** crayons.
pastellmaler painter in crayon el. pastil.
pasteurisere pasteurize.
pasteurisering pasteurization.
pastill pastil, pastille, lozenge.
pastinakk parsnip.
pastor minister; — **B.** the Rev. Mr. B.; **-en** the reverend gentleman.
pastoral pastoral.
pastoralteologi pastoral theology.
pastorat living, parsonage.
patent (adj) unfailing, proof.
patent (subst) patent; (sertifikat) certificate; (åpent brev) letters patent; **ta** — **på** take out a patent for.
patentanmeldelse application for a patent.
patenter|e patent; **-t** patented, registered.
patent|haver patentee. **-kontor** patent-office.
patentlovgivningen the Patent Laws.
patentlås patent lock, safety lock.
pater father.
paternitet paternity, fatherhood, fathership.
patetisk pathetic.
patina patina.
patinere give the appearance of patina.
patologi pathology. **patologisk** pathological.
patos pathos.
patriark patriarch. **patriarkalsk** patriarchal.
patriarkat patriarchate.
patriot patriot. **-isk** patriotic. **-isme** patriotism.
patrisier patrician. **patrisisk** patrician.
I. **patron** (krutthylster) cartridge; **skarp** — ball cartridge; **løs** — blank cartridge.
II. **patron** (skytsherre) patron. **patronat** patronage.
patronhylse cartridge-case.
patrontaske cartridge-box.
patrulje patrol. **-båt** guard-boat.
patruljere patrol. **patruljering** patrol.
patte (subst) nipple, (på dyr) teat, dug, pap; (die) suck; **gi** — suckle, give suck.
patte (vrb) suck.
patte|barn suckling. **-dyr** mammal, mammiferous animal. **-gris** sucking-pig.
pauke kettle-drum; **slå på** — beat the kettledrum. **-slager** kettle-drummer.
Paul Paul. **-ine** Paulina. **paulinsk** Pauline.
paulun pavilion, tent.
Paulus Paul.
pause pause, stop; (musikk) rest.
pausere pause, stop.
pave pope, pontiff, Holy Father; **slåss om -ns skjegg** split straws.
pave|dømme papacy, popedom, Romanism. **-hoff** papal court.
pavelig papal, pontifical. — **bulle** papal bull.
pave|makt papal power. **-mine** lordly air el. mien. **-stol** papal chair. **-sete** papal see. **-valg** election of a pope.
paviljong pavilion.
pd. fork. f. **pund** pound.
pedagog pedagogue, educationist, educator.
pedagogikk pedagogics, pedagogy.
pedagogisk pedagogic(al).
pedal pedal.
pedant pedant. **-eri** pedantry. **-isk** pedantic.
pedell beadle.
peile (mar) set, take a bearing.
peiling bearing; **ta** — **av** take the b. of.
I. **peis** (i dsted) chimney, chimney-place, hearth.
II. **peis** (svepe) cowhide, rawhide.
peise hide, drub; — **på** lay on.
peisestue open-hearth(ed) room el. hall.
peis|hylle chimney-shelf. **-pipe**, se skorsteinspipe.
pek (subst) point of the finger; disservice, bad turn, dodge, trick; **gjøre ham det** — come that dodge on him.
peke point (på: at, to); — **fingrer av** point one's finger) at; — **ut** point out.

peke|finger forefinger, index. **-pinne** pointer.
pekuniær pecuniary. — **erstatning** compensation in money; — **fordel** pecuniary gain.
I. **pel** pole; stake; (stolpe) post; (grunn-) pile; (mindre —) picket.
II. **pel** (glt. mål) half a pint.
pelargonium pelargonium, stork's bill.
pele|bru pile-bridge. **-bygning** pile-building, lake dwelling. **-orm** pile-worm, teredo. **-verk** pile-work, palisade, stockade.
pelikan pelican.
Peloponnes Peloponnese.
pelotong platoon.
pels fur, pelt; (frakk) fur-coat; (pelskåpe) fur-cloak; **få på -en** get a drubbing.
pelsdyr furred animal.
pelsforet fur-lined.
pels|frakk fur-coat. **-handel** fur-trade. **-handler** fur-merchant, furrier. **-hanske** furred glove. **-jeger** trapper. **-kantet** furred. **-kledd** fur-clad; (om dyr ogs.) furry. **-kåpe** fur-cloak. **-støvel** fur-boot. **-verk** furs, peltry, furriery. Se ogs. **skinn** etc.
pemmikan pemmican.
pen handsome, pretty; **en** — **sum** a handsome el. round sum; **det var ikke -t av Dem** that was not well of you; **-t** (adv): **gå nå -t hjem** be good, go home now.
penater Penates, household gods.
pendant pendant.
pendel pendulum.
pendelslag oscillation of a pendulum.
penge|anvisning money-order, check. **-aristokrat** money-prince. **-aristokrati** moneyed aristocracy. **-avpresning** extortion (of hushmoney), black-mail. **-belte** money-belt. **-bidrag** contribution in money. **-bot** pecuniary fine. **-brev** money-letter. **-forhold** monetary el. pecuniary relations, state of the money-market. **-forlegenhet** pecuniary embarrassment, money difficulty. **-forretning** money transaction. **-grisk** greedy, avaricious. **-griskhet** covetousness, avarice. **-hjelp** pecuniary assistance. **-institutt** moneyed institution. **-kasse**, **-kiste** strong-box, strong coffer, (av jern) iron-safe. **-knapphet** dearth of money. **-knipe** money difficulty.
pengekrise financial crisis, money crisis.
pengelens, **pengeløs** moneyless, pennyless, impecunious.
penge|mangel want el. scarcity of money, impecuniosity. **-mann** moneyed man, capitalist. **-marked** money-market. **-nød** pecuniary distress. **-omløp** circulation of money. **-omsetning** money-transaction; circulation of money. **-pose** money-bag. **-puger** miser, hunks, curmudgeon. **-puging** hoarding of money. **-pung** purse.
penger money; **mange** — much money; **rede** — ready money, cash; **falske** — base (el. bad) money; **ikke ha noen** — be out of cash, be short of money; **komme til** — get into money; **leve av sine** — live upon one's income; **tjene** — make money; **det er ingen** — blant folk money is scarce, there is no money stirring; **jeg har ingen** — **på meg** I have no money about me; **gjøre noe i** — turn st. into money; **sette** — **i** invest money in; **gifte seg til** — marry a fortune.
pengesaker money affairs.
penge|seddel note. **-sekk** money-bag. **-sending** remittance of money. **-skap** money-safe, safe. **-skapsfabrikant** safemaker. **-skrin** money-box, cash-box. **-skuff** (i en butikk) till, tiller. **-sorger** pecuniary distress. **-stolt** purse-proud. **-stolthet** purse-pride. **-stykke** piece of money, coin. **-tap** loss of money, pecuniary loss. **-trang** pecuniary distress, scarcity of money. **-transaksjon** money-transaction. **-understøttelse** pecuniary aid. **-utlåner** money-lender. **-utpresning** extortion (of hushmoney). **-velde** plutocracy. **-verd**, **-verdi** value in money. **-vesen** money-matters, matters financial.

penibel painful, distressing.
penn pen; **føre en god** — write well.
pennal pen-case.
penne|feide paper-war. **-fjær** quill. **-holder** pen-holder. **-skaft** pen-handle, pen-holder. **-skisse** pen-and-ink sketch. **-smører** quill-driver. **-splitt** nib of a pen. **-strøk** stroke of the pen. **-tegning** pen-and-ink drawing el. sketch. **-tørker** pen-wiper.
pens (p. jernbanen) points, (amr) switch.
pense shunt, turn the points; switch.
pensel hair-pencil, brush. **-strøk** stroke of a brush el. pencil.
pensjon pension, retiring allowance, (for officerer) half-pay; (kost) board; (skole) boarding school; **ta avskjed med** — retire upon a pension el. upon half-pay.
pensjonat boarding-house. **-skole** boarding-school.
pensjoner|e pension; grant a pension to (one); **-t** pensioned; on half-pay.
pensjonist pensioner, annuitant.
pensjonsalder pensionable age, pension limit.
pensjonsberettiget entitled to a pension.
pensjons|fond, **-kasse** pension fund. **-lov** pensions act. **-rett** right to a pension. **-vesen** matters relative to pensions.
pensjonær (kostgjenger) boarder.
pensle brush; — **en i halsen** brush one's throat.
pensum task, lesson; curriculum.
peon peony.
pepper pepper; **spansk** — Guinea-pepper; **jeg skulle ønske han var der -en gror** I wish he were at Jericho. **pepper|bøsse** pepper-box, pepper-caster, pepper-pot. **-kake** ginger-bread. **-korn** pepper-corn. **-kvern** pepper-quern. **-kysten** the Grain coast. **-mynte** peppermint. **-mynte-sukkertøy** peppermint-drop. **-møy** spinster. **-nøtt** spice-nut, ginger-nut. **-rot** horse-radish.
peppersvenn bachelor.
pepre pepper.
pepsin pepsin. **peptisk** peptic.
Per Peter; — **og Pål** all the world (and his wife), anybody.
per el. **pr.** (merk) by; — **stykke, pund** a piece, a pound; — **dag**, — **mann** per day, per diem, per man; — **Hamburg** via Hamburg; — **damp-skip** by el. per steamer.
perfeksjonere make perfect.
perfekt perfect, famous; (adv) famously.
perfekt|ibel perfectible. **-ibilitet** perfectibility.
perfektum the perfect tense.
perfid perfidious, disingenuous.
perfiditet perfidy.
perforere perforate.
pergament parchment; (fint) vellum.
pergamentaktig parchment-like.
pergamentpapir paper parchment.
pergamentsbind parchment binding.
pergola pergola.
perial (dt.) intoxication; **ha en** — be fuddled, be the worse for liquor.
periferi periphery. **periferisk** peripheric(al).
perikum hypericum.
periode period; (logar.) repetend. **-vis** period-ical; (adv) periodically.
periodisk periodic(al).
periskop periscope.
peristalt|ikk peristalsis. **-isk** peristaltic.
perkusjon percussion.
perle pearl; (av glass osv.) bead; (fig) jewel, treasure, prize.
perle (vrb) sparkle; **svetten -t på hans panne** the sweat stood in beads on his fore-head.
perle|bønne kidney-bean. **-band** string of beads (pearls). **-fisker** pearl-diver, pearl-fisher. **-fiskeri** pearl-fishing, pearl-fishery. **-glans** pearly lustre. **-halsband** pearl-necklace. **-handel** pearl-trade. **-handler** dealer in pearls. **-humør** excellent spirits, the best of humorus. **-høne** Guinea-

fowl el. -hen. **-krans** wreath of pearls. **-løk** pearl onion. **-mor** mother of pearl, nacre. **-mus-ling** pearl-oyster. **-rad** string of pearls el. beads. **-smykke** ornament of pearls. **-snor** string of pearls el. beads. **-stukket** pearl-embroidered. **-venn** intimate friend.
perm board, cover.
permanent permanent; **den -e mellomfolkelige domstol** the permanent court of international justice.
permisjon leave of absence, furlough, (for sykelighet) sick-leave.
permisjoner (bukser) trousers, continuations.
permitter|e furlough, grant leave of absence; **-t on** leave.
perpendik|kel pendulum. **-ulær** perpendicular.
perpleks taken aback.
perrong platform.
pers (dt.) pressure; **måtte til** — be in for it; **nå skal han til** — I'm going to take it out of him.
perse (subst) press.
perse (vrb) press, squeeze; (ved eksamen) screw.
persejern pressing-iron, goose.
perser Persian.
persesylte brawn.
Persia Persia.
persianer(skinn) Persian Astrakhan.
persienne Venetian blind, Venetian, sun-blind, jalousie.
persiflasje quizzing, irony. **persiflere** quizz.
persille parsley; **hakket** — chopped parsley.
persisk Persian.
person person; individual; (i skuespill) actor, character, (pluralis) dramatis personæ, (gram) person; **i egen** — in person; **uten -s anseelse** without respect of persons.
persona: pro — a head.
personale personnel, staff, force, establish-ment.
personalhistorie personal history.
personalia personal history, biographical facts.
personalkunnskap knowledge of individuals.
personasje fellow.
personellkapellan stipendiary curate.
personifikasjon personification.
personifiser|e personify, embody; **han er den -te hederlighet** he is the soul of honour; **den -te høflighet** civility itself.
personifisering personification, embodiment, impersonation.
personlig personal, private, in person; (adv) personally, in person, by bodily presence.
personlighet (egensk.) personality, individua-lity; (person) individual, character, person; (fremragende person) personage; (personlig hen-tydning) personality.
person|takst passenger-tariff. **-tog** passenger-train. **-trafikk** passenger traffic. **-vogn** passenger-car el. carriage.
perspektiv perspective. **-isk** perspective; (adv) perspectively.
perspektivlære science of perspective.
pertentlig precise, finical, prim. **-het** precise-ness, finicality.
Peru Peru, p-aner, p-ansk Peruvian. **p-balsam** balsam of Peru.
pervers perverse, morbid. **-itet** perversity.
pese (puff and) pant.
pesk (Lapp) reindeer cloak.
pessimis|me pessimism **-t** pessimist
pessimistisk pessimist, pessimistic
pest plague, pest, pestilence; **avsky som -en** hate like sin; **sky ham som -en** shun him like a person infected
pestaktig pestilential.
pestbyll plague-sore.
pestfengt infected with the plague.
pestilens pestilence.
pestluft pestilential air.

pest|smitte contagion of the plague. -stank pestilential stench. -tilfelle case of the plague.
petit (typograf.) brevier.
Petrarka Petrarca, Petrarch.
petroleum petroleum, petrol; oil.
petroleumsholdig containing petroleum.
petroleums|omn, -ovn oil stove.
Pfalz the Palatinate. p.-greve Count Palatine.
pianino cottage-piano, cabinet-piano, pianino.
pianist(inne) pianist.
piano (adv. sakte) piano.
piano (subst. klaver) piano, (mindre alm: piano-forte).
pianofabrikant piano-maker.
pianofabrikk manufacture of pianoes.
pianoforte piano, piano-forte.
pianola pianola, piano-player.
piano|skole tutor for the pianoforte, piano-forte primer. -stemmer piano-tuner. -stol music-stool.
pidestall pedestal.
piece piece; (skrift) pamphlet.
pietet piety. pietetsfull reverent.
pietetshensyn: av — from pious considerations.
pietetsløs irreverent.
pie|tisme pietism. -tist pietist.
pietistisk pietistic.
piffpaff! piffpaff, bang.
pigg pike, spike; pinnsvinets -er the quills of the hedge-hog.
pigge spike, prod; (mar.) peak, top; (dt.) — av make off, pack off; — seg fram prod along.
pigget prickly, spiked.
pigg|kjepp, -stav pike-staff. -tråd barbed wire.
piggvar turbot, burt.
pigment pigment.
pikant piquant, pungent, high-flavoured, racy.
pikanteri piquant remark.
piké piqué.
pike girl, maid, lass; (jomfru) maiden; (hus-hjelp) maid (-servant); en -nes Jens a ladies' man. -arbeid maid's work. -barn (motsatt guttebarn) female child, girl child; (ung pike) girl. -dager girlhood. -drakt girl's dress. -jeger wencher. -lønn maid-servant's wages. -navn maiden name, girl's name. -luner girlish whims.
pikert piqued.
pike|skole girl's school; (høyere) ladies' school. -snakk kitchen gossip.
pikespeider girl guide.
piket (spill) piquet.
pikett (vaktpost) picket, outpost.
pike|værelse maid-servant's room. -år girlhood.
pikke tap, rap.
pikkelhue spiked helmet, Prussian helmet.
pikkels pickle.
pikkolo (fløyte) piccolo; (hotellgutt) buttons.
piknik excursion, picnic party.
I. pil (bot.) willow.
II. pil (til bue) arrow, bolt, shaft.
pile hurry, hasten, bolt, speed.
pilegrim pilgrim, palmer. pilegrims|ferd, -gang pilgrimage. -skare party of pilgrims. -stav pilgrim's staff. -vandring pilgrimage.
pile|hekk willow-hedge. -kratt copse of willows. -kvist willow wand.
pile|regn shower of arrows. -skudd arrowshot; (som målsbestemmelse) arrow's flight.
pilk tin-bait, fly-hook, stroke-haul.
pilke fish with a tin-bait, snatch.
pille (vrb), se plukke; — erter shell peas; — med noe busy oneself with a thing; — seg i nesen pick one's nose.
pille (søyle) pillar, column; (i medisin, og fig) pill.
pillert shelled pea.
pilletriller pill-roller.
pilot (v. flyging) pilot.
pilote|re pile. -ring piling; pilework.
pilråtten completely rotten.

pilsener (øl) Pilsener beer.
pimpe topple.
pimpestein pumice, pumice stone.
pinaktig painful. pinaktighet pain.
pine (subst) pain, pang, torture; død og —! by Jove!
pine (vrb) torment, torture.
pine|benk rack; bli lagt på -en be put to the rack. -full tormenting.
ping-pong ping-pong.
pingvin penguin.
pinje stone-pine.
pinlig painful.
pinn (foreldet, nå bare i enkelte uttr.) en — til ens likkiste a nail in one's coffin; det kan du skyte en hvit — etter you may (go) whistle for that.
pinne stick; (i bur) perch; (vagle) roost; (plugg) pin, peg; stå på — for en be at one's beck and call; stiv som en — stiff as a poker.
pinne|stol splinter chair. -ved small-cut faggots.
pinnsvin hedge-hog.
pinse Whitsuntide.
pinsedag Whitsunday; første — Whitsunday; annen — Whit-Monday.
pinseferie Whitsun holidays.
pinse|fest feast of Pentecost. -helg, se pinseferie.
pinsel torture, torment, pang.
pinselilje poetic el. white narcissus.
pinselørdag the Saturday before Whit-Sunday.
pinse|morgen Whitsunday morning. -tid Whitsuntide.
pinsett tweezers, a pair of tweezers.
pinseuke Whitsun-week.
pion peony.
pionér pioneer.
I. pip (sykdom hos høns) pip, gapes.
II. pip (lyd) piping, whistling, fluting, squeaking; (int) peep! pip!
III. pip (på en kjole) pipe, quill.
pip|e (subst) pipe; (soldaterp.) fife; (liten fløyte, damp-) whistle; (til bruk i teat.) cat-call, cat-pipe; kare ut en — unstop a pipe; danse etter en annens — dance as another pipes; -a fikk en annen lyd they all sang another song.
pipe (vrb) pipe, whistle; (klage) whimper, pule, whine; (om kuler osv.) whizz; (om mus) squeak; (om tøy) flute, quill; — ut en skue-spiller hiss a player (off).
pipe|beslag mounting of a tobacco-pipe. -bord pipe-rack (and table). -brann chimney-fire. -hode pipe-bowl. -hylle shelf for tobacco pipes. -konsert hissing. -krage ruff. -legg fluting, quill; ruffles. -leir(e) pipe-clay.
piper piper, fifer; hisser.
pipe|rør pipe-stem. -saks (til legg) egg-iron, gauffering-iron. -spiss mouth-piece, tip. -stilk pipe-stem; (bein) trapsticks, spindle-legs. -strimmel ruche, rucheing.
piple bubble, purl, trickle.
pipp (kvitring) chirp. pippe (kvitre) chirp.
I. pir (liten makrell) spike, young mackerell.
II. pir (utstikkerbrygge) jetty.
pirat pirate.
pirk prod, prodding; se ogs. pirkeri.
pirke poke, prod (i: at); (utføre altfor nøyaktig) friggle, niggle. -ri niggling, niggling thing. pirk|et niggling, pin-pricking. -ing poking etc.
pirre stir; (irritere) irritate, provoke, stimulate; (kildre) tickle.
pirrelig irritable, touchy; gjøre en — fret one's temper.
pirrelighet irritability.
pirringsmiddel stimulant.
piruett pirouette.
pisk whip; (pryl) a flogging, a hiding; (hårpisk) pigtail; være under -en be under one's lash; få av — get a flogging, licking.
piske whip, lash, flog; (egg) beat, whip;

regnet **-r på rutene** the rain patters el. beats against the panes; **som et -t skinn** like winking.
piskesmell smacking el. cracking of a whip.
piskesnert lash.
pisking whipping; flagellation.
piss piss, urine. **-e** piss.
pissoar urinal, lavatory.
pist squeak, whistle; (av fugl) chirp, cheep, pip.
pistasje pistachio(-nut).
pistol pistol; (amr.) gun; (leketøy) popgun.
-duell duel with pistols. **-hylster** pistol case.
-kolbe butt of a pistol.
pistong piston.
pistre squeak; whistle; chirp.
pittoresk picturesque.
pjalt, se **fille**; (fig) coward; contemptible fellow; **slå sine -er sammen** join fortunes, row in the same boat.
pjaster piaster, dollar.
pjatt prittle-prattle, prate, chatter.
pjatte prate, chatter.
pjattet twaddling.
pjekkert pea-jacket.
pjokk (liten gutt) nipper, little el. young shaver, toddler.
pjolter whisky and soda.
pjuske tousle; **-t hår** dishevelled hair.
pladask! bang!
plaff pop. **plaffe** pop.
plafond plafond, ceiling.
plage (subst) torment, worry, infliction, trouble; (støvplagen o. l.) the dust nuisance; **du er en** — you are a worry; **hver dag har nok med sin** — sufficient unto the day is the evil thereof.
plage (vrb) plague, torment, worry; — **livet av en** worry one's soul out; — **seg med** bother oneself about.
plageånd tormentor; (kjedelig person) bore.
plagg article of dress, garment, wear.
plagiat plagiarism. **plagiator** plagiary.
plagiere plagiarize.
plagsom annoying, pestering, troublesome.
plakat placard, bill, poster; (løs) handbill, broadside; (teaterplakat) playbill. **plakat full** dead drunk.
plan (adj) plain, plane.
I. **plan** (subst. en) (utkast, hensikt) plan, design; — **over, til plan** of; **legge en** — lay el. form a scheme; **legge -en til plan**.
II. **plan** (et) plane; (flate, slette) plain; — **med even** with, flush with.
planere level; planish; (papir) size.
planet planet; (dt.) **slå en på -en** knock one on the head.
planetarisk planetary.
planetoider planetoids.
planetsystem planetary system.
plangeometri plane geometry.
planke plank; (av furu el. gran) deal.
planke|gjerde, se **plankeverk**. **-golv** floor of planks el. deals. **-kapp** deal ends, plank cuttings.
plankelegge plank.
plankeverk enclosure of planks, railing, paling.
plankton plancton.
plan|legge, se **legge en plan**. **-legning** design.
-løs planless, designless. **-løshet** want of design el. purpose. **-messig** according to a plan, systematical. **-messighet** regularity of plan.
plansje plate. **-verk** book of plates.
plantasje plantation. **-eier** planter.
plante (subst) plant, herb.
plante (vrb) plant. — **om** transplant; (p. sm. sted) replant; (pottepl.) repot.
plante|etende herbivorous, plantivorous. **-føde** vegetables, vegetable food el. diet. **-gift** vegetable poison. **-liv** vegetable life. (en). **-r** planter. **-rike** vegetable kingdom. **-saft** sap, juice of plants. **-samler** collector of plants, herbalist.

-samling collection of plants; (herbarium) herbal, herbarium. **-skole** nursery. **-stoff** vegetable substance. **-verden** vegetable world el. creation. **-vev** vegetable tissue.
planting (handlingen) planting. **plantning** (plantasje) plantation.
plantrigonometri plane trigonometry.
plapre babble; — **ut** blab out.
plasér amusement, fun.
plasere place; station; (penger) invest.
plask splash.
plaske paddle, splash, plash, dabble.
plaskregn heavy shower.
plaskvåt dripping wet, drenched, plashy.
plass place, position; (ansettelse) situation, place; (på skip) berth; (by o. l.) place; (i en avis o. l.) place; (rikelig plass, rom) room, space; (åpen firkantet plass) square; (rund plass, torg) circus; (fordypet plass foran et hus) area; (husmanns-) cottar's allotment; **dette er min** — this is my seat; **ta** — take a seat; **de tok** — they took their seats; — **til room for; gjør** —! make way! clear the way! **gjøre** el. **gi** — **for** make room for; **gjøre** — **for en** make room for one; **her på -en** in this place, in our place; **på** —! take your places! (fig) **på sin** — appropriate; **ikke på sin** — inappropriate, out of place; **reise på første** — travel first cabin; **annen, tredje** — steerage.
plasskone cottar's wife.
plassmangel want of space.
plassmann, se **husmann**.
plass-søkende applicant for a situation.
plaster plaster; **legge** — **på** apply a plaster.
plastikk plastic art; (kunststoff) plastic. **plastisk** plastic.
platan plane-tree, platane.
plate plate; (bord-) top, slab; (stein-) slab, flag; (tynn metallplate el. l.) sheet; (fotografi) negative; (bedrageri) swindle; (elektrisk) hot **-plate**; **slå -r** swindle; **slå en** — **for en** impose upon one.
platina platina, platinum.
platiner|e platinize. **-ing** platinizing.
platoniker Platonist. **platonisk** platonic.
platt (adj) flat; (i tale el. stil) vulgar, low.
platt (adv) flat; (aldeles) entirely, quite; — **umulig** a sheer el. an utter impossibility; **kaste seg** — **ned** fall el. throw oneself flat.
platt eller krone head or tail; **slå** — **om** toss up for.
platte (subst) plaque, platelet.
platten|slager swindler, cheat. **-slageri** cheating, imposition, imposture.
plattform platform.
plattfot flat foot. **plattfotet** flat-footed.
platthet vulgarity.
plattsøm broad stitch.
plattysk Low German.
platå plateau, table-land.
plausibel plausible.
plebeier, plebeisk plebeian.
plebisitt plebiscite, plebiscitum.
plebs mob, populace.
pledd plaid; (railway) rug. **-re(i)m** rug-straps.
pledere plead.
pleiader the Pleiades, Pleiads.
I. **pleie** (være vant til) be used to, be accustomed to, be wont to, be in the habit of; **som man -r å si** as the saying is; **det -r å gå slik** it will happen so; **han pleide å** he used to.
II. **pleie** (passe) tend, nurse, take care of; — **forhandlinger med** be in negotiation with; — **sin makelighet** take one's ease.
pleie (subst) (pass) nursing; (omsorg) tending, (legemets) care (of), (av blomster osv.) cultivation; **sette i** — put (out) to el. at nurse; **være i** — be (out) at nurse; **ha i** — bring up.
pleie|barn foster-child; (elev e. l.) charge.
-bror foster-brother. **-datter** foster-daughter, adoptive daughter. **-far** foster- el. adoptive

father. **–foreldre** foster- el. adoptive parents.
–hjem nursing home; (for foreldreløse barn)
orphan asylum. **–mor** foster el. adoptive mother.
pleier, –ske caretaker, nurse.
pleie|sønn foster- el. adoptive son. **–søster**
foster- el. adoptive sister.
plen (gras-) lawn.
plent (adv) (dt.) absolutely, fairly.
pleonas|me pleonasm. **–tisk** pleonastic.
I. **plett** (electro-)plate, plated ware.
II. **plett, se flekk;** (sted) spot; (fig) blot; **på –ten**
on the spot; **sette en — på hans rykte** blot
his reputation.
plette, se flekke.
plettere plate. **plettering** plating.
plettfri spotless, stainless, immaculate.
plettfrihet spotlessness, immaculacy.
pli manners.
I. **plikt** duty (mot: to, towards).
II. **plikt** (mar) foresheets (pl). **–anker** sheet-anchor.
plikt|arbeid work of duty. **–begrep** notion
of duty. **–bud** moral precept.
plikt|forglemmelse disloyalty. **–forglemmende**
undutiful, disloyal. **–følelse** sense of duty. **–hensyn** considerations of duty.
plikthogger (som ror forreste åre) bowman.
pliktig bound in duty, obliged.
pliktmenneske slave to duty.
pliktmessig conformable to duty.
pliktoppfyllelse fulfilment of one's duty, discharge of duty.
pliktoppfyllende dutiful, loyal.
pliktsak matter of duty.
plikt|skyldig bound in duty, dutiful. **–skyldigst**
(adv) as in duty bound. **–stridig** at variance
with one's duty, disloyal. **–tro** dutiful, faithful.
–troskap devotion to duty.
plir blink, twinkle, cock of the eye.
plire blink, twinkle. **pliring** blinking, twinkling.
plissé plaiting, pleating.
plog plough. **kjøre –en** lead horses at the
plough. **–får** furrow (made by a plough). **–grep**
plough-handle. **–hest** plough-horse. **–jern** coulter;
plough-share. **–kar** ploughman. **–onn** ploughing
season.
plombe mass (for filling teeth); (merk) (lead)
tally.
plombere seal with lead, lead, tally; **— en
tann** plug el. stop a tooth.
plombering leading etc.; (av tenner) plugging,
stopping.
I. **plomme** (i egg) yolk of an egg; **leve som
plommen i egget** live in clover.
II. **plomme** (frukt) plum; **grønn —** green gage;
gul — mirabelle; **vill —** bullace plum. **–tre**
plum-tree.
pludder (snakk) jabber, gabble, babble, gibberish.
pludre jabber, gabble, babble.
plugg peg; plug; (dt.) (stor, kjekk kar) strapp-
ing fellow, bouncer. **plugge** peg.
plukke pick; (frukter, blomster osv.) gather;
(en fugl) pick, pluck; (en person) fleece; **— noe
bort** pick off; **— på** fidget with, finger; **— noe
(ut) av en** knock st. out of one.
plukkfisk stewed codfish, kedgeree.
plukking picking etc.
plump (rå) coarse, low, vulgar; (klosset)
clumsy.
plump (dump lyd) plump, splash, plunge.
plump (int.) souse, flop!
plumpe plump; **— ut med noe** blurt out a
thing.
plumphet coarseness, vulgarity; clumsiness.
plumpudding plum-pudding.
plun|der (dt.) ado, bother, trouble. **–dre** toil,
have no end of trouble.
plura|lis the plural (number). **–litet** plurality.
pluskvamperfektum the pluperfect tense.

pluss plus.
plutokrati plutocracy.
plutselig sudden; (adv) suddenly, on (of) a
sudden; **stanse —** stop short. **–het** suddenness.
plyndre plunder, pillage, spoil, rifle; (reisende) rob; (tre, juletre) strip; (en by) sack.
plyndring plundering, pillage, rifling, sack.
plysj plush, shag; **–kåpe** cloak of plush.
plystre whistle.
pløse blister, swelling; (i sko) tab, tongue.
pløset bloated, swollen.
pløye plough.
pløye|jord, –land plough-land, arable land.
pløy(n)ing ploughing.
pnevmatisk pneumatic(al).
poda|gra gout. **–grist** gouty person.
pode (subst) graft; (fig) scion, shoot; **den
yngste —** the youngest hope.
pode (vrb) graft, ingraft.
podeks fundament.
pode|kniv grafting-knife. **–kvist** scion, graft.
pod(n)ing grafting.
poeng point, gist; (ved eksamen) mark.
–et i en sak the important point, the gist of
the matter; **forstå et —** ogs.: see the joke.
poengter|e emphasize, point. **–t** pointedly.
poesi poetry, verse. **–løs** unpoetic.
poet poet. **poetikk** poetics. **poetisk** poetic(al).
pokal goblet, (drinking) cup, mazer.
pokker the devil, the deuce; **for —!** hang it!
hva — . . . what the deuce, what the blazes,
what the mischief . . . **— også!** the devil you
are! the devil you do! **gå — i vold!** go to blazes,
out upon you! **— i vold med ham!** confound
him! **som bare —** like anything; **et –s leven**
an infernal noise; **en –s jente** the devil of a
girl; **en –s gutt, fyr** the devil of a boy, fellow;
— så vanskelig deucedly difficult; **de har et
–s hastverk** they are in a devil of a hurry.
pokulere carouse. **pokulering** carousing.
pol pole; **Nordpolen** the North Pole; **Sydpolen** the South Pole; **negativ —** negative pole;
positiv — positive pole.
polakk Pole, Polander. **–inne** Polish lady el.
woman.
polar polar. **polaregner** polar regions; **de
nordlige —** the arctic r.; **de sydlige —** the
antarctic r.
polar|krets polar circle; (nordlige) arctic c.,
(sydlige) antarctic c. **–reise** arctic voyage.
polemiker controversialist.
polemikk controversy, polemic.
polemisere: — mot join issue with, combat.
polemisk polemic, controversial, contentious.
Polen (landet) Poland.
polenta polenta.
poler|e polish, burnish, furbish; **et –t vesen**
polished manners. **en –t nasjon** a polished nation.
polerer polisher.
poler|kritt polishing-powder. **–papir** smooth-
ing-paper. **–stein** burnishing-stone. **–vann** (diluted)
muriatic acid. **–voks** polishing wax.
pol|hav polar sea. **–høyde** latitude.
poliklinikk policlinic, out-patient department.
polise policy, contract of insurance; **tegne en
—** effect a policy.
polisk sly, cunning. **–het** slyness, cunning.
politi police; **–et** the Police force. **–betjent**
se **–konstabel. –funksjonær** police officer, peace-
officer.
politihund police dog.
politikammer police-office.
politiker politician.
politikk (framgangsmåte) policy; line of policy; (statskunst) politics, state-craft; **det er
dårlig —** it is bad policy; **snakke —** talk politics; **det er gått — i saken** politics has got
mixed up with the issue.
politi|konstabel policeman, (police) constable.
–kølle bludgeon.
politirett (domstol) police-court.

polit|isere talk politics. **–isering** talking politics.
politisjef head of police.
politisk political.
politi|skilt policeman's badge. **–spion** police spy, informer. **–stasjon** police station, station-house. **–vedtekt(er)** police by-law el. regulations. **–vesen** police department.
politur polish.
polka polca.
poll (roundish) baylet, **creek.**
polonese polonaise.
polsk Polish.
polstre stuff. **polstring** stuffing.
poly|gami polygamy. **–gamisk** polygamous. **–glott** polyglot. **–gon** polygon. **–histor** polyhistor.
Polynesia Polynesia. **polynom** polynome.
polypp (slags havdyr) polyp; (slags svulst) polypus; (plur. uriktig om adenoide vegetasjoner) adenoids.
polteisme polytheism. **polyteist** polytheist.
polyteknik|er polytechnician. **–k** polytechnics.
polyteknisk polytechnic; **— læreanstalt** polytechnic academy.
pomade pomatum. **–krukke** pomatum pot.
pomadisert pomatumed.
pomerans bitter orange. **–blomst** orange flower.
Pommern Pomerania. **pommersk** Pomeranian.
pomp pomp, state.
Pompeii Pompeii, Pompei.
pompøs pompous, grand, stately.
pongtong pontoon, ponton. **–bru** pontoon-bridge.
ponni pony.
pope pope, (Russian) priest.
poppel poplar.
popularisere popularize. **popularisering** popularization. **popularitet** popularity.
populær popular.
populærvitenskapelig popular scientific.
pore pore.
porfyr porphyry.
pors bog-myrtle, sweet willow.
porselen china, porcelain. **porselens–** china.
porselens|fabrikant china-manufacturer. **–fabrikk** china-manufactory. **–fat** china plate. **–handler** dealer in china. **–jord, –leir** porcelain earth, china-clay. **–maler** china-painter. **–maling** china-painting. **–varer** china-ware.
porsjon portion, share; (forsyning v. bordet) help, helping; **to –er oksestek** roast beef for two.
port gate, doorway; (kanonport) port, port-hole; **den høye — the Sublime Porte; jage på –en** turn away, send packing.
portal porch, ornamental gateway.
portechaise (bærestol) sedan-chair.
portefølje portfolio; **minister uten — minister** without a department.
portemoné (pengepung) purse.
portepé sword-knot.
porter (øl) stout, porter.
porthvelving gateway.
portier hall-porter.
portière curtain, portiére. **–stang** curtain-rod.
portklokke gate-bell.
portner porter, janitor, lodge-keeper. **–bolig** porter's lodge. **–kone** portress, janitress.
portnerske portress, janitress.
portnøkkel door-key, gate-key.
porto postage, carriage. **p–fritt** franked, post-paid, free of. postage. **–nedsettelse** reduction of postage. **–tariff** postage tariff.
portrett likeness, portrait. **–byste** portrait-bust.
portrettere portray.
portrettmaler portrait-painter, face-painter.
portrettmaling portrait-painting.
port|rom doorway, gateway. **–stue** gate-house, (porter's) lodge.
Portu|gal Portugal. **p–giser, –giserinne** Portuguese; **p–giserne** the Portuguese.

portugisisk Portuguese.
portulakk (plante) purslain.
portvakt gate keeper.
portvin port-wine, port.
porøs porous. **–itet** porousness.
pose bag; (som en pung; pose under øynene) pouch; **snakke rent ut av –en** make a clean breast of it; speak flatly, bluntly, frankly; **ha rent mel i –n** have clean hands; **man kan ikke ha både i sekk og i — you cannot eat your cake** and have it.
pose (vrb) (henge løst) bag.
posere pose.
poset (løst hengende) baggy.
posisjon position.
positiv (adj) positive. **positiv** (subst) (gram) the positive (degree).
positiv|isme positivism. **–ist** positivist.
positur posture, attitude.
possementarbeid lace-work.
possementmaker fringemaker, lace-man.
possessiv possessive.
I. **post** (vannpost) pump.
II. **post** (standplass, bestemt sted) post; (stilling; embete, bestilling) appointment, situation; (soldat på post) sentinel, sentry; (punkt) item, entry; **være på sin — be at one's post; (fig) be** on one's guard, on the alert; **stå el. være på — be on duty, stand sentinel.**
III. **post** (postvesen) post; **er –en kommet** has the post come? **sende det med –en** send it by post; **når kommer –en** when is the post due? **med –en i dag** by this day's post; **med omgående — by the next post, by return of post el. mail;** **få, motta i –en** receive through the post.
postal (postlig) postal.
postament pedestal.
postanvisning post-office order, money order.
post|bud postman, letter-carrier. **–båt** mail steamer.
postdirektør postmaster-general.
postei pie, pasty, patty, tart. **–deig** paste.
postekspedisjon branch post-office.
postekspeditør sub-postmaster.
postere station, place, post.
poste restante (to be left at the) post office, to be left till called for.
postering stationing, posting.
postforbindelse postal communication.
postforbund postal union.
postforsendelse conveyance by mail.
postfullmektig post-office clerk.
postfunksjonær (høyere) post-officer.
postfører mail-carrier; mailman.
postgang course of the post.
posthum posthumous.
posthus post-office.
postiljong postilion, post-boy.
postill book of sermons.
post|kasse letter-box, (i en søyle på gata) pillar-box. **–kontor** post office. **–legge** mail, post. **–mann** mail carrier; mailman. **–mester** postmaster.
postoppkrav: mot — payable C. O. D. (ɔ: collect on delivery).
postpakke postal parcel.
postpenger postage. **postporto** postage.
post|saker mail matter. **–sekk** mail-bag, mail-sack.
postskriptum postscript.
poststempel postmark.
postulat postulate.
postvesen post office.
postvogn mail coach.
post|åpner country, (local el. village) post-master. **–åpneri** village post-office. **–åpnerske** village post-mistress.
posør attitudinizer, poseur.
pote (vrb), se **pode**.
pote paw; **vekk med –ne! paws off!**
potens (mat) power; **opphøye i tredje — raise**

to the 3rd power; **a i fjerde** — a to the fourth (power).
potensere raise, intensify; (mat) involve.
potensering raising, involution.
potentat potentate.
potentill(a) (plante) cinquefoil, vefinger.
potet potato. **-gras** potato-shaws. **-nese** bottle-nose. **-opptaker** potato-digger. **-skall, -skrell** potato peel el. skin. **-stappe** mashed potatoes.
potpurri pot-pourri.
pott (glt. mål) quart; **halv** — pint.
pottaske potash.
potte pot; (kammer-) chamber utensil el. vessel.
pottemaker potter. **-arbeid** potter's work, pottery.
potteplante pot-plant, potted plant.
potteskår pot-sherd, piece of a broken pot.
pottøl single el. small beer.
pr., se per.
pragmatisk pragmatic.
Praha, Prag Prague.
praie hail. **-hold** hailing distance.
prakke: — noe på en palm off st. upon one.
praksis practice; **i** — practically.
prakt pomp, magnificence, splendour, grandeur, state.
prakteksemplar admirable specimen.
prakt|elskende splendour-loving, fond of display. **-full** splendid, showy, gorgeous, rich.
prakti|ker, -kus practical fellow, practitioner.
praktisere practise; **få tillatelse til å** — (om en jurist) be admitted to the bar; **en -nde lege** a medical practitioner; — **bort** shuffle away, spirit away.
praktisk (handledyktig, av p. betydning) practical; **-e menn** practical men; — **oppfinnelse** practical invention; (adv) practically; — **talt** practically, virtually.
prakt|stjerne (plante) melandrium. **-stykke** splendid article. **-utgave** splendid edition.
pral ostentation, parade, show.
pralbønne scarlet bean.
prale make a show, make a display (med noe: of a thing), vaunt; (av noe) brag, boast (of a thing); **-nde farger** gaudy colours.
pral|er boaster, braggart, braggadocio. **-erisk** bragging, vaunting, ostentatious. **-hans** boaster, braggart. **-ing** bragging, boasting.
pram lighter, barge.
prange (prunke) shine, glitter; — **med** display, show off.
prat prittle-prattle, prate, jabber; chat, (fig) nonsense. **prate** prate, jabber; chat.
pratmaker prater.
predestinasjon predestination.
predestinere predestine, predestinate.
predikant preacher, pulpit orator.
predikat predicate; (navn) title.
prediker: P-ens bok the Book of the Preacher, Ecclesiastes.
predisponert predisposed.
preferanse preference. **-aksje** preferential share.
preg impression, stamp, impress; (fig) cast, character; **geniets** — the stamp of genius.
prege coin, stamp; (fig) stamp, impress (on); (kjennetegne) mark, characterise. **-t i hukommelsen** impressed on the memory.
pregnans conciseness.
pregnant concise.
prejudisere prejudice.
prek prate, rigmarole.
preke preach; (snakke) prate, hold forth, preachify. — **mot** declaim against, denounce.
prekehest preachifier.
preken sermon; **holde en** — preach a sermon, deliver a sermon.
prekestol pulpit.
preketone sermonizing tone.
prektig splendid, magnificent; (utmerket) capital, excellent.

prekær precarious.
prelat prelate.
preliminarier preliminaries.
preliminær preliminary.
I. **prelle av** glance off, rebound (mot: from).
II. **prelle** (bomme) victimize.
preludium prelude.
premie premium; (belønning) reward; (pris) prize. **-liste** prize list. **premiere** award a prize to.
première first night, first performance.
premierløytnant lieutenant.
premierminister premier, prime minister.
premisser premises.
pren stiletto, bodkin.
prent print; **på** — in print.
prente print.
prepa|rat preparation. **-rere** prepare, dress.
preposisjon preposition.
prerogativ prerogative.
presang present, gift. **-kort** promissory card.
presbyterian|er Presbyterian. **-isme** Presbyterianism. **-sk** Presbyterian.
presedens precedent.
presenning tarpawling, tarpaulin.
presens the present (tense); — **partisipp** the present participle; — **konjunktiv** the present subjunctive.
present|abel presentable. **-asjon** presentation.
presenterbrett tray.
presentere (ved hoffet) present; (ellers) introduce (for: to) **tillat meg å** — **hr. Thomsen for Dem** allow me to introduce Mr. Thomson to you, (eller mindre formelt) this is Mr. Thomson; — **gevær** present arms; — **en regning** present a bill.
preservere preserve.
president president, (i forsamling) chairman; (i underhuset) speaker. **-skap** presidency, presidentship; (i parlament) speakership. **-valg** presidential election. **presidere** preside, hold el. take the chair (på et møte: at a meeting).
presidium chairmanship.
presis precise, punctual; — **kl. 1** at one o'clock sharp. **presisere** define precisely.
presisjon precision.
presjon pressure.
press pressure; strain, stress; — **av seil** press of canvas; **legge blomster i** — dry flowers.
presse (subst) press; **i -n** in (the) press, at press; **legge i -n** put to press; **idet bladet går i -n** as we go to press.
presse (vrb) press, force; squeeze; — **seil** (mar) carry on; — **noe ut av en** extort st. from one; — **penger (ut) av en** (pengeavpresning) blackmail one; **presset** pressed, compressed; **presset arbeid** (met.) chased work.
presse|byrå press bureau. **-folk** pressmen. **pressefrihet** liberty of the press.
presse|jern, se persejern. -lov presslaw. **-mann** journalist, pressman.
presseorgan press organ.
presserende urgent.
presse|sak action for libel or for infringement of the newspaper laws.**-tvang** restrictions on the press.
pressing pressing, straining; (av sjømenn) impressment.
prest clergyman, (katolsk) priest, (sognepr.) parson, rector, vicar; (kapellan) curate; (fengsels-, sjømanns- etc.) chaplain; (mest i Skottl. og om dissenterpr.) minister; (hedensk) priest; **-ene** the clergy; **bli** — take holy orders, take orders, go into orders.
prestasjon performance, achievement.
preste|drakt clerical el. sacerdotal robes. **-embete** clerical office, ministry. **-folk** a clergyman and his lady. **-gjeld** clerical district. **gjerning** ministry. **-gård** parsonage. **-kall** clerical living, church living, benefice. **-kjole** cassock. **-kone** wife of a clergyman. **-krage** clerical collar, clergyman's band. (bot.) (hvit-) moon daisy; (gul-) corn marigold.

prestelig priestly, sacerdotal.
preste|mann clergyman; (ringeakt) pulpeteer. **-offer** offering to the parson. **-ordinasjon** ordination of a clergyman.
prestere furnish, yield, perform; — **prestanda** perform the contract, make good one's engagements.
preste|seminar ecclesiastical seminary. **-stand** priesthood, clerical state el. order. **-velde** hierarchy. **-vie** ordain. **-vielse** ordination of a clergyman. **-vis:** på — in priestly fashion.
prestisje prestige, éclat, glamour.
pretendent pretender. **pretendere** pretend (to), lay claim to. **pretensiøs** pretentious. **pretensjon** pretension.
pretiosa valuables, jewelry.
Preussen Prussia.
prette, se **puss, strek.**
preventiv preventive.
prikk dot; (på skyteskive) bull's eye; **på en** —, **ti punkt og -e** to a turn, to a T, to a tittle, to a nicety; **sette -en over i'en** dot the i; **sette -er under** underdot.
prikke (punktere) dot; (stikke med en nål osv.) prick; **-t** dotted.
prikkenål pricker.
prim (myssmør) whey-cheese.
prima first-class.
primadonna primadonna, leading lady.
primas primate.
primaveksel first (of exchange), first bill.
prime (vrb) talk nonsense, babble.
primitiv primitive.
primo: pro **primo** in the first place.
primtall prime number.
primula primrose, cowslip.
primus (slags kokeapparat) primus.
primær primary.
prins prince. **prinselig** princely.
prinsesse princess.
prinsgemal Prince Consort.
prinsipal (subst) master, employer; chief.
prinsipal (adj) principal.
prinsipalt (adv) in the first instance.
prinsipiell fundamental.
prinsipp principle; **av** — on principle; **i -et** as a principle.
prinsippfast of principle.
prinsippfasthet firmness of principle.
prinsippløs unprincipled.
prinsipp|løshet want of principle. **-rytteri** riding a principle to death, overstraining a principle. **-spørsmål** question of principle.
prinsregent Prince Regent.
prior prior. **priorinne** prioress.
prioritert secured.
prioritet (i alm.) priority, precedence; (pant) mortgage.
prioritets|aksje preferential share, preference share. **-gjeld** mortgage debt. **-haver** mortgagee.
prioritetslån loan on mortgage.
prippen (pirrelig) testy, touchy. **-het** testiness.
I. **pris** price, rate; (forlangt betaling) charge, **faste -er** fixed prices; **nedsatte -er** reduced prices; **ikke for noen** — not for all the world; **til en** — av at the rate of; **til billig** — at a cheap price; **stå høyt i** — stand high in price; **sette** — på value, prize, appreciate.
II. **pris** (belønning osv.) prize; **bære -en** bear away the palm (from); **vinne -en** win the prize, carry the day.
III. **pris** (ros) praise.
IV. **pris** (snus) pinch of snuff.
V. **pris: gi til** — for abandon to the mercy of.
prisavhandling prize-essay.
prisbelønnet prize.
prisbillig cheap. **-het** cheapness.
prisdommer awarder of prizes, adjudicator.
prise (et oppbrakt skip) prize.
prise praise, extol, celebrate; — **seg lykkelig** think oneself fortunate (over å: to).

prise|penger prize-money. **-rett** prize-court.
pris|fall fall in price(s). **-forhøyelse** increase el. rise of price.
prisgi til, for give up to, abandon to the mercy of, leave at the mercy of.
pris|kurant, -liste price-current, price list, priced list.
prismatisk prismatic.
prisme prism; (i lysekrone) drop.
prismedalje prize-medal.
pris|merke (merk) private mark. **-nedsettelse** reduction (of prices), decrease in prices.
prisnivå price level, price.
prisnotering quotation.
prisoppgave prize-question.
prisstigning rise of prices.
prissvingning fluctuation in prices.
prisverdig praiseworthy, commendable.
prisverdighet praiseworthiness.
privat private; — **sak** (søksmål) civil action; **-e** private individuals. **privat-** private.
privat|audiens private audience. **-brev** personal letter. **-forestilling** performance of private theatricals.
privatim privately.
privatist private pupil, outsider.
privatkonto personal account.
privat|livet private life. **-lesning** private lessons. **-mann** private individual. **-rett** civil law. **-sak** private affair. **-skole** private school.
privilegere license, privilege.
privilegium license, privilege.
pro anno per annum; **pro et contra** pro and con.
probat proved, approved, unfailing.
probere, se **prøve.**
problem problem. **problematisk** problematic.
produksjon production, yield; (litterær) performance.
produksjons|evne, -kraft producing power.
produkt product, produce; (mat) product.
produktiv productive.
produktivitet productiveness, productivity.
produsent producer. **produsere** produce.
profan profane. **profanasjon** profanation.
profanere profane.
profesjon trade, business; **av** — by profession, professional. **profesjonell** professional.
profesjonist professional(ist).
professor professor; — **i historie** p. of history.
professorat professorate, professorship; **-et i gresk** the Greek chair.
profet prophet, seer. **profetere** prophesy.
profeti prophecy. **profetinne** prophetess.
profetisk prophetic(al).
profil profile. **profiltegning** drawing in profile.
profitabel profitable. **profitere** profit (av: by).
profitt profit; **med** — at a profit.
proforma (adv) merely as a form, in a perfunctory manner; (adj) simulated, mock, pro forma. **proformaveksel** accommodation bill.
profylakse prophylaxis.
program programme; (teater-) play-bill, theatrical bill; (f. eks. politisk) platform.
programmessig according to the program.
programpost item of one's programme.
progresjon progression.
progressiv progressive.
projeksjon projection. **projeksjonstegning** projective drawing.
projektere project, scheme.
projektør search-light, projector.
proklama legal notice. **-sjon** proclamation.
proklamere proclaim.
prokura procuration; **per** — by procuration.
prokurator (glt.) attorney, solicitor.
prokuratorknep law quibble, pettifogging.
prokurist authorized agent, confidential clerk.
proletar proletarian, proletaire.
proletariat proletariat; **-ets diktatur** proletarian dictatorship.
prolog prologue.

prolongere prolong.
prolongering prolongation, extension.
promenade promenade, walk.
promosjon graduation. **promovere** graduate.
prompt (adj) prompt, punctual; (adv) punctually, promptly; — **utførelse** punctual execution; **ordrer utføres** — orders punctually attended to, orders receive prompt attention.
pronomen pronoun.
propaganda propaganda; **gjøre** — **for** propagate for, carry on a propaganda for.
propell screw (-propeller).
proper tidy, clean. **properhet** tidiness.
propor|sjon proportion. **-sjonal** proportional.
proporsjonalitet proportionality.
proporsjonert proportioned.
propp stopple, stopper; (til å stoppe et hull) plug.
proppe (stoppe) stuff, cram (with), ram into; — **seg** gorge oneself.
proppfull brimful, choke-full, crammed.
proprietær landed proprietor, landowner, country gentleman.
pro rata pro rate, in proportion.
prosa prose; **på** — in prose.
prosaisk prosaic(al); (om person) unimaginative, matter-of-fact, inemotional.
prosaist prosewriter, prose author.
prosedere be at law, go to law; carry on el. conduct a lawsuit, (juridisk) proceed.
prosedyre process, course of proceedings, (way of) conducting a lawsuit.
proselytt proselyte, convert; **verve -er** proselytize. **-maker** proselytizer. **-makeri** proselytism.
prosent per cent, percent; **til fem** — at five percent; **betale visse -er av** pay a percentage on; **ti** — (også) ten in the hundred, two shillings in the pound; **mot -er av utbyttet** at a percentage on the profits; **4 -s obligasjoner** 4 percents. **prosentvis** per cent.
prosesjon procession.
prosess (sak) lawsuit, action; (kjemisk p.; orden i søksmål) process; **fri** — (sakførsel) free legal procedure; **ligge i** — **med** be at law with; **gjøre kort** — cut the matter short.
prosessførsel management of an action, procedure.
prosessomkostninger law expenses, costs.
prositt God bless you!
prosjekt project, scheme.
prosjektil projectile.
prosjektmaker projector, schemer, speculator.
proskri|bere proscribe. **-psjon** proscription.
proskripsjonsliste bill of proscription.
prospekt prospect, view; (plan) prospectus.
prospektkort pictorial postcard, picture card, postcard with view.
prosse: — **av** dismount; — **på** mount.
prost dean. **prosti** deanery.
prostituere disgrace; — **seg** make a fool of oneself, stultify oneself, make an exhibition of oneself.
prostitusjon disgrace, exposure, scandal; (kvinners) prostitution.
prote|gé protégé. **-gere** patronize, favour.
protek|sjon patronage. **-sjonist, -sjonistisk** protectionist. **-tor** protector. **-torat** proctectorate.
protest protest. **-ant** Protestant, **P-antisk** Protestant. **-antisme** Protestantism.
protestere protest el. cry out (mot: against); (en veksel) protest el. dishonour (a bill).
protestmøte meeting of protest.
protestskriv letter of protest.
protokoll record, register, minutes, protocol; **føre -en** hold the register; **diktere noe til -s** have st. minuted down, leave on record.
protokollere register, record. **protokollering** registration. **protokollfører** recorder, actuary.
protokolltilførsel minute.
protokollutskrift extract from records.
protoplasma protoplasma.

prov deposition, evidence.
prove depone, depose.
proveny proceeds.
proviant provisions, victuals, stores; **ta inn** — victual.
proviantere cater, victual.
proviantering victualling, provisioning.
proviantforvalter paymaster; (mar) purser, steward.
provins province, country; **i -en** in the country; in the counties.
provins|by country-town. **-folk** provincials.
provinsiell local, provincial.
provisjon commission.
provisor manager (of a chemist's shop).
provisorisk provisional, provisory, temporary.
provisorium provisional law.
provokasjon provocation.
provokatorisk provocative.
provosere provoke.
prr! (til hest) wo! way!
prunk pomp, parade, show, ostentation.
prunke shine; make a display **(med:** of).
prunkløs unostentatious.
prunkløshet unostentatiousness.
prust snort. **pruste** snort.
prut, se **pruting.**
prute (tinge) chaffer, haggle, higgle. — **av** beat down, cheapen.
pruting chaffery, haggling. **prutingsmonn** margin (for haggling).
pryd ornament, adornment. **-busk** decorative shrub.
pryde adorn, ornament, embellish, decorate.
prydelse ornament, decoration, adornment.
prydplante ornamental plant.
pryl (bank) a thrashing, drubbing, flogging; **ordentlig** — a sound drubbing.
pryle cudgel, cane, flog, thrash, drub, pound.
prylestraff corporal punishment.
prærie prairie.
prøve (subst) trial, proof, test; (av noe) sample, specimen, pattern; (f. eks. på skuespill) rehearsal; (av metaller) assay; **foreta en** —, **gjøre** — **på** make a trial of, try, (skytevåpen, regnstykke o. l.) prove; **bestå -n** stand the test, pass muster; **være på** — be on probation, on trial, on approval, on liking; **svare til -n** be according to the sample; **stå sin** —, **klare -n** stand the test; **ta på** — take on trial; **holde** — **på** (skuespill osv.) rehearse.
prøve (vrb) try, (erfare) experience; (skuespill osv.) rehearse; (metaller) assay; (sette på prøve) prove; — **på** try, essay; — **vin, melk** osv. test wine, milk, (ved å smake på) taste; — **et par sko** try on a pair of shoes; **prøvende** searching, scrutinizing; **prøvet** tried, proved; **han er en prøvet soldat** he is an experienced soldier.
prøve|ark proof(-sheet). **-avtrykk** proof-print. **-bilde** proof. **-bok** pattern-book. **-fart** trial-trip. **-hefte** specimen number. **-klut:** (fig) **være** — serve to experiment upon.
prøvelse trial.
prøvelsestid time of trial, trying time.
prøve|mønster sample, pattern. **-nummer** specimen number. **-nål** touch-needle.
prøveordre sample order.
prøvesamling collection of samples.
prøve|stein touch-stone. **-stund** hour of trial. **-stykke** sample, specimen. **-tid** period of trial el. probation, probation-time, probationary period. **-trykk** proof-impression. **-tur** trial trip. **-valg** preliminary election. **-vekt** standard weight, assaying-weight. **-år** year of probation.
prøyss|er, -isk Prussian.
pås dip; **det gikk en** — **opp for ham** some light dawned at last.
psevdonym (adj.) pseudonymous, (subst) pseudonymous writer, pseudonym, pen-name.
psykiatri psychiatry. **-ker** psychiater, psychiatrist.

psykisk psychic(al).
psykoanalyse psycho-analysis.
psyko|log psychologist. **-ologi** psychology.
psykologisk psychological. **psykose** psychosis.
pu! ugh! oh!
puber|tet puberty. **-tetsalder** age of puberty
publikasjon publication.
publikum the public; (tilhørerne) audience.
publisere publish, (lov o. l.) promulgate.
publisist journalist.
pudder hair-powder, powder. **-dåse** powder
-box. **-kvast** powder-puff.
puddersukker brown sugar, moist sugar.
pudding pudding. **-form** pudding-form el.
-shape.
pudre powder; **— seg** powder.
pueril puerile.
I. **puff** (støt) buffet, thrust, push, shove.
II. **puff** (en) box-ottoman; (på erme) puffing,
puff.
puffe (støte) buffet, thrust, push, shove.
pufferme puffed sleeve, balloon sleeve.
puge scrape money together, hoard up money.
pugg cram, grind. **-e** cram, grind. **-hest**
grinding fellow, plodding student.
I. **pukke** (vi.): **— på noe** insist upon, boast of st.,
plume oneself on st.
II. **pukke** (vt.) break.
pukkel hump, hunch; (dt.) **gi en på -en** dust
one's jacket. **-rygg** hump-back, hunch-back.
-rygget hunch-backed.
pukking: denne -en på egen kraft this boasting
of his own power.
pukkstein broken stone(s), road-metal.
pulje (i spill) pool.
pulk pulkha, pulk.
pull (på hatt) crown.
pulpitur gallery-pews.
puls pulse; **føle en på -en** feel one's pulse;
-en er svak the pulse is low.
pulse|re pulsate, pulse. **-ring** pulsation.
puls|slag pulsation, throb of the pulse. **-vante**
pulse-warmer. **-åre** artery.
pult desk.
pulterkammer lumber-room.
pultost cottage (el. pot-) cheese.
pulver powder. **-heks** hag, beldame.
pulverisere pulverize, levigate, reduce to powder.
puma puma.
pump|e (subst) pump; **-a lenser** the pump
sucks.
pumpe (vrb) pump, (utfritte) draw, bleed.
pumpe|rør pipe of a pump. **-spiker** pump-tack.
-stang pump-spear; pump-brake. **-stempel** piston
of a p. **-verk** pumps. **pumping** pumping.
pund pound; (evner) talent; **et — sterling**
one pound sterling; **åkre med sitt — turn** one's
talent to account. **pundvis** by the pound.
pung purse; (pose) bag; (hos pungdyr) pouch.
pungdyr pouched animal, marsupial.
punge ut med fork out, come down with.
punkt point; (prikk) dot; (fig) point, particular,
head, item, article; **om dette — on** this head;
i dette — in this particular; **på alle -er** everywhere; (fig) in every particular.
punkter|e puncture; **sykkelen -te** the cycle
punctured. **punkterfri** unburstable.
punktering (om sykkelring o. l.) puncture.
punktlig punctual; (adv) punctually.
punktlighet punctuality.
punktum full stop, period.
punktvis point after point.
punsj punch; **kold — cup**.
punsjebolle punch-bowl.
punsjekstrakt essence of punch.
pupill pupil.
puppe nymph, chrysalis, pupa. **-hylster**
cocoon.
pur (ren, skjær) pure; (fig) mere, nothing
but: **det er det -e vrøvl** this is sheer nonsense;
(adv.) **— ung** very young.

puré purée.
purisme purism. **purist** purist.
puritaner Puritan.
puritansk puritan, puritanic; **— enkelhet**
puritan simplicity; **— nidkjærhet** puritan zeal.
purk (sj.) urchin, bit of a boy.
purke sow.
purpur purple.
purpur|farge purple colour. **-farget** purple.
-kåpe p. robe. **-skjell** purple, purple-fish.
purre (subst) leek.
purre (vrb) poke, stir; **han -t opp i håret** he
ran his fingers through his hair; **— ut** (vekke)
rouse, (til sjøs) turn out.
purring (mar) call.
pus pussy; (kjelenavn på barn) chit, ducky,
darling.
puselanker (små barneføtter) trotters, stumps.
pusle (om lyd) rustle; **han går alltid og -r**
med noe he always busies himself with st. **pusle|**
arbeid trifling, trifles. **-ri** trifling employments.
-spill puzzle.
puslet(e) seedy, shabby, not quite well.
pusling manikin, dapperling.
I. **puss** (materie) pus.
II. **puss** (pynt) trim, finery; (på mur) plaster,
fine stuff; **i full — (dt.)** in full fig, in full feather.
III. **puss** (listig påfunn) trick; **spille en et —**
play el. serve one a trick, play a trick with
one.
puss! **— ta ham at him!**
I. **pusse: — en hund på en** set a dog at one.
II. **pusse** clean, polish; finish, rough-coat;
— geværer clean guns; **— metallsaker** polish
metals; **— nesen** blow one's nose; **— en mur**
plaster, finish a wall; **— et lys** snuff a candle;
— lyktene trim the lights; **— støvler** brush el.
clean boots; **— av** clean off, rub off; **— opp**
brush up, touch up.
pusse|garn waste. **-kalk** fine stuff. **-kniv**
(v. garving) currier's knife. **-middel** cleanser.
pussere push.
pusseskinn plate- el. wash-leather.
pussig droll, amusing, queer, funny.
pussighet drollery.
pust (vindpust) puff, blast, (ånde-) breath.
puste breathe, blow, puff; (ånde sterkt) pant;
(hvile for å trekke været) breathe; **— glass** blow,
make glass; **— på varmen** blow the fire; (fig)
add fuel to the fire; **— opp** blow up, inflate;
— seg opp (fig) look big.
pustel (verkholdig blære) pustule.
puster pair of bellows.
pusterom breathing time, respite.
pusterør trunk, pea-shooter.
pute cushion, pillow, pad. **-fyll** stuffing for
pillows etc. **-var** pillow-case, pillow-slip.
putre (om gryte) bubble, simmer.
putte put, stick; **— i lommen** pocket.
pygmé pigmy, pygmy.
pyjamas (nattdrakt) pyjamas.
I. **pynt** (odde) point.
II. **pynt** (stas) finery, dress.
pynte dress, deck, decorate; **— seg** dress,
make oneself smart.
pynte|dokke dressdoll. **-kone** tirewoman.
pyntelig fine, smart. **-het** smartness.
pyntenett (mar) martingale, dolphin-striker
pyramidal|sk) pyramidal.
pyramide pyramid; (mil) pile (of arms);
stille geværene i — pile arms.
Pyreneene the Pyrenees, the Pyrenean mountains; **Den pyreneiske halvøy** the Peninsula.
pyroman pyromaniac.
pyromani pyromania.
pyrrhosseier Pyrrhic victory.
pytisk Pythian.
pytt! (interj.) pshaw! tut! pooh!
pytt (subst.) pool, puddle.
pære pear; (elektrisk) electric bulb.
pære|dansk ultra Danish. **-formet** pear-shaped.

pærefull dead drunk.
pære|skall pear-parings. **-tre** pear-tree.
pærevev utter nonsense.
pøbel populace, mob, rabble. **-aktig** vulgar, mobbish. **-aktighet** vulgarity. **-herredømme** mobocracy, mob rule. **-språk** vulgar language el. slang. **-sverm** mob.
pøl pool, puddle.
pølse sausage; **blod-** black puddings; **som rosinen i -a** last but not least, the pick of the basket; **en — i slaktetiden** a drop in the ocean.
pølse|maker sausage, maker. **-mat** sausage meat. **-pinn** sausage-peg; **koke suppe på en —** spin a long yarn about nothing. **-skinn** sausage--**skin. -snakk** nonsense, bosh, balderdash.
pønitense penitence.
pønse (el. pønske) ponder, muse, meditate, ruminate; **— på** meditate, think on (a thing).
pøs bucket.
pøse pour (with a bucket); **det -r ned** it pours.
på (prep) o n, u p o n: **— bordet** on the table; **— veggen** on the wall; **— betingelse av** on (the) condition that; **spille — et instrument** play on an instrument; **— søndag** Sunday (next); i n; **— dette sted** in this place; **— et torg** in a market-place; **— gata** in the street; **— landet** in the country; **— øya** in the island (ved større øyer, ved mindre alm. on); **— Shet-landsøyene** in the Shetland Islands (ved øy-grupper); **— slottet** in el. at the palace; **— sine gamle dager** in his old age; **— engelsk** in English; **— vers** in verse; **— denne måte** in this way; **ende —** end in; **— marka** in the field (men on the battle-field); **tro — Gud** believe in God; in t o: **ned — gata** down into the street; **reise — landet** go down into the country; a t: **— teateret** at the theatre; **— hjørnet** at the corner; **— ball, kino** at a ball, at the movies; **— den tid at that** time; **— min bekostning** at my expense; t o: **gå — ball, kino** go to a ball, to the movies; **seile el. fare — Ostindia** sail el. trade to the East Indies; **svar — et brev** answer to a letter; **banne —** swear to; **sett det — min regning** place it to my account; **— liv og død** to the death; **lege — et hospital** physician of el. to a hospital; o f: **en kone — 25 år** a woman of twenty-five; **mangel — penger** want of money; **døv — det ene øret** deaf of an ear; **misunnelig —** envious of; a f t e r; **skudd — skudd** shot after shot; t h r o u g h: **— min anbefaling** through my recommendation; b y: **jeg kjenner det — et hemmelig merke** I know it by a private mark; (andre måter): **bygge — et hus** be building a house; **kysse en — hånden** kiss one's hand; **lese — sin lekse** study el. con over one's lesson; **alle — to nær** all except two.
påbegynnelse begin, commence. **påbegynt** in hand.
påberope seg appeal to; plead.
påberopelse appeal; **under — av** appealing to.
på|bud order. **-by(de)** order.
pådra bring on, draw down on, entail on; **— seg ansvar** incur responsibility; **— seg en sykdom** bring on oneself a fit of illness; **— seg en forkjølelse** catch a cold.
pådutte: — en noe impute st. to a person.
påfallende strange, extraordinary; (slående) striking; (adv) strangely, remarkably etc.; **det var meg — å finne ham så forandret** I was struck to find him so much altered.
på ferde, se **ferd.**
på fote, se **fot.**
påfugl peafowl, peacock.
påfugl|fjær peacock's feather. **-hale** tail of a peacock. **-hane** peacock. **-høne** peahen.
påfunn device, invention.
påfølgende following, subsequent.
påføre bring on el. upon, cause; **— krig** wage war against; **— konossement noe** insert st. in the bill of lading.

pågjeldende in question, particular; (sub-stantivisk) the party concerned.
pågripe apprehend, seize.
pågripelse apprehension, seizure, arrest.
pågående forward, pushing.
pågåenhet push, aggressiveness.
påheng hanging on; (fig) importunity; (tiggere) hangers-on. **påhengelig** importunate.
påhitt device, invention.
påholden: med — penn with one's hand at the pen.
påholden(de) sparing, saving, close.
påholdenhet parsimony, closeness.
påhvile be incumbent on, lie upon.
påhør hearing, presence.
påk rod, stick.
påkalle call on, invoke. **påkallelse** invocation; (bibelsk) supplication.
påkjenne (jur.) decide. **påkjennelse** decision.
påkjenning strain, stress.
påkjære appeal; **— en dom** appeal against a sentence.
påkjøre cart upon, drive upon. **påkjøring** carting upon, driving upon; driving against.
påklebet glued on to.
påklistret pasted on. **påklistring** pasting on.
påkledd dressed, attired.
påkledning dressing; (klededrakt) dress, attire; **bruke lang tid til sin —** be long in dressing.
påkledningskone woman dresser.
påkledningsværelse dressing-room.
påkommende: for — tilfelle for emergencies; **— tilfelle** need be.
pålands|vind, -vær sea-wind, sea-breeze.
på langs endlong, lengthwise.
påle pole, stake.
pålegg laying on; (skatt) imposition, impost; (forøkelse) addition, advance; (befaling) in-junction, charge; (på brød) cheese (or meat etc.) laid on bread and butter.
pålegge (fig.) impose on; charge (with), enjoin; **— en noe** enjoin st. on one; **— en å** enjoin one to.
påligge be incumbent on, lie upon.
pålimt glued on.
pålitelig trustworthy, reliable.
pålitelighet trustiness, reliability.
pålydende stated, specified; **obligasjonens — beløp** the sum specified in the bond; **— verdi** facial value.
pålydende (subst) facial value.
påløpende running on; **de — renter** the ac-cruing interest.
påminnelse, påminning admonition, monition, reminder.
påmønst|re engage. **-ring** engagement.
på ny(tt) anew, afresh; **begynne —** recommence.
pånøde press el. force on, obtrude.
påpakning packing on; (fig) pelting with abuse, licking; **få en ordentlig —** be pelted with abuse.
påpasselig vigilant, attentive, careful.
påpasselighet attention.
påpeke point out, indicate, call attention to.
påpekende (gram) demonstrative.
påregne count on, reckon on.
pårørende relation, relative.
påsatt put on, fixed on; (om brann) intentional, incendiary.
påse take care of, attend to; **— at** see that.
påseile run foul of, run against, run into.
påseiling collision, running foul of.
på sinne, se **sinn.**
på skakke aside, askew, aslant, awry.
påske Easter; **-n** Easter; **i -n** at Easter; **til — next** Easter. **-aften** Easter-eve.
påskedag Easter Sunday; **annen — Easter** Monday; **første — Easter** Sunday.
påskeegg Easter egg.
påske|ferie Easter holidays, Easter vacation. **-helg** Easter holidays. **-lam** Easter-lamb; (jø-denes) paschal lamb.

på skeive, se på skakke.
påskelilje daffodil.
påsketid Easter-time.
på skjeve, se på skakke.
påskjønne appreciate.
påskjønnelse appreciation.
på skjøns, se på skakke.
påskott, se påskudd.
påskrift superscription, address; inscription.
påskrive: få passet påskrevet have one's passport visé; (fig.) fikk sitt pass påskrevet got it finely, got a good rap on the knuckles.
på skrå obliquely.
påskudd pretext, pretence, excuse, colour; under — av under (the) pretext of, on el. under pretence of.
påskynde hasten, press, accelerate, quicken.
påskyndelse hastening, acceleration.
påstand assertion, asseveration; contention, theory; (fordring) claim; gjøre — på claim; fremsette en — make el. set up an assertion.
påstrykning spreading on, laying on.
påstrøket spread on, laid on.
påstå insist upon, urge; (en mening) maintain, assert. -(e)lig positive, opinionate, opinionative; -(e)lig menneske dogmatist, dogmatizer. -(e)lighet positiveness, opinionativeness.
påsyn presence, sight; i mitt — in my presence; i alles — in sight of all.
påta assume, put on, affect; (overta) charge oneself with, undertake, take upon oneself; — seg forretningen do the business. — seg et verv take upon oneself a task.

påltagelig, -takelig palpable, tangible, unmistakeable.
påtale (vrb) complain of; — en fornærmelse resent an insult.
påtale (subst) complaint. -myndighet the grand jury, the treasury.
påtatt assumed, affected, put on.
påteg|ne sign; (til bekreftelse) endorse, certificate; (visere) visa, visé; -net broderi traced needlework. -ning signing, signature; endorsement, certificate; visa, visé; (bemerkn.) remark; (bak på veksel) endorsement.
påtenkt intended, comtemplated, in contemplation, proposed.
på tide time.
påtrenge seg (en) obtrude oneself (upon one), intrude (upon one), force oneself (on one).
påtrengende obtrusive, intrusive, importunate; — nødvendig urgent; — nødvendighet urgent el. pressing necessity.
påtrengenhet importunity, obtrusion, intrusion.
påtrykk impulsion, pressure; urgency.
på tverke, — tvers across, crosswise.
påtvinge force upon, press upon, thrust upon; — seg obtrude oneself on, intrude on.
påvente: i — av in anticipation el. expectation of; pending.
påvirke act on, affect, influence; play upon.
påvirkning action, influence; under — av influenced by.
påvis|e point out, show, assign; (bevise) prove, make out. -elig that can be pointed out, assignable, ostensible, traceable.
påvisning pointing out, demonstration.

R

R, r R, r.
ra, se morene.
rabalder noise, hubbub.
rabarbra rhubarb. -grøt rhubarb fool. -stilk rhubarb stalk.
I. rabatt abatement, deduction, discount, tradeallowance; gi 5 prosent — allow a discount of 5 percent.
II. rabatt (blomsterbed) border.
rabb(e) stony hill el. ridge, barren ridge.
rabbel scrawl, scribble.
rabbi, -ner rabbi, rabbin.
rable scrawl, scribble.
rabulist pettifogger. -isk pettifogging.
rad (rekke) rank, row; (losjer o. l.) tier; i — in a row; tre dager på — three days running
radbrekke break on the wheel; han -r det engelske språk he murders the King's English.
radd (krabat) fellow, dog; en lang — a tall fellow, skyscraper.
radere etch; (skrape ut) erase.
radering (bilde) etching; (utskraping) erasing, erasure.
rader|kniv eraser. -nål etching needle. -vann aqua fortis.
radiator (varmeapparat) radiator.
radig (lettvint) handy.
radikal radical; -t (adv) radically.
radikalisme radicalism.
radio radio. -aften wireless evening.
radioaktiv radio-active.
radioantenne antenna, aerial.
radioapparat radio apparatus, (med alt tilbehør) wireless set.
radiokonsert radio concert.
radiolytter listener-in.
radiomot|tager, -taker radio receiver.
radiostasjon radio station; (mottagerstasjon)

receiving station; (utsenderstasjon) transmitting station.
radiotelefoni radio telephony.
radiotelegram radiotelegram, marconigram.
radioutsendelse radio transmission.
radium (metall) radium.
radius radius, semidiameter.
radså sow in rows, drill. radsåmaskin seed drill. radvis in a row, in rows.
raffin|ade refined sugar. -ement refinement. -eri refinery. -ering refining. -ert refined; (i nedsettende bet.) elaborate, accomplished; (om kvinne) sharp. med — grusomhet with elaborate cruelty. -erthet refinement; sharpness.
rafse (rive til seg) grab, snatch.
raft junction of roof and wall; lath.
rage fram jut out, protrude, project, (overhengende) beetle; — opp over overreach, rise above; — ut over overhang, beetle over.
ragg rough hair (især goat's hair); shag.
ragge|sokk hair over-stocking, snow-stocking. -t rough-haired, shaggy.
ragu ragout.
raide (lappisk: rekke) string of draught reindeer.
raigras rye-grass, darnel.
rajah rajah.
rak (subst), se vrakgods.
I. rak (rett) direct, straight, erect, upright.
II. rak (om rakefisk; s. d.) half-fermented, sourish, preserved in earth. -aure corned el. half-fermented trout.
I. rake (angå) concern, regard; — uklar med fall out with; hva -r det deg what's that to you?
II. rake (røre) stir, stir up; (barbere) shave; (m. rive) rake; — i varmen poke the fire; stir up the fire; — seg shave.
rakefisk fish preserved io earth.

rakekniv razor.
rakett (til fyrverkeri) rocket; (små, røde) fire-crackers. **-apparat** rocket-apparatus. **-hylster** rocket-case, rocket-paper. **-line** rocket-line.
rakitis rickets. **rakitisk** rickety.
rakk rabble.
rakke: — ned på noen run one down, throw dirt on one, abuse one; (i skrift) write one down. — til ill-treat, foul; cut up; (i skrift) write down; — ned på noe depreciate a thing.
rakker (glt.) flayer, knacker; (bøddelens hjelper) hangman's assistant, executioner's man; (nå fig.) infamous wretch, villain. **-knekt** flayer's assistant. **-merr** vile jade. **-pakk** rabble.
rakle catkin.
rakne come unsewn or unstitched, give open; (om strømpe) develop ladders; **for å hindre sømmen i å** — to prevent the seam tearing down.
raknefri ladderproof.
rakrygget erect, upright.
raljere banter, rally.
ralle rattle in the throat. **ralling** rattle (in the throat).
ram (om lukt, smak) sharp, acrid, rank; **for -me alvor** in good earnest; **det er mitt -me alvor** I am perfectly serious; — **til å . . .** prone to . . .
I. **ram: få — på en** get one on the hip, hit one (a blow).
II. **ram** (labb, best.: -men) paw.
III. **ram** (gavl, loft — best: -men) loft, upper room.
ramaskrik outcry; **oppløfte et — over** raise an outcry against.
rambukk rammer, pile-driver.
ramle rumble, rattle; — **sammen** burst up, break down; **se rolig på at det hele -r sammen** look calmly at the overthrow of everything.
ramloft half-loft, bed-loft.
ramme hit, strike; (bare fig) befall, overtake; (med rambukk) ram, drive (ned: in); (gjelde om) apply to; (skade) injure; **hardt ramt** hard hit; **ikke** — miss; **-nde** (fig) pertinent, to the point.
ramme (subst) frame; (vindus-) casement; (typograf.) chase; (fig) setting; **i glass og —** framed and glazed.
rammel rattle, rattling noise.
ramn raven.
ramne|far unnatural father. **-krok** petty place, Gotham, rookery. **-mor** unnatural mother. **-reir** raven's nest. **-skrik** croak, croaking of ravens. **ramnunge** young raven.
ramp mob, rabble.
rampe ramp, ascent; (teat.) foot-lights.
rampet(e) (adj) low-bred, low.
ramponere spoil, damage, injure, batter.
rams: lære på — learn el. get by rote.
ramsalta hard salted.
ramse rigmarole, words said by rote.
ramse (vrb) (opp) say by rote, patter out.
ramsvart raven-black.
ran robbery, depredation.
rand (stripe) stripe, streak; (på glass) brim, rim; (på tøy, papir osv.) edge, border, margin; **på gravens** — on the brink of the grave.
randbemerkning marginal note, side-note.
randet(e) streaked, striped.
randnoter marginal notes.
randskrift marginal writing; (p. mynt) legend on the border.
randstat border state.
rand|søm welting. **-tegning** border-drawing.
rane rob, plunder.
rang rank; (forrang) precedence; **av første** — first rate.
rangel revelry; spree, lark.
rangere rank; (om tog) make up; — **foran** take precedence of, take rank above.
rangering (om tog) making-up.
rang|forordning ordinance respecting rank and precedence. **-følge** order of precedence.

rangklasse rank.
rangle (rasle) rattle; (ture) go on the spree, rollic, keep late hours, revel.
rangle (subst) (leketøy) rattle, bells.
ranglefant reveller.
rangsperson man of titular rank.
rangstige hierarchy.
rank straight, erect.
ranke: ride — ride on the knee, be dandled.
ranke (subst) tendril; (vinranke) vine.
ranke seg (rette seg) straighten oneself; — **seg oppover** (slynge seg) cling to, twine round.
rankhet straightness, erectness.
ransake search thoroughly, ransack, overhaul; — **seg selv** examine one's own heart.
ransak(n)ing searching.
ransel knapsack.
ransmann robber, depredator.
ranunkel ranunculus, crowfoot.
rap belch, eructation; (ras) slip.
rape belch, eructate; (gli ut) shift, slip; **steiner -r ut under føttene på ham** stones are slipping from under his feet.
rapert (kanonvogn) gun-carriage, carriage.
raping belching, eructation.
rapp (adj) quick, swift, brisk.
rapp (subst) rap, smart, blow, stripe; **på røde -et** in hot haste; **gi en et** — rap el. slap one.
rappe (vrb) (en mur) plaster roughly, rough cast.
rappe seg make haste, look alive.
rapp|fotet, **-føtt** light of foot, nimble-footed. **-hendt** nimble (el. quick)-handed.
rapp|høne partridge. **-høns** grouse, partridges.
rapport report; (forhold) connection, relation; **sette i** — **med** put in communication with; **være i** — **med** be in touch with; **komme ut av** — **med** lose touch of.
rapportere report.
rapptunget glib-tongued, voluble.
raps (oljeplante) rape.
rapse pilfer, filch, crib. **rapseri** pilfering.
rapskake rape-cake.
raptus fit, access.
rar queer, strange; **vil du se noe -t** will you see a queer sight? **hva -t er det i det?** what is strange in that? **det blir ikke -t igjen** the remainder is not worth much; **jeg er ikke** — (slett ikke frisk) I am not grand; **de var ikke -e sjømenn** they were not much of seamen.
raring character singular, odd fish el. specimen.
raritet rarity, curiosity, novelty.
raritetssamler collector of curiosities.
ras falling down; fall of ground, slide; landslip.
rase (vrb) foam, chafe; (fare vilt avsted) rage; (ta voldsomt på vei) rave; (larme) storm; **stormen, ilden osv. -r** the storm, fire etc. rages; — **ut** spend one's rage, (om utsvevelse) sow one's wild oats; — **ned**, — **ut** (om jord el. stein) fall, slide, slip.
rase (subst) race, breed. **-antipati** racial antipathy. **-biolog** race biologist. **-biologi** race biology.
rasebiologisk: — **spørsmål** question of race biology; — **undersøkelse** investigation into race biology.
rase|blanding crossing, interbreeding. **-hat** race-hatred. **-hest** blood-horse. **-hygiene** race hygiene, eugenics. **-hygienisk** eugenic. **-kamp** war between races. **-merke** race character.
rasende furious, raging, in a rage, infuriated; (uhyre) prodigious, extreme; **som** — furiously; **en** — a madman; **en** — **storm, et** — **angrep etc.** a furious, violent storm, attack etc.; **en** — **smerte** a horrible pain; — **på** in a rage with, furious with; **være** — **over** be in a rage at, be mad at; **det er til å bli** — **over** it is enough to drive one mad; **bli** — go mad, fly out into a rage; (adv) **sulten** ravenously hungry; — **forelsket i** passionately fond of.

rasere raze, level with the ground.
raseri rage, fury, frenzy; **et formelig** — **etter** a perfect fury for.
rasjon ration, allowance; **fordele i -er** ration; **sette på** — ration, put upon rations, put on short allowance.
rasjon|al rational. **-alisme** rationalism. **-alist** rationalist. **-alistisk** rationalistic(al).
rasjonel|l rational; **-t landbruk** scientific husbandry.
rasjonere ration.
rasjonering rationing, rationment. **rasjonerings|kort** rationcard. **-system** rationing system.
rask (fort) quick, active, brisk; **et -t svar** a prompt answer; — **på det** quick; (nesevis) pert, flippant; (framfusende) rash; **raskt** (adv) fast, quickly; **gå -t** walk fast.
rask (avfall) lumber, rubbish; refuse, waste.
raske: — **med seg** snatch up; — **sammen** scrape together.
raskeri, se **rask.**
raskhet quickness, briskness, smartness.
rasle rattle, clatter; (om tørre blader o. l.) rustle; (om sabel, lenke) clank; — **med** (lenker, sabel) clank. **rasling** rattling etc.
rasp rasp.
rasp|e rasp; (med rivjern) grate. **-ing** rasping, grating.
rast rest; **holde** — halt, make a halt. **-dag** day of rest, resting-day, halting-day. **raste** rest.
rastløs restless, active, never-resting; (nervøs) fidgety, fretting. **rastløshet** restlessness.
rata: pro — pro rata, in proportion.
rate instalment.
ratebetaling payment by instalments.
ratevis by instalments.
rati|fikasjon ratification. **-fisere** ratify. **-habere** ratify, sanction. **-habering** sanctioning.
ratin ratteen.
ratt (styrehjul) wheel. **-knagg** spoke of a steering-wheel.
rau (adj), se **rød.**
rauk (av kornband) shock, stook.
raust (dyktig) able, skilful; (gavmild) generous. openhanded.
raut (av ku) low. **raut|e** low. **-ing** lowing.
rav (adv) quite, utterly, stark.
rav (subst) amber.
rave (vakle) totter, reel, stagger.
ravfarget amber-coloured.
ravgal stark mad; (forkjært) completely wrong, quite absurd.
rav ruskende gal utterly absurd; stark mad.
rav|smykke amber ornament. **-spiss** amber mouthpiece; **med** — ambertipped, ambermouthed.
razzia raid, razzia.
re el. **reie:** — **en seng** make a bed; **som man -r, så ligger** man as you brew, you must drink, as we make our bed, so we must lie.
reagens reagent, test. **-glass** test-tube. **-papir** test paper.
reagere react.
reaksjon reaction.
reaksjonær reactionary; **de -e** the reactionaries.
real real; (grei, ærlig) fair-dealing, honest; (dt.) straight; (amr.) white.
realinjurie (jur.) assault.
realisasjon realization; **total** — clearance sale.
realisere realize, dispose of.
realisme realism.
realist realist. **realistisk** realistic.
realiter really, in actual fact.
realitet reality; **i -en** in reality; **sakens** — the merits of the case.
real|kandidat graduate in science. **-linje** (på skole) modern department el. division.
realpolitiker practical politician.
realpolitikk actual politics.
realskole modern el. science school.

reassumere (jur.) resume, reassume.
reassur|andør re-insurer. **-anse** re-insurance.
reassurere re-insure.
Réaumur Réaumur.
rebell rebel. **rebelsk** rebellious.
rebus rebus.
recen|sent reviewer, critic. **-sere** review, criticize. **-sjon** review.
recess recess, statute.
recidiv relapse. **recidivist** previously convicted offender, confirmed criminal.
recitasjon recitation, recital.
recitativ recitative. **recitator** reciter.
red road, roads, roadstead; **på -en** in the roads el. roadstead.
redaksjon editorship el. business of an editor, editorial management; editor; (hele **-en**) the editorial staff; (avfattelse) wording, framing; **som hører til -en** editorial.
redaksjonell editorial; verbal.
redaksjonsartikkel leading article.
redaksjonssekretær sub-editor.
redaktør editor.
redd frightened, afraid; (av sig) timorous; **være** — **for** be afraid of; (engstelig for) afraid for; **bli** — become afraid el. frightened **(for:** of), take fright.
redde save; (befri) rescue.
reddhare coward, poltroon.
reddik radish; **svart** — Spanish radish.
reddsom appalling, frightful, horrible, horrid.
I. **rede,** se **reir.**
II. **rede: finne** — **i en sak** make out a matter; **få** — **på** ascertain, satisfy oneself about; **de hadde ingen** — **på tiden** they had lost all count of time; **gjøre** — **for** render an account of.
rede (vrb), se **re** og **greie;** — **ut,** se **utrede;** — **seg ut av noe** extricate oneself from, make one's way out of.
rede (parat) ready, in readiness; **ha på** — **hånd** have ready at hand; — **penger** ready money, cash.
redegjøre render an account **(for:** of).
redegjørelse account, statement.
redelig upright, honest; (adv) honestly.
redelighet uprightness, rectitude, honesty, integrity, good faith.
reder ship-owner. **rederi** owners, company of ship-owners; (bedrift) ship-owning business.
redigere edit; (avfatte) draft, word.
redning (frelse) saving; rescue; (sikkerhet) safety; **det er ingen** — there is no hope, no help.
rednings|anker (fig) only chance (resource). **-apparat** apparatus for recovering drowning persons. **-belte** life-belt. **-bøye** life-bouy. **-båt** life-boat. **-forsøk** attempt at rescue el. to rescue.
rednings|korps salvage-corps, life-brigade. **-løs** irretrievably lost. **-mann** preserver; (befrier) rescuer. **-mannskap** life-boat crew. **-medalje** silver medal for saving (human) life.
rednings|middel means of safety. **-planke** plank. **-stige** fire escape. **-vest** life-jacket; life-preserver. **-vesen** safety-establishment, Lifeboat Service.
redoble (i kortspill) redouble.
redsel horror, terror; **inngyte** — strike the mind with awe.
redselses|budskap terrible news. **-dag** day of terror. **-full** horrid, dreadful, appalling, terrific.
redselsesherredømme reign of terror.
redselskabinet chamber of horrors.
redselslagen struck with terror, horror-struck.
redsels|scene terrible scene. **-tid** time of terror.
redskap instrument, tool, implement; (fig) (om personer) instrument.
reduksjon reduction.
reduplikasjon reduplication.
reduser|e reduce; — **in absurdum** drive into absurdities; **han ser noe -t ut** he looks rather seedy el. delapidated.

reell real; genuine; honest, fair, trustworthy;

— behandling straightforward dealing; **ha –e hensikter** (dt.) mean business.
referanse reference.
referat report. **referent** reporter.
referere report; **— seg til** appertain to, relate to; **refererende til mitt brev** begging reference to my letter, referring to my letter.
refleks reflection, reflex.
refleksbevegelse reflex motion.
refleksiv reflective, reflexive.
refleksjon reflection, reflective thought.
reflektant applicant.
reflek|tere reflect; **— over** r. on, upon; **— på** attend to, pay attention to. **-terende** reflective; (som substantiv) intending purchasers; intending sellers. **-tert** (self-)conscious. **-tor** reflector.
reform reform.
reforma|sjon reformation. **-tor** reformer.
reformatorisk reformatory.
reform|ere reform; **den –erte kirke** the Reformed Church; **de –erte** the Reformists, Calvinists.
reformering reformation.
reformpartiet the Reform party.
reformvennlig reformist, reformatory.
refreng burden, refrain.
refse chastise, punish.
refselse chastisement, castigation.
refundere refund.
refusjon repayment, reimbursement.
refysere refuse, decline.
regalere regale. **regalier** regalia.
regatta regatta, boat-race.
regel rule, precept; (gram) rule; **gjøre seg til — make** it a rule, a point, make a point of; **mot reglene** against rule; **mot alle regler** contrary to all rule; **i –en** as a (general) rule, as a general thing. **-bundet** regular. **-bundethet** regularity, orderliness. **-messig** regular, regulated; (adv) regularly. **-messighet** regularity. **-rett** regular, according to rule. **-retthet** regularity.
regener|asjon regeneration. **-ator** regenerator. **-ere** regenerate.
regent ruler, regent, sovereign. **–inne** regentess. **–skap** regency, regentship.
regie management, stage-managing.
regime regime.
regiment regiment.
regimente (regjering) rule.
regiments|kirurg surgeon in the army. **–sjef** colonel. **–tambur** drum-major.
region region.
regissør stage manager.
register register; (innholds-) index, table (of contents); (i orgel) stop; **med — indexed**; **uten — unindexed. register|sertifikat** certificate of registry. **-drektighet** register tonnage. **-tonn** ton register, registered ton. **-utskjæring** (fordypninger i forsnittet) thumb index.
regist|rator registrar, abstracter. **-rere** register, enroll, calender, record, docket, inventory. **-rering** registering, drawing up, registration.
regjere govern, reign, rule.
regjering government; (kongelig styre; regjeringstiden) reign; **tiltre –en** accede to the throne; **fratre –en** resign the crown, abdicate the throne; **under denne konges — during el.** in the reign of this king.
regjerings|foranstaltninger governmental measures. **-form** form of government. **-handling** governmental act. **-kretser** ministerial circles. **-kunst** art of governing. **-sjef** Prime Minister, prime minister. **-tid** reign. **-tiltredelse** succession to the reign. **-vennlig** ministerial.
regle rigmarole, jingle.
regle|ment regulations. **-mentert** regulation.
regn rain; **øsende — a** heavy downpour of rain; **det ser ut til — it** looks like rain.
regn|bue rainbow, iris. **-buehinne** iris. **-bye, -bøye** shower, storm of rain. **-dråpe** rain-drop.
I. **regne** rain, (sterkt) pour; **det –r kraftig it**

rains fast; **regnet med buketter over . . . bouquets** were showered on . . .
II. **regne** (med tall) reckon, compute, calculate; **han kan lese, skrive og — he** can read, write and sum (do sums); **— feil** misreckon, miscount, miscalculate; **man -r** it is computed; **uten å — without** taking into account; **man kan — at han tjener . . . you** may estimate his earnings at . . .; **lavt -t** at a low estimate; **blant** class el. count among; **— etter** count over; **det -s for** it is considered; **— i hodet** reckon el. calculate by the head, mentally; **— med** (ta med i beregningen) allow for, take into the account; **vinen er ikke -t med** the wine is not included in the account; **jeg -r det med til det øvrige** I reckon it among the rest; **— over igjen** reckon over; **han har -t alt sammen om igjen** he has made a new calculation; **— opp** recount, enumerate; **— på** (stole) count, calculate, depend el. rely upon; **— sammen** sum up, reckon up; **han -s til dikterne** he is numbered among, ranked el. classed with the poets; **det ble -t ham til last** it was laid to his charge; **— seg til fortjeneste** take merit to oneself for; **— ut** calculate; **— ut en oppgave i hodet** work a question by the head; **-t fra 1. juli** counting from July 1.
regne|bok reckoning el. ciphering book, handbook of arithmetic. **-brett** abacus, ciphering. **-feil** miscalculation. **-kunst** arithmetic. **-lærer** ciphering master, teacher of arithmetic. **-maskin** calculating machine. **-mester** arithmetician. **-måte** mode of calculation. **-oppgave** sum, arithmetical problem.
regne|stykke, se **-oppgave**: **et enkelt — a** simple arithmetical process. **-tabell** arithmetical table. **-time** lesson in arithmetic.
regn|frakk water-proof coat. **-full** rainy. **-hyre** waterproof kit el. outfit. **-høyde** depth of rain.
regning (fag) arithmetic; (regnskap) account; (på varer, arbeid) bill, note of account; (beregning) calculation, computation; **i henhold til — as** per statement; **for egen — on** one's own account, at one's own expense; **strek i -en** disappointment; **føre noe på — put** st. down to one's account; **gjøre — på** reckon el. calculate upon; **ha en — på en** have a bill against one; **holde — med** keep an account with; **sende en — send** in an account; **kjøpe i fast — buy** right out; **gjøre opp en — settle** an account; **skrive på -en** put down in the bill; **skrive på ens — put** down to one's account; **det svarer ikke — it** won't answer, it does not turn to account; **ta på — take** on credit; **gjøre — uten vert** reckon without one's host, be out in one's reckoning el. calculations.
regnings|art branch of arithmetic; **de fire -er** the four rules (of arithmetic). **-blankett** blank bill. **-bud** collector. **-svarende** paying.
regn|kappe water-proof (coat). **-kåpe** raincloak, waterproof cloak. **-løs** rainless, dry. **-mengde** rainfall, amount el. quantity of rain. **-måler** rain-gauge, ombrometer.
regnskap account; **føre — over, holde — med** keep an account of; **gjøre opp et — settle** an account; **gjøre, avlegge — for** render an account of, account for; **fordre — av en, kreve en til — call** one to account; **stå til — be** accountable for.
regnskaps|avleggelse statement of accounts. **-bilag** voucher. **-bok** account book, reckoning -book. **-fører** keeper of account, accountant. **-førsel** keeping of account, accounting. **-kyndig** expert at accounting. **-plikt** accountability. **-utdrag** statement el. abstract of accounts. **-vesen** keeping af accounts, book-keeping; accounts. **-år** financial year.
regn|skur shower of rain. **-skyll** heavy shower, torrents of rain. **-tett** water-proof. **-tid** rainy season. **-vann** rain-water. **-vær** rainy weather. **-værsdag** wet el. rainy day.

regress recourse; **søke — hos** have recourse to; **regler om — for en administrasjon** regulations regarding the right of recourse of an administration.

reguladetri rule of three.

regu|lativ regulation, regulations. **-lator** governor; (dmp.) regulator. **-lere** regulate. **-lering** regulation. **-lær** regular.

rehabiliter|e rehabilitate. **-ing** rehabilitation.

rei (egl. riding); cavalcade, company on horseback; (av overnat. vesener) company of spirits; se **Oskorei**; (dt.) gang, mob on the move.

reie, se **re**.

reim strap; (smal) thong; (i sko) latchet; (driv-) belt. **-fabrikk** belting factory. **-skive** pulley.

rein (adj), se **ren**.

I. **rein**, se **åkerrein**.

II. **rein** (dyr) reindeer. **-avl** reindeer breeding. **-blom** glacier el. icy crowfoot.

reineclaude (slags plomme) greengage.

reinette, se **renett**.

reinfann (plante) tansy.

reinmose reindeer-lichen, reindeer-moss.

reinsdyr, se **rein**. **-kjøtt** rein-flesh, rein-meat.

reir nest, (rovfuglreir) aerie.

reip rope. **-ende** end of a rope. **-slager** rope-maker. **-stige** rope-ladder.

reis, se **reise** (subst).

I. **reise** (vt) (reise opp) raise, set up, erect; **— bust** bristle; **— et minnesmerke** erect a monument; **— penger** raise money; **— et opprør** stir up a rebellion. **— seg** rise, arise, get up, stand to one's feet; (komme seg) recover; **— seg i senga** sit up in bed; **hesten -r seg på bakbena** the horse rears; **hårene reiste seg på hodet mitt** my hair stood on end.

II. **reise** (vi) (fra et sted til et annet) go, (til: to); (avreise) set out, start, leave, depart (til: for); (være på reise) travel; **— utenlands** go abroad; **han reiste i går** he departed, left (here), started on his journey yesterday; **— videre** go on, proceed onward, pursue one's journey; **— bort** go away, set off; **— i forretninger** travel on business; **— med dampskip, jernbane** travel by steamer, by rail; **— til Paris** go to Paris; **— til fots** travel on foot; **— til sjøs, lands** go el. travel by sea, by land.

reise (subst) (en enkelt reise) journey; (lengre sjøreise) voyage; (overreise) passage; (kort reise) trip; (det å reise, ferd) travels; **foreta en —** undertake a journey; **tiltre -n** set out el. proceed on one's journey; **lykkelig — a** pleasant journey to you! **på mine -r** in my travels; **være på en —** be on a journey, be travelling el. on one's travels.

reiseakkreditiv circular letter of credit.

reise|apotek medicine chest. **-beskrivelse** (book of) travels; (om sjøreise) narrative of a voyage. **-byrå** tourist's agency, travelling office. **-drakt** travelling suit. **-ferdig** ready for a start. **-følge** travelling companions. **-gods** luggage. **-håndbok** guide-book. **-kamerat** fellow-traveller, travelling companion. **-kledd** dressed for the journey.

reisende traveller. Se ogs. **handelsreisende**.

reise|penger money for travelling; travelling cash. **-pledd** travelling blanket el. rug. **-rute** route; (bok) tour list; railway guide. **-selskap** travelling company; excursion party. **-stipendium** travelling fellowship. **-tøy** luggage. **-utgifter** travelling expenses. **-veske** suit-case.

reising travelling; (opprettelse) raising, erection.

reisning (oppstand) rising, revolt, rebellion; (mar) rigging; (holdning) carriage.

reiv (til barn) swaddle, swaddling cloth. **-e** swaddle, swathe. **reivebarn** baby in swaddling clothes.

rejisere plough, reject, send back.

rek drifting, floating; (konkr.) driftage, floatage; (jur) flotsam.

rekapitu|lasjon recapitulation. **-lere** recapitulate, sum up.

reke (vrb) drift, float; (gå og drive) lounge about, ramble, stray.

reke shrimp; prawn; **fange -r** catch shrimps; **renske -r** peel shrimps. **-fanger** shrimper.

rekel lout; **lang(t) —** sky-scraper.

I. **rekke** reach, hand, (strekke) stretch; **— en hånden** hold out one's hand to one; **— en hånd** til lend a hand to; **— fram** put out; **— tunge** thrust out one's tongue; **han rakte ut hånden** he stretched out his hand.

II. **rekke** (nå) go, reach; (om skyts) carry, range; (strekke til) go, suffice; (vare) last; **pengene -r ikke til** the money won't go so far; **vi rakk å ... we** managed to ...; **det varte og det rakk** time wore on, and wore on.

III. **rekke: — opp** (f. eks. strikketøy) unravel, ravel out.

rekke (subst) row, series, succession; (mat) series, progression; (tallerken-) rack; (mil) rank; (mar) rail.

rekkefølge series, succession, sequence.

rekkevidde reach, range, bearing, scope.

rekkverk railing, (trappe-) balustrade, banisters; (gitter) trellis.

reklamasjon reclamation, claim; (skriftl.) notice of claim.

reklame trade advertisement, puffing advertisement, self-advertisement, puff; **gjøre — for** advertise.

reklame|maker advertising puffer. **-messig** puffing.

reklame|re reclaim, claim. **-skilt** bill-board.

rekling jerked flounder el. halibut.

rekognosere reconnoitre. **rekognosering** reconnoitring, reconnaissance.

rekommandasjon (av brev) registration.

rekommander|e recommend; **-t brev** registered letter.

rekonstruere reconstruct.

rekonstruksjon reconstruction.

rekonvalesens convalescence. **rekonvalesent** convalescent; **være —** be recovering.

rekord record; **slå en —** beat a record; **sette en —** make (el. put) a record.

rekordinnehaver record-holder.

rekreasjon recreation. **rekreasjonshjem** convalescent home. **rekreere** recreate.

rekrutt recruit. **-ere** recruit. **-ering** recruiting.

rekruttskole recruit's course.

rekt|angel rectangle. **-angulær** rectangular.

rektifisere rectify. **rektifisering** rectification.

rektor headmaster; **universitetets —** rector of the university. **rektorat** headmastership.

rekurs (merk) recourse.

rekvirere requisition.

rekvisisjon requisition.

rekvisisjonsseddel written requisition.

rekvisitt requisite; (til teater) property.

rekyl recoil. **-ere** recoil.

relasjon relation.

relativ relative; **et -t uttrykk** a comaparative term; **et -t begrep** a matter of degree; **alt er -t** all things are by comparison; **-t** (adv) comparatively, proportionately.

relativitetsteorien the theory of relativity.

relegere expel, relegate.

relieff relief, relievo; **sette dem i — throw** them into relief.

religion religion.

religions|filosofi philosophy of religion. **-frihet** religious liberty. **-handling** act of religion, religious act. **-hat** religious hatred. **-iver** religious zeal. **-krig** religious war. **-lære** religious system. **-lærer** religion-master, teacher of religion. **-løs** religionless. **-løshet** want of religion. **-stifter** founder of religion. **-strid** religious controversy, r. dispute. **-tvang** constraint in religious matters. **-undervisning** religious instruction el. teaching. **-øvelse** exercise of religion,

public worship; **fri -øvelse** liberty of worship.
religiøs religious.
religiøsitet religiousness, piety.
relikvie relic.
reling gunwale, gunnel, rail.
rem, se reim; ha en — av huden have the same foible; **skjære brede -mer av annenmanns rygg** cut large thongs of another man's leather, el. large slices of another man's loaf.
remburs reimbursement.
rembursere reimburse.
rembøyle (til gevær) swivel.
remedium (redskap) appliance, device.
reminisens reminiscence.
remise (vognskjul) coach-house.
remisse remittance. **remittere** remit.
remje roar, squall.
remontantrose hybrid perpetual, remontant.
remonte remount. **remontere** remount.
remplasere replace.
remse slip, strip; patch.
ren (adj) clean; (ublandet, ogs. fig) pure; (musikk) in tune; **gjøre -t** (i et værelse) tidy (a room), clean up; **ta -t tøy på** take on clean linen; **bringe på det -e** clear up, ascertain, make certain; **hun er rene barnet** she is a mere child; **-e blader** blank pages; **— fordel** clear profit; **— inntekt, gevinst** net profit(s); **av — medlidenhet** from sheer compassion; **med -e ord** plainly, roundly, in so many words; **-e ord for pengene** plain speaking; **— samvittighet** a clear conscience; **— sannhet** plain truth; **et -t treff, tilfelle** a mere accident; **en — sjeldenhet** quite a rarity. **en — umulighet** a sheer impossibility; **det -e vanvidd** an act of utter insanity; **rent** (adv) cleanly etc.; (musikk) in tune; (ganske, aldeles) quite, completely, clean; **har du — glemt?** have you clean forgotten? **snakke — ut** (av posen) tell a thing bluntly, speak one's mind plainly; **nekter — ut å** refuses pointblank to, declines flatly to.
rendyrk(n)ing (av bakterier) pure cultivation.
renegat renegado, renegade.
renessanse renaissance.
renett pippin.
rengjøring cleaning (up). **rengjøringskone** charwoman.
renhet cleanness, pureness, purity.
renhjertet pure of heart.
renhold cleaning, cleansing. **renholdsverk** cleansing department.
renke intrigue, machination, plot; **smi -r** intrigue, cabal, plot.
renkefull intriguing, designing, artful.
renke|fullhet artfulness. **-smed** intriguer, machinator, plotter. **-spill** machinations.
renkultur pure cultivation.
renlivet chaste. **renlivethet** chastity.
renn run; (sport) race, run, stakes; **der var et forferdelig — hele dagen** there were so many people coming and going the whole day.
renne (subst) conduit, pipe; (takr.) gutter; (i farvann) channel; (i isen) cut, channel, lane of water; (grøft, kanal) canal, drain; (fordypning) groove.
renne (vrb) run; (flyte) run, flow; (om lys) gutter; (om sola) rise; (lekke) leak; **— kården gjennom livet på en** run the sword through one's body; **— hodet mot veggen** (fig) run one's head against a stone wall; **— på dørene hos en** importune one; **— sin vei** run away, take to one's heels; **ha -nde øyne** be blear-eyed.
rennegarn warp.
renne|kule (grovt hagl) slug. **-løkke, -snare** running knot, slip-noose.
rennestein gutter, kennel.
renning (i vev) chain, warp.
renom|mé character, reputation. **-mert** well-known. **-mist** bully, boaster, renowner.
renons: være — have a renounce (f. eks. i hjerter: in hearts); **være — på argumenter** be at a loss for arguments.

renonsere resign, declare off; **— på** give up, dispense with, renounce; **— seg** (i en farge) get out of.
renovasjon (fjernelse av søppel) removal of house-refuse; (fjernelse av ekskrementer) removal of night-soil, sewage disposal.
renovasjons|mann night-man. **-vesen** sanitary system. **-vogn** night-cart; sanitary cart.
rense clean, cleanse, purify; (korn) winnow, fan; **— for mistanke** clear of suspicion; **— for en beskyldning** exculpate from a charge.
renselse cleaning etc., purification.
renselses|ed oath of purgation. **-middel** purgative. **-prosess** cleaning process.
rensemaskin winnowing machine.
renseri cleaning-house.
renske, se rense.
ren|skrift fair copy. **-skrive** copy fair, fair-copy. **-skrivning** copying fair.
renslig cleanly. **renslighet** cleanliness.
rensmakende pure-flavoured.
rens(n)ing, se renselse.
rentabel profitable, remunerative.
rentabilitet profitableness, remunerativeness.
rente interest; **-r** interest; **gi -r** bear interest; **trekke -r** carry interest; **sette, låne ut penger på — put** money out at el. to, lend money on interest. **-bærende** bearing interest. **-fot** rate of interest. **-fri** free from interest. **-frihet** exemption from interest. **-nist** gentleman of private means el. of property.
renteregning percentage, calculation of interest.
rentesrente compound interest.
rentetap loss of interest.
rentier independent gentleman, rentier.
rentrykk clean proof. **rentrykke** work off.
reol shelves, (book-) case.
reorganisasjon reorganization.
reorganisere reorganize.
rep, se reip.
repar|asjon repair(s). **-asjonsverksted** repair(ing) shop. **-ere** repair, mend, refit.
reperbane rope-walk, ropery.
repertoar stock. **-stykke** stock-piece.
repetere repeat.
repetisjon repetition. **-skursus** refresher course.
replikk (jur) replication; (teater) speech. **replikkskifte** exchange of speeches. **replisere** reply.
reportasje reporting. **reporter** reporter.
represalier: ta — make reprisals.
representant representative, deputy; agent; (handelsreisende) commercial traveller, traveller.
representantskap committee.
representasjon representation.
representativ representative.
representere represent, stand for; (parl.) be member for.
reprimande rebuke, reprimand. **gi en — reprimand.**
reprise repetition.
reprodu|ksjon reproduction. **-sere** reproduce.
repslager, se reipslager.
reptil reptile.
republikaner republican.
republikanisme republicanism.
republikansk republican.
republikk republic, commonwealth.
reputasjon reputation.
reseda mignonette, reseda.
resept prescription (oppskrift) recipe; **ekspedere en — make** up a prescription; **gi en — på noe** ogs. prescribe for one. **reseptivitet** receptivity.
reservasjon reservation. **reserve** reserve. **-del** spare part. **-fond** reserve fund. **-forråd** spare stores. **-kapital** capital in reserve; guarantee fund. **-lege** assistant physician. **-mannskap** spare hands. **-offiser** super-

numerary officer. **-porsjon** (mil) emergency ration.
  reservere reserve; — **seg** reserve to oneself; — **seg imot** guard against.
  reserve|styrke, -tropper reserve forces.
  reserveutgang emergency exit.
  reservoar reservoir, basin.
  residens(stad) residence. **resident** resident (minister). **residere** reside.
  resig|nasjon resignation. **-nere** resign.
  resiprok reciprocal.
  resitere recite.
  reskript rescript.
  resolusjon resolution. **resolutt** resolute, determined. **resolvere** resolve (upon).
  resonans resonance. **-bunn** sound-board.
  resong reason; **ta mot** — listen to reason. **reson|nement** reasoning, line of argument. **-nere** reason, argue; **-nere over** consider, ponder; criticize, find fault with. **-nør** fault-finder.
  respekt respect, regard; **sette seg i** — make oneself respected. **respektabel** respectable. **respektere** respect. **respektiv** respective, several; **-e** (adv) severally.
  respekt|løs disrespectful. **-stridig** disrespectful.
  respirator inhaler, respirator.
  respitt respite. **-dager** days of grace.
  respondens the respondent.
  responsum advice of faculty, opinion.
  ressort province, department.
  ressurser resources.
  rest rest, remainder, remnant; **for -en** (for øvrig) for the rest; by the bye; **stå til** — be still due; (om person, m. betalingen) be in arrear(s); **uten** — (mat) without a remainder, and none over.
  restanse arrears.
  restaurant restaurant.
  restaurasjon (restaurant) restaurant; (gjenoppbygging, gjeninnsettelse) restoration.
  restaura|trise (woman) restaurant-keeper; (til sjøs) stewardess. **-tør** restaurant-keeper; (til sjøs) steward; (i visse tilfelle, f. eks. på utstillinger) caterer.
  restaurere restore.
  restbeholdning stock in hand, balance. **restbeløp** remainder. **restere** rest.
  restesalg remnant sale.
  restituere restore, restore to health.
  restitusjon restitution; recovery.
  rest|oppgjør (merk) balance. **-opplag** (publisher's) remainder. **-parti** remainder.
  restriksjon restriction.
  resultat result, upshot, outcome. **resultatløs** resultless. **resultere** result.
  resymé summing up, resumé.
  resymere sum up, recapitulate.
  retirade (klosett) privy, convenience.
  retirere retreat, beat a retreat.
  retning direction; **tankens, sinnets osv.** — tendency of thoughts, of the mind; (fig) **i** — **av** in the way of; **gå i** — **av** (fig) tend towards.
  retorikk rhetoric. **retorisk** rhetorical.
  retorkvere retort. **retorsjon** retort.
  retorte retort.
  retrett retreat. **-post** retreat, post of retreat. I. **rett** (mat) dish.
  II. **rett** (mots. urett) right, rights; (domstol) court of justice, court of law, law-court; (lovgivning) law; **ha** — be right, be in the right; **få** — carry el. gain the point; **med hva** —? by what right? **gi** — **til** entitle to; **stevne en for -en** summon one before a court; **gå -ens vei** go to law; **gi møte for -en** appear in court; **sitte i -en** sit in judgment; **bringe en sak for -en** bring an action; **gå i -e med en**, (bebreide) upbraid one, call to account, expostulate with; **med -e** justly, deservedly; **finne seg til -e** see one's way; **hjelpe en til -e** lend one a helping hand; **komme til -e med noe** find out the proper way of a thing; **ta seg selv til -e** take the law

into one's own hands; **komme bedre til sin** — show to better advantage; **være i sin gode** — be in one's right(s); have a perfect right to do so **med den sterkeres** — by the right of the strongest.
  rett (adj) right, straight; (riktig) right, rightful, true, legitimate, proper; **en** — **vinkel** a right angle; **ikke mer enn** — **og rimelig** only fair; **til -e tid** in due time; **han er nettopp den -e mann** he is the very man; **den -e arving** the lawful (el. rightful) heir; **det -e** what is right.
  rett (adv) right, straight; **det gjør De** — **i** you do right el. well; — **som det var** all of a sudden, just then; (hvert øyeblikk) every now and then; — **og slett** barely, simply; — **fram** straight on; — **på** dead on to.
  rette (vrb) straighten; (gi retning) direct, point; (forbedre) correct; **rett i** (mil) dress (your ranks)! — **seg** come to rights; (om skip) right; **det -r seg nok** that will be all right; — **etter** proportion to; — **seg etter ens luner** humour one; **det -r seg etter** that is regulated by; **alles øyne var -t på meg** all eyes were turned towards me; — **en kanon el. kikkert** (på, imot) point el. level a cannon el. telescope (at, against); — **på en** criticize, censure one; — **ut** straighten; stretch.
  rette (motsatt vrangside) the right side, the face.
  rettelig (adv) rightly, correctly.
  rettelse correction, emendation.
  rettenkende (el. **rett-tenkende**) conscientious, rightminded.
  rettere (komp. av rett): — **sagt** rather, more properly; **eller rettere** or, to put it more exactly; **ikke rettere enn jeg vet** as far as I know; **jeg ser ikke rettere enn at** to the best of my understanding.
  rettergang judicial proceedings, procedure; (prosess) process.
  rettersted place of execution; **føre til -et** lead out for execution.
  rettesnor line; (fig) level, rule, guide.
  rettferdig just, righteous; **sove de -es søvn** sleep the sleep of the just.
  rettferdiggjøre justify, warrant; — **seg** exculpate, disculpate, exonerate oneself.
  rettferdiggjørelse justification.
  rettferdighet justice, righteousness; **la vederfares** — do justice to. **retthaveri** cavilling, special pleading. **retthaversk** cavilling.
  rettighet right, title, privilege.
  rett|lede, -leie direct, guide.
  rettløs lawless. **rettmessig** lawful, legitimate, right. **rettmessighet** lawfulness, legality.
  rettroende (el. **rett-troende**) orthodox. **retttroenhet** orthodoxy.
  retts|akt legal document. **-begrep** notion of right. **-betjent** officer of justice. **-bevissthet** sense of justice. **-dag** court day. **-ferie** vacation. **-forfølgning** legal procedure. **-formann** president of a court of law. **-følelse** sense of justice. **-gyldig** valid, good in law. **-gyldighet** validity in law. **-handling** judicial act. **-historie** history of law. **-hjelp** legal advice. **-hjemmel** legal title.
  rettside, se **rette**.
  rett|sindig upright. **-sindighet, -sinn** uprightness, rectitude. **-skaffen** upright, righteous.
  rettskaffenhet honesty, integrity, uprightness, righteousness.
  rettskraft legal force, validity.
  rettskrivning orthography, spelling.
  rettskyndig, se **lovkyndig**.
  rettslig legal, judicial.
  rettslærd (adj) jurisprudent, learned in law. **rettslærd** (subst) jurist, jurisconsult, lawyer. **retts|lærer** professor of jurisprudence. **-pleie** administration of justice. **-sak** lawsuit, process. **-sal** court(-room). **-sikkerhet** public security. **-stilling** legal status.
  retts|stridig contrary to law, illegal. **-stridighet** illegality. **-system** judicial system.

retts|tilstand state of the law el. of justice. **–vesen** justice. **–vitenskap** jurisprudence, science of law. **–virkning** legal effect. **–vitne** witness appointed by authority.
rettvendt turned the right way.
rettvinklet rectangular, right-angled.
rettvis, se **rettferdig.**
retur return; **tur og** — passage out and home, out and back; **på** — (fig) going down hill, declining; (om utseende) past the prime, on the wane. **–billett** return-ticket.
returnere return.
retur|porto re-postage. **–veksel** redraft.
retusj retouch. **–ere** retouch.
I. **rev** (lavt skjær) reef.
III. **rev** fox; **ha en — bak øret** be up to some trick, play an underhand game.
III. **rev** (i seil) reef; **stikke ut et** — shake out a reef; **ta inn et** — take in a reef; **ta — i seilene** (ogs. fig) shorten sail.
revaksinasjon revaccination.
revaksinere revaccinate.
revaktig foxish, foxlike, vulpine.
revansj(e) revenge; **få — have** one's revenge.
reve (seil) reef.
reve|belg fox's skin, foxcase. **–bjelle** (bot.) digitalis, foxglove.
revehule fox's den, fox-earth.
revelje reveille, morning call.
revepels (fig) old fox.
reverens bow, obeisance.
revers reverse side; counter-bond; **–en av medaljen** the dark side of the picture.
reve|saks fox-trap. **–skinn** fox's skin.
revidere revise; (som revisor) audit.
revier shooting-ground.
revisjon revisal, revision; (revisors) audit.
revisjonsark clean proof, revise.
revisor auditor.
I. **revle** (sandbanke, i Danmark) shoal, bar, sand-bank.
II. **rev|le** (strimmel av vev) shred el. strip of textile. **–linger** spiral wristbands or kneebands.
revmat|isk rheumatic. **–isme** rheumatism.
revne (vrb) crack, split, part, rive, separate, break in two.
revne (subst) crack, chink, cranny, fissure, crevice.
revneferdig nearly bursting.
revolte revolt. **revoltere** revolt.
revolusjon revolution. **–ere** revolutionize. **–ær** revolutionary. **revolusjonsånd** revolutionary spirit, spirit of revolution.
revolver revolver.
revunge fox's cub.
revy review, muster; **holde — over** muster.
Rhinen the Rhine. **Rhinlandet** the Rhineland.
rhinoceros, se **neshorn.**
rhinsk-, se **rinsk.**
Rhodos Rhodes.
Rhone the Rhone.
ri (anfall) fit, spell; paroxysm.
ri (vrb), se **ride.**
I. **ribbe** (subst) rib; (mar) rib.
II. **ribbe** (til gymnastikk) horizontal bars.
ribbe (vrb) pick, pluck.
ribben rib. **–stek** roast rib of pork.
ribbet ribbed.
ricambio (merk) re-exchange.
ridder knight; **vandrende — knight** errant; **slå til — knight; slå seg til — på en** bully sb., walk over sb.
ridderborg castle.
ridderkors cross of an order of knighthood.
ridderlig chivalrous, knightly.
ridderlighet gallantry, chivalrousness.
ridder|orden order of knighthood. **–roman** romance of chivalry. **–sal** knights' hall. **–skap** knighthood; knightage. **–spore** knight's spur; (planten) larkspur. **–stand** knighthood, chivalry. **–vesen** chivalry.

ri(de) ride, go on horseback; **— en tur** take a ride; **— av en storm** (mar) ride out a gale; **— i skritt, trav, galopp, kort galopp** pace, trot, gallop, canter; **— over en** ride one down; **— inn en hest** break in a horse.
ride|bane riding-ground el. -place. **–drakt** riding dress; (bare om dames) riding habit, habit. **–hest** saddle-horse, riding-horse, hackney, hack. **–knekt** groom. **–kunst** horsemanship. **–lærer** riding-master. **–pisk** horsewhip. **–skole** riding-school, manège. **–stell** horse trappings, riding equipage. **–støvler** riding-boots, jockey-boots. **–tur** ride. **ridning** riding.
I. **rifle** (gevær) rifle, rifle-musket. **–kule** rifle-bullet, -ball, -shot.
II. **rifle** (fure) groove, flute. **rifle** (vrb) rifle; **–t kanon** rifled el. rifle cannon el. gun.
rift tear, rent; (spalte) crevice; (på kroppen) scratch; **det er stor — om . . .** there is a great demand for, run on . . .
rigg rigging.
rigge rig. **rigger** rigger.
rigning rigging.
rigor|isme rigorism. **–ist** rigorist.
rigor|istisk, –øs rigorous.
rik rich, wealthy, opulent, affluent, of fortune; **— på** rich in, abounding in; **den –e** the rich man; **de –e** the rich; **i –t mål** abundantly; **–t forgylt** richly gilt.
rikdom riches, abundance; wealth; **–mer** riches; **— på** richness in.
rike empire, kingdom, realm; **komme ditt —** Thy kingdom come.
rikelig plentiful, abundant, liberal, unstinted; **han har sitt –e utkomme** he is well off.
rikfolk rich ones, the rich.
rikholdig rich, copious, abundant.
riking nabob, plute.
rikke move; **— seg** move, stir.
rikmann capitalist, rich man.
rikochettere ricochet. **rikochettskudd** ricochet.
riks|advokat attorney-general; **–arkiv** (public)-records office, state-archives. **–arkivar** master of the rolls, keeper of the public records.
riksdag parliament; (imperial) diet; **–en i Worms** the diet of W. **riksdags|diéter** parliamentary wages. **–mann** member of parliament. **–samling** session.
rikse (knirke) creak.
riks|eple globe, (King's) orb. **–forstander** regent. **–kansler** chancellor of the empire. **–klenodier** regalia. **–mynt** coin of the realm el. kingdom. **–mål** language of the realm; **det norske —** standard Norwegian (now officially called «bokmål», book language). **–råd** (hist) council of the kingdom, senate; (medlem) member of the council. **–regalie,** se **–klenodier. –rett** supreme court of the kingdom. **–rettssak** state trial. **–språk** the written language.
riktig right, correct; **en — slyngel** (o. fl.) a perfect, regular, thorough, unmitigated, villain; **han er ikke — i hodet** he is not in his right sense; **— uttrykk** correct expression; (ganske) **—!** (quite) right, quite so, just so, that's it; (adv) right, rightly, correctly; exactly, quite; **det går ikke — for seg her** there is st. wrong here; **— mottatt** duly received; **skrive, snakke —** write, speak correctly; **hun forstod meg ikke — she** did not exactly understand me; **jeg vet det ikke —** I hardly know, I don't know exactly, I don't know for certain, I can scarcely tell; **— godt** very well, well enough.
riktighet rightness, correctness; justice; **innrømme –en av** admit the justice of; **tingen har sin — it** is quite correct; it is a fact, it is all right.
riktignok certainly, to be sure, indeed.
I. **rim** (rimfrost) hoar frost, white frost, rime (frost).
II. **rim** (i vers) rhyme. **–brev** rhymed epistle.
I. **rime** (av frost) rime.

II. **rime** (i vers) rhyme; — **på** rhyme to; **det –r ikke med** it does not tally with.
rimelig reasonable; (sannsynlig) probable, likely; **til — pris** at a reasonable price.
rimelighet reasonableness; probability.
rimeligvis (adv) probably, in all probability.
rimeri rhyming.
rimfri (vers) blank (verse).
rimfrost hoar frost, white frost.
rim|nød want of a rhyme. **–smed** rhymer, poetaster.
rimtåke frosty fog.
ring ring; (krets) circle; (beslag) hoop, (mindre) ferrule; (i kjede) link; (om månen) halo; (av røyk) wreath; **kjøre i — med en** lead one a life.
ringbane suburban connecting railway.
ringblomst marigold.
ringbrynje chain-mail.
ringdue ring-dove, wood-pigeon.
I. **ringe** (— inn, kringsette) ring; (— ned, ut, krave o. l.) hollow; — **seg i hop** coil oneself up; — **ut en kjole i halsen** cut low the body of a dress.
II. **ringe** (m. klokke) ring; — **av** disconnect; — **på klokka** ring the bell; — **opp** (i telefonen) ring up on the telephone, ring up; — **etter** ring for; — **inn**, — **ut**, ring in, out; **det –r** there is a ring at the bell, at the door; — **på oppvarteren** ring for the waiter; **det –r i ørene mine** my ears tingle.
ringe (kjørel) pan; panful; bowl; bowlful.
ringe (ubetydelig) small, inconsiderable, slight; (uviktig) insignificant; (tarvelig) poor; **av — kvalitet** inferior, of inferior quality; **etter min — evne** to the best of my humble abilities; **ingen –re enn** no less a person than; **intet –re enn** nothing short of; **ikke det –ste** nothing at all, absolutely nothing; **ikke den –ste interesse** not the slightest interest.
ringeakt contempt, disdain; (som vises) slight, disregard; **føle — for** hold in contempt.
ringeakte despise, look down upon; slight, disregard; **–nde** contemptuous; (adv) in contempt.
ringeapparat ringing-apparatus; **elektrisk —** electric bell.
ringer ringer.
ringfinger ring-finger, marriage-finger.
ringhet (spøkende) **min —** my own humble self.
ringle (vi.) tinkle, jingle; coil, curl.
ringorm ringworm.
ringrev atoll, lagoon-island.
ringspill hoop and sticks.
rinne, se **renne**: (om tiden) fly, pass, elapse.
rinskvin Rhenish wine, hock. Flere ord med **ri**, se **rhi**.
rip sheerstrake; (esing) gunnel.
ripe (subst) scratch. **ripe** (vrb) scratch.
ripost return, parry and thrust; (fig) repartee. **–ere** retort.
rippe opp revive, rake up.
I. **rips** (slags tøy) rep.
II. **rips** currant. **–busk** currant bush. **–gelé** currant-jelly. **–saft** currant-syrup.
I. **ris** (papir) ream.
II. **ris** (kratt, kvist) bushes, copse, scrub; (til straff) rod, birch; **gi —** whip, birch; **få —** be whipped.
III. **ris** (kornart) rice; **japansk —** puffed rice.
rise (slå med et ris) birch.
rise (kjempe) giant; (troll) ogre.
risengryn rice. **–grøt** rice-porridge.
ris|fletning wattling. **–fugl** rice-bird.
risgjerde hedgerow, scrub enclosure.
risgrøt rice-porridge.
risikabel risky. **risikere** risk.
risiko risk, peril; **på egen — at** one's own risk; **løpe stor —** run a great risk.
ris|kjerv bundle of fagots. **–kvist** twig.
risle purl, murmur, ripple. **risling** purling etc.
rismel ground rice, rice-flour.
risp slit, slash, tear, scratch.

rispe (vrb) slit, slash, tear; scratch. **–nde gal** stark mad.
rispudding rice-pudding.
riss plan, diagram; (utkast) rough-draught.
risse (vrb) scratch; (tegne) draw, outline.
risse|brett drawing-board. **–fjær**, **–penn** drawing-pen, bow-pen.
I. **rist** (ro) rest; **han har hverken — eller ro** he has not a moment's quiet.
II. **rist** (på foten) instep.
III. **rist** (jernrist, i ovn) grate; grating; (til å riste på) gridiron.
IV. **rist** (fiskeskjell) fish-scales.
V. **rist** (politur, «skåp») shake; alcohol salted and shaken.
I. **riste** (steke) broil, grill. — **brød, ost** toast bread, cheese; **–t brød** toast; **–t kjøtt** grillade.
II. **riste** (skjære el. hogge inn) carve, cut. — **runer** carve runes.
III. **riste = ryste** s. d.
ritt ride.
rittmester captain (of horse).
ritual ritual, service. **ritus** rite(s).
rival, **–inne** rival. **rivalisere** rival. **rivalitet** rivalry, rivalship.
rive pluck; pull; (rive sund) rend, tear; — **brød, pepperrot** grate bread, horse-radish; — **farger** grind colours; — **av en fyrstikk** strike a match; — **seg løs fra** tear oneself from, disengage oneself from; **la seg — med av** be carried away by; — **i** (noe) pull, tear; — **seg i håret** tear one's hair; — **i stykker** tear up, tear to pieces; — **i** (betale for noe) pay for; — **løs** detach; **hun rev publikum med seg** she carried the house el. audience (with her); — **av seg vittigheter** crack jokes; — **ned** tear down, break down; — **ned på** find fault with; revile; **døra blev revet opp** the door was burst open; — **over ende** knock over; — **over** tear asunder; — **på tunga** bite el. burn the tongue; — **seg på noe** scratch oneself on a thing; — **ut av villfarelsen** undeceive, disabuse; **rivende** tearing, rapid; **i rivende fart** at a rapid el. furious rate; **rivende avsetning** rapid sale; **rivende strøm** tearing current, rapid stream.
rive (subst) rake. **–skaft** rake-handle.
Rivieraen the Riviera.
riving tearing etc.; — **i lemmene** rheumatic pains in the limbs.
rivjern grater, rasp; (fig) dragon, rasper.
rivning (fig) collision, friction.
I. **ro** (hvile) rest, repose; (stillhet) quiet; (rolighet) tranquillity; **oppbyhøyd —** serenity; **ha — rest**; **komme til —** get rest; **la meg være i — don't** trouble me; **ta det med —** take it coolly, easy; **han har ingen — på seg** he is never at rest; **slå seg til —** settle (down), rest, compose oneself; **slå seg til — med be** el. rest contented with; **begi seg til — betake** oneself to rest, retire to rest.
II. **ro** (krok) corner.
ro (vrb) row, pull, scull; — **hardt** pull hard; — **smått pull hard**; — **vekk!** pull away!
robber(t) (i spill) rubber.
robe robe.
robust robust.
robåt row-boat.
roe turnip, beet.
roe seg (dt.) go to bed, turn in; settle down.
roer rower, boatman.
roesukker beet-root sugar.
I. **rogn** (av fisk) hard roe, spawn.
II. **rogn** (tre) roan (tree), service-tree. **–ebær** service-berry.
rogn|fisk spawner. **–gyting** spawning.
rojalisme royalism. **rojalist** royalist.
rojalistisk royalist.
rokade (i sjakk) castling. **rokere** castle.
I. **rokk** spinning wheel.
II. **rok(k)** (sjø-) sea-spray, spoon-drift; **sqallu.**
rokke (fisk) ray.

rokke (vrb) (rugge) rock; (flytte) move, shake; **steinen er ikke til å** — the stone cannot be moved; — **seg** move, stir.
rokke|hjul spinning-wheel. **-hode** distaff.
rokoko rococo.
rolig quiet, calm, tranquil; (fredelig) placid; (satt) sedate; (fattet) collected; **holde seg** — keep quiet; **være ganske** — for rest assured that; — **søvn** sound sleep; — **samvittighet** clear conscience.
rolighet tranquillity; quiet, calm, placidity; composedness; composure.
rolle part, character, role; **bli i –n** be in character; **falle ut av –n** be out of character; **få legens** — play the physician, be cast for the physician; **spille en** — play (enact, act) a part, (fig) bear a part; **han spilte en svært ynkelig** — he cut a very pitiful figure; **det spiller ingen** — it is of no consequence, it does not matter; **penger spiller ingen** — money is no object.
rollebesetning cast (of the characters).
I. **rom** room, space; (avdelt) compartment; (i en hylle el. hylle) pigeon-hole; (laste-) hold; **et lufttomt** — a vacuum; **gi** — for give way to, make room for.
II. **rom** (spiritus) rum.
Rom (byen) Rome.
roman novel. romance. **-aktig** romantic.
romanforfatter(inne) novellist, fiction writer.
Romania Romania.
romanlitteratur prose fiction.
romanse romance.
romansk Romanic, Romance.
romantiker romanticist. **romantikk** romance; (litteraturretning) romanticism.
romantisk romantic.
rombe rhomb. **rombisk** rhombic.
romer Roman. **romerinne** Roman (lady).
romer|kirken the Roman (Catholic) church, the Church of Rome. **-retten** civil law.
romersk Roman; — **bad** Turkish bath.
romerskkatolsk Roman Catholic.
romertall Roman numeral.
rom|fang bulk, capacity. **-forhold** proportion.
rom|helg, -jul days intervening between Christmas and Twelfth Day.
romlig of space, relating to space.
romme contain, hold.
rommelig roomy, spacious, capacious.
rommelighet spaciousness, capaciousness.
rompudding rum-pudding.
romstere (rote omkring i) rummage; **hvor dr romsterer!** what a noise you are making!
ro(n)ing rowing, pulling, boating.
rop cry, call, shout.
rope call (out), shout; — **opp** call (out); (på auksjon) put up. — **på noen** call sb.
ropert (mar) speaking-trumpet.
ror rudder, helm; **komme til –et** (fig) come into power; (igjen) be restored to power; **lystre –et** answer the helm.
ror|benk thwart. **-bu** fishermen's booth el. shanty (at a fishing station).
ror|gjenger helmsman. **-kult** tiller. **rors|folk** rowers. **-kar** rower.
ros (pris) praise; **ti hans** — in his praise.
rosa, -farget pink, rose.
rose (vrb) praise, commend, laud; — **seg av** glory in, boast of; **uten å** — **meg** without vanity; **rosende** commendatory, laudatory; (i høy grad) panegyrical, eulogistic.
rose (subst) rose; **ingen –r uten torner** no rose without a thorn; **danse på –r** lie on a bed of roses.
rosen (sykdom) St. Anthony's fire, erysipelas, the rose.
rosen|busk rose-bush. **-flor** bloom of roses. **-kål** Brussels-sprouts. **-knopp** rose-bud. **-krans** (katolsk) rosary, beads; **be sin** — count one's beads. **-olje** rose-oil, otto (el. attar) of roses.
rosenrød rosy, rose-coloured, rose-red.

rosenskjær rosy hue.
rosett rosette.
rosignal (mil.) lights out, tap.
rosin raisin. **-kjerne** seed of a raisin.
roskyss pull, row.
rosmarin rosemary.
rosse squall; eddying wind. **-vær** squally weather.
roste (vrb) mash; (metall) roast, torrefy. **-kar** mash-tub, mash-vat. **-ovn** roasting furnace.
rosverdig praiseworthy.
rosverdighet praiseworthiness, laudableness.
I. **rot** root; **feste** — take root; **slå røtter** strike root; **rykke opp med** — (fig) abolish root and branch; (fig) **utrydde det vonde fra –a** root out, extirpate an evil; **dra ut –a** extract the root; **ord av fremmed** — words of a foreign stock.
II. **rot** (et) disorder, jumble, mess, mix; litter.
rotasjon rotation, revolution. **rotasjonspresse** rotary press. **rotere** rotate, revolve. **roterende** rotatory, rotary.
rotbetennelse (i tann) inflammation of the root.
rote (opp f. eks. i jorda) root (the ground); rummage; — **i gamle saker, papirer osv.** rummage among old things, papers etc.; — **opp i en sak** rip up a matter; — **seg inn i noe** embroil oneself in a thing.
rote (i by) ward, quarter; (soldater) file.
roteforstander quarter registrar.
roteksponent number denoting the root.
rotemester tax-gatherer.
rotende (p. tømmer) butt (el. trunk)-end.
rotet(e) messy, tumbled, confused.
rotfast rooted.
rotfeste (subst) rooting.
rotfestet rooted.
rotfrukt (edible) root.
rot|hogge cut off by the root. **-hogger** (fig) destructionist, leveller. **-løs** rootless.
rotskudd sucker, ground shoot.
rotte: — **seg sammen** conspire.
rotte rat. **-felle** rat-trap. **-fenger** rat-catcher. **-gift** ratsbane. **-hund** terrier. **-krutt** ratsbane, arsenic.
rotting ratan.
rottrevl root-fibre.
rotunde rotunda, rotundo.
rotur row, boating excursion.
rotutdraing evolution.
rotvelte (subst) fallen tree, windfall.
rov prey, spoil, plunder; (røveri) rapine, robbery. **gå ut på** — go in search of prey; **leve av** — live by depredation, by plunder.
rovdrift overworking; spoliation of the future; (om åkerbruk) wasteful cultivation.
rovdyr beast of prey.
rove, se hale.
rov|fisk rapacious fish. **-fiske** wasting fishery. **-fugl** bird of prey, raptorial bird. **-lyst** rapacity, rapaciousness. **-lysten** rapacious. **-mord** robbery attended with murder. **-morder** robber and murderer. **-tann** raptorious tooth.
ru rough, rugged; scabrous.
rubb og stubb bag and baggage.
rubel ruble.
rubin ruby.
rubrikk rubric, head, title, article, column.
rubrisere rubricate.
rudi|ment rudiment. **-mentær** rudimentary.
I. **ruff: i en** — in a trice, in a twinkling.
II. **ruff** round house, deck-house, forecastle.
ruffe bawd, procure.
ruffer pimp, pander, procurer. **-i** pimping, pandering. **-ske** bawd, procuress.
rug rye. **rugaks** ear of rye.
rugbrød rye-bread, brown bread.
rugde woodcock. **-trekk** flight of woodcocks.
ruge brood, hatch; — **over** brood over; **den gjerrige –r over sine penger** the miser hoards his money; — **ut** hatch.

ruge|høne brood-hen. **-kasse** breeding pan, nest. **-maskin** hatching-machine, incubator. **-tid** brooding el. hatching season.·

rugg (stor, svær mann) a thumper.

rugge (vrb) move (se **rokke**); rock, vacillate.

rugge (stor, svær kvinne) fat, roll-about person.

rugle (ligge ustøtt) lie insecurely; (rokke, ryste) shake, move. **-te bokstaver** shaky letters.

rug(n)ing brooding, (process of) incubation.

rugskonrok rye biscuit.

ruhet asperity, roughness.

Ruhr the Ruhr.

ruin ruin.

ruinere ruin, destroy; **-nde for** ruinous to.

rujern (råjern) pig-iron.

rulade roulade.

rulett roulette.

I. **rull**, se **rullepølse**.

II. **rull** (åker-) roller; (noe sammenrullet) roll; (kveil) coil.

rulle (vrb) roll; (om blodet) circulate; (tøy) mangle, calender; **— sammen** roll up; **— opp**, **ned gardinene** draw el. pull the blinds up, down. **-nde materiell** rolling stock.

rulle (valse) roll, roller, cylinder; (logg-) reel; (til tøy) mangle; (liste) roll, list. **stå i -ene** be on the roll, in the books.

rulle|blad defaulter-sheet. **rent — a** clean record. **-bu** mangling room.

rulle|gardin (roller-) blind, sun-blind. **-pølse** collered beef.

rulle|skøyte roller-skate. **-stein** (liten rund stein) pebble (større) boulder. **-steinformasjon** mangling cylinder. **-stol** bath-chair. **-tøy** mangled linen; linen to be mangled. **-vogn** trundle, truck.

rult, -e (dt. tyksak) roll-about, squab.

rumen|er, -sk Romanian.

rumle rumble, roll.

rumling rumbling (in the bowels).

rummel rumble, rumbling noise.

rumpe rump, bottom, posteriors (pl); se **hale. -troll** tadpole.

rund round; **rundt** (adv) round; **-t om, omkring** all round; **det går -t for meg** my head begins to swim.

rund|brenner annular burner. **-buestil** round el. circular style.

runde (subst) round, circuit; (politibetjents) beat.

runde (vrb) round; **— en pynt** round a point; **— av** round.

rundelig (rikelig) abundant, liberal.

rundgang circular movement.

rundhet roundness, rotundity.

rund|hode round-head. **-hodet** roundheaded.

rundholt (mar) spar.

rundhåndet generous, liberal, openhanded.

rundhåndethet generosity, liberality.

runding rounding.

rund|jule maul, thrash. **-juling** mauling etc. **rundkast** somersault; **gjøre et — turn** a s.

rund|krets circle. **-last** round timber. **-pullet** round-crowned.

rundreise circuit, round; circular tour, round trip. **-billett** circular (el. round trip) ticket.

rundrygget round-backed, round-shouldered.

rund|skrift roundhand. **-skriv** circular.

rundstykke roll.

rune Rune, Runic character. **-innskrift** Runic inscription. **-skrift** Runic writing. **-stein** Rune stone, Rune stone.

runge ring (again), resound.

runolog runologist.

rus (beruselse) intoxication, inebriation, debauch; **få seg en — get** drunk; **ha en liten — be** fuddled.

rusdrikk intoxicant.

ruse bow-net, weel.

I. **rusk** mote; **et — i øyet** a mote in one's eye; **— og rask** rubbish.

II. **rusk** (svær kar) bouncer, slapper, strapper; thumping fellow.

rusk (adj) dotty, crazy.

ruske pull, shake; **— en i håret** pull el. tear one by the hair.

rusket nasty, rough, stormy. **— vær** nasty el. rough weather.

rusking (rykk) pull, shake, twitch.

ruskomsnusk hodge-podge, gallimaufry.

rusle jog, potter; **jeg hørte noen — i den andre enden av huset** I heard sb. moving at the further end of the house.

russ (student i det første år) freshman; (in Norway also:) collegians being in for their matriculation degree; **kvinnelig — freshman -girl**.

russer, -inne Russian.

russeår freshman year.

russisk Russian; **det russiske språk** the Russian language.

Russland Russia.

russlær Russia, Russian leather.

rust rust; (på korn) blight, smut.

I. **ruste** (bli rusten) rust, become rusty; **— fast** get fixed by rust.

II. **ruste** (væpne) arm; (folk el. skip) equip; (utstyre) fit out; **— seg arm; — seg til en reise** make preparations for a journey.

rusten rusty; **— stemme** hoarse voice.

rustflekk speck el. stain of rust; (p. tøy) iron-mould; **sette -er** iron-mould, rust.

rustifisert countrified.

rust|kammer armoury. **-mester** armourer.

rustning (til å ta på) armour; **-er** warlike el. military preparations.

rustvogn ammunition-waggon, tumbril.

I. **rute** (vei) route; (for befordringsmiddel) line, service; (jernbane-) railway timetable; (skips-) list of sailing; **holde -n** keep (its) time; **holde -n dårlig** keep bad time; **etter -n** at schedule time; **for sent etter -n** overdue; **gå i — mellom ... og ... run** el. be run between ... and ...; **sette i — run**, commence running.

II. **rute** pane (of glass); (firkant) square, diamond.

rute|bil bus; (motor) char-a-banc, passenger car. **-båt** liner, line steamer.

ruteformet square-shaped, diamond-shaped.

rutepapir section paper.

ruter (kort) diamond. **-konge, -dame** osv. king, queen of diamonds etc.

rutet chequered; (om mønster), check, plaid.

rutine experience; routine.

rutinemessig conventional, jog-trot.

rutinert practised, experienced.

rutsje glide, slide.

rutsjebane gliding hill, switchback.

rutte med spend, squander away.

ruve bulk (large, out).

ry (rykte) rumour, report; (berømmelse) rènown, fame; **ha — for, stå i — for** be renowned for; **komme i — get** into repute.

ry (adj) wild, waste; (altfor likefram) blunt, rough; se også **ujevn**.

rydde clear; **— av veien** remove, clear away, make away with; **— opp** put in order, clear, (hos kjøpmenn) sell off.

ryddig orderly, tidy, clear.

rydning clearing; **rydnings|arbeid** work of clearing; (fig) pioneer work; **-mann** clearer; pioneer.

rye (teppe) rug.

rygg back; (fjell-, jord-, tak-) ridge; **falle i -en** attack in the rear; **vende en -en** turn one's back upon one; **ha noe i -en** be in easy circumstances; **ha en bred — (fig) have a strong back; for å ha -en fri** to secure one's retreat.

ryggbein backbone, spine.

rygge (drive el. gå tilbake) back.

rygg|felt (på bokbind) panel. **-finne** dorsal fin.

ryggesløs profligate, reprobate, abandoned. **ryggesløshet** profligacy, depravity. **rygg|etikett** (på bok) label. **-hvirvel** dorsal vertebra. **-marg** spinal marrow, spinal cord. **-margstæring** dorsal consumption. **-rad** spine, backbone. **-sekk** rucksack. **-skjold** carapax. **-stykke** back. **-stø** support for the back; (fig) backing, support. **-tak** wrestling

ryggtitel lettering; **sette** — **på** letter.

I. **ryke** (fare) rush, dart, fly; (gå i stykker) break, burst, snap; (tape penger) be a loser, go to the bad; — **av pinnen** be turned out of one's place; **den planen røk** the plan came to nothing; — **løs på** fly at; — **ihop** fall to loggerheads; **hammeren røk av skaftet** the hammer flew off the handle.

II. **ryke** (om skorstein) smoke; (dampe) reek; (ulme) smoulder.

rykk tug, jerk, wrench.

rykke (vt.) pull, jerk, pluck; (kreve) dun; (vi.) pull, edge up; hitch, jerk; — **fram** advance; — **inn i et land** march into el. invade a country; — **inn i en avis** insert in a newspaper; — **nærmere** approach, (f. eks. med en stol) draw (one's chair) nearer (to); — **sammen** close; sit closer, move up; — **tilbake** retire, retreat, draw back; — **ut** march out; — **ut med** come out with.

rykker dunner, dun. **rykkerbrev** dunning letter, dun.

rykkevis el. **rykkvis** by jerks, by (fits and) starts.

rykte report, rumour; (frasagn) fame, repute. reputation, character; **-t sier** report says; **ens gode navn og** — one's reputation, character; **et godt** — a good name; **han har ikke det beste** — his reputation is none of the best.

ryktes be rumoured, get wind.

ryktesmed coiner el. spreader of reports.

rynke (subst) wrinkle; (fold) pucker, fold; (legg) tuck, gather.

rynke (vrb) wrinkle, pucker; (legge i legg) gather; — **på nesen av** turn up one's nose at; — **pannen** knit one's brows, frown.

rynket wrinkled, furrowed, corrugated.

rype ptarmigan, white grouse; (den engelske) red grouse. **-jakt** grousing. **-kull** brood el. pack of grouse. **-kylling** grouse chick. **-sekk, se rygg-sekk. -stegg** cock grouse.

rysj ruche.

ryste (el. **riste**) shake; — **av seg** shake off; — **på hodet** shake one's head; **rystende** (fig) harrowing, heart-wringing. **rystelse** shaking, shake, concussion, tremor.

rytme rhythm. **rytmikk** rhythmics.

rytmisk rhythmical.

rytter horsemann, rider, equestrian; (mil) horsesoldier, trooper; **en god** — a good horseman. **rytteri** horse, cavalry. **rytter|statue** equestrian statue. **-veksel** accomodation-bill (of exchange).

rær, pl. av **rå.**

rø, se **snakke.**

rød red, (karmosin) crimson; **bli** — turn red, redden; **bli** — **i hodet** blush, colour (up).

rød|bete red beet, beet-radish. **-blomstret hagtorn** pink-flowered hawthorn, red may. **-blond** (om hår) sandy. **-brun** reddish brown, maroon, (om hest) bay.

rødbøk common beech.

rødegardist red guard.

røde hunder (sykdom) roseola.

Røde Kors Red Cross.

rød|flekket spotted with red, red-flecked. **-glødende** red-hot. **-grøt** red sago-pudding.

Rødhette little Red Ridinghood. **rød|huder** Redskins. **-håret** red-haired. **-kinnet** red-cheeked, rosy-cheeked. **-kjelke** redbreast, robin. **-kløver** purple el. red clover. **-kritt** red chalk, ruddle; **merke med** — ruddle. **-kål** red cabbage.

rød|lett ruddy-faced. **-lig** reddish.

rødme (vrb) redden, blush, colour (up) (av: with).

rødme (subst) blush, flush. **rødming** blushing etc.

rødmusset ruddy (-cheeked), rubicund. **rød|neset** red-nosed. **-rutet** red-chequered. **-skjegget** red-bearded.

rødspette plaice.

rødsprengt florid, blowzy.

rødstripet striped with red.

rød|topp red-haired fellow. **-vin** claret. **-vins-toddy** mulled claret. **-øyd** red-eyed.

røffel blow up. **røfle** blow up.

røk, røke, se **røyk, røyke.**

røkelse incense, frankincense. **-skar** censer

røkt care, tending, keeping.

røkte tend, look to, take care of.

røkter tender, herdsman, cowman.

røllik (plante) milfoil, nosebleed, yarrow.

rømling, se **rømningsmann.**

rømme (vi.) decamp, run away; desert; (vt.) quit, flee from; evacuate; — **en plass** vacate a seat; — **seg** clear one's throat, hum and haw.

rømme (fløte) cream; old cream. **-graut** cream porridge. **-kolle** curdled cream.

rømning flight, escape, decampment; desertion; evacuation. **rømningsmann** runaway, fugitive, deserter.

rønne hovel, dilapidated building.

røntgenfotograf Röntgen photographer, x-ray photographer. **-i** Röntgen photograph, x-ray photograph.

røpe betray, disclose, let out; (legge for dagen) evince; — **seg** betray oneself.

I. **rør** (plante) reed, (til pipe, vann osv.) pipe, tube, funnel; (skorsteins-) flue.

II. **rør** (vås) nonsense, twaddle.

røre (vrb) touch; (sette i bevegelse) move, stir; (våse) talk nonsense; **fiske i rørt vann** fish in troubled water; **rørt smør** butter-sauce; — **seg** stir, move; — **rundt, opp (i)** stir about, up; — **sammen** mix up, stir about; — **ut** rub.

I. **røre** (forvirring) muddle; (sterk bevegelse) stir, commotion.

II. **røre** (i matlaging) batter, paste.

rørelse emotion, agitation.

rørende touching, affecting, pathetic. **røret(e)** (våset) drivelling, nonsensical. **rør|fletning** cane-plaiting; mat of reeds. **-fløyte** reed. **-formet** tubular, cannular.

rørig valid, active; (om mat) heavy; **rask og** — hale and vigorous. **rørighet** vigour. **rør|ledning** conduit (of pipes). **-legger** plumber.

rørlig movable; — **og urørlig gods** real and personal property.

rør|stol cane- el. rush-bottomed chair. **-sukker** cane sugar. **-sete** cane-bottom.

røske pull.

røslig burly, stately.

røsslyng carline heather, heath, ling.

I. **røst** voice; **med høy** — in a loud voice.

II. **røst** (på hus) gable.

røste (stemme) vote.

røstverk (mar) grating.

røtter pl. av **rot.**

røve seize (upon), plunder, steal; **-t gods** plunder.

røver robber, highwayman, brigand; (sjø-) pirate. **-aktig** robber-like, predatory. **-bande** gang of robbers. **-bøle** den of robbers. **-gods** plunder, spoil. **-historie** (dt.) cock-and-bull story, fishy story.

røverhule, se **røverbøle.**

røveri robbery, depredation; piracy. **røver|kaptein** captain of robbers. **-kule:** gjøre sitt hjerte til en **-kule** be double-hearted, insincere, a hypocrite. **-kjøp: jeg fikk det for -kjøp** I had it a dead bargain. **-liv** life of brigandage. **-pakk** pack of robbers. **-reir** thieves' nest.

røversk robberlike, predatory, rapacious.

røver|stat piratical state, community of robbers. **-unge** (dt.) wild monkey. **-vis: på** — like robbers.

røy capercali hen.

røye red char.

røyk smoke; det gikk som en — it was done in a trice; **gå opp i** — be consumed by fire; (fig) come to nothing, end in smoke. **-aktig** smoky.

røyk|e smoke; smoke-dry, (især for smitte) fumigate; (tobakk) smoke; — **med** (røkelse) burn; — **inn en pipe** blacken, brown el. season a pipe; — **ut** (f. eks. en rev) smoke out. **-t flesk** smoke-cured ham; **-t kjøtt** smoke-cured meat; **-t sild** herring dried and smoked, red herring, bloater; **-t skinke** smoke-cured ham.

røykekupé smoking compartment.

røyker smoker. **røykeværelse** smoking-room.

røykeri smoking-place.

røyk|fang flue, uptake; chimney-hood. **-fordrivende** smoke-preventing. **-fortærende** smoke-consuming. **-fri** smokeless. **-fylt** smoky. **-hatt** chimney-hood, turn-cap. **-hette** chimney-cap, turn-cap.

røyking smoking; fumigation; — **forbudt** no smoking (is) allowed.

røyk|nedslag return smoke. **-sky** cloud of smoke. **-søyle** column of smoke.

røynd: i -a in reality, in effect.

røyne try, experience; — **på** tell upon, try.

røynsle experience, practice.

røys heap el. pile of stone; (varde) cairn.

røyskatt stoat; (i vinterdrakt) ermine.

røyte (el. **røte**) moult, shed.

rå (subst) yard.

rå (adj) raw; (fig. ufordøyd) crude; (ikke bearbeidd, uoppdragen) rude; coarse, vulgar; (luft) damp, raw.

rå (vrb): — **med** handle, be a match for; — **seg selv** act for oneself el. on one's own account; **la ham** — **seg selv** let him please himself; — **seg til med** (skaffe seg) provide oneself with. Se ogs. **råde**.

råbarket undertanned; (fig) raw-hide, rawish.

råbukk roebuck.

råd (utvei) means, expedient; (middel til å bøte på noe) remedy; (forlangt, gitt råd) advice, counsel; (rådsforsamling) council; **finne på** — hit upon some expedient, find a way; **jeg vet ikke levende** — I am at my wits' end; **gode** — good advice; **her er gode** — **dyre** this is a difficult case; **følge ens** — take one's advice, be advised by one; **legge** — **opp** (imot) conspire, plot (against); **med** — **og dåd** by word and deed; **jeg har ikke** — **til det** I cannot afford it; **borgermester og** — mayor and aldermen; **et** — a piece of advice; **spørre en om** — consult one, ask advice of one.

rå(de) advise, counsel; (herske over) rule over; la bare meg —, så ... leave it no me, and ...; — over command, dispose of; **her -r han ikke** he has no command el. authority here; — **bot på** remedy.

rådelig advisable.

råderom free scope, liberty of action.

rådføre seg consult, ask advice (**med: of**).

rådgivende advising, counselling; — **stender** consultative estates.

rådgiver adviser, counsellor.

rådhus townhall, council-house.

rådig over master of.

rådighet command, authority; **ha** — **over** have at one's disposal el. command; **stå til min** — be at my command.

rådløs perplexed, puzzled, at one's wit's end, at a loss. **-het** perplexity.

rådmann alderman.

rådsdreng farm foreman.

rådsforsamling meeting of a council.

rådsherre senator, councillor.

råd|slagning conference, consultation, deliberation. **-slå** deliberate el. consult together. **-snar** resourceful, ready el. quick at expedients. **-snarhet** resourcefulness, readiness (of resource).

rådspørre consult.

rådsrepublikk red republic, Soviet republic.

rådstue (glt.) = **rådhus**; (dt.) police-office.

rådvill irresolute, perplexed, puzzled; **aldri** — quick at expedients.

rådvillhet irresolution, perplexity.

rådyr roe, roedeer.

råemne raw material, rough stuff.

råhet rawness; (fig) rudeness, roughness.

råk (spor) track, trail; (fe-) cattle-track; (i isen) cut in the ice; lane el. lead of water.

råke (treffe) hit, strike; (møte) chance to meet, fall in with; — **til å** chance el. happen to.

råke (toppmål) heaped measure.

råkald raw cold.

råkjører road hog.

råmateriale raw material.

råmelk beestings.

råne (hangris) boar.

rånokk yard-arm.

råprodukter raw products, raw produce.

rårand (i brød) watery-streak; **brødet har** — the bread is water-streaked.

rås, se **råk**.

rå|seil square-sail; **føre** — be square-rigged. **-silke** raw silk. **-skrelle** peel while raw. **-stoff** raw material. **-tamp** Goth, yahoo; (amr.) rowdy.

råtne rot, putrefy, decay.

råtten rotten, putrid, decayed, foul.

råttenskap rottenness, decay.

S

S, s s S, s.

sabb lumping fellow.

sabbat Sabbath.

sabbe slouch, shuffle.

sabel sword; (ryttersabel) sabre.

sabel|bajonett sword-bayonet. **-geheng** sabre-belt. **-grep** sword-handle. **-hefte** hilt of a sword. **-hogg** sabre cut. **-klinge** blade of a sabre. **-klirring** clank of swords.

sabotasje sabotage. **sabotere** sabotage.

Sachsen Saxony; i sams. Saxe, f. eks. — **-Meiningen** Saxe-Meiningen. — **-Weimar** Saxe-Weimar.

saffian Morocco-leather.

safir sapphire. **safirblå** sapphirine.

safran saffron.

saft juice; (i trær) sap; (innkokt med sukker)

syrup; (av stekt el. kokt kjøtt) gravy; **uten** — el. **kraft** stale, flat.

saftfull juicy, succulent, sappy.

saftig juicy, sappy; (fig) coarse.

saftighet juiciness, succulence, sappiness.

saftrik juicy, succulent, sappy.

sag saw.

saga Saga; record; **er snart bare en** — is almost traditionary; **han er ute av -en** there is an end of him.

saga|mann Scandinavian bard, saga-man.

sagarbeider sawmill hand.

sagatid age of sagas.

sag|blad blade of a saw. **-bruk** saw-mill.

sage saw.

sag|flis sawdust. **-krakk** saw-horse; (amr) saw-buck. **-mugg**, se **-flis**.

sagn tradition, legend, myth; (folkesnakk, rykte) report, rumour.
sagn|figur legendary personage. **–krets** cycle of traditions. **–messig** traditional, mythic.
sagntid mythical age, heroic era.
sago, –gryn sago. **–mel, –mjøl** sago-powder.
sagopalme sago-palm.
sag|skjærer sawyer. **–takket** saw-toothed, serrate. **–tann** saw-tooth. **–tind** tooth of a saw.
Sahara the Sahara.

sak thing, matter; (interesse, idé) cause; (rettssak) case; (forretning) affair, business; (omstendighet) matter, concern; **anlegge — mot en** bring an action against one; **i en god –s tjeneste** in a good cause; **tale ens —** plead one's cause; **det blir hans —** it's his (own) business, affair, look-out; **det er så sin —** it is an awkward thing; **sikker i sin —** certain that one is right; **for den –s skyld** for the matter of that; **det er (nettopp) –en** that's the thing; **la oss komme til –en** let us come to the point; **holde seg til –en** stick to the subject in hand; **det gjør ingenting til –en** that's nothing to the purpose; **til –en!** to the point! (i parlam.:) Question! **gjøre sine –er godt, dårlig** do one's work, acquit oneself well, poorly; **blande seg i andres –er** intermeddle in other people's concerns.
sakarin saccharin.
sakesløs unoffending, blameless.
sak|fører lawyer; solicitor; (som prosederer for retten) barrister. **–førerbevilling** the right to advocate causes el. maintain pleas; **få –førerbevilling** be called to the bar. **–førerfullmektig** solicitor's clerk. **–førsel** pleading (of a cause).
sakke akterut drop behind.
sak|kunnskap knowledge of the subject, competence. **–kyndig** conversant with the subject, competent, expert. **–kyndighet, se –kunnskap.**
saklig real, pertinent; (om person) concerned about facts. **–het** reality, pertinence.
sakn, sakne, se savn, savne.
sakrament(e) sacrament; **gi –et** administer the sacrament.
sakregister index of subjects, subject-index, index rerum.
sakristi vestry, sacristy.
saks (a pair of) scissors; (stor) shears; (fangst-redskap) steel-trap; **–a** the scissors.
saksanlegg action in the courts, prosecution.
sakser, (–inne) Saxon. **saksisk** Saxon.
saksofon saxophone.
saksomkostninger costs of action (of proceedings of suit).
sak|søke sue, prosecute, action, proceed against, take the law of. **–søker** plaintiff, prosecutor. **–søkning** prosecution.
sakte soft, gentle; slow; (adv) softly, gently; slowly; **uret går 10 minutter for —** the watch is ten minutes slow; **snakk —!** speak low! **han snakket —** he spoke in a low voice, below el. under his breath.
saktelig (adv) softly, gently.
saktens easily, (formodentlig) I dare say.
saktmodig mild, meek, gentle. **saktmodighet** mildness, meekness, gentleness.
saktne moderate; **— sin gang, sine skritt** slacken one's pace.
sakvolder defendant.
I. **sal** (large) room, hall; (selskapsværelse) drawing-room.
II. **sal** (på hest) saddle; **sitte fast i –en** have a firm seat, be firmly seated; **kaste en av –en** unhorse one; **svinge seg i –en** spring into the saddle, spring to one's saddle.
salamander salamander.
salat (plante) lettuce; (rett) salad.
salatfat salad-dish.
sal|bom saddle-tree. **–brutt** galled by the saddle. **–dekken** saddle-cloth, housing.

saldere balance.
saldo balance; **— i vår favør** balance in our favour.
sale saddle; **— av** unsaddle, off-saddle; dt. **— om** change one's opinion el. behaviour, turn coat, come round; **han rir ikke den dag han –r** he is a slow coach. **saling** saddling.
salfast firm in the saddle.
salg sale; (av verdipapirer) negotiation; **til –s** for sale, on sale. **–bar** saleable.
salgs|betingelser terms el. conditions of sale. **–pris** selling price. **–regning** account-sales (fork. A|S). **–vare** sale product.
salig blessed, blest; saved; (lykksalig) blissful; (drukken) glorious, elevated; **min — far, mor** my late (el. poor) father, mother.
salig|gjørelse salvation, beatification. **–gjørende** saving. **–het** salvation, eternal happiness; (lykksalighet) blessedness, bliss, felicity; **den evige —** eternal happiness.
saling (på skip) cross-trees.
salisyl salicyle. **–syre** salicylic acid.
sal|knapp pommel of a saddle. **–maker** saddler. **–makermester, –makersvenn** master-, journeyman-saddler.
salme hymn; (især Davids s.) psalm; **Davids –r** the Book of Psalms.
salme|bok hymn-book. **–dikter** hymnist. **–dikt-ning** hymnography. **–sang** psalm-singing, hymn-singing.
salmiakk sal-ammoniac, ammoniac chloride.
salmiakkspiritus spirit of sal-ammoniac.
salmist psalmist.
Salomo(n) Solomon. **salomonisk** Solomonic.
salong drawing-room; (på dampskip) saloon.
salongfähig fit for the drawing-room.
salonggevær parlour-gun.
salong|helt carpet knight. **–vogn** saloon carriage.
salpeter salpeter, nitre. **–aktig** nitrous. **–holdig** nitrous, nitric. **–syre** nitric acid.
sal|plass (veddeløp) paddock. **–pute** saddle-pad. **–reim** strap. **–rygget** hollow-backed; saddle el. sway-backed.
salt (subst) salt; **engelsk —** (Epsom) salts. **salt** (adj) salt. **saltaktig** saltish, saline.
saltaske saddle-flap.
salt-brott, –brudd salt quarry.
saltdannelse salification.
salte salt, cure; (i lake) pickle; (nedsalte) corn; **–t oksekjøtt** corned beef. **–ri** salting-house. **–trau** salting trough. **–tønne** powdering tub.
saltgruve salt-pit. **salthet** saltness.
salt|holdig saline. **–holdighet** degree of saltness. **–kar** saltcellar; (stort, til kjøkkenet) salt-box. **–kjelde** saltspring. **–koker** salt-manufacturer. **–koking** salt-making. **–korn** grain of salt. **–lake** brine, pickle. **–lut** salt-lye. **–mat** salt meat.
saltomortale somerset, somersault.
sal|tre, se –bom.
salt|støtte pillar of salt. **–sjø** salt-lake. **S–sjø-staden** Salt Lake City. **–syre** muriatic acid. **–tønne** salt-barrel. **–vann** salt-water, sea-water. **–vannsfisk** salt-water fish. **–verk** salt-work, saltern.
salutt a salute. **saluttere** salute, fire a salute.
I. **salve** (geværsalve) volley, salvo; (bifalls-) round (of applause).
II. **salve** (smurning) salve, ointment, unguent.
salve (vrb) anoint; **Herrens –de** the Lord's anointed.
salvekrukke ointment pot.
salvelse anointment, unction; **preke med —** preach with unction. **salvelsesfull** full of unction canting.
salvere seg save oneself.
salvie sage. **–te** sage-tea.
salving anointing, anointment.
salær fee.
samarbeid working together, co-operation.
samarbeide work together, co-operate.

samarie (prestekjole) cassock.
samaritan Samaritan.
samaritt ambulance class man.
samaritt|kursus ambulance class. **-tjeneste** ambulance duty.
sam|band binding tie, connecting link. **-beite** common grazing. **-bladet** gamopetalous.
sambo (krysning mellom neger og indianer) Zambo, Sambo.
sambygding fellow-parishioner.
samdrektig agreeing, unanimous.
samdrektighet harmony, unanimity.
samdrift co-operative business.
same, se **lapp.**
sameie joint-property, joint-possession, joint-ownership, co-ownership.
sameier joint-proprietor, joint-owner.
samfengt mixed, unsorted.
samferdsel communication, intercourse.
samfull: i ti -e år these (el. full) ten years; **-e fem dager** five clear days.
samfunn community, society; **-et** society.
samfunns|farlig dangerous to the community. **-fiende** enemy to society. **-forhold** social conditions. **-klasse** class of society. **-lære** sociology. **-orden** social order. **-sak** social question. **-stilling** social position. **-ånd** social spirit.
samfølelse fellow-feeling, sympathy.
sam|handel commerce. **-hold** concord, union. **-hørig** interdependent, solidary. **-hørighet** solidarity. **-kjensle**, se **-følelse.**
samklang harmony, unison.
samkvem intercourse, communion.
samlag connection, partnership; (brennevins-) trust-company (licensed for selling liquor).
samle collect, gather; — **rikdommer** lay up el. heap up riches; — **inn**, se **innsamle**: — **opp** pick up; — **på (noe)** collect; — **sammen**, se **samle**: — **seg** gather, assemble; — **seg, sine tanker** collect oneself, one's thoughts; **samles** gather (together), assemble, meet, congregate; **mens stortinget er -t** while parliament is sitting; **-t verdi** aggregate value; **-t opptreden** joint action; **samlede verker** complete el. entire works; **samlet** (adv) together, jointly, in the lump.
samleie copulation; **ha** — copulate.
samlending fellow-countryman, **-woman.**
samler collector. **-arbeid** compilation. **-lyst** love of collecting. **-mani** craze of collecting.
samling assembling, collection; (av folk) meeting; (av planter) collection; (av storting) session; **gå fra sans og** — lose one's senses entirely; **være ved full** — be in one's right senses.
samlingsnavn collective noun.
samlingssignal muster-call.
samlings|sted rallying-place. **-tid** time of meeting; length of session.
samliv living together, common life.
sammalt unbolted; — **brød** wholemeal bread.
samme the same; **i el. med det** — at the same time; **det er det** — **for meg** it is the same to me, it is all one to me; **den selvsamme** the very same; **det kan være det** — never mind; **det kan være det** — **for deg** that is nothing to you; **det er det** — **som å si** it is as much as to say.
sammen together; (i forening) jointly, between them; — **med** together with.
sammenbitt: med -e tenner with clenched teeth, with one's mouth hard set.
sammenblande mix together. **sammenblanding** commixture, mingling.
sammenbrakte barn children of different beds.
sammen|brott, -brudd breakdown, collapse.
sammendra draw together, collect; (en sak, fortelling) epitomize, make an abstract of.
sammenfatte comprise, sum up.
sammenfiltre entangle, mat together.
sammenfoldet folded up, doubled up.
sammen|føye join, put together. **-føyning** joining, junction; (stedet) joint, jointing.

sammenheng coherence, cohesion; (fig) connection; **mangel på** — incoherence; **uten** — incoherently; **han forklarte hele -en** he explained the whole affair.
sammenhengende connected, coherent, continuous, consecutive; (adv) coherently.
sammen|hold cohesion, coherence; (fig) union, harmony, concord. **-holde** (fig) compare, confront.
sammenhop(n)ing crowding, conglomeration.
sammenhørende of one set.
sammenkalle call (together), convoke, convene, summon.
sammenkittet cemented.
sammenkjedet chained together, linked together, concatenated.
sammenklumpet conglomerated.
sammenklump(n)ing conglomeration.
sammenknepet contracted.
sammenkomst meeting, interview.
sammenkrøpet crouching.
sammenligne compare (**med:** with, to), liken to; **kunne ikke -s med** could not compare with, could not be compared to. **-nde** comparative.
sammenligning comparison, parallel; **gjøre** **-er** make el. institute comparisons; **i** — **med** in comparison with, (as) compared with, to; **uten** — without c., incomparably, immeasurably, (ved superl.) by far, by many degrees, far and away.
sammenligningsgrad degree of comparison.
sammen|likne, -likning osv., se **-ligne, -ligning.**
sammenpakket packed (up); (fig) crowded.
sammenpresset pressed el. squeezed together.
sammenpressing compression.
sammenrotte seg conspire, plot.
sammenrotting conspiracy, plot.
sammensatt compound; (innviklet) complex; — **ord** compound.
sammensetning composition; (konkret) compound. **sammensette**, se **sette sammen.**
sammenskrapt scraped together.
sammen|skrudd screwed together; **-skrudd is** closely packed ice. **-skruing** screwing.
sammenskudd collection, contribution, subscription.
sammenslutning union, combination.
sammenslynget interwoven, intertwined.
sammenslyngning interweaving.
sammen|smelte melt together; (fig) algamate. **-smelt(n)ing** fusion; amalgamation.
sammensnodd twined together.
sammen|snørt laced together. **-snøring** contraction, constriction.
sammensparte penger savings.
sammenspleiset spliced together.
sammenstablet piled up, heaped up.
sammenstille place together; group; parallel, compare. **sammenstilling** juxtaposition, collocation; comparison.
sammenstimling gathering, crowd.
sammenstuet packed, stowed together.
sammenstøt concussion, collision, conflict; (mar) collision, foul; (fiendtlig) encounter; (av omstendigheter) coincidence, concurrence.
sammenstøtende concurrent.
sammensunket sunk down; sunk into ruin; (fig) prostrate, unnerved.
sammensurium mess, omnium gatherum.
sammensveise weld together.
sammensveis(n)ing welding together.
sammen|sverge seg conspire (om å: to); de **-svorne** the conspirators.
sammensvergelse conspiracy, plot.
sammensydd sewn together, seamed. **sammensyning** sewing together; (søm, syning) seam.
sammentelling summing up.
sammentreff coincidence.
sammentrekke contract; **som lar seg** — contractible.
sammentrekning contraction.

sammen|trengt condensed, compact, concentrated, concise, succinct. **-trengthet** concentration, compactness.
sammentrykning compression.
sammentrykt compressed, squeezed together.
sammenvevd woven together.
sammenviklet rolled together, wrapped up.
sammen|voksing accretion, concretion. **-vokst** coalesced, grown into one.
samme|steds in the same place. **-stedsfra** from the same place. **-stedshen** to the same place.
samnorsk all-Norse, pan-Norwegian.
samrøring mixing up, confusion.
samrå seg consult together, take advice with.
samråd (joint) deliberation.
sams, se enig.
samsang chorus, chorus-singing.
samskipnad organization.
samskole co-education school.
samspill ensemble; **det var utmerket — they played together excellently.
samstem|me harmonize, be in unison, (fig) agree. **-mig** agreeing, concordant; **ikke —** discordant; **-te gemytter** congenial minds. **-thet** agreement, accordance, harmony.
samstilling apposition; (astronomi) conjunction.
samstundes, se samtidig.
sam|svarende, -svarig symmetrical, corresponding.
samt together with; as also, and (at the same time).
samtale (subst) conversation; (lett s.) talk; **føre en —** carry on a conversation; **komme i — med** get (el. fall) into conversation with.
samtale (vrb) converse, talk (med: with).
samtaleemne topic (of conversation).
samtaleform colloquial form.
samtid: hans, vår — his, our contemporaries; the age.
samtidig contemporary, contemporaneous; (som inntreffer s.) simultaneous; **— med** coincident with; **våre -e** our contemporaries.
samtidig (adv) at the same time; contemporaneously.
samtlige one and all, each and all.
samtykke (vrb) consent; **— i** consent to, agree to; **nikke -nde** nod assent; **smilte -nde** smiled adhesion.
samtykke (subst) consent, assent.
samvirke (subst) joint action; (merk. etc) co-operation. **-lag** co-operative association.
samum (tørr ørkenvind) simoom.
samvittighet conscience; **en god, ren — a** quiet, clear conscience; **en rommelig, elastisk — a large el. accommodating c.; **det kan du gjøre med god —** you can do it with a safe c.; **hva har du på -en?** what have you on your mind? **så får du det på -en** you will have that to answer for.
samvittighets|full conscientious, scrupulous, religious. **-fullhet** conscientiousness, scrupulosity. **-kval** pangs of conscience. **-løs** unprincipled, unconscientious, unscrupulous.
samvittighets|nag remorse, compunction. **-sak** matter of conscience. **-skruppel** scruple of conscience. **-spørsmål** question of c.; indiscreet question. **-tvang** restraint of c., intolerance.
samvær being el. living together; (møte) meeting; (selskapelig) convivialities, (social) gathering; **farvel og takk for -et!** this has been a pleasant party indeed . . . good-bye! **etter en times —** after one hour together.
sanatorium sanatorium (pl. -ria).
sand sand, (grov) gravel; **strø — på sand,** (fig) blindly endorse; (fig) **løpe ut i -en** come to nothing, end in smoke. **-aktig** sandy.
sandal sandal.
sand|banke sand-bank, sands (pl.) **-bunn** sand bottom.
sandeltre sandal-wood.

sandet sandy, sanded, sabulous.
sande til be filled with sand.
sand|flukt sand-drift. **-grop** little sand-pit. **-haug** heap of sand. **-jord** sandy soil.
sand|kake sponge-cake. **-korn** grain of sand. **sand|mel** gravel bank, sandy steep. **-mo** sandy plain.
sandpapir sand-paper.
sand|stein sandstone, grit. **-strø** (vrb) sand. **sand|tak** sand-pit. **-øyr** sandy delta. **-ørken** sandy desert.
sang song; (abstrakt) singing; (del av større dikt) canto. **-bar** adapted for singing, melodious. **-barhet** melodiousness.
sangbunn sound-board, sounding-board.
sanger singer, vocalist, vocal performer, professional (man); (fugl) warbler; (fig) poet, bard, minstrel. **sangerinne** singer, vocalist, songstress, (foraktel.) singing girl.
sang|forening singing club, choral union, glee society. **-fugl** singing bird. **-kor** choir. **-lerke** sky-lark. **-lærer(inne)** singing-master, professor of singing.
sangrik melodious.
sangstemme singing voice.
sangundervisning teaching of singing.
sangviniker sanguine person.
sangvinsk sanguine.
sanitet sanitary service el. staff.
sanitetsforening nursing society.
sanitetsvesen sanitary system.
sanitær sanitary; **-e forhold** sanitary conditions.
sanke gather, collect, cull, pick; **— aks** glean.
sanksjon sanction, assent.
sanksjonere sanction; give one's assent to.
sankt Saint, St.
sankthans|aften Midsummer eve. **-bål** fire of Midsummer eve. **-dag** Midsummer day, St. John's day. **-natt** Midsummer night. **-orm** glow-worm.
sanktveisdans the St. Vitus's dance, chorea.
sann|n true; (virkelig) real; **det var en — lykke** it was a piece of real good luck; **det -e the truth; -t å si** to say el. tell the truth; **så -t jeg lever** as I live; **så -t hjelpe meg Gud** so help me God; **det er -t!** by the bye! **ikke et -t ord** not a word of truth; **det er godt, ikke -t?** it is good, isn't it? **du kom der, ikke -t?** you came there, did you not (didn't you)? **han så det, ikke -t?** he saw it, eh?
sanndru veracious, truthful.
sanndruhet veracity, truthfulness.
sanndrømt dreaming true dreams.
sanne find the truth of, verify.
sannelig indeed, truly, verily, in truth, of a truth, in all conscience.
sannferdig veracious. **sannferdighet** veracity.
sannhet truth; **den rene —** the real el. exact truth; **si -en** speak (the) truth; **når jeg skal si -en** to tell the truth.
sannhets|kjærlig veracious. **-kjærlighet** veracity, love of truth. **-vitne** confessor, martyr.
sanning truth. Se også **sannhet.**
sann|si(g)er soothsayer. **-spådd** prophesying true; **jeg var -spådd** I prophesied true, proved a true prophet.
sannsynlig likely, probable.
sannsynlighet likelihood, probability, verisimilitude; **etter all —** in all probability. **-sberegning** calculation of probabilities.
sannsynligvis probably, in all likelihood; **han kommer —** he is likely to come, he will probably come.
sans sense; **sunn —** plain, good sense; **ha — for** have a sense of; **han har ingen — for musikk,** poesi he has no taste for music, poetry; **være fra — og samling** be out of one's senses.
sanse perceive, notice.
sansebedrag illusion el. deception (of the senses). **sansekake** (ørefik) refresher.
sanselig of the sense, belonging to el. affect-

ing the sense, **sensuous**, (legemlig) physical, material, (mest i slett bet.) sensual.
sanselighet sensuousness, sensualism.
sanse|løs senseless, insensible; (forvirret) thoughtless, heedless. **-løshet** senselessness; bewilderment. **-organ** organ of sense, sense-organ. **-rus** intoxication of the senses. **-verden** sensual el. external world.
sanskrit Sanscrit, Sanskrit.
sanskulott sansculotte.
sans(n)ing perception, sensation.
sapør sapper.
sara|sener, -sensk Saracen.
sardell, sardin sardel, sardine.
Sardinia Sardinia. **sardinsk** Sardinian.
sarkasme sarcasm. **sarkastisk** sarcastic(al).
sarkofag sarcophagus.
sart delicate, tender.
Satan Satan. **satanisk** satanic(al).
sateng sateen.
satinere glaze, hot-press.
satire satire. **satiriker** satirist.
satirisere over satirize. **satirisk** satirical.
satisfaksjon satisfaction.
sats (påstand) assertion, proposition; (blanding) mixture, composition, (dt. compo); (typograf.) form, composition, matter in type; (musikk) composition, (avdel.) movement; (på fyrstikk) head; (v. sprang) taking off; **ta –** take off.
satt (adj) sedate, staid, (om vesen) demure, grave.
satyr satyr. **satyraktig** satyr-like.
sau sheep; (søye) ewe; (skjellsord) blockhead, ninny. **–bukk** ram.
saue|fjøs sheep-cot(e). **–grind** sheepcot, -fold, -pen. **–kjøtt** mutton. **–klipping** sheep-shearing. **-kve,** se **–grind. -lett** natural colour (of wool). **-lår** leg of mutton. **-saks** sheep-shears. **-skinn** sheep-skin; (til bokbind) roan. **-skinnspels** sheep-skin jacket el. coat. **-slag** breed of sheep.
sauet (adj) sheepish.
saumfare inspect el. overhaul the nails (of an implement); (fig) overhaul narrowly, go over (very critically), minutely examine.
saus sauce; **– til salat** salad-dressing.
sauseskål sauce-boat.
sauterne (vinsort) Sauterne.
savn want; (tap) loss, privation, bereavement, regret.
savne want, feel the want of, miss; **de -de** the missing men (el. people); **-r all grunn** is devoid of all foundation.
Savoia Savoy. **savoiard** Savoyard.
scene scene; **-n** (teateret) the stage; **sette i –** get up, place on the boards el. scene; **gå over -n** be acted, performed; **gå til -n** go on the stage; **for åpen –** with raised curtain; in public; **det kom til en –** there was a scene.
scene|arrangement stage directions. **-forandring** scene-shifting. **-instruktør** stage-manager. **-vanthet** stage practice el. experience.
scenisk scenic, stage, theatrical.
Schlesien Silesia. **schlesisk** Silesian.
se (ha synsevnen, bli var, innse) see; (rette blikket) look; (flyktig rette blikket) glance; (kike i smug) peep; (se ufravendt) gaze; (stirre) stare; **la meg –** (vent et øyeblikk) let me see; **så vidt jeg kan se** as far as I can see; **se! look!** (høytidelig) lo! behold! **– godt, dårlig** have a good, bad sight; **la seg –** put in an appearance, make one's a.; **se! se! –r man det!** indeed! bless my soul! **han –r mange folk hos seg** he sees many people; **det -r jeg gjerne** I like that **jeg -r gjerne at du kommer** I shall be very glad, if you will come; **du må – til å komme** you must try to come; **vi –(e)s sjelden** we seldom meet; **jeg skal – til** I will see (what I can do); (med prep og adv): **av dette -r** man hence it appears; **– tiden an** wait some time, wait (and see); **– etter** (uten styrelse) look; (med styrelse:

følge med øynene, ta vare på) look after; (søke etter) look for; (om tøy: sette i stand) mend; (med etterfølgende bisetning) see; **jeg kjenner ikke hans telefonnummer, men jeg skal – etter** I do not know his telephone number, but I will look; **han stod og så etter meg** he stood looking after me; **jeg så etter ham i alle værelsene** I looked for him in all the rooms; **jeg skal – om hun er hjemme** I'll see if she is home; **han så etter i boka** he consulted (el. referred to) the book; **– fram til** look forward to; **– seg for** look before one; **– deg for** look about you! **når man -r hen til** considering; **– en i ansiktet** look into one's face; **– igjennom** look through, look over; **han så ikke igjennom regningen** he did not examine the account; **– inn til en** call upon, go el. come and see one; **– seg om** look about one; **– deg om** look behind you; **– seg om på et sted** take a view of a place; **han så seg om i værelset** he looked about the room; **han har -tt seg om i verden** he has seen the world; **jeg må – meg om etter en annen tjener** I must look out for another servant; **– opp til en** look up to one; **– på** (være tilskuer) look on; **– på** look at, regard; **– på sitt eget beste** look to one's own interest; **han så seg sint på dette mennesket** the very sight of this man made him angry; **– til en** give one a call, go to see one; **– mye til en** (ɔ: se en ofte) see much of some one; **– til maten** see to dinner; **– til ovnen** mend the fire; **– skjevt til noe** look black el. blue at a thing; **– seg tilbake** look back; **– ut som** look like; **– godt, dårlig ut** look well, ill; **–, hvordan han –r ut** see how he looks; **hvordan ser han ut** (i alm.) what does he look like? how does he look? what is he like? **hvor det -r ut her!** what a sight the room is! **– ut** (av vinduet) look out (of the window); **det -r stygt ut for ham** his prospects are bad; **det -r ut til regn** it looks like rain; **være vel, ille -tt** hos be in good, bad odour with.
seanse séance.
Sebaot: den Herre – the Lord of Sabaoth.
sebra zebra.
sed (skikk) custom, usage; **gode -er** good morals.
sedat, se **satt.**
sedativ sedative. **-vann** sedative water.
seddel slip of paper; (pengeseddel) (bank-) note. **-bank** bank of issue. **-bok** note-case; (amr) (pocket) wallet. **-katalog** catalogue on slips. **-utstedelse** issue of notes.
sedelig of good morals, moral. **-het** morality, morals. **-hetsattest** certificate of character. **-hetsforbrytelse** offence against decency and morals. **-hetsforening** vigilance society.
sedelære ethics, moral philosophy.
seder (tre) cedar.
sedvane custom, usage, habit, practice, wont.
sedvanemessig customary.
sedvanerett customary law; (engelsk –) common law.
sedvanlig (adj) usual, ordinary, wonted, habitual; **som – as** as usual; (adv) usually.
sedvanligvis (adv) usually, generally.
seende seeing, sighted. **seer** seer.
seer|blikk prophetic eye, eye of a prophet. **-gave** gift of prophecy, prophetic spirit.
sees el. **ses** (av se) see one another el. each other, meet; **hvis vi såes oftere** if we saw more of each other.
sefyr Zephyr. **-garn** Berlin wool.
S. E. & O. fork. f. **salvo errore et omissione** errors and omissions excepted, E. & O. E.
seg oneself, himself, herself, itself, themselves; **han slo –** he hurt himself; **hun slo –** she hurt herself; **de slo –** they hurt themselves.
I. segl (signet etc.) seal, signet.
II. segl, se **seil.**
seglass eyeglass.
segle, se **seile.**

segllakk sealing-wax.
seglsamling collection of seals.
segne sink down, droop, drop.
segneferdig sinking; dropping.
sei (fisk) coalfish, billet.
seid sorcery, witchcraft. **seide** exercise witchcraft.
seidel glass mug, tankard.
seier victory; **vinne — gain the victory,** conquer, be victorious; **en glimrende — a** signal victory.
seierherre conqueror, victor.
seierrik victorious, triumphant; **gå — ut av** prove victorious in.
seier|sikker confident of victory. **-sikkerhet** confidence of victory. **-skjorte** caul.
seiers|krans wreath of victory. **-skrik** shout of victory. **-rus** intoxication of victory.
seier|sæl victorious. **-vinner** victor. **-vinning** victory.
seig tough. **-het** toughness. **-livet** tenacious of life. **-pine** torture slowly. **-pining** slow torture.
seil sail; **heise et — hoist a sail; sette — set** sail; **berge — take in sail; ta inn — furl the** sails; **være under — be under sail; sette alle —** **til crowd sail; seile for fulle — be under a press** of sail, go with all sails set.
seilas sailing, navigation.
seil|båt sailing boat. **-duk** sailcloth, canvas.
seile sail; go, proceed; (dt.) (om gang) jog; reel; **— om sail round,** circumnavigate; (en odde) round, double; **— på (et annet skip)** run into; **la en — sin egen sjø** leave one to his own devices.
seiler sail; **10 -e 10** sail; **en god — a good** sailer.
seilferdig ready to sail, ready for sea.
seilføring amount of sail, spread of canvas.
seil|klar, se **-ferdig, -maker** sail-maker. **-ordre** sailing orders. **-skip** sailing vessel. **-tur** sail water-party; **ta seg en -tur** take a sail.
sein, se **sen.**
seinke, se **sinke.**
seire conquer, gain the victory, be victorious, be triumphant. **-nde** victorious.
seise nipper; (bendsle) seize.
seising (alm.) seizing; (beslag) gasket.
sekel century.
sekk sack, bag.
sekke|gate (blindgate) turn-again-alley. **-lerret** sack-cloth, bagging, sacking. **-pipe** bag-pipe. **-strie,** se **-lerret.**
sekondløytnant sublieutenant.
sekret privy seal; (avsondr.) secretion.
sekretariat secretariat, secretaryship.
sekretær secretary; (møbelet) escritoire, secretaire.
seks six.
seks|dobbelt six-fold, sex-tuple. **sekser** six.
seksfotet six-footed, hexapod; **— vers** hexameter.
seksjon section.
sekskant hexagon.
seks|kantet sex-angular. **-sidet** six-sided.
sekstall six.
sekstant sextant.
seksten sixteen.
sekstende sixteenth.
sekstendedel sixteenth (part); **-s note** semiquaver, demiquaver; **-s pause** semiquaver rest.
sekstenårig of sixteen years.
sekstett sestet, sextet, sextuor.
seksti sixty.
sekstiden: ved — about six.
seksuell sexual.
seksæring six-oar.
seksårig of six years.
sekt sect, denomination. **sekterer** sectarian.
sekterisk sectarian, denominational.
sektvesen sectarianism.
sekund second.
sekunda secondary.

sekundant second.
sekundaveksel second of exchange.
sekundere second.
sekundviser second-hand.
sekundær secondary.
I. **sel** (selhund) seal.
II. **sel** (seterhytte) chalet, cheese-house.
sele (i seletøy) horse-collar; (svømme-) swimming-belt. **-kammer** harness-room. **-pinne** harness-pin. **sele|r** (bukseseler) braces, suspenders. **-tøy** harness.
sel|fanger sealhunter, (ogs. skip) sealer; (skip) sealing vessel. **-fangst** sealing, seal fishing. **-felt** seal-rookery.
selge (el. **selle)** sell; (igjen) resell; **— ut** sell off; **-s til priser som . . .** sell at prices which . . .
selgekone basket-woman. **selgelig** saleable, vendible. **selger** seller, salesman.
selhund seal.
selhundkjøtt flesh of the seal, seal-beef.
selje sallow, palm. **-fløyte** willow-pipe.
selleri celery; (knopp- el. rot) celeriac.
selot zealot. **selotisk** fanatical.
selskap company, society; (selskapelig sammenkomst) party, company; (forening) society, (aksje- o. l.) company; **holde en med — keep,** bear one company; **holde et — give a party;** **gå, komme i — mix el. mingle in society; søke** **— med** keep company with.
selskapelig social; (som liker s.) sociable; (om dyr) gregarious; (om selsk. samvær) convivial; **— dannelse** manners.
selskapelighet sociability.
selskaps|antrekk dress clothes, evening dress. **-dame** (lady's) companion, lady's help. **-drakt** evening dress el. clothes. **-kjole** evening frock. **-livet** social life, society, social intercourse. **-mann** diner-out, society man, man about town.
selskapssal drawing-room.
selskinn seal-skin.
selsom strange, singular, odd.
selsomhet strangeness, singularity.
sel|spekk seal blubber. **-spyd** harpoon el. spear for killing seals.
selters Seltzer(-water).
selunge young seal; (i sin første ham) whitecoat.
selv (pronomen som forsterker substantiv el. pron.) myself, yourself, himself, herself, itself, ourselves, yourselves, themselves; (sammen med et possesiv pron.) own; (i visse forbindelser) of one's own (el. etter person og tall: of my, your, his, her, its, our, your, their own); **jeg** **kom — I** came myself; **han kom — he** came himself; **vi . . . — we. . .** ourselves etc.; **meg —** myself; **henne — herself** osv.; **det kan du —** **være** you are another; **den — samme** the very same, the identical; **om jeg — skal si det though** I say it that should not; **han er ærligheten —** he is honesty itself; **ta seg selv av dage** commit suicide; **han er ikke seg — mer** he is no longer his own self; **han gjorde det av seg — he** was beside himself; **komme til seg — igjen** come to oneself, recover.
selv (adv) even; **— hans fiender** even his enemies, his very enemies.
selv|aktelse self-respect; **som har — self-**respecting. **-angivelse** (til skatt) declaration. **-anklage** self-accusation. **— annen** with another, with a companion. **-antennelse** spontaneous ignition. **-arbeidende** (om maskiner) self-acting. **-avl** spontaneous generation. **-bebreidelse** self -reproach. **-bedrag** self-delusion.
selvbeherskelse self-command, self-control.
selv|bekjennelse self-confession. **-beskatning** self-taxation, voluntary assessment. **-beskuelse** self-contemplation. **-besmittelse** self-abuse. **-be-staltet** self-appointed, self-constituted. **-be-traktning** self-communion. **-bevisst** conscious; arrogant, self-asserting. **-bevissthet** consciousness. **-biografi** auto-biography. **-buden** self-invited.
selvdød dead (a natural death).

selve himself, herself, itself; — **kongen** the king himself.

selv|eier yeoman, freeholder. **–erkjennelse** self-knowledge. **–ervervende** selfmaintaining. **–ervervet** self-acquired. **–forglemmelse** self-oblivion. **–forgudelse** self-worship. **–fornedrelse** self-abasement, self-humiliation. **–fornektelse** self-denial, self-abnegation. **–fornektende** self-denying. **–forskyldt** self-inflicted. **–forsvar** self-defence. **–følelse** feeling of one's own worth, self-esteem.

selvfølge matter of course.

selvfølgelig (adj) matter-of-course, inevitable; (adv) of course, obviously.

selvfølgelighet inevitability, obviousness.

selvgjort self-made. **selvgod** self-sufficient.

selv|godhet self-importance. **–herredømme** self-command. **–hersker** autocrat. **–hevdelse** self-assertion. **–hjelp** self-help. **–hjulpen** self-aided, independent.

selvisk selfish. **selviskhet** selfishness.

selvklok self-conceited, self-wise.

selv|koker tin-kitchen. **–kritikk** self-critique, self-criticism. **–laget** of one's own making. **–lyd** vowel.

selv|mord suicide. **–morder, –morderske** suicide. **–mordersk** suicidal. **–mordforsøk** attempt at suicide. **–motsigelse** self-contradiction. **–motsigende** (self-)contradictory. **–nøyd** self-complacent.

selv om even if; even though.

selv|oppholdelsesdrift instinct of self-preservation. **–oppofrelse** self-sacrifice.

selv|oppofrende self-devoting, self-sacrificing. **–pensjonering** self-superannuation. **–plager** self-tormentor. **–portrett** portrait of oneself. **–prøvelse** self-examination. **–ros** self-praise, self-laudation; — **stinker** self-praise is open disgrace. **–rådig** self-willed, wilful. **–rådighet** wilfulness.

selv|sagt a matter of course, self-evident. **–sikker** cocksure. **–skreven** (egenhendig) autograph; (til noe) the very man.

selv|skyldner security, surety, bondsman. **–skyldnerkausjon** surety. **–starter** self-starter. **–stendig** independent. **–stendighet** independence. **–studium** private study; **til –studium** for private students. **–styre** self-government; home rule.

selvsuggestion auto-suggestion.

selv|supplering co-optation. **–syn** autopsy.

selvtatt self-assumed, self-allotted.

selvtekt taking the law into one's own hands.

selvtilbedelse self-worship.

selvtilfreds self-satisfied, self-approving.

selvtilfredshet self-satisfaction, self-approval.

selvtillit self-confidence, self-reliance; **mangel på** — diffidence, self-distrust.

selvtukt self-discipline.

selvvirkende automatic, self-acting.

semafor semaphore.

sement cement. **–ere** cement. **–ering** cementation.

semester semester, term (of six months).

semikolon semicolon.

seminarist pupil at a seminary.

seminarium seminary, training school, t. college, (spesielt) teachers' seminary.

semitt Shemite.

semittisk Semitic, Shemitic.

semje agreement.

semske shamois, shamoy; **–t skinn** buff, wash-leather.

semulegryn semoule.

sen (adj) (langsom) slow, tardy; (om tid) late; **han var ikke — til å komme** he was not long in coming. **senere** later; **en gang** — on some future occasion; **den — tid** of late, latterly, lately; **hans — liv** his after life; **en — utvikling** an after development; **— etterretninger** later news. **senest** latest, at the latest; **— fredag** on or before Friday, not later than Friday; **han kommer onsdag aften eller — torsdag morgen** he is coming on Wednesday night, or at the latest on Thursday morning. **sent** (adv) late; **komme for — be** late; **komme for — til toget** miss the train; **to timer for — two** hours late.

senat senate. **senator** senator.

sende send, forward, transmit; **— bud til en** send one word; **— bud etter en** send for one. **sendebud** messenger. **sende|lse** sending, mission. **–mann** (gesandt) ambassador, minister. **sending** thing el. present sent; (til skip) shipment. **sendingsgods** goods sent.

sendrektig slow, dilatory.

sendrektighet slowness, dilatoriness.

sene sinew, tendon. **senefull** sinewy.

senehinne fascia; (øyets) sclerotic.

seneknute ganglion.

senere, senest, se **sen**.

senestrekk sprain, strain.

senetrekning contraction of the sinews, spasm.

seng bed; **i — in** bed; **re –a** make the bed; **gå i — el. til –s** go to bed, turn in, (når man er syk) take to one's bed; **ligge til –s av** be in bed, el. laid up, with; **holde –a** keep one's bed, be confined to bed.

senge|forlegger bedside carpet. **–halm** bed-straw. **–hest** bedstaff. **–himmel** tester of a bed. **–rom** bed-accomodation. **–stokk** bed-post. **–stolpe** bed-post. **–teppe** (som bres over senga) coverlid, coverlet, quilt, counterpane; (i senga) blanket. **–tid** bed-time. **–tøy** bedding, bedclothes. **–varme** bed-heat.

seng|kamerat bed-fellow. **–kant** bedside. **–klær** bedclothes.

senhet slowness, dilatoriness.

senhøstes in late autumn.

senior senior. **–at** seniorship, seniors.

seniorsjef senior.

senit zenith.

senk: i — aground, to the bottom; **bore et skip i — sink** a ship; **skyte i — sink** (by a shot).

senke sink; let down, lower; **— blikket** cast down one's eyes; **— seg** sink (down), fall, (om fugl) stoop; **med –t blikk** with downcast eyes, look; **— ned** (i vann) submerge, immerse.

senkning sinking.

senn: smått om — gradually, little by little.

sennep mustard. **senneps|frø** mustard-seed. **–krukke** mustard-pot. **–plaster** sinapism.

sennes|belger senna-pods. **–blader** senna.

sensasjon sensation.

sensasjonell sensational.

sensasjonslysten greedy of sensation.

sensasjonsvekkende sensational.

sensibel sensitive.

sensor censor; (av trykksaker) censor el. licenser (of the press); (teater-) censor (el. licenser) of (stage) plays; (ved eksamen) second examination judge.

sensorat censorship.

sensualisme sensualism.

sensur censorship, critical examination, censure; (bedømmelse) judging; (resultatet av eksamensbedømmelse) marks adjudged, class (el. University) list, pass-list; **–en faller i morgen** the list will be out (el. issued, published) to-morrow; (karakteristikk) character; (presse-) censorship (of the press); **sette under — subject** to a censorship. **sensurere** censor; review, examine.

sent, se **sen**.

sentenkt slow-thoughted, slow.

sentens sentence. **sententiøs** sententious.

senterbor centre-drill; centre-bit.

sentimental sentimental, (latterlig) maudlin.

sentimentalitet sentimentality.

sentral (adj) central; **— beliggenhet** centrality; **sentralt** (adv) centrally; **— beliggende** centrally situated (el. located), centrical; **vi bor — we** are central.

sentral (subst) (centralstasjon, f. eks. for telefon) exchange, central; **–bord** switchboard. **–isasjon** centralization. **–isere** centralize. **–ise–**

ring centralization. **-maktene** the Central Powers. **-oppvarming** central heating. **-punkt** central point; focus. **-varmeapparat** steamheater.
sentri|fugalkraft centrifugal force. **-fuge** centrifuge, centrifugal machine, cream separator. **-petalkraft** centripetal force.
sentrum centre; (politisk) the moderate party. **sentrums|bor** centre-bit. **-mann** centrist. **-parti** Centre (party), Centrists.
separasjon divorce, separation.
separat separate; (adv) separately.
separatavtrykk reprint, excerpt.
separatfred separate peace.
separa|tisme separatism. **-tist** separatist. **-tistisk** separatistic.
separatkonto special account.
separatpris special price.
separere separate.
september September.
septer sceptre.
septett septet, septette, septuor.
septim seventh; **den store, lille** — the major, minor seventh. **-akkord** chord of the seventh.
septiktank septic tank; **septisk** septic.
seraf seraph. **serafisk** seraphic(al).
serber Servian.
Serbia Servia. **serbisk** Servian.
seremoni ceremony, rite, observance. **seremoniell** (subst) ceremonial. **seremoniell** (adj) ceremonious, ceremonial. **seremonimester** master of the ceremonies, M. C.
serenade serenade.
serie series; (av oblig. o. l.) emission.
serk smock, chemise.
serpentin serpentine.
sersjant sergeant. **-post** sergeantship.
sertifikat certificate.
serum serum.
servant wash-stand.
server|e serve (up); — **noe for en** serve one with something; — **suppe** help the soup; **det er -t** dinner is on the table.
serviett napkin, serviette. **-bånd, -ring** napkin holder, napkin ring. **-presse** napkin press.
servil servile. **servilitet** servility.
service service, set.
servitutt servitude, easement.
sesjon session, sittings.
sesong season. **-arbeid** seasonal work.
sesongarbeider seasonal worker.
sesong|billett, -kort contract el. season ticket.
sess (dt.) seat; **er tung i -en** is a slow coach.
sete seat; **ta** — take a seat; **bringe til** — get seated; **få** — **i** obtain a seat in.
setebad hip-bath.
seter summer cheesefarm, outfarm, **seter|bruk** cheesefarming, outfarming. **-bu** shieling, sheal. **-hytte** chalet, cheese-house. **-jente** cheesefarm girl, dairy-woman. **-stø, -støl, -vang, -voll** outfarm enclosure el. loan.
setning (gram) sentence, clause; (typografisk) composition; (påstand) thesis; **innskutt** — intermediate sentence.
setnings|bygning construction of sentences. **-del** part of a sentence. **-lære** syntax.
setre (vrb) summer cattle and sheep at a chalet.
sett (sprang) bound; (dekketøy, porselen) set; (klær) suit (of clothes); (verktøy) gang; (måte) manner, way; **det gav et** — **i ham, han gjorde et** — he started.
sette set, place, put; (typograf.) compose, set up, put in type; (ferdig) **satt** (typograf.) in type; (mar) (om strøm, seil) set; — **fast** arrest; (fig) nonplus; **sett at det skjer** suppose that should happen; — **vondt blod** make bad blood; — **blomst** put forth flowers; — **frukt** set; — **opp en dames hår** do a lady's hair; — **igler, klyster** apply leeches, a clyster; **de satte en minnestøtte på hans grav** they erected el. raised a memorial over his grave; — **et tilfelle** put el. suppose a case; — **seg (synke)** subside,

settle; **sett Dem!** sit down! be seated! take a seat; — **seg fast** get fixed; — **seg et mål** propose an object to oneself; — **av** (til en, til et bruk) leave, set aside; — **av et bein, en arm** amputate a leg, an arm; — **av sted** make off, dart off; — **bort** put aside; — **etter en** go el. set out in pursuit of one; — **vondt for en** prejudice one against a person; — **seg fore** purpose; — **fra** (med båt), push off, shove off; — **fram en stol** place a chair; — **fram** (forslag osv.) propose, propound, advance, state, set forth; (i parlament) bring in (a bill); — **pengene sine i banken** deposit el. lodge one's money in the bank; **han har satt sin formue i** . . . he has vested his money in . . .; — **sin ære i** glory in, pride oneself upon; — **i arbeid** set at work; — **i land** land; — **i led** set; — **i musikk** set to music; — **i pant** pawn, pledge; — **i side** (typograf.) make up; — **seg i gjeld** run into debt; **sett Dem i mitt sted!** put yourself in my place; — **igjennom** carry through, effectuate, achieve; — **vondt i mellom** make mischief between; — **seg imot, se motsette;** — **en inn i** put one up to, give one an idea of; — **seg inn i** make oneself familiar with; realize; identify oneself with; — **inn** (i spill) stake, (i bank) deposit; — **seg ned** sit down, take a seat, seat oneself; — **opp et alvorlig ansikt** put on a grave face; — **opp et barberblad** set a razor-blade; — **opp imot** oppose to; (til jevnførelse m.) contrast with; — **seg opp imot** set oneself against, rise against; — **over** cross; (med et hopp) leap; (sette andre over) convey across, ferry across; **lot hesten** — **over rekkverket** leaped his horse over the rails; — **farge på** colour; **sette hatten på** put on one's hat; — **krydder på** spice; — **smak på** flavour; — **varme på** put fire to; — **på** (dyr) breed, raise; — **på vann** set water over the fire; — **sammen** compose, compound, put el. join together; — **til** waste, spend; — **skipet til** lose the ship; — **livet til** perish, lose one's life; — **til** (en pris) put down at; — **musikk til** set to music; — **en til å** make one; — **tilbake** replace; **dette tap har satt ham mye tilbake** this loss has greatly reduced him; — **ut** (barn) put out to nurse; — **ut av spillet** send to Coventry; — **seg ut over** disregard; — **under avstemning** put to the vote; — **under debatt** bring in question; **han kom settende** he came at full speed.
settedommer commissioned judge.
settemaskin composing machine.
settepotet seed potato.
I. **setter** (hund) setter.
II. **setter** (typograf.) compositor.
setteri composing-room, case-room.
settskipper substitute el. deputy master.
settstykke (teat.) set .
sev, se siv.
severdig worth seeing, worthy of inspection. **severdigheter** sights; **bese** — go sightseeing.
sevje sap. **-full** sappy.
sfinks Sphinx.
sfære sphere. **sfærisk** spherical.
shag shag (tobacco).
shampoo shampoo.
sherry sherry (wine).
shipping shipping.
si say, tell; **det var det han sa til meg dengang** this was what he stated to me on that occasion; — **ja til noe** consent to something; — **god natt, farvel** wish el. bid one good night, goodbye; — **sannheten** speak the truth; **si meg sannheten** tell me the truth! **har ingenting å** — **!** never mind! no matter! **hva sa jeg?** didn't I tell you so? I told you so; **man -r** they say, it is said; **det er blitt sagt meg** I have been told; **la seg** — listen to reason, hear reason, be advised; **nå, det må jeg** — **!** I declare! **hva jeg ville** — what I was going to say; **hva skal det** —**?** what does it mean? **det vil** — that is (to say); **så å** — so to say, so to speak, as it were; **det**

har ikke stort å — it is no great matter; **det har ikke noe å** — it is of no consequence; **som sagt, jeg kan ikke!** as before said (as I said before, I repeat) I cannot; **som sagt, så gjort** no sooner said than done; **mellom oss sagt** between you and me, between ourselves; **det er ikke sagt** it does not follow; — **etter** repeat; — **fram recite,** deliver; **si fram!** say on! **han har mye å** — **hos** he has great influence with; — **imot** oppose; — **om (igjen)** repeat; — **opp** give notice el. warning; **han har ikke noe å** — **over meg** he has no authority over me; **har du noe å** — **på hans oppførsel** do you find fault with his behaviour? — **noe på en** lay (a thing) to one's charge; — **noe til en** say st. to one, tell one st., — **til** drop a hint, give notice; — **til når du er ferdig** when you are ready, say so; — **til seg selv** say to oneself.

sia, se siden.
Siam Siam. **siameser** Siamese.
Sibiria Siberia. **sibirisk** Siberian.
Sicili|a Sicily. **-aner, -ansk** Sicilian.
sid long. **sidde** length.
side side; (om dyr) flank; (av bok) page; (fjell-) flank, face; (av en sak) aspect, point of view, feature, phase; **han har sine gode -r** there are good points in him; **hans svake, sterke** — his weak, strong point; **se en ting fra alle -r** examine a thing in all its bearings; **fra hvilken** — man enn ser saken in any view of the matter; **fra begge -r** (om personer) mutually; **med armene i** —n with arms akimbo; — **om** — side by side; **legge til** — put aside, put on one side, put by; **ved -n av** beside, next to, (fig) along with, collaterally with; **like ved -n av** next door.
side|bane branch-line. **-bein** rib. **-blikk** side-look, side-glance; **kaste et -blikk til** glance at. **-bygning** side-building, wing. **-hogg** back-stroke, side-blow; (fig) hit, back-hander. **-kamerat** neighbour. **-lengs** sideways, sidewise. **-linje** collateral line; **ætlinger i -linjen** collateral descendents. **-lomme** side-pocket.
sidelykt side light.
sidemann neighbour.
I. **siden** (adv) since; (siden etter) afterwards, subsequently; (derpå, dernest) then; (senere) by and by; **like** — ever since; **lenge** — long since; **ikke lenger** — enn i går only yesterday, but yesterday; **jeg skal komme** — (senere) I shall come by and by.
II. **siden** (prep og konj) since; — **hans død** since his death; — **han ønsker å** since it is his wish, that; **det er tre år** — it is three years ago el. since; **for . . . siden** ago; **for to dager** — two days ago; **for mindre enn en halv time** — within this half hour.
sidensvans waxwing.
sideordnet co-ordinate; (adv) co-ordinately.
sider (eplevin) cider.
side|sprang side-leap; (fig) double; shift; aberration. **-stykke** side-piece; (fig) pendant, fellow, parallel, counterpart, companion (piece). **side|vei** side-way. **-vogn** (til motorsykkel) side-car. **-værelse** side-room.
sidlendt low-lying, swampy.
sidrikke drink hard, guzzle.
sie, se **side.**
siffer figure. **-brev** letter in cipher. **-nøkkel** cipher-key. **-skrift** cipher, cryptography.
sifong siphon.
sig (subst) gradual settling, sinking; gradual approach; slow motion, slight headway; (sakteflytende væske) gentle flow, ooze, trickle; **ha** — forever just move ahead; **komme i** — get into motion.
sigar cigar; **tenne en** — light a cigar; **en trekker ikke** the cigar does not draw; **lagret** — matured cigar. **-arbeider** cigar-maker. **-aske** cigar ash. **-dekkblad** wrapper.
sigarett cigarette. **-maskin** cigarette-filler.

-munnstykke c.-holder, c.-tube. **-papir** smoking paper, cigarette paper.
sigar|etui cigar-case. **-handler** tobacconist. **-kasse** cigar-box. **-kniv** cigar-cutter. **-maker, -makerske** cigar-maker. **-munnstykke,** se under **sigarett. -rulling** twisting of cigars. **-røyker** cigar-smoker. **-spiss** cigar-tip. **-stump** cigar-end. **-tenner** cigar-light.
sigd (krumkniv) sickle.
sige settle, sink; sag; just move; ooze, trickle. — **framover** move slowly forward; — **i knærne** give in the knees.
sigende report, rumour; **etter** — according to report; **etter hans** — according to him.
signal signal; **gi** — make a signal.
signalement description (of one's person), personal clue.
signalere signalize, signal.
signalhorn motor-horn.
signalisere signalize, signal.
signalskive (jernb.) disk.
signalsystem signal-code, code of signals.
signalør signaller.
signatur signature.
signe sign the cross on; bless.
signekjerring wise woman.
signere sign.
signet seal, signet.
sigøyner gipsy. **-aktig** gipsy-like, Bohemian. **-bande** set el. gang of gipsies. **-inne** gipsy-woman. **-liv** gipsy life. **-pike** gipsy-girl. **-språk** gipsy dialect, zingarree.
sik (fisk) freshwater herring.
sikkel slobber, slaver, drivel.
sikker (sikret) assured, sure; (viss i sin sak) certain, positive, sure; (trygg) safe; (pålitelig) safe, trusty; (i opptreden) confident; **et -t sted** a safe place; **være** — **på** be sure of; — **for kulene** safe from the balls; — **etterretning** certain intelligence; **en** — **mann** a trusty, reliable man; **være** — **i sin sak** be quite sure.
sikkerhet safety, security; (visshet) certainty; (selvtillit) assurance, confidence, coolness; **for -s skyld** for the sake of security; **stille** — find security; **bringe i** — carry into safety, remove out of harm's way, secure, make safe.
sikkerhets|foranstaltning precautionary measure. **-lenke** safety-chain. **-nål** safe pin, safety pin, baby-pin. **-ventil** safety-valve; (i dampsylinder) escape-valve.
sikkerlig, se **sikkert.**
sikkert (adv) surely, certainly, assuredly, to a certainty.
sikle slobber, slaver, drivel.
siklesmekke bib.
sikori succory, chiccory.-
sikre secure, insure, guarantee (en noe: st. to one); — **seg (imot, for)** shelter, screen, shield oneself (against); — **seg** secure, make sure of st. **sikring** securing, security. **-smiddel** preservative, prophylactic.
siksak zigzag. **-linje** zigzag line. **-lyn** chain (el. forked) lightning.
sikt (merk.) sight; **tre dager fra** — three days sight, at three days' sight; **betale ved** — pay at sight; **på kort** — at short sight.
siktbar clear. **siktbarhet** clearness.
I. **sikte** (vrb) (rette imot) aim, point (på: at); — **til** refer to; — **på** el. (fig) **til en med noe** level st. at one.
II. **sikte** (vrb, beskylde) accuse (of), charge (with).
III. **sikte** (vrb, f. eks. mel) sift, bolt.
I. **sikte** (subst) (mål) aim; (fig) object; (synlighet) sight, view; **ha i** — have in view; **ta** — på take aim at; **tape av** — lose sight of; **ute av** — out of sight; **få i** — get a sight of, come in view of, sight.
II. **sikte** (såld) sieve.
siktebrød bread made of sifted rye.
sikte|korn sight. **-linje** level.

siktelse (beskyldning) accusation, charge.
siktemel bolted flour.
sikte|skåre notch. **-verk** bolter.
sikttratte demand-draft.
siktveksel bill payable at sight.
sil strainer, filter.
sild herring; **så død som en** — as dead as a herring el. a door-nail; **ikke verd en sur** — not worth a straw; **stappet som** — **i en tønne** closely packed, crowded to suffocation.
silde|lake herring-pickle. **-not** herring seine.
silder (sildring) murmur, ripple; tinkling.
silde|salat salad of pickled herring. **-stim** school of herrings. **-tønne** herring-barrel.
sildre (vrb) trickle, murmur, ripple.
sildre (bot.) saxifrage.
sile (vrb) strain, filter.
sile|klede straining cloth. **-pose** jelly-bag. **-sup** taste of new milk.
silhuett silhouette.
silke silk; av — silken; **han spant ikke** — **på det** he did not profit very largely by that. **-aktig** silky. **-fløyel** silk velvet. **-kjole** silk dress. **-orm** silk-worm. **-papir** silk-paper, tissue-paper.
silke|tøy silk(-stuff). **-varer** silks.
sil|regn, -våt, se **siregn, sivåt.**
simle female of the reindeer.
simpel (sj. i det. enkel, likefram) plain, simple (alminnelig) common, ordinary; (ringe, tarvelig) poor, humble, ordinary; inferior, bad; vulgar.
— soldat common soldier; **han er en** — **fyr** he is a vulgar fellow; **det er -t** it is bad taste; **av den simple grunn** for the plain reason that; **simpelt** (adv) (likefram) simply, plainly; (gement) meanly, shabbily; **-t hen** simply. **-het** vulgarity.
simplifi|sere simplify. **-sering** simplification.
simulant simulator, simulant. **simulasjon** simulation. **simulere** simulate, feign.
sin, si, sitt, sine his, her, hers; its, one's, their, theirs; **i sin tid** sometime, once; at the time; (framtid) in due time; **enhver sitt!** every one his own is all fair! **gjøre sitt til noe** do one's best for a thing; **på -e steder** in places; **til -e tider** at times; **av -e grunner** for reasons of my own.
sinders cinder.
sindig temperate, considerate; sedate. **sindighet** temper, considerateness, composure.
sinekyre sinecure.
singel (grov sand) gravel, shingle.
sing(e)l (singling) jingling. **single** jingle.
singularis the singular (number).
sink zinc, zink.
sinke (vrb) retard, detain, delay.
sinke (subst) lag, backward child.
sink|etsing zincography. **-holdig** zinkiferous. **-hvitt** zink-white. **-plate** plate el. sheet of zink.
sinn mind, temper, disposition; **et lett** — a light heart; **skifte** — change one's mind; **i sitt stille** — mentally, privately, within himself; **få i -e** take into one's head; **ha i -e** intend, design, purpose; **han har vondt i -het** he is bent upon el. means mischief; **på -e,** se **hjerte.**
sinna, se **sint. -tagg** hotspur, spitfire.
sinnbillede emblem, symbol.
sinnbilledlig emblematical.
sinne temper, anger; **når -t kommer over ham** when the temper is on him; **fare opp i fullt** — flare up, fly into a passion.
sinnelag disposition, temper.
sinneri fit of anger.
sinnet (mest i sm.setninger) minded, disposed, affected (imot: towards); eks. norsksinnet: pro-Norwegian, of the Norwegian party; kongeligsinnet: loyal.
sinnrik ingenious. **-het** ingeniousness, ingenuity.
sinns|beskaffenhet disposition, temper. **-bevegelse** emotion, excitement, agitation. **-forvirret** deranged, distracted. **-forvirring** derangement (of intellect), insanity, unsound mind. **-likevekt**

(mental) balance. **-opprør** tumult of mind. **-ro** peace, tranquillity el. serenity of mind. **-styrke** strength of mind.
sinnssvak disordered in mind, deranged; **en** — an insane person, a madman, a lunatic.
sinns|svakhet mental derangement. **-svekkelse** mental debility. **-syk,** diseased in mind, deranged. **-sykdom** mental disease el. malady. **-sykeanstalt** mental hospital, lunatic asylum. **-sykelege** alienist.
sinnstilstand condition of mind.
sinober cinnabar. **-rød** vermilion.
sint angry, in a temper (på: with); **bli** — get mad el. wild, get in a temper.
sinus sine.
sippe (vrb) blubber, pule, snivel; **sippe** (subst) blubberer etc. **sipperi** blubbering etc.
sirat ornament.
siregn dead pour, pouring rain.
sirene Siren; (instrum.) siren.
siriss cricket.
Sirius Sirius, the Dog-star.
sirkel circle; **slå en** — draw a circle, describe a circle. **-bue** circular arc. **-flate** circle plane. **-formet** circular. **-periferi** circumference. **-rund** circular.
sirkelsag circular saw.
sirkulasjon circulation. **sirkulere** circulate.
sirkulære (rundskriv) circular.
sirkulærakkreditiv circular letter of credit.
sirkulærveksel circular note.
sirkumfleks circumflex.
sirkus circus, ring, hippodrome.
sirlig elegant, graceful; (altfor —) finical. **sirlighet** elegance; (overdreven —) finicalness.
sirokko sirocco.
sirs print, printed calico.
sirup treacle; (apoteker-s.) syrup. **sirups|krukke** jar of treacle. **-øl** chowder beer.
sisel|ere chase, chisel; **-ert snitt** tooled edges; **-ert** (med stempler) goffered. **-ør** chaser, chiseller.
sisik siskin.
sisselrot common polypody.
sist last; **den -e** (av to) the latter; **for -e gang** for the last time; **til -e mann, dråpe** to the last man, drop; **i den -e tid** lately; **i det -e kvarter** this quarter of an hour; **til det -e** to the last; **de -e dagers hellige** the latter-day saints; **gi den -e olje** administer extreme unction **til** — at last; **da jeg** — **så ham** when last I saw him.
sisten (lek) (the game of) tag, touch, touch-last.
sist|leden last, past. **-nevnte** the last-mentioned; (av to) the latter. **-på,** se **til sist.**
sisyfusarbeid Sisyphean labour.
sitant (jur) plaintiff.
sitar cither(n), cittern.
sitasjonstegn quotation-marks, inverted commas. **sitat** quotation. **sitere** quote.
sitre tremble, quiver. **sitring** trembling.
sitron lemon, (større) citron. **-gul** lemon-coloured. **-presser** lemon-squeezers. **-saft** lemon-juice. **-skall** lemon-peel. **-skive** slice of lemon. **-syre** citric acid.
sitt (eiendomspron.) se **sin.**
sitte sit, be seated; **frakken -r ikke godt** the coat does not fit; — **fast** stick; — **for en maler** sit for one's picture, sit to a painter; — **godt i det** be well off; **vi -r fint i det** (dt.) we are in a nice pickle; — **igjen** (p. skolen) be kept after school, be kept in, detained; — **inne** sit el. remain indoors; (i fengsel) sit, be doing time; — **inne med** have on hand; retain in one's hands; — **ned** sit down; **han bød meg ikke engang å** — **ned** he did not even offer me a chair; — **opp** mount; — **oppe** sit up; — **over** (i dans) not to stand up, get no partner; (i spill) stand out (of the game); **la** — **på seg** pocket, brook, sit down under; — **til hest** be on horseback; — **til doms over** sit in (judg-

ment) upon; **bli sittende (fast)** stick. **sitteplass** sitting.
sitterål electric eel.
situasjon situation; **–en voksen** equal to the occasion; **reddet –en** retrieved the lost game.
situert situated.
siv rush, reed.
sive ooze, filter. **— ut** (fig) creep el. leek out.
sivil civil; **være i** — be dressed in plain clothes. **–t antrekk** civilian clothes, plain clothes. **–domstol** (domst. for sivile saker) court of common pleas. **–etater** Civil Service. **–ingeniør** civil engineer.
sivilisasjon civilization. **sivilisator** civilizer.
sivilisere civilize. **sivilisering** civilization. **sivilist** civilian. **sivil|kledd** in private el. plain clothes. **–liste** civil list. **–prosess** civil proceedings.
sivåt drenched, soaking wet.
sj. fork. f. **sjelden,** (adj.) rare, (adv.) rarely.
sjablon stencil. **–ere** stencil. **–messig** conventional.
sjagreng shagreen.
sjah Shah, Schah.
sjakal jackal.
sjakett cut-away coat, cut-away, morning coat.
sjakk chess; **—!** check! **si** — check, give check, say check; **holde i** — hold one's own against, keep one at bay, keep one in check.
sjakk|brett chess-board. **–brikke** chess-man.
sjakkerjøde street-Jew, Jew-hawker.
sjakkmatt check-mate; **gjøre** — checkmate; (fig) **være** — be knocked up.
sjakk|parti chess match. **–spill** game of chess; (brikker) set of chess-men. **–spiller** chess-player.
sjako shako.
sjakre hawk, peddle.
sjakt shaft.
sjal shawl.
sjalottløk shallot, Welsh onion.
sjalu jealous (**på:** of).
sjalupp (mellomstor båt i et orlogsskip) barge. **–roere** barge-men.
sjalusi (skinnsyke) jealousy; (for vindu) movable blind.
sjampinjong champignon, edible mushroom. **–saus** ketchup.
sjangle shuffle; reel; **full så en –r** reeling drunk.
sjanse chance (**for:** of). **–seilas** random (el. happy-go-lucky) sail el. run.
sjapp drink(ing)-shop, ginnery.
sjarla|tan charlatan, quack, mountebank. **–taneri** charlatanism, charlatanry, quackery.
sjargong (klikkespråk) jargon; (simpelt språk) slang; (tyvespråk, kråkemål, tarvelig klassespråk) cant; (uforståelig tale, kråkemål) gibberish.
sjarmant, sjarm osv., se **charmant, charme.**
sjask flaccid, limp mass. **sjasket** limp; (om person) bedraggled.
sjasmin jasmin, jessamine.
sjatte|re shade, shadow. **–ring** shade.
sjau (dt.) business, operations; (stykke arbeid) job, piece of work; (travelhet) bustle; (hard dyst) job, spell; (støy, forstyrrelse) noise, kick-up, row; **de er i full** — **med våronna** spring farming is in full swing; — **på bryggene** casual quayside jobs.
sjaue do odd jobs; (dt.) make a noise. **sjauer** (brygge-) dock-hand, lumper.
sjef chief, head; (mil) commander; (for forretning) principal; (for orlogsmann) captain. **–redaktør** chief editor, editor-in-chief.
sjefs|kahytt great cabin. **–sjalupp** barge. **–stilling** leadership.
sjeik sheik, sheikh.
sjekk cheque (**på:** for). **–bok** cheque-book.
sjekte funny, skiff.
sjel soul; **på** — **og legeme** in mind and body; **være –en i** the heart and soul of, the life of; **det var ikke tvil i hans** — **om . . .** there was no doubt in his mind as to . . .

sjelatin, se **gelatin.**
sjelden (adj) rare, scarce, unfrequent; **sjeldnere** less frequent; (adv) seldom, rarely; — **eller aldri** seldom (el. rarely), if ever.
sjeldenhet scarceness; rarity, curiosity.
sjeldsynt rarely seen.
sjelé, se **gelé.**
sjele|fryd, se **–glede. –glad** delighted, overjoyed. **–glede** delight, transport of joy. **–hyrde** se **–sørger. –kval** agony of mind.
sjelelig mental; (psykisk) psychical; **–e lidelser** mental sufferings; **det –e** the psychical element.
sjele|liv life of the soul, soul's life, spiritual life. **–lære** psychology, philosophy of the mind. **–messe** requiem, mass for a departed soul. **–nød** mental el. spiritual distress. **–sorg** pastoral care. **–sørger** pastor, clergyman, spiritual guide. **–vandring** transmigration of souls, metempsychosis.
sjelfull instinct with feeling, full of animation, animated, expressive.
sjelfullhet expressiveness, animation, spirit.
sjelløs soulless, lifeless, inanimated, vacant.
sjels|høyhet elevation of soul, high-mindedness. **–storhet** magnanimity, greatness of a mind el. soul. **–styrke** strength of mind, fortitude. **–tilstand** mental state, state of one's soul.
sjenere constrain, cramp, hamper, annoy, embarrass, inconvenience, incommode; — **seg** feel embarrassed, constrained; **sjener Dem ikke** don't put yourself out, don't mind me; make yourself at home; **jeg –r meg for å** I am ashamed to, I am shy of.
sjenerende embarrassing.
sjenert embarrassed, shy, (self-) conscious.
sjenerthet embarrassment, shyness.
sjenerøs generous, liberal.
sjenever gin; Hollands, geneva.
sjeselong longchair, lounge, couch.
sjetlandsk Shetland. **Sjetlandsøyene** the Shetland Isles. **sjetlender** Shetlander; (hest) Shetland pony.
sjette (tallord) sixth; — **bud** seventh commandment (fordi vårt første bud i den engelske katekisme gjøres til to). **–del, –part** sixth (part); **fem –deler** five sixths.
sjevann aqua fortis, nitric acid.
sjeviot (ullent stoff) cheviot.
sjevre (om seil) lift, shiver.
sjikane (fortredelighet) chicane, annoyance; (i bridge) chicane. **–re** (utsette for chikane) annoy, chicane. **–ring** chicane, chicanery.
sjikanøs malicious, vexatious.
sjimpanse chimpanzee.
sjiraff giraffe.
sjirting shirting. **sjirtingsbind** cloth (-boards); **innbundet i** — cloth-bound.
sjofel mean; **sjofilist** blackguard.
sjokk shock; (angrep) charge, onset.
sjokke trudge, jog, shuffle, shamble.
sjokkere shock; offend; pique.
sjokolade chocolate. **–fabrikant** chocolate-maker. **–farget** chocolate-coloured. **–mugge** chocolate pot. **–plate** tablet of c.
sjonglere juggle.
sjonglør balls-man, juggler.
sju (int) shoo!
sju (tallord) seven. **sju|dobbelt,** se **–fold.**
sjuende seventh; **det — bud** the eighth commandment; **for det** — seventhly; **til — og sist** ultimately; last, not least; **i den — himmel** in the seventh heaven of delight. **sjuendedel** seventh. **sjuer** seven.
sjufold, sjufoldig sevenfold, septuple.
sjuk, se **syk.**
sjukling weakling.
sjumilsstøvler seven-league boots.
sjuske (person) slattern, slut.
sjuske, –t, se **slurve** etc.
sju|sover lie-a-bed, slug-a-bed. **–stjerna** the

Seven Stars, the Pleiad(e)s. **-tall** the number seven. **ved -tiden** about seven. **-årig, -års** septennial, seven years, seven years old.

sjy (kjøttsaft) gravy.

sjø (innsjø) lake; (havet) the sea, ocean; (i sammensetninger: sjø-) marine, naval, maritime; **på -en** at sea; **ved -en** at the seaside; **utsikt over -en** sea-view; **svær el. høy** — a heavy sea; **holde -en** keep the sea; **kunne holde -en** (om fartøy) be sea-worthy; **til -s** at sea; **reise til -s** go by sea; **fare til -s** follow the sea, be a seafaring man; **stå til -s** stand (out) to sea; **i åpen, rom** — in the open sea, in the main ocean; (et stykke fra land) in the offing; **vi fikk svær** — **over oss** we shipped a heavy sea; **stikke i -en** put to sea; **la ham seile sin egen** — let him shift for himself; leave him to his own devices.

sjøaure salmon (el. sea)-trout.

sjøassuranse marine insurance.

sjøbad sea-bath; seaside resort.

sjøbilde marine el. sea picture, sea-piece, seascape.

sjøbu warehouse, wharfside shed.

sjøby seaport town; seaside place.

sjødyktig sea-worthy. **-het** sea-worthiness.

sjøetat Royal Navy.

sjø|farende sea faring. **-fart** navigation. **-fartsbok** sailor's certificate. **-folk** seamen, mariners. **-forklaring** (maritime) declaration; (dokum.) extended protest; **la oppta** — extend the protest. **-forsikring** marine insurance. **-forsvar** naval defences.

sjøgang heavy sea; **er det** —? is it rough?

sjøgutt sailor boy el. lad; blue-jacket.

sjøgående sea-going.

sjø|handel maritime commerce el. trade. **-handelsby** seaport (town). **-helt** naval hero. **-hyre** sea-going kit.

sjø|kadett naval cadet. **-kaptein** master, skipper, captain (of a merchant ship); (i marinen) captain of the Royal Navy. **-kart** chart. **-kart-arkiv** hydrographic office. **-krig** maritime war, naval war. **-krigshistorie** naval history.

sjøkyndig acquainted with seamanship, nautical; **-e** nautical men.

sjøkyst sea-coast, sea-margin, seaboard.

sjøl, sjølve, se selv, selve.

sjølov maritime law. **sjøluft** sea-air.

sjøløve sea-lion.

sjømakt naval force; (stat) naval power.

sjømann sailor, seaman, mariner.

sjømannsdyktighet nautical skill.

sjømannshjem sailors' home.

sjømanns|klær seamen's clothes; slops. **-liv** seafaring life; **-messig** seamanlike, sailorly. **-prest** seamen's clergyman. **-skap** seamanship. **-skikk** sailorly usage. **-ssak** sea-language. **-stand** seafaring class. **-uttrykk** nautical phrase el. term. **-vis** på — seaman-like.

sjømerke beacon, sea-mark; buoy.

sjø|mil sea-mile. **-mine** submarine mine. **-minevesenet** submarine mining.

sjø|officer naval officer. **-ord** nautical term. **-ordbok** nautical dictionary. **-orm** sea-serpent **-pass** sea-brief, sea pass.

sjøprotest (ship's) protest, sea protest; **melde** — notify average.

sjøpølse sea slug, trepang.

sjøreise (sea-)voyage.

sjørett (domstol) maritime court; (lovsamling) maritime law. **-ssak** maritime law case.

sjø|rokk sea-spray, smother of spray. **-røyk** sea-smoke.

sjørøver pirate, corsair. **sjørøveri** piracy. **sjørøversk** piratical. **sjørøverskip** pirate (vessel).

sjø|sak naval el. maritime cause. **-side** på -n seaward; fra -n from (the) seaward.

sjøskade damage at sea, sea-damage, sea-risk; (i assuransevesen) average loss.

sjø|skikk maritime usage. **-slag** sea-battle,

naval engagement el battle. **-sprøyt, se -rokk.**

sjøsterk (om skip) sea-worthy; (om mennesker) a good sailor.

sjø|stjerne star-fish. **-styrke** naval force.

sjøsyk sea-sick.

sjø|syke sea-sickness. **-transport** carriage by sea. **-trefning** naval engagement. **-tur** sea voyage; marine excursion.

sjøudyktig unseaworthy; **gjøre** — disable.

sjøulk Jack tar, sea-dog.

sjøuttrykk nautical phrase.

sjøvann sea-water.

sjøvant accustomed to the sea.

sjøvei passage by sea, way by sea; sea-route.

sjøvern defence on the sea-side; (sjømakt) naval force.

sjøvesen maritime matters, nautical affairs.

sjåfør chauffeur, motor-car driver, motor-man.

sjåsé causeway, high-road.

sjåvin|isme jingoism, chauvinism. **-ist** Jingo, chauvinist. **-istisk** Jingo, chauvinistic.

skabb (på sauer) scab; (på hester og hunder) mange; (på mennesker) itch, psora.

skabb|et scabby, mangy.

skabelon (modell) templet; (form i alm.) mould, shape.

skaberakk housing, saddle-cloth.

skade (fortred) hurt, injury, damage, harm, prejudice, detriment, disadvantage; **gammel** — deep-rooted evil; **lide** — (ved utvortes vold) sustain injury el. damage, be damaged el. injured; (lide tap) sustain loss; **komme til** — receive harm, hurt oneself, be hurt el. injured; **komme i** — **for å** have the ill-luck to; **til** — **for** to the injury of; **det er ingen** — skjedd there is no harm done; **det er stor** — it is a great pity; — **at han ikke kom før** what a pity he did not come sooner! **av** — **blir man klok** bought wit is best; once bitten, twice fly; adversity makes wise, though not rich; **skam og** — **følges at** losers are always laughed at.

skade (vrb) (el. ska) hurt, injure, damage, harm, impair, prejudice; **det -r ikke** it does no harm, there is no harm in it.

skade|dyr noxious animal. **-fro** mischievous, mischief-loving, malicious. **-fryd** delight in mischief, mischievousness, spite. **-lidt** sufferer.

skadelig hurtful, injurious, mischievous, harmful, detrimental; (meget skadel.) pernicious; (farlig, giftig) baneful, baleful; (om dyr) noxious; (hindrende) prejudicial.

skadelighet hurtfulness, harmfulness, perniciousness, mischievousness, banefulness.

skadeserstatning indemnification, indemnity, compensation; (juridisk) damages.

skadeskyte wound.

skadesløs indemnified; **holde** — indemnify.

skadesløsholdelse indemnification.

skadevarme destructive el. devastating fire.

I. **skaffe** procure; obtain; — **en noe** procure for one, provide, furnish, supply one with, get one something; (forvolde) cause, give; — **oss mye bryderi** give us el. put us to much trouble; — **av veien** remove, put out of the way; — **til veie** procure.

II. **skaffe** (mar.) eat, mess.

skaffer purveyor, caterer.

skaffetid (mar.) messtime.

skafott scaffold.

skaft handle, haft; (av søyle) shaft; (støvel- og strømpe-) leg; (økse-) helve.

skaftestøvler high boots.

skak|e shake, (om vogn) jolt. **-ing** shaking, jolt.

skakk, se skjev.

skakke (vrb): — **på slant;** — **på hodet** cock one's head, put one's head on one side; **se ogs. på** —.

skakk-kjørt (fig) perverse, wrong-headed.

skakt intetkj. av **skakk.**

skal, se **skall.**
skala scale; **i stor — on** a large scale.
skald (glt) scald, skald. **skalde|dikt** skaldic poem. **-kvad** skaldic lay. **skaldskap** skaldic art, ministrelsy.
I. **skalk,** se **skøyer.**
II. **skalk** (brødskalk) first cut of a loaf.
skalk|aktig, -het, se **skøyer|aktig, -het.**
skalke lukene batten down the hatches.
skalk.skjul blind, false pretext, stalking-horse.
skall shell; (av frukt) peel, rind.
skalldyr testaceous animal.
skalle scull, brain-pan; (støt m. hodet) butt.
skalle (vrb) (støte m. hodet) butt; **— til en** butt at one; **— av** scale (off).
skallepanne bald-pate.
skallet bald (-headed). **skallethet** baldness.
skallfrukt achenium, achene.
skalmeie shawm, shalm.
skalp scalp. **skalpel** scalpel. **skalpere** scalp.
skalte og valte med noe do el. deal with a thing as one likes.
skam shame, disgrace, ignominy, reproach; **stå til -me** be put to shame el. to the blush; **gjøre til — (beregning)** belie, falsify; (anslag) frustrate, foil; **gjøre en —** be a disgrace to one; **gjøre — på** shame; **han har ingen — i livet** he is lost el. dead to all (sense of) shame; **til — for** to the disgrace of; **(med) — å si** to my shame be it spoken; **for -s skyld** for honour's sake, in decency.
skambite bite severely.
skam|bud ridiculous bid el. offer. **-by** make a disgracefully low offer.
skamfere damage, spoil.
skamfile chafe, gall. **skamfiling** chafing.
skamfull ashamed. **skamfullhet** shame.
skamhogge cut severely, maim.
skamløs shameless, impudent, unblushing.
skamløshet shamelessness, impudence.
skamme ut scold sharply.
skamme seg be ashamed (of oneself); **skam deg!** (for) shame! shame on you!
skammekrok corner (of disgrace).
skammel (foot-)stool.
skammelig disgraceful, infamous.
skam|plett stain. **-pris** absurdly low price.
skamrose belard with praise, bepraise.
skamrødme blush of shame.
skamskjenne maltreat, mar, damage.
skamskrift libel, lampoon.
skamslå hurt severely, maim.
skandal|e scandal; scandalous scene. **-historie** scandalous story. **skandaløs** scandalous.
skandere scan. **skandering** scansion.
skandinav Scandinavian. **S-ia** Scandinavia. **-isk** Scandinavian. **-isme** Scandinavism.
skank shank.
skanse redoubt; (mar) quarter-deck.
skansekledning (på skip) bulwarks.
skap press, ward-robe; (finere) cabinet; (vegg-fast) locker; (til matvarer) cupboard; **hun vet hvor -et skal stå** she has a little will of her own.
skapaktig affected. **skapaktighet** affectation.
skapdrikker secret drinker.
skape create, make; (danne) form, fashion; **klær -r folk** fine feathers make fine birds; **— seg** give oneself (ridiculous) airs, behave affectedly.
skapelse creation, formation. **skapelses|dag** day of creation. **-historie** history of creation.
skaper creator, maker.
skaperi affectation, airs.
skaper|makt creative power. **-verk** (work of) creation.
skaping creation.
skapning creature; (noe som er frembrakt) creation; (dannelse) shape, form, make.
skar(d) (i fjellet) gap, gate, glen.

I. **skare** (uordnet mengde) crowd; (mindre flokk, korps) band.
II. **skare** (på snø) (snow)crust. **-føre** sleighing el. walkable snow. **-snø** crusted (el. frozen, hard) snow.
skarevis in crowds.
skarlagen scarlet. **-rød** scarlet.
skarlagensfeber scarlatina, scarlet fever.
skarn dirt, filth; (fig), se **skarv** (slyngel).
skarnsunge, se **skarvunge.**
skarp sharp; keen; (om lyd og åndsevner) acute; **-t syn** sharp sight; **skyte med -t** fire with shot. **skarpt** (adv) sharply; **uttale seg — om** pass severe censure on; **se — på en** look hard at one.
skarphet sharpness, trenchancy, keenness.
skarpladd shotted.
skarpretter executioner.
skarpseiler fast sailer.
skarpsindig acute, sharp-witted, penetrating.
skarp|sindighet acuteness, acumen. **-skodd** rough-shod. **-skytning** (exercise in) shooting at a target el.. mark. **-skytter** sharp-shooter. **-slepet** sharp-edged. **-syn** clear-sightedness. **-synt** sharp-sighted, keen-sighted, sharp-eyed. **-synthet** sharp-sightedness, keen-sightedness.
skarptskåret clear-cut.
skarre burr, pronounce uvularly.
skarring burr.
I. **skarv** (fugl) cormorant.
II. **skarv** (slyngel) scamp, good-for-nothing, wretch.
III. **skarv** (bart fjell) naked rock.
skarve (adj) good-for-nothing, paltry, trumpery. **-bikkje** pyh dog; **-pakk** rabble, mob. **-strek** rascally trick, piece of knavery.
skarvunge vicious child, scapegrace.
skatoll scrutoire, cabinet, bureau.
I. **skatt** (kostbarhet) treasure; **-en min!** my love! (oppsamlede verdier) hoard.
II. **skatt** (avgift til staten) tax, national tax; (avgift til kommunen) rate, local rate; **direkte — assessed** tax; **pålegge — impose** a tax.
skattbar taxable; rat(e)able; assessable. **-het** taxability, ratability.
skatte (verdsette) estimate, value, appreciate, prize; (yte skatt) pay taxes.
skatte|bevilgningsrett right of granting el. voting supplies. **-bok** tax-book. **-evne** tax-paying ability. **-foged** collector of revenue. **-foged-kontor** Inland Revenue Department. **-fri** tax -free, untaxed.
skatte|graver digger for treasure, treasure-hunter. **-graving** digging for treasure, treasure -seeking.
skatte|ligning assessment of taxes. **-nektelse** refusal to pay taxes. **-oppkrever** tax-gatherer, tax-collector. **-pliktig** liable to pay taxes, taxable, rateable. **-pålegg** imposition of taxes, taxation. **-seddel** bill of taxes, demand-note, tax paper; rates bill. **-utskrivning** imposition of taxes. **-vesen** system of taxation.
skattkammer treasury, exchequer.
skattland tributary country.
skattlegge tax.
skattmester treasurer.
skattskyldig liable to pay taxes.
skattyter tax- el. rate-payer.
skattøre rate of assessment.
skaut kerchief.
skav chippings; scrapings, shavings.
skavank hurt, damage; fault, defect.
skave chip; scrape; (lær) skive.
skavl steep snow-drift; (styrtsjø) comber, long crested wave.
skei, se **skje.**
skei(d) (kappløp) heat; (kursus) course, curriculum.
skeie turn aside, deviate; swerve; **— ut** fly out, strike out; (mar) knock off (duty); (fig) lead a dissolute life.
skeine, se **skjene.**

skeis (dt.) worthless.
skeise, se **skøyte.**
skeiv, se **skjev.**
skepsis scepsis, scepticism. **skeptiker** sceptic.
skeptisisme scepticism. **skeptisk** sceptical.
ski ski; **stå (gå) på** — ski.
skibakke ski-ing hill el. slope.
skibbe (dt.) shift. — **vekk** bundle away, shift off.
skibbrudd shipwreck; **lide** — be shipwrecked, be cast away; (fig) **lide** — **på** lose.
skibbrudden shipwrecked.
skibinding ski tie e. fastening.
skifer slate, schist; **tekke med** — slate. **-stein** slate-stone. **-tavle** slate. **-tekker** slater. **-tekt** slated.
skift shift; (t. arbeid) spell of work; (avdeling) gang, relief, relay, shift.
skifte (subst) change, alternation; (deling) partition, division; se ogs. **skift. holde** — divide an inheritance.
skifte (vrb) change; shift; (dele) divide, partition; — **tjenestefolk, klær** change servants, one's clothes; — **rett** administer justice; **skiftes** take turns, do a thing by turns.
skifte|behandling legal division of an inheritance. **-forretning** settlement of an estate.
skiftende changeful, mutable.
skiftenøkkel monkey wrench, adjustable (el. shifting) spanner.
skifte|protokoll record of the settlement of an estate. **-rett** court for the division of inheritances and bankrupts' estates, court of probate, dealing court. **-samling** meeting of heirs and creditors. **-spor** switch-rail, points.
skiftevis by turns, in turn, alternately.
skift(n)ing changing, change.
skiføre ski-ing roads. **-føring** stile of carrying el. managing one's skis.
skigard rail fence, rustic paling.
skikjelke wide-runnered sledge el. sleigh.
skikk custom, habit, usage, practice; — **og bruk** use and wont, common practice; **ha for** — be in the habit of; **han har ingen** — **på seg** he has no manners; **så det hadde (god)** — to good purpose, effectually.
skikke (glt.) se **sende.**
skikke seg, se **oppføre seg og sømme seg.**
skikkelig honest, well-behaved; inoffensive.
skikkelighet good behaviour.
skikkelse form, shape, figure; **i** — **av** in the form of; **ridderen av den bedrøvelige** — the knight of the woful countenance.
skikket fit, qualified, fitted, suitable (for).
skiklubb ski-ing club.
skilderhus sentry-box, watch-box.
skilderi picture.
skildre paint, portray, picture, depict, delineate, describe. **skildrer** portrayer.
skildring picture, description.
skill parting (of the hair).
skille (vrb) separate, part, sever, put asunder; — **at,** se **skille;** — **en av med noe** rid one of a thing; (ta fra) deprive (el. rob) one of a thing; — **fra hverandre** take to pieces, disunite, disjoin; — **fra bord og seng** separate from bed and board; — **seg fra** (el. **la seg** — **fra**) **sin hustru** be divorced from one's wife; — **seg godt, dårlig fra noe** manage, perform well, badly; — **seg med** part with, dispose of; **skilles** separate, part; **-s som venner** part friends; **-s fra** part from el. with; **-s at** part company; **melken har skilt seg** the milk is turned.
skille (subst) demarkation, division, partition.
skille|merke distinguishing mark, criterion. **-mur** partition-wall. **-mynt** small coin, (small) change. **-rom** partition.
skilletegn punctuation- mark, point.
skillevegg partition-wall.
skillevei cross-way, parting of the ways; **stå på -en** have to make one's choice.

skilling (gl. mynt) halfpenny; **ikke en** — not a farthing.
skillinge sammen club (together).
skilnad, se **forskjell.**
skilpadde tortoise; (hav-) turtle; **forloren** — mock-turtle. **-skall** tortoise-shell. **-suppe** turtle-soup.
skilsmisse parting, separation; (ekteskaps-) divorce. **-dom** a decree of divorce. **-lov** divorcive law. **-sak** divorce suit.
skilt (som en person bærer på seg) badge; (på et hus) sign, signboard.
skilte med hang out.
skiltvakt sentry, sentinel; **stå** — stand sentry.
ski|løper skirunner. **-løype** ski-ing course. **-låm** skirunner's track, ski-ing track.
skimlet mouldy.
skimmel (grå hest) grey horse.
skimre (skinne svakt) shimmer.
skimt glimmer, glimmering, glimpse. **skimte** catch a glimpse of, see dimly.
sking|re ring, clang, resound. **skingrende** shrill. **skingring** ringing, clang, clangour.
skinke ham, gammon, leg.
I. **skinn** (hud) skin, fell; (m. ulla på) fleece; (pelsverk) fur; (preparert) leather; **det gylne** — the golden fleece; **bare** — **og ben** mere skin and bone; **holde seg i -et** hold oneself in; **få en ut av sitt gode** — put one out of all patience.
II. **skinn** light, (sterkt) glare, shine, (fig) show, appearance, colour; **-et bedrar ofte** appearances are often deceitful; **dømme etter -et** judge from appearances. **skinn-** pretended, feigned, mock, sham, false.
skinnangrep mock-attack, feint.
skinnbarlig (adj) incarnate, in the body; **den -e djevel** the devil incarnate, the very devil.
skinnbukser leather breeches.
skinndød (adj) apparently dead, asphyxiated.
skinndød (subst) apparent death, asphyxy.
skinne (vrb) shine.
skinne (subst) iron-band; (hjulsk.) tire; (jernbanesk.) rail, (pl) rails, metals; (til brukket ben) splint; (benskinner pl) greaves (pl); **gå av -ne** run off the rails. **-be(i)n** shin, shinbone.
skinne|gang tram-way; (jernb.) rails. **-legger** rail-layer. **-rydder** rail-guard; (amr) pilot.
skinnfektning sham fight.
skinn|fell skin rug. **-foret** fur-lined.
skinnhanske leather-glove.
skinnhellig hypocritical. **-het** hypocrisy.
skinn|kant fur edge. **-kåpe** fur-cloak.
skinnliv seeming life.
skinnlue fur cap.
skinnmager lank-sided, skinny.
skinnpels fur coat.
skinnsyk jealous. **skinnsyke** jealousy.
skinntryte (bot.) whortleberry.
skinn|trøye leather jacket. **-tøy** furs.
skip ship, vessel; (i kirke) nave; (typografisk) galley.
I. **skipe** (ut) ship (off).
II. **skipe** (til) arrange.
skiple disturb, disarrange; displace.
skipning shipping.
skipper master of a vessel, shipmaster, master mariner, skipper. **-eksamen** master's examination. **-løgn** fish-story. **-skjønn** egtl. skipper's judg(e)ment; rough estimate. **-tak** a long stroke in pulling, occasional spurt.
skips|apotek ship's dispensary. **-besetning** (ship's) crew. **-bru** boat-bridge, pontoon (-bridge); pier. **-bygger** ship-builder. **-byggeri** shipwright's yard, dock-yard. **-bygging** ship-building. **-bøkene** the ship's books. **-fart** navigation. **-fartsforholdene** the state of the shipping trade. **-fører** master of a ship, shipmaster. **-handel** shipchandlery. **-handler** ship-chandler, marine -store dealer, (seaman's) outfitter. **-journal** ship's journal. **-kaptein** master el. captain of a ship. **-kjeks** ship-biscuit, sea-biscuit. **-klarerer**

shipping agent. **-kledning** planking of a ship. **-kost** sailor's fare. **-leilighet** shipping opportunity; **få — til** obtain a passage to. **-lege** surgeon. **-mannskap** crew (of a ship). **-megler** ship-broker. **-reder** ship-owner. **-rederi** shipowning business el. trade. **-rulle** station bill. **-side** side of a ship; **fritt ved -side** free over ship's rail. **-skrog** hull (of a ship). **-verft** wharf, dock-yard, ship-yard.
skirenn run on skis; ski-ing match.
skisma schism. **skismatiker** schismatic.
skismatisk schismatic(al).
skispor, se **-låm**.
skisse sketch. **-bok** sketch-book.
skissere sketch, outline.
skistav ski-stick.
skitne (vrb) dirty.
skitt dirt, filth; (fig) trash, rubbish; **skitt** (adv, slett) bad, badly; **det går — it** is but a bad affair! (int) **— la gå!** here goes! never mind! **— i det!** bother! dash it!
skitten dirty, filthy; **-t snakk, skitne ord** coarse, gross language el. words.
skitten|ferdig dirty, slovenly. **-het** dirtiness, filthiness. **-tøy** dirty clothes, soiled linen, washing.
skitt|unge a mere chit. **-viktig** stuck-up.
skitur ski-ing excursion.
skive (vrb) slice.
skive (subst) disk; (til skyting) target; (av brød, kjøtt) slice; (på ur) face, dial; **skyte på —** shoot at a target; **en — for** the butt of; **gjøre til — for** expose to. **skiveskyting** target shooting, ball-practice, target-practice.
skje (vrb) happen, occur, come to pass; be done; **Gud — lov!** thank God! God be praised!
skje (subst) spoon; (om kvantum) spoonful, f. eks. how many tea-spoonfuls did you take? **gi ham det inn med -er** beat it into him; **ta -en i den andre hånden** change one's tactics.
skjeblad bowl of a spoon.
skjebne fate, destiny, fortune; **-n** fate osv.; **finne seg i sin — be** resigned to one's fate; **takk —!** that's like my luck! I like that now!
skjebnesvanger fatal, fateful.
skjebnetro fatalism.
skjede scabbard, sheath, case.
skjefte (subst) stock (of a gun), butt-end.
skjefte (vrb) handle, stock.
skjegg beard; (botan.) barb; (på østers) beard; (på nøkkel) bit; **mumle i -et** murmur in one's beard; **le i -et** laugh in one's sleeve; **la -et vokse** grow a beard.
skjegget bearded.
skjeggløs beardless, unbearded. **-vekst** growth of beard.
skjel: gjøre rett og — give every one his due; **komme til -s år og alder** come to (the) years of discretion.
skjele squint. **— til** look askance at. **skjeling** squinting.
skjelett skeleton. **skjelettere** skeletonize.
I. **skjell** (grense) boundary, bound, limit, term.
II. **skjell** scale; (muslingskall) shell; (musling) shell, mussel.
skjellakk shellac, gumlac.
skjell|dannet scaly, scale-like. **-dekt**, se **skjellet.**
skjelle (ut) abuse, revile, call names.
skjellet scaly, shelly.
skjellig just, reasonable. **— grunn** just el. sufficient cause.
skjellsord abusive term, (term of) abuse.
skjellvinget lepidopterous, scaly-winged.
skjelm (skøyer) rogue. **skjelmeri** roguery, roguishness, waggishness. **skjelmsk** arch, roguish, waggish.
skjelmsstykke knavish el. rascally trick.
skjelne distinguish, discern, make out, discriminate; **— fra** tell from. **-evne** power of discrimination. **-merke** distinctive mark, characteristic. **skjelning** discrimination.
skjelv (subst) tremble, quake. **skjelv** (dt.,

= **skjelvende**); **han er — på hånden** his hand is unsteady.
skjelve tremble, shake. **skjelving** tremble.
skjeløyd(d) squint-eyed.
skjema scheme; (blankett) form.
skjematisk skeleton-like, outlined.
skjemme disfigure, deform, spoil; **— seg** (ta av) fall away el. off; **— seg ut** disgrace oneself.
skjemmes el. **skjems**, se **skamme seg.**
skjemt sport, mirth, jest, joke, pleasantry.
skjemte joke, jest, banter.
skjemte|dikt comic poem. **-full** facetious, sportive, jocose. **-fullhet** jocularity, facetiousness, jocoseness. **-vise** comic song.
skjemt|som jocose. **-vis** (adv) jokingly, jestingly.
skjendig disgraceful, infamous, nefarious, opprobrious. **skjendighet** disgracefulness, infamy, opprobrium; infamous deed.
skjene (om kyr) fly obliquely, swerve.
I. **skjenk** (et møbel) sideboard, buffet; (i vertshus) bar.
II. **skjenk** (gave) gift, present, donation.
III. **skjenk** (drikk) a drink, drinks.
I. **skjenke** (gi) present (with), make a present of, give; **— oppmerksomhet** bestow attention on; **— fortrolighet** admit into one's confidence; **resten -r jeg Dem** never mind the rest.
II. **skjenke** (helle) pour (out); **— te** pour out the tea; **— full fill; — i glasset** fill the glass, pour (wine etc.) into the glass.
skjenke|rett a license (for retailing liquor). **-stue** taproom. **-vert** barkeeper.
skjenk(n)ing pouring; retailing liquor.
skjenn scolding, chiding, rating. **få — be** scolded, get a scolding.
I. **skjenne** (vt.) (ødelegge) spoil, deface; destroy, ruin; **— en pike** violate a maiden; **— og brenne** ravage with fire and sword.
II. **skjenne** (vi.) scold. **— på** scold, chide, rate.
skjennepreken rating.
skjenneri brawling; squabble quarrel.
skjensel infamy, disgrace, dishonour, ignominy. **skjenselsgjerning** infamous deed.
skjeppe bushel.
skjeppe (vrb) (fylle, forslå) yield.
skjerding (til gryte) chimney-hook, pot-hanger.
skjerf scarf, sash; (til halsen) comforter.
skjerm screen; (for øynene, lampe-) shade; (på lue) front-shade; (på bil) dasher, splashboard; (fig) cover, screen. **-blomstret** umbelliferous. **-brett** folding-screen.
skjerme screen, shield, shelter, guard; (beskytte) protect (mot: from).
skjerp (sted hvor malm søkes) prospect-hole, place where metal has been tried for.
I. **skjerpe** (søke etter malm) search for ore, try for metal, prospect.
II. **skjerpe** (gjøre skarp) sharpen; (straff) aggravate; **— appetitten** give an edge to el. whet the appetite; **skjerpende** (omstendigheter) aggravating (circumstances); **skjerpet** (kontroll o. l.) more rigorous.
skjerv mite, portion.
skjev wry; (hellende) oblique; (krum) crooked; (fordreid) distorted; **en — vinkel** an oblique angle; **en — stilling** a false el. wrong position; **la tingene gå sin -e gang** let things slide; **går støvlene sine -e** wears his boots on one side; **skjevt** (adv) awry, aslant, on one side, aslope, obliquely; **se skjevt til** have a dislike to, to turn up one's nose at.
skjevbent crooked-legged.
skjevhalset wry-necked.
skjevhet wryness, obliquity, obliqueness; curvature of the spine; (fig) obliquity, perversity.
skjevsyn warped judgment.
skjevøyd(d) oblique-eyed.
I. **skjold** (flekk) stain, discoloration.
II. **skjold** (et) shield, buckler, target; (dt.) **føre i sitt — be** up to.

skjold|borg rampart of shields. **-brusk** thyroid cartilage. **-bruskkjertel** thyroid gland. **-bule** boss.

skjoldet discoloured, stained.

skjoldlus coccus.

skjoldmøy female warrior, amazon.

skjor, se **skjære.**

skjorte shirt; **i bare -a** in his shirt; **kle av en til -a** strip one naked el. to the skin. **-bryst** shirt-front. **-erme** shirt-sleeve; **i -ermer** in his shirt-sleeves. **-knapp** shirt-button, (løs) stud. **-krage** shirt-collar. **-linning** wristband.

skjul cover, shelter; (skjulested) hiding-place, place of concealment; (ved-) shed; **legge — på noe** make a secret of el. conceal a thing; **ligge i — be** hid.

skjule hide, conceal, secrete **(for:** from); **— seg** hide oneself, conceal oneself; **skjult** hidden, (hemmelig) recondite.

skjulested hiding-place.

skjæker pl. av **skåk.**

I. **skjær** (subst) (lys) gleam, glimmering; (farge) cast, tinge, tint.

II. **skjær** (plogskjær) share.

III. **skjær** (i sjøen) rock, skerry, shelf; **et blind-** a sunken rock.

I. **skjær** (adj) (ren) pure; (om kjøtt) solid, meaty.

II. **skjær** (om åker) cuttable, ready for the sickle.

skjære (subst) magpie, pie.

skjære (vrb) cut; (gjelde) cut; **— ansikter** make faces; **— tenner** grind one's teeth; **— hverandre** (geom.) intersect; **— for** carve; **— i tre** carve in wood; **lyset -r meg i øynene** the light hurts my eyes; **— seg i fingeren** cut one's finger; **det -r meg i hjertet** it cuts me to the heart; **— ned** (bringe ned) reduce, bring down, lower; **— opp** cut open; **— over** cut; **— halsen over på seg** cut one's throat; **— alle over en kam** judge all by the same rule; **— seg på en kniv** cut oneself with a knife; **— seg** (om melk) curdle, turn; **— til** cut out.

skjærende cutting; (fig) (stemme) harsh, (motsetn.) glaring; **— instrument** edge-tool.

skjæretann incisor (tooth).

skjærgård skerries.

skjæring cutting; (jernb.) cut, cutting.

skjærings|linje line of intersection. **-punkt** point of intersection.

skjærmyssel skirmish.

skjærsild purgatory; **i -en** in purgatory.

skjærsliper (knife-, scissor-) grinder.

skjærtorsdag Maundy-Thursday.

skjøke (skjøge) prostitute, harlot, strumpet.

skjølp score, groove, gouge. **skjølpe ut** score.

skjønn (subst) opinion, judgment, estimate; **oppta et — over** estimate; **etter et løst — at** a rough estimate; **handle etter — act** at discretion; **etter beste — to** the best of my understanding.

skjønn (adj) beautiful, beauteous; **den -e** the fair one; **de -e** the fair (sex); **det -e** the beautiful; **de -e kunster** the fine arts.

skjønne perceive, discern; **— på,** se **påskjønne.**

skjønner connoisseur, a good judge.

skjønnhet beauty.

skjønnhetskonkurranse beauty contest.

skjønnhets|middel cosmetic. **-plett** beauty-spot, (face-)patch. **-sans** sense of beauty, beauty sense. **-vann** beauty water, beauty wash.

skjønnlitteratur polite literature.

skjønnsforretning survey, estimate.

skjønn|skrift fine handwriting. **-skrivning** calligraphy.

skjønnsmann surveyor, estimator.

skjønnsom judicious, discreet, discriminating, sensible; (som skjønner på) regardful, grateful

skjønnsomhet discretion, discernment, judiciousness; gratefulness, thankfulness.

skjønnssak matter of judgment.

skjønnsvis at a rough estimate.

skjønnånd wit.

skjønt (enskjønt) though, although.

skjør brittle, fragile; **et -t hode** a weak-headed person.

skjørbuk scurvy; **lidende av — scorbutic; middel mot — anti-scorbutic.**

skjørhet brittleness; fragility.

skjørhodet weakheaded, crazy.

skjørne turn, coagulate.

skjørost curd-cheese, petit Suisse.

skjørt petticoat; (kjole-) skirt; (kvinne) petticoat. **skjørte: — opp** tuck up.

skjørteregimente petticoat-government.

skjørteveien: gå — use female influence.

I. **skjøt** (på frakk) tail, flap, lap.

II. **skjøt** (tau) sheet.

III. **skjøt** (en) eke, eking; (foreningspunkt) junction. **uten — of** one piece.

IV. **skjøt** alm. **fang** (s. d.); (fig) bosom; **legge hendene i -et** sit idle, do nothing.

skjøte (jur.) deed of conveyance.

I. **skjøte** (overdra) convey; (amr) deed.

II. **skjøte** eke el. piece out, lengthen.

skjøtehund lap-dog, toy dog.

skjøteprotokoll register of estates and titles.

skjøtesløs careless, heedless, negligent **(med:** of el. about). **skjøtesløshet** carelessness, heedlessness, negligence.

skjøtesynd favourite sin, bosom sin.

skjøtningsklausul (jur.) habendum.

skjøtsel care, management, tending.

skjøtte mind, take care of, attend (to); **— seg selv** take care of oneself, shift for oneself; **— om** want, like, care for.

skjå, se **skur.**

skli go down a slide.

sklie slide.

sko (subst) shoe; (fig); **over en lav — wholesale,** in a wholesale fashion; **vet hvor -en trykker** knows where the shoe pinches.

sko (vrb) shoe.

skobørste shoe-brush.

skodde fog, mist.

skoft (hviletid) rest; (fravær fra arb.) missing work.

skofte be off el. cut work.

skog wood; (stor) forest; (urskog, i India) jungle, (i Austr.) bush.

skog|bar woodless. **-brann** forest-fire. **-bruk** forestry. **-bryn** edge of a wood. **-bunn** forest -ground. **-bygd** woody district. **-due** stock -pigeon. **skoge: — av** deforest, strip of forests.

skogfredning preservation of woods.

skogger|latter loud laugh, roar of laughter. **-le** roar with laughter, (dt.) guffaw.

skoggrense limit of trees, line of woods; (amr) timber-line.

skog|kledd wood-clad. **-lendt** wooded. **-li** wooded hillside.

skog|plant(n)ing the planting of forests; (konkr.) plantation. **-rabb** woody bank. **-rik** wooded, woody, well timbered. **-rydning** clearing of woods.

skogs|drift, se **skogbruk. -fugl** woodland bird, wild-fowl. **-kar** lumberer.

skog|skjelv the wood's fear. **-slette** glade. **-stjerne** starflower. **-strekning** tract of wood. **-teig** strip of wood, lot of a wood. **-tjern** lake in the forest. **-troll** satyr. **-tur** excursion to the wood, picnic. **-tykning** thicket. **-vokter** forest guard, ranger.

skohorn shoeing-horn, shoe-lift.

skokk threescore; (en hel del) crowd, herd.

skokle trace.

skokrem boot polish.

skolastiker scholastic. **skolastikk** scholasticism.

skolastisk scholastic(al).

skole school; (piano- o. fl.) tutor; **gå i — el. på — go** to school, be at school; **sende en på — put** el. send one to school; **ta ut av -n** take from school; **ta en i — school** one, take one to task.

skole|bestyrer headmaster, school manager, principal of a s. **-bestyrerinne** lady principal of a school. **-benk** form. **-bruk: til -bruk** for school purposes. **-dag** school-day. **-eksamen** school examination. **-elev** pupil (of a school).
skole|film educational film. **-form** form of school. **-gang** schooling; **tvungen -gang** compulsory school attendance. **-gutt** schoolboy. **-hage-arbeid** (som fag i skolen) cottage gardening. **-hest** trained horse. **-hjem** reform school. **-hygiene** school hygiene. **-kamerat** school-fellow, school-mate.
skolekjøkken school kitchen. **-lærerinne** teacher of domestic economy.
skole|lys (fig) college light, school luminary. **-lærer** usher el. teacher, (at el. to a school), school-teacher. **-mann** teacher, school-man, pedagogue. **-mester** school-master. **-penger** school fees. **-pike** school-girl. **-plan** plan el. system of instruction. **-pliktig** bound to attend school. **-pult** desk, school desk.
skolere train.
skole|ritt trick riding. **-rytter** trick rider. **-råd** teachers' council. **-skip** school ship.
skole|stue school-room. **-søkende** attending school; (i motsetn. til kostelever) day boy, daily pupil. **-tid** school-time, school-hours; (skoledager) school-days; **etter -tid** after school. **-time** lesson (in a school). **-tvang** compulsory education. **-utdannelse** schooling. **-vei** road to school. **-vesen** school system, education, schools. **-veske** satchel. **-år** session; the schooldays.
skolisse shoe-string, latchet.
skolm (bot.) husk, pod,.shell.
skolopender (tusenben) scolopendra.
skolt (dt., hode) noddle, pate, sconce.
skomaker shoemaker, bootmaker. **-gutt** shoemaker's apprentice. **-mester** master-shoemaker.
skomakersvenn journeyman shoemaker.
skoning (på skjørt, glt.) bottom lining.
skonnert schooner.
skonrok rye biscuit.
sko|plugg shoemaker's peg. **-pusser** shoeblack, bootblack.
skorpe crust, (på sår) scab; (i pipehode) cake; — **seg** crust.
skorpion scorpion.
skorsonerrot viper's grass.
skorstein chimney; (dmp.) funnel.
skorsteins|feier chimney-sweeper. **-pipe** chimney-top.
skorte: det -r på there is a want of; **det -r ham på** he wants, is wanting in; **la det — på** be wanting in.
skorte (bergkløft) defile, gully, ravine.
skose (subst) taunt, gibe. **skose** (vrb) taunt.
skosverte (shoe-)blacking.
skosåle sole of a shoe.
skotsk Scottish, Scotch.
I. **skott** (skillerom i skip) bulkhead; (akter-) after el. steerage bulkhead; (for-) fore bulkhead.
II. **skott**, se **skudd**.
skotte Schotchman; **-ne** the Schotchmen, the Scotch, the Scots.
skotte glance aside, look sidewise (**bort på**: at).
Skott|land Scotland. **s-lender** Scotchman. **s-lenderinne** Scotchwoman.
skotøy shoes and boots.
skove (subst) crust; pl. ogs. scrapings.
skovl shovel, scoop; (dmp.) (paddle-) float.
skovlblad pan of a shovel. **skovle** shovel.
skovlhjul paddle(-wheel).
skral poor, scanty; (om vinden) scant; (syk) poorly; — **lykke** bad luck, hard lines; **det er -t med ham** he is poorly.
skrall clap, peal, crack.
skralle (vrb) peal, rattle; **en -nde latter** a roar of laughter.
skralle (subst) rattle, clacker.
skramme slash, scratch; scar.
skrammel lumber, trumpery, rubbish. **et gammelt — av et hus** a lumbering old house.

skrammet scarred.
skrangel rattle, rumble.
skrangle jolt, lumber; rattle. **-kjerre** jolting el. lumbering cart. **skranglet**, se **skinnmager**. **skrangle|vei** oldfashioned humdrum way. **-verk** rattletrap.
skranke bar, barrier; (i retten) bar; (på posthus, apotek) counter. **sette -r for** set bounds to; **tre i -n mot en** enter the lists against one; **tre i -n for en** take up the cudgels for one.
skrante be ailing, be in delicate health. **en som -r** a valetudinarian.
skranten (adj) ailing, sickly.
skranting sickliness, weakliness.
skrap (kassert gods) discards; (fig) trumpery, refuse.
skrape scrape, scratch; (om hest) paw; — **ut** (med foten) make a leg, scrape; — **sammen** scrape together; **en -nde lyd** a scratching noise; **en -nde penn** a scratchy pen.
skrape (subst) (irettesettelse) rebuke, reprimand. **-jern** scraper. **-r** (redskap) scraper; (til fangst) scraper, drag, dredge.
skrap|handel old-iron shop, marine store. **-handler** marine-store dealer, old-metal man. **-ing** scraping etc., (på havbunnen) dredging. **-jern** scrap-iron. **-sår** abrasion, scratch. **-ut** scrape.
skras|le roar with laughter. **-sel**, se **skogger-latter**.
skratt chatter; (latter) guffaw.
skratte give a cracked sound; (om fugler) chatter, cockle; **en -nde stemme** a harsh voice.
skratting cracked sound; (om fugl) chattering.
skrattle, se **skrasle**.
skravere hatch. **skravering** hatching.
skravl (snakketøy) talking gear; (snakk) cackle, chatter, gabble, jabber; **la -a gå** chatter away; **-a står aldri på henne** her tongue is never at rest; se ogs. **skravlebøtte**.
skravle prate, jabber.
skravlebøtte chatterbox.
skre (om korn) rough-grind.
skred slip, slide.
skredder tailor. **-arbeid** tailor's work. **-forretning** tailor's shop. **-gutt** tailor's boy. **-kone** tailor's wife. **-lære: sette, være** el. **stå i —** apprentice one to, be apprenticed to, a tailor. **-mester**, se **skredder**. **-regning** tailor's bill. **-saks** tailor's scissors. **-ske** tailoress. **-svenn** journeyman tailor. **-sydd** tailored, tailor-made. **-søm** tailoring. **-verksted** tailor's shop.
I. **skrei** (torsk) (spring, winter) codfish.
II. **skrei** (jule-), se **Oskoreia**; (flokk, f. eks. ulve-) running pack.
skrekk terror, fright, dread; **ha — for** stand in terror el. dread of; **få en — i livet** get a fright.
skrekkelig terrible, terrific, dreadful.
skrekkinnjagende terrifying, formidable.
skrekkregjering reign of terror.
skrekk|slagen terror-struck.
' avskrelt skall) peel, paring, parings.
.. skrell (om lyd), se **skrall**.
I. **skrelle** peel, pare. **skrelling** (avskrelt skall), se **skrell**; (det å skrelle) peeling etc.
II. **skrelle** (smelle) clang, crack, peal, rattle.
skremme (subst), se **skremsel**.
skremme (vrb) scare; frighten, startle; — **livet av** en frighten one out of his life. — **opp** rouse, start, alarm. **-bilde** bugbear. **-skudd** blank shot; (fig) piece of bluff. **skremsel** scare-crow, bug-bear.
skrent slope, declivity; (oppover) acclivity.
skreppe (skryte) brag.
skreppe (subst) bag, knapsack, wallet. **-kar** pedlar. **-kram** pedlary.
skrev interstice between the legs, fork; (skritt) stride.
skreve stride, straddle.
skrevs over astride.

skri glide, slide.
skribent writer, author. (kvinnel.) penwoman, authoress. **skrible** scribble. **skribler** scribbler.
skride advance, proceed; (m. verdige skritt) stalk; — **inn** interfere, interpose; — **inn mot en ad rettens vei** take legal proceedings against one; — **til** proceed to.
I. **skrift** (en) writing; (typograf.) type, letter, fount; **-en** the Scriptures, Holy Writ.
II. **skrift** (et) writing, book, publication, work; **mindre** — paper, tract, treatise; pamphlet.
skriftart sort of type.
skrifte (subst) confession.
skrifte (vrb) confess.
skrifte|barn penitent. **-far** (father-)confessor. **-mål** confession; **hemmelig** — auricular confession; **motta ens** — confess one. **-stol** confessional.
skrift|fortolker interpreter of the Scriptures. **-fortolkning** exegesis. **-kasse** (typograf.) box.
skriftklok scripturist, (bibelsk) scribe.
skriftkyndig expert in handwriting.
skriftlig written, in writing; — **avstemning** poll, polling; — **oppgave** paper; **det -e** the papers; **oppsette** — put in writing; reduce to writing.
skrift|les(n)ing manuscript-reading; reading the Scriptures. **-lærd** scripturist; book-learned, se ogs. **-klok**.
skrift|prøve specimen of penmanship. **-språk** written (el. book el. literary) language; scriptural sentence. **-sted** text, scripture. **-støper** type (el. letter)-founder. **-støperi** type-founding; type (el. letter)-foundry. **-støp(n)ing** founding of types. **-system** system of writing. **-tegn** character.
skrik cry, scream, shriek, screech; **det siste** — (det nyeste nye) the latest thing.
skrike cry; (av skrekk) scream, shriek, screech; — **om hjelp** cry out for help **skrikende** vociferous, screechy; (fig) glaring, flagrant; (om farge) loud. **skrikedokke** squeakingdoll. **skrikerunge** cry-baby, (dt.) squaller. **skrikhals** screamer.
skrin case, box; (lite) casket.
skrinlegge enshrine; (fig) consign to oblivion.
skrinn lean; scraggy; (om jord) barren. **-lende** barren el. poor soil.
skritt pace, step; (i benkl.) fork; **gjøre et** — take å step; **gå i** — pace, walk; **holde** — med keep pace with; — **for** — step by step, at a foot's pace; **holde tre** — **fra livet** keep at arm's length (el. at a distance), make one keep his distance; **tok -et fullt ut** went the whole length.
skritte pace; — **ut** step out.
skritt|gang: i — at a walk(ing pace). **-måler** pedometer.
skrittvis step by step.
skriv letter, communication; memorial.
skrive write; (på maskin) type; **hva -r vi i dag?** what day (of the month) is this? what's the day of the month? — **av** copy, transcribe, write out; — **seg bak øret** keep in mind, make a (mental) note of; **hvor -r han seg fra?** from what place does he come? **det -r seg fra** it is owing to; **det -r seg fra den tid** it dates from that time; — **i et blad** contribute to a paper; — **inn** enter; (i skolesprog) fair-copy; **navnet -s med h** the name is spelt with an h; — **om igjen** rewrite, write over again; — **om noe** write upon a subject; — **opp** write down, make a note of; **han -r på en grammatikk** he is writing a grammar; — **sammen** join in writing; (forfatte) compile; — **til en** write to one, communicate with one; — **under** sign.
skrive|blekk writing ink. **-bok** copy-book. **-bord** writing table. **-hjelp** assistance in doing the clerical work. **-kløe** itch of scribbling, rage for writing. **-krampe** writer's cramp. **-kyndig** able to write.
skrivelse letter, communication; memorial; **Deres ærede** — your favour; **min ærbødige** — my respects.

skrive|lærer writing-master. **-mappe** portfolio. **-maskin** typewriter. **skrive på -maskin** work the type-writer. **-materialer** stationery, writing articles. **-måte** mode of writing, style (of writing); spelling.
skrive|papir writing-paper. **-pult** writing-desk, desk-table; (reise-) writing-case.
skriver writer, scribe; (på kontor) clerk; se ogs. **sorenskriver**.
skriveri writing; (ringeakt.) scribbling.
skriverkar amanuensis, clerk.
skrive|saker writing materials, stationery. **-stell** ink-stand, standish. **-syk** writative. **-syke** se **-kløe**. **-tavle** slate. **-time** writing lesson. **-underlag** blotting pad.
skriv|feil error in writing, slip of the pen. **-ning** writing.
skrofulose scrofula. **skrofuløs** scrofulous.
skrog (av skip) hull, body.
skrot (skrap) rubbish.
skrott carcase; **det kunne gjøre godt i en gammel** — might be acceptable to an old body.
skrov, se **skrog**.
I. **skrubb** (skrubbsår) graze; (skjenn) a scolding; (golv-) scrubber, brush, swab.
II. **skrubb** (en), se **ulv**.
skrubbe (subst) (flyndreart) flounder.
I. **skrubbe** (vrb) scrub; (m. svaber) mop; (huden) graze, rub; (fig) scrub down.
II. **skrubbe** (under aking) check (the way).
skrubbet (ujevn) rough, rugged, scabrous.
skrubbhøvel jack-plane, rough-plane.
skrubbhøvle jack, rough-plane.
skrubbsulten ravenously hungry.
skrubbsår, se under **skrubb**.
skrud garb.
skrue (subst) screw; (dmp.) screw(-propeller), propeller; (biljard) screw, twist; (musikk) peg; (fig) **underlig** — odd fish, eccentric; **ha en** — **løs** be crackbrained, have a soft place in one's head.
skrue (vrb) screw; — **av** unscrew; — **fra** screw off; — **ned lampen** turn down the lamp; — **opp** screw up; (åpne) unscrew.
skrue|damper, **-dampskip** screw steamer. **-gang**, **-gjenge** (screw-)thread el. worm. **-hode** screw-head.
skruestikke vice.
skru|is pack-ice. **-jern** screw-tap.
skrukk(e) (subst) pucker; **slå -er** pucker, wrinkle.
skrukket puckery, puckered.
skrukketroll wood-louse, sow-bug.
skrukoss hummock, pile of ice.
skrull|et crack-brained, crazy; (amr) cranky. **-ing** crack-brain; crank.
skrumle lumber.
skrummel bulky, shapeless object.
skrumor (møtrik) female screw, nut, screw-box.
skrumpe inn, **sammen** shrink, shrivel (up).
skrumpet shrivelled, shrunk.
skruning (is-) pack.
skrunøkkel wrench, spanner, screw-key.
skruppel scruple; **gjøre seg skrupler av** make a scruple of; (av å) scruple to.
skrutrekker turnscrew, screw-driver.
skryt (om esel) bray; (præleri) brag, boast.
skryte (om esel) bray; (prale) brag, boast.
skryter braggart.
skryteri bragging.
skræ (om korn), se **skre**.
skræling (svakelig person) sickly, puny person, weakling; (eskimo, indianer) skraelling.
I. **skrømt** feint, dissimulation; **på** — falsely, feignedly, ironically.
II. **skrømt** (spøkeri) ghosts, goblins.
skrøne (vrb) fable, yarn, fib. **skrøne** (subst) fib. **-maker** bouncer, fibber, fibster.
skrøpelig fragile, brittle; (svak) frail, infirm, feeble; (om karakteren) frail.

skrøpelighet fragility; (fig) frailty, fragility.
I. skrå (artilleri) grape.
II. skrå (tobakk) quid (of tobacco).
III. skrå (lov, glt.) statutes.
I. skrå (tygge skrå) chew tobacco.
II. skrå (ta el. gi en skrå retning) slant, slope; — over cross obliquely.
skrå (adj) sloping, slanting, oblique, inclined; **på —, skrått** (adv) aslope, aslant, slantingly; **skråbjelke** (heraldisk) bar (sinister).
skrål squall, bawl, roar.
skråle squall, bawl, roar.
skråler squaller, bawler, roarer; **skrålhals** bawler, ranter; **politiske -er** political ranters.
skråme, se **skramme.**
skråne slope, slant. **-ning** slope, slant, declivity; (oppover) acclivity. **-plan** inclined plane.
skråpute (i seng) bolster.
skrås overfor nearly opposite.
skråskrift italics. **skråtak** sloping roof.
skråtobakk chew-tobacco.
skråttliggende oblique.
skubb push, thrust.
skubbe shove, push; — **til en** give one a push;
skudd (av plante) shoot, sprout; (mest fig) scion; (med skytevåpen) shot; (ladning) charge; round of ammunition; (i fotball) shot; **et — krutt** a charge of gunpowder; **ikke et — krutt** verd not worth shot and powder; **være i -et** be in luck, a favourite.
skuddag bissextile el. intercalary day, leap-day.
skuddermudder: gå i — go to rack and ruin.
skudd|fast, -fri shot-proof, bullet-proof; **gå -fri** (fig) pass shotfree.
skudd|hold gunreach, range. **komme på** — come within gunshot, get a shot at. **-linje** firing line. **-premie** bonus, money paid for shoot -ing. **-sikker** se **-fast. -sår** (gun-)shot wound. **-vidde** reach el. range (of gunshot); **innenfor** — within gunshot, **utenfor** — out of gunshot.
skuddår leap-year, bissextile.
skue (subst) sight, show; **stille til** — expose to view, exhibit, display, show up; **bære til** — make a display of.
skue|mynt medal. **-plass** stage (of a theatre); (fig) scene. **-retter** show-dishes. **-spill** play; (fig) spectacle, sight. **-spillforfatter** play-writer, playwright, dramatist, dramatic author.
skuespiller actor, (stage-)player, performer. **-inne** actress. **-selskap** company of actors.
skuff (i kommode, skap) drawer.
skuffe (subst) shovel.
I. skuffe (vrb) shovel.
II. skuffe (bedra, narre) disappoint; (forventninger) fall short of; **-nde** delusive; **det er en meget -nde** etterligning it is a splendid illusion; (adv) **etterligne -nde** imitate to nature.
skuffelse disappointment.
skulder shoulder; **trekke på skuldrene** shrug one's shoulders.
skulder|blad shoulderblade, scapula. **-bred** broad-shouldered. **-trekk, -trekning** shrugging of the shoulders, shrug. **skuldre** (vrb) shoulder.
skuldring shouldering.
skule cast down the eyes, scowl; — **bort på** scowl at.
skule|dunk swill tub, waste-butt. **-r** swillings, swills.
skuling scowling, scowl.
skulke shirk; — **skolen** play (the) truant, play hookey. **skulker** truant. **skulke|syk** sham sick; **være -syk** feign illness, malinger, be shirking. **-syke** sham sickness, malingery; **skulking** shirking, truancy.
skulle be obliged; **jeg skal reise imorgen** (det er bestemt) I am to depart to-morrow; (må) I must depart to-m.; (lovende) I will depart to-m.; **jeg skal straffe ham** (truende) I will punish him; **du (han, dere, de) skal gå, bli belønnet, bli straffet** you (he, you, they) shall go, be rewarded, be punished; **det skal ikke mangle noe** there shall be nothing wanting; **jeg skulle (burde) gjøre det** I ought to do it; **jeg visste ikke hva jeg skulle gjøre** I didn't know what to do; **man skulle tro at . . .** one would think that . . .; **det skulle jeg mene** I should think so; **hva skal jeg der** what am I to do there, why should I go there? **hvor skal De hen?** where are you going? **jeg skal hjem** I am going home; **skipet skal til Frankrike** the ship is bound for France; **jeg skal ut å spasere** I am going to take a walk; **skulle det være sant?** can this be true? **jeg skulle forråde min venn?** I betray my friend? **skulle det virkelig være tilfellet?** I wonder if it is really the case? **han skal være hemmelig gift** he is said to be privately married; **— til** (behøves) be needed, be required; **det skal bare lite til for å** it takes but little to.
skulpe (bot) silique.
skulptur sculpture, work of sculpture.
skuls: være — be quits.
skum (mørk) dusk, dusky.
skum scum, froth, foam, spume; (av svette el. såpe) lather; (om munnen) foam; (på øl o. l.) froth, head.
skumdekt covered with foam el. lather.
skumle make ill-natured remarks, grumble.
skumler grumbler.
skumleri ill-natured remarks, grumbling.
I. skumme (vi) foam, froth; (om vin) mantle; **såpa -r** the soap lathers, makes lather; (fig) **— av raseri** foam (at the mouth), chafe with rage.
II. skumme (vt) (f. eks. melk) skim; **-t melk** skim-milk.
skummel gloomy, dismal, lowering, sinister.
skummelhet gloominess, gloom.
skummer, se **skum** (mørk).
skump joggle, jolt. **skumpe** (vi) joggle, jolt; **en vei hvor det -et mye** a jolty road; **— til hverandre** jostle each other; (vt) shake, jolt.
skumpelskudd outcast, scapegoat.
skumple, se **skumpe.**
skumre grow dusk.
skumring dusk, twilight.
skum|skavl foam-crested wave. **-sleiv** skimmer. **-sprøyt** spray, squirt of foam. **-svett** in a lather.
skunk skunk.
I. skur shed, shanty.
II. skur (regn) shower (of rain).
III. skur(d) (korn-) cutting; (av tømmer) sawing.
IV. skur(d) (treskjæring) carvings (pl).
skure (vt) scour; (med skurestein) holystone; scrape, chafe; (vi) (om fartøy) grate, grind.
skure|bøtte scouring-tub. **-fille, -klede, -klut** scouring-clout, floor cloth. **-kone** charwoman.
skur(d)folk harvest-men, reapers.
skuring scouring etc.; grate, grind; (dt.) **det er grei** — that's plain sailing.
skuringsmerke scouring mark, stria (pl. striæ).
skurk scoundrel, villain, knave. **-aktig** villainous, scoundrelly, knavish. **-aktighet** villainy **skurkefjes** hangdog face.
skurkestrek knavish trick, villainy.
skurlast planks and deals, sawn goods.
skur(d)onn reaping season.
skurre grate, jar; (i ørene: on the ear).
skurring grating, jarring.
skurv scurf, scald-head. **skurvet** scurfy.
skusle bort dribble away el. out.
skussmål (written) character (of a servant), testimonial. **skussmålsbok** conduct book.
skute vessel; barge, sloop, smack.
skutte seg shake oneself.
skvadronere talk big, bluster, vapour.
skvadronør blusterer, swaggerer, vapourer.
skvalder babble, noisy talk, verbiage.
skvaldre babble, rant.
skvaldrebøtte babbler, ranter, prater.
skvale rush, spout.

skvallerkål ashweed, goutweed.
skvalp heave, splash; (skvett) spray.
skvalpe heave, splash; lop, wash. **-sjø** loppy sea. **-skjær** rock awash.
skvatre (om skjære) chatter.
skvett plash, sprinkling; (rykk) start; (en liten —) a little drop.
skvette splash; sprinkle; (fare sammen) start, give a sudden start; (om hest) shy.
skvetten skittish, startish.
skvett|gang wash-strake. **-lær** apron. **-skjerm** mudguard.
skvip slipslop, wishywashy stuff.
skvulp ripple. **skvulpe** ripple; (ryste) shake.
skvulping rippling, ripple.
sky (vrb) shun, avoid, eschew.
sky (adj) (om hest) shy, skittish; (fig) shy, timorous, shrinking; **bli** — take fright, shy (at).
I. **sky** (frykt) fear, dread (for: of).
II. **sky** (på himmelen) cloud. **skrike i villen** — cry at the top of one's voice; **heve til -ene** extol to the skies.
skybrudd sudden torrent of rain.
skydekt cloud-covered. **-dott** cloud-fleck, cloudlet. **skyet** cloudy.
skyffel hoe, scraper, paring-shovel.
skyfle hoe, pare, scrape.
skyfri cloudless, unclouded, without a cloud.
skyfull cloudy, overclouded.
skygge (subst) shade; (slagskygge) shadow; (på hatt) brim (of a hat); (på lue) visor, cappeak; **en ren** — a mere shadow; **ikke** — **av** oppstand not the ghost of an insurrection; **en** — **av hva han har vært før** the ghost of his former self; **ligge i -n** lie in the shade; **stille i -n** (fig) throw el. cast into the shade, dwarf; **kaste** — **på** throw a slur on.
skygge (vrb) shade; (passe på som detektiv) shadow; — for obscure, mask; — **for en** stand in one's light; — **for øynene** shade one's eyes; **han ble -t av detektiven** he was shadowed by the detective.
skygge|aktig shadowy. **-bilde** shadow, phantom. **-full** shady, umbrageous. **-liv** life of a shadow, imaginary el. impotent life. **-løs** without shade, shadowless, shadeless.
skygge|riss outline. **-side** shady side; (fig) dark el. unfavourable side, blemish, drawback. **-tilværelse** life of a shadow. **-verden** (innbilt v.) shadowy el. imaginary world; (v. bebodd av skygger) world of shades.
skyhet shyness.
skylag stratum of clouds.
skylapper blinkers, blinds, winkers.
skyld criminality; (i forbindelsen: for... skyld) sake; (forseelse) guilt, blame, fault; (gjeld) debt; (avgift) rent, taxes; **for min** — for my sake; **for pengers** — for money's sake; **for Guds** — for God's sake, for the love of God; **for den saks** — for the matter of that, if it comes to that; **det er ikke min** — it is not my fault; **han har den største** — he is most to blame; **få ha** — **(en)** for noe bear the blame of something; **gi en** — for noe lay something to one's charge; **charge** st. upon one; **være** — **i** be the cause of; **ta -en på seg** take the blame (on oneself); **uten** — blameless, innocent.
skyld|betynget guilty. **-bevisst** conscious (of guilt), guilty. **-bevissthet** consciousness (of guilt). **-bok,** se jordebok. **-brev** bond.
skylde (være i gjeld) owe, be in debt, be indebted for; (beskylde) accuse; **jeg -r ham mye** (fig) I am deeply indebted to him; **jeg -r deg å** I owe it to you that el. (med inf.) to.
skyldes be due, be owing; **den utmerkelse som** — ... the distinction due to; **det** — **et ulykkestilfelle** it is due to an accident.
skyldfolk relations, relatives, kinsfolk.
skyldfri guiltless, blameless.
skyldfrihet guiltlessness, blamelessness.
skyldig guilty; (som er i gjeld) indebted,

owing; (forpliktet til) liable, bound; **være, gjøre seg** — **i** be guilty of; **bli en noe** — remain one's debtor for st.; **bli svar** — return no answer; **juryen kjente ham** — the jury found him guilty, brought in a verdict of guilty.
skyldighet duty, obligation; (det å være forpliktet) liability. **skyldner** debtor; **gjøre en til sin** — lay one under obligation.
skyldsetning taxation, assessment.
skyldsette tax, assess.
skyldskap relationship.
skyll deluge of rain, drencher.
skylle rinse, wash, flush; — **munnen** rinse one's mouth; — **i land** wash ashore; — **i seg, ned** swill (down), wash down; — **mot** wash; **regnet skylte ned** the rain poured down. **skylle|bøtte** swill-pail. **-kar** rinsing-trough. **-kopp** slop-basin.
skylleskål (til fingrene etter middag) finger -bowl, finger-glass.
skyllevann rinse-water, dish-water.
skyllregn heavy downpour of rain, rain falling in torrents. **skyllregne** pour down.
skynde på en urge el. hurry one on; **skynde seg** hasten, haste, hurry, make haste.
skynding haste, hurry.
skyndsom hasty, hurried; **-t** (adv) hastily, in haste; **-st** in the greatest haste.
skypumpe water-spout; land-spout.
skyseil (mar) skysail.
skyskraper sky-scraper.
skyss conveyance; **reise med** — travel post.
skyss|bonde peasant conveying travellers. **-e** convey. **-gutt** postillion, post-boy. **-hest** post-horse. **-kjerre** post-chaise. **-penger** charge (for conveyance). **-skifte, -stasjon** posting -station, stage-house.
skyte (om planter) shoot; (typograf.) lead; (med skytevåpen) shoot, fire; — **med skarpt** fire with ball; — **god fart** make good way; — **ham** cast the slough; — **rygg** raise el. arch the back, set up one's back; — **røtter** strike (root); — **satsen** lead the lines; — **av** shoot off; — **etter** shoot at; — **en kule for pannen** blow out one's brains; — **forbi, feil** miss (the mark): (fig) **skutt forbi!** not a bit of it! — **(seg) fram** project, push forward; — **i hjel** shoot dead; — **inn** insert, put in; (penger) pay in; — **seg inn under** throw oneself upon; — **ned på** pounce el. swoop upon; — **(seg) opp** shoot (up), spring up, crop up; — **på** shoot at; — **på skive** shoot at a target; — **skylden på** lay the blame on; — **sammen** (penger) subscribe, club; — **til** contribute, add; — **ut (i framtiden)** put off (into the future); **skutt** (dt.) smitten (i: with), spoony (on).
skyte|bane shooting gallery. **-bomull** gun-cotton, pyroxyline. **-hull** loophole, embrasure. **skyte|skår,** se **-hull. -skive** target.
skyte|våpen fire-arms. (pl.) **-øvelse** gun practice, shot practice.
skyt(n)ing shooting; (typograf.) leading.
skyts ordnance, artillery.
skyts|engel guardian angel. **-gud** tutelar god el. deity, patron-deity. **-gudinne** tutelar goddess. **-helgen, -patron** tutelar saint, patron saint. **-ånd** guardian spirit, tutelar genius.
skyttel (veveredskap) shuttle.
skytter marksman, shot; **S-en** (astronom.) Sagittarius, the Archer. **-fest** shooting match. **-grav** trench. **-kjede** skirmish line. **-lag** rifle-corps, company of volunteers.
skyve push, shove; (la gli) slide, slip; — **slåen for** draw, slide el. slip the bolt. **-dør** sliding-door. **-lem** slide. **-vindu** sash-window.
skøy fun, mischief; **på** — for fun.
skøyer rogue. **-strek** mischievous prank.
I. **skøyte** (båt) (small) smack.
II. **skøyte** (skeise) skate; **gå på -r** skate.
skøyte|bane skating ice, (kunstig) skating-rink. **-føre** skating, ice (for skating). **-jern** runner. **-løp, -løping** skating. **-løper** skater.

skåk (pl. skjæker) shaft of a carriage; **slå på -a og mene merra** pretend one thing and mean another.

skål bowl, cup; (til kopp) saucer; **drikke ens** — drink one's health; —! your good health! to you! **foreslå en** — give el. propose a toast. **skåld|e** scald. **-het** scalding (hot).

skåldrikking toasting.

skåle (skur) shed, woodshed.

skåle (vrb) drink healths, toast.

skål|formet cup-shaped. **-ing**, se **skåldrikking**. **-penger** gift contributed to the bowl (at rural weddings). **-tale** toast; **holde en** — toast, give a toast. **-vekt** scale balance.

skåne spare, treat with lenience; — **seg** be careful of oneself.

skånsel mercy, lenience, forbearance.

skånseløs unsparing, merciless, remorseless.

skånsom lenient. **-het** lenience.

skår (potteskår) shard, sherd; (hakk) cut; (innsnitt) incision, notch; (i en kniv) hack; **det var et** — **i** that was a draw-back to.

I. **skåre** (i slåtten) windrow.

II. **skåre** (innsnitt) notch, nick.

skårung (måkeunge) young sea-gull; (fig) young lad on his first voyage (esp. to the fisheries at the Lofoten islands), a first voyager.

skåte back astern, back the oars, back water.

skåt|e (for vindu) shutter; (for dør) bar; **skyve -a fra** unbar.

slabbe|dask slapdash fellow el. scamp. **-ras** (ladies') party.

sladder gossip; (ondsinnet) tale-bearing. **-aktig** gossiping. **-aktighet** gossiping propensity. **-hank** informer, telltale. **-hull** place for scandal.

sladre blab, peach, tell tales; — **på** tell on, (baktale) blow on.

sladre|kjerring gossip, talebearer, whisperer. **-kopp** blab, telltale.

slafs splashing, slopping. **slafse** lap, lick; splash. — **i seg** lap up, gobble up.

I. **slag** (handlingen) blow, stroke, hit; (med pisk) cut, lash; (av hest) kick, fling; (hjertets) beating, throbbing; (i krig) battle, action, engagement; (av ur) beat, stroke; (av fugl) warbling; (på klær) cape; (sykdom) apoplexy; (under kryssing) stretch, tack; (fig) blow, shock; stroke; **små** — (mar) go slow! **med ett** — at a blow; — **i** — blow upon blow, without intermission; **fikk** — was struck with apoplexy; **klokka er på -et 12** the clock is on the stroke of 12; **i -et ved Waterloo** at the battle of W.; **her stod -et** here the battle was fought.

II. **slag** (sort) description, kind, sort.

slag|anfall apoplectic fit. **-benk** turn-up bedstead. **-bjørn** cattle-killing bear. **bom** turn-pike. **-bord** folding table.

slag|en (glt. og poetisk partisipp til slå) beaten, stricken; **en** — **mann** a broken-down man; **den -ne landevei** the beaten path, el. track.

slagferdig ready for battle, (fig) quick-witted, ready witted. **slagferdighet** ready wit.

slagfjær main spring; (fugls) beam-feather.

slagg (furnace) cinders, slag, scoria.

slaggaktig scoriaceous, slaggy.

slag|lengde stroke-length. **-linje** line of battle.

slagmaler painter of battle-pieces.

slagmark field of battle.

slag|ord catchword, cry, shibboleth. **-orden** order of battle, battle array. **-plan** plan for battle.

slags sort, kind, description; **den** — **ting** that kind of things; **hva** — **menneske er han?** what sort of man is he?

slagsbror fighter, brawler.

slagside (sjøuttrykk) list; **få** — take a list; **ha** — list.

slagskip battleship.

slagskygge (cast-)shadow. **slagsmål** fighting, fight, fray; **det kom til** — they got to blows.

slagtilfelle fit of apoplexy.

slag|verk (i ur) striking part. **-vidde** striking distance.

slakk slack. **slakke** slacken. — **av** (fig) flag, relax, slacken. — **på roret** ease her helm.

slakne, se **slakke**.

slakt slaughter beast el. cattle.

slakte kill; (især nedsable) butcher, slaughter.

slaktehus slaughterhouse.

slakter butcher. **-benk** shambles (pl.). **-bu** butcher's shop (el. stall).

slakte|ri, se **slaktehus**. (slakt(n)ing) butchering. **-tid** killing season.

slakt|(n)ing butchering. **-offer** victim.

slalåm egtl. ski-ing tracks made down a hill-side or slope; ski-ing in zigzags between pine-trees or upright sticks.

slam mud.

slamp lout, lubber. **-et** loutish, lubberly.

slang slang; **bruke** — talk slang.

slange serpent, snake; (til pumpe, sprøyte) hose. **-bitt** bite of a serpent. **-buktning** serpentine winding. **-linje** serpentine line. **-temmer** snake-charmer.

slank slim.

slanke seg lose flesh. **slankhet** slimness.

slapp (adj) slack, relaxed, loose, flaccid.

slappe slacken, relax, loosen. **slappelse** relaxation. **slapphet** slackness; apathy.

slaps sludge, slush. **slapse** dabble, puddle, paddle. **-føre** sloppy (state of the) road. **det er** — it is sloppy walking. **i** — on a sloppy el. miry road.

slapset sloppy, sludgy, splashy, muddy and wet.

slaraffenland Cockaigne, fools' paradise.

slarke bob, hang loose. **-t** loose; wobbly.

I. **slarv** (person) careless el. negligent fellow, lubber.

II. **slarv** (snakk) idle gossip, tattle; (om arbeid) scamped work.

slarve gossip, tattle; scamp one's work.

slask (dt.) rough. **slasket** limp.

slave slave, bondman; (fange) convict.

slave|fut overseer of slaves; convict-warder. **-handel** slave-trade. **-handler** slave-trader, slave-merchant. **S-kysten** the Slave coast. **-merke** brand of slavery.

slaver (folkenavn) Slav, Sclav.

slaveri slavery; (fengsel) convict-prison.

slaveeskip slaver. **slavinne** (female) slave.

slavisk (adj. til slave) slavish, servile; (adj. til slaver) Slav, Slavic. **slaviskhet** servility.

slede sledge, sleigh, sled; (i artilleri) slide. **-fart** sledging, sleighing. **-føre** sleighing. **-mei** sleigh-runner. **-tur** sleigh-ride.

slegge sledge-hammer.

sleid (dampm.) slide, slide-valve.

sleike lick.

sleip (glatt) gliddery, slippery.

sleiv (øse) ladle; skimmer.

sleivet, se **slurvet**.

slekt race, family, lineage; (generasjon) generation; (naturhist.) genus; **være i** — **med en** be akin to one, be a relation to one; **i nær** — near related.

slekte på take after.

slekt|ledd generation. **-linje** line. **slektning** relation, relative, kinsman (el. kinswoman).

slektskap relationship, consanguinity; (kjemi) affinity.

slektskapsforhold connection.

slekts|merke generic mark. **-navn** family name, surname. **-register** pedigree, genealogy.

slem bad, ill, awkward, sad; (komparativ) worse, (superlativ) worst; **slemt** (adv) badly, sadly.

slem (i kort) slam; **bli** — be el. get slammed; **gjøre** — win a slam.

slemme wash. **slem(m)ing** el. **-ning** washing.

slendrian old custom, ancient routine.

I. **sleng** fling, swing, toss; (p. uttale) turn, twang.

II. **sleng** (flokk) crowd, train.
slengbemerkning casual remark.
slenge (kaste) fling; (henge og —) dangle,
swing; flop; (gå og —) idle, loaf.
slenget dangling, loose, loose-jointed; (om
gang) slouching.
slengevane idling el. loafing habits (pl.).
sleng|kappe Spanish cloak. **-kyss** blown kiss.
slentre saunter, lounge about.
slep (p. kjole) train, trail; (slit og —) toil,
drudgery; **ha, ta på** — have, take in tow.
slepe drag, trail; (arbeide hardt) toil, drudge;
(mar) tow, tug; (med hester) track; — **på
noe** carry a thing heavily; **slepende** slow,
dragging, drawling.
slepe|damper steam tug. **-line** tracking line.
-lønn towage.
slepen (vesen) polished, polite, refined; —
tunge glib tongue. **slepenhet** polish, refinement.
slepenot trawl-net; **fiske med** — trawl.
sleper tug, tow-boat; towline. **slepe|tau**
towing line; (på luftballong) guide-rope. **-trosse**
tow hawser. **sleping** towing, towage, etc.
slepkjole trained dress.
sleppe, se slippe.
slepphendt apt to drop things, butterfingered.
slesk oily, wheedling, fawning, mealy-mouthed.
sleskhet fawning, obsequiousness.
I. **slett** (ond, dårlig) bad, ill; (komparativ)
worse, (superlativ) worst; (adv) ill, badly.
II. **slett** (jevn) level, plane; — **og rett** plain,
common, pure and simple; — **ikke** not at all;
— **ingenting** nothing at all.
slett: klokke— hour, time.
slett(e) (flatt land) plain.
slette (vrb) smooth; (ut-) expunge.
slette|boer plainsman. **-land** level country.
sletthet badness, wickedness.
slett|høvel smoothing plane. **-høvle** clean, try up.
slettvar (flyndre) brill.
slibrig slippery; (fig) indecent, loose, obscene;
en — bok an obscene book.
slibrighet (fig) obscenity.
slik such.
slikk stroke with the tongue; **for en** — for an
old song. **-asparges** full-grown asparagus.
slikke lick. **slikke|pott** (pekefinger i barnespr.)
Pinnikin. **-ri** (søte saker) sweets.
slikkmunn sweet-tooth. **slikkmunnet** sweet-
mouthed.
slim mucus; (hoste- o. l.) phlegm; (av planter)
mucilage; (av snegler, fisk) slime. **slimet**
mucous; slimy. **slimhud** mucous membrane.
slind beam; strip of board for hanging clothes.
slinger, se slingring; (fig) (i valsen) dilly-
dallying, shilly-shally. **slingre** reel; dangle, swing
to and fro; (mar) roll. **slingrekjøl** side-keel.
slingring reeling etc.; (mar) rolling; roll, heel.
slintre fibre, sliver.
slipe grind; (barberblad) hone; (edelstener,
glass) cut; **slepet karaffel** cut-glass decanter.
slipe|brett knife-board. **-maskin** grinding ma-
chine. **-pulver** polishing powder.
slipers (jernb.) sleeper, tie.
slipestein grindstone, whetstone, hone.
I. **slipp** (t. båtbygging) slipway, slip.
II. **slipp: gi** — **på noe** let st. go.
slippe (vt.) let go, leave hold of, release; — **løs**
let loose; — **noe ut** let st. out; (vi.) escape;
(komme fri) get off el. away; **la en** — **lett** let
one off easy; **hvor var det vi slapp?** where did
we stop? — **bort** escape; — **for** be free from,
be spared st.; — **for å** be spared from, escape
-ing; — **fra det get off**; — **vel fra** get well out
of; — **med skrekken** get off for the fright;
— **opp** be used up el. consumed, run short,
give out, run out; — **til** get access, get a chance;
— **ut** get el. slip out; (hemmelighet) ooze out.
slips (neck-) tie. **-nål** tie-pin, pin for the tie.
slir(e) scabbard, sheath; (til bajonett) frog.
-kniv sheath-knife.

sliske (tømmerunderlag) skid, bilgeways.
sliske (vrb) wheedle, fawn (upon).
slit (på ting) wear and tear; (hardt arbeid)
toil, drudgery.
slitasje wear and tear.
slite pull (at), tear; (klær) wear; (og slepe)
toil (and moil), drudge, fag; — **i** pull at; —
(hardt) work hard; — **opp** wear out; — **seg igjennom** keep the wolf from the door; — **seg i hjel**
kill oneself (with work); **slites** wear (out); **slitt**
worn (out), the worse for wear.
sliten done, fagged, worn.
slo (fiske-) entrails.
slodde drag; hand-sleigh.
slokke (vt.) extinguish, quench, put out; —
gassen turn off el. down the gas; **slokkes** go
out; expire, become extinct.
slokne (vi.) extinguish, go out, flicker out;
expire, become extinct.
slokning extinguishing, extinction.
slokningsapparat fire-extinguishing apparatus.
sloppet, av slippe.
sloss, av slåss.
slott palace, castle.
slotts|bygning palace building. **-forvalter**
keeper of a palace, castellan. **-hage** palace-garden.
-kirke palace chapel. **-mur** palace wall. **-plass**
castle square. **-prest** chaplain to a palace chapel.
slu sly, crafty, cunning.
slubbert scamp.
slubre (drikke støyende) imbibe noisily.
sludd sleet.
sludder stuff, fudge, gammon, balderdash.
sludre talk nonsene, jabber, prate.
sluffe two-seated sleigh; sledge-chair.
sluhet slyness, cunning, craftiness.
I. **sluk** (fiskeredskap) tinbait.
II. **sluk** (avgrunn) abyss; (kloak-) gully-hole,
sink.
sluke swallow, devour. **slukhals** glutton.
sluk(k)øret chapfallen, crestfallen.
slukt gorge, ravine, (amr.) canyon.
slum (fattigkvarter) slum.
slummer slumber, doze.
slump (ubestemt mengde) lot, portion; (rest)
remainder; (i glass) heeltap; (tilfeldighet)
chance, hazard, mere accident; **på** — at random, at hap-hazard.
slumpe: — **(til)** stumble, light, chance (upon);
— **til å** chance to. **slumpehell** chance, luck;
a lucky hit. **slumpetreff** matter of chance.
slumre slumber, doze; (fig) lie dormant; —
hen (fig) die; **-nde lidenskaper** dormant passions.
slumset careless, reckless, rough.
slunken lanky. **slunkenhet** lankiness.
sluntre idle; — **unna** shirk (duty).
slupp sloop; (chefs-) barge. **-roer** bargeman.
slurk draught, gulp.
slurpe imbibe noisily.
slurv carelessness, negligence; (m. sin person)
slovenliness; (slurvet person) careless person;
sloven.
slurve (subst.) (slurvet kvinne) slattern, slut.
slurve (vrb) scamp one's work, slur over. **-feil**
slip. **-t** careless, negligent; slovenly, slatternly.
sluse lock; (tverrveggen) sluice. **-mester**
lock-gate man. **-penger** lockage. **-port** lock-gate;
(øverste) flood-gate, sluice. **-verk** lockage.
slusk rowdy, ruffian.
sluske (vrb) slight over.
sluske (subst) slattern, slut. **-ri** slovenliness.
slusket slighted over; (om personer) slovenly.
slutning (ende) termination, conclusion, close,
wind-up; (logisk) inference, conclusion; **til** —
in conclusion, to conclude.
slutningsbemerkning closing remark.
slutt (subst) close, end; **til** — at last.
slutt (endt) finished, at an end.
slutte close; (få i stand) conclude, bring
to a conclusion; (logisk) infer, conclude, judge;

— **et forbund** contract an alliance; — **et kjøp** conclude el. strike a bargain; — **en krets** form a circle; (tett) fit (tightly); — **av el. fra** conclude from; — **seg sammen** unite; — **seg til** (en) attach oneself to one; (en mening osv.) subscribe; (noe) infer, draw a conclusion as to.
sluttelig finally, in conclusion.
slutter jailer, turnkey.
sluttet close, (fig) concentrated; — **selskap** private company; **et** — **bord** a private dining-club.
slutt|kamp final round. **-resultat** final result, outcome.
sluttseddel broker's contract, contract note.
slutt|spurt final spurt. **-stein** keystone, closer.
slyng loop, winding, zigzag. — **på linjen** crossed wires.
slynge (kaste) fling, hurl, pitch, sling; (sno) wind, twine; **-nde** twining; — **seg** wind.
slynge (subst) (våpen) sling. **-kaster** slinger.
slyngel rascal, scoundrel. **-aktig** rascally, scoundrelly. **-aktig oppførsel** rascality. **-alder** hobbledehoy age.
slyngelstrek rascality, scoundrelism.
slyngkraft centrifugal force. **slyngning** turn, winding, zigzag.
slyng|plante creeper, climber. **-tråd** tendril.
I. **slør** veil.
II. **slør** (mar) leading wind. **sløre** run el. sail large.
sløret: — **stemme** husky, muffled voice.
sløse: — (bort) waste. **sløseri** waste.
sløv blunt; (fig) dull, stupid, imbecile.
sløve blunt, dull, (fig. ogs.) stupefy.
sløvhet bluntness; stupidity, imbecility.
sløyd sloyd, woodwork, manual labour.
sløydskole manual labour school.
sløydundervisning manual training.
sløye (om fisk) gut, rough-dress.
sløyfe (subst) bow; (knyttet) (bow-)knot.
sløyfe (vrb) (rasere) raze, demolish, level with the ground; (musikk) slur; (fig) drop, discard; (avskaffe) discontinue. **sløyf(n)ing** razing etc.
slå (subst) (dør-) bolt (of a door); **skyve -a for, fra** bolt, unbolt the door.
slå (vrb) beat, strike, smite, knock, hit; (om fugler) warble, sing; (om hjertet) beat, throb; (om ur, lyn) strike; (med ljå) cut grass, mow; **klokka -r** the clock strikes; — **to glass!** (mar) strike two bells! **det slo meg** it struck me; — **fast** fasten, (fig) establish; — **bukter** turn, bend; — **en sirkel** describe a circle; — **folder** pucker; — **gras** mow grass; — **et hull** make a hole; — **en hær** beat el. defeat an army; — **en knute** tie a knot; — **en medalje** strike a medal; — **takt** beat time; — **seg** hurt oneself, be hurt, injured; (om tre) warp, twist; — **seg løs** (more seg) enjoy oneself — **an** (om vaksinasjon) take (på: with); (gjøre lykke) catch on, make a hit; — **an tonen** (ogs. fig) give the key-note; — **av** (om pris) abate, deduct; (i stykker) break; — **av en passiar** have a gossip, be chatting together; — **av en handel** strike a bargain; — **etter en strike** at one; — **etter i,** se — **opp;** — **fast,** se **fastslå;** — **fra seg** defend oneself; — **et seil fra** unbend a sail; **han slo den her i latter** he turned it off with a laugh; — **døra igjen** slam the door; — **i bordet** strike the table; — **en spiker i veggen** drive a nail into the wall; — **vann i** throw el. pour water into; — **igjen** return the blow; — **gjennom** (om person, f. eks. forfatter) make a name for oneself; (om sak) be a success, turn out a success; **blekket -r igjennom** the ink sinks, runs, strikes through; **slo utmerket igjennom** was very successful; — **seg igjennom** (få det til å strekke til) make both ends meet; — **seg igjennom fienden** cut through the enemy; — **inn** knock in, beat in, (også om sykdom) strike in; — **vinduene inn** smash the windows; — **inn på en vei** take a road; — **inn på et fag** take up a line; — **med blindhet** strike with

blindness; **slo dem med forferdelse** struck dismay among them; — **ned** (om lynet) strike; (om fugler) fall, swoop; — **seg ned** settle; — (om været) el. round; (om været) change, alter; — **øynene ned** cast down one's eyes; — **om wrap** about el. round; (om været) change, alter; — **armene om** throw one's arms around; — **et tau om** pass a rope round; — **om seg** lay about one; (fig) — **om seg med** spout, air; — **opp på en vegg** stick up, post; — **opp i en bok** turn up in, refer to a book; — **opp med en break off a** marriage engagement with one, throw one over; — **opp døra** fling the door open; — **opp, ned en paraply** put up, put down an umbrella; — **opp øynene** open one's eyes; — **seg opp** better one's circumstances, rise in the world; — **en bru over** throw a bridge across el. over; — **over i** fall into; — **armene over kors** cross the arms; — **på tromme** beat the drum; — **seg på noe** go in for; — **seg på drikk** take to drink; — **på at** hint that; — **seg selv på munnen** give oneself the lie; — **på flukt** put to flight, rout; — **stort på** cut a great dash; — **hendene sammen** clasp one's hands; — **seg sammen** combine, join together; — **til** (om kjøp) strike a bargain; — **til en strike** one, let drive at one; — **til jorden** knock down; — **seg til ro** (fig) rest satisfied; — **ut** (f. eks. vann) pour out; (f. eks. om hudsykdom) break out; — **ut av tankene** banish from one's mind; **slående** (f. eks. likhet) striking (resemblance); (overbevisende) convincing; (avgjørende) conclusive; **slått av forbauselse** struck with amazement; **slått av redsel** terror-struck **slåss** fight; — **med** en fight one; — **på pistoler** fight with pistols.
slåbrok dressing-gown, night-gown.
slåmaskin haycutter, mowing machine.
slåpe sloe.
slåpen gaunt, lank, lean.
slåpetorn blackthorn.
slåss, se under **slå. -hanske** brass knuckles. **-kjempe** bully, fighter.
I. **slått** (musikk) air, strain, tune.
II. **slått** (høyonn) cutting, mowing.
slåtte|folk mowers, haymakers. **-kar** hay-cutter, mower. **-teig** strip of meadow.
slåttonn cutting (el. mowing) season (el. operations).
smadder: slå i — smash. **smadre** smash.
smak taste; (særl. velsmak) flavour, relish, savour; (en kunstners, tidsalders) manner, style, way.
smake taste; **det -r godt** it has a good taste; **hvordan -r middagen Dem** how do you enjoy your dinner? **det -r meg ikke** I do not like it; — **av** flavour el. smack of; **det -r fat av denne vinen** this wine has a tang of the cask; — **på** taste, take a taste of.
smakebit sample, specimen, taste.
smakfull tasty, in good taste, elegant.
smakfullhet elegance, good taste.
smakløs in bad taste; (om person) without taste. **smakløshet** bad taste; want of taste.
smaksdommer arbiter of taste, art-critic.
smaks|sak matter of taste. **-sans** sense of taste.
smal narrow; — **kost** scanty fare, short commons.
smale (vrb), se **smalne.**
smale, (subst) se **sau.**
smalhans: det er — i dag there is poor fare to-day; to-day is a banian-day.
smal|het narrowness. **-legg** small of the leg.
smalne (av) narrow, taper.
smal|skuldret narrow-shouldered. **-skygget** narrow-brimmed. **-sporet** narrow-gauge. **-stripet** narrow-striped.
smaragd emerald.
smart smart, clever.
smarthet smartness.
smask smack.
smaske smack the lips when eating.
smatte smack one's lips. — **på hesten** click, cluck to the horse. — **på pipa** suck one's pipe,

smau narrow passage.
smaus treat, junket. **smause** junket.
smed smith; (grov-) blacksmith; **passe på som en** — keep a sharp look-out.
smedarbeid smith's work; forgings.
smede (vrb) (håne) abuse, revile.
smede|dikt libellous poem, lampoon. **-ord** invective, abuse. **-skrift** libel, lampoon.
smed|gutt smith's prentice. **-håndverk** trade of a smith. **-lære:** gå i — be apprenticed to a smith. **-mester** mastersmith. **-svenn** journeyman smith.
smekk rap, smack, flick.
smekke (barne-) bib; (bryst-) stomacher.
smekke, se **smelle.**
smekker slender; slim. **-het** slenderness, slimness.
smekkfeit, se **smelfeit.**
smekk|lås spring-lock, latch. **-låsnøkkel** latch-key.
smekte languish, pine.
smell crack, smack; pop; bang.
smelle (vrb) clap, crack, smack; (svakere) pop; (brake) bang, slam; — **med en pisk** crack a whip; — **igjen døra** slam el. bang the door; **skjelle og** — scold and make a noise; **skjelling og smelling** scolding and abuse.
smelle (subst) (bot.) catchfly.
smell|feit plump, very fat. **-kyss** smacking kiss. **-vakker** thundering fine.
smelte melt, fuse, liquefy; (bare om erts) smelt; (fig) melt; — **sammen med** merge into. **smelte|digel** crucible, melting-pot. **-hytte** smelting-house. **-ovn** (smelting-)furnace. **-punkt** melting point. **-skje** ladle. **-stykke** (leaden) fuse.
smelt(n)ing melting etc.; fusion, liquefaction.
smergel emery. **-lerret** emery-cloth.
smergle rub with emery.
smerte (subst) pain, ache, smart; (sorg) grief affliction; **han har store -r** he is in great pain.
smerte (vi) smart, ache; (vt) pain, grieve. **-fri** free from pain.
smertefrihet painlessness, absence of pain.
smerte|full, -lig painful.
smertestillende soothing el. allaying pain, anodyne, anodynous; — **middel** anodyne.
smette pass, slip; — **av seg** slip off.
smidig limber, supple, agile, active, pliable. **gjøre** — soften. **-het** suppleness, agility.
smi(e) (vrb) forge; work in the smithy.
smie (subst) forge, smithy. **-avl** smith's forge. **-belg** forge bellows. **-kol, -kull** small coal, **smiger** flattery.
smigre flatter; — **for** flatter; — **seg med det håp** at flatter oneself with the hope, indulge in a hope that. **-nde** flattering; **lite -nde** hardly flattering, uncomplimentary.
smigre|r flatterer, adulator. **-ri** flattering, flattery. **-rske** flatterer, adulatress.
smijern wrought iron.
smil smile.
smile smile; — **over** (av) smile at; — **til** smile on.
smilebånd: trekke på -et smile.
smilehull dimple.
sminke (subst) paint, rouge.
sminke (vrb) paint, rouge. **sminkekrukke** rouge-pot.
smiske: — **for** coax, wheedle. **smisking** coaxing, wheedling.
smitt: hver — **og smule** every particle.
smitte (vrb) infect; **bli -t** catch the infection; (uten objekt) be infectious el. contagious; — **av** rub off.
smitte (subst) infection, contagion. **-fri** uninfected. **-stoff** contagious matter, virus, miasma.
smitt|som contagious, infectious, catching, communicative. **-somhet** contagiousness, infectiousness.
smoking dinner jacket.
smokk fingerstall; (flaske-) india-rubber bottle **-sucker.**

I. smug alley, lane, narrow passage.
II. smug: i — secretly, privately, clandestinely, (up)on the sly, on the quiet, by stealth.
smug|brender unlicensed distiller. **-handel** smuggling el. contraband trade.
smugle smuggle, run goods.
smugler smuggler.
smugleri smuggling; smuggling transaction.
smugsalg unlicensed dealing.
smukk, se **vakker; det -e kjønn** the fair sex.
smul smooth, calm; **-t vann** a smooth sea.
smuldre crumble, moulder.
smule particle, bit; (av brød) crumb; **en** — a little, a trifle, a bit, slightly; **den** — **innflytelse han hadde** such influence as he had.
smule (vrb) crumble.
smult (subst) (refined) lard.
smurning grease, lubricant; composition.
smuss filth, dirt. **-blad** low paper. **smusse til** soil, dirty, foul.
smussig soiled, dirty, foul, smutty.
smussighet dirtiness, filthiness, foulness, smuttiness.
smuss|presse gutter-press. **-skrift** libel, lampoon. **-titel** (typograf.) bastard el. half title.
smutte slip, glide; — **bort** slip away; — **fra** slip, give the slip.
smutthull hiding-place; (tilholdssted) haunt.
smyge creep; (fig) cringe, grovel **(for:** to), sneak. — **av seg** slip, slip off.
smykke (subst) ornament, trinket.
smykke (vrb) adorn, deck, decorate.
smykkeskrin trinket-box, casket.
smør butter; **brunet** — browned el. burnt butter; **smeltet** — clarified el. melted butter. **smør|ask** butter-box. **-blomst** butter-cup. **-brød** bread-and-butter; **et (stykke)** — a piece of b.-and-b., a sandwich. **-butt** butter-tub.
smøre smear; (med fett) grease; (med olje) oil; (maskineri) lubricate; (med salve) salve, anoint; (med såpe) soap; (bestikke) bribe, tip; (pryle) lick, thrash; (skrive dårlig) scribble, scrawl; (male dårlig) daub; **det gikk som det var smurt** it went on swimmingly; — **smør på brød** butter bread; (fig) — **tykt på** lay it on thick; — **seg** apply a liniment.
smøre|kanne lubricating can, oil-feeder. **-kopp** oil-cup. **-lse** grease, lubricant; (salve) ointment. **-olje** lubricating oil.
smører oiler. **smøreri** scribble; (maleri) daub.
smør|farge annatto. **-fjerding** butter-firkin. **-handel** butter trade. **-handler** dealer in butter.
smøring (av maskin) lubrication.
smørje (dt.) jumble, mix.
smør|kjøler butter-cooler. **-kløv** butter-pack. **-krukke** butter-jar.
smør|side buttered side. **-stikker** butter-searcher, piercer. **-tønne** butter-barrel. **-øye** lump of butter (in the centre of a plateful of porridge **-øskje,** se **-ask.**
små (plur. av liten) small; (komparativ) **mindre** smaller, less; (superlativ) **minst** smallest, least; (ringe) little, petty, diminutive; **de** — the little ones; **leve i** — **forhold** live in narrow circumstances. **-en** the little one, the kid; **du -en!** little one! **smått** (adv) slowly, gradually; mildly; **begynne** — start with small beginnings; **så** — (dt.) slightly, a little.
små|barn little children. **-borger** petty tradesman. **-bruk** small farms el. holdings. **-bruker** crofter, small farmer. **-by** small town, village. **-dikt** minor poems, small lyrics. **-folk** common people; (barn) small people, little ones.
småfyrster princelets, princelings.
små|gater by-streets. **-gutt** little boy. **-jente** little girl el. lass. **-kaker** (pl.) pastry.
små|kornet small-grained. **-kårsfolk** people of small means. **-le** laugh slily.
smålegemer corpuscles.
smålig narrow-minded, petty.
smålighet narrow-mindedness, pettiness.

småmynt change.
småmønstret small-patterned.
små|ord (pl) particles. **-penger** change. **-piker** little girls. **-skog** coppice, copsewood. **-skrifter** tracts. **-snakke** chatter; mutter. **-stumper,** **-stykker** small pieces el. bits. **-ting** (pl) little things, trifles, small matters; trifling articles.
småtrekk trifles, small matters, minutiæ.
småtærende: være — be a small eater.
småutgifter petty expenses, petties.
småved fagots.
småøyer islets, small islands.
snabb bit, end.
snabel snout, nozzle; (på elefant) trunk, proboscis.
snadde cutty(-pipe); (av tre) brier.
snadre cackle, quack; (fig) gabble, jabber.
snakk talk; (snikksnakk) fudge, stuff, nonsense; **å —! nonsense! gi seg i —** med enter into conversation with.
snakke chat, prate, talk, chatter; **—** seg **fra noe** gloss over st.; **— en fra noe** dissuade one from el. talk one out of something; **— med en** talk to el. with one; **— med** (adv) join in the talk.
snakkesalig loquacious, talkative.
snakkesalighet loquacity, garrulity.
snakketøy talking gear; **ha godt —** be voluble.
snakksom talkative, chatty.
snappe snatch, snap, (etter: at); **— etter været** gasp for breath.
snar quick, swift, fleet; **snart** (adv) soon, quickly, shortly, presently; **-t opp, -t ned** now (el. sometimes) up, now (el. sometimes) down; **snarere** sooner; rather; **det er -ere (må -ere kalles)** ... it is ... if anything; **snarest mulig** as soon as possible; at your earliest convenience;
snar (subst) brushwood, scrub, thicket.
snare snare, gin, springe; **sette opp -r for** lay, set el. spread snares for; **falle i -n** (fig) fall into the trap; **snare|fangst** trapping, **-rype** trapped grouse.
snarlig speedy; (adv) quickly, soon.
snarrådig quick in emergencies, ready, present. **snarrådighet** readiness at need, quickness at expedients, presence of mind.
snart, se **snar.**
snar|tenkt readywitted. **-vei** near way: quick el. short cut. **-ærend** hurried errand.
snau scant, scanty, slender; (skallet) bald; (snauklipt) close-cropped.
snaue crop down close, leave bare.
snau|fjell bare el. naked rock. **-hogge** bare. **-klippe** crop close.
snedig wily, cunning, crafty.
snedighet wiliness, craft, cunning, subtlety.
snegle (med hus) snail; (uten hus) slug.
snegle: — seg avsted move away at a snail's pace.
sneglebelg (plante) lucern(e).
snegleformet spiral, cochlear.
snegle|gang a snail's pace; (på søyle) colute; (i øret) cochlea. **-hus** snail-shell.
snei (avskåret skive) slice; (tykk skive) hunch; (amr) hunk.
snei: på — (på skrå) aslant. **sneiord** taunt.
sneis, se **snes.**
snekke sailboat; (poet) bark.
snekker joiner; (kunst-) cabinet-maker. **-gutt** joiner's apprentice. **-lære: være i —** be apprenticed to a joiner. **-mester** master-joiner. **-svenn** journeyman-joiner. **-verktøy** joinery tools.
snekre do joiner's work.
I. **snelle** reel; **en — tråd** a reel of cotton.
II. **snelle** (bot.) cats-tail, horse-tail.
snerk skin (on top of cream).
snerp (p. korn) awns.
snerpe: — sammen contract, draw together el. up, astringe; **— munnen sammen** purse up the mouth. **-nde** astringent. **snerpe** (subst) prude. **snerperi** prudery. **snerpet** prudish, precise.

snerre snarl, growl.
snert (på pisk) lash, cracker; (fig) wipe, sneer, sarcasm. **snerte** flick, flip, lash; (streife) graze, touch; (fig) sneer at.
snerten (dt.) handy; natty, neat.
snes score. **snesevis: i —** by scores, by the score.
snev dash, smack, touch; **en liten — av influensa** a mere touch of influenza.
snever narrow, strait; **i snevrere forstand** in a more restricted sense.
sneverhet straitness, narrowness, tightness.
sneverhjertet narrow-minded, illiberal.
sneversyn narrowness of view. **-t** lacking in breadth of view, illiberal, prejudiced. **snevring** narrow pass.
I. **snike** (snylte) sponge.
II. **snike** sneak; **— seg** sneak, slink, skulk; **— seg inn** slip in, creep in; **-nde** insidious; **-nde feber** slow el. low fever.
snikksnakk nonsense, fiddle-faddle.
snik|mord assassination. **-morder, -morderske** assassin. **-mordersk** assassin-like. **-myrde** assassinate. **-patrulje** secret patrol. **-skytter** sniper. **-vei** secret path; **på -veier** by underhand means.
snill good-natured, kind; (om barn) good; **vær så — å** please, have the goodness to, be so kind as to; **vær så — å la meg** vite kindly let me know.
snipe (fugl) snipe. **-jakt** snipe shooting.
snipp (om halsen) collar; (av et tørkle) corner of a handkerchief.
snipp|kjole dress-coat. **-losje** stage-box.
snirkel spire, spiral line; (med penn) flourish. **snirklet** scrolled.
snitt cut, incision; (på bok) edge; **han så sitt —** he saw his chance, seized the opportunity.
snitte cut, chip. **-bønne** French bean.
snittflate cut surface.
snive (hestesykdom) glanders.
I. **sno** (vt.) twist, twine; **— seg** twist, twine, wind; (fig) shift and turn; **— seg fra** shuffle off, shirk.
II. **sno** (vi.) blow cold, draw; **det -dde surt** the wind drew strongly.
sno (subst) frosty breeze, biting wind.
snobb snob. **snobbet** snobbish. **-eri** snobbery.
snodig whimsical.
snohale prehensile tail.
snok (ring)snake.
snoning twisting; winding.
snor line, cord, string, lace, braid. **snorbesatt** braided. **— frakk** braided el. laced coat.
snorke snore. **snorking** snoring, snore.
snorksove lie snoring, sleep and snore.
snorrett straight as a line.
snu turn.
snubbe (streife) graze, touch; **— av snip** off short; (fig) snub, snap up short.
snuble stumble (over: over, against); **ligge snublende nær** stare one in the face.
snue cold (in one's head), catarrh.
snufs sniffing, sniff. **snufse** sniff, sniffle.
snurpe (fiske m. snurpenot) purse-fish; **— sammen** pucker up; sew up anyhow.
snurpenot purse net, pod.
snurr: på — tipped on one side, cocked on one side, tilted.
snurre whirl.
snurr(e)bass whirligig, hummingtop.
snurrepiperi gimcrack(s), nicknacks.
snurrig droll, ludicrous, queer, whimsical.
snus snuff; **en klype —** a pinch of snuff.
snusdåse snuff-box.
snuse snuff, sniff; (tobakk) take snuff; **— etter** (fig) rummage for, pry into; **— opp** scent out, discover. **snuser** snuff-taker.
snusfornuft commonplace, prose.
snusfornuftig would-be-wise, wisely-stupid, prosy; **— person** wiseacre. **snushane** prying fellow.

snustobakk snuff.
snute snout, nozzle; (på skotøi) toe.
snutebille weevil-beetle.
snylte sponge, be a parasite.
snylte|dyr parasitic animal, parasite. **-gjest** parasite, sponger, hanger-on, toad-eater. **-liv** parasitism. **-plante** parasitical plant.
snylter parasite. **snylting** parasitism, toad-eating.
snyte (narre) cheat, take in; (nesen) blow (the nose); **— en for noe** cheat one (out) of st.
snyte full quite drunk.
snytepave, snyter cheat, rogue.
snyteri imposition, fraud, swindle.
snære be too tight.
snø (subst) snow.
snø (vrb) snow.
snøball snow-ball; **kaste — play at snow-balls; kaste — på** snow-ball.
snø|balltre laurestinus. **-belte** zone of snow. **-blind** snow-blind. **-bre** snowfield. **-briller** snow-glasses. **-bye** el. **-bøy(e)** snow-squall. **-dekke** cover of snow. **-dekt** snow-covered.
snø|drev drifting snow. **-drive** snow-drift, **-fall** snowfall. **-floke** flake of snow. **-fnugg** flake of snow. **-fok(k)** snow-storm. **-fonn**, se **-bre. -forbygning** snow-shed.
snøft snort.
snøfte snuff, sniff; (om hester) snort.
snøføre available snow, sleighing.
snøgg quick.
snø|grense snow-line. **-hvit, -kvit** snow white. **-kave**, se **-bye.**
snøklokke Candelmas bell, snowdrop.
snø|mann snow-giant, snow-man. **-plog** snow -plough. **-ras** snow-slip.
snøre (subst) cord, string; (især fiske-) line.
snøre (vrb) lace; **— opp** unlace; **— til, sammen** draw together); **— seg** lace one's stays; (til stadighet) wear stays.
snøre|band, -bånd lace. **-fiske** (hook and) line-fishing, hand-lining. **-hull** eyelet-hole, eyelet. **-kjøre** drive a horse while gliding on ski. **-liv** stays; **et — a** pair of stays. **-støvler** (pl) lace(-up) boots.
snø|skjerm (jernb.) snow-shelter, snow-shed. **-skred** snow-slip, snow slide, avalanche of snow. **-slaps** snow-broth. **-storm** snow-storm. **-tykke** thick weather with snow.
snøvle snuffle, talk with a snuffle. **snøvling** snuffling, snuffle.
snøvær snowy weather.
snøye, se **snaue.**
snål (snurrig) droll, odd, queer.
snåve stumble.
soaré soiree, evening entertainment.
sobel sable. **-skinn** sable.
soda (carbonate of) soda. **-pulver** bicarbonate of soda. **-vann** soda-water, seltzer-water.
sodd broth, soup.
sofa sofa, lounge. **-pute** sofa-cushion.
Sofie Sophia, Sophy.
sofis|me sophism. **-t** sophist. **-teri** sophistry.
sofistisk sophistic(al).
sogn parish. **sogne til** be within the parish of . . ., (fig) belong to. **sogne|barn** parishioner. **-bud** sick call. **-folk** parishioners. **-kall** living, rectorate. **-kirke** parish church, parochial church. **-prest** parson, rector, vicar. **-styre** parish council, local board.
sola soy.
solgnert neatly kept, trim.
sokk sock; (dial. strømpe) stocking; (p. hestebein) stocking.
sokkel socle, plinth.
sokkelest stocking foot; **på -en** in one's stockings.
sokn, se **sogn.**
sokne dray, dredge, sweep; (etter: for); **— i elva** drag the river.
sol sun; (fyrv.) Catherine-wheel; **-a står**

opp the sun rises; **-a går ned** the sun sets el. goes down; **ingen kjenner dagen før -a går ned** don't praise a day till it is over; **når en taler om -a, så skinner den** speaking of angels one often sees their wings.
sola-veksel sole (el. single el. only) bill.
solbad sunbath; f. eks. I always take a sunbath before my bathe.
solbelyst sun-lit.
solbrent sun-burnt, tanned.
solbrenthet sunburn, tan.
solbær black currant.
sold (lønning) pay; **halv —** half-pay.
soldat soldier.
soldaterherredømme military government.
soldatermessig soldierly; **lite — unsoldierly.**
sole sun; **— seg** bask in the sunshine.
sole|fall, -glad, se **solnedgang.**
soleie butter-cup, king-cup.
solelhov marsh marigold.
soleklar clear as noon-day, obvious.
sol|flekk solar spot, sun-spot. **-formørkelse** eclipse of the sun, solar eclipse. **-gangsvind** wind shifting with the sun's motion; solar breeze. **-glans** radiance of the sun. **-glimt** gleam of the sun. **-gløtt** glimpse of the sun. **-gud** sungod, Helios. **-hatt** sun-hat; sun-bonnet. **-het** heated by the sun. **-hete** heat of the sun. **-hverv** solstice. **-hvervsdag** solstitial day. **-høyde** altitude of the sun.
solid solid; strong, firm, substantial, sound; (merk) safe, trustworthy, respectable.
solidarisk solidary; (adv) jointly and separately; **— ansvar** unlimited responsibility; **stille seg — med** join interest with.
solidaritet solidarity. **solidaritetsfølelse** feeling of solidarity.
soliditet respectability, stability.
solidum: in — jointly and separately.
solist soloist, solist.
solitær solitaire.
sol|kart heliography chart. **-klar** sunbright, sunny.
soll bannock in milk.
sol|lys (subst) sun-light. **-lys** (adj) sunny. **-nedgang** sunset.
solo solo, solus.
soloppgang sun-rise.
solosanger solo-singer, solo vocalist.
sol|rik sunny. **-ring** halo round the sun. **-seil** (mar) awning. **-side** sunny side. **-sikke** sun-flower. **-sirkel** solar cycle. **-skinn** sunshine. **-skinnsdag** sunshine day. **-skinnsvær** sunshine. **-skjerm** sun-shade, parasol. **-stek** hot, broiling sun. **-stikk** sun-stroke, insolation, siriasis. **-stråle** sun-beam, sun-ray, solar ray. **-tilbedelse** heliolatry. **-tilbeder** heliolater. **-ur** sun-dial. **-varm** sunny. **-varme** warmth of the sun.
solvens solvency. **solvent** solvent.
solår solar year.
som (pron. subjekt) who, which, that; (objekt) whom, which, that; **de — er til stede** those (el. they) who are present; **det — du** så that which you saw.
som (konj) as; (liksom) like; **— om** as if; **— oftest** most frequently; **— svar by** way of answer; **jeg kjenner Dem — en mann som** I know you as el. for a man who; **så mye større — the** greater as (el. because el. in that).
somle dawdle, lounge, be slow at work; **— bort** squander, waste; (forlegge) mislay; (miste) manage to lose.
somme (pron) some.
sommel slowness at work; dawdling, fiddling; confusion.
sommer summer; **om -en** in summer; **i — this** summer; **til -en** next summer.
sommer|bolig summer residence. **-bruk: til — for** summer use. **-dag** summer's day. **-drakt** summer-dress. **-ferie** (mid)summer-holidays, (the) August vacation. **-forkjølelse** summer cold. **-fugl,**

butterfly. **–halvår** summer half-year. **–hete** summer heat. **–kjole** summer-dress. **–kledd** in summer dress. **–kveld** summer evening. **–mål** summer term (14th of April). **–måned** summer -month. **–n 't** summer-night. **–solhverv** summer-solstice **–tid** (sesongen) summertime, summer season; (forandret tid) summer time. **–tøy** summer-stuff; summer things. **–vær** summer -weather.

sommesteds in (some) places, locally. **somme tider** sometimes, at times, now and then.

somnambul (adj) somnambulic. **somnambul** (subst) somnambulist. **–isme** somnambulism.

son, se **sønn.**

sonate sonata.

sonde sound; (især til sår) probe.

sondere sound, probe.

sondre separate; distinguish.

sondring separation; distinction.

sone (vrb) expiate, atone.

sone (subst) zone.

sonett sonnet.

soning atonement, expiation.

sonoffer atoning sacrifice, expiation.

sonor sonorous.

sope besom, broom; clear. **–lime** besom, broom.

sopp fungus (pl fungi).

soppe (legge tømmer i flåte) join (logs) into rafts, lock down.

sopran soprano.

sordin mute, sordine.

sorenskriver country justice, district judge. **–i** cantonal law circuit.

sorg sorrow, grief, affliction, care; (i klededrakt) mourning. **–fri** free from care el. sorrow, sorrowless. **–frihet** comfort. **–full** sorrowful, sad, afflicted, doleful, mournful. **–løs** careless, unconcerned. **–løshet** carelessness. **–tung** sorrow -stricken, heavy with grief.

sort (subst) sort, species, kind, description, denomination, grade; **av første —** first-rate.

sort (adj), se **svart.**

sortere (vt) sort, assort; (vi) **— under come** el. range under, belong to. **sortering** sorting, assorting. **sortermaskin** sorting machine.

sortie exit.

sortiment assortment.

sortimentsbokhandler general bookseller.

S. O. S. (trådløst nødssignal) S. O. S.

sosial social.

sosialdemokrat Social Democrat. **–i** Social Democracy. **–isk** Social Democratic.

sosialisere socialize. **sosialisering** socialization **sosialisme** Socialism.

sosialist Socialist; **venstre — Extreme Socialist.**

sosialistisk socialistic.

sosialminister minister of health, (el. undertiden snarere) minister of labour.

sosietet society; (merk) partnership.

sosiolog sociologist. **–i** sociology.

sosiologisk sociological.

sot soot. **sote** soot. **sotet** sooty, fuliginous.

sot|fille flake of soot. **–rør** blastpipe.

sott sickness, disease. **sotte|død** (glt.): **dø –en** die in one's bed. **–seng** (glt.), se **sykeleie.**

sove sleep, be asleep; **— fast, tungt** el. **hardt** sleep hard; **— trygt** sleep soundly el. securely; **— lett** sleep lightly; **— som en stein** sleep like a post, sleep as fast as a top; **legge seg til å — go** to sleep; **foten min –r** my foot sleeps el. is asleep; **sov godt!** I wish you a good night's rest! **den –nde** the sleeper; **— hos** sleep with; **— på noe** sleep on el. upon st.; **har –t** ut has slept his fill; **— rusen ut** sleep oneself sober.

sove|alkove cubicle, tiny bedroom. **–hjerte: ha et godt — be** a good el. sound sleeper. **–middel** soporific, hypnotic, opiate. **–plass** sleeping accomodation; berth.

sove|sal sleeping-room, dormitory. **–salong**

(mar) sleeping saloon. **–sofa** sofa bed(stead). **–syke** coma, lethargy, sleeping sickness. **–vogn** sleeping-carriage, sleeping-car. **–værelse** sleeping -room.

Sovjet the Sovjet. **–propaganda** Soviet propaganda. **— –Russland** Soviet Russia.

sovne drop el. fall asleep; **— hen** el. **inn** (dø) expire, die.

spa (vrb) spade.

spade (subst) spade; (som mål) a spadeful. **spadeblad** blade of a spade.

spade|skaft handle of a spade. **–stikk: gjøre det første —** put in the first spade.

spak (subst) (hand-) spike.

spak (adj) tractable, quiet, gentle, tame, meek. **spakferdig** gentle, quiet. **spakferdighet** gentleness, meekness. **spakhet** tameness.

spakne become more tractable; subside.

spalier espalier.

spalte (subst) split, slit, cleft, fissure; (typograf.) column. **spalte** (vrb) split. **spaltefyll** filling, padding.

spalt(n)ing splitting; (fig) division, rupture. **spandabel** liberal. **spandere** spend; sacrifice.

Spania Spain. **spanier, –inne,** spanjol Spaniard.

spanke, spankulere strut, stalk.

I. **spann** (melkespann etc.) pail, bucket (de to ord brukes i alm. i fleng, dog alltid: fire-bucket og milk-pail).

II. **spann** (hester) team.

spannevis: i — by the pail, by pailfuls.

spansk Spanish; **— flue** cantharis, Spanish fly; **— pepper** Cayenne pepper; **spanskesyken** the Spanish influenza; **Spanskesjøen** the Spanish Main.

spanskgrønt verdigris.

spanskrør cane. **spanskrørstokk** cane.

spant frame, frame-timber, rib.

spar (i kort) spades; **en — a** spade.

spardame queen of spades.

spare save; **(— på) spare;** (økonomisere) economize, save; (holde godt hus med) husband; (være sparsommelig med) be sparing el. saving of; **— sammen** lay up money.

spare|bank savings bank. **–bøsse** savings-box, thrift-box, money-box. **–kasse** savings-bank. **–kassebok** savings-bank book. **–penger** savings.

sparess ace of spades.

spark kick; (dt.) **få –en** be given boot, be bounced; (fork. for -støtting, s. d.).

sparkel (kittekniv) stopping-knife.

sparke stop (up).

spar|knekt, –konge the knave, king of spades.

sparkstøtting Swedish pedomotive sleigh.

sparre, se **sperre.**

spar|som sparing, scarce. **–somhet** scarcity. **sparsommelig** saving, thrifty, economical, parsimonious. **sparsommelighet** economy, thrift, thriftiness, parsimony.

spartaner, spartansk Spartan.

sparto the two of spades.

spas, se **spøk. spase,** se **spøke.**

spasere walk, take a walk. **spaserdrakt** walking dress.

spaser|stokk walking stick el. cane. **–tur** walk, turn; (for sundh.) constitutional. **–vei** promenade, walk.

spat (mineral) spar.

spatel spatula.

spatiere space out.

spatt (sykdom hos hester) spavin.

spattet spavined.

spe (spott og —) derision, mockery.

spe (adj) tender, delicate, slender, tiny.

spe (spe opp) dilute, thin; **— til** add; (fig) contribute.

spebarn baby, nursling, infant.

spedalsk leprous; **en — a** leper; **hospitalet for –e** the Leper Hospital. **–het** leprosy.

spedisjon transmission el. forwarding (of

goods). **speditør** forwarding agent, commission-agent, forwarder.

speedometer (i bil) speedometer.

spege mortify, chasten; — **seg** mortify one's flesh.

speide spy, watch; reconnoitre.

speider spy, (mil) scout; **-ne** (organisasjon stiftet 1908) the boy scouts.

speider|blikk searching look. **-gutt** boy scout. **-pike** girl guide. **-post** lookout (point). **-skip** scout (vessel). **-tjeneste** scouting. **speiding** spying, scouting.

speiel, se speil.

speil (looking-)glass; (ogs. fig) mirror; (mar) stern; **se seg i -et** look into the glass, look at oneself in the glass.

speil|belegg foil, tinfoiling of a mirror. **-bilde** catoptric image; reflection, image. **-blank** glassy, bright el. smooth as a mirror.

speile (egg) fry; — **seg** be reflected el. mirrored; (se seg i et speil) gaze el. look in a glass; — **seg i en** take an example by el. from one.

speile (subst), se **speil.**

speilegg fried eggs; **steke** — fry eggs.

speil|glass plate-glass. **-glassvindu** plate-glass window. **-glatt** extremely slippery el. smooth.

speilramme frame of a looking-glass.

spekalv sucking-calf, baby calf.

I. **speke** (stivne av frost) freeze.

II. **speke** salt, cure in salt and smoke or dry. **speke|flesk** salt-cured ham. **-pølse** smoked sausage. **-sild** salt el. pickled herring. **-skinke** se **-flesk.**

spekk blubber. **spekke** stuff, lard; **en vel -t pung** a long purse. — **sin tale med sitater** interlard one's discourse with quotations. **-t med opplysninger** primed with intelligence.

spekke|fjøl larding-board. **-flesk** bacon for larding. **-nål** larding-pin.

spekkhogger (hvalart) grampus, killer.

spektralanalyse spectrum analysis. **spektroskop** spectroscope. **spektrum** spectrum.

spekul|ant speculator. **-asjon** speculation, venture; **på** — on speculation, speculatively.

spekulativ speculative, speculatory.

spekulere speculate (i: (vare) in; (en mulighet) on; **over:** on); — **på** meditate.

spelemmet slender-limbed.

spell, spelle, se spill, spille.

spelt spelt, German wheat.

spene dug, pap, teat.

spenn (i bru) span; (spark) kick; **i** — tense, under tension; **sette pistolhane i** — cock the pistol.

spenne (vrb) stretch, strain, tighten; (om) span; (ved spenner) buckle, clasp; (sparke) kick; **spent gevær** a cocked gun; — **ens forventninger** strain one's expectations; — **bein for en** trip one up, trip up one's heels; — **for** put to (the horses); — **fra** take out el. unharness the horses; **spennende** exciting.

spenne (subst) buckle, clasp. **-reim** strap, braces. **-sko** buckled shoes. **-tak** good purchase for the feet. **-tre** (i vev) temple.

spenning tension; (sp. forhold) estrangement; (sinnsstemning) excitement; **holde i** — keep in suspense. **spennings|høyde** pitch of tension. **-måler** voltmeter.

spenn|kraft elasticity; (dampens) tension; (fig) tone. **-trøye** straight-jacket, straight-waistcoat.

spenstig elastic; (fig) buoyant.

spenstighet elasticity; buoyancy; resilience.

spent tense, tensioned, tight; (fig) anxious, eager, on the strain; **et** — **forhold** a strained relation; **i** — **forventning** in tense expectancy. **være** — **på utfallet** anxiously await the result. (adv) tensely etc.; anxiously. **med** — **oppmerksomhet** intently; **i** — **forventning** on the tiptoe of expectation; **være** — be excited; **be on the strain; han var** — **på å vite** he was anxious to learn; **de er på en** — **fot** they are on bad terms.

spermasett spermaceti. **-olje** sperm oil.

sperre (vrb) bar, block up, close; — **veien for en** bar el. obstruct one's passage; — **en inne** shut up, lock up. **-t!** no thoroughfare; — **opp munnen, øynene** open the mouth, the eyes wide.

sperre (subst) rafter. **-tak** raftered ceiling.

sperring barring etc., stoppage.

speseri spice, spicery.

spesialisere specialize. **spesialist** specialist.

spesialitet specialty, speciality.

spesi|ell special, particular; **-elt** (more) especially, particularly. **-fisere** specify, particularize. **-fikk** specific. **-fikasjon** specification.

spetakkel uproar, hubbub, row, racket; (støy) a noise; (moro) fun; **holde** — make a racket, kick up a row; **-maker** noisy, turbulent fellow; jester, joker, wag.

I. **spett** (jern-) bar, crowbar, iron crow.

II. **spett** el. **spette** (fugl) woodpecker.

spetteflyndre plaice.

spettet (adj) spotted.

spidd spit; **sette på** — put on the spit, **spit. spidde** spit.

spik splinter; (tyri-) resinous wood; (hjul-) spoke.

spiker nail; (stor) spike. **-verk** nailery, nail-works.

spikke whittle.

spikre nail; (stifte) tack.

spildre strip (of board).

spile — ut stretch, distend; — **øynene opp** open one's eyes wide.

spile (subst) lath; (i paraply) frame; (i korsett) bone.

spilfekteri humbug, mockery, sham.

spilkum (slop-)basin.

I. **spill** (av tilfellet osv.) play; (med kort osv.) game; (komedie-.) playing, acting; (høyt) gambling; (gang-) capstan, windlass; **et** — **kort** a pack of cards; **et** — (omgang) a hand; **et** — **kjler** a set of nine-pins; **spille et** — **sjakk, biljard, whist** play a game of chess, billiards, whist; **være ute av -et** be played out; **være inne i -et** be up to the game; **med klingende** — drums beating; **sette på** — stake, peril, hazard, put in jeopardy, compromise.

II. **spill** loss, waste; **gå til -e** go to waste.

spilldamp waste steam.

I. **spille** (miste) spill, drop; (forspille) lose; (ødsle bort) waste; **det er spilt på ham** it is thrown away on him.

II. **spille** play; (komedie) act, perform; — **høyt** gamble, play high, deep; — **fallitt** become bankrupt, break, fail; — **hasard** play at hazard; gamble; — **kort, kiler** play (at) cards, at nine-pins; — **en et puss** play one a trick; **la sitt vidd** — show off el. make a display of one's wit; **øynene spilte i hodet på henne** her eyes beamed el. sparkled; — **om penger** play for money; — **opp** strike up; — **fløyte, fiolin** play (on) the flute, violin; — **ut** lead, have the lead; — **under dekke med en** play booty with one.

spille|bord card-table; hazard-table. **-bule** gambling house, gambling hell. **-dåse** musical box, music-box. **-fugl** gambler, gamester. **-gjeld** gambling-debt. **-lærer** music-master. **-lærinne** music-mistress. **-mann** fiddler. **-måte** manner of playing. **-parti** card-party. **-penger** (pl) play-money; card-counters.

spiller player, gamester, gambler.

spillerom scope, margin, latitude.

spilletime music lesson.

spilljakt shooting (wildfowl) in pairing season.

spillkraft waste energy.

spillopp fun, trick(s); **gjøre -er** play tricks, make fun. **-maker** rogue, wag, mischiefmaker.

spilltau (i stall) box, stall.

spillvann waste water.

spinat spinach, spinage.

spindel spindle; (i ur) verge, **spindle.**

spindelvev cobweb.
spinett spinet, virginal.
spinke save, pinch, screw.
spinkel slender, tiny. **-het** slenderness.
spinn yarn; (edderkopps) web.
spinne|lønn wages for spinning. **-maskin** spinning-machine. **-ri** spinning-mill, spinning -factory. **-rokk** spinning-wheel.
spinnerske (female) spinner.
spinnesiden the spindle-side, the distaff, the female line; **på — by** the female line.
spion spy. **spionasje** spying, espionage. **spio**nere spy. **spion|eri**, **-ering** spying, espionage.
spir spire.
spiral spiral. **-fjær** spiral spring.
spiralformig spiral, helical.
I. **spire** (subst) germ, sprout; (fig) germ, root.
II. **spir(e)** (mar) boom, spar.
spire (vrb) sprout, germinate, burgeon.
spirekraft germinating power.
spirea spiræa; ogs. meadow-sweet.
spirit|isme spiritism. **-ist** spiritist. **-ualisme** spiritualism. **-ualist** spiritualist. **-ualistisk** spiritualistic. **-ualitet** spirituality; (åndrikhet) brightness, brilliancy. **-uell** clever, bright, brilliant. **-uosa** (pl) (spirituous) liquors, spirits.
spiritus spirit of wine, spirits. **-lampe** spiritlamp. **spirituøs** spirituous.
spirrevipp little bustling person.
spise eat; **— frokost** breakfast; **— middag** dine; **— aftens** sup; **— seg mett** eat one's fill; **— opp** eat up.
spise (mat) eating, meat, food, victuals.
spise|bord dining-table, dinner-table. **-gjest** diner; (som bor utenfor huset) mealer.
spisekvarter eating-house, ordinary; cook-shop.
spiselig eatable, edible, esculent.
spise|pinne (kinesisk) chop-stick. **-rør** esophagus, gullet. **-sal** dinner-hall, dining-hall. **-seddel** bill of fare, menu. **-skje** table-spoon; (som mål) table-spoonful. **-stell** dinner-service. **-stue** dining-room. **-tid** meal-time; dinner-time. **-vogn** dining -car.
spiskammer larder, pantry, buttery.
spiss (subst) point, tip, end; (på penn) nib; (på berg) top, summit; (hund) Pomeranian dog; **i —en** for at the head of, in the front of; **stå i —en for** head; **sette på —en** carry el. drive to extremities; **sette saken på —en** push matters t o extremes; **-ene** (dt.) the big-wigs, the swells.
spiss (adj) pointed, peaked; (løpende ut i en s piss) tapering; (fig) pointed, sharp, cutting. **en — vinkel** an acute angle.
spiss|borger cit, snob. **-borgerlig** narrow-minded, mechanical, matter-of-fact. **-borgerlighet** narrow-mindedness.
spissbue pointed el. gothic arch.
spissbuestil pointed style.
spisse point; (blyant) mend; **— munnen** draw up the mouth; **— nese, ører, se nese, øre; — til** taper.
spissfindig subtle, captious, sophistical.
spissfindighet captiousness, sophistry.
spiss|hakke pick-axe. **-kål** Yorkshire cabbage. **-mus** shrew-mouse. **-neset** sharp nosed. **-projektil** conic shot.
spisspullet with a conical crown.
spissrot: løpe — run the gantlope el. gantlet.
spiss-slede one-horse sleigh el. sledge.
spissvinklet acute-angled.
spitig, se **spydig.**
Spitsbergen Spitzbergen.
spjeld damper, register; (dmp.) throttle, damper.
spjelke splint up, put into splints.
spjelking splintage.
spjut, se **spyd.**
spjær rent, rip, tear. **spjære** rend, rip, tear. **spjåke seg ut** rig oneself grotesquely. **spjåket** grotesque.

spleen spleen.
spleis splice.
spleise splice; (skyte sammen) club (til: for).
spleiselag slate-club.
splendid grand, liberal, munificent.
splid discord, dissension. **-aktig** disagreeing, at variance; contentious. **-aktighet** dissension.
splint splint, splinter.
splinter: — ny bran-new, altogether new.
splintre splinter, shiver; **-s** splinter, shiver.
splitt slit, split, rent; (p. skjørt) placket.
splitte split, slit; (fig) disintegrate; **-s** split; **— mengden** disperse the crowd; **mengden ble -t** the crowd dispersed. separated.
splittelse cleave, schism, disintegration, split.
splitter: — gal stark mad; (om ting) utterly wrong. **— naken** stark naked.
splittflagg split flag.
spole (subst) spool, hobbin, pirn, cop; (vever-) shuttle, tube. **spole** (vrb) spool.
spole|bein radius. **-garn** spooling yarn.
spolere spoil, ruin.
spolorm roundworm.
spon chip; (høvelsp.) shaving; (pl) (sagsp.) saw-dust; (taksp.) shingle; (filsp.) filings.
spon|fletting plaiting of chips. **-korg** chip -basket. **-matte** chip-mat. **-tak** shingle-roof.
spontan spontaneous.
spor foot-print, footstep; (jakt) track, trail; (hjulspor) rut, track; (fig) track, vestige, trace; (p. jernbane) rails; **tape -et** (om hund) lose the scent; **ikke — av** tvil not the slightest doubt; **(er du redd?) ikke — not** a bit; **komme (ut)av -et** run off the track. **alt kom igjen i det gamle — everything** settled down in the old groove.
sporadisk sporadic.
spor(d) (fiskehale) tail (of a fish).
I. **spore** (vrb) trace, track.
II. **spore** (anspore) spur, prick.
I. **spore** (subst) spur; (fig) stimulus, incentive; **gi en hest -ene** put el. clap spurs to a horse.
II. **spore** (bot.) granule, spore. **-dannelse** sporation.
sporenstreks there and then, full gallop.
sporeplante cryptogam.
sporhund slot-hound, limehound.
spor|løs trackless; **-løst** (adv) tracklessly, leaving no trace, without leaving any track.
sporrenser track-clearer.
sporskifte switch, points; (handl.) shunting.
sporskifter pointsman, switchman, rail-shifter.
sport sport, manly exercise.
sportel perquisite, fee, (dt.) extra.
sports|artikler sporting articles, athletic articles. **-drakt** athletic costume, sporting costume. **-mann** sportsman. **-stevne** sports meeting.
spor|vei tramway, tramroad, street-railway. **-veislinje** tram route. **-vidde** gauge, gage.
sporvogn tram-car, tramway-carriage, tram.
spotsk mocking; **— mine, smil** sneer.
spott mockery, derision, scoff, flouting, jeering.
spotte scoff at, deride, ridicule, mock, jeer, flout; (fig) (f. eks. anstrengelser) frustrate, defeat, baffle; **— med, over** d. s.; **spottende** mocking, derisive.
spotte|dikt lampoon. **-fugl** mocking-bird; (fig) mocker, quizzer. **-glose** gibe, scoff, jeer.
spotter derider, scoffer, mocker.
spottpris absurdly low price, great bargain.
spove (el. spue) curlew.
sprade (vrb) show off, strut, swell.
spradebasse fop, buck, coxcomb, dandy, swell.
spraglet variegated, pied, party-coloured.
sprak flying sparks, splutter of sparks.
sprake crackle, splutter out; (om silke) rustle.
sprang jump, leap, spring, skip, bound; (om hest) plunge; (fig) (avbrytelse) break; **i — (fig)** by fits and starts; **stå på -et** be on the point (til: of).
spre(de) spread; (til alle kanter) scatter, disperse; **-s** scatter, disperse; **— seg for mye**

(fig) be too diffusive. **spreder** rose, spreader.
spredning spreading etc., spread. **spredthet** sparseness.
sprek active, lusty, vigorous.
sprekk crevice, chink, crack, fissure.
sprekke crack, burst; (om hud) chap; — av latter split one's sides with laughing. **sprukne** hender chappy el. chapped hands. **-ferdig** nearly bursting.
sprell flounce, kick; wriggle; struggle; **gjøre** — make a fuss.
sprelle sprawl, flounder, toss the body about.
sprellemann dancing-jack, jumping-jack.
sprelsk boisterous, unruly.
spreng pressure, hot haste; **lese på** — cram for it. **-bombe** high-explosive shell.
I. **sprenge** burst, (i to) part, break; (en troppe-avdeling) defeat, scatter, put to flight; — **en fjellknaus** blow up el. blast a rock; — **døra** burst open el. force the door; — **banken** break the bank; — **en lås** shoot a lock; — **av sted** ride at full speed.
II. **sprenge** (strø med salt) corn, sprinkle with salt; **sprengt kjøtt** corned meat.
spreng|granat percussion shell. **-kraft** bursting power el. force, blasting power. **-krutt** blasting-powder. **-kule** explosive ball, se **-granat**. **-kulde** hard frost. **-lærd** crammed with learning. **spreng(n)ing** bursting, blasting etc. **spreng(n)ingsforsøk** bursting trial. **spreng|pro-jektil** se **-granat**. **-sats** explosive composition. **-stoff** explosive stuff.
sprett kick, bound, pop, start; (om ball) spring; (lauv-) breaking into leaf, leafing; **stå i** — be breaking into leaf;
I. **sprette** (intr. vrb.) pop, bound, leap, kick; start; (om trær) break, come into leaf, shoot; **fisken -r etter allslags fly** the fish will spring at all sorts of flying insects.
II. **sprette** (tr. vrb.): — **av** rip off; — **opp** rip open, unsew, unstitch. — **opp en drakt** pick a dress.
spretten frisky.
spri (mar), se **spristake**.
sprike bristle, stand out stiffly, straggle. — **med armer og bein** sprawl.
spring (vann-) fountain; tap, water-tap.
springar (Norway) roundel.
spring|brett spring-board. **-brønn** (i olje-distrikt) flowing well. **-dans** (Norway) roundel.
springe spring, leap, jump, bound, frisk, skip; (briste) burst, snap, crack; (om vinden) shift (suddenly), chop round el. about; **la en mine** — spring a mine; — **fram** protrude, project, jut out; **skipet sprang i lufta** the ship blew up; — (om yind) chop round el. about; **døra sprang opp** the door flew open; — **opp av skrekk** start up from terror; — **over** jump (ogs. fig); (fig) skip (over); — **ut** (om tre) bud, come into leaf, (om blomst) come out, blossom out, bloom. **springende** (om fremstilling o. l.) disconnected, desultory.
springer (springhval) grampus, springer; (i sjakk) knight.
spring|fjær spring. **-flo** spring flood (tide). **-fyr** spark, fop, beau. **-hval** grampus, springer. **-madrass** spring mattress. **-marsj** run.
spring|stav leaping-pole. **-støvel** elastic-sided boot. **-vann** jet, fountain.
sprinkel bar. **-verk** trellis, lattice, wicker-work.
spristake (mar) spleet, sprit.
sprit spirit.
sprog, se **språk**.
sprosse cross-piece, cross-bar.
sprudle gush, well, bubble.
sprunge crack.
sprut gush, spout, spurt.
sprutbakkels cruller, fried cake.
sprute spout, spurt.
sprutrød (blushing) scarlet.
sprø crackly, crisp, short, brittle, friable;

være — (om mat) eat short; (om kake) eat crisp.
sprøyte (subst) squirt, syringe; (brands.) fire -engine.
sprøyte (vrb) squirt; spurt; (med) syringe, inject; — **vann på et brennende hus** play the engines upon a burning house.
sprøytefull dead drunk.
språk language; (stil) diction; **et levende, dødt** — a living, dead l.; **-et** (i alm.) language; **ut med -et!** speak out! out with it!
språk|bruk usage (of l.). **-feil** blunder against grammar, solecism. **-ferdighet** fluency of speech, volubility; gift for languages. **-forderver** corrupter of the. l. **-forsker** linguist, philologist. **-forskning** philology. **-forvirring** confusion el. corruption of languages. **-gransker** philologist, linguist. **-granskning** philology, study of languages. **-grense** boundary line of the language. **-historie** history of l. **-kjenner** linguist. **-kunn-skap** knowledge of languages; **ha gode -kunn-skaper** be well versed in languages. **-kunst** mastery of language. **-kursus** curriculum of languages. **-kyndig** skilled in languages. **-kyndig-het** knowledge of languages.
språklig linguistic(al).
språklærd learned el. erudite in languages.
språk|lære grammar. **-lærer** teacher of languages, language-master. **-lærerinne** language -mistress. **-mann** linguist. **-renser** purist. **-rensing** purification of a language. **-riktig** correct, grammatical. **-sans** linguistic(al) sense el. genius. **-stamme** stock of languages. **-strid** conflict about a language. **-stridig** incorrect, ungrammatical. **-studium** study of language(s). **-talent** talent for (acquiring) languages. **-under-visning** instruction in languages. **-vitenskap** linguistics (pl), philology. **-ætt** family of languages. **-øvelse**, **-øving** exercise el. practice in a language.
spunning (fuge i skipskjøl) rabbet.
spuns bung. **spunse** bung.
spunshull bung-hole, bung.
spurlag intelligence, tidings.
spurt spurt. **spurte** spurt.
spurv sparrow; **skyte -er med kanoner** break a butterfly on a wheel. **-efugl** passerine bird. **spurve|hagl** small shot. **-hauk** sparrow-hawk.
spy (vrb) spew.
spy (subst) vomit, puke.
spyd spear, lance; (kaste-) javelin.
spydig sarcastic, caustic, satirical.
spydighet sarcasm.
spyflue blue-bottle, blow-fly, meat-fly. **det har vært** — **på kjøttet** the meat is fly-blown.
spygatt (hull i skipssiden) scupper.
spyle wash. **spyling** washing down.
spytt spit, spittle, saliva. **-kjertel** salivary gland. **-slikker** lick-spittle, foot-licker. **-slikkeri** toadeating, toadyism.
spytte spit; (sprute, når man snakker) sputter. **spytte|bakk** spitting-box, spittoon. **-klyse** clot of spittle.
spøk joke, jest, fun, sport, pleasantry; — **til side** without joking; **i** el. **for** — in joke, in jest, for fun; **forstår ikke** — is not to be joked el. trifled with, does not understand a joke.
I. **spøke** (skjemte) jest, joke.
II. **spøke** (gå igjen) haunt (the house); **det -r i huset** the house is haunted.
spøke|fugl joker, wag. **-full** playful, sportive, jocose, jocular. **-fullhet** jocularity.
spøkelse ghost; **se -r ved høylys dag** be easily alarmed. **-aktig** ghostlike, spectral, weird. **-frykt** fear of ghosts. **-historie** ghost-story. **spøkeri** ghosts (pl).
spørger asker, questioner, interrogater, inquierer, querist.
spørre ask, question, demand, interrogate; (i l'hombre) ask leave; **må jeg** — pray, if you please; **etter en** inquire for one, ask for one;

— **seg for** make inquiries; — **en om råd** ask one's advice; (fig) **han spør aldri om hvordan været er** he never cares how the weather is; **det spørs (om)** the question is whether; — **en ut** question one thoroughly; **spørrende** inquiring, interrogative; — **pronomen** interrogative (pronoun).
spørresetning interrogative sentence.
spørreskjema inquiry form, questionary.
spørresyk very inquisitive.
spørsmål question, query, interrogation; **gjøre en et** — ask one a question, ask a question of one; **det er et stort** — it is very questionable; **det er ikke** — om at there is no question but that.
spørsmålstegn (sign of) interrogation.
spøt, se strikketøy.
spå prophesy, predict, foretell, bode, augur; be prophetic of; (uten objekt) tell fortunes; — **i kort** tell fortunes by cards.
spådom prophecy, divination, vaticination, forecast. **spådomsgave** gift of divination.
spåkone prophetess, fortune-teller, sibyl.
spåmann fortune-teller, prophet.
sta jibbing, restive; (fig) obstinate. **være** — jib, (amr) balk. **være** — **på sine meninger** insist upon one's opinions.
stab staff.
stabbe (subst) stump; (hugge-) chopping-block.
stabbe (vrb) stump, trudge (along).
stabbestein roadside curbstone.
stabbur outhouse el. storehouse on pillars. **stabburstrapp** trap-stairs.
stabeis duffer, fogey.
stabel pile; (mar) stocks; **la et skip løpe av** -en launch a ship; **skipet løp av** -en the ship was launched; **på** -en on the stocks; (fig) **ha på** -en have in hand.
stabelavløping launch.
stabil stable. -**isere** stabilize.
stabilisering stabilizing. **stabilitet** stability.
stabie pile, stack.
stabs|kaptein captain on the staff. -**officer** officer on the staff. -**sersjant** sergeant major. -**sjef** chief of the staff, staff commander. -**trompeter** trumpet major.
stad city, town.
stade stand, station; **falle fra det høye** — . . . fall from the high estate . . .
stadfeste confirm, corroborate, ratify.
stadfestelse confirmation, ratification.
stadig steady, constant; (om vær) settled; (adv) constantly.
stadighet steadiness, constancy, staidness.
stadion the Stadium.
stadium stage, phase; **et overvunnet** — a thing of the past.
stads|fysikus chief medical officer. -**ingeniør** city engineer.
stafett estafette, courier, express.
stafettløp relay race.
staffasje accessories, adjuncts.
staffeli easel.
stag stay; **gå over** — tack, go about.
stagge check, curb, restrain; (berolige) hush, soothe.
stagnasjon stagnation. **stagnere** stagnate.
stag|seil stay-sail. -**vending** going about, staving.
stahet jibbing, (fig) restiveness, refractoriness.
stake (subst) pole, stake; (lyse-) candlestick; (sjømerke) spar-buoy. **renne seg en** — **i livet** get into a mess.
stake (vrb) stake, pole; — **seg fram** pole.
stakitt paling, railing. -**port** wicket.
I. **stakk** (korns.) stack, rick.
II. **stakk, se skjørt.**
stakkar poor creature, poor wretch.
stakkars (adj) poor.
stakkato staccato.
stakkåndet short breathed, asthmatic, pursy. -**het** shortness of breath, asthma, pursiness.
stakre (vrb) compassionate, pity.

stalaktitt stalactite.
stall stable. -**bror** companion. -**bygning** stables. -**dør** stable-door. -**fore** stall-feed. -**foring** stall-feeding. -**gutt** stableboy. -**kar** groom; (i vertshus) hostler. -**mester** master of the horse, equerry. -**rom** stable accomodation. -**trev** hay-loft above stables.
stam stammering; **være** — stammer.
stam|bane trunk line. -**bok** book of genealogy -**boksblad** leaf of an album. -**boksvers** poetry in an album. -**far** progenitor, ancestor, founder. -**gjest** regular frequenter el. customer (of an inn etc.). -**gods** (entailed) family estate.
stam|herre heir apparent to an entailed estate. -**hus** entail. -**husbesitter** entail holder.
stamkafé one's regular café.
stamme (subst) (av tre) stem, trunk, stock; (folkestamme) tribe, race.
I. **stamme** (vrb): — **fra** descend, be descended. spring, proceed, originate from.
II. **stamme** (være stam) stammer, stutter.
stamming stammering, stuttering.
stammor first mother, ancestress.
stamn, se stavn.
stamord root-word, primitive word.
stamp (balje) tub.
stampe (vrb) stamp, beat; (klede) mill; (mar) (i sjøen) pitch; (pantsette dt.) dip, pop, spout. — **i jorda** stamp the ground.
stampe (subst) (redskap til å stampe med) stamper; (fig) **stå, være i** — be at a stand el. standstill. -**mølle** stamping mill. **stamper** stamper.
stampesjø head sea.
stampeverk machinery of a stamping mill.
stamping stamping; (mar) pitching.
stamtavle genealogical table.
stamtre pedigree, genealogical tree.
stand (tilstand) state, condition, order; (barom.) reading; (samfunnsstilling) state, station (in life), situation, condition, rank, position, degree; (håndtering) calling, trade, profession; (høy st.) rank, quality, distinction; (pl. stender) rank, class, order; **rikets stender** the states of the kingdom; **holde** — keep el. stand one's ground. make head, be proof (against) **av lav, høy** — of low, high degree; **damer av** — ladies of quality; **i** — in order, in repair; **sette i** — put in order, fit up; **få i** — bring about, set afoot; **gjøre i** — repair; **være i god** — be in good condition; **i dårlig** — (om hus o. l.) in bad repair; **være i** — **til** be able to, be capable of, in a condition el. position to, prepared to; **han er i** — **til** alt he sticks at nothing, is up to everything; **sette i** — **til** enable; **jeg ser meg i** — **til** I am in a position (condition, situation) to,' I find myself able to; **sette ut av** — **til** incapacitate for, disable; **ute av** — **til** incapable of, (til å) unable to, at a loss to.
standard (normalmål; fane) standard.
standart (rytterfane) standard.
stander (vimpel) pendant.
standfugl stationary bird.
standhaftig constant, firm, staunch, resolute.
standhaftighet constancy, firmness, fortitude.
stand|kvarter (fixed) quarters, station (of troops). -**plass** stand, station.
standpunkt stand, position; (høyde) level, standing; (stadium) stage; (synspunkt) standpoint, point of view.
standrett summary el. drumhead court-martial.
stands|fordom class-prejudice. -**forskjell** difference of station. -**messig** suitable to one's station el. condition; (adv) in a way suitable etc.
stands|person person of rank. -**ære** professional honour. -**ånd** spirit of caste.
stang bar; (til vogn, til å bære med osv.) pole; (til fiske) rod; (til bissel) branch; (av gull el. sølv) bar, ingot; (mar) topmast; **på halv** — half-mast high, half-staff; (pl) (p. briller) frame; **en** — **lakk** a stick of sealing wax; **holde en** -**en** be a match for one.

stang|bissel branch-bit, curb-bit; curb-reins. **-bly** bar-lead. **-briller** (pl) temple-spectacles. **-bønner** (pl) kidney-beans.

stange butt, bunt; **væren vil** — the ram will butt.

stangfiske rod-fishing, angling.

stang|jern bar iron, iron in bars. **-sølv** silver in bars. **-tinn** bar-tin. **-såpe** soap in bars.

stangvis (om okse) butting.

stank stench, stink.

stankelbein crane-fly.

stanniol tin-foil.

stans break, intermission, pause; cessation.

stanse (subst) (sl. vers) stanza.

I. **stanse** (vi) stop, pause; — **ved** stop at; stop with; (vt) stop, put a stop to, check; — **blodet** staunch the blood.

II. **stanse** (presse) stamp. **-maskin** stamping-machine.

stans(n)ing stopping etc., stoppage.

stapelplass staple, mart, emporium.

stapp(e) (potet-) mash, pulp.

stappe (vrb) fill, stuff, cram.

stappfull crammed full.

starblind, se **stærblind.**

starr(gras) sedge(-grass).

start start. **starte** start. **starter** starter.

stas state, parade, show; (pynt) finery; **i full** — in great state; **gjøre** — **av** make much of; **bare til** — merely for show; **hele -en** the whole lot.

stasdrakt dress-suit.

staselig showy, splendid, magnificent.

stasjon station; **fri** — board and lodging, all found. **stasjonere** station.

stasjonsmester station-master.

stasjonær stationary.

stas|kar fine el. noble fellow. **-kjole** best dress. **-stue** best drawing-room; (amr) parlour.

stat state, commonwealth, empire; **-ens tjeneste** the public service.

statelig stately. **-het** stateliness.

statikk statics.

statisk static(al).

statist mute, walking gentleman.

statistiker statistician. **statistikk** statistics (pl).

statistisk statistical; **-e opplysninger** statistics.

stativ stand, rack, frame; (til klær) ogs. horse.

stats|advokat Crown prosecutor. **-akt** political act. **-anliggende** state affair, business of state. **-bane** national railway. **-bankerott** national bankruptcy. **-bidrag** subsidy, government grant, state support. **-borger** citizen, subject of a state. **-borgerlig** political. **-drift** public management. **-eiendom** public property. **-embete** public office. **-embetsmann** public functionary. **-fange** state-prisoner. **-fengsel** state-prison. **-forandring** political change. **-forbrytelse** high -treason. **-forbrytersk** treasonable. **-forfatning** constitution. **-form** form of government. **-forvaltning** administration, government of public affairs. **-gjeld** public debt, national debt. **-hemmelighet** state-secret. **-husholdning** administration of the public revenue, finances. **-husholdningslære,** se **-økonomi** **-inntekt** public revenue. **-jernbane** public railway, government railway. **-kalender** office-list. **-kasse** exchequer, revenue. **-kirke** state-church, established church. **-kløkt** policy, political shrewdness. **-kunst** art of governing, politics, statecraft. **-kup** coup d'Etat. **-lære** politics, political science. **-lån** public loan. **-makt** power in the state. **-mann** statesman, politician. **-mannsaktig** statesmanlike. **-mannsblikk** eye of a politician, political foresight. **-mannskunst,** se **-kunst.** **-mannsmessig** statesmanlike. **-minister** prime minister, principal secretary of state. **-myndighet** executive power. **-obligasjoner, -papirer** (pl) stocks, funds, bonds. **-regnskap** public accounts. **-religion** established religion. **-rett** international law, law of nations; constitutional

law. **-rettslig** constitutional; international. **-rettslærer** publicist. **-revisor** Commissioner of Audit, Audit-commissioner. **-ror** helm of the state. **-råd** (et) cabinet council, council of the crown; (en) (cabinet)minister, Secretary of State. **-sak** state el. political affair. **-sekretær** clerk of the council; (i England) Secretary of State. **-sjef** head of the state. **-skatt** (imperial) tax. **-skog** Crown forest. **-telegraf** government telegraph. **-tjener** public servant. **-tjeneste** public service. **-tjenestemann** Civil Servant; **-tjenestemannsforbund** Civil Service Federation; Civil Service Alliance. **-vitenskap** political science. **-økonom** (political) economist. **-økonomi** political economy. **-økonomisk** of political economy.

stattholder governor, vice-regent, vice-roy. **-skap** governorship, vice-regency.

statue statue.

statuere lay down; — **et eksempel på en** make an example of one.

statuette statuette.

statur stature.

status state; (skriftlig) balance(-sheet).

status quo status quo.

statutt regulation; by-law.

statuttmessig regular.

staude perennial.

staup drinking cup, goblet; (dump i en vei) chuckhole. **-et** full of holes, bumpy.

staur pole **-hval,** se **spekkhogger.**

staut fine, noble(-looking), stalwart.

staut (tøy) long-cloth.

stav staff, stick; **bryte -en over** condemn, denounce; (tønne-s.) stave; **falle i -er** be staved; (fig) fall into a revery, be lost in thought.

stavbakterie bacillus (pl. bacilli).

stave (vrb) spell.

stavelse syllable.

stavelsesgåte charade.

stavemåte spelling, orthography.

staving spelling.

stavkirke stave-kirk.

I. **stavn** (hjem-s.) (native) soil, glebe; (fig) dwelling, homestead, home.

II. **stavn, stevn** (for-) stem, (poetisk) prow; (bak-) stern; **fra** — **til** — from stem to stern.

stavnsbundet bound to the soil el. glebe.

stavnsbånd villanage, bondage.

stavre stumble, totter.

stavrim alliterative verse.

stavsprang pole-leaping el. -vaulting.

ste (i tjeneste) engage, hire.

ste (subst), se **ambolt.**

stearin stearine. **-lys** composite candle.

stebarn step-child.

sted place, spot; **-ets beboere** the residents; **han sier et** — he says somewhere; **finne** — take place; come off; **alle -er** everywhere; **ville ikke av -et** would not stir; **rør Dem ikke av -et!** don't budge; **fra det** — **hvor** from where; **i ditt** — in your place; (dt.) in your shoes, **på -et** at el. in the place; (i huset) in the house, on the premises; (straks) on the spot, then and there; **på sine -er** in places; **på høyere -er** in high quarters; **til det** — **hvor** to where; **til stede** at hand, present.

stedatter step-daughter.

stedbetegnelse local el. regional designation.

stedd situated; **være ille** — be badly off, in a sad case.

stede (i forb. m. *for*) admit; — **ham for kongen** admit him to the king. **-s til hvile** be interred, buried.

sted|egen local, peculiar to the locality; **-eget uttrykk** localism. **-finnende** existing. **-forhold** local relation. **-fortreder** deputy, proxy, agent, substitute. **-funnen** having occured, having taken place.

stedig, se **sta. -het,** se **stahet.**

sted|kjent having local knowledge. **-kunnskap** local knowledge. **stedlig** local.

sted|ord (gram) pronoun. **-sans** local sense.
stedsnavn name of a place, place-name.
stedt, se **stedd.**
stefar step-father.
steg (skritt) step.
stegg (hanfugl) cock, male bird.
steik, steike, se **stek, steke.**
steil steep, precipitous; (fig) (om person) brusque.
steile (vrb) rear; (fig) start.
steile: (subst) — (**og hjul**) the wheel; **han ble dømt til — og hjul** he was sentenced to be broken on the wheel.
steilhet steepness; (fig) abruptness in manner.
steilskrift upright el. vertical writing.
stein stone; (liten) pebble; (mur-) brick; **de vises** — the philosophers' stone; **det falt en — fra mitt hjerte** a heavy load was removed from my heart; **kunde røre en** — would touch the heart of a statue; **sove som en** — sleep like a top el. post.
steinaktig stony.
stein|alder stone age. **-bit** wolf-fish. **-brott, -brudd** stone-quarry, stone-pit. **-bru** pavement, stones. **-bryter** quarrier. **-bukk** ibex; S-bukken (stjernebilde) Capricorn; S-bukkens vendekrets the tropic of Capricorn.
steindød stone-dead. **steine** (vrb) stone. **steineik** holmoak. **steinet** stony, pebbly.
steinfrukt stone-fruit, drupe, drupaceous fruit.
steinhogger stone-cutter, stone-mason.
steinkast stone-throw.
steinkiste stone-coffin.
stein|kol, -kull coal; (til knapper o. l.) jet.
stein|røys, se **røys.**
stein|skjærer lapidary. **-skjærerkunst** lapidary's art, art of cutting precious stones. **-smerter** (pl) calculus disease, sufferings from stone. **-skred** rock slide.
steintrapp flight of stone-stairs.
stein|trykk (kunsten) lithography; (et litografi) lithographic print, lithograph. **-trykker** lithographer. **-trykkeri** lithographer's office.
steintøy stone-ware, crockery.
steinskvett (fugl) fallow-chat, stone-chat.
stek roast, joint.
steke roast; — **på rist** broil, grill; — **i en panne** fry; — **i ovn** bake; **-nde hete, sol** broiling heat, sun.
steke|fett drippings, kitchen-stuff. **-gryte** pot for roasting. **-panne** frying-pan; dripping-pan. **-spidd** spit. **-ovn** oven.
stekhete broiling heat. **steking** roasting.
stekke clip el. cut (the wings of a bird).
stele, se **stjele.**
stell proper arrangement; management, manner of doing things; methods, ways; (redskaper) gear, things; (ramme, skrog, skjelett) framework, skeleton; (servise, verktøy) set; f. eks. **spise-** dinner-set; **te-** teaservice, tea-set, tea -things (pl).
stemjern mortise-chisel.
stemme (subst) voice; (i musikk) part, voice; (ved valg) vote, suffrage; (orgel) stop; **han talte med høy** — he spoke in (el. with) a loud voice; **var utmerket pr.** — was in fine el. splendid voice; **avgi sin** — vote; **mot en** — with but one dissentient (vote).
I. **stemme** (vi) (ved valg o. l.) vote; (i lovg. fors.) divide; **det -r ikke** it does not agree; (vt) tune attune; — **en høytidelig** put one in a solemn mood; — for vote for, divide in favour of; **alle de som -r for, rekker hendene i været** all in favour will raise their hands; — **en for** dispose one to, incline one for; — **i (med),** se **istemme;** — **med** agree el. tally with, be consistent with; **ikke å — med** disagree, not agree with; — **overens** agree; **stemt** (musikk) in tune; (språklyd) voiced.
II. **stemme** (stanse) stem, stop; — **føttene imot** thrust one's feet against.

stemme|berettiget eligible to vote; elector. **-band** vocal chord.
stemme|flerhet majority, plurality of votes. **-frihet** liberty of suffrage. **-gaffel** tuning-fork. **-givning** voting. **-hammer** tuning-hammer. **-høyde** pitch.
stemme|kule (-seddel) ballot. **-kveg** voting cattle. **-likhet** an equality of votes, (parl.) an equal division. **-liste** poll-book. **-løs** (kons.) surd, whispered, breath.
stemmenøkkel clef, cliff.
stemmer tuner.
stemme|rett right of voting, franchise. **alminnelig -rett** universal suffrage. **-rettskvinne** lady (el. woman) suffragist. **-risse** glottis. **-seddel** voting paper. **-tall** number of votes. **-telling** counting of votes. **-verving** canvassing (for votes).
stemming (av instr.) tuning, tune.
stemne, se **stevne.**
stemning (lune) mood, humour, temper; feeling, spirit, sentiment.
stemningsfull full of warmth, instinct with feeling.
stemningsmenneske impulsive person.
ste|moderlig like a step-mother; (overført) hard, severe; (adv) stepmotherly. **-mor** step -mother.
stemorsblomst heart's ease; pansy, love-in-idleness.
stempel stamp; (til mynter) die; (dmp., pumpe-) piston.
stempel|avgift stamp-duty. **-gebyr** stamp-duty. **-kontor** stamp-office. **-merke** stamp. **-papir** stamped paper.
stemple stamp, brand; (ved å slå hull igjennom) nick.
stender, se **stand.**
stenderforsamling consultative chamber, states, estates.
steng shot, seine-full; **gjøre et** — shoot a shoal.
stenge (sette stenger ved) pole, stake; (lukke med tverrstang) bar; (en havn) block, close; (låse) lock (up); (med hengelås) padlock; (med slå) bolt; — **inne, ute** shut in, out.
stengel stem, stalk.
stenger pl. av **stang.**
stengsel bar, barrier; fence.
stenk sprinkling, sprinkle; (f. eks. av søle) stain, spot, splash; (sjøvann) spray; (fig) touch, taste, sprinkling, dash.
stenke sprinkle; (overstenke) splash, spatter.
stenograf stenographist, shorthand-clerk. **stenografere** stenograph. **stenografi** stenography.
stenografisk stenographic.
stensil stencil. **stensilere** stencil.
stentorrøst stentorian voice.
steppe savannah, steppe, prairie.
stereo|metri stereometry, solid geometry. **-skop** stereoscope. **-typ** stereotype. **-typere** stereotype. **-typi** stereotypography.
steril sterile. **sterilisere** sterilize.
sterilitet sterility.
sterk strong; (om lyd) loud; **-e drikker** ardent spirits; — **kulde, varme** intense cold, heat; — **strøm** rapid current; — (ansikts-) **farge** deep colour; — **kikkert** powerful telescope; **sterkt** (adv): **det blåser** — it blows hard; **det fryser** — it freezes hard; **vokse** — grow apace; — **interessert** intensely interested. — **fristet** sorely tempted. — **mistenkt** strongly suspected.
sterling sterling.
stesønn stepson. **-søster** stepsister.
steto|skop stethoscope. **-skopere** stethoscope.
stetoskopi stethoscopy.
stetse ever, always. **-varende** everlasting, perpetual.
stett stem (of a glass, of a goblet).
stev stanza; reply stanza in an alternating song. **stevje** el. **stevjes** carry on a verse contest.
stevjing contest in impromptu verses.

stevne (større møte) rally; **sette en** — make an appointment to meet one.

I. **stevne** (styre) head, stand, steer.

II. **stevne** (innkalle) summon, cite.

stevnemøte rendezvous, assignation.

stevnevitne summoner's attendant.

stevning (innkallelse) summons, citation.

stevningsmann summoner, process-server.

stevtone tune or air used in «stevjing» (s. d.)

I. **sti** (vei) path.

II. **sti** (på øyet) sty (on one's eyelid).

I. **stift** (en) pin, tack, flaw.

II. **stift**, se **bispedømme**.

I. **stifte** found, institute, establish; (volde) cause, do; — **fred** make peace; — **forlik** reconcile, bring about a reconciliation; — **gjeld** contract a ᵍdebt.

II. **stifte** (feste m. stift) tack.

stiftelse founding, foundation, establishment, institution; (asyl) almshouse; **velgjørende** —**r** charitable institutions. **stiftelses|brev** foundation charter, deed of foundation. —**dag** day of foundation, anniversary (of a foundation). —**fest**-anniversary-feast, commemoration.

stifter founder; (opphavsmann) author.

stifterinne foundress, institutrix.

stiftprost, se **domprost**.

stigbrett footboard, stepboard.

stigbøyle stirrup; (i øret) stapes.

stige (vrb) mount, rise, ascend; (fig) increase; — **av** alight (from a carriage), dismount (from a horse); — **inn** get up; — **ned** descend; — **opp på et fjell** (bestige) ascend a mountain; — **opp på en stol** mount a chair; — **til hest** mount (a horse); **en vin som** —**r til hodet** a heady wine; — **ut** alight; —**nde inntektsskatt** graduated taxation.

stige (subst) ladder. **stiger** master-miner, surveyor, mining-captain. **stigetrin** rundle, spoke, rung.

stighjul balance-wheel; swing-wheel.

stigning rise; (på vei osv.) gradient, incline, (up) grade; **være i** — be on the rise.

stig|reim stirrup-leather. —**rør** rising-pipe.

stikk (adv) direct, right, due; **vinden var** — **øst** the wind was due east; — **i stavn** right ahead; — **imot** dead el. right against. — **imot** vinden dead in the wind's eye.

stikk (subst) stab; (i kortspill) trick, (mar) hitch; (av et insekt) sting; **holde** — hold good, hold true; **la en i** —**en** leave one in the lurch.

stikkbrev warrant of arrest; **sende** — **etter en** pursue one publicly by a writ of arrest.

stikke (gjennombore) stab; (med knappenåler; om torner) prick; (om insekter) sting; (om lopper) bite; (om sola) burn; (i metall) engrave; (søm) stitch, (om sengeteppe) quilt; (i kort-spill) take, cover; head the trick, win (the trick), (fig) beat, trump, cap; — **et svin, en gris** kill el. stick a hog, pig; — **fast med en nål** fasten with a pin; **skipet** —**r for dypt** the ship bears, the ship draws too much water; **han** —**r ikke dypt** he is no great luminary; **ettersom det** —**r meg** as the fancy takes me; **dette** —**r av imot** ... this forms a contrast to ...; — **av** (fortrekke) de-camp, make off, cut and run, take oneself off, hook it; — **etter en** thrust at one, make a pass at one; — **fram** jut out, stick out, project, pro-trude, be conspicuous el. prominent; **sola** —**r meg i øynene** the sun hurts my eyes; **det stakk henne i øynene** it struck her eyes, it hit her fancy; — **en nøkkel i nøklehullet** put a key in the key-hole; — **noe i lommen** put st. in one's pocket, pocket st.; **stakk min arm inn under hans** slipped my arm through his; — **i brann** set on fire, set fire to, fire; — **seg i fingeren** prick one's finger; — **nesen sin i** poke one's nose into; **jeg vet ikke hva det** —**r i** I don't know what it comes, I don't know the reason; — **til sjøs** put to sea; — **en i hjel** stab one; — **hull på et fat broach** a hogshead; — **hull på en**

byll lance an abscess; — **noe til side** put by put out of the way; — **til seg** pocket; — **en u** cut one out, supplant one; — **et dokumen under stolen** suppress a deed; **det** —**r noe unde** there is something at the bottom of it.

stikke (subst) small stick, splinter of wood (til å tenne opp m.) firelight.

stikkelsbær gooseberry. —**busk** gooseberry bush. —**dreper** mildew. —**vin** gooseberry wine.

stikkontakt plug-connection.

stikkledning branch-connection.

stikk|ord cue, tag, catchword; **falle inn på** — take one's cue. —**penger** a bribe. —**pille** suppository, dry clyster; (fig) wipe, rub, taunt. —**renne** dowr -pipe, leader. —**sag** tenon-saw.

stikle sneer, gibe; — **på** sneer at, taunt.

stikleri sneer, gibe, taunt.

stikling cutting, slip.

stikning (søm) stitching.

stil style; writing; (skolefag) composition; (oppgave) paper, exercise, theme; **bunden og ubunden** — verse and prose; **i stor** — on a large scale.

stilart style.

stile pen, word, compose; — **til address to**; — **høyt** aim high, be ambitious; — **på aim at**; — **henimot** make for.

stilebok exercise-book.

stilett stiletto.

stilfull stylish.

stilisere conventionalize. **stilisert** conventional-ized, conventional.

stilist stylist, elegant writer.

stilistisk of style, of composition.

stilk stem, stalk. **stilket** stalky, petiolate.

stillas scaffold, scaffolding.

stillbar adjustable.

stille (adj) (rolig) still, quiet, tranquil; (taus) hushed, quiet; (mar) calm; **stå** — stand still; (fig) (om forretning) be at a stand-still, stagnant; **tie** — be silent; — **messe** low mass; **den** — **uke** holy week, Passion week; **i mitt** — **sinn** mentally, privately; (om kurs). **sukker** — sugar quiet; — **vann har dyp grunn** still waters run deep.

stille (subst) (stille vær) (mar) calm; **i** — in a calm.

I. **stille** (vrb) (stanse) still; — **smerte** alleviate el. soothe pain; — **sult** appease el. stay hunger.

II. **stille** (vrb) (sette på plass) place, set, post, station; (instrum. o. .) adjust; — **betingelser** make conditions; — **fordringer** lay el. make claims; — **kausjon** give security; — **seilene** trim the sails; — **ur** set a watch (etter: by); — **vitner** call witnesses. **stille** (innfinne seg) meet, make one's appearance; — **seg** (til valg) **i Oslo** stand for Oslo; **saken** —**r seg således** the state of the matter is this; — **opp** set up, put up, arrange, form; **det er ikke noe å** — **opp med ham** he is quite impracticable; — **et ur** tilbake set a watch back; — **tilfreds** content, quiet; — **ut vaktposter** post el. station sentinels. **slik er jeg stilt** this is how I am circumstanced.

stillebelte calm belt.

Stillehavet the Pacific.

Stillehavskysten the Pacific shore.

stillepinne (på fiolin, felle) stay, pin, peg, sound-post.

stillesittende sedentary.

stilleskrue adjusting screw.

stillestående stationary; (om vann) stagnant.

stilferdig gentle, quiet.

stilferdighet gentleness, quietness.

stillhet stillness, silence, calmness, quietness; **i** (all) — secretly, privately, (very) quietly.

stilling (måte legemet anbringes på) attitude, posture; (legemlig stilling i forhold til annet) position; (holdning, standpunkt) attitude; (an-settelse, plass) situation, post; (samtunnsstilling) forhold, omstendigheter) position; **innta en** — take up a position.

stillingsmann (mil.) substitute.

stilliss goldfinch.
stillstand stand-still, stand, stagnation.
stiltiende silent, tacit; (adv) tacitly.
stilverk skeleton clock; (jernb.) central witch-work.
stiløs devoid of style.
stilne abate, calm, slacken, subside; **det -t ult av** it fell a dead calm.
stiloppgave subject for composition.
stilretting correction of papers.
stiltre move along as if raised on stilts; stumble **along.**
stiløvelse book of exercises.
I. **stim** (fiskestim) school, shoal; (stimmel) oncourse, crowd.
II. **stim,** se **tummel.**
stimann highwayman, foot-pad.
stime (bråke) make a noise; (stimle sammen) **throng,** crowd, shoal, swarm (together).
stiming uproar, racket, hubbub.
stimle crowd, throng.
stimmel throng, crowd, concourse.
stimulans stimulant, stimulus. **stimulere** stimu-ate. **stimulering** stimulation.
sting stitch; — **i siden** a stitch in the side.
stinkdyr skunk, zoril.
stinke stink; **-nde** stinking, fetid.
stinn distended; stiffened, stiff; bristling.
stipendiat scholarship holder. **stipendium** scholarship, studentship; (reise-) travelling-aid.
stipulasjon stipulation. **stipulere** stipulate.
stirre stare, gaze. **stirring** staring, gazing.
stiv stiff, rigid; (egensindig osv.) stiff, stub-born, obstinate; (av vesen) stiff, formal, exclu-sive; (av kulde) numb; (av å sitte) cramped; — **som en pinne** stiff as a poker; **en — time** a good hour, a mortal hour; — **i matematikk** well grounded, deep-read in mathematics; **gjøre —** stiffen, (stramme) tighten; **stivt** (adv) stiffly etc.; **se -t på en** look hard (el. stare fixedly) at one; **-t heftet** in boards.
stiv|armet stiff-armed. **-beint** stiff-legged.
stive (m. stivelse) starch; — **stivetøy** starch linen.
stivelse (til tøy) starch; (kjemi) amyl.
stivelsesfabrikk starch-factory.
stiver prop, stay; (i paraply) stretcher.
stive|skjorte dress-shirt. **-tøy** starched linen.
stivfrossen hard-frozen; (om lemmer) be-numbed with cold.
stivhet stiffness, rigidity; (fig) stiffness, for-mality, starch.
stiv|krampe tetanus. **-nakket** stiff-necked.
stivne stiffen, grow el. get stiff; (om flytende ting) coagulate; **får blodet til å — i mine årer** makes my blood run cold; **-t** (uttrykk) set; (i anskuelser) fossilized.
stiv|sinn obstinacy, stubbornness. **-sinnet** obstinate, stubborn. **-stikker** starched fellow.
stjele steal, filch. **stjeler: heleren er ikke bedre enn -en** the receiver is as bad as the thief.
stjerne star; (i skrift) asterisk, star; (om kunstnere) star, luminary; **lese i -ne** read the stars; **ha en høy — hos en** stand high with one; **full av -r** starred.
stjerne|bane orbit of a star. **-banner** star-spangled banner. **-bilde** constellation. **-himmel** starry sky el. heavens, stellar heavens. **-kiker** star-gazer. **-kyndig** versed in astronomy. **-kyn-dighet** (knowledge of) astronomy. **-lys** (adj) starlit. **-lys** (subst) starlight. **-observasjon** stellar observation.
stjerne|skudd shooting star, star-shoot, falling star. **-tyder** astrologer. **-tydning** astrology. **-tåke** nebula.
stjert tail; (mar) (tau) lanyard.
stjålen glt. part av **stjele;** (adj) furtive, stealthy.
stjålne øyekast furtive glances.
sto (hoppeflokk med hingst) stud.
stoff matter, substance; (fig) matter, subject,

theme, topic, argument; (foranledning) cause, reason; (tøy) stuff, fabric; (med blomster, figurer osv.) fancy-cloth; (silkestoff) silken stuff.
stoff|skifte, -veksel change of matter.
stoiker stoic. **stoisisme** stoicism. **stoisk** stoic.
stokk stick, cane; **over — og stein** over stock and stone, at full speed; **den faste — the** regu-lar staff; **av den gamle — a** chip of the old block.
stokkdøv stone-deaf.
stokke|fabrikant stickmaker. **-lag** round of logs. **-pryl** a caning, cudgelling.
stokk|fisk stock-fish, dried cod.
stokkonservativ strictly conservative; a Tory of the Tories. **stokkrose** hollyhock, rose-mallow.
stokkverk story, flat, floor.
stol chair, seat; (uten rygg) stool; (i kirke) pew; (dt. prekestol) pulpit; (vevstol) loom; (på fiolin) bridge; **den pavelige — the** holy see; **sette fram en — place** el. put a chair; **stikke under — hide,** cloak, cushion; **sette en -en for døra** drive one into a corner.
stol|arm arm of a chair. **-bein** leg of a chair.
stole: — på rely el. depend upon, trust; **ikke — på** distrust.
stol|gang stool, motion. **-maker** chair-maker.
stoll level, drift.
stolpe post; **snakke oppover vegger og nedover -r** talk a lot of nonsense.
stolpre stagger, totter.
stol|rygg chair-back, back of a chair. **-sete** seat el. bottom of a chair.
stolt proud, haughty, supercilious; — **av** proud of; **være — av glory in; en — bygning** a grand pile.
stolthet pride; (hovmot) haughtiness; **det var hans — at** his boast was that; **sette sin — i** noe take (a) pride in a thing.
stoltrekk chair-cover.
I. **stopp** (i pute etc.) padding, stuffing.
II. **stopp** (p. strømpe etc.) darn; — **i — all** darn.
III. **stopp** (stans) stoppage; **nå er det — now** there is an end.
stopp! (imperativ av stoppe) hold hand! hold on! hol' soft! stand! stop! **si — call** a halt; (fig) pull up; **maskinen sier — fails** to act; **nå må vi si — we** must stop now, put a stop to!
stoppe (vt) fill, cram, stuff; (stanse) stop; (f. eks. strømper) darn, mend; — **en pipe** fill a pipe; **stopp tyven!** stop thief; (med.) bind, constipate, render costive; (vi) stop; — **opp** stop, bring up; — **munnen på en** silence one.
stoppe|garn darning yarn el. worsted, mend-ing. **-korg** mending basket. **-lapp** darning sampler. **-nål** darning needle.
stopper (mar) stopper; (dmp.) guard, cod; **sette en — for** noe put a stop to a thing.
stoppesignal signal to stop.
stoppested stopping place.
stopping filling, cramming; stopping; dar-ning.
stor great; (i omfang) big; (i utstrekning) large; (av høyde, vekst) tall; (voksen) grown up; **være — på det** carry it high; **både -e og små** both great and small; **de -e** the great; (voksne) the grown up people; **en — A** a capital A; **min -e bror** my big brother; **for en — del** largely; **en — familie** a large family; **den -e masse** the multitude, the mob; **-e ord** big words; **det -e publikum** the general public; **ha -e tanker om** think highly of; **i sine -e trekk** in its broad features; **gjøre -e øyne** stare, open one's eyes wide; **i det -e** on a large scale; **ikke -t annet enn** little more than, scarcely anything but; **slå -t på** live in great style.
storaktig haughty, supercilious.
storaktighet haughtiness, superciliousness.
storarter grand.
stor|blomstret large-flowered el. sprigged. **-bonde** well-to-do farmer el. yeoman.

Storbritannia Great Britain. **storbritannisk** Britannic, British.

stor|båt long-boat. **-dåd** great achievement.

store (mar) main; (f. eks. store boline; mainbowline).

stor|eter glutton. **-folk** great people.

stor|fyrste grand-duke. **-fyrstendømme** grand -duchy. **-fyrstinne** grand-duchess. **-glad** delighted, in great glee. **-gråte** cry loudly el. outright, sob. **-het** greatness. **-hetsvanvidd** megalomania. **-hertug** grand-duke. **-hertugdømme** grand-duchy. **-hertuginne** grand-duchess. **-industri** largescale industry.

stork stork.

storkar big man, swell.

storkenebb stork's beak; (bot.) cranesbill, geranium.

storkors (av orden) grand-cross.

storkunge young stork.

storleik, se størrelse.

storlemmet large-limbed.

stor|losje grand habitation el. lodge. **-luke** main hatch. **-låten** grand, impressive, magnificent.

storm gale (of wind); (leds. av uvær) storm; (voldsomt) tempest; (fig) storm, tempest; **innta med —** take by storm, carry by assault; **løpe —** storm.

stor|makt Great Power. **-mann** grandee, magnate. **-mast** main-mast.

stormdag stormy day. **-dekk** bridge deck.

storme: det **-r** it blows hard, blows a gale, (fare avsted) rush; (fig) (rase) storm; (løpe storm) storm. **stormende** tempestuous, stormy; (fig) tumultuous, uproarious; **det gjorde — lykke** had (el. was) a tremendous success, brought down the house.

stormester Grand-Master.

storm|flod spring-tide. **-full** stormy, tempestuous. **-klokke** alarm-bell. **-kolonne** scaling el. escalading party. **-krok** window hook.

storm|signal storm (warning) signal. **-skritt** double-quick pace, double-march. **-stige** scaling-ladder. **-tromme** alarm-drum.

storm|varsel storm warning. **-vind** tempest, gale of wind. **-vær** stormy weather, tempestuous el. boisterous weather.

stor|mønstret large-patterned. **-nøyd** pretentious, exacting. **-politisk** high politic. **-rengjøring** thorough cleaning.

storr(gras) sedge(-grass).

stor|seil mainsail. **-skryter** bragger, braggadocio, braggart. **-skryting** braggardism. **-slått** grand. **-snutet** insolent, arrogant. **-snutethet** insolence, arrogance. **-spove** curlew. **-stilet** (printed in) large type; (fig) in grand style. **-stue** best parlour.

stortalende grandiloquent, bragging.

stortalenhet grandiloquence, braggardism.

storting parliament, Storthing; **komme på -et** enter parliament, be. returned M. P.

stortings|bygning parliament house. **-dieter** members' payment. **-kart** order paper. **-mann** deputy, member of parliament. **-tidende** parliamentary gazette. **-valg** parliamentary election, election for parliament. **-vedtak** act of parliament. **-verv** a deputyship.

stor|vask a washing-day. **-visir** grandvizier. **-ættet** high-born. **-øyd** large-eyed; wide-eyed.

stotre, stotte, se stamme.

strabas fatigue, toil.

strabasløs fatiguing.

straff punishment, (lovens) penalty; (tuktelse) chastisement, castigation, correction.

straffange convict.

straff|anstalt house of correction. **-arbeid** penal servitude, convict labour. **-bar** penal, punishable.

straffe punish; (tukte) chastise.

straffe|dom penal sentence; **Guds -dommer** the judgments of God. **-lov** penal law. **-lovbok**

penal code. **-middel** means of punishment. **-preken** (severe) lecture. **-rett** right of punishing; (kriminalrett) criminal law. **-sak** criminal action. **straffri** unpunished; (adv) with impunity.

straffrihet impunity.

straff|skyldig deserving (of) punishment, culpable, guilty. **-utmåling** apportionment of punishment.

strak erect, straight, upright; **med -e armer** with outstretched arms; at arm's length.

straks at once, immediately, straightway, forthwith; (oppvarters svar) coming, Sir! **klokka er — tolv** it is nearly twelve o'clock; **— etter** the moment after, presently; **— etterat** immediately after; **— på timen** forthwith, straightway, without delay, this (that) very moment; **— da jeg så det** as soon as I saw it; **— om morgenen** the first thing in the morning.

stram tight, strait, close; (fig) starched, precise; (om pris) stiff; **på — line** on the tight rope; **en — lukt, smak** a rank el. pungent smell, taste; **holde -t** (hester) ride with a tight rein; (fig) hold a strict hand over.

strambuks a breeching.

stramei canvas.

stramhet straitness, tightness, closeness; rankness.

stramme tighten, straiten, stretch; (om pris) enhance, raise; **— opp** (fig) nerve; **— seg opp** brace oneself (up); **knuten -s** the plot thickens.

stramning tightening etc; strain, enhancement, raise, rise; **en — av kullprisene** an enhancement in the prices of coal.

stramtsittende tight-fitting.

strand shore, sea-shore, sea-side, beach, strand, coast. **-bad** bathe on the beach. **-bredd** beach, water-side; se **strand.**

strande be wrecked, run aground, strand; (fig) miscarry, fail; **— på** be frustrated by.

strandhogg (hist) predatory descent, shore raid.

stranding stranding; (fig) failure.

strandings|gods stranded goods, wreck. **-sted** scene of a wreck.

strand|kant seaside, waterside. **-promenade** marine drive. **-sitter** longshoreman. **-snipe** sandpiper. **-vakt** coast-guard. **-vasker** corpse found cast by the sea on the shore. **-vei** seaside road.

strangulasjon strangulation.

strangulere strangle.

strateg strategist. **strategi** strategy. **strategiker** strategist. **strategisk** strategic.

straten|røver highwayman. **-røveri** highway-robbery; **drive —** rob on the high-road.

strebe, se streve; — en etter livet seek el. attempt one's life.

strebe|bue arched buttress. **-pille** buttress.

streber pushing fellow, pusher, place-hunter.

strede narrow street, lane; (sund) strait(s); **-t ved Gibraltar** the straits of Gibraltar.

streif (av lys) gleam, glimmer; (berøring) graze; (fig) touch.

streife graze, glance; **kula -t halsen hans** the bullet grazed his neck; **— om på gatene** saunter about the streets; **— om på landet** stroll about the country; **— om i** roam, rove, scour, range about in, ramble, stroll in; (fig) **— inn på** verge on.

streif|korps flying el. scouting party. **-lys** glimmering (el. faint, unsteady, fitful) light. **-skudd** grazing shot. **-sår** light wound. **-tog** incursion, inroad.

streik strike, turn-out; **gjøre —** strike.

streike (vrb) strike.

streikebryter strike-breaker, ogs. black-leg.

streike|kasse strike-funds. **-vakt** strike picket.

strek line, streak, stroke, stripe, dash; (puss) trick, prank; (på kompass) point; **slå en — draw** a line; **slå en — over** (fig) consign to oblivion, cancel; **gå over -en** go beyond the

line; **det var en — i regningen for ham** he was out in his reckoning; **en dristig —** a bold stroke; **dum —** stupid trick, folly; **gale -er** mad pranks.
streke rule, draw lines; **— over** strike out, cross out, run one's pen through; **— under** underline.
strekk tension; stretch.
strekke draw out, extend, stretch; **— til** suffice, be sufficient; **få inntektene til å — til** make both ends meet.
strekking stretching etc., stretch.
strek|mål, -mat joiner's gauge.
strekning (land) tract, range, extent, distance.
streng (adj) severe, rigorous, strict, austere; **strengt** (adv) severely etc.; **— tatt** strictly speaking.
streng (subst) string, chord.
strengeinstrument stringed instrument.
strengeleik, se **-instrument.**
strenghet severity, rigour, strictness.
strev striving, endeavouring; pursuit, exertion, struggle; plod, toil; strain.
streve work hard, strive, struggle, plod, toil, endeavour.
strevsom industrious, hard-working, hard-worked, plodding. **strevsomhet** industry.
stri rough, coarse, bristly; (av sinn) persistent; headstrong, obstinate; (streng) rigorous; **en — strøm** a rapid el. strong current; **-e tårer** fast flowing tears.
stri, se **streve. mase og — fuss** and pother; se ogs. **stride.**
stribukk (fig) hard-head.
strid strife, combat, contest, struggle; antagonism; (i ord) quarrel, contest, dispute, brawl.
stridbar warlike, martial, combative.
stridbarhet warlike disposition, combativeness.
stri(de) fight, combat, battle; (i ord, skrift) contend, strive, dispute; **det -r imot** it is el. runs contrary to, is at variance with, goes against; **stridende** contending, conflicting; (mil) combatant. **stridende imot** contrary to.
stridig headstrong, obstinate, stubborn; **gjøre en noe —** dispute a thing with one.
stridighet (det å være stridig) obstinacy, stubbornness; (strid) dispute, controversy.
strids|emne controversial question. **-eple** apple of discord. **-hanske** gauntlet. **-hest** war-horse, charger.
strids|krefter military force. **-mann** combatant, warrior, fighting-man. **-punkt** difference, moot case el. point, issue, point in debate. **-skrift** polemical pamphlet. **-øks** battle-axe.
strie canvas, towlinen; pack-cloth; sacking.
strigle (subst) curry-comb.
strigle (vrb) curry, dress.
stri|gråte weep fast-falling tears. **-håret** rough-haired.
strikk elastic band.
strikke (subst) rope, cord, halter.
strikke (vrb) knit. **-garn** knitting cotton el. wool. **-pinne** knitting-needle. **-strømpe** stocking (in progress.) **-tøy** knitting.
strikking knitting; (vrang) purling.
striks strict.
striktur stricture; constriction.
strime stripe, streak. **strimet** striped, streaked.
strimmel slip, strip, ribbon, shred; (kruset) frill; (pipe-) ruff.
stringent stringent.
stripe stripe, streak. **stripet** striped, streaked.
strippe (trekar) piggin.
strips (pryl) a flogging.
stri|regne pour with rain; **-renne** course.
stritte (stå stivt) bristle, stand erect; **— imot** resist; **-nde** (om håret) bristly, erect, on end, (sprikende) wide apart.
strofe stanza, strophe.
stropp strap, strop, loop.
strunk erect, upright.
strupe (subst) throat; **skjære -n over på en**

cut one's throat; **sette en kniven på -n** put one to the last extremity.
strupe (vrb) throttle, choke.
strupe|hode larynx. **-hoste** croup, croop. **-lyd** guttural sound. **-tone** guttural accent.
struts ostrich. **strutsefjær** ostrich-feather.
strutte burst, egtl. bristle; **— av sunnhet** be bursting with health.
stry hards, tow, tows; **snyte opp i —** swindle with a vengeance.
I. **stryk** (pryl) beating, drubbing.
II. **stryk** (i elv) rapid, swift part; (amr) shoot.
stryke stroke, rub, sweep; (m. jern) iron; (til eksamen) fail, fail to pass; (en paragraf) strike out; (gå, løpe) run, pass, shoot; (om vind) sweep; **— en vegg** paint a wall; **— flagget** (mar) strike el. lower the colours; **strøk tårene vekk fra øynene** brushed the tears from his eyes; **— av en fyrstikk** strike a match; **strøk håret fra pannen** brushed the hair off his forehead; **— opp håret** brush up the hair; **— ut** scratch out, efface, erase; **i strykende fart** at a rattling pace.
stryke|bolt heater. **-fjøl** ironing-board. **-instrument** stringed instrument. **-jern** (smoothing) iron, flat-iron, sad-iron. **-klede** ironing blanket. **-kone** ironer. **-kvartett** string quartet. **-orkester** string-band. **-ovn** flat-iron-heater, ironing stove. **-r** (musikk) string performer, (pl. koll.) strings. **-reim** (razor) strap el. strop.
stryknin strychnine, strychnia.
strype, se **strupe.**
strø scatter, spread, strew. **— salt på** sprinkle with salt. **— om seg** scatter broadcast.
strø, strøelse (subst) litter.
strøk stroke, touch, dash; (egn) tract, region, neighbourhood.
strøm river, stream; (strømning) current; (elektr.-) ogs. circuit; **sterk —** a strong current; **med -men imot** with a contrary el. adverse current; **tidens —** the tide of the times; **en — av tårer** a flood of tears; **i -mer** in torrents; **følge -men** (fig) follow the multitude.
strøm|bryter (elektrisk) circuit-breaker. **-forbruk** current consumption. **-fordeler** distributor.
strømkantring turn of the tide.
strømme stream; **regnet har strømt ned** the rain has been pouring down (in torrents); **— over av** overflow with; **det strømte folk til i tusenvis** people thronged in el. flocked to the place by thousands; **blodet strømte til hodet på meg** the blood rushed to my head. **strømmevis** in torrents, in streams.
strømmåler current-gauge, hydrometer; (elektr.) rheometer.
strømning flow, current; **-ene i den offentlige mening** the currents of opinion.
strømpe stocking.
strømpeband garter, (lange) suspenders.
strømpe|holder suspender, stocking suspender. **-lest** stocking foot; **på -en** in one's stockings. **-skaft** leg of a stocking. **-strikking** knitting (of) stockings. **-vever** stocking-weaver. **-veveri** stocking-manufactory.
strøm|skifte change of the current. **-slutning** closing (of) the current. **-styrke** amperage, current, strength of current, electromotive power. **-vender** commutator, rheotrope.
strø|pulver sprinkling powder. **-skei, -skje** dredger, sugar-sifter. **-sukker** powdered sugar. **-tanker** apothegms, desultory thoughts.
strå straw; **trekke det korteste —** get the worst of it; **være høyt på —** be in a high station. **-død** a natural death. **-fletning** straw-plaiting; (en) straw-plait. **-gul** flaxen. **-hatt** straw-hat, straw-bonnet. **-kjøl** false keel.
strål (liten fiskestim) scail.
stråle (subst) ray, beam; (om vann) jet, shoot; (om lyn) flash (of lightning); **en — av håp** a glimmering el. gleam of hope.
stråle (vrb) radiate, beam, shine; **diamanten -r** the diamond sparkles; **strålende** beaming, brilliant, effulgent, radiant.

strålebrytning refraction.
stråle|formig radiated. **-glans** radiance, effulgence, refulgence. **-hav** ocean of light. **-krans** glory, nimbus, halo. **-mester** engine-player.
strå|mann man of straw, dummy. **-matte** straw-mat. **-sekk** straw-mattres. **-sete** straw-bottom. **-stol** straw-chair. **-tak** thatched roof. **-tekke** thatch. **-tekker** thatcher.
stubb stub, stump; (av korn) stubble; **synge en** — sing a snatch of song.
stubbe stub, stump.
stubbe|bryter stump-puller; **-ljå** fagging hook; **-loft** false ceiling.
stubbmark stubble-field.
student university man, college man, undergraduate; **bli** — come up (el. be sent) to college, be entered at the University. **filologisk, juridisk, medisinsk, teologisk** — a student of philology, law, medicine, theology (ogs. divinity student).
studenter|hjem students' hostel. **-liv** college -life. **-lue** college cap. **-samfunn** students' union. **-år** (pl) college-years.
studere study; (jus) read law; **la en** — send one to the university; — **på** meditate; **en studert mann** a man of classical education, a university el. college man. **studerende** student. **studering** study.
studer|lampe reading lamp. **-værelse** study.
studie study; **drive -r** carry on (el. conduct) studies. **-hode** study of a head. **-reise** study tour.
studium study.
stue (subst) room; (staseligere) apartment; (daglig-) sitting-room; (amr) living-room; (hytte) cot, cottage; (på sykehus) ward; **sette stua på taket** throw the house out of the window.
I. **stue** (mat) stew.
II. **stue** (pakke) stow; (mar) (om last) stow, trim. — **ballasten om** shift the ballast.
stue|arrest arrest in one's own rooms. **-gods** stowage goods. **-golv** parlourfloor. **-gris** sit-at-home. **-liv** sedentariness, sedentary life. **-lærd** closet philosopher. **-pike** house-maid, chamber-maid, parlour-maid. **-plante** plant grown indoors.
stuer (mar) stevedore.
stuert steward.
stueur clock.
I. **stuing** stowing; (mar) stowing, trimming.
II. **stuing** (mat) stew; (handlingen) stewing.
stukk stucco; **overtrekke med** — stucco, overlay el. coat with stucco.
stukkatur stucco(-work).
stukkatør stuccoer, worker in stucco.
stukko, stukkmasse stucco.
stulle peddle, potter about.
stum mute, dumb, speechless; — **person** mute; **-t spill** dumb show, byplay. **-het** dumbness, muteness, mutism.
stump (adj) blunt, dull; (vinkel) obtuse; (kjegle) truncated.
I. **stump** (sl. brød) ammunition bread.
II. **stump** (subst) stump, fragment; (rest, levning) remnant; (kjælenavn) pet; **slå i -er og stykker** knock to pieces, smash; **redde -ene** save something out of the wreck. **stumpet** stumpy.
stumpevis by bits el. fragments.
stump|halet dock-tailed. **-het** bluntness. **-nese** snub-nose. **-neset** snub-nosed.
stumtjener dumb-waiter, dummy.
stund time, while; **ennå en** — yet a while; **om en liten** — in a little while; **stunder** (pl) leisure, time; **gi seg gode -er** take one's time; **det har gode -er** med det there is no hurry.
stunde long, yearn; — **etter** be anxious, eager, impatient for. — **hjem til Norge** be homesick for Norway.
stundes|løs bustling, fidgety; **et -løst menneske** a busy trifler, a fidget. **-løshet** bustling, busy trifling.
stundevis at intervals.

stundimellom at intervals.
stundom sometimes, at times.
stup cliff, precipice, steep; (v. svømming) header, plunge head foremost. **-bratt** abrupt precipitous.
stupe fall prone, pitch forward; (i vannet) plunge el. head into the water; (falle) drop fall down.
stupid stupid. **stupiditet** stupidity.
stur dejected, low, moping, sad.
sture mope; pine. **-n,** se **stur.**
stuss (kort) gruff, rough.
I. **stusse** (skjære kort) snip, crop, dock, curtail (om trær) lop, trim; (i toppen) poll. **et -t tre** a pollard.
II. **stusse** (bli forbauset) start, be startled
stussing starting, amazement; cropping, curtailment.
stusslig dejecting, saddening; dull.
stut bullock; ox; (skjellsord) rude fellow.
stute|driver drover. **-handel** trade in bullocks el. oxen. **-handler** dealer in bullocks.
stutt, se **kort.**
stuttenkt unthinking, unwise.
stutteri stud. **-mester** master of the stud.
stutthugsen oblivious, foregetful.
stygg ugly, ill-looking, plain, homely; **en** — (slem) **gutt** a nasty boy; **stygt vær** nasty weather.
stygge|dom horrors, uglies. **-lig** (adv) badly, shockingly. **-mannen** Old Harry. **-vær** nasty, rough weather.
stygghet ugliness.
stygging ugly fellow, fright, scarecrow.
stykke (subst) piece, bit; **bryte i -r** break in el. to pieces; **et** — **vilt** a head of game; **et** — **sukker, såpe** a lump of sugar, a cake of soap; **et** — **klede, silke** a length of cloth, a pattern of silk; **100 -r kveg** 100 head of cattle; **et** — **arbeid** a piece el. stroke of work; **et** — (vei) a little way, some distance; **det nye** — (p. teateret) the new piece el. play; — **for** — piece by piece; **hver mye er det for -t** how much a-piece; **når det kommer til -t** after all; **en alen av samme** — a leaf out of the same book.
stykke (vrb): — **opp** cut up, divide; — **ut** parcel out.
stykkevis by the piece, piecemeal, in detail, by instalments.
stykk|frakt freight by parcels. **-gods** general goods, piecegoods.
stylt(r)e stilt (subst); **gå på -r** walk upon stilts.
stymper poor wretch; (klodrian) bungler. **-aktig** bungling.
I. **styr** (støy, uro) hubbub; **holde** — (vill lek) have romps, make fun; (bråk) kick up a row.
II. **styr: holde** — **på** keep in check; **gå over** — come to nothing; **sette over** — squander, squander away, run through.
styrbar dirigible.
styrbord starboard; — **med roret!** starboard the helm! **styrbords-** starboard.
I. **styre** (vrb) steer; (lede) direct, guide, conduct, manage; (beherske) rule, control; — **etter, imot** make el. stand for; — **en kurs** steer a course; **styrte kursen til** shaped his course to; **gutten vil ikke la seg** — the boy won't submit to control, the boy is unmanageable; **hun -r huset** she runs the house; — **sitt sinne** control one's anger; — **sin lyst** satisfy (også control) one's desire; **-r akkusativ** governs an accusative case.
II. **styre** (bråke) romp, make a noise.
styre (subst) (på sykkel) handle-bar; (på bil) helm; (ledelse) rule, management; (direksjon) board of directors; (i forening) executive committee; **i -t** on the board.
styre|apparat steering apparatus el. gear. **-fart** steerage way. **-hus** pilot-house, wheel -house.
styrelse rule, management, direction; **forsynets** — the direction of providence.

styre|medlem director. **–møte** meeting of directors.

styrer ruler, director. **styresmann** cockswain.

styrestang (dmp.) guide.

styrevalg election of directors.

styring (mar) steerage, steering; (p. bil etc.) control; (dmp) parallel motion; **miste –en** lose control.

styrke (subst) strength; (vindens, krigs-) force; **gi ny — renerve; prøve — med en** try one's strength against one; **han har ikke sin — i latin** Latin is not his force.

styrke (vrb) strengthen, fortify; **–nde midler** corroborants, tonics, restoratives.

styrkeprøve trial of strength; (om kjetting) test-proof of strain.

styrmann mate; **annen —** second mate.

styrmanns|eksamen mate's examination. **–hyre** mate's pay; mate's berth. **–patent, –sertifikat** mate's certificate. **–skole** navigation school.

styrt (dusj) shower-bath, douche.

styrte (vi) fall down, tumble down, topple down; **hesten –t** the horse fell el. dropped down; the horse dropped dead; (vt) precipitate, hurl; (styrte om) subvert, overturn, overthrow; **–t seg i mine armer** threw himself into my arms; **— seg i fordervelse** plunge into ruin, run headlong into destruction el. perdition; **— inn** el. **ut** bolt, dart, rush in or out; **han –t med hesten** the horse fell with him; **regnet –t ned** the rain poured down; **— seg over** fall (el. rush el. pounce) upon; **— sammen** fall el. tumble down, fall to ruin, fall in, collapse; **tårene –t ut of øynene på henne** tears gushed from her eyes.

styrte|bad, se **styrt. –ferdig** ready to drop down. **–gods** goods stowed in bulk. **styrtning,** se **stup.**

styrt|regn pouring rain. **–sjø** heavy sea, topping sea.

styrvol, se **rorpinne.**

I. **styver** (eldre tysk mynt) farthing.

II. **styver** (nese-) knock on the nose, noser.

I. **stær** (fugl) starling.

II. **stær** (øyensykdom): **den grå —** cataract, glaucoma; **den sorte —** amaurosis, drop serene; **operere for —** couch a cataract.

stær|blind purblind. **–briller** spectacles for couched eyes. **–hinne** film of the cataract.

stærkasse starling-box.

stø (subst) hard, landingplace.

stø steady; (adv). **–tt** steadily. **–het** steadiness.

støe (el. **stø**) support.

støkk start, fright, shock. **støkke** (skremme) startle; (bli skremt) start, start up.

stol (subst) egtl. milking-place for cows at an outfarm; se **seter.**

stol (adj) rigid, stiff, stiffened. **stiv og —** very stiff indeed.

stønn moaning, groaning, . moan, groan. **stønne** moan, groan.

støp (el. staup) drinking cup, goblet.

støpe found, cast; (i en form) mould; **— om** recast; **— lys** mould candles; **frakken sitter som om den var støpt på Dem** the coat fits you like a glove.

støpe|form mould. **–gods** cast work, cast-iron ware, castings (pl). **–jern** cast-iron. **–ovn** smelting furnace.

støper founder, caster. **støperi** foundry.

støpe|skje casting ladle. **–stål** cast-steel.

støpning founding, casting; (fig) **av en —** (all) of one piece.

stør sturgeon.

størhus, se **bryggerhus.**

størje tunnyfish.

størk|ne coagulate, curdle, congeal, clot; **–net blod** gore. **–ning** congealing, coagulation.

større komp. til **stor.**

størrelse greatness, magnitude; (i dimensjoner) largeness, size; (i tykkelse, omfang) big-

ness, bulk; (høyde osv.) tallness, height; (i algebra) quantity; (person) notability, star, person of note.

størst superl. til **stor.**

størstedelen the grater part, the best part, the major part el. portion, the generality, most; **for —** for the most part, mostly.

støt push, thrust; (med hodet) butt; (med dolk) stab; (ved sammenstøt, og fig) shock, blow; (mar) (mot grunnen) thump, bump; (av vogn) jog, jolt; (elektrisk) shock; (vind) gust, puff; (i trompet) blast; (virkningen av f. eks. slag) bruise; (fig) (til noe) impulse; **avverge –et** ward off the blow; (fig) **det var et hardt — for ham** that was a hard el. sad blow el. shock to him.

støte (puffe) push, thrust; (fornærme) offend, hurt; (virke -nde på) jar upon; (i mørter) pound, pestle, bray; (om geværer) kick, recoil; (om skip) strike; **bli støtt** be offended, take offence; **— seg** hurt oneself; **— an** offend; **bli støtt over noe** take offence at a thing; **— på** pick up with; **— sammen** come in contact, run el. knock together; **— til** (uhell o. l.) happen, supervene; **støtende** (fig) offensive, harsh, jarring.

støter (i mørter) pestle.

støtpute buffer.

støtt (stadig) ever and always, constantly.

støttann tusk.

støtte (vrb) stay, prop. support, sustain, bear up, (fig) back up, bear out; **— seg på** el. **til** lean upon el. against; (fig) rely on.

støtte (subst) support; (søyle) column, pillar; (billed-) statue; (stiver) shore; (fig) supporter, support. **støtte|punkt** point of support. **–stav** staff, support.

støttesten glottal catch.

støtvis by (fits and) starts, at intervals; (om vind) in gusts.

støv dust; (på sommerfuglens vinger) scales (pl); **tørke — dust; –ets år** the days of our years.

støv|briller goggles. **–drager** stamen.

støve be dusty; **— av** dust, wipe away the dust. **— igjennom** search through. **— opp** ferret el. hunt out; **støve|klut** duster. **–kost** dust-brush.

støvel boot; (lang) blucher, wellington.

støvel|børste blacking-brush. **–knekt** boot-jack. **–lest** boot-last. **–lisse** boot-lace. **–pusser** shoe-black, boot-cleaner. **–skaft** leg of a boot, boot-leg. **–snute** boot-tip, toe. **–stropp** boot-strap, boot -garter.

støver hound, retriever; (liten harehund) beagle.

støvet dusty, covered with dust.

støv|frakk duster, dust-coat. **–grann** atom, mote. **–kåpe** dust-cloak. **–plage** dust nuisance. **–regn** drizzling rain. **–regne** drizzle, missle. **–sky** cloud of dust. **–suger** vacuum cleaner. **–tråd** (i blomst) filament.

støy noise, racket; **lage —** make a noise. **støye** make a noise; **støyende** noisy. **støying** clamour, vociferation.

støype osv., se **støpe.**

støyt, se **støt:** (drikk) drink, pull; **ta seg en — have** a drink.

støyte, se **støte.**

stå stand; **uret –r** the watch has stopped; **det stod et slag** a battle was fought; **når skal bryllupet —?** when is the marriage to come off? **— brud** be married. **— fadder** stand god -father to, stand sponsor for; **— skiltvakt** stand sentinel el. sentry; **— stille** stand still, stop; **hans saker –r dårlig** things do not go well with him; **— seg godt** be well off; **— seg godt med en** be on good terms with one; **— en bi** stand by one, se **bistå; det er umulig å — for** it is irresistible; **— for en** (i ånden) be in one's mind's eye; **det –r Dem fritt å . . .** you are free to . . .; you are at liberty to . . .; **— fram** stand forth el. forward, step forward; present oneself, arise; (rage fram) stand out, jut out, project; **det får — hen** (uvisst) it must remain doubtful; **det -r i avisen** it is in the paper; **-r i akkusativ** is in the accusative; **— i lys lue** be all in flames; **kornet -r høyt i pris** corn sells at high price; **— i brevveksling med** be in correspondence with; **-r i samme forhold til** bears the same relation to; **det -r ikke i min makt** it is not in my power; **— imot** resist, withstand; **kunne stå seg imot** be a match for; **— opp** stand up, arise, rise, get up; **— sent, tidlig opp** be a late, an early riser; **sola -r opp** the sun is rising; **— over** be ahead of, outrank; **— på grunn** (mar) be aground, have struck; **barometeret -r på regn** the barometer indicates rainy weather; **— som på nåler, glør** be on tenterhooks; **— på sin rett** be upon thorns; **— på sin rett** stand on one's right; **hvor lenge vil det — på?** how long will that take? **mens det stod på** while it lasted; **vinden -r på** the wind is el. stands full on the house, is on; **la det nå — til!** now, fire away! **la det bare — til!** never say die! **hvordan -r det til?** how goes it? how are you? **det -r til Deres disposisjon** it is at your service; **han -r ikke til å redde** he is not to be saved el. cannot be saved; **— tilbake for** be inferior el. second to, yield to, be outdone by, be behind; **— ut** (rage fram) jut out, protrude; **— under en** be below one; (tjene) serve under; (under ens befaling) be under the charge of; **— ved sitt ord** stand to one's word, be as good as one's word; **— ved handelen** stand by the bargain; **tør — ved sine meninger** has the courage of his opinions; **på -ende fot** off hand; **-ende vits** standing joke; **jeg har pengene mine -ende i** my money is invested in.

stå: i —, gå i — come to a standstill; **er gått i —** is at a standstill.
ståhei turmoil.
ståk bustle; (strengt arbeid) fag, grind.
ståke bustle, fuss.
ståkort winning card.
stål steel.
stålampe standard lamp.
stålgrå iron-gray. **stålkledd** steel-clad.
stål|orm blind-worm, slow-worm. **-ovn** cementing furnace. **-penn** steel-pen, metallic pen. **-perle** steel-bead. **-satt** steeled. **-sette** steel. **-stikk** steel-engraving. **-tråd** (iron-)wire.
ståplass standing place.
su (dragsu) vortex.
su, se suge.
suav zouave.
subaltern subaltern.
subb (søl) dirt, slop; dirtiness.
subbe (feie, sope) sweep; drag; (m. bena) slouch, shuffle. **sekken -r bakken** the bag-end trails the ground. **— inn penger** sweep up money.
subbevær dirty el. muddy weather.
subjekt subject; **et dårlig —** a bad lot, a black sheep.
subjektiv subjective. **-itet** subjectivity.
subjektsantyder anticipative subject.
sublim sublime. **sublimat** sublimate.
subordin|asjon subordination. **-asjonsfeil** breach of discipline. **subordinere** subordinate.
subsidier subsidies (pl); a subsidy.
subsidiær subsidiary.
subsistens subsistence. **-midler** means of subsistence.
subskribent subscriber. **subskribere på** subscribe to. **subskripsjon** subscription.
subskripsjonsinnbydelse prospectus.
subskripsjonsliste list of subscribers.
substans substance. **substansiell** substantial.
substantiv noun. **substantivisk** substantive.
substituere substitute.
substitusjon substitution. **substitutt** substitute.
substrat substratum.
subtil fine-spun, over-refined.

subtrahend subtrahend. **subtrahere** subtract.
subtraksjon subtraction.
Sudan the Soudan. **sudaneser** Soudanese.
Suderøyene the Sudreys.
Sudetene the Sudetes, the Sudetic range.
Sueskanalen the Suez Canal.
suffiks suffix.
suffisanse self-sufficiency, assertiveness.
suffisant self-sufficient; substantial, stout.
sufflere prompt. **sufflør** prompter.
sufflør|bok prompt-book, prompt-copy. **-kasse** prompter's box. **suffløs** prompter.
sug suction.
suge suck; **— i seg, til seg** suck in, imbibe, absorb; **— seg fast** adhere.
sugg (big) thumping fellow.
sugge sow.
suggestion suggestion.
suging sucking, suction.
suite retinue, attendance, suite; (rekke) suite; (av kort) run, sequence; **à la suite** unattached; **en suite** contiguous.
sujett subject.
sukat succade, candied lemon-peel.
sukk sigh; (tungt) groan.
sukke sigh, (tungt) groan; **— etter** sigh el. groan for el. after; **— over** sigh over el. for.
sukker sugar; **en topp —** a loaf of sugar; **rått —** raw sugar; **raffinert —** refined sugar.
sukkererter sugar-peas, sweet peas.
sukker|holdig sacchariferous. **-karving** sugar-cracknel. **-klype** sugar-tongs (pl) **-kokeri** sugar-boilery. **-kopp** sugar-basin. **-plantasje** sugar-plantation. **-raffineri** sugar-refinery. **-roe** sugar-beet. **-rør** sugar-cane. **-saker** confectionery. **-syke** diabetes. **-søt** sweet as sugar. **-topp** sugar-loaf. **-tøy** confectionery, sweets, sugar-plums. **-unge** (dt) darling, honey. **-vann** sugared water.
sukle gurgle, swish.
sukre sugar; **— ned** preserve in sugar.
suksedere succeed. **suksesjon** succession. **suksess** success. **suksessiv** successive. **suksessivt** successively. **suksessor** successor.
sul meat.
sulfat sulphate.
sulke (vrb), se **søle.**
sull croon. **sulle** croon, hum.
sult hunger.
sultan sultan. **-inne** sultana.
sulte (vi) hunger, starve; (vt) starve, famish; **— i hjel** die of starvation; (med objekt) starve to death, kill by starvation; **— ut** famish, starve (out).
sulte|for insufficient food. **-fø** feed scantily, starve, underfeed. **-kunstner** artist in starving. **-kur** low, strict regimen, fasting cure.
sultelønn starvation wages.
sulten hungry, sharp-set.
sultestreik hunger strike.
sum sum; **hele -men** the sum total.
summa, se sum; — lateris carried forward; **in —** altogether, in short.
summarisk summary; (adv) summarily.
I. **summe opp** sum up, total up.
II. **summe seg** compose one's mind, collect oneself, recover one's balance.
III. **summe** (som bier) buzz, hum.
summere sammen sum up.
sump swamp, fen. **-aktig** swampy, fenny. **-feber** marsh fever. Se forøvrig **myr-.**
sund (subst) sound.
sund (rive —), se **i stykker.**
sunde seg, se summe seg.
sund|mann board-man, ferry-man. **-penger** ferriage. **-sted** ferry. **-toll** (the) sound dues.
sunn (frisk) sound, healthy, healthful; (gagnlig for sunnheten) wholesome, healthy, healthful, salutary, salubrious; **sunt legeme** sound el. hale body; **en — sjel i et sunt legeme** a sane mind in a sane body; **— menneskeforstand** sound (el.

common el. good) sense; — **beliggenhet, sunt klima**, — **beskjeftigelse, mosjon** healthy el. healthful situation, climate, employment, exercise; — **mat** wholesome food; — **luft** (el. **sunt klima**) salubrious air (climate); — **sans** common sense.

sunnhet health; healthfulness, salubrity, wholesomeness; **drikke på ens** — drink one's (good) health.

sunnhets|autoritet the Health Authorities. **-bevis** certificate of health. **-hensyn: av** — from considerations of health. **-kommisjon** board of health, sanitary board el. commission. **-lære** dietetics (pl). **-pass** (mar) bill of health. **-pleie** hygiene. **-politi** sanitary police. **-tilstand** state of health. **-vedtekter** sanitary regulations. **-vesen** sanitary system.

sup nip, sip; (dt) drink.
supe imbibe, suck; (drikke for mye) tipple.
supé el. **souper** supper, evening-party.
superb superb.
superfin superfine.
superfosfat superphosphate (of lime).
superintendent superintendent.
superkargo supercargo, cap-merchant.
superklok overwise.
superlativ superlative.
supinum the supine.
suppe soup, broth; (mel-, gryn-) porridge, gruel.
suppedas (dt): **en fin** — a nice pickle.
suppe|gryte soup-pot. **-sleiv** soup-ladle. **-tallerken** soup-plate. **-terrin** soup-dish, tureen. **-øse** soup-ladle.
supple|ant deputy, substitute. **-ment** supplement. **-ment-** supplementary, supplemental. **-re** supplement, eke out. **-ringsvalg** bye-election.
supplikant petitioner, supplicant, applicant.
suppo|nere suppose. **-sisjon** supposition.
suppurasjon (materiedannelse) suppuration.
suppurere suppurate.
supremat, supremati supremacy.
sur sour, acid; (kjemi) acetous; (om umoden frukt) acerb, sharp; **-t arbeid** hard work; **hun gjorde livet** — **for ham** she led him a sad life of it, made life a burden to him; **sette opp -e miner** frown, look surly; **det var et -t eple han måtte bite i** it was a bitter pill he had to swallow; **gjøre livet -t for seg** embitter one's own life; **surt** (adv): — **fortjent** hard earned.
sur|deig leaven; (fig) **av samme** — **som of** piece with. **-het** sourness, acidity.
surke, se **sukle**.
surkål sour-crout.
surl crooning, humming. **surle** croon, hum.
sur|lynt morose, surly. **-mule** look sour el. sulky, grump. **-muling** sulkiness. **surne** turn sour.
I. **surr: gå** — be confused.
II. **surr** buz, hum; whir.
I. **surre** (summe) hum, buzz.
II. **surre** (binde fast med et tau) lash, secure.
surretau (mar) lashing, frapping.
surring lashing.
surrogat substitute, makeshift, apology.
sursild pickled herring.
surstoff oxygen. **-holdig** oxygenous.
surøyd blear-eyed.
I. **sus: leve i** — **og dus** lead a life of riot and revel.
II. **sus** (susing) whistling, howling; (for ørene) humming, tinkling (in one's ears).
suse whistle, bluster; (om kuler osv.) whistle, whizz; **det -r for ørene mine** my ears tingle; **i humla** — (dt) let things drift. **i -nde fart** at a dizzy speed.
suset(e) whimsical, half-witted.
susing, se **sus**.
suspekt (fordektig) suspicious.
suspendere suspend. **suspensjon** suspension.
suspensorium suspensory, truss.
sut care, concern, solicitude.

sutre whimper, fret. **sutring** whimpering fretting.
sutt sucking-bag. **sutte** suck.
sutur suture, seam.
suvenir souvenir.
suveren sovereign. **-itet** sovereignty.
sva bare rock or mountain slope.
svaber swab; mop.
svaberg bare rock-face, slope of naked rock.
svaber|gast swabber. **-skaft** mop-stick.
svabre swab down, swab.
svada flow of language, oratory.
sval (mar): **ligge på** — be swinging.
svaie swing to and fro; (mar) swing.
svairygget hollow-backed, saddle-backed.
svak weak; (i høyere grad) feeble; (ubetydelig) faint, slight; (om drikker) weak; — **farge, lys,** lyd dull el. faint colour, light, sound; **en** — **støy** a slight noise; **et -t håp** a faint el. forlorn hope; — **helbred** delicate health; **det -e kjønn** the softer sex; **stå på -e føtter** be weak, precarious, in a precarious state; **jeg kjenner hans -e sider** I know his weak point; **svakt** (adv) weakly etc.
svakelig weakly, infirm, delicate.
svakelighet weakness, feebleness.
svakhet (legemlig og åndelig) weakness, feebleness, infirmity; (svakt punkt) infirmity, weak point; **han har en** — **for fine klær** he has a mania for fine clothes; (forkjærlighet) liking; **han har en** — **for deg** he has a liking for you.
svak|hjertet faint-hearted. **-hodet** weakheaded. **-sinnet** imbecile, crazy. **-synt** dimsighted. **-synthet** dim sight.
sval cool.
sval (subst) gallery, balcony.
svale (kjøle) cool.
svale (fugl) swallow; **en** — **gjør ingen sommer** one swallow does not make a summer.
svale|drikk cooling draught. **-maskin** (i mølle) hopper-boy. **-ovn** (i glassverk) leer.
sval|gang, se **sval** (subst). **-het** coolness.
svaling cooling.
svall (passiar) chat, talk. **svalle** chat, confabulate, talk.
svalne cool, become cool.
svamp sponge; **han drikker som en** — he drinks like a fish.
svampaktig spongy. **svampet** spongy.
svane swan. **-dun** swan's down. **-fjær** swan's quill el. feather. **-hals** swan's neck. **-sang** (fig) dying strains (of a swan). **-unge** young swan, cygnet.
svang (adj) (tom, om korn) blighted, empty.
svang: gå i — prevail, be prevalent.
svange (på dyr) flank.
svanger gravid, pregnant; — **med** pregnant with. **-skap** pregnancy. **-skapsperiode** period of gestation. **-skapstegn** symptom of pregnancy.
svans tail. **svanse** wag the tail; (om person) waddle, strut. **svans|skrue** breech pin, thumb -nut. **-stykke** tail-piece.
svar answer, reply; — **betalt** answer prepaid; **bekreftende, benektende** — answer in the affirmative, in the negative (på: to); **gi en** — return el. give one an answer; **få** — get an answer; **som** — **på** in answer to; **til** — **på** in answer to; **han blir aldri** — **skyldig** he is never at a loss for a reply; — **utbes** (s. u.) an answer is requested (R. S. V. P.).
svarbrev written answer, letter of reply.
svar|e answer, reply, respond; (nesevist) answer again; — **toll, leie** pay duty, rent; — **for** (innestå for) answer for, be answerable el. responsible for; — **på** answer el. reply to; — **til** (passe til) agree, correspond, be of a piece with, be in keeping with, answer to; **-te ikke til våre forventninger** did not (quite) come up to our expectations; **og dertil -ende konvolutt** and envelope to correspond.

svare (adj) extraordinary, tremendous, vast. **et — strev** a sore job.

svarskriv, se **svarbrev.**

svart (sort) black; (skitten) dirty; **ha — på hvitt for noe** have a thing in black and white; **være på -elista hos en** be in one's black book, on one's blacklist; (fig) **den -e kunst** the black art, necromancy.

svartaktig blackish, swarthy.

svartalv dark elf, black elf.

svarte|bok black el. conjuring book. **-bror** Black-friar. **-dauen** the Black Death. **-liste** black list. **Svartehavet** the Black Sea. **-kunstner** necromancer.

svartelegram telegram (el. wire) in reply, reply (telegram).

Svartemarja (fangevogn) Black Maria, the King's omnibus.

svart|farget of a black colour. **-flekket** black -spotted. **-het** blackness. **-håret** blackhaired.

svart|kantet black-edged. **-kledd** (dressed) in black. **-kritt** black chalk, drawing-slate. **-krittstegning** drawing in b. chalk.

svartne blacken, grow dark, lower; **det -r for øynene mine** my eyes grow dim, I'm turning giddy.

svart|or black alder. **-smusket** swarthy. **-stripet** black-streaked. **-trost** blackbird. **-øyd** black-eyed.

svarve turn, form in a lathe.

sve burnt land.

sveis (godt lag) knack; (stil) style.

sveisen splendid; ogs. chic, stylish.

sveisbar weldable. **sveise** weld.

sveiser (fjøsmann) cheesemaker, dairyman.

sveis(n)ing welding.

Sveits Switzerland. **s-er** Swiss. **s-erhytte** chalet. **s-erost** Gruyére.

sveitsisk Swiss.

I. **sveiv** curve, sweep, round off.

II. **sveiv** (til å sveive m.) crank, crank-handle, winch.

sveive turn the crank.

sveivespill (mar.) dory winch.

svekk, se **engelsk syke.**

svekke weaken, enfeeble, debilitate, impair.

svekkelse weakening; infirmity.

svekling weakling.

svelg (strupe) throat, gullet, swallow; (avgrunn) abyss, gulf; **betennelse i -et** pharyngitis.

svelgje swallow; **— i** revel in.

svelgkatarr catarrh of the pharynx.

svelle (ut) swell.

svelte, se **sulte.**

svenn (håndverkssvenn) journeyman.

svenne|arbeid journeywork. **-brev** journeyman's certificate. **-prøve, -stykke** journeyman's probation work.

svensk Swedish. **svenske** Swede.

svepe whip, scourge. **-skaft** whiphandle. **-slag** lash of a whip. **-snert** whip-lash.

sverd sword; (mar) lee-board. **-blad** swordblade. **-feste** hilt of a sword. **-fisk** sword-fish. **-lilje** iris, rain-bow flower, flag. **-side** male line. **-slag** stroke with a sword.

sverge swear; **— og banne** swear; **— falsk** take a false oath, forswear oneself; **svorne fiender, venner** sworn enemies, friends.

Sverige Sweden.

sverm swarm; (av mennesker) ogs. crowd.

sverme swarm; (være begeistret) be an enthusiast, rave; **— for** admire, fancy; (sterkere) love, be an enthusiastic admirer of, rave about, worship.

svermer (begeistret mann) enthusiast (for), lover, enthusiastic admirer (of); (fanatiker) fanatic, visionary, transcendentalist; (i fyrverkeri) squib, cracker, serpent. **svermeri** enthusiasm.

svermerisk visionary, fanatical, enthusiastic.

svermerske (female) enthusiast.

sverte (vrb) black, blacken; (fig) blacken, asperse.

sverte (subst) blacking. **-gryte** blacking po **-kost** black brush. **sverting** blacking.

svett sweaty, moist with perspiration.

svette (vi) perspire, sweat; (vt) (mar) stea (planks); **ta inn noe å — på** take a sweat; **—** (fig) unlearn; **svette|bad** sweating-bath, sudator **-kur** course of sudorifics. **-middel** sudorific.

svette (subst) perspiration, sweat; **være bad i —** be in a bath of perspiration. **dampende av -** smoking (with perspiration).

svettedrivende diaphoretic, sudorific.

svettedråpe drop of perspiration.

svette|lukt sweaty smell. **-reim** hat-lining.

sveve (bot) hawkweed.

sveve hang, hover, move, sail, float; (g glide, skim, flit; **— mellom liv og død** be in vering between life and death; **svevende** (o en sak) pending, in suspense; **— form, u trykksmåte** vague form, style. **sveving** hoverin

I. **svi** (vi) smart, pain, ache; (fig) **han får - for det** he must smart for it.

II. **svi** (vt) singe, scorch; **hun har svidd mate** she has burnt the meat; **— av** set fire to.

svibel bulb. **-glass** root-glass.

svie (subst) smart, sharp pain.

svieland, se **sve.**

sviger|datter daughter-in-law. **-far** fathe in-law. **-foreldre** father- and mother-in-la **-inne** sister-in-law. **-mor** mother-in-law. **-søn** son-in-law.

svik fraud, deceit. **-aktig** fraudulent, decei ful. **-aktighet** fraudulence, deceitfulness.

svike deceive, disappoint; (bedra) defrau. **— sitt fedreland** forsake one's country; **— s løfte, sitt ord** break one's promise, one's wor

svikk spigot, vent-peg. **-bor** gimlet. **-hamm** tack-driver.

svikt breach, breakdown, failure.

svikte fail, forsake, abandon, desert, di appoint; (mar) swift; (et seil) balance (a sai mine øyne -r** my sight fails me; **han -r ald sin plikt** he never shrinks from his duty; **— farens stund** be wanting at the time of dange **med aldri -nde iver** with unfailing zeal.

svill (jernb.-) sleeper; (underlag for muren i hus) sill.

svime (av) swoon.

svime: i — in a swoon, unconscious; **slå i - el. —slå** knock unconscious, strike senseless.

svimle be dizzy el. giddy; **det -r for meg** grow dizzy, my head turns el. swims. **svimlenc** dizzy, giddy. **svimling** giddiness.

svimmel giddy, dizzy; **bli — be** taken wi giddiness, turn dizzy. **svimmelhet** giddiness.

svin hog, swine, pig; (fig) beast; **kaste perl for —** throw pearls before swine.

svinaktig swinish, hoggish, piggish; (dt beastly, rascally; (adv) confoundedly.

svinaktighet swinishness, piggishness.

svindel swindle.

svindle swindle. **svindler** swindler.

svine soil. **— til** befoul.

svinebinde tie together all the legs of animal.

svine|be(i)st dirty fellow, beast. **-blod** hog blood. **-blære** hog's bladder. **-bust** (hog bristles. **-fett** hog's lard, pork fat. **-heldig** co foundedly lucky; **han er riktig —** he is a luc dog. **-hell** strange piece of good luck. **-kjø** pork. **-lever** pig's liver. **-lær** hog-skin el. h -leather. **-pels** hoggish fellow. **-pest** swine feve **-ri** swinishness, filthiness. **-rygg** chine of por **-slakter** pork-butcher. **-slakteri** bacon factor

sving swing; (i skrivning) flourish; (fig flight; (dreining) turn; turning point, elbow.

sving|bom swinging-boom. **-bor** centrifug drill. **-bru** swivel-bridge, swing-bridge.

svingdør swing-door.

svinge swing; (om fugler) soar (up); (att

am) oscillate; — **om** wheel about el. round;
(med) **hatten** wave one's hat; — **sverdet**
andish el. flourish the sword; — **seg i salen**
ult into the saddle; — **seg i været** (fig) raise
.eself.
sving|fjær beam-feather. **-hjul** fly-wheel.
.jele swing-kettle. **-kraft** tangential force.
.ran balance-crane.
svingning swinging etc.; swing, vibration,
cillation. **-skrets** oscillatory circuit.
sving|om kickup, step-out, hop; **få seg en**
,m (med) be dancing (with). **-plog** reversible
.ough. **-stang** (gymn.) swing-pole.
svinn shrinking, waste, loss; loss in weight.
svinne (forsvinne) vanish, fade away; (for-
inskes) dwindle (down), diminish, shrink; —
.n waste, be wasted, be consumed.
svinse wriggle; — **omkring** fiddle about; —
.. **svanse** wriggle along.
svinsk hoggish, piggish, swinish.
svint quick, nippy.
svintærend by-errand.
svipp (en) instant, moment; (snert) flick,
.nack; se ogs. **svipptur.**
svippe (fare) whisk, run; (slå lett) crack,
.ick.
svipptur trip, flying visit; **gjøre en** — take
trip.
svir riot and revel, dissipation, carousing;
it) var en ren — for ham was a real treat el.
.d-send to him.
svire revel, riot, carouse.
svire|bror reveller, rioter, carouser. **-gilde,**
.ag drinking-bout, carouse.
svirre whirl (round).
sviske prune, dried plum; **var vekk som en**
- was off like a lamplighter.
sviske|kompott damson cheese. **-prins** split-fig.
suppe plum-porridge.
svivøre disdain, hold in contempt.
svive spin round; hover; ramble, rove.
svoger brother-in-law. **svogerskap** affinity.
svolk bludgeon. **svolke** bang, thrash.
svor(d) (fleskesvor(d)) rind; (stekt) crackling.
svovel sulphur, brimstone; (i stenger) roll-
rimstone; **renset** — washed sulphur.
svovelaktig sulphureous, sulphurous.
svovelbad sulphureous bath, sulphur-bath.
svoveldamp sulphureous vapour.
svovel|fri free from sulphur. **-holdig** sulphu-
.eous, sulphuretted, sulphury.
svovel|kis pyrites. **-kjelde** sulphureous spring.
svovelregn rain of brimstone, sulphurous rain.
svovelsjø lake of fire and brimstone.
svovelsur sulphuric; **-t salt** sulphate; **-t bly,**
Inn sulphate of lead, tin.
svovel|syre oil of vitriol, sulphuric acid. **-syr-**
Ing sulphurous acid. **-vannstoff** sulphuretted
.ydrogen, hydrosulphuric acid, hydric sulphide.
svovle sulphur.
svovlet sulphurous, sulphureous.
I. **svull** (is-) ice, ice-fall.
II. **svull** (hevelse) gathering, swelling, tumor.
.finger, se **verkefinger.**
svullen swelled, swoln, tumid, turgid.
svulme swell; — **opp** swell (out).
svulne swell, become swoln.
svulst (sykelig hevelse) tumour; (oppstyltet
.ale) bombast, turgidity.
svulstig bombastic, turgid.
svulstighet (oppstyltet tale) bombast, tur-
.idity.
svær heavy, ponderous; (om person) big,
.uge; (fig) hard, grievous; difficult; — **sjø**
. heavy sea; **-e sår** grievous wounds; **-e tap**
.eavy losses; **-t tømmer** massive timber; **-e**
.enger a lot of money; **svært** (adv) exceedingly,
.mmensely, hugely.
sværlemmet large-limbed.
sværvekt (om bryter) heavy-weight.
svøm: legge på — start swimming.

svøm|me swim; **hun -te i tårer** she was
bathed in tears; — **i blod** welter in blood;
-mende swimming, afloat; **-mende ladning**
(merk) floating cargo.
svømme|anstalt, se **-skole. -belte** swimming
girdle, lifebelt, life-buoy, life-preserver. **-ben**
natatory leg. **-blære** (hos fisk) swim. **-bukser**
bathing-trousers el. **-drawers. -finne** fin. **-fot**
webbed foot; **forsynt med -føtter** web-footed,
palmiped. **-fugl** web-footed bird, swimmer.
-hinne, -hud web; **med** — webbed; **uten** — not
webbed. **-lærer** swimming-master.
svømmer swimmer.
svømme|sele swimming-rope. **-skole** swim-
ming-school. **-tur** swim. **svømning** swimming.
svøp swaddle, swaddling-cloth.
svøpe (om barn) swaddle, swathe; (om en
hvilken som helst gjenstand) wrap; — **inn**
wrap up.
I. **sy** sew, do sewing, stitch; — **en kjole** make
a gown; la — **en frakk til seg** have a coat made;
— **i en knapp** sew on a button; **hun -r godt**
she is a good needle-woman; — **på noe** be
sewing st., be at work on st.
II. **sy** (bordkle) wainscot.
sybaritt sybarite. **sybarittisk** sybaritical.
sybord work-table.
sydame needle-woman, seamstress.
syde seethe, boil.
Syden (de sydlige land) the South. **sydfrukt**
fruit of the South. **Sydhavet** the South Sea.
sydhavsøyene the South Sea Islands. **Sydis-**
havet the Antarctic Ocean. **Sydkorset** the
Southern Cross. **sydlandsk** southern.
sydlending southerner, inhabitant of the South.
sydlig South, southerly, southern; **i det -e**
England in the South of England; — **bredde**
south latitude; (adv) towards the south, to the
southward. **sydligst** southmost.
Sydpolen the South pole, the Antarctic Pole.
S-polarhavet the Antarctic Ocean, the South
Polar Sea. **-stat** Southern state. **-vest** south
west; (hodeplagg) south-wester.
syerske needle-woman, seamstress.
syk (bare som predikatsord) ill; (med etterfølg.
substantiv) sick; (i mindre grad) indisposed;
(særl. om ting og legemsdeler) diseased; **-e sick**
people; **en** — a sick person, a patient; **bli** —
be taken ill, fall ill; **ligge** — be ill in bed.
sykdom illness, sickness, disease, disorder,
malady; (mindre betyd.) complaint; (mest om
dyr) distemper; (om planter; om sinnet) disease.
syke disease; **engelsk** — the rickets.
syke|attest sick-certificate. **-besøk** visit to a
patient. **-hjelp** medical attendance. **-hjem**
asylum for invalids. **-hus** infirmary. **-leie** bed
of sickness, sick-bed, confinement; **ligge på -t**
keep one's bed, be confined to one's bed. **sykelig**
sickly, infirm, morbid, ailing, valetudinarian.
sykelighet sickliness, morbidness, bad health,
ill-health. **syke|liste** sick-list. **-passer** male nur-
se, man nurse; (soldat) hospital orderly. **-pleie**
nursing of el. attendance on the sick. **-pleier(ske)**
(female) nurse. **-seddel** sick-ticket. **-stol** invalid
chair. **-stue** ward (of an infirmary). **-vatt** medicated cotton-wool. **-vogn** (fra hospital etc.) ambulance. **-værelse** sick-room.
sykkel cycle, bicycle, (dt) bike; **ri** — ride on
bicycle, cycle, bike. **-lykt** cycle-lamp. **-rytter**
cyclist. **-styre** handlebar.
sykle cycle, bicycle, (dt) bike.
syklist cyclist, wheelman, bicyclist.
syklon cyclone.
syklus cycle.
sykmeldt reported ill.
sykne sicken; — **hen** languish, droop.
sykofant sycophant.
sy|korg, -kurv work-basket.
syl awl. **sylblad** (plante) awlwort.
sylfe sylph. **sylfide** sylphid.
sylinder cylinder. **-formet, -formig** cylindri-

form. **–gang** (urm.spr., mots. ankergang) cylinder escapement. **–ur** lever watch. **sylindrisk** cylindric(al).
syllogisme syllogism.
sylspiss (adj) pointed like a shoemaker's awl; (subst) point of a sh.-'s a.
sylte (vrb) preserve; (i sukker) conserve, candy; (i salt el. eddik) pickle.
sylte (subst) brawn, pickled pork, potted ham. **sylte|krukke** pickle-pot, preserve jar, jamjar. **–labb** pickled hog's-foot. **–lake** pickle, souse.
syltetøy sweetmeats, jam; preserves.
syltetøyskrukke jam-pot.
sylting preserving, pickling.
sylønn pay for sewing.
symaskin sewing machine.
symbol symbol. **symbolikk** symbolism.
symbolisere symbolize.
symbolsk symbolic(al).
symfoni symphony.
symfonisk symphonic, symphonious.
symmetri symmetry.
symmetrisk symmetrical.
sympati sympathy. **sympatisere** sympathize; **de som –r med ham** his sympathizers. **sympatisk** congenial, sympathetic.
sympatistreik sympathetic strike.
sympatiuttalelse expression of sympathy.
symptom symptom.
symre anemone; se **blå- og hvit-**.
syn sight, eyesight, (faculty of) vision, eye(s); (noe man ser eller betrakter) sight, spectacle; (synsforretning) survey, view, inspection; (innbilt syn) apparition; vision; **–er** (pl) visions; **ha skarpt —** be sharp-sighted; **miste –et** lose one's eyesight; **— for** an eye for; **tape av –e** lose sight of; **ute av –e** out of sight; **i –e** in sight.
synagoge synagogue.
synd sin; **–en** (i alm.) sin; **det er —** (skade) it is a pity; **det er — på ham** he is to be pitied; **lot ham ikke dø i –en** did not let him off so easily.
synde sin.
synde|bukk scapegoat. **–fall** fall (of man).
syndefull sinful.
synder sinner. **synderegister** list of sins. **synderinne** (female) sinner.
synderlig particular; (adv) particularly; **har ikke — lyst** have no great mind; **ikke — very** little, not greatly, not particularly.
syndflod deluge, flood.
syndfri free from sin.
syndig sinful, wicked. **syndighet** sinfulness.
syndikal|isme Syndicalism. **–ist** Syndicalist. **–istisk** syndicalistic.
syndikat syndicate.
syndsbevissthet consciousness of one's sins.
syndsforlatelse remission of sins.
syne (vise) show; (besiktige) inspect; (om liksynsmann) sit upon, view.
synes (finne) think, find; (ha utseende av) seem, appear; **det — så** so it seems; **som De — as you please;** — **om** like; **som det —** apparently.
synge sing; **— fore** lead off; **— med** join in the singing; **— etter noter** sing by note, from notes.
syngemåte manner of singing.
synge|skole singing-school. **–stykke** opera.
I. **sy(n)ing** sewing; (søm) seam.
II. **syning** inspection; (om liksyn) inquest.
synke (vt) (svelge) swallow; (vi) (falle ned) sink; (om jord o. l.) subside; (litt etter litt) settle (down); (om vannstand, barom.) fall, go down; **skipet er sunket** the ship is gone down; **— i kne** sink down; **— sammen** settle; **hans mot sank** he became disheartened; **hun er sunket dypt** she is fallen very low.
synkeferdig in a sinking state el. condition.
synking sinking; foundering; subsidence, swallowing.
synkverv|e daze, dazzle; hoodwink; **–ing** dazedness; optical delusion.

synlig visible; **bli — come into view.**
synode synod.
synonym (adj) synonymous; (subst) synonym
syns|evne (power of) vision, sight. **–forretning** inspection, survey. **synsk** visionary.
syns|kraft power of vision. **–krets, –linje** horizon. **–lære** optics. **–mann** surveyor, inspector. **–måte** view. **–nerve** optic nerve, visual nerve. **–organ** visual organ, organ of vision. **–punkt** point of view. **–rand** horizon. **–sans** sense of sight, eyesight. **–vidde** range of sight. **–vinkel** optic angle, visual angle.
syntaks syntax. **syntaktisk** syntactic(al).
synte|se synthesis. **–tisk** synthetic(al).
synål needle.
sypike seamstress. **sypose** work-bag, reticule.
sypress cypress.
I. **syre** acid; **— i magen** acidity in the stomach.
II. **syre** (plante) dock, sorrel.
syre (vrb) sour; **— deigen** leaven the dough.
syreholdig acidiferous.
syrer Syrian. **Syria** Syria.
syrin lilac.
syrisk Syrian.
syrlig sourish, subacid. **syrlighet** acidity.
sy|saker sewing materials. **–skrin** work-box.
sysle be busy, occupy oneself (with).
syssel avocation, occupation, business.
sysselmann district judge and revenue officer.
sysselsette busy, employ, occupy.
sysselsettelse employment, engagement.
system system; **sette i — reduce to a system.** **–atisere** systematize. **–atisk** systematic(al); (adv) systematically, on system.
systue sewing-room.
syt whimper, whine. **syte** whimper, whine.
sytråd sewing-thread.
sytten (tallord) seventeen. **–de** seventeenth.
sytti seventy. **–ende** seventieth. **–åring** septuagenarian.
sytøy needle-work, sewing.
syv, se sju.
sæd seed; (frøkorn, såkorn) grain; (korn, voksende el. høstet) crop; (hos mennesker og dyr) semen, sperm.
sæd|flod pollution, involuntary discharge of semen. **–kanal** seminiferous vessel. **–kjertel** spermatic gland. **–legeme** spermatozoid.
sæl (adj) delighted, happy; blessed; **heil og —!** all hail and welcome!
sælde (i såld) sift (meal) **sælding** sifting.
sælebot an act of charity, a humane deed.
sær (gretten) cross, naggy.
særavhandling monograph.
særdeles particularly, peculiarly.
særdeleshet: i — in particular, especially.
særegen peculiar, special, particular.
særegenhet peculiarity, particularity.
særeie separate property.
særinteresser peculiar interests.
særkjenne characteristic, distinctive feature.
særlig separate, distinct; (særegen) especial, particular. **særling** whimsical person, excentric p. **sær|lov** by-law. **–preg** distinctive stamp. **–rettighet** particular privilege. **særskilt** separate, distinct; (adv) separately.
sær|syn phenomenon, prodigy. **–trykk** deprint, reprint.
sødme sweetness.
I. **søke** seek, search for, look for, be in search of; (gå ofte til) resort to, patronize, frequent, attend; **(— å)** endeavour, try, seek (to); (ansøke om) apply for; **dra ut for å — arbeid** go in search of work; **jeg har søkt ham flere ganger** I have called on him several times; **— hen til** resort to; **— hjelp hos en** apply to one for assistance; **— om** solicit, apply for; **— ut** pick out, single out; select; (å komme ut) move out, make off.
II. **søke** (om hund) quarter, quest.
søker seeker, searcher; (på fotografiapparat) finder.

søking search, searching, seeking.
søkk dent, hollow, incavation.
søkke (vrb), se synke og senke.
søkke (subst) sink, sinker, lead.
søkkemyr sinking slough.
søkk|rik superlatively rich. -våt drenched, soaked.
søknad petition, suit, supplication, application.
søknedag week-day.
søkning seeking, etc.; (f. eks. til kafé) custom, patronage, run of customers; (etterspørsel) demand, request.
søksmål prosecution, lawsuit.
søkt (om uttrykk) far-fetched. Se søke.
søl dirt, dirtiness; spill, slop, mess.
søle (subst) mire, mud; slush.
søle (vrb) soil, dirty; (slå ned) make slops; plaske) dabble, splash; — på bordet make a ness on the table. — seg til make a mess of oneself.
søle|bøtte dirt-barrel. -føre dirty el. muddy walking. -pytt puddle. -skvett splash of dirt el. mud. sølet miry, muddy.
sølibat celibacy.
sølje (smykke) filigree brooch.
sølv silver; rent — pure silver; innfatte i — set in silver; beslå med — tip with silver.
sølv- (i sms.) silver.
sølvaktig silvery.
sølv|alder silver-age. -arbeid silver-work.
sølvarbeider worker in silver, silver-smith.
sølv|barre silver-bar. -beslag silver-mounting. -beslått silver-mounted. -blikk plate silver.
sølv|bryllup silver wedding. -dåse silver-box.
sølvglød litharge.
sølv|erts silver-ore. -fot (mynt) silver standard. -gaffel silver-fork. -glans (metall) silver glance. -gruve silver-mine. -holdig argentiferous. -holdighet amount of silver. -kjede silver hain. -klar (bekk el. vann) limpid, pellucid; -klar stemme silver(-toned) voice. -mine silver mine. -mynt silver-coin. -nål silver-pin. -oppøsning solution of silver. -papir silver-tissue. -penger silver, silver-coins, silver-money. -plett plated silver. -prøve assay of silver. -rev silver fox. -rik rich in silver. -saker silver things. -servise service of plate. -skap plate-press. -skei. -skje silver spoon. -skjær silvery lustre. -smed silver-smith. -tråd silver-thread; (ompunnet med sølv) silverwire. -tøy plate, silver. -verdi intrinsic value.
I. søm (spiker) nail.
II. søm (sammensying) seam; (kanting) hem; (botan.) suture.
sømfare (egtl.) inspect the nails of an implement; (fig) overhaul narrowly, minutely examine.
I. sømme (f. eks. et tørkle) hem.
II. sømme seg be becoming, be proper, be decent; — seg for en become, beseem, befit one.
sømmelig becoming, beseeming, decent.
sømmelighet decency, decorum, propriety, suitableness. -følelse a sense of decency. av sømmelighetshensyn for decency's sake.
søndag Sunday, Sabbath; om -en on Sundays, of a Sunday; på -en — on Sunday, next Sunday; forrige — last Sunday.
søndags|barn Sunday-child. -hvile Sunday rest. -jeger make-believe sportsman, would-be sportsman. -klær Sunday-clothes, holiday-clothes. -rytter unskilful rider. -skole Sunday school. -stas (dt.) Sunday best.
sønder (i stykker): — og sammen to bits, to fragments.
sønderjyde South-Jutlander.
Sønderjylland South-Jutland
sønder|knuselse contriteness: contrition. -knust crushed (to pieces). -lemme anatomize; (sønderrive) dismember.
sønder|rive tear asunder, rend asunder, lacerate; (fig) affect deeply with grief; med -revne hjerter broken-hearted.

søndre (sydlige) southern, south.
søndre (vrb) sever. søndring disunion.
sønn son.
sønna South, southern, southerly. -drag a slant of southerly wind. -fjells in the South (of Norway). -fjelsk southern. -for south of. -fra from the south.
sønna|storm southerly gale. -vind south wind.
sønne|barn (pl) son's children, grand-children. -datter son's-daughter, grand-daughter. -kone son's wife, daughter-in-law. -løs sonless.
sønnen|fra, se sønnafra. -om south of.
sønne|sønn grandson. -sønnsdatter great-granddaughter. -sønnssønn great-grandson.
sønnlig filial.
søppel sweepings; riff-raff; rubbish.
søppel|brett dust-pan. -haug dust-heap. -kasse dust-bin. -vogn dust- el. rubbish-cart.
sør south; — for south of; vinden blåser fra — the wind blows south; — til ost, S. t. O. South by East, S. b. E.; S. t. V. S. b. W. etc.
Sør|Amerika South America. s-banen the Southern railway.
sørende south end. Sør-England the south of England. sør for South of, to the South of. sørfra from the South. Sør-Frankrike South-France.
sørge grieve (at el. for), sorrow, mourn (for); — for (ta sig av) take care of, provide for; — for seg selv shift for oneself; — for at see that; — for å take care to.
sørge|budskap sorrowful message. -dikt funeral elegy, dirge. -drakt mourning-suit el. dress. -fest, se -høytid. -flor mourning-crape, black band. -hus house of mourning. -høytid funeral feast. -kledd dressed in mourning.
sørgelig sad, tragical, distressful, dolorous; i en — grad sadly.
sørgemarsj funeral march, dead march. sørgende mourner.
sørge|pil weeping willow. -rand: med — edged in black. -spill tragedy. -tid mourning-time. -tog funeral procession. -år year of mourning.
sørgmodig sad, sorrowful.
sørgmodighet sadness, sorrowfulness.
sørgående going south.
sørkyst south coast.
Sørlandet the South (of Norway). sør|landsk southern. -lending southerner.
sørlig South, southerly, southern; i det -e England in the South of England; — bredde south latitude; (adv) towards the south, to the southward. sørligst southmost.
sør|ost south-east. -ostlig south-east, south-eastern; (adv) to(wards) the south-east. -ostvind south-east wind. -over south-ward.
sørpe sludge, slush.
sør|vest south-west. -vestvind South-western.
søsken brother and sister, brothers and sisters; fem — a family of five.
søskenbarn cousin, first cousin.
søster sister. -barn sister's children, nephews and nieces. -datter sister's daughter, niece.
søsterlig sisterly.
søstermann sister's husband, brother-in-law.
søsterpart (jur) sister's share of an inheritance.
søsterskap sisterhood.
søsterskip duplicate vessel.
søstersønn sister's son, nephew.
søt sweet; (om person) dear, charming; så er du — that's a dear.
søt|aktig sweetish. -het sweetness. -laten bland.
søvn sleep; i søvne — a light sleep, a slumber; falle i — fall asleep; falle i dyp — fall fast asleep; vugge en i — rock one to sleep; dysse en i — lull one asleep; vekke en av -e awaken one out of his sleep; i -e asleep, sleeping, in one's sleep; gå i -e walk in one's sleep; snakke i -e talk in one's sleep.
søvndrukken drowsy, sleep-charged.

søvndyssende soporific, somniferous, narcotic; — **middel** soporific.

søvngjenger somnambulist, sleep-walker.

søvngjengeri somnambulism, sleep-walking.

søvngretten cross from sleepiness.

søvnig sleepy, drowsy. **søvnighet** sleepiness.

søvnløs sleepless; **jeg ligger mye** — I am a bad sleeper.

søvnløshet sleeplessness, insomnia.

søvntung heavy with sleep.

søye ewe.

søyle pillar, column; (voltaisk) pile. **-fot** base of a column el. pillar, pedestal. **-gang** colonnade. **-hall** columnated el. pillared hall; portico. **-helgen** stylite.

så (vrb) sow; seed; disseminate.
I. **så** (stort kar) tub (esp. to be carried by two persons).
II. **så** (på korn) fibril, (chip el. scale) of bran.

så (adv: derpå) then; (adv: altså, følgelig) so; (adv: således) so, thus; (adv: i høy grad) so; (sammenlikning uttrykkes etter nektelse ved) so (med etterfølgende: as); (sammenlikning: så-som) as (med etterfølgende: as); (konj: så at) so that; **først de store,** — **de små** first the great, then the little; — **kunne han ikke komme** he could not come; **jeg er** — **glad over å høre det** I am so glad to hear it; **når det er** — **such** being the case; **om** — **var** if such were the case, if so; — **lala** so—so; — **å si** as it were, so to speak; **de var klokere enn som** — they were wiser than all that; (ja) — indeed? yes? (adjektivisk) **i** — **fall** in this el. that case, if so; (hvor) — **gjerne jeg enn snakker med ham,** — **kan han aldri** . . . much as I like to speak with him, he can never . . .; **bøker,** — **ypperlige de enn er** books, however excellent; (utrop) —, **nå er det nok** there now, that's enough, that will do; **se** —! there! — **hør da** only hear; (foran adj og adv) **for** — **og** — **mye pr. pund** at so much the pound; **han er** — **syk at** . . . he is so ill, that . . .; — **galt er det da ikke** it is not so (el. as) bad as that; — **noenlunde** rather; — **bortimot** well nigh; **en mann av** — **stor fortjeneste** a man of such great merit; — **mange,** — **lite,** — **få som mulig** as many, as little, as few as possible; — **lenge** (som) **han lever** as long as he is alive; — **godt som** as good as, virtually, next thing to; **det er** — **godt som avgjort** it is all but settled; — **vidt jeg vet** as far as I know; — **uskyldig som et barn** as innocent as a child; **den er ikke** — **god som den burde være** it is not so good as it ought to be; **vær** — **snild å** . . . be so kind as to . . .; (ettersaming) **når jeg ser ham igjen,** — **skal**

jeg ikke glemme det when I see him aga[ ] I shall not forget it; **gi meg boka,** — **skal j** lese **for deg** give me the book, and I shall re[ ] to you; — **er du snill** there is a dear; om if (even).

sådan such; **en** — **mann** such a man; — folk such people; **noe -t** such a thing.

så|framt, -fremt provided, granted that.

såkalt so-called, as it is called.

såkorn seed-corn.

såld (grovt) cribble, riddle.

såle (fotsåle, såle på skotøy) sole.

såle (vrb) sole; — **og flikke** sole and he (el. tap).

således so, thus, in this manner, like th[ ] like that; **men** — **forholdt det seg** but the fa[ ] was so.

såle|gjenger plantigrade. **-lær** bend-leathe[ ] sole-leather. **-spar** (boot-)saver.

så lite as little, so little.

så|mann sower. **-maskin** sowing-machine.

så menn indeed, really.

så mye so much, (pekende) thus much; heller, — **mer** so much the more; — **mer so** the more so because; — **mindre** so much t[ ] less; — **mindre som** the less so because.

sånn (jfr. sådan) such; (således) so, thu[ ] **sånt noe som** something like; **eller noe så[ ]** or something like that; — **forholder det se** that's what it is; — **går det i verden tha[ ]** the way of the world; **det er sånt som man si[ ]** it is a conventional expression.

så nær som except, wanting, barring.

såpass so; sufficient.

såpe soap. **såpe** (vrb): — **inn** soap. **såpe|bob[ ]** soapbubble. **-koker** soapboiler. **-kokeri** soa[ ] -manufactory. **-kost** shaving-brush. **-skum** lathe[ ] **-vann** suds.

sår (subst) wound; ulcer.

sår (adj) sore; painful; (fig) sensitive, th[ ] -skinned.

sår|bar vulnerable. **-beint** foot-sore.

såre wound; hurt, injure; (fig) hurt one[ ] feelings; **sårende** painful, cruel; harsh, mort[ ] fying.

sår|feber wound-fever. **-lege** surgeon.

sårt (adv) sorely.

så sant as truly as, as sure as.

så snart as soon as, on -ing.

såte (subst) cock, rick. **såte** (vrb) cock.

såtid seed time, sowing season.

så vel . . . **som** as well . . . as. **så vidt** (som[ ] as far as; **for så vidt som** in so much as; s[ ] vidt mulig as far as possible; **såvidt** (knap[ ] barely, just, very narrowly.

T

T, t T, t.

ta take; (romme) contain, hold; (i betaling) charge; — **avskjed** take leave; — **ende** end, come to an end; — **eksamen** pass one's examination; — **fart** make way, make progress; — **plass** take a seat, sit down; — **skade** suffer damage; — **sete** take a seat; — **båten** go by the steamer; — **båten til H.** take the steamer for H.; **det tok oss fire timer** it took us four hours; — **seg nær av** take to heart; **han tok sin død av det** it was the death of him; — **noe lett** take st. easy; — **av** (forminskes) decrease; (i vekt, tykkelse) lose flesh; (i kortspill) cut; — **av bordet** clear the table; — **hatten av for** take off one's hat to, remove one's hat to, uncover to; — **livet av en** kill one; — **seg av interesse** oneself for; take charge of; — **for seg av rettene** help oneself to what is on the table;

— **noe fra en** deprive one of st.; — **fra hverands[ ]** take to pieces; — **fram** bring el. take ou[ ] produce; — **seg i vare** heed, take care; — e[ ] **i ed** swear one (in); — **i forsvar** defend; — **i hånden** shake hands with; — **i med lend** hand; — **saken i sin hånd** take the matter i[ ] hand; — **i seg** revoke, retract; **tok seg i d[ ]** stopped himself; — **igjen** take back; (innhente catch up, overtake; **ville ikke** — **imot har** would not see him; — **inn** (medisin) take physi[ ] — **inn på et hotell** put up at a hotel; — **inn** ballast take in ballast, ballast; — **med** take alon[ ] with one; **det må -s med i beregningen** it mus[ ] enter into the calculation; — **med seg** brin[ ] carry away; — **avskjed med** take leave of; — d[ ] **strengt med** stand upon; — **mot**, se — **imot**; — **opp** (noe som er falt ned) pick up; (noe som e[ ] sunket) recover, (skip) raise, lift; — **opp e[ ]**

aaske pick up a stitch; — **ille opp** take amiss, take unkindly; **kan — det opp med** is a match or; — **på seg klærne** put on one's clothes; — **på vei** take on; **det –r på kreftene** it is very exhausting; — **hardt på** handle roughly; — **en å ordet** take one at his word; — **seg sammen** ll oneself together; — **til** increase; begin; — **til ange** take prisoner; — **til hustru** take for one's ife; — **til bens** take to one's heels, cut and un, turn tail; — **til hatten** touch one's hat; — **til takke med** put up with, be satisfied with; — **noe til** busy oneself with something; — **øynene til seg** withdraw one's glance; — **til-ake** take back; (ord) revoke, retract; (om igjen) etake, recapture; — **ut (av banken)** withdraw; — **seg (komme seg)** improve; — **seg godt ut** ok el. show well; — **seg ut som** look like; — **under behandling** take in hand.

tabell table; **i -form** in a tabular form.
tabellarisk tabular.
table d'hote table d'hôte, ordinary.
tablett (liten plate) tablet.
tablå picture, tableau.
tabu taboo; **erklære for** — taboo.
taburett tabouret, stool; (fig) seat in the ca-inet.
tafatt awkward, ungainly.
taffel table; **stort** — grand dinner.
taffelberg table-bluff. **T-et** Table Mountain.
taffelformet square.
taffel|musikk music at dinner. **-ur** time-piece, able-clock, bracket-clock.
tafs rag, tatter; tuft el. wisp of hair.
tafset ragged, tattered.
taft taffeta, taffety.
tagal silent, taciturn.
tagg jag; (på metalltråd) barb.
tagget toothed, jagged, indented; barbed.
tagl hair of a horse's mane or tail.
tagne fall silent, hush.
I. tak (med hånd) grasp, hold, gripe, grip; med klo) clutch; (med åre) stroke; (dyst) cuffle; **ta et — i** take hold of; **take a pull of; lippe -et** let go one's hold; **hogge — i** snatch old of.
II. tak (på hus) roof; (i værelse) ceiling; strå-hatch; tegl- tiling; **skifer-** slated roof; **tekke t — med strå, teglstein, skifer** thatch, tile, late a roof; **legge — roof; ta -et av** unroof; nder — under shelter el. cover. **tak|bjelke** ie-beam. **-drypp** drip from the roof. **-halm** hatch.
I. takk thanks; —! thanks! thank you! **mange –! tusen** —! many thanks! thank you very much! nin **beste** — my best thanks; **ja** —! **jo** —! if you) please! **nei** —! no, thank you! thank ou, I'd rather not; **skylde en — for** be much bliged to one for; **si en** — thank one, give one hanks; **jeg sier — for meg** I declare off; **med — motta** noe) gratefully, thankfully; **ta til -e ned hva huset formår** take pot-luck; **det er en** (man har)! there is gratitude!
II. takk (på horn) antler.
takkammer garret.
takke thank, give thanks; **idet jeg på for-ånd -r Dem** thanking you in anticipation; **det an De — Dem selv for** (det er Deres egen kyld) you may thank yourself for that; **takket være** thanks to, owing to; — **av** resign.
takke (til bakst) baxter, griddle.
takke|brev letter of thanks. **-bønn** prayer of hanksgiving.
takkel (runner-)tackle. **takkelasje rigging.**
takket crenate(d), dentate.
takknemlig grateful, thankful.
takknemlighet gratitude, thankfulness.
takknemlighetsgjeld: stå i — til en owe ne a debt of gratitude.
takksigelse thanksgiving.
takkskyldig obliged, indebted
takle rig. **takling** rigging.

tak|luke eyelet-hole. **-papp** carton-pierre (for roofing), asphalt paper. **-renne** roof-gutter. **-rygg** (møne) ridge.
taksameter taximeter.
taksasjon valuation, appraisement; estimate.
taksasjonspris estimated value.
taksator valuer. **taksere** value, appraise. — **om** value over again, revalue.
tak|skjegg eaves. **-spon** shingle.
takst rate, estimated value; set price.
takstein tile.
takstre yew, yew-tree.
takt time; (avdeling i musikk) bar, measure; (finfølelse) tact, discretion; **holde, slå takten** keep, beat time; **⁴/₈ takt ⁴/₈** measure.
tak|tekker slater. **-tekking** slating.
taktfast measured, regularly timed, steady.
takt|full discreet. **-fullhet** tact, discretion.
taktiker tactician. **taktikk** tactics (pl).
taktisk tactical.
taktløs indiscreet, tactless, having no tact.
takt|løshet want of tact, indiscretion. **-slag** beat. **-stokk** baton. **-strek** bar (-line).
tak|vindu dormer-window; (i flukt med taket) sky-light. **-ås** roof-beam.
tal, se **tall** II.
talar robe, gown.
tale (vrb) speak; (samtale) speak, converse, discourse, talk; — **norsk, engelsk** speak Norwegian, English; **-r for** (tyder på) goes to show el. prove; **det -r høyt for** it speaks volumes for; **sannheten -r for seg selv** truth will plead for itself; **han -r godt for seg** he is a fine speaker; **dette -r imot** this tells el. makes against; — **med en** (i alm.) see one, speak to one; **jeg må — under fire øyne med ham** I must speak in private with him; **hvem ønsker De å — med?** whom do you want to see? **De -r med John Smith** (presenta-sjon i telefon) it is John Smith speaking; **-r jeg med John Smith** (i telefon) is that you, John Smith? Are you John Smith? **for ikke å — om** to say nothing of, not to mention, let alone, letting alone; **siden vi -r om** talking of; **jeg har ikke hørt — om det** I have not heard of it; — **sammen** talk togheter, converse; — **ved møtet** speak at el. address the meeting.
talende expressive, significant, suggestive; **den — the** speaker.
tale (subst) speech; (det som sies) speech, talk, discourse; **holde en — make** a speech, deliver an address, oration, (geistlig) sermon; **hun holdt en hel — she** made quite a speech; **han er vanskelig å få i — he** is difficult of access; **det kan ikke være — om** that is out of the question.
taleferdighet fluency.
talefrihet liberty of speech.
tale|gaver oratorical powers el. endowments, rhetorical gifts. **-kunst** art of speaking, oratory.
talemetoden the articulation system.
talemåte mode of expression, phrase; **bare -r** phrases, mere words.
talent talent, faculty, natural gift, natural endowment; accomplishment; **det er en mann med — he** is a talented man, he is a man of talent(s).
talentfull talented, gifted. **talentløs** without talent(s). **talentløshet** want of talent(s).
taler speaker, orator. **taleredskap** organ of speech. **taler|knep** oratorical artifice. **-stol** pul-pit. **talerør** speaking-pipe el. tube; (ropert) speaking-trumpet.
talespråk spoken language; **det engelske — spoken** English. **talestemme** speaking voice.
talg tallow; (nyre-) suet.
talg|lys tallow-candle. **-tit** tomtit.
talisman talisman.
I. talje (heiseinnretning) purchase, tackle.
II. talje (liv) waist.
talkum talcum.
I. tall (furu) red fir, Norway (or red, Scotch) pine.

II. **tall** number, figure; **like, jevne** — even numbers; **ulike, odde** — odd numbers; **i hundre-, i tusen-**, by hundreds, by thousands.
tallerken plate; **dyp** — soup-plate; **flat** — meat-plate; **en** — **suppe** a plateful of soup.
tallerken|rekke dish-shelf, dish-catch, plate-rack.
tallord numeral. **tallrekke** numeral series.
tallrik numerous; **være -ere enn** outnumber.
tall|skive (clock's) face; dial-plate. **-størrelse** number, numeric quantity. **-system** numerical system. **-tegn** numeral character el. figure. **-verdi,** se **-størrelse.**
talløs numberless, countless.
talmigull talmy-gold, Abyssinian gold.
talmud talmud. **-isk** talmudistic.
talong (på obligasjon) counterfoil.
talsmann spokesman, advocate.
tam tame; (bare om dyr) domesticated; **den -me gås** the domestic goose; **gjøre** — (fig) make tractable, manageable.
tamarind tamarind.
tambak tombac, pinch-beck, Bath metal.
tambur (trommeslager) drummer.
tamburin (håndtromme) tambourine.
tamburmajor drum-major.
tamhet tameness.
tamp end, rope's end; (strafferedskap) colt; **få** — get flogged; (fig) **en lang** — a big, thumping fellow; **-en brenner** (fig) we are getting very near the mark.
tampe beat with a rope's end.
tampong (i sykepleie) tampon, plug (of lint).
tandem (sykkel til to) tandem.
tander (fr. tendre) delicate.
tane (vrb), se **løpe.**
I. **tang** (redskap) (pair of) tongs; (liten tang) (pair of) nippers, (pair of) pincers; (leges) forceps.
II. **tang** (plante) sea-weed, tangle, (sea-)tang. **-art** species of sea-weed.
tange spit el. tongue (of land);(på kniv o.l.) tang.
tangens tangent.
tangent tangent; (på piano) key, note.
tangere touch, be tangent to; **-nde** tangent.
tango (dans) the Tango.
tank (beholder, f. eks. i bil; panserbil) tank.
tanke thought, idea; **samle -ne sine** compose el. collect one's thoughts; **-r er tollfrie** thoughts go free; **kjøttet har en** — the meat is touched; **den fri** — free thought; **en** — **av** a suspicion of; **i mine -r er det riktig** in my opinion it is right; **i -n** in idea; **falle i -r** fall into a revery; **stå i -r** be in a brown study; **han har svært høye -r om seg selv** he has a very high opinion of himself; **bare -n (på)** the mere idea (of); **jeg kom på den** — the thought struck me; **komme på andre -r** change one's mind.
tankeeksperiment mere supposition; **som et** — for argument's sake.
tanke|flukt flight of thought. **-forbindelse** association of ideas. **-full** thoughtful, pensive, thought-laden. **-fullhet** thoughtfulness, pensiveness. **-gang** train of ideas, chain of reasoning. **-lek,** se **-spill. -leser** thought-reader. **-lesning** thought-reading. **-liv** meditative el. contemplative life. **-laus, -løs** thoughtless, unthinking, unreasoning, scatter-brained. **-løshet, -løyse** thoughtlessness. **-overføring** thought-transference. **-rik** teeming el. abounding with thought. **-rikdom** abundance el. richness of thoughts. **-riktig** logical. **-riktighet** logic. **-sett** way of thinking. **-spill** witty conceit, witticism, joke. **-sprang** skip of thought, abrupt el. sudden transition of thought. **-språk** apothegm, device. **-strek** dash. **-stridig** contradictory, illogical. **-tom** void of thought, fatuous. **-tomhet** fatuity. **-utveksling** exchange of thought. **-vekkende** suggestive, full of suggestion, thought-producing, thought-compelling. **-vekt** weightiness. **-vektig** weighty, profound, full of thought. **-verden** ideal world. **-øvelse** excercise of thought.

tankskip tanker.
tann tooth; (på rive, kam, gaffel osv.) tooth; prong; tine; (på hjul) cog, tooth; **få tenner** cut teeth; **trekke ut en** — draw a tooth; **tidens** — the tooth of time, the ravages of time; **holde** — **for tunge** keep one's own counsel; **ha vondt for tenner** suffer from teething; **skjære tenner** grind the teeth, gnash the teeth; **tennene mine løper i vann** my mouth waters.
tann|brudd teeth-cutting, dentition, teething. **-byll** gumboil. **-børste** tooth-brush.
tanne (på lys) snuff, cabbage-head; **slokke den rykende** — quench the smoking flax.
tann|felling shedding el. changing of teeth. **-formet** denticulate, dentate. **-gard** row of teeth.
tann|hjul cog-wheel, toothed wheel. **-hjuls-utveksling** toothed gearing.
tannin (garvestoff) tannin.
tann|kitt filling for teeth. **-kjøtt** gum. **-lyd** dental sound. **-lege** dentist, dental surgeon. **-legekunst** dentistry.
tannløs toothless. **tannløshet** toothlessness.
tann|middel remedy for tooth-ache. **-pasta** tooth paste. **-pine** tooth-ache. **-pulver** tooth-powder, dentifrice. **-sett** set of teeth. **-setting** dentition, teething, cutting of the teeth. **-skifte,** se **-felling. -stang** rack. **-stikker** tooth-pick. **-uttrekking** tooth-drawing.
tann|vann tooth-water. **-verk** tooth-ache.
tant trumpery, vanity, nonsense.
tantalisere tantalize.
tantaluskvaler the torments of Tantalus.
tante aunt.
tantieme percentage, commission.
tap loss; **bringe meg stort** — leave me a heavy loss; **lide** — suffer el. sustain a loss; **under** — **av** under pain of losing.
tape lose; **— motet** lose heart; **— av syne** lose sight of; **gå tapt** be lost; **gi tapt** give in el. up, knock under; **— seg** (om toner) die away; (om farger) fade; (bli dårligere) deteriorate; **hun har tapt seg meget** she has fallen off very much; **den tapende** the loser.
tapet hanging; (med vevde figurer) tapestry; (papirs-) paper, paper-hangings, wall-paper; **bringe på -et** bring upon the carpet; **være på -et** be upon the carpet.
tapet|dør jib-door. **-fabrikk** manufactory of paper-hangings. **-maker** paper-stainer. **-mønster** pattern of hangings. **-papir** wall-paper.
tapetsere hang, tapestry; paper. **tapetserer** paperhanger; upholsterer. **tapetsering** papering.
tapioka tapioca.
tapir tapir.
tapp tap, faucet, spigot; (i snekkerarbeid) tenon.
tappe tap, draw; (snekk.) tenon, mortise.
tappenstrek tattoo, drumbeat.
tapper brave, valiant, valorous, gallant; **holde seg** — stand to one's guns.
tapperhet bravery, valour, gallantry.
tapp|kran faucet and spigot. **-lager** axle box. **-rifle** pillar-breech, rifle-musket.
tapsliste list of killed and wounded.
tara (vekt av emballasje) tare.
I. **tarantell** (en art edderkopp) tarantula.
II. **tarantell** (dansen) tarantella.
tararegning tare-account.
tare (tang) alga.
tarere (bestemme taraen av) tare.
tariff tariff. **sette opp** — tariff. **-bestemmelse** tariff ratings. **-sats** tariff rate.
tarlatan (lett bomullstøy) tarlatan.
tarm gut, intestine. **-betennelse** enteritis. **-brokk** enterocele. **-kanalen** the intestinal canal el. tube. **-katarr** catarrh of the intestines. **-nett** caul. **-sekk** peritoneum. **-slyng** twist of a bowel, ileus. **-streng** cat-gut, gutstring.
tartar, -iet, se **tatar.**
tarv behoof, requirements; good, benefit;

vareta ens — look after el. attend to one's interests. **tarvelig** (i levemåte) frugal; (i klededrakt) plain, homely, modest; (simpel) common, ordinary; (fig) scanty, meagre. **tarvelighet** frugality; plainness; scantiness.
taske pouch, wallet; (til bøker o. l.) satchel.
taskekrabbe (høvring) pungar, crab-fish.
taskenspiller juggler, conjurer, prestidigitator. **-kunst** juggling el. conjuring trick, sleight of hand.
tasle walk slowly, toddle; patter.
tass (liten —) bungler, muff.
tasse, se **tasle**.
tast (tangent på klaver) key.
tatar Tartar, Tatar. **tatarisk** Tatarean.
tater gipsy. **-følge** gang of gipsies. **-jente** gipsy girl. **-kvinne** gipsy (woman). **-mål** Rom(m)any.
tatover|e tattoo; tattow. **-ing** tattoo; tattooing.
tau rope; (svært) cable. **-bane** funicular (railway).
taue (buksere) tow. **taukveil** becket el. coil of rope.
taus silent, hushed; (av vane) taciturn, silent, reticent; (som ikke røper hemmeligheter) discreet.
taushet silence; taciturnity; secrecy; **en forventningsfull** — a hush of expectation; **bryte -en** break silence; **bringe til** — silence, still; **under -sløfte** under the promise of secrecy; **-splikt** professional secrecy.
tauverk cordage, rope(s).
tavle (av marmor) table (of marble); (av kopper, bly osv.) plate, sheet; (av tre) board; (til å skrive på) slate; (vegg-) black-board.
tavle|kritt crayon. **-regning** reckoning el. figuring on the slate. **-skifer** slate.
tavlet chequered; (golv) parqueted.
tavto|logi tautology. **-logisk** tautologic(al).
te tea; **drikke** — take el. have tea; **skjenke** — pour out tea; **lage** — make tea; **en kopp** — a cup of tea; **-en er på bordet** tea is ready; **te** (vise) show, display; **— seg** bear oneself, behave.
teaktre teak, teaktree; teak(-wood).
teater theatre, play-house; (skueplass) stage; **være i -et** be at the play; **gå i -et** go to the play.
teater|billett playticket. **-direktør** theatrical manager. **-effekt** stage-effect. **-forestilling** theatrical performance. **-gal** stage-struck. **-gjenger** theatre-goer, play-goer. **-kikkert** opera-glass. **-konfekt** fudge. **-kontrollør** box-keeper. **-kritiker** dramatic critic. **-kup** clap-trap. **-liv** theatrical life. **-maler** scene-painter. **-plakat, -program** play-bill. **-sensor** licenser of plays. **-sesong** theatrical season. **-sjef**, se **-direktør**. **-skurk** stage villain. **-stykke** (stage) play. **-tjeneste** stage duty. **-vesen** theatricals (pl).
teatralsk theatrical, stagy.
teavl cultivation of tea.
te|blad tea-leaf. **-bord** tea-table. **-boks** tea canister. **-brett** tea-board, tea-tray. **-brød** tea-cake. **-busk** tea shrub, tea plant, tea-tree.
teddybjørn Teddy bear.
tedeum Te Deum.
te|duk tea-cloth. **-dåse** tea-caddy.
teft scent, (om hund) ogs. nose; **fin** — a nice scent; **få -en av** get scent of, have wind of; **de har hatt på -en** . . . have detected by instinct el. intuitively.
tege bug.
tegl (til tak) tile; (til murarbeid) brick.
tegl|brenner brick-maker, tile-maker. **-jord** tile- el. brick-clay. **-lagt** paved with bricks. **-ovn** tile-kiln, brick-kiln. **-stein**, se **tegl. -steins-golv** brick-floor. **-tak** tile roof. **-tekker** tiler. **-verk** brick-manufactory.
tegn sign, mark, token, indication; (i sykd.) symptom; (ytring av noe) demonstration; (forvarsel) presage, forebode, omen; (som en

bærer på seg) badge; (billett) ticket, check; **— på el. til** sign of; **gjøre** — til en sign el. make signs to one; **gjorde** — til ham at han skulle sette seg motioned him to take a seat; **være et** — på be indicative of; **til** — på at as a proof that, in token that; **vise** — til show symptoms of.
tegne draw, design; (merke) mark; (gi utsikt til) promise; **— assuranse** effect insurance, take out insurance (**for, på**: for); **— en polise** effect a policy; **-t kapital** subscribed capital; **— etter naturen** draw from life el. nature; **— seg** subscribe, sign, give in one's name, put one's name down; (underskrive seg) sign, underwrite.
tegne|bestikk (case of) drawing instruments. **-bok** drawing-book; (lommebok) pocket-book. **-bord** drawing table. **-brett** drawing-board. **-kritt** drawing chalk. **-kunst** art of drawing. **-lærer, -mester** drawing-master. **-papir** drawing-paper, vellum-paper. **-penn** drawing-pen.
tegner drawer, designer, draughtsman.
tegne|sal designing-room. **-skole** drawing school. **-stift** drawing-pin. **-stump** stump, rubber. **-time** drawing lesson.
tegneundervisning drawing lessons (pl).
tegning drawing, sketching etc.; (kunsten) draughtsmanship; (konkret) drawing, design, sketch, draught; (av abonnement o. l.) subscription; (av assuranse) underwriting; (bot. og zool.) markings (pl).
tegn|setning punctuation. **-skrift** hieroglyphs (pl). **-språk** language of signs, sign language. **-system** system of signs el. signals. **-tyder** interpreter of signs. **-tydning** interpretation of signs.
te|handel tea-trade; (butikken) tea-shop. **-handler** tea-merchant; tea-dealer, teaman.
teiebær stone-bramble.
teig land, slip el. strip of a field. **-bytte** exchange of lands.
tein spindle.
tein (kjemisk stoff) theine; theina.
teine (hummer-) bow-net.
teint complexion, colour.
teisme Theism. **teist** theist. **teistisk** theistic(al).
tekanne tea-pot.
te|kasse tea-chest. **-kjele** tea-kettle.
tekke (vrb) roof; (med strå) thatch.
tekke (subst) grace, charm, attraction.
tekkelig agreable, sweet, attractive, winning, pleasing.
tekkes (ta til takke) put up with; (være til behag) please.
tekkespon shingle.
tekking el. **tekning** roofing, thatching.
tekniker technician. **teknikk** technics (pl); technique, technicalities. **teknisk** technic(al).
teknolog technologist. **teknologi** technology. **teknologisk** technologic(al).
tekopp tea-cup.
tekst text; (i musikk) words; **lese en -en** rebuke one, read one a lecture; **videre i -en!** go on! **anmerkning under -en** footnote.
tekstil|arbeider textile worker. **-industri** textile industry. **-varer** textiles.
tekstkritikk textual criticism.
tekstur texture.
tekstuttale articulation.
tele (frossen jord) ice in the ground, crust of frozen earth. **tele** (vrb) freeze.
telefon telephone; **det er — til Dem** the telephone for you, sir; you are wanted on the phone; **slå på -en** call one upon the telephone.
telefon|abonnenter clients of the telephone system. **-beskjed** telephone message. **-dame** woman telephonist.
telefonere telephone. **telefonisk** telephonic.
telefonist telephonist.
telefonistinne woman telephonist.
telefon|katalog telephone book, telephone directory. **-nummer** telephone number. **-oppringing** telephone call. **-samtale** telephone

conversation. **-sentral** central telephone exchange.

telegraf telegraph; wire; **per** — by telegraph. **telegraf|bestyrer** manager of a telegraph office. **-depesje** telegraphic despatch, message. **telegrafere** telegraph, message; wire; (med undersjøisk t.) cable (**om:** for). **telegrafi** telegraphy. **telegrafisk** telegraphic, by wire, by cable; — **utbetaling** cable-transfer. **telegrafist** telegraphist, telegraph clerk. **telegrafistinne** lady el. woman telegraphist. **telegraf|kabel** telegraph-cable. **-ledning, -linje** line (of telegraphs), telegraph. **-stolpe** telegraph pole. **-stasjon** telegraph station. **-tråd** telegraph **-vesen** telegraphic service.

telegram telegram, wire. **-adresse** telegraphic address. **-befordring** transmission of telegrams. **telegramblankett** telegraph form.

teleløsning thaws of spring. **teleologi** teleology. **teleologisk** teleological. **telepati** telepathy. **telepatisk** telepathic. **teleskop** telescope. **teleskopisk** telescopic. **telgje** whittle. **-kniv** sheath-knife, whittle. **-øks** broad axe.

telle count, number; — **etter** count over; — **opp** add up, sum up, cast up; — **mange år** number many years; — **til tjue** count (to) twenty. **telleapparat** counter; turnstile and counter. **teller** (i bank) teller; (i brøk) numerator. **telling** count, enumeration.

tellur (i kjemi) tellurium. **tellurisk** telluric.

telt tent; **reise et** — pitch a tent. **-by** camp. **-duk** tent-canvas, tent-cloth. **-leir** camp of tents. **-plugg** tent-peg. **-slagning** tent-pitching. **-tak** pavillion-roof.

tema (musikk) theme; (emne) subject.

temaskin tea-urn.

temme tame, domesticate; (hest) break (in); (om ville dyr) reclaim; — **sine lidenskaper** control (el. curb) one's passions.

temmelig rather, fairly, pretty; tolerably; — **kaldt** rather cold, coldish; — **godt** pretty well; — **mye** pretty much; — **dårlige utsikter** rather a bad look-out; **så** — pretty well; pretty much. **temmer** tamer. **temming** el. **temning** taming etc., domestification.

tempel temple; (poet) fane. **-herre** (knight) Templar, Knight of the Temple; (flert. også) Knights Templars. **-herrenes orden** the Order of the Templars. **-skjenner** sacrilegist. **-tjeneste** service at el. in a temple.

tempera distemper, tempera; **a** — in distemper.

temperament temperament, temper.

temperatur temperature; **høy** — high temperature; **lav** — low temperature; **ta ens** — take one's temperature.

temperer|e temper. **-t klima** temperate climate.

tempo time, measure; (mil) movement, time. **temporær** temporary. **tempus** tense.

tendens tendency, bias, drift; (hensikt) purpose; (på markedet) feeling. **tendensiøs** biased, warped, purposeful. **tendensroman** novel of purpose.

tender tender.

tendere tend (**til å:** to).

tenke think; (tro, formode) think, suppose; (akte, skulle til å) be going to; **det -r jeg** I think so; **det kunne jeg** — eller **det tenkte jeg nok** I thought as much; — **seg** imagine, fancy conceive; — **etter** consider; — **om** think of; — **seg om** reflect, consider; f. eks. you should have considered and not have been so foolish; — **over** meditate, reflect on, consider of el. about; — **på noe** think of el. on something; **jeg kom til å** — **på** it occurred to me; — **seg til** guess; **tenkende** thinking, reflective, thoughtful; — **vesen** rational being. **tenke|evne** power of thinking. **-frihet** liberty of thinking. **tenkelig** imaginable conceivable.

tenkemåte way of thinking, mind.

tenker thinker, speculator, reasoner. **tenk-(n)ing** thinking, thought. **tenksom** thoughtful, meditative, reflecting. **tenksomhet** reflection, considerateness, thoughtfulness.

tennbar inflammable, ignitible.

tenne kindle, light, ignite; (bli antent) take fire, ignite; — **opp** light the fire. **tenner** (pl av **tann**) teeth. **tennerskjærende** grinding one's teeth. **tenning** lighting, ignition.

tennis lawn-tennis, tennis. **-bane** tennis-lawn. **tenn|nål** igniting needle. **-plugg** sparking-plug. **-rør** quick-match, spark plug. **-sats** priming (-composition); (på fyrstikk) head.

tenor tenor. **-basun** tenor trombone. **-nøkkel** tenor clef. **-parti** tenor (-part). **-sanger** tenor-singer.

tentamen probation, probational examination. **tentamensstil** probation exercise.

teokrati theocracy. **teokratisk** theocratic(al).

teolog theologian, divine. **teologi** theology, divinity. **teologisk** theologic(al).

teoretiker theorist. **teoretisere** theorize. **teoretisk** theoretical.

teori theory; **sette fram en** — start a theory. **teosof** theosophist. **teosofi** theosophy. **teosofisk** theosophic(al).

teppe (vrb), se **stoppe, stenge.**

teppe (gulv-, o. l.) carpet; (grovere) rug; (i teater) curtain. **-t faller** the curtain descends. **-banker** carpet beater. **-stoff** carpeting.

terapevtisk therapeutic. **terapi** therapeutics.

terge, se **erte.**

termin term; (avdrag) instalment. **terminforretninger** speculation for account. **terminologi** terminology, technicology. **terminus** (uttrykk) term. **terminvis** by instalment(s).

termitt white ant, termit.

termometer thermometer; **hvor høyt står -et?** what is the height of the t.? **-et står på 10°** the t. is at 10°.

termosflaske thermos, vacuumflask, thermosflask.

I. **terne** (= tjenestepike, foreldet, spøkende) handmaid.

II. **terne** (fugl) tern, sea-swallow.

ternet chequered.

terning el. (plur.) dice; (matematikk) cube; **falsk** — loaded die; **spille -er** play at dice; **kaste -ene** throw the dice. **-beger** dice-box. **-kast** throw of a die, of the dice. **-spill** game at dice.

terpe igjennom** toil through.

terpentin turpentine. **-olje** oil of turpentine. **-spiritus** spirits of turpentine.

terrakotta terra cotta.

terrasse terrace. **-formig** terraced.

terreng country, (ogs. fig) ground; **avsøke -et** scour the country; **vinne, tape** — gain, lose ground.

terrier terrier.

terrin tureen. **-lokk** tureen-cover.

territorial|høyhet territorial jurisdiction. **-rett** territoriality. **-rettighet** territorial right.

territorium territory.

terrorisere keep in terror, terrorize (over). **terrorisme** terrorism. **terrorist** terrorist.

ters (i fekting) tierce; (mus) third, tierce; **stor, liten** — major, minor third.

tersett (trestemmig syngestykke) trio.

tersiner (trillingrim) terze rime.

terskel, se **treskel.**

terte tart. **-fin** squeamish, precise; prudish. **tertiaveksel** third of exchange.

tertit, se **talgtit.**

tertiær tertiary. **-bane** light railway, pioneer line.

tesil tea-strainer. **-skei, -skje** tea-spoon; (om mål) tea-spoonful. **-sorter** teas.

tess: lite — of scant value, almost useless;

ikke noe — useless **(til:** for); **ikke stort** — not of much account.

testament|(e) (last) will, testament; **gjøre sitt** — make one's will; **det gamle, det nye** — the old, new testament; **dø og etterlate** — leave a will, die testate. **dø uten å ha gjort** — die intestate. **-arisk** testamentary. **-ere** bequeath, leave by will, will. **testa|tor, -triks** the testator, testatrix.

testikkel testicle, stone.

testimonium certificate.

tête: ta -n take the lead; — **à** — tête-à-tête.

tetne get compact, tighten.

tetning stopping, tightening. **tetningsring** gascheck ring, pad.

tett tight, close; (om tåke) dense; (om skog) thick; (adv) close, closely; **gjøre** — tighten; — **ved** close by, close to; — **sammen** close together; **holde** — be tight; (fig) be silent, keep one's own counsel; **drikke** — drink deep; — **befolket** densely peopled, thickly inhabited.

tette (vrb) stop, tighten; (dør, vindu) list; (vegg) ogs. chink.

tette (subst) addition made to milk (to prevent coagulation), thickening. **-gras** butterwort. **-melk** ropy milk.

tetthet tightness, closeness, density.

tetting tightening. **tettklipt** close-cropped.

tett|skrevet close, closely written. **-sluttende** tight, close, tight-fitting. **-sluttet** (rekke) close, serried (rank).

tev breath; scent, smell.

te|vann tea. **-varmer** tea-cosy.

tevle emulate each other, vie.

tevling competition, emulation.

Themsen the Thames.

ti (konjunksjon) foreldet, se **for.**

ti (tallord) ten.

ti(d) time; (gram) tense; **nå er det** — now is the time; **det er ingen** — **å spille** there is no time to be lost el. to lose; **en tid** one time; **det var en tid da** time was when; **en** — some time, for a time; **tiden** time; **-en og rommet** time and space; **omskifte** — en med evigheten depart this life; **-en går** time runs fast; **når -en kommer** in due time; **fordrive -en, slå -en i hjel** kill time; **tilbringe -en** pass el. spend the time el. one's time; **gamle -er** ancient times; **nyere -er** modern times; **se -en an** wait and see; **kort** — **etter** a short time afterwards; **for -en** at present, pro tem.; **fra** — til annen from time to time; **gammel før -en** prematurely old, old before his time; **i -e** in time; **i rette** — in due time; **i sin** — (fortiden) sometime; (fremtiden) in due time el. course; **i den senere** — of late, of late times; **i disse -er** as times go; **med -en** in time, in the course of time, in process of time, with time; **om et års** —, **en måneds** — in a twelvemonth, month; **om kort** — shortly; **bli over -en** stay behind one's time; **det er på -e** it is (quite) time; **det er på høy** — it is high time; **til rette** — in due course; **til enhver** — at all times; **til en** — for a time; **til sine -er** at times; **gi seg** — til å tenke, overveie stop to think, pause to consider.

tidebolk era, period.

tidende tidings, news; (avis) newspaper.

tidevann tide.

tidfeste determine the time (the date) of.

tidlig early; (adv) (ogs.) betimes, in good time, at an early period; — **moden** precocious, forward; **for** — premature; **så** — **som mulig** også: at your earliest convenience. **-ere** previous, former; (adv) previously, formerly, before; **-st** at the earliest.

tidligdags at an early hour.

tidobbelt tenfold, decuple.

tids|alder age. **-angivelse** date. **i -befraktning** on time-charter. **-besparelse** saving of time.

tidsbesparende time-saving.

tidsbilde picture of the time.

tids|fordriv pastime. **-forhold** times, circumstances, juncture(s). **-frist** space of time. **-følge** chronological order. **-nok** in time, early enough. **-orden** chronological order. **-punkt** moment el. point of time, juncture. **-regning** era. **-rom** period. **-skrift** periodical (publication el. journal el.) magazine, review. **-sparende** time-saving. **-spille** waste of time. **-spillende** time-wasting. **-spørsmål** question of time. **-svarende** suitable el. suited to the times, adapted to the spirit of the age, seasonable, opportune, well-timed. **-ånd** spirit el. genius of the age.

tie be silent, keep silence, hold one's peace, **han kan ikke** — he can't keep a secret; **få til å** — silence, put to silence; — **til** say nothing to, pass in silence; — **i hjel** kill by silence.

tiende (tallord) tenth; **for det** — tenthly, in the tenth place.

tiende (subst) tithe, tenth.

tiendedel tenth (part).

tiendeplikt liability to pay tithes.

tier ten; (pengeseddel) tenner, banknote for ten crowns.

tiere (kompar. av titt) oftener, more frequently; **tiest** (superlativ av titt) oftenest, most frequently; **som** — as often as not; every now and then.

tiger tiger. (huntiger) tigress. **-katt** tiger-cat. **-skinn** tiger's skin. **-unge** young tiger, tiger cub.

tigge beg; — **for hvermanns dør** beg one's bread from door to door; — **ham om det** beg it hard of him, beg him hard for it; — **seg til noe** obtain st. by begging; — **sammen** collect by begging.

tigger beggar, mendicant.

tigger|aktig beggarly. **-brev** begging- el. mendicant-letter. **-gang: gå** — go a-begging. **tiggeri** begging, beggary, mendicity.

tigger|kjerring, -kone beggar-woman. **-munk** mendicant friar. **-pakk** lot of beggars, beggarly set. **-pike** beggar-girl. **-pose** beggar's wallet.

tiggerstav beggar's staff; **han er brakt til -en** he is utterly ruined, reduced to beggary.

tiggerunge beggar's brat.

tikke (om ur) tick.

tikking ticking.

tikk-takk tick-tack.

til (prep) to; **reise** — **London** go to London; **sende** — send to; **fra øverst** — **nederst** from top to bottom; **skrive** — write to; **fri** — propose to; **lytte** — listen to; **vant** — accustomed to; **henfallen** — addicted to; **10** — **20** ten to twenty; — **skade for** to the detriment of; **gå** — **spille** go to waste; **towards: han gikk bortover** — **huset** he went towards the house; **till** (tid): **vent** — **i morgen** wait till to-morrow; **fra morgen** — **kveld** from morning till night; **for: det er** — **brev** — **deg** there is a letter for you; **hva skal vi ha** — **frokost, middag, kvelds** what are we to have for breakfast, dinner, supper? **ta** — **kone** take for one's wife; — **salgs** for sale; **avreise** — departure for; **lyst** — a fancy for; **for stor** — too large for; **god nok** — good enough for; **i n: her** — **lands** in this country; — **hjelp, straff, ære for** in aid, punishment, honour of; — **erindring om** in remembrance of; — **tegn på** in sign of; **i n t o: forvandle** — change into; **o n: fots** on foot; — **hest** on horseback; — **alle sider** on every side; — **høyre** on the right hand; **a t: enhver tid** at all times; — **lav pris** at a low price; **o f: mor** — the mother of; **kjærlighet** — love of; **nøkkelen** — the key of; **b y: lands, vanns** by land, water; **jeg må ha det** — **jul, januar, fredag** I must have it by Christmas, January, Friday; **a s: ta** — **eksempel** take as an example; **w i t h: gi meg litt saus** — **biffen** I want some sauce with this steak; (**a n d r e m å t e r**): — **all ulykke** unfortunately; **ble utnevnt** — **guvernør** was appointed governor; **det er** — **ingen nytte**

it is no use; **se — en** go and see one; **ta — orde** speak, lift one's voice, hold forth; **ønske en — lykke** wish one joy; **lese seg, gjette seg, slutte seg —** read, guess, conclude.

til (adv): **være —** exist; **av og —** now and then; **fra og —** to and fro; **det gjør hverken fra eller —** it's of no moment; **en —** one more; **en halv gang — så lang** half as long again; **— og med** including.

til (konj) till, until.

til akters, se **akter —. til alters: gå — — go** to (el. partake of the) communion. **til ankers**, se **anker.**

tilbake (adv) back, backward(s); **han ble —** he remained behind; **la bli —** leave behind; **være — for sin tid** be behind the day; **fram og —** forward and backward; **han står — i matematikk** he is deficient in mathematics; **gi — på** (veksle) give change for.

tilbakebetale pay back, repay.

tilbakebetaling repayment, return.

tilbakeblikk retrospect, retrospective glance; (fig) **kaste et — på** examine retrospectively.

tilbakefall falling back; (om sykdom) relapse.

tilbakegang retrograde movement, retrogradation, retrogression; decline.

tilbakegående retrograde, retrogressive.

tilbake|holde hold el. keep back, retain; **med –holdt åndedrett** with bated (held, suspended) breath. **–holdelse** retention.

tilbakeholden reserved, backward.

tilbakeholdenhet reserve.

tilbakekalle call back, recall; unsay, repeal, revoke; (en ordre) cancel, countermand, annul (an order). **tilbakekallelse** recall, revocation; retractation, withdrawal.

tilbakekomst return; **ved hans — til** on his return to.

tilbakelegge travel, cover, pass over, traverse, advance; **den tilbakelagte vei** the journey el. distance performed; **et tilbakelagt standpunkt** a thing of the past.

tilbakelent recumbent.

tilbakelevere return, restore.

tilbakelevering return.

tilbakereise return.

tilbakeskritt step backwards, retrogradation. retrogression, retrograde step.

tilbakeslag rebound; (av kanon) recoil.

tilbakestøt back-thrust, repercussion, repulse.

tilbakestøtt repelled, repulsed, discouraged.

tilbaketagelse retaking; recapture.

tilbaketog retreat.

tilbaketredelse retirement, resignation.

tilbaketrengt (fig) repressed, restrained.

tilbaketrukkenhet retiredness, seclusion.

tilbaketrukket retired.

tilbaketur return; passage back, return voyage.

tilbakevei way back, return.

tilbakevendende recurrent.

tilbakevirkende reacting, retroactive; (gram) reflexive; (lov) retrospective, retroactive; **— kraft** retroactive effect.

tilbakevirkning reaction, retroaction.

tilbakevise repulse, reject.

tilbakevisning repulsion, rejection.

tilbakeværende left, remaining; residual.

tilbe adore, worship. **tilbedelse** adoration, worship. **tilbedelsesverdig** adorable.

tilbeder adorer, worshipper; (fig) **hennes tilbedere** her admirers.

tilbehør appurtenances, adjuncts, belongings, surroundings, accompaniment, concomitants.

til be(i)ns, se **bein** og **ben.**

tilberede prepare. **tilberedelse** preparation.

tilblivelse coming into existence, genesis. **tilblivelsesprosess** genesis.

til blods so as to bring blood, till the blood comes (el. came).

til bords: gå — go to dinner (el. supper); **sitte —** be at dinner (el. supper).

tilbrakt: fritt — carriage free.

tilbringe: — tiden spend (the, one's) time, pass (away) time.

tilbud offer, proffer, tender; **— og etterspørsel** supply and demand.

til bunns down, to the bottom; (fig) ogs. thoroughly.

tilby offer, proffer, tender; **— seg** offer oneself; offer.

til bygds: komme — arrive in the neighbourhood; arrive in settled parts.

tilbygg, -bygning addition, building added.

tilbørlig due, proper, suitable.

tilbørlighet suitableness, propriety.

tilbøyelig (til) inclined, disposed, apt, given (to). **tilbøyelighet** inclination, propensity, disposition, tendency, leaning; (for en) affection, attachment; **fatte — for** form an attachment to.

tildanne fashion, form, work.

tildek|ke cover (up). **-ning** covering (up).

til del: bli en — fall to one's share; be extended to one.

tildele allot, assign (to), confer on el. upon.

til dels partly, in part.

til doms: sitte — over sit in judgment upon; **saken er opptatt —** judgment is reserved.

tildra seg come to pass, happen.

tildragelse occurrence, event, adventure.

tilegne: — en en bok dedicate, inscribe a book to one; **— seg** appropriate (to oneself), make one's own; acquire, master, pick up. **tilegnelse** dedication; appropriation; acquirement.

til ekte in marriage.

til ende to an end; (endt) at an end; (uavbrutt) on end; **tre dager —** three days on end.

tilende|bringe bring to a conclusion, finish, accomplish. **–bringelse** conclusion, consummation.

tilfal|le fall to, be devolved on; be forfeited to; **hans andel er -t meg** his share is devolved on me.

til fals for sale, venal, buyable.

tilfangetagelse apprehension, seizure, capture.

tilfeldig accidental, casual, fortuitous, occasional, chance; **— bekjentskap** chance acquaintance.

tilfeldighet casualty, accident accidental circumstance.

tilfeldigvis by chance, accidentally, casually, fortuitously, as it happened el. happens.

tilfelle case, instance; accident, occurrence; (treff) chance; (sykdomsanfall) fit, attack; **for det — at han ... in** case he ...; **i så —** in that case; **i — av** in case of, in the event of; **i ethvert —** at all events, at any rate, in any case; **i verste —** if the worst comes to the worst; **i påkommende — on** an emergency; **for det mulige —** for an emergency; **i det foreliggende —** in the present case; **ved et —** by chance; **hvis det virkelig er —** if it be really the fact; **han har et slemt —** he has a bad complaint.

til felles in common, jointly, conjointly.

tilfellig, tilfellighet, tilfelligvis se **tilfeldig, tilfeldighet, tilfeldigvis.**

tilflukt refuge; **ta sin — til** have recourse to, take refuge in, throw oneself upon, fall back upon, resort to; **finne — hos** find an asylum with.

tilfluktssted place of refuge, asylum.

tilflyte: la noe — en grant el. allow one st.

tilforlatelig reliable, trustworthy; (adv) really. **-het** certainty; (persons) trustworthiness.

tilforordne appoint.

til fots on foot, afoot.

tilfreds content, pleased; (fullt **tilfredsstilt**) satisfied.

tilfredshet content, contentment, satisfaction.

tilfredsstille content, satisfy, gratify.

tilfredsstillelse gratification, satisfaction.

tilfredsstillende satisfactory; gratifying; (adv) satisfactorily; to satisfaction.

tilfriskning rally, recovery; convalescence.
tilfrosset frozen (over).
til fulle fully, completely, to the full.
tilføket: veien er — the road is blocked up by snow-drifts.
til følge: ta — carry into effect.
tilføre carry to, convey to, supply with.
tilførsel supply; (skriftlig) entry.
tilføye add, affix, append: (forårsake) cause, do, bring on, inflict on. — **en et tap** inflict a loss upon one. — **en en fornærmelse** offer one an affront. **tilføyelse** addition; note, observation; (til brev) postscript; (til testament) codicil.
til gagns completely, effectually, to some purpose; (dt) with a vengeance.
tilgang access, approach; (av folk, av varer) inflow, influx; (øking) augmentation, increase.
tilgi forgive, pardon (**en noe:** one st. el. for st.).
tilgift addition, something thrown in.
tilgitre grate, close with a grate.
tilgivelig pardonable, forgiveable.
tilgivelse forgiveness, pardon; **jeg ber Dem om** — I beg your pardon.
tilgjengelig approachable, accessible, available; **lett, vanskelig** — easy, difficult of access; **— for** open to. **tilgjengelighet** approachableness; accessibility.
tilgjort affected, artificial. **-het** affectation, artificiality, posing.
til gode due, owing; **jeg har ennå 100 pund — hos ham** he still owes me 100 pounds; **gjøre seg — med** regale oneself with; **regne en noe** — excuse one.
tilgodehavende due, outstanding debt; **mitt — hos ham** what he owes me.
tilgrensende adjacent, bordering upon.
tilgrodd overrun, overgrown.
til grunne: gå — be ruined, go to ruin.
tilheng (parti) party, adherents (pl); (besværlig) •incumbrance.
tilhenger adherent, follower, votary.
til hest on horseback.
tilhogd fashioned by hewing, rough-hewn.
tilhold injunction; (tilfluktssted) place of resort; stronghold.
tilholdssted haunt, place of resort.
til hope (sammen) together; **alle** — all together; **noen tosker alle** — a pack of fools.
tilhylle veil, wrap up, muffle up.
tilhøre belong to.
tilhørende appurtenent; (som sidestykke) companion.
tilhører, -inne auditor, hearer, listener.
tilhørerkrets audience.
tilhøve chance, opportunity.
tilhøvlet planed. **tilhøvling** planing.
til hånde: gå en — assist one.
tilintet|gjøre annihilate, destroy, demolish; **-gjort** paralysed, crushed, overwhelmed.
tilintetgjørelse annihilation, destruction.
tilje (i båt) floor-board; (glt. og poetisk) ground, floor.
tiljevning levelling; (fig) adaptation; (gram.) assimilation.
tiljuble: — **en bifall** applaud one with cries, cheer one.
tilkalle call (in), summon. **-lse** summoning.
tilkaste cast, fling, throw (to, at); f. eks. **— en forelskede blikk** cast amorous looks at one.
tilkjempe seg gain in fight el. by fighting; (fig) obtain, gain; **— seg prisen** win, carry the prize.
tilkjenne (vrb) adjudge, award, allot.
til kjenne: gi seg — disclose oneself.
tilkjennegi notify, signify, declare, make known; show, evince.
tilkjennegivelse notification, intimation.
tilkjennelse award, adjudication.
tilkjøring carting (home). **tilkjørt: fritt —** carriage free el. paid.
tilklint dirtied.

tilklipping cutting out; **tilklipt** cut out.
tilknappet (fig) reserved.
tilknappethet reserve, aloofness.
tilknytning connection.
tilknytningspunkt connecting point.
tilkomme (skyldes) be due, be owing to; (være ens plikt) be one's duty; **det som -r meg** my due; **det -r ikke meg å** . . . it is no business of mine to . . ., it does not belong to me to . . .
tilkommende coming, to come, future; due; **det** — the future; **min** — **svoger** my brother-in -law that is to be; **min** — **(brud)** my intended.
til kort: komme — be worsted, be foiled, get the worst of it: **jeg kom** — **med pengene** my money ran short.
til køys: gå — turn in.
tillag|et dressed, prepared; **en vel** — **frokost** a well-cooked breakfast. **-ing** dressing, making, preparation.
til lags: gjøre — please, suit; **jeg kan aldri gjøre ham** — I can never do anything to please him; **gjøre alle** — **(dt)** make things pleasant all round: **det er vanskelig å gjøre alle** — it is hard to please everybody.
til lands by land; on land; **her** — in this country.
tillate permit, allow, give leave; **jeg tillater meg herved å meddele Dem** I hereby beg to inform you; **jeg har tillat meg å trekke på Dem for fakturabeløpet** I have taken the liberty to draw on you for the amount of the invoice; **jeg tillot meg å bemerke** I ventured, presumed, took leave el. begged to observe; **-r De?** if you please; **tillatt** allowed, permitted; (etter lovene) legal, lawful.
tillatelig allowable, permissible; (lovlig) lawful.
tillatelse permission; **har** — **til å** is allowed to.
tillegg addition; (til bok el. blad) supplement; (til testament) codicil; — **i lønn** increase of salary.
tillegge (overdra) confer el. bestow upon; (tilregne) ascribe, attribute, assign to; — **viktighet** attach importance to.
tilleggs- additional, supplementary.
tilleggs|avgift surcharge. **-bevilgning** additional grant. **-kursus** supplementary course. **-ord** adjective.
til leie for hire; (om hus etc.) for rent, to (be) let.
tillempe adapt (to), modify (according to).
tillemping adaptation (to); modification.
tilliggende adjacent; belonging; **med** — **rettigheter** with its attached rights.
tillike also, too, withal, moreover. **-med** together with, along with.
tillit confidence (in), trust (in), reliance (on); **ha** — **til** have (place el. repose) confidence in; **nyte alminnelig** — be universally trusted; **i** — **til** trusting to.
tillitsbrudd breach of trust.
tillits|erklæring vote of confidence. **-forhold** relation of confidence. **-full** confident, confiding, full of confidence, trustful, trusting, reliant. **-fullhet** confidence, trustfulness. **-mann** trusted agent, delegate, representative.
tillitspost place of trust, office of trust.
tillitsvekkende confidence-inspiring.
tillitsvotum- se **-erklæring.**
tillitsverv (commission of) trust.
tillokkelse allurement, enticement.
tillokkende alluring, enticing, tempting.
tillukket closed, shut. **tillukning** closing.
tillyse (kunngjøre) publish; (sammenkalle) convene, summon.
tillært acquired; **-e fraser** second-hand phrases.
tilløp (om vann) afflux; (til hopp) run, start; (fig) attempt, effort; **et** — **til lystighet** an attempt at mirth; **gjøre et** — **til samtale** make an effort at conversation. **tilløpskanal** feeder.
til manns a (el. each, per) man, each.

tilmed moreover, besides.
tilmelding notification.
tilmeldt communicated, notified, given notice, apprized of.
til mote: vel, ille — in good, bad spirits; **være — som om** feel as if; **være el. bli underlig** — feel strange.
tilmål|e measure (out) to; (fig) (om tid) allot to. **-ing** measuring, admeasurement.
tilnavn surname; **med** — surnamed.
tilnærmelse approach; (fig) advance. **tilnærmelsesvis** approximately; (adjektiv) approximate, approximative.
tilovers (levnet) left, over; (til overflod) to spare; **ha — for** be partial to; **jeg er — her** I am not wanted here.
til pass suitable, aright; **kom** — came in very well; **han kom riktig** — he came just in due time; **jeg er ikke ganske vel** — I don't feel quite well; **det var** — **for ham** it served him right, (dt) serve him right!
tilpasse fit, suit, adjust.
tilpassing fitting; adjustment.
tilplikte bind (over), oblige.
tilrakke, se rakke til.
tilre(de) treat; **ille tilredt** roughly handled, roughly treated.
tilregne impute, attribute, ascribe, **(en noe st.** to one). **tilregnelig** imputable; (om person) accountable. **tilregnelighet** imputableness; accountableness, accountability.
tilreisende (passenger) arriving; **var kommet** — had arrived.
til rette aright; **sette, legge noe** — set, put something to rights, adjust, arrange; **sette seg** — seat oneself comfortably; **vise en** — direct one, give one directions; **tale en** — make one listen to reason.
tilrettelegge arrange (conveniently), set out, marshal. **tilrettevise** reprimand, rebuke.
tilrettevisning reprimand, rebuke.
tilriding training, breaking (in).
tilrigge, se rigge.
tilrive seg seize upon, usurp, engross.
tilrop cry, shout (to), hail, acclamation.
til rors: stå — be el. stand at the helm.
tilrøykt smoky.
tilrå(de) advise. **tilrådelig** advisable.
til råds: spørre — consult, ask advice of.
tilsagn promise.
tilsammen together, in all; between them.
tilsandet sanded up.
tilsanding filling up with sand.
tilse look to, attend to.
tilsendt sent, transmitted, forwarded.
tilsetning admixture; (krydrende) seasoner; (anstrøk) dash.
tilsi (love) promise; (befale å møte) summon, order to attend.
til side aside, on one side, out of the way. **tilsidesette** pass (one) by, neglect el. slight(one). **tilsidesettelse** passing by, neglect, slight.
tilsig gradual accession, flow, ooze.
tilsigelse summons, order to attend.
tilsikre assure, ensure, secure.
tilsikring assurance.
tilsikte intend, aim at, mean.
tilsiktet intentional.
til sist at last, at length: (ved oppregn.) lastly, finally.
til sjøs: være — be at sea; **fare** — go to sea; **gå** — go to sea.
tilskadekommet hurt, injured, wounded.
til skamme: gjøre — abash, shame.
tilskikke dispense, destine, allot.
tilskikkelse dispensation (of providence).
tilskjærer fashioner, cutter (-out). **tilskjærerske** lady cutter. **tilskjæring** cutting out.
tilskjøting conveyance.
tilskott, se tilskudd.

tilskrift letter, communication; (merk) favour
tilskrive (gi skyld for) attribute, ascribe, set down, impute (st. to one); — **seg seieren** claim the victory; **det kunne ikke –s dem noen skyld** no blame whatever was attributable to them.
tilskudd (bidrag) contribution; (av det offentlige) subsidy, grant.
tilskuer spectator, beholder, looker-on, onlooker; **-ne i teateret** the audience at the theatre.
tilskuerplassen (i teater) the house.
tilskvettet bespattered, splashed over.
tilskynde prompt, stimulate, urge. **tilskyndelse** prompting, stimulus, stimulation, impulse.
tilslag (ved auksjon) knocking down.
tilslutning (bifall) favour, sympathy; (tilhengere) adherents, followers; (møtt antall) attendance; **finne — hos** be favoured by, be joined by.
tilsløre veil; (fig) veil, gloss over.
tilsløring veiling.
tilsmile, se smile til; lykken begynte å — ham good fortune began to smile upon him.
tilsmurt bedaubed, besmeared.
tilsnike seg obtain fraudulently, obtain by underhand practices. **tilsnikelse** fraudulent acquisition, subreption.
tilsnitt cutting out; cut, form, guise.
tilsnødd covered up with snow, snowed up.
tilsnørt laced together el. up.
tilspisse seg come to a point; **situasjonen –t seg** things came to a point.
tilsprang run, start; **ta** — take a run.
tilstand state, condition.
til stede, se sted.
tilstede (vrb) allow, grant.
tilstedekomst appearance, arrival.
tilstedelig allowable, permissible.
tilstedeværelse presence. **tilstedeværende** present; in attendance; **de** — the company.
tilstelling arrangement; (festlig) entertainment.
tilstelt artificial.
tilstille remit, send, hand.
tilstoppe stop up, fill up.
tilstrebe aim at.
tilstrekkelig sufficient, adequate.
tilstrekkelighet sufficiency, adequacy.
tilstrømning afflux, affluxion, influx; (av folk) concourse; **det hadde vært voldsom — til stykket** the play had had an immense run.
tilstussing trimming.
tilstøte happen, befall.
tilstøtende adjacent, adjoining; (omstendighet) unforeseen, supervening.
tilstå confess; (vedgå) admit, own; (bevilge) grant, accord to.
tilståelse confession; admittance; (innrømmelse, bevilling) concession.
tilsvar reply; **på eget ansvar og** — at one's own peril. **tilsvarende** corresponding, parallel, to match; proportionate; **i — grad** correspondingly.
tilsvining soiling, befouling.
tilsyn superintendence, care, supervision; **ha — med** see to, look after.
til syne in sight; **komme** — appear; **komme — igjen** reappear.
tilsynekomst appearance.
tilsynelatende seeming, apparent; (adv) apparently, to all appearance; **den — grunn** the apparent cause.
tilsynshavende in charge.
tilsynslærer subinspector, supervisor.
tilsynsmann inspector, surveyor.
tilsøle soil, dirty.
tilsådd cropped, sown.
I. **tilta** (vokse) grow, increase; **tiltagende** increasing; **i tiltagende** increasing, on the increase.
II. **tilta seg** assume, assume to oneself, usurp.
tiltak attempt, effort, essay; (foretaksomhet) energy, enterprise; (initiativ) initiative; **et nytt** — ogs. a novel departure.

til takke: ta — put up with, be satisfied with.

tiltale (vrb) accost, address; (juridisk) prosecute, sue; (fig) attract; commend itself to; **være tiltalt for** be accused of; **(den) tiltalte** the accused, the defendant; **-nde** pleasing, pleasant, winning, taking, engaging, sympathetic; **lite -nde** unsympathetic.

tiltale (subst) address, (juridisk) prosecution; **han er satt under** — an action has been brought against him; **gi en svar på** — give one tit for tat, return the compliment.

tiltalebenk (felon's) dock.

tiltaleord term el. word of address.

tiltenkt intended for.

tiltepping obstruction, stopping.

tiltre (et embete, arv) step into, enter upon; (et forbund, interessentskap) enter into, join; (mening, ytring) subscribe to, agree with; **— en reise** set out upon (el. start on, proceed on, begin) a journey el. voyage; **— et forslag** second a motion; **en tiltredende bestyrer** a succeeding manager.

tiltredelse (av embete, gods osv.) stepping into, entering on; (av en reise) setting out.

tiltredelsestale inaugural address.

tiltrenge, se **trenge.**

tiltrekke attract; **— seg** attract, draw upon oneself. **tiltrekkende** attractive.

tiltrekning attraction. **tiltrekningskraft** attractive force, (power of) attraction, (fig) charm.

tiltro (subst) confidence, trust, faith; **ha — til** place confidence in, put one's trust in.

tiltro: — en noe give one credit for st.

tiltuske seg obtain by way of exchange.

tiltvinge seg compel, enforce, extort.

til vanns by water; **krigsmakten til lands og — the Army and the Navy.**

tilvant habitual, accustomed.

til veie: skaffe — procure; (penger) raise.

tilveiebringe procure; (penger) raise; (bevirke) bring about, effect; (orden, ro) restore.

tilveiebringelse procurement; bringing about.

tilvekst increase, accession.

tilvende seg obtain by underhand means.

tilvendelse appropriation.

til venns: gjøre seg — med make a friend of.

til venstre to the left; on the left (hand).

til verks: gå — go about it.

tilvirke manufacture; **— klede av ull** el. **bomull** work wool el. cotton into cloth.

tilvirkning manufacture.

til vogns by carriage, driving.

tilvoks|ende growing, increasing. **-t** grown.

tilværelse existence, being; **kampen for -n** the struggle for existence.

til værs up (into the air), skyward; (mar) aloft.

til års advanced in age, advanced in years.

time hour; (undervisnings-) lesson; **-r hos** lessons with; **om en —** in an hour; **for en — siden** an hour ago; **i en —** for an hour; **i -n** an hour, to (in) the hour; (i skoletimen) during the lesson, in class; **hver — på dagen** every hour in the day; **hans — er slått** his hour is come.

time|glass hour-glass, sand-glass. **-kjøring: for —** when hired by time. **timelig** temporal. **det -e** temporal existence.

time|lærer private teacher. **-plan** time-table; table of lessons.

times happen, befall.

time|slag hourstroke. **-vis** (adv) by the hour; **i timevis** for hours (together).

timian thyme.

timotei catstail (el. timothy) grass.

tind, tinde peak (ogs. fig) summit, pinnacle; (fig) acme; (på mur, tårn) battlement.

tindebestiger alpinist.

tindre sparkle, twinkle.

tine (subst) kit, kit-box.

tine (vrb) thaw.

I. **ting** (en) thing; **hva som gjorde -en enda verre** to make matters worse; **kunne sine —** know one's trade.

II. **ting** (et) (sted hvor rett holdes) court, assize; (repr. forsaml.) parliament, house; **på -e** in court, in parliament.

I. **tinge** (prutte) bargain, higgle; (bestille) bespeak; (en plass) book; (abonnere) subscribe (på: for); **— seg i kost hos** board with.

II. **tinge** (forhandle) negotiate, parley.

tingel (liten bjelle) little sleigh-bell.

tinger bargainer; (abonnent) subscriber.

tingest (bit of a) thing, mite.

tingfred peace at the assizes.

tinghus assizehouse.

I. **tinging** bargaining etc.; subscription.

II. **tinging** (forhandling) negotiation, deliberation.

tinglag canton, law circuit, judicial district.

ting|lese notify, record, (legally) register. **-lesning** (legal) notification, recording. **-lyse** notify, record, (legally) register. **-lysning** (legal) notification, recording. **-mann** member of parliament. **-reise** circuit. **-sted** place where assizes are held. **-stut** pettifogger. **tingsvitne** witness.

tinktur tincture, elixir, wash.

tinn tin; (tinnlegering) pewter.

tinn|blikk tin-plate. **-fat** pewter dish.

tinnfolie tinfoil.

tinning temple.

tinn|saker pewter-ware. **-soldat** tin soldier. **-støper** pewterer. **-tallerken** pewter-plate, tin-plate.

tinte bladder-worm; (pl) (hos svin) measles.

I. **tipp** tip.

II. **tipp** (v. veddeløp) tip; **tippe** (vrb) tip.

tippoldefar great-great-grandfather.

tippoldemor great-great-grandmother.

tippvogn tip-cart.

tirade tirade; (ordstrøm) flow of words.

tiral|jere skirmish. **-jør** skirmisher. **-jørfektning** skirmish.

tiritunge lady's slipper.

tirre tease, irritate. **tirring** teasing.

tirsdag Tuesday; **forrige —** last Tuesday; **på —** on Tuesday.

tiske whisper; **hviske og —** buz and whisper.

tispe bitch.

tiss, tisse (barnespr.), se **niss, nisse.**

tist detached fibre; (hår-) straggling strand.

tistel thistle.

titall ten. **-systemet** the decimal system.

I. **titan** (kjempe) Titan.

II. **titan** (stoff) titanium. **-holdig** titaniferous.

titanisk titanic.

titel title; **under — av** under the title of. **-bilde** frontispiece. **-blad** title-leaf, title-page.

titelrolle name-part.

titt often, frequently.

titte peep.

tittel, se **titel.**

titte|lek bopeep. **-skap** peep show.

titulatur titles. **titulere** title, entitle, style, name, address. **titulær** titular.

tiur capercailzie, wood-grouse. **-leik** call and antics of wood-grouse; roosting-place of capercailzie.

ti|år decade, decennium. **-årig, -års** of ten ars, ten years old.

tjafs, se **tafs. tjafset,** se **tafset.**

tjau score.

I. **tjeld** (fugl) oyster-catcher, sea-pie.

II. **tjeld** canvas tent el. hut; curtain.

tjelde spread el. pitch canvas tents; cover with canvas.

tjene serve; (fortjene) earn; **— penger** make money; **— godt** has a good income; **makes a large profit; han -r hos meg** he is in my service; **tjen meg i å** oblige me by, el. do me the favour to . . .; hva kan jeg — Dem med? how can I be of service to you? **det er jeg ikke tjent med** that won't do for me; — **på** profit by; — **så og så mye på** make so much by; **det -r til unnskyldning for ham** it is some excuse for him.

tjener (oppvarter) waiter; (herskapstjener) (man-)servant, footman, groom; **kirkens** — minister; **statens** — public functionary; **Deres ærbødige** — your servant, your obedient servant.

tjenersete (på en vogn) dickey.

tjenerskap domestics, servants (pl).

tjenerstanden the menial class.

tjeneste service; (plass) place; **gjøre** — serve; **gjøre** — **som** serve for el. as, do duty for; assist el. officiate as; **gjøre en en** — do el. render one a service; do one a favour; **gjøre ham den** — **å** be so kind as to, oblige him by, do him the favour to; **ha** — be on duty; **ha** — **ved hoffet** be in waiting; **si opp -n** (om tjenestefolk) give warning; **den ene** — **er den annen verd** one good turn deserves another; **han tok** — **hos meg** he entered my service; **i** -**n** on service; **i utenlandsk** — on foreign service; **hva kan jeg stå til** — **med?** what are your commands? what is for your service? **det står til Deres** — you are welcome to it; **til** — at your service; **uten** — out of place.

tjeneste|anliggender: i — on service. -**folk** servants. -**kar** man(-servant). -**mann** (embetsmann) functionary, civil servant. -**pike** maidservant. -**skriv(else)** official letter. -**tid** time of service. -**udyktig** unfit for duty, inefficient.

tjenlig serviceable, useful.

tjenstaktig ready to serve, obliging, helpful, neighbourly; **altfor** — officious, over-officious.

tjenstaktighet readiness to serve, obligingness, over-officiousness.

tjenst|dyktig fit for service, serviceable, efficient, effective. -**dyktighet** (service) efficiency. -**gjørende** (ved hoff, om tjener osv.) in waiting, in attendance; (mil) on duty. -**iver**, zeal in the service. -**ivrig** assiduous, zealous. **tjenst|lig** by virtue of office. -**villig**, se -**aktig**.

tjenstvillighet readiness to serve.

tjern lakelet, mere, tarn.

tjerneblom, se **vannlilje**.

tjor tether. **tjore** tether.

tjorpåle tether-peg.

tjue (20) twenty. -**dobbelt** twentyfold.

tjuende twentieth. -**del** twentieth part.

tjukk, se **tykk**.

tjuv, se **tyv**.

tjære (vrb) tar.

tjære (subst) tar. -**brenner** tarmaker. -**brenneri** tar-factory. -**bræ** (vrb) tar. -**drev** black oakum.

tjære|kost tar-brush. -**papp** tarred paper. -**pøs** tar-bucket. -**såpe** tar-soap. **tjæret** tarred.

tjønn, se **tjern**.

to (tallord) two; **begge** — both; — **ganger** twice; — **og** — (to om gangen) by twos, two by two; **ett av** — one of two things; **det er så sikkert som at** — **og** — **er fire** it is a dead certainty.

to (stoff) material; **det er godt** — **i ham** he is of good fibre, there is good stuff in him.

toalett (påkledning) toilet; (= W. C.) lavatory; **gjøre** — dress, make one's toilet.

toalett|bord dressing-table. -**bøtte** slop pail, toilet pail. -**skap** wardrobe. -**skrin** dressing-box, dressing-case. -**spell** dressing-glass, toilet-glass, cheval-glass. -**værelse** dressing-room; (på offentlige steder) lavatory.

toarmet two-armed.

tobakk tobacco; **røke** — smoke; **ikke en pipe** — **verd** not worth a button el. farthing.

tobakks|aske tobacco-ashes. -**dåse** tobacco -box. -**fabrikk** tobacco-manufactory. -**fabrikant** tobacconist.

tobakks|handel tobacco-trade, (butikk) tobacconist's shop. -**handler** tobacconist. -**lukt** smell of tobacco. -**pung** tobacco-pouch. -**rull** roll of tobacco. -**røyk** tobacco-smoke. -**røyker** smoker (of tobacco); **en svær** -**røyker** a great smoker. -**røyking** smoking. -**saft**, -**saus** tobacco -juice. -**skrin** tobacco-box.

tobeint two-legged; **et** — **dyr** a biped.

toddi toddy.

todekker two-decker; (flygemaskin) biplane.

todelt bipartite. **todobbelt** double.

toer two; (i kortspill) a deuce. **to-etasjes** two-storied. **tofjerdedels takt** time of two crotchets el. of two fours.

tofold doubly, two-fold.

tofte thwart.

tog (jernbanetog) train; (ferd, reise) expedition; (opptog) procession; (felttog) campaign; **blandet** — mixed train; -**et går** the train starts.

toga toga.

toge march, proceed.

tog|forsinkelse delay of the train. -**fører** guard; (amr) conductor. -**personale** trainmen.

togre(i)nt two-forked, bifurcate.

togstans stopping of the train.

togulykke railway accident.

tohendig for two hands.

tokaier Tokay (wine).

tokammersystem two-chamber system.

I. **tokt** cruise, expedition.

II. **tokt** (ri) fit, spell, paroxysm.

toleranse toleration, tolerance.

tolerant tolerant. **tolerere** tolerate.

tolk interpreter. **tolke** interpret; (uttrykke) express. **tolkning** interpretation.

I. **toll** (tre), se **furu**.

II. **toll** (åretoll) thole, pin.

III. **toll** (avgift) duty (**av**, **på**: on), toll. -**avgifter** customs duties. -**assistent** custom-house officer. -**beskyttelse** protection. -**betjent**, se -**assistent**.

tollbu custom-house.

tolle, se **fortolle**.

tollegang oar-lock, rowlock.

toll(e)kniv sheath-knife; (amr) bowieknife.

tollekspedisjon custom-house.

tollembetsmann officer of the customs.

tollepinne tholepin, thole.

toller receiver of customs; (bibelsk) publican.

toll|etaten the Customs. -**forhøyelse** customs increase. -**forvalter** receiver of the customs, toll-gatherer.

tollfri free from duty, toll-free, duty-free; **tanken er** — thoughts go free.

toll|frihet exemption from duty. -**funksjonær** customs' official. -**godtgjørelse** drawback. -**grense** customs frontier, custom-boundary. -**inspektør** surveyor of the customs. -**kasserer** Collector of Customs. -**klarere** make entry el. clear at the customhouse. -**klarering** (custom-house) clearance. -**klareringsbevis** clearance. -**kontrollør** Controller of Customs. -**krysser** revenue cruiser. -**kutter** revenue cutter. -**kvittering** clearance. -**mur** tariff wall.

tollpliktig liable to duty, dutiable.

toll|reform tariff-reform. -**sted** customhouse. -**svik** defraudation of the customs. -**tariff** tariff (of duties). -**vesen** the customs. -**visitasjon** the Customs' examination.

tolv (tallord) twelve. **tolvte** twelfth; **den** — **januar** the twelfth of January, January the twelfth; **for det** — twelfthly, in the twelfth place. **tolvtedel** twelfth (part); **fem** — five twelfths.

tolvårig, **tolvårs** twelve years old.

tom empty; (fig) void; (meningsløs) inane. **tom** (tønne) rein.

tomaster two-masted vessel.

tomat tomato.

tombola tombola.

tomhendt empty-handed. **tomhet** emptiness, vacuity, inanity; (følelse) void, vacuum.

tomme inch.
tommelfinger thumb, master-finger.
tommeliten Tom Thumb.
tommel|tott the thumb. **-tå** great toe.
tomme|skrue thumb screw. **-stokk** inch-scale.
foot-rule, carpenter's rule. **-tykk** one inch thick.
tommevis by the inch.
tomset crack-brained, half-witted.
tomsing half-wit; fool.
tomskipslinje light water line.
tomt (byggegrunn) site.
tomte–gubbe (nisse) goblin, brownie.
I. **tone** (vrb) (klinge, lyde) sound.
II. **tone** (vrb) (gi f. eks. et fotografi en annen
fargetone) tone.
III. **tone** (vrb) (vise seg) loom; (la se) display,
show; **— fram** appear, loom; **— flagg** display
the colours.
tone (subst) (lyd) sound, tone; (ettertrykk)
accent, emphasis; (levemåte) ton, fashion;
(i maleri) tone; **halv —** semi-tone; **angi –n** give
the tone; **det er ikke god —** it is not bon ton,
not good form. **prise i høye -er** be loud in praise.
tale til meg i denne — speak to me in this
strain.
toneangivende who gives the tone, who leads
the fashion. **toneart** key.
tone|fall accent, emphasis. **–høyde** pitch.
-kunst art of music. **–kunstner** musician. **-skala**
-stige scala, gamut. **–vell** wealth of tones.
tonfikserbad tone fixing bath.
tonika the key-note, the tonic.
tonløs toneless; (om stemme) husky; (uten
ettertrykk) unaccented.
tonn ton; **— dødvekt** ton dead-weight.
tonnasje tonnage.
tonner (i sm.setninger) tonner.
tonsill tonsil.
tonsur tonsure.
topas topaz.
topo|graf topographer. **–grafi** topography.
topografisk topographic.
topp top, summit; (på fugler) tuft, crest;
(v. hogst) toppings; (av mast) masthead; **en —**
sukker a loaf of sugar; **fra — til tå** from head
to foot, from top to toe.
toppe (vrb) top; **— seg** (om bølger) comb, crest.
toppet heaped.
topp|figur crowning-figure. **-hogge** head down,
poll. **-lanterne** masthead light. **-målt** heaped;
(fig) arrant, consummate. **-punkt** summit,
vertex; (geom) apex; (fig) culminating point,
acme, climax.
toppsgast topman. **toppsukker** loaf-sugar.
toradet two-rowed.
torden thunder; **det trekker opp til —** a
thunder-storm is gathering.
torden|brak crash of thunder. **-bye** thunder
-shower, thunder-squall. **-gud** Thunderer. **-luft**
sultry air. **-røst** voice of thunder. **-skrall** clap
of thunder. **-sky** thunder-cloud. **-tale** thundering
speech. **-vær** thunder-storm.
tordivel (dung)beetle.
tordne thunder.
tore, se **torden.**
tore dare; **tør jeg spørre** may I ask; **det tør**
jeg ikke I dare not (do it); **om jeg så tør si**
if I may say so.
toreador toreador.
toreslått, se **tordenbrak.**
torg market, market-place; **til –s** to market.
torg|bu stall el. stand at a market. **-dag**
market day. **-hall** market-hall.
torg|kjerring market-woman, stall-woman.
-kurv market-basket. **-pris** market-price.
torgvogn market-cart.
torn thorn, spine; (barkt.) prickle; (av metall)
pin, spike; **hag-** hawthorn; **nype-** wild brier;
det er en — i øyet på ham it is a thorn in his
side; **ingen roser uten -er** no rose wi thout a thorn.
tornado tornado.

tornblad furze, whin, gorse.
torne|busk thorn-bush, thorn-shrub, bramble,
brier. **-full** thorny, prickly. **-hekk** thorn-hedge.
-kratt bush el. (tett) thicket of brambles and
thorns. **-krone** crown of thorns. **-rose** dogrose;
T-roses slott the palace of the Sleeping Beauty.
tornestrødd thorny.
tornet thorny, prickly, spinous.
tornister knapsack.
torpedere torpedo.
torpedo torpedo. **-båt** torpedo boat.
torpedojager destroyer, torpedo catcher.
torpedovesenet the torpedo service.
torsdag Thursday; **forrige —** last Thursday.
torsk cod.
torske|fiske codfishing. **-hode** cod's head.
-levertran cod-liver oil.
tort injury, disgrace.
tortur torture; **bruke — på** put to torture.
torturkammer torture-chamber.
torturredskap instrument of torture.
I. **torv,** se **torg.**
II. **torv** (på myr) peat; turf.
torv|ild peat-fire. **-jord** turfy el. peaty soil,
peat-soil.
torv|røyk peat-smoke, peat-reek. **-stakk** pile
el. stack of turf. **-strø** peat-dust, peat-moss
litter. **-tak** roof covered with peat.
tosk (skjellsord) fool, booby, ninny, simpleton,
blockhead.
tosket foolish, silly, stupid, idiotic.
tostavelses of two syllables, dissyllabic.
tostavelsesord dissyllable.
tostemmig of two voices, for two voices.
total total. **-avhold** tee-totalism. **-forbud**
total prohibition. **-inntrykk** general impression.
totalisator totalizator.
totalitet totality.
totall the number two.
total|sum (sum) total. **-virkning** general effect.
totoms- two inch.
totschläger life-preserver.
tott tuft; **komme i -ene på hverandre** fall
together by the ears.
tott (mar) taut, tight.
touche (fanfare) flourish.
tove felt, full.
toøre (omtrent d. s. s.) farthing.
toårig, toårs biennial; **et toårs barn** a child
two years old.
tradisjon tradition. **-ell** traditional.
trafikk traffic. **-avbrytelse** interruption of service. **-minister** minister of ways and communications. **-sjef** traffic-manager. **-vesen** traffic
system. **-øy** island. **-åre** artery of traffic.
tragedie tragedy. **-dikter** tragic poet. **tragiker**
tragedian. **tragi|komedie** tragi-comedy. **-komisk**
tragicomic(al). **-tragisk** tragic, tragical.
trakasserier annoyances, vexations.
I. **trakt** (egn) parts, region, tract.
II. **trakt** funnel.
traktat treaty; (religiøs) tract.
I. **trakte** pour through a funnel; (sile)filter.
II. **trakte etter** aim at, aspire to, affect, pursue.
traktepose filtering-bag.
traktere, se **behandle; beverte: — med** treat
to; **stand. traktering, traktement** entertainment; (fig ironisk) treatment.
traktformig funnel-shaped.
traktor tractor.
traktør restaurant-keeper.
traktørsted restaurant, bar.
traleverk, se **tremmeverk.**
tralle (nynne) lilt.
tralle (subst) trolly.
trait (takt) measure; (gangart) pace; (slendrian) rut, routine; **han fortsatte i den gamle**
-en he went on in the old course.
tram doorsteps; (amr) stoop.
tramp (tråkk) tramp, tramping, trample,
trampling.

trampe tramp, trample; — **på** trample upon.
trampoline, se **springbrett.**
tran train-oil, fish-oil; (medisin-) cod-liver oil.
trance trance.
tranchere carve.
trane crane. **-bær** cranberry.
tranedans: en spurv i — a dwarf among giants.
tranet oily.
trang (subst) want, need; **komme i** — come to want; **føler** — **til å** longs to, feels impelled to; **det er** — **til** there is a want of.
trang (adj) narrow, strait. **-e kår** straitened circumstances el. means. **-e tider** hard times.
trangbrystet asthmatic. **tranghet** narrowness, straitness.
trangsyn narrowness of outlook.
trangsynt of narrow views.
tran|kokeri oil refinery. **-lampe** (train-) oil lamp. **-lykt** oil lantern.
transaksjon transaction.
transformator (elektrisk) converter, transformer. **-stasjon** transformer station.
transformere transform.
transitiv transitive.
transitt transit. **transittgods** transit goods.
transitthandel transit-trade.
transittoll transit-duty.
translatør interpreter and translator.
transparent (subst) transparency; (adj) transparent.
transpirasjon perspiration.
transpirere sweat; perspire.
transponer|e transpose. **-ing** transposition.
transport transport, conveyance, transfer; (i bokførsel) brought over el. forward. **transportabel** transportable. **transportbyrå** transport undertaking, carrying agency. **transportere** transport; transfer; (i bok) bring over.
transportmiddel conveyance.
transportomkostninger carrying charges.
trapés (gymn.) trapeze; (matem.) trapezium.
trapeskunstner trapezist.
I. **trapp** (fugl) bustard.
II. **trapp** staircase, stairs; (utenfor dør) (door-) steps; **oppover, nedover -ne** up, down stairs.
trappe|avsats landing. **-gang** staircase. **-gelender** banisters. **-oppgang** staircase. **-stige** set of steps, portable steps, step-ladder. **-trin(n)** step.
trappgås, se **trapp** I.
trappist (en slags munk) trappist.
traske trudge, trot; plod, tramp.
trass: på — spitefully, in sheer defiance. **— i,** se **til tross for.**
trassat drawee. **trassent** drawer.
trasser|e draw (on), value on; **-t veksel** draft.
trassig obstinate. **-het** obstinacy.
tratte draft, draught, valuation; **en — på oss på kr. 1000,00** a draft on us for kr. 1000,00.
trau trough.
traust firm, steady, stalwart, sturdy.
trav trot; **i** — at a trot, at the trot.
trave trot.
travel busy; **ha det -t** be busy; **få det -t** become el. get busy; **ha det svært -t** be in a bustle; **i de travleste timene** during the rush hours.
travelhet bustle, press of business.
traver (match-) trotter, (high-) stepper.
traver|bane trotting-track. **-hingst** trotting stallion.
travest|ere travesty, burlesque. **-ert** travestied, travesty. **-ering** travestying, burlesquing.
travesti travesty, burlesque.
trav|kjøring trotting-match before a sulky. **-løp** trotting.
tre (tallord) three; — **ganger** three times; **alle gode ting er** — It is the third time that tells.
tre (vrb) tread; step; — **av** retire, withdraw; **resign** office; (mil) **tre av!** break your ranks! **— an** take one's position, draw up, fall in rank;

— **fram** step forward; — **istedenfor** replace, take the place of; — **i kraft** come into force; — **i tjeneste** take service, enter into service; — **i møte** come forward to meet one; — **sammen** meet; — **sammen igjen** reassemble; — **til** step up; join; — **tilbake** draw back, stand back; — **til side** stand aside; — **under føtter** trample upon, trample under foot; — **ut** tread out; (av et selskap) retire el. withdraw (from a society). Se ellers **trå.**
tre (subst) tree; (ved) wood; **av** — wooden; **bygd av** — wood-built; wooden-built; **de henger ikke på trærne** (er ikke lette å få fatt i) they do not grow freely.
tre|art species of tree. **-bar** treeless, destitute of trees. **-bein** wooden leg.
trebevokst wooded, arboriferous.
trebrulegning wooden pavement.
tre|dekker threedecker. **-delt** tripartite.
trede|mølle tread-mill. **-pute** pad.
tredevte thirtieth. **tredvtedel** thirtieth part.
tredje third; — **kapitel** the third chapter; **det — bud** the fourth commandment.
tredjedel third; **to tredjedeler** two thirds.
tredjemann a third person el. party.
tredjeprest subdeacon.
tredjesiste the last but two.
tredobbelt three-fold, triple; **den -e krone** the tiara, the triple crown.
tredve thirty.
tredveårskrigen the thirty years' war.
treen stringy.
treenig triune.
treenighet Trinity. **treenighetslæren** the doctrine of the Trinity, Trinitarianism.
treer three.
treet woody, ligneous.
trefarget tricolour(ed).
treff (et) chance, hit, coincidence.
treffe hit; (møte) meet (with). come across; — **en hjemme** find one at home; **kula traff ham ikke** the ball missed him; (fig) **føle seg truffet** find oneself hit, feel oneself culpable, become confused el. disconcerted; — **en på det ømme punkt** strike home; — **forberedelser, et valg** make preparations, a choice; — **på** fall in with, come across, hit upon; — **sammen** meet, (om begiv.) coincide; **treffes** meet; **han -s på sitt kontor** he is to be seen at his office; — **seg** happen, fall out.
treffende (likhet) striking; (bemerkning) appropriate, to the point, pertinent; (adv) **det er særdeles** — **blitt sagt** it has been said with eminent propriety.
treffer hit. **treffsikkerhet** accuracy, certainty in hitting.
trefning (slag) battle, action.
trefold thrice (told), threefold, triple.
trefoldig triplicate; **et — hurra** three cheers.
trefoldighet Trinity.
trefork trident. **trefot** (m. tre føtter) tripod, trevet.
tre|frukt tree-fruit. **-frø** seed of trees.
treg sluggish, slow, tardy. — **mage** a weak digestion.
trege (angre) repent, fret, grieve.
treghet sluggishness, indolence.
tre|golv wooden floor. **-grense** limit of trees. **-hendt** awkward, clumsy. **-hest** wooden horse; (til straff) timber-mare. **-hjulssykkel** tricycle.
trekant triangle. **trekantet** trinagular; three-cornered; — **hatt** cocked el. three-cornered hat.
I. **trekk** (et) pull; (med penn) stroke, dash; (ansikts-) trait, feature; (sjakk o. l.) move; (fugls) roding, roading, passage, flight; (av karakter) trait (of character), feature; (betrekk) cover; **i store** — in its broad features; **3 ganger i** — 3 times running el. in succession; **en hel uke i** — a whole week on end.
II. **trekk** (en) (luft-) draught, current of air; **det er ingen** — **i ovnen** the stove does not draw.

trekk|dyr beast of draught; (fig) drudge.

trekke draw, drag, pull; (i brettspill) move; (ur) wind up; (betrekke) cover; (paraply) recover; **det -r her** there's a draught in here; — **fullt hus** command crowded houses; — **lodd** draw lots, cast lots; **skipet -r vann** the ship makes water; — **frakken, støvlene av** pull off one's coat, boots; — **gardinet for** draw the curtain; — **fra** draw (the curtain, the bolt); (fradra) deduct, subtract; — **noe fra (i en regning)** deduct (from an account); — **i langdrag** spin out; — **(lodd) om** draw for; — **opp** draw up; (narre) cheat, impose upon; **det -r opp til uvær** a storm is coming on; — **opp kunder** fleece customers; — **opp en flaske** uncork a bottle; — **på skuldrene** shrug one's shoulders; — **(en veksel) på** draw (a bill) upon; — **seg tilbake** draw back, retreat, retire, withdraw, recede; — **ut** draw out, extract; **røyken trakk ut** the smoke cleared out; — **tiden ut** procrastinate; — **seg ut av** withdraw from, back out of; **-s med** be troubled with; **-s med en dårlig helbred** labour under ill-health; **jeg har disse barna å -s med** I have these children on my hands.

trekke|band running-string. **-nål** bodkin.

trekkfugl bird of passage.

trekkfull draughty.

trekkpapir blotting-paper.

trekk|penger allotment money. **-plaster** vesicatory; (fig) attraction. **-rute** ventilator in a window. **-spill** accordion, concertina. **-tid** time of migration. **-vind** draught.

treklang triad.

trekloss log of wood.

trekløver trefoil; (fig) trio, triumvirate.

trekning drawing etc.; (i lemmene) spasm; (i ansiktet) twitch. **treknings|dag** day of drawing. **-liste** list of prizes.

tre|kol, -kull, charcoal.

trekt, se **trakt** II.

trekølle mallet.

trelast timber. **-handler** timber-merchant.

trell, se **træl.**

trema diæresis.

tremaktsforbund triple-alliance.

tremanns(bridge) three-handed (bridge).

tremangel scarcity of wood. **-masse** wood-pulp, wood-paste.

tremaster three-masted vessel.

tremenning second cousin.

tremilsgrensen the three-mile limit.

tremme cross-piece, cross-bar; (i gjerde) rail. **-verk** lattice-work, trellis.

tremosaikk inlaid wood-work.

tren (hærens transportvesen) army service corps.

trene train, practise. **trener** trainer.

trenere train. **trenering** training.

I. **trenge** (vt) press, force, drive, push; (vi): — **fram** advance, push on; — **seg fram** press forward; — **igjennom** penetrate; force one's way through; (uten objekt, fig) prevail; — **inn i** enter (into), penetrate into, make one's way el. insinuate oneself into; — **inn på en** (fig) urge one, press one hard; — **på** swarm up; hustle each other; — **tilbake** force back; — **ut** crowd out.

II. **trenge** (mangle, behøve) need, require, want; — **til** waht, be in want el. need (of), need, stand in need of.

trengende indigent, needy, necessitous.

trengsel (av folk) crowd, press, pressure, crush; (motgang) distress, affliction.

trengsels|tid, -år hour, year of distress.

trening training.

trenkusk baggage-waggoner.

trense (mar) snaffle, bridoon.

trensoldat army service man.

treolje wood-oil.

trepan|ere trepan. **-ering** trepanning.

tre|pinne wooden stick, peg. **-planting** planting of trees, woods. **-plantning** plantation. **-propp** wooden plug.

treradet three-rowed, trifarious.

tresidet three-sided, trilateral.

tresk wily, crafty.

treske thrash.

treskel threshold.

treskemaskin thrashing-machine.

treskeverk thrashing-machine el. -mill.

treskhet craft, wiliness.

tre|skjærer wood-engraver, xylographer; (billed-) carver. **-skomaker** maker of wooden shoes. **-slag** (description of) wood. **-sliperi** wood-pulp factory, pulp-mill. **-snitt** wood cut, engraving on wood, xylograph. **-splint** splint of wood. **-sponer** shavings el. chips of wood. **-sprit** methyl alcohol, methylated alcohol.

tresse lace, galloon.

trestamme stem el. trunk of a tree.

trestavelses- trisyllabic.

trestegsprang three jumps.

trestemmig for three voices el. parts.

tre|stol wooden el. wooden-bottom chair. **-stubb** stump of a tree.

trestrenget three-stringed. **-strøket** with three strokes.

tretall (number) three.

tretallerken wooden plate, platter.

tre|tiden: ved — about three. **-toms-** three inch.

tretne fag, knock down, tire.

trett tired, weary (av: of), wearied, fatigued (with); (lei av) weary (of), tired (with).

I. **trette** (gjøre trett) tire, weary, fatigue; **trettende** tiresome, wearisome, tedious.

II. **trette** (stride) quarrel.

trette (strid) dispute, quarrel; **ligge i —** be quarrelling; **komme i —** quarrel; **dømmes for unødig —** be fined for frivolous and vexatious litigation.

trettekjær quarrelsome.

trettelyst quarrelsomeness.

tretten thirteen. **-de** thirteenth.

trettendedel thirteenth (part).

tretthet weariness, fatigue, lassitude.

tretti, se **tredve.**

tre|tøffel clog. **-ull** wood-flock.

trev loft, hay-loft, upper floor of a barn; (pulpitur) gallery(-pews).

tre|varehandel trade in wooden wares; (butikken) woodenware shop. **-varehandler** dealer in wooden wares.

trevekst growth of trees.

treven slow, slack; sullen.

trevenhet slowness, slackness.

tre|verk wood-work. **-virke** wooden materials.

trevl fibre, fibril, filament, thread.

trevle: — **opp, ut** ravel (out). **trevle|bunt** bunch of fibres. **-stoff** fibrous substance; (fibrin) fibrin. **trevlet** fibrous, filamentous.

treårig triennial. **treårs** three years old.

triangel triangle. **triangulær** triangulary.

tribun tribune. **tribunal** tribunal.

tribune (tilskuer-) grand stand.

tributt tribute.

trigonometri trigonometry.

trigonometrisk trigonometrical.

trikin trichina.

trikinsykdom trichiniasis, trichinosis.

I. **trikk** (knep) trick.

II. **trikk,** se **sporvogn.**

trikke go by electric (car), go by trolley.

trikktrakk (brettspill) backgammon.

trikolor tricolour.

trikot tricot.

trikotasje tricot, stockinet. **-varer** hosiery.

I. **trille** (vrb) (rulle) roll, trundle; (om tårer) roll, trickle; (på trillebår) wheel, barrow.

II. **trille** (musikk) trill, shake.

I. **trille** (subst) (i sang) shake; **slå en —** shake;

II. **trille** (lett vogn) light phaeton or chaise.

trillebår wheel-barrow.
trilling triplet; **-er** three at a birth.
trillion trillion.
trilogi trilogy.
trin step; (i stige) round, rung; (fig) stage, development; (i grad, musikk) degree; **— for —** step by step; **stå på et høyt —** stand high; **stå på like — med** be on an equality with.
trinbrett footboard.
trine step, tread.
trinfølge gradual succession, gradation.
trinita|rier Trinitarian. **-risk** trinitarian.
trinn (subst), se **trin.**
trinn round, plump.
trinse (lite hjul under bordbein) caster, castor; (sporehjul) rowel; (v. baking) jagging-iron.
trinvis step by step; successive.
trio trio.
triol triole, triplet.
tripp short step, trip.
trippe trip, pick one's way, mince.
trippel tripoli, rottenstone.
trippelallianse triple alliance.
trippels(e) tripoli; brick-dust (for polishing).
tripp–trapp–tresko tip-tap-toe.
trisse pulley. **-blokk** block of a pulley.
trisseverk mechanism of pulleys.
trist melancholy, depressed, sad; depressing, dreary, lugubrious, cheerless.
tristhet depression, melancholy, sadness.
triton Triton.
tritt step, tread; **holde — keep** time; (fig) **holde — med** keep pace with.
triumf triumph; **i — triumphant(ly). triumfator** triumpher. **triumfbue** triumphal arch.
triumfere triumph, exult (over: at st , over one); **-nde** triumphant.
triumftog triumphal procession.
triumvir triumvir. **-at** triumvirate.
trive (gripe) catch, clutch, grasp; snatch up. **— etter** make a clutch at.
trivelig plump, well-fed. **-het** plumpness.
trives thrive; feel comfortable.
trivialitet commonplace, truism. **triviell** commonplace, hackneyed, tedious, obvious, trite.
trivle fumble grope.
trivsel vigorous growth; thriving, prosperous development.
tro (adj) (trofast) true, faithful, trusty; (undersått) loyal, faithful; **— mot en** faithful to one.
I. **tro** (subst) faith, belief; (tiltro) credence; (relig.) faith; **den kristne — the** Christian faith el. religion; **ha — på** have faith in; **ingen — på** no confidence in; **gi sin — pledge** one's vow; **på — og love** on trust; **i god — in** good faith.
II. **tro** (grise-) trough.
tro (vrb) believe; (tenke) think; (feste lit til) credit, believe, give credit to; (relig.) believe; **ikke — (en, noe)** disbelieve; **det kan du — you** may be sure of that; **ja, det -r jeg** yes, I think so, so I believe; **— på Gud** believe in God; **— en godt** trust one; **ikke til å — not** to be trusted.
troende believing; **en — a** believer; **de — the** faithful; **lite — of** little faith. **troende: stå til — deserve** credit.
trofast faithful, trusty.
trofasthet fidelity, trustiness.
trofé trophy.
trohjertig open-hearted, hearty.
trohjertighet openheartedness.
Troja Troy. **trojaner, trojansk** Trojan; **den trojanske krig** the Siege of Troy.
troké trochee. **trokéisk** trochaic.
trolig (sannsynlig) believable, credible; (stadig, trofast) truly, faithfully.
troll goblin, gnome, troll, ogre.
troll|binde cast a spell on, spellbind. **-bær** baneberry.
trolldom witchcraft, sorcery.
trolldoms|kraft magic power. **-kunst** magic

art. **trolle** (vrb) charm; (dt) conjure, do conjuring tricks. **trollet** naughty, wicked.
troll|folk mountain-sprites. **-heks** witch, sorceress. **-kar** sorcerer. **-kjerring** witch; (av krutt) maroon, devil. **-kvinne** witch. **-kyndig** versed in witchcraft, in the magic art. **-kyndighet** witchcraft. **-mann** sorcerer, wizard. **-pakk** wicked elves, (lot of) goblins. **-unge** young elf el. sprite; (dt) imp, naughty child.
trolove, trolovelse, se **forlove, forlovelse.**
trolsk elfish, magic.
troløs faithless, perfidious; **-e! traitor! traitoress! troløshet** faithlessness, perfidy, bad faith; **en — an** act of perfidy.
tromle (subst) revolving screen; (til jord) roller. **tromle** (vrb) roll.
tromme (subst) drum; **slå på — beat** the drum; **slå på stortromma** (fig) blow the trumpet.
tromme (vrb) drum, beat the drum.
tromme|hinne drum membrane. **-hule** tympanum. **-hvirvel** roll.
trommel(t) barrel, drum; revolving screen.
tromme|skinn drum-skin, drum-head. **-slager** drummer. **-stikke** drumstick. **-syke** tympanitis, tympany.
trompet trumpet; **blåse — blow** the trumpet.
trompeter trumpeter.
trompetstøt flourish (of trumpets).
tronarving heir to the throne, heir apparent.
tronbestigelse accession (to the throne).
trone (subst) throne; **bestige -n** mount, ascend the throne; **komme på -n** come el. succeed to the throne; **støte fra -n** drive from the throne, dethrone.
trone (vrb) throne.
tron|frasigelse resignation of the throne, abdication. **-følge** order of succession (in a kingdom). **-følger** successor, heir to the crown, heir apparent.
tron|himmel canopy. **-pretendent** pretender to the throne. **-røver** usurper (of the throne). **-skifte** accession of the new king.
trontale Royal speech, the King's speech.
trope|hjelm pith-hat, pith-helmet. **-landene** the tropical countries.
tropene the tropics. **tropisk** tropical.
tropp troop; **holde — keep** up.
troppe: — opp muster, troop up. **troppemasse** force.
tropper (pl) troops, forces.
troppetransport conveyance of troops; convoy of troops. **tropps|fører, -sjef** section commander.
troppvis by sections.
tros|artikkel article of faith el. belief. **-bekjennelse** creed, symbol. **-frihet** religious freedom el. liberty. **-iver** religious zeal.
troskap fidelity, faithfulness, loyalty.
troskyldig simple(-hearted), confiding, unsuspecting, unwary. **troskyldighet** simplicity.
I. **tross** (hærens) baggage, camp-train.
II. **tross** defiance, contumacy, obstinacy; **på — in** sheer defiance; **på — av ham** in his despite; **til — for** in defiance of, in spite of.
tross (prep) in spite of; **— alt** in spite of all, for all that.
tros|sak matter of faith. **-samfunn** religious-community. **-sannhet** religious truth.
trosse (vt) defy, bid defiance to, brave, beard, fly in the face of; (vi) be refractory; **— igjennom** carry through; **-r enhver beskrivelse** baffles description.
trosse (tau) rope, hawser, warp.
trossetning dogma (of faith), tenet.
trossig defying, defiant, refractory, froward.
trossighet refractoriness, frowardness.
trossvogn baggage-waggon.
trost thrush.
troverdig worthy of belief el. credit, trust worthy, credible; (ekte) authentic. **troverdighet** trustworthiness; credibility, authenticity.
tru, se **tro.**

trubadur minstrel, troubadour.
true el. **truge** threaten, menace.
trufast faithful, trusty.
truge racket, snowshoe.
trugsmål, se **trusel.**
trulig (sannsynlig) credible.
trulle (vrb), se **rulle.**
trumf trump; **oppfordring til å spille** — a call for trumps; **stikke med** — trump; **ta en med** — drive one into a corner. **trumfe** lead a trump; — **igjennom** push through; — **over** overtrump; — **seg fram** carry it with a high hand; — **ut** outtrump. **trumf ess,** — **knekt,** — **konge** osv. the ace, knave, king of trumps.
trumpet, se **tverr.**
trupp band, company.
trusel threat, menace.
truselbrev threatening letter.
tru|skap, -skyldig, se **troskap, troskyldig.**
trust trust. **-dannelse** formation of trusts. **-vesen** trust system.
trut (dt) chaps, jaw; **sette** — pout, pout one's lips.
trutne bulge, swell.
trutt (adv) faithfully, steadily.
truverdig, se **troverdig.**
trygd (forsikring) insurance. **trygde** insure.
trygdekasse insurance fund.
trygg secure, safe (**for:** from); (**i** sinnet) confiding, confident; **trygt** (adv) safely, with safety, securely; confidently.
trygge make safe, safen.
trygghet security, safety; confidence.
trygle beg, entreat, solicit.
I. **trykk** (et) pressure, squeeze; (for brystet) oppression (of the chest); (avtr.) impression.
II. **trykk** (-en) print; **på** — in print; **i** -en in the press; **fin** — small print; **god** — good type; **skarp** — bold type; **tett** — close print.
trykkark sheet of letterpress.
tryk|ke press, squeeze; (drive) force, thrust; (marked, priser) depress; (typograf.) print; — **på nytt** reprint; — **om** cancel; **la** — print; **kan -kes** for press; **-feil** misprint; **-te tøyer** printed goods; **han -te meg i armene sine** he hugged me in his arms; — **hatten ned i øynene** slouch one's hat; — **på en fjær** touch a spring; **trykkende** heavy; oppressive, grievous; (om luft) close, sultry; **trykket tilstand** depressed state, depression.
trykke|frihet liberty el. freedom of the press, a free press. **-maskin** printing-machine.
trykker printer.
trykkeri printing-house, printing-office.
trykk|feil erratum, misprint. **-ferdig** ready for the press.
trykkfeils|djevel Puck of the Press. **-liste** table of errata.
trykknapp push-button; press-stud.
trykk|papir printing-paper. **-saker** (pl) printed matter, prints. **-sverte** printer's ink.
trykning printing. **trykningsomkostninger** (pl) expenses of printing.
trylle (vt.) enchant, charm, fascinate; (vi.) conjure; — **fram** conjure forth.
trylle|blikk fascinating glance. **-drikk** enchanted potion, philter. **-fløyte** magic flute. **-formular** charm, spell, exorcism. **-klang** magic sound. **-kraft** magic power. **-kunst** magic el. fascinating art. **-midler** magic means, charms, spells.
trylleri enchantment, magic, fascination.
trylle|skrift magic writing. **-slag: som ved et** — as if by magic. **-stav** magic wand.
tryne snout.
træ (en nål) thread (a needle); — **perler på en snor** string pearls el. beads.
I. **træl** (fortykket hud) callosity; callus; (p. stortå) bunion.
II. **træl** thrall, serf, bondsman, slave.
træl|binde enthrall, enslave. **-båren** slave-born.
trældom thraldom, bondage.

træle slave, drudge, toil like a slave.
træle|arbeid work fit for slaves, drudgery. **-født,** se **trælbåren. -kår** condition of a slave. **-liv** slavish life, life of a slave. **-sjel** slavish mind. **-åk** yoke of bondage. **-ånd** slavishness, servility.
trælkvinne bonds-woman.
trælsom toilsome, laborious.
trær pl. av **tre.**
trø, se **tre** og **trå.**
trø cattle-fold.
trøffel truffle.
trøske (på tungen) trush. **-saft** borax honey.
trøst comfort, consolation; (tillit) confidence
I. **trøste** comfort, console.
II. **trøste** — **seg til** (våge) venture, dare, trust oneself (to); (tro seg i stand til) think oneself able.
trøste|brev consolatory letter. **-full** consolatory.
trøster comforter, consoler; (pute) bolster, cushion el. pillow (for chairs); (skjerf) belcher, comforter. **trøsterik** full of comfort, consolatory, consoling. **trøsteløs** inconsolable, disconsolate.
trøstesløshet disconsolateness.
trøstig of good cheer, hopeful.
trøtne fag, knock down, tire.
trøtt, se **trett.**
trøye jacket; (under-) vest.
I. **trå** (jvf. tre) tread, step; — **i** (f. eks. søla) step into, walk in (the mud); — **over** go over; — **feil** make a false step.
II. **trå** (vrb) long, yearn.
trå (harsk) rancid; (langsom, treven) slow, unwilling.
tråd thread; (bomulls-) cotton; (metall) wire; (fiber) fibre, filament; (fig) thread. (lede-) clue; **løs på -en** loose; **-en i ens tale** the thread of one's discourse; **ta -en opp** take up the strain.
tråd|aktig filamentous, thread-like. **-ende** bit of cotton el. thread.
trådløs wireless; **vi hadde** — **om bord** we had a wireless installation onboard; — **telegrafi** wireless telegraphy; — **telefonering** wireless telephony.
trådsnelle cotton reel, thread bobbin.
tråkk tramp, tramping; (plass) well-trodden place; esp. entrance, door-yard.
tråkke step, tread; trample; **han går og -r dagen lang** he isn't off his legs all day.
tråkle baste, tack. **-sting** tack, stitch. **-tråd** tacking thread.
tråkling basting.
trål trawl. **tråle** trawl.
tråler (trålfisker) trawl fisherman; (båt) trawler, trawl-boat.
tråsmak a rancid taste.
tsar czar. **tsardømme** czardom. **tsarevitsj** (tsarens sønn) czarevich. **tsarina** (tsarens gemalinne) czaritsa.
tsaristisk czarist.
tsjekk Czech. **tsjekkisk** Czech.
tsjekkoslovak Czecho-Slovak.
Tsjekkoslovakia Czecho-Slovakia.
tsjekkoslovakisk Czecho-Slovak.
tsjerkess Tcherkess.
tube tube.
tuberkel tubercle. **tuberkulose** phthisis, consumption.
tuberkuløs tuberculous, tubercular, consumptive.
tue knoll, little hillock, mound; (av gras) tuft of grass, tussock; (maur-) ant hill.
tuff (mineral) tufa, tuff.
tufs (lapperi) miserable trifles, trumpery; (dårlighet) poor affair.
tufs(e) (floke) tangle, touzle; (tafs, dusk) tuft, tassel.
tufset touzled.
tufsing bungler, poor wretch.
tuft site.
tufte, -kall goblin.

tuja thuja, thuya.	(f. eks. a wedding); — **bort** spend (on) pleasuring.

tuja thuja, thuya.
tukle bungle; — **med** tamper with.
tukt discipline; (straff) correction; **i — og
ære** in all chastity and honour.
tukte chastise, correct, castigate, chasten, discipline. **tuktelse** chastisement, castigation, correction. **tuktemester** corrector, chastener.
tukthus house of correction, bridewell; **dømme til —** sentence to hard labour; **sitter i –et** is a convict.
tukthus|fange prisoner. **–kandidat** felon.
tukthusstraff hard labour, penal servitude.
tulipan tulip. **–løk** tulip-bulb.
I. **tull** (en) (bylt) bundle; (av hår, ull) lock, roll; (dumrian) fool, whimsical person; **det går (i) — for dem** they get bewildered.
II. **tull** (tøv) nonsense, rubbish, foolery; **snakke — talk** rubbish.
tulle (lita —) toddler, tot.
tulle (vt): — **inn,** — **sammen** bundle up; wrap, huddle. — **seg bort** lose one's way, get lost; — **noe om en** tuck el. wrap something round one.
tulle (vi) (snakke tull) se **tull;** behave like a fool; (rulle rundt) spin round, roll, tumble.
tullet crazy, foolish, silly; **bli — go** crazy.
tulling (subst) fool, silly person.
tulupp topcoat.
tumle tumble, topple; — **med** struggle with; — **seg** disport oneself; riot.
tumleplass place of exercise; (fig) range, field.
tu.nler (delfin) dolphin; (due) tumbler, roller.
I. **tumling** (det å tumle) tumbling etc.
II. **tumling** (lite beger) small tumbler.
tummel tumult, bustle, uproar, racket.
tummelumsk bewildered.
tumult tumult, riot, disturbance.
tun court, court-yard.
tundra tundra.
tunes|er, –isk Tunisian.
tung heavy, ponderous; **–t sinn** gloomy disposition; — **skjebne** a hard fate; — **plikt** a painful duty; — **luft** oppressive air; **tungt** (adv) heavily.
tung|e tongue; (lang-) tongue; (på vektskål) cock; **få –a på gli(d)** give a loose to one's tongue.
tungeband ligament of the tongue; **være godt skåret for –et** have a well oiled tongue.
tungeferdig voluble, fluent of words.
tungeferdighet volubility.
tungeflyndre lemon-sole.
tunge|lyd lingual sound. **–mål** language. **–rot** root of the tongue. **–spiss** tip of the tongue.
tunget tongued.
tunge|tale the gift of tongues, glossolalia. **–taler** glossolalist.
tung|før heavy, slow. **–hendt** heavy-handed. **–hørt** hard of hearing. **–hørthet** difficulty el. hardness of hearing. **–nem** indocile, dull of comprehension, a slow learner. **–nemhet** indocility. **–rodd** pulling heavily. **–sindig** melancholy. **–sindighet** melancholy. **–som** heavyish, saddish.
tungt|lastet heavy-laden. **–væpnet** heavy -armed.
tung|vekt welter-weight. **–vint** clumsy, cumbrous, unwieldy.
tunnel tunnel.
tupp tip.
tur (liten reise) trip, excursion, run; (skips overfart) passage; (til å gjøre ett el. annet) turn; (i dans) figure; **gå, ri, kjøre en —** take a walk, a ride, a drive; **gjøre en —** go a trip; **nå kom –en til oss** now our turn came, now was our turn; **det (arbeidet) gikk etter —** it was taken by turns; **stå for — til tjeneste** be first for duty el. service.
turban turban.
turbin turbine.
turdans figure dance.
ture pleasure; dissipate, go on the spree, revel; (feire) keep (f. eks. Christmas), celebrate

turist tourist, excursionist. **–beger** telescopic (metal) cup. **–forening** touring club. **–hytte** tourists' shelter.
turné tour; **dra på —** be on tour.
turne practise gymnastics. **turner** gymnast.
turnere tilt, joust. **turnering** tournament.
turn|forening gymnastic society. **–hall** gymnasium. **–sko** athletic shoe.
turnips turnip.
turteldue turtle-dove.
turvis (adv) by turns.
tusen a thousand; — **og en natt** the Arabian Nights.
tusenben millepede.
tusende (ordenstall) thousandth.
tusendel thousandth part.
tusen|fold a thousand fold. **–foldig** thousand-fold. **–fryd** daisy. **–kunstner** man of many arts, Jack of all trades. **–stemmig** many-voiced. **–vis: i —** by el. in thousands.
tusenårig thousand years old; **det –e rike** the millennium.
I. **tusj** (musikk), se **touche.**
II. **tusj** (fargestoff) Indian ink, China ink.
tusj|kopp ink saucer. **–tegning** China-ink drawing.
tuske barter, truck.
tuskhandel barter, exchange (trade), truckage.
tusle walk softly, toddle. **tuslet(e)** weak, shaky.
tusmørke dusk, twilight.
tusmørkesvermer hawkmoth.
tusse gnome, goblin, sprite.
tusseladd duffer, fool, muff.
tusset crack-brained, crazy.
tust (dusk) tuft; (treskestokk) flail.
I. **tut** (på kanne) spout.
II. **tut** howl; (av ugle) hoot; (i horn) toot.
tute howl; (om ugle) hoot; (f. eks. i horn) toot; (gråte) cry, whine, pule; — **en ørene fulle** din one's ears; **stikke i å —** have a good cry.
tuting howling etc.
tutt screw (of paper), twist (of paper).
tvang force, compulsion, restraint, restriction, coercion, constraint; **av —** on compulsion; **med — by** constraint, forcibly; **øve — mot en** coerce, put compulsion upon.
tvang|fri, –løs unrestrained, unconstrained.
tvangløshet freedom from restraint.
tvangsakkord compulsory composition.
tvangs|arbeid compulsory el. hard labour. **–arbeidsanstalt** penal workhouse. **–auksjon** executor's sale; **selle ved –auksjon** sell under execution. **–forestilling** imperative idea. **–forholdsregel** coercive measure. **–lov** coercion act. **–lån** forced loan. **–middel** compulsory el. coercive means. **–mulkt** daily fine. **–pass** compulsory passport. **–salg** compulsory sale. **–trøye** strait-jacket.
tvare pot-stick, stirrer, stirring-stick.
tve|bitt double bite el. nibble. **–deling** bipartition, bisection. **–drakt** dissension, discord. **–egget** two-edged. **–hake** double chin. **–kamp** single combat; duel. **–kjønnet** bisexual, hermaphroditic. **–kroket** bent, doubled up; **gå, stå — double** oneself up, stoop double; — **av latter** bent with laughter.
tvelyd diphthong.
tverr cross-grained, sullen, surly, grumpy; perverse.
tverrbane cross-line.
tverrbjelke cross-beam, cross-bar, cross-piece.
tverrbukk self-willed person, obstinate person, wrong-head, snail, slug.
tverrgate cross-street.
tverrhet surliness, morosity; perverseness.
tverr|linje cross line, diagonal line. **–mål** diameter. **–snitt: i —** in section. **–stang** cross-bar.

-strek cross-streak, cross-stripe. **-sum** sum of the digits. **-vei** cross-road, cross-way.

tvers (adv, mar) abeam; — av abreast of; — for across; abreast of; — igjennom right through; **-over** across; på — across, athwart, cross-wise; **på kryss og** — in all directions, every way; **på langs og på** — to and fro, forwards and backwards; **gå** — av break el. snap short (off).

tvert (adv) crossly, transversally, transversely, across. — igjennom straight through; **bryte over** — cut the matter short.

tvert imot (adv) on the contrary; (prep) quite contrary to, right against.

tvesidig bilateral.

tvetunget double-tongued.

tvetungethet double-dealing, duplicity.

tvetydig equivocal, ambiguous; (uviss, mistenkelig) doubtful, questionable; (slibrig) indelicate.

tvetydighet ambiguity; double meaning, equivocalness, equivocation; **-er** indecencies.

tvibrent: leke — play hide-and-seek.

tviholde clutch with both hands, hold tight.

tvil doubt; **nære** — om doubt; — om at doubt that; **være i** — om feel a doubt whether; **dra i** — call in question; **uten** — without doubt, doubtless, undoubtedly, no doubt; **det er hevet over all** — it admits of no doubt whatever.

tvile doubt, call in question, question; **jeg -r ikke på det** I make no doubt el. question of it; **jeg -r ikke på at** I have no doubt but that; **tvilende** doubtful.

tviler doubter, sceptic.

tvilling twin. **-bror** twin-brother. **-par** pair of twins. **-stjerne** double star. **-søster** twin-sister.

tvil|rådig in doubt, in suspense, doubtful, irresolute, in two minds. **-rådighet** irresolution, hesitation. **-som** doubtful, dubious, questionable; **-somt tilfelle** doubtful case. **tvilsomhet** doubtfulness, dubiousness. **i tvilstilfelle** in case of doubt.

tvinge force, compel, constrain, coerce; — fram enforce; **-nde** irresistible, cogent.

tvinne twine, twist, wind.

I. **tvist** (uenighet) dispute, disagreement, difference; litigation; **-ens eple** the apple of discord.

II. **tvist** (bomullsgarn) twist.

tvistavfall white waste.

tviste dispute, contend, contest.

tvistemål dispute.

tvistepunkt matter of dispute, point at issue.

tvungen forced, strained, constrained, laboured; (i oppførsel) stiff, constrained; **le på en** — måte laugh in a strained fashion; — **skolegang** compulsory school attendance; **en — stilling** an unnaturally constrained position.

tvære: — ut spin out.

ty: — hen, til take el. seek refuge (with), have recourse to, resort to.

tyde explain, expound, interpret, decipher; — på augur, bespeak, be suggestive of, argue, go to show, imply, suggest, tell of; **merker som -r på** marks, which are the signs of.

tydelig plain, (å se, høre) distinct; (bare om framstilling) explicit; (adv) plainly etc.; **snakke** — speak plain, make oneself plain; **lese** — read distinctly.

tydelighet plainness, distinctness.

tydeligvis evidently, obviously.

tyd(n)ing explaining etc.; interpretation.

tyende (glt) servant; (kollekt.) domestics, servants, menials (pl).

tyfus typhus (fever).

tygge chew, masticate; (fig) — på noe chew the cud, ponder on. — drøv, se drøv.

tygge|flate grinding surface. **-gummi** chewing-gum. **-redskaper** masticatory organs.

tygging chewing, mastication.

tykk thick; (om personer) corpulent, stout;

(grumset) turbid; (tett) dense; **det er** — **tåke** there is a dense fog; **bli** — (om melk) curdle; **gjennom tykt og tynt** through thick and thin.

tykke (mening) opinion, judgment; (lyst) will pleasure.

tykkelse thickness.

tykkes think, be of opinion, deem.

tykk|fallen stoutish. **-halset** thick-necked.

tykkhodet thick-headed, thick-skulled.

tykk|hudet thick-skinned; (fig) callous, stolid. de -e the pachyderms.

tykk|legg thick part of the calf. **-mavet** big -bellied. **tykkmelk** loppered milk, curdled cream.

tykkpannet thick-skulled.

tykktarm large intestine.

tykne thicken; (trutne) rise; (om melk) curdle; **det -r til** the sky is thickening over.

tykning thicket.

tyksak thickset fellow.

tykt (adv) thick(ly); **smøre** — på lay it on thick.

tyktflytende thick, inspissate.

tylft dozen. **tylftevis** by dozens.

tyll (tøysort) tulle.

tylle; — i seg guzzle.

tyne despatch, murder, pot; (dt) chaw up.

tyngd el. **tyngde** gravity, heaviness, weight; **-n** gravity. **-kraft** force of gravity. **-lov** law of gravitation. **-punkt** centre of gravity; (hovedpunkt) main point.

tynge (vt) weigh upon, oppress; **være -t av sorger** be oppressed by grief; (vi) be el. feel heavy.

tyngre komparativ til **tung**.

tyngsel burden, weight.

tyngst superlativ til **tung**.

tynn thin; (spe) slender; (mots. tett) thin, sparse; (om kunnskaper) weak; (om luft) rare, rarefied.

tynnbrød, se **flabrød**.

tynne thin; — ut (f. eks. neper) thin out.

tynnhåret having thin hair.

tynning thinning.

tynn|kledd thinly dressed. **-slitt** worn thin. **-sålet** thin-soled.

tynntarm small intestine.

tynt (adv) thinly.

type type.

typisk typic(al), representative (for of).

typo|graf typographer. **-grafi** typography. **typografisk** typographic(al).

tyr bull.

tyrann tyrant. **-i** tyranny. **tyrannisere** tyrannize (over). **tyrannisk** tyrannical.

tyre|fekter bull-fighter; (til hest) toreador. **-fektning** bull-fight.

tyri resinous wood (of Norway pine). **-fakkel** pine torch. **-rot** resinous root el. stump.

tyrk Turk. **Tyrkia** Turkey; **det asiatiske Tyrki** Turkey in Asia, Asiatic Turkey.

tyrkis turquois.

tyrkisk Turkish.

Tyrol (the) Tyrol. **tyroler, -inne** Tyrolese.

tyrolsk Tyrolese, Tyrolean.

tysk German. **tysker** German.

tyskfiendtlig anti-German.

tyskhet Germanism. **Tyskland** Germany.

tyskvennlig pro-German.

tyskøsterriksk Austro-German.

tyss! hush!

tysse på en tell one to be silent.

tyst hushed, silent; (adv) silently. **tysthet** silence, hush. **tystne** grow silent.

tyte (ut) filter, ooze.

tyttebær red whortleberry, cowberry.

tyv thief, robber; (innbrudds-) burglar; **stopp -en!** stop thief! **tyvaktig** thievish, thieving.

tyvaktighet thievishness, thieving disposition.

tyve|knekt thief. **-koster** stolen goods, stolen property. **-lykt** dark lantern. **-pakk** set el. lot of thieves.

tyveri theft. **–forsikring** burglary insurance.
tyvespråk thieves' slang el. cant.
tyvsdom conviction for theft or robbery.
tær pl. av **tå**.
tære consume, corrode, fret, waste; — **på** waste; **–s hen** waste away. **–penger** money to live upon.
tæring consuming, corrosion; (sykdom) consumption, decline, phthisis.
tærings|pasient, **–syk** consumptive.
tø (vrb) thaw; — opp thaw.
tøddel jot, tittle, iota.
tøffel slipper; **stå under tøffelen** be henpecked.
tøffel|blomst slipperwort. **–danser**, **–helt** hen-pecked husband. **–regimente** petticoat-government.
tøfle trudge.
tøler (pl) odds and < n >s, trifles kept for use; **se etter i tølene sine s** arch one's lockers.
tølper churl, lout, boor. **–aktig** churlish, loutish. **–aktighet** churlishness, loutishness.
tømme (subst) rein, bridle; **holde en i —** keep one in check.
tømme (vrb) empty, drain; (om postkasse) clear.
tømmer timber; (amerikansk) lumber; (i skip) timber, frame. **–arbeid** carpenter's work, carpentry, timber-work. **–fløter** raftsman; (amr) ogs. lumber-jack. **–fløting** flotage. **–handel** timber-trade. **–handler** timber-merchant. **–haug** jam of logs. **–hogger** feller, logger. **–hogst** felling timber. **–kjører** logger. **–koie** lumber shanty, lumber camp. **–lunne** pile of timber. **–mann** carpenter. **–mannshåndverk** carpenter's craft. **–menn** (etter rangel) hot coppers. **–merker** timber-marker. **–mester** master carpenter. **–plass** timber-yard. **–svenn** journeyman carpenter.
tømming el. **tømning** emptying; (av postkasse) collection. Eks. next collection at six.
tømre carpenter, do carpenter's work; (med objekt) frame, build, make, timber, carpenter.
tømrer carpenter. **tømring** carpentry.
tønder (knusk) tinder.
tønne barrel, cask; (mål) four bushels, half a quarter, comb; (mar) buoy; **nedlegge i –r** barrel; **en — land** measure of land of 56,000 square feet.
tønne|band, **–gjord** hoop.
tønnemål: etter — by the barrel, in barrels.
tønnestav barrel (el. cask) stave.
tønnevis by the barrel.
tør, av **tore**.
tørk drying; **henge (opp) til — hang** (up) to dry.
tørke (subst) drought.
tørke (vt) dry, desiccate; (v. ild) roast; (om kjøtt ogs.) jerk; (vi) dry; **han –t pannen he** mopped his forhead; — **seg** wipe oneself; — **seg i ansiktet, om munnen** wipe one's face, mouth; — av wipe up el. off; — **inn** dry up el. in; — opp dry up; wipe up.
tørke|fille wiper. **–hus** drying house. **–loft** drying-loft. **–middel** drier, siccative. **–ovn** kiln. **–plass** drying-ground; (for klær) tenter-ground. **–ri**, se **–hus**. **tørking** drying, desiccation.
tørn turn; (ved arbeid osv.) spell; (dyst) bout. **en hard — a** hard job. **ta hver sin — take** turns **(til å al -ing).**
tørne mot strike against; — **inn** turn in; — **sammen** collide; — **ut** turn out.
tørr dry; **ha sitt på det –e** be well off, be safe; — **i halsen** parched; **tørt brød** bare bread.
tørr|dokk dry dock. **–fisk** stockfish. **–furu** dead pine-tree. **–het** dryness, aridity.
tørr|legge drain; (i stor målestokk) reclaim. **–legning** draining; (i stor målestokk) reclamation. **–lendt** dry, arid.
tørrmelk dried milk, milk powder.
tørr|skodd dry-shod. **–stoff** dry pulp. **–ved** deadwood. **–vittig** drily humorous.
tørst (subst) thirst.
tørst (adj) thirsty; dry, parched.

tørste be thirsty; (etter) thirst (for); (især fig) be athirst for.
tørstedrikk refreshing beverage.
tøs (ringeakt.) wench, hussy. **tøset(e)** wanton.
tøsne thawy snow.
tøv nonsense, rot, twaddle.
tøve talk nonsense el. rubbish, twaddle. **–kopp** twaddler, nonsensical fellow.
tøvær thawing weather, thaw.
tøy stuff, cloth, fabric; (til en drakt) length, pattern; (klær; vask) clothes; (bagasje) luggage. **ta på seg –et** put on one's things.
tøyblomst artificial flower.
tøye draw out, extend, stretch; (sterkere) strain; — **seg** stretch, give; (fig) — **seg langt for hans skyld** go a long way to oblige him. **tøyelig** elastic, extensible. **en — samvittighet** an accomodating el. elastic conscience.
tøyhus arsenal.
tøyle (subst) rein; **når man gir hesten frie –er** when the horse gets his head; **gi sine lidenskaper frie –er** give a loose to one's passions; (fig) **holde en i stramme –r** hold a tight hand over one.
tøyle (vrb) bridle.
tøyleløs unbridled, licentious.
tøyleløshet licentiousness.
tøyrensing cloth-cleansing.
tøys stuff, trash, trumpery.
tøysekopp fool, twaddler.
tøysko cloth-shoe.
tøyte hussy, minx.
tå toe; **gå på tærne** walk on tiptoe.
tå|gjenger digitigrade. **–hette** toecap.
tåke fog; (lettere) mist. **–bilde** misty form; (fig) airy vision; dissolving views el. figures. **–flekk** nebula. **–lur** fog-horn, fog-siren. **–signal** fog-signal. **–slør** foggy el. misty veil. **–tåket** foggy; (også fig) misty, hazy, dim, nebulous; (fig) vague.
tål: slå seg til –s have el. take patience.
tåle bear, stand, support; suffer, endure; (finne seg i; fordra) bear with, brook, put up with, submit to; tolerate; (kunne bære) (fig) bear, sustain; **jeg kan ikke — vin** wine does not agree with me; **saken –r ingen utsettelse** the business admits of no delay.
tålelig tolerable, supportable, bearable, endurable; (middelm.) passable, tolerable, indifferent; (adv) passably etc.
tål|mod patience. **–modig** patient, long-suffering, uncomplaining. **–modighet** patience; **ha — med** bear with. **–som** patient, tolerant. **–somhet** forbearance, tolerance.
tåpe fool, simpleton. **tåpelig** absurd, silly, foolish, stupid. **tåpelighet** silliness, stupidity, foolishness, folly.
tår drop. **ta seg en — have** a drop of st.; **ta en — over tørsten** have a drop too much.
tåre tear; **felle –r** shed tears; **svømme i –r** be bathed el. dissolved in tears; **–ne trillet nedover kinnene på henne** the tears trickled down her cheeks; **hun fikk –r i øynene** the tears came into her eyes; **lo til jeg fikk –r i øynene** laughed till I cried.
tåreblendet blinded with tears.
tåre|full tearful. **–kanal** lacrymal canal. **–kjertel** lachrymal gland. **–kvalt: med — stemme in** a voice stifled by sobs. **–løs** tearless. **–rik** lachrymose. **–strøm** flood el. torrent of tears. **–våt** tearwet.
tårn tower; (p. kirke) steeple; (i sjakk) rook, castle; (på krigsskip) turret.
tårne pile up, heap up; — **seg** tower.
tårn|fløy vane el. weather-cock on a steeple. **–høy** steeple-high, towering. **–kammer** tower-room. **–klokke** tower-bell. **–skip** turret-ship. **–spir** spire. **–ugle** screech-owl. **–ur** tower-clock, turret clock. **–vekter** watchman (on a tower).
tåspiss tiptoe.
tåte (subst) feeding-bag. **–flaske** feeding-bottle. **–smokk** india-rubber bottle-sucker.
tått (i saga, i tau) strand, thread.

U

U, u U u.

uaktet (prep) despite, in spite of; (konj) though, although, albeit.

uaktsom inattentive, negligent, careless, heedless. **uaktsomhet** inattention, negligence, carelessness, heedlessness, inadvertency.

ualminnelig uncommon, rare; (usedvanlig) unusual, extraordinary; (adv) uncommonly.

uan(e)t unsuspected, undreamt of.

uanfektelig undisturbable; (juridisk) incontestable. **uanfektelighet** incontestableness.

uanfektet unaffected, unmoved (av: by).

uangripelig unassailable, unimpeachable.

uangripelighet unassailable nature.

uanmeldt unannounced, usherless.

uanselig plain-looking, insignificant, unsightly. **-het** insignificance, unsightliness.

uansett (adj) humble, mean, unrespected; (prep) without regard to, notwithstanding.

uanstendig indecent. **-het** indecency.

uansvarlig irresponsible.

uansvarlighet irresponsibility.

uan|tagelig, -takelig unacceptable.

uantastelig unassailable, unattackable, that cannot be touched.

uantastet unassailed, unattacked, untouched.

uanvendelig inapplicable (på: to). **uanvendelighet** inapplicability, uselessness, irrelevancy.

uanvendt unused, unemployed.

uappetittlig uninviting, unsavoury.

uappetittlighet unsavouriness.

uartikulert inarticulate.

uatskillelig inseparable; (uoppløselig) indissoluble. **uatskillelighet** inseparability.

uavbrutt uninterrupted, unintermitting, unintermittent, unbroken, continual, incessant; (adv) incessantly etc., without intermission.

uavgjort unsettled, undecided, unadjusted, undetermined, pending.

uavhendelig inalienable. **uavhendelighet** inalienableness. **uavhendet** unsold; untransferred.

uavhengig independent. **-het** independence.

uavhjelpelig irremediable.

uavkortet uncurtailed, unstinted.

uavlatelig incessant, unceasing, unintermitting; unintermittent; (adv) without intermission, incessantly, continually.

uavlåst unlocked.

uavsettelig (uselgelig) unsaleable, unmarketable, not vendible; (fra embete) irremovable. **-het** irremovability.

uavtalt not agreed upon, unpreconcerted.

uavvendelig inevitable. **-het** inevitableness.

uavvergelig not to be prevented.

uavviselig imperative, peremptory.

uavvitende unknowingly, unwittingly, unintentionally; **meg, deg** osv. — unknown to me, you etc. el. without my, your knowing it.

uban(e)t unbeaten, untrodden.

ubarbert unshaven.

ubarmhjertig unmerciful, merciless, remorseless, uncompassionate. **ubarmhjertighet** unmercifulness, mercilessness, remorselessness.

ubearbeidd unimproved; (fig) crude.

ubebodd uninhabited, unoccupied, tenantless.

ubeboelig uninhabitable.

u(be)bygd not built upon, unbuilt.

ubedekket uncovered.

ubedragelig infallible.

ubedragelighet infallibility, infallibleness.

ubedt unasked, uninvited.

ubeediget unsworn, under no oath.

ubefestet open, unfortified; (flg) unsteadfast,
unsettled. **ubefestethet** (fig) instability; unsettled state of mind.

ubeføyd unauthorized, incompetent.

ubegavet not gifted, incapable.

ubegrenset unbounded, illimitable.

ubegripelig incomprehensible.

ubehag dislike, disgust.

ubehagelig unpleasant, disagreeable.

ubehagelighet unpleasantness; annoyance.

ubeheftet unencumbered.

ubehendig clumsy. **-het** clumsiness.

ubehersket uncontrolled, unrestrained.

ubehjelp|elig, -som awkward, shiftless. **-somhet** awkwardness.

ubehøvlet churlish, rude.

ubekjent unknown; **— med** ignorant of.

ubekjentskap ignorance (med, til: of).

ubekvem uncomfortable.

ubekvemhet inconvenience, discomfort.

ubekymret unconcerned. **-het** unconcern.

ubeleilig unconvenient, inopportune.

ubemerket unnoticed, obscure; (adv) secretly.

ubemerkethet obscurity.

ubemidlet without fortune, poor.

ubendig indomitable, unruly.

ubendighet unmanageableness, unruliness.

ubenevnt (mat) indefinite, abstract.

ubenyttet unavailed of, unemployed, unused.

uberegnelig fickle, capricious.

uberegnelighet capriciousness.

uberettiget unauthorized, not entitled; (påstand o. l.) unwarranted.

uberyktet of good character, unimpeachable.

uberørt untouched, virgin; unconcerned; unaffected. **-het** untouched condition; virginity; unconcern.

ubesatt free, open, unoccupied; (om embete) vacant.

ubeseiret unconquered, unvanquished.

ubesindig imprudent, heedless, rash.

ubesindighet imprudence, rashness.

ubeskadiget unhurt, uninjured, sound.

ubeskjeden immodest, indiscreet; immoderate, pretentious; impertinent. **ubeskjedenhet** immodesty, indiscretion, impertinence.

ubeskjeftiget disengaged, unemployed.

ubeskrevet not written on, blank.

ubeskrivelig indescribable, unspeakable.

ubeskyttet unprotected; unsheltered.

ubeskåret uncurtailed, unimpaired.

ubesluttsom irresolute.

ubesmittet unstained, unpolluted; **den ubesmittede unnfangelse** immaculate conception.

ubestemmelig indeterminable, nondescript.

ubestemt undecided, undetermined, indefinite; (om begreper) vague; (av karakter) irresolute; **den -e artikkel** the indefinite article.

ubestemthet uncertainty; irresolution.

ubestikkelig incorruptible. **ubestikkelighet** incorruptibleness, incorruptibility.

ubestridelig incontestable, indisputable.

ubestridt undisputed, uncontested.

ubesvart unanswered.

ubesørget undone, unperformed; **ubesørgede brev** dead letters.

ubetalelig invaluable, inestimable.

ubetenksom inconsiderate, heedless, rash.

ubetenksomhet rashness, indiscretion.

ubetimelig unseasonable, inopportune, ill-timed.

ubetinget unconditional; (absolutt) unqualified, absolute; (adv) decidedly, absolutely, unconditionally.

ubetont unaccented, unemphasized.

ubetrådt untrodden.
ubetvingelig indomitable, unconquerable; uncontrollable.
ubetydelig insignificant, inconsiderable; unimportant, trifling, trivial, slight.
ubetydelighet insignificance; en — a trifle.
ubevegelig immovable; (ubøyelig) inflexible, inexorable; (som ikke beveger seg) motionless.
ubevegelighet immobility.
ubevisst unconscious, instinctive.
ubevoktet unguarded.
ubevæpnet unarmed.
ubillig unreasonable, unfair, unjust.
ublandet unmixed, unmingled; (om drikkevarer) neat, raw; — glede unmixed joy; — beundring unqualified admiration.
ubleikt unbleached; (i handelsspråk) grey, brown.
ublid inclement, harsh, severe, ungentle.
ublodig bloodless, unbloody.
ublu shameless, impudent, barefaced; en — pris an exorbitant price. ubluferdig shameless, bold, unchaste. -het shamelessness, boldnes, unchastity. ubluhet shamelessness, impudence, barefacedness; exorbitance.
ublyg shameless, bold, unchaste.
ubotelig irreparable.
ubrudden (mat) integral, whole.
ubrukbar, ubrukelig unserviceable, unsuitable, unfit for use; gjøre — disable; bli (gjort) — become disabled.
ubrukelighet uselessness. ubrukt unused.
ubrytelig unbreakable.
ubrødelig inviolable.
ubrøyte (subst) uncleared road, impracticable ground.
ubuden uninvited, unbidden, self-invited.
ubundet unrestrained, unrestricted; — stil prose.
ubygd (subst) desert, uninhabited region, wilds. ubygd (adj), se u(be)bygd.
ubønnhørlig inexorable, inflexible.
ubønnhørlighet inexorableness, inflexibility.
ubøyelig inflexible. -het inflexibility.
u-båt submarine; (om tyske båter også) U-boat. ubåts|angrep submarine attack. -krig submarine war.
udadlelig unblamable, irreproachable.
udannet uncivilized, rude, uneducated. — vesen bad manners.
udelaktig i having no part in, no party to, not participating in.
udelelig indivisible. -het indivisibility.
udelt entire, undivided.
udeltagende indifferent, listless.
udiplomatisk undiplomatic.
udisiplinert undisciplined.
udramatisk undramatic(al).
udrikkelig undrinkable.
udryg el. udrøy unlasting, unsubstantial.
udugelig incapable, unable, unqualified. -het incapability, disqualification.
udyd vice, fault. udydig unvirtuous, vicious.
udyktig incompetent. -het incompetency.
udyr monster.
udyrkelig unfit for cultivation.
udyrket uncultivated.
udødelig immortal. udødelighet immortality.
udøpt unchristened, unbaptized.
udåd misdeed, atrocity, outrage.
uedel ignoble, base.
uedelmodig ungenerous.
ueffen odd; det er ikke så -t that's not amiss.
uegennyttig disinterested.
uegennyttighet disinterestedness.
uegentlig improper; figurative, tropical.
uekte spurious, imitation; — barn natural child, illegitimate child, bastard child; — brøk improper fraction; — diamanter false diamonds; — kniplinger imitation lace; (gram) — sammensetning separable compound. uekthet spuriousness; illegitimacy.

uelskverdig unamiable. uelskverdighet inamiability.
uendelig infinite, endless, interminable; (adv) infinitely; i det -e ad infinitum, indefinitely.
uendelighet infinity, endlessness.
uenig være — med en disagree with one, differ from one in opinion; bli — quarrel, fall out; jeg er — med meg selv I cannot make up my mind.
uenighet disagreement, dissension, difference.
uens unlike; (adv) differently. -artet heterogeneous. uensartethet heterogeneousness.
uens(e)t disregarded.
uer (fisk) Norway haddock, red-fish.
uerfaren inexperienced. -het inexperience.
uerstattelig irreparable. -het irreparability.
ufarbar impassable; (elv) unnavigable.
ufarbarhet impassableness.
ufarlig undangerous.
ufarget not dyed, undyed; (fig) uncoloured.
ufattelig inconceivable, incomprehensible. -het incomprehensibility, inconceivableness.
ufeil|bar infallible, unfailing. -het infallibility, infallibleness. -barlig unfailing; (adv) infallibly, unfailingly, undoubtedly.
uferd unsuccessful expedition, failure; (glt., ulykke) disaster.
uferdig unfinished. -het unfinished state.
uff (interj.) oh, ugh!
ufin coarse, rude, unmannerly, indelicate, vulgar. ufinhet bad taste, indelicacy.
ufjelg unkempt, untidy.
uflidd ill-groomed, unkempt.
uflyg unfledged; — fugl nestling; flapper.
uforanderlig unchangeable, immutable, unalterable, invariable. -het immutability.
uforandret unchanged, unaltered.
uforbederlig incorrigible, inveterate, confirm-ed. -het incorrigibility.
uforbeholden open, free; jeg gjør herved en — unnskyldning I hereby tender a full and free apology.
uforbeholdenhet openness, sincerity.
uforberedt unprepared; (adv) off-hand.
uforberedthet unpreparedness.
ufor|bindende non-committal. -bindtlig disobliging.
uforblommet unambiguous.
uforbrennelig incombustible.
uforbrennelighet incombustibility.
ufordelaktig disadvantageous, unprofitable; (utseende) unprepossessing; det -e ved the disadvantage of. ufordelaktighet disadvantage, unprofitableness.
ufordervelig incorruptible. ufordervet uncorrupted, unspoiled. innocent. ufordervethet incorruptness, innocence.
ufordragelig intolerable; intolerant.
ufordragelighet intolerableness; intolerance.
ufordult undisguised.
ufordunklet undimmed, unclouded.
ufordøyelig indigestible. -het indigestibility.
ufordøyd undigested; (mest fig) crude.
uforenlig incompatible, irreconcilable, inconsistent (with). -het incompatibility.
uforfalsket unadulterated, unsophisticated, genuine. uforfalskethet genuineness.
uforferdet undaunted, intrepid, dauntless.
uforferdethet intrepidity, undauntedness.
uforgjengelig imperishable.
uforgjengelighet imperishableness.
uforglemmelig never-to-be-forgotten; unforgettable, unforgotten.
uforholdsmessig disproportionate; (adv) disproportionately. -het disproportion.
uforklarlig inexplicable, unaccountable.
uforknytt undismayed.
uforkrenkelig imperishable.
uforkrenkelighet imperishableness.
uforlignelig matchless, peerless.
uforlikelig irreconcilable; se uforenlig.

uforlikt at odds, at variance.
uformelig shapeless, amorphous, unshapely.
uformelighet deformity.
uformell informal.
uformerkt unnoticed, unobserved.
uformidlet direct, spontaneous; (adv) ogs. abruptly.
uforminsket unabated, unimpaired.
uformuende fortuneless, impecunious.
uformuenhet want of means; (mangel på evne) inability.
ufornuft absurdity, unreasonableness, unreason. ufornuftig irrational, unreasonable, absurd. -het absurdity, unreasonableness.
ufornøden unnecessary, needless.
ufornøyelig not to be satisfied, hard to please; unpleasant.
uforrettet undone; komme tilbake med — sak return unsuccessful, without accomplishing one's errand.
uforsagt undaunted. -het undauntedness.
uforseglet unsealed.
uforsettlig undesigned.
uforsiktig incautious, imprudent.
uforsiktighet imprudence, incautiousness.
uforskammet insolent, impudent, shameless. -het insolence, impudence, shamelessness.
uforskyldt undeserved, unmerited.
uforsonlig implacable, irreconcilable, uncompromising. uforsonlighet implacability.
uforstand want of sense el. judgment.
uforstandig indiscreet, injudicious.
uforstilt unfeigned, undisguised.
uforstyrrelig imperturbable, cool.
uforstyrrelighet imperturbability.
uforstyrret calm, undisturbed, unvexed.
uforstå(e)lig unintelligible.
uforstående bewildered, puzzled, uncomprehending; (ikke forståelsesfull) uncongenial.
uforsvarlig inexcusable, unjustifiable.
uforsørget unprovided for. tre uforsørgede barn three unprovided children.
ufortapelig (rett) inalienable.
ufortjent undeserved, unmerited.
ufortollet unentered, not duty-paid.
ufortrøden unwearied, indefatigable.
ufortrødenhet indefatigableness.
ufortært unconsumed, entire.
uforutselig that cannot be foreseen.
uforutsett unforeseen, unlooked for.
uforvansket incorrupt, unadulterated.
uforvarende unawares, inadvertently.
uframkommelig impassable, impracticable. -het impassableness, impracticableness.
ufrankert not post-paid, unpaid.
ufravendt intent, fixed; (adv) intently.
ufravikelig unalterable, invariable; (adv) invariably.
ufred troubles (pl), disturbances (pl); dissension; leve i — be at variance.
ufredelig unpeaceable. ufreds|mann mischief-maker. -tid time of war, war-time.
ufri not free, unfree. ufrihet bondage
ufristet (uprøvd) untried.
ufrivillig (adj.) involuntary, unintentional.
ufruktbar unfruitful, barren, sterile, infertile.
ufruktbarhet barrenness, sterility.
ufs (bergvegg) bluff.
ufullbyrdet unfinished, unaccomplished, unperformed, unexecuted.
ufullbåret embryonic, abortive.
ufullendt imperfect, unfinished, unaccomplished.
ufullendthet unfinished el. unaccomplished state.
ufullkommen imperfect. -het imperfection.
ufullstendig incomplete, defective, imperfect.
ufullstendighet incompleteness, defectiveness, imperfectness.
ufundert unfounded; (seddel) unsecured; økning (innskrenkning) av den -e seddelmengde inflation (deflation).
ufyselig forbidding, uninviting, nasty.

ufødt unborn.
ufølsom insensible, apathetic, impassible; unfeeling. ufølsomhet insensibility, apathy, want of feeling.
ufør, se udyktig og vanfør.
uføre impassable road, mire; (fig) mess.
uførhet, se udyktighet og vanførhet.
ugagn mischief. ugagnskråke mischievous thing, imp.
ugalant ungallant, uncomplimentary.
ugarvet untanned.
ugg (brodd, pigg) sting; spike, barb; prickle.
uggen (adj) raw, chilly.
ugidelig listless, indolent. -het listlessness, indolence.
ugift unmarried, single, unwedded.
ugild (jur) disqualified.
ugjendrivelig irrefutable, unanswerable.
ugjenkallelig irrevocable; (adv) irrevocably; (om forestilling o. l.) — siste gang positively last night el. performance.
ugjenkjennelig irrecognizable.
ugjennomførlig impracticable.
ugjennomførlighet impracticability.
ugjennomsiktig intransparent, opaque.
ugjennomsiktighet opaqueness opacity.
ugjennomskuelig impenetrable.
ugjennomtrengelig impenetrable, unpierceable.
ugjennomtrengelighet impenetrability.
ugjerne unwillingly, reluctantly.
ugjerning enormity, outrage.
ugjerningsmann evildoer, malefactor.
ugjestfri inhospitable.
ugjestfrihet inhospitality, inhospitableness.
ugjort undone; la — leave undone.
ugjært unfermented.
ugjørlig impracticable.
uglad melancholy, sad, uncheerful.
ugle: — ut bedizen, rig out.
ugle owl; det er -r i mosen mischief is brewing.
uglebilde fright.
uglese look with an evil eye on.
ugodslig uncomfortable, unpleasant.
ugras weed, (koll.) weeds.
ugrei tangled; (fig) recalcitrant.
ugreie (subst) entanglement, tangle; (fig) difficulty, hitch, trouble; det ble noe — med styreinnretningen something went wrong with the steering gear.
ugreie (vrb) entangle, tangle.
ugrunnet groundless, unfounded.
ugudelig impious, unholy.
ugudelighet impiety, wickedness.
ugunst disfavour, displeasure.
ugunstig unfavourable, adverse; under svært -e vilkår under great disadvantages.
ugyldig invalid, (null and) void. erklære — annul, nullify; gjøre — invalidate.
ugyldighet invalidity, nullity.
uhandterlig, se uhåndterlig.
uharmonisk inharmonious, discordant.
uhederlig dishonourable.
uhederlighet dishonour, dishonourableness.
uhelbredelig incurable; -e incurables.
uheldig unfortunate, unlucky, untoward; (av ytre) ungainly; (ubehagelig) awkward; — stilt placed at a disadvantage.
uheldigvis unluckily, unfortunately.
uhell ill-luck; failure; (enkelt) misfortune, mischance, mishap, accident; til — for unfortunately for; til alt — as bad el. ill luck would have it. -svanger fatal, sinister. -varslende ill-omened, ominous.
uhensiktsmessig inexpedient; inadequate to the purpose. -het inexpediency.
uhevnet unrevenged, unavenged.
uhildet unbiassed, unprejudiced, impartial; (adv) impartially.
uhildethet unprejudicedness, impartiality.
uhindret unhindered, unimpeded, unobstructed; — adgang free acces.

uhistorisk unhistorical.

uhjelpelig unaidable, past help, irremediable.

uhjelpelighet irremediableness.

uhjelpsom unwilling to help.

uhjemlet unauthorized, unauthenticated.

uholdbar (ikke til å opprettholde) untenable, unmaintainable. **en — hypotese** an untenable hypothesis. **uholdbarhet** untenability.

uhu! too-who! tu-whoo!

uhumsk filthy, nasty.

uhumskhet filthiness, nastiness; **–er** filth.

uhygge discomfort, uncomfortableness.

uhyggelig uncomfortable, cheerless, dismal; (illevarslende) sinister; (spøkelsesaktig) ghastly, uncanny, weird. **gjøre det — for meg** render me uncomfortable.

uhyklet unfeigned.

uhyre (adj) enourmous, tremendous, huge, prodigious; (adv) enormously etc. **uhyre** (subst) monster, prodigy.

uhyrlig monstrous stupendous. **–het** monstrosity, stupendousness.

uhøflig uncivil, impolite, discourteous, rude.

uhøflighet incivility, impoliteness, discourtesy, rudeness; **en — an** act of discourtesy.

uhørlig inaudible.

uhørt unheard; (enestående) unheard of, unprecedented.

uhøvisk indecent. **uhøviskhet** indecency.

uhøvlet rough, unplaned, undressed.

uhåndterlig unhandy, awkward, unmanageable, unwieldy.

uhåndterlighet unhandiness, unmanagableness.

uimotsagt uncontradicted.

uimotsigelig incontestable, indisputable.

uimotstå(e)lig irresistible, resistless.

uimotståelighet irresistibility.

uimottagelig el. **uimottakelig** insusceptible (for: of). **–het** insusceptibility.

uinnbudt uninvited.

uinnbundet unbound.

uinnfridd, uinnløst unredeemed; (veksel) unpaid.

uinnskrenket unlimited, unrestricted, unbounded, uncontrolled, absolute; **— herre** sovereign lord. **uinnskrenkethet** absoluteness.

uinntagelig el. **–takelig** impregnable. **–het** impregnableness, impregnability.

uinnvidd (f. eks. jord) unconsecrated; (ikke innvidd i en viten) uninitiated.

uinteres|sant uninteresting. **–sert** disinterested.

uinteresserthet disinterestedness.

ujamn, ujevn uneven, rough. **–het** unevenness, roughness, inequality.

ukallet uncalled.

uke week; **om en — in** a week; **i dag om en — this** day week; **to ganger om –n** twice a week.

ukeblad weekly paper.

ukedag day of the week; (hverdag) week-day.

ukentlig (adj) weekly; (adv) weekly.

ukeskrift weekly (paper el. periodical).

ukevis by the week; **i — for** weeks.

ukjennelig not to be recognised, undistinguishable; **gjøre — disguise.**

ukjennelighet irrecognizableness; **forandret inntil — altered** beyond recognition.

ukjent unknown; ignorant (med: of), unacquainted (with).

ukjærlig unkind. **ukjærlighet** unkindness.

uklanderlig blameless, irreproachable, above reproach.

uklar not clear, turbid, muddy; (fig) indistinct, obscure; (forvirret) confused; (mar) foul; **ryke — med** fall out with; **hadde et –t begrep om** had some dim notion of; **ha en — fornemmelse av** at be vaguely sensible that.

uklarhet turbidness; dimness; confusion; indistinctness, obscurity.

ukledelig unbecoming.

uklok unwise, imprudent.

uklokskap imprudence, indiscretion, impolicy.

ukomplett incomplete, defective, deficient.

ukrenkelig inviolable. **–het** inviolability.

ukrigersk unwarlike.

ukring stiff, unyielding; cramped; (fig) awkward, inconvenient.

ukristelig unchristian. **–het** unchristianness.

ukritisk uncritical.

ukrutt, se ugras. — forgår ikke evil weeds never wither, bad weeds are sure to thrive.

ukuelig indomitable.

ukultivert uncultivated; uncivilised.

ukunstlet artless, inartificial, unaffected.

ukunstlethet artlessness, simplicity.

ukunstnerisk inartistic, bad art.

ukvemsord abusive words, bad language.

ukvinnelig unwomanly. **ukvinnelighet** unwomanly conduct el. manners.

ukyndig ignorant (of), unskilled (in), not conversant (with). **–het** ignorance; unskilfulness.

ukysk unchaste. **ukyskhet** unchastity.

ul (hyl) hooting, hoot; (ulvens, vindens) howling, howl.

ul (bedervet) tainted.

ulage disorder; **bringe i — put** into disorder; **komme i — get** out of order.

ulan Uhlan.

ulastelig unblamable, blameless, irreproachable, irreprehensible. **–het** blamelessness.

ule hoot, howl.

ulegelig incurable.

ulegemlig bodiless, immaterial, incorporeal.

ulegt unhealed.

uleilige trouble, incommode, inconvenience; **— seg med å** take the trouble to.

uleilighet inconvenience, trouble; **komme til — give** trouble; **gjøre en — put** one to inconvenience, give one trouble; **gjøre seg den — å** take the trouble to, be at the trouble of.

ulempe inconvenience, drawback, objection.

ulende rough ground. **ulendt** impracticable, rough, rugged.

ulenkelig ungainly, unwieldy; loose of joint.

uleselig illegible; (ikke leseverdig) unreadable. **–het** illegibility; unreadableness.

ulesket (om kalk) unslaked, quick.

ulidelig intolerable, insufferable.

ulik unlike.

ulike unequal; **et — tall** an uneven el. odd number; **like eller — odd** or even; **— lange** of unequal length; **— store** unequal, of unequal size; **— større, bedre** far greater, better.

ulike|artet heterogeneous. **–sidet** unequalsided.

ulikhet dissimilarity, disparity.

ulivssår fatal el. mortal wound.

ulk (sjø–) tar.

ulk(e) sea scorpion.

ull wool. **ullaktig** woolly.

ullen (adj) woollen.

ull|garn woollen, yarn, worsted. **–hår** woolly hair. **–skjorte** woollen el. flannel shirt. **–skjørt** woollen petticoat. **–spinner, –spinnerske** spinner of wool. **–spinneri** woollen mill. **–strømpe** woollen stocking. **–teppe** woollen blanket. **–trøye** woollen jacket; flannel shirt el. vest. **–tøy** woollen stuff, woollen. **–varefabrikk** woollen mill(s). **–varer** woollen goods, woollens, worsted articles, hosiery. **–vever** woollen weaver.

ulme smoulder.

ulne (bli ul) taint.

ulogisk illogical; **det –e i** the illogicality of.

ulovende(s) (adv) without permission el. leave.

ulovlig unlawful, illegal.

ulovlighet unlawfulness, illegality.

ulster (ytterfrakk) ulster.

ultimatum ultimatum.

ultimo ultimo; **den 5te — on** the 5th ult.

ultra ultra. **–marin** ultramarine. **–montan** ultramontane. **–montanisme** ultramontanism.

ulv wolf. **–aktig** wolfish.

ulve|flokk pack of wolves. **–hi** wolf's den el.

lair. **-hunger** wolfish el. voracious appetite. **-skrei** running pack of wolves. **-stue** pit for trapping wolves.
ulv|inne she-wolf. **-unge** wolf's cub.
ulyd discordant noise, jangle, jar.
ulydig disobedient (mot: to); **være — mot en** disobey one. **-het** disobedience (mot: to).
ulykke misfortune, calamity, disaster; **bringe — bring** ill luck; **fy for all —!** fie for shame! out upon it! **i -n** under misfortunes; **bringe i — bring** trouble el. calamity upon one; **han gjorde en — på seg selv** he made away with himself; **til all — as** ill luck would have it; **komme ut for en — meet** with an accident.
ulykkelig unhappy; (uheldig) unlucky, unfortunate; (hendelse) disastrous, calamitous; **gjøre — ruin. ulykkeligvis** ufortunately, unluckily.
ulykkesbudskap fatal news, bad news.
ulykkes|forsikret insured against accidents. **-forsikring** accidents insurance.
ulykkesfugl bird of ill omen.
ulykkestilfelle (disastrous) accident, casualty.
ulyksalig disastrous, infelicitous, unhappy.
ulyst dislike, disinclination, disgust; **gjøre noe med — do** a thing reluctantly, with reluctance; **ha — til** have a dislike of.
ulægelig, ulægt, se **ulegelig, ulegt.**
ulærd unlearned, unlettered, illiterate.
ulønnsom profitless. **ulønt** unpaid.
ulø(y)selig insolvable, inextricable.
ulø(y)st unsolved.
umak pains, trouble; **bortkastet — labour** in vain; **gjøre seg — for å** take pains to, go out of one's way to; **det er ikke -n verdt** it is not worth while.
umake (adj) not matching, odd.
umakelig inconvenient, uncomfortable, uneasy; (adv) uncomfortably.
umalt unpainted.
umandig unmanly, effeminate.
umandighet unmanliness, effeminacy.
umanerlig unmannerly; (dt.) enormous, immense.
umeddelsom incommunicative.
umedgjørlig unmanageable, intractable, untractable. **umedgjørlighet** intractableness.
umelodisk unmelodious.
umenneske monster, inhuman wretch.
umenneskelig inhuman. **-het** inhumanity.
umerkelig imperceptible, insensible; (adv) imperceptibly. **umerket** unmarked.
umetodisk unmethodical.
umettelig insatiable, unsatiate.
umettelighet insatiableness.
umiddelbar immediate, direct.
umiddelbarhet immediateness.
umiddelbart (adv) directly, immediately (**etter:** after, on).
umild harsh, unkind.
umildhet harshness, unkindness.
uminnelig immemorial; **i** el. **fra -e tider** time out of mind, from time immemorial.
umiskjennelig evident, unmistakable.
umistelig inestimable, priceless.
umistenkelig unsuspicious.
umistenksom unsuspicious, unsuspecting.
umistenksomhet unsuspectingness.
umoden unripe, immature. **-het** immaturity.
umoderne out of fashion.
umoral immorality. **umoralsk** immoral.
umotivert gratuitous, uncalled for.
umulig impossible; **du kan — gå ut** you cannot possibly stir out. **umuliggjøre** render impossible. **umulighet** impossibility.
umusikalsk unmusical; (om person) with no ear for music; **han er — he** is no musician.
umyndig not of age, under age; **han er — he** is a minor, he is not of age; **-es midler** trust funds; **lov om -es midler** trustee act; **gjøre —, -gjøre** declare one incapable of managing his affairs.

umyndighet minority, nonage.
umyntet uncoined.
umælende dumb; **— dyr** dumb animal, brute.
umøblert unfurnished.
umåteholden immoderate, intemperate.
umåtelig immense, enormous; (adv) immensely.
umåtelighet excess, immoderation, intemperance.
unatur, se **unaturlighet. unaturlig** unnatural, contrary to nature; (påtatt) affected. **-het** unnaturalness; forcedness; affectedness.
under (subst.) wonder, marvel, prodigy.
under (prep) **u n d e r: — dags dato** this day, under this date; **— 15. ds.** under the date of 15th inst; **— 15de februar** under date February 15; **— firma ...** under the firm of ...; **— hånd og segl** under (my etc.) hand and seal; **— lås og lukke** under lock and key; **være — seil** be under way; (sted, rang, fortrin, pris) **b e n e a t h, b e l o w: han er — meg** (i nummer osv.) he is below me; **det er — min verdighet** it is beneath me; (om tid) **d u r i n g: — middagsmåltidet** during dinner; **— Frederik den 3djes regjering** during el. in the reign of Frederik the Third; **i n: — pressen** in the press; **— åpen himmel** in the open air; **a m i d s t: — klokkenes klang** amidst the ringing of bells; **b y: han gikk — navnet D.** he went by the name of D.; **o n: — eds ansvar** on (el. upon) oath; **t o: skrive et brev til en — adresse ...** write one a letter to the address of ...; **— en strøm av tårer** (while) shedding a torrent of tears; **— ett** collectively, together.
under (adv): **gå — be** lost, founder; **det stikker noe — there** is something behind, at the bottom of this.
underagent sub-agent. **-ur** sub-agency.
underansikt lower part of the face.
underarm forearm; (i anatomi) cubit.
underavdeling subdivision, subsection.
underbalanse deficit; **en — på** a deficit of.
underbefalingsmann petty officer.
underbenklær drawers.
underbevisst subconscious.
underbevissthet subconsciousness.
underbibliotekar sub-librarian, assistant librarian.
underbind|e tie (up), take up. **-ing** ligature.
underbitt the lower teeth jutting out beyond the upper.
underbud lower offer el. bid.
underbukser drawers.
underby underbid.
underbygge build under; (fig) ground, base.
underbygning substructure, underbuilding.
underdanig submissive; most humble, most obedient. **underdanighet** subjection; submission, deference.
underdyne under feather-bed.
underdønning ground swell, long heavy rollers.
underekstremiteter nether extremities.
undererme under-sleeve.
underernære underfeed.
underernæring underfeeding.
underfeltherre second in command.
underflate lower surface, base.
underforstå imply. **det var stilltiende -tt at** it was tacitly understood that. **-else** implication.
underforvalter submanager.
underfull wonderful, marvellous, wondrous, miraculous.
underfundig crafty, cunning, disingenuous.
underfundighet craft, cunning.
undergang destruction, ruin.
undergi subject (to); **være -tt** be subject to. **undergiven** inferior. **hans undergivne** those under him.
undergjerning wonder, miracle.
under|gjæring sedimentary fermentation. **-gjært** produced by sedimentary fermentation.
undergjørende wonder-working, miraculous.

undergrave undermine, sap.
under|grunn sub-soil, sub-stratum. **-grunns-banen** the Underground; (elektrisk) the Tube.
undergå undergo, suffer, pass through; — **en forandring** undergo a change.
underhandle negotiate, treat. **underhandler** negotiator. **underhandling** negotiation.
underhold support, maintenance, subsistence. **underholde** support, maintain, sustain, subsist; (more) entertain.
underholdende entertaining.
underholdning entertainment, conversation.
under|hus Lower House. **-et** (i England) House of Commons.
underhånden privately.
underjordisk subterranean, subterraneous, underground; **de -e** the elves, the good people.
underkant under side; lower edge.
underkaste submit (to); — **seg (en, noe)** subject oneself (to); **være -t** be subject el. subjected to; **tvil -t** open to doubt.
underkastelse subjection, submission.
underkjenne reverse, overrule, disaffirm.
underkjennelse reversal.
underkjeve lower el. nether jaw.
underkjole under-gown, underskirt.
underkjøpe bribe; (falske vitner) suborn.
underklasse lower class.
underklær under-garments, underwear.
underkropp lower part of the body.
underkue subdue, subjugate; (i vekst) stunt.
underkuelse subjection, subjugation.
underkur miraculous cure.
underkurs discount; **stå i** — be at a discount.
underlag underlayer, support; (av jord osv.) substratum; (typograf.) underlay.
underlaken bottom sheet.
underlege assistant surgeon.
underlegen inferior (to); (i antall) outnumbered. **underlegenhet** inferiority.
underlegge underlay; subject to, assign to. — **seg** reduce, subdue.
underlep(p)e lower lip.
underlig strange, singular, odd, queer; — **nok** for a wonder.
underlighet strangeness, singularity, oddity.
underliv belly, abdomen; (klesplagg) slip-body. **underlivs-** abdominal, hypogastric.
underlivsbetennelse gastritis.
underløpt (blod) extravasated (blood); — **med blod** livid from extravasated blood.
undermann inferior, underling.
undermaskinist assistant engineer.
undermast (mar) lower mast.
underminer|e undermine, sap. **hans helbred ble -t** his health was sapped.
undermunn lower part of the mouth.
undermåler inferior person. **undermåls** undersized; (fig) incapable, inferior, below the average.
underoffiser non-commissioned officer.
underordne subordinate (seg: oneself to.)
underordnet subordinate; (lav) humble; (uviktig) minor, secondary. **de -e funksjonærer** the humbler employees; **et** — **hensyn** a minor consideration; **av** — **betydning** of secondary importance.
underordning subordination.
underpant mortgage.
underrand lower edge.
underretning intelligence, information; intimation; **til** — **for** for the information of.
underrett lower court of law.
underrette inform, acquaint, apprise (om: of); — **feil** misinform; — **en om** at inform one that; **holde en -t om** keep one posted as to; keep one advised of.
underrettsdommer judge of a lower court.
underseil (mar) course, lower sail.
underselge undersell.
undersetsig square-built, square-set, square.
undersetsighet squareness of figure.

underside under side.
undersjøisk submarine.
underskjørt petticoat.
underskog underwood.
underskrift signature; **egenhendig** — sign manual; **uten** — unsigned.
underskrive sign; (fig) endorse.
under|skudd, -skott deficit **(på:** of).
underskyte insert surreptitiously, substitute.
underslag, -slep embezzlement, peculation, malversation, defalcation.
underslå (seil, bende s.) bend; (betrodd gods) divert, embezzle; (et brev) intercept.
underspist fed up.
underst undermost, lowermost, lowest; **at** the bottom.
understemme counterpart; base, bass.
understell base-frame.
understikk trick short el. in defect.
understrek|e underline, underscore; (fig) emphasize. **-ning** underlining; (fig) emphasizing.
understukket: et — **barn** a surreptitious child; **et** — **brev** a substituted letter.
understrøm under-current, under-tow.
understøtte prop; (fig) support, succour, assist, second, back; (med penger ogs.) subsidize.
understøttelse support, aid, assistance.
understøttelsesfond relief fund.
understøttelsesforening relief association.
understå seg presume, dare.
undersøke examine (into), investigate, inquire into, search into, look into; (sondere) probe; — **på nytt** re-examine; — **nøye** scrutinize, scan, overhaul; (om tollv.) search.
undersøkelse examination, investigation, inquiry, scrutiny, search; **foreta en** — set on foot an inquiry el. investigation.
undersøkelses|dommer examining judge el. magistrate. **-kommisjon** committee of inquiry, commission of inquiry.
undersått subject.
undersåttlig as a subject; **mine -e plikter** my duties as a subject.
undertallig deficient, short.
undertann lower tooth.
undertegne, se underskrive; -de the undersigned; **-t** signed.
undertiden sometimes, at times.
undertitel sub-title.
undertrykke stifle; (tilbakeholde) restrain, repress; (brev, bok o. l.) suppress; (opprør) crush, suppress; (underkue) oppress.
undertrykkelse suppression; oppression.
undertrykker oppressor.
undertrøye vest, under-jacket.
undertvinge subdue, subjugate, conquer.
undertvingelse subjection, subjugation.
undertvinger subduer, subjugator.
undertøy under-garments, under-clothing.
undervanns- submarine. **-båt** submarine. **-krig** submarine warfare. **-skjær** sunken rock.
underveis on el. by the way, on the road; (om ladning) on the water.
undervekt under-weight, short weight, light weight. **undervektig** short in weight; being under-weight.
underverden lower el. infernal regions.
underverk wonder, miracle.
undervest under-waistcoat.
undervise instruct (one in st.), teach (one st.); (uten objekt) give lessons, teach.
undervisning instruction; **gi** — give lessons.
undervisnings|anstalt educational establishment. **-fag** branch of learning. **-inspektør** inspector of schools. **-metode** method of instruction. **-minister** minister for education. **-plan** course el. system of instruction. **-vesenet** education, educational matters.
undervurdere underrate, under-estimate, undervalue. **undervurdering** underrating, undervaluation, underestimate.

undre surprise, astonish; **dette -t meg** this surprised me; **det -r meg at** I wonder, I am astonished that; — **seg, -s (over)** wonder, marvel, be surprised (at); **-nde** wondering, astonished.
undring wonder, astonishment.
unektelig undeniable.
unevnelig unnamable, unmentionable; (usigeig) inexpressible. **unevnt** unnamed, anonymous.
ung young, youthful.
ungar Hungarian. **Ungarn** Hungary.
ungarsk Hungarian.
ungdom youth; (unge mennesker) young people. **ungdommelig** youthful, juvenile.
ungdommelighet youthfulness.
ungdoms|alder youthful el. juvenile age. **-dager** youthful days. **-kraft** youthful vigour. **-mot** youthful courage. **-skole** continuation school **-tid** (time of) youth. **-venn** early friend. **-år** (pl) early el. young years.
unge young one; (av bjørn, rev, tiger) cub; (dt) brat, kid, urchin.
ungersvenn (glt., poetisk) young man, swain.
ung|fe young cattle. **-gutt** youngster.
ung|kar bachelor. **ungkars|bolig** (bachelor's) chambers. **-gilde, -lag** bachelor's party. **-leilighet** (bachelor's) chambers, bachelor's flat. **-liv** bachelor's life.
ungmøy young maiden.
ungpikeaktig girlish.
ungskog young wood.
ungsosialist Junior Socialist.
ungtyrk Young Turk.
uniform uniform, regimentals (pl); (daglig) undress. **uniformere** uniform; (gjøre ensartet) uniformise. **uniformering** clothing; uniformising.
uniformsfrakk regimental coat.
union union. **unions|fiende** anti-unionist; (i Irland) home-ruler. **-flagg** union flag; (gjøs) union jack.
unison unisonous; **-t** in unison.
unitar, unitarier, unitarisk Unitarian.
univers universe. **universal** universal.
universalarving residuary legatee, heir general; (ifølge slektskap) heir at law.
universalitet universality.
universal|leksikon encyclopedia. **-middel** sovereign remedy, panacea, cure-all.
universell universal.
universitet university; **ligge ved -et** be at college. **universitets|kamerat** college friend. **-liv** college-life. **-lærer** university professor. **-utdannelse** university education. **-utdannet** university-taught.
unna aside, away, off; clear; **for langt —** too far out of the way; **gå —** stand, clear; **holde — keep off; komme —** clear away; **gjøre —** get done.
unna|gjemt sequestered. **-renn** off-run, run (track) below the big jump.
unndra withdraw, deprive (of); **— en fra straff** screen one from punishment; **— seg (fra)** avoid, shun; (sin plikt o. l.) shirk, evade.
unne allow, grant; **ikke —** grudge; **— en det beste** wish one every success; **det er Dem vel unt** you are welcome to it.
unnfallen pliable, yielding.
unnfange conceive. **-lse** conception.
unnfly escape; (unngå) evade, elude; (sky) shun, avoid.
unngjelde pay, suffer, smart (for).
unngå shun, avoid; eschew; **hvis jeg kan — det if** I can help it; **— oppmerksomhet** escape notice.
unnkomme escape (**fra:** from).
unnlate omit, forbear; fail (to). **jeg skal ikke — å påpeke** I beg to point out.
unnlatelse ommission.
unnløpe escape, run away.
unnse seg (for) be ashamed (of), blush (at, for); **unnse seg for å** be ashamed to.
unnseelse bashfulness.

unnselig bashful, shy, shamefaced; **— over** ashamed of.
unnselighet bashfulness.
unnsetning relief; **komme ham til —** come to his relief. **unnsette** relieve.
unnsi denounce, threaten with deadly revenge. **unnsigelse** denunciation, threat.
unnskylde excuse (**hos** el. **for en:** to one); — **seg** excuse oneself, apologize, make an apology el. make excuses; **— seg for noe** excuse oneself for st.; (ønske seg fritatt for) from st.; **— seg med** plead; **unnskyld, jeg kommer for sent** excuse me for being late; **ha en unnskyldt** hold one excused; **unnskyld!** (i anledning av en feiltagelse eller forseelse) sorry, I am sorry;(foran et spørsmål) excuse me, are you Mr. Smith? **-skyldende** apologetical; (formildende) extenuating.
unnskyldelig excusable.
unnskyldning excuse, apology; exculpation; **gjøre en —** make an apology; **dårlig —** poor (el. lame) excuse; **be om —** beg one's pardon; **anføre til sin —** plead (as an excuse).
unnslippe escape; **unnslapp med nød og neppe** had a narrow escape.
unnslå seg beg to be excused (from), refuse, decline.
unnta except.
unntagelse exception; **med — av** with the e. of; **en — fra** an exception from el. to. **unntagelses-** exceptional. **unntagelsesvis** rarely, by exception, as a rare exception; (adj) exceptional.
unntagen except, excepting, excepted, save, barring; (etter nektelse) but.
unntak, se **unntagelse.**
unntatt, se **unntagen.**
unnvike escape, elude; (sky) avoid; (ved utflukter) evade. **-lse** escape. **-nde** evasive.
unnvære do without, dispense with. **unnværlig** dispensable. **unnværlighet** dispensableness.
unote bad habit.
unse ounce. **i unsevis** by the ounce.
unytte uselessness; **til -s** uselessly.
unyttig useless, unprofitable.
unødig unnecessary; (overflødig) superfluous.
unøyaktig inaccurate, incorrect.
unøyaktighet inaccuracy, incorrectness.
unøysom hard to satisfy, greedy.
unøysomhet greediness.
unåde disgrace, disfavour; **falle, være i —** be disgraced; **falle i — hos** incur the disgrace of. **unådig** ungracious.
uomgjengelig unsociable, inconversable; (uunngåelig) unavoidable; **— nødvendig** absolutely necessary. **-het** unsociableness.
uomstøtelig irrefragable, incontestable incontroversible. **uomstøtelighet** incontestability, incontestableness.
uomtvistelig indisputable, incontestable, incontrovertible. **-het** indisputableness.
uoppdragen uneducated, rude, ill-bred, ill-mannered, unmannerly, underbred.
uoppdragenhet unmannerliness, rudeness.
uoppdyrket uncultivated.
uoppfordret unsolicited, uninvited.
uoppholdelig without delay, immediate.
uopphørlig incessant, unceasing, unintermitting, unremitting; (adv) incessantly.
uoppklart uncleared, obscure. **en — forbrytelse** an unsolved crime.
uopplagt indisposed, disinclined.
uopplagthet indisposedness.
uopplyst unlighted; unexplained; unenlightened.
uoppløselig insoluble, indissoluble, irresolvable; **en — knute** an inextricable knot. **-het** insolubility. **uoppløst** undissolved.
uoppmerksom inattentive (**mot:** to) unobservant (**på:** of). **uoppmerksomhet** inattention.
uoppnå(e)lig unattainable. **-het** unattainableness. **uoppnådd** unattained; unrivalled.
uopprettelig irreparable, irremediable, irretrievable. **uopprettelighet** irreparability.

uoppsettelig admitting of no delay, urgent, pressing. **uoppsettelighet** urgency.

uoppsigelig irrepealable; (om penger) not to be called in; — **obligasjon** unredeemable bond.

uoppsigelighet irrepealability; **med flere års** — not to be called in for several years.

uoppskåret uncut, unopened.

uoppslitelig imperishable.

uorden disorder, derangement; untidiness; **i** — out of order; (hær) in confusion; (affærer) deranged; **komme i** — get out of order; **bringe i** —, **bringe** — **i** put out of order, derange, throw into confusion.

uordentlig disorderly; untidy; — **liv** irregular life. **-het** disorderliness, want of order.

uordholden untrustworthy.

uordnet unordered, unarranged.

uorganisk inorganic(al).

uortografisk unorthographic, misspelt.

uoverdragelig untransferable, inalienable.

uoverensstemmelse disagreement, incongruity, discrepancy. **uoverensstemmende** disagreeing, incongruous, discordant.

uoverkommelig insuperable, insurmountable.

uoverlagt ill-advised, unpremeditated, rash.

uoversettelig untranslatable.

uoverskuelig interminable, exceeding the range of vision.

uovertreffelig unsurpassable.

uovertreffelighet unrivalled superiority.

uovertruffet unsurpassed.

uoverveid ill-considered, rash.

uovervinnelig invincible; insurmountable, insuperable. **uovervinnelighet** invincibility, insuperability. **uovervunnet** unconquered.

upar, upar(r)et unpaired, se ogs. **umake.**

uparlamentarisk unparliamentary.

upartisk impartial. **upartiskhet** impartiality.

upasselig indisposed, unwell.

upasselighet indisposition.

upassende improper, unseemly.

upatriotisk unpatriotic.

upersonlig impersonal, non-personal.

upersonlighet impersonality.

uplettet unstained, unblemished, immaculate.

upolert unpolished.

upolitisk impolitic, unpolitical.

upopulær unpopular.

upraktisk not practical, unpractical.

upresis unprecise.

uprioritert unsecured.

uprivilegert non-privileged.

uproduktiv unproductive.

upåaktet unnoticed, disregarded.

upåanket unappealed from.

upåklagelig unexceptionable, creditable, irreproachable.

upåkledd undressed.

upålitelig not to be relied on, unreliable.

upålitelighet unreliableness.

upåpasselig inattentive, heedless. **-het** inattentiveness, heedlessness.

upåtagelig impalpable.

upåtalt uncensured, unchallenged.

upåvirkelig insensible, impassible.

upåviselig untraceable.

ur- first, primitive, original, primeval.

I. **ur** (lomme-) watch; (større) clock; **armbånds-** wristlet watch; **etter mitt** — by my watch; **trekke et** — wind (up) a watch.

II. **ur** (stein-) slope of large boulders, rock-falls, rock-strewn slope.

uraffinert unrefined.

uransakelig inscrutable, unsearchable.

urbilde archetype, prototype.

urcelle primitive cell.

I. **uredd** (om seng) unmade.

II. **uredd** (modig) dauntless, fearless, unafraid.

urede disorder, confusion, entanglement, intricacy; **bringe i** — throw into confusion, entangle, embroil.

uredelig dishonest, unfair.

uredelighet dishonesty, unfairness.

uregelmessig irregular, anomalous.

uregelmessighet irregularity, anomaly.

uregjerlig ungovernable, unruly, intractable, unmanageable. **uregjerlighet** intractableness, intractability, unruliness.

urein, uren unclean, impure, foul; (tone) out of tune; false. **-het** uncleanness, impurity.

urenset uncleaned. **urenslig** uncleanly, filthy. **-het** uncleanliness, filthiness.

urett (subst) injustice; **med -e** unjustly; **med rette eller -e** right or wrong; **man har gjort meg** — I have been wronged.

urett (adj) wrong; **han var kommet til den** — (dt) he had got the wrong sow by the ear.

urettferdig unjust, iniquitous.

urettferdighet injustice, iniquity.

urettmessig unlawful, illegal, unjust.

urettmessighet unlawfulness, illegality.

urfjær mainspring of a watch.

urfolk aboriginal people.

urform original el. primitive form.

urgere urge, insist upon.

urglass watch-glass, crystal.

urgrunn first el. primeval cause.

Urias Uriah. **u-post** forlorn post.

uridderlig unchivalrous.

uriktig wrong, incorrect. **-het** incorrectness.

urimelig absurd, preposterous; (ubillig) unreasonable. **-het** absurdity; unreasonableness.

urimt not rhymed.

urin urine. **urinaktig** urinary. **urinal** urinal.

urinere urinate.

urin|glass urinal. **-rør** urethra. **-syre** uric acid.

urkasse watch el. clock-case.

urkjede watch-chain, watch-guard; (om halsen) guard-chain.

urkraft primitive force.

urmaker watch- el. clock-maker.

urmenneske primitive man.

urne urn; (valg-) ballot-box; (aske-) cinerary urn. **-hall** columbarium.

urnøkkel watch-key.

uro disturbance, disquiet, disquietude, unrest; (fig) uneasiness, anxiety, alarm.

uro(e) disquiet, disturb, trouble.

urokkelig firm, immovable, unshaken; determined. **urokkelighet** firmness, fixedness.

urokket unshaken.

urolig turbulent; restless, uneasy, anxious **(for:** for, about); (vær) stormy, rough, boisterous; — **søvn, -e drømmer** troubled sleep, dreams; **jeg er** — **over hans fravær** I am uneasy at his absence.

urolighet commotion, disturbance, trouble, turbulence.

urostifter quareller; rioter.

urskive dial(-plate), face of a watch el. clock.

urskog primeval forest.

urslim protoplasm.

urspråk primitive language.

urt herb, plant. **urtaktig** herbaceous.

urtepose poultice of boiled herbs.

urtid primeval ages.

urtilstand primitive condition.

urverden primeval world.

urverk watch-work, clock-work.

urviser hand of a watch, hand of a clock.

uryddig disorderly, untidy. **-het** disorderliness.

urørlig immovable, stationary; — **gods** immovables (pl), real estate.

urørt untouched, intact; (ubeveget) unmoved.

urøykelig unsmokeable.

uråd (umulighet) impossibility; **ane** — suspect mischief; (amr) sense danger; **det er** — **å . . .** it is impossible to . . ., there is no . . . ing . . .; **råd for** — a way out of a difficulty.

usagt unsaid, not said.

usakkyndig incompetent.
usal(e)t unsaddled, bare-backed.
usalig unblessed; baleful, hapless, luckless.
usammenhengende incoherent, disconnected.
usammensatt uncompounded, simple.
usams at odds; **bli —** fall out.
usance trade custom.
usann untrue, false.
usannferdig not veracious. **-ferdighet** unveracity.
usannhet untruth, falsehood, falsity; **si en — tell** a falsehood.
usannsynlig improbable, unlikely.
usannsynlighet improbability, unlikelihood.
usans nonsense.
usanselig incorporeal, immaterial.
usedelig immoral, licentious.
usedelighet immorality, licentiousness.
usedvanlig unusual, uncommon.
useilbar innavigable.
uselgelig unsaleable. **-het** unsaleableness.
uselskapelig unsociable. **-het** unsociability.
uselvstendig dependent, subordinate; (karakt.) pliant, yielding. **-het** dependency, pliancy.
usett unseen.
usigelig unspeakable, unutterable, ineffable.
usikker unsafe, insecure, precarious; (tvilsom) doubtful, uncertain; (blikk, gang) unsteady; **gjøre en —** make one falter el. hesitate. **veien er gjort —** av røvere the road is infested with robbers. **usikkerhet** unsafety, insecurity; uncertainty; unsteadiness.
usiktbar thick, hazy.
usivilisert uncivilized.
usjenert free-and-easy, at one's ease; cool, unconcerned; (adv) coolly, quietly, unconcernedly. **usjenerthet** ease, free-and-easy behaviour.
uskadd unhurt, unharmed, uninjured.
uskadelig harmless, innocuous, innoxious. **-gjøre** render harmless.
uskadelighet harmlessness, innocuousness.
uskaplig shapeless, unshapely.
uskattelig invaluable, priceless.
uskiftet undivided; **sitte i — bo** retain the undivided estate.
uskikk bad habit, bad custom; nuisance.
uskikkelig ill-behaved, naughty. **-het** naughtiness.
uskikket unfit, unqualified, unsuited (**til:** for).
uskikkethet unfitness.
uskjedd undone, not happened.
uskjønn ungraceful, inelegant, unhandsome.
uskjønnhet inelegance, ungracefulness.
uskjønnsom ungrateful. **-het** ungratefulness.
uskrømtet sincere, unfeigned.
uskyld innocence, guiltlessness.
uskyldig innocent, guiltless (of); unoffending. **uskyldighet,** se **uskyld.**
uslepen (glt., i egtl. betydn. nå: uslipt) (fig) unpolished, unrefined, rude; **en — diamant** a rough diamond. **uslepet vesen** (fig) rudeness, roughness, impoliteness.
usling wretch.
uslipt not ground, not polished.
uslitelig everlasting, indestructible.
uslukkelig inextinguishable, unquenchable.
usmak disagreeable flavour el. taste, tang. **usmakelig** insipid, tasteless, unsavoury; **et — tema** an unsavoury subject.
usmeltet unmelted; unfused.
usminket unpainted; (fig) unvarnished.
usnakket untalked, unspoken; **jeg har noe — med ham** I wish to have it out with him.
uso (merk) usance.
usolid unsafe, unsound.
usol(g)t unsold.
usont unexpiated, unatoned.
usortert unsorted.
uspiselig uneatable, inedible.
ussel poor, wretched, miserable, paltry, pitiful. **usselhet** misery, wretchedness, paltriness.

ustadig unsteady, unstable, unsettled, changeable, inconstant, wavering, variable.
ustadighet instability, inconstancy, changeableness, unsteadiness.
ustand disorder disrepair; **i — out of repair** el. order.
ustanselig checkless; incessant.
ustell mismanagement, disorder.
ustemplet unstamped.
ustemt untuned, out of tune.
ustraffelig (skyldfri) irreproachable, blameless. **-het** irreproachableness, blamelessness.
ustraffet unpunished, with impunity.
ustudert unstudied, not university taught; (om ting) natural, unstudied.
ustyrlig ungovernable, unruly, intractable, out of hand. **-het** unruliness, intractability.
ustyrtelig (dt) enormous, excessive, immense.
ustø unsteady; (dt) shaky; (fig) unstable. **-het** unsteadiness etc; (fig) instability.
usunn unhealthy, sickly, insalubrious.
usunnhet unhealthiness, insalubrity.
usurpator usurper. **usurpere** usurp.
usvekket unimpaired; **— interesse** unflagging el. unabated interest.
usvikelig faithful, unfailing.
usymmetrisk unsymmetrical.
usympatisk uncongenial.
usynlig invisible, unseen. **-het** invisibility.
usyrt unleavened, azymous.
usystematisk unsystematical.
usømmelig unseemly, indecent, indecorous. **-het** unseemliness, indecorousness, indecency.
usørgende(s) unconcerned (**for:** about).
usårlig invulnerable; **være — ogs.** bear a charmed life. **usårlighet** invulnerableness, invulnerability.
ut out (of), forth; **uken — to** the end of the week; **brakte ham — av seg selv** made him beside himself; **— for** (mar) off; **— fra** starting from, taking one's departure from; **år —, år inn** year by year; **jeg vet hverken — eller inn** I am quite bewildered; **— over** beyond; **til langt — på natta** till late in the night.
utabords on the outside; outboard, overboard.
utad, se **utetter. -gående,** se **utgående.**
utadvendt turned outward.
utafor (adv) outside, without; (prep) out of outside. Se også **utenfor.**
utakk reproach, blame.
utakknemlig ungrateful, unthankful; (arbeid o. l.) thankless. **utakknemlighet** ingratitude, unthankfulness; thanklessness.
utakt: komme i — fall out of time; (mil. etc. fall el. get out of step. _
utall awful number, no end of. **utallig** innumerable, numberless, unnumbered, countless. **utallighet** innumerability, innumerableness.
utalt uncounted, untold.
utapå outside.
utarbeide|e compose, prepare; **en -d tale** an elaborate speech. **-else** composing; (en skriftlig) composition, written exercise, paper.
utarmet impoverished, poverty-stricken.
utarte degenerate; **-t** degenerate.
utart(n)ing degeneration.
utaskjærs in open waters.
utast knocked up, dead beat, jaded.
utbasunere trumpet, blazon (forth el. abroad).
utbe seg request; **svar -s** the favour of an answer is requested; **Deres svar -s pr. telegraf** your answer is requested by wire.
utbedre repair, mend; (maleri) restore.
utbedring repair, mending, restoration.
utbetale pay (out), disburse.
utbetaling paying out, disbursement; **vekselen forfaller til — neste onsdag** the bill falls due Wednesday week.
utblø(y)te macerate, soak, steep.
utblåsing (av forbrukt gass) exhaust.
utblåsningsventil exhaust valve.

utbre(de) spread, extend; (et rykte) divulge, circulate; — **seg** spread, extend; — **seg om en sak** expatiate, dilate upon a matter; — **seg** (som et rykte) spread, get abroad; **utbredt** wide-spread.

utbredelse spread, extension, extent.

utbrent burned out; (renset) cleansed by burning; (kirurgi) cauterized; — **vulkan** extinct volcano.

utbringe (brev) deliver; — f. eks. **kongens skål** propose, give, drink the health of the king.

utbrudd outbreak, breaking out; (om vulkan) eruption; (om lidenskaper) burst, outburst; **komme til** — break out.

utbrukt worn out.

utbryte break out; (med uttrykk for sinnsbevegelse f. eks. glede eller vrede) exclaim, burst out; (si, ytre) cry; **det utbrøt ild, krig** a fire, a war broke out.

utbud offer for sale; (av varer) supply; (ledings-) call to arms.

utbuet convex.

utby (merk) offer, put up; (innkalle) call in, summon.

utbygd (subst) distant parish.

utbygge (foss) dam.

utbygning additional structure; projecting part (of a building).

utbytning utilization; (overdreven utnyttelse) grinding, sweating.

utbytte (vrb) make the most of, utilize, exploit.

utbytte (subst) clear profit proceeds, earnings, yield; (av bank osv.) dividend; (fig) result, outcome, gain; **bekjentgjøre** — declare dividend; **en bok man vil lese med** — a book which may be read with advantage.

utbytting, se **utbytning.**

utbæring carrying out; (av brev) delivery.

utdanne form, finish, perfect; (åndel.) cultivate, train, improve, educate; — **seg** train, prepare oneself, serve an apprenticeship.

utdannelse perfection, finish; cultivation, improvement; training, education.

utdele distribute, deal, portion (out), serve out, issue (**til:** to), dispense (to).

utdeling distribution, dispensation, issue.

utdra draw out, educe, extract.

utdrag extract; (kort) abstract, summary.

utdragning extraction; eduction.

utdrive drive out, expel, displace.

utdrivelse driving out; expulsion.

utdunsting exhalation, evaporation.

utdype deepen, make deeper.

utdypning deepening.

utdø become extinct. **utdødd** extinct.

ute out; (forbi) at an end, finished, over; **han er — av seg selv (av glede)** he is beside himself, out of his mind (with joy).

utearbeid out-door work.

utebli stay away, fail to come, fail to appear.

uteblivelse staying away, absence, non-arrival, non-attendance; (fra retten) default.

uteglemt left out (by inadvertency).

utekkelig disagreeable.

utekkelighet disagreeableness.

utelate leave out, omit. **-lse** omission.

uteliv out-door life.

utelukke shut out, lock out; (fig) exclude, debar. **-lse** exclusion; expulsion. **-nde** exclusive; (adv) exclusively entirely, wholly.

utemmelig untameable, irreclaimable, indomitable. **utemt** untamed.

uten without; **ingen** — none but, nobody but; **intet** — nothing but; — **å vite det** without knowing it; — **tvil** without doubt, no doubt; — **videre** (uten omstendigheter) without further ceremony; (selvfølgelig) as a matter of course; (straks) at once.

utenat: lære noe — learn something (off) by heart.

utenbys out of town; not resident in town; — **medlemmer** country-members.

utenfor (adv) outside, without; (prep) out of, outside; **utenfor byen** out of town. **uten forstående** outside; outside person, outsider (— tilskuer) impartial spectator.

utenfra from without, from outside.

utenkelig unimaginable, inconceivable.

utenlands abroad. **utenlandsk** foreign; (u. o, underlig) outlandish. **utenlandsreise** foreig journey el. tour.

utenom round about, outside of; **gå** — **sake** elude the subject. **utenomhensyn** extraneou consideration. **utenomsnakk** irrelevant talk.

utenpå outside.

utenpåskrift (p. brev) superscription, address (p. flaske, krukke) label.

utenriks abroad, out of the kingdom. **-fart** -**handel** foreign trade, oversea trade.

utenriksdepartement ministry of foreign affairs, foreign office.

utenriksk foreign.

utenriks|minister minster for foreign affairs -**politikk** foreign politics, foreign policy.

utenrikspolitisk relating to foreign politics.

utenverden outside el. outer world.

utenverker outer works.

uterlig impure, obscene.

uterlighet impurity, obscenity.

uteske, se **utfordre** (til kamp).

utestengt shut out.

utestående (mellomværende) account, score (krav) claim; **ha noe** — **med en** be at odd with one; — **penger** money due.

utett leaky; — **sted** leak. **-het** leakiness.

utetter outward.

utfall issue, result, upshot; (mil) sally, sortie (i fektekunst) pass; **heldig** — success; **ulykkelig** — failure, failing, miscarriage; **få e dårlig** — fail; **få et annet** — turn out differently

utfart exit; (utflukt) excursion; (i masse, exodus. **utfartssted** picnic place, resort.

utfattig destitute, penniless.

utferd departure.

utferdige draw up, prepare, expedite, dispatch. **utferdigelse** drawing up etc., preparation, expedition.

utfinne find out, make out.

utflod discharge, flux.

utflukt flight; (tur) excursion, outing, trip (unnskyldning) shuffle, evasion, shift; excuse **komme med -er** shuffle, evade

utfold|e unfold; (f eks. fane) unfurl; (f. eks. blad) expand; (fig) unfold; (legge for dagen osv.) display; (utvikle) develop. **-else, -(n)ing** unfolding etc.; expansion; development; display.

utfor (adv og prep) over; **falle** — fall over; **gled** — **brygga** slipped off the pierhead; — **bakken** downhill.

utfor|dre challenge, call out; (trosse) defy, dare; (kreve) require, call for. **-drende** defiant; **den** — the challenger. **-dring** challenge.

utforme form.

utforsk|e find out, trace; (egn o. l.) explore; (en) sound. **-(n)ing** exploring etc., exploration.

utfrakt outward freight.

utfri deliver, set free, liberate.

utfrielse deliverance, liberation.

utfritte question closely.

utfylle fill up, fill out; (skjema) fill in; (fig) (plass) fill. **utfylling** filling up.

utfyllingsvalg bye-election.

utføre carry out; (bringe til utførelse) carry into effect; (varer) export; (arbeid) execute, accomplish, perform; (musikk) execute, play; — **en ordre** execute an order, fill an order.

utførelse carrying out, execution, accomplishment, performance.

utførlig (fullstendig) full, copious, detailed, explicit; (adv) fully etc., at length, in extenso; **svært** — at great length; **temmelig** — in some detail. **utførlighet** fulness, detail, explicitness.

utførsel exportation, export.

utførsels|artikkel (staple of) export; (pl) export goods. –forbud prohibition of exportation. -premie bounty. –toll export-duty. –varer export goods.

utgammel in extreme old age, old and decrepit.

utgang going out, departure; (slutning) issue, end; (skuespillers; typograf.) exit; (sted) outlet, issue, passage out.

utgangs|billett check, pass-check. –dag one's day out. –dør door of egress. –punkt starting -point, (point of) departure. –replikk exit. –sau unhoused sheep. –tillatelse leave of absence. -ventil (dmp.) eduction valve.

utgave edition.

utgi (bøker osv.) publish, issue, (om utgiver) edit; (om forfatter) bring out; — på nytt republish; — seg for noe, for en annen person pass oneself off as something, for another.

utgift expense, expenditure; store -er heavy expenses; (merk.) føre til — carry to the expenditure; sette seg i — for go to the expense of.

utgifts|post item of expenditure. –side debit.

utgivelse publication. under — in course of publication.

utgiver publisher, (som besørger utgivelsen; redaktør) editor.

utgjort: det er som — just like my luck.

utgjøre constitute, compose. make, form; (om gjeld o. l.) amount to, come to.

utglidning landslide, slip.

utgranskning, se utforskning.

utgraving digging out, exhumation, excavation. utgravingsmaskin excavator.

utgrunne penetrate, fathom.

utgyte pour out; — tårer, blod shed tears, blood; — sitt hjerte (for) unbosom oneself (to).

utgytelse pouring out, effusion, outpouring.

utgå issue; (utelates) be omitted, be struck out; — av regnskapet pass out of the accounts.

utgående (adj) out-going; (om skip) outward bound; — tidevann offward tide.

utgående (subst) departure; for — outward -bound.

I. utgått: et — tre a decayed tree.
II. utgått: en — sko a walked-out shoe.

uthaler rake, dissipated fellow, old rip.

uthaling equipment, outfit.

uthamn, uthavn outport.

uthengs|skap street show-case. –skilt overhanging sign el. sign-board.

utheve (typogr.) distinguish by italics; (fig) emphasize, point. uthevelse setting off; emphasizing. –ne er gjort av oss the italics are ours.

uthogd hewn out, cut (out). uthogst cutting, felling; (ødeleggende) exhaustion of forests.

utholde bear, stand, endure, support, sustain, go trough with, bear up against.

utholdende persevering.

utholdenhet perseverance, endurance.

uthule hollow, scoop (out), excavate.

uthuling hollowing (out), excavation.

uthungring starving, famishing, subduing by hunger.

uthus out-house, (out-) office.

uthvilt rested (up).

utid unseasonable time; i -e untimely, unseasonably, out of time; i tide og -e in season and out of season.

utidig untimely, unseasonable, premature, illtimed, misplaced; (urimelig) troublesome, unreasonable.

utidighet unseasonableness; troublesomeness.

utilbørlig improper, undue; (adv) improperly, unduly. utilbørlighet impropriety.

utilbøyelig disinclined, indisposed.

utilbøyelighet disinclination.

utilfreds dissatisfied, discontented; — med at displeased that. utilfredshet dissatisfaction, discontent. utilfredsstillende dissatisfactory, unsatisfactory. utilfredsstilt unsatisfield.

utilgivelig unpardonable.

utilgjengelig inaccessible, unapproachable. utilgjengelighet inaccessibility.

utilisme utilitarianism. –ist, –istisk utilitarian.

utillatelig illicit, inadmissible; i — grad beyond excuse; (adv) extravagantly unjustifiably.

utilnærmelig unapproachable.

utilpass: være — feel ill, feel unwell.

utilregnelig irresponsible. utilregnelighet irresponsibility.

utilslørt unveiled.

utilstrekkelig insufficient. –het insufficiency.

utiltalende uncongenial, unpleasant.

uting absurdity, nuisance.

utjamning, se utjevning.

utjenlig unsuitable. –het unsuitableness.

utjevne smooth; (jevne) even, level; (fig) adjust, settle. utjevning smoothing etc.; settlement, adjustment.

utkant extremity, outskirts, skirts.

utkast draught, sketch, design (til: of).

utkaste (en plan) devise, lay down.

utkaster chucker-out.

utkik look-out; holde — look out; stå på — be on the look-out (etter: for).

utkjempe (en strid) fight out.

utkjørt knocked up, dead beat.

utklarer|e clear. –ing clearance.

utklekke hatch; (fig) hatch, plot.

utklekning hatching. utklekningsapparat hatching-machine, incubator.

utklipp slip, cutting, snipping; scrap.

utkledd dressed up.

utkommandere call out, order away.

utkomme (vrb) (om bok o. l.) be published, appear. boka –r hos . . . the book appears through . . . –t hos . . . published by . . .

utkomme (subst) competence, competency, subsistence, livelihood; et rikelig — an ample competency; ha sitt gode — have an easy competency; ha sitt knappe — make both ends meet; det er ikke noe — med ham there is no dealing with him.

utkreve call for, need, require, want.

utkroting scrolls, flourishes.

utkåre choose, elect, select.

utladning discharge.

utlandet foreign countries, foreign parts; i — abroad; fra — from abroad; sende til — send abroad; handel med — foreign trade.

utlate seg discharge oneself; (fig) express oneself.

utledd laughed at, derided, ridiculed.

utlede deduce, derive, evolve.

utlegg outlay, advance, disbursement; (juridisk) execution; ta — i take in execution, distrain; få sine — dekket recover one's expenses.

utlegge (forklare) explain, interpret, construe; — en som barnefar father a child upon one.

utlegging (av bøyer etc.) placing.

utleggs|forretning act of execution, fieri-facias. –tager distrainor.

utlegning explanation, interpretation.

utleie let; (framleie) sub-let.

utlendighet exile. –lending foreigner, alien.

utlevd superannuated, decrepit, decayed.

utlever|e deliver up, give up, surrender; (ammunisjon o. l.) serve out; planer –es plans may be had. –ing delivery, reddition, restitution; (av forbrytere) extradition; — av bo discharge.

utleverings|ordre delivery order. –seddel bill of delivery. –traktat extradition treaty.

utligne asses; (avgjøre, klare) settle, balance; — konti settle accounts.

utligning assessment; (betaling) settlement, payment; til — av in payment of; til — av vårt mellomværende to balance our accounts, in settlement of our accounts.

utlodning (v. loddtrekning) lottery.

utlove offer, promise.

utluft(n)ing airing, ventilation.

utlyd final sound; i — at the end of words, when final. utlydende final.

utlært having served one's apprenticeship.

utløe outlying barn.

utløp running out, flow; (av elv) outlet, issue, mouth; (av tid) expiration. utløpe (om tid) expire; (komme til ende) end, come to a close. utløper (bot.) offshoot, runner; (av fjellkjede) spur, counterfort.

utløps|rør discharge-pipe. -tid expiration. -ventil delivery el outlet valve

utlø(y)se ransom; (frigjøre) release; (pantsatte saker) redeem utløsning, utløysing ransoming; releasing; redeeming.

utlån loan. utlåns|bibliotek circulating el. lending library. -rente interest on loans.

utmaiet tawdry.

utmale (i ord) depict; — seg picture (to oneself).

utmarget enervated, enfeebled.

utmark hill el. forest pasture.

utmattelse exhaustion, prostration.

utmattet exhausted, fatigued.

utmeldelse withdrawal.

utmeldt (av skolen) taken out; se ogs. melde seg ut.

utmerke distinguish; — seg distinguish oneself, gain distinction, make one's mark.

utmerkelse distinction.

utmerket excellent, distinguished, of note, high-class; (adv) eminently.

utmynte coin. utmynting coining.

utmønstring discarding, rejection.

utmåling measuring out.

utnavn nickname.

utnevn|e nominate, appoint; ble -t til minister was appointed minister.

utnevnelse nomination, creation, appointment; (utnevnelsesbrev) letters of creation, patent; bekjentgjøre ens — gazette one; hans — til minister his appointment as a minister el. to the ministry.

utnytte turn to account, utilise; exhaust, use up, wear out. utnyttelse utilisation.

utopi utopianism. utopisk utopian.

utover (adv) out, outward; (mar) offward, seaward, off; (prep) beyond.

utover|hengende, -lutende overhanging, pendent.

utpakking unpacking.

utpant(n)ing distraining, execution, distress.

utparsellere parcel out (into lots).

utpeke point out, indicate, designate.

utpenslet elaborate.

utpensling elaboration of detail.

utpepet, se pipe ut.

utpint impoverished, stripped, fleeced; (jord) exhausted.

utpiping hissing; (av et skuespill) damning.

ut|plukk pick, pickings. -plukking culling, picking, selection.

utplyndre plunder, pillage.

utplyndring plundering.

utpost out-sentinel, out-sentry; out-post.

utpreget marked, emphatic, pronounced.

utpressing (av penger) extortion.

utpresser blackmailer, extortionist.

utpyntet dressed out, decked out; (fig) embellished.

utpønse excogitate.

utrangere cast, cast off, discard.

utrasing fall of ground, slide.

utrede furnish, supply, pay.

utredsel contribution, rate, tax.

utregning calculation, computation.

utreise journey el. trip out; passage out; outward route.

utrengsmål i — without necessity, gratuitously.

utrens(k)e purge away el. off; cleanse, purify.

utrette do, effect, perform; — et ærend execute a commission.

utrettelig indefatigable, unwearied. utrettelighet indefatigableness, unweariedness.

utrigger outrigger.

utringet (om kjole) low, low-necked.

utrivelig comfortless, uncomfortable.

utro unfaithful, false (mot: to).

utrolig incredible.

utrop outcry, exclamation, shout.

utrope proclaim; bli utropt til konge be proclaimed king.

utroper proclaimer, herald, (public) crier.

utropsord interjection.

utropstegn note of exclamation.

utror pull out; run, (fishing excursion) to the outlying grounds.

utroskap unfaithfulness, infidelity.

utruge hatch. utrug(n)ing hatching.

utrulig incredible.

utruste fit out, equip; (på ny) re-equip; (om soldater) equip, accoutre; (fig) equip, furnish (med: with). utrustning equipment, accoutrement, outfit.

utrydde eradicate, root out, extirpate.

utryddelse eradication, extirpation.

utrygg insecure, unsafe. -het insecurity.

utrykning (mil.) march out; (utfall) sally; (av vakt etc.) turnout.

utrykt unprinted, unpublished.

utrømming evacuation.

utrørt mixed, stirred out.

utrøstelig inconsolable, disconsolate (over: at).

utrøstelighet disconsolateness.

utsagn saying, statement, assertion.

utsalg sale; shop; —! selling off!

utsalgs|pris selling-price. -sted shop, store.

utsatt exposed, open, liable, subject (for: to): (typograf.) finished. utsatthet liability.

utse select, mark (out), pitch upon.

utseende appearance, exterior, look, aspect, complexion, face; jeg kjenner ham av — I know him by sight; å dømme etter — to judge by appearances; gi seg — av affect.

utsendelse, utsending despatch, sending; (pr. radio) broadcasting.

utsending delegate, deputy.

utsette (f. eks. for fare) expose (to); se oppsette; (dadle) find fault with, censure, criticise, blame (something in el. somebody for); (musikk) transcribe, adapt, arrange; han har utsatt seg for fare he has exposed himself (to danger); — seg for å run the risk of.

I. utsettelse, utsetting (av musikk) transcription, adaptation, arrangement; (for fare) exposure; (av vakter) posting.

II. utsettelse (oppsettelse) adjournment, delay, postponement.

utsettelsesforslag motion for adjournment.

utside outside.

utsikt prospect, view, look-out, outlook, opening, vista; (sted) outlook; med — til facing; (fig) stille i — hold out a prospect of; har den beste — til stands a fair chance of.

utsiktspunkt point of view, outlook.

utskeielser excesses.

utskeiende dissolute.

utskifte (bytte om) replace; (dele) apportion, divide. utskift(n)ing replacement, division, partition.

utskille separate; (utsondre) secrete; (kjemisk) disengage.

utskillelse separation; secretion; disengagement.

utskipe (eksportere) export, ship; (losse) unship; (landsette) disembark, debark. utskipning shipment; disembarkation, disembarkment, debarkation.

utskjelling abuse.

utskjemt spoiled.

utskjenk(n)ing pouring out; (salg i glassevis) retail(ing).

utskjæring cutting; (kunstnerisk) carving,

sculpture; (kirurgisk) excision, extirpation; **kjole med dyp — foran** dress cut low in front.
   utskott projection; shed.
   utskrift (avskrift) copy, transcript.
   utskrive (skatter o. l.) levy, impose; (soldater, sjøfolk) raise, enlist; **utskrevet** (fra hospitalet) discharged.
   utskrivning conscription, enlistment. **utskrivningsalder** conscription age.
   utskudd refuse; rubbish, trash; (av folket) refuse, scum, dregs. **menneskehetens** — the rabble of mankind.
   utskyte (vrake) reject; (jurymann) set aside, strike off; (typograf.) impose; (oppsette) delay.
   utskytning (m. skytevåpen) discharge, shooting; (av torpedo) expulsion, launching.
   utskåret cut out; (i tre) carved.
   utslag (i vekt) turn, turning; (pendels) oscillation; (resultat) outcome, outcrop; **gjøre —et** turn the scales el. balance, decide the matter.
   utslagsbord folding table.
   utslett eruption, tetter, rash.
   utslette efface, obliterate, wipe out.
   utslitt worn out.
   utslukt extinguished.
   utslynge hurl, fling out, dart.
   utslått (om hår) floating, dishevelled; (v. meslinger etc.) broken out, come to the surface; (om pasienten) having eruptions on the skin.
   utsmykke embellish, set off, deck.
   utsmykning embellishment.
   utsnitt cut, cutting; (mat) section.
   utsol(g)t out of stock, sold off el. out; (om bok) out of print.
   utsondre separate, pick (out), single out; se **utskille. utsondring** separation.
   utsone atone for, expiate.
   utsoning expiation, reconciliation.
   utsovet: være — have slept enough el. one's fill.
   utspeide spy out, pry upon; explore, scour. **utspeiding** spying, espionage.
   utspekulert (om person) crafty, designing.
   utspiling stretching out, distension.
   utspill lead; (i fotball) kick off.
   utspilt stretched out, distended, dilated.
   utspionere spy on, spy out.
   utspjåket, se **utmaiet.**
   utspre(de) (rykter) circulate, spread, divulge.
   utspring source, head-waters; (opphav) origin.
   utsprunget: en — **rose** a full-blown rose; **blåveisen er** — the blue anemones are out; **trærne er** — the trees are (out) in leaf; **fullt** — in full leaf.
   utspydd vomited, belched forth.
   utspørre (close-)question, pump.
   utstaffere garnish, trim (up); (særl. ironisk) rig (out), caparison, dress up.
   utstede issue, draw; — **en sjekk** draw a cheque; — **en veksel** draw a bill. **utstedelse** issue; drawing. **utstedelsesdag** date of issue.
   utstigning alighting, dismount.
   utstikkerbrygge pier.
   utstikning alignment, staking, tracing.
   utstille exhibit; hold an exhibition; — **varer** expose goods. **utstiller** exhibitor.
   utstilling exhibition, exposition.
   utstillings|gjenstand exhibit, object exhibited, -**kasse** showcase. -**vindu** show-window.
   utstopping stuffing. **utstoppet** stuffed.
   utstrakt extensive, wide; **i** — **betydning** in a larger sense.
   utstrekke stretch out; extend; — **seg** extend. **utstrekning** extension; (omfang) extent; **i stor** — extensively, largely.
   utstridd: en har — one's struggles are at an end.
   utstryk(n)ing blotting out; sponging out; rubbing out.
   utstrøing scattering, strewing; (fig) dissemination.

utstrøket blotted out; sponged out; rubbed out.
   utstrømning efflux, flow; exhaustion; (fig) emanation.
   utstråle radiate, beam forth.
   utstråling radiation.
   utstykking parcelling out; subdivision.
   utstyr endowment, dowry, portion; (til brud) trousseau; (særl. til reise) outfit, equipment; (til bok o. l.) get-up, make-up; (i rom) furniture, decoration.
   utstyr|e portion, endow; establish; (værelse o. l.) furnish; **boka er prektig —t** the book is splendidly got up, mounted; **—t med radiotelefoni** equipped with radio-telephony.
   utstyrs|forretning outfitting el. furniture establishment. -**stykke** sceneful drama el. piece.
   utstøte (av selskap) expel; — **et skrik** set up a cry; — **et sukk** heave a sigh.
   utstå (gjennomgå) undergo, experience; (fordra) bear; — **en straff** suffer a punishment.
   utsuge (fig) fleece, shear; (med skatter) overtax. **utsugelse** extortion, exaction.
   utsuger fleecer, extortioner, blood-sucker.
   ut|sultet famished. -**sult(n)ing** starving.
   utsvevelser debauch, debauchery.
   utsvevende debauched, dissolute, licentious.
   utsydd embroidered.
   utsyn outlook, prospect.
   utsæd seed (sown).
   utsøkt choice, select, exquisite, picked.
   utta: — stevning mot serve a writ on, summon.
   uttak (av bank) withdrawal.
   utta(k)ing withdrawal; selection; (av stevning) issue of process.
   uttale (vrb) pronounce; — **et ønske** express a wish; — **at** declare that; **h —s ikke** h is not sounded: — **seg** express oneself; — **seg for** recommend, advocate.
   uttale (subst) pronunciation.
   uttalebetegnelse system of notation.
   uttalelse utterance, declaration, observation.
   uttelling counting out; disbursement, payment.
   uttenkt invented, devised, thought out.
   uttjent having served one's time; (uskikket til tjeneste) unfit for service; **gammel — soldat** veteran.
   uttog (f. eks. av en bok) abstract, epitome, summary.
   uttredelse retirement, withdrawal; secession; (av blod) extravasation.
   uttrykk expression; (ansikts- ogs.) look; (ord ogs.) term; (talemåte ogs.) phrase.
   uttrykke express; tell of; **uttrykt: (ens) —e bilde** the exact el. very picture of, the express image of.
   uttrykkelig express; (adv) expressly, distinctly, on purpose, in set terms.
   uttrykks|full expressive, suggestive, meaning. -**løs** having no expression, expressionless.
   uttrykksløshet want of expression.
   uttrykksmåte mode of expression.
   uttvære beat el. spin out.
   uttværet prolix, tedious.
   uttært emaciated.
   uttømme exhaust; (med) evacuate. **uttømmelse** exhaustion; evacuation. **uttømmende** exhaustive, full; (med) evacuative.
   utterke dry up, exsiccate; (om myr) drain. **utterking** drying up, exsiccation; draining.
   utukt unchastity, lechery, lewdness.
   utuktig lewd, unchaste, indecent.
   utvalg selection, choice, pick; (i storting osv.) (select) committee.
   utvandre emigrate. **utvandrer** emigrant.
   utvandring emigration.
   utvanning freshening, unsalting; (fig) diluting.
   utvasking washing; (av sår) bathing.
   utve out-longings, a roving spirit.
   utvegg outer wall.
   utvei way out of (a difficulty), means, expedient, resource; compromise.

utveksle exchange. **utveksling** exchange.
utvekst excrescence, protuberance.
utvelge choose, select, elect, pick out; **utvalt** choice, select, picked; **de utvalte** the elect.
utvelgelse selection, election.
utvendig outward, external, exterior; (adv) externally, (on the) outside; — **side** outside; **det -e** the exterior.
utvetydig unequivocal, unmistakable.
utvetydighet unequivocal character.
utvide widen, enlarge, extend, amplify, dilate, expand; — **seg** expand, dilate; widen, broaden, develop (**til:** into). **utvidelse** enlargement, extension, dilatation, expansion. **utvidelseskraft** extensible el. expansive power.
utvikle develop, evolve; (f. eks. en plan) explain, set forth; **fullstendig -t** full-grown; — **seg** develop, evolve.
utvikling development; (fysikk) evolution; (kjemi) emission, escape; (forklaring) explanation, exposition.
utviklingsdyktig capable of development.
utviklingslæren the doctrine of evolution.
utvilsom undoubted. **-t**·(adv) undoubtedly.
utvinne extract, gain, get; — **et metall fra malmen** gain a metal from its ore.
utvirke effect, obtain.
utvise turn out, expel, order out; (legge for dagen) show, exhibit, evince, manifest, put forth. — **grov uaktsomhet** be guilty of a grave oversight. — **av skolen** expel one from school.
utvisning expulsion.
utvisningsordre order of expulsion.
utvokst fully grown, fullgrown, full-sized.
utvortes (adj) exterior, outside, external; (adv) outwardly; for outward application.
utvortes (subst) exterior, externals (pl).
utvotere vote out; blackball.
utvungen unforced, uncompelled; (naturlig, fri) unconstrained, easy, free. **-het** ease.
utvær distant el. outlying fishing camp.
utvåkt exhausted with watching.
utydelig indistinct. **-het** indistinctness.
utyske sprite, ogre.
utørk, utørken remote desert, waste.
utørst not thirsty; **drikke seg** — drink enough, satisfy one's thirst.
utøse pour out; — **blod** shed blood; — **sitt hjerte (for)** unbosom oneself (to); — **sin vrede** vent one's anger.
utøve exercise, practise; (om noe vondt) perpetrate; **den -nde makt** the executive (power).
utøvelse exercise, practice, discharge; perpetration.
utøy vermin.
utøylet unbridled.
utålelig intolerable, insufferable, insupportable, aggravating, past endurance.
utålmodig impatient (**over:** at; **etter:** for; **etter å:** to). **utålmodighet** impatience.
utålsom intolerant (**overfor:** of, towards) **-het** intolerance.
utånde (dø) expire; (ånde ut) breathe forth el. out; exhale.
uunngå(e)lig unavoidable, inevitable.
uunnværlig indispensable.
uunnværlighet indispensability.
utforskelig inscrutable.
uutgrunnelig unfathomable.
uutholdelig intolerable, unbearable, unendurable.
uutryddelig ineradicable.
uutsigelig unutterable, unspeakable.

uutslettelig ineffaceable, indelible.
uutslukkelig inextinguishable.
uuttømmelig inexhaustible.
uutviklet undeveloped; rudimentary.
uvalgbar ineligible.
uvand easy, simple.
uvane bad habit.
uvant unaccustomed, unused (**med:** to).
uvanthet want of practice.
uvarig unlasting.
uvederheftig insolvent, irresponsible.
uvederheftighet insolvency, irresponsibility.
uvedkommende foreign, irrelevant; **en meg -sak** an affair in which I am not concerned; —(personer) persons not concerned, strangers intruders; — **forbys adgang!** no admittance
uvegerlig: en — plikt an absolute duty (adv) (uunngåelig) inevitably; (alltid, uten unn tagelse) invariably.
uveisom trackless, pathless, impervious.
uveisomhet impassableness, imperviousness.
uvel unwell, uncomfortable.
uvelkommen unwelcome.
uvenn enemy. **bli -er** fall out, quarrel. **gjør** seg **-er med** make an enemy of.
uvennlig unfriendly, unkind. **uvennlighet** un friendliness, unkindness. **uvennskap** enmity.
uventet unexpected, unlooked-for.
uverdig unworthy, undeserving (**til:** of).
uverdighet unworthiness.
uvesen disorder, disturbance, nuisance.
uvesentlig unessential, immaterial.
uvett folly, unwisdom; (besvimelse) swoon **ligge i** — be in a swoon.
uvettig foolish, injudicious; reckless.
uviktig immaterial, insignificant, unimpor tant.
uvilje ill-will; (ulyst) reluctance, aversion (mishag) displeasure, disgust, indignation. **få** — **mot** take a dislike to.
uvilkårlig involuntary.
I. **uvillig** (jur) impartial, unprejudiced.
II. **uvillig** unwilling; (adv) grudgingly. **uvil lighet** unwillingness.
uvirkelig unreal, unsubstantial.
uvirksom inactive, idle; (virkningsløs) in efficacious, ineffective, inefficient.
uvirksomhet inactivity; idleness, inefficiency
uvisnelig imperishable, unfading.
uviss uncertain, doubtful, undecided.
uvisshet uncertainty.
uvitende ignorant (**om:** of).
uvitenhet ignorance.
uvitenskapelig unscientific, unscholarly.
uvittig unwitty, dull, stupid.
uvurderlig invaluable, inestimable.
uvæpnet unarmed.
uvær storm, rough (el. bad) weather. **uværs-bolk** spell of bad weather. **-natt** rough el. stormy night. **-sky** storm-charged cloud.
uvøren careless, reckless, bold, daring; (i sir tale) rough; — **kjøring** reckless driving **uvørenhet** carelessness, recklessness, boldness daring; roughness.
uærbødig disrespectful, irreverent.
uærbødighet disrespect, irreverence.
uærlig dishonest. **uærlighet** dishonesty.
uøkonomisk wasteful; (om person) thriftless.
uøvd unexercised, unpractised, untrained, raw.
uåpnet unopened.
uår bad crop(s) el. harvest, bad (el. scarce) year.

V

', **v** V, v.
va wade; — over ford.
vabbe paddle el. splash about.
vable blister, vesicle.
I. **vad** (not) fishing-net, net, seine.
II. **vad** (vadested) ford, fording place.
vade, se va.
vade|fugl wading-bird. **-sted** ford.
vadmel, vadmål frieze, russet.
vadsekk portmanteau, travelling bag.
vaffel waffle, wafer. **-jern** waffle-irons.
vag vague.
vagabond vagabond, vagrant. **vagabondere**
agabondize. vagabondering vagrancy.
vagge rock; waddle.
vaghet vagueness.
vagle (til høns) perch, roost.
vagong (el. wagon) railway-carriage.
vaie fly, float, wave.
vaisenhus orphan asylum, orphan house.
vaisenhusbarn orphan-house child.
vak light-sleeping; (årvåken) watchful; (sky,
m dyr) wary.
vakanse vacancy. **-tilfelle: i** — on a vacancy,
n case of vacancies.
vakant vacant; **oppslå** — declare vacant.
I. **vake** (på sjøen) float lightly; be floating.
II. **vake** wake, be awake. Se også **våke**.
vaken awake, waking. Se også **våken**.
vaker (sjømerke) beacon, buoy; (vinnfløy)
ane.
vakker pretty, handsome, fine.
vakle shake, totter; (være uviss) waver, fluc-
uate, vacillate. **vakling** shaking, tottering;
acillation, fluctuation.
vakne wake, awake.
vaksinasjon vaccination.
vaksinasjonsattest vaccination certificate.
vaksine vaccine matter, lymph.
vaksinere vaccinate.
vakt watch, guard; (mar) watch; (mann)
guard, sentinel; (lokale) guard- el. watchhouse;
være el. stå på —, **ha** — be on guard el. duty;
stille, sette på — put on guard; **holde** — keep
watch el. guard.
vakt (pts) awakened. **de -e** the awakened
nes.
vaktavløsning guard mount.
vaktel quail.
vakthavende on guard, on watch, on duty,
n charge.
vakt|hund watch-dog. **-mann** caretaker, guard.
-mannskap (men on) guard el. watch. **-mester**
caretaker, keeper; (portner) janitor.
vakt|parade parade of the soldiers on guard.
-post watch sentinel. **-skifte** change of the
guard. **-skip** guard ship. **-skudd** watch-gun, gun
-fire. **-stue** guardroom. **vaktsom** watchful,
vigilant.
vaktsomhet vigilance.
vakuum vacuum. **-bremse** vacuum-brake.
vakuumventil vacuum valve.
valen benumbed, numb (with cold); (fig)
feeble, half-hearted.
val|fart pilgrimage. **-farte** make a pilgrimage.
valg choice, option, selection; (mellom to
ting) alternative; (av fyrste) election; (av de-
putert) election, return, poll; **etter hans** — at
his option; **treff Deres** — make your choice.
valg|agn bait for voters. **-bar** eligible. **-barhet**
eligibility.
valg|brev certificate of election. **-dag** election
day. **-deltagelse: liten (stor)** — a low (heavy)

poll. **-etterretninger** election news. **-fri** optional.
-fusk electious fraud.
valg|handling election. **-kamp** contested elec-
tion. **-kampanje** election campaign, electioneering campaign. **-kandidat** candidate. **-klage** election petition. **-knep** electioneering trick. **-krets**
constituency, elector(al) district, (parliamentary)
borough. **-liste** register of electors el. voters.
-lokale polling-place. **-lov** law of elections.
-mann elector. **-menighet** free congregation.
-måte manner of election. **-protokoll** pollbook.
-rett (elective) franchise, electoral rights el.
privileges. **-rike** elective kingdom. **-seier** election
victory, victory at the polls. **-slektskap** elective
affinity. **-språk** motto. **-sted** place of election.
-styre presiding officers (at a polling station).
-styrer returning officer, presiding officer. **-tale**
electoral speech, candidate's address. **-tribune**
hustings. **-trykk** pressure on electors. **-urne**
ballot-box.
Valhall the Valhalla.
valiser Welshman. **valisisk** Welsh.
valk pad, roll; (av kunstig hår) frisette.
valke full, mill. **valke|jord** fuller's earth
-mølle fulling mill fullery. **valker** fuller.
valkyrje battle-nymph, valkyr, valkyria.
vallak gelding.
valle, se myse.
vallon (fransktalende belgier) Walloon.
vallonsk Walloon.
valmue poppy. **valmue|frø** poppy-seed. **-saft**
poppy-juice, opium.
valnøtt walnut.
valplass battle-field, field of battle.
vals waltz. **valse** (danse vals) waltz.
vals(e) (subst) cylinder, roller. **valse** (vrb) roll.
valseverk rolling mill.
valthorn French-horn, bugle.
valuta (verdi) value; (kurs) currency, exchange, rate of exchange; — **i kontanter** value
in cash; — **i meg selv** (i egenveksel) value in
myself; — **i regning** value in account; — **mottatt** value received; **få** — **for pengene** get value
for one's money, get a good value; **de små
lands** — **er sikker nok** the currency of the small
countries is safe enough.
valuta|fall fall in the rate of exchange. **-for-
hold** state of exchanges. **-kurs** rate of exchange.
-marked foreign exchange market. **-spekulasjon**
speculation in foreign currency.
valør value.
vammel mawkish, nauseous, sickly.
vammelhet mawkishness, nauseousness.
vampyr vampire.
vanart wickedness. **vanarte**, se **vanslekte**.
vand (vanskelig) difficult.
vandal Vandal. **-isme** vandalism.
I. **vandel** conduct; **handel og** — trade and
commerce, business, common intercourse.
II. **vandel** (høyvisk) wisp of hay.
vandig hydrous, watery; (fig) insipid.
vandle bundle up hay or straw for cattle.
vandre wander, walk, roam, perambulate;
-nde itinerant; erratic; **en -nde ridder** a knight
errant.
vandre|drift instinct of migration. **-kran**
bridge crane.
vandre|liv itinerant life. **-lyst** roaming pro-
pensity. **-lærer** visitant teacher. **-pokal** (floating)
challenge cup.
vandrer wanderer, way-farer, rambler.

vandrevet mismanaged.
vandreår travelling year.
vandring wandering etc. (se **vandre**), ramble, peregrination, perambulation.
vandrings|mann wanderer, way-farer, traveller. **-stav** walkingstaff, pilgrim's staff.
vane custom, habit; **av** — from habit. **-dyr** (fig) slave of custom. **-kristen** conventional Christian. **-messig** habitual, of routine.
vanesak (matter of) habit.
vanfør crippled, lame, disabled; **hjem for -e** cripples' home. **vanførhet** lameness, infirmity.
vang field, lawn; (jvr. **seter-**).
vanhedre disgrace, dishonour.
vanhell misfortune, disaster.
vanhellig profane. **vanhellige** profane, desecrate. **vanhelligelse** profanation, desecration.
vanhjulpen left in the lurch.
vanilje vanilla. **-stang** vanilla pod.
vanke stroll, roam, wander, rove; — **hos** visit with; — **i** visit in; **det -r god mat og drikke** there will be a treat.
vankelmodig fickle, inconstant.
vankelmodighet fickleness, inconstancy.
vankle misbecome, sit ill upon.
vankundig ignorant. **-het** ignorance.
vankunne ignorance.
vanlig usual, customary, habitual.
vann water; (tinktur etc.) wash; (luktende) essence; **vann-** water, aquatic; **stille** — **har dyp grunn** still waters run deep; **ta inn** — (mar) water, take in water; **late -et** make water; **trå -et** tread (in the) water; **av reneste** — of the first water; **gå i -et** bathe, go bathing; (fig) (dt) go wrong, come off second best, be sold; **fiske i rørt** — fish in troubled waters; **en storm i et glass** — a tempest in a teacup; **hans tenner løper i** — his mouth waters; — **i hodet** hydrocephalus, water on the brain; **slå kaldt** — **i blodet** take it coolly; **legge tøy i** — soak washing; **oven -e** above water; **holde seg oven -e** (fig) keep one's head above water; **fengsel på** — **og brød** imprisonment on bread and water; **det er** — **på hans mølle** that is grist to his mill; **bli satt på -et** (om båt) be launched; **sette under** — flood.
vannaktig watery, aqueous, waterish.
vannavløp drainage.
⚓ **vann|balje** water-tub. **-basseng** waterpond, water reservoir. **-beholder** reservoir, cistern, tank. **-beholdning** stock el. supply of water. **-damp** (aqueous) vapour.
vanne (vrb) water; irrigate; (kveg o. l.) water.
vann|farge water-colour; **male med -r** paint in water-colours. **-fat** basin. **-flate** surface of the water; sheet of water; **i -n** at the water's edge. **-flygemaskin** seaplane.
vannforbruk consumption of water.
vannforsyning supply of water.
vann|fugl water-fowl, aquatic bird. **-fylling** watering. **-gang** (mar) waterline; (fig) blunder, failure, defeat. **-glass** (glass) tumbler; (stoff) water-glass. **-holdig** watery, aqueous, hydrous. **-holdighet** amount of water (contained in st.).
vanning watering, irrigation.
vann|kalv water-beetle. **-kanten** the water's edge. **-kappe** (i bil) water-jacket. **-karaffel** (water-)decanter, water-bottle. **-karse** water -cresses. **-kjemmet** water-combed. **-kjøler** water -cooler, refrigerator. **-klosett** water-closet, W. C. **-kopper** water-pox, chicken pox. **-kraft** hydraulic power, water-power. **-kran** water-cock, hydrant. **-kunst** water-works, fountain. **-kur** hydropathic cure, water-cure. **-kuranstalt** hydropathic establishment, water-cure (establishment). **-ledning** aqueduct, conduit. **-linje** (mar) water-line; (i papir) wire line. **-mangel** scarcity of water. **-mann** water-carrier; (himmeltegn) water-bearer. **-melon** water-melon.
vann|merke water-mark, paper-mark. **-mugge** water-jug, ewer. **-mølle** water-mill. **-nymfe**

water-nymph. **-omslag** (pl) water-dressings. **-pipe** hookah. **-plante** aquatic plant. **-post** pump. **-pute** (i sykepleien) water-bed. **-pytt** puddle. **-pøs** water-bucket.
vannrett horizontal, level.
vannrik abounding with water. **-dom** abundance of water.
vann|rotte water-rat. **-rør** conduit-pipe; (i rørkjele) water-tube.
vann|skade damage by water. **-skatt** water-tax. **-skille** water-shed, divide. **-skorpa** the surface of the water, the water's edge. **-skrekk** hydrophobia. **-slange** (zool.) watersnake; (brann-, hage) water-hose.
vann|spill waste of water. **-spring** fountain. **-sprøyte** (til hagebruk) watering- el. water-pot. **-stand** height of the water; **høy** — high water; **lav** — low water. **-stoff** hydrogen.
vannstøvler water-proof boots.
vannsyk oozy, sour, swampy.
vann|tett water-proof, watertight; **gjøre** — waterproof; — **tøy** waterproof; — **rom** watertight compartment. **-tønne** water-cask.
vannverk water works (pl).
vannåre vein of water.
vanry, vanrykte ill repute, disrepute, discredit; **komme i** — get into bad repute.
vanrøkt bad tending, neglect.
vanrøkte tend ill, neglect.
vansaltet undersalted, insipid.
vansire disfigure.
vanskapning monster.
vanskapt deformed, disfigured, monstrous.
vanskapthet deformity, monstrosity.
vanskelig difficult, hard; (person) hard to please; (adv) with difficulty, not easily; **ha** — **for å have** (some) difficulty in.
vanskeliggjøre impede, render difficult.
vanskelighet difficulty; **-en ved** the difficulty of.
vanskjebne adverse el. hard fate, fatality.
vanskjøtte mismanage, neglect.
vanslekte degenerate.
vansmekte languish, grow faint.
vanstell bad management.
vanstyre (vrb) misgovern, misrule; (subst) misgovernment, misrule.
vant (adj) accustomed, used.
vant (på skip) shroud; shrouds (pl).
vante (subst) mitten.
vante (vrb) want, lack, be destitute of.
vantreven unhealthy; (kuet i veksten) stunted.
vantrives thrive ill, pine away. **vantrivning** piner, stunt.
vantro (adj) incredulous, disbelieving; (ikke ortodoks) unbelieving. **vantro** (subst) incredulousness, incredulity, disbelief, infidelity, unbelief
vanvare inadvertence; **av** — inadvertently, from inadvertence.
vanvidd insanity, madness, mental derangement, lunacy; **drive en til** — drive one mad.
vanvittig insane, lunatic, mad, deranged.
vanvøre contemn; neglect; scoff at.
vanverddom contempt; neglect; scoffing.
vanære (subst) dishonour, infamy, disgrace.
vanære (vrb) dishonour, disgrace. **-nde** ignominious, disgraceful, infamous.
var (til sengklær) cover, case.
I. **var** vigilant, wakeful; cautious, wary; shy; sensitive.
II. **var: bli** — become aware of, perceive.
vara|formann deputy-chairman. **-mann** deputy, substitute. **-spire** (mar) rough tree, spare spar. **-stang** (mar) spare topmast.
varbind (loose) paper cover.
varde (subst) cairn of stones; (sjømerke) beacon.
varde (vrb) build a cairn el. cairns. — **opp** cairn out el. up.
varde|penger beaconage. **-vakt** (glt.) watch kept near a cairn.

vardøger double, fetch, wraith of a living person.

I. **vare** (handelsvare) article, commodity; **-r** goods; ta **for god** — put up with, accept; **skadde -r** damaged goods.

II. **vare: ta seg i** — for beware of, be on one's guard against; **ta** — **på** take care of; attend to, observe, watch, have an eye upon.

I. **vare** (advare) warn; — **seg** take care, take heed, beware.

II. **vare** (v. ved) last, endure; **det vil ikke** — **lenge** it will not be long.

vare|balle bale of goods. **-beholdning** stock (in trade).

vare|heis goods el. parcel lift. **-hus** stores.

vare|lager stock(-in-trade), store. **-lagring** warehousing. **-leksikon** commercial dictionary. **-merke** trade mark.

vareopptelling (til status) stocktaking.

vare|prøve sample. **-skur** goods shed.

vareta attend to, look after, take care of; **har nok å** — has enough upon his hands.

varetagelse attending to, care.

varetekt care; **ta i (sin)** — take charge of.

varetekts|arrest custody; (lokalet) house of detention. **-fange** remanded prisoner.

varetrekk cover, housing.

varg, se **ulv**.

varhet vigilance; wariness; shyness; sensitiveness.

variabel variable. **variasjon** variation; range.

variere vary. **varietet** variety.

varieté–teater theatre of varieties, music-hall.

varig lasting, permanent.

varighet duration, permanence, continuance.

varlig (adv) cautiously, gently, tenderly; **fare** — med deal tenderly by.

varm warm; (sterkere) hot; **-t bad** hot bath; **-t vann** hot water; **det er -t i dag** it is hot today, the day is hot.

varmblodig warm-blooded; (fig) hotblooded.

varme (subst) warmth, heat; (fig) fervour, ardour. **ti graders** — ten degrees of heat.

varme (vrb) warm, heat.

varme|apparat warming apparatus, steamheater, radiator. **-bølge** hot el. warm wave. **-flaske** hot-water bottle, warming bottle. **-grad** degree of heat. **-kasse** heater. **-ledende** heat-conducting. **-leder** conductor of heat; **dårlig** — bad conductor (of heat), non-conductor. **-lære** theory of heat. **-måler** calorimeter, thermometer.

varmerør pipe for hot air (or steam).

varme|stråle heat ray. **-stue** warming room.

varmeutstråling radiation of heat.

varmhjertet warm-hearted.

varmhjertethet warm-heartedness.

varmtvannsbeholder hot-well.

varmtvannsrør hot-water pipe.

varp warp. **varpe** warp; (ved hjelp av anker) kedge; (kaste) heave. **varpetrosse** warp.

varsel (advarsel) warning; (lovl.) notice, summons; (forvarsel) omen, foreboding; **på et øyeblikks** — at a moment's notice.

varsku (vrb) warn (om: of). **varsku!** look out! **ake care!** make way! **varsku** (subst) warning.

varsle (bebude) presage, bode, augur; (stevne) summon; — **om** augur, bode.

varsom cautious, circumspect. **varsomhet** caution, cautiousness, circumspection.

varte opp wait (upon), attend.

vartpenger allowance; (officers) half-pay.

varulv were-wolf.

vas nonsense, rubbish.

vasall vassal. **-tjeneste** feudal service.

I. **vase** (blomster-) vase.

II. **vase** (floke) jumble, tangle; (av tømmer) am.

vase (tøve) talk nonsense. **-kopp** rattle.

vaselin vaseline. **vaselinolje** vaseline oil.

vask wash; laundry-work; (det tøy som er til vask) washing; (i kjøkken) sink; **gå i -en** come to nothing; **være på** — be at wash.

vaskbar washable.

vaske wash; (blande kort) mix; — **opp** wash up; **som kan -s** washable; **den ene hånd -r den andre** one hand washes another, one good turn deserves another; **noe som har vasket seg** (noe imponerende) a stunner.

vaske|balje wash-tub.

vaske|bjørn racoon. **-kjole** washing dress. **-klut** dish cloth, wash-rag. **-kone** laundress, washer woman. **-liste** list of things to be washed. **-regning** wash bill, laundry bill.

vaskeri laundry.

vaske|rom (f. eks. i toget) lavatory. **-servant** wash-stand. **-skinn** wash-leather. **-skinnshansker** wash-leather gloves. **-tøy** washing; (stoff) washable material, washing fabric. **-vann** water for washing. **-vannsbolle** wash-hand basin.

vass|arv chickweed. **-blande** milk-and-water. **-bøtte** water-bucket. **-drag** water-course.

vasse wade; plash, splash.

vassen washy, watery; sloppy.

vass|fall waterfall; (svært stort) cataract; (mindre) cascade. **-inntak** (water) intake; (mar) watering-place. **-krukke** water-jug. **-renne** water -pipe.

vass–sele (watercarrier's) yoke.

vass|trukken sodden, water-soaked. **-velling** water-gruel.

vater: i — horizontal; **stille i** — level; **bringe ut av** — unlevel.

vaterpass level; (tømmermanns) plumb-rule.

Vatikanet the Vatican.

vatn (innsjø) lake; (tjern) lakelet. Se ellers **vann**.

vatre water. **vatring** watering.

vatt wadding; **renset** — medicated cotton-wool. **en plate** — a sheet of wadding.

vattere wad, stuff (with wadding).

vattering wadding.

vattersott dropsy. **vattersottig** dropsical.

vattfabrikant manufacturer of wadding.

vatt|fabrikk wadding manufactory. **-teppe** wadded quilt.

ve pain, ache, anguish; (sorg) woe; **folkenes** — **og vel** the welfare of nations; **i** — **og vel** in weal or woe; **veer** throes el. pains of child -birth. **ve! woe!** — **meg ulykkelige!** woe is me.

ved (prep) by, at, on, in. b y: **tett** — close by, hard by; — **lys** by candlelight; — **et tilfelle** by chance el. accident; — **navn** by el. of the name of; **føre** — **hånden** lead by the hand; — **å arbeide** by working; — **Gud!** by God! — (el. på) **min ære** by el. upon my honour; **hva forstår man** — . . . what is meant by . . .? what is the meaning of . . .? a t: — **døra** at the door; **professor** — **et universitetet** professor at (in) a university; — **daggry** at daybreak; — **synet av** at the sight of; — **hånden** at hand; o n: — **Themsen** on the Thames; **byen ligger** — **sundet** the town stands on the sound; **et hotell** — **en sjø i Italia** a hotel on an Italian lake; — **denne leilighet** on this occasion; o f: **slaget** — **Leipzig** the battle of Leipzig; t o: **henge fast** — **cleave to; lege** — **et hospital** physician to a hospital; **tenke** — (el. for) **seg selv** think to oneself; i n: **en annen eiendommelighet** — **mannen** another peculiarity in the man; **det var ikke noe for-bausende** — **dette faktum** the fact had in it nothing surprising; **(a n d r e m å t e r):** **det er ikke noe** — **ham** he is not good for much; **han befant seg vel, ille** — **det** it agreed with him, it disagreed with him; **jeg kunne ikke gjøre** — **det** I could not help it; **røre** — **noe** touch a thing; **være** — (tilstå) **own,** acknowledge.

ved (adv): **det kommer ikke meg** — it is no business of mine; **snakkes** — speak together; **tett** — close by, hard by.

ved (subst) wood.

vedbend ivy.

vedbli continue, go on, keep on, persevere; — **å arbeide** keep working, continue working, continue to work; — **å være venner** remain friends.

vedblivende continued, persistent; (adv) still.

vedde wager, bet, lay a wager; **jeg vil —** hva som heist at I'd lay any wager that; **jeg -r med Dem ti mot en** I'll bet you ten to one.

vedde|kamp contest for a wager, match. **-kjørsel** driving-match. **-løp** race, foot-race, horse-race; **løpe -løp** run a race, race. **-løpsbane** race-course el. -ground. **-løpshest** racer, race -horse. **-løpsstall** racing stables.

vedde|mål wager, bet. **-ritt** riding-match, race. **-strid** contest for a wager.

vederfares happen, befall; **la en — rettferdighet** do one justice.

vederheftig responsible, reliable, solvent.

vederheftighet responsibility, solvency.

vederkvege refresh.

vederkvegelse refreshment, recreation.

vederlag compensation, requital; commutation; **gi —** compensate; **til — for** in compensation for, in return for; **uten —** gratis, gratuitously.

vederlagsfri costfree, gratuitous, free.

vederstyggelig abominable.

vederstyggelighet abomination.

vedett vedette, vidette.

ved|famn cord of wood. **-fang** armful of firewood.

vedføy|e annex, subjoin, **affix; til -de priser** at the prices affixed.

vedgå admit, own, acknowledge, confess.

vedgåing admission.

vedhefte attach.

vedheng appendage.

ved|hengende appendent, adhesive. **henging** adherence, attachment (ved: to).

ved|hogger wood-chopper, wood-cutter. **-hogst** wood-chopping, wood-cutting.

vedholdende persevering, continuous, prolonged. **vedholdenhet** perseverance.

vedkasse wood-box.

vedkjenne seg own, own to, acknowledge; **ikke — seg** disown.

vedkjennelse recognition; acknowledgment.

vedkomme concern, regard, respect, bear on; **se komme ved; (ikke) — saken** be (ir)relevant to the matter.

vedkommende concerned; **— forfatter** the author in question; **— ansøker** the party applying; **(de) —** those concerned; **rette —** the proper person el. persons.

vedkommende (subst): **for mitt —** for my part, personally; **for Norges —** as to, with respect to, in the case of Norway.

vedkubbe log of (fire)wood.

vedlagt (adj) accompanying, annexed, subjoined; **— sender jeg** inclosed, etc., under this cover, I send. **— sendes Dem liste over** please, find inclosed a list of; **ifølge -e nota** as per statement enclosed; **-e** the inclosed.

vedlegg accompanying document el. paper annexed; (i brev) enclosure; **hermed to —** 2 Encs.

vedlegge annex; (i brev) inclose.

vedliggende annexed, subjoined, accompanying.

vedlikehold keeping in repair; preservation, maintenance.

vedlikeholde el. **holde ved like** (bygninger) keep in repair; (bevare) preserve; support, maintain, keep up; (fortsette) carry on, continue; **de er godt vedlikeholdt** they are well preserved el. in good condition el. repair.

ved|mann woodman. **-pinne** stick of firewood.

vedrøre, se **angå.**

ved|ski stick of firewood. **-skjul, -skjå** woodshed. **-stabel** pile el. stack of fire-wood.

vedstå maintain, stand by.

vedta agree (on), resolve, adopt, vote, sanction, pass; (en dom) acquiesce in; **beslutninge ble enstemmig vedtatt** the resolution wa carried unanimously; **— å agree to. vedtagels** agreeing etc.; adoption; (av lov) passage.

vedtak resolution, vote; (lov) enactmen **vedtaksfør** in sufficient numbers to pass resolu tions: **være —** form a quorum.

vedtekt convention, established custom, habit standing rule el. order; **-er** by-laws (of a so ciety). **vedtektsmessig** customary, establishe by custom.

vedtre stick of firewood.

vedvare endure, continue; **vedvarende** con tinual, unceasing, constant; (adv) still.

veft woof.

veg, se vei.

vegelsinn fickleness, vacillation.

vegelsinnet fickle, wavering, vacillating.

veget|abil vegetable. **-abilsk** vegetable. **-ari aner** vegetarian. **-arianisme** vegetarianism **-asjon** vegetation. **-ativ** vegetative. **-ere** vege tate. **-ering** vegetating.

vegg wall; **sette til -s** drive into a corner.

vegge|dyr, se **-lus. -lav** (plante) wall feathe **-moss. -lus** bed bug, house-bug. **-pryd** (på ball wall-flower.

veggfast forming a part of the wall.

veggimellom from wall to wall.

vegg|kart wall-map. **-lampe** wall-lamp. **-maler wall**-painting. **-pille** pier. **-skap** wall-cupboard **-speil** pier-glass. **-tavle** black-board.

vegne: på mine, hans, hennes — on my, his her behalf el. account.

vegre seg refuse, decline (to do a thing).

vegring refusal.

vei (anlagt vei, landevei) road; (strekning retning, veilengd) way; (avstand) distance way; (stor landevei) highroad, highway; (regel messig benyttet vei, rute) route; **den korteste — the** nearest way; the shortest cut; **halve -en** halfway; **hele -en** all the way; **et stykke —** some distance; **en mils — herfra** at a mile's distance **finne -en** find one's way; **bane seg —** make el force one's way; **reiser samme — (som jeg)** is travelling my way, in my direction; **gå ret tens —** go to law; **gå, ride sin —** go off, go one's way, ride off; **gå din —** get you gone go about your business; **han kommer ingen —** he makes no headway; **den -en (by)** that way av **-en out** of the way; **gå av -en** get out of the way; **det var ikke av -en** it would not be amiss, would be as well, no bad thing; **rydde av -en** make away with; **gå langs -en** along the road; **hva er det i -en** what is the matter? **være, stå i -en for en** be, stand in one's way; **sette en i — start** one in life; **gi seg på —** set out; (mar) **på -en til** on her passage to, en route for; **på rett —** on the right road; **komme på gale -er** go astray el. wrong; **ta på —** take on; **bringe el. skaffe til -e,** se **tilveiebringe.**

vei|anlegg road-making. **-arbeider** navvy, road-labourer. **-bom** turnpike.

veide kill, shoot, catch.

veidehår tactile bristle, smeller.

veie (vrb) weigh; (fig) balance; **— av** weigh off (and set aside); **mon kan ikke — det opp med penger** it is not to be had for love or money; **— opp imot** counterbalance, be equal to; **det -r ikke lite** it is rather heavy.

veiegods weight goods. **veier** weigher.

veieredskap weighing implement.

veifarende wayfaring; traveller, passenger.

veigrind gate across a public road.

veigrøft roadside ditch.

vei|inspektør road surveyor. **-kant** roadside.

veik (myk) flexible, pliant; (fig) ogs. yielding (svak) weak; (forsakt) poor-spirited.

veike, se **veke.**

veikhet weakness.

veikjent familiar with the roads.

veikrygg small of the back.
veilede guide, lead, conduct; instruct; **-nde** rd word of guidance el. instruction. **veileder** iide, conductor. **veiledning** guidance, con- uct; instruction; (bok) guide; **til — for** for the iidance of; **til — for deg** for your guidance.
veilegeme road-bed.
veilengd(e) distance.
veining weighing.
veiovergang (jernb.) crossing, crossover.
veilpenger turnpike-money. **-skille** dividing ways, fork. **-stolpe** finger-post. **-sving** bend a road.
veit ditch, drain; (smal gate) alley, lane.
veite (vrb) ditch, drain.
veitsle (gammelnorsk ord) coshering; **ta —** xact entertainment, quarter oneself on a enant.
veiundergang subway, underpass.
veiv crank, crankhandle, winch.
veivals(e) (steam) road-roller.
veive turn a crank.
veivesen Road Board.
veiviser (fører) guide; (på vei) direction- ost; (bok) directory.
veivokter caretaker, man in charge.
I. **veke** wick.
II. **veke,** se **uke.**
vekk (borte) away, gone; (bort) away, off; å nå — get off now; **— med fingrene!** hands ff! snakk **—!** speak away! fire away! **jeg er —, ganske —** I am enraptured, quite enrap- ured; **i ett —** incessantly; **— med** away with.
I. **vekke** awaken, wake, awake; (etter avtale) all; (fig) create, raise, excite, rouse; **— fore- tillingen om** suggest; **— den f. at** suggest that.
II. **vekke** (fare sm.) start, give a start.
III. **vekke** (f. eks. i is) open, cut a passage n (the ice).
vekke (bjelle) bell, jingle.
vekkelse stimulus, awakening; (religiøs) re- vival. **vekkelse|møte** revivalist meeting. **-pre- dikant** revivalist preacher. **-ånd** revivalism.
vekkende awakening, inspiring.
vekke(r)ur alarm-clock; **stille -et på sju** set he alarm-clock to seven.
I. **veksel** (omskiftning) change.
II. **veksel** (tratte) bill (of exchange), draught, iraft; (egen, innenbys) promissory note, note of hand; **— på kort tid** short bill; **— på lang id** long bill; **trekke, utstede en —** draw, issue a bill (on); **akseptere, endossere, protestere en —** accept, endorse, protest a bill; **honorere en —** honour a bill; **ikke innløse en —** dishonour a bill; (fig) **trekke veksler på** make some draft on. **trekke store veksler på** draw heavily on.
veksel|aksept acceptance of a bill of exchange. **-arbitrasje** arbitration of exchanges. **-blankett** blank draught, bill-form. **-bruk** rotation of crops. **-debitor** party of a bill. **-diskonto** bill-discount. **-drift,** se **-bruk.**
vekseler exchanger, money-changer.
veksel|falsk forging of bills. **-gjeld** bill-debt. **-konto** account of exchange. **-kurs** (rate of) exchange. **-kurtasje** bill-brokerage. **-lov(givning)** law of bills of exchange. **-megler** bill-broker, exchange-broker. **-omkostninger** bill-charges. **-omsetning** circulation of bills of exchange. **-protest** protest. **-provisjon** exchange. **-regning** calculation of exchange. **-rett** right of exchange; se **-lov. -ristorno** redrawing. **-rytter** bill-jobber. **-rytteri** cross-accommodation, cross-acceptance, kiteflying system; **drive —** be engaged in accom- modation-bills, fly the kite. **-sang** alternative song. **-spill** alternative play. **-stempel** bill -stamp.
vekselstrøm (elckt.) alternate current.
vekselutsteder drawer.
vekselvirkning reciprocal action.
vekselvis alternating; (adv) alternately, in turns.

veksle change; (utveksle) **exchange. med -nde hell** with varying success.
vekslepenger change.
veksling exchange, exchanging.
vekst growth; (høyde, skikkelse) stature; (plante) herb, plant; **skyte — grow; -grense** limit of vegetation; **-liv** flora, vegetation.
vekt weight; (veieinnretning) pair of ba- lances, (pair of) scales, balance; (stor) weighing- machine; **etter — by** weight; **legge — på lay** stress on; attach importance el. weight to; **hva — ligger det på . . . ?** what signifies . . .?
vekter watchman. **-gang** watchman's gallery.
vektfabrikant scale-maker.
vektig weighty. **vektighet** weightiness.
vekt|lodd weight. **-skål** balance, scale. **-stang** lever. **-tap** loss of weight. **-tunge** tongue (of a balance). **-økning** increase in weight.
vel (subst) welfare, good, benefit, weal.
vel (adv) well; **befinne seg —** be well; **jeg er ikke riktig —** I am not quite well, rather unwell. out of sorts; **ville en —** wish one well; **gjøre —** do good; **og det gjorde han — i** and he was right; **gid det var så —!** that would be good news, I wish he would (etc.); **gjøre — imot** be kind to, befriend; **— møtt!** well met; **kom du — hjem?** did you get home safe? **— rodd!** (mar) rowed off all! way enough! **—! nå —!** well! well then! **ja —!** certainly, to be sure; **(r i k e l i g, f o r) kjolen er — vid** the gown is rather wide; **(godt og) — åtte tommer** fully el. quite eight inches; **— så stor som** rather larger than; **da de — var ute av byen** once out of the town; **(n o k, f o r m o d e n t l i g) kan (kunne) — være . . .** may (might) be; **han gjør det — når man ber ham om det** I dare say he will do it when he is asked; **tror du — at han tilgir meg** do you think (indeed) that he will pardon me? **du har ikke gjort det, — ?** you haven't done it, have you? **det er — ikke mulig** you don't say so? **han kan — være 40 år** I fancy he may be about 40; **(r i k t i g n o k) vel . . . men** certainly, it is true, indeed, no doubt . . . but.
velan well! go to! **velanstendig** proper, decor- ous. **velanstendighet** propriety, decorum.
velassortert well assorted.
velbefinnende health, healthiness.
velbeføyd well-grounded, legitimate.
velbegavet gifted, talented.
velbehag delight, complacency, pleasure.
vel|behagelig pleasing, agreeable, gratifying. **-beholden** safe and sound. **-beregnet** well cal- culated. **-berget** safe; prosperous. **-berådd: med — hug** deliberately. **-besatt** well filled. **-be- staltet** (spøkende) duly appointed. **-betenkt** well considered, well-advised. **-båren** wellborn; (titu- latur) honourable. **-bårenhet: Deres —** your Honour.
velde (makt) power, might.
veldedig charitable, benevolent. **i — øyemed** for (purposes of) charity. **-het** charity, bene- volence.
veldig powerful, mighty.
velferd welfare. **velferds|komité** committee of public safety. **-sak** matter of vital importance. **-tap** material loss.
vel|flidd tidy, trim, well-kept. **-forsynt** well- provided, well-stocked. **-fortjent** well-deserved, well-merited; (straff) condign.
velge choose, select; (til en post osv.) elect; (til stortingsmann) elect, return; **— ved hånds- opprekning** elect by show of hands. **— til konge** choose as (their) king, for their king.
velger elector, voter, constituent.
velger|folk body of electors. **-forening** voters' association, caucus. **-møte** meeting of elec- tors.
velgjerning benefit, benefaction, charitable deed; **vise en -er** confer benefits upon one.
velgjort well done.

velgjørende (sunn) beneficial, saluraty; (velldedig) beneficent, benevolent, charitable; **i — øyemed** for benevolent objects, for a b. object.
velgjørenhet beneficence, charity.
velgjørenhetsanstalt charitable institution.
vel|gjører benefactor. **-gjørerinne** benefactress.
velgrunnet well-grounded, well-founded.
velgående (velferd) welfare; (hell) prosperity; **drikke på ens —** drink to one's health.
velhavende well-to-do, prosperous, substantial.
velhavenhet easy circumstances, opulence, ample means.
velig fiery, high-mettled, high-spirited.
velighet spirit, mettle.
velin vellum paper, wove paper.
velklang harmony, melody, euphony.
velkledd well-dressed.
velklingende euphonic, euphonious, harmonious.
velkommen welcome, acceptable; **være —** (om person) be welcome; **by, hilse —** welcome, bid welcome.
velkomst welcome.
velkomst|beger cup of welcome. **-hilsen** welcome. **-tale** address of welcome.
velkonservert well-kept, in good condition.
vell spring; **— av toner** flood of harmony.
vellagret well-seasoned.
velle (sprudle) well, spring forth, issue forth.
vellevnet luxurious living, luxury.
velling gruel.
vellukt perfume, scent, odour. **velluktende** odorous, sweet-scented, fragrant; perfumed.
vellyd pleasing sound euphony, harmony.
vellydende harmonious.
vellyk(ke)t successful; **var svært — was a** great success.
vellyst sensual rapture; voluptuousness, sensuality, lust.
vellystig voluptuous, sensual; lascivious, wanton. **vellystighet** lasciviousness.
vellysting voluptuary, sensualist.
vellønt well paid. **vel|makt** vigour, strength; prosperity. **-maktsdager** days of vigour el. power; days of prosperity. **-ment** well-meant, well-intended. **-nært** well-fed.
veloppdragen well-bred.
veloppdragenhet good manners.
velproporsjonert well-proportioned.
velrettet well-aimed.
velsett looked upon with favour, popular.
velsigne bless; **i -de omstendigheter in the** family way.
vel|signelse blessing; (bare i egl. bet.) benediction; **guds — av** any amount of, no end of. **-signelsesrik** blessed, rich in blessing, beneficial.
vel|sinnet well-intentioned, well-disposed, well -affected. **-skapt** well-shaped, well-made, well -formed.
velskbind half-calf.
vel|skikket well qualified (**til:** for). **-skolet** well schooled, well trained.
velsmak fine (el. agreeable) taste el. flavour, palatableness. **velsmakende** savoury, palatable.
velspekket: — pung heavy, well-filled purse.
velstand prosperity, prosperous circumstances.
velstands|mann person of substance. **-messig** prosperous-looking.
velstekt properly roasted el. done.
velstudert of extensive reading.
velstående well-to-do, prosperous.
velt: være i -en be in vogue.
veltalende eloquent. **veltalenhet** eloquence, (power of) oratory; (kunst) rhetoric.
velte (vt) upset, turn over, overturn, overset; (vi) tumble over, be upset; (komme -nde) pour, rush, stream; **— skylden på** throw the blame upon; **han -t (med vognen)** his carriage was upset; **— seg** roll.
velte (tømmerv.) pile.
vel|tenkende right-minded. **-tilfreds** well-satis-

-fied. veltilfredshet satisfaction; (med seg selv) self-complacency.
vel|tjent old and deserving, of long standing. **-truffet** well taken. **-underrettet** well informed.
velur (til hatter) velours.
vel|utrustet well equipped. **-valt** well-chosen, well-selected.
velvilje benevolence, kindness, good-will.
velvillig benevolent, kind, kindly.
velvoksen well-grown, good-sized.
vel|være well-being. **-ynder** well-wisher, patron. **-ynderinne** well-wisher, patroness.
velærverdig reverend.
velærverdighet reverence; **hans — pastor** N. N. the Rev. N. N.
veløvd practised, well-trained.
vemmelig nauseous, disgusting, loathsome.
vemmelse disgust, nausea.
vemmes be disgusted; **— ved** loathe.
vemod sadness, sorrowfulness. **vemodig** sad, sorrowful, melancholy.
ven (adj), se **vakker**.
vend (p. vevde tøyer) right side; **med dobbelt — with** double chain.
vende turn; **— en ryggen** turn one's back upon one; **— seg** turn; (om vinden) change, shift, come round; **— ansiktet bort** turn one's face away; **— om** turn (back); **vend om!** turn over! over! **— seg om** turn round; **— seg om imot, — seg mot (i alm.)** turn to, turn towards; (vennlig) turn upon, turn on; (fiendtlig) turn against; **— opp ned på** turn topsy turvy; **disse vinduene -r (ut) til gata** these windows look (out) upon el. into the street, face the street; **— seg til en** turn to one; **— tilbake** return.
vende|krets tropic. **-kåpe** turn-coat, time -server. **-punkt** turning point.
vending turning, turn; (i stil) turn (of phrase), mode of expression; **i en snever — at** a pinch; **rask i -en** quick (in emergencies); **være sen i -en** be slow.
vene vein. **-blod** veinous blood.
Venedig Venice.
venerasjon veneration; **nære — for** hold in v.
venerisk venereal; **— sykdom** venereal disease.
venetianer Venetian. **venetianerinne** Venetian lady. **venetiansk** Venetian.
veng wing, pinion. Se også **vinge.**
venn friend; **en — av meg** a friend of mine; **gode -er** great friends; **gjøre seg gode -er med** make friends with.
venne accustom; **— en av med noe** break one of a thing; **— fra (brystet)** wean; **— seg av med** break oneself of; **— seg til accustom** oneself to, get accustomed to; **— seg til å get** into the habit of.
venne|hilsen friendly greeting. **-krets** circle of friends, friendly circle. **-løs** friendless, unfriended. **-møte** meeting of friends. **-ord** friend's word. **-råd** friend's advice. **-sæl** liked, beloved; kindly, amicable. **-sælhet** popularity. **-tjeneste** act of friendship, friendly turn.
venninne friend, lady friend.
vennlig kind, kindly, friendly; (by, værelse) pleasant; (adv) kindly, with kindness; **vær så — å underrette meg** please inform me.
vennlighet kindness, goodness; kindliness.
vennligsinnet friendly (**mot:** towards).
vennskap friendship; **slutte — contract** a friendship, form a friendship (**med:** with); **føle — for** feel friendship for.
vennskapelig friendly, amicable.
vennskapelighet friendliness.
vennskapsbevis proof el. mark of friendship.
vennskapstegn token el. mark of friendship.
vennskapstjeneste friendly act, act of friendship.
venstre left; **til — (på — side)** on the left, **(over til —)** to the left; **— om!** the left! face to the left; **på — side** on the left-hand side;

— hånd the left hand; **giftermål til — hånd** left-handed marriage.
venstre (subst) the Liberal party; the moderate liberals.
venstre|blad democratic paper. **-mann** moderate, liberal. **-ministerium** liberal cabinet.
vente (vi) wait, stay; (vente på) wait for; (vt) (ha forventning om) expect, anticipate; (avvente) wait for; (være forbeholdt) await; — seg noe expect st.; **-r seg** is near her confinement; **jeg vil** — I will wait; **det kan** — there is no hurry about that; — **etter** wait for; — **med noe** delay a thing; — **på en** wait for one; **det -r meg et vanskelig arbeid** a difficult task awaits me; **la en** — (**på seg**) keep one waiting.
vente: i — in expectation, in prospect.
ventelig to be expected; (adv) probably, likely. **ventende** (dt. som kan ventes) expected, due.
vente|sal waiting apartment el. -room. **-tid** waiting time. **-værelse** waiting-room.
ventil air-hole, scuttle; (maskin.) valve, escape-valve. **-asjon** ventilation.
ventilasjonsapparat ventilating apparatus.
ventilator ventilator; fan.
ventilere ventilate.
venting waiting etc., expectancy.
venøs venous.
veps wasp.
vepsebol wasp's nest, (fig) nest of hornets; **stikke hånden i et** — poke one's head into a hornet's nest; put one's hand into a bee-hive.
vepse|stikk wasp's sting. **-talje** wasp-waist.
veranda veranda.
verbal verbal.
verbal|injurie libel. **-substantiv** verbal noun.
verbum verb.
verd (adj) worth; (verdig) worthy; **det er ikke -t** you had better not; **er ham ikke** — is not worthy of him.
verd (subst) worth, value; **det får stå ved sitt** — it may go for what it is worth; **tillegge stort** — attach great value to.
verden world; **hele** — all the world, the whole world; **den annen** — the next el. other world; **ta** — **som den er** take things as they are; **det er -s gang** so goes the world, that's the way of the world; **all -s rikdom** all the riches in the world; **til ingen -s nytte** to no earthly use el. purpose, perfectly useless; **ingen -s ting** no earthly thing; **ikke for alt i** — not for the world, not for worlds; **ingen ting i** — nothing on earth; **hva i all —?** what in the name of wonder? what on (the) earth? what in the world? **bringe til** — bring into the world, bring forth; **komme til** — come into the world, be born.
verdens|alt universe. **-anskuelse** view of the world. **-barn** worldly-minded person. **-berømt** far-famed; world-famed, world-famous, world-renowned. **-berømthet** world-wide fame. **-beskrivelse** cosmography. **-borger** citizen of the world. **-del** part of the world. **-egn** region of the world.
verdens|erfaring experience of the world. **-forakt** contempt of the world. **-herredømme** empire of the world. **-historie** history of the world, universal history. **-historisk** of universal history, in the history of the world. **-hjørne** quarter of the globe. **-kart** map of the world. **-klok** worldly wise, having knowledge of the world. **-klokskap** knowledge of the world, worldly wisdom.
verdens|kongress world's congress.
Verdenskrigen (krigen 1914—18) the Great War.
verdens|krise world crisis. **-kunnskap** knowledge of the world. **-litteratur** universal literature. **-mann** man of the world. **-omseiler** circumnavigator. **-omseiling** circumnavigation. **-orden** system of the world. **-rommet** space. **-språk** universal language. **-stad** world-city.

verdenstrett world-wearied; world-worn.
verdensutstilling universal exhibition.
verdi value, price; **store -er** large sums; **til en** — **av** to the value of.
verdi|angivelse statement of value. **-fall** decrease in value. **-forsendelse** parcel of value. **-forøkelse** increased value.
verdifull valuable.
verdig worthy; (om vesen) dignified; — **til** worthy of; **som var en bedre sak** — deserving of a better cause.
verdige think worthy of; **han -t meg ikke et svar** he did not deign el. condescend to answer me; **-s å** deign (el. condescend) to.
verdighet dignity; (til noe) worthiness.
verdigjenstand article of value, pl. også valuables.
verdiløs valueless, worthless.
verdi|løshet worthlessness. **-papirer** bonds, stocks and shares, papers. **-post** treasure mails. **-saker** valuables. **-stigning** increment value. **-stigningsskatt** increment tax.
verdsette estimate, value; — **for høyt, lavt** overvalue, undervalue. **verdsettelse** valuation.
verdslig temporal, secular, worldly, mundane; **den -e makt** the secular power.
verdslighet temporality, secularity, worldliness.
verdsligsinnet worldly-minded.
verft shipbuilding yard, dock-yard. **marinens** — naval dockyard, navy yard.
verge (vrb) (forsvare) defend; — **seg** defend oneself.
I. verge (subst) (formynder) guardian; (bestyrer av myndlings gods) trustee.
II. verge (varetekt): **ha i sitt** — have in charge, have in trust.
III. verge (subst) (våpen) weapon of defence, sword.
vergeløs defenceless. **-het** defencelessness.
verifisere verify. **verifisering** verification.
verje, se **verge.**
I. verk (arbeid) work; (litterært etc.) performance, work; (musikk) opus; (bruk) factory, mill. **sette i** — set on foot; **skride til -et** set to work.
II. verk (smerte) ache; (revmatisme) rheumatism; (materie) gathering, matter.
verkbrudden palsical, palsied.
verke ache, pain; (sette verk) matter.
verkefinger swelled (el. swoln) finger.
verken linsey-woolsey.
verks|drift factory business. **-eier** factory owner, millowner. **-mester** foreman, manager of a factory.
verk|sted workshop, shop. **-tøy** tool, implement. **-tøyfutteral** tool-holder. **-tøykasse** tool -box, tool-chest.
verktøymaskin machine tool.
vermut vermouth, vermuth.
vern defence.
verne defend, protect.
verne|plikt liability to military service; conscription, compulsory enlistment; **alminnelig** — general military service; **tjene sin** — serve one's time as a soldier. **-pliktig** liable to serve.
verneskog protecting belt of trees.
verne|ting venue. **-toll** protective duty.
veronal veronal.
verop howl of woe, lamentation.
verpe lay. **-høne** laying hen. **-tid** period of laying.
verre worse; (dt.) **det var** — that beats everything.
vers verse; **han synger på sitt siste** — he is drawing near his end; **på** — in verse; **skrive** — write el. compose poetry el. verses.
Versailles-traktaten the treaty of Versailles.
versart kind of verse.
versemaker verse-maker, versifier.
versemakeri verse-making, rhyming.

versemål metre.

versere circulate, be abroad; **-r for retten** is before the court, is pending.

versform: i — in the form of verse.

versfot (metrical) foot.

versifi|kasjon versification. **-sere** versify.

versjon version.

vers|kunst (art of) versification. **-kunstner** versifier. **-lære** prosody, rules of versification.

verst worst; **er — mot seg selv** is his own worst enemy; **i -e fall** at (the) worst, if the worst came (comes) to the worst.

' **vert** (i vertshus) landlord, host, innkeeper; (i selskap) host, entertainer; (eier) landlord; **fungere som —** do the honours.

vertikal vertical.

vertinne (i vertshus) landlady; (i selskap) hostess; (eierinne) landlady; **fungere som —** do the honours.

vertsfolk entertainers.

vertshus public house, inn.

vertshusholder publican, innkeeper.

vertskap entertainers, host and hostess.

I. **verv** task, commission, duties.

II. **verv,** se **verft.**

verve enlist; recruit; **— stemmer** canvass (for votes); **la seg —** enlist. **-r** recruiting officer; canvasser. **verv(n)ing** recruiting etc.

vesel weasel.

vesen being, (filos.) entity; (dt.) creature; (egenart.) essence, substance; (natur) nature; (opptreden) manners, address. Som led i mange sammensetn. gjengis vesen bl. a. ved pl. av vedkommende ord, f. eks. schools, telegraphs; **ved:** affairs el. matters of el. relating to; **ved: department** (intelligence department); **ved: board** (road board) **ved:** establishment (lighthouse establishment); **ved:** service (signalling service); **ved:** system (education system).

vesensforskjell essential difference.

vesentlig (adj) essential; **i det -e** substantially, in substance; **i alt —** in all essentials; **det -e innhold** the substance.

vesentlig (adv) essentially, substantially; (for størstedelen) chiefly, mostly; (så godt som) practically, virtually.

vesir (tyrkisk minister) vizier.

veske bag, handbag.

vesle little; (bitteliten) tiny, wee.

veslevoksen precocious.

I. **vest** (kledesplagg) waistcoat; (amr) vest; (dame-) vest, cardigan.

II. **vest** (verdenshjørne) west; **rett i —** due west; **— t. N. W. by N.; V. N. V. W. N. W.; N. V. t. v. N. W. by W.** etc.; **rett — from** (the) west; **i —** (in the) west; **— for** west of; **mot — towards** the west, westward; **vinden er slått om til —** the wind has shifted to the west.

vesta|fjells west of the mountains. **-fjelsk** western. **-for** west of, to the westward of.

vestalinne vestal virgin.

Vest-Asia Western Asia.

vestavind west-wind, westerly wind.

Vesten the West.

vestende west end.

vestenfor, se **vestafor.**

vestenfra (adv) from the west el. westward.

vestenvind, se **vestavind.**

vester|landene the Occident el. West. **-landsk** occidental, western.

vestetter (towards the) west, westward.

Vest-Europa Western Europe.

vestfronten the West Front.

vestgående bound (going, running, sailing) west, westward bound.

vestibyle hall, entrance-hall.

Vest-India the West-Indies. **v-indier** West Indian. **v-indisk** West-Indian, West India.

vestkant west side. **-en** (som bydel) the West End.

vestkyst west-coast, western coast.

Vestlandet Western Norway **vestlandsk** western. **vestlending.** Westerner, a native of W. N.

vestlig western, westerly, west; (adv) towards the west.

vestmaktene the western powers.

vest|over to the west, towards the west. **-på** westward.

vestre western; west.

veteran veteran.

veterinær veterinarian, veterinary surgeon. **veterinærskole** veterinary school.

veto veto.

vett brains, gumption, sense; (bevissthet) senses, wits; **stort hode, lite —** great head with little wit. **han har ikke bedre —** he knows no better. **være fra -et** be off one's head; **gå fra — og sans** lose one's wits.

vette (i folketroen) genius, spirit.

vett|løs unreasonable, witless. **-skremme** scare the senses out of.

vev (vevstol) loom; (det som veves) web, texture, tissue; (fig) tissue; (løst snakk) idle chatter, twaddle.

veve weave; (fig) (dt.) twaddle, prose.

vever (adj) (rask, livlig) agile, nimble, active.

vever (subst) weaver. **-håndverk** weaver's craft el. trade.

veveri weaving manufactory. **veverindustri** textile industry. **veverske** (female) weaver.

vev|kjerring, se **edderkopp. -knute** weaver's knot.

vevle (mar) rattle down.

vevling ratling. **-line** ratlin(e) line.

vev|nad textile. **-(n)ing** weaving.

vev|skei, -skje weaver's reed(s). **-skutt, -skyttel** weaver's shuttle. **-spole** quill. **-stol,** se **vev.**

vi we; **vi . . . selv** we . . . ourselves; **— alle** we all, all of us.

via (over) by, via.

viadukt viaduct.

vibrasjon vibration. **vibrere** vibrate; **-nde** vibratory. **vibrering** vibration.

vid wide, ample, large; (komparativ). **-ere** wider; (ytterligere) farther, further; **inntil -ere** till further notice; **uten -ere** without further ceremony, as a matter of course, just. Se **vidt.**

vidd (forstand) wits, sense; (vittighet) wit;

vidd(e) width; wide expanse, vast space.

vide ut broaden, enlarge, expand, widen; generalise; (om hansker) stretch.

viderebefordring re-conveyance; **til — to** be forwarded, t. b. f.

videreforhandling resale.

videreforsendelse reforwarding.

videre|gående further, ulterior; more extensive, more thorough-going. **-komne** advanced. **-komne** advanced pupils; **lærebøker for begynnere og —** textbooks introductory and advanced.

videresende reforward, deliver through.

viderverdighet adversity, trouble.

videst, se **vidt.**

videstgående most advanced, most radical.

vid|farende far-faring, much-travelled. **-gjeten** far-famed, renowned.

vidimasjon legalization. **vidimere** legalize.

vidisse legalized copy.

vidje willow. **-band** withe, withy, osier-band.

vidjefletning osier-work, wicker-mat.

vidløftig prolix, diffuse, long-winded, prolonged, elaborate; (utsvevende) dissipated. **-het** prolixity, diffuseness; (pl) difficulties, ado, unnecessary delay.

vid|spurt, se **vidgjeten. -synt** far-seeing.

vidt (adv) far, widely; **videre** farther, further; **videst** farthest, furthest; **— og bredt** far and wide; **tale — og bredt** expatiate, enlarge; **— forskjellig** differing widely. **bringe det — attain** eminence; **drive noe for —** this is too bad, this is going too far; **for så — som** in as far as, so far as; **videre: hva så —?** what more?

gå — go on; **vi må** — we must be on; **les** —! read on! **og så** — and so on, et cetera; **ikke** — not particularly; **inntil** — for the present, **so far**, till further notice, provisionally, for a time.

vidt|bereist travelled. **-berømt** far-famed, far-renowned. **-forgre(i)nt** widely spread, widebranching. **-gående** far-going, extreme.

vidt|omfattende extensive. **-rekkende** far-reaching. **-skuende** far-looking. **-svevende** diffuse.

vidunder wonder, prodigy. **-barn** child prodigy, infant phenomenon.

vidunderlig wondrous, prodigious, wonderful, marvellous; (adv) wonderfully, to a miracle.

vidått|e wide expanse; wilderness, wilds. **ut på -a** into the wide world; (fig) far afield.

vie consecrate, dedicate; (ektefolk) marry, wed; (en prest) ordain (a clergyman); **la seg borgerlig** — go before the registrar; (fig) — **til** devote to; — **seg til** devote oneself to, give oneself up to; — **sine krefter til** devote one's efforts to.

vielse wedding ceremony.

vielsesattest marriage certificate.

vielsesformular marriage service.

vier willow, withy. **-kjerr** osiery.

vievann holy-water.

vievanns|kar holy-water basin. **-kost** holy-water sprinkle, aspergill.

vift breath, puff (of air, of wind); whiff; (dt.) **gå på** — go on the spree.

vifte (vrb) flutter, wave; (om lys) flicker; — **med hånden, med et tørkle** wave one's hand, a handkerchief; waft; (med vifte) fan.

vifte (subst) fan. **-vifteformet** fanshaped.

viftepalme fan-palm.

vigle, se **oppvigle**.

vignett vignette.

vigsel consecration. **vigsle** consecrate.

vigør vigour; **være i** — ennå be still active.

vik creek, cove, inlet.

vikar substitute, deputy. **-iat** vicariate, vicarship. **vikariere** act as (one's) substitute.

I. **vike** yield, give way (**for:** to) — **for fienden** retreat before the enemy; — **fra** depart, leave; — **tilbake** draw back, recede, retreat, recoil, flinch (**for:** from); — **til side** step aside; — **plass** cede el. give up one's place; — **sete** resign one's seat; **vikende: kursene er** — exchanges are declining.

II. **vike** (— en hest) turn; — **av** swerve, turn off, **vike|plikt** duty to keep clear. **-spor** siding, shunt.

viking viking. **fare i** — go el. sail a viking. **-skip** viking ship. **-tid** viking age. **-tog** viking cruise, viking's raid.

vikke vetch.

vikle wrap, twist; — **inn i papir** wrap up in paper; — **om** wind; — **sammen** roll el. wrap up; — **seg om** twist itself round; — **seg ut** extricate oneself.

vikse wax.

vikte seg give oneself airs, pose; — **med** show off.

viktig (betydningsfull) important, of importance, momentous; (om person: ledende) leading, considerable; (innbilsk) conceited, stuck-up, self-important; **-st** principal; **det -ste** the main thing.

viktig|het importance; (innbilskhet) conceit. **-maker** coxcomb. **-makeri** consequentialness. **-per, -pære** se **-maker**.

viktualier provisions, victuals.

vildre wander, wilder; — **seg bort** go astray, get lost.

Vilhelm William. **-ine** Wilhelmina.

vilje will; (i filosofi) volition; (ønske) pleasure; **den fri** — free-will; **min siste** — my last will and testament; **ha den beste** — have the best intentions; **sette sin** — igjennom carry

one's point; **få sin** — have one's will el. way; **av egen fri** — of one's own free will; **med** — on purpose, purposely; **ikke med min gode** — not willingly.

vilje|kraft energy of will, will-power. **-løs** having no will of one's own. **-løshet** want of will.

viljes|akt act of the will, volition. **-sak** matter of free will.

vilje|sterk firm. **-styrke** firmness. **-svak** weak, pliable.

viljesytring manifestation of the will.

vilkår conditions, terms; (omstendigheter) circumstances; **på el. under disse** — on these terms.

vilkårlig (egenmektig) arbitrary, high-handed.

vilkårlighet arbitrariness.

vilkårsfolk, se **føderådsfolk**.

vill wild; (barbarisk) savage, wild; (glupsk) fierce, ferocious, savage; **en** — **gutt** rompish boy; **-e** (mennesker) savages; **-e dyr** wild beasts; **et vilt liv** a dissolute life; **i** — **tilstand** in a state of nature; **fare** — lose one's way, stray; **føre en** — lead one astray, mislead; **over -e fjellet** across desolate mountain wastes; **på** — **flukt** in rout; **vilt** (adv) wildly etc.; **vokse vilt** grow wild el. naturally.

villa cottage, country-house, villa.

villaby villa suburb, garden city.

villand wild duck. **villbasse** madcap.

ville be willing; (ønske) wish, want; **jeg vil** I will; **jeg ville** I would; **jeg har -t** I have wished (meant, intended) to; **som du vil** as you like el. please; **om Gud vil** if it please God, God willing; **det får nå være som det vil** be that as it may; **uten å** — **det** unintentionally, unawares; **man kan hva man vil** where there is a will, there is a way; **gjør hva De vil!** do whatever you please! **hva ville han her?** what did he want here? **han vil meg vel** he wishes me well; **hva vil du (meg)** what do you want (of me el. with me); **jeg vil ikke gå** I don't want el. choose to go; **jeg ville gjerne gå** I want to go; **jeg vil gjerne det** I am willing el. ready to do it; **jeg vil ikke gjerne gjøre det** I am unwilling to do it, I should not like to do it; **jeg ville gjerne ha den boka** I should like to have that book; **jeg vil heller bli** I had rather stay; **vil du være så snill å si meg** please tell me; **tell me, if you please; det er noen som vil snakke med Dem** you are wanted; **jeg vil gjerne vite** I want to know; **jeg ville ønske** I wish; **hva vil du at jeg skal gjøre?** what will you have me do? what do you want me to do? **han vil ikke av med det** he does not want to part with it; **han vil forbi** he wants to pass; **hvor vil han hen?** where is he going? (fig) what is he driving at? what is he up to; **vil du være med?** will you come with us? will you be of the party? will you join us? **hva vil du med det?** what are you going to do with that? **jeg vil til England** I am going to England; **han ville til å gå** he was about to go; **han vil nødig til pers** he is unwilling to do it.

villelse delirium; **snakke i** — be delirious.

villeple crab-apple.

villfarelse error, delusion; **rive ut av -n** undeceive; **sveve i** — be under a delusion.

villfarende having lost one's way; (om dyr) stray.

villfremmed utterly strange, a perfect stranger.

villhet wildness, savageness, fierceness.

villig willing; ready; (adv) willingly, readily, freely; (mar) apace, roundly. **villighet** willingness; (tjeneste) favour, service, a good turn.

villkatt wild cat; (fig) tomboy, romp.

vill-lede lead astray, mislead, misguide; **-nde** misleading.

vill|mann savage. **-mark** wilderness, wilds. **-nis** wilderness.

villrede perplexity, confusion; **være i —** be perplexed, puzzled, confused.
vill|skap wildness. **–skudd** straggler. **–som** intricate.
villspor wrong track el. scent; **på —** on a false scent, off the track; **være på —** be at fault; **sette en på —** put one on a wrong el. false scent, throw one off the scent.
villstrå: komme på — stray.
villstyring madcap.
villsvin wild boar.
villvin Virginia(n) creeper, American ivy.
vilske wildness, delirium, light-headedness.
vilt game; (dyrekjøtt) venison.
vilter giddy, wild, boisterous.
vilt|handel dealing in game; (butikken) poulterer's shop, game shop. **–handler** game -dealer; poulterer and fruiterer. **–smak** flavour of game; **som har —** gamy. **–tyv** poacher. **–tyveri** poaching.
vimpel pennant, pendant, streamer.
vimre stray, wander, fool; (fig) vacillate.
vims (subst) scatterbrain.
vimse whisk, fuss, bustle. **–bøtte, –kopp,** se **vims. vimset** birdwitted, scatterbrained.
vin wine. **vin|avl** wine-growing, viniculture. **–berg** vineyard.
vind (skjev) warped.
vind (luftstrøm) wind; (i magen) flatulence, wind; **god —** fair wind; **dårlig —** adverse wind; **kraftig —** high el. strong wind; **svak —** light wind; **flau, løy —** light air; **slippe en —** break wind; **for –en** (mar) before the wind; **blåser –en fra den kant?** : the wind in that quarter? **være i –en** (fig) be in great request, much sought after; **få — i seilene** catch the wind; **unna –en** off the wind.
vind|bar bleak (and exposed). **–bolk** spell of blowy weather. **–bye** squall of wind.
vinde (subst) (heiseverk) windlass, winch; (garnvinde) reel.
vinde (sno, vikle) wind; (heise med en vinde) hoist up.
vinde|bom (mar) capstan-bar. **–bru** draw -bridge.
vindegg egg without a shell; wind-egg.
vindeltrapp winding stairs.
vinde|pinne winder. **–reip** capstan-rope.
vind|fall wind-fall, fallen tree el. trees. **–fang** windscreen. **–flake** flaw el. gust of wind. **–fløy** weather vane.
vindig blowy, windy; (fig) flothy, windy.
vindikasjon vindication.
vinding (snoning) winding, twist.
vindisere vindicate.
vind|kast squall, gust of wind. **–maker** humbug. **–mølle** windmill. **–måler** wind-gauge.
vind|pipe air-pipe. **–pust** breath of wind.
vindrose card of the compass.
vindrue grape. **–klase** bunch of grapes.
vindsel thread-paper, winder.
vind|ski barge- el. verge-board. **–skjerm** (på bil) windglass. **–skjev,** se **skjev.**
vindstille calm. **vindstøt** gust of wind.
vind|tørke dry in the wind. **–tørket** air-dried. **–tørr** gaunt, shrivelled.
vindu window;(på hengsler) casement; (skyve-) sash.
vindus|forhøyning window-bench, -seat. **–karm** window-frame. **–nisje** window-recess. **–post** (window) sill. **–rute** window-pane. **–utstilling** show, display. **arrangere en —** dress a shop-window.
vindyrker wine-grower.
vindøyd(d) squint-eyed.
vineger vinegar.
vin|fat wine-cask. **–flaske** wine-bottle.
vinge wing, pinion; **slå med –ne** flap el. beat the wings.
vingeben wing-bone; **ta ved –et** catch by the ear.
vinge|brutt broken-winged. **–fang** breadth

(stretch, sweep) of wing. **–skutt** winged. **–slag** stroke of the wings.
vinget winged.
vinglass wine-glass.
vingle flutter about; stray, wander; (være ubestemt) be neither on nor off. **vingleri** fickleness, vacillation. **vinglet** fickle, inconstant.
vingling trifling backwards and forwards, fickleness.
vin|gud god of the grape el. of wine. **–gård** vineyard. **–gårdsmann** vine-dresser; (bibl.) husbandman.
vinhandel wine-trade; (butikken) vintner's (el. wine) shop.
vinhandler wine-merchant, vintner.
vink (tegn) sign, signal; (antydning) hint; (opplysning) hint, inkling, suggestion.
vin|kanne wine-can. **–karaffel** wine-decanter. **–kart** wine card.
vinke beckon; **— til** beckon to; **–t med hånden til dem** waved my hand to them; **— en av** wave one off.
vinkel angle; (verktøy) square; **rett —** right angle; **spiss, stump —** acute, obtuse angle; **under en — på 45°** at an angle of forty-five; **i rett —** med at a right angle to. **vinkel|dannet** angular. **–hake** square; (typograf.) composing -stick. **–jern** angle iron.
vinking winking, nodding, beckoning.
vin|kjeller (privat) wine-cellar; (utsalg) wine -vaults. **–kjenner** judge of wine. **–kjøler** wine -cooler. **–lager** store of wines. **–land** wine country. **–lauv** vine-leaves (pl). **–monopol** monopoly of wine.
vinn: legge — på apply oneself to.
vinne (oppnå) gain, win; (om premie) også carry off; (erobre) conquer, win; (makte, orke) be equal to, manage; **— en for en sak** gain one over, enlist one in a cause; **— en for seg** interest a person in one's favour; **— inn på** gain upon; **han –r ved nærmere bekjentskap** he improves upon acquaintance; **— bifall** gain approbation.
vinne (subst), se **onn.**
vinnende winning, (fig) prepossessing.
vinner gainer; winner.
vinne|syk covetous, greedy of gain. **–syke** covetousness, cupidity.
vinning (inntekt) gain, profit.
vinnskipelig industrious. **–het** industry.
vin|produksjon wine-produce. **–ranke** vine.
vinsj winch.
vin|smak winy taste el. flavour. **–sort** growth el. sort of wine. **–stein** argal, tartar. **–stokk** vine, vine-plant, grape-vine. **–stue** wine-house, wine -room. **–syre** acid in wine. **–tapper** vintner.
vinter winter; **i —** this winter; **om –en** in el. during (the) winter; **til –en** next winter; **–en over** throughout the winter; **midt på –en** in the depth of winter.
vinter|bruk: til — for winter use; (om klær) for winter wear. **–drakt** winter costume. **–dvale** hibernation, winter-sleep; **ligge i —** hibernate. **–foring** wintering. **–forråd** winter supply. **–frakk** great-coat, winter over-coat. **–føre: på — on** the snow, on the winter roads. **–grønn** winter-green. **–hage** winter-garden(s), conservatory. **–hi** winter lair. **–kvarter** winter-quarters. **–kåpe** winter-cloak. **–landskap** wintry scenery.
vinterlig wintry.
vinter|morgen winter morning. **–natt** winter night. **–opplag: ligge i —** be laid during the winter. **–solhverv** winter solstice. **–sæd** winter -crop. **–tøy** winter garments.
vintervei: vise en –en send one about his business; turn one out of doors. **vintervær** winter-weather; (vinterlig vær) wintry weather.
vipe lapwing, peewit.
vipp bob, rapid el. short movement; flicker; cant, tilt.
vippe (vrb) see-saw, bob up and down, rock; **— opp** raise; (dt.) **— av pinnen** put down, worst.

vippe (subst) (til brønn) swipe; (fig) **stå på -n** hang in the balance.

vippe|brett see-saw. **-måler** (elektr.) current limiter.

vips pop! whip!

virak frankincense, incense; (fig) incense.

virakduft (perfume of) incense.

virke act (upon), work (upon), influence; (gjøre virkning) take effect, tell; (om legemidler) operate; — **på sansene** affect the senses; — **for en** make interest for one; — **tilbake på** react on; **han -t høy** he gave the effect of tallness. I. **virke** (subst) material, stuff; (især om tre) timber, building materials. II. **virke** (arbeid), se **yrke**.

virke|evne efficacy. **-felt** field of activity, province. **-kraft** power of action, active power. **-krets** sphere of action, of labour.

virkelig (adj) real, actual; (sann) veritable, bonafide; (absolutt) positive; **som stemmer med det -e forhold** in accordance with fact.

virkelig (adv) really, actually; veritably, positively, indeed, in fact; **han kom** — he did come. **-gjøre** realize. **-gjørelse** realization.

virkelighet reality; **i -en** in reality, in effect; **bli til** — be realized; **gjøre til** — realize.

virkelighets|bilde picture of real life. **-fjern** detached from the realities of life. **-preg** (stamp of) reality. **-sans** realism. **-tro** realistic.

virke|lyst desire for action, activity of mind. **-lysten** active, indefatigable. **-måte** mode el. manner of action el. operation.

virkerom space el. scope for action.

virkning effect, operation; **gjøre** — take effect, tell. **virknings|full** effective, telling. **-løs** ineffective, inoperative. **-løshet** inefficacy.

virksom (om person, liv, forholdsregel, motstand, vulkan) active; (om legemiddel) effective, successful.

virksomhet activity; (virkning) agency; (arbeid) operations, efforts, labours; (livsstilling) profession; **i full** — in full activity; **tre i** — be carried into effect.

virre wire; (hatte-) ribbon-wire.

virre (vrb, = surre, omvikle) wind about; — **med hodet** roll el. wriggle one's head.

virtuos master. **-itet** mastership, eminent skill. **-messig** masterly.

virvar confusion, mess.

vis (adj) wise, sage, sapient; **de -es stein** the philosopher's stone.

vis (måte) way, manner; **på det -et** in that way; **det var hennes — å . . .** it was her practice to . . .

visdom wisdom.

visdoms|kilde source of wisdom. **-ord** word of wisdom. **-tann** wisdomtooth; wise tooth; **få -tenner** cut one's wise teeth.

I. **vise** show; (legge for dagen) exhibit, evince, display; (bevise) prove, demonstrate; (angi) indicate; (klokkeslett) point to; — **en oppmerksomhet** pay one attention; **termometeret -r 10⁰** the thermometer is at 10'; — **fram** show, exhibit; — **en et sted hen** direct one to a place; — **ham til Dem** refer him to you; — **en inn** take el. show one in; — **en ned** show one the way down; — **en om(kring) i huset** show one all over the house; **uret -r tolv** the watch points to twelve; — **tilbake på** (om relativ) relate to; bear upon; — **en døra** el. — **en ut** turn one out, show one the door, order one out of the room. II. **vise seg** appear, make one's appearance; show (oneself), become apparent; (ta seg ut) show oneself off, show off, display oneself; (dukke opp) turn up; (vise seg å være) prove (oneself); **det vil** — we shall see, it remains to be seen; **det viste seg å være riktig** it proved (el. turned out) to be right; **han viste seg som en sann venn** he proved (himself) a true friend; — **til sin fordel** show best.

vise (subst) song, ditty; (gatevise) ballad;

forstå en halvkvedet — take a hint; **den gamle -n** the usual song, the old story; **enden på -en** the end of it.

vise- vice-, deputy-. **-admiral** vice-admiral.

vise|bok song-book. **-dikter** ballad-maker, ballad-monger.

vise|konge viceroy. **-konsul** vice-consul.

viselig wisely.

visepresident deputy-chairman.

viser index; (p. ur) hand.

visere (om pass, også: la visere) visa, visé; (måle) gauge.

visergutt errand (el. message)-boy. **-kontor** express office.

visering viséing.

viserpike errand (el. message)-girl.

visesamling collection of ballads.

vise|sanger balladsinger, balladist. **-stubb** snatch of a ballad el. song.

visevert (i selskap) (dt.) vice; (v. offentl. middag) assistant chairman; (husvert) deputy landlord, house agent.

visibel at home, to be seen.

visir (p. hjelm) beaver, visor; **med åpent** — with the visor up.

visitas visitation. **visitasjon** inspection, visit.

visitere inspect, search.

visitering inspection, examination.

visitt visit; **avlegge** — pay a visit.

visittkort (visiting-, calling-) card. **-bok** card-case. **-skål** card-basket, card-tray.

visjon vision. **visjonær** visionary.

visk (dott) wisp.

viske rub. **viskelær** india rubber. **visker** (artilleri) sponge.

visle hiss. **vislelyd** hissing sound, hiss; (fonet.) sibilant.

visling hissing, sibilation.

vismann wise man, sage.

vismut bismuth.

visne wither, fade.

visp beater, whisk. **vispe** beat, whisk.

viss (sikker) certain, sure; **være** — **på** be certain el. positive of, be sure of; **det er -t og sant** and that's a fact; **være** — **i sin sak** be sure of what one says; **vite for -t** know for certain el. for a fact; **en** — **dr. N.** a (certain) Dr. N., one Dr. N.; **noe -t** a certain something; **det er den -e død å** it is certain death to; **være den -e ruin for** bring sure destruction on; **visst** (adv), se nedenfor.

visselig certainly, surely, to be sure.

vissen withered. **vissenhet** withered state.

visshet certainty; **vite med** — know for certain; **få** — **for** ascertain, get certain intelligence that; **skaffe seg** — (om) make sure (of) ha — be sure; **en til** — **grensende sannsynlighet** a moral certainty.

visst (adv) certainly; **han vil** — **ikke gjøre det mer** I am sure he won't do it any more; **du visste det** — **ikke** you did not know it, I suppose; **jo** —! dare say! indeed! the idea! **se** — **på en** look fixedly (el. hard el. steadily) at one.

visstnok (visst) no doubt; (riktignok) it is true, no doubt, certainly.

visum (av pass) visa, visé.

visvas nonsense; (som utrop **nonsense!** fiddlestick! fiddle dee-dee!

vital vital. **vitalitet** vitality.

vitamin vitamin, vitamine.

vite know, be aware; **ikke det jeg vet** not that I am aware of, not that I know; **vet du hva!** I tell you what! **få** — learn; **la en** — **noe** acquaint one with el. inform one of a thing; **jeg gad** — I should like to know, I wonder; **man kån ikke** — there, no knowing; **han vet seg aldri sikker** he never feels secure; **jeg vil ikke** — **av det** I'll have none of it; — **av erfaring** know from experience; **hvordan vet du det** how do you know that? **før han visste ordet av det** before he was aware of it, in no

time; — **forut** know beforehand; — **med seg
selv** be conscious of; — **om** know of el. about;
han vet hverken ut el. inn he does not know
which way to turn; **vitende: et — blikk** a significant glance; **være — om** know of, be aware of.
  vitebegjærlig desirous of knowledge, inquiring. **vitebegjærlighet** love of knowledge, inquisitiveness.
  viten knowledge, science.
  vitende knowledge; **med mitt — with** my consent, with my will; **uten mitt —** without my
knowledge; **med — og vilje** deliberately; **mot
bedre —** against his own better conscience.
  vitenskap science, knowledge.
  vitenskapelig scientific(al), philosophical; (adv)
scientifically; **— nøyaktighet** philosophical exactness; **en — dannet mann** a scholar.
  vitenskaps|mann man of science, philosopher,
scientific man, scientist. **-selskap** scientific
society.
  vitne (vrb) give evidence, depose; **— (om)
sannheten** bear witness to (el. bear testimony
to, testify) the truth; **— om** evince, speak to.
  vitne (subst) witness; (edsvorent) deponent;
(vitnesbyrd) evidence; **føre -r** call el. produce
witnesses; **kalle til —** call to witness; **ta -r på**
call witnesses to; **ha — på** have a witness to;
være — til be a witness of, witness; **(til å:** that);
bære — om bear witness to, give an evidence of;
i -rs påhør in the presence of witnesses.
  vitne|avlukke witness-box. **-fast** that can be
proved by valid witnesses, legal. **-forklaring**
deposition.
  vitne|førsel production of evidence. **-mål** se
vitnesbyrd. -plikt the duty of giving evidence.
  vitnesbyrd evidence; testimony; (attest) testimonial, certificate, attestation; **til —** in witness; **avlegge — om** bear testimony to; **gi en
et godt —** give one a good testimony.
  vitneutsagn evidence.
  vitriol vitriol.
  vits joke, witticism.
  vitskap osv., se **vitenskap.**
  vitterlig known publicly, generally known,
notorious; (adv) notoriously; **— synd** a known
sin; **— gjeld** acknowledged debt; **gjøre —** do to
wit; **herved gjøres —** know all men by these
presents. **vitterlighet: underskrive til —** sign
one's name as a witness; **til —** witness to the
signature. **vitterlighetsvitne** witness (at signing), (attesting) witness.
  vittig witty, clever.
  vittighet (egenskapen) wittiness; (en) joke,
witty saying, witty thing; (søkt) witticism; **si
-er** say witty things, be witty; (dt.) **rive -er av
seg** crack jokes.
  vittighets|blad comic paper. **-jageri** affectation
of wit. **-jeger** wit-snapper, would-be wit.
  viv (bare i poesi) wife.
  vivat! long live! **-rop** (pl) cheers.
  vivi|sekere vivisect. **-seksjon** vivisection.
  vlies: den gylne — the golden fleece.
  Vliessingen Flushing.
  Vogesene the Vosges mountains.
  vogge (subst) cradle.
  vogge (vrb) rock; **— på armen** nurse.
  voggegave christening gift; (fig) dower.
  voggegjenge rocker of a cradle.
  vogge|pute cradle-cushion. **-sang** lullaby,
cradle ditty.
  vogn carriage; (firhjulet arbeids-) waggon;
(stor, dekket transport-) van; (tohjulet arbeids-) cart; (lav firhjulet arbeids-) dray; (på
småhjul) lorry; (jernbanevogn i England)
carriage, (i Amerika) car; (jernbanegodsvogn i
England) waggon, (i Amerika) freight-car;
(herskaps-) carriage, chariot, drag, phaeton,
brougham, break; (karét) coach; (drosje) cab;
— med seks hester for a carriage and six;
hester og — carriage and horses; **han er ikke
tapt bak en —** he is no fool.

vogn|bremse brake. **brett** foot-board. **-dør**
carriage-door. **-fabrikk** carriage-factory, coach
-manufactory. **-fabrikant** carriage-builder, coach
-maker. **-fating** body of a carriage. **-ferdsel**
carriage traffic. **-fører** car-conductor; (p. sporvogn) tram-driver, driver. **-lakk** coach colours.
-lass waggon-load, cart-load. **-lykt** carriage
lantern. **-maker** coach-maker el. builder; **cart**
-wright, waggon-wright. **-mann** coach-master,
hack(ney)-man.
  vognmanns|hest hackney(-horse). **-kusk** cabman; waggoner.
  vogn|rammel din el. rumble of carriages.
-remisse, -skjul coach-house, cart-house. **-skyss**
conveyance by carriage. **-smørelse** cart-grease.
-smører (jernbane) lubricator. **-spor** rut. **-stang**
pole of a waggon el. carriage.
  vogntrin(n) carriage-step.
  voile (tynt stoff) voile.
  vokal (subst) vowel. **vokal** (adj) vocal.
  vokalforandring vowel-change.
  vokalisere vocalize. **vokalisk** vocalic.
  vokal|lyd vowel-sound. **-musikk** vocal music.
  vokativ the vocative.
  voks wax; **overtrekke med —** wax, cere.
  voksavstøpning wax cast. **voksavtrykk** wax-
impression.
  voks|bønne wax-bean. **-duk** oil-cloth, wax-
cloth, American cloth, oil-skin. **-dukspapir**
oil-cloth paper.
  I. **vokse** (gni inn med voks) cere, wax.
  II. **voks|e** grow, wax; (tilta) increase; **— frodig**
luxuriate; **— det av seg** grow out of it; **han er
-t meg over hodet** he has outgrown me, (fig)
he has grown upon me; **han er -t fra sine bukser**
he has grown out of his breeches; **— sammen**
coalesce; **-t til med ugras** overgrown with
weeds; **voksende** growing. **voksedyktig** capable
of growth.
  voksekraft power of growth.
  voksen grown, full-grown, grown-up, adult;
de voksne the adults; **en — kvinne** (quite) a
woman! **være en —** be a match for one; **være
en oppgave —** be equal to a task.
  voks|farge wax-like colour. **-farget** wax-
coloured. **-figur** wax-figure, (pl) wax-works.
-fyrstikke vesta.
  voks|kabinett wax-work show. **-kake** wax
-comb. **-lerret** oil-cloth. **-lys** wax-candle, taper.
-maske wax-mask. **-papir** waxed paper. **-stabel**
wax-taper. **-tavle** wax-tablet.
  vokster, se **vekst.**
  vokte watch, guard; **— en for noe** guard;
one from; **— kveg** tend cattle; **— på watch**
— seg for take care, take heed, guard against
have a care, beware of; **vokt deg for å** take care
not to, take care how you.
  vokter keeper; (gjeter) herdsman, cowherd;
(sauegjeter) shepherd.
  vokter|hund shepherd's dog. **-hus** keeper's
lodge. **voketske** keeper.
  volapyk Volapuk.
  vold (makt, kraft) power; (overlast) violence, force; **med — by** force; **ta med — ravish;**
bruke — use violence; **gjøre — på** do violence
to, put violence upon; **med — og makt** with
all one's might; **i ens —** in one's power; **gi seg
Gud i —** commend oneself to God.
  volde (forårsake) cause, occasion.
  voldelig (adj) forcible; (adv) forcibly, by force.
  voldgift arbitration; **avgjøre ved — arbitrate;**
la avgjøre ved — refer el. submit to arbitration;
  voldgifts|domstol arbitral tribunal, arbitration
court. **-kjennelse** award of arbitrators. **-mann**
arbitrator. **-rett** court of arbitration. **-traktat**
arbitration treaty.
  volds|dåd, -gjerning act of violence, outrage.
  voldsherre usurper. **-dømme** tyranny.
  voldsmann perpetrator of violence.
  voldsom violent. **voldsomhet** violence.
  voldssak action for assault.

voldta ravish, rape, violate.
voldtekt rape. **voldtektsmann** ravisher.
voll (jordvoll) mound, dike; (til festningsverk)
wall, rampart; (gras-) grassy plain, green field.
vollgrav fosse, moat.
vollhøy hay of natural grasses, meadow-hay.
volontør (merk.) apprentice.
volt (mål for elektrisk spenning) volt.
volta-søyle Volta's pile, voltaic pile.
volte volt; (fig) dodge.
voltigere practise gymnastics, vault.
voltigering gymnastics. **voltigør** gymnast.
voltmeter voltmeter.
volum volume. **-inøs** voluminous.
volve (spåkvinne) prophetess, sibyl.
vom paunch, belly.
vombat (punggnager) wombat.
vomitiv (brekkmiddel) emetic.
vomfyll filling.
von expectation, hope; a chance, a prospect.
vonbrott, se skuffelse.
vond bad, evil, wicked; (sint) angry, cross;
(folkevond) dangerous, vicious; **være — på** be
angry with. **gjøre -t** hurt, pain, be painful;
hvor har du -t where do you feel pain? **ha det
-t** have a hard time of it; be badly off. **jeg har
-t i hodet** I have a headache. **slite -t** experience
hardships. **godt og -t** good and evil. **ønske -t
over en** wish one evil; **det gjør meg -t for ham**
I am sorry for him; **snakke -t om** speak badly
of; **det er ikke noe -t i det** there is no harm in
that; **man må ta det -e med det gode** you must
take the lean with the fat.
vond|ord angry words. **-vær** hard weather.
vone hope, expect. **vonlig** likely, as likely
as not.
vorde (pres pts. vordende ennå i bruk, ellers
foreldet). **-nde** that is to be, future. **-nde mødre**
mothers to be.
vorden (litt.) genesis; **i sin —** in an embryo state.
vorte wart; (bryst-) nipple; (veterinær) horny
excrescence. **vorteaktig** warty.
vorte|gras lust-wort. **-svin** wart-hog.
voter|e vote. **-ing,** se **avstemning.**
votiv- votive. **-gave** votive offering.
vott mitten, muffler.
votum vote.
vove (poet. for bølge) billow, wave.
vovet (adj) bold, daring; (om historier o. l.)
risky.
vrak wreck; **er fullstendig — is** a total loss;
kaste — på reject. **et menneskelig —** a wreck of
humanity.
vrake (forkaste) reject; (sortere) sort.
vraker sorter; gauger. **-bu** sorter's office.
vrakgods (utskuddsvarer) refuse-goods, goods
of inferior quality; (strandingsgods) stranded
goods, wreck, wreckage.
vralte waddle. **vralting** waddling.
vrang (vrengt) inverted, reversed, pulled
inside out; (forkjært) wrong, erroneous, incorrect;
(vanskelig) intricate, tangled; **slå seg —** become
restive; **strikke -t** purl.
vrange (vrangside) wrong side, seamy side;
vende -en ut turn the wrong side outward, pull
inside out.
vrangforestilling delusion, wrong idea.
vranglære erroneous doctrine, heterodoxy.
vranglærer heretic, false teacher.
vranglås: døra gikk i — the lock caught.
vrangmaske close stitch.
vrangside the wrong side.
vrangstrupe: få i -n swallow the wrong way.
vrangvilje disobligingness, perverseness.
vrangvillig perverse, disobliging.
vred angry; **bli — over** get angry at; **bli
— på en** get angry with one.
vredaktig passionate, choleric, irascible.
vredaktighet irascibility.
vrede anger, wrath, ire, choler, resentment;
— over anger at.

vrenge invert, pull el. turn inside out, reverse;
(belgflå) slip; **— etter** caricature, ridicule.
vrengebilde caricature. **vrenging** inverting etc.;
mocking, sneering; making mouths (at).
vri (subst) writhing; wringing; (i underlivet)
griping pain in the stomach.
vri (vrb) twist, wring; **— sine hender** wring
one's hands; **— av (løs)** wrench off; **— seg**
writhe; **— seg ved å gjøre noe** shrink from
doing a thing.
vridning torsion.
vrien (om person) wayward, wrongheaded;
(om ting) intricate, hard. **-t** (adv) twistedly,
awkwardly.
vrier (på dør) door-handle.
vrieri cavils (pl.), strainings (pl.)
vrikke wriggle; (med åre) scull; (forvri)
contort, sprain.
vrikkeåre scull.
vrimaskin wringer.
vrimle swarm, shoal (av: with).
vrimmel swarm, shoal.
vringel cavil, chicanery, quibbles. **vringle**
cavil, chicane, prevaricate, quibble. **vringler**
caviller, chicaner, quibbler. **vringlet** cavilling,
quibbling; intricate.
vrinsk neighing, neigh. **vrinske** neigh.
vriompeis (vrang og umedgjørlig person)
wronghead; se **vringler.**
vrist, se **rist.**
vriste wrest, wrench.
vræl roar, bawl. **vræle** roar, bawl.
vrøvl nonsense, stuff, bosh; **det er noe —**
that is all nonsense; (dt) **gjøre — raise** needless
objections.
vrøvle prate, twaddle, talk nonsense. **tilbøyelighet til å — twaddling** propensity.
vrøvlebøtte prater, twaddler.
vrå (krok) nook, corner.
vugge, se **vogge.**
vulkan volcano. **vulkanisere** vulcanize. **vul-
kanisering** vulcanization. **vulkansk** volcanic.
vunde (poet. for sår) wound.
vurdere value, appraise, estimate **(til:** at);
(skatte) appreciate, value; **— etter fortjeneste**
do justice to.
vurdering valuation, appraisement.
vurderings|mann valuator, appraiser. **-sum**
appraised value; (ved auksjon) upset price.
vy (utsikt) view; (langt perspektiv) vista.
væpne arm; **— seg** arm (oneself), take arms.
væpner esquire. **væpning** arming; militia.
I. **vær** (saubukk) ram.
II. **vær** (fiske-) egtl. place, station; især fishing
camp, (encampment, station, village); (fugle-)
rookery; jfr. dun-, egg-, fugle-, fiske-.
III. **vær** weather; (ånde) breath; (vind) wind
godt — fair (el. fine) weather; **dårlig — bad** (el.
foul) weather; **hardt, stormende — heavy** (el. severe, rough, boisterous) weather; **hvis -et tillater**
det weather permitting; **i -et** up, aloft; **med
bunnen i -et** bottom up; **med nesen i -et** with
his nose in the air; **få -et igjen** recover one's
breath; **til -s** (mar) aloft; **svinge seg i -et** rise;
det tok nesten -et fra meg it nearly took away
my breath; **trekke -et** draw breath; **trekke -et
dypt** draw a long el. low breath; **snakke om —
og vind** converse upon indifferent subjects;
be om godt — cry mercy; **komme under —
med noe** get scent of a thing.
værbitt weatherbeaten.
værbror, se **svoger.**
værdatter, se **svigerdatter.**
I. **være** (lukte) scent, get scent of, wind; **—
hen, bort** blow away, waft away.
II. **være** be; **dersom han ikke var** but for him;
når så er such being the case; **til et første forsøk å — for** a first attempt; **det er sagt** it has
been said; **det er ham** it his he; **det var riktig!**
that is right! **det er mennesker som** there are
people who; **det er dem som** there are those

who; **det måtte da** — unless; **det** — **nå som det vil** be that as it may, however that may be; **la** — have done; don't; **la meg** — let me alone; **la så** —! be it so! — **av med** be rid of; — **etter en** press one hard; — **fra seg selv** be beside oneself; **jeg har vært hos Dem** I have called on you; **hvordan er det med Dem?** how are you? **det fikk** — med det nå it couldn't be done now; **har vært med på** has had a hand in, has taken a part in; — **lenge om** be long about; — **om seg** be up and doing, look sharp, know on which side one's bread is buttered; **måte å** — **på** manner of being; — **til** exist.

værelse room, apartment. **-kamerat** chamber fellow.

væremåte manner, way, ways.

værfar, se **svigerfar**.

værfast wind-bound, weather-bound.

vær|fløy vane. **-forandring** weather change, change of el. in the weather.

værforeldre, se **svigerforeldre**.

vær|forhold atmospheric conditions. **-hane** weather-cock. **-hard** exposed, unsheltered.

værhår, se **veidehår**.

-væring (i sm.setn. f. eks. lomværing) native, inhabitant of . . .

værkart weather-chart.

værkyndig weather-wise. **værlag** weather, climate.

vær|melding weather forecast, prognostic of weather, weather prognostic.

værmor, se **svigermor**.

vær|omslag, se **-forandring**. **-profet** weather -prophet, weather-spy. **-skifte** change of weather. **-slått** weatherbeaten. **-spådom** forecast of the weather, weather forecast.

værsøster, se **svigerinne**.

vær så god (idet noe rekkes) here (it is), here you are, there (it is); (tillatelse) yes, do, by all means, all right; (begynn) go ahead; (fortsett) go on; (kom inn) come in!

vær|telegram telegraphic weather intelligence. **-utsikter** weather outlook. **-varsel**, se **-melding**.

væske liquid, fluid, moisture, humor; (saft hos dyr og planter) juice; (i legemet) humor.

væske (vrb) secrete a humor, run; **-nde:** — **sår** running sore. **væskeform** a fluid form.

væte (vrb) wet, moisten.

væte (subst) wet, moisture.

vøle (kav) fisherman's buoy el. float.

vøle (vrb, = bøte) mend, repair, patch.

vøre appreciate, value; heed, mind.

vørnad regard, deference.

vørsløs careless, negligent.

vørter sweet-wort, wort; (gjæret) wash. **-kake** Norway wort-cake.

våde danger, peril; accident.

våde|ild accidental fire. **-skudd** chance shot.

vådeville vaudeville.

I. **våg**, se **vekt**.

II. **våg** (bukt) bay, inlet.

III. **våg** (materie) gathering, pus.

vågal audacious, daring, dare-devil.

våge venture; (sette på spill) risk; — **(på)** å venture to; — **seg til** venture upon, risk.

vågehals desperado. **vågelig** bold, daring, hazardous. **vågestykke** daring el. venturesome deed. **våget** hazarded, bold, risky.

vågmor (i verk) core of a boil.

vågsom (om ting) adventurous, bold, hazardous, risky.

våk (i is) hole el. opening (in the ice).

våke wake, be awake; — **over** watch (over); — **hos en syk** sit up with a sick person.

våkekone night nurse.

våken awake, waking; **våkne netter** wakeful (el. sleepless) nights; **ha et -t øye med** keep a watchful eye on.

våkne wake, awake **(av:** from).

vånd (poet. om kvist) wand, rod.

vånde distress, embarrassment; pain.

vånde seg groan, moan.

våningshus dwelling-house.

våpen weapon; arms (pl); (familie-) arms, coat of arms, escutcheon; **gripe til** — take (up) arms, rise (up) in arms.

våpen|art arm (of service). **-bilde** armorial bearings. **-bror** brother in arms. **-brorskap** brotherhood in arms. **-bruk** the use of arms.

våpendrager armour-bearer, (e)squire.

våpen|fabrikant sword-cutler; gunsmith. **-fabrikk** manufactory of arms. **-ferdighet** dexterity el. skill in arms. **-før** ablebodied. **-handler** armorer. **-herold** herald at arms. **-hvile** armistice, truce. **-kjole** coat (of arms). **-klirr** rattle of arms. **-kyndig** skilled in heraldry. **-løs** unarmed, weaponless.

våpenmakt military power el. force; **med** — by force of arms.

våpen|maler blazoner. **-merke** device. **-sal** armory. **-samling** collection, (depot, museum), of arms. **-skjold** coat of arms, shield of arms. **-smed** armorer. **-stillstand** truce, armistice, cessation of hostilities. **-øvelser** military drill, training.

vår (adjektivisk) our; (substantivisk) ours; **vi skal gjøre -t** we shall do ours; **denne** — **innbilning** this fancy of ours.

vår (årstiden) spring.

vår|aktig vernal. **-bud** harbinger of spring. **-flom** spring flood. **-frakk** light overcoat (for spring wear). **-frisk: alting er -friskt** there is the freshness of spring about everything.

Vårherre the Lord, Heaven, the Saviour.

vår|jevndøgn the vernal equinox. **-kåpe** cloak for spring wear. **-luft** vernal air. **-onn** spring business el. work. **-regn** spring rain. **-rengjøring** spring cleaning. **-sol** vernal sun. **-sæden** the spring-sown grain. **-tid** spring-time. **-vinne**, se **-onn**. **-vær** spring-weather.

vås nonsense, rubbish. **våse** talk nonsense.

våsekopp driveller, twaddler. **våset** nonsensical.

våt wet; **gjøre** — wet; **få en** — **trøye** get a wet jacket; **-e varer** liquor; **han hadde hverken fått -t eller tørt** he had had nothing, nothing had passed his lips.

våt|lende fen, marshy (swampy) land. **-lendt** fenny, marshy, swampy.

W

W, w W, w.

wagon (el. vagong) railway-carriage.

Wales Wales.

wallon, wallonsk Walloon.

Warsawa Warsaw.

watt (mål for elektrisk forbruk) watt.

W. C. W. C., water-closet.

whig whig. **-partiet** the Whig party.

whiskers (kinnskjegg) whiskers.

whisky whisky. **-pjolter** whisky and soda.

whist whist. **et parti** — a game of whist.

Wien Vienna. **wiener** Viennese.

wienerinne Viennese (woman el. lady).

wiener|brød Vienna bread. **-Weinerkongressen** the Congress of Vienna. **-vals** Viennese waltz.

wiensk Viennese.

X

X, x X, x.
xantin xanthin.
Xantippe Xantippe, shrew, vixen.

xylograf xylographer, wood-engraver. **xylografere** engrave on wood. **xylografi** xylography, wood-engraving. **xylografisk** xylographic.

Y

Y, y Y, y.
yacht yacht. **-klubb** yachting-club. **-seilas** yachting; (en som driver denne sport) yachtsman.
yankee Yankee.
ydmyk humble, lowly.
ydmyke humble, humiliate; **— seg for en** humble oneself before one; **-nde** humiliating.
ydmykelse humiliation.
ydmykhet humility, humbleness, lowliness.
ymse various; **det kan være så — med deres frisinn** they are liberal more or less; **til — kanter** different ways.
ymt hint, inkling, whispered rumour.
ymte whisper, talk secretly (**om**: of).
ynde (vrb) like, be fond of, be partial to; **yndet** liked, favourite; **en -t sport** a popular sport; **gjøre seg -t av** ingratiate oneself with.
ynde (subst) grace, charm.
yndefull charming, graceful. **ynder** lover.
yndest favour, good graces; **i — hos en** in favour with one, in one's good graces; **sette seg i — hos** ingratiate oneself with.
yndig graceful; (deilig) charming, delightful.
yndighet charm.
yndling favourite. **yndlings-** favourite, pet.
yngel brood; (fiske-) fry.
yngle breed, multiply, propagate.
yngling youth, young man.
ynglingalder adolescence, youth.
yngre younger; (temmelig ung) youngish; (av senere dato) later.
yngst youngest.
ynk misery, wretchedness; (medynk) pity. **det var en — å se** it was a pitiful sight.
ynke pity. **— seg** moan. **ynkes over** have pity on, commiserate, pity.
ynkelig pitiful, pitiable, miserable. **ynkelighet** pitifulness, miserableness. **ynkverdig** pitiable, pitiful. **ynkverdighet** pitiableness.
yppe (vekke) stir (up); (hisse, egge) incite, instigate; **— kiv (trette)** stir up a quarrel, pick a quarrel.
ypperlig excellent, capital. **ypperst** supreme, highest, chief. **yppersteprest** high priest, pontiff.
yppig (frodig) luxuriant, exuberant; (overdådig) luxurious.
yppighet luxury; luxuriancy, exuberance.
yr (adj) giddy, mad, wanton, wild.
yr (duskregn) drizzling rain, drizzle, mizzle.
I. yre (duskregne) drizzle, mizzle.
II. yre (kry) teem, swarm; **— av utøy** crawl with vermin.

yrhet giddiness, madness etc., se **yr.** (adj)
yrke (arbeid) art, craft, trade, work.
yrkedag work-day.
yrkeskvinne a self-maintaining woman.
yrsnø drizzling snow.
yste curdle; **— ost** make cheese; **— seg** curdle.
ystel curds; (myse, pultost) hard curds.
yster cheese-maker, dairyman. **-i** cheese-factory, (-dairy, -farm), cheesery. **-ske** dairymaid, (-woman). **yst(n)ing** cheese-making.
yte yield, render; **— anerkjennelse** do justice to; **— motstand** offer resistance. **yteevne** capacity, yielding power. **ytelse, yting** yielding etc.; (det som ytes) prestation, contribution.
yter yielder, bestower; (bidrags-) contributor; (skatt-) ratepayer.
ytre (adj) outer, outward; exterior, external; **det —** the outward appearance, the exterior; **— bekvemmeligheter** offices, sanitaries.
ytre (subst) the exterior el. externals; **ens —** one's exterior, (outward) appearance, presence.
ytre (vrb) utter, express; **sykdommen har ennå ikke -t seg** the disease has not yet broken out.
ytring uttering; expression, saying, remark; (av kraft osv) manifestation.
ytringsfrihet liberty el. freedom of speech.
ytter|del exterior. **-dør** outer door. **-ende** outer end. **-frakk** great-coat, over-coat. **-kant** extreme verge, outskirt. **-led** extreme.
ytterlig extreme, excessive; (utvortes) outward; (adv) near the edge; (i høy grad) extremely, excessively; **-ere** further, additional; (adv) further, in addition.
ytterliggående extreme, ultra.
ytterlighet extreme, extremity; **drive til —** push to an extreme; **la det komme til -er** carry things to extremities.
ytterlomme outer pocket.
yttermur outer wall.
ytterpunkt extreme. **ytterside** outside.
ytterst (adj) outmost, extreme; (grad) utmost, extreme; **den -e dag** the day of judgment; **av -e viktighet** of the last importance el. consequence; **det -e øyeblikk** the last moment; **være** el. **ligge på sitt -e** be at the last extremity; **det er kommet til det -e med ham** he is reduced to extremity; **til det -e** to the utmost.
ytterst (adv) farthest out, on the outside, at the very edge; (grad) extremely, exceedingly; **— til høyre** farthest to the right.
yttertøy outer el. outdoor things.
yttervegg outer el. external wall.
ytterverdenen the outer el. external world.

Z

Z, z Z, z.
zeppeliner (luftskip) Zeppelin.
Zevs Zeus.
zodikallys zodical light.

zoolog zoologist. **zoologi** zoology. **zoologisk** zoological; **den -e have** the Zoological Gardens.
zulu, -kaffer Zulu. **Z-landet** Zululand.
Zürich Zurich.

Æ

æra era.

ærbar modest. ærbarhet modesty.

ærbødig respectful, deferential; Deres –e (brevstil) Yours faithfully, Yours sincerely; min –e skrivelse my respects; ærbødigst (brevstil) Yours truly, Yours sincerely, Yours (most) respectfully.

ærbødighet respect, deference.

ærdun eider down.

ære (subst) honour; (heder) glory; gjøre en — be creditable to one, be a credit to one; gjøre en liten — be discreditable to one; gjør meg den — å do me the honour to; jeg skal ha den — I shall do myself the honour; jeg har den — å underrette Dem om at . . . I have the honour to inform you that . . .; vise en den siste — pay one the last honours; en mann av — a man of honour, an honourable man; han har stor — av det it does him great honour el. credit; i tukt og — in all honour and decency; sette sin — i take a pride in, think it an honour, glory in; han setter sin — i it is his ambition to; på — upon my honour! honour bright! på — og samvittighet in honour and in conscience; — den som –s bør honour to whom honour is due.

ære (vrb) honour; den –de leser the (gentle) reader; Deres –de (skrivelse) your favour.

ærefrykt awe, veneration; ha — for reverence, revere; ærefryktinngytende awe-inspiring; (ærverdig) venerable.

ærefull honourable, glorious. –kjær jealous of one's honour. –krenkelse defamation. –krenkende defamatory, libellous. –løs ignominious, infamous. –løshet ignominy, infamy.

ærend errand; commission; gå — do errands, run (on) errands, be sent (on) messages; han har utrettet sitt — he has done his errand; hva er Deres —? what is your business? jeg har et — I have something to do; gjorde seg

et — der found some pretext for going there; gå ens — (fig) play into one's hands.

ærendsvenn messenger.

æreport triumphal arch el. gateway.

æresbevisning demonstration of honour.

æresborger honorary citizen el. freeman; gjøre en til — av byen present one with the freedom of the town.

æres|doktor doctor honoris causa. –følelse (sense of) honour. –gave complimentary gift. –gjeld debt of honour. –gjest guest of honour.

æreskjenner defamer, slanderer.

æres|legion legion of honour. –medlem honorary member. –oppreisning (honourable) satisfaction. –ord (word of) honour; på –ord on my honour; on parole; jeg gir Dem mitt –ord på at I pledge you my honour that; han ble løslatt på — he was released on parole. –president honorary chairman. –sak point of honour; affair of honour. –tap disgrace.

æresyk morbidly ambitious.

ærfugl eider duck.

ærgjerrig ambitious. ærgjerrighet ambition.

ærlig honest, fair, upright; (adv) honestly; — talt honestly; mene det — med en mean well by one; som han — fortjener as he amply el. richly deserves.

ærlighet honesty, fairness; — varer lengst honesty is the best policy.

ærstegg eider-drake.

ærverdig venerable. –het venerableness.

æser (pl) av ås.

ætling descendant.

ætt family, race, stock.

ætte|far ancestor, founder. –gård family estate. –saga family saga. –tavle genealogical table, genealogy.

ætt|god well-born, of (respectable) family. –ledd generation. –lede adopt. –legg line, succession of generations. –stor highborn.

Ø

øde (forlatt) deserted, desolate; (udyrket) waste; legge —, se ødelegge.

øde (vrb) waste, lavish.

øde|legge ruin, destroy; (legge øde, om et land) lay waste, waste; (forarme) ruin, impoverish; –leggende ruinous, destructive, devastating; — for destructive to el. of; –lagt ruined; (utmattet) knocked up.

ødeleggelse ruin, destruction; (herjing o. l.) havoc, devastation, desolation.

ødeleggelseslyst destructive instinct.

ødemark waste land, wilderness.

ødsel prodigal, lavish; wasteful, extravagant; (overflødig) profuse; omgås –t med be prodigal of, waste. ødselhet prodigality, lavishment, lavishness, wastefulness, extravagance, profuseness; (overflødighet) profusion.

ødsle be wasteful el. prodigal; — bort squander; — med lavish, be lavish el. prodigal of. ødslig bleak, desolate, dreary.

øgle small lizard, newt, eft; (mest om utdødde arter, pl.) saurians, sauria; (fig) viper. øgle|reir nest of vipers. –yngel brood of vipers.

øk (work-)horse, jade; (jvf. øyk).

øke el. auke add to, enlarge, increase; eke (out); (vi) increase.

økenavn nickname.

øk(n)ing el. auking growth, increase, eking.

økonom (på hospital osv.) steward; (sparsommelig mann) economist, manager. økonomi economy. økonomisere economize. økonomisk economical.

øks axe, hatchet. økse|hammer axe-head. –hogg blow of an axe. –skaft handle of an axe.

økt spell(of work),interval of time between meals.

økumenisk ecumenical.

I. øl (varme) heat, warm air.

II. øl beer; (sterkt, lyst) ale; (dt.) vise en hvor David kjøpte –et give one a lesson, teach one manners.

øl|brygger beer-brewer. –bryggeri brew-house; –brygging brewing of beer.

ølet (adj) tipsy, beery.

øl|fat beer-cask. –flaske beer-bottle. –glass tumbler. –kagge beer-anker. –kjeller beer-cellar. –kjører a brewer's drayman. –krus beer-jug, beer-mug.

ølrøyk (varmedis) heat-haze.

øl|sjapp ale-house, beershop. –tapper ale-house keeper, keeper of a beer-shop. –tønne beer-barrel.

øm tender; (som gjør vondt) sore; røre ved det –me punkt touch the sore point.

ømfintlig sensitive (for: to). **-het** sensitiveness. **ømhet** soreness; (fig) tenderness.
ømhjertet tender-hearted.
ømskinnet delicate, (også fig) thinskinned, sensitive. **ømskinnethet** sensitiveness.
ømtålig delicate, sensitive; **et — emne** også a sore subject.
ønske (subst) wish, desire; **nære — om** have a desire to, be desirous of; **alt går etter —** everything succeeds to one's wishes; **for å imøtekomme Deres -r** to meet your wishes.
ønske (vrb) wish, desire; want; **det er en som -r å tale med Dem** you are wanted, Sir; **det er å — it** is to be desired; **later intet tilbake å —** leaves nothing to be desired; **en alt godt** wish one well; **— seg** wish for, wish to have.
ønske|hatt wishing cap. **-kvist** divining twig.
ønskelig to be wished, desirable; (som går etter ønske) wished for; **mindre —** undesirable.
ønskemåte (gramm.) the optative.
ønskeseddel list of desiderata.
ønskesetning optative clause.
ør confused, giddy in the head; (av drikk)boozed; **jeg blir — i hodet av det** it makes my head swim.
I. øre ear; (p. gryte, kar) ear, lug; **spisse -ne** prick up one's ears; **holde -ne stive** look sharp, have all one's wits about one; **put a bold face** on it, brave it out; **være lutter — (spøkende)** be all ear(s) el. attention; **han har en rev bak -t** he is after some mischief; **skrive seg noe bak -t** note, make a note of a thing; **komme en for —** reach one's ear, reach one; **det er å snakke for døve -r** it's talking to the wind; **ha — for** have an ear for; **ha vondt i -ne** have a pain in one's ears; **trekke i -t** pull by the ear, pull one's ears; **holde en i -ne** keep one in order; **være i gjeld til oppover -ne** be over head and ears in debt; **slå en på -t** give one a box on the ear; **låne — til** listen to.
II. øre (mynt) a hundredth part of a krone, about half a farthing.
ørebetennelse inflammation of the ear, otitis.
øredøvende deafening.
øre|fik box on the ear. **-flipp** tip el. lobe of the ear, earlap. **-flod** discharge from the ear, otorrhoea. **-gang** auditory passage. **-hule** concha, alveary. **-klaff** ear-lap.
ørekyte (liten karpefisk) minnow.
ørelapp, se **-flipp**.
ørelege aural surgeon, aurist.
ørenerve auricular nerve.
ørenslyd: her er ikke — for alt levenet there's no hearing a word for all that noise.
øre|pine ear-ache. **-ring** earring; pl. eardrops. **-skje** ear-pick. **-speil** auricular speculum. **-sprøyte** syringe.
øre|sus tingling, singing el. ringing in the ear. **-tuter, -tuterske** scandal-monger, tale-bearer, whisperer. **-tuteri** scandal, slander, tale-bearing. **-tvist** earwig. **-vitne** ear-witness.
ørevoks ear-wax, cerumen.
ørfin very fine; (fig) subtle.
ørhet confusion, giddiness.
ørken desert; wilderness, waste; **gjøre til en — lay** waste; **det var en røst i -en** it was preaching to the wind.
ørkensand sand of the desert.
ørkesløs idle. **ørkesløshet** idleness.
ørliten (pl. ørsmå) puny, tiny, wee.
ørn eagle. **-aktig** aquiline.
ørne|blikk sharp el. eagle eye. **-flukt** eagle flight. **-ham** eagle's skin (and feathers). **-klo** talon of an eagle. **-nebb** eagle's beak. **-nese** aquiline nose, hooknose; **med —** aquiline-nosed. **-reir** eagle's nest. **-øye** eagle-eye.
ørnunge eaglet.
ørsk (adj) bewildered, confused, dazed.
ørske (vrb) be delirious; muddle.
ørsk|e (subst), se **ørhet; i — in** a dazed fashion. **gå i —** walk about dazedly; **svare i -a** answer at random.

øse el. **ause** bale, dip, scoop; (av brønn og fig) draw; **— lens** bale out; **— ut penger** squander away money; **regnet øste ned** the rain poured down, fell in torrents; **— opp** (suppe) help the soup; **et øsende regn** a pouring rain.
øse el. **ause** (subst) scoop; (til suppe) ladle.
øsekar baler, dipper, scoop.
øs|regn downpour of rain. **-regne: det -r** the rain falls in torrents.
øst East, east; **— til nord** East by North (osv.); **fra — from** the east; **i — in** the east; **rett i — due** east; **— for** east of; **mot — towards** the east, (to the) eastward. **øst-** eastern, east.
østetter eastward, east. **-Østen** (subst) the East.
østa from the east. **østa|fjells, -fjelsk** east of the mountains.
østa|for east of. **-fra** (adv) from the east (ward). **østa|storm** easterly gale. **-strøm** easterly current. **-vind** eastwind.
østenom eastward of.
Øster|land (Orienten) the East. **ø-landsk** oriental. **-lender, -lending** Oriental.
Østerrike Austria. **østerriker** Austrian. **østerriksk** Austrian.
østers oyster.
østers|avl oyster-culture. **-banke** oyster-bank. **-fiske** oyster-fishing. **-handel** oyster-trade.
Østersjøen the Baltic. **østersjøisk** Baltic. **østersjøprovins** Baltic province.
østers|skall oyster-shell. **-skraper** scraper. **-skraping** dredging for oysters. **-tiden** the oyster-season. **-yngel** oyster-spat.
Øst-Europa Eastern Europe.
østfronten the East Front.
østgrense eastern frontier.
østgående easterly; (fartøy) eastward bound.
øst|kant eastern side. **-en** (bydel) the East end. **-kyst** eastern coast.
Østlandet (i Norge) South-Eastern parts.
øst|landsk (i Norge) South-Eastern. **-lending** Easterner.
østlig eastern, easterly; **det -e England** the East of England.
østnordøst East North East.
øst|over (to the) east, (to the) eastward. **-på** eastward; in the east.
østre eastern, east.
øst|side East side. **-sydøst** East South East.
øve (lære ved øvelse, utøve) practise; (utdanne, utvikle) exercise, train; **— tiltrekningskraft** exercise an attraction; **— vold** use violence; **— seg i dans** practise dancing; **— seg på piano** practise (on) the piano; **øvd** practised, skilled, expert.
øvelse practice, exercise; **— gjør mester** practice makes perfect, use makes perfectness; **jeg· er ute av —** I am out of practice; **holde seg i —** keep one's hand in.
øverst uppermost, topmost, top, highest; (fig) supreme, highest; **det -e** the top; **-e klasse** the top form; **-e dekk** the upper el. main deck; **i -e etasje** at the top of the house; **— ved bordet** at the head of the table; **sitte — i klassen** be at the head of one's class el. form; **stå — på listen** head the list; **— står** (fig) chief among these is; **fra — til nederst** from top to bottom; **from head to foot.**
øverstbefalende, øverstkommanderende commander in chief.
øving, se **øvelse.**
øvre upper.
Øvre-Italia Upper Italy.
øvrig remaining; **det -e** the rest, remainder; **en av døtrene er gift, de -e** osv. one of her daughters has married, the others etc.; **for —, i —** (as) for the rest; besides; otherwise, in other respects.
øvrigheten magistrates, authorities.
øvrighetsperson magistrate.
øy island; **-a Man** the Isle of Man; **-a Wight** the Isle of Wight.

øy(d)e, se **øde.**

øy(d)elegge, øy(d)emark, se **ødelegge, ødemark.**

øye eye; (sekraft) sight; (på kort og terning) pip; **øynene mine renner** my eyes water; **jeg har ikke lukket et — hele natten** I did not sleep a wink last night; **gjøre store øyne** stare. open one's eyes in surprise; **kom ikke mer for mine øyne** let me never see you again; **binde en for øynene** blindfold one; **ha for —** keep in view; **ha — for** have an eye for; (fig) **lukke øynene for** shut one's eyes to; **få øynene åpne for** become alive to; **i mine øyne** to my mind in my eyes, in my opinion; **rett opp i øynene på meg** to my face; **se en rett inn i øynene** look one straight in the face; **se noe i øynene** face; **det er ham en torn i -t** it is an eyesore to him; **jeg fikk tårer i øynene** the tears came into my eyes; **sette et par øyne i** en look daggers at one; **man kan se det med et halvt —** you may see that with half an eye; **ha, holde — med** have el. keep an eye upon, watch; **ha et våkent — med** watch closely; **han har øynene med seg** he has (all) his eyes about him; **slå øynene ned** cast down one's eyes; **jeg fikk øynene opp** my eyes were opened; **holdt hånden over øynene** shaded his eyes; **være blind på det ene —** be blind of (el. in) an eye; **få — på** discover, become aware of, catch sight of; **ha et godt —** til look with favourable eyes on; **under fire øyne** among ourselves, privately, in private, alone; **en samtale under fire øyne** a private conversation; **gå en under øynenene** flatter one.

øyebetennelse inflammation of the eye.

øyeblikk twinkling (of an eye), moment, instant, minute; **om et —** in a moment, this el. that very minute; **for -et** at present; **for et — siden** this moment; **i dette —** at this moment; **i det rette —** in the nick of time; **i hans lyse —** in his lucid intervals; **hvert — every** now and again.

øyeblikkelig momentary, instantaneous, immediate; (adv) this instant, immediately.

øyeblikksfotografi snapshot.

øye|bryn eyebrow. **-eple** eye-ball.

øye|forblendelse optical illusion. **-hule** orbit, socket of the eye. **-hår** (pl) eyelashes. **-kast** glance; **ved første —** at first sight. **-lege** oculist, eye-doctor. **-lokk** eyelid.

øyemed object, aim, end; **i det — å** for the purpose of.

øyemål measure by the eye.

øyenerve optic nerve.

øyensynlig (adj) evident, obvious. **øyensynlig** (adv) evidently.

øyen|tjener eye-servant. **-tjeneri** eye-service. **-trøst** (bot.) eyebright.

øye|operasjon operation on the eye. **-par** pair of eyes. **-skjerm** shade for the eyes. **-speil** ophthalmoscope.

øyestein apple of the eye, eye-ball, pupil of the eye; (fig) **ens —** the apple of one's eye.

øyestikker dragon-fly.

øyesykdom disease of the eye.

øyesyn eyesight; **ta i —** view, inspect, take a view of.

øyetann eye-tooth, dog-tooth.

øye|vann eye-water. **-vipper** eyelashes. **-vitne** eye-witness.

øyk horse, gee; (jvf. øk).

øyklima insular climate.

øyne (vrb) descry, spy, espy; see, behold.

øyr delta, sandbank, sands at the mouth of a river.

øyrike kingdom of islands; insular kingdom.

Å

å (inf.-merke) to; **jeg vil prøve å gjøre det** I will try to do it; **det er lett å se** it is easy to see; **det er ikke noe å se** there is nothing to be seen; **for å** to; **for ikke å** not to; **etter, i, med ,om** osv. **å** after etc. -ing; **tør jeg bry Dem med å** may I trouble you to; **til å** to; **vil De ha meg til å vaske . . .** would you have me wash . . .; **ikke til å beskrive** not to be described; **ved å arbeide** (middel) by working; **ved å se meg om** (ɔ: idet) looking round.

å (elv) rivulet, brook; **mange bekker små gjør en stor å** many a little makes a mickle.

å (interj) (sorg, misbilligelse, bønn) Oh! O! (forundring, smerte) Ah! Oh! — Gud O dear! —, **ikke annet!** pooh! — **pytt!** pshaw! bah! —, **gi meg boka!** pray, (just) give me the book! give me the book, (if you) please! —, **hold opp med det!** stop that, please! (el. will you); — **hør!** I say! look here! — **ja!** rather; well, yes.

åbit, se **frokost.**

åbor perch.

åbot upkeep, repairs; (jur.) compensation (to be paid by a tenant for disrepair of the farmhouses).

åger usury; drive **— practise** usury; **leve av —** live upon usury. **-aktig** usurious. **-forretning** usury, usurer's business. **-kar(l)** usurer. **-lov** usury law. **-rente** usury, usurious interest.

ågre practise usury, lend money upon usury; (fig) **— med sitt pund** make the most of one's talents, put one's talent to usury. **ågring** money -lending, usuries.

åk yoke; **kaste -et av** shake off the yoke; **bringe under -et** bring under the yoke; **bøye seg under -et** bow one's neck to the yoke; **gå under -et** pass under the yoke; **la gå under -et** send under the yoke; **spenne i -et** yoke, put to the yoke; **spenne fra -et** unyoke.

åker field. **-bruk** agriculture, husbandry, farming, tillage. Jvf. jordbruk, landbruk.

åkerdyrk|er agriculturist. **-(n)ing** agriculture.

åker|flekk field, piece (little patch) of arable land. **-fly** (zool.) cutworm, dart. **-får** furrow. **-høne — rapphøne** partridge. **-jord,** se **-land. -kål** charlock, wild cabbage. **-land** arable land. **-lapp,** se **-flekk. -mynte** corn mint. **-nellik** blue cornflower. **-redskap** field implement. **-rein** balk, headland, strip of sod (fringing a cultivated field). **-rikse** corn|crack, -crake, -crow, crake, landrail. **-rydning** clearing. **-sennep** charlock. **-skjell** field-boundary. **-snegl, -snile** common slug. **-teig** ridge (of a field). **-tistel** corn sow -thistle.

åkle carpet, cover, (woven) rug.

I. **ål** (boktrykkersyl) bodkin.

II. **ål** (fisk) eel; **så glatt som en —** as slippery as an eel; **strømpene hans hang i — rundt anklene** his stockings hung loose el. in wrinkles, el. about his heels.

åle|dam eel-pond. **-fangst** eel-fishing, eeling. **-gras** bell-ware, furtle. **-hode** eel's head. **-kiste** eel-box, -trunk. **-lyster** eel-spear, eel-fork. **-stanging** eel-spearing. **-teine** eel-bick, -pot. **-vad** net for catching eels. **-vandring** eel-fare.

åme antler, grass-moth.

åmot confluence, junction.

ånd spirit; (sjel) soul; (spøkelse) ghost, spectre, phantom; (forstand, geni) mind, intellect, intelligence, genius; (i en hær etc., dens moralske kraft) morale; **-en og materien** mind and matter; **den menneskelige** — the human mind; **den hellige** — the Holy Ghost, the Holy Spirit; **ens gode, onde** — one's good, evil spirit; **ond** — demon, evil spirit; **store -er** great minds; **språkets** — the genius of language; **lovens, tidens** — the spirit of the laws, of the time el. age; **oppgi -en** give up the ghost, expire, draw one's last breath.

ånde (subst) breath; **illeluktende** — foul el. rank breath; **få en i** — draw one out; **holde en i** — keep one at it; **holde folk i** — keep attention on the alert; **komme i** — become warm, warm to one's work; **være i** — be inspired, be in, be in vein.

ånde (vrb) breathe, respire; — **dypt** draw a deep breath; — **tungt** gasp, pant; — **inn** draw in, inhale, breathe.

åndeaktig ghostly, ghost-like.

ånde|besvergelse conjuration, incantation; exorcism. **-besverger** exorcist.

ånde|drag, -drett breath, breathing, respiration; **til siste** — to the last gasp; **i ett og samme** — at a breath, with the same breath. **-dretts-system** respiratory system. **-fotografi** spirit photograph. **-hull** breathing-hole, spiracle. **-legeme** astral body.

åndelig intellectual, mental, spiritual; ghostly; — **anspennelse** mental tension; — **anstrengelse** exertion of mind; **-e betraktninger** religious meditations; **-e evner** intellectual el. mental faculties; — **føde** intellectual food; **-e gaver** spiritual gifts; **i** — **henseende** intellectually el. mentally; — **likevekt** mental balance; **-e sanger** divine el. sacred songs; — **slektskap** congeniality, affinity; **-e skrifter** (traktater) religious, holy el. sacred tracts; — **trøst** spiritual el. ghostly comfort. **-gjøre** spiritualize. **-het** spirituality, ghostliness.

åndelyd aspiration.

åndelære pneumatology, doctrine of spirits, (om onde ånder) demonology.

åndeløs breathless, out of breath.

ånde|maner conjurer, necromancer. **-maning** necromancy. **-medium** spirit medium.

ånde|nød difficulty of breathing. **-pust** breath.

ånde|røst ghostly el. spectral voice, spirit voice. **-seer, -seerske** visionary, visionist, ghostseer.

ånde|stemme spectral voice. **-syn** vision, apparition. **-time** ghostly hour of midnight. **-verden** invisible world, ghost-world.

åndfull, se **åndrik.**

åndig spiritual, spirituous.

åndløs spiritless, shallow, dull, prosaic, insipid. **åndløshet** shallowness, dullness, insipidity.

åndrik clever, highly intellectual, brilliant.

åndrikhet clever saying, flash of wit; (søkt innfall) conceit.

åndsanlegg abilities, parts.

ånds|arbeid mental work, intellectual work el. labour. **-aristokrati** intellectual aristocracy. **-armod,** se **-fattigdom.** **-beslektet** congenial. **-dannelse** mental el. intellectual cultivation el. culture, improvement. **-dannende** cultivating, improving, educating. **-egenskap** mental quality. **-evne** (mental) faculty, pl. også parts, mentality. **-fattig** poor, empty, dull. **-fattigdom** intellectual poverty. **-felle** brother spirit. **-forlatt** shallow, dull in spirit. **-fornektelse** materialism. **-fornekter** materialist. **-fortærende** stultifying, tiresome. **-foster** production (of the mind), creation; lucubration. **-fraværelse** absence of mind, abstraction, preoccupation. **-fraværende** absent (in mind), absent-minded, abstracted, preoccupied; **et** — **blikk** a vacant stare. **-frembringelse,** se **-foster. -fri** free in mind. **-frihet** mental el. intellectual freedom el. liberty. **-frisk** mentally alert; of unimpaired mental faculties; sane. **-friskhet** sanity, soundness of mind, mental activity. **-fylde** a full mind. **-føde** food for the mind. **-gaver** gifts of the mind, parts. **-innhold**

spirit, mind. **-kraft** mental power el. energy. **-kraftig** strong minded, of vigorous mind. **-liv** intellectual life. **-nytelse** intellectual enjoyment. **-nærværelse** presence of mind, self-possession, resourcefulness. **-nærværende** resourceful, ready -witted, self-possessed, quick in emergencies. **-oppløftende** elevating (the mind), exalting. **-overlegenhet** superiority of mind. **-retning** bent of the mind, tendency. **-slektskap** congeniality, affinity, sympathy. **-sløv** idiotic, imbecile, obtuse. **-sløvende** stupefying. **-sløvhet** idiocy, imbecility. **-svak** feeble-minded, imbecile, weak of mind. **-svakhet** imbecility, weakness of mind. **-svekkelse** mental debility. **-utvikling** mental development. **-virksomhet** mental activity.

åpen open: (fig) frank, vacant; **-t endossement** blank indorsement el. endorsement; — **fiende** declared (professed) enemy; **under** — himmel in the open air; **i** — **mark** in the open field; — **plass** (i skrift) a blank; **holde** — **for** keep open for; **la plass stå** — **til** . . . leave . . . in blank; **hans plass står** — his place is vacant; — **red** open el. wild road; **-t spørsmål** open question; **åpne steder** (i trykk, skrift) blanks, (i skogen) clear spots, glades; — **sjø** the open sea, the offing.

åpen|bar manifest, evident, obvious, plain. **-bart** (adv) evidently (osv.) **-bare** reveal, disclose, discover, manifest, unfold, make known; — **en hemmelighet for en** reveal a secret to one; **den -barte religion** revealed religion; — **seg** appear (for: to). **-barelse, -baring** manifestation, unfolding, disclosure; (tilsynekomst) appearance; apparition.

åpenbaringen (Johannes' Å.) the Revelation (of St. John).

åpenhet openness; (fig) frankness, candour.

åpen|hjertig open(hearted), frank, candid, confiding. **-hjertighet** openheartedness, frankness. **-lys** manifest, undisguised; **-lyst** (adv) openly, avowedly. **-munnet** talkative, garrulous. **-munnethet** talkativeness, garrulity.

åpne open (for to); (på høytidelig måte) inaugurate; — **igjen** reopen; — **en butikk** set up a shop; — **et fat** broach a cask; — **en sekk** untie a bag; — **ilden** open (the) fire (mot: on); — **en korrespondanse** open a correspondence; — **en kreditt** open a credit (på et beløp: to an amount; hos en: with sb); **dørene -s kl. 7** doors open at seven; **jeg har -t en konto for Dem** I have opened you an account; — **seg** open (for: to); — **seg igjen** reopen.

åpning opening; (høytidelig) inauguration; (konkret) opening, hole, aperture; (i skog) glade; (i postkasse) letter-slit; (smal sprekk) slit.

åpnings|fest inaugural banquet. **-tale** inauguration address.

år year, twelvemonth; **et halvt** — six months; **hvert annet** — every two years, every other year; — **og dag** a year and a day; (dt.) (lang tid) an age; **han er ikke tjue** — he is not twenty, he is in his teens; **dette** —, d. å. (= i år) this year; **dette års** of this year; **forrige års** of last year; **neste** — next year; **-et etter** next year; **for mange** — **siden** years ago; — **for** —, **fra** — **til** — year by year, annually, yearly; **i** — this year; **-et 1815** the year (sj. of) 1815; **han er i sine beste** — he is in the prime of life, in the flower of his age; **det gir seg med -ene** that will come with the years; **mellom** — **og dag** in the course of a year; **om -et a** (per) year, per annum, per ann.; **om et** — in a year; **i dag om et** — this day twelvemonth; **han er over tjue** — he is above twenty, he is out of his teens; **til -s** advanced in years; **et to -s barn** a two years old child. **siste** — last year.

årbøker annals.

I. **åre** (i legeme, tre, blad, insektvinge osv., også om varmåre, anlegg, tendens) vein; (puls) artery; (min.) grain, vein.

II. **åre** (til å ro med) oar, (mindre) scull; **hvile**

på -ne lie on one's oars; **trekke på -ne** pull el. tug at the oars; **legge -ne inn** el. **opp** unship the oars; **legge -ne ut** ship the oars.
III. **åre** (ildsted) hearth.
åre|betennelse phlebitis. **-bind** bandage.
åreblad oar-blade, wash of an oar.
åreforkalkning phlebolite.
åre|grep oar-handle. **-keip** row-lock, crutch.
åreknute varicose vein, varix (pl. varices), (pulsåresvulst) aneurism.
årelang of (several) years; **ved -t arbeid** by the labour of years.
årelate bleed, let blood, blood, phlebotomize.
årelat(n)ing letting of blood, bleeding, blood -letting, phlebotomy, venesection.
åremål term of years.
årestue open-hearth room el. hall.
åre|svulst (pulsåre-) aneurism. **-system** venal el. arterial system. **året** veined, veiny.
åre|tak stroke; **-toll(e)** thole, thole-pin, row -lock.
årevis: i — for years.
år|følge chronological order. **-gang** (av tidsskrift) annual series el. set, year's course year's file; (av årsskrift) annual publication; (av vin, spøkende også om mennesker) vintage. **-gangsvann** a perennial supply of water.
århundre century. **århundreskifte** century end.
-årig -year-old. **den ni-årige Karl** nine-year -old Charles. **-åring** -year-older. **en tolv-åring** a twelve-year-older.
åringer years; **gode — good** crops.
årlig yearly, annual; **— rente** annual interest.
årmann steward.
år|merke, se **-ring**, **-rekke** series of years. **-ring** circle, yearly ring (of a tree).
årsak cause, reason, occasion; **for visse -ers skyld** for certain reasons; **av den — for** that reason, on that account; **-en til at** the cause why; **har vært — til at** has been (the) cause of; **ingen — don't** mention it, no matter, all right, you are quite welcome, no thanks required.
årsaks|- causal. -begrep idea of cause. **-forhold** relation of cause, causation. **-konjunksjon** causal conjunction. **-setning** causal proposition.
års|angivelse date of the year. **-beretning** annual report. **-dag** anniversary. **-fest** annual festival, anniversary; wake; (for en skole) prize day, speech-day. **-gammel** (unge) yearling, year-old, of one year. **-grøde** produce of a year, a year's crop.
årskort annual ticket, (is. v. jernbanen) pass-ticket.
års|lønn annual salary el. wages. **-regnskap** yearly el. annual account. **-skifte** turn of the year, new year. **-skrift** annual. **-tall** year, date.

-tid time of (the) year, season (of the year). **-unge** yearling; (fig) **han er ingen — he** is no chicken. **-vekst** crop.
år|ti decade (of years), decennium, decennary. **-tusen** a thousand years, millennium.
årvak, se **årvåken.**
årvei crops of a year; **utsiktene for -en** the harvest prospects.
årviss unfailing; perennial.
årvåken vigilant, watchful, alert, on the alert. **-het** vigilance, watchfulness, wakefulness, alertness.
I. **ås** (mountain) ridge; (bjelke) beam.
II. **ås** (pl. æser) As, pl. Ases.
Asator Thor the As.
åsete possession; estate, property. **åsetesrett** right of retaining possession of the paternal estate.
åsetroen the religion of the Ases.
ås|lendt ridgy. **-rygg** crest, ridge.
åsted place of perpetration, spot in question, locus in quo; **besøke -et** visit the locus. **åstedsbefaring** local inquest.
åsyn face, visage, countenance; **for Guds — in** the face, sight, presence of God; **bort fra mitt — out** of my sight.
åsynje (myt.) goddess.
åt (prep) se **til**: (adv) se **at.**
åt (i sjøen) brit, whale's food. Se ogs. **åte.**
åtak attack.
åte bait, lure; (levende) kill; (åtsel) carcase; **legge ut — i** (på) bait.
åtferd, se **atferd.**
åtsel carcass, carcase, carrion. **-etende dyr** carrion-eater. **-flue** carrionfly. **-fugl** carrion -bird.
åtselgribb vulture.
åtte (tallord) eight; **i dag — dager** this day week; **i morgen — dager** tomorrow week; **om en — dagers tid** in a week; **— timers arbeidsdag** eight hours' working-day.
åttekant octagon.
åttekantet octagonal, octangular.
åttende eighth; **for det — eighthly**; **— bud** ninth commandment.
åttendedel eighth part, eighth; **-s note** quaver; **-s pause** quaver rest.
åttesidet eight-sided.
åttetall figure of eight.
åttetimersdagen the eight hour day.
åtte|fold octuple, eight-fold. **-årig**, **-års of** eight years, eight years old.
åtti eighty. **-ende** eightieth. **-årig** octogenarian
åttring eight-oar.
åtvare, **åtvaring**, se **advare**, **advarsel.**
åverk (jur.) damage done to property.
åvirke fell (and work), as applied to timber.

VERBAL-LISTE

abide (vente på)	abode	abode
arise (oppstå, reise seg)	arose	arisen
awake (våkne)	awoke	awaked, awoke
be (være)	was, pl. were	been
bear (bære)	bore	borne
bear (føde)	bore	born
beat (slå)	beat	beaten
beget (avle)	begot	begot
begin (begynne)	began	begun
bend (bøye)	bent	bent
bereave (berøve)	bereaved, bereft	bereaved, bereft
beseech (bønnfalle)	besought	besought
bet (vedde)	betted, bet	betted, bet
betide (times)	betid	betid
bid (by(de))	bade, bid	bid, bidden
bind (binde)	bound	bound
bite (bite)	bit	bit, bitten
bleed (blø)	bled	bled
blow (blåse)	blew	blown
break (sprenge, bryte, brekke)	broke	broken
breed (avle)	bred	bred
bring (bringe)	brought	brought
build (bygge)	built	built
burn (brenne)	burned, burnt	burned, burnt
burst (briste)	burst	burst
buy (kjøpe)	bought	bought
can (kan)	could	(been able)
cannot (kan ikke)	could not	(been unable)
cast (kaste)	cast	cast
catch (fange)	caught	caught
chide (skjenne på)	chid, chided	chid, chidden
choose (velge)	chose	chosen
cleave (klebe)	clave, cleaved, clove	cleaved
cleave (kløyve)	cleft, clove	cleft, cloven
cling (henge ved)	clung	clung
come (komme)	came	come
cost (koste)	cost	cost
creep (krype)	crept	crept
cut (hogge)	cut	cut
dare (tore; våge)	dared, (gml.) durst	dared
dare (utfordre)	dared	dared
deal (handle)	dealt	dealt
dig (grave)	dug	dug
dive (dukke)	dived, undert. dove	dived
do (gjøre)	did	done
draw (trekke)	drew	drawn
dream (drømme)	dreamed, dreamt	dreamed, dreamt
drink (drikke)	drank	drunk
drive (drive)	drove	driven
dwell (dvele, bo)	dwelled, dwelt	dwelled, dwelt
eat (spise)	ate, eat	eaten
fall (falle)	fell	fallen
feed (fø)	fed	fed
feel (føle)	felt	felt
fight (kjempe)	fought	fought
find (finne)	found	found
flee (fly, flykte)	fled	fled
fling (slenge)	flung	flung

fly (fly(ge))	flew	flown
fly (flykte)	fled	fled
forget (glemme)	forgot	forgotten, forgot
forsake (svikte)	forsook	forsaken
freeze (fryse)	froze	frozen
get (få)	got	got
gild (forgylle)	gilded, gilt	gilded, gilt
gird (omgjorde)	girded, girt	girded, girt
gird at (spotte)	girded at	girded at
give (gi)	gave	given
go (gå)	went	gone
grave (utskjære)	graved	graved, graven
grind (male (korn o. l.))	ground	ground
grow (vokse)	grew	grown
hang (henge)	hung	hung
hang (henge i galge)	hanged	hanged
have (ha)	had	had
hear (høre)	heard	heard
heave (løfte; hive)	heaved, hove	heaved, hove
hew (hogge)	hewed	hewed, hewn
hide (skjule)	hid	hid, hidden
hit (ramme)	hit	hit
hold (holde)	held	held
hurt (gjøre vondt)	hurt	hurt
keep (holde, gjemme)	kept	kept
kneel (knele)	knelt	knelt
knit (strikke)	knit, knitted	knit, knitted
know (vite)	knew	known
lade (belesse, laste)	laded	laded, laden
lay (legge)	laid	laid
lead (føre)	led	led
lean (lene)	leaned, leant	leaned, leant
leap (hoppe)	leaped, leapt	leaped, leapt
learn (lære)	learnt, learned	learnt, learned
leave (forlate)	left	left
lend (låne)	lent	lent
let (late)	let	let
lie (ligge)	lay	lain
light (tenne)	lighted, lit	lighted, lit
load (belesse, laste, lade)	loaded	laden, loaded
lose (tape)	lost	lost
make (gjøre)	made	made
may (kan)	might	(been allowed)
mean (tenke)	meant	meant
meet (møte)	met	met
mow (slå, om gras)	mowed	mowed, mown
must (må)	must	(been obliged)
ought (bør)	ought	(been obliged)
pay (betale)	paid	paid
pen (ha i kve, innestenge)	penned, pent	penned, pent
put (legge)	put	put
read (lese)	read	read
reave ((be)røve)	reft	reft
rend (rive i stykker)	rent	rent
rid (befri)	rid	rid
ride (ri)	rode	ridden
ring (ringe)	rang	rung
rise (reise seg)	rose	risen
rive (kløyve)	rived	rived, riven
run (løpe)	ran	run
saw (sage)	sawed	sawed, sawn
say (si)	said	said
see (se)	saw	seen
seek (søke)	sought	sought
seethe (koke)	seethed, sod	seethed, sodden
sell (selge)	sold	sold
send (sende)	sent	sent
set (sette)	set	set
sew (sy)	sewed	sewed, sewn
shake (riste)	shook	shaken
shall (skal)	should	(been obliged)
shear (klippe)	sheared, (gml.) shore	sheared, undert. shorn
shed (utgyte)	shed	shed
shine (skinne)	shone	shone
shoe (sko)	shod	shod
shoot (skyte)	shot	shot
show (vise)	showed	showed, shown
shrink (krype, krympe)	shrank, shrunk	shrunk
shrive (skrifte)	shrived, shrove	shriven
shut (lukke)	shut	shut
sing (synge)	sang, sung	sung

sink (synke)	sank, sunk	sunk
sit (sitte)	sat	sat
slay (slå i hjel)	slew	slain
sleep (sove)	slept	slept
slide (gli)	slid	slid, slidden
sling (slynge)	slung	slung
slink (luske)	slunk	slunk
slit (skjære opp)	slit	slit
smell (lukte)	smelled, smelt	smelled, smelt
smite (slå)	smote	smitten
sow (så)	sowed	sowed, sown
speak (tale)	spoke	spoken
speed (ile)	sped, speeded	sped
speed (la ile)	sped, speeded	sped, speeded
spell (stave)	spelled, spelt	spelled, spelt
spend (bruke)	spent	spent
spill (spille)	spilled, spilt	spilled, spilt
spin (spinne)	spun	spun
spit (spytte)	spat, spit	spit
split (kløyve)	split	split
spread (spre(de))	spread	spread
spring (springe)	sprang, sprung	sprung
stand (stå)	stood	stood
stave (slå hull på)	staved, stove	staved, stove
stay (stanse)	staid, stayed	staid, stayed
steal (stjele)	stole	stolen
stick (klebe, sitte fast)	stuck	stuck
sting (stikke m. brodd)	stung	stung
stink (stinke)	stank	stank
strew (strø)	strewed	strewed, strewn
stride (skride)	strode	stridden
strike (slå)	struck	struck
string (spenne)	strung	strung
strive (streve)	strove	striven
strow (strø)	strowed	strown
swear (sverge)	swore	sworn
sweat (svette)	sweat, sweated	sweat, sweated
sweep (feie)	swept	swept
swell (svulme)	swelled	swelled, swollen, swoln
swim (svømme)	swam	swum
swing (svinge)	swung	swung
take (ta)	took	taken
teach (lære, undervise)	taught	taught
tear (rive)	tore	torn
tell (fortelle)	told	told
think (tenke)	thought	thought
thrive (trives)	thrived, throve	thriven
throw (kaste)	threw	thrown
thrust (støte)	thrust	thrust
tread (tre)	trod	trod, trodden
wake (våkne; vekke)	woke, waked	waked, woke
wear (bære)	wore	worn, wore
weave (veve)	wove	woven
weep (gråte)	wept	wept
wet (væte)	wet, wetted	wet, wetted
will (vil)	would	(been willing)
win (vinne, oppnå)	won	won
wind (vinde, sno)	wound	wound
wring (vri; knuge)	wrung	wrung
write (skrive)	wrote	written

ENGLISH-NORWEGIAN

By B. Berulfsen

FOREWORD

In this new edition the material has been substantially revised. The Norwegian spelling introduced by law in 1938 is used, and special stress has been laid on giving the definitions a more Norwegian and up-to-date stamp. Over the long period of years that the dictionary has been in use, a certain volume of experience has been gained as to words and phrases that might be lacking in former editions or have proved to be without any particular viability. It has been possible to eliminate some material without detriment to the whole, and thus make room for the great number of new words and expressions resulting from the language growth of recent years. In that respect World War II brought vast additions that, assuredly, will become a permanent part of the English language.

Wherever feasible, we have endeavored to incorporate that additional vocabulary in the present edition, with the result that it has increased somewhat in volume.

PRONUNCIATION

(Diacritical marks and phonetic symbols appear in brackets [ ] at the beginning of each explanation.)

['] signifies stress (accent) ; it precedes the strongly accented syllable ; e.g., *city* ['siti] with the stress on the first syllable ; *insist* [in'sist] with the stress on the second syllable. If the mark appears twice, it means a uniform or uncertain accentuation, as in *inside* ['in'said] with the stress on the first or the second syllable (or on both syllables).

[·] marks the length of sound ; e.g., *seat* [si·t], whereas the vowel in *sit* is short.

[a·] as in *far* [fa·ə], *father* ['fa·ðə].

[ai] as in *eye* [ai].

[au] as in *how* [hau].

[ä] as in *hat* [hät].

[b] as in *bed* [bed], *ebb* [eb].

[d] as in *do* [du·], *bed* [bed].

[ð] as in *then* [ðen].

[þ] as in *thin* [þin].

[e] as in *let* [let].

[eⁱ] as in *hate* [heⁱt].

[ë] wavering between [e] and [i] as in *basket* ['ba·-skët = 'ba·sket, 'ba·skit].

[ə·] as in *hurt* [hə·t], *her* [hə·].

[ə] as in *inner* ['inə], *about* [ə'baut], *hear* [hiə].

[ə] the same sound, but weaker, as in *far* [fa·ə], *vary* ['væ·əri].

[f] as in *find* [faind].

[g] as in *go* [goᵘ].

[h] as in *hat* [hät].

[i·] as in *feel* [fi·l].

[i] as in *fill* [fil].

[j] as in *you* [ju·].

[k] as in *can* [kän].

[l] as in *low* [loᵘ], *ell* [el].

[m] as in *man* [män].

[n] as in *no* [noᵘ].

[ŋ] as in *singer* ['siŋə], *finger* ['fiŋgə].

[oᵘ] as in *no* [noᵘ].

[o] the same, but weaker, as in *phonetic* [fo'netik].

[oi] as in *boy* [boi].

[p] as in *pea* [pi·].

[r] as in *red* [red], *vary* ['væ·əri].

[s] as in *so* [soᵘ].

[ʃ] as in *she* [ʃi·], *chin* [tʃin].

[t] as in *toe* [toᵘ].

[u·] as in *fool* [fu·l].

[u] as in *full* [ful].

[v] as in *vivid* ['vivid].

[w] as in *we* [wi·].

[z] as in *zeal* [zi·l].

[ʒ] as in *measure* ['meʒə] ; *join* [dʒoin].

[æ·] as in *hair* [hæ·ə], *vary* ['væ·əri].

[å·] as in *caught* [kå·t], *court* [kå·ət].

[å] as in *cot* [kåt].

[ʌ] as in *cut* [kʌt].

[~] over a vowel signifies a nasal pronunciation.

( ) enclose phonetic marks that may be pronounced or not, as in *every* ['ev(ə)ri], *empty* ['em(p)ti].

(·) indicates alternative length, as in *soft* [så(·)ft] pronounced either with a long or a short [å].

Where a word is listed with two or more pronunciations, the first is preferred.

LIST OF MARKS AND ABBREVIATIONS

— (long dash) indicates repetition of a word: account; on — of.

- (hyphen) indicates repetition of a word as a compound word without a hyphen or preceding a derivational ending: any, -body (= anybody), approach, -ing (= approaching).

— - (a long dash and a hyphen) indicate repetition of a word with a hyphen: carving, — -knife (= carving-knife).

| (a vertical line) indicates that only the part of the word preceding the mark is to be repeated in the following word indicated by - or — -, for instance: cross|bar, -beam, — -bearer, — -bench (= crossbar, crossbeam, cross-bearer, cross-bench), cross|-piece, — -purpose, — -question, -road (= cross-piece, cross-purpose, cross-question, crossroad), approbat|e, -ion (= approbation).

adj.	adjective	merk.	business expression
adv.	adverb	m. h. t.	in regard to
alm.	common	mots.	contrary
amr.	American	nml.	namely (*viz.*)
ark.	architecture	ogs.	also
bet.	sense, meaning; designation, term	o. l.	and such like
		osv.	and so forth
bil.	figurative, metaphorical	ovf.	above
bl. a.	among other things, *inter alia*	oppr.	originally
dial.	dialect	p.	on, upon; person
d. s. s.	the same as	perf.	the perfect tense
egtl.	proper, true sense of a word	pl.	plural
etc.	*et cetera* (etc.)	poet.	poetic
f.	for	prep.	preposition
fig.	figurative	pres.	the present tense
fk.	abbreviated	pts.	participle; participles
flgd.	following	relig.	religious, religiously
forb.	the connection	s.	like, as
fork.	abbreviation	sb.	somebody
fr.	French	s. d.	see this
gml.	old	sg.	singular
imperf.	imperfect (past) tense	sl.	slang
ind.	indicative tense	smnl.	compare
inf.	infinitive	smstn.	compound(s)
iron.	ironical	srl.	special, especially
istf.	instead of	st.	something
jfr.	*cf.*	subst.	noun
jur.	legal expression	sv.	corresponding
lat.	Latin	t.	to
lign.	similar	v.	verb; by, near
m.	with	vulg.	vulgar
mar.	maritime expression	årh.	century
med.	medicine		

4

A

A, a [e¹] A, a.
A fk. f. **Academician; Academy; America; Associate. A 1** [e¹ wʌn] **(first-class, No. 1)** første klasses skip i Lloyd's register. **A flat** ass; **A major** A-dur; **A minor** a-moll; **A sharp** aiss.
a. fk. f. **acre; adjective; anno; ante.**
A. A. fk. f. **Associate in Arts; American Academy; Automobile Association.**
a [e¹; oftest ubetont ə], **an** [än, oftest ubetont ən], en, et; undertiden én, ett; om; **two at a time** to på én gang; **at a blow** med ett slag; **a shilling a day** en shilling om dagen.
a [ə] på, i, til; oftest sammenskrevet med det følgende ord; **aflame** i flammer, i lys lue.
A. B. fk. f. **able-bodied (seaman).**
aback [ə¹bäk] bakk; **take — bakke** seil; forvirre, klumse, gjøre målløs.
abacus [¹äbəkəs], pl. **-i** [¹äbəsai] abakus (øverste del av søylekapitél); kuleramme, regnetavle.
abaft [ə¹ba·ft] akter(ut); aktenfor, bak.
abandon [ə¹bändən] forlate, svikte; oppgi; avstå (skip); løssloppenhet, overgivenhet, villskap. **-ed** [ə¹bändənd] forlatt, herreløs; forvorpen, ryggesløs. **-ment** [ə¹bändənmənt] oppgivelse, forlatthet; avståelse.
abase [ə¹be¹s] ydmyke, fornedre, nedsette. **-ment** [ə¹be¹sment] ydmykelse, fornedrelse.
abash [ə¹bäʃ] gjøre skamfull. **-ment** [-mənt] skam, skamfølelse, skamkjensle.
abate [ə¹be¹t] nedslå, minske, sløve, døyve; slå av (om prisen); (jur.) omstøte, gjøre ugyldig, vrake; avta, minke. **-ment** [-mənt] minking, mink; avslag, rabatt.
abatis [sg. ə¹bäti(s), pl. ə¹bätiz] forhogning; bråte.
abb [äb] renning (i en vev).
abbacy [¹äbesi] abbeds verdighet el. område.
abbatial [ə¹be¹ʃəl] abbed-, som hører til en abbed.
abbé [¹äbe¹] pastor. **abbess** [¹äbis] abbedisse.
abbey [¹äbi] abbedi, klosterkirke. **abot** [¹äbət] abbed. **abbotship** [¹äbətʃip] abbedverdighet.
abbr. fk. f. **abbreviated, abbreviation.**
abbreviate [ä¹bri·vie¹t] forkorte. **abbreviation** [äbri·vi·e¹ʃen] forkorting; abbreviatur.
ABC abc, alfabet.
A. B. C. fk. f. **aerated bread company,** se **aerated;** (alfabetisk) jernbane-rute.
abdicate [¹äbdike¹t] frasi seg (trone el. embete), nedlegge, abdisere, **abdication** [äbdi¹ke¹ʃən] fratredelse, tronfrasigelse.
abdomen [äb¹do·ᵘmən] underliv, buk. **abdominal** [äb¹dåminəl] buk-, underlivs-.
abduct [äb¹dʌkt] bortføre, kidnappe. **abduction** [äb¹dʌkʃən] bortføring.
abeam [ə¹bi·m] tvers, tverrskips.
abecedarian [e¹bi·si·¹dä°riən] alfabetisk; elementær; nybegynner.
abed [ə¹bed] i seng.

Aberd|een [äbə¹di·n]. Aberdeen. **-onian** [äbə-¹do·ᵘnjən] (en) som er fra Aberdeen.
aberration [äbə¹re¹ʃən] avvik, villfarelse.
abet [ə¹bet] tilskynde, hjelpe. **-ment** [ə¹betment] tilskynding. **-ter, -tor** [ə¹betə] tilskynder, medskyldig.
abeyance [ə¹be¹ə s] midlertidig herreløs; **in — i** bero, i ro så lenge, midlertidig herreløs.
abhor [äb¹hå·°] avsky, se på med forakt. **-rence** [äb¹hårəns] avsky, vemmelse. **-rent** [äb-¹hårənt] avskyelig, ekkel, vemmelig; uforenelig **(to** med).
abide [ə¹baid] bli; bo; holde fast **(by** ved); rette seg **(by** etter); vente på, avvente; utstå, tåle. **abiding** [ə¹baidiŋ] vedvarende, permanent.
Abigail [¹äbige¹l] Abigail; kammerpike.
ability [ə¹biliti] evne, dugelighet, dyktighet; (pl.) talenter, (ånds)evner.
abject [¹äbdʒekt] lav, foraktelig, ynkelig, krypende. **-ion** [äb¹dʒekʃən] ydmykelse. **-ness** [¹äbdʒiktnés] nedrighet, lavhet, servilitet.
abjuration [äbdʒu¹re¹ʃen] avsverging.
abjure [äb¹dʒuə] avsverge.
ablative [¹äblativ]: **— case** ablativ; **— absolute** dobbelt ablativ.
ablaut [¹äblaut] avlyd, lydsprang.
ablaze [ə¹ble¹z] i lys lue.
able [¹e¹bl] dugelig, dyktig; **be — to** kunne. **able-bodied** [¹e¹bl¹bådid] rask, rørig, arbeidsfør; helbefaren (om sjømann).
ablet [¹äblit] løye (fisk).
abloom [ə¹blu·m] i blomst.
ablution [äb¹lu·ʃen] rensing, vask, vasking.
ably [¹e¹bli] dyktig; **— edited** godt redigert.
abnegate [¹äbnige¹t] nekte, fornekte. **abnegation** [äbni¹ge¹ʃen] fornekting.
abnormal [äb¹nå·°ml] abnorm, uregelmessig; vanskapt, unaturlig, sykelig. **abnormity** [äb-¹nå·°miti] uregelmessighet; vanskapthet.
aboard [ə¹bå·°d] ombord; ombord på.
abode [ə¹bo·ᵘd] bolig, bustad.
abode [ə¹bo·ᵘd] imperf. og perf. pts. av **abide.**
abolish [ə¹båliʃ] avskaffe, få bort. **abolishment** [ə¹båliʃmənt], **abolition** [äbo¹liʃən] avskaffing. **abolitionist** [äbo¹liʃənist] abolisjonist (motstander av negerslaveriet).
abominable [ə¹båminəbl] avskyelig, fæl. **abominate** [ə¹båmine¹t] avsky. **abomination** [əbåmi-¹ne¹ʃən] avsky, avskyelighet; styggedom.
aboriginal [äbo¹ridʒinəl] opprinnelig, opphavlig; urinnvåner. **aborigines** [äbo¹ridʒini·z] opprinnelige innbyggere, urinnvånere, urfolk.
abort [ə¹bå·°t] abortere. **-ion** [ə¹bå·°ʃən] abort; misfoster. **-ive** [ə¹bå·°tiv] som framkaller abort; for tidlig født, mislykt.
abound [ə¹baund] være rik på; ha overflod **(in** el. **with** av, på).
about [ə¹baut] omkring; på, hos; omtrent;

nærheten, ved hånden; omkring i el. på; omtrent ved; angående, om; **all** — overalt; **be** — **to være** i begrep med, være i ferd med, skulle til å; **how** — hvordan går det med?
about-sledge [ə'bautsledȝ] storslegge.
above [ə'bʌv] over, ovenfor; ovenpå; fig. over, mer enn; — **all** framfor alt; **he was** — **suspicion** han var hevet over all mistanke; **hardly** — **his breath** neppe hørlig.
above-board [ə'bʌv'bå·ᵊd] uten fusk, ærlig. **above-deck** på dekk; ærlig. **above-mentioned** [ə'bʌv'menʃənd] ovennevnt, før nevnt.
abrade [-'ge¹ʃən] skrape av, gnure.
Abraham ['e¹brəhäm] Abraham.
abrasion [ə're¹ʒən] avskraping; skramme.
abreast [ə'brest] ved siden av hverandre, side om side; — **of à jour med**; **keep** — **of** (el. **with**) **the times** følge med tiden.
abridge [ə'bridȝ] forkorte, sammendra.
abridgement [-mənt] forkorting; utdrag.
abroach [ə'bro⁰tʃ] anstukket (om tønne).
abroad [ə'brå·d] ute; utenlands; **at home and** — **ute og hjemme; from** — fra utlandet.
abrogate ['äbroge¹t] oppheve, avskaffe. **abrogation** [-'ge¹ʃən] opphevelse, avskaffing.
abrupt [əb'rʌpt] avbrutt; (stup)bratt, steil; brå, plutselig. **-ness** [-nēs] bratte, bratthet.
abscess ['äbsis] svull, svulst, byll.
abscond [äb'skånd] lure seg unna, rømme.
absence ['äbsəns] fravær; uteblivelse; mangel, skort; åndsfraværelse. **absent** ['äbsənt] fraværende, borte; atspredt, åndsfraværende, distré. **absent** [äb'sent] holde seg borte. **absentee** [äbsən-'ti·] (embetsmann) som er mye borte fra sitt embete, (godseier) som ikke bor på sitt gods. **absenteeism** [äbsən'ti·izm] varamanns-styre. **absent-minded** ['äbsənt'maindid] åndsfraværende. **-ly** i distraksjon. **-ness** åndsfraværelse.
absinth ['äbsinþ] malurt; absint.
absolute ['äbsəl(j)u·t] absolutt, uinnskrenket; egenmektig; fullstendig, hel, ubetinget. **-ly** aldeles, plent, ubetinget. **absolution** [äbsə'l(j)u·ʃən] frikjenning; absolusjon; tilgivelse. **absolutism** ['äbsəljutizm] enevelde; predestinasjonslæren. **absolutist** ['äbsəljutist] tilhenger av eneveldet; absolutistisk.
absolve [əb'zålv] frikjenne (**from** fra), løse.
absorb [əb'så·ᵊb] suge inn, sluke, oppta (i seg); **-ed in** (el. **with** el. **by**) helt opptatt av; **-ed in thoughts** i dype tanker; **of -ing interest** som helt opptar ens interesse. **absorbent** [əb'så·ᵊbənt] absorberende, som suger opp (el. i seg).
absorption [əb'så·ᵊpʃən] innsuging.
absquatulate [äb'skwåtjule¹t] stikke av.
abstain [äb'ste¹n] avholde seg, holde seg borte fra.
abstainer [äb'ste¹nə] avholdsmann.
abstemious [äb'sti·mjəs] måteholdende.
abstention [äb'stenʃən] avholdenhet, avhold; det å stå utenfor noe, ikke bruke sin stemme.
abstinence ['äbstinəns] avhold; **total** — totalavhold. **abstinent** ['äbstinənt] avholdende.
abstract ['äbsträkt] abstrakt begrep; utdrag; abstrakt; **in the** — in abstracto, i sin rene alminnelighet; **an** — **of the accounts** et utdrag av regnskapene; — **number** ubenevnt tall.
abstract [äb'sträkt] utdra, fradra; abstrahere, skille ut; stjele, kvarte. — **from** ta fra. **-ed** [äb'sträktid] fradratt; abstrakt; lutret, forfinet; atspredt. **-ion** [äb'sträkʃen] avsondring, abstraksjon; atspredthet, distraksjon.
abstruse [äb'stru·s] dunkel, uforståelig, dyp.
absurd [əb'se·d] absurd, urimelig, meningsløs, tåpelig. **-ity** [əb'sə·diti] urimelighet, meningsløshet.
abt. fk. f. **about.**
Abukir [äbu'kiə] Abukir.
abundance [ə'bʌndəns] overflødighet, overflod (**of** på). **abundant** [ə'bʌndənt] rikelig, rik; som det er nok el. mer enn nok av.

abuse [ə'bju·z] misbruke; skjelle ut.
abuse [ə'bju·s] misbruk, skjellsord.
abusive ['əbju·siv] uriktig; grov. **abusiveness** [-nēs] grovhet, grov munn.
abut [ə'bʌt] støte el. grense (**on** til); hvile.
abysm [ə'bizm] avgrunn. **-al** bunnløs.
abyss [ə'bis] avgrunn, bunnløst dyp. **-al** dypvanns-, mer enn 300 favner under havflaten.
Abyssinia [äbi'sinjə] Abessinia (= Etiopia).
A. C. fk. **Aero Club**; **Ante Christum** før Kristi fødsel; **Alpine Club.**
a|c fk. f. **account.**
acacia [ə'ke¹ʃə] akasie.
academic [äkə'demik] akademisk; akademiker.
academician [əkädi'miʃən] akademiker, medlem av et akademi, især av the **Royal Academy of Fine Arts**; **Royal Academician** medlem av the Royal Academy.
academy [ə'kädimi] akademi, høyskole, høyere fagskole f. eks. **Royal Military A.**; selskap for vitenskap el. kunst, især the **Royal Academy of Fine Arts**; dette selskaps årlige utstilling i Burlington House.
acanthus [ə'känþəs] akantus.
acatalectic [äkätə'lektik] akatalektisk.
acatalepsy [ä'kätəlepsi] uforståelighet.
accede [äk'si·d] tiltre (ogs. **accede to an office**); samtykke, innvilge (**to** i).
accelerate [äk'seləre¹t] framskynde, påskynde. **acceleration** [äkselə're¹ʃen] akselerasjon.
accent ['äksnt] aksent, trykk; lesetegn; tonelag, uttale; tonefall; uttrykk, ordlag, ordleiing.
accent [äk'sent] aksentuere, betone.
accentuate [äk'sentjue¹t] betone, framheve.
accentuation [äksentju'e¹ʃen] aksentuasjon.
accept [äk'sept] motta; godta; si ja (til); akseptere. **-ability** [äkseptə'biliti] antakelighet. **-able** [äk'septəbl] antakelig. **-ance** [äk'septəns] mottaking; godtaking, bifall, aksept; akseptert veksel. **acceptation** [äksəp'te¹ʃən] betydning, mening (et ords). **acceptor** [äk'septə] akseptant.
access ['äkses, äk'ses] adgang; vei (til); tilgjengelighet; anfall, ri; **easy of** — lett å komme til, lett å få i tale.
accessary [äk'sesəri] medskyldig, f. eks. — **to a crime.**
accessibility [äksesi'biliti] tilgjengelighet.
accessible [äk'sesibl] tilgjengelig.
accession [äk'seʃən] tiltredelse, tronbestigelse, forøking, auke, tilvekst; anfall, ri.
accessory [äk'sesəri] underordnet, bi-; delaktig, medskyldig (**to** i); pl. **accessories** tilbehør.
accidence ['äksidəns] formlære, bøyningslære.
accident ['äksidənt] tilfelle, slump, uhell, ulykkestilfelle; **railway** — jernbaneulykke; **by** — tilfeldigvis. **accidental** [äksi'dentl] tilfeldig; uvesentlig. **accidentally** [äksi'dentəli] tilfeldigvis.
acclaim [ə'kle¹m] hilse med bifallsrop, fagne.
acclamation [äklə'me¹ʃən] akklamasjon, bifallsrop, håndklapp, fagning. **acclamatory** [ə'klämətəri] bifalls-.
acclimat|isation [əklaimət(a)i'ze¹ʃən] akklimatisering. **-ise** [ə'klaimətaiz] akklimatisere.
acclivity [ə'kliviti] motbakke, stigning.
accolade [äko'le¹d] ridderslag; (i musikk) klamme.
accommodate [ə'kåməde¹t] tillempe, tilpasse; bilegge, forlike; forsyne; huse, skaffe husrom. **accommodating** [ə'kåmədə¹tin] imøtekommende, hjelpsom. **accommodation** [əkåmə'de¹ʃən] tilpassing, innretning, bekvemmelighet, husrom, losji. **-bill** akkommodasjonsveksel, proformaveksel. **-ladder** fallrepstrappe. — **-train** somletog.
accomodative [ə'kåmodeitiv] adj. lempelig, rimelig.
accompaniment [ə'kʌmpənimənt] ledsagelse, akkompagnement. **accompany** [ə'kʌmpəni] ledsage, følge, akkompagnere. **accompanyist** [ə'kʌmpə-niist] akkompagnatør (ogs. **accompanist**).
accomplice [ə'kåmplis] medskyldig (**in, of** i).

accomplish [ə'kåmpliʃ] fullføre, utføre; oppnå. **-ed** [ə'kåmpliʃt] dannet, talentfull. **-ment** [-mənt] fullføring. fullending; utrettelse; (pl.) talenter, selskapelige evner (især i musikk, sang, dans). **accord** [ə'kå·ºd] samklang, akkord; overensstemmelse, samsvar; forlik; **of his own** — av egen drift. **accord** [ə'kå·ºd] stemme; forsone; stemme overens; tilstå, innvilge i. **-ance** [-əns] overensstemmelse, samsvar; **in** — **with** ifølge. **according** to [ə'kå·ºdiŋ] etter, i samsvar med, ifølge; **the Gospel** — **Saint John** Johannes evangelium; **according as** liksom, etter. **accordingly** [ə'kå·ºdiŋli] i samsvar med det, deretter; følgelig, altså. **accordion** [ə'kå·ºdjən] trekkspill. **accost** [ə'kåst] henvende seg til; snakke til. **accouch·ur** [åku'ʃə·] fødselshjelper. **accoucheuse** [åku'ʃə·z] jordmor. **account** [ə'kaunt] beregning, regning, utregning; konto, regnskap; beretning; grunn; hensyn; omsyn, kunde; **call to** — kreve til regnskap; **render an** — avlegge regnskap; **as per** — ifølge regning; **pay to account** b tale à konto, betale i avdrag; **turn to** — dra fordel av; **on that** — derfor, av den grunn; **on our** — for vår skyld; **on** — **of** på grunn av; **on no** — på ingen måte; **take into** — ta i betraktning, ta omsyn til, regne med. **account** [ə'kaunt] beregne, regne; gjøre avregning; mene: — **for** gjøre regnskap for, gjøre greie for; forklare seg. **accountability** [əkaunta'biliti] ansvar, ansvarlighet. **accountable** [-əbl] ansvarlig. **accountan-** [-ənt] regnskapsfører, revisor, bokholder. **accountant-general** hovedbokholder. **account-book** regnskapsbok. **account-current** kontokurant. **account-sales** salgsregning. **accoutre** [ə'ku·tə] ruste ut, stase opp. **-ments** [-mənts] utrustning, utstyr, bunad, mundur. **accredit** |ə'kredit] akkreditere, bemyndige, gi fullmakt. **-ed** ansatt, offiselt godkjent. **letter of accredit tion** [åkredi'te!ʃən] kreditiv. **accretion** [ə'kri·ʃən] tilvekst, forøkelse, auke. **accrue** [ə'kru·] (til)flyte, tilfalle; **accruing interest** påløpende renter; **advantages accruing from this** derav flytende fordeler; — **to** tilfalle, tilhøre. **accumulate** [ə'kju·mjule!t] dynge sammen, hope opp; ta flere universitetsgrader samtidig; tilta. **accumulation** [əkju·mju'le!ʃən] opphoping. **accumulative** [ə'kju·mjuletiv] ivrig etter å erverve. **accumulator** [ə'kju·mjule!tə] opphoper; akkumulator. **accuracy** ['åkjurəsi] nøyaktighet. **accurate** ['åkjurét] nøyaktig. **accursed** [ə'kə·sid, ə'kə·st] forbannet, nederdrektig. **accusable** [ə'kju·zəbl] lastverdig, som kan anklages. **accusation** [åkju'ze!ʃən] beskyldning, anklage, klagemål. **accusative** [ə'kju·zətiv] akkusativ. **accusatory** [ə'kju·zətəri] anklagende, klage-. **accuse** [ə'kju·z] anklage, beskylde (of for); **the accused** anklagede. **accuser** [ə'kju·zə] anklager. **accustom** [ə'kʌstəm] venne. **-ed** vant; tilvant, vanlig, sedvanlig; **he is -ed to** han pleier. **ace** [e!s] ess (i kortspill); — **of diamonds** ruter ess; **within an** — på et hengende hår, nær ved; **not an** — ikke det minste. **acephalous** [ə'sefələs] hodeløs; som mangler første staving. **acerbity** [ə'sə·biti] bitterhet, skarphet. **acetose** ['åsitous], **acetous** ['åsitəs] sur, eddik-. **acetylene** [ə'sitəli·n] asetylén. **ache** [e!k] smerte; verke, gjøre vondt; **my head aches** jeg har vondt i hodet; **with an aching heart** med sorg i hjertet. **ache** [e!tʃ] (bokstaven) h; **drop one's -s** ikke uttale h på de riktige steder, tale halvemål; tale udannet. **achievable** [ə'tʃi·vəbl] som kan utføres, oppnåelig. **achieve** [ə'tʃi·v] utføre, fullende; oppnå. **-ment** [-mənt] utførelse; bedrift, storverk, dåd. **Achil(l)** ['åkil], **Achilles** [ə'kili·z] Akilles. **achromatic** [åkro'måtik] fargeløs.

acid ['åsid] sur; syre. **acidity** [ə'siditi] surhet. **acidulate** [ə'sidjule!t] gjøre syrlig. **acidulous** [ə'sidjuləs] syrlig; sur, gretten. **ack** [åk] (signaleringsspråk) a; **ack-ack gun** (for **anti-aicraft gun**) luftvernkanon. **acknowledge** [ə'knålidʒ] anerkjenne; innrømme, vedgå, gå med på; kvittere for. **acknowledgment** [-mənt] innrømmelse; anerkjennelse; erkjentlighetsbevis. **acme** ['åkmi] topp; topp-punkt; krise. **acne** ['åkni] filipens, finne, kveise. **acolyte** ['åkolait] akolytt, messehjelper. **aconite** ['åkonait] stormhatt (en giftplante). **acorn** ['e!kå·ºn] eikenøtt. **acoustic** [ə'kaustik] akustisk. **acoustics** [ə'kaustiks] akustikk, (læren om) lydforhold. **acquaint** [ə'kwe!nt] gjøre kjent, underrette. **acquaintance** [-əns] bekjentskap, kjennskap; kunnskap; bekjent, kjenning. **acquaintanceship** [-ʃip] kjennskap. **acquainted** [-id] bekjent. **acquest** [å'kwest] vinning, ervervelse. **acquiesce** [åkwi'es] akkviescere (in ved), slå seg til ro (in med), samtykke, finne seg (in i). **acquiescence** [-əns] innvilgning, samtykke. **acquiescent** [-nt] føyelig. **acquirable** [ə'kwai·ºrəbl] oppnåelig. **acquire** [ə'kwaiə] erverve, erverve seg, oppnå; — **knowledge** lære noe; **he -d his letters** han lærte alfabetet. **-ment** [-mənt] ervervelse, dugelighet, dugleik; **-ments** kunnskaper; talenter. **acquisition** [åkwi'ziʃən] ervervelse; vinning, akkvisisjon. **acquisitive** [ə'kwizitiv] ivrig etter å erverve, havesyk. **acquit** [ə'kwit] frikjenne, frita, frigjøre; betale; — **oneself** skille seg ved el. fra (of); sikre seg for (from). **-tal** [ə'kwitl] frikjenning. **-tance** [ə'kwitəns] klarering, betaling (av gjeld), kvittering. **acre** ['e!kə] acre (engelsk flatemål 4046,29 m²;) **broad acres** stor eiendom; **God's** — kirkegården. **acreage** ['e!kəridʒ] flateinnhold. **acrid** ['åkrid] skarp, bitende, besk. **-ity** [å'kriditi] skarphet, beskhet; (fig.) eiter, galle. **acrimonious** [åkri'mo¹nəs] skarp, bitter. **acrimony** ['åkrimøni] skarphet; bitterhet. **acrobat** ['åkrobåt] akrobat. **-ic** [åkro'båtik] akrobatisk. **Acropolis** [å'kråpəlis] Akropolis. **across** [ə'krå(·)s] på tvers; tvers over, over; tvers for, overfor; **come** — **one** treffe en, støte på **acrostic** [ə'kråstik] akrostikon. **act** [åkt] virke, fungere; handle, opptre; innvirke (**on** på); spille, opptre (som skuespiller), forstille seg; framstille (på scenen), oppføre; handling, gjerning; forordning, vedtak, lov; akt (i skuespill); avhandling, disputas; dokument; — **a part** spille en rolle; **-ing copy** eksemplar til bruk for skuespillerne; **-ing manager** aktiv (virkelig fungerende) direktør; **on your advice** rette seg etter ditt råd; **caught in the** — grepet på fersk gjerning; **Act of God** uforutsett hending, force majeure; **the Acts of the Apostles** Apostlenes Gjerninger; **Act of Parliament** lov. **act-drop** ['åktdråp] mellomaktsteppe. **actinia** [åk'tinjə] aktinie, sjøanemone. **actinic** [åk'tinik] aktinisk, kjemisk virksom. **action** ['åkʃən] handling, gjerning; bevegelse, gang; trefning, slag; prosess, klage, søksmål; **take** — skride til handling. **actionable** [-əbl] som kan påtales, som det kan reises sak om. **active** ['åktiv] virksom, sprek; rask, flink; praktisk, aktiv. **activity** [åk'tiviti] virksomhet; raskhet; aktivitet, drift, tak. **actor** ['åktə] skuespiller. **actress** ['åktrés] skuespillerinne. **actual** ['åktjuəl, 'åktʃuəl] virkelig, egentlig, likefram; nåværende, aktuell. **-ity** [åktju'åliti, åktʃu'åliti] virkelighet, aktualitet. **-ly** virkelig, i virkeligheten. **actuary** ['åktjuəri, 'åktʃuəri] aktuar. **actuate** ['åktjue¹t, 'åktʃue¹t] drive, sette i gang, påvirke.

acuity [ə'kju·iti] skarphet, kvasshet.
acumen [ə'kju·mən] skarpsindighet, gløggskap.
acute [ə'kju·t] spiss; fin, gløgg, skarpsindig, hissig, akutt. **-ness** [-nès] skarphet; skarpsindighet; gløggskap; heftighet.
ad [äd] fk. f. **advertisement**.
ad [äd] (lat.) ad, til; **ad libitum** etter behag. **A. D.** fk. f. **Anno Domini** i det Herrens år.
adage ['ädidʒ] ordspråk, ordtak, ordtøke.
adagio [ə'da·dʒio⁰] adagio.
Adam ['ädəm] Adam; **I don't know him from** — jeg aner ikke hvordan han ser ut. **-'s ale** vann. **-'s apple** adamseple.
adamant ['ädəmənt] diamant. **adamantine** [ädə'mäntain] av diamant; hard som flint.
adapt [ə'däpt] avpasse, innrette etter, lempe til, bearbeide (**from** etter). **-ability** [ə'däptə'biliti] anvendelighet. **-able** [ə'däptəbl] anvendelig. **-ation** [ädäp'te¹ʃən] tillemping, avpasning; bearbeiding; brukbarhet.
A. D. C. fk. f. **Aide-de-Camp** adjutant.
add [äd] tilføye, skjøte på; legge sammen, addere; — **to** forøke, øke, auke, utvide.
addendum [ə'dendəm], i plur. **addenda** [ə'dendə] addend, tilføyelse, tillegg.
adder ['ädə] hoggorm. —**-fly** gullsmed, libelle.
addict [ə'dikt] hengi; — **oneself to** hengi seg til, slå seg på; **-ed to** især: forfallen til (f. eks. **whisky** el. **drink**). **-edness** [-idnès], **-ion** [ə'dikʃən] tilbøyelighet, hug.
addition [ə'diʃən] tilføyelse, tillegg; addisjon; **in** — dessuten, omfram, attpå. **-al** [-əl] forøket, ekstra, ny. **-ally** [-əli] som tilføyelse, i tilgift, attpå.
addle ['ädl] fordervet; tom, hul; gold; forderve. — **-brain**, — **-head**, — **-pate** fehode, tosk. **-d egg** råttent egg.
address [ə'dres] henvende, vende seg til; tiltale, adressere; — **oneself to** gi seg i kast med, legge i vei med. **address** [ə'dres] henvendelse, adresse; behendighet; vesen, kur; **pay one's addresses to** gjøre kur til. **addressee** [ädre'si·] adressat. ːt
adduce [ə'dju·s] legge fram, føre fram, anføre.
adduction [ə'dʌkʃən] framføring, anførelse.
Adelaide ['ädile¹d] Adelaide (kvinne el. by).
Adelphi [ə'delfi] teater og kvarter i London.
Aden ['e¹dn] Aden.
adenoids ['ädinoidz] adenoide vegetasjoner.
adept [ə'dept] adept, gullmaker; kunsterfaren, helt innvidd (**in** i).
adequacy ['ädikwəsi] riktig forhold; nøgd.
adequate ['ädikwèt] som holder mål, passende, formålstjenlig, fullgod.
adhere [əd'hiə] henge fast, henge ved. **adherence** [əd'hiərəns] det å henge fast, det å holde fast; troskap. **adherent** [əd'hiərənt] vedhengende; tilhenger.
adhesion [əd'hi·ʒən] vedheng, adhesjon, det å holde (fast) på; **give in one's** — to gi sin tilslutning til. **adhesive** [əd'hi·siv] vedhengende, klebrig; — **plaster** heftplaster; — **envelope** gummiert konvolutt.
adiaphora [ädi'äfərə] adiafora.
adieu [ə'dju·] far vel; farvel, avskjed.
adipose ['ädipo⁰s] fet, fettholdig; fett, nyrefett.
adit ['ädit] gang, inngang, stoll.
adjacency [ə'dʒe¹sənsi] beliggenhet like ved, grannelag. **adjacent** [ə'dʒe¹sənt] tilgrensende; — **angle** nabovinkel.
adjective ['ädʒektiv] adjektiv; adjektivisk.
adjoin [ə'dʒoin] legge el. sette til, tilføye; grense til, støte til; **the -ing room** værelset ved siden av.
adjourn [ə'dʒə·n] oppsette, utsette, heve møtet. **adjournment** [ə'dʒə·nmənt] utsettelse; mellomtid mellom parlamentsmøter, tingferie.
adjudge [ə'dʒʌdʒ], **adjudicate** [ə'dʒu·dike¹t] tildømme, tilkjenne; dømme. **adjudication** [ədʒu·di·'ke¹ʃən] tilkjennelse; dom, kjennelse, orskurd.

adjunct ['ädʒʌŋkt] tilføyd, tilleggs-; tillegg; medhjelper, hjelpesmann. **-ion** [ä'dʒʌŋkʃən] tilføyelse. **-ive** [ä'dʒʌŋktiv] tilføyd, tilleggs-; tillegg.
adjuration [ädʒu're¹ʃən] besvergelse.
adjure [ə'dʒuə] besverge, bønnfalle.
adjust [ə'dʒʌst] beriktige; greie, skipe, ordne; bringe i overensstemmelse; stille; — **things to our point of view** ordne forholdene slik at de tilfredsstiller våre synspunkter. **-able** [ə'dʒʌstəbl] som kan avpasses; stillbar. **-er** [ə'dʒʌstə] beriktiger. **-ment** [-mənt] beriktigelse; stilling; ordning.
adjutancy ['ädʒutənsi] adjutantpost. **adjutant** ['ädʒutənt] adjutant; marabustork (også kalt **adjutant bird**).
adjuvant [ä'dʒuvənt] hjelpende, hjelpes-; medhjelp, hjelperåd.
admeasure [äd'meʒə] tilmåle. **admeasurement** [-mənt] tilmåling; mål, størrelse.
administer [əd'ministə] administrere, forvalte, styre, utdele, meddele, gi, yte; bruke, nytte; — **to** bidra til, avhjelpe. **administration** [ədmini-'stre¹ʃən] styrelse, forvaltning. **administrative** [əd'ministrətiv] forvaltende, styrings-. **administrator** [əd'ministre¹tə] bestyrer, administrator.
admirable ['ädmirəbl] beundringsverdig, framifrå.
admiral ['ädmirəl] admiral (de 4 grader ovenfra: **A. of the Fleet, Admiral, Vice-A., Rear-A.**). **admiralship** [-ʃip] admiralsverdighet. **Admiralty** [-ti] admiralitet, marineministerium, bestående av 7 Lords Commissioners, hvorav the **First Lord of the Admiralty** er marineminister. **A. knot** engelsk sjømil: 5900 fot.
admiration [ädmi're¹ʃen] beundring (**of** for); **note of** — utropstegn; **do it to** — gjøre det utmerket. **admire** [əd'maiə] beundre. **admirer** [əd'mai⁰rə] beundrer. **admiringly** [əd'mai⁰riŋli] med beundring.
admissibility [ädmisi'biliti] antagelighet; adgangsrett. **admissible** [əd'misibl] tillatelig, antagelig; som har adgangsrett.
admission [əd'miʃən] adgang; innrømmelse; **pay for** — betale entré; **by general** — som det innrømmes fra alle sider. — **-port** dampport.
admit [əd'mit] gi adgang, slippe inn; innrømme, vedgå.
admittance [əd'mitəns] adgang; **no** — adgang forbudt.
admixture [əd'mikstʃə] blanding, tilsetning.
admonish [əd'måniʃ] påminne; formane, advare. **admonition** [ädmo'niʃən] påminning. **admonitory** [əd'mänitəri] advarende, formanings-.
ado [ə'du·] ståk, kluss, bry, besvær; ståhei; **much** — about nothing stor ståhei for ingenting.
adobe [ə'do⁰bi] ubrent soltørket murstein.
adolescence [ädo'lesəns] ungdomsalder.
adolescent [ädo'lesənt] i oppveksten.
Adolphus [ə'dålfəs] Adolf.
adopt [ə'däpt] adoptere, ta til seg, ta i barns sted; anta. **-ion** [è'däpʃən] adopsjon; antagelse. **-ive** [ə'däptiv] adoptiv-, foster-.
adorable [ə'då·rəbl] tilbedelsesverdig, guddommelig. **adoration** [ädä're¹ʃən] tilbedelse. **adore** [ə'då·⁰] tilbe, dyrke, forgude, (i daglig tale) holde mye av. **adorer** [ə'då·rə] tilbeder.
adorn [ə'då·n] smykke, pryde. **-ment** [-mənt] prydelse, smykke.
adrenalin [ə'drenəlin] adrenalin.
Adriatic [e¹dri'ätik, äd-]; **the** — Adriaterhavet.
adrift [ə'drift] i drift, drivende for vind og vær; på lykke og fromme; **turn** — la seile sin egen sjø.
adroit [ə'droit] behendig, hag.
adulation [ädju'le¹ʃən] smigreri, smisking. **adulator** ['ädjule¹tə] smigrer. **adulatory** ['ädjulətəri] smigrende.
adult [ə'dʌlt] voksen; voksen person.
adulter|ate [ə'dʌltəre¹t] forfalske. **-ation** [ədʌl-te¹re¹ʃən] forfalskning. **-er** [ə'dʌltərə] horkar. **-ess**

[ə'dʌlt(ə)rès] horkvinne. -ous [ə'dʌltərəs] skyldig i hor. -y [ə'dʌltəri] ekteskapsbrudd, hor.

adumbrat|e [ə'dʌmbreʲt] ymte om, slå på. **-ion** [ädʌm'breʃən] ymt, løst henkastet bilde.

advance [əd'va·ns] framskritt, framsteg, framgang; framrykning; avansement, forfremmelse; forskudd; avanse, stigning, pristillegg; **in** — på forhånd. **advance** gå fremad, rykke fram; (om pris) stige; heve; forfremme, framskynde; nærme seg; framføre; gi på forskudd, forstrekke. **-ment** [-mənt] forfremmelse, avansement; fremme, framhjelp. — **-money** forskudd. — **-sheets** prøveark.

advantage [əd'va·ntidʒ] fordel, føremonn, nytte; gunstig leilighet; gagne, hjelpe; **something greatly to his** — noe meget fordelaktig for ham; — **of the ground** terrengforhold; **take** — **of** benytte seg av; snyte; **you have the** — **of me** De kjenner meg og jeg kjenner ikke Dem; **sell to** — selle med fordel; **to the best** — med størst fordel, i det fordelaktigste lys. **advantageous** [ädvən-'teʲdʒəs] fordelaktig.

advent ['ädvent] komme, tilkomst; advent. **adventitious** [ädven'tiʃəs] som kommer til, attpå-; tilfeldig.

adventur|e [əd'ventʃə] hending; vågestykke; eventyr; spekulasjon. **-er** [əd'ventʃərə] vågehals; eventyrer; lykkeridder. **-ess** [əd'ventʃərès] eventyrerske. **-ous** [əd'ventʃərəs] dristig, vågsom, forvoven; eventyrlig.

adverb ['ädvə·b] adverbium, adverb. **adverbial** [äd'və·bjəl] adverbiell.

advers|ary ['ädvəsəri] motstander; fiende; **the Adversary** djevelen. **-ative** [əd'və·sətiv] motsetnings-, mot-. **-e** ['ädvə·s] motsatt, som er imot; fiendtlig, ugunstig; — **fortune** motgang. **-ity** [äd'və·siti] motgang, ulykke.

advert [əd'və·t] akte, henvende sin oppmerksomhet (**to** på). **-ence** [əd'və·təns], **-ency** [əd-'və·tənsi] oppmerksomhet.

advertise ['ädvətaiz] bekjentgjøre, kunngjøre, avertere, lyse; — **for** avertere etter; — **oneself** gjøre reklame for seg selv.

advertisement [äd'və·tizmənt] avertissement, annonse, reklame. **advertiser** ['ädvətaizə] averterende; lysingsblad. **advertising** ['ädvətaiziŋ] reklame. — **agency** reklamebyrå.

advice [əd'vais] råd; advis, melding; etterretning; **a piece** (el. **bit**) **of** — et råd; **obtain medical** — søke legehjelp. — **-boat** avisobåt.

advis|ability [ədvaizə'biliti] tilrådelighet. **-able** [əd'vaizəbl] rådelig. **advis|e** [əd'vaiz] underrette (**of** om); råde; advisere, gi melding om; overlegge; — **with** rådføre seg med; **be advised** ta imot råd. **-edly** [əd'vaizidli] med vilje, med velberådd hug. **-edness** [əd'vaizidnès] betenksomhet. **-er** [əd-'vaizə] rådgiver; **legal** — juridisk konsulent. **-ory** [əd'vaizəri] rådgivende.

advocacy ['ädvokəsi] forsvar. **advocate** ['äd-vokét] talsmann; advokat, forsvarer; **Lord Advocate** (i Skottland) riksadvokat. **advocate** ['äd-vokeʲt] være talsmann for, forsvare. **advocateship** ['ädvokétʃip] advokatur, sakførsel; forsvar.

advowee [ädvau'i·] kirkepatron (med kallsrett). **advowson** [əd'vauzn] kallsrett.

adynamic [ädai'nämik] kraftløs, veik.

adytum ['äditəm] helligdom.

adz(e) [ädz] teksel, diksel, bøkkerøks.

aeger ['i·dʒə] sykeattest.

ægis ['id·ʒis] egide; skjold, vern.

Æneid ['i·niid, 'injid] Eneiden.

Æolian [i·oʷljən] eolisk; — **harp** eolsharpe.

æon ['i·ən] evighet.

aerate ['eʲəreʲt, 'æ·ʲreʲt] forbinde med kullsyre; **-d bread** kullsyrehevet brød; **Aerated Bread Company** selskap som driver **A.B.C.-shops**, billige restauranter; **-d water** kullsyreholdig vann.

aerial ['æ·ʲrial] luftig; eterisk; høy; lett; antenne. **aerial railway**, luftbane, ogs. løypestreng.

aerie ['æ·ʲri, 'iəri] ørnereir.

aeriform ['æ·ʲrifä·ʲm] luftformig. **aerify** ['æ·ʲ-rifai] forvandle til luft; forbinde med luft.

aero- ['ä·ʲro] i smstn. luft- (jfr. **air-**).

aerodrome ['æ·ʲrodroʷm] flyplass.

aerodynamics [æ·ʲrodai'nämiks] aerodynamikk.

aerofoil ['æ·ʲrofoil] aeroplans bæreflate.

aerogram ['æ·ʲrogräm] trådløst telegram.

aerogun ['æ·ʲrogʌn] antiluftkanon.

aerolite ['æ·ʲrolait] meteorstein.

aerology [æ·ʲ'rälədʒi] luftlære.

aerometer [æ·ʲ'rämitə] luftmåler.

aeronaut ['æ·ʲronä·t] luftskipper, flyver.

aeronautical [æ·ʲro'nä·tikl] som har med luftseilas å gjøre, luftfarts-.

aeronautics [æ·ʲro'nä·tiks] luftseilas, luftfart.

aeroplane ['æ·ʲropleʷn] flyvemaskin, fly.

aerostat ['æ·ʲrostät] luftballong.

aerostatics [æ·ʲro'stätiks] aerostatikk.

æruginous [iə'ru·dʒinəs] eiret, eir-. **ærugo** [iə'ru·goʷ] eir, irr.

'aery ['æ·ʲri] d. s. s. **aerie**.

Æsop ['i·sop] Æsop.

aesthete ['i·spi·t] estetiker. **aesthetic** [i·s'þetik] estetikk. **aesthetics** [i·s'þetiks] estetikk.

æstival [i·s'taivəl] sommer-, sommerlig.

afar [ə'fa·ʲ] fjernt, langt borte.

affability [äfə'biliti] vennlighet, nedlatenhet. **affable** ['äfəbl] omgjengelig, hyggelig; nedlatende.

affair [ə'fæ·ʲ] forretning, sak, greie, affære, anliggende, ting; fektning; **that is my** — det blir min sak.

affect [ə'fekt] strebe etter, virke på, angripe, affisere; berøre; like; affektere, hykle. **-ation** [äfek'teʲʃən] affektasjon; påtatt vesen. **-ed** affektert, kunstlet. **-ing** gripende.

affection [ə'fekʃən] affeksjon; sinnsbeskaffenhet; sinnsbevegelse; kjærlighet, godhug, hengivenhet; **demonstrative of** — som viser sin hengivenhet. **-ate** [ə'fekʃənet] kjærlig, hengiven; **Yours affectionately** Deres hengivne.

affiance [ə'faiəns] forlove; forlovelse.

affidavit [äfi'deʲvit] beediget erklæring.

affiliate [ə'filieʲt] ta til seg, knytte (**to** til). **affinity** [ə'finiti] svogerskap, slektskap; likhet.

affirm [ə'fə·m] påstå; bekrefte, sanne, stadfeste. **-ance** [-əns] stadfesting. **-ation** [äfə'meʲ-ʃən] bekreftelse; stadfesting, forsikring. **-ative** [ə'fə·mətiv] bekreftende; **in the** — bekreftende. **-atory** [ə'fə·mətəri] stadfestings-.

affix [ə'fiks] tilføye, feste, knytte til, vedføye. **afflict** [ə'flikt] bedrøve; hjemsøke, plage, tynge. **affliction** [ə'flikʃən] sorg, lidelse.

afflu|ence ['äfluəns] tilstrømning; overflod; rikdom. **-ent** ['äfluənt] overflødig; sideelv, tverr-elv.

affluks ['äflʌks] tilstrømning.

afford [ə'fä·ʲd] frambringe, yte, gi, levere; makte, greie, ha råd til: kunne selle (for en viss pris); **cannot** — it har ikke råd til det.

afforest [ə'färist] plante til med skog.

affranchise [ä'fräntʃaiz] frigjøre, gi fri.

affray [ə'freʲ] slagsmål, tumult, oppløp.

affright [ə'frait] skremme; skrekk, støkk.

affront [ə'frʌnt] fornærme; fornærmelse, krenking.

Afghan ['äfgän] afgansk. **-istan** [äf'gänistän] Afganistan.

afield [ə'fi·ld] i el. ut på marka, i felten; på villstrå.

afire [ə'faiə] i brann; **set** — stikke i brann.

aflame [ə'fleʲm] i flammer, i lys lue.

afloat [ə'floʷt] flott; ombord, til sjøs; i fart; i drift; i full gang.

afoot [ə'fut] til fots; i gjære, på beina, på ferde.

afore [ə'fä·ʲ] før; forut. **-mentioned** [-menʃənd] førnevnt. **-said** [-sed] førnevnt, bemeldt. **-thought** [-þå·t] overtenkt. **-time** [-taim] før i tiden.

a fortiori [eʲfä·ʲʃi'ärai] (latin) med så mye mer grunn, enn mer, så mye mer, ikke å tale om.

afraid [ə'freɪd] redd (**of** for); — **for** engstelig, bekymret for; — **of death** redd for å dø; — **of doing it** el. **to do it** redd for å gjøre det; — **for his life** redd for livet sitt.

afreet ['äfriːt] troll (i muhamedansk mytologi).

afresh [ə'freʃ] på ny, på nytt lag, igjen.

Afric ['äfrikə] Afrika.

African ['äfrikən] afrikansk; afrikaner.

Africander [äfri'kändə] afrikander (etterkommer av hollandske kolonister i Sør-Afrika).

aft [aːft] akter, akterut.

after ['aːftə] etter; etterat; baketter, senere. — **all** når alt kommer til alt; **in** — **times** senere. — **-ages** etterverdenen. — **-birth** etterbyrd. — **-body** akterskip. — **-clap** ettersmekk, etterspill. — **-damp** kullos (etter sprengning i gruve). — **-dinner speech** skåltale. **-glow** aftenrøde. — **-grass** hå, etterslått. — **-hours** fritid. **-math** ['aːftəmaˑþ] hå, etterslått. **-most** akterst. **-noon** [aːftə'nuˑn; i smstn. 'aːftənuˑn] ettermiddag. **-pains** etterveer. **-thought** tanke en kommer på senere (for sent). **-wards** ['aːftəwədz] baketter, etterpå, senere. **-wise** ['aːftəwaiz] bakklok, etterpåklok.

again [ə'geɪn, ə'gen] igjen, atter; på den andre siden; dessuten; **as much** — en gang til så mye; — **and** — gang på gang, om og om igjen; **now and** — nå og da; **ring** — gi gjenlyd, atterljom, lyde sterkt, ljome, drønne.

against [ə'geɪnst, ə'genst] mot, imot; bortimot (om tiden); **over** — like overfor.

agape [ə'geɪp] gapende, kopende.

agate ['ägət, 'ägit] agat.

agave [ə'geɪvi] agave.

age [eɪdʒ] alder, menneskealder, alderstrin; alderdom, tidsavsnitt; tidsalder, tid; hundreår; lang tid, evighet; **full** — myndighetsalderen (21 år); **be of** — være myndig; **come of** — bli myndig; **of an** — jamgamle; **under** — umyndig, mindreårig; **the Middle Ages** mellomalderen; **the present** — nåtiden; **I have not seen you for ages** jeg har ikke sett deg på lange tider, på år og dag.

aged [eɪdʒd] **twenty** 20 år gammel. **aged** ['eɪdʒid] gammel, tilårskommet.

agency ['eɪdʒənsi] virksomhet; middel; agentur; kontor; **Reuter's Agency** Reuters byrå.

agenda [ə'dʒendə] notisbok; dagsorden.

agent ['eɪdʒənt] agent, forretningsfører, fullmektig; virkemiddel.

agglomerate [ə'glåməreɪt] hauge opp, klumpe sammen, bli sammendynget, klumpe seg sammen.

agglomeration [əglåməˈreɪʃən] sammenhoping.

agglutinate [ə'gluˑtinét] sammenlimt; agglutinerende. [ə'gluˑtineɪt] lime sammen, klumpe i hop; bli til lim el. klister. **-ion** [əgluti'neɪʃən] sammenliming, agglutinasjon.

aggrandize ['ägrəndaiz] forstørre, utvide. **-ment** [ə'grändizmənt] forstørrelse, utvidelse.

aggravate ['ägrəveɪt] forverre; overdrive; ergre. **aggravating** ergerlig, harmelig. **aggravation** [ägrə'veɪʃən] forverrelse; overdrivelse.

aggregate ['ägrigeɪt] samle; samlet. ['ägrigét] samling, aggregat. **-ion** [ägri'geɪʃən] samling.

aggression [ə'greʃən] angrep. **-ive** [ə'gresiv] angripende, pågående. **-or** [ə'gresə] angriper.

aggrieved [ə'griˑvd] foruretet, krenket.

aghast [ə'gaːst] forferdet, forstøkt, fælen.

agile ['ädʒail] rask, kvikk, lett og ledig.

agility [ə'dʒiliti] raskhet.

Agincourt ['ädʒinkåˑət] Azincourt.

agio ['ädʒiouⁿ] agio.

agiotage ['ädʒətidʒ] børsspill, børsspekulasjoner.

agitate ['ädʒiteɪt] bevege, ryste; opphisse, skake opp; agitere; drøfte. **-ion** [ädʒi'teɪʃən] bevegelse; opphisselse, oppskaking. **-or** ['ädʒiteɪtə] agitator.

aglare [ə'glæˑə] strålende.

aglet ['äglit] dopp på frynse eller snor, aiguillette, dupp, adjutantsnor.

agley [ə'gliˑ] (skotsk) skjevt, galt, på skjeve.

aglow [ə'glouⁿ] glødende, i glo.

agnail ['ägneɪl] neglesvull; neglerot.

agnate ['ägneɪt] beslektet på farssiden; agnat.

agnation [äg'neɪʃən] slektskap på mannssiden.

Agnes ['ägniz] Agnes.

agnomen [äg'noᵘmən] oppnavn, utnavn.

agnostic [äg'nåstik] agnostisk; agnostiker.

agnosticism [äg'nåstisizm] agnostisisme.

ago [ə'gouⁿ] for... siden; **long** — for lenge siden.

agog [ə'gåg] ivrig, oppsatt (**on** på).

agone [ə'gån] for... siden.

agonize ['ägənaiz] pines, pine; **-d** forpint; **agonizing** pinefull.

agony ['ägəni] dødsangst, sjeleangst; kval, pine, smerte; — **column** avisspalte med lysing etter bortkomne venner og skyldfolk; **an** — **of tears** en fortvilet gråt.

agrarian [ə'græˑəriən] agrarisk; agrar.

agree [ə'griˑ] stemme overens; passe sammen; bli enig (**upon** om), være enig; gå med (**to** på). **-able** [-əbl] overensstemmende; behagelig. **-ably** [-əbli] i overensstemmelse, i samsvar (**to** med). **-ment** [-mənt] overensstemmelse, samsvar; forlik, overenskomst; **come to an -ment** slutte forlik.

agrestic [ə'grestik] landlig; bondsk, rå.

agricultur|al [ägri'kʌltʃərəl] jordbruks-. **-e** ['ägrikʌltʃə] jordbruk, landbruk. **-ist** [ägri-'kʌltʃərist] jordbruker, bonde, agronom.

aground [ə'graund] på grunn.

ague ['eɪgju] koldfeber; kuldegysning, kuls(ing).

ah [aː] ah! akk! **aha** [a'haˑ] aha!

Ahab ['eɪhäb] Akab.

Ahasuerus [ähäzju'iˑrəs] Ahasverus.

ahead [ə'hed] forut; fremad, fram, framover; **go** — gå på, klem i vei.

aheap [ə'hiˑp] i én haug, under ett.

ahoy [ə'hoi] ohoi!

aid [eɪd] hjelpe; hjelp, bistand, tilskudd; **by (the)** — of med hjelp av (el. fra), takket være. **aide-camp** ['eɪddəkâŋ] adjutant (hos general).

aigrette ['eɪgret] heire; hodepynt av fjær, blomster eller edelsteiner; fjærbusk.

aiguillette [eɪgwi'let] aiguillette, adjutantsnor.

ail [eɪl] plage; være syk, hangle. **what ails you?** hva feiler deg? **ailing** skrantende, skral, upasselig.

aileron ['eɪlərän] aileron, balanseror anbrakt på flyets bæreflater.

ailment ['eɪlmənt] illebefinnende, sykdom.

aim [eɪm] sikte (**at** på); trakte, strebe (**at** etter); sikte; mål, formål, hensikt.

aint [eɪnt] fk. f. **am not, is not, are not, have not, has not.**

air [æˑə] luft, luftning; lufte (ut), gi luft, tørke; **open** — fri luft; **castles in the** — luftkasteller; **take the** — trekke frisk luft; — **oneself** få seg frisk luft, gå (kjøre, ri) en tur.

air [æˑə] melodi, arie.

air [æˑə] mine, utseende; pl. **airs** viktig vesen; **give oneself airs** el. **put on airs** gjøre seg viktig, — **ball** leketøysballong. — **bladder** luftblære, svømmeblære. — **borne** flybåren. — **brake** vakuumsbremse. — **craft** luftskip, fly; — **cushion** luftpute. — **engine** luftmaskin.

Air Force: the Royal — luftvåpnet.

air-gun luftbørse.

air|ified luftig, høyttravende. **-iness** luftighet, letthet. **-ing** utflukt, spasertur. **-man** flyver.

Air Marshal flyvermarsjal (øverste leder av luftvåpnet).

airplane flyvemaskin, fly.

air|-pocket tilsynelatende tomrom i lufta, som gjør at flyet faller et stykke. — **port** lufthavn. — **-pump** luftpumpe. — **-raid** flyangrep. — **-raid alarm** flyalarm. — **-ship** luftskip. — **-spring** pnevmatisk bremse. — **-threads** kingelvev. — **-tight** lufttett. — **-trunk** ventilasjonsrør.

Air Vice-Marshal nest øverste leder av luftvåpnet.

airy luftig, lett, tom.

aisle [ail] sideskip (i en kirke); gang.

ait [eɪt] liten øy, holme (srl. i en elv).

ajar [ə'dʒɑ·ə] på klem, på gløtt.
akimbo [ə'kimbou] med hendene i siden.
akin [ə'kin] beslektet, skyldt (**to** med).
Alabama [ælə'bɑ·mə] Alabama.
alabaster ['æləbɑ·stə] alabast.
alack [ə'læk] akk!
alacrity [ə'lækriti] livlighet, sprekhet, djervskap.
alarm [ə'lɑ·əm] alarm; skrekk, angst; uro, bekymring; vekker (i et ur), vekkerur; alarmere; forurolige, uroe, engste, skremme; **give the —** gjøre anskrik; **take** (el. catch) **—** bli urolig.
alarm-|bell alarmklokke. **— -clock** vekkerur.
alarum [ə'lærəm] vekkerur.
alas [ə'lɑ·s] akk! dessverre!
alb [ælb] (katolsk) messeserk.
Albania [əl'beinjə] Albania. **-n** albaner, albansk.
albatross ['ælbətrɔs] albatross.
albeit [ɔl'bi·it] enskjønt.
albert ['ælbət] kort klokkekjede.
Albert ['ælbət] Albert.
albinism ['ælbinizm] albinisme.
albino [æl'bi·nou] albino.
Albion ['ælbjən] Albion, England.
album ['ælbəm] stambok; album.
albumen [æl'bju·mən] eggehvite.
alchem|ist ['ælkimist] alkymist. **-istic** [ælki'mistik] alkymistisk. **-y** ['ælkimi] alkymi, gullmakeri.
alcohol ['ælkəhɔl] alkohol. **-ic** [ælkə'hɔlik] alkoholisk, alkoholholdig. **-ism** ['ælkəhɔlizm] alkoholisme. **-ization** [ælkəhɔlai'zeiʃən] alkoholisering. **-ize** ['ælkəhɔlaiz] alkoholisere. **-ometer** ['ælkəhɔ'lɔmitə] alkoholometer.
alcove ['ælkouv] alkove, kleve; lysthus.
alder [ɔ'ldə] older, or.
alderman [ɔ'ldəmən] rådmann, formannskapsmedlem.
Aldershot ['ɔ·ldəʃɔt] Aldershot.
Aldgate ['ɔ·ldg(e)it] Aldgate.
Aldwych [ɔ·ldwitʃ] Aldwych.
ale [e'l] (engelsk) øl.
a-lee [ə'·i] i le.
alembic [ə'lembik] destillerkolbe.
alert [ə'lə·t] rask, årvåken; alarm, flyalarm; **on the —** på post.
Alexandria [æleg'zɑ·ndriə] Alexandria. **alexandrine** [ælig'zɑ·ndrain] aleksandriner.
alfa ['ælfə] alfagras.
alga ['ælgə] alge; **freshwater alga** grønske; **sea** (el. **maritime**) **alga** tang og tare (pl. **algæ**).
algebra ['ældʒibrə] algebra.
Algeria [æl'dʒiəriə] Algerie.
Algiers [æl'dʒiəz] Alger.
alias ['eiljəs] alias, ellers; falsk navn.
alibi ['ælibai] alibi.
Alice ['ælis] Alice.
alien ['eiljən] fremmed, utenlandsk; utlending, innflytter. **-able** [-əbl] avhendelig. **-ate** [-e't] avhende; skille seg med; støte fra seg. **-ation** [e'ljə'neiʃən] avhending; **— of mind** galskap.
alight [ə'lait] stige ned, stige av (hesten), stige ut av (vognen); dale, falle ned.
alight [ə'lait] opplyst; i brann.
align [ə'lain] stille opp i linje.
alike [ə'laik] på samme måte, ens, i samme grad, like mye.
aliment ['ælimənt] næring, føde; underholdningsbidrag. **alimental** [æli'mentl] nærende. **alimentary** [æli'mentəri] nærings-. **alimentation** [ælimen'teiʃən] næring; ernæring.
alimony ['æliməni] underhold(ningsbidrag).
aline se **align.**
alive [ə'laiv] i live, levende; mottagelig; oppmerksom; yrende full; **look — rapp deg.**
alkal|escent [ælkə'lesənt] lett alkalisk. **-i** ['ælkəlai] alkali. **-ine** ['ælkəlain] alkalisk. **-oid** ['ælkəlɔid] alkaloid.
Alkoran [ælkɑ'rɑ·n] koranen.
all [ɔ·l] all, hel; helt; ganske, aldeles; alt; **it is — one** det kommer ut på ett; **above —** framfor alt; **after —** når alt kommer til alt; **at — i**

det hele tatt; **first of — først** og fremst; **not at — slett** ikke; ingen årsak; **— about** overalt; **— the same** likevel; **it is — the same to me** det er det samme for meg; **— but** nesten; **på . . . . .** nær; **— day, — the day** hele dagen; **— at once** med en eneste gang; **— of us** alle vi; **be — that is amiable** være ytterst elskverdig; **be — affability** være lutter elskverdighet; **— over** overalt (i); **by — means** framfor alt, endelig; **— right i** orden, ferdig; riktig; ja vel; det er godt; **I am — right** jeg har det godt; **— that** alt det som; **— the better** så mye bedre; **with — his eyes** med store øyne; alt hva han kunne.
Allah ['ælə] Allah.
allay [ə'lei] dempe, lindre; legge seg, stilne av.
all-clear ['ɔ·l'kliə] avblåsing av flyalarm, faren over.
allege [ə'ledʒ] anføre; hevde; vise til.
Alleghany [ə'ligeini] Allegany.
allegiance [ə'li·dʒəns] troskap, lydighet.
allegor|ic(al) [æligɔ·rik(l)] allegorisk. **-ize** ['æligɔraiz] forklare el. framstille allegorisk; allegorisere. **-y** ['æligəri] allegori.
allegr|etto [æli'gretou] allegretto. **-o** [ə'le'grou] allegro.
alleviate [ə'li·vie't] lette, lindre.
alleviation [əlivi'eiʃən] lettelse, lindring.
alley ['æli] allé; smug; **skittle-alley** kilebane.
alley-tor ['æli'tɔ·ə] kiksekule.
All Fools' Day 1. april.
alliance [ə'laiəns] forbund, forbindelse, allianse; giftermål; slektskap, svogerskap.
allied [ə'laid, (attributivt) 'ælaid] alliert.
alligation [æli'geiʃən] forbindelse, legering.
alligator ['æligeitə] alligator, kaiman.
alliterat|e [ə'litərei't] allitterere. **-ion** [əlitə'reiʃən] alliterasjon.
allocution [ælo'kju·ʃən] tale, henvendelse.
allodi|al [ə'loudiəl] odels-; **— farm** odelsgård; **— law** odelsrett. **-um** [-əm] odel, odelsjord.
allot [ə'lɔt] tildele ved lott; dele ut; skifte ut; tilstå, skjenke. **-ment** [-mənt] tildeling ved lott; del; lott; tilskikkelse; jordlott, parsell.
allow [ə'lau] tillate; innrømme; tilstå; gi; godkjenne, ta til følge; **— for ta** omsyn til; **be allowed** få lov til, ha lov til. **-able** [-əbl] tillatelig; rettmessig. **-ance** [-əns] innrømmelse; tilståelse; det som innrømmes til underhold; rasjon, porsjon; lønn; rabatt.
alloy [ə'lɔi] legering, tilsetning; blande.
All Saints' Day helgemess, allehelgensdag (1. november).
All Souls' Day allesjelesdag (2. november).
allspice ['ɔ·lspais] allehånde.
allude [ə'lju·d] hentyde, alludere (**to** til), ymte (**to** om), slå (**to** på).
allure [ə'ljuə] lokke; forlokke. **-ment** [-mənt] tillokking; lokkemiddel, lokkemat.
allusion [ə'lju·ʒən] hentydning, ymt, allusjon.
allusive [ə'lju·siv] hentydende, ymtende.
alluvial [ə'lju·vjəl] oppskylt, alluvial.
ally [ə'lai] forbinde, forene, alliere; ['ælai] forbundsfelle, alliert.
Almack's ['ælmæks] selskapslokale i London.
almanac(k) ['ɔ·lmənæk] almanakk.
almighty [ɔ·l'maiti] allmektig.
almond ['ɑ·mənd] mandel.
almoner ['ælmənə, 'ɑ·mnə] almisse-utdeler.
almost ['ɔ·lmoust] nesten.
alms [ɑ·mz] (pl. = sg.) almisse.
almshouse ['ɑ·mzhaus] fattighus.
aloe ['ælou] aloë.
aloft [ə'lɔ·ft] høyt, i været; til værs.
alone [ə'loun] alene; **let me — ta** la meg være; **let — enn** si, for ikke å tale om.
along [ə'lɔŋ] langs, langs med; av sted, fram; **all — hele** veien, hele tiden, helt igjennom; **come — kom** med! kom nå! **— with sammen** med, med.
alongside [ə'lɔŋsaid] side om side.
aloof [ə'lu·f] på avstand, langt borte, reservert.

aloud [ə'laud] lytt, høyt; **read** — lese høyt.
alp [älp] berg; **the Alps** Alpene.
alpen|horn ['älpenhå·°n] lur; **-stock**[-ståk] -alpestokk, fjellstav.
alpestrian [äl'pestriən] fjellklatrer.
alpha ['älfə] alfa.
alphabet ['älfəbet] alfabet; ordne etter alfabet. **-ic(al)** [älfə'betik(l)] alfabetisk.
Alpine ['älpain] alpe-.
already [å·l'redi] allerede, alt.
Alsace ['älsäs] Alsace.
also ['å·lsoᵘ] også, og, au.
altar ['å·ltə] alter. **-piece** altertavle.
alter['å·ltə] forandre, endre, brigde, forandre seg. **-able** foranderlig. **-ability** [ältərə'biliti] foranderlighet. **-ation** [ältè're'ʃən] forandring.
altercate ['ältəke't] kives, trette.
altercation [ältə'ke'ʃən] trette, ordstrid.
alternate ['ältəne't, 'å·lt-] alternere, skifte, veksle, avveksle; skiftes.
alternate [äl'tə·nèt, ält-], vekselvis, gjensidig; — **angles** vekselvinkler; **on** — **nights** hverannen aften.
altern|ately [äl'tə·nitli] skiftevis; **-ateness** avveksling. **-ation** [ältə'ne'ʃən, ält-] omskifting, avveksling. **-ative** [äl'tə·nətiv, ält-] vekslende; alternativ; valg; **there was no -ative left to us** vi hadde ikke noen annen utvei.
althea [äl'þi·ə] altea, vill kattost.
although [å·l'öoᵘ] skjønt, enskjønt, uaktet.
altitude ['ältitju·d] høyde.
alto ['ältoᵘ] alt (stemme).
altogether [å(·)ltə'geðə] aldeles, ganske; i det hele tatt.
altruism ['ältruizm] altruisme, uegennytte.
altruist ['ältruist] altruist. **altruistic, altruistically** altruistisk.
alum ['äləm] alun.
aluminium [älju'minjəm] aluminium.
aluminous [ə'lju·minəs] alunaktig, alunholdig.
always ['å·lwiz] alltid, støtt.
am [äm, əm] 1. person presens av **to be; I** — jeg er; **I** — **to say nothing** jeg skal ikke si noe; **I** — **not one to** (med infinitiv) jeg hører ikke til dem . . .
A. M. ['e''em] fk. f. **anno mundi** (i året . . .) etter verdens skapelse; (i Skottland) **Master of Arts** (egl. artium magister; i England: M. A.); **ante meridiem** ['änti mi'ridjəm] før middag, om formiddagen.
amadou ['ämədu·] knusk.
amain [ə'me'n] av alle krefter, av all makt.
amalgam [ə'mälgəm] amalgam. **-ate** [-e't] amalgamere, blande, blande seg. **-ation** [əmälgə'me'ʃən] amalgamasjon. **-ator** [ə'mälgəme'tə] sammensmelter.
amanuens|is [əmänju'ensis] pl. **-es** [-i·z] privatsekretær, skriver, amanuensis.
amaranth ['äməränþ] amarant.
amass [ə'mäs] dynge sammen, hauge opp, samle.
amateur ['ämətə·] kunstelsker, dilettant, amatør; **he is an** — **musician** han dyrker musikk; — **photographer** amatørfotograf.
amative ['ämətiv] erotisk.
amaze [ə'me'z] forbause, forstøkke. **-ment** [-mənt] bestyrtelse, forbauselse, undring.
amazon ['äməzən] amasone.
ambassador [äm'bäsədə] ambassadør.
amber ['ämbə] rav. **-gris** ['ämbəgri·s] ambra.
ambidexter ['ämbi'deksta] som bruker begge hender like godt; som heller til begge sider.
ambient ['ämbjənt] omgivende, omsluttende.
ambiguity [ämbi'gju·iti] tvetydighet.
ambiguous [äm'bigjuəs] tvetydig, dunkel.
ambition [äm'biʃən] ærgjerrighet. **ambitious** [äm'biʃəs] ærgjerrig; begjærlig (of etter).
amble ['ämbl] passgang; gå (el. ri) i passgang.
ambler ['ämblə] passgjenger.
ambulance ['ämbjuləns] ambulanse.
ambulatory ['ämbjulətəri] vandrende, flakkende, omgangs-.

ambuscade [ämbə'ske'd] = **ambush** ['ämbuʃ] bakhold, ligge (legge) i bakhold.
ameer [ə'miə] emir.
ameliorate [ə'mi·ljəre't] bedre, forbedre.
amelioration [ə'mi·ljə're'ʃən] forbedring, bedring.
amen ['a·'men, e''men] amen.
amenable [ə'mi·nəbl] ansvarlig; medgjørlig; — **to reason** mottagelig for fornuft. **amenability** [əmi·nə'biliti] ansvarlighet; føyelighet.
amend [ə'mend] rette på, forbedre; endre; forbedre seg. **-able** [-əbl] forbederlig. **-ment** [-mənt] forbedring; endring, endringsforslag.
amends [ə'mendz] erstatning, oppreisning; skadebot; **make** — **for** gjøre godt igjen.
amenity [ə'meniti] behagelighet, skjønnhet.
amerce [ə'mə·s] idømme en bot, mulktere. **-ment** [-mənt] pengebot, mulkt.
America [ə'merikə] Amerika.
American [ə'merikən] amerikansk; amerikaner.
Americanism [ə'merikənizm] amerikanisme.
amethyst ['ämiþist] ametyst.
AMGOT, fk. f. **Allied Military Government of Occupied Territory** alliert militærstyre av besatt område.
amiability [e'mjə'biliti] elskverdighet.
amiable ['e'mjəbl] elskverdig.
amicable ['ämikəbl] vennskapelig; fredelig.
amice ['ämis] (prests) skulderklede, akselklede.
amid [ə'mid], **amidst** [-st] midt; midt iblant.
amir [ə'miə] emir.
amiss [ə'mis] uriktig; feil; **not** — ikke av veien; **to do** — handle uriktig.
amity ['ämiti] vennskap.
ammonia [ə'moᵘnjə] ammoniakk.
ammunition [ämju'niʃən] ammunisjon. — **boots** militærstøvler.
amnesty ['ämnisti] amnesti.
among [ə'mʌn], **amongst** [-st] iblant, blant.
amoral [ä'märəl] amoralsk.
amorous ['ämərəs] forelsket; som lett blir forlibt; kjærlighets-.
amortizable [ə'må·°tizəbl] amortisabel.
amortization [ə'må·°ti'ze'ʃən] amortisasjon.
amortize [ə'må·°tiz] amortisere.
amount [ə'maunt] beløp, mål, sum; beløpe seg, stige; bety; **this** — **of confidence** denne store tillit; — **to** beløpe seg til.
ampere [äm'pæ·ə] ampère.
ampersand [ämpə'sänd] tegnet &.
amphibious [äm'fibjəs] amfibisk. **amphibium** [äm'fibjəm], pl. **amphibia** [äm'fibiə] amfibium.
amphitheatre [ämfi'þi·ətə] amfiteater. **amphitheatrical** [ämfiþi'ätrikl] amfiteatralsk.
amphora ['ämfərə] amfora.
ample ['ämpl] vid, stor, utførlig; rikelig, drus, raust. **amplification** [ämplifi'ke'ʃen] utviding; utførlig skildring. **amplify** ['ämplifai] utvide; øke; være vidløftig; forøkes.
amplitude ['ämplitju·d] vidde, utstrekning; evne; amplityde.
ampulla [äm'pʌlə] ampulle.
amputate ['ämpjute't] amputere.
amputation [ämpju'te'ʃən] amputasjon.
amuck [ə'mʌk] amok.
amulet ['ämjulet] amulett.
amuse [ə'mju·z] more, underholde; oppholde (med løfter). **-ment** [-mənt] underholdning, morskap, fornøyelse. **amusing** [ə'mju·ziŋ] underholdende, morsom.
an [än, ən] (ubestemt artikkel) en, et.
anabaptism [änə'bäptizm] anabaptisme.
anabaptist [änə'bäptist] anabaptist.
anabasis [ə'näbəsis] anabasis.
anachronism [ə'näkronizm] anakronisme. **anachronistic** [ənäkro'nistik] anakronistisk.
anaconde [änə'kåndə] anakonda.
anacreontic [änäkri'åntik] anakreontisk.
anæmia [ə'ni·mjə] anemi, blodmangel.
anæmic [ə'ni·mik] anemisk.
analog|ic(al) [änə'lådʒik(l)] analogisk. **-ism**

[ə'nälodʒism] analogisk slutning. **-ous** [ə'näləgəs] analog. **-y** [ə'nälədʒi] analogi, overensstemmelse.

analy|se ['änəlaiz] analysere. **-sis** [ə'nälisis] analyse. **-tic** [änə'litik] analytisk.

ananas [ə'na·nəs] ananas.

anarchic(al) [ə'na·ᵒkik(l)] anarkisk, lovløs.

anarchist ['änaᵒkist] anarkist.

anarchy ['änaᵒki] anarki.

anathema [ə'näþimə] bann; forbannelse. **ana-thematize** [ə'näþimətaiz] bannlyse.

anatomic(al) [änə'tåmik(l)] anatomisk.

anatomist [ə'nätəmist] anatom.

anatomy [ə'nätəmi] anatomi; skjelett.

ancestor ['änsistə] stamfar; (pl.) forfedre, aner. **ancestral** [än'sestrəl] fedrene, nedarvet. **— estate** fedregård. **ancestry** ['änsistri] aner; ætt, herkomst, byrd.

anchor ['äŋkə] anker; ankre; **drop —** kaste anker; **weigh —** lette anker. **-age** ['äŋkərėdʒ] ankerplass; avgift.

anchoret ['äŋkərėt] anakoret, eremitt, eneboer.

anchovy [än'tʃoᵘvi] ansjos.

ancient ['eᶦnʃənt] gammel, fra gamle tider; **the -s** de gamle, folk i oldtiden.

and [änd, ən] og.

andante [än'dänti] andante.

andiron ['ändaiən] bukk (til et stekespidd).

Andrew ['ändru·] Andreas. **St. Andrew's cross** andreaskors: ×.

anecdote ['änekdoᵘt] anekdote.

anemia [ə'ni·mjə] anemi.

anemone [ə'neməni] anemone; symre. **blue —** blåveis; **white —** hvitveis.

anent [ə'nent] likeoverfor; angående, om.

anew [ə'nju·] på ny, på nytt.

anfractuosity [änfräktju'ásiti] buktning, krok.

angel [ᵉ'ndʒəl] engel.

angelic [än'dʒelik] engleaktig, engle-.

angelus ['ändʒiləs] angelus, angelusklokke.

anger ['äŋgə] vrede, sinne; gjøre sint.

angina [än'dʒainə] angina.

angle ['äŋgl] vinkel.

angle ['äŋgl] angel; fiske med snøre, angle.

angler ['äŋglə] fisker, stangfisker.

Angles ['äŋglz] angler (folkenavn).

Anglican ['äŋglikən] som hører til den engelske statskirke, høykirkelig. **Anglicanism** ['äŋgli-kənizm] anglikanisme. **anglicism** ['äŋglisizm] anglisisme. **anglicize** ['äŋglisaiz] anglisere.

Anglo-Norse Society norsk-britisk forening.

Anglo-Norwegian engelsk-norsk.

Anglo-Indian engelskmann i India.

Anglo-Saxon ['äŋgloᵘ-'säksən] angelsaksisk; angelsakser.

angry ['äŋgri] vred, sint (**at** over, **with** på).

anguish ['äŋgwiʃ] angst, kval, pine, smerte.

angular ['äŋgjulə] vinkeldannet; kantet. **-ity** [äŋgju'läriti] kantethet. **angulate** [-lėt] kantet.

aniline ['änilain] anilin.

animadversion [äniməd'və·ʃən] irettesetting, dadel. **animadvert** [äniməd'və·t] dadle, laste.

animal ['äniməl] dyr; dyrisk; **the — kingdom** dyreriket; **— spirits** livskraft.

animate ['änime't] besjele, gjøre levende, oppildne, animere. **-d** ivrig, livlig.

animate ['änimėt] levende.

animation [äni'meᶦʃən] levendegjøring; liv.

animosity [äni'måsiti] hat, fiendskap, heftig uvilje. **animus** ['äniməs] ånd; uvilje, agg, nag.

anise ['änis] anis. **aniseed** ['änisi·d] anis (frukten). **anisette** [äni'zet] anislikør.

anker ['äŋkə] anker (som mål); kagge, dunk.

ankle ['äŋkl] ankel.

ankus ['äŋkəs] piggstav (til elefant).

annals ['änəlz] årbøker, annaler.

Anne [än] Anna.

anneal [ə'ni·l] utgløde (om metall); avkjøle (om glass); herde.

annex [ə'neks] knytte til; legge ved; forene,

annektere. **-ation** [änek'se'ʃən] tilknytting, vedlegging; forening, innlemming.

annex(e) ['äneks] anneks, tilbygg; tillegg, bilag.

annihilate [ə'naiəle't] tilintetgjøre. **annihilation** [ənaiə'le'ʃən] tilintetgjøring.

anniversary [äni'və·səri] årsdag, årsfest; årlig. **Anno Domini** ['änoᵘ 'dåminai] Anno Domini.

annot|ate ['änote't] skrive merknader til. **-ation** [äno'te'ʃən] anmerkning, merknad.

announce [ə'nauns] forkynne, tilkjennegi, melde, kunngjøre, gjøre kjent. **-ment** [-mənt] tilkjennegivelse, bekjentgjørelse, kunngjøring. **-r** hallomann (i radio).

annoy [ə'noi] plage, bry; erte, ergre; irritere; sjenere, forulempe. **-ance** [-əns] plage; bry. **annoyed** fortredelig, misnøyd.

annual ['änjuəl] årlig.

annuitant [ä'nju·itənt] livrenteeier, pensjonist. **annuity** [ä'nju·iti] livrente.

annul [ə'nʌl] tilintetgjøre, oppheve, annullere.

annular ['änjulə] ringformet, ring-.

annulated ['änjule'tid] forsynt med ringer.

annulment [ə'nʌlmənt] opphevelse, annullering.

annum ['änəm] år; **per —** om året.

annunciation [ənʌnsi'e'ʃən] bebudelse; **the A.** Marias budskapsdag, maria-messe (25. mars). **annunciator** [ə'nʌnsie'tə] forkynner; nummertavle.

anode ['änoᵘd] anode, positiv pol.

anodyne ['änodain] smertestillende; smertestillende middel.

anoint [ə'noint] salve. **-ment** [-mənt] salving.

anomalous [ə'nåmələs] uregelmessig, uregelrett, avvikende. **anomaly** [ə'nåməli] anomali, uregelmessighet, avvik.

anon [ə'nån] snart, straks, øyeblikkelig; **ever and —** nå og da; i ett vekk.

anon. fk. f. anonymous.

anonymity [äno'nimiti] anonymitet.

anonymous [ə'nåniməs] unevnt, anonym.

anormal [ə'nå·ᵒməl] anormal.

another [ə'nʌðə] en annen, en ny; en til, enda en; **one —** hinannen, hverandre; **many — battle** mange flere slag; **you are an Englishman, . . . I am another** De er engelskmann, . . . det er jeg også.

answer ['a·nsə] svar; svare; svare seg; svare på, besvare; svare til; stå til ansvar for; **in —** to som svar på; **— to the name of** lyde navnet; **— the bell** lukke opp når det ringer; **— the helm** lystre roret; **— for** svare for, innestå for.

answerable ['ansərəbl] ansvarlig.

ant [änt] maur.

antagon|ism [än'tägənizm] strid, motsetningsforhold. **-ist** [än'tägənist] motstander. **-ize** [än'tägənaiz] motvirke, motarbeide; støte fra seg, pådra seg fiendskap hos.

antarctic [än'ta·ᵒktik] antarktisk, sydpols-.

ant-bear ['äntbæ·ə] maurbjørn.

ante ['änti] foran, før. **-act** [-äkt] foregående handling. **-cedence** [änti'si·dəns] det å gå forut; presedens. **-cedent** [änti'si·dənt] foregående; det foregående. **-cessor** [änti'sesə] forgjenger; tidligere eier. **-chamber** ['äntitʃe'mbə] forværelse. **-date** ['äntide't] oppgi for tidlig datum for, gå forut for, foregripe. **-diluvian** [äntidi'lju·vjən] antediluviansk.

antelope ['äntiloᵘp] antilope.

antemeridian ['äntimi·ridjən] før middag.

ante meridiem ['änti mi'ridjəm] før middag, om formiddagen.

antemundane [änti'mʌnde'n] som var før verden ble skapt.

antenna [än'tenə] pl. **-ae** [-i·] følehorn; antenne.

antepenult(imate) ['äntipi'nʌlt(imit)] tredje siste staving.

anterior [än'tiəriə] foregående, tidligere.

anteroom ['äntiru(·)m] forværelse.

anthem ['änþem] kirkesang; hymne; **the national —** nasjonalsangen.

ant-hill ['änthil] maurtue.

anthology [än'þålədʒi] antologi.
Anthony ['äntəni]; **St. -'s fire** rosen.
anthracite ['änþrəsait] antrasitt.
anthropology [änþro'pålədʒi] antropologi.
anti ['änti] imot, mot. **anti-aircraft** luftvern.
Antichrist ['äntikraist] Antikrist.
anticipate [än'tisipe't] antesipere, foregripe; forutføle; glede seg til.
anticipation [äntisi'pe'ʃən] antesipering, foregriping; forutfølelse, forsmak, forutnyting.
antics ['äntiks] narrestreker, krumspring.
antidotal ['äntido"tl] som inneholder motgift.
antidote ['äntido"t] motgift.
Antilles [än'til(i·)z]: **the —** Antillene.
antimacassar [äntimə'käsə] antimakassar.
antimony ['äntiməni] antimon.
antipathetic [äntipə'þetik] antipatisk.
antipathy [än'tipəþi] antipati.
antiphony [än'tifəni] vekselsang.
antipodal [än'tipodəl] antipodisk, motsatt.
antipodes [än'tipodi·z] antipoder; motsetning.
antiquarian [änti'kwæ·°riən] om angår oldgransking. **antiquarianism** interesse for oldsaker.
antiquary ['äntikwəri] oldgransker.
antiquated ['äntikwe'tid] antikvert, foreldet.
antique [än'ti·k] fra oldtiden, antikk; gammeldags; kunstverk fra oldtiden.
antiquity [än'tikwiti] elde; oldtid; antikvitet.
anti-Semite [änti'si·mait] antisemitt. **anti-Semitic** [äntisi'mitik] antisemittisk. **anti-Semitism** [änti'semitizm] antisemittisme.
antiseptic [änti'septik] antiseptisk.
antithesis [än'tiþisis] motsetning, antitese.
antitype ['äntitaip] motbilde, den til bildet svarende virkelighet.
antler ['äntlə] hjortetakk, takk på horn.
anvil ['änvil] ambolt.
anxiety [äŋ'zaiiti] iver; engstelse, uro.
anxious ['äŋkʃəs] ivrig (**for** etter; **to do** etter å gjøre); engstelig, urolig (**about** for); engstende, urovekkende.
any ['eni] noen, noen som helst, hvilken som helst; enhver, enhver som helst; **hardly —** nesten ingen; **at — rate** i hvert fall; **— way** på noen måte, i hvert fall; **— longer** lenger; **— more** mer. **-body** [-bådi] noen, noen som helst; enhver, enhver som helst; hvem som helst; **-how** [-hau] på enhver el. noen som helst måte, i ethvert tilfelle; **-one** [-wʌn] noen som helst; enhver som helst; **— one** en (hvilken som helst) enkelt; **-thing** [-þiŋ] noe; alt (**anything but** alt annet enn); **-way** [-we'] på noen måte; på hvilken som helst måte; i ethvert tilfelle; **-where** [-hwæ·ə] hvor som helst, alle steder, overalt; **-wise** [-waiz] på noen måte.
Anzac ['änzäk] fk. f. **Australian and New Zealand Army Corps**; (soldat) i hæren fra Australia el. New Zealand.
aorta [e'¹å·tə] aorta.
apace [ə'pe's] rask, snøgg, hurtig.
Apache [ä'pätʃi] apasjeindianer.
apache [ə'pa·ʃ] apasje, utskudd og forbrytere i Paris' underverden.
apanage se appanage.
apart [ə'pa·°t] avsides, avsondret; atskilt fra hverandre; **— from** bortsett fra.
apartment [ə'pa·°tmənt] værelse, rom; **-s** leilighet; husvære; **-house** leiehus (hus med mange leiligheter med visse ting felles).
apathetic [äpə'þetik] følelsesløs, kald; sløv.
apathy ['äpəþi] apati.
ape [e'p] ape; etteraper; ape, ape etter, herme.
apeak [ə'pi·k] (rett) opp og ned.
Apennines [ä'pinainz]; **the —** Apenninene.
aperient [ə'piəriənt] avføringsmiddel. **aperitive** [ə'peritiv] avføringsmiddel.
aperture ['äpətʃə] åpning; hull.
apex ['e'peks] topp, spiss, høgd.
aphasia [ä'fe'ziə] afasi.
aphis ['äfis] bladlus.

aphorism ['äfərizm] aforisme.
aphoristic [äfə'ristik] aforistisk.
apia|n ['e'piən] bie-. **-rian** [e'pi'æ·°riən] birøkter. **-ry** ['e'piəri] bigård, bikube.
apiece [ə'pi·s] for stykket; til hver person, hver.
apish ['e'piʃ] ape-; etterapende; narraktig.
apocalypse [ə'påkəlips] åpenbaring.
apocope [ə'påkəpi] apokope.
apogee ['äpodʒi] punkt fjernest fra jorda; høyde, topp.
apollinaris [əpåli'næ·°ris] apollinaris.
apolog|etic [əpålə'dʒetik] forsvarende, unnskyldende. **-etically** [əpålə'dʒetikəli] til sin unnskyldning, unnskyldende. **-ize** [ə'pålədʒaiz] gjøre unnskyldning. **-y** [ə'pålədʒi] forsvar, unnskyldning; surrogat, nødhjelp, som skal gjelde for.
apophthegm ['äpoþem] fyndord, tankespråk.
apoplectic [äpə'plektik] apoplektisk.
apoplexy ['äpəpleksi] apopleksi.
aport [ə'på·°t] babord.
apostasy [ə'påstəsi] frafall. **apostate** [ə'påstet] apostat, frafallen.
a posteriori ['eipåsteri'å·rai] a posteriori.
apostle [ə'påsl] apostel. **apostolic** [äpo'stålik] apostolisk.
apostrophe [ə'påstrəfi] apostrof; apostrofe. **apostrophize** [ə'påstrəfaiz] apostrofere.
apothecary [ə'påþikəri] apoteker (som også har lov til å ordinere medisin); **-'s shop** apotek.
apotheosis [äpoþi'o"sis] apoteose.
appal(l) [ə'på·l] forskrekke, skremme, forferde.
appanage ['äpənidʒ] appanasje.
apparatus [äpə're'təs] apparat, innretning, hjelpemidler, hjelperåder; apparatsamling; **teaching —** skolemateriell.
apparel [ə'äpərəl] kledning, drakt; klede; kle.
apparent [ə'pæ·°rənt, ə'pärənt] øyensynlig; tilsynelatende; **heir —** nærmeste arving; tronarving. **-ly** tilsynelatende; øyensynlig.
apparition [äpə'riʃən] tilsynekomst; syn, skikkelse; gjenferd, skrømt.
appeal [ə'pi·l] berope seg på; appellere, innanke (**to** til); henvendelse; appell; innanking, anke, kjæremål; **— to the country** (appellere til velgerne ved å) skrive ut nye valg.
appealable [ə'pi·ləbl] appellabel.
appear [ə'piə] vise seg, komme fram; komme ut (om en bok); bli tydelig, finnes; stå (i en avis); synes, forekomme. **-ance** [ə'piərəns] tilsynekomst, framkomst, opptreden; nærvær, tilstedeværelse; møte (for retten); syn, åpenbaring; utseende; skinn, sannsynlighet; **make one's —** vise seg, tre inn, komme til stede; **put in an —** komme til stede, møte; **save -s** redde skinnet; **judge from —** dømme etter utseendet; **keep up -s with** holde gode miner til; **to all —** etter alt å dømme.
appease [ə'pi·z] berolige, formilde, forsone, dempe, døyve, stille.
appell|ant [ə'pelənt] appellant. **-ation** [äpe-'le'ʃən] benevnelse. **-ative** [ə'pelətiv] felles-; fellesnavn, appellativ. **-ee** [äpe'li·] innstevnte.
append [ə'pend] henge på, feste ved, tilføye. **-age** [ə'pendidʒ] vedheng, tillegg, underbruk (**under** to). **-ant** [ə'pendənt] som følger med. **-icitis** [əpendi'saitis] blindtarmbetennelse. **-ix** [ə'pendiks] bilag, tillegg; vedheng; **the vermiform —** blindtarmens ormeformede vedheng.
appertain [äpə'te'n] tilhøre.
appetence, appetency ['äpitəns, -si] begjær, lyst.
appetise ['äpitaiz] gi appetitt. **appetising** appetittlig, fristende. **appetite** ['äpitait] begjærlighet, begjær, lyst, hug; appetitt.
applaud [ə'plå·d] klappe i hendene, applaudere; rose, prise. **applause** [ə'plå·z] applaus, bifall; ros.
apple ['äpl] eple; **— of the eye** øyeeple; øyestein; **— of discord** stridens eple. **— dumpling** eple bakt i deig. **— -pie bed** seng med laken lagt dobbelt, så en ikke kan få strakt ut beina.

— **-pie** order fullkommen orden. — **-sauce** eplemos.
appli|able [ə'plaiəbl] anvendelig. **-ance** [ə'plaiəns] anvendelse; innretning, redskap.
applic|ability [äplikə'biliti] anvendelighet. **-able** ['äplikəbl] anvendelig. **-ant** ['äplikənt] ansøker; reflekterende. **-ation** [äpli'keɪʃən] anbringelse; omslag; søknad; flid; åndsanstrengelse. **-ative** ['äplikeɪtiv] anvendelig, praktisk. **-atory** ['äplikətəri] utøvende.
applied [ə'plaid] anvendt. — **art** brukskunst.
apply [ə'plai] sette el. legge på, anbringe; bruke; anvende; (hen)vende seg (**to** til); søke; passe (**to** på); — **for** søke; — **oneself to** legge seg etter; — **to me for help** be meg om hjelp; — **myself to her assistance** tilby henne min hjelp.
appoint [ə'point] bestemme, fastsette; ansette, utnevne; anvise; utruste. **-ee** [əpoin'ti·] (den) utnevnte. **-ment** [ə'pointmənt] bestemmelse, avtale, anordning, tilvising; utnevning; ansettelse, oppnevning; foranstaltning; avtale; forslag; utrustning, utstyr; lønning; **by** — etter avtale; **purveyor by** — hoffleverandør; **when you make an** — **keep it** når du gjør en avtale, så hold den.
apportion [ə'pɔ·əʃən] fordele; tilmåle. **-ment** [-mənt] fordeling; tilmåling.
apposite ['äpozit] passende, skikket.
apposition [äpo'ziʃən] tillegg, økning; apposisjon.
appraise [ə'preɪz] vurdere, taksere.
appreci|able [ə'pri·ʃjəbl] merkbar, kjennelig. **-ate** [ə'priʃie't] vurdere, skatte; sette pris på. **-ation** [ə'pri·ʃi'eɪʃən] vurdering, verdsetting; skjønn; påskjønnelse. **-ative** [ə'pri·ʃiətiv] el. **-atory** [ə'pri·ʃiətəri] som påskjønner; skjønnsom.
appre|hend [äpri'hend] ta fatt på; gripe; pågripe, anholde; fatte, oppfatte, forstå, skjønne, begripe; frykte for, frykte; anta, mene. **-hensible** [äpri'hensibl] begripelig, fattelig. **-hension** [-ʃən] pågripelse, fatteevne, begrep; frykt, engstelse. **-hensive** [-siv] lærenem; følsom; redd.
apprentice [ə'prentis] læresvenn, læregutt; sette i lære; **bind one** — **to** sette en i lære hos. **-ship** [ə'prentiʃip] lære, læretid, læreår.
apprise [ə'praiz] underrette (**of** om).
apprize [ə'praiz] prise, verdsette.
approach [ə'proʷtʃ] nærme seg, komme nær; bringe nær; henvende seg til; det å nærme seg; anmarsj; adgang; innkjørsel; tilnærming; **-ing** forestående, nær.
approbat|e ['äprobeit] godta, gå med på. **-ion** [äpro'beɪʃən] bifall, samtykke; bekreftelse. **-ive** ['äprobeɪtiv] som billiger, samtykker.
appropriat|e [ə'proʷprie't] tilegne seg; overdra, bestemme (til et visst bruk); gjøre særegen; særegen, egen; passende, skikket. **-ion** [əproʷpri-'eɪʃən] tilegnelse; anvendelse; bestemmelse; bevilling. **-ive** [ə'proʷpriətiv] det som kan tilegnes.
approval [ə'pru·vəl] bifall, billigelse, approbasjon; **on** — til prøve, til gjennomsyn.
approve [ə'pru·v] billige; bifalle; approbere; — **of** bifalle.
approximate [ə'präksimét] omtrentlig; **-ly** tilnærmelsesvis. **approximate** [ə'präksime't] nærme, bringe nær; nærme seg. **approximation** [əpräksi'meɪʃən] tilnærming. **approximative** [ə'präksimátiv] som nærmer seg (sannheten), nesten nøyaktig.
appulse [ə'pʌls] sammenstøt, berøring.
appurtenance [ə'pə·tinəns] tilbehør.
apricot ['eɪprikät] aprikos.
April ['eɪpril] april; — **fool** aprilsnarr.
a priori ['ei-prai'á·rai] à priori.
apron ['eɪprən] forkle; fangskinn; skvettlær (på en vogn). **-string** [-striŋ] forklebånd.
apropos ['äprəpoʷ] apropos, beleilig; det faller meg inn; hva jeg vil si; — **of** angående.
apt [äpt] skikket, høvelig, passende (**for** til, **to** m. inf.: til å); (om bemerkning) treffende; dyktig, flink (**at** i, **to** m. inf.: til å); tilbøyelig (**to** m. inf.: til å); — **to forget** glemsom. **-itude**

[-itju·d]. **-ness** [-nès] skikkethet; tilbøyelighet; hang; anlegg; dugelighet.
aqua ['eɪkwə] vann. — **fortis** [-fâ·ətis] sjevann. — **marine** [-mə'ri·n] akvamarin, beryll (sjøgrønn edelstein). — **regia** [-'ri·dʒə] kongevann. — **vitæ** [-'vaiti·] akevitt.
aquarium [ə'kvæ·əriəm] akvarium.
aqueduct ['äkwidʌkt] vannledning, akvadukt.
aqueous ['eɪkwiəs] vannrik; vannaktig.
aquiline ['akwilain] ørne-.
A. R. A. fk. f. **Associate of the Royal Academy.**
Arab ['ärəb] araber; (især om befolkningen) arabisk; — **sheikh** a. sjeik; — **horse** a. hest; (**City** el. **street**) **Arabs** hjemløse gategutter.
arabesque [ärə'besk] arabesk.
Arabia [ə'reɪbjə] Arabia.
Arabian [ə'reɪbjən] arabisk; araber; — **bird** føniks; — **nights** tusen og én natt.
Arabic ['ärəbik] arabisk (om språk, skrift og litteratur); arabisk.
arable ['ärəbl] som kan pløyes; oppdyrket.
Aragon ['ärəgán] Aragonia.
arbiter ['a·əbitə] voldgiftsmann; dommer.
arbitrage ['a·əbitridʒ] arbitrasje, kursspekulasjon.
arbit|rariness [a·ə'bitrərinés] vilkårlighet. **-rary** ['a·əbitrəri] arbitrær, vilkårlig; egenmektig. **-rate** ['a·əbitre't] avgjøre, dømme. **-ration** [a·əbi'treɪʃən] voldgift. **-rator** ['a·əbitre'tə] voldgiftsmann, makthaver. **-ress** ['a·əbitris] kvinnelig voldgiftsdommer.
arboreal [a·ə'bâ·riəl] som lever på trær, tre-.
arbour ['a·əbə] lauvhytte, lysthus.
arc [a·ək] bue.
arcade [a·ə'keɪd] buegang.
Arcadian [a·ə'keɪdjən] arkadisk; land'ig.
arcanum [a·ə'keɪnəm] arkanum.
arch [a·ətʃ] bue; hvelving; bue, hvelve, bue seg, hvelve seg. (**Court of**) **Arches** høyeste geistlige rett.
arch [a·ətʃ] erke-, hoved-; skjelmsk.
archaeologer [a·əki'á-lədʒə] arkeolog.
archaeological [a·əkiə'lâdʒikl] arkeologisk.
archaeologist [a·əki'álədʒist] arkeolog.
archaeology [n·əki'álədʒi] arkeologi.
archaic [a·ə'keɪik] foreldet, gammeldags.
archaism ['a·əkeɪizm] gammeldags uttrykk.
archaistic [a·əke'istik] arkaiserende.
archangel ['a·əkʲeɪndʒəl] erk·engel.
arch|bishop ['a·ətʃ'biʃəp] erkebiskop. **-bishopric** erkebispedømme. **-deacon** erkedegn, -diakon (i geistlig rang nærmest under bispene). **-duchess** erkehertuginne. **-duke** erkehertug.
archer ['a·ətʃə] bueskytter.
archery ['a·ətʃəri] bueskyting.
archetype ['a·əkitaip] forbilde, mønster, original.
archipelago [a·ə'kipeləgoʷ] arkipel; **the Archipelago** Egeerhavet.
architect ['a·əkitekt] byggmester, arkitekt. **-onic** [a·əkitek'tânik] arkitektonisk. **-ure** ['a·əkitektʃə] bygningskunst, arkitektur. **-ural** [a·əki-'tektʃurəl] arkitektonisk.
archives ['a·əkaivz] arkiv; dokumenter. **archival** [a·ə'kaivl] arkiv-.
archway ['a·ətʃweɪ] overhvelvet gang, hvelv, portrom, æresport.
arc-lamp ['a·əklämp] buelampe.
arc-light ['a·əklait] buelys.
arctic ['a·əktik] arktisk, nordlig, nord-.
ardency ['a·ədnsi] varme, inderlighet; iver.
ardent ['a·ədnt] het, brennende, fyrig, ivrig; — **spirits** brennevin.
ardour ['a·ədə] varme; iver; begjærlighet.
arduous ['a·ədjuəs] bratt, steil; vanskelig, besværlig.
are [a·ə, ə; foran vokal a·r, (ə)r] er (pl. og 2. person sg. av **to be** å være).
area ['æ·əriə] flateinnhold, areal; innhegnet plass; lite inngjerdet rom mot gata foran et hus

(lavere enn gatelegemet). — **-bell** klokke til kjøkkenet. — **-steps** trapp ned til kjøkkenet.
arena [ə'ri·nə] kampplass, arena.
argand ['a·ᵊgənd] argandbrenner.
argent ['a·ᵊdʒənt] sølv-; sølvklar.
Argentin|a [a·ᵊdʒən't(a)inə] Argentina. **-e** ['a·ᵊ-dʒəntain] argentinsk; argentiner.
argentine ['a·ᵊdʒəntain] sølv-: av sølv.
argil ['a·ᵊdʒil] pottemakerleir.
argillaceous [a·ᵊdʒi'leiʃəs] leiret.
argon ['a·ᵊgən] argon (luftformig grunnstoff).
argosy ['a·ᵊgəsi] rikt lastet skip.
argot ['a·ᵊgoⁿ] argot.
argu|e ['a·ᵊgju] bevise; strides om; drøfte; gjøre innvendinger, si imot. **-ment** ['a·ᵊgjumənt] bevis, prov, argument, slutning; drøfting; strid. **-mentation** [a·ᵊgjumen'teiʃən] bevisføring, argumentasjon. **-mentative** [a·ᵊgju'mentətiv] som skal bevise el. som tjener til bevis (**of** for); stridslysten.
Argyle [a·ᵊ'gail] Argyle, skotsk grevskap.
aria ['a·riə, æ·ᵊriə] arie.
Arian ['æ·ᵊriən, 'a·riən] arier; arisk.
arid ['ärid] tørr, skrinn, uttørret, tørrlendt. **-ity** [ə'riditi] tørrhet, tørke.
aright [ə'rait] riktig, rett.
arise [ə'raiz] reise seg, stå opp; oppstå (fra de døde); opptre, framtre; komme opp.
arisen [ə'rizn] perf. pts. av **arise**.
aristocracy [äri'ståkrəsi] aristokrati.
aristocrat ['äristəkrät] aristokrat.
aristocratic [äristə'krätik] aristokratisk.
Aristotle ['äriståtl] Aristoteles.
arithmetic [ə'riþmitik] regning; aritmetikk.
arithmetical [äriþ'metikl] aritmetisk; — pro-gression aritmetisk rekke.
ark [a·ᵊk] ark; (amerikansk) flodbåt; **Noah's** — Noahs ark; også et slags leketøy med dyr i en ark; **the Ark of the Covenant** paktens ark.
arm [a·ᵊm] arm; kraft, velde; **infant in -s** spebarn som ennå må bæres, også reivebarn; **keep at -'s length** holde seg fra livet.
arm [a·ᵊm] (som subst. oftest i pl.) våpen, våpenart, våpenskjold; bevæpne, væpne; ruste ut; forsyne; ruste seg, gripe til våpen; **small -s** håndskytevåpen; **in -s** væpnet, kampberedt; **under -s** under våpen; **companion in -s** våpen-bror; **coat of -s** våpenskjold; **-ed neutrality** væpnet nøytralitet.
armada [a·ᵊ'me¹də] krigsflåte, armada.
armadillo [a·ᵊmə'dilo¹] beltedyr.
Armageddon [a·mə'gedn] armageddon.
armament ['a·ᵊməmənt] krigsmakt, rustning.
armature ['a·ᵊmətʃə] bevæpning, våpen; beslag; armatur.
arm-chair ['a·ᵊm'tʃæ·ə] armstol, lenestol.
Armenian [a·ᵊ'mi·njən] armensk; armener.
armistice [a·ᵊ'mistis] våpenstillstand. **Armistice Day** den festligholdte årsdag for våpenstillstanden (11. nov. 1918).
armlet ['a·ᵊmlét] liten arm, f. eks. fjordarm, armbånd, armring.
armorial [a·ᵊ'må·riəl] våpen-, heraldisk; — **bearings** våpenmerke.
armory [a·ᵊ'məri] heraldikk, vitenskapen om våpenmerker; (amr.) våpenfabrikk.
armour ['a·ᵊmə] bevæpning; hærbunad, harnisk; rustning; panser (et skips). — **-clad** pansret; panser(skip). **-er** ['a·ᵊmərə] våpensmed; rust-mester.
armoury ['a·ᵊməri] rustkammer, arsenal.
armpit ['a·ᵊmpit] armhule.
army ['a·ᵊmi] hær. — **chaplain** feltprest. — **-corps** armékorps. — **-list** liste over offiserene i hæren. — **-officer** landoffiser. **(Royal) Army Service Corps** trenkorpset.
arn't [a·ᵊnt] sammentrukket av **are not**.
aroma [ə'ro¹mə] duft, ange, aroma. **-tic** [äro¹mätik] aromatisk.
arose [ə'ro¹z] imperf. av **arise**.

around [ə'raund] rundt, rundt omkring; om.
arouse [ə'rauz] vekke.
arow [ə'ro¹] i rekke, på rad.
arrack ['äräk] arrak.
arrah ['ärə] (irsk utrop) kjære! ja så!
arraign [ə're¹n] stevne for retten; sikte, anklage; beskylde. **-ment** anklage.
arrange [ə're¹ndʒ] ordne, bringe i orden, stille opp, arrangere. **-ment** [-mənt] ordning; **make -ments** for treffe foranstaltninger til, få i stand; **arrant** ['ärənt] åpenbar, vitterlig; beryktet. erke-, toppmålt.
array [ə're¹] kle, smykke; stille i orden, fylke, stille opp, klededrakt; orden, slagorden, fylking.
arrear [ə'riə] restanse, etterskudd.
arrest [ə'rest] stanse; arrestere, fengsle; ta arrest i; arrestasjon; arrest, beslag; — **of judgment** innsigelse mot dom (atter at lagretten har sagt skyldig. Er dommeren enig i innsigelsen, blir det ikke avsagt dom). **put under** — arrestere.
arrival [ə'raivəl] ankomst (NB. med påsted-preposisjon). **an** — en (noen) som kommer.
arrive [ə'raiv] komme (**at,** en i til).
arrogance ['ärəgəns] hovmod, anmasselse.
arrogant ['ärəgənt] hovmodig, hoven, stolt.
arrogate ['ärəge¹t] anmasse seg; kreve.
arrow ['äro¹] pil; **the broad** — den brede pil (statens merke på dens eiendeler, også på fange-tøy).
arrow-root ['äro¹ru·t] salep.
A. R. S. A. fk. f. **Associate of the Royal Scottish Academy.**
arsenal ['a·ᵊsənəl] arsenal.
arsenic ['a·ᵊsnik] arsenikk. **arsenic** [a·ᵊ'senik] som inneholder arsenikk, arsenikkholdig. **arsenicate** [a·ᵊ'senike¹t] blande med arsenikk.
arson ['a·ᵊsən] brannstiftelse, ildspåsetting.
art [a·ᵊt]: **thou** — du er (høyere stil), av **to be**.
art [a·ᵊt] kunst; kunstferdighet; list, knep; **the -s** de skjønne kunster, kunst(en); **have the** — to være listig nok til; **have no** — **nor part in** it ingen som helst andel ha i det; **master of -s** magister (også om lag svarende til cand. philol.).
arterial [a·ᵊ'tiəriəl] arteriell, pulsåre-.
artery ['a·ᵊtəri] pulsåre, arterie.
Artesian [a·ᵊ'ti·ʒən] artesisk.
artful ['a·ᵊtful] kunstig; sinnrik, listig, slu.
art-handicraft kunsthåndverk, kunstindustri.
arthritic [a·ᵊ'þritik] giktbrudden.
artichoke ['a·ᵊtitʃoⁿk] artisjokk.
article ['a·ᵊtikl] ledd, del; vare; punkt; artikkel, (flertall:) vilkår, betingelser; beskylde, anklage; sette i lære; **at clerk** sakførerfull-mektig.
articulate [a·ᵊ'tikjulét] ledd-; tydelig. **articulate** [a·ᵊ'tikjule¹t] uttale tydelig; artikulere.
articulation [a·ᵊ'tikju'le¹ʃən] tydelig uttale; artikulasjon; leddannelse.
artifice ['a·ᵊtifis] kunstgrep, list, knep; kunst, ferdighet, håndverk. **artificial** [a·ᵊ'ti'fiʃəl] kunstig; kunstlet.
artillerist [a·ᵊ'tilərist] artillerist. **artillery** [a·ᵊ'tiləri] artilleri.
artisan [a·ᵊ'ti'zän, 'a·ᵊtizən] håndverker. **artist** ['a·ᵊtist] kunstner. **artiste** [a·ᵊ'tist] artist. **artistic** [a·ᵊ'tistik] kunstnerisk.
artless [a·ᵊtles] ukunstlet, naturlig. **-ness** [-nés] naturlighet, naivitet.
art-master [a·ᵊ'tma·stə] tegnelærer.
Aryan ['æ·ᵊrian, 'a·riən] arier; arisk.
A. S. [e¹ es] fk. f. **Anglo-Saxon.**
as [äz, əz] liksom, som, da, idet; ettersom; så sant; etter hvert som; som om; likså; **as soon as, as well as** etc. så snart som, så vel som osv.; — **if** som om; — **if** to som for å; — **it were** to meet som for å møte; **as for,** as to hva angår, med hensyn til; **as it were** så å si; **as though** som om; **as yet** ennå, hittil; **fool** — **he was** tosk som han var; **help such** — **are poor** hjelp dem

som er fattige; **so kind — to** så vennlig å; — **I live** så sant jeg lever.
asbestos [äz'bestås] asbest.
ascend [ə'send] stige opp; heve seg; stige opp etter el. på, bestige. **-ant** [ə'sendənt] oppstigende, oppgående; overlegen; overveiende; overlegenhet, innflytelse, overmakt; ascendent, slektning i oppstigende linje. **-ency** [ə'sendənsi] overlegenhet, innflytelse, makt.
ascension [ə'senʃən] oppstigning; himmelfart; **A. (Day)** [-deⁱ] Kristi himmelfartsdag.
ascent [ə'sent] oppstigning; oppgang, opptur; hall, motbakke; høyde, høgd, høyt sted. **a steep** — en brekke.
ascertain [äsə'teⁱn] bringe på det rene; forvisse seg om, få full greie på, få fastslått. **-ment** [-mənt] bestemmelse, det å få noe fastslått, konstatering.
ascetic [ä'setik] asketisk; asket.
asceticism [ä'setisizm] askese.
Ascot ['äskət] Ascot, sted med veddeløp.
ascribable [ə'skraibəbl] som kan tilskrives.
ascribe [ə'skraib] tilskrive, henføre (**to** til).
asexual [eⁱ'seksjuəl] kjønnsløs.
ash [äʃ] ask; asketre.
ash [äʃ] oftest i pl. **ashes** aske. **ashes to ashes, dust to dust** av jord er du kommet, til jord skal du bli.
ashamed [ə'ʃeⁱmd] skamfull; **be** — skamme seg (**of** over).
ashen ['äʃən] aske-; askegrå.
ashlar ['äʃlə] kvaderstein; støtte under loftsbjelke.
ashore [ə'ʃå·ə] i land; **run** — sette på grunn.
ash-pan ['äʃpän] askeskuff.
ash-tray ['äʃtreⁱ] askebeger.
Ash-Wednesday askeonsdag.
Asia ['eⁱʃə] Asia. — **Minor** [-'mainə] Lilleasia.
Asiatic [eⁱʃi'ätik] asiatisk; asiat.
aside [ə'said] til side; avsides; **set** — fjerne; **put** — legge på hylla, oppsette; **stand** — stå utenfor.
asinine ['äsinain] eselaktig, dum.
ask [a·sk] forlange; spørre om; be om; innby; be; spørre; — **for** be om, spørre etter, spørre om; — **a question** gjøre et spørsmål; — **someone's leave** be en om lov; — **one's way** spørre seg fram; — **the banns** lyse til ekteskap; **they were -ed in church** det ble lyst for dem i kirken.
askance [ə'skäns, ə'ska·ns] på skjeve, til siden; **look** — skotte; **look** — at se skjevt til.
askew [ə'skju·] skjevt; **hang** — henge skjevt.
aslant [ə'sla·nt] på skrå, på snei.
asleep [ə'sli·p] i søvn; sovende; **fall (fast)** — falle i (dyp) søvn; **go** — falle i søvn; **be** — sove.
aslope [ə'sloᵘp] hellende, på hall, skrånende.
asp [äsp] osp.
asp [äsp] giftslange (srl. egyptisk brilleslange).
asparagus [ə'spärəgəs] asparges.
aspect ['äspekt] utseende; side (av en sak), synspunkt; beliggenhet; **have a southern** — vende mot sør.
aspen ['äspən] osp; ospe-; — **leaf** ospelauv.
asperge [as'pə·dʒ] skvette, vanne, srl. med vigslevann.
asperity [ə'speriti] ujevnhet; barskhet.
asperse [ə'spə·s] stenke; bakvaske. **aspersion** [ə'spə·ʃən] overstenkning; bakvasking.
asphalt ['äsfält] asfalt; asfaltere.
asphyxiate [äs'fiksieⁱt] kvele; **-d** skinndød; **asphyxiating gas** giftig gassart.
aspic ['äspik] gelé; — **of eggs** egg i gelé.
aspirant [ə'äspirənt] aspirant.
aspiration [äspi're'ʃən] aspirasjon, (inn)ånding; lengsel, attrå. **aspire** [ə'spaiə] håke, trakte, strebe, stunde (**to** etter); stige; gjøre krav (**to** på).
aspirin ['äspirin] aspirin.
asquint [ə'skwint] skjevt, skjelende.
ass [a·s, äs] esel; (fig.) esel; tosk.
assagai ['äsəgai] assagai.

assail [ə'seⁱl] angripe. **-ant** [-ənt] angriper.
assassin [ə'säsin] (snik)morder. **-ate** [-eⁱt] (snik)myrde. **-ation** [əsäsi'neⁱʃən] (snik)mord.
assault [ə'så·lt] angripe; overfalle; angrep; overfall; storm; **carry by** — ta med storm.
assay [ə'seⁱ] prøve; probere; prøve; probering; justering. **-er** [ə'se'ə] myntguardein.
assembl|age [ə'semblidʒ] samling; sammenkomst. **-e** [ə'sembl] samle (seg); komme sammen til møte; montere. **-y** [ə'sembli] forsamling.
assent [ä'sent] samtykke, bifall; samtykke; **the royal** — kongelig sanksjon; — **to** samtykke i, være med på.
assert [ə'sə·t] påstå; forfekte; hevde; forsvare. **-ion** [ə'sə·ʃən] påstand. **-ive** påståelig.
assess [ə'ses] pålegge skatt, ligne, beskatte. **-ment** [-mənt] beskatning, skattlegging; skatteligning. **-or** [-ə] dommer, bisitter; ligningsmann.
asset ['äsèt] aktiv; oftest i pl.: en persons (et firmas, selskaps) bruttoformue; **-s and liabilities** aktiva og passiva; i aviser brukes **asset** ofte i bet. fordel, verdi, nyttig egenskap.
asseverate [ə'sevəreⁱt] høytidelig forsikre. **asseveration** [ə'sevə're'ʃən] høytidelig forsikring.
assiduity [äsi'dju·iti] stadig flid; i pl. oppmerksomhet, ære, hyllest.
assiduous [ə'sidjuəs] flittig, iherdig.
assign [ə'sain] anvise; utpeke; bestemme, overdra; avhende; en som en fordring er overdratt til; — **motives** tillegge motiver. **-able** som kan anvises, utpekes. **-ation** [äsig'neⁱʃən] avtale å møtes, stevnemøte; anvisning; avhending; overdraing. **-ee** [äsi'ni·] fullmektig. **-or** [äsi'nå·ə] den som anviser el. overdrar; avhender.
assimilable [ə'similəbl] som kan assimileres; fordøyelig. **assimilate** [ə'simileⁱt] assimilere; assimilere seg. **assimilation** [əsimi'le'ʃən] assimilasjon; fordøyelse; likhet.
assist [ə'sist] hjelpe; — **at** være til stede ved. **-ance** [ə'sistəns] hjelp, bistand; **lend -ance** yte hjelp. **-ant** [ə'sistənt] medhjelper, assistent.
assize [ə'saiz] sesjon, rett, lagrette; forordning; pris el. takst (på matvarer); i flertall: (distrikts-)ting, rett(s-møte), (som holdes på regelmessige tingreiser rundt om i England av dommere i High Court of Justice). **assizor** [ə'saizə] jurymann, lagrettemann.
associable [ə'souⁿʃəbl] forenlig; omgjengelig.
associate [ə'souⁱʃieⁱt] knytte til, assosiere; forbinde, forene; slutte seg sammen (**with** med). **associate** [ə'souⁱʃièt] tilknyttet, med-; kamerat, felle, medhjelper; medlem.
association [əsouⁿʃi'eⁱʃən] forening; selskap, klubb; forbund; idéassosiasjon; — **-football** alminnelig fotballspill (forskjellig fra Rugby football).
assoil [ə'såil] frita, tilgi, frikjenne.
assonance ['äsənəns] assonans, halvrim.
assort [ə'så·ət] ordne, sortere; assortere, forsyne med varesorter; stemme overens; egne seg. **-ment** [-mənt] sortering; forråd av mange slag.
assuage [ə'sweⁱdʒ] lindre. **-ment** [-mənt] lindring.
assume [ə's(j)u·m] anta, tro, mene; tilta seg; påta seg; anmasse seg; være anmassende, være stor på det. **assumption** [ə'sʌmpʃən] antagelse, tro; påtagelse; viktighet; forutsetning; (jomfru Maria) himmelfart.
assur|ance [ə'ʃuərəns] forsikring, trygd; forvissning; tillit; selvtillit, suffisanse. **-e** [ə'ʃuə] forsikre, trygde; forvisse; sikre; tilsikre. **-edly** [ə'ʃuəridli] sikkert. **-er** [ə'ʃuərə] assurandør; livsforsikret person.
Assyria [ə'siriə] Assyria.
aster ['ästə] asters.
astern [ə'stə·n] akterut.
asthma ['äsmə] astma. **-tic** [äs'mätik] astmatisk.
astir [ə'stə·] i bevegelse, på beina.
astonish [ə'ståniʃ] forbause, gjøre bestyrtet. **-ment** [-mənt] forbauselse, bestyrtelse, undring.

astound [ə'staund] gjøre forbauset, forfjamset, forbløffet, målløs.

astrakhan [ästrə'kän] astrakan(skinn).

astral ['ästrəl] stjerneformig; stjerne-.

astray [ə'streiˈ] på villstrå; **go** — fare vill, komme bort; **lead** — føre på villspor.

astriction [ə'strikʃən] sammentrekning.

astride [ə'straid] på skrevs, skrevs.

astringe [ə'strindʒ] trekke sammen. **astringent** [-ənt] sammensnerpende; astringerende middel.

astrologer [ä'strålədʒə] astrolog, stjernetyder.

astrological [ästro'lådʒikl] astrologisk. **astrology** [ä'strålədʒi] astrologi.

astronomer [ä'strånəmə] astronom. **astronomical** [ästro'nåmikl] astronomisk. **astronomy** [ä'strånəmi] astronomi.

astrophysics ['ästroˈfiziks] astrofysikk.

astute [ə'stjuˈt] slu, gløgg, listig.

asunder [ə'sʌndə] i stykker, i sund; atskilt.

asylum [ə'sailəm] asyl, fristed, tilfluktssted; **orphan** — barnehjem; **lunatic** — sinnssykeasyl.

at [ät] bet. for A. T. S. (s. d.); **an** — **secretary** en sekretær som tilhører A. T. S.

at [ät, ət] til, ved, i, på; **at best** i beste fall; **at last** til sist; **at least** i det minste; **at length** omsider, til sist; **at once** på én gang, straks; **at worst** i verste fall.

ate [et, eˈt] imperf. av **to eat**.

atheism ['eiˈþjizm] ateisme. **atheist** ['eiˈþjist] ateist. **atheistic** [eiˈþi'istik] ateistisk.

Athena, Athene [ä'þiˈnə, -ni] Atene.

Athenian [ä'þiˈnjən] atensk; atener.

Athens ['äþinz] Athen.

athirst [ə'þəˈst] tørst (**for** etter).

athlete ['äþliˈt] bryter, atlet, kjempe.

athletic [äþ'letik] atletisk; kjempemessig. **athletics** [äþ'letiks] legemsøvelser, idrett, gymnastikk.

at-home [ət'houˈm] mottagelse, mottagelsesdag.

athwart [ə'þwåˈət] tvers over; tvers for.

Atkins ['ätkinz] Atkins; **Tommy** — den britiske soldaten.

Atlantic [ät'läntik] atlantisk; **the** —, **the** — **ocean** Atlanterhavet.

atlas ['ätləs] atlas (samling av kart el. bilder).

atmosphere ['ätməsfiə] atmosfære. **atmospheric(al)** [ätməs'ferik(l)] atmosfærisk. **atmospherics** atmosfæriske forstyrrelser (i radio).

atoll [ə'tål] atoll, ringøy, laguneøy.

atom ['ätəm] atom. **-ic** [ə'tåmik] atom-; **-ic bomb** atombombe; **-is theory** atomteori; **-ic weight** atomvekt.

atone [ə'touˈn] sone; — **for** bøte for, utsone. **-ment** [-mənt] soning, utsoning; **make -ment for** gjøre godt igjen.

atrocious [ə'trouˈʃəs] fryktelig, avskyelig.

atrocity [ə'tråsiti] avskyelighet, grusomhet.

atrophy ['ätrəfi] atrofi, svinn.

A. T. S. fk. f. **Auxiliary Territorial Service** bet. for de engelske lotter som er tilknyttet hæren, flåten og luftvåpnet; lottekorps.

attach [ə'tätʃ] sette fast, beslaglegge; feste, knytte; fengsle, tiltrekke, vinne.

attaché [ə'täʃeˈ] attaché. — **case** attachétaske. **-ship** attachépost.

attachment [ə'tätʃmənt] hengivenhet, sympati; beslaglegging, arrest.

attack [ə'täk] angripe; anfalle; angrep, åtak.

attain [ə'teiˈn] nå til; oppnå.

attainable [ə'teiˈnəbl] oppnåelig.

attainder [ə'teiˈndə] skamplett, vanære, ærestap.

attainment [ə'teiˈnmənt] oppnåelse; talent, ferdighet.

attaint [ə'teiˈnt] besmitte, sette en skamplett på.

attar ['ätə] rosenolje.

attempt [ə'tem(p)t] prøve, forsøke; gjøre attentat på; forsøk; prøve (**at** på); attentat; — **his life** strebe ham etter livet; — **upon his life** attentat på ham.

attend [ə'tend] legge merke til; varte opp; passe; pleie; betjene :besørge; forrette; ledsage,

følge; være til stede ved; vente på; skjenke oppmerksomhet, gi akt; innfinne seg, besøke, frekventere; vente. **-ance** [-əns] oppmerksomhet, pleie; oppvartning, betjening; nærvær; følge, oppvartende personer; møte (for retten). **-ant** [-ənt] oppvarter, tjener; deltager; ledsager; tilstedeværende. **-ants** betjening.

attention [ə'tenʃən] oppmerksomhet; **he was all** — han var lutter øre. **attentive** [ə'tentiv] oppmerksom, aktpågivende.

attenuate [ə'tenjueˈt] fortynne, pulverisere.

attest [ə'test] bevitne; ta til vitne, vitnemål. **-ation** [äte'steiˈʃən] vitnesbyrd; vitnemål, bevitnelse.

Attic ['ätik] attisk.

attic ['ätik] kvist; kvistværelse.

attire [ə'taiə] kle; pynte, smykke; klær, drakt; **change of** — sett tøy.

attitude ['ätitjuˈd] stilling, holdning; **strike an** — innta en teatralsk stilling, gjøre seg til.

attorney [ə'təˈni] fullmektig; (foreldet om) sakfører. **Attorney-general** regjerings-advokat.

attract [ə'träkt] tiltrekke, tiltrekke seg; (fig.) henrive. **-ion** [ə'träkʃən] tiltrekning(skraft); tillokking, tiltrekkende egenskap. **-ive** [ə'träktiv] tiltrekkende, tillokkende.

attributable [ə'tribjutəbl] som kan tilskrives el. tillegges. **attribute** [ə'tribjut] tilskrive, tillegge. **attribute** ['ätribjut] egenskap; attributt, kjennetegn. **attribution** [ätri'bjuˈʃən] tillagt egenskap. **attributive** [ə'tribjutiv] som tillegg, attributiv.

attrition [ə'triʃən] slit; sønderknuselse, anger.

attune [ə'tjuˈn] stemme, stille, bringe i harmoni.

auburn ['åˈbən] brun, kastanjebrun.

auction ['åˈkʃən] auksjon. **auction bridge** auksjonsbridge. **auctioneer** [åˈkʃə'niə] auksjonarius; selle ved auksjon.

audacious [å'deiˈʃəs] dristig, vågsom, vågal; frekk. **audacity** [å'däsiti] dristighet; frekkhet.

audible ['åˈdibl] hørlig, tydelig, tydelig.

audience ['åˈdjəns] audiens; tilhørere, tilskuere, publikum.

audit ['åˈdit] revisjon. **-or** ['åˈditə] tilhører; revisor. **-ory** ['åˈditəri] høre-; tilhørere; auditorium.

Aug. fk. f. **August**.

Augean [å'dʒiˈən]: **cleanse the** — **stables** rense augiasstallen.

auger ['åˈgə] bor, naver.

aught [åˈt] noe; **for** — **I know** for alt det jeg vet.

augment [åg'ment] forøke; øke, vokse. **augment** ['åˈgmənt] forøkelse, økning, tilvekst, auke. **-ation** [åˈgmənt'teiˈʃən] forøkelse, økning, auke.

augur ['åˈgə] augur; forutsi ved tegn; spå, varsle. **-y** ['åˈgjuri] spådom, varsel.

August ['åˈgəst] august (måned).

august [å'gʌst] ærverdig, opphøyd.

Augustan [å'gʌstən] augusteisk (som angår keiser Augustus); **the** — **Confession** den augsburgske bekjennelse.

Augustin(e) [å'gʌstin] Augustinus; augustinermunk.

Augustus [å'gʌstəs] August(us).

auk [åˈk] alke; **great** — geirfugl.

auld [åˈld] gammel; — **lang syne** [läŋ sain] de gode gamle dager, for lenge siden.

aunt [aˈnt] tante, faster, moster; **Aunt Sally**, en markedslek (man kaster til måls mot et kvinnehode av tre).

auntie, aunty ['aˈnti] kjære (gode, søte, snille) tante.

aura ['åˈrə] aura, luftning, utstråling, lysning; utdunstning.

aural ['åˈrəl] øre-. — **surgeon** ørelege.

aureola [å'riˈələ], **aureole** ['åˈrioˈl] glorie.

auricular [å'rikjulə] øre-.

aurist ['åˈrist] ørelege.

Aurora [å'råˈrə]Aurora; morgenrøde. — **borealis** nordlys; — **australis** sydlys.

auscultation [åˈskʌl'teiˈʃən] auskultasjon.

auspice ['åˈspis] varsel, auspisium; **under his**

-s under hans auspisier. **auspicious** [å'spiʃəs] lykkevarslende.

austere [å'stiə] streng. **austerity** [å'steriti] strenghet.

austral ['å·strəl] sydlig, sørlig.

Australasia [å·strəl'eiʃə] Australia (ɔ: fastland med omliggende øyer). **Australia** [å'strei'ljə] Australia (fastlandet).

Austria ['å·striə] Østerrike. **Austrian** ['å·striən] østerriksk, østerriker.

authentic [å'þentik] pålitelig, autentisk; ekte. **-ate** [å'þentike't] stadfeste, lovfeste. **-ation** [åþenti'kei'ʃən] stadfesting, legalisasjon. **authenticity** [å·þən'tisiti] ekthet, pålitelighet.

author ['å·þə] opphavsmann; forfatter. **-ess** [-rès] forfatterinne. **-itative** [å'þårite'tiv] autoritativ, som har autoritet, offisiell; myndig, bydende. **-ity** [å'þåriti] autoritet, myndighet; anseelse, innflytelse; vitnesbyrd; kilde; gyldighet; hjemmel; bemyndigelse, fullmakt. **-ize** ['å·þeraiz] bemyndige, gi fullmakt; gjøre rettsgyldig, autorisere; **authorized version** autorisert oversettelse, bibeloversettelsen av 1611. **-ship** ['å·þəʃip] forfatterskap.

auto ['å·to**u**] automobil, bil.

autobiography [å·tobai'ågrəfi] selvbiografi.

autocar ['å·toka·ə] automobil, bil.

autochthon [å·'tåkþən] autokton.

auto|cracy [å'tåkrəsi] autokrati, enevelde. **-crat** ['å·tokrät] selvhersker, enevoldsherre. **-cratic** [å·to'krätik] uinnskrenket, autokratisk.

auto-da-fé [å·todə'fe**i**, au-] autodafé.

autograph ['å·togra·f] autograf, egen håndskrift, egenhendig skrivelse; egenhendig. **-ic** [å·to-'gräfik] egenhendig. **-y** [å'tågrəfi] egenhendig skrift, original; litografering; litografi.

automatic [å·to'mätik] automatisk.

automaton [å·'tåmətən], i pl. også **automata** automat.

automobile ['å·tomobi·l] automobil, bil; bile.

autonomy [å'tånəmi] autonomi, selvstyre.

autumn ['å·təm] høst.

autumnal [å'tʌmnəl] høst-, høstlig.

auxiliary [åg'ziljəri] hjelpe-; hjelper. **auxiliaries** hjelpetropper.

avail [ə'vei**l**] nytte, være til nytte, gagne, hjelpe; nytte, fordel, gagn; — **oneself of** benytte seg av. **-ability** [-ə'biliti] anvendelighet, nytte. **-able** [-əbl] disponibel, ledig, tilgjengelig; anvendelig, gyldig, som gjelder.

avalanche ['ävə'la·nʃ] lavine, snøskred.

avarice ['ävəris] griskhet; gjerrighet. **avaricious** [ävə'riʃəs] gjerrig; havesyk.

avaunt [ə'vå·nt] bort! gå fra meg!

avenge [ə'vendʒ] hevne.

avenue ['ävinju] vei; allé; (amr.) bred gate.

aver [ə'və·] forsikre, forsikre.

average ['ävəridʒ] middeltall, gjennomsnitt; havari; gjennomsnittlig, gjennomsnitts-; **on an** — i gjennomsnitt, gjennomsnittlig; — **marks** ho-

vedkarakter; general (el. **gross**) — grosshavari; **particular** — partielt havari; **statement of** — dispasj; **state -s** dispasjere.

averment [ə'və·mənt] erklæring, forsikring.

averse [ə'və·s] utilbøyelig, uvillig. **-ness** [-nés] uvilje. **aversion** [ə'və·ʃən] uvilje, avsky; gjenstand for avsky.

avert [ə'və·t] vende bort; avvende.

aviary ['ei·vjəri] fuglehus, stort fuglebur.

aviate ['ei·vie·t] drive flyvning.

aviation [ei·vi'ei·ʃən] flyvning, flyteknikk. **aviator** ['ei·vie·tə] flyver, aviatiker.

avid ['ävid] grisk.

avidity [ə'viditi] griskhet, begjærlighet.

avocation [ävo'kei·ʃən] beskjeftigelse, yrke.

avoid [ə'void] sky, unngå, unnvike. **-able** [-əbl] unngåelig. **-ance** [-əns] unngåelse; ledighet (srl. av presteembete).

avoirdupois [ävədə'poiz] handelsvekt.

Avon ['ei·vən]; **the Swan of** — Shakespeare.

avouch [ə'vautʃ] erklære, påstå; stadfeste.

avow [ə'vau] erklære åpent, tilstå, vedkjenne seg. **-al** [-əl] åpen erklæring, tilståelse. **-edly** [-idli] åpent, uforbeholdent.

await [ə'wei·t] bie, vente på, avvente, oppebie; vente, forestå.

awake [ə'wei·k] vekke; våkne, vakne; våken, vaken; **wide** — lys vaken. **awaken** [ə'wei·kn] vekke; vakne.

award [ə'wå·**ə**d] tilkjenne, tildømme; tildele; kjennelse; bedømmelse; karakteristikk.

aware [ə'wæ·ə] vitende (**of** om), merksam (**of** på); **be** — vite; **be** — **of** kjenne; **become** — **of** bli oppmerksom på.

awash [ə'wåʃ] i vass-skorpa.

away [ə'wei·] bort; unna; borte; av sted! bort!

awe [å·] ærefrykt, age, hellig redsel; respekt; inngyte ærefrykt; imponere.

awful ['å·ful] fryktinngytende, imponerende; frykteslig; ['å·fl] skrekkelig, fæl.

awfully ['å·fuli] frykteslig; ['å·fli] meget; — **nice** forferdelig hyggelig.

awhile [ə'hwail] en stund.

awkward ['å·kwəd] keitet, ubehendig, klosset; kjedelig. **-ness** [-nés] keitethet; klossethet.

awl [å·l] syl.

awning ['å·nin] solseil; markise.

awoke [ə'wo**u**k] imperf. og perf. pts. av **awake**.

awry [ə'rai] skjevt, til siden, på skakke.

axe [äks] øks. **-head** økseblad, øksehammer.

axiom ['äksiəm] aksiom.

axis ['äksis] akse. **the** — **Powers** aksemaktene.

axle ['äksl] aksel, hjulaksel.

ay(e) [ai] ja; **the ayes** (i Parlamentet) stemmene for; **the ayes have it** forslaget er vedtatt.

aye [ei·] bestandig.

azalea [ə'ze·ljə] asalea.

azimuth ['äzimʌþ] asimut.

azure ['ei·ʒə, 'äʒə] asur-, himmelblå.

B

B [bi·] b; (tonen) h. **B flat** b; **B flat major** b-dur; **B flat minor** b-moll; **B sharp** hiss.

B. A. fk. f. **Bachelor of Arts**, laveste akademiske grad i England.

baa [ba·] breke; breking, brek.

Baal ['be·əl] (guden) Baal.

babble ['bäbl] bable, pludre; pjatte.

babe [be**i**b] pattebarn, spebarn.

Babel ['be·bl] Babel, Babylon.

baboo ['ba·bu] (indisk) herr.

baboon [ba'bu·n] bavian.

baby ['be·bi] pattebarn, spebarn. — **-calf** spekalv. — **-farm** barnehjem, — **-farmer** en som tar barn i pleie for betaling; englemaker. — **-farming**

englemakeri. **-hood** første barndom. **-ish** barnaktig. — **-linen** barnetøy.

Babylonian [bäbi'lo**u**njən] babylonisk; babylonier.

bacchanal ['bäkənəl] bakkant, bakkantinne; bakkantisk; bakkanal, svirelag. **bacchant** ['bäkənt] bakkant. **bacchante** [bə'känt(i)] bakkantinne.

baccy ['bäki] for **tobacco** tobakk.

bachelor ['bätʃilə] ungkar; kandidat (den laveste akademiske grad).

bacillus [bə'siləs], pl. **bacilli** [bə'silai] basill.

back [bäk] bak, rygg, bakside, bakdel, baktropp; akterkant; back (i fotball); bak-, bakre,

tilbake-; etterliggende; bevege (skyve, trekke) tilbake, rygge, hope (en hest); bakke (maskin, seil); kaste (anker); stige opp på (en hest); hamle, skåte. **-bite** [-bait] baktale. **-biter** [-baitə] baktaler. **-board** [-bå·ºd] ryggstøe. **-bone** [-boⁿn] ryggrad; **to the -bone** helt igjennom. **- door** bakdør; bakdørs-.
   backgammon [bäk'gämən] trikktrakk.
   back|ground [-graund] bakgrunn. **-hand, -hand-**led bakvendt, med handbaken, indirekte. — **-house** do. — **kitchen** oppvaskrom. — **-number** eldre nummer (av avis); foreldet metode o. l. — **-pedal** bremse. — **-rent** resterende avgift. — **-seat** baksete; **take a — -seat** tre i bakgrunnen. — **-settlements** grensekolonier.
   backsheesh [bäkʃi·ʃ] (indisk) drikkepenger, gave.
   back|slide [bäk'slaid] falle fra. **-slider** frafallen. **-stairs** [-stæ·ºz] baktrapp. **-stay** [-stei] bardun. **-ward** [bäkwəd] bakvendt; som slår tilbake; tungnem, langsom, sen, uvillig; unnselig.
   backwards [bäkwədz] tilbake, baklengs.
   backwash motsjø, dragsug.
   backwater [bäkwå·tə] evje, lon; bakevje, høl; hamle, skåte.
   backwoods [bäkwudz] urskog (i det vestl. Nord-Amerika).
   backwoodsman [bäkwudzmən] rydningsmann, nybrottsmann, pionér.
   bacon [be'kn] flesk.
   bacteria [bäk'tiəriə] flertall av: **bacterium.**
   bacteriology [bäk'tiəri'ålədʒi] bakteriologi.
   bacterium [bäk'tiəriəm] bakterie.
   Bactrian [bäktriən] baktrisk.
   bad [bäd] vond, slett, slem; skadelig; syk, dårlig; — **language** skjellsord, banning.
   bade [bäd] imperf. av **bid.**
   Baden [ba·dn] Baden.
   badge [bädʒ] kjennetegn, merke, ordenstegn.
   badger [bädʒə] grevling. **-legged** [-legd] låghalt.
   badinage [bädi'na·ʒ] skjemt, spøk.
   badly [bädli] slett; slemt; dårlig; — **wounded** hardt såret; **I want it** — jeg trenger hardt til det.
   badminton [bädmintən] et slags fjærballspill.
   badness [bädnès] sletthet, ondskap.
   Baedeker [beidikə] Baedeker. — **raids** (slang) tyske luftangrep våren 1942 som hevn for Lübeck, fortrinsvis rettet mot de engelske byer med to stjerner i Baedeker.
   baffle [bäfl] narre, drive gjøn med; forpurre; trosse.
   bag [bäg] sekk; pose; veske; taske; legge i sekk; skyte (vilt), nedlegge; svulme opp, pose; pose seg.
   bagatelle [bägə'tel] bagatell.
   baggage [bägidʒ] tross; tøyte; (især i amr.) reisetøy; **bag and** — (med) rubb og stubb.
   bagging [bägin] sekkestrie.
   baggy [bägi] poset, pløset, som henger i løse folder.
   bagman [bägmən] handelsreisende.
   bagpipe [bägpaip] sekkepipe.
   bagpiper [bägpaipə] sekkepiper.
   bah [ba·] pytt! blås! snakk!
   Bahama [be'ha·mə] Bahama.
   bail [be'l] kausjon; kausjonist; løslate mot kausjon; gå god for; — **out** få løslatt ved å stille kausjon.
   Bailey [be'li]; **the Old** — rettslokale i London.
   bailiff [be'lif] lensmann, underordnet gårdsbestyrer.
   bailment [be'lmənt] løslating mot kausjon.
   bairn [bæ·ən] (skotsk) barn.
   bait [be'l] lokkemat, beite, agn, åte; sette agn på, agne, egne; egge, terge.
   baize [be'z] bai (slags flanell).
   bake [be'k] bake; steke.
   baker [be'kə] baker; —**'s dozen** tretten. **-legged** [be'kəlegd] kalvbeint.
   balalaika [bälə'laikə] balalaika.
   balance [bäləns] vektskål; likevekt; balanse; sammenligning; overskudd, saldo; svinghjul (i et ur); veie; holde i likevekt; gjøre opp, saldere

(regnskap); overveie; være rådvill; **a pair of balances** en vekt.
   balcony [bälkəni] altan, balkong.
   bald [bå·ld] skallet; naken.
   baldness [bå·ldnès] skallethet.
   baldachin [bå·ldəkin] baldakin, tronhimmel.
   balderdash [bå·ldədäʃ] lapskaus; tøv, tull, vrøvl.
   baldric [bå·ldrik] belte.
   Baldwin [bå·ldwin].
   bale [be'l] balle; pakke inn.
   bale [be'l] øse (en båt), lense.
   bale [be'l] kval, elendighet. **-ful** [-ful] forvolvelig, ødeleggende; giftig.
   Balfour [bälfuə] Balfour.
   Baliol [be'ljəl] Baliol.
   balk [bå·k] skuffe, narre; spotte; bjelke; ås; åkerrein.
   Balkan [bå·lkən] Balkan.
   ball [bå·l] ball, kule; jark, ball (på fot, hånd); kneskjell; nøste; **the — of the eye** øyeeplet.
   ball [bå·l] ball; danselag.
   ballad [bäləd] ballade, folkevise; gatevise. — **-monger** [mʌŋgə] viseselger. **-poetry** [po"itri] visediktning.
   ballast [bäləst] ballast; gruslag, grusing (på jernbanelinjen); ballaste, gruse.
   ballet [bäle'] ballett.
   ballistics [bə'listiks] ballistikk.
   balloon [bə'lu·n] ballong.
   ballot [bälət] stemmekule, stemmeseddel, skriftlig avstemning; stemme med sedler; **vote by** — stemme med sedler. — **-box** valgurne.
   ball-room [bå·lrum] ballsal.
   balm [ba·m] balsam; balsamere; lindre.
   balmy [ba·mi] veIIuktende; legende.
   balsam [bå·lsəm] balsam. **-ic** [bå·l'sämik, bäl-] balsamisk.
   Baltic [bå·ltik] baltisk; **the** — Østersjøen.
   Baltimore [bå·ltimå·ª] Baltimore.
   baluster [bäləstə] trem i rekkverk. **balustrade** [bälə'stre'd] rekkverk, gelender.
   bamboo [bäm'bu·] bambus.
   bamboozle [bäm'bu·zl] snyte, jukse, bedra.
   ban [bän] bann; lysing, kunngjøring; bannlyse.
   banana [bə'na·nə] banan.
   band [bänd] bånd; bind; flokk, bande; forbindelse, forening; band, musikk-korps.
   bandage [bändidʒ] bind, bandasje, forbinding; forbinde.
   bandbox [bändbåks] hatteske, pappeske.
   banderole [bändərəl] vimpel, banderole.
   bandit [bändit] banditt, røver. **banditti** [bän-'diti] røvere, røverfølge.
   bandmaster [bändma·stə] musikkdirigent.
   bandog [bändåg] bandhund.
   bandoleer [bändo'liə] skulderreim, bandolær.
   bandy [bändi] balltre; et ballspill; kaste fram og tilbake; diskutere; utveksle.
   bandy-legged [bändilegd] hjulbeint.
   bane [be'n] gift; bane, banesår; undergang.
   bang [bäŋ] banke, slå; dundre med; denge; pryle; slag, dunder. **bang!** bum!
   Bangkok [bäŋkåk] Bangkok.
   bangle [bäŋgl] armring; ankelring.
   banian [bäniən] kjøpmann (i India); (indisk) kjortel; indisk fikentre. — **day** fastedag. — **ho-**spital dyrehospital.
   banish [bäniʃ] bannlyse; forvise. **-ment** [-mənt] landlysing, utlegd.
   banister [bänistə] se **baluster.**
   banjo [bändʒoⁿ] banjo.
   bank [bäŋk] banke, haug, bakke, voll; kant, bredd; bank. **-bill** [-bil] bankveksel; (amr.) pengeseddel. — **-book** bankbok. — **-draft** bankanvisning. **banker** [bäŋkə] bankier.
   bank-holiday [bäŋk'hälide'] alminnelig fridag (dager da bankene er lukket, i England: 2. påskedag, 2. pinsedag, første mandag i august og 2. juledag; i Skottland: nyttårsdag, første mandag i mai og første mandag i august).

banking ['bäŋkin] bankvesen, bankforretninger. **banknote** ['bäŋkno⁸t] pengeseddel. **bankrupt** ['bäŋkrəpt] fallent. **bankruptcy** ['bäŋkrəpsi] bankerott, fallitt.

banner ['bänə] banner, merke, fane.

bannock ['bänək] lefse, flatbrød.

banns [bänz] lysing (til ekteskap).

banquet ['bäŋkwét] gjestebud, gilde, fest; beverte, feste. **-inghall** festsal.

banquette [bäŋ'ket] skyteavsats (i skyttergrav).

banshee ['bänʃi·] spøkelse, draug.

bant [bänt] ta avmagringskur.

bantam ['bäntəm] dverghøne; (i boksing) vektklasse som ikke overstiger 116 pounds; — **battalion** (av særlig små menn i verdenskrigen).

banter ['bäntə] spøke med; erte; godmodig gjøn, erting.

baptism ['bäptizm] dåp; — **of fire** ilddåp. **baptismal** [bäp'tizməl] dåps-, døpe-. **baptist** ['bäptist] baptist. **St. John the Baptist** Johannes døperen. **baptistery** ['bäptistəri] dåpskapell, (bl. baptister) baptisterium. **baptize** [bäp'taiz] døpe.

bar [ba·ª] stang, slå, bom, skranke; tverrtre; sprosse; stengsel, hindring; sandaur, sandbanke; rettsskranke; skjenk, disk; bar, skjenkestue; taktstrek; tverrbjelke (heraldisk); spak; stenge, sette slå for; hindre, forby; stenge ute; unnta; underbinde; unntatt, så nær som; **below the** — nedenfor skranken (i Underhuset); **a** — **of soap** en stang såpe; **examination for the** — juridisk eksamen; **go to (study for) the** — studere jus; **be admitted (be called el. go) to the bar** bli advokat.

barb [ba·ªb] skjegg el. snerp (på plantedeler); stråle (på fjær); mothake, agnor (på en krok el. pil); **barbed wire fence** piggtrådsgjerde.

Barbados [ba·ª'be¹do⁸z] Barbados.

barbarian [ba·ª'bæ·riən] barbarisk; barbar. **barbaric** [ba·ª'bärik] barbarisk. **barbarism** ['ba·ªbə·rizm] barbari. **barbarous** ['ba·ªbərəs] barbarisk.

Barbary ['ba·ªbəri] Berberiet (i Nord-Afrika).

barbel ['ba·ªbəl] skjeggkarpe.

barber ['ba·ªbə] barber. **barber's block** parykkblokk. **barber's pole** barberskilt (en broket farge).

bard [ba·ªd] barde, skald.

bare [bæ·ª] bar, naken, snau; barhodet; blottet; **lay** — blotte. **-backed** uten sal. **-faced** frekk. **-foot(ed)** barbeint. **barely** neppe.

bargain ['ba·ªgin] handel, kjøp; god handel, godt-kjøp; spottpris; tinge, kjøpslå; bli enig. **into the** — attpå kjøpet; **make, strike a** — gjøre en handel, slutte en overenskomst. — **away** handle bort, tinge bort.

barge [ba·ªdʒ] sjefsbåt (på orlogsskip), lystbåt; pram, lekter. **bargee** [ba·ª'dʒi·] lektermann.

bar-iron ['ba·rai(r)ən] stangjern.

baritone ['bärito⁸n] baryton.

bark [ba·ªk] bark; barkskip.

bark [ba·ªk] gjø, bjeffe, søke; gjøing, glam.

bark [ba·ªk] bark; kinabark; avbarke.

barkeeper ['ba·ki·pə] barkeeper, vertshusholder.

barker ['ba·ªkə] (sl.) pistol.

barley ['ba·ªli] bygg. — **corn** [-kå·n] byggkorn; **John Barleycorn** ølet, drikken. — **sugar** brystsukker, kandis.

barm [ba·ªm] berme, gjær.

barmaid ['ba·ªme¹d] oppvartningspike.

barman ['ba·ªmən] oppvarter (i bar).

barn [ba·ªn] lade, løe, låve.

barnacle ['ba·ªnäkl] andeskjell (langhals); fagergås; pl. nesejern (til hest), (sl.) neseklemmer.

barometer [bə·ªråmitə] barometer.

baron ['bärən] baron (laveste grad av nobility). **-ess** [-nés] baronesse. **-et** [-nét] baronett (høyeste grad av gentry).

baroque [ba·ª'råk] barokk.

barouche [bə·ªru·tʃ] firhjult kalesjevogn.

barrack(s) ['bärək(s)] kaserne, brakke.

barrage ['bära·ʒ, 'bäridʒ] demning, stengsel; sperreild. — **balloon** sperreballong.

barratry ['bärªtri] svik, forfalskning; baratteri.

barrel ['bärəl] tønne; hul ting; løp (på en børse); trommel; valse; legge el. pakke i tønne. **-led** med løp.

barren ['bärən] gold; ufruktbar.

barricade [bäri'ke¹d] barrikade; barrikadere.

barrier ['bäriə] barriere; bom; grense.

barring ['ba·riŋ] unntatt; — **accidents** om ikke noe uforutsett hender.

barrister ['bäristə] advokat, sakfører.

bar-room skjenkestue.

barrow ['bäro⁸] trillebår.

bar-tender (amr.) oppvarter.

barter ['ba·ªtª] tuske, bytte; tuskhandel, byttehandel.

Bartholomew [ba·ª'þålomju·] Bartolomeus.

barytone ['bärito⁸n] baryton.

basalt ['bäsalt, bə'så·lt] basalt.

base [be¹s] lav; dyp (om toner); uedel (om metaller); lav, simpel; nedrig, foraktelig. **base** [be¹s] basis; grunnflate; fotstykke; nederste ende; base; basere, grunnlegge; gjøre ringere. **-ment** [-mənt] kjelder-etasje. **-ness** [-nés] dybde (en tones); ringhet; nedrighet, sletthet, låk atferd.

base-ball ['be¹s bå·l] amerikansk ballspill.

bashful ['bäʃful] skamfull, unnselig, sjenert.

basic ['be¹sik] basisk; grunn-.

basilisk ['bäzilisk] basilisk (et fabeldyr).

basin ['be¹sn] kum; vannfat; basseng, kulp, dam.

basis ['be¹sis] basis; fotstykke; (fig.) grunnvoll, grunnlag.

bask [ba·sk] bake, varme seg; sole, varme.

basket ['ba·skét] kurv, korg; pakke i korg. **basketry, basket-work** kurvarbeid.

bas-relief [ba·(s)ri'li·f] basrelieff.

bass [be¹s] bass.

Bass [bäs] slags øl (etter fabrikanten).

bassinet ['bäsi'net] barnevogn, babykurv.

bassoon [bə'su·n] fagott.

bastard ['bästəd] uekte barn, bastard; uckte. **baste** [be¹st] dryppe (en steik).

baste [be¹st] neste, tråkle.

baste [be¹st] pryle, smøre opp.

bastinado [bästi'ne¹do⁸] bastonade; stokkeslag, pryl; pryle.

bastion ['bästiən] bastion.

bat [bät] balltre; stykke (mursten); kølle (i cricket); slå med el balltre.

bat [bät] flaggermus.

Batavia [bə'te¹vjə] Batavia.

batch [bätʃ] bakning, bakst; samling, flokk; lag; sleng, slump.

bate [be¹t] forminske, minke på, slå av.

bath [ba·þ] bad; badekar; badeværelse; badeanstalt; badested; bade (i badekar).

Bath [ba·þ]:—**brick** pussestein;—**chair** rullestol.

bathe [be¹ð] bade; bade seg; bad (i det fri).

bathing-machine ['be¹ðinma·ʃi·n] badevogn.

bathos ['be¹þás] antiklimaks, flau avslutning.

batiste [bə'tist] batist (slags stoff).

batman ['bätmən] opp-passer for rytteroffiser.

baton ['bätən] taktstokk; kommandostav.

batsman ['bätsmən] slåer i cricket.

battalion [bə'täljən] bataljon.

batten ['bätn] meske, gjø, fete, meske seg.

batten ['bätn] planke; skalke.

batter ['bätə] slå; skamslå; beskyte; **battered** medtatt (bulet).

batter-pudding ['bätəpudiŋ] en slags pudding laget av mel, egg og melk.

battery ['bätəri] batteri; (jur.) overfall, vold.

battle ['bätl] slag; kamp; kjempe, stride; **fight a** — levere et slag; **lose the** — tape slaget, forspille seieren; **pitched** — ordentlig slag; **recover the** — gjenvinne seieren. **-array** [-ª're¹] slagorden. — **axe** [-äks] stridsøks. — **bowler** (sl.) soldats stålhjelm. **-cruiser** slagkrysser. **-dore** [-då·ª] ketsjer. **-field** [-fi·ld] slagmark. **-ment** [-mənt] murtind; brystvern. — **piece** slagmaleri. — **plane** stort kampfly. **-ship** slagskip.

battue [bə'tu·] klappjakt.

bauble ['bå·bl] barneleke, tufs.

bauxite ['bå·ksait] bauxitt.
Bavaria [bə'væ·ºriə] Bayern. Bavarian [-n] bayersk; bayrer.
bawbee [bå·'bi·] halvpenny (skotsk).
bawd [bå·d] rufferske.
bawdy ['bå·di] slibrig. — -house horehus.
bawl [bå·l] skråle, gaule; skrål, gaul.
bay [be¹] bukt, vik; kverndam; dør- el. vindusåpning.
bay [be¹] rødbrun; rødbrun hest.
bay [be¹] gjø; halse; gjøing; nødverge; nød; be (el. stand) at bay gjøre fortvilet motstand (om vilt, som vender seg mot hundene); keep at — holde unna, fra seg, holde fra livet.
bay [be¹] laurbærtre, laurbær.
bayadere [ba·jə'diə] bajadere.
bayonet ['be¹ənit] bajonett.
bay-window ['be¹windoᵘ] karnappvindu. — -yarn [-ja·n] ullgarn.
bazaar [bə'za·ᵊ] basar.
B. C. fk. f. British Broadcasting Corporation.
B. C. fk. f. before Christ
B. C. L. fk. f. bachelor of civil law.
B. D. fk. f. bachelor of divinity.
be [bi·] være, være til; bli (srl. til å danne passiv); — in være hjemme; — in for it ha innlatt seg på det; — right, wrong ha rett, urett; I must — off jeg må av sted.
B. E. fk. f. British Empire.
B. E. F. fk. f. British expeditionary force.
beach [bi·tʃ] strand, strandbredd, fjære; sette på land, legge til land. -comber ['bi·tʃkoᵘmə] stor, lang bølge som ruller inn fra havet mot stranda; løsgjenger som lever av å bomme sjøfolk i havnebyer.
beacon ['bi·kən] sjømerke, båke; baun; varde; fyr; lyse for.
bead [bi·d] liten kule; perle; rosenkrans; knopp; siktekorn; tell one's -s lese sin rosenkrans; draw a — on sikte på, ta på kornet.
beadle ['bi·dl] kirketjener; universitetspedell.
bead-roll ['bi·droᵘl] liste, fortegnelse.
beadsman ['bi·dzmən] forbeder, munk.
beady ['bi·di] perleaktig; perlende.
beagle ['bi·gl] liten harehund.
beak [bi·k] nebb; snabel; snyteskaft.
beaker ['bi·kə] beger.
beam [bi·m] bjelke; ås; veverbom; vektstang; vognstang; skåk; dekksbjelke, dekksbredde; stråle; kick the — vippe i været, bli funnet for lett; on the weather — tvers til lovart.
beam ends skipsside; on her — på siden, ligge helt over; være nedfor.
beamy ['bi·mi] bred, brei, svær; strålende.
bean [bi·n] bønne; -s (sl.) gryn, penger; give him -s (sl.) straffe ham, skjenne på ham. —feast prinsipals årlige fest for arbeiderne.
bear [bæ·ə] bjørn; baissespekulant; the Great Bear (stjernebi!det) Den store bjørn.
bear [bæ·ə] bære; bringe; føre; støtte; utholde, tåle; oppføre seg; føde (perf. pts. borne; i betydn. født: born, unntatt etter have og foran by); I was born in 1914 jeg er født i 1914; born of, borne by født av; — one a grudge bære nag til en; — witness to vitne om; — one company holde en med selskap: he bore himself han førte seg, hans holdning var; — down overvelde; renne i senk; — down upon seile mot; — in mind huske på; — out støtte; stadfeste; — up holde oppe, ikke fortvile; — up under afflictions holde seg oppe i motgang; — with bære over med.
bearable ['bæ·ºrəbl] utholdelig.
beard ['bi·ºd] skjegg (især om hakeskjegg; ogs. om skjegg på aks, snerp); trosse. -ed [-éd] skjegget. -less [-lés] skjeggløs.
bearer ['bæ·ºrə] bærer (f. eks. av kiste); overbringer (f. eks. av brev el. anvisning), ihendehaver.
bearing ['bæ·ºrin] holdning; retning; peiling; lager (i maskin); the question in all its -s saken

fra alle sider; have lost my -s kan ikke orientere meg.
bearish ['bæ·ºriʃ] som ligner en bjørn, plump.
bear-leader ['bæ·ə'li·də] bjørnetrekker.
beast [bi·st] dyr (firbent); best, udyr. -liness [-linês] råskap. -ly dyrisk, bestialsk; avskyelig; -ly drunk full som et svin.
beat [bi·t] slå; pryle; banke; bane (sti el. vei); slag; distrikt (en politimanns), runde; overvinne; slå på; gjennomstreife; treske; hamre ut; — a way bane seg vei; — about prøve på forskjellige måter; — about the bush gå som katten om den varme grøten; — down slå til jorda, slå over ende; beaten down nedslått; the sun was beating down on my head sola brente hett på hodet mitt; — into innprente; — time slå takt.
beaten ['bi·tn] perf. pts. av beat; the — track den slagne landevei.
beater ['bi·tə] klapper (på jakt).
beatify [bi'ätifai] gjøre lykkelig; erklære (en avdød) for salig.
beating ['bi·tin] banking; bank; drakt pryl.
beatitude [bi'ätitju·d] salighet; saligprisning.
beau [boᵘ] laps, sprett, motenarr.
beauteous ['bju·tiəs] skjønn, fager.
beautiful ['bju·tiful] skjønn, fager, deilig, fin.
beautify ['bju·tifai] forskjønne, smykke.
beauty ['bju·ti] skjønnhet; — -sleep søvnen før kl. 12. — -spot skjønnhetsplett.
beaver ['bi·və] bever; beverskinn; kastorhatt (av beverhår); hjelmgitter, visir.
becalm [bi'ka·m] berolige; be -ed få vindstille.
became [bi'ke¹m] imperf. av become.
because [bi'kå·z] fordi; — of på grunn av.
Bechuana [betʃu'a·nə] Bechuana.
beck [bek] bekk.
beck [bek] vink.
beckon ['bekən] vinke, vinke til.
become [bi'kʌm] bli; sømme seg; kle; passe seg. becoming [-iŋ] passende; kledelig.
bed [bed] seng; bed; elvefar; lag; vange (i dreiebenk); underlag; plante i bed; in — i senga; go to — gå til sengs; keep one's — holde senga; take to one's — gå til sengs (om en syk); make a — reie opp en seng; you must lie in the — you have made som man reier, så ligger man; be brought to — of bli forløst med; nedkomme med; the — of the sea havbunnen; the — of coal kull-leie; — of ashes askelag.
bedaub [bi'då·b] søle til, smøre til.
bedchamber sovekammer.
bed-clothes sengklær.
bedding ['bedin] sengklær; underlag; bedding.
Bede [bi·d] Beda.
bedevil [bi'devl] forhekse.
bedew [bi'dju·] dogge.
bedim [bi'dim] fordunkle, dimme.
bedlam ['bedləm] sinnssykeanstalt, galehus.
bedlamite ['bedləmait] sinnssyk, forrykt person.
bed|maker gangkone. — -pan (syke)bekken. — -post sengestokk; in the twinkling of a — -post på røde rappet.
bedraggle [bi'drägl] søle til, rakke til.
bed-ridden sengeliggende. -rock grunnfjell; det faste grunnlag. -room soveværelse, soverom. -side sengekant; at the -side ved senga. -sore liggesår. —-spread sengeteppe. -stead ['bed-sted] seng. —-straw (plante) fegre. —-strings stropper (som bærer madrassen). -tick dynevar. -time sengetid.
bee [bi·] bie; (amr.) sammenkomst til felleshjelp (dugnad, dønning) el. i velgjørende øyemed; have a — in one's bonnet ha en skrue løs. —-bread biebrød.
beech [bi·tʃ], -tree bøk.
beef [bi·f] oksekjøtt.
beefeater ['bi·fi·tə] oppsynsmann (i Tower), livgardist.
beefsteak ['bi·f'ste¹k] biff.
beef-tea ['bi·f'ti·] kjøttekstrakt, sodd, buljong.
bee-hive ['bi·haiv] bikube.

bee-line ['bi·'lain] luftlinje, beinvei.
Beelzebub [bi'elzibʌb] Beelzebub.
been [bi·n, bin] perf. pts. av **be.**
beer [biə] øl; **small** — tynt øl; småting.
beestings ['bi·stiŋz] råmelk.
beeswax ['bi·zwäks] bievoks; bone (med voks).
beet [bi·t] bete (plante).
beetle ['bi·tl] bille, tordivel; kølle; jomfru (til brulegging); rage fram, true. **-browed** med buskete øyebryn.
beet|radish alm. bete (plante). — **-root** rødbete, sukkerroe, forbete.
befall [bi'få·l] tilstøte, times, hende, vederfares.
befit [bi'fit] passe for, sømme seg.
befool [bi'fu·l] holde for narr.
before [bi'få·ə] før, foran; i nærvær av; overfor; fram for; førenn; — **Christ** for Kristi fødsel; — **God** ved Gud; **sail** — **the mast** være menig matros. — **long** om en liten stund. **come** — **the House** tre fram for tinget; **this war which is** — **Europe** denne krig, som Europa står overfor.
beforehand [bi'få·əhänd] på forhånd; i forveien; **be** — **with** komme i forkjøpet.
beforementioned [bi'få·ə'menʃənd] før nevnt.
befoul [bi'faul] sulke til, gjøre uren.
befriend [bi'frend] vise velvilje imot; hjelpe.
beg [beg] be om, anmode om, utbe seg; tigge; — **one's leave** be en om tillatelse; **I** — **you a thousand pardons** jeg ber Dem tusen ganger om forlatelse; **(I)** — **your pardon** unnskyld; hva behager? — **the question** ta som selvsagt nettopp det som skulle bevises; **I** — **to** . . . jeg tillater meg å . . .
begad [bi'gäd] min santen, sannelig.
began [bi'gän] imperf. av **begin.**
beget [bi'get] avle.
beggar ['begə] tigger; bringe til tiggerstaven; **poor little** — stakkars liten; — **all description** være over all beskrivelse. **-ly** fattig, ussel.
beggary ['begəri] armod.
begin [bi'gin] begynne, begynne på, ta til med. **-ner** begynner. **-ning** begynnelse, førstning.
begone [bi'gån] ut! gå med deg!
begonia [bi'go⋻njə] begonia.
begot [bi'gåt] imperf. av **beget.**
begrime [bi'graim] grime til, søle til.
beguile [bi'gail] skuffe; fordrive (tiden).
begum ['bi·gəm] (ostindisk) fyrstinne.
begun [bi'gʌn] perf. pts. av **begin.**
behalf [bi'ha·f] nytte, beste; vegne; **in his** — til hans beste; **on his** — på hans vegne.
behave [bi'he¹v] oppføre seg; **ill behaved** uoppdragen; **well behaved** veloppdragen. **behaviour** [bi'he¹vjə] oppførsel, atferd; holdning.
behead [bi'hed] halshogge.
beheld [bi'held] imperf. og perf. pts. av **behold.**
behest [bi'hest] bud, påbud, befaling.
behind [bi'haind] bak, bakved, baketter, tilbake; **leave** — la bli tilbake; **from** — bakfra.
behindhand [bi'haindhänd] tilbake, i etterhånden, til akters i pengesaker.
behold [bi'ho⁴ld] se, skue, betrakte, iaktta.
beholden [bi'ho⁴ldn] forbunden, takk skyldig.
behoof [bi'hu·f] gagn, nytte, beste, interesse.
behove [bi'ho⁴v] behøves, sømme seg.
being ['bi·in] være, tilværelse, tilvære, liv, skapning, vesen; nærværende.
belabour [bi'le¹bə] bearbeide, slå løs på.
belated [bi'le¹tid] sent ute, forsinket.
belaud [bi'lå·d] lovprise.
belch [beltʃ] rape, gurpe; rap, gurp; oppstøt.
beldam ['beldəm] heks, gammel hurpe.
beleaguer [bi'li·gə] beleire, kringsette.
belfry ['belfri] klokketårn.
Belgian ['beldʒiən] belgisk; belgier.
Belgium ['beldʒəm] Belgia.
Belial ['bi·ljəl] Belial.
belie [bi'lai] lyve på en, gjøre til skamme.
it does not — **its name** det svarer til sitt navn.
belief [bi'li·f] tro; **beyond** — utrolig.

believable [bi'li·vəbl] trolig.
believe [bi'li·v] tro; **I** — **you** det skulle jeg mene; — **in tro på** (eksistensen, tilrådeligheten, virkningen av, f. eks. — **in God**; — **in ghosts**).
bell [bel] klokke; bjelle; (mar.) glass, halvtime; henge bjelle på; **ring the** — ringe; **the** — **rings** det ringer; **answer the** — lukke opp (når det ringer); **bear the** — vinne prisen.
belladonna [belə'dånə] belladonna.
belle [bel] skjønnhet (ɔ: skjønn kvinne).
belligerent [be'lidʒərənt] krigførende.
bellman ['belmən] utroper.
bellow ['belo⁴] brøle; raute, larme; brøl, raut.
bellows ['belo⁴z] blåsebelg, puster.
bell-pull ['belpul] klokkestreng, klokkesnor.
bell-wether ['belweðə] bjellevær, bjellesau.
belly ['beli] buk, mage, underliv; svulme.
belong [bi'låŋ] to tilhøre, vedkomme; høre til.
belongings [bi'låŋiŋz] eiendeler, habengut; pårørende.
beloved [bi'lʌv(i)d] elsket; avholdt.
below [bi'lo⁴] under, nedenunder, nede; ned under dekket, ned i kahytta.
belt [belt] belte; drivreim, reim; omgjorde; **strike below the** — slå nedenfor beltestedet, bruke uhederlige kampmidler.
bemoan [bi'mo⁴n] gråte for, jamre seg for, jamre over.
Ben fk. f. Benjamin. **Big Ben** tårnklokka i parlamentsbygningen.
bench [ben(t)ʃ] benk; dommersete; dommere, domstol; benke; **King's Bench Division** hovedavdelingen av overretten. **bencher** ['ben(t)ʃə] ledende medlem av juristkollegiet.
bend [bend] spenne (en bue); bøye, krøke; rette; bøye el. bukke seg; bøyning, krumning; **bent** on oppsatt på, ivrig etter.
bender ['bendə] (sl.) sixpence.
beneath [bi'ni·þ] under; nede; nedenunder.
benediction [beni'dikʃən] velsignelse, signing, vigsel.
benefaction [beni'fäkʃən] velgjerning. **benefactor** [beni'fäktə] velgjører. **benefactress** [beni'fäktrɛs] velgjører (kvinnelig).
benefic|e [beni'fis] prestekall. **-ence** [bi'nefisəns] godgjørenhet. — ɘnt [bi'nefisənt] godgjørende. **-ial** [beni'fiʃəl] velgjørende, heldig, gagnlig.
benefit [beni'fit] velgjerning, gagn, nytte, beste; benefise; gagne; **the** — **of my intention** det gagn man kan ha av min hensikt; **give him the** — **of doubt** regne ham det tvilsomme (i den foreliggende sak, anklage el. l.) til gode.
benevolence [bi'nevələns] velvilje; velgjerning. **benevolent** [bi'nevələnt] velvillig, menneskekjærlig.
Bengal [beŋ'gå·l, ben'gå·l] Bengalen. **Bengalee** el. **Bengali** [beŋ'gå·li, ben'gå·li] bengalsk; bengaleser; bengali.
benighted [bi'naitid] overrasket av natten, sent ute; uopplyst, i åndelig mørke.
benign [bi'nain] mild, kjærlig; gunstig; godartet. **benignity** [bi'nigniti] mildhet, vennlighet; velgjørende virkning.
benison ['benisən] (poet.) velsignelse.
Benjamin ['bendʒəmin] Benjamin.
bent [bent] av **bend**; retning, tilbøyelighet.
bent [bent] stritt gras, kvein.
Benthamism ['bentəmizm] nyttemoralen.
benumbed [bi'nʌmd] valen, nommen, stivnet.
benzine ['benzi·n] bensin.
benzoin ['benzo⁴in] bensoe.
bepraise [bi'pre¹z] lovprise.
bequeath [bi'kwi·ð, bi'kwi·þ] testamentere.
bequest [bi'kwest] testamente, arv, legat.
Berber ['bə·bə] berber; berberspråk.
bere [biə] bygg.
bereave [bi'ri·v] berøve; **the -d parents de** sørgende foreldre. **-ment** smertelig tap, sorg.
bereft [bi'reft] imperf. og perf. pts. av **bereave.**
berg [bə·g] isfjell.

bergamot['bə·gəmåt]bergamott-pære (-tre,-olje).
beriberi ['beri'beri] beriberi.
Berks [ba·ᵊks] fk. f. Berkshire ['ba·ᵏʃiə].
Berlin [bə·'lin, 'bə·'lin] Berlin; en slags vogn;
(i pl.) trådhansker; — blue ['bə·lin'blu·] ber-
linerblått.
Bermuda [bə'm(j)u·də]; the -s Bermudasøyene.
berry ['beri] bær; hente, plukke bær.
berth [bə·þ] ankerplass; hugar; køyplass; (fig.)
plass, stilling; give a wide — gå langt utenom.
beryl ['beril] beryll.
beseech [bi'si·tʃ] be innstendig, bønnfalle (om).
beseem [bi'si·m] sømme seg for.
beset [bi'set] beleire; kringsette, omringe;
-ting sin skjøtesynd.
beshrew [bi'ʃru·]: — me if Gud straffe meg
om . . .
beside [bi'said] ved siden av, ved; utenfor;
be — oneself være fra seg selv.
besides [bi'saidz] dessuten; foruten; something — dessuten noe annet.
besiege [bi'si·dʒ] beleire, kringsette.
besmear [bi'smiə] smøre til, kline til.
besom ['bi·zəm] kost, sopelime; feie, sope.
besot [bi'såt] gjøre sløv (ved drikk); fordumme.
besought [bi'så·t] imperf. og perf. pts. av
beseech.
bespatter [bi'spätə] overstenke, søle til.
bespeak [bi'spi·k] bestille, tinge; betinge seg;
tyde på, bære vitne om. — -night benefisefore-
stilling. bespoke department bestillingsavdeling.
bespoke imperf. av bespeak. bespoken perf. pts.
av bespeak.
Bess [bes] fk. f. Elisabeth.
best [best] best; mest, høyest; vinne over,
lure; to the — of my ability etter beste evne;
at — i det høyeste; like — like best; make the —
of nytte på beste måte, utnytte; — man forlover.
bestial [,bestjəl] dyrisk. -ity [besti'äliti] dyriskhet. -ize ['bestjəlaiz] gjøre til et dyr.
bestir [bi'stə·] oneself ta seg sammen.
bestow [bi'stoᵘ] overdra, skjenke; gi; vise.
-al [-əl] overdragelse.
bestride [bi'straid] skreve over, ri på.
bestrode [bi'stroᵘd] imperf. av bestride.
bet [bet] veddemål; vedde.
betake [bi'teⁱk] oneself begi seg; ty.
betaken [bi'teⁱkn] perf. pts. av betake.
betel ['bi·tl] betelpepper.
bethel ['beþəl] bedehus.
bethink [bi'þiŋk] oneself of komme til å tenke
på, huske.
betide [bi'taid] times; woe — him ve ham.
betimes [bi'taimz] i tide, betids.
betoken [bi'toᵘkn] antyde, betegne, varsle.
betook [bi'tuk] imperf. av betake.
betray [bi'treⁱ] forråde, svike, røpe; forlede.
betrayal [bi'treⁱəl] forræderi.
betroth [bi'troᵘð] trolove, forlove seg med.
betrothal [bi'troᵘðəl] troloving, forlovelse.
better ['betə] bedre; mer; overhånd, overtak;
forbedre, bedre, overgå; overtreffe; i pl. overmenn; had — gjør best i å; gjorde best i å;
like — like bedre; be — off stå seg bedre; be —
than one's word gjøre mer enn man har lovet;
get the — of beseire, ta ved nesen; for — for
worse i medgang og i motgang, hvordan det enn
går; be the — for it ha godt av det; think —
of it ombestemme seg; — oneself slå seg opp.
better ['betə] en bedre.
betterment ['betəmənt] forbedring.
betting [' betiŋ] veddemål.
between bi'twi·n] imellom, mellom; between
them i forening, ved felles hjelp; — ourselves el.
— you and me (and the gatepost) mellom oss
sagt; they are far — de forekommer sjelden; — the
devil and the deep sea mellom barken og veden.
betwixt [bi'twikst] imellom; — and between
midt imellom.
bevel ['bevl] skjev vinkel; skjevmål; skjev, skeiv;
gi skrå retning. -led glass glass med fasettkanter.

beverage ['bevəridʒ] drikk.
bevy ['bevi] flokk.
bewail [bi'weⁱl] begrete, klage over, jamre over.
beware [bi'wæ·ə] passe seg (of for).
bewilder [bi'wildə] føre vill; forvirre; -ed fortumlet, forfjamset, uforstående. -ment forvirring.
bewitch [bi'witʃ] forhekse, trylle, forgjøre.
bey [beⁱ] bey; tyrkisk stattholder.
beyond [bi'jånd] hinsides, på den andre siden,
forbi; over, utover, mer enn; — measure over
all måte; — me over min forstand; the — det
hinsidige.
B. F. B. S. fk. f. British and Foreign Bible
Society.
bi [bai] som forstaving: to, to ganger, dobbelt.
bias ['baiəs] skjevhet, avvikende retning;
hang, tilbøyelighet; partiskhet; dra til en eller
annen side; påvirke; forut innta.
bib [bib] smekke, siklesmekke.
bib [bib] pimpe, supe.
bibacious [bi'beⁱʃes] fordrukken, drikkfeldig.
bible ['baibl] bibel. biblical ['biblikl] bibelsk.
bibliographer [bibli'ågrəfə] bibliograf. -ic
[biblio'gräfik] bibliografisk. -y [bibli'ågrəfi]
bibliografi.
bibliomania [biblio'meⁱnjə] galskap etter bøker.
bibliophile ['bibliofail] bibliofil, bokelsker.
bibulous ['bibjuləs] drikkfeldig; porøs.
biceps ['baiseps] biceps; muskel i overarmen.
bicker ['bikə] kjeftes; kjekle; dure, blaffe, kjekl;
bicycle ['baisikl] sykkel; sykle.
bicyclist ['baisiklist] syklist.
bid [bid] by, byde, befale; be; tilby, gjøre bud;
ønske; bud; — fair tegne godt, være lovende;
— welcome by velkommen; — defiance by tross;
make a — for gjøre bud på; no — (i bridge) pass.
bidden perf. pts. av bid.
bidder ['bidə] byder. bidding bud, befaling.
bide [baid] bie på, tåle, bære; — one's time se
tiden an; vente og se.
biennial [bai'enjəl] toårig (plante).
bier [biə] likbåre, båre.
biffin ['bifin] slags eple.
bifurcate ['baifə·keⁱt] tvegreinet.
big [big] stor, tykk, svær; svanger; oppblåst;
viktig.
bigamy ['bigəmi] bigami.
bight [bait] bukt, kveil (av et tau); havbukt.
bigot ['bigət] blind tilhenger. bigoted ['bigə-
tid] bigott. bigotry ['bigətri] religiøs forblindelse.
bigwig ['bigwig] storkar, kakse.
bike [baik] sykkel; sykle.
bilateral [bai'lätərəl] tosidet, tosidig; på begge
sider.
bilberry ['bilberi] blåbær.
bile [bail] galle.
bilge [bildʒ] bunn (av fat, el. skipsskrog);
gjøre lekk, bli lekk i bunnen.
bilge-water ['bildʒwå·tə] slagvann, kjølvann,
grunnvann.
bilingual [bai'liŋgwəl] bilingval.
bilious ['biljəs] gallesyk, grinete; galle-.
bilk [bilk] snyte, jukse; snyter.
Bill [bil] fk. f. William.
bill [bil] nebb; nebbes; — and coo utveksle
kjærtegn.
bill [bil] øks; hakke.
bill [bil] seddel; dokument; regning; veksel;
plakat; fortegnelse; lovforslag; find a true —
finne klagen berettiget; — of exchange veksel;
— of fare spiseseddel; — of health helsepass;
— of lading konnossement; — of parcels faktura;
the B. of Rights den lov, som sikret engelskmen-
nene en fri forfatning etter at stuartene var for-
drevet; — of sale skjøte. — -book vekselbok.
— -broker vekselmekler.
billet ['bilit] billett; innkvarteringsseddel;
kvarter; stilling, stykke arbeid; innkvartere.
billet ['bilit] vedtre, vedskie.
billet-doux ['bile'du·] kjærlighetsbrev.
billiard-ball ['biljədbå·l] biljardkule.

billiard-marker [-ma·°kə] markør.
billiard|s ['biljədz] biljard. — -stick [-stik] kø.
— -table [-'te¹bl] biljard(bord).
Billingsgate ['biliŋzge¹t] fisketorg; pøbelspråk.
billion ['biljən] billion; (amr.) milliard.
billow ['bilo⁰] bølge, båre. -y bølgende, båret.
bill|-poster ['bilpo⁰stə], — -sticker [-stikə]
plakatklistrer.
Billy ['bili] forkorting for William. — cock
[-kåk] bløt hatt. — -goat geitebukk.
bimetallism [bai'metəlizm] bimetallisme.
bin [bin] binge, bøle, beholder.
bind [baind] binde; forbinde; binde inn; forplikte; forstoppe; — up binde; forbinde. binder
bokbinder; bind, bindemiddel. binding bind; innbinding; bokbind.
binnacle ['binåkl] natthus, kompasshus.
binocle ['binåkl] dobbeltkikkert.
biographer [bai'ågrəfə] biograf, levnetsskil-
drer. biographical [baio'gräfikl] biografisk.
biography [bai'ågrəfi] biografi.
biologic(al) [baio¹'lådʒik(l)] biologisk.
biology [bai'ålədʒi] biologi, læren om livet.
biped ['baipéd] toføtt dyr.
birch [bə·tʃ] bjørk; ris; gi ris. -en ['bə·tʃen]
bjørke-.
bird [bə·d] fugl; fange fugler. — -cage fuglebur.
— -fancier fuglehandler. — -lime fuglelim. - 's eye
view fugleperspektiv. -'s nest fuglereir; go bird's-
nesting plyndre fuglereir.
birth [bə·þ] byrd, fødsel; herkomst; a man of
— en fornem mann, av god ætt.
birth-control ['bə·þ-kən'tro⁰l] fødselsregulering.
bir th|day fødselsdag. — -mark føflekk. — -place
fødested.
Biscay ['biske¹] Biscaya.
biscuit ['biskit] kjeks; (skips)kjeks; beskøyt;
biscuit.
bisect [bai'sekt] halvere.
bisexual ['bai'sekʃuəl] biseksuell.
bishop ['biʃəp] biskop, bisp; løper (i sjakk);
bisp (drikk). -ric ['biʃəprik] bispedømme.
bismuth ['bizməþ] vismut.
bison ['baisn] bison, bøffel.
bissextile [bi'sekstail] skuddår.
bistoury ['bisturi] skalpel.
bit [bit] bit, bete, stump; stykke, munnbitt,
kjeft (på tang); bissel; skjær (på nøkkel); (amr.)
liten sølvmynt; a — litt; be a — on (sl.) være litt
pussa.
bit [bit] imperf. av bite.
bitch [bitʃ] tispe; teve; hore.
bite [bait] bite; narre; bitt; the biter (has been)
bit han er blitt fanget i sitt eget garn.
bitten ['bitn] perf. pts. av bite.
bitter ['bitə] bitter; bitende, barsk; a — cold
en bitende kulde; bitter ting, bitter (drikk).
bittern ['bitən] rørdrum.
bitterness ['bitənès] bitterhet, skarphet.
bitumen [bi'tju·mən] jordbek, asfalt.
bivouac ['bivuäk] bivuakk; bivuakere.
bi-weekly ['bai'wi·kli] hver 14de dag.
bizarre [bi'za·°] bisarr, underlig.
B/L fk. f. bill of lading.
blab [bläb] sladre, plapre, buse ut med. -ber
sladderhank.
black [bläk] sort, svart, mørk; svart farge, sørgedrakt; neger; sverte. the Black Country kull-
distriktene; in — and white svart på hvitt.
-amoor morian; dunkjevle. — -and-tan især
en art terrier (svart og rødfarget); the Black and
Tans, styrke sendt til Irland for å kue Sinn Fein
(disse i Irland alm. forhatte soldater var i khaki
med svart hodetøy). — -ball svart kule (ved ballotering) nei-stemme, stemme mot ens opptagelse.
-berry bjørnebær. -bird svarttrost. — -board
veggtavle. — -book svartebok. — cap svart
lue som dommeren bærer, når han avsier døds-
dommen. — currant solbær. — draught, et avføringsmiddel.
blacken ['bläk(ə)n] sverte; besudle.

blacketeer [bläki'ti·°] svartebørshandler, svartehandler.
black eye «blått» øye. the Black Forest Schwarz-
wald. — frost barfrost. -guard ['blägəd] skarv,
slyngel; skjelle ut, bruke seg på; pøbelaktig; —
-heads hudormer. — hole «hullet», arresten.
-ie svarting, neger. -ing sverte. -leg spillefugl,
falsk spiller; streikebryter. — -list svartelista
(over firmaer som det ikke må handles med);
sette på svartelista; — -mail brannskatt; avgift
til røvere; pengeavpressing; avpresse penger.
Black Maria [Svartemarja] (vogn til fangetrans-
port). — market svartebørs. — marketeer
[ma·°ki'ti·°] svartebørshandler, svartehandler.
— -out mørklegging; mørklegge. — pudding blod-
pølse; Black Rod: Gentleman usher of the Black
Rod kongelig overseremonimester i Overhuset
(som har en svart embetsstav). — -smith grov-
smed. -thorn slåpetorn.
bladder ['blädə] blære (også om person).
blade [ble¹d] blad (på gras, kniv, åre o. l.);
klinge; en «løve» (kjekk kar).
blain [ble¹n] blemme.
blamable ['ble¹məbl] lastverdig, daddelverdig.
blame [ble¹m] daddel; skyld; dadle, laste. -less
ulastelig, daddelfri. -worthy daddelverdig.
blanch [bla·nʃ] gjøre hvit; bleike; skålde (f. eks.
mandler); koke ut (f. eks. sølv); bli hvit, bleikne.
blancmange [blə'mångʒ] blancmange (en slags
dessert).
bland [bländ] mild, blid.
blandish ['bländiʃ] smigre, kjærtegne.
blank [bläŋk] blank, ubeskrevet, ikke utfylt;
utelatt fornavn el. forbokstav; rimfri (om vers);
ren, fullstendig; forbløffet, forstyrret, forvirret;
ubeskrevet papir; åpent rom, tomrom; blankett;
blanko; nitte; — cartridge løs patron; point —
rent ut; in — in blanco; — verse urimede vers,
især 5-fotede jambiske. eighteen hundred —,
atten hundre og den tid.
blanket ['bläŋkét] ullteppe; legge teppe i; leke
himmelsprett med; put a wet — on legge en
demper på.
blare [blæ·ə] gjalle (om trompet); brøl.
Blarney ['bla·°ni] flekke og slott i Cork; have
kissed the — stone ha store talegaver. blarney
innsmigrende tale; smigre.
blasé [bla·'ze¹] blasert.
blasphem|e [bläs'fi·m, bla·s-] spotte; spotte
Gud, banne. -ous ['bläsfiməs, 'bla·s-] bespottelig. -y ['bläsfimi, 'bla·s-] gudsbespottelse.
blast [bla·st] vindkast; blåst; støt (i blåseinstrument); sprengning, lufttrykk; sott, landeplage; smitte; svie, brenne; ødelegge, sprenge; at
full — for full fres; — it! pokker ta det! blasted
helvetes, fordømt. — -furnace masovn.
blatant ['ble¹tənt] høyrøstet, snakkesalig.
blaze [ble¹z] flamme; lysning; blink (på tre);
bles (på hest); like blazes som bare pokker. blaze
blusse, flamme; lyse, skinne; utbasunere; merke,
blinke; — away! brenn løs! klem på!
blazer ['ble¹zə] flanellsjakke.
blazon ['ble¹zən] kolorere; vise fram, skildre;
pryde; utbasunere; tyde (heraldiske figurer); heraldikk; våpenskjold, våpenmerke. -ry våpen-
kunst; heraldikk.
bleach [bli·tʃ] bleike; bleikne.
bleak [bli·k] kald, råkald, trist, ødslig. -ness
kulde, tristhet.
blear [bliə] rennende, dim (om øyne); skumme,
mørk; gjøre mørk, bringe til å renne. -eyed surøyd, med rennende øyne.
bleat [bli·t] breke, mekre, raute (om kalv);
brek, rauting.
bleb [bleb] blemme, y- [-i] blemmet.
bled [bled] imperf. og perf. pts. av bleed.
bleed [bli·d] blø; årelate. -ing blødning; årelating.
blemish ['blemiʃ] lyte, skavank; plett; sette
plett på, vanære.
blench [blenʃ] gyse tilbake, vike.

blend [blend] blande; blande seg; blanding.
Blenheim ['blenim] Blenheim.
bless [bles] velsigne; også: forbanne; — me! el. God — my soul! herregud! without a sixpence to — oneself with uten så mye som en rød øre. -ed ['blesid] velsignet; salig; the -ed de salige; the whole -ed night hele den lange natt. -edness lykksalighet; single -edness den lykksalige ugifte stand. -ing velsignelse, signing; a -ing in disguise en uvelkommen, men gagnlig opplevelse; by the -ing of God med Guds hjelp.
blew [blu·] imperf. av blow.
blight [blait] sykdom på planter som: meldugg, rust, brann; (fig.) skade, ødeleggelse; forderve, ødelegge.
blighter ['blaitə] (sl.) fjols.
Blighty (soldaterslang) hjemmet, England; a — et sår som en blir sendt hjem for.
blind [blaind] blind; skjult; blinde; synkverve; blende; — of blind på; — to blind for; — alley blindgate; — coal antrasitt; — door blinddør (tilmurt, tildekt); — letter offisic kontor for brev med mangelfull adresse; — wall blindvegg.
blind [blaind] rullegardin, persienne, sjalusi, skylapp, skalkeskjul.
blind|fold ['blaindfoᵘld] med bind for øynene; binde for øynene. -man's-buff [-mənz'bʌf] blindebukk. -man's holiday tusmørke. -ness blindhet. -worm stålorm, slo.
blink [blink] blinke; blunke, glippe med øynene; lyse svakt; blink; glimt.
blinker ['blinkə] skylapp.
bliss [blis] lykksalighet. -ful lykksalig, sæl.
blister ['blistə] vable, blære, blemme; trekkplaster, spansk flue; trekke vabler; legge trekkplaster på; heve seg i vabler.
blithe [blaiδ], **blithesome** ['blaiδsəm] livsglad, fornøyd.
blitz [blits] (tysk ord) lynkrig; ogs. brukt om den tyske bombingen av England høsten 1940; bombe.
blizzard ['blizəd] snøstorm.
bloat [bloᵘt] blåse opp; bli tykk, svulme opp; -ed svullen; oppblåst, mesket.
bloat [bloᵘt] røyke (sild). -er røykt sild; Yarmouth -er økenavn for innbygger i Yarmouth.
block [blåk] blokk, hoggestabbe, retterblokk, parykkblokk, hatteblokk, støvelblokk, skriveblokk; kloss; heiseblokk, trisse; tretavle utskåret til trykning; blokkintervall (på jernbane); kvartal, bygningskompleks; sperring, hindring (av ferdsel); melding om at et lovforslag vil møte motstand; blokke ut; sperre, innelukke, blokere; — letters bokstaver skrevet som trykte bokstaver (vanligvis store bokstaver).
blockade [blå'keᵢd] blokade; blokere.
block-book bok trykt med utskårne tretavler.
blockhead ['blåkhed] dumrian. **blockhouse** ['blåkhaus] blokkhus. **blockish** tung, klosset.
bloke [bloᵘk] (sl.) fyr.
Blokes [bloᵘks]: Mr. — herr N. N., herr noksagt.
blond [blånd] lys, blond. **blonde** [blånd] blondine; blonde. **blond-lace** [-le¹s] blonder.
blood [blʌd] blod; slekt, ætt; venne til blod; gi blod på tann; her flesh-and- — life hennes jordiske liv.
blood-horse fullblodshest.
blood-hound blodhund; detektiv. -less blodløs, bleik. — -letting årelating. — orange blodappelsin. — -poisoning blodforgiftning. — -red blodrød. — relation blodsfrende, blodsbeslektet.
blood|shed blodsutgytelse. — shot blodunderløpen, blodsprengt. — -stained blodig, blodstenket. -stone blodstein (mineral), — -sucker blodsuger, igle. — -thirsty blodtørstig. — -vessel blodkar. **bloody** ['blʌdi] fandens, helvetes, fordømt (i denne alm. bet. er ordet meget vulgært); blodig; plette med blod.
bloom [blu·m] blomst, blome, blomsterflor; frisk dåm; rødme, glød, friskhet, dun på hud el. frukt; blomstre; in the — of youth i ungdommens vår; the — of health sunnhetsroser.

bloom [blu·m] smijernsblokk.
bloomers ['blu·məz] sykkelbukser, bukseskjørt.
blooming ['blu·min] blomstring; blomstrende; velsignet, forbannet (sl.).
Bloomsbury ['blu·mzbəri] strøk i London.
Bloomy ['blu·mi] blomstrende.
blossom ['blåsəm] blomst; blomstre.
blot [blåt] klatt, flekk; plett; flekke, plette, skjemme; bruke trekkpapir på, stryke ut; slå igjennom (om blekk).
blotch [blåtʃ] blemme, kveise; plett, flekk.
blotchy ['blåtʃi] flekkete, kveisete.
blotting-book ['blåtin'buk] skrivemappe. — -pad underlag av trekkpapir.
blotting-paper ['blåtinpe¹pə] trekkpapir.
blouse [blauz] bluse.
blow [bloᵘ] slag, støt; at a — med ett slag; come to -s komme i slagsmål.
blow [bloᵘ] springe ut, blomstre; blomstring.
blow [bloᵘ] blåse; blåse på (et instrument); pusse nesen; røpe, utspre; sprenge i lufta; gjennomhegle. -er blåser; belgetreder; tinnstøper. **blow|fly** ['bloᵘflai] spyflue. — -hole blåsterhull, sprøytehull.
blown [bloᵘn] perf. pts. av blow.
blow-off cock utblåsingshane. **blow-out** utblåsing; (sl.) rikelig måltid. **blow-pipe** blåserør; pusterør; utblåsingsrør. **blow-up** overhaling.
blubber ['blʌbə] hvalspekk; sutre, sippe, flepe.
bluchers ['blu·tʃəz, 'blu·kəz] (en slags) snørestøvler.
bludgeon ['blʌdʒən] kort kølle; lurk, svolk, påk.
blue [blu·] blå; (fig.) nedtrykt, melankolsk; som hører til torypartiet, lærd (om kvinner); blått, blå farge, konservativ; politibetjent; (i pl.) tungsinn, tunglynne, blåstrømpe; gjøre blå; (sl.) ødsle, feel — føle seg nedtrykt; things look — alt ser håpløst ut; win (el. get) one's — bli valt til å representere sitt universitet ved sportskamp. be in the blues være nedtrykt. **Bluebeard** blåskjegg. **bluebell** blåklokke. **bluebook** blåbok (offisiell beretning). **bluebottle** spyflue; kornblomst. **bluecoat boy** vaisenhusgutt (srl. fra Christ's Hospital). **blue devils** melankoli. **blue funk** (sl.) stor redsel. **bluejacket** orlogsgast. **bluelight** blålys. **once in a blue moon** meget sjelden. **Blue Peter** avgangssignal (et blått flagg). **blue ribbon** blått bånd; tegn for hosebåndsordenen og for avholdsforening. **blue rock** bergdue. **blue-stocking** blåstrømpe. **blue-stone** blåstein, kobbervitriol. **blue-water school**, om dem som anser flåten for tilstrekkelig vern for Storbritannia.
bluff [blʌf] steil, bratt; djerv, endefram; morsk, barsk; bratt skrent, ufs; påtatt selvsikkerhet, skryt, bløff; skremmeskudd; bløffe, skremme.
bluish ['blu·iʃ] blålig.
blunder ['blʌndə] forseelse, bommert; gjøre en bommert; vase; famle seg fram, vase, tumle (av sted). -buss muskedunder.
blunt [blʌnt] skjemt, sløv; likefram, endefram grov; sløve; døyve. -ness sløvhet; usjenerthet.
blur [blə·] plette, sulke, sette plett på; dimme; plett; uklarhet, tåke.
blurt [blə·t] out buse ut med.
blush [blʌʃ] rødme, bli rød; rødme; flyktig, blikk, øyekast. -less skamløs.
bluster ['blʌstə] bruse, suse; larme; skryte; brus, sus; laım; skryt. -er ['blʌstərə] storskryter.
bo, boh! [boᵘ] bø! cannot say — to a goose tør ikke si kitt in i katten, er en stakkar.
boa ['boᵘə, bå·ə] kjempeslange; boa (pelskrage).
boar [bå·ə] råne; villsvin.
board [bå·əd] bord, brett, fjel; (vegg)tavle; (spise-)bord; kost, kostpenger; kollegium, råd, utvalg, nemnd; styre; (i pl.) scenen; (skips)side; slag, baut; papp, kartong, perm; bordkle; ha i kost; sette i kost, sette bort på for; være i kost; borde, entre (et fiendtlig skip); bed and — bord og seng (ekteskapelig forhold); — and lodging kost og losji. above — åpent og ærlig; on — ombord, (amr.) med toget; B. of Agriculture land-

bruksdepartement; — of directors direksjon, styre. **B. of Education** undervisningsdepartement; **B. of Trade** handelsdepartement; **Local Government B.** (har vesentlig med fattigvesenet å gjøre). **School B.** skolestyre; **the B. of Admiralty** marinestyret. **-er** kostgjenger; entregast. **-ing-house** pensjonat. **-ing-school** kostskole (mots. **day-school**). — **-school** folkeskole (under School-Board).

board-wages ['bå·ºd'we¹dʒiz] kostpenger.

boarish ['bå·rif] grisete; plump, rå.

boast [boᵘst] skryte, kyte; rose seg av, være byrg av; kyt, skryt, stolthet. **boaster** storskryter. **boastful** skrytende. **boasting** kyting.

boat [boᵘt] båt; ferjebåt; skip; dampskip; **be in the same** — være i samme stilling. — **-house** båtshake. — **-house** båthus. **-ing** rotur, roning, seilas. **-man** ferjemann, båtutleier. — **-race** kapproing. **-swain** ['boᵘsn] båtsmann.

Bob [båb] kjælenavn for Robert; konstabel.

bob [båb] rykke (i, med); slå, dulte til; stubbe, stusse, stutte; rykke; dingle; duppe; duve; neie; hile, pilke; — **a curtsey** neie; — **one's head in at the door** stikke hodet kjapt gjennom døra; **-bed hair** pasjehår, «cutting»; **bob** [båb] noe som henger og dingler, f. eks. lodd på en loddline; **dingeldangel**; agn, makk; omkved; rykk, kast, støt; (sl.) shilling.

bobbin ['båbin] snelle; spole; kniplepinne; håndtak; klinkesnor; tynn snor.

bobbish ['båbif] rask, sprek, kry.

Bobby ['båbi] kjælenavn for Robert; konstabel. **bob-sleigh** ['båbslei] tømmerslede; drag, drog. **bob-tail** ['båbteᶦl] kort hale, spæl; **tag-rag and** — pøbel. **bob-tailed** korthalet.

Boche [båf] (sl.) tysker.

bode [boᵘd] varsle.

bodice ['bådis] snøreliv, korsett; kjoleliv.

bodily ['bådili] legemlig; fysisk; fullstendig.

boding ['boᵘdin] varsel.

bodkin ['bådkin] syl; ål; trekkenål; **sit** — **sitte** inneklemt mellom to andre.

Bodleian [båd'li·ən, 'bådliən]: **the** — **library**, bibliotek i Oxford.

body ['bådi] legeme; kropp; lik; person; substans; korps; samling, samlet masse; samfunn; hele, helhet; hovedstyrke; stamme (på et tre): skrog (et skips); fating; forme, danne. — **-guard** livvakt. — **-snatcher** liktyv.

Boer [buə] boer.

bog [båg] myr, myrlende; søkke ned i en myr.

bogey ['boᵘgi] busemann, skremsel.

boggle ['bågl] fare sammen, skvette, støkke, kvekke; tvile, nøle.

boggy ['bågi] myrlendt.

bogie ['boᵘgi] boggi.

bogle [boᵘgl] spøkelse, skremsel.

bogus ['boᵘgəs] uekte, falsk, jukse-.

Bohemia [bo'hi·mjə] Bøhmen. **Bohemian** [bo-'hi·mjən] bøhmisk; tater-, bøhmer; bohem.

boil [boil] byll.

boil [boil] koke. **-er** dampkjele. **-ing** kokende; **keep the pot -ing** holde det gående; **the whole -ing** (sl.) hele stasen; **-ing-point** kokepunkt.

boisterous ['boistərəs] voldsom; framfus(ende); larmende, bråkende. **-ness** voldsomhet; høyrøstethet.

bold [boᵘld] dristig, djerv, kjekk; frimodig, freidig; frekk; fri; **make** — fordriste seg. **-faced** frekk. **-ness** dristighet.

bole [boᵘl] trestamme, bol.

bolero [bo'læ·ºroᵘ] bolero (spansk dans).

Boleyn ['bulin] Boleyn.

boll ['boᵘl] frøhus, skolm.

Bologna [bə'loᵘnjə] Bologna.

Bolchevik ['bålfəvik] bolsjevik. **-ism** ['bålfə-vizm] bolsjevisme. **-ist** ['bålfəvist] bolsjevik, bolsjevistisk.

bolshie, bolshy ['bålfi] (sl.) bolsjevik.

bolster ['boᵘlstə] bolster, underdyne; pute,

underlag; salpute; kompress (på sår); legge pute under; støtte oppunder, hjelpe fram.

bolt [boᵘlt] bolt; slå; lyn; stenge (m. slå el. skåte); lenke, legge i bolt og jern; buse ut med; sluke (uten å tygge); styrte fram el. ut; stikke av. **bolt** [boᵘlt] bent; — **upright** rett opp og ned. **bolt** [boᵘlt] sælde, sikte (korn, mel); (fig.) drøfte, prøve. **-er** siktemaskin.

bolus ['boᵘləs] stor pille.

bomb [båm] bombe, slippe bomber ned på.

bomb alley ['båm'äli] stripe som bomben (V-bomben) etterlater seg på himmelen.

bombard [båm'ba·ºd] bombardere. **-ier** [båmbə-'diə] bombarder, artilleriersjant. **-ment** [båm'ba-ºdmənt] bombardement.

bombardon [båm'ba·dn] bombardon.

bombasine [båmbə'zi·n] bombasin.

bombast ['båmbəst] svulst, ordbram. **bombastic** [båm'bästik] svulstig, høyttravende.

Bombay [båm'beᶦ] Bombay.

bomber ['båmə] bombefly.

bomb blast ['båm'bla·st] lufttrykk fra bombeeksplosjon.

bomb disposal ['båm di'spoᵘzəl] uskadeliggjøring av tidsinnstilt bombe.

bomb-proof ['båmpru·f] bombesikker. — **-raid** bombeangrep. — **-shell** bombe.

bonafide ['boᵘnə'faidi] i god tro, ekte.

bonanza [bo'nänzə] (spansk ord) lykke; rikt ertsfunn, rik gullgruve; rik, fordelaktig, lønnende.

Bonaparte [bo'ᵘnəpa·ºt] Bonaparte.

bond [bånd] bånd; forband; obligasjon, forskrivning; gjeldsbrev; forpliktelse; tollopplag, frilager; bunden, fangen; legge i tollopplag; **-ed goods** transittgods. **-ed warehouse** tollopplag, frilager. **-age** ['båndidʒ] trelldom. **-man** ['båndmən] trell. **-sman** ['båndzmən] slave; kausjonist.

bone [boᵘn] ben, bein, knokkel; fiskeben (i kjoleliv), fribillett; (i pl.) spiler (i paraply); kastanjetter; terninger; renske for ben; sette fiskeben el. spiler i; kvarte, redde; **bred in the** — medfødt; **have a** — **to pick with** ha en høne å plukke med; — **of contention** stridens eple. **-less** benfri. — **-setter** ledd-doktor. — **-shaker** gammeldags sykkel med massive ringer.

Boney ['boᵘni] fork. f. Bonaparte.

bonfire ['bånfaiə] festbluss, bål.

bonne [bån] bonne (fransk barnepike).

bonnet ['bånit] lue; damehatt; ta hatt på; slå hatten ned i pannen (på en).

bonny ['båni] (skotsk) vakker, gild; glad.

bonus ['boᵘnəs] bonus; gratiale.

bony ['boᵘni] beinet, knoklet.

boo [bo·] bø! bu! pytt! raut; si bø, raute; **si bø til**, true; pipe ut.

booby ['bu·bi] havsule; tosk; fuks (i en klasse).

book [buk] bok; 6 stikk (i whist); skrive, føre til boks, bokføre, engasjere; løse billett til, tinge på; **bring to** — kreve til regnskap; **speak by the** — tale som en bok. **-binder** bokbinder. **-case** bokreol, bokskap. **-ie** ['buki] (sl.) veddemålsagent. **-ing-office** billettkontor. **-ish** ['bukif] pedantisk, stuelærd. — **-keeper** bokholder. — **-keeping** bokføring. — **-learned** stuelærd. — **-maker** veddemålsagent, profesjonell veddemålsspekulant (ved hesteveddeløp). **-man** litterat. — **-mark** bokmerke. — **-post** korsbånd; **by** — **-post** som korsbånd, *trykksaker*. **-seller** bokhandler; **-shelf** bokhylle. — **-stall** åpent bokutsalg, kiosk. — **-stand** liten bokhylle. — **-store** (amr.) bokhandel. — **-worm** bokorm, lesehest.

boom [bu·m] bom; dønn, drønn; reklame; prisstigning, oppsving, høykonjunktur; drønne; reklamere for, drive prisen opp; blomstre opp.

boomerang ['bu·məräŋ] bumerang.

boon [bu·n] gave, velgjerning; gunst; lystig, glad; **a** — **companion** svirebror.

boor [buə] tølper, bondelamp. **-ish** ['buərif] bondsk, tølperaktig.

boost [bu·st] reklamere for; hjelpe; forsterke (batteris spenning).

boot [bu·t] gagne, hjelpe; fordel, gagn; **to —** attpå, på kjøpet.

boot [bu·t] støvel; vognskrin (under kuske-setet); skvettlær; (pl.) skopusser, hotellgutt; trekke støvler på. **-ee** ['bu·ti] damestøvel; barne-sokk.

booth [bu·þ] bu, fjelebu.

bootjack ['bu·tdʒäk] støvelknekt.

bootlace ['bu·tleis] støvelreim, støvellisse.

bootless ['bu·tlès] unyttig, gagnløs, fåfengt

bootmaker ['bu·tme¹kə] skomaker.

boot-tree ['bu·t-tri] støvelblokk.

booty ['bu·ti] bytte, rov, hærfang; **to play —** tape med forsett; spille under dekke.

booze [bu·z] (sl.) svire; fyll, drikkevarer. **boozer** (sl.) svirebror; bevertning. **boozy** (sl.) omtåket.

bo-peep [bou'pi·p] tittelek, gjemme-kikke.

boracic [bo'räsik] bor-; **— acid** borsyre.

borax ['bå·°ræks] boraks.

border ['bå·°də] rand, kant; bord; grense(land); kante; avgrense; grense (**upon** til). **-er** grenseboer.

bore [bå·°] imperf. av **bear**.

bore [bå·°] bore; utbore; plage, kjede; (bore)-hull; plageånd, plage; løp (på børse), kaliber; **it is a —** det er ergerlig, kjedelig.

bore [bå·°] flobølge, springflo.

boreal ['bå·°riəl] nordlig, norda-.

born [bå·°n] født, perf. pts. av **bear**.

borne [bå·°n] båret, perf. pts. av **bear**.

Borneo ['bå·°njou] Borneo.

borough ['bʌrə] kjøpstad, by; valgkrets; **close — eller pocket —** valgkrets, der velgerne var avhengig av godseieren (før 1832); **rotten —** valgkrets, som, enda velgertallet var ganske lite, sendte egen representant til Parlamentet (før 1832).

borough-English ['bʌrə'iŋgliʃ] system i visse deler av England, hvoretter all jord og eiendom tilfaller den yngste sønnen.

borrow ['båro¹] låne (av andre). **-er** låntager.

boscage ['båskidʒ] kratt, tykning.

bosh [båʃ] vrøvl, sludder.

bosom ['buzəm] barm; bryst. **— -friend** hjer-tevenn, bestevenn.

boss [bås] mester, sjef, prinsipal; styre, rå.

boss [bås] bule, kul; knott, knapp; bossere.

bot [båt] verre, bremselarve.

botanic(al) [bo'tänik(l)] botanisk. **botanist** ['båtənist] botaniker. **botanize** ['båtənaiz] bota-nisere. **botany** ['båtəni] botanikk.

botch [båtʃ] svulst: bot, lapp, lappverk; be-fenge med svulster; bøte, lappe i hop; skjemme bort. **-er** lappeskredder; fusker.

both [bouþ] begge; **we . . . both of us** vi . . . begge to; **— and** både . . . og.

bother ['båðə] plage, bry; umake, bry(deri); **oh —!** det var da ergerlig! **— him!** gid pokker hadde ham! **be bothered** ha ubehageligheter. **-ation** [båðə're¹ʃən] plage, mas, kav. **-some** ['båðəsəm] brysom, plagsom.

Bothnia ['båþniə], **Gulf of —** Bottenvika.

bothy ['båþi] (skotsk) bu, hytte.

bottle ['båtl] bunt; **look for a needle in a — of hay** lete etter en knappenål i et høylass.

bottle ['båtl] flaske; fylle på flasker. **— -green** flaskegrønn. **— -holder** (i bokser) sekundant.

bottom ['båtəm] bunn, botn; grunn; nederste del; bakdel, ende; dal; skip; kjøl; (fig.) kraft, ut-holdenhet; sette bunn i; grunne, basere, grunnleg-ge; **at the —** på bunnen; ved foten (av en bakke); nedenfor; **he is at the — of it** han står bak det. **-less** bunnløs; **-ry** ['båtəmri] bodmeri; pant-sette.

boudoir ['bu·dwa·°] budoar.

bough [bau] grein.

bought [bå·t] imperf. og perf. pts. av **buy**.

boulder ['bo¹ldə] rullestein, kampestein.

Boulogne [bu'lo¹n] Boulogne.

bounce [bauns] spring, byks, sprett; støt; skryt, overdrivelse; trusel; løgn; sprette, bykse,

komme settende; bråke; skryte. **bouncer** stor, svær rusk; storskryter; diger skrøne.

bound [baund] bykse, hoppe; sprett, byks.

bound [baund] grense, skranke; begrense.

bound [baund] bestemt (**for** til), reiseferdig, på veien; **homeward —** på hjemveien.

bound [baund] imperf. og perf. pts. av **bind**.

boundary ['baundəri] grense.

bounden ['baundən]: **my — duty** min simple plikt.

bounder ['baundə] (sl.) simpel person.

boundless ['baundlès] grenseløs.

bounteous ['bauntiəs, -tjəs] gavmild, raus.

bountiful ['bauntiful] gavmild; rikelig. **bounty** ['baunti] gavmildhet; gave; barmhjertighet; pre-mie.

bouquet ['buke¹] bukett; aroma, buké.

bourgeois ['buəʒwa·] bursjoa.

bout [baut] tur, tak, dyst, tørn; drikkelag.

bovine ['bo¹vain] hornkveg, okse-.

bovril ['båvril] kjøttkraft, buljong.

bow [bau] bøye; bukke; bukke seg; bukk; baug (på skip); **— one to the door, carriage** følge en bukkende til døra, vognen.

bow [bo¹] bue; sløyfe; bøye, krumme, krøke. **Bow-bells** ['bo¹belz] klokkene i **Bow-Church** ['bo¹tʃə·tʃ] Bowkirken omtrent midt i London; **he is born within the sound of —** han er en ekte londoner.

bowels ['bauəlz] innvoller, indre; medliden-het, sympati; **have your — moved** har De hatt avføring; **— of the earth** det indre av jorda.

bower ['bauə] lauvhytte, lauvsal, lysthus; kabi-nett; kove.

bowie-knife ['bo¹inaif] (amr.) tollekniv.

bowl [bo¹l] ball, kule; bolle, kum, skål; terrin; pipehode; skjeblad; trille; slå (i spill); spille ball, slå kiler. **-er** kilespiller; ballspiller; stiv hatt. **-ing-alley** kilebane, ballplass. **-ing-green** ballplass.

bowlder ['bo¹ldə] se **boulder**.

bow-legged ['bo¹legd] hjulbeint.

bowler-hat ['bo¹lähät] rund, stiv hatt, skalk.

bowline ['bo¹lain] buline.

bow-sprit ['bo¹sprit] baugspryd.

Bow Street ['bo¹stri·t] gate i London, tidligere sete for politiets hovedkontor; **— officer** el. **— runner** oppdagelsesbetjent (i gamle dager).

bow-string ['bo¹striŋ] buestreng.

bow-window ['bo¹'windo¹] karnappvindu (i rundt karnapp).

bow-wow ['bau'wau] vovvov.

box [båks] buksbom.

box [båks] eske, ask, skrin; kasse; koffert; jule-gave (**Christmas —**); bukk, kuskesete; losje; av-lukke; kove; spiltau; jakthytte (**hunting —**); bøs-sing; legge i eske el. kasse; **go a -ing** gå omkring og ønske gledelig jul; **— the compass** lese (gå) kompasset rundt.

box [båks] bokse, fike, slå; slag, fik, lusing; **on the ear** ørefik. **boxer** ['båksə] bokser.

boxhaul ['båkshå·l] bakke for.

Boxing-day ['båksiŋde¹] annen juledag.

box-iron strykejern (m. bolt). **box-keeper** bil-lettkontrollør (på teater). **box-office** billettkon-tor (på teater).

boy [boi] gutt, guttunge; tjener.

boyar [bå¹ja·°, ¹boiə] bojar.

boycott ['boikət] boikotte; boikott.

boyhood ['boihud] gutteår, barndom.

boyish ['boiiʃ] guttaktig, gutte-. **-ness** gutt-aktighet.

Boz [båz] psevdonym for Charles Dickens.

Bp fork. f. **bishop**.

brabble ['bräbl] kjekle; kjekl.

brace [bre¹s] bånd, reim; gjord, belte; støtte, knekt; borsveiv; parentes, klammer; bras; par (i jaktspr.); binde, gjorde, styrke, stramme, spenne; brase; **-s** seler; **— his feet against** ta spenntak i.

bracelet ['bre¹slèt] armbånd.

brachycephalic [bräkise'fälik] kortskallet.

bracing ['bre¹siŋ] forfriskende, nervestyrkende.
bracken ['bräkn] bregne, einstape.
bracket ['bräkit] konsoll; liten benk (som er gjort fast i veggen); klamme (parentes); støtte med konsoll; sette i klammer; sammenstille. **square** — [], **round** — ().
brackish ['bräkiʃ] brakk; — **water** brakkvann.
brad [bräd] nudd, dykkert. **-s**(sl.) penger. **-awl** [-å·l] pinnesyl.
brae [bre¹] (skotsk) bakke, hall, skrent.
brag [bräg] prale, skryte, braute; kyt, skryting; et slags kortspill. **-gadocio** [brägə¹do⁻ʃo⁻] skryt. **-gart** ['brägət], **bragger** ['brägə] storskryter.
Brahma ['bra·mə] Brama.
Brahman ['bra·mən], **Brahmin** ['bra·min] braman, bramin.
braid [bre¹d] flette, tvinne; besette med snorer; snor; flette.
brail [bre¹l] gitau; gi opp.
brain [bre¹n] hjerne; hode, vett, forstand (også **brains**); slå hodet inn på; **rack** (el. **puzzle**) **one's brains** legge sitt hode i bløyt.— **-fever** ['bre¹n'fi·və] hjernebetennelse. **-less** enfoldig. **-sick** ikke riktig i hodet; tankeløs.
brake [bre¹k] (lin)brakk; bremse; bråke, bremse.
brake [bre¹k] kratt; einstape.
bramble ['brämbl] klunger(kjerr), bjørnebær (ris). **brambly** ['bræmbli] tornet.
bran [brän] kli.
branch [bra·nʃ] grein; arm; avsnitt; avdeling, bransje; læregrein, fag; filial; greine seg.— **line** sidelinje. **-y** ['bra·nʃi] greinet.
brand [bränd] brann (et brennende stykke tre); sverd; brennemerke, skamplett; (merk.) stempel; merke, kvalitet, kvalitetsmerke, fabrikat; brennemerke; merke, stemple. **-iron** brennjern.
brandish ['brändiʃ] svinge (f. eks. sverd).
brand-new ['brändnju·] splinterny.
brandy ['brändi] brennevin, konjakk; blande med konjakk. — **-and-water** grogg. — **pawnee** (i anglo-indisk) grogg.
bran-new ['brännju·] se **brandnew**.
brash [bräʃ] kvist, kvas, rusk.
brass [bra·s] messing; messingtøy; messinginstrument; mynt, penger; pryd, ornament; uforskammethet. **-band** musikk-korps med blåseinstrumenter. — **farthing** en døyt. — **hat** (soldatslang) høytstående offiser. — **plate** messingplate, navneplate(på dør). **-y** messingaktig; messinggul; frekk.
brat [brät] unge.
bravado [brə¹va·do⁻] kyt, skryt.
brave [bre¹v] modig, tapper; gjev; storartet; gild; vågehals, slåsskjempe; trosse, sette seg opp imot. **-ly** tappert, motig; prektig; til gagns, dyktig. **bravery** ['bre¹vəri] tapperhet; prakt.
bravo ['bra·vo⁻] bravo! bravorop; banditt, leiemorder.
bravura [brə¹v(j)urə] bravur, bravurarie.
brawl [brå·l] larme, krangle; ståk, klammeri.
brawn [brå·n] grisesylte; muskelkraft, svære muskler. **brawny** ['brå·ni] sterk, muskuløs.
bray [bre¹] støte, finstøte; rive.
bray [bre¹] skrall, drønn; skryting (et esels); drønne, skralle; skryte.
braze [bre¹z] lodde; beslå med messing; (fig.) forherde; herde.
brazen ['bre¹zən] messing-, malm-, bronse-; frekk, uforskammet. **-faced** [-feist] uforskammet.
brazier ['bre¹ʒə] messingsmed, gjørtler.
brazier ['bre¹ʒə] glopanne, fyrfat.
Brazil [brə¹zil] Brasil. **brazil** brasiltre, rødtre.
Brazilian [brə¹ziljən] brasiler, brasilsk. **Brazils** [brə¹zilz]: **the** — Brasil.
breach [bri·tʃ] brudd; bresje; — **of promise** brudd på ekteskapsløfte.
bread [bred] brød; panere; — **and butter** smørbrød (tynne brødsnitter med smør, men uten pålegg); **quarrel with one's** — **and butter** spolere sitt levebrød.
breadth [bredþ] bredde, breidd.
bread-winner ['bredwinə] familieforsørger.

break [bre¹k] brekke, bryte, nedbryte, bryte i sund; ruinere, ramponere, ødelegge; sprenge; springe, briste, ryke sund; bryte løs, bryte fram; gry; ri inn, temme (en hest); avbryte; åpne; begynne; gå fallitt; svekkes, avta; ikke holde seg; — **the news to a person** meddele lempelig, forberede en på et budskap; — **one's heart** gjøre en hjertesorg; — **down** bryte ned; mislykkes, slå feil; miste fatningen; **-down** uhell, nederlag; — **in falle inn** (i talen), utbryte; — **in upon** avbryte; her cheeks broke into dimples hun fikk smilehull i kinnene; — **up** bryte opp; oppløse; hogge opp; klarne (om været); **-up** oppløsning; — **oneself of a habit** venne seg av med noe.
break [bre¹k] brudd; frambrudd; avbrytelse, stans, ombrøyte; friminutt; avsats. **-able** ['bre¹kəbl] skrøpelig. **-age** ['bre¹kidʒ] brudd, beskadigelse; erstatning for ramponert gods. **-er** ['bre¹kə] en som bryter osv.; brottsjø, skavl, brenning.
breakfast ['brekfəst] åbit, frokost; spise frokost.
breakwater ['bre¹kwå·tə] bølgebryter, molo.
bream [bri·m] brasen, brasme (fisk).
breast [brest] bryst, bringe, barm; hjerte; sette brystet imot; stemme imot; trosse; **make a clean** — tilstå. **-work** brystvern.
breath [breþ] ånde; åndedrag, åndedrett; pust; luftning; liv; pusterom; munnsvær; **at a** — i samme åndedrett; **out of** — andpusten; **half under her** — halvt dempet, halvhøyt; **draw one's** — puste. **breathe** [bri·ð] ånde, puste, dra pusten; hvile litt; innånde; blåse inn; puste ut; hviske, kviskre; **one's last** dra sitt siste suk. **breather** ['bri·ðə] en som ånder; en som innånder, innblåser. **breathing** ['bri·diŋ] ånde; gust, luftning; innblåsning. **breathless** ['breþlės] åndeløs, andpusten.
bred [bred] avlet; — **in the bone** medfødt, av **breed**.
breech [bri·tʃ] bakstykke (på skytevåpen); gi en gutt bukser på. **-es** ['britʃiz] pl. slags knebukser; **she** (l. **the wife**) **wears the -es** det er kona som har buksene på. **-ing** ['bri·tʃiŋ] bakreim; strambuks. **-loader** bakladningsbørse el. -kanon.
breed [bri·d] avle; ale, fostre; oppdra; frambringe; yngle, formere seg; avkom, rase; yngel; art, slag. **-ing** avl, al, oppdrett; utklekking; oppdragelse.
breeze [bri·z] kullavfall.
breeze [bri·z] bremse, klegg.
breeze [bri·z] bris. **breezy** ['bri·zi] luftig, frisk.
brethren ['breðrėn] (høyere stil) brødre.
Breton ['bretn] bretagner, bretagnisk.
breviary ['bri·viəri] breviarium.
brevity ['breviti] korthet.
brew [bru·] brygge; trekke opp (om uvær); være i gjære. **-age** [-idʒ] brygg, blanding. **-er** ['bru·ə] brygger. **-ery** [-əri] bryggeri.
briar ['braiə] se **brier**.
bribe [braib] bestikkelse, stikkpenger; bestikke, mute. **bribery** ['braibəri] bestikkelse.
brick [brik] murstein; teglstein; brikke; byggekloss; kjernekar; mure. **-bat** stykke murstein. **-burner** teglbrenner. **-field** teglverk. **-kiln** teglovn. **-layer** murer. **-maker** teglbrenner. **-nogging** bindingsverk. **-yard** teglverk.
bridal ['braidəl] brude-, bryllups-.
bride [braid] brud. **-groom** [-gru·m] brudgom. **brides|maid** ['braidzme¹d] brudepike. — **-man** brudesvenn.
bridewell ['braidwel] tukthus.
bridge [bridʒ] bru, kommandobru; stol (på en fiolin); neserygg; bygge bru over.
bridge [bridʒ] bridge, bridsj (kortspill).
bridge-board ['bridʒbå·d] vange (i trapp).
bridgehead ['bridʒhed] bruhode, befestningsverk til beskyttelse av bru, pass el. lign. overgang.
bridle ['braidl] bissel; tømme, tom, tøyle; bisle; tøyle; kneise. — **-path**, — **-way** ridevei.
bridoon [bri¹du·n] bridon.
brief [bri·f] kort, kortfattet; kort uttog av en

rettssak, resymé utarbeidd av the solicitor til bruk for the barrister; rettsordre; diplom; bevilling til innsamling; låneseddel. **-s** juridiske saker. **briefless** uten praksis (jur.).**briefly** kort, i korthet.
brier ['braiə] vill rose; klunger; tornebusk; snadde.
brig [brig] brigg.
brigade [bri'ge'd] brigade.
brigadier [brigə'diə], **-general** brigade-general.
brigand ['brigənd] røver.
brigantine ['brigəntain, -ti·n] brigantin.
bright [brait] blank, klar, funklende; lys; opplyst; gløgg; **honour bright!** på ære! — **red** høyrød. **-en** ['braitn] lysne, gjøre lysere; **as the day -ened** etter som det lysnet. **-ness** klarhet, glans; skarpsindighet.
Brighton ['braitn] Brighton.
brilliance ['briljəns] glans; åndrikhet. **brilliancy** ['briljənsi] glans, lysstyrke. **brilliant** ['briljənt] glimrende, skinnende; briljant (diamant).
brim [brim] rand, kant; brem (på hatt); fylle til randen, være breddfull. **-ful** breddfull.
brimstone ['brimstən] svovel. **brimstony** ['brimstəni] svovelaktig, svovel-.
brinded ['brindid], **brindled** ['brindld] spettet, stripet, brandet, droplet.
brine [brain] saltvann; salt vann; saltlake, lake; (fig.) hav; tårer; legge i saltlake, salte.
bring [briŋ] bringe (især til den talende); skaffe; innbringe; ta, bringe med, ha med; **to — word** bringe bud el. etterretning; — **about** få i stand, utvirke, volde; — **down the house** høste stormende applaus; — **one down a peg** legge en demper på en; — **forth** frambringe, føde; — **home** overbevise, gjøre det klart; — **in** innføre, innbringe; sette fram; — **to** dreie bi; — **to mind** gjenkalle i minnet; — **up** bringe opp; oppdra; bringe på bane; stanse; forankre.
bringer ['briŋə] overbringer, budbærer.
brink [briŋk] stup, kant; **on the — of the grave** på gravens rand.
briny ['braini] salt. **the — ** havet.
briquet ['brikət], **briquette** [bri'ket] brikett. **brisk** [brisk] frisk, livlig, rask, sprek.
brisling ['brizliŋ] brisling.
bristle ['brisl] bust; reise seg, stritte, stå stivt; **set up the -s** reise bust.
Britain ['britn], **Great Britain** Storbritannia. **Greater Britain** «større Britannia» (om det britiske verdensrike). **North Britain** Skottland.
Britannia [bri'tänjə] Britannia. **britannia** britanniametall. **Britannic** [bri'tänik] britisk.
Brit|ish ['britiʃ] britisk; **-isher** [-iʃə] brite.
Briton ['britən] brite. **North —** skotte.
Brittany ['britəni] Bretagne.
brittle ['britl] skjør, sprø, skrøpelig.
broach [broʊtʃ] stekespidd; stikke an; ta hull på, begynne å bruke; begynne å diskutere.
broad [brå·d] bred, brei, vid, stor; grov, drøy; — **awake** lysvåken; — **daylight** høylys dag; **B. Church** frisinnet retning i den engelske kirke. **broad|cast** ['brå·dka·st] håndsådd, strødd vidt og bredt; kringkaste. — **cloth** fint klede. **-ly speaking** stort sett. **-sheet** ark trykt på den ene side, plakat. **-side** bredside; glatt lag. **-sword** pallask. **broaden** ['brå·dn] gjøre bred; utvide seg. **broadness** bredde, vidde.
broadwise ['brå·dwaiz] etter bredden.
Brobdingnag ['bråbdiŋnäg] kjempelandet i Swift's **Gulliver's Travels.**
brocade [bro'ke'd] brokade.
brocket ['bråkət] spisshjort (toårig hjort).
brogan ['broʊgən, 'brågən] tykk sko.
brogue [broʊg] irsk uttale av engelsk; slags sko.
broil [broil] steke, riste; stekes; oppstyr, leven.
broke [broʊk] imperf. av **break.**
broken ['broʊkn] perf. pts. av **break.** — **meat** kjøttrester. — **-hearted** med knust hjerte, nedslått. **-ly** avbrutt, rykkvis. — **-spirited** nedbrutt, motløs. — **-winded** stakkåndet.

broker ['broʊkə] mekler; marsjandiser; auksjonarius, inkassator. **-age** ['broʊkəridʒ] meklerlønn, kurtasje, provisjon.
brome [broʊm] brom. **bromide** ['broʊmaid] bromid; — **of potassium** bromkalium.
bronchia ['bråŋkiə] **bronchiæ** [bråŋkii·] bronkier, luftveier. **bronchitis** [bråŋ'kaitis] bronkitt.
Brontë ['brånti, -te'] Brontë.
bronze [brånz] bronse; figur av bronse; bronsere; forherde, barke.
brooch [broʊtʃ] brosje, brystnål; smykke.
brood [bru·d] unger, yngel; avkom; ruge; ruge ut, klekke ut.
brook [bruk] tåle, finne seg i.
brook [bruk] bekk, å. **-let** ['bruklit] liten bekk.
broom [bru·m] (slags) lyng, gyvel; sopelime, feie, koste, sope.
broomstick ['bru·mstik] kosteskaft.
Bros. ['brʌðəz] brødrene (i firmanavn).
broth [brå·þ] sodd, kjøttsuppe; — **of a boy** flink fyr.
brothel ['bråþl, 'bråðl] bordell, horehus.
brother ['brʌðə] bror; (fig.) kollega; svoger. — **in arms** krigskamerat. **brother-in-law** ['brʌðərin'lå·] svoger. **-hood** [-hud] brorskap. **-ly** broderlig.
brougham [bru·m] lett landauer.
brought [brå·t] imperf. og perf. pts. av **bring.**
brow [brau] bryn, kant; ås; (fig.) panne; mine; **knit one's -s** rynke pannen.
browbeat ['braubi·t] skremme, hundse.
brown [braun] brun; brunt, brun farge; brune, brunsteke; — **bread** brød av usiktet hvetemel, grovbrød; — **Holland** et slags ublekt stivt lerret; — **paper** gråpapir; — **study** dype tanker.
brownie ['brauni] nisse; en slags kamera.
Browning ['brauniŋ] Browning.
browse [brauz] gnage, bite av; gresse, beite.
Bruce [bru·s] Bruce.
Bruges [bru·ʒ] Brügge.
Bruin ['bru·in] bamse. **(Master)** — Bamse Brakar.
bruise ['bru·z] kveste; forslå, støte; knuse; kvestelse; støt, slag, skramme.
bruit [bru·t] gjøre kjent, utspre; **the word is -ed about** that det går det rykte at.
Brummagem ['brʌmədʒəm] Birmingham; imitasjon, juks; uekte; — **buttons** falske penger.
brunette [bru·'net] brunette.
Brunswick ['brʌnzwik] Braunschweig.
brunt [brʌnt] hissighet, hete; støt, strid; **bear the — of the battle** bære dagens byrde og hete.
brush [brʌʃ] børste; kost; pensel; hale (på en rev); kamp; kratt; kvas; børste, koste, streife; stryke; — **away** viske bort, jage fra seg; — **up** det å gjøre seg litt i stand (etter reise e.l.). — **-wood** kratt; kvas.
brusque [brusk, brʌsk] brysk, brå; morsk.
Brussels ['brʌslz] Bryssel; — **sprouts** rosenkål.
brutal ['bru·təl] dyrisk; brutal. **-ity** [bru·'täliti] dyriskhet, råskap, brutalitet.
brute [bru·t] dyrisk; rå; dyr; rått menneske, umenneske. **brutish** ['bru·tiʃ] dyrisk, rå.
bryony ['braiəni] gallebær.
B. S. A. fk. f. **British South Africa.**
Bt. fk. f. **baronet.**
bubble ['bʌbl] boble; humbug; boble; putre; snyte; **blow -s** blåse såpebobler.
buccaneer [bʌkə'niə] sjørøver; drive sjørøveri.
Buchanan [bju·(')känən]
buck [bʌk] hannen av forskj. dyr, geite-, sau-, reins-bukk; sprett, sprade; (amr.) sagkrakk; parre seg, løpe, gjøre bukkesprett; steile; — ta seg sammen; — **off** kaste (rytter av). **bucket** ['bʌkit] bøtte, spann, pøs, vassbøtte; øse; slå vann på; skamri; ro ujevnt, plaske.
Buckingham ['bʌkiŋəm] Buckingham.
buckle ['bʌkl] spenne, spenne fast, gjorde på; krøke, krumme; krølle seg. — **to** legge seg i selen, ta fatt for alvor.

buckler ['bʌklə] skjold; beskytter.
buckram ['bʌkrəm] stivt lerret, innleggsstrie.
Bucks. fk. f. **Buckinghamshire.**
buck-shot ['bʌkʃåt] dyrehagl. **buck-shot rule** styre av Irland ved væpnet politi.
buckskin ['bʌkskin] hjorteskinn; buckskinn.
buckwheat ['bʌk'wi·t] bokhvete.
bucolic [bju'kålik] bukolisk, som hører til hyrdelivet; hyrdedikt.
bud [bʌd] knopp; springe ut, skyte knopper; inokulere; **nip in the** — kvele i fødselen.
Buddha ['budə] Buddha. **buddhism** ['budizm] buddhisme. **buddhist** ['budist] buddhist.
budge [bʌdʒ] røre seg av stedet, lee på seg.
budget ['bʌdʒit] pose, veske, taske; budsjett; budsjettere.
Buenos Aires ['bwenəs 'aiəriz].
buff [bʌf] bøffellær, semsklær; lærbrynje; lærfarget, brungul; **-coat** lærbrynje.
buffalo ['bʌfəlou] bøffel; (amr.) bison.
buffer ['bʌfə] støtpute, buffer; stabeis, fysak; **a** — **state** bufferstat.
buffet ['bʌfit] puff, støt; puffe, støte; skubbe.
buffet ['bʌfit] buffet, skjenk, framskap.
buffet ['bufe'] slags restaurant f. eks. på jernbanestasjon, buffet.
buffoon [bʌ'fu·n] bajas. **-ery** narrestreker.
bug [bʌg] veggelus; (amr.) insekt, bille.
bugbear ['bʌgbæ·ə] busemann, skremsel.
bugger ['bʌgə] sodomitt.
buggy ['bʌgi] slags lett vogn.
buggy ['bʌgi] full av veggelus.
bugle ['bju·gl] jakthorn, valthorn, signalhorn.
bugle ['bju·gl] lang perle.
buhl [bu·l] innlagt arbeid.
build [bild] bygge; bygningsform, bygning; fasong, snitt (på klær). **-er** byggmester. **-ing** bygning.
built [bilt] imperf. og perf. pts. av **build.**
bulb [bʌlb] rund innretning; elektrisk pære; løk, svibel; svelle ut.
bulb [bʌlb] løk; kul; lyspære; kule (på gradestokk); svelle ut.
Bulgaria [bʌl'gæ·ᵊriə] Bulgaria. **-n** bulgar(sk).
bulge [bʌldʒ] kul; buk (av et fat el. en tønne); bulne ut. **bulgy** ['bʌldʒi] oppsvulmet.
bulk [bʌlk] framstikkende del, utbygg, sval; hovedmasse, størstedel; mengde, majoritet; last; ruve; **break** — brekke lasten (for å losse). — **cargo** styrtegods, gods i løs masse. **-head** skott (på skip). **-y** svær, stor.
bull [bul] tyr, stut, okse; hausse-spekulant.
bull [bul] bulle, pavebrev.
bull [bul] meningsløshet, mistak.
bulldog ['buldåg] bulldogg.
bullet ['bulit] (liten) kule.
bulletin ['bulitin] bulletin.
bull-fight ['bulfait] tyrefektning.
bull-finch ['bulfinʃ] dompap; hinder, høy hekk.
bullion ['buljən] umyntet gull el. sølv; sølvbarre, gullbarre.
bullock ['bulək] stut, okse.
bull's-eye ['bulzai] skipsvindu, kuøye; blindlykt, blink (i skive); slags stripet sukkerkule.
bully ['buli] dominere; tyrannisere; rå, hoven person; tyrann; bølle; grepa, kjempefin.
bulrush ['bulrʌʃ] siv.
bulwark ['bulwək] bolverk, bastion; skanse-kledning; (fig.) forsvar, vern, sikkerhet.
Bulwer ['bulwə] Bulwer.
bum [bʌm] rumpe, ende.
bum-bailiff [bʌm'be'lif] underlensmann, lensmannsbetjent.
bumble-bee ['bʌmbl-bi] humle (insekt).
bumboat ['bʌmbou°t] bombåt, kadreierbåt.
bump [bʌmp] støt, slag, dask, dult; bule; støte, dunke; — **of locality** stedsans. **bumper** ['bʌmpə] breddfullt glass; fullt hus (teater).
bumping-race kapproing på elv, der det gjel-

der for hver båt å innhente og røre den båten som ligger foran.
bumpkin ['bʌm(p)kin] slamp, kloss.
bumptious ['bʌmpʃes] viktig, innbilsk, selvgod.
bun [bʌn] bolle (ofte m. korinter i).
bunch [bʌn(t)ʃ] pukkel; bunt, knippe; klase, klynge. **-backed** pukkelrygget, krylrygget.
buncombe ['bʌŋkəm] floskler, valgflesk.
bundle ['bʌndl] bunt, bylt, knytte, pakke; bunte; pakke sammen; pakke seg (**off** bort).
bung [bʌŋ] spuns; spunse. **-hole** spunshull.
bungalow ['bʌŋgəlou] bungalow.
bungle ['bʌŋgl] klusse, kludre, forkludre, skjemme bort; fuskeri; mistak. **bungler** fusker.
bunion ['bʌnjən] trell, liktorn.
bunk [bʌŋk] slagbenk; fast køy; køye; stikke av.
bunker ['bʌŋkə] kistebenk; binge; kullboks, bunker; grop, hindring (på golfbane).
bunkum se **buncombe.**
bunting ['bʌntiŋ] flaggduk, flaggskrud.
bunting ['bʌntiŋ] (gul)spurv, snøspurv.
Bunyan ['bʌnjən] Bunyan.
buoy [boi] bøye, merke; legge ut bøyer, merke opp; holde flott; svømme, flyte. **-ancy** ['boiansi] evne til å flyte; oppdrift; (fig.) letthet, livlighet. **-ant** ['boiənt] flytende, svømmende; livfull.
bur [bə·] se **bur(r).**
burberry ['bə·bəri] et vanntett stoff, frakk av dette.
burden ['bə·dn] byrde; drektighet; omkved, etterstev, ettersleng; lesse, legge på, tynge ned. **-some** tyngende, byrdefull.
burdock ['bə·dåk] borre.
bureau [bju'ro°] byrå; (amr.) kommode, skrivepult. **-cracy** [bju'råkrəsi] byråkrati. **-crat** ['bjuərokrät] byråkrat. **-cratic** [bjuəro'krätik] byråkratisk.
burgeon ['bə·dʒən] knopp, springe ut.
burgess ['bə·dʒis] borger; tingmann for en kjøpstad.
burgh ['bʌrə] (skotsk) by (jvf. **borough**). **-er** ['bə·gə] borger. **-master** ['bə·gma·stə] borgermester.
burglar ['bə·glə] innbruddstyv. **-y** ['bə·glari] innbrudd. **burglarious** [be-'glæ·ᵊriəs] innbrudds-. **burgle** ['bə·gl] gjøre innbrudd, bryte seg inn
Burgundy ['bə·gəndi] Burgund, Bourgogne; burgunder.
burial ['beriəl] begravelse, gravferd. — **-ground** begravelsesplass, kirkegård.
Burke [bə·k] Burke. **burke** [bə·k] myrde ved kvelning, snikmyrde; stikke unna.
burlesque [bə·'lesk] overdrevent komisk; burlesk; parodi, travesti; gjøre latterlig, travestere.
burly ['bə·li] tykk, svær, røslig.
Burma ['bə·mə] Burma, Birma.
burn [bə·n] (sc.) bekk; låg (srl. i brygging).
burn [bə·n] brenne; brannsår; brennemerke.
burnish ['bə·niʃ] polere, bli blank; skinne.
Burns [bə·nz] Burns.
burnt [bə·nt] imperf. og perf. pts. av **burn.**
bur(r) [bə·] borre.
burrow ['bʌro°] hule; gang (i jorda); grave ganger i jorda, grave seg ned.
bursar ['bə·sə] kasserer, universitetskvestor, stipendiat.
burst [bə·st] briste, springe; fare, springe (fram, ut); sprenge; utbrudd; brak, revne, brudd; range'.
burthen ['bə·ðən] se **burden.**
bury ['beri] begrave, nedsenke, glemme.
bus [bʌs] buss.
bush [buʃ] bøssing, foring.
bush [buʃ] busk, kjerr; dusk, kvast; (i Australia og Sør-Afrika) villmark, utbygd; (amr.) småskog. **beat about the** — bruke kroker.
bushel ['buʃəl] bushel, engelsk skjeppe (i Storbr. og Irl. = 36,368 l, i U. S. A. og Canada = 35,24 l).
bushman ['buʃmən] buskmann; nybygger (i Australia).

bushranger ['buʃre'ndʒə] røver (i villmarka).
bushy ['buʃi] busket; som gror tett.
business ['biznés] forretning, forretninger, butikk, foretagende; beskjeftigelse; sak; arbeid, yrke; greie. **this is no — of theirs** dette vedkommer ikke dem; **mind your own — pass deg selv. -like** forretningsmessig.
buskin ['bʌskin] koturne; halvstøvel.
buss [bʌs] kyss, smask; kysse.
bust [bʌst] byste.
bustle ['bʌsl] ha det travelt, fare omkring, mase, vimse om; travelhet, as, mas, hastverk; røre.
busy ['bizi] beskjeftige, sysselsette; travel, beskjeftiget, opptatt; urolig; **be —** ha det travelt; **— oneself about** beskjeftige seg med, gi seg av med, ta vare på. **-body** vims.
but [bʌt, bət] men; unntagen, uten, så nær som, bare; at; **— for him** hadde ikke han vært. **the last — one** den nest siste.
butcher ['butʃə] slakter; slakte. **-y** slakteri.
butler ['bʌtlə] kjellermester, hovmester.
butt [bʌt] skyteskive; merke, mål; skive; fat, tønne; tykkende, skaft, kolv; støt (med hode eller horn); støt (i fektning); støte, stange; **come full — against** løpe bus på.
butter ['bʌtə] smør; lage til med smør, smøre smør på; være smørblid mot, smigre, smiske, gjøle. **bread-and- — smørbrød. -boat** smørnebbe, sausenebbe. **-cup** smørblomst. **-fingered** klosset, slepphendt. **— -fingers** klodrian. **-fly** sommerfugl. **-milk** kjernemelk. **-print** smørstempel.
buttery ['bʌtəri] matkott, matbu; matutsalg.
buttock ['bʌtək] rumpeballe, seteballe.
button ['bʌtn] knapp; knappe. **-hole** knapphull(sblomst); klenge seg på, hekte seg fast i. **buttons** ['bʌtnz] (pl. av **button**) pikkolo.
buttress ['bʌtris] framspring, støttepille, murstiver, støtte; avstive, støtte.
buxom ['bʌksəm] trivelig, ferm; livlig, rask.
buy [bai] kjøpe. **-er** kjøper. **-ing department** innkjøpsavdeling. **buying price** innkjøpspris.
buzz [bʌz] summe, surre, hviske om; drikke ut (siste slanten); surr, summing.
buzzard ['bʌzəd] musvåk.

buzz-bomb ['bʌzbåm] flyvende bombe (brukt om V-bombene).
B. W. T. A. fk. f. British Women's Temperance Association.
by [bai] ved siden av, ved, langs(med), forbi; innen, i, etter, gjennom, med; etter, ifølge; av; **— oneself** for seg selv, alene; **— 6 o'clock** innen kl. 6. **— the sack** i sekkevis; **— the score** i snesevis; **little — little** litt etter litt; smått om senn; **day — day** dag for dag; **— railway, steamer** med jernbane, dampskip; **— telegram, telegraph** telegrafisk; **multiply — three** multiplisere med tre; **— forced marches** i ilmarsj; **a novel — Dickens** en roman av D.; **— all means** ja visst; **— no means** på ingen måte; **— chance** tilfeldig; **— heart** utenat; **— and —** snart; **— land** til lands; **— sea** til sjøs, sjøveien; **— the bye** el. **— the way** i parentes bemerket, à propos; **— this time** nå el. imidlertid; **— now** iallfall, nå om ikke før; **— day** (night) om dagen (natten); **— larger — a half** en halv gang til så stor; **taller — three inches = three inches taller; six — two** is three to i seks er tre; **six feet — three** seks fot lang og tre fot bred; **younger — years** yngre av år; **all — himself** ganske for seg selv, alene.
by-blow slengeslag, slumpeslag; lausunge.
by(e) [bai] i smstn. bi-, side-, omfram-, ekstra-.
bye-bye [bai'bai] farvel! (i barnemålet) na-na; bye, bysse, seng, søvn.
by-election ['bai'lekʃən] suppleringsvalg.
bye-law, by-law ['bailå·] vedtekt, statutt.
by-gone ['baigån] forbigangen, framfaren; **let by-gones be by-gones!** la det være glemt.
by-name ['baine'm] økenavn, utnavn.
by-path ['bai·pþ] tverrvei.
by-play ['baiple'] stumt spill.
by-product ['baiprådəkt] biprodukt.
byre ['baiə] (skotsk) fjøs.
Byron ['bairən] Byron.
Bysshe [biʃ] Bysshe.
bystander ['baistændə] hosstående, tilstedeværende, tilskuer.
by-street ['baistri·t] sidegate, bakgate.
by-word ['baiwə·d] ordspråk, ordtak.
Byzantine [bi'zäntain, bai'zänti·n] bysantinsk; bysantiner.

C

C [si·] C.
C. fk. f. Centigrade.
c. fk. f. caught, cent, cents, century, chapter circa, colt, cubic.
C. A. fk. f. Chartered Accountant.
cab [käb] drosje.
cabal [kə'bäl] kabal; klikk; intrige; bruke renker, intrigere; **the Cabal;** [kə'bäl] Cabalministeriet (1671).
cabbage ['käbidʒ] kål, kålhode.
cabby ['käbi] drosjekusk.
cabin ['käbin] kahytt; hyttekabin.
cabinet ['käbinit] kabinett, kove, kammer; skap; ministerium, statsråd. **-council** statsråd. **-maker** møbelsnekker.
cable ['ke'bl] kabel; trosse; kabellengde (kabel)telegram; telegrafere (pr. kabel). **-gram** (kabel)telegram.
cabman ['käbmən] drosjekusk, vognmann.
caboose [kə'bu·s] kabysse, bysse.
cabriolet [käbrio'le'] kabriolett.
cab-stand ['käbständ] drosjeholdeplass.
ca'canny [kə'käni] se **canny.**
cacao [kə'ke'o, kə'ka·o] kakaotre.
cache [käʃ] skjulested for matvarer, ulovlige våpen o. l.; forråd.
cachinnation [käki'ne'ʃən] skoggerlatter.
cackle ['käkl] kakle; fnise, knegge, skratte; kakling; skravling. **cackler** kakler; skravlekopp.

cacophony [kä'kåfəni] kakofoni.
cactus ['käktəs] kaktus.
cad [käd] tarvelig fyr, pøbel.
cadaver [kə'de'və] kadaver, lik. **cadaverous** [kə'dävərəs] lik-; likblek.
caddie ['kädi] køllebærer (for golfspiller).
caddish ['kädiʃ] simpel, ufin, pøbelaktig.
caddy ['kädi] tedåse.
cade [ke'd] dunk, kagge.
cadence ['ke'dəns] kadens; tonefall.
cadet [kə'det] yngste, yngre bror; kadett.
cadge [kädʒ] fekte, tigge; luske omkring; fiske (for etter). **cadger** ['kädʒə] kramkar, gateselger; plattenslager.
cadi ['ka·di, 'ke'di] kadi.
Cadiz ['ke'diz] Cadiz.
cæcum ['si·kʌm, -əm] blindtarm.
Cædmon ['kädmən] Cædmon.
Cæsar ['si·zə] Cæsar.
café ['käfe', 'käfi] kafé.
Caffre ['käfə] se **Kaffir.**
caftan ['käftən] kaftan.
cage [ke'dʒ] bur; fangebur; heis; sette i bur.
caiac ['ke'jäk, 'kaiak] kajakk.
caiman ['ke'mən] kaiman.
Cain [ke'n] Kain.
cairn [kæ·ən] steinrøys, steindysse.
Cairo ['kaiəro] Kairo.
caitiff ['ke'tif] skurk, usling.

cajole [kə'dʒoʰl] smigre, snakke rundt. **cajolery** [-(ə)ri] smiger, smisking.

cake [keʰk] kake; **the land of -s** ɔ: Skottland; — of soap såpestykke; **you cannot eat your** — **and have it en kan ikke få både i pose og sekk. cake** bake sammen; kline til.

Cakewalk ['keʰkwɑ·k] en slags negerdans.

Cal. fk. f. **California.**

calabash ['kǽləbæʃ] flaskegresskar; kalebass.

calaboose [kǽlə'bu·z] kasjott.

Calais ['kǽlei] Calais.

calamitous [kə'lǽmitəs] ulykkelig, bedrøvelig.

calamity [kə'lǽmiti] ulykke, elendighet.

calash [kə'lǽʃ] kalesje, kalesjevogn; hette.

calcination [kǽlsi'neʰʃən] forkalking. **calcine** ['kǽlsain, kǽl'sain] forkalke; forkalkes.

calculable ['kǽlkjuləbl] beregnelig. **calculate** ['kǽlkjuleʰt] beregne, regne ut. **calculated** beregnet, skikket, egnet; **calculating-machine** regnemaskin. **calculation** [kǽlkju'leʰʃən] regning, beregning. **calculator** ['kǽlkjuleʰtə] regnemester, regnskapsfører; regnemaskin.

calculous ['kǽlkjuləs] gruset, sandet; som lider av stein.

Calcutta [kǽl'kʌtə] Calcutta.

caldron ['kɔ·ldrən] se **cauldron.**

Caledonia [kǽli'doʰnjə] Kaledonia, Skottland. **Caledonian** [kǽli'doʰnjən] skotsk; skotte.

calefactory [kǽli'fǽktəri] varmende, varme-.

calendar ['kǽləndə] kalender; føre inn, bokføre; lage liste over.

calender ['kǽləndə] kalander; (damp)presse, glatte.

calf [kɑ·f] kalv; kalveskinn; kalve; tykklegg. **-'s-foot** ['kɑ·vzfut] kalvedans.

Caliban ['kǽlibæn].

caliber ['kǽlibə] kaliber, størrelse, slag.

calico ['kǽlikoʰ] kaliko, fint, tett, lerretsvevd bomullstøy. **-printer** kattuntrykker.

calif ['keʰlif] se **caliph.**

California [kǽli'fɔ·ʰnjə] Kalifornia. **-n** kalifornisk; kalifornier.

caliph ['keʰlif] kaliff. **-ate** ['keʰlifit] kalifat.

calk [kɔ·k] kalkere.

calk [kɔ·k] kalfatre; grev el. hake (på hestesko); brodd; sette haker (grev, brodder) på; skarpsko. **calker** ['kɔ·kə] kalfatrer; driver.

call [kɔ·l] kalle, kalle på; rope; påkalle; henvende seg; nevne, benevne, kalle; besøke, se innom; gjøre et kort besøk; — **one names** skjelle en ut; — **after** kalle (opp) etter; — **at** besøke (et sted), gå innom, anløpe; — **for** kalle på; la spørre etter (en); forlange; hente; — **forth** framkalle, oppby; — **in** kalle inn; kreve inn; tilbakekalle; — **on** besøke (en person); oppfordre; — **over** lese opp; — **out** rope; utfordre; — **to** rope til; — **to mind** huske, minnes; — **upon** (**on**) kalle på; påkalle, anrope; besøke; **the military have been called out** innkalt; **to be left till called for** poste restante.

call [kɔ·l] rop; kalling; kall; navneopprop; oppfordring, innkalling; befaling; kort (regelmessig) besøk; båtsmannspipe; lokkepipe; — **of the house** Parlamentets sammenkalling (ved særlige anledninger); **to give one a** — besøke en; **telephone** — telefonoppringning, -samtale. **-ing** roping, kalling; kall; stand, håndtering, yrke; **money at** (**on**) — penger på anfordring.

calligraphy kä'ligrəfi] kalligrafi.

Calliope [kə'laiəpi·] Kalliope.

calliper ['kǽlipə]: — **compasses** el. **callipers** krumpasser, hullpasser.

callisthenic [kǽlis'θenik] som gir ynde og styrke. **-s** taktmessige legemsøvelser, mellomting mellom dans og gymnastikk.

callosity [kä'ləsiti] hard hud, trell; følesesløshet.

callous ['kǽləs] hard, forherdet; ufølsom.

callow ['kǽloʰ] bar, naken, fjærløs; myrlendt.

calm [kɑ·m] stille, rolig; klar; stillhet, ro;

stille vær, havblikk; berolige, roe, formilde. **-ness** stillhet, mildhet, ro.

caloric [kə'lɑrik] hete-, varme-; varmestoff. **calorifere** [kə'lɑrifiə] varmeapparat. **calorific** [kǽlo'rifik] som gir varme el. varmer, varme-. **calory** ['kǽləri] kalori.

calque [kɑ·k, kǽlk] se **calk** kalkere.

calumet ['kǽljumət] indiansk fredspipe.

calumniate [kə'lʌmnieʰt] baktale. **-iator** [kə-'lʌmnieʰtə] baktaler. **-ious** [kə'lʌmniəs] bakvaskende, baktalerisk. **-y** ['kǽləmni] baktaling.

Calvary ['kǽlvəri] Golgata.

calve [kɑ·v] kalve, bære.

calves [kɑ·vz] flertall av **calf.**

Calvinism ['kǽlvinizm] kalvinisme. **Calvinist** ['kǽlvinist] kalvinist.

calyx ['kǽliks, 'keʰliks] beger.

cam [kǽm] kam (på hjul).

camber ['kǽmbə] kuv, bøy, krumning.

Cambrian ['kǽmbriən] valiser, valisisk.

cambric ['keʰmbrik] kammerduk (fint tøy).

Cambridge ['keʰmbridʒ] Cambridge.

Cambs. fk. f. **Cambridgeshire.**

came [keʰm] imperf. av **come.**

camel ['kǽməl] kamel.

cameleer ['kǽmə'liə] kameldriver.

camellia [kə'mi·liə] kamelia.

camelopard ['kǽmiləpa·d, kə'mələpa·d] sjiraff.

camelry ['kǽməlri] tropper som rir på kameler.

Camembert ['kǽməmbæ·ə] camembertost.

cameo ['kǽmioʰ] kamé, gemme.

camera ['kǽmərə] kamera.

camisole ['kǽmisoʰl] underliv (alm. brodert).

camlet ['kǽmlət] kamelott.

camomile ['kǽməmail] kamille. — **tea** kamillete.

camouflage ['kǽmufla·ʒ] kamuflasj; kamuflere.

camp [kǽmp] leir; slå leir; ligge i leir.

campaign [kǽm'peʰn] slette; felttog; ligge i felten. **campaigner** [kǽm'peʰnə] gammel kriger.

camp-bed ['kǽmp'bed] feltseng.

Campbell ['kǽmbl].

Campeachy [kǽm'pi·tʃi] Campeche, blåtre.

camphor ['kǽmfə] kamfer.

camp-meeting ['kǽmpmi·tiŋ] amr. religiøst (srl. metodistisk) friluftsmøte. — **-stool** [-stu·l] feltstol.

can [kǽn] kanne, (hermetikk)dåse, eske, boks; legge, koke ned (hermetisk).

can [kǽn, kən] kan.

Can. fk. f. **Canada.**

Canaan ['keʰnən, 'keʰniən] Kanaan.

Canada ['kǽnədə] Kanada.

Canadian [kə'neʰdjən] kanadisk; kanadier.

canal [kə'nǽl] kanal (kunstig); kanal (i legemet), gang, rør.

Canaries [kə'næ·əriz] the — Kanariøyene.

canary [kə'næ·əri] kanarifugl; kanarivin.

cancel ['kǽnsəl] streke ut, stryke; kassere; oppheve, annullere, tilbakekalle ordre. **-lation** [kǽnse'leʰʃən] opphevelse, annullering.

cancer ['kǽnsə] krabbe; Krepsen (himmeltegn); kreft; **the tropic of Cancer** Krepsens vendekrets. **-ous** ['kǽnsərəs] kreft-.

candelabrum [kǽndi'leʰbrəm] kandelaber.

candescent [kǽn'desnt] hvitglødende.

candid ['kǽndid] oppriktig, åpen, ærlig.

candidate ['kǽndideʰt] ansøker, kandidat.

candidature ['kǽndiditʃə] kandidatur.

candle ['kǽndl] lys; **he is not fit to hold** a — **to you** han kan slett ikke måle seg med deg; **burn the** — **at both ends** ødsle med (el. ødsle sine krefter (el. sine midler); **the game is not worth the** — det er ikke umaken verd.

Candlemas ['kǽndlməs] kyndelsmess.

candle-power ['kǽndl'pauə] lysstyrkeenhet) lys.

candlestick ['kǽndlstik] lysestake.

candour ['kǽndə] oppriktighet.

candy ['kǽndi] kandis; (amr.) konfekt, sukkertøy; kandisere; sukre; krystalliseres.

cane [keɪn] rør; sukkerrør; spanskrør; stokk; pryle med stokk. — -bottom rørsete. — -chair rørstol. — -sugar rørsukker. — -trash sukkerrøravfall.

Canicula [kəˈnikjulə] Sirius, Hundestjerna.

canicular [kəˈnikjulə]: — days hundedagene.

canine [ˈkänain] hundeaktig, hunde-.

caning [ˈkeɪniŋ] drakt pryl.

canister [ˈkänistə] blikkdåse. — -shot kardeske.

canker [ˈkäŋkə] kreft (også på trær); sår, etende væske; ete; tære på; forderves.

canner [ˈkänə] hermetikkfabrikant. cannery [ˈkänəri] hermetikkfabrikk.

cannibal [ˈkänibəl] kannibal, menneskeeter. -ism [-izm] menneskeeteri; grusomhet.

cannon [ˈkänən] karambolasje; karambolere. cannon [ˈkänən] kanon; artilleri; skyts. -ade [känəˈneɪd] skyte med kanoner; kanonade. -ball [ˈkänənbả·l] kanonkule. -eer [känəˈniə] kanonér.

cannot [ˈkänȧt, ka·nt] kan ikke; — but kan ikke annet enn; — help kan ikke annet enn.

canny [ˈkäni] slu, var; forsiktig; trygg. ca'canny (skotsk) far med lempe (om fagforeningspolitikk som går ut på å innskrenke produksjonen).

canoe [kəˈnuˑ] kano.

canon [ˈkänən] kirkelov; kanon; fortegnelse over helgener; kannik, korsbror.

cañon [ˈkänjən] se canyon.

canonize [ˈkänənaiz] kanonisere.

can-opener boksåpner, hermetikkåpner.

canopy [ˈkänəpi] tronhimmel.

canorous [kəˈnåˑrəs] velklingende, melodiøs.

can't [kaˑnt] d. s. s. cannot.

cant [känt] helling, hall, snei; sette på hall, på kant, på snei; velte; endevende; hogge en kant av; helle, vippe over på siden; svinge rundt.

cant [känt] affektert tale; hyklerisk tale, frasemakeri, fraser; dialekt; slang; pøbelspråk, gatespråk; tale affektert.

Cantab [ˈkäntäb] fk. f. Cantabrigian [käntəˈbridʒiən] akademiker fra Cambridgeuniversitet.

cantankerous [känˈtäŋkərəs] trettekjær, kranglevoren, stri, krakilsk.

cantata [känˈtaˑtə] kantate.

canteen [känˈtiˑn] marketenteri; feltflaske.

canter [ˈkäntə] kort galopp; gå, ri i kort galopp.

Canterbury [ˈkäntəbəri] Canterbury.

cantharides [känˈpäridiˑz] spansk flue.

canticle [ˈkäntikl] kort sang, salme, en av salmene i Prayer-Book; i pl. Salomos høysang.

canto [ˈkäntoⁿ] sang (avdeling av et dikt).

canton [ˈkäntən] distrikt, kanton; avdeling.

canton [känˈtuˑn] innkvartere (soldater).

cantonment [känˈtuˑnmənt] kantonnement.

Canuck [kəˈnʌk] (sl.) kanadier, kanadisk.

Canute [kəˈnjuˑt] Knut.

canvas [ˈkänvəs] lerret; strie, seilduk, teltduk; seil, telt, maleri.

canvass [ˈkänvəs] drøfte, undersøke, prøve, verve stemmer, agitere; drøfting, undersøkelse, agitasjon, srl. husagitasjon. canvasser [ˈkänvəsə] stemmeverver; (hus)agitator.

canyon [ˈkänjən] dyp, trang elvedal i fjellgrunn med nesten loddrette vegger, elvegjel.

caoutchouc [ˈkautʃuk] kautsjuk, viskelær.

cap. fk. f. chapter.

cap [käp] kappe; hue, lue; hette; fenghette, knallperle; bedekke; sette hette, lue osv. på; ta hatten av; the — fitted bemerkningen ramte; set her — at legge an på, søke å erobre; — and bells narrelue; — and gown akademisk drakt; — in hand ydmykt.

capability [keɪpəˈbiliti] evne; dugelighet.

capable [ˈkeɪpəbl] mottagelig (of for); i stand (of til); dugelig, dyktig.

capacious [kəˈpeɪʃəs] rommelig; omfattende.

capacitate [kəˈpäsiteɪt] sette i stand til. capacity [kəˈpäsiti] vidde; rom, lasteevne, kapasitet; dugelighet; fag; egenskap, stand; karakter.

cap-à-pie [käpəˈpiˑ] fra topp til tå.

caparison [kəˈpärisən] saldekken, skaberakk; legge saldekken på.

cape [keɪp] cape, overstykke, slag (på kappe).

cape [keɪp] forberg, nes, odde; the Cape Kapp.

caper [ˈkeɪpə] kapers.

caper [ˈkeɪpə] bukkesprang, kast, sprett; danse, hoppe; cut -s springe, hoppe, gjøre bukkesprett.

capercailzie [käpəˈkeɪlji, -ˈkeɪlzi] tiur.

Capetown [ˈkeɪptaun] Kappstaden.

capias [ˈkeɪpiäs] arrestordre.

capillary [kəˈpiləri] hår-, hårfin; hårrør.

capital [ˈkäpitəl] hoved-, viktigst; fortreffelig; kriminell; hovedstad; kapital; kapitél; stor bokstav; a — crime en forbrytelse som straffes med døden; — letters store bokstaver: — punishment dødsstraff; the — point hovedpunktet, det vesentlige; — sentence dødsdom; capital! storartet!

capitalism [ˈkäpitəlizm] kapitalisme.

capitalist [ˈkäpitəlist] kapitalist.

capitalize [ˈkäpitəlaiz] kapitalisere.

capitation [käpiˈteɪʃən] folketelling; koppskatt.

Capitol [ˈkäpitl] Kapitol; (amr.) kongressbygning, senatsbygning.

capitulary [kəˈpitjuləri] samling lovbud, lovbok.

capitulate [kəˈpitjuleɪt] kapitulere. capitulation [kəpitjuˈleɪʃən] kapitulasjon, oppgivelse.

capon [ˈkeɪpən] kapun.

capote [kəˈpoⁿt] slags lang kappe med hette.

caprice [kəˈpriˑs] grille, lune, kaprise.

capricious [kəˈpriʃəs] lunefull, lunet.

Capricorn [ˈkäprikåˑⁿn] Steinbukken (stjernebildet); the Tropic of — S. vendekrets.

capsicum [ˈkäpsikəm] spansk pepper.

capsize [käpˈsaiz] kantre, kullseile; kantring.

capstan [ˈkäpstən] gangspill, spill.

capsular [ˈkäpsjulə] kapselformet, kapsel-.

capsule [ˈkäpsjul] kapsel; kapsle; innkapsle.

Capt. fk. f. Captain.

captain [ˈkäptin] kaptein; feltherre, skipskaptein, skipper; fører, bas.

captious [ˈkäpʃəs] vrang, vrien; kritikksyk.

captivate [ˈkäptiveɪt] fortrylle, bedåre.

captive [ˈkäptiv] fanget; fange; lead — føre bort som fange; — balloon fastgjort ballong.

captivity [käpˈtiviti] fangenskap. capture [ˈkäptʃə] pågripelse; tilfangetagelse; fange, kapre (skip).

capuchin [käpjuˈ(t)ʃiˑn] kåpe med hette; kapusiner.

car [kaˑⁿ] vogn, bil; gondol (på luftballong); (amr.) jernbanevogn; the Car Karlsvognen.

carabineer [kärəbiˈniə] karabinier.

carafe [kəˈraˑf, kəˈräf] vannkaraffel.

caramel [ˈkärəmel] karamell.

carat [ˈkärət] karat.

caravan [kärəˈvän, ˈkärəvän] karavane; stor vogn, sirkusvogn.

caraway [ˈkärəweˑ] karve.

carbide [ˈkaˑⁿbaid] karbid.

carbine [ˈkaˑⁿbain] karabin.

carbolic [kaˑəˈbålik] karbol-; — acid [-ˈäsid] karbolsyre; solution of — acid karbolvann.

carbon [ˈkaˑⁿbon] kullstoff; kullspiss.

carbonate [ˈkaˑⁿbonét] karbonat, kullsurt salt.

carbon-paper karbonpapir.

carborundum [kaˑⁿbəˈrʌndəm] karborundum.

carbuncle [ˈkaˑⁿbʌŋkl] karbunkel; brannbyll.

carburett|ed [ˈkaˑⁿbjuretid] forbundet med kullstoff. -or [ˈkaˑⁿbjuretə] karburator; forgasser.

carcass [ˈkaˑⁿkäs] død kropp, skrott; åtsel; korpus, skrog; stumper, rester.

card [kaˑⁿd] (subst. og v.) karde.

card [kaˑⁿd] kort, spillkort, visittkort; a big — matador; lucky at -s heldig i spill; on the -s ikke urimelig, ikke utenkelig; play at -s spille kort; speak by the — veie hvert ord; tell fortunes by -s spå i kort; leave one's — gi sitt kort (visittkort), legge sitt kort.

cardamom [ˈkaˑⁿdəmåm] kardemomme.

card-board [ˈkaˑⁿdbå·ⁿd] kartong, papp.

card-case [ˈkaˑⁿdkeˑs] visittkortbok.

cardiac ['ka·ºdiäk, -djək] hjerte-; hjertestyrkende, opplivende; hjertestyrkning.
cardialgy ['ka·ºdiäldʒi] kardialgi.
cardigan ['ka·digən] ullvest.
cardinal ['ka·ºdinəl] viktigst, fornemst, hoved-;
kardinal: — numbers grunntall.
cardoon [ka·'du·n] artisjokk.
card-sharper ['ka·ºdʃa·ºpə] falskspiller.
card-trick kortkunst.
care [kæ·ə] sorg, sut, bekymring; omsorg, pleie,
omhu; omhyggelighet; — of (el. fk. c|o) adressert;
take — of sørge for; ta vare på. care [kæ·ə]
bekymre seg, syte, bry seg (for om); dra omsorg.
cared for pleiet, velholdt. careful omhyggelig;
forsiktig, varsom. careless ['kæ·ºlis] likegyldig;
skjøtesløs; likeglad. carelessness skjøtesløshet.
careen [kə'ri·n] kjølhale; krenge, ligge over.
career [kə'riə] bane; løp; løpebane, karrière;
renne, ruse, fare, ha stor fart.
caress [kə'res] kjæle for; kjærtegn.
caret ['kärit] utelatelsestegn (ʌ).
caretaker ['kæ·əte'kə] oppsynsmann, tilsynsmann.
careworn ['kæ·əwå·ºn] forgremmet.
Carey ['kæ·ºri]: mother —'s chickens storm-
fugler.
cargo ['ka·ºgoᵘ] ladning, last — -steamer lastebåt.
Carribbean [käri'bi·ən] karib-.
caricature [kä'rikətʃuə] karikatur; karikere.
caries ['kæ·ºrii·z] karies, kronisk beinbetennelse;
tannråte.
Carinthia [kə'rinþiə] Kärnten.
carious ['kæ·ºriəs] angrepet av karies, råtten.
Carlisle ['ka·ºlail] Carlisle.
Carlton ['ka·ºltn] Carlton.
Carlyle ['ka·ºlail] Carlyle.
carman ['ka·ºmən] vognmann.
carmine ['ka·ºmain] karmin, høyrød.
carnage ['ka·ºnidʒ] blodbad, nedslakting.
carnal ['ka·ºnəl] kjødelig; sanselig.
carnation [ka·ºne'ʃən] kjøttfarge; nellik.
Carnegie [ka·ºˈri·gi, -'ne'gi] Carnegie.
carnelian [ka·ºni·ljən] karneol (en rødlig stein).
Carniola [ka·ºni·ºoᵘlə] Krain.
carnival ['ka·ºnivəl] karneval, fastelavnsmoro.
carnivorous [ka·ºnivərəs] kjøttetende.
carol ['kärəl] lov; ᵘng, sang; lovsynge; synge;
Christmas carol julesang.
Carolina [kärə·lai'nə] Carolina (i Nord-Amerika).
Caroline ['kärələin] Karoline (kvinnenavn).
carousal [kə'rauzəl] drikkelag, kalas.
carouse [ke'rauz] svire, drikke, ture; drikkelag.
carp [ka·ºp] karpe.
carp [ka·ºp] klandre, dadle, utsette (på).
Carpathians [ka·ºˈpe'þjənz] Karpatene.
carpenter ['ka·ºpəntə] tømrer. carpentry ['ka· º-
pəntri] tømmerhåndverk; tømmerarbeid.
carpet ['ka·ºpét] teppe; legge teppe på. —
-bag vadsekk. -bagger politisk lykkeridder, en
fremmed som valgkandidat. — dance uformell
dans. — -beater teppebanker. -ing (golv)tep-
per. — -knight soldat som holder seg hjemme
fra krigen, pikenes Jens. — -rod stang til å
feste trappeløper med.
carriage ['käridʒ] transport; kjøretøy; vogn;
lavett; atferd, holdning; frakt, jernbanefrakt;
— and four vogn med fire hester; — forward
frakt ubetalt; — paid frakt betalt.
carriageable ['käridʒəbl] farbar.
carrier ['käriə] bærer, bybud, bud, overbringer;
kommisjonær. — -pigeon brevdue.
carrion ['käriən] åtsel.
carronade [kärə'ne'd] kort grovkalibret skips-
kanon.
carrot ['kärət] gulrot. -y ['käreti] rødhåret.
carry ['käri] føre, bære, bringe; transportere;
utføre; oppnå; oppføre seg, bære seg at; erobre;
føre igjennom; vedta; rekke, nå; — a bill vedta
en lov; — his point sette sin vilje igjennom; —

off bortføre; rive bort; — on fremme; føre; drive
(f. eks. forretning); fortsette; — out utføre, følge
(instrukser); sette igjennom.
carrying capacity lasteevne. carrying trade
fraktfart. carrying trafic godstrafikk.
carryings-on ['käriinz'ån] atferd, framferd.
cart [ka·ºt] kjerre; arbeidsvogn, vogn; føre på
vogn; frakte.
cartage ['ka·ºtidʒ] kjøring, vognleie.
carte-blanche ['ka·ºt'bla·nʃ] carte blanche.
carte-de-visite ['ka·ºtdəvi'zi·t] visittkort; fotografi i visittkortformat.
cartel ['ka·ºtəl] utvekslingskontrakt angående
krigsfanger; kartell; sammenslutning av fabri-
kanter, syndikat.
carter ['ka·ºtə] kjører.
Cartesian [ka·ºˈti·zjən] kartesiansk.
Carthage ['ka·ºþidʒ] Kartago.
cart-horse ['ka·ºthå·ºs] arbeidshest, brygger-
hest.
Carthusian [ka·ºb(j)u·zjən] karteuser.
cartilage ['ka·ºtilidʒ] brusk.
cart-load ['ka·ºtloᵘd] vognlass.
carton ['ka·ºtən] hvit prikk i blinken, pappeske.
cartoon [ka·ºtu·n] mønstertegning, kartong;
tegne, karikere.
cartridge ['ka·ºtridʒ] kardus, patron; blank —
patron uten kule, løspatron. -box patrontaske.
-paper karduspapir.
cart('s)-tail baksiden av kjerre; flog at the —
binde bak en kjerre og piske.
cartwright ['ka·ºtrait] vognmaker, kjerre-
maker.
carve [ka·ºv] skjære ut, hogge ut; skjære for, til.
carvel-built ['ka·ºvəlbilt] kravellbygd.
carver ['ka·ºvə] billedskjærer; forskjærer.
carving billedskjæring; utskåret arbeid, billed-
skjærerarbeid. — -knife forskjærkniv. — -table
anretningsbord.
caryatid [käri'ätid] karyatide.
cascade [kä'ske'd] (liten) foss.
case [ke's] tilfelle; høve; stilling; sak, rettssak;
kasus; in — of i tilfelle av.
case [ke's] kasse; stiv håndkoffert, veske,
skrin; hylster; stikke i et futteral, overtrekke.
casein ['ke'siin] kasein, ostestoff.
casemate ['ke'sme't] kasematt.
casement ['ke'smənt] vindusramme; vindu (på
hengsler).
caseous ['ke'siəs] osteaktig, oste-.
casern [kə'zə·n] kaserne, brakke.
cash [käʃ] kontanter; kasse; innkassere; heve
penger; betale; — on delivery etterkrav; hard
— klingende mynt; — down mot kontant betaling; — a cheque heve penger på en sjekk;
be in — ha penger for hånden; out of — pengelens. — -book kassebok.
cashier [kə'ʃiə] kasserer(ske).
cashier [kə'ʃiə] avskjedige, kassere, vrake.
cashmere ['käʃmiə] kasjmir, kasjmirsjal.
casing ['ke'siŋ] hylster, futteral, overtrekk.
cask [ka·sk] fat, tønne; fylle på fat.
casket ['ka·skit] skrin, smykkeskrin.
casque [ka·sk] hjelm.
cassation [kä'se'ʃən] kassasjon; court of —
øverste ankedomstol (i utlandet).
Cassiopeia [käsio'pi·ə] Kassiopeia.
cassock ['käsək] prestekjole, samarie.
cassowary ['käsəwəri] kasuar (en fugl).
cast [ka·st] kaste; overvinne; støpe, forme; beregne, gjøre overslag; overveie; la seg forme; slå
seg; fordele (rollene i et stykke); kast; rollebesetning; støpning, avstøpning; beregning; karakter, form, preg; anstrøk; farge; blingsing;
be — tape saken; be — away lide skibbrudd; —
down nedslå, gjøre motløs.
castanet [kästa'net] kastanjett.
castaway ['ka·stəwe'] forstøtt, utstøtt, skibbrudden, paria.
caste [ka·st] kaste; lose — bli utstøtt av sin
kaste; gjøre seg umulig.

caster ['ka·stə] kaster, støper; pepper- el. sukkerbøsse; oppsatsflaske; trinse (under bordbein); (amr.) oppsats; **(a set of) -s** bordoppsats.

castigate ['kästige¹t] refse, tukte. **castigation** [kästi'ge¹ʃen] tukting, refsing.

casting ['ka·stiŋ] kasting; støpning. **— -vote** avgjørende stemme.

cast-iron ['ka·st'aiən] støpejern.

castle ['ka·sl] befestet slott, borg; herregård; tårn (sjakk); rokere (i sjakk); **build -s in the air, in the clouds, in Spain** bygge luftkasteller.

Castlereagh ['ka·slrei] Castlereagh.

cast-off ['ka·st'å·f] avlagt, kassert.

castor ['ka·stə] bever; hatt; oppsatsflaske.

castor-oil ['ka·stəroil] lakserolje.

castrate ['kästre¹t] kastrere, skjære, gjelde. **castration** [kä'stre¹ʃen] kastrering, gjelding. **castrato** [kä'stra·to⁰] kastrat (kastrert sanger).

casual ['käzjuəl, 'käzuəl] tilfeldig; **Casual Ward** natteherberge (for husville, i fattighus).

casualty ['käzjuəlti, 'käzuəlti] tilfelle; ulykkestilfelle; **— ward** mottagelsesstue på hospital; **list of casualties** tapsliste, liste over falne.

casuist ['käzjuist] kasuist. **-ry** [-ri] kasuistikk.

cat [kät] katt, kjette; dobbelt trefot; (mar.) katt; katte (ankret); **let the — out of the bag** plumpe ut med hemmeligheten; **a — of nine tails** nihalet katt (til å piske med).

cataclasm ['kätəkläzm] sønderriving, sprengning.

cataclysm ['kätəklizm] oversvømmelse, storflom, syndflod.

catacomb ['kätəko⁰m] katakombe.

catafalque ['kätəfälk] katafalk.

catalectic [kätə'lektik] katalektisk.

catalepsy ['kätəlepsi] katalepsi.

catalogue ['kätəlåg] katalog; katalogisere.

catamaran [kätəmə'rän] tømmerflåte; trettekjær kvinne, troll.

cataplasm ['kätəpläzm] grøtomslag.

catapult ['kätəpʌlt] katapult, slynge.

cataract ['kätəräkt] vannfall, foss; grå stær (sykdom).

catarrh [kə'ta·ə, kä'ta·ə] snue, katarr.

catastrophe [kə'tästrəfi] katastrofe.

catcall ['kätkå·l] piping, pipekonsert, utpiping.

catch [kätʃ] fange, gripe, ta, fatte; innhente; nå, rekke, komme med **(the train)**; overraske; fengsle; (opp)fatte; pådra seg; smitte; gripe inn, få tak, hake seg fast; **— a cold** forkjøle seg; **— me doing it** det skal jeg passe meg vel for å gjøre; **— the chairman's (the speaker's) eye** få ordet; **the lock has caught** døra er gått i baklås; **the play never caught on** stykket gjorde ikke lykke; **— sight of** få øye på, få se. **catch** [kätʃ] grep, fangst; tak; hake, hekte; lyte; rykk; fordel; felle; listig spørsmål; flerstemmig vekselsang.

catcher ['kätʃə] fanger, håv.

catching ['kätʃiŋ] smittsom.

catchpenny godtkjøps-, anlagt på (el. laget for) å tjene penger.

catchpole (underordnet) rettsbetjent, lensmannsbetjent.

catchword (i boktrykk) kustode; slagord; oppslagsord.

catechetic(al) [käti'ketik(l)] kateketisk. **catechise** ['kätikaiz] katekisere; spørre ut. **catechism** ['kätikizm] katekisme.

categorical [käti'gårikl] kategorisk. **category** ['kätigəri] kategori.

cater ['ke¹tə] firer (på kort og terninger).

cater ['ke¹tə] skaffe mat **(for** til).

cater-cousin ['keitəkʌzn] fortrolig venn.

caterer ['ke¹tərə] proviantmester, skaffer.

catepillar ['kätəpilə] larve, åme, kålorm.

caterwauling ['kätəwå·liŋ] katteskrik; kattemusikk.

Catharine ['käþərin] Katrine.

Cathay [kä'þe¹] gammelt navn for China.

cathedral [kə'þi·drəl] katedral, domkirke; dom; katedral-, dom-.

Catherine ['käþərin] Katrine.

catherine-wheel ['käþərinwi·l] hjulrakett; rosevindu; **turn -s** slå hjul.

Catholic ['käþəlik] alminnelig; fordomsfri, tolerant; katolsk; katolikk. **Catholicism** [kə'þålisizm] katolsk religion, katolisisme.

Catiline ['kätilain] Catilina.

catkin ['kätkin] rakle.

catlike ['kätlaik] kattaktig.

Cato| ['ke¹to⁰] Cato. **-nian** [ke¹'to⁰niən] katonisk, streng.

cat-o'-nine tails ['kätə'nainteilz] nihalet katt, se **cat.**

cattle ['kätl] fe, kveg, hornkveg, krøtter, naut. **— -dealer** fekar, driftekar. **— -plague** kvegpest, busott. **— -show** dyrskue, fesjå. **— -truck** kuvogn.

Caucasian [kå·'ke¹ziən] kaukasisk; kaukasier. **Caucasus** ['kå·kəsəs] Kaukasus.

caucus ['kå·kəs] forberedende partimøte.

caudal ['kå·dl] hale-.

caudle ['kå·dl] varm drikk med vin.

caught [kå·t] imperf. og perf. pts. av **catch.**

caul [kå·l] tarmnett; seierskjorte; **be born with a —** være født med seierskjorte.

cauldron ['kå·ldrən] (stor) kjel.

cauliflower ['kåliflauə] blomkål.

caulk [kå·k] se **calk** kalfatre.

causal ['kå·zəl] kausal. **-ality** [kå·'zäliti] kausalitet, årsakssammenheng. **-ation** [kå·ze¹ʃən] forårsaking.

'cause [kå(·)z] fk. f. **because** fordi.

cause [kå·z] årsak, grunn; sak; rettssak; forårsake, ta. **-less** ugrunnet, grunnløs.

causeway ['kå·zwe¹] landevei, chaussé, fortau. **causey** ['kå·ze¹] d. s. **causeway.**

caustic ['kå·stik] kaustisk, etsende; bitende, skarp; etsemiddel: **lunar —** helvetesstein.

cauter ['kå·tə] brennjern. **cauterization** [kå·tərai'ze¹ʃən] kauterisasjon, etsing. **cauterize** ['kå·təraiz] kauterisere.

caution ['kå·ʃən] forsiktighet, varsomhet; advarsel, åtvaring; kausjon; kausjonist; advare.

cautious ['kå·ʃəs] forsiktig, varsom.

cavalcade [kävəl'ke¹d] kavalkade. **cavalier** [kävə'liə] rytter, ridder; kavalér; ridderlig; anmassende, hoven; **cavalry** ['kävəlri] kavaleri. **-man** kavalerist.

cave [ke¹v] hule, heller; hule ut, grave ul; ligge i en hule; falle sammen; **— in** falle sammen, styrte sammen; gå over styr.

caveat ['ke¹viät] protest; (amr.) patentanmeldelse; advarsel.

cavern ['kävən] hule, heller. **-ous** ['kävənəs] full av huler.

caviar(e) ['kävia·] kaviar; **— to the general** perler for svin.

cavil ['kävil] sjikanere, kritisere; sofisteri, spissfindighet, sjikane. **-ler** sofist.

cavity ['käviti] hulhet, kløft, grop, kavitet.

caw [kå·] skrike (som en ramn eller kråke); ramneskrik, kråkeskrik, skrik.

Caxton ['käkstən] Caxton.

cayenne [ke¹'en] el. **Cayenne pepper** ['ke¹en-'pepə] kajennepepper.

cayman ['ke¹mən] kaiman, alligator.

C. B. fk. f. **Companion of the Bath; confinement to barracks; construction battalion.**

C. B. E. fk. f. **Commander of the order of the British Empire.**

C. C. fk. f. **County Council(lor); cricket club.** cc. fk. f. **chapters.**

C. C. C. fk. f. **Corpus Christi College.**

C. C. S. fk. f. **Ceylon Civil Service.**

C. D. Acts fk. f. **contagious-diseases Acts.**

C. E. fk. f. **Church of England; Civil Engineer.**

cease [si·s] opphøre, holde opp; la være, holde

opp med; — **fire** stoppe (skytingen); **without** — uten opphør.
ceaseless ['si·sles] uopphørlig, uavlatelig.
Cecil ['sesl, 'sesil, 'sisl] Cecil. **Cecilia** [si'siljə] Cecilia. **Cecily** ['sesili] Cecilia.
cedar ['si·də] seder.
cede [si·d] avstå, oppgi.
cedilla [si'dilə] cedille.
cee-spring ['si·spriŋ] vognfjær (formet som en c).
ceil [si·l] kle et loft, himling.
ceiling ['si·liŋ] loft, tak, himling. — **price** maksimalpris.
Celebes [se'li·bez, 'selibi·z] Celebes.
celebrate ['selibre·t] prise; feire, høytideligholde, gjøre ære på. **-ed** berømt. **celebration** [seli'bre·ʃen] høytideligholdelse; lovprising. **celebrity** [si'lebriti] berømthet; berømt menneske.
celerity [si'leriti] hurtighet.
celery ['seləri] selleri.
celestial [si'lestjəl] himmelsk; himmelboer.
celibacy ['selibəsi] sølibat, ugift stand.
celibate ['selibét] ungkar, ugift kvinne.
cell [sel] celle, arrest; hytte; grav; **the condemned** — de dødsdømtes celle.
cellar ['selə] kjeller.
cellist ['tʃelist] cellist. **-o** ['tʃelo⁰] cello.
cellular ['seljulə] celle-.
celluloid ['seljuloid] celluloid.
Cels. fork. f. **Celsius.**
Celsius ['selsjəs].
Celt [selt, kelt] kelter.
celtic ['seltik, 'keltik] keltisk.
cement [si'ment] bindingsmiddel; sement; (fig.) bånd; sammenkitte; sementere. **-ation** [si·men'te·ʃən] sementering; stålherding.
cemetery ['semitəri] kirkegård.
cenotaph ['senota·f] kenotaf, tom grav.
censor ['sensə] sensor; sensurere.
censorious [sen'sɔ·riəs] kritikksyk, kritisk.
censorship ['sensəʃip] sensorstilling, sensur.
censure ['sanʃə] daddel, klander; laste, klandre, dømme; **vote of** — mistillitsvotum.
census ['sensəs] telling, folketelling.
cent [sent] hundre; (amr.) cent, ¹/₁₀₀ dollar; **per** — prosent.
Cent. fk. f. **Centigrade.**
centaur ['sentɔ·ə] kentaur.
centenarian [senti'nɛ·ᵊriən] hundreåring. **centenary** ['sentinəri] hundreår; hundreårsfest.
centennial [sen'tenjəl] hundreårsfest.
centigrade ['sentigre·d] som er inndelt i hundre grader; celsius. **centimeter** ['senti'mi·tə] centimeter.
centiped(e) ['sentiped] tusenbein.
central ['sentrəl] sentral, midt-; viktigst; — **exchange** sentral; — **heating** sentralvarme. **centralisation** [sentrəlai'ze·ʃən] sentralisering. **-ize** ['sentrəlaiz] sentralisere.
centre ['sentə] midtpunkt, sentrum. **-piece** bordoppsats. **centre** sette i sentrum; konsentrere; samle seg, være samlet; være i sentrum.
centrifugal [sen'trifjugəl] sentrifugal. — **machine** sentrifuge, separator.
centripetal [sen'tripitəl, 'sentripi·tl] sentripetal.
centuple ['sentjupl] hundrefold.
century ['sentʃuri] århundre, hundreår.
'cept (**except**) unntagen.
ceramic [si'rämik] keramisk, keramikk-, pottemaker-. **ceramics** [si'rämiks] keramikk.
Cerberus ['sɔ·bərəs] Kerberos.
cereal ['siəriəl] korn-; kornslag.
cerebellum [seri'beləm] lille hjerne. **cerebral** ['seribrəl] hjerne-; — **inflammation** hjernebetennelse. **cerebrum** ['seribrəm] hjerne.
cerecloth ['siəklɔθ] voksduk, vokslaken.
cerement ['siəmənt] vokslede, likklede.
ceremonial [seri'mo⁰njəl] seremoniell, høytidelig; seremoniell. **ceremonious** [seri'mo⁰njəs] seremoniell, seremoniøs; formell, stiv.

ceremony ['seriməni] seremoni; høytidelighet; formaliteter, omstendigheter; **on occasions of** — ved høytidelige anledninger; **stand on** — gjøre omstendigheter; **without** — uten videre.
certain ['sə·tn, 'sə·tin] viss, sikker, bestemt; **I feel** — jeg føler meg overbevist om; **he is** — **to come** han kommer sikkert; **for** — sikkert. **-ly** sikkert, ganske visst, visselig, ja vel, ja.
certainty ['sə·tnti] visshet, bestemthet; **for a** —, **of a** —, **to a** — sikkert.
certificate [sə·'tifikét] bevis, attest, vitnemål, sertifikat **certificate** [sə·'tifike·t] bevitne. **certification** [sə·tifi'ke·ʃən] attestering; attest, pass.
certify ['sə·tifai] bevitne; **this is to** — herved bevitnes.
certitude ['sə·titju·d] visshet, visse.
cerulean [si'ru·ᵊliən] himmelblå.
ceruse ['siəru·s, si'ru·s] blyhvitt.
cervine ['sə·vain] hjorte-.
cessation [se¹se'ʃen] opphør, ende, stans.
cession ['seʃən] avståelse. **-ary** ['seʃənəri] befullmektiget.
cesspool ['sespu·l] kloakk-kum.
C. E. T. S. fk. f. **Church of England Temperance Society.**
Ceylon [si'lån] Ceylon.
cf. fk. f. **confer** (= **compare**).
C. F. fk. f. **Chaplain of the Forces.**
cg. fk. f. **centigram.**
C. H. fk. f. **Companion of Honour.**
ch., chap. fk. f. **chapter.**
chafe [tʃe·f] gni for å varme, varme; gni sår; opphisse; bli forbitret; skure, gnage; tirre, ergre; rase; fnyse; gnidning, skuring; varme; hissighet, forbitrelse.
chaff [tʃa·f] agner; hakkelse; skjemt, skøy, ap; skjemte, ape, erte, drive gjøn (med).
chaffer ['tʃäfə] prutte; kjøpslå; tinge; tinging.
chaffinch ['tʃa·finʃ] bokfink.
chafing-dish ['tʃe·findiʃ] glopanne, fyrfat.
chagrin [ʃä'gri·n] ergrelse; ulag; ergre.
chain [tʃe·n] kjede, lenke; kjetting; lenke; sperre med lenker; (fig.) fengsle. — **armour** ringbrynje; — **bridge** hengebru. — **gang** lenkegjeng, tukthusfanger.
chair [tʃæ·ə] stol; talerstol; lærestol; dommersete; forsete; bærestol; president, dirigent, ordstyrer; **take the** — være dirigent.
chairman ['tʃæ·əmən] formann, dirigent, ordstyrer. **-ship** ['tʃæ·əmənʃip] presidentstilling.
chaise [ʃe'z] lett vogn, gigg.
chaldron ['tʃä·ldrən] kullmål (36 bushels).
chalet ['ʃäle)i] sveitserhytte; fjellhytte, fjellstue.
chalice ['tʃälis] beger, kalk.
chalk [tʃå·k] kritt; poeng; regning; kritte. **-pit** krittbrudd. — **stone** forkalkninger (hos giktpasienter); giktknute. **chalky** ['tʃå·ki] krittaktig.
challenge ['tʃälən(d)ʒ] utfordre; oppfordre; uteske; fordre, kreve; gjøre innsigelse; utfordring; oppfordring; uteskring; fordring.
chalybeate [kə'libi¹t] jernholdig.
cham [käm] kan, tatarfyrste; **the great C. of literature** litteraturens store høvding (om Samuel Johnson).
chamade [ʃə'ma·d] signal til underhandling el. overgivelse.
chamber ['tʃe·mbə] kammer, værelse, stue; kontor; rettssal, rett; **live in -s** bo til leie. — **counsel** privat rådgiver, som ikke fører saker. — **music** kammermusikk.
chamberlain ['tʃe·mbəlin] kammerherre; kemner; **the Lord C.** hoffmarskalk, sensor.
chamber-maid ['tʃe·mbəme·d] kammerpike, stuepike.
chamelon [kə'mi·ljən] kameleon.
chamfer ['tʃämfə] skråkant; skjev vinkel; grop; rifle; sette skråkant på, rifle.
chamois ['ʃämwa·] gemse; vaskeskinn.
champ [tʃämp] tygge, bite.

champagne [ʃäm'peˈn] champagne.
champaign ['tʃämpeˈn] slette.
champignon [ʃäm'pinjən] sjampinjong.
champion ['tʃämpiən] kjemper; forkjemper, ridder; (i sport) champion, mester; forsvare; forfekte, ta seg av; være ens ridder.
chance [tʃaˈns] sjanse, tilfelle; slump; høve; mulighet: risiko; leilighet; utsikt; utsikter; tilfeldig; hende, treffe seg, bære til; **by** — tilfeldig; **all our** — was vår eneste sjanse var; **on** — på må få, på det uvisse, på vona; **stand a good** — ha en god anledning.
chancel ['tʃaˈnsəl] kor (del av kirke).
chancellor ['tʃaˈnsələ] kansler; — **of the exchequer** finansminister; **Lord (High) Chancellor** lordkansler (justisminister, president i overhuset og i kanslerretten).
chance-medley ['tʃaˈns'medli] uaktsomt drap.
Chancery ['tʃaˈnsəri] kanslerretten (avdeling av the High Court of Justice); **in chancery** i klemme (om bokser, hvis hode er under motstanderens arm, slik at denne, så lenge det skal være, kan hamre løs på det).
chancre ['ʃäŋkə] sjanker.
chandelier [ʃändi'liə] lysekrone.
chandler ['tʃaˈndlə] lysestøper, lyseselger; detaljhandler, småhandler, høker.
'change [tʃeˈn(d)ʒ] børs (d. s. s. **exchange**).
change [tʃeˈn(d)ʒ] forandring, omskifte, skifte, brigde, bytte; småpenger; børs; forandre, bytte, skifte, veksle; forandre seg, skifte; — **of attire** klær til skift, sett klær; — **for** ombytte med.
changeable ['tʃeˈn(d)ʒəbl] foranderlig.
changeling ['tʃeˈn(d)ʒəliŋ] bytting.
channel ['tʃänəl] (naturlig) kanal; renne; **the Channel** Kanalen (mellom England og Frankrike).
chant [tʃaˈnt] synge; messe; besynge, synge om; sang; messe.
chantey el. **chanty** ['tʃaˈnti] oppsang.
Chanticleer ['tʃaˈntikliə] hane.
chantry ['tʃaˈntri] sjelegave (til sjelemesser); kapell; prest, alter (for sjelemesser).
chaos ['keˈäs] kaos. **chaotic** [ke'ˈätik] kaotisk.
chap [tʃäp] sprekke, kløvne, revne; få til å sprekke; sprekk.
chap [tʃäp] kjeve, kinn, kjake; **-s** kjeft.
chap [tʃäp] fyr (gutt el. mann).
chapel ['tʃäpəl] dissenterkirke, mindre kirke, kirke knyttet til en institusjon, f. eks. slottskirke; — **of ease** hjelpekirke, annekskirke. **-ry** ['tʃäpəlri] anneks.
chaperon ['ʃäpəroun, -rån] hette; chaperone, anstandsdame; ledsage (som anstandsdame).
chapfallen ['tʃäpfä·ln] lang i fjeset; motfallen.
chaplain ['tʃäplin] prest (ved en institusjon); feltprest, skipsprest; hoffprest.
chaplet ['tʃäplet] krans; rosenkrans.
chapman ['tʃäpmən] kramkar.
chapter ['tʃäptə] kapitel (i bok), domkapitel, ordenskapitel. **-house** kapitelbygning, kapitelhus.
char [tʃaˈ] brenne (tre) til kull; svi; svartne.
char [tʃaˈ] sjaue, ha løsarbeid.
char-à-banc ['ʃärəbäŋ] turistbil.
character ['käriktə] skrifttegn, bokstav; eiendommelighet, særmerke, egenskap; karakter; rolle; person; ry, rykte; vitnesbyrd, vitnemål, skussmål; **he has the** — **of a miser** han har ord for å være en gnier; **a street** — en gatefigur; **I know him only by** — bare av omtale; **in the** — **of the King** i kongens rolle; **a girl of** — en uberyktet (bra) pike. **characteristic** [käriktə'ristik] karakteristisk; eiendommelighet. **characterize** ['käriktəraiz] karakterisere, betegne; prege, særprege.
charade [ʃə'raˈd] charade, stavelsesgåte; **act -s** leke ordspråkslek.
charcoal ['tʃaˈkouˈl] trekull.
charge [tʃaˈˈdʒ] lese, belesse, pålegge; forlange (som betaling); beregne; ta el skytevåpen); overdra; beskylde; angripe; ladning, last, lass; pålegg; befaling; omsorg, varetekt; omkostning; betaling,

pris; gebyr; pleiebarn; protesjé; beskyldning, anklage; angrep; **what's your** — hva er Deres pris? **without** — gratis; **have** — of ha i forvaring; **who had** — **of these things** som disse ting var betrodd; **make the** — that anføre, gjøre gjeldende at; **sound the** — blåse til angrep; **at a certain** — til en viss betaling; **be in** — ha kommando; **in** — of under bevoktning av; **give in** — of a policeman overlevere til en konstabel, la anholde (av en konstabel); — **at**, — **on** rette angrep på, angripe. **-able** ['tʃaˈˈdʒəbl] som kan pålegges, tilskrives, anklages.
chargé d'affaires ['ʃaˈˈʒeˈdä'fæˈə] chargé d'affaires.
charger ['tʃaˈˈdʒə] ganger, stridshest.
chariness ['tʃæˈˈrinés] forsiktighet, sparsommelighet.
Charing Cross ['tʃärin 'kråˈs] en plass og en jernbanestasjon i London.
chariot ['tʃäriət] stridsvogn; lett herskapsvogn.
charitable ['tʃäritəbl] godgjørende; barmhjertig.
charity ['tʃäriti] kjærlighet (til nesten); kjærlighetsgjerning, velgjerning; miskunn, sælebot; godgjørenhet; medlidenhet; godhet; velvilje; almisse; **it would be quite a** — det ville være en ren velgjerning; — **begins at home** enhver er seg selv nærmest; — **school** fattigskole; **bread of** — nådesnsbrød.
charivari ['ʃaˈri'vaˈri] kattemusikk; pipekonsert.
charlatan ['ʃaˈˈlətän] sjarlatan.
Charlemagne ['ʃaˈˈlimeˈn] Karl den store.
Charles [tʃaˈˈlz] Karl. **-'s-wain** Karls-vognen.
Charley, Charlie ['tʃaˈˈli].
charlock ['tʃaˈˈlåk] åkersennep.
Charlotte ['ʃaˈˈlåt] Charlotte; eplegrøt.
charm [tʃaˈˈm] tryllemiddel, trylleri, trylleformel; yndighet, elskverdighet, sjarm; fortrylle, henrive, henrykke, dåre, vinne. **the -ed circle** tryllesirkel; **he bears a -ed life** han er usårlig. **charmer** trollmann; en som tryller. **-ing** elskverdig, henrivende, yndig.
charnel(-house) ['tʃaˈˈnəl(haus)] likhus.
Charon ['kæˈˈrån] Charon.
chart [tʃaˈˈt] sjøkart; kart; tabell; kartlegge.
charta se **Magna Charta**.
charter ['tʃaˈˈtə] dokument; frihetsbrev, privilegium; befraktning; fraktbrev; privilegere; frakte: **the Atlantic** — Atlanterhavserklæringen (mellom Churchill og Roosevelt 1941); **the Great Charter** d. s. s. **Magna Charta. the people's** — chartistenes program. **-ed accountant** autorisert revisor.
Charterhouse ['tʃaˈˈtəhaus] Charterhouse.
charter-party ['tʃaˈˈtəpaˈˈti] serteparti, fraktbrev.
chartism ['tʃaˈˈtizm] chartisme (engelsk radikal bevegelse etter reformloven 1832).
chartist ['tʃaˈˈtist] chartist.
charwoman ['tʃaˈˈwumən] kone som arbeider for daglønn, skurekone, vaskekone.
chary ['tʃæˈˈri] forsiktig; sparsom, økonomisk.
chase [tʃeˈs] drive, siselere; skjære gjenge på.
chase [tʃeˈs] jage, forfølge; jakt; forfølgelse; jaktdistrikt.
chase [tʃeˈs] formramme.
chasm [kä·zm] kløft, gap, avgrunn.
chassis ['ʃäsi] chassis, understell til bil.
chaste [tʃeˈst] kysk; ren.
chasten ['tʃeˈsn], **chastise** [tʃä'staiz] tukte, refse. **chastisement** ['tʃästizmənt] tukt, refsing.
chastity ['tʃästiti] kyskhet; renhet.
chasuble ['tʃäzjubl] messehakel.
chat [tʃät] passiar, snakk, prat; passiare, prate, snakke.
Chatham ['tʃätəm] Chatham.
chattels ['tʃätlz] løsøre.
chatter ['tʃätə] pjatte, skravle, klapre; skravl, klapring. **-box** ['tʃätəbåks] skravlebøtte.
chatty ['tʃäti] snakksom, pratsom.
Chaucer ['tʃaˈsə] Chaucer.
chauffer ['tʃaˈfə] fyrfat, glopanne.

chauffeur [ʃoᵘ'fəˑ, 'ʃoᵘfə] sjåfør.
chaw [tʃåˑ] tygge; skrå, buss.
cheap [tʃiˑp] billig. - **Jack** (or **John**) godt-kjøpshandler ved marked el. l.; **to do it on the —** leve på billigste måte. **-en** ['tʃiˑpn] by på, prute; slå av; (fig.) nedsette.
cheat [tʃiˑt] bedrageri; snyter, bedrager; be-dra, snyte. **cheater** bedrager.
check [tʃek] hindring, stansing, stans; kontroll; merke; garantiseddel; utgangsbillett; rute (i tøy); anvisning; sjakk; hindre, stanse, stagge; kontrol-lere; irettesette; sette i sjakk; **put a — upon** legge **en** demper på; **keep him in —** holde ham i sjakk.
checker ['tʃekə] gjøre rutet (se **chequer**).
checkmate ['tʃek'meˑt] matt (i sjakk), neder-lag; gjøre sjakkmatt, tilføye neder'lag.
cheddar ['tʃedə] cheddarost.
cheek [tʃiˑk] kinn; (sl.) frekkhɛt, freidighet, uforskammethet; **— by jowl** side om side. **cheeky** ['tʃiˑki] frekk, nesevis, nebbet.
cheep [tʃiˑp] pip, pistring; pipe, pistre.
cheer [tʃiə] (sinns)stemning, mot, lag, hug; glede, munterhet; bevertning, mat og drikke; hurra, bifallsrop, fagning; oppmuntre; tiljuble; rope hurra for, fagne; **-io** ['tʃiəri'oᵘ] hallo, hei på deg! **— up** fatte mot; **how — you?** hvorledes går det med deg? **-ful** ['tʃiəful] glad, munter, for-nøyd. **-fulness** munterhet, lystighet. **-less** ['tʃiə-lès] gledeløs; bedrøvelig. **-y** ['tʃiəri] munter, glad.
cheese [tʃiˑz] ost. **-monger** [-mʌŋgə] oste-handler, fetevarehandler. **— -paring**[- pæˑ⁹ring] osteskorpe; flisespikkeri; knussel; smålig, knuslet.
cheetah ['tʃiˑtə] tsjita, slags leopard.
chef [ʃef] overkokk.
chela ['tʃeˑlə] disippel, lærling.
Chelsea ['tʃelsiˑ] Chelsea (del av London).
chemical ['kemikl] kjemisk. **-s** kjemikalier.
chemis|e [ʃiˑmiˑz] chemise, linnet, serk. **-ette** [ʃemi'zet] chemisette, underliv, livstykke.
chemist ['kemist] kjemiker; apoteker; **chemist's** (**shop**) apotek. **-ry** ['kemistri] kjemi.
cheque [tʃek] sjekk. **-book** sjekkbok.
chequer ['tʃekə] gjøre ternet el. rutet; gjøre avvekslende.
cherish ['tʃeriʃ] kjæle for; pleie; oppelske; be-skytte; holde av.
cheroot [ʃə'ruˑt] cheroot, (mindre) sigar som er tvert avskåret i begge ender.
cherry ['tʃeri] kirsebær(tre); kirsebærfarget. **— -brandy** kirsebærlikør. **— -pie** heliotrop.
cherub ['tʃerəb] kjerub; **cherubs** el. **cherubim(s)** ['tʃerubim(z)] kjeruber.
chervil ['tʃəˑvil] kjørvel.
chess [tʃes] sjakk. **— -board** sjakkbrett. **— -man** sjakkbrikke. **— -player** sjakkspiller.
chest [tʃest] kiste; bryst; **— of drawers** drag-kiste, kommode.
chesterfield ['tʃestəfiˑld] chesterfield.
chest-note ['tʃestnoᵘt] brysttone.
chestnut ['tʃes(t)nʌt] kastanje.
cheval-glass [ʃə'vaˑl,] 'väl] toalettspeil, dreie-speil.
cheviot ['tʃevjət] sjeviot (slags tøy).
chew [tʃuˑ] tygge; (fig.) tygge på; skrå, buss; **— the cud** tygge drøv.
chewing-gum ['tʃuˑiŋʌm] tyggegummi.
chic [ʃiˑk] chic, elegant.
Chicago [ʃi'kaˑgoᵘ, amr.: ʃi'kåˑgoᵘ] Chicago.
chicane [ʃi'keˑn] sjikane, knep, (i bridge) hånd uten trumf; sjikanere, bruke knep. **chicaner** [ʃi'keˑnə] sjikanør. **chicanery** [ʃi'keˑnəri] sjikane.
Chichester ['tʃitʃistə] Chichester.
chick [tʃik] kylling; unge, pjokk.
chicken [tʃikn] kylling; unge, småbarn. **-hearted** forsagt, stakkarslig.
chicken-pox ['tʃiknpåks] vannkopper.
chicory ['tʃikəri] sikori.
chid [tʃid] imperf. og perf. pts. av **chide**.
chidden ['tʃidn] perf. pts. av **chide**.
chide [tʃaid] irettesette, laste, skjenne på.

chief [tʃiˑf] først, fornemst, viktigst, høyest, øverst; hode; høvding, sjef, anfører, overhode; **— friends** nærmeste venner; **Lord Chief Justice** ju-stitiarius (rettsformann) i King's Bench Division; **in —** øverst, først og fremst; **commander in —** øverstbefalende; **editor in —** sjefredaktør.
chiefly ['tʃiˑfli] især, hovedsakelig.
chieftain ['tʃiˑftin, 'tʃiˑftən] høvding, fører.
chignon ['ʃiˑnjəŋ] nakkeknute,oppsattnakkehår.
chilblain ['tʃilbleˑn] frostknute.
child [tʃaild] barn (i poesi: junker); **with —** fruktsommelig. **child-bed** ['tʃaildbed] barselseng.
childe [tʃaild] junker.
Childermas ['tʃildəmäs] barnedag (28. desbr.).
childhood ['tʃaildhud] barndom.
childish ['tʃaildiʃ] barnlig, barnslig, barnaktig.
childless ['tʃaildlès] barnløs.
childlike ['tʃaildlaik] barnlig, barnslig.
children ['tʃildrən] pl. av **child** barn.
Chile ['tʃili] Chile. **Chilian** ['tʃiliən] chilener; chilensk.
chill [tʃil] kald, sval, kjølig; kulsen; nedslått; kulde, kjølighet; kulsing; gjøre kald, få til å fryse; nedslå; **take the — off** kuldslå, temperere. **-iness** ['tʃilinès] kulde.
chilly ['tʃili] kjølig, kald. **— -body** frysepinne.
Chiltern Hundreds ['tʃiltən 'hʌndrədz] engelsk kronland i Buckinghamshire, hvis styrelse for-melt som embete overdras til dem som vil oppgi sitt sete i Parlamentet; **to take** (el. **to accept**) **the —** å oppgi sitt sete i Parlamentet.
chime [tʃaim] samklang; kiming, klokkering-ing; stemme sammen; ringe, kime.
chimera [ki'miərə, kai'miərə] kimære, hjerne-spinn, drømmeri.
chimere [tʃi'miə] bispesamarie.
chimerical [ki'merikl, kai'merikl] kimæreaktig, fantastisk.
chimney ['tʃimni] skorstein, peis, kamin. **— -piece** kaminstykke, kamingesims, kaminhylle. **— -pot** skorsteinspipe. **— -stack** murblokk med en rad av skorsteinsrør; skorsteinspipe. **— -sweep(er)** skorsteinsfeier.
chimpanzee [tʃim'pänziˑ] sjimpanse.
chin [tʃin] hake.
China [tʃiˑnə] China.
china ['tʃiˑnə] porselen.
Chinaman ['tʃiˑnəmən] kineser, kinafarer.
chinaware ['tʃiˑnəwæˑ⁹] porselen.
chincough ['tʃiŋkåˑf] kikhoste.
Chinee [tʃaiˑniˑ] (vulg.) kineser.
Chinese [tʃai'niˑz] kineser; kinesisk.
chink [tʃiŋk] revne, sprekk; sprekke.
chink [tʃiŋk] klirre; ringle (med); klirring; penger.
Chink [tʃiŋk] kineser.
chinky [tʃiŋki] sprukken, full av sprekker.
chintz [tʃints] chintz, slags sirs.
chip [tʃip] snitte, flise opp, hugge; slå småstyk-ker av; hogge, skave, telgje til el. av; sprekke; miste småstykker; spon; flis; (sl.) mynt; tømmer-mann; **'tis a — of the old block** det er faren opp av dage; **chips** ogs. slags stekte potetskiver.
Chippendale ['tʃipəndeˑl] engelsk møbelstil.
chippy ['tʃipi] fliset; tørr, uinteressant.
chirography [kai'rågrəfi] skrivekunst; hånd-skrift.
chiromancer ['kairomänsə] kiromant. **chiro-mancy** [-si] kiromanti, kunsten å spå i hendene.
chiropodist [tʃi'råpədist] liktornoperatør.
chirp [tʃəˑp] kvitre, pistre; kvitring, pip; riksing.
chirpy ['tʃəˑpi] livlig, kipen, kåt.
chirrup ['tʃirəp] d. s., ogs. klappe, applaudere for betaling.
chisel ['tʃizəl] meisel, beitel; meisle; snyte.
Chiswick ['tʃizik] Chiswick.
chit [tʃit] barn, unge (foraktel.); spire; (i eng-elske kolonier) brev, billett.

chitchat ['tʃit-tʃät] småsnakk, prat.
chivalrous ['ʃivəlrəs, 'tʃ-] ridderlig. chivalry
['ʃivəlri, 'tʃ-] ridderskap; ridderverdighet; ridderlighet.
chive [tʃaiv] purre (løk), grasløk.
chlor|al ['klå·rəl] kloral. -ic ['klå·rik] klor-.
-ine ['klå·r(a)in] klor. -odyne ['klå·rodain]
smertestillende midde!. -oform ['klå·rofå·əm]
kloroform.
chlorosis [klå'rousis] bleksott.
chock [tʃåk] ki!e, klamp; krabbe, krakk (under
båt, vannfat); kile fast; sette krabbe under.
chocolate ['tʃåkəlet] sjokolade.
choice [tʃois] valg; utvalg; (fig.) kjerne; utsøkt;
make — of velge; for — fortrinsvis; men of —
utsøkte folk.
choir ['kwaiə] sangkor (i kirke); kor (i dom-
kirker); synge i kor.
choke [tʃouk] kvele; stoppe, undertrykke,
døyve; kveles; kovne; kvelning. choker ['tʃoukə]
kveler; stort halstørkle.
choler ['kålə] galle; sinne. cholera ['kålərə]
kolera. choleric ['kålərik] hissig, kolerisk.
choose [tʃu·z] velge (ut), kåre; foretrekke; ha
lyst, ønske, ville, finne for godt, skjøtte om; I
cannot — but jeg kan ikke annet enn; beggars
must not be choosers tiggere må ikke være kresne.
chop [tʃåp] hogge, kutte, hakke; kappe; slå
om, vende seg (om vind); — in hogge inn i (et
ordskifte); — up hogge opp; hogg, hakk, avhogd
stykke; kotelett; -s krappe bølger, krapp sjø.
chop [tʃåp] bytte, skifte; — logic disputere;
— and change være vinglete.
chop [tʃåp] kinn, kjake; (pl.) kjeft; munning;
the Chops of the Channel kanalgapet (mot
Atlanterhavet).
chop [tʃåp] (i India) kvalitet, sort, slag.
chop-house ['tʃåphaus] spisekvarter.
chopping-block ['tʃåpiŋblåk] hoggestabbe.
chopping-knife ['tʃåpiŋnaif] kjøttkniv, hakke-
kniv.
choppy ['tʃåpi] krapp (om havet); vinglet, ustø.
chopstick ['tʃåpstik] spisepinne (et par, brukt
som gaffel i China).
choral ['kå·rəl] kor-; koral, salmemelodi.
chord [kå·əd] streng; akkord; korde; sporv.
chore ['tʃå·ə] arbeid; husstell.
chorister ['kåristə] korsanger.
chorus ['kå·rəs] kor (i drama); korverk; rope
i kor; stemme i med.
chose [tʃouz] imperf. av choose.
chosen ['tʃouzn] perf. pts. av choose.
chouse [tʃauz] snyte, narre; svindler.
chowchow ['tʃau'tʃau] slags kinesisk grøt-
blanding.
chrism [krizm] hellig olje; salving.
Christ [kraist] Kristus.
Christabel ['kristəbəl] Christabel.
christen ['krisn] døpe. -dom ['krisndəm] kri-
stenhet, kristendom. -ing ['krisniŋ] dåp.
Christian ['kristjən, -tʃən] kristelig; kristen;
— name døpenavn, fornavn. -ism, -ity ['kristjən-
izm, kristi'äniti] kristendom. -ize ['kristjənaiz]
kristne.
Christmas ['krisməs] jul. —box julegave. —
-carol julesang. —day .første juledag. —
-eve [-i·v] julaften. —tree juletre.
Christopher ['kristəfə] Kristoffer.
Christy ['kristi] — Minstrels varietésangere,
som opptrer som negrer.
chromatic [kro'mätik] kromatisk.
chrome [kroum] krom. chromic ['kroumik]
krom-.
chronic ['krånik] (kld-, tids-; kronisk, langvarig. chronicle ['krånikl] krønike, årbok; nedskrive, opptegne; the Chronicles Krønikebøkene (i
Bibelen). chronicler ['kråniklə] krønikeskriver,
kronikør.
chronological [krånə'lådʒikl] kronologisk. chro-
nology [krə'nålədʒi] kronologi, tidsregning.

chronometer [krə'nåmitə] kronometer.
chrysalis ['krisəlis] puppe.
chrysantemum [kri'sänpəməm] krysantemum.
chubby ['tʃʌbi] buttet, tykk, lubben.
chuck [tʃʌk] kakle, lokke på; klappe, daske
(under haken); kaste, slenge, oppgi; kakling;
lett dask, klapp; sleng, kast; get the — (vulg.)
få sin avskjed, ‹sparken›. — farthing kaste på
stikka.
chuckle ['tʃʌkl] klukke, le innvendig; innvendig latter, klukklatter.
chuckle-head ['tʃʌklhed] stut, tosk.
chum ['tʃʌm] venn, kamerat, busse, kontubernal; være gode venner, dele værelse; new
— nyinnvandret i Australia; — together bo
sammen.
chummy ['tʃʌmi] kameratslig.
chump [tʃʌmp] trekloss; kubbe; hode, skolt;
kjøtthue, naut; — end tykkende; off one's —
gal, toskete.
chunk [tʃʌŋk] tykk stump, skive, klump.
church ['tʃə·tʃ] kirke; be at — være i kirke;
go to — gå i kirke; as safe as a — fullstendig
sikker. — -goer kirkegjenger. — -going kirkegang.
Churchill ['tʃə·tʃil] Churchill.
church|ing ['tʃə·tʃiŋ] inngang (en barselskones).
— -man ['tʃə·tʃmən] tilhenger av statskirken. —
-mouse: as poor as a — -mouse så fattig som
en kirkerotte. — -rate kirkeskatt. — -servi e
gudstjeneste. — -time kirketid.
churchwarden ['tʃə·tʃ'wå·ədn] kirkeverge; lang
krittpipe.
churchyard ['tʃə·tʃ'ja·əd] kirkegård (ɔ: plass
omkring kirke).
churl [tʃə·l] bonde; tølper, slamp; gnier, lus.
-ish [-iʃ] bondeaktig; tølperaktig.
churn [tʃə·n] kjerne; spann, kjerne.
churr [tʃə·] knarr; knarre, mekre.
chute [ʃu·t] stryk; vann-, tømmerrenne; akebakke.
C. I. fk. f. Channel Islands.
cicada [si'ke¹də, si'ka·də] cikade.
cicatrice [si'ke¹tris], cicatrix ['sikətriks] pl.
cicatrices [sikə'traisi·z] arr, merke.
Cicero ['sisərou] Cicero.
C. I. D. fk. f. Criminal Investigation Dept;
Committee of Imperial Defence.
cider ['saidə] sider, eplemost, fruktvin.
C. I. E. fk. f. Companion of the Indian Empire.
c. i. f. [sif] cif, fritt levert (fk. f. cost, insurance
and freight ɔ: kostnader, assuranse og frakt
betalt).
cigar [si'ga·ə] sigar. — -case sigarfutteral.
cigarette [sigə'ret] sigarett.
cigar-holder [si'ga·ə'houldə] sigarmunnstykke.
C. I. G. S. fk. f. Chief of Imperial General
Staff.
cilia ['siljə] øyehår, randhår.
Cimbric ['simbrik] kimbrisk.
Cincinnati [sinsi'na·ti] Cincinnati.
cincture ['siŋktjuə-, -tʃə] belte.
cinder ['sində] slagg; glødende kull; sinders.
Cinderella [sində'relə] Kari trestakk.
cinema ['sinimə] kino, kinematograf; — -goer
kinogjenger; — star filmstjerne.
cinematograph [sinə'mätəgra·f] kinematograf.
cinerary ['sinirări] aske-.
Cingalese [siŋgə'li·z] singaleser; singalesisk.
cinnabar ['sinəba·] sinober.
cinnamon ['sinəmən] kanel.
cinque [siŋk] femmer (i kort og på terninger).
-ports fem havner på Englands kyst: Hastings,
Dover, Hythe, Romney, Sandwich.
cipher ['saifə] sifferskrift; navnesiffer; null,
tall, siffer; regne. -ing ['saifəriŋ] regning.
Circassian [sə·'käʃən] tsjerkessisk; tsjerkesser.
circle ['sə·kl] sirkel, ring; krets; ringe, ringe
inne, inneslutte; gå rundt i ring. circlet ['sə·klet]
liten sirkel, ring.
circuit ['sə·kit] kretsløp; omkrets; elektrisk

ledning, strøm; en dommers reise i sitt distrikt for å holde rett, tingferd; retts-distrikt; omvei.

circuitous [sə·'kjuitəs] som går omveier; vidløftig; ugrei; — **road** omvei, krok.

circular ['sə·kjulə] sirkelrund, ring-, rund-; sirkulære, rundskriv; — **note** pengeanvisning, anvisning.

circulate ['sə·kjulə't] sirkulere, være i omløp; la sirkulere, bringe i omløp; **circulating library** leiebibliotek. **circulation** [sə·kju'le'ʃən] omløp, sirkulasjon; utbredelse.

circum|ambient [sə·kəm'æmbiənt] som går rundt, i ring. **-ambulate** [sə·kəm'æmbule't] gå rundt, i ring.

circumcise ['sə·kəmsaiz] omskjære.

circumference [sə·'kʌmfərəns] periferi; sirkel.

circumjacent ['sə·kəm'dʒe'sənt] omliggende.

circumlocution [sə·kəmlo'kju·ʃən] omskrivning; omsvøp.

circumnavigat|e [sə·kəm'nävige't] seile rundt. **-ion** [sə·kəmnävi'ge'ʃən] omseiling.

circum|scribe [sə·kəm'skraib] omskrive; (fig.) innskrenke, begrense. **-scription** [sə·kəm'skripʃən] omskrivning; begrensning, innskrenkning.

circumspect ['sə·kəmspekt] omtenksom, forsiktig, varsom. **-ion** [sə·kəm'spekʃən] omsikt, forsiktighet. **-ive** [sə·kəm'spektiv] omtenksom, var, gløgg.

circumstance ['sə·kəmstəns] omstendighet, tilfelle; tilstand; kår; bringe i visse omstendigheter. **circumstantial** [sə·kəm'stänʃəl] som ligger i omstendighetene; som beror på enkelthetene; omstendelig; **circumstantial evidence** indisiebevis.

circumvent [sə·kəm'vent] gå rundt om; overliste, bedra. **-ion** [sə·kəm'venʃən] bedrageri.

circus ['sə·kəs] sirkus; runding, rund plass i en by (**Oxford** —, **Piccadilly** —, i London).

Cirencester ['sairənsestə, 'sisi(s)tə] Cirencester.

cirrus ['sirəs] fjærsky.

cist [sist] steingrav; kiste for hellige kar.

cistern ['sistən] sisterne (beholder).

cit [sit] spissborger.

citadel ['sitədel] citadell.

citation [si'te'ʃən, sai'te'ʃən] stevning; anføring, sitat, henvisning. **cite** [sait] stevne; sitere.

citizen ['sitizən] borger. **-ship** borgerskap, borgerrett.

citron ['sitrən] sitron.

citern ['sitə·n] sitar, gitar.

city ['siti] stad, (stor) by; **of this** — her; **of your** — der; **of that** — der (i omtale); **the City** den opprinneligste del av London, forretningskvarteret der. — **article** artikkel om forretningslivet.

civet-cat ['sivitkät] desmerkatt.

civic ['sivik] by-, borger-, kommunal.

civil ['sivil] by-, borger-, borgerlig; sivil; sivilisert, høflig; — **engineer** sivilingeniør; — **list** (den kongelige) sivilliste; appanasje; — **marriage** borgerlig vielse; **C. Servant** sivil embetsmann; **C. Service** statsadministrasjonen (bortsett fra hær og flåte); — **war** borgerkrig.

civilian [si'viljən] sivil, sivil person.

civility [si'viliti] høflighet; folkeskikk.

civil|ization [sivil(a)i'ze'ʃən] sivilisasjon. **-ize** ['sivilaiz] sivilisere.

C. J. fk. f. Chief Justice.

cl. fk. f. centilitre; class.

clack [kläk] klapring; klapre.

clad [kläd] kledde, kledd, av **clothe.**

claim [kle'm] fordring, krav, påstand; lodd; skjerp; fordre, gjøre krav på, kreve. **-ant** ['kle'mənt] en som gjør fordring; pretendent.

clairvoyance [klæ·ə'voiəns] clairvoyance.

clam [kläm] (mat)skjell, sandskjell.

clamant ['klämənt] bråkende, høymælt.

clamber ['klämbə] klavre, klyve, klatre.

clammy ['klämi] klam, kaldvåt.

clamorous ['klämərəs] skrikende, larmende.

clamour ['klämə] skrik; skrike, larme, ståke.

clamp [klämp] klamp; krampe; klemme, tvinge; kjeng, klemskrue; skruestikke; feste med klamp osv.

clamp [klämp] haug, dynge; stakk.

clan [klän] klan, stamme, ætt m. høvding.

clandestine [klän'dest(a)in] hemmelig; smug-.

clang [kläŋ] klirre, single, rasle; klirre, rasle med; klirr, rasling. **clangour** ['kläŋ(g)ə] klang, skrall. **clangorous** ['kläŋgərəs] klingende.

clank [kläŋk] klirre; klirr.

clap [kläp] slå sammen, klappe; sette, stikke, legge i en fart; gripe; klappe for; klapre; banke (på en dør); fare av sted; klapp, slag, smell, skrall; dryppert. — **them in (to) prison** sette dem i fengsel; — **a pistol to his breast** sette pistolen for brystet på ham; — **one's hands** klappe i hendene.

clapper ['kläpə] kolv.

claptrap ['kläpträp] forberedt teatereffekt, effektjageri; fraser, slagord, store ord.

Clara ['klæ·ərə], **Clare** [klæ·ə] Klara.

Clarence ['klärəns] Clarence.

Clarendon ['klärəndən] Clarendon.

claret ['klärit] rødvin, srl. bordeauxvin.

clarification [klärifi'ke'ʃən] klaring, avklaring.

clarify ['klärifai] klare, klare opp, avklare; klares.

clarinet [kläri'net] klarinett.

clarion ['klärien] trompet; — **-call** kampsignal.

clarity ['kläriti] klarhet.

clash [kläʃ] klaske, klirre; støte sammen med; klirring, smell, brak; sammenstøt.

clasp [kla·sp] hekte, spenne; omfavnelse; fangtak; hekte; folde (hendene); holde fast, omfavne.

clasp-knife ['kla·sp'naif] foldekniv.

class [kla·s] klasse, skeid, kursus; deler i klasser, klassifisere, ordne, sette i klasse med.

classic ['kläsik] klassisk, fortrinlig; klassiker.

classical ['kläsikl] klassisk. **classicism** ['kläsisizm] klassisisme. **classification** [kläsifi'ke'ʃən] klassifikasjon. **classify** ['kläsifai] klassifisere, inndele i klasser.

clatter ['klätə] klapre, skrangle, plapre; klapring, plapring, skrangling.

clause [klå·z] klausul, paragraf; setning.

clave [kle'v] imperf. av **cleave.**

clavecin ['klävisin] klavecin.

clavichord ['klävikå·əd] klavikord.

clavicle ['klävikl] nøklebein, kragebein.

clavier ['kläviə] klaviatur; [klə'viə] klavér.

claw [klå·] klo; krasse, krafse.

clay [kle'] leir, leirjord; kline; gjødsle med leir. **claymore** ['kle'må·ə] gammelt skotsk tveegget sverd.

clean [kli·n] ren; pen, feilfri; rent, ganske, fullkommen; rense, **to make a** — **confession** komme med full tilståelse. — **-cut** klar, skarp; velstøpt.

cleanliness ['klenlinès] renslighet; — **is next to godliness** ren i skinn, ren i sinn. **cleanly** ['klenli] (adj.) renslig. **cleanly** ['kli·nli] (adv.) ren, renslig. **cleanness** ['kli·nnès] renhet. **cleanse** [klenz] rense; renske; pusse.

clear [kliə] klar, lys; ren; ryddig; tydelig; fullkommen, ganske; gjøre klar, klare; rense; få bort, ta bort; rømme, rydde; selge ut, realisere; klarne. **clear** [kliə] klarere, tollbehandle; — **away** ta bort, rydde bort; — **up** klare opp, oppklare, opplyse, forklare. **-ance** ['kliərəns] klarering; oppryddning. **-ance sale** utsalg, realisasjon; **-ing** rydning, ryddet land; avregning srl. av veksler

Clearing-House ['kliəriŋhaus] avregningskontor.

clearness ['kliənès] klarhet.

cleave [kli·v] (imperf.: **cleaved** el. **clave**, perf. pts. **cleaved**) henge ved, henge fast, holde fast (to på, ved).

cleave [kli·v] (imperf.: **clove** el. **cleft**; perf. pts.: **cloven** el. **cleft**) kløve; spalte; **cloven** kløvne (klovne).

clef [klef] nøkkel (i musikk).

cleft [kleft] imperf. og perf. pts.; **in a** — **stick** i klemme.

cleft [kleft] kløft; spalte, åpen gane.
clematis ['klematis, kli'me¹tis] klematis.
clemency ['klemənsi] mildhet, skånsel.
clench [klenʃ] klinke; nøve; fatte fast, stramme, klemme sammen, knytte; slå fast; fast tak, hold, grep; — **one's fist** knytte neven; — **the teeth** bite tennene sammen.
Cleopatra [kli·o'pa·trə] Kleopatra.
clergy ['klə·dʒi] geistlighet, presteskap.
clergyman ['klə·dʒimən] geistlig, prest.
clerical ['klerikl] geistlig; — **error** skrivefeil.
clerk [kla·ᵊk] skriver; kontorist; sekretær; fullmektig; klokker, kirkesanger.
Clerkenwell ['kla·ᵊkənwel] Clerkenwell.
clever ['klevə] dyktig, flink, kvikk, begavet, kløktig, evnerik; (amr.) elskverdig. **-ness** dyktighet osv.
clew [klu·] nøste; ledetråd; nøkkel (fig.); lede, anvise.
cliché [kli'ʃe¹] klisjé; forslitt litterær talemåte.
click [klik] tikke, pikke; smelle, klikke med; knepp, pikk, klikk; sperrhake.
client ['klaiənt] klient.
cliff [klif] fjellskrent, hammer, stup.
cliffsman øvd klatrer.
climacteric [klaimäk'terik] klimakterisk, kritisk; kritisk år i menneskenes liv; **the grand** — det store klimakteriske år, det 63. år.
climate ['klaimit] klima, værlag; himmelstrøk.
climatic(al) [klai'mätik(l)] klimatisk.
climax ['klaimäks] klimaks.
climb [klaim] klatre, entre, bestige. **-er** ['klaimə] klatrer, tindebestiger; slyngplante.
clime [klaim] se **climate.**
clinch [klinʃ] se **clench.**
clincher ['klinʃə] svar, ord, prov som avgjør spørsmålet.
cling [kliŋ] klynge seg, henge fast; holde fast.
clinic ['klinik] sengeliggende; klinisk; sengeliggende pasient; klinikk. **clinical** ['klinikl] klinisk.
clink [kliŋk] klinge, klirre; klang, klirring.
clink [kliŋk] fengsel, «hullet».
clinker ['kliŋkə] klinke (sl. hardbrent murstein); størknet slagg.
clinker ['kliŋkə] grepa kar, kløpper.
Clio ['klaioᵘ] Klio.
clip [klip] klemme, papirklype; klype.
clip [klip] klippe; beklippe; stekke; stusse; klipp; klipping. **-fish** klippfisk. **-per** klipper; **-per, -per-ship** klipperskip. **-ping** klipping; avklipt stykke, stump; utklipp.
clippy ['klipi] fra 1940 bet. for kvinnelige buss- og trikkekonduktører.
clique [kli·k] k ikk.
Clive [klaiv] Clive.
cloak [kloᵘk] kappe, kåpe; (fig.) skalkeskjul, påskudd; dekke med kappe; (fig.) skjule.
cloak-room ['kloᵘkrum] garderobe; oppbevaringssted (for reisegods på jernbanestasjon).
clock [klåk] silkemønster på siden av strømpe.
clock [klåk] stueur, tårnur, ur, klokke; **what o'clock is it?** hva er klokka? **it is two o'clock** klokka er to; **there goes four o'clock** nå slår klokka fire. **-face** urskive, tallskive. **-maker** urmaker. **-work** urverk.
clocking ['klåkiŋ] klukk; klukking, ligging.
clod [klåd] klump; jordklump, slamp; kaste jordklumper på.
clog [klåg] tynge, bebyrde, hindre; klatte seg sammen; bli hindret; stappe, stoppe til; byrde, hemsko, hindring; tresko; kloss, klamp (om foten).
cloister ['klɔistə] kloster; klostergang, søylegang (dekt gang langs kloster, kollegium eller domkirke); innesperre i et kloster.
close [kloᵘs] lukket, tillukket; sluttet, tettsluttet, tett; nøye, nøyaktig, streng; skjult; lummer; nær; **come to** — **quarters** komme inn på livet, komme i håndgemeng; — **by** nær ved, tett ved; — **-fisted** påholden, knipen — **on** i nærheten av, like ved.

close [kloᵘs] innhegning, inngjerdet plass.
close [kloᵘz] slutning, avslutning, ende; avgjørelse.
close [kloᵘz] lukke, stenge; slutte, ende; indeslutte; lukke seg; slutte seg sammen, samle seg; nærme seg, rykke sammen; komme overens med (**with**); gå løs på.
closely ['kloᵘsli] tett, kloss, nøye; hemmelig.
-ness ['kloᵘsnés] tillukkethet; tetthet; lummerhet; hemmelighet; tilbakeholdenhet; fasthet; forbindelse. **closequestion** utspørre.
closet ['klåzit] lite værelse, kammer, skap (i veggen); do; **be -ed with** holde hemmelig rådslagning med.
closure ['kloᵘʒə] lukning; lukke; slutning, ende.
clot [klåt] størknet masse, klump; klumpe seg, levre seg, størkne.
cloth [klåþ, klå·þ] klede; tøy; duk; bordduk; (fig.) geistlig stand. **clothe** [kloᵘð] klæ; forsyne med klær; (fig.) bekle. **clothes** [kloᵘðz] klær; klesplagg. **clothes-brush** klesbørste. **clothes-peg** (el. **-pin**) klesklype. **clothes-press** klesskap.
clothier ['kloᵘðiə] tøyfabrikant; kledehandler.
clothing ['kloᵘðiŋ] kledning. **cloths** [klåþs, klå·þs, klåðz] tøyer; tøystykker; duker.
cloud [klaud] sky, skye, skye for, formørke, fordunkle; skye over, bli overskyet. **-less** ['klaudlés] skyfri. **-y** ['klaudi] skyfull, overskyet.
clough [klʌf] fjellkløft, gjel.
clout [klaut] klut, lapp; lusing; lappe; slå, dra til.
clove [kloᵘv] imperf. av **cleave.**
clove [kloᵘv] kryddernellik, nellik; løk.
cloven ['kloᵘvən] kløyvd, spaltet; se **cleave; the** — **foot** hestehoven; **show the** — **foot** stikke hestehoven fram.
clover ['kloᵘvə] kløver; **live in** —, **be in** — ha det som kua i den grønne enga.
clown [klaun] bonde; slamp; klovn, bajas. **-ish** ['klauniʃ] bondsk; klovneaktig.
cloy [klɔi] overmette, overfylle, stappe.
C. L. R. fk. f. **Central-London Railway.**
club [klʌb] klubbe; kløver (i kort); klubb; slå, klubbe; slå, skyte sammen; slå seg sammen. — **-foot** klumpfot. — **-haul** vende ved hjelp av anker.
clubland ['klʌbländ] klubbstrøket (i London).
club-law ['klʌb'lå·] neverett; selvtekt.
cluck [klʌk] klukke.
clue [klu·] holdepunkt (for en undersøkelse), nøkkel (til forståelse), tråden (i en framstilling).
clump [klʌmp] klump, kloss; klynge, gruppe.
clumsy ['klʌmzi] klosset; tung.
clung [klʌŋ] imperf. og pf. pts. av **cling.**
cluster ['klʌstə] klynge; klase; knippe; samle i klynge; vokse i klaser, vokse i klynge; flokkes.
clutch [klʌtʃ] gripe; grep, tak, kopling.
clutter ['klʌtə] forvirring, røre, larm, ståk, støy; støye; ståke, lage rot i.
Clyde [klaid] Clyde.
clyster ['klistə] klystér.
cm. fk. f. **centimetre.**
cmd. fk. f. **command paper.**
C. M. G. fk. f. **Companion of the Order of St. Michael and St. George.**
C. O. fk. f. **Colonial Office; commanding officer; conscientious objector.**
Co. [koᵘ] fk. f. **Company, County.**
c|o fk. f. **care of.**
coach [koᵘtʃ] karét; postvogn, diligence; manuduktør; jernbanevogn; kjøre; manudusere; få manuduksjon; — **-box** bukk, kuskesete. — **-fare** takst. — **-house** vognskjul. **-man** kusk. — **-office** skyss-skifte; stasjon.
coadjutor [koᵘ'ädʒutə] medhjelper.
coadventure [koᵘəd'ventʃə] fellesforetagende.
coagency [koᵘ'e¹dʒənsi] samvirke. **coagent** [koᵘ'edʒent] medagerende.
coagulate [koᵘ'ägjule¹t] koagulere, løpe sammen, størkne; få til å løpe sammen el. størkne.
coak [koᵘk] metallbøssing (i en blokk).
coal [koᵘl] kull, kol; forsyne med kull; fylle kull;

kulle; carry -s to Newcastle gi bakerens barn brød haul el. call over the -s skjelle ut, irettesette.
— -bed kull-leie, kull-lag.
coalesce [koᵘəˈles] vokse sammen, forene seg.
coal-field [ˈkoᵘlfi·ld] kullfelt.
coal-heaver [ˈkoᵘlhi·və] kull-lemper, kullsjauer.
coalition [koᵘəˈliʃən] forening; forbund.
coal measures kull-leier. — -pit kullgruve. — -scuttle kullboks. — -trimmer, -whipper kull-lemper; -y kull-lignende, kullholdig.
coaming [ˈkoᵘmiŋ] lukekarm.
coarse [kɑ·əs] grov; rå, plump. — -grained [-greˈnd] grovkornet, grovskåren. coarsen [ˈkɑ·əsn] forgrove, forråe. coarseness grovhet, råhet.
coast [koᵘst] kyst; seile langs kysten; gå i kystfart. -al [ˈkoᵘstəl] kyst-. -er [ˈkoᵘstə] kystbåt. -ing [ˈkoᵘstiŋ] kyst-. -wise [ˈkoᵘstwaiz] kyst-, som foregår langs kysten.
coat [koᵘt] frakk; jakke, trøye; bekledning; pels, skinn, hud, hinne, ham, dekke; strøk (maling); (be)kle; dekke, overtrekke, stryke (m. maling). cut one's — according to one's cloth sette tæring etter næring. — -collar frakkekrage. — of mail ringpanser, panserskjorte.
coating bedekning, overtrekk; hinne.
coax [koᵘks] smigre; godsnakke for.
cob [kåb] klump, kule, ball; knapp, rund topp; slags ridehest; hode; maiskolbe; blanding av leir og halm (til bygging); måse, havmåke.
cobalt [koˈbålt, ˈkoᵘbålt] kobolt.
cobble [ˈkåbl] lappe, bøte, vøle.
cobble [ˈkåbl] rullestein, brustein; brulegge; -s større kull.
cobbler [ˈkåblə] lappeskomaker; fusker; svaledrikk, f. eks. sherry —.
cobnut [ˈkåbnʌt] hasselnøtt (av dyrket hassel).
cobra [ˈkoᵘbrə] brilleslange.
cobweb [ˈkåbweb] spindelvev, kingelvev.
cocaine [kɑˈkeˈn] kokain.
coccus [ˈkåkəs] kokke, kuleformet bakterie.
Cochin China [ˈkåtʃinˈtʃainə] Cochin-China.
cochineal [ˈkåtʃini·l] kochenille.
cochlea [ˈkåkliə] ørets sneglegang.
cochleary [ˈkåkliæ·əri], cochleate(d) [ˈkåkliˈ-tid] skrueformet, snegleformet.
cock [kåk] hane; han (av forskj. fugler); hane (på børse); værhane; høysåte, stakk; tunge (på vekt); tapp, kran (på tønne); oppbrett (på hatt); pliring med øynene, blink; spenn (av geværhane); kast, kneising; biks, bas, førstemann; spenne hanen på; brette opp (en hatteskygge); brette på nesen, kaste med nakken; spisse ører; sette hatten på snurr; plire; såte; cock-and-bull (-story) røverhistorie; cock of the walk hane eneste hane i kurven; cocked hat trekantet hatt.
cockade [kɑˈkeˈd] kokarde.
cockadoodledoo [ˈkåkadu·dlˈdu·] kykeliky.
Cockaigne [kɑˈkeˈn] slaraffenland; Cockneyland, London.
cockatoo [kåkɑˈtu·] kakadu.
cockatrice [ˈkåkətr(a)is] basilisk.
cock-boat [ˈkåkboᵘt] liten båt, pram, jolle.
cock-chafer [ˈkåktʃeˈfə] oldenborre.
cocker [ˈkåkə] få godt; gjø; forkjæle.
cockerel [ˈkåkərəl] hanekylling.
cock-eyed [ˈkåkaid] skjeløyd; skjev.
cock-fight [ˈkåkfait] hanekamp.
cock-horse [ˈkåkˈhå·s] kjepphest.
cockle [ˈkåkl] saueskjell; klinte; krølle(s).
cock-loft [ˈkåklåft] øverste loft.
cockney [ˈkåkni] ekte londoner; londonerspråk.
cockpit [ˈkåkpit] hanekampplass; (på krigsskip) lasarett; cockpit.
cockroach [ˈkåkroᵘtʃ] kakerlakk.
cockscomb [ˈkåkskoᵘm] hanekam.
cocksure [ˈkåkˈʃuə] skråsikker, brennsikker.
cokswain [ˈkåksən, ˈkåksweˈn] se coxswain.
cocktail [ˈkåktcˈl] halvtemt hest, halvdannet

person; cocktail, drikk av forskj. slags bittere, konjakk, gin m. m.
cocky [ˈkåki] viktig, hoven.
coco [ˈkoᵘkoᵘ] kokospalme. -nut kokosnøtt.
cocoa [ˈkoᵘkoᵘ] kakao.
cocoon [kɑˈku·n] kokong.
cod [kåd] torsk; belg, skolm; testikkelpung; fyr, kar.
C. O. D. fk. f. cash on delivery etterkrav.
coddle [ˈkådl] forkjæle; forkjælet person.
code [koᵘd] lovbok; kodeks; system; kode.
codex [ˈkoᵘdeks] pl. codices [ˈkoᵘdisi·z] kodeks.
codfish [ˈkådfiʃ] torsk.
codger [ˈkådʒə] (gammel) særling; gnier, knark.
codices se codex.
codicil [ˈkådisil] kodisill (tilleggsbestemmelse i testamente). codification [kådifiˈkeˈʃən] kodifikasjon (samling av lover i en lovbok). codify [ˈkådifai] kodifisere.
codling [ˈkådliŋ] småtorsk.
codling [ˈkådliŋ] slags avlangt eple; mateple.
cod-liver-oil [ˈkådlivərˈoil] levertran, medisintran.
co-education [ˈkoᵘedjuˈkeˈʃen] fellesskole.
coefficient [ˈkoᵘéˈfiʃənt] medvirkende; koeffisient.
coerce [koᵘˈə·s] tvinge. coercion [koᵘˈə·ʃen] tvang. coercive [koᵘˈə·siv] tvingende.
Cœur de Lion [kə·dəˈlaiən] Løvehjerte.
coeval [koᵘˈi·vəl] samtidig, jevnaldrende.
coexist [ˈkoᵘigˈzist] være til på samme tid.
coexistence [ˈkoᵘigˈzistəns] samtidig eksistens.
coffee [ˈkåfi] kaffe. — -bean kaffebønne. — -berry kaffebær. — -grounds (pl.) kaffegrut. — -house kafé. — -pot kaffekanne. — -room kafé (i hotell).
coffer [ˈkåfə] kiste, (penge)skrin; kasett.
coffin [ˈkåfin] likkiste; legge i kiste, skrinlegge.
cog [kåg] tann, kam (på hjul); sette tenner på; fuske, narre; — a die forfalske en terning.
cogency [ˈkoᵘdʒənsi] tvingende kraft, styrke; overbevisende kraft.
cogent [ˈkoᵘdʒənt] tvingende; overbevisende.
cogitate [ˈkådʒiteˈt] tenke. cogitation [kådʒiˈteˈʃən] ettertanke; tenkning.
cognac [ˈkoᵘnjäk, ˈkånjäk] konjakk.
cognate [ˈkågneˈt] beslektet, skyld; slektning.
cognition [kågˈniʃən] erkjennelse.
cognizance [ˈkågnizəns] kunnskap; kompetense, jurisdiksjon; forhør, undersøkelse for retten.
cognomen [kågˈnoᵘmən] tilnavn, etternavn.
cogwheel [ˈkåghwi·l] tannhjul, kamhjul.
cohabit [koᵘˈhäbit] bo sammen; leve sammen som ektefolk. -ation [koᵘhäbiˈteˈʃen] samliv.
coheir [koᵘˈæ·ə] medarving.
cohere [koᵘˈhiə] henge sammen, i hop.
coherence [koᵘˈhiərəns], cohesion [koᵘˈhi·ʒən] sammenheng; kohesjon. coherent [koᵘˈhiərənt], cohesive [koᵘˈhi·siv] sammenhengende. cohesiveness [koᵘˈhi·sivnēs] sammenheng; kohesjon.
cohort [koᵘˈhå·ət] kohort.
coif [koif] hue; advokathue.
coign [koin] of vantage fordelaktig stilling.
coil [koil] legge sammen i ringer el. bukter, rulle sammen; kveile; rulle seg sammen (også — up); ring, spiral, rull, bukt, kveil.
coin [koin] mynt; pengestykke; prege, mynte; slå; dikte opp, lage, finne på. -age [ˈkoinidʒ] mynting; mynt; oppdiktning, påfunn.
coincide [koᵘinˈsaid] treffe sammen, falle sammen. coincidence [koᵘˈinsidəns] sammentreff.
coincident [koᵘˈinsidənt] sammentreffende.
coiner [ˈkoinə] mynter; falskmyntner.
coir [ˈkoiə] kokosbast.
coke [kouk] koks; brenne til koks.
col [kål] skar (i fjell).
Col. fk. f. colonel; colonial; Colorado; Colossians; column.
colander [ˈkʌləndə] dørslag.

Colchester ['koultʃistə] Colchester.
cold [kould] kald; kaldblodig; rolig; kulde; forkjølelse, snue; **I am** — jeg fryser; **catch** —, **get a** — forkjøle seg; — **in the head** snue; **give the** — **shoulder to one** behandle en med kulde. — **-blooded** kaldblodig. **-ness** ['kouldnês] kulde. **-short** kaldskjør — **-storage** fryserom.
Coleridge ['koulridʒ] Coleridge.
colibri ['kálibri] kolibri.
colic ['kálik] kolikk, magekrampe.
collaborate [kå'läbəre't] være medarbeider. **collaboration** [kåläbə're'ʃən] samarbeid. **collaborationist** [kåläbə're'ʃənist] samarbeidsmann (med tyskerne). **collaborator** [kå'läbəre'tə] medarbeider.
collapse [kå'läps] falle sammen; sammenbrudd.
collar ['kålə] halsbånd; krage, snipp; bogtre (på seletøy); gripe i kragen; koble; legge halsbånd på; få fatt i.
collar-bone ['kåləbou n] kragebein.
collate [kå'le't] sammenligne, sikte; kalle (som prest).
collateral [kå'lätərəl] som løper jamsides med; side-, tilleggs-; parallell; slektning i en sidelinje.
colleague ['kåli·g] embetsbror, kollega.
collect [kə'lekt] samle (inn); kreve opp; samle seg.
collect ['kålekt] kollekt, alterbønn.
collected [kə'lektid] fattet, rolig, med sinnsro.
collection [kə'lekʃən] innsamling; samling; innkreving. **-ive** [kə'lektiv] samlet, sam-, felles. **-or** [kə'lektə] samler; inkassator; innsamler.
college [kå'lidʒ] kollegium; fakultet; universitetsavdeling; høyere skole; gymnasium, college.
collegian [kå'li·dʒən] student i et college.
collegiate [kå'li·dʒiét] kollegial, akademisk; medlem av et kollegium; **non** — som ikke bor på et college.
collet ['kålit] krage, ring; flange [uttal: flændsj], flens.
collide [kə'laid] støte sammen, kollidere.
collie ['kåli] (skotsk) fårehund.
collier ['kåljə] kullgruvearbeider; kullskip. **colliery** ['kåljəri] kullgruve.
collision [kə'liʒən] sammenstøt, kollisjon.
collocate ['kåloke't] sette sammen, stille opp, ordne.
collodion [kə'lou djən] kollodium.
collop ['kåləp] kjøttskive; snei, remse.
colloq. fk. f. **colloquial.**
colloquial [kə'lou kwiəl] som hører til hverdagsspråket el. alminnelig samtale, i dagligtale. **colloquialism** [kə'lou kwiəlizm] hverdagsuttrykk. **colloquy** ['kålokwi] samtale.
collude [kə'lju·d] være i hemmelig forståelse, spille under dekke. **collusion** [kə'lju·ʒən] hemmelig forståelse. **collusive** [kə'lju·siv] avtalt i hemmelighet.
collywobbles ['kåliwåblz] ramling i magen.
colocynth ['kålosinþ] kolokvint.
Cologne [kə'lou n] Köln; eau-de-Cologne.
colon ['kou lån] kolon; tykktarm.
colonel ['kə·nəl] oberst; **Colonel Commandant,** en offiserspost, som trådte istedenfor Brigadier General; **lieutenant-colonel** oberstløytnant. **colonelcy** ['kə·nlsi] oberstrang, oberststilling.
colonial [kə'lou njəl] kolonial, koloni-; **Colonial Office** kolonialdepartementet.
colonist ['kålənist] kolonist, nybygger. **colonization** [kålənai'ze'ʃən] kolonisasjon. **colonize** ['kålənaiz] kolonisere, anlegge kolonier; slå seg ned som kolonist.
colonnade [kålə'ne'd] søylegang, kolonnade.
colony ['kåləni] koloni, nybygd.
Colorado [kålo'ra·do] Colorado.
coloration [kʌlə're'ʃən] fargelegging.
colorature ['kʌlərətʃə, 'kå-] koloratur.
colorific [kålə'rifik] s. setter farge; sterkt farget.
colossal [kə'låsəl] kolossal. **colossus** [kə'låsəs] koloss.
colour ['kʌlə] farge; rødme; pynt; påskudd;

skinn; beskaffenhet; **off** — av ringere verd (især om edelsteiner); (i pl.) fane; flagg. **colour** ['kʌlə] farge; kolorere; smykke; rødme:**-able** rime lig, berettiget; plausibel. **-blind** fargeblind. **-e** farget, neger-. **-ing** ['kʌləriŋ] fargegivning, kolo ritt. **-ist** ['kʌlərist] kolorist. **-less** ['kʌlelès fargeløs; gjennomsiktig. **-man** fargehandler **-y** ['kʌləri] som har en farge som viser go kvalitet.
colt [koult] føll; (ung)fole; folunge; (fig.) un; narr; tamp (til sjøs).
colter ['koultə] ristel (i plog).
columbary ['kåləmbəri] dueslag; urnehall.
Columbia [kə'lʌmbjə] Columbia.
columbine ['kåləmbain] akeleie.
Columbine ['kåləmbain] Columbine.
Columbus [kə'lʌmbəs] Kolumbus.
column ['kåləm] søyle; kolonne; spalte (i en bok) **coma** ['koumə] sovesyke; taKe (om en komet) **comb** [koum] kam; vokskake; kjemme; grei combe [ku·m] se **coomb.**
combat ['kåmbät] kamp; kjempe; bekjempe **-ant** ['kåmbətənt] stridsmann; forkjemper. **-iv** ['kåmbətiv] stridslysten.
combination [kåmbi'ne'ʃən] forbindelse, sam band, forening; komplott; **-s** kombination (under tøy). **combine** [kəm'bain] forbinde, forene; for binde seg, forene seg.
combustibility [kəmbʌsti'biliti] brennbarhet **combustible** [kəm'bʌstibl] brennbar; brennba ting. **combustion** [kəm'bʌstʃən] forbrenning.
come [kʌm] komme; spire (om malt); — **to pas** hende, bære til; — **and see** se innom til, besøke **the years to** — de kommende år; — **abou** vende seg; skje; forandre seg, vende om; — **across møte;** — **along** skynde seg; — **at** få fat på; oppnå; — **away** skilles; — **by** komme forbi komme til, få fatt på; — **down** komme ned falle ned; ydmykes; — **forward** melde seg; — **in** komme inn; komme til målet; komme opp bli mote; bli valt; — **in for** komme med en for dring på; få andel i; — **into a fortune** arve e formue; — **of** komme av, nedstamme fra; — **of age** bli myndig; — **off** komme bort fra; slipp fra (noe); gå av; foregå, finne sted; falle ut (god el. dårlig); **she would have** — **off worse** det vill ha gått henne dårligere; — **on** komme fram komme på, falle på; trives, lykkes; — **over** g over; gå over til et annet parti; gjøre seg t herre over; — **out** komme ut, bli kjent; komm fram, bli oppdaget; debutere i selskapslivet; — **out no.** x komme inn som nr. 1; — **round** vend seg (om vinden); komme på bedre tanke komme seg; komme til seg selv; — **short** komm til kort, ikke nå; ikke være lik; — **to** innvilg beløpe seg til; falle ut, ende; — **under** komme in under; — **up** komme på mote; — **up to** nærm seg til, komme hen til; komme opp imot; beløp seg til; — **up with** nå, innhente; kunne må seg med; — **upon** treffe på; komme over; fall over, overfalle.
come [kʌm] perf. pts. av **come.**
comedian [kə'mi·djən] skuespiller, komike **come-down** ['kʌm'daun] fall, tilbakegang, fo andring til det verre.
comedy ['kåmədi] lystspill, komedie.
comeliness ['kʌmlinés] tekkelighet. **come** ['kʌmli] tekkelig, nett, tiltalende.
comestible [kə'mestibl] spiselig; **-s** matvare **comet** ['kåmit] komet.
comfit ['kʌmfit] sukkertøy, konfekt.
comfort ['kʌmfət] trøst, vederkvegelse, ve være; bekvemmelighet, behagelighet, hygg styrke, vederkvege; trøste, opplive. **-able** ['kʌm f(ə)təbl] trøstende; behagelig, makelig, hyggeli koselig; be **-able** ha det koselig, føle seg vel, h et sorgfritt utkomme; **make yourself -able** gjø Dem det bekvemt! — **er** ['kʌmfətə] trøster; skjer stukket teppe. **-less** ['kʌmfətlès] trøsteløs; hagelig, ubekvem.

comfrey ['kʌmfri] vollgras.
comfy ['kʌmfi] fk. f. **comfortable.**
comic ['kåmik] komisk; — **paper** vittighets-blad. **-al** ['kåmikəl] komisk, morsom. **-ality** [kåmi'käliti] morsomhet.
coming ['kʌmiŋ] kommende, tilkommende, framtidig; komme.
Comintern ['kåmintə·n] Komintern.
comity ['kåmiti] høflighet; — **of nations** vennskapelig forståelse mellom nasjonene.
comma ['kåmə] komma; **inverted commas** anførselstegn, hermetegn, gåseøyne.
command [kə'ma·nd] befale, by; føre, kommandere; styre; beherske; ha utsikt over; befaling; anførsel, kommando; makt, herredømme. **-ant** [kåmən'dänt] kommandant. **-er** [kə'ma·ndə] befalingsmann; kaptein (i marinen), kommandør (av en orden). **-er-in-chief** [kə'ma·ndərin'tʃi·f] øverstbefalende. **-ment** [kə'ma·ndmənt] bud; **the ten -ments** de ti buᴅ.
commando [kə'ma·ndoᵘ] kommando, troppestyrke under en kommando.
commemorate [kə'memərei't] feire; minnes; være et minne om. **commemoration** [kəmemə'rei'ʃən] ihukommelse; minnefest. **commemorative** [kə'memərətiv] minne-, til minne (**of** om).
commence [kə'mens] begynne, ta til. **-ment** [kə'mensmənt] begynnelse, opphav.
commend [kə'mend] overgi, betro; rose, prise; anbefale; — **me** to hils fra meg. **-able** [kə'mendəbl] prisverdig; verd å anbefale. **-atory** [kə'mendətəri] anbefalende; rosende.
commensur|ability [kə'menʃərə'biliti] kommensurabilitet. **-able** [kə'menʃərəbl] kommensurabel. **-ate** [kə'menʃərit] som er i samsvar med.
comment ['kåment] (kritisk) bemerkning, merknad; folkesnakk; kommentar, tolking, tyding; gjøre bemerkninger, skumle; skrive kommentar (**on** til). **-ary** ['kåməntəri] fortolkning, kommentar. **-ator** ['kåməntei'tə] kommentator.
commerce ['kåməs] handel; omgang, samkvem. **commercial** [kə'mə·ʃəl] kommersiell, handels-; — **traveller** handelsreisende.
comminate ['kåminei't] true, fordømme.
commingle [kå'miŋgl] blande (seg).
comminute ['kåminju·t] krase, smuldre, dele i småstykker.
commiserate [kə'mizərei't] ynke, synes synd på, ha medlidenhet med. **commiseration** [kəmizə're'ʃen] medlidenhet, medynk.
commissariat [kåmi'sæ·ᵊriət] intendantur.
commissary ['kåmisəri] kommissær, ombudsmann; intendant. — **-general** generalintendant.
commission [kə'miʃən] oppdrag, verv; ombud; bestalling, utnevning; offiserspost; kommisjon; provisjon; utøving; tjeneste; utstyre med fullmakt; gi et verv, pålegge, gi i kommisjon; **-ed officer** offiser; **non-commissioned officer** underoffiser.
commissioner [kə'miʃənə] kommissær; **High C.** øverste representant for den britiske regjering i visse kolonier e. l.
commit [kə'mit] betro, overgi; utøve, begå; — **for trial** sette under tiltale· — **to prison** fengsle; — **to writing** skrive ned; — **oneself** avsløre seg, kompromittere seg. **-tee** [kə'miti] komité, nemnd, utvalg; — **of the whole house** underhuset som komité (under en særlig ordstyrer, ikke the speaker) til vedtak av innstillinger (ikke lover); **the house went into -tee** underhuset gikk over til komitémessig forhandling.
commix [kå'miks] blande sammen.
commodious [kə'moᵘdjəs] bekvem; rommelig.
commodity [kə'måditi] vare, handelsvare. — **price** varepris.
commodore ['kåmədå·ᵊ] eskadresjef; kommandør.
common ['kåmən] alminnelig, vanlig, sedvanlig; simpel; menig; sams, felles; almenning; **in** — sammen, felles; **in** — **with** i fellesskap med, lik-

som; — **gender** felleskjønn; — **law** sedvanerett; — **sense** sunn sans, folkevett.
commoner ['kåmənə] borgerlig; underhusmedlem; (i Oxford) student, som betaler for seg.
commonplace ['kåmənple's] trivialitet; hverdagslig, banal, fortersket.
common-room ['kåmənrum] lærerværelse.
commons ['kåmənz] borgerlige folk, borgere, almue; kost; **on short** — på smal kost; **the (House of) Commons** underhuset.
commonwealth ['kåmənwelþ] stat, republikk; **the Commonwealth (of England)** republikken (under Cromwell); **the Commonwealth of Australia** Australia; **the British Commonwealth of Nations** Det britiske samvelde (= **the British Empire**).
commotion [kə'moᵘʃən] bevegelse; røre, oppstyr.
communal ['kåmjunəl, kə'mju·nəl] kommunal.
commune ['kåmju·n] kommune.
commune [kə'mju·n, 'kåmju·n] samtale.
communicable [kə'mju·nikəbl] meddelelig.
communicate [kə'mju·nikei't] melde, meddele (**this to him** ham dette); stå i forbindelse; gå til alters. **communication** [kəmju·ni'ke'ʃən] meddelelse; forbindelse, samband. **communicative** [kə'mju·nikətiv] meddelsom; åpen.
communion [kə'mju·njən] forbindelse; omgang; samfunn; kommunion, altergang. **communion-cup** alterkalk. **communion-rails** alterring.
communiqué [kə'mju·nike'] kommuniké.
communism ['kåmjunizm] kommunisme.
communist ['kåmjunist] kommunist; kommunistisk. **-ic** [kåmju'nistik] kommunistisk.
community [kəm'ju·niti] fellesskap; samfunn.
commutable [kə'mju·təbl] som kan ombyttes; avhendelig. **commutation** [kåmju·te'ʃən] forandring; bytte; — **of tithes** tiendeavløsning.
commute [kəm'ju·t] ombytte, gjøre om, lage om; formilde (en straff).
compact [kəm'päkt] tett, kompakt; kortfattet.
compact ['kåmpäkt] overenskomst, pakt.
companion [kəm'pänjən] kamerat; ledsager (-inne); ridder (av en orden); kahyttskappe; ledsage, følge. **-able** kameratslig, omgjengelig. **-ship** kameratskap.
company ['kʌmpəni] selskap, forening, lag, kompani; **a ship's** — et skips mannskap; **keep** — **with** være kjæreste med; **keep** (eller **bear**) **me** — holde meg med selskap.
comparable ['kåmpərəbl] som kan sammenlignes. **comparative** [kəm'pärətiv] forholdsmessig; sammenlignende; komparativ. **-ly** forholdsvis.
compare [kəm'pæ·ə] sammenligne; kunne sammenlignes med; komparere, gradbøye. **comparison** [kəm'pärisən] sammenligning; komparasjon, gradbøyning.
compartment [kəm'pa·ᵊtmənt] avdeling, fag, rom; kupé; felt.
compass ['kʌmpəs] omgi; omfatte; inneslutte; oppnå, bringe i stand; volde; legge plan til; omfang; omkrets; rom; omvei; kompass; passer; **a pair of -es** en passer.
compassion [kəm'päʃən] medlidenhet (**on** med). **compassionate** [kəm'päʃənit] medlidende; [kəm'päʃənei't] ha medlidenhet, synes synd i.
compatibility [kəmpäti'biliti] forenlighet, samsvar. **compatible** [kəm'pätibl] forenlig, overensstemmende.
compatriot [kəm'pätriət] landsmann.
compeer ['kåm'piə] likemann, like.
compel [kəm'pel] tvinge; tiltvinge seg.
compendious [kəm'pendjəs] kort, kortfattet.
compendium [kəm'pendjəm] utdrag.
compensate ['kåmpənsei't] erstatte, godtgjøre; gi erstatning. **compensation** [kåmpen'se'ʃən] erstatning, godtgjørelse.
compete [kəm'pi·t] konkurrere, tevle (**for** om).
competence ['kåmpitəns], **competency** ['kåmpitənsi] tilstrekkelighet; utkomme; kompetanse.

competent ['kåmpitənt] tilstrekkelig, fullgod; passende; beføyd; sakkyndig; kompetent.
competition [kåmpi'tiʃən] konkurranse, tevling.
competitor [kəm'petitə] konkurrent, medbeiler.
compilation [kåmpi'leiʃən] kompilasjon, samlerarbeid, utdrag (av forskjellige bøker). **compile** [kəm'pail] samle; kompilere. **compiler** [kəm'pailə] samler, kompilator.
complacence [kəm'pleisəns], **complacency** [kém'pleisənsi] velbehag; tilfredshet; selvtilfredshet; elskverdighet. **complacent** [kəm'pleisənt] tilfreds, selvtilfreds; vennlig forekommende.
complain [kəm'plein] klage; beklage seg (of over). **-ant** [-ənt] klager. **complaint** [kəm'pleint] klage, klagemål, anke; lidelse, sykdom, feil.
complaisance [kəm'pleizəns] føyelighet, elskverdighet. **complaisant** [kəm'pleizənt] føyelig; elskverdig.
complement ['kåmplimənt] fullendelse, utfylling; komplement; fullstendig bemanning (av et skip). **-ary** [kåmpli'mentəri] utfyllende.
complete [kəm'pli·t] fullstendig, komplett; fullende fullstendiggjøre. **completion** [kəm'pli·ʃən] fullendelse; fullstendiggjøring.
complex ['kåmpleks] innviklet, sammensatt.
complexion [kəm'plekʃən] ansiktsfarge, hudfarge, utseende; gemytt, lynne, temperament.
complexity [kəm'pleksiti] innviklet beskaffenhet, floke.
compliance [kəm'plaiəns] innvilgelse; ettergivenhet, føyelighet; **in — with** i samsvar med, etter. **compliant** [kəm'plaiənt] føyelig, ettergivende.
complicate ['kåmplikeit] sammenfiltre, gjøre floket.
complicate ['kåmplikét] floket, innviklet.
complication [kåmpli'keiʃən] forvikling, floke.
complicity [kəm'plisiti] medskyld.
compliment ['kåmplimənt] kompliment; hilsen; **give** (eller **take**) **my compliments to** bring min ærbødige hilsen til.
compliment ['kåmpliment] komplimentere, lykkønske (**on** med), si komplimenter.
complimentary [kåmpli'mentəri] komplimenterende; høflig, smigrende. **— ticket** fribillett.
complot ['kåmplåt] sammensvergelse, komplott. **complot** [kəm'plåt] sammenrotte seg.
comply [kəm'plai] føye seg (**with** etter); samtykke, innvilge (**with** i), etterkomme.
compo ['kåmpoᵘ] fk. f. **composition,** især om en blanding av sand og sement.
component [kəm'poᵘnənt] som utgjør en del; bestanddel; emne; **— parts** bestanddeler.
comport [kəm'på·ət] stemme overens, passe; høve; **— oneself** oppføre seg. **comportment** [kəm'på·ətmənt] oppførsel, framferd.
compose [kəm'poᵘz] sette sammen; danne, forfatte; komponere; berolige; sette (typ.). **-posed** [kəm'poᵘzd] fattet, rolig. **composer** [kəm'poᵘzə] forfatter; setter; komponist.
composing [kəm'poᵘziŋ] bl. a. komposisjon; sats (typ.); **— powder** beroligende pulver. **— -room** setteri (typ.). **— -stick** vinkelhake (typ.).
composite ['kåmpəzit] sammensatt; sammensetning. **composition** [kåmpə'ziʃən] sammensetning; komposisjon; stil; verk; skrift; konsept; tonediktning; oppsetning; sats (typ.); forlik, akkord; sammenheng. **compositor** [kəm'pázitə] setter.
compost ['kåmpåst] kompost, blandingsgjødsel; gjødsle med kompost.
composure [kəm'poᵘʒə] ro, fatning.
compote ['kåmpoᵘt] kompott.
compound ['kåmpaund] sammensatt; blanding; sammensetning; (i India og China) innhegnet gård med beboelsesleilighet; **— interest** rentes rente.
compound [kəm'paund] sette sammen; blande; bilegge; avfinne seg med; forlike seg.
comprehend [kåmpri'hend] innbefatte; begripe;

fatte. comprehensible [kåmpri'hensibl] begripelig, fattelig. **comprehensibly** omfattende; fattelig **comprehension** [kåmpri'henʃən] innbegrep; oppfatning, forståelse; fatteevne. **comprehensive** [kåmpri'hensiv] omfattende; sammentrengt.
compress [kəm'pres] presse sammen; trenge sammen. **compress** ['kåmpres] kompress. **-ion** [kəm'preʃən], **-ure** [kəm'preʃə] sammentrykning, fortetning.
comprise [kəm'praiz] innbefatte, omfatte.
compromise ['kåmprəmaiz] kompromiss, overenskomst, forlik; bilegge, avgjøre i minnelighet; gå på akkord, gjøre innrømmelser; avsløre, kompromittere, binde (til en bestemt framgangsmåte); **no compromising step had been taken** ikke noe avgjørende skritt var gjort.
comptroller [kən'troᵘlə] kontrollør (i visse titler); **the C. and Auditoɪ General** leder av statsrevisjonen.
compulsion [kəm'pʌlʃən] tvang.
compulsory [kəm'pʌlsəri] tvungen; obligatorisk; **— service** tvungen krigstjeneste.
compunction [kəm'pʌŋkʃən] samvittighetsnag.
computable [kəm'pju·təbl] beregnelig.
computation [kåmpju'teiʃən] beregning.
compute [kəm'pju·t] beregne, anslå.
comrade ['kåmrid, -reid] kamerat.
con [kån] lære, studere; (som forkorting av det latinske contra) imot; **the pros and cons** hva det kan sies for og imot.
Conan ['koᵘnən] Conan.
conation [koᵘ'neiʃən] viljestyrke.
concatenate [kən'kätineit] sammenkjede. **concatenation** [kənkäti'neiʃən] sammenkjeding.
concave ['kånkeiv, 'kån'keiv] hul, konkav; hulhet; hvelv.
concavity [kən'käviti] hulhet.
conceal [kən'si·l] skjule, gjemme. **-ment** [-mənt] fordølgelse; hemmeligholdelse: skjul; tilfluktssted.
concede [kən'si·d] innvilge i, innrømme.
conceit [kən'si·t] idé, forestilling; innfall, grille; innbilskhet, selvtilfredshet; **be out of — with** være misnøyd med. **-ed** [kən'si·tid] innbilsk.
conceivable [kən'si·vəbl] forståelig. **conceive** [kən'si·v] unnfange, komme på, fatte; tenke seg; avfatte.
concentrate ['kånsəntreit] konsentrere, samle, fortette. **concentration** [kånsən'treiʃən] sammendraing, konsentrasjon. **concentrative** ['kånsəntreitiv] samlings-, konsentrerende. **concentric** [kån'sentrik] konsentrisk (som har felles midtpunkt).
concept ['kånsəpt] begrep. **conception** [kən'sepʃən] unnfangelse; begrep, forestilling.
concern [kən'sə·n] angå, vedkomme; forurolige, bekymre; andel; sak, ting, anliggende; viktighet, betydning; bekymring; forretning, bedrift, foretagende, bruk, verk, konsern, firma; **be —ed** være bekymret; ha å gjøre (med); være interessert (i); **as far as good fighting was -ed** hva dyktig kamp angikk, med hensyn til å kjempe godt; **it is no — of mine** det raker ikke meg, det er ikke min sak; **the whole —** hele historien, hele herligheten. **concerning** angående.
concert [kən'sə·t] innrette, ordne, planlegge, avtale. **concert** ['kånsət] konsert; forståelse, forbindelse; avtale. **the European Concert** de europèiske makters enighet, de enige makter.
concertina [kånsə'ti·nə] trekkspill.
concerto [kən'tʃə·toᵘ] konsertstykke, stykke for solo instrument med orkesterledsagelse.
concession [kən'seʃən] innrømmelse; bevilling, konsesjon. **-ionary** [kən'seʃənəri] konsesjons-.- **ive** [kən'sesiv] innrømmende.
conch [kåŋk] konkylie.
conchy ['kåntʃi] (fk. f. **conscientious objector**) militærnekter (av samvittighetsgrunner).
conciliate [kən'silieit] vinne, forsone, forlike.
conciliation [kənsili'eiʃən] forsoning. **conciliator**

[kən'silie'tə] fredsmekler. **conciliatory** [kən-siljətəri] meklende.

concise [kən'sais] kortfattet, konsis.

conclave ['kånkle'v] konklave (den kardinalforsamling som velger paven, og dens lokale).

conclude [kən'klu·d] slutte, ende, avslutte; dra en slutning; beslutte. **conclusion** [kən-'klu·ʒən] slutning, ende; avslutning; **try -s** gjøre el. våge et forsøk. **conclusive** [kən'klu·siv] slutnings-, avgjørende; følgeriktig.

concoct [kən'kåkt] sette el. lage sammen; finne på, utspekulere; **-ion** [kən'kåkʃən] utklekking, påfunn, plan.

concomitant [kən'kåmitənt] ledsagende, medvirkende; ledsager.

concord ['kåŋkå·ˀd, 'kån-] endrektighet; samsvar; samhold; overensstemmelse; samklang. **-ance** [kən'kå·ˀdəns] samsvar, overensstemmelse; konkordans, alfabetisk ordnet fortegnelse over de enkelte ord i et verk med angivelse av de steder hvor de fins. **-ant** [-ənt] overensstemmende; enstemmig.

concourse ['kåŋkå·ˀs, 'kån-] sammenstimling, tilstrømmende masse, forsamling, sverm.

concrescence [kən'kresəns] sammenvoksing.

concrete [kən'kri·t] bli hard, størkne; herde, gjøre til en masse. **concrete** ['kånkri·t, 'kån-] sammenvokst, hard, fast; konkret; sammensatt fast masse; konkret begrep; betong; dekke med betong. **concretion**[kån'kri·ʃən] størkning; masse.

concubinage [kən'kju·binidʒ] konkubinat. **concubine** ['kåŋkjubain] konkubine.

concupiscence [kən'kju·pisəns] lystenhet. **concupiscent** [-ənt] lysten.

concur [kən'kə·] stemme overens; hende samtidig; falle sammen; medvirke. **-rence** [kən-'kʌrəns] sammentreff; forening, overensstemmelse; medvirkning; bifall; konkurranse. **-rent** [kən'kʌrənt] medvirkende; samtidig.

concussion [kən'kʌʃən] risting, skaking. **concussive** [kən'kʌsiv] ristende, skakende.

condemn [kən'dem] dømme; fordømme; forkaste; kondemnere. **condemning** [kən'demiŋ]. **condemnable** [kən'demnəbl] forkastelig. **condemnation** [kåndém'ne'ʃən] fordømming, domfellelse; forkasting. **condemnatory** [kən'demnətəri] fordømmende.

condensable [kən'densəbl] s. lar seg fortette. **condensation** [kåndən'se'ʃən] fortetting. **condense** [kən'dens] fortette, kondensere; kondensere seg, fortettes. **condenser** [kən'densə] kondensator.

condescend [kåndi'send] nedlate seg. **-ing** [kåndi'sendiŋ] nedlatende. **condescension** [kåndi-'senʃən] nedlatenhet.

condign [kən'dain] fortjent.

condiment ['kåndimənt] krydderi.

condition [kən'diʃən] betingelse, vilkår; tilstand, forfatning; stand, rang; betinge; **on — of** på betingelse av; **on — that** på den betingelse at. **conditional** [kən'diʃənəl] betingelses-, betinget. **-ly** betingelsesvis; med forbehold.

condole [kən'do⁰l] bevitne sin deltagelse; — **with one on** kondolere en i anledning av. **condolence** [kən'do⁰lǝns] kondolanse.

condonation [kåndo'ne'ʃən] tilgivelse. **condone** [kən'do⁰n] tilgi; la gå upåtalt hen.

condor ['kåndå·ˀ] kondor.

conduc|e [kən'dju·s] bidra, tjene, virke (**to** til). **-ive** [kən'dju·siv] tjenlig, som bidrar (**to** til).

conduct ['kåndəkt] føring; bestyrelse; oppførsel, framferd. **conduct** [kən'dʌkt] føre, lede; føre an, dirigere, styre; — **oneself** oppføre seg. **-ible** [kən'dʌktibl] som leder, har ledningsevne. **-ion** [kən'dʌkʃən] ledning. **-ive** [kən'dʌktiv] som leder, lednings-. **-or** [kən'dʌktə] fører, leder, anfører; styrer; konduktør; orkesterdirigent; (i fysikk) leder, konduktor.

conduit ['kåndit, 'kåndjuit] vannledning, rør, kanal; — **of pipes** rørledning.

cone [ko⁰n] kjegle; lyskjegle; kile; kongle; kjeglesnegl; (meteorologisk) signal for styggvær fange en flyver inn i lyskjeglen.

confabulate [kən'fåbjule't] snakke, prate.

confabulation [kənfåbju'le'ʃən] passiar, snakk.

confection [ken'fekʃən] sukkertøy, konfekt; sylting; ferdigsydde klær.

confectioner [kən'fekʃənə] konditor. **confectionary** [kən'fekʃənəri] konditorvarer, sukkertøy, konfekt; konditori.

confederacy [kən'fedərəsi] forbund; samlag. **confederate** [kən'fedøre't] forbinde; forene seg, slutte forbund; **confederate** [kən'fedərit] forbundet, forbunds-; forbundsfelle; medskyldig; hørende til de konfødererte amerikanske sydstater, sydstats- (motsatt **Federal** Nordstats-). **confederation** [kənfədə're'ʃən] forbund.

confer [kən'fə·] jamføre, konferere; rådslå, rådlegge; meddele, overdra, gi. **conference** ['kånfərəns] overveielse; underhandling; konferanse.

confess [kən'fes] bekjenne, tilstå; vedgå, innrømme; skrifte. **-edly** |kən'fesidli] åpenbart, ubestridelig. **-ion** [kən'feʃən] konfesjon, bekjennelse, tilståelse; skriftemål, skrifte; trosbekjennelse. **-onal** [kən'feʃənəl] konfesjons-; skriftestol. **-or** [kən'fesə] bekjenner; skriftefar.

confetti [kən'feti] konfekt; konfetti (små runde biter papir).

confidant, confidante [kånfi'dänt] fortrolig (venn, venninne).

confide [kən'faid] stole, lite (**in** på), ha tillit (**in** til); betro (**to** til). **confidence** ['kånfidəns] tillit; tillitsfullhet, fortrolighet; hemmelighet; selvtillit; **repose — in** feste lit til; **take him into my —** betro meg til ham, skjenke ham min fortrolighet; **in —** i fortrolighet; — **trick** bondefangeri. **confident** ['kånfidənt] overbevist; tillitsfull; selvtillitsfull, sikker, trygg; — er stolende på, i tillit til. **confidential** [kånfi'denʃəl] fortrolig; betrodd; — **clerk** prokurist.

configuration [kənfigjə're'ʃən] sammenstilling, form.

confine [kən'fain] grense, avgrense, begrense innskrenke; inneslutte, innesperre; holde fanget, fengsle; **be confined** være syk; ligge i barselseng. **-ment** [kən'fainmənt] innesperring; innskrenkning, fangenskap, arrest; sykdom, upasselighet; barselseng, nedkomst. **confines** ['kånfainz] grenser.

confirm [kən'fə·m] sikre, befeste; sanne, bekrefte, stadfeste; bestyrke; konfirmere. **-ation** [kånfə'me'ʃən] stadfesting, bekreftelse; konfirmasjon. **confirmed** ogs. forherdet, uforbederlig, inngrodd; f. eks. **a confirmed bachelor.**

confisc|able ['kånfiskəbl] konfiskabel. **-ate** [kån-fi'ske'ʃən] konfiskasjon, inndraging, kverrsetting.

confiteor [kån'fitiå·] syndsbekjennelse.

conflagration [kånflə'gre'ʃən] brann.

conflict [kən'flikt] kjempe, stride. **conflict** ['kånflikt] kamp, strid.

confluence ['kånfluəns] sammenløp; tilstrømning, konfluks. **confluent** ['kånfluənt] sammenflytende. **conflux** [kån'flʌks] sammenløp.

conform [kən'få·ˀm] føye, tilpasse, tillempe; rette seg (etter), handle etter (**to**). **-able** [kən-'få·ˀməbl] overensstemmende, passende; lydig, føyelig. **-ation** [kånfå·ˀ'me'ʃən] dannelse, skikkelse, bygning; overensstemmelse, samsvar. **-ist** [kən'få·ˀmist] konformist (tilhenger av den engelske kirke). **-ity** [kən'få·ˀmiti] overensstemmelse, samsvar.

confound [kən'faund] blande sammen; forvirre, forvildre; gjøre til skamme. **confound it!** pokker også! **-edly** forbistret, forbasket, skammelig.

confraternity [kånfrə'tə·niti] brorskap.

confront [kən'frʌnt] stå, stille seg ansikt til ansikt med; stå like overfor; konfrontere.

Confucius [kən'fju·ʃəs] Confucius (Konfutse).
confuse [kən'fju·z] forvirre; blande sammen; **confused** forvirret, rotet. **confusion** [kən'fju·ʒən] uorden, forvirring; sammenblanding, forveksling; forlegenhet, bestyrtelse; ødeleggelse. — **worse confounded** verre og verre.
confutable [kən'fju·təbl] som kan gjendrives.
confutation [kənfju·'te·ʃən] gjendriving. **confute** [kən'fju·t] gjendrive.
congé ['kɔ̃ʒe'] avskjed.
congeal [kən'dʒi·l] få til å fryse; få til å størkne, stivne; fryse, størkne, stivne.
congelation [kɔ̃ndʒi'le'ʃən] frysning, stivning, størkning.
congener ['kɔ̃ndʒinə] jamlike, skylding, slektning.
congenial [kən'dʒi·njəl] likeartet, av samme natur, beslektet; åndsbeslektet; sympatetisk; høvelig, tekkelig, hyggelig. **-ity** [kəndʒi·ni'äliti] ensartethet, åndsslektskap; sympati.
congenital [kən'dʒenitəl] medfødt.
conger-eel ['kɔ̃ŋɡə'ri·l] havål.
congestion [kən'dʒestʃən] kongestion, blodstigning; opphoping, trafikk.
conglobate ['kɔ̃ŋɡlobe't] lage til kule.
conglomerate [kən'ɡlɔ̃məre't] rulle sammen, sammenhope: dynge, hop. **conglomerate** [kən-'ɡlɔ̃mərət] sammenklumpet. **conglomeration** [kənɡlɔ̃mə're'ʃən] sammenklumping; konglomerat.
conglutinate [kən'ɡlu·tine't] klistre sammen, klebe sammen; limes sammen, vokse sammen.' **conglutination** [kənɡlu·ti'ne'ʃən] sammenliming; sammenvoksing.
Congo ['kɔ̃ŋɡoʊ] Kongo.
congratulate [kən'ɡrätjule't] lykkønske, gratulere ((up)on med). **-ion** [kəngrätju'le'ʃən] lykkønskning. **-ory** [kən'grätjulətəri] lykkønsknings-, gratulasjons-.
congregate ['kɔ̃ŋɡriɡe't] samle; samle seg.
congregation [kɔ̃ŋɡri'ge'ʃən] kongregasjon, samling; forsamling; menighet. **-al** [kɔ̃ŋɡri'ge'ʃənəl] menighets-, selvstyrt. **-alism** [kɔ̃ŋɡri'ge'ʃənəlizm] kongregasjonalisme, den kirkelige retning som gjør de enkelte menigheter uavhengige.
congress ['kɔ̃ŋɡres] møte; kongress. **congressman** kongressmedlem; tingmann.
Congreve ['kɔ̃ŋɡri·v] Congreve.
congruence ['kɔ̃ŋɡruəns] overensstemmelse; kongruens, samfall, samsvar. **-gruent** ['kɔ̃ŋɡruənt] overenstemmende; kongruent. **-gruity** [kɔ̃ŋ'gru·iti] overensstemmelse, samsvar; kongruens; følgeriktighet. **-gruous** ['kɔ̃ŋɡruəs] passende, samsvarende; fornuftig.
conic(al) ['kɔ̃nik(l)] kjegle-; kjegleformet, konisk; **conics** kjeglesnitt, læren om kjeglesnitt.
conifer ['koʊnifə] nåletre, bartre.
conjectural [kən'dʒektʃərəl] bygd på gjetning, uviss. **conjecture** [kən'dʒektʃə] gjetning, gisning, konjektur; gjette, gjette seg til.
conjoin [kən'dʒɔin] forbinde; **-t** forent.
conjugal ['kɔ̃ndʒuɡəl] ekteskapelig.
conjugate ['kɔ̃ndʒuɡe't] konjugere. **conjugate** ['kɔ̃ndʒuɡit] par-, parvis sammenstilt. **conjugation** [kɔ̃ndʒu'ge'ʃən] konjugasjon, bøyning.
conjunction [kən'dʒʌŋkʃən] forbindelse, forening, konjunksjon. **conjunctive** [kən'dʒʌŋktiv] nær forbundet; binde-; konjunktivisk; konjunktiv.
conjunctivitis [kəndʒʌŋkti'vaitis] konjunktivitt.
conjuncture [kən'dʒʌŋktʃə] konjunktur, tidspunkt; sammentreff, omstendigheter, forhold.
conjuration [kɔ̃ndʒu're'ʃən] besvergelse.
conjure [kən'dʒuə] besverge.
conjure ['kʌndʒə] mane; hekse, trolle.
conjurer ['kʌndʒərə] taskenspiller, tryllekunstner.
conjuror se **conjurer**.
conk [kɔ̃ŋk] nese, snyteskaft.
connate ['kɔ̃ne't] medf⸳dt.

Connaught ['kɔ̃nå·t], Connaught.
connect [kə'nekt] forbinde, sette sammen; stå i forbindelse med.
connectedly [kə'nektidli] i sammenheng.
Connecticut [kə'nektikʌt] Connecticut.
connection [kə'nekʃən] forbindelse, sammenheng; slektskap, bekjentskap. **connective** [kə-'nektiv] forbindende; bindeledd, bindeord.
connexion se **connection**.
conning-bridge ['kɔ̃niŋbridʒ] kommandobru.
conning-tower ['kɔ̃niŋtauə] utkikstårn, pansertårn (på et krigsskip).
connivance [kə'naivəns] det å se igjennom fingrer med, stilltiende samtykke.
connive [kə'naiv] se igjennom fingrer (**at** med).
connoisseur [kɔ̃ni'sə·] kjenner, skjønner.
connotation [kɔ̃nå'te'ʃən] bibetydning; [kå'noʊt] også betegne, dessuten bety; inneholde.
connubial [kə'nju·bjəl] ekteskapelig.
conoid ['koʊnåid] kjegleformet.
conquer ['kɔ̃ŋkə] erobre, beseire; seire, vinne. **-able** ['kɔ̃ŋkərəbl] overvinnelig, inntagelig. **-or** ['kɔ̃ŋkərə] erobrer, seierherre.
conquest ['kɔ̃ŋkwist] erobring, seier; **the Conquest** især **the Norman Conquest** (1066).
consanguin|e [kɔ̃n'säŋgwin] skyldt, beslektet. **-eous** [kɔ̃nsäŋ'gwinjəs] nærbeslektet, nærskyldt. **-ity** [kɔ̃nsäŋ'gwiniti] blodsslektsskap; skyldskap.
conscience ['kɔ̃nʃəns] samvittighet; **in all** —, **on one's** — på ære og samvittighet. **have the** — **to** være frekk nok til å. **conscientious** [kɔ̃n-ʃi'enʃəs] samvittighetsfull; samvittighets-; — **objector** militærnekter (av samvittighetsgrunner).
conscionable ['kɔ̃nʃənəbl] samvittighetsfull, billig, rett, rettvis.
conscious ['kɔ̃nʃəs] bevisst, ved bevissthet, selvbevisst, sjenert; **be** — of være seg bevisst. **consciousness** ['kɔ̃nʃəsnès] bevissthet.
con|scribe [kɔ̃n'skraib] skrive ut. **-script** [kɔ̃n-skript] utskreven (soldat). **-scription** [kən-'skripʃən] utskrivning, verneplikt.
consecrate ['kɔ̃nsikre't] innvie, vigsle. **consecration** [kɔ̃nsi'kre'ʃən] innvielse, vigsel. **consecratory** ['kɔ̃nsikre'təri] innvielses-.
consecutive [kən'sekjutiv] som følger på hinannen, komme etter hverandre; følgende; sammenhengende.
consent [kən'sent] samtykke; — **to** samtykke i, innvilge i, finne seg i; **-ing party** medviter. **-aneous** [kɔ̃nsen'te'njəs] overensstemmende.
consequence ['kɔ̃nsikwəns] følge, resultat, konsekvens; innflytelse, viktighet, betydning; **in** — som følge av det, følgelig; **in** — of som følge av.
consequent ['kɔ̃nsikwənt] følgende; slutning, følge. **-ly** følgelig, altså.
consequential [kɔ̃nsi'kwenʃəl] følgende; følgeriktig, konsekvent; innbilsk.
conservable [kən'sə·vəbl] som kan oppbevares, som holder seg.
conserv|ancy [kən'sə·vənsi] vern, vedlikehold, tilsyn. **-ation** [kɔ̃nsə·'ve'ʃən] vedlikehold, bevaring.
conservatism [kən'sə·vətizm] konservatisme.
conservative [kən'sə·vətiv] bevarende; konservativ; høyremann.
conservatoire [kən'sə·vətwa·] musikk-konservatorium. **conservator** ['kɔ̃nsə·ve'tə] bevarer, vedlikeholder; konservator. **conservatory** [kən-'se·vətəri] drivhus; konservatorium.
conserve [kən'sə·v] syltet frukt; bevare, sylte, legge ned.
consider [kən'sidə] betrakte, overveie, betenke, granske, ta i betraktning, anse for, holde for; tro, anta, mene; tenke seg om, betenke seg. **-able** [kən'sidərəbl] anselig, betydelig; **a** — **heiress** en rik arving. **-ate** [kən'sidərèt] hensynsfull, omtenksom. **-ation** [kənsidə're'ʃən] betraktning; overveielse; synspunkt, hensyn(sfullhet); viktighet; erkjentlighet, vederlag, lønn; aktelse. **-ing** [kən'sidəriŋ] i betraktning av, med tanke på

consign [kən'sain] overdra; betro; konsignere. -ation [kånsig'ne¹ʃən] overdragelse; konsignasjon. -ee [kånsai'ni·] (vare-)mottaker, konsignatar. -er [kən'sainə] (vare-)avsender, overdrager. -ment [kən'sainment] overdragelse; konsignasjon, sending. -ment note fraktbrev. -or [kən'sainə] se consigner.

consist [kən'sist] bestå (in i, of av); stemme overens (with med). -ence [kən'sistens] tetthet. -ency [kən'sistənsi] tetthet, fasthet; konsekvens; overensstemmelse, samsvar. -ent [kən'sistənt] overensstemmende; følgeriktig, konsekvent.

consistory [kən'sistəri] konsistorium, kirkeråd. consol|able [kən'souləbl] som lar seg trøste. -ation [kånso'le¹ʃən] trøst. -atory [kən'sålətəri] trøstende, til trøst. -e [kən'sou¹l] trøste.

console ['kånso⁰l] konsoll.

consolid|ate [kən'sålide¹t] gjøre fast, grunnfeste, trygge; forene, samle; forene seg, bli fast. -ation [kånsåli'de¹ʃən] fast forening, grunnfesting, styrking, sammensveising; konsolidering. consols ['kånsålz] fk. f. consolidated annuities konsoliderte (engelske) statsobligasjoner.

consonance ['kånsənəns] samklang; overensstemmelse. consonant ['kånsənənt] medlyd, konsonant; samsvarig, overensstemmende.

consort ['kånså·⁹t] kamerat; ektefelle, make, gemal, gemalinne; medfølgende skip; prince — prinsgemal, regjerende dronnings ikke-regjerende gemal. consort [kən'så·⁹t] omgås, leve sammen; følge, ledsage.

conspicuous [kən'spikjuəs] klar, tydelig, iøynefallende; ansett, velkjent, framtredende; make oneself — gjøre seg bemerket; be — by one's absence glimre ved sitt fravær.

conspiracy [kən'spirəsi] sammensvergelse; conspirator [kən'spirətə] sammensvoren, konspirator. conspire [kən'spaiə] sammensverge seg; legge planer mot; samvirke. conspirer se conspirator.

constable ['kʌnstəbl] politibetjent, konstabel; chief — (fylkes) politimester; Lord High Constable riksmarskalk (nå bare en tittel). special — borgersoldat; outrun the — komme i gjeld. constabulary [kən'stäbjuləri] politistyrke, politikorps.

Constance ['kånstəns] Konstanse; Constantsa Lake of — Bodensjøen.

constancy ['kånstənsi] trofasthet; standhaftighet. constant ['kånstənt] bestandig, stadig; standhaftig, stø, fast.

Constantine ['kånstəntain] Konstantin. Constantinople [kånstänti'nou¹pl] Konstantinopel.

constantly ['kånstəntli] støtt, stadig, bestandig. constellation [kånste'le¹ʃən] stjernebilde. consternation [kånstə·'ne¹ʃən] bestyrtelse, støkk.

constipate ['kånstipe¹t] forstoppe. constipation [kånsti'pe¹ʃən] forstoppelse. constitu|ency [kən'stitjuənsi] valgkrets; velgere. -ent [kən'stitjuənt] utgjørende; velgende; grunnlovgivende; bestanddel; velger, mandant. constitute ['kånstitju·t] utgjøre; innrette; fastsette; utnevne, velge; he constituted himself her protector han oppkastet seg til hennes beskytter. constitution [kånsti'tju·ʃən] innretning, beskaffenhet; legemsbeskaffenhet, natur; forfatning, statsforfatning, konstitusjon; forordning. constitutional [kånsti'tju·ʃənəl] naturlig; forfatningsmessig, konstitusjonell; lovmessig; spasertur for sunnhetens skyld, mosjon. constitutionalist [-ist] grunnlovsmann. constitutive [kən'stitju·tiv] vesentlig; fastsettende, grunnleggende.

constrain [kən'stre¹n] tvinge; nøde; innskrenke. constraint [kən'stre¹nt] tvang.

constrict [kən'strikt] trekke sammen, presse sammen, snøre sammen. -ion [kən'strikʃən] sammentrekning, sammensnøring. -or [kən'striktə] ringmuskel; kvelerslange.

constringe [kən'strindʒ] trekke sammen. constringent [-ənt] bindende, sammentrekkende. construct [kən'strʌkt] oppføre, bygge, sette sammen, konstruere. construction [kən'strʌkʃən] oppførelse, bygning; konstruksjon; forklaring, mening. — battalion bet. for flåteingeniørtropper. constructive [kən'strʌktiv] ordnende; bygnings-, konstruktiv. construe [kån'stru·] konstruere, utlegge, tolke, tyde.

consul ['kånsul] konsul. -ar ['kånsjulə] konsul-. -ate ['kånsjulət] konsulat. -ate-general generalkonsulat. — -general generalkonsul. -ship ['kånsəlʃip] konsulrang, konsuls ombud.

consult [kən'sʌlt] rådslå, rådlegge, rådføre seg med, rådspørre, ta hensyn til. consultation [kånsʌl'te¹ʃən] rådlegging; rådslagning. consultative [kån'sʌltətiv] rådslående; rådgivende.

consume [kən'sju·m] tære opp; forbruke, øyde. consummate ['kånsəme¹t] fullende; fullbyrde. consummate [kən'sʌmit] fullendt. consummation [kånsə'me¹ʃən] fullending, fullføring; ende. consumption [kən'sʌm(p)ʃən] fortæring; forbruk; tæring; article of household — gjenstand til bruk i husholdningen. consumptive [kən-'sʌm(p)tiv] fortærende, ødeleggende; tæringssyk.

contact ['kåntäkt] berøring, kontakt.
contagion [kən'te¹dʒən] smitte; smittestoff.
contagious [kən'te¹dʒəs] smittsom.
contain [kən'te¹n] inneholde; — oneself beherske seg, styre seg.
contaminate [kən'tämine¹t] besmitte, søle til.
contamination [kəntämi'ne¹ʃən] besmittelse.
contemn [kən'tem] forakte, vanvøre.
contemplate ['kåntəmple¹t] granske; betrakte; overveie, studere på; gruble. contemplation [kåntəm'ple¹ʃən] betraktning; beskuelse. contemplative [kən'templətiv] ettertenksom, dypsindig; — faculty tenkeevne. contemplator ['kåntəmple¹tə] iakttager, betrakter; tenker.

contemporaneous [kəntempə're¹njəs] samtidig. contemporary [kən'tempərəri] samtidig.
contempt [kən'tem(p)t] forakt. -ible [kən-'tem(p)tibl] foraktelig; elendig. -ous [kən-'tem(p)tjuəs] hånlig; stolt.
contend [kən'tend] stride; forfekte; påstå, hevde, holde på.
content ['kåntent] (rom-)innhold.
content [kən'tent] tilfreds; (ved avstemning i overhuset) ja (motsetning: non-content eller not content); tilfredsstillelse; tilfredshet; tilfredsstille; stemme for (et forslag i overhuset); be — with la seg nøye med; to his heart's — av hjertens lyst; — oneself la seg nøye (with med).
contented [kən'tentid] tilfreds. -ness tilfredshet.
contention [kən'tenʃən] strid, tvist; stridspunkt; påstand.
contentious [kən'tenʃəs] trettekjær, kranglevoren; omstridt; — issues stridsspørsmål.
contentment [kən'tentmənt] tilfredshet.
contents ['kåntents, kən'tents] (pl.) innhold; table of — innholdsfortegnelse.
conterminous [kən'tə·minəs] med samme grenser; tilgrensende.
contest [kən'test] bestride; gjøre stridig; strides. contest ['kåntest] strid, konkurranse. -able [kən'testəbl] omtvistelig, tvilsom.
context ['kåntekst] sammenheng. contexture [kən'tekstjuə, -tʃə] forbindelse, bygning, system.
contiguity [kånti'gju·iti] berøring, nærhet.
contiguous [kən'tigjuəs] tilstøtende, nær.
continence ['kåntinəns] måteholdt; avholdenhet. continent ['kåntinənt] måteholdende; avholdende, kysk; fastland; on the Continent på Europas fastland, i utlandet (motsatt England). continental [kånti'nentəl] som hører til fastlandet, kontinental, utenlandsk; utlending.
contingency [kən'tindʒənsi] mulighet; tilfelle; slump.
contingent [kən'tindʒənt] tilfeldig, mulig; eventuell, foreløpig; avhengig av (upon); fram-

tidsmulighet; tilskudd; troppekontingent; **be paid for — services** få betaling for eventuelle tjenester. **continual** [kən'tinjuəl] uavbrutt, bestandig, stadig, uopphørlig. **continuance** [kən'tinjuəns] vedvarenhet; vedvarende opphold. **continuation** [kəntinju'e'ʃən] fortsettelse. **continue** [kən'tinju] fortsette, la vedvare; bli, vedbli; vedvare, vare. **continuity** [kåntin'ju·iti] sammenheng. **continuous** [kən'tinjuəs] nøye forbundet, sammenhengende; fortsatt.
contort [kən'tå·ºt] forvri. **-ion** [kən'tå·ºʃən] forvridning. **contortioner** [kən'tå·ºʃənə], **contortionist** [kən'tå·ºʃənist] slangemenneske.
contour ['kåntuə] omriss, kontur.
contra ['kåntrə] mot-, kontra-.
contraband ['kåntrəbänd] ulovlig, forbudt; smuglergods. **-ist** ['kåntrəbändist] smugler.
contrabass ['kåntrə'be's] kontrabass.
contract [kən'träkt] trekke sammen, forkorte; pådra seg; venne seg til; bringe i stand, slutte; forlove; trekke seg sammen; slutte forlik, kontrahere; forlove seg; sammentrukket. **contract** ['kånträkt] overenskomst, kontrakt; forlovelse; **place a — for** kontrahere. **-ible** [kən'träktibl] som kan trekkes sammen. **-ion** [kən'träkʃən] sammentrekning; forkorting. **-or** [kən'träktə] kontrahent; entreprenør, byggmester.
contradict [kåntrə'dikt] motsi. **-ion** [kåntrə'dikʃən] motsigelse, uoverensstemmelse. **-ory** [kåntrə'diktəri] motsigende; motsigelse.
contradistinction [kåntrədi'stiŋkʃən] motsetning, atskillelse ved motsatte egenskaper. **contradistinguish** [kåntrədi'stiŋwiʃ] atskille ved motsatte egenskaper.
contralto [kån'trälto"] kontra-alt, kontralto (dyp kvinnestemme).
contraposition [kåntrəpə'ziʃən] motsetning.
contraption [kən'träpʃən] innretning, påfunn, påhitt.
contrapuntal [kåntrə'pʌntl] kontrapunktisk.
contrariety [kåntrə'raiity] uforenelighet, motsetning, motstrid.
contrary ['kåntrəri] motsatt; forskjellig; imot; det motsatte; motsetning; **— to** stridende imot, imot; **on the — tvert** imot, tvert om; **to the —** i motsatt retning.
contrast ['kåntra·st] kontrast, motsetning. **contrast** [kən'tra·st] stille i motsetning.
contravene [kåntrə'vi·n] handle imot, overtrede, motvirke.
contravention [kåntrə'venʃən] overtredelse, strid; **in — with** i strid med.
contribute [kən'tribjut] bidra, medvirke. **contribution** [kåntri'bju·ʃən] bidrag; skatt; krigsskatt. **contributive** [kən'tribjutiv] s. hjelper til, s. medvirker. **contributor** [kən'tribjutə] skattyter, bidragsyter. **contributory** [kən'tribjutəri] som gir tilskudd, en som bidrar.
contrite ['kåntrait] angerfull, sønderknust.
contrition [kən'triʃən] anger, sønderknuselse.
contrivance [kən'traivəns] oppfinnelse; påfunn, påhitt; innretning. **contrive** [kən'traiv] oppfinne; tenke ut; finne på, pønske ut, finne middel til, oppnå; lage det så; **I — to** det lykkes meg.
contriver [kən'traivə] oppfinner; opphavsmann.
control [kən'tro"l] kontroll, tilsyn; innskrenkning, tvang; makt, herredømme, myndighet; kontrollere, styre, beherske. **-lable** [kən'tro"ləbl] som kan beherskes. **-ler** [kən'tro"lə] kontrollør.
controversial [kåntro'vo·ʃəl] polemisk. **controversy** ['kåntrovə·si] strid, polemikk. **controvert** ['kåntrovə·t] bestride, benekte, nekte. **controvertible** [kåntro'və·tibl] omtvistelig.
contumacious [kåntju'me'ʃəs] hardnakket, halsstarrig, trassig, ulydig. **contumacy** ['kåntjuməsi] gjenstridighet; uteblivelse tross lovlig varsel.
contumelious [kåntju'mi·ljəs] fornærmelig; hånlig. **contumely** ['kåntjumili] hån, fornærmelse.
contuse [kən'tju·z] støte, kveste. **contusion** [kən'tju·ʃen] kvestelse, kontusjon, støt.

conundrum [kə'nʌndrəm] ordspill, ordspillgåte.
convalesce [kånvə'les] friskne til, komme seg (av sykdom). **convalescense** [kånvə'lesəns] bedring, rekonvalesens. **convalescent** [-ənt] som er i bedring; rekonvalesent.
convection [kånvek'ʃən] overføring, ledning.
convenance ['kå·nvinä·ns] sed, skikk.
convene [kən'vi·n] komme sammen; kalle sammen, forsamle; innkalle.
convenience [kən'vi·njəns] bekvemmelighet, behagelighet, mak; **at your earliest —** så snart det er beleilig for Dem. **public -s** offentlige toalettrom, «underjordisk». **convenient** [kən'vi·njənt] høvelig; bekvem, passende, skikket.
convent ['kånvənt] kloster.
conventicle [kən'ventikl] forsamling, religiøs sammenkomst (især av dissentere).
convention [kən'venʃən] sammenkomst, forsamling; overenskomst. **-al** [kən'venʃənəl] avtalt, bestemt, vedtatt, konvensjonell. **-alism** [kən'venʃənəlizm] vedtekt, sedvanlig bruk. **-ality** [kənvenʃə'näliti] skikk og bruk, konveniens. **-ary** kontraktfast, etter avtale; leilending.
conventual [kən'ventʃuəl] kloster-, klosterlig; munk; klosterbror; nonne.
converge [kən'və·dʒ] løpe sammen, konvergere. **convergence** [kən'və·dʒəns] konvergens. **convergent** [-ənt] konvergerende, sammenløpende.
conversable [kən'və·səbl] omgjengelig, selskapelig, konversabel. **-ance** kjennskap. **-ant** [kən'və·sənt] bevandret. kyndig; fortrolig (**with** med). **-ation** [kånvə'se'ʃən] samtale; konversasjon. **-ational** [kånvə'se'ʃənəl] samtale-; underholdende, pratsom, selskapelig. **-azione** [kånvəsätsi'o"ni] aftenselskap, soaré (for lærde el. kunstnere).
converse [kən'və·s] underholde seg, konversere, samtale. **converse** ['kånvə·s] omgang; samtale, konversasjon; (matematisk) omvendt forhold; omvendt. **conversely** omvendt. **conversion** [kən'və·ʃən] forvandling, omvendelse, konvertering.
convert ['kånvə·t] omvendt, proselytt. **convert** [kən'və·t] forvandle; omvende; konvertere. **-ibility** [kånvə·ti'biliti] evne til å kunne forvandles. **-ible** [kən'və·tibl] som kan forvandles. **— husbandry** vekselbruk.
convex ['kånveks] konveks, utbuet.
convey [kən've'] føre, bringe, frakte, føre bort; overdra, tilskjøte; bibringe, meddele. **-ance** [kən've'əns] befordring, transport; befordringsmiddel, vogn; befordringsvei; leilighet; overlevering; overdragelse; bevilling; overdragelsesdokument, skjøte. **-ancer** [kən've'ənsə] dokumentskriver, skjøteskriver. **-er** [kən've'ə] overbringer.
convict [kən'vikt] overbevise; erklære for skyldig, dømme. **convict** ['kånvikt] forbryter; straff-fange. **conviction** [kən'vikʃən] overbevisning; domfelling.
convince [kən'vins] overbevise, overtyde.
convivial [kən'vivjəl] selskapelig, festlig.
con\vocation [kånvo'ke'ʃən] sammenkalling; prestemøte; geistlig synode (i England); akademisk forsamling. **-voke** [kən'vo"k] kalle sammen.
convolute(d) [kånvəlu·t(id)] sammenrullet.
convolution [kånvə'l(j)u·ʃən] sammenrulling, omvinding. **convolve** [kən'vålv] sammenrulle.
convolvulus [kən'vålvjuləs] vindel.
convoy ['kånvoi] ledsagelse, eskorte, konvoi. **convoy** [kən'voi] eskortere, konvoiere.
convulse [kən'vʌls] volde krampetrekninger; skake voldsomt, bringe i krampelatter. **-ion** [kən'vʌlʃən] krampetrekning. **-ary** krampe-; **-ive** [kən'vʌlsiv] krampaktig.
Conway ['kånwe'] Conway.
cony ['ko"ni] kanin.
coo [ku·] kurre; kurring; **-ing** ['ku·iŋ] kurring.

cook [kuk] kokk, kokkepike; tilberede, lage (mat); (fig.) lage i stand; forfalske, fingre med; **too many -s spoil the broth** jo flere kokker jo mer søl.

cooker ['kukə] stekeovn, kokeapparat; frukt som er lett å koke; en som dikter sammen noe.

cookery ['kukəri] kokekunst, matlaging. — **-book** kokebok.

cook|maid kokkepike. **-room** kjøkken, kabyss. **-shop** spisekvarter.

cool [ku·l] kjølig, sval; kald, rolig; uforskammet; kjølighet; kjøle, svale; kjølne, bli kjølig, avkjøles; bli rolig; **a — hand** en freidig herre; — **one's heels** måtte vente.

cooler ['ku·lə] vinkjøler.

cool-headed kald, rolig.

coolie ['ku·li] kuli, fattig dagarbeider srl. i Øst- og Sør-Asia.

cool|ly ['ku·lli] kjølig, koldblodig, rolig, sindig; usjenert. **-ness** ['ku·lnəs] kjølighet; kaldt blod, ro; kulde; kaldblodighet; usjenerthet.

coomb [ku·m] et mål (145,4 liter).

coomb, combe [ku·m] dyp, trang dal, dokk.

coon [ku·n] (amr. fork. **racoon**) vaskebjørn; **a gone —** en som er oppgitt, ferdig.

coop [ku·p] hønsebur, hønsekorg; teine; sperre inne.

cooper ['ku·pə] bøkker, tagger; blanding av øl og porter. **-'s knife** båndkniv. **-age** ['ku·pəridʒ] bøkkerlønn; bøkkerverksted; bøkkerarbeid.

co-operate [kouˈápəreˈt] medvirke; samvirke. **co-operation** [kouˈápəˈreˈʃən] medvirking; samarbeid, samvirke, kooperasjon. **co-operative** [kouˈápərətiv] medvirkende; samvirkende; samvirke-; — **association** forbruksforening; — **bakery** fellesbakeri; — **society** forbruksforening; samvirkelag; — **stores** utsalg for samvirkelag. **co-operator** [kouˈápəreˈtə] medarbeider, medlem av samvirkelag.

co-opt [kouˈápt] supplere seg med, velge inn.

co-ordinate [kouˈáˈədineˈt] sideordnet, jamstilt.

co-ordination [kouˈáˈədiˈneˈʃən] sideordning, likestilling, koordinasjon.

coot [ku·t] blisshøne, sothøne.

cop [káp] topp; spole; (sl.) polis, purk; ta, fange, arrestere.

copaiva [koˈpaivə] kopaivabalsam.

copal ['koupəl] kopal (et slags harpiks).

copartner ['kouˈpa·ʔtnə] deltager, kompanjong.

cope [koup] korkåpe; hvelving; dekke.

cope [koup] kappes (**with** med), prøve å klare, prøve krefter med.

copeck ['koupek] kopek (russisk mynt).

Copenhagen [kouˈpnˈheˈgən] København.

coper ['koupə] hestehandler; brennevinsfartøy (i Nordsjøen).

Copernican [kouˈpəˈnikən] kopernikansk.

copestone ['koupstoˈn] mønestein, toppstein, sluttstein; kronen på verket.

copier ['kápiə] avskriver, kopist; etterligner.

coping ['koupiŋ] murtak, (mur-)avdekning. — **-stone** d. s. s. **cope-stone.**

copious ['koupjəs] rik, flus, i overflod, rikelig; vidløftig. **-ness** mengde, overflødighet; vidløftighet.

copper ['kápə] kopper; bryggepanne, kopperkjel; koppermynt; (sl.) polis, purk; **hot coppers** tømmermenn (etter rangel).

copperas ['kápərəs] jernvitriol.

copper|-beech blodbøk. — **-bit** loddebolt med kopperegg; **-bottomed** kopperforhudet.

Copperfield ['kápəfiˈld] Copperfield.

copper|-plate kopperplate, kopperstikk. — **-print** kopperstikk. — **-sheathing** kopperforhudning. — **-smith** koppersmed. — **-works** kopperverk.

coppice ['kápis] krattskog, kratt.

copra ['káprə] kopra, kokoskjerner.

copse [káps] d. s. s. **coppice**; frede, beskjære, plante småskog. **copsy** ['kápsi] bevokst med småskog.

Copt [kápt] kopter. **-ic** ['káptik] koptisk.

copul|a ['kápjulə] kopula, bindeledd. **-ate** ['kápjuleˈt] parre (seg). **-ation** [kápjuˈleˈʃən] parring, grammatisk el. logisk sammenheng. **-ative** ['kápjulətiv] binde-; sideordnet konjunksjon.

copy ['kápi] avskrift; kopi; manuskript; eksemplar; avtrykk; forskrift; skrive av, kopiere; etterligne; **fair** (el. **clean**) — renskrift; **foul** (el. **rough**) — kladd.

copy|-book skrivebok. **-head** forskrift. **-hold** arvefeste(gård), bygslejord, leilendingsjord. **-holder** arvefester, leilending. **-ing-ink** kopiblekk. **-ingpress** kopipresse.

copyist ['kápiist] avskriver; plagiator.

copy|paper konseptpapir. **-right** forlagsrett.

coquet [koˈket] kokettere. **coquetry** ['koˈketri] koketteri. **coquette** [koˈket] kokette. **coquetish** [koˈketiʃ] kokett.

coral ['kárəl] korall; tannring (for småbarn til å bite i). **-laceous** [kárəˈleˈʃəs] korallaktig. **-line** ['kárəlain] korall-; korallmose. — **-reef** korallrev.

Coran [kà·ra·n] Koranen.

cord [kà·ʔd] strikke, reip, snor, streng, bånd; favn (ved); binde, snøre; sette i favn.

cordage ['kà·ʔdidʒ] snøre; tauverk.

corded ['kà·ʔdid] randet, stripet; senet.

Cordelia [kà·ʔˈdi·ljə] Cordelia.

cordial ['kà·ʔdjəl] hjertelig; hjertestyrkende; hjertestyrkning, forfriskning; likør. **-ity** [kà·ʔˈáliti] hjertelighet. **-ly** ['kà·ʔdjəli] hjertelig.

cordon ['kà·ʔdən] snor; kordong.

Cordova ['kà·ʔdovə] Cordoba.

corduroy ['kà·ʔdjuroi] korderoy, et slags tykt og sterkt, stripet bomullsfløyel.

cordwain ['kà·ʔdweˈn] korduan (slags tykt skinn). **-er** ['kà·ʔdweˈnə] skomaker.

cord-wood ['kà·ʔdwud] favneved.

core [kà·ʔ] det innerste, indre del, kjerne; (fig.) hjerterot; ta kjernehuset ut av; **to the —** helt igjennom, til hjerterota.

Corea [koˈriə] Korea.

co-regent ['kouˈri·dʒənt] medregnet.

co-respondent ['kouˈriˈspándənt] medinnstevnet ved skilsmisseprosess.

Corfu [kà·ʔˈfu·] Korfu.

coriaceous [kà·riˈeˈʃəs] lær-; læraktig.

Corinth ['kà·rinθ] Korint.

Corinthian [kà·ʔrinθjən] korinter; korintisk.

Coriolanus [kà·rio·leˈnəs] Koriolan.

cork [kà·ʔk] kork; flaskekork; korke; sverte med en brent kork; få korksmak. **-age** ['kà·ʔkidʒ] korkepenger. **-screw** korketrekker. **corky** ['kà·ʔki] kork-; korkaktig; med korksmak.

cormorant ['kà·ʔmərənt] skarv.

corn [kà·ʔn] korn; sæd; i Amerika især mais; i Skottland især havre, i England især hvete.

corn [kà·ʔn] salte, sprenge; **corned beef** saltsprengt, preservert kjøtt.

corn [kà·ʔn] liktorn, liktå.

corn|-chandler kornhandler. — **-cob** maiskolbe. **-crake** åkerrikse (fugl).

corn-cutter ['kà·ʔnkʌtə] meiemaskin.

corn-cutter ['kà·ʔnkʌtə] liktornoperatør.

cornea ['kà·ʔniə] hornhinne (i øyet).

cornel ['kà·ʔnəl] kornelltre.

corneous ['kà·ʔniəs] hornaktig, hornet.

corner ['kà·ʔnə] vinkel, hjørne, krok; ytterste ende; avkrok; oppkjøperspekulasjon; oppkjøperkonsortium, ring; sette til veggs, sette i klemme; kjøpe opp. — **-stone** hjørnestein. — **-wise** på skrå.

cornet ['kà·ʔnet] kornett; sekondløytnant i kavaleriet; kremmerhus. **-cy** ['kà·ʔnitsi] kornettpost; **he was gazetted to a —** han ble utnevnt til kornett.

corn|-field kornåker. **-flower** er kornblomst.

cornice ['kà·ʔnis] karniss, gesims; gardinstang.

Cornish ['kà·ʔniʃ] fra Cornwall.

cornucopia [kà·ʔnjuˈkoupjə] overflødighetshorn.

Cornwall ['kà·ʔnwəl, 'kà·ʔnwà·l] Cornwall.

corny ['kå·ᵊni] korn-; kornrik; kornet; kjernefull; hard som horn; liktorn-.
corolla [kə'råla] krone (på blomst).
corollary [kə'råləri] logisk konsekvens.
Coromandel [kåro'mändəl] Coromandel.
corona [kə'roᵘnə] korona, krone, krans.
coronation [kåro'neⁱʃən] kroning.
coroner ['kårənə] kronbetjent (embetsmann, som med en jury på åstedet anstiller undersøkelser og avholder likskue i anledning av dødsfall, hvis årsak er ukjent); -'s inquest likskue.
coronet ['kårənét] liten krone, adelskrone.
corporal ['kå·ᵊpərəl] korporal.
corporal ['kå·ᵊpərəl] legemlig, kroppslig, korporlig. -ity [kå·ᵊpə'räliti] legemlighet. corporate ['kå·ᵊpərét] innlemmet, opptatt (i en korporasjon); — body samfunn, lag, korporasjon; person. corporation [kå·ᵊpə're'ʃən] korporasjon, lag; juridisk person; kommunestyre, bystyre.
corporeal [kå·ᵊ'på·riol] legemlig. -ist [kåᵊ-'på·riəlist] materialist. corporeity [kå·ᵊpə'ri·iti] legemlighet, legemlig tilværelse.
corposant ['kå·əpəzänt] elmsild; nålys.
corps [kå·ᵊ, i pl. kå·ᵊz] korps.
corpse [kå·ᵊps] lik.
corpulence ['kå·ᵊpjulens] førhet, korpulense.
corpulent ['kå·ᵊpjulənt] før, tykkfallen, korpulent.
corpuscle ['kå·ᵊpʌsl] blodlegeme.
corral [ko'ra·l] kve, innhegning til kveg (i Sør-Amerika); vognborg; drive inn i en innhegning, sette i kve.
correct [kə'rekt] forbedre, bedre, rette, korrigere; tukte, straffe; bøte på; riktig, rett, korrekt. correction [kə'rekʃən] forbedring; retting; irettesetting; tuktelse, straff; korrektiv; house of — tukthus. corrective [kə'rektiv] forbedrende, rettende; korrigerende, nøytraliserende; straffende; forbedringsmiddel, korrektiv. correctness [kə-'rektnis] riktighet; nøyaktighet. corrector [kə-'rektə] forbedrer; refser; korrekturleser; korrektiv.
correlat|e ['kårile'ⁱt] korrelat, motstykke; svare til; sette i forbindelse, sette i sammenheng. -ion [kåri'le'ʃən] gjensidig forhold, korrelasjon. -ive [kå'relətiv] korrelativ, samsvarende.
correspond [kåri'spånd] svare (til); veksle brev, korrespondere. -ence [kåri'spåndəns] overensstemmelse, samsvar; korrespondanse, brevveksling, brevbytte; forbindelse. -ent [-ənt] svarende (til); brevskriver, korrespondent.
corridor ['kåridå·ə] gang, korridor. — -carriage gjennomgangsvogn.
corrigenda [kåri'dʒendə] rettinger.
corrigible ['kåridʒibl] forbederlig.
corrobor|ant [kə'råbərənt] styrkende; styrkemiddel. -ate [kə'råbəre'ⁱt] bekrefte, stadfeste. -ation [kərəbə'reⁱʃən] bekreftelse, stadfesting. -ative [kə'råbərətiv] styrkende; bekreftende; styrkemiddel.
corrode [kə'roᵘd] gnage, ete på, tære på, fortære. corrodent [kə'roᵘdənt] etende, gnagende, etsende; etsende middel. corrosion [kə'roᵘʒən] oppløsning, opptæring. corrosive [kə'roᵘsiv] som tærer, gnager el. løser opp, etsende, fortærende; etsende middel.
corrugate ['kåruge'ⁱt] rynke, falde, rifle; -d iron bølgeblikk; -d wood grips riflete trehåndtak. corrugation [kåru'ge'ʃən] rynking.
corrupt [kə'rʌpt] skjemme, forderve; forfalske; forføre; korrumpere, bestikke; forderves, bli skjemt, råtne; fordervet, råtten; lastefull; forført; bestukket, korrupt, bestikkelig. -er forderver, forfalsker; bestikker. -ibility [kərʌpti-'biliti] bestikkelighet. -ible [kə'rʌptibl] forkrenkelig, forgjengelig; bestikkelig; -ibleness forkrenkelighet osv. -ion [kə'rʌpʃən] fordervelse; forråtnelse; bestikkelse; forfalskning; korrupsjon. -ive [kə'rʌptiv] fordervende, korrumperende.

corsage [kå·ᵊ'sa·ʒ] kjoleliv.
corsair ['kå·ᵊsæ·ə] sjørøver, viking, korsar; sjørøverskip.
corselet ['kå·ᵊslet] brynje, kyrass.
corset ['kå·ᵊset] korsett, snøreliv.
Corsica ['kå·ᵊsikə] Korsika. Corsican [-kən] korsikansk; korsikaner.
cortege [kå·ᵊ'te·ʒ] opptog, følge.
Cortes ['kå·ᵊtiz] cortes, storting (i Spania og Portugal).
cort|ex ['kå·ᵊteks] bark, hjernebark. -ical ['kå·ᵊtikl] barkaktig; bark-, kortikal; ytre.
coruscate ['kårəske'ⁱt] glimte, glitre. coruscation [kårə'ske'ʃən] funkling, glimting.
corvette [kå·ᵊ'vet] korvett.
coryphaeus [kåri'fi·əs] fører, koryfé.
C. O. S. fk. f. Charity Organization Society.
cos [kås] slags salat.
cosher ['kåʃə] forkjæle, fagne, gjøre krus for.
cosignatory ['koᵘ'signətəri] medunderskriver.
cosily ['koᵘzili] hyggelig, koselig.
cosine ['koᵘsain] kosinus.
cosmetic [kåz'metik] kosmetisk, forskjønnende; forskjønnelsesmiddel.
cosmic(al) ['kåzmik(l)] kosmisk, verdens-.
cosmogony [kås'mågəni] læren om verdens opprinnelse, kosmogoni.
cosmographer [kåz'mågrəfə] verdensbeskriver.
cosmographical . [kåzmo'gräfikl] kosmografisk.
cosmography [kåz'mågrəfi] verdensbeskrivelse.
cosmopolitan [kåzmo'pälitən] kosmopolitisk; kosmopolitt, verdensborger. cosmopolite [kåz-'måpolait] kosmopolitt.
cosmorama [kåzmo'ra·mə] kosmorama.
cosmos ['kåzmås] kosmos.
coss [kås] indisk mål (ca. 2 kilometer).
Cossack ['kåsäk] kosakk.
cosset ['kåsit] deggelam, kopplam, kjæledegge; forkjæle.
cost [kå·(·)st] omkostning, pris; innkjøpspris; koste; I know it to my — det har jeg fått føle; at all costs for enhver pris; at less — of life med oppofring av færre menneskeliv; — me dear blir meg en dyr lek, får jeg svi for.
coster ['kåstə] fk. f. coster-monger.
coster-monger ['kåstəmʌŋgə] gateselger.
costive ['kåstiv] forstoppet, som har treg mage. -ness [-nés] forstoppelse, treg mage.
costliness ['kå(·)stlinés] kostbarhet. costly ['kå(·)stli] kostbar, dyr.
cost-price ['kåstprais] innkjøpspris, selvkostende.
costume ['kåstju·m] kostyme.
costume [kå'stju·m] kostymere.
cosy ['koᵘzi] koselig, hyggelig; tevarmer.
cot [kåt] hytte, bu; kve, skjul; lett seng; barneseng, vogge; smokk; hengekøye.
co-tangent ['koᵘ'tändʒənt] kotangens.
cote [koᵘt] skur, hus, skjul, kve.
coterie ['koᵘtəri] koteri, klikk.
cothurnus [ko'pə·nəs] koturne; svulstig stil.
cotill(i)on [ko'tiljən] kotiljong.
cottage ['kåtidʒ] hytte; landsted, villa. —-organ husorgel; — -piano opprettstående piano. cottager ['kåtidʒə] hytteboer, husmann. cottar ['kåtə], cotter ['kåtə], cottier ['kåtiə] husmann.
cotton ['kåtn] bomull; bomullstøy; bomullstråd; bli ullen, reise to; stemme; passe sammen; være enig; få godhug for; kjæle for. — -cake bomullsfrøkake. —-gin egreneringsmaskin. -lord bomullsmagnat. -mill bomullsspinneri. printed cotton, cottonprint sirs.
cotton-wool ['kåtnwul] rå bomull, vatt.
couch [kautʃ] legge ned (srl. be -ed være nedlagt, ligge), legge malt til groning; felle (en lanse); fjerne, operere vekk (— a cataract operere vekk stær); uttrykke, avfatte; tilsløre; legge seg, krøke seg, huke seg ned; legge seg på lur. couch [kautʃ] løybenk, sofa, sjeselong; lag; grunn (i maleri); kveke (plante).

cougar ['ku·ga·ə, -gə] kuguar, puma.
cough [kåf] hoste. **-drop** [-dråp] hostepastille.
could [kud, kəd] imperf. av **can**.
couldn't ['kudnt] fk. f. **could not**.
coulisse [ku'li·s] kulisse.
council ['kaunsl] rådsmøte, råd; **County Council** grevskapsråd; fylkesting, bystyre (i London); **Town Council** bystyre som ut av sin midte velger **mayor** og **aldermen**, således at resten danner **the Common Council**, representantskapet; **Privy Council** geheimeråd (over 400 menn, og blant dem har **the Cabinet**, statsrådet, sete).
council-board ['kaunsl'bå·°d] rådsbord; rådsmøte, råd.
councillor ['kaunsilə] rådsherre; bystyremedlem, rådsmedlem.
counsel ['kaunsəl] råd; rådslagning; hensikt; juridisk konsulent; sakfører; juridisk bistand; gi råd, råde; rådlegge; **a piece of** — et råd; **keep one's** — holde noe hemmelig, holde tann for tunge. **Counsel for the Plaintiff** klagerens advokat; **Counsel for the Defendant** anklagedes advokat; **Counsel for the Crown** el. **Counsel for the Prosecution** anklager (i kriminalsaker); **Counsel for the Defence** forsvarer (i kriminalsaker); **King's Counsel** (fork. **K. C.**) kongelig advokat, kronadvokat.
counsellor ['kaunsələ] rådgiver; sakfører.
count [kaunt] greve (i utlandet, sv. til **earl**).
count [kaunt] tall; regning; klagepunkt; telle, regne; regne med; anse for; tilskrive; — **upon** gjøre regning på.
countenance ['kauntinəns] ansikt, mine; yndest; understøttelse, beskyttelse; fatning, kontenanse; **change** — skifte farge; **put out of** — bringe ut av fatning, forfjamse. **countenance** ['kauntinəns] oppmuntre, støtte; begunstige; billige. **countenancer** [-ə] befordrer, velynderbeskytter.
counter ['kauntə] regnepenger, tellepenger, sjetong; disk; teller.
counter ['kauntə] motsatt, imot; met·; parere.
counteract [kauntər'äkt] motvirke. **-ion** [-'äkʃən] motvirkning, motstand, hindring; ['kauntəräkʃən] mottrekk, svar. **-ive** [-'äktiv] motvirkende.
counterbalance [kauntə'bæləns] oppveie.
counterbalance ['kauntəbæləns] motvekt; [kauntə'bäləns] veie opp, være motvekt mot.
countercharge ['kauntətʃa·°dʒ] motangrep, motbeskyldning; [kauntə'tʃa·dʒ] gjøre motangrep.
counterfeit ['kauntəfit] etterligne, ettergjøre; forfalske; hykle; ettergjort, forfalsket, oppdiktet, falsk; etterlizning; bilde; forfalsket ting. **-er** ettergjører, forfalsker; hykler.
counterfoil ['kauntəfoil] talong i sjekkbok.
counterfort ['kauntəfå·°t] skråpille, strever, kontrefort.
counter-hopper ['kauntəhåpə], **counter-jumper** 'kauntədʒʌmpə] diskenspringer.
countermand ['kauntə'ma·nd] gi kontraordre, avlyse, sende atterbud om. **countermand** ['kauntəma·nd] kontraordre, atterbud.
countermarch ['kauntəma·°tʃ] kontramarsj.
countermarch [kauntə'ma·°tʃ] marsjere tilbake.
countermessage ['kauntəmesidʃ] avbud.
countermine ['kauntəmain] kontramine.
countermine [kauntə'main] kontraminere.
counterpane ['kauntəpe'n] sengeteppe; åkle; patchwork — lappeteppe.
counterpart ['kauntəpa·°t] gjenpart; tilsvarende stykke, motstykke.
counterpoint ['kauntəpoint] kontrapunkt.
counterpoise ['kauntəpoiz] motvekt; veie opp.
counterpoison ['kauntəpoizn] motgift.
counterscarp ['kauntəska·p] kontreskarpe, ytre vollgravside.
countersign ['kauntəsain] kontrasignere; løsen; feltrop; kontrasignatur.

countersink [kauntə'sink] forsenke (bore hul til skruehode osv.
countertenor ['kauntə'tenə] alt (altstemme).
countervail ['kauntəve'l] veie opp.
countess ['kauntés] grevinne (gift med **earl** eller **count**).
counting-house ['kauntiŋhaus] kontor.
countless ['kauntlès] utallig.
countrified ['kʌntrifaid] rustifisert, bondsk.
country ['kʌntri] land; egn; land (motsatt by); fedreland; terreng, lende; **in the** — på landet; **into the** — ut på landet; **throw** (el. **put**) **oneself upon the** — kreve å bli stilt for en jury; **go** (el. **appeal**) **to the** — appellere til velgerne. — **-cousin** slektning fra landet; gudsord fra landet. — **-dance** kontradans. — **-folk** landsfolk, bygdefolk. — **-house** gård, landsted. **-man** landsmann; landmann, bonde. **-seat** landsted. **-side** bondebygd, landsbygd, land; egn, omegn. **-town** kjøpstad. **-woman** landsmanninne; bondekone.
county ['kaunti] grevskap (betegnelse for de provinser som England er oppdelt i, til vanlig det samme som **shire**). — **council** se **council**. — **court** lokal rett (for sivile småsaker). **-family** godseierfamilie, adelsætt med ættegods i fylket. — **town** hovedstaden i et grevskap. **the Midland Counties** de mellomengelske grevskaper.
coup [ku·] kup. — **d'état** ['ku·de''ta·] statskup.
coupé ['ku·pe'] kupé.
couple ['kʌpl] koppel; par; kople; parre; forbinde; parre seg. **couplet** ['kʌplet] par; verspar. **coupling** ['kʌpliŋ] kopling. **coupling|-pin** [-pin] eller **-rod** [-råd] koplingsjern.
coupon ['ku·pån] kupong.
courage ['kʌridʒ] mot, tapperhet; **have the** — **of one's conviction** ha sine meningers mot. **courageous** [kə're'dʒəs] motig, tapper.
courier ['kuriə] ilbud, kurér.
course [kå·°s] løp; løpebane; kurs; gang, framskritt; kursus; rekke; vandel, framgangsmåte, sedvane, skikk, måte; naturmessig virkemåte, naturens gang; rett (ved et måltid), anretning; menstruasjon; **of** — naturligvis, selvsagt; **in due** — i rette tid; **in the** — of i løpet av, under; **a matter of** — en selvfølgelighet; **a** — **of lectures** forelesningsrekke. **course** [kå·°s] forfølge, jage.
courser ['kå·°sə] hest, ganger.
court [kå·°t] gård; tun, gårdsplass; veit, smug; krokketplass, tennisplas:s hoff; oppvartning, kur; rett; rettssal; — **of justiəo** domstol, rett; **the Law-Courts** rettslokalene; **at** — ved hoffet; **have a friend at** — ha fanden til morbror; **before the** — for retten; **in** — i retten; **in** — i rettssalen; **bring into the** — bringe for retten; **make** — **to** gjøre kur til. — **-day** rettsdag; tingdag. — **-dress** hoffdrakt.
courteous ['kə·tiəs, 'kå·tiəs] høflig; vennlig. **-ness** høflighet, elskverdighet, vennlighet.
courtesan ['kå·°tizən] kurtisane, skjøge.
courtesy ['kə·tisi] høflighet, elskverdighet; oppmerksomhet; belevenhet. **courtesy** ['kə·tsi] neiing; neie; **drop a** — neie.
court|-guide ['kå·°tgaid] hoff- og statskalender. **-hand** kanselliskrift. **-house** tingstue.
courtier ['kå·°tjə] hoffmann.
courtly ['kå·°tli] høflig, høvisk, beleven.
court|-martial ['kå·°t'ma·°ʃəl] krigsrett; dømme ved krigsrett. **-plaster** heftplaster.
courtship ['kå·°tʃip] kur, frieri.
courtyard ['kå·°t'ja·°d] gårdsplass.
cousin ['kʌzn] fetter, kusine, søskenbarn; slektning. **-german** el. **first** — (kjødelig) søskenbarn, kjødelig fetter el. kusine; **second** — tremenning. **cousinship** ['kʌznʃip] fetterskap.
cove [ko°v] bukt, fjord, vik, våg; hvelve.
cove [ko°v] kar, fyr.
covenant ['kʌvinənt] pakt, overenskomst, avtale; slutte pakt; **the Covenant** en overenskomst

mellom skottene i det 16. og 17. århundre til vern for deres protestantiske kirke. **covenanter** ['kʌvinəntə] tilhenger av **the Covenant.**

Covent Garden ['kåvənt' ga·ᵊdn] Covent Garden (sted i London).

coventrate ['kåvəntre¹t] (laget etter tysk «coventrieren») ødelegge en by ved bombing (slik som Coventry ble det i november 1940).

Coventry ['kåvəntri] Coventry (en by); **send a man to** — ikke ville ha omgang med en mann, boikotte en person.

cover ['kʌvə] dekke, dekke til; skjule; beskytte; bedekke (parre seg med); tilbakelegge; reise gjennom; sikte bent på; dekke; kuvert; deksel; lokk; skjul; påskudd, skinn; perm, bind, konvolutt; beskyttelse; kratt, tykning; et dyrs leie; **covered-in** tildekt, overdekt; **under separate** — særskilt, med særskilt post. **under this** — innlagt. — **note** interimsbevis.

covering ['kʌvəriŋ] bedekning; ly, skjul.

coverlet ['kʌvəlet] sengeteppe, åkle.

Coverley ['kʌvəli] Coverley.

coverlid ['kʌvəlid] sengeteppe, åkle.

covert ['kʌvət] skjul, ly, tilfluktssted, smutthull; tykning; dekt, skjult; forblomme; (jur.) **gift** (under en ektemanns beskyttelse).

covert-coat ['kʌvət'koᵘt] slags kort, lett frakk.

coverture ['kʌvətʃuə, -tʃə] bedekning, vern, livd; (jur.) en kones ekteskapelige stilling.

covet ['kʌvət] begjære, trå, hike etter. **-ous** ['kʌvətəs] begjærlig (**of** etter). **-ousness** begjærlighet, griskhet, lyst.

covey ['kʌvi] yngel; flokk, kull.

cow [kau] ku.

cow [kau] kue, forkue, gjøre motløs.

coward ['kauəd] kujon, reddhare; feig, forsagt. **-ice** ['kauədis] feighet, forsagthet. **-ly** feig.‿

cowbane ['kaube¹n] selsnepe.

cow-boy ['kauboi] gjeter, cowboy.

cow-catcher ['kaukätʃə] kufanger, skinnerydder.

cower ['kauə] sitte på huk, sette seg på huk, huke seg ned, krype sammen.

Cowes [kauz] Cowes (by på Wight).

cowherd ['kauhə·d] hjuring, gjeter.

cowhide ['kauhaid] kuhud; pisk, piske.

cow-house fjøs, flor.

cowl [kaul] munkehette, munkekutte; røykhette.

Cowley ['kauli] Cowley.

co-worker ['koᵘ'wə·kə] medarbeider.

Cowper ['ku·pə, 'kaupə] Cowper.

cowpox ['kaupåks] kukopper.

cowslip ['kauslip] kusymre, marianøkleband.

cox [kåks] d. s. s. **coxswain;** styre; være kvartermester el. båtstyrer.

coxcomb ['kåkskoᵘm] narr, laps.

coxcombical [kåks'koᵘmikl] lapset, narraktig.

coxcombry ['kåkskəmri] lapsethet, narraktighet.

coxswain ['kåkswe¹n, 'kåksn] kvartermester (i marinen); båtstyrer (på robåt).

coy [koi] bluferdig, blyg, ærbar. **-ish** ['koiiʃ] litt tilbakeholden, blyg.

coyote [ko'joᵘti] prærieulv.

coz [kʌz] fetter, kusine; forkortet av **cousin.**

cozen ['kʌzn] narre, lure, bedra.

cozy ['koᵘzi] se **cosy.**

c. p. fk. f. **candle power.**

cp. fk. f. **compare.**

C. P. R. fk. f. **Canadian Pacific Railway.**

Cr. fk. f. **creditor.**

C. R. fk. f. **Caledonian Railway.**

crab [kräb] krabbe; villeple, sureple; tverrdriver; sur; gretten; klore; rakke ned på, plukke sund. **the Crab** Krepsen (stjernebilde); **catch** (eller **cut) a** — gjøre et galt åretak.

Crabbe [kräb] Crabbe.

crabbed ['kräbid] sur, gretten; uklar, ugrei, floket; gnidret.

crabby ['kräbi] sur, gretten.

crab-louse ['kräblaus] flatlus.

crab-pot ['kräbpåt] hummerteine.

crack [kräk] knaking, braking, brak, slag, smell; knekk; brudd, brott, sprekk, brist, revne; skryt; innbrudd, innbruddstyv; knake, brake, smelle; knekke; knalle med, smelle med; sprekke, revne, sprenge; skryte; **a** — **shot** mesterskytter; **a** — **regiment** eliteregiment; — **a bottle** knekke halsen på en flaske; **a -ed voice** en sprukken stemme; — **jokes** rive vittigheter av seg.

crack-brained ['kräkbre¹nd] tomset, skrullet.

cracker ['kräkə] nøtteknekker; knallbonbon, (tynn, hard) kjeks; piskesnert; (i slang) løgn.

crackle ['kräkl] knitre, sprake. **crackling** ['kräkliŋ] spraking; brunstekt fleskesvor.

cracknel ['kräknəl] kjeks.

cracksman ['kräksmən] innbruddstyv.

Cracow ['kra·koᵘ] Krakau.

cradle ['kre¹dl] vogge; rede, reir; skinne, spjelk; bøyle (over sår); avløpningspute; sl. renske el. skilletrau (for malm); meiebøyel (på en ljå); legge i vogge; vogge; ale opp, fostre.

craft [kra·ft] hendighet; håndverk, yrke, kunst; list, bedrageri, kunstgrep; skip, fartøy, farkost. **-sman** ['kra·ftsmən] håndverker; fagmann. **-iness** ['kra·ftinés] behendighet, snedighet, list. **-y** ['kra·fti] listig, slu.

crag [kräg] fjellknaus, berghammer. **-ged** ['krägid], **-gy** ['krägi] ujevn, knudret, knauset, berglendt.

crake [kre¹k] åkerrikse.

cram [kräm] stappe, proppe, presse inn; fylle seg, stappe seg, proppe seg; fylle med løgner; proppe (med kunnskaper), manudusere; terpe, pugge; eksamenslesning; terping; løgn, skrøne.

crambo ['krämboᵘ] rimlek, rimord.

crammer ['krämə] pugghest; manuduktør; løgn, skrøne; løgnhals.

cramp [krämp] krampe (sykdom); krampe (i mur osv.); skruestikke; hindring, innskrenkning; volde krampe; gjøre stiv; tvinge, innskrenke; gjøre fast, klemme fast; gjøre det trangt, vanskelig for.

cramp-iron ['krämpaiən] jernkrampe.

crampon ['krämpən] klo, hake; brodd (under sko).

cran [krän] mål for sild = 37¹/₂ gallons.

cranage ['kre¹nidʒ] kranleie, kranpenger.

cranberry ['kränbəri] tranebær.

crane [kre¹n] trane; kran; løfte med en kran; tøye seg, strekke halsen, strekke; — **at** betenke seg, før man forsøker.

crane's-bill ['kre¹nzbil] storkenebb.

cranium ['kre¹niəm] kranium, hjerneskall.

crank [kräŋk] krok, krumtapp, krank: sveiv, veiv; bukt, krok; påhitt; ordspill; særling, skrue; frisk, sprek, livlig; rank; krank, skrøpelig; vende og dreie seg; bukte og sno seg. **crankle** ['kräŋkl] sno seg; krumme; krok, krumning.

crannied ['kränid] full av sprekker.

cranny ['kräni] revne, sprekk; få revner.

crape [kre¹p] krepp, (sørge-)flor; kruse; kreppe.

crapulence ['kräpjuləns] fyllesyke; fyll, umåteholdenhet.

crash [kräʃ] knak, brak, bulder; nedstyrtning; krakk, fallitt; brake, styrte sammen.

crass [kräs] tykk, grov, drøy, dryg, krass. **-itude** ['kräsitju·d] drøyhet, grovhet.

crate [kre¹t] pakk-korg, tremmekasse.

crater ['kre¹tə] krater.

cravat [krə'vät] (gammeldags) halsbind, (også om:) slips; **hempen** — bøddels reip.

crave [kre¹v] kreve, forlange; be om; hike etter; **a craving appetite** en glupende appetitt.

craven ['kre¹vən] kujon, kryster, stakkar; feig.

craw [krå·] krel, krås.

crawfish ['krå·fiʃ] kreps.

crawl [krå·l] kravle, krabbe; ha krypende fornemmelser; kravling; — **with** myldre av.

crawler ['krå·lə] kryp, lus; ledig bil (som kjører langsomt for å få passasjer).

cray-fish ['kreɪfiʃ] kreps.

crayon ['kreɪən] tegnekritt; stift; tegning.

craze [kreɪz] gjøre forrykt, skrullet, være forrykt; sprekke, slå sprekker; sprekk, revne; mani, galskap, grille, fiks idé. **craziness** ['kreɪzinès] brøstfeldighet, forrykthet. **crazy** ['kreɪzi] brøstfeldig, falleferdig, avfeldig; skrullet, tullet, gal, vanvittig.

creak [kri·k] knirke, knake; knirk.

cream [kri·m] fløte; rømme; krem; det beste; — of tartar renset vinstein, kremor-tartari. **cream** [kri·m] sette fløte; skumme fløte; ha fløte i.

creamery ['kri·məri] meieri; melkehandel.

crease [kri·s] fold, fald, brett, rynke; brette, folde. **creasy** ['kri·si] foldet.

create [kri'e·t] skape; frambringe; utnevne. **creation** [kri'e·ʃən] skapelse; det skapte, skapning; utnevnelse. **creative** [kri'e·tiv] skapende. **creator** [kri'e·tə] skaper. **creatress** [kri'e·très] skaperinne. **creature** ['kri·tʃə] skapning, menneske, vesen; dyr; kreatur.

crèche [kreʃ] barnekrybbe.

credence ['kri·dəns] tro, tillit, tiltro; **letter of** — kreditiv. **credenda** [kri'dendə] trosartikler. **credentials** [kri'denʃəls] kreditiver; legitimasjonsskrivelse. **credibility** [kredi'biliti] troverdighet. **credible** ['kredibl] trolig, troverdig.

credit ['kredɪt] tillit, tiltro; kreditt; godt navn, anseelse, anerkjennelse, ære; troverdighet; innflytelse; tro, lite på, skjenke tiltro; kreditere. **-able** ['kreditəbl] aktverdig; ærefull, hederlig. **-or** ['kreditə] kreditor.

credulity [kri'dju·liti] lett-troenhet. **credulous** ['kredjuləs] lett-troende, godtroende.

creed [kri·d] tro, trosbekjennelse.

creek [kri·k] krik; vik; bukt; (amr.) sideelv, bekk.

creel [kri·l] kurv, korg, kipe, teine.

creep [kri·p] krype, liste seg; være krypende. **-er** ['kri·pə] kryper; kryp; slyngplante; trekryper; **Virginia creeper** villvin. **-y** ['kri·pi] uhyggelig.

creese [kri·s] kris (malaiisk dolk); dolke.

cremate [kri'me·t] brenne (især lik). **cremation** [kri'me·ʃən] likbrenning. **crematorium** [kremə'tå·riəm] krematorium. **Cremona** [kri'moʷnə] Cremona; kremonaserfiolin. **Cremonese** [kri·mo'ni·z] kremonesisk; kremoneser.

crenated [kri'ne·tid] takket, tagget. **crenelated** ['krenile·tid] krenelert, forsynt med skyteskår.

Creole ['kri·oʷl] kreol.

creosote ['kri·osoʷt] kreosot.

crepe de Chine ['kre·pdə'ʃi·n] crêpe de Chine. **crepitate** ['krepite·t] sprake, knitre. **crepitation** [krepi'te·ʃən] knitring, spraking.

crepon ['krepå·n, 'krepån] krepong.

crept [krept] imperf. og perf. pts. av **creep**.

crepuscule ['krepəskju·l] tusmørke. **crepuscular** [kri'pʌskjulə] tusmørke-, demrende.

crescendo [kri'ʃendoʷ] crescendo.

crescent ['kresənt] voksende; månesigd, halvmåne; halvrund plass.

cress [kres] karse; **water-** — brønnkarse.

cresset ['kresit] baun; fakkel, skunde; lanterne.

crest [krest] kam, topp; fjærtopp, hjelmbusk; hjelm (over et våpenskjold), våpenmerke. **-fallen** motfallen, slukøret.

Crete [kri·t] Kreta.

cretin ['kri·tin] kretiner (vanskapt idiot).ˉ**-ism** ['kri·tinizm] kretinisme, idioti.

cretonne [kre'tån, 'kretån] kretong.

crevice ['krevis] sprekk.

crew [kru·] (skips-)mannskap, besetning; flokk, bande.

crib [krib] krybbe, bås; barneseng; binge; hus, leilighet; stilling; oversettelse (av klassikere, som brukes til å fuske med i skolen); sperre inne; stjele, naske; **stimle sammen**; være stuet sammen; fuske (i skolen).

cribbage ['kribidʒ] pukk, et slags kortspill.

cribbing ['kribin] krybbebit; fusk (i skolen). **crib-biter** ['kribbaitə] krybbebiter; grinebiter. **cribble** ['kribl] grovt såld; sælde.

crick [krik] stivhet (i ryggen el. halsen), hold.

cricket ['krikit] siriss.

cricket ['krikit] cricketspill; spille cricket; **not** — ikke ærlig spill. **-er** ['krikitə] cricketspiller. — **-match** cricketkamp.

cried [kraid] imperf. og perf. pts. av **cry**.

crier ['kraiə] roper, utroper.

cries [kraiz] 3. pers. sing. presens av **cry**.

cries [kraiz] pl. av **cry**.

crime [kraim] forbrytelse; ulovlighet.

Crimea [krai'mi·ə]; **the** — Krim. **Crimean** [krai'mi·ən] Krim-, krimsk.

criminal ['kriminəl] forbrytersk, kriminell; forbryter. **-ity** [krimi'näliti] forbrytersk beskaffenhet; straffskyldighet; kriminalitet. **criminate** ['krimine·t] anklage, beskylde. **crimination** [krimi'ne·ʃən] beskyldning, anklage.

crimp [krimp] verver; hyrebas; verve. **crimp** [krimp] kruse, krølle.

crimple ['krimpl] krympe; kruse, krølle.

crimson ['krimzn] karmosinrød; høyrød; farge karmosinrød; rødme; — **rambler** rød slyngrose.

crinal ['krainl] hår-.

cringe [krin(d)ʒ] kryperi, smisking; bøye seg, krype sammen; krype (for en). **cringer** ['krin(d)ʒə] kryper. **cringing** kryping.

cringle ['kringl] løyer.

crinkle ['krinkl] bøye; sno, tvinne; kruse; bøye seg; sno seg; kruse seg; tvinning; krusning; krøll.

crinoline ['krinəli·n, krinə'li·n] krinoline.

cripple ['kripl] krøpling; gjøre til krøpling; lemleste, skamfere, helseslå.

crises ['kraisi·z] pl. av **crisis**.

crisis ['kraisis] vendepunkt, krise, krisis.

crisp [krisp] kruset; brunet; stekt; skjør, sprø; fast; musserende; kruse, krølle; flette; kruse seg. **crispate(d)** ['krispe·t(id)] kruset, krøllet.

criss-cross ['kriskrå·s] på kryss og tvers; kors. **criterion** [krai'tiəriən] kriterium, kjennemerke, særkjenne.

critic ['kritik] kritiker, dommer, klandrer. **-al** ['kritikl] kritisk; klandresyk; avgjørende: betenkelig, farlig. **criticise** ['kritisaiz] kritisere, bedømme; klandre. **criticism** ['kritisizm] kritikk. **critique** [kri'ti·k] kritikk, anmeldelse, melding.

croak [kroʷk] kvekke (som frosk); skrike (som ramn); knurre (om innvollene); knurre; brumme; kvekking, skriking, knurring. **croaker** ['kroʷkə] griner; menneskehater; ulykkesprofet.

Croat ['kroʷət] kroat. **Croatia** [kroʷ'e·ʃ(i)ə] Kroatia. **Croatian** [kroʷ'e·ʃ(i)ən] kroatisk.

crochet ['kroʷʃə'] hekle; hekling; hekletøy. **crocheting** ['kroʷʃe'in] hekling; hekletøy. **crochet-hook** ['kroʷʃihuk] heklenål.

crock [kråk] krukke;. skarveøyk, skottgamp; svak (utslitt el. udyktig) person. **crockery** ['kråkəri] leirvarer, steintøy.

crockshop ['kråkʃåp] porselens- og glasshandel. **crocky** ['kråki] sotet.

crocodile ['kråkədail] krokodille.

crocus ['kroʷkəs] krokus, safran.

Cræsus ['kri·səs] Krøsus.

croft [krå·ft] bø, inngjerdet markstykke; husmannsplass.

crofter ['krå·ftə] husmann, leilending.

cromlech ['kråmlek] dolmen, steindysse.

Cromwell ['kråmwel] Cromwell.

crone [kroʷn] gammel kjerring.

crony ['kroʷni] gammel venn, busse.

crook [kruk] hake, krok; krumstav; krumning, bukt; uærlig person, snyter. **by hook or by** — med rett el. urett, på enhver måte. **-back** pukkelrygg; kryl. **crook** krumme, krøke; fordreie. **crooked** ['krukid] kroket, skjev, skeiv, fordreid, uærlig. **-ness** krumhet; forkjærthet, uærlighet.

croon [kru·n] trall, nynning; tralle, nynne.

crop [kråp] krel, krås; topp (f. eks. på plante); høst, avling, grøde; snauklipt hår, snauklipping;

skjære av, stusse. — **-eared** ['kråpiəd] med stussede ører, snauklipt.

cropper ['kråpə] kroppdue; fall; fiasko; **to go a** — falle, styrte; gjøre fiasko.

croquet ['kroᵘkeⁱ] krokket; krokere.

croquette [kro'ket] slags kjøttkake med ris o. m.

crore [krå.ᵊ] 10 mill. rupi (indisk).

crosier ['kroᵘʒə] bispestav.

cross [krå·s, krås] kors; kryss; krysning (av kveg); (fig.) kors, lidelse; bedrageri, svindel; **take up the** — bære sitt kors med tålmodighet; **to play — and pile** spille mynt og krone; **the Southern Cross** sydkorset.

cross [krå·s, krås] på tvers, skrå, skjev; forkjært; tverr; gretten; sint; — **questions and crooked answers** spørsmål og svar (selskapslek).

cross [krå·s, krås] krysse, gå tvers over; gå over, gå igjennom, dra over, dra igjennom (på en eller annen måte; gående, kjørende osv.); sette over, komme over, komme igjennom; motvirke, motarbeide, hindre; motsi; sette kors ved; slå kors over (stryke); legge over kors; — **one's arms** legge armene over kors; — **one's mind** falle en inn; **be -ed in love** ha uhell i kjærlighet; — **a fortune-teller's hand with silver** gi en spåmann penger.

cross-action ['kråsˈäkʃən] motsøksmål.

cross|bar tverrtre, tverrstang. **-beam** tverrbjelke, tverrås. — **-bearer** korsbærer. — **-bench** tverrbenk (i det engelske underhus de nederste tverrbenker, der de uavhengige el. nøytrale sitter). **-bencher** partiløs, nøytral.

crossbill ['kråsbil] korsnebb (fugl).

cross|-bones korslagte dødningeben. — **-bow** armbrøst. — **-breed** krysning, blanding. — **-bun** korsbolle, langfredagsbolle. — **-country** tvers over landet el. markene, som ikke holder seg til veiene. — **-cut** tverrskurd, beinvei. — **-examine** kryssforhøre. — **-eyed** skjeløyd. — **-fire** kryssild. — **-grained** vrien (om ved); vanskelig, tverr, gretten.

crossing ['krå·siŋ] korsvei; gatekryss. — **-sweeper** gatefeier.

cross-legged ['kråslegd] med beina over kors.

crosslet ['kråslit] lite kors.

cross|light dobbeltbelysning; gransking fra forskjellige synspunkter. **-line** tverrlinje.

crossness ['kråsnes] vranghet, tverrhet, grettenhet.

crosspatch ['kråspätʃ] tverrdriver, sinnatagg, vriompeis.

cross|-piece tverrstykke, tverrbjelke. — **-purpose** formål som kommer på tverke; motsetning; misforståelse (**be at cross-purposes** komme på tverke for hinannen, komme til å motvirke hinannen). — **-question** kryssforhøre. **-road** korsvei. — **-row** tverr-rad. — **-stitch** korssting. — **-street** tverrgate. — **-trees** tverrsaling, tverrstang på masten.

crosswise ['kråswaiz] over kors.

cross-word ['kråswə·d] kryssord. — **puzzle** kryssordoppgave.

crotch [kråtʃ] kløft, gaffel.

crotchet ['kråtʃit] stiver; fjerdedelsnote; klammer (i trykte el. skrevne ting); grille. **crotchety** ['kråtʃiti] full av griller, sær, vimet.

crouch [krautʃ] bukke seg, huke, bøye seg ned, bøye seg sammen, legge seg ned, krype sammen, ligge sammenkrøpet; krype, smiske.

croup [kru·p] kryss, korsrygg, lend (på hest); strupehoste.

croupier ['kru·piə] croupier, bankholderens medhjelper i spillehus; visepresident (ved festmåltid).

crow [kroᵘ] kråke; galing, hanegal; brekkjern, kubein; **as the — flies** i like linje; luftlinje; **eat (boiled)** — bite i det sure eple; **pluck** (el. **pull**) **a** — slåss om bagateller; **have a — to pluck** (el. **pull** el. **pick**) **with one** ha en høne å plukke med en.

crow [kroᵘ] gale; prale, braute; hovere.

crow|bar ['kroᵘba·ᵊ] kubein, spett, brekkjern. **-berry** krekling (slags bær). **-bill** slags doktortang til å trekke ut kuler med.

crowd [kraud] hop, mengde, oppløp; fylle, trenge sammen, trenge seg, flokkes, stimle; — **all sail** sette alle seil til; **play to a -ed house** spille for fullt hus.

crown [kroᵘn] perf. pts. av **crow.**

crown [kraun] krone, krans; engelsk mynt = fem shillings; isse; topp; pull; krone, kranse, dekke, bedekke; sette kronen på verket; gjøre dam; — **king** krone til konge; **the hill, which was -ed by the standard** bakketoppen som banneret vaide over.

crown-imperial keiserkrone (blomst).

crown|-lands doméne, krongods. **-law** straffelov. **-officer** kronbetjent. **-prince** kronprins (i andre land enn England).

crow's-foot ['kroᵘzfut] rynker ved øynene; ogs. ranunkel.

crow's-nest ['kroᵘznest] utkikstønne (ved mastetopp).

crucial ['kru·ʃəl] korsdannet; kors-; kryssstreng, gjennomtrengende; avgjørende.

crucible ['kru·sibl] smeltedigel.

cruciferous [kru'sifərəs] korsbærende: korsblomstret. **crucifier** ['kru·sifaiə] korsfester. **crucifix** ['kru·sifiks] krusifiks. **crucifixion** [kru·si'fikʃən] korsfesting. **cruciform** ['kru·sifå·ᵊm] korsdannet. **crucify** ['kru·sifai] korsfeste.

crude [kru·d] rå, ukokt, umoden; ufordøyd. **-ness** ['kru·dnis], **crudity** ['kru·diti] råhet, umodenhet; ufordøyelighet; noe ufordøyd.

cruel ['kru·əl] grusom, ubarmhjertig, hjerteløs. **-ty** ['kru·əlti] grusomhet, ubarmhjertighet.

cruet ['kru·it] flaske (i bordoppsats). **-stand** [-ständ] bordoppsats, platmenage.

Cruikshank ['krukʃäŋk] Cruikshank.

cruise [kru·z] krysse, være på krysstokt; seiltur; krysstokt. **cruiser** ['kru·zə] krysser.

crumb [krʌm] krumme; brødsmule; bestrø med smuler, panere; **to a** — helt nøyaktig, på en prikk; **pick up one's -s** begynne å komme seg.

crumble ['krʌmbl] smuldre, smuldre bort; smule.

crumby ['krʌmi] bløt; smulet.

crumpet ['krʌmpit] slags bløt kake. **-face** kopparret ansikt.

crumple ['krʌmpl] krympe, krølle; bli krøllet, skrukne. **crumpling** ['krʌmpliŋ] slags skrukket eple.

crumpy ['krʌmpi] skjør.

crunch [krʌnʃ] knase; knasing.

crupper ['krʌpə] korsrygg; lend; bakol, bakreim.

crural ['kru·rəl] bein-.

crusade [kru'seⁱd] korstog; være el. dra på korstog. **crusader** [kru'seⁱdə] korsfarer.

crush [krʌʃ] støt; sammenstøt; knusing; trengsel; soaré; knuse, mase; presse; tilintetgjøre; presses sammen. **-er** ['krʌʃə] støter; knuser; fall; slag; politibetjent.

crush-hat ['krʌʃ'hät] bløt hatt; chapeau claque.

crush-room ['krʌʃrum] garderobe, teaterfoajé.

Crusoe ['kru·soᵘ] Crusoe.

crust [krʌst] skorpe; skare (på snø); overtrekke med skorpe, skorpelegge; sette skorpe; **-ed port** gammel, vel avlagret portvin. **-acea** [krʌ'steⁱʃiə] krepsdyr, **-aceous** [krʌ'steⁱʃəs] **animal** krepsdyr. **-ated** [krʌ'steⁱtid] med skorpe, med skall. **-ation** [krʌ'steⁱʃən] skorpe. **-ily** ['krʌstili] vrantent. **-iness** grettenhet. **-y** ['krʌsti] med skorpe; fortredelig, gretten, sur, vranten.

crutch [krʌtʃ] krykke; rogaffel.

crux [krʌks] (fig.) kors; floke, knute.

cry [krai] skrike, rope; utbryte; gråte; gi los (om jakthunder); rope ut (på gata); etterlyse; kunngjøre; lyse til ekteskap; — **down** rakke ned på; — **off** si seg løs fra, si pass; — **out** rope ut, klage høyt; skrike; — **up** rose, heve til skyene.

cry [krai] skrik, rop; gråt, klage; los, gjøing; utroping, kunngjøring; **a far** — et drygt stykke vei; **have a — over** gråte for el. over.

cryolite ['kraiəlait] kryolitt.
crypt [kript] krypt (kapell under kirke); gravhvelving. -ic ['kriptik] skjult, hemmelig. cryp-
togram ['kriptogräm] kryptogram, sifferskrift.
cryptography [krip'tågrəfi] lønnskrift.
crystal ['kristəl] krystall; krystallglass. -line
['kristəl(a)in] krystallinsk, krystallklar. -lization
[kristəlai'ze¹ʃən] krystallisasjon, krystallisering.
-lize ['kristəlaiz] krystallisere; krystallisere seg.
-logography [kristə'lågrəfi] krystall-lære.
c/s fk. f. case.
C. S. C. S. fk. f. Civil-Service Co-operative Stores.
C. S. I. fk. f. Companion of the Order of the
Star of India.
C. S. M. fk. f. Company Sergeant-Major.
ct. fk. f. cent.
C. T. C. fk. f. Cyclists' Touring Club.
C. U. fk. f. Cambridge University.
C. U. A. C. Cambridge University Athletic Club.
cub [kʌb] hvalp, unge; yngle, hvalpe.
Cuba ['kju·bə] Cuba. Cuban ['kju·bən] ku-
bansk; kubaner.
cubature ['kju·bətʃə] utregning av kubikkinnhold; kubikkinnhold.
cube [kju·b] kubus, terning; kubikktall. -root
kubikkrot. cubic(al) ['kju·bik(l)] kubisk.
cubicle ['kju·bikl] sovekammer, sengekove.
cubiform ['kju·bifå·ºm] terningdannet.
cubism ['kju·bizm] kubisme.
cubist ['kju·bist] kubist.
cubit ['kju·bit] underarm; engelsk alen (18 til
22 tommer).
cucking-stool ['kʌkiŋstu·l] stol som uhederlige
forretningsfolk ble bundet til og dukket i vannet.
cuckold ['kʌkəld] hanrei; gjøre til hanrei.
cuckoo ['kuku·] gauk. — -flower engkarse,
gaukesyre.
cucumber ['kju·kəmbə] agurk.
cucurbi(te) [kju·kə·bit] gresskar, destillerkolbe.
cud [kʌd] drøv; (sl.) skråtobakk, chew the —
tygge drøv, jorte; (fig.) tygge drøv på.
cudbear ['kʌdbæ·ə] rød indigo.
cuddle ['kʌdl] omfavne, kjæle, ligge lunt og
godt; omfavnelse, kjæling.
cuddy ['kʌdi] kahytt; kott; skap; asen, escl.
cudgel ['kʌdʒəl] svær stokk, påk, lurk; cross
the -s erklære seg for overvunnet; take up the -s
ta parti, gripe til våpen.
cudgel ['kʌdʒəl] pryle; — the brains bryte hodet.
cue [kju·] hale; pisk (i nakken); stikkord (på
teatret); vink; lune; kø (biljard).
cuff [kʌf] slag, dask, klaps; slå, daske; slåss.
cuff [kʌf] oppslag (på erme); mansjett.
cuibono ['kaibo·no] til hva nytte? hvortil?
cuirass [kwi'räs] harnisk, kyrass, brynje.
cuirassier [kwirə'siə] kyrasér.
cuisine [kwi'zi·n] kjøkken, matstell.
culinary ['kju·linəri] som hører til kokekuns-
ten, kulinarisk.
cull [kʌl] søke ut, velge ut; samle, plukke (ut).
cullender ['kʌlində] dørslag.
cullet ['kʌlit] glass-skår (til omsmelting).
cullis ['kʌlis] buljong; gjelé; renne, takrenne.
Culloden [kə'lådn, kə'loºdn] Culloden.
cully ['kʌli] troskyldig fyr, godfjott.
culm [kʌlm] kullstøv; stengel, halmstubb,
helme.
culminate ['kʌlmine¹t] kulminere.
culmination [kʌlmi'ne¹ʃən] kulminasjon.
culpability [kʌlpə'biliti] straffskyld, straffbarhet.
culpaple ['kʌlpəbl] straffskyldig, fordømmelig.
culprit ['kʌlprit] den tiltalte; skyldig, forbryter; synder, misdeder.
cult [kʌlt] kultus, gudsdyrking.
cultivable ['kʌltivəbl] som kan dyrkes; som
kan pløyes. cultivate ['kʌltive¹t] dyrke; avle; utvikle, utdanne; foredle; sivilisere. cultivation
[kʌlti've¹ʃən] dyrking; utdannelse; dannelse;
kultur. cultivator ['kʌltive¹tə] dyrker; utdanner;
foredler; kultivator (en slags harv).

cultural ['kʌltʃərəl] kultur-, kulturell.
culture ['kʌltʃə] dyrking, åkerdyrking; dannelse, kultur; dyrke; danne, sivilisere.
culver ['kʌlvə] skogdue, blådue.
culvert ['kʌlvət] avløpsrenne, stikkrenne.
cumber ['kʌmbə] bebyrde, besvære; overlesse.
Cumberland ['kʌmbələnd] Cumberland.
cumbersome ['kʌmbəsəm] byrdefull, besværlig.
Cumbrian ['kʌmbriən] kumberlandsk, kum-
brisk.
cumbrous ['kʌmbrəs] besværlig, tung. -ness
bry, brysomhet.
cum d., (el.) cum div. fk. f. cum dividend iberegg-
net dividenden.
cumin, cummin ['kʌmin] karve.
cummer ['kʌmə] gudmor, skravlekjerring, kjerring.
cummerbund ['kʌməbʌnd] livskjerf.
cumshaw ['kʌmʃå·] dusør (engelsk-kinesisk).
cumulate ['kju·mjule¹t] dynge opp, dynge sammen. cumulation [kju·mju'le¹ʃən] oppdynging,
sammendynging. cumulative ['kju·mjulətiv] sammendynget, opphopet; som øker i styrke.
cumulus ['kju·mjuləs] haug; skyfloke, haugsky.
Cunard [k(j)u'na·ºd]; — Line en dampskips-
linje.
cunctation [kʌŋk'te¹ʃən] nøling, somling.
cuneal ['kju·njəl] kiledannet.
cun(e)iform ['kju·n(i)ifå·ºm] kiledannet, kile-.
cunning ['kʌniŋ] kyndig; listig, forslagen, slu;
listighet, list, sluhet.
cup [kʌp] kopp, beger, pokal, kalk; blomsterbeger; pris, gevinst (ved veddeløp og annen
sport); kopp (til koppsetting); kald punsj (blandet på forskjellig måte av viner og andre ting);
koppsette, koppe; be in one's -s være beruset.
— and ball bilboquet. — -bearer munnskjenk.
-board ['kʌbəd] skap, matskap; the skeleton in
the -board den uhyggelige familiehemmelighet.
cupboard-love matfrieri, pengefrieri.
cupel ['kju·pəl] prøvedigel; skille ut.
Cupid ['kju·pid] Kupido; -s amoriner.
cupidity ['ju'piditi] begjærlighet, trå.
cupola ['kju·pələ] kuppel.
cupreous ['kju·priəs] kopperaktig, kopper-.
cupri'ercus [kju'prifərəs] kopperholdig.
cur [kə·] kjøter.
cur. ιк. . current.
curab.'ity [kjuərə'biliti] helbredelighet; bote-
von.
curable ['kjuərəbl] helbredelig.
curaçao [k(j)uərə'soº] curaçao (slags likør).
curacy ['kjuərəsi] kapellani.
curate ['kjuərét] kapellan. -ship kapellani.
cura'ive ['kjuərətiv] lægende; læge-.
curator [kju're¹tə] verge, verje, kurator; konservator, direktør (for en samling f. eks.).
cur'b [kə·b] stang i stangbissel; tømmer, tom;
tøyle, hindring; brønninnfatning; randstein.
curb [kə·b] holde i tømme, temme, styre.
curbstone ['kə·bstoºn] kantstein, randstein.
curd [kə·d] sammenløpet melk, opplagt melk,
ost, ystet; i pl. dravle, hagtette. curds and cream
tykkmelk. curdle ['kə·dl] løpe sammen; oste seg;
kjørne; størkne; stivne; la løpe sammen; bringe
til å stivne. curdy ['kə·di] sammenløpet.
Curdistan, se Kurdistan.
cure [kjuə] kur, helbredelse; sjelepleie; helbrede, kurere; salte, nedsalte.
cure [kjuə] underlig skrue, raring.
curfew ['kə·fju·] aftenklokke.
curio ['kjuərioº] kuriositet. curiosity [kjuəri-
'åsiti] nysgjerrighet; vitebegjærlighet; sjeldenhet, merkverdighet, raritet, kuriositet.
curious ['kjuəriəs] nysgjerrig, vitebegjærlig;
nøyeregnende; kunstig; merkelig, besynderlig, rar.
curl [kə·l] krøll; krusning; kruse, krølle; sno seg;
kruse seg. — oneself up rulle seg sammen; — one's
moustache snurre bartene; -ed hair krøllet hår.
curlew ['kə·l(j)u·] stor spove, spue.
curling ['kə·liŋ] et skotsk spill på isen.

curling-irons, curling-tongs krølltang. **curl-paper** papiljott. **curly** ['kə·li] krøllet.

curmudgeon [kə·'mʌdʒən] gjerrigknark, gnier.

currant ['kʌrənt] korint; **red** — rips; **black** — solbær. — **jelly** ripssjelé.

currency ['kʌrənsi] løp (f. eks. tidens); omløp, sirkulasjon; gangbarhet, kurs; verdi; papirpenger; gangbar mynt; letthet (i tale).

current ['kʌrənt] løpende; gangbar, gyldig, almen, gjengs; inneværende, løpende (år, måned); løp; strøm.

curricle ['kʌrikl] tohjult tvibeite.

curriculum [kə·'rikjuləm] kursus (på skole el. ved universitet); fagkrets; pensum, studieplan.

currier ['kʌriə] fellbereder (hvitgarver).

currish ['kə·riʃ] kjøteraktig; bisk.

curry ['kʌri] tilberede (skinn); skrape, strigle; gjennompryle; — **favour** innsmigre seg.

curry ['kʌri] karri; tillage med karri.

currycomb ['kʌrikoᵘm] strigle, hesteskrape.

curse [kə·s] forbannelse, ed; forbanne, banne.

cursed ['kə·sid] forbannet.

cursedly ['kə·sidli] forbannet, nederdrektig.

cursive ['kə·siv] hurtig, flytende; kursiv.

cursory ['kə·səri] hurtig, flyktig, løselig.

curst [kə·st] forbannet.

cursus ['kə·səs] kurs; pensum; ritual.

curt. fk. f. **current.**

curt [kə·t] mutt, kort på det.

curtail [kə·'teᵘl] forkorte, innskrenke, beskjære. **-ment** [kə·'teᵘlmənt] avkorting; beskjæring.

curtain ['kə·tn] forheng; gardin; teppe (i teater); portière; forsyne med gardiner, dekke; **draw the** — trekke forhenget for; **drop the** — la teppet falle; — **rises** teppet går opp. **iron** — el. **fireproof** — jernteppe (i teater). — **-fire** sperreild. — **-lecture** gardinpreken. — **-raiser** forspill (kort innledende skuespill). — **-rod** gardinstang.

curts(e)y ['kə·tsi] neiing; neie.

curvation [kə·'veᵘʃən], **curvature** ['kə·vətʃə] krumning, bøyning; krok.

curve [kə·v] krum; krumning, kurve; krumme, bøye; krøke seg.

curvet ['kə·vit, kə·'vet] gjøre krumsprang; kurbettere; la kurbettere; krumsprang; lystighet.

curvilineal [kə·vi'liniəl] kroklinjet, buet.

curvity ['kə·viti] krumhet.

cushion ['kuʃən] pute; bande (biljard); legge på puter; legge puter på; berolige; stikke under stolen. **cushionet** ['kuʃənət] liten pute.

cusp [kʌsp] spiss; horn (månens).

cuspidor(e) ['kʌspidã·ᵉ] spyttebakk.

cuss [kʌs] fyr, fysak, knekt.

cussed ['kʌsid] forbistret, forbasket, ondskapsfull, utgjort. **-ness** ondskap, forkjærthet.

custard ['kʌstəd] eggemelk, eggekrem.

custodian [kə·'stoᵘdjən] oppsynsmann; bestyrer; bevarer, konservator. **custody** ['kʌstədi] forvaring; arrest; oppsyn, bevoktning, varetekt.

custom ['kʌstəm] sedvane, skikk, bruk; søkning; kunder; toll. **-ary** ['kʌstəməri] brukelig, sedvanlig. **-er** ['kʌstəmə] kunde; fyr; **-house** ['kʌstəmhaus] tollbu. **-house-officer** tollbetjent. **customs** ['kʌstəmz] toll; tollvesen.

cut [kʌt] skjære, skjære til; felle; skjære; meie; såre, krenke; ignorere; klippe; hogge; ta av (i kortspill); slipe (glass osv.); løpe sin vei, stikke av, gjøre seg usynlig, skulke; — **down** ogs. skjære ned (utgifter); — **teeth** få tenner; — **short** gjøre kort, avbryte, knappe av, gjøre kortfattet; — **one's acquaintance** avbryte omgangen med en; — **a man** ignorere en mann; — **away** hogge bort, skjære bort; — **and run** løpe sin vei, stikke av, gjøre seg usynlig; — **in** falle inn, falle i talen; — **in pieces** hogge i sund, hogge ned; — **off** skjære av; avspise; — **out** skjære til; komme fram (om tann); stikke av.

cut [kʌt] imperf. og perf. pts. av **cut.**

cut [kʌt] snitt, hogg, skramme; slag; fornærmelse, tilsidesettelse; innsnitt; kanal; stykke; lodd (som trekkes); tresnitt; illustrasjon; avtaing (i kortspill); måte, mote, snitt, art; **short** — beinvei, snarvei; — **glass** slipt glass.

cutaneous [kju'teᵘnjəs] hud-.

cut-away ['kʌtəweᵘ] sjakett.

cute [kju·t] skarp, gløgg, klok, fk. f. **acute.**

cut-glass ['kʌtglɑ·s] slipt glass.

cuticle ['kju·tikl] overhud. **cuticular** [kju-'tikjulə] hud-.

cutlass ['kʌtləs] hoggert.

cutler ['kʌtlə] knivsmed. **cutlery** ['kʌtləri] knivsmedhandel; knivsmedvarer.

cutlet ['kʌtlét] kotelett.

cutpurse ['kʌtpə·s] lommetyv.

cutter ['kʌtə] tilskjærer (hos skredder); freser (skjære-apparat); framtann; kutter; **paper-** — papirkniv.

cut-throat ['kʌtþroᵘt] snikmorder.

cutting ['kʌtiŋ] skjærende; skarp, bitende; skjæring; gjennomskjæring; innsnitt; strimmel; utklipp; stikling; skurd, kornskurd; **a** — **wind** en bitende kald vind; — **of the teeth** tennenes frambrudd, tannsprett.

cuttle ['kʌtl], **cuttlefish** blekksprut.

cutty ['kʌti] (skotsk) kort: kort for hodet; tøyte, tøs, jåle; snadde, kort pipe.

cutwater ['kʌtwã·tə] skjegg (på skip); nese, nebb.

cutworm ['kʌtwə·m] slags åme.

C. V. O. fk. f. **Commander of the Victorian Order.**

c. w o. fk. f. **cash with order.**

C. W. S. fk. f. **Co-operative Wholesale Society.**

cwt ['hʌndrədweᵘt] fk. f. **hundredweight.**

cyanic [sai'änik] cyan-.

cyanide ['saiənaid] **of potassium** cyankalium.

cyanosis [saiə'noᵘsis] blåsott.

Cybele ['sibili·] Kybele.

cyclamen ['sikləmən] alpefiol.

cycle ['saikl] krets; periode; syklus; sykkel; sykle. **cyclist** ['saiklist] syklist.

cyclone ['saikloᵘn] syklon, hvirvelstorm.

cyclopedia ['saiklo'pi·djə] encyklopedi.

cyclops ['saiklåps] kyklop.

cygnet ['signit] ung svane.

cylinder ['silində] vals, sylinder. **cylindric(al)** [si'lindrik(l)] sylindrisk.

cymbal ['simbəl] cymbel; bekken.

Cymbeline ['simbili·n] Cymbeline.

Cymri ['kimri, 's-] kymrere, valisere. **Cymric** ['kimrik, 's-] kymrisk, valisisk.

cynic ['sinik] kynisk; kyniker. **-al** ['sinikl] kynisk. **cynicism** ['sinisizm] kynisme.

cynosure ['sinəzjuə, 'sainəzjuə] Den lille bjørn Polarstjerna; ledestjerne.

cypress ['saiprés] sypress.

Cyprus ['saiprəs] Kypros.

Cyrene [sai'ri·ni] Kyrene. **Cyrenian** [sai'ri·njən] kyrenaisk; kyrenaiker, epikureer.

cyst [sist] blære; svulst. **cystocele** ['sistosi·l] blæresvulst. **cystotomy** [si'ståtomi] blæresnitt.

czar [zɑ·ᵘ] tsar.

czardas ['zɑ·däs] tsardas (ungarsk folkedans).

czarevitch ['zɑ·rivitʃ] tsarevitsj (tsarens sønn).

czarevna [zɑ·'revnə] tsarevna (tsarens datter).

czarina [zɑ·'ri·nə] tsarina (tsarens hustru).

czaritsa [zɑ·'ritsə] tsaritsa (tsarens hustru).

Czech [tʃek] tsjekk; tsjekkisk.

Czechian ['tʃekjən], **Czechish** ['tʃekiʃ] tsjekkisk.

Czecho-Slovak ['tʃekoᵘslo"väk] tsjekkoslovak; tsjekkoslovakisk.

Czecho-Slovakia ['tʃekoᵘslo"va·kiə] Tsjekkoslovakia.

D

D [di] D. **d.**: tegn for **denarius, denarii** = penny, pence; **5 d.** vil altså si 5 pence. **D.** fk. f. **David; Deus; division; Doctor; Domini; dose; Dowager; Dublin; duchess; duke; Dutch. D.** el. d. fk. f. **date; daughter; day; degree; deputy; died.**

d — fk. f. damn.
D sharp diss. **D flat** dess. **D major** d-dur. **D minor** d-moll. **D flat major** dess-dur. **D flat minor** dess-moll.

dab [däb] slå lett el. bløtt; daske; dynke, væte; stryke lett over; lett slag, klapp; pikking; skvett, stenk; våt klut el. fille; kløpper, mester; ising.

dabber ['däbə] svertepute el. -ball.

dabble ['däbl] dynke, skvette til; plaske, susle; — **in** (el. at) fuske med. **dabbler** ['däblə] fusker.

dabster ['däbstə] kløpper, mester, adept.

da capo [da'ka·po] dakapo.

Dacotah [də'koutə] Dakota.

dactyl ['däktil] daktyl.

dad [däd] pappa.

daddle ['dädl] skjage, sjangle, stavre.

daddy-long-legs [dädi'låɲlegz] stankelben, myhank, helge høgbeina.

dado ['de¹dou] brystpanél; midtstykke.

Dædal|us ['di·dələs] Daidalos. **-ian** [di'de¹ljən] innviklet, labyrintisk.

daffadowndilly ['däfədaun'dili], **daffodil** ['däfədil], **daffodilly** ['däfədili] påskelilje.

daft [da·ft] fjollet, vill, gal. **-ness** toskeskap.

dag [däg] gammeldags lang pistol.

dagger ['dägə] daggert, dolk; kors; **look -s** se forbitret ut; **look -s at one** se på en med et gjennomborende blikk.

daggle ['dägl] søle til, skitne ut.

daguerreotype [də'gerotaip] daguerreotypi; daguerreotypere.

dahlia ['de¹ljə] georgine (plante).

Dahomey [də'houme¹] Dahome.

Dail Eireann ['dail'æərən] underhuset i Den irske fristat.

daily ['de¹li] daglig; dagblad, blad.

daintiness ['de¹ntinés] finhet; lekkerhet; kresenhet. **dainty** ['deinti] fin; lekker; kresen; lekkerbisken, godbit.

dairy ['dæə·ri] melkebu; meieri. **-farm** meieri. **-maid** meierske. **-man** meieribestyrer, meierist.

mountain — seter.

dais ['de¹is] forhøyning, pall, tram, estrade; tronhimmel; høysete.

daisy ['de¹zi] tusenfryd. **ox-eye** — hvit prestekrage.

dale [de¹l] dal.

dalliance ['däliəns] fjas. **dally** ['däli] fjase; dryge, somle, drunte.

Dalmatia [däl'me¹fə] Dalmatia. **-n** [däl'me¹fən] dalmatisk. **Dalmatic** [däl'mätik] dalmatisk; dalmatika (katolsk messehakel).

daltonism ['då·ltənizm] fargeblindhet.

dam [däm] mor (om dyr).

dam [däm] dam, demning, dike; demme (**in** el. **up** opp).

damage ['dämidʒ] skade, men; skadesløsholdelse, erstatning; tilføye skade, ska, beskadige, ta skade; **estimate damages** fastsette skadeserstatning; **lay one's damages at £ 200** kreve 200 pund i skadeserstatning.

damascene [dämə'si·n] damascere; damascener-.

damask ['däməsk] damask, damaskere (veve med opphøyde figurer; etse inn figurer i stål).

dame [de¹m] (foreld.) dame; (fornem) frue (tittel for hustruen til en **knight** el. **baronet** nå

alm. lady); husmor (husfar el. husmor ved Eton pensjonatskole).

damn [däm] fordømme; forbanne; forkaste; hysse ut, pipe ut (om skuespill); banne. **damnability** [dämnə'biliti] fordømmelighet; forkastelighet. **damnable** ['dämnəbl] fordømmelig; forkastelig. **damnation** [däm'ne¹fən] fordømmelse. **damnatory** ['dämnətəri] fordømmende. **damned** [dämd, poet. og relig. 'dämnid] fordømt. **damnify** ['dämnifai] gjøre skade på. **damning** ['däm(n)iɲ] fellende.

Damocles ['däməkli·z] Damokles.

damp [dämp] tåke; fuktighet; (fig.) demper; rå, fuktig, klam; fukte, væte; nedslå, dempe.

damper ['dämpə] sordin; spjeld.

damsel ['dämzəl] jomfru, ungmøy, terne.

damson ['dämzən] damaskusplomme.

Dan [dän] fork. f. Daniel.

Danaides [dä'ne¹idi·z] danaider.

dance [da·ns] dans; danse; la danse; **I'll lead you a pretty** — du skal få med meg å bestille. **St. Vitus's** — sanktveitsdans. **dancer** ['da·nsə] danser, danserinne.

dancing ['da·nsiɲ] dansing, dans. — **-master** danselærer.

dandelion ['dändilaiən] løvetann.

dander ['dändə] sinne; **he got his** — **up** sinnet tok han.

dandie ['dändi] sl. terrier.

dandify ['dändifai] gjøre lapset.

dandle ['dändl] gynge, ri ranke med; leke med; kjæle for, fjase. **dandler** ['dändlə] barnevenn.

dandriff ['dändrif] flass (i hodet).

dandy ['dändi] laps; fin, nydelig; spretten. **-ism** ['dändiizm] lapseri.

Dane [de¹n] danske; dane. **great Dane** grand danois. **-lagh, -law** ['de¹nlå·] Danelag.

danger ['de¹n(d)ʒə] fare. — **-light** faresignal; signallanterne. **dangerous** ['de¹n(d)ʒərəs] farlig.

dangle ['däɲgl] dingle; la dingle; følge ydmyk. **dangler** kvinnejeger.

Daniel ['dänjəl] Daniel.

Danish ['de¹nif] dansk; dansk (språket).

dank [däɲk] rå, fuktig. **-ish** [-if] noe fuktig.

Danube ['dänju(·)b]: **the** — Donau.

dapper ['däpə] livlig, vever; nett, knøten.

dapple ['däpl] spettet, droplet; gjøre spettet. — **-bay** rødskimlet. — **-gray** apalgrå, gråskimlet.

darbies ['da·²biz] (slang) håndjern.

Dardanelles [da·²də'nelz]: **the** — Dardanellene.

dare [dæ·ə] tore, våge, driste seg til; trosse; utfordre; **he dare not do it** eller **he does not dare to do it** han tør ikke gjøre det; **I** — **say** jeg tror nok; visstnok; uten tvil, utvilsomt; — **somebody to do something** uteske en til å gjøre noe; **I** — **you** to ja, våg du bare å.

dare-devil ['dæ·ədevl] vågehals.

daring ['dæ·²riɲ] djervskap, dristighet; forvågen, modig, dristig, djerv.

dark [da·²k] mørk; mørke; mørkning; **the** — **ages** den uopplyste tidsalder, mellomalderen; — **blues** representanter for Oxford i sportskamp; **keep in the** — holde utenfor; **a** — **horse** en ukjent hest (i veddeløpsspråk), en ukjent politiker; — **lantern** blendlykt; — **room** mørkekammer; — **saying** dunkel uttalelse.

darken ['da·²kn] mørkne, skumre, formørke, gjøre mørk; — **one's doors** trå ned dørstokkene hos en.

darkish ['da·²kif] noe mørk, mørkladen.

darkling ['da·²kliɲ] i mørke.

darkness ['da·²knés] mørke; **Prince of** — mørkets fyrste, djevelen; **deeds of** — synd.

darky ['da·²ki] neger, svarting, svart.

darling ['da·ᵊliŋ] yndling, kjæledegge, øyesten; som adj. yndlings-.

darn [da·ᵊn] d. s. s. **damn.**

darn [da·ᵊn] stoppe (huller); stopping. **-ing-needle** stoppenål. **-ing-yarn** stoppegarn.

dart [da·ᵊt] kastespyd, kastepil; skyte, kaste, sende (plutselig), trive; fare, sette av sted.

Dartmoor ['da·ᵊtmuə, -má·ᵊ] Dartmoor.

Dartmouth ['da·ᵊtməþ] Dartmouth.

dartre ['da·ᵊtə] ringorm.

Darwin ['da·ᵊwin] Darwin. **Darwinism** ['da·ᵊwinizm] darwinisme. **Darwinist** ['da·ᵊwinist] darwinist.

dash [däʃ] splintre, knuse, slå i knas; daske til; slynge, kyle; skvette, stenke, fortynne, blande; tilintetgjøre; fare, styrte av sted; kaste seg; — **out** stryke ut.

dash [däʃ] støt, slag, klask; skvett; tilsetning, iblanding; stenk; anstrøk, snev; fart, futt; plutselig bevegelse, anfall; flotthet; tankestrek.

dash-board ['däʃbå·ᵊd] skvettbord.

dashing ['däʃiŋ] flott, feiende, sveisen, rask.

dastard ['dästəd] kryster, reddhare, kujon; feig, stakkarslig.

dastardly ['dästədli] feig.

dat. fk. f. **dative.**

data ['deitə] data, pl. av **datum.**

date [de¹t] daddel.

date [de¹t] dato; tid, år, årstall; **out of —** foreldet; **up to —** moderne, tilsvarende.

date [de¹t] datere; regne; datere seg fra, skrive seg fra.

dative ['de¹tiv] dativ.

datum ['de¹təm], plur.: data kjensgjerning, faktum. **datum-line** grunnlinje (ved landmåling).

daub [då·b] søle til; smøre sammen; smøreri; smisking. **-er** ['då·bə] smører. **-ery** ['då·bəri] smøreri.

daughter ['då·təl] datter. **— -in-law** svigerdatter. **-ly** datterlig.

daunt [då·nt] kue; gjøre redd, skremme. **nothing daunted** uforferdet. **-less** [-lès] uforferdet.

davenport ['dävənpå·ᵊt] skrivepult.

David ['de¹vid] David.

davit ['dävit] davit.

Davy ['de¹vi] David.

Davy Jones's locker ['de¹vi'dʒoᵘnziz'låkə] havsens bunn. **be in —** være gått nedenom og hjem.

Davy-lamp ['de¹vi lämp] sikkerhetslampe.

daw [då·] kaie; slamp.

dawdle ['då·dl] nøle, somle, spille tiden, drive. **dawdler** ['då·dlə] somlekopp.

dawn [då·n] gry, dages, lysne; daggry, dagning, grålysning; **it dawned upon him** det gikk opp for ham.

day [de¹] dag, døgn; dagslys; tid; **by —** om dagen; **— by —** dag for dag; hver dag; **to-day** i dag; **to-day's paper** avisen for i dag; **the — before yesterday** i forgårs; **now-a-days** nå til dags; **the other —** forleden dag, her om dagen; **this — week** åtte dager i dag; **one of these — s** en av dagene; **he is fifty years if he is a —** han er minst 50 år; **carry (gain, win) the —** vinne seier; **lose the —** tape slaget, forspille seieren; **make a —** of it ta seg en glad dag.

day|-bed sjeselong. **— -boarder** elev, som spiser på skolen, men ikke bor der. **— -book** journal, kladdebok. **-boy** elev, som ikke bor på skolen. **— -break** daggry, dagning. **— -dream** dagdrøm; luftslott. **— -labour** dagarbeid. **— -labourer** dagarbeider, leiekar.

daylight ['de¹lait] dagslys; **broad —** høylys dag.

daylong ['de¹låŋ] dagen lang.

day|-school dagskole, skole der elevene bor hjemme (mots. **boarding-school**). **— -spring** dagning. **— -star** morgenstjerne.

daytime ['de¹taim] dag; **in the —** om dagen.

daze [de¹z] forvirre, fortumle; fortumlethet.

dazzle [däzl] blende; blendende glans.

D. C. L. [di·si·'el] fk. f. **Doctor of Civil Law** dr. juris.

D. C. M. fk. f. **distinguished-conduct medal.**

D. D. ['di·'di·] fk. f. **Doctor of Divinity** dr. theol.

d—d fk. f. **damned.**

d/d fk. f. **days after date.**

D-day ['di·de¹] D-dagen, invasjonsdagen 5. juni 1944.

deacon ['di·kn] diakon, i den eng. statskirke den laveste klasse geistlige; i Skottland: fattigforstander.

deaconess ['di·kənès] diakonisse.

dead [ded] død, avdød, livløs; sloknet; som ikke gjelder lenger; mørk, glansløs, maktløs, dempet, stagget; uvirksom, ufølsom; glemt, forbigangen; ørkesløs, doven; øde; fullstendig; sørgelig; vissen, flau, matt; dødsstillhet; **the — de døde. a — bargain** spottpris; **— beat** dødstrett; **— calm** blikkstille. **— capital** død kapital; **it is a — certainty** det er skråsikkert; **— drunk** døddrukken, pærefull; **— fire** (sankt)elmsild, nålys. **— hand,** se **mortmain**; **— heat** dødt løp, kapprenn hvor to el. flere vinnere kommer til målet samtidig. **— language** dødt språk; **— letter** uanbringelig brev (som en ikke finner adressaten til); lov som ikke lenger enses; **— level** vannrett plan, uavbrutt slette; alminnelig middelmådighet; **— loss** rent tap; **be a — man** være dødsens; **— march** sørgemarsj; **step into a — man's shoes** tiltre en arv; **at the — of night** i nattens mulm og mørke; **— pull** el. **lift** altfor tung byrde; **the D.** the Dødehavet; **a — shot** blinkskudd; **— stock** uselgelig vare; **come to a — stop** gå helt i stå; **stop — bråstoppe; — on the target** rett i blinken; **— tired of** inderlig lei av; **flog — horse** skvette vann på gåsa; **cut one —** ignorere en, behandle en som luft.

dead|-alive livløs; kjedelig. **— -beat** dødstrett. **— -colouring** grunnfarge.

deaden ['dedn] avdempe, forminske, døyve (f. eks. smerte), gjøre flau; avdempes, miste kraft el. følelse.

dead|-eye (mar.) jomfru. **— -head** gratispassasjer el. -tilskuer, fribillett. **— -heat** uavgjort veddeløp. **— -light** lenseport; **-lock** stillstand;; **be at a -lock** være kjørt fast.

deadly ['dedli] dødelig, dødbringende; uforsonlig, død-.

deadness ['dednès] livløshet, dødhet.

dead|-reckoning utregning av skips posisjon ved hjelp av kompass og logg (når observasjon er umulig). **— -water** dødvann, blikkstille. **— -weight** dødvekt. **— -wind** motvind.

deaf [def] døv; tunghørt; **— as a post** stokkdøv; **— and dumb** døvstum. **deafen** ['defən] gjøre døv, døve, bedøve. **deafmute** ['defmju·t] døvstum.

deafness ['defnès] døvhet.

deal [di·l] furu- el. grantre.

deal [di·l] del; antall; kortgivning; dele ut; tildele; fordele; gi (kort); handle; mekle; oppføre seg, handle; **a good —, a great —** en hel del; **— by** eller **with** behandle; — in handle med; gi seg av med; **— with** oppføre seg imot; ha å gjøre med; ta seg av, ordne med, behandle; stri med; **it is your —** det er deg til å gi. en som gir seg av med noe; handlende, kjøpmann; en som gir kort; **plain dealer** ærlig mann; **double dealer** bedrager. **-ing** ['di·liŋ] handlemåte, ferd; handel; behandling; omgang.

dealt [delt] imperf. og perf. pts. av **deal.**

dean [di·n] dekan; domprost, stiftsprost; prost. **-ery** ['di·nəri] prosteembete, prosti; prostebolig.

dear [diə] dyr; dyrebar; kjær; kjære, elskede. **O —!** bevares vel! **— me!** du store min! **do, that's (there's) a —** gjør det, så er du snill! **— -bought** dyrekjøpt. **-ly** ['diəli] dyrt; ømt. **-ness** ['diənès] dyrhet; ømhet, kjærlighet.

dearth [də·þ] dyrtid; uår; mangel.

deary ['diəri] kjær; elsket.

death [deþ] død; dødsfall; dødsmåte; **put to — slå i hjel; it was the —** of him han tok sin død av det; — **-agony** dødskamp — **-bed** dødsleie; — **-blow** banehogg. — **-duty** arveavgift. **-less** ['deþlès] uforgjengelig, udødelig. **-ly** ['deþli] dødlignende. — **-rate** dødelighet, dødelighetsprosent. — **-rattle** dødsralling. **-'s head** dødningehode. — **-warrant** dødsdom. — **-watch** dødningeur; veggesmed (insekt).

débâcle [de'¹ba·kl] isgang; forvirring, katastrofe, krakk.

debar [di'ba·ə] utelukke, stenge ute, forby.

debark [di'ba·ək] gå i land; utskipe. **-ation** [dibaə'ke¹ʃən] landgang; utskiping.

debase [di'be¹s] nedverdige; forfalske; gjøre ringere. **-ment** [-mənt] nedverdigelse; forfalskning; forringelse.

debatable [di'be¹təbl] omtvistelig; omtvistet.

debate [di'be¹t] ordskifte, debatt; drøfte, debattere.

debauch [di'bå·tʃ] forføre; svire; svir; rangel; utsvevelse. **debauchee** [debå·¹tʃi·] svirebror; utsvevende menneske. **debauchery** [di'bå·tʃəri] utsvevelse, uordentlig levnet.

debenture [di'bentʃə, də¹b-] gjeldsbrev, obligasjon, debenture.

debilitate [di'bilite¹t] svekke, utarme. **debilitation** [dibili'te¹ʃən] svekkelse. **debility** [di'biliti] svakhet.

debit ['debit] debet; gjeld; debetside; debitere.

debonair [debå'næ·ə] vennlig; høflig.

debouch [di'bu·ʃ, di'bautʃ] munne ut; rykke ut, marsjere ut; utmunning.

debris ['debri·] beter, rester, ruiner.

debt [det] gjeld; **run into —, contract -s** stifte gjeld. **debtless** [detlès] gjeldfri. **debtor** ['detə] debitor, skyldner.

debut ['de¹bu·] debut, første opptreden.

Dec. fk. f. December.

decade ['dekəd, 'deke¹d] dekade; tiår.

decadence ['dekədəns], **decadency** [-si] forfall.

decadent ['dekədənt] som er i tilbakegang.

decagon ['dekəgən] tikant.

decalogue ['dekəlåg] de ti bud.

decamp [di'kämp] bryte opp med leiren; forsvinne, fortrekke. **-ment** [-mənt] oppbrudd.

decant [di'känt] avklare, helle forsiktig, dekantere. **-ation** [di·kän'te¹ʃən] avhelling, avklaring.

decanter [di'käntə] karaffel.

decapitate [di'käpite¹t] halshogge. **decapitation** [dikäpi'te¹ʃən] halshogging.

decay [di'ke¹] forfalle; gå tilbake, avta; visne; forarmes; forfall; tilbakegang, nedgang, oppløsning; forarming.

decease [di'si·s] bortgang, død; avgå ved døden; dø. **the deceased** den avdøde.

deceit [di'si·t] bedrageri, svik. **-ful** [-f(u)l] bedragersk. **-fulness** [-f(u)lnès] svikaktighet.

deceivable [di'si·vəbl] lett å bedra.

deceive [di'si·v] bedra, svike. skuffe, narre. **deceiver** [di'si·və] bedrager; forfører.

December [di'sembə] desember.

decency ['di·sənsi] sømmelighet; anstendighet.

decennial [di'seniəl] tiårs-. **decennium** [di-'seniəm] tiår.

decent ['di·sənt] sømmelig, anstendig; passende, rimelig.

decentralization [di·'sentralai'ze¹ʃən] desentralisasjon.

deception [di'sepʃən] bedrag; skuffelse. **deceptive** [di'septiv] skuffende; **appearances are often —** skinnet bedrar ofte.

dechristianise [di'kristʃənaiz] avkristne.

decide [di'said] avgjøre; beslutte. **decided** [di-'saidid] avgjort, bestemt, klar.

decimal ['desimal] desimal; desimal-. **decimate** ['desime¹t] desimere; ta bort hver tiende av; herje voldsomt blant. **decimation** [desi-'me¹ʃən] desimering.

decimetre ['desimi·tə] desimeter.

decipher [di'saifə] dechiffrere, tyde.

decision [di'siʒən] avgjørelse; vedtak; kjennelse; dom; bestemthet. **decisive** [di'saisiv] avgjørende.

deck [dek] dekke, kle, smykke, pynte.

deck [dek] dekk, skipsdekk; **— of cards** kortstokk. **below —** under dekk, i kahytta; **on —** på dekket.

declaim [di'kle¹m] tale ivrig; deklamere. **-er** [di'kleimə] ivrig taler; deklamator. **declamation** [deklə'me¹ʃən] deklamasjon. **declamatory** [di-'klämətəri] deklamatorisk, stortalende, retorisk.

declaration [deklə're¹ʃən] erklæring, kunngjøring, deklarasjon, angivelse (f. eks. av skatt); klageskrift. **declarative** [di'klärətiv], **declaratory** [di'klärətəri] forklarende; erklærende. **declare** [di'klæ·ə] erklære; kunngjøre; melde (i kort); deklarere, angi (til fortolling); erklære seg; **I — det må jeg si! I -d to myself** jeg sa til meg selv.

declension [di'klenʃən] forfall; nedgang; avslag; deklinasjon, bøyning av substantiver.

declination [dekli'ne¹ʃən] bøyning; forfall; avvik; misvisning, deklinasion. **decline** [di''lain] helle, avvike; avta, forfalle, være i forfall; bøye; vende seg bort fra; avslå; avvikelse, avvik, helling; daling; tilbakegang; forfall· tæring; **— all responsibility** fralegge seg ethvert ansvar; **the sun is declining** sola holder på å gå ned; **his business had been a declining one** det var gått tilbake med hans forretning.

declivity [di'kliviti] skråning, helling, hal'. **declivous** [di'klaivəs] skrå, hellende.

decoct [di'kåkt] koke, avkoke; fordøye. **-ion** [di'kåkʃən] avkoking; avkokt, dekokt.

decode ['di·ko¹d] dechiffrere.

decoloration [dikʌlə're¹ʃən] avfarging; falmethet; skjold. **decolour** [di'kʌlə] avfarge; falme.

decompose [di·kəm'po¹z] oppløse, dekomponere; oppløse seg. **decomposite** [di'kåmpozit] dobbelt sammensatt. **decomposition** [di·kåmpo-'ziʃən] oppløsning.

decorate ['dekəre¹t] pryde, smykke, dekorere. **decoration** [dekə're¹ʃən] prydelse; dekorasjon. **decorative** ['dekərətiv] dekorativ; prydende.

decorous [di'kårəs, 'dekərəs] sømmelig, passende.

decorum [di'kå·rəm] sømmelighet, dekorum.

decoy [di'koi] lokke; forlokke; lokking; lokkemat; lokkefugl.

decrease [di'kri·s] avta, minke; forminske. **decrease** ['di·kri·s] minking, mink, nedgang.

decree [di'kri·] forordne, bestemme; forordning, dekret; kjennelse.

decrement ['dekrimənt] forminsking, nedgang, minking.

decrepit [di'krepit] utlevd, avfeldig.

decrepitude [di'krepitjud] avfeldighet.

decrescent [di'kresənt] avtagende, minkende; avtagende måne.

decrial [di'kraiəl] nedriving, nedrakking, dårlig rykte. **decrier** [di'kraiə] en som rakker ned. **decry** [di'krai] rakke ned på, laste, bringe i vanry.

decumbent [-bənt] liggende.

decuple ['dekjupl] tidobbelt; tidoble.

dedicate ['dedike¹t] innvie; hellige; tilegne. **dedication** [dedi'ke¹ʃən] innvielse, vigsel, helligelse, helging; tilegning, dedikasjon.

deduce [di'dju·s] utlede, slutte. **deducible** [di'dju·sibl] som kan utledes el. sluttes.

deduct [di'dʌkt] ta ifra, trekke fra. **-ion** [di-'dʌkʃən] utledelse; slutning; avdrag; rabatt. **-ive** [di'dʌktiv] som kan utledes og sluttes, deduktiv.

dee [di·] banne, forbanne (i st. f. **damn**).

deed [di·d] dåd, gjerning; udåd; dokument, skjøte, tilskjøte, overdra; **by word and —** med råd og dåd.

deem [di·m] tenke, mene; anse for.

deemster ['di·mstə] dommer (på øya Man).

deep [di·p] dyp; dypt; dyptgående, dypsindig; grundig; listig; mørk (om farge); **the men came, four —** mennene kom, fire mann høy.

deepen ['di·pn] utdype, gjøre dyp; formørke; bli dypere og dypere.
deep-laid klokt uttenkt, dypt anlagt.
deep|-mouthed grovmælt (om hund). **-read** belest. **-rooted** inngrodd. **-sea** havdyp. **-seated** dyptgående, inngrodd.
deer [di·ə] dyr (av hjorteslekten). — **-stalking** jakt (på hjort).
deface [di'fe's] skjemme; ødelegge. **-ment** [-mənt] beskadigelse, ødelegging.
de facto [di·'fäktoⁿ] faktisk.
defalcate ['difäl'ke't] dra fra, trekke fra; underslå, begå underslag; **defalcation** [difäl-'ke'ʃən] fradrag; underslag, kassesvik.
defamation [di·fə'me'ʃən, def-] baktalelse, bakvaskelse. **defamatory** [di'fämətəri] ærekrenkende. **defame** [di'fe'm] baktale. **defamer** [di'fe'mə] baktaler.
default [di'få·lt] forseelse; forsømmelse, etterlatenhet; mangel; uteblivelse (fra retten); ikke holde sitt ord, ikke oppfylle en plikt; utebli; in — of i mangel av. **-er** [-ə] en som ikke møter; bedrager, kassesviker, dårlig betaler, fallent.
defeasance [di'fi·zəns] opphevelse. **defeasible** [di'fi·zibl] som kan oppheves el. omstøtes.
defeat [di'fi·t] overvinne; slå; tilintetgjøre; nederlag; tilintetgjørelse. **-ism** [di'fi·tizm] defaitisme, nederlagsstemning.
defecate ['defike't] lutre, rense. **defecation** [defi'ke'ʃən] rensing.
defect [di'fekt] mangel, lyte, feil; **he has the -s of his qualities** han har de feil som (ofte) følger med hans gode egenskaper.
defect|ion [di'fekʃən] frafall, svikt. **-ive** [di-'fektiv] mangelfull, ufullstendig. **-iveness** [di-'fektivnès] mangelfullhet, ufullstendighet.
defence [di'fens] forsvar; vern; defensorat; **appear for the** — møte som defensor; **in** — **of** til forsvar for; **Defence of the Realm Act** (lov av aug. 1912); **Counsel for the Defence** forsvarer, defensor (i kriminalsak).
defenceless [di'fenslès] forsvarsløs.
defend [di'fend] forsvare. **-ant** [di'fendənt] innstevnte. **-er** [di'fendə] forsvarer.
defensible [di'fensibl] som kan forsvares; forsvarlig. **defensive** [di'fensiv] forsvars-, defensiv; **the** — defensiven; **stand on the** — stå ferdig til forsvar, stå rede til å møte et angrep.
defer [di'fə·] utsette; overlate, henstille (til en annens avgjørelse); bøye seg for. **deference** ['defərəns] aktelse; hensynsfullhet, ettergivenhet. **deferential** [defə'renʃəl] ærbødig.
defiance [di'faiəns] utfordring; tross; **bid** — by tross; **he sets all rules at** — han trosser alle regler; **in** — **of** til tross for, trass i. **defiant** [di'faiənt] trossig; utfordrende.
deficiency [di'fiʃənsi] mangel; ufullkommenhet; underskudd; (fig.) hull. **deficient** [di'fiʃənt] mangelfull, utilstrekkelig; manglende; **mentally** — abnorm i sjelelig henseende.
deficit ['defisit, 'di·-] defisit, underskudd.
defier [di'faiə] en som trosser; en som utfordrer.
defilade [defi'le'd] beskytte mot ild fra siden.
defile [di'fail] pass, trang sti, skar, defilé; marsjere rotevis, defilere.
defile [di'fail] besmitte, skjemme, vanhellige, besudle. **-ment** besmittelse; besudling.
definable [di'fainəbl] som kan bestemmes. **define** [di'fain] forklare, definere; begrense. **definite** ['definit, 'defnit] bestemt; begrenset. **definition** [defi'niʃən] bestemmelse, forklaring, definisjon. **definitive** [di'finitiv] bestemt; avgjørende.
deflagration [deflə'gre'ʃən] forbrenning.
deflect [di'flekt] avvike, bøye av. **deflection** [di-'flekʃən] avvikelse; bøy, krok, sving.
defloration [deflo're'ʃən] det å ta blomsten av; det å ta møydommen, krenking.
deflower [di'flauə] rive blomsten av; krenke.
Defoe [di'foⁿ] Defoe.

deform [di'få·əm] misdanne, vanskape, vansire. **-ed** [di'få·əmd] vanskapt. **-ation** [difä·ə-'me'ʃən] misdannelse; vansiring. **-ity** [di'få·ə-miti] misdannelse vanskapthet; feil, lyte.
defraud [di'frå·d] svike, snyte. **-er** [-ə] bedrager.
defray [di'fre'] bestride (omkostninger, utgifter). **defrayal** [di'fre'əl] bestriding. **defrayer** [-ə] en som bestrider (omkostningene). **defrayment** [di'fre'mənt] bestriding, betaling.
deft [deft] flink, hendig, netthendt. **-ness** ['deftnès] flinkhet, hendighet, netthet.
defunct [di'fʌŋkt] avdød.
defy [di'fai] utfordre, uteske, trosse; **I** — **him** jeg byr ham tross; jeg tiltror ham det ikke; **I** — **him to do that** jeg tør innestå for at han ikke kan gjøre det.
deg. fk. f. **degree**.
degeneracy [di'dʒenərəsi] utarting, vanslekting. **degenerate** [di'dʒenəre't] utarte, vanslekte; som adjektiv: [di'dʒenərèt] vanslektet. **degeneration** [didʒenə're'ʃən] degenerasjon, utarting. **degenerative** [di'dʒenərətiv] vanslektende.
deglutinate [di'glu·tine't] løse, la gå opp i limingen, oppløse.
deglutition [di·glu'tiʃən] svelgjing.
degradation [degrə'de'ʃən] nedverdigelse; avsetting, degradasjon; tilbakegang; nedgang, forfall; forminskelse, mink.
degrade [di'gre'd] nedverdige; avsette, degradere; utarte.
degree [di'gri·] grad; rang, verdighet; klasse, orden; eksamen (ved universitet); **by -s** gradvis, litt etter litt.
dehisce [di'his] sprette opp (om skolm).
dehortative [di'hå·ətativ] som fraråder.
deicide ['di·isaid] gudedrap; gudedreper.
deification [di·(i)fi'ke'ʃən] guddommeliggjøring, apoteose. **deify** ['di·ifai] gjøre til gud, oppta blant gudene.
deign [de'n] verdiges, nedlate seg til.
Dei gratia ['di·ai'gre'fə] av Guds nåde.
deism ['di·izm] deisme. **deist** ['di·ist] deist. **deistic(al)** [di·'istik(l)] deistisk. **deity** ['di·iti] guddom, guddommelighet.
deject [di'dʒekt] nedslå. **-ed** [di'dʒektid] nedslått, motløs. **-edness, -ion** [di'dʒekʃən] motløshet.
de jure [di·'dʒuəri] etter loven.
delapse [di'läps] falle, sige, dale ned.
delate [di'le't] anklage. **delation** [di'le'ʃən] angivelse; anklage; — **of the sound** lydens forplantning.
Delaware ['delawæ·ə] Delaware.
delay [di'le'] oppsette, utsette, forhale. vente med å; oppholde; nøle, dryge, drunte; oppsetting, forhaling; opphold; **without** — uten å nøle, uoppholdelig.
delayed-action bomb [di'le'd 'äkʃən båm] tidsinnstilt bombe.
del credere [del'kre'dərə] delkredere (at en agent borger for riktig oppfylling av en annens forpliktelser).
dele ['di·li] ta ut, stryke ut, utelate.
delectable [di'lektəbl] yndig, liflig. **delectation** [di·lek'te'ʃən] lyst, fornøyelse, fryd.
delegacy ['deligəsi] beskikkelse, representasjon; utvalg.
delegate ['delige't] sende ut, gi fullmakt, beskikke. **delegate** ['deligèt] beskikket; utsending, befullmektiget. **delegation** [deli'ge'ʃən] utsending, utnevning; beskikkelse; delegasjon, sendelag; delegerte.
delete [di'li·t] utslette, stryke ut.
deleterious [deli'tiəriəs] ødeleggende, skadelig.
deletion [di'li·ʃən] utsletting, utskraping.
delf(t) [delf(t)] fajanse (fra Delft, Nederland).
Delhi ['deli] Delhi.
deliberate [di'libəre't] overveie; betenke seg.
deliberate [di'libərèt] betenksom, forsiktig; overlagt; rolig. **-ness** [di'libərètnès] betenksom-

het, forsiktighet; ro. **deliberation** [di'libə're'ʃən] overveielse, betenkning; forhandling. **deliberative** [di'libərətiv] overveiende; rådslående.

delicacy ['delikəsi] finhet; finfølelse; kjælenhet; kresenhet; lekkerbisken; svakhet, skrøpelighet.

delicate ['delikét] fin; fintfølende; sart, klek, svakelig; vanskelig; delikat, lekker.

delicious [di'liʃəs] delikat, lifllg; yndig; lekker.

delict ['di·likt] lovbrudd.

delight [di'lait] glede, fryd; behag; fryde, glede; glede seg (in ved, over).

delighted [di'laitid] glad, lykkelig, henrykt; **he will be** — **with it** han vil være henrykt over det; **he will be** — **to come** det vil være ham en glede å komme.

delightful [di'laitf(u)l] deilig, yndig, fornøyelig, inntagende; morsom, interessant.

delimit [di'limit] avgrense, sette grenser for. **delineate** [di'linie't] tegne; skildre. **delineation** [di'lini'e'ʃən] tegning; skildring. **delineator** [di·'linie'tə] tegner; skildrer.

delinquency [di'liŋkwənsi] forseelse. **delinquent** [di'liŋkwənt] som forser seg; skyldig, delinkvent.

delirious [di'liriəs] delirerende, fantaserende.

delirium [di'liriəm] fantasering, ørske, villelse, delirium; — **tremens** [di'liriəm'tri·menz] delirium tremens, drankergalskap, dilla.

deliver [di'livə] levere, overlevere, avlevere, overgi; utlevere; slynge ut; befri; redde; forløse; si fram, holde (en tale f. eks.); — **us from evil** fri oss fra det onde.

deliver|ance [di'livərəns] befrielse, redning; forløsning. **-er** [di'livərə] befrier, frelser. **-y** [di'livəri] overlevering; levering; overgivelse; befordring, ombæring (av post), ekspedisjon; befrielse; forløsning, nedkomst; foredrag; **give** — levere.

dell [del] liten dal; dalsøkk.

Delos ['di·lås] Delos.

Delphi ['delfai] Delfi. **Delphian** ['delfiən], **Delphic** ['delfik] delfisk.

delta ['deltə] delta; øyr.

delude [di'l(j)u·d] bedra. **deluder** bedrager. **deluge** ['delju·dʒ] oversvømmelse; syndflod; oversvømme; **the Deluge** syndfloden (bibelsk).

delusion [di'l(j)u·ʒən] blendverk; illusjon, villfarelse; forblindelse, synkverving; optical — synsbedrag. **delusive** [di'l(j)u·siv], **delusory** [di'l(j)u·-səri] skuffende; illusorisk.

delve [delv] grave, spa opp; granske.

dely fk. f. **delivery.**

demagogic(al) ['demə'gådʒik(l), -gågik(l)] demagogisk. **demagogue** ['deməgåg] demagog.

demand [di'ma·nd] fordre, kreve, forlange; spørre; fordring; bønn; spørsmål; etterspørsel; **much in** — meget søkt, etterspurt. **-ant** [di·'ma·ndənt] klager.

demarcation [di·ma·ə'ke'ʃən] avgrensing, grense; **line of** — grenselinje, demarkasjonslinje.

demean [di'mi·n] **oneself** oppføre seg; nedverdige seg, nedlate seg.

demeanour [di'mi·nə] oppførsel, atferd; ytre.

demented [di'mentid] avsindig, tullet.

Demerara [demə'ræ·rə] Demerara.

demerit [di'merit] feil; **merits and -s** fordeler og mangler.

demesne [di'mi·n] doméne, hovedbøle; selveie; **royal** — krongods.

demi ['demi] halv-. **-god** halvgud. **-john** ['demidʒən] damejeanne, demisjang, glassballong med kurvfletning. — **-monde** ['demimånd] demimonde.

demi-rep ['demirep] tvilsom dame.

demise [di'maiz] bortgang, død (fyrstelig); overdraging; tronskifte; avgå ved døden; overdra.

demission [di'miʃən] nedlegging; oppgivelse; abdikasjon; nedverdigelse.

demit [di'mit] oppgi, nedlegge.

demiurge ['demiə·dʒ, 'di·m-] verdensskaper.

demob fk. f. **demobilize.**

demobilization [di·mo^n bilai'ze'ʃen] hjemsending,

demobilisering. **demobilize** [di'mo^n bilaiz] demobilisere, hjemsende.

democracy [di'måkrəsi] demokrati. **democrat** ['demokrät] demokrat. **democratic(al)** [demo·'krätik(l)] demokratisk. **democratize** [di'måkrətaiz] demokratisere.

demography [di'mågrəfi] demografi.

demol|ish [di'måliʃ] rive ned, sløyfe; ødelegge. **-ition** [demo'liʃən] nedriving, sløyfing; ødelegging.

demon ['di·mən] demon, vette, ond ånd, djevel. **demonetize** [di'må·nitaiz] sette penger ut av kurs, inndra.

demoniac [di'mo^n niək], **demoniacal** [di·mo·'naiəkl], **demonic(al)** [di'månik(l)] demonisk, djevelsk; besatt. **demonolatry** [di·mo'nålətri] demondyrking, djevledyrking. **demonology** [di·mo·'nålədʒi] læren om demoner, om djevler.

demonstrable [di'månstrəbl] bevislig. **demonstrate** ['demənstre't] bevise, forevise. **demonstration** [demən'stre'ʃən] bevisføring; bevis; forevisning; tilkjennegivelse av stemning, (offentlig) demonstrasjon. **demonstrative** [di'månstrətiv] klargjørende, som påviser; bevisende; som viser sine følelser, demonstrativ, åpen; påpekende; **not** — tilbakeholdende; **a little too** — **of** affection som viser sin hengivenhet litt for mye. **demonstrator** ['demənstre'tə] demonstrant; prosektor.

demoralization [dimårəlai'ze'ʃən] demoralisasjon. **demoralize** [di'mårəlaiz] demoralisere.

Demosthenes [di'måsþini·z] Demostenes.

demotic [di'måtik] folkelig.

demulcent [di'mʌlsənt] beroligende (legemiddel).

demur [di'mə·] gjøre innsigelse; nære betenkeligheter; nøle, tvile; betenkelighet; tvil; oppsettelse.

demure [di'mjuə] alvorlig; stø; ærbar; from (ofte om disse egenskaper, når de er påtatt).

demurrage [di'mə·ridʒ] overliggedager; overliggedagspenger.

demurrer [di'mə·rə] innsigelse.

demy [di'mai] stipendiat (ved Magdalen College, Oxford); sl. papirformat.

den [den] hule (dyrs); hybel (om værelse).

denarius [di'næ·ə riəs] denar, romersk mynt; penny (fork. **d.**).

denationalize [di'näʃənəlaiz] denasjonalisere.

denature [di'ne'tʃə] denaturere (om sprit).

dendrology [den'drålədʒi] trærnes naturhistorie.

dene [di·n] dyne, sandhaug, klett, sandbakke.

dengue ['dengi] denguefeber (tropefeber).

deniable [di'naiəbl] som kan nektes. **denial** [di'naiəl] nekting, benektelse; fornekting.

denizen ['denizən] naturalisert utlending; borger; naturalisere. **-ship** borgerskap.

Denmark ['denma·ək] Danmark.

denomin|ate [di'nämine't] benevne, kalle, peke. ut. **-ation** [dinåmi'ne'ʃən] benevnelse; sekt; klasse. **-ational** hørende til en sekt el. klasse. **-ative** [di'nåminətiv] benevnende. **-ator** [di'nå·mine'tə] navngiver; nevner (i brøk).

denote [di'no^n t] betegne, merke ut.

denounce [di'nauns] forkynne truende, true med; fordømme, si opp; dra voldsomt til felts mot; angi. **-ment** forkynnelse; anklage. **denouncer** [di'naunsə] forkynner; angiver.

dense [dens] tett. **density** ['densiti] tetthet.

dent [dent] hakk, hull, grop, hult merke, bule, bunk; gjøre hakk (merke) i, slå bule i.

dental ['dentəl] dental, tann-; tannlyd. **dentate** [di'dente't(id)] tannet, takket. **dentifrice** ['dentifris] tannpulver (-krem, -pasta, -vann).

dentist ['dentist] tannlæge. **dentistry** ['dentistri] tannlægevitenskap. **dentition** [den'tiʃən] tennenes frambrudd, tannsprett; tannsystem, tanngard.

denudation [denju'de'ʃən] blotting. **denude** [di'nju·d] blotte, gjøre naken.

denunciation [dinʌnsi'e'ʃən] fordømming; trusel; hard daddel; oppsigelse; angivelse. **denun-**

ciator [di'nʌnsie'tə, -'nʌnʃi-] fordømmer, streng dommer; angiver. **denunciatory** [di'nʌnsiətəri, -'nʌnʃi-] truende; anklagende.
deny [di'nai] nekte; avslå; fornekte.
deodorization [diou'dorai'ze'ʃən] desinfeksjon.
deodorize [di'ouᵘdoraiz] desinfisere, rense.
Deo volente ['di'ouᵘ vo'lenti] om Gud vil.
depart [di'pa·ᵊt] gå bort, reise bort; gå bort, dø; **we cannot — from our rules** avvike fra; — **with** avstå fra. **departed** avdød.
department [di'pa·ᵊtmənt] avdeling; krets; fag; bransje; departement.
departure [di'pa·ᵊtʃə] bortgang; avreise; avvik; død; **a new** — noe ganske nytt, ny framgangsmåte; **next** — neste avgående skip, tog; — **platform** avgangsperrong.
depasture [di'pa·stʃə] (v.) beite.
depend [di'pend] henge ned; komme an på; — **on** avhenge av, bero på; stole på. **dependant** [di'pendənt] undergiven; tilhenger. **dependence** [di'pendəns] avhengighet; sammenheng; tillit; støtte. **dependency** [di'pendənsi] avhengighet; forbindelse; tillit; tilbehør; biland. **dependent** [di'pendənt] nedhengende; avhengig, underordnet; tilhenger.
depict [di'pikt] male; skildre.
depilation [depi'le'ʃən] fjerning av hår. **depilatory** [di'pilətəri] hårfjerningsmiddel.
deplete [di'pli·t] tømme.
depletion [di'pli·ʃən] tømming, uttømming.
deplorable [di'plå·rəbl] beklagelig; sørgelig.
deplore [di'plå·ᵊ] beklage, synes synd i.
deploy [di'ploi] utfolde, deployere; deploycring. **deployment** [-mənt] deployering.
deplume [di'plu·m] plukke, ribbe.
depone [di'poᵘn] bevitne; vitne.
depopulate [di'påpjule't] avfolke. **depcpulation** [dipåpju'le'ʃən] avfolking.
deport [di'på·ᵊt] deportere; — **oneself** oppføre seg, forholde seg. **-ment** [di'på·ᵊtment] holdning; oppførsel; forhold; plastikk; **lessons in** — anstandsøvelser.
deposable [di'poᵘzəbl] avsettelig.
depose [di'poᵘz] avsette; avgi forklaring; vitne.
deposit [di'påzit] nedlegge; avsette, avleire; deponere, anbringe; sette inn (penger); betro; avleiring, grums, berme, bunnfall; betrodd gods, depositum; pant; innskudd. **deposition** [di·po-'ziʃən] avsetning; avleiring; avsettelse; vitnes forklaring. **depository** [di'påzitəri] gjemmested, opplagssted.
depot ['depoᵘ] depot; (amr.) jernbanestasjon.
depravation [diprə've'ʃən, dep-] fordervelse; utarting. **deprave** [di'pre'v] forderve. **depravity** [di'präviti] fordervelse; utarting.
deprecate ['deprike't] be seg fri for, be om befrielse fra; avverge; være meget imot; frabe seg. **deprecation** [depri'ke'ʃən] bønn om befrielse, om tilgivelse; innvending; misbilligelse. **deprecative** ['deprike'tiv] bedende; unnskyldende. **deprecator** ['deprike'tə] en s. ber seg fri el. er imot. **deprecatory** [deprike'təri] bedende, bønnlig.
depreciate [di'pri·ʃie't] nedsette, forringe; undervurdere; falle i verdi. **depreciation** [dipri·ʃi-'e'ʃən] nedsetting, forringelse; undervurdering. **depreciative** [di'pri·ʃiativ] nedsettende. **depreciatory** [di'pri·ʃiətəri] nedsettende.
depredate ['depride't] plyndre; herje. **depredation** [depri'de'ʃən] plyndring. **depredator** ['depride'tə] plyndrer. **depredatory** [di'predətəri] plyndrende, herjende, rans-.
depress [di'pres] trykke ned; trykke; nedslå; tynge ned. **-ion** [di'preʃən] nedtrykking; senkning; depresjon. **-ive** [di'presiv] trykkende, tyngende. **-or** [di'presə] nedtrykker, undertrykker.
deprivable [di'praivəbl] som kan berøves. **deprivation** [depri've'ʃən] berøvelse; tap, avsetting.
deprive [di'praiv] berøve; avsette; — **him of it** berøve ham for det.
dept. fk. f. **department.**

depth [depþ] dybde; dyp; **in the — of night** midt på natten; **in the — of winter** midt på vinteren, på svarteste vinteren; **swim beyond one's** — svømme lenger ut enn man kan bunne. — **-charge** dypvannsbombe.
depurate [di'pjuəre't, 'depjure't] lutre, rense, renske. **depuration** [depju're'ʃən] lutring. **depuratory** [di'pjuərətəri] rensende.
deputation [depju'te'ʃən] beskikkelse; sending med fullmakt, sendelag, deputasjon; beskikke.
depute [di'pju·t] velge, kåre, gi fullmakt.
deputy ['depjuti] representant, målsmann, varamann, (i smstn. vara-, vise-); fullmektig.
De Quincey [di'kwinsi] De Quincey.
derail [di're'l] avspore; gå av sporet. **-ment** avsporing.
derange [di're'n(d)ʒ] forvirre, forstyrre; gjøre sinnsforvirret. **-ment** [di're'n(d)ʒmənt] forvirring, forstyrrelse; sinnsforvirring.
Derby ['da·əbi] Derby; **the — races** Derbyveddeløpene (ved Epsom, sør for London, innstiftet av en jarl av Derby).
derelict ['derilikt] forlatt, folketom; herreløst gods; menneskevrak. **-ion** [deri'likʃən] oppgivelse.
deride [di'raid] håne, spotte, gjøre narr av. **derider** spotter. **derision** [di'riʒən] bespottelse, hån. **derisive** [di'raisiv], **derisory** [di'raisəri] spottende.
derivable [di'raivəbl] som kan avledes. **derivation** [deri've'ʃən] avledning; utledning; **derivative** [di'rivətiv] avledet; noe avledet; avledning.
derive [di'raiv] avlede, utlede; motta, få.
derm [də·m] hud, underhud.
dermatology [də·mə'tålədʒi] dermatologi.
derogate ['deroge't] svekke, innskrenke; nedsette; utarte; — **from oneself** nedverdige seg. **derogation** [dero'ge'ʃən] innskrenking; forkleinelse, nedsetting. **derogatory** [di'rågətəri] innskrenkende; forkleinende, nedsettende.
derrick ['derik] lastebom, lastekran.
derringer ['derin(d)ʒə] lommepistol.
dervish ['də·viʃ] dervisj.
descant ['deskänt] diskant, variasjon; utvikling, utlegging. **descant** [di'skänt] synge variasjoner over; utbre seg, legge (omstendelig) ut.
descend [di'send] gå ned; synke; flyte. strømme med; komme ned. gå ned, stige ned; gjøre landgang; nedlate seg; nedstamme; — **upon** slå ned på, angripe voldsomt; **be -ed from** nedstamme fra, ætte fra. **-ant** [di'sendənt] etterkommer. **-ent** [di'sendənt] nedstigende; nedstammende. **-ibility** [disendi'biliti] arvelighet. **-ible** [di'sendibl] framkommelig; arvelig. **descension** [di'senʃən] nedstigning; forfall. **descent** [di'sent] nedstigning; landgang; (fiendes) innfall; herkomst, avstamning, ætt; avkom; grad, trin.
describable [di'skraibəbl] beskrivelse.
describe [di'skraib] beskrive. **description** [di·'skripʃən] beskrivelse; beskaffenhet; art, slag.
descriptive [di'skriptiv] beskrivende.
descry [di'skrai] øyne; oppdage.
Desdemona [dezdi'moᵘnə] Desdemona.
desecrate ['desikre't] vanhellige. **desecration** [desi'kre'ʃən] vanhelligelse, vanhelging.
desert ['dezət] øde; ørken, ubebodd sted.
desert [di'zə·t] forlate; falle fra; desertere.
desert [di'zə·t] fortjeneste.
deserter [di'zə·tə] frafallen; rømling, desertør.
desertion [di'zə·ʃən] frafall; desertering.
deserve [di'zə·v] fortjene; gjøre seg fortjent. **deservedly** [di'zə·vidli] fortjent, med rette. **deserving** [di'zə·viŋ] fortjent; verdig.
deshabille ['dezäbi·l] neglisjé.
desiccate ['desike't] tørre; tørke. **desiccation** [desi'ke'ʃən] uttørring, tørk. **desiccative** ['desike'tiv] tørrende, tørk tørrende middel.
desiderate [di'zidəre't] savne; ønske. **desideratum** [dizidə're'təm] savn; ønske; noe som var å ønske.

design [di'zain] gjøre utkast, tegne; skissere; legge plan til; tenke ut; bestemme; spekulere; tegning; plan, mønster; forehavende, hensikt. **-able** [di'zainəbl] bestemmelig, påviselig, kjennelig; merkelig. **designate** ['dezigne¹t] betegne, bestemme, merke ut, utpeke (**to, for** til). **designate** ['dezignét] utpekt, utvalt. **designation** [dezig'ne¹ʃən] betegnelse, bestemmelse. **designative** ['dezigne¹tiv] betegnende; bestemmende. **designedly** [di'zainidli] med vilje. **designer** [di'zainə] tegner, konstruktør, en som legger planer; renkesmed. **designing** [di'zainiŋ] listig, renkefull, lumsk, falsk, slu.

desilverize [di·'silvəraiz] ta sølvet av.

desirability [dizairə'biliti] ønskelighet. **desirable** [di'zairəbl] attråverdig, ønskelig. **-ness** [di'zairəblnés] ønskelighet. **desire** [di'zaiə] forlangende, begjæring, ønske; attrå; bønn; forlange, begjære, be, ønske, attrå. **desirous** [di'zairəs] begjærlig (**of** etter); ønskende.

desist [di'zist] avstå (**from** fra); stanse opp (**from** med).

desk [desk] pult; kateter; lesepult; prekestol. **desolate** ['desolét] ubebodd, øde, forlatt; ensom; ulykkelig. **desolate** ['desole¹t] avfolke, snøye, ødelegge. **desolation** [deso'le¹ʃən] avfolking; ødelegging; ørken; trøstesløshet; forlatthet, ensomhet. **despair** [di'spæ·ə] fortvilelse; fortvile; oppgi håpet (**of** om). **-ingly** [di'spæ·ərinₗli] fortvilet. **despatch** [di'spätʃ] se **dispatch.** **desperado** [despə're¹do⁰] vågehals, uvøre. **desperate** ['desp(ə)rét] fortvilet; dumdristig; uvøren. **desperation** [despə're¹ʃən] fortvilelse. **despicable** ['despikəbl] foraktelig, låk. **despise** [dè'spaiz] forakte. **despiser** foraktar. **despite** [dè'spait] ondskap; tross; **in** — **of** til tross for, trass i; **in one's own** — mot ens egen vilje. **despite** [dè'spait] (prep.) tross, trass i. **despoil** [di'spoil] plyndre. **-er** [di'spoilə] plyndrer. **despoliation** [dispo⁰li'e¹ʃən] plyndring.

despond [di'spånd] fortvile, oppgi håpet. **-ency** [di'spåndənsi] håpløshet, vonløyse, fortvilelse; motfallenhet. **-ent** [di'spåndənt] fortvilet; motfallen.

despot ['despåt] enevoldshersker, despot. **despotic(al)** [de'spåtik(l)] despotisk. **despotism** ['despətizm] despotisme.

desquamation [deskwa·me¹ʃən] avskalling.

dessert [di'zə·t] dessert, knask.

destination [desti'ne¹ʃən] bestemmelse; bestemmelsessted. **destine** ['destin] bestemme, etle. **destiny** ['destini] skjebne, lagnad; i flertall ogs. skjebnegudinner; norner.

destitute ['destitjut] blottet (**of** for) fattig. **destitution** [desti'tju·ʃən] fattigdom, armod, skort. **destroy** [dè'stroi] ødelegge. **-er** [dè'stroiə] ødelegger; torpedojager.

destructible [di'strʌktibl] forgjengelig. **destruction** [di'strʌkʃən] ødelegging; undergang. **destructive** [di'strʌktiv] ødeleggende, skadelig. **destructor** [di'strʌktə] forbrenningsovn.

desudation [dis(j)u·de¹ʃən] svetting.

desuetude ['di'sju·itju·d, 'deswitjud, 'di·switjud] glemsel, det å gå av bruk; **fall into** — gå av bruk.

desultoriness ['desəltərinés] planløshet. **-y** ['desəltəri] planløs, springende, spredt; flyktig. **detach** [di'tätʃ] skille, avsondre; sende, detasjere. **detached** avsondret, frittliggende. — **house** enebolig. **detachment** [di'tätʃmənt] atskillelse; avsondring; løsrivelse; fri stilling; detasjement.

detail [di'te¹l] fortelle omstendelig, berette inngående om; beordre til særtjeneste. **detail** ['di·te¹l] detalj, enkelthet; omstendelig beretning; soldater uttatt til særtjeneste; **in** — punkt for punkt; **go into -s** gå i detaljer. **-ed** [di'te¹ld] omstendelig, utførlig, detaljert.

detain [di'te¹n] forholde; holde tilbake; oppholde; holde i forvaring, holde fengslet. **-ee** [dite¹n'i·] bet. for personer (f. eks. Sir Oswald

Mosley) som ble tatt i forvaring ved krigsutbruddet. **-er** [di'te¹nə] en som holder tilbake; tilbakeholdelse. **-ment** [di'te¹nmənt] tilbakeholdelse.

detect [di'tekt] oppdage; spore opp. **-ion** [di'tekʃən] oppdagelse. **-ive** [di'tektiv] oppdagelsesbetjent, oppdager; oppdagelses-. **-or** [di'tektə] oppdager, .detektor.

detent [di'tent] stopper. **detention** [di'tenʃən] tilbakeholdelse; forvaring, arrest.

deter [di'tə·] avskrekke, skremme. **detergent** [di'tə·dʒənt] rensende middel. **deteriorate** [di'tiəriəre¹t] forringe; bli forringet. **deterioration** [di'tiəriə're¹ʃən] forringelse. **determinable** [di'tə·minəbl] som kan bestemmes. **determinant** [di'tə·minənt] bestemmende. **determinate** [di'tə·minét] bestemt. **determination** [dita·mi'ne¹ʃən] bestemmelse; avgjørelse, mening, forsett; bestemthet; — **of blood to the head** blodstigning til hodet. **determine** [di'tə·min] bestemme; avgjøre; beslutte. **determinism** [di'tə·minizm] determinisme. **determinist** [-ist] determinist.

deterrent [di'terənt] avskrekkende; avskrekkende middel.

detersive [di'tə·siv] rensende.

detest [di'test] avsky. **-able** [-əbl] avskyelig. **-ation** [di·tes'te¹ʃən] avsky.

dethrone [di'bro⁰nənt] styrte fra tronen; avsette. **-ment** [di'bro⁰nmənt] detronisering; avsetting.

detonate ['detone¹t] eksplodere; knalle; la eksplodere. **detonation** [deto'ne¹ʃən] detonasjon, eksplosjon; knall.

detour ['de¹tuə, de''tuə, di'tuə] omvei, krok.

detract [di'träkt] ta bort; — **from** nedsette, forringe. **-ion** [di'träkʃən] forringelse; baktalelse. **detractor** [di'träktə] bakvasker. **-ory** [di'träktəri] nedsettende, baktalersk.

detrain [di'tre¹n] få ut av toget; gå av toget.

detriment ['detrimənt] skade. **detrimental** [detri'mentl] skadelig.

detrition [di'triʃən] avsliting, avskuring.

deuce [dju·s] to (i spill); stå likt (i tennis); fanden, pokker. **deuced** [dju·sid] fandens, pokkers. **Deut.** fk. f. **Deuteronomy.**

deuteronomy [dju·tə'rånəmi] femte mosebok. **devastate** ['devəste¹t] ødelegge, herje. **devastation** [devə'ste¹ʃən] ødelegging.

develop [di'veləp] utvikle, utfolde; framkalle (et fotografi); utvikle seg; bli synlig. **-ment** [di'veləpmənt] utvikling, utfolding; (fotografisk) framkalling.

deviate ['di·vie¹t] avvike; forse seg. **deviation** [di·vi'e¹ʃən] avvikelse; avvik; villfarelse; deviasjon.

device [di'vais] oppfinnelse, påfunn; plan; list; motto, valgspråk; fyndord; devise, merke; **leave him to his own -s** la ham seile sin egen sjø.

devil ['devl] djevel, demon; ondskapsfull, ondsinnet, snedig, listig menneske (el. dyr); forkommen stakkar; volfemaskin; sterkt krydret kjøttrett, sterkt krydderi; visergutt (i trykkeri) (ogs. printer's —); — **a bit** aldri det grann; **the** — **you did** (nei) så fanden om du gjorde; **between the** — **and the deep sea** mellom barken og veden; **give the** — **his due** gjøre rett og skjel; **beat the -'s tattoo** tromme (el. trampe) som besatt; **a** — **of** a fellow en fandens fyr; — **a one** ikke en eneste (sjel); **the** — **on two sticks** djevlespill; **play the** — **with** gjøre kål på; **devil-may-care** ['devl-me¹'kæ·ə] fandenivoldsk; **devil** krydre sterkt og steike; volfe. **-ish** ['devliʃ] djevelsk, fandens. **-ment** ['devlmənt] djevelskap; djevelsk strek. **-ry** ['devlri] djevelskap.

devious ['di·vjəs] avvikende; forkjært; villsom. **devise** [di'vaiz] finne opp, opptenke, tenke ut; overveie; testamentere; testamente, arv, legat. **devisee** [divai'zi·] arving (etter testamente). **devisor** [devi'zå·ə, di'vaizå·ə] arvelater.

devitalize [di·'vaitəlaiz] ta livslysten fra.

devoid [di'void] fri, blottet (**of** for).

devolution [devo'l(j)u·ʃən] overgang (**on** til), overføring, hjemfall. **devolve** [di'vålv] rulle fram, rulle ned; overdra (**on** til); gå i arv (**on** til), tilfalle; **it -s upon me to** det påhviler (el. faller på) meg å.
Devon ['devn] Devon. **Devonian** [di'voᵘnjən] devonisk.
Devonshire ['devnʃə] Devonshire.
devote [di'vout] hellige, hengi, vie. **devoted** [di'voᵘtid] vigd til undergang, ulykkelig; hengiven; selvoppofrende. **devotedness** [di'voᵘtidnės] hengivenhet, oppofring. **devotee** [devoᵘ'ti·, devo'ti·] en som helliger seg til noe; hengehode, svermer, tilbeder. **devotion** ['divoᵘʃən] innvielse; hengivelse, oppofrelse; hengivenhet; fromhet; andakt, gudsfrykt. **devotional** [di'voᵘʃənl] andektig, gudelig, oppbyggelig. **devotionalism** [di'voᵘʃənəlism] tilbøyelighet til overdreven hengivelse, skinnhellighet. **devotions** [di'vouʃənz] andaktsøvinger, andakt.
devour [di'vauə] sluke, kjøre i seg.
devout [di'vaut] from, religiøs; andektig; oppriktig.
dew [dju·] dugg, dogg; dogge. **mountain** — whisky, som er brent i smug. — **-berry** en slags bjørnebær. **-fall** doggfall. — **-lap** kjøttlapp. — **-point** doggpunkt.
dexterity [deks'teriti] hendighet, ferdighet, godt lag. **dexterous** ['dekst(ə)rəs] hendig, hag, god, øvet; listig.
dextrin(e) ['dekstrin] dekstrin.
dextrose ['dekstroᵘs] druesukker.
dey [deⁱ] dei (tyrkisk guvernør).
D. F. C. fk. f. **Distinguished Flying Cross.**
D. F. M. fk. f. **Distinguished Flying Medal.**
D. G. fk. f. **Dei Gratia** av Guds nåde; **Dragoon Guards.**
dg fk. f. **decigram.**
diabetes [daiə'bi·tiz] sukkersyke.
diabolic(al) [daiə'bålik(l)] djevelsk.
diabolo [di'äboloᵘ] djevlespill.
diadem ['daiədem] diadem.
diagnose [daiəg'noᵘz] diagnostisere. **diagnosis** [daiəg'noᵘsis] diagnose. **diagnostic** [daiəg'nåstik] diagnostisk; kjennetegn (på en sykdom), symptom. **diagnosticate** [daiəg'nåstikeⁱt] diagnostisere.
diagonal [dai'ägənəl] diagonal.
diagram ['daiəgräm] diagram, riss, figur.
dial ['daiəl] solskive, solur; urskive, skive (f. eks. på automatisk telefon); (sl.) ansikt; måle, vise med en skive; dreie (et telefonnummer).
dialect ['daiəlekt] dialekt, målføre. **dialectal** [daiə'lektl] dialektisk. **dialectic(al)** [daiə'lektik(l)] dialektisk, som hører til en dialekt el. til dialektikken. **dialectician** [daiəlek'tiʃən] dialektiker. **dialectics** [daiə'lektiks] dialektikk.
dialogue ['daiəlåg] samtale, dialog.
diameter [dai'ämitə] diameter, tverrmål. **diametral** [dai'ämitrəl] diametral. **diametrical** [daiə'metrikl] diametrisk; diametral. **diametrically opposite** diametralt motsatt.
diamond ['dai(ə)mənd] diamant; ruter (i kortspill); — **cut** — hauk over hauk; **black -s** svarte diamanter: steinkull; **king of -s** ruter konge. **-cutter** diamantsliper. — **wedding** diamantbryllup.
Diana [dai'änə] Diana.
diapason [daiə'peⁱzən] oktav; omfang (av stemme, instrument); tonehøyde, kammertone; stemmegaffel.
diaper ['daiəpə] dreiel; bleie; veve figurer inn i; ta bleie på.
diaphanous [dai'äfənəs] gjennomsiktig.
diaphragm ['daiəfrəm] mellomgulv; skillevegg; hinne. **-atic** [daiəfräg'mätik] mellomgulvs-.
diarist ['daiərist] dagboksforfatter.
diarrhoea [daiə'ri·ə] diaré, magesyke.
diary ['daiəri] dagbok.
diastole [dai'ästəli] utviding (av hjertet).
diatonic [daiə'tånik] diatonisk.
diatribe ['daiətraib] vidløftig avhandling, lang lekse; heftig utfall.
dibble ['dibl] plantestikke; gjøre huller i; plante.
dice [dais] (plur. av **die**) terninger; spille med terninger. — **-box** terningbeger. **dicer** ['daisə] terningspiller.
dichotomy [dai'kåtomi] tvedeling.
Dick [dik] Dick (fk. f. **Richard**).
dick [dik]: **take one's** — sverge (**to** på); **up to** — med på notene, gløgg.
Dickens ['dikinz] Dickens.
dickens ['dikinz] fanden, pokker.
dickey el. **dicky** ['diki] tjenersete på en vogn; baksete; skjortebryst; liten fugl; dårlig; ussel.
dictaphone ['diktəfoᵘn] diktafon.
dictate [dik'teⁱt] diktere; si til; befale. **dictate** ['diktėt] befaling, påbud. **dictation** [dik'teⁱʃən] diktat. **dictator** [dik'teⁱtə] diktator. **dictatorial** [diktə'tå·riəl] diktatorisk. **dictatorship** [dik'teitəʃip] diktatur.
diction ['dikʃən] stil, språk, diksjon.
dictionary ['dikʃənəri] ordbok, leksikon.
dictograph ['diktəgra·f] diktograf, diktafon.
dictum ['diktəm] utsagn; (jur.) betenkning.
did [did] imperf. av **do.**
didactic [di'däktik] belærende, didaktisk; — **poem** læredikt. **didactics** pedagogikk.
diddle ['didl] dingle, vakle, stavre; skake, riste; sumle, søle; snyte; snyteri. — **-daddle** snikksnakk. **diddler** ['didlə] plattenslager.
didn't ['didnt] **did not.**
Dido ['daidoᵘ] Dido.
dido ['daidoᵘ] puss, spikk, strek; **cut up -es** gjøre mudder, holde leven.
die [dai] dø; omkomme; visne; dø bort, opphøre; **be dying** holde på å dø, ligge for døden, være døden nær; — **of illness** dø av sykdom; — **by the sword** falle for sverdet; **be dying for** lengte seg i hjel etter; — **in harness** arbeide like inn i døden; **do and** — handle og dø; **never say** — frisk mot!
die [dai] (i plur.: **dice**) terning; (i plur.: **dies**) myntstempel; **the** — **is cast** terningene er kastet.
die-hard ['daiha·ᵊd] stri, en som motstår tvang til det ytterste (om Ulster-unionistene).
diet ['daiət] riksdag, riksforsamling, ting.
diet ['daiət] kost, diét; holde med kosten; sette på diét; spise; holde diét.
dietary ['daiətəri] forpleinings-, diet-; kost, diét.
dietetic [daiə'tetik] dietetisk. **dietetics** dietetikk.
differ ['difə] være forskjellig, være ulik, avvike; være av forskjellig mening.
difference ['dif(ə)rəns] forskjell, forskjellighet, ulikskap; avvikelse; uenighet; stridspunkt.
different ['dif(ə)rənt] forskjellig (**from** fra), ulik.
differential [difə'renʃəl] differensial.
differentiate [dif(ə)'renʃieⁱt] differensiere.
difficult ['difikəlt] vanskelig, vrang. **difficulty** ['difikəlti] vanskelighet, vanske; forlegenhet.
diffidence ['difidəns] mistro, mistillit; fryktsomhet, mangel på selvtillit. **diffident** ['difidənt] mistroisk (**of** like overfor); forknytt, redd av seg.
difform [di'få·ᵊm] uregelmessig.
diffuse [di'fju·z] utøse; utbre; spre. **diffuse** [di'fju·s] spredt, utspredt; vidløftig. **diffusible** [di'fju·zibl] flyktig. **diffusion** [di'fju·ʒən] spredning; utbredelse. **diffusive** [di'fju·siv] spredende seg; utbredt; vidløftig. **diffusiveness** [di'fju·sivnės] utstrakthet; utbredelse; vidløftighet.
dig [dig] i uttrykket **infra dig.** fk. f. infra dignitatem (latin), under ens verdighet.
dig [dig] grave; terpe; graving; støt; dult; terping.
digest ['daidʒest] oversikt; lovbok.
digest [d(a)i'dʒest] ordne; fordøye, melte; la seg fordøye; modnes. **digester** [d(a)i'dʒestə] en som ordner; fordøyelsesmiddel; digestor; Papins gryte. **digestible** [d(a)i'dʒestibl] fordøyelig. **digestion** [d(a)i'dʒestʃən] ordning; fordøyelse; digestion, digerering; modning; forståelse. **digestive** [d(a)i'dʒestiv] som fremmer, er god for fordøyelsen;

(i kjemi) digererende; digestiv, middel, som fremmer fordøyelsen, modningen.
digger ['digə] graver; gullgraver. **digging** ['digiŋ] graving; gullgraving; bolig, losji.
dight [dait] sette i stand; smykke.
digit ['didʒit] tå, finger (i zoologi); fingerbredde; siffer, tall. **digitalis** ['didʒi'te'lis] revebjelle, digitalis. **digitigrade** ['didʒitigre'd] tågjenger.
dignification [dignifi'ke'ən] opphøyelse. **dignified** ['dignifaid] opphøyd; verdig. **dignify** ['dignifai] opphøye; utmerke, hedre, bære. **dignitary** ['dignitəri] høy geistlig, høy embetsmann, dignitar. **dignity** ['digniti] høyhet; verdighet, rang, embete.
digraph ['daigra·f, 'daigräf] to bokstaver for én lyd (f. eks. rd for tykk l).
digress [di'gres, dai-] avvike; komme bort fra emnet; skeie ut. **digression** [di'greʃən, dai-] digresjon, avvikelse. **digressive** [di'gresiv, dai-] vikende bort fra, skeiende ut fra, side-.
digs [digz] bolig, losji, hybel.
dike [daik] dike, dam, demning; grav, grøft; åre (i mineralogi); demme inn; grøfte ut.
dilapidat|e [di'läpide't] fare ille med, forsømme, vanskjøtte. **-ed** [di'läpide'tid] forsømt, forfallen, skrøpelig. **-ion** [diläpi'de'ʃən] brøstfeldighet, forfall.
dilatability [d(a)ile'tə'biliti] utvidingsevne. **dilatable** [d(a)i'le'təbl] utvidelig. **dilatation** [dailə-'te'ʃən] utvidelse, utviding. **dilate** [d(a)i'le't] utvide, tøye; utvide seg; tøye seg; utvikle vidløftig. **dilation** [d(a)i'le'ʃən] utvidelse. **dilatory** ['dilətəri] nølende; forhalende.
dilemma [d(a)i'lemə] dilemma; forlegenhet.
dilettante ['dilé'tänti] pl. **dilettanti** [-ti·] dilettant. **dilettantism** [dilé'täntizm] dilettanteri.
diligence ['dilidʒəns] flid; diligence.
diligent ['dilidʒənt] flittig.
dill [dil] dill.
dilly-dally ['dili'däli fjase; somle, gå og slenge.
diluent ['diljuənt] fortynnende; fortynnende middel. **dilute** [di'l(j)u·t] fortynne, spe opp, vanne ut; la seg fortynne; fortynnet. **dilution** [di'l(j)u·ʃən, dai-] fortynning.
diluvi|al [d(a)i'l(j)u·vjəl] diluvial, oversvømmelses-, flom-. **-an** [d(a)i'l(j)u·vjən] storflod-, syndflods-.
dim [dim] dim, mørk, dunkel, matt, svak; formørke, dimme.
dim. fk. f. diminuendo, diminutive.
dime [daim] tiendedel av en dollar, ticent.
dimension [d(a)i'menʃən] dimensjon, omfang, vidde, mål.
dimidiate [d(a)i'midiét] halvert, halvt.
diminish [di'miniʃ] forminske, minke på; forminskes, minke. **-able** [di'miniʃəbl] som kan forminskes.
diminuendo [diminju'endo⁰] diminuendo.
diminution [dimi'nju·ʃən] forminskelse, mink, minking. **diminutive** [di'minjutiv] ørliten; forminskelsesord, diminutiv.
dimissory [di'misəri] dimisjons-, avgangs-.
dimity ['dimiti] slags blomstret bomullstøy.
dimple ['dimpl] liten fordypning, dokk, smilehull, kløft i haken; krusning; danne små fordypninger; kruse; kruse seg. **dimpled** med smilehull. **dimply** ['dimpli] med små fordypninger, med smilehull, kruset.
din [din] larm, drønn, brak; bedøve ved støy; dønne, brake. — **st. into sb.** hamre noe inn i en.
Dinah ['dainə] Dina.
dine [dain] spise middag; — **off** (on) få .... til middag. **diner** ['dainə] middagsgjest; **diner -out** en som ofte spiser ute, selskapsmann.
ding [diŋ] slå, kaste; banke; larme; ringe. **ding-dong** [diŋ'däŋ] klingklang, dingdang.
dingey el. **dinghy** ['diŋgi] jolle.
dinginess ['din(d)ʒinés] mørke, mørk farge, mørkebrunt; skitt, saur, smussighet.

dingle ['diŋgl] dal, dalsøkk.
dingo ['diŋgo⁰] vill hund (i Australia).
dingy ['din(d)ʒi] mørk, mørkebrun, skitten.
dingy ['diŋgi] jolle.
dining-car ['daininka·ə] spisevogn.
dining-room ['daininrum] spisestue.
dining-table ['daininte'bl] spisebord.
dinky ['diŋki] nett, pen, fin, lekker.
dinner ['dinə] middag, middagsmat; — **-jacket** smoking; — **party** middagsselskap.
dint [dint] merke av slag el. støt, hakk, bunk; gjøre bulet; **by** — **of** ved hjelp av.
diocesan [dai'ásisən] som hører til bispedømme, stifts-.
diocese ['daiəsis] stift, bispedømme.
Dionysus [daiə'naisəs] Dionysos.
dioptric [dai'áptrik] dioptrisk. **dioptrics** [dai-'áptriks] dioptrikk, læren om lysets brytning.
diorama [daiə'ra·mə, 'daiərə·mə] diorama.
dip [dip] dyppe; øse; farge; støpe lys; låre flagg, dukke; synke, skråne, helle ned; kikke på, bla igjennom, trenge inn i; dukkert; dypping; helling, hall; magnetnålens inklinasjon; talglys. — **of the horizon** (**needle**) kimmingdaling.
dipetalous [dai'petələs] tobladet.
diphtheria [dif'þiəriə] difteri. **diphtheritic** [difþe-'ritik] difterittisk.
diphthong ['difþäŋ, 'dipþäŋ] tvelyd, diftong.
diploma [di'plo⁰mə] diplom. **diplomacy** [di-'plo⁰məsi] diplomati. **diplomat** ['diplomät] diplomat. **diplomatic** [diplo'mätik] diplomatisk. **diplomatics** [diplo'mätik, diplomvitenskap. **diplomatist** [di'plo⁰mətist] diplomat.
dipper ['dipə] dykker; bademann; gjendøper; sleiv, øse; fossekall; lommetyv; (amr.) **big** — Store bjørn; **little** — Lille bjørn.
dipping-needle inklinasjonsnål.
dipsomania [dipso'me'njə] drikkesyke.
dipter ['diptə] pl. **diptera** ['diptərə] tovinget insekt. **dipteral** ['diptərəl] tovinget. **dipterous** ['diptərəs] tovinget.
dire [daiə] skrekkelig, sørgelig, fæl. **-ful** ['daiəf(u)l] skrekkelig, sørgelig. **-ness** ['daiənés] skrekkelighet, gru.
direct [di'rekt, dai-] ben, bein, rett, rak, strak; direkte, uten omvei el. stans; umiddelbar; endefram; rette, styre, rettleie, anvise; by, befale, gi ordre; adressere; anordne.
direction [di'rekʃən, dai-] retning; ledelse; direksjon, styre, styring; anvisning; adresse. — **-post** veiviser. **directive** [di'rektiv, dai-] ledende, som rettleier. **directly** [di'rektli, dai-] direkte; umiddelbart, straks; så snart som, med det samme. **directness** [di'rektnés, dai-] benhet; umiddelbarhet. **director** [di'rektə] leder; veileder; bestyrer, direktør. **directorate** [di'rektərét] direktorat, styre. **directorial** [direk'tá·riəl, dai-] ledende el. direktorial-. **directory** [di'rektəri] veiledende; adressebok, katalog, veiviser. **directress** [di'rektrés], **directrix** [di'rektriks] bestyrerinne, direktrise.
direful ['daiəful] fæl, skrekkelig.
dirge [də·dʒ] klagesang, sørgesang.
dirk [də·k] dolk; dolke.
dirt [də·t] smuss, skitt, lort; boss. — **-cheap** for røverkjøp. **-iness** [də·tinés] smussighet; skittenhet, tarvelighet. — **track** «sølebane» (til motorsykkelveddeløp). **dirty** ['də·ti] skitten, sølet; skitne, rakke til; bli sølet.
dis|ability [disə'biliti] svakhet; udugelighet, mangel på evne; inhabilitet. **-able** [dis'e'bl] gjøre udugelig, gjøre ufør til strid, gjøre til krøpling; avkrefte, lamme; **disabled soldier** krigsinvalid, stridsudyktig. **-ablement** [dis'e'blmənt] udyktiggjøring; hjelpeløshet; vanførhet; ukampdyktighet.
disabuse [disə'bju·z] bringe ut av villfarelse.
disaccustom [disə'kʌstəm] venne av.
disacknowledge [disək'nälidʒ] fornekte.
disadvantage [disəd'va·ntidʒ] skade, lyte,

ulempe, uheldig forhold; tap. **disadvantageous** [disädvən'te¹dʒəs] ufordelaktig, ulaglig.

disaffect [disə'fekt] gjøre utilfreds, vekke misnøye. **-ion** [disə'fekʃən] utilfredshet, misnøye.

disaffirm [disə'fə·m] nekte, si mot, avsanne; kullkaste.

disagree [disə'gri·] være uenig, ikke stemme overens; bekomme ille, ikke ha godt av (om mat og drikke). **disagreeable** [disə'gri·əbl] ubehagelig. **disagreement** [disə'gri·mənt] uoverensstemmelse; uenighet; misforståelse.

disallow [disə'lau, 'disə'lau] forkaste; misbillige. **-ance** [disə'lauəns] forkasting; misbilligelse.

disappear [disə'piə] forsvinne, komme bort. **disappearance** [disə'piərəns] forsvinning.

disappoint [disə'point] skuffe (**in** i), svike, narre (of for). **disappointment** [disə'pointmənt] feilslått håp, skuffelse, vonbrott.

disappreciate [disə'pri·ʃie¹t] undervurdere.

disapprobation [disäpro'be¹ʃən] misbilligelse. **disapprobatory** ['disäpro'be¹təri] misbilligende.

disapproval [disə'pru·vəl] misbilligelse. **disapprove** [disə'pru·v] misbillige, mislike.

disarm [dis'a·°m, diz-] avvæpne, desarmere. **disarmament** [dis'a·°məmənt] avvæpning, desarmering, nedrusting.

disarrange [disə're¹n(d)ʒ] bringe i uorden, skiple. **-ment** [disə're¹n(d)ʒmənt] uorden, ugreie, forvirring.

disarray [disə're¹] avkle; løse opp, bringe i uorden; uorden, forvirring; neglisjé.

disassociate [disə'souʃie¹t] atskille.

disaster [diz'a·stə] ulykke. **disastrous** [diz-'a·strəs] ulykkelig, sørgelig.

disavow [disə'vau, 'disə'vau] desavouere; fragå. **disavowal** [disə'vauəl] desavouering.

disband [dis'bänd] gi avskjed, avskjedige; sende hjem; oppløse seg. **-ment** hjemsending.

disbelief [disbi'li·f] vantro, tvil.

disbelieve [disbi'li·v, 'disbi'li·v] ikke tro, tvile på. **-r** [-ə] en som ikke tror; vantro.

disbranch [dis'bra·nʃ] brekke greinene av; hogge av.

disburden [dis'bə·dn] fri for en byrde; lette.

disburse [dis'bə·s], betale ut. **disbursement** [dis-'bə·smənt] utbetaling, uttelling.

disc [disk] se **disk**.

discard [dis'ka·əd] kaste (i kortspill); kassere, vrake; avsette, avskjedige; **-ed theory** forlatt teori.

discern [di'zə·n] skjelne; skjønne; oppdage, bli var. **discernible** [di'zə·nibl] som kan skjelnes. **discerning** [di'zə·niŋ] forstandig; skarpsindig, gløgg. **discernment** [di'zə·nmənt] skjelning; dømmekraft; skarpsindighet, gløggskap.

discharge [dis'tʃa·°dʒ] lesse av; losse; avfyre; gi fra seg; frikjenne; frigi; løslate; gi avskjed; utføre; oppfylle; betale; kvittere; bortskaffe, fjerne; avkaste en byrde, lette seg; avlessing; lossing; avfyring, salve; fjerning; avskjedigelse; befrielse, løslating, frikjenning; frigivelse, avmønstring; oppfylling; betaling; kvittering.

disciform ['disifä·°m] skiveformet.

disciple [di'saipl] disippel. **discipleship** [di-'saiplʃip] disiplers stilling el. forhold.

disciplinable ['disiplinəbl] mottagelig, lærvillig; straffskyldig. **disciplinarian** [disipli'næ·°riən] disiplinær; læremester, tuktemester. **disciplinary** ['disiplinəri] disiplinær. **discipline** ['disiplin] undervisning; kunst; disiplin, mannstukt; fag; undervise; disiplinere; tukte; holde i age.

disclaim [dis'kle¹m] ikke erkjenne; fralegge seg; forkaste; frasi seg. **disclaimer** [dis'kle¹mə] forkaster; fraleggelse; avkall; fornekting.

disclose [dis'klo°z] åpne; oppdage; åpenbare; åpne seg. **disclosure** [dis'klo°ʒə] åpning; åpenbaring; oppdaging.

discoloration [diskʌlə're¹ʃən, -kål-] fargeskifte; flekk. **discolour** [dis'kʌlə] gi annen farge, forandre fargen; farge av; sette flekker på.

discomfit [dis'kʌmfit] slå på flukt; skuffe; gjøre det av med; gjøre motløs, gjøre ulykkelig, forfjamse. **-ure** [dis'kʌmfitʃə] nederlag; forvirring; forstyrrelse; skuffelse, uhell.

discomfort [dis'kʌmfət] ubehagelighet, bry, sorg, plage; gjøre urolig.

discommend [diskə'mend]· dadle, misbillige, laste.

discompose [diskəm'po°z] bringe i uorden, forstyrre; forurolige, uroe, bringe ut av fatning. **discomposure** [diskəm'po°ʒə] uorden, ulag, forvirring, forstyrrelse.

disconcert [diskən'sə·t] gjøre forlegen, forfjamse, bringe ut av fatning; tilintetgjøre, forpurre; uroe.

disconnect [diskə'nekt] atskille.

disconsolate [dis'kånsəlèt] trøstesløs.

discontent [diskən'tent] misfornøyd, misnøgd; gjøre misnøgd; misnøye. **-ed** [-id] misfornøyd, misnøgd.

dis|continuance [diskən'tinjuəns], **-continuation** [diskəntinju'e¹ʃən] avbrytelse; stans, opphør. **-continue** [diskən'tinju] holde opp med, avbryte gjøre ende på. **-continuous** [diskən'tinjuəs] usammenhengende.

dis|cord ['diskå·°d] disharmoni, dissonans, mislyd; splid. **-cord** [dis'kå·°d] være uenig, disharmonere. **-cordance** [dis'kå·°dəns], **-cordancy** [dis-'kå·°dənsi] disharmoni, mislyd; uoverensstemmelse. **-cordant** [dis'kå·°dənt] uharmonisk; uoverensstemmende.

discount [dis'kaunt] diskontere, slå av på, trekke fra, gjøre fradrag i. **discount** ['diskaunt] avdrag, rabatt, diskonto; **be at a** — stå under pari; ogs. være billig to salgs. **discounter** [dis-'kauntə] diskontør.

discountenance [dis'kauntinəns] bringe ut av fatning, forfjamse, ikke støtte; motarbeide.

discourage [dis'kʌridʒ] ta motet fra; gjøre motløs; avskrekke; søke å hindre. **-ment** [dis'kʌridʒmənt] avskrekkelse; motløshet; hindring.

discourse ['diskå·°s] samtale; tale; foredrag; preken! [dis'kå·°s] samtale, tale, holde foredrag om; forhandle, tale om.

discourteous [dis'kʌ·°tjəs, -kə·-] uhøflig. **discourtesy** [dis'kå·°tisi, -kə·-] uhøflighet.

discover [dis'kʌvə] vise, åpenbare; oppdage. **discoverable** [dis'kʌv(ə)rəbl] som kan oppdages; synlig. **discoverer** [dis'kʌvərə] oppdager. **discovery** [dis'kʌvəri] oppdaging.

discredit [dis'kredit] vanry, skam, miskreditt; bringe i miskreditt; ikke tro. **discreditable** [dis-'kreditəbl] vanærende, beskjemmende.

discreet [dis'kri·t] forsiktig, var, betenksom; taktfull, diskret.

discrepancy [dis'krepənsi] uoverensstemmelse, motsigelse. **discrepant** [dis'krepənt] uoverensstemmende, motsiende, stridende.

discrete [dis'kri·t] avsondret; særskilt; atskillende.

discretion [dis'kreʃən] betenksomhet, forsiktighet, varsomhet, klokskap, forstand, skjønn; diskresjon, takt; **years of** — skjels år og alder; **at** — på nåde og unåde; **by** —, **on** — etter skjønn; — **is the better part of valour** forsiktighet er en dyd; **follow his own** — handle etter eget skjønn. **discretional** [dis'kreʃənəl], **discretionary** [dis-'kreʃənəri] etter skjønn.

discriminate [dis'krimine¹t] skjelne; gjøre forskjell på; skille. **discriminate** [dis'kriminèt] atskilt; særskilt. **discrimination** [diskrimi'ne¹ʃən] skjelning; forskjell; takt, skjønn; skillemerke. **discriminative** [dis'kriminətiv] karakteristisk; skjelnende, kritisk.

discrown [dis'kraun] ta kronen av, avsette.

discursive [dis'kə·siv] springende, spredt, ujamn, resonnerende, slutnings-.

discus ['diskəs] pl. **disci** ['diskai] diskos. **-thrower** [dis] diskoskaster.

discuss [dis'kʌs] drøfte, forhandle om, disku-

tere, debattere; spise, fortære, nyte; fordele (i lægevitenskap). **discussion** [dis'kʌʃən] drøfting, forhandling.
disdain [dis'deˈn] forakt, ringeakt; forsmå, forakte. **-ful** [-f(u)l] ringeaktende.
disease [di'ziˑz] sykdom; sykelighet; gjøre syk; smitte. **diseased** [di'ziˑzd] syk; sykelig.
disembark [disim'baˑᵒk] skipe ut, landsette; gå i land, gå fra borde. **disembarkation** [disembaˑə-'keˈʃən] utskiping, landsetting.
disembarrass [disim'bärəs] befri, fri. **-ment** [disim'bärəsmənt] befrielse, frigjøring.
disembody ['disim'bådi] frigjøre fra legemet; oppløse, sende hjem (en hæravdeling).
disembogue [disim'boᵘg] utgyte; løpe ut (i havet f. eks.).
disembowel [disim'bauəl] ta innvollene ut av; sprette magen opp på.
disembroil [disim'broil] utrede, greie ut.
disenchant [disin'tʃaˑnt] løse fra fortryllelse.
disencumber [disin'kʌmbə] befri (fra en byrde). **disencumbrance** [disin'kʌmbrəns] befrielse.
disendow [disin'dau] ta gavene fra.
disenfranchise ['disin'frän(t)ʃaiz] ta borgerrett el. stemmerett fra.
disengage [disin'geˈdʒ] gjøre fri, gjøre løs, befri. **disengaged** [disin'geˈdʒd] fri, ledig, ikke opptatt; uforlovet. **disengagement** [disin'geˈdʒmənt] befrielse; utfrielse; frihet.
disentangle [disin'täŋgl] greie ut; vikle løs; frigjøre. **disentanglement** [disin'täŋglmənt] utredning, utgreiing; befrielse.
disenthral(l) [disin'bråˑl] befri, løse fra trelldom.
disentitle [disin'taitl] berøve en rettighet.
disentomb [disin'tuˑm] ta opp av grava.
disestablish [disi'stäbliʃ] oppløse, opphave. **-ment** [disi'stäbliʃmənt] oppløsning, opphevelse.
disesteem [disi'stiˑm] ringeakte; gjøre ringeaktet; ringeakt; miskreditt. **disestimation** [disesti-'meˈʃən] ringeakt; miskreditt.
disfavour [dis'feˈvə] ugunst; unåde; disfavør.
disfiguration [disfigju'reˈʃən] vansiring, lyte; beskadigelse. **disfigure** [dis'fig(j)ə] vansire, skjemme, lyte, beskadige.
disfranchise ['dis'frän(t)ʃaiz] ta borgerrett, stemmerett el. representasjonsrett fra.
disgorge [dis'gåˑᵒdʒ] spy ut, gulpe opp; gi fra seg. **-ment** [-mənt] utspying, oppgulping.
disgrace [dis'greˈs, diz-] unåde, skam, skjensel; bringe i unåde; vanære. **-ful** [-f(u)l] vanærende; skjendig, skammelig.
disgruntled[dis'grʌntld]misfornøyd,misnøgd,lei.
disguise [dis'gaiz] forkle, kle ut; maskere, dølge; forkledning, utkledning; forstillelse; **-d as** eller **-d like** eller **in the — of** forkledd som; **-d in liquor** beruset; **-d hand** fordreid håndskrift.
disgust [dis'gʌst] avsmak, usmak, vemmelse, motbydelighet; avsky; volde vemmelse, vekke motbydelighet. **disgusting** [dis'gʌstiŋ] motbydelig, vemmelig; frastøtende.
dish [diʃ] fat, skål; rett; hulhet, dokk, grop; legge på fat, servere, anrette; styrte, gjøre kål på, ødelegge; anrette; gjøre hul.
dishabille [disə'biˑl] neglisjé.
disharmonious [dis(h)aˑᵒ'moᵘnjəs] uharmonisk. **disharmony** [dis'haˑᵒməni] disharmoni.
dish|cloth ['diʃklå(·)þ] el. **-clout** [-klaut] fateklut, vaskefille.
dishearten [di'haˑᵒtn] ta motet fra; gjøre motløs. **-ed** [di'haˑᵒtnd] forsagt, motløs.
dishevel [di'ʃevəl] ruske opp (håret), bringe i uorden; **-led** oppløst, utslått, i uorden, pjusket.
dish-mop vaskeklut, -fille.
dishonest [di'zånist, dis-] uærlig. **dishonesty** [di'zånəsti, dis-] uærlighet.
dishonour [di'zånə, dis-] skam; vanære; ikke honorere, la protestere (en veksel f. eks.). **dishonourable** [di'zånərəbl, dis-] vanærende; vanæret, æreløs.
dish-rag vaskefille.

dish-water oppvaskvann.
disillusion [disi'l(j)uˑʒən] desillusjonering; desillusjonere, befri for illusjoner.
disinclination [disinkli'neˈʃən] utilbøyelighet, ulyst. **disincline** [disin'klain] gjøre utilbøyelig til.
disincorporate [disin'kåˑᵒpareˈt] oppløse (et samfunn); utelukke (av et samfunn).
disinfect [disin'fekt] rense, desinfisere. **disinfectant** [disin'fektənt] desinfeksjonsmiddel. **disinfection** [disin'fekʃən] desinfeksjon.
disingenuous [disin'dʒenjuəs] falsk, uærlig, underfundig.
disinherit [disin'herit] gjøre arveløs.
disintegrate [dis'intigreˈt] oppløse, smuldre opp. **disintegration** [disinti'greˈʃən] oppløsning.
disinter [disin'təˑ] grave opp, bringe for lyset.
disinterested [dis'intərestid] uegennyttig, uhildet, upartisk.
disinterment [disin'təˑmənt] oppgraving.
disjoin [dis'dʒoin] splitte, atskille.
disjoint [dis'dʒoint] vri av ledd; dele opp.
disjunction [dis'dʒʌŋkʃən] atskillelse.
disjunctive [dis'dʒʌŋktiv] atskillende; disjunktiv.
disk [disk] skive.
dislike [dis'laik] mishag; avsky; ikke like, ikke kunne like, misbillige, avsky; **-d** ille likt.
dislocate ['dislokeˈt] forrykke; bringe av ledd.
dislocation [dislo'keˈʃən] forrykkelse, forskyvning, forvridning.
dislodge [dis'lådʒ] fordrive, drive bort, drive ut, jage opp (vilt); flytte; ta ut (kule av sår).
disloyal [dis'loiəl] illojal; utro, ulydig. **disloyalty** [-ti] illojalitet; utroskap, svik.
dismal [dis'mal] forferde, gjøre redd, gjøre fælen, nedslå; forferdelse, skrekk; motløshet; sorg.
dismast [dis'maˑst] avmaste.
dismay [dis'meˈ] forferde, gjøre redd, gjøre fælen, nedslå; forferdelse, skrekk; motløshet; sorg.
dismember [dis'membə] sundlemme; stykke ut. **dismemberment** [-mənt] sundlemming; utstykking.
dismiss [dis'mis] sende bort, la gå; avvise; skaffe seg av med, bli av med; avskjedige. **dismissal** [dis'misəl], **dismission** [dis'miʃən] fjerning; avskjedigelse, bortvising.
dismount [dis'maunt] kaste av hesten; demontere (en kanon); stige av hesten, stige av; stige ned.
disobedience [diso'biˑdjəns] ulydighet. **disobedient** [diso'biˑdjənt] ulydig (**to** imot). **disobey** [diso'beˈ] være ulydig, ikke adlyde, ikke lystre.
disobligation [disåbli'geˈʃən] uvillighet, tverrhet, mangel på forekommenhet, uvennlighet, fornærmelse. **disoblige** [diso'blaidʒ] vise seg uvillig mot, være tverr mot, fornærme. **disobliging** uvillig.
disorder [dis'åˑᵒdə] uorden, forvirring, forstyrrelse; sykdom; bringe i uorden; gjøre syk; påvirke. **-ed** i uorden, sky. **-ly** uordentlig; i uorden; udisiplinert; syk.
disorganization [disåˑᵒgənai'zeˈʃən] oppløsning.
disorganize [dis'åˑᵒgənaiz] oppløse, bringe i uorden.
disown [dis'oᵘn] fornekte.
disparage [dis'päridʒ] nedsette, laste, forkleine. **-ment** nedsettelse, forkleinelse.
disparate ['dispərét] ganske forskjellig, ulik; **-s** ganske forskjellige ting.
disparity [dis'päriti] ulikhet, ulikskap.
dispart [dis'paˑᵒt] skille, skjøve.
dispassionate [dis'päʃənét] rolig, sindig.
dispatch [dis'pätʃ] avsendelse, sending, ekspedisjon, hurtig besørgelse, fortgang, hurtighet, hast; depesje, ilbrev; sende; ekspedere; utferdige; gjøre det av med, ta av dage. **— -box** dokumentmappe. **— -rider** rytterordonnans. **— -money**

godtgjørelse som et skip betaler en varemottaker for å få lasten losset på kortere tid enn de liggedager som er bestemt i certepartiet.
dispel [di'spel] spre, fordrive, drive bort.
dispensable [di'spensəbl] som kan utdeles; unnværlig, uviktig.
dispensary [di'spensəri] apotek. **dispensation** [dispen'se¹ʃən] utdeling; tilskikkelse; fritagelse, dispensasjon. **dispensative** [di'spensətiv] fritagende. **dispensator** ['dispense¹tə] utdeler; fritager. **dispensatory** [di'spensətəri] fritagende; farmakopø. **dispense** [di'spens] utdele, fordele; frita **(from** for), gi dispensasjon; — **with** unnvære. **dispenser** utdeler; provisor.
dispeople [dis'pi·pl] avfolke.
disperse [di'spə·s] spre; atspre; spre seg. **dispersedly** [di'spə·sidli] spredt. **dispersion** [di-'spə·ʃən] spredning; utbredthet. **dispersive** [di-'spə·siv] spredende.
dispirit [di'spirit] berøve motet, nedslå. **-ed** motløs. **-edness** motløshet.
displace [dis'ple¹s] flytte, fjerne; avsette, forjage. **-ment** [dis'ple¹smənt] flytting, forskyvning; deplasement.
display [dis'ple¹] framstilling, framsyning, skue, framvising, pranging; utfolde; vise fram, bre ut, stille ut, legge fram, vise; — **to view** vise fram.
displease [dis'pli·z] mishage. **displeased** misfornøyd. **displeasure** [dis'pleʒə] misnøye, mishag.
displume [dis'plu·m] ribbe, plukke.
disport [di'spå·ᵊt] forlystelse; forlyste seg, more seg, tumle seg.
disposable [di'spoᵘzəbl] som står til rådighet, disponibel.
disposal [di'spoᵘzəl] rådighet, disposisjon. **at one's** — til ens disposisjon. **dispose** [di'spoᵘz] ordne, innrette, bestemme; gjøre tilbøyelig til; lede, styre; disponere; råde, herske. — **of** ha rådighet over; skille seg av med, kvitte seg med; gjøre av, gjøre ende på. **disposer** ordner; leder, styrer. **disposition** [dispo'ziʃən] ordning; anordning; anlegg; tilbøyelighet, stemning, tenkemåte; natur. **dispossess** [dispə'zes] berøve; fordrive fra. **dispossession** [dispə'zeʃən] fordrivelse; berøving.
dispraise [dis'pre¹z] daddel, last; laste.
disproof [dis'pru·f] gjendrivelse, motprov.
disproportion [dispro'på·ᵊʃən] misforhold; uforholdsmessighet; utilstrekkelighet; bringe i misforhold. **disproportional** [dispro'på·ᵊʃənəl] uforholdsmessig; utilstrekkelig. **disproportionality** [dispropå·ᵊʃə'näliti] misforhold, uforholdsmessighet; utilstrekkelighet. **disproportionate** [dispro-'på·ᵊʃənét] uforholdsmessig, utilstrekkelig.
disprovable [dis'pru·vəbl] som kan gjendrives.
disprove [dis'pru·v] motbevise, gjendrive.
disputable ['dispjutəbl, di'spju·təbl] omtvistelig. **disputant** ['dispjutənt] disputator. **disputation** [dispju'te¹ʃən] strid; disputas. **disputatious** [dispju'te¹ʃəs] trettekjær. **dispute** [di'spju·t] strides, disputere; drøfte; bestride; strid; ordstrid, konflikt. **in** — omtvistet. **disputer** [dis'pju·tə] disputant.
disqualification [diskwålifi'ke¹ʃən] uskikkethet, uheldig egenskap. **disqualify** [dis'kwålifai] gjøre uskikket, gjøre inhabil.
disquiet [dis'kwaiət] uro; urolig; forurolige, uroe.
disquisition [diskwi'ziʃən] undersøkelse, avhandling.
Disraeli [diz're¹li] Disraeli.
disrate [dis're¹t] degradere, sette ned.
disregard ['disri'ga·ᵊd] ringeakt; ringeakte, overse.
disrelish [dis'reliʃ] ulyst, utilbøyelighet, ha avsmak for; gjøre ekkel.
disrepair [disri'pæ·ᵊ] forfall, dårlig tilstand.
disreputable [dis'repjutəbl] skammelig; beryktet, ille omtalt. **disrepute** ['disri'pju·t] slett rykte.
disrespect [disri'spekt] mangel på aktelse, uærbødighet. **-ful** [-f(u)l] uærbødig.

disrobe [dis'roᵘb] kle av.
disruption [dis'rʌpʃən] brudd, sprengning.
dissatisfaction [dis(s)ätis'fäkʃən] utilfredshet; misfornøyelse, misnøye. **dissatisfactory** [dis(s)ätis-'fäktəri] utilfredsstillende. **dissatisfied** [di(s)-'sätisfaid] misfornøyd, misnøgd, utilfreds. **dissatisfy** [di(s)'sätisfai] gjøre misfornøyd.
dissect [di'sekt] sønderlemme, sundlemme, dissekere; obdusere. **dissection** [di'sekʃən] sønderlemmelse; disseksjon; obduksjon. **dissector** [di-'sektə] dissektor; prosektor; obdusent.
dissemble [di'sembl] skjule, dølge; forstille seg. **dissembler** hykler. **dissembling** forstilt; hyklersk.
disseminate [di'semine¹t] så, strø ut. **dissemination** [disemi'ne¹ʃən] utstrøing.
dissension [di'senʃən] tvist, splid, uenighet, tvedrakt. **dissent** [di'sent] være av en annen mening; avvike (særlig i kirkelig henseende); meningsforskjell; avvikelse fra statskirken. **dissenter** [di'sentə] dissenter. **dissentient** [di'senʃənt] avvikende, uenig; annerledes tenkende.
dissert [di'sə·t] skrive en avhandling, komme med en utgreiing. **-ation** [disə'te¹ʃən] avhandling, utgreiing, undersøkelse.
dissever [di'sevə] skille, rive fra hverandre.
dissidence ['disidəns] uenighet. **dissident** ['disidənt] uenig; dissenter-.
dissimilar [di'similə] ulik, forskjellig, ymse. **dissimilarity** [disimi'läriti]. **dissimilitude** [dis;-'militjud] ulikhet, forskjellighet.
dissimulat|e [di'simjule¹t] forstille seg, skape seg. **-ion** [disimju'le¹ʃən] forstillelse.
dissipate ['disipe¹t] atspre; forøde, sette til spre seg. **dissipated** ['dispe¹tid] utsvevende. **dissipation** [disi'pe¹ʃən] atspredelse, spredning utsvevelser, ageløyse.·
dissociate [di'soᵘʃie¹t] skille, løse opp. **dissociation** [disoᵘʃi'e¹ʃən] atskillelse.
dissolubility [di'sälju'biliti] oppløselighet. **dissoluble** ['disəljubl, di'säljubl] oppløselig.
dissolute ['disəljut] utsvevende, agelaus. **-ness** utsvevelse. **dissolution** [disə'l(j)u·ʃən] oppløsning.
dissolvability [dizälvə'biliti] oppløselighet. **dissolvable** [di'zälvəbl] oppløselig. **dissolve** [di'zälv] løse opp; løse seg opp; smelte; bråne; **dissolving views** tåkebilder. **dissolvent** [di'zälvənt] oppløsende; oppløsende middel. **dissolver** oppløser; oppløsningsmiddel.
dissonance ['disənəns] mislyd, dissonans. **dissonant** ['disənənt] skurrende, illelydende; uoverensstemmende.
dissuade [di'swe¹d] rå ifra. **dissuasion** [di-'swe¹ʒən] fraråding. **dissuasive** [di'swe¹siv] frarådende.
dissyllabic [disi'läbik] tostavings-. **dissyllable** [di'siläbl] tostavingsord.
distaff ['dista·f] håndtein; rokkehode; spinneside, kvinnen.
distance ['distəns] avstand, frastand, distanse; fjernhet; tidsrom; tilbakeholdenhet; **at a** — langt borte; et stykke borte; **in the** — i det fjerne; **keep one's** — holde seg unna, være reservert. **distance** [di'distəns] fjerne, rykke fra hverandre; la tilbake, distansere; **be -d** bli distansert. **distant** ['distənt] fjern; grissen; tilbakeholdende; **at this** — **period** nå så lang tid etterpå.
distaste [dis'te¹st] avsmak, utilbøyelighet. **distasteful** [dis'te¹stf(u)l] ubehagelig, usmakelig.
distemper [dis'tempə] sykdom, især hvalpesyke; gjøre syk; bringe i uorden; opphisse.
distemper [dis'tempə] limfarge, vannfarge (til kalkvegger).
distend [dis'tend] strekke, spile ut, utvide; utvide seg. **distensive** [di'stensiv] utvidende; som kan utvides. **distention** [di'stenʃən] utstrekning, utvidelse; vidde.
distil [di'stil] dryppe; sildre; destillere, brenne. **distillable** [di'stiläbl] som kan destilleres. **distillation** [disti'le¹ʃən] drypp; destillasjon. **distillatory**

[di'stilətəri] destillasjons-. **distiller** [di'stilə] destillatør, brennevinsbrenner. **distillery** [di'stiləri] destillasjon, brenneri.

distinct [di'stiŋ(k)t] forskjellig; tydelig atskilt; særskilt; tydelig, avgjort. **distinction** [di'stiŋkʃən] forskjell; atskillelse; utmerkelse, anseelse. **distinctive** [di'stiŋ(k)tiv] eiendommelig; utpreget, særs, særlig. **distinctly** tydelig, bestemt. **distinctness** tydelig atskillelse; tydelighet.

distinguish [di'stiŋgwiʃ] atskille; skjelne; utmerke. **distinguishable** [di'stiŋgwiʃəbl] som kan skilles el. skjelnes. **distinguished** [-t] utmerket, framragende, fornem, navngjeten.

distort [di'stå·ət] fordreie, forvri. **distortion** [di'stå·əʃən] fordreiing, forvridning.

distract [di'sträkt] forvirre; plage; drive fra vettet, gjøre gal. **-ed** [di'sträktid] forstyrret, forrykt, gal, rasende. **distraction** [di'sträkʃən] bortledning; forvirring, forstyrrelse; sinnsforvirring.

distrain [di'streˈn] ta utlegg i; pante ut; legge beslag på. **distraint** [di'streˈnt] utpanting.

distrait [di'streˈ] distré, fortenkt.

distraught [di'strå·t] vanvittig (av sorg etc.).

distress [di'stres] nød, ulykke; sorg, utpanting; bringe i nød; pine; bedrøve; pante. **distressful** [di'stresful] ulykkelig; **the — country:** Irland.

distribute [di'stribjut] dele ut, fordele; bringe omkring. **distribution** [distri'bju·ʃən] utdeling; fordeling; utbredelse; ombæring. **distributive** [di'stribjutiv] utdelende, fordelende. **distributor** [di'stribjutə] fordeler, utdeler; ombærer.

district ['distrikt] distrikt, egn.

distrust [dis'trʌst] mistro, ikke tro, mistenke, ha mistillit til; mistro, mistillit **(of** til). **-ful** mistroisk; fryktsom.

disturb [di'stə·b] forstyrre; forvirre; forurolige, uroe, skiple. **disturbance** [di'stə·bəns] forstyrrelse; forvirring; opphisselse; oppløp; opprør; oppstyr. **disturber** [di'stə·bə] fredsforstyrrer.

disunion [dis'ju·njən] atskillelse, løsriving, uenighet. **disunite** [disju'nait] skille; skilles.

disusage [dis'ju·zidʒ] det å gå av bruk. **disuse** [dis'ju·z] ikke bruke mer, slutte å bruke, holde opp med, avvenne. **disuse** [dis'ju·s] det å gå av bruk; ledighet; avskaffelse; ubrukelighet; opphør.

disyllabic ['disi'läbik] tostavings-. **disyllable** [di'siləbl] tostavingsord.

ditch [ditʃ] grøft, veit, grav (slang) Kanalen, Nordsjøen; grøfte, veite, forsyne med grøft; nødlande, styrte i havet. **ditcher** ['ditʃə] grøftegraver.

dither ['diðə] skjelve; gyse; skjelving; gysning.

dithyramb ['diþiräm] dityrambe, drikkevise. **dithyrambic** [diþi'rämbik] dityrambisk, oppglødd.

dittany ['ditəni] bredbladet karse.

ditto ['ditoˈ] ditto; det omtalte, det samme; **I say — to him** (spøkende) jeg er enig med ham; **a suit of -es, a — suit** hel drakt av samme stoff. **ditty** ['diti] vise, stubb.

ditty|-bag ['ditibäg] el. **-box** [-båks] skrin, syskrin.

diuresis [daiju'ri·sis] urinavsondring. **diuretic** [daiju'retik] urindrivende; urindrivende middel.

diurnal [dai'ə·nəl] dag-, daglig.

div. fk. f. **dividend.**

diva ['di·və] stor sangerinne, diva.

divagation [daivə'geˈʃən] digresjon.

divan [di'vän] divan, tyrkisk statsråd; divan (løybenk), røykeværelse.

dive [daiv] dukke, stupe; trenge inn i, trenge ned; dukkert, bad; svipptur. **dive-bomber** ['daivbåmə] stupbombefly, stupbomber. **diver** ['daivə] dykker.

diverge [di'və·dʒ, dai-] gå til forskjellige sider, gå fra hverandre, vike av, divergere. **divergence** [di'və·dʒəns, dai-], **divergency** [di'və·dʒəns] divergens. **divergent** [-ənt] divergerende.

divers [di'daivəz] forskjellige, atskillige; flere.

diverse [d(a)i'və·s, 'daivəs] forskjellig, ulik, mangfoldig. **diversification** [d(a)ivə·sifi'keˈʃən]

forandring, avveksling; forskjellighet, variasjon. **diversify** [di'və·sifai, dai-] forandre, variere. **diversion** [di'və·ʃən, dai-] avledning; bortdraging; fornøyelse, atspredelse; diversjon. **diversity** [di'və·siti, dai-] forskjellighet; mangfoldighet.

divert [di'və·t, dai-] avlede, vende bort, bortlede; atspre, more.

divest [di'vest, dai-] kle av, avføre; blotte, berøve, snøye.

dividable [di'vaidəbl] delelig.

divide [di'vaid] dele, kløyve; inndele; dividere; være uenig; stemme; **— the House** la foreta avstemning i underhuset. **dividend** ['dividénd] dividende, dividend. **divider** [di'vaidə] deler, utdeler.

dividers [di'vaidez] passer; **a pair of —** en passer.

divination [divi'neˈʃən] spådom, varsel, anelse. **divinator** ['divineˈtə] spåmann. **divine** [di'vain] spå; ane, gjette; guddommelig; teologisk; **— right** guddommelig rett (om kongens rett til å regjere); **— service** gudstjeneste. **divine** geistlig, teolog. **— diviner** [di'vainə] spåmann. **divineress** [di'vainərès] spåkvinne.

divining-rod ønskekvist (til å vise vann).

divinity [di'viniti] guddommelighet; guddom; teologi, teologisk fakultet; **Doctor of Divinity** dr. theol.

divisibility [divizi'biliti] delelighet. **divisible** [di'vizibl] delelig.

division [di'viʒən] deling; inndeling; avdeling; uenighet, stridighet; avstemning; **— lobby** forhall i parlamentet, som blir brukt ved avstemning; **— of labour** arbeidsdeling.

divisor [di'vaizə] divisor.

divorce [di'vå·ºs] skilsmisse; separasjon; skilsmissedom; skille (ektefolk); separere; la seg skille fra; skilles; separeres. **-able** [di'vå·ºsəbl] som kan skilles. **divorcee** [divå·ºsi·] fraskilt. **divorcement** [di'vå·ºsmənt] skilsmisse.

divulge [di'vʌl(d)ʒ, dai-] åpenbare, bekjentgjøre, kunngjøre, la sive ut.

dizen ['daizn] spjåke til, stase til.

dizziness ['dizinès] svimmelhet. **dizzy** ['dizi] svimmel; gjøre svimmel.

D. L. fk. f. **Doctor of Law** dr. juris.

dl fk. f. **decilitre.**

D. Lit. fk. f. **Doctor of Literature.**

D. M. fk. f. **Daily Mail.**

dm fk. f. **decimetre.**

D. N. fk. f. **Daily News.**

d—n fk. f. **damn.**

D. N. B. fk. f. **Dictionary of National Biography.**

do [du·] (imperf. **did;** perf. pts. **done;** 3. p. sg. pres.: **does).** 1. (transitivt selvstendig v.) gjøre, utføre, bevirke, fullføre; drive (handel); sone, lide, sitte; tilberede, ordne; snyte. 2. (intransitivt selvstendig v.) gjøre, handle; klare, greie seg, gå an, være nok, passe; leve, ha det. 3. (hjelpeverb) brukt i usammensatte tider i setninger benektet med «not», i spørrende hovedsetninger unntatt hvor et spørrende ord står som subjekt, og for å gi ettertrykk. 4. brukt som stedfortreder for et verbum eller lengre uttrykk. Eksempler: 1. **— oneself well** godgjøre seg; **do one's best** gjøre sitt beste, gjøre seg umak; **do credit** gjøre ære; **do one's duty** gjøre sin plikt; **do me a service** gjør meg en tjeneste; **do good; do harm; do wrong; do right; do me the honour; do me the favour; do justice to** la vederfares rettferdighet; **the work is done** arbeidet er ferdig; **I have done eating** jeg er ferdig med å spise; **done!** la gå! så er det en avtale; **do bills** drive vekselforretninger; **do one's hair** stelle håret; **do one's lessons** lære leksene sine; **a well done chop** en godt stekt kotelett; **do a room** gjøre et værelse i stand; **do a sum** regne ut stykke; **do the town** se (severdighetene i) en by; **they will do you** de kommer til å snyte deg; **he does himself very well** han holder seg

selv med kost, og det går meget godt; **do away with** avskaffe; vrake; **do by others as you would be done by** gjør imot andre som du vil at de skal gjøre imot deg; **do into Norwegian** oversette til norsk; **do out** gjøre i stand; — **up** sette i stand; sette opp; pakke inn. 2. **there is nothing doing** det foregår ingenting; **he did well to refuse** det var best om han sa nei; **do or die** seire eller falle; **be up and doing** være i full virksomhet; **have to do with** ha å gjøre med; **a great to do** et stort spetakkel; **that will do** det er nok; **that won't do** den går ikke; **will this do?** kan De bruke denne? **this will do for him** dette vil gjøre det av med ham; **I am done for** det er ute med meg; **how do you do?** god dag! god aften! god morgen! (hilsen, når man møtes; svaret er likelydende: how do you do?); sjeldnere, hvordan har du det? (som alm. uttrykkes ved: How are you?); **a well-to-do man** en velstående mann; **do without** unnvære. 3. **I do not like it** jeg liker det ikke; **he did not see me** han så meg ikke; **he does not smoke** han røyker ikke; **don't do it** ikke gjør det; **don't la være!** **do you speak English?** snakker (kan) du engelsk? **did he speak with you?** talte han med deg? **I do like London** jeg liker godt London; **I do think he is crying** jeg tror virkelig at han gråter; **do come á,** kom nå; **vær så snill å komme; don't you know** du forstår nok (det brukes også som fylleord uten noen egentlig betydning). 4. **did you see him?** — **Yes, I did** så du ham? — ja jeg gjorde; **you like him, don't you?** du liker ham, ikke sant? **you don't smoke, do you?** du røyker ikke vel?
do. fk. f. **ditto.**
dobbin ['dåbin] øyk.
docile ['dåsil, 'dou sil] lærvillig; lærenem; føyelig. **docility** [do'siliti] lærvillighet; føyelighet.
dock [dåk] syre (plante).
dock [dåk] dokk; forbryterens plass i en rettssal. **dock dokke;** gå i dokk.
dock [dåk] stump, avhogd hale, stubberumpe; skjære av, stusse; trekke fra (i lønn o. l.).
dockage ['dåkid3] dokkplass; dokkpenger.
docker ['dåkə] dokkarbeider, havnearbeider, sjauer.
docket ['dåkit] innholdsliste, sakliste; merke; utdrag (av dom el. protokoll); dagsorden. **docket** ['dåkit] merke, sette merkelapp på; gjøre utdrag av, sette opp liste over.
dockize ['dåkaiz] bygge dokker i. **dockyard** ['dåkja·°d] dokk, verft.
doctor ['dåktə] doktor, lege; doktor (innehaver av en universitetsgrad); vinblander, vinforfalsker; doktorere, praktisere; forfalske (vin), forgifte; **send for the** — sende bud etter legen; **who shall decide when -s disagree** hvem skal avgjøre det, når de lærde er uenige. **doctoral** ['dåktərəl] doktor-. **doctorate** ['dåktərét] doktorat, doktorgrad.
doctrinaire [dåktri'næ·ə] doktrinær (politiker).
doctrinal ['dåktrin] lære-, tros-.
doctrine ['dåktrin] doktrin, læresetning.
document ['dåkjumənt] skriftlig bevis; dokument; forsyne med bevis, med papirer; dokumentere, prove. **documental** [dåkju'mentl] dokument-, brev-, som bygger på brev. **documentary** [dåkju'mentəri] dokument-, brev-; — **credit** remburs.
dodder ['dådə] snyltetråd, cuscuta.
dodder ['dådə] skjelve, vakle, rugle.
dodge [dåd3] springe til side, skvette unna; sno seg, gjøre krumspring; unngå behendig, lure seg unna; krumspring, list, knep. **dodger** ['dådʒə] snyter; rev.
dodo ['dou do] dronte (fugl).
doe [dou] dåkolle; hunhare, hunkanin.
doer ['du·ə] gjerningsmann; handlingens mann.
does [dʌz] 3 p. sg. pres. ind. av **do.**
doeskin ['dou skin] dådyrskinn; slags buckskinn.
doest ['du·ist] gml. 2 p. sg. pres. ind. av **do.**
doff [dåf] ta av, avføre seg.
dog [dåg] hund, bikkje; han (av flere dyr);

krampe; dogg; forfølge, følge hakk i hæl, lure seg etter; **a lucky** — en heldig gris; **an odd** — en underlig skrue; **a sly** — en luring, rev; **give** el. **send to the -s** kaste bort; **go to the -s** gå i hundene; **let sleeping -s lie** ikke rippe opp i gamle stridsspørsmål; **let loose the -s of war** slippe krigsråskapen løs.
dog|-berry rød kornell. — -**biscuit** hundekjeks. — -**box** hundevogn (på jernbane). — -**cart** dogcart; jaktvogn. — -**cheap** svinaktig billig. — -**days** hundedager.
doge [dou dʒ] doge.
dog|-eared eseløre, brett (på bok). — -**fancier** hundeoppdretter.
dogged ['dågid] egensindig; trassig; sta.
dogger ['dågə] tomastet hollandsk fiskefartøy.
doggerel ['dåg(ə)rəl] slett, uregelmessig (om vers), burlesk; burlesk vers.
doggie ['dågi] bisken (kjælenavn for **dog**).
doggish ['dågif] hundsk; bisk.
doggo ['dågo°]: **lie** — vente ubevegelig.
doggy ['dågi] = **doggie;** som liker hunder.
dog|-grass kveke. — -**hole** hundehull (dårlig værelse). — -**hutch** hundehus. — -**latin** dårlig latin. — -**lead** hundelenke.
dogma ['dågmə] trossetning, dogme. **dogmatic** [dåg'mätik], **dogmatical** [dåg'mätikl] dogmatisk; selvsikker. **dogmatics** [dåg'mätiks] dogmatikk. **dogmatism** ['dågmətizm] selvsikkerhet. **dogmatist** ['dågmətist] selvsikker person. **dogmatize** ['dågmətaiz] tale med selvsikkerhet, være skråsikker i sine påstander.
dog|-rose ['dågro°z] nyperose. — -**'s-ear** eseløre, brett (på blad i bok), legge bretter i. — -**sleep** urolig søvn. **lead one a** — -**'s life** plage en. — **'s -meat** hundemat. — **'s -nose** blanding av brennevin og øl. — -**star** Sirius, Hundestjernen. — -**tired** dødstrett. — -**tooth** hjørnetann; sl. ornament i gammel engelsk bygningskunst. — -**trot** dilt. — -**watch** kort ettermiddagsvakt på skip. — -**whip** hundepisk. -**wood** rød kornell, brakal, trollhegg.
doily ['doili] dessertserviett (under skylleskål).
doing ['du·iŋ] gjerning, handling, verk, dåd. **-s** gjerninger, handlinger; oppførsel, atferd.
doit [doit] døyt, grann.
doldrums ['dåldrəmz] det stille belte i Atlanterhavet; **be in the** — være i dårlig humør, i ulag, nedtrykt; kjede seg.
dole [dou l] arbeidsløshetsunderstøttelse, forsorg, gave, skjerv; dele.
dole [dou l] sorg, sut, kvide.
doleful ['dou lful] sorgfull; sørgelig; sturen.
dolichocephalic ['dåliko°se'fälik] langskallet.
doll [dål] dukke, dokke.
dollar ['dålə] dollar.
doll-house ['dålhaus] dukkestue.
dollop ['dåləp] stykke, bit, porsjon (av pudding e. l.).
Dolly ['dåli] = **Dorothy.**
dolly ['dåli] dukkeaktig. **dolly** dukke. **dolly-shop** klutehandel; ulovlig pantelånerforretning.
dolman ['dålmən] dolman (tyrkisk kjortel; husartrøye; damekåpe).
dolorous ['dålərəs] smertelig, sørgelig.
dolphin ['dålfin] delfin.
dolt [dou lt] tosk, dåsemikkel. **doltish** ['dou ltif] dum, klosset, tosket.
D. O. M. fk. f. **Deo Optimo Maximo.**
domain [do'me'n] område; besittelse; egn.
Dombey ['dåmbi] Dombey.
dome [dou m] dom, kuppel.
domesday ['du·mzde'] dommedag; **Domesday Book** Englands jordebok fra Vilhelm Erobrers tid.
domestic [do'mestik] hus-, huslig; hjemmegjort; indre, innenriks-; tam; tjener. **domesticate** [do'mestike't] venne til huset, gjøre husvant; temme. **domesticated** (især:) huslig. **domestication** [domesti'ke'ʃən] tilvenning; temming; lag til å stelle i huset; **domesticity** [do°me'stisiti] husvanthet; huslighet; tamhet.

domicile ['dåmisil, -sail] bopel; hjemsted;domisil;bosette. **domiciliary**[dåmi'siljəri]hus-;domisil-; — **visit** husundersøkelse. **domiciliate** [dåmi'silie't] bosette; domisiliere.
dominant ['dåminənt] herskende; dominant (i musikk). **dominate** ['dåmine't] herske, rå; beherske. **domination**[dåmi'ne'ʃən]herredømme,rådvelde. **dominator** ['dåmine'tə] hersker, behersker.
domineer [dåmi'niə] herske, dominere.
Domini ['dåminai]: **anno** — i det Herrens år.
dominical [do'minikəl] som angår Herren, søndags-.
Dominican [do'minikən] dominikansk; dominikaner.
dominie ['dåmini] skolemester, lærer.
dominion [do'minjən] herredømme, makt; koloni med selvstyre (om: Canada, Australia, New Zealand, Sør-Afrika og Irland).
domino ['dåminoᵘ] domino; dominospill.
don [dån] don, herre (spansk); spanjer; storborger; ved engelske universiteter kalles magistrer og kandidater **the dons**.
don [dån] ta på, iføre seg (motsatt **doff**).
Donald ['dånəld] Donald.
donation [do'ne'ʃən] gave; gavebrev. **donative** ['dånətiv] skjenket; gave-.
done [dʌn], perf. pts. av **do**, gjort, utført; ferdig, forbi; la gå! så er det en avtale. **I have** — jeg er ferdig; — **up** lagt sammen, pakket inn; gjort i stand; ruinert; utmattet; **I am** — **for** jeg er ferdig; **I have** — **Italy** jeg har reist gjennom hele Italia; — **with you!** la gå!
donee [doᵘ'ni·] mottager av en gave.
donjon [dʌndʒən, 'dån-] slottstårn.
Don Juan [dån'dʒu·ən] Don Juan.
donkey ['dåŋki] esel, asen. — **engine** donkeymaskin (liten dampmaskin til heising). — **man** mann som passer donkeymaskin.
Donnybrook ['dånibruk] irsk by; — **fair** slagsmål, hurlumhei.
donor ['doᵘnə, -nå·ə] giver.
do-nothing ['du·nʌþiŋ] ledig; dagdriver.
Don Quixote [dån 'kwiksoᵘt] Don Quíxote.
don't [doᵘnt] fk. f. **do not**.
doodle ['du·dl] dåsemikkel, tosk; fk. f. **doodle-bug**.
doodle-bug ['du·dlbʌg] flyvende bombe (brukt om V-bombene).
dooly ['du·li] bærestol. — **-box** bærestol.
doom [du·m] dom; lodd; ulykke; dømme; fordømme. **doomsday** ['du·mzde'] se **domesday**.
door [då·ə] dør; **the fault lies wholly at my** — det er utelukkende min skyld; **in** -s innendørs; **out of -s** ut av huset, ute, utenfor; utendørs. — **-bell** dørklokke. — **-case** dørkarm; — **-chain** sikkerhetskjede. — **-frame** dørkarm. — **-keeper** dørvokter, portner. — **-knocker** dørhammer. — **-nail** den knapp som dørhammeren slår på; **as dead as a -nail** så død som en sild. — **-post** dørstolpe. — **-step** trappetrin (utenfor huset); dørterskel, dørstokk. — **-way** døråpning; portåpning; **in the doorway** i døra, i porten.
dope [doᵘp] saus, smurning; vognsmøring; oppsugingsmiddel; bedøvende middel; behandle med (ta) noe bedøvende.
doper ['doᵘpə], **dopper** ['dåpə] dykker (fugl); gjendøper.
dor [då·ə] tordivel.
Dora ['då·ərə] Dora (kvinnenavn).
Dora = **D. O. R. A.** fk. f. **Defence·of the Realm Act** forsvarsloven av 1914.
dorado [do'ra·doᵘ] dorade (fisk).
dorbeetle ['då·əbi·tl] tordivel.
Dorcas ['då·əkas] Dorcas; godgjørende kvinne. derav mange sammensetninger som: — **association**, — **society** kvinneforening i velgjørende øyemed.
Dorian ['då·riən] dorisk; dorer. **Doric** ['dårik] dorisk.
Dorking ['då·əkiŋ] Dorking, en by i Surrey, kjent for sine høns. **dorking** dorking-høne.

dormancy ['då·əmənsi] hvile, dvale. **dormant** ['då·əmənt] slumrende, hvilende; — **partner** passiv kompanjong, stille medinteressent.
dormer ['då·əmə] ark (på hus), takvindu; **dormer-window** (framspringende) takvindu.
dormice ['då·əmais] pl. av **dormouse**.
dormitive ['då·əmitiv] søvndyssende; sovemiddel.
dormitory ['då·əmitəri] soveværelse; sovesal.
dormouse ['då·əmaus] sjusover, hasselmus.
Dorothea [dårə'þi·ə], **Dorothy** ['dårəþi] Dorothea.
dorothy ['dårəþi] **bag** liten damehåndveske.
dorsal ['då·əsəl] rygg-, på ryggsiden.
Dorset ['då·əsit] Dorset.-**shire** [-ʃiə] Dorsetshire.
dorter el. **dortour** ['då·tə] d. s. s. **dormitory**.
dory ['då·ri] dory, slags jolle.
dose [doᵘs] dosis; foreskrive lægemidler; gi en doser; forgi en med lægemidler.
doss [dås] seng, køy; sove, losjere. — **-house** (simpelt og billig) losjihus.
dost [dʌst] 2. p. pres. sg. i høyere stil av **do**.
dot [dåt] prikk, punkt; desimaltegn; prikke, punktere; sette prikk over; bestrø; **describe him to a** — beskrive ham på en prikk; **off his** — forrykt; — **and go one** halte; **people dotted the fields** rundt omkring på markene så man folk; **a landscape dotted with cottages** oversådd med.
dotage ['doᵘtidʒ] alderdomssløvhet; **he is in his** — han går i barndommen.
dotal ['doᵘtəl] som hører til medgift.
dotard ['doᵘtəd] mann som går i barndommen.
dotation [do'te'ʃən] gave; medgift, utstyr.
dote [doᵘt] gå i barndommen; — **(up)on** forgude.
doth [dʌþ] (gammelt) = **does**.
dott(e)rel ['dåtrəl] boltit, fjell-lo; tosk.
dottle ['dåtl] urøykt tobakksrest (i en pipe).
dotty ['dåti] prikket; forrykt, bløt, sløv.
double ['dʌbl] dobbelt; fordoble; legge dobbelt; omseile; dublere; fordobles; fordoble seg; gjøre krumspring; gjøre seg skyldig i knep; gå i stormskritt; — **up** knytte neven. **double** det dobbelte; krumspring; knep; gjenpart; dublett; dobbeltgjenger; vardøger; stormmarsj. — **-barrelled** dobbeltløpet. — **-bass** kontrabass. — **-breasted** dobbeltknappet (om jakke). — **cross** narre, svindle, bedra. — **-dealer** falsk menneske. — **-dealing** falskhet. — **-Dutch** labbelendsk. — **-dyed** farget to ganger; durkdreven, erke-. — **eagle** amerikansk 20-dollar. — **-edged** tveegget. — **entendre** [-'ta·ndr] tvetydig. — **-entry** dobbelt (om bokføring). — **-faced** falsk. — **-ganger** [-gänger] dobbeltgjenger, vardøger. — **-lock** låse forsvarlig. — **-minded** vaklende, vinglet. — **-quick** hurtigmarsj; i hurtigmarsj.
doublet ['dʌblit] dublett, tvillingform; stuttrøye.
double-tongued ['dʌbl'tʌŋd] tvetunget, falsk.
doubling ['dʌbliŋ] fordobling; kunstgrep.
doubloon [dʌ'blu·n] dublon (spansk gullmynt).
doubly ['dʌbli] dobbelt.
doubt [daut] tvile; tvile på; frykte for; tvil, uvisshet, betenkelighet; mistanke; **no** — uten tvil, utvilsomt, ganske visst. **doubted** ['dautid] tvilsom. **doubter** ['dautə] tviler. **doubtful** ['dautf(u)l] tvilrådig; tvilsom. **doubting** ['dautiŋ] tvil. **doubtingly** tvilsomt. **doubtless** ['dautlès] utvilsom, uten tvil; utvilsomt.
douceur [du·'sə] dusør.
douche [du·ʃ] styrtebad, dusj; dusje.
dough [doᵘ] deig. **-baked** dødstekt. — **-boy** kokt bolle; amerikansk soldat (især infanterist). **-face** godfjott, dott. **-faced** dottet. — **-nut** smultbolle.
doughy ['doᵘi] deiget; — **complexion** gråbleik hudfarge.
doughtiness ['dautinès] mandighet, tapperhet.
doughty ['dauti] tapper, mandig; djerv, gjev.
Douglas ['dʌgləs] Douglas.
dour [duə] (skotsk) hard, ubøyelig, stri.

douse [daus] se **dowse.**
dove [dʌv] due. — **-cot** [-kåt] dueslag; **flutter the** — **-cots** bringe uro i leiren, sette støkk i godtfolk.
dovelet ['dʌvlit] liten due, ung due.
Dover ['douvə] Dover; — **court** støyende forsamling, polsk riksdag.
dovetail ['dʌvte'l] sinketapp; sinke sammen; passe sammen.
dowager ['dauidʒə] fornem el. rik enke, enkefrue; **Queen Dowager** enkedronning.
dowdy ['daudi] gammeldags el. sjusket kledd kvinne; slusket, slurvet.
dowel ['dauil] blindnagle, dimling; feste med blindnagle osv.
dower ['dauə] enkes boslodd, enkesete; medgift; begavelse; begave (**with** med).
dowlas(s) ['daulǝs] slags grovt lerret.
down [daun] dun, hy, fnugg, fnokk.
down [daun] klett, dyne, sandbanke; banke; **the Downs** dynene, sandbankene (flere steder f. eks. i Sussex).
down [daun] ned; nede; nedad; ned igjennom; — **here** her ned(e); — **stairs** ned trappa; ned; nedenunder, nede; — **there** der ned(e); **come** — komme ned, falle ned; **cut** — hogge ned, felle; meie; **go** — gå under; synke, falle (i kamp), velte; **lie** — legge seg (ned); **sit** — sette seg (ned); **be** — **on one** være etter en; **be** — **for** være tegnet for; ha i vente. **be** — **and out** ute av stand til å gjenoppta boksekampen, beseiret i livskampen; gjort av med. **-cast** nedslått, motfallen. **-draught** nedslag. **-fall** fall. **-hearted** motfallen. **-hill** hellende; unnabakke; skrent.
Downing ['dauniŋ]; — **Street,** gate i London hvor statsministeren bor; regjeringen.
down|pour ['daunpå·ə] skyllregn, øsregn. **-right** likefram, endefram; fullstendig. **-stairs** ned trappene, ned, i stua, nedenunder. — **-train** tog fra London. **-trodden** nedtrukket; tråkket under fot. **-ward** ['daunwəd] nedadgående. **-wards** ['daunwədz] nedad, nedover.
downy ['dauni] dunet; dunbløt; listig.
dowry ['dau°ri] medgift; talent.
dowse [daus] skvette vann på, slokke (lys), fire (seil) ned; nytte ønskekvist til å finne vann; — **the glim** slokke lyset. **dowser** ['dauzə] en som bruker ønskekvist til å finne vann. **dowsing-rod** ønskekvist.
doxology [dåk'sålǝdʒi] lovprisning, lovsang.
doxy ['dåksi] kjæreste, fente.
doyen ['dwaiǎn] eldstemann.
Doyle [doil] Doyle.
doz. fk. f. **dozen.**
doze [douz] døse, dorme, slumre; døs, blund, lur.
dozen ['dʌzn] dusin, tylft; **half-a-** — et halvt dusin, fem-seks, **dozens of** i dusinvis av.
doziness ['douzinès] døsighet. **dozy** ['douzi] døsig.
D. P. I. fk. f. **Director of Public Instruction.**
D. R. fk. f. **District Railway.**
Dr. fk. f. **doctor, debtor.**
dr. fk. f. **drachm.**
drab [dräb] sjuske, slurve; skjøke.
drab [dräb] et slags gulbrunt klede; gulbrun farge; **-boots** gule støvler.
drabbet ['dräbit] slags grovt lerret.
drabble ['dräbl] søle, skitne til.
drachm [dräm], **drachma** ['dräkmə] drakme.
Draconian [drə'kounjən], **Draconic** [drə'kånik] drakonisk, meget streng.
draff [dra·f] bunnfall, berme, avfall, utskudd.
draffish ['dra·fiʃ], **draffy** ['dra·fi] bermet; slett.
draft [dra·ft] trekning; tapning; veksel, tratte; detasjement; grunnriss, plan, tegning (se **draught**); avsette, tegne; gjøre utkast til; detasjere. **draftsman** [-smən] tegner.
drag [dräg] dra, trekke, drasse, slepe (bortover bakken); sokne; harve, slepe, dra seg; — **on** trekke ut. **drag** [dräg] harv; vogn; dregg; sokn;

dragnot; muddermaskin; drass, hindring; slep; slepjakt; hemsko.
draggle ['drägl] dra i sølen; søle til; skitne; slepes, søles til, skitnes til. **-tail** sjuske. **-tailed** sjusket, slurvet.
dragnet ['drägnet] dragnot.
dragoman ['drägomən] orientalsk tolk.
dragon ['drägən] drake. **dragonet** ['drägənét] liten drake; fløyfisk. **dragon-fly** gullsmed, libelle.
dragoon [drə'gu·n] dragon; tvinge ved dragoner, bruke soldatervold.
drain [dre'n] lede bort noe flytende; tørre ut; drenere; tømme; filtrere, sile; tappe; veite, grøfte; flyte, renne, sige bort; tømning; avledningskanal; tapping. **drainage** ['dre'nidʒ] bortledning; uttapping; drenering; rørlegging; kloakkvesen. **drainpipe** ['dre'npaip] drenrør.
drake [dre'k] andrik; andestegg.
dram [dräm] drakme; smule; dram, støyt, knert; supe, pimpe.
drama ['dra·mə] drama. **dramatic(al)** [drə'mätik(l)] dramatisk. **dramatis personæ** ['drämetis pə·'soⁿni·] de opptredende personer. **dramatist** ['drämətist, 'dra·-] dramatisk forfatter. **dramatize** ['drämətaiz, 'dra·-] dramatisere. **dramaturgy** ['drämətə·dʒi, 'dra·-] dramaturgi.
drank [dräŋk] imperf. av **drink.**
drape [dreip] bekle, drapere; tjelde; pryde. **draper** ['dre'pə] kledeshandler, manufakturist. **drapery** ['dre'p(ə)ri] drapering, draperi; kledehandel; klær; manufakturvarer.
draping ['dre'piŋ] drapering; draperi.
drastic ['drästik] drastisk; kraftig virkende middel.
drat [drät]: — **it** så for pokker!
drattle ['drätl] se **drat.**
draught [dra·ft] trekning, dragning; tapping; trekk, trekkvind; slurk, drikk; fiskedrett; varp, kast; grunnriss; veksel; (se **draft**); dybde; **-s** damspill; **beer on** — øl på fat. — **-board** dambrett. — **-horse** arbeidshest. **-sman** tegner, planlegger; dambrikke. **-smanship** tegnekunst, avfattingskunst. **-y** ['dra·fti] trekkfull.
drave [dre'v] sjelden imperf. av **drive.**
draw [drå] dra, trekke; tegne; avfatte, sette opp skriftlig; oppebære, heve (penger); strekke, tøye; utlede, utvinne; suge; øse; tømme; tappe; erverve; lokke; fordreie; ta ut, renske innvollene; trekke for; bevege seg; trekke blank; trekke, trassere; trekkes for; trekkes til side; trekking, trekk; gevinst; skuff; kassestykke (om skuespill el. lign. som går godt); **the ship draws too much water** skipet stikker for dypt; — **back** trekke seg tilbake; — **near** nærme seg; — **off** utdra; avlede; — **on** nærme seg; trekke veksler på, ty til, ta tilflukt til; trekke blank imot; — **out** trekke ut, forhale; velge ut; — **up** stille opp, fylke; stanse; sette opp; — **upon one** trekke (en veksel) på en. **drawback** ['drå·bäk] avbrekk, hindring; ulempe, ubehagelighet, lyte, skyggeside; tilbakebetaling av innførselstollen, når varene utføres igjen. **-bridge** vindebru. **drawee** [drå·'i·] trassat. **drawer** ['drå·ə] trekker; tegner; tapper; trassent; skuff. **drawers** underbenklær; kommode (**chest of drawers**).
drawing ['drå·iŋ] trekning; trassering; tegning; **out of** — fortegnet; **-s** inntekter. — **board** tegnebrett. — **master** tegnelærer. — **pen** tegnepenn; rissefjær. — **pin** tegnestift. — **room** sal, salong, bestestue; selskap; hoff-fest (for både herrer og damer); tegnekontor.
drawl [drå·l] være sendrektig, tale el. lese slepende; sendrektig uttale, drag.
drawn [drå·n] perf. pts. av **draw;** stram, skarp (i ansiktet); smeltet (smør); — **battle** uavgjort slag; — **game** uavgjort spill.
draw-well ['drå·wel] heisebrønn.
dray [dre'] sluffe; slodde; ølvogn. **-man** ølkjører.
dread [dred] skrekk, redsel, frykt; skrekkelig,

fryktelig; mektig, høy, fryktinngytende; frykte, reddes. **dreadful** ['dredf(u)l] fryktelig; **a penny —** el. **a shilling —** en røverroman.

dreadnought ['drednå·t] vågehals; tykt frakketøy, tykk frakk; slags stort krigsskip, slagskip.

dream [dri·m] drømme; drøm; **a — of a face** et nydelig ansikt. **dreamer** ['dri·mə] drømmer. **dreaminess** ['dri·minēs] drømmerier. **dreamt** [dremt], imperf. og perf. pts. av **dream. dreamy** ['dri·mi] drømmende.

dreary ['driəri] sørgelig, trist, uhyggelig.

dredge [dredʒ] dregg; østersskrape; bunnskrape; muddermaskin; skrape (østers); mudre opp; drysse, bestrø. **dredger** ['dredʒə] skraper; muddermaskin; strødåse. **dredging box** strødåse.

dredging-machine muddermaskin.

dree [dri·] tåle; **— my weird** finne meg i min skjebne.

dregginess ['dreginēs] gjørmet beskaffenhet; bunnfall. **dreggish** ['dregiʃ], **dreggy** ['dregi] mudret, uklar, gjørmet. **dregs** [dregz] berme, bunnfall.

drench [drenʃ] gjennombløyte, gjøre dyvåt; mette med drikk; gi medisin inn med makt; drikk; lægedrikk. **drencher** ['drenʃə] øsregn.

dress [dres] kledning, drakt; damekjole; galla. **— -boots** selskapsstøvler. **— circle** balkong (i teatret). **— -clothes** selskapsdrakt. **— coat** snippkjole. **— improver** kø, «løytnant». **-maker** dameskredder(ske). **— -rehearsal** generalprøve. **— -shirt** mansjettskjorte.

dress [dres] stelle til, bringe i stand; garve; kle, kle på; pynte; kle på seg; kle seg om; rette; rette seg; gjøde, gjødsle; **— the salad** lage salaten; **— a wound** forbinde et sår; **— a horse** strigle en hest; dressere en hest; **— the ground** gjødsle; **— fish** renske fisk; **— flax** hekle lin; **— a tree** beskjære et tre.

dresser ['dresə] en som tilbereder osv.; forbinder (på hospital); påkleder; pyntekone; kjøkkenbord, anretningsbord; tallerkenrekke.

dressing ['dresiŋ] forbinding; gjødning, gjødsel; tilberedning; tilbehør (til en rett); påkledning; appretur; farse; refselse. **— -case** toalettskrin, -veske, forbindingstaske. **— -gown** slåbrok. **-room** påkledningsværelse. **— -table** toalettbord.

dressy ['dresi] pyntesyk; pyntelig, fjong.

drew [dru·] imperf. av **draw.**

dribble ['dribl] dryppe; sikle; drible (i fotball); drypp; sikl; støvregn, duskregn. **driblet** ['driblit] drypp; liten smule; liten sum penger.

drier ['draiə] tørrer; tørremiddel; se **dry.**

drift [drift] drift; drivkraft; retning; snødrive, snødrev; snøfonn, drivis; drivgarn; hensikt, øyemed. **drift** [drift] drive; fyke; dynge sammen.

drill [dril] drille, bore; innøve; inneksersere (soldater); avrette; så i rad; spille (tiden); drill, drillbor; radsåmaskin; rad, fure; eksersis. **-harrow** gymnastikkllærer, eksersermester.

drily ['draili] tørt.

drink [driŋk] drikk; drikke, være fordrukken; **have a —, take a —** drikke et glass, få seg et glass; **— to drikke på; — to one** skåle med en, for en. **drinkable** ['driŋkəbl] drikkelig; **drinkables** drikkevarer. **drinker** ['driŋkə] en som drikker; dranker. **drinking** ['driŋkiŋ] drikking, sidrikking; **drinking-bout** drikkegilde, drikkelag, rangel.

drink-offering ['driŋkåfəriŋ] drikkoffer.

drip [drip] dryppe; drypp; gesims. **-stone** kransliste; gesims. **dripping** ['dripiŋ] drypping; stekefett.

drive [draiv] drive; jage; tvinge; ramme ned; slå i; kjøre; styre, føre; kjøre omkring, jage med, fare hurtig av sted, ile; sikte (til: at); **— a bargain** gjøre en handel; **— at** sikte til; ha i sinne, ha i kikkerten, gå løs på. **drive** [draiv] driving, drift, fedrift, tømmerdrift osv.; kjøretur; kjørevei.

drivel ['drivl] sikle, sleve; vrøvle; sikl; vrøvl. **driveller** ['drivlə]· siklesvin; vrøvlekopp.

driven ['drivn] perf. pts. av **drive; — snow** nyfalt snø.

driver ['draivə] kjører, kusk, vognstyrer, lokomotivfører; driver (av dyr etc.); drivverk, drivhjul; golfkølle.

drizzle ['drizl] duskregne, småregne, duske; stenke; duskregn. **drizzling rain** støvregn. **drizzly** ['drizli] rusket, musket.

droit [droit] avgift, sportel, rett, krav.

droll [droᵘl] pussig, snodig, rar; spøkefugl, spasmaker; klovn; farse; marionettspill. **drollery** ['droᵘl(ə)ri] pussighet, morsomt påfunn.

dromedary ['dråmidəri, 'drʌm-] dromedar.

drone [droᵘn] drone; lat person, tverrblei; brumming, dur; basspipe; brumme, surre, dure; mulle; lire av seg.

droop [dru·p] henge ned; lute; la henge; falle sammen; synke, segne, helle. **-ing** ['dru·piŋ] hellende, lut, slut.

drop [dråp] dråpe; øredobbe; drops, snop, bonbon; teppe (for scenen); fall; senkning, nedgang; fall-lem; **takes a — sometimes** er ikke fri for å drikke; **has taken a — too much** er drukken; **a — in the ocean** en dråpe i havet.

drop [dråp] dryppe, la falle; falle; slippe seg ned; synke, sige; sakke; holde opp; komme uventet; tape, miste; senke; ytre, ymte; forlate, utelate; sende med posten; drive (f. eks. av vann), falle fra, dø; forgå, forsvinne; **— an acquaintance** oppgi et bekjentskap; **let us — the subject** la oss ikke snakke mer om den ting; **— a courtesy** neie; **— in** komme uventet, se innom en; **— off** falle ned; avta; falle fra, dø.

drop-curtain ['dråp'ka·tin] mellomaktsteppe.

drop-scene ['dråpsi·n] mellomaktssteppe.

dropsical ['dråpsikl], **dropsied** ['dråpsid] vattersottig. **dropsy** ['dråpsi] vattersott.

droshky ['dråʃki] drosje.

drosometer [dro'såmitə] doggmåler.

dross [drås] slagg; avfall, skrap; berme. **drossy** ['dråsi] slaggaktig; uren.

drought [draut] tørke; tørketid; skort, mangel; tørst. **droughtiness** ['drautinēs] tørke. **droughty** ['drauti] tørr; tørst.

drove [droᵘv] drift, flokk (fe); stime; driftevei, buvei, sti. **drover** ['droᵘvə] fekar, driftekar. **drove** [droᵘv] drev, imperf. av **drive.**

drow [drau] yr, musk.

drown [draun] drukne (intransitivt bare i formen **drowning**); døyve; overdøyve; **be -ed** drukne.

drowse [drauz] slumre, døse; dorme; gjøre døsig, sløve. **drowsiness** ['drauzinēs] søvnighet, døsighet. **drowsy** ['drauzi] søvnig, døsig; søvndyssende.

drub [drʌb] banke, denge, pryle, jule; **— something into** en banke noe inn i en. **drub** [drʌb] slag, støt. **drubbing** ['drʌbiŋ] drakt pryl; juling, bank.

drudge [drʌdʒ] flittig arbeider, sliter; slite og slepe. **drudgery** ['drʌdʒəri] trellearbeid; slit og slep; «negerarbeid».

drug [drʌg] kjemikalier, medisin, apotekervare, drogeri; vare som det er vanskelig å bli av med; blande med el bedøvende stoff el. gift; forfalske; bedøve, svimeslå; **— in the market** uavsettelig vare; **— oneself with morphine** bedøve seg med morfin.

drugget ['drʌgit] grovt ulltøy, golvteppetøy, teppeskåner.

druggist ['drʌgist] drogist; apoteker (amr.). **drugstore** ['drʌgstå·ə] apotek (amr.).

druid ['dru·id] druide, keltisk prest.

drum [drʌm] tromme; trommeslager; trommehule (i øret); larmende aftenselskap; tromle; valse; tromme; tromme på; tromme sammen, verve (rekrutter, politiske partifeller); gjenta; **beat the —** slå på tromme; **— something into one's ears** banke noe inn i hodet på en.

drum|fire ['drʌmfaiə] trommeild (voldsom artilleriild forut for infanterrangrep). **-head** ['drʌmhed] trommeskinn; trommehinne; standrett; spill-

hode. — -major [-'me'dʒə] korpstambur, regimentstambur.
drummer ['drʌmə] trommeslager, tambur; en som fanger kunder, handelsreisende.
drumstick ['drʌmstik] trommestikke.
drunk [drʌŋk] perf. pts. av drink; drukken, full; rangel, rus, fyll; full mann. drunkard ['drʌŋkəd] dranker. drunken ['drʌŋkən] drukken, full (bare som tilføyd adjektiv); drikkfeldig. drunkenness ['drʌŋkə(n)nés] drukkenskap; drikkfeldighet.
drupe [dru·p] steinfrukt.
Drury ['druəri] Lane gate (og teater) i London.
dry [drai] tørr; gjeld (om ku); tørst; tørre; tørke. — up tørke ut; opphøre helt; holde kjeft.
dryad ['draiəd] dryade, skognymfe.
dry-as-dust ['draiəzdʌst] meget tørr; tørr, stuelærd, pedant. drybeat ['draibi·t] mørbanke.
Dryden ['draidn] Dryden.
dry-goods ['draigudz] manufakturvarer. dryly ['draili] tørt (også drily). drynurse amme som passer men ikke gir barnet bryst; flaske opp; være barnepike for (figurlig). -pile tørrelement. dry-rot tørråte. drysalter ['draiså·ltə] drogist, fargehandler. drysaltery ['draiså·ltəri] drogeri, fargehandel. dryshod ['draiʃåd] tørrskodd.
D. S. C. fk. f. distinguished service cross.
D. Sc. fk. f. Doctor of Science.
D. S. M. fk. f. distinguished service medal.
D. S. O. fk. f. distinguished service order.
D. T. fk. f. Daily Telegraph; delirium tremens.
dual ['djuəl] dobbelt; dual monarchy dobbeltmonarki; dualis.
dualism ['dju·əlizm] dualisme. -istic [dju·ə-'listik] dualistisk.
dub [dʌb] slå; slå til ridder; betitle, utnevne; pusse, stelle til; smøre inn.
dubious ['dju·bjəs] tvilende; tvilsom.
dubitation ['dju·bi'teiʃən] tvil, tvilsmål.
dubitative ['dju·bite'tiv] tvilende.
Dublin ['dʌblin] Dublin.
ducal ['dju·kəl] hertugelig.
ducat ['dʌkət] dukat.
duchess ['dʌtʃis] hertuginne. duchy ['dʌtʃi] hertugdømme.
duck [dʌk] dukke (kjæleord), engel.
duck [dʌk] seilduk; (pl.) lerretsbukser.
duck [dʌk] and; make (el. play at) -s and drakes skeine, kaste en flat stein bortover vannflaten; play at ducks and drakes with money øse penger ut.
duck [dʌk] dukke, væte, bl..yte. -ing ['dʌkiŋ] dukkert; dåp (første gang man passerer linjen).
duck-legged ['dʌklegd] kortbeint.
duckling ['dʌkliŋ] andunge.
duck-meat ['dʌkmi·t], duckweed ['dʌkwi·d] andemat.
ducky ['dʌki] yndig, søt, god; skatt, engel.
duct [dʌkt] kanal, rør, gang.
ductile ['dʌkt(a)il] tøyelig, smidig. ductility [dʌk'tiliti] tøyelighet, smidighet.
dud [dʌd] granat som ikke springer; unyttig forehavende, unyttig person; unyttig, ubrukelig.
duds (gamle) klær, filler.
dude [dju·d] laps, sprett (amr.).
dudgeon ['dʌdʒən] vrede, sinne, harme; take in — ta ille opp.
due [dju·] skyldig; passende, tilbørlig; nøyaktig, riktig; punktlig; forfallen (f. eks. om veksel); skyldighet; rett; avgift; come (fall) — forfalle (til betaling); in — time i rette tid; the steamer is — to-day damperen skal komme i dag; — north beint nord.
duel ['dju·əl] tvekamp, duell; duellere; fight a — with pistols duellere med pistoler. duellist ['dju·əlist] duellant.
duenna [dju'enə] duenna, anstandsdame.
duet [dju·'et] duett; stevjing.
duff [dʌf] deig; melpudding; bløt skogbunn; snyte i handel (med dårlige varer).

duffel ['dʌfl] dyffel.
duffer ['dʌfə] kramkar; en som handler med innsmuglede eller stjålne varer, svindler; idiot; fusker; pedant, filister; uekte stas; falsk mynt.
dug [dʌg] patte; spene.
dug [dʌg] imperf. og perf. pts. av dig.
dug-out ['dʌgaut] utgravd; jordhytte, oppholdssted for tropper under jorda; uthult tre, eike; avskjediget offiser, som blir kalt til tjeneste igjen.
duke [dju·k] hertug; doge. dukedom ['dju·kdəm] hertugdømme.
dulcamara [dʌlkə'mæ·°rə] søtvier.
dulcet ['dʌlsit] søt, liflig, blid.
dulcify ['dʌlsifai] forsøte; gjøre blid, tine opp.
dulcimer ['dʌlsimə] hakkebrett, cymbel.
Dulcinea [dʌlsi'ni·ə] Dulcinea.
dull [dʌl] dunkel, dim, matt, dump; stump; sløv; dum; langsom, treg, kjedsommelig; flau; trist; gjøre uklar; sløve; sløves; — of hearing tunghørt. dullard ['dʌləd] dumrian, staur. -minded åndssløv, halvfjollet, innskrenket. dullness ['dʌlnés] dunkelhet; sløvhet; dumhet; søvnighet; kjedsommelighet. dull-witted dum, enfoldig.
dully ['dʌli] matt, sløvt, tregt, kjedelig.
duly ['dju·li] tilbørlig, i rett tid.
Duma ['du·mə] (russisk) duma.
dumb [dʌm] umælende, målløs, stum. — -barge lekter, pram. -bells manual. -found gjøre forvirret, forfjamse, gjøre målløs. -show pantomime. -waiter stumtjener.
dumdum ['dʌmdʌm] dumdumkule.
dum(b)found [dʌm'faund] gjøre målløs.
Dumfries [dəm'fri·s] Dumfries.
dummy ['dʌmi] stum person; statist; dumming, fehode; attrapp; blindvindu, blinddør; hallingmann; fugleskremsel; parykkblokk; stumtjener; blindmann (i kortspill); stråmann.
dump [dʌmp] klinkeskilling; søppelhaug, søppelplass; styrte ut, velte, tømme ut; dumpe, kaste ut på markedet til en lav pris; (i plur.) melankoli; I don't care a — jeg bryr meg ikke en døyt.
dumpish ['dʌmpiʃ] nedtrykt, sturen, motfallen.
dumpling ['dʌmpliŋ] innbakt frukt.
dumps [dʌmps] (pl. av dump) melankoli; in the — nedtrykt, sturen.
Dumpty se Humpty-dumpty.
dumpy ['dʌmpi] liten og tykk.
dun [dʌn] gråbrun, mørkebrun; mørk, trist.
dun [dʌn] plage, kreve, rykke; rykker.
Dunbar [dʌn'ba·°] Dunbar.
dunce [dʌns] dumrian, fe, tosk; fuks (i en klasse). The Dunciad ['dʌnsiäd] (dikt av Pope).
Dundee [dʌn'di·] Dundee.
dunderhead ['dʌndəhed] kjøtthue, naut.
Dundreary [dʌn'dri·əri] whiskers langt kinnskjegg.
dune [dju·n] sandklett, sandbanke.
dung [dʌŋ] møkk, gjødsel; gjødsle.
dungaree [dʌŋgəri·] dongeri, tynt blått tøy brukt til arbeidsklær.
dung-beetle ['dʌŋbi·tl] tordivel.
dungeon ['dʌndʒən] fangetårn, fengsel, fangehull; innesperre i et fangehull.
dung|fork ['dʌnfå·°k] møkkgreip. dunghill ['dʌŋhil] møkkdynge.
dungy ['dʌŋi] møkket, skitten.
dunlin ['dʌnlin] strandvippe (fugl).
Dunlop ['dʌnlåp] dunlopring, dunlopgummi.
dunnage ['dʌnidʒ] underlag, garnering, bedding.
dunner ['dʌnə] rykker.
dunnish ['dʌniʃ] mørklaten.
duo ['d(j)u·o] duo, duett.
duodecimo [dju·o'desimo°] duodes (bokformat hvor arket deles i 12 blad).
dupe [dju·p] narre, bedra, føre bak lyset; en som lar seg narre, narr, lettroende menneske.
duple ['dju·pl] dobbelt; -ratio 2 : 1; -time ³/₄takt.

duplex ['dju·pleks] dobbelt.
duplicate ['dju·plike't] fordoble; legge sammen; ta gjenpart av. duplicate ['dju·pliket] dobbelt; dublett; gjenpart; pantelånerseddel. duplication [dju·pli'ke'ʃən] fordobling; sammenlegging.
duplicity [dju'plisiti] dobbelthet; falskhet.
durability [djuªrə'biliti] varighet, hold. durable ['djuərəbl] varig, holdbar.
durance ['djuərəns] varighet; uslitelig bekledningsstoff; fangenskap; in — vile i forsmedelig fangenskap.
duration [dju're'ʃən] varighet, vedvarenhet.
durbar ['də·ba·ª] audienssal (i Ostindia); audiens; utøvende myndighet.
duress [dju'res] fengsling, urettmessig tvang.
Durham ['dʌrəm] Durham.
during ['djuəriŋ] i løpet av, under, i.
durn [də·n] fordømt, forbannet.
durra ['durə, 'dʌrə] durra, indisk hirse.
durst [də·st] torde, imperf. av dare.
dusk [dʌsk] dunkel, mørk, skum; halvmørk; mørk farge; skumring, tusmørke.
duskiness ['dʌskinəs] mørklatenhet.
dusky ['dʌski] mørk, dunkel.
dust [dʌst] støv; dust, føyke, gyv; penger, mynt; gullstøv; støve til, støve av, rense for støv; gjennombanke; bestrø; bite the — bite i graset; kick up a — gjøre spetakkel; throw — in some one's eyes kaste en blår i øynene. — -bin søppelkasse. — -brush støvekost. — -cart søppelkjerre. — -cloak støvkappe. — -coat støvfrakk, støvkåpe. — -contractor [-kən'träktə] entreprenør som besørger dagrenovasjonen bortkjørt. — -man søppelkjører. — -pan søppelbrett.
duster ['dʌstə] støveklut; støvekost; soll.
dusty ['dʌsti] støvet; not so dusty el. none so dusty ikke så galt, ikke så ueffent.
Dutch [dʌtʃ] hollandsk; hollandsk (språket); the — nederlenderne; — auction hollandsk auksjon hvor varer ropes opp til høye priser, som reduseres til det blir gjort bud; — clock schwarzwalderur; varmedunk; — comfort, — consolation dårlig trøst; — concert konsert, hvor alle synger eller spiller, men hver sin melodi; — courage kunstig mot (især tildrukket); — feast et gilde hvor verten blir full før gjestene; — gold bladgull; flittergull; — toys nürnbergerkram; — uncle ubehagelig moralpredikant.
Dutchman ['dʌtʃmən] nederlender; i Amerika også: en tysker, en skandinav; the Flying — den

flyvende hollender; iltoget mellom London og Exeter; I'm a — if . . . du kan kalle meg en krakk hvis . . .
Dutchwoman ['dʌtʃwumən] nederlandsk kvinne.
duteous ['dju·tiəs] lydig, ærbødig; plikttro.
dutiable ['dju·tiəbl] tollpliktig.
dutiful ['dju·tif(u)l] lydig, ærbødig, tro.
duty ['dju·ti] plikt, skyldighet; hilsen, ærbødighet, aktelse; avgift, toll; tjeneste, vakt (militær); as in — bound pliktskyldigst; be on — være på vakt, gjøre tjeneste; officer on — vakthavende offiser; off — fri for tjeneste. — -free tollfri.
dux [dʌks] duks, bestemann.
D. V. fk. f. Deo volente om Gud vil.
d. w. el. dw. fk. f. dead weight.
dwarf [dwɔ·ªf] dverg; hindre i veksten, forkrøple. dwarfish ['dwɔ·ªfiʃ] dvergaktig.
dwell [dwel] dvele, dryge, slå seg til; bo; pause, stans. dweller ['dwelə] beboer.
dwelling ['dweliŋ] opphold, stans; bolig. — -house våningshus. — -place bopel.
dwelt [dwelt] imperf. og perf. pts. av dwell.
dwindle ['dwindl] svinne; svinne inn, skrumpe sammen, minke. — away svinne bort.
dwt. fk. f. pennyweight.
dye [dai] farge, lett; farge. — -house fargeri.
dyeing ['daiiŋ] farging. dyer ['daiə] farger. dyery ['daiəri] fargeri. dye-stuff fargestoff.
dying ['daiiŋ] pres. pts. og verbalsubstantiv av die dø; — bed dødsleie; — day dødsdag.
dyke [daik] se dike.
dyn. fk. f. dynamics.
dynamic [d(a)i'nämik] dynamisk.
dynamics dynamikk, kraftlære.
dynamite ['dainəmait] dynamitt. dynamitard ['dainəmita·ªd], dynamiter ['dainəmaitə], dynamitist ['dainəmaitist] dynamittmann, bombekaster.
dynamo ['dainəmoᵘ] dynamo. dynamometer [dainə'mämitə] dynamometer, kraftmåler.
dynast ['dainäst] styrer, høvding.
dynasty ['dinəsti, 'dai-] dynasti, herskerfamilie.
dysenteric(al) [disən'terik(l)] dysenterisk. dysentery ['disəntəri] dysenteri, blodgang.
dyspepsia [dis'pepsiə], dyspepsy [dis'pepsi] dyspepsi, dårlig fordøyelse.
dyspeptic [dis'peptik] dyspeptisk; dyspeptiker.
dyspnæa [disp'ni·ə] åndenød.
dysury ['disjuri] urintvang.
dziggetai ['dzigətai] vilt esel (asiatisk).

E

E. [i·] e; E. fk. f. earl; East, Eastern.
E sharp eiss; E flat ess; E major e-dur; E minor e-moll.
each [i·tʃ] hver især, hver enkelt (av et antall); they cost sixpence — de koster 6 pence stykket; — other hinannen, hverandre.
eager ['i·gə] ivrig, livlig; spent; bitter, sårende (om ord); kald (om lufta). eagerness ['i·gənəs] iver, begjærlighet, trå.
eagle ['i·gl] ørn; amerikansk mynt (10 dollars). — -eyed ørnøyd, skarpsynt. — -owl hubro, bergugle.
eagless ['i·glis] hunørn. eaglet ['i·glét] ørnunge.
eagre ['e'gə, 'i·gə] springflo, stormflo.
E. & O. E. fk. f. errors & omissions excepted.
ear [iə] øre; box on the — ørefik; set a flea in one's — gjøre en mistenksom; noise in one's — øresus; be all ears være lutter øre; keep a promise to the — oppfylle et løfte etter ordlyden (ikke etter meningen); lend (el. turn) a deaf — to vende det døve øre til; fall (out, together) by the ears komme i tottene på hverandre; prick up one's ears spisse ørene; set people (together)

by the ears pusse folk på hverandre; have about one's ears ha om ørene, ha om halsen; I have something for your private — jeg har noe å si Dem i enrom; go in at one — and out at the other gå inn gjennom det ene øre og ut av det andre; lead by the ears ha i ledebånd; over (head and) ears opp over ørene; speak in the — hviske.
ear [iə] aks.
ear [iə] pløye.
ear-ache ['iəre'k] øreverk.
ear-drum ['iədrʌm] trommehule i øret, trommehinne.
earing ['iəriŋ] nokkbendsel.
earl [ə·l] jarl; greve (om engelske grever).
Earl's Court forlystelsessted i London.
ear-lap ['iəläp] øreflipp, ytre øre, ørebrusk.
earldom ['ə·ldəm] grevskap; jarledømme.
earliness ['ə·linəs] tidlighet, det å være tidlig.
early ['ə·li] tidlig; tidlig moden; at an — age i en ung alder; at an — date i nær framtid; the — boat morgendamperen; — to bed and — to rise, makes a man healthy, wealthy, and wise morgenstund har gull i munn; as — as May

allerede i mai; — **bird**, — **riser** morgenfugl; **the — bird catches the worm** morgenstund har gull i munn; **the** — **church** oldkirken; — **habits** den vane å gå tidlig i seng og stå tidlig opp; **keep** — **hours** gå tidlig i seng og stå tidlig opp.
ear-mark ['iəma·ᵊk] merke (hakk) i øret (på sauer); merke øret på.
earn [ə·n] tjene, fortjene, erverve.
earnest ['ə·nist] alvorlig; ivrig, inntrengende; alvor; **are you in** —? er det ditt alvor? **in good** — for ramme alvor.
earnest ['ə·nist] festepenger, pant; avdrag; forsmak. — **-money** festepenger.
earnestness ['ə·nistnés] alvor, alvorlighet.
earnings ['ə·niṇz] fortjeneste.
ear-pick ['iəpik] øreskje.
ear-shot ['iəʃåt] hørevidde.
ear-splitting ['iəsplitiṇ] øredøvende.
earth [ə·þ] jord, jordklode, jorden; land; jordslag; hule, hi; utgang i hi; **what (where) on** —? hva (hvor) i all verden? **earth** grave ned; bedekke med jord; hyppe; grave seg ned; gå i hi.
earthen ['ə·þn] jord-; leir-. — **ware** leirvarer; steintøy.
earthiness ['ə·þinés] jordaktig beskaffenhet.
earthliness ['ə·þlinés] jordiskhet.
earthling ['ə·þliṇ] jordisk menneske, jordens barn; moldtrell.
earthly ['ə·þli] jordisk; opptenkelig; **no** — **reason why** ingen verdens grunn til; — **-minded** verdsligsinnet.
earthquake ['ə·þkwe¹k] jordskjelv.
earthworm ['ə·þwə·m] regnorm, beitemark.
earthy ['ə·þi] jordaktig; jordisk; jordbunden.
ear-trumpet ['iətrʌmpit] hørerør.
earwig ['iəwig] saksedyr; påvirke en ved øretuteri, smiske for.
ease [i·z] rolighet, ro; makelighet, behagelighet; tvangsfrihet; lediggang; lindring, lettelse; letthet, frihet; lindre, lette; befri; løsne, slappe, la gå med sakte fart, slakke (seilskjøtet); **at** — i ro, i ro og mak, bekvemt; **ill at** — ille til mote; **put at** — berolige; **stand at** — stå på stedet hvil; **take one's** — gjøre seg det makelig; **with** — med letthet.
easel ['i·zl] staffeli.
easement ['i·zmənt] lettelse; rettighet; fordel.
easily ['i·zili] med letthet, lett; utvungen.
easiness ['i·zinés] letthet; mak, ro; føyelighet; — **of belief** lettroenhet.
East eller **east** [i·st] øst; Østen; Østerland; Orienten; øst, østlig; **to the** — of øst for.
Easter ['i·stə] påske; — **Day** (første) påskedag; — **Monday** annen påskedag.
easterly ['i·stəli] østlig. **eastern** ['i·stən] fra øst; østerlandsk; østerlender.
East Indies [i·st'indiz]: **the** — Ostindia.
easting ['i·stiṇ] østseiling, østlig kurs.
eastward ['i·stwəd] mot øst, østlig, østre; østpå.
easy ['i·zi] rolig, behagelig; makelig; lett, ikke vanskelig; jevn; usjenert; villig; lettvint; fri, utvungen, naturlig; — **circumstances** gode kår; **on** — **terms** på rimelige vilkår; — **of belief** lettroende; **make** — berolige. — **-chair** lenestol. — **-going** sorgløs, makelig, medgjørlig.
eat [i·t] ete, spise; fortære; **the meat eats well** kjøttet smaker godt; — **one's head off** ete seg i hjel; kjede seg fordervet; — **one's fill** spise seg mett; — **one's words** ta sine ord tilbake.
eat [et] imperf. av **eat**.
eatable ['i·təbl] spiselig; **-s** matvarer.
eatage ['i·tidʒ] beiterett.
eaten ['i·tn] perf. pts. av **eat**.
eau-de-Cologne ['oᵘdako'loᵘn] eau de Cologne.
eaves [i·vz] takskjegg. **-drop** [-dråp] lytte, lure. **-dropper** [-dråpə] lytter, lurer.
ebb [eb] ebbe, fjære; avta, gå tilbake. **-tide** ['ebtaid] ebbe, fjære.
E. b. N. fk. f. **East by North.**

E-boat ['i·boᵘt] fk. f. **enemy boat** E-båt, pansret motorbåt.
ebon ['ebən] ibenholt.
ebony ['ebəni] ibenholt.
ebriate ['i·briit] drukken, full.
ebriety [i'braiiti] drukkenskap.
E. b. S. fk. f. **East by South.**
ebullition [ebju'liʃən] koking; oppkoking; oppbrusning.
E. C. fk. f. **East Central (London postal district).**
eccentric [ek'sentrik] eksentrisk; overspent, besynderlig, sær; eksentrisk sirkel, eksentrisk skive; eksentrisk person, særlig. **eccentricity** [eksən'trisiti] eksentrisitet, besynderlighet.
Ecclesiastes [ikli·zi'ästi·z] Predikerens bok.
ecclesiastic(al) [ikli·zi'ästik(l)] kirkelig, kirke-; geistlig.
Ecclesiasticus [ikli·zi'ästikəs] Jesu Siraks bok.
echinus [e'kainəs] sjøpinnsvin, kråkebolle.
echo ['ekoᵘ] gjenlyd, ekko; gjenlyde; gjenta; si etter. **echometer** [e'kåmitə] lydmåler.
eclectic [ek'lektik] ᴄklektisk, utvelgende, utsøkende; eklektiker. **eclecticism** [ek'lektisizm] eklektisisme.
eclipse [i'klips] formørking; fordunkling; formørke; fordunkle, trenge i bakgrunnen. **ecliptic** [i'kliptik] ekliptikk (jordens bane om sola).
eclogue ['eklåg] hyrdediktt.
economic(al) [i·kə'nåmik(l)] økonomisk, sparsom. **economics** [i·'kə'nåmiks] økonomi. **economist** [i·'kånəmist] økonom. **economize** [i'kånəmaiz] holde hus med, økonomisere. **economy** [i'kånəmi] husholdning; økonomi; sparsommelighet; hensiktsmessig innretning.
ecstasy ['ekstəsi] henrykkelse, begeistring, ekstase; **be in ecstasies** være i den sjuende himmel.
ecstatic [ek'stätik] ekstatisk, henrykt, henrevet.
E. C. U. fk. f. **English Church Union.**
Ecuador [ekwə'då·ə] Ecuador.
ecumenic(al) [ekju'menik(l)] alminnelig, økumenisk.
eczema ['ekzimə, 'eksimə] eksem.
edacious [i'deiʃəs] grådig, hol.
E. D. D. fk. f. **English Dialect Dictionary.**
eddish [ediʃ] etterslått, hå.
eddy ['edi] hvirvel, malstrøm; bakevje; hvirvle.
Eddystone ['edistən] Eddystone.
edelweis ['i·dlvais] edelweiss (alpeblomst).
Eden ['i·dn] Eden; Paradis.
edentate [i'dente¹t] tannløs; gomler.
edge [edʒ] egg, odd, spiss; rand; kant; søm, skur, snitt (på en bok); skarphet; skjerpe; rykke; flytte seg; **set the teeth on** — få det til å ise i tennene; **with gilt edges** med gullsnitt; — **on** egge; — **in a word** få lirket inn et ord.
edgeways ['edʒwe¹z], **edgewise** ['edʒwaiz] på kant; **get in a word** — få kilt inn et ord, få lirket inn et ord.
edging ['edʒiṇ] rand, kant, kanting, bord, innfatning; smale kniplinger.
edgy ['edʒi] skarp; hissig, brå, oppfarende; ivrig etter.
edibility [edi'biliti] spiselighet.
edible ['edibl] spiselig.
edict ['i·dikt] edikt, forordning, kunngjøring.
edification [edifi'ke¹ʃən] oppbyggelse, oppbygging. **edifice** ['edifis] bygning. **edifier** ['edifaiə] en som oppbygger. **edify** ['edifai] oppbygge; belære. **edifying** oppbyggelig.
edile ['i·dail] edil.
Edinburgh ['ed(i)nbərə] Edinburg.
Edison ['edisən] Edison.
edit ['edit] gi ut, stå for utgivelsen av, redigere.
Edith ['i·diþ] Edith.
edition [i'diʃən] utgave; opplag. **editor** ['editə] utgiver; redaktør. **editorial** [edi'tå·riəl] redaksjonell, utgiver-. **editorship** ['editəʃip] redaksjon; redaktørpost; utgiverstilling. **editress** ['editrés] kvinnelig redaktør; utgiverinne.

Edmund ['edmənd] Edmund.
E. D. S. fk. f. **English Dialect Society.**
educ|ability [edjukə'biliti] nemme. -able ['edjuk-əbl] nem, som kan oppdras.
educate ['edjuke⁴t, 'edʒ-] oppdra; utdanne.
education [edju'ke⁴ʃən, edʒ-] oppdragelse; utdannelse, undervisning; skolevesen; **Primary** — folkeskolevesen; **Secondary** — høyere skolevesen; **the Elementary** — **Act** folkeskoleloven (av 1870); **board of E.** undervisningsdepartement. **educational** oppdragelses-; pedagogisk. **educationalist** [edju'ke⁴ʃənəlist, edʒ-] oppdrager, pedagog. **educationist** [edju'ke⁴ʃənist, edʒ-] pedagog. **educator** ['edjuke⁴tə, 'edʒ-] pedagog.
educe [i'dju·s] utlede, dra fram, få fram, lokke fram. eduction [i'dʌkʃən] utledelse; utvinning; utstrømning, utløp, avløp.
Edward ['edwəd] Edvard.
E. E. F. fk. f. **Egyptian Expeditionary Force.**
eel [i·l] ål; fange ål. — **-buck** åleteine. — **-pout** ålekone. — **-spear** ålelyster. — **-trunk** ålekiste.
e'en [i·n] fk. f. even.
e'er [æ·ə] fk. f. ever.
eerie [i'əri], eery ['iəri] uhyggelig, nifs; vill.
E. E. T. S. fk. f. **Early English Text Society.**
effable ['efəbl] som kan uttales, som kan sis.
efface [è'fe⁴s] slette ut, viske ut, stryke ut, tilintetgjøre. **-ment** [-mənt] utsletting.
effect [i'fekt] virkning, følge; effekt; utførelse, fullbyrdelse; hensikt, øyemed; -s effekter, innbo, løsøre; **take** — gjøre virkning, virke; tre i kraft; **carry into** — virkeliggjøre; **to that** — i den retning, som går ut på det. **effect** bevirke, utrette, fullbyrde, sette i verk. **-ible** [-ibl] gjørlig, mulig. **-ive** [-iv] virksom; effektiv; brukbar, tjenstdyktig, stridsfør. **effectual** [i'fektjuəl, -tjuəl] virksom, kraftig. **effectuation** [ifektju'e⁴ʃən, -tʃu-] iverksettelse, gjennomføring.
effeminacy [è'feminəsi] kvinneaktighet, bløtaktighet. **effeminate** [è'feminét] kvinneaktig, bløtaktig, feminin; [è'femine⁴t] gjøre bløtaktig.
effervesce [efə'ves] bruse opp.
effervescence [efə'vesəns] oppbrusning.
effervescent [efə'vesənt] brusende.
effete [è'fi·t] utlevd, utslitt, uttjent; gold; gjeld.
efficacious [èfi'ke⁴ʃəs] virksom, kraftig. **efficacy** ['efikasi] virksomhet, kraft; evne.
efficiency [e'fiʃənsi] virksomhet, effektivitet, kraft. **efficient** [e'fiʃənt] virksom; dyktig, dugelig; fullgod; virkende årsak.
effigy ['efidʒi] bilde; **in** — in effigie.
effloresce [eflo'res] blomstre, sprette ut; slå ut, blomstre ut i krystaller. **efflorescence** [eflo'resəns] blomstring; utslett. **efflorescent** [eflo'resənt] framblomstrende.
effluence ['efluəns] utflyting, utstrømning.
effluent ['efluənt] utflytende, utstrømmende; utløp, avløp.
effluvium [è'flu·vjəm], flertall: effluvia [è'flu·vjə] utstrømning, utdunstning, tev.
efflux ['eflʌks] utstrømning. **effluxion** [e'flʌk-ʃən] utstrømning, utgang, forløp.
effort ['efət] anstrengelse, bestrebelse, strev, møye; prestasjon; forsøk.
effrontery [e'frʌntəri] uforskammethet, skamløyse.
effulgence [è'fʌldʒəns] glans; skinn. **effulgent** [è'fʌldʒənt] glinsende, strålende.
effuse [é'fju·z] utgyte, sende ut, stråle ut; strekke ut. **effusion** [è'fjuʒən] utgytelse. **effusive** [è'fju·siv] utgytende; strømmende; overstrømmende, hjertelig.
eft [eft] salamander, firfirsle.
e. g. fk. f. **exempli gratia = for instance.**
egad [i'gäd] for pokker! min sel!
egest [i'dʒest] kaste ut, tømme ut. -ion [i'dʒest-ʃən] uttømmelse, avføring, avfall, skarn.
egg [eg] egg; (i krigsslang) bombe fra fly; **bad** — plan som ikke fører til noe; **have all one's -s in one basket** sette alt på ett kort; **as**

sure as **eggs** is **eggs** så sikkert som to og to er fire.
egg [eg] egge, tilskynde, sette opp; — **on** egge. **egg**|-cup eggeglass. **-glass** eggeglass, (lite) timeglass (til å koke egg etter). **-nog** eggedosis. **-shaped** eggformet, oval. **-shell** eggeskall. **-trot** smått trav, lunk. **-whisk** eggepisker.
eglantine ['eglənt(a)in] vinrose; klunger.
ego ['ego⁴] jeg, selv, sjøl. **egoism** ['ego⁴izm] egoisme, gjennomført egenkjærlighet. **egoist** ['ego⁴ist] egoist. **egoistic** [ego⁴'istik], **egoistical** [ego⁴'istikl] egoistisk.
egotism ['ego⁴tizm] for mye snakk om seg selv, selvopptatthet, innbilskhet, egoisme. **egotistic** [ego⁴'tistik], **egotistical** [ego⁴'tistikl] egoistisk. **egotize** ['ego⁴taiz] snakke mye om seg selv
egregious [i'gri·dʒəs] overordentlig, framifrå, grepa; — **fool** stor tosk; — **folly** erkedumhet.
egress ['i·gres] utgang; utløp; slutt. **-ion** [i'greʃən] utgang.
egret ['i·gret] silkeheire; fnokk.
Egypt ['i·dʒipt] Egypt. **Egyptian** [i'dʒipʃən] egyptisk; egypter. **egyptologist** [i·dʒip'tålədʒist] egyptolog. **egyptology** [i·dʒip'tålədʒi] egyptologi.
eh? [e⁴] hva?
eider ['aidə] ær, ærfugl. — **-down** [-daun] ærdun. — **-duck** [-dʌk] ærstegg.
eidolon [ai'do⁴lən] fantom, skyggebilde; skrømt.
eight [e⁴t] åtte, åttetall. **eighteen** ['e⁴ti·n] atten. **eighteenth** ['e⁴ti·nþ] attende; attendedel. **eighth** [e⁴tþ] åttende; åttendedel; oktav. **eighthly** ['e⁴tþli] for det åttende. **eightieth** ['e⁴tiiþ] åttiende; åttiendedel. **eightsquare** åttekantet. **eighty** ['e⁴ti] åtti.
eisteddfod [e⁴'steðvåd] valisisk dikterstevne.
either ['aiðə, 'i·ðə] en (av to): den ene el. den andre; begge; enten; either . . . **or** enten . . . eller; **not** . . . either ikke . . . heller.
ejaculate [i'dʒäkjule⁴t] utstøte, sende ut, ytre plutselig; rope ut. **ejaculation** [idʒäkju'le⁴ʃən] utbrudd, utrop; uttømming. **ejaculatory** [i'dʒäkjulätəri] utstøtt, plutselig ytret.
eject [i'dʒekt] kaste ut, støte ut, fordrive; avsette. **ejection** [i'dʒekʃən] utkasting, utstøting. **ejectment** [i'dʒektmənt] fordriving, utkasting.
eke [i·k] out forøke; skjøte på; utfylle, fullstendiggjøre; skrape sammen (med besvær); — **one's income** hjelpe på sine inntekter.
elaborate [i'läbore⁴t] forarbeide, utarbeide. **elaborate** [i'läborét] utarbeidd, raffinert; forseggjort; omhyggelig innstudert; fullendt. **elaboration** [iläbə're⁴ʃən] utarbeiding; forfinelse; tilberedelse.
eland ['i·lənd] elgantilope.
elapse [i'läps] forløpe, lide, gå (om tid).
elastic [i'lästik] elastisk; spenstig, tøyelig; elastikk, strikk; — **boots** springstøvler.
elasticity [elä'stisiti] elastisitet; spennkraft.
elate [i'le⁴t] overmodig, oppblåst; løfte opp, gjøre overmodig.
elation [i'le⁴ʃən] overmot, oppblåsthet.
Elbe [elb], **the** — Elben.
elbow ['elbo⁴] albue; bøyning, sving, krok; **be at one's** — være ved hånden; **out at -s** med hull på albuene, forkommen, raka fant. — **-chair** armstol. — **-grease** slit, hardt arbeid, f. eks. — **-room** alburom.
elbow ['elbo⁴] skubbe; stå ut; bøye av, svinge; — **one's way** albue seg fram, skubbe seg fram.
elder ['eldə] eldre; eldst (av to); gamling; eldste. — **hand** førehand (i kort).
elder ['eldə] hyll; — **berry** hyllebær.
elderly ['eldəli] eldre, aldrende, tilårskommen.
eldern ['eldən] av hyll.
eldest ['eldist] eldst.
El Dorado [eldo'ra·do⁴] Eldorado.
eldri(t)ch ['eldritʃ] spøkelsesaktig, uhyggelig.
Eleanor ['elinə] Eleonore.
elecampane ['elikäm'pe⁴n] alantrot.
elect [i'lekt] kåre, velge; kåret, valt, utvalt.

election [i'lekʃən] valg; utvelging. **general** — (alm.) valg (til parlamentet). **electioneer** [ilekʃə-'niə] drive valgagitasjon. **electioneering** valgagitasjon. **elective** [i'lektiv] valg-, velgende; **elective monarchy** valgrike. **elector** [i'lektə] velger, valgmann; kurfyrste. **electoral** [i'lektərəl] valg-; kurfyrstelig. **electorate** [i'lektərét] kurfyrsteverdighet; kurfyrstendømme. **electress** [i'lektrés] kurfyrstinne.

electric [i'lektrik] elektrisk. **electrical** [i'lektrikl] elektrisk. **electrician** [i·lek'triʃən] elektriker. **electricity** [i·lek'trisiti] elektrisitet. **electrification** [i'lektrifi'ke'ʃən] elektrifisering, omlegging til elektrisk drift. **electrify** [i'lektrifai] elektrifisere; legge om til elektrisk drift. **electro** [i'lektro] i sammensetninger; elektro-, galvano-. **electrocute** [i'lektrokju·t] henrette ved elektrisitet. **electrocution** [ilektro'kju·ʃən] henrettelse ved elektrisitet. **electrode** [i'lektro"d] elektrode. **electrodynamic** [i'lektro"dai'nämik] elektrodynamisk. **electrolyse** [i'lektrolaiz] spalte kjemisk ved en elektrisk strøm. **electrolysis** [i·lek'trálisis] elektrolyse. **electrolytic** [ilektro'litik] elektrolytisk. **electro-magnet** [i'lektro'mägnét] elektromagnet. **electro-magnetism** [i'lektro'mägnitizm] elektromagnetisme. **electrometer** [ilek'trâmitə] elektrisitetsmåler. **electromotion** [ilektro'mo"ʃən] elektrisk bevegelse. **electromotor** [i'lektro'mo"tə] elektromotor. **electron** [i'lektrån] elektron. **electrophorus** [ilek'trâfərəs] elektrofor. **electroplate** [i'lektrople't] galvanisk forsølve. **electroscope** [i'lektrosko"p] elektroskop. **electrotype** [i'lektrotaip] elektrotypi.

electuary [i'lektjuəri, -tʃ-] latverge.

eleemosynary [elii'måsinəri] almisse-; fattig-; som lever av almisse; almisselem.

elegance [eligəns] eleganse, finhet, smakfullhet, skjønnhet. **elegant** ['eligənt] smakfull, elegant; fin.

elegiac [eli'dʒaiək] elegisk, klagende, vemodig; elegisk vers. **elegist** ['elidʒist] elegisk dikter. **elegize** ['elidʒaiz] skrive elegi (om). **elegy** ['elidʒi] klagesang, elegi.

element ['elimənt] element, grunnstoff, emne; livsbetingelse;(pl.)begynnelsesgrunner,elementer. **elemental** [eli'mentəl] element-. **elementary** [eli-'mentəri] elementær, enkel. — **school** folkeskole.

elephant ['elifənt] elefant; **white** — en dyr og nytteløs ting; **show the** — vise en stor bys severdigheter; **have seen the** — kjenne de nyeste knep; være durkdreven. **elephantiasis** [elifän-'taiəsis] elefantiasis. **elephantine** [eli'fänt(a)in] elefantaktig, uhyre, stor, stolpet. **elephantoid** [eli'fäntoid] elefantaktig.

Eleusinian [elju'sinjən] eleusinsk.

elevate ['elive't] heve, løfte; opphøye; oppmuntre,gjørebegeistret; gjøre hovmodig. **elevated** ['elive'tid] høytliggende; opphøyd; i løftet stemning, «glad». **elevation** [eli've'ʃən] opphøyelse; høyhet, verdighet; høyde; elevasjon. **elevator** ['elive'tə] løftemuskel; heisegreie, løfteredskap; kornsilo; (amr.) elevator.

eleven [i'levn] elleve; lag (som består av elleve spillere, i cricket og fotball). **eleventh** [i'levnþ] ellevte; ellevtedel.

elf [elf] alv. — **-bolt** [-bo"lt] flintepil. **elfin** ['elfin] liten alv; småtroll; alv. **elfish** ['elfiʃ] alveaktig, ondskapsfull, trolsk. **elfshot** ['elffåt] alvskott.

Elgin [i'elgin] Elgin; **the** — **marbles** greske marmorverker, som lord Elgin brakte til England, nå i British Museum.

Elia ['i·ljə], psevdonym for Charles Lamb.

Elias [i'laiəs] Elias.

elicit [i'llsit] lokke fram, bringe for dagen. **elicitation** [ilisi'te'ʃən] framlokking.

elide [i'laid] elidere, støte ut.

eligibility [elidʒi'biliti] valgbarhet; fortrinlig-

het. **eligible** ['elidʒibl] valgbar; verd å velge; attråverdig, ønskelig, antagelig.

Elijah [i'laidʒə] Elias (profeten).

eliminate [i'limine't] skaffe bort, støte ut, skyte ut, få bort, eliminere, borteliminere. **elimination** [ilimi'ne'ʃən] bortskaffelse, utstøting; eliminering, borteliminering.

Elinor ['elinå·ə, -nə] Elinor.

Eliot ['eljət] Eliot.

Elisabeth [i'lizəbeþ] Elisabeth.

Elisha [i'laiʃə] Elisa (profeten).

elision [i'liʒən] elisjon, utelating.

élite [e"'li·t] elite.

elixir [i'liksə] eliksir; kvintessens.

Eliza [i'laizə] Elisa.

Elizabeth [i'lizəbəþ] Elisabeth.

Elizabethan [ilizə'bi·þən] fra Elisabeth-tiden (1558—1603).

elk [elk] elg.

ell [el] alen (gml. mål, omkring 1,14 meter); **give him an inch and he'll take an** — når man gir en viss mann (el. fanden) lillefingeren, tar han hele hånden.

ellipse [é'lips] ellipse (i geometri). **ellipsis** [é'lipsis] ellipse, utelating (i grammatikk). **elliptic(al)** [é'liptik(l)] elliptisk.

elm [elm] alm.

Elmo ['elmo"]: **Elmo's fire** elmsild.

elmy ['elmi] bevokst med alm.

elocution [elo'kju·ʃən] framføring; foredrag; (ut)talekunst; språkbehandling. **elocutionary** [elo-'kju·ʃənəri] som vedrører uttalen eller foredraget. **elocutionist** [elo'kju·ʃənist] lærer i opplesning (deklamasjon).

elongate ['i·långe't, i'långe't] forlenge, tøye; forlenges. **elongation** [i·lån'ge'ʃən] forlenging; fortsettelse; avstand; forstrekning (i kirurgi).

elope [i'lo"p] løpe bort, rømme (især med elsker). **-ment** [i'lo"pmənt] rømning; bortførelse.

eloquence ['elokwəns] veltalenhet.

eloquent ['elokwənt] veltalende.

else [els] ellers; **any one** — hvilken som helst annen; **nothing** — intet annet; **no one** — ingen annen; **nowhere** — ikke noe annet sted; **somewhere** — et annet sted; **what else** hva annet; **who else** hvem andre.

elsewhere ['els'wæ·ə] annensteds.

Elsie ['elsi] Else.

Elsinore [elsi'nå·ə] Helsingør.

elucidate [i'l(j)u·side't] opplyse, forklare. **elucidation** [il(j)u·si'de'ʃən] forklaring, opplysning. **elucidatory** [i'l(j)u·sidátəri] opplysende, forklarende.

elude [i'l(j)u·d] unnvike, unngå; omgå. **elusion** [i'l(j)u·ʃən] unngåelse; omgåelse. **elusive** [i'l(j)u·siv] unngående, unnvikende; slu, listig. **elusory** [i'l(j)u·səri] unngående, unnvikende, slu.

elves [elvz] pl. av **elf**.

elvish ['elviʃ] se **elfish**.

Ely ['i·li] Ely.

Elysian [i'lizjən] elysisk, elyseisk, himmelsk.

Elysium [i'lizjəm] Elysium.

'em [əm] dem (**them**).

emaciate [i'me'ʃie't] avmagre. **emaciation** [ime'ʃi'e'ʃən] avmagring.

emanate ['eməne't] flyte, strømme ut; springe ut, utgå. **emanation** [emə'ne'ʃən, i·-] utflyting, utstrømning.

emancipate [i'mänsipe't] emansipere, frigjøre. **emancipation** [imänsi'pe'ʃən] frigjøring; emansipasjon. **emancipationist** [imänsi'pe'ʃənist] talsmann for opphevning av negerslaveriet. **emancipator** [i'mänsipe'tə] befrier. **emancipatory** [i'mänsipətəri] emansipasjons-, frigjørende.

emarginate [i'ma·'dʒinét] utskåret i kanten, utrandet.

emasculate [i'mäskjule't] kastrere; gjelde, svekke. **emasculate** [i'mäskjulét] berøvet manndommen; svak, veik. **emasculation** [imäskju'le'ʃən] kastrering; gjelding; avkrefting.

embalm [èm'ba·m] balsamere, salve; holde frisk i minnet. -ment [èm'ba·mmənt] balsamering.

embank [èm'bäŋk] demme inne, demme opp.

embankment [èm'bäŋkmənt] inndemming; oppdemming; demning; kai; fylling; **the (Victoria) Embankment** Victoriakaien i London.

embarcation [èmba·ə'ke'ʃən] innskiping.

embargo [èm'ba·ºgoᵘ] beslag, arrest (på skip og ladning); legge beslag på.

embark [èm'ba·ºk] skipe inn; innskipe seg; innlate seg. -ation [èmba·ə'ke'ʃən] innskiping.

embarrass [èm'bärəs] forvirre, forfjamse, sette i forlegenhet; gjøre forlegen; bringe i uorden. embarrassment [èm'bärəsmənt] forvirring; forlegenhet, besvær, vanske, knipe; **financial —** økonomiske vansker.

embassy ['embəsi] gesandtskap, sendeferd; gesandtskapsbolig.

embattle [èm'bätl] stille (seg) i slagorden, fylke; forsyne med tinder (en mur).

embay[èm'be'] drive inn i en bukt, inneslutte.

embed [èm'bed] legge inn, feste, leire; ligge rundt.

embellish [èm'beliʃ] forskjønne, smykke ut, pryde, stase. embellishment [èm'beliʃmənt] forskjønnelse, prydelse.

ember ['embə] glo, aske. embers ['embəz] glør, ildmørje. -days temperdager.

embezzle [èm'bezl] begå underslag, gjøre kassesvik, underslå, forgripe seg på. embezzlement [èm'bezlmənt] underslag, kassesvik. embezzler [èm'bezlə] en som begår underslag.

embitter [èm'bitə] gjøre bitter, forbitre.

emblaze [èm'ble'z] smykke, pryde, male med våpenfigurer, illuminere, utmale. emblazon [èm'ble'zn] dekorere med våpenfigurer, male med glimrende farger; utmale, stase opp. emblazonry [èm'ble'znri] våpenmaleri; våpenfigurer; heraldisk utsmykking.

emblem ['embləm] sinnbilde, emblem, merke. emblematic(al) [èmbli'mätik(l)] sinnbilledlig.

embodiment [èm'bɔdimənt] legemliggjøring, inkarnasjon; innrullering, innlemming; samling til et hele.

embody[èm'bɔdi] legemliggjøre, inkarnere; innrullere, innlemme; samle til et hele; oppta, samle.

embolden [èm'boᵘlden] gjøre dristig, gjøre motig.

embolus ['embɔləs] stempel (i pumper osv.).

embonpoint [ånbån'pwæŋ] embonpoint.

embosom [èm'buzəm] ta til sitt bryst; omgi.

emboss [èm'bås] utføre i opphøyd arbeid, bossere. embossed [èm'båst] utført i opphøyd arbeid, drevet, bossert. embossment [èm'båsmənt] opphøyd arbeid.

embouchure [èmbu'ʃuə] munning, os, gap; munnstykke på blåseinstrument; den blåsendes munnstilling ved frambringelsen av tonen.

embowed [èm'boᵘd] hvelvet.

embowel [èm'bauil] ta innvollene ut, sløye, skjære opp.

embower [èm'bauə] omgi, pryde med lauv.

embrace [èm'bre's] omfavne, slå armene om; omfatte; gripe; anta, knesette; omfavne hverandre; omfavning,favntak,fangtak. embracement [èm'bre'smənt] omfavning.

embrasure [èm'bre'ʒə] skyteskår; vindusfordypning; dørfordypning.

embrocate ['embroke't] gni inn. embrocation [embro'ke'ʃən] lægemiddel (som gnis inn).

embroglio [èm'broᵘljoᵘ] floke, vase.

embroider [èm'broidə] brodere. embroidery [èm'broidəri] broderi; — **frame** broderramme.

embroil [èm'broil] innvikle; forvirre, forstyrre. embroilment [èm'broilmənt] forvikling.

embrue [èm'bru·] se **imbrue.**

embryo ['embrioᵘ] embryo, kim, spire. embryology [èmbri'ålədʒi] embryologi. embryonic [èmbri'änik] embryonisk.

embue [èm'bju·] se **imbue.**

6 — Engelsk-norsk.

embus [em'bʌs] anbringe på en lastebil.

emend [i'mend] rette på, vøle. -able[i'mendəbl[som kan bøtes, rettes på. -ate ['i·mende't] rette, bedre, gjøre rettinger i. -ation [i·mən'de'ʃən] forbedring, beriktigelse, retting. -ator ['i·mande'tə] forbedrer, tekstkritiker. -atory[i'mendətəri,i·men'de'təri] forbedrende.

emerald ['em(ə)rəld] smaragd; **the Emerald Isle** den smaragdgrønne øy, Irland.

emerge [i'mə·dʒ] dukke opp, komme opp; komme fram. emergence [i'mə·dʒəns] oppdukking; tilsynekomst. emergency [i'mə·dʒənsi] uventet begivenhet; uheldig sammenstøt av omstendighetene; kritisk stilling, ytterste nød; **in case of —** i nødsfall; **on an —** i nødsfall; **— -brake** nødbremse; **— -door** eller **— -exit** nødutgang (f. eks. i et teater); **— man** en mann som hjelper en i nødstilfelle.

emeritus [i'meritəs] emeritus, uttjent.

emersion [i'mə·ʃən] tilsynekomst; emersjon (et himmellegemes, etter formørkelse).

emery ['eməri] smergel. **— -wheel** smergelskive.

emetic [i'metik] brekkmiddel. emetic(al) [i'me-tik(l)] som får en til å brekke seg.

emigrant ['emigrənt] utvandrer-, utvandrende; utvandret; utvandrer, emigrant. emigrate ['emigre't] utvandre, emigrere; sende ut av landet. emigration [emi'gre'ʃən] utvandring, emigrasjon. émigré ['emigre'] emigrant (om fransk roya'ist, landflyktig under revolusjonen).

Emily ['emili] Emilie.

eminence ['eminəns] høyde, forhøyning; høy rang; berømmelse, ære; eminens (kardinalenes titel); **by way of —** par excellence. eminent ['eminənt] høy; framragende; anselig, utmerket. eminently ['eminəntli] i framragende grad; særdeles.

emir [è'miə] emir.

emissary ['emisəri] utsending.

emission [i'miʃən] utsending; utstedelse, utstråling.

emit [i'mit] ende ut; emittere, utstede.

emma gee ['·mə'dʒi·] maskingevær (se **m. g.**).

Emmanuel [i'mänjuəl] Emmanuel.

Emmaus [e'me'əs] Emmaus.

emmet ['emit] maur.

emollescence [emo'lesəns] bløthet før smeltningen. emollient [i'måliənt] bløtgjørende; bløtgjørende middel. emollition [emo'liʃən] bløtgjøring.

emolument [i'måljumənt] fordel, lønn, inntekt.

emotion [i'moᵘʃən] sinnsbevegelse, rørelse. emotional [i'moᵘʃənəl] bevegelses-, følelses-; stemningsfull, følelsesfull; **an — being** et stemningsmenneske.

emotive [i'moᵘtiv] følelses-, stemnings-.

empale [èm'pe'l] se **impale.**

empanel [èm'pänəl] oppføre som lagrette; oppnevne.

emperor ['empərə] keiser; **the Emperor Alexander** keiser Alexander.

emphasis ['emfəsis] ettertrykk, fynd, klem. emphasize ['emfəsaiz] legge ettertrykk på, framheve. emphatic [èm'fätik] ettertrykkelig, kraftig. emphatically [èm'fätikəli] ettertrykkelig, i framtredende grad.

emphysema [emfi'si·mə] emfysem.

empire ['empaiə] rike, velde, keiserrike; **the Empire** ofte: Det britiske samvelde.

empiric [èm'pirik] erfaringsmessig, empirisk; empiriker; sjarlatan, kvaksalver. empiricism [em'pirisizm] empirisme; kvaksalveri.

employ [èm'ploi] beskjeftige, sysselsette, gi arbeid, ansette, ste, feste, bruke, nytte, anvende; tilbringe; beskjeftigelse, arbeid; ansettelse, tjeneste. employable [èm'ploiəbl] anvendelig. employé [èm'ploie'], employee [èm'ploii·] funksjonær, arbeidsmann, handelsbetjent. employer [èm'ploiə] arbeidsgiver, prinsipal; husbond; reder. employment [èm'ploimənt] beskjeftigelse, arbeid, sysselsettelse; anvendelse; ansettelse, tjeneste.

emporium [em'pɔ·riəm] handelsplass, stabelplass; opplag; (amr.) varehus, stor butikk.

empower [em'pauə] bemyndige, gi fullmakt; dyktiggjøre, sette i stand.

empress ['empres] keiserinne; **the Empress Alexandra** keiserinne Alexandra.

emprise [em'praiz] tiltak; foretagende; djervskap.

emptier ['em(p)tiə] uttømmer. **emptiness** ['em(p)tinès] tomhet. **empty** ['em(p)ti] tom (**of** for); tom emballasje, tomgods; tømme (**of** for), tømmes, renne ut.

empyema [ɛmpai'i·mə] empyem.

empyreal [einpi'ri·əl] ildklar, himmelsk. **empyrean** [empi'ri·ən] ildhimmel; den sjuende himmel.

emu ['i·mju] emu (australsk fugl).

emulate ['emjuleɪt] kappes med, måle seg med, tevle. **emulation** [emju'leɪʃən] kappelyst, tevling, strid. **emulative** ['emjulətiv] kappelysten. **emulator** ['emjuleɪtə] medbeiler, medtevler, rival. **emulatress** ['emjuleɪtrès] medbeilerinne. **emulous** ['emjuləs] rivaliserende.

emulsion [i'mʌlʃən] emulsjon, svaledrikk. **emulsive** [i'mʌlsiv] melkeaktig, formildende, lindrende.

emunctory [i'mʌŋktəri] utførselsgang.

enable [e'neɪbl] sette i stand til.

enact [e'näkt] gi lovskraft; vedta en lov; forordne; foreta (en seremoni); spille, utføre (en rolle); sette i scene. **enactive** [e'näktiv] forordnende, lovgivende, lov-. **enactment** [e'näktmənt] vedtagelse, vedtak; forordning, lov, lovbestemmelse. **enactor** [e'näktə] lovgiver.

enamel [e'näməl] emalje; glassur; emaljere; glassere. **enameller** [e'nämələ] emaljør.

enamour [i'nämə] gjøre forelsket (**of** i).

enc. fork. f. **enclosure.**

encaenia [en'si·njə] minnefest, årsfest.

encage [èn'keɪdʒ] sette i bur; innesperre. **encagement** [èn'keɪdʒmənt] innesperring.

encamp [èn'kämp] leire, slå leir, leire seg. **encampment** [èn'kämpmənt] leir.

encase [èn'keɪs] overtrekke; gi overtrekk, legge i futteral el. kasse, pakke inn.

encash [èn'käʃ] innkassere, heve penger på. **encashment** [èn'käʃmənt] innkassering.

encaustic [èn'kå·stik] enkaustikk, voksmaling; — **tiles** teglstein med innbrente farger.

enceinte [ä·ŋ'sæ̀·nt] enceinte; fruktsommelig.

encephalic [ensi'fälik] hjerne-.

enchain [èn'tʃeɪn] lenke, fengsle; kjede sammen. **enchainment** [èn'tʃeɪnmənt] lenkebunden tilstand, sammenknytting; rad, rekke.

enchant [èn'tʃa·nt] fortrylle, trolle, trollbinde. **enchanter** [èn'tʃa·ntə] trollmann. **enchantment** |èn'tʃa·ntmənt] fortryllelse. **enchantress** [èn'tʃa·ntrès] trollkvinne, trollkjerring; tryllerinne.

enchase [èn'tʃeɪs] innfatte; ramme inn; siselere, grave.

enchiridion [enkai'ridjàn] håndbok.

encircle [èn'sə·kl] omringe; omslutte, inneslutte; omfavne.

enclasp [èn'kla·sp] omfatte; favne.

enclave ['enkleɪv] enklave.

enclose [èn'kloʊz] innhegne; inngjerde; inneslutte; innlegge; legge ved. **enclosure** [in'kloʊʒə] innhegning; inngjerding; inneslutning; innlegg, vedlegg, bilag; hekk, gjerde.

encomiast [en'koʊmiàst] lovtaler. **encomiastic(al)** [enkoʊ'mi'àstik(l)] lovprisende. **encomium** [en'koʊmjəm] lovtale.

encompass [èn'kʌmpəs] omgi; omfatte; cm-ringe, ringe inn.

encore [àŋ'kå·ə] dakapo; rope dakapo.

encounter [èn'kauntə] sammenkomst, sammenstøt, kamp, basketak; treffe sammen med, møte, råke; tørne sammen med; møtes; motstå.

encourage [èn'kʌridʒ] oppmuntre, inngyte mot;

opplive, hjelpe fram, befordre; frede. **encouragement** [èn'kʌridʒmənt] oppmuntring, oppmoding, befordring, framhjelp, fremme; fredning. **encourager** [-ə] oppmuntrer, befordrer, fremmer.

encroach [èn'kroʊtʃ] gjøre inngrep (**upon** i); anmasse seg. **encroacher** [-ə] en som gjør inngrep; en som fornærmer. **encroachment** [-mənt] inngrep, overgrep; anmasselse.

encrust [in'krʌst] trekke over med skorpe, belegge.

encumber [èn'kʌmbə] bebyrde, bry, plage, belemre, hefte; beliefte, pantbinde. **encumbrance** [èn'kʌmbrəns] byrde, hindring, kloss om beinet; gjeld, pant, hefte, heftelse.

encyclic(al) [en'saiklik(l)] sirkulerende, rund-, sirkulære-; — **epistle** rundskriv (især pavelig), encyklika.

encyclopedia [ensaiklo'pi·djə] encyklopedi, konversasjonsleksikon. **encyclopedian** [-djən] encyklopedisk. **encyclopedic(al)** [ensaiklo'pi·dik(l)] encyklopedisk. **encyclopedist** [ensaiklo'pi·dist] encyklopedist.

encyst [en'sist] innkapsle.

end [end] ende; opphør; slutt, slutning; endelikt, død; stubb, stykke, bete; hensikt, øyemed, mål; ende, slutte, opphøre; gjøre ende på; **in the** — til sist; **be at an** — være til ende, være forbi; **come to an** — stoppe, stanse, opphøre; **the line of our native kings came to an** — vår innfødte kongerekke utdøde; **make both ends meet** få endene til å møtes. **put an** — **to** el. **make an** — of stagge, gjøre ende på; **there is an** — dermed får det være slutt, dermed basta; **such was the** — of slik endte (døde); **odds and ends** stumper og stykker, likt og ulikt; — **of a cigar** sigarspiss; sigarstump; **no** — of en masse; **for an hour on** — en time i trekk; **stand on** — stritte, reise seg (om håret); **all's well that ends well** når enden er god, er allting godt.

endamage [èn'dämidʒ] beskadige, ska.

endanger [èn'deɪn(d)ʒə] sette i fare, sette på spill, våge.

endear [èn'diə] gjøre elsket eller kjær; **he -ed himself to them** han vant deres hengivenhet. **-ing** [èn'diəriŋ] vinnende; elskverdig, kjærlig. **endearment** [èn'diəmənt] kjærtegn.

endeavour [èn'devə] bestrebelse, strev; bestrebe seg for, søke, strebe, streve.

endemic [en'demik] endemisk; endemi.

ender ['endə] tilendebringer.

endermic [en'də·mik] endermisk, som anbringes på el. gjennom huden.

ending ['endiŋ] slutning; endelse, ending.

endive ['endiv] endivie (en plante).

endless ['endlès] endeløs; formålsløs.

endlong ['endlàŋ] på langs, endelangs.

endmost ['endmoʊst] fjernest.

endogamy [en'dågəmi] inngifte.

end-on ['end'àn] med enden først.

endorsation [èndå·ə'seɪʃən] påtegning. **endorse** [èn'då·əs] endossere; påtegne; kausjonere; gå god for; **endorsee** [èndå·ə'si·] endossat. **endorsement** [en'då·əsmənt] endossement, påtegning; godkjenning, bekreftelse. **endorser** [en'då·əsə] endossent.

endow [èn'dau] utstyre; stifte, dotere, gi gave til. **endowment** [èn'daumənt] dotasjon; stiftelse; pengemidler; utstyr; **-s** evner, begavelse.

end-paper ['endpeɪpə] forsatspapir.

endue [èn'dju·] iføre seg, ta på, bekle.

endurable [èn'djuərəbl] utholdelig. **endurance** [èn'djuərəns] utholdenhet; varighet, vedvarenhet; tålmodighet. **endure** [èn'djuə] holde ut, tåle, døye, holde ut; vare.

endways [èn'endweɪz] på kant, på ende; med enden foran.

endwise [èn'endwaiz] på kant, på ende; med enden foran.

Endymion [en'dimjən] Endymion.

Eneid ['i·niid], **the** — Eneiden.

enema ['enimə, i'ni·mə] klystér.

enemy ['enimi] fiende, uvenn. **how goes the —?** hva er klokka?

energetic(al) [enə'dʒetik(l)] kraftig, energisk, virksom. **energize** ['enədʒaiz] gjøre kraftig.

energumen [enə·'gju·mən] svermer, fanatiker.

energy ['enədʒi] kraft, energi, framferd.

enervate ['enəveɪt] enervere, svekke. **enervation** [enə'veɪʃən] svekkelse, avkrefting.

enfeeble [en'fi·bl] svekke, avkrefte. **enfeeblement** [en'fi·blmənt] avkrefting.

enfeoff [en'fi·f] forlene. **enfeoffment** [en'fi·fmənt] forlening; lensbrev.

enfilade [enfi'leɪd] sidebestrykning (med skudd); beskyte langs lengderetningen.

enfold [en'foʊld] innhylle, folde, sveipe inn.

enforce [en'fɑ·ɹs] støtte, styrke; tvinge, tiltvinge seg; sette igjennom; innskjerpe; hevde. **enforcement** [en'fɑ·ɹsmənt] bekreftelse, bestyrkelse; tvang; makt; håndhevelse; tvangsmiddel.

enfranchise [en'fræntʃaiz] befri; oppta som borger, gi stemmerett; gi kjøpstadsrett.

enfranchisement [en'fræntʃizmənt] befrielse; opptagelse i samfunn, tildeling av stemmerett; **the — of women** innføring av stemmerett for kvinner.

engage [en'geɪdʒ] forplikte, binde; feste, engasjere, ansette, verve; sette i pant; vinne; beskjeftige, sysselsette, oppta; forplikte seg til, påta seg, love; innlate seg (i kamp), gi seg av med; gripe inn i (hverandre); innestå for, svare for; feste seg, forlove seg; **engaged** beskjeftiget (in med); forlovet (**to** med); innviklet, dradd inn, i kamp (**with** med). **engagement** [en'geɪdʒmənt] forpliktelse; avtale; løfte; sysselsettelse, yrke, engasjement; forlovelse; slag, trefning; inngriping, tak. **engaging** [en'geɪdʒiŋ] vinnende, inntagende.

engender [en'dʒendə] avle, dra etter seg.

engine ['endʒin] maskin; drivverk; lokomotiv; brannsprøyte; (fig.) middel, redskap; sette maskin i. **-driver** lokomotivfører. **engineer** [endʒi'niə] maskinmester; maskinist; ingeniør; maskinbygger; lokomotivfører (amr.). **engineering** [endʒi'niəriŋ] maskinvesen; ingeniørarbeid, ingeniørvitenskap.

engineman ['endʒinmən] maskinist; brannmann.

engirdle [en'gə·dl] omgi, spenne rundt.

England ['iŋglənd] England. **-er** ['iŋləndə] engelskmann; **Little Englander** antiimperialist.

English ['iŋliʃ, 'iŋliʃ] engelsk; engelsk, engelsk språk; oversette til engelsk; **the — engelsk-mennene. -man** ['iŋliʃmən] engelskmann.

Englishry ['iŋliʃri] engelsk befolkning, engelsk koloni; engelsk vesen.

Englishwoman ['iŋliʃwumən] engelsk kvinne, englenderinne.

engraft [en'grɑ·ft] pode, innpode.

engraftment [en'grɑ·ftmənt] poding; pode.

engrailed [in'greɪld] takket i kanten.

engrain [en'greɪn] farge i ulla; rotfeste.

engrave [en'greɪv] gravere, stikke (i metall), skjære (i tre); grave; prege. **engraver** [en'greɪvə] gravør. **engraving** [en'greɪviŋ] gravering, gravørkunst; kobberstikk.

engross [en'groʊs] forstørre; kjøpe opp; trekke til seg, legge beslag på, oppta; skrive med store bokstaver, renskrive. **engrosser** [en'groʊsə] oppkjøper; renskriver. **engrossment** [en'groʊsmənt] oppkjøp; opptatthet; tilegnelse; renskrivning, renskrift.

engulf [en'gʌlf] sluke opp.

enhance [en'hɑ·ns] forhøye, forøke, auke, forstørre; gjøre dyrere; øke, forøkes. **enhancement** |en'hɑ·nsmənt] forhøyelse, forøkelse, auke, forstørring.

enigma [i'nigmə] gåte. **enigmatic(al)** [i·nig·'mätik(l)] gåtefull. **enigmatize** [i'nigmətaiz]· tale i gåter.

enjambment [in'dʒämmənt] enjambement.

enjoin [en'dʒoin] pålegge; påby, innskjerpe.

enjoy [en'dʒoi] glede seg ved, synes godt om, synes om; nyte; more seg over; **— oneself** more seg, glede seg, like seg, befinne seg vel. **enjoyable** [en'dʒoiəbl] gledelig, behagelig. **enjoyment** [en'dʒoimənt] nytelse, fornøyelse, morskap.

enkindle [en'kindl] kveike, oppflamme, glø opp.

enlace [en'leɪs] omslynge.

enlarge [en'lɑ·dʒ] forstørre; utvide; overdrive; utvide seg; **— the payment of a bill** prolongere en veksel; **— upon** legge ut om, utbrede seg over. **enlargement** [en'lɑ·dʒmənt] forstørrelse; utvidelse, utstrekning.

enlighten [en'laitn] opplyse.

enlightenment [en'laitnmənt] opplysning.

enlist [en'list] føre opp på en liste; verve; vinne; la seg verve. **enlistment** [en'listmənt] verving, innrullering. **enliven** [en'laivn] opplive, sette kveik i, oppmuntre. **-er** oppmuntrer, opplivende middel.

enmesh [en'meʃ] innvikle (som i et nett).

enmity ['enmiti] fiendskap, uvennskap.

enneagon ['eniəgɑn] nikant.

ennoble [e'noʊbl] adle; foredle. **ennoblement** [e'noʊblmənt] adling, opptagelse i adelsstanden.

ennui [a·n'wi·] livslede.

Enoch ['i·nɑk] Enok.

enormity [i'nɑ·ɹmiti] overordentlighet, regelløshet; forbrytelse, udåd; avskyelighet, uhyrlighet. **enormous** [i'nɑ·ɹməs] overordentlig, uhyre, umåtelig; gresselig.

enough [i'nʌf] nok, tilstrekkelig; **— and to spare** mer enn nok; **be good — to tell us** være så vennlig å si oss, gjør så vel å si oss; **a nice — fellow** en ganske kjekk kar.

enounce [i'nauns] uttale, legge fram; artikulere.

enquire [en'kwaiə] se **inquire.**

enrage [en'reɪdʒ] gjøre rasende, drive fra vettet.

enrapture [en'räptʃə] henrykke, henrive.

enrich [en'ritʃ] berike, gjøre rikere; pryde.

enrichment [en'ritʃmənt] berikelse.

enrobe [en'roʊb] bekle, kle.

enrol [en'roʊl] innrullere; skrive inn. **enrolment** [en'roʊlmənt] innrullering; innskrivning.

ENSA fk.f. **Entertainment National Service Association** organisasjon til underholdning og forpleining av soldatene.

ensample [en'sɑ·mpl] eksempel.

ensanguine [en'säŋgwin] plette med blod.

ensconce [en'skɑns] forskanse, dekke.

ensemble [fr.: ɑŋ'sɑŋbl] hele, ensemble.

enshrine [en'ʃrain] legge i et skrin; oppbevare som en relikvie; frede om.

enshroud [en'ʃraud] innhylle, sveipe inn.

ensiform ['ensifɑ·əm] sverddannet.

ensign ['ensain] tegn; fane; merke; fenrik; sekondløytnant. **— -bearer** fanebærer. **ensigncy** [-si], **ensignship** [-ʃip] fenriks el. sekondløytnants stilling el. rang.

ensilage [en'sailidʒ] surhå, surhøy; oppbevaring av grønnfor i silo; oppbevare grønnfor i silo. **ensile** [en'sail] legge ned grønnfor i silo.

enslave [en'sleɪv] gjøre til slave, trelke, trellbinde.

enslaver [en'sleɪvə] tryllerinne, flamme.

ensnare [en'snæ·ə] fange (i snare), dåre.

ensoul [in'soʊl] fylle med sjel.

ensue [en's(j)u·] følge, påfølge, følge på.

ensure [en'ʃuə] sikre, trygge, betrygge (**against,** **from** mot); **— to** tilsikre.

entablature [en'täblətʃə] entablement (omfattende arkitrav, frise og gesims).

entail [en'teɪl] stamgods, ættegods, fideikommiss; arvegangsorden, arvefølge; cut off an — oppheve et fideikommiss. **entail** ['en'teɪl] opprette et fideikommiss, testamentere som stamgods; foranledige, pådra. **entailment** [en'teɪlmənt] oppretting til stamgods; bestemmelse angående arvefølgen.

entangle [ɛn'tæŋgl] forvikle, gjøre floket, fløkje inn, innvikle; besnære; bli innviklet. **entanglement** [ɛn'tæŋglmənt] forvikling; innvikling; floke, ugreie; ståltrådnett; **barbed wire entanglement** piggtrådgjerde.

enter ['entə] tre inn i, gå inn, komme inn; innlate seg; føre inn, oppta; innskrive; angi til fortolling; begynne, la seg innskrive; tiltre; — a scholar skrive inn en studerende (ved universitetet); — **into** forstå; innlate seg på, ta del i; — **into one's mind** falle en inn; — **into partnership with** gå i kompani med; **he entered warmly into the cause of his native land** han tok seg varmt av (tok varmt del i) sitt fedrelands sak; — **upon** ta fatt på, begynne, foreta; innlate seg på. **enterable** ['entərəbl] som må innføres, ikke forbudt (om varer).

enteric [en'terik] innvoll-, tarm-, som angår innvollene; — **fever** tyfoidfeber.

enterocele ['entərəsi·l] tarmbrokk.

enterology [entə'rålədʒi] læren om innvollene.

enterprise ['entəpraiz] foretagende; tiltak; foretaksomhet. **enterpriser** ['entəpraizə] entreprenør. **enterprising** foretaksom, tiltaksom.

entertain [entə'te¹n] nære; more, underholde; beverte; ta under overveielse. **entertainer** [-ə] vert. **entertaining** [-in] underholdende. **entertainment** [entə'te¹nmənt] underholdning; bevertning; fest; gjestebud; **dramatic** — teaterforestilling; **musical** — musikalsk aftenunderholdning.

enthrall [ɛn'þrɔ·l] gjøre til slave, trelke, trellbinde.

enthrone [ɛn'þro⁹n] sette på tronen; innsette (f. eks. en biskop). **enthronement** [-mənt] det å sette på tronen; innsetting. **enthronization** [enþro⁹nai'ze¹ʃən] innsetting.

enthuse [ɛn'þju·z] vise begeistring, gjøre (være) oppglødd. **enthusiasm** [ɛn'þ(j)u·ziäzm] begeistring, henrykkelse, entusiasme; svermeri. **enthusiast** [ɛn'þ(j)uziäst] begeistret, entusiast; svermer. **enthusiastic** [ɛnþ(j)u·zi'ästik] begeistret, oppglødd, entusiastisk, henrykt, svermerisk.

entice [ɛn'tais] lokke, forlokke, forlede. **enticement** [-mant] forlokkelse, lokking, lokkemiddel. **enticer** [-ə] forlokker, forfører.

entire [ɛn'taiə] hel, udelt, fullstendig. **entirely** [-li] helt, ganske. **entireness** [-nés] helhet. **entirety** [ɛn'taiəti] helhet; hele.

entitle [ɛn'taitl] benevne, titulere; berettige; gi atkomst, rett (**to** til).

entity ['entiti] vesen.

entomb [ɛn'tu·m] begrave, gravlegge, jorde. **entomological** [entomo'lådʒikl] entomologisk. **entomologist** [ento'målədʒist] entomolog, insektkjenner. **entomology** [ento'målədʒi] entomologi, insektlære.

entrails ['entre¹lz] innvoller.

entrain [ɛn'tre¹n] anbringe på et tog; ta plass i et tog.

entrammel [in'träməl] hindre, hefte.

entrance ['entrəns] inntredelse; inngang; innløp; tiltredelse; begynnelse; adgang, opptagelse; innskrivning; (toll)deklarering. — **-duty** innførselstoll.

entrance [ɛn'tra·ns] henrykke, henrive.

entrap [ɛn'träp] lokke i felle, hilde, narre, fange.

entreat [ɛn'tri·t] be, bønnfalle, trygle. **entreating** [ɛn'tri·tiŋ] bedende, bønnfallende. **entreaty** [ɛn'tri·ti] bønn.

entrée ['äntre¹] mellomrett.

entremets ['äntrəme¹] mellomrett.

entrench [ɛn'trenʃ] forskanse (bak løpegrav). **entrenchment** [ɛn'trenʃmənt] forskansning.

entrepot ['äntrəpo⁹] lagerplass, opplagssted.

entresol ['äntrəsål] mesaninetasje, mellometasje.

entrust [ɛn'trʌst] betro, overlate; — **it to him** eller — **him with it** betro ham det.

entry ['entri] inngang; inntredelse; inntog;

innskriving; tiltredelse (av en eiendom); tollangivelse; post (innført i en bok); notis; innførsel; bokføring; **bill of** — varefortegnelse (på tollbu).

ent. Sta. Hall fk. f. **entered at Stationers' Hall.**

entwine [ɛn'twain] flette sammen, tvinne (seg) sammen, fløkje inn.

entwist [ɛn'twist] surre, tvinne om.

enucleate [i'nju·klie¹t] plukke ut kjernen; utvikle.

enumerate [i'nju·məre¹t] regne, telle opp. **enumeration** [inju·mə're¹ʃən] oppregning, opptelling. **enumerative** [i'nju·mərətiv] som regner opp. **enumerator** [i'nju·məre¹tə] oppregner, oppteller.

enunciate [i'nʌnʃie¹t] uttale; erklære, bekjentgjøre, kunngjøre. **enunciation** [inʌnʃi'e¹ʃən] utsigelse; erklæring, bekjentgjørelse, kunngjøring; uttrykk; foredrag. **enunciative** [i'nʌnʃiətiv] erklærende; uttale-.

envelop [ɛn'veləp] svøpe inn, innvikle, sveipe inn, hylle inn; pakke inn; legge i konvolutt. **envelope** ['enviloup] konvolutt; hylster, dekke. **envelopment** [ɛn'veləpmənt] innvikling; innhylling; hylster; omslag.

envenom [ɛn'venəm] forgifte.

enviable ['enviəbl] misunnelsesverdig. **envier** ['enviə] misunner. **envious** ['enviəs] misunnelig.

environ [ɛn'vairən] omringe, omgi. **environment** [ɛn'vairənmənt] omgivelse(r), grannelag. **environs** ['envirənz] omegn, omgivelser, grannelag.

envisage [in'vizidʒ] se i ansiktet, se i øynene; møte; betrakte.

envoy ['envoi] slutningsstrofe, etterstev, ettersleng.

envoy ['envoi] gesandt; sendebud. **envoyship** en gesandts stilling, sendemanns ombud.

envy ['envi] misunnelse, gjenstand for misunnelse; misunne.

enwrap [ɛn'räp] hylle inn, sveipe inn; forvikle.

enwreathe [ɛn'ri·ð] kranse.

eocene ['iosi·n] som hører til eldre avsnitt av tertiærtiden.

E. & O. fk. f. **errors and omissions excepted.**

epaulette [ɛn'pälet] epålett.

E. P. D. fk. f. **Excess Profits Duty.**

epergne [i'pə·n] frukt- el. blomsteroppsats.

ephemera [é'femərə] endagsfeber; døgnflue. **ephemeral** [é'femərəl], **ephemeric** [efi'merik] som bare varer en dag; flyktig, kortvarig, døgn-. **ephemeris** [é'feməris] dagbok.

Ephesian [é'fi·ʒən] efeser; efesisk.

Ephesus ['efisəs] Efesus.

ephod ['i·fåd, 'efåd] messehakel.

epic ['epik] episk; episk dikt, epos.

epicure ['epikjuə] epikureer. **epicurean** [epikju'ri·ən] epikuréisk; epikureer. **epicureanism** [epikju'ri·ənizm] epikureisme. **epicurize** ['epikjuraiz] leve som epikureer.

Epicurus [epi'kjuərəs] Epikur.

epidemic [epi'demik] epidemisk, herskende, omgangs-; omgangssyke, farsott, farang, epidemi. **epidermis** [epi'də·mis] epidermis, overhud. **epiglottis** [epi'glåtis] epiglottis, strupelokk. **epigones** ['epigo⁹nz], **epigoni** [é'pigonai] epigoner. **epigram** ['epigräm] epigram. **epigrammatic** [epigrə'mätik] epigrammatisk; fyndig, poengtert. **epigraph** ['epigra·f] innskrift, gravskrift. **epilepsi** ['epilepsi] epilepsi, fallsyke. **epileptic** [epi'leptik] epileptisk; epileptiker; middel mot epilepsi.

epilogue ['epilåg] epilog, etterord.

Epiphany [i'pifəni] helligtrekongersdag.

Epirus [i'pairəs] Epirus.

episcopacy [i'piskopəsi] episkopal kirkeforfatning, biskoppelig forfatning. **episcopal** [i'piskopəl] episkopal, biskoppelig. **episcopalian** [ipisko·pe¹ljən] episkopal, biskoppelig; medlem, tilhenger av episkopal kirke. **episcopalianism** [ipisko·pe¹ljənizm] biskoppelig kirkestyre. **episcopate** [i'piskopét] bispeembete, bispeverdighet; bispedømme; bispesete.

episode ['episoᵘd] episode.
episodic [epi'sådik] episodisk.
epistle [i'pisl] skrivelse, epistel, brev. **epistolar(y)** [e'pistolə(ri)] skriftlig; brev-.
epitaph ['epita·f] gravminne; gravskrift.
epithalamium [epiþə'leᶦmjəm] bryllupsdikt.
epithet ['epiþét] tilleggsord, tilnavn, epitet.
epitome [i'pitəmi] uttog, utdrag. **epitomize** [i'pitəmaiz] lage utdrag; gi utdrag av.
epizoon [epi'zoᵘån] snyltedyr. **epizootic** [epizo'åtik] snyltedyr-; kvegpest.
epizooty [epi'zoᵘoti] kvegpest.
epoch ['i·påk] epoke, tidsskifte.
epopee ['epopi·] heltedikt.
epos ['epås] epos.
Epsom ['epsəm] by med hesteveddeløp; — **salt** engelsk salt.
equability [i·kwə'biliti] jevnhet, jamne, likhet.
equable ['i·kwəbl, 'ek-] likelig, ensformig, ens, jevn, jamn, stø.
equal ['i·kwəl] like; jevn, jamn, stø, rolig, likelig, ens; ensformig; billig, upartisk; likemann, like, make; gjøre lik; nå; være lik med, svare til; **be — to a task** være en oppgave voksen; — **to my expectations** svarende til mine forventninger. **equality** [i'kwåliti] likhet; likeberettigelse, likestilling, jamstelling; **on an — with** på like fot med. **equalization** [i·kwəlai'zeᶦʃən] utjevning, utjamning; likestilling. **equalize** ['i·kwəlaiz] utjevne; stille på like fot; gjøre like. **equally** ['i·kwəli] i samme grad, likså; — **with** likså meget (godt) som; — **guilty with** likså skyldig som . . .
equanimity ['i·kwə'nimiti] sinnslikevekt, sinnsro.
equate [i'kweᶦt] redusere til middeltall; utjevne, jamne ut. **equation** [i'kweᶦʃən] ligning.
equator [i'kweᶦtə] ekvator.
equatorial [ekwə'tå·riəl] ekvator-, ekvatorial.
equerry ['ekwəri] stallmester.
equestrian [i'kwestriən] ridende, hest-, ride-, rytter-; ridder-; rytter, rytterske.
equiangular [i·kwi'äŋgjulə] likevinklet.
equidistant [i·kwi'distənt] i like avstand, parallell.
equilateral [i·kwi'lätərəl] likesidet.
equilibrate [i·kwi'l(a)ibreᶦt] bringe el. holde i likevekt. **equilibration** [i·kwil(a)i'breᶦʃən] likevekt, jamvekt. **equilibrious** [i·kwi'libriəs] i likevekt. **equilibrist** [i'kwilibrist] linedanser. **equilibrium** [i·kwi'libriəm] likevekt, jamvekt.
equine ['i·kwain] heste-, som angår hester.
equinoctial [i·kwi'nåkʃəl, -ek-] jevndøgns-, ekvinoktial; vår- el. høststorm; himmelens ekvator. -ly i retning av ekvator.
equinox ['i·kwinåks, 'ek-] jevndøgn, jamdøger.
equip [i'kwip] utstyre, utruste, ekvipere. **equipage** ['ekwipidʒ] rustning; ekvipasje. **equipment** [i'kwipmənt] utrustning, ekvipering.
equipoise ['i·kwipoiz] likevekt, jamvekt; holde i likevekt.
equiponderance [i·kwi'påndərəns] likevekt.
equitable ['ekwitəbl] billig, rettferdig, upartisk.
equitation [ekwi'teᶦʃən] ridning.
equity ['ekwiti] billighet, rettferdighet, upartiskhet; **court of** — billighetsrett (en engelsk domstol).
equivalence [i'kwivələns] like gyldighet, like kraft, like verd. **equivalent** [i'kwivələnt] av samme verdi, likeverdig, enstydende, tilsvarende; ekvivalent, vederlag, enstydende ord.
equivocal [i'kwivokl] tvetydig. **equivocate** [i'kwivokeᶦt] tale tvetydig. **equivocation** [ikwivo'keᶦʃən] tvetydighet, tvetydig tale. **equivocator** [i'kwivokeᶦtə] en som taler tvetydig. **equivoque** ['i·kwivoᵘk, 'ek-] tvetydighet; tvetydig tale.
E. R. fk. f. **East Riding, Edwardus Rex** (= **King Edward**).
era ['iərə] tidsregning, periode, tidebolk, æra.
eradiate [i're'dieᶦt] stråle ut.
eradiation [ire'di·e'ʃən] utstråling; glans.

eradicate [i'rädikeᶦt] rykke opp med rota, røske opp; utrydde. **eradication** [irädi'keᶦʃən] opprykking med rot; utrydding. **eradicative** [i'rädikətiv] utryddende; radikal.
erasable [i're'səbl] som kan raderes. **erase** [i're's] radere bort, skrape ut; stryke ut. **erasement** [-mənt] utradering; utsletting. **eraser** [i're'sə] en som raderer, utsletter; raderkniv; radergummi. **erasion** [i're'ʃən] utradering; utsletting. **erasure** [i're'ʒə] radering, utsletting.
ere [æ·ə] før, førenn; — **long** innen kort tid, snart; — **now** før.
'ere [iə] vulgært for here her; **this — chum of mine** denne herre kameraten min.
erect [i'rekt] reise, reise opp, oppføre; opprette, stifte, grunne; oppreist, rett opp, rak, motig, fast, standhaftig. **erecter** [i'rektə] oppreiser; oppfører. **erectile** [i'rektil] som kan reises; som kan reise eg. **erection** [i'rekʃən] reising; oppføring; bygging; oppretting; oppløfting, oppstramming, oppvekking. **erective** [i'rektiv] reisings-. **erector** [i'rektə] grunnlegger, stifter, maskinmontør.
eremite ['erimait] eneboer, eremitt (poetisk for hermit). **eremitic** [eri'mitik] eremitt-, eneboer-.
ergo ['ə·goᵘ] ergo, altså.
ergot ['ə·gåt] sopp på korn, meldrøye, «mjølauke».
ergotism ['ə·gotizm] meldrøyesott.
Erin ['erin, 'iərin] Erin, Irland.
ermine ['ə·min] hermelin, røyskatt, røyskattskinn; dommerverdighet (etter dommerens kappe som er fort med hermelin); kle i hermelin.
erne [ə·n] ørn, havørn.
erode [i'roᵘd] fortære; gnage på. **erosion** [i'roᵘʒən] erosjon, fortæring; kreft. **erosive** [i'roᵘsiv] tærende.
erotic [e'råtik] erotisk; erotisk dikt. **-ism** [e'råtisizm] erotikk.
err [ə·] ta feil, feile, ta i miss, fare vill.
errand ['erənd] ærend; **go** (eller **run**) (**on**) **an** — gå et ærend; **do an** — utføre et ærend.
errand-boy ['erəndboi] visergutt, ærendssvenn.
errant ['erənt] farende, omflakkende. **errantry** ['erəntri] flakking, omflakking.
errata [e're'tə] trykkfeil (flertall av **erratum**).
erratic [e'rätik] omflakkende; uregelmessig. **erratum** [e're'təm] trykkfeil.
errhine ['erain] scm snuses; nysemiddel.
erroneous [e'roᵘnjəs] feilaktig, gal, uriktig, villfarende, falsk.
error ['eɪə] feiltagelse, villfarelse, forseelse, feil; **commit an** — begå en feil; **in** — ved en feiltagelse; **you are in** — De tar feil; **errors and omissions excepted** med forbehold av mulige feil og forglemmelser.
ersatz [er'zats] (tysk ord) ersatz, erstatning.
Erse [ə·s] gælisk.
erst [ə·st], **erstwhile** ['ə·sthwail] i gamle dager.
erubescence [eru'besəns] rødme.
erubescent [eru'besənt] rødmende; rødlig.
eructation [irʌk'teᶦʃən] oppstøt, raping; utbrudd.
erudite ['erudait] lærd.
erudition [eru'diʃən] lærdom.
erupt [i'rʌpt] være i utbrudd; sprute, sende ut.
eruption [i'rʌpʃən] utbrudd; ri; utslett; utfall. **eruptive** [i'rʌptiv] som bryter fram; eruptiv.
erysipelas [eri'sipiläs] rosen (sykdommen).
escalade [eska'le'd] angrep med stormstiger, stormløp; bestige ved hjelp av stormstiger, storme.
escalator ['eskələ'tə] rullende trapp.
escallop [is'kåləp] kammusling.
escapade [eskə'peᶦd] eskapade, flukt; galskap.
escape [e'ske'p] unnløpe, unnslippe, rømme, løpe bort, unnvike; unngå; rømning, unnvikelse, flukt; redning; brannstige; utflukt; utbrudd; skjøtesløshet; **he had a narrow** — det var så vidt han slapp fra det. **escapee** [eske'pi·] en som er sloppet unna (fangenskapet). **escapement** [e'ske'p-

mənt] echappement, gang (i et ur). **escapevalve** [ė'ske'pvälv] sikkerhetsventil.
escarp [ė'ska·ᵊp] eskarpere. **escarpment** [ė'ska·ᵊpmənt] skråning, stupbratt hall, eskarpe.
eschalot [eʃə'låt] sjalottløk.
eschatology [eskə'tålådʒi] eskatologi, læren om de siste ting.
escheat [ės'tʃi·t] hjemfall, heimfall; hjemfalt gods; hjemfalle, heimfalle.
eschew [ės'tʃu·] fly, unngå, sky.
escort ['eskå·ət] bedekning, eskorte.
escort [i'skå·ᵊt] ledsage, eskortere.
escritoire [eskri'twå·ᵊ] skrivepult, skrivebord.
Esculapios [eskju'le'piås] Æskulap.
esculent ['eskjulənt] spiselig; mat.
escutcheon [ė'skʌtʃən] skjold, våpenskjold, våpen.
E. S. E. fk. f. **East South-east.**
Eskimo ['eskimoᵘ] eskimo.
esophagus [ė'såfəgəs] spiserør.
esoteric [eso'terik] hemmelig, esoterisk, forbeholdt en utvalt krets. **esoterics** hemmelig lærdom.
espalier [ė'späljə] espalier.
esparto [ė'spa·ᵊtoᵘ] espartogras.
especial [i'speʃəl] særlig, spesiell; fortrinlig. **especially** [i'speʃəli] særlig, spesielt, især.
Esperantist [espə'räntist] esperantist. **Esperanto** [espə'räntoᵘ] esperanto.
espial [ė'spaiəl] speiding, utspionering.
espionage [espiə'na·ʒ] spionering.
esplanade [esplə'ne'd] esplanade; åpen plass.
espousal [ė'spauzəl] forlovelse; antagelse.
espouse [ė'spauz] forlove, trolove; ekte; gi til ekte; ta seg av; forsvare, anta (en mening). **espouser** [ė'spauzə] forsvarer, forfekter.
esprit ['espri·] livlighet, esprit; — **de corps** ['espri·də'kå·ᵊ] korpsånd.
espy [ė'spai] øyne, få øye på, oppdage.
Esq. [ė'skwaiə] fk. f. **Esquire** herr (på brev: **T. Brown, Esq.** herr T. Brown).
Esquimau ['eskimoᵘ] eskimo.
esquire [ė'skwaiə] fk. til **Esq.** herr (på brev); herremann, godseier, fornem mann, i rang under knight; (gammel betydning: væpner).
essay ['ese'] prøve; forsøk; essay, avhandling, utgreiing.
essay [ė'se'] forsøke; prøve.
essayist ['ese'ist] essayist, essayforfatter.
essence ['esəns] tilværelse; vesen; kjerne; essens; gjøre velluktende, parfymere.
essential [i'senʃəl] vesentlig; fin; uunnværlig, absolutt nødvendig; avgjørende, om å gjøre; — **oil** etérisk olje. **essential** tilværelse, vesen; **f** hovedpunkt, det viktigste. **essentiality** [esenʃi'älitti vesentlighet, viktighet.
Essex ['esiks] Essex.
establish [ė'stäbliʃ] fastsette, opprette; innrette; grunne, anlegge, etablere; stadfeste; bevise, fastslå, fastsette, bestemme; **the Established Church** statskirken (særlig om Englands); **recently -ed in business** som nylig har (hadde) slått seg ned. **establishment** [ė'stäbliʃmənt] fastsettelse; bestemmelse; stiftelse, etablissement; forretning hus, husholdning; nedsettelse; anordning, form, innretning; organisasjon.
estafet [ė'stə'fet] stafett, ilbud.
estate [ė'ste't] bo, formue; gård, gods, eiendom; tilstand; rang stand, klasse; **man's —** manndomsalder; **Estates of the Realm** rikssten der; **personal —** rørlig gods, løsøre; landgods på bestemt åremål; **real —** fast eiendom, grunneiendom.
esteem [ė'sti·m] sette pris på, skatte, vurdere, akte, ære; mene, holde for; vurdering, aktelse.
esthete [ė'esþi·t] estetiker. **estheti·:** [es'þetik, i·s-] estetisk. **esthetical** [es'þetikl, i·s-] estetisk. **esthetician** [e þe'tiʃən, i·s] estetiker. **estheticism** [es'þetisizm, i·s-] estetisering. **es tics** [es'þetiks, i·s-] estetikk.
estimable ['estiməbl] aktverdig. **estimate**

['estime't] vurdere; beregne, taksere, anslå (**at** til).
estimate ['estimėt] vurdering; overslag, beregning; budsjett. **estimation** [esti'me'ʃən] vurdering; anslag, overslag, skjønn, beregning; aktelse; mening. **estimator** ['estime'tə] taksasjonsmann.
estop [ė'ståp] hindre, stanse (juridisk uttr.).
estrade [es'tra·d] estrade, pall, forhøyning.
estrange [ė'stre'n(d)ʒ] gjøre fremmed; fjerne; stille i et kjølig forhold.
estrangement [ė'stre'n(d)ʒmənt] det å ta avstand; kjølig forhold, kulde.
estrapade [estrə'pe'd] sprett av en hest for å kaste rytteren av.
estray [ė'stre'] streife omkring; herreløst dyr.
estreat [ė'stri·t] gjenpart; ta utskrift av.
estuary ['estjuəri] os, munning, elvemunning, fjordgap.
esurient [i'sjuəriənt] sulten.
etc. fk. f. **et cetera.**
etcetera [it'setrə] og så videre. **etceteras** andre ting, andre poster, ekstrautgifter.
etch [etʃ] etse, radere. **etching** ['etʃiŋ] etsekunst; radering; **etching needle** radernål.
eternal [i'tə·nəl] evig, endeløs. **eternalize** [i'tə·nəlaiz] forevige, gjøre udødelig. **eternity** [i'tə·niti] evighet. **eternize** [i'tə·naiz] forevige, gjøre udødelig.
etesian [ė'ti·ʒən] regelmessig, periodisk (om vind).
Ethel ['eþəl] Edel.
ether ['i·þə] eter.
ethereal [i'þiəriəl] etérisk, overjordisk.
etherealize [i'þiəriəlaiz] forvandle til eter.
ethical ['eþikl] etisk, moralsk.
ethics ['eþiks] moral, sedelære, etikk.
Ethiop ['i·þiåp] etiopier.
Ethiopean [i·þi'oᵘpʃən] etiopisk; etiopier.
ethnic ['eþnik] etnologisk; hedensk.
ethnographer [eþ'någrəfə] etnograf. **ethnographic(al)** [eþno'gräfik(l)] etnografisk. **ethnography** [eþ'någrəfi] etnografi. **ethnological** [eþno'lådʒikl] etnologisk. **ethnologist** [eþ'nålədʒist] etnolog. **ethnology** [eþ'nålədʒi] etnologi.
ethyl ['eþil] etyl.
etiolate ['i·tjole't] bleike; bleikne, falme. **etiolation** [i·tjo'le'ʃən] bleiking, bleikhet.
etiology [i·ti'ålədʒi] etiologi, årsakslære.
etiquette [eti'ket] etikette, skikk og bruk.
Eton [i·tən] Eton, by ved Themsen, med en berømt skole. **Etonian** [i'toᵘnjən] gutt, mann fra Eton college.
et seq. fk. f. **et sequentia** (= **and what follows**).
E. T. U. fk. f. **Electrical Trades Union.**
etui [e'twi·], **etwee** [e'twi·] etui.
etymological [etima'lådʒikl] etymologisk.
etymologist [eti'målədʒist] etymolog.
etymologize [eti'målədʒaiz] etymologisere.
etymology [eti'målədʒi] etymologi.
etymon ['etimån] etymon, stamord.
eucalyptus [ju·kə'liptəs] evkalyptus.
Eucharist ['ju·kərist] nattverdens sakrament.
euchre ['ju·kə] amerikansk kortspill; overliste; slå.
Euclid ['ju·klid] Evklid; **I know my —** jeg kan mine klassikere.
eudæmonism [ju'di·mənizm] lykkemoral.
Eugène ['ju·dʒi·n, ju(d)ʒi·n] Eugène.
eugenics [ju·'dʒeniks] rasehygiene, vitenskapen om rasekultur.
eulogist ['ju·lədʒist] lovpriser, lovtaler. **eulogistic(al)** [julo'dʒistik(l)] prisende, rosende. **eulogium** [ju'loᵘdʒ(j)əm], **eulogy** ['ju·lədʒi] lovtale.
eunuch ['ju·nək] evnukk, gjelding, kastrat.
eupepsy ['ju·pepsi] evpepsi; god fordøyelse. **eupeptic** [ju'peptik] evpeptisk, med god fordøyelse.
euphemism ['ju·fimizm] evfemisme, formildet uttrykk. **euphemistic** [ju·fi'mistik] evfemistisk, formildende. **euphemize** [ju·fimaiz] formilde, tilsløre.

euphonic [ju'fånik], **euphonious** [ju'fo⁽u⁾njəs] velklingende, vellydende. **euphony** ['ju·fəni] velklang, vellyd.

euphrasy ['ju·frəsi] øyentrøst (plante).

Euphrates [ju'fre'ti·z] Evfrat.

Euphues ['ju·fjui·z] Euphues (roman av Lyly).

euphuism ['ju·fjuizm] euphuisme, søkt sirlighet i språk og stil. **euphuist** ['ju·fjuist] euphuist. **euphuistic**[ju·fju'istik]euphuistisk;affektertsirllg.

Eurasia [ju're'ʃə] Eurasia, Europa og Asia tilsammen. **Eurasian** [ju'reiʃən] eurasiatisk; barn av en europeer og en asiat.

eureka [ju'ri·kə] heureka! jeg har funnet det!

Euripides [ju·'ripidi·z] Evripides.

Europe ['juərəp] Europa.

European [juᵊrə'pi·ən] européisk; europeer.

Eurydice [ju'ridisi·] Eurydike.

eurythmy [ju'riþmi] symmetri, harmoni.

Eustachian [ju'ste'kjən] eustakisk; **the** — **tube** det eustakiske rør.

Euston ['ju·stən], — **station** jernbanestasjon i London.

euthanasia [ju·þə'ne'ziə] lett og rolig død.

Euxine ['ju·ksain], **the** — Svartehavet.

evacuant [i'väkjuənt] avførende; avførende middel. **evacuate** [i'väkjue't] tømme ut; rømme, forlate, evakuere. **evacuation** [iväkju'e'ʃən] uttømming; avføring; rømning, evakuering. **evacuee** [iväkju'i·] evakuert.

evade [i've'd] unngå, omgå, unnvike, lure seg unna; bruke utflukter; skulke.

evaluate [i'väljue't] vurdere, taksere, verdsette.

evaluation [ivälju'e'ʃən] vurdering, taksering.

evanesce [i·və'nes] forsvinne. **evanescence** [i·və'nesəns] forsvinning, flyktighet. **evanescent** [i·və'nesənt] forsvinnende, kortvarig.

evangel [i'vändʒəl] evangelium. **evangelic** [i·vən'dʒelik] evangelisk. **evangelical** [i·vən'dʒelikl] evangelisk; protestantisk kristen, som hevder frelsen ved tro (motsatt gode gjerninger). **evangelicalism** [i·vən'dʒelikəlizm] den læren at frelsen ved tro er det sentrale i kristendommen. **evangelism** [i'vändʒəlizm] forkynnelse av evangeliet. **evangelist** [-ist] evangelist; predikant. **evangelize** [i'vändʒəlaiz] preke evangeliet.

Evans ['evəns] Evans.

evaporable [i'väpərəbl] som kan fordampe. **evaporate** [i'väpəre't] fordampe; dunste bort; la fordampe; forsvinne. **evaporation** [iväpə're'ʃən] fordamping; avdamping. **evaporative** [i'väpərətiv] som bevirker fordampning. **evaporator** [i'väpəre'tə] avdampningsapparat.

evasion [i've'ʒən] det å unngå, omgåelse; unndragelse; utflukt; kunstgrep. **evasive** [i've'siv] unnvikende; som søker utflukter.

Eve [i·v] Eva; **daughter of** — evadatter.

eve [i·v] aften, kveld (i poesi); helligaften; Christmas eve julaften; **on the** — **of** (om tiden nærmest før en begivenhet) like før.

evection [i'vekʃən] uregelmessighet i månens bane.

Evelyn ['evəlin] Evelyn.

even [i·vən] aften, kveld (poetisk).

even ['i·vən] nettopp, just, endog, selv, jamvel, allerede, alt, enda; endatil; helt, like; — **if** (eller **though**) selv om; — **bigger** enda større; **not** — ikke engang; — **then** allerede da, alt dengang; — **to** helt til, like til, inntil.

even ['i·vən] jevn, jamn; glatt, slett; ensartet, ensformig; rolig, upartisk, rettvis; som går opp i opp, like, kvitt, skuls; like (om tall); hel; jevne, jamne ut, utjevne.

even-handed ['i·vən'händid] upartisk.

evening ['i·vnin] aften, kveld; **this** — i aften; **yesterday** — i går aftes, i går kveld; **in the** — om aftenen; **good** — god aften. — **-dress** selskapsantrekk. — **-party** aftenselskap. — **-service** aftengudstjeneste, aftensang.

even-minded ['i·vənmaindid] rolig, behersket.

evenness ['i·vənnès] jevnhet, rolighet, upartiskhet.

evensong ['i·vənsån] aftensang.

event [i'vent] begivenhet, tilfelle, hending, utfall, følge, resultat; **at all -s** i ethvert tilfelle, iallfall. **-ful** [i'ventf(u)l] begivenhetsrik.

eventide ['i·vəntaid] kveld.

eventless [i'ventlès] begivenhetsløs.

eventual [i'ventʃual, -tjuəl] mulig, eventuell; endelig. **eventuality** [ventʃu'äliti, -tju-] mulighet. **eventually** [i'ventʃuali, -tjuəli] endelig, til sist. **eventuate** [i'ventjue't] ende, resultere.

ever ['evə] noensinne (i nektende, spørrende og betingende setninger); alltid, støtt, bestandig, på noen mulig måte; i høyest mulig grad (forsterkende, især brukt foran **so**); **did you** — **see the like?** har De noensinne sett maken? **hardly** — nesten aldri; — **since** alltid siden; helt fra; **for** — for bestandig; **liberty for** — leve friheten! **for** — **and a day** eller **for** — **and** — (i spøk) evig og alltid, støtt og stadig; **for** — **and again** atter og atter; **be as amusing as** — **you can** vær så underholdende som De bare kan; **we thank you** — **so much** tusen takk; — **so often** utallige ganger; **let him be** — **so poor** la ham være aldri så fattig. **-burning** evig brennende. **-glade** myrlende (især i Florida).

evergreen ['evəgri·n] eviggrønn; eviggrønn plante.

everlasting [evə'la·stin] evig, evinnelig; evighet; evighetsblomst; et slags tøy.

evermore [evə'må·ᵊ] støtt, stadig; **for** — **for** alltid, i all evighet.

eversion [i'və·ʃən] utvrengning.

evert [i'və·t] vrenge ut.

every ['ev(e)ri] enhver, hver, alle; — **now and then** rett som det er (el. var) nå og da; — **here and there** d. s. — **one of you** hver eneste en av dere; **his** — **word** hvert ord han sier; — **way** i enhver henseende, på alle måter; — **other** (eller **second**) **day** hver annen dag, annenhver dag; — **one** enhver.

everybody ['ev(ə)ribådi] enhver.

everyday ['ev(ə)ride'] hverdags-.

everyone ['evriwʌn] enhver.

everything ['ev(ə)riþiŋ] alt.

everyway ['ev(ə)riwe'] på alle måter.

everywhere ['ev(ə)rihwæ·ə] overalt.

evict [i'vikt] utsette, kaste ut.

eviction [i'vikʃən] utsletting, utkasting.

evidence ['evidəns] evidens, visshet, tydelighet, klarhet; vitnesbyrd, prov, vitneprov; bevis; bevismateriale; vitne; gjøre innlysende, bevise, godtgjøre, prove; **give** — avgi vitneforklaring, vitne; **the taking of** — vitneførsel; **in** — forhånden; framlagt; iøynefallende; godtgjort.

evident ['evidənt] øyensynlig, tydelig, klar, håndgripelig. **evidential** [evi'denʃəl] som beviser; som bygger på prov. **evidentiary** [evi'denʃəri] som har beviskraft. **evidently** ['evidəntli] øyensynlig, åpenbart.

evil ['i·vl, 'i·vil] ond, vond, låk, slem, slett; onde; ulykke; **the** — **one** den onde; **the King's** — kjertelsyke (folk trodde kongen kunne helbrede den).

evil-doer ['i·vl'duə] misdeder, illgjerningsmann.

evil-eye ['i·vl'ai] ondt øye.

evilly ['i·vili] ondt.

evil-minded ['i·vl'maindid] ondsinnet, vondlyndt.

evince [i'vins] vise, tilkjennegi, røpe.

evincible [i'vinsibl] påviselig.

evince [i'vinsiv] som beviser.

eviscerate [i'visəre't] ta innvollene ut av, skjære opp, sløye, gane. **evisceration** [ivisə're'ʃən] oppspretting.

evitable ['evitəbl] unngåelig.

evoke [i'vo⁽u⁾k] mane fram, framkalle, vekke.

evolution [evo'l(j)u·ʃən] utvikling; evolusjon; rotutdraging. **evolutionary** [evᵊ'l(j)u·ʃənəri] evolusjons-, utviklings-. **evolutionist** [evo'l(j)u·- ʃənist] tilhenger av utviklingslæren.

evolve [i'vɔlv] utvikle, utfolde, utarbeide.

evulsion [i'vʌlʃən] opprykking, utriving.

ewe [ju·] søye, sau. **-lamb** gimmerlam.

ewer ['ju·ə] krukke, vaskevannsmugge.

ex [eks] ex (latin), fra; eks, som har vært, tidligere; **sell — ship** selle fra skip.

exacerbate [ėk'säsəbe't] forverre, tirre, terge, erte. **exacerbation** [ėksäsə'beiʃən] forverring.

exact [ėg'zäkt] nøyaktig; punktlig; **I remembered the exact spot where** jeg husket nøyaktig det stedet hvor; **— sciences** eksakte vitenskaper.

exact [ėg'zäkt] inndrive; avtvinge, avpresse; fordre, kreve. **exacting** [ėg'zäktiŋ] fordringsfull; streng.

exaction [ėg'zäkʃən] inndriving; fordring, krav. **exactitude** [ėg'zäktitjud] nøyaktighet; punktlighet. **exactly** [ėg'zäktli] nøyaktig, nøye, ganske; nettopp; egentlig, riktig, nettopp; **not — a ghost story** ikke nettopp noen spøkelseshistorie.

exaggerate [ėg'zädʒəre't] overdrive. **exaggeration** [ėgzädʒə're'ʃən] overdrivelse. **exaggerative** [ėg'zädʒərətiv] som overdriver, overdreven.

exalt [ėg'zå·lt] oppløfte; opphøye; lovprise; fornøye, henrykke. **exaltation** [ėgzål'te'ʃən] oppløfting; fryd; opphøyning; lutring. **exalted** [ėg'zå·ltid] opphøyd; lutret. **exaltedness** [ėg'zå·ltidnės] opphøydhet.

exam [ėg'zäm] eksamen.

examination [ėgzämi'ne'ʃən] undersøkelse; eksamen; eksaminasjon, avhøring, forhør; **pass an — ta** en eksamen; **— paper** eksamensoppgave.

examine [ėg'zämin] undersøke; eksaminere; forhøre, avhøre, holde forhør over.

examinee [ėgzämi'ni·] eksaminand, kandidat. **examiner** [ėg'zäminə] undersøker, gransker; eksaminatoŕ; forhørsdommer; revisor, sensor.

example [ėg'za·mpl] eksempel, døme; **for — for** eksempel, til dømes; **make an —** of statuere et eksempel på; **set the —** tjene som forbilde; **take — by** (eller **from**) ta eksempel av, ta lærdom av.

exanimate [ėg'zänimėt, ėk's-] livløs; skinndød.

exanthemata [ėksän'þi·mata] utslett; feber med utslett. **exanthematic** [ėksänþi'mätik] eksantematisk.

exarch ['eksa·ᵊk] eksark, stattholder i det bysantinske rike, patriark (biskop) i den greske kirke.

exasperate [ėg'zäspəre't, -za·s-] forbitre; forverre, terge, erte. **exasperation** [ėgzäspə're'ʃən, -za·s-] forbitrelse, terging; forverring.

exc. fk. f. **except.**

excavate ['ekskəve't] hule ut; grave ut, grave fram. **excavation** [ekskə've'ʃən] uthuling; utgraving; hulning. **excavator** [eks'kəve'tə] jordarbeider, ekskavator, gravemaskin; muddermaskin.

exceed [ėk'si·d] overgå; overskride, overstige; gå for vidt. **exceeding** [ėk'si·diŋ] overordentlig, betydelig; veldig, framifrå; i høy grad. **exceedingly** i høy grad, overmåte.

excel [ėk'sel] overgå; utmerke seg. **excellence** ['eksələns] fortrinlighet; fortrin. **excellency** ['eksələnsi] eksellense (tittel); **his — hans** eksellense.

excellent ['eksələnt] fortreffelig, fortrinlig, glup.

excelsior [ek'selsiå·ᵒ] høyere, lenger oppe; **the — state** staten New York.

eccentric [ėk'sentrik], se **eccentric.**

except [ėk'sept] unnta; gjøre innsigelse, motmæle (**to** el. **against** mot); unntagen; med mindre, uten. **excepting** unntagen, unntatt, med unntagelse av.

exception [ėk'sepʃən] unntagelse, unntak; innsigelse, motmæle, motlegg; **with the — of** med unntak av; **an — to the rule** et unntak fra regelen; **take — against** (**at, to**) ta ille opp; reise innvending imot.

exceptionable [ėk'sepʃənəbl] omtvistelig.

exceptional [ėk'sepʃənəl] ualminnelig. **-ly** unntagelsesvis, unntaksvis, omfram.

exceptive [ėk'septiv] unntagelses-, unntaks-.

excerpt [ėk'sə·pt] utdra, ekserpeie, gjøre utdrag. **excerption** [ėk'sə·pʃən] utdrag.

excess [ėk'ses] overmål; overdrivelse; overskridelse; umåtelighet, utskeielse; **carry to — overdrive; be in — of** overgå; **— of luggage** overvekt. **excessive** [ėk'sesiv] overordentlig, overvettes, overdreven; heftig.

exchange [ėks'tʃein(d)ʒ] utveksle; tuske, bytte, ombytte, veksle; gå i bytte; utveksling; ombytting; bytte; veksel; kurs; børs; sentral (for telefon); **bill of —** veksel; **in — i** bytte. **exchangeable** [ėks'tʃe'n(d)ʒəbl] som kan byttes. **exchange-broker** [ėks'tʃe'ndʒ'broᵘkə] vekselmekler.

exchange-list kursliste.

exchequer [ėks'tʃekə] finansdepartement, skattkammer; **the Chancellor of the Exchequer** finansministeren; **court of —** skattkammer-rett (en avdeling av **the High Court of Justice**). **—bill, — -bond** statsobligasjon.

excipient [ėk'sipiənt] bindemiddel.

excisable [ėk'saizəbl] aksisepliktig, avgiftspliktig.

excise [ėk'saiz] aksise, avgift til stat el. kommune ved salget av særl. innenlandske varer; avgift; aksisekontor; beskatte.

excision [ėk'siʒən] bortskjæring, fjerning.

excitability [ėksaitə'biliti] pirrelighet. **excitable** [ėk'saitəbl] pirrelig; nervøs. **excitant** [ėk'saitənt, 'eksitənt] pirrende; stimulans, oppstiver. **excitation** [eksi'te'ʃən] pirring; egging. **excitative** [ėk'saitətiv], **excitatory** [ėk'saitətəri] stimulerende, pirrende.

excite [ėk'sait] vekke, framkalle, egge, opphisse, sette kveik i, bringe i sinnsbevegelse; beta. **excited** [ėk'saitid] betatt; begeistret; nervøs. **excitement** [ėk'saitmənt] tilskyndelse; oppfisselse; spenning; sinnsbevegelse; uro. **exciting** [ėk'saitiŋ] spennende.

excl. fk. f. **exclusively.**

exclaim [ėks'kle'm] utbryte; rope ut; skrike, ivre (imot).

exclamation [ekskla'me'ʃən] rop, utrop; utropstegn; **mark** (el. **note** el. **point** el. **sign**) **of —** utropstegn.

exclamatory [ėks'klämətəri] utrops-; utroper-.

exclude [ėks'klu·d] utelukke; unnta.

exclusion [ėks'klu·ʒən] utelukkelse, utestenging; unntagelse.

exclusive [ėks'klu·siv] utelukkende; eksklusiv; avvisende; aristokratisk, strengt sluttet, fornem; **— of** fraregnet. **exclusively** utelukkende, med utelukkelse; eksklusive. **exclusiveness** fornem tilbakeholdenhet, avvisende holdning.

excogitate [ėks'kådʒite't] tenke, grunde, pønske ut, opptenke. **excogitation** [ėkskådʒi'te'ʃən] oppfinnelse, utspekulering.

excommunicable [ekskə'mju·nikəbl] som fortjener å bannlyses.

excommunicate [ekskə'mju·nike't] bannlyse. **excommunication** [ėkskəmju·ni'ke'ʃən] bann.

excoriate [ėks'kå·rie't] flå, **excoriation** [ėkskå·ri'e'ʃən] flåing; hudløst sted.

excrement ['ekskrimənt] ekskrement, møkk. **excremental** [ekskri'mentl] ekskrement-, avførings-.

excrescence [ėks'kresəns] utvekst. **excrescent** [ėks'kresənt] utvoksende; overflødig.

excretal [ėks'kri·təl, 'ekskritəl] ekskrement-.

excrete [ėks'kri·t] skille ut, avsondre. **excretion** [ėks'kri·ʃən] avsondring; utførmning.

excretive [ėks'kri·tiv] avførende.

excruciate [ėks'kru·ʃie't] pine, martre. **excruciation** [ėkskru·ʃi'e'ʃən] pine, kval.

exculpate [ėks'kʌlpe't, 'eks-] unnskylde; rettferdiggjøre. **exculpation** [ekskʌl'pe'ʃen] unn-

skyldning; rettferdiggjøring. **exculpatory** [ėks-'kʌlpətəri] unnskyldende; rettferdiggjørende.
excursion [ėks'kə·ʃən] ekspedisjon; tur, utferd, lysttur, utflukt. — **train** tog som til nedsatt takst befordrer passasjerer på lysttur, billigtog.
excursionist [ėks'kə·ʃənist] lystreisende, turist.
excursive [ėks'kə·siv] springende.
excursus [ėks'kə·səs] ekskurs.
excusable [ėks'kju·zebl] unnskyldelig.
excusatory [ėks'kju·zətəri] unnskyldende.
excuse [ėks'kju·z] unnskylde; frita, forskåne; — **me** unnskyld, om forlatelse; — **me for being late** unnskyld at jeg kommer for sent; — **me from coming** frita meg for å komme; **excused** school fritatt fra skolegang.
excuse [ėks'kju·s] unnskyldning; påskudd; surrogat; **an — for a breakfast** en lett frokost.
execrable ['eksikrəbl] avskylig. **execrate** ['eksikreˡt] forbanne; avsky. **execration** [eksi-'kreˡʃən] forbanning; gjenstand for avsky; **hold in** — forbanne, avsky. **execratory** [eksi'kreˡtəri] forbannings-.
executant [ėg'zekjutənt] eksekutør, utøvende kunstner.
execute ['eksikju·t] utføre, fullbyrde; utstede; henrette; ekskvere; spille (på et instrument).
execution [eksiˡkju·ʃən] utførelse, fullbyrding; henretting; ødelegging, nederlag; utpanting, innførsel, eksekusjon; fingerferdighet (i musikk); — **ground** rettersted; — **sale** tvangsauksjon.
executioner [eksiˡkju·ʃənə] skarpretter, bøddel.
executive [ėg'zekjutiv, -ks-] utøvende, fullbyrdende, eksekutiv; **the** — den utøvende makt.
executor [ėg'zekjutə] utfører, fullbyrder; eksekutor (av et testament). **executorial** [ėgzekju'tå·riəl, -ks-] eksekutiv. **executorship** [ėg'zekjutəʃip] eksekutors ombud el. stilling. **executory** [ėg'zekjutəri, -ks-] eksekutrise.
exegesis [eksiˡdʒi·sis] eksegese. **exegete** ['eksidʒi·t] ekseget, fortolker.
exegetic [eksiˡdʒetik] fortolkende, eksegetisk.
exemplar [ėg'zemplə] mønster, eksemplar, ideal.
exemplary [ėg'zempləri] eksemplarisk.
exemplification [ėg'zemplifi'keˡʃən] belysing ved eksempler; bekreftet avskrift. **exemplify** [ėg'zemplifai] belyse ved eksempler; ta en attestert avskrift av.
exempli gratia [ėg'zemplai 'greˡʃə] f. eks.
exempt [ėg'zem(p)t] frita; forskåne (**from** for); fri, tollfri; fritatt, forskånet; immun; gardekorporal. **exemption** [ėg'zem(p)ʃən] fritaing; immunitet.
exequatur [eksiˡkweˡtə] eksekvatur, regjeringens anerkjennelse av en fremmed konsul.
exequies ['eksikwiz] jordfesting, begravelse.
exercise ['eksəsaiz] øve; utøve; eksersere; sette i bevegelse, sette i verk; øve seg; bevege seg, ta mosjon; øving; legemsbevegelse; mosjon, eksersis; skoleøving, utarbeiding, stil; utøving; andaktsøving; **do an** — skrive en stil; **take** — ta mosjon.
exercitation [egzə·siˡteˡʃən] øving.
exert [ėg'zə·t] anstrenge; bestrebe; streve.
exertion [ėg'zə·ʃən] anstrengelse, strev.
exes ['eksiz] utgifter (fk. f. **expenses**).
Exeter ['eksitə] Exeter.
exeunt ['eksiʌnt] de går ut (i skuespill).
exfoliate [ėks'fouˡlieˡt] miste bladene; skalle av, flekke, flakne. **exfoliation** [ėksfouˡliˡeˡʃən] flakning, avskalling.
exhalation [eksəˡleˡʃən, egz-] utånding, utdunsting; flyktighet; dunst, eim, ange, tev.
exhale [ėk's(h)eˡl] dunste ut, ange ut; få til å dampe bort; trekke (om sola).
exhaust [ėg'zå·st] tømme ut; utmatte, avkrefte, slite ut; ekshaust, eksos. **exhaustible** [ėg'zå·stibl] uttømmelig. **exhaustion** [ėg'zå·stʃən] uttømming, utmatting. **exhaustive** [ėg'zå·stiv] uttømmende.
exhaustless [ėg'zå·stlės] uuttømmelig.

exhibit [ėg'zibit] legge fram, tilstille; utstille; framstille; vise, syne, vise seg; utstillingsgjenstand.
exhibition [eksiˡbiʃən] framlegging; framvisning; utstilling; stipendium; **make an** — of oneself gjøre seg til narr; **world's** — verdensutstilling. **exhibitioner** [eksiˡbiʃənə] stipendiat. **exhibitive** [ėg'zibitiv] framstillings-, utstillings-. **exhibitor** [ėg'zibitə] utstiller. **exhibitory** [ėg'zibitəri] framstillings-.
exhilarant [ėg'zilərənt] oppmuntrende; oppmuntring. **exhilarate** [ėg'ziləreˡt] oppmuntre; live opp. **exhilaration** [ėgzilə're'ʃən] oppmuntring; munterhet.
exhort [ėg'zå·ət] formane, oppmuntre. **exhortation** [egzå·ə'teˡʃən] formaning, oppmuntring. **exhortative** [ėg'zå·ətativ], **exhortatory** [ėg'zå·ətətəri] formanings-.
exhumation [eks(h)ju'meˡʃən] oppgraving.
exhume [eks'(h)ju·m] grave opp, grave fram.
exigence ['eksidʒəns], **exigency** ['eksidʒənsi] kritisk stilling, nød, knipetak, behov. **exigent** ['eksidʒənt] presserende. **exigible** ['eksidʒibl] som kan inndrives.
exiguity [eksiˡgju·iti] litenhet, ubetydelighet. **exiguous** [ėg'zigjuəs] liten, ubetydelig.
exile ['eksail, -gz-] landsforvisning, landlysing, landflyktighet, utlegd; landflyktig, forvist, utleg; landsforvise; landlyse.
exility [ėg'ziliti, -ks-] litenhet, svakhet.
exist [ėg'zist] være, være til, eksistere; finne sted; **her existing pleasure** hennes glede her i livet.
existence [ėg'zistəns] eksistens, tilværelse; tilstedeværelse; vesen. **existent** [ėg'zistənt] eksisterende, bestående.
exit ['eksit] i skuespill: (han, hun) går, forlater scenen; utgang, sortie; avferd, bortgang.
Exmouth ['eksməþ] Exmouth.
exodus ['eksodəs] utvandring; annen Mosebok.
ex officio [eks å'fiʃioᵘ] på embets vegne.
exogamy [ek'någəmi] ekteskap utenfor ætten.
exon [ek'ksån] gardekorporal.
exonerate [ėg'zånəreˡt] befri, lette, frita, frigjøre, frifinne.
exoneration [ėgzånə're'ʃən] lettelse, befrielse.
exonerative [ėg'zånərətiv] befriende.
exor. fk. f. **executor**.
exorbitance [ėg'zå·əbitəns], **exorbitancy** [ėg-'zå·əbitənsi] urimelighet; ytterlighet; ubillighet.
exorbitant [ėg'zå·əbitənt] overdreven, ublu.
exorcise ['eksə·əsaiz] besverge, mane, drive ut onde ånder. **exorcism** ['eksə·əsizm] (ånde)besvergelse, bortmaning av djevelen el. onde ånder.
exorcist ['eksə·əsist] en som driver ut djevler ved bønn og seremonier.
exordial [ėg'zå·ədjəl] innledende.
exordium [ėg'zå·ədjəm] innledning.
exoteric [eksoˡterik] populær, almenfattelig.
exotic [ėg'zåtik] fremmed, utenlandsk, eksotisk.
expand [ėks'pänd] folde ut; bre ut; utvide; folde seg ut, vide seg ut; **my heart expands** mitt hjerte svulmer.
expanse [ėks'päns] vidstrakt rom, vid utstrekning; — **of heaven** himmelrom. **expansibility** [ėkspänsi'biliti] evnen til å vide seg ut. **expansible** [ėks'pänsibl] utvidelig.
expansion [ėks'pänʃən] utfoldelse; utbredelse; utvidelse; vidt utstrakt rom, vidde.
expansive [ėks'pänsiv] utvidende; utvidelig, tøyelig; vidstrakt; gemyttlig, åpenhjertig, raust.
expatiate [ėks'peˡʃieˡt] bre seg ut (**on** over).
expatiation [ėkspe'ʃieˡʃən] vidløftig omtale.
expatriate [ėks'peˡtrieˡt] forvise, landlyse; — oneself utvandre. **expatriation** [ėkspe'tri'eˡʃən] forvisning, utvandring, landlysing.
expect [ėks'pekt] vente; forvente; vente seg; anta; tro; **she is expecting** hun venter seg (venter sin nedkomst). **expectancy** [ėk'spektənsi] for-

ventning; ekspektanse. **expectant** [ék'spektənt] ventende, forventningsfull, vordende. **expectation** [ekspék'te¹ʃən] forventning, framtidshåp.
expectorant [ek'spektərənt] slimløsende; slimløsende middel. **expectorate** [ek'spektəre¹t] hoste opp, spytte opp; hoste, spytte. **expectoration** [ekspekto're¹ʃən] det å hoste, spytte opp; spytt.
expediency [ek'spi·djənsi] formålstjenlighet; hensiktsmessighet; gagn; egoistiske hensyn. **expedient** [ek'spi·djənt] hensiktsmessig, passende, tjenlig; middel, utvei, råd.
expedite ['ekspidait] framskynde; utferdige, ekspedere.
expedition [ekspi'diʃən] raskhet; ekspedisjon.
expeditionary [ekspi'diʃənəri] ekspedisjons-.
expeditious [ekspi'diʃəs] hurtig, rask, kjapp.
expel [ek'spel] drive ut, kaste ut; utvise; ekskludere; **the boy was -led from the school** el. **was -led the school** gutten ble vist ut av skolen.
expellable [ek'speləbl] som kan vises bort.
expend [ek'spend] gi ut, legge ut, nedlegge, anvende, ofre; bruke, forbruke. **expenditure** [ek'spenditʃə] utgift, utlegg, forbruk.
expense [ek'spens] utgift, utlegg, omkostning; bekostning, kostnad; **the expenses of the war** krigsomkostningene; **at my —** på min kostnad. **expensive** [ek'spensiv] kostbar, dyr. **expensiveness** [ek'spensivnès] kostbarhet.
experience [ek'spiəriəns] erfaring, røynsle, opplevelse; forsøke, prøve; erfare, røyne, føle, fornemme; få å føle, gjennomgå; **from** (eller **by**) — av erfaring. **experienced** [ek'spiəriənst] erfaren, røynd. **experiential** [ekspiəri'enʃəl] erfaringsmessig, empirisk.
experiment [ek'sperimənt] forsøk, eksperiment; forsøke, prøve, røyne, eksperimentere. **experimental** [eksperi'mental] erfaringsmessig, erfarings-; eksperimental. **experimentalist** [eksperi'mentəlist] eksperimentator. **experimentalize** [eksperi'mentəlaiz] eksperimentere. **experimentally** eksperimentalt; forsøksvis. **experimenter** [ek'sperimantə] se **experimentalist**. **experimentize** [iks'perimentaiz] eksperimentere.
expert ['ekspə·t] øvd, røynd, erfaren, kyndig, hag.
expert ['ekspə·t] sakkyndig, fagmann, ekspert. **expertness** [ek'spə·tnès] erfaring; dyktighet.
expiab'e ['ekspiəbl] som kan utsones. **expiate** ['ekspie¹t] sone, utsone, bøte. **expiation** [ekspi·'e¹ʃən] utsoning, bot, sonemiddel. **expiator** ['ekspi·e¹tə] soner, utsoner. **expiatory** ['ekspiätəri] utsonings-, son-, sonende.
expiration [ekspi're¹ʃən] utånding; utdunsting; død; opphør; utløp, forløp, ende, slutt; forfallstid. **expiratory** [ek'spaira¹təri] utåndings-.
expire [ek'spaiə] utånde, puste ut, utdunste; dø; forløpe, utløpe, gå til ende; opphøre.
expiry [ek'spairi] utløp, ende, slutt; død; forfall.
explain [ek's'ple¹n] forklare, tyde, tolke, greie ut, gjøre greie for; **— away** bortforklare; **— oneself** forklare seg. **explainable** [ek's'ple¹nəbl] forklarlig. **explainer** [ek's'ple¹nə] forklarer. **explanation** [ekspla·'ne¹ʃən] forklaring, uttydning, utlegging, utgreiing. **explanatory** [ek'splänətəri] forklarende.
expletive [èks'pli·tiv] utfyllende; fylleord; fyllekalk. **expletory** ['eksplitəri] utfyllende, fylle-.
explicable ['eksplikəbl] forklarlig. **explicate** ['eksplike¹t] utfolde, forklare. **explication** [ekspli'ke¹ʃən] utvikling, utgreiing, forklaring. **explicative** ['eksplike¹tiv el. iks'plikətiv] forklarende. **explicator** ['eksplike¹tə] forklarer. **explicatory** ['eksplikətəri] forklarende.
explicit ['eksplisit] tydelig, grei, klar, bestemt, uttrykkelig; likefram, endefram. **-ly** beint fram, med rene ord. **-ness** klarhet; likeframhet.
explode [ek's'plo⁰d] få til å eksplodere, sprenge; eksplodere, springe; bringe i miskreditt; pipe ut, hysse ut; bryte ut, fare opp, briste i latter. **exploding cotton** skytebomull.

exploit ['eksploit, iks'ploit] storverk, dåd, bedrift. **exploit** [iks'ploit] utbytte, utnytte. **exploitation** [eksploi'te¹ʃən] utnytting, utbytting.
exploration [eksplo're¹ʃən] utforsking, undersøkelse. **explorative** [èks'plå·rətiv] forskings-. **explorator** ['eksplore¹tə] forsker. **exploratory** [èk'splårətəri] undersøkende, undersøkelses-.
explore [ek'splå·ᵊ] forske ut, granske ut, undersøke; gjøre oppdagelsesreise; skjerpe. **explorer** [ek'splå·ᵊrə] utforsker; oppdagelsesreisende.
explosion [ek'splo⁰ʒən] eksplosjon; utbrudd. **explosive** [ek'splo⁰siv] eksplosiv; bråsint; sprengstoff; **— air** knallgass; **— cotton** skytebomull.
exponent [ek'spo⁰nənt] eksponent; representant, talsmann, målsmann.
export ['ekspå·ᵊt] utførsel, eksport; eksportartikkel; **prohibition of —** eksportforbud. **export** [ek'spå·ᵊt] utføre, føre ut, eksportere. **exportable** [èk'spå·ᵊtəbl] som kan utføres. **exportation** [ekspå·ᵊ'te¹ʃən] utførsel, eksport. **exporter** [ek·'spå·ᵊtə] eksportør.
expose [ek'spo⁰z] utsette, stille ut; blottstille, blotte; våge; avsløre, avdekke. **-d situation** utsatt stilling.
exposé [ekspo⁰'ze¹] framstilling, utgreiing.
exposition [ekspo'ziʃən] utstilling; utvikling, forklaring. **expositive** [ek'späzitiv] forklarende.
expositor [ek'späzitə] fortolker, utlegger. **expository** [ek'späsitəri] forklarende.
ex post facto [eks po⁰st 'fäkto⁰] etter at gjerningen er gjort; **— law** lov med tilbakevirkende kraft.
expostulate [eks'påstʃule¹t] gjøre forestillinger, gjøre bebreidelser; **— with** gå i rette med, bebreide. **expostulation** [ekspåstʃu'le¹ʃən] bebreidelse. **expostulator** [eks'påstʃule¹tə] en som gjør forestillinger. **expostulatory** [eks'påstʃulətəri] bebreidende.
exposure [ek'spo⁰ʒə] blottelse, beskjemmelse; utsatt stilling, ubeskyttethet, nød.
expound [ek'spaund] legge ut, forklare, tolke, uttyde. **expounder** [ek'spaundə] uttyder, fortolker.
express [ek'spres] presse ut; uttrykke, ytre; gi uttrykk for; uttrykkelig; ekspress; ilbud; iltog; **— oneself** uttrykke seg; **— train** iltog. **expressible** [ek'spresibl] som kan presses ut; som kan uttrykkes. **expression** [ek'spreʃən] uttrykking; uttrykk; framstilling. **expressionless** uttrykksløs. **expressive** [ek'spresiv] uttrykksfull; **— of** som gir uttrykk for. **expressly** [ek'spresli] uttrykkelig. **express-train** [èks'prestre¹n] iltog.
expropriate [èks'pro⁰prie¹t] ekspropriere, ta eiendomsretten.
expropriation [ékspro⁰pri'e¹ʃən] ekspropriasjon.
expulsion [eks'pʌlʃən] fordrivelse, utvising, relegasjon. **expulsive** [eks'pʌlsiv] som driver bort el. ut.
expunge [eks'pʌn(d)ʒ] stryke ut, slette ut.
expurgate ['ekspə·ge¹t] rense. **expurgation** [ekspə·'ge¹ʃən] renselse. **expurgator** ['ekspə·ge¹tə, èks'kspə·gətə] renser. **expurgatory** [eks'pə·gətəri] rensende.
exquisite ['ekskwizit] utsøkt, fortreffelig, framifrå; ualminnelig; sterk, heftig, intens (f. eks smerte); laps, sprett. **-ness** ['ekskwizitnès] utsøkthet, finhet; styrke, kraft.
exsanguinous [eks'säŋgwinəs] blodløs.
exscind [ek'sind] skjære bort.
exsect [ek'sekt] skjære bort. **-ion** [ek'sekʃən] utskjæring, bortskjæring.
ex-service man en som tidligere (især i verdenskrigen) har tjent i hær eller flåte, forhenværende soldat.
exsiccant [ek'sikənt] uttørrende. **exsiccate** ['eksike¹t] tørre ut. **exsiccation** [eksi'ke¹ʃən] uttørring. **exsiccative** [ek'sikativ] tørrende.
exsuction [ek'sʌkʃən] utsugning.
exudation [eksu'de¹ʃən] utsvetting.

extant [ĕks'tänt, 'ekstənt] bevart, i behold.
extemporaneous [ĕkstempə're!njəs]. **extempo-rary** [ĕks'tempərəri] ekstemporert, ekstempore.
extempore [eks'tempori] uforberedt, på stående fot, ekstempore. **extemporize** [ĕks'temporaiz] ekstemporere, improvisere. **extemporizer** [ĕks-'temporaizə] en som ekstemporerer, improvisa-tor.

extend [ĕk'stend] strekke ut; strekke; utvide, forlenge, tøye; spe opp, tynne; yte, skjenke, vise; strekke seg. **extendible** [ĕk'stendibl] strekkelig, tøyelig, utvidelig. **extensibility** [ĕkstensi'biliti] strekkelighet, utvidingskraft. **extensible** [ĕks-'tensibl] utstrekkelig, utvidelig. **extensile** [ĕk-'stensil] se **extensible**. **extension** [ĕk'stenʃən] ut-strekning, utvidelse; **University Extension** popu-lærvitenskapelig foredragsserie. **extensional** [ĕk-'stenʃənəl] vidt utstrakt. **extensive** [ĕk'stensiv] utstrakt, vid, stor. **extensor** [ĕk'stensɔ·ɔ, -sə] strekkemuskel.

extent [ĕk'stent] utstrekning, omfang, monn; område; **to a certain** — til en viss grad; **to a great** — i vid utstrekning.

extenuate [ĕks'tenjue!t] avkrefte, minke, svekke; smykke, pynte på, formilde, døyve; **extenuating circumstances** formildende omsten-digheter. **extenuation** [ĕkstenju'e!ʃən] avkrefting; det å pynte på; unnskyldning. **extenuatory** [ĕk'stenjue!təri] unnskyldende, formildende.

exterior [ĕks'stiəriə] ytre, utvendig; utvortes. **-ize** [ĕk'stiəriəraiz] gi ytre form; se tydelig.

exterminate [ĕks'tə·mine!t] rydde ut. **extermi-nation** [ĕkstə·mi'ne!ʃən] utrydding. **extermina-tor** [ĕks'tə·mine!tə] utrydder. **exterminatory** [ĕks'tə·minətəri] utryddings-.

external [ĕk'stə·nəl] ytre, utvendig; — **evidence** bevismateriale fra andre kilder enn det under-søkte; — **remedies** midler til utvortes bruk. **externalize** [ĕk'stə·nəlaiz] gi ytre form. **externals** [ĕk'stə·nalz] ytre, utvortes.

exterritorial [ĕksteri'tå·riəl] eksterritorial, som ikke er undergitt myndighetene i et land. **-ity** [ĕksteritå·ri'äliti] eksterritorialitet.

extinct [ĕk'stiŋkt] slokt, sløkt, sloknet; opp-hevd, avskaffet; utdødd. **extinction** [ĕk'stiŋkʃən] slokning, sløkking, opphevelse, avskaffelse; ut-døing; tilintetgjøring.

extinguish [ĕk'stiŋgwiʃ] slokke; sløkke; be-legge. **extinguishable** [ĕk'stiŋgwiʃəbl] som kan slokkes osv. **extinguisher** [ĕk'stiŋgwiʃə] lyseslok-ker; slokningsapparat. **extinguishment** [ĕk'stiŋg-wiʃmənt] slokking, ødeleggelse, stansing.

extirpate ['ekstə·pe!t] rydde ut, tyne, ødele. **extirpation** [ĕkstə·'pe!ʃən] utrydding. **extirpator** ['ekstə·pe!tə] utrydder.

extol [ĕk'sto·l] opphøye, heve opp i skyene, prise.

extort [ĕks'tå·ət] fravriste, presse ut, pine ut, tvinge fram. **extortion** [ĕks'tå·ɔʃən] ut-pressing; pengeavpressing, flåing, utsugn̄ig; brannskatte. **extortionary** [ĕks'tå·ɔʃənəri] ut-sugende, utpressings-. **extortionate** [ĕks'tå·ɔʃənét] hard, ublu. **extortioner** [ĕks'tå·ɔʃənə] utsuger, opptrekker.

extra ['ekstrə] ekstra; omfram; noe ekstra; ekstrablad, ekstraforestilling o. l.; **extras** ekstra-utgifter.

extract [ĕks'träkt] dra ut; trekke ut; trekke fram; ta fram; hale ut. **extract** ['eksträkt] utdrag, ekstrakt; utvalg. **extractable** [ĕks'träktəbl] som kan utdras. **extraction** [ĕks'träkʃən] utdraing; utdrag, uttrekk; avstamning, ætt, herkomst; ekstraksjon; **extraction of roots** rotutdraing (i matematikk). **extractive** [ĕks'träktiv] som kan ut-dras. **extractor** [ĕks'träktə] ekstraktor;fødselsklype.

extradite ['ekstrədait] utlevere (en forbryter). **extradition** [ekstrə'diʃən] utlevering (av for-brytere).

extrajudicial [ekstrədʒu·'diʃəl] ekstrajudisiell, utenrettslig (som skjer utenfor retten).

extraneous [ĕks'tre!njəs] fremmed, uvedkom-mende; — **to the subject** emnet uvedkommende.
extraordinary [ĕk'strå·ɔdinəri, -dnri] overor-dentlig; usedvanlig, merkverdig, merkelig. **ex-traordinaries** noe ualminnelig; tilfeldige utgifter.
extraparochial [ekstrəpə'roukjəl] utenbygds.
extravagance [ĕk'strävəgəns] urimelighet; over-drivelse; ekstravaganse, overspenthet; ødselhet.
extravagant [ĕk'strävəgənt] urimelig; over-dreven; ekstravagant, overspent; ødsel.
extravaganza [ekstråvə'gänzə] regelløs kompo-sisjon; fantastisk stykke.
extreme [ĕk'stri·m] ytterst; ytterlig; sist; me-get stor, overordentlig; ytterste ende; ytterlighet, ekstrem; høyeste grad.
extremely [ĕk'stri·mli] ytterst, høyst, overor-dentlig, omfram.
extremity [ĕk'stremiti] ytterste ende; ytterste; ytterlighet; verste knipe; nød, ulykke; i pl. ekstremiteter, hender og føtter.
extricable ['ekstrikəbl] som kan greies ut. **extricate** ['ekstrike!t] utvikle, utrede, greie ut; befri. **extrication** [ekstri'ke!ʃən] utvikling, utred-ning, utgreiing, befrielse.
extrinsic(al) [ĕk'strinsik(l)] utvortes, ytre.
extrude [ĕk'stru·d] støte, drive, trenge ut.
extrusion [ĕk'stru·ʒən] utstøting, utdriving.
exuberance [ĕg'z(j)u·bərəns] overflod, fylde, yp-pighet. **exuberant** [ĕg'z(j)u·bərənt] overstrøm-mende, frodig, yppig, rik, flus.
exudation [eks(j)u'de!ʃən] utsvetting.
exude [ĕg'zju·d] svette ut.
exult [ĕg'zʌlt] juble; hovere, triumfere.
exultant [ĕg'zʌltənt] jublende; hoverende.
exultation [egzʌl'te!ʃən] jubel; hovering.
exuviæ [ĕg'z(j)u·vii·] felt ham el. hud el. skall (av dyr). **exuviate** [ĕg'z(j)u·vie!t] skifte ham el. hud el. skall. **exuviation** [ĕgz(j)u·vi'e!ʃən] skifte av ham, hud, skall el. tenner.

exx. fk. f. **examples.**
eyas ['aiəs] falkunge.
eye [ai] øye, blikk; øye (på nål, potet etc.); løkke, malje; syn, synsevne; se på, betrakte, iaktta, mønstre; **set eyes on** se (for sine øyne); **see eye to eye** with være enig med; **find favour in his eyes** finne nåde for hans øyne; **open one's eyes** stirre forbauset; **open a person's eyes to the truth** få en til å se sannheten; **his eyes are bigger than his belly** magen blir før mett enn øynene; **eyes right!** se til høyre! **have all one's eyes about one** ha øynene med seg, ha et øye på hver finger; **any one with half an eye in his head might have seen** enhver kunne ha sett med et halvt øye; **my eye!** du store tid! **have an eye for** ha sans for; **keep an eye on** holde øye med; **make eyes** bruke øynene, kokettere; **it is a sight for bad eyes to see** det gjør ens gamle øyne godt å se Dem; **in my mind's eye** for mitt indre øye; **stand eye to eye** stå ansikt til ansikt; **up to one's eyes** til opp over ørene; **mind your eye** (slang) pass på; **all my eye** (slang) sludder; **he has an eye to her money** han har et godt øye til pengene hennes; **the glad eye** (slang) kokett el. forelsket blikk.
eye|ball øyeeple, øyestein. **-brow** ['aibrau] øye-bryn. **-flap** skylapp. **-glass** lorgnett; lorgnettere. **-lashes** øyehår.
eyelet ['ailet] snørehull; liten åpning; takluke. **-ted** forsynt med et lite hull.
eyelid ['ailid] øyelokk.
eye-opener overraskende kjensgjerning.
eye-piece okular.
eye|-salve øyesalve. — **-servant** øyentjener. — **-service** øyentjeneste. — **-shot** synsvidde. **-sight** syn, synsvidde, — **-sore** torn i øyet. — **-tooth** øyetann, hjørnetann. — **witness** øyevitne.
eyot ['e!ət] liten øy, holme.
Eyre [æ·ə] Eyre.
eyre [æ·ə] omgang, rundferd.
eyrie, eyry ['æ·ɔri] rovfuglreir, ørnereir.

F

F [ef] F; **F sharp** fiss; **F flat** fess; **F major** f-dur; **F minor** f-moll.

F., f. fk. f. **Fahrenheit; farthing; fellow; following; fort; forte; Flemish; French; Friday.**

F. A. fk. f. **Football Association.**

F. A. A. fk. f. **free of all average.**

Fabian ['fe¹biən] klokt nølende (som Fabius, Hannibals motstander); — **Society** sosialistforening som hyller en forsiktig iherdig politikk.

fable ['fe¹bl] fabel; sagn; skrøne; fabulere; oppdikte, dikte i hop, lyve. **fabled** ['fe¹bld] berømt; omtalt i fabelen el. sagnet.

fabric ['fäbrik] indre sammensetning, vevning; fabrikat, (vevd) stoff; bygningsverk; bygning. **fabricate** ['fäbrike¹t] bygge; dikte; fabrikere, lage. **fabrication** [fäbri'ke¹ʃən] bygning; oppdikting, falskneri, fabrikasjon. **fabricator** ['fäbrike¹tə] bygger; oppdikter; fabrikant.

fabulist ['fäbjulist] fabeldikter. **fabulize** ['fäbjulaiz] dikte el. fortelle fabler. **fabulosity** [fäbju-'låsiti] fabelaktighet. **fabulous** ['fäbjuləs] fabelaktig; — **age** sagntiden.

façade [fə'sa·d] fasade, forside.

face [fe¹s] overflate; forside; ansikt; fjes; tallskive; mine; dristighet; uforskammethet; kunstig farge; **face to face** ansikt til ansikt; **throw oneself face down** kaste seg nesegrus; **full face** en face; **carry two faces** bære kappen på begge skuldrer; **in the face of** beint mot, opp i ansiktet på; **have the face to** være dristig nok til å; **lose face** bli ydmyket; **make faces** skjære ansikter; geipe; **pull a long face** bli lang i ansiktet; **put a good face on the matter** gjøre gode miner til slett spill; **fly in the face of danger** løpe like i løvens gap, trasse; **in the very face of** like for nesen på; **on the very face of the matter** straks på forhånd; **save a person's face** redde en fra åpenlys skam; **set one's face against it** motsette seg det; **he told him to his face** han sa ham like opp i ansiktet. **face** [fe¹s] stille seg ansikt til ansikt med, vende ansiktet mot; se like i øynene; trosse, trasse; være like overfor, vende ut mot; bedekke, bekle, belegge; besette, kante, forsyne med oppslag; hykle; vende seg om, dreie seg, snu seg; — **the music** ta mot kritikken; — **the question** ta spørsmålet opp; **right** —! høyre om! — **about** gjøre helomvending.

face-ache ['fe¹se¹k] nevralgi, ansiktssmerter.

facer ['fe¹sə] slag i ansiktet, strek i regningen.

facet ['fäsit] fasett; fasettere.

facetiæ [fə'si·ʃii·] vittige innfall, vitser.

facetious [fə'si·ʃəs] munter, skjemtsom; vittig.

face value pålydende verdi.

facial ['fei¹ʃəl] ansikts-.

facile ['fäsail] lett (ikke vanskelig); tilgjengelig, godslig, vennlig; lett å overtale, bøyelig.

facilitate [fə'silite¹t] lette. **facilitation** [fəsili-'te¹ʃən] lettelse. **facility** [fə'siliti] letthet; ferdighet; omgjengelighet; **facilities** lettelser, fordeler; hjelpemidler; lett adgang.

facing ['fe¹siŋ] oppslag, kant; vending; **put a person through his facings** prøve hva en duger til.

facsimile [fäk'simili] faksimile; faksimilere.

fact [fäkt] kjensgjerning, hending, faktum; sak; **in** — i virkeligheten, faktisk, endog, ja; **as a matter of** — i virkeligheten; **matter of** — kjensgjerning; nøktern, prosaisk; **the** — **is that** saken er at, nemlig.

faction ['fäkʃən] parti; klikk; uenighet, strid. **factionist** ['fäkʃənist] partimann, partigjenger. **factious** ['fäkʃəs] parti-; misfornøyd, misnøgd, urolig.

factitous [fäk'tiʃəs] kunstig, tillært, tilgjort.

factor ['fäktə] agent, ombudsmann, kommisjo-

nær; faktor (i regning og fig.). **factorage** ['fäktəridʒ] kommisjon.

factorship ['fäktəʃip] agentur; kommisjon.

factory ['fäktəri] fabrikk; faktori, handelskoloni. — **-made** fabrikkarbeid.

factotum [fäk'to·təm] høyre hånd, faktotum.

facultative ['fäk(ə)lte¹tiv] fakultativ, valgfri; fakultets-.

faculty ['fäkəlti] evne, dyktighet, kraft; makt, myndighet; fakultet (ved universitetet, især de lægevitenskapelige); **one of the** — medisiner, som har tatt eksamen, lege.

fad [fäd] innfall; kjepphest, mani. **faddish** ['fädiʃ] besatt av en idé el. mani, monoman. **faddism** ['fädizm] monomani. **faddist** ['fädist] monoman.

fade [fe¹d] falme; visne, bleikne; svinne; **fade away** svinne hen; forsvinne. **faded** visnet, falmet.

fadeless ['fe¹dlès] uvisnelig.

fæcal ['fi·kəl] som angår ekskrementer, (se fecal).

fæces ['fi·si·z] bunnfall; ekskrementer.

faery ['fä·°ri] se fairy.

fag [fäg] trelle, slite og slepe; bli trett; la trelle; trell, tjener, mindre elev som må oppvarte de eldre; slit; (slang) sigarett; **-ged out** utkjørt. **fag-end** ['fäg'end] matt avslutning, stump, rest. **faggot** ['fägət] riskjerv; risbunt; knippe, bunt; myrmann (i politikk). **faggot-vote** ['fägətvo·t] myrmannsstemme. **fagottist** [fə'gåtist] fagottist. **fagotto** [fə'gåto·] fagott.

Fahr. fk. f. **Fahrenheit.**

Fahrenheit ['färin(h)ait, 'fa·r-] Fahrenheit.

faience [fr.; fə'jåns] fajanse.

fail [fe¹l] feile, mislykkes, slå feil; gå fallitt; la i stikken, svikte, skorte; unnlate, forsømme; ikke makte; **he failed** det slo feil for ham; **had I failed in this** hadde det ikke lykkes meg; **that failing** el. **failing that** i mangel herav; **fail one's promise** svikte sitt løfte; **fail to appear** utebli; **I fail to see** jeg kan ikke innse; **he failed in the examination** han dumpet til eksamen.

fail [fe¹l] skort, svikt, svikting; **without** — ganske sikkert, uten tvil.

failing ['fe¹liŋ] skavank; svakhet; mangel, skort, lyte; mistak; fallitt; i mangel av.

failure ['fe¹lja] mangel, skort, uteblivelse; det å slå feil; uhell; fåfengt strev; fiasko; misvekst; det å avta, svikting, svekkelse; unnlatelse, forsømmelse; fallitt; mislykt individ.

fain [fe¹n] glad, fornøyd, nøgd; glad til, nødt til (bare etter **would**) gjerne; **he was** — **to do it** han var nødt til å gjøre det.

faint [fe¹nt] bli svak, falle i avmakt, besvime, dåne; la motet falle; svinne hen; svak, matt, utmattet; kraftløs; dårlig; dåneferdig; fryktsom; avmakt; besvimelse; — **away** besvime; **-ing fit** besvimelsesanfall; **I have not the -est idea** jeg har ikke den fjerneste idé. **-hearted** forsagt. **faintly** ['fe¹ntli] svakt, matt, utydelig. **faintness** svakhet, matthet; motløshet.

fair [fä·ə] skjær, ren, fin, plettfri, klar; blond, lys; fager, skjønn, smukk; billig, rettferdig, rettvis; ærlig; god; antagelig; (på barometer) pent vær; **the** — **sex** det smukke kjønn; **a** — **one** en kvinne; **the** — **Venetian** venetianerinnen; **if it were** — **to judge of** . . . hvis man da kunne dømme om . . .; — **copy, draft** renskrift; — **fight** ærlig kamp; **a** — **impression** et rentrykk; — **play** ærlig spill; **in a** — **way to** på god vei til å; — **wind** god bør; **bid** — love, tegne til; **speak him** — tale ham tilfreds; — **and square** ærlig og redelig.

fair [fæ·ə] marked; kjøpstevne; basar; **a day after the** — (en postdag) for sent, post festum. **Vanity Fair** forfengelighetens marked (bok av Thackeray).

fair-faced ['fæ·əfeˈst] lyslett, fager.

Fairfax ['fæ·əfäks] Fairfax.

fair-haired ['fæ·əˈhæ·əd] lyshåret.

fairing [ˈfæ·əriŋ] markedsgave.

fairish [fæ·əriʃ] ganske pen; tålelig bra, ikke verst.

fairl [ˈfæ əli] klart; greitt; åpent; tydelig; like fram; auske, fullkomment. **fair-minded** [ˈfæ·ə-ˈmaindid] rettsindig.

fairness ['fæ·ənès] skjærhet, klarhet; blondhet; åpenhet, ærlighet, rimelighet; **in** — når rett skal være. **fair-spoken** ['fæ·əspoˈuken] beleven, forekommende.

fairway ['fæ·əweˈ] skipslei, farlei, farvann.

fair-weather ['fæ·əweðə] godværs-; — **friend** upålitelig venn.

fairy ['fæ·əri] fe, hulder, alvkone, alv; feaktig, trolldomsaktig, fe-, alv-. — **-circle** alvedans. **-land** eventyrland. — **-ring** alvedans. — **-tale** eventyr.

faith [feˈþ] løfte, ord; troskap; tro; tillit; **the Christian** — den kristne tro. **faith!** min santen! **faithful** ['feˈþf(u)l] tro, trofast, redelig; troende; **yours faithfully** ærbødigst, vørsamt (under brev). **faithless** ['feˈþlès] troløs; vantro. **faithlessness** ['feˈþlèsnès] troløshet; vantro.

fake [feˈk] bukt, kveil; kveile opp.

fake [feˈk] pynte på, ettergjøre, forfalske; stjele, knabbe; forfalskning, svindel. — **up** ettergjøre, pynte på. **fakement** ['feˈkmənt] knep; falskt tiggerbrev.

fakir ['fa·kiə, 'feˈkiə, fə'kiə] fakir (muhamedansk tiggermunk).

falcated ['fälkeˈtid] sigdformet.

falchion ['få·lʃən] kort sabel; sverd.

falciform ['få·lsifå·əm] sigdformet.

falcon ['få·kən, 'få·lkən] falk. **falconer** ['få·k(ə)nə] falkonér. **falconry** ['få·kənri] falketemming.

falderal ['fäldə'räl] småting; småpynt; vas. **faldstool** ['få·ldstu·l] en slags skammel.

Falkirk ['fa·(l)kə·k] Falkirk.

Falkland ['få·klənd] Falkland.

fall [få·l] falle, dette, sige, synke, gå ned; legge seg (om vind); bli (plutselig), inntreffe; fødes (om visse dyr); fall; synking, nedgang; tone-fall; helling; hall, brekke, li; vassfall, (amr.) høst; trin; høgst; **his face fell** han ble lang i ansiktet; **his heart fell** motet hans sank; **the wind fell** vinden løyde av, spaknet; — **about** gå for seg, gå til, bære til; — **asleep** falle i søvn; — **astern** bli akterutseilt; — **away** tape seg, bli svakere, falle fra; — **back** trekke seg tilbake (**upon** til); falle tilbake (**upon** på); — **behind** sakke akterut; — **calm** stilne av; — **due** forfalle til betaling; — **flat** falle virkningsløs til jorda; — **foul of** ryke uklar med; — **ill** bli syk; — **in** falle inn, styrte sammen (om tak etc.); stille seg på plass, gå på plass, stille (om soldater); utløpe, opphøre (f. eks. om pensjon); tre i kraft; bifalle; — **in love** bli forelsket (**with** i); — **in with** treffe sammen med; falle sammen med, stemme overens med; — **in line** stille seg opp (i geled), tre på linje (**with** med); — **into** munne ut i (om **elv**), tiltre (en mening); — **off** falle fra, svikte; falle av (for vinden); tape seg; gå av bruk; — **off from** svikte; — **on** (eller **upon**) overfalle; komme i; — **on** (on adv.) ta fatt (f. eks. på måltid); — **out** falle ut; hende; bli uvenner, ryke uklar (**with** med); — **over** styrte ned; — **short** slippe opp; — **short of** ikke fylle, ikke nå opp til; — **through** gå i stykker, gå over styr; — **to** (to adv.) gi seg i kast med, ta fatt (f. eks. på måltid); — **to** (to prep.) henfalle til; gi seg til; tilfalle; — **to blows** komme i slagsmål; ryke i hop; — **to pieces** falle sammen; — **to work** ta fatt; — **under** falle inn under, høre til; **have a** — falle; **the falls of**

Niagara N. fossen. **try a** — **with** prøve en dyst med.

fall [få·l] hval (i Skottland).

fallacious [fə'leˈʃəs] bedragersk, villedende, misvisende.

fallacy ['fäləsi] villfarelse; sofisme, falsk slutning.

fal-lals ['fäl'lälz] flitter, dingeldangel, stas.

fallen ['få·l(ə)n] perf. pts. av **fall**.

fallibility ['fäli'biliti] det å kunne ta feil.

fallible ['fälibl] som kan ta feil.

falling-sickness epilepsi, fallesyke, fang.

falling-star ['få·liŋ'sta·ə] stjerneskudd, stjernerap.

fallow ['fälouˈ] blakk, gulbrun; brakk; oppløyd men ikke tilsådd; brakkmark, brakkpløyning; legge brakk; **lie** — ligge brakk; **be in** — ligge brakk. — **-deer** dådyr.

Falmouth ['fälməþ] Falmouth.

false [få·(·)ls] falsk; usann, ikke sann; uekte, forloren; uærlig, utro; uriktig; **play** — spille et puss, bedra. **falsehood** ['få·(·)lshud] usannhet, løgn, svik; uriktighet. **falsely** ['få·(·)lsli] falskt, usant; uærlig.

falsetto [få·l'setoˈu] falsett, fistelstemme.

falsification [få·lsifi'keˈʃən] forfalskning; gjendriving. **falsifier** ['få·(·)lsifaiə] forfalsker; løgner. **falsify** ['få·(·)lsifai] forfalske; gjendrive; gjøre til skamme; svikte. **falsity** ['få·(·)lsiti] falskhet; usannhet, usanning; uvederheftighet.

Falstaff ['få·(·)lsta·f] Falstaff.

falter ['få·(·)ltə] riste, skjelve, vakle, bli usikker; stamme. **falteringly** stammende, usikkert.

fame [feˈm] rykte; ry, gjetord, berømmelse, fregd.

famed [feˈmd] berømt, navngjeten, freg.

familiar [fə'miljə] bekjent, velkjent, fortrolig; fri, utvungen; endefram; fortrolig venn, gammel kjenning; demon, tjenende ånd; inkvisisjonstjener, familiær. **familiarity** [fəmili'äriti] fortrolighet. **familiarize** [fə'miljəraiz] gjøre fortrolig med.

family ['fämili] familie, huslyd, husstand; ætt, slekt; **her little** — hennes små barn; — **doctor** huslæge; — **man** familiefar; **in a** — **way** uten krus, i all enkelhet; **be in the** — **way** være fruktsommelig.

famine ['fämin] hungersnød, sult; — **prices** dyrtidspriser. **famish** ['fämiʃ] sulte ut, tvinge ved sult, ta sulte i hjel; sulte, forsmekte; **famishing** ogs. skrubbsulten.

famous ['feˈməs] berømt, navngjeten, vidgjeten; utmerket; ypperlig.

fan [fän] vifte; rensemaskin, kornrenser; kasteskovl; fjærvinge; fjærvifte; ventilator; stryke bort over (om vind); vifte; rense; egge, oppflamme; (fig.) puste til.

fanatic [fə'nätik] fanatisk; fanatiker.

fanatical [fə'nätikl] fanatisk.

fanaticism [fə'nätisizm] fanatisme.

fancied ['fänsid] innbilt, tenkt; yndet.

fancier ['fänsiə] ynder, libhaber, oppdretter; **dog-** — hundeoppdretter.

fanciful ['fänsif(u)l] fantastisk; forunderlig; narraktig; eventyrlig.

fancy ['fänsi] innbilningskraft, fantasi; innbilning, forestilling, tanke; innfall, grille, lune; lyst, smak; elsk; forkjærlighet, tilbøyelighet; svermeri; kjærlighet; inklinasjon; **take a** — **to** legge elsk på, få sans for, få lyst til.

fancy ['fänsi] tro, mene; tenke seg, forestille seg; sverme for; ha lyst til.

fancy|-articles motevarer. — **-ball** kostymeball. — **-butter** fint smør. — **-cloth** mønstret tøy. — **-dress** fantasidrakt; kostyme. — **-fair** basar (i velgjørende øyemed). — **-free** uberørt av kjærlighet. — **-goods** luksusartikler, galanterivarer. — **-man** kjæreste; alfons. — **-picture** fantasibilde. — **-price** eventyrlig pris. — **-shop** galanterihandel, broderihandel. — **-skater** kunstskøyteløper. — **-work** fint håndarbeid, kniplinger.

fandango [fän'däŋgoᵘ] fandango.
fane [feⁱn] helligdom, tempel.
fanfare ['fänfæ·ə] fanfare.
fanfaronade [fänfäro'neⁱd] skryt, fanfare.
fang [fäŋ] fange, gripe; hoggtann; tannrot; klo.
fanlight ['fänlait] viftefoi met vindu over en dør.
fanner ['fänə] vifte, rensemaskin.
Fanny ['fäni] Fanny.
fanny ['fäni] medlem av F. A. N. Y. (s. d.)
fan-palm ['fänpa·m] viftepalme.
fantail ['fänteⁱl] høystjert (fugl).
fantasia [fäntə'zi·a, fän'ta·zia] fantasi (i musikk). **fantasm** ['fäntäzm] se **phantasm. fantastic** [fən'tästik], **fantastical** [fən'tästikl] innbilt; fantasi; fantastisk; lunefull. **fantasticality** [fəntästi'käliti] fantastisk beskaffenhet; fantasteri; lunefullhet. **fantasy** se **phantasy.**
F. A. N. Y. fk. f. **First Aid Nursing Yeomanry** bet. for en organisasjon som sørger for troppenes forpleining.
faqueer, faquir [fə'kiə] se **fakir.**
far [fa·ə] fjern, langt borte, som ligger langt unna; lang, vid; fjernt, langt; vidt; meget, mye; — **away** langt borte; — **off** langt borte, langt bort; — **and near** nær og fjern; — **and wide** vidt og bredt; **I am — from wishing** jeg ønsker absolutt ikke; — **from it!** langtfra! — **be it from me to** det være langt fra meg å; **few and — between** få og sjeldne; — **and away the best** uten sammenligning den beste; **as — as** inntil, like til; for så vidt som, ikke rettere; **make it go** — få det til å slå godt til; **he is — gone in drink** han er meget full; — **on in the day** langt på dag; **by** — i høy grad; **too difficult by** — altfor vanskelig; **from the — end of the room** fra den motsatte del av værelset; **the — side of the horse** den høyre side av hesten; **a — journey** en lang reise; **a — cry** en lang vei; **is London** — er det langt til London; **so — as to** i den grad at.
farad ['färəd] farad (elektrisk kraftenhet).
Faraday ['färədi, 'färədei].
far-away ['fa·rə'weⁱ] fjern, (om utseende) drømmende.
farce [fa·əs] farsere, fylle; farse, fyll; farse (teaterstykke). **farcical** ['fa·əsikl] farseaktig.
farcy ['fa·əsi] utslett (hos hester), snive.
fardel ['fa·ədl] byrde.
fare [fæ·ə] fare, ha det, befinne seg; spise og drikke, leve; ferjepenger, frakt, skyssbetaling, billettpris, takst; fortjeneste (for kjøring); passasjer; kost, mat; **you may go further and — worse** en kan lete lenge uten å finne noe bedre; vær tilfreds med det du har; **I had fared very hard** det hadde gått meg meget dårlig; **it fared well with us** det gikk oss godt; — **well** leve godt, spise og drikke godt; **table of fares** taksttariff; **bill of** — spiseseddel; **coarse** — grov kost; **ordinary** — husmannskost.
farewell ['fæ·ə'wel] farvel; avskjeds-.
far-famed ['fa·əfeⁱmd] navngjeten, vidgjeten.
far-fetched ['fa·əfetʃt] søkt, unaturlig.
far-gone ['fa·ə'gån] langt nede eller ute m. h. t. sykdom, galskap, drikk, gjeld.
farina [fə'rainə] mel; blomsterstøv.
farinaceous [färi'neⁱʃəs] melet, melen, melaktig.
farinose ['färinoᵘs] melet.
farm [fa·əm] gård, gard, bondegård, avlsgård; forpakte bort; forpakte, ta i forpaktning, bygsle; dyrke (jorda), drive (en gård osv.). **farmer** ['fa·əmə] forpakter, bygselmann, leilending; bonde, landmann. **farmeress** ['fa·əmərės] forpakterske. **farmhouse** forpakterbolig; bondegård; **farming** ['fa·əmiŋ] landbruk, jordbruk.
farmost ['fa·əmoᵘst] fjernest, som ligger lengst borte.
farmstead ['fa·əmsted] bondegård.
farm-yard ['fa·əm'ja·əd] gårdsrom, tun.
faro ['fæ·əroᵘ] et slags kortspill.
Faroe Islands ['fæ·əroᵘ'ailəndz], **the — eller the Faroes** Færøyene. **Faroese** [fæ·əro'i·z, -'i·s] færøysk, færøying.
far-off ['fa·råf] fjerntliggende, fjern.
Farquhar ['få·ək(w)ə] Farquhar.
farrago [fə'reⁱgoᵘ] blanding, røre, miskmask.
far-reaching ['fa·əri·tʃiŋ] vidtrekkende.
farrier ['färiə] hovslager; dyrlege. **farriery** ['färiəri] grovsmedhåndverk, skosmie.
farrow ['färoᵘ] grise, få griser; kull grisunger.
far-seeing ['fa·əsi·iŋ] vidtskuende, vidsynt.
far-sighted ['fa·əsaitid] vidtskuende; langsynt.
farther ['fa·əðə] fjernere; lenger bort(e); videre; lenger. **farthest** ['fa·əðist] fjernest, lengst.
farthing ['fa·əðiŋ] kvartpenny; dust, grann, døyt.
farthingale ['fa·əðiŋgeⁱl] fiskebeinsskjørt.
f. a. s. fk. f. **free alongside ship.**
F. A. S. fk. f. **Fellow of the Antiquarian Society; Fellow of the Society of Arts.**
fasces ['fäsiz] riskjerv, risknippe, fasces.
fascia ['fäʃiə] bind, forbinding; bånd, flat list; senehinne.
fascicle ['fäsikl] knippe, bunt; hefte.
fascinate ['fäsineⁱt] fjetre, fortrylle. **fascination** [fäsi'neⁱʃən] fortryllelse, trylling, fjetring.
fascine [fä'si·n] faskin, risknippe, riskjerv.
fascism ['fäʃizm] fascisme. **fascist** ['fäʃist] fascist; **the — movement** fascistbevegelsen.
fash [fäʃ] drille; bry, plage; ergre seg; bli kjed av; plage; ergrelse; bekymring, bry; ubehagelig person.
fashion ['fäʃən] form; fasong; mote, snitt; skikk, skikk og bruk, vedtekt; lag, vis, måte; danne, forme; avpasse, innrette; **be (become) the** — være (bli) mote; **after a** — på en måte; **in (the)** — på moten, moderne; **out of** — gått av mote, gammeldags, umoderne; **the latest** — siste mote; **a man of** — en fin mann. **fashionable** ['fäʃənəbl] fin; moderne; moteherre. **fashion-book** motejournal. **fashionist** ['fäʃənist] motenarr, spjert.
Fashoda [fə'ʃoᵘdə] Fashoda.
fast [fa·st] fast; sterk, holdbar, varig; hurtig, rask; flott, lettlyndt; lettsindig, utskeiende; emansipert; dyp (om søvn); feste, tau; **make** — gjøre fast, lukke forsvarlig, fortøye; **play — and loose with** behandle uhederlig, utnytte og svikte; ikke ta det så nøye med, leke med. — **freight** ilgods; — **friends** svorne venner; — **train** iltog; **my watch is** — klokka mi går for fort; — **girl** lettsindig pikebarn; — **liver,** — **man** levemann; — **lady** emansipert (for fri) dame; **he goes too** — han dømmer for overilt; **live too** — leve for sterkt; **he went — asleep** han falt i en dyp søvn; — **coloured** ekte i fargen.
fast [fa·st] faste. **-day** fastedag.
fasten ['fa·sn] gjøre fast, feste; stenge; sammenføye; feste seg. **fastener** ['fa·snə] befester; festemiddel. **fastening** ['fa·sniŋ] feste; holder.
fastidious [fə'stidjəs] kresen, fin på det. **-ness** [fə'stidjəsnės] kresenhet.
fasting ['fa·stiŋ] faste.
fastness ['fa·stnės] fasthet, støhet; troskap; befestet sted, festning.
fat [fät] fet, feit; svær, tykk, tjukk ; fruktbar; fett, det fete, fedme; fete, meske, fetne, tykne. **to cut it** — overdrive; slå stort på; **cut up** — dø rik; **a — lot** en farlig masse, (også ironisk) svært lite; — **types** fete typer; **live on the — of the land** ete av landets fedme; **the fat's in the fire** det blir leven; **kill the fatted calf for** slakte den fete kalven for.
fatal ['feⁱt(ə)l] skjebnesvanger, lagnadstung; ødeleggende, drepende, dødelig. **fatalism** ['feⁱtəlizm] fatalisme. **fatalist** ['feⁱtəlist] fatalist; fatalistisk. **fatalistic** [feⁱtə'listik] fatalistisk. **fataliy-** [fə'täliti] uunngåelig skjebne; fare; ulykke; dødelighet.
fata morgana ['fa·tə må·ə'ga·nə] fatamorgana, luftspeiling, hildring.
fate [feⁱt] skjebne, lagnad; **the Fates** skjebne

gudinnene, parserne, nornene. **fated** ['fe'tid] av skjebnen bestemt. **fateful** [-ful] skjebnesvanger. **fathead** ['fäthed] dumrian, kjøtthue, naut. **fatheaded** ['fäthedid] «tjukk i hue», nauten.
father ['fa·ðə] far, fader; væ1e far til; ta til seg som barn; — **upon (on)** leggè ut som far; tillegge forfatterskapet av; tilskrive; **she -ed the child upon him** hun la ham ut som barnefar. **-hood** farskap; forfatterskap. — **-in-law** svigerfar; stefar. **-land** fedreland. **-less** farløs. **-liness** farkjærlighet. **-ly** faderlig.
fathom ['fäðəm] favn (lengdemål, 1,828 meter); måle dybden av, lodde; utgrunde. **fathomable** ['fäðəməbl] som kan måles; utgrundelig. **fathomless** ['fäðəmlès] bunnløs; uutgrundelig. **-line** loddline.
fatigue [fə'ti·g] tretthet; anstrengelse, besværlighet; leirarbeid; trette, utmatte, anstrenge; — **party** arbeidskommando.
fatling ['fätliŋ] tykkfallen; gjøkalv.
fatness ['fätnès] fedme.
fatten ['fätn] fete, feite opp, gjø; gjødsle; fetne, tykne, bli fet, meske seg.
fatty ['fäti] fet, feit; tykksak.
fatuity [fə'tju·iti] enfoldighet, tåpelighet, toskeskap. **fatuous** ['fätjuəs] enfoldig, tåpelig; innbilt, uvirkelig.
fat-witted ['fätwitid] «tjukk i hue», tungnem.
faubourg ['fo"buəg] forstad (især til Paris).
faucal ['fä·k(ə)l] svelg-. **fauces** ['fä·si·z] svelg.
faucet ['fä·sit] tapp, kran, hane, ture, rørmuffe.
faugh [fä·] fy! isj!
fault [få(·)lt] feil, lyte, forseelse, mistak; **it is my** — det er min skyld; **for** (el. **in**) — of i mangel av; **be at** — være på villspor, ha tapt sporet; **find** — **with** dadle, bebreide, ha noe å utsette på, laste; **to a** — altfor mye, for mye av det gode. — **-finder** ['få(·)ltfaində] dadler, kritiker. **-finding** kritikksyke, daddel; kritikksyk. **faultily** ['få(·)ltili] mangelfullt; uriktig. **faultiness** ['få·ltinès] mangelfullhet, uriktighet. **faultless** ['få·ltlès] feilfri. **faulty** ['få(·)lti] lytefull, full av feil, ufullkommen.
faun [få·n] faun, skoggud.
fauna ['få·nə] fauna; dyrerike; dyreliv.
fauteuil ['fo"tø·i] lenestol; orkesterplass, parkettplass.
faux-pas ['fo"pa·] feiltrin.
favour ['fe'və] gunst, yndest, velvilje, gunstbevisning; tjeneste; gave; ærede skrivelse (i forretningsbrev); sløyfe e. l. (som bæres som tegn, f. eks. **wedding** —); forkjærlighet; partiskhet; begunstige, støtte; bære; gjøre en en tjeneste; **in** — of til fordel for; velvillig mot; heldig for; **be in** — **with** være yndet av; **in one's** — til fordel for en; **out of** — i unåde; by (the) — of ved hjelp av; **your** — of **the 6th inst.** Deres ærede skrivelse av 6. d. m.; **in your** — i Deres favør.
favourable ['fe'v(ə)rəbl] gunstig, heldig.
favourite ['fe'v(ə)rit] yndling; favoritt; yndlings-; — **dish** livrett; — **reading** yndlingslektyre. **favouritism** ['fe'v(ə)ritizm] begunstigelse.
Fawkes [få·ks]. **Guy Fawkes's day** 5. nov.
fawn [få·n] dåkalv; råkalv; lysebrun; blakk, brunblakk; — **-coloured** lysebrun.
fawn [få·n] kalve (om dådyr).
fawn [få·n] logre for, smigre; bøye seg, smiske, krype (**upon** for).
fay [fe'] fe, hulder, alv.
F. B. A. fk. f. **Fellow of the British Academy.**
F. B. I. fk. f. **Federation of British Industries.**
F. C. fk. f. **football club.**
fcap., fcp. fk. f. **foolscap.**
F. D. fk. f. **fidei defensor** (= **defender of the faith**).
fealty ['fi·əlti] lenslydighet, troskap.
fear [fiə] frykt, otte, skrekk, ank; frykte, ottes, være redd (for); **no fear!** det er det ingen fare for. **fearful** ['fiəf(u)l] fryktsom, bange, redd, ottefull; fryktelig, skrekkelig. **fearfully** ['fiəfəli]

fryktelig. fearless ['fiəlès] uten frykt, uforferdet. **fear-monger** ['fiəmʌŋgə] kryster. **fearnought** ['fiənå·t] vågehals; vadmel. **fearsome** ['fiəsəm] gruelig, skremmelig.
feasibility [fi·zi'biliti] gjørlighet, mulighet. **feasible** ['fi·zibl] gjørlig, mulig.
feast [fi·st] fest; festmåltid, gilde, lag, gjestebud; holde gilde, spise og drikke godt, godgjøre seg; beverte, traktere, fornøye, fagne. **feaster** ['fi·stə] gjest; vert. **feasting** gilde, traktement, festlighet.
feat [fi·t] dåd, heltegjerning, bedrift, karsstykke; ferdighet, kunst, kunststykke.
feather ['feðə] fjær; fuglevilt; sette fjær i, dekke med fjær; fjærkle; vaie som fjær, spre seg, frynse seg, skjene. **in high** — i løftet stemning; **I haven't got a** — **to fly with** jeg har ikke en øre i lommen; **a** — **in one's hat** en fjær i hatten, noe å være stolt av; **be in full** — være i full puss; **you might have knocked him backwards with a** — han var på nippet til å gå bakover; **show the white** — være feig; **fine feathers make fine birds** klær skaper folk; **birds of a** — **will flock together** like barn leker best; — **one's nest** mele sin egen kake.
feather|-bed fjærdyne, dyne. — **-brained** tankeløs; vimset. — **-broom** fjærkost, fjærving. — **-brush** støvekost. — **-driver** fjærrenser. — **-duster** fjærkost, fjærving. — **-edge** tynn kant, lauvkant (når en planke er tynnere på den ene siden enn på den andre). — **-game** fuglevilt. — **-head** tankeløst menneske, vims. — **-headed** vimset, tankeløs.
feather|ing ['feðəriŋ] fjærham, fjærkledning; fjærskifte, fjærfelling. **-less** ['feðəlès] fjærløs, uten fjær. **-let** ['feðəlèt] liten fjær.
feather-weight ['feðəwe't] fjærvekt; fjærvektsbokser.
feathery ['feðəri] fjærkledd; fjærlett.
featly ['fi·tli] nett, knøten, snerten.
feature ['fi·tʃə] form, skikkelse; ansiktstrekk; drag, mine, trekk (også figurlig); ligne, svipe på, ha samme ansikt som; **features** ansiktstrekk, ansikt. **featured** ['fi·tʃəd] med trekk; **ill-featured** grim. **featureless** ['fi·tʃəlès] uten bestemte trekk.
feaze [fi·z] trevle opp, rekke opp.
Feb. fk. f. **February.**
febrifuge ['febrifju·dʒ] feberstillende; febermiddel.
febrile ['fi·brail] febersyk; febril.
February ['februəri] februar.
fec. fk. f. **fecit** (= **made**).
fecal ['fi·kəl] bermet, tykk, gjørmet, skitt-.
feces ['fi·si·z] berme; gjørme, skarn.
feckless ['feklès] kraftløs, doven, dårlig.
feculence ['fekjuləns] bunnfall, grums; gjørme.
feculent ['fekjulənt] grumset, gjørmet, grugget.
fecund ['fekənd, 'fi·-] fruktbar. **fecundate** ['fekənde't, 'fi·-] gjøre fruktbar; befrukte. **fecundation** [fekən'de'ʃən, fi·-] det å gjøre fruktbar; befruktning. **fecundity** [fi'kʌnditi] fruktbarhet.
fed [fed] imperf. og perf. pts. av **feed.**
federal ['fedərəl] forbunds-, sambands-. **federalism** ['fedərəlizm] føderalisme. **federalist** ['fedərəlist] føderalist. **federate** ['fedəre't] forene; forene seg; ['fedərèt] alliert, forbunden. **federation** [fedə're'ʃən] føderasjon, forbund. **federative** ['fedərətiv] føderativ.
fee [fi·] betaling, lønn, honorar, salær, skolepenger, gebyr; len, gods; full eiendomsrett, selveiendom; betale, lønne, gi drikkepenger; — **simple** el. **absolute** — selveiendom.
feeble ['fi·bl] svak, veik. — **-minded** vaklende, vinglet, svak; forsagt; åndssvak. **feebleness** ['fi·blnès] svakhet. **feebly** ['fi·bli] vakt; matt.
feed [fi·d] fore, nære, gi føde, mate, gi mat; beite; spise, ete; leve (**on** av); fór, næring, beite; måltid; rasjon; føde. **feeder** ['fi·də] fórer; eter, spiser; gjøkalv; tilførselskanal; bielv, sideelv; sidebane; smekke. **feeding** fór, føde osv. **feeding-bottle** tåteflaske. **feedpipe** føderør. **feedpump** fødepumpe.

fee-faw-fum ['fiˑ'fåˑ'fʌm] bø! interjeksjon som særlig bruˑˑs i eventyr av troll og kjemper; skremsel.

Feejee ['fiˑdʒi]: **Fiji: the — Islands** Fidsjiøyene.

feel [fiˑl] føle, kjenne, få en fornemmelse av; føle seg, kjenne seg, være til mote, befinne seg; følelse; — **cold** fryse; **the hall feels cold** forstua gjør et kaldt inntrykk; — **cordially with** sympatisere hjertelig med; **it feels soft** det er bløtt å ta på.

feeler ['fiˑlə] følehorn, veidehorn, værhorn, veidehår, værhår; prøveballong.

feeless ['fiˑles] uten salær, uten pasienter.

feeling ['fiˑlin] følende; medfølende, følsom; varm; levende; følelse, kjensle. **-ly** med følelse.

feet [fiˑt] føtter; fot (som mål).

feign [feˑn] fingere, late som, forstille, forstille seg, hykle; oppdikte; **make a feigned submission** underkaste seg på liksom.

feignedly ['feˑnidli] forstilt; på liksom.

Fein: Sinn Fein ['ʃin'feˑn] et irsk parti.

feint [feˑnt] list, forstillelse, knep; finte; skinnangrep; **make a — of doing** late som om en gjør.

feldspar ['feldspaˑº] feltspat (mineral).

felicitate [fi'lisiteˑt] lykkønske.

felicitation [filisi'teˑʃən] lykkønskning.

felicitous [fi'lisitəs] lykkelig; heldig; velvalt.

felicity [fi'lisiti] lykke, hell; lykkelig evne.

feline ['fiˑlˑ(a)in] katteaktig, katte-.

Felix ['fiˑliks] Felix.

fell [fel] imperf. av **fall**.

fell [fel], fæl, grusom, umenneskelig.

fell [fel] berg, knaus, fjell; hei, mo.

fell [fel] skinn, hud, fell; pels.

fell [fel] felle; hogge ned.

fellah ['felə] pl. **fellaheen** [felə'hiˑn], **fellahs** ['feləz] fellah.

feller ['felə] vulg. for **fellow**.

fell-monger ['felmʌŋə] skinnhandler.

felloe ['feloʉ] hjulfelg.

fellow ['feloʉ] felle, kamerat, felage, følgesvenn; kollega; medlem (av et selskap osv.); lagsmann; stipendiat; like, jamlike, make; svenn, medhjelper, kollega, embetsbror; fyr, kar; **my dear** — kjære venn; **old** —! gamle venn! — **citizen** medborger; — **commoner** student som sigrer sammen med **fellows;** — **countryman** landsmann. — **-creature** medskapning, medmenneske. — **-feeling** medfølelse.

fellowship ['feloʉʃip] fellesskap, kameratskap, forbindelse; hopehav, delaktighet, andel; likhet; selskap, omgang; universitetslegat, stipendium; selskapsregning, delingsregning.

felly ['feli] hjulfelg.

felo-de-se ['feloʉ di 'siˑ] selvmorder, selvmord.

felon ['felən] verkefinger.

felon ['felən] forbryter, brottsmann. **felonious** [fe'loʉnjəs] forbrytersk, skjendig. **felony** ['feləni] forbrytelse; stor forbrytelse, som straffes med fengsel el. døden.

felt [felt] imperf. og perf. pts. av **feel.**

felt [felt] filt; filthatt, hatt; filte.

felucca [fe'lʌkə] felukk (lettbygd, hurtiggående seil- og rofartøy, alm. i Middelhavet).

fem. fk. f. **feminine.**

female ['fiˑmeˑl] kvinnelig; kvinne; hun (om dyr); — **friend** venninne; — **slave** slavinne; — **screw** møtrik, mutter, skrumor.

feme [fem] kvinne (juridisk uttrykk); — **covert** ['kʌvət] gift kone; — **sole** ugift kvinne, enke.

femineity [femi'niˑiti] kvinnelighet.

feminine ['feminin] kvinnelig; kvinneaktig; hunkjønns-; — **gender** hunkjønn; — **rhyme** kvinnelig rim (rim på to stavinger, hvorav den siste er ubetont); — **ending** linjeavslutning med siste stavelse ubetont.

femininity [femi'niniti] kvinnelighet, hunkjønn.

feminism ['feminizm] feminisme. **feminist** ['feminist] feminist.

femoral ['femərəl] lår-.

fen [fen] myr. **-berry** tranebær.

fen [fen] forby (i barnespråk); — **larks!** ingen dumheter!

fence [fens] hegn, gard, gjerde; vern; fektning, fektekunst; heler; helers gjemmested; innhegne, gjerde inn; forsvare; forsvare seg; fekte; selge til heler; komme med utflukter, omgå sannheten. **fenceless** ['fenslés] åpen, uten vern. **fencer** ['fensə] fekter. — **-months** fredningstid. **fencible** ['fensibl] landvernsmann; i flertall: landvern.

fencing ['fensin] fekting. **fencing-master** fektemester. **fencing-school** fekteskole.

fend [fend] avverge, ta av for; streve, stri; — **for oneself** klare seg selv; — **off** avverge, ta av for, **fender** ['fendə] kamingitter; fender, støtfanger. **fenestral** [fi'nestrəl] vindus-.

Fenian ['fiˑnjən] fenier-; fenier; **the — brotherhood** et samfunn, stiftet i Amerika for å styrte engelskmennenes makt i Irland.

fennel ['fenil] fennikel.

fennish ['feniʃ] myr-, myrlendt.

fenny ['feni] myr-, myrlendt.

fen-reeve ['fen'riˑv] myroppsynsmann.

fen-runners ['fen'rʌnəz] et slags skøyter.

fenugreek ['fenjugriˑk] fillegrek (plante).

feod [fjuˑd] len (se **feud**).

feoff [fiˑf] len; gi til len, gi len. **feoffee** [fiˑ'fiˑ] lensmann, vasall. **feoffer** ['fiˑfə] lensherre. **feoffment** ['fiˑfmənt] len, forlening.

feral ['fiərəl] vill, utemt; udyrket; rå.

feretory ['feritri] helgenskrin.

ferial ['fiəriəl] ferie-.

ferine ['fiərain] vill; barbarisk; villdyr.

Feringhee [fi'riŋgi] europeer særl. portugiser (engelsk-indisk).

ferment [fə'ment] sette i gjæring; gjære, ese, gå. **ferment** ['fəˑmənt] gjær; gjæring, esing, gang. **fermentable** [fə'mentəbl] som kan gjære. **fermentation** [fəmən'teˑʃən] gjæring, esing, gang. **fermentative** [fə'mentətiv] gjærende, som forårsaker esing, gang.

fern [fəˑn] bregne, burkne. **fernery** ['fəˑnəri] bregneplantning. **ferny** ['fəˑni] full av bregner.

ferocious [fi'roʉʃəs] vill, sint, olm, glupsk. **ferocity** [fi'råsiti] villhet, glupskhet osv.

ferreous ['feriəs] jern-, jernholdig.

ferret ['ferit] (bomulls- eller silke-) bånd.

ferret ['ferit] en slags ilder el. mår som brukes til rottejakt og kaninjakt; forfølge; ettersporre, støve etter; — **eyes** røde øyne.

ferriage ['feriedʒ] ferjepenger.

ferric ['ferik] jern-.

ferriferous [fe'rifərəs] jernholdig.

ferro ['feroʉ, 'ferro] sammensetninger: jern-, f. eks. **ferro-concrete** ['fero(ʉ)'kåŋkriˑt] jernbetong; jernblåsyre-. **ferrugineous** [feru'dʒiniəs] jernholdig; rustfarget. **ferruginous** [fe'ruˑdʒinəs] jernholdig; rust (på planter). **ferrugo** [fe'ruˑgoʉ] jernrust; rust (på planter).

ferrule ['feruˑl, 'ferəl] doppsko, holk; bøssing.

ferry ['feri] ferje, ferjested; ferje. **-boat** ferje. ferjebåt. **-man** ferjemann.

fertile ['fəˑtil, 'fəˑtail] fruktbar. **fertility** [fəˑ'tiliti] fruktbarhet. **fertilization** [fəˑtilai'zeˑʃən] det å gjøre fruktbar; befruktning. **fertilize** ['fəˑtilaiz] gjøre fruktbar; befrukte. **fertilizer** ['fəˑtilaizə] gjødsel, gjødningsstoff.

ferule ['feruˑl] ferle; slå med en ferle.

fervency ['fəˑvənsi] fyrighet, varme, inderlighet, iver. **fervent** ['fəˑvənt] varm, brennende, fyrig, ivrig, inderlig.

fervid ['fəˑvid] het, brennende.

fervour ['fəˑvə] hete, varme, heftighet, inderlighet.

fescue ['feskju] pekepinne; svingel (grasart).

festal ['festəl] fest-, festlig.

fester ['festə] bolne, svelle ut, verke, avsondre seg; råtne, ete om seg, gnage, fortære; svull, verk, vågsår.

festival ['festival] fest-, festlig; festdag, høytid; fest. **festive** ['festiv] lystig, festlig, glad. **festivity** [fe'stiviti] feststemning, festlighet, fest.

festoon [fe'stu·n] girlander, pryde med girlander.

fetal ['fi·tl] foster-.

fetch [fetʃ] dobbeltgjenger, vardøger.

fetch [fetʃ] hente; innbringe, komme opp i (ved salg); gjøre inntrykk på, gjøre virkning på, bite på; forbause; — **a blow** deise til en; — **a sigh** sukke; — **and carry** apportere (om hunder). **fetch** [fetʃ] kunstgrep, knep, list, fiff. **fetcher** ['fetʃə] en som henter; — **and carrier** hund som apporterer; lydig slave. **fetching** ['fetʃiŋ] fengslende, fortryllende.

fête [fe¹t] fest; navnedag; gjøre fest for; fetere. **fetich** ['fi·tiʃ, 'fetiʃ] osv. se **fetish.**

feticide ['fi·tisaid, 'fet-] fosterdrap; fosterfordrivelse.

fetid ['fetid, 'fi·tid] stinkende.

fetish ['fi·tiʃ, 'fetiʃ] fetisj. **-ism** [-izm] fetisjdyrking.

fetlock ['fetlåk] hovskjegg; ankelledd (på hest). **fetor** ['fi·tə] tev, stank.

fetter ['fetə] lenke, legge i lenker; binde; tjore; lenke, fotlenke, helde, tjor; tvang, bånd.

fettle ['fetl] orden, god stand; sette i stand.

fetus ['fi·təs] føtus, foster.

feu [fju·] (skotsk) bygsel, forpakting; grunn; bortfeste, bortforpakte, bygsle, forpakte.

feud [fju·d] feide, ufred, strid; len. **feudal** ['fju·d(ə)l] feudal, lens-. **feudalism** ['fju·dəlizm] lensvesen, feudalsystem. **feudality** [fju·däliti] lensforhold, feudalsystem. **feudary** ['fju·dəri] lensmann, vasall. **feudatary** ['fju·dətəri], **feudatory** ['fju·dətəri] feudal, lens-; lensmann, vasall; len. **feudist** ['fju·dist] kjenner av lensvesenet.

feuilleton ['fə·jətåŋ] føljetong.

fever ['fi·və] feber; få feber; bringe i feber; **ravings of** — feberfantasier. **feverish** ['fi·vəriʃ] febersyk; feberaktig.

few [fju·] få; **a few** noen få, et par. **fewer** ['fju·ə] færre. **fewest** ['fju·ist] færrest. **fewness** ['fju·nès] det å være få, fåtallighet.

fewtrils ['fju·trilz] bagateller.

fey [fe¹] døden nær.

fez [fez] fess (muhamedansk lue).

ff. fk. f. **fortissimo.**

F. G. fk. f. **Foot Guards.**

F. G. S. fk. f. **Fellow of the Geological Society.**

fiancé, fiancée [fi'ãŋse¹, fi'aŋse¹] forlovede.

fiasco [fi'äsko⁰] fiasko.

fiat ['faiət] (jur.) ordre, befaling; samtykke, fullmakt.

fib [fib] fabel, usannhet, skrøne, løgn; slag; lyve; slå. **fibber** ['fibə] løgnhals.

fibre ['faibə] fiber, trevl, tråd. **fibril** ['faibril] liten fiber, fin trevl. **fibrin(e)** ['faibrin] fibrin. **fibrous** ['faibrəs] trevlet, trådet.

fibster ['fibstə] løgnhals, skrønemaker.

fibula ['fibjulə] spenne; leggbein; synål (i kirurgi). **fibulated** ['fibjule¹tid] spenneformet.

fichu ['fi·ʃu·] fichu.

fickle ['fikl] vaklende, ustø, vankelmodig, ubestemt. **-ness** foranderlighet, vankelmodighet.

fictile ['fiktil] formet; pottemaker-.

fiction ['fikʃən] oppfinnelse, oppdikting, dikt, oppspinn, fiksjon; **a work of** — en diktning, roman. **fictionist** ['fikʃənist] romanforfatter.

fictitious [fik'tiʃəs] diktet, oppdiktet; fingert, uekte, forloren; — **gem** uekte edelstein.

fid [fid] spleishorn; slutthtolt.

fid. def. fk. f. **fidei defensor.**

fiddle ['fidl] fiolin, fele; gautjuv, bondefanger; **fiddles** ogs. slingrebretter. **fiddle** spille fiolin, spille på fele; fjase; lure, snyte. **fiddle-de-dee** [fidldi'di·] vas, tøv, tull, vrøvl. **fiddle-faddle** ['fidlfädl] fjas, tøv, vrøvl.

fiddler ['fidlə] fiolinspiller; spillemann; bondefanger; somlekopp; sixpence; **drunk as a** — full som en alke.

fiddlestick ['fidlstik] fiolinbue; **fiddlesticks!** snakk! vas! tøv!

fidelity [fi'deliti] troskap.

fidget ['fidʒit] være urolig; være rastløs; ikke ha ro på seg, være nervøs, vimse omkring; uro, vimsing, en som ikke kan holde seg i ro, vims. **fidgety** ['fidʒiti] urolig, nervøs; vimset.

fiducial [fi'dju·ʃəl], **fiduciary** [fi'dju·ʃəri] betrodd; tillitsmann, verje.

fie [fai] fy! — **upon you!** — **for shame** fy! fy for fanden!

fief [fi·f] len.

field [fi·ld] mark; jorde; åker; eng; løkke; felt, valplass; feltslag; område; spilleplass (i sport); alle spillerne; alle veddeløpshestene; jaktselskap; grunn, bakgrunn (i maleri); synsfelt; felt (i våpen); rykke i marka; (i cricket) være markspiller; **in the** — på marka, ute på landet; **on the** — på slagmarka; — **of battle** valplass; slagmark; **keep the** — kumpere i felten; fortsette felttoget; holde valplassen; **take the** — rykke i felten, dra i krigen; — **the ball** (i cricket) gripe ballen og kaste den inn til gjerdet. **field|-bed** feltseng. — **-book** landmålers noteringsbok. — **-day** mønstringsdag, stor anledning; viktig debatt (ogs. — **-night**).

fielder ['fi·ldə] (i cricket) utespiller (en av det parti, som er ute, unntagen bowler og wicketkeeper).

fieldfare ['fi·ldfæ·ə] kramsfugl, gråtrost. **field-glass** ['fi·ldgla·s] feltkikkert, reisekikkert. **field-greys** ['fi·ldgre¹z] feltgrå (tyske soldater). **field-gun** ['fi·ldgʌn] feltkanon.

Fielding ['fi·ldiŋ] Fielding.

field-marshal feltmarsjal. **field-mouse** markmus. **field-officer** stabsoffiser, (i frelsesarméen: feltoffiser). **field-piece** feltkanon. **field-practice** felttjeneste.

fieldsman ['fi·ldzmən] utespiller (i cricket).

field-sports ['fi·ldspå·⁰ts] friluftsidrett (især jakt og fiskeri).

field-work ['fi·ldwə·k] feltskanse.

fiend [fi·nd] djevel. **-ish** djevelsk.

fierce [fiəs] vill, barsk, rasende, bister, heftig. **fieri-facias** ['faiərai'fe¹ʃiäs] utpantingsordre (jur.).

fieriness ['fai³rinés] hete; heftighet, fyrighet. **fiery** ['faiⁿri] ild-; het, brennende; heftig; fyrig; — **red face** ildrødt ansikt.

fife [faif] pipe, pikkolofløyte; pipe. **fifer** ['faifə] piper.

fifteen ['fif'ti·n] femten.

fifteenth ['fif'ti·nþ] femtende; femtendedel.

fifth [fifþ] femte; femtedel; kvint (i musikk). **fifth-columnist** ['fifþ'kåləmnist] medlem av femte kolonne.

fifthly ['fifþli] for det femte.

fiftieth ['fiftiiþ] femtiende; femtiendedel.

fifty ['fifti] femti.

fig [fig] fiken; fiken; **a** — **for him!** blås i ham. **I don't care a** — **for it** jeg bryr meg aldri det grann om det.

fig. fk. f. **figure, figuratively.**

fig [fig] puss, stas; pynte; **in full** — i fineste puss; — **out** pynte; — **up a horse** kvikke opp en hest. **fight** [fait] kjempe, stride (**against, with** mot, med; **for** for, om), slåss; bekjempe; kjempe for, slåss for; prosedere; konkurrere om; — **a battle** levere et slag.

fight [fait] strid, kamp, slagsmål; kamplyst, mot; **free** — alminnelig slagsmål; **show** — sette seg til motverge.

fighter ['faitə] kjemper; stridsmann; slagsbror. **fighting** ['faitiŋ] kampdyktig, stridsfør.

fig-leaf ['figli·f] fikenblad.

figment ['figmənt] oppdikting, påfunn.

figurant ['figjurant] ballettdanser. **figurante** ['figjurant, figju'ränt] ballettdanserinne. **figurate** ['figjurèt] figurert (om musikk). **figuration** [figju·'re¹ʃən] figurering. **figurative** ['figjurətiv] billedlig, figurlig, symbolsk; billedrik, blomstrende. **figure** ['figə] figur; form, skikkelse; siffer,

figure 98 finish

tall; gallionsfigur; forbilde, type; figur, mønster (i tøy); **cut** el. **make a** — gjøre figur, spille en rolle; **what's the** — hva er prisen, hva har jeg å betale; **at a low** — til lav pris; **speak in -s** tale billedlig.

figure ['figə] forme, danne; avbilde, framstille; figurere, pryde med figurer; tenke el. anvende figurlig; be*r*egne, regne (i matematikk); spille en rolle, figurere.

figure|-head gallionsfigur. — **-man** kunstløper, kunstskøyteløper. — **-skating** kunstløp på skøyter. — **-stone** agalmatolitt, billedstein.

Fiji ['fi(·)dʒi·] se **Feejee.**

filament ['filəmənt] tråd, trevl, fiber.

filamentous [filə'mentəs] trådaktig, trevlet.

filature ['filətjuə, -tʃə] silkehesping; hespetre, snelle; sted hvor silken blir hespet.

filbert ['filbət] dyrket hasselnøtt.

filch [fil(t)ʃ] stjele, rapse, kvarte. **filcher** ['filʃə] tyv.

filching ['filʃiŋ] rapserier.

file [fail] tråd; metalltråd; dokumentholder, brevordner, regningskrok; ordnet bunke (av brev etc.), arkiv, samling av dokumenter, aviser o. lign.; fortegnelse, liste; rote; **rank and file** de menige soldater; rekke; **by files** rotevis; **move in Indian (or single) file** gå en og en, gå gåsegang.

file [fail] hefte sammen; ordne; legge på sin plass; legge til aktene; sende inn (om søknad o. l.); legge fram i retten; marsjere rotevis; defilere; — **a bill** inngi en klage. — **a petition of bankruptcy** overlevere sitt bo til konkurs.

file [fail] fil; luring, fuling; lommetyv; **a sly old** — en utspekulert fyr. **file** [fail] file; **a gun, half filed down** en børse som er halvt avfilt. **-cutter** filhogger. **-dust** filspon.

filer ['failə] filer.

filial ['filjəl] sønnlig, datterlig, barnlig, barne-.

filiate ['filie¹t] adoptere. **filiation** [fili·e¹ʃən] barns forhold; adopsjon; utlegging som barnefar.

filibeg ['filibeg] (skotsk) kort skjørt.

filibuster ['filibʌstə] fribytter, sjørøver, viking; drive fribytteri.

filiform ['failifå·ºm] tråddannet, tråd-.

filigrane ['filigre¹n], **filigree** ['filigri·] filigran.

filings ['failiŋz] filsponer.

filipeen [fili'pi·n] filipine.

fill [fil] fylle; utfylle, oppfylle; oppta; plombere; mette; bekle (f. eks. et embete); besette (f. eks. et embete); utføre; fylles; full forsyning, mette; fyll; **eat your** — spis deg mett.

fillet ['filit] hårbånd, pannebånd; list, kant; skive; filet; rulade; mørbrad; sette bånd på etc.; ta bein ut (av fisk o. l.).

fillibeg ['filibeg] se **filibeg.**

filling ['filiŋ] fylling, plombe; plombering.

fillip ['filip] knipse; knips; stimulans, oppstrammer; kveik. **give one a** — egge en.

filly ['fili] fole, hoppeføl, ungmerr; galneheie.

film [film] hinne, film; overtrekke med en hinne; filme (ɔ: oppta i levende bilder).

filmy ['filmi] overtrukket med en hinne; hinneaktig; hinne-.

filoselle ['filosel] florettsilke.

filter ['filtə] sile, filtrere; filtreres, sive, trenge (igjennom); filter, filtrerapparat.

filtering ['filtəriŋ] filtrering; — **bag** filtrerpose; — **paper** filtrerpapir.

filth [filþ] smuss, skitt.

filthy ['filþi] smussig, skitten.

filtrate ['filtre¹t] filtrere; filtrert væske.

filtration [fil'tre¹ʃən] filtrering.

fimble-famble ['fimblfämbl] tom unnskyldning, utflukt.

fimbriate(d) ['fimbrie¹t(id)] frynset.

fin [fin] finne, svømmefinne; hånd, neve; **tip us your** — gi meg din hånd. **fin** skjære opp fisk. **-footed, -toed** med svømmeføtter.

finable ['fainəbl] som en kan få mulkt for.

final ['fainəl] endelig, avgjørende; slutt-, sist; avsluttende konkurranse.

finale [fi'na·lē] finale, slutt.

finality [fai'näliti] endelighet; avgjørelse; resultat.

finally ['fainəli] endelig, til sist, til slutt.

finance [fi'näns, fai-] finansvitenskap; (mest i flertall): statens inntekter; **finances** inntekter (privatfolks). **finance** [f(a)i'näns] gjøre pengeforretninger; utarbeide el. styre finansielt; forsyne med inntekter, finansiere. **financial** [fi'nänʃəl, fai-] finansiell, finans-, penge-. — **report** kredittopplysning. **financier** [fi'nänsiə, fai-] finansmann, pengemann. **financier** [finən'siə, fai-] utføre finansoperasjoner.

finback ['finbäk] rørhval, sildehval.

finch [finʃ] finke (en fugl).

find [faind] finne; treffe; råke; finne ut, skjønne, merke; yte, forsyne, forsørge, bestride omkostningen ved; skaffe til veie; avsi (en kjennelse); funn; finnested; — **a true bill** anta en klage (som grunnet); beslutte tiltale reist; — **oneself** befinne seg; ha det, sørge for seg selv; **the jury found him guilty** juryen erklærte ham skyldig; — **for the plaintiff** erklære den anklagede for skyldig; **he -s me in money and clothes** han holder meg med penger og klær; **50 pounds a year and everything found** 50 pund om året og alt fritt; — **one business** skaffe en arbeid; — **one in a lie** gripe en i en løgn; **I cannot** — **in my heart** jeg kan ikke bringe det over mitt hjerte; **I could** — **in my heart** jeg kunne ha lyst til; — **fault with** dadle, ha noe å utsette på; — **out** oppdage.

finder ['faində] finner; søker, siktekikkert.

finding ['faindiŋ] kjennelse; resultat.

fine [fain] bot, mulkt; mulktere; idømme en bot.

fine [fain] fin; smukk, skjønn; staut; ren, klar; tynn, grann; rense, klare, lutre; avklares; bli finere; svinne hen; — **day** fint vær; **the** — **arts** de skjønne kunster; **a** — **fellow** en kjernekar, en prektig fyr; (spottende) en deilig fyr; — **feathers** fine klær; **a** — **friend you have been** du har vært en nydelig venn; **one of these** — **days** en vakker dag.

fine-draw ['fain'drå·] sy fint sammen.

fine-grained ['fain'gre¹nd] finkornet.

finely ['fainli] fint; smukt.

fineness ['fainnès] finhet, lødighet.

finery ['fainəri] stas, pynt.

finespoken ['fainspo⁰ken] veltalende, beleven.

fine-spun ['fain'spʌn] fint spunnet; fint uttenkt.

finesse [fi'nes] kunstgrep; list; gjøre kunstgrep; snyte; bruke list el. kroker.

Fingal ['fiŋgəl] Fingal.

finger ['fiŋgə] finger; fingerbredde; fingerferdighet; fingre med; berøre lett; gripe; fingre, bruke fingrene; **have at one's fingers' ends** kunne på fingrene. — **-alphabet,** — **-and-sign-language** fingerspråk (for døvstumme). — **-basin** skylleskål (i middagsselskap). — **-board** gripebrett (på fiolin osv.); klaviatur, manual (på orgel). — **-bowl** [-bo⁰l] skylleskål.

fingerer ['fiŋgərə] klåfinger.

finger-glass ['fiŋgəgla·s] skylleskål. **fingering** ['fiŋgəriŋ] fingersetning; stoppegarn. **fingerpost** ['fiŋgəpo⁰st] veiviser (stein el. stolpe). **fingerprint** ['fiŋgəprint] fingeravtrykk. **fingerstall** ['fiŋgəstå·l] smokk.

finical ['finikl] sirlig, pertentlig. **finicality** [fini'käliti] sirlighet, pertentlighet.

finicking ['finikiŋ] sirlig, pertentlig.

finikin ['finikin] se **finicking.**

finis ['fainis] ende, finis.

finish ['finiʃ] ende, gjøre seg ferdig med, bli ferdig med, slutte; fullende; legge siste hånd på; apretere (tøy); finpusse; spise opp; drikke ut; sette til livs; gjøre det av med en; holde opp; slutning; slutt; avpussing; siste hånd (på verket); slutningsscene (i skuespill); slutningskamp (i

sport); **war to a** — krig på liv og død. **finished**
['finiʃt] fullendt. **finishing establishment** høyere
dannelsesanstalt. **finishing stroke** nådestøt.
finite ['fainait] endelig, avgrenset.
Finland ['finlənd] Finnland, Suomi. **Finlander**
['finləndə] finne, finnlending. **Finlandish** ['fin-
ləndiʃ] finsk. **Finn** [fin] finne; finnlending; finn,
kven.
finner ['finə] finnehval, sildehval.
Finnic ['finik], **Finnish** ['finiʃ] finsk.
finny ['fini] finnet.
fiord [fjå·ᵊd] fjord (især norsk).
fir [fə·] bartre, nåletre; gran; furu, toll. **spruce**
— alminnelig gran. — **-apple,** — **-cone** kongle.
fire ['faiə] ild, eld, varme, fyr; brann; flamme,
lue, lidenskap; bål; nying; ildprøve; **catch (eller
take)** — fenge; **light (el. make) a** — gjøre opp varme på, legge i kakkelovnen; **set — to (el. set on —)**
sette fyr på; **smell of** — brannlukt; **he will
never set the Thames on** — han har ikke funnet
opp kruttet; **no smoke without** — ingen røyk
uten ild; **between two fires** mellom dobbelt ild.
by the — foran kaminen, borte ved peisen.
fire ['faiə] tenne; sette ild på; avfyre; fyre,
tenne opp, fyre under; brenne; komme i brann;
oppildne; — **away!** ogs. snakk fra leveren; ut med
det; — **the boilers** fyre under kjelene; — off
avfyre; — **out** hive ut, sette på porten. — up
komme i fyr og flamme.
fire|-alarm brannalarm; brannsignalapparat.
— **-arms** ildvåpen, skytevåpen. — **-board** peis-
spjeld. — **-brand** brann; urostifter. — **-brick** ildfast murstein. — **-brigade** brannvesen. — **-bucket**
brannspann. — **-clay** ildfast leire. — **-cock** brannkran. — **-damp** gruvegass. — **-dog** brannjern. —
-drill brannvernøvelse. — **-eater** ildsluker; pral-
hans; slagsbror; sinnatagg. — **-engine** brannsprøyte. — **-escape** redningsapparat, brannstige. —
-extinguisher brannslokkingsapparat. — **-fly**
ildflue. — **-guard** kamingitter. — **-hook** brann-
hake. — **-hose** brannslange.
fire|-insurance brannforsikring. — **-irons** ild-
tøy. **-less** uten ild. — **-man** brannmann; fyrbøter. **-new** splinter ny. — **-office** brannassu-
ranse-kontor. — **-pan** fyrfat; panne (på et gevær).
-place ildsted, arne, åre, grue, peis, kamin, fyr-
sted. — **-plug** brannkran. — **-policy** brannpolise.
-proof ildfast, brannsikker. — **-raising** brannstiftelse. — **-risk** brannfare. — **-screen** kamin-
skjerm. — **-set** ildtøy. — **-ship** brannskip. **-side**
åre, peis, arnested, arne; (fig.) hjem, heim. —
-station brannstasjon. — **-steel** fyrstål. — **-water**
ildvann, brennevin. **-wood** ved. **-work** fyrverkeri.
— **-worship** ildtilbedelse. — **-worshipper** ildtilbeder.
firing ['faiəriŋ] brensel; antennelse; avfyring,
skyting, fyring. — **-iron** brennejern. — **-party**
avdeling som har til oppgave å sprenge en mine
eller salutere ved en begravelse. — **-step** trin
som en soldat i løpegrav står på for å skyte.
firkin ['fə·kin] fjerding; anker, kagge, dunk,
butt.
firm [fə·m] fast, stø, traust; bli fast.
firm [fə·m] firma, handelshus.
firmament ['fə·məmənt] firmament, himmelhvelving. **firmamental** [fə·məˈmentəl] himmel-.
firman ['fə·män], østerlandsk monarks forordning.
first [fə·st] først; for det første; før, heller;
første stemme; første karakter; første premie;
at (the) — i begynnelsen, i førstningen, først og
fremst; **from the** — fra begynnelsen av, fra først
av; **in the** — place for det første; **on** — **coming**
straks når en kommer; **on the** — **approach of
a stranger** straks en fremmed nærmer seg;
when — straks da . . .; — **aid** førstehjelp; **chapter
the** — første kapitel; — **cousin** søskenbarn; —
floor annen etasje; — **form** nederste klasse (i
skole); — **name** fornavn; **the** — **thing** straks;
come — **thing to-morrow** kom ganske tidlig i

morgen; — **come,** — **served** den som kommer
først til mølla, får først malt; — **of all** først
og fremst; — **and foremost** aller først; — **of
exchange** prima-veksel.
first|-begotten førstefødt. — **-born** førstefødt. —
-class utmerket, prima. — **-foot** (skotsk) første
gjesten på nyåret. — **-fruit** førstegrøde. — **-hand**
førstehånds; umiddelbart.
firstling ['fə·stliŋ] førstefødt avkom.
firstly ['fə·stli] for det første.
first-night première.
first-rate ['fə·st're·t] førsterangs, fortrinlig.
firth [fə·þ] fjord.
fisc [fisk] statskasse. **fiscal** ['fiskəl] fiskal.
fish [fiʃ] fisk; fyr; spillemerke; fiske; fiske opp;
fiske i; **a pretty kettle of** — en nydelig suppe;
drink like a — drikke som en svamp; **all is**
— **that comes to net** alle monner drar; **feed the
fishes** drukne; være sjøsyk; **have other** — **to
fry** ha annet å greie med; **an odd (el. queer)** —
en snurrig fyr; — **in troubled waters** fiske i rørt
vann.
fishable ['fiʃəbl] som kan fiskes.
fish|-ball fiskebolle. — **-carver** fiskespade.
fisher ['fiʃə] fisker. **fisherman** ['fiʃəmən] fisker.
fishery ['fiʃəri] fiskeri.
fish|-fag fiskerkjerring, hurpe. — **-glue** fiske-
lim. — **-hook** fiskekrok. **fishing** ['fiʃiŋ] fiskeri.
fishing|-line fiskesnøre. — **-rod** fiskestang.
-station fiskevær. — **-tackle** fiskeredskaper.
fish|-ladder laksetrapp. — **-monger** fiskehandl-
er. — **-pot** (hummer)teine. — **-slice** fiskespade.
— **-turtle** forloren skilpadde. — **-woman** fiskekone.
fishy ['fiʃi] fiskaktig; fiskerik; utrolig, overdreven; usikker (om spekulasjon), mistenkelig.
fissile ['fisil] som kan spaltes el. kløyves. **fissil-
ity** [fi'siliti] det å kunne la seg kløyve. **fission**
['fiʃən] kløyving, spalting. **fissiparous** [fi'si-
pərəs] som forplanter seg ved spalting.
fissure ['fiʃ(u)ə] spalte, splitte, kløyve; spalte,
revne.
fist [fist] neve; **the mailed** — den pansrede
neve. **fist-fight** ['fistfait] nevekamp. fiske ['fistik]
neve-, bokser-. **fisticuffs** ['fistikʌfs] nevekamp,
slagsmål, boksing.
fistula ['fistjula] rør; fistel. **fistular** ['fistjulə]
rørformig. **fistulate** ['fistjule·t] gjøre til et rør;
bli til en fistel. **fistulous** ['fistjuləs] fistelaktig.
fit [fit] anfall, ri, flage, kramperi; innfall,
lune; **go off in a** — få krampe; **a** — **of laughter**
et latteranfall; **beat him all to -s** slå ham sønder
og sammen; **for a** — en tid lang; **by -s** nå og da,
rykkevis.
fit [fit] tjenlig, skikket, passende, høvelig,
laglig; som passer godt; dyktig, dugelig; det å
passe, passing; gjøre tjenlig, gjøre skikket til;
avpasse; utstyre; gjøre i stand, innrette; montere; være tjenlig til, være egnet til; passe, sitte;
a — **person** den rette mann; **be** — **for a sailor**
duge til å være sjømann; — **for use** brukelig;
brukbar; **she cried** — **to break her heart** hun
gråt som hennes hjerte skulle briste; **well
fitted** godt sammenpasset; **the key fits the lock**
nøkkelen passer i låsen; — **on** prøve; anbringe
på; **the shoes are just your fit** skoene passer
nettopp til foten Deres; **be a bad fit** ikke passe;
— **out** utruste, forsyne med; — **up** innrette.
fit [fit] vers, stev.
fitch [fitʃ] mår; mårskinn.
fitchew ['fitʃu·] mår.
fitful ['fitʃ(u)l] rykkvis, ustadig, ustø, ujamn.
fitly ['fitli] passende.
fitness ['fitnəs] skikkethet; dugelighet; **it is
but in the** — **of things that** det ligger i sakens
natur at.
fit-out ['fit'aut] utrustning; utstyr.
fitter ['fitə] montør. —
fitting ['fitiŋ] passende; montering; utrustning; rørdel, fitting; apparat, rekvisitt. **metal** —
beslag. **boiler** — **-s** armatur.

fitting-out ['fitiŋ'aut] utstyr; utrustning. — **berth** monteringsplass.

fitting-shop ['fitiŋʃáp] maskinverksted.

Fitzgerald [fits'dʒerəld] Fitzgerald.

five [faiv] fem; femmer; femtall.

five|fold ['faiv'fo⁰ld] femfold, femdobbelt. — **-o'clock tea** ettermiddagste. **fiver** ['faivə] fempundseddel, (i Amerika:) femdollarseddel.

fives [faivz] slags ballspill.

fix [fiks] klemme, knipe.

fix [fiks] feste, gjøre fast, hefte; nistirre på; avtale; fiksere; fastsette; bestemme, slutte; sette seg fast; nedsette seg; bli fast, størkne; (amr.) ordne; — **on** bestemme seg til.

fixation [fik'seiʃən] fastgjøring, fastsetting fasthet; bestemmelse; fiksering.

fixative ['fiksətiv] fiksermiddel. **fixature** ['fiksə-tjə, -tjuə] stangpomade.

fixed [fikst] fast, stø, bestemt; determinert; — **air** kullsyre; — **day** bestemt dag; mottagelsesdag; — **fact** fait accompli; — **idea** fiks idé; — **oil** fet olje; — **prices** faste priser; — **star** fiksstjerne.

fixedly ['fiksidli] fast; stivt, ni-, bestemt.

fixedness ['fiksidnès] fasthet.

fixing ['fiksiŋ] festing, ordning, tillaging; (især amr. og især i pl.) tilbehør, pynt, besetning (på kjole); — **bath** fiksérbad.

fixity ['fiksiti] fasthet, støhet.

fixture ['fikstʃə] fast tilbehør; stamgjest; slutning; **fixtures** naglefaste ting.

fizgig ['fizgig] harpun; rakett; flokse, jåle; sporenstreks, ratt.

fizz [fiz] bruse, frese, sprake, putre, mussere; brus, putring; musserende drikk.

fizzle ['fizl] visle, sprute, frese; gjøre fiasko; falle gjennom; rejisert; fresing.

fizzy ['fizi] sprutende, fresende, brusende.

fjord se **fiord**.

fl. fk. f. florin.

Fla. fk. f. Florida.

flabbergast ['flæbəga·st] forbløffe, forfjamse.

flabby ['flæbi] slapp, slakk, pløset, lealaus; klam, kaldvåt.

flaccid ['flæksid] slapp, slakk, pløset. **flaccidity** [flæk'siditi] slapphet.

flag [flæg] henge slapp; slakne; bli matt, bli sløv.

flag [flæg] flagg; — **of truce** parlamentærflagg; **white** — parlamentærflagg; **black** — sjørøverflagg; **yellow** — karanteneflagg; **fly the** — la flagget vaie; **lower the** — stryke flagget; **strike the** — stryke flagget.

flag [flæg] sverdlilje.

flag [flæg] flise: steinhelle; fliselegge, hellelegge.

flagellant ['flædʒilənt] flagellant. **flagellate** ['flædʒəle¹t] piske. **flagellation** [flædʒə'le¹ʃən] pisking.

flageolet [flædʒo'let] flageolett.

flaggy ['flægi] slapp, slakk; matt; flau.

flaggy ['flægi] full av sverdliljer.

flagitious [flə'dʒiʃəs] avskylig; skjendig.

flag-list ['flæg'list] liste over flaggoffiserer.

flagman ['flægmən] flaggmann; banevokter.

flag-officer ['flæg'áfisə] flaggoffiser.

flagon ['flægən] flaske.

flagrancy ['fle¹grənsi] vitterlighet; avskylighet; åpenbar skjendighet, skamløshet. **flagrant** ['fle¹grənt] vitterlig, åpenbar; avskylig.

flag-ship ['flægʃip] admiralskip.

flagstaff ['flægsta·f] flaggstang.

flagstone ['flægsto⁰n] flise, hellestein. **-d** fliselagt.

flagwagging ['flægwägiŋ] signalering med flagg; uteskende tale.

flail [fle¹l] flygel, sliul, slagvol.

flair [flæ·ə] teft.

flak [fläk](egl.fk.f.tysk Flieger-Abwehr-Kanone) flak, luftvernskyts.

flake [fle¹k] flak, hinne, tynt lag, tynn skive; fnugg; snøfille. — **off** skalle av.

flaky ['fle¹ki] fnuggaktig; skjellet, i lag.

flam [fläm] trommeslag; oppdiktet historie; lyve for.

flambeau ['flämbo⁰] fakkel.

Flamborough ['flämbərə] Flamborough.

flamboyant [fläm'boiənt] flammet; bølgende; (fig.) blomstrende.

flame [fle¹m] flamme, lue; flamme, kjæreste; flamme, lue; **-coloured** ildrød, rødgul.

flame-projector ['fle¹mpro'dʒektə] flammekaster.

flame-thrower ['fle¹m'þro⁰ə] flammekaster.

flamingo [flə'miŋgo⁰] flamingo.

flammiferous [flä'mifərəs] som frambringer flamme. **flammivomous** [flä'mivoməs] ildspyende.

flamy ['fle¹mi] flammende, flammet.

Flanders ['fla·ndəz] Flandern (NB. sing.).

flange [flän(d)ʒ] framstående kant; flange.

flank [fläŋk] side; slagside, svangside (på fe), flanke; dekke sidene, flankere. **turn his** — falle ham i flanken. **flanker** ['fläŋkə] flankrør; sideverk.

flannel ['flän(ə)l] flanell; kledningsstykke av flanell; tørre el. gni med flanell; kle i flanell. **flannels** flanellsdrakt, sportsklær. **flannelled** kledd i flanell.

flap [fläp] klaff; bordklaff; lapp; lepp, snipp; flik; frakkeskjøt; spennetamp; smekk, klask, dask; dasking; klaske, daske; slå; baske (med vingene); henge slapp ned. **-doodle** store ord; vås, nonsens. — **-door** falldør. — **-eared** med hengende ører; slukkøret. — **-jack** pannekake.

flapper ['fläpə] skralle; vifte; klaps; ung (ikke flygeferdig) fugl; ung villand; backfisch; hånd, pote, fluesmekker.

flare [flæ·ə] ustadig lys; praleri; flagre; flimre, flakke; flamme ustadig; glimre, glimte; lyse med blendende glans, glore. **-up** oppblussing, oppbrusing; heftig klammeri; bråkende lag.

flash [fläʃ] glimt, blink, lyn; flott; smakløs; simpel; falsk; glimte, blinke; lyne; la blusse opp; sende ut glimtvis; gjøre hvitglødende (kullspisser); prale med, flotte seg med; **it suddenly flashed (up) on me** det slo meg plutselig, det gikk plutselig opp for meg; — **in the pan** klikke, gå opp i røyk; — **a message along the wires** sende med telegrafen.

flashy ['fläʃi] påfallende; flimrende, broket; smakløs; uekte; hissig, brå.

flask [fla·sk] flaske; kurvflaske; krutthorn.

flat [flät] flat, jevn, jamn, matt, svak, flau; nedslått; likefram, endefram; fullkommen, ganske, rent ut; med b foran (i musikk); liten (om ters); moll (om tonearten); tosk, naut; flathet; jevnhet; flate, slette; grunne; langgrunne, lang fjære; bakgrunn (i teater); pram; åpen godsvogn; (amr.) bredskygget damestråhatt; etasje; leilighet; **fall** — falle til jorda; **flat** [flät] gjøre flat; gjøre flau; sette en halv tone ned; (amr.) gi en kurv; bli flau; synke (i musikk).

flat|bottomed flatbunnet. — **-catcher** bondefanger. — **-catching** bondefangeri. — **-chested** flatbrystet. — **fish** flyndre, kveite. — **-footed** som har plattfot. — **-iron** strykejern. — **-milk** skummet melk.

flatten ['flätn] gjøre flat; jevne; slå flat, hamre flat; glatte ut; trykke; gjøre flau; gjøre en halv tone dypere; bli flat osv.

flatter ['flätə] planerer; planeringsredskap.

flatter ['flätə] smigre; flattere. **flatterer** ['flätərə] smigrer. **flattery** ['flätəri] skamrosing, smiger.

flatulent ['flätjulənt] plaget av vind i magen; oppblåst, truten.

flatwise ['flätwaiz] på flatsiden.

flaunt [flå·nt] flagre, vaie; kneise; briske seg; prunke, prange.

flautist ['flå·tist] fløytespiller, fløytenist.

flavour ['fle¹və] aroma, vellukt, duft; velsmak, smak; buké (om vin); sette smak (el. duft) på, krydre.

flavouring ['fle¹vəriŋ] krydder, smakstilsetning.

flavourless ['fleɪvəlès] uten duft, uten smak.
flaw [flå·] revne, knekk, sprekk; mangel, lyte, feil, svakhet, ufullkommenhet; flage, vindstøt; oppbrusing, spetakkel; knekke; slå revner i; bryte. **a — in a will** en feil (et svakt punkt) ved et testament. **flawless** ['flå·lès] uten mangler, feilfri. **flawy** ['flå·i] sprukken; mangelfull.
flax [flåks] lin. **-comb** linhekle. **flaxen** [flåksən] av lin, lin-; — **hair** lyst hår. **flaxy** ['flåksi] linaktig; blond.
flay [fle¹] flå. **flayer** ['fleɪə] flåer.
flea [fli·] loppe; **put a — in his ear** hviske ham en djevel i øret. **— -beetle** jordloppe. **— -bite** loppestikk; ubetydelighet, knappenålsstikk. **-bitten** bitt av lopper; plettet, fregnet; ussel.
fleam [fli·m] bild, årelatejern.
fleck [flek] plett, flekk, stenk; plette; stenke. **flecker** ['flekə] stenke, marmorere. **fleckless** ['fleklès] plettfri.
flection ['flekʃən] bøyning.
fled [fled] imperf. av **flee.**
fledge [fledʒ] forsyne med fjær, gjøre flygeferdig. **fledged** flygeferdig; **newly — graduates** nybakte kandidater. **fledgling** ['fledʒliŋ] nettopp flygeferdig unge.
flee [fli·] fly, flykte.
fleece [fli·s] ull; skinn, fell; klippe (sau); flå, suge ut; overtrekke med ull; **the golden —** det gylne skinn; den gylne Vlies (en orden); **fleecer** ['fli·sə] flåer.
fleecy ['fli·si] ullen; ullaktig; ullrik, lodden; a **— sky** en himmel med makrellskyer.
fleer [fliə] spotte; flire; spott, flir.
fleet [fli·t] flåte (samling av skip).
Fleet [fli·t], **the —** tidligere bekk, også fengsel, i London; — **Street** gate i London med pressekontorer; pressen.
fleet [fli·t] hurtig, snøgg, rapp, lett; ile av sted; sveve. **fleeting** flyktig. **fleetness** raskhet, hurtighet, flyktighet.
Fleming ['flemiŋ] flamlender. **Flemish** ['flemiʃ] flamsk; **the Flemish** flamlenderne.
flench [flenʃ], **flense** [flens] flense.
flesh [fleʃ] kjøtt (også på frukt); muskler; hold; menneskehet; syndig menneske; sanselig lyst; — **and fell** hud og hår; — **and blood** den menneskelige natur; **his own — and blood** hans egne barn (eller nære slektninger); **be in —** være i godt hold; **be in the —** være i live; **lose —** bli tynn, mager; **put on —** bli fet, legge seg ut.
flesh [fleʃ] gi (hunder) rått kjøtt (el. blod); gi blod på tann, innvie; øve, herde; mette; gi kjøttfarge; **men -ed in cruelty** folk som er herdet i grusomhet.
flesh|-brush hudbørste, frottérbørste. **— -colour** kjøttfarge; hagenellik. **--creeper** gruoppvekkende roman. **— -eater** kjøtteter.
flesher ['fleʃə] (skotsk) slakter.
flesh|-fly spyflue. **— -glove** frottérhanske.
fleshings ['fleʃiŋz] (kjøttfarget) trikot.
flesh|less ['fleʃlès] kjøttløs, skrinn, beinet. **-ly** ['fleʃli] kjødelig; kjøttfull, tykk; sanselig, vellystig.
flesh-pot kjøttgryte.
fleshy ['fleʃi] kjøttrik, kjøttfull, kjøtt-.
fletcher ['fletʃə] buemaker.
flew [flu·] imperf. av **fly.**
flews [flu·z] hengeflabb (på hund).
flex [fleks] bøye, krøke.
flexibility [fleksi'biliti] bøyelighet. **flexible** ['fleksibl] bøyelig. **flexile** ['fleksil] bøyelig.
flexion ['flekʃən] bøyning. **flexional** ['flekʃənəl] bøynings-, **flexor** ['flekså·ə] bøyemuskel. **flexuous** ['fleksjuəs] buktet; ustadig; ustø. **flexure** ['flekʃə] bøyning.
flibberdigibbet [flibədi'dʒibit] skravlekopp, skravlebøtte; vinglehode.
flick [flik] svippe, slå, snerte, smekke; knipse; snert, smekk.
flicker ['flikə] flagre, vifte, blafre, flakke (om

lys og flamme); flakring; flyktig oppblussing. **flickering** flakring, blafring.
flier ['flaiə] flyger; desertør, rømling; hurtigtog; svinghjul (i maskin); **-s** rett trapp.
flight [flait] flukt, flyging; flokk, sverm; — **of arrows** pileregn; — **of steps,** — **of stairs** trapp; **take to —** gripe flukten; **put el.** turn to — jage på flukt; **the birds winged their —** fuglene fløy. **flightily** ['flaitili] flyktig; overspent. **flightiness** flyktighet; overspenthet. **flighty** ['flaiti] flyktig, vinglet, ustø; fantastisk, overspent; fjollet.
flimflam ['flimfläm] grille, innfall; knep; skrøne.
flimsiness ['flimzinès] tynnhet; svakhet, overfladiskhet. **flimsy** ['flimzi] tynn; svak, usolid; løs, intetsigende; tynt kopipapir; noteblad; pengeseddel.
flinch [flinʃ] vike tilbake, trekke seg tilbake; svikte, gripe til utflukter; — **from duty** svikte sin plikt; **without -ing** uten å blunke.
flinch se flench og flense.
flinders ['flindəz] stumper, stykker.
fling [fliŋ] slynge, kaste, hive, kyle; velte, beseire; ile, fly, styrte; bevege seg urolig; slå bakut (om hester); bli ustyrlig; være grov; stikle; kast, slag; snert, stikleri; hang, lyst; ubunden frihet, vilt liv; — **down** kaste ned; ødelegge; — **off** kaste av; føre på villspor; skille seg av med; — **out** slå ut (om hester); utstøte (ord); utbre, strø ut (skrifter); — **oneself out** fare heftig opp; — **one out of a thing** narre noe fra en; — **the door to** smelle døra igjen; — **up** oppgi; **have a — at one** gi en en støt; **have one's —** få styrt sin lyst, rase ut; **give one his —** la en få styrt sin lyst.
flint [flint] flint. — **-glass** krystallglass.
flintiness flinthardhet.
flint-lock flintelås. **flintstone** flintestein.
flinty ['flinti] flint-, flinthard, steinhard.
flip [flip] sjømanns-drikk (øl, brennevin og sukker).
flip [flip] lite slag; knipse; vippe; slå.
flip-flap ['flipfläp] kollbøtte.
flippancy ['flipənsi] flåsethet, flabbethet.
flippant ['flipənt] kåt, flabbet, nesevis.
flipper ['flipə] luffe; (i slang) hånd.
flirt [flə·t] kaste, slenge; vifte med, svinge, løpe fram og tilbake, vimse; kokettere, flørte **(with med);** kast, sleng; kokette; kurmaker. **flirtation** [flə·'te¹ʃən] koketteri, flørt, kurtise. **flirtatious** [flə·'te¹ʃəs] kokett, flørtende, kurtiserende. **flirty** ['flə·ti] kokett; kurtiserende, flørtende.
flit [flit] fly; flagre; vandre; flytte.
flitch [flitʃ] fleskeside; bakhun.
flitter ['flitə] fille; flagre; flakse.
flittermouse ['flitəmaus] flaggermus.
flitting ['flitiŋ] flyktig; flytning.
float [flo"t] flyte, svømme; drive, reke; være flott; sveve; vaie (om fane); sette i gang, starte, få flott; flåte (tømmer); oversvømme; tømmerflåte; kavl, flå, flytholt; flyter; **be -ed** komme flott. **floatage** ['flo"tidʒ] flyting; flytende gjenstander.
float-board ['flo"tbå·d] hjulskovl.
floater ['flo"tə] noe som flyter; sikkerhet.
floating ['flo"tiŋ] flytende; — **anchor** drivanker; — **bridge** flytebru, flytebrygge, ferjepram. — **capital** flytende kapital; — **cargo** svømmende ladning; — **dock** flytedokk; — **light** fyrskip, lysbøye.
flock [flåk] flokke seg, samle seg; flokk; hop; hjord (især om sauer).
flock [flåk] ulldott, tust. — **-bed** seng med ullmadrass.
floe [flo"] stort isflak.
flog [flåg] piske, slå, banke, denge, jule.
flogging ['flågiŋ] pisking; bank; **get (el. come in for) a good —** få en ordentlig drakt pryl.

flood [flʌd] høyvanne, flo (motsatt fjære); flom, oversvømmelse; overflødighet; strøm; oversvømme; overskylle; **the Flood** syndfloden; **a — of light** et lyshav; **when the -s are out** i flodtiden. **-gate** sluseport. **-light** flomlys; belyse med flomlys. **-mark** høyvannsmerke. **— -tide** høyvanne, flo.

floor [flå·ə] gulv, golv, stokkverk, etasje; bunn (inne i et skip); i Amerika: kongressens sal; retten til å tale i kongressen; **have** el. **get the — ha** el. få ordet; **ground — første etasje; first — annen etasje.

floor [flå·ə] legge golv i; legge (el. slå) i golvet el. bakken; slå, målbinde; **— the paper** ta eksamen med glans; **be -ed** ryke, dumpe til eksamen; (om bilder på en utstilling:) bli hengt lavest.

floorage ['flå·ridʒ] golvflate. **floor-cloth** linoleum. **floorer** ['flå·rə] knusende slag, svimeslag. **flooring** ['flå·riŋ] golv; materiale til golv. **floorwalker** (amr.) butikkinspektør.

flop [flåp] slå, bakse (med vingene o. l.); la henge; klaske; plumpe ned; falle sammen; tungt fall.

floppy ['flåpi] slapt nedhengende; slakk.

flor. fk. f. **floruit** (= **flourished).**

flora ['flå·rə] flora, blomsterrike. **floral** ['flårəl] blomster-. **floreated** ['flå·rie'tid] blomsterprydd; blomstret.

Florence ['flårəns] Firenze; ogs. kvinnenavn.

Florentine ['flårəntain] florentiner, florentinerinne; florentinersilke; florentinsk.

florescence [flå'resəns] blomstring, bløming.

floret ['flå·rét] liten blomst.

floriated ['flå·rie'tid] se **floreated.**

floricultural [flå(·)ri'kʌltʃərəl] blomsterdyrkings-. **floriculture** ['flå·rikʌltʃə] blomsterdyrking. **floriculturist** [flå(·)ri'kʌltʃərist] blomsterdyrker.

florid ['flårid] blomstrende; av frisk rød farge. **Florida** ['flåridə] Florida.

floridity [flå'riditi], **floridness** ['flåridnès] blomstrende farge; frisk rødme; sirlighet el. snirklethet (i stil). **floriferous** [flå'rifərəs] som bærer blomster.

florin ['flårin] florin (engelsk sølvmynt: 2 shillings); gylden.

florist ['flå(·)rist] blomsterhandler; blomsterdyrker; blomsterkjenner.

floss [flås] dun på planter; floss, flokksilke; bekk, å. **-silk** flokksilke. **flossy** ['flåsi] dunet; silkebløt.

flotage ['floutidʒ] se **floatage.**

flotation [flo'teiʃən] flyting; oppdrift; **power of — flyteevne.**

flotilla [flo'tilə] flotilje.

flotsam ['flåtsəm] havrekst.

flounce [flauns] bakse, kave, sprelle; garnere; rykk, kast, sleng; plask; garnering, kappe.

flounder ['flaundə] flyndre, skrubbe.

flounder ['flaundə] sprelle, tumle, bakse, kave. **flour** [flauə] mel, siktemel, mjøl; male til mel; mele.

flourish ['flʌriʃ] florere, trives, blomstre; stå på høyden av sin makt; bruke blomstrende språk; preludere, fantasere: spille støyende; blåse en fanfare; svinge (f. eks. sverd); prale, rose seg; briske seg; pryde med blomster og snirkler; skrive med kruseduller; pryde med sirlige ord; utstaffere overdådig; utarbeide omhyggelig; forskjønne; smykke; blomstrende tilstand; glans, smykke, skjønnhet; forsiring, forskjønnelse, blomster (i stil); snirkel, sving; kruseduJle; forspill; fanfare; svingende bevegelse, sving; det å slå ut med hånden.

floury ['flauri] melen; melet, mjølet.

flout [flaut] spotte, håne; spott, spe, hån.

flow [flou] flyte, strømme; stige (om vannet); oversvømme, flyte over; **— with** være fylt med; flyte, gli blidt av sted; henge løst og bølgende ned; miste blod.

flow [flou] flo (motsatt fjære); stigning; tilløp (av vann); (fig.) strøm; **he has a fine — of**

language han uttrykker seg flytende; **his great — of spirits** hans store livlighet. **flowage** ['flouidʒ] flom, oversvømmelse.

flower ['flauə] blomst, blome; blomstring; det fineste, det beste; pryd, glans; aroma, ange; buké (av vin); vignett; blomstre, smykke med blomster; **the — of the flock** crème de la crème; **the — of youth** ungdommens vår; **-s of speech** retoriske blomster; **-s of sulphur** svovelblomme. **flower-de-luce** [flauədi'lu·s] iris.

floweret ['flauərét] liten blomst. **floweriness** ['flauərinès] blomstervrimmel; blomsterflor.

flower-picture, — -piece blomsterstykke. **-pot** blomsterpotte. **— -show** blomsterutstilling. **— -stand** blomsterstativ.

flowery ['flauəri] blomsterrik; blomstrende.

flown [floun] perf. pts. av **fly.**

F. L. S. fk. f. **fellow of the Linnaean Society.**

flu [flu·] influensa.

fluctuant ['flʌktjuənt] vankelmodig, ustø, uviss. **fluctuate** ['flʌktjue't] bølge; strømme fram og tilbake. **fluctuation** ['flʌktju'eiʃən] bølging; vakling, ubestemthet; fluktuering; stigning og fall.

flue [flu·] luftgang; skorstein, skorsteinspipe, skorsteinsrør; rørkanal.

flue [flu·] fnugg, dun, bløte hår.

flue [flu·] influensa, spanskesyke.

fluency ['flu·ənsi] letthet, tungeferdighet.

fluent ['flu·ənt] flytende; **speak fluently** tale flytende.

fluey ['flu·i] dunet, dunmyk.

fluff [flʌf] bløte hår, dun; fnugg; lo. **fluffy** ['flʌfi] dunaktig, bløt.

flugelman ['flu·glmän] leder; forbilde.

fluid ['flu·id] flytende; væske; fluidum. **fluidity** [flu·'iditi] flytende tilstand.

fluke [flu·k] ankerfli; flygg; lykketreff, slumpehell, (i biljardspill:) svin; være svineheldig.

fluke [flu·k] saueigle.

flume [flu·m] kanal (gravd), vassrenne, gjel (som en elv renner gjennom).

flummery ['flʌməri] en slags grøt; smiger; vrøvl, tøv.

flummox ['flʌməks] sette i beit.

flung [flʌŋ] imperf. og perf. pts. av **fling.**

flunkey ['flʌŋki] lakei, spyttslikker.

flunkeyism ['flʌŋkiizm] lakeivesen, spyttslikkeri.

fluor ['flu·ə] fluss-spat.

fluorescence [fluə'resəns] fluorescens. **fluorescent** [fluə'resənt] fluorescerende.

flurried ['flʌrid] forfjamset, befippet, nervøs.

flurry ['flʌri] vindrose, flage; hastverk; befippelse; sette i bevegelse; kave, ase ut; gjøre befippet, forfjamse.

flush [flʌʃ] strømme, flyte voldsomt; rødme, bli plutselig rød; bli flytende; fly plutselig opp (om fugler); synge triller, koloraturer; få til å rødme plutselig; farge, spyle, sprøyte (kloakk o. l.); oppmuntre, oppflamme; gjøre oppblåst; jage opp; frisk, blomstrende, kraftig; full, svulmende; rikelig; flust med; vel forsynt; ødsel, gavmild; raust; som ligger i flukt med; rødme plutselig; glød; oppbrusing, storm (av følelser); blomstring, kraft; triller, koloraturer; force (i kortspill); **-ed with joy** berust av glede; **— up** bli blussende rød; **in the — of victory** i den første seiersrus; **money was — der** var overflod av penger; **— of money** velbeslått med penger; **I came — upon him** jeg kom like over ham.

Flushing ['flʌʃiŋ] Vlissingen.

fluster ['flʌstə] varme, hete; beruse; forvirre; være varm; kave, vimse; være overlesst; hete; beruselse, forvirring; overlessing.

flute [flu·t] fløyte, orgelpipe; fure; langt franskbrød; blåse på fløyte; rifle; pipe (om tøy). **flutist** ['flu·tist] fløytespiller, fløytenist, fløytist.

flutter ['flʌtə] bølge, svaie; flagre; vimse, bevege seg urolig fram og tilbake el. opp og ned; skjelve, banke (om hjerte); fare i siksak; være opphisset;

være nervøs; være i sinnsbevegelse; vakle; sette i bevegelse; få til å flagre; skremme; gjøre angst; bringe i forvirring; hurtig og uregelmessig bevegelse, flagring; banking (av hjertet); svingning, vakling, bølging; opphisselse, uro, forvirring; **be in a** — være ganske nervøs.
fluty ['flu·ti] fløytelignende, fløyte, myk og ren.
fluvial ['flu·vjəl], **fluviatic** [flu·vi'ätik] flod-.
flux [flʌks] flyting; flod; flo; framkalle en uttømming; få til å purgere; rense; smelte, bringe til å flyte; — **of money** pengeomløp; — **and reflux** flo og fjære; — **of blood** blodgang. **fluxibility** [flʌksi'biliti] smeltelighet. **fluxible** ['flʌksibl] smeltelig. **fluxion** ['flʌkʃən] flyting; flod; **-s** differensialregning. **fluxional** ['flʌkʃənəl], **fluxionary** ['flʌkʃənəri] integral; foranderlig.
fly [flai] flyve, flyge; fly, flykte; springe i stykker (om glass o. l.); vaie; la vaie (om flagg), sette opp (om draker o. l.); flagre; kjøre i drosje; **let** — skyte ut (en pil); — **at** fly imot, fare inn på, anfalle; slå løs på; — **in the face of** fare løs på; trosse; — **into a passion** bli forbitret, fare opp; se også **flying.**
fly [flai] flue; svinghjul; **break a** — **on the wheel** skyte spurver med kanoner.
fly [flai] drosje (plur. især: **flys**).
fly [flai] våken, oppvakt, gløgg.
fly-away ['flaiəwe'] flyktig; flagrende.
fly-blow ['flaiblo"] spy; legge spy. **fly-blown** ['flaiblo"n] belagt med fluespy; tilsmusset.
fly-catcher ['flai'kätʃə] fluesnapper (en ugl).
flyfish ['flaifiʃ] fiske med flue.
fly-flap ['flaifläp] fluesmekker.
flying ['flaiiŋ] flygende, lett, hurtig; flyging, flukt. — **-boat** flygebåt. — **bomb** flyvende bombe (brukt om V-bombene). — **buttress** streverbue. — **colours** flygende faner. **Flying Dutchman** flygende hollender (spøkelsesskip; ogs. om hurtigtog på linjen Exeter—London). — **fish** flygefisk; person fra Barbadoes. — **-jib** jager (slags skip). — **machine** flygemaskin, fly. — **-squirrel** flygeekorn. — **visit** fransk (ɔ: rask) visitt.
flyleaf ['flaili·f] forsatsblad.
flyman ['flaimən] drosjekusk, maskinmann (på teater).
fly-paper ['flai'pe'pə] fluepapir.
fly-sheet flygeblad. **fly-wheel** svinghjul.
F. M. fk. f. **Field Marshal.**
F. M. S. fk. f. **Federated Malay States.**
F. O. fk. f. **Foreign Office.**
fo. fk. f. **folio.**
foal [fo"l] føll; fole; følle, fole, kaste føll.
foam [fo"m] skum, fråde; skumme, fråde.
foamy ['fo"mi] skummende.
f. o. b. fk. f. **free on board.**
fob [fåb] liten lomme, urlomme.
fob [fåb] fiff, knep; narre, lure, snyte; — **off** bli kvitt på en behendig måte; spise en av.
focal ['fo"kəl] brennpunkt-. **foci** ['fo"sai] flertall av **focus. focus** ['fo"kəs] brennpunkt, fokus; bringe i fokus; innstille.
fodder ['fådə] fôr; fôre.
foe [fo"] fiende. **foeman** ['fo"mən] fiende.
fœtal ['fi·təl], **fœtus** ['fi·təs] se **fetal, fetus.**
fog [fåg] tåke, skodde; hylle inn i tåke; bringe i forlegenhet; **-bank** tåkebanke.
fog[fåg] hå, etterslått.
fogey ['fo"gi]; **old** — gammel knark, stabeis.
foggage ['fågidʒ] etterslått.
fogginess ['fåginès] tåkethet, tåke, skodde.
foggy ['fågi] tåket; omtåket; uklar.
fog-horn ['fåghå·ən] tåkelur.
fogie ['fo"gi] se **fogey.**
fogle ['fo"gl] silketørkle.
fogy ['fo"gi] se **fogey.**
foh! [fo"] fy!
foible ['foibl] svakhet, svak side.

foil [foil] folie (tynt metallblad); bakgrunn; **be a** — **to** tjene til å framheve; **tinfoil** ['tin'foil] tinnfolie.
foil [foil] sløve, svekke; tilintetgjøre (ens planer); narre; krysse (ens planer); overvinne; komme på tverke for; florett; far, spor (av vilt); nederlag; uhell.
foiling ['foiliŋ] folie; speilbelegg.
foin [foin] støte, stikke (i kamp); støt, stikk.
foison ['foizn] fylde, overflødighet.
foist [foist] lure inn, stikke inn; sette til; — **something upon somebody** prakke noe på en.
Fokker ['fåkə] fokker (slags fly).
fold [fo"ld] fold; i sammensetninger med tallord, f. eks. **ninefold** nifold, nidobbelt.
fold [fo"ld] fold, sauekve; folde, brette, legge sammen (hendene, et brev osv.); legge over kors (armene); — **up** legge sammen; false.
folder ['fo"ldə] falser; falsbein (hos bokbinder); falsejern.
folding ['fo"ldiŋ] sammenlegging; falsing. **folding]-bed** feltseng, slagseng. — **-chair** feltstol. — **-cot** feltseng. — **-door** fløydør, dobbelt dør. — **-screen** skjermbrett. — **-stick** falsbein.
foliaceous [fo"li'e'ʃəs] blad-, lauv-.
foliage ['fo"ljidʒ] blad, lauv; lauvverk; pryde med lauvverk. **foliate** ['fo"lie't] foliere, utstyre med bladsirater, pryde med lauvverk.
foliate ['fo"liit] bladaktig, med blad.
foliation [fo"li'e'ʃən] bladutvikling, bladvokster; uthamring til blad; foliering.
folio ['fo"ljo"] folio; foliant.
folious ['fo"ljəs] bladrik; bladaktig, tynn.
folk [fo"k] folk, mennesker; ofte også **folks; little folks** barn; **the old folks** de gamle (far og mor).
Folkestone ['fo"kstən] Folkestone.
folklore ['fo"klå·ə] folkeminneforskning, folklore, folkeminne; sagn, folketradisjon. **folklorist** ['fo"klå·rist] folklorist. **folkloristic** [fo"klå·'ristik] folkloristisk.
foll. fk. f. **following.**
follicle ['fålikl] belgkapsel, skolm; pose, sekk; **hair** — hårsekk.
follow ['fålo"] følge, komme el. gå etter; (fig.) følge; fatte, forstå; være kjæreste med; strebe etter (f. eks. et mål); adlyde (f. eks. en fører); bekjenne seg til (f. eks. en lære); slå lag med, rette seg etter (f. eks. en mote); være følgen av; — **other men's business** bry seg om andre folks saker; — **-me-lads** lange krøller eller sløyfer i nakken; — **-my-leader** gåsegang, hermeleik; etterdilting; — **suit** følge farge, bekjenne kulør (i kortspill); — **one's nose** gå like etter nesen; — **the hounds** delta i parforsejakt; — **up one's victory** forfølge sin seier; — **the sea** være sjømann.
follower ['fålo"ə] følgesvenn, ledsager; tilhenger; kjæreste.
following ['fålo"iŋ] følgende (NB. artikkelen: **the** — **story** følgende historie); følge; tilslutning; parti, tilhengere.
folly ['fåli] dårskap, dumhet, fjollethet.
foment [fo"'ment] bade (med varm væske); oppmuntre; nære, oppelske. **fomentation** [fo"mən-'te'ʃən] bading (med varmt omslag); omslag; næring; oppelskning. **fomenter** [fo"'mentə] oppmuntrer.
fond [fånd] tåpelig, godtruen; kjærlig, øm; svak i sin ømhet; **a** — **parent** en svak, uforstandig far (mor); **be** — **of** være glad i, være forelsket i; **get** — **of** bli glad i. **fondle** ['fåndl] kjæle, kjæle for. **fondling** ['fåndliŋ] kjælebarn, kjæledegge. **fondly** ['fåndli] tåpelig; kjærlig. **fondness** ['fåndnès] tåpelighet; kjærlighet; ømhet.
font [fånt] kasse med typer.
font [fånt] kilde, kjelde; font, døpefont.
food [fu·d] føde, mat, kost, næring; **plant-** — plateføde; **articles of** — fødevarer, matvarer;

— **for powder** kanonføde, kanonmat; — **for reflection** stoff til ettertanke; — **for worms** ormemat.

food|-card matkort. — **-controller** rasjoneringsminister. — **-stuff** næringsstoff. — **-value** næringsverdi.

fool [fu·l] fruktgrøt: f. eks. **gooseberry —** stikkelsbærgrøt.

fool [fu·l] tosk, naut, tåpe, fåvetting; narr, spasmaker; narre, bedra, fjase bort; **make a —** **of** holde for narr, ta ved nesen; **go (send) on a -'s errand** bli narret (narre) april.

foolery ['fu·ləri] narrestreker. **foolfarmer** ['fu·l-fa·²mə] bondefanger. **foolhardiness** ['fu·lha·dinès] dumdristighet. **foolhardy** ['fu·lha·²di] dumdristig, uvøren. **fooling** ['fu·liŋ] narrestreker, fjas.

foolish ['fu·liʃ] dum, tåpelig, tosket, narraktig, latterlig. **foolishness** dumhet, tåpelighet.

foolscap ['fu·lzkäp] folioark.

foot [fut] fot (flertall **feet** føtter); fot (som mål, i flertall **feet** fot); fotfolk, infanteri; det som er på bunnen (av sukker-, oljefater osv.); den nederste del (f. eks. av en side, et berg, et glass o. l.); — **-and-mouth disease** munn- og klovsyke; **at —** nedentil, nedenunder, nederst på siden; **on —** til fots; **knock** (el. **throw**) **one off his feet** velte en; **be on foot** være i gang; være på beina; **get on one's feet** komme på beina; **he helped her to her feet** han hjalp henne på beina; **she started to her feet** hun fór (sprang) opp; **go on foot** gå til fots; **set on foot** sette i gang.

foot [fut] danse, hoppe; sparke; (amr.) summere opp; beløpe seg til; sette fot på, strikke ny fot i; (amr.) betale en regning; kausjonere.

football ['futbå·l] fotball; fotballspill.

footballer ['futbå·lə] fotballspiller.

foot|-bath fotbad. — **-board** stigbrett, trin. — **-boy** lakei. — **-bridge** gangbru, klopp. **-fall** fottrin; feiltrin. **-hold** fotfeste.

footing ['futiŋ] fotfeste; fotlag; dans; nederste del; oppsummering; **keep one's —** holde seg på beina; **on the same —** på like fot.

foot-lights ['futlaits] rampe, lamperekke i teater.

foot|man ['futmən] lakei, tjener. **-mark** fotspor, fotefar. **-muff** fotpose. **-note** fotnote. **-pace** skritt. **-pad** stimann, røver. **-page** pasje. **-path** sti, fotsti. **-print** fotspor. **-race** kappløp, veddeløp. **-rope** underlik, pert.

foot|-rule ['futru·l] tommestokk. — **-soldier** infanterist.

foot|sore ['futså·²] sårføtt, sårbeint. **-step** fotspor. **-stool** fotskammel. **-way** fortau. **-wear** fottøy, skotøy.

foozle ['fu·zl] kludre, forkludre, tull; gammel knark, sullik.

fop [fåp] laps, sprett. **fopling** ['fåpliŋ] liten laps. **foppery** ['fåp(ə)ri] lapseri. **foppish** ['fåpiʃ] lapset. **foppishness** ['fåpiʃnès] lapseri.

for [(alm. ubetont uttale:) fə; (foran vokal:) fər; (med ettertrykk:) få·²; (foran vokal:) får] 1. ti, for; 2. for, i stedet for; 3. for, til beste for, til hjelp mot; 4. for, etter, til (om mål eller bestemmelse); 5. for (om rekkefølge); 6. i, på (om utstrekning i tid og rom); 7. på grunn av, for; 8. til tross for, trass i; 9. med hensyn til, i forhold til, for; 10. (foran et ord som er forbundet med en infinitiv); eksempler: 2. **member — Liverpool** medlem (av underhuset) for L.; **once — all** en gang for alle; **give change —** veksle; gi igjen på; **eye — eye** øye for øye; **know — certain** vite sikkert; **take —** oppfatte som; **mistake —** forveksle med; — **one thing** for det første, for eksempel; blant annet; 3. **there is nothing — it but** to gjøre er intet annet for enn; ingen annen råd enn; **they live — each other** de lever for hverandre; **a remedy —** et middel mot; 4. — **instance,** — **example** for eksempel; **a letter — you** et brev til deg; **bound — China** som skal

til China, bestemt til China; **ask —** spørre etter; **hope —** håpe på; **long —** lengte etter; **look —** se etter; **send —** sende bud etter; **wish —** ønske; **an instrument — cutting** et instrument til å skjære med; **good — nothing** ingenting verd, ubrukelig; 5. **word — word** ord for ord; 6. **he has lived there — three years** han har bodd der i tre år (el. . . . bodd der tre år); — **years** i årevis; — **miles i mils** omkrets; milevidt; — **life** på livstid; — **ever** bestandig; — **the most part** for største delen; — **once** for en gangs skyld; — **once in a way** for en gangs for denne ene gang; — **once in a way** for en gangs skyld; 7. — **fear of** av frykt for; — **love of** av kjærlighet til; — **this reason** av denne grunn; — **want of** av mangel på; **he wept — joy** han gråt av glede; **but — him** hvis han ikke hadde vært; — **my sake** for min skyld; **fie — shame!** fy, skam deg! (etter komparativ med the) **be the better —** it ha godt av det; **he will be none the worse —** it han vil ikke ha noe vondt av det; **her eyes were the brighter —** having wept hennes øyne var desto klarere, fordi hun hadde grått; 8. — **all** that trass i alt, likevel; — **all** (el. **aught** el. **anything**) **I know** så vidt (el. for alt det) jeg vet; — **all I care** det er meg likegyldig; — **all I do** trass i alt jeg gjør; — **all her scolding** hvor mye hun enn skjente; 9. **well written — a boy of his age** godt skrevet av en gutt på hans alder; **clever — his age** klok for sin alder; **as —** med hensyn til, med omsyn til; **as — me** hva meg angår; 10. — **him to do that would be the correct thing** det ville være riktig at han gjorde det; **he halted his carriage — me to jump in** han stanset vognen så jeg kunne hoppe oppi.

f. o. r. fk. f. **free on rail.**

forage ['fåridʒ] fôr; furasjere, skaffe fôr. — **-cap** leirlue. **foraging** ['fåridʒiŋ] furasjering.

foramen [fo're¹mən] lite hull.

forasmuch [fårəz'mʌtʃ] ettersom; når det gjelder.

foray ['fåre¹] plyndringstog; plyndre, herje.

forbade [fə'bäd] imperf. av **forbid.**

forbear ['få·²bæə] (skotsk) ættefar.

forbear [få·¹bæ·²] la være, unnlate; ha tålmodighet; avholde seg fra, styre seg. **forbearance** [få·¹bæ·²rəns] tålmodighet, overbærenhet; mildhet.

forbid [fə'bid] forby; hindre; bannlyse, forvise. **forbidden** [fə'bidn] perf. pts. av **forbid. forbidding** [fə'bidiŋ] frastøtende, ubehagelig.

forbore [få·¹bå·²] imperf. av **forbear.**

forborne [få·¹bå·²n] perf. pts. av **forbear.**

force [få·²s] kraft, styrke; makt; tvang, nødvendighet; politistyrke, politikorps; tropper, stridsmakt; tvinge, nøde; tiltvinge seg; gjøre vold på; ta med makt, innta med storm; voldta; fordrive; rive, støte, sprenge; anstrenge; forsterke; legge vekt på; forsere; drive fram (frukter, blomster o. l.); — **a door** sprenge døra; — **wine** klare vin hurtig; — **out** avtvinge, avnøde; — **upon** påtvinge, pånøde.

forced [få·²st] tvunget, forsert osv.; — **jest** forsert spøk; — **sale** tvangssalg, tvangsauksjon. **forcedly** ['få·²sidli] tvunget. **forcedness** ['få·²sidnès] tvungenhet, forserthet.

force majeure [få·²sma·²ʒə·] uovervinnelig hindring (f. eks. krig) for oppfylling av kontrakt.

forcemeat ['få·²smi·t] farse, fyll.

forceps ['få·²seps] tang (især kirurgisk).

force-pump ['få·²spʌmp] trykkpumpe. **forcer** ['få·²sə] en som tvinger osv.; pumpestempel.

forcible ['få·²sibl] kraftig, sterk; voldsom, heftig. **forcibly** ['få·²sibli] kraftig; voldsomt.

forcing-frame ['få·²sinfre¹m] mistbenk. — **-house** drivhus. — **-pump** trykkpumpe.

ford [få·²d] vadested; vasse, vade over.

fordable ['få·²dəbl] som en kan vasse over.

fordo [få·²du·] ødelegge.

fore [få·²] foran, forrest; for-; forut, fortil; fortropp; **at the —** i fronten; **to the —** foran; ved hånden, til stede; i live; **come to the** — vise seg, tre fram; bli berømt.

fore-and-aft ['få·ʰrən'da·ft] for og akter; over hele skipet, i skipets lengderetning.

forearm [få·r'a·əm] forut væpne; **forewarned** **forearmed** (om lag:) forord bryter trette.

forearm ['få·ra·ʰm] underarm.

forebode [få·ʰ'boᵘd] varsle; ane, kjenne på seg.

foreboding [få·ʰ'boᵘdiɳ] varsel; anelse.

forecast ['få·ʰka·st] værvarsel, værmelding, forutsigelse. **what's the** — **for to-day** hva sier meteorologisk institutt for i dag?

forecast [få·ʰ'ka·st] planlegge, forutse.

forecastle ['foᵘksl] bakk; ruff (på skip). **fore-close** [få·ʰ'kloᵘz] hindre, stanse; utelukke; realisere. **foreclosure** [få·ʰ'kloᵘzə] utelukkelse.

fore|-deck ['få·ʰdek] fordekk. **-design** forutbestemme. **-doom** [få·ʰ'du·m] dømme (på forhånd). **-father** ættefar. **-fend** [få·ʰ'fend] forebygge, avvende, avverge. **-finger** pekefinger. **-foot** forfot, framfot. **-front** forgrunn; forside; forreste linje.

forego se **forgo.**

forego [få·ʰ'goᵘ] gå forut; **foregoing** [få·ʰ-'goᵘiɳ] førnevnt, forutgående; **foregone** [få·ʰ-'gån] tidligere; på forhånd bestemt; **a foregone conclusion** noe som er avgjort på forhånd; noe en kunne vite i forveien.

foreground ['få·ʰgraund] forgrunn.

forehand ['få·ʰhänd] frampart på en hest, bog.

forehead ['fårɛd] panne; (fig.) frekkhet.

foreign ['fårin] fremmed, utenlandsk, utenriks-; — **-made** utenlandsk, laget i utlandet; — **office** utenriksdepartement.

foreigner ['fårinə] fremmed, utlending.

fore-imagine [få·ri'mädʒin] forestille seg forut.

foreknow [få·ʰ'noᵘ] vite forut.

foreknowledge [få·ʰ'nålidʒ] forutviten.

forel ['fårəl] pergament.

foreland ['få·ʰələnd] odde, nes, pynt, forberg.

foreleg ['få·ʰleg] forbein.

forelock ['få·ʰlåk] lugg, pannehår; **take time by the** — nytte tiden, nytte høvet, gripe leiligheten, være om seg.

foreman ['få·ʰmän] formann, arbeidsformann.

foremast ['få·ʰma·st] fokkemast.

foremost ['få·ʰmoᵘst, -məst] forrest; først; **first and** — først og fremst; **feet** — på føttene; **head** — på hodet, hodestupes.

forenoon ['få·ʰ'nu·n] formiddag.

forensic [fo'rensik] retts-, juridisk.

fore-ordain [få·rå·ʰ'de'n] bestemme forut.

forerunner ['få·ʰrʌnə] forløper.

foresail ['få·ʰse'l] fokk.

fore|see [få·ʰ'si·] forutse. **-seer** seer. **-shadow** ['få·ʰʃädoᵘ] forutanelse; [få·ʰ'ʃädcᵘ] forut antyde, bebude. **-shore** strand, fjære. **-shorten** [få·ʰ-'få·ʰtn] forkorte. **-sight** framsyn, forutviten; forsiktighet. **-skin** forhud.

forest ['fårist] skog (større); kongelig jaktdistrikt; skogkle.

forestall [få·ʰ'stå·l] oppta i forveien, kjøpe opp forut; komme i forveien, i forkjøpet. **forestaller** oppkjøper. **forestalling** oppkjøp.

forester ['få·ristə] forstmann; en som bor i skogen; **forestry** ['få·ristri] forstvesen, forstvitenskap.

fore|taste [få·ʰ'te'st] smake forut; få en forsmak på. **-tell** [få·ʰ'tel] forutsi. **-thought** ['få·ʰþå·t] framtanke, betenksomhet, velberådd hug. **-token** [få·ʰ'toᵘkn] varsle; varsel. **-top** fokkemers, formers. **-top-mast** forstang.

forewarn [få·ʰ'wå·ʰn] advare; forut meddele.

foreyard ['få·ʰja·ʰd] fokkerå.

forfeit ['få·ʰfit] forseelse, feiltrin; forbrytelse; gjenstand el. gods som er forbrutt; bot, mulkt; pant (i panteleik); (pl.) panteleik; hjemfallen, forspilt, forbrutt; forbryte; forspille, tape, miste; — **one's credit** forspille sitt gode navn og rykte; **game of -s** panteleik; **pay the** — gi pant, betale boten; **pay the** — **of one's life** bøte for det med

livet; **cry the -s** rope pantene opp; **play at -s**; leike panteleik. **forfeitable** ['få·ʰfitəbl] som kan forbrytes, som kan forspilles. **forfeiture** ['få·ʰfitʃə] forbrutt gods; fortapelse; pengebot.

forfend [få·ʰ'fend] forby, avvende.

forgave [fə'ge'v] imperf. av **forgive.**

forge [få·ʰdʒ] esse, smieavl, smie; smi; ettergjøre, forfalske, skrive falsk. **forger** falskner, forfalsker. **forgery** ['få·ʰdʒəri] ettergjøring; forfalskning; falsk, falskneri; falsum.

forget [fə'ɡet] glemme; ikke huske, ikke kunne komme på; — **oneself** glemme seg; forløpe seg. **forgetful** [fə'ɡetf(u)l] glemsk, glemsom; som gjør glemsom; uaktsom. **forgetfulness** [-nēs] forglemmelse; glemsomhet; etterlatenhet. **forget-me-not** [fə'ɡetminåt] forglemmegei.

foregive [få·ʰ'ɡiv] tilgi, forlate; ettergi (gjeld el. straff). **forgiven** [fə'ɡivn] perf. pts. av **forgive.** **forgiveness** [-nēs] tilgivelse, forlatelse; ettergivelse; ettergivenhet. **forgiving** ettergivende, forsonlig, barmhjertig.

forgo [få·ʰ'goᵘ] oppgi, gi avkall på.

forgot [fə'ɡåt] imperf. og perf. pts. av **forget** **forgotten** [fə'ɡåtn] perf. pts. av **forget.**

fork [få·ʰk] fork; gaffel; greip; spiss; skillevei; gren, grein, arm (f. eks. av en flod); dele seg, kløyve seg; forke, gafle; kaste med greip; grave med greip; ta med gaffel; — **out** punge ut, betale regningen; utlevere; **forked** [få·ʰkt] gaffelformig; greinet, forgrenet; tvetydig; — **lightning** siksaklyn. **forky** ['få·ʰki] gaffelformet; forgrenet; takket; kløftet.

forlorn [få·ʰ'lå·ʰn] ulykkelig, hjelpeløs, fortvilet; forlatt; — **hope** tropper som går først i ilden uten håp om å seire; stormkolonne; håpløst foretagende; svakt håp. **forlornness** [-nēs] forlatt, hjelpeløs tilstand.

form [få·ʰm] form; skikkelse; system, metode, orden; formel; formular, skjema, blankett; formalitet, skikk og bruk; måte, vis; fantom; benk, skolebenk; klasse i skole; leie (et dyrs); satt form (typograf.); høflighetsform, manér; kondisjon (sport); prestasjon (sport); forme, danne, utgjøre, forferdige; ordne, oppstille, formere (mil.); innrette; utvikle; utkaste (en plan); anta form, forme seg, utvikle seg, stille seg opp; formere seg (mil.); **in due** — i tilbørlig form, tilbørlig; **set** — mønster, forbilde; **a mere** — of **words** en ren frase; **good** — god tone; **bad** — dårlig tone, uhøflighet; **in bad** — i dårlig kondisjon; **the first** — første (laveste) klasse; — **an acquaintance** stifte bekjentskap.

formal ['få·ʰməl] i tilbørlig form, tilbørlig; tvungen, stiv; pedantisk; skolemessig, akademisk, teoretisk; utvortes, ytre; tilsynelatende, skinn-.

formalism ['få·ʰməlizm] formalisme.

formalist ['få·ʰməlist] formalist.

formality [få·ʰ'mäliti] formvesen; riktighet i formen; formalitet, form; formfullhet, høytidelighet; stivhet, pedanteri. **formally** ['få·ʰməli] formelt osv.; for formens skyld; høytidelig, stivt.

format ['få·ʰmæt] format.

formation [få·ʰ'me'ʃən] dannelse, skikkelse; lag, flo. **formative** ['få·ʰmætiv] dannende, plastisk; avledet ord. **formed** [få·ʰmd] utviklet.

former ['få·ʰmə] former; skaper.

former ['få·ʰmə] foregående, forrige, tidligere, førstnevnt, første, hin; forbigangen.

formerly ['få·ʰməli] før i tiden, tidligere, fordum.

formic ['få·ʰmik] maur-. — **acid** maursyre.

formication [få·ʰmi'ke'ʃən] mauring, krisling.

formidable ['få·ʰmidəbl] fryktelig, skrekkelig.

formless ['få·ʰmlis] formløs.

form-master ['få·ʰmma·stə] klasselærer.

formula ['få·ʰmjulə] formel; (pl.) **formulæ** [-li·].

formulary ['få·ʰmjuləri] formular. **formulate** ['få·ʰmjule't] formulere.

fornicate ['få·ʰnike't] drive utukt. **fornication**

[få·ᵊni'ke'ʃən] utukt. **fornicator** ['få·ᵊnike'tə] utuktig person.

forray ['fåreᵊ] røvertog.

forsake [fə'se'k] svikte; forlate. **forsaken** [fə-'se'kn] imperf. av **forsake**. **forsook** [fə'suk] perf. pts. av **forsake**.

forsooth [fə'su·þ] i sannhet, sannelig.

forswear [fə'svæ·ᵊ] forsverge; avsverge; sverge falsk. **forswore** [fə'swå·ᵊ] imperf. av **forswear**. **forsworn** [fə'swå·ᵊn] perf. pts. av **forswear**.

Forsyte ['få·ᵊsait] Forsyte.

fort [få·ᵊt] fort, festning, borg.

fortalice ['få·ᵊtəlis] blokkhus, lite fort.

forte [få·ᵊt] styrke, sterk side, forse.

forte ['få·ᵊtė] forte (i musikk).

forth [få·ᵊþ] fram, fremad, videre; ut; **from this time** — fra nå av; **and so** — og så videre.

forthcoming ['få·ᵊþ'kamin] på rede hånd, ved hånden; til stede; forestående.

forthright ['få·ᵊþ'rait] likefram, endefram; oppriktig; øyeblikkelig; på flekken; straks.

forthwith ['få·ᵊþ'wiþ, -ð] straks, uoppholdelig.

fortieth ['få·ᵊtiiþ] førtiende.

fortifiable ['få·ᵊti'faiəbl] som kan befestes.

fortification [få·ᵊtifi'ke'ʃən] befestning, befestningskunst.

fortify ['få·ᵊtifai] styrke, forsterke, befeste.

fortitude ['få·ᵊtitjud] kraft; mot; sjelsstyrke.

fortnight ['få·ᵊtnait] fjorten dager; **every** — hver fjortende dag; **this day** — fjorten dager i dag; i dag for fjorten dager siden. **fortnightly** fjortendags; hver fjortende dag.

fortress ['få·ᵊtris] festning.

fortuitous [få·ᵊ'tju·itəs] tilfeldig, slumpe-.

fortunate ['få·ᵊtʃənėt] lykkelig; heldig. **fortunately** lykkeligvis.

fortune ['få·ᵊtʃən] skjebne, lagnad, lodd; lykke; formue; medgift; godt parti; **by** — tilfeldigvis; **soldier of** — lykkejeger; **tell a person's** —, **tell -s** spå; **he had made his** — han hadde gjort seg en formue; **a man of** — en formuende mann; **the tide of** — **has set in again** tingene har tatt en gunstig vending igjen.

Fortune ['få·ᵊtju·n] Fortuna (lykkegudinnen).

fortune|-book ['få·ᵊtʃənbuk] spåbok. **-hunter** lykkejeger. **-teller** spåmann, spåkone.

forty ['få·ᵊti] førti, førr; **take** — **winks** ta seg en liten blund; **the forties** førtiårene.

forum ['få·ᵊrəm] forum.

forward ['få·ᵊwəd] (adv.) fram, fremad, videre; **be** — være i gjære; **look** — to vente, glede seg til; **put** — sette fram; **put oneself** — stikke (holde) seg fram; **straight** — like ut; **from this time** — fra nå av; **carried** — overført; transport.

forward ['få·ᵊwəd] (adj.) forrest; langt kommet; tidlig moden; fremmelig, for seg; vel utviklet; imøtekommende, ivrig; overilet, kåt, nesevis; kjekk; uforskammet. **a** — **order** en ordre til framtidig (senere) levering.

forward ['få·ᵊwəd] (subst.) forward, løper, spiller i løperrekken (i fotball).

forward ['få·ᵊwəd] (verbum) sende, befordre, ekspedere; fremme, framskynde; begunstige, oppmuntre; — **on** sende videre; **letter to be -ed** brevet sendes etter.

forwarder ['få·ᵊwədə] sender; speditør.

forwarding ['få·ᵊwədin] også: spedisjons-. — **agent** speditør. — **clerk** ekspeditør.

forwardness ['få·ᵊwədnės] beredvillighet; iver; nesevishet; dristighet.

forwards ['få·ᵊwədz] fremad osv. se **forward**.

fosse [fås] grav (mil.).

fossil ['fåsil] oppgravd, funnet i jorda, fossil; forsteinet; fossil; forsteining. **fossiliferous** [fåsi-'lifərəs] som inneholder fossiler. **fossilification** [fåsilifi'ke'ʃən] forsteining. **fossilize** ['fåsilaiz] forsteine; (fig.) stivne; størkne; forsteines.

foster ['fåstə] fostre, oppfostre, oppføde, ale opp; nære, pleie, begunstige. **fosterage** ['fåstəridʒ] oppfostring,

foster|-brother fosterbror. — **-child** pleiebarn. **fosterer** ['fåstərə] pleiefar, pleiemor. **foster-mother** fostermor; rugemaskin.

fother ['fåðə] **a leak** stoppe en lekk.

fother ['fåðə] fôr (se **fodder**); lass (især av bly, kalk osv.).

fought [få·t] imperf. og perf. pts. av **fight**.

foul [faul] uren, skitten, stygg, fæl, vond, ubehagelig, motbydelig; skadelig; dårlig, rusket (om vær); mot (om vind); stinkende; mudret; fordervet; full av ting som ikke bør være der; full av ugras (om hage), full av sot (om skorstein) o. l.; i uorden (om mage); farlig (om kyst); innviklet, i uorden; ulovlig; som strir mot reglene; uriktig, uærlig, falsk; slett, ond; ryggesløs, rå; sårende, uanstendig (om ord); søle, grise til, besudle; plumre; bringe i uorden; innvikle; hindre; bli skitten el. gjørmet; bli innviklet; — **air** dårlig luft; — **breath** dårlig ånde; — **copy** kladd; — **disease** venerisk sykdom; **the** — **fiend** den onde, djevelen; — **language** stygt snakk, råprat; — **pipe** sur pipe; — **play** uærlig spill; — **sky** overskyet himmel; — **weeds** ugras; **fall** — **of** ryke uklar med; **run** — **of** seile på (mot).

foul-mouthed ['faul'mauðd] grov (i munnen), plump, rå.

foulness ['faulnės] urenslighet, skitt; heslighet; uredelighet.

foul-spoken ['faul'spoᵘkən] kynisk i sin tale, rå, grov.

foumart ['fu·ma·ᵊt] ilder, mår.

found [faund] imperf. og perf. pts. av **find**; **50 pounds a year and everything found** 50 pund om året og alt fritt.

found [faund] grunnlegge; grunne; stifte; bygge; innrette, fastsette; stole (**on** på).

found [faund] støpe, smelte, bre.

foundation [faun'de'ʃən] grunnlegging, fundamentering; grunn, fundament; oppretting, stifting; dotasjon; stipendium; anstalt, stiftelse; **be on a** — ha et stipendium; — **school** legatskole; — **stone** grunnstein.

foundationer [faun'de'ʃənə] stipendiat; frielev.

founder ['faundə] grunnlegger, stifter.

founder ['faundə] støper.

founder ['faundə] synke, gå til bunns; ramle ned; være uheldig, mislykkes.

founder ['faundə] skamri, gjøre halt; dette, snåve.

foundry ['faund(ə)ri] støperi.

foundling ['faundlin] hittebarn.

foundress ['faundrės] kvinnelig stifter, grunnlegger.

fount [faunt] kilde, vell, oppkomme.

fountain ['fauntin] kilde; oppkomme; fontene, springvann; (fig.) opphav, opprinnelse. — **head** kildevell; opprinnelse; første opphav. — **-pen** fyllepenn.

four [få·ᵊ] fire; firetall; **fours** båter med fire årer, færing; **by fours** fire og fire; **on all fours** på alle fire; **four-and-twenty** fire og tjue; **a coach and four** firspann, firbeite; **well-matched four** firspann som passer godt sammen.

four|-cornered firkantet. **-fold** firefold, firedobbelt. — **-handed** firemanns-; firhendig (i musikk). **-in-hand** med fire hester; firspann; firbeite; — **-legged** firbeint. — **-poster** himmelseng. — **-score** fire snes, åtti.

foursome ['få·ᵊsəm] fire og fire, spill mellom to par (i golf).

fourteen ['få·ᵊ'ti·n] fjorten.

fourteenth ['få·ᵊ'ti·nþ] fjortende; fjortendedel.

fourth [få·ᵊþ] fjerde; fjerdedel, kvart; fjerdemann; **the** — **estate** fjerdestanden; pressen.

fourthly ['få·ᵊbli] for det fjerde.

fourwheeler ['få·ᵊ'wi·lə] firehjulsvogn.

fowl [faul] fugl; fugler; høns, fjærkre; fange fugl; skyte fugl. **fowler** ['faulə] fuglefenger.

fowling-piece ['faulinpi·s] fuglebørse.

fowl-run ['faulrʌn] hønsegård,

fox [fåks] rev; (fig.) rev, fuling, slu person; spionere; (i slang) snyte; **he-fox** hanrev; **she -fox** hunrev. **arctic fox, blue fox, polar fox** blårev, polarrev. **fox and geese** revespill. — **-brush** revehale. — **-earth** revehule, revehi — **-evil** en sykdom som ytrer seg ved at hårene faller av; røyting, håravfall. — **-glove** revebjelle. — **-hound** revehund; **master of -hounds** den som forestår revejakten, formann for revejakten. — **-hunt** revejakt; gå på revejakt. **-like** reveaktig. — **-sleep** lensmannssøvn, høneblund, tilsynelatende uoppmerksomhet. — **-tail** revehale. — **-terrier** foksterrier. — **-trap** revefelle. — **-trot** foxtrot, navn på en dans.

foxy ['fåksi] reveaktig, reve-; snedig, lumsk; rødlig, rødbrun; rødhåret; ramtluktende; sur.

foyeı ['foie¹] foyer.

Fr. fk. f. **French.**

fr. fk. f. **francs.**

fracas ['fräka¹] ståk, styr, trette.

fraction ['fräkʃən] brudd; bruddstykke; brøk.

fractional ['fräkʃənəl] brøk-, brudden.

fractious ['fräkʃəs] sær, prippen, vanskelig.

fracture ['fräkt(ə] brudd; brekke.

fragile ['frädzail] skjør; skrøpelig.

fragility [frə'dʒiliti] skjørhet, skrøpelighet.

fragment ['frägmənt] fragment, bruddstykke.

fragmental [fräg'mentəl] bruddstykkeaktig.

fragmentary ['frägməntəri] fragmentarisk.

fragrance ['fre¹grəns] duft, vellukt, ange.

fragrant ['fre¹grənt] duftende, velluktende.

frail [fre¹l] svak, skrøpelig, skral, klekk, kløkk.

frail [fre¹l] sivkorg; korg med fiken, rosiner o. l.; siv.

frailty ['fre¹lti] skrøpelighet.

frame [fre¹m] form, skıkkelse; legeme, kropp; bygning; tilstand; ramme, karm; innretning. system; skjelett, bjelkeverk, bındingsverk, spant; danne; bygge; sette sammen, passe til; ramme inn, innrette, lage; tenke ut, utkaste, oppfinne; passe, stemme; — **well** love godt, peke godt i vei. — **an estimate** gjøre et overslag; — **of an umbrella** paraplystell; — **of mind** sinnsstemning; **out of** — i uorden; upasselig; forstemt. — **-built** bindingsverks-.

frame|-house bindingsverkshus. — **-saw** rammesag.

framework ['fre¹mwə·k] indre bygning, bindingsverk, skjelett.

framing ['fre¹miη] bygning; formnıng; avfattelse; form; ramme, rammeverk.

franc [fräηk] franc (fransk mynt).

France [fra·ns] Frankrike.

Frances ['fra·nsis, -siz] Frances, Franciska.

franchise ['fräntʃaiz, -iz] frihet, rettighet, privilegium; fribrev; valgrett; stemmerett; fristed, asyl; frigjøre.

Francis ['fra·nsis] Frans, Franciskus.

Franciscan [frän'siskən] fransiskaner (munk); fransiskansk.

Franco-German ['fräηkoᵘ'dʒə·mən] fransk-tysk.

Franconia [fräη'koᵘnjə] Franken.

frangibility [frändʒi'biliti] skrøpelighet.

frangible ['frändʒibl] skrøpelig, skjør.

frangipane ['frändʒipe¹n] sjasminparfyme; slags bakverk.

frangipanni [frändʒi'päni] sjasminparfyme.

Frank [fräηk] franker; Frank (navn).

frank [fräηk] oppriktig, åpen, åpenhjertig, frimodig; utvetydig, utvilsom; sende portofritt; frankere; frita; frankert brev; — **ignorance** åpenbar uvitenhet; — **poverty** usminket fattigdom.

Frankfort ['fräηkfət] Frankfurt; **F. on the Main** Frankfurt am Main.

frankincense ['fräηkinsens] virak, røykelse.

Frankish ['fräηkiʃ] frankisk.

Franklin ['fräηklin] Franklin.

franklin ['fräηklin] jordeier av fri men ikke adelig byrd.

frankly ['fräηkli] oppriktig, åpent.

frankness ['fräηknés] oppriktighet, åpenhet.

frantic ['fräntik] avsindig, vanvittig, rasende.

frantically ['fräntikəli] avsindig, vanvittig.

F. R. A. S. fk. f. **Fellow of the Royal Astron. Soc.**

Frascati [frä'ska·ti] Frascati.

fraternal [frə'tə·nəl] broderlig, bror-. **fraternity** [frə'tə·niti] brorskap; brorfølelse, brorkjensle. **fraternization** [frätə·nai'ze¹ʃən] broderlighet, broderlig forhold; brorskap. **fraternize** ['frätə·naiz] omgås som brødre, fraternisere; ha broderlige følelser.

fratricidal ['frätrisaidl] brodermorderisk, brormorder-. **fratricide** ['frätrisaid] brormord; brormorder.

fraud [frå·d] svik, bedrageri; bedragær, svindler; **this wine is a perfect** — denne vinen er det rene juks.

fraudulence ['frå·djuləns] svik, svikferd.

fraudulent ['frå·djulənt] svikaktig.

fraught [frå·t] fraktet, ladet, lastet; vel forsynt, fylt, svanger **(with** med); — **with danger** faretruende.

fray [fre¹] gni; gnure; slite tynn; tafse opp; gni seg; flosse; slagsmål; oppløp; kamp; tynnslitt sted, frynse (av slit).

F. R. C. O. fk. f. **Fellow of the Royal College of Organists.**

F. R. C. P. fk. f. **Fellow of the Royal College of Physicians.**

F. R. C. S. fk. f. **Fellow of the Royal College of Surgeons.**

freak [fri·k] grille, lune, innfall; strek.

freakish ['fri·kiʃ] lunefull, lunet.

freckle ['frekl] fregne; gjøre (el. bli) fregnet.

freckly ['frekli] fregnet; flekket.

Fred [fred] fk. f. **Frederick.**

Freddie ['fredi] Rikke. **Freddy** ['fredi] lille Frits.

Frederic(k) ['fredrik] Fredrik.

free [fri·] fri; uavhengig, selvstendig, ledig; utvungen, tvangfri; oppriktig, åpen; dristig, djerv, hensynsløs, uforskammet; tøylesløs; uanstendig; offentlig, tilgjengelig for alle; gratis; tollfri; skattefri; gavmild, høymodig, raust; befri, frigjøre. gjøre fri; — **fight** slagsmål som alle tilstedeværende tar del i; **give one** (el. **have) a** — **hand** gi en (el. ha) frie hender (til å handle etter skjønn); — **thought** fri tanke; — **will** fri vilje; **have the** — **run of a house** kunne gå som en vil i et hus; **he is** — **to do it** han har lov til å gjøre det; **make** — **with a thing** skalte og valte med noe; sette noe på spill; blande seg i noe; **make** — **with a person** tillate seg friheter mot en; **se;** — befri, løslate; **be** — snakke like ut av posent **be** — **and easy** gjøre seg det makelig; — **church** kirke hvor man ikke betaler noe for stolene; — **library** offentlig bibliotek; — **on board** (forkortet til f. o. b. el. **F. O. B.**) levert fritt ombord; **make a person** — **of a city** gi en borgerrett.

free-and-easy ['fri·ən(d)i·zi] flott, usjenert; gemyttlig sammenkomst, klubbaften o. l.

freeboard ['fri·bå·ᵈd] fribord.

free|booter ['fri·bu·tə]fribytter, sjørøver, viking. **-booting** [-bu·tiη] fribytteri.

freedom ['fri·dəm] frihet, fridom, rettighet, forrettighet, privilegium; utvungenhet; for stor fortrolighet; djervskap, dristighet, hensynsløshet; letthet, ferdighet; (merk.) livlighet (på markedet); — **of the press** pressefrihet; — **of a city** borgerrett; **take out one's** — få borgerrett.

free|hand ['fri·händ]: **in** — på frihånd. — **-handed** rundhåndet, gavmild, raust. — **-hearted** åpenhjertig; edelmodig, gavmild. **-hold** selveiendom, selveiergård. **-holder** selveier. — **-lance** (i middelalderen) leiesoldat; (i moderne politikk) løsgjenger.

freely ['fri·li] fritt; åpent; beredvillig, gavmildt; ivrig, livlig; rikelig; **live too** — leve for flott.

free|man ['fri·mən] fri mann; borger; lagsmann. **-mason** ['fri·me¹sən] frimurer. **-masonry** frimureri. — **-minded** sorgfri. — **-spoken** fri i sin tale, djervmælt. **-stone** kvaderstein. **-thinker** fritenker. **-thinking** fritenkersk; fritenkeri. — **-trade** frihandel. — **-trader** frihandelsmann (motstander av tollbeskyttelse); frihandler (en som handler utenom handelskompaniene).
free-wheel ['fri·wi·l] frihjul.
freeze [fri·z] fryse; størkne, stivne av kulde; være iskald, bli iskald; fryse i hjel; få til å fryse; drepe ved kulde.
freezer ['fri·zə] fryseapparat, ismaskin.
freezing iskald; frysning. — **-point** frysepunkt.
freight [fre¹t] frakt; ladning, last, gods; fraktpenger; frakttransport; frakte. **freightage** ['fre¹-tidʒ] frakt. **freighter** ['fre¹tə] befrakter; lastebåt. **freight-train** (amr.) godstog.
French [frenʃ, frentʃ] fransk; **the** — franskmennene; **know** — kunne fransk; — **brandy** konjakk; — **disease** el. **gout·syfilis;** — **horn** valdhorn; **take** — **leave** forsvinne i stillhet fra et selskap; stikke av uten å betale sin gjeld; — **plums** katrineplommer; — **polish** møbelpolitur; — **red** rød sminke; — **roll** langt franskbrød; — **roof** mansardtak; — **vinegar** vineddik; — **wheat** bokhvete; — **window** glassdør.
frenchify ['fren(t)ʃifai] forfranske, gjøre fransk, danne etter fransk mønster.
Frenchman ['fren(t)ʃmən] franskmann.
Frenchwoman ['fren(t)ʃwumən] fransk kvinne.
Frenchy ['fren(t)ʃi] franskmann (spøkefullt el. ironisk); overdreven fransk i sitt ytre, smak, stil.
frenzied ['frenzid] fra vettet, avsindig, gal.
frenzy ['frenzi] vanvidd, raseri, vettløst sinne.
frequenzy ['fri·kwənsi] hyppighet, frekvens.
frequent ['fri·kwənt] hyppig.
frequent [fri'kwent] besøke hyppig, søke, frekventere; — **a café** være stamgjest på en kafé.
frequentation [fri·kwən'te¹ʃən] hyppig besøk.
frequentative [fri'kwentətiv] frekventativ.
frequenter [fri'kwentə] hyppig gjest.
frequently [fri'kwəntli] hyppig, ofte.
fresco ['freskoᵘ], maling på våt kalk, freskomaleri; **paint in** — (el. **al** —) male al fresco. **fresco** male al fresco.
fresh [freʃ] frisk; sval; sprek, sunn, ny, blomstrende, ungdommelig, «grønn»; nybakt; livlig; forfrisket, usaltet (om kjøtt, smør osv.); fersk (om vann); uerfaren; anløpen, beruset; kjekk, kåt; påtrengende; friskt, kjølig; for kort tid siden; bekk, kilde; oversvømmelse, høyvanne; **as** — **as a daisy, as** — **as paint** så blomstrende som en rose.
freshen ['freʃən] gjøre frisk, stramme opp; gjøre fersk; utvanne; bli frisk, bli fersk.
fresher ['freʃə] nybakt student, russ.
freshet ['freʃit] flom, overstrømning.
freshly ['freʃli] frisk; — **painted** nymalt.
freshman ['freʃmən] nybakt student, russ.
freshwater ['freʃwå·tə] ferskvann.
fret [fret] ete opp, tære på, gnure, gnage på; gni i stykker, kruse; sette i sterk bevegelse; ergre, krenke, såre, gjøre sint; gjøre bekymret, gjøre urolig; bli tært på, bli slitt på; ete om seg; ete seg inn i, trenge seg inn i; kruse seg; ergre seg; være sint; være bekymret; klynke; sutre; krote ut; gnidning, gnuring, eting; et såret sted; utslett; ornament à la grecque; krusning; oppbrusing; sutring, grin, ergrelse, vrede, heftighet, lidenskapelighet; — **for lengte** utålmodig etter; — **and fume** skumme av raseri. **fretting** irritabel.
fret [fret] bånd på gripebrett på gitar.
fretful ['fretf(u)l] ergerlig, sær, gretten, irritabel.
fretfulness ['fretf(ə)lnés] grettenhet, pirrelighet.
fret-saw ['fretså·] lauvsag, stikksag; dekupørsag. **-ing** lauvsagarbeid.
fretty ['freti] gretten, grinet, sutret, vanskelig.

fretwork ['fretwɑ·k] lauvsagarbeid, utskåret arbeid, à la grecque (-arbeid).
Freudian ['froidiən] som angår Freud og hans verk; disippel av Freud; psykoanalytiker.
F. R. G. S. fk. f. **Fellow of the Royal Geographical Society.**
friability [fraiə'biliti] sprøhet, skjørhet.
friable ['fraiəbl] løs, sprø, skjør.
friar ['fraiə] klosterbror, srl. munk.
friary ['fraiəri] munkekloster.
F. R. I. B. A. fk. f. **Fellow of the Royal Institute of British Architects.**
fribble ['fribl] fjase; fjaset, vaset; narr; laps.
fricandeau ['frikəndoᵘ] fricandeau.
fricassee [frikə'si·] fricassé.
friction ['frikʃən] gnidning, gnuring, stryking, friksjon; frottering. **frictional** ['frikʃənəl] gnidnings-, friksjons-.
Friday ['fraidi, 'fraide¹] fredag; **Black** — Tycho Brahes dag; **Good** — langfredag; — **face** bededagsansikt.
fried [fraid] imperf. og perf. pts. av **fry.**
friend [frend] venn, venninne; **friends** venner venninner; nærmeste, familie; bekjent, kjenninger; **the Friends, the Society of F.** kvekerne; a **friend of mine** en venn av meg; **a** — **of my father's** en venn av min far; **he is no** -— **to me** han er ikke vennligsinnet imot meg; **be -s with** være gode venner med; **have a** — **at court** ha bispen til morbror; **keep good -s with** holde seg gode venner med; **make a** — **of** gjøre til venn, slutte vennskap med; **make -s** bli (være) gode venner igjen, forlike seg; **lady** — venninne; **my honourable** — det ærede medlem (om et annet medlem av underhuset); **my learned** — min kollega (om en annen sakfører).
friendless ['frendlis] venneløs.
friendliness ['frendlinès] vennskapelighet; godhet. **friendly** ['frendli] vennskapelig; god; hjelpsom; gunstig. **the Friendly Islands** Vennskapsøyene.
friendship ['fren(d)ʃip] vennskap.
frieze [fri·z] fris, vadmel.
frieze [fri·z] frise.
frigate ['frigit] fregatt.
fright [frait] skrekk, støkk, frykt; skremmebilde, skremsel; skremme; **he looks a perfect** — han ser fæl ut.
frighten ['fraitn] støkke, skremme.
frightful ['fraitf(u)l] skrekkelig.
frigid ['fridʒid] kald, iskald; **the** — **zone** den kalde sone. **frigidity** [fri'dʒiditi] kulde.
frigorific [frigo'rifik] som frambringer kulde; svalende.
frill [fril] kruset el. rynket strimmel, pipestrimmel; krage; kalvekryss; mansjett; rynke, pipe; **put on -s** gjøre seg viktig. **frilling** strimler osv., rynket strimmel el. blonde.
fringe [frin(d)ʒ] frynse, pannehår, lugg; kant, rand; besette med frynser. **fringy** ['frin(d)ʒi] frynset.
frippery ['fripəri] ordstas, kruseduller, tom stas.
'Frisco ['friskoᵘ] fk. f. **San Francisco.**
Frisian ['friʒən, -zjən] frisisk; friser.
frisk [frisk] springe, sprette, bykse, hoppe; sprett, hopp.
frisky ['friski] spretten, lystig, kåt, sprek.
frit [frit] glassmasse; glasur (ved pottemakeri); gløde, smelte.
frith [friþ] fjord, vik.
fritter ['frita] epleskive; fjase, somle bort; — **away** ødsle bort litt etter litt, klatte bort.
frivol ['frivl] tøve, fjase. **frivolity** [fri'væliti] ubetydelighet, verdiløshet; frivolitet, lettsindighet, lettferdighet. **frivolous** ['frivələs] betydningsløs, verdiløs; overfladisk, intetsigende; frivol, lettsindig, lettferdig. **frivolousness** av **frivolity.**
friz [friz] krølle, kruse; krøll, krus.
frizzle ['frizl] krølle, kruse; krøll; steke, brase.

frizzly ['frizli] kruset.

fro [frouˈ]: **to and** — fram og tilbake, att og fram.

frock [fråk] bluse, kittel; blusekjole, barnekjole; damekjole; diplomatfrakk.

frockcoat el. frock-coat ['fråk'kouˈt] diplomatfrakk.

frog [fråg] frosk; kvast; knapp; kråke (i hestehov). — -eater (hånlig om) franskmann. -ged snorebesatt.

froggy ['frågi] froskaktig; franskmann.

frog-in-the-throat håshet.

froise [froiz] fleskepannekake.

frolic ['frålik] lystighet, spøk; være lystig, holde leven, skjemte; (poetisk) lystig. frolicked imperf. av frolic. frolicking ['frålikiŋ] lystig. frolicsome ['fråliksəm] lystig.

from [fråm, frəm] fra, ut fra; på grunn av, av; å dømme etter, etter; — **above** ovenfra; — **behind** bakfra; — **beneath** nedenfra; **conclude** — slutte av; **draw** — **nature** tegne etter naturen; — **a child**, — **childhood** fra barndommen av; — **home** ikke hjemme, bortreist; **safe** — sikker mot; **defend** — forsvare mot; **hide** — skjule for; **absent** — illnes fraværende på grunn av sykdom; **cry** — **pain** skrike av smerte; — **his dress I should think** å dømme etter hans drakt skulle jeg tro; **he stepped** — **behind the tree** han trådte fram fra treet som han hadde stått bak; **the thief came** — **under the bed where he had been lying** tyven kom fram under senga, hvor han hadde ligget.

frond [frånd] bregneblad, burkneblad.

frondescence [från'desəns] lauvsprett.

Frondeur [fr.; från'dəˑ] opposisjonsmann.

front [frʌnt] panne, ansikt; frekkhet, djervskap, uforskammethet; forside; fasade; front, forreste rekke, viktigste plass, krigsskueplass; forstykke i skjorte; løst skjortebryst, krage; falskt pannehår; forrest, front-; gjøre front mot; vende fasaden mot, vende, snu; pryde med fasade; **change** — foreta en frontforandring; **show a bold** — sette opp en dristig mine; **have the** — **to say** ha den uforskammethet å si; **the** — **bench** den forreste benk (i underhuset ministerbenken); **a two-pair** — et gateværelse i tredje etasje. — **door** gatedør; — **gate** hovedport; — **hall** forstue, entré; — **parlour** stue ut til gata; — **rank** første rekke; — **room** værelse til gata; — **tooth** fortann; **in** — i fronten, foran; **in** — of foran; **bring to the** — bringe fram i første rekke; **come to the** — komme fram i første rekke; **go to the** — gå til fronten.

frontage ['frʌntidʒ] forside, fasade; forhage.

frontal ['frʌntəl] panne-; fasade-; front-; pannebånd; omslag på panne eller hode; antemensale.

frontier ['frʌntiə, 'fråntiə, 'frʌntʃə] grense.

frontispiece ['frʌntispiˑs] vignett.

frontless ['frʌntlès] uforskammet.

frontlet ['frʌntlèt] pannebånd.

frost [frå(·)st] frost; tele; rim; skuffelse, fiasko; skade ved frost; brodder (hestesko); dekke med rim; strø sukker på; gjøre matt (f. eks. glass); **white** —, **hoar** —, rimfrost; **black** — barfrost (uten rim). **Jack Frost** personifikasjon av frosten.

frost|-bitten frosset; skamfrosset.—-bound frosset fast, innefrosset; telet. frostiness iskulde, frost.

frost|-nail isbrudd. — -nipped frostskadd.

frosty ['frå(·)sti] frossen, frost-; kald; dekt med rim; — face kopparret ansikt.

froth ['frå(·)þ] fråde, skum; få til å skumme; skumme. frothiness ['frå(·)binès] skumming; ubetydelighet. frothy ['frå(·)þi] skummende; tom, intetsigende.

Froude [fruˑd] Froude.

frou-frou ['fruˑfruˑ] rasling (av kjole).

frow [frau] (hollandsk el. tysk) kvinne.

froward ['frouˈ(w)əd] gjenstridig, vrang.

frown [fraun] rynke pannen (el. brynene), sette nyver; se mørk ut; — **upon** el. **at** se truende på;

skremme med truende blikk. **frown** rynking av pannen; rynket panne; mørk mine, truende blikk. **frowningly** med rynket panne; med truende blikk; sint.

frowzy ['frauzi] stinkende, ekkel; lurvet, pjusket.

froze [frouˈz] imperf. av **freeze**.

frozen ['frouˈzn] perf. pts. av **freeze**; — **ocean** ishav; — **zone** kald sone.

F. R. S. fk. f. **Fellow of the Royal Society**.

fructiferous [frʌk'tifərəs] frukt-, som bærer frukt. fructification [frʌktifiˈkeˈʃən] befruktning; befruktningsorganer; frukt. fructify ['frʌktifai] befrukte; gjøde, gjødsle; bære frukt.

frugal ['fruˈgəl] måteholden, sparsommelig, økonomisk; tarvelig, nøysom.

frugality [fruˈgäliti] sparsommelighet, god økonomi; tarvelighet, nøysomhet.

frugivorous [fruˈdʒivərəs] fruktetende.

fruit [fruˈt] frukt, grøde; trefrukt; bær; følge, resultat; avkom; bære frukt; **forbidden** — forbuden frukt; **small fruits** bær. — -**grower** [-groˈə] fruktdyrker.

fruitage ['fruˈtidʒ] frukt.

fruiter ['fruˈtə] fruktbåt; frukttre.

fruiterer ['fruˈtərə] frukthandler.

fruitery ['fruˈtəri] frukt.

fruitful ['fruˈtf(u)l] fruktbar. fruitfulness ['fruˈtf(u)lnès] fruktbarhet.

fruition [fruˈiʃən] nyting, bruk.

fruitless ['fruˈtlès] ufruktbar; barnløs; fruktesløs; gagnløs.

fruit-show ['fruˈtʃouˈ] fruktutstilling.

fruit-stand ['fruˈtständ] fruktvase.

fruit-tree ['fruˈt-triˑ] frukttre.

fruity ['fruˈti] fruktaktig; med fruktsmak.

frumentaceous [frumən'teˈʃəs] kornaktig, korn-.

frumenty ['fruˈmənti] risvelling; grynsodd, grynsuppe.

frump [frʌmp] gammel (gammeldags) kjerring, hurpe. -y ['frʌmpi] gammeldags.

frustrate ['frʌ'streˈt, 'frʌstreˈt] krysse el. tilintetgjøre (planer); komme på tverke for; gjøre ugyldig; skuffe, narre.

frustration [frʌ'streˈʃən] tilintetgjøring, skuffelse.

frustum ['frʌstəm] bruddstykke, stump.

frutescent [fruˈtesənt] buskaktig.

fruticose ['fruˈtikoˈˈs] buskaktig, busk-.

fry [frai] steike, steike i panne; bli stekt, brase; stekt mat; **fried eggs** speilegg.

fry [frai] fiskyngel; flokk, stim; småunger.

frying-pan ['fraiiŋpän] stekepanne; **fall out of** the — into the fire komme fra asken i ilden.

F. S. fk. f. **Fleet Surgeon**.

F. S. A. fk. f. **Fellow of the Society of Antiquaries**.

ft. fk. f. **feet, foot**.

fubby ['fʌbi], fubsy ['fʌbzi] tykk, buttet.

fuchsia ['fjuˈʃ(j)ə] fuksia, Kristi blodsdråpe.

fuchsine ['fuˈksin] rødt anilinfargestoff.

fuddle ['fʌdl] gjøre beruset, drikke full; rangle, ture, svire, pimpe; drikkevarer, fyll, beruselse, rangel.

fudge [fʌdʒ] løgn, sludder, vanvidd, humbug; dessert av sjokolade; smøre sammen, dikte opp.

fuel ['fjuˈəl] ved, brensel; lidenskap; forsyne med brensel; **add** — **to the fire** gyte olje i ilden.

fug [fʌg] mugg, muggenhet, boss.

fugacious [fjuˈgeˈʃəs] flyktig, kortvarig, forgjengelig.

fugacity [fjuˈgäsiti] flyktighet, forgjengelighet.

fugitive ['fjuˈdʒitiv] flyktig; upålitelig; (om farge) uekte; flytende; flyktning; rømling.

fugleman ['fjuˈglmän] fører, leder.

fugue [fjuˈg] fuga.

fulcrum ['fʌlkrəm] støtte; dreiningspunkt; vågmat.

fulfil [ful'fil] oppfylle, fullbringe, fullbyrde; — a promise holde et løfte.

fulfilment [ful'filmənt] oppfyllelse, fullbyrding.
fulgency ['fʌldʒənsi] glans, skinn.
fulgent ['fʌldʒənt] glansfull, strålende.
fulguration [fʌlgju're'ʃən] glimt, lyn.
Fulham ['fuləm] eller — palace, biskopen av Londons residens.
fuliginous [fju'lidʒinəs] sotet; røykaktig; mørk.
full [ful] 1. adj. full (of av), oppfylt (of av), hel, fullstendig, uinnskrenket, fyldig; 2. adv. helt, fullstendig, fullt; like; 3. subst. fullstendighet, helhet; eksempler: 1. — of water full av vann; — house opptatt; we are — her er opptatt; his mind was — han var overveldet; — of business overlesst med forretninger; — of his subject helt opptatt av sitt emne; of — age myndig; a — beard fullskjegg; — brothers and sisters helsøsken; — dress galla; at — length i hele sin lengde; a — hour en hel time; — stop punktum; — in the face med et fyldig ansikt; — up opptatt; — moon fullmåne; a — meal et rikelig måltid; — speed full fart; 2. look one — in the face se en like i ansiktet; — back back (i fotball); 3. in — fullstendig, fullt ut; to the — i fullt mål, fullstendig; name in — fulle navn; the moon is in the — månen er full.
full [ful] valke, stampe; la seg valke el. stampe.
fullage ['fulidʒ] valkelønn.
full-aged ['fule'dʒd] myndig.
full|-blooded ['ful'blʌdid] blodfull; fullblods.
-blown helt utsprunget; fullblods. — -bodied svær.
— -bottom allongeparykk. — -bred fullblods. —
-built svær. — -dress selskapsdrakt, galla. —
-dressed fullt påkledd; i selskapsdrakt, i galla.
fuller ['fulə] valker, stamper; fuller's earth valkejord.
fullery ['fuləri] valkeri, stampeverk, stampe.
full-face ['fulfe's] en face; (typograf.) fet skrift.
— -faced ['fulfe'st] med rundt, fyldig ansikt.
fulling ['fuliŋ] valking, stamping.
full|-length i legemsstørrelse; et bilde i legemsstørrelse. — -moon fullmåne.
fullness ['fulnis] fylle, fullhet; the — of time tidens fylle.
full|-rigged fullrigget. — -sized i legemsstørrelse. — -swing fritt løp, fritt spillerom.
fully ['fuli] fullt, fullstendig, helt, ganske; utførlig.
fulmar ['fulma·ə] havhest.
fulminate ['fʌlmine't] lyne og tordne; dundre; skjelle; eksplodere; la eksplodere; slynge bannstråle imot; knallsalt; fulminating cap fenghette; fulminating cotton skytebomull.
fulmination [fʌlmi'ne'ʃən] lyn og torden, dundring, smell; bannstråle.
fulness ['fulnés] se fullness.
fulsome ['fulsəm] motbydelig, vammel. fulsomeness ['fulsəmnés] motbydelighet.
Fulton ['fultən] Fulton.
fulvous ['fʌlvəs] gulbrun.
fumatory ['fjumətəri] jordrøyk (plante).
fumble ['fʌmbl] famle, rote, trivle (for etter); leike (with med), tukle, fikle (with ved); stamme; finne ved å famle omkring; ta kluntet på, krølle; — -fisted kluntet.
fume [fju·m] røyk, os, eim; virak; damp, dunst, tev, ange; lidenskapelighet, sinne, vrede; innbilning, hjernespinn; ryke; dampe, ose; rase, skumme, fnyse; røyke; farge mørk; be in a — være oppbrakt; fykende sint; fumed oak mørkt eiketre; — away fordampe, fordunste.
fumet ['fju·mét] viltlukt; lort, møkk.
fumigate ['fju·mige't] røyke; desinfisere ved røyk; parfymere. fumigation [fju·mi'ge'ʃən] røyking; damp, røyk.
fumitory ['fju·mitəri] jordrøyk (plante).
fun [fʌn] moro, spøk, gammen, ap; skjemte, drive ap; for —, in — for spøk; like — flott; the — of the fair vitsen med det; I do not see the — of it (også:) jeg skjønner ikke vitsen med

det; have good — more seg godt; make — of a person, poke — at a person ha en til beste, drive ap med en; there is not much — to be got out of him han forstår ikke spøk.
funambulate [fju'nämbjule't] danse på line.
funambulation [fju'nämbju'le'ʃən] linedans.
funambulist [fju'nämbjulist] linedanser.
function ['fʌnkʃən] funksjon, virksomhet, bestilling, gjøremål, yrke; fest; festmåltid; (mat.) funksjon; fungere. functional [-əl] funksjons-, embetsmessig. functionary [-əri] funksjonær.
fund [fʌnd] fond, kapital; sette i statsobligasjoner. funds statspapirer, obligasjoner; have money in the funds ha penger i statsobligasjoner; be in funds være pr. kasse.
fundament ['fʌndəmənt] bakdel, ende, sess.
fundamental [fʌndə'mentəl] fundamental, grunn-; grunnlag, grunntrekk.
fund-holder ['fʌndhoᵘldə] eier av statspapirer.
Funen ['fju·nən] Fyn.
funeral ['fju·nərəl] begravelse, jordfesting, likferd; begravelses-, lik-, sørge-; — expenses begravelsesomkostninger; — march sørgemarsj; — sermon liktale.
funereal [fju'niəriəl] begravelses-; trist, sørgelig.
fungi ['fʌndʒai] pl. av fungus.
fungous ['fʌngəs] soppaktig.
fungus ['fʌngəs] (pl.: fungi el. funguses) sopp; skyte opp som sopp.
funicle ['fju·nikl] tråd, streng.
funicular [fju'nikjulə] trådaktig; snor, streng-; — railway taubane, fjellbane.
funk [fʌnk] støkk, kvekk, skrekk; feighet; kryster; reddhare; være redd, kvekke; be in a blue — være livende redd; — out trekke seg feigt tilbake, stikke av. funkify ['fʌŋkifai] gjøre redd.
funky ['fʌŋki] redd, blaut, stakkarslig.
funnel ['fʌnil] trakt; røykkappe; skorstein (på dampskip og lokomotiv).
funniment ['fʌnimənt] morsomhet.
funning ['fʌniŋ] spøk, skjemt; gale streker.
funny ['fʌni] morsom, pussig; the — gentleman komikeren; klovnen (på teater og i sirkus).
funny ['fʌni] liten båt, skjekte, snekke.
funny-bone ['fʌniboᵘn] albuknoke, albuspiss.
fur [fə·] pels, skinnfell; pelsverk; pelsvilt; dun (f. eks. på fersken); vinstein; belegg på tunga; kjelestein; skinn-, pelsverk-; fore med skinn, bedekke, belegge.
furbelow ['fə·biloᵘ] garnering, kappe på kjole; sette garnering på.
furbish ['fə·biʃ] blankskure; polere. furbisher polerer.
fur-cap ['fə·kăp] pelslue.
furcate ['fə·két], furcated ['fə·ke'tid] kløftet, greinet, gaffeldelt.
furcation [fə·'ke'ʃən] gaffelform, forgreining.
fur-coat ['fə·koᵘt] pels, pelskåpe.
furious ['fjuəriəs] rasende. furiousness raseri.
furl [fə·l] beslå (seil); rulle sammen, lukke (paraply, vifte).
furlong ['fə·lăŋ] (veimål, 201,166 meter, ca. ⅛ engelsk mil).
furlough ['fə·loᵘ] orlov, permisjon; gi orlov.
furnace ['fə·nés] ovn, masovn, smelteovn; ildsted.
furnish ['fə·niʃ] forsyne, ruste ut; møblere, utstyre; levere, skaffe, yte; -ed apartments møblerte værelser. furnisher leverandør.
furniture ['fə·nitʃə] møbler, møblement; utstyr; tilbehør; a piece of — et møbel; much — mange møbler; her mental — hennes åndelige innhold. — -remover flyttemann.
furore [fu'a·ré] furore; make a — gjøre furore.
furrier ['fʌriə] buntmaker. furriery ['fʌriəri] pelsverk; pelsverkhandel, buntmakerforretning.
furrow ['fʌroᵘ] får, plogfår, fure; fure. furrowy ['fʌro'i] furet.
furry ['fə·ri] pelskledd; skinnkledd; pels-, pelsverk; belagt (om tunge).

further ['fə·ðə] fje:nere, lenger borte; videre, ytterligere, nærmere, mer; **I may — mention** jeg kan enn videre nevne; **nothing — ikke mer; what —?** hva så mer?; **demand a — explanation** forlange en nærmere forklaring; **wish a man — ønske en mann dit pepperen gror; I'll see you — first** det kunne aldri falle meg inn.
further ['fə·ðə] fremme, befordre.
furtherance ['fə·ðərəns] fremme, befordring.
furtherer ['fə·ðərə] en som fremmer.
furthermore ['fə·ðəmå·ə] dessuten, ennvidere.
furthermost ['fə·ðəmoᵘst] fjernest, lengst borte.
furthest ['fə·ðist] fjernest; lengst.
furtive ['fə·tiv] stjålen, hemmelig.
furuncle ['fjuərʌŋkl] byll, kong, kveise.
fury ['fjuəri] raseri; furie; **paroxysms of mad — anfall** av vilt raseri.
furze [fə·z] tornblad.
fuscous ['fʌskəs] mørk; brun.
fuse [fju·z] smelte; brannrør; lunte.
fusee [fju·zi·] spindel; lunte, brannrør; storm-fyrstikk (til å tenne sigarett i blåst).
fusel ['fju·zəl]; **— oil** fusel.
fusibility [fju·zi'biliti] smeltelighet.
fusible ['fju·zibl] smeltelig.
fusileer, fusilier [fju·zi'liə] musketér; grenader.
fusillade [fju·zi'le'd] geværsalve; skyte ned.
fusion ['fju·ʒən] smelting; flytende tilstand; sammensmelting; fusjon.
fuss [fʌs] larm, ståk, bråk, mas, blest, krus; ståhei, oppstuss, vesen; forvirring; ha det travelt, vimse omkring; gjøre store opphevelser, gjøre

mye vesen; **— and fret** skumme og rase; **make — of** gjøre krus for.
fussy ['fʌsi] maset; stundesløs; geskjeftig; opp-kavet, hesblesende; brysom.
fust [fʌst] søyleskaft.
fustian ['fʌstjən] sterkt bomullstøy; (fig.) bom-bast, svulst; bombastisk, svulstig.
fustic ['fʌstik] gult brasilietre.
fustigation [fʌsti'ge'ʃən] pryl.
fustiness ['fʌstinès] muggenhet, skimlethet.
fusty ['fʌsti] muggen, myglet, stinkende.
fut. fk. f. **future.**
futile ['fju·tail] intetsigende; unyttig, verdiløs; gagnløs; fåfengt.
futility [fju'tiliti] unyttighet, gagnløshet.
future ['fju·tʃə] framtidig, tilkommende; fram-tid, futurum; **— tense** futurum; **— perfect (tense)** futurum eksaktum; **— prospects** framtidsutsikter; **in (the) —** i framtiden; **for the —** for framtiden.
futurism ['fju·tʃərizm] futurisme. **futurist** ['fju·tʃərist] futurist.
futurity [fju'tʃuᵊriti, -tʃu-] framtid; framtidig begivenhet; kommende tilstand.
fuz [fʌz] dun; støv, gyv; krøllhår; røyksopp. **— -ball** røyksopp.
fuze [fju·z] brannrør.
fuzz se **fuz.**
fuzzy ['fʌzi] dunet, loet.
fylfot ['filfåt] hakekors.
fy [fai] fy!
F. Z. S. fk. f. **Fellow of the Zoological Society.**

G

G [dʒi·] g; g (i musikk); **— sharp** giss; **— flat** gess; **— major** g-dur; **— minor** g-moll; **— clef** g-nøkkelen, fiolin-nøkkelen.
G., g. fk. f. **genitive; George; German; God; Gospel; gram(me); guide.**
Ga. fk. f. **Georgia.**
G. A. fk. f. **general assembly.**
gab [gäb] snakk, sludder; **he has got the gift of the —** han har et godt snakketøy.
gabardine ['gäbədi·n] kaftan, talar; gabardin.
gabble ['gäbl] sludre, plapre; skvalder, plapring; skravlebøtte.
gabbler ['gäblə] skravlebøtte.
gaberdine se **gabardine.**
gaberlunzie [gäbə'lʌnzi] (skotsk) ligger.
gabion ['ge'bjən] skansekorg.
gable ['ge'bl] gavl. **gabled** ['ge'bld] forsynt med gavl; **a — roof** tak med gavl mot gata.
gablet ['ge'blèt] liten gavl.
Gabriel ['ge'briəl] Gabriel.
gaby ['ge'bi] fjols, idiot, dåsemikkel.
Gad [gäd] Gud (slang for: **God**).
gad [gäd] meisel, bergsjern, skarp metallspiss; brodd; piggstav; bremse, klegg; drive omkring, reke; vokse her og der. **— about** farte om; **be on the —** drive omkring.
gadabout ['gädəbaut] flyfille, dagdriver.
gadfly ['gädflai] bremse, blinding; klegg.
gadget ['gädʒit] innretning, greie.
gadzooks ['gädzuks] å du gode Gud!
Gael [ge'l] gæler; gælisk.
Gaelic ['ge'lik] gælisk.
gaff [gäf] kjeks, klepp, lyster; (mar.) gaffel; kjekse, kleppe, lystre.
gaff [gäf] gjøglerbu; kneipe; **blow the — (up)on** angi, forråde.
gaffer ['gäfə] gamling, gamlen; arbeidsformann, bas.
gag [gäg] kneble, målbinde; lyve; improvisere; legge ord inn i rollen sin.
gag [gäg] knebel; munnkorg, muleband, kve-

lende munnfull; løgn, skrøne, improvisert til-føyelse til en rolle.
gage [ge'dʒ] mål (se **gauge**).
gage [ge'dʒ] pant; trygd, sikkerhet; hanske; utfordring.
gage [ge'dʒ] slags plomme, se **greengage.**
gagger ['gägə] bedrager; en skuespiller som dikter til i rollen sin.
gaglaw munnkorglov.
gaiety ['ge'(i)ti] munterhet, lystighet; pynt.
gaily ['ge'li] muntert, lystig; prektig.
gain [ge'n] gevinst, vinning; fordel, nytte; profitt; overskudd; vinne; tjene, fortjene; få, oppnå; forskaffe; dra seg (om ur); bli rik, vokse, tilta; bli bedre; **make -s** vinne; **clear —** netto-inntekt; **— the day** vinne seier; **we had -ed our point** vi hadde nådd vårt mål, vi hadde opp-nådd vår hensikt; **— ground** vinne terreng; **the ocean -s on the land** havet skyller landet bort; **— over** vinne for sitt parti; **— strength** komme til krefter; **— upon** vinne inn på, få makt over.
gain [ge'n] tapphull; sinkehull.
gainful ['ge'nf(u)l] fordelaktig; lønnsom.
gainings ['ge'ninz] vinning; profitt.
gainsay [ge'n'se'] motsi. **gainsayer** motsier.
Gainsborough ['ge'nzb(ə)rə] Gainsborough.
'gainst [genst, ge'nst] fk. f. **against.**
gairish ['gæ·ᵊriʃ] se **garish.**
gait [ge't] gang, måte å bevege seg på; gang-lag; holdning.
gaiter ['ge'tə] gamasje; forsyne med gamasjer.
gal [gäl] (vulg. for **girl**) tøs.
gala ['ge'lə] festlighet. **— -dress** galla.
galactic [gə'läktik] melke-; melkeveis-.
galactometer [gälək'tåmitə] melkeprøver.
galantine ['gälənti·n] kaldt kjøtt i sjelé.
galanty-show [gə'läntiʃoᵘ] skyggebilder.
galaxy ['gäləksi] melkevei; strålende forsam-ling.
gale [ge'l] pors (en plante).
gale [ge'l] blåst, kuling, storm.

galeate(d) ['gälie¹t(id)] hjelmformet.
galena [gə'li·nə] blyglans.
Galicia [gə'liʃ(i)a] Galicia.
Galician [gə'liʃən] galisier.
Galilean [gäli'li·ən] galileisk; galileer.
Galilee ['gälili·] Galilea.
Galilei [gäli'le¹i] Galilei.
galimatias [gäli'me¹ʃəs] galimatias, tull, vrøvl.
galiot ['gäliät] galiot (et lite enmastet skip).
galipot ['gälipät] furuharpiks.
gall [gå·l] galle; bitterhet, hat, ilske.
gall [gå·l] galleple.
gall [gå·l] gni huden av, gnage, skrubbe, gjøre hudløs; skade; såre; ergre, forbitre; plage, sjenere; gnagsår, gnag.
gallant ['gälənt] kjekk, djerv, tapper; edelmodig, høymodig, ridderlig; prektig, glimrende.
gallant [gə'länt] galant; galan; gjøre kur til; ledsage som kavalér. **gallantly** ['gäləntli] tappert osv. **gallantly** [gə'läntli] galant. **gallantry** ['gäləntri] kjekkhet, tapperhet; edelmodighet, høysinn, ridderlighet; galanteri; lefleri.
galleas ['gäliäs] galei.
galleon ['gäliän] galleon (spansk krigsskip).
gallerian [gə'liəriən] galeislave.
gallery ['gäləri] galleri; søylehall; korridor; billedgalleri; **in the** — på galleriet; **play to the** — spille for galleriet, jage etter mengdens bifall.
galley ['gäli] galei; kabyss; skip (i trykkeri).
galley-slave ['gälisle¹v] galeislave.
galliard ['gäljəd] lystig; lystig fyr; slags dans.
gallic ['gälik] galleple; — **acid** gallussyre.
Gallic ['gälik] gallisk. **Gallican** ['gälikən] gallikansk; gallikaner. **gallice** ['gälisi·] på fransk. **gallicism** ['gälisizm] gallisisme. **gallicize** ['gälisaiz] forfranske.
galligaskins [gäli'gäskinz] slags benklær.
gallimaufrey [gäli'må·fri] miskmask, røre, rot.
gallinaceous [gäli'ne¹ʃəs] hønse-.
gall-insect ['gå·linsekt] gallveps.
gallipot ['gälipät] apotekerkrukke.
gallivant [gäli'vänt] fjase; drive omkring, slenge.
gall-louse ['gå·llaus] bladlus.
gall-nut ['gå·lnʌt] galleple.
gallomania [gälo'me¹njə] gallomani. **gallomaniac** [gälo'me¹njək] galloman.
gallon ['gälən] gallon (= 4,544 liter; i Amerika 3,785 liter).
galloon [gə'lu·n] galon, tresse, snor. **-ed** [ge-'lu·nd] galonert.
gallop ['gäləp] galoppere; få til å galoppere; galopp.
gallopade [gälo'pe¹d] galoppade.
gallophobe ['gälofo⁰b] franskhater. **gallophobia** [gälo'fo⁰bjə] hat til alt fransk.
gallow-grass ['gälogra·s] hamp (med hentydning til galgen).
gallows ['gälo⁰z] galge.
gallows|bird ['gälo⁰z-] galgenfugl. **-face** galgenfjes.
gallows-poor lutfattig.
gall-sickness ['gå·lsiknés] gallefeber.
gall-stone ['gå·lsto⁰n] gallestein.
gally ['gäli] galei (typ.); kabyss (se **galley**).
gally ['gäli] skremme.
galop ['gäləp] galopp (dansen); danse galopp.
galore [gə'lå·⁹] mengde, overflod; i massevis, fullt opp, flust.
galosh [gə'låʃ] kalosje.
galumph [gə'lʌmf] (av gallop triumphant) briske seg, kjekke seg.
Galvani [gäl'va·ni] Galvani.
galvanic [gäl'vänik] galvanisk; — **battery** galvanisk batteri; — **belt** giktbelte; — **induction** galvanisk induksjon; — **pile** voltasøyle.
galvanization [gälväni'ze¹ʃən] galvanisering.
galvanism ['gälvənizm] galvanisme. **galvanize** ['gälvənaiz] galvanisere.
galvanometer [gälvə'nåmitə] galvanometer.
gam [gäm] (amr.) forsamles; avlegge besøk; flokk, forsamling; besøk.

gambado [gäm'be¹do⁰] tverrbyks, hopp, sprett, kast.
gambit ['gämbit] gambit (i sjakk).
gamble ['gämbl] spille, spille høyt, spille hasard; — **with dice** spille terning; — **in stocks** spekulere i aksjer; — **away** spille bort.
gambler ['gämblə] spiller; falskspiller.
gambling ['gämblin] høyt spill; hasard. — **hell**, — **house** spillebule.
gamboge [gäm'bu·ʒ] gummigutt (tørret saft av et østasiatisk tre).
gambol ['gämbəl] sprett, byks, kast, hopp; hoppe.
gambrel ['gämbrəl] has (på en hest); krok, som man henger slakt på.
game [ge¹m] spill, lek, leik, morskap, spøk; spill (med kort); kampleik; måte å spille på; vinning, fordel; de stikk eller poeng som hører til for å vinne et spill; plan, hensikt; intrige, knep; jakt; vilt; tyveri (i tyvespråk); motig, bestemt; dyktig; halt; spille; **a** — **at** (el. of) **chess** et parti sjakk; **a** — **of billiards** et parti biljard; — **of chance** hasardspill; **round** — selskapsleik, selskapsspill; **make** — **of** gjøre narr av; **play the** — spille etter reglene, opptre hederlig; **give up el. throw up the** — oppgi partiet; **the** — **is not worth the candle** det er ikke umaken verd; **he is playing a losing** — han er i en fortvilt situasjon; **two can play at that** — jeg vil gjerne ha et ord med i lage; **I know his** — jeg gjennomskuer ham; **what** — **is he after?** hva har han i sinne? **he is up to every** — han kjenner alle knep; **winged** — vilt fjærkre; **a** — **old gentleman** en motig gammel mann; **he's** — **for anything** han er rede til alt; **are you** — **for a shilling** tør De våge en shilling; **die** — ikke gi seg, holde ørene stive; **the** — **is up** spillet er tapt.
game|-bag jakttaske. — **-cock** kamphane.
gamekeeper ['ge¹mki·pə] skogfut.
game-law ['ge¹mlå·] jaktlov.
gamesome ['ge¹msəm] lystig, munter, kåt.
gamester ['ge¹mstə] spiller.
gaming ['ge¹miŋ] hasardspill. **-house** spillehus.
gammer ['gämə] gammel kone; gamla, mor.
gammon ['gämən] juks, fanteri, luring, humbug; lure, skrøne.
gammon ['gämən] røykeskinke; salte og røyke skinke.
gammoner ['gämənə] svindler.
gamp [gämp] paraply (etter Mrs. Gamp i Martin Chuzzlewit av Dickens).
gamut ['gämət] skala; omfang.
gamy ['ge¹mi] viltrik; som smaker av vilt.
gander [gä'ändə] gasse; fe; **what's good** (el. sauce) **for the goose is good** (el. sauce) **for the** — det som gjelder for én, bør gjelde for en annen.
gander-faced ['gändəfe¹st] med et dumt fjes.
gang [gäŋ] bande; hop; avdeling, skift, gjeng; sett; — **of thieves** tyvebande; — **of workmen** arbeidslag.
gang [gäŋ] (skotsk) gå; — **agley** gå galt.
gang-board ['gänbå·⁹d] (smal) landgang.
ganger ['gänə] arbeidsformann, bas.
Ganges ['gändʒi·z] Ganges.
ganglion ['gäŋgliən] ganglie, nerveknute.
ganglionic [gäŋgli'änik] nerveknute-.
gangrene ['gäŋgri·n] koldbrann; angripe med koldbrann, gå over til koldbrann. **gangrenous** ['gäŋgrinəs] angrepet av koldbrann, gangrenøs.
gangster ['gäŋstə] gangster, medlem av en forbryterbande.
gangway ['gäŋwe¹] landgang; gang mellom stolrekker; tverrgang (mellom benkene i underhuset); **members below the** — uavhengige medlemmer (av underhuset).
ganja ['gändʒə] hampplante.
gantlet se **gauntlet**.
Ganymede ['gänimi·d] Ganymedes; oppvarter.
gaol [dʒe¹l] fengsel; fengsle. **gaolbird** ['dʒe¹lbə·d] fange. **gaoler** ['dʒe¹lə] fangevokter.

gap [gäp] åpning, gap, spalte; kløft, skar, hakk, avbrytelse; bresje; åpne.
gape [ge'p] gape, gjespe, glo med åpen munn, måpe; gaping, gjesp, måping; — **after** el. **at** glo på; — **for** el. **on** sikle etter.
gar [ga·ə] horngjel, nebbesild.
garage [gä'ra·ʒ, 'gäridʒ] garasje.
garb [ga·əb] drakt, kledning; mote, snitt; ytre.
garbage ['ga·əbidʒ] slo; kjøkkenavfall.
garble ['ga·əbl] forvanske, forkludre. **garbler** ['ga·əblə] forfalsker.
garden ['ga·ədn] hage; gjøre hagearbeid, drive gartneri; **back** — hage bak huset; **front** — forhage; — **city** hageby.
garden-engine ['ga·ədnendʒin] hagesprøyte.
gardener ['ga·ədnə] gartner.
garden-frame drivbenk, drivkasse.
garden-hose hageslange. — **-house** lysthus.
gardening ['ga·ədnin] hagearbeid; gartneri.
garden-party ['ga·ədnpa·əti] selskap, som holdes i det fri, hageselskap.
garden-stand blomsterstativ.
garden-stuff hagevekster.
garfish ['ga·əfiʃ] se **gar**.
gargarism ['ga·əgərizm] gurglevann.
gargantuan [ga·'gäntjuən] svær, uhorvelig stor.
gargle ['ga·əgl] gurgle; gurglevann.
gargoyle ['ga·əgoil] tut på takrenne.
Garibaldi [gäri'bäldi] Garibaldi; garibaldibluse.
garish ['gæ·əriʃ] påfallende, skrytende, skrikende, grell.
garland ['ga·ələnd] krans; kranse.
garlic ['ga·əlik] hvitløk.
garment ['ga·əmənt] klesplagg; kledebon.
garn [ga·ən] for pokker!
garner ['ga·ənə] kornloft; magasin; samle inn.
garnet ['ga·ənit] granat (edelstein).
garnish ['ga·əniʃ] smykke, pryde; garnere, besette; forsyne; beslå; stevne; legge beslag på; prydelse; garnering; lenker; drikkepenger. **garnishment** [-mənt] garnering, prydelse.
garniture ['ga·ənitʃə] garnityr; pynt, pryd.
gar-pike ['ga·əpaik] horngjel.
garran ['gärən] liten skotsk hest.
garret ['gärit] kvistværelse.
garrison ['gärisən] garnison besetning; legge garnison, besette; ligge som garnison.
garrotte [gə'råt] kvelning, garottering; kvele, garottere. **garrotter** [gə'råtə] garottør.
garrulity [gä'ruliti] snakkesalighet.
garrulous ['gäruləs] snakkesalig.
garter ['ga·ətə] strømpebånd; binde med strømpebånd; gjøre til ridder av hosebåndsordenen; (mar.; **-s** jern, lenker; **the Order of the Garter** hosebåndsordenen (Englands høyeste ridderorden); **Knight of the Garter** ridder av hosebåndsordenen.
garth [ga·əþ] hage, hegn, gård.
gas [gäs] gass; dumt, unyttig snakk; kyt; svi med gass; gassforgifte, gasslegge, innbille en noe; skvadronere; **turn on the great amount of** — **about something** si mye unødvendig sludder om noe; **give one** — skjelle en ut; pryle en; **lay on the** — legge en gassledning, legge inn gass; **turn on (off) the** — åpne (lukke) for gassen; **turn down (up) the** — skru gassen ned (opp).
gas-bag ['gäsbäg] gassbeholder; vrøvler; (hånlig) luftskip.
gas-bracket ['gäsbräkit] gassarm.
gasburner gassbrenner.
Gascon ['gäskən] gaskogner; storskryter; gaskognisk.
gasconade [gäskə'ne·d] skryt, skryte.
Gascony ['gäskəni] Gascogne.
gaselier [gäsə'liə] gasskrone.
gas-engine gassmotor.
gaseous ['ge·ziəs, 'gäsiəs] gassaktig.
gas|-fitter ['gäsfitə] gassarbeider; gassmester; gassrørlegger. — **-flue** gassrør.— **-furnace** gassovn.— **-gauge** gass- trykkmåler. — **-governor** gassregulator.
gash [gäʃ] flenge, gapende sår; flenge.

gas-helmet ['gäshelmit] gasshjelm (gassmaske).
gasification [gäsifi'ke'ʃən] gassutvikling.
gasify ['gäsifai] omdanne til gass.
gas-jet ['gäsdʒet] gassbluss.
Gaskell ['gäskəl] Gaskell.
gasket ['gäskit] beslagseising.
gas|-lamp gasslampe. — **-lantern** gasslykt. — **-light** gassbelysning; gassblus. — **-lighter** lyktetenner. — **-main** gasshovedrør. — **-manager** gassverksdirektør.
gas-mask ['gäsma·sk] gassmaske.
gas-meter ['gäsmi·tə] gassmåler.
gasolene ['gäsoli·n], **gasoline** [-li(·)n] gassolin, (am.) bensin.
gasometer [gä'såmitə] gassbeholder.
gasp [ga·sp] puste tungt, stønne, snappe etter været; hikste; stønn, tungt åndedrag; — **for breath** snappe etter luft; — **for life** ligge på det aller siste; **may I** — **my last, if** . . . jeg vil dø på at . . .; **to the last** — til det siste åndedrett.
gaspipe ['gäspaip] gassrør.
gas-stove ['gäs'sto"v] slags gassovn til oppvarming av værelse.
gassy ['gäsi] gassaktig; snakkesalig.
gastric ['gästrik] gastrisk, mage-; — **fever** gastrisk feber; — **juice** magesaft.
gastriloquist [gä'strilokwist] buktaler.
gastritis [gä'straitis] magekatarr.
gastronomer [gä'strånomə] gastronom. **gastronomic(al)** [gästro'nåmik(l)] gastronomisk. **gastronomy** [gä'strånəmi] gastronomi.
gastrotomy [gä'strätomi] magesnitt.
gas-works ['gäswə·ks] gassverk.
gate [ge't] port, led, grind; trang gjennomgang; veg, vei, inngang; entré, adgang; forsyne med port; gi stuearrest, nekte utgangstillatelse; **free** — gratis adgang; **Golden Gate** innløp i San Franciskobukta; **the Iron Gates of the Danube** Jernporten, pass ved Donau; **Gate of Tears** Bab-el-Mandeb.
gate|-house portnerhus; portstue; vokterhus (ved jernbaneoverskjæringer). — **-keeper** portvakt; banevokter. — **-money** entré. — **-post** portstolpe; **between you and me and the** — strengt fortrolig. — **-way** porthvelving, port.
gather ['gäðə] samle, sanke, samle inn; høste; plukke; velge ut; oppdynge; slutte, oppfatte, oppfange, forstå; forsamle; samle seg, samles; vokse; flyte sterkere; trekke sammen; rynke, snurpe sammen; modnes (om byll); — **breath** få pusten igjen; — **dust** bli støvet; sluke støv; — **flesh** bli tykk; — **ground upon one** innhente en, få forsprang for en; — **information** innhente opplysninger; — **in debts** innkassere gjeld; — **up one's crumbs** komme til krefter; — **in the grain** kjøre inn kornet; **the clouds are -ing** det trekker opp (med skyer).
gatherer ['gäðərə] en som samler, plukker osv.
gathering ['gäðərin] samling; forsamling; høst; kollekt; svull, byll.
Gatling ['gätlin] slags maskingevær.
gauche [go"ʃ] keitet, klosset.
gaucho ['gautʃo"] gaucho; europeisk-indiansk gjeter.
gaud [gå·d] stas, flitter.
gaudiness ['gä·dines] prakt, flitterstas.
gaudy ['gä·di] prunkende, utmaiet; fest, lag, gilde. — **-night** festaften.
gauffer ['gå(·)fə] se **goffer**.
gauge [ge'dʒ] mål, måleredskap; strekmål; strekmål; sporvidde; måle, måle innholdet av et fat. **gauger** ['ge'dʒə] måler, aksisebetjent.
Gaul [gå·l] Gallia; galler, (for spøk) franskmann; gallisk kvinne. **Gaulish** ['gå·liʃ] gallisk.
gaunt [gå·nt] mager, skrinn; uttært; slank.
gauntlet ['gå·ntlet] stridshanske; hanske; halvhanske; forbinding om hånden; spissrot; **throw down the** — kaste sin hanske (utfordre); **take up the** — ta hansken opp (motta utfordringen); **run the** — løpe spissrot.

gaur ['gauə] gaurokse.
gauze [gå·z] gas; moe, varmedis.
gauzy ['gå·zi] gasaktig.
gave [ge¹v] imperf. av **give**.
gavel ['gävəl] dirigent(klubbe).
gavial ['ge¹vjəl] gavial (art krokodille).
gavotte [gə'våt] gavotte (en dans).
Gawain ['gäwe¹n] Gawain.
gawk [gå·k] kloss, dåsemikkel, staur. **gawky**
['gå·ki] klosset; kloss.
gay [ge¹] livlig, munter, lystig; prangende, strålende, broket; pyntet; levelysten; utsvevende.
gayety ['ge¹(i)ti] se **gaiety. gayly** se **gaily.**
gaze [ge¹z] stirre, glo, se stivt (**at** på); stirring; stand **at** — stå som fortapt.
gazelle [gə'zel] gasell.
gazette [gə'zet] kunngjørelsestidende, lysingsblad, offisiell tidende; bekjentgjøre, kunngjøre, lyse. **be -d** stå i avisen som utnevnt.
gazetteer [gäzi'tiə] geografisk leksikon.
gazing-stock ['ge¹ziŋståk] noen eller noe som man ser på med nysgjerrighet eller avsky.
gazogene ['gäzodʒi·n] apparat til å lage kullsyreholdig vann.
G. B. fk. f. Great Britain.
G. B. E. fk. f. Knight Grand Cross of the Order of the British Empire.
G. C. B. fk. f. Grand Cross of the Bath.
G. C. F. fk. f. greatest common factor.
G. C. I. E. fk. f. Grand Commander of the Order of the Indian Empire.
G. C. M. fk. f. greatest common measure.
G. C. R. fk. f. Great Central Railway.
gear [giə] stoff, plagg, tøy; utstyr; pynt; apparat; tilbehør, greier; kledning; kjøkkentøy, seletøy; (i Skottland) formue, gods; krigsutrustning; gir, utveksling (på sykkel); spenne for; forsyne med drivverk; sette i gang; gripe inn i (om tannhjul); **be in** — være i gang; **throw into** — sette i gang; **out of** — i ustand; i uorden; **travelling** — reisegods.
gearing ['giəriŋ] inngrep, inngripning; utveksling (på sykkel). **gear-wheel** drivhjul, tannhjul.
gecco, gecko ['geko⁰] gekko, slags firfisle.
gee [dʒi·] hypp (til hesten), til høyre.
gee-gee ['dʒi·dʒi·] fole, ptroa (i barnespråk).
geese [gi·s] gjess, flertall av **goose.**
gee-up ['dʒi·'ʌp] hypp (til hest).
Gehenna [gi'hennə] Gehenna.
geisha ['ge¹ʃə] geisha.
gelatinate [dʒě'lätine¹t] gjøre til sjelatin; bli til sjelatin. **gelatine** ['dʒelətin] sjelatin. **gelatinize** [dʒě'lätinaiz] se **gelatinate.**
geld [geld] gjelde, skjære, kastrere.
gelding ['geldiŋ] kastrering, gjelding, gjelk.
gelid ['dʒelid] iskald.
gelidity [dʒě'liditi] iskulde.
gelt [gelt] imperf. og perf. pts. av **geld.**
gem [dʒem] edelstein; pryde med edelsteiner.
gemel ['dʒeməl] tvilling-.
geminate ['dʒeminét] par-, tvilling-.
Gemini ['dʒeminai] Tvillingene (stjernebildet); **oh, gemini!** Herre Jemini.
geminous ['dʒeminəs] dobbelt, parret.
gemma ['dʒemə] knopp (på trær).
gemmaceous [dʒě'me¹ʃəs] knoppaktig.
gemmate(d) [dʒě'me¹t(id)] prydd med edelsteiner, juvélbesatt.
gemmation [dʒě'me¹ʃən] knoppskytning.
gemmeous ['dʒemiəs] edelsteinaktig.
gemmiferous [dʒě'mifərəs] knoppskytende.
gemmiparous [dʒě'mipərəs] knoppskytende.
gemmy ['dʒemi] edelsteinaktig; strålende.
Gen. fk. f. General.
gen. fk. f. general; genitive.
gendarm ['ʒa·nda·°m] gendarm, politisoldat.
gender [dʒendə] kjønn (grammatisk).
genealogic(al) [dʒenə·¹lådʒik(l), dʒi·-] genealogisk. **genealogist** [dʒeni'älədʒist, dʒi·-] genealog. **genealogy** [dʒeni'älədʒi, dʒi·-] genealogi; avstamning; stamtavle.

genera ['dʒenərə] slekter; flertall av **genus.**
general ['dʒen(ə)rəl] almen, alminnelig, vanlig; sams; framherskende, rådende; general-, hoved-; over-; vag, ubestemt, svevende. — **appearance** det hele ytre; — **assembly** generalforsamling; (amr.) lovgivende forsamling; — **bookseller** sortimentsbokhandler; — **cargo** stykkgodsladning; — **cook** kokkepike som forstår seg på både alminnelig og fin matlaging; — **court** lovgivende forsamling; — **dealer** kremmer; — **direction** hovedretning; — **effect** totalvirkning; — **goods** stykkgods; — **hospital** alminnelig sykehus; — **invitation** innbydelse en gang for alle; **lieutenant-general** generalløytnant; **major-general** generalmajor; — **manager** generaldirektør; — **meeting** generalforsamling; — **post office** hovedpostkontor; — **practitioner** praktiserende læge (ikke spesialist); **the** — **public** det store publikum; — **readers** alminnelige lesere; — **servant** enepike; **speak in a** — **way** tale så løselig.
general ['dʒen(ə)rəl] hele; general, feltherre; generalmarsj; enepike; anføre, lede; **in** — i alminnelighet.
generalissimo [dʒenərə'lisimo⁰] generalissimus, øverstbefalende.
generality [dʒenə'räliti] alminnelighet; hele; største del, storpart, største tall; flertall; generalitet; generalstab; **the** — **of people** folk i alminnelighet; **the** — **of readers** alminnelige lesere.
generalization [dʒenəräl(a)i'ze¹ʃən] alminneliggjøring, generalisering; induksjon; (sl.) frase. **generalize** ['dʒen(ə)rəlaiz] generalisere, alminneliggjøre.
generally ['dʒen(e)rəli] i alminnelighet; i det hele tatt; hyppig; — **speaking** i det hele tatt.
generalship ['dʒen(ə)rəlʃip] generalsverdighet; feltherretalent; behendighet, list.
generate ['dʒenəre¹t] avle, ale fram, frambringe, utvikle; **generating station** kraftstasjon.
generation [dʒenə're¹ʃən] avl; frambringelse, utvikling; avkom, ætt, ættlegg, generasjon, slektledd, ættledd.
generative ['dʒenərətiv] avle-; fruktbar; — **organs** forplantningsorganer. **generator** ['dʒenəre¹tə] avler; generator, damputvikler.
generic [dʒi'nerik] slekts-; — **name** slektsnavn. **generically** med et felles navn.
generosity [dʒenə'råsiti] edelmodighet, høysinn; gavmildhet.
generous ['dʒenərəs] edelmodig, gjev, høysinnet; gavmild; raust; motig, kjekk; åndrik; sterk, kraftig (om vin); — **diet** rikelig ernæring.
Genesaret(h) [gě'nesəret] Genesaret.
genesis ['dʒenisis] skapelse, opphav, tilblivelse; tilblivelseshistorie; **genesis** (1. mosebok).
genet [dʒenit] genette (slags katt).
genetic [dʒě'netik] tilblivelses-, opphavs-.
Geneva [dʒi'ni·və] Genf, Genève. — **Convention** Genferkonvensjonen; the — **Cross** det røde kors.
geneva [dʒi'ni·və] sjenever.
Genevan [dzi'ni·vən] genfer; genfisk.
Genevese [dʒenə'vi·z] genfer; genfisk.
genial ['dʒi·njəl] mild, lun; godslig, gemyttlig.
geniality [dʒi·ni'äliti] mildhet; gemyttlighet.
genie ['dʒi·ni] ånd; fylgje, vette.
genii ['dʒi·njai] genier, skytsånder (flertall av **genius**).
genitals ['dʒenitlz] genitalia.
genitive [dʒenitiv]: **the** —, **the** — **case** genitiv.
genius ['dʒi·njəs] genius, fylgje, vette, skytsånd (flertall: **genii**); geni; talent (flertall: **geniuses**); — **loci** skytsånd; **a man of** — en genial mann; **the** — **of a language** et språks ånd; **the** — **of the times** tidens ånd.
Genoa ['dʒenoə] Genua.
Genoese [dʒeno'i·z] genuesisk; genueser.
gent [dʒent] fk. f. **gentleman.**
genteel [dʒen'ti·l] fin.
gentian ['dʒenʃən] søte (en plante.)

gentile ['dʒentail] hedensk; hedning; — **noun** folkenavn.

gentility [dʒen'tiliti] fornemhet, finhet.

gentle ['dʒentl] maddik.

gentle ['dʒentl] fornem; fin, yndefull; vennlig, blid; gunstig sinnet; lett virkende (medisin); svak, jevn (om skråning); saktmodig; nennsom; blid, sakte, dempet (om musikk); a — **breeze** en lett bris; **the — passion** kjærligheten; **the — reader** den gunstige leser; **the — sex** det svake kjønn.

gentle ['dʒentl] formilde; berolige (en hest).

gentlefolk(s) fornemme, fine folk. **gentle-hearted** godhjertet.

gentleman ['dʒentlmən], flertall: **gentlemen** ['dʒentlmən] fornem mann, fin herre, dannet mann, mann av ære, gentleman, kavalér; mann; trumfkonge (i kortspill); **the old** — den onde, fanden; **the old — helps his own** fanden hjelper sine; **be born a** — være av god familie; **the first — of Europe** et tilnavn som ble gitt kong Georg IV.; **there is nothing of the — about him** han eier ikke folkeskikk; **independent** — rentier; **private** — privatmann; **attendant** oppvartende kavalér; **single** — ungkar; — **commoner** student av høyere rang; — **dog** hanhund; — **farmer** proprietær; — **jockey** amatørveddeløpsrytter; — **player** (el. **rider**) amatørspiller (-rytter); **gentlemen's boots** herrestøvler; **gentlemen's companion** lus; **gentlemen's lavatory** toalett for menn; **a gentleman's piece** et tynt delikat stykke; **gentlemen's walk** (el. **toilet**) toalett for menn! **(place for) gentlemen!** for menn! **gentleman in velvet** moldvarp; **gentleman of the gown** jurist; **gentleman of the green baize** bordefanger; **gentleman's gentleman** kammertjener; **gentleman of the bedchamber** kammerjunker.

gentlemanlike ['dʒentlmənlaik] fin, dannet.

gentlemanliness ['dʒentlmənlinés] fint vesen.

gentlemanly ['dʒentlmənli] fin, dannet.

gentleness ['dʒentlnés] blidhet, mildhet.

gentlewoman ['dʒentlwumən] fin dame, dannet dame; kammerfrue; — **of the Queen** hoffdame.

gentry ['dʒentri] storfolk (de fineste etter nobility); (spottende) fine folk, folk.

genuflect ['dʒenjuflekt] bøye kne. **genuflection** [dʒenju'flekʃən] knebøyning, knefall.

genuine ['dʒenjuin] ekte, uforfalsket; virkelig.

genuineness ekthet, uforfalskethet.

genus ['dʒi·nəs] slekt, pl. **genera**.

geocentric [dʒi·o'sentrik] geosentrisk.

geodesic [dʒi·o"'desik] geodetisk. **geodesy** [dʒi'ǎdisi] geodesi, landmåling. **geoditic** [dʒio'detik] geodetisk. **geodetics** geodesi.

Geoffrey ['dʒefri] Gottfred.

geog. fk. f. **geography; geographer**.

geognost ['dʒi·ǎgnåst] geognost. **geognostic** [dʒi·åg'nåstik] geognostisk. **geognosy** [dʒi'ǎgnosi] geognosi, læren om formingen av jordskorpa.

geogonic [dʒi·o'gånik] geogonisk. **geogony** [dʒi·'ǎgəni] geogoni, læren om jordens dannelse.

geographer [dʒi'ǎgrəfə] geograf. **geographical** [dʒi·o'gräfikl] geografisk. **geography** [dʒi'ǎgrəfi] geografi.

geol. fk. f. **geology**.

geologic(al) [dʒi·o'lådʒik(l)] geologisk. **geologist** [dʒi'ålədʒist] geolog. **geology** [dʒi'ålədʒi] geologi.

geom. fk. f. **geometry**.

geometer [dʒi'ǎmitə] geometer, matematiker; måler (insekt).

geometric(al) [dʒio'metrik(l)] geometrisk; — **drawing** geometrisk tegning, projeksjonstegning.

geometrician [dʒiǎmə'triʃən] se **geometer**.

geometry [dʒi'ǎmitri] geometri.

Geordie ['dʒǎ·ədi] diminutiv av **George**.

geordie ['dʒǎ·ədi] sikkerhetslampe; kullgruvearbeider; kullskip; guinea (mynten).

George [dʒǎ·ədʒ] Georg; bilde av St. Georg

til hest, som hosebåndsridderne bærer; **the four Georges** de fire engelske konger Georg; **St.** — St. Georg, Englands skytspatron.

Georgia ['dʒǎ·dʒə] Georgia.

Georgian ['dʒǎ·ədʒən] georgisk (om et folk i Kaukasus); georgier; som hører til Georgenes tid.

Georgie ['dʒǎ·ədʒi] diminutiv av **George** el. **Georgina**.

Georgina [dʒǎ·ə'dʒi·nə] Georgine, Jørgine.

G. E. R. fk. f. **Great Eastern Railway**.

Gerald ['dʒerəld] Gerald, Gerhard.

geranium [dʒi're'njəm] geranium.

Gerard ['dʒerəd, -a·əd] Gerard.

gerfalcon ['dʒə·få·lkən] jaktfalk.

germ [dʒə·m] kim, spire.

german ['dʒə·mən] nærskyldt; **cousin** — kjødelig søskenbarn.

German ['dʒə·mən] tysk; tysker; — **flute** tverrfløyte; — **gold** flittergull; **the — Ocean** Nordsjøen; — **silver** nysølv; — **text** fraktur; — **toys** nyrnbergerkram; **High** — høytysk; **Low** — plattysk.

germane [dʒə·'me'n] som har med saken å gjøre.

Germania [dʒə·'me'niə] Germania.

germanic [dʒə·'mänik] germansk.

germanism ['dʒə·mənizm] germanisme.

germanize ['dʒə·mənaiz] germanisere.

Germany ['dʒə·məni] Tyskland.

germen ['dʒə·mən] kim, spire.

germicidal ['dʒə·misaidəl] spiredrepende.

germinal ['dʒə·minəl] spire-.

germinate ['dʒə·mine't] spire, brydde, skyte.

germination [dʒə·mi'ne'ʃən] spiring, brydding.

gerrybuilder ['dʒeribildə] bygningsspekulant.

gerrymander [geri'mändə] omlegge valgkretsene vilkårlig, fuske med.

Gertie ['gə·ti] diminutiv av **Gertrude**.

Gertrude ['gə·tru·d] Gjertrud.

gerund ['dʒerənd] gerundium, verbalsubstantiv. — **-grinder** (slang) latinlærer.

gerundive [dʒi'rʌndiv] gerundiv.

gest [dʒest] bedrift; beretning, krønike.

gestate ['dʒeste't] være fruktsommelig med.

gestation [dʒe'ste'ʒən] fruktsommelighet; svangerskapsperiode.

geste [dʒest] se **gest**.

gestic ['dʒestik] sagnaktig, sagn; bevegelses-; **the — art** dansekunsten.

gesticulate [dʒe'stikjule't] gestikulere. **gesticulation** [dʒestikju'le'ʃən] gestikulering; fakter.

gesticulatory [dʒe'stikjulətəri] gestikulerende.

gesture ['dʒestʃə] fakte, gestus.

get [get] få; oppnå; skaffe seg; formå, bevege; (amr.) bringe i forlegenhet; (amr.) lage; gripe; avle; samle; nå, komme til, begi seg til; bli; — **angry** bli int; — **the better of** få bukt med, mestre. — **one's bread** tjene sitt brød; — **a cold** bli forkjølt; — **the day** vinne seier; — **dinner ready** gjøre middagsmaten ferdig; — **drunk** bli full; — **hold of** få fatt i; — **information** innhente opplysninger; — it oppnå det; få en drakt pryl; — it **hot** få sitt, få det hett; **I wish you may** — it! jeg skal nok ta meg i akt! velbekomme! — **to know** (el. **hear** el. **learn**) erfare, få greie på; — **a language** lære et språk; — **a living** få sitt utkomme; — **a mile** gå en mil; — **the pig by the tail;** — **the wrong sow by the ear** ta feil; — **your places** (el. **seats**) ta plass! stig inn! — **possession of** ta i besittelse; — **a slip** falle igjennom, få en kurv; — **the start** få forsprang; — **the worst** trekke det korteste strå; **have you got a light** har De fyr(stikker)? **I have got it** nå sitter jeg nett i det; " **have got no money** jeg har ingen penger; **he . s got to do it** han må gjøre det; — **one's hair** cut ta seg klippe; — **him a situation** skaffe ham en stilling; — **you gone!** kom deg av sted, av gårde! — **aboard** bringe ombord; gå ombord; — **abroad** bringe ut; utbre, gjøre kjent; bli kjent; — **afloat** gjøre flott; bli flott; — **aground** strande; sitte på bar bakke, ikke ha penger; — **ahead** komme fram; gjøre gode forretninger; — **along** greie seg, komme igjennom; komme ut av det; gjøre framskritt; — **along with you** av sted med deg! — **at** komme til, nå til, få fatt i; **what are you -ting at?** hva sikter De til? — **away** skaffe bort; fjerne seg; stikke av; løpe løpsk; — **back** få tilbake; komme tilbake; — **behind** komme baketter; sette seg opp bakpå (en vogn); — **behind a man** endossere en manns veksel; — **by** komme forbi; — **one's living by** tjene sitt utkomme ved; — **even with** hevne seg på; **what can I — for you?** hva ønsker De? (i butikk); — **home** komme hjem; — **in** få inn, bringe inn; innkassere; trenge inn; bli valt (til Parlamentet o. l.); komme til målet; — **in with** innsmigre seg hos; — **into** bringe inn i; — **with** innsmigre seg hos; — **into** bringe inn i; trenge inn i; — **a man into trouble** bringe en mann i forlegenhet; — **a thing into one's head** sette seg noe i hodet; innprente seg noe; — **into debts** komme i gjeld; — **off** ta av; bli av med, skaffe bort; ta av sted; løsrive seg fra; slippe bort; stige ut el. av; — **off false coin** anbringe falske penger; — **off with a fright** slippe med skrekken; — **off the rails** løpe av skinnene; — **clear off** slippe uskadd fra; — **off with you** av sted med deg! — **on** ta på klær; drive framover; stige opp; gjøre framskritt; — **on the steam** få dampen opp; — **on horseback** stige til hest; — **on one's feet** komme på beina; **how are you -ting on?** hvordan har De det? — **on!** av sted! videre! — **on together** komme ut av det med hverandre; — **out** få ut; komme ut; gå ut (om flekker); — **out of shape** miste formen; — **out (with you)!** tøys! — **over** bringe over, trekke over; gjøre seg løs fra; vinne, bestikke; overvinne; overrumple, overliste; behandle hensynsløst; gjøre ende på noe; komme over, overstå; — **ready** gjøre i stand, gjøre ferdig; — **rid of** bli kvitt; rive seg løs fra; skaffe seg av med; — **round** snakke rundt; lure seg unna; — **round a difficulty** gå av veien for en vanskelighet; — **to** få; nå; bringe det til; — **to land** gå i land; — **to sleep** falle i søvn; — **together** få sammen; samle seg; — **oneself together** ta seg sammen; — **under** overvelde, beseire; — **up** få opp; vekke; innrette; sette i verk; forberede; sette i scene; utstyre (bøker); oppmuntre; avfatte; studere; bearbeide; hope opp; stå opp (av senga); — **up by heart** lære utenat; — **up the steam** få dampen opp; — **up** bli vred; — **up to** (el. **with**) **one's back up** bli vred; — **up to** (el. **with**) **a man** innhente en; — **well** bli frisk; — **with child** gjøre gravid.

getatable [get'ätəbl] tilgjengelig.
Gethsemane [geθ'semən'] Getsemane.
getter-up ['getərʌp] en som arrangerer.
getting ['getiŋ] ervervelse; gevinst.
get-up ['getʌp] arrangement; utstyr.
gewgaw ['gju·gå·] stas, unyttig leketøy.
geyser ['ge'za] geiser, varm springkjelde.
gharri ['gäri] okse- el. ponnivogn (i India).
ghastliness ['ga·stlinès] likbleikhet; forferdelse.
ghastly ['ga·stli] likbleik, nåbleik; forferdelig; uhyggelig.
gha(u)t [gå·t] fjellskar; trapp ned til en flod (i India).
ghazi ['ga·zi] muhamedansk troshelt.
Gheber ['ge'bə, 'gi·bə] ildtilbeder, parser.
ghee [gi·] smør, fett (i India).
Ghent [gent] Gent.
gherkin ['gə·kin] liten sur agurk.
ghetto ['geto°] getto, jødekvarter (plur. **-s**).
Ghibelline ['gibəlin,- ain] ghibelliner; ghibellinsk.
ghost [go°st] ånd, spøkelse; draug; spor, skygge; **the Holy Ghost** den Hellige Ånd; **give** (el. **yield**) **up the** — oppgi ånden; **as pale as a —** likbleik; (i teaterspråk:) **the** — **walks** det er gasjeutbetaling; **we want no** — **to tell us that** det vet hvert barn;

I have not the — **of a chance** jeg har ikke den minste sjanse.
ghostlike ['go°stlaik] spøkelsesaktig.
ghostly ['go°stli] åndelig; spøkelsesaktig; geistlig; — **hour** åndetimen.
ghost|seer åndeseer. — **-show** framvising av ånder (ved spiritistiske møter). — **story** spøkelseshistorie.
ghoul [gu·l] varulv (i Østen).
ghoulish ['gu·liʃ] demonisk, uhyggelig.
G. H. Q. fk. f. **General head-quarters.**
giant ['dʒaiənt] kjempe, rise, jotun, gigant; kjempemessig, rise-.
giantess ['dʒaiəntès] kjempekvinne, gyger.
giaour ['dʒauə] vantro, især kristen (tyrkisk).
gibber ['dʒibə] snakke uforståelig; skravle, tøve.
gibberish ['dʒibəriʃ] uforståelig snakk, javl, vås.
gibbet ['dʒibit] galge; henge i galge; stille i gapestokken.
Gibbon ['gibən] Gibbon (srl. eng. historiker).
gibbon ['gibən] gibbon, langarmet ape.
gibbose [gi·bo°s] pukkelrygget, krylrygget.
gibbous ['dʒibəs] pukkelrygget, krylrygget. **gibbousness** [-nès] pukkelryggethet.
Gibbs [gibz] Gibbs.
gibe [dʒaib] hån, spott, stikleri; håne, spotte, geipe til.
Gibellin ['gibəlin] se **Ghibelline.**
giber ['dʒaibə] spotter.
giblets ['dʒiblits] kråser (og annen innmat av fugl). **giblet-soup** kråsesuppe.
Gibraltar [dʒi'brå(·)ltə] Gibraltar; hardt kandissukker; **Straits of** — Gibraltarstredet.
Gibson ['gibsən] Gibson.
giddiness ['gidinès] svimmelhet, ørske; vankelmodighet, flyktighet.
giddy ['gidi] svimmel, ør; svimlende; vankelmodig; flyktig, vinglet, tankeløs; lettsindig, forfløyen; gjøre svimmel; dreie seg hurtig, hvirvle om; **I feel** — det løper rundt for meg; **turn** — bli svimmel; — **as a goose** meget lettsindig el. tankeløs. — **-head** usedvanlig menneske.
Gideon ['gidiən] Gideon.
gift [gift] gave; naturgaver, begavelse; rett til å gi, til å overdra, kallsrett; hvit flekk under neglen; begave; **new-year's -s** nyttårsgaver; — **of the gab** godt snakketøy; **deed of** — gavebrev.
gifted ['giftid] begavet. **giftedness** ['giftidnès] begavelse.
gig [gig] gigg (tohjult vogn); gigg (lett båt); kardemaskin.
gigantic [dʒai'gäntik] kjempemessig, gigantisk, uhorvelig.
giggle ['gigl] fnise; knis. **giggler** en som fniser.
giglamps ['giglämps] (i slang:) briller.
gigmil ['gigmil] stampemølle.
gigot ['dʒigät] sauelår; — **sleeve** skinkeerme.
Gilbert ['gilbət] Gilbert.
Gilchrist ['gilkrist] Gilchrist.
gild [gild] gylle, forgylle; — **the pill** ha sukker i de beske dråpene; sukre pillen. **Gilded Chamber** overhus; gilded el. **gilt spurs** riddersporer.
gilder forgyller. **gilding** ['gildiŋ] forgylling.
Gill [dʒil] diminutiv for: **Julia; Juliana; Jack and** — Hans og Grete, gutt og jente.
gill [dʒil] gjelle, tokn, gan; kjøttlapp under fuglenebb; underansikt, tvihake; **pale about the -s** bleik om nebbet; **rosy about the -s** rødmusset; **grease one's -s** gjøre seg rett til gode; **lick one's -s** slikke seg om munnen.
gill [gil] gjel, kløft, hulvei.
gill [dʒil] hulmål på 0,14 l.
gill-cover ['gilkʌvə] gjellelokk.
gillie ['gili] oppr. høyskotsk tjener, nå: jaktbetjent.
gillyflower [dʒi'gliflauə] gyllenlakk; levkøy.
gilt [gilt] imperf. og perf. pts. av **gild;** forgylling; **that takes the** — **off the gingerbread** det river ned illusjonen.
gilt-edge gullsnitt; med gullsnitt.

gilt-edged ['giltedʒd] med gullsnitt; ekstrafin; første klasses.

gimbals ['dʒimbəlz] slingrebøyler (til kompass).

gimcrack ['dʒimkräk] leketøy; snurrepiperi; ubetydelig; uekte; overlesse med stas. **gim-crackery** ['dʒimkräkəri] snurrepiperier; dårlig stas.

gimlet ['gimlit] bor, naver; bore.

gimmer ['gimə] gimmer, sau som ennå ikke har hatt lam.

gimmer ['dʒimə] hengsel.

gin [dʒin] sjenever.

gin [dʒin] maskin; gangspill; heisekran; jern-blokk; pinebenk, torturredskap; done, fugle-snare; fange i snare.

gin [gin] dersom, om, hvis.

gin [dʒin] (australsk) gammel kone.

gin-foundered ['dʒinfaundəd] ødelagt av drikk.

ginger ['dʒindʒə] spe, skrøpelig.

ginger ['dʒindʒə] ingefær; lys rødgul farge; to, spenn, futt; gulbrun.

gingerale ['dʒindʒə're³l] ingefærøl.

gingerbeer ['dʒindʒə'biə] ingefærøl.

gingerbread ['dʒindʒəbred] honningkake; **the gilt is off the** — forgyllingen er gått av.

gingerly ['dʒindʒəli] forsiktig, varsom, sirlig.

ginger-nut ['dʒindʒənʌt] peppernøtt.

ginger-pop ['dʒindʒəpåp] ingefærøl.

gingham ['giŋəm] slags lett tøy; paraply.

gingival [dʒin'dʒaivəl] tannkjøtt-.

gin-palace ['dʒinpälis] fin skjenkestue.

ginseng ['dʒinseŋ] ginseng (plante, slags ved-bend).

gin-sling ['dʒinsliŋ] sjeneverpjolter.

Giovanni [dʒio'va·ni], **Don** — Don Juan.

gip [dʒip] oppvarter, tjener (hos studenter).

gip [gip] rense fisk, gane, sløye.

gippo ['dʒipoᵘ] (soldaterslang) suppe, saus.

gippy ['dʒipi] (soldaterslang) egyptisk soldat.

gipsy ['dʒipsi] tater, sigøyner, sigøynerinne; heks; tøs; sigøynerspråk; sigøyneraktig; streife om i det fri; leve på tatervis; gjøre en utflukt på landet; — **-bonnet,** — **-hat** hatt med bred skygge.

giraffe [dʒi'ra·f] giraff.

girandole ['dʒirandoᵘl] armstake; ildhjul (fyr-verkeri); øredobbe.

gird [gə·d] omgjorde; omgi; innhegne; hån, geip; — **at** håne; geipe til. **girder** ['gə·də] en som håner; bandstokk, bærebjelke; ås; slind, bete.

girdle ['gə·dl] omgjorde, sette belte omkring, omgi; omseile; gjord, belte; omfang; bakstehelle, takke; **have** (el. **hold**) **someone's head under one's** — ha en i sin makt.

girkin ['gə·kin] se **gherkin.**

girl [gə·l] pike, jente, tjenestepike, tjenes-tejente, hushjelp; toårs råbukk; — **graduate** kvinnelig kandidat; — **guide** speiderpike; — **machinist** maskinsyerske; **servant** — tjenestepike.

girlhood ['gə·lhud] pikestand, pikeår; **she had grown from** — **into womanhood** hun var fra pike blitt kvinne.

girlish ['gə·liʃ] jenteaktig, barnslig.

Girondist ['dʒi'rändist] girondiner.

girt [gə·t] imperf. og perf. pts. av **gird.**

girth [gə·þ] gjord, livreim; omfang; omgjorde, omgi; måle omfanget av.

girton ['gə·tn] Girton; — **College** skole for kvinnelige studenter nær Cambridge. **Gir-tonian** [gə·'toᵘnjən], **Girtonite** ['gə·tənait] kvin-nelig student fra Girton.

gist [dʒist] hovedpunkt; kjerne.

gittern ['gitən] gitar.

give [giv] gi; gi etter; slå seg (om tre); tø; føre (**on, into** til); — **attention** (el. **heed**) **to** skjenke oppmerksomhet; — **battle** levere et slag; — **a bill of exchange** utstede en veksel; — **bonds** (el. **bail**) stille kausjon; — **content** tilfredsstille; — **countenance** oppmuntre, støtte; — **one his due**

gi en det som tilkommer ham; — **ear to** lytte til; — **evidence** vitne, avlegge vitneforklaring; — **fire!** fyr! — **the horse his head** (el. **rein** el. **line**) gi hesten frie tøyler; — **it him!** gi ham! la ham få (juling)! — **joy** ønske til lykke; — **the lie to** someone beskylde en for løgn; — **like for like** gi like for like; — **one a look** tilkaste en et blikk; — **a look to a thing** passe på; — **mouth** snakke; — **notice** si opp; — **offence** fornærme; — **place to** gi etter for; — **a reading** holde en fore-lesning; — **a start** fare opp; — **suck** die; — **and take** la vinning og tap gå opp i opp; **a** — **-and -take fight** en kamp som de to motstandere slipper like godt fra. **would you** — **me the time?** vil De si meg hva klokka er? — **tongue** gi los; — **the wall** gå av veien; — **way** gi etter, vike; — **a person good day** si god dag til en; — **one's love** (el. **kind regards**) **to** sende vennlig hilsen til; — **my respects to your mother** hils Deres mor fra meg; — **one's mind** (el. **oneself**) **to a thing** ofre seg for en sak; — **us a song** syng en sang for oss; — **a judgment** (**sentence**) avgi en kjen-nelse; — **thanks** takke; — **a toast** utbringe en skål; — **trouble** volde uro; **I am given to under-stand** jeg har hørt; **I** — **you the ladies!** skål for damene; — **away** røpe, melde; — **away the bride** være brudens forlover; — **away for** anse for; — **back** vike tilbake; — **forth** bekjentgjøre, kunn-gjøre, uttale; — **from** rive seg løs; — **in** innlevere, overrekke; slå av (på prisen); erklære; gi seg, gi etter; — **in one's name** la seg innskrive; — **in one's verdict** avgi sin stemme som edsvoren; — **into** henvende seg til; føre til (vei); gi inn på; — **on** vende ut til, ha utsikt til (om vindu o. l.); — **out** utdele; bekjentgjøre, kunngjøre; — **out the hymns** nevne de salmene som skal synges; — **out a play** meddele at man vil oppføre et skue-spill; — **out** utbre (rykter); sende ut (røyk); opp-stille (påstand); — **out for** anse for; — **oneself out for** utgi seg for; — **out** framstille; (i cricket) avgjøre at spilleren er «**out**»; — **over** overlate; oppgi (en syk); — **oneself over** hengi seg til; — **up** oppgi; renonsere på; utlevere; inngi (andra-gende); tilstå, bevilge; — **up one's effects to one's creditors** erklære seg for insolvent; — **up the ghost** oppgi ånden; — **oneself up** hengi seg.

given [givn] perf. pts. av **give; tilbøyelig,** for-fallen.

giver ['givə] giver; vekselutsteder, trassent; god bokser.

gizzard ['gizəd] mave (især hos fugler), kräs; stemning; **fret one's** — pine seg, ergre seg; **grumble in the** — være misfornøyd; **stick in one's** — ergre en.

Gk. fk. f. Greek.

glabrous ['gle³brəs] glatt, skallet.

glacé [gla·'se³] glasé, glans-; glasert.

glacial ['gle³ʃəl] is-; — **epoch** istiden.

glacinte ['gle³ʃie³t] dekke med is. **glaciation** [gle³si'e³ʃən] isbredannelse; is.

glacier ['gläsjə, 'gle³ʃə] isbre.

glacis ['gläsis] glacis.

glad [gläd] glad, fornøyd, nøgd; **I am** — **to hear it** det gleder meg å høre det; **I am** — **of it** det gleder meg; **I am** — **that you are here** det gleder meg at du er her; — **news** gledelige nyheter; **the** — **eye** forelskede øyekast; — **rags** (slang) besteklær, kisteklær.

gladden ['glädn] glede, oppmuntre, fryde.

glade [gle³d] lysning i skog, glenne.

gladiate ['gle³die³t] sverdformet.

gladiator ['glädie³tə] gladiator.

gladiatorial [glädjə'tå·riəl] gladiator-.

gladly ['glädli] med glede, gjerne.

gladness ['glädnés] glede.

gladsome ['glädsəm] glad, deilig.

gladstone ['glädstən] håndkoffert.

Gladstone ['glädstən] Gladstone; håndkoffert, reisetaske. **Gladstonian** [gläd'stoᵘnjən] som slut-ter seg til Gladstone.

glair [glæ·ə] eggehvite; bestryke med egge-hvite.

glaireous ['glæ·ᵊriəs] eggehviteaktig.

glaive [gleⁱv] sverd, glavin.

glamour ['glämə] trolldom, blendverk; syn-kverving; fortryllelse; fortrylle; synkverve.

glance [gla·ns] glimt; øyekast, blikk; flyktig tanke, hentydning, antydning; (i mineralogi) glans; glimte; kaste et blikk; vise seg et øye-blikk; streife; hentyde til, berøre lett; kaste til-bake (et skjær); at a —, at the first — ved første øyekast; straks; a — of the eye et blikk; catch a — of få et glimt av; take (el. cast) a — at se flyktig på, kikke på; — over (el. through) kikke igjennom.

glance-coal ['gla·nskoᵘl] antrasitt.

gland [gländ] kjertel.

glandered ['gländəd] snivet. **glanders** ['glän-dez] snive (sykdom hos hester).

glandiform ['gländifä·ᵊm] kjertelformet.

glandular ['gländjulə] kjertelaktig, kjertel-. **glandule** ['gländjul] liten kjertel. **glandulous** ['gländjuləs] kjertelaktig, kjertel-.

glare [glæ·ə] stråle, skinne, blende, skjære i øynene; være avstikkende; stirre, glo, se skarpt; blendende lys, ɡlans, skinn; gjennomborende blikk; glimtende flate.

glaring ['glæ·ᵊriŋ] blendende, strålende; skri-kende, skjærende, grell; a — crime en skamløs forbrytelse.

Glasgow ['gla·sgoᵘ, 'gläs-] Glasgow.

glass [gla·s] glass; timeglass; speil; kikkert; lorgnett; barometer; termometer; glassaktig, glass-; dekke med glass; speile; glasere; se på med en lorgnett; **-es** kikkert, briller; **broken** — glasskår, glassbrott; **cut** — slepet glass; **sheet** — vindusglass; **stained** — glassmaleri; **wine** — vin-glass; — **of wine** glass vin; **I had a** — **of brandy** jeg fikk meg et glass konjakk; **crush a** — **with** drikke et glass med; **he is fond of his** — han liker godt å ta seg et glass; **get a** — **in one's head** få et glass for mye; **he that loves a glass without a G(lass), take away L(ass), and that is he** den som renner etter pikene, er et fe; **dressing** — toalettspeil; **burning** — brennglass; **eye** — lorgnett; **magnifying** — forstørrelsesglass. **glass|-blower**['gla·sbloᵘə] glassblåser. — **-cement** glasskitt. — **-chimney** lampeglass. — **-chord** glass-harmonika. — **-cloth** glasshåndkle, glasslerret. — **-coach** fin karét. — **-cutter** glasssliper. — **-eye** glassøye.

glassful ['gla·sful] glass; a — of gin et glass sjenever.

glass-house ['gla·shaus] glasshytte; drivhus; glasshus; **they who live in glass-houses should not throw stones** en skal ikke kaste med stein når en sitter i glasshus.

glassiness ['gla·sinés] glassaktighet.

glassworks ['gla·swə·ks] glassverk.

glassy ['gla·si] glassaktig; speilblank; speilklar.

Glaswegian [gläs'wi·dʒən] person fra Glasgow.

Glauber ['glå·bə] **salts** glaubersalt.

glaucoma [glå·'koᵘmə] grønn stær. **glaucosis** [glå·'koᵘsis] grønn stær. **glaucous** ['glå·kəs] blå-grønn.

glave [gleⁱv] glavin.

glaze [gleⁱz] sette glass i, sette ruter i; gi en glatt, blank overflate, glasere; lasere (legge gjennomsiktig farge over); polere; lakkere; glitte; satinere; få et glassaktig uttrykk (om øyet); glasur; glasering; politur; glass, lasering; (sl.) vindu.

glazed [gleⁱzd] glasert, med glasur; blank; skinnende; — **paper** satinert papir; — **starch** glansstivelse.

glazer ['gleⁱzə] glaserer; polerer; polerskive.

glazier ['gleⁱzə] glassmester; (i pottemakeri) glaserer; (sl.) en som stjeler fra butikkvinduer; **your father wasn't a glazier!** faren din var ikke glassmester! ikke stå i lyset for meg!

glazing ['gleⁱziŋ] glasur; lasur(farger).

gleam [gli·m] glimt; lys; stråle; lysstråle; stråle, lyse, funkle, glimte; lyne. **gleamy** ['gli·mi] strålende, funklende.

glean [gli·n] sanke (f. eks. aks), samle inn; erfare, fatte, skjønne; bemerke; etterhøst, etter-rakst; **what did you** — **from them?** hva fikk du greie på av dem? **gleaner** ettersanker; inn-samler. **gleaning** ['gli·niŋ] sanking; innsamling.

glebe [gli·b] prestegårdsjord, kirkegods.

glee [gli·] lystighet, glede, munterhet; musikk, flerstemmig sang. — **-club** sangforening, kvartett.

gleeful ['gli·ful] glad, lystig.

gleg [gleg] gløgg, skarp, kvass.

glen [glen] skar, kløft, fjelldal.

glengarry [glen'gäri] skotsk lue.

glib [glib] glatt; kjapp, lett; munnrapp; hår-lugg; — **speech** flytende tale; a — **tongue** en slepen tunge.

glib-tongued ['glibtʌnd] munnrapp.

gliddery ['glidəri] slibrig, sleip, glatt; lumsk.

glide [glaid] gli, sveve; glidning, sveving.

glim [glim] lys, lampe; **douse the** — slokke lyset.

glimmer ['glimə] glimte, flimre; glimting, flimring; glimmer (i mineralogi); **put the lamp on a** — skrue lampen langt ned.

glimpse [glim(p)s] glimt; skimt, glytt; vise seg som et glimt; kaste et flyktig blikk på; se flyktig.

glint [glint] glimt; blinke.

glisk [glisk] glitre; glimt.

glissade [gli'sa·d, gli'seⁱd] ski; skliing.

glisten ['glisn] funkle, stråle; glans.

glitter ['glitə] glitre, funkle, stråle; glitring, glans.

gloaming ['gloᵘmiŋ] skumring, tusmørke.

gloat [gloᵘt] fryde seg, hovere, være skadefro (**over** el. **on** over); hovering, skadefryd.

globate ['gloᵘbêt, 'gloᵘbeⁱt], **globated** ['gloᵘ·beⁱtid] kuleformet.

globe [gloᵘb] kule; klode; globus; noe rundt; rikseple; glasskule; lampekuppel; øyeeple; danne som en kule; bli kuleformet; **parts of the** — verdensdeler.

globe-trotter ['gloᵘbtråtə] jordomreiser.

globose ['gloᵘboᵘs] kuleformet. **globosity** [glo-'bäsiti] kuleform. **globous** ['gloᵘbəs] kule-formet. **globular** ['gläbjulə] kuleformet. **globule** ['gläbjul] liten kule. **globy** ['gloᵘbi] rund.

glomerate ['glåməreⁱt] tvinne sammen i et nøste; se **conglomerate**. **glomeration** [glåmə-'reⁱʃən] sammenrulling til et nøste.

gloom [glu·m] mørke; tyngsel, tungsindighet, tungsinn; formørke; se mørk ut. **gloomily** ['glu·-mili] mørkt; tungsindig. **gloomy** ['glu·mi] mørk, døkk, skummel; tungsindig, nedtrykt, sturen.

glorification [glå·rifi·keⁱʃən] forherligelse; lov-prising; (religiøst) forklarelse. **glorify** ['glå·rifai] forherlige; lovprise; forklare.

glorious ['glå·riəs] ærefull, freg, vidgjeten; her-lig, storartet; a — **time** en herlig tid.

glory ['glå·ri] heder; glans, herlighet; glorie; glede seg; være stolt av; **in all his** — i all sin herlighet; **in the field of** — på ærens mark; **go to** — dø; **send to** — drepe; **he is in his** — han er riktig i sitt element. — in være stolt av.

glory-hole ['glå·rihoᵘl] rotet skuff eller værelse.

gloss [glå(·)s] glans; gi glans, gi en overfladisk glans; besmykke, stase opp; — **cloth** presse klær; **remove the** — dekatere klær; (fig.) ta for-gyllingen av.

gloss [glå(·)s] glose, anmerkning, merknad, for-klaring; forklare, kommentere; bortforklare; be-smykke; satirisere. **glossarist** ['glåsərist] kommen-tator. **glossary** ['glåsəri] glossar. **glosser** ['glåsə] polerer; kommentator. **glossic** ['glåsik] lydskrift.

glossiness ['glåsinés] glans.

glossitis [gli·'saitis] tungebetennelse.

glossy ['glåsi] skinnende, glinsende, blank.

glottal ['glɔ̃tl] som angår stemmerissen.
glottis ['glɔ̃tis] stemmerisse.
Gloucester ['glɔ̃stǝ] Gloucester, ost fra Gloucestershire; **double** — særlig feit ost fra G.
glove [glʌv] hanske; gi hanske på; **kid** — glaséhanske; **the fellow of a** — maken til en hanske; **a pair of -s** et par hansker; gave til damer (f. eks. ved tapt veddemål; gave for å bestikke; **be hand and** — **with** stå på en meget fortrolig fot med; **excuse my** —! unnskyld at jeg beholder hansken på! **go for the -s** vedde uten å ha penger; **handle without -s** ikke legge fingrene imellom; **stretch a** — blokke ut en hanske; **throw down the** — kaste hansken, utfordre; **take up the** — motta utfordringen; **tie up the knocker with a** — vikle en hanske om dørhammeren (som tegn på at det er en barselkone el. en pasient i huset).
glove-fight ['glʌvfait] boksekamp med hansker.
gloveless ['glʌvlés] uten hansker; hensynsløs.
glover ['glʌvǝ] hanskemaker. **gloving** ['glʌv-iŋ] hanskefabrikasjon.
glove-stretcher ['glʌvstretʃǝ] hanskeblokk.
glow [glou] gløde; glød, rødme; opphisselse, heftighet; **be all in a** — være ganske opphisset.
glower ['glauǝ] stirre sint, glo; fiendtlig stirring.
glowing ['glouiŋ] glødende.
glow'-lamp glødelampe. **-worm** sankthansorm.
glcxinia [glɔk'sinjǝ] gloxinia (plante).
gloze [glouz] smykke, pynte på, stase opp.
glucose ['glu·kous] stivelsesukker, druesukker.
glue [glu·] lim; lime; sitte fast. — **-boiler** limkoker. **gluey** ['glu·i] limaktig, klebrig.
glum [glʌm] barsk, ergerlig, mørk, trist, sturen, bister.
glume [glu·m] hams.
glut [glʌt] mette, overfylle; overmetting, mette, overfylling.
gluten ['glu·tǝn] gluten. — **-bread** glutenbrød. **glutinous** ['glu·tinǝs] klebrig.
glutton ['glʌtn] eter, fråtser, slukhals; jerv; grådig, forsluken. **gluttonize** ['glʌtǝnaiz] sluke, fråtse, svelge i. **gluttonous** ['glʌtǝnǝs] grådig, forsluken. **gluttony** ['glʌtǝni] grådighet, forslukenhet, fråtseri.
glycerin(e) [glisǝ'ri·n, 'glisǝri·n] glyserin.
glycine ['glisin], **glycocine** ['gl(a)ikosin], **glycocoll** ['gl(a)ikokɔ̃l] glycin, glykokoll, glykol.
glyn [glin] se **glen**.
glyptic ['gliptik] glyptisk. **glyptics** [-s] glyptikk, steinskjærerkunst.
glyptography [glip'tɔ̃grǝfi] steinskjærerkunst.
glyptotheca [glipto'þi·kǝ], **glyptotheke** ['gliptoþi·k] glyptotek.
G. M. T. fk. f. **Greenwich mean time.**
gnar [na·ǝ] knurre.
gnarl [na·ǝl] knort, kvist; fure; knurre, brumme.
gnarled ['na·ǝld], **gnarly** ['na·ǝli] kvistet, vrien.
gnash [næʃ]: — **one's teeth** skjære tenner.
gnat [næt] mygg. — **-flower** gyllenlakk.
gnaw [nå·] gnage; nage; — **one's lips** bite seg i leppa; — **the ground** bite i graset. **gnawer** ['nå·ǝ] gnager.
gneiss [nais] gneis. **gneissic** ['naisik] gneis-.
gnome [noum] gnom, jordånd, alv, vette; dverg; fyndord, ordspråk. **gnomic(al)** ['noumik(l)] gnomisk.
gnomon ['noumǝn] viser på solur.
gnosis ['nousis] vitenskap. **gnostic** ['nɔ̃stik] gnostisk; gnostiker.
G. N. R. fk. f. **Great Northern Railway.**
gnu [nu·] gnu (slags sørafrikansk okse).
go [gou] gå, dra, dra av sted, reise, ta (et sted hen), begi seg; gå av (om skytevåpen); lyde, ringe (om klokke); slå (om ur); være i omløp (om rykte); anses for; ha til formål; nå, føre til; finne sted; lykkes; befinne seg; gå ut på; foreta, ha til hensikt; ta tilflukt til; gå (om varer); være drektig; gang; hending; omstendighet, tempo; mot; forsøk, sjanse; glass

(brennevin); eksamen (i Cambridge); **here -es!** nå går det løs! **here we** — **again!** nå har vi det igjen! **I can't** — **it** jeg kan ikke holde det ut; — **it** handle energisk; **call a** — velge seg en annen kundekrets, et annet sted til utsalg på gata; — **about** gi seg i ferd med, gi seg til; — **about your business** pass deg selv; **what do you** — **about?** hva har De fore? — **about the bush** gjøre omsvøp; **this goes against** . . . dette taler imot . . .; **it goes against my principles** det strir imot mine prinsipper; — **ahead** gå foran; gå fram; gjøre framskritt; — **ahead!** klem på! driv på! — **along** gå bort; — **along!** av sted med deg! gå med deg! — **along with a man** følge med en mann; holde med en mann; **as we** — **along** undervels; på veien; — **aside** trekke seg tilbake; gå feil; — **asleep** falle i søvn; — **astray** fare vill; begå et feiltrin; — **at** angripe, gå løs på; — **at large** ferdes i frihet; være frikjent; **I am going away for my holidays** jeg skal reise på ferie; — **back** vende om; gå tilbake; — **back from** (el. **upon**) **one's word** ta sitt ord tilbake; — **between** gå imellom; være mekler; — **by** gå forbi; gå hen, gå (om tiden); finne seg i; rette seg etter; (amr.) ta inn, se inn til; — **by the board** gå over bord; gå tapt; — **by the name of** gå under navn av; — **by train** reise med jernbane; — **by the worse** (el. **worst**) trekke det korteste strå; **I am gone by** det er ute med meg; **in times gone by** i svunne tider; — **down** gå under, synke; falle (i kamp); velte; synke (i pris); gå nedover bakke (fig.); — **down into the country** dra ut på landet; — **down to town** gå fra forstaden inn til byen; **this won't** — **down** dette går ikke; **this won't** — **down with him** dette finner han seg ikke i; — **far** slå godt til; ha innflytelse; **he is far gone** han har det meget dårlig, han er ødelagt økonomisk; **as far as that -es** hva det angår; — **fast** gå for fort (om ur); leve flott; — **for** gå etter, hente; — **for a trip** gjøre en utflukt; — **for a walk** gå en tur; **that -es for nothing** det er det ingen mening i; — **for a soldier** bli soldat; — **for oneself** arbeide for egen regning; — **for the gloves** vedde uten å ha penger; — **in** inntreffe (etterretning); stå for tur til å slå (i sport); — **in and win** oppta kampen og seire; — **in for** gi seg av med; tre i skranken for; — **in for an examination** gå opp til eksamen; — **in for cycling** sykle; — **in for dress** legge stor vekt på sitt toalett; — **in for money** søke å tjene mange penger; — **into mourning** kle seg i sorg; — **into partnership with one** gå i kompani med en; — **near** nærme seg; være i begrep med; gå til hjertet; — **as near as possible** leve så økonomisk som mulig; selge så billig som mulig; — **off the rails** løpe av skinnene; — **off** holde opp; dø; finne avsetning; gå av (om skytevåpen); visne; falle i avmakt, dåne, besvime; bli demoralisert; — **off at score** komme i harnisk over noe; — **off into** fits få anfall, bli ute av seg selv; — **off one's nut** gå fra vettet, få en skrue løs; — **on** dra videre, ta videre, gå videre, reise videre, fortsette reisen; gå for seg; bli ved, fortsettes; gå over til; gjøre framskritt; være heldig; oppføre seg; — **on!** snakk! — **on in that way** bære seg slik, ta slik på vei; **we did not** — **on together quite pleasantly** vi kom ikke riktig godt ut av det med hverandre, vi hadde det ikke riktig behagelig sammen; **I must** — **on upon my journey** jeg må fortsette reisen; — **on one's last legs** synge på det siste vers; — **on one's knees** falle på kne; — **on horseback** ri; — **on a journey** gjøre en reise; — **on shore** gå i land; — **on the stage** gå til scenen; — **on strike** gå til streik; — **on tick** ta på kreditt; — **out** gå ut; gå i selskap; kjempe, fekte; dø; bli kjent; — (**out**) **doctor** bli doktor; — **out at a salary** feste seg bort; — **out of fashion** gå av mote; — **out of one's mind** bli gal, gå fra vettet; — **out of the**

way gå av veien; fare vill; gjøre seg særlig umak; skeie ut; — **over** lese igjennom, se gjennom; overveie; undersøke; (amr.) — **over the range** dø; — **round** gå en omvei; — **through** gå gjennom; gjennomgå; utføre, foreta; undersøke nøye; ødsle bort; — **through the mill** gjøre ubehagelige erfaringer, bli klok av skade; (amr.) — **through a man** blottstille en, vise en manns dårlige sider; utplyndre en; — **to!** å tøv! kom ikke med det der! — **to** vedrøre; — **to it** ta fatt, gå løs på hverandre; gå på; ta tilflukt til; — **to grief** bli såret; blamere seg; — **to pieces** gå i stykker, forfalle; ha en ødelagt helbred; **he has gone to pot** han er fullstendig ødelagt; **I won't** — **to the price of it** så mye vil jeg ikke spandere; — **together** gå sammen; passe sammen, stemme overens; — **under** gå under, bli ødelagt, omkomme; — **under an ill reputation** ha et dårlig rykte; — **up to town** reise til hovedstaden; — **up** (amr.) bli hengt; — **up for one's examination** gå opp til eksamen; — **up the line** bli sendt til fronten; — **upon** støtte seg til; foreta, overta; — **upon the tick** kjøpe på kreditt; — **west** (soldaterslang) falle, bli drept; — **with** ledsage; holde med; passe til; — **with the life** slippe fra det med livet; — **without** savne; ikke å ha noe å spise og drikke; — **without!** la være! **that goes without saying** det følger av seg selv; — **wrong** mislykkes; ta feil, ha urett; komme på avveie; gå fallitt; (om ting) virke dårlig; **two in four goes twice** to i fire er to; **the lock goes wrong** låsen er dårlig; **set going** sette i gang; **the play goes** skuespillet gjør lykke; **how goes it?, how goes the world?** hvordan står det til? **the world is going wrong with him** det går dårlig med ham; — **a-hunting** gå på jakt; — **a-pleasuring** være forlystelsessyk; — **a-wool-gathering** være adspredt; — **to see** besøke; — **in quest** oppsøke; — **to borrowing** gi seg til å låne; — **to the country** appellere til velgerne; — **to law** gå til rettssak; — **bail** bli kausjonist, gå i borg; — **blind** bli blind; — **mad** bli gal; — **a long way about** gjøre en stor omvei; — **a great way about** gjøre en stor omvei; — **a great way** ha stor innflytelse; bidra mye til; — **it** gå på! — **it alone** gjøre noe uten hjelp; ta ansvaret selv; — **it blind** handle overilt; **always on the** — i stadig bevegelse; **that's the** — slik går det i verden; **well, that is a** —! det var en slem historie! **here's a fine** —! det er en fin historie! **a rum** — en snodig historie.

goad [go^ud] piggstav; (fig.) spore; drive fram med piggstav; spore, egge.

go-ahead ['go^uə'hed] fremadstrebende, energisk, framdjerv.

goal [go^ul] mål. — **-keeper** målmann.

go-along(er) ['go^uə'lɔ́ŋ(ə)] en dum fyr som lar seg bruke som redskap.

go-ashores ['go^uə'ʃɔ́·əz] landgangsklær, søndagsklær.

goat [go^ut] geit; **he-** geitebukk; **she-** geit (hun).

goa'ee [go^u'ti·] bukkeskjegg.

goatish ['go^utiʃ] bukkeaktig; vellystig.

goatskin ['go^utskin] geiteskinn.

goatsucker ['go^utsʌkə] kveldknarr, nattramn.

gob [gɔb] klump; spytt; spytte.

gobang [go^u'bäŋ], **gobang** (japansk brettspill).

gobbet ['gɔ́bit] bit, munnfull.

gobble ['gɔbl] sluke begjærlig; pludre (om kalkun). **gobbler** ['gɔ́blə] slukhals; kalkun.

gobelin ['gɔ́bəlin] gobelin.

go-between ['go^ubitwi·n] mellommann, mekler.

goblet ['gɔ́blit] beger, pokal.

goblin ['gɔ́blin] nisse, dverg, tomte(gubbe), tuftekall.

goby ['go^ubi] suter (fisk).

go-by ['go^ubai] det å unnslippe, unngå; **give the** — ignorere; **get the** — bli ignorert.

go-cart ['go^uka·^ət] gangstol; barnevogn; lett vogn.

god [gåd] gud; avgud; **the -s** galleriet (i teatret); **God bless her!** Gud velsigne henne! **God forbid!** Gud forby det! **God willing** om Gud vil; **I wish to God, would to God, God grant it!** Gud gi! **God knows** Gud vet (ɔ: vi vet ikke); **Gud skal vite** (ɔ: det er sikkert); **thank God** Gud være lovet.

godchild ['gådtʃaild] gudbarn.

God-damn ['gåd'däm] fordømt; for satan.

goddaughter ['gåddå·tə] guddatter.

goddess ['gådès] gudinne; gydje.

godfather ['gådfa·ðə] gudfar; fadder.

godfearing ['gådfiəriŋ] gudfryktig.

godforsaken ['gådfəsei̯kn] gudsforlatt.

godhead ['gådhed] guddom.

godhood ['gådhud] guddom.

godless ['gådlès] gudløs.

godlike ['gådlaik] guddommelig.

godliness ['gådlinès] gudfryktighet.

godling ['gådliŋ] liten gud.

godly ['gådli] gudfryktig, from.

godmother ['gådmʌðə] gudmor.

godown ['go^udaun] pakkhus.

god's-acre ['gåds'ei̯kə] kirkegård.

godsend ['gådsend] uventet hell.

godson ['gådsʌn] gudsønn.

godwit ['gådwit] langnebbe.

god-speed ['gåd'spi·d] hell; lykke på reisen.

goer ['go^uə] en som går; fotgjenger; **he is a fast** — han går fort; **this horse is a good** — denne hest går fort.

goffer ['gåfə] rynke, kruse, pipe.

goggle ['gågl] skjele, blingse, rulle med øynene; glo; rullende, gloende (om øyne); rulling med øynene; gloing; **goggles** støvbriller, snøbriller; skylapper.

goggle-eyed ['gåglaid] med framstående øyne.

gogs [gågz] se **goggles**.

go-in ['go^uin] begynnelse.

going ['go^uiŋ] gående osv.; i gang; som løper godt (om hest); på mote; **the greatest rascal** — den største slubbert som fins; **be** — to være i begrep med, skulle til; —, —, **gone** (ved auksjon) første, annen, tredje gang. **going** gang, avreise; (amr.) føre; **-s** atferd, oppførsel; verker (Guds); **let us be going** la oss komme av sted; **keep** — holde i gang; **set** — sette i gang; **I am** — **to read** jeg skal til å lese, jeg vil lese nå; **I am not** — **to tell him** jeg vil ikke si ham det. — **-out** det å gå ut; avgang. **goings-on** atferd; **pretty goings-on!** det er fine greier.

goitre ['gɔitə] kversill; struma.

gold [go^uld] gull; rikdom; gyllen farge; sentrum (i en skive); — **-bearing** gullholdig. — **-beater** gullslager (en som lager bladgull). — **-chain** gullkjede.

gold-digger ['go^ulddigə] gullgraver, eventyrer. **golden** ['go^uldn] av gull, gull-, gyllen. — **-crested** gulltoppet.

gold|-field gull-leie. — **-finch** stilliss. — **-hammer** gulspurv. — **-laced** gullgalonert.

goldsmith ['go^uldsmiθ] gullsmed.

Goldsmith ['go^uldsmiθ] Goldsmith.

gold-worked gullbrodert.

golf [gålf] golfspill; golfspille; spille golf. **golf-club** ['gålfklʌb], **-gåf-**] golfklubb; golfkølle. **golfer** ['gålfə, 'gåf-] golfspiller. **golf-links** ['gålfliŋks, 'gåf-] golfterreng.

Golgatha ['gålgəθə] Golgata.

Golia(t)h [go'laiəθ] Goliat.

golliwog ['gåliwåg] slags dukkemann.

golly ['gåli]: **by** — ved Gud!

golore [go'lå·ə] se **galore**.

golosh [go'låʃ] se **galosh**.

goluptious [go'lʌptʃuəs] lekker, delikat.

G. O. M. fk. f. **grand old man** (ɔ: Gladstone).

gombeen [gåm'bi·n] åger.

gomeral, gomeril ['gåmrəl] tosk, fåming.

gondola ['gåndolə] gondol.

gondolier [gåndo'li·ə] gondolfører.

gone [gå(·)n] gått; borte, vekk; ødelagt, håpløs; vekk (i betydningen: meget forelsket); **he has** — han er gått; **he is** — han er borte; **be** —, **get you** —! kom deg av gårde! **let us be** — la oss komme av sted; **in times** — by i svunne tider; **not long** — **eight** litt over åtte; **this woman is six months** — denne kvinne er fruktsommelig på sjette måned; **a** — **man** en ødelagt mann; **it is a** — **case with him** det er ute med ham; **dead and** — død og borte; **far** — **in years** til års, (meget) gammel; **far** — **in drink** beruset.

goneness ['gånnés] matthet.

goner ['gånə] en, det er ute med, en som er ferdig.

gonfalon ['gånfələn] banner. **gonfaloneer** [gånfəlo'ni·ə] fanebærer. **gonfanon** ['gånfənən] banner.

gong [gåŋ] gongong; klokke, bordklokke.

goniometer [gouni'ámitə] vinkelmåler.

gonorrhea [gåno'ri·ə] dryppert.

good [gud] god; pålitelig; velvillig; passende, egnet; gyldig, ekte; dyktig, flink; munter; solvent; snill (om barn); sunn, ufordervet; noe godt, det gode; lykke, velferd; **make** — **cheer** spise godt; **a** — **deal** en hel del; — **fellow** bra kar, flink fyr; — **speed** god lykke! **hold** — holde stikk; **be as** — **as one's word** holde sitt ord; — **nature** godmodig natur; — **words** belærende ord, kjærlige ord; god etterretning; **will you be so** — **as to let me know** vil De være så vennlig å underrette meg om; — **for nothing** udugelig; **be** — **at** jokes forstå en spøk; **be** — **at sums** kunne regne godt; **a** — **many** en hel del; **that is a** — **one** den er god; det er en fin fyr; den var verre! **a** — **fire** en ordentlig ild; **have a** — **mind to** ha god lyst til; **a** — **while** temmelig lenge; **in** — **time** i rette tid; **all in** — **time** alt til sin tid; **it will come to no** — det ender ikke godt; **much** — **may it do you!** velbekomme! (mest ironisk); **clothes to the** — og klær attpå (foruten lønn); **he has gone to America for** — han er reist til Amerika for godt; **for** — **and all** fullstendig, en gang for alle.

goodbye [gud'bai] farvel.

good-day [gud'dei] farvel; (sjeldnere: god dag).

good-for-nothing ['gudfə'nʌþiŋ] udugelig; unyttig; **a** — **fellow** en døgenikt.

Good-Friday [gud'fraidi, -dei] langfredag.

good-humoured ['gud'hju·məd] munter, godmodig.

goodies ['gudiz] slikkerier, gotter.

goodish ['gudiʃ] antagelig, tålelig god; betydelig.

good-looking ['gud'lukiŋ] skjønn, vakker, pen.

goodly ['gudli] vakker, staut, staselig; behagelig, gledelig; betydelig.

goodman ['gudmən] husfar, husbond.

good-nature ['gud'nei'tʃə] godmodighet, godhjertethet, elskverdighet. **good-natured** ['gud'nei'tʃəd] godlyndt, godhjertet, snill, elskverdig.

goodness ['gudnés] godhet; fortreffelighet; dyd; **my** — du store tid! **for goodness' sake** for Guds skyld; — **knows** gudene skal vite.

goods [gudz] gods, varer; godstog. — **-train** godstog.

good-tempered ['gud'tempəd] godmodig, godlyndt.

good-templar [gud'templə] goodtemplar.

good-wife ['gud'waif] husmor, matmor.

good-will ['gud'wil] velvilje, gunst; god hensikt; kundekrets, kunder; **buy the** — **of the house** kjøpe forretningen med dens kunder.

Goodwin ['gudwin] Goodwin; **the** — **Sands** beryktet sandbanke ved kysten av Kent.

goodwoman ['gudwumən] husmor.

goody ['gudi] god kone, mor.

goody ['gudi] from i det ytre, moraliserende, sentimental.

go-off [gou'å·f] begynnelse.

gooroo ['gu·'ru·] lærer, sjelelig veileder (i India).

goose [gu·s] gås; gåsestek; pressejern; pipe ut; **roast** — gåsestek; **get the** — bli pepet ut; **be sound** (el. **all right**) **on the** — (amr.) være en ivrig partigjenger; **cook a man's** — **for him** ødelegge en mann; **it's a gone** — **with him** han er ferdig; **the** — **is hanging high** aksjene står høyt.

gooseberry ['guzb(ə)ri, 'gu·z-] stikkelsbær; **play old** — **with a person** ta ordentlig fatt på en; **play** (el. **do** el. **pick**) — være forkle for to elskende; — **fool** stikkelsbærgrøt.

goose|-flesh ['gåsekjøtt; gåsehud (hud som er nuppet og blek av kulde). — **-herd** gåsegjeter. — **-quill** gåsepenn.

gooser ['gu·sə] avgjørende støt, nådestøt (hos boksere).

goose|-skin ['gu·sskin] gåsehud. — **-step** marsj på stedet.

goosey-gander ['gu·sigåndə] dumrian.

gopher ['gou'fə] (amr.) vånd, jordrotte.

Gordian ['gå·ədiən] gordisk; **cut the** — **knot** hogge over den gordiske knute.

Gordon ['gå·ədn] Gordon.

gore [gå·ə] (størknet) blod.

gore [gå·ə] kile; danne til en kile; stange; gjennombore.

gorge [gå·ədʒ] strupe, svelg; hulvei, kløft, skar; sluke; proppe; proppe seg; fråtse.

gorgeous ['gå·ədʒəs] strålende, prektig; praktelskende.

gorger ['gå·ədʒə] fråtser; fin mann, laps; prinsipal; teaterdirektør.

gorgio ['gå·ədʒou] kristen (i sigøynerspråk).

gorgon ['gå·əgən] gorgo, medusa.

gorgonian [gå·ə'gou njən] gorgonisk, medusa-.

gorgonize ['gå·əgonaiz] forsteine.

gorilla [go'rilə] gorilla.

gormand ['gå·əmənd] storeter. **gormandize** ['gå·əməndaiz] fråtse, sette i seg. **gormandizer** storeter.

gorse [gå·əs] tornblad.

gory ['gå·ri] blodig, blodet.

goshawk ['gåshå·k] hønsehauk.

Goshen ['gou'ʃən] Gosen.

gosherd ['gåzəd] gåsegjeter.

gosling ['gåzliŋ] gåsunge, rakle.

gospel ['gåspəl] evangelium.

gossamer ['gåsəmə] fin kingelvev (som henger løs i lufta); fint vevd stoff; silkehatt; (amr.) tynn regnkappe.

Gosse [gås] Gosse.

gossip ['gåsip] slarvekopp, sladrebøtte; sladder, vås; sladre. **gossiping** ['gåsipiŋ] sladring.

gossipy ['gåsipi] lett kåserende.

gossoon [gå'su·n] (irsk) gutt.

got [gåt] imperf. og perf. pts. av **get**.

Goth [gåþ] goter; barbar.

Gotham ['gåtəm] en by i Nottinghamshire; ['gou'þəm] New York; **the wise men of Gotham** ['gåtəm] molboene. **Gothamist** ['gåtəmist] heimføing.

Gothic ['gåbik] gotisk; barbarisk. **gothicism** ['gåþisizm] gotisisme; gotikk; barbari. **gothicize** ['gåþisaiz] føre tilbake til barbarisk tilstand.

gotten ['gåtn] gammel perf. pts. av **get**.

Gottingen ['gåtiŋən, 'gʌt-] Göttingen.

gouge [gaudʒ, gu·dʒ] skjøljn, skjølpejern; (amr.) bedrageri; bedrager; hule ut; (amr.) bedra.

Goulard [gu·la·əd] Goulard; **-'s extract** en slags blyvann.

Gould [gu·ld] Gould.

gourd [gå·əd, guəd] gresskar.

gourmand ['guəmənd; fr.] gourmand; storeter, matkrok.

gourmet ['guəmei] gourmet; en som skjønner seg på mat el. vin.

goût [gu·] smak, skjønn.

gout [gaut] gikt, podagra; (gammelt) dråpe.

gouty ['gauti] giktsvak, podagristisk, giktaktig, gikt-; svullen, oppustet; framstående.

Gov. fk. f. **governor; government.**

govern ['gʌvən] styre, lede, greie med, regjere. **governess** ['gʌvənês] lærerinne, guvernante.

government ['gʌvənmənt] styrelse, styre, ledelse; riksstyring; regjering; riksstyre; riksråd, statsråd, guvernement. — **-house** guvernementsbolig. — **-office** guvernementskontor, regjeringskontor.

governor ['gʌvənə] styrer, leder; hersker, regent; guvernør, stattholder; direktør; hovmester; gammel'n, den gamle (om ens far el. sjef); regulator (på dampmaskin). — **-general** generalguvernør.

gowan ['gauən] (skotsk) tusenfryd.

Gower ['gauə] Gower.

gowk [gauk] gauk; dumrian, tosk.

gown [gaun] embetskappe; prestekjole; kvinnekjole, kjole; slåbrok; gi kjole på; ta kjole på; **he is a disgrace to his** — han gjør skam på sin stilling; **he will lose his** — han blir avsatt.

gown(s)man ['gaun(z)mən] en som går med kappe; jurist; akademiker (i motsetning til **townsman** filister).

gozzard ['gåzəd] gåsegjeter.

G. P. O. fk. f. **General Post Office.**

G. R. fk. f. **General Reserve; Georgius Rex** (kong Georg).

gr. fk. f. **grains; grammar.**

Graal [gre'l] gral, det hellige nattverdsbeger iflg. middelalderske sagn.

grab [gräb] gripe, trive, snappe, grafse til seg; grep; grafsing; tilegnelse på uhederlig måte, noe man har tilegnet seg på uhederlig måte; likrøver; grabb, klo.

grab [gräb] et slags to- el. tremastet skip.

grab-bag ['gräb'bäg] forundringspose på basarer o. l., som man mot betaling har lov til å snappe en av gjenstandene opp av.

grabber ['gräbə] kniper, gnier; gautjuv.

grabble [gräbl] fomle, trivle, rote; trive, grave til seg.

grace [gre's] ynde; gratie; tekke; elskverdighet; skaperi; utsmykning (i musikk); ringspill; gunst; hyllest; nåde; privilegium; frist; bordbønn; pryde, smykke; begunstige; utmerke; benåde; **His Grace** Hans nåde; **with a good** — med anstand; **sue for** — be om nåde; **five days'** — fem dagers frist; **let us say** — la oss be bordbønn.

graceful ['gre'sf(u)l] yndefull, smukk.

graceless ['gre'slês] uten ynde; fordervet, lastefull; uforskammet, gudløs.

graceosities [gre'ʃi'äsitiz] nedlatende talemåter.

gracious ['gre'ʃəs] nådig; **good** — du gode Gud! **most** — allernådigst.

gradate [grə'de't] la gå gradvis over i hverandre.

gradatim [grə'de'tim] gradvis, trinvis.

gradation [grə'de'ʃən] gradasjen; trin; nyansering; avlyd.

grade [gre'd] grad, trin, rang, klasse; skråning, stigning, hall, fall; **down** — nedover; **high** — **school for girls** høyere pikeskole. **grade** gradere; sortere; krysse (om fe); planere.

Gradgrind ['grädgraind] tørrpinne, fantasiløst menneske (etter en mann i **Hard Times** av Dickens).

gradient ['gre'djənt] hellende; hellings-; helling, hall, stigning.

gradual ['grädjuəl, -dʒuəl] gradvis, trinvis.

gradually ['grädjuəli, -dʒ-] gradvis, etterhånden, litt etter litt, smått om senn.

graduate ['grädjue't] gradere, inndele; graduere, tildele en akademisk grad; gå gradvis over til; ta en akademisk grad, en eksamen.

graduate ['grädjuét] graduert, en som har tatt en eksamen; trinvis ordnet.

graduation [grädju'e'ʃən, -dʒ-] gradering; tildeling av en akademisk grad.

graffage ['gra'fidʒ] skråning.

graft [gra'ft] podekvist; poding; stykke vev som blir ført over fra en organisme til en annen; arbeid; pode; arbeide, føre over; grafse til seg.

Graham-bread ['gre'əmbred] sunnhetsbrød.

Grail [gre'l] se **Graal.**

grain [gre'n] korn, frøkorn; gran; grann; kornaktig ting; kornaktig beskaffenhet av noe; mask, drav; tekstur, fibrer, tråd, trevl, gåre; larve; narv (på lær); korne; korne seg; åre; marmorere; **with a** — **of salt** med litt sunn sans, cum grano salis; **in** — helt igjennom; **against the** — mot ens ønske.

grainage ['gre'nidʒ] kornavgift.

gram. fk. f. **grammar.**

gram [gräm] gram.

gramary(e) ['gräməri] trolldom.

gramercy [grə'mə·si] mange takk (foreldet).

gramineous [grə'miniəs, gre'-] grasaktig; gras-.

graminivorous [grämi'nivərəs] grasetende.

grammar ['grämə] grammatikk; språkvitenskap; riktig språkbruk; grammatisk riktig uttrykk; elementarbok; begynnelsesgrunner, elementer (i en kunst eller vitenskap); **analytical** — vitenskapelig grammatikk; **fault in** — grammatisk feil; **rule of** —, — **-rule** grammatisk regel; **comparative** — sammenliknende språkvitenskap; **bad** — språkstridig; **this is not** — dette er galt i grammatisk henseende; **speak** el. **use bad** — tale galt i grammatisk henseende; — **of political economy** ledetråd i statsøkonomien; — **school** latinskole.

grammarian [grə'mæ·əriən] grammatiker.

grammatical [grə'mätikl] grammatisk.

gramme [gräm] gram.

grammophone ['gräməfoʷn] grammofon.

grampus ['grämpəs] slags grindhval, staurhynning; en som puster høyt.

Granada [grə'na·də] Granada.

granary ['gränəri] kornmagasin.

grand [gränd] stor, storartet; herlig, prektig; fornem, fin; **the Grand Old Man** er betegnelse for Gladstone; — **piano** flygel (også **grand** alene).

grandam ['grändəm], **grandame** ['grände'm] bestemor.

grand-aunt ['grända·nt] grandtante.

grandchild ['gründtʃaild] barnebarn.

grand-cross ['gründkrås] storkors.

grand-dad ['gründdäd] bestefar. — **-daddy** [-dädi] bestefar.

granddaughter ['gründdå·tə] sønnedatter, datterdatter.

grand¦-duchess ['gründdʌtʃis] storhertuginne, storfyrstinne. — **-duke** storhertug, storfyrste.

grandee [grän'di·] grande; fornem adelsmann, storslagenhet, storsnomann; (amr.) snobb.

grandeur ['gründjə, -dʒə] storhet, storslagenhet, høyhet; prakt, glans.

grandfather ['gründ)fa·ðə] bestefar; **great** — oldefar.

grandiloquence [grän'dilokwəns] patos, svulst, store ord, stortalenhet. **grandiloquent** [grän'd¦lokwənt] patetisk, svulstig, skrytende.

grandiose ['grändio°s] grandios; stortalende.

grandiosity [grändi'äsiti] storartethet; skryt.

grandly ['gründli] storartet; flott, viktig.

grandma ['gränma·] bestemor.

grandmama ['gränd)məma·] bestemor.

Grand-Master ['gründma·stə] stormester.

grandmother ['gründ)mʌðə] bestemor; **great** — oldemor; **see one's** — ha meritt; **teach your** — **to suck eggs** egget vil lære høna.

grandness ['grändnés] storhet, storartethet, prakt.

grand¦-papa ['gränd)pəpa·] bestefar. — **-parents** ['gränd)pæ·ərənts] besteforeldre.

grand piano [gränd pi'äno°] flygel.

grandsire ['gränd)saiə] bestefar; stormester.

grandson ['gränd)sʌn] sønnesønn, dattersønn.

granduncle ['grändʌŋkl] grandonkel.

grange [gre¹n(d)ʒ] avlsgård; utflyttergård.
granger [¹gre¹n(d)ʒə] forvalter.
granite [¹gränit] granitt. **Granite City** Aberdeen. **Granite State** New Hampshire i De forente stater.
granivorous [grə¹nivorəs] kornetende.
grannam [¹gränəm] bestemor.
granny [¹gräni] bestemor; gammel kone.
grant [gra·nt] gi, skjenke, yte, innrømme, tilstå, være ved; bevilling, innrømmelse, tilståelse; gave; gavebrev; **God** — Gud gi! **-ing it to be true** om vi går ut fra at det er sant; **-ed** it had happened sett at det hadde hendt; **take something for -ed** anse noe for gitt; **state** — statsbidrag.
granular [¹gränjulə] kornet.
granulate [¹gränjule¹t] korne, prikke; korne seg. **granulate** [¹gränjulèt] kornet. **granulation** [gränju¹le¹ʃən] korning, prikking. **granule** [¹gränjul] lite korn. **granulous** [¹gränjuləs] kornet.
Granville [¹gränvil] Granville.
grape [gre¹p] drue; skrå, kardeske (mil.); **a bunch of -s** en klase vindruer; **grapes** ogs. mugg (en hestesykdom). **grape-fruit** [¹gre¹pfru·t] grapefrukt.
grapery [¹gre¹p(ə)ri] vinanlegg; vinespalier.
grape-shot [¹gre¹pʃåt] kardeske.
graphic(al) [¹gräfik(l)] grafisk; skrive-, skrift-; tydelig tegnet, anskuelig framstilt, malende; livaktig; illustret; — **art** skrivekunst.
graphite [¹gräfait] grafitt.
graphology [grä¹fålədʒi] grafologi.
graphometer [grə¹fåmitə] vinkelmåler.
grapnel [¹gräpnəl] dregg; anker.
grapple [¹gräpl] entrehake, entredregg; fast tak, grep; brytning, kamp; håndgemeng; gripe; holde fast; klamre seg til; kjempe, brytes; gi seg i kast (**with** med); **close** — nærkamp. **grappling -iron** entredregg.
grapy [¹gre¹pi] drueaktig; drue-.
Grasmere [¹gra·smiə] Grasmere.
grasp [gra·sp] gripe, trive, ta fatt i, holde fast ved, ettertrakte; begripe, skjønne, fatte; grep, tak; makt, vold; fatteevne, nemme; forståelse; **all** —, **all lose** den som vil ha alt, får ingenting; — **of iron**, **iron** — jerntak. **grasper** [¹gra·spə].en som griper osv.; gnier, grisk menneske. **grasping** [¹gra·spin] gjerrig, begjærlig.
grass [gra·s] gras; eng; beite; bleikeplass; grønnfôr; dagen (i gruvespråk); hjelpesetter (typ.); midlertidig arbeid; graskle; kle med grastorv; slå til jorda; legge i bakken, overvinne (om bryter, bokser); skyte (en fugl); hale en fisk i land; fôre med friskt gras; drive ut på beitet; legge på bleik; **blade of** — grasstrå; **bring, drive, put (out), send (out), turn to** — sette på gras; **go to** — gå på gras; dø, bite i graset; vente på jobb; **go to** —! gå pokker i vold! (amr.) **hunt** — stikke av, smette unna; **while the** — **grows, the steed starves** mens graset gror, dør kua; **piece of** — grasplett; **he did not let the grass grow under his feet** han gikk straks i gang med sitt forehavende.
grass-cutter [¹gra·skʌtə] slåttekar.
grass-grown bevokst med gras, grasvokst.
grasshopper [¹gra·shåpə] grashoppe.
grass-plot [¹gra·s¹plåt] grasplen.
grass-widow [¹gra·s¹widou] gressenke.
grass-widower [¹gra·s¹widoᵘə] gressenkemann.
grassy [¹gra·si] graskledd, grasrik.
grate [gre¹t] gitter; rist; kaminrist; kamin; tilgitre; forsyne med rist.
grate [gre¹t] gni, nive, gnure, skure; knirke, skurre, rasle, hvine; tilgitre; berøre smertelig, såre; — **the teeth** skjære tenner.
grateful [¹gre¹tf(u)l] takknemlig; behagelig, gledelig.
grater [¹gre¹tə] rivjern, rasp.
Gratiano [gre¹ʃi¹a·noᵘ] Gratiano.
gratification [grätifi¹ke¹ʃən] tilfredsstillelse; glede, fornøyelse, nytelse; gratiale, belønning.

gratify [¹grätifai] tilfredsstille; glede, fornøye; belønne, lønne.
grating [¹gre¹tin] skurrende, raslende, hvinende; gnell; ubehagelig, pinlig; skurring.
grating [¹gre¹tin] gitter, gitterverk; rist.
gratis [¹gre¹tis] gratis.
gratitude [¹grätitju·d] takknemlighet; **I owe him a deep debt of** — jeg står i stor takknemlighetsgjeld til ham.
gratuitous [grə¹tju·itəs] gratis; frivillig; vilkårlig, grunnløs; ufortjent.
gratuity [grə¹tju·iti] gratiale; drikkepenger.
gratulation [grätju¹le¹ʃən] se **congratulation**.
gravamen [grə¹ve¹mən] klage, klagepunkt (jur.). flertall: **gravamina** [grə¹ve¹minə].
grave [gre¹v] gravere; skjære ut.
grave [gre¹v] bunnskrape (et skip i dokk).
grave [greiv] alvorlig, veldig, høytidelig; (om klær, farge) jevn, mørk; (om tone) dyp; (fig.) betydningsfull, alvorlig; — **accent** accent grave.
grave [gre¹v] grav. — **-clothes** likklær. — **-digger** graver.
gravel [¹grävəl] aur, grus, singel; gruslag; nyregrus; gruse; forvirre, bringe i forlegenhet. — **-car,** **-cart** grusvogn. — **-drive** grusvei.
gravelly [¹grävəli] gruset; grus-, aur-.
gravel-pit [¹grävəlpit] grustak.
gravel-walk [¹grävəl¹wá·k] grusgang.
grave-mound [¹gre¹vmaund] gravhaug.
graven [¹gre¹vən] perf. pts. av **grave**.
graves [gre¹vz] grever, fettholdig avfallsprodukt som blir igjen når fettet smeltes ut av svineister (**greaves**).
Gravesend [¹gre¹v¹end] Gravesend.
gravestone [¹gre¹vstoᵘn] gravstein.
graveyard [¹gre¹vja·ªd] kirkegård.
gravid [¹grävid] gravid, svanger.
gravimeter [grə¹vimitə] tyngdemåler.
graving [¹gre¹vin] gravering, utskjæring; gravert arbeid; utskåret arbeid; bunnskraping; — **dock** tørrdokk.
gravitate [¹grävite¹t] strebe mot tyngdepunktet, graviteres; (fig.) strebe med ytterste kraft; bli sterkt tiltrukket.
gravitation [grävi¹te¹ʃən] gravitasjon, tyngdekraft; **centre of** — tyngdepunkt; **law** (el. **principle**) **of** — tyngdelov.
gravity [¹gräviti] alvor, verdighet, høytidelighet; gravitet; betydning, vekt; tyngde; dybde (om tone).
gravy [¹gre¹vi] kjøttkraft; sky, sjelé; saus. — **-boat** sausekopp. — **-soup** kraftsuppe.
gray [gre¹] grå; se **grey**.
graybeard [¹gre¹biəd] gråskjegg, gamling, gubbe.
grayhaired [¹gre¹hæ·əd] gråhåret. **gray-headed** [¹gre¹hedid] gråhåret.
grayish [¹gre¹iʃ] gråaktig.
graylag [¹gre¹läg] villgås.
Gray's Inn [¹gre¹z¹in] Gray's Inn.
graze [gre¹z] gresse; beite på, fore med gras; gjete; gå på beite; streife, snerte; beiting; streifing; streifsår, streifskudd. **grazer** [¹gre¹zə] beitende dyr.
grazier [¹gre¹ʒə] fealer; kveghandler.
grazing {¹gre¹zin] beiting; hamnegang; streifing, snerting; **send a man to** — gi en mann avskjed. — **-ground** beite, hamnegang.
grease [gri·s] fett; smurning; vognsmøring; mugg (en hestesykdom). **grease** [gri·z] smøre; søle til; smøre, bestikke (også: — **a person's palm**); **like greased lightning** som et olja lyn, lynsnart.
grease-box [¹gri·sbåks] smøredåse. — **-cock** smørekran. — **-cup** smørekopp.
grease-proof [¹gri·spru·f] som fett ikke trenger gjennom.
greaser [¹gri·zə] smører; (amr., sl.) skjellsord mot meksikanere.
greasy [¹gri·si, -zi] fettet; sleip; oljeaktig;

gjørmet; (mar.) tjukk, skyet (om været); befengt med mugg (om hester).

great [gre¹t] stor, storartet, mektig, anselig, fornem, betydelig, betydningsfull, av betydning; høymodig, edel; fruktsommelig; meget benyttet; innflytelsesrik; et ættledd lenger tilbake; — **age** høy alder; **Great Britain** Storbritannia; **Greater Britain** England og dets kolonier i forening; — **corn** mais; a — **deal** (el. **many**) en hel del (mengde); **the Great Duke** et tilnavn for hertugen av Wellington; — **enemy** (of mankind) den onde; djevelen; **the** — **forty days** de førti dager mellom påske og Kristi himmelfartsdag; — **friends** gode venner; **the Great Ocean** Stillehavet; a — **pity** synd og skam; — **Powers** stormakter (især: Frankrike, Russland, Storbritannia og De forente stater); **Great Scott** å, du store min! a — **way** en lang vei; **go a** — **way with one** ha stor innflytelse på en; **the** — **week** den stille uke.

great|-aunt [¹gre¹ta·nt] grandtante. **-coat** [¹gre¹t-¹ko⁴t] overfrakk, vinterfrakk, ytterfrakk.

greaten [¹gre¹tn] bli større; forstørre; forhøye. **great¹-grandfather** oldefar. **-grandson** sønnesønns sønn. **-hearted** høysinnet.

greatly [¹gre¹tli] i høy grad, høylig, meget.

great-nephew grandnevø.

greatness [¹gre¹tnès] størrelse; betydning; høy verdighet; storhet; høysinn; berømthet; innbilt storhet; herlighet; heftighet.

great-uncle [¹gre¹tʌŋkl] grandonkel.

greaves [gri·vz] beinskinner.

greaves [gri·vz] se **graves**.

grebe [gri·b] topplom (fugl).

Grecian [¹gri·ʃən] gresk; greker(inne), hellén.

Greece [gri·s] Hellas.

greed [gri·d] begjærlighet, grådighet.

greediness [¹gri·dinès] se **greed**.

greedy [¹gri·di] begjærlig, grådig; gjerrig; — **of gain** begjærlig etter vinning; — **of honour** ærgjerrig.

greegree [¹gri·gri] amulett (i Afrika).

Greek [gri·k] hellén, greker, grekerinne; gresk; kaudervelsk; bedrager, bondefanger; **St. Giles's** — tyvespråk; **as merry as a** — sjeleglad.

green [gri·n] grønn; frisk; ung, ny; blomstrende, kraftig; umoden (f. eks. om frukt); fersk; rå (om mat); (fig.) umoden, grønn; grønt (fargen); grasvoll, grasbakke; grønt lauv; (sl.) grønn te; grønt eple; uerfarenhet; grønnes, bli grønn; gjøre grønn; **-s** (plur.) grønnsaker; — **knight** ridder av tistelordenen; — **complexion** blomstrende teint; — **old age** blomstrende alderdom; — **hand** uøvd arbeider; **as** — **as duckweed** så dum som en gås; **send a horse to Dr. Green** sende en hest ut på beite.

greenback [¹gri·nbäk] pengeseddel (i U. S. A.).

greener [¹gri·nə] uøvd arbeider; grønnskolling.

greenery [¹gri·n(ə)ri] voksterhus; grønt.

green-eyed [¹gri·naid] grønnøyd; mistroisk, skinnsyk.

green|finch [¹gri·nfin(t)ʃ] svenske (fugl). **-fly** [-flai] bladlus. **-frog** [-fråg] lauvfrosk. **-gage** [¹gri·n¹ge¹dʒ] reineclaude, slags fine plommer. **-grocer** [-gro⁴sə] grønthandler. **-grocery** [-gro⁴səri] grønthandel; grønnsaker. **-horn** [-hå·ən] grønnskolling; heimføing. **-house** drivhus, voksterhus.

greenish [¹gri·niʃ] grønnlig; grønn av seg.

Greenland [¹gri·nlənd] Grønland; grønlandsk; **to come from** — være grønn. **Greenlander** [-ə] grønlender, grønlending; grønnskolling. **Greenlandman** grønlandsfarer.

greenness [¹gri·nnès] grønnhet, grønske.

greenroom [¹gri·nru·m] fojé.

greensick [¹gri·nsik] bleksottig. **-ness** [-nès] bleksott.

greensward [¹gri·nswå·əd] grønnsvær.

Greenwich [¹grinidʒ] Greenwich.

greenwood [¹gri·nwud] grønn skog; **under the** — **tree** (poet.) i skogen den grønne.

greet [gri·t] gråte (skotsk).

greet [gri·t] hilse, helse. **greeting** [¹gri·tiŋ] hilsen, helsing.

gregarious [gri¹gæ·əriəs] som lever i flokk, selskapelig; — **animal** hordedyr.

Gregorian [gri¹gå·riən] gregoriansk.

Gregory [¹gregəri] Gregor.

grenade [gri¹ne¹d] håndgranat, granat.

grenadier [grenə¹diə] grenader.

Grendel [¹grendəl] Grendel (uhyre i Beowulf).

Gresham [¹greʃəm] Gresham.

Gretna Green [¹gretnə ¹gri·n] landsby i Skottland, hvor forlovede, som ellers ikke kunne bli gifte, kunne la seg vie av fredsdommeren.

grew [gru·] imperf. av **grow**.

grey [gre¹] grå, gråhåret; (om tøy o. l.) ubleikt; (om ild) gått ut, slokt; grått, grå farge; grålysning; gråskimmel; **the** — **mare is the better horse** kona førrer regimentet, kona er herre i huset. — **-hen** orrhøne.

greyhound [¹gre¹haund] mynde; hurtigseilende (passasjer-)damper.

greyish [¹gre¹iʃ] grålig.

griddle [¹gridl] kakejern; (liten) bakstehelle; stråltrådsåld (i gruvene).

griddle [¹gridl] synge (på gata).

griddler [¹gridlə] gatesanger.

gride [graid] gni skurrende mot hverandre; skurre, knirke.

gridiron [¹gridaiən] stekerist; rist, lunner (til landsetting av skip).

grief [gri·f] sorg; sut, smerte; **come** (el. **go) to** — komme i ulykke; ha uhell med seg; komme til skade; blamere seg; bli uenige med hverandre; gå til grunne; (mar.) forlise.

grievance [¹gri·vəns] besværing, ankemål, klagemål, grunn til klage; onde; plage.

grieve [gri·v] gjøre sorg; sørge, syte.

grievous [¹gri·vəs] svær, slem, tung, hard; bitter, stri, streng. **-ly** svær, hardt. **-ness** sværhet, hardhet.

griff [grif] ny mann, nyankommen (især i India og China); mulatt (i Amerika); ny hest.

griffin [¹grifin] griff (bevinget løve med ørnehode); lammegribb; ny mann, nyankommen (især i India og China).

griffinage [¹grifinidz], **griffinhood** [¹grifinhud] læretid.

griffon [¹grifən] griff.

grig [grig] ålunge; siriss; **as merry as a** — sjeleglad.

grill [gril] stekerist; mat stekt på rist; stekerom; griljere, steke på rist; pine, plage.

grillade [gri¹le¹d, -¹la·d] ristet kjøtt.

grille [gril] gitter; rist.

grill-room [¹grilrum] værelse, der kjøtt tilberedes og serveres.

grilse [grils] ung laks, tart, svele.

grim [grim] mørk, barsk; grusom, streng; uhyggelig, fæl.

grimace [gri¹me¹s] grimase; geip; gjøre grimaser.

grimalkin [gri¹mälkin] gammel kjette.

grime [graim] smuss; sulke til, sverte. **griminess** [¹graiminès] saur, smuss.

Grimsby [¹grimzbi] Grimsby.

grimy [¹graimi] smussig; skitten; svertet.

grin [grin] grine, glise, vise tenner; le, smile bredt; grin, glis, bredt smil; **to** — **and bear it** gjøre gode miner til slett spill.

grind [graind] knuse, male; slipe; kvesse; rive (farger o. l.); gni sterkt mot hverandre; glatte, polere; dreie, sveive (på kaffekvern, på lirekasse); plage, kue, undertrykke, mishandle; sprenglese med, terpe inn i en (i skole, til eksamen); håne, gjøre latterlig; la seg male; la seg slipe osv.; slite, streve (f. eks. til eksamen); terpe, pugge; knusing, maling; sliping; kvessing; skuring; slit (og slep), strev, pugg; eksamenslesing; sprenglesing; lesehest; pugghest; spøkefugl; — one's teeth skjære tenner; være rasende; take a — gå (el. ri) en tur.

grinder ['grainda] en som maler, knuser; møllestein, slipemaskin; en som sliper; skjærsliper; en som river farger; jeksel; manuduktør, privatlærer; driver.

grindery ['graindari] sliperi; skomakersaker.

grinding ['graindiŋ] knusing osv.; hard; tyngende. — **-mill** håndkvern; sliperi; manuduksjon.

grindstone ['graindstoᵘn] slipestein; slit (og slep); **be a tight-fisted hand at the** — et jern til å henge i; **be kept with one's nose to the** — måtte henge kraftig i, måtte legge seg overordentlig i selen.

gringo ['griŋgoᵘ] fremmed, engelskmann, anglo-amerikaner (i Sør-Amerika).

griner ['grina] grinebiter.

grip [grip] gripe, ta fatt i; tak; grep (f. eks. på en kårde); influensa (i Amerika); **be at grips with** være i heftig kamp med; **lose one's** — tape fatningen.

gripe [graip] gripe, ta fatt i; holde fast; knipe (om smerter i maven); pine, plage; være gjerrig, skrape penger sammen); ha maveknip; grep, tak; håndtak, grep; kolikk, maveknip.

griper ['graipa] en som griper; blodsuger.

griping ['graipiŋ] gjerrig, grisk.

grippe [gri(·)p] influensa.

gripper ['gripa] gnier.

gripple ['gripl] ta fatt i; som tar fatt i; begjærlig.

gripsack ['gripsäk] (amr.) reisetaske.

Griqua ['gri·kwa] griqua, barn av en boer og en hottentottkvinne i Sør-Afrika.

grisamber ['grisämba] ambra.

grisly ['grizli] uhyggelig, gyselig.

grist [grist] melder; korn, som skal males på én gang; mel; (fig.) fordel; **that's** — **to his mill** det er vann på hans mølle; det er noe for ham.

gristle ['grisl] brusk.

gristly ['grisli] brusket, bruskaktig.

grit [grit] sandstein; grus, sand; (steins) struktur; fasthet; mot; **he is clear** — ham er det fatt i. **grits** [grits]havregryn. **Grit** (i Canada) radikal.

grit knirke; gnurre; slipe, pusse.

gritstone ['gritstoᵘn] hard kornet sandstein.

gritty ['griti] sandet, gruset; bestemt, motig.

grizzle ['grizl] jamre, klynke; være ergerlig.

grizzle ['grizl] grått, grå farge.

grizzled ['grizld] gråsprengt.

grizzly ['grizli] grålig; grå bjørn; — **bear** grå bjørn.

groan [groᵘn] sukke (**for** etter); stønne; knurre, brumme; knake (om tre) få en til å tie ved å brumme (f. eks. i parlamentet, især — **down**): stønning; mishagsytring.

groat [groᵘt] grot (gammel engelsk sølvmynt, 4 pence verd); (fig.) dust, grann; **I don't care a** — **for him** jeg bryr meg aldri det grann om ham.

groats [groᵘts] (større) gryn, havregryn.

grocer ['groᵘsa] kolonialhandler; materialist; **-'s shop,** (amr.) **-'s store** kolonialhandel, landhandel. **grocery** ['groᵘsari] kolonialvarer; (amr.) kolonialhandel.

grog [gråg] grogg, brennevin og vann; **he has** — **on board** han er full. — **-blossom** rød nese.

groggery ['grågari] kneipe.

groggy ['grågi] omtåket; usikker, ustø.

grogram ['grågram] grogram (et slags tøy).

grog|-shop kneipe. **-tub** drammeflaske.

groin [groin] lyske; (ark.) grat, gratbue; ribbe; parallellverk.

grommet ['gråmit] stropp, løkke; kaus.

gromwell ['gråmwal] steinfrø (plante).

groom [gru·m] stallkar; kongelig kammertjener; brudgom (**bridegroom**); croupier (i spillehus); passe, soignere, pleie, stelle; **well-groomed** soignert; — **of the stole** overkammertjener; — **of**

---

the great chamber kongelig kammertjener; — **in waiting** tjenstgjørende kammerherre.

groomsman ['gru·mzman] brudesvenn.

groove [gru·v] grop; renne, fure; fals; slendrian; fure, danne renne i, grave; **he keeps in the same** — han lar alt gå i den gamle gjenge.

groover ['gru·va] falsejern.

groovy ['gru·vi] ensidig.

grope [groᵘp] famle, trivle, føle seg for; — **one's way** famle seg fram.

grosbeak ['groᵘsbi·k] kirsebærfugl.

gross [groᵘs] stor, svær, tykk, før, dryg; grov, plump; brutto; hovedmasse, hovedstyrke; gross (tolv dusin); — **injustice** skammelig urettferdighet; — **insult** grov fornærmelse; — **amount** bruttobeløp, totalsum; — **average** gross-havari; **the** — **of the people** folkets store masse; **in (the)** — i det hele; **en gros; dealer in (the)** — engroshandler.

grossly ['groᵘsli] plumpt, grovt.

grossular ['gråsjula] stikkelsbær-.

gross-weight ['groᵘs'weᵗt] bruttovekt.

Grosvenor ['groᵘvna] Grosvenor.

grotesque [gro'tesk] grotesk, underlig.

grotto ['gråtoᵘ] grotte, heller; flertall: **grottoes.**

ground [graund] imperf. og perf. pts. av **grind.**

ground [graund] jord; grunn, jordbunn; mark; terreng, lende; grunnlag, grunn, bunn; golv; område; egn; jordstykke, jorde, eng; bakke; rom, tuft; grunn, grunnfarge; jordledning, ledning; grunn, grunnlag, grunnvoll; stilling, årsak, begrunnelse, grunn, motivering; **-s** bunnfall, grugg, berme; anlegg; begynnelsesgrunner; premisser; **on the** — **of** på grunn av; **change one's** — skifte standpunkt; **fall to the** — falle til jorda; slå feil; **gain** — vinne terreng; **keep (el. hold el. stand) one's** — holde stand; holde seg (om priser); **lose** — miste innflytelse; vike tilbake; **to see how the** — **lies** se terrengforholdene an, se hvordan landet ligger; **it was a low building, one story above the** — det var en lav bygning, to etasjer høy (el. på to etasjer); **he had gone over the** — **again** between the farmhouse and his mill han hadde igjen tilbakelagt veien mellom gården og mølla si; **this suits me down to the** — dette passer meg glimrende.

ground [graund] sette el. legge på jorda; legge i bakken; grunne, grunnlegge; (mar.) sette på grunn; undervise i begynnelsesgrunnene; lede ned i el. sette i forbindelse med jorda (om elektrisitet); grunne (ved maling); begrunne, motivere; komme på grunn.

groundage ['graundidʒ] havnepenger.

ground|-bait fly (lokkemat). — **-beetle** skrukketroll. **-floor** første etasje. **-game** hare og kanin.

grounding ['graundiŋ] grunnstøting; grunning.

groundless ['graundlés] grunnløs. **groundlessness** ['graundlésnés] grunnløshet.

groundling ['graundlin] bunnfisk.

ground|-nut ['graundnʌt] jordnøtt. — **-plan** grunnplan. — **-plate** (jern)svill. — **-plot** byggegrunn, tuft, tomt. — **-sea** grunnbrott.

groundsel ['graunsal] svineblom.

ground-swell ['graundswel] dønning.

group [gru·p] gruppe, flokk; gruppere. **grouping** gruppering.

grouse [graus] rype; skyte ryper; **white** — fjellrype; **black** — orrfugl; **wood** (el. **great**) — tiur; **ruffed** — præriehøne; **hazel** — jerpe. **grousing** ['grausiŋ] rypejakt.

grouse [gra·s] knurre, mukke, murre.

grout [graut] grovt mel; (skotsk) grøt, graut; gipsblanding, tynn murblanding; bunnfall.

grouty ['grauti] sur, gretten.

grove [groᵘv] lund, holt.

grovel ['gråvl] krype, kravle; (fig.) ligge på maven, være krypende; ha et lavt tenkesett.

groveller ['gråvlə] kryper; kryp.
grovelling ['gråvliŋ] krypende, lav, småskåren.
grow [groᵘ] gro, vokse; bli, bli til; la vokse, dyrke; — **angry** bli sint; — **dark** mørkne; — **easy** bli beroliget; — **hot** bli ilter; **it is -ing late** det blir sent; — **less** avta; — **light** lysne; — **pale** bli bleik, blekne; **while the grass -s, the steed starves** mens graset gror, dør kua; **as the week -s old** i løpet av uken; mot slutningen av uken; — **well** bli bedre, besne; — **worse** bli verre; — **from** oppstå av, følge av; — **in bulk** tilta i omfang; — **in favour** vinne anseelse; — **in flesh** legge seg ut; — **in love with a thing** bli forelsket i noe; — **in years** bli gammel; — **into fashion** bli mote; — **into a habit** bli til vane; — **on** vedbli å vokse, trives, nærme seg; — **on** (e . **upon**) **one** få makt over en; vokse en over hodet; — **out of** oppstå av; være følge av; etterhånden oppgi; — **out of fashion** gå av mote; — **out of favour** with falle i unåde hos; — **out of all recognition** forandre seg, så man ikke er til å kjenne igjen.
grower ['groᵘə] en (el. noe) som vokser; dyrker, produsent; **slow -s** langsomt voksende trær. **growing** ['groᵘiŋ] voksende; vekst; avl.
growl [graul] knurre, murre; brumme; brumming, knurring. **growler** ['graulə] en som knurrer el. brummer; knurrende hund; brumlebasse; (sl.) firhjult drosje.
growlery ['grauləri] mannens værelse i huset, studerkammer.
grown [groᵘn] perf. pts. av **grow;** voksen.
grown-up voksen; **a** — **person** en voksen; — **people** voksne; **the grown-ups** de voksne.
growth [groᵘþ] vekst, vokster; dyrking, avling, produksjon; produkt; sort; **of one's own** — av egen avling.
groyne [groin] tømmermolo.
grub [grʌb] grave; rote; slite, trelle; spise; ete; fore; fø på; mark, makk, åme, larve, mat, fór, kost; arbeid, hardt slit; — **and bub** mat og drikke; **dead on the** — sulten som en skrubb; **in** — beskjeftiget. — **-ıxe** hakke, grev.
grubber ['grʌbə] sliter; eter; kultivator.
grubbery ['grʌbəri] spisekvarter; fattighus.
grubbing ['grʌbiŋ] spisning.
grubby ['grʌbi] smussig, skitten; slarvet.
grub|-stake fri kost; holde med kost. **-stealer** tigger som stjeler mat fra andre tiggere.
Grubstreet ['grʌbstri·t] Grubstreet; fattige forfattere; dusinbøker.
grub-wages ['grʌbweidʒiz] kostpenger.
grudge [grʌdʒ] knurre, være uvillig over; misunne; knipe på, nekte; være misunnelig; uvilje, vrede, nag, agg; **bear** (el. **owe**) **one a** —, **have a** — **against one** bære nag til en, ha et horn i siden til en. **grudger** ['grʌdʒə] en som misunner; uvenn.
grudgingly ['grʌdʒiŋli] motstrebende.
grue [gru·] gyse (skotsk).
gruel ['gru·il] havresuppe, velling.
gruelling ['gru·iliŋ] gruelig, forferdelig.
gruesome ['gru·səm] gyselig, uhyggelig.
gruff [grʌf] barsk, morsk; grov (i mælet).
gruffish ['grʌfiʃ] noe barsk. **gruffness** ['grʌfnès] barskhet; grovhet (i mælet).
grum [grʌm] gretten, sur.
grumble ['grʌmbl] knurre, murre, brumme; knurring; brumming.
grumbler ['grʌmblə] brumlebasse; knurr (fisk).
grumous ['gru·məs] klumpet, tykk.
grumph [grʌmf] grynt.
grumpy ['grʌmpi] gretten, sær, ergerlig, sur.
Grundy ['grʌndi]; **Mrs.** — folkesnakk; **what will Mrs.** — **say?** hva vil folk si til det.
grunt [grʌnt] grynte; grynting, grynt.
gruntle ['grʌntl] grynte; grynting, grynt.
gruyere ['gru·jææ] sveitserost.
gryphon ['grifən] griff (se **griffon**).
gs. fk. f. **guineas.**
Guadalquivir [gwa·dəl'kwivə] Guadalquivir.

guana ['gwa·na] leguan, slags firfisle.
guano ['gwa·no] guano, fuglegjødsel.
guarantee [gärən'ti·] garanti, trygd; garant, kausjonist; garantere, gå god for. — accounts stå delkredere. **guarantor** [gärən'tå·º] garant. **guaranty** ['gärənti] garanti, trygd; garantere.
guard [ga·ºd] vokte, beskytte, verge, passe, forsvare; eskortere; bevare; vake, våke over, holde vakt; være på sin post; passe seg for; være forsiktig; gardere seg (**against** mot); vakt, livvakt, garde; beskyttelse, vern; konduktør, vognfører; forbehold; urkjede; kuppel; rekkverk; gitter; parérplate (på kårde); håndbøyle (på gevær); bukseklemme (for syklist); skjerm (på sykkel); **-s garde,** livvakt, vakt; — **against** forebygge; **keep under a strong** — passe omhyggelig på; **be** (el. **stand**) **on one's** — være på sin post; ta seg i akt; **off one's** — uforsiktig, sorgløs; **take** (el. **throw**) **off one's** — overrumple; bortlede ens oppmerksomhet; gjøre trygg; **go on** (el. **mount**) — gå på vakt, troppe på.
guard boat vaktbåt.
guard-chain ['ga·ºdtʃeˡn] urkjede.
guarded ['ga·ºdid] forsiktig, varsom; reservert.
guardhouse gardekaserne, vaktstue; «kakebu».
guardian ['ga·ºdjən] formynder; verje; beskytter; oppsynsmann; bestyrer, forstander; **Board of Guardians** fattigstyre; — **angel** skytsengel; — **spirit** skytsånd; **parish -s** sogneråd.
guardianlike ['ga·ºdjənlaik] formynderaktig.
guardianship ['ga·ºdjənʃip] formynderskap.
guardless ['ga·ºdlès] vergeløs, ubeskyttet.
guardroom ['ga·ºdru·m] vaktstue. **guardship** ['ga·ºdʃip] vaktskip.
guardsman ['ga·ºdzmən] gardeoffiser; gardist.
Guatemala [gwa·ti'ma·lə] Guatemala.
guava ['gwa·və] guajava(tre).
gubbings ['gʌbiŋz] avfall (især av fisk).
gudgeon ['gʌdʒən] grunnling (liten karpefisk); dumrian; tapp, pinne; rørløkke.
Guelderland ['geldəländ] Geldern.
guelderrose ['geldərᵒuz] snøballtre.
Guelders ['geldəz] Geldern (byen).
Guelf, Guelph [gwelf] welfer.
guerdon ['gə·dən] lønn; lønne.
guerilla [gə'rilə] gerilja; — **warfare** geriljakrig.
Guernsey ['gə·nzi] Guernsey.
guernsey ['gə·nzi] matrostrøye, genser.
guess [ges] gjette; amerikanerne bruker ofte **I** — som innskudd i setningen i betydningen «formodentlig»; — **at** gjette på; gjette, oppfatte riktig. **guess** gjetning; gisning; (skotsk) gåte; **give** (el. **make**) **a** — gjette, formode. **guesser** ['gesə] en som gjetter. **guessing** ['gesiŋ] gjetting.
guesswork gjetninger.
guest [gest] gjest; (i zoologi i sammensetningen) parasitt; tyv (i lyset). — **-chamber** gjesteværelse.
guffaw (gə'få·] skrallende latter; le høyrøstet.
guggle ['gʌgl] se **gurgle.**
Guiana [gi'a·nə] Guiana.
guidable ['gaidəbl] som kan ledes; villig.
guidance ['gaidəns] ledelse; rettesnor.
guide [gaid] lede, føre, rettleie; fører; veileder; fremmedfører; reisehåndbok; veiledning, rettleiing; **a London** — en reisehåndbok for London; **girl** — speiderpike. — **-post** veiviser (på en vei).
guide-rod ['gaidråd] styrestang.
guidon ['gaidən] standart; fanebærer.
guild [gild] gilde, lag, laug.
guilder ['gildə] gylden (hollandsk sølvmynt).
guildhall ['gildhå·l] gildehus, laughus. **Guildhall** Guildhall, rådhuset i the City of London.
guile [gail] svik, falskhet; list; bedra; besnære. **guileful** ['gailful] svikefull, ful. **guileless** ['gaillès] uten svik.
guillemot ['gilimåt] teiste (fugl).
guillotine [gilə'ti·n] giljotine; giljotinere. — **-window** giljotinevindu (det alminnelige engelske **sash-window**).

guilt [gilt] brøde, skyld; straffbarhet, straff-skyld. **guiltiness** ['giltinés] skyld, straffverdighet.
guiltless ['giltlès] skyldfri, uskyldig.
guilty ['gilti] skyldig; straffverdig; brødefull; skyldbevisst; — **of** skyldig i; **bring a man in** — dømme en mann skyldig; **plead** — erkjenne seg (for) skyldig.
Guinea ['gini] Guinea (på Afrikas vestkyst).
guinea ['gini] guinea (en eldre, ikke lenger gangbar gullmynt; nå brukes ordet som verdibetegnelse for 21 shillings).
guinea|-corn negerhirse, durra. — **-dropper** bedrager. — **-fowl**, — **-hen** perlehøne. — **-pig** marsvin (liten gnager); (sl.) stråmann; styremedlem får én guinea pr. møte; medstifter av en svindelforretning. — **-wheat** mais.
Guinevere ['g(w)ini'viə].
guise [gaiz] skikkelse, form; lag, måte; maske.
guitar [gi'ta·ə] gitar. **guitarist** [gi'ta·rist] gitarspiller.
gulch [gʌltʃ] bergkløft, geil; elvefar.
gulden ['guldən] se **guilder.**
gules [gju·lz] rødt (i heraldikk).
gulf [gʌlf] golf, vik, havbukt; avgrunn, gap, svelg; malstrøm, sluk, strømhvirvel.
Gulfstream ['gʌlfstri·m]: **the** — Golfstrømmen.
gulfy ['gʌlfi] rik på havbukter.
gull [gʌl] måke, måse.
gull [gʌl] dumrian, tosk; narre; bedra.
guller ['gʌlə] gautjuv.
gullet ['gʌlit] spiserør; vassrenne; (pl.) ulvetenner på en sag.
gullibility [gʌli'biliti] dumhet, lettroenhet.
gullible ['gʌlibl] dum, lettroende.
Gulliver ['gʌlivə] Gulliver.
gully ['gʌli] uttørret elvefar; renne, rennestein, avløpskanal; uthule; skvulpe; (skotsk) stor kniv. — **-hole** kloakksluk. — **-raker** kvegtyv. — **-trap** rennesteinsavløp.
gulosity [gju'làsiti] forslukenhet, grådighet.
gulp [gʌlp] slurk, jafs, drag; sluke, svelgje, tylle i seg; **at one** — i en eneste munnfull; — **out** hikste fram.
gulpin ['gʌlpin] lettroende menneske.
gum [gʌm]: **by** — ved Gud, min sel.
gum [gʌm] gom, tannkjøtt. **old mother Gum** gammel tannløs kjerring.
gum [gʌm] gummi; (amr.) kalosjer; våg (i øyet); ha gummi på; klebe; narre, pusse; — **elastic** gummi elasticum, kautsjuk. — **arabic** gummi arabicum.
gumboil ['gʌmboil] tannbyll.
gumlac ['gʌmläk] gummilakk.
gummiferous [gʌ'mifərəs] som gir gummi.
gumminess ['gʌminès] klebrighet.
gummous ['gʌməs] gummiaktig, klebrig; tykk.
gummy ['gʌmi] gummiaktig; klebrig; feit.
gump [gʌmp] tosk, idiot.
gumption ['gʌm(p)ʃən] forstand, omløp i hodet, godt vett.
gumptious ['gʌm(p)ʃəs] skarp, dyktig, med omløp i hodet.
gum|resin ['gʌmrezin] gummiharpiks. **-stick** (gammeldags) narresutt.
gum-sucker ['gʌmsʌkə] ung australier av européisk opprinnelse.
gumtree gummitre.
gun [gʌn] tyv, bondefanger; utspionere.
gun [gʌn] kanon, gevær, børse; skudd; skyte med børse; **a big** (el. **great**) — en storkar; **it is blowing great -s** det blåser en kraftig storm.
gun|-barrel ['gʌnbärəl] børseløp, børsepipe. — **-boat** kanonbåt. — **-carriage** lavett. — **-cotton** skytebomull. — **-deck** batteridekk, kanondekk. — **-fire** skyting; signalskudd, vaktskudd.
gun-metal ['gʌnmetl] kanonmetall.
gunnage ['gʌnidʒ] antall av kanoner (på et krigsskip).
gunnel ['gʌnəl] se **gunwale.**
gunner ['gʌnə] konstabel; kanonér; **kiss the**

-'s daughter bli bundet til en kanon og få tamp.
gunn(e)y ['gʌni] jute (en slags grovt pakklerret), jutestrie, sekk.
gunport ['gʌnpå·ət] kanonport.
gunpowder ['gʌnpaudə] krutt; — **factory** kruttverk; **the Gunpowder Plot** kruttsammensvergelsen (5. nov. 1605).
gunreach ['gʌnri·tʃ] skuddvidde.
gun-room ['gʌnru·m] kadettmesse.
gun-running ['gʌnrʌniŋ] ulovlig innføring av våpen i et besatt område.
gunshot ['gʌnʃåt] skudd, skott; skuddvidde.
gunsmith ['gʌnsmiθ] børsemaker.
gun-stock ['gʌnståk] børseskjefte, børsestokk.
Gunter ['gʌntə] engelsk matematiker; (amr.) landmålerkjede; **according to** — et uttrykk som betegner noe riktig, selvfølgelig.
gun-wad ['gʌnwåd] forladning.
gunwale ['gʌnəl] reling, esing, rip.
gurge [gə·dʒ] malstrøm.
gurgle ['gə·gl] gurgle, klukke; skvulpe; gurgling, klukking; skvulping.
gurnard ['gə·nəd] knurr (en fisk).
gurrah ['gʌrə] gurrah (et slags grovt musselin).
gurrawaun ['gʌrəwå·n] kusk (i India).
Gurton ['gə·tn] Gurton; **Gammer -'s Needle** tittelen på en gammel komedie.
guru ['gu·ru·] åndelig veileder (i India).
Gus eller **Guss** [gʌs] diminutiv av: **Augustus** og **Gustavus** [gʌ'ste'vəs].
gush [gʌʃ] strømme, fosse, bruse, flømme; snakke overspent, strømme over i følelser; utgyte; strøm; sprøyt; utgyting, svermerisk hjerteutgyting; oppsiktsvekkende avisartikkel.
gusher ['gʌʃə] noe som strømmer fram; (amr.) petroleumskjelde; overstrømmende menneske.
gushing ['gʌʃiŋ] strømmende; ildfull; overstrømmende.
gusset ['gʌsit] skjøt, kile (i klær); stråle (i hanske); vinkelplate (i dampkjele).
Gussie, Gussy ['gʌsi] diminutiv av: **Augusta.**
gust [gʌst] vindstøt, vindrose, flage, kast; utbrudd (av lidenskap).
Gustavus [gʌ'ste'vəs] Gustav.
gusto ['gʌsto°] smak, velbehag.
gusty ['gʌsti] stormfull, byget.
gut [gʌt] tarm; innvoller (plur.), slo; grådighet; trangt sund; strede (f. eks. Gibraltar); ta innvollene ut (især av fisk), sløye, gane; tømme; plyndre; ødelegge; sluke begjærlig, ete og drikke; **more -s than brains** lykka bedre enn forstanden; **he has plenty of -s but no bowels** han er hard og ufølsom.
gut-scraper ['gʌtskre'pə] felegnikker.
gut-string ['gʌtstriŋ] tarmstreng.
gutta|-percha ['gʌtə'pə·tʃə] guttaperka.
guttate ['gʌtét], **guttated** ['gʌte'tid] med stenk i, spettet, dråplet.
gutter ['gʌtə] renne; takrenne; rennestein; fure, grop; lage renne i; hule ut, fure; gi avløp gjennom en renne; strirenne; renne (om lys). — **-bred** oppvokst på gata. — **-chanter** gatesanger.
gutter-hotel bu med forfriskninger på gata.
guttering ['gʌtəriŋ] renner; renning, drypping.
gutter press smusspresse.
gutter-snipe ['gʌtəsnaip] gategutt.
guttle ['gʌtl] sluke, fråtse.
guttulous ['gʌtjuləs] dråpeformet.
guttural ['gʌt(ə)rəl] guttural, strupe-; guttural, strupelyd.
Guy [gai] Guy-Fawkes-figur (som blir båret omkring den 5. november og brent); fugleskremsel, spjåk, julebukk.
guy [gai] bardun; feste med bardunner.
guy-rope ['gairo°p] støttetau.
guzzle ['gʌzl] sidrikke, fylle i seg; fråtse, stoppe seg. **guzzler** fyllebøtte, dranker.
Gwendolen, Gwendoline ['gwendolin].

G. W. R. fk. f. **Great Western Railway.**
gwyniad ['gwiniəd] sik.
gyall ['gaiɑ·l] gayalokse.
gybe [dʒaib] jibbe, se også **gibe.**
gyle [gail] brygg; vørter; bryggekar, bryggeså.
gym [dʒim] gymnastikksal, gymnastikk.
gymkhana [dʒim'ka·nə] idrettshus; sports-stevne, kappleik.
gymnasium [dʒim'ne¹zjəm] gymnastikksal; gymnasium; — **shoes** gymnastikksko.
gymnast ['dʒimnäst] gymnast, turner.
gymnastic [dʒim'nästik] gymnastisk.
gymnastics [dʒim'nästiks] gymnastikk; **prac-tise** — gymnastisere.
gymno i smstn. naken.
gymnosophist [dʒim'nåsofist] gymnosofist, naken vismann (asketisk indisk filosof).
gymshoes ['dʒimʃu·z] gymnastikkske, turnsko.
gynarchy ['dʒinaⁿki] kvinneherredømme. **gy-**

necocracy [dʒini'kåkrəsi] kvinnestyre. **gyneco-logist** [dʒini'kålədʒist] gynekolog. **gynecology** [dʒini'kålədʒi] gynekologi.
gyp [dʒip] oppasser, tjener (i universitetsspråk); svindler; bedra.
gyp [dʒip] (slang); **give one** — skjenne på, straffe el. sjenere en.
gypseous ['dʒipsiəs] gipsaktig, gipsholdig; gips-.
gypsum ['dʒipsəm] gips.
gypsy ['dʒipsi] sigøyner, se **gipsy.**
gyrate ['dʒaire¹t] svive rundt. **gyration** [dʒai-'re¹ʃən] omdreining; rotasjon. **gyratory** ['dʒairə-təri] roterende; som sviver rundt.
gyrfalcon ['dʒə·få·kən] jaktfalk.
gyromancy ['dʒiromänsi] gyromanti.
gyroscope ['dʒairoskoⁿp] gyroskop.
gyrus ['dʒairəs] hjernevindinger.
gyve [dʒaiv] lenke, fotlenke; lenkebinde.

H

H [e¹tʃ] H; **to drop one's h's** ikke uttale h'ene, snakke «halvemål».
H. el. **h.** fk. f. **harbour; hard; height; high; hour(s); husband; hail.**
ha [ha·] å, hå.
H. A. fk. f. **Horse Artillery.**
h|a. fk. f. **his account.**
hab. corp. fk. f. **habeas corpus.**
Habeas-Corpus ['he¹bjəs'kå·ᵊpəs]: — **Act** en lov fra 1679, som beskytter en engelsk borger mot å bli fengslet eller holdt fengslet uten undersøkelse og dom; **writ of** — ordre til å framstille en anholdt for retten.
haberdasher ['häbədäʃə] kremmer (som handler med sysaker, bånd osv.), trådhandler. **ha-berdashery** ['häbədäʃəri] mindre manufaktur-varer (sysaker og bånd).
haberdine ['häbədi(·)n] klippfisk.
habergeon ['häbədʒən] brystharnisk.
habiliments [hə'bilimənts] kledning, klær.
habit ['häbit] sedvane, lag, vis, vane; drakt, dameridedrakt; (legems-)konstitusjon; tilstand; kle; **be of a full** — være i godt hold; **be of a spare** — være mager; **be in the** — of pleie; get **into bad -s** få dårlige vaner; **it grows into a** — with him det blir ham en vane; **leave** (el. **break) off an inveterate** — oppgi en inngrodd vane; **by** (el. **from)** — av vane.
habitability [häbitə'biliti] beboelighet. **habit-able** ['häbitəbl] beboelig. **habitant** ['häbitənt] be-boer; ['häbitå·ŋ] fransk innbygger i Canada. **habitat** ['häbität] hjemsted; bosted, oppholdssted; beliggenhet. **habitation** [häbi'te¹ʃən] beboelse; bolig.
habit|-cloth lett klede (særlig til damerided-rakt). — **-gloves** ridehansker (damers). — **-maker** skredder, som syr dameridedrakter.
habitual [hə'bitjuəl, -tʃuəl] tilvant; vanemes-sig; sedvanlig, alminnelig, vanlig; — **drinker** vanedranker. **habituate** [hə'bitjuə¹t, -tʃu-] venne. **habitude** ['häbitju·d] vane, lag, vis, måte; om-gang, fortrolighet. **habitué** [hə'bitjue¹] stamgjest.
H. A. C. fk. f. **Honourable Artillery Co.**
hacienda [äsi'endə] gård, plantasje (i Sør-Amerika).
hack [häk] hakke; gjøre hakk i, hakke sund; radbrekke (ord); harke; hakke tenner, hakke, grav; hakk.
hack [häk] leiehest; skottgamp, øyk; sliter, sleper, lønnsslave srl. en som skriver for føden; leie-; forslitt, utslitt; fortersket.
hackbut ['häkbʌt] hakebørse.
hack|-carriage drosje. — **-cough** hard, tørr hoste. — **-horse** leiehest, drosjehest, skysshest.

hacking-cough ['häkiŋkåf] hard, tørr hoste.
hackle ['häkl] hekle; rive sund; hakke, skam-hogge; hekle; råsilke; nakkefjær på hane; flue (til fisking); **show** — reise bust.
hackly ['häkli] opphakket, ujevn, ru.
hackman ['häkmən] vognmann.
hackney ['häkni] brukshest; leiehest; leievogn, gjøre forslitt, fortersket, slite ut. — **-coach** leievogn, drosje. — **-coachman** drosjekusk.
hack|-watch observasjonsur. — **-work** slave-arbeid.
had [häd, (h)əd] imperf. og perf. pts. av **have; you** — **better go** du gjør (el. gjorde) best i å gå; **I** — **rather go** jeg vil (el. ville) heller gå.
haddock ['hädək] kolje, hyse.
Hades ['he¹di·z] Hades.
hadji ['hädʒi·] pilegrim til Mekka.
hadn't sammentrukket av: **had not.**
hadst [hädst] gl. 2. pers. sing. imperf. av **have.**
hæ. Når ord med denne forstavelse ikke fins her, se under **he.**
hæmal ['hi·məl] hæmal, blod-. **hæmatogen** [he-'mätodʒən] hæmatogen. **hæmatosis** [hi·mə'toⁿsis] hæmatose, bloddannelse. **hæmoglobin** ['hi·moglo-bin] hæmoglobin.
haft [häft] håndtak, skaft, skjefte.
hag [häg] hurpe, trollkjerring, heks; pirål.
hagberry ['hägbəri] hegg; heggebær.
Haggard ['hägəd] Haggard.
haggard ['hägəd] vill; uhyggelig; mager, skrinn, uttært; forgremmet; utemmet falk.
haggis ['hägis] slags hachis.
haggish ['hägiʃ] trollslig, trolldomsaktig.
haggle ['hägl] tinge, prute. **haggler** pruter; oppkjøper.
hagiography [hägi'ågrəfi] hagiografi. **hagio-grapher** [-fə] hagiograf.
hag-ridden ['hägridn] pint av mareritt.
Hague [he¹g] the — Haag (byen).
Haidee [hai'di·] Haidee (i Byrons Don Juan).
hail [he¹l] hagl; hagle; la det hagle med.
hail [he¹l] hilse; praie; rope; praiing, rop; — **from** angi det sted et skip kommer fra; komme fra. **hail!** heil! vel møtt!
hail-fellow(-well-met) ['he¹lfeloⁿ('welmet) ka-merat, god busse; kameratslig.
hail|-shower haglbyge. **-stone** haglkorn. **-storm** haglstorm, haglskur.
haily ['he¹li]; — **weather** haglvær.
hair [hæ·ə] hår; få hår til å vokse; **he has combed my** — **the wrong way** han har ergret meg; **dress one's** — greie, sette opp håret; **a fine head of** — godt hår; **keep your** — **on!** ta det rolig! ikke så hissig! **he pulled his** — **for him**

han holdt en riktig straffepreken for ham; **split** -s være hårkløyver.

hair|bag hårpung. — **-brained** flyktig, tankeløs. — **-breadth** hårsbredd; **have a hair-breadth escape** slippe unna med nød og neppe. — **-brush** hårbørste. — **-cloth** hårduk. — **-cutter** frisør; barber. — **-cutting** klipping, frisering. — **-dress** hårpynt. — **-dresser** frisør; barber. — **-dressing** frisering. — **-dye** hårfargemiddel. — **-glove** frotterhanske.

hairiness ['hæ·ᵊrinès] hårethet.

hairless ['hæ·ᵊlès] hårløs, snau.

hair|-pencil pensel. — **-pin** hårnål. — **-powder** pudder. **-raising** hårreisende. **-splitter** hårkløyver. **-splitting** hårkløyvende, hårkløyver-. **-trigger** [-'trigə] snellert (i geværlås). **-wash** hårvann.

hairy ['hæ·ᵊri] håret, lodden.

Haiti ['he¹ti] Haiti.

hake [he¹k] lysing (fisk).

Hal [häl] diminutiv av: **Harry, Henry.**

halberd ['hälbəd] hellebard. **halberdier** [hälbə'diə] hellebardist.

halcyon ['hälsiən, -ʃiən] kongefisker (fugl); fredelig, stille. — **-days** lykkelige dager.

hale [he¹l] hale, dra; slepe.

hale [he¹l] sunn, rask, kraftig, sterk.

half [ha·f] halv; halvt, halvveis; halvdel; semester, halvår; **a — year** et halvt år; — **the year** halve året; — **a pound** et halvt pund; a — **-pound** et halvpundsstykke; **three hours and a** — 3¹/₂ time; **at — past 6** klokka halv sju; **it is — past** klokka er halv; **every one with — an eye in his head might have seen** enhver kunne ha sett med et halvt øye; — **a moment** et lite øyeblikk; **you are not — a fellow!** you are not — up to snuff! du er en fin fyr! du er ikke riktig inne i forholdene. **I have — a mind to do it** jeg har nesten lyst til å gjøre det; **he is too clever by — han** er altfor dreven; **come in — gå** i stykker; **cut in — skjære** midt over; **not — well** temmelig dårlig; **not — bad** temmelig god, slett ikke så ille.

half-and-half ['ha·fənd'ha·f] halvparten av hver(t), halvblandet; blanding av ale og porter.

half-back ['ha·f'bäk] (i fotball) halfback.

half|-baked halvstekt, rå o. l.; halvtomset. — **-baptize** hjemmedøpe. — **-binding** halvbind. — **-blooded** halvblods. — **-boarder** halv kostgjenger. — **-bound** innbundet i halvbind. — **-brained** halvtomset, halvgal. — **-bred** halvblods, halvdannet. — **-breed** blandingsrase; bastard. — **-brother** halvbror. — **-caste** halvkaste, barn av hindu og europeer. — **-cock** halvspenn. — **-cracked** halvtullet. — **-crown** halvkrone (en sølvmynt, verdt 2¹/₂ shillings). — **-done** halvgjort; halvkokt o. l. — **-feed** sultefore. — **-foolish** halvtullet. — **-gone** halvgal; bedugget. — **-grown** halvvoksen. — **-hearted** sjofel, gjerrig; lunken, likegyldig. — **-holiday** halv fridag (fri om ettermiddagen). — **-hour** halv time. it wants ten minutes to the — den mangler ti minutter på halv. — **-length** brystbilde. — **-mast: at — -mast** på halvstang. — **-measure** halv forholdsregel. — **-moon** halvmåne. — **-mourning** halvsorg.

halfness ['ha·fnès] halvhet.

half|past halv. — **-pay** halv gasje, pensjon, ventepenger. **-pence** ['he¹pəns] halvpence. **three -pence** 1¹/₂ d. **-pennies** ['he¹pəniz] halvpennystykker. **-penny** ['he¹pəni] halvpenny; **sixpence halfpenny** seks og en halv penny; **a twopenny halfpenny stamp** et frimerke til to og en halv pence (20 øre). — **-price** halv pris, **children — -price** barn det halve! — **-rocked** halvtomset. — **-scholar** halvdannet. — **-seas-over** halvfull. — **-sighted** kortsynt. — **-sister** halvsøster. — **-step** halvtone. — **-sword: be at — komme** i håndgemeng. — **-thought** overfladisk mening. — **-timer** arbeider som bare arbeider halve tiden; skolegutt som bare er på skolen halve tiden. — **-turn** halv dreining. — **-way** ['ha·f'we¹] på halv-

veien; halvveis; midtveis. — **-witted** fjollet, halvtullet. — **-year** halvår, semester. — **-yearly** halvårlig, halvårs-.

halibut ['hälibʌt] helleflyndre, kveite.

halidom ['hälidəm] salighet, helligdom (foreldet).

Halifax ['hälifäks] Halifax.

hall [hå·l] hall, sal; vestibyle, forstue, gang, entré; herresete; rettssal; kneipe; varieté (for: **music hall**); (i universitetsspråk): kollegium; spisesal; **this is liberty — her** er vi i frihetens land, her kan vi gjøre som vi vil.

hallelujah [häli'lu·jə] halleluja.

halliard ['häljəd] fall (tau el. talje til å heise en rå, gaffel el. et seil opp med).

hall-mark ['hå·lma·ᵊk] (gull- el. sølv-) stempel; preg; stemple.

hallo [hə'lo⁾ᵘ] hallo!

halloo [hə'lu·] rope (hallo); huie, heie; rope oppmuntrende til; praie; hallo; **don't — till you are out of the wood** gled deg ikke for tidlig.

hallow ['hälo⁾ᵘ] hellige, innvie.

Halloween ['hälo⁾ᵘ'i·n] allehelgensaften.

Hallow-Eve ['hälo⁾ᵘ'i·v] allehelgensaften, helgemessaften. **Hallowmas** ['hälomäs] allehelgensdag, helgemess.

hall|stand [hå·lständ] paraplystativ (med speil og knaggrekke). — **-time** middagstid (for studenter).

hallucination [hälu·si'ne¹ʃen] hallusinasjon, sansebedrag, synkverving; feiltagelse.

halm [ha·m] halm.

halma ['hälmə] halma, slags brettspill.

halo ['he¹lo⁾ᵘ] glorie, strålekrans; ring (om sola el. månen); omgi med glorie.

halt [hå·lt] halt; halting; halte; dryge, vakle.

halt [hå·lt] holdt, stans; stane, stanse, gjøre holdt; la stanse, la gjøre holdt; **make a — gjøre** holdt, stanse.

halter ['hå·ltə] en som halter.

halter ['hå·ltə] grime; strikke, reip; legge grime på; legge reipet om.

halve [ha·v] halvere, kløyve; (i golf:) **a hole with him** nå et hull med det samme antall slag som han.

halves [ha·vz] halvdeler; av **half.**

halyard ['häljəd] se **halliard.**

Ham [häm] Kam (i Bibelen).

ham [häm] skinke; hase.

hamadryad ['hämə'draiəd] hamadryade.

Hamburg ['hämbə·g] Hamburg.

Hamburgh ['hämbərə] slags drue; slags høns.

Hamite ['hämait] hamitt, **Hamitic** [hə'mitik] hamittisk.

hamlet ['hämlit] liten landsby; grend.

hammer ['hämə] hammer; geværhane; hamre, banke, slå; **bring to the — bringe** under hammeren, selge ved auksjon; **come (el. go) to the —** bli solgt ved auksjon; **be -ed** bli erklært for insolvent (børsspråk); **work at — and tongs** arbeide av all kraft; **live (like) — and tongs** leve sammen som hund og katt; — **it into one's head** banke det inn i hodet på en. — **-beam** stikkbjelke. — **-cloth** stasklede, dekken på kuskebukk. — **-hard** herdet ved hamring. — **-harden** kaldhamre. — **-head** hammerhai (fisk). — **-smith** hammersmed.

Hammersmith ['häməsmiþ] (kvarter i London): **he has been at — han** har fått ordentlig bank. **hammer-works** ['häməwə·ks] hammerverk.

hammock ['hämək] hengekøy. — **chair** liggestol. — **-netting** finkenett.

hamper ['hämpə] stor kurv, stor korg, torgkorg, kleskorg, flisekorg; legge i korg; **clothes —** kleskorg.

hamper ['hämpə] hindring; bringe i uorden; hindre, hefte; belemre, bry, tynge, lesse.

Hampshire ['hämpʃə] Hampshire.

Hampstead ['hämstèd] Hampstead.

Hampton ['häm(p)tən] Hampton; — **Court** Hampton slott, i nærheten av London.

hamshackle ['hämʃäkl] binde et dyr med hodet til det ene forbeinet; tømme, tøyle.

hamster ['hämstə] hamster (en gnager).

hamstring ['hämstriŋ] hasesene; skjære hasene over på, skamfere. **hamstrung** ['hämstrʌŋ] imperf. og perf.pts. av **hamstring**.

hand [händ] hånd, hand (hos ape, hauk og hest) fot; (hos kreps) saks; håndsbredd; side, retning; handlag; behendighet; mann, kar, arbeider, matros; håndskrift; håndkort; spiller; urviser (**long, short** — langviser, lilleviser); levere; rekke, fli, lange; beslå (seil); lede, ledsage, leie (ved hånden); **a light** — en lett hånd; mildhet; **slack** — (fig.) treghet, sorgløshet; **heart and** — inderlig, hjertelig; **in the turn of a** — i en håndvending; **at** — for hånden, nær; **I was at his right** — jeg var for hånden; **he has got the book (at) second** — han har kjøpt boka brukt; **I only demand justice at your -s** jeg krever bare rettferdighet av Dem; **by** — med hånden; **the child is brought up by** — barnet blir flasket opp; **he died by his own** — han døde for egen hånd; **by the strong** — med makt; **for one's own** — på egen hånd, for egen regning; **from good -s** fra en sikker kilde; **from** — **to mouth** fra hånden til munnen; **in** — i hende; **the matter in** — den foreliggende sak; **money in** — rede penger; — **in** — hånd i hånd; **heavy in** — vanskelig å styre; **be in** — være under arbeid; **give money in** — gi penger på hånden; **have money in** — ha penger mellom hendene; **off** — på flekken, med det samme; uten vanskelighet; på stedet, improvisert; **off one's -s** ferdig, kvitt; **-s off** vekk med fingrene; **on** — i hende, på lager; til rådighet; **on all -s** på alle kanter; **on the other** — på den annen side, sett fra den annen kant; derimot, men; **heavy on** — tung i hånden; vanskelig å behandle; **he has this difficulty on his -s** han har denne vanskelighet å stri med; **on the mending** — på bedringens vei; **money out of** — kontante penger; — **over head** hodekulls; **have one's** — **out** være ute av øvelse; ikke ha noe å gjøre med; **to one's** — rede, til rådighet; **fight** — **to** — kjempe i håndgemeng; **under** — underhånden, hemmelig; **hands up!** opp med hendene! **be** — **and glove with** stå på en fortrolig fot med; ha mye å gjøre med; **buy at the best** — kjøpe billig; **carry it with a high** — leve flott, slå stort på; **change -s** skifte eier; **come to** — komme til rette, komme fram; bli mottatt; **your letter has come to** — jeg har mottatt Deres brev; **force one's** — tvinge en; **get one's** — **in** arbeide seg inn i, få øvelse; **have one's** — **in** ha en finger med i spillet; **hold** — **with** være likestilt med; **join -s** gi hverandre hånden; **kiss one's** — **to** sende fingerkyss til; **lay one's** — **upon the book** avlegge ed; **live by one's -s** leve av sine henders arbeid; **make a poor** — at gjøre lite inntrykk på; **make no** — ikke være i stand til, gjøre ringe framskritt; **put one's** — **to** stjele; gi seg av med; **shake -s** ta hverandre i hånden, handtas; **strike -s** treffe en overenskomst; slå lag; **take my** — ta kortene mine; **take by the** — ta i sin beskyttelse, ta under armene; **take one through -s** holde en straffepreken for en; **all -s on deck!** alle mann på dekk! **be a good** — være en dyktig arbeider; **he is a good** — **at cards** han er en dyktig kortspiller; **I am an old** — **at it** jeg er en gammel erfaren mann; **send by** — sende med bud; **a cool** — et kaldblodig el. uforskammet menneske; **a knowing** — en luring; **elder** — forhånd; **younger** — bakhånd; **have a good** — ha lykke i spill, ha gode kort; **you have the (first)** — De er i forhånd, De spiller ut; **take a** — **at whist** spille et parti whist; **good** — god håndskrift; **round** — rundskrift.

hand|bag håndtaske, pose; håndkoffert. —

-ball kasteball. — **-barrow** båre; trillebår. — **-basket** håndkorg. — **-basket portion** de penger som mannen får av sin kones foreldre. — **-bell** bordklokke. — **-bill** flyveblad; billett; program; gjeldsbevis. — **-book** håndbok. — **-breadth** håndsbredd. — **-car** dresin. — **-cart** håndkjerre, dragkjerre. — **-cuff** håndjern; sette håndjern på. **Handel** ['händəl] Händel.

hander ['händə] en som overleverer el. overrekker; sekundant; slag over hånden.

hand|fire-engine håndsprøyte. **-ful** ['händful] håndfull. — **-gallop** [-'gäləp] kort galopp. — **-glass** glassklokke (til å sette over planter); håndspeil. — **-glasses** (amr.) lorgnett, neseklemmer, briller. — **-grenade** ['händgrine'd] håndgranat. — **-grip** håndtrykk. — **-hold** grep.

handicap ['händikäp] handicap (et gammelt kortspill); i sport: løp, hvor forskjellighetene mellom de deltagende blir utjevnet ved vekt eller ved at man gir de svakere forsprang; utjevne; hemme, hindre; **they want a favourable** — **upon their trade** de ønsker begunstigelse for sin handel; **they are heavily -ped** de er meget uheldig stilt. **handicapper** (['händikäpə] oppmann, som bestemmer betingelsene for handicapløpet. **handicraft** ['händikra·ft] håndarbeid; håndverk. **handicraftsman** [-smən] håndverker.

handiness ['händinés] behendighet, fingernemhet; hensiktsmessighet.

handiwork ['händiwə·k] håndarbeid; kunstverk.

handkerchief ['häŋkətʃif] tørkle, lommetørkle.

handle ['händl] ta fatt på, fingre på, ta på; håndtere; behandle; lede, føre; manøvrere (et skip); gjøre bruk av; ha å gjøre med, greie med; skjefte; sekundere (ved brytekamp); håndgrep; håndtak, skaft; hank; **they were vigorously -d** det ble tatt kraftig fatt på dem; — **without gloves** ikke ta på med silkehansker; — **money freely** gi ut mange penger; **give a** — gi el. by en gunstig leilighet; **take by the right** — ta fatt i den riktige enden; **a** — **to one's name** en tittel. **hand|line** ['händlain] snøre, djupsagn. **-liner** snørefisker.

handling ['händliŋ] berøring; behandling, handsaming, medferd; penselføring.

hand|lining ['händlainiŋ] snørefisker. — **-loom** håndvev. — **-made** gjort med hånden; håndsydd. **-maid** jente, tjenestepike, hushjelp. **-maiden** se **-maid**. — **-maker** tyv. — **-me-downs** ['händmi-'daunz] brukte klær. — **-mill** håndkvern. — **-organ** lirekasse. — **-paper** bøttepapir. **-saw** håndsag; knivhandler på gata; **not to know a hawk from** a **handsaw** ikke å kunne telle til to. **hand's-breadth** håndsbredd.

handsel ['hän(d)səl] hansel; håndpenger; gi hansel; bruke første gangen, krympe. **Handsel Monday** første mandagen i det nye året. **handseller** ['händselə] gateselger.

handshake ['händʃe'k] håndtrykk, håndtak.

handsome ['hänsəm] smukk, skjønn, vakker, pen; anselig, staut, betydelig; edel, fin; gavmild; **come down -ly** vise seg gavmild; **do the** — **thing** være gavmild, være meget høflig.

hand|span spann. — **-spike** håndspak, våg. — **-spring** kollbøtte, rundkast. — **-to-hand** mann mot mann. — **-vice** skrueste, skruestikke. **-writing** håndskrift.

handy ['händi] behendig, fingernem; bekvem, nem, praktisk; for hånden, nær ved; nyttig; til passende tid; **be** — **with** være flink med; **come** — komme beleilig. — **-blow** neveslag — **-book** håndbok. — **-cuff** ['händikʌf] neveslag. — **-dandy** ['händi'dändi] en barnelek hvor barnet skal gjette i hva for en hånd en gjemmer noe godt. e. l.

hang [häŋ], (i imperf. og perf. pts. **hung** unnt. i betydning: drepe ved hengning), henge; henge opp; behenge; henge (i galgen); bringe i galgen; ta henge; henge med (f. eks. hodet); holde i spenning, holde i uvirksomhet; hemme

en bevegelse; (fig.) hylle til; være hengt opp; være hengt (i galgen); sveve; sveve i uvisshet, dryge, somle, vakle; være omkring; være i likevekt; skråning; hall; innretning, orden; hang, tilbøyelighet; **go and — yourself, you be -ed** gå fanden i vold! **— a jury** hindre de edsvorne i å avgi en kjennelse ved som edsvoren å nekte sitt samtykke til kjennelsen; **— fire ikke gå av** straks, klikke (om børse); (fig.) være vaklende, dryge, somle; **get the — of a thing** komme på det rene med noe; **I don't care a —** jeg bryr meg pokker om det; **— about** drive omkring; **— back** kvie seg, ville nødig; **— on** henge ved; henge fast; tynge på; være avhengig av; se forundret på; lytte spent til; holde ut; bli til besvær; **— up** henge opp; dryge med, dryge ut; **— up one's fiddle** oppgi noe; trekke seg tilbake fra forretningene; **— it up!** skriv det på regning! (amr.) glem det ikke! **— up one's hat in a house** innrette seg hos en, som om man er hjemme; **— a room with paper** tapetsere et værelse.
hangar ['häŋə, 'häŋgə, 'häŋgaˑ] hangar. **-ship** hangarskip.
hang-dog ['häŋdåg] en fyr av et skurkaktig og skyldbevisst utseende, fark, galgenfugl; galgenfuglaktig.
hanger ['häŋə] en som henger opp; bøddel; tapetserer; hempe; grytekrok; rabbel; jaktkniv; bratt skogli.
hanger-on ['häŋər'ån] tilhenger; snyltegjest.
hangfire shot skudd som ikke går av.
hanging ['häŋiŋ] hengende; hengning; omheng, gardin, draperi; **marriage and — go by destiny** ingen kan unngå sin skjebne; **— affair** (el. matter) en sak som kan bringe en i galgen; **— committee** opphengingskomité (ved maleriutstillinger); **— market** flau forretning.
hangman ['häŋmən] bøddel.
hangnail ['häŋneˑl] neglerot.
hank [häŋk] dukke (garn); hårlokk; tak; hegde; **catch a — on** hevne seg på; **have a — on a man** el. **have a man on the —** ha en mann i sin makt; **have a great — over** ha stor innflytelse hos.
hanker ['häŋkə] hike, lengte, stunde **(after** etter).
hankering ['häŋkəriŋ] attrå, lengt, lengsel.
hanky ['häŋki] (i barnespråk) lommetørkle.
hanky-panky ['häŋki'päŋki] knep, hokuspokus.
Hanover ['hänovə] Hannover. **Hanoverian** [häno'viəriən] hannoveransk; hannoveraner.
Hansa ['hänsə] se **Hanse.**
Hansard ['hänsəd] parlamentstidende, de trykte parlamentsforhandlinger (etter boktrykkerens navn).
Hanse [häns] Hansa; **the — towns** hansestedene.
Hanseatic [hänsi'ätik] hanseatisk, hanse-.
hansel ['hänsəl] se **handsel.**
hansom ['hänsəm] el. **-cab** tohjultˑdrosje.
han't [(h)eˑnt] fk. f. **has not** el. **have not.**
hantle ['häntl, 'haˑntl] mengde, god slump.
Hants [hänts] fork. f. **Hampshire.**
Hanwell ['hänwəl] Hanwell; **— asylum** en sinnssykeanstalt.
hap [häp] hendelse, tilfelle; lykke; lykketreff; hende; **good — lykke; ill — ulykke; ulykkes**tilfelle; **by good — til alt hell; by ill — til alt** uhell.
hap [häp] (provinsielt og skotsk) dekke, hylle inn; kåpe, dekke.
ha'-penny ['heˑpəni] se **halfpenny.**
hap-hazard ['häp'häzəd] lykke, slump, lykketreff; tilfeldig, vilkårlig, slumpe-. **at** el. **by — på** slump.
hapless ['häpləs] ulykkelig.
haply ['häpli] tilfeldigvis.
ha'porth ['heˑpəþ] en halvpennys verdi; **a — of cheese** for en halv penny ost; (fig.) **a poor — o' cheese** en svekling.

happen ['häpn] hende, bære til, treffe seg; **I happened to be there** jeg var der nettopp, jeg var der tilfeldigvis; (amr.) **to — on** treffe tilfeldigvis. **happening** ['häpniŋ] hendelse, hending.
happily ['häpili] lykkelig; heldigvis.
happiness ['häpinés] lykke; lykksalighet; skjønnhet, ynde; heldig valg av uttrykk.
happy ['häpi] heldig; lykkelig; lykksalig; glad; passende, treffende; behendig, slagferdig; **(I am) — to see you** det gleder meg å se Dem; **she would make herself quite —** hun ville gjøre seg det riktig hyggelig, hun ville ha det riktig koselig; **in a — hour, in — time** i en heldig stund.
happy-go-lucky ['häpigoᵘ'lʌki] ubekymret, sorgløs; på må få, det gå som det vil.
Hapsburg ['häpsbəˑg] Habsburg.
hara-kiri ['haˑrə'kiri] harakiri, japansk selvmord ved oppspretting av maven.
harangue [hə'räŋ] tale; ordskvalder, prek; holde tale til; preke. **haranguer** [hə'räŋə] taler; ordgyter; skvaldrebøtte.
harass ['härəs] trette, utmatte; pine, plage; mase på; forstyrrelse, uro. **harasser** ['härəsə] plageånd. **harassment** ['härəsmənt] forstyrrelse, uro; utmatting.
harbinger ['haˑᵊbindʒə] bebuder, forløper; bebude, melde; **— of spring** vårbud.
harbour ['haˑᵊbə] havn, hamn; huse, gi ly; nære (følelser, tanker); finne havn, ankre i havn; være til huse. **— captain** havnekaptein. **— commissioners** havnekommisjon. **— -dues** havneavgifter.
harbourless ['haˑᵊbələs] uten havn.
harbour|-light havnefyr. **-master** havnefoged. **-works** havneanlegg.
Harcourt ['haˑᵊkət, -kåᵊt] Harcourt.
hard [haˑd] stø, landingssted.
hard [haˑd] hard; stri; streng, grusom; vanskelig, tung; pinlig, smertelig; sterk (om regn, drikk o. l.); forherdet; gjerrig; sårende; flittig, utholdende; praktisk; grov (om trekk); stiv, tvungen (om stil, kunst); tarvelig (f. eks. om kost); sur (om drikk); berusende; som adverb: hardt, strengt; med anstrengelse, møysommelig, ivrig; skarpt, nøye; vanskelig; tungt; nær, tett; **I thought it — upon me** jeg synes det var hardt mot meg; **— cash** (el. **money**) rede penger, kontanter; **a horse in — condition** en hest i god kondisjon; **— of digestion** tungt fordøyelig; **— egg** hardkokt egg; **— to please** vanskelig å tilfredsstille; **— labour** straffarbeid, tukthusstraff; **— lines** harde vilkår; **— drinker** dranker; **a — student** en flittig student; et jern til å studere; **beg — be** inntrengende; **— names** økenavn; sterke uttrykk; **— words** vanskelige uttrykk; **— by tett ved; — -fought battle** hardnakket slag; **it is — upon one** klokka er nesten ett; **look one — in the face** se en rett i ansiktet; **they tried very — de prøvde av all makt; — up** opprådd, i pengeknipe. **— -and-fast** urokkelig; av alle krefter. **— -bake** mandelknekk. **— -bitted, — -bitten** hardkjeftet; seig; stri (om hest). **— -boiled** hardkokt.
harden ['haˑᵊdn] gjøre hard, herde; forherde, bli hard, hardne; bli forherdet.
hard|-faced, — -favoured, — -featured med grove, frastøtende trekk; barsk. **— -fisted** med harde, grove hender; ubehøvlet; gjerrig. **— -fought** se under **hard. — -frozen** stivfrossen. **— -handed** se **— -fisted. — -headed** klok; gløgg; listig; forstandig; kaldt beregnende.
Hardicanute ['haˑᵊdika'njuˑt] Hardeknut.
hardihood ['haˑᵊdihud] dristighet, djervskap.
hardily ['haˑᵊdili] tappert, uforferdet.
hardiness ['haˑᵊdinés] utholdenhet, hardførhet; (sjelden: tapperhet, uforferdethet).
Harding(e) ['haˑᵊdiŋ] Hardinge.
hardly ['haˑᵊdli] hardt; neppe, snautt, nesten ikke; **— anybody** nesten ingen; **— anything**

nesten ingenting; — **ever** nesten aldri; **hardly** . . . **when** neppe . . . før.
hard-mouthed ['ha·ᵊdmauðd] hardkjeftet (om hest); stri, vrang; gjerrig.
hardness ['ha·ᵊdnės] hardhet osv., se **hard**.
hard|nibbed hard (om penn). — **-reared** vant til grov kost.
hards [ha·ᵊdz] stry, drev.
hard-set sterkt betrengt; streng, ubøyelig.
hardship ['ha·ᵊdʃip] undertrykkelse, overlast, urett; besværlighet, byrde, strabas, gjenvordighet.
hardware ['ha·ᵊdwæ·ᵊ] isenkram, jernvarer.
— **dealer** jernvarehandler. **hardwareman** ['ha·ᵊdwæ·ᵊmən] jernvarehandler.
hardwood ['ha·ᵊdwud] hardt, tettfibret treslag; lauvtre.
hardy ['ha·ᵊdi] dristig, djerv; hardfør.
hare [hæ·ᵊ] hare; **kiss the -'s foot** komme for sent; — **and hounds** papirjakt, jaktlek med utstrødde papirbeter.
harebrained ['hæ·ᵊbreᵗnd] flyktig, tankeløs.
hare|hearted feig. — **-lip** haremunn. — **-lipped** haremynt.
harem ['hæ·ᵊrəm] harem.
haricot ['härikou] snittebønne; ragout.
hark [ha·ᵊk] lytte, høre etter; — **back!** kom tilbake! kom hit! (til hunder som er kommet på et galt spor); — **back** komme tilbake til utgangspunktet for en samtale e. l.
harkee ['ha·ᵊki], **harkye** ['ha·ᵊkji] hør! hør nå!
harl [ha·ᵊl] slepe; bringe i forvirring; floke; slepes; slepe seg; sleping; trevler (av lin); uhederlig vinning; hundekobbel.
Harleian ['ha·ᵊljən] som angår Harley.
harlequin ['ha·ᵊlikwin] bajas, skalk, narr; trylle bort.
harlequinade [ha·ᵊlikwi'neᵗd] del av pantomime hvor harlequin spiller hovedrollen.
Harley ['ha·ᵊli] Harley; — **street** gate i London, hvor der bor mange læger.
harlot ['ha·ᵊlət] skjøke, hore, ludder.
harlotry ['ha·ᵊlåtri] skjøkelevnet.
harm [ha·ᵊm] vondt, skade, mén, fortred; ska, gjøre fortred; **what** — **has he done to you?** hva har han gjort Dem? **I meant no** — det var ikke så vondt ment; **there's no** — **done** har ikke noe å si. — **watch**, — **catch** den som graver en grav for andre, faller selv i den; **out of harm's way** i sikkerhet.
harmful ['ha·ᵊmful] skadelig; vond.
harmless ['ha·ᵊmlės] uskadelig, harmløs.
harmonic [ha·ᵊ'månik] harmonisk.
harmonica [ha·ᵊ'månikə] harmonika; munnspill.
harmonics [ha·ᵊ'måniks] harmonilære.
harmonious [ha·ᵊ'mouⁿjəs] harmonisk; fredelig, vennskapelig.
harmonist ['ha·ᵊmonist] harmonist; komponist.
harmonium [ha·ᵊ'mouⁿjəm] harmonium, husorgel.
harmonization [ha·ᵊmonai'zeᵗʃən] harmonisering; (fig.) samklang, harmoni.
harmonize ['ha·ᵊmonaiz] harmonisere; (fig.) bringe i samklang; synge flerstemmig; harmonere; komme overens.
harmony ['ha·ᵊməni] harmoni; (fig.) samdrektighet, samsvar, fredelighet.
harness ['ha·ᵊnis] harnisk, rustning; seletøy; hovold; gi rustning på; sele på, spenne for; **die in** — henge i selen til det siste. — **-maker** salmaker.
harns [ha·ᵊnz] (skotsk) hjerne.
Harold ['härəld] Harald.
harp [ha·ᵊp] harpe; spille på harpe; (fig.) alltid komme tilbake til det samme, alltid spille på den samme streng, gnåle om el. på.
harper ['ha·ᵊpə], **harpist** ['ha·ᵊpist] harpespiller. harpist.
harpoon [ha·ᵊ'pu·n] harpun; harpunere.
harpooner [ha·ᵊ'pu·nə] harpunér.
harpress ['ha·ᵊprės] harpespillerske.

harpsichord ['ha·ᵊpsikå·ᵊd] klavecin.
harpy ['ha·ᵊpi] harpy, grisk person.
harquebus ['ha·ᵊkwibəs] (gml.) hakebørse.
harridan ['häridən] heks, gammel hurpe.
harrier ['häriə] harehund, støver.
Harriet ['häriet] Harriet.
harrikari ['härika·ri] se **hara-kiri**.
Harrogate ['härogeᵗt] Harrogate.
Harrovian [hä'rouⁿvjən] elev fra skolen i **Harrow** ['härouⁿ].
harrow ['härouⁿ] harv; harve;(fig.)rive sund; pine.
Harry ['häri] kjælenavn for **Henry; Old** — fanden, Gamle-Erik; **play Old** — **with a man** behandle en mann fryktelig.
harry ['häri] herje, plyndre; pine. **harrying** ['häriiŋ] herjing, plyndring.
harsh [ha·ᵊʃ] harsk, trå, stram; hard, skurrende; hard, rå, barsk; plump, frastøtende, ubehagelig. **harshen** ['ha·ᵊʃən] gjøre harsk, hard osv. **harshness** stramhet; hardhet, strenghet; barskhet, grettenhet.
hart [ha·ᵊt] hjort.
hartal ['ha·ᵊtəl] arbeidsstans, boikott (i India).
hart-royal ['ha·ᵊtroiəl] en hjort som kongen forgjeves har jagd, og som siden er fredet.
hartshorn ['ha·ᵊtshå·ᵊn] hjortehorn, hjortetakk; hjortetakkspiritus; **salt of** — hjortetakksalt.
harum-scarum ['hæ·ᵊrəm'skæ·ᵊrəm] vill, ubesindig; vill person, galning; kåthet.
Harvard ['ha·ᵊvad] Harvard; — **College** det eldste universitetet i De forente stater.
harvest ['ha·ᵊvist] høst; avl; (av)grøde; høste, høste inn; **owe some one a day in** — være en stor takk skyldig; **reap a golden** — gjøre en rik høst; **sow for a** — gjøre noe av egennytte.
harvester ['ha·ᵊvistə] høstkar, skurmann; skurmaskin, selvbinder.
harvest festival høsttakkefest.
harvest home høstgilde, skurgilde, høstfest.
harvest moon fullmåne nærmest høstjevndøgn.
harvest mouse liten markmus, dvergmus.
Harwich ['häridʒ] Harwich (eng. havn).
has [häz, svakt (h)əz] 3. p. sg. pres. av **have**.
hash [häʃ] hakke, skjære i stykker; hakkemat; lapskaus; hachis; virvar, rot, røre.
hasheesh, hashish ['häʃiʃ, hə'ʃi·ʃ] hasjisj, orientalsk nytelsesmiddel.
Haslemere ['he·ᵗzlmiə] Haslemere.
hasn't ['häznt] sammentrukket av **has not**.
hasp [ha·sp] hasp, hempe, vinduskrok; spenne; hespel; hespetre; lukke med hasp el. spenne.
hassock ['häsək] fotskammel, knelepute.
hast [häst] (gml. 2. p. sg. pres. av **have**).
hastate ['hästeᵗt] spydformet.
haste [heᵗst] hast, fart, il; **make** — skynde seg; **be in** — ha det travelt; **the more** —, **the less speed** hastverk er lastverk.
hasten ['heᵗsn] haste, ile, skynde seg; framskynde, skynde på.
hastily ['heᵗstili] hurtig, skyndsomt.
hastiness ['heᵗstinès] hurtighet, hastighet; overilelse, hissighet; iver.
hasting ['heᵗstiŋ] tidlig moden; **hastings** tidlig modne grønnsaker.
Hastings ['heᵗstiŋz] Hastings.
hasty ['heᵗsti] hastig, brå, hurtig; brålyndt, hissig; hastverks-; — **pudding** grøt.
hat [hät] hatt; **opera** — chapeau claque; **under one's own** — på egen hånd; **change**, -s hilse på hverandre; **I'll eat my** — **first** jeg vil heller la meg henge; **he hangs his** — **up there** han er som hjemme der; **have a brick in one's** — være full; **iron a** — presse opp en hatt; **put one in a** — få en i sin makt; **talk through one's** — snakke borti veggene.
hatable ['heᵗtəbl] som fortjener å bli hatet, avskyelig.
hatband ['hätbänd] hattebånd, hattesnor; sørgeflor om hatten; **it fits like Dick's** — det passer som en knytteneve til et blått øye.

hatbox ['hætbåks] hatteske.

hatch [hætʃ] halvdør; (mar.) luke; sluseport; **under -es** (mar.) ikke i tjeneste, ikke på dekket; suspendert; i nød; vel forvaret; død.

hatch [hætʃ] ruge ut, klekke ut; ruge; ruges ut; klekkes ut; utruging; utklekking; yngel, kull; **count one's chickens before they are -ed** selge skinnet før bjørnen er skutt.

hatch [hætʃ] skravere; skravering.

hatchel ['hætʃəl] hekle; hekle, skrubbe, plage, terge.

hatcher ['hætʃə] en som ruger ut, klekker ut.

hatchery ['hætʃəri] utklekkingsanstalt.

hatchet ['hætʃit] håndøks, liten øks; hogge; **bury the —** slutte fred; **sling the —** smette unna; **take** (el. **dig**) **up the —** begynne krig; **throw the — skrøne; send** (el. **throw**) **the helve after the — oppgi alt; — -face** langt ansikt med skarpt-skårne trekk.

hatching ['hætʃiŋ] utruging, utklekking.

hatching ['hætʃiŋ] skravering.

hatching-apparatus rugemaskin.

hatchment ['hætʃmənt] våpen, våpenskjold (ofte om en avdøds våpen, som ble anbrakt på huset ved begravelsen og hang der i 6—12 måneder, deretter i kirken).

hatchway ['hætʃweɪ] luke (om åpningen).

hate [heɪt] hate; (poet.) hat; **— worse hate** mer.

hateful ['heɪtf(u)l] forhatt, avskylig (sjelden: hatefull).

hater ['heɪtə] hater.

hat|ful ['hætful] en hel del. **— -guard** snor i hatten.

hath [hæþ] gml. form for **has** av **have**.

Hathaway ['hæþəweɪ] Hathaway.

hatless ['hætlès] uten hatt, barhodet.

hatmoney ['hætmʌni] kaplak (frakttillegg, som tilfaller skipperen).

hatred ['heɪtrid] hat (**of** el. **for** til).

hatter ['hætə] hattemaker; **mad as a —** splittergal; sint som en tyrk.

hat-touching hilsende; **have a — acquaintance with** være på hatt med.

hauberk ['hå·bə·k] ringbrynje.

haught [hå·t] stolt, kaut, hovmodig (foreldet).

haughtily ['hå·tili] hovmodig, stolt.

haughtiness ['hå·tinès] hovmod, stolthet.

haughty ['hå·ti] hovmodig, kaut, stolt.

haul [hå·l] hale, dra; haling; rykk; drett; kast; varp, fangst; **get a fine —** gjøre et godt kup. **haul-net** ['hå·lnet] kastenot, dragnett.

haulm [hå·m] halm; stilk.

haunch [hå·nʃ] hofte; bakfjerding; bakdel, ende; **— of sheep** sauelår.

haunt [hå·nt] tilholdssted; oppholdssted; besøke ofte, frekventere; hjemsøke i; plage, besvære; **the house is -ed** det spøker i huset.

haunter ['hå·ntə] stamgjest.

hautboy ['houboɪ] obo; slags jordbær.

hauteur [oᵘtə·, ᵒᵘtə·] stolthet, hovmod.

Havana [hə'vänə] Havana; havanasigar, havaneser.

Havanese ['hævə'niːz] havanesisk; havaneser.

have [hæv, (h)əv] ha; besitte; få; la; **as Shakespeare has it** som det står hos Shakespeare; **what would you — me do** hva vil du at jeg skal gjøre; **I won't — it** jeg vil ikke vite av det; **I — had my hair cut** jeg har fått klipt håret mitt; **— something done** få gjort noe, la noe gjøre; **— some wine** drikk litt vin; **he had his head broken** han fikk hodet knust; **— by heart** kunne utenat; **you — it right** det er riktig; **you had better** (el. **best** el. **rather**) **du gjør** (el. gjorde) best i, du burde **I — had a friend of your Mr. Irving's** en venn av Deres Irving har besøkt meg; **he had the bishopric given him** hanfikk bispedømmet overdratt,bispedømmet ble gitt ham. **I would — you write** jeg ville gjerne De skulle skrive; **what answer would you — me return?**

hva vil De jeg skal svare? **what would you —?** hva ønsker De? **— a care** passe på, ta seg i akt; **— a mind for** ha lyst til; **— after** følge etter, forfølge; **— at angripe; begynne på; — at** oneself se seg for; **— at you** nå er det deg! se deg for! **— away** fjerne, skaffe av veien; **you — to** du må; **I don't want to go. But I tell you, you will — to** (go) jeg vil ikke gå. Men jeg sier deg, du må; **— it out** få en ende på det. **— upon me** ha på meg (f. eks. penger).

havelock ['hævlåk] havelock, hodeduk mot solstikk.

haven ['heɪvn] havn, ly (mest i overført bet.).

havenage ['heɪvnidʒ] havneavgift.

haven't ['hævnt] sammentrukket av **have not**.

haver ['hævə] havre.

haver ['heɪvə] vrøvle; vås, tøv, vrøvl (skotsk).

haverel, haveril ['heɪvril] vrøvlekopp, tosk.

haversack ['hævəsäk] brødpose (soldats).

havildar ['hævəldɑ·] sersjant i regiment av innfødte i den indiske armé.

havoc(k) ['hævək] ødelegging; nederlag; blodbad; ødelegge; massakrere; **make — of** ødelegge; massakrere.

haw [hå·] innhegning, hegn, hage, gård.

haw [hå·] hagtorn; hagtornbær.

haw [hå·] blinkhinne.

haw [hå·] stamme, kremte, hakke; stamming, kremt.

Hawaii [hə'waɪiː] Hawaii. **Hawaiian** [he'waɪən] havaiisk; havaier.

Hawarden ['ha·ədn] Hawarden.

hawbuck ['hå·bʌk] idiot, tosk.

hawfinch ['hå·finʃ] kirsebærfugl.

haw-haw ['hå·'hå·] ha-ha; skratt, latter; storle.

hawk [hå·k] hauk; falskspiller, bedrager; jage med falk; jage; **it is neither — nor buzzard** det er hverken fugl eller fisk; **ware** (**the**) **— pass på!**

hawk [hå·k] renske halsen, harke; harking.

hawk [hå·k] høkre, rope ut, sjakre.

hawk [hå·k] kalkbrett.

hawker ['hå·kə] gateselger.

hawking ['hå·kiŋ] falkejakt; sjakring.

hawse ['hå·z] klyss (hull i skipsbaugen.)

hawser ['hå·zə] pertline, trosse.

hawtorn ['hå·þå·ən] hagtorn.

Hawthorne ['hå·þå·ən] Hawthorne.

hay [heɪ] hei! hallo!

hay [heɪ] høy; **make — høye; (amr.) between — and grass** for tidlig til det ene og for sent til det andre; (amr.) **neither — nor grass** hverken fugl eller fisk; **look for a needle in a bottle of —** lete etter en nål i høylass; **he made — of my books and papers** han kastet bøkene og papirene mine om hverandre; **make — while the sun shines** smie mens jernet er varmt.

hay-asthma høyfeber. **-bag** kvinnfolk. **-box** høykasse. **-cart** høyvogn.

haycock ['heɪkåk] høysåte.

Haydn ['haɪdn] Haydn.

hay|-fever høyfeber. **-field** eng. **--fork** høygaffel. **-loft** høyloft. **-maker** slåttekar.

Haymarket ['heɪma·əkit] gate i London.

hay|-mow ['heɪmau] høystakk. **-rake** høyrive. **-rick** høystakk. **-seed** høyfrø; høyrusk; (amr.) bonde. **-stack** høystakk.

hazard ['hæzəd] tilfelle, treff; fare, vågestykke; hasard, vågespill; hull (i biljard og ballspill); våge; sette på spill; løpe en risiko.

hazardous ['hæzədəs] vågelig, vågal.

haze [heɪz] tåke, dis, moe.

haze [heɪz] pine, plage, terge; dørhale.

hazel ['heɪzl] hassel; nøttebrun.

hazelly ['heɪzl-i] nøttebrun.

hazel-nut ['heɪzlnʌt] hasselnøtt.

haziness ['heɪzinès] disighet; omtåkethet.

Hazlitt ['häzlit] Hazlitt.

hazree ['häzri·] frokost (i India).

hazy ['heɪzi] disig, tåket; dunkel, ubestemt; omtåket, anløpen.

H. B. fk. f. hard black (om blyant).
H. B. M. fk. f. His Britannic Majesty.
H. C. fk. f. House of Commons.
H. C. F. fk. f. highest common factor.
he [hi, (h)i] han; den, det; **he who** den som.
H. E. fk. f. His Excellency; high explosive.

head [hed] hode, forstand, vett; overhode; høvedsmann, øverste; hovedperson, leder; hovedpunkt, punkt, post, sak; naut; det øverste, øverste del, øverste ende, topp, åsrygg, fjellkam; kilde, kjelde, oppkomme, opphav; fallhøyde, vanntrykk; forreste del, forstavn, forside, forende; spiss, nes, odde; overskrift; først; forrest, hovedsakelig; hoved-, over-, for-; **sette hode på**; spiss o. l.; lede, føre, sette seg i spissen for; innta forsetet; innhente, komme forut for, gå i forvelen; holde tilbake; stå i spissen, stå øverst; **få et hode; vende; ta kursen; føre** (om vei); springe ut; gå hodekulls løs på noe; **on that** — i den henseende; **back of the** — nakke; **crown of the** — isse; — **over heels** hodekulls, hodestupes, hulter til bulter; **over** — **and ears til** opp over ørene, fullstendig; **neither** — **nor tail** hverken fugl eller fisk; **get** (el. **take**) **into one's** — sette seg i hodet; **give one's** — **a toss, toss up one's** — slå med nakken; **keep one's** — bevare fatningen; **turn** — dreie seg om, gjøre front; **an idle** — **is the devil's workshop** lediggang er rota til alt vondt; **be off one's** — være fra forstanden, fra vettet; **gather** — samle styrke; **give a horse the** — gi en hest tøylen; **make** — **against** gjøre motstand, sette seg tvert imot; **make** — (up)on vinne forsprang for; **take** — være sta (om hest); **a beautiful** — **of hair** vakkert hår; **she threw herself at his** — hun kastet seg rett i armene på ham; **at the** — **of** i spissen for; øverst i (ved); — **of the table** æresplassen; **head(s) or tail(s)** krone eller mynt; **make** — **to** sette kursen imot; **twenty** — **of cattle** tjue naut.

headache ['hedeᴵk] hodepine. **headachy** ['hedeᴵkj] som har el. lett får hodepine; som forårsaker hodepine.
head|band hodebånd, pannebånd. — **-beetler** første mann (på et verksted). **-borough** lensmannsdreng. — **-boy** duks. — **-cook** overkokk. — **-cook and bottle-washer** enepike. — **-dress** hodepynt, hodeplagg.
header ['hedə] en som setter hode på; dukkert; stup, hodekulls fall el. sprang.
headfast ['hedfɑ·st] landtau fra skipets forstavn.
head|first hodestupes, på hodet; — **-gear** hodeplagg.
headily ['hedili] ubesindig.
headiness ['hedinés] voldsomhet; stridighet, stivsinn; berusende egenskap (av en drikk).
heading ['hediŋ] tittel, hode, overskrift.
headland ['hedlənd] pynt, nes, odde.
headless ['hedlés] hodeløs; tosket.
headlight ['hedlait] forlanterne (på lokomotiv).
headline ['hedlain] overskrift.
head|long ['hedlåŋ] hodekulls, på hodet; ubesindig; voldsomt. — **-man** ['hed'män] hovedmann, høvding, fører, formann; skarpretter. **-master** ['hed'mɑ·stə] skolebestyrer, rektor. **-mastership** rektorat, skolebestyrerstilling. **-mistress** (kvinnelig) rektor, skolebestyrerinne. — **-money** koppskatt; pris som blir satt opp for hver fange som blir tatt.
headmost ['hedmoᵘst] forrest, fremst.
head-nurse ['hed'nə·s] oversøster.
head-over-heels hodekulls, hodestupes.
head-piece ['hedpi·s] hjelm; hodeplagg; forreste stykke, hodestykke, (fig.) hode.
head-quarters ['hed'kwɑ·ᵊtəz] hovedkvarter.
headship ['hedʃip] førerstilling; rektorat.
headsman ['hedzmən] skarpretter.
headspring ['hedspriŋ] kilde, oppkomme; opphav.

headstone ['hedstoᵘn] hjørnestein; gravstein.
headstrong ['hedstråŋ] stri, sta; hissig.
head|waiter overtjener. — **-waters** utspring.
headway ['hedweᴵ] bevegelse framover; framskritt; forsprang; fart; **fetch** — komme i gang; **make** — komme av sted; gjøre framskritt; **be under** — være i full fart.
head|wind ['hedwind] motvind. — **-work** tankearbeid.
heady ['hedi] stivsinnet, egensindig; selvrådig, overilet, voldsom; berusende; omtåket.
heal [hi·l] lege, kurere, helbrede; bilegge, forsone; leges, heles, gro igjen.
heal-all ['hi·lå·l] baldrian.
healer ['hi·lə] lege; legemiddel.
healing ['hi·liŋ] legende.
health [help] helse, sunnhet; helbred; skål; **bill of** — helsepass; **board of** — sunnhetskommisjon; **be in good (bad)** — ha det godt (dårlig); **drink one's** — drikke en skål for; **your (good)** —! Deres skål! **here's a** — **to** ...! skål for ...!
healthful ['helpful] sunn, frisk, rask; god for helbreden. **-ness** sunnhet.
health-giving sunn, helsebringende.
healthily ['helpili] sunt.
healthiness ['helpinés] sunnhet.
health|-officer karanteneembetsmann. — **-resort** sanatorium.
healthy ['helpi] sunn.
heap [hi·p] hop, haug, bunke, dynge; masse; hope opp, dynge på; **a** — **of** mange, en masse, en hel dynge med; **all of a** —, **all on a** — i én klump; forvirret, forbløffet; **strike all of a** — gjøre rent målløs; **sit in a** — sitte forknytt, sammenkrøpet; **live at full** — leve i overdådighet.
heapy ['hi·pi] som ligger i bunker, i dynger.
hear [hiə] høre; erfare, få vite; høre på.
heard [hə·d] imperf. og perf. pts. av **hear**.
hearer ['hiərə] tilhører.
hearing ['hiəriŋ] høring; hørsel; påhør; forhør; **within** — innenfor hørevidde. — **-trumpet** hørerør.
hearken ['hɑ·ᵊkən] lytte, lye etter.
hearsay ['hiəseᴵ] forlydende, rykte; folkesnakk; omtale.
hearse [hə·s] likvogn; likbåre; sette på likvogn, sette på båre; kjøre til kirkegården.
heart [hɑ·ᵗt] hjerte; mot; kraft; det innerste, midte; alved, malm; marg; **the** — **beats** (el. **palpitates**) hjertet banker; **disease of the** — hjertesykdom; **bless my** — å du gode gud; **by** — utenat; **for one's** — inderlig gjerne; om det så skulle koste livet; **be all** — være godheten selv; **find it in my** — bringe det over mitt hjerte, få meg til, orke det; **in my heart of hearts** i mitt innerste hjerte, innerst inne; **wear one's** — **on one's sleeve** mangle tilbakeholdenhet, vise enhver sine følelser; **with all one's** — hjertens gjerne; — **of the matter** sakens kjerne; — **of an apple** kjernehus; **he is a good fellow at** — han er i grunnen et godt menneske; **speak one's** — snakke fritt ut; **my** — **fails** motet svikter meg; **out of** — motløs; **take** — fatte mot.
heart|-ache ['hɑ·ᵊteᴵk] hjertesorg. — **-beat** hjerteslag; hjertebank. — **-breaker** hjerteknuser. — **-breaking** hjerteskjærende. — **-broken** med knust hjerte, sorgtynget. — **-burn** halsbrann; kardialgi. — **-burning** misnøye; nag, skinnsyke. — **-cheering** oppmuntrende. — **-complaint**, **-disease** hjertesykdom.
hearten ['hɑ·ᵗtn] oppmuntre, sette mot i.
heart|felt ['hɑ·ᵊtfelt] inderlig, hjertelig. **-free** ikke forelsket.
hearth ['hɑ·ᵊp] arne, arnested; skorstein; kamin; åre, peis, grue. — **-rug** kaminteppe. — **-stone** gruestein; årestein; arne; hjem; skurestein; skure, polere.
heartily ['hɑ·ᵊtili] hjertelig, varmt; ivrig; kraftig; dyktig; varig; muntert, glad; meget.

heartless ['ha·ᵊtlės] hjerteløs. heartlessness hjerteløshet.

heart-rending ['ha·ᵊtrendiŋ] hjerteskjærende.

heart-rent ['ha·ᵊtrent] sønderknust.

hearts [ha·ᵊts] hjerter (i kort); queen of — hjerterdame.

heart's-ease ['ha·ᵊtsi·z] stemorsblomst.

heartsick ['ha·ᵊtsik] hjertesyk, sorgtynget.

heartsome ['ha·ᵊtsəm] oppmuntrende; munter.

heartsore ['ha·ᵊtså·ᵊ] sorgtynget; hjertesorg.

heart|spasm brystkrampe. — -spoon brystbein. — -stirring gripende. -stricken ramt i hjertet; sorgtynget.

hearth-whole ['ha·ᵊthoᵘl] ikke forelsket.

heart-wood ['ha·ᵊtwud] alved, malm.

hearty ['ha·ᵊti] hjertelig; ivrig; sunn, kraftig; fast, sterk, solid, varig; munter, glad; my — vennen min (i tiltale); my hearties! guttene mine! a — meal et rikelig måltid.

heat [hi·t] hete, varme; (sport): enkelt løp; varme, gjøre het; legge i; bli het, hetne, bli varm; at a — på én gang, i ett kjør; be in — renne (om hunder); dead — uavgjort løp; final — avgjørende løp. — -apoplexy solstikk.

heater ['hi·tə] heter, varmer; fyrbøter; varmeinnretning, ovn; strykejern, bolt.

heath [hi·þ] mo, hei; lyng. — -bell lyngklokke. — -bramble blåbær. — -cock orrhane.

Heathcote ['hi·þkət] Heathcote.

heathen ['hi·ðn] hedning; hedensk. heathendom [-dəm] hedenskap. heathenish [-iʃ] hedensk. heathenism [-izm] hedenskap. heathenize [-aiz] gjøre til hedning. heathenry [-ri] hedenskap.

heather ['heðə] lyng, røsslyng, bustelyng; set the — on fire stifte ufred. heathery ['heðəri] lyngaktig, lyng-; lyngbevokst; lyngbevokst sted. heath|game ['hi·þge¹m] orre. — -pea jordnøtt. heathy ['hi·þi] lyng-; mo-.

heating ['hi·tiŋ] varmende; opphissende; oppheting, oppvarming; steam — sentralfyring; — apparatus varmeapparat.

heat|lightning kornmo. -spots fregne; heteblemmer. -stroke heteslag, solstikk.

heat-wave ['hi·twe¹v] hetebølge.

heave [hi·v] heve, løfte; hive; heve seg; stige; stige og synke (f. eks. om bryst); båre; svulme; ha vondt, streve, arbeide, brekke seg, slite seg; hevning, løft, tak; bølging; duving, dønning, båregang; tung pust, sukking; — a sigh sukke dypt; — the lead hive loddet; — in sight komme i sikte; — to legge bi.

heaven ['hevn] himmel(en), himmerike; (især pluralis også:) himmelhvelving (alm. sky). heaven-born ['hevnbå·ᵊn] himmelfødt.

heavenly ['hevnli] himmelsk; — bodies stjerner; the — city Paradis.

heavenward(s) ['hevnwəd(z)] mot himmelen, til himmels.

heavily ['hevili] tungt; svært; besværlig, langsomt; tungsindig, bedrøvet; sterkt, heftig, meget; se heavy.

heaviness ['hevinės] tunghet, tyngde, vekt.

heavy ['hevi] tung, svær; solid; besværlig; tungvint; heftig, kraftig, sterk; plump; trettende; kjedelig; fornem, viktig; — of sale vanskelig å selge; — to the stomach vanskelig å fordøye; — debt trykkende gjeld; — expenses store utgifter; — with sleep søvndrukken. — -armed tungt væpnet. — -laden tungt lastet. — -weight sværvektsbokser (-rytter, -bryter, -hest); viktig personlighet.

hebdomadal [heb'dåmədəl] ukentlig; uke-.

Hebe ['hi·bi·] Hebe.

hebetate ['hebite¹t] sløve, døyve. hebetation [hebi'te¹ʃən] døyving; sløvhet. hebete ['hebi·t] sløv. hebitude ['hebitjud] sløvhet.

Hebraic(al) [hi'bre¹k(l)] hebraisk. hebraism ['hi·bre¹izm] hebraisk eiendommelighet.

Hebrew ['hi·bru(·)]hebreer; hebraisk. Hebrewess ['hi·bruės] hebraisk kvinne.

Hebridean [hi'bridjən] hebridisk; hebrider.

Hebrides ['hebridi·z]: the — Hebriderne; Suderøyene.

hecatomb ['hekətəm] hekatombe.

heck [hek] hekk, høygrind; dørklinke; buktning (av en elv).

heckle ['hekl] hekle; interpellere strengt, plage med spørsmål.

hectic ['hektik] hektisk; hektisk feber; tæring.

hectogram(me) ['hektogräm] hektogram.

hectograph ['hektogra·f] hektograf; hektografere.

hectolitre ['hektoli·tə] hektoliter.

hectometre ['hektomi·tə] hektometer.

hector ['hektå·ᵊ] skryte; true; tyrannisere.

he'd [hi·d] sammentrukket av: he had eller he would.

hedge [hedʒ] hegn, gjerde, hekk; omhegne, sette gjerde omkring, omgjerde; gjemme seg, liste seg bort; vri seg unna; vedde på begge parter (i sport); be on the wrong side of the — ta feil; sit on the —, be on both sides of the — lefle med begge partier.

hedgeborn ['hedʒbå·ᵊn] av lav ætt; simpel. hedgehog ['hedʒ(h)åg] pinnsvin. hedge|-lawyer lovvrier, vinkelskriver. — -marriage hemmelig ekteskap.

hedger ['hedʒə] en som setter gjerder; en som klipper hekker; luring, slu rev.

hedgerow ['hedʒroᵘ] hekk.

hedge|school skole under åpen himmel (tidligere i Irland); tarvelig skole. — -sparrow gjerdesmutt. — -tavern kneipe. — -writer obskur forfatter.

hedonism ['hi·donizm] hedonisme (læren om nytelsen). hedonist ['hi·donist] hedonist. hedonistic [hi·do'nistik] hedonisk.

heed [hi·d] akte, ense, gi akt på, bry seg om; akt, oppmerksomhet; omhug; forsiktighet; give eller pay eller take — to ense, passe på, legge merke til; take — passe seg.

heedful ['hi·df(u)l] oppmerksom; forsiktig.

heedless ['hi·dlės] likegyldig, ubekymret; likesæl; ubetenksom. heedlessness ubesindighet, skjøtesløshet.

heehaw ['hi·hå·] remje, skryte (om et esel).

heel [hi·l] hæl; skorpe (på brød, ost); slagside; sette hæl på; følge hakk i hæl; (mar.) krenge; legge seg over; -s over head el. head over -s el. over head and -s hodekulls, hulter til bulter; come (down) to — gi etter; ◊være snill gutt◊; cool the -s vente stå'modig; kick one's -s vente utålmodig; kick up one's -s slå bakut, være kåt; lay by the -s kaste i fengsel; pick up one's -s ta beina på nakken; stikke av; take to one's -s stikke av; have one's heart at one's -s stå med hjertet i halsen; throw up a man's -s overvinne en; grow out at -s ha hull på strømpene.

heeltap ['hi·läp] bakflikk, hællapp; skvett (i et glass); flikke, lappe.

heft [heft] håndtak, skaft; tak; tyngde; løfte.

hefty ['hefti] svær, kraftig.

hegemony [hi'geməni] hegemoni.

hegira ['hedʒira, hi'dʒaiərə, hə'dʒaiərə] Muhameds flukt fra Mekka til Medina i 622.

hegoat ['hi·goᵘt] geitebukk.

heifer ['hefə] kvie; (amr. ogs.) kone, kvinne.

heigh-ho ['he¹'hoᵘ] akk! akk ja!

height [hait] høyde, høgd; lengde; legemsstørrelse; haug, fjell, ås; høydepunkt, toppunkt; høy rang; høyeste makt.

heighten ['haitn] forhøye, heve; forskjønne; bli høyere, sterkere osv.

heinous ['heinəs] avskylig, skjendig; fryktelig. heinousness avskylighet, skjendighet.

heir [æ·ə] arving; arve; — apparent rettmessig arving, nærmeste arving, tronarving; — general universalarving.

heiress ['æ·ᵊrés] kvinnelig arving; godt parti,

heirless ['ɛə·əlĕs] uten arvinger.
heirloom ['ɛə·ɔlu·m] arvestykke.
heirship ['ɛə·əʃip] arverett.
hejira se **hegira**.
held [held] imperf. og perf. pts. av **hold.**
Helen ['helin] Helene.
Helena ['helinə] Helena; **St.** — [snt (h)i'li·nə] St. Helena.
heliacal [hi'laiəkl] helisk, heliotisk.
helical ['helikl] skrueformet, spiral-.
Helicon ['helikån] Helikon.
helicopter ['helikáptə] helikopter.
Heligoland ['heligoländ] Helgoland.
heliocentric ['hi·ljoᵘ'sentrik] heliosentrisk.
heliograph ['hi·ljogra·f] heliograf; heliografere.
heliographic [hi·ljo'gräfik] heliografisk. **heliography** [hi·li'ågrəfi] heliografi.
heliolater [hi·li'ålətə] soltilbeder. **heliolatry** [-tri] soldyrking.
heliometer [hi·li'åmitə] heliometer, solmåler.
Helios ['hi·liås] Helios (gresk solgud).
helioscope ['hi·ljəskoᵘp] helioskop, solkikkert.
heliotrope ['heljətroᵘp] heliotrop.
heliotype ['hi·ljətaip] fotografi.
helispheric(al) [heli'sferik(l)] helisfærisk.
helium ['hi·ljəm] helium.
helix ['hi·liks] skruelinje, spiral.
he'll [hi·l] sammentrukket av **he will.**
hell [hel] helvete; spillehus; den kasse som skredderen kaster lapper i; en kasse til kasserte typer i boktrykkerier; (i barnelek) det sted hvor fangene blir anbrakt.
Hellas ['helås] Hellas.
hellebore ['helibå·ə] nyserot.
Hellene ['heli·n] hellen. **Hellenian** [he'li·njən], **Hellenic** [he'li·nik] hellensk, gresk. **hellenism** ['helinizm] hellenisme. **hellenist** ['helinist] hellenist, kjenner av gresk språk; gresk jøde. **hellenistic** [heli'nistik] hellenistisk. **hellenize** ['helinaiz] hellenisere.
Hellespont ['helispånt] Hellespont.
hell-fire ['hel·faiə] helvetes ild.
Hellgate ['helge't] Hellgate, det trangeste sted ved innseilingen til New York.
hell-hound ['helhaund] helveteshund.
hellcat ['helikät] (skotsk) ondt vesen.
hellier ['heljə] taktekker.
hellish ['heliʃ] helvetes, djevelsk.
helm [helm] hjelm.
helm [helm] rorpinne, ratt, ror; styrvol.
helmet ['helmit] hjelm. **helmeted** ['helmitid] hjelmkledd. **helmet-flower** stormhatt (planten).
helminth ['helminþ] innvollsorm.
helminthic [hel'minþik] ormdrivende middel. **helminthoid** [hel'minþoid] ormeaktig. **helminthology** [helmin'þålədʒi] ormelære.
helmsman ['helmzmən] rorgjenger, rorsmann.
helot ['helåt] helot; træl, trell.
helotism ['helətizm] helotisme; trældom.
helotry ['helətri] slaveri, trældom; heloter.
help [help] hjelp, bistand; hjelper, hjelpesmann, støtte; (amr.) tjener, pike; råd, hjelpemiddel; hjelpe; støtte; forhindre; hjelpe for, la være med; hjelpe seg; forsyne seg; hjelpe til; duge; **be of** — være til hjelp; **by the** — of ved hjelp av; **there's no** — **for it** det er ikke noe å gjøre ved det; **so** — **me God!** så sant hjelpe meg Gud! — **yourself to some claret, please** forsyn Dem med rødvin; **he helped me to a glass of wine** han skjenkte et glass vin til meg; — **the soup** øse opp suppa; **I cannot** — **it** jeg kan ikke la være med det; **how can I** — **it?** hva kan jeg gjøre for det? **what's done cannot be** -**ed** gjort gjerning står ikke til å endre; **I cannot** — **laughing** jeg kan ikke holde meg for å le; — **down** hjelpe ned; bidra til undergang; — **forward** (fig.) fremme; — **off the time** fordrive tiden; — **on** hjelpe, fremme; hjelpe med å ta på (tøy); — **me on with this coat** hjelp meg på med denne frakken; — **out**

hjelpe ut av nød o. l.; understøtte; **this helps out the picture** dette framhevet bildet; — **a lame dog over a stile** hjelpe en ut av en forlegenhet.
helper ['helpə] hjelper, hjelperske.
helpful ['helpf(u)l] hjelpsom; behjelpelig; gagnlig.
helping ['helpiŋ] forsyning, servering.
helpless ['helplĕs] hjelpeløs.
help-mate ['helpme't] medhjelp; hjelper(ske).
helterskelter ['heltə'skeltə] over hals og hode; hodestupes; hulter til bulter.
helve [helv] økseskaft; skjefte.
Helvetia [hel'vi·ʃ(j)ə] Helvetia, Sveits. **Helvetic** [hel'vetik] helvetisk, sveitsisk.
hem [hem] søm; fald, brett, kant; sømme; kante; falde; inneslutte; — **in** innestenge.
hem [hem] kremte; kremt.
hemal ['hi·məl] blod-, hemal; se **hæmal.**
Hemans ['hi·mənz] Hemans.
hematine ['hemətin, 'hi·m-] hematin.
hematogen [hĕ'mätodʒən] hematogen.
hemeralopia [hemərə'loᵘpjə] nattblindhet.
hemicrania [hemi'kre'njə], **hemicrany** ['hemi-kre'ni] vondt i den ene siden av hodet, migréne.
hemicycle ['hemisaikl] halvring.
hemisphere ['hemisfiə] halvkule. **hemispheric(al)** [hemi'sferik(l)] halvkuleformet.
hemistich ['hemistik] halvvers.
hemlock ['hemlåk] skarntyde; hundekjeks; selsnepe; hemlockgran (en slags kanadisk gran); skarntydeekstrakt.
hemoptysis [hĕ'måptisis] blodspytting.
hemorrhage ['hemoridʒ] blodstyrtning, blodtap.
hemorrhoids ['hemoroidz] hemorrhoider.
hemp [hemp] hamp. **hempen** ['hempən] av hamp; hampe-; **die of a** — **fever** dø i galgen; — **rogue** galgenfugl; — **widow** enken etter en hengt.
hemp-nettle ['hemp'netl] dåe (plante).
hemp-seed ['hempsi·d] hampefrø.
hemstitch ['hemstitʃ] hullsøm; sy hullsøm.
hen [hen] høne; hun (av fugl); **grey** — orrhøne.
henbane ['henbe'n] bulmeurt, villrot.
hence [hens] herfra; fra nå av; herav, derfor, av dette følger; **twenty-four hours** — om fire og tjue timer.
henceforth [hens'få·əþ] fra nå av, for fremtiden.
henceforward [hens'få·əwəd] fra nå av, for fremtiden.
henchman ['hen(t)ʃmən] drabant, tjener, håndgangen mann.
hencoop ['henku·p] hønsebur.
hendecagon ['hen'dekəgån] ellevekant.
hendecasyllable ['hendikə'siləbl] ellevestavelsesvers.
Hendon ['hendən] (by og lufthavn).
hen-driver ['hendraivə] hønsehauk.
Hengist ['hengist] Hengist.
hen-harrier ['hen'häriə] hønsehauk.
hen-house ['henhaus] hønsehus.
Henley ['henli] Henley.
henna ['henə] henna (fargestoff av alkanna).
hennery ['henəri] hønseri, hønsehus.
Henny ['heni] Henny, diminutiv av **Henrietta.**
henpeck ['henpek] ha under tøffelen; **a** -**ed husband** en tøffelhelt.
Henry [henri] Henrik.
hepatic [hi'pätik] hepatisk, lever-.
hepatite ['hepətait] hepatitt, leverstein.
hepatitis [hepə'taitis] leverbetennelse.
hepatology [hepə'tålədʒi] læren om leveren.
Hephæstus [hi'fi·stəs] Hefaistos.
heptagon ['heptəgån] sjukant.
heptarchy ['heptəᵏki] heptarki.
her [hə·, hə] henne; seg; hennes; sin, sitt, sine.
Heracles ['herəkli·z] Herakles.

herald ['herəld] herold; våpenkyndig; forkynne, melde, innvarsle. heraldic [he'räldik] heraldisk. heraldry ['herəldri] heraldikk; heroldverdighet.

Herat [hə'rät] Herat.

herb [hə·b] urt, plante. herbaceous [hə'be'ʃəs] urteaktig, urte-. herbage ['hə·bidʒ] urter, planter. herbal ['hə·bəl] plantebok, botanikk, herbarium. herbalist ['hə·bəlist] plantekjenner; plantesamler. herbarium [hə·'bæ·əriəm] herbarium.

Herbert ['hə·bət] Herbert.

herbescent [hə·'besənt] planteaktig.

herbivorous [hə·'bivərəs] planteetende.

herblet ['hə·blėt] liten plante.

herborize ['hə·boraiz] botanisere.

herbous ['hə·bəs] rik på planter, grasrik.

Herculaneum [hə·kju'le'niəm] Herculaneum.

Herculean [hə·'kju·ljən, hə·kju'li·ən] herkulisk.

Hercules [hə·'kjuli·z] Herkules.

herd [hə·d] hjord, flokk; buskap, bøling; mengde; gjeter; gå i flokk, samle seg, stue seg sammen; samle i flokk; være gjeter, gjete. herdsman ['hə·dzmən] gjeter, hjuring.

here [hiə] her, hit; kom her! hei da! hei! from — herfra; leave — reise herfra; — and there her og der; that's neither — nor there det hører ikke noe sted hjemme; det kommer ikke saken ved; — goes! la gå! nå får det våge seg; — you are vær så god (når man gir en noe); here's to you skål!

hereabout(s) [hiərə'baut(s)] her omkring, på disse kanter.

hereafter [hiə'ra·ftə] heretter; det hinsidige, livet etter dette.

hereby [hiə'bai] herved, herigjennom.

hereditable [hi'reditəbl] arvelig.

hereditary [hi'reditəri] arvelig, arve-.

heredity [hi'rediti] arvelighet, arv.

Hereford ['herifəd] Hereford.

herein ['hiə'rin] heri. hereof [hiə'råv] herom; herav.

heresiarch ['herisia·ºk, hi'ri·si-] erkekjetter.

heresy ['herisi] kjetteri. heretic ['herətik] kjetter; kjettersk. heretical [hi'retikl] kjettersk.

hereto ['hiə'tu·] hertil.

heretofore ['hiətə'få·ª] hittil, før; tidligere; fortid.

hereupon ['hiərə'pån] herpå, derpå.

herewith ['hiə'wið] hermed.

heritable ['heritəbl] arvelig; arveberettiget.

heritage ['heritidʒ] arv.

hermaphrodite [hə·'mäfrodait] hermafroditt, tvetulle. hermaphroditic ['hə·mäfro'ditik] hermafrodittisk.

Hermes ['hə·mi·z] Hermes.

hermetic [hə·'metik] alkymi-; hermetisk; the — art alkymien. hermetically [hə·'metikəli] hermetisk.

Hermia ['hə·miə] Hermia.

Hermione [hə·'maioni·] Hermione.

hermit [hə·'mit] eremitt. hermitage ['hə·mitidʒ] eneboerhytte; eremitasje; slags fransk vin. hermitess ['hə·mitès] eneboerske.

hernia ['hə·njə] brokk. hernial ['hə·njəl] brokk-.

hero ['hiəroª] heros; helt.

Herod ['herəd] Herodes.

Herodias [hi'roudjäs] Herodias.

Herodotus [hi'rådətəs] Herodot.

heroic [hi'roªik] heroisk; heltemessig; hestekur (medisin); heltediktets versemål; — treatment hestekur. heroics (plur.) heltestil, høyttravende uttrykksmåte. heroically [hi'roª kəli] heltemodig.

heroine ['heroªin] heltinne.

heroism ['heroªizm] heltemot.

heron ['herən] hegre. -ry hegrekoloni.

Herostratos [hi'rástrətås] Herostrat.

hero-worship ['hiərowə·ʃip] heltedyrking.

herpes ['hə·pi·z] herpes (en hudsykdom).

Herrick ['herik] Herrick.

herring ['heriŋ] sild; red — røykesild; en list for å få motstanderne bort fra sporet; draw a red — across the trail of the war avlede oppmerksomheten fra krigen; king of the herrings sildekonge; gulhå; hågylling, sjøkatt; laksestørje; --bone sildebein; sildebeinssting, fiskebeinssting; aksdannet (el. sildebeins-) murverk (opus spicatum); sy med heksesting. herringer ['heriŋə] sildefisker. herring-gull gråmåke. herring-pond spøkende uttrykk for Atlanterhavet; be sent across the herring-pond bli deportert.

hers [hə·z] hennes; sin, sitt, sine.

herse [hə·s] fallgitter som likner en harv.

herself [hə·'self] hun selv, henne selv; seg selv, seg; selv, sjøl.

hership ['hə·ʃip] hærverk; bytte.

Hertford ['hə·ªfəd; amr. 'hə·tfəd] Hertford.

Hertfordshire ['ha·ªfədʃə], Herts [ha·ªts] Hertfordshire.

he's [hi·z] sammentrukket av he is el. he has.

Hesiod ['hi·siåd] Hesiod.

hesitancy ['hezitənsi] nøling, uvisshet; stamming. hesitant ['hezitənt] nølende; stammende. hesitate ['hezite't] nøle; nære betenkeligheter; stamme, hakke i det. hesitatingly ['hezite'tiŋli] nølende; usikkert. hesitation [hezi'te'ʃen] nøling; vingling, usikkerhet; stamming. hesitative ['hezite'tiv] nølende; vinglete; usikker.

Hesperia [he'spiəriə] Hesperia (•Vesterlandet•) Italia eller Spania. Hesperian [he'spiəriən] hesperisk, vestlig. Hesperides [he'speridi·z] hesperider (gudinner hos grekerne, boende i vest). Hesperus ['hespərəs] aftenstjerne.

Hesse ['hesi] Hessen. Hessian ['hesjən] hessisk; hesser; — boots el. Hessians skaftestøvler.

hest [hest] befaling, bud.

Hester ['hestə] Ester.

hetæra [he'tiərə] hetære, frille.

hetaira [he'tairə] hetære. hetairia [he'tairiə] et hemmelig gresk forbund for å befri Hellas fra tyrkernes åk. hetairism [he'tairizm] hetærisme; prostitusjon.

heteroclitic(al) [hetəro'klitik(l)] uregelmessig.

heterodox ['hetərodåks] heterodoks, annerledestenkende; kjettersk. heterodoxy ['hetərodåksi] heterodoksi; kjetteri.

heterogeneous [hetəro'dʒi·njəs] uensartet.

hetman ['hetmən] hetman, kosakkhøvding, fører.

hew [hju·] hogge; hogge til. hewer ['hju·ə] hogger.

hewn [hju·n] perf. pts. av hew.

hexagon ['heksəgən] sekskant. hexahedral [heksə'hi·drəl] kubisk. hexahedron ['heksə'hi·drən] kubus.

hexameter [hek'sämĭtə] heksameter.

hey [he'] hei! hva?

heyday ['he'de'] heida! hopsa!

heyday ['he'de'] blomstringstid, beste tid, velmaktsdager; storm (f. eks. lidenskapenes); in the — of youth i ungdommens vår.

Heywood ['he'wud] Heywood.

Hezekiah [hezi'kaiə] Esekias.

hf. bd. fk. f. half-bound.

hf. cf. fk. f. half-calf.

H. G. fk. f. High German; Holy Ghost; Horse Guards.

hg fk. f. hectogram.

H. H. fk. f. His (el. Her) Highness.

HH fk. f. double-hard (om blyant).

hhd. fk. f. hogshead.

HHH fk. f. treble-hard (om blyant).

hi! [hai] ei! hei!

hiah! ['haia·] ei! hva! (i engelsk-kinesisk).

hiatus [hai'e'təs] åpning, gap, kløft, lakune; hiatus.

Hiawatha [haiə'wåþə] Hiawatha.

hibernal [hai'bə·nəl] vinterlig, vinter-. hibernate ['haibənet] ligge i vinterdvale, i hi. **hibernation** [haibə'ne'ʃən] overvintring; vinterdvale. **Hibernia** [hai'bə·niə] Irland. **Hibernian** [hai-'bə·niən] irsk; irlender.

hiccough ['hikəp], **hiccup** ['hikəp] hikke, hikste; hikke. **hiccupy** ['hikəpi] hikkende.

hic jacet ['hik 'dʒe'sét] (latin) her ligger; gravskrift.

hick [hik] (amr.) bonde.

hickory ['hikəri] hickory, nordamerikansk valnøtt-tre.

hickup ['hikəp] se **hiccough**.

hid [hid] imperf. og perf. pts. av **hide**.

hidalgo [hi'dälgoᵘ] hidalgo, spansk adelsmann.

hidden ['hidn] perf. pts. av **hide**.

hide [haid] hud, skinn.

hide [haid] skjule, gjemme; gjemme seg.

hide-and-seek [haidn'si·k] gjemsel, «gjømmekikke».

hidebound ['haidbaund] trangskinnet; trangbrystet, stivsinnet, fordomsfull.

hideous ['hidiəs] fryktelig, skrekkelig, heslig.

hiding ['haidiŋ] pryl; bank; **he gave him a good** — han gav ham ordentlig juling.

hiding ['haidiŋ] gjemsel, gjemmested.

hiding-place ['haidiŋple's] skjulested.

hie [hai] ile, skynde seg; — **oneself** ile.

hiera-picra ['haiərə·'pikrə] et avføringsmiddel av aloe og kanel.

hierarch ['haiərə·ᵊk] hierark, kirkefyrste. **hierarchal** ['haiə'ra·ᵊk]] eller **hierarchic(al)** [haiə·'ra·ᵊkik(l)] hierarkisk. **hierarchy** ['haiərə·ᵊki] hierarki, prestevelde; rangforordning. **hieratic** [haiə'rätik] hieratisk; geistlig, prestelig.

hieroglyph ['haiəroglif] hieroglyff. **hieroglyphic** [haiəro'glifik] hieroglyffisk; hieroglyff. **hieroglyphical** [haiəro'glifikl] hieroglyffisk. **hierophant** ['haiərofänt] overprest.

higgle ['higl] prange, drive gatehandel; prute, tinge.

higgledy-piggledy ['higldi'pigldi] hulter til bulter, rotet; kaos.

higgle-haggle ['higlhägl] tinge.

higgler ['higlə] sjakrer; tinger; gateselger.

high [hai] høy, høg, opphøyd, fornem; sterk, stri, heftig, stor; høytliggende; litt råtten, som har en snev (om kjøttmat, f. eks. vilt); i stemning; høyt; **the sun is** — sola står høyt på himmelen; **smell** — ha en snev (om vilt); **on the** — i det høye, høyt oppe; — **colour** sterk (livlig) farge; — **day** høylys dag; — **and dry** på land (om fartøy); — **feeding** kraftig næring; **with a** — **hand** med kraft eller strenghet eller vilkårlighet; — **level** høyslette; — **life** den fornemme verden; — **looks** stolt mine; — **priest** yppersteprest; — **sea** sterk sjøgang; **the** — **seas** det åpne havet; **it is** — **time for me to be off** det er på høy tid jeg kommer av sted; **a** — **school** en høgre skole; **be on the** — **ropes** være sterkt eksaltert; oppføre seg anmassende; **be in** — **spirits** være i godt humør; — **summer** høysommer; — **tea** te med kjøttretter; — **wind** hard vind; — **words** vrede ord.

high|altar høyalter; — **-and-dry** [haiən'drai] på det tørre; strandet; — **-bailiff** foged; — **-binder** uforskammet fyr, bølle; pengeutpresser. — **-blown** oppblåst, hoven, kaut; — **-born** høybåren; — **-bred** fint dannet; fornem.

High-Church ['hai'tʃə·tʃ] høykirke; høykirkelig. **High-Churchman** ['hai'tʃə·tʃmən] høykirkelig.

high|-coloured sterkt farget; overdreven. — **-day** festdag, gledesdag. — **-designing** høytstrebende.

higher ['haiə] høyere.

high|falutin(g) ['haifə'lu·tin, -iŋ] høyttravende snakk; svulstig, affektert. — **-fed** velnært, gjødd. — **-flier** høytflyvende person el. ting, svermer; noe ualminnelig; sprett, flottas; stor gynge; hurtig vogn, hurtigtog o. l.; plattenslager. — **-flown** høytflyvende; oppblåst. — **-flyer** se — **-flier**. — **-flying** høytflyvende.

Highgate ['haigét] Highgate (del av London) **high-handed** anmassende; myndig.

highland ['hailənd] høyland, fjellbygd; **the Highlands** især: høylandene i Skottland. **Highlander** høylender, fjellbu; høyskotte. **high|-life** den fornemme verden; livet i den fornemme verden. — **-lived** ['hailivd] fornem. — **-low** halvstøvel, ankelsko.

highly ['haili] høylig, høyt, i høy grad, i stor monn, meget, sterkt; **think** — **of** ha store tanker om; **speak** — **of** snakke i høye toner om, prise.

high|-mettled ['hai'metld] hissig, fyrig, sprek. — **-minded** høysinnet; kaut, hovmodig. — **-neck(ed)** høyhalset.

highness ['hainés] høyhet; **His Royal Highness** hans kongelige høyhet.

high|-placed høytstilt. — **-pressure** høytrykk. — **-priest** yppersteprest. — **-principled** med edle grunnsetninger. — **-proof** sterkt alkoholholdig, nesten ublandet, ren, sterk. — **-road** landevei, chaussé; (fig.) slagen vei; **be on the -road to perdition** ile sin undergang i møte. — **-souled** høysinnet. — **-sounding** høyttravende. — **-spirited** høysinnet, stolt; trossig, irritabel; sprek. — **-stepper** stortraver — **-street** hovedgate i en kjøpstad. — **-strung** stri; oppspilt; trassig; oppblåst.

hight [hait] (foreldet og poetisk) by; love; kalle, nevne; omtale; hete, kalles.

high|-tasted pikant; krydret. — **-tide** høyvanne. — **-toned** høystemt; opphøyd. — **-treason** høyforræderi.

highty-tighty ['haiti'taiti] se **hoity-toity**.

high-water ['hai'wå·tə] høyvanne. **high-water mark** (ofte billedlig:) kulminasjonspunkt. **highway** se **high-road**. **highwayman** landveisrøver. **high-wrought** fint utarbeidd; oppløst, oppspilt.

H. I. H. fk. f. **His** (el. **Her**) **Imperial Highness.**

hike [haik] dra; dra seg, gå fottur i landet; — **off** stikke av.

hilarious [hi'læ·ᵊriəs] munter, lystig.

hilarity [hi'läriti] munterhet, lystighet.

Hilary ['hiləri] Hilarius; Hilaria; — **mass 13.** januar; — **term** rettssesjon fra 11. til 31. jan.; fastetermin (ved Oxford universitet).

hill [hil] haug, ås, hei, berg; **up** — **and down** — oppfor bakke og nedfor bakke. — **country** høyland, kupert og bølgende landskap.

hill-folk ['hilfoᵘk] haugfolk, hulderfolk, underjordiske.

hilli-ho [hili'hoᵘ] hallo!

hilliness ['hilinés] bakket lende.

hillman ['hilmän] fjellbygg; fjellmann; haugkall.

hilloa [hi'loᵘ] hallo! rope hallo!

hillock ['hilək] liten haug; tue.

hill|people underjordiske. **-side** ['hilsaid] skrent, bakke, skråning, hall; li.

hilly ['hili] bakket; åslendt; bakke-; ås-, fjell-; **the** — **range** høydedraget.

hilt [hilt] sverdfeste, hjalt; **up to the** — fullstendig, ubetinget; **live up to the** — leve i sus og dus. **hilted** ['hiltid] forsynt med feste.

him [him, im] ham; den, det; seg.

H. I. M. fk. f. **His** (el. **Her**) **Imperial Majesty.**

Himalaya [hi·mə'le'ja] Himalaya.

himself [(h)im'self] han selv, selv, sjøl; seg selv, seg; **he is not** — han er ikke riktig i hodet; **he is beside** — han er ute av seg selv.

hind [haind] hind, dyrkolle, hjortkolle.

hind [haind] bakre, bak-; bakerst; bakerste del.

hind [haind] tjener, dreng, gårdsgutt.

hindberry ['hainbəri] bringebær.

hinder ['haində] bakre; bakerst; bak-.

hinder ['hində] hindre, forhindre; hemme, avbryte; være til hinder; hindring.

hinderance ['hind(ə)rəns] hindring.

hindermost ['haindəmoᵘst] bakerst, sist.

hindleg ['haindleg] bakbein.

hindmost ['haindmoᵘst] bakerst, sist.
Hindoo osv. se Hindu.
Hindostan se Hindustan.
hind quarters bakende, rumpeball.
hindrance ['hindrəns] hindring.
Hindu [hin'du·] hindu. Hinduism ['hinduizm] hinduisme (hinduenes religion). Hindu-Kush ['hindu'ku·ʃ] Hindukɯsj. Hindustan [hindu'sta·n] Hindustan. Hindustanee, Hindustani [hindu'stäni, hindu'sta·ni] hindustansk, hindustani.
hinge [hin(d)ʒ] hengsel; gangjern; hovedpunkt, hovedsak; forsyne med hengsel; dreie seg om, bero på; off the -s av lage; a -d sash vindu på hengsler.
hinny ['hini] mulesel.
hint [hint] vink, ymt, antydning, forslag; insinuasjon; gi vink, antyde, ymte om; insinuere; take a — ta seg noe ad notam; forstå en halvkvedet vise; — at hentyde til, antyde.
hinterland ['hintəländ] oppland.
hip [hip] hofte; catch on the — få i sin makt; have on the — ha i sin makt, overvinne.
hip [hip] nype.
hip-bath ['hipba·þ] setebad.
hip-joint ['hipdʒoint] hofteledd.
hipper ['hipə] vidje.
hippic ['hipik] som hører til hesten, heste-.
hippocamp ['hipokämp] havhest.
hippocentaur [hipo'sentä·ᵊ] hippokentaur (halvt menneske, halvt hest).
hip-pocket baklomme (i benklær).
hippocras ['hipokräs] kryddervin.
Hippocrates [hi'påkrəti·z] Hippokrates; '-sleeve en slags filtrerpose.
Hippocrene ['hipokri·n] Hippokrene.
hippodrome ['hipodroᵘm] hippodrom, sirkus.
hippogryph ['hipogrif] hippogriff, vinget hest.
Hippolyta [hi'pälitə] Hippolyta.
hippopathology [hipopə'pålədʒi] hippopatologi, læren om hestesykdommer.
hippophagous [hi'påfəgəs] som spiser heste-kjøtt.
hippopotamus [hipo'påtəməs] flodhest.
hip-shot ['hipʃåt] med hoften av ledd.
hire [haiə] hyre, leie, leiesum; ste; bygsle bort; hyre, leie, lønn, bygslepenger.
hireling ['haiəliŋ] leiesvenn.
hirsute [hə·'sju·t] håret, bustet.
his [hiz] svakt ofte iz] hans; sin, sitt, sine.
Hispano- [hi'späno] i sammensetn.: spansk-.
hispid ['hispid] strihåret.
hiss [his] visle, hvese; frese, frøse; hysse; pipe; hysse ut; pipe ut; visling, hvesing; hyssing; piping. hissing ['hisiŋ] vislende osv.; visling osv.
hist [st, hist] hyss! hysj!
histogeny [hi'stådʒini] vevdannelse.
histological [histo'lådʒikl] histologisk. histology [hi'stålədʒi] histologi, vevlære.
historian [hi'stå·riən] historiker, historieskriver.
historic [hi'stårik] historisk; — present histo-risk presens.
historical [hi'stårikl] historisk; — novel histo-risk roman.
historiographer [histå·ri'ågrəfə] historiker, historiograf. historiography [histå·ri'ågrəfi] historieskrivning; historiografi.
history ['hist(ə)ri] historie, saga; beretning. — of the world verdenshistorie; matter of — historisk faktum; natural — naturhistorie.
histrionic [histri'ånik] skuespill-, skuespiller-, teater-; teatralsk. histrionism ['histriånizm] skuespillervesen; skuespillkunst; spill.
hit [hit] treffe, råke, ramme; støt, slag; treffer, heldig tilfelle, slump; god idé, godt inn-fall, sarkasme; — off gi et godt bilde av, ta på kornet; lage, rive av seg; finne; — it off være enige; — on eller upon komme på; tilfeldig treffe eller oppdage; komme over; — out utdele slag; — together holde sammen; — it

in his teeth! sleng det i ham! that is meant to — me det sikter til meg; — a man home vise en mann vinterveien; look to one's — se hen til sin fordel; make a — ha hell; more by — than by wit lykken er bedre enn forstanden.
hit [hit] imperf. og perf. pts. av hit.
hitch [hitʃ] hufse, humpe av sted, hinke; hake, klenge seg fast; stryke seg; (amr.) stemme overens; trekke opp, rykke; hekte fast, hake fast; gjøre et stikk; (amr.) spenne for (hester); (amr.) tjore; rykk, hufs, støt; hindring, stans; floke, ugreie, vanskelighet; stikk; give one's trousers a — hufse opp i buksene sine; there is a — somewhere det er en hake ved saken; have a — in one's gait halte.
hither ['hiðə] hit, herhen; nærmest. hithermost ['hiðəmoᵘst] nærmest.
hitherto ['hiðə'tu·] hittil.
hitherward ['hiðəwəd, -wə·ᵊd, -wå·ᵊd] hitover. Hittite ['hitait] hetitt; bokser; hetittisk.
hive [haiv] bikube; fange bier i kube; samle honning i bikube; samle inn; bo sammen; — off sverme (om bier). — -bee honningbie. hiver ['haivə] biskjøtter, birøkter.
hives [haivz] strupehoste; utslett, alvegust, alveblåst.
hizz [hiz] se hiss.
H. L. fk. f. House of Lords.
hl fk. f. hectolitre.
H. L. I. fk. f. Highland Light Infantry.
H. M. fk. f. His (el. Her) Majesty.
hm fk. f. hectometre.
H. M. A. fk. f. His Majesty's airship.
H. M. S. fk. f. His (el. Her) Majesty's ship.
ho [hoᵘ] pro! ptro! (til hest); rope, praie.
ho. fk. f. house.
H. O. fk. f. Home Office.
hoa [hoᵘ] se ho.
hoaky ['hoᵘki]: by the —! for pokker!
Hoangho ['hoᵘäŋ'hoᵘ] Hoangho.
hoar [hå·ᵊ] hvitgrå, hvit; grånet, hvit av elde; hvithet, gråhet; elde; rim; tåke.
hoard [hå·ᵊd] plankeverk (rundt et bygg).
hoard [hå·ᵊd] forråd; skjult forråd; skatt; sammensparte penger; samle sammen, dynge opp, hamstre, samle skatter, muge sammen.
hoarder [hå·ᵊdə] pengepuger.
hoarding [hå·ᵊdiŋ] plankeverk.
hoarfrost ['hå·ᵊfrå(·)st] rimfrost.
hoariness ['hå·rinès] hvitgråhet, gråhet.
hoarse [hå·ᵊs] hås, hes. hoarsely [-li] håst. hoarseness [-nés] håshet, heshet.
hoary ['hå·ri] grå, hvit av elde; grånet; hvit-håret. — -headed grånet; hvithåret.
hoax [hoᵘks] puss, spøk, mystifikasjon; avis-and; narre, mystifisere. hoaxer ['hoᵘksə] en som mystifiserer.
hob [håb] hjulnav; kaminplate (på hver side av risten; her settes ting som skal holdes varme).
hob-and-nob ['håbən'nåb] drikke med; være gode busser med.
hobbadehoy, hobbadyhoy ['håbədihoi], hob-, bardde-hoy ['håbəddihoi] ung fyr, gutt i slyngelalderen.
Hobbes [håbz] Hobbes.
hobbetyboy ['håbitiboi] se hobbadehoy.
Hobbism ['håbizm] hobbisme (filosofen, Hobbes' lære). Hobbist ['håbist] tilhenger av Hobbes.
hobble ['håbl] humpe; halte; helde (en hest); lenke forbeina (på en hest); humping, halting; helde; forlegenhet, knipe; floke. — over a thing jaske noe unna; I've got into a nice — der er jeg kommet godt opp i det.
hobbledehoy ['håbldihoi] se hobbadehoy.
hobbler ['håblə] en som halter; fusker.
hobbly ['håbli] hullet, ujevn (om vei).
hobby ['håbi] lerkefalk.
hobby ['håbi] kjepphest; have a — for ha en mani for.

hobby-horse ['håbihå·°s] kjepphest, gyngehest.
hobgoblin ['håb'gåblin] nisse, tomte, tunkall.
hobidehoy ['håbidihoi] se **hobbadehoy**.
hobnail ['håbne¹l] nudd, hesteskosøm; bonde-slamp; sette nudder under.
hobnob ['håbnåb] være fine busser med; drikke sammen.
hob-or-nob ['håbå°'nåb] drikke sammen.
hobson-jobson ['håbsən'dʒåbsən] (engelsk-in-disk) festlighet, seremoni; — **dictionary** ordbok over engelsk-indiske ord og uttrykk.
hock [håk] hase, haseledd; den tynne del av en skinke; **hocks** også føtter.
hock [håk] rinskvin (oppr. Hochheimer).
hockey ['håki] hockey (et slags ballspill).
hockle ['håkl] skjære hasene over på.
hocus ['ho⁪kəs] bedrager; vin med tilsetning (for å gjøre en beruset); bedra, narre; blande noe i vinen for å bedøve.
hocus-pocus ['ho⁪kəs'po⁪kəs] hokuspokus, tas-kenspilleri; narre, bedra.
hod [håd] brett (en murers); kalktrau; kull-boks.
hoddengrey ['hådngre¹] ufarget ulltøy.
hoddle ['hådl] humpe, vralte.
Hodge [håd͡ʒ] bonde; uvitende mann.
hodgepodge ['håd͡ʒpåd͡ʒ] suppe, sammen-surium, mølje, rot.
hodman ['hådmən] murerhåndlanger; hånd-langer.
hodometer [hå'dåmitə] odometer.
hoe [ho⁪] hakke; grev (**draw-hoe**); skyffel (**thrust-hoe**); pigghai; hakke; hyppe; (amr.) slite i det; (amr.) — **one's own row** passe sine egne saker; (amr.) **have a hard row to** — for-berede, ha planer om. — **-cake** ['ho⁪ke¹k] maiskake (i Amerika).
hoer ['ho⁪ə] hakke.
hog [håg] svin, råne, galt; (fig.) svin, gris; **a** — **in armour** en gris i snippkjole; **bring one's -s to a fine market** gjøre en god forret-ning; **go the whole** — ta skrittet helt ut; **like a** — **in a squall** fra sans og samling.
hog [håg] stusse, klippe.
Hogarth ['ho⁪ga·°b] Hogarth.
hog|cholera ['hågkålərə] svinepest. — **-cote** ['hågko⁪t] grisehus.
hoggerel ['håg(ə)rəl] toårig sau.
hoggish ['hågiʃ] svinsk.
hoghair ['håghæ·ə] grisebust; bustpensel.
hog|herd grisegjeter. — **-louse** skrukketroll.
hogmanay ['hågmə'ne¹] (skotsk) nyttårsaften; nyttårsfest.
hog-mane stusset manke.
hogsbean ['hågzbi·n] bulmeurt.
hogshead ['hågzhed] oksehode (stort hulmål; for øl og vin er det 245,353 liter).
hogskin ['hågskin] svinelær.
hog|sty grisehus. — **-wash** skyllevann; sku-ler, skyller, grisemat.
hoi! [hoi] hopp!
hoiden ['hoidn] galneheie, villkatt, vilter.
hoi(c)k [hoik] tvinge fly til plutselig stigning.
hoist [hoist] heise; heising; heiseapparat, heis, elevator. — **-man** elevatorfører.
hoity-toity ['hoiti'toiti] hå; nei hør på den! lystig, kåt, overgiven.
hokey-pokey ['ho⁪ki'po⁪ki] verdiløs, dårlig.
Holborn ['ho⁪bən] Holborn (gate i London).
hold [ho⁪ld] hold, tak, grep; støttepunkt, støtte, fotfeste; (skips-)last; **catch** (el **lay el. seize** eller **take**) — **of** ta fatt i; **let go one's** — gi slipp, slippe taket.
hold [ho⁪ld] holde; fastholde; holde tilbake; inneholde, romme; opprettholde, fortsette; ha i besittelse; holde for, anse for; påstå; forsvare; understøtte; støtte; holde, ikke gå i stykker; stå stille, gjøre holdt; holde stand; vare ved, vedbli å gjelde; holde seg (om pris); holde med; — **water** være vanntett; (fig.) gjelde,

duge; **that doesn't hold water** det holder ikke stikk; — **an action** fortsette en prosess; **he should** — **the crown of him** han skulle bære kronen under hans overhøyhet; — **good** (el. **true**) stadfeste seg; — **hard!** stopp! vent! — **one's own** hevde seg; — **a meeting** holde møte; **have and** — besitte; — **the market** beherske markedet; — **an office** ha et embete; — **the bent** holde stand; — **in chase** forfølge; — **in contempt** forakte; — **in hatred** hate; — **on** holde fast, vedbli; — **on to** holde fast i; — **out** holde ut, holde seg; — **out against** hevde seg overfor; **I couldn't** — **up any longer** jeg kunne ikke holde ut lenger.
hold|all ['ho⁪ldål] reiseteppe, som en kan gjemme alle mulige småting i. — **-back** hindring.
holden ['ho⁪ldn] gl. perf. pts. av **hold**; **a meeting will be** — et møte vil bli holdt.
holder ['ho⁪ldə] holder; beholder; forpakter, leilending; innehaver, besitter; håndtak, skaft; arbeider i lasten.
holder-forth ['ho⁪ldə'få·°b] taler; predikant.
holding ['ho⁪ldiŋ] hold (fig.) etc.; besittelse, forpaktet gård; gårdsbruk; innflytelse, makt.
hole [ho⁪l] hull, grop; høl; hi; knipe, klemme; hulle, gjøre huller i; gjøre en ball (i biljard); **put one into a** — sette en i knipe; **make a** — **in the water** springe i vannet; drukne seg.
holibut ['hålibʌt] helleflyndre, kveite.
holiday ['hålidi, -de¹] helligdag, helg; fridag, ferie; **-s ferie**. — **-maker** lystreisende. — **-mak-ing** på lystreise, på ferietur; fornøyelsesreise.
holily ['ho⁪lili] hellig.
holiness ['ho⁪linès] hellighet; fromhet.
Holinshed ['hålinʃed] Holinshed.
holla ['håla; 'hå'la·] hallo! rope; praie, kaue.
holla balloo [hålə bə'lu·] helvetes spetakkel.
Holland ['håland] Holland, Nederland. **holland** ['håland] ubleikt lerret. **hollands** sjenever.
Hollander ['håləndə] hollender, nederlender.
hollo ['hålo⁪], **holloa** ['hålo⁪] se **holla**.
hollow ['hålo⁪] se **holla**.
hollow ['hålo⁪] hulning; hule, grop, søkk; hull, gruve, hul; dump; falsk; gjøre hul, hule ut; hult; dumpt; fullstendig, ganske, helt; **the** — **of the hand** den hule hånd; **hold a thing in the** — **of one's hand** ha noe i sin makt; **beat (all)** — slå helt av marka.
hollow|-backed svairygget. — **-eyed** huløyd. **-hearted** falsk.
hollowness hulhet.
holly ['håli] kristtorn. — **-hock** ['hålihåk] stokkrose. — **-oak** kristtorn.
holm (ho⁪m] kristtorn.
holm [ho⁪m] holme.
Holmes [ho⁪mz] Holmes.
holm|-oak, **-tree** steineik.
holocaust ['hålokå·st] brennoffer.
holocryptic [hålo'kriptik] hemmelig; uløselig.
holograph ['hålogra·f] egenhendig skrevet do-kument. **holographic** [hålo'gräfik] egenhendig skrevet.
Holsatia [hål'se¹ʃ(j)ə] Holstein.
Holstein ['hålstain] Holstein; holsteinsk. **Hol-steiner** [-ə] holsteiner.
holster ['ho⁪lstə] pistolhylster.
holt [ho⁪lt] skog, lund, holt; hull, hulning, smutthull.
holus-bolus ['ho⁪ləs'bo⁪ləs] over hals og hode.
holy ['ho⁪li] hellig; **the Holy Ghost** den hel-lige ånd; — **ground** innvigd jord; **the Holy Land** Det hellige land; — **Office** inkvisisjonen; — **orders** presteembete, prestevigsel; **take** — **orders** la seg ordinere; **the** — **week** den stille uke; **Holy Writ** den hellige skrift, Bibelen. **holyday** ['ho⁪lide¹] helligdag, helg.
Holyrood House ['håliru·d'haus] slott i Edin-burgh.
holystone ['ho⁪listo⁪n] skurestein; skure.

Holy-Thursday ['ho^uli'þə·zdi] Kristi himmelfartsdag.

homage ['hámidʒ] lenshylling, hyllest; **do** (eller **pay**) — hylle, vise hyllest; **owe** — to stå i vasallforhold til. **-able** lenspliktig.

home [ho^um] hjem, heim; (i sport) mål; hjemme, heime; hus-; innenlandsk; ettertrykkelig, grundig; hjem, heim; til målet, ved målet; bo, ha et hjem; finne hjem (om brevduer); bringe hjem, sende hjem; **at** — hjemme, heime; **be at** — **on a subject** være hjemme i en sak; **make oneself at** — late som om man er hjemme; **Mrs. Smith is at** — **on Tuesdays** fru Smith tar imot om tirsdagen; **go to one's long** — ligge for døden; **from** — hjemmefra; ikke hjemme, bortreist; **charity begins at** — enhver er seg selv nærmest; — **affairs** indre anliggender; **Home Department, Home Office** innenriksdepartementet; **Home Secretary** innenriksminister; **the Home land** moderlandet; — **trade** innenrikshandel; **arrive** — komme hjem; **a** — **thrust** et velrettet støt; **bring** — gjøre noe klart for; overbevise om; **it comes** — **to me** det er meg kjent; **it will come** — **to you** det vil falle tilbake på Dem; **see a man** — følge en mann hjem; **carry an argument** — dra de ytterste konsekvenser av et bevis; **drive** — slå i (om spiker); **go** (el. **get**) — treffe, råke; **lay** — legge på hjerte; **pay** — gjengjelde; **screw** — skrue fast; **he pushes his inquiries** — han gjør sine undersøkelser grundig, til gagns; **strike** — ramme spikeren på hodet; **take** — legge seg på sinne.

home|**bird** stuegris. — **-bred** hjemmeavlet; udannet; medfødt, naturlig. — **-brewed** hjemmebrygget. — **-coming** hjemkomst. **-farm** hovedgård. **-felt** dypfølt. **-keeping** vant til å være hjemme. **-like** hjemlig.

homeliness ['ho^umlinès] tarvelighet; simpelhet; stygghet.

homely ['ho^umli] tarvelig, jevn, enkel; stygg; **home is home, be it ever so** — hjemmet er nå hjem om det er aldri så tarvelig; — **living** husmannskost.

home|**-made** hjemmelaget. —**-mission** indremisjon. — **-office** innenriksdepartementet.

homeopath ['ho^umiopäþ] homøopat.
homeopathic [ho^umjo'päþik] homøopatisk.
homeopathist [ho^umi'áþəþist] homøopat.
homeopathy [ho^umi'áþəþi] homøopati.
Homer ['ho^umə] Homer. **Homeric** [ho'merik] homerisk.

home|**-rule** ['ho^um'ru·l] homerule, selvstyre (især for Irland). — **-ruler** tilhenger av (Irlands) selvstyre.

homesick ['ho^umsik] som lengter hjem. **-ness** hjemlengsel, hjemve.

homespun ['ho^umspʌn] hjemmespunnet, hjemmevevd, hjemmegjort; hjemmevevd tøy, et slags sjeviot.

home|**stead** ['ho^umsted] bondegård, gården, bøen, hjemmehusene; (amr.) gård, selvstendig småbruk (srl. en gård på 160 acres som nybrottsfolk har fått seg overlatt av statsjorda); hjem. **-steader** småbruker, gårdbruker.

homethrust ['ho^umþrʌst] slag som sitter; bemerkning som sitter.

homeward ['ho^umwəd] hjem, hjemover.—**bound** som skal hjem. **homewards** ['ho^umwədz] hjemover.

homey ['ho^umi] hjemlig.

homicidal [hámi'saidl] draps-; morderisk.
homicide ['hámisaid] drap; drapsmann.
homiletic(al) [hámi'letik(l)] homiletisk. **homiletics** homiletikk. **homilist** ['hámilist] predikant.
homily ['hámili] homilie, preken.
homing ['ho^umiɲ] det å vende hjem (især om brevduer).
hominy ['hámini] maisgrøt.
hommock ['hámək] liten haug el. høgd.

homogeneity [håmodʒi'ni·iti] ensartethet.
homogeneous [håmo'dʒi·njəs] ensartet.
homologate [ho'mologeⁱt] billige; stadfeste.
homologous [ho'máləgəs] overensstemmende.
homomorphism [håmo'má·əfizm] likedannethet. **homomorphous** [-'má·əfəs] likedannet.
homonym ['håmonim] homonym. **homonymous** [ho'mániməs] homonym, likelydende.
homophony [ho'máfoni] samklang.
homunculus [ho'mʌɲkjuləs] mannsling.
homy ['ho^umi] hjemlig.
Hon. fk. f. **honorary; honourable.**
Honduras [hån'd(j)uəräs] Honduras.
hone [ho^un] hein, brynestein; heine, bryne.
hone [ho^un] jamre; lengte etter.
honest ['ánist] ærlig, redelig, rettskaffen, bra; — **Injun** ['ánist'indʒən] på ære! **make an** — **woman of** gifte seg med (en forført kvinne).
honestly ['ánistli] ærlig, redelig, ærlig talt.
honesty ['ánisti] ærlighet, redelighet; — **is the best policy** ærlighet varer lengst.
honey ['hʌni] honning; vennen min, gullet mitt! — **-bag** honningsekk, honningmave (utvidelse av biens fordøyelseskanal). — **-bee** honningbie. — **-comb** vokskake. — **-combed** hullet. — **-dew** honningdogg (utsondring av bladlus), søttobakk.
honeyed ['hʌnid] honning-, honningsøt.
honey|**-guide** honninggauk (en liten fugl som ved sin sang og sine bevegelser viser vei til bikuber). **-month, -moon** hvetebrødsdager; **they were on their honeymoon** de var på bryllupsreise. **-moon** tilbringe hvetebrødsdagene. —**-mouthed** [-mauð] innsmigrende, søtt-talende. —**-sack** honningsekk, honningmave. **-suckle** [-sʌkl] vivendel, kaprifolium. — **-sweet** honningsøt. — **-tongued** innsmigrende, søtt-talende.
hong [håɲ] kinesisk pakkhus; faktori i China; europeisk handelshus i· China.
Hongkong ['håɲ'kåɲ] Hongkong.
honied ['hʌnid] se **honeyed.**
honk [håɲk] skriket til villgåsa, tuting av automobilhorn.
Honolulu [håno'lu·lu] Honolulu.
honorarium [(h)ånə'ræ·əriəm] honorar.
honorary ['ånərəri] æres-, heders-. — **arch** æresport. — **member** æresmedlem. — **secretary** ulønt sekretær.
honorific [ånə'rifik] æres-.
honour ['ánə] ære, heder; rang, rangspost, verdighet; æresfølelse, æresbevisning, æresport; hederstegn; honnør (de beste kort i whist og bridge); ære, hedre, bære; prise; honorere (veksel o. l.); motta, si ja takk til (innbydelse o. l.); **maid of** — hoffdame; **meet with** — honoreres (om veksel); — **and glory** ære og berømmelse; **your Honour** deres velbårenhet (især til dommere i county courts); — **bright** på ære! **I have three by** — s jeg har tre honnører (i kortspill); **in** — **of** til ære for; **-s of rank and station** æresbevisninger i rang og stilling; **pass in first-class -s, get through the examination with full -s** ta eksamen med glans; **meet with due** — bli tilbørlig honorert (om veksel); **do the -s** gjøre honnør, presidere ved bordet, opptre som vert-(inne).
honourable ['án(ə)rəbl] ærlig, hederlig; ærefull; som tittel: velbåren, høyvelbåren (fast tittel for yngre barn av earls, alle barn av viscounts og barons og for Underhusets medlemmer); **the** — **member for** det ærede medlem for; **Most Honourable** høyvelbårne (brukes om markis); **Right Honourable** høyvelbårne (især om medlemmer av the Privy Council samt adelsmenn under markis); **his intentions are** — han har redelige hensikter (ɔ: ekteskap).
Hon. Sec. fk. f. **Honorary Secretary.**
Hood [hud] Hood.
hood [hud] hette; lue, kyse; røykhette; trekke en hette over.

hoodlum ['hudləm] (amr.) bølle, slamp, slusk.
hoodoo ['hu·du·] (amr.) trollmann, sykdomsbesverger; en som bringer ulykke; utyske, trollskap; nonsens, humbug; bringe ulykke, forhekse.
hoodwink ['hudwiŋk] binde for øynene; skjule, dekke til; narre, forblinde.
hoof [hu·f] hov, (spøkende) fot; sparke; **beat the** — gå; — **it** gå som kveg.
hook [huk] hake, krok; angel; stabel (til et hengsel); sigd; hagekniv; krumkniv; få på kroken; fange med krok; huke; spidde med horna; fange med knep; forføre; stjele, nype, nappe; krøke; bøye seg, kroke seg; stikke av; **-s and eyes** hekter og maljer; **with a** — **at the end** med en hake ved, med et spørsmålstegn; **by** — **or by crook** på den ene eller på den andre måten; **off the -s** i uorden, av lage; ferdig, vekk; **drop** (el. **go**) **off the -s** dø, stryke med; **on one's own** — på egen hånd, på egen regning; **take** (el. **sling**) **your -s** stikke av med deg; — **it** stikke av; pakke seg; — **on** hake seg fast til.
hooka(h) ['hukə] huka, orientalsk vannpipe med lang slange.
hook-and-eye hekte.
hook|-bill ['hukbil] hakelaks. — **-bolt** [-'bouͯlt] hakebolt. — **-bone** [-'bouͯn] halestykke.
hooked [hukt, 'hukid] kroket, krum.
hooker ['hukə] hukkert (lite fartøy); skute.
hookey ['huki] et slags kulespill; **do** — gjøre lang nese til en; **by** — **ved gud! play** — skulke fra skolen: — **Walker** det kan du innbille bønder, den må du lenger på landet med.
hookum ['hu·kəm] tjenstlig ordre (i India).
hooky ['huki] kroket; full av haker; **play** — skulke fra skolen.
hooligan ['hu·ligən] bølle, forbryter, fark. **-ism** [orbrytervesen, røveruvesen.
hoop [hu·p] bånd, gjord, tønnebånd; ring; bøyle; fiskebein (i skjørt); fiskebeinsskjørt; gjure, gjorde, bande, sette bånd el. ring om (på); innfatte; **croquet** — krokettbøyle; **go through the** — melde seg fallitt, overgi sitt bo til skifteretten.
hoop [hu·p] huie, hauke, rope; huiing, hauking.
hooper ['hu·pə] bøkker; lagger.
hooper ['hu·pə] sangsvane (en fugl).
hooping-cough ['hu·piŋkå·f] kikhoste.
hoop-iron båndjern.
hoopoe, hoopoo ['hu·pu·] hærfugl.
hoop-petticoat, hoop-skirt fiskebeinsskjørt.
hoora, hooray [hu're¹] hurra.
Hoosier ['hu·ʒə] beboer av Indiana (i Amerika).
hoot [hu·t] skrike; tute; ule; huie etter; hysse ut, pipe ut; huiing, skrik, tuting. **hoot(s)** [hu·t(s)] (skotsk) fy!
hooter ['hu·tə] signalhorn, alarmhorn, signalpipe, sirene.
hoove(n) ['hu·v(n)] trommesyke (hos sauer).
hop [håp] hoppe, bykse, hinke; danse; hopp; dans; — **the twig** renne vekk, smette unna; **be always on the** — svinse omkring.
hop [håp] humle; høste humle; sette til humle.
hop-bine humleranke.
hope [houͯp] egl. hop, flokk; **forlorn** — avdeling soldater som ofres, især stormkolonner.
hope [houͯp] håp, von; håpe; håpe på, vone; — **in God** stole på Gud; **in -s of** i håp om; — **for** håpe på.
hopeful ['houͯpf(u)l] forhåpningsfull; håpefull; lovende.
hopeless ['houͯplès] håpløs, vonlaus. **hopelessness** håpløshet, vonløyse.
hoplite ['håplait] hoplitt.
hop-merchant humlehandler; dansemester.
hop-o'my-thumb ['håpomiþ^m] pusling, tommeliten.
hopper ['håpə] hopper; ostemark; såkasse; fødeapparat; mølletrakt; kvernteine; selvtømmende mudderpram.
hopper ['håpə] humlehøster.
hop-picking humlehøst.

hopping ['håpiŋ] hopping; dans.
hopping ['håpiŋ] humlehøst.
hopple ['håpl] helde; sette helde på.
hoppo ['håpouͯ] (pidgin-engelsk) kasserer; handelsinspektør.
hopscotch ['håpskåtʃ] paradis (barneleiken).
hopvine ['håpvain] humleranke.
Horace ['hårəs, -is] Horats.
Horatio [ho're¹ʃiouͯ] Horatio.
horde [hå·əd] horde, bande; leve i flokk.
horizon [hə'raizn] horisont, synskrets. **horizontal** [håri'zåntl] horisontal, vannrett; sylindergang. **horizontality** [hårizån'täliti] vannrett stilling. **horizontally** [håri'zåntəli] horisontalt.
hormone ['hå·ⁿmouͯn] hormon (indre sekresjon).
horn [hå·ⁿn] horn; jakthorn; drikkehorn; krutthorn; sparkel; sette horn på, (fig.) sette horn i pannen; **draw (pull, haul) in one's -s** ta følehorna til seg; **lower one's -s** nedlate seg. **horn|beak** horngjel. **-beam** avnbøk; kvitbøk. **-book** abc.
horned ['hå·ⁿn(i)d] hornet; hornformet.
horner ['hå·ⁿnə] hornarbeider; hornhandler.
hornet ['hå·ⁿnit] geitehams, bedrum; **bring** (el. **raise**) **a nest of -s about one's ears, poke one's head into a -'s nest** stikke hånden i en vepsebol.
horn|fish horngjel. — **-fisted** med barkede never.
Hornie ['hå·ⁿni], **Auld-Hornie** (skotsk) fanden.
hornish ['hå·ⁿniʃ] hornaktig.
hornless ['hå·ⁿnlès] uten horn, kollet.
horn|owl bergugle, hubro. **-pipe** hornpipe (et blåseinstrument); hornpipe (en matrosdans). — **-player** hornblåser.
horn-work ['hå·ⁿnwə·k] hornverk (et framskutt befestningsverk med to lange tilbakegående greiner).
horny ['hå·ⁿni] horn; hornaktig; hard som horn.
horography [ho'rågrəfi] timeberegning.
horologer [ho'rålədʒə], **horologist** [ho'rålədʒist] urmaker. **horology** [ho'rålədʒi] urmakerkunst.
horometry [ho'råmitri] tidsmåling.
horoscope ['håroskouͯp] horoskop; **cast** (el. **draw** el. **erect**) **a person's** — tyde ens skjebne etter stjernenes stilling da han ble født.
horrent ['hårənt] strittende, bustet.
horrible ['håribl] skrekkelig, fryktelig, forferdelig; avskyelig.
horrid ['hårid] redselsfull; avskyelig.
horrific [hå'rifik] forferdelig, skrekkinnjagende.
horrify ['hårifai] forferde, skremme, støkke.
horror ['hårə] gysning; redsel, støkk; avsky; stygg; avskyelighet, grufullhet; **-s** tungsindighet; drankergalskap; **give one the -s** inngyte en avsky; **have the -s** ha delirium; **Chamber of Horrors** redselskabinett (i et panoptikon); **the horror of it all!** hvor avskyelig! — **-stricken**, — **-struck** redselsslagen.
horse [hå·s] hest; hingst; grahest; gjelk; hestfolk; rytter, kavaleri, trehest (strafferedskap); sagbukk; stillas; løygang, løybom; pert; bukk, (på skolen) oversettelse som man fusker med, forbudt hjelpemiddel, fuskelapp; (arbeiderspråk) **(dead)** — forskudd; (sl.) fempundsseddel; **(the old) Horse** tukthus i Horsemonger-Lane; (amr.) energisk mann; forsyne med hester; spenne hesten for; bedekke (en hoppe); piske; fuske (på skolen); **the -s are to** be spent for; **take** — stige til hest; bedekkes; **a dark** — en ukjent størrelse (egl. fra veddeløpsspråket); **get on** (el. **mount**) **the high** — sette seg på den høye hest; **gentleman** (eller **master**) **of the** — stallmester; **flog a dead** — søke å vekke ny interesse for noe forslitt; **they cannot set their -s together** de kan ikke forlikes; **a regiment of** — et kavaleriregiment; **5000** — 5000 mann kavaleri; **lieutenant of** — kavaleriløytnant.
horse|-artillery ridende artilleri. **-back** hesterygg; **on -back** til hest; i salen. — **-bean** hestebønne. — **-breaker** hestedressør, hestetemmer, be-

rider. — -breaking hestedressur. — -buss smell-kyss. — -chaunter (sl.) hestehandler. — -chestnut hestekastanje. — -cloth hestedekken. — -comb strigle, skrape. — -deal hestehandel. — -dealer hestehandler. — -dealing hestehandel. — -drench hestemedisin.—-face langt, plumpt ansikt. —-fair hestemarked. — -faker (sl.) hestehandler; vogn-mann. — -flesh hestekjøtt; hester; be a judge of -flesh forstå seg på hester. — -fly klegg, blinding. — -fool leirfivel, hestehov (planten).—-godmother stor, svær kvinne. — -guard livvakt (til hest). — -guards hestegarde. the Horse-Guards den byg-ningen i London hvor den øverstbefalende general i den britiske hær bor; derfor betyr det ofte: gene-ralkommando, krigsministerium. -hair krøllhår; hestetagl. — -keeper hesteholder; stallkar. —-lati-tudes (mar.) stille belte. — -laugh rå latter, gap-skratt. — -leech hesteigle; blodigle; blodsuger. horse|man ['hɔ·ɔsmən] rytter. —-manship ride-kunst. —-marine (i spøk) flåtekavalerist, kavaleri-sjømann; landkrabbe, fisk på land, dumrian; tell it to the -marines det kan du innbille bøn-der; den må du lenger på landet med. -nail hesteskosøm. —-play grov spøk.—-police ridende politi.—-power hestekraft; hestekrefter (60 horse-power). — -race hesteveddeløp. — -radish pepper-rot. — -railway hestesporvei. — -rider berider. — -rug hestedekken. —-sense (amr.) sunn menn-eskeforstand. -shoe hestesko. —-show hesteskue. — -soldier kavalerist. — -stealer hestetyv. -way kjørevei; hestevandring. —-whip ridepisk, svepe; bruke ridepisken på, piske, banke. —-whipping pryl med ridepisken. -woman rytterske.

horsy (eller horsey) ['hɔ·ɔsi] heste-; hesteaktig; hestehandler-; sportsmessig, jockeyaktig.

hortative ['hɔ·ɔtətiv] formanende, styrkende, oppmuntrende. hortatory ['hɔ·ɔtətəri] forma-nende, styrkende, oppmuntrende.

horticultural [hɔ·ɔti'kʌltʃərəl] hage-, hage-bruks-; — exhibition (el. show) blomsterutstil-ling; — society hageselskap. horticulture ['hɔ·ɔti-kʌltʃə] hagebruk; hagekunst. horticulturist [hɔ·ɔti'kʌltʃərist] gartner.

Horton ['hɔ·ɔtn] Horton.

hortus siccus ['hɔ·ɔtəs 'sikəs] herbarium.

hosanna [hoʊ'zänə] hosianna.

hose [hoʊz] strømper, hoser, sokker; hage-slange; oversprøyte.

Hoshea [ho'ʃi·ə] Hoseas.

hosier ['hoʊʒə] trikotasjehandler.

hosiery ['hoʊʒəri] trikotasje, ullvarer.

hospice ['håspis] hospitium (tilfluktssted for reisende i Alpene), hospits, herberge.

hospitable ['håspitəbl] gjestfri.

hospital ['håspitəl] hospital, sykehus; flying — feltlasarett; lying-in — fødselsstiftelse; Magdalen — Magdalenestiftelse. —-fever hospitalstyfus.

hospitality [håspi'täliti] gjestfrihet.

hospitaller [hå'spitələ] Johannitterridder.

host [hoʊst] hær, krigshær; skare; Lord of Hosts hærskarenes Gud.

host [hoʊst] vert; count (el. reckon) without one's — gjøre regning uten vert; -s vertsfolket.

host [hoʊst] hostie.

hostage ['håstidʒ] gissel, pant.

hostel(ry) ['håst(ə)l(ri)] gjestgiveri, herberge; studenthjem (f. eks. King's College Hostel i London).

hostess ['hoʊstès] vertinne.

hostile ['håstail] fiendtlig; fiendtligsinnet.

hostility [hå'stiliti] fiendskap, fiendtlighet.

hostler ['(h)ås(t)lə] stallkar (i et vertshus).

hostlery ['håstlri] gjestgiveri, vertshus.

hot [håt] het, varm; hissig, stri, brå, heftig, sint; ivrig; bitende, skarp (om smak); krydret, pepret; lidenskapelig, ildfull; sterkt sanselig; L. is becoming too — for him det blir for hett for ham i L., jorda begynner å brenne under føttene hans i L.; he'll get it — and strong han får en ordentlig overhaling, han blir ordentlig

gjennombanket; make a place too — for a man gjøre helvete hett for en mann; boiling — ko-kende hett; red — rødglødende; white — hvit-glødende; — brandy konjakktoddy; — cockles (hist.) landlig leik hvor en person med bind for øynene gjetter hvem som slo ham; — coppers tømmermenn (etter rangel); — tiger varmt øl med sherry; we had a — time yesterday i går gikk det hett for seg; be in — water være i en opphisset, nervøs tilstand; være i forlegenhet; get into — water with somebody komme i strid med en; tildra seg en irettesettelse av en; be — upon a thing være sterkt oppsatt på noe; være sint for noe; there is — work there det går varmt til der; in — haste i en flyvende fart; a — patriot en ivrig fedrelandsvenn; en kraftpatriot; — tobacco sterk tobakk.

hot-air ['håtæ·ə] varm luft.

hot-and-hot meget varm mat.

hotbed ['håtbed] mistbenk, drivbenk; (fig.) arnested; a — of vice et arnested for lasten.

hot-blooded ['håt'blʌdid] varmblodig.

hotchpot(ch) ['håtʃpåt(ʃ)] miskmask, suppe, mølje, sammensurium.

hot|cockles ['håt'kåklz] se under hot. — -cop-pers tømmermenn (etter rangel).

hotel [hoʊ'tel] hotell. — -keeper [hoʊ'tel'ki·pə], — -manager hotellvert.

hot|foot ['håtfut] i største hast, på røde rappet. — -head brushode, sinnatagg. — -headed hissig. — -house ['håthaus] drivhus. — -livered irri-tabel; varmblodig. — -mouthed hardmunnet; halsstarrig.

hotness hete; hissighet, brålynne, voldsomhet. hot|pot ragout av fårekjøtt og poteter. — -press satinere. — -short rødskjør (skjør i glø-dende tilstand). — -spirited hissig, heftig. — -spur ['håtspə·] villstyring; hissig. — -spurred hissig. — -tempered hissig.

Hottentot ['håtntåt] hottentott.

hot-water varmtvanns-; — bottle varmeflaske. hot-well varmtvannsbeholder.

hough [håk] hase; skjære hasene over på.

hound [haund] hund; jakthund; jage, hisse; pusse (on på); ride to hounds drive sprengjakt, drive revejakt.

Houndsditch ['haundzditʃ] gate i London. hound's-tongue ['haundztʌn] hundetunge (plante).

hour [auə] time, tid, klokkeslett; timeslag; keep good (bad) -s komme tidlig (seint) hjem, gå tidlig (seint) til sengs; by the — for timen (f. eks. om å ta en drosje); i timevis; for -s (together) timevis; an — and a half halvannen time; a quarter of an — et kvarter; business -s forretningstid; small -s de små timer; it strikes the — den slår hel; it strikes the half — den slår halv; what's the —? hva er klokka?

hour|-glass ['auəgla·s] timeglass. —-hand lille-viser.

houri ['hu·əri] huri.

house [haus], fl.: houses ['hauziz] hus; også i betydninger som: kongehus, hus, kammer, ting, kollegium (ved universitetet), skuespillhus, tea-ter, handelshus, firma, fattiggård, børs; country — landsted; public — vertshus; religious — kloster; the White House den amerikanske presi-dents embetsbolig i Washington; — of call arbeidsanvisningskontor; — of correction for-bedringsanstalt; — of ill fame bordell; keep — holde hus, føre hus; keep the — holde seg hjemme; as safe as -s ganske sikkert; raise the — sette hele huset på ende; set up — for oneself begynne sin egen husholdning; the Lower House, the House of Commons underhuset (i det engelske parlament); the House of Lords, the House of Peers, the Upper House overhuset (i det engelske parlament); the House of Parliament parlamen-tet; (amr.) the House of Representatives den amerikanske kongress; call of the House navneopprop; **be in the House, be a member of the House** være medlem av parlamentet; **be in possession of the House** ha ordet i parlamentet; **there is a House** det er møte i parlamentet; **bring down the house** ta publikum med storm; — **full!** utsolgt! **a full** — fullt hus; **a thin** — dårlig hus, lite folk.

house [hauz] få under tak, i hus; installere; huse; beskytte, dekke; bo i hus, holde til.

house|-agent ['hause'dʒənt] gårdsbestyrer; innehaver av leiebyrå. — **-bell** portklokke. — **-boat** flytende sommerhus, husbåt (båt som er innrettet til beboelse). **-breaker** innbruddstyv. **-breaking** innbrudd. **-carl** ['hauska·əl] huskall (kriger av de angelsiksiske og nordiske kongers livvakt). — **-door** gatedør. — **-farmer** husvert som for høye priser leier dårlige leiligheter ut til fattigfolk. **-flag** firmaflagg.

household ['haus(h)oʊld] husholdning; husstand, hus, familie; tjenerskap; — **bread** hjemmebakt brød; — **drudge** kone som sliter seg opp i huset; — **gods** husguder, penater; — **medicine** husråd; — **stuff** bohave; — **suffrage** valgrett for husleiere; — **troops** livvakt, gardetropper; — **words** daglig vending, ordtak; — **worship** husandakt.

house|holder ['haushoʊldə] familiefar, husfar, en som har stemmerett. **-keeper** husmor; husholderske; oldfrue. **-keeping** husholdning; **we started -keeping** vi begynte å føre hus.

house|leek ['hausli·k] taklauk. **-less** husvill. **-line** hyssing. **-linen** lintøy, vasketøy. **-lot** byggegrunn. **-maid** stuepike. **-painter** maler (i motsetning til kunstmaler). — **-physician** reservelege. **-place** dagligstue (skotsk og på landet). — **-rent** husleie. **houserent free** med husleiegodtgjørelse. **-room** husrom. **-rule** husorden. — **-sparrow** gråspurv. — **-steward** hushovmester, første tjener i et hus. — **-surgeon** reservelege. **-top** hustak; **cry from the housetops** preke fra hustakene. — **-warming** hjemkommerøl.

housewife ['hauswaif] husmor; [hʌzif] syskrin. **housewifely** ['hauswaifli] husmoderlig. **housewifery** ['hʌzifri, 'hauswaifəri] husholdning, husstell.

housing ['hauziŋ] saldekken.

the housing problem boligspørsmålet.

Houyhnhnms ['hu'i(n)mz] de fornuftige vesener i skikkelse av hester i Swifts Gulliver's travels.

hove [hoʊv] imperf. av **heave**.

hovel ['håvəl] skur, halvtekke, skjå; elendig hytte, rønne; kornstakk; anbringe i skur; bringe under tak. **-ler** bergingsmann.

hoven ['hoʊvən] hoven.

hover ['håvə] sveve; dvele, sverme, vandre; vingle; — **about** kretse om; **drive om i nærheten.**

how [hau] hvorledes, hvordan; hvor, i hvilken grad; hvor! å; (således) som; — **are you?** hvorledes har De det? — **do you do?** ['haudju'du·] god dag! **know** — **to do it** forstå å (el. kunne) gjøre det; — **is it that** hvordan kan det være at; **do it** — **you can** gjør det så godt du kan; — **hot it is!** hvor varmt det er.

howadji [hau'ådʒi] kjøpmann (i Orienten).

Howard ['hauəd] Howard.

howbeit [hau'bi·(i)t] likevel, enda.

howda(h) ['hauda] elefantsal (helst med telt og med rom til flere).

how-do [hau'du·] god dag!

how-d'ye-do [haudi'du·] god dag! fine greier; oppstyr.

howel ['hauəl] bøkkerøks.

however [hau'evə] hvorledes enn, hvordan enn; hvor — enn; hvordan i all verden; likevel, dog, imidlertid.

howf(f) [hauf] (skotsk) tilholdssted; ha tilhold et sted.

howitzer ['hauitsə] haubits.

howk [hauk] (skotsk) grave.

howl [haul] hyle, ule, tute; ul, hyl, tuting.

howler ['haulə] hyler, bommert, leitt mistak; **go a** — tape svært.

howlet ['haulit] nattugle.

howling ['hauliŋ] hylende; skrekkelig.

howsoever [hauso'evə] hvorledes enn; skjønt.

hoxter ['håkstə] innvendig sidelomme.

hoy [hoi] hei!

hoyden ['hoidn] se **hoiden**.

h. p. fk. f. **horse-power**.

H. Q. fk. f. **head-quarters**.

hr. fk. f. **hour**.

H. R. H. fk. f. **His** (eller **Her**) **Royal Highness**.

hrs. fk. f. **hours**.

H. S. H. fk. f. **His** (el. **Her**) **Serene Highness**.

huanaco [hwa'na·koʊ] guanako (en slags lama).

hub [hʌb] hjulnav; midtpunktet for ens interesse; kjælenavn for ektemann (**husband**): (amr.) **the** — **of the universe** spøkefull benevnelse for Boston; verdens midtpunkt; **the Hub** et sportstidsskrift.

hubbie (e. **hubby**) ['hʌbi] liten mann (kjælenavn for ektemann).

hubblebubble ['hʌblbʌbl] snakk i munnen på hverandre; javl, vås, tøv; virvar; vannpipe.

hubbly ['hʌbli] knudret.

hubbub ['hʌbʌb] larm, ståk, styr, lurveleven.

hubby ['hʌbi] knudret.

huck [hʌk], **huckaback** ['hʌkəbäk] dreiel.

huckle ['hʌkl] hofte; pukkel, kryl. **-backed** pukkelrygget. **-berry** (amr.) blåbær; **red huckleberry** tyttebær.

huckster ['hʌkstə] høker; gatehandler; høkre.

huckstress ['hʌkstrés] høkerkjerring.

hud [hʌd] belg, hylse.

huddle ['hʌdl] stuve sammen i et rot; røre sammen, dynge sammen; slenge; kaste (klærne på seg); trenge seg sammen; gjøre ferdig i en fei, smøre sammen, sjaske fra seg; stimle, flokke seg; hop, dynge; røre; stimmel, trengsel; — **oneself up** (el. **together**) krype sammen; — **over** (el. **through**) fare igjennom; — **together** kaste i en dynge; stimle sammen.

huddler ['hʌdlə] stymper.

Hudson ['hʌdsən] Hudson.

hue [hju·] farge, lett, lød; anstrøk, dåm.

hue [hju·] skrik; **make** — **and cry after a person el. raise a** — **and cry against a person** forfølge en med huiing og skrik; forfølge en med stikkbrev eller etterlysning.

huel ['hjuəl] gruve (i Cornwall).

hueless ['hju·lés] fargeløs.

huer ['hju·ə] utkiksmann.

huff [hʌf] blåse opp; heve seg (om deig); blåse seg opp; larme, fnyse; behandle grovt, hundse; fornærme; blåse (**at** av); fornærmelse; sinne; skryter, knep, puss.

huffer ['hʌfə] praler, skryter; tyrann.

huffish ['hʌfiʃ] hoven.

huffy ['hʌfi] hoven, oppblåst, hårsår, lett støt.

hug [hʌg] favne, omfavne; favntak, fangtak, omfavnelse, klem; — **oneself** glede seg, gotte seg, fryde seg; — **oneself in bed** krype sammen i senga av kulde; (mar.) — **the land** holde seg tett oppunder land; (mar.) — **the wind** knipe tett til vinden.

huge [hju·dʒ] stor, uhyre, umåtelig, veldig.

hugeness ['hju·dʒnés] uhyre størrelse.

huggermugger ['hʌgə'mʌgə] hemmelighet; forvirring, rot, røre; gnier; hemmelig; uordentlig; ynkelig; gå hemmelig til verks; holde hemmelig.

Hugh [hju·] Hugo.

Hughes [hju·z] Hughes.

Huguenot ['hju·gənət] hugenott.

hukeem [hə'ki·m] læge (i India).

hulk [hʌlk] skrog (av et skip); losjiskip; brye; anbringe i losjiskip; sprette opp; drive; **-ing** tykk, klosset, ulenkelig.

Hull [hʌl] Hull.

hull [hʌl] hylster; belg, skolm; hams; skrog (av skip); skalle, renske; pille (erter); hamse; ramme i skroget.

hullabaloo [hʌləbə'lu·] ståk, oppstyr, lurveleven.

hullo ['hʌ'lou] hallo! hei!

hulloa ['hʌ'lou] hallo! hei!

hullock ['hʌlək] del av et seil.

hully ['hʌli] skolmet, skallet.

hully ['hʌli] åleruse, åleteine.

hum [hʌm] surre, summe; mumle; mulle; brumme; humre; nynne bifall til; få til å brumme, nynne; stamme; føre bak lyset; surring, summing; murring; mumling; brumming; bifallsytring; nynning; spøk; humbug; hm! — and haw hakke og stamme i det, dra på det; make things — sette liv i tingene, få sveis på det; the — of the city byens liv og larm; she -med of her happiness det sang i henne av glede.

human ['hju·mən] menneskelig, menneske-; — being menneske.

humane [hju'me'n] human, menneskekjærlig; humanistisk; the Humane Society et menneskekjærlig selskap i London som særlig har til formål å treffe anstalter til redning av druknende.

humanely [hju'me'nli] menneskekjærlig.

humanist ['hju·mənist] humanist; klassisk filolog.

humanitarian [hjumäni'tæ·ᵊriən] menneskevenn, filantrop; menneskekjærlig.

humanity [hju'mäniti] menneskelighet; menneskehet, mennesker; humanitet, menneskekjærlighet; the humanities humaniora, humanistiske fag, særlig latinske og greske klassikere.

humankind ['hju·mən'kaind] menneskeslekten.

humate ['hju·mèt] humussurt salt.

Humber ['hʌmbə] Humber.

humble ['hʌmbl] ringe; ydmyk, beskjeden, smålåten, spakferdig gjøre ringere, nedsette, ydmyke; my — self min ringhet.

humble-bee ['hʌmblbi·] humle.

humble-pie ['hʌmblpai] postei av innmat; tjenerkost; eat — spise nådsensbrød, ydmyke seg, bite i det sure eple.

humbly ['hʌmbli] ringe; ydmykt, beskjedent.

humbug ['hʌmbʌg] humbug, jugl, juks, fusk og fanteri; humbugmaker; bedrager; narre, bedra, jukse. humbugger ['hʌmbʌgə] humbugmaker.

humbuggery ['hʌm'bʌgəri] bedrageri, svindel.

humdrum ['hʌmdrʌm] kjedelig, hverdagslig; kjedsommelighet, hverdagslighet; samme gnålet; dødbiter; staur.

Hume [hju·m] Hume.

humective [hju'mektiv] fuktende; våt.

humeral ['hju·mərəl] skulder-.

humgruffin [hʌm'grʌfin] heslig, frastøtende person, stygt troll.

humhum ['hʌmhʌm] grovt, glatt bomullstøy (i India).

humid ['hju·mid] fuktig. humidity [hju'miditi] fuktighet. humidness ['hju·midnés] fuktighet.

humiliate [hju'milie't] ydmyke.

humiliation [hju·mili'e'ʃən] ydmykelse; day of — alminnelig bededag.

humility [hju'militi] ydmykhet.

humming ['hʌmiɲ] summende; summing. -bird kolibri; sprengstykke av granat. — -top rumlepotte, snurrebass.

hummock ['hʌmək] liten bakke, haug; skruis.

hummocky ['hʌməki] bakket.

humor ['(h)ju·mə] væske, væte; (se humour).

humoral ['(h)ju·mərəl] humoral, væske-, væte-. humorist ['(h)ju·mərist] humorist; raring. humoristic (h)ju·mə'ristik] humoristisk. humorous ['(h)ju·mərəs] humoristisk.

humour ['hju·mə; 'ju·mə] væske, væte; stemning; humør; lune; skjemt, vidd, humor; føye, rette seg etter, gå inn på; be out of — være i dårlig humør; be in the — for være opplagt til; please one's — følge sin lyst; put one in good —

sette en i godt humør; put one out of — sette en i dårlig humør; the — takes me jeg får lyst til; take one in the — benytte ens gode humør; do a thing for the — of it gjøre noe for spøk; children must not be -ed too much man må ikke være for ettergivende mot barn.

hump [hʌmp] pukkel, kryl; kuv; haug; (sl.) dårlig humør; gjøre krylrygget; samle; (sl.) ergre; (sl.) ødelegge; ta seg sammen. — -back pukkelrygg; pukkelrygget. -backed rundrygget; krylrygget; pukkelrygget.

humph [hmf] hm!; si hm, brumme, kremte.

Humphrey ['hʌmfri] Humphrey.

hump-shouldered ['hʌmpʃoᵘldəd] rundrygget.

humpty ['hʌm(p)ti] pukkelrygget.

humpty-dumpty ['hʌm(p)ti'dʌm(p)ti] liten og tykk; tjukken; Humpty-dumpty sat on a wall et lite barnerim hvor h. er et egg.

humpy ['hʌmpi] puklet; bulet.

humpy ['hʌmpi] hytte (i Australia).

humstrum ['hʌm'strʌm] dårlig instrument; lirekasse.

humus ['hju·mas] moldjord.

Hun [hʌn] huner (også brukt hånlig om tyskere).

hunch [hʌnʃ] pukkel, kul, kryl, kuv; klump; puff; krumme, krøke; puffe. -back pukkelrygg, krylrygg; pukkelrygget person. -backed ['hʌnʃbäkt] pukkelrygget.

hundred ['hʌndrəd] hundre; by -s i hundrevis; 4 in the — 4 prosent. -fold hundre fold. hundredth ['hʌndrədþ] hundrede (ordenstall), hundrededel.

hundredweight ['hʌndrədwe't] centner (i England: 112 lbs. (50,802 kg); i Amerika: 100 lbs. (45,359 kg).

hung [hʌɲ] imperf. og perf. pts. av hang.

Hungarian [hʌɲ'gæ·ᵊriən] ungarsk; ungarer.

Hungary ['hʌɲgəri] Ungarn.

hunger ['hʌɲgə] sult, hunger; sulte, være sulten, hungre; sulte ut. — -strike hungerstreik.

hungrily ['hʌɲgrili] grådig, begjærlig.

hungry ['hʌɲgri] sulten, hungrig, hol, grådig; — as a hunter sulten som en skrubb.

hunk [hʌɲk] stort, tykt stykke.

hunk [hʌɲk] (amr.) ved målet; be on — være ved målet; være i sikkerhet.

hunker ['hʌɲkə] (amr.) stokk-konservativ hunkerism ['hʌɲkərizm] stokk-konservatisme.

hunks [hʌɲks] gnier.

hunt [hʌnt] jage, veide; jage etter, gå på jakt etter; jakt; forfølgelse; alt det som hører til jakten; jaktselskap; jaktrevier; — down jage til døde; — down a criminal forfølge og pågripe en forbryter; — up (el. out) finne, snuse opp.

hunter ['hʌntə] jeger; jakthund; jakthest.

hunting ['hʌntiɲ] jakt, veiding; jakt-; — -box jakthytte. — -cog overtallig tann (i et sett tannhjul). — -crop jaktpisk. — -lodge jakthytte. — -meet [-mi·t] jaktmøte. — -watch jaktur, ur med varksasse.

huntress ['hʌntrés] kvinnelig jeger.

Hunts [hʌnts] Huntingdonshire.

huntsman ['hʌntsmən] jeger, overpikør, jaktfører (ved parforsejakt). huntmanship jegerkunst; overpikørstilling.

hur-bur ['hə·bə·] borre.

hurdle ['hə·dl] flyttbart gjerde, risgard, risgjerde, traleverk; ståltrådsgjerde; hinder (ved veddeløp). — -race veddeløp med forhindringer, hekkeløp.

hurdler ['hə·dlə] hekkeløper.

hurds [hə·dz] drev, stry.

hurdygurdy ['hə·di'gə·di] lirekasse, lire.

hurkara [hə·'ka·rə], hurkaru [hə·'ka·ru] bud, kurér (i India).

hurl [hə·l] kaste, slynge, slenge.

hurlyburly ['hə·li'bə·li] larm, tummel, virvar.

Huron ['hjuərån] Huron.

hurr-burr ['hə·bə·] borre, klåtegras.
hurricane ['hʌrikən] orkan; engelsk flytype; — deck stormdekk.
hurried ['hʌrid] hurtig, hastig, skyndsom, kort.
hurriedly ['hʌridli] hurtig, hastig, skyndsomt.
hurry ['hʌri] il, hast, hastverk; ile, haste; skynde på; føre hurtig av sted, drive på, få av gårde; skynde seg; **be in a** — ha hastverk, ha det travelt; **in the** — i skyndingen; i farten; — oneself forhaste seg; — **up** skynde seg, rappe seg, svinte seg; **there is no** — det haster ikke; — away ile bort; føre hurtig bort; **he hurried on his clothes** han fór i klærne.
hurry-skurry ['hʌri'skʌri] forvirring, virvar; hodekulls, hodestupes, i forvirring.
hurst [hə·st] lund, holt, kjerr; øyr.
hurt [hə·t] gjøre fortred, skade, såre, krenke, gjøre vondt; fortred, skade, men, sår, støt; — oneself slå seg; **I feel** — jeg føler meg såret; — **one's feelings** såre ens følelser.
hurtful ['hə·tf(u)l] skadelig.
hurtle ['hə·tl] støte mot, tørne sammen; hvirvle, suse; rasle, klirre.
hurtless ['hə·tlès] uskadelig, uskadd.
husband ['hʌzbənd] ektefelle, ektemann, mann; god økonom; holde godt hus med; spare på; handle som ektemann mot; overta ansvaret for, ta seg av.
husbandage ['hʌzbəndidʒ] skipsagents provisjon.
husbandman ['hʌzbəndmän]jordbruker, bonde.
husbandry ['hʌzbəndri] landbruk, jordbruk, kultur.
hush [hʌʃ] hyss! hysj! stille!; stille, rolig; stillhet; stille, døyve; få til å tie; berolige, roe; være stille, tie; — **up** dysse ned.
hushaby ['hʌʃəbi] barnesull, bånsull, båntull.
hush-money ['hʌʃmʌni] penger for å tie.
husk [hʌsk] belg, kapsel, skolm, skall; hams; agne; skalle, skolme, skrelle, pille, hamse, renske.
huskiness ['hʌskinés] håshet.
husky ['hʌski] skallet, skolmet; rusten, sløret (om stemmen).
Husky ['hʌski] eskimo, eskimospråk, eskimohund.
hussar [hu'za·ᵒ] husar.
hussif ['hʌsif] sypose, syskrin.
Hussite ['hʌsait] hussitt.
hussy ['hʌzi] tøs, førkje, galneheie.
hustings ['hʌstiŋz] talertribune, talerstol.
hustle ['hʌsl] ryste sammen; støte, trenge, skubbe; skubb.
huswife ['hʌzif, 'hʌzwaif] se **hussif.**
hut [hʌt] hytte; skjul; brakke; legge i brakker; bo i brakker.
hutch [hʌtʃ] kasse (f. eks. til kaniner).
huzza [hʌ'za·, hu'za·] hurra!; rope hurra; hilse med hurra.
hy [hai] hei!
hyacinth ['haiəsinþ] hyasint.
hyacinthine [haiə'sinþ(a)in] hyasintaktig.
hyæna [hai'i·nə] hyene.
hyaline ['haiəl(a)in] glassklar, krystallklar gjennomsiktig; glassklar substans el. flate; (poet.) klar himmel, blank sjø.
hyalite ['haiəlait] hyalitt, glassopal.
hyaloid ['haiəloid] gjennomsiktig, glassaktig.
hybernate ['haibəneʰt] ligge i vinterdvale.
hybrid ['haibrid] bastard; bastardaktig.
hydatid ['haidətid, 'hid-] vannblære; blæreorm.
Hyde Park ['haid 'pa·ᵒk] Hyde park (i London).
hydra ['haidrə] hydra, vannslange (i mytologi).
Hydrabad ['haidrəbäd] Hydrabad.
hydranger [hai'dreʰndʒə] hortensia.
hydraulic [hai'drå·lik] hydraulisk; — **press** hydraulisk presse.
hydraulically [hai'drå·likəli] med vannkraft.
hydraulics [hai'drå·liks] hydraulikk, vannkraftlære.

hydric ['haidrik] vannstoff-.
hurra(h) [hu're¹] hurra; rope hurra; -'s **nest** stor forvirring; huskestue (Amerika).
hydro ['haidro] i sammensetninger: vann-.
hydrocele ['haidrosi·l] vannbrokk.
hydrocephalus [haidro'sefələs] vann på hjernen.
hydrogen ['haidrədʒən] vannstoff.
hydrographer [hai'drågrəfə] hydrograf.
hydrographical [haidro'gräfikl] hydrografisk.
hydrography [hai'drågrəfi] hydrografi (havbeskrivelse og havmåling).
hydromel ['haidromel] honningvann, mjød.
hydrometer [hai'dråmitə]hydrometer,flytevekt.
hydropathic [haidro'päþik] hydropatisk, vann-kur-. **hydropathist** [hai'dråpəþist] hydropat.
hydropathy [hai'dråpeþi] hydropati, vannkur.
hydrophobia [haidro'foᵘbjə] vannskrekk.
hydrophone ['haidrofoᵘn] hydrofon.
hydropic [hai'dråpik] middel mot vattersott.
hydropsy ['haidråpsi] vattersott.
hydroscopy [hai'dråskopi] hydroskopi.
hydrostat ['haidrostät] hydrostat. **hydrostatic** [haidro'stätik] hydrostatisk; -**s** hydrostatikk, læren om væskers likevekt.
hydrous ['haidrəs] vannholdig.
hydrus ['haidrəs] vannslange.
hyemal [hai'i·məl] vinterlig.
hyemation [hai'meʰʃən] overvintring.
hyena [hai'i·nə] hyene.
hyetograph ['haiətogra·f] regnkart.
Hygeia [hai'dʒi·ə] Hygea. **hygiene** ['haidʒii·n] hygiene. **hygienic** [hai'dʒi·nik] hygienisk. -**s** hygiene. **hygienist** ['haidʒiənist, 'hidʒ-] hygieniker.
hygrometer [hai'gråmitə] hygrometer, fuktighetsmåler.
hygroscope ['haigroskoᵘp] hygroskop, fuktighetsviser. **hygroscopic** [haigro'skåpik] hygroskopisk.
Hymen ['haimən] Hymen, møydom.
hymeneal [haimi'ni·əl], **hymenean** [haimi'ni·ən] bryllups-.
hymn [him] hymne; salme; lovsang; lovprise, lovsynge. — -**book** salmebok. **hymnal** ['himnəl] hymneaktig, hymne-; salmeaktig, salme-; salmebok. **hymnic** ['himnik] hymneaktig; salmeaktig.**hymnody**['himnodi]salmesang; salmekomposisjon. **hymnologist** [him'nålədʒist] hymnedikter; salmedikter. **hymnology** [him'nålədʒi] hymnedikting; salmedikting.
hyperæmia [haipə'ri·mja] blodoverføring.
hyperbola [hai'pə·bolə] hyperbel (i stereometri).
hyperbole [hai'pə·boli] overdrivelse.
Hyperborean [haipə'bå·riən] hyperboreer, nordbo; hyperboreisk, nordligst.
hypercritic [haipə'kritik] overdrevent kritisk.
hypercriticism ['haipə'kritisizm] overdreven kritikk.
Hyperion [hai'piəriən] Hyperion (solgud).
hypertrophy [hai'pə·trofi] hypertrofi, et organs overdrevne fyldighet.
hyphen ['haifən] bindestrek; sette bindestrek.
hypnosis [hip'noᵘsis] hypnose. **hypnotic** [hip-'nätik] hypnotisk; sovemiddel. **hypnotism** ['hipnotizm] hypnotisme. **hypnotize** ['hipnətaiz] hypnotisere.
hypochondria[haipo'kåndriə]hypokondri,tungsinn. **hypochondriac** [haipo'kåndriäk] hypokonder, hypokondrisk.
hypocrisy [hi'påkrisi] hykleri; skinnhellighet. **hypocrite** ['hipokrit] hykler. **hypocritic(al)** [hipo'kritik(l)] hyklersk; skinnhellig.
hypodermic [haipo'də·mik] som ligger under huden; innsprøyting under huden.
hypogynous [hai'pådʒinəs] som sitter under fruktemnet.
hypotenuse [hai'påtənju·z] hypotenus.
hypothec [hai'påþek] hypotek, pant. **hypothecate** [hai'påþikeʰt] pantsette.
hypothesis [hai'påþisis] hypotese forutsetning

vitenskapelig gjetning. **hypothetic(al)** [haipo-'þetik(l)] hypotetisk, betinget, tvilsom.
hyson ['haisən] hyson, grønn te.
hyssop ['hisəp] isop.
hysteria [hi'stiəriə] hysteri. **hysteric(al)** [hi-

'sterik(l)] hysterisk. **hysterics** [hi'steriks] anfall av hysteri; **go off into** — bli hysterisk.
hysteron proteron ['histərån'pråtərån] uttrykk hvor det settes først, som normalt kommer sist.
hysterotomy [histə'råtəmi] keisersnitt.

I

I, i [ai] I, i (bokstav).
I. fk. f. **Island; Isle; imperator** (keiser); **imperatrix** (keiserinne); **Victoria, R. I.** (regina, imperatrix, dronning og keiserinne).
I [ai] jeg; **it is** — det er meg; — **say hør!** **between you and** — **and the lamp-post** mellom oss sagt.
i' [i] i; — **the morning** om morgenen.
Iago ['ja·go^u] Iago.
iamb ['aiämb] jambe. **iambic** [ai'ämbik] jambisk.
iambus [ai'ämbəs] jambe.
.ati [ai'e'ti], — **wood** tik (tre).
ex ['aibeks] steinbukk.
i idem [i'baidəm] samme, sted.
ibis ['aibis] ibis (fugl).
Icarian [ai'kæ·ə·riən] ikarisk; høytflyvende.
Icarus ['ikərəs] Ikaros.
ice [ais] is; dekke med is, ise, ha is på; få til å fryse; legge på is; glasere (med sukker). **ice|berg** ['aisbə·g] isberg. — -**blink** isblink. -**bolt** istapp. -**bound** innefrosset; tilfrosset. — -**box** isskap. — -**breaker** isbryter. — -**cream** iskrem, is (fruktis o. l.). — -**escape** redningsapparat ved ulykkestilfelle på isen. -**foot** isbelte.
Iceland ['aisland] Island; islandsk. **Icelander** ['aisləndə] islending. **Icelandic** [ais'ländik] islandsk.
ice|leaf kongelys. — -**pack** pakkis. -**safe** isskap.
ichneumon [ik'nju·mən] ikneumon, faraorotte. **ichneumon-fly** snyltevepps.
ichnography [ik'någrəfi] iknografi, grunnriss.
ichor ['aikə] gudenes blod; blodvæske.
ichthyic ['ikþiik] fiske-. **ichthyocol(la)** ['ikþiokål, ikþio'kålə] fiskelim. **ichthyography** [ikþi'ågrəfi] beskrivelse av fiskene. **ichthyolog:st** [ikþi'ålədʒist] fiskekjenner.·**ichthyology** [ikþi'ålədʒi] iktyologi, læren om fiskene.
icicle ['aisikl] istapp, jøkel.
icily ['aisili] iskaldt.
iciness ['aisinés] iskulde.
icing-machine ['aisinmə'ʃi·n] frysemaskin.
iconoclasm [ai'kånokläzm] billedstorming. **iconoclast** [ai'kånokläst] billedstormer. **iconoclastic** [aikåno'klästik] billedstormende, revolusjonær.
I. C. S. fk. f. **Indian Civil Service.**
icteric [ik'terik] gulsottig; som fordriver gulsott; middel mot gulsott. **icterus** ['iktərəs] gulsott.
icy ['aisi] iset; iskald.
I'd [aid] for **I had** el. **I would.**
idad [i'däd] min santen!
Idaho ['aidəho^u] Idaho (nordamerikansk stat).
ide [aid] idmort (fisk).
idea [ai'diə] idé, begrep, forestilling; tanke; **my** — **would have been to** det hadde vært min tanke å; **the Turks have no** — **of travelling for amusement** tyrkerne forstår ikke (kan ikke tenke seg) at en kan reise for sin fornøyelses skyld; **the** — **of such a thing** skulle du ha hørt på maken! var det likt seg! **the** —! tenke seg! hvor kan det falle Dem inn?
ideal [ai'diəl] ideal, mønster, forbilde; ideal, tanke-; tenkt; mønstergyldig, fullendt; ideell, idealistisk. **idealism** [ai'diəlizm] idealisme. **idealist** [ai'diəlist] idealist. **idealistic** [aidiə'listik] idealistisk. **ideality** [aidi'äliti] idealitet. **idealize** [ai'diəlaiz] idealisere; danne seg idealer.

idé fixe ['i·de''fi·ks] fiks idé.
identic(al) [ai'dentik(l)] identisk, ens med, samme.
identification [ai'dentifi'ke'ʃən] identifisering.
identify [ai'dentifai] gjøre ens med, identifisere; — **oneself** bevise at en er den person en gir seg ut for, bevise sin identitet.
identity [ai'dentiti] identitet.
Idez [aidz] Idus (i romersk kalender).
id est [id est] det er, det vil si (fork. **i. e.**).
idiocy ['idjəsi] idioti.
idiom ['idjəm] idiom, dialekt, målføre; språkeiendommelighet. **idiomatic** [idjo'mätik] idiomatisk.
idiosyncrasy [idjo'siŋkrəsi] idiosynkrasi (særegenhet).
idiot ['idjət] idiot; tåpe, tosk, naut, fé; — **asylum** idiotanstalt. **idiotic** [idi'åtik] idiotisk. **idiotism** ['idjətizm] idioti; idiotisme (et for et språk eiendommelig uttrykk). **idiotize** ['idjətaiz] gjøre til idiot; bli idiot.
idle ['aidl] ledig, ørkesløs, uvirksom; doven; tom, unyttig; intetsigende; ubetydelig; dovne; late seg; — **Monday** blåmandag; — **rumour** grunnløst rykte; — **time away** slunte tiden bort.
idleheaded ['aidlhedid] tom i hodet.
idleness ['aidlnés] ledighet, ørkesløshet; dovenskap, lathet.
idle-pated ['aidlpe'tid] tom i hodet.
idler ['aidlə] lediggjenger; dagdriver.
idol ['aidl] avgudsbilde; avgud. **idolater** [ai-'dålətə] avgudsdyrker; forguder, tilbeder. **idolatrize** [ai'dålətraiz] drive avguderi; forgude. **idolatrous** [ai'dålətrəs] avguderisk. **idolize** ['aidolaiz] drive avguderi; forgude. **idolizer** ['aidolaizə] avgudsdyrker; forguder, tilbeder.
idyl, idyll ['aidil] idyll. **idyllic** [ai'dilik] idyllisk.
i. e. ['ai'i·; 'ðät'iz] fk. f. **id est** det er, det vil si.
if [if] hvis, dersom; om; om også, selv om; **as if** som om; **if but** når bare; **if so** i så fall; **if anything** nærmest; **even if** selv om; **he is thirty years, if he is a day** han er minst 30 år gammel; **if I were you** i Deres sted.
ifags [i'fägz] min santen!
ifakins [i'fe'kinz] død og pine!
ifecks [i'feks] min santen!
igloo ['iglu] snøhytte (hos eskimoene).
Ignatius [ig'ne'ʃ(j)əs] Ignatius.
igneous ['igniəs] av ild; vulkansk.
ignis ['ignis] ild; — **fatuus** ['fätjuəs] lyktemann, blålys; flertall; **ignes fatui** ['igni·z 'fätjuai].
ignite [ig'nait] tenne, sette i brann; fenge, komme i brann. **ignitible** [ig'naitibl] antennelig. **ignition** [ig'niʃən] tenning; brenning; gløding.
ignoble [ig'no^ubl] av lav ætt; uedel, lav.
ignominious [igno'minjəs] skjendig; vanærende. **ignominy** [ig'nämini] skjensel, vanære.
ignoramus [igno're'məs] ignorant.
ignorance ['ignərəns] uvitenhet. **ignorant** ['ignərənt] uvitende. **ignore** [ig'nå·ə] ikke ta hensyn til, ignorere; ikke tenke på, overse.
iguana [i'gwa·nə] leguan.
I. H. P. fk. f. **indicated horse-power** indisert hestekraft.
ihram [i'ra·m] muhammedansk pilegrimsdrakt.
I. H. S. fk. f. **Jesus; In hoc signo** i dette tegn; **Jesus Hominum Salvator** Jesus, menneskenes frelser.

ile [ail] (provinsielt og amerikansk:) olje; **the nine -s** populært inngnidningsmiddel; (i Amerika:) **strike** — ha hell med seg.

ileum ['iliəm] krumtarm, mellomtarm.

ileus ['iliəs] tarmslyng, tarmgikt.

ilex ['aileks] kristtorn, steineik, beinved.

Iliad ['iliäd] Iliaden.

ilk [ilk] (skotsk) samme; enhver; **of that** — fra godset av samme navn (ɔ: godseierens og godsets navn er det samme); av samme slags, av samme ulla; **of the same** — av samme slags. **ilka** ['ilkə] (skotsk) enhver.

I'll [ail] fk. f. **I shall** el. **I will.**

ill [il] syk; dårlig; låk; vond, slett; ille, vondt; onde; ulykke, lidelse; **be** — være syk; **be** — **in bed** ligge syk; **be taken** —, **fall** — bli syk; **as** — **luck would have it** uheldigvis; **she is as** — **as a witch** hun har en fin nese; — **weeds grow apace** ukrutt forgår ikke så lett; **it's an** — **wind that blows nobody good** ingenting er så galt at det ikke er godt for noe; **with an** — **grace** ugjerne; it would go — **with him** det ville gå ham galt; — **at ease** ille til mote; **speak** — **of** snakke vondt om; **return** — **for good** gjengjelde godt med vondt.

ill|-advised [iləd'vaizd] dårlig betenkt; ubetenksom. — **-affected** illesinnet.

illation [i'leiʃən] slutning. **illative** [i'leitiv] slutnings-, følge-, årsaks-.

ill|-behaved ['ilbi'heivd] uskikkelig. — **-boding** illevarslende. — **-bred** uoppdragen, udannet. — **-conditioned** som har det leitt; av dårlig beskaffenhet; ondartet (f. eks. om sykdom). — **-considered** uoverveid. — **-disposed** illesinnet, uvillig, vrang, lei. — **-doing** som gjør urett; dårlig atferd; forseelse.

illegal [i'li·gəl] ulovlig. **illegality** [ili'gäliti] ulovlighet. **illegalize** [i'li·gəlaiz] gjøre ulovlig.

illegibility [iledʒi'biliti] uleselighet. **illegible** [i'ledʒibl] uleselig.

illegitimacy [ili'dʒitiməsi] urettmessighet, ugyldighet; uekte fødsel. **illegitimate** [ili'dʒitimét] urettmessig; uekte født; uriktig. **illegitimate** [ili'dʒitime¹t] erklære for uekte eller ulovmessig.

ill|-fated ['il'fe¹tid] ulykkelig, ugunstig. — **-favoured** stygg, heslig, fæl. — **-featured** stygg. — **-found** dårlig utrustet (om skip). — **-gotten** ervervet på urettmessig vis. — **-humoured** i dårlig humør.

illiberal [i'libərəl] gjerrig, knipen; ukjærlig; smålig, småskåren, trangsynt; knuslet. **illiberality** [ilibə'räliti] gjerrighet; ukjærlighet; smålighet.

illicit [i'lisit] utillatelig; ulovlig. **illicitness** [-nés] ulovlighet.

illimitable [i'limitəbl] ubegrenset, uinnskrenket.

illinition [ili'niʃən] innsmøring; salve.

Illinois [ili'noi, -'noiz] Illinois.

illiquation [ili'kwe¹ʃən] sammensmelting.

illision [i'liʒən] sammenstøt.

illiteracy [i'litərəsi] uvitenhet, udannethet; trykkfeil; mistak. **illiteral** [i'litərəl] ikke bokstavelig. **illiterate** [i'litərét] uvitende; udannet; ikke lesekyndig; **absolute illiterate** analfabet.

ill|-judged ubetenksom, ufornuftig, forkjært. — **-looking** som ser dårlig ut, usunn, mistenkelig ut; stygg. — **-luck** ulykke, uhell. — **-management** vanstell, vanstyre. — **-mannered** uoppdragen, udannet. — **-nature** grettenskap; ondskap. — **-natured** gretten; ondskapsfull.

illness ['ilnés] sykdom.

illogical [i'lådʒikəl] ulogisk. **illogicalness** [-nés] fornuftstridighet.

ill|-omened ['iloᵘmənd] illevarslende. — **-paid** dårlig betalt. — **-pleased** misfornøyd. — **-seasoned** umoden; ubetimelig. — **-sorted** som passer dårlig sammen. — **-spoken** grov. — **-starred** født under en uheldig stjerne, ulykkelig, uheldig. — **-tempered** gretten, sur, kranglet. — **-timed** ubetimelig; umoden. — **-treat** behandle dårlig, mishandle, fare ille med. — **-treatment** mishandling.

illude [i'l(j)u·d] narre, dåre, gjekke.

illume [i'l(j)u·m] opplyse, kaste lys over. **illuminant** [i'l(j)u·minənt] belysningsmiddel. **illuminate** [i'l(j)u·mine¹t] opplyse, belyse; illuminere; begeistre; forklare; kolorere, illustrere. **illumination** [il(j)u·mi'ne¹ʃən] opplysning, belys. ning; illuminasjon; lys, glans; illustrasjon, illustrering. **illuminative** [i'l(j)u·minətiv] opplysende-belysende. **illuminator** [i'l(j)u·mine¹tə] opplyser, belyser; kolorerer, maler; opplysningsapparat. **illumine** [i'l(j)u·min] se **illume** og **illuminate.**

ill-usage ['il'ju·zidʒ] mishandling.

ill-use ['il'ju·z] mishandle.

illusion [i'l(j)u·ʒən] illusjon; blendverk; et slags gjennomsiktig tøystoff. **illusionist** [-ist] tryllekunstner. **illusive** [i'l(j)u·siv] illuderende, skuffende. **illusory** [i'l(j)u·səri] illusorisk, skuffende.

illustrate ['iləstre¹t, i'lʌstre¹t] opplyse, belyse; forherlige; forklare; illustrere (med bilder). **illustration** [ilə'stre¹ʃən] opplysning, belysning, forklaring; illustrasjon. **illustrative** [i'lʌstrətiv] opplysende, forklarende; **be** — **of** forklare. **illustrator** ['iləstre¹tə] opplyser; illustrator.

illustrious [i'lʌstriəs] strålende, utmerket, berømt; navngjeten, fræg; opphøyd, høy, høg (om fyrstelige personer).

ill-will ['il'wil] uvilje; nag; fiendskap.

Illyria [i'liriə] Illyria. **Illyrian** [i'liriən] illyrisk; illyrier.

I. L. P. fk. f. **Independent Labour Party.**

I'm [aim] fk. f. **I am.**

image ['imidʒ] bilde; avbilde; gjenspeile; forestille seg, tenke seg.

imagery ['imidʒri] billedverk; bilder; billedrikdom; anskuelig framstilling, billedstil, billedspråk.

imaginable [i'mädʒinəbl] tenkelig, som tenkes kan.

imaginary [i'mädʒinəri] innbilt, tenkt; fingert; imaginær (i matematikk); imaginær størrelse. **imagination** [imädʒi'ne¹ʃən] innbilningskraft, fantasi; innbilning, forestilling. **imaginative** [i'mädʒine¹tiv, -nətiv] fantasi-, innbilt; fantasirik; oppfinnsom. **imagine** [i'mädʒin] forestille seg, tenke seg, tenke, tro.

Imam [i'ma·m], **Iman** [i'ma·n] muhammedansk prest, muhammedansk fyrste.

imaret ['imərét, i'ma·rét] muhammedansk herberge for pilegrimer og reisende.

Imaum [i'ma·m] se **Imam.**

imbecile ['imbisi(·)l] imbesill, åndssvak, tomset, sløv; idiot. **imbecility** [imbi'siliti] åndssvakhet, idioti.

imbed [im'bed] leire.

imbibe [im'baib] drikke, suge, suge inn.

imbitter [im'bitə] gjøre bitter, forbitre.

imbosk [im'båsk] skjule; skjule seg.

imbricate [im'brikét] taklagt (som teglstein over hverandre).

imbroglio [im'broᵘljoᵘ] innviklet forhold, floke, ugreie, knute (i drama eller roman).

imbrue [im'bru·] væte, fukte; flekke.

imbrute [im'bru·t] gjøre til dyr; bli som et dyr.

imbue [im'bju·] impregnere, mette; farge sterkt; gjennomtrenge.

imitability [imitə'biliti] det å være etterlignelig. **imitable** ['imitəbl] etterlignelig. **imitate** ['imite¹t] etterligne. **imitation** [imi'te¹ʃən] etterligning; imitasjon; uekte. **imitative** ['imite¹tiv] etterlignende, som tar etter; etterlignet. **imitator** ['imite¹tə] etterligner.

immaculable [i'mäkjuləbl] ubesmittelig. **immaculate** [i'mäkjulét] ubesmittet, ren.

immalleable [i'mäljəbl] som ikke kan smis.

immanent ['imənənt] iboende.

Immanuel [i'mänjuəl] Emanuel.

immaterial [imə'tiəriəl] immateriell; uvesenlig, tom, ubetydelig. **immaterialism** [-izm] immaterialisme. **immaterialist** [-ist] immaterialist. **immateriality** [imətiəri'äliti] ulegemlighet. **immaterialize** [imə'tiəriəlaiz] gjøre ulegemlig.

immature [imə'tjuə] umoden. **immaturity** [imə'tjuəriti] umodenhet.
immeasurable [i'meʒ(ə)rəbl] som ikke kan måles; umåtelig. **-ness** [-nés] umåtelighet, endeløshet.
immediacy [i'mi·djəsi] umiddelbarhet; umiddelbar nærhet.
immediate [i'mi·djət] umiddelbar; øyeblikkelig; umiddelbart nær, nærmest; endefram, beinleies; presserende, uoppsettelig, påtrengende. **in the — future** i nærmeste framtid. **immediately** [i'mi·djətli] umiddelbart; straks; øyeblikkelig; beinleies.
immemorial [imi'må·riəl] uminnelig, eldgammel; **from time(s) — i** uminnelige tider, fra arilds tid; **— usage** eldgammel skikk og bruk.
immense [i'mens] umåtelig, uendelig; storartet. **immensely** [-li] umåtelig. **immensity** [i'mensiti] uendelighet, kolossal utstrekning.
immensurable [i'menʃərəbl] som ikke kan måles.
immerge [i(m)'mə·dʒ] dyppe ned, senke ned. **immerse** [i'mə·s] senke ned; fordype. **immersion** [i'mə·ʃən] nedsenking, neddypping; fordypelse.
immethodical [imi'þådikl] umetodisk, planløs.
immigrant ['imigrənt] innvandrer, innflytter. **immigrate** ['imigre't] innvandre, flytte inn. **immigration** [imi'gre'ʃən] innvandring, innflytting.
imminence ['iminəns] truende nærhet. **imminent** ['iminənt] overhengende, truende.
immiscible [i'misibl] som ikke kan blandes.
immission [i(m)'miʃən] innføring, innsprøyting.
immit [i(m)'mit] sprøyte inn.
immitigable [i(m)'mitigəbl] som det er uråd å formilde; uforsonlig.
immobility [imo'biliti] ubevegelighet.
immobilize [i'mo**u**bilaiz] gjøre ubevegelig; feste, binde.
immoderate [i'måd(ə)rét] overdreven; umåtelig; voldsom. **immoderation** [imådə're'ʃən] umåtelighet; voldsomhet.
immodest [i'mådist] ubeskjeden, ublu; usømmelig. **immodesty** [i'mådisti] ubeskjedenhet; usømmelighet, usedelighet.
immolate ['imole't] ofre. **immolation** [imo-'le'ʃən] ofring; offer; oppofrelse.
immoral [i'mårəl] umoralsk. **immorality** [imo-'räliti] umoral, umoralskhet.
immortal [i'må·ətəl] udødelig. **immortality** [imå·'täliti] udødelighet. **immortalize** [i'må·'ətə-laiz] gjøre udødelig, forevige.
immortelle [imå·'tel] evighetsblomst.
immovability [imu·və'biliti] ubevegelighet.
immovable [i'mu·vəbl] ubevegelig; urokkelig; **-s** urørlig gods, fast eiendom.
immune [i'mju·n] fri, priviligert; immun, uimottagelig, som ikke angripes. **immunity** [i'mju·niti] frihet (for forpliktelser); immunitet.
immure [i'mjuə] mure inne; stenge inne.
immutability [imju·tə'biliti] uforanderlighet. **immutable** [i'mju·təbl] uforanderlig.
Imogen ['imodʒen] Imogen.
imp [imp] pode; renning; unge; smådjevel, djevelunge; pode; skjøte på.
impact [im'päkt] presse inn; klemme; drive fast; **impact** ['impäkt] støt, trykk, anslag.
impair [im'pæ·ə] forringe, minke, svekke; avta, forverres. **impairment** [im'pæ·əmənt] forringelse, svekkelse.
impale [im'pe'l] spidde; omgi (med peler). **impalement** [im'pe'lmənt] spidding; peleinnhegning.
impalpability [impälpə'biliti] ufølbarhet. **impalpable** [im'pälpəbl] ufølbar, ufølelig; upåtagelig, ugripelig.
impanel [im'pänəl] forfatte en liste over (særlig jurymedlemmer).
imparity [im'päriti] ulikhet; misforhold.

impark [im'pa·**ə**k] omgjerde, inneslutte.
impart [im'pa·**ə**t] tildele, gi; meddele.
impartial [im'pa·**ə**ʃəl] upartisk. **impartiality** [im'pa·**ə**ʃi'äliti] upartiskhet. **impartially** [im-'pa·**ə**ʃəli] upartisk.
impartibility [impa·**ə**ti'biliti] udelelighet; meddelelighet. **impartible** [im'pa·**ə**tibl] udelelig; meddelelig.
impassability [impa·sə'biliti] uframkommelighet, uføre; uoverstigelighet. **impassable** [im-'pa·səbl] uframkommelig; uoverstigelig, ufør.
impasse [im'pa·s] uføre, klemme, knipe.
impassibility [impäsi'biliti] ufølsomhet, uimottagelighet. **impassible** [im'päsibl] ufølsom.
impassioned [im'päʃənd] lidenskapelig.
impassive [im'päsiv] kald, uberørt. **impassivity** [impä'siviti] ufølsomhet.
impatience [im'pe'ʃəns] utålmodighet; heftig attrå (**of** etter); heftighet. **impatient** [im'pe'ʃənt] utålmodig (**at, of** over); begjærlig etter; brå, fus; utrøstelig (**at** over).
impavid [im'pävid] fryktløs, uredd.
impawn [im'på·n] pantsette.
impeach [im'pi·tʃ] dra i tvil; nedsette; bestride (f. eks. et vitnes troverdighet); anklage (f. eks. en embetsmann for uforsvarlig embetsførsel); anklage for riksretten. **impeachable** [im'pi·tʃəbl] som kan anklages; daddelverdig. **impeacher** [im'pi·tʃə] anklager. **impeachment** [im'pi·tʃmənt] det å reise tvil; det å bestride; anklage; anklage for riksretten.
impeccability [impekə'biliti] syndefrihet. **impeccable** [im'pekəbl] syndefri. **impeccancy** [im'pek-ənsi] syndefrihet. **impeccant** [im'pekənt] syndefri.
impecuniosity [impikju·ni'äsiti] pengemangel; fattigdom. **impecunious** [impi'kju·njəs] pengeløs; fattig.
impede [im'pi·d] hindre, forhindre.
impediment [im'pedimənt] hindring, forhindring; **have an — in one's speech** lide av en talefeil.
impel [im'pel] drive fram; tilskynde, skyve på. **impellent** [im'pelənt] framdrivende; drivfjær, drivende kraft. **impeller** [im'pelə] en som tilskynder; drivfjær; drivkraft.
impend [im'pend] henge over; forestå, true.
impenetrability [im'penitrə'biliti] ugjennomtrengelighet. **impenetrable** [im'penitrəbl] ugjennomtrengelig.
impenitence [im'penitəns] ubotferdighet, forstokkethet. **impenitent** [im'penitənt] ubotferdig, forstokket; forstokket synder.
impennate [im'penét] vingeløs; kortvinget.
imperat. fk. f. **imperative.**
imperatival [impərə'taivəl] imperativisk. **imperative** [im'perətiv] bydende, befalende; imperativisk; imperativ, bydemåte.
imperceptibility [impəsepti'biliti] umerkelighet. **imperceptible** [impə'septibl] umerkelig; ørliten, hårfin; usanselig, ufattelig.
imperence ['impərəns] (sl.) uforskammethet; De uforskammede fyr! **imperent** ['impərənt] (sl.) uforskammet.
imperf. fk. f. **imperfect.**
imperfect [im'pə·fikt] ufullkommen; ufullstendig, mangelfull; ufullendt; imperf. (**the — el. the — tense**). **imperfection** [impə·'fekʃən] ufullkommenhet; mangelfullhet, ufullstendighet; svakhet, skrøpelighet. **imperfectly** [im'pə·fiktli] ufullkomment; ufullstendig.
imperforate(d) [im'pə·forét, -re'tid] ikke gjennomboret, uten huller; uten porer. **imperforation** [impə·fo're'ʃən] imperforasjon, sammengroing (av ellers åpne legemsdeler).
imperial [im'piəriəl] riks-; keiser-, keiserlig, konge-, kongelig, suverén; som vedkommer det britiske rike, britisk; imperial (en slags russisk gullmynt); spisskuppel, spisskuppeltak; diligencetak; napoleonsskjegg; imperialpapir; — **city** fri tysk riksdag; — **diet** riksdag; — **Government**

riksstyre; — **purposes** rikets øyemed; — **section** keisersnitt; **the** — **interests** Det britiske samveldes interesser; — **Parliament** Det britiske samveldes parlament. **imperialism** [im'piəriəlizm] imperialisme, stormakts-stilling, stormaktspolitikk. **imperialist** [-list] imperialist; keiserligsinnet; storenglender.

imperil [im'peril] bringe i fare, sette i fare, våge. **imperilment** [-mənt] det å bringe i fare, utsettelse for fare.

imperious [im'piəriəs] bydende; myndig; herskesyk; **imperiously** **required** absolutt påkrevd. **imperiousness** [-nəs] bydende atferd, herskesyke.

imperishable [im'periʃəbl] uforgjengelig.

impermeability [impə·mjə'biliti] ugjennomtrengelighet. **impermeable** [im'pə·mjəbl] ugjennomtrengelig; — **to air** lufttett; — **to water** vanntett. **impermeator** [im'pə·mje'tə] fortetningssmøreapparat.

impersonal [im'pə·sənəl] upersonlig; noe upersonlig; upers. verbum. **impersonality** [impə·sə-'näliti] upersonlighet.

impersonate [im'pə·səne't] personifisere; framstille (på teater o. l.). **impersonation** [impə·sə-'ne'ʃən] personifikasjon; framstilling. **impersonator** [im'pə·səne'tə] framstiller.

imperspicuity [impə·spi'kju·iti] uklarhet, utydelighet; uoverskuelighet. **imperspicuous** [impə-'spikjuəs] uklar, utydelig; uoverskuelig.

impersuasible [impə'swe'sibl, -zibl] ikke til å overtale, urokkelig.

impertinence [im'pə·tinəns] noe som ikke hører til saken, det som er saken uvedkommende; bagatell; uforskammethet; nesvishet; **Miss** — frøken nesvis. **impertinent** [im'pə·tinənt] som ikke vedkommer saken, uvedkommende; uforskammet, nesevis.

imperturbability [impətə·bə'biliti] urokkelig ro. **imperturbable** [impə'tə·bəbl] urokkelig rolig, kald. **impervious** [im'pə·vjəs] ugjennomtrengelig; — **to the air** lufttett; — **to the water** vanntett. **impetuosity** [impetju'äsiti] heftighet, voldsomhet. **impetuous** [im'petjuəs] heftig, voldsom.

impetus ['impətəs] drivkraft, fart; **give an impetus to** sette fart i.

imphee ['imfi] afrikansk sukkerrør.

impi ['impi] troppeavdeling (hos kafferne). **impiety** [im'paiiti] ugudelighet.

impignorate [im'pignore't] pantsette.

impinge [im'pindʒ] renne, støte (**on** mot). **impious** ['impiəs] ugudelig; vantro; pietetløs. **impish** ['impiʃ] trollaktig; djevelsk; ondskapsfull.

implacability [impläkə'biliti] uforsonlighet. **implacable** [im'pläkəbl] uforsonlig.

implant [im'pla·nt] innplante; innpode. **implantation** [impla·n'te'ʃən] innplanting; innpoding.

implate [im'ple't] belegge med plater.

implement ['implimənt] redskap, verktøy; forsyne med verktøy; oppfylle betingelser; utføre. **implemental** [impli'mental] anvendt som verktøy; mekanisk. **impletion** [im'pli·ʃən] fylling;fylde.

implicate ['implike't] innvikle; dra inn med (i en sak), implisere, trekke med i anklage. **implication** [impli'ke'ʃən] innvikling; indraing; stilltiende slutning. **implicative** ['implike'tiv] impliserende; stilltiende underforstått. **implicit** [im'plisit] stilltiende, innbefattet, underforstått; ubetinget. **implied** [im'plaid] forutsatt, selvfølgelig.

implore [im'plå·ə] anrope, bønnfalle, be inntrengende om, trygle om. **implorer** [im'plå·rə] en som bønnfaller osv. **imploring** [im'plå·riŋ] bedende, bønnfallende; det å be, bønnfalle, trygle. **imply** [im'plai] inneslutte i seg, innbefatte, inneholde; tyde på; antyde, gi å forstå, la (det) komme fram; **as your words would imply** som Deres ord lar formode (synes å antyde); **implied** indirekte, tilhyllet, skjult.

impo ['impoᵘ] ekstraarbeid (som straff på skolen).

impolicy [im'pälisi] dårlig politikk; uklokskap, mangel på politikk.

impolite [impa'lait] uhøflig, uhøvisk, uslepen. **impolitic** [im'pälitik] upolitisk; uklok.

imponderability [impändərə'biliti] vektløshet. **imponderable** [im'pändərəbl] vektløs.

import [im'pä·ᵊt] importere, innføre; betegne, bety; være av viktighet for, ha noe å si for, vedrøre; være av viktighet. **import** ['impå·ᵊt] importartikkel, innførselsvare; import, innførsel; betydning; viktighet, vekt; **I am not sure of the** — **of his reply** jeg er ikke sikker på hvor han egentlig ville hen med sitt svar. **importable** [im'pä·ᵊtəbl] som kan importeres. **importance** [im'på·ᵊtəns] betydning, viktighet; viktigmakeri; **give** — **to** legge vekt på. **important** [im'pa·ᵊtənt] viktig, av viktighet, maktpåliggende, betydningsfull; hoven, innbilsk. **importation** [impa·ᵊ-'te'ʃən] import, innførsel. **importer** [im'pa·ᵊtə] importør; **the free importers** frihandelsmennene.

importunate [im'pa·ᵊtjunét] påtrengende, brysom, besværlig. **importune** [im'på·ᵊtju·n, impå·ᵊtju·n] falle til besvær, til bry; plage, bestorme med bønner; gnåle, mase, trygle; tigge. **importunity** [impa·ᵊ'tju·niti] påtrengenhet, overheng, gnål, gnag, trygling.

impose [im'poᵘz] pålegge; utgi (**as** for); — **upon** narre, bedra, dupere, vildre, ta ved nesen, imponere. **imposing** [im'poᵘziŋ] ærefryktinngytende, imponerende. **imposingness** [im'poᵘziŋnəs] det imponerende. **imposition** [impo'ziʃən] pålegging; utskriving (av skatter); skattepålegg; skatt; bedrageri; opptrekkeri; ekstraarbeid (i universitetsspråk).

impossibility [impäsi'biliti] umulighet, uråd. **impossible** [im'päsibl] umulig; — **of attainment** uoppnåelig.

impost [im'poᵘst] pålegg, skatt; impost (arkitektonisk uttrykk).

impostor [im'pästə] bedrager. **imposture** [im-'påstʃə] bedrageri.

impotence ['impotəns], **impotency** ['impotənsi] kraftløshet, svakhet; avmakt; impotens. **impotent** ['impotənt] kraftløs, svak; avmektig; impotent; gagnløs.

impound [im'paund] lukke inne, sperre inne, sette inn (især fe); beslaglegge.

impoverish [im'påvəriʃ] forarme; utpine (f. eks. en mark). **impoverishment** [-mənt] forarming, utpining.

impracticability [im'präktikə'biliti] uutførlighet. **impracticable** [im'präktikəbl] uutførlig, umulig; umedgjørlig; ufarbar, ufør.

imprecate ['imprike't] ønske el. kalle ned ondt over; forbanne. **imprecation** [impri'ke'ʃən] nedkalling; forbannelse. **imprecatory** ['imprike'-təri, -kət-] forbannende.

impregnability [impregnə'biliti] uinntagelighet, uovervinnelighet. **impregnable** [im'pregnəbl] uinntagelig, uovervinnelig.

impregnate [im'pregne't] befrukte; impregnere, mette. **impregnation** [impreg'ne'ʃən] befruktning; impregnering.

impresario [impre'za·rioᵘ] impresario.

impress [im'pres] påtrykke, prente inn, stemple; innprege, innprente; presse, verve med makt (i krigstjeneste); — **oneself** gjøre inntrykk; **it impresses me as** det står for meg som.

impress ['impres] avtrykk, merke, preg. **impressibility** [impresi'biliti] mottagelighet. **impressible** [im'presibl] mottagelig; nem. **impression** [im'preʃən] inntrykk; merke, søkk, far, preg; virkning, innflytelse; avtrykk, opplag. **impressionable** [im'preʃənəbl] mottagelig for inntrykk. **impressionism** [im'preʃənizm] impresjonisme. **impressionist** [-ist] impresjonist; impresjonistisk. **impressionistic** [impreʃə'nistik] impresjonistisk.

impressive [im'presiv] som gjør inntrykk; virkningsfull, slående; imponerende, betagende.

impressment [im'presmənt] pressing (til hær), tvangsverving.

imprest ['imprest] forskudd, lån (av en offentlig kasse).

imprimis [im'praimis] først, framfor alt, især.

imprint [im'print] merke, prege; trykke inn, prente; ['imprint] avtrykk; merke; tittelfot (trykkested og forleggerfirma på boks tittelblad).

imprison [im'prizn] fengsle.

imprisonment [im'priznmənt] fengsling, fangenskap; **false** — ulovlig fengsling; — **before trial** varetektsarrest.

improbability [impråbə'biliti] usannsynlighet. **mprobable** [im'pråbəbl] usannsynlig.

improbity [im'pråbiti] uredelighet.

impromptu [im'pråm(p)tju] impromptu; laget på stående fot.

improper [im'pråpə] upassende, utilbørlig; uriktig, uheldig, feilaktig. — **fraction** uekte brøk.

impropriety [impro'praiiti] usømmelighet; uriktighet; feilaktighet.

improvable [im'pru·vəbl] som kan forbedres; som egner seg til dyrking; god, nyttig, brukelig.

improve [im'pru·v] forbedre, bøte, forskjønne, foredle; nytte ut, dra fordel av; bli bedre, besne, forbedre seg, gjøre framskritt; stige (om pris); — **on** innføre forbedringer i. **improvement** [im'pru·vmənt] forbedring; framskritt.

improvidence [im'pråvidəns] uforsiktighet, ubetenksomhet. **improvident** [im'pråvidənt] uforsiktig, ubetenksom.

improvisate [im'pråvize't] improvisere. **improvisation** [improvai'ze'ʃən] improvisasjon. **improvisator** [im'pråvize'tə] improvisator. **improvise** ['improvaiz] improvisere. **improviser** ['improvaizə] improvisator.

imprudence [im'pru·dəns] mangel på klokskap, uklokskap; uforsiktighet; ubetenksomhet. **imprudent** [im'pru·dənt] uklok; uforsiktig, ubetenksom.

impudence ['impjudəns] uforskammethet. **impudent** ['impjudənt] uforskammet.

impugn [im'pju·n] bekjempe, bestride. **impugnable** [im'pju·nəbl] som kan bestrides, tvilsom. **impugner** [im'pju·nə] angriper, motsiger. **impugnment** [im'pju·nmənt] bekjempelse; bestridelse, motsigelse, motlegg, motmæle.

impuissance [impju'isəns] svakhet, gagnløyse. **impulse** ['impʌls] støt, trykk; impuls, tilskynding, beveggrunn; innskytelse. **impulsion** [im-'pʌlʃən] støt, trykk; tilskynding; innskytelse. **impulsive** [im'pʌlsiv] bevegende, tilskyndende; brå, impulsiv, umiddelbar; drivkraft; beveggrunn.

impunity [im'pju·niti] straffløshet, frihet for straff; **with** — ustraffet.

impure [im'pjuə] uren; ukysk; full av feil. **impurity** [im'pjuəriti] urenhet; ukyskhet.

impurple [im'pə·pl] farge rød, purpurfarge.

imputable [im'pju·təbl] som kan tilskrives; tilregnelig, skyldig. **imputation** [impju'te'ʃən] beskyldning; bebreidelse; hentydning. **imputative** [im'pju·tətiv] tilskrevet, tillagt; underlagt. **impute** [im'pju·t] tilregne, regne, tillegge, beskylde.

imputrescibility [impjutresi'biliti] uforråtnelighet. **imputrescible** [impju'tresibl] uforråtnelig.

imrig ['imrig] (skotsk) oksekjøttsuppe.

in [in] i, på; til; under; om; inn, inne; hjemme; i og med at, ved å. **in the country** på landet; **in town** i byen; **in Shakespeare** hos Shakespeare; **in the sky** på himmelen; **in the university** ved universitetet; **in health** frisk; **be in love** være forelsket; **in the afternoon** om ettermiddagen; **in two hours** om to timer; **in the reign of Elizabeth** under Elisabeths regjering; **in time** i rette tid; i sin tid; **in his travels** på hans reiser; **trust in God** stole på Gud; **in answer** (el. **reply**) **to** som svar på; **in obedience to** av lydighet mot; **in pity of** av

medlidenhet med; **in this manner** på denne måte; **in vain** forgjeves; **in as far as** for så vidt som; **in appearance** etter det ytre å dømme; **in my opinion** etter min mening; **in all probability** etter all sannsynlighet; **in boots** med støvler på; **five in hundred** fem prosent; **two in the four goes twice** to i fire er to; **be in for it** ha påtatt seg det, ha innlatt seg på det.

in [in] medlem av regjeringen el. det herskende parti; passasjer inne i vognen; **the ins and outs** regjeringen og opposisjonen; de som er med i spillet, og de som er utenfor; alle kroker og kriker.

in. fk. f. **inch.**

inability [inə'biliti] udyktighet, udugelighet.

inaccessibility [inäksesi'biliti] utilgjengelighet. **inaccessible** [inak'sesibl] utilgjengelig.

inaccuracy [in'äkjurəsi] unøyaktighet, slurv. **inaccurate** [in'äkjurét] unøyaktig.

inaction [in'äkʃən] uvirksomhet. **inactive** [in-'äktiv] uvirksom; treg. **inactivity** [inäk'tiviti] uvirksomhet; treghet.

inadequacy [in'ädikwəsi] utilstrekkelighet. **inadequate** [in'ädikwét] utilstrekkelig, mangelfull; uskikket.

inadmissibility [in ·'misi'biliti] utillatelighet, uantagelighet. **inadmissible** [inäd'misibl] utilstedelig, uantagelig.

inadvertence [inəd'və·təns], **inadvertency** [-tən-si] uaktsomhet; forseelse, feil, feiltagelse. **inadvertent** [-tənt] uaktsom, uoppmerksom, forsømmelig.

inalienability [in'e'liənə'biliti] uavhendelighet. **inalienable** [in'e'ljənəbl] uavhendelig, umistelig.

in-and-in ['inən(d)'in]: **breeding** — innavl.

inane [i'ne'n] tom; tomhet.

inanimate [in'änimét] livløs. **inanimated** [in-'änime'tid] livløs. **inanimation** [inänl'me'ʃən] livløshet; mangel på liv, flauhet.

inanition [inə'niʃən] tomhet; avkreftelse. **inanity** [i'näniti] tomhet.

inappetence [in'äpitəns] mangel på appetitt. **inappetent** [in'äpitənt] matlei.

inapplicability [inäplika'biliti] uanvendelighet. **inapplicable** [in'äplikəbl] uanvendelig. **inapplication** [inäpli'ke'ʃən] mangel på flid.

inapposite [in'äpozit] uhøvelig, uskikket.

inappreciable [inə'pri·ʃ(j)əbl] uberegnelig; ringe, ørliten.

inapproachable [inə'pro"tʃəbl] utilgjengelig, utilnærmelig.

inappropriate [inə'pro"priét] som lite høver; uskikket.

inapt [in'äpt] uskikket; upassende; tungnem. **inaptitude** [in'äptitju·d] uskikkethet; tungnemhet.

inarch [in'a·ətʃ] pode inn (således at podekvisten står på mortrêet til den er vokst fast i det nye).

inarticulate [ina·ə'tikjulét] uartikulert. **inarticulation** [ina·ə'tikju'le'ʃən] mangel på artikulasjon.

inartificial [ina·əti'fiʃəl] ikke kunstig; ukunstlet.

inasmuch [inəz'mʌtʃ]: — **as** for så vidt som; ettersom, da.

inattention [inə'tenʃən] uoppmerksomhet, forsømmelighet. **inattentive** [inə'tentiv] uoppmerksom; forsømmelig.

inaudibility [ina·di'biliti] uhørlighet. **inaudible** [in'a·dibl] uhørlig.

inaugural [in'a·gjurəl] innvielses-, åpnings-; innsettelses-; innvielsestale; — **address** åpningstale; — **sermon** tiltredelsespreken. **inaugurate** [i'na·gjure't] innvie; høytidelig innsette; innvarsle; begynne lykkelig. **inauguration** [inä·gju-'re'ʃən] innvielse; høytidelig innsettelse. **inauguratory** [i'na·gjurətəri] se **inaugural**.

inaurate [i'na·re't] forgylle. **inaurate** [i'na·rét] forgylt.

inauspicious [inå'spiʃəs] uheldig, ugunstig.
in-being ['inbi·iŋ] iboen, immanens, inhærens.
inboard ['inbå·ᵊd] innabords. inboards [-z] innabords, om bord.
inborn ['inbå·ᵊn] medfødt.
inbread ['inbred] tilgift på brød, brød på kjøpet.
inbred ['inbred] medfødt, naturlig; kommet av innavl.
inbreed ['inbri·d] avle; avle ved innavl.
Inca ['iŋkə] inka (peruansk konge).
incage [in'ke'dʒ] sperre inne.
incalculable [in'kälkjuləbl] uberegnelig.
incandescence [inkän'desəns] hvitglødning.
incandescent [inkän'desənt] hvitglødende; — lamp glødelampe.
incantation [inkän'te'ʃən] besvergelse; maning; trolling, gand; besvergelsesformular; fess, trollbønn, gandvise, incantatory [in'käntətəri] besvergende; magisk.
incapability [inke'pə'biliti] udyktighet, udugelighet. incapable [in'ke'pəbl] udugelig, ute av stand (of til); udyktig, undermåler.
incapacious [inkə'pe'ʃəs] ikke rommelig, snever; trangbrystet.
incapacitate [inkə'päsite't] gjøre udyktig (for til). incapacity [inkə'päsiti] udyktighet; udugelighet.
incarcerate [in'ka·ᵊsəre't] fengsle, sperre inne. incarceration [inka·ᵊsə're'ʃən] fengsling, innesperring.
incarn [in'ka·ᵊn] dekke med kjøtt; inkarnere; legemliggjøre; hele; heles, gro igjen. incarnadine [in'ka·ᵊnədin, -dain] kjøttfarget, blekrød; rød; kjøttfarge; blekrød; farge rødt. incarnate [in'ka·ᵊne't] inkarnere; legemliggjøre; heles. incarnate [in'ka·ᵊnét] inkarnert; legemliggjort. incarnation[inka·ᵊ'ne'ʃən]kjøttdannelse; inkarnasjon; heling; legemliggjørelse; blekrød nellik. incarnative [in'ka·ᵊnətiv] helende; helende middel.
incase [in'ke's] inneslutte; bedekke, omgi, overtrekke; ligge rundt. incasement [in'ke'smənt] inneslutning; bedekning; overtrekk.
incask [in'ka·sk] ha på fat.
incautious [in'kå·ʃəs] uforsiktig.
incavation [inkə've'ʃən] søkk, huling; fordypning.
incendiarism [in'sendjərizm] brannstifting, mordbrann. incendiary [in'sendjəri] brannstiftings-, mordbranns-, brann-; opphissende, opprørsk; brannstifter, mordbrenner; noe opphissende; opphissende artikkel; brannfakkel; brannbombe; opphisser, mytteristifter; — bomb brannbombe. — fire påsatt ildebrann.
incense ['sens] egge opp, oppflamme.
incense ['insens] røykelse, virak; ofre røykelse til; burn (el. offer) — to strø virak for. incensive [in'sensiv] oppflammende, eggende. incensory [in'sensəri] røykelseskar.
incentive [in'sentiv] oppflammende, eggende; spore, oppmuntring, kveik; motiv.
inception [in'sepʃən] begynnelse, tiltak, inceptive [in'septiv] begynnende; begynnelses-.
incertitude [in'sə·titju·d] uvisshet.
incessant [in'sesənt] uopphørlig. incessantly [in'sesəntli] uopphørlig.
incest ['insest] blodskam. incestuous [in-'sestjuəs, -stʃ-] skyldig i blodskam.
inch [inʃ] tomme; bagatell, hårsbredd; tommelang, tommebred, tommetykk; inndele i tommer; tildele smått; rykke tomme for tomme fram (el. tilbake); by -es tommevis; — by — tomme for tomme; every — a gentleman en kavaler til fingerspissene; flog one within an — of his life pryle en halvt i hjel.
inchmeal ['inʃmi·l] tommevis, smått om senn.
inchoate ['inkoᵘit] i emning, påbegynt. inchoate ['inkoᵘe't] ta til med, begynne.
incidence ['insidəns] innfall; virkning; angle of

— innfallsvinkel; the — of the tax skatteforholdene; den som får bære skattetrykket.
incident ['insidənt] tilstøtende; som kan inntreffe tilfeldig, ved leilighet; forbundet med; begivenhet, tilfelle, tildragelse, hendelse, hending; biting; episode; innskudd.
incidental [insi'dentəl] tilfeldig; bi-; innskudd; — expenses tilfeldige utgifter. incidentally [insi-'dentəli] tilfeldig, leilighetsvis, for øvrig.
incinerate [in'sinəre't] brenne til aske. incineration [insinə're'ʃən] forbrenning til aske; likbrenning.
incipient [in'sipiənt] begynnende; innledende.
incise [in'saiz] skjære ut. incision [in'siʒən] innskjæring; skur; innsnitt; skår; skar, hakk; flenge.
incisive [in'saisiv] skjærende, kvass, gnell; — tooth fortann. incisiveness [-nés] skarphet. incisor [in'saisə] skjæretann, fortann, incisory [-səri] skjærende. incisure [in'siʒə] innsnitt.
incitant [in'insitənt, in'saitənt] eggende, sporende middel, incitament, kveik. incitation [insi'te'ʃən] tilskyndelse; spore, incitament, kveik, beveggrunn. incite [in'sait] spore, egge, tilskynde; opphisse. incitement [in-'saitmənt] tilskyndelse; spore, incitament, beveggrunn. inciter [in'saitə] en som tilskynder osv.
incivility [insi'viliti] uhøflighet.
incivism [''insivizm] mangel på borgerånd.
incl. fk. f. inclusive.
inclemency [in'klemənsi] barskhet.
inclement [in'klemənt] barsk, hard.
inclinable [in'klainəbl] tilbøyelig; gunstig, vennlig (to mot).
inclination [inkli'ne'ʃən] bøyning; inklinasjon, tilbøyelighet (to el. for til; to do til å gjøre).
incline [in'klain] bøye; gjøre tilbøyelig, stemme; helle, lute; ha tilbøyelighet; ha anstrøk (to av); helling, skråplan; hall, bakke. inclined [in'klaind] tilbøyelig (to til); skrå.
inclose [in'kloᵘz] innhegne, inngjerde; inneslutte; legge inn i; legge ved. inclosure [in'kloᵘʒə] innhegning, inngjerding; jorde; inneslutning; innlegg; bilag, vedlegg; gjerde.
include [in'klu·d] inneslutte; inneholde; innbefatte; — in brackets sette i parentes. inclusion [in'klu·ʒən] inneslutning; innbefatning.
inclusive [in'klu·siv], — of inklusive. pages 7 to 26 — fra og med side 7 til og med side 26.
incog [in'kåg] inkognito.
incogitable [in'kådʒitəbl] utenkelig. incogitance, incogitancy [in'kådʒitəns(i)] tankeløshet; utenkelighet. incogitative [in'kådʒite'tiv] som ikke kan tenke.
incognita [in'kågnitə] ukjent dame, dame som reiser inkognito. incognito[in'kågnitoᵘ] inkognito; ubekjent; inkognito. incognizable [in'kågnizəbl] ukjennelig.
incoherence, incoherency [inko'hiərəns(i)] mangel på sammenheng.
incoherent [inko'hiərənt] usammenhengende, våsete; speak -ly snakke i vilske.
incombustible [inkəm'bʌstibl] uforbrennelig, ildfast.
income ['inkəm] inntekt. incomer ['inkʌmə] tiltredende leier el. forpakter. income-tax ['inkʌmtäks] inntektsskatt.
incoming['inkʌmiŋ] innkommende, tiltredende, ankommende; -s innkomst.
incommensurability [inkə'menʃərə'biliti] inkommensurabilitet. incommensurable [inkə'menʃurəbl] inkommensurabel, uensartet.
incommode [inkə'moᵘd] uleilige, umake, bry. incommodious [inkə'moᵘdiəs] ubekvem; brysom, besværlig.
incommunicable [inkəm'ju·nikəbl] umeddelelig. incommunicative [inkə'mju·nikətiv] umeddelsom; som skyr samkvem, som holder seg for seg selv.

incomparable [in'kåmpərəbl] som ikke kan sammenlignes; uforlignelig, enestående, makeløs.
incompatibility [inkəmpäti'biliti] uforenelighet; uforlikelighet. **incompatible** [inkəm'pätibl] uforenelig; uforlikelig.
incompetence, incompetency [in'kåmpitəns(i)] inkompetanse; udyktighet, udugelighet; utilstrekkelighet. **incompetent** [in'kåmpitənt] inkompetent; uskikket, udugelig, ugild; utilstrekkelig.
incomplete [inkəm'pli·t] ufullstendig, ufullendt, mangelfull, defekt. **incompletion** [inkəm'pli·ʃən] ufullstendighet osv.
incompliance [inkəm'plaiəns] ubøyelighet, umedgjørlighet. **incompliant** [inkəm'plaiənt] umedgjørlig, ubøyelig.
incomposite [in'kåmpozit] usammensatt, enkelt; — **numbers** primtall.
incomprehensibility [inkåmprihensi'biliti] ubegripelighet, ufattelighet. **incomprehensible** [inkåmpri'hensibl] ubegripelig, ufattelig.
incomprehensive [inkåmpri'hensiv] ikke omfattende; uforstående.
incompressible [inkåm'presibl] som ikke kan trykkes sammen, ikke kan klemmes sammen.
inconceivable [inkən'si·vəbl] ufattelig.
inconclusive [inkəŋ'klu·siv] ikke overbevisende, ikke avgjørende; uvirksom, resultatløst; ubestemt.
incondite [in'kåndit] dårlig utarbeidd, plump.
incongruence [in'kåŋgruəns] uoverensstemmelse; forkjærthet; urimelighet; motsigelse. **incongruent** [in'kåŋgruənt] uoverensstemmende, inkongruent; upassende; fornuftstridig, forkjært.
incongruity [inkån'gru·iti, -kåŋ'g-] uoverensstemmelse; forkjærthet; urimelighet; motsigelse.
incongruous [in'kåŋgruəs] uoverensstemmende, inkongruent; upassende; fornuftstridig, forkjært.
inconsequence [in'kånsikwəns] inkonsekvens, selvmotsigelse. **inconsequent** [in'kånsikwənt] inkonsekvent, selvmotsigende. **inconsequential** [inkånsi'kwenʃəl] uviktig; inkonsekvent.
inconsiderable [inkən'sid(ə)rəbl] ubetydelig.
inconsiderate [inkən'sidərėt] ubetenksom, brå, tankeløs; lite hensynsfull.
inconsistence, inconsistency [inkən'sistəns(i)] motsigelse; uoverensstemmelse; inkonsekvens. **inconsistent** [inkən'sistənt] selvmotsigende; uoverensstemmende; inkonsekvent.
inconsolable [inkən'souləbl] utrøstelig.
inconsonance [in'kånsənəns] uoverensstemmelse; inkonsekvens; disharmoni, misklang. **inconsonant** [in'kånsənənt] uoverensstemmende (**with, to** med).
inconspicuous [inkən'spikjuəs] ikke til å skjelne, umerkelig.
inconstancy [in'kånstənsi] mangel på standhaftighet; ustadighet. **inconstant** [in'kånstənt] ustadig; ustø, vinglet.
inconsumable [inkən'sju·məbl] som ikke kan fortæres, som ikke kan brukes opp.
incontaminate [inkən'täminėt] ubesmittet, ren; ekte.
incontestable [inkən'testəbl] ubestridelig.
incontiguous [inkən'tigjuəs] som ikke berører; atskilt, separat.
incontinence [in'kåntinəns] mangel på avholdenhet; ukyskhet; inkontinens; — **of urine** urinflod. **incontinent** [in'kåntinənt] ikke avholdende; villstyring; ukysk; som lider av inkontinens.
incontrovertible [inkåntro'və·tibl] uomtvistelig.
inconvenience [inkən'vi·njəns] uleilighet, umak, strev, bry, besværlighet, ulempe, forlegenhet; uleilige, besvære, bry, bringe i forlegenhet, forstyrre; være til bry (el. ulempe) for. **inconvenient** [-jənt] ubekvem, ubeleilig, besværlig, brysom, lei, vrang.
inconvertible [inkən'və·tibl] uforanderlig; som ikke kan byttes om, som ikke kan omsettes.
inconvincible [inkən'vinsibl] som ikke lar seg overbevise, stivsinnet.
incorporate [in'kå·əpəre'ˡt] blande; legemliggjøre; legere; oppta, innlemme; inkorporere; gi kjøpstadsrettigheter; få kjøpstadsrettigheter; forbinde seg, forene seg. **incorporate** [in'kå·əporėt] inkorporert, opptatt i; forent til en korporasjon; som danner en korporasjon; sterkt blandet om hverandre; sterkt forbundet, inderlig; ulegemlig; ikke inkorporert; uten korporasjonsrettigheter.
incorporation [inkå·əpə'reˡʃən] blanding; legemliggjøring; opptagelse, innlemmelse; inkorporasjon; tildeling av kjøpstadsrettigheter; oppnåelse av kjøpstadsrettigheter. **incorporeal** [inkåə'på·əriəl] ulegemlig. **incorporeity** [inkå·əpə'ri·iti] ulegemlighet.
incorrect [inkə'rekt] unøyaktig, uriktig, urett, feilfull. **incorrection** [inkə'rekʃən] unøyaktighet, uriktighet.
incorrigibility [in'kåridʒi'biliti] uforbederlighet. **incorrigible** [in'kåridʒibl] uforbederlig.
incorrupt [inkə'rʌpt] ufordervet; ikke bestukket; ubestikkelig. **incorruptibility** [inkərʌpti'biliti] ufordervelighet, uforgjengelighet; ubestikkelighet. **incorruptible** [inkə'rʌptibl] ufordervelig, uforgjengelig; ubestikkelig. **incorruption** [inkə'rʌpʃən] ufordervet tilstand; uforkrenkelighet.
incrassate [in'kräseˡt] fortykke, gjøre tykkere; bli tykk, tykne. **incrassation** [inkrä'seˡʃən] fortykkelse. **incrassative** [in'kräsətiv] fortykkende; fortykkende middel.
increase [in'kri·s] tilta, vokse, øke, auke; formere seg; formere, forsterke, forøke, forhøye, forstørre. **increase** ['inkri·s] forøkelse, auke, vekst.
increasingly [in'kri·siŋli] tiltagende, voksende, stigende, mer og mer.
incredibility [inkredi'biliti] utrolighet. **incredible** [in'kredibl] utrolig. **incredibly** [-bli] utrolig.
incredulity [inkri'dju·liti] vantro. **incredulous** [in'kredjuləs] vantro.
incremation [inkri'meˡʃən] likbrenning.
increment ['inkrimənt] vokster, tilvekst, forøkelse, auke, verdauke. — **-tax** verdaukeskatt.
increscent [in'kresənt] tiltagende; (heraldikk voksende; voksende måne.
incriminate [in'krimineˡt] anklage, beskylde.
incrust [in'krʌst] bedekke med et lag, overtrekke; belegge, kle, **incrustation** [inkrʌ'steˡʃən] dekning; belegg; dekke, lag; kjelestein.
incubate ['inkjubeˡt] ruge, ligge på egg; varme, klekke ut; utvikle seg (om sykdom). **incubation** [inkju'beˡʃən] ruging, utklekking; inkubasjon; **period of** — inkubasjonstid. **incubator** ['inkjubeˡtə, 'iŋ-] utklekkingsapparat, rugemaskin. **incubus** ['inkjubəs, iŋ-] mare, mareritt.
inculcate [in'kʌlkeˡt, 'inkəl-] innprente, innskjerpe. **inculcation** [inkəl'keˡʃən] innprenting, innskjerping.
inculpate [in'kʌlpeˡt, 'inkəl-] dadle, kaste skylden på, bebreide; anklage. **inculpation** [inkəl'peˡʃən] daddel, klander, beskyldning. **inculpatory** [in'kʌlpətəri] dadlende; som inneholder en beskyldning.
incumbency [in'kʌmbənsi] forpliktelse; byrde; (det å inneha) geistlig embete.
incumbent [in'kʌmbənt] påliggende; påhvilende; innehaver av et prestekall; **it is — on you to** det er din plikt å.
incunabula [inkju'näbjulə] inkunabler, paleotyper, eldste trykkverker.
incur [in'kə·] utsette seg for; pådra seg, våge seg ut for; — **debts** stifte gjeld; — **losses** lide tap.
incurability [inkjuərə'biliti] uhelbredelighet.
incurable [in'kjuərəbl] uhelbredelig.
incuriosity [inkjuəri'åsiti] likegyldighet, mangel på vitebegjærlighet, uoppmerksomhet, sorgløshet. **incurious** [in'kjuəriəs] likegyldig, likesæl, uoppmerksom, sorgløs.
incursion [in'kə·ʃən] fiendtlig innfall, streiftog.
incursive [in'kə·siv] fiendtlig, angripende.
incurvate ['inkə·veˡt] krumme. **incurvation**

[inkə've'ʃən] krumning. **incurve** [in'kə·v] krumme. **incurvity** [in'kə·viti] krumning. **incus** ['iŋkəs] ambolt (i øret). **incuse** [in'kju·z] prege; preget; preg, stempel. **Ind** [ind] India (i høyere stil). **ind. fk. f. indicative.** **indebted** [in'detid] som skylder, som står i gjeld; forpliktet; I am — to him for it jeg skylder ham det. **indebtedness** [-nès] det å stå i gjeld; gjeld. **indecency** [in'di·sənsi] usømmelighet, uanstendighet. **indecent** [in'di·sənt] usømmelig, uanstendig. **indecipherable** [indi'saif(ə)rəbl] ikke til å tyde, uleselig. **indecision** [indi'siʒen] ubestemthet, rådvillhet. **indecisive** [indi'saisiv] ubestemt, uavgjørende; rådvill, vinglet. **indecisiveness** [-nès] ubestemthet, vakling. **indeclinable** [indi'klainəbl] ubøyelig. **indecorous** [in'dekərəs] usømmelig, uanstendig. **indecorum** [indi'kårəm] usømmelighet, uanstendighet, uoppdragenhet. **indeed** [in'di·d] i virkeligheten, virkelig; ja, ja visst; så menn; ganske visst, sant å si; nok, riktignok; vel, saktens; for resten, da; nei virkelig? så? **indefatigability** [indifätigə'biliti] utrettelighet, trott. **indefatigable** [indi'fätigəbl] utrettelig, trottig. **indefeasibility** [indifi·zi'biliti] uomstøtelighet; ugjenkallelighet; uavhendelighet. **indefeasible** [indi'fi·zibl] uomstøtelig; ugjenkallelig; uavhendelig. **indefectibility** [indifekti'biliti] feilfrihet; ufeilbarlighet; uforgjengelighet. **indefectible** [indi·'fektibl] feilfri; ufeilbar; uforgjengelig. **indefective** [indi'fektiv] ganske feilfri, fullkommen. **indefinite** [in'def(i)nit] uklar, ugrei; ubegrenset; ubestemt; — **payment** betaling på avdrag. **indelibility** [indeli'biliti] uutslettelighet. **indelible** [in'delibl] uutslettelig. **indelicacy** [in'delikəsi] mangel på finfølelse, ufinhet; taktløshet. **indelicate** [in'delikét] ufin, udelikat, taktløs. **indemnification** [indemnifi'ke'ʃən] skadesløsholdelse, skadebot, sikkerhet, erstatning. **indemnify** [in'demnifai] holde skadesløs, sikre. **indemnity** [in'demniti] skadeløsholdelse, skadebot, sikkerhet, skadesløshet, erstatning; benådning. **indemonstrable** [indem'månstrəbl] ubeviselig, påviselig. **indent** [in'dent] skjære hakk i, gjøre hakk i, gjøre tagget; stemple; sette merke i; duplisere; sette i lære; innsnitt, hakk; preg; dokument. ordre. **indentation** [inden'te'ʃən] innsnitt, hakk, skar, søkk; ny linje (typ.) **indenture** [in'dentʃə] duplikat; binde ved kontrakt, sette i lære. **independable** [indi'pendəbl] upålitelig. **independence** [indi'pendəns] uavhengighet, selvstendighet; tilstrekkelig utkomme; **Independence Day** (amer.) frihetsdagen, 4. juli. **independency** [indi'pendənsi] selvstendighet; frikirkepolitikk; selvstendig stat. **independent** [indi'pendənt] uavhengig (of av), fri, ubunden; selvstendig; formuende. **indescribable** [indi'skraibəbl] ubeskrivelig. **indestructibility** [indi'strʌkti'biliti] uforgjengelighet. **indestructible** [indi'strʌktibl] uforgjengelig. **indeterminable** [indi'tə·minəbl] ubestemmelig, ugrei, som ikke kan avgjøres. **indetermination** [indita·mi'ne'ʃən] ubestemthet. **index** ['indeks] en som påpeker el. anviser; viser; pekefinger; eksponent (mat.); register, innholdsfortegnelse, indeks; fingerpek; forsyne med register; sette på indeks; **the Index** listen over forbudte bøker. **indexterity** [indeks'teriti] ubehendighet. **India** [indjə] India; Ostindia, Forindia; —

Office departement for India; — **paper** indiapapir (tynt trykkpapir); — **rubber** viskelær. **Indiaman** ['indjəmən] indiafarer. **Indian** ['indjən; 'indʒən] indisk, india-; indiansk; inder; indianer; — **bread** maisbrød; — **cane** bambus; — **corn** mais; — **gift** gave, som tas tilbake; — **ink** tusj; — **summer** ettersommer; sensommer (omkring helgemess); — **weed** tobakk; **Red** — el. **American** — indianer; **honest** — på ære! (egentlig: så sant jeg er en ærlig indianer; en forsikring i barneleik). **Indiana** [indi'änə] Indiana. **india-rubber** ['indjərʌbə] viskelær. **indican** ['indikən] indikan, indigostoff. **indicant** ['indikənt] som angir, anviser. **indicate** ['indike't] anvise, tilkjennegi, syne, bestemme; bebude, tyde på; indisere. **indication** [indi'ke'ʃən] anvisning; kjennetegn; antydning; tegn; symptom; indikasjon. **indicative** [in'dikətiv] som antyder, som er tegn på; indikativisk; **the** — el. **the** — **mode** indikativ. **indicator** ['indike'tə] angiver, anviser; indikator; dynamometer, kraftmåler. **indicatory** [in'dikətəri, '-ke'·təri] som angir, tyder på. **indices** ['indisi·z] (flertall av **index**) eksponenter. **indicia** [in'dif(j)ə] indisier. **indict** [in'dait] anklage, sette under tiltale (for for). **indictable** [in'daitəbl] som kan anklages. **indictee** [indai'ti·] anklagede. **indictment** [in'daitmənt] anklage; tiltalebeslutning. **Indies** [in'di·z]: **the** — India; **the West** — Vestindia; **the East** — Ostindia. **indifference** [in'dif(ə)rəns] likegyldighet; middelmåtighet. **indifferent** [in'dif(ə)rənt] likegyldig; likesæl; middelmåtig; middels, tarvelig. **indifferentism** [in'dif(ə)rəntizm] indifferentisme, likegyldighet. **indifferentist** [-'tist] indifferentist; indifferentistisk. **indifferently** [in'dif(ə)rəntli] likegyldig; middelmåtig. **indigence** ['indidʒəns] trang, armod. **indigene** ['indidʒi·n] innfødt, innenlandsk; innfødt dyr el. plante. **indigenous** [in'didʒinəs] innfødt; innenlandsk; medfødt; virkelig, sann. **indigent** ['indidʒənt] trengende, fattig. **indigested** ['indi'dʒestid] ufordøyd; uordnet, uordentlig; umoden. **indigestibility** [indidʒesti·'biliti] ufordøyelighet. **indigestible** [indi'dʒestibl] ufordøyelig. **indigestion** [indi'dʒestʃən] dårlig fordøyelse. **indigestive** [indi'dʒestiv] med dårlig fordøyelse. **indignant** [in'dignənt] harmfull, oppbrakt, sint; — **at** sint for; — **with** sint på. **indignation** [indig'ne'ʃən] harme, vrede, forbitrelse. **indignity** [in'digniti] skammelig behandling, uverdighet, skjendighet, beskjemmelse. **indigo** ['indigo⁰] indigo(farge). **indirect** [indi'rekt] ikke likefram; kroket, skjev; indirekte. **indirection** [indi'rekʃən] skjevhet; omvei; krokvei. **indirectly** [indi'rektli] ikke likefram, ved omveier, indirekte. **indirectness** [indi-'rektnès] se **indirection**. **indiscernible** [indi'zə·nibl] umerkelig. **indisciplinable** [in'disiplinəbl] uregjerlig. **indiscipline** [in'disiplin] mangel på disiplin, ageløyse, vantukt . **indiscreet** [indis'kri·t] ubetenksom, tankeløs, åpenmunnet, indiskret, taktløs. **indiscretion** [indi'skreʃən] ubetenksomhet; indiskresjon, taktløshet. **indiscriminate** [indis'kriminét] i fleng, på slump; ikke forskjellig, uten forskjell. **indiscriminating** [indis'krimine'tiŋ] som ikke gjør forskjell, hensynsløs, kritikkløs. **indiscrimination** ['indiskrimi'ne'ʃən] kritikkløshet. **indispensability** [indispensə'biliti] uunnværlighet. **indispensable** [indi'spensəbl] uunnværlig, absolutt nødvendig. **indispose** [indi'spo⁰z] gjøre uskikket; sette i ulag; gjøre upasselig; gjøre utilbøyelig; stemme ugunstig. **indisposed** [indi'spo⁰zd] uskikket; uopplagt, ikke disponert. **indisposedness** [indi'spo⁰-zidnés] uskikkethet; utilbøvelighet; indisposisjon, upasselighet; uonplagthet; uvilie. **indisposition** [indispo'ziʃən] utilbøvelighet; indisposisjon, upasselighet; uonplagthet; ulag; uvilje.

indisputable [in'dispjutəbl] ubestridelig, klar.

indissociable [indi'so⁰fəbl] uatskillelig.

indissolubility [indi'sâlju'biliti, in'disəlju-] u-oppløselighet. **indissoluble** [indi'sâljubl, in'disə-ljubl] uonpløselig. **indissolvable** [indi'zâlvəbl] uonpløselig.

indistinct [indi'stin(k)t] utvdelig, uklar, ugrei. **indistinctness** [-nés] utvdelighet, uklarhet.

indistinguishable [indi'stingwiʃəbl] ikke til å skjelne.

indite [in'dait] diktere, målbære, forfatte, skrive.

individual [indi'vidjuəl, -dʒu-] enkelt; individuell, personlig; særegen, eiendommelig; individ, person, menneske; enkeltmann; vedkommende. **individualism** [indi'vidjuəlizm, -dʒu-] individualisme, egoisme; individualitet. **individuality** [individju'äliti, -dʒu-] individualitet. **individualize** [indi'vidjuəlaiz, -dʒu-] individualisere, kjennetegne.

indivisibility [indivizi'biliti] udelelighet. **indivisible** [indi'vizibl] udelelig.

indo- ['indo⁰-] indo-, indisk.

indocile [in'do⁰sail] ulærvillig; tungnem; umedgjørlig, stri, vrang. **indocility** [indo'siliti] ulærvillighet; tungnemhet; umedgjørlighet.

indoctrinate [in'dâktrine⁰t] undervise, lære opp. **indoctrination** [indâktri'ne⁰ʃən] undervisning.

Indol-English ['indo⁰'ingliʃ] indo-engelsk. — European [indoiuəro'pi·ən] indoeuropeisk; indoeuropeer. — -Germanic [indodʒə'mänik] indogermansk, indoeuropeisk.

indolence ['indoləns] lathet, latskap. **indolent** ['indolənt] treg, lat; smertefri.

indomitable [in'dâmitəbl] utemmelig, utstyrlig.

indoor ['indå·⁰] innendørs, hjemme, inne; — relief understøttelse på fattiggården og på de velgjørende anstalter som er knyttet til forsorgsvesenet, i motsetning til **outdoor-relief**, forsorgsunderstøttelse utenfor den slags anstalter; — work innendørs arbeid, innearbeid.

indoors [in'då·⁰?] innendørs, inne; hjemme.

indorsation [indå·⁰se'ʃən], **indorse** [in'då·⁰s] se endorsation osv.

indubitable [in'dju·bitəbl] utvilsom.

induce [in'dju·s] innføre; medføre, forårsake, bevirke; overtale, bevege, formå, få til; forlede; indusere. **inducement** [-mənt] foranledning, beveggrunn; motiv; lokkemiddel, overtalelsesmiddel. **inducible** [in'dju·sibl] som man kan slutte seg til (from av); som kan bevirkes osv.

induct [in'dʌkt] innføre; presentere; innsette (f. eks. i et embete).

inductance [in'dʌktəns] induksjon. **inducteous** [in'dʌktiəs] indusert.

inductile [in'dʌktail] ustrekk › r, utøyelig, ustrekkelig.

induction [in'dʌkʃən] innføring; innsetting; introduksjon, innledning; induksjon.

inductive [in'dʌktiv] som beveger, som bevirker; induktiv; induksjons-; — circuit induksjonsstrøm; — philosophy eksperimentalfysikk.

indue [in'dju·] iføre, bekle, utruste.

indulge [in'dʌldʒ] føye, se gjennom fingrene med, benke seg etter, la få sin vilje; tilfredsstille; hengi seg til; gi fritt løp; begunstige, smigre; — in hengi seg til; tillate seg, forfalle til, nyte i fulle drag. — oneself in tillate seg. **indulgence** [in-'dʌldʒəns] overbærenhet; tilfredsstillelse; nytelse (in av); begunstigelse, frihet; henstand (merk.); avlat. **indulgent** [in'dʌldʒənt] overbærende, skånsom, mild, svak.

indument [in'dju·mənt] fjærkledning.

induna [in'du·nə] anfører (i Sør-Afrika).

indurate ['indjure⁰t] herde; forherde; bli forherdet; hard, forherdet. **induration** [indju-'re⁰ʃən] herding; hardhet; forherding.

Indus ['indəs] Indus.

industrial [in'dʌstriəl] industriell; nærings-, yrkes-; industridrivende; — exhibition industriutstilling; — maintenance system, hvoretter hver industri sørger for sine egne arbeidsløse; — school fagskole; oppdragelsesanstalt for forsømte el. vanartede barn. **industrialism** [in'dʌstriəlizm] industridrift. **industrialist** [in'dʌstriəlist] industridrivende. **industrious** [in'dʌstriəs] flittig. **industry** ['indəstri] flid, driftighet; industri, kunstflid; industrigrein, erverv, ervervsgrein, næringsvei; **cottage** — husflid.

indwell [in'dwel] bo i; bebo. **indweller** ['indwelə] beboer; innbygger. **indwelling** ['indwelin] iboende; det å bo i.

inebriant [in'i·briənt] berusende; berusende middel. **inebriate** [in'i·brie⁰t] beruse, gjøre beruset; beruset, drukken; dranker. **inebriation** [ini-bri'e⁰ʃən] beruselse. **inebriety** [ini'braiiti] drukkenskap, rus, fyll.

inedited [in'editid] utrykt, ikke utgitt; ny.

ineffability [inefə'biliti] uutsigelighet. **ineffable** [in'efəbl] uutsigelig; -s unevnelige, bukser.

ineffaceable [ine'fe⁰səbl] uutslettelig.

ineffective [ini'fektiv] uvirksom, kraftløs, virkningsløs, fåfengt.

ineffectual [ini'fektjuəl, -tʃuəl] uvirksom, frukteløs, kraftløs; unyttig. **inefficacious** [inefi-'ke⁰ʃəs] se **ineffectual**. **inefficacy** [in'efikəsi] virksomhet, virkningsløshet, unyttighet. **inefficiency** [inè'fiʃənsi] uvirksomhet, virkningsløshet, unyttighet; mangel på driftighet. **inefficient** [inè-'fiʃənt] uvirksom, kraftløs, ubrukbar.

inelegance [in'eligəns] mangel på eleganse, smakløshet; platthet. **inelegant** [in'eligənt] ikke elegant, smakløs.

ineligibility [in'elidʒi'biliti] ikke-valgbarhet; uhensiktsmessighet, uskikkethet. **ineligible** [in-'elidʒibl] ikke valgbar; uhensiktsmessig, uheldig.

ineluctable [ini'lʌktəbl] uovervinnelig.

inept [i'nept] uskikket; tåpelig, tosket, urimelig. **ineptitude** [in'eptitju·d] uskikkethet; tåpelighet.

inequality [ini'kwâliti] ulikhet; uoverensstemmelse; ujevnhet; utilstrekkelighet; urettferdighet. **inequation** [ini'kwe⁰ʃən] ulikhet.

ineradicable [ini'rädikəbl] som ikke kan utryddes.

inerrable [in'erəbl] ufeilbar.

inert [i'nə·t] treg, lat, trå, uvirksom. **inertia** [i'nə·ʃ(j)ə] treghet, slapphet. **inertitude** [i'nə·ti-tju·d] treghet. **inertly** [i'nə·tli] tregt, trått, slapt.

inessential [ini'senʃəl] uvesentlig, uviktig.

inestimable [in'estiməbl] uvurderlig, makeløs. **inevitability** [inevitə'biliti] uunngåelighet. **inevitable** [i'nevitəbl] uunngåelig, ikke til å slippe unna.

inexact [ineg'zäkt] unøyaktig. **inexactitude** [ineg'zäktitju·d] unøyaktighet, slurv.

inexcusable [ineks'kju·zəbl] uunnskyldelig, utilgivelig.

inexecutable [inek'sekjutəbl] uutførlig. **inexecution** [ineksi'kju·ʃən] misligholdelse.

inexhaustibility [inèg'zä·sti'biliti] uuttømmelighet. **inexhaustible** [inèg'zä·stibl] uuttømmelig.

inexistence [inèg'zistəns] ikke-tilvær; iboen. **inexistent** [inèg'zistənt] ikke eksisterende; iboende.

inexorability [ineksorə'biliti] ubønnhørlighet. **inexorable** [i'neksorəbl] ubønnhørlig.

inexpediency [inèk'spi·djənsi] uhensiktsmessighet. **inexpedient** [-ənt] uhensiktsmessig.

inexpensive [inèk'spensiv] ikke kostbar, billig.

inexperience [inèk'spiəriəns] uerfarenhet. **inexperienced** [inèk'spiəriənst] uerfaren.

inexpert [ineks'pə·t] ukyndig.

inexpiable [in'ekspiəbl] usonelig, ubotelig.
inexplicability [i'neksplikə'biliti] uforklarlighet.
inexplicable [i'neksplikəbl] uforklarlig; inexplicables unevnelige, bukser.
inexplosive [inèk'splo^{u}siv] som ikke eksploderer; ikke eksploderende stoff.
inexpressible [inèk'spresibl] ubeskrivelig, uutsigelig; inexpressibles unevnelige, bukser. inexpressive [inèk'spresiv] uttrykksløs.
inexpugnable [inèks'pʌgnəbl] uinntagelig.
inexstinguishable [inèk'stingwiʃəbl] uutslokkelig.
inextirpable [inèk'stə·pəbl] som ikke kan utryddes.
inextricable [in'ekstrikəbl] uoppløselig; innviklet, floket.
ineye [in'ai] okulere.
inf. fk. f. infinitive; infra (under).
infallibility [infäli'biliti] ufeilbarlighet.
infallible [in'fälibl] ufeilbarlig.
infamous ['infəməs] beryktet; skjendig, infam; æreløs. infamy ['infəmi] skjensel, vanære.
infancy ['infənsi] barndom; umyndighet, mindreårighet.
infant [infənt] lite barn, småbarn, spebarn; (jur.) umyndig, mindreårig; barne-, barnslig.
infanta [in'fäntə] infantinne (spansk el. portugisisk prinsesse). infante [in'fäntè] infant. infanticide [in'fäntisaid] barnemord; barnemorder (-ske). infantile ['infəntail] barne-; barnlig. infantine ['infəntin, -tain] barne-; barnslig. infantlike ['infəntlaik], infantly [-li] barnslig, barnaktig.
infantry ['infəntri] infanteri, fotfolk.
infare ['infäə] hjemkommersøl.
infatuate [in'fätjue^{i}t] bedåre, dåre, forblinde.
infatuation [infätju'e^{i}ʃən] dåring, det å forblinde(s); forgapelse.
infeasibility [infi-zi'biliti] umulighet. infeasible [in'fi-zibl] umulig, ugjørlig.
infect [in'fekt] smitte, infisere; besmitte; forpeste. infection [in'fekʃən] smitte, infeksjon; besmittelse. infectious [in'fekʃəs] smittsom.
infelicitous [infi'lisitəs] uheldig, ulykkelig. infelicity [infi'lisiti] ulykke; ulykkelig tilstand.
infelt ['infelt] dyptfølt.
infer [in'fə·] slutte, dedusere; syne, vitne om, føre med seg. inferable [in'fə·rəbl] som kan sluttes. inference ['infərəns] slutning. inferential [infə'renʃəl] som kan sluttes; slutnings-.
inferior [in'fiəriə] lavere, nedre, ringere, mindre (to enn); underordnet, undergiven. inferiority [infiəri'äriti] lavere stand; underordning; underlegenhet; ringere kvalitet; mindreverdighet.
infernal [in'fə·nəl] helvetes; djevelsk; som hører til underverdenen; — machine helvetesmaskin.
infertile [in'fə·tail] ufruktbar. infertility [infə-'tiliti] ufruktbarhet.
infest [in'fest] hjemsøke, plage. infestation [infes'te^{i}ʃən] hjemsøkelse, befengthet.
infidel ['infidəl] vantro. infidelity [infi'deliti] vantro; utroskap.
infiltrate [in'filtre^{i}t] sive inn (i), sive igjennom. infiltration [infil'trei ʃən] infiltrering, gjennomsiving.
infinite ['infinit] uendelig. infinitesimal [infini-'tesiməl] uendelig liten; uendelig liten størrelse. infinitival [infini'taivəl] infinitivisk. infinitive [in'finitiv] ubegrenset; infinitiv. infinitude [in-'finitju·d] uendelighet. infinity [in'finiti] uendelighet, endeløyse.
infirm [in'fə·m] svak, veik, skral, svakelig; usikker, skrøpelig, vaklende. infirmary [in-'fə·məri] sykehus. infirmity [in'fə·miti] svakhet, svakelighet, skrøpelighet.
infix [in'fiks] feste, innprente; infiks.
inflame [in'fle^{i}m] stikke i brann; kveike opp; hete opp, oppflamme, egge; betenne, inflammere; flamme. inflammability [inflämə'biliti] lett antennelighet, brennbarhet. inflammable [in-

'flämabl] lett antennelig, brennbar, ildsfarlig. inflammation [inflə'me^{i}ʃən] antennelse; inflammasjon, betennelse; opphisselse. inflammatory [in-'flämətəri] betennelses-; opphissende.
inflate [in'fle^{i}t] blåse opp, puste opp, fylle med luft; gjøre oppblåst; drive prisene i været. inflated [in'fle^{i}tid] oppblåst; svulstig. inflation [in-'fle^{i}ʃən] oppblåsing, fylling; oppblåsthet; svulstighet; inflasjon, kunstig hausse. inflatus [in-'fle^{i}təs] innblåsing; oppblåsing, inspirasjon.
inflect [in'flekt] bøye; modulere. inflection [in-'flekʃən] bøyning; (stemmes) modulasjon. inflectional [in'flekʃənəl] bøynings-. inflective [in-'flektiv] bøyelig. inflex [in'fleks] bøye. inflexibility [infleksi'biliti] ubøyelighet. inflexible [in'fleksibl] ubøyelig. inflexion [in'flekʃən] bøyning. inflexure [in'flekʃə] bøyning.
inflict [in'flikt] tilføye, bibringe, påføre. infliction [in'flikʃən] tilføyelse, det å påføre; tildeling; lidelse; straff. inflictive [in'fliktiv] som pålegger lidelse, straff osv.; skjebnesvanger.
inflorescence [inflo'resəns] oppblomstring; bløming; blomsterstand.
inflow ['inflo^u] innstrømming, tilstrømming; tilgang, tilførsel.
influence ['influəns] innflytelse; ha innflytelse på, påvirke. influential [influ'enʃəl] innflytelsesrik.
influenza [influ'enzə] influensa.
influx ['inflʌks] innstrømming, tilførsel.
infold [in'fo^{u}ld] innhylle; omfavne.
infoliate [in'fo^{u}lie^{i}t] bedekke med blad.
inform [in'fä·^{ə}m] underrette, opplyse, melde, gjøre kjent; — (against el. on) angi, anklage; — him of it underrette ham om det; — him that si ham at; -ed opplyst.
informal [in'fä·^{ə}məl] uformell, formløs, fri, uregelmessig; fordringsløs. informality [infä·^{ə}'mäliti] uregelmessighet; formfeil.
informant [in'fä·^{ə}mənt] meddeler, hjemmelsmann.
information [infä·^{ə}'me^{i}ʃən] underretning, opplysning(er), meddelelse, melding, viten, kunnskap(er); tiltale (rettslig); a man of various — en mann med allsidige kunnskaper el. erfaringer; general — alminnelige kunnskaper; to the best of my — etter hva jeg har erfart, så vidt jeg vet. informationist [infä·^{ə}'me^{i}ʃənist] en oppdrager som legger hovedvekten på solide kunnskaper.
informative [in'fä·^{ə}mətiv] opplysende, belærende. informatory [in'fä·^{ə}mətəri] lærerik, belærende. informer [in'fä·^{ə}mə] angiver; kronvitne.
infra ['infrə] nedenfor, under; infra dig. under ens verdighet.
infract [in'fräkt] bryte, krenke. infraction [in-'fräkʃən] brudd, krenkelse. infractor [in'fräktə] en som bryter, krenker.
infrangibility [infrändʒi'ɦiliti] ubrytelighet; ubrødelighet. infrangible [in'frändʒibl] ubrytelig; ubrødelig.
infrequency [in'fri-kwənsi] sjeldenhet, ualminnelighet. infrequent [in'fri·kwənt] sjelden, sjeldsynt, ualminnelig.
infringe [in'frin(d)ʒ] bryte, overtre, krenke; gjøre inngrep i. infringement [-mənt] brudd, overtredelse, krenkelse; inngrep. infringer [in-'frin(d)ʒə] en som bryter osv.
infuriate [in'fjuərie^{i}t] gjøre rasende (against på).
infuscate [in'fʌske^{i}t] gjøre mørk; formørke.
infuse [in'fju·z] gyte; inngyte; infundere; gjøre låg på, trekke (f. eks. te). infusibility [infju·zi-'biliti] usmeltelighet. infusible [in'fju·zibl] usmeltelig. infusion [in'fju·ʒən] inngyting, inngytelse, inngivelse; infusjon.
infusoria [infju'så·riə] infusjonsdyr, infusorier. infusory [in'fju·səri] infusorisk; infusjonsdyr.
ingate ['inge^{i}t] inngang; hals, svelg (på støpeform).
ingather [in'gäðə] høste inn, samle inn.
ingeminate [in'dʒemine^{i}t] fordoble; gjenta.

ingeminate [-nèt] fordoblet; gjentatt. ingemination [indʒemi'neɪʃən] fordobling; gjentagelse.
ingenious [in'dʒi·njəs] sinnrik, skarpsindig, oppfinnsom, klok; genial.
ingenue [fr.; änʒə'nju·] ingénue.
ingenuity [indʒi'nju·iti] sinnrikhet, skarpsindighet; genialitet.
ingenuous [in'dʒenjuəs] åpen, åpenhjertig, ærlig; naiv, troskyldig. -ness åpenhet, ærlighet; troskyldighet.
ingest [in'dʒest] innføre (især næring i magen).
ingesta [in'dʒestə] stoffer som er innført i en organisme. ingestion [in'dʒestʃən] innføring (av stoffer i en organisme).
ingle ['iŋgl] ild; arne, åre, peis, skorstein. — -nook kakkelovnskrok, peiskrå.
inglorious [in'glå·riəs] uberømt, ukjent; skammelig, skjendig, vanærende.
ingoing ['ingo⁰iŋ] tiltredende.
ingot ['iŋgət] stang, barre (av metall).
ingraft [in'gra·ft] pode; innpode. ingraftment [-mənt] podning; innpoding; podekvist.
ingrain [in'greɪn] farget i ulla; rotfestet; inngrodd, innbarket; farge i ulla; impregnere; innplante; rotfeste.
ingrate ['ingreɪt] utakknemlig.
ingratiate [in'greɪʃieɪt] bringe i yndest (with hos); — oneself with innynde seg hos.
ingratitude [in'grätitju·d] utakknemlighet.
ingredient [in'gri·djənt] ingrediens, bestanddel.
ingress ['ingres] inntredelse, inngang; innstrømning (av luft el. vann osv.); adgang. ingression [in'greʃən] inntredelse; inngang.
Ingria ['iŋgria] Ingermanland.
ingrowing ['ingro⁰iŋ] inngrodd, som vokser inn (om negl).
inguen ['ingwən] lyske. inguinal ['iŋgwinəl] ingvinal, lyske-.
ingulf [in'gʌlf] oppsluke; styrte i en avgrunn.
ingurgitate [in'gə·dʒiteɪt] sluke grådig. ingurgitation [ingə·dʒi'teɪʃən] sluking.
inhabit [in'häbit] bebo, holde til i; bo. inhabitable [in'häbitəbl] beboelig. inhabitancy [in'häbitənsi] beboelse.
inhabitant [in'häbitənt] beboer; innbygger.
inhalant [in'heɪlənt] innåndende. inhalation [inhə'leɪʃən] innånding. inhale [in'heɪl] innånde. inhaler [in'heɪlə] innåndingsapparat.
inharmonic [inhaə⁰'mänik], inharmonious [inhaə⁰'mo⁰njəs] uharmonisk.
inhaul(er) ['inhå·l(ə)] innhaler.
inhere [in'hiə] henge ved; høre med til. inherence [in'hiərəns], inherency [-rənsi] det å henge ved; forekomst. inherent [-rənt] vedhengende; iboende, naturlig; uatskillelig fra; inngrodd, fast; knyttet (in til).
inherit [in'herit] arve. inheritable [in'heritəbl] arvelig. inheritance [in'heritəns] arv. inheritor [-tə] arving. inheritress [-très], inheritrix [-triks] kvinnelig arving.
inhesion [in'hi·ʒən] det å henge ved; forekomst.
inhibit [in'hibit] hindre (from i), forby. inhibition [in(h)i'biʃən] hindring, forbud. inhibitory [in'hibitəri] hindrende; forbuds-, hefte-.
inhospitable [in'håspitəbl] ugjestfri. inhospitality [inhåspi'täliti] ugjestfrihet.
inhuman [in'hju·mən] umenneskelig, barbarisk, hjerteløs, grusom. inhumanity [inhju'mäniti] umenneskelighet. inhumanly [in'hju·mənli] umenneskelig, grusomt.
inhumate ['inhjume·t] begrave, jorde, jordfeste. inhumation [inhju'me·ʃən] begravelse; jordfesting; inhumasjon (kjemisk uttrykk). inhume [in'hju·m] begrave, jorde, jordfeste.
inial ['iniəl] inial, som hører til nakken.
inimical [i'nimikl] fiendtlig; uforenelig (to med).
inimitability [i'nimitə'biliti] uetterlignelighet; uforlignelighet. inimitable [i'nimitəbl] uetterlignelig; uforlignelig.

inion ['iniån] nakke (anatomisk uttrykk).
iniquitous [i'nikwitəs] ubillig, urettferdig; urettvis; syndig, lastefull. iniquity [i'nikwiti] ubillighet, urettferdighet; synd, forbrytelse, mis gjerning.
init. fk. f. initio (i begynnelsen).
initial [i'niʃəl] begynnende, begynnelses-, først; begynnelsesbokstav, forbokstav, initial; sette forbokstav ved; undertegne med forbokstav; merke. initiate [i'niʃie·t] åpne, ta til med, sette i gang, innlede; innvie; oppta (i et selskap); ta initiativet; sette fram forslag. initiate [-ie·t] begynt; innvidd. initiation [iniʃi'e·ʃən] åpning, begynnelse, innledning; innvielse; opptagelse; elementærundervisning.
initiative [i'niʃ(i)ətiv] første, begynnelses-, innlednings-; initiativ; take the — in doing it ta initiativet til å gjøre det; have the — ha rett til å ta initiativet.
initiatory [i'niʃ(i)ətəri] første begynnelses-, innlednings-; innvielses-; opptagelses-.
inject [in'dʒekt] sprøyte inn; inngi, inngyte. injection [in'dʒekʃən] innsprøytning; injeksjon; klyster.
injudicious [indʒu'diʃəs] uforstandig, uoverlagt.
injunction [in'dʒʌŋ(k)ʃən] pålegg, påbud, innskjerping.
injure [in'dʒə] gjøre urett; gjøre ondt; såre, fornærme; gjøre skade, beskadige, forderve; ska, skade, sverte. injurious [in'dʒuəriəs] skadelig, ødeleggende (to for); ondskapsfull; farlig; fornærmelig, urettvis, sårende; skammelig. injury ['indʒəri] urett; krenkelse; fornærmelse; skade, beskadigelse, fortred.
injustice [in'dʒʌstis] urettferdighet; urett.
ink [iŋk] blekk; boktrykkersverte; tusj; besmøre med blekk (el. sverte, tusj); as black as — svart som blekk; dull as — skrekkelig kjedelig; (amr.) sling — skrive mye, smøre opp; clever at reading — dyktig til å lese skrift; written in — skrevet med blekk. — blot blekklatt. — -bottle blekkflaske; blekkhus. — -eraser blekkviskelær.
inkfish ['iŋkfiʃ] blekksprut.
inkhorn ['iŋkhå·⁰n] blekkhorn (gammeldags).
inkle ['iŋkl] gjette.
inkle-weaver possementmaker.
inkling ['iŋklin] vink, ymt, antydning, mumling; ønske, lyst, attrå; get an — of få nyss om; høre et ymt om.
in-kneed ['inni·d] kalvbeint.
ink-slinger (amr.) blekksmører.
ink-spiller blekksmører.
inkstand ['iŋkständ] blekkhus; skrivestell.
ink-well (fast) blekkhus.
inky ['iŋki] blekk; blekket; kullsort. — -black beksvart, svart som blekk.
inland ['in'le·d] innlagt; — floor parkettgolv; — work, — wood-work tremosaikk; be (well) — ha sitt på det tørre.
inland ['inlənd] innlands-, indre (som er, som ligger osv.) inne i landet, i det indre; innenlandsk; inn i landet; i landet; innland, opp-land; — trade innenrikshandel. inlander ['inləndə] en som bor i det indre av landet.
inlay ['in'le·] innlegge; parkettere; innlegg; innlagt arbeid, mosaikk. inlayer ['inle·ə] mosaikk-arbeider. inlay-work ['inle·'wə·k] innlagt arbeid, mosaikk.
inlet ['inlet] inngang; innløp; fjord, sund, vik.
inly ['inli] i det indre; hemmelig.
inmate ['inme·t] husfelle, beboer.
in memoriam [in mi'må·riəm] til minne.
inmesh [in'meʃ] få i garnet.
inmost ['inmo⁰st] innerst.
inn [in] gjestgiveri, vertshus, herberge; juridisk kollegium, juridisk skole. Inns of Court juristkollegier, der jurister får utdannelse.
innard ['inəd] indre (korrumpert av: inward);

fill one's — fylle magen; **there's something wrong with my** — jeg har en innvendig sykdom.
innate ['in'ne't] medfødt; naturlig.
innavigable [in'nävigəbl] ufarbar, useilbar.
inner ['inə] indre, innvendig.
innervation [inə've'ʃən] nervevirksomhet; stimulering. **innerve** [i(n)'nə·v] styrke, kveike.
innings ['ininz] tur til å spille (i cricket), tur til å ha makten, maktperiode, god tid; **have one's** — ha sin tur, skulle til; **it is your** — now nå er det Deres tur, vis nå hva De duger til; **he has had long** — han har lenge hatt gode sjanser.
innkeeper ['inki·pə] vertshusholder, gjestgiver.
innocence ['inəsəns] uskyldighet; harmløshet; troskyldighet; enfoldighet.
innocent ['inəsənt] uskyldig; uskadelig, harmløs; troskyldig; enfoldig; naiv; uskyldig person; heimføing; **the murder of the Innocents** barnemordet i Betlehem; **Innocents' Day** 28. desember (minnedag for barnemordet i Betlehem); **The Innocents Abroad** «Naive reisende» (en bok av Mark Twain); **he was innocent of any attempt of a joke** det var ikke hans mening å forsøke på å si noe morsomt.
innocuity [ino'kju·iti] uskadelighet. **innocuous** [i(n)'nåkjuəs] uskadelig.
innovate ['inove't] forandre, omdanne; innføre som noe nytt; bøte, vøle. **innovation** [ino-'ve'ʃən] forandring, omdannelse; innføring av noe nytt. **innovationist** [ino've'ʃənist] tilhenger av forandringer. **innovator** ['inove'tə] en som innfører forandringer, en som omdanner.
innoxious [i(n)'nåkʃəs] uskadelig.
Innsbruck ['inzbruk] Innsbruck.
innuendo [inju'endo⁰] antydning, ymt, hentydning, insinuasjon.
Innuit ['in(j)uit] eskimo.
innumerability [inju·mərə'biliti] utallighet. **innumerable** [i'nju·mərəbl] utallig, tallos.
innutritious [innju'triʃəs], **innutritive** [in'nju·tritiv] ikke nærende, av liten næringsverdi.
inobservant [inåb'zə·vənt] uoppmerksom.
inoculate [i'nåkjule't] okulere; innpode, vaksinere; **inoculation** [inåkju'le'ʃən] okulering; innpoding.
inodorous [in'o⁰dərəs] luktløs, luktfri.
inoffensive [inə'fensiv] uskadelig, uskyldig, harmløs; beskjeden, smålåten.
inofficial [inə'fiʃəl] ikke offisiell, privat.
inoperative [in'åpərətiv] virkningsløs, gagnløs.
inopportune [inåpə'tju·n] ubeleilig.
inordinate [i'nå·ⁱdinét] uordentlig, uregelmessig; overdreven.
inorganic [inå·ⁱ'gänik] uorganisk; — **chemistry** uorganisk kjemi.
inorganised [in'å·ⁱgənaizd] ikke organisert.
inosculate [in'åskjule't] forbinde seg; forbinde. **inosculation** [inåskju'le'ʃən] forbindelse.
in-patient ['inpe'ʃənt] sykehuspasient.
inquest ['inkwest] undersøkelse; rettslig undersøkelse; likskue; **coroner's** — rettslig liksyn; **the last (el. great)** — dommedag.
inquietude [in'kwaiətju·d] uro, ank, otte.
inquirable [in'kwairəbl] som kan undersøkes.
inquire [in'kwaiə] spørre, forhøre seg (**for** om); spørre om; undersøke, anstille undersøkelse; — **of a person about a thing** spørre en om noe; — **after him** el. — **for him** spørre etter ham; — **the way** spørre om veien; — **the reason** spørre om grunnen; — **into** etterforske, undersøke.
inquiry [in'kwairi] etterspørsel, forespørsel; etterlysning, etterforskning, undersøkelse; forskning. puzzled — spørrende forvirring; **private** — **agents** agenter for private undersøkelser, sjefer for et opplysningsbyrå. — **agency** opplysningsbyrå. — **office** opplysningsbyrå, forespørselsbyrå.
inquisition [inkwi'ziʃən] undersøkelse; kjennelse (rettslig); skjønn, skadebot; inkvisisjon. **in-**

quisitive [in'kwisitiv] spørresyk; nysgjerrig. **inquisitiveness** [-nés] spørresyke; nysgjerrighet. **inquisitor** [in'kwizitə] undersøker; eksaminator; forhørsdommer; inkvisitor. **inquisitorial** [inkwizi-'tå·riəl] undersøkelses-; inkvisisjons-; inkvisitorisk.
I. N. R. I. fk. f. **Jesus Nazarenus Rex Judaeorum** Jesus fra Nasaret, jødenes konge.
inroad ['inro⁰d] innfall, streiftog; overfall.
inrush ['inrʌʃ] innstrømning, inntrenging.
insalivate [in'sälive't] blande med spytt. **insalivation** [insäli've'ʃən] fødens blanding med spytt.
insalubrious [insə'l(j)u·briəs] usunn. **insalubrity** [-briti] usunnhet.
insanability [insänə'biliti] uhelbredelighet. **insanable** [in'sänəbl] uhelbredelig.
insane [in'se'n] vanvittig, fra vettet, avsindig, gal; — **asylum**, — **hospital** sinnssykeanstalt.
insanitary [in'sänitəri] usunn, sunnhetsfarlig.
insanity [in'säniti] avsinn, vanvidd, sinnssyke.
insatiability [inse'ʃ(j)ə'biliti] umettelighet. **insatiable** [in'se'ʃ(j)əbl] umettelig. **insatiate** [in-'se'ʃiét] umettelig. **insatiety** [insə'taiiti] umettelighet.
inscribe [in'skraib] innskrive; inngravere; innføre (i en liste); forsyne med påskrift; tilegne, dedisere; innprente (i hukommelsen: **on the memory**); innskrive (matematisk). **inscription** [in-'skripʃən] innskrivning; innføring; innskrift, påskrift, overskrift; tilegnelse; dedikasjon. **inscriptive** [in'skriptiv] med innskrift; innskrift-.
inscrutability [inskru·tə'biliti] uutgrunnelighet, uransakelighet. **inscrutable** [in'skru·təbl] uutgrunnelig, uransakelig.
insect ['insekt] insekt; foraktelig liten tingest. **insecticide** [in'sektisaid] insektmiddel. **insectile** ['insektil] insektaktig, insekt-.
insection [in'sekʃən] snitt, innsnitt.
insectivorous [insek'tivorəs] insektetende.
insecure [insi'kjuə] usikker, utrygg. **insecurity** [insi'kjuəriti] usikkerhet.
insensate [in'sensét] ufølsom; ufornuftig;vettløs.
insensibility [insensi'biliti] følelsesløshet; ufølsomhet; uimottagelighet, sløvhet. **insensible** [in-'sensibl] følelsesløs; ufølsom; likesæl, hjerteløs, hard; umerkelig; bevisstløs.
inseparability [insepərə'biliti] uatskillelighet. **inseparable** [in'sep(ə)rəbl] uatskillelig; -**s** uatskillelige venner.
insert [in'sə·t] skyte inn, innføre, innsette, felle inn; rykke inn (**in el. into** i). **insertion** [in'sə·ʃən] innføring, innsetting; innrykking (i avis); innsendt stykke, inserat; mellomverk.
inset ['inset] noe som settes inn, innlegg, vedlegg.
inseverable [in'sevərəbl] uskillelig.
inshore ['in'ʃå·ⁿ] pålands-; inne ved land, tett ved land; mot land, under land; kyst-.
inside ['in'said] innerside, innside, innvendig del, det innvendige; passasjer inne i en vogn; innvendig; inneni, innenfor, inne, inn, indre; inne i. **from the** — innenfra; **turned** — **out** vendt ut inn på.
insider ['in'saidə] lagsmann; en som er inne i saken.
insidious [in'sidjəs] underfundig, lumsk, innful.
insight ['insait] innblikk; innsikt, kjennskap, vett.
insignia [in'signiə] insignier, verdighetstegn.
insignificance [insig'nifikəns] ubetydelighet, betydningsløshet. **insignificant** [insig'nifikənt] ubetydelig, betydningsløs; ringe.
insincere [insin'siə] uoppriktig, falsk; hyklersk. **insincerity** [insin'seriti] uoppriktighet, falskhet.
insinuate [in'sinjue't] smøre inn, lure inn; insinuere; antyde, hentyde, ymte om. **insinuation** [insinju'e'ʃən] innlisting, innsmigring, insinuasjon. **insinuative** [in'sinjuətiv] insinuant, ful.
insipid [in'sipid] flau. **insipidity** [insi'piditi] flauhet.

insist [in'sist] hevde, holde på sitt, påstå, forestille; — **on** el. **upon** stå på, holde på, fordre, ville bestemt, ville absolutt. **insistence** [in'sistəns] hevding, det å holde på; vedholdenhet.

insnare [in'snæ·ə] snare, fange i snare; besnære.

insobriety [inso'braiəti] uavholdenhet, drukkenskap, drikkfeldighet.

insolate ['insole't] sole, bake i sola. **insolation** [inso'le'ʃən] soling, solbak; solstikk.

insolence ['insoləns] uforskammethet. **insolent** ['insolənt] uforskammet.

insolubility [insålju'biliti] uoppløselighet. **insoluble** [in'såljubl] uoppløselig.

insolvency [in'sålvənsi] insolvens. **insolvent** [in'sålvənt] insolvent.

insomnia [in'såmniə] søvnløshet. **insomnious** [in'såmniəs] søvnløs.

insomuch [inso'mʌtʃ]: — **that** så at; — **as** for så vidt som; idet, da nemlig, så som.

inspan [in'spän] spenne for.

inspect [in'spekt] ha oppsyn med; undersøke nøye, inspisere. **inspection** [in'spekʃən] ettersyn, oppsyn, undersøkelse, inspeksjon. **inspector** [in'spektə] inspektør. **inspectress** [in'spektrés] inspektrise.

inspirable [in'spairəbl] som kan innåndes. **inspiration** [inspi're'ʃən] innånding; innskytelse; inspirasjon. **inspiratory** [in'spairətəri] innåndings-. **inspire** [in'spaiə] innånde; inngi, inngyte; inspirere.

inspirit [in'spirit] flamme opp, opplive, kveike.

inspissate [in'spise't] fortykke. **inspissation** [inspi'se'ʃən] fortykkelse.

inst. fk. f. instant (i denne måned).

instability [instə'biliti] ubestandighet, usikkerhet. **instable** [in'ste'bl] ubestandig, ustø, usikker.

instal(l) [in'stå·l] anvise (sete, plass); innsette (f. eks. i et embete); innrette, stille opp, installere.

installation [instə'le'ʃən] innsettelse; anbringelse; installasjon (især av elektrisk apparat).

instalment [in'stå·lmənt] innsettelse; rate, avdrag; **payable by** (el. **at**) **-s** kan betales i rater.

instance ['instəns] tilfelle, fall, leilighet; eksempel; instans; begjæring, inntrengende anmodning; anføre som eksempel; **at the** — for foranlediget av, etter krav fra; **for** — for eksempel; **in the first** — for det første; først; **in the last** — i siste instans; til sist, til slutt.

instant ['instənt] øyeblikkelig; innstendig, inntrengende; dennes, denne måned; øyeblikk; **the 7th inst.** den sjuende dennes; **on the** — straks; **in an** — om et øyeblikk.

instantaneous [instən'te'njəs] øyeblikkelig; snøgg, brå; — **photograph** øyeblikksfotografi. **instantaneously** [-li] øyeblikkelig.

instanter [in'stäntə] øyeblikkelig, straks, på timen.

instantly ['instəntli] øyeblikkelig, straks; inntrengende (foreldet).

instate [in'ste't] innsette.

instead [in'sted] isteden, i stedet; — **of** istedenfor; **this will do** — the dette kan brukes isteden; — **of him** el. **in his stead** istedenfor ham.

instep [in'step] rist (på foten).

instigate ['instige't] opphisse, egge; anstifte. **instigation** [insti'ge'ʃən] opphisselse; anstiftelse, tilskyndelse. **instigator** ['instige'tə] opphisser, anstifter, opphavsmann.

instil [in'stil] dryppe inn, helle dråpevis; inngyte, bibringe, gi, gi inn smått om senn. **instillation** [insti'le'ʃən] inndrypping; inngytelse; inngivelse.

instinct [in'stiŋkt] drevet, opplivet, besjelet, fylt. **instinct** ['instiŋkt] instinkt, drift, naturdrift. **instinctive** [in'stiŋktiv] instinktmessig, uvilkårlig. **instinctively** [-li] instinktmessig, uvilkårlig. **instinctivity** [instiŋk'tiviti] det instinktmessige, uvilkårlighet.

institute ['institju·t] stifte, opprette; få til, få i gang; anordne, fastsette; innsette (f. eks. en regjering); innlede (f. eks. en undersøkelse); undervise (foreldet); innretning, ordning; forordning, lovprinsipp; institutt; **-s** også: lærebok. **institution** [insti'tju·ʃən] oppretting, stiftelse; innretning, lov; anstalt; innsetting, kallelse; institusjon; **charitable** — velgjørende stiftelse. **institutional** [insti'tju·ʃənəl] fastsatt; elementær. **institutionary** [insti'tju·ʃənəri] institusjons-. **institutive** ['institju·tiv] innrettende, grunnleggende; institusjonsmessig. **institutor** ['institju·tə] stifter, grunnlegger; prest som innsetter en annen; lærer.

instruct [in'strʌkt] undervise; belære; instruere. **instruction** [in'strʌkʃən] undervisning; lære; råd; anvisning, forskrift, forholdsordre, instruksjon. **instructional** [in'strʌkʃənəl] undervisnings-, pedagogisk. **instructive** [in'strʌktiv] belærende, lærerik. **instructiveness** [-nés] lærerikhet. **instructor** [in'strʌktə] lærer, instruktør.

instrument ['instrumənt] redskap; instrument; dokument; **musical** — musikkinstrument. **instrumental** [instru'mentəl] tjenlig; virksom; medvirkende, behjelpelig; instrumental; — **case** instrumentalis. **instrumentalist** [instru'mentəlist] instrumentalist.

instrumentality [instrumən'täliti] virksomhet, råd, medvirkning, hjelp. **instrumentally** [instru'mentəli] som redskap, som middel; med instrumenter. **instrumentation** [instrumən'te'ʃən] instrumentering.

insubordinate [insə'bå·°dinét] insubordinert, oppsetsig, ulydig, trassig. **insubordination** [insə·'bå·°di'ne'ʃən] insubordinasjon, oppsetsighet, trassighet, ulydighet.

insuetude ['inswitju·d] uvanthet.

insufferable [in'sʌf(ə)rəbl] utålelig.

insufficiency [insə'fiʃənsi] utilstrekkelighet; udugelighet, udyktighet. **insufficient** [-ʃənt] utilstrekkelig, snau; udugelig, uskikket, gagnløs.

insufflation [insʌ'fle'ʃən] innblåsing.

insular ['insjulə] øy-; trang, trangsynt, avstengt; øybu, øyboer. **insularity** [insju'läriti] det å være øy, det å være avgrenset til øyer; isolerthet; avsondring, trangsyn. **insulate** ['insjule't] isolere. **insulation** [insju'le'ʃən] isolasjon. **insulator** ['insjule'tə] isolator.

insult ['insʌlt] fornærmelse, forhånelse. **insult** [in'sʌlt] fornærme, forhåne, krenke.

insuperability [ins(j)u·pərə'biliti] uovervinnelighet. **insuperable** [in's(j)u·pərəbl] uovervinnelig. **insupportable** [insə'på·°təbl] utholdelig.

insurable [in'ʃuərəbl] som kan forsikres.

insurance [in'ʃuərəns] forsikring, trygding, assuranse; forsikringssum; trygdesum; forsikringspremie; trygdepremie; **effect** el. **make an** — tegne en forsikring; **accident and fire** — ulykkesog brannforsikring; — **-policy** forsikringspolise.

insure [in'ʃuə] sikre; sikre seg; forsikre, assurere. **insurer** [in'ʃuərə] assurandør.

insurgent [in'sə·dʒənt] opprørsk; opprører, insurgent.

insurmountability [insə·mauntə'biliti] uoverstigelighet. **insurmountable** [insə·'mauntəbl] uoverstigelig.

insurrection [insə'rekʃən] opprør, oppstand. **insurrectional** [-əl], **insurrectionary** [-əri] opprørsk, opprørs-. **insurrectionist** [-ist] opprører.

insusceptibility [insəsepti'biliti] uimottagelighet. **insusceptible** [insə'septibl] uimottagelig. **insusceptive** [insə'septiv] uimottagelig.

inswathe [in'sweɪð] svøpe inn.

int. fk. f. interjection.

intact [in'täkt] uberørt; ubeskadiget, uskadd.

intactible [in'täktibl] uføIbar.

intagliated [in'tälje'tid] inngravert. **intaglio** [in'ta·ljo°, in'täljo°] inngravert arbeid; gjemme.

intake ['inte'k] inntak (ved vannledning), innsnevring; nybrott, nylende; lastet mengde.

intangible [in'tændʒibl] umerkelig; ulegemlig.
integer ['intidʒə] det hele, helhet; helt tall.
integral ['intigrəl] hel, udelt; integrerende; det hele, helhet; — calculus integralregning. integrate ['intigreit] gjøre fullstendig; integrere. integration [inti'greiʃən] fullstendiggjøring; integrering. integrity [in'tegriti] helhet, fullstendighet; ufordervethet, renhet; rettskaffenhet, ærlighet.
integument [in'tegjumənt] dekke, hud, skinn, skjå.
intellect ['intilekt] intelligens, forstand, vett, åndsevne. intellection [inti'lekʃən] oppfatning, oppfattelse; tankevirksomhet. intellectual [inti-'lektʃuəl] forstandsmessig, forstands-, intellektuell; sjelelig, åndelig, ånds-. intellectuality [inti-'lektʃu'äliti] forstand, intelligens; åndrikhet.
intelligence [in'telidʒəns] innsikt, etterretning(er), underretning(er), melding(er); meddelelse(r); intelligens, forstand, vett; — department militært etterretningsvesen; — -office opplysningsbyrå; festekontor. intelligencer [in'telidʒənsə] en som bringer meldinger, reporter, aviskorrespondent; bud; spion.
intelligent [in'telidʒənt] forstandig, klok, intelligent. intelligibility [in'telidʒi'biliti] forståelighet, tydelighet. intelligible [in'telidʒibl] forståelig, tydelig.
intemperance [in'temp(ə)rəns] mangel på måtehold, utskeielse; fylleri; umåtelighet i drikk. intemperate [in'temp(ə)rёt] umåteholden; stri; utskeiende; lidenskapelig; umåteholden i drikk.
intenable [in'tenəbl] uholdbar.
intend [in'tend] ha i sinne, tilsikte, esle, ha til hensikt, akte; bestemme; we — to do it el. we — doing it vi har i sinne å gjøre det; what was this -ed for? hva var hensikten med dette? his words were -ed as a warning hans ord var ment som en advarsel; -ed to do for . . . bestemt til å skulle gjelde for . . .
intendancy [in'tendənsi] overoppsyn; intendantur; intendantembete; intendanturdistrikt. intendant [in'tendənt] tilsynshavende; intendant.
intended [in'tendid] påtenkt; — husband tilkommende mann; — wife tilkommende hustru; her — hennes kjæreste.
intense [in'tens] spent; heftig, stri, sterk. intensification [intensifi'keiʃən] anspennelse; forsterkning; skjerping. intensify [in'tensifai] spenne; forsterke, forøke, skjerpe; øke; spennes; forsterkes osv. intension [in'tenʃən] spenning; forsterkning, forøkelse, auke, skjerping, styrke, heftighet, intensitet. intensity [in'tensiti] intensitet, anspennelse; styrke; heftighet; anstrengelse; iver. intensive [in'tensiv] intensiv, sterk; forsterkende; forsterkende ord.
intent [in'tent] forehavende, akt; hensikt, spent, begjærlig, oppsatt (on på); through an — med forsett, forsettlig; to all -s and purposes praktisk talt, i virkeligheten.
intention [in'tenʃən] mening, formål, hensikt. intentional [in'tenʃənəl] forsettlig. intentionality [in'tenʃə'näliti] forsettlighet. intentioned [in-'tenʃənd] -sinnet i smstn. f. eks. well-intentioned velmenende.
intently [in'tentli] spent, oppmerksomt.
inter [in'tə·] begrave, jordfeste.
inter ['intə] (latin) imellom, mellom.
inter|act ['intəräkt] virke på hverandre. -action [intər'äkʃən] gjensidig påvirkning.
interblend [intə'blend] blande.
interbreed [intə'bri·d] krysse (om raser).
intercalar [in'tə·kələ] innskutt; — day skudddag; feberfri dag. intercalary [in'tə·kələri; intə-'käləri] se intercalar. intercalate [in'tə·kəleit] innskyte. intercalation [intə·kə'leiʃən] innskyting, innskudd.
intercede [intə'si·d] komme mellom, tre mellom, gå i forbønn, be for; she -d for him with the king hun gikk i forbønn for ham hos kongen. interceder [intə'si·də] talsmann.

intercept [intə'sept] snappe opp, oppfange; avskjære; hindre, stemme, stanse. interception [intə'sepʃən] oppsnapping; avskjæring; hindring, stansing.
intercession [intə'seʃən] mellomkomst; forbønn. intercessor [intə'sesə] megler, talsmann. intercessory [intə'sesəri] meglende.
interchange [intə'tʃe·n(d)ʒ] veksle, utveksle, bytte; utveksling; veksling, skifte, bytte; handel, handelsforbindelse. interchangeable [intə-'tʃe·n(d)ʒəbl] som kan utveksles; vekslende, skiftende; som kan ombyttes.
interchapter ['intətʃäptə] mellomkapitel.
intercollegiate [intəkə'li·dʒёt] mellom kollegiene.
intercolonial [intəkə'lo·njəl] mellom koloniene.
intercommunicate [intəkə'mju·nikёt] stå i samkvem. intercommunication [intəkə'mju·ni-'keiʃən] forbindelse, samkvem, samband.
intercommunion [intəkə'mju·njən] innbyrdes forbindelse.
intercommunity [intəkə'mju·niti] innbyrdes forbindelse.
intercostal [intə'kåstəl] mellom ribbeina; mellom spantene.
intercourse ['intəkå·ºs] samkvem; forbindelse, handelsforbindelse.
intercurrent [intə'kʌrənt] som kommer mellom.
inter|dependency [intədi'pendənsi] gjensidig avhengighet. -dependent [intədi'pendənt] gjensidig avhengig.
interdict [intə'dikt] forby; belegge med interdikt. interdict ['intədikt] forbud; interdikt; put an — upon forby; lay el. put under an — belegge med interdikt. interdiction [intə'dikʃən] forbud; (juridisk) umyndiggjøring; forbud; interdikt. interdictory [intə'diktəri] forbydende.
interest ['intrist, 'intərest] interesse; rente; innflytelse; makt, velde; interesse; the common — det felles beste; feel el. take (an) — in ha interesse for, interessere seg for; make — for gjøre seg til talsmann for (with hos); use one's — gjøre sin innflytelse gjeldende; have an — in ha andel i; — per annum, annual —, yearly — årlige renter; bear — at the rate of 5 per cent el. bear 5 per cent — gi 5 prosent rente; compound — rentesrente; rate of — rentefot; lend out money at — låne ut penger mot renter; put out money at — sette penger på rente; — oneself in interessere seg for.
interested ['intərestid] interessert; egennyttig. interesting ['intərestiŋ] interessant.
interfere [intə'fiə] støte sammen, kollidere, komme i kollisjon, legge seg mellom; blande seg (with i); stryke seg (om hest). interference [intə-'fiərəns] sammenstøt, kollisjon, innblanding, inngrep (with i). interflow ['intəflo·ᵘ] det å gli over i hverandre. interfoliate [intə'fo·lie·t] interfoliere (se interleave).
interim ['intərim] mellomtid. interimistic [intəri'mistik] interimistisk.
interior [in'tiəriə] indre; innvendig, innlands-; interiør, innland, oppland. (i Amerika) Department of the Interior innenriksdepartement; Secretary of the Interior innenriksminister.
interjacent [intə'dʒe·sənt] mellomliggende.
interject [intə'dʒekt] kaste el. stille mellom; skyte inn. interjection [intə'dʒekʃən] innskudd; interjeksjon, utropsord. interjectional [intə-'dʒekʃənəl] innskutt; interjeksjons-.
interlace [intə'le·s] slynge (el. flette) sammen; blande; flette inn; være sammenflettet. interlacement [-mənt] sammenfletting, sammenslynging.
interlard [intə'la·ºd] spekke, stappe, blande; — with foreign words spekke med fremmedord.
interleave [intə'li·v] skyte gjennom rene blad i en bok (se interfoliate).
interline [intə'lain] skrive mellom linjene; skrive i skiftende linjer; (typ.) skyte. interlineal

[intə'linjəl], **interlinear(y)** [intə'linjə(ri)] skrevet el. trykt mellom linjene, interlinear. **interlineation** [intəlini'e'ʃən] mellomskrivning; mellomtrykning; (typ.) skytning. **interlining** [intə-'lainiŋ] se **interlineation**.

interlink [intə'liŋk] kjede sammen.

interlock [intə'låk] gripe inn i hverandre; la gripe inn i hverandre, føye sammen.

interlocution [intəlo'kju·ʃən] samtale; interlokutoriekjennelse. **interlocutor** [intə'låkjutə] deltager i en samtale. **interlocutory** [intə'låkjutəri] som er i form av en samtale; samtale-.

interlope [intə'lo"p] gjøre inngrep i andres forretning; kjøpe opp på markedet; drive smughandel, «gauke». **interloper** [intə'lo"pə] en som gjør inngrep i andres forretning; smughandler, «gauk».

interlude ['intəl(j)u·d] mellomspill.

interlunar(y) [intə'l(j)u·nə(ri)] ved nymåne.

intermarriage [intə'märidʒ] innbyrdes giftermål, inngifte (mellom to stammer eller familier).

intermarry [intə'märi] gifte seg innbyrdes.

intermeddle [intə'medl] blande seg inn (**with, in** i). **intermeddler** [intə'medlə] en som ukallet blander seg i andres affærer.

intermediary [intə'mi·djəri] mellom-; mellomledd, formidler.

intermediate [intə'mi·djèt, -dʒ-] mellomliggende, mellom-; — **school** middelskole, mellomskole, **intermedium** [intə'mi·djəm] mellommann; bindemiddel.

interment [in'tə·mənt] begravelse, jordfesting.

intermezzo [intə'medzo"] intermesso.

interminable [in'tə·minəbl] uendelig, endeløs.

interminate [in'tə·minèt] uendelig, ubegrenset.

intermingle [intə'miŋgl] blande; blande seg.

intermission [intə'miʃən] opphør, avbrytelse, stansning, stans. **intermissive** [intə'misiv] uavbrutt, med mellomrom.

intermit [intə'mit] avbryte, stanse, la holde opp for en tid; bli avbrutt, stanse, holde opp for en tid. **intermittence** [intə'mitəns] opphør, avbrytelse, stansning. **intermittent** [intə'mitənt] som kommer med mellomrom, som kommer rykkevis, intermitterende; — **light** blinkfyr.

intern [in'tə·n] internere.

internal [in'tə·nəl] indre, innvortes; innenlandsk.

international [intə'näʃənəl] internasjonal, mellomfolkelig; internasjonalen (det internasjonale arbeiderforbund).

internationale [intənäʃə'na·l] internasjonalen (sosialistisk sang).

internationalize [intə'näʃənəlaiz] gjøre internasjonal.

interne [in'tə·n] indre.

internecine [intə'ni·sain] gjensidig ødeleggende, dødbringende; — **war** blodig krig.

internment [in'tə·nmənt] internering.

internuncio [intə'nʌnʃ(j)o"] internuntius, pavens representant i republikker og ved mindre hoff.

inter-office telephone omstillingstelefon.

interpellate [in'tə·pele't] interpellere, stille spørsmål til. **interpellation** [intə·pe'le'ʃən] interpellasjon. **interpellator** [in'tə·pe'le'tə] interpellant.

interpolate [in'tə·pole't] innskyte; interpolere. **interpolation** [intə·po'le'ʃən] innskyting; innskudd, interpolasjon. **interpolator** [in'tə·pole'tə] skriftforfalsker, interpolator.

interposal [intə'po"zəl] mellomkomst. **interpose** [intə'po"zə] sette (el. legge) mellom; legge seg mellom, mekle; gå i forbønn (**in behalf of** for).

interposer [intə'po"zə] mellommann, mekler. **interposition** [intəpə'ziʃən] stilling mellom; det å stille mellom; mellomkomst, mekling.

interpret [in'tə·prèt] fortolke, tyde, forklare. utlegge; tolke; være tolk. **interpretable** [in'tə·pritəbl] som kan fortolkes. **interpretation** [intəpri·'te'ʃən] fortolkning, forklaring, tydning; tolkning, oversettelse. **interpretative** [in'tə·pritətiv] for-

tolkende, forklarende. **interpreter** [in'tə·pritə] fortolker, tolk. **interpretress** [in'tə·pritrès] kvinnelig tolk.

interregnum [intə'regnəm] interregnum.

interrelationship [intəri'le'ʃənʃip] innbyrdes slektskap.

interrogate [in'terəge't] spørre; avhøre, forhøre. **interrogation** [intərə'ge'ʃən] spørring; avhøring; spørsmål; spørsmålstegn; — **point, mark** el. **note** el. **sign of** — spørsmålstegn. **interrogative** [intə'rågətiv] spørrende; spørreord. **interrogator** [in'terəge'tə] en som spør. **interrogatory** [intə'rågətəri] spørrende; spørsmål.

interrupt [intə'rʌpt] avbryte; forstyrre. **interrupter** [intə'rʌptə] avbryter. **interruption** [intə-'rʌpʃən] avbrytelse; forstyrrelse. **interruptive** [intə'rʌptiv] avbrytende; forstyrrende.

intersect [intə'sekt] gjennomskjære, overskjære, gjennombryte, dele. **intersection** [intə'sekʃən] gjennomskjæring. **intersectional** [intə'sekʃənəl] skjærings-.

interspace ['intəspe's] mellomrom. **intersperse** [intə'spə·s] strø inn, sette inn imellom (her og der), strø ut. **interspersion** [intə-'spə·ʃən] innstrøing, utstrøing.

interstice [in'tə·stis] mellomrom; hull. **interstitial** [intə'stiʃəl] med mellomrom.

intertie [in'intətai] losholt.

intertropical [intə'tråpikl] som ligger mellom tropene.

intertwine [intə'twain], **intertwist** [-'twist] sammenflette.

interval ['intəvəl] mellomrom; mellomtid, pause; interval; frikvarter; **at -s** med visse mellomrom, nå og da.

intervene [intə'vi·n] komme mellom; hjelpe; hindre. **intervention** [intə'venʃən] mellomkomst.

interview ['intəvju·] sammenkomst, møte; intervju; ha sammenkomst med; intervjue, besøke for å innhente opplysninger. **interviewer** ['intə-vju·ə] intervjuer.

interweave [intə'wi·v] veve sammen; innblande.

intestable [in'testəbl] uberettiget til å gjøre testament. **intestacy** [in'testəsi] mangel på testament. **intestate** [in'testèt] død uten å ha gjort testament.

intestinal [in'testinəl] innvolls-, tarm-. **intestine** [in'testin] indre, innvortes; tarm; **the large** — tykktarmen; **the small** — tynntarmen; **-s** (plur.) innvoller, tarmer.

inthral [in·θrɑ·l] gjøre til trell, trelke. **inthralment** [-mənt] trelking; trelldom.

intimacy ['intiməsi] intimitet, fortrolighet, fortrolig forhold. **intimate** ['intimèt] fortrolig; fortrolig venn, bestevenn. **intimate** ['intime't] gi å forstå, ymte om, antyde, tilkjennegi, melde, bebude. **intimately** ['intimétli] fortrolig; nøye. **intimation** [inti'me'ʃən] antydning, ymt, vink; tilkjennegivelse.

intimidate [in'timide't] gjøre forskrekket, skremme. **intimidation** [intimi'de'ʃən] skremming, støkk.

into [intu (foran vokallyd), 'intə (foran konsonantlyd)] inn i, i; ut i, ut på, på; opp i; ned i; over i; til; **translate** — **English** oversette til engelsk; **go** — **the park** gå inn i parken; **grow** — **a habit** bli en vane; **flatter him** — **doing** it ved smiger få ham til å gjøre det; **far** — **the night** langt ut på natten.

in-toed ['in'to"d] med tærne innad, bjørneføtt.

intolerable [in'tål(ə)rəbl] utålelig. **intolerance** [in'tålərəns] intoleranse, utålsomhet; mangel på evne til å kunne tåle. **intolerant** [-ənt] intolerant, utålsom (**of, towards** like overfor). **intoleration** [intålə're'ʃən] se **intolerance**.

intonate ['intone't] istemme, intonere; la tone; synge eller spille skala; messe; resitere, si fram syngende. **intonation** [into'ne'ʃən] intonering,

toneangivelse; modulasjon; messing. **intone** [in-'to^un] istemme, intonere; angi tonen; messe. **intorsion, intortion** [in'tå·^əʃən] dreining, vridning.
intoxicant [in'tåksikənt] berusende middel el. drikk, rusdrikk.
intoxicate [in'tåksikeⁱt] beruse, ruse, drikke full; **-d with** berust av. **intoxication** [intåksi-'keⁱʃən] beruselse, rus.
intr. fk. f. **intransitive.**
intractability [inträktə'biliti] uregjerlighet, umedgjørlighet, stridighet. **intractable** [in'träktəbl] uregjerlig, umedgjørlig, ustyrlig, stridig, stri, vrang.
intransigent [in'tränsidʒənt] uforsonlig.
intransitive [in'tränsitiv, -tra·n-] intransitiv.
intrant ['intrənt] inntredende; tiltredende.
intrench [in'trenʃ] forskanse; gjøre inngrep i. **intrenchment** [-mənt] forskansning; inngrep (**on** i), **intrepid** [in'trepid] uforferdet, uredd, uforsagt. ikke skjelven. **intrepidity** [intri'piditi] uforferdethet.
intricacy ['intrikəsi] forvikling, floke, forvirring; innviklet beskaffenhet. **intricate** [in'trikét] innviklet, forvirret, floket, vrien.
intrigue [in'tri·g] intrige, renke; elskovsforhold; intrigere; smi renker; stå i forhold. **intriguer** [in'tri·gə] intrigant, renkesmed.
intrinsic [in'trinsik] indre, vesentlig.
introcession [intro'seʃən] innsynkning.
introd. fk. f. **introduction.**
introduce [intrə'dju·s] innføre; presentere, forestille (**to** for); innbringe; innlede. **introducer** [-'dju·sə] innfører; innleder. **introduction** [-'dʌkʃən] innførelse; forestilling, presentasjon; anbefaling; innledning; **letter of** — anbefalingsbrev. **introductory** [-'dʌktəri] innledende.
introit [in'tro^uit] inngang; gudstjenestens begynnelse; inngangssalme.
intromission [intrə'miʃən] innsending; innkalling. **intromit** [-'mit] sende inn; slippe inn.
introspect [intro'spekt] se inn i, prøve. **introspection** [intro'spekʃən] innblikk. **introspectionist** [intro'spekʃənist] selviakttager. **introspective** [intro'spektiv] som ser innetter, selvgranskende.
introvert [intro'və·t] vende innover.
intrude [in'tru·d] trenge (seg) inn; falle til besvær; forstyrre, gjøre inngrep; — **oneself** trenge (klenge) seg inn på. **intruder** [-də] påtrengende menneske, ubuden gjest. **intrusion** [in'tru·ʒən] inntrenging; påtrengenhet; inngrep. **intrusionist** [-ʒənist] påtrengende menneske; talsmann for patronatsretten (i Skottland). **intrusive** [in'tru·siv] påtrengende.
intrust [in'trʌst] betro (**sth. to sb.** en noe.)
intuition [intju'iʃən] intuisjon, anskuelse, umiddelbar oppfattelse. **intuitive** [in'tju·itiv] intuitiv, umiddelbart erkjennende.
intumesce [intju'mes] svulme opp, trutne, svelle. **intumescence** [-'mesəns] svulming, trutning.
inturbidate [in'tə·bideⁱt] gjøre mørk, plumre.
inumbrate [in'ʌmbreit] kaste skygge på, skygge over.
inundate ['inʌndeⁱt] oversvømme, flø. **inundation** [inʌn'deⁱʃən] oversvømmelse, flom.
inure [in'juə] herde (**to** mot), venne (**to** til); komme til anvendelse, tjene til beste. **inurement** [-mənt] vane, vanthet, herdethet, øvelse.
inurn [in'ə·n] legge i urne, begrave, jordfeste.
inutility [inju'tiliti] unyttighet.
invade [in'veⁱd] falle inn i, trenge seg inn i, gjøre innfall i, overfalle; tilrive seg, rane til seg. **invader** [in'veⁱdə] en som faller inn i, angriper, voldsmann; en som gjør inngrep i.
invalid [in'välid] ugyldig.
invalid [in'vali·d] syk, svak, helseløs; vanfør; pasient; sette på sykelisten, fjerne fra aktiv tjeneste som utjenstdyktig, bli utjenstdyktig. **invalidate** [in'välideⁱt] avkrefte; gjøre ugyldig.

invalidation [invali'deⁱʃən] ugyldiggjøring. **invalidism** ['invəlidizm] sykelighet, utjenstdyktighet. **invalidity** [invə'liditi] ugyldighet; utjenstdyktighet.
invaluable [in'välju(ə)bl] uvurderlig.
invariability [invæ·^əriə'biliti] uforanderlighet. **invariable** [in'væ·^əriəbl] uforanderlig; ufravikelig, gjengs; (i matematikk) konstant.
invasion [in'veⁱʒən] innfall, angrep; inngrep. **invasive** [in'veⁱsiv] angripende; angreps-.
invective [in'vektiv] hån, hånsord, sneiord.
inveigh [in'veⁱ] bruke seg på, skjelle.
inveigle [in'vi·gl] forlede, narre, forlokke (**into** til). **inveiglement** [-mənt] forledelse, forlokkelse. **inveigler** [in'vi·glə] forleder, forfører.
invendible [in'vendibl] uselgelig.
invent [in'vent] oppfinne; hitte på; dikte opp. **invention** [in'venʃən] oppfinnelse; oppdikting; løgn; oppfinnsomhet; **necessity is the mother of** — nød lærer naken kjerring å spinne. **inventive** [in'ventiv] oppfinnsom. **inventiveness** [-nés] oppfinnsomhet. **inventor** [in'ventə] oppfinner.
inventory ['inventri] inventarliste, katalog; ta opp fortegnelse over; **make** el. **take** el. **draw up an** — ta opp en fortegnelse.
inventress [in'ventrés] oppfinnerske.
Inverness [invə'nes] Inverness; ermeløs mannskappe med løst slag.
inverse [in'və·s] omvendt.
inversion [in'və·ʃən] omstilling; inversjon, omvendt ordstilling.
invert [in'və·t] vende, vende opp ned på; vrenge; **-ed commas** anførselstegn, gåseøyne. **invertebral** [in'və·tibrəl] hvirvelløs. **invertebrate** [-brét] hvirvelløs; holdningsløs; vinglet, lealaus.
invest [in'vest] bekle; kle; pryde, innsette (i et embete); gi; skjenke; innslutte (som ved beleiring); anbringe (**money in** penger i); gjøre fruktbringende (f. eks. penger).
investigable [in'vestigəbl] som kan oppspores, som kan utforskes. **investigate** [in'vestigeⁱt] oppspore, utforske; undersøke. **investigation** [investi'geⁱʃən] utforskning, undersøkelse. **investigative** [in'vestigətiv] forskende. **investigator** [in-'vestigeⁱtə] forsker, gransker; undersøker. **investigatory** [in'vestigətəri] forskende.
investiture [in'vestitʃə, -tjuə] innsetting (i et embete); investitur, innsettingsrett.
investment [in'vestmənt] kledning; cernering, beleiring; anbringelse (av penger); fruktbargjøring (av penger); anbrakt kapital. **investor** [in'vestə] innsetter; en som har penger å anbringe el. har anbrakt penger i noe.
inveteracy [in'vetərəsi] inngroddhet, hardnakkethet; inngrodd hat, agg. **inveterate** [in-'vet(ə)rét] inngrodd; kronisk, vanskelig å helbrede; forherdet; **an** — **drunkard** en uforbederlig dranker.
invidious [in'vidjəs] odiøs; vanskelig, lei, slem; **an** — **affair** en betenkelig sak. **invidiousness** [-nés] kilden (el. betenkelig) art.
invigorate [in'vigəreⁱt] gi kraft, styrke, kveike. **invigoration** [invigə'reⁱʃən] styrking, ny kraft.
invincibility [in'vinsi'biliti] uovervinnelighet. **invincible** [in'vinsibl] uovervinnelig.
inviolability [in'vaiələ'biliti] ukrenkelighet; ubrødelighet, **inviolable** [in'vaiələbl] ukrenkelig; ubrødelig. **inviolacy** [in'vaiələsi] ukrenkelighet; ubrødelighet.
invisibility [in'vizi'biliti] usynlighet.
invisible [in'vizibl] usynlig; **make oneself** — gjøre seg usynlig.
invitation [invi'teⁱʃən] innbydelse, invitasjon. **invite** [in'vait] innby, invitere; oppfordre, be; oppfordre til; innbydelse; — **to dinner** innby til middag; — **to dine** innby til å spise til middag. **inviting** innbydende, fristende.
inviter [in'vaitə] innbyder.
invocate ['invokeⁱt] påkalle. **invocation** [in-

vo'ke'ʃən] påkalling. **invocatory** [in'våkətəri; 'invo-] påkallende.
invoice ['invois] faktura; (amr.) tollfortegnelse; fakturere, utferdige faktura over. — **-book** fakturabok.
invoke [in'voᵘk] påkalle, anrope.
involucre ['invəlju·kə] svøp, sporegjemme (i planter).
involuntarily [in'våləntərili] ufrivillig; uvilkårlig. **involuntary** [in'våləntəri] ufrivillig; uvilkårlig.
involution [invo'l(j)u·ʃən] innvikling, innrulling; innfiltrethet, floke; bedekning, hylster; potensering; involusjon; innskyting av et setningsledd mellom subjektet og verbet.
involve [in'vålv] innvikle; synkverve; innhylle, inneholde; medføre; potensere; **-d and enigmatical** innviklet og gåtefull; **-d in debt** forgjeldet; **a quantity -d to the third power** en størrelse i tredje potens.
invulnerability [in'vʌlnərə'biliti] usårlighet. **invulnerable** [in'vʌlnərəbl] usårlig.
inward ['inwəd] indre, innvendig, innvortes; inn(ad)gående; innad; innetter; indre; (i plur.) innvoller; — **correspondence** inngående korrespondanse.
inwardly ['inwədli] innvendig, i ens stille sinn; **her heart bled** — hjertet blødde i henne.
inwardness ['inwədnès] indre tilstand; fortrolighet; egentlig betydning.
inwards ['inwədz] innad, innover, innetter, i ens indre.
inwrap [in'räp] se **enwrap**.
Io ['aioᵘ] Io.
io ['aioᵘ] gledesrop; hei! hurra!
iodate ['aiodèt] jodsurt salt. **iodic** [ai'ådik] jodholdig. **iodid(e)** ['aiod(a)id] jodforbindelse; — **of potassium** jodkalium; — **of sodium** jodnatrium. **iodine** ['aiod(a)in] jod. **iodism** ['aiodizm] jodforgiftning. **iodize** ['aiodaiz] preparere med jod, bruke jod på. **iodoform** [ai'ådofå·ᵉm] jodoform.
I. of M. fk. f. **Isle of Man.**
I. of W. fk. f. **Isle of Wight.**
Iolanthe [aio'länþi] Jolante.
iolite ['aiolait] iolitt.
Ionia [ai'oᵘnjə] Jonia.
Ionian [ai'oᵘnjən] jonisk; joner.
iota [ai'oᵘtə] jota; bagatell, tøddel.
IOU ['aioᵘ'ju·] (= **I owe you**) gjeldsbrev.
Iowa ['aioᵘə, 'aiəwə] Iowa.
ipecac ['ipikäk] fk. f. **ipecacuanha.**
ipecacuanha [ipikäkju'änə] brekkrot.
Iphigenia [ifidʒi'naiə] Iphigenia.
Ipswich ['ipswitʃ] Ipswich.
Ir. fk. f. **Irish.**
Irak ['ira·k] Irak, Mesopotamia.
Iran [i'ra·n] Iran, Persia. **Iranian** [ai're'njən] iransk, persisk.
irascibility [airäsi'biliti] vredaktighet, ilske, hissighet. **irascible** [ai'räsibl] vredaktig, ilsk, hissig, brå. **irate** [ai're't] vred, sint.
I. R. B. fk. f. **Irish Republican Brotherhood.**
ire [aiə] vrede, harme, forbitrelse; vredes. **ireful** ['aiəf(u)l] vred, forbitret, harm, sint.
Ireland ['aiələnd] Irland.
Irene [ai'ri·ni] Irene.
irestone ['aiəstoᵘn] hard stein.
Iricism ['airisizm] irsk språkegenhet.
iridal ['airidəl] regnbue-. **iridectomy** [iri'dektomi] utskjæring av en del av iris. **iridescence** [iri'desəns] spill i regnbuens farger, fargespill. **iridescent** [iri'desənt] spillende i regnbuens farger. **iridian** [ai'ridiən] iris-, regnbuehinne-. **iridium** [ai'ridiəm] iridium. **iridize** ['iridaiz] iridisere.
Iris ['airis] Iris.
iris ['airis] regnbue; iris, regnbuehinne; sverdlilje. **irisated** ['airise'tid] regnbuefarget; regnbueaktig.
Irish ['airiʃ] irsk; (fig.) uforskammet; dum;

irsk (språket); **the** — irlenderne, irerne; — **apricots** poteter; — **assurance** dumdristighet; — **bull** språkfeil; dum vittighet; nonsens; — **cockney** londoner av irsk opprinnelse; — **daisy** fivel, løvetann; **the** — **Free State** Den irske fristat (offisielt navn for Sør-Irland); — **horse** salt kjøtt; — **night** en natt i 1688, da man i London og andre engelske byer fryktet for at irlenderne ville myrde protestantene; — **stew** en rett som lages av sauekjøtt med poteter og løk; — **theatre** arrestlokale. **Irishism** ['airiʃizm] irisisme. **Irishman** ['airiʃmən] irlender, irer. **Irishry** ['airiʃri] irsk befolkning. **Irishwoman** ['airiʃwumən] irlenderinne.
iritis [ai'raitis] iritis, regnbuehinnebetennelse.
irk [ə·k] ergre; trette; kjede; smerte.
irksome ['ə·ksəm] trettende; lei, kjedsommelig.
iron ['aiən; 'airən] jern; (fig.) kraft, styrke; hardhet, grusomhet; strykejern; av jern; fast, urokkelig; hard, grusom; frekk, uforskammet; legge i lenker; kle med jern; stryke (med strykejern), presse, perse; **irons** lenker; **put in -s** legge i lenker; **stand on hot -s** stå som på glør; **the Iron Duke** et tilnavn til Wellington; **he wants an** — **rod over him** han må tas hardt. — **-band** jernband; jernbeslag. — **-bar** jernstang. — **-bound** jernbeslått; fjell-lendt, bratt; hard, ubøyelig. **-clad** pansret; panserskip.
ironer ['aiənə] en som stryker.
ironical [ai'rånikl] ironisk.
ironing ['aiəniŋ] strykning; pressing, persing. — **-board** strykebrett. — **-cloth** strykeklede.
ironist ['airənist] ironiker.
iron-liquor ['aiənlikə] jernsverte.
ironmaster ['aiən'ma·stə] jernverkseier, jernvarehandler.
iron|monger ['aiənmʌŋgə] jernvarehandler. **-mongery** [-mʌŋgəri] jernvarer, isenkram; jernvarehandel. — **-mould** [moᵘld] rustflekk. — **-plate** [-ple't] jernplate, jernblikk. — **-rod** [-råd] jernstang. — **-safe** [-se'f] jernskap. — **-scrap** [-skräp] skrapjern.
ironside ['aiənsaid] jernside, srl. brukt om Cromwell's tropper.
iron-stone ['aiənstoᵘn] jernmalm.
iron|ware ['aiən wæ·ə] jernvarer. **-work** [-wə·k] jernarbeid; jernbeslag; i pl. jernverk.
irony ['aiəni] jernhard; jern-.
irony ['airəni] ironi; ironisering.
Iroquois ['irokwoi] irokeser; irokesisk.
irradiate [i're'die't] bestråle, belyse; opplyse (ånden, forstanden); bringe liv i (ved varme og lys); pryde; stråle. **irradiation** [ire'di'e'ʃən] stråling, utstråling; stråleglans; (fig.) opplysning.
irrational [i'räʃ(ə)nəl] ufornuftig, irrasjonell. **irrationality** [iräʃə'näliti] ufornuft.
irreclaimable [iri'kle'məbl] ugjenkallelig; uforbederlig.
irrecognisable [i'rekəg'naizəbl] ugjenkjennelig. **irreconcilability** [i'rekənsailə'biliti] uforsonlighet; uforenelighet. **irreconcilable** [i'rekən'sailəbl] uforsonlig, uforenelig.
irrecoverable [iri'kʌv(ə)rəbl] ubotelig, uerstattelig; ikke til å få igjen.
irredeemable [iri'di·məbl] uinnløselig; ugjenkallelig; uunngåelig; uforbederlig.
irredentist [iri'dentist] forkjemper for gjenforening med moderlandet av italiensk-sinnede områder under fremmed herredømme.
irrefragability [i'refrəgə'biliti] uomstøtelighet. **irrefragable** [i'refrəgəbl] uomstøtelig, ugjendrivelig.
irrefutable [iri'fju·təbl] ugjendrivelig.
irregular [i'regjulə] uregelmessig, uregelrett; uordentlig; pl. irregulære tropper. **irregularity** [iregju'läriti] uregelmessighet.
irrelative [i'relətiv] uten gjensidig forhold, uten forbindelse, uvedkommende; absolutt.

irrelevance [i'relivəns], **irrelevancy** [i'relivənsi] uanvendelighet. **irrelevant** [i'relivənt] uanvendelig, uvedkommende, likegyldig.

irreligion [iri'lidʒən] religionsløshet; irreligiøsitet. **irreligious** [-dʒəs] religionsløs; irreligiøs.

irremediable [iri'mi·djəbl] ulegelig, uhelbredelig, uavhjelpelig; ubotelig.

irremissible [iri'misibl] utilgivelig.

irremovability [iri'mu·vəibiliti] uavsettelighet; fasthet. **irremovable** [iri'mu·vəbl] uavsettelig; fast.

irreparability [i'repərə'biliti] uerstattelighet. **irreparable** [i'repərəbl] uopprettelig, ubotelig.

irrepealable [iri'pi·ləbl] ugjenkallelig.

irreplaceable [iri'ple¹səbl] uerstattelig.

irrepressible [iri'presibl] ubetvingelig, ustyrlig. **irreproachable** [iri'proⁿtʃəbl] ulastelig.

irresistance [iri'zistəns] motstandsløshet, underkastelse. **irresistibility** [iri'zisti'biliti] uimotståelighet. **irresistible** [iri'zistibl] uimotståelig.

irresolute [i'rezəl(j)ut] ubesluttsom, vinglet. **irresolution** [irezə'l(j)u·ʃən] ubesluttsomhet, vakling, vingling.

irresolvability [iri'zɑlvə'biliti] uoppløselighet. **irresolvable** [iri'zɑlvəbl] uoppløselig.

irrespective [iri'spektiv] uten hensyn (**of** til); uansett.

irresponsibility [iri'spɑnsi'biliti] uansvarlighet. **irresponsible** [iri'spɑnsibl] uansvarlig.

irresponsive [iri'spɑnsiv] ikke svarende; uten sympati, uten øre (**to** for).

irretentive [iri'tentiv] som ikke kan beholde; upålitelig (f. eks. om hukommelse).

irretrievable [iri'tri·vəbl] uopprettelig, ubotelig.

irreverence [i'rev(ə)rəns] mangel på ærbødighet (**of** for). **irreverent** [-rənt] uærbødig; pietetsløs.

irreversible [iri'və·sibl] uomstøtelig.

irrevocable [i'revokəbl] ugjenkallelig.

irrigate [i'rige¹t] overrisle, vanne.

irrigation [iri'ge¹ʃən] overrisling; **turn to the purpose of** — benytte til overrisling.

irrigator [i'rige¹tə] vanningsmaskin; irrigator, utskyllingsapparat.

irritability [iritə'biliti] pirrelighet, irritabilitet. **irritable** [i'ritəbl] pirrelig, irritabel, sær. **irritant** [i'ritənt] pirrende; pirringsmiddel. **irritate** [i'ri·te¹t] pirre, irritere; erte, terge; egge. **irritation** [iri'te¹ʃən] pirring, irritasjon; opphisselse; vrede. **irritative** [i'iritətiv] pirrende, irriterende; opphissende.

irruption [i'rʌpʃən] innbrudd; overfall, overrumpling. **irruptive** [i'rʌptiv] som bryter seg inn.

Irving [i'ə·viŋ] Irving.

Irvingite [i'ə·viŋait] irvingiansk; irvingianer.

Irwell [i'ə·wəl] Irwell (sideelv til Mersey).

is [iz] er, 3. p. sg. pres. av **be**.

Isaac [i'aizək] Isak.

Isabel [i'izəbl] Isabella. **isabel** [i'izəbl] isabellafarge; isabellafarget hest. **Isabella** [izə'belə] Isabella. — **-coloured** [-'lʌləd] isabellafarget, grågul.

Isaiah [ai'zaiə] Jesaia.

ischiadic [iski'ädik] som angår hoften, hofte-; — **passion el. disease** hofteverk, isjias. **ischiatic** [iski'ätik] se **ischiadic**. **ischion** [i'iskiän], **ischium** [i'iskiəm] hoftebein.

ischury [i'iskjuri] urinstansning.

Ishmael [i'iʃmiəl] Ismael. **Ishmaelite** [i'iʃmiəlait] ismalitt; araber; en som er i krig med samfunnet.

isinglass [i'aiziŋla·s] gelatin; fiskelim.

Isis [i'aisis] Isis; **the Isis** Themsen ved Oxford.

Islam [i'izla·m] Islam. **Islamism** [i'izləmizm] islamisme. **Islamite** [i'izləmait] muhammedaner. **Islamitic** [izlə'mitik] islamittisk, muhammedansk.

island [i'ailənd] øy, refuge, tilfluktssted for fotgjengere; **in the** — på øya (om større øyer). **on the** — på øya (om mindre øyer). **islander** [i'ailəndə] øybu, øyboer.

Islay [i'aile¹] Islay (en av Hebridene).

isle [ail] øy (brukes især poetisk eller i navn f. eks. **the Isle of Man; the Isle of Wight; the British Isles**).

islet [i'ailet] liten øy, småøy, holme.

Islington [i'izliŋtən] Islington.

ism [izm] (ironisk) teori, lære.

I. S. O. fk. f. **Imperial Service Order**.

isobar [i'aisoba·ə] isobar, liketrykkslinje.

isobathytherm [aiso'bäþiþə·m] isobatyterm, linje for like varme punkter i jorda eller havet.

isocheim [i'aisokaim] linje for samme middeltemperatur om vinteren. **isochimene** [aiso-'kaimi·n] se **isocheim**.

isochromatic [aisokro'mätik] ensfarget.

isochronal [ais'äkronəl] som tar like lang tid, isokron. **isochronism** [ai'säkronizm] like lang tid, tidslikelengde. **isochronous** [ai'säkronəs] som følges i tid.

isogonal [ai'sägonəl], **isogonic** [aiso'gänik] likevinklet, ensvinklet.

isohyetal [aiso'haiətəl] med samme regnmengde.

isolate [i'aisəle¹t] isolere, avsondre. **isolation** [aisə'le¹ʃən] isolering, avsondring.

isometric [aiso'metrik] isometrisk, av samme mål.

isopod [i'aisopåd] isopode, en slags ringkreps.

isosceles [ai'säsili·z] likebe(i)nt; likebe(i)nt figur.

isotherm [i'aisoþə·m] isoterm, likevarmelinje. **isothermal** [aiso'þə·məl] isotermisk.

Ispahan [ispə'ha·n] Ispahan. **Ispahanee** [ispə'ha·ni] ispahansk; ispahaner.

Israel [i'izriəl] Israel. **Israelite** [i'izriəlait] israelitt. **Israelitic** [izriə'litik], **Israelitish** [-'laitiʃ] israelittisk.

issuable [i'iʃuəbl] som kan utstedes; som fører til avgjørelse. **issuance** [i'iʃuəns] utstedelse.

issue [i'isju·, 'iʃu·] utgang; os, munning; avkom; resultat, utfall, følge; utstedelse, levering; utlån; utgivelse (f. eks. av en bok); utgave, opplag; nummer (av blad); kjennelse (av edsvorne); spørsmål, kjerne, stridspunkt; uttømmelse; fontanelle (kunstig frambrakt sår); komme ut; strømme ut; stamme (**from** fra); ha sitt opphav i; ende (in med); føre til resultat; utlevere; utstede; utgi (f. eks. bok); **at** — omstridt; **amount at** — det beløp det dreier seg om; **cause at** — sak som skal avgjøres; **raise an** — reise et juridisk spørsmål el. bringe et sådant til avgjørelse.

isthmian [i'ismiən, -stm-, -sþm-] istmisk. **isthmus** [i'ismos, -stm-, -sþm-] istme, eid.

is-to-be [i'iztəbi·] tilkommende.

Istria [i'istriə] Istria.

it [it] den, det; (ubetont personlig pronomen) **it is my hat** det er min hatt; **give it me** gi meg den; **the child lost its way** barnet for vill; (ubestemt, som subjekt) **who is it?** hvem er det? **what time is it?** hva er klokka? **it is two o'clock** klokka er to; **that's it** det er riktig; **that's it, give us a song** det var rett, syng litt; **it seems to me** jeg synes; **it is natural that he should complain** det er naturlig at han klager; (i upersonlige uttrykk om været etc.) **it is raining** det regner; **it is cold** det er kaldt; **it looks like rain** det ser ut til regn; (om avstand) **it is a long way to Oxford** det er langt til O.; **it is 6 miles to O.** det er 6 mil til O.; **it is no way there** det er ganske kort dit; (om tid) **it is long since I saw him** det er lenge siden jeg har sett ham; (ubestemt, som objekt) **you are going it** du slår stort på det; **you'll catch it** du vil få svi for det; **cab it** kjøre i drosje; **foot it** gå til fots; **lord it** spille herre; **have done it** er kommet galt av sted; **we had a good time of it** vi morte oss godt.

Italian [i'täljən] italiensk; italiener; — **hand** kursivskrift; — **iron** pipejern; — **juice** lakrissaft; — **store**, — **warehouse** olje-, såpehandel; sydfrukthandel. **Italianism** [i'täljənizm] italianisme. **italianize** [i'täljənaiz] italienisere, spille italiener.

Italic [i'tälik] italisk; kursiv; **italics** [i'täliks] kursiv. **italicize** [i'tälisaiz] kursivere.

Italy ['itəli] Italia.

itch [itʃ] klø; klå; klø etter; kløe, klåe; fnatt, skabb; sterk attrå; lengt; **my fingers — to box his ears** fingrene mine klør etter å gi ham en lusing. **itchy** ['itʃi] fnattet, skabbet.

item ['aitəm] item, likeledes.

item ['aitəm] artikkel, punkt, post; opptegne, notere. **itemise** ['aitəmaiz] føre opp de enkelte poster.

iterate ['itəreit] gjenta. **iteration** [itə're'ʃən] gjentagelse. **iterative** ['itərətiv] gjentagende.

itinerancy [i'tinərənsi] omflakkende virksomhet; flakking; **itinerant** [i'tinərənt] reisende, omvandrende; reisende; vandrer; omflakkende lærer; omreisende predikant; skreppekar. **itinerary** [i'tinərəri] reisende, reisebeskrivelse; rute; reisehåndbok. **itinerate** [i'tinəreit] reise om, vandre om; flakke.

its [its] dens, dets; sin, sitt, sine.

it's [its] sammentrukket av: **it is, it has.** **itself** [it'self] den selv, det selv; seg selv, seg; selv, sjøl; **the thing** — selve tingen; **he was civility** — han var høfligheten selv; **a house standing by** — et hus som ligger for seg selv; **good in** — god i seg selv.

Ivanhoe ['aivənhoᵘ] Ivanhoe.

I've [aiv] sammentrukket av: **I have.** **ivied** ['aivid] kledd med vedbend.

ivory ['aivəri] elfenben; ting av elfenben; fribillett; av elfenben, elfenbens; **ivories** elefanttenner; terninger; biljardkuler; tenner. **ivory|-black** ['aivəri'bläk] elfenbe(i)nsvart; beinkull. — **-nut** elfenbensnøtt.

ivy ['aivi] vedbend, eføy, bergflette.

I. W. fk. f. **Isle of Wight.**

I. W. T. D. fk. f. **Inland Water Transport Department.**

I. W. W. fk. f. **Industrial Workers of the World.**

J

J [dzeⁱ] j.

J. fk. f. **Judge; Julius; Justice.**

Ja. fk. f. **James.**

J|A fk. f. **joint account** felles regning.

jab [dʒäb] støte, stikke; pirke; støt; stikk.

jabber ['dʒäbə] pludre, skravle, sludre; pludring, skravl.

jabiru ['dʒäbiru·] slags tropisk amerikansk stork.

jabot ['ʒäboᵘ] halskrus.

jacal ['dʒäkl] (amr.) trehytte.

jacala ['dʒa·kəla·] krokodille (hindusk).

jacamar ['dʒäkəma·ᵊ] jakamar (en fugl).

jacaranda [dʒäkə'rända] jakaranda (et brasiliansk tre).

jacinth ['dʒeⁱsinþ, 'dʒäsinþ] hyasint.

Jack [dʒäk] Jack, Ola; ung fyr; tjener, arbeidskar; hverdagsmenneske; enfoldig fyr; frekk fyr; uoppdragen fyr; matros, jan; knekt, trumfknekt, fil (i kortspill); han (om dyr); betegnelse for forskjellige redskaper som: støvelknekt; donkraft; stekvender; lærflaske; hammer (i klaver); sagkrakk; trekile; vinde; regnepenger; gjøs; —, **Tom and Harry** Per og Pål; — **and Gill** (el. **Jill**) han Ola og ho Kari (mann og kone); — **fool dumrian;** — **Sprat** spirrevipp; **every man** — hver kjeft; — **in the water** bryggeslusk; **Yellow** — den gule feber; **Union Jack** det britiske unionsflagget; — **in office** storsnutet embetsmann; — **on both sides** overløper; — **of all trades, master of none** en som gir seg av med alt, men ikke kan noe grundig; tusenkunstner; — **of all work** faktotum, altmuligmann; **play the** — **with some one** holde en for narr; **before you could say** — **Robinson** før man kunne telle til tre; **boot-jack** støvelknekt; **Cheap Jack** omreisende gateselger, markskriker; **lifting-jack** donkraft; **sawing-jack** sagbukk, sagkrakk.

jack [dʒäk] jacktre, helbladet brødfrukttre.

jack [dʒäk] skrubbhøvle; løfte med donkraft.

Jack-a-dandy [dʒäkə'dändi] viktigper.

jackal ['dʒäkå·l] sjakal; håndlanger.

jack-all-general ['dʒäkå·l'dʒenərəl] faktotum.

jackanapes ['dʒäkəneⁱps] galfrans, apekatt, narr, utange.

jackass ['dʒäkäs] han-esel; (fig.) ['dʒäka·s] esel, idiot, naut.

Jack-at-a-pinch ['dʒäkətə'pinʃ] en som hjelper i nøden.

jackboot ['dʒäkbu·t] militær ridestøvel, langstøvel; **the** — **politicians of Berlin** militærpartiet i Berlin.

jackdaw ['dʒäkdå·] kaie.

jacket ['dʒäkit] jakke, trøye, skinnfell; skrell (på poteter); gi jakke (el. trøye) på. **jacketing** ['dʒäkitiŋ] drakt pryl.

jackey ['dʒäki] sjenever.

jackfish ['dʒäkfiʃ] fiske gjedde.

Jackie ['dʒäki] kjælenavn for **Jack;** ofte for **Jack-Tar; the jackies** sjøguttene.

Jack-in-a-box ['dʒäkinə'båks] esketroll.

Jack-in-office byråkratisk viktigper.

Jack-in-the-green ['dʒäkinðə'gri·n] en lauvkledd figur som man danser omkring ved maifesten.

Jack-in-the-water ['dʒäkinðə'wå·tə] mann som hjelper til på dampskipsbruer o. l., bryggeslusk.

jack-knife ['dʒäknaif] stor follekniv.

Jack-of-all-trades ['dʒäkəv'å·ltre'dz] tusenkunstner.

Jack-o'-Lantern ['dʒäko'läntən] lyktemann, blålys, vettelys.

jack-plane ['dʒäkpleⁱn] skrubbhøvel.

jack-pudding ['dʒäk'pudiŋ] bajas.

jack-screw ['dʒäkskru·] hånddonkraft.

jack-snipe ['dʒäksnaip] bekkasin, myrsnipe.

Jackson ['dʒäksən] Jackson.

jack-staff ['dʒäksta·f] gjøsstake.

jack-stay ['dʒäkste'] strekktau.

Jack-tar ['dʒäk'ta·ə] matros, sjøgutt.

jack-towel ['dʒäktauəl] håndkle som går over en rull.

Jacky ['dʒäki] kjælenavn for **Jack;** kaie.

jacky ['dʒäki] slags skråtobakk.

Jacob ['dʒeⁱkəb] Jakob.

Jacobin ['dʒäkobin] jakobiner; dominikaner; parykkdue.

Jacobite ['dʒäkobait] jakobitt; tilhenger av Jakob 2. og hans sønn.

Jacob's ladder ['dʒeⁱkəbz'lädə] fjellflokk, fjellfnokk (plante); vantleider (på skip).

Jacobus [dʒə'koᵘbəs] jakobus; gullmynt = 20—24 sh. preget under Jakob 1.

jaconet ['dʒäkənet] jakonett, en slags fint bomullstøy.

jacquerie [ʒäkə'ri·] bondeoppstand, bondereisning.

jade [dʒeⁱd] skottgamp, fillemerr; tøs, galneheie, villkatt; utmatte, ase ut, slite ut; utmattes.

jade [dʒeⁱd] nefritt (en slags grønn stein).

jadish ['dʒeⁱdiʃ] ondskapsfull; løs (på tråden).

jaeger ['je'gə] jäger (ulltøy).

jag [dʒäg] takk; tagg, spiss, tann; gjøre takket.

jagger ['dʒägə] kakejern, bakkelsspore.

jaggy ['dʒägi] sagtakket.
jaguar ['dʒägwa·ᵊ, 'dʒägjua·ᵊ] jaguar.
Jahve ['dʒa·ve'] Jahve, Jehova.
jail [dʒe'l] fengsel; fengsle, sette fast, arrestere.
— -**bird** fange, en som ofte har vært i fengsel, «gammel kjenning av politiet». — -**delivery** utlevering av anholdte personer til assiseretten; frigivelse av fangene. **jailer** ['dʒe'lə] slutter, fangevokter. **jail-keeper** = **jailer**.
jalap ['dʒäləp] jalaprot.
jalousie ['ʒälu·zi·] sjalusi, persienner.
jam [dʒäm] trengsel, stim, stimmel; trykke, presse, klemme, kile fast; sitte fast.
jam [dʒäm] syltetøy.
Jamaica [dʒə'me'kə] Jamaica; rom.
jamb [dʒäm] dørstolpe; vange; beitski.
jamboree [dʒämbo'ri·] drikkelag, lystighet; speiderstevne.
James [dʒe'mz] Jakob.
jampot ['dʒämpåt] syltekrukke.
Jan. fk. f. January.
Jane [dʒe'n] Johanne. **Janet** ['dʒänét] Hanna.
Janeiro [dʒə'niəroⁿ].
jangle ['dʒängl] skurre; skravle; kives, kjekle; la skurre; rasle med; kjekl; strid; rasling.
janitor ['dʒänitə] portner; skolepedell.
janizary ['dʒänizəri] janitsjar.
jant se jaunt.
January ['dʒänjuəri] januar.
Jap [dʒäp] japaner; japansk. **Japan** [dʒə'pän] Japan; japansk; japansk arbeid; lakere (på japansk vis). **Japanese** ['dʒäpə'ni·z; -ni·s] japansk; japaner. **japanned** [dʒə'pänd] lakert. **japanner** [dʒə'pänə] lakerer.
jape [dʒe'p] spøk, gjøn; spøke, gjøne, skjemte.
jar [dʒa·ᵊ] skurre i ørene på en, kvine, rikse, knirke; være uenig, kives, kjekle, skurre; gjøre falsk; forstyrre, ryste, skake, bringe mislyd i; skurring, mislyd, strid; **it jarred upon my ears** det skurret i ørene mine; **every nerve was jarring** hver nerve dirret; — **upon** (el. **with, against**) skrape mot.
jar [dʒa·ᵊ] leirkrukke, steinkrukke; pakke ned i krukke; **tobacco** — tobakksdåse (av krukkeform).
jar [dʒa·ᵊ]; **on the** — på gløtt (**ajar**).
jardiniere [ʒa·ᵊdin'jæ·ᵊ] blomsterstativ.
jargon ['dʒa·ᵊgən] kråkemål, sjargong.
jarnut ['dʒa·ᵊnʌt] jordnøtt.
jarvey ['dʒa·ᵊvi] (irsk) kusk, vognmann.
jasmine ['dʒäsmin] sjasmin.
jasper ['dʒäspə] jaspis.
jaundice ['dʒä·ndis] gulsott. **jaundiced** [-st] gulsottig; misunnelig, avindsyk, mistenksom.
jaunt [dʒå·nt] gjøre utflukter, streife om; **take a jaunt** ta en tur; tur, utflukt.
jauntily ['dʒä·ntili] muntert, flott. **jauntiness** [-tinés] munterhet, flotthet, flyktighet, lettferdighet. **jaunty** ['dʒä·nti] munter, flott, spretten,
Java ['dʒa·və] Java. **Javanese** ['dʒävə'ni·z] javansk; javaner; javanesisk.
javelin ['dʒävlin] kastespyd.
jaw [dʒå·] kjeve, kjake, munn, gap, kjeft; skravl, skjelling, praling; kjefte (om), bruke kjeften (på); **the jaws of death** dødens gap; **his jaw dropped** han fikk et fortvilet uttrykk i ansiktet; **his jaws were set** han bet tennene sammen (hadde et uttrykk av sammenbitt energi); **hold your** — hold munn; **there is too much** — **about him** han snakker for mye; **give us none of your** — hold opp med den kjeftingen din; **I gave her a bit of my** — jeg sa henne ordentlig beskjed; **don't you** — **me in that way** plag meg ikke med det snakket ditt. -**bone** kjevebein, kjakebein. -**breaker** langt ord som er vanskelig å uttale. -**tooth** kinntann, jeksel.
jay [dʒe'] nøtteskrike.
ᵣ jazz [dʒäz] jazz (sl. musikk og dans); bråk; jazze (spille el. danse j.); bråkende; gloret.
J. B. fk. f. John Bull.

J. C. fk. f. Jesus Christ; Julius Caesar; juris consult; justice clerk.
jealous ['dʒeləs] årvåken, årvak, var, mistenksom (**of** over for, med hensyn til); nidkjær, sjalu, skinnsyk, avindsyk (**of** på).
jealousy ['dʒeləsi] (skinnsyk) årvåkenhet; avindsyke; skinnsyke; brennhug; nidkjærhet; sjalusi, persienner.
jeer [dʒiə] håne, spotte; hån, spott. **jeerer** ['dʒiərə] spotter. **jeeringly** ['dʒiəriŋli] hånlig.
Jehu ['dʒi·hju·] Jehu; kusk som kjører vilt.
jejune [dʒi'dʒu·n] tørr, åndløs; skrinn, mager.
Jekyll ['dʒi·kil].
jellied ['dʒelid] klebrig, geléaktig.
jelly ['dʒeli] gelé; tykk saft; **beat a person into a** — slå en til plukkfisk.
jellyfish ['dʒelifiʃ] gople, manet, kobbeklyse.
Jem [dʒem] = **James**.
Jemima [dʒi'maimə] alm. navn for tjenestejente.
jemmy ['dʒemi] brekkjern, kubein.
jennet ['dʒenit] liten spansk hest.
jenneting ['dʒenitiŋ] tidlig sommereple.
Jenny ['dʒini, 'dʒeni] Jenny, Johanne; spinnemaskin; gjerdesmutt. — -**ass** hunesel.
jeopard ['dʒepəd] våge, sette på spill. **jeopardize** ['dʒepədaiz] våge. **jeopardous** ['dʒepədəs] farlig, vågelig, vågal. **jeopardy** ['dʒepədi] fare, våg; **put one's life in** — sette livet på spill.
Jer. fk. f. Jeremiah.
jeremiad [dʒeri'maiəd] jeremiade.
Jeremiah [dʒeri'maiə] Jeremias.
Jericho ['dʒerikoⁿ] Jeriko; **go to** —! gå pokker i vold, reis og ryk; **I wish you were in (at)** — gid du satt på Blokksberg.
jerk [dʒə·k] støte (plutselig), rykke, kaste, trive, kyle, slenge, kippe, gjøre et rykk; plutselig støt; rykk, puff, kast; **by jerks** rykkevis.
jerkin ['dʒə·kin] jakke, korttrøye, stutt-trøye.
jerky ['dʒə·ki] støtvis.
Jerome ['dʒerəm] Hieronymus; [dʒə'roᵘm] Jerome (etternavn).
jerque [dʒə·k] tollvisitere; også **jerk. jerquer** ['dʒə·kə] tollbetjent.
jerry-builder ['dʒeribildə] byggespekulant. **jerry-built** bygd på spekulasjon, skrøpelig.
Jersey ['dʒə·zi] Jersey; fint ullgarn; jerseyliv.
Jerusalem [dʒi'ru·sələm] Jerusalem; — **pony** esel.
jessamine ['dʒesəmin] sjasmin.
jest [dʒest] spøke, si i spøk; spøk, skjemt, morsomhet, vits; **in jest** i spøk; **take a jest** forstå spøk. **jest-book** anekdotesamling. **jestee** [dʒe'sti·] den som er · gjenstand for spøken. **jester** ['dʒestə] spøkefugl; hoffnarr, **jestingly** ['dʒestinli] i spøk. **jesting-stock** = **jestee**.
Jesuit ['dʒezjuit, -ʒuit] jesuitt. **jesuitic(al)** [dʒezju'itik(l), -zu-] jesuittisk.
Jesus ['dʒi·zəs] Jesus.
jet [dʒet] jet, gagat (slags fint steinkull). -**black** kullsvart.
jet [dʒet] springe fram, spy ut, sprøyte ut; sprute, strømme, velle; stråle, sprut, sprøyt; tut; innløpstapp (ved støpning); gassbrenner; gassbluss.
jetsam ['dʒetsəm], **jetson** ['dʒetsən], **jettison** ['dʒetsən] strandingsgods; utkasting av gods i havsnød.
jetty ['dʒeti] gagatlignende, kullsvart.
jetty ['dʒeti] framspringende kant på en bygning, framskott, utbygning, utbygg; demning, molo, landinsplass.
Jew [dʒu·] jøde; lure, narre, bedra; **be as thick as two Jews on a pay-day** være meget intime; **the Wandering** —den evige jøde; **to** — **down** prutte, sjakre. — -**baiting** jødeforfølgelse.
jewel ['dʒu·il; -əl] juvel, edelstein, perle; smykke; skatt; smykke med juveler; **mock** — uekte edelstein; -**led** juvelbesatt; **her richly jewelled hand** hennes hånd som var besatt med

prektige ringer. — -case juvelskrin; smykkeskrin. **jeweller** ['dʒuˑilə] juvelér, gullsmed. **jewellery, jewelry** ['dʒuˑilri] edelsteiner, kostbarheter; smykker.

Jewess ['dʒuˑès] jødinne.

Jewish ['dʒuˑiʃ] jødisk; jødeaktig. **jewishness** [-nès] jødisk vesen, jødisk utseende.

jewry ['dʒuˑəri] getto, jødekvarter; jødefolket.

Jezebel ['dʒezibel] Jesabel; arrig, frekk kvinne.

jib [dʒib] sky (**at** for); bli sta, tverrstanse; slå seg vrang; steile, protestere.

jib [dʒib] klyver; jibb; jibbe.

jibber ['dʒibə] sky hest, sta hest.

jiff [dʒif] øyeblikk; **in a** — i en fei, håndvending; **wait a** — vent et lite øyeblikk.

jiffy = **jiff.**

jig [dʒig] jigg (musikkstykke og dans); etterspill ved de gamle skuespill, oppført av narren; pilk; sprette, danse, hoppe, huske seg; pilke; harpe (i vann); **the** — **is up** spillet er ferdig; det er forbi med en; — **one's legs** sparke med beina. **jig-clog** tresko til å danse jigg med. **jigger** ['dʒigə] jigg-danser.

jigger ['dʒigə] skreddertalje; pottemakerskive; (amr.) liten hestesporvogn uten konduktør; prisviser (på børs); arrestlokale; pilk (fiskeredskap); hoppe, rykke; — **oneself free** sprelle seg fri (om fisk).

jiggle ['dʒigl] hoppe omkring; huske, hufse.

Jill [dʒil] Julie; ung pike; **Jack and Jill** Ola og Kari. — **-flirt** lettferdig pike.

jilt [dʒilt] lettferdig kvinne, kokette; bedra (i kjærlighet), slå opp med, narre for en dans.

Jim [dʒim] fk. f. **James;** — **Crow car** negerjernbanevogn.

jimjams ['dʒimdʒämz] dilla.

jimp [dʒimp] nett, slank; knapp.

jims [dʒimz] delirium, dilla.

jingle ['dʒiŋgl] klirre, single, rasle; la klirre, rasle med; klirring, rasling; remse, regle, rispe; rangle.

Jingo ['dʒiŋgoᵘ] (måskje forvanskning av Jesus); **by** (**the living**) — Guds død, død og pine; økenavn for en krigsbegeistret konservativ. **-ism** [-izm] kraftpatriotisme.

jink [dʒiŋk] fare, sette, sprette, smette unna; sprett, skvett, bråkast; **jinks** moro, leven.

jinrik(i)sha [dzin'rik(i)ʃə] japansk tohjulsvogn som trekkes av de innfødte.

jiu-jitsu se **jujitsu.**

Jn. fk. f. **junction.**

Joan [dʒoᵘn] Johanne; — **of Arc** Jeanne d'Arc.

Job [dʒoᵘb] Job; -**'s comfort** dårlig trøst.

job [dʒäb] slag, støt, stikk; bestemt stykke arbeid, akkordarbeid, (tilfeldig) arbeid, sjau, jobb, forretning; affære, greie, historie; aksidensarbeid (i boktrykkerspråk); korrupsjon, nepotisme; **occasional** — tilfeldig arbeid; **odd -s** tilfeldige jobber; **a soft** — et makelig arbeid, en smal sak; **what a** — det er jo til å fortvile over; **work by the** — arbeide på akkord. **job** [dʒäb] slå, støte, stikke; pikke; rykke (i tømmene); arbeide (på akkord); sette bort på akkord, leie, hyre; spekulere, jobbe, handle med aksjer; mele sin egen kake, sko seg; ågre. **job** [dʒäb] leie-; — **carriage** leievogn; — **horse** leiehest; — **lot** en slump varer.

jobber ['dʒäbə] akkordarbeider, daglønner, leiekar, lauskar; børsspekulant, jobber; — **in bills** vekselrytter.

jobbery ['dʒäbəri] spekulering, jobbing; misbruk av politisk makt til egen fordel.

joc. fk. f. **jocose; jocular.**

jockey ['dʒäki] jockey, rideknekt; hestehandler; bedrager; ri; ta ved nesen; snyte; lirke og lure seg fram; — **a person out of his money** narre pengene av en; — **-boots** ridestøvler. — **-club** jockeyklubb. **jockeyism** ['dʒäkiizm] jockeyvesen. **jockeyship** ['dʒäkiʃip] ridekunst.

jocko ['dʒäkoᵘ] sjimpanse; apekatt.

jocose [dʒo'koᵘs] munter, spøkefull. **jocular** ['dʒäkjulə] spøkefull. **jocularity** [dʒäkju'läriti] munterhet. **jocularly** ['dʒäkjuləli] i spøk.

jocund ['dʒäkənd] lystig. **jocundity** [dʒo'kʌnditi] lystighet.

Joe [dʒoᵘ] Josef; — **Miller** forfatter av en bok med vittigheter; **a** — **Miller** en gammel vittighet.

jog [dʒäg] ryste, skumple (om en vogn); nugge i; dilte, rusle, lunke; støt, skubb, puff; **give his memory a** — få en til å huske på noe.

joggle ['dʒägl] skubbe, støte; skumpe; riste; bli skubbet; støt.

jogtrot ['dʒägtråt] dilt; gammel slendrian.

Johannesburg [dʒoᵘ'hänisbəˑg] Johannesburg.

John [dʒän] Johannes, Jon; — **Bull** alm. navn på engelskmannen; **St. John's day** sankthansdag, jonsokdag; — **Doe** Peder Ås (juridisk).

Johnny ['dʒäni] Vesle-Jon; fyr, kar; spjert, sprett. — **Raw** nybegynner, jypling.

Johnson ['dʒänsən] Johnson. **Johnsonese** ['dʒånsə'niˑz] johnsonsk (etter dr. Samuel Johnson).

join [dʒoin] forbinde, forene, skjøte, sammenføye; slutte seg til, slå lag med, være med, forene seg; **what God hath joined together, let no man put asunder** hva Gud har sammenføyd, skal mennesket ikke atskille; — **battle** begynne slag; — **hands** ta hverandre i hånden; — **interest with** gjøre felles sak med, holde med; — **the army** tre inn i hæren; **let us** — **the ladies** la oss gå inn til damene. **join** [dʒoin] sammenføyning, skjøt.

joinder ['dʒoində] forbindelse.

joiner ['dʒoinə] snekker. **joinering** ['dʒoinəriŋ], **joinery** ['dʒoinəri] snekkerarbeid.

joint [dʒoint] sammenføyning, skjøt, hengsle; ledd; stek, stykke (av slakteskrott); **dinner off** (**from**) **the** — middag med en hel stek på bordet; **put out of** — vri av ledd; **set into** — sette i ledd; **the time is out of** — tiden er av lage.

joint [dʒoint] forent, felles, sams; **on** (**for**) — **account** for felles regning; — **concern** interessentselskap.

joint [dʒoint] sammenpasse, felle el. skjøte sammen, forbinde; passe inn i. **jointed** ['dʒointid] forbundet; leddet.

jointer ['dʒointə] skotthøvel, kanthøvel.

jointly ['dʒointli] felles, sams. — **and severally** en for alle og alle for en.

joint-stock [dʒoint'ståk] aksjekapital; — **company** aksjeselskap.

joke [dʒoᵘk] spøk, skjemt, vittighet, vits; spøke, spøke med, skjemte, vitse; **in** — for spøk; **bear** (**take**) **a** — forstå spøk; **crack** (**cut**) **a joke** rive av seg en vittighet; **play a practical** — **upon** him ha ham grovt til beste.

joker ['dʒoᵘkə] spøkefugl, spasmaker.

joking ['dʒoᵘkiŋ] spøk; **there is no** — **with** him han forstår ikke spøk; — **apart** ett spøk, et annet alvor; spøk til side. **jokingly** [-li] for spøk.

jole, joll [dʒoᵘl] se **jowl.**

jollification [dʒälifi'keˑʃən] lystighet, moro, muntert lag. **jollily** ['dʒälili] muntert. **jolliness** ['dʒälinès], **jollity** ['dʒäliti] lystighet, munterhet.

jolly ['dʒäli] livlig, munter, lystig, glad, kipen; trivelig; meget, temmelig; **it was a** — shame det var en stor skam; **we had a** — **spree, a** — **lark** vi morte oss storartet; **we had a** — **bad time of it** vi hadde det temmelig vondt; **he is a** — **good fellow** han er en prektig fyr.

jolly-boat ['dʒäliboᵘt] jolle.

jolt [dʒoᵘlt] skake, skrangle, riste; risting, skumpling.

jolterhead [dʒoᵘltəhed] dumrian, naut, kjøtthue.

Jonah ['dʒoᵘnə] Jonas.

Jonathan [dʒo'nånəbən; -än] Jonatan; **Brother** — alm. navn på en amerikaner.

Jones [dʒoᵘnz] Jones.

jorum ['dʒåˑrəm] stor drikkebolle, skål.

Joseph ['dʒoᵘzéf] (forkortet: **Jos.**) Josef.

joskin ['dʒåskin] bondeslamp.
joss [dʒås] kinesisk gudebilde. **-house** kinesisk tempel.
jostle ['dʒåsl] skubbe, støte, dunke.
jot [dʒåt] jota; prikk, punkt, minste grann; notere, opptegne; rable ned; **not a** — ikke det minste grann; — **down** rable ned. **jotting-book** notisbok.
jounce [dʒauns] skumple, skake, riste.
journal ['dʒə·nəl] journal, dagbok; dagblad, tidsskrift; (aksel-)tapp. **journalise** ['dʒə·nəlaiz] journalisere, føre inn i dagbok, bokføre; drive bladvirksomhet. **journalism** ['dʒə·nəlizm] journalistikk. **journalist** [-list] journalist, bladmann. **journalistic** [dʒə·nə'listik] journalistisk; dagblads-.
journey ['dʒə·ni] reise, ferd (mest til lands); reise; — **on business** forretningsreise; **a pleasant** — god tur; **go (make) a** — foreta en reise. **journeyer** ['dʒə·niə] reisende.
journey-man ['dʒə·nimən] lauskar; håndverkssvenn. **journey-men's school** håndverkerskole.
joust [dʒu·st] turnering; turnere.
Jove [dʒoᵘv] Jupiter; **by** — min santen; sannelig.
jovial ['dʒoᵘvjəl] munter, gladlyndt, hyggelig. **joviality** [dʒoᵘvi'äliti] munterhet.
jowl [dʒaul, dʒoᵘl] kjake, kinn; tvehake; hode (på fisk); **cheek by jowl** i fortrolig nærhet, side om side.
joy [dʒoi] glede, fryd, lykke; **wish him** — ønske ham til lykke. **joyful** ['dʒoiful] lystig, glad. **joyfully** med glede. **joyfulness** [-nés] glede. **joyless** ['dʒoilés] gledeløs, uglad. **joyous** ['dʒoiəs] glad, munter; gledelig. **joyousness** [-nés] glede.
J. P. ['dʒei'pi·] fk. f. **Justice of the Peace** fredsdommer.
Jr. fk. f. **junior.**
jubilant ['dʒu·bilənt] jublende.
jubilee ['dʒu·bili·] jubileum, jubelfest, jubelår; jubel.
Judaic [dʒu'de'ik] jødisk.
Judaism ['dʒu·dəizm] jødedom.
Judas ['dʒu·dəs] Judas.
judge [dʒʌdʒ] dommer; skjønner, kunstkjenner; sakkyndig; **Book of Judges** Dommernes bok; **be a** — **of pictures** ha forstand på malerier.
judge [dʒʌdʒ] dømme; felle dom; bedømme, anse for; dømme etter; slutte; — **for yourself** du kan selv dømme; — **not that ye be not judged** døm ikke, at I ikke selv skal dømmes; **you may** — (**of) my astonishment** De kan tenke Dem min forundring. **judgment** ['dʒʌdʒmənt] dom; mening; dømmekraft; skjønn, forstand; **day of judgment** dommedag. **judgment-seat** dommersete.
judicatory ['dʒu·dikətəri] dømmende; rettslig; rett, domstol; rettspleie. **judicature** ['dʒu·dikətʃə, -tjuə] jurisdiksjon.
judicial [dʒu'difəl] rettslig; dommer-; doms-; — **murder** justismord; — **sale** tvangsauksjon. **judicially** [dʒu'difəli] rettslig. **judiciary** [dʒu·'difiəri] dømmende; dømmende myndighet, domstol. **judicious** [dʒu'difəs] klok, skjønnsom. **judiciousness** [-nés] forstandighet, klokskap, innsikt.
Judith ['dʒu·diþ] Judit. **Judy** ['dʒu·di] Judy, Mr. Punchs hustru i dukkekomedien.
jug [dʒʌg] mugge, krukke; fexgsel, «kakebu»; koke i vannbad.
Juggernaut ['dʒʌgənå·t] indisk avgud.
juggle ['dʒʌgl] gjøre tryllekunster; narre; tryllekunst; — **people out of their money** narre pengene fra folk. **juggler** ['dʒʌglə] tryllekunstner, taskenspiller. **jugglery** ['dʒʌgləri] taskenspillerkunst; bedrageri.
Jugo-Slav ['ju·gosla·v] jugoslav, jugoslavisk. **Jugo-Slavia** Jugoslavia.
jugular ['dʒu·gjulə] hals-; halsåre.
jugulate ['dʒu·gjule't] stanse en sykdom med hestekur.
juice [dʒu·s] saft; væske; (sl.) motorolje el.

elektrisk kraft til maskin. **juiceless** [-lés] saftløs. **juiciness** ['dʒu·sinés] saftfullhet. **juicy** ['dʒu·si] saftfull, saftig.
jujitsu [dʒu·'dʒitsu·], **jujutsu** [dʒu·dʒət'su·] jiujitsu (japansk brytning).
jujube ['dʒu·dʒu·b] brystbær; brystbærdråper; brystsukker.
julep ['dʒu·lip] søt drikk, srl. som skal gjøre det lettere å ta besk medisin; (amr.) krydret pjolter.
Julia ['dʒu·ljə] Julia, Julie. **Julian** ['dʒu·ljən] juliansk, Julian; — **account** juliansk tidsregning. **Juliet** ['dʒu·ljət] Julie. **Julius** ['dʒu·ljəs] Julius. **July** [dʒu·'lai, dʒu'lai] juli; — **flower** gyllenlakk, hagenellik.
jumble ['dʒʌmbl] kaste sammen, rote sammen, blande sammen; blanding; virvar, røre, rot. — **-sale** salg av forskjellige billige ting på basar.
jump [dʒʌmp] hoppe, bykse, springe, sprette; skvette, kvekke, støkke, stemme overens; la springe; kaste seg over, slå under seg, tilegne seg. — **at** gripe til (el. etter) med begge hender; — **at conclusions** dra forhastede slutninger; — **for joy** danse av glede. **jump** [dʒʌmp] hopp, byks; skvett, støkk; dilla, ølkveis. **jumper** ['dʒʌmpə] gammelt økenavn på metodister; løstsittende lang trøye, kittel, busserull; jumper. **jumping-jack** sprellemann, hallingmann. **jumpy** ['dʒʌmpi] hoppende, urolig, nervøs.
jun., junr. fk. f. **junior.**
junction ['dʒʌŋkʃən] forening, forbindelse; møtested; stasjon hvor jernbanelinjer møtes og forenes; knutepunkt for jernbanen.
juncture ['dʒʌŋktʃə] sammenføyning; forening; tidspunkt, øyeblikk, kritisk øyeblikk.
June [dʒu·n] juni.
jungle ['dʒʌŋgl] jungel, krattskog (i India). **jungly** ['dʒʌŋgli] tettvokst med kratt.
junior ['dʒu·njə] yngre, yngst, junior; **he is my** — **by some years** han er noen år yngre enn jeg. **juniority** [dʒu·ni'äriti] yngre alder, ungdom. **juniper** ['dʒu·nipə] brisk, einer.
junk [dʒʌŋk] gammelt tauverk; skrap, filler; salt kjøtt.
junk [dʒʌŋk] djunke (kinesisk fartøy).
junket ['dʒʌŋkét] dravle, gumme; lystighet, fest, kalas; feste.
Juno ['dʒu·noᵘ] Juno. **Junonian** [dʒu'noᵘnjən] junonisk.
junto ['dʒʌntoᵘ] hemmelig forsamling.
Jupiter ['dʒu·pitə] Jupiter.
juridical [dʒu'ridikl] juridisk, rettslig. **jurisdiction** [dʒuəris'dikʃən] jurisdiksjon, rettsområde. **jurisprudence** [-'pru·dəns] lovkyndighet. **jurisprudent** [-'pru·dənt] lovkyndig. **jurist** ['dʒuərist] jurist, rettslærd. **juristic** [dʒu'ristik] juridisk.
juror ['dʒuərə] edsvoren, jurymann, lagrettesmann, domsmann.
jury ['dʒuəri] jury; samtlige medlemmer av en jury, lagrette; **grand** — anklagejury (som avgjør om det er grunn til å reise anklage), anklagemyndighet; **petty** — eller **common** — lagrette (av inntil 12 medlemmer, for hvem saken føres); **the** — **brought him in guilty** lagretten fant ham skyldig; **be (sit) on the** — være medlem av juryen; — **man** jurymann, lagrettemann.
jury-mast ['dʒuərima·st] nødmast.
just [dʒʌst] rettskaffen, rettvis, rettferdig; redelig; riktig; tilbørlig; just, nettopp, kun, bare; **it is** — **the thing for you** det er nettopp noe for Dem; — **now** nettopp nå; — **by** like ved, tett ved; — **tell me à,** si meg en gang.
just [dʒu·st] turnering; holde turnering.
justice ['dʒʌstis] rettferdighet, rett, rett og skjel; billighet; dommer; **the** — **of his claims** det berettigede i hans krav; **do** — **la** vederfares rettferdighet; **bring to** — anklage, påføre prosess; — **of the peace** fredsdommer (ulønt dommer uten juridisk utdannelse); **Lord chief** — rettspresident (for King's Bench division). **justiceship** ['dʒʌstisʃip] dommerembete; dommerverdig-

het. **justifiable** ['dʒʌstifaiəbl] forsvarlig; bevislig. **justification** [dʒʌstifi'ke'ʃən] rettferdiggjøring, forsvar. **justifier** ['dʒʌstifaiə] forsvarer. **justify** ['dʒʌstifai] rettferdiggjøre, forsvare; berettige.
justle ['dʒʌsl] skubbe, se **jostle.**
justly ['dʒʌstli] med rette, med god grunn.
justness ['dʒʌstnès] rettferdighet, rettferd; riktighet.

jut [dʒʌt] rage fram, springe fram; framspring, framskott, utskott, nov.
jute [dʒuːt] jute, jutehamp.
Jute [dʒuːt] jyde. **Jutish** ['dʒuːtiʃ] jysk.
Jutland ['dʒʌtlənd] Jylland; jysk. **Jutlander** ['dʒʌtləndə] jyde.
juvenile ['dʒuːvinail] ungdommelig; ungdoms-.
juxtaposition [dʒʌkstəpo'ziʃən] sidestilling.

K

K. k [ke'l] k; fk. f. **king; knight.**
Kaffir ['käfə] kaffer.
kail [ke'l] se **kale.**
kailyard ['ke'lja·ᵊd] kålhage, kjøkkenhage; **the Kailyard School** el. **the kailyard novelists,** en skotsk forfattergruppe.
kainite ['ke'nait] kainitt.
Kaiser ['kaizə] tysk keiser.
kakhi ['ka·ki] se **khaki.**
kale [ke'l] kål, srl. grønnkål.
kaleidoscope [kə'laidoskoᵘp] kaleidoskop. **kaleidoscopic** [kəlaido'skåpik] kaleidoskopisk.
kali ['ke'l(a)i, 'ka·li] salturt.
kalium ['ke'liəm] kali.
kangaroo [kängə'ru·] kenguru.
kaolin ['ke'olin] kaolin, porselensleir.
kapok ['ka·påk] plantedun (til putefyll).
karma ['ka·mə] gjerninger som avgjør ens skjebne etter døden; skjebne.
kar(r)oo ['kə'ru·] tørr høyslette (i Sør-Afrika).
kaross [kə'rås] kasteplagg av skinn (i Sør-Afrika).
Kate [ke't] Kari. **Katharine** ['käþərin] Katarina.
katydid ['keitidid] amerikansk skoggrashoppe.
kauri ['kauri] et slags bartre på New Zealand.
kava ['ka·va] slags rusdrikk, laget av en polynesisk vokster.
kavass [kə'väs] tyrkisk politisoldat.
kayak ['kaiäk] kajakk.
K. B. fk. f. **Knight of the Bath; King's Bench.**
K. C. B. E. fk. f. **Knight Commander of the Order of the British Empire.**
K. C. fk. f. **King's Counsel: King's College.**
K. C. B. fk. f. **Knight Commander of the Bath.**
K. C. I. E. fk. f. **Knight Commander of the Order of the Indian Empire.**
K. C. M. G. fk. f. **Knight Commander of the Order of St. Michael and St. George.**
K. C. S. I. fk. f. **Knight Commander of the Order of the Star of India.**
K. C. V. O. fk. f. **Knight Commander of the Victorian Order.**
kea ['keiə] slags grønn papegøye på New Zealand.
Keble ['ki·bl] Keble (personnavn).
keck [kek] ville brekke seg.
kedge [kedʒ] varpanker; varpe, kjekke.
kedgeree [kedʒə'ri·] indisk rett av kokt ris, fisk og egg.
keel [ki·l] kjøl; lekter, kullpram; kjegle; **from the — to the truck** fra kjøl til flaggknapp; fra øverst til nederst. **keel** [k'·l] forsyne med kjøl; seile; vende kjølen i været, kappseise; — **over** kullseile. **keelage** ['ki·lidʒ] havneavgift. **keeler** ['ki·lə] lektermann.
keelman ['ki·lmən] lektermann.
keen [ki·n] heftig, ivrig; skarp; kvass; bitende, gjennomtrengende; nøye; punktlig; skjerpe, kvesse; **be — on** være ivrig etter. **keen-eyed** ['ki·naid] skarpsynt. **keenness** [-nès] ivrighet; skarphet; — **of sight** skarpsynthet.
keen [ki·n] irsk klagesang.
keep [ki·p] holde (beholde, bevare det man har), beholde, besitte; underholde; overholde;

holde ved like; gjemme; ha liggende, ta vare på¦ oppbevare; føre; holde (sitt ord, løfte); holde seg; bli ved med; — **one's bed** holde senga; — **hold of** (on) holde fast på; — **good (bad) hours** komme tidlig (sent) hjem; — **pace with** holde skritt med; — **the peace** holde seg i ro; — **silent** være stille; — **a term** være et semester ved universitetet; — **time** holde takt; — **the country** leve på landet; — **money with a banker** ha penger stående hos en bankier; — **the cash** føre kassen, være kasserer; — **aloof** holde seg borte; — **down** trykke ned; holde i lav pris; — **in** holde inne; la sitte igjen; — **in money** forsyne med penger; — **up appearances** bevare skinnet; **how long did you — it up last night** hvor lenge holdt dere ut i går kveld; — **up with** holde tritt, holde skritt med; **she kept crying** hun ble ved med åt gråte.
keep [ki·p] tilstand; forfatning; bevaring; omsorg; forpleining; slottsfengsel; fangetårn.
keeper ['ki·pə] en som besitter, holder osv.; bevarer, vokter; fangevokter, slutter; bokholder; **K. of the Great Seal, Lord K.** storseglbevarer. — **of the rolls** statsarkivar.
keeping ['ki·piɳ] forvaring; besittelse; underhold; overensstemmelse, samsvar; **be in — with** stemme overens med; **be in good** — være i godt hold.
keepsake ['ki·pse'k] erindring, minne; **by way of** —, **as a** — til minne.
keg [keg] kagge, dunk.
kelp [kelp] tang, tare; tangaske.
kelson ['kelsn] kjølsvin.
Kelt [kelt] se **Celt.**
ken [ken] vite, kjenne; kjennskap; synskrets.
Kenilworth ['kenilwə·þ] Kenilworth.
kennel ['ken(ə)l] rennestein.
kennel ['ken(ə)l] hundehus, hule, hi; oppholde seg i hule; holde i hundehus.
Kensal ['kensəl] **Green** kirkegård i London.
Kensington ['kenziɳtənþ del av London.
Kent [kent] grevskap i det sørøstlige England.
Kentish ['kentiʃ] kentisk, fra Kent.
kentledge ['kentledʒ] ballastjern.
Kentucky ['ken'tʌki] Kentucky.
kept [kept] imperf. og perf. pts. av **keep.**
kerb [kə·b] fortaukant. — **-stone** ['kə·bstoⁿn] kantstein, fortaustein.
kerchief ['kə·tʃif] hodeplagg, tørkle.
kerf [kə·f] skur, skar.
kermes ['kə·mi·z] kermes, rødt fargestoff.
kermis ['kə·mis] marked (i Nederland).
kern [kə·n] fotsoldat i den gamle irske hær.
kern [kə·n] håndkvern; kjerne.
kernel ['kə·n(ə)l] kjerne; sette kjerne.
kerosene ['kerosi·n] petroleum, bakuolje.
kersey ['kə·zi] slags ulltøy, kjersi.
kerseymere ['kə·simiə] kasjmir.
Keswick ['kezik] Keswick (by i England).
ketch [ketʃ] tomastet fartøy.
ketchup ['ketʃəp] en slags sjampinjongsaus.
kettle ['ketl] kjele, gryte; **a fine (pretty)** — **of fish** fine greier.
kettledrum ['ketldrʌm] pauke. **-mer** paukeslager.

kettle-holder ['ketlhoᵘldə] gryteklut.
kettlemender ['ketlmendə] kjelflikker.
kevel ['kevl] kryssholt.
Kew [kju·] Kew.
key [ki·] nøkkel (også i overført bet.); tangent; klaff; toneart; splint, kile; kai; **keep under lock and** — holde under lås og lukke, gjemme omhyggelig; **he has the** — **of the street** han har ikke noen gatedørsnøkkel; han må bli på gata; **the House of Keys** underhuset på øya Man; **and much more to the same** — og så videre i samme duren.
key [ki·] feste, kile fast; stemme, stille; — **up** stemme (instrument); stramme opp.
keyage ['ki·idʒ] havnepenger.
key|board ['ki·bå·ᵊd] tangenter; klaviatur. — **-bugle** ['ki·'bju·gl] klaffhorn. **-hole** nøklehull. **-note** grunntone. — **-plate** låsskilt, nøkleskilt. — **-ring** nøklering. **-stone** ['ki·stoᵘn] sluttstein (i bue); hovedprinsipp.
K. G. fk. f. Knight of the Garter.
kg fk. f. **kilogramme.**
K. G. C. B. fk. f. **Knight of the Grand Cross of the Bath** (storkors av Bathordenen).
khaki ['ka·ki] kakitøy (brukt til militære uniformer).
khan [ka·n, kän] herberge; kan (fyrste).
Khartum [ka·ᵊ'tu·m].
Khedive [ke'di·v] visekonge av Egypt.
kibble ['kibl] jerntønne (til å heise malm opp med); grovhogge (stein).
kibe [kaib] frostsvull.
kibosh [ki'båʃ] vrøvl, vås, tøv; **put the** — **on** gjøre det av med.
kick [kik] sparke, spenne, slå (om hester); spenne (om geværer); slå bakut; — **the beam** bli veid og funnet for lett; — **up a row** gjøre bråk; — **the bucket** krepere. **kick** [kik] spark, spenn.
kickshaw ['kikʃå·] lekkerbisken; bagatell.
kid [kid] narre; narreri.
kid [kid] kje; barn; unge; **-glove** tertefin; **-s** glacéhansker; — **skin** kjeskinn.
kidgloves ['kidglʌvz] glacéhansker.
kidnap ['kidnäp] stjele, røve barn; med list verve folk, huke, slå kloa i. **kidnapper** ['kidnäpə] en som stjeler, røver mennesker.
kidney ['kidni] nyre; art, slags; **all of a** — alle av samme kaliber.
kill [kil] drepe; slakte, slå i hjel; tilintetgjøre; felle, veide, skyte; drap (av vilt); **killer** ['kilə] drapsmann; **killing** ['kiliŋ] drepende, morderisk; drap.
Killarney [ki'la·ᵊni].
kiln [kil(n)] badstue; tørkeovn; kullmile. **-brick** ildfast stein. **-dried** ovntørket.
kilo ['ki·loᵘ] kilo. **kilogramme** ['kilogräm] kilogram. **kilometer, kilometre** ['kilomi·tə] kilometer. **kilowatt** ['kiloẁåt] kilowatt.
kilt [kilt] skottenes skjørt; kiltre opp, brette opp.
kimbo ['kimboᵘ] bøyd, krum; **arms a-** med hendene i siden.
kimono [ki'moᵘnoᵘ] kimono.
kin [kin] slektskap, slekt, ætt, skyldfolk; art; beslektet; **are you any**—**to him** er De skyldt ham? **the next of** — de nærmest beslektede.
kinchin ['kintʃin] barn, unge; — **lay** det å stjele penger fra barn.
kind [kaind] art, slags; naturlig tilstand; **these** **(those)** — **of things** denne (den) slags ting; **the human** — menneskeslekten; **pay in** — betale i varer; **betale** med samme mynt; **taxes paid in** — avgifter betalt in natura; **nothing of the** — aldeles ikke, på ingen måte, var det likt; **what** — **of thing is this** hva slags ting er det; **he is a** — **of fool** han er noe narraktig; **that is** — **of good** det er temmelig godt; **it kinder (kind of)** seemed to me det forekom meg nesten.
kind [kaind] god, snill, vennlig, kjærlig; velvillig; velment; **be so** — **as to, be** — **enough to**

være så vennlig; **with** — **regards yours affectionately** med vennlig hilsen din hengivne; **send one's** — **regards to** sende vennlig hilsen til.
kindergarten ['kindəga·ᵊtn] barnehage.
kind|-hearted ['kaind|ha·ᵊtid] godhjertet. — **-heartedness** [-nès] godmodighet, godt hjerte.
kindle ['kindl] tenne, kveike; gjennomgløde; tennes, fate, fenge.
kindliness ['kaindlinès] vennlighet, blidhet.
kindly ['kaindli] vennlig, kjærlig. **kindness** ['kaindnès] vennlighet, godhet.
kindred ['kindrid] slektskap, skyldskap, slektninger, skyldfolk; ætt; likhet; beslektet.
kine [kain] kyr. **-pox** [-påks] kukopper.
kinema ['kainimə] kinematograf, kino, teater.
kinematograph [kaini'mätogra·f] kinematograf, kino.
king [kiŋ] konge; dam (i damspill); **the Kings** Kongenes bok; **King's Bench Division** overrettens hovedavdeling; **King's Counsel** kongelig advokat, kongelige advokater (et utvalg av barristers); **cotton** —, **iron** — stor bomulls-, jernfabrikant; — **of diamonds, hearts** ruter-, hjerterkonge; **King's Cross** jernbanestasjon i London; **King's (Queen's) evidence** (kronvitne som tidligere ved å angi sine medskyldige ble fri for straff); **a** — **or a beggar** alt eller intet; **there spoke a** — det var kongelige ord; **God save the** — Gud bevare kongen (nasjonalsangen). **king** [kiŋ] gjøre til konge; — **it** spille konge. **king-craft** regjeringskunst; kongelist. **kingdom** ['kiŋdəm] kongedømme, kongerike. **kingly** ['kiŋli] kongelig. **king's-cushion** ['kiŋzkuʃən] gullstol. **king's-evil** ['kiŋz'i·vəl] kjertelsvakhet, skrofulose. **kingship** ['kiŋʃip] kongeverdighet.
kink [kiŋk] kink (bukt på tau), krøll; grille, knep, fiff; slå bukter, danne krøller på. **kinky** ['kiŋki] full av bukter, tettkruset; full av griller.
kinsfolk ['kinzfoᵘk] slektninger, skyldfolk. **kinship** ['kinʃip] slektskap, skyldskap. **kinsman** ['kinzmən] slektning, frende. **kinswoman** kvinnelig slektning, frenke.
kiosk [ki'åsk] kiosk.
Kipling [ki'pliŋ] Kipling.
kipper ['kipə] flekt røykesild; salte og røyke.
kirk [kə·k] (skotsk) kirke.
kirkman ['kə·kmən] medlem av den skotske kirke **(Kirk of Scotland).**
kirk session (skotsk) menighetsråd.
kismet ['kismet] skjebne.
kiss [kis] kysse, kysse hverandre; — **the dust** bite i graset; — **the rod** kysse riset; underkaste seg en straff. **kiss** [kis] kyss. **kisser** ['kisə] kysser. **kissing** ['kisiŋ] kyssing.
kit [kit] kar, butt, ambar, holk; utstyr, (især soldats) utrustning, klær, vadsekk; **in civilian** — sivilkledd.
kitchen ['kitʃin] kjøkken; kabyss. — **-apple** mateple. — **-boy** kjøkkengutt.
kitchener ['kitʃənə] komfyr.
kitchen|-garden ['kitʃin'ga·ᵊdən] kjøkkenhage. **-maid** kjøkkenpike. **-midden** kjøkkenmødding, avfallsdynge, skjelldynge. **-range** komfyr. — **-stairs** kjøkkentrapp (ned fra the hall). — **-steps** kjellertrapp; gardintrapp.
kite [kait] glente; drake (leketøy); **as the** — **flies** bent fram; **fly a** — leke med drake; sette en drake til værs; **fly the** — ri på veksler; drive vekselrytteri; **kiting transactions** vekselrytteri. **kiteflier** vekselrytter. **kite-flying** vekselrytteri.
kith [kiþ] bekjentskap; slektskap; — **and kin** slekt og venner. **kithless** ['kiþlès] frendeløs, som står alene i verden.
kitten ['kitn] kattunge; få kattunger; kisle.
kittle ['kitl] kilden, vanskelig; kile, kildre.
kittlish ['kitliʃ] kilen; vanskelig.
kitty ['kiti] kattunge; pus.
kleptomania [klepto'me'niə] kleptomani. **kleptomaniac** [klepto'me'niäk] kleptoman.

K. L. I. fk. f. **King's Light Infantry.**
Klondike eller **Klondyke** ['klåndaik] Klondike.
km fk. f. **kilometre.**
knack [näk] nips, leketøy; ferdighet, knep, handlag; **you must know the** — **of it** du må kjenne knepet; **he has no** — **in him** han har ikke det rette grepet; **have a** — of ha det med å.
knacker ['näkə] utslitt hest; hestehandler; hesteslakter.
knag [näg] knast, knort, knute; idelig skjenne på. **knaggy** ['nägi] knortet.
knap [näp] slå, smekke; pukke; drøse, skravle; bakkekam, klett.
knapsack ['näpsäk] ransel, skreppe, vadsekk, ryggsekk.
knar [na·ɔ] knort.
knave [ne¹v] knekt, fil (i kortspill); gautjuv; kjeltring; **he is more** — **than fool** han er mer slu enn en tror. **knavery** ['ne¹v(ə)ri] kjeltringstrek. **knavish** ['ne¹viʃ] kjeltringaktig, skalkaktig. **knavishness** [-nés] kjeltringaktighet.
knead [ni·d] elte, kna deig. **-ing-trough** ['ni·diŋ-trå·f] deigtrau.
knee [ni·] kne; fang; **go on one's** **-s** falle på. kne; **housemaid's** — betennelse i kneskjellet **in-kneed** kalvbeint, **out-kneed** hjulbeint.
knejoint ['ni·dʒoint] kneledd.
kneel [ni·l] knele. **kneeler** ['ni·lə] knelende.
kneepan ['ni·¹pän] kneskjell.
knell [nel] klemting, likringing; ringe, klemte.
Knickerbocker ['nikəbåkə] new-yorker (især av gammel hollandsk familie); **knickerbockers** [-z], **knickers** ['nikəz] vide knebukser; (nu alm.) damebenklær.
knick-knack ['niknäk] leketøy; nips.
knife [nai‍f] kniv; **war to the** — krig på kniven; **erasing** — raderkniv; **play a good** — **and fork** spise godt; — **it** hold opp! —**board** pussebrett; benk på taket av buss. —**-rest** kniv-bukk (til å legge kniver på for å skåne duken).
knight [nait] ridder; nå en som har rang nærmest under baronett og rett til tittelen **Sir;** springer, hest (i sjakkspill); slå til ridder, utnevne til ridder; — **of the brush** maler; skopusser; skorsteinsfeier; — **of the napkin** oppvarter; — **of the wheel** syklist; — **of the whip** kusk.
knight-errant ['nait'erənt] vandrende ridder.
knighthood ['naithud] ridderskap.
Knightsbridge ['naitsbridʒ] gate i London.
Knight-Templar ['nait'templə] tempelherre.
knit [nit] knytte, binde, strikke; knytte sammen, forene; rynke; bunding, strikning; — **the brows** rynke pannen. **knitter** ['nitə] en som strikker. **knitting** strikketøy. **knitting-needle** strikkepinne.
knob [nåb] knopp, knute; knott, dørhåndtak; slå knuter på, knope; **press the** — trykke på den elektriske knappen. **knobby** ['nåbi] knudret; knutet; knubbet, trassig.
knock [nåk] banke, hamre, slå, dunke; kakke; **somebody -s** det banker; — **about** drive (el. reke) omkring, slenge; — **down** slå til jorda; slå til, gi tilslag på (på en auksjon); — **up** vekke ved å banke på døra; ase ut; slag, støt; dunk, banking; — **at the door** banke på døra; **there is**

a — **at the door** det banker; **double** — kort dobbeltslag med dørhammeren; **single** — enkeltslag (av arbeidere, tjenere o. l.). — **-about hat** bulehatt. — **-about work** løsarbeid.
knocker ['nåkə] en som banker; dørhammer; **muffled** — omviklet dørhammer (til tegn på at det er en syk i huset). **knocking** ['nåkiŋ] banking.
knock-kneed ['nåk'ni·d] kalvbeint.
knoll [no⁹l] haug; koll; fjellknaus.
knoll [no⁹l] ringe, klemte; ringing, klemting.
knot [nåt] knute; løkke, sløyfe; knop, stikk; gruppe, klynge, samling; knort; kvist; ledd; klump; knop (kvartmil i timen); knytte; slå knute på; forvikle: knope; rynke (brynene); **Admiralty** — engelsk sjømil (1854,965 meter); **knotted** ['nåtid] knutet, knortet. **knottiness** ['nåtinés] knudrethet, forvikling, vanskelighet. **knotty** ['nåti] knudret, innviklet, floket, vanskelig.
knout [naut] knutt, russisk pisk.
know [no⁹] vite, kjenne, kjenne til, vite om, kjenne igjen; få vite, bli kjent med; forstå seg på; — **a person by sight** kjenne en av utseende; **come to** — få greie på; — **better** vite bedre; **there is no -ing** en kan ikke vite; — **of** kjenne til; — **a lesson** kunne en lekse. **knowable** ['no⁹əbl] som kan vites. **knower** ['no⁹ə] kjenner; som vet. **knowing** ['no⁹iŋ] kyndig, erfaren; gløgg; slu; **a knowing one** en kjenner. **knowingly** [-li] forstandig.
knowledge ['nålidʒ] kunnskap, kjennskap, erfaring; **to my** — så vidt jeg vet; **much** — mange kunnskaper; — **of** kjennskap til.
Knox [nåks] Knox.
Knt. fk. f. **knight.**
knuckle ['nʌkl] knoke; skank (av en kalv); kjøttknoke; ledd; banke, slå med knokene. — **-bones** en slags spill el. leik med bein. — **-duster** jernknoke, slåsshanske.
kobold ['ko⁹bo⁹ld] nisse, dverg.
kodak ['ko⁹däk] kodak, fotografiapparat; fotografere; skildre livlig.
Kohinoor [ko⁹i'nuə] Kohinoor (en briljant).
kop [kåp] haug, kolle, topp.
kopje ['kåpji] = **kop.**
Koran [ko'ra·n, kå·'ra·n, 'kå·rän] koranen.
K. O. S. B. fk. f. **King's Own Scottish Borderers.**
kotow ['ko⁹tau] kaste seg nesegrus (kinesisk hilsen); ligge på maven, smiske for.
K. O. Y. L. I. fk. f. **King's Own Yorkshire Light Infantry.**
K. P. fk. f. **Knight of St. Patrick.**
kraal [kra·l] kra(a)l, sørafrikansk landsby.
kraken ['kra·kən] krake (fabeldyr i sjøen).
K. R. R. fk. f. **King's Royal Rifles.**
K. T. fk. f. **Knight of the Thistle.**
K. fk. f. **knight.**
Ku-Klux-Klan ['kju·'klʌks'klän] Kukluxklanen (hemmelig selskap i sørstatene med det oppr. hovedformål å holde negrene nede).
Kurd [kə·d] kurder(inne); kurdisk.
Kurdistan [kə·di'sta·n] Kurdistan.
Ky. fk. f. **Kentucky.**

L

L, 1 [el] L, l. **L.** fk. f. **libra** ɔ: pound(s) sterling, pund i penger (især stilt således: 25 l. eller £ 25).
the three L's (lead blylodd; **latitude** breddegrad; **lookout** utkik), som er av betydning for sjømannen.
l. fk. f. **lake; left; lane; latitude; league; libra** (pund); **lire; litre(s).**
l. a. fk. f. **last account** siste regning.

L. A. fk. f. **Law Agent.**
laager ['la·gə] leir, srl. vognborg; sette i vognborg.
label ['le¹bl] seddel, merkelapp, merke, etikett; tillegg til dokument, kodisill; stykke papir som seglet henges ved; merke; etikettere, sette merkelapp på.
labial ['le¹biəl] lepe-, leppe-, labial; leppelyd. **-ize** [-aiz] labialisere, runde.

labiodental ['leɪbioʊˈdentl] labiodental, leppe-tannlyd.

laboratory ['læb(ə)rətəri; man hører også lä-ˈbårətəri] laboratorium.

laborious [ləˈbáˑriəs] møysommelig; slitsom, strevsom, arbeidsom. **laboriousness** [-nĕs] besværlighet; arbeidsomhet.

labour ['leɪbə] arbeid; anstrengelse, besvær, strev, slit; fødselssmerter; arbeiderne, arbeider-klassen, arbeiderpartiet; arbeid; streve, slite, stri med; arbeide på, bearbeide; **Labour Exchange** arbeidsanvisningskontor; — **leaders** arbeiderførere (især fagforeningsførere). — **-market** arbeidsmarked. — **of Hercules** kjempearbeid. — **of love** kjært arbeid. **Knights of Labour** arbeidets riddere (amerikansk arbeiderforening). — **party** arbeiderpartiet; **hard** — tvangsarbeid; **lost** — spilte anstrengelser; — **at a thing** arbeide på noe; — **on the way** arbeide seg framover veien; — **under** lide under, ha å kjempe med; streve med; — **under difficulties** kjempe med vanskeligheter; **you** — **under a strange mistake** De befinner Dem i en merkelig misforståelse.

labourage ['leɪbəridʒ] arbeidspenger.

laboured ['leɪbəd] kunstlet, anstrengt, forseggjort.

labourer ['leɪbərə] arbeider, arbeidskar; håndlanger.

Labrador ['læbrədåˑ⁹] Labrador.

laburnum [ləˈbəˑnəm] gullregn.

labyrinth ['læbirinþ] labyrint. **labyrinthic** [læbiˈrinþik] labyrintisk. **labyrinthine** [læbiˈrinþain] labyrintisk.

L. A. C. fk. f. **London Athletic Club.**

lace [leɪs] snor; lisse; tresse; distinksjoner; kniplinger; snøre; kante, sette tresser el. kniplinger på; snøres; snøre seg. **-d boots** snørestøvler. **lace-pillow** ['leɪsˈpiloʊ] kniplepute.

lacerate ['læsəreɪt] rive sund, flerre, rive opp. **laceration** [læsəˈreɪʃən] sundriving; rift, flerre. **laches** ['lætʃiz] forsømmelse.

lachrymal ['lækriməl] tåre-; — **duct** tåregang; — **gland** tårekjertel.

lachrymatory ['lækrimətəri] tåreflaske (fra antikke graver); — **shell** tåregassbombe.

lachrymose ['lækrimoʊˢs] tårefull; begretelig; **be** — være en tåreperse.

lacing ['leɪsiŋ] snorer, snøreband, lisser; border, tresser.

lack [læk] mangel, skort, trang, nød; vante, mangle, lide mangel på; skorte; **there was no** — **of** det skortet ikke på; **for** — **of** av mangel på; **be -ing** in mangle.

lackadaisical [lækəˈdeɪzikl] søtlaten, affektert (overlegen, fin, sart).

lackaday ['lækədeɪ] akk!

lackey ['læki] se **lacquey.**

Lackland ['læklænd], **John** — Johan uten land.

lack-lustre ['læklʌstə] glansløs, dim; glansløshet, dimme.

laconic [ləˈkænik] lakonisk; kort og fyndig. **laconically** [ləˈkánikəli] lakonisk.

lacquer ['lækə] lakkferniss, lakering; fernisere, lakere. **lacquerer** ['lækərə] lakerer.

lacquey ['læki] lakei; være tjener, oppvarte.

lacrosse [ləˈkrås] lakrosse (et ballspill).

lactate ['læktert] melkesurt salt; gi die.

lactation [læk'te'ʃən] diegivning.

lacteal ['læktiəl] melke-, lymfe-; — **fever** melkefeber; — **vessel** lymfekar.

lactescent [læk'tesənt] melkaktig; som skiller ut melk.

lactic ['læktik] melke-.

lactometer [læk'tåmitə] melkeprøver.

lactose ['læktoʊˢs] melkesukker.

lacuna [ləˈkjuˑnə] lakune, hull, tomrom.

lacustrine [leɪˈkʌstrin, ləˈkʌstrain] innsjø-; — **dwelling** pålebygning.

lacy ['leɪsi] kniplingaktig.

lad [læd] unggutt, gutt; skotsk: kjærest.

ladder ['lædə] stige; trapp; leider. **companion** — **kahyttstrapp.**

laddie ['lædi] gutt; kjæreste.

lade [leɪd] laste, belesse; besvære; øse. **laden** ['leɪdn] perf. pts. av **lade.**

lading ['leɪdiŋ] ladning, last; lass.

ladle ['leɪdl] sleiv, potasjeskje, øse, støpeskje; skovl (på møllehjul); øse.

ladrone ['lædrən] (skotsk) skarv, fark, fant. **ladrone** [ləˈdroʊⁿ] røver, tyv.

lady ['leɪdi] tittel for damer av en viss rang; frue; husfrue, matmor, hustru, dame; **Our Lady** vår frue, jomfru Maria; **a young** — en ung dame, frøken; **boarding-school for young ladies** pensjonatskole for unge piker; **court** — hoffdame; **ladies and gentlemen** mine damer og herrer; **she is quite the** — hun er fullendt dame; **old** — **of Threadneedle Street** (spøkefullt) navn for Bank of England; — **author** forfatterinne.

lady|-bird, -bug marifly, marihøne.

lady-chair gullstol; **carry in a** — bære på gullstol.

Lady|-chapel Maria-stuke. — **-day** Marias budskapsdag, marimess (25. mars).

ladylike ['leɪdilaik] fin, kvinnelig; **ladylove** ['leɪdilʌv] kjæreste. **lady's-bower** klematis. **lady's companion** eller **lady-companion** selskapsdame. **lady's eardrop** fuksia. **lady's** (el. **ladies'**) **man** kavalér, helt i dameselskap. **lady's-mantle** marikåpe (plante). **lady's-slipper** marisko. **lady's-smock** engkarse.

ladyship ['leɪdiʃip] rang som **lady; her L. was present** hennes nåde var til stede.

lag [læg] som kommer baketter, etternøler; den nederste på en skole; laveste klasse; komme baketter, nøle, slunte, ligge etter.

lag [læg] tønnestav; dekke med staver.

lag [læg] forbryter, straff-fange, fakke, knipe; sette på straffarbeid.

lagan ['leɪgən] vrakgods (som det ligger vakt over).

lager-beer ['laˑgəˈbiə] el. **lager** lagerøl.

laggard ['lægəd] lat, seig, trå, doven; etternøler.

lagging ['lægiŋ] langsom, nølende.

lagoon [ləˈguˑn] lagune, grunn vik.

laic ['leɪik] lek; lekmann.

laid [leɪd] imperf. og perf. pts. av **lay.**

lain [leɪn] perf. pts. av **lie.**

lair [lɛˑə] leie, bol, hi; sete; havn.

laird [læˑəd] godseier, herremann (i Skottland).

laissez-faire ['leɪseɪˈfæˑə] det at regjeringen ikke blander seg inn i privat foretaksomhet.

laity ['leɪiti] lekfolk.

lake [leɪk] lakkfarge.

lake [leɪk] sjø, innsjø, fjord, kanal; **the Lake District** sjødistriktet i Nordvest-England; — **dwelling** pålebygning. — **-poet** sjødikter, forfatter av sjøskolen. **Lake-School** sjøskolen (romantisk dikterskole, hvortil hører: Wordsworth, Coleridge og Southey). **Lakist** ['leɪkist] dikter av sjøskolen.

lam [læm] (slang) slå, denge, jule.

lama ['laˑmə] lama (prest i Tibet).

lama ['laˑmə] lama (dyr) (ogs. **llama**).

lamb [læm] lam, lammekjøtt; lamme.

Lamb [læm] Lamb (eng. forfatter).

lambent ['læmbənt] slikkende, spillende (om ild), bjart; lysende, klar (om vidd, øyne).

Lambeth [læmbeþ] del av London; — **Palace** residens i London for erkebispen av Canterbury.

lambkin ['læmkin] ungt lam.

lamblike ['læmlaik] lamaktig; spak.

lamb-skin ['læmskin] lammeskinn (med ull eller som lær), slags plysj.

lamb's-wool ['læmzwul] lammeull.

lame [leɪm] lam, halt, vanfør; skrøpelig, skral; lamme, gjøre halt; — **in** (el. **of**) **a foot** halt; — **in** (el. **of**) **one arm** med en ubrukelig arm; **a** — **duck** en insolvent person.

lamella [ləˈmelə] tynt blad el. plate.

lameness [-nès] vanførhet; halting.
lament [lə'ment] jamre, klage, syte, beklage seg; beklage; gråte for; klage, jamring; klagesang; **lamented** avdød, salig, **lamentable** ['lämintəbl] beklagelig, ynkelig. **lamentably** ['lämintəbli] sørgelig; jammerlig. **lamentation** [lämin'teɪʃən] klage. **lamenter** [lə'mentə] klagende, sørgende.
lamina ['läminə] tynn plate, tynn hinne. **laminate** ['lämineɪt] valse ut, kløyve i skiver; ['läminèt] lagdannet.
lamish ['leɪmiʃ] noe halt, noe vanfør.
Lammas ['läməs] en fest for brød av den nye høst; 1. august; **at latter** — (for spøk) = aldri.
lamp [lämp] lampe, (faststående) lykt; **ex-tinguish (put out) a** — slokke en lampe; **light a** — tenne.
lamp|black ['lämp'bläk] kjønrøk. — **-chimney** lampeglass. — **-cotton** lampeveike.
lamplight ['lämplait] lampelys, kunstig lys, kveldslys.
lamp-lighter ['lämplaitə] lyktetenner.
lampoon [läm'puˑn] smededikt.
lampooner [läm'puˑnə] smededikter.
lamp-post ['lämppuˑst] lyktestolpe.
lamprey ['lämpri] niøye.
Lancashire ['läŋkəʃə] Lancashire.
Lancaster ['läŋkəstə] Lancaster.
lance [laˑns] lanse, spyd; lansedrager; gjen-nombore. **lancer** ['laˑnsə] lansenér; i plur. the lancers lanciers (en dans).
Lancs. fk. f. **Lancashire.**
land [länd] land, landjord; åkerteig; land, folk, rike; jord, jordsmonn; gods; **lord of lands** jord-drott; **go by** — reise til lands; **native** — hjemland; — **of promise** det forjettede land; **see how the** — lies se hvorledes sakene står. **land** [länd] bringe i land, landsette; losse; sette av (en vogn); lande, havne; **landed** grunneier-, som eier grunn, grunn-; **landed proprietor** godseier. **land-agent** eiendomsmekler; gårdsbestyrer. **land-breeze** fra-landsbris, landgule. **landfall** ['ländfåˑl] jordras; landkjenning. **land-forces** landtropper. **land-grabber** en som krafser til seg jord på ulovlig vis; (i Irland) en som tar land etter bortjagd leilending.
land|grave ['ländgreˑv] landgreve. **-gravine** ['ländgrəviˑn] landgrevinne. **-holder** ['ländhoˑuldə] jordeier, grunneier.
landing ['ländiŋ] landing; landgang; stø, lan-dingsplass; trappegang, trappeavsats; — **charges** omkostninger ved ilandbringing. — **place** andgangssted; trappeavsats. — **-stage** brygge.
landlady ['länleˑidi] vertinne (som leier ut væ-relser el. har gjestgiveri el. pensjonat). **landlocked** ['ländläkt] omgitt av land. **landloper** ['ländloˑupə] landstryker. **landlord** ['länlåˑəd] godseier; vert (især husvert el. hotellvert). **landlordism** ['länlåˑə-dizm] godseiersystemet. **landlubber** ['ländlʌbə] landkrabbe. **landmark** ['ländmaˑək] dele, grense-merke; landmerke, landkjenning; milepel.
landscape ['länskeˑip] landskap; — **painting** landskapsmaleri.
Landseer ['länsiə] Landseer.
Land's End ['ländz'end] sørvestligste odde av England, i Cornwall.
landslide ['ländslaid] jordskred.
landsman ['ländzmən] landkrabbe.
land-steward ['länd'stjuˑəd] godsforvalter.
land-tax ['ländtäks] grunnskatt.
lane [leˑin] smal vei (mellom gjerder e. l.), gutu, geil, strede, smal gate; gang; espalier; råk.
lang syne ['läŋ'sain] (skotsk) for lenge siden.
language ['läŋgwidʒ] språk, mål, tunge; **in a** — på et språk; **finger** — fingerspråk; — **of flowers** blomsterspråk; — **of signs** tegnspråk; **teacher of -s** språklærer; **use bad** — banne; **strong** — kraft-uttrykk, eder.
languid ['läŋgwid] treg, matt, blasert; flau; **trade is in a very** — **state** handelen er meget flau.

languish ['läŋgwiʃ] bli matt, sykne bort, dovne, slakne, sløves; smekte, vansmekte; **languishment** [-mənt] matthet, slapphet; smekting. **languishing-ly** [-inli] smektende. **languor** ['läŋgwə, 'läŋgə] matthet, kraftløshet, vanmakt.
lank [läŋk] tynn, skrinn, mager, slank; slapp, hengslet, lealaus; matt. **lankish** ['läŋkiʃ] noe slank, noe slapp. **lankly** ['länkli] slunkent, slapt. **lankness** [-nès] tynnhet, magerhet. **lanky** ['läŋki] mager, tynn, skranten, skranglet, opp-løpen.
lanolin(e) ['länolin] lanolin.
lansquenet ['länskinet] landsknekt, leiesoldat.
lantern ['läntən] lanterne, lykt; **dark** — blend-lykt. — **-slides** lysbilder. — **views** lysbilder.
lanyard ['länjəd] taljereip.
lap [läp] kepje, slikke, sleike, skvulpe, skvalpe; skvalping, skval, skvip, søl.
lap [läp] flik, flak, snipp; fang, skjøt; overleg-ning; — **of the ear** øreflipp; **everything falls in her** — hun kommer sovende til alt; **in the** — **of luxury** i rikdommens skjøt. **lap** [läp] folde, brette, vikle, tulle omkring; — **over** ligge over, være brett over. **lap-dog** skjøtehund. **lap-eared** med hengeører.
lapel [lə'pel] oppslag på frakk; **-led** med opp-slag.
lapidary ['läpidəri] kjenner av edelsteiner; stein-skjærer; lapidar, hogd i stein; kort og treffende, fyndig; **lapidify** [lə'pidifai] forsteine, forsteines.
lapis-lazuli [läpis'läzjulai] lasurstein.
Lapland ['läpländ] Lappland; (spøkende) fang. **Laplander** ['läpländə] lapplending. **Lapp** [läp] lapp, finn, lappekvinne; lappisk.
lappet ['läpit] flik, snipp, flak; brett; ørelapper.
Lappish ['läpiʃ] lappisk.
lapse [läps] fall; feil, mistak; forløp (av tid); forfall; falle, gli; begå en feil; bli ugyldig.
lapwing ['läpwiŋ] vipe.
larboard ['laˑˑbåˑəd] babord, babords- (nå av-løst av ordet **port**).
larcener ['laˑəsinə], **larcenist** ['laˑəsinist] tyv. **larcenous** ['laˑəsinəs] tyv-, tyvaktig.
larceny ['laˑəsni] tyveri.
larch [laˑətʃ] lerketre.
lard [laˑəd] flesk, smult; spekke, stappe. **larder** ['laˑədə] spiskammer. **larderer** ['laˑədərə] provi-antmester.
larding ['laˑədiŋ] stapping. — **-bacon** stappe-flesk. — **-pin** stappenål.
lardy ['laˑˑdi] full av fett, smult-.
large [laˑədʒ] stor, bred, brei, tykk; utstrakt, vid, rommelig; raust, gjev; omfattende; tallrik; **as — as life** i legemsstørrelse; **on a** — **scale** i stor målestokk; **be in a** — **way (of business)** drive forretning i stor stil; **go at** — gå fritt omkring, på frifot. **set at** — frigi; **talk at** — tale vidt og bredt; **the world at** — hele verden; **sail** — gå for en slør. — **-featured** med grove trekk. — **-hearted** edel, gjev, høysinnet. — **-limbed** sværlemmet.
largely [-li] i stor utstrekning. **largeness** [-nès] betydelig størrelse, stor utstrekning, størrelse.
largish [laˑədʒiʃ] stor, stor av seg.
lariat [läriät] lasso, renneløkke.
lark [laˑək] lerke; fange lerker.
lark [laˑək] moro, leven; holde moro el. leven; **they were up to their -s** de var ute med sine gale streker; **wasn't that a** — var det ikke moro.
larkspur ['laˑəkspəˑ] torskemunn; ridderspore.
larum ['lärəm] larmsignal; vekkerur.
larva ['laˑəvə], plur. **larvae** ['laˑˑviˑ] larve, åme.
laryngal [lə'riŋgl], **laryngeal** [lə'rindʒiəl] strupe-.
laryngitis [lərin'dʒaitis] laryngitis.
laryngoscope [lə'riŋgəskoˑup] strupespeil.
larynx ['läriŋks] strupehode.
Lascar ['läskə] indisk sjømann.
lascivious [lə'sivjəs] lysten, vellystig.
lash [läʃ] piskeslag; smekk; snert; svepe; rapp, slag; øyehår; piske; snerte; gjennomhegle; surre; — **out** slå seg løs, sparke bakut. **lasher** ['läʃə]

en som pisker; skyllregn. **lashing** ['läʃiŋ] surring.
lass [läs, la·s] pike, jente; tøs. **lassie** ['läsi] ung pike, småjente.
lassitude ['läsitju·d] utmattelse, tretthet.
lasso ['läsoᵘ] lasso, rennesnare; fange med lasso.
last [la·st] lest; **stick to one's** — bli ved sin lest.
last [la·st] sist, ytterst, nest foregående, forrige; det siste; ende; — **of all** aller sist; — **but one** nest sist; — **but two** tredje sist; **our** — **respects** vår siste skrivelse; —, **(but) no least** sist, men ikke minst; ikke å forglemme; — **night** i går kveld; — **week** forrige uke; — **year** i fjor; **at** — til sist, endelig; **breathe one's** — dra sitt siste sukk, dø; **to the very** — til det aller siste; **this time** — **year** i fjor på denne tiden; **the** — **importance** den største viktighet.
last [la·st] vare, vedvare, holde seg; varighet, holdbarhet, utholdenhet; **he cannot** — **much longer** han gjør det ikke stort lenger.
lasting ['la·sting] varig; holdbar; varighet; lasting (slags tøy). **lastingly** [-li] varig; **lastingness** [-nès] varighet.
lastly ['la·stli] endelig, til sist (i oppregning).
lat. fk. f. **latitude.**
latch [lätʃ] klinke, slå; smekklås; lukke med klinke.
latchet ['lätʃit] skoreim.
latch-key ['lätʃki·] gatedørsnøkkel, entrénøkkel.
late [le·t] sen, sein; for sen; forsinket; forhenværende; nylig; avdød, salig; **be (too)** — komme for sent; **keep** — **hours** bli lenge oppe, komme sent hjem; **the** — **Mr. N.** avdøde hr. N.; **of** — nylig, for kort tid siden; **of** — **years** i de senere år; **it is** — klokka er mange; **sit up** — sitte lenge oppe; **sit** — **at dinner** sitte lenge til bords.
lateen [lə'ti·n]; — **sail** latinerseil.
lately ['le·tli] nylig; i den senere tid.
lateness ['le·tnès] senhet, sen tid.
latent ['le·tənt] skjult; latent, bunden.
later ['le·tə] senere, nyere; — **on** senere.
latest ['le·tist] senest, sist, nyest; **at** — det siste; — **fashion** nyeste mote.
lath [la·þ] lekte; forskallingsbord; slå lekter over.
lathe [le·ð] dreiebenk; slagbom (i vevstol).
lather ['lä·ðə] skumme; såpe inn; bli skumsvett; skumming, skum; såpeskum; skumsvette.
Latin ['lätin] latin, latiner; latinsk. **Latinism** ['lätinizm] latinsk uttrykk. **Latinist** ['lätinist] latiner. **Latinity** [lə'tiniti] (korrekt) latin.
latitude ['lätitju·d] bredde; polhøyde; frihet, spillerom, utstrekning.
latitudinarian [lätitju·di'næ·°riən] frisinnet, frilynt, tolerant. —**ism** [-izm] toleranse.
latten [lätn] messing. —**brass** messingblikk.
latter ['lätə] sist (av to), senere, nyere, sistnevnte; **the** — (motsatt **former**) denne, dette, disse; **the** — **end** slutningen. — **day** nåtids-; **the Latter-day Saints** de siste dagers hellige, mormonene. **latterly** [-li] i den senere tid; nylig.
lattice ['lätis] gitter; forsyne med gitter; — **window** gittervindu; blyinnfattet vindu. **-d window** gittervindu; blyinnfattet vindu.
lattice-work ['lätiswə·k] gitterverk.
Latvia ['lätviə] Latvia.
laudable ['lå·dəbl] rosverdig; godartet.
laudanum ['lå·dənəm] opiumsdråper.
landation [lå·'de¹ʃən] lov, pris, ros, lovprising.
laudatory ['lå·dətəri] lovprisende; lovprising.
laugh [la·f] le; smile; si leende; latter. — **at** le av; le ut; — **in one's sleeve** le hemmelig, le i skjegget; — **to scorn** le ut, gjøre to latter; — **out** le av full hals; **he -s best who -s last** den som ler sist, ler best; **have the** — **of** triumfere over; **the** — **was turned against her** latteren vendte seg mot henne; **break out into a loud** — le høyt opp.

laughable [la·fəbl] latterlig.
laugher ['la·fə] en som ler.
laughing ['la·fiŋ] latter. — **-gas** lystgass. — **-gull** hettemåke. **this is no** — **matter** dette er ikke noe å le av. — **-stock** skive for latter.
laughter ['la·ftə] latter.
launch [lå·n(t)ʃ, la·n(t)ʃ] slynge ut, kaste ut; sette på vannet, la gå av stabelen; gå av stabelen; utbre seg vidløftig; legge i vei; avløpning; barkasse; **the** — **into life** første skritt ut i livet; **launching** ['lå·n(t)ʃiŋ, 'la·n(t)ʃiŋ] utskytning; avløpning.
launder ['lå·ndə] vaske.
laundress ['lå·ndrès] vaskekone.
laundry ['lå·ndri] vask, vasking; vaskeri. **-man** vasker. **-works** vaskeri.
laureate ['lå·riét] laubærkronet el. -kranset; kronet; **poet** — hoffdikter. **-ship** stilling som hoffdikter.
laurel ['lårəl] laurbær, laurbærtre; krone med laurbær.
lava ['la·və] lava.
lavabo [lə'veʲboᵘ] håndvask (i kirke el. kloster); vaskefat.
lavatory ['lävətəri] toalett, W. C., vaskerom.
lavender ['lävində] lavendel; lavendelfarget; parfymere med lavendel; **lay up in** — legge bort (tøy) med lavendler; gjemme omhyggelig.
lavish ['läviʃ] ødsel; raust; rundhåndet; ødsle med, sløse med. **lavishly** ['läviʃli] med ødsel hånd. **lavishment** ['läviʃmənt] sløsing. **lavishness** [-nès] ødselhet, sløseri.
law [lå·] jøss!
law [lå·] lov, rett, prosess; rettsvitenskap, jus; **-s catch flies but let hornets go free** de små tyvene henger man, de store lar man gå; **necessity has no** — nød bryter alle lover; **be at** — føre prosess; **go to the** — studere jus; **go to** — **with** anlegge sak, anklage; **have the** — **of** anklage; **civil** — borgerlig rett; **ten minutes'** — ti minutters forsprang; **give** — **to a person** gi en en frist.
law|-abiding ['lå·əbaidiŋ] lovlydig. — **-agent** (skotsk) sakfører, prokurator. —**-breaker** lovovertreder. —**-court** rettslokale, i plur.: justisbygning.
lawful ['lå·f(u)l] lovlig, rettmessig. **lawfully** ['lå·fuli] lovlig. **lawfulness** ['lå·f(u)lnès] lovlighet, rettmessighet.
law-giver ['lå·givə] lovgiver.
lawless ['lå·lès] ulovlig; lovløs.
law|-lord ['lå·lå·ºd] juridisk kyndig medlem av overhuset. — **-maker** lovgiver.
law merchant handelslovgivning.
lawn [lå·n] lawn (en slags fint lerret), lawnermer (på biskops ornat); bispeembete.
lawn [lå·n] åpen grasflekk i skogen; grasplen. — **-mower** plenklipper (maskin).
lawn-sleeves ['lå·nsli·vz] lawnermer, bispeembete.
lawn-sprinkler ['lå·n'spriŋklə] plenvanner.
lawn-tennis ['lå·n'tenis] lawntennis.
lawny ['lå·ni] jevn, jamn, plenaktig.
law-suit ['lå·sju·t] prosess, rettssak, søksmål.
lawyer ['lå·jə] jurist, sakfører.
lax [läks] løs, slapp, slakk. **laxative** ['läksətiv] avførende; avførende middel. **laxity** ['läksiti] slapphet, løshet. **laxness** [-nès] slapphet.
lay [leʲ] legge, sette, stille; legge i bakken, få til å legge seg; dempe; døyve; — **the table,** — **the cloth** dekke bordet; **I'll** — **ten** to one jeg holder 10 mot 1; — **about one** slå om seg; — **aside** legge til side, legge av; — **by** legge bort; legge opp; — **down the law** legge ut, forklare loven; — **in** forsyne seg med, ta inn, hauge opp, samle; — **off** avlegge; — **on** legge på, legge inn, anlegge; slå, banke; — **out** legge fram; legge ut; anlegge; kik tok legg det til skue; gi ut (penger); — **up** legge opp, samle; stenge inne, tvinge til å holde senga.
lay [leʲ] imperf. av **lie** i betydningen «ligge».

lay [le¹] lag; retning, stilling; lott; lur, søvn; fag, spesialitet; arbeid, jobb, yrke.
lay [le¹] sang, kvad, dikt, vise.
lay [le¹] lek, ulærd; lekmanns-; — **habit** verdslig drakt; — **lords** ikke juridiske lorder i parlamentet. **lay-brother** lekbror.
lay-day ['le¹de¹] liggedag.
layer ['le¹ə] en som legger; verpehøne; deltager i veddemål.
layer ['le¹ə] lag, flo; avlegger.
layette [le¹'et] tøy etc. til nyfødt.
lya-figure ['le¹¹figə] trefigur med bevegelige ledd, til å henge draperier på; stråmann.
layman ['le¹mən] lekmann.
lazaretto [läze¹reto] lasarett.
Lazarus ['läzərəs] Lasarus.
laze [le¹z] late seg, dovne seg. **lazily** ['le¹zili] dovent. **laziness** ['le¹zinès] dovenskap.
lazuli ['läzjulai] lasurstein.
lazy ['le¹zị] doven, lat. — **-bones** ['le¹zibo²nz] dovenlars, lathans. — **-tongs** gripetang (innretning av siksaktenger til å nå fjerne ting med).
lazzarone [läzə'ro²ni] lasaron.
lb. [paund] fk. f. **libra** pund.
lbs. [paundz] plur. av **lb.**
L. B. S. C. R. f k. f. **London Brighton and South Coast Railway.**
L. C. C. ['el si·'si·] fk. f. **London County Council.**
L. C. J. fk. f. **Lord Chief Justice.**
L. C. M. fk. f. **lowest common multiple.**
Ld. fk. f. **Lord, limited.**
Ldp. fk. f. **Lordship.**
L. D. S. fk. f. **Licentiate of Dental Surgery.**
lea [li·] eng, mark, voll, slette.
lead [led] bly; blylodd; blysøkke; tekke, overtrekke med bly.
lead [li·d] føre, lede, anføre; spille ut (i kortspill); ha utspillet, munne ut; gå foran; — **the** way gå først; — **a life** føre (leve) et liv. **lead** [li·d] forrang, forsprang; forhånd; førelse; ledelse, anførsel, rettledning; råk.
leader ['li·də] fører, anfører.
leading ['li·diŋ] ledende, førende; hoved-, viktigste; — **article** leder (i avis); — **fashion** herskende mote; — **hand** forhånd; — **lady** primadonna; — **man** første elsker; — **motive** ledemotiv; — **part** hovedrolle; — **question** suggestivt spørsmål, hvorved man søker å framkalle et bestemt ønsket svar; brennende spørsmål.
leading ['lediŋ] blyvarer.
leading-screw ['li·diŋskru·] ledeskrue (i dreiebenk). **-strings** ledebånd.
lead-pencil ['led'pensil] blyant.
lead poisoning blyforgiftning.
leaf [li·f] blad, lauv; blad (i en bok); fløy, dørfløy; klaff, bordlem; **a** — **out of the same book** alen av samme stykke; **take a** — **out of his book** etterligne ham; **turn over a new** — ta skjeen i en annen hånd, begynne et nytt og bedre liv; **fall of the** — lauvfall. **leaf** [li·f] få blad; lauves, springe ut.
leafage ['li·fidʒ] lauv, lauvverk, blad. **leafiness** ['li·finès] lauvrikdom. **leafing** ['lifiŋ] lauvsprett. **leafless** ['liflès] bladløs. **leaflet** ['li·flèt] lite blad; piece; seddel.
leafy ['li·fi] bladrik, bladlignende; lauvkledd.
league [li·g] mil; 3 engelske sjømil.
league [li·g] forbund, liga; inngå i forbund, slå seg sammen; forene; **L. of Nations** Folkeforbundet.
leaguer ['li·gə] forbundsmedlem.
leak [li·k] lekk; lekkasje; lekke, være lekk; **spring a** — springe lekk; — **out** sive ut, bli kjent.
leakage ['li·kidʒ] lekk; lekkasje.
leaky ['li·ki] lekk, utett; sladderaktig.
leal [li·l] trofast, ærlig.
lean [li·n] lene, lene seg; støtte, helle; forlate seg.
lean [li·n] mager, tynn, tørr, skrinn; det magre;

you must take the — **with the fat** man må ta det onde med det gode.
leaning ['li·niŋ] tendens, tilbøyelighet.
leanness ['li·nnès] magerhet.
leant [lent] imperf. og perf. pts. av **lean.**
leap [li·p] springe, bykse, hoppe; spring; — **at an excuse** gripe en unnskyldning begjærlig; **by -s and bounds** med forbausende hurtig framgang.
leap-frog ['li·pfråg] det å hoppe bukk; **play at** — hoppe bukk.
leapt [lept] imperf. og perf. pts. av **leap** (ogs. **leaped).**
leap-year ['li·pjə·] skuddår; — **proposal** en dames frieri til en mann (tillatt i skuddår).
learn [lə·n] lære, få vite, få greie på, erfare, høre. **learned** ['lə·nid] kyndig, lærd; **the** — de lærde. **learner** ['lə·nə] lærling, elev. **learning** ['lə·niŋ] lærdom, erfaring, kyndighet.
lease [li·z] sanke aks'.
lease [li·s] leie, forpaktning, bygsel, feste; leiekontrakt, bygselbrev; forpaktningstid; frist; **a long** — leie på 99 år; — **for life** leie for livet; **take a new** — **of life** forynges, gi (få) nytt livsmot.
lease [li·s] leie bort, bygsle bort, forpakte, feste.
leasehold ['li·sho²ld] bygsel, feste; leid, forpaktet. **leaseholder** leier, forpakter, bygselmann.
leash [li·ʃ] kobbel; reim, line, snor; hovold; tre stykker (av jakthunder, harer osv.); binde sammen; **hold in** — beherske.
least [li·st] minst; **at** — i det minste; **not in the** — ikke det aller minste, aldri det grann; **to say the** — **of it** mildest talt; — **said soonest mended** jo mindre det sies om det, dess bedre.
leastways ['li·stwe¹z] i det minste.
leather ['leðə] lær, huder, skinn; kle med lær; jule, denge, peise. — **-dresser** feldbereder. — **-head** dumrian. **leathern** ['leðən] av lær; lær-. **leathery** ['leðəri] læraktig, seig (som lær).
leave [li·v] lov, tillatelse; permisjon; frihet; avskjed; **be on** — være fri, ha permisjon. — **ashore** landlov; **sick** — sykepermisjon. **ask** — be om lov; **take** — **of** si farvel til.
leave [li·v] forlate, etterlate, gå fra, la ligge, la være; overlate; opphøre, holde opp; forlate et sted, reise bort; (i biljard) den stilling som en spiller etterlater kulene i; — **much to be desired** la mye tilbake å ønske, være langt fra fullkommen; **six from seven leaves one** seks fra sju er én; — **alone** la være (i fred); — **behind** etterlate seg; ha etter seg; legge tilbake etter seg; glemme (igjen); **he left off smoking** han vente seg av med å røyke, han slnttet å røyke; — **out** utelate; forbigå; — **for** reise til.
leaved [li·vd] med blad, med klaffer.
leaven ['levn] surdeig; syre; gjennomsyre.
leaves [li·vz] plur. av **leaf.**
leave-taking ['li·vte¹kiŋ] avskjed, farvel.
leavings ['li·viŋz] levninger, rester.
Lebanon ['lebənən] Libanon.
lecher ['letʃə] vellysting. **lecherous** ['letʃərəs] utuktig; vellystig; liderlig. **lechery** ['letʃəri] utukt, liderlighet, vellyst.
lectern ['lektən] lesepult, pult.
lection ['lekʃən] lektie (forelest stykke av Bibelen).
lecture ['lektʃə] foredrag, forelesning; lekse, tekst, straffepreken; holde forelesning; holde straffepreken. — **-list** forelesningskatalog. **lecturer** ['lektʃərə] foredragsholder, lektor; hjelpeprest. **lectureship** ['lektʃəʃip] lektorat; stilling som hjelpeprest.
led [led] impf. og perf. pts. av **lead.**
ledge [ledʒ] kant, pall, hjell, rand; klippeavsats, bergskår.
ledger ['ledʒə] hovedbok. — **-line** bilinje, hjelpelinje.

lee [li·] ly, le, livd; **under the — of** i le av; **on the — beam** tvers i le.

leech [li·tʃ] igle; blodsuger; (gammelt) lege; sette igler på; **sticks like a —** suger seg fast som en igle, er ikke til å riste av.

Leeds [li·dz] Leeds.

leek [li·k] purre(løk); **eat the —** ete i seg, bite i seg en fornærmelse.

leer [liə] sideblikk, (ondt el. uanstendig) øyekast, skjeve el. gløtte (ondskapsfullt el. uanstendig; **at** til), skotte.

leery ['liəri] gløgg, ful, slu.

lees [li·z] berme; **drain to the —** tømme til siste dråpen.

leeward ['ljuəd, 'li·wəd] le; i le.

left [left] venstre; **to the —** til venstre; **right and — til** høyre og venstre. **— -handed** keivhendt, klosset, tvilsom, venstrehånds-.

left [left] forlatt, latt tilbake (imperf. og perf. part. av leave); **to be — till called for** til avhentning, poste restante.

left-luggage office kontor for glemte saker.

leg [leg] ben, bein, lår; sauelår; baut; ramme i beinet; **fetch a very long —** ta en stor omvei; **fall on his -s** komme ned på beina; slippe heldig fra det; **pull one's —** holde en for narr, drive gjøn med. **— it** bruke beina, ta beina fatt.

legacy ['legəsi] legat, gave, arv. **— -hunter** arvejeger.

legal ['li·gəl] lovlig, rettsgyldig, rettmessig; **— adviser** juridisk rådgiver, advokat; **— tender** lovlig betalingsmiddel. **legality** [li'gäliti] lovgyldighet. **legalization** [li·gəlai'ze'ʃən] legalisering. **legalize** ['li·gəlaiz] legalisere, gjøre lovgyldig. **legally** ['li·gəli] lovgyldig, i samsvar med loven.

legate ['legét] legat, sendebud, sendemann, utsending. **legatee** [legə'ti·] arving. **legateship** ['legétʃip] legatpost. **legation** [li'ge'ʃən] sending, misjon; sendebud; legasjon; gesandtskapsbolig.

legator [li'ge'tå·ə] testator.

legend ['ledʒənd] legende, sagn; innskrift, inskripsjon; **the — says; it is in the —** sagnet forteller. **legendary** ['ledʒəndəri] fabelaktig; legendesamling.

leger ['ledʒə] hovedbok.

legerdemain [ledʒədə'me'n] taskenspillerkunst; jugl; knep.

legged [legd] -be(i)nt (i smstn.).

legging ['legiŋ] legging; lang gamasje.

Leghorn ['leg'hå·ən] Livorno.

legibility [ledʒi'biliti] leselighet.

legible ['ledʒibl] leselig.

legion ['li·dʒən] legion; mengde; **their name is —** deres tall er legio; **foreign —** fremmedlegion (avdeling av fremmede frivillige i moderne hær); **the L. of Honour** æreslegionen.

legionary ['li·dʒənəri] legionær.

legislate ['ledʒisle't] gi lover. **legislation** [ledʒis'le'ʃən] lovgivning. **legislative** ['ledʒisle'tiv] lovgivende. **legislator** ['ledʒisle'tə] lovgiver. **legislature** ['ledʒisle'tʃə] lovgivningsmakt.

legist ['li·dʒist] lovkyndig.

legitimacy [li'dʒitiməsi] legitimitet; rettmessighet; ekte fødsel; ekthet; berettigelse.

legitimate [li'dʒitimét] rettmessig; lovlig; ektefødt; berettiget.

legitimate[li'dʒitlme't]gjørelovlig, erklære ekte.

legitimation [lidʒiti'me'ʃən] legitimasjon, gyldighetserklæring, forsvar, rettferdiggjøring.

leguminous [le'gju·minəs] belg; **— plants** belgplanter.

Leicester ['lestə] Leicester.

Leics. fk. f. **Leicestershire.**

Leighton ['le'tən] Leighton.

Leinster ['lenstə] Leinster.

leisure ['leʒə] fritid, tid, leilighet, ro; **be at — ha** tid; **at his —** når han får tid; **— hour** ledig stund; **— time** fritid. **leisured** ['leʒəd] som har god tid, makelig, rolig; økonomisk uavhengig. **leisurely** ['leʒəli] makelig; i ro og mak.

Leith [li·þ] Leith.

lemming ['lemiŋ] lemen (slags gnager).

lemon ['lemən] sitron.

lemonade [lemə'ne'd] limonade, sitronbrus.

lemon|-coloured ['lemənkʌləd] sitrongul. **—-drop** sitrondrops. **— -juice** sitronsaft. **—-peel** sitronskall. **—-sole** ising, sandflyndre. **—-squash** lemonsquash (presset sitron med sukker og vann). **— -squeezer** sitronpresser. **— -yellow** sitrongul.

lemony ['leməni] sitronaktig (farge el. smak).

lemur ['li·mə] lemur, maki (slags halvape).

lend [lend] låne ut, låne til; **— an ear** låne øre; **— a hand** el. **— a helping hand** hjelpe, rekke en hjelpende hånd; **— oneself to** vie seg til; egne seg for. **lender** ['lendə] långiver. **money lender** pengeutlåner. **lending** ['lendiŋ] lån. **lending library** leiebibliotek.

length [leŋþ] lengde, strekning, vidde; **at —** i hele sin lengde; utførlig; omsider; langt om lenge; **at full —** i legemsstørrelse; **at great —** meget utførlig; **ten feet in —** 10 fot i lengden; **win by three -s** vinne med tre hestelengder; **go the — of saying** gå så vidt at man sier; **she gave him the — of her tongue** hun gav ham ordentlig inn; **I cannot go that —** with you jeg kan ikke være enig med deg i det; **go the whole —** ta skrittet fullt ut.

lengthen ['leŋþn] forlenge, utvide; bli lengre; **lengthened** ['leŋþnd] lengre, langvarig.

lengthways ['leŋþwe'z], **lengthwise** [-waiz] på langs.

lengthy ['leŋþi] vidløftig, langdryg, langtrukken.

leniency ['li·njənsi] mildhet, lemfeldighet.

lenient ['li·njənt] formildende, mild; lemfeldig.

Leningrad ['leningra·d] Leningrad.

lenity ['leniti] mildhet; lemfeldighet.

lens [lenz] linse; **burning —** brennglass.

Lent [lent] faste, fastetid.

Lenten ['lentən] faste-; **— fare** tarvelig kost.

lentil ['lentil] linse (frukt).

Leo ['li·o·u] Leo; stjernebildet Løva.

Leonard ['lenəd] Leonard.

leonine ['li·on(a)in] løve-.

leopard ['lepəd] leopard.

leper ['lepə] spedalsk. **lepered** ['lepəd] spedalsk.

leprosy ['leprosi] spedalskhet.

leprous ['leprəs] spedalsk.

Lerwick ['lə·wik, 'lerik; på stedet 'lerwik] Lerwick på Shetlandsøyene.

lesion ['li·ʒən] skade, lesjon.

less [les] mindre, ringere; minus; **none the —** ikke desto mindre; **no — than £ 100** hele 100 pund! **not — than £ 100** minst 100 pund.

lessee [le'si·] leier, forpakter, leilending.

lessen ['lesn] forminske, nedsette; minke, avta, bli svakere.

lesser ['lesə] mindre, ringere.

lesson ['lesn] lektie; bibelstykke; lekse; leksjon; lærdom; undervisningstime, time; irettesetting; undervise, belære; lese teksten; **take lessons from** (el. of cl. **with**) **somebody** ta timer hos en.

lessor [le'så·ə, 'le'så·ə] jorddrott, grunneier; utleier.

lest [lest] for at ikke, for at (etter fryktsverber).

-let [-lét] diminutivending (hamlet).

let [let] hindring, hinder, hefte; (gammelt) hindre; **without — or hindrance** uten minste hindring.

let [let] la (tillate, bevirke); forpakte bort, leie ut, sette bort; **apartments to (be) —** værelser til leie; **— go** slippe løs, la gå; slippe tanken på; **— alone** la være i fred; oppgi, utelate; ikke tale om; for ikke å tale om; **— down** senke ned, fire ned; la slippe; **— him down as easily as you can** døm ham så mildt som mulig; **— fly** at slå løs på; gå løs på; **— in** lukke inn; snyte, la i stikken; **— into a secret** innvie i en hemmelighet; —

loose løslate; slippe løs; — off la slippe fra det,
slippe løs; fyre av; — out lukke ut; røpe; he —
it all out han røpet alt; he knew what rents the
houses — at han visste til hvilke priser husene
ble utleid.
lethargic [li'pa·ᵊdʒik] døsig; tung; sovesyk;
dvaleligende. **lethargy** ['leþədʒi] sovesyke; døsighet; dvale.
Lethe ['li·þi] Lethe; glemsel; død.
Lett [let] latvier, letter.
letter ['letə] utleier.
letter ['lete] bokstav; brev, skriv; skrift; -s
vitenskap, litteratur; forsyne med bokstaver;
sette tittel på ryggen av en bok; to the — bokstavelig; — of credit kreditiv; man of -s litterat.
— -bag brevsekk. — -book kopibok. — -box
brevkasse, postkasse. — -card brevkort. —
-carrier brevbud. — -case brevtaske, lommebok.
lettered ['letəd] merkt, med ryggtittel; boklærd, litterær.
letter|-paper brevpapir. — -perfect sikker i sin
rolle. — -press kopipresse.
letterpress ['letəpres] trykte ord, tekst.
letter|-weight brevpresse, brevholder; brevvekt.
— -writer brevskriver, brevbok.
Lettish ['letiʃ] latvisk, lettisk.
lettuce ['letis] salat (planten).
levant [li'vänt] stikke av, fordufte.
Levant [li'vänt] Østen, Levanten.
levee ['levi] kur, morgenoppvartning.
levee ['levi] kai; demning, dam; floddike.
level ['levl] jevn, jamn, like, flat, vannrett;
jevngod, jamgod, jevnhøy, jevnstilt; planere,
jevne, jamne, jevne med jorda, rette mot, sikte,
legge an på; plan, vannrett linje; nivå; flate,
slette; jevnhøyde; siktelinje; vaterpass; one —
teaspoonful en strøket teskje; do one's — best
gjøre sitt aller beste; — against el. at sikte på;
above the — of the sea over havet; on a — with
på høyde med. — crossing jernbaneovergang
(uten bru eller viadukt).
level-headed ['levlhedid] sindig, stø, vettig.
leveller ['levlə] planerer, nivellør. **levelling**
['levlin] planering, utjevning, utjamning.
lever ['li·və] vektstang; våg, håndspak, handspik; pinsebein; løftestang; håndtak. **lever** ['li·və]
løfte. — -watch ankergangsur.
leviable ['levjəbl] som kan utskrives.
leviathan [li'vaiəþən] leviatan, uhyre.
levitate ['levite't] lette, løfte; løfte seg. **levitation** [levi'te'ʃən] letting; lettelse; (spiritistisk)
det å sveve bort.
Levite ['li·vait] levitt.
Leviticus [li'vitikəs] tredje Mosebok.
levity ['leviti] letthet; flyktighet; lettsindighet.
levy ['levi] oppby, reise (en hær); utskrive
(soldater); oppkreve (avgifter); oppbud, reisning,
utskrivning; oppkreving.
lewd [l(j)u·d] utuktig, stygg, grisete. **lewdness**
[-nès] utuktighet; utsvevelse.
Lewis ['l(j)u·is] Lewis, Ludvig.
lexical ['leksikl] leksikalsk, ordboks-.
lexicographer [leksi'kågrəfə] ordboksforfatter;
the Great L. om dr. Samuel Johnson. **lexicon**
['leksikən] leksikon, ordbok (mest om gresk,
hebraisk, syrisk el. arabisk, ellers brukes dictionary).
Leyden ['le'dn] Leyden; — jar leydenerflaske.
L. G. fk. f. **Low German; Life Guards.**
L. G. B. fk. f. **Local-Government Board.**
L. G. O. C. fk. f. **London General Omnibus
Company.**
L. I. fk. f. **Light Infantry.**
liability [laiə'biliti] ansvarlighet, skyld, ansvar; utsatthet; tilbøyelighet; forpliktelse; **liabilities** forpliktelser; passiver, gjeld.
liable ['laiəbl] ansvarlig, bunden, forpliktet;
skyldig; utsatt for; tilbøyelig; — to duty tollpliktig.
liaison [li'e'zn] illegitimt forhold; overføring

(av konsonant til ord som begynner med vokal);
— officer offiser som virker som mellommann
mellom allierte styrker.
liana [li'a·nə] lian.
liar ['laiə] løgner, løgnerske.
libation [lai'be'ʃən] drikkoffer.
libel ['laibl] smedeskrift, nidskrift; klageskrift;
skrive smedeskrift; injuriere; innstevne.
liberal ['lib(ə)rəl] fribåren, frisinnet; frilynt;
edel; gjev, gavmild, raust, rundhåndet; liberal,
demokrat, venstremann; the — arts de frie
(skjønne) kunster; — education høyere dannelse;
Liberal Unionists de som i 1886 skilte seg ut
fra det liberale parti i Homerulepolitikken («frisinnede unionsvenner»).
liberalism ['lib(ə)rəlizm] frisinn. **liberality**
[libə'räliti] gavmildhet; frisinnethet; fordomsfrihet. **liberalize** ['lib(ə)rəlaiz] frigjøre; gjøre frilynt. **liberate** ['libəre't] frigi, sette i frihet.
liberation [libə're'ʃən] frigivelse. **liberationist**
[libə're'ənist] tilhenger av statskirkens opphevelse. **liberator** ['libəre'tə] befrier.
Liberia [lai'biəriə] Liberia.
libertarian [libə'tæəriən] (en) som tror på den
fri vilje.
libertine ['libətain] fri, tøylesløs, utsvevende;
frigiven; utsvevende menneske, vellysting, libertiner. **libertinism** ['libətinizm] ryggesløshet.
liberty ['libəti] frihet, privilegium. — -day
fridag. — -man landlovgast.
Liberty ['libəti] Liberty (forretning i London).
libra ['laibrə] pund; pund sterling (£); skålpund (lb.).
librarian [lai'bræ·ᵊriən] bibliotekar; assistant
— underbibliotekar, bibliotekassistent.
library ['laibrəri] bibliotek, lesesalong (undertiden: herreværelse); circulating — leiebibliotek.
librate ['laibre't] veie, holde i likevekt; balansere, sveve. **libration** [lai'bre'ʃən] veiing;
likevekt, balansering.
libretto [li'breto"] liten bok; operatekst.
lice [lais] lus (pl. av louse).
licence, license ['laisəns] bevilling, tillatelse,
løyve, rett, samtykke; kjørekort; frihet, tøylesløshet; autorisere, gi bevilling til; gi løyve til;
tillate, tåle; marriage — kongebrev; letter of —
tillatelse av kreditor til å fortsette en forretning, akkord; — to practise medicine licentia
practicandi, tillatelse til å praktisere som lege
licensee [laisən'si·] innehaver av et privilegium, en som har løyve. **licenser** ['laisənsə] utsteder av et privilegium, en som gir løyve.
licentious [lai'senʃ(i)əs] fri, frekk, tøylesløs;
uanstendig. **licentiousness** [-nès] tøyslesløshet.
lichen ['laikən] lav; ringorm.
licit ['lisit] lovlig.
lick [lik] sleike, slikke, slikke på; pryle, smøre
opp, banke; slikk, sleik; slag; — the dust bite i
graset; it -s me det går over min forstand.
licker ['likə] slikker; that's a — to me det går
over min forstand.
lickerish ['likəriʃ] kresen; fristende, lekker.
licking ['likin] sleiking; juling.
lickspittle ['lik'spitl] spyttslikker.
licorice ['likəris] lakris.
lictor ['liktə] liktor.
lid [lid] lokk; deksel; øyelokk. -less [-lés] udekt;
uten øyelokk.
lie [lai] løgn, usannhet, dikt; lyve; — with
a hatchet lyve åpenlyst; white — nødløgn; give
the — to gjøre til løgner; fornekte; tell lies
lyve.
lie [lai] ligge; how -s the land hvordan står
sakene; her talents do not — that way hennes
anlegg går ikke i den retning; — about ligge
og flyte; — by ligge unyttet, hvile, være vanfør,
være i nærheten; — down legge seg (ned);
legge seg; take something lying down finne seg
i noe uten å kny. — in ligge i barselseng; —
low ligge syk; holde seg skjult; — over ikke bli

honorert ved forfall (veksler); — to ligge bi
(om skip); — up gå til sengs, holde seg inne, gå
i dokk; — with ligge med; pålegge, stå til.
lie [lai] leie; beliggenhet; **lie-abed** sjusover;
the — **of the land** situasjonen.
lie-by ['lai'bai] elskerinne.
lief [li·f] gjerne; **I would as** — **go as not jeg**
kan gjerne gå.
liege [li·dʒ] håndgangen, tro; lens-; vasall,
lensmann; fyrste, lensherre. **-man** [-mən] vasall,
undersått.
lien ['li·ən] retensjonsrett; krav.
lieu [l(j)u·]: **in** — **of** i stedet for.
Lieut.-Col. fk. f. **Lieutenant-Colonel.**
lieutenancy [lef'tenənsi] løytnantspost. **lieutenant** [lef'tenənt] løytnant; stattholder; varamann. — **colonel** oberstløytnant. — **-general**
generalløytnant. **Lord L.** tittel på visekongen i
Irland. **the L. of the Tower** kommandanten i
Tower.
Lieut.-Gen. fk. f. **Lieutnant-General.**
Lieut.-Gov. fk. f. **Lieutnant-Governor.**
life [laif] liv, levetid, levnet, livsførsel; levnets-
beskrivelse; **choice of** — valg av livsstilling; **the**
— **to come** det kommende liv; **not for the** — **of**
me ikke for alt i verden; **for** — på harde livet;
på livstid; **many lives were lost** mange mennesker strøk med; **as large as** — i legemsstørrelse; **by the** — etter naturen; **come to** —
livne opp igjen, komme til seg selv; **bring to** —
bringe til live igjen, få liv i igjen; live opp igjen;
to the — aldeles livaktig; **at my time of** — i
min alder; **high** — den fornemme verden; **such**
is — slik er livet; — **is not all jam** livet er ikke
bare dans på roser.
life|-annuitant en som nyter livrente. — **-an-
nuity** livrente. — **-belt** livbelte. — **-blood** hjerteblod.
-boat livbåt. — **-buoy** livbøye. — **-estate** eiendom
på livstid. — **-guard** livgarde; livvakt. — **-insurance**
livsforsikring, livstrygding. — **-interest** livrente.
lifeless ['laifləs] livløs. **-ness** [-nès] livløshet,
livløyse.
lifelike ['laiflaik] livaktig. **-ness** [-nés] livaktighet.
lifelong ['laiflåŋ] hele livet, livsvarig.
life|-office livsforsikringsanstalt. — **-peerage**
adelskap for livet, ikke arvelig. — **-preserver** liv-
bergingsapparat; blytamp, totschläger.
life|r ['laifə] en som er dømt på livstid, livs-
slave. — **-rent** livrente. — **-size** legemsstørrelse;
i legemsstørrelse. **-time** levetid. — **-weary** livs-
trett.
lift [lift] løfte, heve, lette; stjele; ta opp (poteter); lette (tåke); frakte; løft; løfting, hevning;
vekt; elevator, heis; **give (lend) a person a** —
la en få sitte på med; gi en en håndsrekning;
another — **in life for you** leilighet til å begynne
et nytt liv. **liftable** ['liftəbl] som kan løftes.
lifter ['liftə] elevator; tyv.
ligament ['ligəmənt] bånd; sene.
ligature ['ligətʃə] bånd, bind; sammenbinding;
ligatur, dobbelttype.
light [lait] lys; dagslys, dag; belysning, opplysning; **he is no great** — han har ikke oppfunnet
kruttet; **the** — **went out** lyset gikk ut; **may I**
trouble you for a — tør jeg be en en fyrstikk;
in the — **of** som; i egenskap av; **I look on him**
in the — **of father** jeg betrakter ham som min far.
light [lait] lys, blond.
light [lait] lyse; tenne, kveike, nøre; opplyse,
lyse for; — **a fire** nøre opp ild, gjøre opp varme.
light [lait] stige av, komme ned, stige ned;
— **on** treffe, støte på, råke på.
light [lait] lett; ringe, ubetydelig; lett (om
vekt); fri, sorgløs; lettsindig; — **reading** mor-
skapslesning; — **sleeper** en som sover lett (som
lett våkner); **make** — **of** ikke gjøre noe oppstyr;
gjøre lite av; ta som om det ikke var noe.
lightable ['laitəbl] som kan opplyses.
lighten ['laitn] lysne; opplyse; lyne.

lighten ['laitn] lette, oppmuntre; letne.
lighter ['laitə] tenner.
lighter ['laitə] pram, lekter; føre i lekter.
pramme. lighterage ['laitəridʒ] lekterpenger.
lighterman ['laitəmən] lektermann.
light|-fingered ['laitfiŋgəd] langfingret. — **-foot**
(**-ed**) lett på foten, sprek. — **-handed** lett på
hånden. — **-headed** tankeløs; fra seg, ør. — **-hearted**
lett om hjertet, med lett hjerte.
light|-house fyr, fyrtårn. — **-keeper** fyrvokter.
lightly ['laitli] lett, lettsindig.
light-minded ['laitmaindid] lett, ustadig, flyktig.
lightness ['laitnès] lyshet, klarhet.
lightness ['laitnès] letthet.
lightning ['laitniŋ] lyn, lynild; **flash of** — lynglimt; **sheet** — flatelyn (som viser seg som en
utbredt lysning i skyene); **summer** — kornmo;
like — med lynets fart; — **strike** overrumplings-
streik.
lightning|-conductor ['laitniŋkən'dʌktə] lynav-
leder. — **-rod** lynavleder.
light-ship ['laitʃip] fyrskip.
lightsome ['laitsəm] lys, munter, glad.
light-wave ['laitweɪv] lysbølge.
light-weight ['laitweɪt] (sportsspråk) lettvekt.
ligneous ['ligniəs] tre-, treaktig, treen.
likable ['laikəbl] hyggelig, tekkelig, likendes.
like [laik] lik, like, lignende; i begrep med,
opplagt, i rette laget; sannsynlig; **such** — den
slags; **be** — ligne; **they are as** — **as two peas**
de er så like som to dråper vann; **what is he** —
hvordan ser han ut; **not anything** —, **nothing** —
ikke tilnærmelsesvis; **that's something** — det
lar seg høre; **the weather looks** — **clearing
up** det ser ut til å bli godt vær; **I feel** — **taking**
a walk jeg har lyst til å gå en tur; **I am** — **to**
jeg vil sannsynligvis. **like** [laik] lignende, samme,
slikt; like; make; **I never saw the** — **of you**
jeg har aldri sett din make. **like** [laik] liksom;
sannsynligvis; — **a drunken man** som en beruset;
som et overflødig slutningsord i daglig tale, over-
settes ofte ikke; **they encouraged us** — de liksom oppmuntret oss; **frightened** — forskrekket.
like [laik] like; ønske; synes om, ville helst;
I rather — **him** jeg liker ham ganske godt; **I** — **him**
jeg synes om ham; **I should** — **to know** jeg
skulle gjerne vite; **as you** — som De ønsker.
like [laik] sympati; **likes and dislikes** sympa-
tier og antipatier.
likelihood ['laiklihud] sannsynlighet; **in all** —
høyst sannsynlig.
likely ['laikli] sannsynlig, rimelig; behagelig,
tekkelig; **there is** — **to be some trouble** det blir
rimeligvis en del ugreie; **he is** — **to come** han
kommer sannsynligvis; **he is not a very** —
candidate han har ikke store sjanser.
likeminded ['laikmaindid] likesinnet.
liken ['laikən] sammenligne, ligne, likne.
likeness ['laiknès] likhet; bilde; **in the** —
of a friend under vennskaps maske; **have one's**
— **taken** bli fotografert.
likening ['laikəniŋ] sammenligning.
likewise ['laikwaiz] likeså, likeledes, like ens.
liking ['laikiŋ] smak, behag, forkjærlighet;
to my — etter min smak; **have a** — **for it** ha
forkjærlighet for det.
lilac ['lailək] syrin; lilla, lillafarget.
Lilliput ['lilipʌt] Lilliput (i Gulliver's Travels).
Lilliputian [lili'pju·ʃiən] lilliputianer; lilliputi-
ansk, ørliten.
lilt [lilt] tralle, synge muntert; munter vise,
rytme, liv, sving, trall, slått, tone.
lily ['lili] lilje. — **-iron** harpun med løs spiss.
— **-livered** feig, blaut. — **of the valley** liljekonvall.
limb [lim] rand, kant.
limb [lim] lem; be(i)n; tilhørende del; hoved-
gren, uskikkelig unge (egl. **limb of the devil**); forsyne med lemmer; sønderlemme; **-ed** -lemmet.
limber ['limbə] bøyelig, smidig, myk, sprek.

limber ['limbə] framstell (til kanon); prosse på.
limbo ['limbo"] forgård til helvete; fengsel.
lime [laim] lind, lindetre.
lime [laim] fuglelim; murkalk, kalk; overstryke med lim; ha kalk på.
lime [laim] sur sitron.
lime-kiln ['laimkiln] kalkovn.
lime-light ['laimlait] kalklys, slags sterkt lys; — views (gl.) lysbilder; in the — på scenen; for offentlighetens øyne (i sterk belysning).
lime-mortar ['laim'må·tə] murkalk.
limerick ['limərik] slags småvers på fem linjer der 1., 2. og 5. er lange og rimer, 3. og 4. er korte og rimer. (Kjent fra Lear's Book of Nonsense).
lime|stone ['laimsto"n] kalkstein, limstein. -wash ['laimwåʃ] murkalk. -water ['laimwåtə] kalkvann (slags mineralvann).
limit ['limit] grense; utkant; prisgrense, limitum; avgrense, begrense, innskrenke; without — grenseløs; set —s to begrense; that is the — det er toppen, det er det verste en skulle ha sett; — man deltaker i løp, som får det størst mulige forsprang. limitable ['limitəbl] avgrensende. limitary ['limitəri] grense-. limitation [limi'te'ʃən] begrensning, avgrensing; frist.
limited ['limitid] begrenset; med begrenset ansvar; a — company selskap med begrenset ansvar; — monarchy innskrenket monarki.
limitless ['limitlés] ubegrenset, grenseløs.
limn [lim] tegne, skildre, male.
limner ['limnə] tegner, maler.
limousine['limuzi·n]limousine,slagsautomobil.
limp [limp] hinke; halte; hinking; halting.
limp [limp] svak; slakk, blaut, kraftløs; slasket, slarket; — cloth bøyelig bind på bøker.
limpet ['limpit] albueskjell (dyr); en som ikke er til å riste av, en som suger seg fast; stick like a — holde iherdig fast (f. eks. på et embete), suge seg fast som en igle.
limpid ['limpid] klar, gjennomsiktig. -ity [lim'piditi] klarhet, gjennomsiktighet.
limy ['laimi] klebrig; kalk-.
linage ['lainidʒ] linjetall, linjebetaling.
linchpin ['lintʃpin] lunstikke (på hjul).
Lincoln ['liŋkən] Lincoln.
Lincs. fk. f. Lincolnshire ['liŋkənʃiə].
linden ['lindən] lind, lindetre.
line [lain] line, snor, snøre; linje; strek; verslinje; framgangsmåte, retning; grunnsetning; grenselinje; lodd, skjebne; bransje, fag; varesort, kvalitet; cross the — passere linjen (ekvator); that is hard -s det er harde vilkår; artificial — hjelpelinje; dotted — punktert linje; — of argument bevisførsel; — of conduct framgangsmåte, holdning; what — are you in hva er Deres beskjeftigelse; be in the cloth — høre til kledesbransjen; that's not in my — det ligger ikke for meg, jeg kan ikke med det; we do nothing in that — vi arbeider ikke i den bransjen; drop me a — send meg et par ord; the — must be drawn somewhere et sted må en trekke grensen; take the -s of gå samme vei som, følge ens eksempel; go beyond the -s gå over streken; in the talking — i retning av å tale; a shop in the general — en detaljhandel.
line [lain] streke; linjere opp; stille opp på linje; rynke, fure; fore, kle; trees — the roads trær står i rekker langs veien.
lineage ['linjidʒ, -nié̄dʒ] linje; slekt, ætt, avstamning, stamme.
lineal ['linjəl] linje-, som nedstammer i rett linje fra.
lineament ['linjəmənt] trekk, ansiktstrekk, drag.
linear ['linjə] linjeformig; førstegrads.
lineation [lini'eiʃən] tegning, skildring.
linen ['linin] lerret, lin, lintøy; linnet, lerrets-. — -cloth lerret. — -draper hvitevarehandler. — -drapery hvitevarer. — -press linnetskap. —

-prover trådteller. — -thread lintråd. — -weaver lerretsvever.
line-of-battle ship ['laino'bätlʃip] linjeskip, (nå: battleship).
liner ['lainə] rutedamper; linefisker.
linesman ['lainzmən] soldat (som står i linjen); linjemann (hjelper for dommeren i visse ballspill).
ling [liŋ] røsslyng, bustelyng.
ling [liŋ] lange, longe (fisk).
linger ['liŋgə] bie, dryge, drunte, nøle, dvele, tøvre; lide lenge, pines; forhale; he lingered on for some years han levde enda noen år. lingerer ['liŋgərə] nøler. lingering [-riŋ] langvarig; nøling.
lingo ['liŋgo"] uforståelig språk, kråkemål; kaudervelsk.
lingua ['liŋgwə] språk. linguist ['liŋgwist] lingvist, språkmann, målgransker, språklærd. linguistic [liŋ'gwistik] språklig, språkvitenskapelig. linguistics [liŋ'gwistiks] språkvitenskap.
liniment ['linimənt] tynn salve.
lining ['lainiŋ] innvendig kledning, for, foring, panel, kant; every cloud has a silver lining bakom skyene er himmelen alltid blå.
link [liŋk] ledd, ring, kjede; forbindelsesledd; bånd; kjede sammen; knytte sammen; forbindes; gå arm i arm; links lenkeknapper; the missing — det manglende mellomledd (mellom ape og menneske).
link [liŋk] fakkel. — -boy fakkelbærer.
link [liŋk] el. links [liŋks] golfterreng.
link-buttons ['liŋkbʌtənz] lenkeknapper.
linn [lin] vannfall; dam, høl; stup, juv.
linnet ['linit] irisk.
linoleum [lai'no"ljəm, li'no"ljəm] linoleum.
linotype ['lainotaip] linjesettemaskin.
linseed ['linsi·d] linfrø.
linsey ['linsi] verken. — -woolsey verken; verkens-.
lint [lint] charpi, især engelsk charpi; shredded — tysk charpi.
lintel ['lintl] overligger (over dør el. vindu), dekkstein.
lion ['laiən] løve; berømthet; berømt mann; sprett; severdighet; the lion's share brorparten; the British — Storbritannia; show a person the lions and tombs å vise en stedets severdigheter. — -ant maurløve. lionel ['laiənel] løveunge.
lioness ['laiənés] løvinne.
lion|-hearted ['laiən'ha·ˀtid] motig som en løve; Richard the L. Rikard Løvehjerte. — -hunter løvejeger; en som jager etter berømte personer, som frir etter fine bekjentskaper.
lionize ['laiənaiz] gjøre stas av, gjøre krus for.
lion's-foot ['laiənzfut] edelweiss, kattefot.
lip [lip] leppe, lepe, lippe; kant, rand; tut; grov kjeft, grovheter; kysse; synge, mulle; upper — overleppe; lower —, under — underleppe; hang on one's lips lytte beundrende til en; none of your — vær ikke uforskammet; — a chant synge en sang. — -deep bare med munnen. — -devotion gudsfrykt i munnen. — -labour munnsvær. — -service tomme ord, munnsvær. -salve leppesalve; smiger. — -wisdom visdom i ord.
liquation [lai'kwe'ʃən, li'-] smeltet tilstand; smelting. liquefaction [likwi'fäkʃən] smelting; smeltet tilstand. liquefy ['likwifai] smelte; bli flytende, bråne.
liqueur [li'kjuə] likør.
liquid ['likwid] væske, flytende, smeltende; gjennomsiktig, klar. liquidate ['likwide'ˀt] gjøre flytende; gjøre klar; avvikle, likvidere; avgjøre. liquidation [likwi'de'ʃən] avvikling. liquidity [li'kwiditi] flytende tilstand.
liquor ['likə] væske; saft; ь rk drikk, brennevin; drikke; skjenke; what's your — hva vil du drikke; be in — være beruset. — -dealer brennevinshandler.
liquorice ['likəris] lakris. — -lozenge lakrispastill.
lira ['liərə] lire (italiensk mynt).

Lisbon ['lizbən] Lisboa, Lissabon.

lisp [lisp] lespe; lespe fram; lesping.

lissome ['lisəm] myk, smidig.

list [list] liste, fortegnelse, rulle; innrullere, verve; la seg verve; **be on the active** — stå i rullene; — **of quotations** prisliste.

list [list] skranke, kampplass; **enter the -s** tre i skranken.

list [list] hall; slagside; halle, ha slagside.

list [list] lyste, ha lyst til.

listen ['lisn] lytte, lye, høre etter; — **in** høre radio; — **to** lytte til. **listener** ['lisnə] en som lytter, hører til; lytter; **good** — en som hører etter med interesse.

listless ['listlès] likegyldig, likesæl; treg; udeltagende. **listlessness** [-nès] likegyldighet, likesæle, ulyst.

lit [lit] imperf. og perf. pts. av **light**.

litany ['litəni] litani.

literacy ['litərəsi] evne til å lese og skrive.

literal ['lit(ə)rəl] bokstavelig, ordrett; — **translation** ordrett oversettelse; — **truth** ord for ord sannheten.

literalism ['litərəlizm] bokstavtrelldom.

literally ['litərəli] bokstavelig; — **tired to death** bokstavelig talt trett inntil døden.

literary ['lit(ə)rəri] boklig, litterær.

literate ['lit(ə)rèt] en som kan lese og skrive; prest uten universitetseksamen; boklærd; kjenner av litteratur, belest mann.

literatim [litə'rɛ'tim] bokstav for bokstav, etter bokstaven.

literature ['lit(ə)rətʃə; -tjuə] litteratur.

litharge ['liþa·dʒ] glette (blyoksyd).

lithe [laið] smidig, myk, bøyelig. **-some** [-səm] smidig; lett, sprek.

lithograph ['liþogra·f] litografi. **lithographer** [li'þågrəfə] litograf. **lithographic** [liþo'gräfik] litografisk. **lithography** [li'þågrəfi] litografi.

lithotype ['liþotaip] litotypi.

Lithuania [liþju'e'njə] Litauen. **-n** [liþju'e'njən] litauer; litauisk.

Lit. Hum. fk. f. **Literae humaniores** gammelspråklig kursus til en eksamen ved universitetet i Oxford.

litigable ['litigəbl] omtvistelig, tvilsom. **litigant** ['litigənt] stridende; prosederende part. **litigate** ['litige't] ligge i strid om, føre prosess om; føre prosess. **litigation** [liti'ge'ʃən] rettsstrette, tvistemål. **litigious** [li'tidʒəs] trettekjær; omtvistelig.

litmus ['litməs] lakmus (blått fargestoff); — **paper** lakmuspapir.

litre ['li·tə] liter.

Litt. D. fk. f. **literarum doctor** (— **doctor of Letters).**

litter ['litə] bærebår, båre; strø, boss, halm;· kull (griser o. l.); uorden, svineri, rot, røre; strø, strø under; ligge strødd utover; strø utover, slenge utover; få unger.

little ['litl] liten; **a** — **one** en liten en, et barn; **the** — **ones** barna; **a** — litt; — **better** lite bedre; **a** — **better** litt (noe) bedre; **make** — **of** ikke bry seg om; **after a** — om litt, litt etter; — **by** — litt etter litt; **by** — **and** — litt etter litt; **he** — **thought** han ante ikke. **Little-Ease** navnet på en celle i Tower. — **Englander** ['litl'iŋləndə] anti-imperialist. — **-go** ['litlgoᵘ] første del av eksamen for B. A. graden i Cambridge, forberedende prøve; — **man** gutt (vennlig). — **Mary** (spøkende om) maven. **littleness** ['litlnès] litenhet.

littoral ['litərəl] strand-; havstrand, kyst.

liturgic [li'tə·dʒik] liturgisk.

liturgy ['litədʒi] liturgi, kirkeskikk.

live [liv] leve, være til; livberge seg; bo; holde seg; føre et . . . liv; **to** — **to see** oppleve; **no boat could** — **in such a sea** ingen båt kunne greie seg i slik sjø; **he -s by himself** han bor alene; — **by one's wits** leve av å slå plater; — **to a great age** oppnå en høy alder; — **up to** leve i overens-

stemmelse med; — **by** livberge seg med, leve av **(chasing, fishing);** — **on** leve av; spise; — **a roving life** leve et omstreifende liv; — **down** bringe i glemsel.

live [laiv] levende; — **coals** glør.

livelihood ['laivlihud] utkomme; livsopphold; levebrød.

liveliness ['laivlinès] liv, livlighet.

livelong ['livlåŋ] lang; **the** — **day** den utslagne dag.

lively ['laivli] levende; livlig; livaktig, kvikk.

liver ['livə] en som lever, beboer.

liver ['livə] lever. — **-oil** levertran.

Liverpool ['livəpu·l] Liverpool.

Liverpudlian [livə'pʌdliən] innbygger av Liverpool.

livery ['livəri] overdragelse; overdragelsesdokument; tjenerdrakt, livré; laugsdrakt; iføre livré. **-coat** livréfrakk. — **-servant** tjener. — **-stables** leiestall.

lives [laivz] pl. av **life;** [livz] av v. **live.**

live-stock ['laivståk] besetning, buskap.

livid ['livid] blyfarget, blygrå, blå (som følge av slag), blodunderløpen; likbleik. **lividness** ['lividnès] blygrå farge.

living ['liviṇ] levende; liv, levnet; levebrød, livsopphold; kall; **make a** — tjene sitt brød; — **wage** lønn som en kan leve av.

living-room ['liviṇru·m] dagligstue.

living-space ['liviṇspe's] (brukt for å gjengi tysk Lebensraum) livsrom.

Livingstone ['liviṇstən] Livingstone.

Livonia [li'voᵘnjə] Livland.

Livy ['livi] Livius; Livia.

lizard ['lizəd] firfisle.

L. J. fk. f. **Lord Justice.**

ll. fk. f. **lines.**

llama ['la·mə] lama (dyr).

llano ['l(j)a·noᵘ] llano, steppe (i Sør-Amerika).

L. L. B. fk. f. **legum baccalaureus** (= **bachelor of Laws).**

L. L. D. fk. f. **legum doctor** (= **doctor of Laws).**

L. L. J. fk. f. **Lords Justices.**

L. L. L. fk. f. **Love's Labour's Lost.**

Lloyd [loid] Lloyd's, skipsassuransekontor i London; **Lloyd's List** skipsfartstidende i London; **Lloyd's Register** årlig skipsliste.

L. M. S. fk. f. **London Missionary Society.**

L. M. S. (R.) fk. f. **London Midland & Scottish (Railway).**

L. N. E. (R.) fk. f. **London & North-Eastern (Railway).**

L. N. W. (R.) fk. f. **London & North-Western (Railway).**

lo! [loᵘ] se!

load [loᵘd] byrde, vekt; lass, last, ladning; bæreevne; belesse, lesse på, la, laste; overlesse; **take a** — **off my mind** ta en stein fra mitt hjerte; **loads of** masser av, i haugevis; **-ed cane** stokk med bly i spissen (som våpen); **-ed dice** forfalskede terninger; **-ed table** bugnende bord.

loader ['loᵘdə] lagreie (til bøsse).

loading ['loᵘdiṇ] byrde; last, ladning.

load-line ['loᵘdlain] lastelinje.

loadstar ['loᵘdsta·ə] ledestjerne, srl. Polarstjernen.

loadstone ['loᵘdstoᵘn] magnetjernstein.

loaf [loᵘf] masse, klump; brød; **a** — **of bread** et brød; — **of sugar** sukkertopp; **half a** — **is better than no bread** smuler er også brød; — **of cabbage, of lettuce** kålhode, salathode; **loaves and fishes** fordel, vinning.

loaf [loᵘf] drive dank, gå og slenge, late seg; driveri, sleng. **loafer** ['loᵘfə] dagdriver, løsgjenger, vagabond, slusk.

loaf-sugar ['loᵘfʃu·gə] toppsukker.

loam [loᵘm] leir, leire; dekke med leir; fylle med leir. — **-earth** leirjord. **loamy** ['loᵘmi] leiret; leir-.

loan [loᵘn] lån, utlån; låne ut; **put out to** —

låne ut; **interest on** — utlånsrente; **to** — **on interest** låne mot rente. — **-collection** sammenlånt billedsamling. — **-office** lånekontor.
loath [louþ] uvillig, lei.
loathe [louð] føle motbydelighet, vemmelse for, hate, avsky, vemmes ved. **loathful** ['louðful] avskyelig, vemmelig. **loathing** ['louðiŋ] vemmelse, avsky. **loathsome** ['louðsəm] heslig, motbydelig.
loaves [louvz] pl. av **loaf** (brød).
lob [låb] kloss, staur, tosk; høy ball (i tennis); sandmakk, fjæremark; kaste langsomt, la falle (sakte); henge slapp.
lobby ['låbi] forværelse; korridor; forsal (i parlamentet); **they voted (went into) the same** — stemte for samme parti.
lobe [loub] lapp, flik, snipp.
lobster ['låbstə] hummer; rødtrøye (økenavn for en soldat).
local ['loukl] stedlig, lokal, på stedet; **Local Government Board** det ministerium som inntil 1919 hadde oppsynet med kommunalbestyrelsen. **locale** [lo'ka·l] lokale, sted. **localism** ['loukəlizm] lokal natur. **locality** [lo'käliti] det å høre til på et sted; beliggenhet. **localization** [loukəlai'zei'ʃən] lokalisering; stedfesting. **localize** ['loukəlaiz] anbringe; stedfeste.
Locarno [lå'ka·°nou] Locarno.
locate [lo'keit] anbringe; bestemme stedet for; bosette seg.
location [lo'keiʃən] anbringelse, beliggenhet; plass, sted, rom; utstikking; utleie.
loch [låk] sjø, innsjø; vann; fjord, bukt.
lock [låk] lås, lukke; sluse; avlukke; floke, vase; lokk, hårlokk; låse, sperre, stenge; være til å låse; låse inne; binde (kapital), inneslutte; sette bremse på (hjul); **keep under** — **and key** forvare under lås og lukke, gjemme omhyggelig; **the street was closed by a** — **of carriages** gata var sperret av vogner; **the Rape of the Lock** Lokkeranet (dikt av Pope); **be -ed in prison** bli innesperret i fengsel; — **up** låse ned, låse inne.
lockable ['låkəbl] som kan låses. **lockage** ['låkidʒ] slusepenger. **lockchamber** ['låk'tʃe¹mbə] slusekammer.
Locke [låk] Locke (engelsk filosof).
locker ['låkə] skap, kiste; kistebenk.
locket ['låkit] medaljong, kapsel.
lock-gate ['låk'geit] sluseport.
lock-jaw ['låkdʒɔ·] stivkrampe.
lock-keeper ['låkki·pə] slusevokter.
lockout ['låk'aut] lockout, arbeidsstans.
lock-picker ['låkpikə] dirk.
lock|smith ['låksmiþ] kleinsmed. — **-up** arrest.
locomotion [loukə'mouʃən] bevegelse, befordring, befordringsmåte.
locomotive ['loukəmoutiv, loukə'moutiv] som kan bevege seg, bevegelig; lokomotiv.
locum ['loukəm] vikar. — **-tenens** [-'ti·nenz] vikar.
locust ['loukəst] grashoppe, engsprette; johannesbrødtre.
locution [lo'kju·ʃən] tale, talemåte, ordlag.
locutory ['låkjutəri] samtalerom.
lode [loud] gang, åre; veit. **lodestar, lodestone,** se **load-.**
lodge [lådʒ] hytte, hus, (jakt-) villa; portnerhus; losje; leie; samling, gruppe; gi losji, anbringe; gi i forvaring, deponere; oppbevare; framføre (klage mot en); slå ned; losjere, bo, ta inn; **to** — **in the warehouse** ta inn på lager. — **-gate** ['lådʒgeit] innkjørsel, hovedport (til park). — **-keeper** ['lådʒki·pə] portner.
lodgement ['lådʒmənt] anbringelse, opphoping; besettelse. **lodger** ['lådʒə] losjerende, leier.
lodging ['lådʒiŋ] losji, bolig, kvarter; **live in -s** bo til leie; **take -s** leie værelser.
lodginghouse ['lådʒiŋhaus] losjihus, natteherberge.
lodgment ['lådʒmənt] anbringelse, innsetting, opphoping; besettelse.

loft [lå·ft, låft] loft, loftsrom; trev; galleri; dueslag, duehus.
loftily ['lå·ftili, 'låf-] høyt; stolt, overlegent. **loftiness** ['lå·ftines, 'låf-] høyde, høyhet; stolthet. **lofty** ['lå·fti, 'låfti] høy, anselig, opphøyd, høyreist, stolt.
log [låg] tømmerstokk, kloss, kubbe; logg; loggbok; felle, hogge tømmer; føre inn i loggbok.
loganberry ['lougənberi¹] loganbær, en krysning av bjørnebær og bringebær.
logan-stone ['lågənstoun] ruggestein.
logarithm ['lågəriþm] logaritme.
log-book ['lågbuk] loggbok. **-cabin** [käbin] tømmerhytte.
logger ['lågə] tømmerkjører.
loggerhead ['lågəhed] kloss, staur, kjøtthue; **be at -s** være i tottene på hverandre; **fall to -s** komme i hårene (el. kladdene) på hverandre.
loggerheaded ['lågəhedid] dum, klosset.
log-house ['låghaus] tømmerhus.
log-hut ['låghʌt] tømmerhytte.
logic ['lådʒik] logikk. **logical** [-l] logisk.
logician [lå'dʒiʃən] logiker.
log-line ['låglain] loggline.
logman ['lågmən] skogsarbeider.
logomachist [lå'gåməkist] ordkløyver.
log-rolling ['lågro¹liŋ] gjensidig reklame; tømmerlunning (som arbeiderne hjelper hverandre med).
log-wood ['lågwud] blåtre, Campêche-tre.
loin [loin] lend, lendestykke; — **-cloth** lendklede. — **of veal** kalvenyrestek.
loiter ['loitə] driva, slentre, nøle; somle, gi seg god tid; slenge, reke. **loiterer** ['loitərə] etternøler, dagdriver. **loiteringly** [-riŋli] langsomt.
loll [lål] lene seg makelig, ligge og dovne seg; henge ut, la henge ut (om tunga).
Lollard ['lålad] lollard, økenavn på Wicliffs tilhengere.
lollipop ['lålipåp] slags sukkergodt.
lollop ['låləp] slenge, reke.
Lombard ['lʌmbəd, 'låmbad] longobarder, lombarder, lombardisk; — **Street,** sentrum for Londons pengemarked. **-ic** [låm'ba·°dik] lombardisk. **-y** ['lʌmbədi, 'låmbədi] Lombardi.
Lon., lon fk. f. **longitude.**
London ['lʌndən] London; londoner-, londonsk.
Londoner ['lʌndənə] londoner.
lone [loun] enslig, ensom; stusslig. **loneliness** [-lines] ensomhet. **lonely** ['lounli] ensom. **lonesome** ['lounsəm] ensom.
long [låŋ] lang, dryg; langvarig; langtrekkende, langtskuende; omstendelig; lenge; **in the** — **run** i lengden; til sist; **a** — **time since** for lenge siden; **a** — **way** about stor omvei; **bill at a** — **date** veksel på lang tid; **he is** — **in doing a thing** det varer lenge før han får gjort noe; **will it be** — varer det lenge? **he won't be** — han vil ikke bli lenge borte; **a** — **dozen** 13 stk.; **all day** — hele dagen; **the** — **and the short of it** summa summarum, sannheten kort og godt.
long [låŋ] lengte, lenges etter, ønske; — **for,** — **after** lengte etter; — **to see him** lengte etter å se ham; **longed for** ønsket.
long. fk. f. longitude.
longanimity [låŋgə'nimity] langmod, langmodighet.
Long Acre ['låne¹kə] gate i London.
longe [lʌndʒ] støt, utfall; gjøre utfall.
longeval [lån'dʒi·vəl] langlivet.
longevity [lån'dʒeviti] høy alder.
Longfellow ['lånfelou] Longfellow.
longhand ['lånhänd] vanlig skrift (mots. **shorthand).**
long-headed ['lån'hedid] langskallet; gløgg, klok, vaken.
longing ['låŋiŋ] lengselsfull; lengsel, lengt.
longish ['låŋiʃ] langaktig.

longitude ['låndʒitju·d] lengde.
longways ['låŋwe¹z] på langs.
longwise ['låŋwaiz] på langs.
loo [lu·] et slags kortspill; gjøre storeslem; beseire.
looby ['lu·bi] staur, kloss, treneve.
loof [lu·f] lo, lovart; loffe; luffe.
loofah ['lu·fa·] frotterhanske, frottersvamp (av lufatrevler), lufa (et slags gresskar).
look [luk] se; se ut, se ut til, synes; vende ut til; — all wonder se ganske forbauset ut; — black sette opp et sørgelig fjes; — like ligne; my windows — into the garden mine vinduer vender ut mot hagen; — about you se Dem for; — after se etter (følge med øynene); passe på, ta seg av; — at se på; betrakte; — for se etter; vente; forutse; what are you looking for hva ser De etter; not looked for uventet; — on se på, se til, være tilskuer; betrakte; — out se ut; holde utkik; — out there pass på; — over se igjennom; se over; overse, tilgi; — sharp skynde seg; passe på; — to passe på; se hen til; lite på; I shall — to you for the payment jeg skal henvende meg til Dem for å få betalingen; — up se opp; gå opp; stige (varer); slå opp (i en ordbok); he does not — his age han ser ikke ut til å være så gammel som han er; — daggers at a person gjennombore en med øynene.
look [luk] blikk, øyekast, mine, utseende; I don't like the — of it jeg syns ikke det ser bra ut; her good -s hennes deilige ansikt; I can see by the — of you jeg kan se på ansiktet ditt.
looker-on ['lukər'ån] tilskuer.
looking ['lukin] utseende.
looking-glass ['lukingla·s] speil.
look-out ['luk'aut] utkik; vakt; utsyn; utkiksmann, it is his own — det får han greie selv, det blir hans sak.
loom [lu·m] vevstol; årelom.
loom [lu·m] vise seg, heve seg i avstand, rage opp, ruve, se stor ut.
loom [lu·m] teiste (fugl).
loon [lu·n] lømmel, skarv, slamp.
loon [lu·n] lom, imbre (fugl).
loony ['lu·ni] fk. f. lunatic.
loop [lu·p] løkke, bukt; stropp; hempe; sløyfe; krumning; slå løkke på; feste med en løkke; ligge i løkke; looping the — sløyfekjøring (på sykkel e. l.), sløyfeflyging.
looper ['lu·pə] måler (slags larve).
loophole ['lu·phoᵘl] skyteskår, skytehull; smutthull.
loopholed ['lu·phoᵘld] med skyteskår.
loop-line ['lu·plain] sløyfespor.
loose [lu·s] løse, løse opp, åpne; slippe løs.
loose [lu·s] løs, vid; løssloppen; løsaktig, slibrig; at — ends i uorden, forsømt; ledig (uten arbeid). loose-limbed slåpen, lealaus. loosen [lu·sn] gjøre løs, løse opp; løsne. looseness ['lu·snês] løshet; løsaktighet; løs mage.
loot [lu·t] plyndring, bytte, hærfang, rov; streife om, plyndre, herje, røve.
lop [låp] hogge av, kappe, skjære, klippe; henge med, henge ned; skat, toppende av tre, kvister.
lop-eared ['låpiəd] med hengende ører.
lopper ['låpə] en som hogger av, kapper.
lopping ['låpin] avkapping; skat, kvister.
lop-sided ['låpsaidid] skjev.
loquacious [lo'kwe¹ʃəs] snakkesalig.
loquacity [lo'kwäsiti] snakkesalighet.
Lor [lå·ᵊ] josses!
Loraine [lo're¹n] Lorraine.
lord [lå·ᵊd] herre, hersker, lensherre, overherre, lord (medlem av overhuset; tittel); ektemann; gjøre til lord, adle; gi lordtittelen; — spiritual geistlig medlem av overhuset; — temporal verdslig medlem av overhuset; the -s of (the) creation skapningens herrer, det sterke kjønn; the Lord Herren, Vårherre; the Lord's day søndag; Lord's

prayer fadervår; Lord's supper alterens sakrament, nattverden; Lord's table alterbordet; the day of the Lord den ytterste dag; in the year of our Lord i det Herrens år; the House of Lords overhuset; in the Lords i overhuset; lord it spille herre(r).
lordlike ['lå·ᵊdlaik] fornem.
lordliness ['lå·dlinês] fornemhet; adelskap; høy stilling.
lordling ['lå·ᵊdlin] svekling av en adelsmann.
lordly ['lå·ᵊdli] fornem; høy, edel; hovmodig, kaut.
lord-mayor ['lå·ᵊd'mæ·ə] overborgermester, lord-mayor.
lordship ['lå·ᵊdʃip] herskap; herredømme; his Lordship hans herlighet.
lore [lå·ᵊ] lære, lærdom, vitenskap, kunnskap.
lorgnette [lå·ᵊn'jet] teaterkikkert; stanglornjett.
lorgnon ['lå·ᵊnjån] lornjett; monokkel; teaterkikkert.
lorn [lå·ᵊn] forlatt, enslig.
Lorraine [lo're¹n] Lorraine.
lorrie ['låri] flatvogn, grusvogn, lastebil.
losable ['lu·zəbl] som kan mistes.
Los Angeles [lås'ändʒiliz, lås'äŋgiliz].
lose [lu·z] tape, miste, fortape, gå tapt; spille, skusle bort; be lost komme bort; gå tapt; fare vill; forlise; — oneself gå vill; there is no love lost between them de er ikke særlig begeistret for hverandre; his anger lost him many friends hans sinne skilte ham av med mange venner; — the train komme for sent til toget; my watch -s five minutes a day uret mitt saktner 5 minutter i døgnet; all hands lost hele besetningen omkommet; the bill was lost in the Lords lovforslaget ble forkastet i overhuset.
loser ['lu·zə] tapende, en som taper.
losing ['lu·ziŋ] tapende; som bringer tap.
loss [lå·ᵊ)s] tap; skibbrudd, skibrott; bortgang (=død); be at a — være i villrede; at a — med tap.
lost [lå·st] tapt, mistet, bortkommet; be — in thought være i dype tanker.
lot [låt] lodd, skjebne; parti (varer), masse; mengde, bråte; lodd (jordlodd; lotterilodd); tildele, fordele. -s of money masser av penger; such a — for en mengde; a — of harm meget vondt; cast -s kaste lodd; draw -s trekke lodd; it fell to his — det falt i hans lodd; cast in one's — with sta last og brast med; sell by small -s selge i småpartier; a bad — en dårlig fyr; a poor — en stakkar.
loth [loᵘþ] uvillig; nothing — gjerne.
Lothian [lo·ᵊðiən].
lotion ['loᵘʃən] vasking, bading; vask, bad.
lottery ['låtəri] lotteri. — -ticket loddseddel.
lotus ['loᵘtəs] vannlilje, lotus, lotustre.
loud [laud] høy; lydelig, skrikende, høyrøstet, larmende; høyt, lytt; don't speak so — ikke tal så høyt; who laughed -est? hvem to høyest? loudly ['laudli] lydelig; høyt og lytt. loud-mouthed ['laudmauðd] høyrøstet. loudness ['laud-nês] høyde, styrke. loud-speaker ['laud'spi·kə] høyttaler. loudvoiced (-voist] høyrøstet.
lough [låk] d. s. s. loch.
lounge [laundʒ] slentre, drive omkring, reke, gå og slenge; lene seg makelig; slå tiden i hjel med å drive; driving, slentring; makelig stilling; makelig dagligstue, salong; promenade; liggestol; sjeselong; støt, utfall (i fekting). lounger ['laundʒe] en som driver, dagdriver. lounging-chair ['laundʒinʧæ·ə] makelig stol.
lour [lauə] henge truende, true; formørkes. -ing skummel. loury ['lauəri] truende, mørk.
louse [laus] (pl. lice) lus. louse [lauz] luse, avluse. lousy ['lauzi] luset.
lout [laut] slamp, kloss, staur; lute seg.
loutish ['lautiʃ] slampet, klosset.
louver, louvre ['lu·və] lufthette (med persienne-

formede sideåpninger). — -window lydåpning (i klokketårn).

lovable ['lʌvəbl] elskelig; elskverdig.

love [lʌv] kjærlighet (for, of, to til); elsk, elskhug, elskov, elske, holde av, være glad i, like; my — vennen min; for the — of God for Guds skyld; marry for — gifte seg av kjærlighet; in — with forelsket i; fall in — with forelske seg i; make — to gjøre kur til; send one's — hilse så mye; with much — yours med vennlig hilsen Deres ... (brevslutning); there is no — lost between them de er ikke svært begeistret for hverandre; play for — spille om ingen ting (uten innsats); do it for — gjøre det gratis; for — or money for gode ord og betaling; what a — of a dog! for en snill (pen) hund! I — my wife jeg elsker min kone; I — to do it jeg liker svært godt å gjøre det.

love|-affair ['lʌvəfæ·ə] kjærlighetshistorie. — -child elskovsbarn, uekte barn. — -knot kjærlighetssløyfe. — -letter kjærlighetsbrev. -lorn forlatt av sin elskede.

lovely ['lʌvli] yndig, deilig; storartet, glupt.

love-making ['lʌvme'kiŋ] kurmakeri.

love-match ['lʌvmätʃ] inklinasjonsparti.

lover ['lʌvə] elsker, tilbeder, kjæreste.

love-sick ['lʌvsik] elskovssyk.

loving ['lʌviŋ] kjærlig, øm.

loving-cup ['lʌviŋkʌp] festpokal (som går fra munn til munn i et selskap).

loving-kindness ['lʌviŋ'kaindnės] kjærlig hensynsfullhet; godvilje.

low [loᵘ] lav, låg; sakte; dempet, hul; simpel, tarvelig; ydmyk, dyp; ringe; ussel; låk; a — bow et dypt bukk; the L. Countries Nederlandene; reduced to a — condition temmelig meget på knærne; buy at a — rate kjøpe billig; be in — spirits, be — in spirits være i dårlig humør; be — in cash ha smått med penger; bring — redusere; cut — nedringe (på kjole); lay — slå ned, drepe; begrave.

low [loᵘ] raute (om kuer); raut(ing).

low|-born ['loᵘbå·ᵊn] av lav ætt. — -church lavkirke, lavkirkelig.

lower ['lauə] = lour.

lower ['loᵘə] lavere, nedre, under-; the Lower House Underhuset; the — orders underklassen; the — world underverdenen.

lower ['loᵘə] gjøre lavere, senke, senke ned, fire ned; forminske; synke, avta, minke.

lowermost ['loᵘəmoᵘst] lavest.

lowland ['loᵘlənd] lavland; the Lowlands det skotske lavland.

Lowlander ['loᵘləndə] innbygger i det skotske lavland.

lowliness ['loᵘlinės] beskjedenhet, ringhet.

lowly ['loᵘli] beskjeden, ydmyk, smålåten, beskjedent.

low-lying lavtliggende. low-minded lavsinnet. low-necked nedringet. lowness lavhet. low-priced billig. low-spirited ['loᵘspiritid] nedslått, nedrykt. low-spiritedness nedtrykthet.

low-water ['loᵘ'wå·tə] lavvanne, lavvanns-. — mark lavvannsmerke.

loyal ['loiəl] lojal, tro (mot bestående myndigheter); trofast, redelig; lydig. loyalist ['loiəlist] lovlydig borger, regjeringsvennlig. loyalty ['loiəlti] lojalitet; trofasthet, lydighet.

lozenge ['låzindʒ] rute, rombe (likesidet, sk jevvinklet firkant); drops, pastill, brystsukker.

L. R. A. M. fk. f. licentiate of the Royal Academy of Music.

L. R. C. fk. f. London Rowing Club; Labour Representation Committee.

L. R. C. P. fk. f. licentiate of the Royal College of Physicians.

L. R. C. S. fk. f. licentiate of the Royal College of Surgeons.

£'s. d. el. l. s. d. el. L. S. D. ['eles'di·] fk. f. rae (ɔ: pounds), solidi (ɔ: shillings), denarii

(ɔ: pence); a question of — et pengespørsmål; it is only a matter of — det kan gjøres (klares), har en bare de nødvendige pengene.

L. S. W. R. fk. f. London & South-Western Railway.

Lt. fk. f. Lieutenant.

L. T. A. fk. f. London Teachers' Association.

ltd., Ltd. fk. f. limited.

lubbard ['lʌbəd], lubber ['lʌbə] kloss, staur, slamp; klein sjømann.

lubberly ['lʌbəli] klosset, slampet, slåpen.

Lübeck ['lu·bek] Lübeck.

lubricant ['l(j)u·brikənt] smørelse; smurning. lubricate ['l(j)u·brike't] gjøre glatt; smøre. lubrication [l(j)u·bri'ke'ʃən] smøring. lubricator ['l(j)u·brike'tə] smøreapparat; smørekopp. lubricity [l(j)u·'brisiti] glatthet, hålke; slibrighet.

Lucas ['l(j)u·käs] Lukas.

luce [l(j)u·s] gjedde.

lucerne [lu·'sə·n] luserne (plante).

lucid ['l(j)u·sid] skinnende, klar, bjart, lys, lysende; gjennomsiktig; overskuelig. lucidity [lu'siditi] klarhet.

Lucifer ['l(j)u·sifə] morgenstjernen; Lusifer; satan. lucifer fyrstikk. luciferous [lu'sifərəs] lysende, lysgivende; opplysende.

luck [lʌk] tilfelle, treff, lykketreff, slumpehøve, slumpelykke, lykke, hell; by — ved et slumpetreff; be in — ha hell med seg; that's my usual —, that's just my — slik skal det alltid gå meg; try one's — forsøke lykken; more — than judgment lykken er bedre enn forstanden; be down on one's — være i vanskeligheter; as — would have it heldigvis.

luckily ['lʌkili] lykkelig, heldig; heldigvis.

luckless ['lʌklės] ulykkelig, uheldig.

Lucknow [lu'snə·n] Lucknow (by i India).

lucky ['lʌki] lykkelig, heldig; a — hit et lykketreff.

lucky-bag eller lucky-tub forundringspakke.

lucrative ['l(j)u·krətiv] innbringende, fordelaktig, lønnsom.

lucubrate ['l(j)u·kjubre't] studere ved lys (om natten). lucubration [lu·kju'bre'ʃən] (nattlig) studium; lærd verk.

Lucy ['lu·si, 'lju·si] Lucie.

lud [lʌd] herre (for: lord); du store tid.

luddite ['lʌdait] luddist (som søkte å hindre innføring av dampvevstoler).

Ludgate Hill ['lʌdgit'hil] gate i London.

ludicrous ['l(j)u·dikrəs] latterlig; pussig, morsom.

luff [lʌf] lo, lovart; forlik (på skonnertseil); luffe.

lug [lʌg] hale, trekke, rykke, ruske; øre, øresnipp; klakk, nakke (på takstein).

luggage ['lʌgidʒ] reisegods, bagasje; føring. — -label merkelapp. — -ticket garantiseddel. — -train godstog. — -van bagasjevogn.

lugger ['lʌgə] lugger (lite skip).

lugubrious [lu'gju·briəs] sorgfull, trist, stusslig.

Luke [l(j)u·k] Lukas. St. Luke's sinnssykeasyl i London.

luke, lukewarm ['l(j)u·k], ['l(j)u·kwå·ᵊm] lunken. lukewarmness [-nės] lunkenhet.

lull [lʌl] lulle, sulle, bye, bysse; berolige, roe, døyve; stilne, roe seg; stans, opphold; døs; stille, havblikk.

lullaby ['lʌləbai] voggesang; barnetull, barnesull, bånsull.

lumbago [lʌm'be'goᵘ] hekseskudd, lumbago.

lumber ['lʌmbə] tømmer; skrammel, skrap, skrot, rask; fylle opp; skrangle, ramle; være skogsarbeider; it came -ing down with a crash det kom styrtende ned med et brak.

lumberer ['lʌmbərə] tømmerhandler.

lumbering ['lʌmbəriŋ] tung, klosset; ramling; skogsarbeid; tømmerhandel.

lumberman ['lʌmbəmən] skogsarbeider, tømmerhandler.

lumber-mill ['lʌmbəmil] sagbruk.
lumber-room ['lʌmbərum] pulterkammer, skraploft.
luminary ['l(j)u·minəri] lysende; lysende legeme; **he is no great** — han har ikke oppfunnet kruttet.
luminous ['l(j)u·minəs] lysende, strålende.
lummy ['lʌmi] prektig, herlig, grom, glup.
lump [lʌmp] klump, masse; stykke; slå sammen; ikke synes om, mislike; **a — of a fellow** en stor rusk; **I felt a — in my throat** jeg kjente en klump i halsen; **I swallowed a great — in my throat** jeg svelgde en klump, som kom opp i halsen på meg; **a — was rising in his throat** han kunne ikke tale (av bevegelse); **sell by the —** selge rubb og stubb; **work by the —** arbeide på akkord; **lumps** sukkerklumper; **if you don't like it you may —** it hvis du ikke synes om det, kan du la være; **— the lighter** bli deponert; — it down drikke i én slurk.
lumper ['lʌmpə] bryggesjauer.
lump-fish ['lʌmpfiʃ] rognkjeks, steinbit (fisk).
lumping ['lʌmpiŋ] kluntet, klosset, svær.
lumpish ['lʌmpiʃ] kluntet, svær, treg, seig.
lump-sugar ['lʌmp'ʃugə] stykkesukker, raffinade.
lump-work akkordarbeid.
lumpy ['lʌmpi] kluntet, klosset; krapp.
lunacy ['l(j)u·nəsi] månesyke, sinnssyke, galskap.
lunar ['l(j)u·nə] måne-, måneformig; distanseobservasjon.
lunatic ['l(j)u·nətik] sinnssyk, gal; **— asylum** sinnssykeasyl.
lunch [lʌn(t)ʃ] lunsj, annen frokost; spise lunsj.
luncheon ['lʌn(t)ʃən] lunsj (især om en festlig el. offisiell lunsj).
lune [l(j)u·n] halvmåneformet gjenstand; halvmåne.
lunette [lu'net] lunette (slags befestningsverk); flatt urglass; halvsirkelformet hull.
lung [lʌŋ] lunge.
lunge [lʌn(d)ʒ] støt, utfall; langtom, langreip; leie i langtom; gjøre utfall.
lunged [lʌŋd] forsynt med lunger.
lupin ['l(j)u·pin] lupin.
lupine ['lu·pain] ulvaktig; ['lu·pin] lupin.
lupus ['l(j)u·pəs] lupus.
lurch [lə·tʃ] overhaling, krengning; krenge over; tumle; **leave in the —** la i stikken; **lie upon the —** ligge på lur; lure.
lurcher ['le·tʃə] kjeltring; krypskytterhund.
lure [l(j)uə] lokkemat; lokke.

lurid ['l(j)uərid] bleik, gusten, uhyggelig; mørk, døkk.
lurk [lə·k] ligge på lur, lure på, lure; **— about** snike seg omkring, luske. **lurking-place** ['lə·kiŋ ple's] skjulested, smutthull.
luscious ['lʌʃəs] søt; vammel.
lush [lʌʃ] saftig, yppig.
lush [lʌʃ] sterk drikk; drikke; full, drukken.
lust [lʌst] lyst, begjær, lystenhet; føle begjær. **lustful** lysten, vellystig. **lustfulness** lystenhet. **lustihood, lustiness** kraft, friskhet.
lustration [lʌ'stre'ʃən] renselse.
lustre ['lʌstə] glans; prakt; berømmelse; lysekrone. **lustreless** [-lès] glansløs, matt.
lustrine ['lʌstrin] lystring (slags silkestoff).
lustrous ['lʌstrəs] skinnende.
lustrum ['lʌstrəm] femårsperiode.
lusty ['lʌsti] kraftig, sterk, sprek.
lute [l(j)u·t] lutt; spille på lutt.
Luther ['l(j)u·þə] Luther. **Lutheran** ['l(j)u·þərən] luthersk, lutheraner. **Lutheranism** ['lu·þərənizm] lutherdom.
luxate ['lʌkse't] forvri, bringe ut av ledd; **luxation** [lʌk'se'ʃən] forvridning.
luxe [luks] luksus.
Luxemburg ['lʌksəmbə·g] Luxembourg.
luxuriance [lʌg'ʒuəriəns, -gzj-], **luxuriancy** [-si] yppighet, frodighet. **luxuriant** [lʌg'ʒuə riənt, -gzj-] yppig, fyldig, rik.
luxuriate [lʌg'ʒuərie't, gzj-] vokse frodig; fråtse, fråsse i.
luxuriation [lʌgʒuəri'e'ʃən, -gzj-] frodig vekst.
luxurious [lʌg'ʒuəriəs, -gzj-] luksuriøs, yppig, overdådig. **luxuriousness** [-nès] overdådighet.
luxury ['lʌkʃəri] overdådighet, luksus, behagelighet; nytelse, delikatesse; **live in —** leve omgitt av luksus.
lyceum [lai'si·əm] lyceum; lærd skole, latinskole.
lyer-in ['laiər'in] barselkone.
lying ['laiiŋ] løgnaktig, løgn.
lying ['laiiŋ] ligging. **— -day** liggedag.
lying-in ['laiiŋ'in] barselseng; **lying-in hospital** fødselsstiftelse.
lymph [limf] vannaktig legemsvæske, lymfe.
lymphatic [lim'fätik] lymfekar.
lyncean [lin'si·ən] gaupe-, gaupeaktig; skarp.
lynch [linʃ] lynche. **— -law** lynchjustis.
lynx [liŋks] gaupe.
Lyons ['laiənz] Lyons; Lyon (by i Frankrike).
lyre ['laiə] lyre.
lyric ['lirik] lyrisk; lyrisk dikt; lyrikk; **— poem** lyrisk dikt; **— poet** lyriker.
lyrical ['lirikl] lyrisk.

M

M, m [em] M fk. f. **madam, majesty, married, masculine, metre.**
M. fk. f. bl. a. **monsieur.**
'm fk. f. **madam, am.**
M' det samme som Mac (i navn).
M. A. fk. f. **Master of Arts.**
ma [ma·] mamma, mor.
Ma'am [məm; ma·m] frue (brukt i tiltale av tjenere).
Mab [mäb] Mab (fk. f. Mabel); **Queen —** alvedronningen.
M. A. B. fk. f. **Metropolitan Asylums Board.**
Mac [mäk, mək] forstaving i skotske navn, -son, -sen, -søn.
macadam road [mək'ädəm ro·d] makadamisert vei (oppkalt etter oppfinneren Mac Adam). **macadamization** [məkädəmai'ze'ʃən] makadamisering. **macadamize** [mə'kädəmaiz] makadamisere.
macaroni [mäkə'ro·ni] makaroni; (gammelt:)

sprett, sjpert; **— cheese**, en pudding med makaroni og ost.
macaronic [mäkə'rånik] makaronisk vers (vers i blandingsspråk, f. eks. med latinske ord el. engelske ord med latinske endinger).
macaroon [mäkə'ru·n] makron.
macassar [mə'käsə] makassarolje.
Macaulay [mə'kå·li] Macaulay.
macaw [mə'kå·] ara (slags papegøye).
Macbeth [mək'beþ] Macbeth (skotsk fyrste).
mace [me's] kølle, stav, septer, septerbærer.
mace [me's] muskatblomme.
Macedonia [mäsi'do·njə] Makedonia.
macerate ['mäsəre't] bløte; avmagre, uttære **maceration** [mäsə're'ʃən] avmagring.
machinate ['mäkine't] planlegge, klekke ut, finne på, tenke ut. **machination** [mäki'ne'ʃən] planlegging, renke, meinråd. **machinator** ['mäkine'tə] renkesmed.

machine [mə'ʃi·n] maskin; arbeide på (el. med) maskin. **machinelike** [mə'ʃi·nlaik] maskinmessig. **machinery** [mə'ʃi·n(ə)ri] maskineri. **machine-gun** maskingevær. **machine-tool** verktøysmaskin **machinist** [mə'ʃi·nist] maskinbygger, maskinist.
mackerel ['mäkərəl] makrell. — **-gale** sterk kuling.
mackintosh ['mäkintåʃ] mackintosh; slags vanntett tøy; regnfrakk; vanntett.
Maclaren [mək'lärən] Maclaren.
macula ['mäkjulə] plett, flekk. **maculate** ['mäkjuleit] plette, flekke. **maculation** [mäkju'leiʃən] makulering, flekking; flekk.
mad [mäd] avsindig, gal, rasende, fra vettet; — **with** joy ute av seg selv av glede; — **after** (**for, upon**) gal etter, forhippet på; — **as a March hare** sprøyte gal; — **as a hatter** gal som en tyrk; **like** — som en gal; **drive** — gjøre gal; **go** — bli gal.
Madagascar [mädə'gäskə] Madagaskar.
madam ['mädəm] frue, frøken (i tiltale).
madame ['mädəm] fru (tittel foran utenlandsk dames navn); **Madame Tussaud's** [tu'souz] vokskabinett i London.
madcap ['mädkäp] galfrans, galning.
madden ['mädn] gjøre rasende, drive fra vettet; bli gal.
madder ['mädə] krapplante; sl. rød farge av denne.
madding ['mädiŋ] avsindig, rasende, vill.
mad-doctor ['mäddåktə] sinnssykelege.
made [meid] imperf. og perf. pts. av **make**; — dishes lapskaus, litt av hvert; **he is a** — **man** hans lykke er gjort.
Madeira [mə'diərə] Madeira; madeira (vin).
mademoiselle [mädəm'zel] frk. (tittel brukt om fransk dame, ofte om fransk guvernante).
made-up ['meidʌp] kunstig, laget, sminket.
madhouse ['mädhaus] sinssykeasyl, galehus.
madman ['mädmən] sinnssyk person, gal.
madness ['mädnes] sinnssyke, galskap.
Madonna [mə'dånə] madonna.
Madras [mə'dräs, -a·s] Madras (indisk by).
madrepore ['mädripå·ə] stjernekorall.
Madrid [mə'drid] Madrid.
madrigal ['mädrigəl] madrigal, elskovsdikt.
maelstrom ['meilstroum] malstrøm.
Mafeking ['mäfikiŋ] Mafeking (i Sør-Afrika).
maffick ['mäfik] juble.
mag [mäg] halvpenny; snakk, snakketøy; pludre, skravle, snakke; **hold your** — hold snavl.
magazine [mägə'zi·n] magasin, tidsskrift; magasinere, oppsamle. — **-rifle** magasingevær. **magazinist** [-'zi·nist] medarbeider ved tidsskrift.
Magdalen ['mägdəlin] Magdalene; — **College** 'må·dlin'kålidʒ] Magdalen College (i Oxford).
Magellan [mə'gelən] Magellan; **Strait of** — Magellanstredet.
maggot ['mägət] larve, maddik, mark, makk; innfall, lune, grille; **just as the** — **bites her** etter om det stikker henne.
magotty ['mägəti] full av makk; lunefull.
magi ['meidʒai] magere (plur. av **magus**). **magian** ['meidʒən] magisk: mager.
magic ['mädʒik] tryllekunst, trolldom; magisk; — lantern laterna magica; — **wand** tryllestav.
magical ['mädʒikl] magisk. **magician** [mə-'dʒiʃən] tryllekunstner, trollmann.
magisterial [mädʒi'stiəriəl] øvrighets-; skolemester-, overlegen, hoven. **magistracy** ['mädʒistrəsi] embetsverdighet, magistrat. **magistrate** ['mädʒistrét] øvrighetsperson; fredsdommer, politidommer.
Magna Charta ['mägnə'ka·ətə] det store engelske frihetsbrevet fra 1215; frihetsbrev.
magnanimity [mägnə'nimiti] høymodighet.
magnanimous [mäg'nänimə s] høymodig.
magnate ['mägneit] stormann, storkar, magnat.
magnesia [mäg'ni·ʃə] magnesia.

magnesium [mäg'ni·ziəm] magnesium — **light** magnesiumslys.
magnet ['mägnèt] magnet. **magnetic** [mäg-'netik] magnetisk. **magnetics** [mäg'netiks] læren om magnetisme. **magnetism** ['mägnitizm] magnetisme, tiltrekningskraft. **magnetize** ['mägnitaiz] magnetisere. **magnetizer** ['mägnitaizə] magnetisør.
magneto [mäg'ni·tou] magnet (i motor).
magnificence [mäg'nifisəns] prakt, herlighet. **magnificent** [mäg'nifisənt] storartet, praktfull.
magnefier ['mägnifaiə] forstørrelsesglass, lupe.
magnify ['mägnifai] forstørre, forøke; overdrive; lovprise. **magnefying-glass** ['mägnifaiiŋ-'gla·s] forstørrelsesglass, lupe.
magniloquence [mäg'nilokwəns] svulstighet, kyt, store ord. **magniloquent** [mäg'nilokwənt] svulstig.
magnitude ['mägnitju·d] størrelse; viktighet, vekt.
magnolia [mäg'nouljə] magnolia.
magnum-bonum ['mägnəm-'bounəm] magnum bonum (slags stor potet, plomme osv.).
magpie ['mägpai] skjor, skjære; skravlekopp.
Magyar [mə'dʒa·ə] madjar; madjarsk.
Maharaja [ma·hə'ra·dʒə] indisk fyrste.
Maharanee [ma·hə'ra·ni] indisk dronning.
mahatma [mə'hätmə] stor sjel, mahatma.
Mahdi ['ma·di] Mahdi (muhamedansk Messias).
mahlstick ['ma·lstik] malerstokk.
mahogany [mə'hägəni] mahogni, mahognitre.
Mahomet [mə'håmèt] Muhamed. **Mahometan** [mə'håmitən] muhamedansk; muhamedaner. **Mahometanism** [mə'håmitənizm] muhamedanisme.
mahout [mə'haut] elefantfører.
Mahratta [mə'rätə] mahratta.
maid [meid] jomfru; jente, pike, hushjelp; — **of all work** enepike; — **of honour** hoffdame.
maiden ['meidn] jomfru, pike, jente; jomfruelig, uberørt, ren; — **name** pikenavn; — **speech** jomfrutale, et medlems første tale. — **trip** jomfrutur, første reise.
maidenhair ['meidnhæ·ə] burkne, murburkne; bjørnemos, romegras.
maidenhead ['meidnhed] jomfrudom, møydom. **maiden|hood** ['meidnhud] jomfruelighet, jomfrustand. **-like** ['meidnlaik] jomfruelig; jomfrunalsk. **maidenliness** ['meidnlinès] jomfruelighet. **maidenly** ['meidnli] jomfruelig, ærbar.
maidhood ['meidhud] = **maidenhood**.
maid-servant ['meidsə·vənt] tjenestepike, hushjelp.
mail [meil] panser, brynje; pansre; **coat of** — panserskjorte; **-ed fist** pansret neve.
mail [meil] postsekk, brevsekk; brevpost, post; sende med posten; **by to-day's** — med posten i dag; **by return of** — omgående.
mailable ['meiləbl] som kan sendes med posten. **mail|bag** ['meilbäg] postsekk. **-cart** postvogn; barnevogn (for noe større barn), promenadevogn. — **-coach** postvogn. — **-guard** postfører.
mail-train ['meiltrein] posttog.
maim [meim] lemleste, skəmslå, skamfere.
main [mein] kraft, makt, styrke; hovedledning; hovedel, hovedmasse; hovedsak; hav, verdenshav; fastland, kontinent; **with might and** — av all makt, av alle krefter, anspent; **for the** —, **in the** — for største delen; i hovedsaken; hoved-, vesentligst, viktigst; **the** — **chance** egen fordel, et godt parti; — **line** hovedlinje (av jernbane); **the** — **opinion** den rådende mening; **by** — **force** med makt; — **sea** rom sjø; **the** — **stress** hovedvekten; — **-brace** storbras. — **-deck** hoveddekk; øverste dekk. — **-drain** hovedkloakk.
mainland ['mei·n'länd] fastland.**mainly** ['meinli] hovedsakelig. **mainmast** ['mei·nma·st] stormast. **main|-plot** hovedhandling. — **-sheet** storskjøt. — **-spring** hovedfjær, drivfjær.
maintain [men'tein, mən-, mei·n-] holde, opprettholde, vedlikeholde, hevde, holde i hevd,

fastholde, forsvare; underholde, understøtte, ernære. **maintainable** [-əbl] holdbar. **maintainer** [-'te'nə] forsvarer, hevder, forsørger. **maintenance** ['me'ntinəns] vedlikehold; forsvar; underhold, understøttelse, opprettholdelse.
main|-top ['me'ntåp] stormers. **-yard** [-ja·d] storrå.
maize [me'z] mais.
majestic [mə'dʒestik] majestetisk. **majesty** ['mædʒisti] majestet. **His Majesty** hans majestet.
majolica [mə'jålikə] majolika (slags fajanse.)
major ['me'dʒə] større, eldre; størst (av to); major; fullmyndig. — **-domo** ['me'dʒə'do"mo"] major domus, rikshovmester, drottsete. — **-general** ['me'dʒə'dʒə'nərəl] generalmajor.
Majorca [mə'dʒå·kə, mə'jå·-] Majorca.
majority [mə'dʒåriti] stilling som major; fullmyndighet; majoritet; **have a** — være i majoritet, ha flertall; **join the** — gå all kjødets gang; dø.
majorship ['me'dʒəʃip] majors rang, stilling.
majuscule [mə'dʒʌskju.l] majuskel, stor bokstav.
make [me'k] gjøre; lage, fabrikere, gjøre i stand, få til, få isammen, forferdige, skape, danne, tilberede; la bringe til; gjøre til, utnevne til; utgjøre, framstille; tjene; bli; **made in England** engelsk fabrikat; — **the cards** stokke, blande og gi kort; — **cheer** være munter; — **good cheer** spise godt; — **a hit** gjøre lykke, slå igjennom; — **one's mark** bli berømt; — **a mess of it** ødelegge det hele; — **money** tjene penger, bli rik; — **the most of** få mest mulig ut av; — **much of** sette stor pris på, sette høyt, like godt; — **a night of it** more seg hele natten; **he -s nothing** of han regner det ikke for noe at; — **peace** slutte fred; — **a point of** legge stor vekt på; — **reply** svare; — **a speech** holde en tale; — **war** føre krig; — **good** syne, bevise; holde, oppfylle; virkeliggjøre, utføre, rinne inn igjen. — **good a charge** bevise en anklage; — **oneself scarce** stikke av; **how much does it** — hvor mye beløper det seg til; — **believe** få til å tro; **I** — **the sum** larger than you do** jeg regner beløpet for større enn De gjør; **what time may you** — it hvor mange er Deres klokke; — **friends** bli gode venner; **he will never** — **an officer** han blir aldri offiser; — **out** greie, skjønne; tyde, tolke, legge ut; få fram; få ut av; skaffe; **I cannot** — him out jeg vet ikke hva jeg skal tro om ham; **he was not able to** — out the money han var ikke i stand til å skaffe pengene til veie; — **over** overdra, avhende; — **up** samle, lage; lage til; legge sammen; bilegge, slutte fred; innhente; **we made it up** vi ble gode venner igjen; — **up one's mind** ta en beslutning, bestutte seg til; — **up the lost time** innhente det forsømte; — **for** ta retning, sette kursen for; — **as if** late som om; — **off** skynde seg bort, løpe bort; **he is not so bad as people** — out han er ikke så slem som folk vil ha ham til.
make [me'k] fabrikasjon, fabrikat; form, bygning, lag, snitt.
make [me'k] (i skotsk) kamerat, felle, like.
makeable ['me'kəbl] gjørlig.
make-believe ['me'kbili·v] skinn, påskudd.
maker ['me'kə] fabrikant, produsent.
makeshift ['me'kʃift] nødmiddel, surrogat, midlertidig hjelpemiddel.
make-up ['me'kʌp] utstyr, ytre; maske, forkledning, sminke.
making ['me'kiŋ] dannelse, laging, fabrikasjon; **that was the** — **of him** det grunnla hans lykke; **there is the** — **of a good soldier in him** det er stoff til en god soldat i ham.
Malacca [mə'läkə] Malakka.
malachite ['mäləkait] malakitt (grønt mineral)
maladjustment ['mälə'dʒʌstmənt] dårlig ordning.
maladministration ['mälədmini'stre'ʃən] vanstyre.

maladroit ['mälədroit] ubehendig, trehendt.
malady ['mälədi] sykdom.
mala fide ['me'lə'faidi] ikke i god tro.
Malagasy [mälə'gäsi] madagassisk; madagasser.
malaise [mä'le'z] illebefinnende.
malapert ['mäləpə·t] nesevis.
Malaprop ['mäləpråp] latterlig feilbruk av ord. **Mrs. Malaprop** person i Sheridans The Rivals som bruker ordene galt. **malapropism** ['mäləprápizm] d. s. s. **malaprop**.
malapropos ['mäl'äprəpo"] malapropos, i utide, på urette sted.
malar ['me'lə] kinnbein.
malaria [mä'læ·əriə] malaria, sumpfeber. **malarial** [mä'læ·əriəl], **malarious** [-riəs] som hører til malaria, usunn.
Malay [mə'le'] malaier. **Malayan** [mə'le'n] malaiisk.
Malcolm ['mälkəm] Malcolm.
malcontent ['mälkən'tent] misfornøyd,misnøyd.
malcontented [mälkən'tentid] misfornøyd, misnøyd. **malcontentedness** [-nès] misnøye.
male [me'l] mannlig, han-; mannfolk, han; — **child** guttebarn.
malediction [mäli'dikʃən] forbannelse, våbønn.
malefactor [mäli'fäktə] forbryter, illgjerningsmann.
malepractice [mäl'präktis] feilgrep, feil, misbruk.
malevolence [mə'levoləns] uvilje, ondskap.
malevolent [mə'levolənt] ondskapsfull.
malfeasance ['mälfi·zəns] mislighet.
malformation ['mälfå·ə'me'ʃən] misdannelse.
malformed [mäl'få·əmd] vanskapt.
malice ['mälis] ondskap, hat.
malicious [mə'liʃəs] ondskapsfull.
maliferous [mə'lifərəs] ondartet, farlig.
malign [mə'lain] ondskapsfull, ond, vond; tale ille om, hate, skade. **malignancy** [mə'lignənsi] ondskap. **malignant** [mə'lignənt] ondskapsfull; ondartet. **maligner** [mə'lainə] baktaler. **malignity** [mə'ligniti] ondskap.
malinger [mə'liŋgə] simulere, skulke.
malism ['meilizm] pessimisme, den læren at verden i grunnen er ond.
malison ['mälizən, -sən] forbannelse.
malkin ['må·(l)kin] skureklut; fugleskremsel.
mall [mel, mäl] spasergang, allé; **the M.** en allé i St. James's park i London.
mall [må·l] langskaftet klubbe, trehammer; banke med trehammer.
mallard ['mäləd] villandrik; villand, stokkand.
malleable ['mäljəbl] som kan smies, strekkes; bøyelig, plast sk. **malleate** ['mälie't] hamre
malleation [mäli'e'ʃən] uthamring.
mallet ['mälit] klubbe, trehammer.
mallow ['mälo"] kattost, malva.
malmsey ['ma·mzi] malvasier (slags vin)
malnutrition ['mälnju'triʃən] dårlig kost, dårlig ernæring.
malt [må(·)lt] malt; øl; malte, melte.
Malta ['må(·)ltə] Malta.
malt-dust [må'ltdäst] maltspirer.
Maltese ['må·l'ti·z, mål'ti·z] maltesisk, malteser-; malteser.
malt-floor ['må·ltflå·ə] maltloft; maltlag.
malt-house ['må·lthaus] malteri.
Malthus ['mälþəs] Malthus. **-ian** [mäl'þju·ʒən] malthusiansk; malthusianer.
maltreat [mäl'tri·t] mishandle. **maltreatment** [-mənt] mishandling.
maltster ['må·ltstə] malter. **malty** ['må·lti] malt-, maltlignende.
malversation [mälvə'se'ʃən] slett oppførsel; utroskap; bestikkelighet; underslep.
Ma'm [məm] frue (i tiltale).
mam [mäm], **mama** [mə'ma·] se **mamma**.
mamma [mə'ma·] mamma.

mamma ['mämə] spene, patte. mammal ['mä-məl] pl. mammalia [mä'me¹liə] pattedyr.

mammon ['mämən] mammom. mammonist ['mämənist], mammonite ['mämənait] mammon-dyrker.

mammoth ['mäməþ] mammutdyr.

mammy ['mämi] mor, mamma; negerkvinne (især om aldrende negerkvinne).

man [män] menneske, mann; tjener; brikke (i spill); bemanne; manne opp; the old — den gamle, gamlen = faren; — of business forretningsmann; — of colour neger; — of letters lærd; forfatter; — -of-all-work faktotum, altmuligmann, tusen-kunstner; — of many words en som bruker mange ord; — of his word som en kan stole på; — of the world verdensmann; to a — alle som en; — and boy fra barndommen av; when I am a — når jeg blir voksen; the fall of — syndefallet; the rights of — menneskerettighetene. Man [män] Man; the Isle of — øya Man.

manacle ['mänəkl] håndjern; sette håndjern på.

manage ['mänidʒ] håndtere, lede, styre, be-handle, manøvrere, klare, greie, overkomme, spare på, holde hus med; temme, ride til, av-rette; I suppose it can be -d det kan nok la seg ordne; they all -d to get out det lyktes alle å slippe ut.

manageability [mänidʒə'biliti] medgjørlighet; påvirkelighet. manageable ['mänidʒəbl] med-gjørlig.

management ['mänidʒmənt] behandling, be-tjening; bestyrelse, styre, ledelsé; takt, klokskap.

manager ['mänidʒə] leder, bestyrer, avdelings-sjef, disponent, direktør; en som manøvrerer med takt og klokskap; impressario, arrangør. managerial [mäni'dʒiəriəl] bestyrelses-, styre-.

managing ['mänidʒiŋ] ledende, bestyrende; managing director administrerende direktør.

man-at-arms ['mänət'a·mz] krigsmann; tungt-væpnet soldat.

Manchester ['mäntʃistə] Manchester; the — school ɔ: frihandelspartiet.

man-child ['mäntʃaild] guttebarn.

Manchu [män'tʃu·] mandsju; mandsjuisk.

Manchukuo ['mäntʃu·ku'oᵘ] Mandsjukuo.

Manchuria [män'tʃuəriə] Mandsjuria.

manciple ['mänsipl] leveringsmann, en som skaffer forsyninger til et college osv.

mandamus [män'de¹məs] (jur.) ordre; utstede ordrer til.

mandarin ['mändərin] mandarin.

mandatary ['mändətəri] fullmektig, ombuds-mann.

mandate ['mände¹t] pålegg, ombud, befaling; fullmakt.

mandible ['mändibl] kjeve, kjake(bein).

mandolin ['mändolin] mandolin.

mandragora [män'drägərə] alrune.

mandrake ['mändre¹k] alrune.

mandrel ['mändrəl] spindel (på dreiebenk); dor; kilhakke. — -stock spindeldokk.

mandrill ['mändril] mandrill (slags bavian).

manducable ['mändjukəbl] som kan tygges, spises. manducate ['mändjuke¹t] tygge; spise.

mane [me¹n] manke, man, faks. -d med manke.

man-eater ['mäni·tə] menneskeeter; menneske-etende tiger.

manege [mə'ne¹ʒ] ridekunst; ridebane.

manes ['me¹ni·z] maneser, de avdødes sjeler.

manful ['mänf(u)l] mandig, karslig, tapper.

manganese [mäŋgə'ni·z] mangan.

mange [me¹n(d)ʒ] skabb (utslett).

manger ['me¹n(d)ʒə] krybbe.

manginess ['me¹n(d)ʒinés] skabbethet.

mangle ['mäŋgl] lemleste, sønderrive, rive sund.

mangle ['mäŋgl] rulle, mangle (tøy); rulle.

mango ['mäŋgoᵘ] mango (indisk frukt).

mangrove ['mäŋgroᵘv] mangrovetre.

mangy ['me¹n(d)ʒi] skabbet.

manhater ['mänhe¹tə] menneskehater.

manhole ['mänhoᵘl] mannhull (i dampkjele).

manhood ['mänhud] menneskelighet; mann-dom, manndomsalder; grow to — vokse opp til mann.

mania ['me¹njə] vanvidd, galskap; mani.

maniac ['me¹niäk], maniacal [mə'naiəkl] van-vittig, gal, avsindig.

manicure ['mänikjuə] pleie av hender og neg-ler; manikyrist; pleie hender og negler; mani-curing ['mänikjuəriŋ] håndpleie.

manifest ['mänifest] tydelig, klar, grei, åpen-bar; nøyaktig liste over skipslast, tolloppgivelse; åpenbare, legge for dagen, kunngjøre, anmelde (varer for tollvesenet). manifestable ['mäni'festəbl] som kan angis. manifestant [mäni'festənt] de-monstrant. manifestation [mänifes'te¹ʃən] åpen-baring, demonstrasjon, utslag. manifesto [mäni-'festoᵘ] manifest, erklæring.

manifold ['mänifoᵘld] mangfoldig, mangfoldig-gjøre; — writer hektograf, duplikator.

manikin ['mänikin] mannsling, leddedukke.

Manila [mə'nilə] Manila; manilasigar.

maniple ['mänipl] manipel; romersk kompani.

manipulate [mə'nipjule¹t] behandle, håndtere, utføre; manipulere. manipulation [mənipju'le¹-ʃən] håndtering, behandling, manipulasjon.

Manitoba [mänito'ba·, mäni'toᵘbə] Manitoba.

manitou ['mänitu·] manitu, slags guddom el. fylgje hos indianerne.

mankiller ['mänkilə] drapsmann.

mankind [mən'kaind] menneskehet, menneske-slekt; [ogs. 'mänkaind] mannkjønn(et).

Manks = Manx.

manlike ['mänlaik] som en mann, mannlig : mandig, karslig; mannhaftig.

manliness ['mänlinés] mandighet.

manly ['mänli] mandig.

man-mountain ['mänmauntin] kjempe.

manna ✦[mänə] manna.

mannequin ['mänikwin] mannequin.

manner ['mänə] manér, skikk, vis, måte, lag, framferd, sedvane, stil; -s oppførsel, folkeskikk, manérer; all — of things alle mulige ting; by no — of means på ingen måte, under ingen om-stendigheter, slett ikke; in a (certain) — på en måte; in a — of speaking i parentes bemerket; in this — på denne måte; he has no -s han eier ikke folkeskikk; ways and -s skikk og bruk. mannered ['mänəd] med . . . seder; av . . . seder; kunstlet, tilgjort, maniert.

mannerism ['mänərizm] manér, unatur; manert-het. mannerist ['mänərist] manierist.

mannerless ['mänəlés] uoppdragen, ubehøvlet. mannerliness ['mänəlinés] god tone, folkeskikk. mannerly ['mänəli] veloppdragen, høflig.

mannikin ['mänikin] mannsling, dverg; (kunst-ners) leddedukke; fantom; mannequin, prøve-dame.

mannish ['mäniʃ] maskulin, mannhaftig.

manoeuvre [mə'nu·və] manøver; manøvrere.

man-of-war [mänə(v)'wå·ə] krigsskip, orlogs-skip.

manometer [mə'nämitə] trykkmåler.

manor ['mänə] landgods, hovedgård; lord of the — godseier. —-house herregård.

manorial [mə'nå·riəl] herskapelig, herregårds.

mansard ['mänsa·ᵃd, -səd] el. mansard roof mansard-tak; brutt tak.

manse [mäns] (skotsk:) prestegård.

mansion ['mänʃən] våning, herregård, herskaps-bolig. the Mansion-house embetsbolig i London for lord Mayor.

manslaughter ['mänslå·tə] drap.

manslayer ['mänsle¹ə] drapsmann.

mansuetude ['mänswitju·d] mildhet.

mantel ['mäntl] kamingesims. — -piece, — -shelf kamingesims, kaminhylle, peishylle.

mantilla [män'tilə] mantilje, kort silkekå

mantle ['mäntl] kappe, kåpe; glødenett (i lamper); dekke til, bedekke, innhylle; skjule.

mantlet ['mäntlèt] liten kåpe; skuddsikkert skjermtak.

mantrap ['mänträp] fotangel, saks.

manual ['mänjuəl] manuell, kropps-, hånd-; håndbok; — **alphabet** fingeralfabet; — **exercise** håndgrep; — **goods** avsettelige varer; — **labour** kroppsarbeid, håndkraft; — **letters** fingeralfabet.

manufactory [mänju'fäktəri] fabrikk, fabrikasjon. **manufactural** [mänju'fäktʃərəl] fabrikk-. **manufacture** [-fäktʃə] fabrikasjon, fabrikat, industri, industrivare; fabrikere, tilvirke, lage. **manufacturer** [-'fäktʃərə] fabrikant. **manufacturing industry** fabrikkindustri, industrinæring.

manumission [mänju'miʃən] frigivelse (av slave). **manumit** [mänju'mit] gi (slave) fri.

manurable [mə'njuərəbl] som kan gjødsles, dyrkes. **manure** [mə'njuə] dyrke, gjøde; gjødsle; gjødning, gjødsel. **manurial** [mə'njuəriəl] gjødnings-.

manuscript ['mänjuskript] håndskrevet, i manuskript; håndskrift, manuskript.

Manx [mäɲks] mansk, fra Man.

Manxman ['mäɲksmən] beboer av Man.

many ['meni] mang en, mangt, mange; mengde; **this** — **a day, for** — **a long day** på lange tider; **as** — **again** en gang til så mange; **he is one** **too** — for me han er meg for sterk; **I have not** **seen him these** — years jeg har ikke sett ham på mange år; **the leaves reflected back the light** **as if so** — **little mirrors had been scattered . . .** som om bare småsmått . . .; **we were packed up** **like so** — **herrings** vi var stuet sammen som sild i en tønne; **the** — flertallet, mengden; **a good** —, **a great** — en mengde. — **-coloured** mangefarget. — **-cornered** mangekantet. **manyheaded** ['menihedid] mangehodet. **manysided** mangesidet; mangesidig.

Maori ['mauri] maori; maori-.

map [mäp] kart; lendkart; tegne kart; kartlegge; planlegge.

mapping ['mäpiɲ] karttegning.

maple ['meipl] lønn (tre). — **-tree** lønn.

Maquis [ma'ki·] betegnelse for den franske hjemmefrontbevegelse, hjemmefronten.

Maquisard [maki'sa·r] medlem av maquis'en.

mar [ma·ə] skjemme, lyte, vansire, spolere; **make or** — **him** bestemme hans skjebne, skape eller ødelegge hans framtid.

marabou ['märəbu·] marabustork.

maraschino [märə'ski·no"] maraskino (en likør).

maraud [mə'rå·d] marodere, plyndre, streife om på rov; plyndretog. **marauder** [mə'rå·də] marodør. **marauding** [-diɲ] plyndring; plyndrende.

marble ['ma·əbl] marmor, kunstverk av marmor; kiksekule; marmorere; åre.

marbleize ['ma·blaiz] marmorere.

March [ma·ətʃ] mars; — **hare** ung hare; — **mad** sprøyte gal.

march [ma·ətʃ] grense, grensebygd; avgrense.

march [ma·ətʃ] marsjere, rykke fram; la bryte opp; marsjere fram med, bryte opp med; marsj; **forced** — ilmarsj; **steal a** — **upon** komme ubemerket i forkjøpet, snike seg til en fordel over.

marching ['ma·ətʃiɲ] marsj-; **marching-order** marsjordre; marsjorden; **in full marching-order** med full opp-pakning.

marchioness ['ma·əʃənès] markise, markifrue.

marchpane ['ma·ətʃpe'n] marsipan.

marconigram [ma·ə'ko"nigräm] radiotelegram.

mare [mæ·ə] mare, nattmare.

mare [mæ·ə] hoppe, merr; **money makes the** — **go** pengene regjerer verden.

mare's-nest ['mæ·əznest] innbilt funn, skrinet med det rare i.

mare's-tail ['mæ·əzte'l] hestehale (plante); lang fjærsky.

Margaret ['ma·əg(ə)rit] Margrete.

margarine [ma·ədʒə'ri·n, ma·əgə'ri·n] margarin.

Margate ['ma·əgit] engelsk havn og badested.

marge [ma·ədʒ] rand, kant, jare, brem.

Margery ['ma·ədʒəri], **Marget** ['ma·ədʒit] Margit.

margin ['ma·ədʒin] rand, kant, marg, bredd; spillerom, forskjell; prutningsmonn; overskudd; forskjell mellom innkjøps- og utsalgspris; forsyne med rand, begrense; sette marg; forsyne med randbemerkninger; **as per** — som anført i margen; **allow (leave) a** — levne et spillerom; **£ 20 leave a fair** — **for enjoyment** med 20 pund kan en more seg ganske bra. **marginal** ['ma·ədʒinəl] rand-. **marginalia** [ma·ədʒi'ne'ljə] randbemerkninger. **marginate** ['ma·ədʒine't] forsyne med rand.

margravate ['ma·əgrəvèt] markgrevskap. **margrave** ['ma·əgre'v] markgreve. **margraviate** [ma·ə'gre'vjèt] markgrevskap. **margravine** ['ma·ə-grəvi·n] markgrevinne.

Maria [mə'raiə] Marie.

Marian ['mæ·əriən] Mariane.

marigold ['märigo"ld] marigull; ringblomst; — **window** rundt vindu med forsiringer.

marine [mə'ri·n] som hører til havet, sjøen; sjø-; hav-; flåte; marine; sjøbilde; marinesoldat; **mercantile** (el. **merchant**) — handelsflåte.

mariner ['märinə] matros, sjømann, sjøfarende.

marine-store [mə'ri·nstå·ə] et sted hvor det handles med gammelt skipsinventar.

mariolater [mæ·ə'ri'ålətə] mariadyrker.

mariolatry [mæ·ə'ri'ålətri] məriədyrking.

marionette [märiə'net] marionett, dukke.

marish ['märiʃ] myr; sumpig, myrlendt.

marital ['märitəl] ektemanns-.

maritime ['märitaim] maritim, som hører til sjøen, kysten; — **law** sjørett; — **war** sjøkrig.

marjoram ['ma·ədʒərəm] merian (plante).

mar-joy ['ma·ədʒoi] fredsforstyrrer.

Mark [ma·ək] Markus.

mark [ma·ək] merke, tegn; landmerke; fabrikkmerke, stempel, kvalitet; karakter (på skolen); betydning, viktighet; mål; **he will leave his** — han vil vinne seg et navn; **a** — **of favour** en gunstbevisning; **get high -s** få gode karakterer; **a man of** — en betydelig, fremragende mann; **make one's** — skape seg et navn; **hit the** — treffe det rette; **be below the** — være under gjennomsnittet; **be up to the** — holde mål, gjøre fyldest; **fall short of the** — forfeile målet; **mark** [ma·ək] merke, tegne, betegne, markere; gi karakter, sensurere; legge merke til, iaktta; — **time** holde takt; marsjere på stedet. — **-book** karakterbok. **marked** [ma·əkt] merket, mørkert, utpreget. **markedly** ['ma·əkidli] utpreget.

marker ['ma·əkə] merker; markør; sjetong.

market ['ma·əkit] torg; marked, avsetning; **poor (scanty)** — dårlig forsynt marked; — **for** **cattle** kvegmarked; **be at the** — være på markedet; **go to the** — gå på torget; **home** — innenlandsk marked; **foreign** — utenlandsk marked; **dull** — flau avsetning; **find a** — for kunne anbringe, selge, få solgt (varer); **find a ready** —, **meet with a ready** — finne god avsetning; **put on the** — by fram til salgs; **put out of the** — utkonkurrere. **be in the** — for være kjøper av. **market** [ma·ə'kit] sende til torgs, handle med; handle.

marketable ['ma·əkitəbl] avsettelig, kurant.

market-accommodation torgplass. **market-day** torgdag. **market|garden(s)** handelsgartneri. — **-hall** torghall. **marketing** ['ma·əkitiɲ] torghandel; torgkjøp. **market|place** torgplass. — **-prices** torgpriser; kurser. — **-report** markedsmelding. — **-town** kjøpstad.

marking ['ma·əkiŋ] merking; avtegning.
marking-ink merkeblekk.
marksman ['ma·əksmən] sikker skytter. marksmanship [-ʃip] kunstskyting.
marl [ma·əl] mergel; mergle.
Marlborough ['mǻ·lbrə] Marlborough.
Marlow ['ma·əloᵘ] Marlow.
marmalade ['ma·əmələ¹d] marmelade, syltetøy (især appelsin-).
Marmora ['ma·əmərə], the Sea of — Marmarahavet.
marmorate ['ma·əmərét] broket som marmor, marmorert. marmoreal [ma·ə¹må·riəl], marmorean [ma·ə¹må·riən] marmor-, av marmor.
marmoset ['ma·əməzet] silkeape.
marmot ['ma·əmət] murmeldyr.
maroon [mə¹ru·n] rødbrun; slags fyrverkeri.
maroon [mə¹ru·n] møronneger, rømt neger; matros som er latt tilbake på en øy; la tilbake på et ubebodd sted. marooner [mə¹ru·nə] etterlatt matros; bortrømt slave.
marplot ['ma·əplåt] ugagnskråke, ulykkesfugl.
marque [ma·ək] kaperbrev.
marquee [ma·ə¹ki·] telt; teltdekke.
Marquesas [ma·ə¹ke¹säs]; the — Marquesasøyene.
marquess ['ma·əkwis] marki.
marquessate ['ma·əkwisét] marki-rang.
marquetry ['ma·əkitri] innlagt arbeid.
marquis ['ma·əkwis] marki, markgreve.
marquisate ['ma·əkwisét] marki-rang.
marrer ['ma·rə] ugagnskråke.
marriage ['märidʒ] giftermål, ekteskap, bryllup; — articles ektekapskontrakt; — licence kongebrev, ektekapstillatelse; ask in — fri til; give in — gifte bort.
marriageable ['märidʒəbl] gifteferdig, voksen.
married ['märid] gift; her — name hennes navn som hustru; the — state ektestanden.
marrow ['märoᵘ] marg; indre kraft; fylle med marg eller fett; vegetable — slags gresskar.
marrow ['märoᵘ] kamerat, make.
marrowbone ['märoᵘboᵘn] margbein; (i pl. spøkende) kne; bring one to his -s få en til å gi seg.
marrow-fat ['märoᵘfät] slags ert.
marrowless margløs. marrow-pudding margpudding; gresskarpudding. marrowy margfull.
marry ['märi] mare (en ed).
marry ['märi] vie, gifte bort; gifte seg med, ekte; — below oneself gifte seg under sin stand.
Mars [ma·əz] Mars (krigsguden og planeten).
Marseilles [ma·ə¹se¹lz] Marseille.
marsh [ma·əʃ] myrlende, myrland, myr, sump.
marshal [ma·ə¹ʃl] marsjal, marskalk; stille opp, fylke, ordne, føre i rekke. marshaller ['ma·əʃlə] fører, en som stiller opp eller leder. marshalship ['ma·əʃlʃip] marsjal-rang.
Marshalsea ['ma·əʃlsi·] fengsel i London.
marshy ['ma·əʃi] sumpet, myrlendt.
marsupial [ma·ə¹s(j)u·piəl] pungdyr.
mart [ma·ət] marked, torg, markedsplass.
martello [ma·ə¹teloᵘ] tower lite rundt fort bygd på kysten for å hindre fiendtlig landgang.
marten ['ma·tin] mår.
Martha ['ma·əθə] Martha.
martial ['ma·əʃl] krigs-, krigersk, morsk, militær, martialsk; court — krigsrett. martialize ['ma·əʃəlaiz] gjøre krigersk.
martin ['ma·tin] taksvale.
Martin ['ma·ətin] Martin, Morten.
martinet [ma·əti¹net] streng offiser; domestic — hustyrann.
martingale ['ma·ətiŋeᵘl] springreim (på ridehest); fordobling av innsats.
martini [ma·ə¹ti·ni] Martini-rifle.
Martinmas ['ma·ətinməs] mortensdag, d. 11. november.
martlet ['ma·ətlét] taksvale.
martyr ['ma·ətə] martyr, blodvitne; die a — to one's principles dø som martyr for ...; I am

quite a — to gout jeg lider fryktelig av gikt.
martyr ['ma·ətə] la dø som martyr, gjøre til martyr; pine. martyrdom [-dəm] martyrium.
marvel ['ma·əvəl] vidunder; forundring, forbauselse; bli forundret, bli forbauset, undre seg. marvellous ['ma·əvələs] vidunderlig, ganske merkverdig. marvellousness [-nés] vidunderlighet.
Mary marvellousness [-nés] vidunderlighet.
Mary ['mæ·əri] Marie, Maria.
marzipan [ma·ə¹zi¹pän] marsipan.
mascot ['mäskət] maskott, talisman, amulett, lykkebringende person eller ting.
masculine ['mäskjulin] mannlig, maskulin hankjønns-; mandig.
mash [mäʃ] knuse, mase, male sund, meske (malt); -ed potatoes potetstappe. be -ed on være forelsket i. mash [mäʃ] blanding; røre, stappe; forvirring, uorden, miskmask; skatt, kjæreste.
masher ['mäʃə] hjertekuser, løve.
mashie ['mäʃi] slags golfkølle.
mash-tub ['mäʃtʌb] meskekar.
mask [ma·sk] trekke (te).
mask [ma·sk] maske; maskerade, maskespill; skalkeskjul, påskudd; maskere; maskere seg; -ed ball maskerade. masker ['ma·skə] maskert person, maskeskuespiller.
maslin ['mäzlin] blandkorn.
mason ['me¹sn] murer; steinhogger; frimurer; mure. masonic [mə¹sånik] frimurer-. masonry ['me¹snri] muring; murerhåndverk; frimureri.
masque [ma·sk] = mask.
masquerade [mäskə¹re¹d] maskerade; oppføre en maskerade; være maskert. masquerader [mäskə¹re¹də] deltager i en maskerade, utkledd person.
mass [mäs] masse; samle i masse, dynge (seg) opp.
mass [mäs, ma·s] messe.
Mass. fk. f. Massachusetts.
Massa ['mäsə] herre (i negerspråk).
Massachusetts [mäsə¹tʃu·sets].
massacre ['mäsəkə] massakre, blodbad, nedsabling; nedsable, myrde; the — of the innocents barnemordet i Betlehem.
massage ['mäsə·ʒ] massasje; massere.
masseur [mä·sə·] massør.
masseuse [mä·sə·z] massøse.
massive ['mäsiv] massiv, svær, diger, traust
mass-meeting ['mäs¹mi·tiŋ] massemøte.
massy ['mäsi] massiv, svær, tett, diger.
mast [ma·st] mast; before the — forut, som simpel matros; ship before the — ta hyre som simpel matros.
mast [ma·st] eike- el. bøkenøtter, åkorn.
master ['ma·stə] mester, herre, husbond, hersker; håndverksmester, leder, sjef, bestyrer; lærer, skolestyrer; kaptein, skipsfører, skipper; ung herre; magister; over-, hoved-; — of the field herre over slagmarka; be — of oneself beherske seg; be one's own — være sin egen herre; a — of (in) his business en mester i sitt fag; the old -s de gamle mestere; M. of the Horse hoffstallmester; — of the Rolls riksarkivar. master ['ma·stə] mestre, beherske, betvinge, få bukt med; when once all these facts are well -ed når en først har lært alt dette godt; — the language mestre språket.
master-builder ['ma·stə¹bildə] byggmester.
masterful ['ma·stəful] mesterlig; myndig.
master-hand ['ma·stəhänd] mesterhånd.
master|less herreløs; ustyren. -liness mesterlighet, mesterskap. -ly mesterlig, virtuosmessig; myndig; egenmektig. — -mind overlegen ånd. — -piece mesterverk. mastership mesterskap.
master|stroke mestertrekk; mesterverk. — -work hovedverk, mesterstykke. — -workman verksmester.
masthead ['ma·sthed] mastetopp.
mastic ['mästik] mastikstre, mastiksgummi.
masticable ['mästikəbl] som kan tygges. ma-

sticate ['mästikeⁱt] tygge. **mastication** [mästi-'keⁱʃən] tygging.

mastiff ['mästif, 'ma·s-] stor engelsk hund.

mastodon ['mästədån] mastodont (utdødd kjempeelefant).

mat [mät] matte; binde (matter), sammenflette, sammenslynge; **-ted hair** sammenfiltret hår.

matador ['mätedå·ə] matador (i tyrekamp; i kortspill).

match [mätʃ] kamerat, like, likemann; tilsvarende, jevnbyrdig; make; ekteskap, parti; veddekamp, sportsstevne; **he is more than a — for you** han er deg overlegen; **he has not his —** han har ikke sin like; **it's a — la** gå; **will it be a —** blir det et parti ut av det; **she made a good —** hun har gjort et godt parti; **a wrestling —** en brytekamp.

match [mätʃ] forbinde, skaffe maken til; kunne måle seg med, kunne settes ved siden av; komme opp mot, avpasse, bringe i harmoni med; forenes, være par, være make, parre seg; **we tried to — a vase** vi prøvde å kjøpe en vase av samme slags; **they are ill -ed** de passer dårlig sammen; **he cannot — him** han kan ikke greie ham; **a pair of shoes that did not —** som ikke var make.

match [mätʃ] fyrstikk; lunte; **strike a —** tenne en fyrstikk.

matchable ['mätʃəbl] som en kan oppdrive maken til; **not —** makeløs, uten make.

match-board ['mätʃbå·əd] pløyd bord.

match-box ['mätʃbåks] fyrstikkeske, fyrask.

matchless ['mätʃlés] makeløs.

matchlock ['mätʃlåk] luntebørse; luntelås.

match-maker ['mätʃmeⁱkə] giftekniv (en som stifter partier); fyrstikkfabrikant.

matchwood ['mätʃwud] fyrstikkved; **smash to —** slå i småbeter.

mate [meⁱt] felle, kamerat, den ene av et par, ektefelle, make; styrmann; (mar.) mat; forbinde, forene; formæle, gifte, parre.

mate [meⁱt] matt (i sjakk); gjøre matt.

mater ['meⁱtə] (i skoleguttspråk) mor, gamla.

material [mə'tiəriəl] stofflig, legemlig, sanselig, materiell; alvorlig, vektig; emne, materiale, stoff, tilfang. **materialism** [-izm] materialisme. **materialist** [-ist] materialist. **materialistic** [mətiəriə-'listik] materialistisk. **materialize** [mə'tiəriəlaiz] legemliggjøre, materialisere.

matériel [mətiəri'el] materiell.

maternal [mə'tə·nəl] moderlig, moder-, mors-. **maternity** [mə'tə·niti] moderskap, moderlighet.

mathematical [mäþə'mätikl] matematisk. **mathematician** [mäþəmə'tiʃən] matematiker. **mathematics** [mäþə'mätiks] matematikk.

Mathew ['mäþju·] Matteus, Matias.

matin ['mätin] morgen-.

matinée ['mätineⁱ] matiné (tidlig ettermiddagsunderholdning). **matins** ['mätinz] morgengudstjeneste, ottesang, ottemesse.

matric. fk. f. **matriculation.**

matricidal [mätri'saidl] modermordersk. **matricide** ['mätrisai.l] modermord; modermorder.

matriculate [mə'trikjuleⁱt] innskrive, immatrikulere. **matriculation** [mətrikju'leⁱʃən] innskriving, immatrikulering; studenteksamen, eksamen artium.

matrimonial [mätri'mo^unjəl] ekteskapelig, ekteskaps-. **matrimony** ['mätriməni] ekteskap, ektestand.

matrix ['meⁱtriks, 'mät-] livmor; matrise; klisjé; underlag (i lokkemaskin); skrumor, mutter.

matron ['meⁱtr^ən] gift kone, matrone; rådskone, husmor; forstanderinne, f. eks. oldfrue, pleiemor, oversøster.

matronly ['meⁱtrənli] matroneaktig, satt, verdig; matrone-.

Matt. fk. f. **Matthew.**

matter ['mätə] stoff, to, emne, sak, ting, materie; materiale; manuskript, sats; anliggende, grunn, årsak, gjenstand; **— of business** forretningsanliggende; **— of consequence** viktig sak; **— of course** selvfølge; **— of doubt** tvilsom sak; **— of fact** kjensgjerning, realitet; **as a — of fact** i virkeligheten, ja; **the — in hand** den foreliggende sak; **— of joy** grunn til glede; **no -s** det gjør ingenting; bry Dem ikke om det; **it's no — of mine** det kommer ikke meg ved; **no — what I might say** hva jeg så enn ville si; **what's the —** hva er det i veien; **what's the — with him** hva feiler det ham; **make much — of** legge stor vekt på; **he does not mince -s** han tar bladet fra munnen, legger ikke fingrene imellom; **a — of seven miles** omtrent sju mil.

matter ['mätə] være av betydning, ha noe på seg; **it does not —** det gjør ingenting, det har ikke noe å bety; **what does it —?** hva gjør det? **it -ed little whether** det hadde lite å si om; **not that it -s** ikke at det betyr noe; det er nå det samme.

matterful ['mätəful] innholdsrik. **matterless** [-lés] innholdsløs. **matter-of-course** selvfølgelig. **matter-of-fact** prosaisk.

Matthew ['mäþju·] Matteus.

matting ['mätiŋ] matter; mattelaging.

mattock ['mätək] hakke.

mattress ['mätris] madrass.

mature [mə'tjuə] moden, fullstendig, utviklet, voksen; modne, modnes; forfalle til betaling. **maturity** [mə'tjuariti] modenhet, forfallstid; **at (on) —** på forfallsdagen.

matutinal [mätju'tainəl] morgen-, tidlig.

Maud [må·d] fk. f. **Magdalene** eller **Mathilda.**

Maudlin ['må·dlin] Magdalena.

maudlin ['må·dlin] beruset, sentimental.

maugre ['må·gə] til tross for, trass i.

maul [må·l] trehammer, treklubbe; slå, skamslå, pryle, mishandle.

maulstick ['må·lstik] malerstokk.

maunch ['må·nʃ] erme.

maunder ['må·ndə] klynke, jamre, seg; snakke usammenhengende, ørske, tulle, snakke i vilske.

Maundy Thursday ['må·ndi þə·zdi] skjærtorsdag.

Mauser ['mauzə], slags magasinrifle.

mausoleum [må·sə'li·əm] mausoleum, gravminne.

mauve [mo^uv] lilla, lillafarget.

mavis ['meⁱvis] måltrost.

maw [må·] krel, mage; **hold your —** hold munn!

mawkish ['må·kiʃ] kvalmende, ekkel; søtlaten, sentimental.

maxillar(y) [mäk'silə(ri)] kjeve-, kjake-.

maxim ['mäxim] grunnsetning, regel.

Maxim ['mäksim] maximkanon.

maximum ['mäksiməm] maksimum, det høyeste; **— price** maksimalpris.

May [meⁱ] mai, mai måned.

May [meⁱ] Maia.

may [meⁱ] må, kan, kan kanskje, tør; **the young — die, but the old must** barn kan dø, gamle må dø; **it — be** kanskje; **come what — —** komme hva det vil; **— I trouble you for some bread** vil De være så vennlig å rekke meg noe brød; **— I never** (nml. be saved el. l.) if så sant jeg lever! **that they might not** for at de ikke skulle.

maybe ['meⁱbi·] kanskje, kan hende.

may|-bug ['meⁱbʌg] oldenborre. **-day** første mai. **-flower** maiblomst, hagtorn.

may-fly ['meⁱflai] døgnflue; vårflue.

mayhap ['meⁱhäp] kan hende.

maying ['meⁱiŋ], **go —** gå ut og plukke maiborgerblomster.

May-lady ['meⁱleⁱdi] maidronning.

May-lord ['meⁱlå·əd] maigreve.

mayonnaise [meⁱə'neⁱz] majones.

mayor [mæ·ə] borgermester. **mayoress** ['mæ·ə-rés] borgermesterfrue. **mayorship** ['mæ·əʃip] borgermestrembete.

maypole ['mei poul] maistang.
may-queen ['mei kwi·n] maidronning.
maze [meiz] labyrint; forvirring; I felt in a —
jeg var ganske ør i hodet. maze [meiz] forvirre,
forfjamse. maziness ['mei zinés] forvikling, forvirring, forrykthet.
mazurka [ma'za·kə] masurka.
mazy ['mei zi] forvirret, floket, innviklet.
M. C. fk. f. master of ceremonies; member of
Congress; Military cross.
M. D. fk. f. Medicinae doctor (= doctor of
Medicine) dr. med.
Md. fk. f. Maryland.
me [mi·, mi] meg.
M. E. fk. f. middle English.
mead [mi·d] mjød.
mead [mi·d] eng.
meadow ['medou] eng. — -bouts hestehov,
smørblomst. — -hay vollhøy. — -sweet mjødurt.
meadowy ['medoui] eng-.
meagre ['mi·gə] mager, tynn, skrinn; fattig,
tarvelig. meagreness ['mi·gənés] magerhet.
meal [mi·l] måltid, mål. — time spisetid.
meal [mi·l] (usiktet) mel; mele; male, pulverisere. mealiness [-nés] melenhet.
meal|man ['mi·lmən] melhandler. — -moth
melmøll. — -tub meltønne. — -worm melorm.
mealy ['mi·li] melet, melen. — -mouthed forsiktig i sin tale, slesk.
mean [mi·n] ringe, simpel, lav, låk, slett, foraktelig; gnieraktig, knuslet; no — foe en motstander som ikke må undervurderes.
mean [mi·n] middel-, mellom-, gjennomsnittlig; mellomting, middelvei; in the — i mellomtiden, imidlertid; in the meantime, in the meanwhile i mellomtiden, imidlertid, imens.
mean [mi·n] ha i sinne, tenke, esle, mene, ville
si, bety; I meant no harm jeg mente ikke noe
vondt med det; you don't — it det er ikke
Deres alvor; I — business det er mitt alvor; does
he — business tenker han på å fri; you don't
— to say De mener da vel ikke; that word -s det
ordet betyr; he -s well by you han mener det
godt med deg.
mean-born ['mi·nbá·ən] av lav ætt.
meander [mi'ændə] buktning, bukt, løkke,
sving; bukte seg, gjøre sidespring (i en fortelling).'
meaning ['mi·niŋ] betydningsfull; megetsigende.
meaning ['mi·niŋ] mening, hensikt, øyemed;
betydning. meaningless [-lés] meningsløs, intetsigende. meaningly [-li] betydningsfull.
mean-looking ['mi·nlukiŋ] av simpelt utseende.
meanly ['mi·nli] simpelt, tarvelig.
meanness ['mi·nnés] tarvelighet, simpelhet,
lavhet, usselhet; gnieraktighet.
means [mi·nz] midler, råd, utvei, middel;
formue; by all — naturligvis; så gjerne, endelig,
for alt i verden; by no — på ingen måte; by
any — på noen måte; by (the) — of ved hjelp
av; ways and — inntektskilder; live beyond
one's — leve over evne (det motsatte: live up
to one's —); he is a man of considerable — han
har en betydelig formue.
mean-spirited ['mi·nspiritid] feig, forsakt.
meant [ment] imperf. og perf. pts. av mean.
meantime ['mi·n'taim] mellomtid, in the —
imidlertid.
meanwhile ['mi·n'wail] imidlertid, i mellomtiden.
measles ['mi·zlz] meslinger, krilla; tinter.
measly ['mi·zli] syk av meslinger; elendig, jammerlig.
measurable ['meʒ(ə)rebl] som kan måles, be-
regnes; ikke meget stor; within — distance i kort
avstand; i en overskuelig framtid.
measure ['meʒə] mål, målesnor, måleband;
grad; takt; forholdsregel, lovforslag; måte; versemål; greatest common — største felles mål; —

for — like for like; — of length lengdemål;
beyond all — overordentlig; over all måte; in
a — til en viss grad; in good — i fullt mål;
coat made to — frakk sydd etter mål; frakk som
passer godt; take a person's —, have a person's —
taken ta mål av en; in — with i samme grad
som, side om side med; take -s ta forholdsregler.
measure ['meʒə] måle, ta mål av, holde et
visst mål, avpasse, tilbakelegge; he -d his length
han falt så lang han var; — by one's own yard
dømme etter seg selv; — a person for a suit
of clothes ta mål av en til en dress.
measured ['meʒəd] avmålt, taktfast; måteholden; gjennomtenkt.
measureless ['meʒəlés] uendelig, umåtelig.
measurelessness ['meʒəlésnés] umåtelighet,
uendelighet.
measurement ['meʒəmənt] måling; mål.
measurer ['meʒərə] måler.
measuring-tape ['meʒəriŋteip] måleband.
measuring-worm ['meʒəriŋwə·m] måler (larve).
meat [mi·t] kjøtt, kjøttmat; (nå bare i enkelte forbindelser) mat; butcher's — kjøtt; —,
game, and fish kjøtt, vilt og fisk; — and drink
mat og drikke; sit down to — sette seg til bords;
one's — is another's poison den enes død den
andres brød. — -ball kjøttbolle. — -bill (amr.)
spiseseddel. — -carrier matspann. — -chopper
[-tʃápə] kjøttkvern. — -pie kjøttpostei. — -safe
matskap, flueskap. — -tea te og en kjøttrett.
meaty ['mi·ti] kjøttfull.
mechanic [mi'känik] mekaniker, håndverker;
mekanisk.
mechanical [mi'känikl] mekanisk, maskinmessig, maskin-; — engineer maskintekniker; —
sweeper feiemaskin. mechanician [mekə'niʃən]
mekaniker. mechanics [mi'käniks] mekanikk.
mechanism ['mekənizm] mekanisme. mechanist
['mekənist] maskinbygger, mekaniker. mechanize
['mekənaiz] utføre mekanisk.
Mechlin ['meklin] Mecheln; — lace Mecheln
kniplinger.
med. fk. f. medic ne.
medal ['medl] medalje. medalist ['medəlist]
medaljør, medaljekjenner; gravør. medallion [mi-
däljən] medaljong.
meddle ['medl] blande seg i, legge seg borti;
— with (in) other people's affairs blande seg i
andre folks saker; don't — with him bland deg
ikke borti ham; you are always meddling du
stikker nesen din opp i alt.
meddler ['medlə] kláfinger, nesevis person.
meddlesome ['medlsəm] nesevis, som blander
seg i alt. meddling ['medliŋ] innblanding.
Mede [mi·d] meder. Media ['mi·djə] Media.
medial ['mi·djəl] middel-.
Median ['mi·djən] medisk.
median ['mi·djən] midt-.
mediate ['mi·djét] mellomliggende; indirekte.
mediate ['mi·die·t] mekle, megle. mediately
['mi·djétli, -dʒ-] middelbart. mediation ['mi·di-
'eiʃən] mekling; middel. mediator ['mi·die·tə]
mekler-, mediatorial [mi·djə'tá·riəl] meklende,
mekler-, meklings-. mediatorship ['mi·die'teiʃip]
meklerstilling. mediatory ['mi·djətəri] = mediatorial.
medical ['medikl] medisinsk, lege-; we sent
for our — man vi sendte bud etter huslegen
vår; — care legekyndig pleie.
medicament ['medikəmənt] legemiddel.
medicate ['medikeit] behandle; -d baths medisinsk bad; -d cotton-wool renset bomull; -d paper
toalettpapir; -d waters mineralske vann.
medication [medi'keiʃən] medisinering.
medicative ['medikətiv] legende.
Medicean [medi'si·ən] mediséisk.
medicinal [mi'disinəl] legende, medisin; —
springs sunnhetskjelder; — treatment legebe-
handling.

medicine ['medsin] medisin, medisinsk vitenskap.
medieval [medi'i·vl, mi·d-] middelalderlig; the — ages middelalderen. medievalism [-izm] begeistring for middelalderen; middelalderens skikk el. ånd.
mediocre ['mi·diouˈkə] middelmådig.
mediocrity [mi·di'åkriti; med-] middelmådighet.
meditate ['mediteˈt] tenke over, grunne på, gruble, anstille betraktninger; overlegge, ha i sinne. -d påtenkt.
meditation [medi'teˈʃən] overveielse, ettertanke, meditasjon; book of -s andaktsbok; leave a person to his own -s overlate en til hans egne betraktninger.
meditative ['mediteˈtiv] tenksom, spekulativ.
Mediterranean [meditəˈreˈniən] Middelhavs-; the — Middelhavet.
medium ['mi·djəm] medium; midte, mellomting, middeltall; gjennomsnitts-; middel, middels-. a — of communication meddelelsesmiddel; hit upon the happy — treffe den gylne middelvei; there is a — in all things det er måte med alt. — -sized [-saizd] av middels størrelse, middelstor.
medlar ['medlə] mispel.
medley ['medli] blanding; miskmask, røre, rot; håndgemeng; blandet, forvirret.
medulla [mi'dʌlə] marg. medullar [mi'dʌlə] marg-, fylt med marg.
Medusa [mi'dju·zə] Medusa.
medusa [mi'dju·zə] manet, gople.
meed [mi·d] lønn, belønning, pris.
meek [mi·k] ydmyk, spakferdig, saktmodig.
meekness [-nés] ydmykhet, saktmodighet.
meerschaum ['miəʃəm] merskum(spipe).
meet [mi·t] passende, høvelig, egnet, skikket.
meet [mi·t] møte, møtes, råke (på), treffe sammen med, komme i berøring med, treffe på; støte sammen med; etterkomme, oppfylle (forpliktelse); dekke, honorere (veksel); — due protection finne beskyttelse; bli prompte innfridd (om veksel); — his fate kjekt gå sin skjebne i møte; his eyes met hans øyne falt på; go to — a person gå en i møte; till we — again på gjensyn; — with møte tilfeldig, treffe; få, komme ut for, oppleve; — with an accident ha et uhell. meet [mi·t] møtested, møte (ved jakt o. l.).
meeter ['mi·tə] møtende.
meeting ['mi·tin] møte; gjensyn; sammenløp (av elver). — -house bedehus. — -place møtested.
M. E. F. fk. f. Mesopotamian Expeditionary Force.
Meg [meg] fk. f. Margaret.
megalomania [megəlo'meˈnjə] stormannsgalskap.
megaphone ['megəfouˈn] megafon.
megilp ['megilp] blanding av linolje og mastiksferniss.
megrim ['mi·grim] migréne, hodepine.
melancholia [melənˈkouˈljə] melankoli. melancholic [melən'kålik] melankolsk, tungsindig, tunglynt. melancholy ['melənkəli] melankolsk, sørgmodig, sturen, tungsindig; melankoli, tungsinn.
mélange [fr.] blanding.
Melba ['melbə] berømt sangerinne; peach — dessertrett av ferskener.
Melbourne ['melbən] Melbourne.
mêlée ['meleˈ] håndgemeng.
meliorate ['mi·ljoreˈt] forbedre, bøte, foredle, besne. -ion [mi·liəˈreˈʃən] bedring, framgang.
melliferous [me'lifərəs] som gir honning. mellific [me'lifik] som gir honning. mellification [me·lifi'keˈʃən] frambringelse, tillaging av honning. mellifluent [me'lifluənt], mellifluous [me'lifluəs] honningsøt, søttflytende.
mellow ['melouˈ] bløt, myk, mør, moden, saftig; mild; dyp, rik (om farge); mildnet (av tiden), modnet, avdempet, fin; modne, gjøre bløt, mod-

nes; a well-mellowed meerschaum en godt tilrøykt merskumspipe. mellowness [-nés] bløthet, modenhet; avdempet farge, patina.
melodeon [mi'louˈdiən] melodion (slags orgel); harmonika.
melodious [mi'louˈdjəs] melodisk, velklingende.
melodiousness [-nés] velklang, musikk. melodist ['melədist] sanger. melodrama [melo'dra·mə] melodrama. melodramatic [-drə'mätik] melodramatisk, høyttravende.
melody ['melədi] melodi, velklang, musikk.
melon ['melən] melon.
Melpomene [mel'påmini·] Melpomene.
melt [melt] smelte, bråne, mykne, tø opp; tine.
melting ['meltin] smelting. -point smeltepunkt. -pot smeltedigel.
mem. fk. f. memento.
member ['membə] lem; del, ledd; medlem, representant (jvf. M. P.); be — for representere. membership ['membəʃip] medlemskap, medlemmer.
membranaceous [membrə'neˈʃəs] hinneaktig.
membrane ['membreˈn] membran, hinne.
membraneous [mem'breˈnjəs] hinneaktig.
memento [mi'mentoˈu] memento, minnelse, påminning, minning, erindringstegn, souvenir.
memoir ['memwa·ᵊ, 'memwå·ᵊ] notis, opptegnelse; pl.: memoarer, erindringer.
memorabilia [memərə'biliə] minneverdige be givenheter, erindringer.
memorable ['mem(ə)rəbl] minneverdig. memorandum [memə'rändəm] pl. -da [-də] anmerkning, note, uttog. — -book notisbok.
memorial [mi'må·riəl] som vedlikeholder minnet, til minne; erindring, minne, minnesmerke; utgreiing; andragende. memorialist [mi'må·riəlist] forfatter av et andragende. memorialize [mi'må·riəlaiz] ansøke, sende søknad til. memorize ['meməraiz] feste i hukommelsen, memorere, lære utenat.
memory ['meməri] hukommelse, minne, erindring; from —, by — etter hukommelsen; a good — en god hukommelse; a bad — en dårlig hukommelse; I have no — of it jeg har ingen erindring om det; it is but a — det er bare et minne; to the best of my — så vidt jeg husker; call to — minnes; in — of til minne om; within the — of men, within living — i manns minne.
mems [memz] opptegnelser, notiser.
memsahib ['mem'sa·ib] (indisk) européisk frue (egl. madam sahib).
men [men] (pl. av man) menn, mennesker.
menace ['menəs, 'menis] true; true med; trusel, trugsmål.
ménage [me'na·ʒ] menasje; husholdning.
menagerie [me'na(d)ʒəri] menasjeri.
mend [mend] sette i stand, reparere, rette, forbedre, vøle; forbedre seg; besne; lappe, stoppe; bedring; reparasjon, stopping; we cannot — it det er ikke noe å gjøre ved det; matters at worst are sure to — når nøden er størst, er hjelpen nærmest; in the end things will — tiden læger alle sår; be on the — være i bedring.
mendable ['mendəbl] som kan repareres.
mendacious [men'deˈʃəs] løgnaktig.
mendacity [men'däsiti] løgnaktighet.
mendicancy ['mendikənsi] tiggeri, tigging.
mendicant ['mendikənt] tigger.
mendicity [men'disiti] tiggeri, tigging.
mending ['mendin] reparasjon.
menhir ['menhiə] bautastein.
menial ['mi·njəl] leid, tjenende; tjener-, ringe, simpel; tjener; krypende person.
meningitis [menin'dʒaitis] meningitt.
men-of-war ['menəˈwå·ᵊ] pl. av man-of-war.
menology [me'nålədʒi] månedskalender, srl. kalender med helgenbiografi i den greske kirke.
menses ['mensi·z] månedlig renselse, menstruasjon.

Menshevik ['menʃəvik] mensjevik.

menstrual ['menstruəl] månedlig; menstruasjons-.

menstruation [menstru'eiʃən] menstruasjon.

mensurability [menʃərə'biliti] målelighet.

mensurable ['menʃərəbl] målelig.

mensuration [menʃu're¹ʃən] måling.

mental ['mentəl] mental, forstands-, sinns-, ånds-, åndelig; — **arithmetic,** — **computation** hoderegning; — **condition** mental tilstand; — **reservation** stilltiende forbehold.

mentality [men'täliti] mentalitet, åndsvirksomhet; forstand, ånd; sjeleliv.

mentation [men'te¹ʃən] åndsvirksomhet.

menthol ['menþål] mentol.

mention ['menʃən] omtale; tale om, nevne; **don't — it** ingen årsak, ikke noe å takke for; snakk aldri om det; **above -ed** ovennevnt; **not to —** for ikke å tale om, enn si da.

mentionable ['menʃənəbl] nevneverdig.

mentor ['mentå·ə] mentor, veileder.

menu ['menju·] spiseseddel, meny.

mercantile ['mə·kəntail]merkantil, kjøpmanns-, handels-; — **class** handelsstand; — **law** handelslov; — **man** kjøpmann; — **reports** handelsberetninger; — **term** handelsuttrykk.

mercenary ['mə·sinəri] leid; salgbar, til fals; egennyttig; vinnesyk; leiesvenn; leiesoldat; i pl. leietropper.

mercer ['mə·sə] manufakturhandler, (nå især) silkevarehandler.

mercerize ['mə·səraiz] mercerisere (gjøre bomull silkeglinsende).

mercery ['mə·səri] manufakturforretning, silkevarehandel; silkevarer.

merchandise ['mə·tʃəndaiz] varer.

merchant ['mə·tʃənt] kjøpmann, handelsmann, grossist, handlende. **merchantable** ['mə·tʃəntəbl] salgbar. **merchant-man** handelsskip, koffardiskip. **merchant-marine** handelsflåte. **merchant-ship** handelsskip.

merchant-tailor ['mə·tʃənt'te¹lə] medlem av Merchant Taylors' Company (et laug); elev av the Merchant Taylors' School (i denne betydning vanlig **a Merchant Taylor**).

Mercia ['mə·ʃiə] Mercia.

merciful ['mə·sif(u)l] barmhjertig, nådig.

merciless ['mə·silés] ubarmhjertig.

mercurial [mə'kjuəriəl] livlig, full av liv; kjøpmannsmessig; som inneholder kvikksølv. **mercurialise** [-laiz] behandle med kvikksølvpreparat. **mercurify** [mə'kjuərifai] utvinne kvikksølv.

Mercury ['mə·kjuri] Merkur; budbringer, avis. **mercury** ['mə·kjuri] kvikksølv.

Mercutio [mə'kju·ʃioᵘ] Mercutio.

mercy ['mə·si] barmhjertighet, nåde, miskunn; medlidenhet; **beg for —, cry for —** be om nåde; **— on me; for -'s sake** barmhjertige Gud, for Guds skyld; **it is a — he did not . . .** det er en Guds lykke at han ikke . . .; **be at the — of** somebody være i ens makt.

mercy-seat ['mə·sisi·t] nådestol.

mere [miə] tjern, dam; myr.

mere [miə] grense, merkestein.

mere [miə] blott, ren, bare; **a — boy** bare barnet; **for the — purpose** ene og alene for å.

Meredith ['merədiþ, 'meridiþ] Meredith.

merely ['miəli] kun, alene, bare.

meretricious [meri'triʃəs] skjøkeaktig; uekte.

merganser [mə·'gänsə] stor fiskand.

merge [mə·dʒ] senke ned, søkke, dukke; synke; bli oppslukt; **be-d in** gå opp i, smelte sammen med.

merger ['mə·dʒə] sammensmelting (av handelsselskaper).

meridian [mi'ridjən] høyde, høyeste punkt; middagshøyde, meridian; — **of life** kulminasjonspunkt. **meridional** [mi'ridjənəl] meridian-, sørlig. **meridionality** [miridjə'näliti] kulminasjon, sørlig beliggenhet.

meringue [mə'ræŋ] marengs (slags småkaker).

merino [mə'ri·noᵘ] merinosau; merino (slags tøy).

merit ['merit] fortjeneste, fortreffelighet, dyd, god side, gagn, fortrin; **-s** fortjeneste, verd; **make a — of, take — to oneself** regne seg til fortjeneste; **make a — of necessity** gjøre en dyd av nødvendighet; **ugly to a —** stygg som en ulykke.

merit ['merit] fortjene; gjøre seg fortjent, gjøre gagnsverk.

meritedly ['meritidli] med rette, etter fortjeneste.

meritorious [meri'tå·riəs] fortjenstfull. **meritoriousness** [-nés] fortjenstfullhet.

merle [mə·l] svarttrost, sysvorte.

merlin ['mə·lin] dvergfalk, steinfalk.

mermaid ['mə·me¹d] havfrue.

merman ['mə·mən] havmann.

merrily ['merili] lystig.

merriment ['merimənt] munterhet, gammen, moro.

merry ['meri] munter, rask, livlig, spøkefull; **make —** more seg, holde leven; **a — Christmas (to you)!** gledelig jul; — **dancers** nordlys; **make — with** ha til beste, drive gjøn med.

merry-andrew ['merri'ändru·] bajas.

merry-go-round ['merigoᵘraund] karusell.

merry-making ['merime¹kin] moro, leven.

merrythought ['meriþå·t] kragebein, nøklebein (på en fugl).

mésalliance [me'zäliəns] mesallianse.

mesdames [me¹'da·m] pl. av **madame.**

mesdemoiselles [me¹dmwa'zel] pl. av **mademoiselle.**

meseems [mi'si·mz] (arkaisk) meg tykkes.

mesh [meʃ] maske, nett, garn; drev; fange i garn, innvikle, hilde. **meshy** ['meʃi] masket, nettformet.

mesmeric [mez'merik] mesmerisk.

mesmerism ['məzmərizm] mesmerisme.

mesmerist ['məzmərist] mesmerist.

mesmerize ['mezməraiz] hypnotisere.

mesne [mi·n] (jur.) mellom-; — **lord** underlensherre, undervasall.

Mesopotamia [mesəpə'te¹mjə] Mesopotamia. **Mespot** ['mespåt] (slang) Mesopotamia.

mess [mes] blanding, forvirret masse, uorden, røre, rot, suppe, sammensurium; **the house was in a pretty —** huset var i den villeste uorden; **be in a pretty —** sitte nett i det; **make a — of** bringe i forvirring; søle til; **he got into a — with his accounts** det var uorden i hans regnskaper.

mess [mes] rote i, forplumre, ødelegge, søle til; rote, klusse.

mess [mes] rett, servering, porsjon; messe; spise (i samme messe); bespise; skaffe; — **of pottage** rett linser; **dine at —** spise i messen; **divide the men into -es** fordele mannskapet i bakker (bakksvis). — **-boy** messegutt. — **-man** marketenter. — **-mate** messekamerat, bakkskamerat. — **orderly** kokk. — **-room** offisersmesse.

message ['mesidʒ] bud, budskap; depesje, telegram; **go -s** gå ærender; **send a — of excuse** sende avbud. — **-form** telegramblankett. — **-lad** visergutt.

messenger ['mesindʒə] bud, sendebud, forløper, kurér.

Messiah [mè'saiə] Messias.

messieurs ['mesəz] de herrer, herrer.

Messrs. ['mesəz] fk. f. **Messieurs.**

messuage ['meswidʒ] (jur.) gård, jord, eiendom.

messy ['mesi] forvirret, rotet, sølet, griset.

met [met] imperf. og perf. pts. av **meet.**

metabolism [me'täbəlizm] stoffskifte.

metacarpus [metə'ka·əpəs] mellomhånd.

metage ['mi·tidʒ] måling (av kull); måleavgift.

metal ['metl] metall; (fig.) malm; pukk, pukkstein, glassmasse; metallforhude; makadamisere; **-s** skinner; **leave the —** gå av sporet.

metallic [mi'tälik] metallisk, metall-.
metalliferous [metə'lifərəs] metallholdig.
metalline ['metlin, -ain] metallinsk.
metallize ['metlaiz] metallisere.
metalloid ['metəloid] metalloid.
metallurgy [me'tälədʒi] metallurgi.
metalman ['metlmən] metallarbeider.
metamorphic [metə'må·°fik] metamorfisk.
metamorphose [metəmå·°'fo°z] forvandle.
metamorphosis [metə'må·°fəsis] forvandling.
metaphor ['metəfə] billedlig talemåte.
metaphoric(al) [metə'fårik(l)] billedlig.
metaphysic(al) [metə'fizik(l)] metafysisk, over-sanselig.
metaphysician [metəfi'ziʃən] metafysiker.
metaphysics [metə'fiziks] metafysikk.
metathesis [mé'täbəsi·z] metatese.
mete [mi·t] måle; mål.
metempsychosis [metempsi'ko°sis] sjelevandring.
meteor ['mi·tjə] meteor. **meteoric** [mi·ti'årik] meteorisk. **meteorological** [mi·tjərə'lådʒikl] meteorologisk. **meteorologist** [mi·tjə'rålədʒist] værkyndig. **meteorology** [mi·tjə'rålədʒi] meteorologi.
meter ['mi·tə] måler, måleredskap; meter.
metheglin [mə'beglin] en slags mjød.
methinks [mi'biŋks] det synes meg.
method ['mebəd] måte, framgangsmåte; plan, metode; **reduce to —** bringe metode i.
methodic(al) [mi'bådik(l)] metodisk.
methodics [mi'bådiks] metodikk.
methodism ['mebədizm] metodisme. **methodist** ['mebədist] metodist; metodistisk. **methodistic** [mebə'distik] metodistisk.
methodize ['mebədaiz] bringe metode i.
methought [mi'bå·t] det syntes meg.
Methuselah [mé'bju·sələ] Metusalem.
methyl ['mebil] metyll.
methylated ['mebile¹tid] som inneholder metyll-alkohol; **— spirit** denaturert sprit.
meticulous [mé'tikjuləs] engstelig omhyggelig.
métier ['metje¹] metier, fag, yrke.
metonymy [me'tånimi] metonymi.
Met. R. fk. f. **Metropolitan Railway.**
metre ['mi·tə] meter; metrum, versemål. **metric** ['metrik] metrisk. **metrical** ['metrikl] metrisk. **metrics** ['metriks] metrikk.
metronome ['metrəno°m] taktmåler.
metropolis [mi'tråpəlis] hovedstad: **the —** (især) London, Stor-London.
metropolitan [metro'pålitən] hovedstads-, metropolitan-, londoner-; metropolitt, erkebiskop; **the M.** Railway jernbane i London.
mettle ['metl] metall; liv, mot, fyrighet, futt, iver; stoff, to, malm; materie; **now show your —** vis nå hva du kan; **put one on his —** få en til å gjøre sitt beste.
mettlesome ['metlsəm] livlig, modig, fyrig; sprek.
mew [mju·] måke, måse.
mew [mju·] myte, røyte; skifte drakt.
mew [mju·] bur (is. for falk som myter); skjul.
mew [mju·] mjaue; mjauing.
mewl [mju·l] skrike, sutre; skrik, sutring.
mews [mju·z] stallbygninger, staller; bakgate, smug; (oppr. pl. av **mew** falkebur; men nå gjerne brukt som singularis: **a mews,** pl. **mewses**).
Mexican ['meksikən] meksikansk; meksikaner.
Mexico ['meksiko°] Mexico.
mezzaine ['mezəni·n] mesanin(etasje).
mf. fk. f. **mezzo forte** middelssterkt.
M. G. fk. f. **Order of St. Michael and St. George.**
m. g. fk. f. **machine gun.**
mg. fk. f. **milligram.**
M. G. C. fk. f. **machine gun Corps.**
M. I. fk. f. **mounted infantry.**
miaow [mi'au] mjaue; mjauing.
miasma [mai'äzmə] miasma, smittestoff.

miaul [mi'å·l] mjaue; mjauing.
mica ['maikə] glimmer; kråkesølv
micaceous [mi'ke¹ʃəs] glimmeraktig.
Micawber [mi'kå·bə], person i David Copperfield.
mice [mais] (plur. av **mouse**) mus.
Michael ['maikl] Mikael, Mikkel.
Michaelmas ['miklməs] mikkelsmess, den 29. september.
Michigan ['miʃigən] Michigan.
mickle ['nikl] (gammelt el. dialekt) megen, stor; mengde.
microbe ['maikro°b] mikrobe, bakterie.
microcosm ['maikrokázm] mikrokosmos, liten verden.
micrography [mai'krågrəfi] beskrivelse av mikroskopiske gjenstander.
micrometer [mai'kråmitə] mikrometer.
micron ['maikrån, -rən] mikron, my.
Micronesia [maikrə'ni·ʃə] Micronesia (visse øygrupper i Stillehavet).
microphone ['maikrəfo°n] mikrofon, hørerør på telefon.
microscope ['maikrosko°p] mikroskop. **microscopic** [maikro'skåpik] mikroskopisk, meget liten.
mid [mid] midt-, mid-, mellom.
'mid; mid [mid] midt iblant, under.
Midas ['maidäs] Midas.
mid-day ['midde¹] middag, kl. 12.
midden ['midn] (dial.) mødding.
middle ['nidl] mellom-, middel-, midt-; **at the — of last week** midt i siste uke; **in the — of** midt i; midt på; **— age** alder mellom 40 og 60; **the — ages** middelalderen; **— article** avisartikkel, som hverken dreier seg om politikk eller litteratur; **— finger** langemann; **the Middle Kingdom** China.
middle-aged ['midl'e¹dʒd] halvgammel.
middle-class ['midl'kla·s] middelklasse, middelstand.
middleman ['midlmän] mellommann.
middlemost ['midlmo°st] midterst.
Middlesex ['midlseks] Middlesex.
middle'-sized middelstor. **-tint** mellomfarge, **-watch** hundevakt. **— weight** mellomvekt.
middling ['midliŋ] middels, middelmådig, temmelig. **middlings** ['midliŋz] mellomkvaliteter; en slags grovere mel, fint hvetekli, kliblanding (brukt som hønsefor).
midge [midʒ] mygg; liten mann.
midget ['midʒit] liten mygg, ørliten mann, fotografi i minste format
midland ['midlənd] innland; indre; **the Midlands** det indre av England.
midmost ['midmo°st] midterst.
midnight ['midnait] midnatt.
midriff ['midrif] mellomgulv.
midship ['midʃip] midtskips. **-man** sjøkadett.
midships ['midʃips] midtskips.
midst [midst] midte; midt, midterst; **in the — of** midt i; **in our —** midt iblant oss.
midsummer ['midsʌmə] midtsommer; **— day** sankthansdag, jonsokdag. **— holidays** sommerferie; **— night** sankthansnatt.
midway ['midwe¹] midtvei, mellomvei; midtveis, halvveis.
midwife ['midwaif] jordmor; fødselshjelper; bistå, opptre som jordmor.
midwifery ['midw(a)ifri] jordmor-kunst, -yrke.
mien [mi·n] mine, lag, framferd.
miff [mif] fornærmelse; småkjekl; **they have had a —** det er kommet en knute på tråden.
might [mait] imperf. av **may. — -be** kanskje.
might [mait] makt, kraft, evne; **by — or by sleight** ved makt eller list; **with — and main** el. **with all his —** av all makt, av alle krefter.
mightily ['maitili] mektig, omfram, svært.
mightiness ['maitinés] høyhet, mektighet. **mighty** ['maiti] mektig, kraftig; svært, i høy grad.
mignonette [minjə'net] reseda.

migrant ['maigrənt] vandrende; trekkfugl. **migrate** [mai'greit] flytte, vandre ut, trekke bort. **migration** [mai'greiʃən] utflytning, vandring. **migratory** ['maigrətəri] vandrende; — **bird** trekkfugl.

Mikado [mi'ka·douɴ] Mikado (keiser i Japan). **Mike** [maik] Mikkel. **mike** [maik] slentre, drive om. **mil.** fk. f. **military.** **Milan** ['milən, mi'län] Milano. **milch** [milt)ʃ] som gir melk, som melker. — **cattle** melkekuer. **-er** melkeku. **mild** [maild] mild; lind; blid, saktmodig; lett. **mildew** ['mildju·] meldugg, mygl, jordslag; mygle. **mildewy** ['mildju·i] jordslått. **mildness** ['maildnés] mildhet. **mild|spoken** mild i ordene. — **-tempered** mild. **mile** [mail] (engelsk) mil; (= 1609,3 m.); for **-s** milevidt. **mileage** ['mailidʒ] mil, miletall; skyssgodtgjørelse pr. mil. **Milesian** [mai'li·ziən] irsk; irlender; milesisk. **milestone** ['mailstouɴ] milepel. **Miletus** [mai'li·təs] Milet. **milfoil** ['milfoil] røllik (plante). **miliary** ['miljəri] hirsekornlignende; — **fever** frisler. **militant** ['militənt] stridende; stridbar. **militarism** ['militərizm] militarisme. **military** ['militəri] militær, krigersk, krigs-, militær; — **man** militær. **militate** ['milite't] stri(de), virke for. **militia** [mi'liʃə] milis, landvern. **militiaman** [mi'liʃəmən] landvernsmann. **milk** [milk] melk; forsyne med melk; ha melk i; melke; **it is no use crying over** (el. **for**) **spilt** — gjort gjerning står ikke til å endre; — **-and-water** tynn, kraftløs. — **-can** melkedunk. **-er** melker, melkeku, melkemaskin. — **-gauge** [-ge'dʒ] melkemåler. — **-glass** melkeglass (slags hvitt glass). **-ing-stool** melkekrakk. **milk|-jug** melkemugge. — **-livered** blaut, redd, feig. **-maid** budeie. — **-pail** melkespann. — **-pan** melkebøtte. — **-sop** brød som er bløtt i melk; stakkar. — **-tooth** melketann. **milky** ['milki] melkeaktig, melke-; melkemann. **mill** [mil] mølle, kvern, fabrikk; male, valse ut, prege, mynte; piske; **he has been through the** — han har selv prøvd det; **no** — **no meal** uten arbeid ingen mat; **-ed edges** maskinpregede kanter, opphøyde (og riflete) kanter (på mynter). **millboard** ['milbå·əd] tykk papp. **mill-dam** ['mildäm] mølledam, mølledemning. **millenarian** [mili'næ·əriən] tusenårig; millennarier. **millenary** ['milinəri] tusen-, tusenårs; årtusen; tusenårsfest. **millennial** [mi'lenjəl] tusenårs-. **millennium** [mi'lenjəm] årtusen; tusenårsrike. **milleped** ['miliped] tusenbein. **miller** ['milə] møller; fresemaskin. **millet** ['milit] hirse. **mill|-hand** fabrikkarbeider. — **-head** overvann (oppdemt drivvann til en mølle). **milliard** ['miljəd] milliard. **millibar** ['miliba·ə] millibar. **milligramme** ['miligräm] milligram. **millilitre** ['mililitə] milliliter. **millimetre** ['milimi·tə] millimeter. **milliner** ['milinə] motehandler. **millinery** ['millinəri] motepynt. **milling** ['milin] mølledrift. — **-machine** fresemaskin. **million** ['miljən] million. **millionaire** ['miljə'næ·ə] millionær. **millionth** ['miljənþ] milliontedel. **mill|-owner** mølleeier. — **-pond** mølledam, kverndam. — **-race** kvernbekk, møllevann. **-stone** mølle-

stein. — **-stream** kvernbekk. — **-tail** spillvann (fra møllehjulet). — **-wheel** møllehjul. **millwright** ['milrait] kvernbygger. **milt** [milt] milt; melke (hos hanfisk); befrukte. **Milton** ['milt(ə)n] Milton. **mime** [maim] mime; slags farse; komiker. **mimeograph** ['mimiogra·f] mimeograf. **mimic** ['mimik] (pres. pts. **mimicking,** imperf. og perf. pts. **mimicked**) etterlignet, etterapet; mimisk; mimiker, etteraper; etterligne, etterape, herme. **mimicry** ['mimikri] etterligning, etteraping. **mimosa** [mi'mouzə] mimose. **min.** fk. f. **mineralogy.** **minaret** ['minərét] minaret. **minatory** ['minətəri] truende. **mince** [mins] hakke smått, skjære fint; forminske, beklippe, pynte på; snakke affektert, småtrippe; hakket kjøtt, hakkemat; **not to** — **matters** for å ta bladet fra munnen. **mincemeat** ['minsmi·t] finhakket kjøtt; **make** — **of you** gjøre hakkemat av dere, gjøre kål på dere. **mince-pie** ['mins'pai] kjøttpostei. **mind** [maind] sinn, hug, sinnelag, gemytt; sjel, ånd; forstand, vett, mening, tanke; tilbøyelighet, lyst; erindring, minne; **make up one's** — beslutte seg til; fatte en bestemt mening; bringe det over sitt hjerte; **my** — **misgives me** jeg har bange anelser; **absence of** — åndsfraværelse; **presence of** — åndsnærværelse; **lose one's** — miste forstanden; **change one's** — komme på andre tanker; **give a person a bit of one's** — si en sin mening; **I was in two -s about it** jeg kunne ikke beslutte meg; **be of a** — **with somebody** dele ens anskuelser: **it is not to my** — det er ikke etter mitt hode; **have a good** — **to** ha god lyst til; **I have half a** — **to** jeg kunne nesten ha lyst til; **bear in** — huske; **bring (call) to** — erindre, minnes. **mind** [maind] iaktta, ense, akte på, legge merke til; bekymre seg om, bry seg om; ha noe imot; innvende imot; huske, passe på; ha i sinne; — **one's book** passe sin lesning; — **your own business!** pass deg selv; — **a child** passe et barn; **never** — him bry deg ikke om ham; **never** — —! bry Dem ikke om det! det gjør ikke noe; jeg ber; ingen årsak; pass Dem selv: **I don't** — **a few pounds more or less** jeg tar det ikke så nøye med et par pund mer eller mindre; **if you do not** — it hvis De ikke har noe imot det; **do you** — **my smoking a cigar** har De noe imot at jeg røyker en sigar; — **and come in good time** sørg for å komme i god tid; — **your eye!** pass på! — **that!** husk det! **minded** ['maindid] til sinns; av ... karakter. **mindful** ['maindf(u)l] oppmerksom, omhyggelig. **mindless** ['maindlés] sjelløs; likeglad, likesælmine** [main] min, mitt, mine (brukt substantiv. isk); **the box is** — esken er min; **a friend of** — en venn av meg. **mine** [main] gruve, bergverk, mine; grave gruver; drive gruver; drive bergverksdrift; minere, grave; undergrave; utvinne, drive. **mine-field** ['mainfi·ld] minefelt. **mine|layer** ['mainle'ə] mineutlegger (skip eller menneske). **-laying** [-le'iɴ] minelegging. **miner** ['mainə] gruvearbeider, bergmann; minegraver, minør. **miner's elbow** hygrom i albuen. **mineral** ['minərəl] mineral. **mineralize** ['minərəlaiz] forvandle til mineral. **mineralogic** [minərə-'lådʒik] mineralogisk. **mineralogist** [minə'rälədʒist] mineralog. **mineralogy** [minə'rälədʒi] mineralogi. **mineral-water** ['minərəl 'wåtə] mineralvann, brus. **Minerva** [mi'nə·və] Minerva. **mine-sweeper** ['mainswipə] minefeier. **minever** ['minivə] d. s. s. **miniver.** **mingle** ['miɴgl] blande; blande seg.

miniature ['minjətʃə] miniatyr, miniatyrportrett; **in** — en miniature, i miniatyr.

minify ['minifai] forminske, minske, nedsette.

minikin ['minikin] yndling, kjæledegge; bitte liten.

minim ['minim] bitte liten; 0,06 centiliter; halvnote.

minimal ['miniməl] minimal, minste-.

minimise ['minimaiz] bringe ned til det minst mulige.

minimum ['miniməm] lavmål, minimum.

mining ['mainiŋ] gruvedrift, bergverksdrift, mine-.

minion ['minjən] (hånlig) yndling, favoritt, gromgutt; kreatur; kolonell (liten skriftsort).

minish ['miniʃ] forminske.

minister ['ministə] tjener; minister, statsråd; sendemann; prest (især om dissenterprest); levere, yte, gi, bringe; tjene, hjelpe, behandle. **ministerial** [mini'stiəriəl] tjenende, tjenlig; minister-, ministeriell; prestelig, geistlig. **ministerialist** [-ist] regjeringsvennlig.

ministrant ['ministrənt] tjenende, underordnet; tjener. **ministration** [mini'streiʃən] tjeneste, virksomhet; medvirkning.

ministry ['ministri] tjeneste, virksomhet; medvirkning; riksstyre, ministerium (i bet. regjering; utenfor England om enkelt ministers fagområde), ministerstilling; geistlig stilling; presteskap, geistlighet.

minium ['minjəm] mønje.

miniver ['minivə] gråverk, ekornskinn.

mink [miŋk] mink, oter.

Minneapolis [mini'æpəlis] Minneapolis.

Minnesota [mini'soʷtə] Minnesota.

minnow ['minoʷ] ørekyte, gorrkyte.

minor ['mainə] mindre; mindreårig, umyndig; — canon prest ved domkirke, men ikke medlem av domkapitlet; — **premise** undersetning (i slutning). **Asia Minor** Lilleasia.

Minorca [mi'nå·kə] Minorca.

minority [mi'nåriti, mai-] mindreårighet, umyndighet; minoritet, mindretall; **be in a** — være i minoritet.

M. Inst. C. E. fk. f. member of the Institution of Civil Engineers.

minster ['minstə] domkirke, klosterkirke.

minstrel ['minstrəl] skald, sanger; **negro** — el. **Christy** — negersanger (sanger utkledd som neger).

minstrelsy ['minstrəlsi] sang, skaldskap.

mint [mint] mynt, myntverk; **he is worth a** — **of money** han er grunnrik. **mint** [mint] mynte, slå, smelte, lage.

mint [mint] mynte; **crisped** (el. **curled**) — krusemynte.

mintage ['mintidʒ] mynting; mynt, penger, nylaging; myntpreg, preg; pregningsomkostninger.

mint-master ['mint'ma·stə] myntmester.

mint-sauce ['mint'så·s] krusemyntesaus (eddiksaus med hakkede krusemynteblad).

mint-warden ['mintwå·ədn] myntguardein.

minuet [minju'et] menuett.

minus ['mainəs] mindre; minus; negativ; uten. **minuscule** [mi'nʌskju·l] minuskel, liten bokstav. **minute** [mi'nju·t, mai-] liten, liten, ørliten, ubetydelig; nøyaktig, minutiøs.

minute ['minit] minutt; opptegnelse, (især i pl.) referat, forhandlingsprotokoll; gjøre utkast til, opptegne, protokollere; **this** — straks; **I knew him the** — **I saw him** jeg kjente ham straks, da jeg så ham; **to the** — på minuttet; **wait a** — vent et øyeblikk.

minute-book ['minitbuk] forhandlingsprotokoll.

minute-gun ['minitgʌn] minuttskudd.

minute-hand ['minithänd] minuttviser, langviser.

minutely ['minitli] hvert minutt, hvert øyeblikk.

minutely [mi'nju·tli, mai-] nøye, minutiøst.

minx [miŋks] villkatt, vilter pike.

miny ['maini] underjordisk; rik på miner.

miracle ['mirəkl, -rikl] mirakel, vidunder, undergjerning; mirakel-skuespill; **as if by** — som ved et under. **miraculous** [mi'räkjuləs] mirakuløs, vidunderlig.

mirage [mi'ra·ʒ] luftspeiling, fatamorgana.

mire ['maiə] mudder, dynd, søle, gjørme; senke ned i dynd; synke ned i dynd; føre opp i uføre. **miriness** ['ma rinés] det å være gjørmet.

mirk [mə·k] mørk. **mirky** ['mə·ki] mørk.

mirror ['mirə] speil; bilde; avspeile, speile.

mirth [mə·þ] munterhet, moro, latter. **mirthful** ['mə·þf(u)l] lystig. **mirthfulness** [-nés] lystighet. **mirth-moving** [-mu·viŋ] lattervekkende.

miry ['mairi] gjørmet, mudret.

mis [mis] (forstavelse) feil-; uriktig.

misadventure ['misəd'ventʃə] uhell; **homicide by** — uforsettlig drap.

misadvice ['misəd'vais] dårlig råd. **misadvise** ['misəd'vaiz] råde ille; vill-lede.

misalliance ['misə'laiəns] mesallianse.

misanthrope ['mizənþroʷp] misantrop, menneskehater. **misanthropic** [mizən'þräpik] menneskefiendsk. **misanthropy** [miz'änþropi] misantropi. **misapplication** ['misäpli'keiʃən] misbruk, uriktig anvendelse.

misapply ['misə'plai] anvende feil, misbruke.

misapprehend ['misäpri'hend] misforstå. **misapprehension** ['misäpri'henʃən] misforståelse.

misappropriation ['misəproʷpri'eiʃən] urettmessig tilegnelse, uriktig anvendelse.

misbecoming ['misbi'kʌmiŋ] upassende.

misbegotten ['misbi'gåtn] uekte født.

misbehave ['misbi'heiv] oppføre seg dårlig. **misbehaviour** ['misbi'heivjə] dårlig oppførsel.

miscalculate ['mis'kälkjule¹t] beregne feil; forregne seg. **miscalculation** ['miskälkju'leiʃən] feilregning.

miscall [mis'kå·l] kalle uriktig, sette galt navn på.

miscarriage [mis'käridʒ] dårlig utfall; uhell; misfall; ulykke; (brevs) bortkomst; for tidlig fødsel, abort. **miscarry** [mis'käri] slå feil; mislykkes; være uheldig; forulykke; komme bort; nedkomme for tidlig, abortere.

miscellaneous [misi'le¹njəs] blandet.

miscellany ['misələni] blanding, samling av blandet innhold; **miscellanies** ['misələniz] artikler av forskjellig innhold; blandede skrifter.

mischance [mis'tʃa·ns] ulykke, uhell.

mischarge [mis'tʃa·²dʒ] oppføre feilaktig; uriktig fordring.

mischief ['mistʃif] fortred, ugagn, skade; puss; ulykke; **get into** — komme ille opp i det; no — **has happened** det er ingen skade skjedd; **he means** — han har vondt i sinne; **make** — stifte ufred; **what the** — **are you doing** hva pokker bestiller du. — **-maker** ufredsstifter; ugagnskråke. — **-making** som gjør ugagn, stifter ufred.

mischievous ['mistʃivəs] skadelig; skadefro, ondskapsfull, skjelmsk; — **child** liten spillopp-maker.

misconceive ['miskən'si·v] oppfatte forkjært, mistyde. **misconception** ['miskən'sepʃən] misforståelse, mistyding.

misconduct ['mis'kåndʌkt] uriktig oppførsel; feilgrep. **misconduct** ['miskən'dʌkt] lede dårlig; oppføre seg dårlig.

misconjecture ['m,skən'dʒektʃə] gjette feil; feilgjetning.

misconstruction ['miskən'strʌkʃən] mistyding. **misconstrue** ['miskån'stru·] mistyde, misforstå.

miscount ['mis'kaunt] telle feil; feiltelling.

miscreant ['miskriənt] skurk, skarv.

misdate ['mis'de¹t] datere feil; feil datum.

misdeed ['mis'di·d] udåd, misgjerning.

misdelivery ['misdi'livəri] feilaktig avlevering.
misdemean ['misdi'mi·n] forse seg. **misdemeanant** [-'mi·nənt] forbryter. **misdemeanour** [-'mi··nə] forseelse, feil; mindre forbrytelse.

misdirect ['misdi'rekt] vill-lede; adressere feil, **misdirection** [-'rekʃən] feilretning; vill-ledelse; feilaktig adressering.

misdo ['mis'du·] feile, forse seg. **misdoer** ['mis-'du·ə] en som feiler· misdeder. **misdoing** ['mis-'du·iŋ] feil, forseelse, misgjerning.

misdoubt [mis'daut] mistenke, tvile på, ha mistillit til; mistanke, mistvil.

misemploy ['misèm'plɔi] misbruke, nytte galt.

misentry [mis'entri] feilaktig innføring (i en bok).

miser ['maizə] gnier, gjerrigknark.

miserable ['miz(ə)rəbl] elendig, ynkelig, ulykkelig; jammerlig, ussel; — **sinner** arm synder.

miserere [mizə'riəri] miserere, botssalme.

miserly ['maizəli] gnieraktig, gjerrig, knipen.

misery ['miz(ə)ri] elendighet, ulykke.

misesteem ['misè'sti·m] ringeakt. **misestimate** [mis'estimei't] miskjenne.

misfeasance ['mis'fi·zəns] embetsmisbruk.

misfit ['mis'fit] noe som ikke passer; vankle.

misfortunate [mis'fâ·ətʃənét] ulvkkelig.

misfortune [mis'fâ·ətʃən] ulvkke, uhell.

misgive [mis'giv] fvlle med bange anelser.

misgiving [mis'giviŋ] bange anelse, tvil, otte, uro, bekymring.

misgovern ['mis'gʌvən]regiere slett. **misgovernment** ['mis'gʌvənmənt] dårlig regjering.

misguidance ['mis'gaidəns] vill-ledelse. **misguide** ['mis'gaid] vill-lede.

mishandle ['mis'händl] behandle dårlig, fare ille med.

mishap ['mishäp, mis'häp] uhell.

mishear ['mis'hiə] høre feil.

mishmash ['miʃmäʃ] sammensurium, røre, rot.

misimprove ['misim'pru·v] misbruke. **misimprovement** misbruk.

misinform ['misin'fâ·əm] underrette feil. **misinformation** ['misinfâ·ə'meiʃən] feil underretning.

misinterpret ['misin'tə·prét] mistyde. **misinterpretation** ['misintə·pri'teiʃən] mistyding.

misjudge ['mis'dʒʌdʒ] dømme feil.

mislay [mis'lei] forlegge.

mislead [mis'li·d] forlede; vill-lede.

mismanage ['mis'mänidʒ] forplumre, forkludre. **mismanagement** [-mənt] dårlig ledelse.

misname [mis'neim] benevne feilaktig.

misnomer ['mis'noⁿmə] misvisende benevnelse.

misplace ['mis'pleis] mislegge, anbringe forkjært. **misplacement** forkjært anbringelse.

misprint [mis'print] trykke feil; trykkfeil.

misprision [mis'priʒən] lovstridig fortielse; — **of felony** fortieise av forbrytelse.

mispronounce ['mispro'nauns] uttale galt. **mispronunciation** ['mispronʌnsi'eiʃən] feilaktig uttale.

misrepresent ['misrepri'zent] framstille uriktig, fordreie, oppgi galt el. unøyaktig; baktale. **misrepresentation** ['misrepriʒən'teiʃən] feilaktig framstilling, fordreiing; baktalelse.

misrule ['mis'ru·l] vanstyre; vanstell, uorden, forvirring.

miss [mis] frøken; **the Misses Smith, the Miss Smiths** frøknene Smith.

miss [mis] savne, sakne, unnvære, mangle, gå glipp av, forsømme; feile, ta feil av, ikke treffe, bomme på, feilskudd, feilslag; — **fire** klikke (om gevær); — **the train** komme for sent til toget; — **the mark** skyte forbi, bomme.

missal ['misəl] messebok, missale.

misshapen ['mis'ʃeipən] vanskapt, misdannet.

missile ['misail] kastevåpen, prosjektil.

missing ['misiŋ] forsvunnet, manglende; som savnes, savnet, sakna; **the — link** det manglende mellomledd mellom ape og menneske; **be — savnes**, mangle.

mission ['miʃən] misjon, sending, bud, ærend; verv, kall, oppgave; gesandtskap, sendelag, sendeferd; **on a — i** en sendelse, i et ærend.

missionary ['miʃənəri] misjonær, lekpredikant; utsending.

missis ['misiz] frue (brukt av tjenerne).

Mississippi [misi'sipi] Mississippi.

missive ['misiv] sende-; kaste-; sendebrev.

Missouri [mi'suəri] Missouri.

mis-spell ['mis'spel] stave feil.

mis-spend ['mis'spend] forøde, skusle bort, anvende ille; **a mis-spent youth** en forspilt ungdom.

misstate ['mis'steit] framstille uriktig. **misstatement** [-'steitmənt] uriktig framstilling.

missus ['misəs, -əz] frue (brukt av tjenerne).

missy ['misi] jomfrunalsk, affektert; sentimental; veslefrøken.

mist [mist] tåke, skodde, moe; støvregn, duskregn, yr; snøtykke.

mistake [mis'teik] ta feil; misforstå, forveksle, feiltagelse, feil, mistak; misforståelse, forveksling; **I mistook him for his brother** jeg forvekslet ham med hans bror; **and no — det** er visst og sant, det kan du ta gift på; **make a — ta** feil; **by — ved** en feiltagelse.

mistaken [mis'teikn] misforstått; forfeilet; **be mistaken** ta feil.

mister ['mistə] herr.; si herr til; **Mr. B.** herr B.

misterm [mis'tə·m] kalle feilaktig, nevne galt.

mistimed [mis'taimd] ubetimelig, ulugom.

mistiness ['mistines] tåkethet.

mistitle [mis'taitl] benevne feilaktig.

mistletoe ['misltoᵘ, 'mizltoᵘ] misteltein.

mistook [mis'tuk] imperf. av **mistake**.

mistral ['mistrəl] mistral, nordvestvind (i Sør-Frankrike).

mistranslate ['mistra·ns'leit] oversette galt. **mistranslation** gal oversettelse.

mistreat [mis'tri·t] behandle dårlig.

mistress ['mistris] herskerinne; frue, husfrue, matmor; lærerinne; elskerinne; kjæreste; **Mrs. Brown** ['misiz 'braun] fru Brown.

mistrust ['mis'trʌst] ha mistillit til, mistro. **mistrustful** [-f(u)l] mistroisk.

misty ['misti] tåket, skoddet; omtåket.

misunderstand ['misʌndə'ständ] misforstå. **misunderstanding** [-iŋ] misforståelse, uenighet.

misusage ['mis'ju·zidʒ] misbruk, mishandling.

misuse ['mis'ju·z] misbruke, mishandle.

misuse ['mis'ju·s] misbruk.

mite [mait] midd, mit (i ost, mel).

mite [mait] liten mynt; liten smule; grann, døyt, skjerv; liten pjokk, gryn, stump; **it ain't a — of use** det er ikke til ringeste nytte.

mithridate ['miþrideit] motgift.

mitigant ['mitigənt] formildende; lindrende.

mitigate ['mitigeit] formilde, demne, døyve, lindre. **mitigation** [miti'geiʃən] formildelse, lindring, formildende omstendighet. **mitigator** ['mitigeitə] en som formilder, lindrer.

mitrailleuse [mitrai'ə·z] mitraljøse, kulesprøyte.

mitre ['maitə] mitra, bispehue, bispeverdighet; (i snekkerspråk) gjæring (slags fugning), gjæringsfuge; bekle med bispehua; gjøre til bisp; gjære sammen. — **-joint** gjæringsfuge. — **-wheel** konisk hjul (om tannhjul, med akse som danner en vinkel på 45°).

mitt [mit] se **mitten**.

mitten ['mitn] belgvott, lovott, halvhanske, ermebeskytter, (i pl. slang) boksehansker; **give the — gi** en kurv, avskjedige; **get the — få** reisepass.

mittimus ['mitiməs] arrestordre.

mix [miks] blande, lage; blande sammen; blande seg, ha omgang, omgås; — **a glass** brygge et glass; **he was mixed up in a conspiracy** han var innviklet i en sammensvergelse; — **with the world** ferdes ute i verden.

mixable ['miksəbl] som kan blandes.

mixed [mikst] blandet, forvirret; — **bathing** fellesbading (for herrer og damer); — **company** blandet selskap; — **marriage** ekteskap mellom protestant og katolikk; — **mathematics** anvendt matematikk; — **school** fellesskole (for gutter og piker).

mixen ['miksən] mødding.

mixture ['mikstʃə] blanding, oppblanding; mikstur.

mizzen ['mizn] mesan, mesanmast. — **-mast** mesanmast. — **-sail** mesanseil.

mizzle ['mizl] duskregne, muske; dusk, yr.

ml fk. f. **millilitre.**

Mlle fk. f. **mademoiselle.**

Mlles fk. f. **mesdemoiselles.**

M. M. fk. f. **military** medal.

M. M. fk. f. **Messieurs.**

mm fk. f. **millimetre.**

Mme fk. f. **madame.**

Mmes fk. f. **mesdames.**

mnemonic [ni'mánik] mnemonisk, som hjelper på hukommelsen; **-s** hukommelseskunst. **mnemonician** [nimo'niʃən] hukommelseskunstner.

mo [moᵘ] (slang) øyeblikk; **wait half a** — vent et lite øyeblikk.

Mo. fk. f. **month.**

M. O. fk. f. **medical officer.**

moan [moᵘn] klage, stønne, anke seg; klage, anking.

moat [moᵘt] festningsgrav, borggrav; omgi med en grav.

mob [måb] pøbel. pøbelhop; hjord, flokk; stimle sammen, lage oppløp.

mobbish ['måbiʃ] pøbelaktig, rå.

mobcap ['måbkäp] nattkappe, hylk.

mobile ['moᵘbail] bevegelig. **mobility** [mo-'biliti] bevegelighet. **mobilization** [moᵘbilai-'ze'ʃən] mobilisering. **mobilize** ['moᵘbilaiz] mobllisere.

mob-law ['måblå·] pøbeljustis.

mobocracy [må'båkrəsi] pøbelherredømme.

mobsman ['måbzmən] plattenslager, snyter, velkledd tyv.

moccasin ['måkəsin] indianersko, mokkasin.

Mocha ['moᵘkə] mokkakaffe.

mock [måk] ape etter, herme etter, gjøre latterlig, spotte over. spotte, skuffe; etterligning; spott, spe, latterliggjøring; forloren, uekte, falsk, forstilt. **mocker** ['måka] spotter. **mockery** ['måkəri] etterligning, herming; spott, spe latterliggjøring.

mocking ['måkiŋ] spottende, spotsk. — **-bird** hermekråke, spottefugl.

mock-turtle ['måk'tə·tl] forloren skilpadde.

mod. fk. f. **modern.**

modal ['moᵘdl] formell, modal. **modality** [moᵘ-'dåliti] modalitet, måte, form. **mode** [moᵘd] måte, mote, vis, lag, beskaffenhet, skikk, bruk.

model ['mådl] mønster, modell; eksemplar, forbilde; mønster-, mønstergyldig; modellere, avbilde, danne; **a** — **husband** en eksemplarisk ektemann. **modeller** ['mådlə] modellør. **modelling** ['mådliŋ] modellering.

Modena [mo'de'nə] Modena.

moderate ['måd(e)rét] måteholden, moderat; tarvelig, lempelig, middelmådig; **at a** — **price** til en rimelig pris.

moderate ['mådəre't] legge bånd på, betvinge, beherske; moderere, holde måte med; være ordstyrer ved forhandlinger.

moderation [mådə're'ʃən] betvingelse, beherskelse; måtehold, moderasjon; sindighet; annen eksamen ved Oxford.

moderator ['mådre'tə] betvinger, demper; dirigent, ordstyrer.

modern ['mådən] moderne, nyere, nymotens, ny, nåtids-; **the -s** nåtidsmennesker; — **languages** nyere språk. **modernism** ['mådənizm] ny skikk, nyere smak. **modernist** ['mådənist] beundrer av det nyere. **modernity** [mo'də·niti] ny-

het; det å henge ved det nye. **modernization** [mådənai'ze'ʃən] modernisering. **modernize** ['må-dənaiz] modernisere,· omforme.

modest ['mådist] beskjeden, fordringsløs, små-låten; sømmelig, anstendig, ærbar, blyg. **modesty** ['mådisti] beskjedenhet, fordringsløshet; anstendighet, ærbarhet. — **-piece** fichu, brystduk (over en nedringet kjole).

modicum ['mådikəm] liten smule, grann, knapt mål.

modifiable ['mådifaiəbl] som kan forandres, tillempes; omformelig. **modification** [mådifi-'ke'ʃən] modifikasjon, omforming, omdanning, omlyd. **modificatory** ['mådifi'ke'təri] endrende. **modify** ['mådifai] modifisere, omforme, omdanne; begrense, innskrenke.

modish ['moᵘdiʃ] moderne, nymotens, sveisen. **modishness** [-nés] motesyke; modernitet. **modist** ['moᵘdist] en som følger moten. **modiste** [mo-'di·st] motehandlerske, dameskredderske, sydame.

modulate ['mådjule't] avpasse (stemmen), modulere. **modulation** [mådju'le'ʃən] toneskifte, modulasjon. **modus** ['moᵘdəs] modus, måte; godtgjørelse for tiende, erstatning.

Mogul [mo'gʌl] mogul, mongol.

M. O. H. fk. f. **medical officer of health.**

mohair ['moᵘhæ·ə] angoraull, kamelhår.

Mohammedan [mo'hämədən] muhamedansk.

Mohawk ['moᵘhå·k] mohawkindianer.

Mohican ['moᵘikən] mohikaner; **the last of the -s** den siste mohikaner, ættens siste.

Mohock ['moᵘhåk], slags londonsk pøbel.

moidore ['moidå·ə] moidor, en portugisisk gullmynt, verd ca. 25 kr.

moiety ['moiiti] halvdel.

moil [moil] søle til, flekke; slite, slepe; flekk, klatt; slit, strev.

moire [mwa·ə] moarering; silkemoaré.

moist [moist] rå, fuktig. **moisten** ['moisn] fukte, væte. **moistener** ['moisnə] fukter, fuktemiddel. **moistness** ['moistnés] fuktighet, væte. **moisture** ['moistʃə] fuktighet, væte.

moke [moᵘk] maske (i nett); esel; dumrian.

moky ['moᵘki] mørk, skummel.

molar ['moᵘlə] som tjener til å male el. knuse; kinntann, jeksel. — **-tooth** kinntann, jeksel.

molasses [mə'läsiz] sirup; melasse.

mold [moᵘld] se **mould.**

Moldavia [mål'de'vjə] Moldau.

mole [moᵘl] føflekk.

mole [moᵘl] molo, havnedemning, steindemning.

mole [moᵘl] moldvarp; — **out** grave fram.

mólecast ['moᵘlka·st] moldvarpskudd.

molecricket ['moᵘl'krikit] jordkreps.

molecular [mo'lekjulə] molekylar, molekylær, molekyl-.

molecule ['moᵘlikju·l] molekyl, småpartikkel.

molehill ['moᵘlhil] moldvarpskudd; **make a mountain of a** — gjøre en mygg til en elefant.

molerat ['moᵘlrät] blindmus.

moleskin ['moᵘlskin] moldvarpskinn; moleskin (slags tykt bomullstøy); (i pl.) bukser av moleskin.

molest [mo'lest] besvære, molestere, plage, bry, forulempe; **be -ed** li overlast.

molestation [moᵘle'ste'ʃən] overlast; fortred, bry.

moletrack ['moᵘlträk] moldvarpgang.

mollah ['målə] mollah (arabisk prestetittel).

mollient ['måljənt] bløtgjørende, lindrende.

mollification [målifi'ke'ʃən] bløtgjøring, lindring, stagging. **mollify** ['målifai] lindre, bløtgjøre, myke. **be mollified** la seg formilde.

molluscan [må'lʌskən] bløtdyr.-.

mollusk ['målʌsk] bløtdyr.

Molly ['måli] Marie.

mollycodle ['målikådl] veikling, svekling, stuegris, kjerring.

Moloch ['mo^ulåk] Molok.

molten ['mo^ultən] smeltet; støpt.

Moluccas [mo'lʌkəz], **the** — Molukkene.

moly ['mo^uli] slags løk.

moment ['mo^umənt, -mint] øyeblikk, moment; drivkraft; beveggrunn; vekt, viktighet; betydning; **the** — **I saw him** straks jeg så ham; **it is of no** — det har ikke noe å si.

momentary ['mo^uməntəri] øyeblikkelig, som varer et øyeblikk; forbigående.

momently ['mo^uməntli] for et øyeblikk, hvert øyeblikk.

momentous [mo'mentəs] betydningsfull, viktig; kritisk, skjebnesvanger.

momentum [mo'mentəm] drivende kraft, fart, bevegelse; moment, viktig punkt; vekt.

monachal ['mänəkl] klosterlig, kloster-, munke-.

monachism ['mänəkizm] munkeliv, munkevesen.

Monaco ['mänəko^u] Monaco.

monad ['månäd] monade.

monarch ['månək] monark, hersker, enevoldsherre; konge, fyrste. **monarchic(al)** [mo'na·^əkik(l)] monarkisk. **monarchist** ['månəkist] monarkist.

monarchy ['månəki] monarki, kongedømme, keiserdømme.

monasterial [månə'stiəriəl] klosterlig, kloster-. **monastery** ['månəstəri] kloster. **monastic** [må'nästik] klosterlig, kloster-, munke-; munk. **monasticism** [må'nästisizm] munkevesen; klosterliv.

Monday ['mʌndi] mandag.

monde [månd, månd] verden, folk; **beau** — den fine verden.

monetary ['mʌnitəri] mynt-, penge-.

money ['mʌni] mynt, penger; **much** — mange penger; **piece of** — pengestykke; **for love or** — for gode ord og betaling; **keep a person in** — forsyne en med penger; **keep a person out of his** — la en vente på betalingen; **lend (put, place)** — **on interest** sette penger på rente; **make** — tjene penger, bli rik.

money|-agent vekselér. — **-bag** pengesekk. — **-belt** pengebelte. — **-bill** lovforslag om penger (til sivillisten). — **-box** pengeskuff, pengeskrin; sparebøsse. — **-broker**, — **-changer** vekselér. — **-drawer** pengeskuff.

moneyed ['mʌnid] bemidlet, velhavende.

money|-grubber pengepuger, gnier, flåer. — **-lender** pengeutlåner, diskontør. — **-lending** pengeutlån, diskontering. — **-market** pengemarked. — **-order** pengeanvisning; postanvisning.

monger ['mʌngə]-handler, -kremmer.

Mongol ['mångål] mongol; mongolsk.

Mongolia [mån'go^uliə] Mongolia.

Mongolian [mån'go^uljən] mongol; mongolsk.

mongoose [mʌn'gu·s] mungo, mongus (slags indisk desmerdyr).

mongrel ['mʌngrəl] blandet, uekte, bastard, fillebikkje.

'mongst [mʌŋst] blant.

monism ['månizm] monisme. **monist** ['månist] monist. **monistic** [må'nistik] monistisk.

monition [mə'niʃən] advarsel, åtvaring, påminning.

monitor ['månitə] påminner, formaner; monitor (betrodd elev som har oppsyn med yngre elever); monitor (slags krigsskip).

monitorial [måni'tå·riel] påminnende; tilsyns-; — **school** skole som nytter monitorsystemet. **monitory** ['månitəri] advarende, formanende. **monitress** ['månitrəs] kvinnelig monitor.

monk [mʌŋk] munk.

monkery ['mʌŋkəri] munkeliv, munkevesen.

monkey ['mʌŋki] ape (især laverestående ape), apekatt; rambukk, maskin til å ramme ned peler el. drive inn bolter med; (i slang) £ 500; herme etter, drive gjøn, drive ap; **put his** — **up** gjøre ham sint.

monkey|-board stigbrett på en omnibus til konduktøren. — **-boat** kanalbåt. — **-bread** apebrød.

monkeyism ['mʌŋkiizm] apekattstreker, ap.

monkey|-jacket kort, tettsittende sjømannstrøye, pjekkert. — **-nut** jordnøtt. — **-puzzle** en slags araukaria. — **-trick** apekattstrek.

monkhood ['mʌŋkhud] munkestand.

monkish ['mʌŋkiʃ] munkaktig.

Monmouth ['månməþ] Monmouth.

monocle ['månåkl] monokkel.

monocracy [mo'nåkrəsi] eneherredømme.

monocrat ['månokrät] eneversker.

monocular [mo'nåkjulə] enøyd, for ett øye.

monodon ['månodån] narhval.

monodrama [måno'dra·mə] monodrama.

monody ['månodi] sørgesang.

monogamist [mo'någəmist] monogamist.

monogamy [mo'någəmi] monogami.

monogram ['månogräm] monogram, navnetrekk.

monography [mo'någrəfi] særavhandling, monografi, skisse.

monolith ['månoliþ] bautastein, støtte av én stein, monolitt.

monologue ['månolåg] monolog, enetale.

monomania [måno'meⁱnje] monomani, fiks idé. **monomaniac** [måno'meⁱnjäk] en som lider av en fiks idé.

monometallism [måno'metəlizm] monometallisme, enkeltmyntfot.

monoplane ['månopleⁱn] monoplan, endekker.

monopolist [mə'nåpolist] innehaver av et monopol, enehandler. **monopolistic** [monåpo'listik] monopolmessig. **monopolize** [mə'nåpəlaiz] få monopol på, ha enerett til; tilvende seg enehandel; kjøpe opp alt; oppta for seg alene. **monopolizer** [mə'nåpəlaizə] monopolhaver, enebesitter; eneberettiget.

monopoly [mə'nåpəli] monopol, enehandel, embetsbesittelse; **have a** — **of** ha monopol på. **monorail** ['månoreⁱl] énskinnet jernbane.

monosyllabic [månosi'läbik] enstavings-. **monosyllable** [måno'siləbl] enstavingsord.

monotheism ['månoþi·izm] læren om en eneste Gud. **monotheist** ['månoþi·ist] en som tror på en eneste Gud.

monotone ['månoto^un] ensformig tone. **monotous** [mə'nåtənəs] monoton, enstonig; ensformig. **monotony** [mə'nåtəni] ensformighet.

Monroe [mən'ro^u] Monroe; **the** — **doctrine** Monroedoktrinen (ingen europeisk innblanding i Amerikas forhold).

monseigneur [månseⁱn'jə·] monseigneur, Deres nåde. **monsieur** [må'sjə·] monsieur.

monsoon [mån'su·n] monsun (vind).

monstrance ['månstrəns] monstrans (kapsel hvor hostien stilles ut).

monstrosity [mån'stråsiti] vanskapthet; vanskapning.

monstrous ['månstrəs] uhyre, unaturlig stor; avskyelig; vanskapt.

montane ['månteⁱn] berg-, fjell-.

monte ['månti] et slags kortspill.

Montenegrin [månti'ni·griən] montenegrinsk, montenegriner. **Montenegrin** [månti'nigrin] montenegrinsk, montenegriner. **Montenegro** [mânti'ni·gro^u] Montenegro.

month [mʌnþ] måned; **at three months' date** 3 måneder fra dato; **for -s** i månedsvis; **that day** — en måned fra den dag; **a** — **of Sundays** en evighet. **monthly** ['mʌnþli] månedlig; månedsskrift.

monticle ['måntikl] lite fjell, knatt, haug.

Montreal [måntri'å·l] Montreal.

monument ['månjumənt] monument, minnesmerke; minnestein; **the Monument**, en søyle (el. et tårn) i London (til minne om brannen 1666). **monumental** [månju'mentl] som hører til et monument; monumental.

moo [mu·] raute, si »bø« (som en ku; brukes av barn); raut.

mooch [mu·tʃ] skulke, liste seg vekk (uten å betale); være på utkik etter fordel.

moo-cow ['mu·kau] ku.

mood [mu·d] modus; måte, form; toneart.

mood [mu·d] sinnsstemning, humør; lag; lune, egensindighet; **be in one's -s** være i dårlig humør; **be in a drinking** være opplagt til å drikke.

moody ['mu·di] lunet; nedslått, tunglynt; gretten.

moon [mu·n] måne; måned; drømme, vandre drømmende omkring, gå og drømme. **the — increases (waxes)** månen tiltar. **the — decreases (wanes)** månen avtar; **cry for the —** forlange urimeligheter; **at the full —** ved fullmåne.

moon-beam ['mu·nbi·m] månestråle.

mooncalf ['mu·nka·f] misfoster; idiot, naut.

mooner ['mu·nə] drømmer. **moon-eyed** ['mu·naid] dimsynt. **mooning** ['mu·niŋ] drømming, drømmeri. **moonish** ['mu·niʃ] måneaktig, ustadig.

moonless ['mu·nlès] uten måne, månemørk.

moonlight ['mu·nlait] måneskinn; måneskinns-; månelys; begå overfall om natten; **— flitting** det å stikke av ved nattetid.

moonlighter ['mu·nlaitə] en som begår overfall om natten.

moonlit ['mu·nlit] månelys, månebelyst.

moonrise ['mu·nraiz] måneoppgang.

moonshine ['mu·nʃain] måneskinn; snakk, sludder; smuglersprit, heimebrent; **that's all —** det er ganske urimelig, bare tøv.

moonshiner ['mu·nʃainə] spritsmugler, hjemmebrenner.

moon-stone ['mu·nstoⁿn] månestein (slags feltspat).

moon-struck ['mu·nstrʌk] gal; vanvittig forelsket.

moony ['mu·ni] måneaktig; drømmende; tåpelig.

Moor [mu·ə] maurer; mor, morian.

moor [muə] hei, mo, vidde.

moor [muə] fortøye, legge for anker.

moorage ['muəridʒ] fortøyningsplass.

moor-cock ['muəkåk] rypestegg.

moor-fowl ['muəfaul] morype.

moor-game ['muəgeⁱm] moryper.

moor-hen ['muəhen] hunrype; bleshøne.

mooring ['muəriŋ] fortøyning; **let go the -s** kaste fortøyningen løs.

Moorish ['muəriʃ] maurisk.

moorish ['muəriʃ] moaktig; myrlendt.

moorland ['muələnd] hei, lyngmo.

moose [mu·s] amerikansk elg.

moot [mu·t] avhandle, diskutere, drøfte, disputere; omstridt, omtvistet, uavgjort; diskusjon, drøfting, disputas; møte. **mootable** ['mu·təbl] omtvistelig. **moot-case, moot-point** oppkastet stridsspørsmål. **mooter** ['mu·tə] en som de tar i en disputas. **mooting** ['mu·tiŋ] diskusjon, drøfting.

mop [måp] geip, grimase; geipe.

mop [måp] svaber, skureklut på skaft; skrubbe, tørre, slå (av marka); **I feel all -s and brooms** jeg føler meg aldeles elendig; **— one's brow** tørke (svetten av) pannen.

mope [moⁿp] sture, være nedfor; gjøre sturen; sette i ulag; en som sturer, daubiter; **get the -s** bli i dårlig humør.

mope-eyed ['moⁿpaid] stærblind; nærsynt.

mopish ['moⁿpiʃ] nedslått, sturen, sløv.

moppet ['måpit] tøydukke, dukkebarn (som kjælenavn).

mops [måps] mops.

mopstick ['måpstik] kosteskaft.

mopus ['moⁿpəs] skilling, slant.

moraine [mo·reⁱn] morene.

moral ['mårəl] moralsk, dydig, sedelig; moral (i en fabel o. l.); ogs. moralsk kraft (= morale); **the moral el. morale of the troops** troppenes moral. **morals** moral, moralske grunnsetninger; **bad morals** dårlige seder.

morale [må·ra·l] moralsk kraft (til å utholde vanskeligheter og farer), mannstukt.

moralist ['mårəlist] moralist, moralpredikant.

morality [mo·räliti] moralsk forhold, moral, dyd; moralitet (ɔ: gammeldags allegorisk skuespill).

moralization [mårəl(a)iˈzeⁱʃən] moralsk betraktning. **moralize** ['mårəlaiz] moralisere, bruke i moralsk hensikt; utdra en moral av; snakke moral.

morass [mə·räs] morass, myr.

moratorium [mårəˈtå·ⁿriəm] moratorium.

Moravia [mə·reⁱvjə] Mähren.

Moravian [mə·reⁱvjən] mährisk; herrnhutisk; **— brethren** mähriske brødre, herrnhutere.

morbid ['må·ⁿbid] sykelig, syk.

morbidity [må·ⁿbiditi] sykelighet, vanhelse.

morbific [må·ⁿbifik] som forårsaker sykdom.

mordacious [må·ⁿdeⁱʃəs] bitende, skarp, kvass. **mordacity** [-ˈdäsiti]skarphet. **mordant** ['må·ⁿdənt] bitende; beisende; beis; beise.

mordent ['må·dənt] (mus.) mordent.

more [må·ⁿ] mer, flere; **one pound —, one —** pound et pund til; **— fool you to marry** hvordan kunne du være så dum å gifte deg; **— or less** mer eller mindre; **and — than that** og hva mer er; **so much the —** så meget desto mer; **the — . . . the —** jo mer . . . desto mer; **— to pay** ɔ: utilstrekkelig frankert (skrives på brever av postvesenet); **as much —** en gang til så mye; **we have not heard of him any —** since vi har ikke hørt noe til ham senere; **once —** en gang til; **no —** aldri mer.

moreen [mo·ri·n] morin, ullmoaré.

morel [mo·rel] morell (kirsebær).

morello [mo·reloⁿ] el slags lite kirsebær.

moreover [må·ⁿroⁿvə] dessuten, enn videre.

Moresque [mo·resk] maurisk; arabesker.

morganatic [må·ⁿgə·nätik] morganatisk; **— marriage** ekteskap til venstre hånd.

morgue [må·ⁿg] likhus; hovmod.

moribund ['måribənd] døende.

Morisco [mo·riskoⁿ] = **Moresque.**

morish ['må·riʃ], **it tastes —** det har mersmak.

morling ['må·ⁿliŋ] ull fra selvdød sau.

Mormon ['må·ⁿmən] mormon.

Mormonism ['må·ⁿmənizm] mormonisme.

morn [må·ⁿn] morgen (dikterisk).

morning ['må·ⁿniŋ] morgen, formiddag; **in the —** om morgenen; **to-morrow —** i morgen tidlig; **this —** i morges, i dag tidlig; **I wish you good —, good —** to you god morgen! **one —, some fine —** en vakker dag.

morning-call ['må·ⁿniŋkå·l] visitt (avlagt om ettermiddagen mellom 4 og 6).

morning-coat ['må·ⁿniŋˈkoⁿt] sjakett.

morning-dress ['må·ⁿniŋˈdres] formiddagsdrakt.

morning|-gift morgengave, benkegave. **— -gown** slåbrok; morgenkjole; friserkåpe. **— -room** dagligstue. **— -service** høymesse. **— -star** morgenstjerne. **— -tide** (poet.) morgenstund.

morning-watch ['må·ⁿəniŋˈwåtʃ] dagvakt (fra 4 til 8 morgen).

Moroccan [mə·råkən] marokkansk; marokkaner. **Morocco** [mə·råkoⁿ] Marokko.

morocco [mə·råkoⁿ] saffian, tyrkisk lær.

morose [mo·roⁿs] gretten, sur, sær.

Morpheus ['må·ⁿfiəs, -fju·s] Morfeus.

morphia ['må·ⁿfjə] morfin.

morphine ['må·ⁿfi·n] morfin.

morphinism ['må·ⁿfinizm] morfinisme.

morphi(n)omaniac [må·ⁿfi(n)o·meⁱniäk] morfinist.

morphology [må·ⁿfålədʒi] morfologi.

morris ['måris] maurisk dans, narredans; **nine men's —** slags møllespill.

morris ['måris] danse; stikke av.

morrow ['måroⁿ] følgende dag, morgendag;

to- — i morgen; **the day after to-** — i overmorgen; **to-morrow morning** i morgen tidlig.

morse [mȧ·ˑs] hvalross.

morsel ['mȧ·ˑsl] bit, bete; smule, grann.

mort [mȧ·ˑt] bråte, stor mengde, haug.

mortal ['mȧ·ˑtl] dødelig; dødbringende, ulivs-, bane-; menneskelig; døddrukken; dødelig; menneske; — **enemy** dødsfiende; **four** — **hours fire** forferdelige lange timer; **any** — **thing** alt mulig; **it must be** — **hard** det må være forferdelig tungt.

mortality [mȧ·ˑˑtäliti] dødelighet; mennesker.

mortally ['mȧ·ˑtəli] dødelig; — **wounded** dødelig såret.

mortar ['mȧ·ˑtə] mørtel, kalk; kalke.

mortar ['mȧ·ˑtə] morter; mørser (svær kanon).

mortar-board ['mȧ·ˑtəbȧ·ˑd] kalkbrett; (firkantet, flat) studenterlue.

mortgage ['mȧ·ˑgėdʒ] panteheftelse, pant, pantobligasjon; prioritet; pantsette. — **-deed** pantobligasjon. **mortgagee** [mȧ·ˑgėˈdʒi.] panthaver. **mortgager** ['mȧ·ˑgėdʒə] pantsetter.

mortification [mȧ·ˑtifiˈkeˈʃən] gangren, brann, koldbrann; speking; ydmyking; krenking, skuffelse, sorg; — **set in** det gikk koldbrann i såret.

mortify ['mȧ·ˑtifai] framkalle koldbrann i; speke; krenke; ydmyke; ergre, plage; forderves; angripes, dø bort av koldbrann; **mortifying** ['mȧ·ˑtifaiiŋ] krenkende.

mortise ['mȧ·ˑtis] hull til en tapp; hogge ut tapphull i; tappe sammen, tappe inn.

mortise-chisel ['mȧ·ˑtisˈtʃizəl] hoggjern.

mortmain ['mȧ·ˑtmeˈn] korporasjons besittelse av uavhendelig gods; **hold in** — besitte som uavhendelig gods.

mortuary ['mȧ·ˑtjuəri] som hører til lik eller begravelse; gravsted, begravelse; likhus.

Mosaic [moˈzeˈik] mosaisk, Mose-.

mosaic [moˈzeˈik] mosaikk.

moschatel ['mȧskətel] desmerurt.

Moscow ['mȧskoᵘ] Moskva.

moselle [məˈzel] moselvin.

Moses ['moᵘziz] Moses.

Moslem ['mȧzlem] muselman; muhamedaner; muhamedansk.

mosque [mȧsk] moské.

mosquito [mȧˈskitoᵘ] moskito. — **-bar** moskitoramme. — **-craft** torpedobåter. — **-net** moskitonett.

moss [mȧs] myr, torvmyr.

moss [mȧs] mose; mosekle. — **-agate** dendritisk agat. — **-berry** tranebær. — **-grown** mosegrodd. **mossiness** ['mȧsinės] det å være mosegrodd. — **-rose** moserose.

moss-troopers røvere i grensedistriktene mellom England og Skottland i det 17. hundreår.

mossy ['mȧsi] mosegrodd.

most [moᵘst] mest, flest, høyst; de fleste; — **people** folk flest; **make the** — **of** utnytte så godt som mulig, dra størst mulig nytte av; **as good as** — **people** slett ikke så gal; — **of all** allermest; — **willingly** hjertens gjerne; **at (the)** — i høyden.

mostly ['moᵘstli] for det meste, mest, som regel.

mot [moᵘ] fyndord; vits.

mote [moᵘt] møte.

mote [moᵘt] støvgrann, sandkorn; (bibelsk:) splint.

motet [moᵘˈtet] motett, flerstemmig kirkelig sang.

moth [mȧþ] møll; nattsommerfugl.

moth-eaten ['mȧþi·tn] møllett, møllspist.

mother ['mʌðə] moder, mor; være mor for (til), ta seg moderlig av; **become a** — føde; bli mor; **necessity is the** — **of invention** nød lærer naken kvinne å spinne; **he -ed it upon her** han gav henne ansvaret for det; **Mother Carey's chicken** stormpetrell (fugl): **mother's help** barnefrøken; **mother's mark** føflekk; **mother's meeting** møte for mødre; **every mother's son** hver levende sjel.

mother ['mʌðə] eddikmor (hinne på eddik), slim (i eddik).

mother-bee bidronning. **mother-cell** modercelle. **mother-church** moderkirke. **mother-country** moderland.

motherhood ['mʌðəhud] moderskap, moderverdighet.

Mothering ['mʌðəriŋ] **Sunday**, morsdag, den fjerde søndag i fasten, da man etter gammel skikk besøker sin mor med gaver.

mother-in-law ['mʌðərinlå·] svigermor, (i dialekt) stemor.

motherless ['mʌðəlės] morløs.

motherly ['mʌðəli] moderlig.

mother-of-pearl ['mʌðərəvˈpə·l] perlemor.

mother-queen ['mʌðˈkwi·n] enkedronning.

mother-ship moderskip (for fly etc.).

mothersill ['mʌðəsil] mothersill, et middel mot sjøsyke.

mother-tongue ['mʌðəˈtʌŋ] morsmål.

mother-wit ['mʌðəwit] naturlig vidd, medfødt forstand.

motherwort ['mʌðəwə·t] løvehale (planten: leonurus cardiaca).

mothery ['mʌðəri] mudret, grumset

mothy ['mȧþi] møllett, møllspist.

motif [moᵘˈti·f] motiv (i musikk).

motion ['moᵘʃən] bevegelse, rørsle, gang; rørelse; vink; forslag; andragende; avføring; verk, mekanisme; gi tegn til, vinke til; foreslå, stille forslag; **of one's own** — av egen drift; **carry a** — vedta et forslag; **the** — **was withdrawn** forslaget ble tatt tilbake; **he -ed them to be taken away** han gjorde tegn til at de skulle føres bort.

motionless ['moᵘʃənlės] ubevegelig.

motive ['moᵘtiv] bevegende, bevegelses-, drivbeveggrunn, motiv; motivere, begrunne. **motiveless** [-lès] umotivert. **motivity** [moᵘˈtiviti] bevegelseskraft.

motley ['mȧtli] broket, spraglet, mangefarget; blandet; broket drakt; narredrakt.

motor ['moᵘtə] motor; automobil, bil; bevegende, motorisk, motor-; kjøre i bil, bile; — **cab** drosjebil; **rides in motors** bilturer; — **nerve** bevegelsesnerve.

motor-boat ['moᵘtəboᵘt] motorbåt.

motor|-bus ['moᵘtəbʌs] motoromnibus, rutebil. — **-car** automobil, bil. — **-cycle** motorsykkel. — **-drome** bilbane.

motor|ing ['moᵘtəriŋ] bilkjørsel, biling. **-ist** ['moᵘtərist] bilkjører, bilist.

motor|-man ['moᵘtəmän] vognstyrer, lokomotivfører; sjåfør. — **-ship** motorskip. — **-vessel** motorskip, motorbåt.

mottled ['mȧtld] broket, spraglet, droplet, marmorert. **mottling** ['mȧtliŋ] marmorering.

motto ['mȧtoᵘ] valgspråk, devise, motto.

mouch [muˈtʃ] skulke, lure seg unna; skulking.

moujik ['muˈʒik] musjik, russisk bonde.

mould [moᵘld] form, støpeform; skikkelse, type, preg; skabelon; forme, danne, støpe; **to** — **candles** støpe lys.

mould [moᵘld] muld, mold; stoff, emne; mulde, molde.

mould [moᵘld] mugg, mygl; mugne, mygle. **mouldable** ['moᵘldəbl] plastisk, som kan formes.

mould|-board formbrett; plogvelte. — **-candle** formlys.

moulder ['moᵘldə] smuldre, smuldre bort.

moulder ['moᵘldə] former.

mouldiness ['moᵘldinės] mugg, mygl.

moulding ['moᵘldiŋ] støping, forming, list- (verk).

mouldy ['moᵘldi] muggen, myglet.

moult [moᵘlt] myte; skifte ham; røyte, røyte; myting; røyting, skifting.

moulter ['moᵘltə] fugl som myter.

mound [maund] jordhaug; demning, koll, voll; demme, forskanse, beskytte med en voll.

mount [maunt] berg (især bibelsk, poetisk el. med egennavn, f. eks. Mount Etna); **the Sermon of the M.** bergprekenen.

mount [maunt] stige, klyve opp, gå opp, stige til hest; beløpe seg til, utgjøre; la stige, heve; bestige; sette på en hest; skaffe hest til; pryde med forsiringer, besette, beslå, innfatte, skefte, montere; kartong, papir (til å klebe bilder på); beslag; skoning; monterng; hest, ridehest; — **too high** forregne seg; bli overmodig; — **the breach** løpe storm; — **guard** troppe på vakt; — **the high horse** sette seg på den høye hest, skryte; **be -ed** være bereden; **the troops were miserably -ed** troppene hadde elendige hester; — **a piece** sette et stykke i scene; — **a gun** legge en kanon på lavett; — **a gaslight** anbringe et gassbluss.
mountable ['mauntəbl] som kan bestiges.
mountain ['mauntin] fjell, berg; **the M.** Berget (under den franske revolusjon); **a** — **of flesh et** kjøttberg, et meget tykt menneske; **make a** — **of a molehill** gjøre en mygg til en elefant; **a** — **is raised off my spirits** det falt en stein fra hjertet mitt; **it was a** — **on my breast** det hvilte tungt på meg. — **-ash** rogn, rognetre. — **-chain** fjellkjede, fjelldrag. — **-climber** bergbestiger, tindebestiger.
mountaineer [maunti'niə] fjellbu, fjellbygg, tindestiger; være tindebestiger.
mountainous ['mauntinəs] berglendt, fjell-lendt.
mountain-range ['mauntinrei'ndʒ] fjellkjede.
mountain-slide bergskred, fjellras.
mountebank ['mauntibäŋk] markskriker; jukse, narre; kvaksalver; storskryter. **mountebankery** [-əri] kvaksalveri; markskrikeri.
mounted ['mauntid] ridende, bereden; oppstilt, montert, oppklebet.
mounting ['mauntiŋ] montering, oppklebing, innfatning, beslag.
mourn [må·ən] sørge; sørge over, gråte for; — **for** bære sorg for, sørge for; — **over** sørge over.
mourner ['må·ənə] sørgende; en som følger lik, som hører til likfølget; **the chief** — den som går like etter kisten, nærmest pårørende.
mournful ['må·ənf(u)l] sorgfull, sørgmodig, sørgelig.
mourning ['må·əniŋ] sorg, sørgedrakt; sørgende, sørge-. **year of** — sørgeår; **be in** — **for a person** gå i sorg for en; **put on** —, **take to** — anlegge sorg; **put off** — kaste sorgen.
mouse [maus] mus; (sl.) blått øye; **when the cat's away, the mice will play** når katten er ute, danser musene på bordet; **a man or a** — alt eller intet; **as poor as a church** — så fattig som en kirkerotte.
mouse [mauz] fange mus.
mouse|-coloured ['maus'kʌləd] musgrå, musblakk. — **-hawk** musvåk. — **-hunt** musejakt; musefanger. **mouser** ['mauzə] musefanger. **mouse-trap** musefelle. **mousing** ['mauziŋ] musejakt.
mousseline [mu·s(i)'li·n] musselin.
moustache [mu'sta·ʃ] mustasje. **moustached** [-t] med mustasjer.
mouth [mauþ] munn; mule, kjeft; munning, os; hals; åpning; stemme, mæle; halsing; los; grimase, geip; **by (word) of** — muntlig; **roof of the** — gane; **be down in the** — være nedfor, henge med hodet; **foam at the** — skumme av raseri; **make up one's** — **with a thing** mele sin egen kake; **give it** — ! ut med det, snakk høyere; **make -s** at geipe til; **out of the full heart the** — **speaks** hva hjertet er fullt av, løper munnen over av.
mouth [mauð] deklamere, ta i munnen, bite på; snakke affektert, kysse; skjære ansikter, geipe.
mouther ['mauðə] en som deklamerer affektert.
mouthful ['mauþful] munnfull.
mouth-harmonica ['mauþha·ə'mänikə] munnspill.
mouthing ['mauðiŋ] svulst; svulstig.
mouth-organ ['mauþ'å·əgən] munnspill.

mouthpiece munnstykke.
mouthy ['mauði] fraseaktig.
movable ['mu·vəbl] bevegelig, rørlig; **-s** rørlig gods, løsøre.
move [mu·v] flytte, bevege; sette i gang; drive; bevege seg, flytte seg, lee på seg; røre på seg; røre; forflytte; foreslå; sette fram forslag, gjøre framlegg om; — **a person from his purpose** bringe en bort fra hans forsett; **I -d him in your favour** jeg fikk ham gunstig stemt for Dem; **black is to** —svart skal trekke (i sjakk); **it is well -d** det er et godt forslag; **I** — **we go** jeg foreslår at vi går; **to** — **an amendment** stille et endringsforslag; — **on!** gå videre, ikke stå stille (politiordre).
move [mu·v] bevegelse, flytning, forflyttelse; trekk (i sjakk o.l.); **a wrong** — feiltrekk; et misgrep; **be on the** — være i bevegelse; være på farten; **is always on the** — har kvikksølv i enden; **be up to every** —, **be up to a** — or **two**, **know every** — kjenne knepene, ikke være for katten. **moveless** ['mu·vlès] ubevegelig.
movement ['mu·vmənt] bevegelse, rørsle, gang, tempo; **watch a person's -s** holde øye med en; **upward** — kursstigning; **party of** — framskrittsparti. — **-cure** sykegymnastikk.
mover ['mu·və] forslagsstiller; en som beveger, tilskynder; **prime** — primus motor.
movies ['mu·viz] film, levende bilder, kinematograf, kino. **movietone** talefilm. **moving** ['mu·viŋ] bevegende, bevegelig; rørende. **movingness** [-nès] evne til å bevege.
mow [mou] grimase, geip; geipe.
mow [mau, mou] høystål, høystakk, høytrev.
mow [mou] slå, meie, skjære. **mower** ['mouə] slåttekar. **mowing** ['mouiŋ] slått.
mown [moun] slått.
M. P. ['em'pi·] fk. f. **member of Parliament.**
mp. fk. f. **mezzo piano** middels svakt.
m. p. h. fk. f. **miles per hour.**
M. P. S. fk. f. **member of the Pharmaceutical Society.**
M. R. fk. f. **Master of the Rolls; Midland Railway.**
Mr. ['mistə] herr (foran egennavn og noen titler); — **Jones** herr Jones, (i hustrus omtale) min mann; — **President** herr president.
M. R. C. P. fk. f. **member of the Royal College of Physicians.**
M. R. C. S. fk. f. **member of the Royal College of Surgeons.**
M. R. C. V. S. fk. f. **member of the Royal College of Veterinary Surgeons.**
Mrs. ['misiz] fru (foran gift kvinnes navn, sedvanligvis etternavn); — **Jones** fru J.; — **Henry** Jones el. **Mrs. Henry,** Henry Jones's hustru.
m. s. fk. f. **motor-ship.**
Ms. fk. f. **manuscript.**
MSS. fk. f. **manuscripts.**
Mt. fk. f. **Mount.**
much [mʌtʃ] megen, meget, mye; en stor del; **he is too** — **for me** han er for slu for meg; **he said as** — det var meningen med det han sa; **I feared as** — det var det jeg var redd for; **I thought as** — jeg tenkte det nok; **as** — **as to say** som om man ville si; **as** — **more** én gang til så mye; **he did not as** — **as offer us a dinner** han ikke engang så mye som tilbød oss middag; **so** — **the better** så mye desto bedre; **so** — **for the present** det er tilstrekkelig for øyeblikket; **how** — **is it** hva koster det, hvor mye er det; **how** — **is it to** . . .? hva koster det til . . .? (sier man til drosjesjåføren); **make** — **of** gjøre mye av, sette høyt, gjøre stas av; **nothing** — ikke videre, ikke mye. **muchness** ['mʌtʃnès] kvantum, mengde.
mucid ['mju·sid] myglet, muggen. **mucidness** [-nès] mygl, mugg.
mucilage ['mju·silidʒ] slim, planteslim.

muck [mʌk] møkk, gjødsel, skitt, lort, søle; penger; gjødsel; **the nasty little** — den vemmelige skittungen; **it's all** — det er det rene vrøvl; **to** — **out** måke; plukke, ribbe (i spill).

muck [:mʌk], **run a** — bli rasende, gå berserkergang.

mucker ['mʌkə] fall (i søla); **come a** — dette over ende.

muck-heap ['mʌkhi·p] mødding, møkkdynge.

mucky ['mʌki] møkket, skitten.

muckle ['mʌkl] stor, meget.

mucous ['mju·kəs] slimet, seig; — membrane slimhinne. mucus ['mju·kəs] slim.

mud [mʌd] mudder, gjørme, dynd; begrave i dynd, søle til, skitne.

mud|bath ['mʌd'ba·þ] gytjebad.

muddiness ['mʌdinės] gjørme, grumsethet.

muddle ['mʌdl] rot, røre, søl, ugreie, uføre; grumse; gjøre omtåket; sløve; forplumre, beruse; rote i søla, røre, slarke i vei; — -headed vrøvlet, uklar.

muddy ['mʌdi] mudret, tykk, gjørmet, sølet; mørk, dunkel, forvirret; dum; søle til, grumse, formørke, omtåke.

mud|engine muddermaskin. -guard skvettskjerm. -head vrøvlehode.

Mudie's ['mju·diz], et leiebibliotek.

mud|lark ['mʌdla·ᵉk] kloakkrenser; en som roter i strand- el. kloakkgjørma etter brukbare gjenstander. — -lighter mudderpram. — -pie sølekake. — -student landbruksskoleelev. — -wall leirvegg, klint vegg.

muezzin [mu'ez·in] muezzin (muhamedansk utroper av bedetimen).

muff [mʌf] muffe (til bekledning og som del av rør).

muff [mʌf] fe, treneve; forkludre, tulle bort; klusse.

muffin ['mʌfin] bolle. — -bell klokke som ‹bollemannen› ringer med. muffineer [mʌfi'niə] fat (til boller). muffin-man mann som selger boller.

muffle ['mʌfl] innhylle, tulle inn, dekke, svøpe; binde for øynene; omvikle for å dempe lyden; stagge, legge en demper på; **in a -d tone** i dempet tone; **he was so -d up** han var så innpakket; **be -d up to a blind obedience** å være tvunget til blind lydighet; **-d drums** dempede trommer.

muffler ['mʌflə] hylster; slør; sjal, skjerf; vante.

mufti ['mʌfti] mufti (muhamedansk rettslærd); sivilt antrekk.

mug [mʌg] krus; fjes, ansikt; tulling, fe; **cut -s** skjære ansikter, geipe; **make a** — **of oneself** gjøre seg latterlig.

mug [mʌg] slite med (for å lære), pugge; — **up** sminke seg, spjåke seg ut.

mugginess ['mʌginės] lummervarme.

muggy ['mʌgi] fuktig, tung, lummer, varm.

mugwump ['mʌgwʌmp] (amr.) viktigper, blære; politisk løsgjenger.

mulatto [mju'lätoᵘ] mulatt.

mulattress [mju'lätrės] mulattinne.

mulberry ['mʌlb(ə)ri] morbær, morbærtre.

mulch [mʌl(t)ʃ] halvråtten, fuktig halm; talle; dekke med fuktig halm.

mulct [mʌlt] bot, mulkt; mulktere.

mule [mju·l] muldyr; bastard, blanding; tverrdriver, fe; sta person; mule (spinnemaskin). — -driver muldyrdriver. — -headed sta. muleteer [mju·li'tiə] muldyrdriver. mulish ['mju·liʃ] muldyraktig; sta.

mull [mʌl] svikt; mistak; **make a** — **of it** spolere det hele, gjøre fiasko.

mull [mʌl] dempe, forsøte, mildne, avbrenne (vin); **-ed wine** avbrent vin, kryddervin.

mullein ['mʌlin] kongelys (plante).

mullet ['mʌlit] multefisk; mulle.

muligatawny [mʌligə'tå·ni] sterkt krydret brun suppe.

ullion ['mʌljən] post (i vindu o. l.).

mullock ['mʌlək] avfall, søppel, skitt, skrot.

multangular [mʌl'täŋgjulə] mangekantet.

multi ['mʌlti] mange- (i smstn.). multifarious [-'fæ·ᵉriəs] mangfoldig. multiflorous [mʌlti'flå·rəs] mangeblomstret. multilateral [-'lätərəl] mangesidet, mangesidig. multimillionaire [mʌlti'miljə-'næ·ə] mangemillionær. multiped ['mʌltiped] mangefotet.

multiple ['mʌltipl] mangfoldig; multiplum. multiplex ['mʌltipleks] mangfoldig. multipliable ['mʌlti'plaiəbl] flerdoblelig. multiplicand ['mʌlti-plikänd] multiplikand. multiplication ['mʌltipli-'keᵗʃən] mangfoldiggjøring; multiplikasjon. multiplicity [mʌlti'plisiti] mangfoldighet. multiplier ['mʌltiplaiə] multiplikator. multiply ['mʌltiplai.] forøke, formere, mangfoldiggjøre; multiplisere; vokse, formere seg.

multitude ['mʌltitju·d] mengde, masse, mangfoldighet; the — den store hop. multitudinous [mʌlti'tju·dinəs] mangfoldig, mangedobbelt; stor.

multure ['mʌltʃə] maling av korn; mølletoll.

mum [məm] frue (i tarvelig språk).

mum [mʌm] taus, tagal, stille; hyss! spille i pantomime; **mum's the word** dette er en hemmelighet; **be** — tie stille.

mumble ['mʌmbl] mulle, mumle; mumle fram: mumling. — -news sladderhank. mumbler ['mʌmblə] mumler. mumblingly ['mʌmbliŋli] mumlende.

Mumbo-Jumbo ['mʌmboᵘ 'dʒʌmboᵘ] busemann hos afrikanske negerfolk.

mumchance ['mʌmtʃa·ns] taushet; stille, taus.

mummer ['mʌmə] maskert person, maske.

mummery ['mʌməri] maskerade; narrespill.

mummiform ['mʌmifå·ᵉm] mumieaktig.

mummify ['mʌmifai] balsamere.

mummy ['mʌmi] mumie; gummiaktig væske; podevoks; **beat to a** — mørbanke, slå sønder og sammen.

mummy ['mʌmi] (i barnespråk) mamma.

mump [mʌmp] være gretten og stille.

mumpish ['mʌmpiʃ] gretten.

mumps [mʌmps] dårlig humør; kusma.

mun [mʌn] må, måtte.

munch [mʌnʃ] maule, tygge, jafse (i seg).

Munchausen [mʌn'tʃå·zn] Münchhausen.

mundane ['mʌndeⁱn] verdens-, verdslig, jordisk.

munge [mʌndʒ] mimre, klynke.

mungoos ['mʌŋgu·s] se mongoose.

Munich ['mju·nik] München.

municipal [mju'nisipl] kommunal, by-, stads-, stats-; — town kjøpstad. municipality [mjuni-si'päliti] by, kommune; landdistrikt.

munificence [mju'nifisəns] gavmildhet, rundhåndethet. munificent [-sənt] gavmild, raust, rundhåndet.

muniment ['mju·nimənt] forsvar; festningsforsvarsmiddel; hjelpemiddel; dokument, bevis. — -house el. — -room arkiv.

munition [mju'niʃən] ammunisjon.

munnion ['mʌnjən] = mullion.

mural ['mjuərəl] mur-; loddrett, steil, stupbratt; — crown murkrone.

murder ['mə·də] mord; myrde; tilintetgjøre; forderve, tyne, forvanske; **the** — **is out** hemmeligheten er oppklart. murderer ['mə·dərə] morder. murderess ['mə·dərés] morderske. murderous ['mə·dərəs] morderisk.

mure [mjuə] mure, innemure.

muriate ['mjuəriėt] klorid; — of soda koksalt.

muriatic [mjuəri'ätik] acid saltsyre.

murk [mɔ·k] mørke.

murky ['mə·ki] mørk, skummel.

murmur ['mə·mə] mumling, dur, sus, risle, mulle, brusing; mumle, knurre, bruse, risle; mulle. murmurer ['mə·mərə] en som knurrer, misfornøyd. murmuring ['mə·məriŋ] knurring. murmurous ['mə·mərəs] knurrende; som vekker misnøye.

murphy ['mə·fi] potet.
murrain ['mɑrin] kvegpest, munn- og klovsyke;
a — upon him! pokker ta ham!
mus. fk. f. music.
Mus. B. el. Mus. Bac. fk. f. musicae baccalaureus (= bachelor of Music).
muscadel ['mʌskədəl] se muscatel.
muscatel [mʌskə'tel] muskateller (vin); muska-
telldrue; muskatellpære; -s and almonds rosiner
og mandler.
muscle ['mʌsl] muskel. muscling ['mʌsliŋ]
muskulatur.
Muscovite ['mʌskovait] moskovitt.
Muscovy ['mʌskovi] Russland; — duck mos-
kusand.
muscular ['mʌskjulə] muskuløs; muskel-.
muscularity [mʌskju'läriti] muskelstyrke.
Mus. D. el. Mus. Doc. fk. f. musicae doctor
(= doctor of Music).
muse [mju·z] muse (gudinne for diktekunst
etc.).
muse [mju·z] grubling; studere, gruble, grunne,
tenke, være fordypet i; be in a — sitte (stå, gå)
i dype tanker.
muser ['mju·zə] grubler, drømmer. musing
['mju·ziŋ] grublende, tankefull; grubling, åndsfraværelse.
museum [mju'zi·əm] museum.
mush [mʌʃ] paraply; grøt. mushfaker ['mʌʃ-
fe'kə] en som reparerer paraplyer.
mushroom ['mʌʃru·m] sopp; sjampinjong;
paraply; parveny, oppkomling; soppaktig.
music ['mju·zik] musikk; noter; face the —
spytte i nevene og ta fatt; make — spille.
musical ['mju·zikl] musikalsk; — box spilledåse; — glasses glassharmonika, avstemte glass.
music|-book notebok. — -hall variete.
musician [mju'ziʃən] musikant; musikalsk
person.
music|-paper notepapir. — -rest notestol. —
-stand notestol, notehylle. — -stool pianokrakk.
musk [mʌsk] moskus; moskusdyr. — -cat
desmerkat. — -deer moskusdyr.
musket ['mʌskit] gevær, muskett; ung spurve-
hauk.
musketeer [mʌski'tiə] musketér.
musketproof ['mʌskitpru·f] skuddfri, skuddfast.
musketry ['mʌskitri] musketter; infanteri; mu-
skettild.
musket-shot geværskudd; geværkule.
musk-rat ['mʌskrät] moskusrotte.
musk-rose ['mʌskro·z] moskusrose.
musky ['mʌski] moskusaktig, moskusduftende.
muslin ['mʌzlin] musselin; ung jente.
mussel ['mʌsl] blåmusling, blåskjell.
Mussulman ['mʌsəlmən] muselman, muhamedaner.
must [mʌst] må, måtte (nødvendigvis), få; —
you go away already skal du alt gå; you — not
smoke here det er ikke tillatt å røyke her; that's
a case of — det må til.
must [mʌst] most.
must [mʌst] vill, gal, rasende; villhet.
must [mʌst] mygl; mygle, tråne; gjøre trå
el. harsk.
mustache [mu'sta·ʃ] se moustache.
mustachio [mu'sta·ʃo·] se moustache.
mustachioed [mu'sta·ʃo·d] med mustasj·r.
mustang ['mʌstäŋ] mustang, vill præriehest.
mustard ['mʌstəd] sennep. — -plaster sennepe-
kake. — -pot sennepskrukke. — -poultice sen-
nepsomslag. — -seed sennepskorn.
mustee [mʌ'sti·] mestis.
muster ['mʌstə] mønstre, samle, reise; oppdrive;
mønstring, revy; mannskapsrulle; — in mønstre
på; — out mønstre av; -ing all his strength med
oppbydelse av alle krefter; pass — stå for kritikk.

muster-roll ['mʌstəro·l] styrkeliste, mannskapsrulle.
mustiness['mʌstinés] muggenhet, kjedelighet:
mygl.
mustn't ['mʌsnt] = must not.
musty ['mʌsti] muggen, tra, harsk; kjedelig.
Muswell Hill ['mʌswəl'hil] del av London.
mutability [mju·tə'biliti] foranderlighet, ustadighet. mutable ['mju·təbl] foranderlig, skiftende;
ustadig. mutation [mju'te'ʃən] forandring, omskiftelse; omlyd; mutasjon.
mute [mju·t] fugleskitt; skite (om fugler).
mute [mju·t] stum, målløs; stum person; statist; betjent hos begravelsesentreprenører; stum
bokstav, stum lyd; eksplosiv; demper. muteness
['mju·tnés] stumhet.
mutilate ['mju·tile't] lemleste; skamfere; forvanske. mutilation [mju·ti'le'ʃən] lemlestelse,
skamfering. mutilator ['mju·tile'tə] lemlester
skamferer.
mutineer [mju·ti'niə] opprører, opprørsstifter.
mutinous ['mju·tinəs] opprørsk.
mutiny ['mju·tini] mytteri; gjøre mytteri; raise
a — stifte mytteri.
mutoscope ['mju·tosko·p] mutoskop, apparat
til levende fotografier.
mutter ['mʌtə] mumle; mulle; mumling.
mutton ['mʌtn] sau, får; fårekjøtt, sauekjøtt;
return to one's -s komme tilbake til saken; leg
of — sauelår.
mutton-chop ['mʌtntʃåp] lammekotelett; —
whiskers rundt avklippede bakkenbarter.
mutton|-cutlet lammekotelett. — -hst tykk, rød
neve. — -ham spekelar. — -head sau, tosk.
mutual ['mju·tjuəl] gjensidig, innbyrdes, sams,
felles; by — consent etter felles overenskomst.
mutuality [mju·tju'aliti] gjensidighet.
muzzle ['mʌzl] mule, snute; nunning; munnkurv, muleband; files; legge munnkurv på; stenge
munnen på; malbinde; kvele. — -loader forlad-
ningsgevær, forladningskanon.
muzzy ['mʌzi] tomset, omtåket, søvnig, ør.
m. v. fork. f. motor vessel.
M. V. O. fk. f. member of the Victorian Order.
M. W. B. fk. f. Metropolitan Water Board.
Mx. fk. f. Middlesex.
my [mai] min, mitt, mine; Oh —! du store
min!
Mylord [mai'lå·ᵈd, mi-] Deres herlighet; hans
herlighet (i omtale); titulere ‹Deres herlighet›.
Mynheer [main'hiə] (hollandsk) min herre;
nederlender (i spott).
myope ['maio·p] nærsynt. myopic [mai'åpik]
nærsynt. myopy ['maiopi] nærsynthet.
myriad ['miriəd] myriade; utall; mangfoldige.
myriapod ['miriəpəd] tusenbein.
myrmidon ['mə·midən] (lydig) håndlanger.
myrrh [mə·] myrra. myrrhic ['mə·rik] av
myrra.
myrtle ['mə·tl] myrt.
myself [mai'self; mi-] jeg selv, selv; meg selv,
meg; I did not believe it —, I — did not believe
it jeg trodde det ikke selv; I wash — jeg vasker
meg.
mysterious [mi'stiəriəs] hemmelighetsfull.
mystery ['mistəri] mysterium, hemmelighet,
gåte; hemmelighetsfullhet; mysterieskuespill;
(gammelt) kunst, håndverk.
mystic ['mistik] mystisk, hemmelighetsfull;
mystiker. mystical [-kl] = mystic. mysticism
['mistisizm] dunkelthet, mystikk.
mystification [mistifi'ke'ʃən] mystifikasjon.
mystify ['mistifai] narre, mystifisere.
myth [miθ] myte. mythic ['miθik] mytisk. mythical ['miθikl] mytisk. mythological [miθo-
'lädʒikl] mytologisk. mythologist [mi'θalədʒist]
mytolog. mythology [mi'θalədʒi] mytologi; sagn-
lære.

N

N, n [en] N, n.
N. fk. f. North, Northern; Nitrogen.
n. fk. f. name; neuter; noon, number.
Na. fk. f. Nebraska.
N. A. fk. f. North America; National Academy.
N|A. fk. f. non-acceptance manglende aksept.
NAAFI fk. f. Navy Army and Air Force Institutes bet. for organisasjon til underholdning og forpleining av soldatene.
nab [näb] trive, nappe; — the rust bli fornærmet.
nab [näb] bergnabb, fjelltopp; haug
nabob ['ne¹båb] nabob; stattholder; rikmann som har samlet seg en formue i India.
nacre ['ne¹kə] perlemor.
nacreous ['ne¹kriəs] perlemors-.
nadir ['ne¹diə] nadir.
naffy ['näfi] kantine under NAAFI (s. d.)
nag [näg] liten hest, pony, hest; kjæreste, elsker.
nag [näg] skjenne, plage, gnage på; skjenne på.
naiad ['naiäd] najade, vann-nymfe.
nail [ne¹l] negl, klo; nagle, spiker, søm; nagle, spikre; holde fast, fange, gripe, slå fast; on the — på stedet; pay on the — betale på flekken; hit the — on the head treffe spikeren på hodet; — in one's coffin pinne til ens likkiste; nails in mourning «sørgerand», svarte negler; — up spikre til, spikre ned. nailbrush ['ne¹lbrʌʃ] neglebørste.
nailer ['ne¹lə] spikersmed; kjernekar, kløpper, storartet eksemplar.
nailery ['ne¹ləri] spikerfabrikk, spikerverk.
nail-file ['ne¹lfail] neglefil.
nailing ['ne¹liŋ] første klasses; — good storartet.
naive [nai'i·v, na·'i·v] godtroende, naiv; naturlig; likefrem, endefram. naiveté [nai'i·vte¹, na·'i·vte¹] naivitet; naturlighet.
naked ['ne¹kid] naken, blottet, snau, bar; ubevæpnet; the — eye det blotte øye; the — truth den nakne sannhet. nakedness [-nés] nakenhet.
namable ['ne¹məbl] som kan nevnes.
namby-pamby ['nämbi'pämbi] affektert, smektende, klisset, sentimental; søtlatenhet, kliss.
name [ne¹m] navn; rykte, berømmelse; to call names skjelle ut, kalle; by — ved navn; by the — of ved navn; Christian (el. first el. given) — fornavn; family — etternavn; maiden — pikenavn; his — has escaped me, has slipped from my memory jeg husker ikke navnet på ham; how in the — of fortune hvordan i all verden; send in one's — la seg melde; take in one's — melde; what's your — hva heter De? my — is jeg heter; a man of (great) — en berømt mann. name [ne¹m] benevne, kalle, oppnevne, oppkalle.
nameable ['ne¹məbl] som kan nevnes. name-day navnedag. nameless ['ne¹mlés] navnløs; unevnelig; uberømt. namely ['ne¹mli] nemlig.
namesake ['ne¹mse¹k] navne, navnefetter.
Nancy ['nänsi] Nancy.
nankeen [nän'ki·n] nanking; -s nankingsbukser.
Nanny ['näni] Anna, nanny-goat geit.
nap [näp] nappe, gripe; trive; kvarte.
nap [näp] lur, liten blund; blunde, dorme, sove; have a — after dinner ta seg en middagslur; catch napping gripe i uaktsomhet, komme uforvarende på.
nap [näp] slags kortspill; go — by seg til å ta alle stikkene.
nap [näp] lo (på tøy); dun (på planter).
nape [ne¹p] nakke; nape of the neck nakke.

napery ['ne¹p(ə)ri] dekketøy.
naphtha ['näfþə, 'näpþə] nafta. -lene [-li·n], -line [-lin] naftalin.
napkin ['näpkin] serviett. — -ring serviettring.
Naples ['ne¹plz] Neapel.
napless ['näplés] glatt, slett, loslitt.
Napoleon [nə'pouljən] Napoleon.
napoleon [nə'pouljən] napoleondor, tjuefrankstykke.
Napoleonic [nə'pouli'änik] napoleonsk.
napoo [na·'pu.] (slang i hæren) ferdig, forb (av: il n'y a plus).
nappy ['näpi] flosset, loet.
nappy ['näpi] berusende; omtåket.
narcissus [na·ə'sisəs] narsiss, nå især: pinselilje.
nacosis [na·ə'kousis] bedøvelse. narcotic [-'kåtik] bedøvende; bedøvelsesmiddel. narcotism ['na·ə'kotizm] bedøvelse. narcotize ['taiz] bedøve.
nard [na·d] narde, nardus; nardussalve.
narghile ['na·ə'gili] nargile, tyrkisk vannpipe.
narrate [nä're¹t] fortelle, melde, berette. narration [nä're¹ʃən] fortelling. narrative ['närətiv] fortellende, berettende; fortelling, beretning. narrator [nä're¹tə] forteller.
narrow ['närou] snever, smal, trang, liten, snau; snevring; innsnevre; innsnevres; he had a — escape from being killed han holdt på å bli drept; a — fortune en liten, ubetydelig formue.
narrow-breasted ['närou'brestid] trangbrystet.
narrow-gauge ['närouge¹dʒ] smalsporet.
narrow-hearted ['närou'ha·ətid] tranghjertet.
narrowly ['närouli] snevert, nøye; escape — slippe fra det med nød og neppe; examine — undersøke nøyaktig.
narrow|-minded ['närou'maindid] smålig, trangsynt, sneversinnet. — -mindedness smålighet. narrowness ['närounés] smalhet, sneverhet; smålighet. narrow-souled nevnhjertet.
narwhal ['na·əwəl] narhval.
nasal [ne¹zl] nese-, nasal; neselyd. nasality [nə'säliti] nasalitet. nasalization [ne¹zalai'ze¹ʃən] nasalering. nasalize ['ne¹zlaiz] nasalere, tale gjennom nesen.
nascency ['näsənsi] tilblivelse, fødsel.
nascent ['näsənt] begynnende, voksende.
Naseby ['ne¹sbi] Naseby.
nastiness ['na·stinés] ekkelhet, vemmelighet.
nasty ['na·sti] ekkel, vemmelig; a — affair en stygg historie.
natal ['ne¹tl] fødsels-, føde-.
Natal [nə'täl] Natal.
natant ['ne¹tənt] svømmende. natation [ne¹-'te¹ʃən] svømming, svøm. natatores [ne¹ta'tå·riz] svømmefugl. natatorial [-'tå·riəl] svømme-. natatory ['ne¹tətəri] svømme-.
natheless ['ne¹ðéles], nathless ['ne¹ðles; 'näþ-] (gammelt) ikke desto mindre.
nation ['ne¹ʃən] nasjon, folk, folkeslag.
national ['näʃənəl] nasjonal, folke-, frederlandsk; the — anthem nasjonalsangen (God save our gracious King); — church folkekirke; — convention nasjonalkonvent; — debt statsgjeld; National Gallery Nasjonalgalleriet i London; National Insurance folketrygd, folkeforsikring (tvungen forsikring mot sykdom og arbeidsløshet).
nationality [näʃə'näliti] nasjonalitet. nationalization [näʃənalai'ze¹ʃən] nasjonalisering, nationalize ['näʃənalaiz] nasjonalisere, gjøre folkelig, gjøre til folkeeie.
native ['ne¹tiv] føde-; naturlig, medfødt, innfødt; slags engelsk østers; — country fedreland; a — of en mann (kone) fra.

nativity [nə'tiviti] fødsel; **calculate (cast) his — stille** hans horoskop; **the Nativity** Kristi fødsel; juledag.

natron ['ne⁴trən] kullsurt natron, soda.

natty ['näti] nett, fin, netthendt.

natural ['nätʃərəl] naturlig; **— history** naturhistorie; **— philosophy** fysikk; **— science** naturvitenskap; **die a — death** dø en naturlig død; **it does not come — to me** det faller meg ikke naturlig. **naturalism** ['nätʃərəlizm] naturtilstand; naturalisme. **naturalist** [-list] naturforsker; naturalist. **naturalistic** [nätʃərə'listik] naturalistisk. **naturalization** [nätʃərəlai'ze⁴ʃən] naturalisasjon. **naturalize** ['nätʃərəlaiz] naturalisere; gjøre naturlig.

naturally ['nätʃərəli] naturlig, naturligvis.

naturalness ['nätʃərəlnés] naturlighet.

nature ['ne⁴tʃə] natur, art, slags, beskaffenhet, egenskap; **beside —** unaturlig; **beyond —** overnaturlig; **by —** av naturen; **draw from —** tegne etter naturen; **in the — of things** ifølge tingenes natur; **it has become part of his —** det er gått ham i blodet; **die in the course of —** dø av alderdom; **in the order of —** etter naturens orden; **in a state of —** i dypeste neglisjé, naken; **imitate to —** etterligne livaktig. **-natured** ['ne⁴tʃəd] (i smstn.) av . . . natur.

naught [nå·t] ingenting, intet; null; **put (set) at —** redusere til ingenting, ringeakte; **come to — mislykkes,** bli til ingenting.

naughtiness ['nå·tinés] uskikkelighet.

naughty ['nå·ti] slem, uskikkelig.

nausea ['nå·ʃ(i)ə] sjøsyke, kvalme.

nauseate ['nå·ʃie⁴t] være sjøsyk, ha kvalme; vemmes ved; gjøre sjøsyk, gjøre kvalm.

nauseous ['nå·ʃ(i)əs] kvalm; vemmelig.

nauseousness [-nés] vammelhet, vemmelighet.

nautch [nå·tʃ] slags ballettforestilling av indiske danserinner.

nautical ['nå·tikl] nautisk; sjø-, sjømanns-.

nautilus ['nå·tiləs] nautil, papirsnekke.

naval ['ne⁴v(ə)l] flåte-, skips-, sjø-; **— army** krigsflåte; **— officer** sjøoffiser.

nave [ne⁴v] skip (i en kirke), midtskip.

nave [ne⁴v] hjulnav.

navel ['ne⁴v(ə)l] navle; midte. **— -string** ne⁴vlestreng.

navicular [nə'vikjulə] båtformet.

navigability [nävigə'biliti] seilbarhet. **navigable** ['nävigəbl] seilbar. **navigate** ['nävige⁴t] seile, fare; seile på el. over, befare; navigere. **navigation** [nävi'ge⁴ʃən] seilas; navigasjon. **navigator** ['nävige⁴tə] sjømann; navigatør.

navvy ['nävi] anleggsarbeider slusk.

navy ['ne⁴vi] flåte; krigsflåte, marine; marineblå; **the British** (el. **Royal**) **—** den britiske marine.

nawab [nə'wa·b] nabob, indisk stattholder.

nay [ne⁴] nei (i denne betydning sjelden); ja, ja endog; **my — is just as good as your** ay mitt nei er likså godt som ditt ja.

Nazarean [näzə'riən] nasareisk. **Nazarene** [-'ri·n] nasareer. **Nazareth** ['näzərep] Nasaret.

naze [ne⁴z] nes; **the Naze** Neset, Lindesnes.

nazi ['na·tsi·] nazi, nasjonalsosialist. **naziism** ['na·tsi·izəm] nazisme, nasjonalsosialisme.

N. B. fk. f. **North Britain** (ɔ: Skottland); **North British; New Brunswick; nota bene.**

n. b. fk. f. **no ball.**

N. b. E. fk. f. **North by East.**

N. B. R. fk. f. **North British Railway.**

N. b. W. fk. f. **North by West.**

N. C. fk. f. **North Carolina.**

N. C. C. V. D. fk. f. **National Council for Combating Venereal Diseases.**

N. C. O. fk. f. **non-commissioned officer.**

n. d. fk. f. **no date** udatert.

N. D. L. fk. f. **Nord-Deutscher Lloyd.**

N. E. fk. f. **North-east.**

neap [ni·p] nipptid; **— tide** nippflo. **neaped**

[ni·pt] komme på grunn ved flotid; som ligger tørt.

Neapolitan [niə'pålitən] neapolitansk; neapolitaner.

near [niə] nær; nærliggende; nærstående, kjær; gjerrig; nærme seg; **lose all that is — and dear to one** miste alt det som står en nærmest; **the -est way** den korteste vei; **you are very —** du er en gnier; **a — old fellow** en gnier; **the -est price** den nøyaktigste pris; **have a — escape** slippe fra det med nød og neppe (også: **have a — shave**); **— side** nærmeste side, venstre side; **far and — vidt og bredt; come — to** omtrent beløpe seg til; **it will go — to ruin him** det vil nesten ruinere ham; **I lost — upon twenty pounds** jeg mistet omtrent tjue pund; **we were -ing land** vi nærmet oss land.

nearly ['niəli] nesten; nær; **not — ikke på** langt nær.

nearness ['niənés] nærhet; nært forhold, nært slektskap; nærighet. **near-sighted** ['niə'saitid] nærsynt. **near-sightedness** [-nés] nærsynthet.

neat [ni·t] nett, ren, pen, fjelg, nydelig; netto; **drink brandy —** drikke ren konjakk.

neat [nit·t] kveg, hornkveg, storfe, naut. **-cattle** hornkveg.

'neath [ni·þ] under.

neat-handed ['ni·thändid] nevenyttig, netthendt.

neat-herd ['ni·thə·d] gjeter, hjuring.

neatness ['ni·tnés] netthet.

neb [neb] nebb, tut.

N. E. b. E. fk. f. **North-east by East.**

N. E. b. N. fk. f. **North-east by North.**

Nebraska [ni'bräskə] Nebraska.

Nebuchadnezzar [nebjukəd'nezə] Nebukadnesar.

nebula ['nebjulə] tåkeplett, stjernetåke; flekk på hornhinnen.

nebular ['nebjulə] tåket.

nebulosity [nebju'låsiti] tåkethet.

nebulous ['nebjuləs] tåket, skoddet.

necessarily ['nesisərili, -särili] nødvendigvis.

necessariness ['nesisərinés] nødvendighet.

necessary ['nesisäri, 'nesésri] nødvendig, fornøden; fornødenhet, nødtørft, nødvendighetsartikler; klosett; **be without the necessaries of life** unnvære livets alminneligste fornødenheter; **if — om** nødvendig, i nødsfall.

necessitarian [nisesi'tæ·əriən] determinist.

necessitate [ni'sesite⁴t] nødvendiggjøre.

necessitous [ni'sesitəs] nødlidende. **necessitousness** [-nés] nød; nødtørft.

necessity [ni'sesiti] nødvendighet, nødtørft, fornødenhet; **there is no — for (of)** det er absolutt ikke nødvendig å . . .; **find oneself under the — of** se seg tvunget til; **make a virtue of — gjøre** en dyd av nødvendighet; **— has no law** nød bryter alle lover; **— is the mother of invention** nød lærer naken kvinne å spinne; **in case of — i** nødsfall.

neck [nek] hals; halsstykke; **— and crop** el. **— and heels** med hud og hår; **go — and heels into a thing** gi seg i kast med noe med liv og sjel; **— or nothing** halsbrekkende, dumdristig; koste hva det vil; **he rides — or nought** han rir alt det remmer og tøy kan holde; **on the — of** umiddelbart etter; **one mischief comes on the — of the other** en ulykke kommer sjelden alene; **break one's — brekke** halsen; **break the — of the business** få unnagjort det meste (det grøvste); **win by a — vinne** med en halslengde; **tread on the — of a person** sette foten på nakken av en; **save one's — redde** livet.

neckband ['nekbänd] halslinning.

neck-cloth ['nekklå·þ] halsduk.

neckerchief ['nekətʃif] halstørkle.

neck-handkerchief ['nekhäŋkətʃif] halstørkle.

necking ['nekiŋ] halstørkle. **neckinger** ['ne-kindʒə] halstørkle. **necklace** ['neklis] halsbånd.

necklet ['neklét] halsbånd. **necktie** ['nektai] slips. **neckwear** ['nekwæ·ə] halstørkle. **neckweed** hamp.

necrological [nekro'lådʒikl] nekrologisk.
necrologist [ne'krålədʒist] nekrologforfatter.
necrology [ne'krålədʒi] nekrolog.
necromancer ['nekromänsə] åndemaner, trollmann. **necromancy** ['nekromänsi] åndemaning, trolldom. **necromantic** [nekro'mäntik] trolldoms-, besvergende; besvergelse, tryllemiddel.
necropolis [ne'krápəlis] kirkegård.
necrosis [ne'krousis] koldbrann i knoklene.
nectar ['nektə] nektar, gudedrikk. **nectareal** [nek'tæ·əriəl] nektar. **nectarean** [-riən] nektarsøt, liflig. **nectared** ['nektəd] nektarblandet. **nectareous** [nek'tæ·əriəs] nektarsøt.
nectarine ['nektərin] nektarin.
nectarous ['nektərəs] nektarsøt, liflig.
nectary ['nektəri] honninggjemme (i blomst).
Ned [ned] Ned, Edward.
N. E. D. fk. f. **New English Dictionary.**
neddy ['nedi] esel, asen.
née [neɪ] født (foran gift kvinnes pikenavn); **Mrs. A. née B.** fru A. født B.
need [ni·d] nødvendighet; nød, mangel, trang; **if — be** i nødsfall; **in case of —** i nødsfall; **be (stand) in — of, have — of** behøve, trenge til; **there's no — for** you to go du behøver ikke å gå; **what — of** hesitating hvorfor nøle; **a friend in — is a friend** indeed i nøden skal man kjenne sine venner.
need [ni·d] (imperf.: **needed** el. **need**) behøve, trenge, trenge til, ha bruk for; **it -s not to go** there det er ikke nødvendig å gå dit; **it -s but to become known** det trengs bare å bli kjent; **I — not have walked** jeg behøvde ikke å ha gått.
needfire ['ni·dfaiə] signalild, varde, bål.
needful ['ni·df(u)l] nødvendig, fornøden; **the one thing — det** ene fornødne; kontante penger; **show the — komme** fram med kontantene.
neediness ['ni·dinés] trang, nød, armod.
needle ['ni·dl] nål, synål, magnetnål, strikkepinne; nut, tind, horn; obelisk; **I have pins and -s in my foot** foten min sover; **hit the — ramme** spikeren på hodet; **navigate by the — styre** etter kompasset; **cop the — føle** seg krenket; **have the — være** opphisset.
needle ['ni·dl] ergre, plage; smyge seg fram; sy; danne krystaller som nåler.
needle|-bar nålestang (i symaskin). **— -bath** fin dusj. **— -book** nålebrev. **— -case** nålehus. **-fish** horngjel. **— -gun** tenn-nålsgevær. **— -lace** sydde kniplinger. **— -shell** igelkjær, kråkebolle.
needless ['ni·dlés] unødvendig, unødig. **— -ly** i utrengsmål.
needle|telegraph nåletelegraf. **-woman** syerske. **-work** håndarbeid, sytøy.
needments ['ni·dmənts] nødvendighetsartikler.
needn't ['ni·dnt] = **need not.**
needs [ni·dz] nødvendigvis, endelig, plent; (bare i forbindelsen) **needs must** eller **must needs; if it needs must** be når det endelig skal være; **men must needs** be laughing menn skal absolutt le. **— must when** the devil drives nød lærer naken kvinne å spinne.
needy ['ni·di] trengende, nødlidende.
ne'er ['næ·ə] aldri.
ne'er-do-well ['næ·əduwel] døgenikt.
nefarious [ni'fæ·əriəs] avskyelig, skjendig.
negation [ni'geiʃən] nektelse, nekting, benektelse.
negative ['negətiv] nektende; negativ; nektelse, nekting, avslag, forbud; **reply in the — svare** benektende; svare med nei, avslå; nektende svar.
negativeness ['negətivnés], **negativity** [negə'ti·viti] negativitet.
neglect [ni'glekt] forsømme, neglisjere, tilsidesette, ringeakte; vanvøre; forsømmelse, likegyldighet, etterlatenhet; **fall into — forsømmes.**
neglectable [ni'glektəbl] som kan tilsidesettes.

neglectedness [ni'glektidnés] vanrøkt, forsømmelse; liten etterspørsel. **neglectful** [ni'glektf(u)l] forsømmelig, likegyldig. **neglection** [ni 'glekʃən] forsømmelse. **negligé** ['negli·ʒeɪ] mor gendrakt, morgenkjole. **negligence** ['neglidʒənsɪ] forsømmelighet, skjøtesløshet.
negligent ['neglidʒənt] forsømmelig, skjøtesløs; **be — of** være likegyldig med.
negligible ['neglidʒibl] ganske liten.
negotiability [nigouʃiə'biliti] salgbarhet.
negotiable [ni'gouʃiəbl] salgbar, omsett lig.
negotiate [ni'gouʃieɪt] forhandle; underhandle, tinge, kjøpslå; forskaffe seg, utvirke; avslutte, slutte, formidle, avhende, selge, omsette.
negotiation [nigouʃi'eɪʃən] forretninger; salg; forhandling, underhandling; avslutning (av lån, traktater). **negotiator** [ni'gouʃieɪtə] underhandler, mellommann.
negress ['ni·grés] negress, negerkvinne.
negro ['ni·grou] neger. **— -traffic** slavehandel.
negus ['ni·gəs] vintoddy, bisp; **claret-negus** rødvinstoddy.
neigh [neɪ] knegge; knegging.
neighbour [ni'beɪbə] nabo, granne; sidemann, neste; være granne til, grense til; bo i nærheten; passe, stemme; **next — nærmeste** nabo, sidemann; **opposite — gjenbo.**
neighbouress ['neɪbərés] naboerske, grannekone.
neighbourhood ['neɪbəhud] naboskap, nabolag, nærhet; grannelag; grend; **in the — of** i omegnen av; **in our — på** våre kanter. **neighbouring** ['neɪbəriŋ] nærliggende, tilgrensende, nabo, granne-. **neighbourly** ['neɪbəli] som gode naboer. **neighbourship** ['neɪbəʃip] naboskap, granneskap.
neither ['naiðə, 'ni·ðə] ingen (av to), ingen av delene, hverken den ene eller den andre; heller ikke; **I am on — side** jeg er nøytral; **he does not like him, — do I** han liker ham ikke, og det gjør ikke jeg heller; **nor that — (vulg.)** heller ikke det; **— .. nor** hverken ... eller.
nem. con. fk. f. **nemine contradicente** uten at noen talte imot.
nem. dis. fk. f. **nemine dissentiente** enstemmig.
Nemesis ['nemisis] Nemesis; straffende gudinne; nemesis.
nenuphar ['nenjufa·ə] nøkkerose, tjerneblom.
neolith ['ni·o(u)liþ] neolitt. **-ic** [ni·o(u)'liþik] neolittisk.
neologism [ni·'ålədʒizm] neologisme, nylaging.
neophyte ['ni·ofait] nyomvendt, begynner.
Nepa(u)l [ni'på·l] Nepal.
nephew ['nevju] nevø, brorsønn, søstersønn.
nephrite ['nefrait] nefritt, nyrestein.
nephritis [ni'fraitis] nyrebetennelse.
nepotism ['nepətizm] nepotisme, det å foretrekke slekt og venner. **nepotist** ['nepətist] nepotist.
Neptune ['neptju·n] Neptun.
N. E. R. fk. f. **North-eastern Railway.**
nereid ['niəriid] nereide, havnymfe.
Nero ['niərou] Nero.
nerve [nə·v] nerve, nerver; sene, muskel; kraft, fasthet, mot; **war of nerves** nervekrig; **he has not got the — to do it** han har ikke mot til å gjøre det; **that waiter is getting on my -s** den tjeneren går meg på nervene.
nerve [nə·v] styrke, stålsette, gi kraft.
nerveless ['nə·vlés] kraftløs; veik.
nerver ['nə·və] oppstrammer, hjertestyrkning.
nervous ['nə·vəs] sterk, senesterk; nerve-; nervøs, nervesliten; **— centre** nervesentrum; **— debility** nervesvekkelse; **— fever** tyfus, nervefeber; **— system** nervesystem; **— about** urolig for; **he was — of his reception** han var spent på å se hvilken mottagelse han ville få.
nervousness ['nə·vəsnés] nervøsitet.
nervy ['nə·vi] sterk, kraftig, djerv; nervesliten.
nescience ['neʃ(i)əns] uvitenhet.
nescious ['neʃ(i)əs] uvitende

nesh [neʃ] bløt, øm, klekk, svak.

ness [nes] nes, forberg, odde, pynt.

nest [nest] reir, rede; oppholdssted, bolig, bo, bol, bøle; sett (av gjenstander, som kan settes inn i hverandre; skuffer, esker e. l.); bygge reir; hekke; lete etter fuglereir; legge i reir; — of thieves tyvereir; — of vice lastens hule; a — of drawers and pigeonholes en reol med skuffer og fag; — themselves slå seg ned.

nest-egg reiregg; spareskilling. **nesting-box** rugekasse.

nestle ['nesl] ligge lunt; putte seg ned; huse, anbringe; lune om, pleie.

nestling ['neslin] nyutklekket; fugleunge.

net [net] netto; innbringe netto; tjene netto.

net [net] nett, garn, not, vad, snare; binde, knytte; fange i garnet. — -cap hårnett. — -fishing garnfiske.

nether ['neðə] nedre, underste, under-; — garments benklær; the — man beina; the — world underverdenen, helvete.

Netherlander ['neðələndə] hollender, nederlender.

Netherlandish ['neðəländiʃ] nederlandsk.

Netherlands ['neðələndz], the — Nederlandene, Nederland, Holland.

netherlings ['neðəlinz] strømper.

nethermost ['neðəmoᵘst] nederst, dypest.

netting ['netin] nett, netting, nettverk; ståltrådnett; filering.

netting-needle ['netin̩ni·dl] filernål.

nettle ['netl] nesle, brennenesle; brenne som en nesle, svi, irritere, ergre; common (great eller stinging) — stor nesle; small — brennenesle; blind (eller dead) — døvnesle; -d at ergerlig over. — -fish brennmanet. — -rash neslefeber, elveblest.

netty ['neti] nettaktig.

net-winged ['netwind] nettvinget.

network ['netwə·k] nettverk; nett, filering.

neural ['njuərəl] nerve-, som hører til nervesystemet. **neuralgia** [nju'räldʒə] nevralgi, nervesmerter. **neurasthenia** [njuräsþi'naiə] nervesvakkelse. **neurotic** [nju'råtik] nerve-, nervestyrkende middel.

neuter ['nju·tə] nøytral; stand — holde seg nøytral; the — intetkjønn.

neutral ['nju·trəl] nøytral, likegyldig; keep (remain) — holde seg nøytral. **neutrality** [nju·'träliti] nøytralitet. **neutralization** [nju·trəl(a)i-'zeiʃən] nøytralisering, motvirkning. **neutralize** ['nju·trəlaiz] nøytralisere, veie opp, uskadeliggjøre. **neutralizer** ['nju·trəlaizə] motvirkning; motvekt.

never ['nevə] aldri; ikke; well, I — ! nå har jeg aldri hørt maken; — heard of uhørt; — say die gi deg aldri; godt mot; — mind det gjør ikke noe, bry deg ikke om det; — a one ikke en eneste. — -ceasing uopphørlig. — -fading uvisnelig.

nevermore ['nevə'må·ᵒ] aldri mer, aldri.

nevertheless [nevəðə'les] ikke desto mindre.

new [nju·] ny, frisk, fersk, ubrukt, moderne; nyoppdaget; — bread ferskt brød; — milk nysilt melk; the — woman den moderne kvinne; a — man oppkomling; there's nothing — under the sun det er ikke noe nytt under sola.

newborn ['nju·bå·ᵒn] nyfødt.

Newcastle ['nju·'ka·sl] Newcastle.

new|-come [nju·kʌm] nylig kommet; nykomling. — -comer nykomling.

New England [nju·'inglənd] Ny-England (de seks nordøstlige stater i U. S. A.).

new|-fallen nyfallen. — -fangled [-'fängld] nyoppfunnet, nymotens. — -fangledness ny smak, ny mote. — -fashioned nymotens, moderne.

Newfoundland [nju·fənd'länd, nju·'faundlənd] Newfoundland.

Newgate ['nju·git] Newgate (tidligere fengsel i London).

newish ['nju·iʃ] temmelig ny.

new-laid ['nju·le¹d] nylagt (om egg).

newly ['nju·li] nylig, nettopp, ny-; — married nygift.

Newman ['nju·mən] Newman.

Newmarket ['nju·ma·ᵊkit] Newmarket (sted i England, hvor det holdes hesteveddeløp).

new|-model omforme. — -mown nyslått. **newness** ['nju·nés] nyhet, ferskhet.

New-Orleans [nju·'å·ᵊliənz, nju·å·ᵊli·nz] New-Orleans.

news [nju·z] nyhet, nyheter; etterretning, tidende, blad, avis; a piece of — en nyhet; no — is good — ikke noe nytt er godt nytt. — -agent avisselger. -boy avisgutt. -editor nyhetsredaktør. -man avisbud. — -monger nyhetskremmer.

newspaper ['nju·spe¹pə, 'nju·z-] avis, blad; the Times newspaper bladet Times.

newsprint ['nju·zprint] avispapir.

newsreel ['nju·zri·l] lydfilmavis, filmnytt.

news|-room leseværelse. — -sheet nyhetsblad. **Newstead** ['nju·sted] Newstead.

news|vendor ['nju·zvendə] avisselger. -woman aviskone.

newsy ['nju·zi] full av nytt, interessant.

newt [nju·t] salamander.

Newton ['nju·tən] Newton.

new-year ['nju·jiə] nyttår, nyår; a happy — ! godt nyttår! New Year's Day nyttårsdag.

New York [nju·'jå·ᵊk] New York.

New-Zealand [nju·'zi·länd] New Zealand.

next [nekst] nest, nærmest, førstkommende; he is in the — room han er i værelset ved siden av; he lives — door han bor i huset ved siden av; he is — door to a fool han er ikke langt fra å være en tosk; — door but one det andre huset herfra; — to nothing nesten ingenting; — year neste år; Monday (eller on Monday) next neste mandag; — best nestbest; he lives — to me han er nærmeste grannen min; who follows — hvem kommer så; what — nå har jeg hørt det med; the gentleman — me at table min sidemann ved bordet.

nexus ['neksəs] sammenbinding, bånd, samband, sammenheng.

N. F. fk. f. Newfoundland.

N. H. fk. f. New Hampshire.

Niagara [nai'ägərə] Niagara.

nib [nib] spiss, pennesplitt; nebb; spisse, kvessə, sette spiss på.

nibble ['nibl] nippe, smånappe etter, smågnage på; bite varsomt i; nappe, nype, kvarte; kritisere, dadle; gnaging, napp. **nibbler** ['niblə] en som biter; skumler.

Nicaragua [nikə'rägjuə] Nicaragua.

Nice [ni·s] Nizza.

nice [nais] lekker, delikat; kresen, vanskelig; vakker, pen, fin, nett, nydelig, god, gild; elskverdig, tiltalende, snill; a — distinction en fin forskjell; a very — case en meget delikat historie; **niceness** ['naisnès] lekkerhet; godhet; finhet. overdreven nøyaktighet; vanskelighet.

nicety ['naisiti] finhet; ømhet; delikatesse; nøyaktighet, akkuratesse; kresenhet, vanskelighet; netthet; to a — nøyaktig, på en prikk; niceties of words ordkløveri; stand upon niceties ta det altfor nøye.

niche [nitʃ] nisje, fordypning i muren, liten krok.

Nicholas ['nikələs] Nikolai, Nils.

nick [nik] hakk, snitt, skår; kup, heldig kast; rette øyeblikk; skjære hakk i; ramme, treffe det rette øyeblikket; he came in the — of time han kom i rette øyeblikk, i siste liten; be on the — vare ute på fangst. **nicker** ['nikə] tyveknekt; nattlig fredsforstyrrer.

Nick [nik] ond ånd; old — fanden.

nickel ['nikl] nikkel. **nickel-plate** ['niklple¹t] fornikle. **nickel-plating** fornikling.

Nickleby ['niklbi] Nickleby.

nickname ['niknelm] økenavn, oppnavn; fortrolig forkorting; gi klengenavn; **was -d** hadde oppnavnet.

nicnac ['niknäk] leketøy; nips, nipsgjenstand; **-s** nips. **nicnackatory** ['niknäkətəri] leketøybutikk.

nicotine [nikə'ti·n, 'nikəti·n] nikotin.

nicotinism ['nikətinizm] nikotinforgiftning.

nictate, nictitate ['nikte¹t], ['niktite¹t] blunke med øynene.

nidering ['n(a)idərin] æresløs, nedrig.

nidificate ['nidifike¹t, ni'difike¹t] bygge reir. **nidification** [nidifi'ke¹ʃən] reirbygging.

nidus ['naidəs] reir; utklekkingssted.

niece [ni·s] niese, brordatter, søsterdatter.

Niger ['naidʒə], **the** — Niger.

Nigeria [nai'dʒiəriə] Nigeria.

niggard ['nigəd] gnier; gjerrig; knipen, gnieraktig; **be a** — **of** something være knuslet med noe; **play the** — være gnieraktig. **niggardliness** [-linès] gjerrighet. **niggardly** [-li] gnieraktig, gjerrig.

nigger ['nigə] neger (brukt med forakt); **work like a** — arbeide som en hest; **there is a** — **in the woodpile** (el. **fence**) det ligger noe under, det henger ikke riktig sammen; **where the good -s go** fanden i vold.

niggerhead ['nigəhed] (amr.) grastue, myrtue; en slags skråtobakk.

niggle ['nigl] fjase; pusle, pirke; skrive gnidret skrift; gnidret skrift.

nigh [nai] nær, nesten, nær ved; **he was well** — **starved** han var nesten utsultet; **winter is** — **at hand** vinteren står for døra; **draw** — rykke nærmere; — **but** nesten; — **upon** nesten.

night [nait] natt, aften, kveld; **at (by, in the)** — om natten; **in the dead of (the)** — i nattens stillhet; **-'s lodging** nattekvarter; **late at** — sent på kvelden; **last** — i går kveld, i natt; **make a** — **of it** ha seg en glad aften; rangle hele natten; **sit up at** — våke hele natten; **a first** — **première**, første oppførelse av et stykke; **the piece had a run of** 100-**s** stykket gikk 100 ganger; **on the** — **of the** 11th **to the** 12th natten mellom den 11. og 12.; **the day after the** — **before** dagen derpå (tømmermenn etter rangel); **tonight** el. **to-night** i aften, i kveld, i natt.

night|-bird nattfugl, ugle etc. — **-blindness** nattblindhet. — **-cap** ['naitkäp] nattlne; nattkappe; aftentoddy. — **-cart** renovasjonsvogn. **-dress** nattkjole, nattdrakt.

night|fall ['naitfå·l] skumring, mørkning. — **-fire** nattbål; lyktemann, blålys. — **-glass** nattkikkert. — **-gown** nattkjole; slåbrok. — **-house** nattkafé.

nightingale ['naitiŋge¹l] nattergal.

night|jar ['naitdʒa·⁹] natteravn, kveldknarr. — **-lamp** nattlampe. — **-light** nattlampe. **-ly** ['naitli] nattlig, natt-; hver natt, hver aften. — **-man** nattmann, renovasjonsmann. **-mare** mare, mareritt. — **-owl** nattugle. — **-piece** nattstykke, nattbilde. — **-rest** nattero. — **-revel** natterangel. — **-reveller** natterangler. — **-rule** leven om natten. — **-school** aftenskole, kveldskole. — **-shade** søtvier. — **-shift** nattkjole. — **-shirt** nattskjorte. — **-stool** nattstol. — **-time** natt, nattetid. — **-walk** nattevandring, aftentur. — **-walker** søvngjenger(ske); gatetøs. — **-watch** nattevakt. — **-watchman** nattvekter. — **-work** nattarbeid; renovasjon. — **-yard** renovasjonsplass.

nigrification [nigrifi'ke¹ʃən] sverting.

nihilism ['naiilizm] nihilisme. **nihilist** ['naiilist] nihilist. **nihilistic** [naii'listik] nihilistisk. **nihility** [nai'hiliti] intethet.

nil [nil] intet, ingenting, null.

Nile [nail]: **the** — Nilen.

nilgai ['nilge¹], **nilg(h)au** ['nilgå·] nilgai (en slags stor indisk antilope).

nilly-willy [nili'wili] el. **nill-ye will-ye** ['nilji 'wilji] enten man (du) vil eller ei.

14 — Engelsk-norsk.

nimbed ['nimbd] omgitt av en nimbus.

nimbiferous [nim'bifərəs] regnførende.

nimble ['nimbl] lett, rapp, rask, kvikk, sprek. — **-footed** rappfotet. **nimbleness** [-nès] hurtighet, sprekhet.

nimbus ['nimbəs] nimbus, glorie, glans.

nimiety [ni'maiiti] overmål.

niminy-piminy ['nimini'pimini] pertentlig, tertefin.

nincompoop ['ninkəmpu·p] tull, tullebukk, tosk, naut.

nine [nain] ni; nitall; **he has** — lives like a cat han er seiglivet; **look** — ways skjele; **he is** up to the **-s** han kjenner knepene; **be dressed up** to the **-s** være i puss; **the Nine** de ni muser; — corns en pipe tobakk. **-fold** nifoldig, av ni slags. **-pence** ['nainpəns] ni pence. **-pin** kile; **play at -pins** spille kiler, slå kiler.

nineteen ['nain'ti·n] nitten; **talk** — **to the dozen** sludre, la munnen gå som en pepperkvern. **nineteenth** ['nain'ti·nþ] nittende. **ninetieth** ['nain-tiiþ] nittiende; nittiendedel. **ninety** ['nainti] nitti. **ninny** ['nini] tosk. **-hammer** tullebukk.

ninth [nainþ] niende, niendedel; — **part of a** man ɔ: en skredder. **ninthly** [-li] for det niende.

Niobe ['naiobi] Niobe.

nip [nip] nippe, knipe, knipe, klemme, klype, svi, bite, angripe, forderve; ødelegge (ved frost el. ild); nappe, kvarte; knip, klyp, bit, napp; avskåret stykke; — **in the bud** klype av i knoppen; kvele i fødselen.

nip [nip] slurk, dram, liten støyt; smådrikke, ta seg en tår.

nipper ['nipə] fortann, framtann (på hest); frostdag; liten gutt, guttunge; knipetang, neseklemme; klo; **a pair of -s** sukkersaks.

nipple ['nipl] brystvorte; tåtesmokk; nippel; pistong. — **-wort** haremat (plante).

nippy ['nipi] bitende, kald; kvikk, rapp.

Nirvana [niə'va·nə] Nirvana.

nisi ['naisai] (latin, egentlig: hvis ikke); **a rule** — en kjennelse som kan påankes; **a decree** — en betinget dom (især skilsmissedom); — **prius** ['praiəs] assiserett for sivilsaker.

nitrate ['naitrét] nitrat, salpetersurt salt. **nitrate** ['naitre¹t] blande med salpeter; **-d** cotton skytebomull.

nitre ['naitə] salpeter.

nitric ['naitrik] salpetersur; salpeter; — **-acid** salpetersyre, sjevann.

nitrogen ['naitrodʒen, -in] kvelstoff.

nitroglycerine [naitro'glisərin] nitroglyserin.

nitrous ['naitrəs] salpeterholdig.

nival ['naivəl] snøfull, snørik, vinter-.

nix [niks], **nixie** ['niksi] nøkk.

nix [niks] ingenting; hysj! stille! (når læreren kommer); **for** — gratis, fritt. **nixey** nei, ikke.

N. J. fk. f. New Jersey.

N. L. C. fk. f. National Liberal Club.

N. L. F. fk. f. National Liberal Federation.

N. Mex. fk. f. New Mexico.

N. N. E. fk. f. North North-east.

N. N. W. fk. f. North North-west.

no [no⁹] nei, ikke; neistemme, avslag; ingen, ikke noe; **I can't say** whether or no jeg kan hverken si ja eller nei; **he will do it** whether or no han vil gjøre det under alle omstendigheter; **is your mother no better?** er ikke din mor bedre? **no less than** ten hele ti; **no more** ikke mer; **no more of your tricks** ikke flere dumheter; **that's no business of yours** det kommer ikke deg ved; **no such matter** absolutt ikke; **to no purpose** forgjeves; **there are no such things as** . . . det er ikke noe som heter; **the ayes and noes** stemmer (i Parlamentet) for og imot; **the noes have it** forslaget er forkastet.

N. O. fk. f. natural order; New-Orleans. **No.**, **no.** fk. f. numero (number).

Noah ['no⁹ə, 'nå·ə] Noa; **Noah's ark** Noas ark, også en slags leketøy.

nob [nåb] storfant, bikse; adelig; **one for his** — (i cribbage „pukkspill") en for trumfknekt.

nob [nåb] hode, skolt; streikebryter; **a fellow of little** — tosk, dumrian; **bob a** — en shilling pr. snute; **do a** — gå omkring med hatten (og samle inn penger).

nobble ['nåbl] bedra, lure, jukse; overtale, vinne for seg; stjele. **nobbler** ['nåblə] bedrager; medviter. **nobbly** ['nåbli] pen, vakker.

nobby ['nåbi] fin, staselig, elegant, grom.

nobilitate [no'bilite¹t] adle.

nobility [no'biliti] adel, adelstand, adelskap (som består av fem grader: **duke, marquis, earl, viscount, baron,** og hvis medlemmer har sete i overhuset); **the** — **and gentry** den høyere og lavere adel.

noble ['noubl] edel, stolt, gjev, herlig; adelig, adelsmann; **the Most Noble** den høyedle (om hertug eller marki); — **style** opphøyd stil. — **-looking** med fornemt utseende, vesen. **-man** [-mən] adelsmann. — **-minded** høysinnet. **nobleness** ['noublnès] adel.

noblesse [nou'bles] adel (i utlandet); — **oblige** [å'bli·ʒ] adel forplikter, rettigheter medfører ansvar. **noblewoman** ['noublwumən] adelsdame.

nobody ['noubədi, -bådi] ingen; ubetydelig person; **a mere** — en ganske ubetydelig person.

nock [nåk] hakk, innskjæring (i bue el. pil til buestrengen); klo (på gaffelseil).

noctambulation [nåktämbju'le¹ʃən], **noctambulism** [nåk'tämbjulizm] søvngjengeri. **noctambulist** [-list] søvngjenger(ske). **nocturnal** [nåk'tə·nl] nattlig, natte-. **nocturne** ['nåktə·n] nokturne, nattestemning (om maleri eller musikkstykke).

nod [nåd] nikke, duppe; nikke med; nikke til; nikk, dupp; vink; **nod one's assent** nikke bifallende; **go to the land of Nod** falle i søvn.

N. O. D. fk. f. Naval Ordnance Department.

nodal ['noudl] knutet; knute-

noddle ['nådl] hode, skolt; kasse; **cracked in the** — skjør i hodet.

noddy ['nådi] tosk, fe, dumrian; havsule.

node [noud] knute, knutepunkt. **nodose** ['nou-'dous] knutet, leddet. **nodosity** [no'dåsiti] knutethet. **nodular** ['nådjulə] knuteformet. **nodule** ['nådjul] liten knute. **nodulous** ['nådjuləs] småknutet.

nog [någ] lite krus, trekanne; trenagle; kloss, klamp.

noggin ['någin] kanne.

nogging ['någin] (skillerom av) bindingsverk.

nohow ['nouhau] på ingen måte, slett ikke; **look** — se forkommen ut.

noise [noiz] lyd, ståk, bråk, larm, spetakkel, skriking; — **of feet** tramping; **hold your** — hold munn; **make a** — **at a person** skjelle en ut; **make a** — **about a thing** gjøre mye bråk; **there is a** — **abroad** det går det rykte; **this made a great** — **in the world** dette vakte stor oppsikt; **noise abroad** utspre, la ryktes; **when it became -d abroad** da det ryktedes. **noiseless** ['noizlès] lydløs. **noisiness** ['noizinès] larm, ståk, styr, bråk. **noisome** ['noisəm] skadelig, usunn; motbydelig. **noisy** ['noizi] bråkende.

nolens-volens ['nou'lenz'vou'lenz] enten en vil eller ei.

noli-me-tangere ['noulaimi·'tändʒəri·] springfrø; lupus (sykdommen).

nolt [noult] storfe; naut.

nom. fk. f. nominative.

nomad ['nåməd] nomade. **nomadic** [no'mädik] nomadisk. **nomadize** ['nåmədaiz] leve som nomader, flytte omkring.

nomenclature ['noumənkle¹tʃə] navneliste, nomenklatur.

nominal ['nåminəl] nominell, bare av navn, i navnet, navne-. **nominalism** ['nåminəlizm] nominalisme (en filosofisk lære). **nominate** ['nåmine¹t] nevne, kalle, utnevne.

nomination [nåmi'ne¹ʃən] utnevning, benev-

nelse; innstilling, forslag; **be in** — **for** være oppstilt som kandidat for.

nominative ['nåm(i)nətiv] nevneform, nominativ. **nominator** ['nåmine¹tə] en som utnevner. **nominee** [nåmi'ni·] innstilt, oppstilt.

non [nån] ikke. — **-ability** ['nånə'biliti] uskikkethet. — **-acceptance** ['nånək'septəns] manglende aksept (av veksel).

nonage ['nounidʒ, 'nånidʒ] umyndighet.

nonagenarian [nounədʒi'næ·'riən, nån-] nittiårsgammel; nittiåring.

non|-appearance ['nånə'piərəns] uteblivelse. — **-attendance** fraværelse, fravær.

nonce [nåns] anledning, høve; **for the** — i den anledning, for den(ne) ene gangen. — **-word** ord laget for anledningen.

nonchalance ['nånʃələns] nonchalanse, skjøtesløshet. **nonchalant** [-lənt] skjøtesløs, likesæl. **non-com. fk. f. non-commissioned officer.**

non-combatant ['nån'kåmbətənt] nonkombattant, ikke-stridende.

non-commissioned ['nånkə'miʃənd] officer underoffiser.

non|-committal ['nånkə'mitl] ikke bindende. — **-compliance** vegring. — **-condensing** ['nånkəndensin] engine høytrykksmaskin. — **-conducting** som ikke leder (varme el. elektrisitet). — **-conductor** isolator. — **-conforming** avvikende, dissenter-. **-conformist** utgått av statskirken, dissenter. **-conformity** avvikelse, avvik, uoverensstemmelse med statskirken. **-content** ['nånkən'tent] nei, stemme imot forslaget (i overhuset).

nondescript ['nåndiskript] ny, ubestemmelig, ugrei, underlig, rar; allehånde; noe ubestemmelig; altmuligmann.

none [noun] (srl. i pl.) nonsmesse.

none [nʌn] ingen, intet (i forbindelse med of eller etter nylig nevnt substantiv); (slett) ikke (foran the, fulgt av komparativ, og foran too); **he is** — **of our company** man hører ikke til oss; **here are** — **but friends** her er bare venner; **it is** — **of your business** det kommer ikke deg ved; **I am** — **the wiser for it** jeg er ikke det plukk klokere; — **the less** ikke desto mindre; — **too soon** ikke et minutt for tidlig. — **too well** mindre godt.

non-electric ['nåni'lektrik] uelektrisk (legeme).

nonentity [nån'entiti] ikke-tilværelse; intet, ingenting, null, intetsigende person.

non-essential ['nåni'senʃəl] uvesentlig (ting).

nonesuch ['nʌnsʌtʃ] enestående, makeløs.

non|-execution misligholdelse. — **-existence** ikke-eksistens. — **-existing** som ikke eksisterer. — **-intoxicant** alkoholfri. — **-juring** som ikke har svoret troskap (nml. til William og Mary), jakobittisk. — **-juror** ['nån'dʒuərə] jakobitt. — **-member** ikke-medlem.

nonpareil ['nånpərel] uforlignelig, makeløs, uten like; uforlignelighet; nonpareille (slags epler); mindre skrift hos boktrykkerne.

non|-parishioner en som ikke bor i sognet. — **-payment** uteblivelse med betaling. — **-performance** forsømmelse, misligholdelse.

nonplus ['nån'plʌs] rådvillhet, forlegenhet, knipe; forbløffe; gjøre opprådd; **he was at a** — han var i en lei klemme; **catch a person on the** — overraske en.

non|-residence fraværelse fra det sted hvor man burde oppholde seg, fra embetskrets, eiendom. — **-resident** fraværende. — **-resistance** ikkemotstand; blind lydighet. — **-resisting** som ikke gjør motstand, som viser blind lydighet.

nonsense ['nånsəns] vas, vås, tøv, tøys, nonsens; **I shall stand none of your** — jeg vil ikke høre på det vrøvlet ditt. **nonsensical** [nån'sensikl] urimelig, tåpelig.

non|-sensitive ufølsom. — **-sexual** kjønnsløs. — **-society** som ikke hører til noen fagforening. — **-sparing** ubarmhjertig. — **-success** manglende hell.

nonsuch ['nʌnsʌtʃ] se **nonesuch.**
nonsuit ['nåns(j)u·t) avvisning av en prosess;
avvise.
non-user ['nånju·zə] ikke-benyttelse, vanhevd,
forsømmelse.
noodle ['nu·dl] tosk, naut, kjøtthue.
noodle ['nu·dl] nudel (om små deigfigurer).
nook [nuk] krok, hjørne, krå, ro.
noon [nu·n] non;middag; blomstring, blomstringstid; hvile middag. **-day** middag; middagshøyde, høyeste. — **-tide** middagstid.
noose [nu·s] løkke, rennesnare; fange med
snare, lage til rennesnare; fange.
nor [nå·ə] (etter nekting, især **neither**) eller;
(i andre tilfelle) heller ikke, og heller ikke.
og ... ikke; (vulgært) enn (**than**); **neither gold
nor silver** hverken gull eller sølv; **she has no
money, nor has he** hun har ikke penger, og det
har ikke han heller; **I thought of him, nor did
I forget you** jeg tenkte på ham, og jeg glemte
ikke deg heller.
Norfolk ['nå·əfək] Norfolk. — **-jacket** sports-
trøye med belte.
norm [nå·əm] norm, mønster, rettesnor.
normal['nå·əməl] normal, regelmessig, naturlig;
vinkelrett, loddrett; — **school** lærerskole, seminar. **normalization** [nå·əməlai'ze¹ʃən] norme-
ring. **normalize** ['nå·əməlaiz] normere, normalisere.
Norman ['nå·əmən] normannisk, normanner; —
architecture normannisk bygningsstil (rundbuestil). **Normandy** ['nå·əməndi] Normandi.
Norn [nå·ən] norne.
Norse [nå·əs] gammelnorsk, norrøn; nynorsk;
-man nordbo, nordmann.
north, North [nå·əþ] nord; nord-, nordlig; **the
wind is at** (el. in) **the** — vinden er nordlig; **in
the** — **of England** i det nordlige England; **to the**
— **mot nord;** — **by East** nord til øst.
Northampton [nå·ə'þämtən] Northampton.
Northants. fk. f. **Northamptonshire.**
Northcliffe ['nå·əþklif] Northcliffe.
northcock ['nå·əþkåk] snøspurv.
North-country ['nå·əþkʌntri] Nord-England;
nordengelsk.
northeast ['nå·əþ'i·st] nordost; nordost-, nordøstlig. **-erly** [-əli] nordøstlig, nordost-.
northerly ['nå·əðəli] nordlig, mot nord.
northern ['nå·əðən] nordisk, nordlig; — **lights**
nordlys; **the most** — **point** det nordligste punkt.
northerner ['nå·əðənə] nordbo, nordlending; beboer i Nordstatene.
Northman ['nå·əþmən] nordbo; nordmann.
northmost ['nå·əþmo̶ust] nordligst.
north-north-east ['nå·əþnå·əþ'i·st] nord-nordost
(of for).
north-north-west ['nå·əþnå·əþ'west] nord-nord-
vest (of for).
north-polar ['nå·əþ'po̶ulə] nordpols-, arktisk.
the North-Sea ['nå·əþsi·] Nordsjøen.
the north-star ['nå·əþstɑ·] Nordstjernen.
Northumberland [nå·ə'þʌmbələnd] Northumberland. **Northumbrian** [nå·ə'þʌmbriən] northum-
brisk.
northward(s) ['nå·əþwəd(z)] mot nord, nord-
etter.
northwest [nå·əþ'west, nå·ə'west] nordvest.
northwind ['nå·əþwind] nordavind.
Norton ['nå·ətn] Norton.
Norway ['nå·əwe¹] Norge. **Norwegian** [nå·ə-
'wi·dʒən] norsk; nordmann; norsk (språket).
Norwich ['nårid̶ʒ] Norwich.
Nos. nos. fk. f. **numbers.**
nose [no̶uz] nese; lukt; spion, angiver; **bleeding at the** — neseblod; **bridge of the** — neserygg; **blow one's** — pusse nesen; **lead by the** —
lede etter sin egen vilje, ha i lommen, vikle om
fingeren; **put a person's** — **out of joint** stikke en
ut; **speak through the** — snøvle, snakke i nesen;
pay through the — betale i dyre dommer.

nose [no̶uz] lukte, være, få teften av; snuse;
angi (for politiet); — **out** snuse opp; snøvle fram.
nose-bag ['no̶uzbäg] mulepose, fôrpose.
nose-band ['no̶uzbänd] nesereim (på heste-
grime).
nosed [no̶uzd] -neset.
nose-dive ['no̶uzdaiv] det at flygemaskinen
dukker ned, stup.
nosegay ['no̶uzge¹] bukett.
noseless ['no̶uzlés] neseløs.
noser ['no̶uzə] sterk motvind; nesestyver.
nose-rag ['no̶uzräg] (i slang) snytefille.
nose-ring ['no̶uzriŋ] nesering.
nose- armer nesevarmer (en kort pipe).
nosing ['no̶uziŋ] tilspisset framspring (i arkitektur); trappebeslag.
nostalgia [nå'stäldʒiə] sykelig hjemve.
nostril ['nåstril] nesebor.
nostrum ['nåstrəm] arkanum, vidundermedisin.
nosy ['no̶uzi] storneset.
not [nåt] ikke; — yet ennå ikke; — **at all** aldeles ikke, på ingen måte; **I could** — **but** jeg
kunne ikke 'annet enn; — **in the least** ikke det
minste; aldri det grann; **he had better** — det
burde han helst la være; **I think** — jeg mener nei.
nota bene ['no̶utə'bi·ni] nota bene, vel å
merke.
notability[no̶utə'biliti] merkelighet, notabilitet.
notable ['no̶utəbl] merkelig, bemerkelsesverdig,
merkbar; tydelig; bekjent, kjent, vidgjeten;
notabilitet, størrelse. **notably** ['no̶utəbli] særlig.
notarial [no'tæ·əriəl] notarial, utferdiget av en
notarius.
notary ['no̶utəri] notarius; — **public** ['pʌblik]
notarius publicus.
notation [no'te¹ʃən] betegnelse, notering, opptegnelse; **the decimal** — desimalsystemet.
notch [nåtʃ] innsnitt, skåre, hakk; skår; skar;
gjøre innsnitt, karve, skjære skår i; lafte.
notching ['nåtʃiŋ] innsnitt, hakk, skår; lafting
note [no̶ut] tegn, merke; særdrag; tonetegn,
note, tone; notis, opptegnelse; billett, lite brev;
seddel, bevis; banknote, pengeseddel; regning;
anseelse, betydning, viktighet; merke, bemerke,
legge merke til, ta notis av, merke seg, skrive
opp; forsyne med merknader; **he changed his** —
han talte i en annen tone; **a man of** — en ansett
mann; **speak without -s** tale uten forberedelse;
— **of conjunction** bindetegn; — **of exclamation**
utropstegn; — **of interrogation** spørsmålstegn;
as per — ifølge nota; **cause a bill** (**of exchange**) **to
be -d** la en veksel protestere. — **-book** notisbok.
noted ['no̶utid] bekjent.
noteless ['no̶utlés] ubekjent, ubemerket. **note-
paper** ['no̶utpe¹pə] brevpapir i lite format. **noteworthy** ['no̶utwə·ði] verd å legge merke til.
nothing ['nʌþiŋ] intet, ikke noe, ingenting;
ubetydelighet, null; **a mere** — en ren bagatell;
for — gratis; **next to** — nesten ingenting; —
but ikke noe annet enn, bare; **that's** — **to me** det
kommer ikke meg ved, det raker ikke meg; **he
is** — **to us** han er oss likegyldig; **there's** — **in it**
det har ikke noe å si; **come to** — ikke bli
noe av; **make** — **of** ikke bry seg om, ikke gjøre
noe av; **I can make** — **of it** jeg kan ikke bli
klok på det; — **like** ikke tilnærmelsesvis; —
loath slett ikke lei; — **short of** intet mindre enn.
nothingness ['nʌþiŋnés] intethet, betydningsløshet; småting.
notice ['no̶utis] iakttagelse, bemerkning; underretning, varsel, oppslag, melding, bekjentgjørelse, kunngjøring; oppsigelse; oppmerksomhet, høflighet; **the child takes** — barnet begynner
å kunne skjønne: **this is to give** — that hermed
bekjentgjøres; **give a person** — å si en opp;
until further — inntil nærmere ordre, inntil
videre; **without** — uten oppsigelse; **attract** —
vekke oppmerksomhet; **he took no** — **of us** han
tok ingen notis av oss, vørte oss ikke.

notice ['noutis] bemerke, være, legge merke til, merke seg; skjønne; ta hensyn til.

noticeable ['noutisəbl] verd å legge merke til, bemerkelsesverdig, merkelig.

notification [noutifi'keiʃən] kunngjøring, melding, bekjentgjørelse, varsel. notify ['noutifai] bekjentgjøre, kunngjøre, varsle (om); berette.

notion ['nouʃən] begrep, forestilling, tanke; nykke, innfall, idé, lune; (amr.) småting, srl. i pl.: kortevarer, småartikler; he hasn't a — of doing it det faller ham ikke inn å gjøre det; form a true — of danne seg en riktig forestilling om; I had no — of it jeg hadde ikke noen anelse om det; I've got a — jeg har en idé; the horse has -s hesten har nykker; put -s into her head sette fluer i hodet på henne. notional ['nouʃənəl] tenkt, innbilt, abstrakt. notionist ['nouʃənist] fantast.

notoriety [noutə'raiəti] vitterlighet; berømmelse, navnkundighet; beryktethet; berømt personlighet.

notorious [nou'tå·riəs] alminnelig bekjent, åpenbar, vidgjeten, vitterlig, notorisk; beryktet; become — komme i folkemunne; a — case en celeber sak. notoriousness [-nès] vitterlighet; beryktethet.

Nottingham ['nåtiŋəm] Nottingham.
Notts. fk. f. Nottinghamshire.

notwithstanding [nåtwið'ständiŋ] tross, trass i, til tross for; dessuaktet, ikke desto mindre; uaktet, enskjønt.

nougat [nu·'ga·] nougat (en slags sukkertøy med mandler).

nought [nå·t] intet; ingenting, null; (sifret 0 leses oftest slik; jfr. naught;) set at — ringeakte, slå bort.

noun [naun] substantiv, navnord.

nourish ['nʌriʃ] nære, gi næring, føde, styrke, ernære, underholde; ale opp, ale fram; — a hope nære håp om. nourishable ['nʌriʃəbl] som kan næres. nourisher ['nʌriʃə] ernærer; næringsmiddel. nourishment ['nʌriʃmənt] næring.

nous [naus] (sunn) fornuft, vett, omløp.
Nov. fk. f. November.

Nova Scotia ['nouvə'skouʃə] Nova Scotia, Ny-Skottland.

novel ['nåv(ə)l] ny, ualminnelig, uvanlig, hittil ukjent; roman; a — departure noe ganske nytt. novelese [nåvə'li·z] romanstil. novelette [nåvə'let] novellett, liten fortelling. novelist ['nåv(ə)list] romanforfatter. novelty ['nåv(ə)lti] nyhet.

November [nou'vembə] november.

novice ['nåvis] novise; nybegynner; uøvd. noviciate, novitiate [no'viʃiét] prøvetid.

now [nau] nå; — before — tidligere, før; but — nettopp nå; he will be here just — han er her straks; now . . . now snart . . ., snart; now that nå da.

nowadays ['nauədeiz] nåtildags, nå for tiden. noway(s) ['nouwei(z)] på ingen måte, slett ikke.

nowhence ['nouhwens] ingenstedsfra. nowhere ['nouhwæ·ə] ingensteds. nowhither ['nouhwiðə] ingenstedshen. nowise ['nouwaiz] på ingen måte, slett ikke.

noxious ['nåkʃəs] skadelig, usunn.

nozzle ['nåzl] tut, trut; nese, spiss.
n. p. or d. fk. f. no place or date.
N. R. A. fk. f. National Rifle Association.
n. s. fk. f. not sufficient.
N. S. A. fk. f. National Skating Association.
N. S. P. C. C. fk. f. National Society for the Prevention of Cruelty to Children.
N. S. W. fk. f. New South Wales.
N. T. fk. f. New Testament.
-n't [-nt] fk. f. not (især etter hjelpeverber).

nuance [nju·'ä·ns, nju'a·ns] nyanse.

nub [nʌb] klump, stykke; knute. nubbly ['nʌbli] knutet, klumpet; i småklumper.

nubile ['nju·bil] gifteferdig, gifteferdig alder.
nuciferous [nju'sifərəs] som bærer nøtter.
nuciform ['nju·silä·m] nøtteformet.
nucleus ['nju·kliəs] kjerne; grunnstamme; — of a screw skruespindel.
nudation [nju'deiʃən] blottelse.
nude [nju·d] naken, blottet; ikke lovformelig, ugyldig; akt (i kunst). nudeness [-nès] nakenhet.
nudge [nʌdʒ] skubbe, dulte (med albuen); puff.
nudification [nju·difi'keiʃən] blottelse.
nudity ['nju·diti] nakenhet.
nugatory ['nju·gətəri] betydningsløs, gagnløs.
nuggar ['nʌgə] egyptisk fraktbåt.
nugget ['nʌgit] klump, gullklump.
nuisance ['nju·səns] uvesen, besværlighet, plage, ulempe, ubehagelighet; that's a — det er kjedelig; don't be a — ikke plag meg da; a public — en landeplage, pestilens; commit no — urenslighet forbydes; inspector of -s sunnhetsinspektør; necessary -s nødvendige onder.
null [nʌl] ugyldig, intetsigende; — and void (jur.) ugyldig.
nullification [nʌlifi'keiʃən] opphevelse. nullify ['nʌliiai] oppheve, gjøre ugyldig.
nullity ['nʌliti] ugyldighet, intethet, null; — suit søknad om å få et ekteskap erklært ugyldig.
numb [nʌm] forfrossen, valen, nommen, stiv; gjøre stiv, følelsesløs; -ed stivfrossen.
number ['nʌmbə] tall, nummer, antall, mengde numérisk styrke; versemål; telle, nummerere; plural — flertall; even — like tall; odd — ulike tall, oddetall; take care of — one sørge godt for seg selv; out of —, without — utallig, talløs; -s of times atter og atter; double the — det dobbelte antall; come in -s utkomme heftevis; -s rytmer; he is -ed among han regnes blant. numberless ['nʌmbəles] utallig, talløs.
Numbers ['nʌmbəz] Numeri, fjerde mosebok.
numerable ['nju·mərəbl] som kan telles.
numeral ['nju·mərəl] som angår, består av tall, tall-; tallord, talltegn, tall. numerary ['nju·mərəri] som angår et visst nummer. numerate ['nju·məreit] nummerere; telle, regne. numeration [nju·mə're'ʃən] telling; tall, antall; tallesning. numerator ['nju·məreitə] teller (også i brøk). numeric(al) [nju·merik(l)] numérisk, tall-, som hører til eller inneholder tall.
numerous ['nju·mərəs] tallrik, mannsterk; harmonisk. numerousness [-nès] tallrikhet, mengde.
numismatic [nju·mis'mätik] numismatisk, myntvitenskapelig; -s numismatikk, myntvitenskap.
nummary ['nʌməri] mynt-, penge-.
nummy ['nʌmi] dosmer.
numskull ['nʌmskʌl] dosmer, fæ, dåsemikkel.
nun [nʌn] nonne; blåmeise.
nuncio ['nʌnʃou] nuntius, pavelig sendebud.
nundinal ['nʌndinəl] torg-, markeds-.
nunnery ['nʌnəri] nonnekloster. nunnish ['nʌniʃ] nonneaktig.
nuptial ['nʌpʃəl] brude-, bryllups-; -s bryllup.
N. U. R. fk. f. National Union of Railwaymen.
Nuremberg ['njuərəmbə·g] Nürnberg.
nurse [nə·s] amme, barnepleierske, sykepleier-(ske); våkekone; fostre; nære, amme opp, die, gi bryst; pleie, passe; nære, framelske; trained (eller hospital) — (hospitalsutdannet) sykepleierske; be at — være i pleie; put to — gi, sette i pleie; one's wrath nære sin vrede. — child spebarn. — -maid barnepike. — -pond fiskedam for fiskyngel. nurser ['nə·sə] den som underholder (eller ernærer, pleier).
nursery ['nə·s(ə)ri] barnekammer; planteskole. — -garden planteskole. — -governess lærerinne for små barn. — -house drivhus. — -jingel barnerim. — -maid barnepike. — -man handelsgartner. — -rhyme barnerim, barneregle. — -school barnehage. — -tale barneeventyr.
nursling ['nə·sliŋ] pleiebarn, fosterbarn.

nurture ['nə·tʃə] næring; oppfostring, oppdragelse; oppfostre, oppdrage; opptukte; nature passes — naturen går over opptuktelsen.

nut [nʌt] nøtt; hasselnøtt; mutter, skrumor; møtrik; nøttekull; vanskelig problem; hode, skolt; moderne laps; plukke nøtter; be off one's — være gal; a hard — to crack en hard nøtt å knekke; I have a — to crack with him jeg har en høne å plukke med ham; it is -s to him det er vann på hans mølle; be -s on a person være sterkt forelsket i en. N. U. T. fk. f. National Union of Teachers.

nut-brown ['nʌtbraun] nøttebrun.

nutcracker ['nʌtkräkə] nøtteknekker.

nut-gall ['nʌtgå·l] galleple.

nuthatch ['nʌthätʃ] nøttvekke, spettmeise.

nutmeg ['nʌtmeg] muskat, muskatnøtt.

nutoil ['nʌtoil] valnøttolje.

nutrient ['nju·trɪənt] nærende; næringsstoff.

nutriment ['nju·tr.mənt] næring. nutrimental [nju·tri mentəl] næ¹rende. nutrition [nju'triʃən] ernæring. nutritions [nju'triʃəs] nærende. nutritive ['nju·tritiv] nærende.

nutshell ['nʌtʃel] nøtteskall; in a — sammentrengt i få ord, kort sagt. Nuttall ['nʌta·l] Nuttall.

nutting ['nʌtiŋ] nøttesanking, nøtteplukking.

nut-tree ['nʌttri·] nøttetre, hasselbusk.

nutty ['nʌti] rik på nøtter, med nøttesmak.

nut-wood nøttetre.

N. U. W. S. S. fk. f. National Union of Women's Suffrage Societies.

nuzzle ['nʌzl] anbringe; ligge lunt; grave seg godt ned; snuse, rote i jorda.

N. W. fk. f. North-west.

N. W. b. N. fk. f. North-west by North.

N. W. b. W. fk. f. North-west by West.

N. W. T. fk. f. North-Western Territories.

N. Y. fk. f. New York.

nylghau ['nilgå·] indisk antilope.

nymph [nimf] nymfe, hulder; puppe. nymphal ['nimfəl] nymfe-. nymphlike ['nimflaik] nymfelett.

N. Z. fk. f. New Zealand.

O

O, o [oᵘ] O.

O [oᵘ] null, 0.

O [oᵘ] å! o! akk! O the rich reward! å, hvilken rik belønning!

O¹[oᵘ, o] forstavelse i irske navn: sønn av.

o [o, ə] fk. f. of eller on.

O. fk. f. Ohio; oxygen.

o|a. fk. f. on account of.

oaf [oᵘf] bytting; tomsing; klodrian. oafish ['oᵘfiʃ] dum, nauten, enfoldig.

oak [oᵘk] eik, eiketre; ytterdør (for studentenes værelse i et kollegium); heart of — alved av eik; traust kar, fast karakter; sport his — stenge ytterdøra og frabe seg visitter. — -apple galleple. — -bark eikebark. oaken ['oᵘkən] av eiketre, eike-. oak-gall ['oᵘkgå·l] galleple. oakling ['oᵘkliŋ] ung eik.

Oaks [oᵘks] sted ved Epsom i Surrey; the — veddeløp ved Oaks.

oakum ['oᵘkəm] drev (opplukket tauverk). — — -picker drevplukker(ske). — -picking drevplukking.

oar [å·ə] åre; put in one's —, shove in an — blande seg i andre folks saker; rest upon one's -s hvile seg på sine laurbær. oared [å·əd] -året, forsynt med årer. oarsman roer. oarswoman roerske.

oases [oᵘ¹e¹si·z] pl. av oasis [oᵘ¹e¹sis] oase.

oast [oᵘst] kjone, badstue, bastue, tørkeovn.

oat [oᵘt] havre. -bread havrebrød. oaten ['oᵘtn] havre-, av havre.

oath [oᵘþ] ed; banning; take an — avlegge ed.

oaths [oᵘðz] pl. av oath.

oatmeal ['oᵘtmi·l] havremel; havregryn; havregrøt.

oats ['oᵘts] havre; wild — floghavre; sow one's wild — rase ut, renne horna av seg.

ob. fk. f. obiit døde.

obduracy ['åbdjurəsi] hardhet, forstokkethet.

obdurate ['åbdjurèt] hard, forherdet, forstokket; stiv, stri, strilyndt, umedgjørlig.

O. B. E. fk. f. Officer of the Order of the British Empire.

obeah ['oᵘbiə] negertrolldom.

obedience [o'bi·djəns] lydighet (to mot).

obedient [o'bi·djənt] lydig (to mot).

obeisance [o·be¹(i)səns, -bi·s-] reverens, bukk.

obelisk ['åbilisk] obelisk, støtte; kors.

Oberon ['oᵘbərən] Oberon.

obese [o'bi·s] mesket, tykk, feit.

obesity [o'bi·siti] fettsyke, korpulense.

obey [o'be¹] adlyde, lyde, lystre; I will be -ed jeg forlanger lydighet.

obfuscate ['åblʌske¹t] formørke, forvirre. obfuscation [åbfəs'ke¹ʃən] formørkelse.

obiit ['åbiit] døde (v.).

obit ['oᵘbit, 'åbit] død, begravelseshøytidelig-heter, årlig sjelemesse.

obitual [o'bitjuəl] som angår død, døds-. — days dødsdager. obituary [o'bitjuəri] nekrologisk; nekrolog, fortegnelse over dødsfall.

obj. fk. f. object.

object ['åbdʒikt, -ekt] gjenstand, hensikt, mål, øyemed, tanke; salary no — på lønnen ses ikke; the — of my wishes mine ønskers mål; — lesson anskuelsesundervisning.

object [əb'dʒekt, åb-] innvende, gjøre motlegg (that at; to el. against imot); protestere, ha noe å innvende (to imot); if you don't — hvis du ikke har noe imot det.

objection [åb'dʒekʃən, åb-] innvending, innsigelse, motlegg; motmæle; I have no — to your going jeg har ikke noe imot at du går.

objectionable [əb'dʒekʃənəbl] ubehagelig, lei, forkastelig.

objective [əb'dʒektiv, åb-] objektiv; akkusativ; — case akkusativ. objectivity [åbdʒik'tiviti] objektivitet. objectless ['åbdʒiktlés] hensiktsløs, fånyttig. objector [əb'dʒektə, åb-] innsiger, motsiger, motmann, opponent.

objurgation [åbdʒə·'ge¹ʃən] skjenn, irettesetting, skiape, bebreidelse, straffetale.

oblate ['åble¹t] person vigd til munkeliv el. religiøst liv el. arbeid.

oblation ['åbligənt] forpliktet, oblig'ate ['åblige¹t] forplikte. obligation [åbli'ge¹ʃən] forpliktelse, skyldnad. obligatory ['åbligətəri] bindende, tvingende, tvungen, obligatorisk.

oblige [o'blaidʒ] binde, nøde, tvinge, forplikte, forbinde, gjøre forbunden el. takkskyldig, tjene; I am -d to you for it jeg er Dem takknemlig for det; an answer by return of post will — me De bes vennligst svare meg omgående; will any gentleman — a lady er det en av herrene som vil overlate plassen sin til en dame; — me by leaving the room vær så vennlig å forlate værelset; be -d to være nødt til; I am much -d to you jeg er Dem meget takknemlig, jeg skylder Dem stor takk, mange takk. obligedly [o'blaidʒidli] yours Deres forbundne (i brev).

obligee [åbli'dʒi·] fordringshaver.

obliging [o'blaidʒiŋ] forbindtlig, forekommende, tjenstvillig. **obligingness** [-nès] imøtekommenhet, tjenstvillighet.

obligor [åbli'gå·ə] skyldner.

oblique [o'bli·k] hellende; skrå, skakk, skjev; indirekte, forblommet; uredelig; bevege seg skjevt, skråne; — **angle** skjev vinkel; — **speech** indirekte tale; **in — terms** i forblommede uttrykk; — **-angled** skjev-vinklet.

obliquity [o'blikwiti] hall, skjevhet; uredelighet.

obliterate [åb'litəre·t] utslette, stryke ut, tilintetgjøre. **obliteration** [åblitə're·ʃən] utsletting, tilintetgjøring, tyning. **obliterative** [åb'litərətiv] utslettende, tilintetgjørende.

oblivion [o'blivjən] forglemmelse, glemsel; ettergivelse, amnesti; **fall (pass) into** — gå i glemme; **gå i glemmeboka; save from** — bevare for etterverdenen. **oblivious** [o'blivjəs] som får til å glemme; glemsom, glemsk. **obliviousness** [-nès] glemsomhet.

oblong ['åblåŋ] avlang, langaktig; avlang figur. **oblongish** [-iʃ] noe avlang.

obloquy ['åbləkwi] daddel, lastord, bebreidelse.

obnoxious [əb'nåkʃəs] forkastelig, daddelverdig, forhatt, ubehagelig, anstøtelig, upopulær; **make oneself** — gjøre seg forhatt, vekke anstøt. **obnoxiousness** [-nès] straffskyldighet; forhatthet.

oboe ['oᵘboi, 'oᵘboᵘ] obo. **oboist** ['oᵘboᵘist] oboist.

O'Brien [oᵘ'braiən,o-] O'Brien.

obs. fk. f. observation, obsolete.

obscene [åb'si·n] obscøn, smussig, heslig, fæl, uanstendig. **obscenity** [åb'si·niti] smussighet, utuktighet, uanstendighet.

obscurant [åb'skjuərənt] opplysningsfiende. **obscurantism** [-izm] obskurantisme, lysskyhet. **obscuration** [åbskju're·ʃən] formørkelse.

obscure [åb'skjuə] mørk, døkk, dunkel, uklar, ugrei; skjult, ubemerket, ringe, ubekjent; fordunkle, formørke; **be of — origin** av ringe herkomst; **he lives an — life** han fører et tilbaketrukket liv; **in some — locality** på et eller annet ukjent sted.

obscurity [åb'skjuəriti] mørke, dunkelhet, dimme, uklarhet; ubemerkethet, utydelighet, uberømthet; **obscurities** ukjente personer.

obsecration [åbsi'kre·ʃən] besvergelse, trygling, inntrengende bønn.

obsequial [åb'si·kwiəl] begravelses-; grav-. **obsequies** ['åbsikwiz] begravelse, likferd.

obsequious [åb'si·kwiəs] servil, underdanig, krypende. **obsequiousness** [-nès] underdanighet.

observable [əb'zə·vəbl, åb-] som kan (el. må) overholdes, merkbar, bemerkelsesverdig.

observance [əb'zə·vəns, åb-] oppmerksomhet, regel, praksis, skikk; **according to old** — etter gammel vedtekt.

observant [əb'zə·vənt, åb-] oppmerksom, iakttagende, omhyggelig, lydig, underdanig.

observation [åbzə've·ʃən] iakttagelse, bemerkning; observasjon; **keep a person under** — holde en under oppsikt. **observational** [åbzə've·ʃənəl] observasjons-. **observator** ['åbzəve·tə] observator. **observatory** [åb'ze·vətəri, åb-] iakttagelses-; observatorium.

observe [əb'zə·v, åb-] iaktta, legge merke til, bemerke; høytidligholde, holde, overholde, følge; gjøre en bemerkning, si. **observer** [əb'zə·və, åb-] iakttager, betrakter, en som overholder (en lov, skikk); observator. **observing** [əb'zə·viŋ, åb-] oppmerksom.

obsess [åb'ses] besette, beleire; idelig plage. **obsession** [åb'seʃən] beleiring; anfektelse, besettelse, fiks idé.

obsolescence [åbso'lesəns] foreldethet, det å gå av bruk, foreldelse. **obsolescent** [-sənt] som holder på å gå av bruk, bli foreldet. **obsolete** ['åbsoli·t] gått av bruk, foreldet, gammeldags. **obsoleteness** [-nès] foreldethet.

obstacle ['åbstəkl] hindring; **put -s in the way** legge hindringer i veien.

obstetric(al) [åb'stetrik(l)] som hører til fødselsvitenskapen. **obstetrician** [åbsti'triʃən] fødselshjelper.

obstinacy ['åbstinəsi] gjenstridighet, egensindighet, hårdnakkethet, stridighet. **obstinate** ['åbstinét] hårdnakket, stri(lyndt), vrang, lei, egensindig, ubøyelig.

obstipation [åbsti'pe·ʃən] forstoppelse.

obstreperous [åb'strepərəs] bråkende, larmende; uregjerlig. **obstreperousness** [-nès] ståk, bråk, larm.

obstriction [åb'strikʃən] forpliktelse.

obstruct [åb'strʌkt] sperre, stenge, teppe, forstoppe, stoppe til; hindre; forsinke, sinke. **obstruction** [åb'strʌkʃən] sperring, tilstopping, hindring, forsinkelse; obstruksjon, hindringspolitikk. **obstructionist** [-ist] en som driver obstruksjon; obstruksjonistisk. **obstructive** [åb'strʌktiv] sperrende, stoppende, hindrende, forsinkende. **obstruent** ['åbstruənt] forstoppende, hindrende.

obtain [əb'te·n, åb-] erholde, få, oppnå, vinne, utvirke, skaffe, forskaffe, skaffe seg, skaffe til veie; holde seg, bestå, gjelde, herske, være i bruk, ha framgang; **this rule -s in most cases** denne regel gjelder i de fleste tilfelle. **obtainable** [əb'te·nəbl, åb-] oppnåelig, erholdelig; som kan erholdes, fås, utvirkes. **obtainer** [əb'te·nə, åb-] en som oppnår. **obtainment** [-mənt] oppnåelse, erholdelse.

obtest [åb'test] påkalle som vitne, anrope, bønnfalle; protestere; forsikre. **obtestation** [åbtès-'te·ʃən] påberopelse, forsikring, erklæring.

obtrude [əb'tru·d, åb-] påtrenge, påtvinge, pånøde; trenge seg inn, være påtrengende. **obtruder** [əb'tru·də, åb-] påtrengende person. **obtrusion** [əb'tru·ʒən, åb-] påtrengenhet, påtvinging. **obtrusive** [əb'tru·siv, åb-] påtrengende.

obtund [əb'tʌnd] avstumpe, dempe, døve. **obturate** [åb'tju(ə)re·t] stoppe til, stoppe. **-ion** [åbtju(ə)'re·ʃən] tilstopping.

obtuse [åb'tju·s] sløv, stump, dump. **obtuseness** [-nès] sløvhet, avstumpethet. **obtusion** [åb'tju·ʒən] sløvelse, avstumping, sløvhet.

obverse [åb'və·s] omvendt, som smalner mot grunnen (om bladform). **obverse** ['åbvə·s] avers, forside av en mynt. **obversion** [åb'və·ʃən] vending. **obvert** [åb'və·t] vende fram.

obviate ['åbvie·t] møte; forebygge, avvende, rydde av veien, få bort. **obviation** [åbvi'e·ʃən] forebygging, avvending, fjerning. **obvious** ['åbviəs] motvendt; utsatt for; iøynefallende, tydelig, grei, innlysende, klar, opplagt, selvfølgelig, likefram, endefram. **obviousness** [-nès] tydelighet.

ocarina [åkə'ri·nə] okarina (musikkinstrument).

occasion [ək'ke·ʒən, å-] tilfelle, (gunstig) leilighet, anledning, høve, tilhøve, gang; foranledning, (ytre) årsak, (ytre) grunn; trang, bruk, behov; foranledige, forårsake, gi anledning til, bevirke; **we met him on a former** — vi har truffet ham ved en tidligere leilighet, før en gang; **if — offers** hvis leilighten byr seg; **on that** — ved den leilighet, ved det høve, den gang; **equal to the** — situasjonen voksen; **there is no** — **for you to speak English** De behøver ikke å snakke engelsk; **for this** — for tilfellet; **on some slight** — for en ubetydelig årsaks skyld.

occasional [ə'ke·ʒənəl, å-] leilighetsvis; tilfeldig; tilveiebrakt ved en viss leilighet, leilighets-, slenge-, slumpe-; **occasionally** [-i] leilighetsvis, av og til.

Occident ['åksidənt], **the** — Vesten, Oksidenten. **occidental** [åksi'dentəl] vestlig, vesterlandsk. **occidentally** [-təli] i vest; etter sola.

occipital [åk'sipitəl] bakhode-, nakke-. **occiput** ['åksipət] bakhode, nakke.

occlude [å'klu·d] stenge, dytte, stenge inne el. ute; absorbere, suge i seg.

occlusion [å'klu·ʒən] stengsel, tillukking.

occult [å'kʌlt] skjult, hemmelig, lønnlig. occultation [åkəl'te'ʃən] usynlighet; fordølgelse; okkultasjon. occulted [å'kʌltid] bedekket, gjemt. occultism ['åkʌltizm] okkultisme. occultness [-nĕs] skjulthet, hemmelighet.

occupancy ['åkjupənsi] det å ta i besittelse; okkupasjon: besittelse. occupant [-pənt] en som tar i besittelse, okkupant, besitter, innehaver.

occupation [åkju'pe'ʃən] det å ta i besittelse, bemektigelse, inntagelse, okkupasjon; besittelse; beskjeftigelse, arbeide; — bridge forbindelsesbru over eller under en jernbane. occupier ['åkjupaiə] besitter, innehaver. occupy ['åkjupai] ta i besittelse, innta, okkupere, oppta, besette; besitte, sitte inne med; bebo; beskjeftige, sysselsette.

occur [ə'kə·, å-] forekomme, bære til, hende, inntreffe; komme i tankene, falle inn, komme for en; this never -red to me det har aldri falt meg inn; what has -red hva har hendt. occurrence [ə'kʌrəns, å-] hendelse, tilfelle, hending, forekomst.

ocean ['o·ʃən] osean, hav, verdenshav; uhyre utstrekning; he has got -s of money han har masser av penger.

Oceania [o·ʃi'e'niä] Oceania. oceanic [o·ʃi-'änik] oʌean,- hav:- stor som et osean.

ochre ['o·kə] oker, gult fargestoff.

o'clock [ə'klåk] klokka; at five — klokka fem; it is five — klokka er fem; what — is it hva er klokka?

Oct. fk. f. October.

octagon ['åktəgån] åttekant. octagonal [åk-'tägənəl] åttekantet. octangular [åk'tängjulə] åttekantet. octant ['åktənt] oktant. octave ['åk-te'v] åtte; oktav. octavo [åk'te'vo·] oktav, bok i oktav. octennial [åk'tenjəl] åtteårig, åtteårlig. October [åk'to·bə] oktober.

octogenarian [åktodʒi'næ·'riən] åttiårs, på åtti år; åttiåring.

octopod ['åktopåd] åttearmet blekksprut. octopus ['åktopʌs] blekksprut; (oldtidens) polypp; mangearmet uhyre.

octosyllable [åkto'siløbl] ord med åtte stavinger. octroi ['åktrwa·] monopol, enerett.

ocular ['åkjulə] øye-, syns-, som avhenger av øyet, som man ser med sine egne øyne, øyensynlig; — demonstration synlig bevis, syn for saken; — witness øyenvitne; — intercourse øyenspråk. oculiform ['åkjulifå·əm] øyeformig. oculist ['åkjulist] øyenlæge.

odalisque ['o·dəlisk] odalisk (kvinnelig haremsslave).

odd [åd] ulike; umake, parløs; overskytende; noen få; enkelt; sær; underlig, besynderlig, snurrig, rar; slem; — number ulike tall; play at — or even spille par eller odde (en gjetteleik); eighty — years noen og åtti år; — jobs tilfeldig arbeid; ten pounds — money 10 pund og derover; there is some — money det er enda noen penger til overs; an — glove en umake hanske; an — volume et enkelt bind av et verk; how — hvor besynderlig; an — kind of man en rar mann; in an — sort of way på en merkelig måte, tilfeldig. — -boy reservegutt, visergutt.

Odd-Fellow ['ådfelo·] Odd-Fellow, medlem av et hemmelig selskap.

oddish ['ådiʃ] underlig av seg, litt rar.

oddity ['åditi] særhet, besynderlighet; oddities merkelige innfall.

oddlooking ['ådlukiŋ] merkelig, rar, som ser underlig ut. odd-man ['ådmän] reservemann, ekstramann; reserveroer; en som kan brukes til alt mulig på en gård e. l., altmuligmann; oppmann.

oddment ['ådmənt] overskudd, rest, slump; ubetydelighet; især i pl.: rester.

odds [ådz] forskjell, skilnad, ulikhet, (tilstått) fordel, begunstigelse, største utsikt; uenighet, strid; ulike vilkår; fordel, overlegenhet, overmakt; what's (where's) the — hva gjør det? it is no —

det betyr ikke noe; it's no — of mine meg kan det være det samme; I'll lay you any — jeg vil holde, hva det skal være; at heavy — mot stor overmakt, på ulike vilkår; it is within the — det er en mulighet for det; the — are on his side han har fordelen på sin side, han har de beste sjanser; be at — with somebody ligge i strid med en; — and ends stumper og stykker, likt og ulikt.

ode [o·d] ode.

odeum ['o·di·əm] konsertlokale.

odious ['o·diəs, 'o·djəs] hatet, forhatt; odiøs, hatefull; avskylig, motbydelig. odiousness [-nĕs] forhatthet; avskylighet.

odium ['o·djəm] hat, motvilje, uvilje, stygg.

odorator ['o·dəre'tə] dusj. odoriferous [o·də-'rifərəs] velluktende, duftende. odorous ['o·dərəs] duftende. odour ['o·də] lukt, duft, vellukt. odourless [-lĕs] uten duft.

Odysseus [o'disju·s] Odyssevs.

Odyssey ['ådisi] Odysséen.

O. E. fk. f. old English.

O. E. D. fk. f. Oxford English Dictionary.

o'er [å·ə] fk. f. over.

of [åv, əv, ə] (preposisjon) av, fra, i; the work — Shakespeare Shakespeares verker (genitiv); the children of your uncle and aunt barna til din onkel og tante; a boy of ten years en gutt på 10 år; — an afternoon om ettermiddagen; en ettermiddag; — late i det siste; — old fra gammel tid; — the name — ved navn; a wall — six feet high en mur 6 fot høy; be all — a tremble skjelve over hele kroppen; — necessity nødvendigvis; be — the party høre til selskapet; — all things framfor alt; all — them alle; the three — you dere tre; tall — one's age høy etter alderen; the Queen — England dronningen av England; the King — Norway Norges konge; the town — N. byen N; a glass — water et glass vann.

O. F. fk. f. old French.

off [å·f, åf] (adverbium el. adjektiv) bort, av sted, av gårde, vekk, borte, fri; (om hest) som går på høyre side av vogn el. plog; av; ut for, på høyden av; — street sidegate; — and on, on and — av og til, med avbrytelser, — til forskjellige tider; I must be — jeg må av sted; be — være hevet, være forbi; sove; he was fast — han sov fast; be badly — være ille ute; be well — være velstående; a great way — et langt stykke borte; — one's guard uoppmerksom; throw a person — his guard avlede en persons oppmerksomhet; the ship is — hire befrakteren betaler ikke noen leie for skipet; he was not — the horse the whole day han var ikke av hesten hele dagen; — the stage utenfor scenen, i kulissen; — day fridag; a little parlour — his bedroom en liten dagligstue ved siden av soveværelset hans.

offal ['åfəl] avfall; åtsel; skrap, søppel.

off-and-on ['å(·)fən(d)'ån] vankelmodig, vegelsinnet, vinglet.

offence [ə'fens, å-] fornærmelse, krenking, forbrytelse, forseelse; forargelse; vrede, sinne; take — at ta anstøt av; no — det var ikke ment som noen fornærmelse; give — vekke anstøt, fornærme.

offend [ə'fend, å-] fornærme, krenke, støte, støte mot, fortørne; synde, feile; angripe; forse seg; støte an; offended [-did] fornærmet, støtt (at over; with på). offender [ə'fendə, å-] fornærmer, overtreder, synder.

offensive [ə'fensiv] offensiv, angreps-; fornærmelig, anstøtelig; motbydelig, utålelig; skadelig, besværlig, lei; offensiv, angrep, angrepsstilling; act on the — gå angrepsvis fram, ta offensiven. -ness offensiv beskaffenhet; anstøtelighet; motbydelighet.

offer ['åfə] by fram, tilby, gi, inngi, innlevere; oppstille, utsette, utlove; forsøke; tilby seg, framby seg; ofre; tilbud, bud, forsøk; this -s few advantages dette byr bare på få fordeler; this

was the sacrifice -ed dette var den ofring som ble brukt; **if an occasion -s** hvis leilighet byr seg; **he -ed to strike me** han gjorde mine til å slå meg; — **of marriage** ekteskapstilbud; **wool on** — tilbud på ull, offerert ull; **-s and demand** tilbud og etterspørsel. **offerable** ['åf(ə)rəbl] som kan tilbys. **offerer** ['åfərə] en som tilbyr, tilbyder, tilbydende; ofrer, ofrende. **offering** ['åfəriŋ] offer, gave. **offertory** ['åfətəri] offersang, offertorium.

offhand ['å·f'händ] på stedet, på flekken, uten forberedelse, ekstempore; improvisert, rask, kjapp, snøgg, ikke gjennomtenkt, flott. **off-horse** borteste hesten.

office ['åfis] bestilling, forretning, tjeneste, verv, embete, yrke, kall, gjerning, ombud, post; kontor, ekspedisjon; ministerium; gudstjeneste, ritual; **-s** kjøkken og ytre rom, uthus; **be in** (el. **hold an**) — bekle et embete, være minister; **resign** — gå av (som minister); **take** — overta en ministerpost; **Foreign Office** utenriksdepartement; **in virtue of my** — i kraft av min stilling; **good** — vennetjeneste. — **-bearer** embetsmann. — **-clerk** kontorist. — **-hours** kontortid.

officer ['åfisə] betjent, bestillingsmann, funksjonær, tjenestemann, rettsbetjent, politikonstabel; tillitsmann, styremedlem; styrmann; offiser; forsyne med offiserer; kommandere, føre; **the regiment is well -ed** regimentet har dyktige offiserer. **office-seeker** embetsansøker, embetsjeger.

official [ə'fiʃəl, å-] som hører til et embete, embets-, offisiell; tjenestemann, bestillingsmann, embetsmann; offisial (biskops vkiar i rettssaker). **officially** [ə'fiʃəli, å-] på embets vegne, offiselt. **officiate** [å'fiʃie·t] fungere, utøve en bestilling, forrette, gjøre tjeneste; vikariere. **officina** [åfi'sainə] verksted. **officinal** [å'fisinəl] som has ferdig på et apotek; lægende. **officious** [ə'fiʃəs, å-] tjenstaktig; geskjeftig, påtrengende. **officiousness** [-nés] tjenstaktighet; påtrengenhet.

offing ['å(·)fiŋ] rom sjø; **gain** (el. **get**) **an** — komme ut i rom sjø; **in the** — under oppseiling. **stand for the** — stå til sjøs.

offish ['å·fiʃ] fornem, stiv, kald.

officense ['å(·)flaisens] skjenkerett.

off-night ['å·fnait] friaften.

off-print ['å·fprint] særtrykk; særtrykke.

offsaddle ['å·fsädl] ta salen av.

off|scourings ['å·fskauriŋz] avfall, utskudd. **-scum** skum, slagg, avfall, skrap, smuss. **-season** tid utenfor sesongen.

offset ['å(·)fset] boktrykk ved hjelp av avsmitting (overføring) fra gummiduk; rotskudd, renning, avlegger; forgrening; avsats, terrasse, pall; krok, kne (på rør); hjelpelinje; motkrav (fordring som går opp mot en annen sum); vederlag, motvekt. **offset** ['å(·)f'set] balansere, oppveie.

offshoot ['å(·)tʃu·t] utløper, sidegrein.

offshore ['å(·)ʃʃå·ə] fra land; ikke langt fra land; fralands-.

offside ['å·f'said] høyre side (av hest el. kjøretøy); borteste side; offside (i fotball).

offspring ['å·fspriŋ] avkom, slekt, etterkommere.

O. F. S. fk. f. **Orange Free State.**

oft [å(·)ft] ofte, titt.

often ['å(·)fn, 'å(·)ften] ofte, titt; **as** — **not** ikke så sjelden. **oftenness** [-nés] hyppighet. **oftentimes** [-taimz] ofte, mang en gang.

ogee ['oᵘdʒi·; oᵘdʒi·] listverk formet som en S; ark; S-formet.

ogival [oᵘ'dʒaivəl] spissbueformet, gotisk; spiss (på spisskule). **ogive** ['oᵘdʒaiv, oᵘ'dʒaiv] spissbue; anordning (i dreiebenk).

ogle ['oᵘgl] skotte, gløtte, bruke øynene, gi øyekast, kokettere (med), kaste forelskede blikk på, betrakte, mønstre; øyekast, sideblikk; forelsket blikk. **ogler** ['oᵘglə] en som ser med forelskede blikk. **ogling** ['oᵘgliŋ] ømme blikk, øyekast.

ogre ['oᵘgə] troll, utyske, menneskeeter. **ogreish** ['oᵘgəriʃ] trollaktig. **ogress** ['oᵘgrés] gyger. **Oh!** [oᵘ] o! å! akk!; **oh me!** å jøye meg! **oh no** nei selvfølgelig; — **yes** ja visst.

ohm [oᵘm] ohm.

O. H. M. fk. f. on His (el. **Her**) **Majesty's Service.**

Ohio [o'haioᵘ] Ohio.

oho [oᵘ'hoᵘ] åhå!

oil [oil] olje; bomolje; petroleum; smøre, olje, overstryke med olje; **mineral** — petroleum; **whale** — tran; **sweet** — olivenolje; **strike** — finne petroleum, bli plutselig rik; **-ed canvas** voksduk; **-ed paper** oljepapir. **oil|-bag** ['oilbåg] oljekjertel, oljepose (på dyr). — **-box** smørekopp. **-cake** oljekake. — **-can** oljekanne, smørekanne. **oilcloth** ['oilklåþ] voksduk; oljetøy. **oil-colour** ['oilkʌlə] oljefarge. **oil|er** ['oilə] oljehandler; smørekopp, oljekanne. **-ery** ['oiləri] oljehandel. **oil|-field** ['oilfi·ld] oljefelt. — **-fuel** brenselolje. — **-gauge** oljemåler. — **-hole** smørehull. **oilman** ['oilmən] oljehandler; arbeider i oljefabrikk; smører. **oil|-meal** ['oilmi·l] oljekakemel. — **-mill** oljefabrikk, oljeraffineri. — **-nut** avlang valnøtt. — **-paint** oljefarge; maling. — **-painting** oljemaling; oljemaleri. — **-refinery** trankokeri. — **-paper** oljepapir. **oilskin** ['oilskin] oljelerret; i pl. oljeklær, oljehyre. **oilstone** ['oilstoᵘn] oljestein, fin slipestein. **oil-well** ['oilwel] oljekjelde, oljebrønn. **oily** ['oili] oljet, oljeaktig, oljeglatt, slesk, sleip. **ointment** ['ointmənt] salve.

O. K. ['oᵘ'ke¹] fiks og ferdig, fin.

old [oᵘld] gammel; fiffig, dreven, klok; — **age** høy alder, alderdom; — **maid** gammel jomfru, peppermøy; — **song** gammel sang; lav pris; **give for an** — song for en ubetydelighet; **my** — **man** gamlen min; **of** —, in times of —, in days of — i gamle dager, fordum; **grow** — eldes. **Old-Age Pensions** alderdomsunderstøttelse, alderstrygd, alderspensjon.

old-clothes man ['oᵘld'kloᵘ(ð)zmən] en som handler med gamle klær.

olden ['oᵘldn] fordums, gammel; eldes; elde. **older** ['oᵘldə] eldre. **oldest** ['oᵘldist] eldst.

old|-established ['oᵘldi'stäbliʃt] gammel, hevdvunnen. — **-familiar** ['oᵘldfə'miljə] gammelkjent. — **-fangled** ['oᵘld'fäŋgld]. — **-fashioned** [-'fäʃənd] gammeldags. — **-fogeyism** [-'foᵘgiizm] stokkkonservatisme. **oldish** ['oᵘdiʃ] gammelaktig, aldrende. **oldness** ['oᵘldnés] elde, alderdom. **oldster** ['oᵘldstə] eldre, veteran. **old|-time** ['oᵘldtaim] gammeldags, gammel. — **-timer** veteran. — **-womanish** ['oᵘld'wuməniʃ] kjerringaktig. — **-world** ['oᵘldwə·ld] fra gammel tid, gammel.

oleander [oᵘli'ändə] oleander, nerium. **oleiferous** [oᵘli'ifərəs] oljeførende. **oleomargarine** [oᵘlio°ma·ᵈdʒə'ri·n] margarin. **olfactory** [ål'fäktəri] luktesans, lukte-. **oligarch** ['åliga·ᵒk] oligark, oligarchy ['åliga·ᵒki] oligarki, fåmannsstyre. **olio** ['oᵘlioᵘ] lapskaus, ruskomsnusk, blanding. **olive** ['åliv] oliventre, oljetre. **-branch** olivengrein, oljegrein; fredssymbol; i pl. (til dels) barn. **-oil** olivenolje. **Olive** ['åliv] Olivia. **olived** ['ålivd] prydd med oljetrær. **Oliver** ['ålivə] Oliver. **Olivia** [o'livjə] Olivia. **Olympia** [o'limpiə] Olympia. **olympiad** [-piäd] olympiade. **Olympian** [-pjən] olympisk. **Olympic** [o'limpik] olympisk; — **games** olympiske leiker. **Olympus** [-pəs] Olymp.

O. M. fk. f. Order of Merit.

ombre ['åmbə] l'hombre.

omega ['oumigə] omega.

omelet ['åmlèt] omelett, eggekake; savoury — omelett med urter; make — without breaking eggs nå sitt mål uten å benytte midlene.

omen ['oumen] omen, varsel; varsle (om).

ominous ['åminəs] varslende, varsels-; illevarslende, illespående, uhellsvanger, nifs.

omissible [o'misibl] som kan unnlates,· som kan utelates.

omission [o'miʃən] unnlatelse, utelatelse, forsømmelse; sins of — unnlatelsessynd.

omit [o'mit] unnlate, forsømme; utelate, springe over, glemme; — to lock the door glemme å låse døra; omittance [o'mitəns] unnlatelse.

omnibus ['åmnibəs] omnibus, rutebil.

omnifarious [åmni'fæ·əriəs] av alle slags, ymse.

omnipotence [åm'nipotəns] allmakt.

omnipotent [åm'nipotənt] allmektig.

omnipresence [åmni'prezəns] allestedsnærværelse. omnipresent [-zənt] allestedsnærværende.

omniscience [åm'niʃ(i)əns] allvitenhet. omniscient [-ʃ(i)ənt] allvitende.

omnium gatherum ['åmniəm'gäðərəm] sammensurium, broket blanding.

omnivorous [åm'nivərəs] altetende.

omphalos ['åmfələs] navle; skjoldknapp; midtpunkt.

on [ån] på; om; over; ved; videre, framover, tett innpå; (om tid) straks etterpå, ved, på, om; — the earth på jorden; — earth i all verden; — foot til fots; — hand på hånden, på lager; I lay — the red jeg holder på rødt; — her arrival ved hennes ankomst; — the first of April den første april; — Friday fredag var, om fredagen, på fredag; — Friday next på fredag; — Friday last fredag var; — this occasion ved denne leilighet, ved dette høve; — a sudden plutselig, uventet, brått; live — bread and cheese leve av brød og ost; — business i forretninger; act — principle handle etter faste prinsipper; — purpose med forsett, med vilje; he is sweet — her han er forelsket i henne; — my word på mitt ord; — the whole i det hele tatt, egentlig; be — fire være i brann; discourse — avhandling om; I am — la gå; he is neither — nor off han vet ikke hva han selv vil; read — lese videre; get — gjøre framskritt; lead — gå i forveien; and so — og så videre; on to (også onto) (opp eller ned, over, ut, inn) på; — reaching the river da han nådde elva.

O. N. fk. f. Old Norse.

onager ['ånədʒə] vill-asen.

onanism ['ounənizm] onani.

once [wʌns] en gang; engang; en eneste gang; at — straks; på én gang (samtidig); all at — med ett, plutselig; — upon a time there was a king det var en gang en konge; — more en gang til, enda en gang; — again en gang til; enda en gang; — and again gjentatte ganger; for — for en gangs skyld, unntagelsesvis; this — denne gang; — for all en gang for alle; — or twice et par ganger; — he was roused no one could stop him når han først var blitt tirret, kunne ingen stanse ham.

oncome ['ånkʌm] nedbør, regn, snøfall, snøkave; begynnelse; tur; utbrudd. oncoming ['ånkʌmiŋ] som nærmer seg, som er i anmarsj.

oncost ['ånkåst] utgift, ekstrautgift.

on-dit [ån'di·] rykte, forlydende.

one [wʌn] én, ett, eneste; en, noen, man; — another hverandre; — and all alle og enhver, alle som én; you're — too many for me du er meg overlegen; — fine morning en vakker dag; a large dog and a little — en stor hund en liten; little -s de små, barn; it is all — to me det er ganske det samme for meg, det er meg likegyldig; go — by — gå en for en; be at — with være enig med; make — of the party være med; like — o'clock så det står etter.

O'Neal [ou'ni·l] O'Neal.

one-eyed ['wʌn'aid] enøyd; (sl.) ubillig.

one-horse ['wʌn'hå·s] enspenner.

O'Neil(l) [ou'ni·l] O'Neil(l).

one-legged ['wʌn'legd] med ett bein.

oneness ['wʌnnès] enhet.

oner ['wʌnə] ener; avgjørende slag; a — en kløpper, kjernekar, grepa kar.

onerous ['ånərəs] byrdefull, besværlig, tung.

oneself [wʌn'self] seg, seg selv, selv, en selv; of — av seg selv; to do right — is the great thing det viktigste er at en selv gjør det som er rett.

onesided ['wʌnsaidid] ensidig.

one's self = oneself.

onfall ['ånfå·l] angrep, åtak.

ongoing ['ångou̇iŋ] framgang; (i pl.) framferd, atferd; hendinger.

onion ['ånjən] løk, lauk; rødløk; vinterløk.

onlooker ['ånlukə] tilskuer. onlooking som står og ser på.

only ['ounli] 1. adj.: eneste. 2. adv.: kun, blott, bare, alene; først, ikke før, ennå, ikke lenger siden enn. 3. konjunksjon: unntagen å, bare å. Eksempler: 1. adj.: an only child et eneste barn; the only instances de eneste eksempler; only bill solaveksel. 2. adv.: only you can guess it. you only can guess bare du kan gjette; you can only guess du kan bare gjette (ikke gjøre annet); I not only heard it, but saw it jeg ikke bare hørte det, jeg så det; if only hvis bare, gid; he came only yesterday han kom først i går. 3. konjunksjon: he makes good resolutions, only that he never keeps them han tar gode beslutninger; det er bare det at han aldri holder dem.

onomatopoetic[ånomätopou'etik]onomatopoietisk, lydbetegnende.

onrush ['ånrʌʃ] framstøt.

onset ['ånset] angrep, anfall.

onslaught ['ånslå·t] anfall, stormløp.

onto ['ʌntu, -tə] på, opp på, bort på.

ontology [ån'tålədʒi] ontologi, læren om tingenes vesen.

onus ['ounəs] byrde, plikt, ansvar, skyldnad.

onward ['ånwəd] fram, framover, fremad; fremadgående, fremrykket. onwards ['ånwəd(z)] fram, framover, videre fram.

onyx ['åniks, 'ouniks] onyks (agat med forskjelligfargede lag).

oof [u·f] (sl.) penger, mynt, gryn.

ooze [u·z] sige; sive igjennom, flyte tregt, piple fram, tyte; evje, mørje, dy, slam, mudder; garverlut; the secret -d out hemmeligheten sivet ut.

oozy ['u·zi] mudret, dyndet.

O. P. fk. f. opposite prompt side.

o. p. fk. f. out of print; overproof.

op. fk. f. opus.

opacity [o'päsiti] ugjennomsiktighet.

opal ['oupəl] opal (edelstein med et sterkt spill av regnbuefarger). opalesce [oupə'les] spille i regnbuefarger. opalescence [oupə'lesəns] fargespill. opalescent [-ənt] som spiller i regnbuefarger.

opaque [o'pe·k] ugjennomsiktig.

ope [oup] åpne; åpen.

open ['oupn] åpen, rom, grissen; utbredt, fri, udekt, ubeskyttet, utsatt; åpenbar, klar, øyensynlig; fritt uttalt; ikke avgjort, åpenstående; — question et åpent spørsmål; — verdict jurys uttalelse at de ikke er kommet til et enig resultat; keep — house holde åpent hus, være gjestfri; in the — air i fri luft; I am — to jeg er tilbøyelig til; in the — om dagen, på åpne marka, under åpen himmel.

open ['oupn] åpne, lukke opp, vide ut, begynne, åpenbare, fortolke, forklare; åpnes, åpne seg, begynne; springe ut; — a credit åpne en kreditt; the exchange -ed very flat børsen åpnet meget flaut. — on vende ut til; — out on vende ut til; — up åpne tilgjengelig.

open-air ['oupn'æ·ə] ute-, frilufts-; — games friluftsleiker; — theatre friluftsteater; — treatment luftkur.

opener ['oᵘpnə] en som åpner, innleder.
open|-eyed ['oᵘpn'aid] med åpne øyne, vak, årvåken, årvak; — **-handed** rundhåndet, gavmild, raust; — **-hearted** åpenhjertig, åpen, grei.
opening ['oᵘpniŋ] åpnings-, begynnelses-; første; åpning, glugg, hull; glenne; sjanse, lovende mulighet, god anledning, utvei, råd.
open-mouthed ['oᵘpn'mauðd] med åpen munn; flåkjeftet. **openness** ['oᵘpnnès] åpenhet. **openwork** gjennombrutt arbeid.
opera ['åpərə] verker; opera. — **-cloak** teaterkåpe, slags lett aftenkåpe. — **-girl** ballettdansernne — **-glass** teaterkikkert. — **-hat** chapeau claque. — **-house** opera, operabygning.
operate ['åpəre't] virke; operere; bevirke; drive, sette i gang; betjene (en maskin); — **on him** operere ham; — **a typewriter** skrive på skrivemaskin.
operatic [åpə'rätik] opera-.
operation [åpə're'ʃən] virksomhet, operasjon, drift, gang; utførelse, virkning; framgangsmåte; **the act comes into** — **this day** loven trer i kraft i dag; **watch his -s** holde øye med hva han foretar seg; **perform an** — utføre en operasjon; **undergo an** — underkaste seg en operasjon; la seg operere.
operative ['åp(ə)rətiv] virkende, virksom; kraftig; praktisk, utøvende; arbeider, svenn; håndverker. **operator** ['åpəre'tə] virkende; virkemiddel; operatør; spekulant; telegrafist, telefonist.
operculum [o'pə·kjuləm] lokk, gjellelokk.
operetta [åpə'retə] operette.
operose ['åpəroᵘs] besværlig, tung.
Ophelia [o'fi·ljə] Ofelia.
ophthalmia [åf'bålmiə; åp-] øyenbetennelse.
ophthalmic [åf'bålmik; åp-] øyen-. **ophthalmologist** [åfbäl'målədʒist] øyenlæge. **ophthalmology** [-'målədʒi] oftalmologi. **ophthalmy** [åf'bälmi; åp-] øyenbetennelse.
opiate ['oᵘpjét] sovemiddel. **opiated** ['oᵘpie'tid] opiumholdig; bedøvet med opium.
opine [o'pain] holde for, mene.
opinion [ə'pinjən, o-] mening; skjønn, syn; god mening, anskuelse; rykte, godt navn, vørnad; **if I were to give my real** — hvis jeg skulle uttale min virkelige mening; **in my** — etter min mening; **it is a matter of** — det er en skjønnssak; **public** — offentlige mening; **received** — alminnelig antatt mening; **be of** — være av den mening, mene; **I have no** — of jeg nærer ikke høye tanker om. **opinionated** [o'pinjəne'tid] påståelig, stri.
opinioned [o'pinjənd] stivsinnet; innbilsk. **opinionist** [o'pinjənist] stivsinnet menneske.
opium ['oᵘpjəm] opium. — **-eater** opiumsspiser. — **-master** opiumsvert. — **-poppy** opiumsvalmue.
opossum [o'påsəm] opossum, virginsk pungrotte; **play** — (eller **possum**) forstille seg, ligge død.
oppidan ['åpidən] elev i Eton, som bor utenfor skolen, skolesøkende elev.
opponent [å'poᵘnənt] motstander, motmann.
opportune ['åpatju·n] betimelig, beleilig, høvelig, opportun. **opportunism** ['åpatju·nizm] opportunisme. **opportunist** ['åpatju·nist] opportunist.
opportunity [åpə'tju·niti] (gunstig) leilighet, el. høve; beleilig tid; **at the first** — ved første leilighet; **I have little** — of speaking English jeg har bare liten anledning til å snakke engelsk; **take** el. **seize the** — gripe leiligheten, nytte høvet; **miss** (el. **lose**) **the** — la leiligheten gå fra seg.
opposable [å'poᵘzəbl] motvirkende, som kan stilles imot, som kan anføres imot.
oppose [ə'poᵘz, å-] sette imot, stille imot; motstå, gjøre motstand mot, bekjempe, gjøre motmæle; motsette seg, gjøre innvendinger, opponere; **several members -d the bill** atskillige medlemmer bekjempet lovforslaget. **opposed** [-d] motstilt, motsatt, stridende, fiendtlig.
opposer [ə'poᵘzə, å-] fiende, motstander, opponent. **opposing** [ə'poᵘziŋ, å-] motsatt, stridende.

opposite ['åpəzit] motsatt, som ligger bent overfor, på den motsatte side; overfor; motsetning; **on the** — **side of the river** på den andre siden av elva; — **angles** toppvinkler.
opposition [åpə'ziʃən] motstand; det å stå bent overfor; strid, motstrid; motsetningsforhold, opposisjon; motparti, opposisjonsparti; motpart; motforslag; **start an** — **shop** åpne en konkurrerende forretning; **make** — gjøre motstand; drive opposisjon.
oppositionist [åpə'ziʃənist] opposisjonsmann.
oppress [ə'pres, å-] trykke, trykke ned, tynge på, undertrykke, trælke, overvelde. **oppression** [ə'preʃən, å-] trykk, undertrykkelse; fortrykthet, nedtrykthet, tyngsel.
oppressive [ə'presiv, å-] trykkende, hard, tung; **the air is very** — luften er meget trykkende.
oppressor [ə'presə, å-] undertrykker.
opprobrious [ə'proᵘbriəs] forsmedelig, vanærende; skammelig; æreløs, vanæret. **opprobrium** [ə'proᵘbriəm] vanære, skam, ukvemsord.
oppugn [å'pju·n] bekjempe; angripe; reise tvil om.
opt [åpt] velge; — **for** velge.
optative ['åptətiv] optativ, ønske-, som uttrykker et ønske.
optic ['åptik] syns-, optisk; synsorgan, øye. **optician** [åp'tiʃən] optiker, instrumentmaker. **optics** ['åptiks] optikk (læren om lyset).
optimates [åpti'me'ti·z] optimater, stormenn, aristokrati. **optime** ['åptimi] (ved Cambridge universitet) en som går i annen klasse (**senior optime**) eller tredje klasse (**junior optime**), mots. **wrangler. optimism** ['åptimizm] optimisme. **optimist** ['åptimist] optimist. **optimistic** [åpti'mistik] optimistisk. **optimize** ['åptimaiz] være optimist.
option ['åpʃən] valg, valgrett; ønske; kallsrett; opsjon; **it is at your** — to do the one or the other det står deg fritt å gjøre det ene eller det andre; **if he had been allowed an** — hvis han hadde fått valget; **at** — etter eget valg. **optional** ['åpʃənəl] overlatt til ens valg; valgfri; frivillig.
opulence ['åpjuləns] velstand, rikdom. **opulent** [-lənt] velstående, rik.
opus ['oᵘpəs] opus, arbeid, verk.
opuscle [o'pʌsl], **opuscule** [o'pʌskjul], **opusculum** [-kjuləm] opuskel, mindre arbeid, verk.
or [å·ə, å] eller; ellers; **white or black** hvit eller svart; **either white or black** enten hvit eller svart; **one or two** en å to; **two or three to—tre**; make haste, or you will be late skynd deg, ellers kommer du for sent.
or [å·ə] gull; gull-.
O. R. fk. f. **Orderly Room.**
oracle ['årəkl, 'årikl] orakel, orakelsvar; gi orakelsvar, tale i gåter. **oracular** [o'räkjulə] orakelmessig, gåtefull.
oral ['å·rəl] muntlig.
orang [o'räŋ] orangutang.
Orange ['årin(d)ʒ] Orania; **the House of** — huset Orania; — **River** Oranjeelva; — **Free State** Oranje-Fristaten.
orange ['årin(d)ʒ] orange, pommerans, appelsin, appelsintre; appelsinfarget, orange. **orangeade** ['årin'dʒe'd] appelsinsaft.
orange|-blossom ['årin(d)ʒbläsəm] orangeblomst; orangeblomster (som bruden pyntes med til bryllup liksom hos oss med myrt). **-coloured** orangegul.
Orangeman ['årindʒmən] orangist (medlem av et protestantisk selskap i Irland).
orange-man ['årindʒmən] appelsinhandler.
orange-peel ['årindʒpi·l] appelsinskall.
orangery ['årindʒəri] orangeri.
orange-tree ['årin(d)ʒtri·] orangetre.
Orangist ['årin(d)ʒist] se **Orangeman.**
orang-outang [o'räŋu·täŋ], **orang-outan** [-tän] orangutang.
orate [å're't] holde tale(r), tale. **oration** [o're'ʃən] tale. **orator** ['årətə] taler. **oratorical** [årə'tårikl]

oratorisk, taler-. **oratorio** [årə'tå·rioᵘ] oratorium, slags bibelsk musikkdrama. **oratory** ['årətəri] talekunst, veltalenhet, svada; bedekammer, bedehus.

orb [å·ᵊb] klode, kule, runding, sfære; krets, hjul, ring, sirkel; himmellegeme; øye; kretsløp, kretsbane, periode; omringe, omkranse, omgi; **the bright -s of heaven** de strålende himmellegemer. **orbed** [å·ᵊbd] klodeformig, kuleformet; ringformet, rund, kuledannet; måneformet. **orb -fish** pinnsvinfisk. **orbicular** [å·ᵊ'bikjulə], **orbiculate** [å·ᵊ'bikjulėt] = **orbed**.

orbit ['å·ᵊbit] bane. **orbital** ['å·ᵊbitəl] bane-. **orc** [å·ᵊk] spekkhogger, staurhval, staurhynning.

Orcades ['å·ᵊkədi·z] Orknøyane. **Orcadian** [å·ᵊ'ke'djən] orknøyisk; orknøying.

orchard ['å·ᵊtʃəd] frukthage, hage. — **-grass** hundegras. — **-house** drivhus til frukttrær. **orcharding** [-iŋ] fruktavl. **orchardist** [-ist] fruktavler.

orchestra ['å·ᵊkistrə] orkester; musikktribune. **orchestral** [å·ᵊ'kestrəl] orkester-. **orchestrate** ['å·ᵊkistre't] instrumentere. **orchestration** [å·ᵊki-'stre'ʃən] instrumentering.

orchestrion [å·ᵊ'kestriən] spilledåse.

orchid ['å·ᵊkid] orkidé (plante av marihåndfamilien). **orchis** ['å·ᵊkis] marihånd.

ordain [å·ᵊ'de'n] ordne, innrette, forordne, fastsette, bestemme; beskikke, ordinere, prestevie. **ordainable** [å·ᵊ'de'nəbl] som kan ordnes, ordineres. **ordainer** [å·ᵊ'de'nə] som ordner, bestemmer; en som innsetter, ordinant. **ordainment** [å·ᵊ'de'nmənt] ordning, anordning, bestemmelse; ordinasjon.

ordeal [å·ᵊ'diəl, -'di·l] gudsdom, uskyldsprøve, prøve; ildprøve, prøvelse; — **by fire** ildprøve, jernbyrd; — **by water** vannprøve; — **of the bier** båreprøve; — **of the combat** gudsdom ved tvekamp.

order ['å·ᵊdə] orden, ro; skikk; ordning, anordning, rekkefølge, oppstilling; stand, rang, klasse, lag; ordenstegn; anvisning, forskrift, befaling; ordre, bestilling, tinging; fribillett, adgangskort; anvisning til utbetaling; postanvisning (også: **money-order, postal order, post-office-order**); **out of** — i uorden, i ulag, ufullkommen; upasselig; **the higher -s of society** samfunnets øverste klasser; **be in (holy) -s** tilhøre den geistlige stand; **take -s** inntre i den geistlige stand; **bli ordinert**; — **of the day** dagsbefaling; **marching** — marsjordre; **in** — **that, in** — to for at; for å; **get out of** — komme i uorden; **to** — etter bestilling; **call to** — kalle til orden.

order ['å·ᵊdə] ordne, bestemme, befale; forordne, ordinere; bestille, tinge, foreskrive; — **about** kommandere hit og dit; — **the coach la** vognen spenne for, kjøre fram; bestille vognen; — **away** sende bort.

order-book ['å·ᵊdəbuk] ordrebok. **orderer** ['å·ᵊdərə] ordner, styrer; befalende. **order-form** bestillingsblankett. **ordering** ['å·ᵊdəriŋ] ordning, anordning; bestyrelse. **orderless** ['å·ᵊdəlės] uordentlig; mot reglene.

orderliness ['å·ᵊdəlinės] orden. **orderly** ['å·ᵊdəli] ordentlig, velstelt, grei, stille, rolig; tjenstgjørende; ordonnans; gatefeier. — **-man** ordonnans. — **-officer** jourhavende offiser. — **-room** kompanikontor. — **-sergeant** ordonnans.

ordinal ['å·ᵊdinəl] ordens-, ordenstall. **ordinance** ['å·ᵊdinəns] forordning, bestemmelse, anordning; kirkeskikk.

ordinary ['å·ᵊdinəri] ordinær, ordentlig, regelmessig, regelrett, fast; alminnelig, vanlig, sedvanlig; tarvelig, simpel, ubetydelig, middelmådig; ordinær dommer; middagsstevne, spisekvarter, table-d'hote; en slags heraldisk figur; **in** — ordinær, ordentlig, regelmessig, hoff-, liv- (motsatt: extraordinary, tilkalt, eller honorary, titu-

lær); **physician in** — **to the King** kongens livlæge; **ambassador in** — ordentlig gesandt; **chaplain in** — hoffpredikant; **professor in** — professor ordinarius; **in** — **life** til dagiig; — **sailor** (el. **seaman**) lettmatros, jungmann, halvbefaren matros. — **-looking** ubetydelig (tarvelig) utseende. — **-sized** av alminnelig størrelse.

ordinate ['å·ᵊdinėt] ordinat; ordentlig, regelmessig. **ordination** [å·ᵊdi'ne'ʃən] ordning; anordning; prestevielse.

ordnance ['å·ᵊdnəns] svært skyts, artilleri; **a piece of** — kanon. — **-map** generalstabskart. — **-office** tøyhusdepartement. — **-survey** [-'sə·ve¹] geografisk oppmåling. **master-general of the** — generalfelttøymester.

ordonnance ['å·ᵊdənəns] fordeling, disposisjon.

ordure ['å·ᵊdjuə] skarn, smuss, lort. **ore** [å·ᵊ] erts, malm; metall. **ore-weed** ['å·ᵊwi·d] blæretang.

organ ['å·ᵊgən] organ; orgel; lirekasse; **the** Protectionist **-s** proteksjonistiske blad; **American** (el. **cottage**)· — amerikansk stueorgel (el. harmonium); **barrel** — lirekasse. — **-blower** belgetreder. — **-builder** orgelbygger. — **-grinder** lirekassemann.

organdy ['å·ᵊgəndi] organdi, musselin. **organic** [å·ᵊ'gänik] organisk. **organism** ['å·ᵊgə-nizm] organisme. **organ** [-nist] organist. **organization** [å·ᵊgən(a)i'ze'ʃən] organisasjon, organisme. **organize** ['å·ᵊgənaiz] organisere; innrette, bygge. **organizer** ['å·ᵊgənaizə] organisator. **organ-pipe** orgelpipe.

orgasm ['å·ᵊgäzm] orgasme; heftig bevegelse; opprør.

orgiastic [å·ᵊdʒi'ästik] orgiastisk, vill. **orgy** ['å·ᵊdʒi] orgie, vilt svirelag. **oriel** ['å·ᵊriəl] karnapp, karnappvindu. **Orient** ['å·ᵊriənt]; **the** — Østen, Orienten. **orient** ['å·ᵊriənt] oppstående, østlig; østerlandsk; strålende; vende mot øst; orientere. **oriental** [å·ri'entəl] østlig, østerlandsk,orientalsk. **Oriental** orientaler, østerlender. **orientalism** [å·ri'entəlizm] orientalisme. **orientalist** [-list] orientalist. **orientate** ['åriənte't] orientere. **orientation** [å·rien'te'ʃən] orientering. **orientator** ['å·riente'tə] orienteringsinstrument.

orifice ['å·ᵊrifis] munning, åpning, munn.

orig. fk. f. original.

origin ['å·ᵊridʒin] opprinnelse, herkomst, opphav; **certificate of** — opprinnelsesbevis.

original [ə'ridʒinəl] opprinnelig, opphavlig, original; første; ekte; original, originalverk; grunnspråk; type; særling; — **sin** arvesynd; **the** — **text** grunnteksten. **originality** [əridʒi'näliti] originalitet.

originally opprinnelig, opphavlig, fra først av.
originate [ə'ridʒine't] grunnlegge, skape, være skaperen av; gi anledning til, oppstå, begynne, komme fra. **origination** [əridʒi'ne'ʃən] skapelse, oppkomst, opprinnelse, opphav, framkomst. **originative** [ə'ridʒinətiv] skapende, oppfinnsom. **originator** [ə'ridʒine'tə] skaper, opphav; forslagstiller.

oriole ['å·rioᵘl] pirol, gullpirol. **Orion** [o'raiən] Orion. **orison** ['å·rizən] (gml.) bønn. **Orkney** ['å·ᵊkni] Orknøyene. **Orleanist** ['å·ᵊ'liənist] orleansk; orleanist. **Orleans** ['å·ᵊliənz, -li·nz] Orleans. **orleans** kjoletøy av ull og bomull.

orlop ['å·ᵊlåp] banjerdekk (undre dekk på orlogsskip).

ormolu ['å·ᵊmolu·] gullbronse (en gull-lignende legering).

ornament ['å·ᵊnəmənt] prydelse, smykke, krot, ornament; pryd; pryde, smykke, utsmykke, krote, dekorere.

ornamental [å·ᵊnə'mentəl] ornamental, dekorativ, som tjener til pryd; — **painter** dekorasjonsmaler.

ornamentation [å·ºnəmən'te¹ʃən] utsmykking, dekorasjon, pynt.
ornate [å·º¹ne¹t; 'å·º-] utsmykket, pyntet. orateness [-nès] pryd, stas.
ornithological [å·ºniho'lådʒikl] ornitologisk.
ornithologist [å·ºni'bålədʒist] ornitolog, fuglekjenner. ornithology [-dʒi] læren om fuglene.
orotund ['årátund] svulmende, pompøs, stortalende, bombastisk.
orphan ['å·ºfən] foreldreløs, foreldreløst barn; gjøre foreldreløs, dø fra. orphanage ['å·ºfənidʒ] foreldreløshet; vaisenhus. orphanhood ['å·ºfənhud] foreldreløshet.
Orpheus ['å·ºfju·s] Orfeus.
orpin(e) ['å·ºpin] smørbukk (plante).
orra ['årə] (skotsk) overflødig; tilfeldig.
orris [åris] sverdlilje; fiolrot.
orthodox ['å·ºþədåks] ortodoks, rettroende.
orthodoxy ['å·ºþədåksi] rettroenhet.
orthographer [å·º¹þågrəfə] ortograf, rettskriver.
orthographic ['å·ºþo'gräfik] ortografisk.
orthographical ['å·ºþo'gräfikəl] ortografisk.
orthographist [å·º¹þågrəfist] rettskriver.
orthography [å·º¹þågrəfi] rettskrivning.
orthopædy ['å·ºþəpi·di] ortopedi.
ortolan ['å·ºtələn] hortulan (fugl).
os [ås] bein, knokkel.
O. S. fk. f. old stvle; ordinary seaman.
O. S. A. fk. f. of the Order of St. Augustine.
O. S. B. fk. f. of the Order of St. Benedict.
oscillancy ['åsilənsi] svingninger fram og tilbake. oscillate ['åsile¹t] svinge. oscillation [åsi-'le¹ʃən] oscillasjon, svingning. oscillatory ['åsilətəri] svingende, skiftende.
osculant ['åskjulənt] tett sammenhengende, umiddelbart mellomliggende. osculate ['åskjule¹t] kysse. osculation [åskju'le¹ʃən] berøring; kyssing. osculatory ['åskjulətəri] kysse-. oscule ['åskjul] liten munn; sugemunn.
osier ['o⁴ʒə] vidje, pil. — -basket vidjekurv. — -bed pilplantning. — -bottle kurvflaske. osiered ['o⁴ʒəd] dekt med vidjekratt. osierholt ['o⁴ʒəho⁴lt] vidjekratt. osiery ['o⁴ʒəri] vidjeskog; kurvarbeid.
Osiris [o'sairis] Osiris.
osmosis [åz'mo⁴sis] osmose.
ospray, osprey ['åspri] fiskejo, fiskeørn.
ossein ['åsiin] beinvev, beinbrusk.
osselet ['åsilet] beinutvekst.
Ossian ['åʃ(i)ən] Ossian.
ossicle ['åsikl] lite bein, småbein. ossific [å'sifik] forbenende. ossification [åsifi'ke¹ʃən] beindannelse. ossify ['åsifai] forbene; forbenes. ossuary ['åsjuəri] beinhus.
ostensibility [ostensi'biliti] påviselighet, sannsynlighet. ostensible [o'stensibl] iøynefallende, synlig; sannsynlig; erklært. ostensive [o'stensiv] påvisende; prunkende. ostentation [åsten'te¹ʃən] det å stille til skue, framsyning, praling, praleri. ostentatious [åsten'te¹ʃəs] brammende, pralende.
osteology [åsti'ålədʒi] osteologi.
ostiary ['åstiəri] dørvokter.
ostium ['åstiəm] elvemunning, os.
ostler ['åslə] stallkar, stallgutt.
ostracism ['åstrəsizm] ostrakisme, forvisning ved folkeavstemning i det gamle Aten.
ostracize ['åstrəsaiz] forvise.
ostreaceous [åstri'e¹ʃəs] østersaktig.
ostrich ['åstridʒ, -itʒ] struts. — -feather strutsefjær.
O. T. fk. f. Old Testament.
O. T. C. fk. f. Officers' Training Corps.
Othello [o⁴'belo⁴] Othello.
other ['ʌðə] annen, annet, andre; the — day forleden dag, her om dagen. give me some book or — gi meg en eller annen bok; every — day hver annen dag; on the — hand på den annen side, derimot; the — place helvete; (i parlamentsspråk): det andre huset; no — than ingen annen enn, ikke annerledes enn; on the — side på den

andre siden, omstående; if he doesn't like it he may do the — thing hvis han ikke liker det, kan han la være; of all -s framfor alle; somehow or — på den ene eller andre måten.
otherwise ['ʌðəwaiz] annerledes, på annen måte; ellers, i motsatt fall; alias, også kalt; unless you are — engaged hvis De ikke er opptatt; such as think — annerledes tenkende; rather than — helst; nærmest.
otherworldly ['ʌðə'wə·ldli] overjordisk.
Otho ['o⁴þo⁴] Otho; Otto.
otiose ['o⁴ʃio⁴s] ledig, lat, ørkesløs. otiosity [o⁴ʃi'åsiti] dovenskap. otium ['o⁴ʃiəm] fritid.
Ottawa ['åtəwə] Ottawa.
otter ['åtə] oter.
Ottoman ['åtomən] osmansk, tyrkisk; osman; tyrk: ottoman, slags løvbenk.
O. U. fk. f. Oxford University.
O. U. A. C. fk. f. Oxford University Athletic Club.
O. U. A. F. C. fk. f. Oxford University Association Football Club.
O. U. B. C. fk. f. Oxford University Boat Club.
oubliette [u·bli'et] (gml.) oubliette, hemmelig fengsel.
Oudhe [aud] Oudh, provins i Forindia.
ought [å·t] noe d. s. s. aught.
ought [å·t] bør, burde; you — to do it du burde gjøre det; those who — to know it folk som absolutt må kjenne til det.
Ouida ['wi·də] Ouida.
ounce [auns] unse (28.35 gram i alm. handelsvekt, 31.10 gram i apotekervekt).
ounce [auns] snøleopard; (gml.) gaupe.
our [auə] (attributivt) vår, vårt, våre.
ours [auəz] (substantivisk) vår, vårt, våre; a friend of — en venn av oss.
ourself [auə'self] (pluralis majestatis) vi selv, oss selv, oss.
ourselves [auə'selvz] oss selv, vi selv, vi, oss selv.
oust [aust] fjerne; drive ut, jage bort.
ouster ['austə] utkasting, utsetting.
out [aut] ute, ut, utenfor; you must have been — very late du må ha kommet meget sent hjem; on our way — på veien ut; he turned his cap inside — han vendte foret ut på lua si; right — like ut; be — ikke lenger være medlem av regjeringen, være ute av spillet; være sloppet opp; you are — there der tar du feil; my dream is — min drøm er gått i oppfyllelse; the moon is — det er måneskinn; the last novel — den nyeste roman; she is (come) — hun er innført i selskapslivet; the murder is — mordet er oppdaget; the fire is — varmen er sloknet; — at the elbows med hull på albuene; read — lese høyt; be — of cash være pengelens; — of breath åndeløs, andpusten; time — of mind fra uminnelige tider; — of print utsolgt fra forlaget; — of the ordinary utenfor det vanlige; — upon him fy! han burde skamme seg. out [aut] ta ut, ta fram, komme fram med; overvinne.
out-act [aut'äkt] overgå, ta luven fra.
out-and-out ['autand'aut] helt igjennom, ut og inn, i alle henseender; grundig, gjennomført; durkdreven; ubetinget, absolutt, ekte; fullstendig; an — Yankee en fullblods Yankee.
out-and-outer ['autand'autə] en som gjør tingene grundig, storartet fyr; grepa kar.
out'balance [aut'bålans] veie mer enn. -bid [aut'bid] by over. -board ['autbå·ºd] utenbords. -bound ['autbaund] bestemt til utlandet, for utgående. -brag [-'bräg] døyve med (el. i) kyt. -brave [aut'bre¹v] overtrumfe; trosse. -break utbrudd, ri. -breathe puste ut; ta pusten fra. -bredding utsprettning, knapping. -building uthus(-bygning). -burst [-bə·st] utbrudd, ri. -cast ['autka·st] forstøtt. -class være av ved bedre slag; slå ut. -climb [-'klaim] klatre bedre enn. -come ['autkʌm] utslag, resultat. -crier ['autkraiə] utroper. -cry

skrik, rop, nødskrik; oppstyr. -distance [aut-'distəns] distansere, løpe fra. -do [-'du·] overgå; stikke ut. -door ['autdå·°] utendørs. -doors uten-dørs, utenfor huset, ute. -drink [-'driŋk] kunne drikke mer enn.

outer ['autə] ytre, ytter-; an — barrister en advokat som plederer utenfor skranken; his — man hans ytre, utseende. -most ['autəmo°st] ytterst.

out|face [aut'fe¹s] få til å slå øynene ned; se rett i øynene; trosse, trasse. -fall ['autfå·l] ut-løp, avløp. -field utmark, utbø. -fit ['autfit] ut-rustning, ekvipering, utstyr. -fitter ekviperings-handler. -fitting ekvipering, utrustning. -flank [aut'flæŋk] omgå. -flow ['autflo°] utstrømning. -fly [aut'flai] fly hurtigere enn, fly fra. -fly ['autflai] utflyvning; utbrudd. -foot [aut'fut] distansere. -giving [aut'giviŋ] beretning, forly-dende. -go ['autgo°] utgift, utlegg, utgifter. -goer ['autgo°ə] avgående, utgående. -going avgående, fratredende; avgang, fratredelse. -goings utlegg, utgifter. -grow [aut'gro°] overgå i vekst, vokse fra. -growth ['autgro°b] utvekst; (bil.) frukt, skudd. -guard ['autga·°d] forpost. -gush [aut'gʌʃ] strømme ut.

out-herod [aut'herəd] i forb. — Herod overgå Herodes i grusomhet; overdrive, gjøre altfor mye av.

outhouse ['authaus] uthus.

outing ['autiŋ] utgang, spasertur, tur; utflukt; rihet; 'fridag: ekspedisjon, tog.

outish ['autiʃ] lapset, pyntet, utstaffert.

out|jump [aut'dʒʌmp] hoppe bedre enn. — -jutting [-'dʒʌtin] utstikkende, framstående. -kneed ['autni·d] hjulbeint.

outlander ['autländə] utlending, fremmed.

outlandish [aut'ländiʃ] aparte, fremmedartet; underlig.

out|lash ['autläʃ] utbrudd. -last [aut'la·st] vare lenger enn. -laugh [-'la·f] le mer enn.

outlaw ['autlå·] fredløs, utleg. outlaw [aut'lå·] lyse utleg; gjøre fredløs. outlawry ['autlå·ri] fredløshet, utlegd.

outlay ['autle¹] utlegg, utgifter; legge ut. out|let ['autlet] utløp, avløp; marked, avset-ningssted. -lie ['autlai] utestående penger. -line ['autlain] omriss, kontur; tegne i omriss, gi omriss av. -live [aut'liv; 'aut'liv] overleve; leve bedre enn.

outlook ['autluk] utkik, utsikt; be on the — for være på utkik etter.

out|lying ['aut'laiin] som ligger utenfor, fjernt-liggende. -manoeuvre [autmə'nu·və] utmanøvrere, overliste. -march [-'ma·°tʃ] marsjere fra, distan-sere. -match [-'mätʃ] være . . . overlegen, over-treffe. -most ['autmo°st, -məst] ytterst. -number [aut'nʌmbə] være overlegen i antall.

out-of-date ['autəv'de¹t] umoderne, gammel-dags; ikke lenger gyldig.

out-of-door ['autəvdå·°] ... outdoor. out-of-the-way ['autə(v)ðə'we¹] avsides, avsidesliggende; usedvanlig. out-of-pocket ['autəv'på·kit] person-lig, av sin egen lomme. out-of-work ['autəv'wə·k] arbeidsløs.

outpace [aut'pe¹s] gå fortere enn, gå forbi.

outpatient ['autpe¹ʃənt] poliklinisk pasient.

out-pensioner ['autpenʃənə] pensjonær utenfor anstalten, kostganger.

out|play ['aut'ple¹] spille bedre enn, slå. -point [-'point] seile høyere opp i vinden. -port ['aut-på·°t] uthavn. -post ['autpo°st] utpost. -pour ['autpå·°] utgyting; flom, rikdom, fylde; la renne, la flomme. -put ['autput] produksjon, utbytte.

outrage ['autre¹dʒ, 'autridʒ] øve vold mot, voldta, forurette, fornærme, krenke; vold, grov forurettelse, fornærmelse, krenkelse; ondskap; voldshandling; voldtekt.

outrageous [aut're¹dʒəs] skjendig; grov, opp-rørende.

outraid ['autre¹d] tog, ekspedisjon.

outrange [aut're¹nʒ] gå, skyte lenger enn.

outrank [aut'räŋk] rangere over.

outré ['u·tre¹] outrert, overdreven.

out|reach [aut'ri·tʃ] strekke seg utover, nå lenger enn. -reign styre lenger enn. -relief fattig-hjelp til folk som ikke er på fattighus. -ride [aut'raid] ri fra. -ride ['autraid] utritt. -rider forrider. -rigger ['autrigə] utlegger; utriggerbåt (kapproningsbåt med tollegangene anbrakt på et stativ utabords. -right ['autrait] straks, på stedet, helt og holdent, fullstendig; he laughed -right han formelig lo. -rival [aut'raivl] ta luven fra, fordunkle, stille i skyggen. -run [aut'rʌn] løpe fra, løpe hurtigere enn; overgå. -sail [-'se¹l] seile fra. -score [-'skå·°] ta luven fra. -sell [-'sel] selge mer; selge til høyere priser. -set ['autset] oppbrudd, start, avreise; begynnelse; utgivelse; utkomst; medgift. — -settlement ['autsetlmənt] avsides koloni, utbygd. -shine [-'ʃain] overstråle.

outside ['aut'said] utvendig, ytterst, utenpå, ovenpå, på bukken, hos kusken; utvortes; ut-side, ytterside; utvendig passasjer; — and all med hud og hår; on the — utenpå, utenfor.

outsider ['aut'saidə] fremmed; utenforstående; uinnvigd.

out|sit [aut'sit] sitte lenger enn. -skirt ['aut-skə·t] grense, utkant, ytterkant; forpost; forstad. -sleep [aut'sli·p] sove lenger enn. -span ['aut-'spän] spenne fra; slå leir; ligge i leir. -speak [aut'spi·k] tale mer (el. høyere) enn. -spoken ['autspo°kn] frimodig, dristig; djerv, endefram. -spokenness frimodighet; djervhet. -spread [aut-'spred] utbrede, utspre. -stand [-'ständ] stå ut, stå fram; utebli. -standing framtredende; uav-gjort, utestående. -standing charges uoppgjorte poster. -stay [aut'ste¹] bli lenger enn, bli over tiden; holde ut lenger enn. -street forstadsgate. -strip [aut'strip] distansere. -talk [-'tå·k] bringe til taushet, tale i hjel. -turn ['auttə·n] utbytte, produksjon; losset mengde. -vie [aut'vai] overgå, overby. -vote ['aut'vo°t] overstemme. -walk [-'wå·k] gå fra. -wall ['autwå·l] yttermur.

outward ['autwəd] ytre, utvendig, utvortes, utgående; utad, utetter, ut; — bound for utgå-ende (om skip); — correspondence utgående enn; — passage utreise.

out|wear [aut'wä·°] slite ut; utholde; vare lenger enn. -weather [-'weðə] ri av, utholde. -weigh [-'we¹] veie mer enn; gjelde mer enn. -wit [-'wit] overliste. -work [-'wə·k] ta luven fra, arbeide bedre enn. -workman [-'wə·k] utenverk; utearbeid.

ouzel ['u·zl] ringtrost, fossekall, kvernkall.

ova ['o°və] egg (pl. av ovum).

oval ['o°vəl] eggformig, oval; oval plass.

ovary ['o°vəri] ovarie, eggstokk; fruktknute.

ovation [o°'ve¹ʃən] ovasjon, hyldest.

oven ['ʌvn] bakerovn, bakerovn, ovn; Dutch — en slags løs stekeovn.

oven-tender ['ʌvntendə] ovnpasser.

over ['o°və] over, utover; forbi, omme; till overs, tilbake, igjen; i koll, over ende; all — the world hele verden over; — the way på den andre siden av gata; — night natten igjennom; — and — igjen; twice — to ganger, om igjen; — and — gang gå gang; — against like overfor; — here herover; hit; — there der borte, derover; — and — again atter og atter; it is all — with him det er forbi med ham; talk it — drøfte; knock — velte.

over|abound [o°və'raund] finnes i stor meng-de. -act [o°və'räkt] overdrive, karikere. -acting ['o°və'räk-l(z)] arbeidsbluse, kit-tel; ytterbukser, ytterkjole. -arch [o°və'å·tʃ] hvelve seg over. -awe [o°və'rå·] skremme, impo-nere, holde i age. -bake [-'be¹k] steke for mye. -balance [-'bäləns] veie mer enn; bringe ut av likevekt, vippe opp. -balance ['o°və'bäləns] over-vekt, overskudd. -bear [-'bä·ə] overvelde, nedslå, overvinne. -bearing [-'bä·°riŋ] overveldende; anmassende; hovmodig. **-bearingness** [-nés] anmasselse, overmot. **-bid** [-'bid] by over. **-board** ['oᵘvəbå·ᵊd] overbord; utabords. **-boot** [-bu·t] botfor, snøsokk. **-bridge** [-bridʒ] overgangsbru. **-brim** renne over, flomme over. **-burden** [-'bə·dn] overlesse. **-burn** [-'bə·n] forbrenne. **-cast** [-'ka·st] formørke, overskye; overtrukken, overskyet; sy med kastesting; overvurdere. **-cautious** [-'kå·ʃəs] for forsiktig. **-charge** [-'tʃə·ᵊdʒ] overlesse; beregne for mye for, trekke opp. **-charge** ['oᵘvətʃə·ᵊdʒ] for stor byrde, for stort lass; overdrevent prisforlangende. **-cloud** [oᵘvə'klaud] skye over. **-coat** [-koᵘt] overfrakk, ytterfrakk, kappe. **-come** [oᵘvə'kʌm] overvinne, beseire, overvelde. **-confidence** ['oᵘvə'kånfidəns] overdreven (selv-)tillit. **-crow** [oᵘvə'kroᵘ] triumfere over. **-crowd** [-'kraud] overlesse; overfylle, fullstappe. **-do** [-'du·] gjøre for mye av; koke for mye; steke for mye; brenne for mye; overanstrenge. **-dose** ['oᵘvadoᵘs] for stor dosis. **-dose** ['oᵘvə'doᵘs] gi for stor dosis. **-draft** ['oᵘvədra·ft] for stor tratte; **a gigantic -draft upon his credulity** en for stor veksel å trekke på hans godtroenhet. **-draw** [oᵘvə'drå·] overtrekke, heve for mye (på en konto); overdrive. **-dress** [-'dres] overpynte, spjåke ut, overlesse; ['oᵘvədres] overkledning, overkjole; ['oᵘvə-'dres] overlessing med pynt. **-drive** [-'draiv] overanstrenge. **-due** [-'dju·] manglende; for lengst forfallen; forsinket, for sent ute. **-eat** [o·və'ri·t] forspise seg. **-eating** forspising. **-excited** [-ik'saitid] overopphisset; overspent. **-exhaustion** [-ig'zå·st-ʃən] overanstrengelse. **-fatigue** matte helt ut, sprenge. **-feed** [-'fi·d] fø for godt, gi for mye mat. **-flow** [-'floᵘ] flyte over; gå over sine bredder; oversvømme. **-flow** ['oᵘvəfloᵘ] oversvømmelse; overflod. **-flowing** [oᵘvə'floᵘiŋ] overflod. overmål. **-grow** [-'groᵘ] gro over, vokse over. **-grown** [-'groᵘn] overgrodd; oppløpen. **-hand** ['oᵘvəhänd] med håndflaten ned; **-hand bowling** overarmkasting (ɔ: med armen over skulderen) i cricket og baseball. **-hang** [oᵘvə'häŋ] henge ut over, rage opp over. **-hang** ['oᵘvəhäŋ] utheng. **-hanging** [-'häŋiŋ] hengende, lutende; framspringende; overhengende. **-haul** [oᵘvə'hå·l] overhale; etterse, mønstre nøye; seile opp, hale inn på. **-haul** ['oᵘvəhå·l] overhaling, ettersyn, mønstring. **-hauling** [-hå·liŋ] overhaling. **-head** [-'hed] over hodet, oppe, ovenpå; **heels -head** med beina i været. **-head charges** slike kostnader som skatter, leie, assuranse, gebyr osv. **-hear** [-'hiə] overhøre, høre (tilfeldig, ubemerket), komme til å høre; lytte til, utspionere. **-heat** [-'hi·t] overhete. **-indulgence** [oᵘvərin'dʌldʒəns] svakhet; overdreven nytelse. **-joyed** [-'dʒoid] overstadig glad. **-land** [oᵘvə'länd] til lands. **-lander** ['oᵘvələndə] en som reiser over land. **-lap** [oᵘvə'läp] delvis dekke, gripe over. **-lay** [-'lei] belegge, bedekke, overtrekke. **-leaf** [-'li·f] omstående. **-leap** [-'li·p] hoppe over. **-lie** [-'lai] ligge over; ligge i hjel. **-load** [-'loᵘd] overlesse. **-look** [-'luk] overskue, se over; gi utsikt over, dominere; se; se gjennom, gjennomgå; overse. **-looking** med utsikt over. **-man** ['oᵘvəmən] oppmann, voldgiftsmann; (arbeids-)formann. **-mantle** ['oᵘvəmäntl] kaminoppsats (dekorativ overdel). **-march** [-'ma·ᵊtʃ] overanstrenge ved marsj. **-match** [-'mätʃ] være for sterk for; overtreffe, overgå. **-match** ['oᵘvəmätʃ] mester. **-much** [oᵘvə'mʌtʃ] for mye. **overnight** ['oᵘvə'nait] natten over; kvelden før. **over|paint** [oᵘvə'peint] male med for sterke farger, sminke for mye. **-pass** [-'pa·s] overse, forbigå; overskride; gå over. **-pay** [-'pei] betale for mye; betale for mye for; mer enn oppveie. **-people** [-'pi·pl] overbefolke. **-pleased** ['oᵘvə-'pli·zd] altfor fornøyd; **not —** mellomfornøyd. **-plus** ['oᵘvəplʌs] overskudd. **-poise** ['oᵘvəpoiz] overvekt. **-polish** [-'påliʃ] polere for mye. **— -polite** ['oᵘvəpəlait] altfor forekommende. **-populousness** [-'påpjuləsnés] overbefolkning. **-pour** [-'på·ᵊ] strømme over. **-power** ['oᵘvə'pauə] over-

velde, overmanne; være overlegen over. **-rate** [-'reit] overvurdere; overbeskatte, ligne for høyt. **-reach** [-'ri·tʃ] strekke seg ut over; innhente; overvinne ved list, narre, bedra. **-rent** [-'rent] betale for høy leie; forlange for høy avgift. **-ride** [-'raid] ri for hardt, skamri; ri hurtigere enn, ri forbi; trampe ned; tilsidesette, sette seg ut over; underkjenne; vanvøre. **-right** ['oᵘvərait] like overfor, tvers over. **-roast** [-'roᵘst] steke for mye. **-rule** [-'ru·l] beherske, råde over; overstemme; underkjenne; herske, gå av med seieren. **-ruling** altstyrende. **-run** [-'rʌn] løpe forbi; gro over, bre seg over; oversvømme; strømme over. **-score** ['oᵘvə'skå·ᵊ] overstreke, overstryke. **-sea** [-'si·] oversjøisk; atlanterhavs-; over havet. **-seas** over havet; oversjøisk, på den andre siden av havet. **-season** [-'si·zn] krydre for sterkt. **-see** [-si·] ha tilsyn med, etterse, tilse. **-seer** [-'siə] oppsynsmann; en slags kommunal funksjonær (sognestyret velger to overseers og en assistant overseer, hvis arbeid bl. a. består i å ta seg av det kommunale skattevesen, men ikke mer av fattigvesenet, som er overlatt board of guardians). **— -set** [-'set] velte, rive over ende; omstyrte, kullkaste. **-set** ['oᵘvəset] velting; kullkasting. **-shade, -shadow** [-'ʃe'd], [-'ʃädoᵘ] overskygge, skygge for. **-shoe** ['oᵘvəʃu·] oversko; kalosje. **-shoot** [-'ʃu·t] skyte forbi; skyte over målet; **-shoot oneself** ta munnen for full. **-shot** drukken; **-shot wheel** overfallshjul. **-sight** ['oᵘvəsait] oppsyn, tilsyn; forglemmelse, uaktsomhet. **-sleep** ['sli·p] sove lenger enn: forsove seg, sove over **-spread** [-'spred] bre seg over, strekke seg over; utbre over. **-state** [-'steᵗt] angi for høyt; overdrive. **-stay** [-'steᵗ] bli lenger borte enn. **-step** [-'step] overskride. **-stock** [-'ståk] overfylle. **-store** [-'stå·ᵊ] forsyne for mye, overfylle. **-strain** [-'streᵗn] forstrekke seg, forløfte seg; overanstrenge. **-string** [-'striŋ] overspenne. **-subscribe** [oᵘvəsəb'skraib] overtegne (lån osv.).
overt ['oᵘvət] åpen; åpenlys, åpenbar; **letters —** åpent brev, patent.
over|take [oᵘvə'te·k] innhente, nå (ta) igjen; overraske, overrumple, komme over, gripe, klare. **-take** ['oᵘvəteᵗk] overraskelse, overrumpling. **-task** [-'ta·sk] overlesse, overanstrenge; stille for store krav til. **-throw** [-'broᵘ] kaste over ende, kaste i koll; kullkaste, ødelegge; styrte, kaste. **-throw** ['oᵘvəbroᵘ] kullkasting, omstyrting; styrting; undergang, fall. **-time** ['oᵘvətaim] overarbeid; ekstratid (over den fastsatte arbeidstid). **-top** [-'tåp] rage opp over; overgå; beseire. **-tower** ['-tauə] kneise over. **-trade** [-'tre'd] ruinere ved for stor handel; drive forretninger med for lite kapital; anskaffe for mange varer; **-trading** [-'tre'diŋ] vidløftige spekulasjoner.
overture ['oᵘvətʃə] forslag; tilbud; ouverture; **make -s** søke en tilnærmelse; tre i forhandlinger, innlede underhandlinger (to med).
overturn = overthrow.
over|valuation [oᵘvəvälju'eᵗʃən] for høy verdsetting; overvurdering. **-value** [-'välju] overvurdere. **-watched** [-'wåtʃt] forvåket. **-ween** [-'wi·n] ha for høye tanker. **-weening** anmassende, overmodig; overdreven, overstadig. **-weight** ['oᵘvə-we't] overvekt. **-weight** [-'we't] overbelaste. **-whelm** [-'hwelm] overvelde. **-wind** [-'waind] trekke et ur for mye opp. **-word** [-'wə·d] si med for mange ord. **-work** ['oᵘvawə·k] overanstrenge. **-work** ['oᵘvawə·k] ekstraarbeid; overarbeid; overanstrengelse; overarbeide. **-wrought** [-'rå·t] overanstrengt; innvirket, brodert.
Ovid ['åvid] Ovid.
oviform ['oᵘvifå·ᵊm] eggformet, eggrund.
ovum ['oᵘvəm] (pl. ova) egg.
owe [oᵘ] skylde; være skyldig; **— him a debt** eller **— a debt to him** stå i gjeld til ham; **— him a grudge** ha et horn i siden til ham, bære agg til ham.
owing ['oᵘiŋ] skyldig; tilgodehavende; **it is —**

to det skyldes; det kommer av; — to på grunn av.
owl [aul] ugle; drunk as an — full som en alke.
owl [aul] luske, snike seg; drive ulovlig handel.
owler ['aulə] smughandler.
owlet ['aulet] liten ugle, ugleunge.
owlish ['aulif] ugleaktig; stærblind.
owl-light ['aullait] tusmørke, skumring.
own [oⁿn] egen, eget, egne; kjødelig; name your — day bestem selv dagen; of its — accord av seg selv; he cooks his — meals han lager maten sin selv; he stands in his — light han skygger for seg selv; have a reason of one's — ha sin særlige grunn; my ownest min helt og holdent; give him his — la ham få sin rett; hold his — holde stand; klare seg; hold his — with him hamle opp med ham; he still keeps his — han hevder fremdeles sin plass; pay every one his — svare hver sitt; she has a fortune of her — hun har privat formue; he has no idea of his — han har ingen selvstendig mening; — cousin to kjødelig fetter av; — brother kjødelig bror; helbror (motsatt: half-brother).
own [oⁿn] eie; anerkjenne, vedkjenne seg, stå ved, kjennes ved; erkjenne, innrømme; være eier; it must be -ed det må innrømmes; — to

bekjenne, innrømme, vedkjenne seg; — up tilstå, gå til bekjennelse; — up to tilstå, bekjenne.
owner ['oⁿnə] eier; eiermann; reder, skipsreder.
ownerless ['oⁿnəlès] herreløs. ownership [-ʃip] eiendomsrett.
ox [åks] (pl. oxen ['åksn]) okse, stut, tyr.
ox-eye ['åks-ai] prestekrage; marigull.
Oxford ['åksfəd] Oxford.
oxidable ['åksidəbl] som kan oksyderes. oxidate ['åksideⁱt] oksydere. oxidation [åksi'deⁱʃən] oksydering. oxidize ['åksidaiz] oksydere.
ox-lip ['åkslip] engelsk kusymre (eg. blanding av kusymre og marinøkkelband).
Oxon. fk. f. Oxfordshire; of Oxford.
Oxonia [åk'soⁿnjə] Oxford. Oxonian [åk'soⁿnjən] fra Oxford, Oxford-.
ox-tail ['åksteⁱl] oksehale; — soup oksehale-suppe.
ox-tongue ['åkstʌŋ] oksetunge (også planten).
oxygen ['åksidჳèn] surstoff, klorkalk.
oyer ['oiə] forhør.
oyes [oⁿjes], oyez [oⁿjes, 'oⁿjes, 'oⁿjez] hør! (rettsbetjents rop for å påby stillhet).
oyster ['oistə] østers. — -bed østersbanke. — -brood østersyngel. — -catcher tjeld (fugl). — -knife østersåpner. — -man østershandler.
oz. fk. f. ounce(s).
ozone ['oⁿzoⁿn] ozon.

P

P. p. [pi·.] P p; mind (eller be on) one's P's and Q's (eller p's and q's) passe godt på, være på sin post; stand upon one's P's and Q's (eller p's and q's) holde strengt på formene.
p. fk. f. page (side); participle.
P. & O. eller P. and O. ['pi·ənd 'oⁿ] fk. f. the Peninsular and Oriental Steam Navigation Company det spansk-orientalske dampskipsselskap; dette selskaps skip.
Pa. fk. f. Pennsylvania.
p. a. fk. f. participial adjective.
P. A. fk. f. (the) Press Association.
pa [pa·] pappa.
pabulum ['påbjuləm] føde, mat; næring.
pace [pe's] skritt, steg; gang, ganglag, fotlag; passgang, skritt; be going the — leve lystig; hold (keep) — with holde skritt med; make — skritte ut; at a great — med svær fart; put a person through his -s få en til å vise sine kunster.
pace [pe's] gå, skride, gå passgang; gå bortover, gå opp og ned, gå att og fram; skritte opp.
pace ['pe'si] med tillatelse av; — the freetraders med frihandelsmennenes tillatelse.
paced [pe'st] som har en viss gang; -gående; dressert.
pacemaker ['pe'sme'kə] pacer; leder.
pacer ['pe'sə] gående; passgjenger.
pacha [pa'ʃa·] pasja, tyrkisk stattholder.
pachyderm ['påkidə·m] tykkhudet dyr.
pachydermatous [påki'də·mətəs] tykkhudet.
pacific [pə'sifik] fredelig, fredsstiftende, meklende, beroligelse. the Pacific Stillehavet.
Pacifics aksjer i Pacificbanen.
pacifically [pə'sifikəli] på fredelig vis.
pacification [påsifi'ke'ʃən] pasifikasjon, mekling, beroligelse, gjenoppretting av fred.
pacificator ['påsifike'tə] fredsstifter.
pacificatory [pə'sifikətəri] som stifter fred.
pacifier ['påsifaiə] fredsstifter.
pacifist ['påsifist] fredsvenn.
pacify ['påsifai] stille tilfreds, roe, berolige; stemme blidere; døyve, stille; tilfredsstille; stifte fred i; forsone.
pack [påk] pakke, balle, bylt; kløv; kortstokk; mengde, flokk, hurv; kobbel, bande; a — of

thieves en tyvebande; a — of wool 240 pd. ull; in -s flokkevis.
pack [påk] pakke, pakke sammen, legge ned, stue, emballere; sende av sted, jage på porten; pakke inn, gjøre seg reiseferdig; pakke seg sammen; — a jury samle en jury av partiske medlemmer; — one's traps gjøre seg reiseferdig; -ed up like so many herrings stuet sammen som sild i en tønne.
package ['påkidჳ] pakning; pakke, balle.
pack-animal ['påkånimə] lastdyr, kløvdyr.
pack-cloth ['påkklåþ] pakklerret.
packet ['påkit] pakke, bunt; pakett; bunte sammen, bunte; sende med postbåt. — -boat pakettbåt. — -day postdag. — -line postrute.
pack|-horse pakkhest, kløvhest; trekkdyr. — -ice pakkis. -ing ['påkiŋ] pakning, emballasje; nedlegning. — -load byrde. -man kramkar, skreppekar. — -saddle pakksal; kløvsal. — -thread seilgarn, hyssing. — -waggon bagasjevogn.
paco ['pa·koⁿ, 'peⁱ-] pako, alpakka.
pact [påkt] pakt, forbund, avtale.
pactional ['påkʃənəl] kontraktmessig.
Pad [påd] (økenavn for) irlender.
pad [påd] underlag, pute, valk; hynde; bløt sal; tredepute; skamfilingsmatte; stoppe ut, fylle; beise (kattun); padded room værelse med polstrede vegger (for sinnssyke).
pad [påd] stin.ann; go on the — være landeveisrøver; sit —, stand — sitte og tigge ved veien (med plakat på brystet).
pad [påd] betre; vandre langsomt, traske.
padder ['pådə] landeveisrøver.
padding ['pådin] utstopping, stopp; fyllekalk; lettere stoff i ukeskrift.
Paddington ['pådinən] Paddington.
paddle ['pådl] pagaie, padle, ro med en tobladet åre; plaske, vasse, susle; fingre. — about drive omkring; — his own canoe stå på egne bein.
paddle ['pådl] tobladet åre; pagai; skovl på et vannhjul. -board skovl på et vannhjul. -box hjulkasse.
paddler ['pådlə] pagairoer.
paddle|-steamer hjuldamper. — -vessel hjulfartøy. — -wheel skovlhjul.

paddock 224 palm

paddock ['pädək] hage, gjerde, innhegning, hestehage, salplass (ved veddeløpsbane).
paddock ['pädək] (gml.) padde, frosk. — **-pipe** myrsnelle. — **-stool** sopp.
Paddy ['pädi] Paddy (av Patrick), økenavn for irlender.
paddy ['pädi] ris (som ikke er avskallet).
padishah ['pa·diʃa·] hersker (om sjahen av Persia, sultanen av Tyrkia, keiseren av India).
padlock ['pädlåk] hengelås; lukke med hengelås.
padnag ['pädnäg] passgjenger.
padre ['pa·dre] prest (i hær el. flåte).
Padua ['pädjuə] Padua. **Paduan** ['pädjuən] paduansk; paduaner.
pæan ['pi·ən] festhymne; seiersang.
paedobaptism [pi·do'bäptizm] barnedåp.
paedobaptist [pi·do'bäptist] tilhenger av barnedåp.
pagan ['pe'gən] hedensk; hedning. **paganish** ['pe'gəniʃ] hedensk. **paganism** [-izm] hedenskap.
paganize [-aiz] gjøre hedensk; avkristne; oppføre seg som hedning.
page [pe'dʒ] pasje; følge og tjene som pasje.
page [pe'dʒ] side (i bok); paginere.
pageant ['pädʒənt] skuespill, forestilling, komedie; skuespillvogn; praktopptog; prunk. **pageantry**]'pädʒəntri] skuespill; praktopptog; prunk.
paginal ['pädʒinəl] som har sidetall, side-. **paginate** ['pädʒine't] paginere. **pagination** [pädʒi-'ne'ʃən] paginering. **paging** ['pe'dʒiŋ] paginering.
pagoda [pə'go"də] pagode, gudshus; gammeldags indisk mynt; **shake the — -tree** komme hurtig til rikdom, sope inn penger.
pah! [pa·] uff! fy! esj! pytt!
paid [pe'd] imperf. og perf. pts. av **pay**.
pail [pe'l] spann. **pailful** ['pe'lful] spannfull.
paillasse [päl'jäs] se **palliasse**.
pain [pe'n] straff; smerte; lidelse; sorg, sut; **on (upon) — of** under straff av; **put him out of — gjøre ende på hans lidelser; pains** [pe'nz] smerter; fødsels-smerter; umak; møye, uleilighet, bry, flid; **take pains** gjøre seg umak; **much pains** stor umak.
pain [pe'n] gjøre vondt, smerte; bedrøve.
painful ['pe'nf(u)l] smertelig; pinefull; tung, besværlig, møysommelig, slitsom; pinlig.
pain-killer smertestillende middel.
painless ['pe'nlés] smertefri.
painstaker ['pe'nzte'kə] flittig arbeider.
painstaking ['pe'nzte'lkiŋ] flid, samvittighetsfullhet; flittig, strevsom, samvittighetsfull.
paint [pe'nt] maling, farge, sminke; male, sminke; skildre, fremstille, beskrive; sminke seg; **as fresh as — så frisk som en rose; wet —! fresh -ed!** nymalt (plakat til advarsel). — **-box** malerkasse; fargeskrin. — **-brush** malerkost, pensel.
painter ['pe'ntə] maler, kunstmaler.
painter ['pe'ntə] fangline til en båt, feste.
painting ['pe'ntiŋ] malerkunst; maleri, maling.
paintress ['pe'ntrés] malerinne.
painty ['pe'nti] overlesst med farger; som hører til maling.
pair [pæ·ə] (oftest uforandret i pl. etter tallord) par (om to sammenhørende, forskjellig fra couple); sett, tospann; slå seg sammen to og to, parre seg, parre; **a — of boots** et par støvler; **that's another — of sleeves (trousers, shoes)** det er en annen historie; **there's a — of them** det er et nydelig par (ironisk); — **of glasses** briller; — **of scissors** saks; **a — of stairs** en trapp; **a two-pair back (front)** et værelse i tredje etasje til gården (til gata); **a pair of steps** en (utvendig) trapp, en kjøkkentrapp; **a carriage and pair** en vogn med to hester; **in pairs** to og to.
pairing ['pæ·ʰriŋ] parring. — **-season** parringstid. — **-time** parringstid.
pal [päl] (slang) kamerat, busse.
palace ['päləs, -is] palass, slott; **the Palace** ofte for **the Crystal Palace; Peoples' Palace** en stor bygning med lokaler til underholdning, be-

læring o. l. **for fattigere folk** i Londons East-End. — **-car** amr. salongvogn. — **-court** slottsrett (gml. rett, som dømte i sivile saker i 12 miles omkrets om Whitehall). — **-yard** slottsgård.
paladin ['pälədin] omstreifende ridder, eventyrer; jevning.
palæography [pe'li'ágrəfi, päli-] paleografi; kunnskap om paleografi. **palæologist** [pe'li-'ålədʒist, päl-] oldkyndig. **palæology** [-dʒi] arkeologi, kunnskap om den gamle tiden. **palæontology** [päliån'tålədʒi] pateontologi. **palæotype** ['päliotaip] paleotyp. **palæozoic** [pälio'zo"ik] paleozoisk. **palaestra** [pə'lestrə] bryteplass. **palanquin** [pälən'ki·n] bærestol, palankin. **palatable** ['pälətəbl] velsmakende. **palatableness** [-nés] velsmak. **palatal** ['pälətəl] ganelyd, palatal. **palatalize** ['pälətəlaiz] palatalisere. **palate** ['pälət, -it] gane. **palatial** [pə'le'ʃəl] palassaktig, palassmessig. **palatinate** [pə'lätinét] pfalzgrevskap: **the Palatinate** Pfalz, Kur-Pfalz med biland. **palatine** ['pälətain] pfalzgrevelig; **count — pfalzgreve; the Elector Palatine** kurfyrsten av Pfalz.
palaver [pə'la·və] forhandling, forhandlingsmøte; tomt snakk; forhandle; snakke, skravle; smigre.
pale [pe'l] pel, påle, staur; grense; gjerde; enemerke, område; sette peler el. gjerde omkring; **beyond the — of civilisation** utenfor sivilisasjonens grenser.
pale [pe'l] ble(i)k; gjøre blek; blekne, falle igjennom (ved sammenligning); **turn — bli blek; as — as death** dødblek; — **ale** en slags lyst bittert øl. **pale-face** blekansikt, hvit mann. **pale-faced** hvit. **paleness** ['pe'lnés] blekhet.
Palestine ['pälistain] Palestina. **Palestinean** [päli'stinjən] palestinsk.
palestra [pə'lestrə] palestra, bryteplass; bryteøvelser.
paletot ['pälto"] paletot, overfrakk.
palette ['pälit] palett. — **-knife** palettkniv.
palfrey ['på·lfri] ridehest, især damehest.
Pali ['pa·li] pali, palispråk.
palification [pälifi'ke'ʃən] peling, påling, peleramming, inngjerding.
palimpsest ['pälimpsest] palimpsest.
paling ['pe'liŋ] peler, påler, peleverk; grenser, enemerke.
palisade [päli'se'd] palisade, peleverk, påleverk; palisandre; palisandertre.
palish ['pe'liʃ] blekaktig.
pall [på·l] pallium, talar; likklær, sorte klær over en kiste; innhylle i likklær, dekke til.
pall [på·l] dovne, miste sin kraft, svekkes, svinne; gjøre doven; svekke, matte, gjøre motløs.
Palladian [pə'le'djən] i Palladios stil.
palladium [pə'le'djəm] palladium, bilde av Pallas Atena; bollverk, vern, beskyttelsesmiddel.
Pallas ['päləs] Pallas Atena.
pallbearer ['på·lbæ·ʰrə] sørgemarskalk.
pallet ['pälit] simpel seng, halmmadrass.
pallet ['pälit] palett; dreieskive (hos pottemakere); liten pel (i vågen); ventil (i orgelpipe).
palliasse [päl'jäs] halmmadrass.
palliate ['pälie't] smykke, pynte på, unnskylde; lindre, døyve. **palliation** [päli'e'ʃən] unnskyldning, besmykkelse; lindring. **palliative** ['päljətiv] unnskyldende; lindrende; lindrende middel.
pallid ['pälid] blek, gråblek, gusten. **pallidity** [pə'liditi] blekhet. **pallidness** ['pälidnés] blekhet.
pallium ['päliəm] gammel gresk kappe, filosofkappe; pallium.
Pall Mall [pæl'mel] Pall Mall (gate i London).
pallor ['pälə] blekhet.
palm [pa·m] håndflate, love, håndsbredd; ankerfli; stryke håndflaten over, berøre, føle; gjemme i hånden; — **it off on him** narre det på

ham; — a lie upon him binde ham en løgn på ermet; — himself off as utgi seg for.
palm [pa·m] palme; carry off the — gå av med seieren, bære prisen.
palma ['pälmə] palme.
palmaceous [päl'meiʃəs] palmeaktig.
palmated [päl'meitid] palmformet, hånddelt.
palmer ['pa·mə] pilegrim; sommerfugllarve.
Palmerston ['pa·məstən] Palmerston.
palmery ['pa·məri] palmehus.
palmetto [päl'metoⁿ] dvergpalme.
palmist ['pa·mist] en som spår i håndflaten.
palmistry [-ri] kiromanti.
palmoil ['pa·moil] palmeolje; bestikkelse; ‹bein›.
Palm-Sunday ['pa·m'sʌndi] palmesøndag.
palm-tree ['pa·mtri·] palme.
palm-wine ['pa·mwain] palmevin.
palmy ['pa·mi] palmevokst, palmelignende; seierrik, lykkelig, stor, velmakts-.
palp [pälp] føletråd, følehorn. palpability [pälpə'biliti] håndgripelighet. palpable ['pälpəbl] håndgripelig. palpation [päl'peiʃən] beføling.
palpitate ['pälpiteit] banke, pikke, klappe; sitre. palpitation [pälpi'teiʃən] skjelving, hjertebank.
palsgrave ['på·lzgreiv] pfalzgreve.
palsied ['på·lzid] lam; verkbrudden.
palsy ['på·lzi] lamhet; hjelpeløshet; lamme.
palter ['på(·)ltə] være underfundig, bruke knep, fuske; fjase; misbruke ens tillit.
paltriness ['på(·)ltrinês] usselhet, lumpenhet.
paltry ['på(·)ltri] ussel, stakkarslig, lumpen.
paludal [pə'l(j)u·dəl, 'päljudəl] sumpet, myr-.
palustrual [pə'lʌstrəl] sumpet, myr-.
paly ['peili] noe blek.
pampas ['pämpəs] pampas.
pamper ['pämpə] overmette, stappe; gjø, fete; forkjæle, skjemme bort.
pamphlet ['pämflét] piece, hefte, brosjyre; flyveskrift; skrive, gi ut en brosjyre. pamphleteer [pämfli'tiə] brosjyreforfatter; skrive brosjyrer.
Pan [pän] Pan; a set of -'s pipes hyrdefløyte.
pan [pän] panne, stekepanne; saltpanne; gryte, kasserolle; skle, ringe; skalle, skolt; aurhelle.
panacea [pänə'siə] universalmiddel, mirakelråd.
Panama [pänə'ma·] Panama.
Pan-American [pänə'merikən] panamerikansk (omfattende alle stater i Nord- og Sør-Amerika).
Pan-Anglican [pän'änglikən] pananglikansk (omfattende alle grener av den anglikanske kirke).
panary ['pänəri] brød-, som hører til brød.
pancake ['pänkeik] pannekake. — Tuesday fetetirsdag (tirsdag etter fastelavnssøndag).
pancreas ['pänkriəs] bukspyttkjertel.
pandar, se pander.
pandect ['pändekt], the Pandects pandektene, Justinians samlinger av rettslærdes betenkninger.
pandemic [pän'demik] pandemisk; epidemisk.
pandemonium [pändi'moⁿnjəm] pandemonium, de onde ånders bolig; helvete.
pander ['pändə] kobler, ruffer; koble, ruffe.
panderage ['pändəridʒ] kobleri, rufferi.
Pandora [pän'då·rə] Pandora.
Pandours ['pänduəz] slags brutale soldater.
pandy ['pändi] pandy, økenavn for en indisk soldat.
pane [pein] felt, stykke, avdeling, flate, side, tavle; rute, vindusrute. -less [-lês] uten ruter.
panegyric [päni'dʒirik] lovtale. panegyric(al) [-l] lovprisende, rosende, smigrende. panegyrist ['pänidʒirist] lovpriser, lovtaler. panegyrize ['pänidʒiraiz] berømme, rose; holde lovtaler.
panel ['pänl] felt, fag; avdeling; speil, fylling (i dør); pute (i sal); pergamentrull, liste (især over lagrettesmenn); jury.
panel ['pänl] pryde med felter, panele.
panelling ['pän(ə)liŋ] panelverk, felter, fyllinger. panel-work felter, fyllinger.

15 — Engelsk-norsk.

pang [päŋ] smerte, kval, stikk, styng, støt trykke, presse, trenge; pakke.
panic ['pänik] panikk; panisk skrekk; panisk, plutselig, ustyrlig (frykt). panicky ['päniki] panikkaktig. panic|-monger ['pänikmʌŋgə] panikk-, som setter støkk i folk. -stricken [-strikn], -struck [-strʌk] vettskremt, fælen, skrekkslagen; motløs.
pannier ['pänjə] meis, bakmeis; kløvmeis.
pannikin ['pänikin] metallkrus, tinnkrus.
panorama [pänə'ra·mə] panorama, kringsjå. panoramic [pänə'rämik] panoramatisk.
Panslavic ['pän'slävik, -sla·-] panslavisk.
Panslavism ['pän'slävizm, -'sla·-] panslavisme.
pansy ['pänzi] stemorsblomst.
pant [pänt, pa·nt] trekke pusten kort og fort, puste, stønne, pese; pesing, snapping etter pusten, stønn; stormgang.
pantalet(te)s [päntə'lets] damebenklær.
pantaloon [päntə'lu·n] latterlig person i komedier og pantomimer; i pl.: benklær.
pantechnicon [pän'teknikən] flytteomnibus.
pantheism ['pänþiizm] panteisme. pantheist [-ist] panteist. pantheistic [pänþi'istik] panteistisk.
pantheon ['pänþiån] panteon, tempel for alle guder.
panther ['pänþə] panter. pantherine [-r(a)in] panteraktig, flekket.
panto ['päntoⁿ] pantomime.
pantomime ['päntomaim] pantomime; slags eventyrskuespill med forvandlingsscene. pantomimic [päntoˈmimik] pantomimisk. pantomimist ['päntoˈmaimist] pantomimiker.
pantry ['päntri] spiskammer, anretningsrom.
pants [pänts] benklær; underbenklær.
pap [päp] pappa.
pap [päp] barnemat; grøt, grøtaktig masse.
pap [päp] brystvorte.
papa [pə'pa·] pave; prest.
papa [pə'pa·] pappa, far.
papacy ['peipəsi] pavedømme; paveverdighet.
papal ['peipəl] pavelig.
papaver [pə'peivə] valmue.
papaw [pə'på·] melontre.
paper ['peipə] papir, papp; tapet; blad, avis; foredrag; avhandling; nummer av et skrift; oppgave; eksamenspapir; verdipapir, veksel; read a — on holde forelesning om; on — skriftlig, svart på hvitt; printed -s trykksaker; the house is full of — de fleste tilskuere har fribillett; commit to — skrive ned; write to the -s skrive i avisene.
paper ['peipə] kle med papir, tapetsere; legge i papir. — -bag pappose. — -cap papirlue. — -carrier avisbud. — -chase ›hares and hounds› (en slags leik). — -cover papiromslag. — -currency papirpenger. — -cutter ›papirkniv. — -folder falsben; papirkniv. — -hanger tapetserer. — -hangings tapeter, tapet. — -hunts, se paper-chase. papering ['peipəriŋ] innpakning, emballering; tapetsering.
paper|-knife ['peipənaif] papirkniv. — -maker papirfabrikant; klutesamler. — -padded papirforet. — -pulp papirmasse. — -reed papyrus. — -ribbon papirstrimmel; telegrafpapir. — -shawings papiravfall. — -stainer tapetfabrikant. — -weight brevvekt. — -worker viseselger. papery ['peipəri] papir, papiraktig.
papier-maché ['päpjeiⁿma·ʃei] pappmasjé.
papillote ['päpiloⁿt] papiljott.
papist ['peipist] papist. papistical [pə'pistikl] papistisk. papistry ['peipistri] papisteri.
papoose [pə'pu·s] indianerbarn.
pappy ['päpi] grøtaktig, bløt.
papyrus [pə'paiərəs] papyrus.
par [pa·] likhet, likestilling; pari; be on a par — with være likestilt med; put on a — with likestille med; above — over pari; at — til pari; below — under pari.

par. fk. f. **paragraph.**

parable ['pärəbl] parabel, lignelse; tale, foredrag; uttrykke ved en lignelse.

parachute ['pärəʃuˑt] fallskjerm. — **-flare** lysbombe.

parade [pə're¹d] parade; paradeplass; promenade; prakt, prunk, stas; paradere med, vise, stille til skue; la paradere; paradere i; **make a** — **of** paradere med, prale med. — **-ground** paradeplass. — **-step** paradeskritt.

paradigm ['pärədaim] paradigma, mønster.

paradise ['pärədais] paradis.

paradox ['päredåks] paradoks; tilsynelatende motsigelse. **paradoxical** [pärə'dåksikl] paradoksal, paradoks. **paradoxist** ['pärədåksist] paradoksmaker. **paradoxy** ['pärədåksi] paradoksal beskaffenhet.

paraffin ['pärəfi(·)n] parafin; parafinere; — **-oil** parafinolje.

paragon ['pärəgån] mønster; — **of virtue** dydsmønster.

paragraph ['pärəgraˑf] paragraf, avsnitt, stykke, notis, artikkel (i et blad); paragrafere, behandle, omtale i en avisnotis.

Paraguay ['pärəgwe¹, 'pärəgwai] Paraguay.

parakeet ['pärəki·t] parakitt (slags papegøye).

parallax ['pärəläks] parallakse.

parallel ['pärəlel, -ləl] parallell, likeløpende; tilsvarende; parallell; likhet; sammenligning; sidestykke; trekke parallell, gjøre parallell; løpe parallell med; svare til, kunne måle seg med; komme opp mot. **parallelism** ['pärəlelizm] parallellisme, likhet, parallell; sammenligning, sammenstilling.

parallelogram [pärə'lelogräm] parallellogram.

paralyse ['pärəlaiz] lamme; lamslå, fjetre.

paralysis [pə'rälisis] lammelse, lamhet.

paralytic [pärə'litik] lam.

paramount ['pärəmaunt] øverst, som står over alt annet, framherskende; overhode.

paramour ['pärəmuə] elsker; frille, elskerinne.

parapet ['pärəpet] brystvern; rekkverk; forsyne med brystvern.

paraphernalia [pärəfə'ne¹ljə] parafernalier; kones særeie; personlig utstyr, smykker; tilbehør, utstyr.

paraphrase ['pärəfre¹z] omskrivning; omskrive.

paraphrastic [pärə'frästik] omskrivende.

parasite ['pärəsait] parasitt, snyltegjest, snylter; snylteplante, snyltedyr. **parasitic** [pärə'sitik] snyltende.

parasol [pärə'sål] parasoll.

parboil ['pa·°boil] halvkoke; skålde, steke.

parcel ['pa·°sl] kvantum, parti (varer); stykke, pakke; parsell, del; fordele, stykke ut; **by -s** stykkevis; **-s' delivery** pakkebefordring; **by -s'** **post** med pakkeposten. — **-office** pakkeekspedisjon. — **-post** pakkepost. — **-van** vogn til utbringing av varer.

parcener ['pa·sənə] medarving.

parch [pa·°tʃ] brenne; svi, tørke bort. **parchedness** ['pa·tʃidnės] avsvidd tilstand. **parching** ['pa·°tʃiŋ] brennende.

parchment ['pa·°tʃmənt] pergament.

pard [pa·°d] leopard.

pardner ['pa·°dnə] (vulgært for **partner**) kompanjong, kamerat, «kompis».

pardon ['pa·°dn] tilgi; benåde; tilgivelse, forlatelse; benådning; — **me** unnskyld! **I beg** **your** — om forlatelse; hva behager; **beg** — unnskyld, hva behager! **I beg you a thousand -s** (eller **I beg your pardon a thousand times**) jeg ber tusen ganger om forlatelse.

pardonable ['pa·°dnəbl] tilgivelig.

pardoner ['pa·°dnə] (gammelt) avlatskremmer.

pardoning ['pa·°dniŋ] barmhjertig.

pare [pæ·ə] skrelle; klippe, skave, sneie, skjære (en negl); skrape; beskjære, beklippe.

parent ['pæ·°rənt] far; mor; **-s** foreldre. **pa-**

rentage ['pæ·°rəntidʒ] herkomst, opphav, byrd, slekt, ætt. **parental** [pə'rentəl] faderlig; moderlig; foreldre-.

parenthesis [pə'renþisis] parentes. **parenthesize** [-þisaiz] skyte inn i en parentes.

parenthetic [pärən'þetik] parentetisk.

parenthood ['pæ·°rənthud] foreldres stilling el. verdighet.

parentless ['pæ·°rentlės] foreldreløs.

parer ['pæ·°rə] redskap til å skrelle med.

parget ['pa·°dʒét] mørtel, murpuss, stukkatur.

pariah ['päriə, 'pa·riə, 'pæ·°riə] paria.

paring ['pæ·°riŋ] skrelling; skrell.

Paris ['päris] Paris.

parish ['päriʃ] sogn, herred, kommune; sogne-. — **-clerk** degn, klokker. — **council** sognestyre. **parishioner** [pə'riʃənə] som hører hjemme i sognet el. herredet; sognebarn. **parish**-**meeting** herredsting. — **-minister** sogneprest. — **-officer** kommunal bestillingsmann. — **-pauper** person som underholdes av fattigvesenet, av forsorgsvesenet. — **-pay, -relief** fattigunderstøttelse, forsorgsbidrag.

Parisian [pə'riʒən] parisisk; pariser(inne).

parisyllabic [pärisi'läbik] med like mange stavelser.

parity ['päriti] likhet; pari.

park [pa·°k] park; skog; anbringe i park; spasere i park; parkere (biler); **cars must not be -ed** parkering forbudt.

parlamentarian [pa·°ləmen'tæ·°riən] parlamentariker.

parlance ['pa·°ləns] talebruk; språkbruk.

parley ['pa·°li] tale, forhandle; samtale, forhandling; underhandling.

parliament ['pa·°ləmənt] parlament, storting. **parliamentarian** [pa·°ləmən'tæ·°riən] parlamentarisk; på parlamentets side (i 17. årh.); parlamentariker. **parliamentarism** [pa·°lə'mentərizm] parlamentarisme. **parliamentary** [pa·°lə'mentəri] parlamentarisk; — **train** et av de tog som før Verdenskrigen ifølge en parlaments-lov befordret 3. klasses passasjerer en takst av 1 penny pr. mile.

parlour ['pa·°lə] taleværelse i kloster; stue, dagligstue; gjestestue; privatkontor. — **-boarder** pensjonær som mot høyere betaling spiser ved familiens eget bord. — **-car** amr. salongvogn. — **-carpet** golvteppe. — **-gun** salonggevær. — **-maid** stuepike. — **-skates** rulleskøvter.

parlous ['pa·°ləs] (spøkende uttrykk) farlig.

Parmesan [pa·°mi'zän] **cheese** parmesanost.

Parnell ['pa·°nel; pa·°'nəl] Parnell.

Parnellite ['pa·°nəlait] tilhenger av Parnell.

parochial [pə'rou¹kjəl] sogne-, herreds-, kommunal.

parodic(al) [pə'rådik(l)] parodisk, parodierende. **parodist** ['pärədist] parodiker. **parody** ['pärədi] parodi; parodiere.

parole [pə'rou¹l] parole, feltrop; æresord; frigi, løslate på æresord.

paronomasia [pärəno'me¹ʒə] ordspill.

parotid [pe'rátid] ørekjertel, spyttkjertel ved øret.

paroxysm ['pärəksizm] paroksysme, anfall; **she burst into a** — **of tears** hun brast i krampegråt.

parquet [pa·°'ket] parkettgolv; legge inn parkettgolv, innlegge med trearbeid. **parquetry** ['pa·°kétri] parkettgolv, parkettplater.

parricidal [päri'saidəl] fadermordersk; modermordersk. **parricide** ['pärisaid] fadermorder, modermorder; fadermord, modermord.

parrot ['pärət] papegøye; snakke etter; etterape. **parroter** ['pärətə] ettersnakker, etteraper, skravlekopp. **parrotry** ['pärətri] etteraping.

parry ['päri] avparere; parere, komme seg unna; parade.

parse [pa·°s] analysere (i grammatikk).

Parsee ['pa·°si·] parser, ildtilbeder.

parsimonious [pa·°si'mou¹njəs] knipen, knuslet,

altfor sparsommelig. **parsimony** ['pa·ᵊsimǝni] på- holdenhet, kniping, knussel.
parsley ['pa·ᵊsli] persille. — **-bed** persillebed; **the doctor brought him from the** — (brukes over- for barn som vårt:) storken er kommet med ham.
parsnip ['pa·ᵊsnip] pastinakk.
parson ['pa·ᵊsn] sogneprest, prest.
parsonage ['pa·ᵊsnidʒ] sognekall; prestegård.
parsties ['pa·ᵊstiz] (i slang) bakverk.
part [pa·ᵊt] del, part, stykke; andel, lut, del av et skrift, hefte, avdrag: stemme, parti; rolle; **-s** begavelse, evner; egn, kant (av landet); — **of speech** ordklasse; **the most** — de fleste; **for the most** — for største delen; **for my** — hva meg angår; **take in good** — oppta godt; **on his** — fra hans side; **in foreign -s** i utlandet; **do one's -s** gjøre sitt; **a man of -s** et talentfullt menneske; **don't play me any of your -s** kom ikke med dine kunster; **he would take her** — han ville ta parti for henne; **take** — **with** ta parti for; **in** — delvis.
part [pa·ᵊt] dele; atskille; skille; dele seg, gå i stykker; revne, springe, sprenges; skilles; skille seg; **we -ed with him** vi skiltes fra ham; **our routes -ed** våre veier skiltes; **I won't** — **with my property** jeg vil ikke skille meg av med min eiendom.
partake [pa·ᵊ'te¹k] delta, ta del, være med; — **of** nyte, innta; besitte noe av; — **too freely of** ta for mye til seg av. **partaker** [pa·ᵊ'te¹kǝ] deltager. **partaking** [pa·ᵊ'te¹kin̩] deltagelse; del- aktighet.
parter ['pa·ᵊtǝ] deler, atskiller.
parterre [pa·ᵊ'te·ǝ] parterre (i fransk teater).
Parthia ['pa·ᵊþjǝ] Partia. **Parthian** [-n] partisk; parter; — **arrow** (el. bolt el. shot) partisk pil; et rammende svar avlevert idet man går.
partial ['pa·ᵊʃǝl] partiell, delvis; særskilt; par- tisk; **be** — **to** være partisk til fordel for; være inntatt i, ha en svakhet for. **partiality** [pa·ᵊʃi- 'äliti] partiell beskaffenhet; partiskhet; ensidig- het; svakhet; forkjærlighet. **partially** ['pa·ᵊʃǝli] delvis, for en del.
partibility [pa·ᵊti'biliti] delelighet. **partible** ['pa·ᵊtibl] delelig, delbar.
participant [pa·ᵊ'tisipǝnt] deltager; deltagende. **participate** [pa·ᵊ'tisipe¹t] delta, ta del i. **par- ticipation** [pa·ᵊtisi'pe¹ʃǝn] deltagelse. **participator** [pa·ᵊ'tisipe¹tǝ] deltager.
participial [pa·ᵊti'sipjǝl] partisipial. **participle** ['pa·ᵊtisipl] partisipp. **past** — perfektum parti- sipp. **present** — presens partisipp.
particle ['pa·ᵊtikl] liten del; partikkel, atom; **not a** — ikke det minste; **there wasn't a** — **of truth in it** der var ikke et grann av sannhet i det.
particular [pǝ'tikjulǝ; pa·ᵊ-] særegen, særskilt; bestemt, enkelt, spesiell, viss; viktig; nøyaktig; detaljert; nøyeregnende, fordringsfull, kresen; merkelig, rar; enkelthet, detalj; spesialitet; **he is** — **in his eating** han er kresen med hva han spiser; **for a** — **purpose** i et bestemt øyemed; **they're nobody** — det er ganske alminnelige folk; **it's** — det er av viktighet; **be** — **about** være nøyeregnende med; **in** — især, i særdeleshet; **in that** — i den henseende; **(further) -s** nærmere opplysninger, utførlige opplysninger. **particularity** [pǝtikju'läriti; pa·ᵊ-] særegenhet, omstendighet; eiendommelighet.
particularize [pǝ'tikjulǝraiz] nevne særskilt, oppføre enkeltvis; gå i det enkelte.
parting ['pa·ᵊtin̩] delende, kløyvende, skillende; avskjeds-; deling, atskillelse; avdeling; avskjed; oppbrudd; skilsmisse; skill i håret. — **-comb** kam. — **-cup** avskjedsbeger.
partisan [pa·ᵊti'zän] partisan (slags hellebard). **partisan** [pa·ᵊ'ti'zän] partigjenger, tilhenger; partitraver, partifanatiker; partisan. **partisanship** [pa·ᵊ'ti'zänʃip] partiånd; partitrav, partifana- tisme; partisanvirksomhet.

partition [pa·ᵊ'tiʃǝn] deling; skille, skjell; skillerom, skillevegg; skar, hakk; dele, avdele (i rom).
partitive ['pa·ᵊtitiv] delende, delings-.
partizan ['pa·ᵊtizän, pa·ᵊti'zän] se **partisan**.
partly ['pa·ᵊtli] til dels, delvis.
partner ['pa·ᵊtnǝ] deltager; parthaver, interes- sent, kompanjong; makker, medspiller; ekte- felle; **acting** (**active, working**) — aktiv deltager; **silent** (**sleeping**) — passiv deltager; **be admitted as a** — bli opptatt som kompanjong; **take -s** engasjere.
partnership ['pa·ᵊtnǝʃip] kompaniskap, felles- skap; firma; **enter into** — gå i kompaniskap.
part-owner ['pa·ᵊto̍ʰnǝ] medeier, parthaver.
partridge ['pa·ᵊtridʒ] åkerhøne, åkerrikse; rapp- høne.
part-singing [pa·ᵊ'tsiniŋ] flerstemmig sang.
part-song ['pa·ᵊtsåŋ] flerstemmig sang.
parturition [pa·ᵊtju'riʃǝn] fødsel.
party ['pa·ᵊti] parti; selskap, lag; kommando, avdeling, deling; flokk; deltager; part, person; **the offended** — den fornærmede part; **give a** — holde et selskap; **a jolly** — et lystig lag; **go to a** — gå i selskap; **be of the** — være med; **I will be no** — **to this affair** jeg vil ikke ha noe å gjøre med denne sak; **a third** — en tredjemann, en upartisk; **this here** — denne fyren; **there will be no** — (ved innbydelser) i all tarvelighet; **I resolved to make her a** — jeg besluttet å innvie henne i saken. — **-coloured** ['pa·ᵊtikʌlǝd] spraglet. — **-end** partiformål. — **-man** parti- mann. — **-spirit** partiånd. — **-wall** skillemur, skillevegg (mellom to hus).
pas [pa·] trin; fortrin; **have the** — **of** gå foran. **paschal** ['pa·skǝl] påske-.
pasha ['pa·ʃǝ, 'pȧʃǝ, pǝ'ʃa·] pasja.
pasquil ['päskwil], **pasquin** ['päskwin] smede- skrift. **pasquinade** [päskwi'ne¹d] smedeskrift.
pass [pa·s] passere (gå, komme, kjøre, dra, ri); passere forbi, gå forbi, gå over, gå hen, falle, forsvinne; bestå, greie, ta (en eksamen); vedtas (om lover); tilbringe; forbigå; la passere; anta; vedta; rekke, levere; utgi; — **an examina- tion** bestå en eksamen; **bring to** — iverksette, gjennomføre; **come to** — hende; — **by** gå forbi; — **on** passere videre, gå videre; sende videre; — **over** gå hen over; gå over; forbigå; **by way of** -ing **the time** for å fordrive tiden; **it -es my comprehension** det går over min forstand; **he -es his hand across his eyes** han strøk seg med hånden over øynene; — **away** fordrive tiden; — **by in silence** forbigå i taushet; **he -ed it off as genuine** han gav det ut for å være ekte; — **it on** sende det videre; **he is -ing himself as an unmarried man** jeg gir seg ut for å være ugift.
pass [pa·s] passasje, gang, vei, overgang; skar, pass, snevring; seddel el. brev som gir rett til å passere, fribillett; pass; abonnementsbillett; eks- amensbevis; **matters have come to a bad** — det står dårlig til; **be at a fine** — sitte fint i det.
pass. fk. f. **passive**.
passable ['pa·sǝbl] framkommelig, farbar; an- tagelig; tålelig, noenlunde bra.
passacaglia [pȧsǝ'ka·ljǝ] passacaglia.
passage ['päsidʒ] passasje, gang; overkjørsel; overreise; gjennomreise, forbigang, forbikjørsel; vei, lei; atkomst; begivenhet, tildragelse; sted (i en bok); gjennomføring, vedtagelse; **bird of** — trekkfugl; **the following** — is told **of him** det gjende trekk fortelles om ham; **the public have a right of** — folk har rett til å benytte en gangsti. — **-boat** ferjebåt. — **-money** reisepenger; frakt.
pass|-bill ['pa·sbil] tollpass. **-book** ['pa·sbuk] kontrabok, bankbok. **-check** utgangsbillett.
passé ['päse¹] foreldet, passé, falmet.
passenger ['päs(i)ndʒǝ] passerende; forbigå- ende; forbireisende; passasjer. — **-ship** passasjer- skip. — **-train** persontog.

passe-partout ['päspa·'tu·ə] hovednøkkel.
passer ['pa·sə] passerende; forbigående; forbireisende. — **-by** forbigående. — **-through** gjennomreisen de.
passibility [päsi'bíliti] mottagelighet. **passible** ['päsibl] mottagelig. **passibleness** [-nés] mottagelighet.
passim ['päsim] på forskjellige steder.
passing ['pa·sin] forbigående, forbipasserende, forbiseilende; (gml.) overordentlig, forbigående; avgang; vedtagelse. — **-bell** likklokke.
passion ['päʃən] lidelse; pasjon, stemning, sinnsbevegelse; vrede, sinne, forbitrelse; lidenskap; **be in a** — være sint, være rasende; **burst into a** — **of tears** bryte ut i voldsom gråt; **fly into a** — bli fykende sint. **passionate** ['päʃənët] lidenskapelig; pasjonert. **passionateness** [-nés] lidenskapelighet. **passioned** ['päʃənd] lidenskapelig.
passion-flower ['päʃənflauə] pasjonsblomst.
passion|-play ['päʃənple¹] pasjonsskuespill. **-tide** fasten. **-week** den stille uke.
passive ['päsiv] passiv, uvirksom; **the** — **voice** passiv (grammatisk); **the** — passiv.
passivity [pə'siviti] passivitet.
pass-key ['pa·ski·] hovednøkkel.
passman ['pa·smän] en som tar en gjennomsnittseksamen ved universitetet; middelhavsfarer.
passport ['pa·spá·ət] pass.
pass-ticket ['pa·stikit] fribillett; abonnement.
password ['pa·swə·d] feltrop, løsen.
past [pa·st] forbigangen, forløpen, fortidig; tidligere; fortid; forbi, over, ut over, utenom; **for the** — **fortnight** i de siste 14 dager; **his** — **life** hans fortid; **the** — **tense** fortid (i grammatikk); **he is** — **help** han står ikke til å hjelpe; — **hope** håp løs; **he is** — **saving** han står ikke til å redde; **it is exactly 20 minutes** — klokka er nøyaktig 20 minutter over.
paste [pe¹st] masse, deig; leirmasse; pasta, kitt; klister; falsk(e) edelstein(er); klebe, klistre; mørbanke. **-board** ['pe¹stbå·əd] papp; visittkort. — **-roller** kjevle.
Pasteur [pä'stə·] Pasteur. **pasteurization** [pästərai'zə¹ʃən] pasteurisering. **pasteurize** ['pästəraiz] pasteurisere.
pastille [pə'sti·l] røkelseskule; pastill; røyke.
pastime ['pa·staim] tidsfordriv, morskap.
past-master ['pa·st'ma·stə] forhenværende mester (især blant frimurere), mester (i sitt fag).
pastor ['pa·stə] hyrde, sjelesørger, prest. **pastorage** ['pa·staridʒ] pastorat, prestekall. **pastoral** ['pa·st(ə)rəl] hyrde-; prestelig; hyrdedikt.
pastorate ['pa·storët] pastorat; prestekall.
pastry ['pe¹stri] butterdeig, butterdeigskaker, konditorkaker, kaker, bakverk. **-board** bakstebord. **pastrycook** ['pe¹strikuk] konditor.
pasturable ['pa·stʃərəbl] tjenlig til beite.
pasturage ['pa·stʃəredʒ] beiting; beiteland, hamn.
pasture ['pa·stʃə] gras, beite, hamnegang; sette på beite, la beite; beite, gå på gras, på beite. — **-land** beiteland, beitesmark.
pasty ['pe¹sti] deigaktig, klisteraktig; klisterpotte; bokbinder; kjøttpostei.
Pat [pät] navn for en irlender, fk. f. Patrick.
pat [pät] klappe; klapp; klatt, klakk.
patch [pätʃ] lapp, bot, flikk, grime, flekk, skjønnhetsplett; stykke i mosaikkarbeid; mosaikkstift; siktekorn; lappe, bøte, flikke. **he patched up a quarrel** han glattet over tretten.
patcher ['pätʃə] lapper, fusker.
patchouli ['pätʃuli] patchouli.
patch|pocket utvendig påsydd lomme. **-work** lappverk, flikkverk; **-work quilt** lappeteppe.
patchy ['pätʃi] lappet; gretten.
pate [pe¹t] (i søpk) hode, haus, skolt, skalle.
pâté [pä'te¹] postei.
patella [pə'telə] liten skål; kneskjell.
patent ['pe¹tənt, 'pätənt] åpen, åpenbar; framtredende; klar, grei, villig; patentert; patent; patentere; gi patent på, ta patent på; —

letter patentbrev; take out a — løse patent. **patentable** ['pe¹təntəbl, 'pät-] som lar seg patentere. **patentee** [pe¹tən'ti·, pät-] patenthaver. **patent-fuel** briketter. **patent-leather shoes** lakksko. **patent-right** patentrett.
pater ['pe¹tə] opphav, far.
patera ['pätərə] fat, skål.
paternal [pə'tə·nəl] fader-, faderlig, fedre-, fedrene. **paternity** [pə'tə·niti] paternitet, farskap. **paternoster** [pätə'nåstə] fadervår.
path [pa·þ] pl. **paths** [pa·ðz] sti, gangsti.
path. fk. f. **pathology.**
pathetic [pə'þetik] patetisk, gripende, rørende. **pathetical** [pə'þetikl] rørende. **pathetics** [pə'þetiks] det rørende; rørende opptrin.
pathfinder ['pa·þfaində] stifinner; foregangsmann.
pathology [pə'þålədʒi] patologi, sykdomslære.
pathos ['pe¹þås] patos, følelse, lidenskap, varme.
pathway ['pa·þwe¹] fortau; gangsti, vei, bane.
patience ['pe¹ʃəns] tålmodighet, utholdenhet, langmodighet; kabal (i kort); engelsk spinat; **I have no** — **with him** jeg kan ikke utstå ham; **be out of** — **with** være trett av; være meget sint på; **lose (one's)** — miste tålmodigheten; — **cards** kabalkort; **play at** — legge kabaler.
patient ['pe¹ʃənt] tålmodig; lidende, pasient.
patois ['pätwa·] patois, folkespråk; dialekt, målføre.
patrial ['pe¹triəl] patrial, familie-; folke-.
patriarch ['pe¹tria·ək] patriark. **patriarchal** [pe¹tria·əkl] patriarkalsk. **patriarchism** ['pe¹tria·əkizm] patriarkvelde, patriarkalsk styre. **patriarchship** [-a·əkʃip], **patriarchy** [-a·əki] patriarkat.
patrician [pə'triʃən] patrisisk, adelig; patrisier. **patricianism** [-izm] egenskap, rang som patrisier. **patriciate** [pə'triʃiét] patrisiat, patrisiere.
patricide ['pätrisaid] fadermord, fadermorder.
Patrick ['pätrik] Patricius; **St.** —, Irlands skytshelgen.
patrimonial [pätri'mo¹njəl] arvet (fra fedrene), arve-. **patrimony** ['pätriməni] fedrenearv.
patriot ['pe¹triət, 'pät-] patriot, fedrelandsvenn; patriotisk, fedrelandssinnet; fedrelandsk. **patriotic** [pätri'åtik] patriotisk. **patriotism** ['pätriátizm] patriotisme, fedrelandskjærlighet.
patrol [pə'tro¹l] patrulje; runde; avpatruljere; patruljere, gå runden.
patron ['pe¹trən, 'pät-] patron, beskytter, velynder. **patronage** ['pätrənédʒ] beskyttelse, proteksjon; yndest, støtte; kallsrett. **patroness** ['pe¹trənés, 'pät-] beskytterinne, velynder, skytshelgen. **patronize** ['pätrənaiz] beskytte, støtte, være velynder av, ynde; være kunde el. gjest hos, søke; behandle nedlatende. **patronizer** [-ə] beskytter, velynder, venn.
patronymic [pätro'nimik] familie-, slekts-; familienavn, etternavn, srl. laget fra farsnavnet.
patten ['pätin] tresko; fotstykke, svillstokk.
patter ['pätə] hagle, knitre, larme, piske, trommeme; la hagle, tromme; mumle, mumle fram; plapre, ramse opp; hagling, knitring, larm, larming, pisking, tromming; klapring; snakk, skravl.
pattern ['pätən] modell, mønster; prøve; slag, type; forme; pryde (med et mønster); **set him a** — foregå ham med et godt eksempel; **take** — **by** ta til mønster av; **a** — **with** i smak med: **to** — etter modell, etter mønster; **a** — **young man** et eksempelaktig ungt menneske. — **-card** prøvekort.
patty ['päti] liten postei. — **-pan** posteifat.
paucity ['på·siti] fåtallighet; knapphet.
Paul [på·l] Paul; **St. Paul** Paulus; **St. Paul's (Cathedral)** Paulskirken (i London).
Paulina [på·'lainə, -'li·nə] Pauline.
paunch [på·nʃ] buk; vom; skamfilingsmatte.
pauper ['på·pə] fattig, fattiglem. **pauperism**

[-rizm] armod. **pauperization** [på·pəri'ze'ʃən] utarming. **pauperize** ['på·pəraiz] forarme.

pause [på·z] stans, stansning, tankestrek; pause; betenkelighet, uvisshet; gjøre pause; betenke seg, stanse, nøle; **give — to** gjøre betenkelig.

pave [pe'v] brulegge; bane, jevne, jamne. **pavement** ['pe'vmənt] brulegning; fortau.

paver ['pe'və] brulegger.

pavilion [pə'viljən] telt, paviljong; dekke med telt; gi ly, spenne sitt telt over.

paving ['pe'viŋ] brulegning. — **-beetle** bruleggerjomfru. — **-brick** brulegningsfliser. — **-stone** brustein.

pavior ['pe'vjə] brulegger.

pavo ['pe'voᵘ] påfugl.

paw [på·] pote, labb; hånd, neve; fot; skrape, stampe med foten; skrape, stampe på; grapse, handvalke. **keep his -s off** holde fingrene av fatet.

pawed [på·d] med poter; bredlabbet.

pawn [på·n] bonde (i sjakk); brikke (i dam).

pawn på·n] pant; pantelåner; pantsette.

pawn |**broker** ['på·nbroᵘkə] pantelåner. **-broking** pantelånervirksomhet. **pawnee** [på·'ni·] panthaver. **pawner** ['på·nə] pantsetter. **pawnshop** ['på·nʃåp] pantelånerbutikk. **pawn-ticket** panteseddel.

pay [pe'] betale; lønne; svare seg; avlevere; vise, gjøre; — **a bill** el. **draft** innfri en veksel; **it did not — cost** det dekte ikke omkostningene; **there's the devil to — nå** er fanden løs; **it won't — det** svarer seg ikke; — **one's way** betale for seg; **I'll — you off for this** det skal du nok få svi for, få igjen; — **for** betale for, betale; **he will — for it very dearly** det vil han få svi ꜰor; — **a compliment** si en kompliment; — **attention** være oppmerksom; — **a visit** avlegge et besøk.

pay [pe'] betaling, lønning, gasje; sold; hyre; **draw —** heve gasje; **take into his —** ta i sin tjeneste.

payable ['pe'əbl] betalbar, å betale, som kan betales; forfallen; som svarer seg; **bill** (el. **note**) — **to bearer** veksel lydende på ihendehaveren, ihendehaverveksel.

pay|-bill lønningsliste. — **-boy** betalende elev. — **-day** gasjedag.

payee [pe'i·] den som pengene skal betales til, mottager, remittent. **payer** ['pe'ə] utbetalende, betaler. **paying** ['pe'iŋ] lønnende, som svarer seg, som svarer regning.

paymaster ['pe'ma·stə] kasserer; kvartermester; proviantforvalter; **take care who is your —** se til at De får pengene Deres.

payment ['pe'mənt] betaling; innfriing (av en veksel).

pay|-office ['pe'åfis] kassekontor, hovedkasse. — **-roll** lønningsliste.

P. B. fk. f. **Prayer Book.**

P. C. fk. f. **post-card; police constable; Privy Council; Privy Councillor.**

p. c. fk. f. **per cent.**

pd. fk. f. **paid.**

pea [pi·] (pl. **peas** eller kollektivt: **pease**) ert; **they are as like as two -s** de ligner hverandre som to dråper vann.

peace [pi·s] fred; fredsslutning; **for the sake of — for** husfredens skyld; **make — stifte** fred (**between** imellom), slutte fred (**with** med); **I am at — jeg** har funnet fred; **at** (**by**) **the — of** ved (i) freden i; **justice of the — fredsdommer** (uløn lavere dommer uten juridisk utdanning).

peaceable ['pi·səbl] fredelig, fredsommelig. **peace|-breaker** fredsforstyrrer.—**establishment** fredsstyrke. — **-footing** fredsfot.

peaceful ['pi·sf(u)l] fredelig, fredfull, stille, rolig.

peace|-loving fredelig, fredselskende. **-maker** fredsmegler, fredsstifter; **blessed are the -makers** salige er de fredsommelige. — **-offering** takk-

offer, sonoffer. — **-officer** politifunksjonær. — **-party** fredsparti. — **-policy** fredspolitikk.

peach [pi·tʃ] fersken; ferskentre.

peach [pi·tʃ] sladre, fisle; sladderhank, fisletut.

peach-blow ['pi·tʃbloᵘ] fin, lyserød farge (på porselen).

peachy ['pi·tʃi] ferskenaktig, ferskenfarget.

peacoat ['pi·koᵘt] pjekkert.

peacock ['pi·kåk] påfugl. **peacockery** [-kå·kri] overmot, overlegenhet, stolthet. **peacocky** stolt, kry, viktig.

peafowl ['pi·faul] påfugl.

pea-green ['pi·'gri·n] ertegrønn.

peahen ['pi·hen] påfuglehøne.

peajacket ['pi·dʒäkit] pjekkert.

peak [pi·k] spiss, topp, bergtinde; være (el. bli) tynn, mager, se sykelig ut, skrante.

peaked [pi·kt] spiss, skarp, tynn.

peaking ['pi·kiŋ] klynkende; krypende; klynk.

peaklet ['pi·klèt] liten tinde.

peaky ['pi·ki] som løper spisst ut; mager, skrinn, spiss.

peal [pi·l] brak, drønn, skrell, skrall; klang, ringing, kiming; **a — of laughter** en lattersalve; **the -s of the organ** orgelbrus.

peal [pi·l] brake, drønne,skrelle, skralle,tordne; ringe, kime, bruse; la brake, ringe.

peanut ['pi·nʌt] jordnøtt.

pear [pæ·ə] pære.

pearl [pə·l] perle; hvit flekk i øyet, stær; besette med perler; avskalle; **mother of — perlemor.** **-aceous** [pə·'le'ʃəs] perleaktig, perlemoraktig.

pearl-ash ['pə·läʃ] perleaske (slags pottaske).

pearl|-barley ['pə·l'ba·ᵘli] perlegryn. — **-button** perlemorsknapp. — **-diver** perlefisker. — **-diving** perlefiske.

pearled [pə·ld] perlebesatt, perlelignende.

pearl|-embroidered perlestukken. — **-fisher** perlefisker. — **-grass** bevergras. — **-grey** perlegrå. — **-oyster** perlemusling. — **-shell** perleskjell. — **-string** perlesnor. **-white** hvit sminke.

pearly ['pə·li] perlerik, perleklar; perle-.

Pears [pæ·əz]: **Pears' soap** Pears' såpe.

pear-tree ['pæ·ətri·] pæretre.

peasant ['pezənt] bonde (om småbønder og landarbeidere). — **-farmer** bonde. — **-like** bondsk. — **-man** bondemann. **peasantry** ['pezəntri] bondestand, bønder.

peascod ['pi·zkåd] erteskolm, ertebelg.

pease ['pi·z] erter. — **-blossom** erteblomst. — **-meal** ertemel.

pea-shell ['pi·ʃel] ertebelg.

pea-shooter ['pi·ʃu·tə] pusterør.

pea-soup ['pi·su·p] ertesuppe, gule erter.

peat [pi·t] torv, brenntorv. — **-bog** torvmyr. — **-hag**, — **-moss** torvmyr. — **-reek** ['pi·tri·k] torvrøyk. **peaty** ['pi·ti] torvrik; torvaktig.

pebble ['pebl] liten rullestein, fjærestein, kiselstein, stein, småstein. — **-crystal** bergkrystall. — **-glasses** krystallbriller.

pebbly ['pebli] full av småstein, steinet.

peccability [pekə'biliti] syndighet. **peccable** ['pekəbl] syndig. **peccadillo** [pekə'diloᵘ] liten synd, liten forseelse. **peccancy** ['pekənsi] syndefullhet, forseelse. **peccant** ['pekənt] syndig, syndefull; sykelig. **peccavi** [pe'ke'vai] jeg har syndet, syndstilståelse, syndserkjennelse.

peck [pek] halvskjeppe 9,087 l; mengde, haug, bråte; **be in a — of troubles** sitte i vanskeligheter til opp over ørene.

peck [pek] pikke, hakke; pikke på; spise; arbeide; tjene sitt brød; mat, føde.

peck [pek] falle, snuble.

peckage ['pekidʒ] for, mat.

pecker ['pekə] pikker, hakker; pikkende, hakkende; (hakke)spett; matlyst; mot, humør; **keep up one's —** ikke miste motet. **pecket** ['pekit] pikke. **peckish** ['pekiʃ] sulten.

Pecksniff ['peksnif] salvelsesfull hykler (fra Dickens' roman Martin Chuzzlewit).

pectinate ['pektinėt] kamformig.
pectination [pekti'ne'ʃən] kamform, kam.
pectoral ['pektərəl] bryst-; brystplate, bryststykke.
peculate ['pekjule't] begå underslag, stjele av kassen. peculation [pekju'le'ʃən] underslag, kassesvik. peculator ['pekjule'tə] kassetyv.
peculiar [pi'kju·ljə] egen, eiendommelig, særegen; særlig; underlig, rar; særeie, særrett. peculiarity [pikju·li'äriti] egenhet, eiendommelighet, særegenhet.
pecuniary [pi'kju·njəri] pekuniær, penge-.
pedagogic [pedə'gågik, pedə'gådʒik] pedagogisk; pedagogikk. pedagogical [pedə'gågikl, -'gådʒikl] pedagogisk. pedagogics [-iks] pedagogikk. pedagogism ['pedəgågizm] pedagogs arbeid; pedanteri. pedagogue ['pedəgåg] pedagog; pedant. pedagogy ['pedəgågi, -gådʒi] pedagogikk.
pedal ['pedəl, 'pi·dəl] pedal, fot-.
pedal ['pedəl] pedal; bruke pedalen; sykle.
pedant ['pedənt] pedant. pedantic [pi'däntik] pedantisk. pedantical [-kl] pedantisk. pedantry ['pedəntri] pedanteri.
peddle ['pedl] være kramkar, fare med skreppa, drive småhandel, høkre, reise omkring og høkre ut. peddler = pedlar. peddling ['pedliŋ] høkeraktig; handel som kramkar.
pedestal ['pedistəl] fotstykke, pidestall.
pedestrian [pi'destriən] fot-; til fots; gående; fotgjenger. pedestrianism [-izm] fotvandring; fotturer; fotsport. pedestrianize [-aiz] bruke føttene; gjøre fotturer.
pedicure ['pedikjuə] fotlege, liktornoperatør; fotpleie.
pedigree ['pedigri·] stamtavle, stamtre, herkomst, ætt.
pediment ['pedimənt] gavl over dør el. vindu.
pedlar ['pedlə] kramkar, skreppekar, kremmer. pedlaress ['pedlorès] kvinnelig kremmer. pedlary [-ri] skreppehandel; kram.
pedometer [pi'dåmitə] skrittmåler.
peel [pi·l] grissel, brødspade.
peel [pi·l] firkantet borgtårn (i skotsk grenseområde).
peel [pi·l] skrelle, skalle, flekke; avbarke; plyndre; kle av; la seg skrelle av; skall, skinn, skrell.
Peel [pi·l] Peel.
peeler ['pi·lə] en som skaller, skreller; røver, plyndrer.
peeler ['pi·lə] politibetjent (etter Robert Peel).
peeling ['pi·liŋ] skrell, skall; skinn, bark.
peep [pi·p] kike, gløtte, titte fram; pipe; pip; titting; kik, gløtt; tilsynekomst, frambrudd; innblikk. peep-bo ['pi·pboⁿ] titteleik. peeper ['pi·pə] spion: øye. peep(ing)-hole kikhull.
peep-show ['pi·pʃoⁿ] perspektivkasse.
peer [piə] stirre, kike, gløtte, speide; stirre på; komme til syne, bryte fram.
peer [piə] likemann, like; jevning; pair; overhusmedlem; House of Peers overhuset; create him a — opphøye ham i adelstanden.
peerage ['piəridʒ] pairs verdighet; adelskap; adel; adelskalender.
peeress ['piərès] pairs frue.
peerless ['piəlès] uforlignelig, makeløs. peerlessness [-nès] uforlignelighet.
peery ['piəri] stirrende, nysgjerrig (om blikk).
peeved [pi·vd] irritert, plaget, ergerlig.
peevish ['pi·viʃ] sær, gretten. peevishness [-nès] grettenhet.
Peg [peg] (kjælenavn for Margaret) Grete.
peg [peg] pinne; nagle, tapp; plugg; knagg; holder; klesklype; skrue; konjakk og vann; shilling; nagle; plugge; binde; stikke; markere; arbeide ivrig; come down a — slå av litt; take him down a — bringe ham, gjøre ham myk; use it as a — bruke det som middel; move one's -s gå bort; — out stikke opp, avmerke (med pinner).

peggingawl ['pegiŋå·l] pluggsyl.
Peggotty ['pegøti] Peggotty.
Peggy ['pegi] Grete.
pegtop ['pegtåp] snurrebass.
peignoir ['pe'nwa·] peignoir, frisérkåpe.
pejorative ['pi·dʒərətiv] nedsettende; nedsettende bemerkning.
pekan ['pekən] pekan, slags mår.
Pekin [pi·'kin]; Peking [pi·'kiŋ] Peiping.
pelagic [pi'lädʒik] pelagisk, hav —.
pelargonium [pelə'goⁿnjəm] pelargonium.
pelerine ['peləri·n] pelerine, dameskulderslag.
pelf [pelf] rikdom, mammon, mynt.
pelican ['pelikən] pelikan.
pelisse [pi'li·s] damepaletot, kåpe.
pell [pel] skinn; pergamentrull; clerk of the -s bokholder i skattkammeret.
pellet ['pelit] liten kule, pille, hagl.
pell-mell ['pel'mel] hulter til bulter.
pellucid [pel'l(j)u·sid] klar, gjennomsiktig. pellucidity [pel(j)u'siditi], pellucidness [pe'l(j)u·sidnès] gjennomsiktighet, klarhet.
Peloponnesian [peləpo'ni·ʃən] peloponnesisk; peloponneser.
pelt [pelt] fell, pels, skinn med hårene på.
pelt [pelt] dynge over, overdenge, bombardere; kaste med; kaste, hive; piske; øse ned, halje (om regn); kast, slag; set off full — sette av sted i fullt trav.
pelter ['peltə] kaster; angriper; skur, hagl, regn.
peltmonger ['peltmʌŋgə] pelsvarehandler.
peltry ['peltri] pelsverk, pelsvarer.
pelvics ['pelviks] bekken (i anatomi).
pemmican ['pemikən] pemmikan (slags konservert kjøtt).
pen [pen] kve; innelukke; sauegrind, hønsegård; stenge inne, sperre inne; inneslutte; kvee, sette i kve; — up the water demme opp for vannet.
pen [pen] penn, stil; skrive, føre i pennen.
penal ['pi·nəl] straffe-, kriminal; straffbar, kriminell; — code straffelov; — servitude straffarbeid.
penalize ['pi·nəlaiz] gjøre straffbart, sette straff for; belaste med ekstravekt; stille ugunstig.
penally ['pi·nəli] under straff.
penalty ['pen(ə)lti] straff, bot, pengebot, mulkt; the — of death dødsstraff; impose a — idømme en mulkt; pay the — of bøte for; on — of under straff av.
penance ['penəns] bot, botsøving.
pen-and-ink ['penəndiŋk] drawing pennetegning.
Penang [pi'näŋ] Penang. — -nut betelnøtt.
pen-case ['penke's] pennehus, pennal.
pence [pens] pence, pl. av penny.
penchant [fr., 'pa·nʃa·n] hang, tilbøyelighet.
pencil ['pensl] pensel; blyant; griffel, stift; male, tegne, skrive med blyant; rable ned.
pencil-box ['penslbåks] pennal.
pencil-case ['penslke's] blyantholder.
pencilled ['pensld] skrevet med blyant; stråleformig. penciller ['penslə] veddemålsagent. pencilling ['pensliŋ] blyantskrift; blyantskisse. pencil-sharpener ['penslʃa·pnə] blyantspisser.
pendant ['pendənt] hengende; tilheng, tillegg; pendant; ørering; dobbe, vimpel, stander.
pendency ['pendənsi] henging (utover); det å være uavgjort; during the — of the suit mens saken står på.
pendent ['pendənt] hengende; ragende utover.
pending ['pendiŋ] hvilende, svevende, uavgjort; verserende, gående; forestående; truende; (preposisjon om tiden:) under, i løpet av; i påvente av.
pendulous ['pendjuləs] hengende; svingende.
pendulum ['pendjuləm] pendel.
pendulum-clock ['pendjuləmkliŋk] pendelur.
Penelope [pi'neləpi] Penelope.

penetrability [penitrə'biliti] gjennomtrengelighet. **penetrable** ['penitrəbl] gjennomtrengelig; sårbar, tilgjengelig. **penetralia** [peni'tre'liə] innerste; hemmeligheter. **penetrancy** ['penitrənsi] inntrengenhet, gjennomtrenging; skarphet. **penetrant** ['penitrənt] inntrengende, gjennomtrengende, skarp.

penetrate ['penitre't] trenge inn i, trenge igjennom, gjennomtrenge, gjennombore; røre, gjøre inntrykk på; utgrunne, gjennomskue; trenge inn, bane seg vei. **penetrating** ['penitre'tiŋ] gjennomtrengende; skarp; skarpsindig. **penetration** [peni-'tre'ʃən] inntrenging, gjennomtrenging; skarpsindighet. **penetrative** ['penitrətiv] inntrengende, gjennomtrengende; skarp; skarpsindig. **penetrativeness** [-nés] inntrenging, skarphet. **penfold** ['penfo·ld] kve, innhegning. **penguin** ['peŋgwin] pingvin. **pen-holder** ['penho·ldə] penneskaft. **peninsula** [pé'ninsjulə] halvøy; **the Peninsula** (især:) Pyreneerhalvøya. **peninsular** [pé'ninsjulə] halvøy-; halvøyformet; på Pyreneerhalvøya; **the Peninsular War** Englands krig på Pyreneerhalvøya mot Napoleon.

penitence ['penitəns] anger. **penitent** ['penitənt] angrende, angerfull, botferdig; skriftebarn. **penitential** [peni'tenʃəl] anger-; angrende, botferdig. **penitentiary** [peni'tenʃəri] bots-, pønitense-; angrende; fengsel.

penknife ['pennaif] pennekniv. **penman** ['penmən] skribent; kalligraf. **penmanship** ['penmənʃip] skrivedyktighet. **pen-name** ['penne'm] påtatt forfatternavn, psevdonym. **pennant** ['penənt] vimpel. **pennies** ['peniz] pennyer, pennystykker. **penniform** ['penifå·əm] fjærformet. **penniless** ['penilés] fattig, uten en skilling; **a — beggar** en fattig lus. **pennilessness** [-nés] fattigdom.

pennon ['penən] vinge; vimpel, stander. **penn'orth** ['penəþ] = pennyworth. **Pennsylvania** [pensil've'nje] Pennsylvania, forkortet: **Penn.** **penny** ['peni] penny, ca. 7 øre; penger, skilling; **a — for your thoughts!** den som visste hva De tenker så på; **I'll bet you a —** jeg skal vedde; **make a —** tjene penger; **he thinks his — silver** han har høye tanker om seg selv; **turn an honest —** tjene seg en skilling på ærlig vis; **in for a —, in for a pound** når man har sagt A, må man også si B; **take care of the pence, and the pounds will take care of themselves!** vær sparsommelig i småting! **he that will not keep a — shall never have many** den som ikke sparer på skillingen, får aldri daleren; **a — saved is a — got** penger spart er penger tjent. **penny|-a-liner** ['penia'lainə] bladneger. **— -bank** ørebank. **— -dreadful** røverroman, fillebok. **— -drive** pennytur. **— -gaff** fjelebodsteater; kneipe. **— -in-the-slot-machine** automat. **— -pig** sparegris. **— -post** pennypost. **— -postage** pennyporto. **— -roll** sjuøres franskbrød. **— -stamp** pennyfrimerke. **— -weight** et vektlodd. **— -wise** sparsommelig i småting; **be — -wise and pound-foolish** spare på skillingen og la daleren gå. **pennyworth** ['penəþ, 'peniwə·þ] pennys verdi, så mye som fås for en penny; full verdi for pengene, godt kjøp; liten smule; **have a good — of a thing** få noe svært billig. **penology** [pi'nålədʒi] straffelære. **pension** ['penʃən] understøttelse, stønad, pensjon; tiendepenger; føderåd; pensjonat, pensjon; pensjonere, sette på pensjon; not for a — ikke for alt i verden; **retire on a full-pay —** trekke seg tilbake med sin fulle gasje i pensjon; **old-age —** alderdomspensjon, alderspensjon. **pensionary** ['penʃənəri] pensjonert; pensjons-; pensjonist; tidligere, i Nederlandenes større byer:

borgermester; **Grand —** premierminister, statssekretær. **pensioner** ['penʃənə] pensjonist, føderådsmann, student av 2. klasse i Cambridge; **the King's —s** kongelig æresvakt. **pensive** ['pensiv] tankefull, fortenkt, tungsindig. **pensiveness** [-nés] tankefullhet. **penstock** ['penståk] stigbord; pumperør. **pent** [pent] innelukket, innesperret. **pentacapsular** [pentə'kæpsjulə] med fem rom. **pentachord** ['pentəkå·əd] femstrenget instrument. **pentagon** ['pentəgån] femkant. **pentameter** [pen'tämitə] pentameter, femfotsvers. **pentangular** [pen'täŋgjulə] femvinklet. **Pentateuch** ['pentətju·k] de fem mosebøkene. **Pentecost** ['pentikåst] (jødenes) pinse. **pentecostal** ['penti'kåstəl] pinse-. **penthouse** ['penthaus] halvtekke, utskott, sval, bislag. **pentroof** ['pentru·f] halvtak. **pent-up** ['pent'ʌp] innelukket, innesperret; inneklemt, innestengt, oppdemt; undertrykt. **penultimate** [pi'nʌltimit] nest sist, nest siste staving. **penurious** [pi'njuəriəs] fattig, knapp, snau, sparsom. **penuriousness** [-nés] fattigdom, knapphet. **penury** ['penjuri] armod, fattigdom, trang. **pen-wiper** ['penwaipə] pennetørker. **peon** ['pi·ən] dagleier; leiekar; (i Mexico:) gjeldsfange; (i India:) bud, politibetjent. **peony** ['pi·əni] bonderose, peon. **people** ['pi·pl] folk, folkeslag; mennesker; befolke; **the -s of Europe** Europas nasjoner; **the —** folket, den store masse; **a man of the —** en mann av folket; **— of quality** standspersoner; -**'s edition** folkeutgave; **People's Palace,** londonsk institusjon til folkeopplysning. **pep** [pep] kraft, mot. **pepper** ['pepə] pepper; stryk, pryl; pepre; overdenge; beskyte. **— -and-salt** gråmelert. **— -box** pepperbøsse. **— -cake** pepperkake. **— -caster** pepperbøsse. **— -corn** pepperkorn; småting. **— -cress** hagekarse. **pepperer** ['pepərə] peprer; brushode. **peppering** ['pepəriŋ] skarp; sint. **pepper|mint** ['pepəmint] peppermynte. **— -pot** pepperbøsse. **— -wort** karse. **peppery** ['pepəri] hissig, brå, irritabel. **pepsin** ['pepsin] pepsin (stoff i mavesaften). **peptic** ['peptik] peptisk, fordøyelses-; lettfordøyelig; fordøyelsesmiddel. **Pepys** [pi·ps, peps, 'pepis] Pepys. **per** [pə·] igjennom; ved, om, pr.; **— annum** pro anno, for året; **— bearer** ved overbringer; as **— account** ifølge regning; **— cent** prosent, pr. hundre; as **— usual** som sedvanlig. **peradventure** [pərəd'ventʃə] kan hende, kanskje. **perambulate** [pə'rämbjule't] gjennomvandre; bereise; undersøke. **perambulation** [pərämbju-'le'ʃən] gjennomreise; inspeksjonsreise. **perambulator** ['prämbjule'tə, pə'rämbjule'tə] barnevogn. **perceivable** [pə'si·vəbl] kjennelig, merkbar. **perceive** [pə'si·v] fornemme, merke, oppfatte, føle, se, bemerke. **per cent** [pə'sent] prosent. **percentage** [pə'sentidʒ] prosent, prosentsats, prosenttall; tantième; prosentvis. **perceptibility** [pəsepti'biliti] det å oppfatte; merkbarhet. **perceptible** [pə'septibl] kjennelig, merkbar. **perception** [pə'sepʃən] oppfatting, erkjennelse; oppfatningsevne; nemme. **perceptive** [pə'septiv] oppfattende; oppfattings-; **— faculty** oppfattingsevne. **perceptivity** [pəsep'tiviti] oppfattingsevne; nemme. **perch** [pə·tʃ] stang; pinne, vagle, hønsehjell; høy plass, høyt stade; (lengdemål) 5½ yards; (flatemål) 40¼ yards; sette seg, slå seg ned; sitte (om fugler); anbringe, sette, legge (på et høyere

sted); **the convent is -ed on a crag** klostret ligger på en bergknaus.
perch [pə·tʃ] åbor, tryte.
perchance [pə'tʃɑ·ns] kanskje.
percher ['pə·tʃə] sittefugl.
percipient [pə'sipjənt] fornemmende, oppfattende.
percolator ['pə·kəle'tə] sil, filter.
percussion [pə'kʌʃən] støt, slag, sammenstøt, rystelse; — **of the brain** hjernerystelse. — **-cap** fenghette, knallperle. — **-shell** sprenggranat.
percussive [pə'kʌsiv] støt-.
perdition [pə·'diʃən] fortapelse, undergang.
perdu [pə·dju·] skjult.
peregrinate ['perigrine't] vandre; leve i utlandet. **peregrination** [perigri'ne'ʃən] vandring; opphold i utlandet.
peregrine ['perigrin] farende, flakkende; vandrefalk; — **falcon** vandrefalk.
peremptorily ['perəmtərili] avgjørende.
peremptory ['perəmtəri, pə'remtəri] avgjørende, bestemt, sikker, ugjenkallelig.
perennial [pə'renjəl] stetsevarig; uopphørlig, uuttømmelig; flerårig; flerårig plante, staude.
perennity [pə'reniti] flerårighet.
perfect ['pə·fikt] fullkommen; fullstendig, formelig; **the** — perfektum; **practice makes** — øvelse gjør mester; **he's a** — **horror** det er et fryktelig menneske.
perfect [pə'fekt] fullkommengjøre, utvikle, utdanne; **perfect oneself** perfeksjonere seg, dyktiggjøre seg.
perfectation [pə·fek'te'ʃən] fullkommengjøring. **perfecter** [pə·fektə, pə'fektə] utvikler. **perfectibility** [pəfekti'biliti] utviklingsevne. **perfectible** [pə'fektibl] som kan utvikles, bli fullkommen.
perfection [pə'fekʃən] fullkommenhet; **in** —, **to** — fortreffelig, utmerket; **she acts to** — hennes spill er fortreffelig.
perfectionist [pə'fekʃənist] en som foregir å være fullkommen; svermer (religiøs, politisk).
perfective [pə'fektiv] utviklende.
perfectly ['pə·fiktli] fullkommen, til fullkommenhet.
perfectness ['pə·fiktnes] fullkommenhet.
perficient [pə'fiʃənt] fullbyrder, stifter.
perfidious [pə'fidiəs] troløs, falsk; utro. **perfidiousness** [-nês], **perfidy** ['pə·fidi] troløshet, falskhet; svik, utroskap.
perforate ['pə·fore't] gjennombore, perforere; **perforated stockings** gjennombrutte strømper.
perforate ['pə·fərit] gjennomboret, med huller.
perforation [pə·fo're'ʃən] gjennomboring, perforering. **perforator** ['pə·fore'tə] bor, boremaskin.
perforce [pə'få·°s] nødtvungen; nødvendigvis.
perform [pə'få·°m] gjennomføre, fullende, utføre; oppfylle (plikt, løfte); gi til beste; opptre, komme med noe, utføre et parti, spille, synge; **he -s well** han spiller godt; — **on the piano** spille piano.
performable [pə'få·°məbl] gjennomførlig, gjørlig, mulig, som lar seg utføre, oppfylle.
performance [pə'få·°məns] utførelse; oppfyllelse; prestasjon; verk, arbeid; forestilling, nummer av en forestilling.
performer [pə'få·°mə] utfører, opptredende, rollehavende; **be the principal -s** utføre hovedrollene.
performing [pə'få·°miŋ] som kan utføre. — **seals** dresserte selhunder.
perfume ['pə·fju·m] duft, vellukt, parfyme.
perfume [pə'fju·m] parfymere.
perfumery [pə'fju·məri] parfymer; parfymeri.
perfunctoriness [pə'fʌŋktərinês] overfladiskhet, skjøtesløshet. **perfunctory** [pə'fʌŋktəri] skjøtesløs, slurvet, overfladisk, mekanisk.
pergamentaceous [pə·gəmən'te'ʃəs] pergamentaktig, som pergament.
pergola ['pə·gələ] pergola (åpen lauvgang).

perhaps [pə'häps, präps] kanskje; — **so, and** — **not,** kanskje, og kanskje ikke.
peri ['piəri] peri, fe i persisk mytologi.
peri [peri] i smstn.: omkring.
perianth ['periänþ] blomsterdekke.
pericarp ['perika·°p] frøgjemme.
periclean [peri'kli·°n] perikleisk. **Pericles** ['perikli·z] Perikles.
perigee ['peridʒi·] perigeum (planetbanes punkt nærmest jorden).
perihelion [peri'hi·liån] perihelium (planetbanes punkt nærmest solen), høydepunkt.
peril ['peril] fare, vågnad; sette på spill, våge; **at his own** — på eget ansvar; **do it at your** —! gjør det om du tør; **be in** — **of one's life** være i livsfare.
perilous ['periləs] farlig, vågelig, vågal.
period ['piəriəd] omløp, periode; slutning; slutt, ende; stans; punktum; **put a** — **to** gjøre ende på; **a girl of the** — moderne pike.
periodic [piəri'ådik] periodisk.
periodical [piəri'ådikl] tidsskrift.
peripatetic [peripə'tetik] omvandrende; peripatetisk; vandrende, reisende; peripatetiker.
periphery [pə'rifəri] periferi, omkrets.
periphrasis [pe'rifrəsis] perifrase, omskrivning.
periphrastic [peri'frästik] omskrivende.
periscope ['periskoʷp] periskop (kikkert, brukt ved styring av undervannsbåt).
perish ['periʃ] forgå, omkomme, forkomme, gå til grunne, forulykke, forlise; forderves, visne; fortapes; ødelegge. **perishability** [periʃə'biliti] forgjengelighet. **perishable** ['periʃəbl] forgjengelig; lett fordervelig.
peristalsis [peri'stälsis] peristaltikk.
peristaltic [peri'stältik] peristaltisk.
peristyle ['peristali] peristyl, søylegang.
periwig ['periwig] parykk; gi parykk på, ta parykk på. — **-pated** med parykk på.
periwinkle ['periwiŋkl] havsnegl; gravmyrt.
perjure ['pə·dʒə] sverge falsk; **perjured** mensvoren.
perjurer ['pə·dʒərə] meneder.
perjury ['pə·dʒəri] mened, falsk ed.
perk [pə·k] kneise, briske seg; pynte.
perky ['pə·ki] viktig, kry, staselig.
permanence ['pə·mənəns] standhaftighet, stadighet, støhet. **permanency** [-nənsi] stadighet, støhet. **permanent** [-nənt] bestandig, blivende, fast, stadig, stødig, varig.
permeate ['pə·mie't] gjennomtrenge, gå igjennom. **permeation** [pə·mi'e'ʃən] gjennomtrenging, gjennomgang.
permissible [pə'misibl] tillatelig, tillatt.
permission [pə'miʃən] tillatelse, lov, løyve.
permissive [pə'misiv] som tillater; tillatt.
permit [pə'mit] tillate, gi lov, la.
permit ['pə·mit] passerseddel, tollpass.
permittee [pəmi'ti·] en som har fått tillatelse(n).
permutable [pə'mju·təbl] ombyttelig.
permutation [pə·mju·'te'ʃən] ombytting.
pernicious [pə'niʃəs] fordervelig, skadelig, pernicious.
perniciousness [-nês] fordervelighet.
pernickety [pə'nikiti] småpirket.
pernoctation [pənåk'te'ʃən] overnatting.
peroration [pero're'ʃən] slutningsavsnitt av en tale.
perpend [pə·'pend] overveie.
perpendicular [pə·pen'dikjulə] perpendikulær, loddrett; loddrett linje. **perpendicularity** ['pə·pəndikju'läriti] lodrett stilling.
perpetrate ['pə·pitre't] iverksette, begå, forøve. **perpetration** [pə·pi'tre'ʃən] iverksetting, begåelse, forøvelse; dåd; udåd. **perpetrator** ['pə·pitre'tə] forøver, gjerningsmann.
perpetual [pə'petjuəl] bestandig, stetsevarende; fast; idelig; — **motion** perpetuum mobile; rastløshet; **-screw** skruen uten ende. **perpetuate** [pə'petjue't] fortsette uavbrutt, forplante, vedlikeholde, forevige.

perpetuation [pəpetʃu'eiʃən] fortsettelse, forevigelse.

perpetuity [pə·pi'tju·iti] evighet, uavbrutt varighet; for a —, in — for bestandig.

perplex [pə'pleks] forvikle, gjøre innviklet, forplumre; forvirre, sette i forlegenhet; plage, ergre. perplexity [-iti] forvikling; forvirring, forlegenhet, vånde.

per pro. fk. f. per procuration pr. prokura.

perquisite ['pə·kwizit] sportel, bifortjeneste; (i pl.) aksidenser, tilfeldige inntekter.

perquisition [pə·kwi'zifən] etterforsking.

perruque [pə'ru·k] parykk.

perruquier [pə'ru·kiə] parykkmaker.

perry ['peri] pærevin.

perse [pə·s] gråblå; gråblå farge.

persecute ['pə·sikju·t] forfølge (mest om religiøs forfølgelse). persecution [pə·si'kju·ʃən] forfølgelse. persecutive ['pə·sikju·tiv] forfølgelses-. persecu‹r ['pə·sikju·tə] forfølger.

perse erance [pə·si'viərəns] utholdenhet. persevere [pə·si'viə] vedbli, fortsette med, persevering [pə·si'viərin] iherdig, utholdende.

Persia ['pə·ʃə] Persia. Persian ['pə·ʃən] persisk; perser; angorakatt.

persiennes [pə·ʃi'enz] utvendige persienner.

persiflage [pə·si'fla·ʒ] spott, persiflasje, fjas.

persimmon [pə·simən] daddelplomme, svart daddel.

persist [pə'sist] vedbli, fortsette med, ture fram; fastholde. persistency [-ənsi] det å vedbli el. å fastholde, iherdighet, hårdnakkethet; framturing. persistent [-ənt] iherdig, utholdende, hårdnakket, persistingly [-inli] vedblivende, iherdig.

person ['pə·s(ə)n] person; legemsskikkelse, ytre; in — personlig, selv. personable ['pə·s(ə)nəbl] nett, tekkelig. personage [pə·s(ə)nidʒ] personlighet. personal ['pə·s(ə)nəl] personlig; personlig pronomen. personality [pə·sə'näliti] personlighet; person.

personalty ['pə·snlti] løsøre, rørlig gods.

personate ['pə·səne·t] framstille, etterligne, utgi seg for, påta seg; personated devotion påtatt fromhet. personation [pə·sə'neiʃən] framstilling, det å gi seg ut for. personator ['pə·s(ə)ne·tə] framstiller.

personification [pə'sånifi'keiʃən] personliggjøring, personifikasjon. personify [pə'sånifai] personliggjøre.

personnel [pə·så'nel] personale, personell.

perspective [pə'spektiv] perspektivisk; perspektiv; — drawing perspektivtegning.

perspicacious [pə·spi'keiʃəs] skarpsynt, skarpsindig. perspicaciousness [-nés], perspicacity [pə·spi'käsiti] skarpsynthet, skarpsindighet.

perspicuity [pə·spi'kju·iti] klarhet, anskuelighet. perspicuous [pə'spikjuəs] klar.

perspirate ['pə·spire't] svette, transpirere. perspiration [pə·spi'reiʃən] svette, transpiration. perspirative [pə·'sp(a)irətiv] svette-, transpirasjons-. perspire [pə'spaiə] svette ut, svette; tyte ut, transpirere. perspiring [pə·spaiərin] svett, varm.

persuade [pə·swe'd] overtale, overbevise; — oneself bli overbevist; be -ed of være overbevist om. persuader [pə'swe'də] overtaler, overtalingsmiddel, motiv; (i kuskespråk) pisk.

persuasion [pə·swe'ʒən] overtaling, overbevisning; tro. persuasive [pə'swe'siv] overtalende, overbevisende; overtalingsmiddel. persuasiveness [-nés] overtalingsevne.

pert [pə·t] nesevis, kjepphøy, kry; nesevis person.

pertain [pə·te'n] tilhøre, høre til; angå.

Perth [pə·þ] Perth.

pertinacious [pə·ti'ne'ʃəs] hårdnakket, stiv; iherdig, seig, standhaftig. pertinaciousness [-nés], pertinacity [pə·ti'näsiti] hårdnakkethet, stivhet; iherdighet, standhaftighet.

pertinence ['pə·tinəns] anvendelighet, passelig-

het. pertinent [-nənt] anvendelig, høvelig, treffende; saklig; — to angående.

pertness [pə·tnés] nesevishet.

perturb [pə·tə·b] forstyrre, uroe, forurolige; bringe forstyrrelse i. perturbation [pə·tə'be'ʃən] forstyrrelse; uregelmessighet. perturbedly [pə'tə·bidli] urolig.

pertuse [pə·tju·s] gjennomhullet, hull i hull.

Peru [pə'ru·] Peru.

peruke [pə'ru·k, pi'ru·k] parykk.

perusal [pə'ru·zəl] gjennomlesing, lesning.

peruse [pə'ru·z] lese grundig igjennom.

Peruvian [pi'ru·vjən] peruaner, peruansk; — bark kinabark.

pervade [pə·'ve'd] gå igjennom, trenge igjennom. pervasion [pə·'ve'ʃən] gjennomtrenging, det å gå gjennom. pervasive [pə·'ve'siv] gjennomtrengende, gjennomgående.

perverse [pe(·)və·s] forkjært, fordervet; forstokket, bakvendt, vrang, lei. perverseness [-nés] forkjærthet, fordervethet. perversion [pə'və·ʃən] forvrenging, forvansking; fordervelse. perversity [pə'və.siti] forkjærthet, fordervelse. perversive [pə'və.siv] forvrengende; fordervelig, skadelig.

pervert [pə'və·t] frafallen.

pervert [pə'və·t] forvrenge, forvanske, fordreie; fordervet forføre.

pervious ['pə·viəs, -vjəs] tilgjengelig, farbar.

pesky ['peski] (amr.) trettende, plagsom, lei, vond.

pessimism ['pesimizm] pessimisme. pessimist [-mist] pessimist. pessimistic [pesi'mistik] pessimistisk.

pest [pest] sykdom, sott; plage, pestilens, skadedyr; a — upon him! skam få han!

pester ['pestə] besvære, plage, bry.

pestiferous [pe'stifərəs] smitteførende, usunn; fordervelig. pestilence ['pestiləns] pest, smitte. pestilent [-lənt] pestaktig, skadelig. pestilential [pesti'lenʃəl] pestaktig, forpestende; fordervelig; avskyelig.

pestle ['pesl] støter (til morter); støte, knuse.

pet [pet] ulune, grettenskapsri; in a — i et dårlig lune; take — bli fornærmet, furte.

pet [pet] kjælebarn, kjæledegge, yndling, favoritt; kjæle-, yndlings-; kjæle for, gjøre stas av, forkjæle; make a — of gjøre til sin kjæledegge; — name kjælenavn.

petal ['petl] blomsterblad, kronblad.

peter ['pi·tə] out begynne å slippe opp, minke.

peter ['pi·tə] Peter; -('s)pence peterspenger.

peterman ['pi·təmən] fisker på Themsen.

petit ['peti] liten, mindre.

petition [pə'tifən] bønn; ansøkning, søknad, andragende; be; ansøke, sende en søknad til; protestere, klage; file his — overlevere sitt bo (til skifteretten).

petitionary [pə'tifən(ə)ri] bedende; bede-, bønne-. petitioner [pə'tifənə] andrager, søker; klager (især i skilsmissesak).

Petrarch ['pi·tra·k] Petrarka.

petre ['pi·tə] salpeter.

petrean [pi'tri·ən] klippe-, stein-.

petrel ['petrəl] stormfugl, petrell.

petrifaction [petri'fäkʃən] forsteining. petrifactive [petri'fäktiv] forsteinende. petrific [pi·'trifik] forsteinende. petrification [petrifi'keiʃən] forsteining. petrify ['petrifai] forsteine; forsteines.

Petrograd ['petrogräd] Petrograd (nå Leningrad).

petrol ['petrål, 'petr(ə)l] petroleum; forsyne med petroleum.

petroleum [pi'tro"ljəm, pə'tro"ljəm] petroleum.

petticoat ['petiko"t] underskjørt; ta på skjørter; — government skjørteregimente; Petticoat Lane gate i London.

petties ['petiz] småting, ubetydeligheter.

pettifog ['pétifåg] bruke lovtrekkerier, lovkroker, opptre smålig el. sjikanøst. pettifogger

|-ə] vinkelskriver, lovtrekker; rev, fuling. **pettifoggery** [-əri] lovkroker, lovtrekkerier.
pettiness ['petinès] litenhet, ubetydelighet.
pettish ['petiʃ] gretten, ergerlig. **pettishness** [-nés] lunethet, grettenhet.
pettitoes ['petitoᵘz] griselabber.
petto ['petoᵘ], **in** — i sitt eget bryst, i hemmelighet, for seg selv.
petty ['peti] liten, mindre; ubetydelig; — **jury** mindre jury, bestående av 12 mann.
petulance ['petjuləns] grettenhet, pirrelighet.
petulant ['petjulənt] gretten, grinet, vrang, pirrelig, furten; lunefull; kåt, overgiven.
pew [pju·] kirkestol, lukket stol i en kirke.
pew-opener ['pju·oᵘpnə] kirketjener.
pewter ['pju·tə] britanniametall; tinnkrus; sølv; penger. **pewterer** ['pju·tərə] blikkenslager. **pewtery** ['pju·təri] britanniametall.
pf. fk. f. **piano forte** svakt, dernæst sterkt.
phaeton ['feᵗtən] faeton, en høy, åpen, lett vogn, trille; (amr.) jaktvogn.
phalanx ['fäläŋks] falanks, fylking.
phantasm ['fäntäzm] fantasibilde, synkverving, syn, drøm, hjernespinn.
phantasy ['fäntəsi] fantasi.
phantom ['fäntəm] fantasibilde, syn; gjenferd, spøkelse, vardøger, fantom. — **-ship** spøkelsesskip.
Pharaoh ['fæ·ᵒrɔᵘ] Farao.
pharisaic [färi'seᵗik] fariseisk. **pharisaical** [färi-'seᵗikl] fariseisk. **pharisaism** ['färiseᵗizm] fariseisme. **pharisee** ['färisi·] fariseer.
pharmaceutic [fa·ᵒmə's(j)u·tik] farmasøytisk. **pharmaceutical** [-kl] farmasøytisk. **pharmaceutics** [-ks] farmasi. **pharmacist** ['fa·ᵒməsist] farmasøyt. **pharmacologist** [fa·ᵒmə'kålədʒist] farmakolog. **pharmacology** [-dʒi] farmakologi, læren om lægemidler. **pharmacopoeia** [fa·ᵒməkə'pi·ə] farmakopø, apotekerbok. **pharmacy** ['fa·ᵒməsi] farmasi; apotek.
phase [feᵗz] fase, skifte.
phases ['feᵗsi·z] faser; **phasis** ['feᵗsis] fase.
phasma ['fäzmə, -s-] spøkelse.
Ph. D. fk. f. **philosophiae** doctor dr. philos.
pheasant ['fez(ə)nt] fasan. **pheasantry** ['fezentri], **pheasant-walk** fasangård, fasaneri.
phenacetin [fi'näsitin] fenacetin.
Phenicia [fi'niʃə] Fønikia.
Phenician [fi'niʃən] fønikisk; føniker.
Phenix ['fi·niks] Føniks.
phenomena [fi'nåminə] fenomener. **phenomenal** [-nəl] fenomenal, enestående. **phenomenon** [fi'nåminən] fenomen, forekomst, foreteelse.
phial ['faiəl] medisinflaske, flaske; ha på glass, på flasker.
Phil. [fil] fk. f. **Philip**.
Philadelphia [filə'delfjə] Filadelfia.
philander [fi'ländə] gjøre kur, flørte; fjase, **philandering** [-riŋ] kurmakeri, flørting, flørt.
philanthropic [filän'þråpik], **philanthropical** [-kl] filantropisk, menneskekjærlig. **philanthropist** [fi-'länþropist] filantrop, menneskevenn. **philanthropy** [fi'länþropi]filantropi, menneskekjærlighet.
philatelic [filə'telik] filatelistisk, frimerke-. **philatelist** [fi'lätilist] frimerkesamler; filatelist. **philately** [fi'lätili] filateli.
philharmonic [fil(h)a·ᵒ'månik] filharmonisk, musikkelskende.
Philip ['filip] Filip.
Philippian [fi'lipjən] mann el. kvinne fra Filippi.
philippic [fi'lipik] tordentale, filippika.
Philippine ['filipain, 'filipi·n], **the — Islands** el. **the Philippines** Filippinene.
philippine ['filipi·n] filippine, filippinegave.
philistine ['filistain] filister, spissborger.
philological [filo'låadʒikl] filologisk, språkvitenskapelig. **philologist** [fi'lålədʒist] filolog, språkgransker, **philology** [fi'lålədʒi] filologi, språkvitenskap.

philomel ['filomel] (poetisk:) nattergal. **philomela** [filo'mi·lə] nattergal.
philopine [filo'pi·n] el. **philop(o)ena** [filo'pi·nə] filipine; filipinegave: **eat** — **with** spise filipine med.
philosopher [fi'låsəfə] filosof. **philosophical** [filo'såfikl; -zåf-] filosofisk. **philosophism** [fi-'låsəfizm] sofisteri. **philosophist** [-fist] sofist. **philosophize** [-faiz] filosofere.
philosophy [fi'låsəfi] filosofi, filosofisk system el. lære; **moral** — etikk; **natural** — naturfilosofi; fysikk.
philter ['filtə] elskovsdrikk.
phiz [fiz] fjes, ansikt.
phlebitis [fli'baitis] årebetennelse.
phlegm [flem] slimvæske i blodet; flegma, koldsindighet; dorskhet.
phlegmatic [fleg'mätik] flegmatisk.
phlox [flåks] floks (plante).
phone [foᵘn] telefonere; telefon.
Phoenicia, Phoenician s e **Phenicia, Phenician**.
phonetic [fo'netik] fonetisk, lyd-; — **spelling** lydskrift. **phonetical** [fo'netikl] lyd-. **phonetician** [foᵘni'tiʃən] fonetiker. **phonetics** [fo'netiks] fonetikk.
phonic ['foᵘnik] fonisk, lyd-; **the** — **method** lydmetoden.
phonograf ['foᵘnogra·f] fonograf.
phonological [foᵘno'låadʒikl] fonetisk. **phonologist** [fo'nålədʒist] fonetiker. **phonology** [fo'nålədʒi] fonologi.
phosphate ['fåsfeᵗt, -fit, -fet] fosfat.
phosphorate ['fåsfəreᵗt] forbinde med fosfor. **phosphoreous** [fås'få·riəs] lysende. **phosphorescence** [fåsfo'resəns] fosforglans, morild. **phosphoric** [fås'fårik] fosforaktig. **phosphorous** ['fås-fərəs] fosfor. **phossy** ['fåsi] fosfor-, fosforaktig.
photo ['foᵘtoᵘ] fotografi. **photochrome** ['foᵗtakroᵘm]fargefotografi.**photo-engraving**[-èn gre'viŋ] fotogravyr. **photograph** ['foᵘtəgra·f, -gräf] fotografi; fotografere. **photographer** [fo'tågrəfə] fotograf. **photographic** [foᵘto'gräfik] fotografisk. **photographist** [fo'tågrəfist] fotograf. **photography** [fə'tågrəfi] fotografi. **photogravure** [foᵘtogrə-'vjuə] fotogravyr.
phrase [freᵗz] frase, forbindelse, setning, uttrykk, ordlag, vending, ord; uttrykke, kalle, benevne; **empty -s** tomme talemåter; **in your own** — for å bruke Deres egne ord. **phrase-book** parlør. **phraseologic** [freᵗzio'lådʒik] fraseologisk. **phraseologist** [freizi'ålədʒist] fraseolog, frasesamler. **phraseology** [-dʒi] språk, fraseologi, uttrykksmåte. **phrasing** ['freᵗziŋ] uttrykk, ordvalg, språk.
phrenologic(al) [freno'lådʒik(l)] frenologisk. **phrenologist** [fre'nålədʒist] frenolog. **phrenology** [-dʒi] frenologi (den lære som av kraniets ytre form vil bestemme de sjelelige evners sete i hjernen).
Phrygia [fi'ridʒiə] Frygia.
Phrygian ['fridʒiən] frygisk; fryger.
phthisic ['tizik] tæringssyk, tærings-. **phthisical** [-kl] tæringssyk. **phthisis** ['þaisis, 'taisis, 'þisis, 'tisis, -z-] tæring.
phys. fk. f. **physics; physician; physiology**.
physic ['fizik] legekunst; legemiddel; medisin, legemidler; behandle, pleie; kurere. **physical** ['fizikl] fysisk; legemlig; naturvitenskapelig.
physician [fi'ziʃən] læge, doktor.
physicist ['fizisist] fysiker.
physics ['fiziks] fysikk.
physiognomic [fizio'nåmik] fysiognomisk. **physiognomics** [-s] fysiognomikk. **physiognomist** [fizi-'ånəmist] ansiktskjenner. **physiognomy** [fizi-'ånəmi] fysiognomi, ansikt, ansiktsuttrykk.
physiography [fizi'ågrəfi] fysisk geografi.
physiologic(al) [fizio'lådʒik(l)] fysiologisk. **physiologist** [fizi'ålədʒist] fysiolog. **physiology** [fizi'ålədʒi] fysiologi.

physique [fi'zi·k] konstitusjon, legemsbygning, ytre.
pi [pai] pi, π (i matematikk 3,14).
piaffe [pjäf] lunke, smådilte, småtrave.
pianist [pi'änist] pianist.
piano [pi'a·noᵘ] piano, svakt.
piano [pi'änoᵘ, pi'a·noᵘ] piano; grand — flygel.
pianoforte [pjäno'få·ᵊti] pianoforte.
pianola [piə'noᵘlə] pianola.
piano-organ [pjänoᵘ'å·ᵊgən] mekanisk piano.
piano-player ['pjänoᵘ ple'ə] mekanisk klavér.
pianotuner ['pjänoᵘ tju·nə] pianostemmer.
piassava [pi'äsəvə] piassava (trevler av bladstilker på palmer, benyttet til koster).
piastre [pi'ästə] pjaster (i Spania, ca. 4 kr.).
piazza [pi'ädzə] piazza, åpen plass; (amr.) veranda.
pibroch ['pi·bråk] sekkepipe(musikk).
picaroon [pikə'ru·n] sjørøver, pirat.
piccadilly [pikə'dili] slags høy pipekrage.
Piccadilly [pikə'dili] gate i London.
piccolo ['pikoloᵘ] pikkolo (en fløyte).
piceous ['pisiəs, 'pifəs] beksvart.
pick [pik] hakke, stikke, pirke i; plukke; pille, rense; velge, velge ut, plukke ut, søke ut; sanke, samle, samle opp; — one's way lete seg fram, kjenne seg for; fare varsomt; I shall have to — a bone with him jeg har en høne å plukke med ham; — a hole in a person's coat kritisere en sterkt, ha noe å utsette på en; — oakum plukke drev; sitte i forbedringsanstalten; — a pocket begå lommetyveri; — weed luke; — and choose velge og vrake; — words være kresen i valget av ord; — off plukke av, bort, skyte ned en for en; — out hakke ut; ble ut; finne ut; velge; velge ut; utheve, framheve; — up hakke, pikke, pille opp; plukke opp; oppta; tilegne seg; he has -ed up strange acquaintances han har gjort merkelige bekjentskaper; he -s up a few pence now and then han tjener noen få skillinger nå og da; — up courage fatte mot; — up one's living slå seg igjennom; — up with gjøre bekjentskap med.
pick [pik] spisst redskap; hake, krok; hakke; the — of det beste av, eliten av; have one's — kunne velge.
pick-a-back ['pikəbäk] på skuldrene, på ryggen.
pickaback ['pikəbäk] på skuldrene, på ryggen.
pickaxe ['pikäks] hakke, kilhakke.
picked [pikt] utsøkt. picker ['pikə] plukker; liten tyv; sanker; hake, krok; hakke. pickery ['pikəri] småtyveri, raskeri.
picket ['pikit] pel, påle; staur, stake; tjorpåle; pikett; forpost; feltvakt; streikevakt; omgi med stakitt; tjore; blokere. — -fence pelegjerde. — -guard pikettvakt.
pickings ['pikinz] småplukk; biinntekter.
pickle ['pikl] lake, saltlake, eddik; pickles; villstyring, vill krabat; knipe, klemme; legge i lake, sylte; be in a — sitte fint i det; I have a rod in — for him det skal han komme til å unngjelde for.
pickle|-cured saltet i lake. -d rogue erkekjeltring. — -pot syltekrukke. pickler ['piklə] nedlegger.
pickling ['piklin] nedlegging; sylting. — -season syltetid. — -tub saltetønne.
picklock ['piklåk] dirk.
pick-me-up ['pikmiʌp] oppstrammer, hjertestyrkning, oppstiver, dram.
pickpocket ['pikpåkit] lommetyv.
pickthank ['pikpänk] øyentjener.
Pickwick ['pikwik] person hos Dickens.
Pickwickian [pik'wikiən] pickwickiansk; pickwickianer; in a — sense i spesiell betydning.
picnic ['piknik] landtur, utflukt (med måltid i det fri), dra på landtur, gjøre utflukt.
Pict [pikt] pikter. Pictish ['piktif] piktisk.
pictorial [pik'tå·riəl] maler-; billed-; malende; illustrert.
picture ['piktfə] maleri; malerkunst; lerret,

bilde; male, avbilde; utmale; animated (living el. moving) -s levende bilder; she is the living — of her mother hun er sin mors uttrykte bilde; she is as beautiful as a — hun er billedskjønn. — -book billedbok. — -gallery malerisamling. — -hat schæferhatt (bredskygget). — -house kino. — -palace kino. — -postcard prospektkort. — -puzzle rebus, billedgåte; fiksérbilde; billedklosser.
picturesque [piktfə'resk, -tjə-] malerisk; malende; naturskjønn. picturesqueness [-nés] maleriskhet.
Pidgin-English ['pidʒin'inglif] kineserengelsk, kaudervelsk.
Pidgin-English ['pidʒin'inglif] kineserengelsk, kaudervelsk.
pie [pai] skjære (fugl).
pie [pai] postei, pai.
pie [pai] fisk (som typografuttrykk); røre, rot; go to — falle i fisk.
piebald ['paibå·ld] broket, flekket, spraglet.
piece [pi·s] stykke; lapp; fille; skjøt; bete, stump; skuespill; pengestykke; kanon; gevær; threepence a — tre pence stykket (pr. stykk); work by the — arbeide på akkord; take to -s ta fra hverandre; a — of domestic furniture et stykke innbo; møbel; a — of artillery en kanon; a — of advice et råd; a — of news en nyhet; a — of information en meddelelse, en melding; a — of needlework et håndarbeid; a — of good fortune et hell, en lykke; give him a — of my mind si ham sannheten; by the — stykkevis; tear in(to) -s rive i stykker; of a — av samme stykke, av samme slags; of one — i ett stykke.
piece [pi·s] bøte, lappe, utbedre; forene, forbinde; forbinde seg, vokse sammen.
pièce de résistance [pie'sdøre'zi·sta·ŋs] den solide rett, noe solid el. viktig.
piece-goods ['pi·sgudz] alenvarer. pieceless ['pi·slés] hel, som består av ett stykke. piece-meal ['pi·smi·l] stykkevis, stykke for stykke; oppstykket; enkelt, atskilt. piece-work stykkarbeid. piece-worker stykkarbeider.
pied [paid] spraglet, flekket (især om hest).
pie-man ['paimən] posteibaker.
pier [piə] molo, bru, skipsbru, landingsbru; brupel, brukar; stolpe, dørstolpe.
pierage ['piəridʒ] bryggepenger.
pierce [piəs] gjennombore, gjennomtrenge; gjennomskue; bore seg inn, trenge fram. piercer ['piəsə] gjennomborende; boringsredskap.
piercing ['piəsin] gjennomtrengende; bitende, skarp, kvass, inntrengende. piercingness [-nés] skarphet.
pier-glass ['piəgla·s] konsollspeil (stort).
pier-table ['piəte'bl] konsoll, speilbord.
pietism ['paiitizm] pietisme. pietist [-tist] pietist. pietistic(al) [paii'tistik(l)] pietistisk.
piety ['paiiti] fromhet, gudfryktig kjærlighet.
piffle ['pifl] skravl, tull, sludder; vrøvle, tøve.
pig [pig] gris, svin; flesk; smeltet klump, blokk; -s smelt fly det er jo helt umulig; buy — in a poke kjøpe katten i sekken; keep a — holde gris; dele sitt losji med en annen student.
pig [pig] grise; få grisunger; ligge som griser.
pig [pig] blue —; cock — duestegg; hen — hundue; milk a — (bl. spillere) plukke en grønnskolling; as fond as -s forelsket som duer.
pigeon ['pidʒən] plukke (bl. spillere).
pigeon ['pidʒən] plukke (bl. spillere).
pigeon-breast ['pidʒənbrest] duebryst; fuglebryst, framstående brystbein (en misdannelse, som kan skyldes engelsk syke).
Pigeon-English ['pidʒən'inglif] = Pidgin-English.
pigeon|-express ['pidʒəniks'pres] duepost — -fancier [-'fänsjə] duehandler, dueelsker. — -hearted fryktsom. — -hole hull i dueslag; fag, rom; reol; legge i særskilte rom, oppbevare, legge på hylla; forsyne med rom. — -house dueslag. — -livered feig, redd, med harehjerte.
pigeonry ['pidʒənri] duehus, dueslag.

pig-eyed ['pigaid] grisøyd. **piggery** ['pigəri] grisehus, svineri. **piggish** ['pigiʃ] griset, svinsk.
pig|headed ['pighedid] stivsinnet. **-headedness** stivsinnethet. — **-iron** råjern.
pigling ['piglin] grisunge.
pigment ['pigmənt] farge, fargestoff.
pigmental [pig'mentəl] farge-.
pignut ['pignʌt] jordnøtt.
pig|pen grisehus. **-skin** svinelær. — **-sticker** svine-slakter. **-sty** svinesti. **-tail** grisehale, hårpisk.
pike [paik] gjedde.
pike [paik] spyd, pigg, brodd, lanse; høygaffel; veibom.
piked [paikt] pigget, pigg-, spiss.
pikeman ['paikmən] bommann.
pikestaff ['paiksta·f] spydskaft; piggstav; **call a — a —** kalle tingen med dens rette navn; **it is all as plain as a —** det er som fot i hose, sole-klart, klart som blekk.
pilaster [pi'lästə] pilaster, halvpille, (delvis i muren innbygd, firkantet pille).
pilchard ['piltʃəd] pilchard, sardell, sardin.
pile [pail] stabel, dynge, haug, hop; bål, likbål; bygning, bygningskompleks; — **of arms** gevær-kobbel; — **of buildings** bygningskompleks; funeral — likbål.
pile [pail] stable (opp), dynge (opp); fylle, starpe, kcble (ρεværene).
pile [pail] grunnpel, påle; pilotere, pele.
pile [pail] hår, ull, lo; forsyne med lo.
pile-driver ['paildraivə] rambukk.
piles [pailz] hemorroider.
pile-work ['pailwə·k] peleverk
pile-worm ['pailwə·m] peleorm.
pilfer ['pilfə] rapse, raske, naske, småstjele. **pilferer** ['pilfərə] rapser, nasker. **pilfering** [-riŋ] rapseri, raskeri, nasking. **pilferi** [-ri] rapseri, raskeri, nasking.
pilgrim ['pilgrim] pilegrim; valfarte; **Pilgrim's Progress** bok av Bunyan; **the — Fathers** de engel-ske puritanere som i 1620 forlot England med The Mayflower for å bosette seg i Amerika.
pilgrimage ['pilgrimidʒ] pilegrimsferd.
piling ['pailiŋ] oppstabling; pilotering.
pill [pil] pille; kule; læge; gi piller; lage til piller.
pillage ['pilidʒ] plyndring, bytte, rov; plyndre, røve.
pillar ['pilə] pille, søyle; stolpe; støtte. — **-box** postkasse anbrakt på en støtte. **pillared** ['piləd] som hviler på piller; søyleformig.
pill-box ['pilbåks] pilleeske; liten vogn.
pillion ['piljən] baksete på motorsykkel; ride-pute (som plass for en person bak rytteren).
pillory ['piləri] gapestokk; sette i gapestokk.
pillow ['pilo⁰] hodepute, pute; legge på pute. — **-bier** putevar. — **-case** putevar. — **-slip** putevar. **pillowy** ['pilo⁰i] puteaktig, myk.
pilot ['pailət] los; flyger (— **of aeroplane**); lose. **pilotage** ['pailətidʒ] lospenger; losing, le-delse. **pilot|balloon** prøveballong. — **-bread** be-skøyter. — **-cloth** en slags tøy til bruk for sjø-menn og til kåper og overfrakker. — **-engine** et lokomotiv som sendes ut for å holde linjen klar for et tog. — **-fish** losfisk. — **-jacket** pjekkert.
Pimlico ['pimliko⁰] fint kvarter i London.
pimp [pimp] ruffer; drive rufferi, holde horehus.
pimpernel ['pimpənel] pimpinelle; arve (plante).
pimple ['pimpl] kveise, kvise, filipens. **pimpled** ['pimpld], **pimply** ['pimpli] full av filipenser, kveiset, kviset.
pin [pin] nål (til å feste med), knappenål; stift, nudd, splint, bolt, tapp, trenagle, plugg, pinne, sinketapp; kleskype; strikkepinne, bunding-stikke; kjevle; skrue (på strenginstrument); viser (på solur); kile; (i slang) grann, dust; feste med nåler. feste med stifter; **hairpin** hårnål; **hat-pin** hattenål; **broach-pin** brystnål; **scarf-pin** slipsnål; **safety pin** sikkerhetsnål;

curtain pin gardinholder; **tent pin** teltplugg; **clothes-pin** klesklype; **rolling-pin** kjevle; **I don't care a —** about it jeg bryr meg ikke det grann om det; — **him to the earth** spidde ham til jorda, holde ham fast.
pinafore ['pinəfå·⁰] ermeforkle, barneforkle.
pin-case ['pinke¹s] nålehus.
pince-nez [fr., 'pänsne¹] pince-nez, stang-lorgnett.
pincers ['pinsəz] knipetang, tang.
pinch [pin(t)ʃ] knipe, klemme; klype; trykke, presse; pine, smerte; bringe i knipe; knappe av, nekte seg det nødvendigste, spare, spinke. — **oneself** nekte seg det nødvendige; **every man knows best where his shoe -es** . . . hvor skoen trykker; **they were -ed for room** det knep med plassen; **with the most -ing economy** med den mest knepne sparsommelighet.
pinch [pin(t)ʃ] knip, kniping, klemming; trykk; nød; klemme; pris (snus); **I see where your —** **lies** jeg ser hvor skoen trykker; **on (at) a —** i knipe; **if ever it comes to a —** om det skulle komme til stykket, om det skulle knipe.
pinchbeck ['pin(t)ʃbek] tambak; uekte, etter-gjort.
pinched [pinʃt] sammenknepen; tynn; forpint.
pincher ['pinʃə] gnier; brekkjern, pinsebein, spett.
pin-cushion ['pinkuʃən] nålepute.
Pindar ['pində] Pindar (gresk dikter).
pin-drill ['pindril] tappbor.
pine [pain] næletre, furu, furutre; ananas; **Norway —** alminnelig gran; **Scotch —** alminnelig furu; **dwarf —** dvergfuru; **(Italian) stone —** pinje.
pine [pain] tæres bort, ta av, forsmekte; for-tæres av lengsel, lengte sårt (for etter); — **away** tæres bort, — **for one's country** lide av hjemlengsel.
pineal ['piniəl] kongleformet; — **body** (el. **gland**) pinealkjertel (i hjernen).
pine|apple ['painäpl] ananas (planten og fruk-ten). — **-barren** ['pain'bärən] furumo. — **-beauty** furuspinner. — **-bullfinch** konglebit. — **-bur**, — **-cone** kongle. — **-house** ananas-drivhus. — **-marten** skogmår.
pinery ['pain(ə)ri] ananas-hage; -anlegg.
pine-tree ['paintri·] nåletre. **pinetum** [pai-'ni·təm] nåleskog. **pine-wood** nåleskog.
piney ['paini] vegetabilsk talg.
pin-fire ['pinfaiə] tenn-nåls-; — **-cartridges** tenn-nåls-patroner.
ping [piŋ] visle.
ping-pong ['piŋpåŋ] bordtennis, ping-pong.
pinhead ['pinhed] nålehode, knappenålshode.
pining ['painiŋ] vantreven.
pinion ['pinjən] vinge; vingespiss; drev på et hjul; armlenke; binde vingene på; stekke vingene på; (bak)binde, lenke.
pink [piŋk] lite øye; nellik; blekrød farge; fullkommenhet; ideal; blekrød, lyserød, rosa; gjennombore, stikke huller el. tunger i; farge rød; **the — of perfection** fullkommenheten selv; — **coat** rød frakk; jegerdrakt. — **-eye** ['piŋkai] lite øye. — **-eyed** småøyd; rødøyd. **pinking** ['piŋkiŋ] uthogging. — **-eye** hoggjern; kakejern.
pinkish ['piŋkiʃ] blekrød, lyserød.
pinky ['piŋki] liten; rødlig.
pin-money ['pinmʌni] nålepenger.
pinnace ['pinis] tomastet skip; slupp.
pinnacle ['pinəkl] lite tårn, spir, tinde; topp; bygge med spisstårn; sette spir el. småtårn på.
pinnate ['pinet] fjærformet; finnet.
pinner ['pinə] nålemaker.
pinnock ['pinək] meis (fugl).
pint [paint] halvpott; halvflaske.
pintle ['pintl] liten pinne, liten stift, rortapp.
pinworm ['pinwə·m] barneorm.
piny ['paini] rik på nåletrær, furukledd.
pioneer [paiə'niə] bane, bryte vei for; være

banebrytende; pionér; banebryter, foregangsmann.

piony ['paiəni] peon.

pious ['paiəs] kjærlig, from, gudfryktig.

pip [pip] kvitre, pistre, pipe (om fugleunge).

pip [pip] kjerne, fruktkjerne.

pip [pip] pip (fuglesykdommen); **have the** — (om mennesker) være i dårlig humør.

pipe [paip] fløyte, pipe; sekkepipe, rør, ledningsrør; tobakkspipe; luftrør; skattkammer; pipe, blåse på fløyte, fløyte, plystre; **clear his** — kremte; **fill a** — stoppe en pipe; **the -s played** sekkepipene spilte opp; **put his** — **out** krysse hans planer, la det hele ryke over ende; gjøre ende på ham; **put that in your** — **(and smoke it)** merk Dem det! forstår De det! **clerk of the** — fullmektig i dómenekontoret. — **-bowl** pipehode.

pipeclay ['paipkle¹] pipeleire; rense med pipeleire, pusse; klarere, kvitte.

pipe-cleaner ['paipkli·nə] piperenser.

piped [paipt] pipet, rørformet.

pipeful ['paipful] pipefull, pipestopp.

pipe|-layer ['paiple'ə] rørlegger. — **-laying** rørlegging. — **-light** fidibus. — **-line** rørledning. — **-man** strålemester.

pip emma [pip'emə] (i slang) ... **post meridiem** ettermiddag.

piper ['paipə] piper, spillemann; sekkepiper; knurr (fisk).

pipe|-rack pipehylle. — **-roll** skattkammerrull. — **-shank** pipestilk. — **-stem, -stick** piperør. — **-tube** piperør.

piping ['paipiŋ] besetning av snorbroderi på damekjoler; **pipings** (pl.) rørledning.

pipit ['pipit] piplerke.

Pippa ['pipə] navn på en italiensk fabrikkpike i et dikt; — **Passes** (dikt av Robert Browning).

piquancy ['pi·kənsi] skarphet, pikant beskaffenhet, pikanteri. **piquant** ['pi·kənt] skarp, pirrende; bitende; pikant.

pique [pi·k] fornærmelse, såret stolthet; pik kere, såre, støte; pirre, egge; **be -d** bli støtt på mansjettene.

piquet [pi'ket] pikett (slags kortspill).

piquet ['pikit] pikett, feltvakt, vakt.

piracy ['pairəsi] sjørøveri; ulovlig ettertrykk.

pirate ['pairét] sjørøver, pirat, sjørøverskip; drive sjørøveri; plagiere; ettertrykke; — **buses** pirat-omnibuser (som lever av rov; kusk og konduktør lønnes med prosenter).

piratical [pai'rätikl] sjørøversk, sjørøver-.

pirouette [piru'et] piruett (sving med foten i dans, vending på samme flekken).

piscary ['piskəri] fiskerett. **piscator** [pi'ske'tə] fisker. **piscatorial** [piskə'tå·riəl] fiske-, fiskeri-. **piscatory** ['piskətəri] fiske-, fiskeri-. **pisciculture** [pisi'kʌltʃə] fiskeutklekking. **pisciform** ['pisifå·ᵐm] av form som en fisk. **piscina** [pi'sainə] piscina (vaskebekken for presten i katolsk kirke). **piscine** ['pisain] fiske-. **piscivorous** [pi'sivərəs] fiskeetende, fiskespisende.

pish [p(i)ʃ] pytt! blåse av; si pytt.

pistachio [pi'sta·ʃio⁰] pistasie.

pistil ['pistil] støvvei.

pistol ['pistəl] pistol; skyte ned, skyte med pistol.

pistole [pi'sto⁰l] pistol (spansk mynt). **piston** ['pistən] stempel; pistong. — **-rod** stempelstang. — **-stroke** stempelslag. — **-valve** stempelventil; sylinderglider.

pit [pit] hull, grav, grop, gruve, hule; sjakt; avgrunn; fallgruve; dyregrav; armhule; hjertekule; parterre; kampplass for haner; gjøre fordypninger, huller i; grave i; stille opp; hisse sammen; **have the power of** — **and gallows** ha makt til å dømme til døden; **a face -ted by the small-pox** et kopparret ansikt.

pitapat ['pitəpät] klapp-klapp, tikk-takk; banking.

pitch [pitʃ] bek; beke; formørke.

pitch [pitʃ] slå ned, drive ned, feste i jorda, slå (f. eks. telt, leir); stille opp i slagorden, fylke, ordne; kaste, hive, kyle; stemme, fastsette tonehøyden av; steinlegge; slå leir, stille ut, legge fram (til salgs); styrte, falle; skråne, halle; stampe, duve; høyde, trin, tonehøyde, tone, høydepunkt; skrues stigning, skruegang; tannhjulsdeling; helling, hall, skråning (f. eks. av tak); kast; sted, plass; **a -ed battle** et regulært slag, feltslag; — **into skjenne på,** gi en inn, «gi en på pukkelen»; **at its highest** — på høydepunktet; — **of a screw** skruegang; the — of the roof hellingen på taket.

pitch-and-toss ['pitʃən'tås] kaste på stikka; mynt og krone.

pitch|-black ['pitʃbläk] beksvart. **-blende** [-blend] bekblende. **-coal** ['pitʃko⁰l] bekkull, gagat. **-dark** ['pitʃdɑ·ᵒk] bekmørk, belgmørk. **pitched** [pitʃt] ogs. hellende; **a high-pitched** roof et bratt tak.

pitcher ['pitʃə] kaster osv.; gatestein.

pitcher ['pitʃə] krukke; (amr.) kanne, mugge; little pitchers **have long ears** små gryter har også ører; **pitchers have ears** veggene har ører; **the pitcher goes so often to the well that it comes home broken at last** krukka går så lenge til vanns at den kommer hankeløs hjem.

pitch-farthing ['pitʃ'fɑ·ᵒδin] klink. **pitch-fork** ['pitʃfå·ᵒk] fork, høygaffel, greip; stemmegaffel; kaste, sende, hive.

pitchiness ['pitʃines] bekaktighet, beksvart farge; belgmørke.

pitching ['pitʃiŋ] gatesalg, utstilling til salg; steinlegging; stamping, duving. **pitch-pine** ['pitʃpain] bekfuru, amerikansk feitfuru.

pitchy ['pitʃi] bekaktig, beket; beksvart, belgmørkt.

pitcoal ['pitko⁰l] steinkull. **piteous** ['pitiəs, -tjəs, -tʃəs] medlidende; sørgelig; bedrøvelig; ynkelig; ussel. **piteousness** [-nés] sørgelighet.

pitfall ['pitfå·l] fallgruve; dyregrav, felle, snare.

pith [piþ] marg; styrke, kraft; kjerne. **pithy** ['piþi] marg-, margfull; kraftig; fyndig. **pitiable** ['pitiəbl, -tjəbl] ynkverdig, elendig. **pitiful** ['pitif(u)l] medlidende; ynkverdig; jammerlig, sørgelig. **pitiless** [-lés] ubarmhjertig; hard. **pitilessness** [-nés] ubarmhjertighet.

pitman ['pitmən] bergmann, gruvearbeider.

pittance ['pitəns] porsjon, tilmålt del; ussel lønn; smule; almisse.

pitter ['pitə] plaske; tromme. — **-patter** klapring; klapre.

pity ['piti] medlidenhet, medynk; barmhjertighet; **it is a** — det er skade, synd; **the** — of it! så sørgelig; **take** — **on** ha medlidenhet med; for -'s sake for Guds skyld.

pity ['piti] føle (ha) medlidenhet med; ynkes over, synes synd på, beklage, ynke.

pivot ['pivət] tapp, aksel, gjenge; hengsel; fløymann; sette på en tapp, dreie på en tapp; svinge. **pivotal** ['pivətəl] svingende, roterende; vesentlig, viktig.

pixie el. **pixy** ['piksi] hulder. **pizzicato** [pitsi'ka·to⁰] pizzicato. **pl.** **fk.** **f. plate;** plural. **P. L. A.** fk. f. **Port of London Authority.** **placability** [pläkə'biliti] forsonlighet. **placable** ['pläkəbl] forsonlig. **placard** ['pläkɑ·ᵒd] plakat, oppslag; slå opp, kunngjøre.

place [ple¹s] plass, sted, rom; stilling, post, tjeneste; stand, rang; stille, sette, legge; **it is not my** — **to** ... det tilkommer ikke meg å ...; **take** — finne sted; **in the first** — for det første; **be in his right** — være på sin rette hylle. — **-hunter** embetsjeger, levebrødspolitiker. — **-kick** (i fotball) spark til liggende ball.

placeman ['ple'smən] tjenestemann, funksjonær.

place-name ['ple'sne'm] stedsnavn.

placenta [plə'sentə] morkake; blomsterbunn.

placer ['ple'sə] gull-leie, gullgruve.

placid ['pläsid] stille, fredelig, blid, rolig. **placidity** [plə'siditi] blidhet, stillhet, tilfredshet.

placket ['pläkit] skjørtesplitt, stakklomme.

plagiarism ['ple'dʒərizm] plagiat. **plagiarist** [-rist] plagiator. **plagiarize** [-raiz] plagiere. **plagiary** [-ri] plagiator; plagiat.

plague [ple'g] pest; plage; landeplage, svartedauen, pestilens; plage, pine, hjemsøke; være til plage; a — upon him pokker ta ham! **plaguer** ['ple'gə] plageånd. **plaguy** ['ple'gi] forbannet, fordømt.

plaice [ple's] rødspette, kongeflyndre.

plaid [pläd] pledd (slags skotsk rutet skjerf eller kappe); reisepledd; skotsk rutet.

plain [ple'n] klage.

plain [ple'n] jevn, jamn, slett, flat, åpen; tydelig, klar, åpenbar; usmykket, simpel, enkel; middelmådig, ordinær; glatt; ukunstlet, likefrem, endefram, åpenhjertig, oppriktig, ærlig; tarvelig; plan; flate, slette, jevn mark; kampplass; planere, jevne, slette, glatte, utjevne, jamne; in — clothes i sivil. — **cooking** daglig matlaging. — **-dealer** ær.ig person. — **-dealing** oppriktig, ærlig; oppriktighet, ærlighet, åpenhet. — **-looking** stygg. **-ness** ['ple'nnés] jevnhet. — **-speaking** oppriktighet, åpenhet. — **-spoken** oppriktig, åpen, måldjerv.

plaint [ple'nt] klage. **plaintiff** ['ple'ntif] sitant, saksøker, klager. **plaintive** ['ple'ntiv] klagende; melankolsk, sørgelig. **plaintiveness** [-nés] klagende karakter. **plaintless** ['ple'ntlès] klageløs.

plait [plät] fletning; flette.

plan [plän] plan, grunnriss, utkast; råd; hensikt; legge planer.

planchette [pla·n'ʃet] plansjett, brett på støtter brukt til psykiske forsøk.

plane [ple'n] plan, flate; aeroplan, fly; høvel; plan; flat, jevn, jamn; jevne, jamne, glatte; høvle. — **-iron** høveljern.

planer ['ple'nə] høvelmaskin.

planet ['plänit] planet. **planetarium** [pläni-'tæ·ºriəm] planetarium. **planetary** ['plänit(ə)ri] planetarisk.

plane-tree ['ple'ntri·] platan (slags lønnetre).

planing ['ple'niŋ] høvling.

planing-bench ['ple'ninbenʃ] høvelbenk.

planing-machine ['ple'ninmə'ʃi·n] høvelmaskin.

planing-mill ['ple'ninmil] høvleri.

planish ['pläniʃ] planere; jevne, glatte, slette.

plank [pläŋk] planke; plankekle, plankelegge.

plant [pla·nt] vokster, plante; renning, stikling, avlegger; plantning; inventar; materiell; anlegg; avtalt bedrageri; gjemmested for stjålne varer; plante, beplante; anlegge; grave ned, skjule; transmission — kraftoverføringsanlegg; electric light — lysanlegg; school — skolemateriell. **plantable** ['pla·ntəbl] som kan plantes (til).

Plantagenet [plän'tädʒinet] Plantagenet.

plantain ['pläntin] kjempe (plante); pisang.

plantation [plän'te'ʃən] plantasje, plantning, planteskole.

planter ['pla·ntə] plantasjeeier; planter; såredskap.

plantigrade ['pläntigre'd] sålegjenger.

planting ['pla·ntiŋ] plantasje; plantning.

plantless ['pla·ntlès] ubevokst, bar, gold.

plant-louse ['pla·ntlaus] bladlus.

plaque [pla·k] platte; flekk.

plash [plaʃ] flette greiner sammen, flette gjerde. **plash** [pläʃ] skvette, skvalpe, plaske; plasking. **plashing** ['pläʃiŋ] plasking. **plashy** ['pläʃi] våt, tilskvettet; sumpet.

plasma ['pläzmə] plasma; protoplasma, celleslim; serum.

Plassey ['pläsi] Plassey.

plaster ['pla·stə] (mur)puss, kalk; gips; plaster; kalk; pusse; gipse; legge plaster på; **adhesive** (el. sticking) — heftplaster; — of Paris gips. — **-cast** gipsavstøpning. **plasterer** ['pla·stərə] gipser, gipsarbeider. **plasterfigure** gipsbilde. **plastering** ['pla·stəriŋ] gipsing, pussing, kalking; kalkpuss. **plaster-work** gipsarbeid. **plastery** gipsaktig, gipsholdig.

plastic ['plästik] formende, dannende; plastisk; — art plastikk; — arts bildende kunster; — clay pottemakerleire.

plasticity [plä'stisiti] formende kraft; plastisitet.

plastron ['plästrən, 'pla·strən] brystharnisk; fekters kyrass; skilpaddes bukskjold.

plat [plät] flette; fletning.

plat [plät] jevn, jamn, flat; flat plass; jordstykke, lapp, flekk.

plat [pla·] rett (på spisekart).

plate [ple't] skive, tavle, plate, metallplate; skilt; sølvtøy, sølv; plett, plettsaker; tallerken; premie; dekke med metallplater; pansre; plettere; hamre; **-d frigate** panserfregatt. — **-armour** platerustning.

plateau ['plätou] vidde, høyslette.

plate-basket ['ple'tba·skit] korg (el. kasse) til kniver og gafler.

plateful ['ple'tful] (en full) tallerken.

plate|-glass ['ple'tgla·s] speilglass. — **-glazed** forsynt med speilglass. — **-goods** plettvarer. — **-iron** jernblikk. — **-layer** skinnelegger. — **-mark** stempel, prøvemerke. — **-printer** koppertrykker. — **-printing** koppertrykk. **plater** ['pleitə] pletterer, elektropletthandler.

plate|-rack ['ple'träk] tallerkenrekke. — **-warmer** tallerkenvarmer.

platform ['plätfå·ºm] plattform, perrong; forhøyning; talerstol; politisk program; standpunkt; oppfatning; holde tale fra plattform. — **-speaker** folkemøtetaler.

plating ['ple'tiŋ] panser.

platinum ['plätinəm] platina.

platitude ['plätitju·d] platthet, smakløshet; flauhet. **platitudinize** ['pläti'tju·dinaiz] gjøre flaue bemerkninger.

Platonic [plə'tånik] platonisk. **platonism** ['ple'tənizm] platonisme. **platoon** [plə'tu·n] pelotong. **platter** ['plätə] tretallerken. **platy** ['ple'ti] plateaktig, plate-. **plaudit** ['plå·dit] bifallsytring. **plauditory** ['plå·ditəri] bifalls-; bifallende. **plausibility** [plå·zi'biliti] antagelighet, tilsynelatende riktighet; behagelig vesen. **plausible** ['plå·zibl] plausibel, antagelig, trolig, tiltalende.

play [ple'] spille (ut); le(i)ke, fjase, spøke; framstille, utføre en rolle, agere; sette i virksomhet, la spille; spill; bevegelse; virksomhet, forlystelse, leik, spøk; skuespill; handlemåte, framgangsmåte; at what spille whist; two can — at that det skal vi være to om; — off on her føre henne bak lyset; — of colours fargespill; — of features minespill; what's the — to be? hva går det på teatret? at the — i teatret; fair — ærlig spill; foul — uærlig spill; cheat at — bedra i spill. **playable** ['ple'əbl] som det er råd (el. verdt) å spille.

play|-actor ['ple''äktə] skuespiller (nedsettende). — **-actress** skuespillerinne (nedsettende). — **-bill** program, plakat. — **-book** tekst til teaterstykke. — **-day** fridag. — **-debt** spillegjeld. **play-fellow** leikekamerat. **playful** ['ple'f(u)l] opplagt til leik, le(i)ken; spøkefull, gladlyndt, spøkende. **playfulness** lyst til å leike; spøkefullhet, spøk.

play|-goer ['ple''gonə] teatergjenger. — **-going** teatersøkende. **-ground** leikeplass. **-hour** leiketid. fritid; spilletid.

playing ['ple'iŋ] le(i)k, spill. — **-card** spillkort.

play|night teateraften. **-thing** leketøy. **-wright** skuespillforfatter.

plea [pli·] rettssak; sakførsel; forsvar; påstand; unnskyldning; partsinnlegg; påskudd, bønn; on the — that med påberopelse av at . . ., idet man gjør gjeldende at . . .; **put in a** — nedlegge innsigelse; **put in a** — for legge et ord inn for.

plead [pli·d] tale i en sak for retten; føre en sak, pledere; påberope seg, anføre som unnskyldning; — **guilty** erkjenne seg skyldig etter tiltalen; — **not guilty** erklære seg ikke skyldig. **pleadable** ['pli·dəbl] som kan gjøres gjeldende. **pleader** ['pli·də] sakfører; forsvarer, talsmann, forfekter. **pleading** ['pli·diŋ] bedende, bønnlig; forsvar; innlegg; bønner.

pleasance ['plezəns] moro, gammen, behagelighet, lyst, fornøyelse, forlystelse; lysthage. **pleasant** ['plezənt] behagelig; elskverdig; hyggelig; lystig, munter, gemyttlig. **pleasantness** [-nès] behagelighet. **pleasantry** ['plezəntri] spøk, skjemt; munterhet.

please [pli·z] behage, være til lags, tiltale; — God om Gud vil; **to** — **him** for å gjøre ham til lags; **there's no pleasing some folks** noen mennesker er det umulig å gjøre til lags; **I am to** — **myself** jeg kan gjøre som jeg selv vil; **pass me the book** —! vær så vennlig å rekke meg boka; **if you** — om forlatelse, unnskyld; **(a cup of tea?) if you** —! ja takk! **pleased** [pli·zd] glad, tilfreds, fornøyd; **I shall be** — **to** det skal glede meg å . . ., jeg skal med glede . . . **pleasing** ['pli·ziŋ] tiltalende, behagelig. **pleasingness** [-nès] behagelighet.

pleasurable ['pleʒərəbl] behagelig. **pleasure** ['pleʒə] behag, velbehag, glede, fornøyelse, gammen, moro; lyst, ønske; befaling; fornøye; behage; være til lags; **what's your** — hva kan vi så til tjeneste med? **have a** — in synes gildt i; **I take** — **in sending you** el. **I have the** — **of sending you** jeg har den glede å sende Dem; **at** — etter behag, etter eget tykke; **a man of** — en levemann.

pleasure|-boat ['pleʒəbo⁺t] lystbåt. — **excursion** lysttur. — **-going** fornøyelse. — **-grounds** (offentlig) park. — **-house** lysthus. **pleasureless** [- ès] gledeløs. **pleasurer** ['pleʒərə] en som er ute for å more seg. **pleasure|-reading** morskapslesning. — **-seeker** en som er ute for å more seg. — **-seeking** forlystelsessyk. — **-trip** fornøyelsestur, rekreasjonsreise. **pleasuring** ['pleʒəriŋ] fornøyelse, fornøyelser.

pleat [pli·t] fold, legg; folde, plissere. **plebeian** [pli'bi·ən] plebeiisk; plebeier. **plebiscite** ['plebisit] folkebeslutning, -vedtak. **plectrum** ['plektrəm] plektrum.

pledge [pledʒ] pant; pantsetting; garanti; forpliktelse; løfte; gissel; skål; pantsette, sette i pant; innestå for; skål med (el. for) en. **I was -d in honour not to** jeg var på ære forpliktet til ikke. **pledgee** [ple'dʒi·] panthaver. **pledger** ['pledʒə] pantsetter, pantstiller. **pledget** ['pledʒit] dott (f. eks. vatt), kompress.

Pleiades ['plaiədi·z] pleiader (Atlas' 7 døtre i gresk mytologi); the **Pleiades** Pleiadene, Sjustjernen.

plenary ['pli·nəri] full, hel, fullstendig. **plenipotentiary** [plènipo'tenʃəri] befullmektiget (utsending), som har fullmakt, fullmektig. **plenteous** ['plentiəs, -tjəs] overflødig, rikelig; vel forsynt. **plenteousness** [-nès] overflod. **plentiful** ['plentif(u)l] overflødig, rik, rikelig, fruktbar, grøderik. **plenty** ['plenti] fylle, overflod, overflødighet, rikdom; — **of** ['plentjəv] fullt opp av, flust opp av, nok av; — **of time** god tid. **pleonasm** ['pli·ənäzm] pleonasme. **pleonastic** [pliə'nästik] pleonastisk. **plesiosaurus** ['pli·siə'så·rəs] plesiosaurus (et fossilt dyr). **plethora** ['pleþərə] blodoverfylling; overflod.

plethoric [ple'þårik, pli-] blodrik, blodfull; overlesst.

pleurisy ['pluərisi] brysthinnebetennelse; plevritt. **pleuritic** [pluə'ritik] som har brysthinnebetennelse, som har plevritt. **pleuritis** [pluə'raitis] se **pleurisy**.

plexus ['pleksəs] nettverk, flettverk, vev, plexus.

pliability [plaiə'biliti] bøyelighet, smidighet; føyelighet, svakhet. **pliable** ['plaiəbl] bøyelig, smidig; myk; svak. **pliancy** ['plaiənsi] se **pliability**. **pliant** ['plaiənt] bøyelig; bløt; myk. **pliers** ['plaiəz] nebbetang, **flatnosed** — flattang. **plight** [plait] løfte; love; binde, gi; sette i pant.

plight [plait] forfatning, tilstand, knipe, klemme.

Plimsoll ['plimsəl] Plimsoll.

plinth [plinþ] pl int, søylesokkel.

Pliny ['plini] Plinius.

pliocene ['plaiəsi·n] pliocen formasjon; pliocen. **plod** [plåd] traske, trakke, labbe; henge i, slite i; slepe; seigt arbeid, slit. **plodder** ['plådə] sliter, trekkdyr; arbeidstræl, lesehest. **plodding** ['plådiŋ] seig, strevsom; iherdighet, tålmodig slit.

plot [plåt] jordstykke, lapp, flekk, hageflekk, kolonihage, (gras)plen; plan, kart; gjøre et grunnriss av; kartlegge.

plot [plåt] plan, sammensvergelse, komplott; anslag; intrige; handling, gang (i et skuespill); legge planer; smi renker, intrigere. **plotter** ['plåtə] renkesmed. **plotting** ['plåtiŋ] intrigant, renkefull; planer, anslag, renker.

plough [plau] plog, snøplog; ploghøvel, nothøvel; bokbinderhøvel; pløye; beskjære; la dumpe til eksamen, stryke; the **Plough** Karlsvogna; — in pløye ned; — **over again** pløye om igjen; — **up** (el. out) pløye opp, pløye opp av jorda; — **and tongue together** pløye sammen med fjær og not; **be -ed** dumpe, ryke, stryke. **ploughable** ['plauəbl] som kan pløyes. **plougher** ['plauə] pløyer. **ploughing** ['plauiŋ] pløying; våronn, plogonn.

plough|-beam ['plaubi·m] plogås. **-iron** ['plauaiən] plogjern, ristel. **-land** plogland, akerland. **-man** plogkar, landmann, bonde. **-share** plogskjær, plogjern. **-wright** plogmaker, plogsmed.

plover ['plʌvə] brokkfugl; regnpiper; heilo. **pluck** [plʌk] rive, nappe, trive, rykke, trekke; plukke, ribbe; rejisere, stryke; rykk, grep, tak, napp; mot, mannsmot, bein i nesen; innmat; — **up** ta mot til seg, manne seg opp. **pluckiness** ['plʌkinès] mot. **plucky** ['plʌki] modig, kjekk, tapper, djerv.

pluffy ['plʌfi] svampet, porøs; slapp; bleikfeit. **plug** [plʌg] plugg, propp, tapp; spuns, nagle; plate av skråtobakk; plombere; proppe til.

plum [plʌm] plomme, rosin; godbit, det beste.

plumage ['plu·midʒ] fjær, fjærkledning.

plumb [plʌm] bly, blylodd, lodd; loddrett; bent, ende, pladask; plombere; bringe i lodd; lodde; måle, lodd; være i lodd.

plumbago [plʌm'be'go⁺] grafitt, blyant; fjærekoll (plante).

plumbean ['plʌmbiən], **plumbeous** ['plʌmbiəs] bly-, blyaktig, blyholdig.

plumber ['plʌmə] blyarbeider, blytekker; rørlegger; blykule. **plumbery** ['plʌməri] blyarbeid, blytekking; rørlegging. **plumbic** ['plʌmbik] bly-. **plumbiferous** [plʌm'bifərəs] blyholdig, blyførende. **plumbing** ['plʌmiŋ] blyarbeid; blytekking. **plumb|-line** ['plʌmlain] loddline, loddsnor; loddrett linje. **-rule** vaterpass. **plum-cake** ['plʌmke⁺k] plumkake, formkake med rosiner. **plum-duff** ['plʌmdʌf] melpudding med rosiner. **plume** [plu·m] fjær; fjærdusk; pusse, pynte, stelle fjærene sine; plukke; ribbe; — **oneself** være stolt, briske seg, gjøre seg til. **plumelet** ['plu·mlèt] dunfjær.

plummet ['plʌmit] lodd; blysøkke (på fiske-snøre); loddsnor.

plummy ['plʌmi] full av rosiner; utmerket, førsterangs, framifrå.

plumose ['plu·moᵘs] fjæraktig, fjær-, fjæret.

plump [plʌmp] rund, tykk, lubben, trivelig, fyldig, før; uten videre, bent ut, endefram, bums, lukt; klump, klynge; fylle, utfylle, utvide; gjøre fyldig, gjøre lubben; utvide seg, tykne, legge seg ut; buse ut med.

plumper ['plʌmpə] stemmeseddel (med bare ett navn); diger løgn, diger skrøne.

plum-pudding ['plʌm'pudiŋ] plumpudding.

plum-tree ['plʌmtri·] plommetre.

plumy ['plu·mi] fjæret, fjærkledd.

plunder ['plʌndə] plyndre, røve; plyndring; plyndret gods; rov, bytte. **plunderer** ['plʌndərə] plyndrer.

plunge ['plʌn(d)ʒ] styrte, kaste, slenge, støte; dukke ned, kaste seg, stupe, styrte seg; plutselig fall; dukk, dukkert, dukking; styrt, renn, forlegen-het, vanskelighet, ulykke, vågestykke.

plunger ['plʌn(d)ʒə] dukker, dykker; plunger-stempel; veddemålsspekulant, jobber.

pluperfect ['plu·'pə·fikt] pluskvamperfektum.

plural ['pluərəl] som inneholder flere, flertalls-; flertall. **pluralism** ['pluərəlizm] pluralisme, det å ha flere prestekall samtidig. **pluralist** [-list] pluralist. **plurality** [plu'räliti] pluralitet, flerhet, majoritet, flertall.

plus [plʌs] pluss; positiv; addisjonstegn.

plus-fours ['plʌs'fɔ·ᵊz] lange, vide knebukser, først brukt av golfspillere, nikkers.

plush [plʌʃ] floss, plysj.

Plutarch ['plu·ta·ᵊk] Plutark.

plutocracy [plu·'tåkrəsi] plutokrati, rikmanns-styre; rikmannsaristokrati, pengeadel. **plutocrat** ['plu·tokrät] plutokrat, pengefyrste. **plutocratic** [plu·to'krätik] plutokratisk.

Plutonian [plu·'toᵘnjən] plutonisk (som angår Pluto); vulkansk.

Plutonic [plu·'tånik] plutonisk.

pluvial ['plu·vjəl] regnfull.

pluvious ['plu·vjəs] regn-, regnfull.

ply [plai] folde; bearbeide; nytte, bruke, drive på med; drive, utføre; gå løs på; henge i; gå (i rute); baute, krysse; fold; tråd; eiendommelig utvikling, retning; tilbøyelighet; — **with questions** bombardere med spørsmål; — **with drink** få til å drikke tett, traktere flittig; **the small steamers that** — **on the lake** de små dampere som går i rute på sjøen.

plyer ['plaiə] (i plur.) nebbetang.

Plymouth ['plimə) Plymouth.

P. M. fk. f. Prime Minister; Police Magistrate; postmaster; post meridiem.

p. m. fk. f. post meridiem, at 3 p. m. kl. 3 em.; post-mortem.

P. M. G. fk. f. Pall-Mall Gazette; Paymaster General; Postmaster General.

pneumatic [nju'mätik] pnevmatisk; — **engine** luftpumpe; — **tyre** luftring, luftslange.

pneumonia [nju'moᵘnjə] lungebetennelse. **pneumonic** [nju'månik] lunge-, lungesyk.

P. O. fk. f. postal order; Post Office.

poach [poᵘtʃ] lage forlorne egg (koke dem uten skall); trampe ned; bli nedtrampet; drive krypskytteri, drive ulovlig jakt (el. fiske); lure seg til en fordel (i kappløp); slå til ballen mens den er på medspillerens grunn (i tennis); krypskytteri; **-ed eggs** forlorne egg (ɔ: kokt uten skall i vann). **poacher** ['poᵘtʃə] vilttyv. krypskytter. **poaching** ['poᵘtʃiŋ] vilttyveri, krypskytteri.

pock [påk] pustel, kopp; syfilis.

pocket ['påkit] lomme, pose, sekk; grop, for-dypning; dalsøkk; putte eller stikke i lommen; — **up** stikke til seg, skjule; tie stille til, tåle, bite i seg, finne seg i. — **-book** tegnebok, notebok. — **-glass** lommespeil, lommekikkert. — **-handker-chief** lommetørkle. — **-knife** lommekniv. —

-money lommepenger. — **-picker** lommetyv. — **-picking** lommetyveri. — **-piece** lommepenger, lykkeskilling. — **-pistol** lommepistol; lommelerke. — **-volume** bok i lommeformat.

pock-marked ['påkma·əkt] kopparret.

pod [påd] belg, skjelm, skolm; flokk, (fiske-stim; skjelme, skolme.

podagra ['pådəgrə] podagra, **podagrical** [po'dägrikl] podagristisk.

podded ['pådid] velhavende, velberget.

podgy ['pådʒi] buttet, tykk, klumpet.

podium ['poᵘdjəm] podium.

Poe [poᵘ] Poe.

poem ['poᵘim] dikt.

poesy ['poᵘisi] (gml.) poesi, diktekunst, skaldskap.

poet ['poᵘit, -et] dikter. **poetaster** [poᵘi'tästə] rimsmed, versemaker. **poetess** ['poᵘités] dikter-inne. **poetic** [poᵘ'etik] dikterisk, poetisk. **poetical** [poᵘ'etikl] dikterisk, poetisk. **poetics** [poᵘ'etiks] lærebok i diktekunst, poetikk. **poetry** ['poᵘitri] poesi, diktning, diktekunst.

pogo ['poᵘgoᵘ] el. **pogo-stick** kengurustylte.

pogrom [på'gråm, 'pågråm] jødeforfølgelse.

poignancy ['poinənsi] skarphet; brodd; pirre-lighet. **poignant** ['poinənt] skarp, kvass, bitter, besk; skjærende.

point [point] spiss; støt, stikk; punkt, prikk; odde, nes; poeng; klarhet, skarphet; hovedsak; formål, endemål; strek, kompasstrek; komma ved desimalbrøk; skilletegn, punktum; **bad** — svak-het; smakløshet; **good** — god egenskap, dyd; **the great** — hva det især kommer an på; — **of honour** æressak; — **of view** synspunkt; **gain a** — nå sitt mål; **make a** — of legge vekt på; **in** — of med hensyn til; — **of exclamation** ut-ropstegn; **in** — **of fact** i virkeligheten; vesentlig; **on this** — hva dette angår; **be on the** — of stå i begrep med, være på nippet til; **let us come to the** — la oss komme til saken.

point [point] spisse, sette spiss på; skjerpe; sikte; peke; sette skilletegn; poengtere; framheve; understreke, markere.

point-blank ['point'bläŋk] likefrem, bent ut.

point-duty ferdselstjeneste (politibetjents ar-beid med å dirigere trafikken osv. på et bestemt sted).

pointed ['pointid] spiss, tilspisset; poengtert; skarp, kvass; punktlig. **pointedness** [-nês] spiss-het; skarphet; likefremhet.

pointer ['pointə] pekestokk; viser (på ur); pointer, korthåret fuglehund. **pointing-lace** sydde kniplinger.

pointsman ['pointsmən] sporskifter.

poize [poiz] vekt; likevekt; veie, sette, holde i likevekt; balansere; veie, vurdere.

poison ['poizn] gift; forgifte; forgi; forderve. **poisoner** ['poiznə] giftblander; giftblanderske. **poison-fang** gifttann, **poison-gas** giftgass, **poison-ing** ['poizniŋ] forgiftning; giftblanding; giftmord. **poisonous** ['poiznəs] giftig. **poisonousness** [-nês] giftighet.

poke [poᵘk] stikke, støte, skyve, puffe, rote i, stikke fram; rote, kare, grave i; snuse (**about** om-kring); stikke hodet fram; stikk, støt, dunk, dytt, dult; spark; — **one's nose into** stikke nesen sin i.

poke [poᵘk] (gl.) pose, lomme; **buy a pig in a** — kjøpe katten i sekken.

poke [poᵘk] framstående hatteskygge. **-bonnet** kysehatt.

poker ['poᵘkə] ildrake, glorake; nål til bren-ning i tre, brannmaling; **have swallowed a** — se ut som en har slukt en linjal.

poker ['poᵘkə] poker, kortspill.

poker|-drawing, -painting, -picture brann-maleri.

pokerwork brannmaling.

poky ['pouki] (om plass) trang, liten; (om virksomhet) ubetydelig, dau.

Poland ['poᵘlənd] Polen.

polar ['poᵘlə] polar; polar-, pol-; — **bear** isbjørn. — **explorer** polarforsker.
Pole [poᵘl] polakk.
pole [poᵘl] pol.
pole [poᵘl] stang, stake; påle; staur; målestang (f. eks. erter); stake fram (en båt); bære på påler el. stenger; (**carriage-**)**pole** vognstang; (**fish-**)**pole** fiskestang; (**curtain-**)**pole** gardinstang; (**flag-**)**pole** flaggstang; (**hanging-**)**pole** stang (til gymnastikk).
pole-axe ['poᵘläks] stridsøks; hogge med stridsøks.
pole-cat ['poᵘlkät] ilder, slags mår.
polemic [po'lemik] polemiker, polemisk; **polemics** polemikk.
polenta [po'lentə] polenta, maisgrøt.
police [pə'li·s, po-] politi; føre politioppsyn med; holde orden blant, holde styr på. — **case** politisak. — **constable** politikonstabel. — **court** politirett. — **force** politistyrke. **-magistrate** dommer.
policeman [pə'li·smən] politibetjent, konstabel. **notice office** politikammer. — **officer** politifunksjonær. — **sergeant** overbetjent.
police station [po'li·s'ste'ʃən] politistasjon.
policlinic [påli'klinik] poliklinikk.
policy ['pålisi] politikk; statsvitenskap; statsklokskap; framgangsmåte; sluhet, list; **honesty is the best** — ærlighet varer lengst.
policy ['pålisi] polise, forsikringsbrev. **—broker** assuransemekler. — **-holder** innehaver av en polise, forsikret.
Polish ['poᵘliʃ] polsk.
polish ['påliʃ] polere, blankslipe, blanke, blankskure, glatte, forfine, smykke, pryde; politur, glatthet; finhet; — **off** gjøre det av med en; bli ferdig i en fart. **polisher** ['påliʃə] polerer; sliperedskap. **polishment** politur.
polite [pə'lait, po'-] høflig, fin, dannet; — **literature** skjønne vitenskaper; skjønnlitteratur. **politeness** [-nès] forfinelse, finhet, høflighet. **politesse** [påli'tes] belevenhet, høflighet.
politic ['pålitik] politisk, stats-; fornuftig, forsiktig; — **economy** nasjonaløkonomi. **political** [pə'litikl, po-] politisk, stats-; politiker, statsmann. **politician** [påli'tiʃən] politiker, statsmann. **politics** ['pålitiks] politikk, statsvitenskap; statskunst; politiske anskuelser.
polity ['påliti] regjeringsform; samfunn; skipnad.
polka ['pålkə, 'poᵘlkə] polka.
poll [pål] kjælenavn på papegøye.
poll [poᵘl] skolt, haus; nakke; bakhode; manntall; manntallsprotokoll; valgprotokoll; stemmeopptelling; valg; valgdag; koppskatt; **when the** — **was declared** da utfallet av valget ble kunngjort; **decline the** — oppgi sitt kandidatur; **come out at the head (at the bottom) of the** — få det største (det minste) stemmetall; **a** — **was demanded** da det ble krevd skriftlig avstemning; **go to the** — gå til valg.
poll [poᵘl] kylle, topphogge; snauklippe, skjære av, kappe av; innskrive; innføre; avgi (sin stemme); bringe til valgurnen; få, samle (et antall stemmer); telle opp stemmene.
pollack ['pålək] lyr; **green** — sei.
poll|-book manntall; manntallsprotokoll. — **-clerk** valgsekretær. **polled** [poᵘld] kollet.
pollen ['pålin] pollen, blomsterstøv; pollinere, bestøve.
poller ['poᵘlə] kapper; manntallsfører; stemmeberettiget, velger.
pollinate ['påline't] pollinere.
polling ['poᵘliŋ] avstemning; valghandling. **-day** valgdag. — **-station** valgsted.
poll-parrot ['pål'pärət] papegøye; pludre.
pollute [på'l(j)u·t] forurense, skjemme; besmitte; krenke, vanære. **polluter** [-ə] besmitter.
pollution [på'l(j)u·ʃən] besmittelse.
polo ['poᵘloᵘ] polo.
polonaise ['pålo'ne'z] polonese.

Polonese [poᵘlo'ni·z] polsk.
poltroon [pål'tru·n] reddhare, kujon; krysteraktig, feig. **poltroonery** [pål'tru·nəri] feighet, kujoneri. **poltroonish** [-iʃ] krysteraktig, feig.
polygamist [po'ligəmist] polygamist. **polygamy** [-mi] polygami. **polyglot** ['påliglåt] som taler mange språk; som er på mange språk; polyglott. **polypode** ['pålipoᵘd] tusenbein. **polypous** ['pålipəs] polyppaktig. **polypus** ['pålipəs] polypp; koralldyr. **polyspermal** [påli'spə·məl] mangefrøet. **polysyllable** [påli'siləbl] mangestavingsord. **polytechnic** [-'teknik] polyteknisk; polyteknisk skole. **polytechnics** [-ks] polyteknikk.
pomaceous [po'me'ʃəs] som består av epler, eple-.
pomade [pə'ma·d] pomade; pomadisere.
pomatum [po'me'təm] pomade; pomadisere.
pome [poᵘm] eplefrukt, kjernefrukt. — **-citron** sitroneple. — **-granate** ['påmgränét] granateple.
Pomerania [påmə're'njə] Pommern. **-n** pommersk; pommeraner; pommersk spisshund.
pommel ['pʌməl] knapp; kule; knott; kårdeknapp; banke, rundjule, denge.
pomp [påmp] praktopptog; pomp; prakt, stas, bram, prunk.
Pompeian [påm'pi·ən] pompeiansk.
Pompeii [påm'pi·ai] Pompeii.
Pompey ['påmpi] Pompeius; (i sjømannsslang:) Portsmouth.
pompon ['påmpån, fr.] pompong (pyntekvast).
pomposity [påm'påsiti] praktfullhet; høytidelighet.
pompous ['påmpəs] pompøs, praktfull; høytidelig, staselig, høyttravende.
pond [pånd] dam; demme opp; **the big** — Atlanterhavet. — **-lily** nøkkerose.
ponder ['påndə] overveie, overlegge; grunde, tenke etter. **ponderable** ['påndərəbl] veielig, som lar seg veie. **ponderal** ['påndərəl] ponderal, vekt-, veid. **pondering** ['pånderiŋ] grundende, ettertenksom. **ponderosity** [påndə'råsiti] tyngde, vekt. **ponderous** ['påndərəs] tung, diger, svær, vektig; viktig, betydningsfull. **ponderousness** [-nès] tyngde, vekt.
poniard ['pånjəd] dolk; dolke, stikke.
pontage ['påntidʒ] brupenger, brutoll.
pontiff ['påntif] overprest; pontifeks; pave. **pontific** [pån'tifik] pontifikal; pavelig; **pontificate** [pån'tifikét] pontifikat; pavestol; paves embetstid. **pontify** ['påntifai] spille pave, late som en har greie på alt.
pont-levis [pånt'levis] vindebru.
pontoon [pån'tu·n] pongtong. — **-bridge** pongtongbru.
pony ['poᵘni] ponni; (i slang) £ 25.
poodle ['pu·dl], puddelhund.
pooh [pu·] pytt!
pooh-pooh ['pu·'pu·] blåse av, blåse i, flire av.
pool [pu·l] dam; pytt; høl, kulp; **The Pool** Londons havn nedenfor London Bridge.
pool [pu·l] pulje, innsats; sammenslutning, ring; samle, skyte sammen.
poop [pu·p] popp, hytte, bakerste opphøyde del av et skipsdekk; slå inn over (om en sjø); seile på bakfra. **pooping-sea** svær sjø over akterskipet.
poor [puə] fattig, trengende, stakkars, arm, ringe; mager, skrinn; ussel; salig, avdød. — **-box** fattigbøsse. — **-farm** fattiggård, pleiehjem. — **-house** fattighus. — **-law** fattiglov.
poorly ['puəli] tarvelig, fattig; dårlig; skral, skrøpelig. **poorness** ['puənəs] fattigdom; tarvelighet, smått stell; magerhet.
poor|-rate ['puəre't] fattigskatt. — **-relief** fattigunderstøttelse, forsorgsbidrag. — **-spirited** forsagt; feig.
pop. fk. f. **popular; population**.
pop [påp] puff, smell, knall; futte, plaffe, knalle; — **the question** fri; — **in** smutte inn, komme inn; — **off** stikke av, smutte bort;

avvise; — out smutte ut; — up fare opp. **pop paff, vips!**
pop [påp] folkekonsert (fk. f. **popular**).
Pope [po^up] Pope (engelsk dikter).
pope [po^up] pave. **popedom** [-dəm] pavedømme.
popery ['po^up(ə)ri] papisme; papistisk lære.
popinjay ['påpindʒei] papegøye; srl. papegøye til å skyte til måls på; grønnspette.
popish ['po^upiʃ] pavelig, papistisk.
poplar ['påplə] poppel.
popple ['påpl] gynge, duve; krapp sjø; poppel.
poppy ['påpi] valmue; **Flanders** — flandernvalmue (helliget minnet om dem som døde i verdenskrigen); **Poppy day,** d. 11. nov., da det selges Flanders poppies.
populace ['påpjulis] almue, hop. **popular** ['påpjələ, 'påpjulə] folke-; folkets; folkelig; populær; lettfattelig; folkekjær. **popularity** [påpju-'läriti] popularitet. **popularization** [påpjuläri-'zeiʃən] popularisering. **popularize** ['påpjuləraiz] popularisere.
populate ['påpjuleⁱt] befolke; bo i.
population [påpju'leⁱʃən] befolkning; folkemengde, folketall. — **-returns** folketellingslister.
populous ['påpjuləs] folkerik, tett befolket. **populousness** [-nés] folkerikdom, tett befolkning.
porcelain ['på^əslin] porselen.
porch [på^ətʃ] portal; søylegang, buegang; bislag, utskott, sval.
porcine ['på^əsain] svine-, grise-, som hører til svina.
porcupine ['på^əkjupain] hulepinnsvin, afrikansk pinnsvin; maurpinnsvin.
pore [på^ə] stirre; henge over bøkene, grave seg ned, fordype seg **(over** i).
pore [på^ə] pore.
poriness ['på·rinés] porøs beskaffenhet.
pork [på^ək] svinekjøtt, flesk, svin. — **-chop** svinekotelett. **porker** ['på^əkə] fetesvin, gjøgris.
pornography [på^ə'någrəfi] pornografi.
porosity [påsi'råsiti] porøsitet; pore.
porous ['på·rəs] porøs.
porpoise ['på^əpəs] nise.
porridge ['påridʒ] suppe; velling; grøt.
porringer ['pårindʒə] fat, skål, bolle.
port [på^ət] havn, sjøhavn; havneby; **naval port** sjøby; **free port** frihavn; **port of call** anløpssted.
port [på^ət] port; kanonport; by- el. festningsport.
port [på^ət] holdning, føring, lag, ytre; holde, føre.
port [på^ət] portvin.
port [på^ət] babord; **to** — til babord.
portable ['på^ətəbl] som kan bæres; transportabel.
portage ['på^ətidʒ] førsel, bæring; bærepenger.
portal ['på^ətəl] portal; port, dør; porthvelving.
portcrayon [på^ət'kreⁱən] blyantholder.
portcullis [på^ət'kʌlis] fallgitter.
Porte [på^ət]; **the** — el. **the Ottoman** — el. **the Sublime** — Porten (den tyrkiske regjering).
portend [på^ə'tend] varsle, tyde på, varsle om, spå.
portent ['på^ətent] varsel, forvarsel, forbud, dårlig varsel; vidunder.
portentous [på^ə'tentəs] varslende, ildevarslende; uhyre, vidunderlig.
porter ['på·tə] portner, dørvokter; portier.
porter ['på·^ətə] bærer, fast bybud.
porter ['på·^ətə] porter (slags øl).
porterage ['på·təridʒ] portnerstilling.
porterage ['på·^ətəridʒ] bærepenger, budpenger.
portfolio [på^ət'fo^ulio^u] mappe; portefølje.
porthole ['på^ətho^ul] port, glugge.
portico ['på^ətiko^u] søylegang.
portion ['på^əʃən] del, andel, part, lodd, porsjon; arvedel, arvepart; medgift; dele, dele ut, fordele; skifte ut; utstyre. **portioner** ['på·^əʃənə] utdeler, fordeler. **portionist** ['på·^əʃənist] stipendiat.
portionless [-lés] uten andel; uten medgift; fatig.

portliness ['på·^ətlinês] anstand, verdighet; korpulense, førhet. **portly** ['på·^ətli] anselig; korpulent, før, svær.
portmanteau [på·^ət'mänto^u] koffert, håndkoffert.
portrait ['på·^ətrét] portrett, bilde. **portraiture** ['på·^ətretʃə] portrett; skildring. **portray** [på·^ə'treⁱ] avbilde, male; skildre, tegne. **portrayal** [-əl] avbilding; framstilling, skildring. **portrayer** [-ə] portrettmaler; framstiller, skildrer.
portress ['på·^ətrés] portnerske, dørvokterske.
Portsmouth ['på·^ətsməþ] Portsmouth.
Portugal ['på·^ətjugəl] Portugal. **Portuguese** [på·^ətju'gi·z] portugisisk; portugiser(inne); portugisisk.

P. O. S. B. fk. f. Post-Office Savings Bank.
pose [po^uz] stilling; positur, attityde, oppstilling; stille opp; stille seg i positur, skape seg; sitte (modell); sette i forlegenhet. **poser** ['po^uzə] vanskelig spørsmål; posør, en som skaper seg, gjør seg til.
poseur [po'zə·] posør, en som skaper seg.
position [po'ziʃən] stilling; posisjon; **hold the** — of ha stilling som.
positive ['påsitiv] positiv, virkelig; uttalt, uttrykkelig, bestemt, grei, med rene ord; avgjørende; direkte; uomtvistelig; sikker, viss; det positive, virkelighet; positiv. **positiveness** [-nès] virkelighet, bestemthet, sikkerhet.
possess [pə'zes] besitte, sitte inne med; besette.
possessed [pə'zest] fylt, behersket; besatt; **be — of** være i besittelse av, ha forståelse av.
possession [pə'zeʃən] besittelse; djevlebesettelse.
possessive [pə'zesiv] eiendoms-, eie-; eiendomspronomen; genitiv; — **case** genitiv; — **pronoun** possessivt pronomen, eiendomspronomen.
possessor [pə'zesə] besitter, innehaver, eier.
possessory [pə'zesəri] besittelses-; besittende.
posset ['påsit] ølost.
possibility [påsi'biliti] mulighet, von.
possible ['påsəbl, 'påsibl] mulig.
possibly ['påsibli] muligens, kanskje; på noen mulig måte; **I cannot — do it** jeg kan umulig gjøre det.
possum ['påsəm] opossum, pungrotte; **(act) play** — forstille seg, hykle uvirksomhet, hykle likegyldighet.
post [po^ust] post, pel, påle, stolpe; stilling; embete; bestilling; befordringsvesen; postbefordring; postbud; slå opp (plakater), kunngjøre, sette, stille; ansette, postere; føre inn poster; skrive av, overføre; poste; reise med posten; reise hurtig; ta skyss; ile, skynde seg; sende hurtig; hurtig, fort, ilsomt.
postage ['po^ustidʒ] porto. — **-stamp** frimerke.
postal ['po^ustəl] postal, post-; — **card** brevkort; — **parcel** postpakke; — **order** postanvisning.
post|-bag ['po^ustbäg] postsekk. — **-boy** postiljong. — **-card** brevkort. — **card with view** prospektkort. — **-chaise** ekstraskyss, postskyss. **-date** senere datum; postdatere.
posted ['po^ustid] underrettet; **be** — ha god greie på tingene; **keep oneself** — holde seg à jour.
post-entry ['po^ustentri] senere angivelse; senere innføring.
poster ['po^ustə] avsender, kurér, ilbud; skysshest; plakatoppsetter; plakat.
poste-restante [po^ustre'sta·nt] poste restante.
posterior [på'stiəriə] senere (to enn); bakdel.
posteriority [påstiəri'åriti] det å komme til, hende senere.
posterity [på'steriti] etterslekt(en), ettertid(en); etterkommere; **go down to** — bevares for etterslekten.
postern ['po^ustə·n, 'po^ustən] bakdør, lønndør.
post-free ['po^ust'fri·] portofri.
post-haste ['po^ustheⁱst] hast; i bråhast.
post-hour ['po^ustauə] innleveringstid.

post-house ['poᵘsthaus] poststasjon, posthus; skyss-stasjon.

posthumous ['påstjuməs] posthum; født etter farens død; etterlatt.

postil ['påstil] randbemerkning; preken; prekensamling.

postillion [pə'stiliən] postiljong.

posting ['poᵘstiŋ] innlevering.

post|man ['poᵘs(t)mən] postbud. — -mark poststempel. — -master postmester. — -master-general post- og telegrafdirektør, postminister.

postmeridian ['poᵘstmə'ridjən] ettermiddags-.

post meridiem ['poᵘst mi'ridjəm] etter middag, ettermiddag (srl. p. m. el. P. M.).

post-mortem [poᵘst'må·ᵊtəm] etter døden; obduksjon.

post-obit [poᵘst'åbit] gjeldsbrev med sikkerhet i en kommende arv.

post-office ['poᵘståfis] postkontor; postdepartement, poststyre; General Post-Office hovedpostkontoret (i London).

post-paid ['poᵘstpe'd] frankert, franko.

postpone [poᵘst'poᵘn] utsette, oppsette, dryge med; ombestemme. postponement [-mənt] utsetting; ombestemmelse.

post|position [poᵘstpo'zifən] etterstilling. -positive [poᵘst'påzitiv] etterhengt, etterstilt.

postscenium [poᵘst'si·njəm] rom bak scenen.

postscript ['poᵘstskript] etterskrift.

postulant ['påstjulənt] ansøker.

postulate ['påstjulėt] postulat, påstand.

postulate ['påstjule'␣t] påstå, forutsette.

postulation [påstju'le·ʃən] forutsetning. postulatory ['påstjulətəri] forutsatt, antatt.

posture ['påstʃə] stilling, lag, positur; plasere, stille, sette; stille seg i positur, skape seg, gjøre seg til.

posy ['poᵘzi] devise, inskripsjon, motto; dikt sendt med en bukett; bukett.

pot [påt] potte, kar, gryte, kanne, digel, krukke; pott; beger; sekspence; teine; keep the — boiling holde gryta i kok, skaffe utkomme, holde det gående; make -s and pans of his property ødsle bort sin formue; go to — gå i hundene.

pot [påt] oppbevare i en krukke, sylte ned, legge ned, salte ned.

potable ['poᵘtəbl] drikkelig; (i flertall) drikkevarer.

potage [poᵘ'ta·ʒ] suppe.

potash ['påtäʃ] pottaske.

potassium [pə'täsjəm] kalium; carbonate of — pottaske; chloride of — klorkalium.

potation [poᵘ'te'ʃən] drikking; drikkelag.

potato [poᵘ'te'toᵘ, po-] potet. — -blight potet-syke, tørr-råte. — -flour potetmel. — -peel potetskall. — -skin potetskrell. — -trap munn.

pot-belly ['påtbeli] tykk mage.

pot-boiler ['påtboilə] kunstverk som er laget bare for pengenes skyld.

pot-boy ['påtboi] kjellergutt.

poteen [po'ti·n] (hjemmebrent) irsk whisky.

potency ['poᵘtənsi] kraft, makt; innflytelse.

potent ['poᵘtənt] sterk, mektig, innflytelsesrik.

potentate ['poᵘtənte'␣t, -ėt] fyrste, makthaver, potentat. potential [po'tenʃəl] mektig, mulig, potentiality [potenʃi'äliti] mulighet.

pot-hanger ['påt'häŋə] grytekrok, skjerding.

pot-hat ['påthät] stiv filthatt, skalk.

pothecary ['påþikəri] apoteker.

potheen [po'þi·n] whisky, brennevin.

pother ['påðə] travelhet; ståk, styr; oppstyr, tumult; larme, ståke, bråke, plage, mase med.

pot-herb ['påthə·b] kjøkkenvekster.

pot-hole ['påthoᵘl] jettegryte.

pothook ['påthuk] grytekrok, skjerdingkrok; rund strek (i skriveøvelse); kråketær, rabbel.

pot-house ['påthaus] ølstue, sjapp, kneipe.

potion ['poᵘʃən] lægedrikk, mikstur.

pot-luck ['påtlʌk] hva som faller; take — ta til takke med hva huset formår.

potman ['påtmən] kjellersvenn.

pot-pourri ['poᵘ'puəri] potpourri.

potsherd ['påtʃə·d] potteskår, skålbrott.

pot-shot ['påt'ʃåt] skudd for å få noe i gryta, skudd fra bakhold, slengeskudd.

pottage ['påtidʒ] (gml.) kjøttsuppe; nå bare: a mess of — en rett linser (fra Bibelen).

potter ['påtə] pottemaker.

potter ['påtə] arbeide så smått, pusle, somle.

pottery ['påtəri] leirvarer; pottemakerindustri; leirvarefabrikk.

potting ['påtiŋ] sylting.

pottle ['påtl] kanne (mål); kurv; play at — hoppe paradis.

pouch [pautʃ] pose, taske; lomme; pung; stikke i lommen; bite i seg, finne seg i.

poule [pu·l] innsats.

poult [poᵘlt] kylling.

poulterer ['poᵘltərə] vilthandler, fjærfehandler.

poultice ['poᵘltis] grøtomslag; legge omslag på.

poultry ['poᵘltri] fjærfe, høns. — -farm hønseri. — -farmer fjærfeavler. — -house hønsehus. -man fjærfehandler.

pounce [pauns] slå ned, slå kloa (on i).

pounce [pauns] raderpulver, pimpsteinspulver.

pound [paund] pund (vekt); pund (= 20 shillings); in for a penny in for a — har man sagt A, får man si B; — weight pundsvekt, pundlodd.

pound [paund] innhegning, kve; ta i forvaring; sette inn; få i fella.

pound [paund] banke løs på, banke, gjennompryle; støte (i en morter); hamre; støte; ri tungt.

poundage ['paundidʒ] prosenter; sportler.

pounder ['paundə] (i smstn.) -punding; five-pounder fempunding.

pounder ['paundə] støter.

pour [på·ə] helle, skjenke; slå; øse, tømme ut, la strømme; strømme, styrte, øse med; styrtregn, øsregn; it never rains but it -s en ulykke kommer sjelden alene. pourer ['på·rə] heller, øser; øsc.

pouring ['på·riŋ] øsende.

pout [paut] surmule, sette trut, furte; geipe, sette fram, skyte ut; surmuling; be in the — surmule. pouter ['pautə] surmule. pouting ['pautiŋ] surmulende, furten; surmuling.

poverty ['påvəti] fattigdom. — -stricken, — -struck forarmet.

powder ['paudə] pulver; krutt; pudder; forvandle til pulver, pulverisere; pudre, strø, overstrø; sprenge med salt; -ed sugar strøsukker. — -cart kruttvogn. — -horn krutthorn. powdering ['paudəriŋ] pudring; sprengning; salting.

powder|-magazine ['paudəmägəzi·n] kruttmagasin. — -mill kruttmølle. — -puff pudderkvast. — -room kruttkammer. — -smoke kruttrøyk. — -works kruttverk.

powdery ['paudəri] smuldrende; støvet; melet; pudderaktig.

power ['pauə] makt, velde, kraft; evne; gave; begavelse; styrke; fullmakt; makthaver; krigsmakt, hær; potens (i matematikk); the great -s of Europe Europas stormakter. powerful [-f(u)l] mektig, kraftig, sterk. powerless [-lės] kraftløs; avmektig, maktesløs. powerlessness avmektighet, maktesløshet; power-loom maskinvevstol.

power-station ['pauə'ste'ʃən] kraftstasjon.

pow-wow ['pau'wau] møte av indianere, konferanse, spetakkel, lurveleven.

P. P. fk. f. parish priest.

p. p. fk. f. past participle; per procuration.

pp. fk. f. pages; pianissimo.

P. P. C. fk. f. pour prᵉ re congé (for å ta avskjed).

P. P. S. fk. f. post-postscriptum (etter-etterskrift).

P. R. A. fk. f. President of the Royal Academy.

practicability [präktikə'biliti] gjørlighet, utførlighet; mulighet.

practical ['präktikl] praktisk; a — joke en

nærgående spøk, spikk. **practicality** [präkti'käliti] praktisk natur; praktisk innretning. **practically** ['präktikəli] i praksis; praktisk talt.

practice ['präktis] bruk, skikk; øvelse; anvendelse; praksis; framgangsmåte; list, kunstgrep, knep; **he is in** — han praktiserer; **put in** —, **reduce to** — bringe til utførelse; **run into evil -s** komme på gale veier; **by way of** — til øvelse, for å få øvelse.

practise ['präktis] drive, bruke, øve, utøve, sette i verk; innøve, øve seg på, i; praktisere, drive forretninger; utnytte, spekulere i.

practitioner [präk'tiʃənə] praktiker, praktiserende lege; praktiserende jurist.

pragmatic [präg'mätik] pragmatisk; forretningsmessig; praktisk materiell; nesevis; forordning.

Prague [pre'g] Praha.

prairie ['præ·°ri] eng, prærie, grassteppe.

praise [pre'z] ros, pris; rose, berømme, prise. **praiseless** [-lès] urost, uten ros. **praiser** ['pre'zə] lovpriser, berømmer. **praiseworthy** ['pre'zwə·ði] rosverdig, prisverdig.

pram [präm] fk. f. **perambulator** barnevogn.

pram [pra·m] pram.

prance [pra·ns] danse, steile; ri stolt; spanke. **prancer** ['pra·nsə] fyrig hest. **prancing** ['pra·nsiŋ] dansing, steiling.

prank [präŋk] strek, spikk; utstaffere, stase opp, spjåke til. **pranker** ['präŋkə] laps. **prankish** ['präŋkiʃ] kåt.

prate [pre't] pludre, sludre; skravle, prate; prat; sludder; snakk. **prater** ['pre'tə] skravlekopp.

prattle ['prätl] sludre, skravle, pludre; snakk, sladder. **prattler** ['prätlə] vrøvler; sladrer.

pravity ['präviti] fordervelse, sletthet.

prawn [prå·n] reke.

praxis ['präksis] øvelse, eksempel; praksis.

pray [pre'] be, bønnfalle, anrope; be til, be om; nedbe; **I** — om jeg tør spørre. **prayer** ['pre'ə] bedende.

prayer ['præ·ə] bønn; **family -s** husandakt; **say his -s** lese (el. be) bønnene sine. — **-book** bønnebok. — **-meeting** bønnemøte. **praying** ['pre'iŋ] det å be, bønn.

P. R. B. fk. f. **Pre-Raphaelite Brotherhood.**

preach [pri·tʃ] kunngjøre; preke; legge ut. **preacher** ['pri·tʃə] predikant, prest. **preachership** [-ʃip] presteembte. **preaching** ['pri·tʃiŋ] preken.

preachment ['pri·tʃmənt] preken.

preamble ['pri·ämbl, pri'ämbl] fortale, forord, innleiing; innlede.

preapprehension ['pri·äpri'henʃən] forutfattet mening; fordom.

prearrangement ['pri·ə're'ndʒmənt] ordning på forhånd, forhåndsavtale.

prebend ['prebənd] prebende (kanniks særinntekter av domkirkens gods). **prebendary** ['prebəndəri] prebendarius, domherre, kannik.

precarious [pri'kæ·°riəs] prekær, usikker, utrygg, mislig, vaklende. **precariousness** [pri'kæ·°riəsnès] usikkerhet.

precatory ['prekətəri] bedende, bønnlig.

precaution [pri'kå·ʃən] forsiktighet; forsiktighetsregel, forholdsregel; advare; **take -s against** ta sine forholdsregler mot. **precautionary** [-əri] advarende; forsiktighets-.

precede [pri'si·d] gå foran, komme foran, gå forut for, rangere foran. **precedence** [pri'si·dəns, 'presidəns] forrang, prioritet; fortrin. **precedency** [pri'si·dənsi, 'presidənsi] forrang. **precedent** [pri·'si·dənt, 'president] foregående, forutgående. **precedent** ['president] presedens, tidligere tilfelle, sidestykke. **precedented** ['presidəntid] ikke uten sidestykke; hevdet (ved praksis).

precept [pri'sept] forskrift. **preceptive** [pri·'septiv] foreskrivende, bydende. **preceptor** [pri·'septə] lærer. **preceptorial** [prisep'tå·riəl] lærer. **preceptress** [pri'septrès] lærerinne.

precession [pri'seʃən] forutgang; framgang; presesjon.

precinct ['pri·siŋ(k)t] grense, distrikt; **precincts** enemerker, område; plass, tun.

precious ['preʃəs] kostelig, dyrebar; (ironisk:) nydelig, deilig; være affektert åndrik, snakke tilgjort fint. — **metals** edle metaller. **-ness** [-nès] kostelighet.

precipice ['presipis] avgrunn, skrent, stup.

precipitance [pri'sipitəns], **precipitancy** [-tənsi] bråhast; framfusenhet; overilelse.

precipitate [pri'sipite't] kaste, slynge, stupe, styrte; framskynde; påskynde; skynde seg med; falle, ruse, styrte; forhaste seg.

precipitate [pri'sipitèt] som kommer styrtende el. rusende, hodekulls; brå, hastig; framfusende, ubesindig.

precipitation [prisipi'te'ʃən] styrting, rusing; bråhet, hast; framfusenhet; ubesindighet, overilelse.

precipitous [pri'sipitəs] bratt, stupbratt, steil; hastig, brå, ubesindig, framfusende.

précis ['presi·] resymé; resymere.

precise [pri'sais] nøyaktig; sikker, nøyeregnende; striks, pertentlig. **precisian** [pri'siʒən] pedant. **precision** [pri'siʒən] nøyaktighet; sikkerhet.

preclude [pri'klu·d] utelukke, forebygge, avskjære. **preclusion** [-'klu·ʒən] utelukking; avskjæring. **preclusive** [-'klu·siv] som stenger ute, avskjærende; forebyggende.

precocious [pri'ko·ʃəs] tidlig moden, tidlig utviklet; vèslevoksen. **precocity** [pri'kåsiti] tidlig utvikling, fremmelighet.

precognition [pri·kåg'niʃən] forutgående kjennskap.

preconceive [pri·kən'si·v] forut oppfatte; gjøre seg opp en mening på forhånd; **-d notions** forutfattede meninger. **preconception** [-'sepʃən] forutfattet mening.

preconcert [pri·kən'sə·t] avtale forut.

preconsent [pri·kən'sent] forutgående samtykke.

precursor [pri'kə·sə] forløper. **precursory** [-səri] forutgående; som bebuder el. varsler.

predatorily ['predətərili] plyndrende, på røveres vis. **predatory** ['predətəri] plyndre-, plyndrings-; plyndrende, røverisk.

predecease [pri·di'si·s] avgå ved døden før; tidligere død.

predecessor [pri·di'sesə] forgjenger, formann.

predestinarian [pri·desti'næ·°riən] tilhenger av læren om forutbestemmelsen. **predestinate** [pri·'destine't] forutbestemme. **predestination** [pri(·)desti'ne'ʃən] forutbestemmelse. **predestine** [pri·'destin] forutbestemme.

predeterminate [-'ne'ʃən] forutbestemt. **predetermine** [pri·di'tə·min] forutbestemme. **predeterminate** [-'ne'ʃən] forutbestemmelse. **predetermine** [pri·di'tə·min] forutbestemme.

predicability [predikə'biliti] det å kunne utsis. **predicable** ['predikəbl] som kan utsis; egenskap. **predicament** [pri'dikəmənt] forlegenhet; knipe; kategori, begrepsklasse.

predicant ['predikənt] preker; prekende. **predicate** ['predike't] utsi, erklære. **predicate** ['predikèt] predikat, omsagn. **predication** [predi'ke'ʃən] omsagn, utsagn; predikat. **predicative** [pri'dikətiv] predikativ, som predikat.

predict [pri'dikt] forutsi, spå. **prediction** [pri·'dikʃən] forutsiing, spådom. **predictive** [pri·'diktiv] forutsiende. **predictor** [pri'diktə] spåmann, en som forutsier.

predilection [pri·di'lekʃən] forkjærlighet (for for). **predispose** [pri·dis'po·z] predisponere (to til), gjøre mottagelig. **predisposition** [pri·dispo'ziʃən] predisposisjon, tendens (to til).

predominance [pri'dåminəns] overtak, overmakt, overvekt. **predominant** [-nənt] overlegen; framherskende. **predominate** [-'ne't] være framherskende; ha overhånd. **predomination** [pri·dåmi·'ne'ʃən] overtak, overlegenhet, overmakt.

pre-elect [pri·i'lekt] velge ut på forhånd.
pre-eminence [pri'eminəns] forrang; overlegenhet. **pre-eminent** [-nənt] framragende, fortrinlig, grepa, framifrå. **pre-eminently** i særlig framragende grad, framifrå.
pre-emption [pri·'em(p)ʃən] forkjøp, forkjøpsrett.
preen [pri·n] pusse, fjelge (om en fugl osv.)
pre-engage [pri·in'geidʒ] forut forplikte; forutbestille. **pre-engagement** [-mənt] tidligere forpliktelse; tidligere løfte; forutbestilling.
pre-establish [pri·i'stäbliʃ] forut fastsette, innrette. **pre-establishment** [-mənt] forutgående fastsettelse, innretning.
pre-exist [pri·ig'zist] være til tidligere, finne sted forut. **pre-existence** [-stəns] preeksistens, foruttilværelse. **pre-existent** [-stənt] forut bestående; tidligere.
preface ['prefis] forord, fortale, innleiing; innlede; si noe til innleiing, skrive en fortale. **prefatory** ['prefətəri] innledende.
prefect ['pri·fekt] prefekt (især: fransk fylkesmann, romersk embetsmann; skolegutt som har tilsyn med de lavere klasser).
prefecture ['pri·fektjuə, -tʃə] prefektur, forstanderskap.
prefer [pri'fə·] foretrekke (**to** for), ville heller, begunstige; forfremme, befordre (**to** til); sette fram, legge fram, føre fram; — **water to wine** foretrekke vann for vin; — **working to doing nothing** foretrekke å arbeide framfor ikke å gjøre noe; **preferred shares** preferanseaksjer; **preferred claim** priviligert fordring; — **a claim** fremsette et krav.
preferable ['prefərəbl] til å foretrekke, som bør ha fortrinet, bedre.
preference ['prefərəns] forkjærlighet, svakhet; det å foretrekke; begunstigelse; fortrin, forrang; prioritet, preferanse; by — heller; helst; in — to heller enn, framfor. — **-share** preferanseaksje. — **-stock** preferanseaksjer.
preferential [prefə'renʃəl] preferanse-, fortrinsberettiget.
preferment [pri'fə·mənt] forfremmelse, befordring, avansement; kall; forrett.
prefiguration [prifig(j)ə're'ʃən] forbilledlig betegnelse. **prefigurative** [pri'fig(j)ərətiv] forbilledlig. **prefigure** [pri'fig(j)ə] betegne forbilledlig. **prefigurement** [-mənt] forbilde.
prefix [pri'fiks] sette foran.
prefix ['pri·fiks] prefiks, forstaving, førefeste.
pregnable ['pregnəbl] inntagelig.
pregnancy ['pregnənsi] svangerskap, fruktsommelighet; fruktbarhet, fylde, rikdom.
pregnant ['pregnənt] svanger, fruktsommelig; vektig, betydningsfull.
prehensible [pri'hensibl] som lar seg gripe. **prehensile** [pri'hensail] gripende, gripe-. **prehension** [pri'henʃən] griping.
prehistoric [pri·hi'stärik] forhistorisk.
prejudge [pri·'dʒʌdʒ] dømme på forhånd; avgjøre på forhånd. **prejudgment** [-mənt] forhåndsdom; forhåndsavgjørelse.
prejudice ['predʒudis] fordom (**against** imot); skade; gjøre partisk; ska; **without** — uten forbindtlighet. **prejudiced** ['predʒudist] forut inntatt.
prejudicial [predʒu'diʃəl] skadelig (**to** for).
prelacy ['preləsi] prelatembete; høy geistlighet; høyere prestevelde. **prelate** ['prelét] prelat.
prelect [pri'lekt] holde en forelesning. **prelection** [pri'lekʃən] forelesning. **prelector** [-ə] foreleser.
preliminary [pri'limin(ə)ri] foreløpig; innledende; innleiing, forberedelse, førebuing; **preliminaries of peace** fredspreliminarier.
prelude ['prelju·d] preludium; innleiing; innlede, være forspill til; preludere.
premature [premə'tjuə, 'pri·mə'tjuə] for tidlig moden, framkommet før tiden; forhastet. **prema-**

tureness [-nés], **prematurity** [premə'tjuəriti] tidlig modenhet; forhastethet.
premeditate [pri'medite't] overlegge, tenke over. **premeditately** [-tétli] med overlegg. **premeditation** [primedi'te'ʃən] overlegg; forsettlighet, forsett.
premier ['premiə] først; fornemst; statsminister, førsteminister. **premiership** ['premiəʃip] stilling som statsminister.
premise [pri'maiz] forutskikke, si forut.
premise ['premis] premiss, forutsetning; **premises** ['premisiz] premisser; eiendom, gård, tomt, lokale.
premiss ['premis] d. s. s. **premise**.
premium ['pri·mjəm] premie; belønning, godtgjørelse, assuransepremie; mellomlag; agio, overkurs; **at a** — over pari.
premonition [pri·mo'niʃən] advarsel; forvarsel, tegn; forutfølelse, forutanelse.
premonitory [pri'mänitəri] varslende (**of** om), advarende, varslende.
prentice ['prentis] lærling, læregutt; uøvd; **her hand** hennes uøvde hånd.
preoccupation [priåkju'pe'ʃən] besettelse i forveien; opptatthet (med andre ting); åndsfraværelse.
preoccupy [pri'åkjupai] forut besette, ta i besittelse først; oppta på forhånd, helt legge beslag på, fylle; **preoccupied** opptatt (av andre ting), fordypet (i tanker), tankefull, åndsfraværende.
preoption [pri'åpʃən] rett til å velge først, fortrinsrett.
preordain [pri·å·ə'de'n] forut bestemme.
prep. fk. f. **preposition; preparation.**
prep [prep] (i skoleslang:) lekselesing.
prepaid ['pri·'pe'd] forut betalt, franko.
preparation [prepə're'ʃən] forberedelse (**for** til); tilberedelse; utrusting; tilberedning.
preparative [pri'pärətiv] forberedende.
preparatory [pri'pärətəri] forberedende; — **school** forberedelsesskole.
prepare [pri'pæ·ə] forberede (**for** på, til); tilberede, lage; innrette; forberede seg, gjøre seg ferdig, holde seg beredt. **preparedness** [pri'pæ·əridnés] beredthet, beredskap. **preparer** [pri'pæ·ərə] forbereder, tilbereder.
prepay ['pri·'pe'] betale i forveien, frankere. **prepayment** [-mənt] forutbetaling.
prepense [pri'pens] forsettlig, gjennomtenkt, overlagt.
preponderance [pri'påndərəns] overvekt, overtak, overmakt. **preponderant** [-rənt] som har overvekten, som veier mest. **preponderate** [-re't] ha overtaket over; være overveiende.
preposition [prepə'ziʃən] preposisjon.
prepositional ['prepo'ziʃənl] som preposisjon.
prepositive [pri'pázitiv] foranstilt.
prepossess [pri·pə'zes] ta i besittelse først; forut innta; fylle, gjennomtrenge. **prepossession** [-'zesin] inntagende, vinnende. **prepossessing** [-'zeʃən] det å være opptatt i forveien, forutfattet mening, forkjærlighet.
preposterous [pri'påstərəs] bakvendt, meningsløs, fullkommen absurd.
prepotent [pri'po"tənt] overmektig.
Preraphaelism [pri'räf(i)əlizəm] prerafaelisme (en retning i engelsk malerkunst). **Preraphaelite** [pri'räf(i)əlait] prerafaelitt, prerafaelittisk.
prerogative [pri'rågətiv] prerogativ, forrett.
Pres. fk. f. **President.**
pres. fk. f. **present.**
presage ['presidʒ] forvarsel, varsel; anelse.
presage [pri'se'dʒ] varsle om, spå.
presbyter ['prezbitə] presbyter, kirkeforstander. **presbyterian** [prezbi'tiəriən] presbyteriansk; presbyterianer. **presbyterianism** [prezbi'tiəriənizm] presbyterianisme. **presbytery** ['prezbitəri] kirkeråd; prestegård (i katolske land).
prescience ['preʃəns] forutviten.

prescient ['preʃiənt] forutvitende, framtenkt.

prescribe [pri'skraib] foreskrive; ordinere; skrive resepter; foreldes; gjøre krav på hevdsrett (for på).

prescript ['pri·skript] forskrift.

prescription [pri'skripʃən] resept; hevd; foreldelse. **prescriptive** [pri'skriptiv] hevdvunnen.

presence ['prez(ə)ns] tilstedeværelse, nærværelse; overværelse; audiens; audiensværelse (gammelt); (høytstående) personlighet, overnaturlig vesen, ånd; person; ytre; stilling; — of mind åndsnærværelse; **usher into** (eller **admit to**) **the** — of gi foretrede for, stede for; **never enter my** — again la meg aldri se deg mer. — **-chamber,** — **-room** audiensværelse.

present ['prez(ə)nt] nærværende, tilstedeværende; nåværende, denne; ferdig, på rede hånd; — **persons always excepted** selvsagt snakker jeg ikke om dem som er her. **the persons** — eller **those** — de tilstedeværende; **the** — nåtid, presens; **the purport of the** — is to . . . vi (jeg) skriver dette for å . . .; **be** — at være til stede ved, overvære; **at** — for nærværende; for øyeblikket; **at the** — moment i øyeblikket; **for the** — for tiden, foreløpig; **in the** — nå, for tiden; **by the** — eller **by these presents** herved, ved nærværende skrivelse.

present ['prezənt] gave, presang; **make him a** — of it forære ham det.

present [pri'zent] forestille, presentere; framsette, framstille, syne fram; overlevere, overrekke; innbringe, innlevere; forære, gi; presentere (en veksel); holde fram, rette (at mot); — **arms!** presenter gevær! — **to a living** kalle (også innstille) til et presteembete.

presentable [pri'zentəbl] presentabel, anstendig, antagelig.

presentation [prezn'teiʃən] presentasjon, framstilling; overlevering, overrekking; innlevering; innstillingsrett; **on** — ved sikt, ved forevisning.

presenter [pri'zentə] innstiller; giver.

presentient [pri'senʃiənt] forutfølende. **presentiment** [-'sentimənt] forutfølelse, forutanelse.

presently ['prezntli] snart, på timen; litt etter.

presentment [pri'zentmənt] framstilling, framførelse (f. eks. av skuespill); presentasjon (av veksel).

preservable [pri'zə·vəbl] holdbar.

preservation [prezə've'ʃən] bevaring; vedlikehold; fredning; vern, beskyttelse; oppbevaring. nedlegging, sylting; redning, sikkerhet.

preservative [pri'zə·vətiv] bevarende, sikrende; konserveringsmiddel.

preserve [pri'zə·v] bevare, verne, sikre; frede; redde, berge; nedlegge, preservere, sylte; vedlikeholde; syltet frukt, syltetøy; innhegning til vilt; -s syltetøy, hermetisk nedlagte matvarer. — **-jar** syltekrukke.

preserver [pri'zə·və] bevarer, beskytter, redningsmann, frelser; nedlegger; bevaringsmiddel. **preserve-tin** [pri'zə·vtin] hermetikkboks.

preside [pri'zaid] innta forsetet, presidere.

presidency ['prezidənsi] forsete; presidentskap. **president** [-dənt] formann, president. **presidential** [prezi'denʃəl] formanns-. **presidentship** ['prezidəntʃip] formannsplass.

press [pres] presse, perse, trykke, kryste, klemme; presse ut; trenge på, tilskynde, tvinge, nøde; presse (til krigstjeneste); presse, perse, boktrykkerpresse; litteratur; blad; avis; journalister; skap, linnetskap, klesskap; det å trenge på, jag, renn; trengsel. — **-cutting** avisutklipp. — **-gang** flokk matrospressere.

pressing [pri'sin] presserende, overhengende; påtrengende, inntrengende; pressing, presning; press, overtalelser. — **-iron** pressejern.

pression ['preʃən] trykk, press.

press|man ['presmən] pressemann; bladmann. — **-money** håndpenger. — **-proof** siste korrektur.

pressure ['preʃə] trykk, press; — of space trangt om rom; — of business forretningstravelhet; **head of** — trykkhøyde. — **-gauge** ['preʃə·geidʒ] trykkmåler. — **-pump** trykkpumpe.

prestige [pre'sti·ʒ] prestisje, anseelse, vørnad.

prest-money ['prestmʌni] håndpenger, vervepenger.

presto ['prestoʊ] presto, hurtig; snøgg; vips! **presumable** [pri'z(j)u·məbl] antagelig, ventelig.

presume [pri'z(j)u·m] anta, formene, formode, forutsette; understå seg; gå for vidt; våge (seg for langt); ta seg friheter; **don't** —! bli ikke innbilsk; — on stole for mye på, trekke veksler på; være innbilsk av.

presumedly [pri'zju·midli] formentlig, ventelig.

presumption [pri'zʌm(p)ʃən] antagelse, forutsetning, formodning; sannsynlighet; anmasselse; innbilskhet; dristighet.

presumptive [pri'zʌm(p)tiv] antatt, trolig, forutsatt; **heir presumptive** presumptiv arving (vordende arving under forutsetning av at det ikke fødes arvelateren barn).

presumptuous [pri'zʌm(p)tjuəs, -ʃəs] anmassende, overmodig, uvøren, dumdristig; formastelig. **presuppose** [pri·sə'poʊz] forutsette, gå ut fra. **presupposition** [prisʌpə'ziʃən] forutsetning.

pretence [pri'tens] foregivende, påskudd; krav, fordring; **on** (eller **under**) **(a)** — of under skinn av; **under false pretences** under falsk forutsetning; **make** — of foregi.

pretend [pri'tend] foregi, gi som påskudd; påstå; hykle; kreve; — **to** gi seg skinn av; — **to learning** ville passere for lærd; **pretended** [-did] hyklet, falsk.

pretender [pri'tendə] kandidat; kongsemne; pretendent; hykler. **pretendership** [-ʃip] kandidatur.

pretension [pri'tenʃən] krav, fordring; pretensjon.

pretentious [pri'tenʃəs] fordringsfull.

preterite ['pretərit] forgangen, fortids-; — **tense** fortid.

preternatural [pri·tə'nätʃərəl] overnaturlig, unaturlig.

pretext ['pri·tekst] påskudd; **under** (el. **on**) **the** — of under påskudd av; **find a** — **for delay** finne et påskudd til oppsettelse.

pretor ['pri·tə] pretor. **pretorial** [pri'tå·riəl] pretorial. **pretorian** [-riən] pretorianer.

prettiness ['pritinés] netthet, penhet, finhet.

pretty ['priti] fin, pen, nett, nydelig; temmelig.

prevail [pri've'l] få overhånd, seire; herske, råde, rå, være herskende; gjøre seg gjeldende; — **upon** formå til, bevege til; overtale. **prevailing** [-iŋ] framherskende, alminnelig, vanlig.

prevalence ['prevələns] overvekt, overtak; seier: makt, innflytelse. **prevalent** [-lənt] seirende; (fram)herskende, rådende, alminnelig (utbredt); kraftig.

prevaricate [pri'värikeit] bruke utflukter, vringle. **prevarication** [priväri'ke'ʃən] utflukter, vringel, misbruk av tillit, det å spille under dekke. **prevaricator** [pri'värike'tə] mester i å bruke utflukter.

prevent [pri'vent] hindre (**from doing** i å gjøre), forebygge; være i veien for; være til hinder.

preventable [pri'ventəbl] til å hindre.

prevention [pri'venʃən] forhindring, hindring, forebygging.

preventive [pri'ventiv] hindrende, forebyggende; **preventive service** krysstollvesen; **preventive officer** krysstollbetjent.

previous [pri·vjəs] foregående, forutgående, forrige; tidligere. **previously** ['pri·vjəsli] før, tidligere. **previousness** [-nés] det å gå forut.

prevision [pri'viʒən] forutseenhet, framsyn; forutanelse.

prey [pre'] bytte; rov; røve, plyndre; **animal of** — rovdyr; **bird of** — rovfugl; — **upon** anfalle, angripe, etterstrebe; gnage, tære på.

price [prais] pris, verd, verdi; belønning: lønn; bestemme prisen, vurdere. — **-current** priskurant. **-less** uvurderlig. — **-list** priskurant.

prick [prik] prikke, stikke; stikke fast; spore, ri på spreng; (opp)reise; prikke ut, punktere (mønster); sette merke ved, velge (til); spiss, brodd, odd, stikk; — **his ears** spisse (el. reise) ørene; **his conscience -ed him** han hadde samvittighetsnag.

pricker ['prikə] brodd, spiss, torn, syl.

prickle ['prikl] pigg, torn; prikke, stikke, maure

prickliness ['priklinès] det å være tornet.

prickly ['prikli] tornet, pigget.

pride [praid] stolthet, hovmod; prakt; **to —** oneself **on** være stolt av, bryste seg av.

prier ['praiə] snuser, snushane.

priest [pri·st] prest, geistlig, især katolsk prest; **high —** yppersteprest. — **-craft** prestelist, prestebedrag. **priestess** ['pri·stés] prestinne. **priest-hood** [-hud] presteembete, presteyrke, presteskap. **priestly** prestelig.

prig [prig] tyv; stjele, kvarte, knipe.

prig [prig] innbilsk narr, forfengelig pedant. **priggish** ['prigiʃ] innbilsk, pedantisk, narraktig, snobbet, lapset. **priggishness** [-nès], **priggism** ['prigizm] innbilskhet, selvklokskap.

prim [prim] pertentlig, tertefin, stiv, pen; gjøre sirlig; pynte. stramme.

primacy ['praiməsi] primat, erkebiskoppelig verdighet; overlegenhet, forrang, første plass.

prima-donna ['pri·mə¹dånə] primadonna.

prima facie ['praimə'fei'ʃii·] straks, ved første øyekast.

primage ['praimidʒ] kaplak (tillegg til frakten som tilfalt skipperen).

primal ['praiməl] først, viktigst, opphavlig.

primarily ['praimərili] for det første, opprinnelig, opphavlig, fra første ferd; først og fremst.

primary ['praiməri] første; opprinnelig, opphavlig; elementær, forberedende, lavere; størst, viktigst; hovedsak; — **colours** grunnfarger; — school elementærskole, forskole, folkeskole.

primate ['praimét] primas, øverste geistlig; **Primate of all England** erkebiskopen av Canterbury; **Primate of England** erkebiskopen av York.

prime [praim] først, opprinnelig, opphavlig; fornemst, fremst; fortrinlig; prima; prim- (matematikk); beste del, beste tid; velmaktsdager, blomstring, blomstrende alder; opphav; primtall; legge fengkrutt på; stive opp; stramme seg opp ved drikk; sette i gang, inspirere, instruere; — **of the moon** nymåne; **he is in his —** of life han er i sin beste alder; **past his —** ut over sin beste alder; — **minister** statsminister; — **number** primtall.

primely ['praimli] fortrinlig, storartet.

primeness ['praimnès] fortreffelighet.

primer ['primə] slags boktrykkerskrift; **great —** tertia; **long —** korpus.

primer ['praimə] elementarbok, begynnerbok.

primer ['praimə] antennelsesmiddel, fengrør, fenghette, tenn-nål, brannrør; instruktør; oppstiver.

primeval [praim'i·vəl] først, eldgammel, opphavlig, opprinnelig; ur-.

primitive ['primitiv] opprinnelig, opphavlig; ur-; primitiv, gammeldags, simpel, uutviklet; stamord. **primitiveness** [-nés] opprinnelighet.

primness ['primnès] pertentlighet, stivhet.

primordial [prai'mâ·ədjəl] først, opprinnelig, opphavlig, ur-, uberørt, til: grunnelement.

primrose ['primro°z] kusymre, primula; **Primrose Day** primuladagen, den 19. april, lord Beaconsfields dødsdag; **Primrose League** et konservativt selskap, hvis kjennetegn er en bukett primula, lord Beaconsfields yndlingsblomst.

primula ['primjulə] primula.

primus ['praiməs] første; primus (kokeapparat).

prince [prins] fyrste, prins; **Prince Consort** [-'kånsət] prinsgemal (regjerende dronnings ektefelle); **Prince Regent** prinsregent; **Prince of Wales** prins av Wales, den engelske kronprins; **Crown Prince** kronprins (i noen land, ikke England). **princedom** ['prinsdəm] fyrsterang; fyrstedømme. **princelike** fyrstemessig, fyrstelig. **princely** fyrstelig, prinselig, prinse-.

princess ['prin'ses] prinsesse, fyrstinne; **Princess Royal** tittel for den engelske konges eldste datter: **Princess of Wales** prinsen av Wales's gemalinne, kronprinsesse (i England); **Crown Princess** kronprinsesse (utenfor England).

principal ['prinsipl] først, hoved-, høyest, viktigst, vesentligst; hovedperson; hovedmann, bestyrer, skolebestyrer; hovedsum, hovedstol; kapital; **principality** [prinsi'päliti] suverenitet; fyrstedømme.

principle ['prinsipl] kilde, opprinnelse, opphav; bestanddel, grunnsetning, prinsipp; **on —** av prinsipp; **-s** begynnelsesgrunner. **principled** ['prinsipld] med . . . prinsipper.

print [print] trykke, prente, trykke av, kopiere, prege av; la trykke, utgi, få trykt; merke, søkk, avtrykk, preg, trykk; spor, far; trykt skrift; blad, avis; stikk, kopperstikk; sirs; stempel, merke; **-ed matter** trykksaker; **coloured -s** fargetrykk; **in —** på trykk, på prent; i bokhandelen; i den skjønneste orden; **out of —** utsolgt fra forlaget.

printer ['printə] trykker, boktrykker.

printing ['printiŋ] trykning; boktrykk; boktrykkerkunst. — **-establishment** trykkeri. — **-press** boktrykkerpresse. **print|seller** kunsthandler. — **-shop** kunsthandel. — **-works** trykkeri; kattuntrykkeri.

Prior ['praiə] Prior.

prior ['praiə] tidligere, forrige, eldre; prior, klosterforstander. — **to** førenn. **priorate** ['prai-ərêt] priorat. **prioress** [-rés] priorinne. **priority** [prai'âriti] fortrin, forrett; prioritet.

prise [praiz] bryte, brekke; brekkjern; våg.

prism [prizm] prisme.

prismatic [priz'mätik] prismatisk.

prismatical [priz'mätikəl] se **prismatic**.

prison ['prizn] fengsel; (poetisk) fengsle. **prisoner** ['priznə] fange, arrestant, anklagede (i kriminell sak); **prisoner's base** (el. egl. bars) en gutteleik med avmerkte frieteder og «fengsler». **prison-house** ['priznhaus] fengselsbygning. **prison-ship** ['priznʃip] fangeskip. **prison-yard** ['priznja·°d] fengselsgård.

pristine ['pristain] opprinnelig, opphavlig; primitiv.

prithee ['priði·] **(pray thee)** jeg ber deg, kjære deg, snille deg.

prittle-prattle ['pritl'prätl] snikksnakk.

privacy ['praivəsi; priv-] avsondring; ensomhet, ro, stillhet; tilflukt, tilfluktssted; hemmeligholdelse, taushet; **in —** i enrom, under fire øyne.

private ['praivit] privat, stille, alene, hemmelig; menig; — **arrangement** ogs. underhåndsakkord; **in — clothes** sivilkledd; **in —** privat.

privateer [praivi'tiə] kaperskip, kaper. **privateering** [-'tiəriŋ] kaperi, kapring.

privation [prai've'ʃən] savn, skort.

privative ['privətiv] berøvende, nektende; negativ.

privet ['privit] liguster.

privilege ['privididʒ] privilegium, særrett(ighet), begunstigelse; privilegere, gi forrett.

privily ['privili] i all stillhet; hemmelig.

privy ['privi] privat. hemmelig, geheime-: deltager; privet, klosett; — **council** geheimeråd; councillor geheimeråd; — **seal** geheimesegl; **Lord keeper of the — seal** geheimeseglbevarer.

prize [praiz] fangst, prise; pris, premie; gevinst; skatt; lønn; bestemme prisen på; sette

pris på, skatte, vurdere; premie-; prisbelønt, premiert.
prize [praiz] brekkjern; bryte opp.
prizeable ['praizəbl] som fortjener å skattes.
prize|-court priserett. — **-day** årsfest, eksamensfest; — **-essay** prisavhandling. — **-fight** premiekamp; boksekamp. — **-fighter** profesjonell bokser. — **-fighting** premieboksing; profesjonell boksekamp. — **-list** premieliste, prisliste. — **-money** prisepenger. — **-question** prisespørsmål; prisoppgave.
prize-ring (plass til) premieboksing.
prize-winner premievinner, prisvinner.
pro [prouˈ] pro, for; **pros & cons** grunner for og imot.
pro. fk. f. **procuration.**
probability [prɔbəˈbiliti] sannsynlighet, rimelighet, von; **in all** — etter all sannsynlighet.
probable ['prɔbəbl] sannsynlig, rimelig, trolig.
probably ['prɔbəbli] sannsynligvis, ventelig.
probate ['proubét] stadfestende (med hensyn til testamente); testamentstadfesting; kopi av stadfestet testamente: — **court** skifterett; — **duty** stempelavgift av testamente, (eldre) arveavgift.
probation [proˈbeiʃən] vitnemål, prov; prøve; prøvetid.
probationer [proˈbeiʃənə] person på prøve; aspirant, sykepleieelev; munk.
probative ['proubətiv] som skal prøve; prøvende, prøve-.
probe [proub] sonde; sondere, prøve.
probity ['prɔbiti] rettsindighet, redelighet.
problem ['prɔbləm] oppgave, spørsmål, problem. **problematic(al)** [prɔbliˈmätik(l)] problematisk, tvilsom, vrang.
proboscis [proˈbɑsis, prəˈbɑsis] snabel.
procedure [proˈsiːdʒə, -djuə] framgangsmåte, framferd rettergang, forretningsorden.
proceed [proˈsiːd] gå framover; begi seg, legge i vei; dra videre; fortsette, vedbli; gå til ve ks; bære seg at, gå fram; foreta rettslige skritt, reise tiltale, anlegge sak, prosedere; ta eksamen (ved universitet).
proceeding [proˈsiːdiŋ] framferd, framgang, framgangsmåte, skritt, atferd; saksanlegg, prosess, sak, sakførsel; forhandlingsprotokoll; **watch the -s** iaktta hva som foregår; **in -s at law** ved rettergang, for domstolene; **in the case of legal -s** om det skulle komme til sak.
proceeds ['prouˈsiːdz] vinning, utbytte, avdrått, avkastning; **gross** — bruttoutbytte. **net** — nettoutbytte.
process ['prouses, 'prɑses, -is] framgang; gang; forløp; prosess; framgangsmåte; behandling; utvekst; reproduksjon; **in** — **of time** i tidens løp, med tiden; reise sak mot; sterilisere, koke; reprodusere.
procession [proˈseʃən] prosesjon; ferd; tog; opptog; gå i prosesjon. **processional** [-ʃənəl] prosesjons-. **processive** [proˈsesiv] fremadskridende.
procidence ['prɑsidəns] framfall, nedsiging.
proclaim [proˈkleim] bekjentgjøre; kunngjøre; erklære, lyse, proklamere, forkynne, bebude; erklære fredløs; — **him king** utrope ham til konge; — **the banns** lyse til ekteskap; — **war** erklære krig. **proclaimer** [-ənt] forkynner, utroper.
proclaimant [-ə] = **proclaimant.**
proclamation [prɑkləˈmeiʃən] bekjentgjørelse, lysing, kunngjøring; proklamasjon.
proclivity [proˈkliviti] tilbøyelighet, lag, hang; nemme, anlegg (to for).
proclivous [proˈklaivəs] som står på skrå, haller.
proconsul [prouˈkɑnsəl] prokonsul. **proconsulate** [prouˈkɑnsjulét] prokonsulat.
procrastinate [proˈkrästineit] oppsette, somle, dryge. **procrastination** [prokrästiˈneiʃən] oppsetting. **procrastinator** [proˈkrästineitə] en som oppsetter, somlekopp.
procreant ['proukriənt] avlende, avle-; avler. **procreate** ['proukrieit] avle, frambringe. **procrea-**

tion [proukriˈeiʃən] avling, frambringelse. **procreator** ['proukrieitə] far, stamfar, opphav.
proctor ['prɑktə] prokurator, fullmektig; sakfører; proktor (i universitetsspråk, en **fellow**, som har oppsyn med disiplinen blant studentene).
procumbent [proˈkʌmbənt] liggende, krypende.
procurable [proˈkjuərəbl] som kan fås, som det er råd å få tak i. **procuration** [prɑkjuˈreiʃən] tilveiebringelse; fullmakt, prokura. **procurator** ['prɑkjureitə] fullmektig, forretningsfører.
procure [proˈkjuə] skaffe, tilveiebringe; oppdrive, få tak i; forskrive; utvirke. **procurement** [-mənt] tilveiebringing, det å skaffe til veie. **procurer** [proˈkjuərə] tilveiebringer; ruffer.
prod [prɑd] pigg, brodd, spiss; stikk; stikke, pirre.
prodigal ['prɑdigəl] ødsel; ødeland; **the** — **son** den fortapte sønn. **prodigality** [prɑdiˈgäliti] ødselhet, ødsling.
prodigious [proˈdidʒəs] vidunderlig, forbausende; uhyre. **prodigy** ['prɑdidʒi] under; vidunder; uhyre, monstrum.
produce [proˈdjuːs] føre fram; framstille; oppføre, framlegge; ta fram; frambringe, produsere, lage, tilvirke.
produce ['prɑdjuːs] frambringelser, produkter, naturprodukter; avling, utbytte; utvinning; resultat. **producer** [proˈdjuːsə] produsent, tilvirker. **producible** [proˈdjuːsibl] som kan frambringes.
product ['prɑdʌkt] frambringelse; avling, produkt.
production [proˈdʌkʃən] framførelse; framstilling; frambringelse, produksjon, produkt. **productive** [proˈdʌktiv] frambringende, skapende, som produserer; fruktbar, rik. **productiveness** [-nés] fruktbarhet; nytte. **productivity** [proudʌkˈtiviti] yteevne.
proem ['prouem] fortale, innledning, innleiing.
profanation [prɑfəˈneiʃən] profanasjon, vanhelligelse, misbruk. **profane** [proˈfein] profan, verdslig; bespottelig; profanere, vanhellige, besmitte, skjemme, krenke, bespotte; misbruke. **profaneness** [proˈfeinnis] vanhellighet; bespottelighet; bespottelig tale. **profaner** [proˈfeinə] vanhelliger, krenker, spotter. **profanity** [proˈfäniti] bespottelse, spott.
profess [proˈfes] erklære, bekjenne seg til; tilstå; bevitne, forsikre; utøve, praktisere; **professed** [proˈfest] erklært; erklært; faglært; profesjonell; **a** — **nun** nonne som har avlagt løftet; **a** — **smoker** en ivrig røyker.
profession [proˈfeʃən] erklæring; bekjennelse; forsikring; stilling, yrke, fag, kall, stand; **the learned -s** ɔ: teologi, jus, legevitenskap; **a** — **of faith** en trosbekjennelse; **a beggar by** — en profesjonell tigger.
professional [proˈfeʃənəl] fagmessig, faglig, yrkes-, fag-, kalls-, profesjonell; fagmann; profesjonist: — **man** orfer: akademiker.
professor [proˈfesə] bekjenner, forkynner; lærer, professor, universitetslærer. **professoress** [-rés] kvinnelig professor. **professorial** [profeˈsɑːriəl] professor-.
proffer ['prɑfə] framføre, by fram, tilby; tilbud.
proficiency [proˈfiʃənsi], **proficiency** [proˈfiʃənsi] kyndighet, ferdighet; standpunkt; framskritt. **proficient** [-ʃənt] kyndig, dyktig, vel bevandret; viderekommen, mester, fagmann.
profile ['proufiːl] omriss, kontur, profil; tegne i omriss.
profit ['prɑfit] fordel, gagn, nytte, vinning, gevinst, avanse, fortjeneste; **at a** — med fortjeneste. **profit** ['prɑfit] gagne, være til gagn for, være en vinning for; ha gagn av, vinne, profitere, tjene; **excess profits tax** merinntektskatt.
profitable ['prɑfitəbl] gagnlig, nyttig; fordelaktig, lønnsom, innbringende.

profiteer [pråfi'tiə] gulasjgrosserer, krigsmillionær, jobber. **profitless** ['pråfitlés] ufordelaktig.

profligacy ['pråfligəsi] ryggesløshet, lastefullhet, ryggesløst liv, laster. **profligate** [-gét] ryggesløs, lastefull; ryggesløst menneske.

pro(-)forma [prouˈfåˑᵃmə] pro forma, for et syns skyld.

profound [pro'faund] dyp; grundig; dypsindig; dyp. **profoundness** [-nés] dybde, dyp.

profundity [pro'fʌnditi] dybde; dyp.

profuse [pro'fjuˑs] gavmild, raust, flus; ødsel; overflødig; overstrømmende, overvettes, rikelig. **profuseness** [-nés] ødselhet; overflødighet, overflod.

profusion [pro'fjuˑʒən] stor gavmildhet, ødselhet; overflod, overflødighet.

prog [pråg] tigge, stjele (mat); matvarer.

progenitor [pro'dʒenitə] stamfar, ættefar.

progeny ['prådʒini] avkom; etterkommere; slekt; resultater, følger.

prognostic [pråg'nåstik] varslende; tegn, merke, symptom. **prognosticate** [-'nåstikeˈt] forutsi, spå, varsle. **prognostication** [-nåsti'keˈʃən] forutsigelse, spådom; tegn, merke, varsel. **prognosticator** [-'nåstikeˈtə] varsler; værprofet.

programme ['prouˈgräm] program; plan.

progress ['prouˈgres, 'prågres, -is] det å skride fram, framgang, gang; framrykking; framskritt, framsteg; vokster, utvikling; ferd, reise, gjestereise (især om kongers høytidelige rundreise); **in** — i emning; under utarbeiding; under utgivelse; **make** — bevege seg fram; **The Pilgrim's Progress** Pilegrimsvandring (Bunyans allegori); **triumphal progress** triumftog.

progress [pro'gres] gå fram, gå, skride fram; gjøre framgang, gjøre framskritt; stige (om pris).

progression [pro'greʃən] det å skride fram; framgang; progresjon; **arithmetical** — aritmetisk rekke; **geometrical** — geometrisk rekke.

progressional [pro'greʃənəl] fremadskridende.

progressive [pro'gresiv] progressiv, fremadskridende; tiltagende, voksende; framskrittsvennlig; framskrittsmann; — **income-tax** progressiv inntektsskatt.

prohibit [pro'hibit] forby; hindre.

prohibition [prouhi'biʃən] forbud.

prohibitionist [prouhi'biʃənist] tilhenger av sterk beskyttelsestoll; forbudsmann (ɔ: tilhenger av forbud mot alkoholholdige drikker). **prohibitive** [pro'hibitiv] forbydende; sterkt beskyttende. **prohibitory** [pro'hibitəri] = **prohibitive**.

project [pro'dʒekt] framkaste; utkaste; tenke på, utkaste plan om; planlegge; projisere (framstille ved tegning); rage fram, stikke ut.

project ['prådʒékt] plan, påhitt, prosjekt.

projectile [pro'dʒektil] framdrivende; drevet fram; kaste-; prosjektil.

projection [pro'dʒekʃən] kasting; utslynging; planlegging, plan; framstående del, framskott, utskott; projeksjon.

projector [pro'dʒektə] planlegger, opphavsmann; prosjektmaker; prosjektør, lyskaster, laterna magica.

projecture [pro'dʒektʃə] det å springe fram.

prolapse [pro'läps] framfall.

prolegomena [prouli'gåminə] innledning, innleiing, forord.

proletarian [prouli'tæˑᵃriən] proletar. -**ism** proletartilstand.

proletariat(e) [prouli'tæˑᵃriét] proletariat; **the dictatorship of the** — proletariatets diktatur.

prolific [pro'lifik] fruktbar.

prolix ['prouliks, pro'liks] langtrukken.

prolixity [pro'liksiti] langtrukkethet.

prologue ['prouˈlåg] fortale, prolog.

prolong [pro'lån] forlenge, prolongere.

prolongation [prouˈlåŋˈgeˈʃən] forlenging, utsetting, frist. **prolonger** [pro'lånə] forlenger.

promenade [pråmə'naˑd] spasertur; spaservei; spasere, promenere.

Prometheus [pro'miˑþjuˑs] Prometevs.

prominence ['pråminəns] framståenhet; framskott; kul; utmerkelse. **prominent** [-nənt] framstående; utpreget; framragende, grepa, framskutt, promiscuity [prouˈmisˈkjuˑiti] sammenblanding; tilfeldighet. **promiscuous** [pro'miskjuəs] blandet, forvirret, broket; i fleng, tilfeldig. ymse.

promise ['pråmis] løfte, tilsagn; forjettelse; love, tilsi; gi forventning om; tegne til; **of (great)** — (meget) lovende; **the land of** — det forjettede land. **promiser** ['pråmisə] en som lover, gir løfte. **promising** [-iŋ] lovende; håpefull. **promissory** ['pråmisəri] lovende; — **note** sola veksel, promesse; egenveksel.

promontory ['pråməntəri] forberg, odde; nes. forhøyning, kul (anatomisk).

promote [pro'mout] befordre, fremme; hjelpe opp el. fram: vekke; flytte opp, forfremme. **promoter** [pro'moutə] fremmer; beskytter; stifter. **promotion** [pro'mouʃən] fremme, befordring; opphjelp; oppflytting, forfremmelse; **be on (one's)** — **promotion** stå for tur til forfremmelse; strebe etter å oppnå forfremmelse. **promotive** [pro'moutiv] som forfremmer, befordrer.

prompt [pråm(p)t] hurtig, snar, snøgg, rask; villig; prompte; betalingsfrist; sufflering; påvirke, tilskynde, inngi; sufflere; tilsi; **orders receive** — **attention** ordrer utføres prompte; **at two** — kl. to presis. — -**book**, — -**copy** sufflørbok. **prompter** ['pråm(p)tə] påvirker, tilskynder; rådgiver; sufflør. **prompting** påvirkning, tilskyndelse, hugskott, råd.

promptitude ['pråm(p)titjuˑd] raskhet; beredvillighet

promptness se **promptitude.**

promulgate ['pråməlgeˈt] kunngjøre.

promulgation [pråməl'geˈʃən] kunngjørelse.

promulgator ['pråməlgeˈtə] kunngjører.

pron. fk. f. **pronoun.**

prone [proun] liggende gruve, foroverbøyd, utstrakt; skrå; tilbøyelig. **proneness** [-nés] tilbøyelighet; helling.

prong [prån] spiss, brodd, odd, klo; tind (på en gaffel); stikke, spidde (på en klo, gaffel). **prong-horn** ['trånhåˑᵃn] prærieantilope.

pronominal [pro'nåminəl] pronominal.

pronoun ['prouˈnaun] pronomen.

pronounce [pro'nauns] uttale; avsi, felle; holde; erklære; uttale seg. **pronounceable** [pro'naunsəbl] som lar seg uttale. **pronounced** [pro'naunst] uttalt, tydelig, grei, umiskjennelig. **pronouncement** [pro'naunsmənt] uttalelse, erklæring, utsagn; dom. **pronouncing** [pro'naunsiŋ] uttale-.

pronunciation [pronʌnsi'eˈʃən] uttale.

proof [pruˑf] prøve, bevis; styrke, styrkegrad; prøvebilde, avtrykk; korrektur; fast, trygg, som holder stand; usvikelig; skuddfri, skuddsikker; tett; **fire-** — ildfast; **water-** — vanntett **be** — **against** kunne motstå, ikke angripes av. — -**charge** prøveladning. — -**impression** prøveavtrykk; korrekturavtrykk. — -**reading** korrekturlesning. — -**sheet** korrekturark.

prop. fk. f. **properly; proposition.**

prop [pråp] støtte, støtte under, stive av; støtte; stiver; strever, bukk; **props** gruvestøtter, props; **prop-word** støtteordet **one, ones,** f. eks. i **the** little **one, his** little **ones.**

propædeutic [proupˈjduˑtik] propedevtisk, forberedende; propedevtikk, forskole.

propagable ['pråpəgəbl] som kan forplante seg, bre seg. **propaganda** [pråpə'gändə] propaganda. **propagate** ['pråpəgeˈt] forplante; utbrede; avle, frambringe. **propagation** [pråpə'geˈʃən] forplantning, utbredelse.

propel [prə'pel] drive fram; -**ling power** drivkraft.

propeller [prə'pelə] propell (på fly), propell, skrue (på dampbåt); skruebåt.

propensity [pro'pensiti] hang, tilbøyelighet.

proper ['pråpə] egen, særegen, eiendommelig; egnet, passende, høvelig; anstendig, sømmelig; ordentlig; riktig, rett, korrekt; — **fraction** ekte brøk; **Italy** — selve Italia.

properly ['pråpəli] egentlig, riktig, passende; meget; **do it** — gjøre det riktig; **behave** — oppføre seg ordentlig; — **speaking** strengt tatt.

property ['pråpəti] eiendommelighet; egenskap; eiendom; formue; rekvisitt. — **-qualification** valgcensus. — **-tax** formueskatt.

prophecy ['pråfisi] profeti, spådom. **prophesier** [-saiə] profet, spåmann. **prophesise** [-saiz] spå.

prophesy ['pråfisai] spå, profetere.

prophet ['pråfit, -et] profet, spåmann.

prophetic(al) [pro'fetik(l)] profetisk.

prophylactic [pråfi'läktik] forebyggende; forebyggende middel.

propinquity [pro'piŋkwiti] nærhet.

propitiate [prə'pifie¹t] forsone, formilde; stemme gunstig; bøte. **propitiation** [propifi'e¹fən] forsoning, formildelse. **propitiator** [pro'pifie¹tə] forsoner. **propitiatory** [-fiətəri] forsonende.

propitious [prə'pifəs] gunstig; nådig, blid.

proponent [pro'poʷnənt] forslagsstiller.

proportion [pro'på·əfən] proporsjon, forhold; høve, samsvar; symmetri; avmåle, avpasse; danne symmetrisk. **proportionable** [-nəbl] som lar seg avpasse; forholdsmessig; proporsjonal. **proportional** [-nəl] forholdsmessig, symmetrisk, proporsjonal; forholdstall. **proportionality** [propå·əfə'näliti] forholdsmessighet, forhold.

proposal [pro'poʷzl] forslag, framlegg; ekteskapstilbud, frieri; ansøkning.

propose [pro'poʷz] foreslå; forelegge; legge fram; ha i sinne; legge planer; tenke; fri.

proposition [pråpo'zifən] framlegging; framlegg, forslag, tilbud; setning.

propound [pro'paund] forelegge, legge fram.

proprietor [pro'praiitə] eier; eiendomsbesitter.

propriety [pro'praiiti] riktighet; berettigelse; hensiktsmessighet; anstand, velanstendighet, sømmelighet, folkeskikk; vørnad; sans for velanstendighet; **play propriety** agere skjermbrett.

propulsion [prə'pʌlfən] framdrift.

propulsive prə'pʌlsiv] drivende, driv-.

pro rata [proʷ're¹tə] pro rata, forholdsmessig.

prorogation [pråro'ge¹fən, proʷ-] forlenging; avbrytelse; oppløsning (ved slutten av en parlamentsamling). **prorogue** [prə'roʷg] forlenge; utsette; avbryte, oppløse, sende hjem.

prosaic [pro'ze¹ik] prosaisk.

proscenium [pro'si·njəm] proscenium (forreste del av scenen). — **-box** prosceniumslosje.

proscribe [pro'skraib] lyse fredløs, gjøre utleg, proskribere. **proscription** [pro'skripfən] proskripsjon; fordømmelse; forbud.

prose [proʷz] prosa; skrive prosa; snakke kjedelig; være langdryg i snakket; — **works** prosaverker; **the** — **of life** livets prosa.

prosecute ['pråsikju·t] forfølge, utøve, drive på med, søke å sette igjennom; saksøke, anklage; fortsette; **trespassers will be prosecuted** overtredelser vil bli meldt.

prosecution [pråsi'kju·fən] forfølgelse; utøvelse; saksøkning; anklage, søksmål; **counsel for the** — aktor.

prosecutor ['pråsikju·tə] en som forfølger, utøver; anklager; saksøker.

proselyte ['pråsilait] proselytt; gjøre til proselytt; omvende.

proser ['proʷzə] prosaskriver; tørrpinne. **prosiness** ['proʷzinés] åndløshet, kjedsommelighet. **prosing** ['proʷziŋ] langtrukken.

prosody ['pråsodi] prosodi, verslære.

prospect ['pråspekt] utsikt; prospekt; skjerp. **prospect** [prə'spekt] søke; skjerpe **(for** etter).

prospective [prə'spektiv] framsynt, framtenkt; som en har i utsikt, ventet; eventuell; framtidig; — **candidates** vordende kandidater. **prospectively** i framtiden, engang.

prospectus [pro'spektəs] plan, program.

prosper ['pråspə] begunstige; være heldig; ha hell med seg, trives; lykkes, ha framgang.

prosperity [prås'periti] hell, framgang; gode konjunkturer; velstand, velvære.

prosperous ['pråspərəs] heldig; velstående.

prostate ['pråste¹t] **(gland)** prostata, blærehalskjertel.

prostitute ['pråstitju·t] prostituere, vanære; prostituert, lav; skjøke. **prostitution** [pråsti-'tju·fən] prostitusjon.

prostrate ['pråstrét] utstrakt; ydmyket, ydmyk; som ligger i støvet; utmattet; nesegrus. **prostrate** [prå'stre¹t] felle, strekke til jorda, legge i bakken; kullkaste, omstyrte, ødelegge; matte, svekke, maktstjele, lamme; — **oneself** kaste seg i støvet, bøye seg dypt.

prostration [prå'stre¹fən] nedkasting, kneling, knefall; nedtrykthet; avkrefting, vanmakt.

protect [pro'tekt] beskytte, verne; gardere (i sjakk); honorere (en veksel); **-ed cruiser** beskyttet krysser (med delvis pansring).

protection [pro'tekfən] beskyttelse, vern; fredning; leidebrev; pansring; tollbeskyttelse, vernetoll; honorering (av veksel). **protectionist** [-ist] beskyttelses-; proteksjonist.

protective [pro'tektiv] beskyttende.

protector [pro'tektə] beskytter; riksforstander. **Lord P.** Cromwell's tittel. **protectoral** [-rel] beskyttende. **protectorate** [-rét] beskyttelse, vern, protektorat. **protectorship** [pro'tektəfip] protektorat.

protégé ['proʷteʒe] protegé (myndling el. yndling).

pro tem. fk. f. **pro tempore** for tiden, p. t.

protest [pro'test] protestere, gjøre innsigelse, gjøre motmæle, gjøre innvendinger; påstå, forsikre; protestere (en veksel). **protest** ['proʷtest] innsigelse, innvending; protest, motmæle.

protestant ['pråtistənt] protestantisk; protestant. **protestantism** [-izm] protestantisme.

protestation [proʷte'ste¹fən] forsikring, erklæring; protest, motmæle, innsigelse. **protester** [pro-'testə] forsikrer; protesterende.

Proteus ['proʷtju·s] Protevs (gresk gud).

proteus ['proʷtju·s] hulepadde.

protocol ['proʷtokål] protokoll; protokollere. **-ise** ['proʷtəkålaiz] protokollere. **-ist** ['proʷtəkålist] protokollfører.

protoplasm ['proʷtoplāzm] protoplasma, celleslim.

prototype ['proʷtotaip] forbilde, original, mønsterbilde.

protozoon [proʷto'zoʷən] urdyr, protozo.

protract [pro'träkt] forlenge, trekke ut, forhale, trekke i langdrag. **protracted** [-id] langvarig. **protraction** [pro'träkfən] forhaling; langvarighet. **protractive** [pro'träktiv] som forlenger, hefter, trekker i langdrag. **protractor** [pro'träktə] hefter, forhaler.

protrude [pro'tru·d] skyte fram, stikke fram. **protrusion** [-'fən] framskytning, framspring. **protrusive** [-'tru·siv] framskytende.

protuberance [pro'tju·bərəns] framståenhet; hevelse, kul. **protuberant** [-rənt] framstående.

proud [praud] stolt, kry, byrg.

proudish ['praudif] kry, stor på det.

provable ['pru·vəbl] bevislig.

prove [pru·v] prøve, erfare; bevise, godtgjøre; syne seg, vise seg; bli; — true slå til.

provedor(e) ['prāvidå·ə] leverandør.

proven ['pru·vən] bevist (skotsk).

provenance ['prāvinəns] opprinnelse, opphav.

provenience [pro'vi·njəns] se **provenance**.

proverb ['pråvə(·)b] ordspråk, ordtak, ordtøke; ordstev; ordspråklek; **the Proverbs** Salomos ordspråk.

proverbial [pro'və·bjəl] ordspråklig, som er blitt til et ordtak, velkjent.

proverbialism [pro'vǝ·bjǝlizm] ordspråklig forbindelse, talemåte. **proverbialist** [-list] en som bruker ordspråk.

provide [pro'vaid] sørge for, syte for, besørge, skaffe, tilveiebringe; forsyne; foreskrive, bestemme; dra omsorg for, ta forholdsregler, sikre seg. **provided** [pro'vaidid] forutsatt.

providence ['prǎvidǝns] forsorg, forsynlighet; forsyn. **provident** [-ǝnt] omtenksom, forsynlig.

providential [prǎvi'denʃǝl] forsynets, bestemt av forsynet; **he had a** — **escape** det var et Guds under at han slapp unna.

providentially [prǎvi'denʃǝli] ved forsynets styrelse, ved et under.

provider [pro'vaidǝ] leverandør.

province ['prǎvins] provins, egn; område, distrikt; fag, felt. **provincial** [pro'vinʃǝl] provinsiell, provins-. **provincialism** [-ʃǝlizm] provinsialisme. **provincialist** [-ʃǝlist] provinsmann.

provision [pro'viʒǝn] forsorg; omsut; anskaffelse; forsørgelse; proviant; bestemmelse; (i pl.) fetevarer; forsyne, proviantere, niste ut; **make** — **treffe** forholdsregler (**for** for: **against** imot). **provisional** [-ʒǝnǝl] midlertidig, foreløpig; provisorisk. **provisionary** [-ʒǝnǝri] = **provisional**. **provision-dealer** fetevarehandler. **provisioner** [pro-'viʒǝnǝ] proviranthandler. **provisioning** [-iŋ] proviantering.

proviso [pro'vaizou] klausul, forbehold. **provisory** [prǝ'vaizǝri] foreløpig; betinget. **provocation** [prǎvo'keiʃǝn] utfordring, uteskng, tirring, erting. **at small (on the slightest)** — **ved den minste anledning, for et godt ord.**

provocative [pro'vǎkǝtiv] utfordrende, uteskende; pirringsmiddel.

provoke [pro'vouk] framkalle, vekke, egge, pirre; utfordre, uteske, oppirre; fornærme. **provoking** uteskende, tirrende; ergerlig, harmelig.

provost ['prǎvǝst] domprost; rektor (ved visse universitetskollegier); (skotsk) borgermester; — **sergeant** profoss (fangevokter ved en kaserne).

prow [prau] forstavn, baug.

prowess ['praués] djervhet, manndom, tapperhet.

prowl [praul] snuse om i; luske om på rov; røve. **prowler** ['praulǝ] luskende tyv.

prox. [prǎks] fk. f. **proximo**.

proximate ['prǎksimét] nærmest.

proximity [prǎk'simiti] nærhet; — **of blood** nært slektskap.

proximo ['prǎksimou] i neste måned.

proxy ['prǎksi] fullmakt; fullmektig, varamann, stedfortreder; prokurist. **proxyship** [-ʃip] fullmektigstilling.

P. R. S. fk. f. **President of the Royal Society**.

prude [pru·d] snerpe; **play the** — spille den dydige.

prudence ['pru·dǝns] klokskap, omtanke; forsiktighet; **as a matter of** — for sikkerhets skyld. **prudent** ['pru·dǝnt] klok; forsiktig, varsom. **prudential** [pru·'denʃǝl] klokskaps-; forsiktighets-; forsiktig; klokskapsregel.

prudery ['pru·d(ǝ)ri] snerperi, affektasjon.

prudish ['pru·diʃ] snerpet, tertefin, affektert.

prune [pru·n] beskjære, stusse (trær, planter). **prune** [pru·n] sviske. **prunes and prims** affektert snakk.

prunella [pru'nelǝ] prunell (ullstoff); blåkoll (plante). **pruner** ['pru·nǝ] beskjærer; hagekniv. **pruning-knife** gartnerkniv. **pruning-shears** hagesaks.

Prussia ['prʌʃǝ] Preussen. **Prussian** ['prʌʃǝn] prøyssisk; prøysser.

prussic ['prʌsik] blåsur.

pry [prai] snuse, spotte, spionere; snusing, speiding, spionering. **prying** ['praiiŋ] snusende, nyfiken; snusing.

P. S. fk. f. **postscript; prompt side**.

Ps. fk. f. **psalms**.

psalm [sa·m] salme (især om Davids salmer);

the **(Book of) Psalms** Davids salmer. **psalmist** ['sa·mist] salmist; salmedikter.

psalter ['så(·)ltǝ] Davids salmer.

pseudo ['s(j)u·do(u)] i smstn.: falsk, uekte; psevdo.

pseudonym ['s(j)u·donim] psevdonym. **pseudonymity** [s(j)u·do'nimiti] psevdonymitet. **pseudonymous** [s(j)u·'dånimǝs] psevdonym.

pshaw [(p)ʃå·] pytt; si pytt til, blåse av (el.i).

psora ['så·rǝ] skabb, fnatt.

psoriasis [so'raiǝsis] psoriasis (hudsykdom).

psychanalysis [saikǝ'nälisis] psykoanalyse.

Psyche ['saiki] Psyke; sjel.

psychiater [sai'kaiǝtǝ] sinnssykelæge.

psychologic(al) [saiko'lådʒik(l)] psykologisk. **psychologist** [sai'kålǝdʒist] psykolog. **psychology** [sai'kålǝdʒi] psykologi.

psychoanalyse [saiko·u'änǝlaiz] psykoanalysere. **-analysis** [saiko·u'nälǝsis] psykoanalyse.

Pt. fk. f. 'Part; Port.

pt. fk. f. **pint**.

ptarmigan ['ta·ǝmigǝn] fjellrype.

ptisan ['tizǝn] tisane (avkok av bygg el. legeplanter).

P. T. O. fk. f. **please turn over.**

Ptolemaic [tåli'me·ik] ptolemeisk.

ptomaine ['to·ume·in] ptomaïn, likalkaloid.

pub [pʌb] (fk. f. **public house**) kafé, vertshus.

public ['pʌblik] offentlig; alminnelig; sams, felles: offentlighet, almenhet, publikum; — **conveniences** offentlige toalett-rom (i regelen underjordiske); — **house** vertshus, kneipe, sjapp; — **school** 1) i England brukt om visse gamle, dyre latinskoler som Eton, Rugby og Harrow; 2) i Amerika: offentlig skole (gratis og med adgang for alle).

publican ['pʌblikǝn] skatteforpakter; toller; vertshusholder.

publication [pʌbli'ke·ʃǝn] offentliggjøring, kunngjøring; forkynnelse; utgivelse; skrift, blad; — **-price** bokhandlerpris.

publicist ['pʌblisist] folkerettslærer; politisk journalist, publisist.

publicity [pʌ'blisiti] offentlighet.

publish ['pʌbliʃ] offentliggjøre, kunngjøre; røpe; forkynne, bekjentgjøre, gjøre kjent; utgi; utgi bøker, forlegge bøker.

publisher ['pʌbliʃǝ] kunngjører, forkynner; forlegger; utgiver.

publishing ['pʌbliʃiŋ] offentliggjøring; forlag. **-firm**, — **-house** forlagsbokhandel.

Puck [pʌk] nisse, tunkall, tuftekall; puke; puck. **pucker** ['pʌkǝ] rynke; snurpe, spisse munnen; rynke; spiss munn; **he is in a terrible** — han er ille stedt, i en lei knipe.

pud [pʌd] lanke, labb, pote.

pudding ['pudniŋ] vile, fender.

pudder ['pʌdǝ] ståhei, oppstyr; gjøre kvalm. **pudding** ['pudiŋ] pudding; vile, vurst, fender. **-faced** med månefjes. **—headed** stjukk i hue, tosket. **—sleeves** vidt ome (på pudding tidligere var første rett), rette øyeblikk, den ellevte time, grevens tid.

puddingy ['pudiŋi] puddingaktig.

puddle ['pʌdl] pøl, sølepytt; rote, grumse, røre opp i; pudle (leire); elte. **puddly** ['pʌdli] mudret, gjørmet.

pudgy ['pʌdʒi] buttet, tykk, klumpet.

puerile ['pjuerail] barnaktig.

puerperal [pju·'ǝ·pǝrǝl] barsel-.

puff [pʌf] pust, vindpust, gufs, blaff; drag (av en sigar), pudderkvast i røyksopp: terte, bakkels; puff (på kjole): reklame; pudre, blåse, blaffe; pese; gjøre blest; reklamere; spile opp; rose, skryte av; gjøre reklame for; — **off** få avsatt ved god reklame.

puff-ball ['pʌfbå·l] røyksopp.

puff-box ['pʌfbåks] puddereske, pudderdåse.

puffer ['pʌfə] markskriker, humbugmaker, reklamemaker.
puffery ['pʌfəri] praling; reklame.
puffiness ['pʌfinés] oppspilthet.
puffy ['pʌfi] oppustet, oppblåst, andpusten.
pug [pʌg] blande, elte (leire); fylle.
pug [pʌg] kjælenavn for en ape; mops. — -dog ['pʌgdàg] mops. — -face ['pɪ gfe's] apefjes.
puggree ['pʌgri·] musselinskjerf (om hatten til beskyttelse mot sola).
pugilism ['pju·dʒilizm] nevekamp, boksing.
pugilist ['pju·dʒilist] nevekjemper, bokser.
pugnacious |pʌg'ne'ʃəs] stridbar, trettekjær.
pugnacity [pʌg'näsiti] stridbarhet.
pug-nose ['pʌgnoᵘz] brakknese, oppstoppernese.
puisne ['pju·ni] yngre; underordnet.
puissance ['pju·isəns] makt.
puissant ['pju·isənt] mektig.
puke [pju·k] spy, kaste opp; oppkasting; oppkast.
pule [pju·l] klynke, pipe, tyte, pistre, sutre.
pull |pul] trekke, dra, hale, rive; plukke; rykke; ro; trekk, rykk, tak; kamp, dyst, strid; slurk; rotur; — along ro av sted; holde det gående; klare seg; — round ta seg sammen; — up holde an, stanse. puller ['pulə] som trekker osv.
pullet ['pulit] ung høne; backfisch.
pulley ['puli] trisse, blokk, reimskive; cone — trappeskive; single — enkelt reimskive.
Pullman ['pulmən] Pullman; pullmanvogn.
pulmonary ['pʌlmənəri] lunge-.
pulp [pʌlp] bløt masse; fruktkjøtt; papirmasse; pulpa; mase, støte; chemical — cellulose; mechanical — tremasse. pulpiness ['pʌlpinés] bløthet, kjøttfullhet.
pulpit ['pulpit] prekestol.
pulpiteer [pulpi'tiə] prekehest, storpreker.
pulp-mill ['pʌlpmil] cellulosefabrikk.
pulpous ['pʌlpəs] bløt, kjøttfull, saftig.
pulpy ['pʌlpi] bløt, kjøttfull.
pulsate [pʌl'se't] banke, pikke, pulsere, slå.
pulsation [pʌl'se'ʃən] slag, banking.
pulsative ['pʌlsativ], pulsatory ['pʌlsətəri] bankende, slående, pulserende.
pulse [pʌls] slag, pulsslag, puls; banke, pikke, slå, pulsere; feel his — føle ham på pulsen; føle ham på tennene.
pulse [pʌls] belgfrukter.
pulverization [pʌlvərai'ze'ʃən] pulverisering.
pulverize ['pʌlvəraiz] finstøte, pulverisere; pulveriseres.
pumice ['pʌmis] pimpstein; polere (el. slipe) med pimpstein.
pump [pʌmp] pumpe; lense, pumpe; utspørre.
pump [pʌmp] dansesko.
pumpkin ['pʌm(p)kin] gresskar.
pun [pʌn] ordspill; lage ordspill.
punch [pʌnʃ] punsj (en drikk).
punch [pʌnʃ] (fork. f. Punchinello) polichinell, bajas; a P. and Judy show et dukketeater; Punch (eller The London Charivari) et vittighetsblad.
punch [pʌnʃ] dor, lokkedor (til å slå huller med i jern); neveslag, kilevink; stikke eller slå huller, gjennombore; slå, dra til.
punch-bowl ['pʌnʃboᵘl] punsjebolle.
Punchinello [pʌnʃi'neloᵘ] Polichinell (figur i den italienske maskekomedie).
punching-machine ['pʌnʃinˌmaʃin]lokkemaskin.
punctilio [pʌn(k)'tilioᵘ] finesse, overdreven punktlighet; stand upon -s ta det altfor nøye.
punctilious [pʌn(k)'tiliəs] smålig nøyaktig, ytterst nøye; stivt korrekt punctiliousness [pʌn(k)-'tiliəsnés] nøyaktighet; smålighet.
punctual ['pʌn(k)tjuəl, -tʃuəl] punktlig, nøyaktig; ordentlig. punctuality [pʌn(k)tʃu'äliti, -tju-] punktlighet, nøyaktighet, orden.
punctuate ['pʌn(k)tjue't, -tʃu-] sette skilletegn i; poengtere. punctuation [pʌn(k)tju'e'ʃən, -tʃu-] interpunksjon. punctum ['pʌnktəm] punkt.

puncture ['pʌŋ(k)tʃə] stikk; punktering; stikke i; stikke hull i; punktere.
pundit ['pʌndit] (egl. indisk) lærd.
pungency ['pʌn(d)ʒənsi] skarphet.
pungent ['pʌn(d)ʒənt] skarp, ram, skjærende.
Punic ['pju·nik] punisk, kartagisk; troløs.
puniness ['pju·ninés] litenhet.
punish ['pʌniʃ] straffe, avstraffe; legge i seg av (mat).
punishable ['pʌniʃəbl] straffverdig; straffbar.
punishment ['pʌniʃmənt] straff, avstraffelse; dårlig medfart; capital punishment dødsstraff.
punitive ['pju·nitiv] straffende; straffe-.
Punjab [pʌn'dʒa·b] Punjab.
punster ['pʌnstə] vitsemaker.
punt [pʌnt] flatbunnet båt, lorje; stake (seg) fram; føre i pram.
punt [pʌnt] ponto (i kort); vedde, sette innsats.
punt [pʌnt] spenne til fotballen, som en har sloppet, før den når bakken; spark.
punter ['pʌntə] en som staker seg fram i en flatbunnet pram; spiller.
punt-hook ['pʌnthuk] båtshake.
puny ['pju·ni] bitte liten, ørliten, ubetydelig.
pup [pʌp] hvalp; hvalpe, få hvalper.
pupa ['pju·pə], pl. pupæ ['pju·pi·] puppe.
pupil ['pju·pl, -pil] pupill; myndling, elev, disippel. pupilage ['pju·pilidʒ] læretid; umyndighet. pupilarity [pju·pi'läriti] umyndighet, umyndig alder. pupilary ['pju·piləri] pupill-; som angår en elev.
pupil-teacher ['pju·pilti·tʃə] læreremne, vordende lærer (som arbeider under ledelse av en eldre lærer).
puppet ['pʌpit] dukke, marionett.
puppetish ['pʌpitiʃ] dukkeaktig.
puppet!-man, — -master marionettmann. — -play dukkespill.
puppetry['pʌpitri]dukkeaktigutseende, dukkeaktighet; formaliteter; skinn.
puppet-show['pʌpitʃoᵘ]dukketeater, marionetteater.
puppy ['pʌpi] hvalp; laps, sprett; få hvalper.
puppyhood [-hud] hvalpetid; grønn ungdom.
puppyish [-iʃ] hvalpaktig. puppyism [-izm] lapsethet, flabbethet.
purblind ['pə·(')blaind] stærblind.
purchasable ['pə·tʃəsəbl] til fals, til kjøps.
purchase ['pə·tʃəs] kjøpe, erverve, forskaffe seg; bevege, hive, lette; ervervelse; kjøp, innkjøp, anskaffelse; heiseverk, gein, plass (for a stroke) til å slå ut med armen; tak.—book kreditt-kladd. — -deed kjøpekontrakt. — -money innkjøpspris. — -price innkjøpspris. purchaser ['pə·tʃəsə] kjøper; erverver; kunde.
purdah ['pə·da·] (indisk) forheng.
pure [pjua] ren; klar, skjær.
pureness ['pjuənés] renhet.
purgation [pə·'ge'ʃən] renselse; avføring. purgative ['pə·gətiv] avførende. purgatory ['pə·gətəri] rensende, sonende; skjærsild.
purge [pə·dʒ] rense; skaffe avføring; renses, lutres; rensing, utrensing; avførende middel. purger ['pə·dʒə] renser; avførende middel. purgery ['pə·dʒəri] sukkerraffineri. purging ['pə·dʒiŋ] rensing.
purification [pjuərifi'ke'ʃən] renselse; rettfer-diggjøring. purifier ['pjuərifaiə] renser; rensingsmiddel. purify ['pjuərifai] rense; renses.
purism ['pjuərizm] purisme, språkrensing.
purist ['pjuərist] purist, språkrenser.
Puritan ['pjuəritən] puritansk; puritaner.
Puritanism ['pjuəritənizm] puritanisme.
purity ['pjuəriti] renhet.
purl [pə·l] sildre, skvulpe, risle; risl, surl.
purl [pə·l] krydderol (med sukker og ingefær).
purl [pə·l] bremme, kante; strikke vrangt; brodert kant, rcid.
purlieu ['pə·lju·] grensedistrikt, utkant, omegn.

purloin [pəˈloin] tilvende seg, stjele, rapse.
purloiner [-ə] tyv; plagiator.

purple [ˈpəˑpl] purpurfarget; fiolett, blåfiolett; purpurfarge; blårødt; purpur; farge(s) rød (fiolett, blå). **purplish** [ˈpəˑpliʃ] purpuraktig, lett blåligrød.

purport [ˈpəˑpət, -påˑət] hensikt, mening, betydning; innhold; inneholde, ha å bety, gå ut på, gi seg ut for.

purpose [ˈpəˑpəs] hensikt, formål, øyemed; forsett; saken, det det gjelder om; virkning, retning; ha til hensikt, akte; **on** — med forsett, med vilje; **on** — **that** i den hensikt å; **for** (eller **to**) **that** — i den hensikt; **to the** — saken vedkommende, på sin plass; **to some** — med virkning; **to no** — til ingen nytte, forgjeves, fåfengt.
purposeless [ˈpəˑpəslês] hensiktsløs, formålsløs.
purposely [ˈpəˑpəsli] med hensikt, forsettlig.
purr [pəˑ] male; maling (om katten).

purse [pəˑs] portemoné, pung; penger, pengesum; gevinst, premie; rikdom, velstand; stikke i pungen; rynke; snurpe sammen; **a** — **was made up** det ble foretatt en innsamling; **the keeper of the national** — den bevilgende myndighet. — **-penny** lykkeskilling. — **-pride** pengestolthet. — **-proud** pengestolt.
purser [ˈpəˑsə] proviantforvalter, intendant.
purslane [ˈpəˑslin] portulakk.
pursuable [pəˈs(j)uˑəbl] som lar seg forfølge.
pursuance [pəˈs(j)uˑəns], **in** — of ifølge.
pursuant [pəˈsjuˑənt] overensstemmende; — **to** overensstemmelse med, i samsvar med.
pursue [pəˈs(j)uˑ] forfølge, sette etter; strebe etter, strebe hen til; tilstrebe; følge; drive, sysle med; fortsette.
pursuer [pəˈsjuˑə] forfølger; etterstreber.
pursuit [pəˈs(j)uˑt] forfølgelse; etterstrebelse; jakt; beskjeftigelse, syssel; interesse; fortsettelse.
pursuivant [ˈpəˑswivənt] persevant, underherold (funksjonær i **College of arms**).
pursy [ˈpəˑsi] astmatisk, tungpusten; tykk; rynket; pengesterk.
purtenance [ˈpəˑtinəns] tilbehør.
purvey [pəˈveⁱ] forsyne; skaffe, forskaffe; proviantere. **purveyance** [pəˈveⁱəns] forsyning; tilveiebringelse. **purveyor** [pəˈveⁱə] leverandør; **Purveyor to His Majesty** hoffleverandør.
purview [ˈpəˑvjuˑ] lovtekst; bestemmelser; sfære, område.
pus [pʌs] våg, materie, verk.
Pusey [ˈpjuˑzi] Pusey.
push [puʃ] støte, skubbe, puffe (til), drive; trenge inn på: drive på, framskynde; støt, skubb, puff; framdrift; trykk; tak; anstrengelse; — **his fortune** slå seg opp; — **off goods** få avsatt varer; — on drive på; framskynde; hjelpe fram. — **-button** eller — **-contact** trykkontakt.
pushful [ˈpuʃf(u)l] foretaksom, påtrengende.
pushing [ˈpuʃin] foretaksom, pågående.
push-pin [ˈpuʃpin] en barneleik med knappenåler.
pusillanimity [pjuˑsiləˈnimiti] forsagthet, feighet. **pusillanimous** [pjuˑsiˈläniməs] forsagt, feig.

puss [pus] pus, kiss; — **in the corner** bytte sete, låne varme (leik).
Puss-in-Boots [ˈpusinˈbuˑts] den bestøvlede katt.
pussy [ˈpusi], **pussy-cat** pus, pusekatt.
pustule [ˈpʌstjuˑl] kveise, filipens.
put [put] putte, sette, stille, stikke, legge, bringe; framstille, sette fram, uttrykke; to — **it** mildly mildest talt; — **about** la sirkulere; utbre; gå baut, baute; plage; — **along** sette i fart; — **by** legge til side; — **down** legge fra seg; skrive ned, notere; undertrykke; kue, døyve, kvele; ydmyke; bringe til taushet; — **forth** sette fram; utgi; stille fram; utstede; — **forward** forfremme, fremme, sette fram med; — **in** legge inn; skyte inn; komme fram med; — **in mind of** (eller **that**) minne om; — **off** legge vekk; utsette, oppsette; — on legge på, sette på, ta på; — **out** legge ut, sette ut; sette fram; slukke; forvri; utfolde, oppby; forvirre, forville; stikke ut; skyte (knopper, røtter); **be** — **out about** være ute av det over, bli brekt i forlegenhet; — **to** spenne for; **be** — **to it** bli nødt (til det); — **to bay** sette, stille (på jakt); — **to sea** stikke til sjøs; — **to death** avlive. drepe, la henrette; — **up** heve; — **up at** ta inn hos; — **up with** finne seg i, tåle.
put [pʌt] (gml.) staur, slamp.
put-off [ˈputˈåˑ)f] utflukt, påskudd.
put-on [ˈputˈån] påtatt.
putrefaction [pjuˑtriˈfäkʃən] forråtnelse.
putrefy [ˈpjuˑtrifai] forråtne, forpeste; råtne.
putrid [ˈpjuˑtrid] råtten.
puttee [ˈpʌtiˑ] slags gamasjer av tøy (som vikles om leggen fra ankel til kne).
putter [ˈpʌtə] slags golfkølle til å slå ballen i hull med.
putty [ˈpʌti] kitt; kitte.
puzzle [ˈpʌzl] forvirre, sette i forlegenhet, forbløffe; spekulere, tenke over, bry hjernen med; finne ut; gåte, knute, floke, vanskelighet, vanskelig spørsmål; puslespill. **puzzled** [ˈpʌzld] forlegen, rådvill, rådløs. **puzzler** [ˈpʌzlə] gåte, knute.

P. W. D. fk. f. **Public Works Department.**
pyæmia [paiˈiˑmiə] blodforgiftning.
pygmean [pigˈmiˑən] pygmeisk; dvergaktig.
pygmy [ˈpigmi] dverg.
pyjamas [pəˈdʒaˑməz] pyjamas (nattdrakt).
pyramid [ˈpirəmid] pyramide. **pyramidal** [piˈrämidəl] pyramideformet, pyramidestor.
pyre [ˈpaiə] likbål.
Pyrenean [piriˈniˑən] pyreneisk. **the Pyrenees** [ˈpiriniˑz] Pyreneene.
pyromania [paiəroᵘˈmeⁱniə] pyromani. **pyromaniac** [paiəroᵘˈmeⁱniäk] pyroman.
pyrotechnics [p(a)iroˈtekniks] fyrverkeri.
Pythagoras [piˈbägəräs] Pytagoras.
Pythia [ˈpiⁱⁱa] Pytia.
python [ˈpaiþən] pyton, en slags kjempeslange.
pyx [piks] pyksis (sølvskål til oppbevaring av hostien); eske med prøvemynter.

Q

Q, q [kjuˑ] Q, q.
Q. fk. f. **query; question.**
Q. B. fk. f. **Queen's Bench.**
Q. C. fk. f. **Queen's Counsel; Queen's College.**
q. e. fk. f. **quod est** (latin: som betyr).
Q. M. fk. f. **Quartermaster.**
qr. fk. f. **quarter.**
Qt., **qt.** fk. f. **quantity, quart.**
Q. T. fk. f. **quiet; on the Q. T.** i all hemmelighet.
qua [kweⁱ] i egenskap av, som.
quack [kwäk] snadre, skryte; drive kvaksalveri; snadring; kvaksalver. **quackery** [ˈkwäkəri] kvak-

salveri; sjarlataneri. **quackish** [ˈkwäkiʃ] kvaksalveraktig.
quacksalver [ˈkwäksälvə] kvaksalver.
quad [kwåd] fk. f. **quadrat; quadrangle.**
quadragenarian [kwådrədʒiˈnäˑᵊriən] mellom 40 og 49 år gammel.
Quadragesima [kwådrəˈdʒesimə] første søndag i fasten; faste.
quadrangle [ˈkwådrängl] firkant; plass, gård.
quadrangular [kwåˈdrängjulə] firkantet.
quadrant [ˈkwådrənt] kvadrant.
quadrat [ˈkwådrét] utslutning (en blind type).

quadrate ['kwådrét] kvadrat-, kvadratisk, firkantet; firkant, kvadrat. quadrature ['kwådrət-ʃə] kvadratur.
quadrille [kwå'dril] kvadrilje (en turdans av 4 par; også et slags kortspill, spilt av 4 personer).
quadrisyllabic [kwådrisi'läbik] firstavings-.
quadroon [kwå'dru·n] kvarteron, barn av mulatt og hvit.
quadruped ['kwådruped] firføtt (dyr).
quadruple ['kwådrupl] firdobbelt; firdoble.
quaff [kwå·f] drikke (ut).
quaggy ['kwägi] gyngende (om myr); myrlendt, sumpig. quagmire ['kwägmaiə] hengemyr.
quail [kwe'l] synke sammen, bli forsagt, tape motet; knuse, tilintetgjøre; kue.
quail [kwe'l] vaktel.
quaint [kwe'nt] gammeldags; original; eiendommelig, underlig. quaintness [-nés] særhet, underlighet, gammel stil.
quake [kwe'k] ryste, riste, skjelve, beve; skjelving, rystelse, risting.
Quaker ['kwe'kə] kveker. quakerism [-rizm] kvekertro.
quakiness ['kwe'kinés] skjelv, skjelving. quaky ['kwe'ki] skjelvende.
qualifiable ['kwålifaiəbl] som kan modereres; som kan begrenses. qualification [kwålifi'ke'ʃən] dyktiggjøring; dyktighet; kvalifikasjon, forutsetning, atkomst, berettigelse; omdanning; innskrenkning, nærmere bestemmelse, avdemping· qualified ['kwålifaid] skikket, dyktig, berettiget; blandet; betinget, forbeholden.
qualify ['kwålifai] gjøre skikket, dyktiggjøre, kvalifisere; innskrenke, modifisere, begrense; svekke; erverve seg atkomst.
quality ['kwåliti] egenskap, beskaffenhet, karakter, rang, verdighet; stand; kvalitet; people of — standspersoner, fornemme folk.
qualm [kwa·m, kwå·m] kvalme, (plutselig) illebefinnende; skruppel, betenkelighet. qualmish ['kwåmiʃ, 'kva·miʃ] syk, som føler kvalme.
quandary ['kwåndəri] forlegenhet, knipe.
quant [kwånt] stake, båtstake; stake (seg) fram.
quantify ['kwåntifai] begrense med hensyn til mengde; taksere. quantitative ['kwåntitətiv] kvantitativ. quantity ['kwåntiti] kvantum, mengde, kvantitet.
quarantine ['kwårənti·n] karantene(stasjon).
quarrel ['kwårəl] strid, trette, kiv, uenighet; grunn til å klage, utestående sak; trette, strides, ligge i klammeri. quarrelsome [-səm] trettekjær, stridslysten.
quarry ['kwåri] vilt, fangst, bytte; gjøre bytte, jage.
quarry ['kwåri] brott, steinbrott, marmorbrott; bryte.
quarry ['kwåri] (firkantet) glassrute; firkantet flise.
quarryman ['kwårimən] steinbryter.
quart [kwå·°t] pott; kvart.
quarter ['kwå·°tə] kvart, fjerdedel, fjerdepart; kvarter; kvartal; fjerdingår; egn, strøk, himmeltegn; kvarter, bolig; nåde; dele i fire deler; innkvartere; partere, sønderlemme; kvadrere, anbringe i et (kvadrert) våpenskjold; være innkvartert hos; streife, fare hit og dit, kjøre ut og inn; vike til siden; in the highest -s på høyeste sted. — -day kvartalsdag, termin. — -deck skanse. quartering ['kwå·°tərin] firdeling; innkvartering; partering.
quarterly ['kwå·°təli] fjerdedels; kvartals-; kvartalsvis; kvartalsskrift.
quarter|master ['kwå·°təma·stə] kvartermester. — -sessions kvartalsting. underrett. — -staff piggstav; fektestav (som føres med begge hender, den ene hånd en fjerdedel inne på staven).
quartet [kwå·°'tet] kvartett.
quarto ['kwå·°toⁿ] kvartformat.
quartz ['kwå·ts] kvarts.
quash [kwåʃ] kassere; forkaste, omstøte.

quaternion [kwə'tə·niən] kvaternion; gruppe av fire; firstavingsord.
quatrefoil ['kätəfoil, 'kätrəfoil] firkløver.
quaver ['kwe'və] dirre, skjelve; trille; dirring, skjelving.
quay [ki·] bolverk, kai: forsyne med bolverk.
quayage ['ki·idʒ] kaiavgift.
quean [kwi·n] tøs, taske; jente.
queasy ['kwi·zi] som har kvalme; blasert, kræsen.
Quebec [kwi'bek] Quebec.
queen [kwi·n] dronning; dame (i kort); Q. Mab alvedronningen; Queen's Counsel kronjurist; Queen's English korrekt engelsk; Queen's shilling håndpenger (for vervet soldat); Queen's weather strålende vær; queen it spille dronning. — -bee biedronning. — -dowager, — -mother -like, -ly dronningaktig.
Queensland ['kwi·nzlənd] Queensland.
queer [kwiə] merkelig, underlig, rar, snodig; tvilsom; utilpass; be in Queer street være i knipe. queer [kwiə] gjøre underlig; latterliggjøre, spolere; — the pitch for hemmelig ødelegge sjansene for.
queerish ['kwiəriʃ] litt rar.
quell [kwel] knuse, få bukt med; dempe, døyve, stille.
quench [kwenʃ] slokke, sløkke, stille. quenchable ['kwenʃəbl] som lar seg slokke. quencher ['kwenʃə] slokker, slokkingsmiddel. quenchless ['kwenʃlés] uslokkelig, ubetvingelig.
querimonious [kweri'mo"njəs] klynkende, syten. querulous ['kwer(j)uləs] klagende, klynkende. gretten. querulousness [-nés] klaging, klynking.
query ['kwiəri] spørsmål; spørsmålstegn: spørre om, undersøke, betvile.
quest [kwest] leting; ønske; bønn; søke: in — of søkende.
question ['kwestʃən, -tʃən] spørsmål; debatt, forhandling, undersøkelse; tvil; forhør, tortur; regnskap; spørre, spørre ut; undersøke; dra i tvil; ask a — gjøre et spørsmål; call for the — forlange slutt på debatten; the matter in — den foreliggende sak; out of — utenfor tvil; out of the — som det ikke kan være tale om. questionable ['kwestʃənəbl] tvilsom, uviss, problematisk; mistenkelig. questionary [-(ə)ri] spørrende, spørre-. questioner [-ə] spørger, eksaminator. questioning [-in̩] spørring, spørsmål; eksaminasjon.
queue [kju·] hårpisk, flette; kø.
quibble ['kwibl] spissfindighet; brander, ordspill, vits; bruke spissfindigheter, utflukter. quibbler ['kwiblə] vringler, sofist; vitsmaker.
quick [kwik] levende; kvikk, snøgg, livlig, rask; hurtig; tin, skarp, gløgg; levende kjøtt; ømt punkt; levende hegn; hagtorn; to the — ned i kjøttet, til marg og bein, på det føleligste. quicken ['kwikn] gjøre levende, gi liv, anspore, sette fart i; framskynde, påskynde; bli levende, få liv, kvikne til.
quicken ['kwikn] rogn (tre), asal.
quickening ['kwiknin̩] framskynding, påskynding.
quickens ['kviknz] kveke.
quicklime ['kwiklaim] ulesket kalk.
quickness ['kwiknés] kvikkhet, livlighet, raskhet; — of parts hurtig fattevne.
quicksand ['kwiksånd] kvikksand.
quick|-scented ['kwik|'séntid] som har fin nese, god teft. -set levende hegn. -sighted skarpsynt. -silver kvikksølv. -tempered hissig, brålyndt. -witted snarrådig, oppfinnsom.
quid [kwid] noe.
quid [kwid] skrå, buss; pund (sovereign).
quiddity ['kwiditi] spissfindighet, ordkløyving, vringel.
quiescence [kwai'esəns] hvile, ro. quiescent [-ənt] hvilende, i ro; passiv, uvirksom.
quiet ['kwaiət] rolig, stille, fredelig; ro, fred;

berolige, roe, stagge, stille; **on the** — i smug, hemmelig. **quieter** [-ə] en som beroliger. **quietism** [-izm] kvietisme; ro. **quietness** [-nés] ro, stillhet. **quietude** ['kwaiətju·d] ro, fred.

quill [kwil] pennefjær, (fjær)penn; fjærpose; plektrum; pigg (på pinnsvin); spole.

quill [kwil] fold (i pipekrage); pipe, kruse.

quilt [kwilt] stukket teppe, vattert (el. dunfylt) teppe; stoppe ut, polstre, vattere. **quilting** [-iŋ] utstopping, polstring, vattering.

quina ['kwainə] kinabark.

quince [kwins] kvede (frukt).

quinine [kwi'ni·n] kinin.

quinsy ['kwinzi] halsbetennelse, halsbyll.

quintessence [kwin'tesəns] kvintessens.

quire ['kwaiə] bok (24 ark).

quire ['kwaiə] kor; synge i kor.

quirk [kwɔ·k] utflukt, spissfindighet; innfall; kast, sveis, sving.

quit [kwit] oppgi, forlate; fratre, legge ned; kvitt, fri; — **cost** bære seg, svare seg; — **scores** gjøre opp, gjøre avregning; jevne ut; **give notice to** — si opp.

quite [kwait] ganske, helt, fullstendig; **when I was** — **a child** da jeg enda var barn; — **the contrary** tvert imot.

quits [kwits] kvitt, skuls; **be** — være kvitt.

quittable ['kwitəbl] som kan forlates.

quitter ['kwitə] en som forlater; usling, forræder.

quiver ['kwivə] kogger, pilekogger.

quiver ['kwivə] dirre, sitre, skjelve; dirring, sitring, skjelving.

Quixote ['kwiksət] Quijote. **quixotic** [kwik-ˈsåtik] don-quijotisk.

quiz [kwiz] raring; gjøner; gjøn, ap, spikk; drive gjøn med, spotte, gjøre narr av, fiksere.

quizzical ['kwizíkl] spottende, ertende, gjønende; komisk.

quizzing-glass ['kwiziŋgla·s] monokkel.

quod [kwåd] (i slang) fengsel; putte i «hullet».

quoin [koin] hjørne, hjørnestein; kile.

quoit [koit] kastering; -s kastering-spill.

quondam ['kwåndäm] fordums.

quorum ['kwå·rəm] beslutningsdyktig antall.

quota ['kwoᵘtə] kvotadel, forholdsmessig andel.

quotable ['kwoᵘtəbl] som kan anføres, siteres.

quotation [kwo'te¹ʃən] anførsel, sitat; notering. — **-marks** anførselstegn.

quote [kwoᵘt] anføre, sitere; notere.

quoth [kwoᵘþ] mælte, sa, sier.

quotidian [kwo'tidjən] hverdags-, daglig.

quotient ['kwoᵘʃənt] kvotient.

q. v. fk. f. *quod vide* (= **which see**) se dette.

qy. fk. f. query.

R

R, r [a·ə, a·r] R, r; **The three R's** (= **reading, (w)riting, and (a)rithmetic**).

R. fk. f. rex (latin: konge); **regina** (latin: dronning); **Réaumur; recipe.**

R. A. fk. f. Royal Academy (eller **Academician**); **Royal Artillery.**

rabbet ['räbit] fals; (inn)false.

rabbin ['räbin] rabbi, rabbiner.

rabbit ['räbit] kanin; fange kaniner; **Welsh** — ristet brød med ost kokt i øl og krydret med spansk pepper. — **-burrow** kaningang. — **-mouth** haremunn. **-ry,** — **-warren** [-wårən] kaningård.

rabble ['räbl] pøbel, mobb, utskudd, pakk; berme; stimle sammen om, danne oppløp om. — **-charming** som henriver pøbelen. **rabblement** [-mənt] pøbel.

rabid ['räbid] rasende, vill, gal. **-ness** (hunde-)galskap.

rabies ['re¹bii·z] rabies, galskap.

R. A. C. fk. f. Royal Automobile Club.

race [re¹s] rase, slekt, kolkeferd; friskhet.

race [re¹s] gang, fart, løp; veddekamp; kapproing, kappseilas, kappløp; ile, jage, løpe, renne; kappløpe; drive på, sette i sterk fart. **-boat** kapproingsbåt. **-course** veddeløpsbane. — **-cup** pokal, sportspremie. **-horse** veddeløpshest.

racer ['re¹sə] kappløper, kapproer; veddeløpshest, veddeløpsmaskin; kappseiler.

racial ['re¹ʃəl] rase-.

rack [räk] drivende skymasser.

rack [räk] strekke, spenne, utspenne; legge på pinebenken; martre, pine; — **his brains** b₀yte sitt hode, legge sitt hode i bløt.

rack [räk] strekkeredskap, pineredskap; pinebenk; høyhekk; hylle, reol, nett (i kupé til lettere bagasje); rekke, stativ, henger.

racker ['räkə] strekker; bøddel.

racket ['räkit] racket (til bruk i tennis); truge; spetakkel; lurveleven, huskestue; holde spetakkel; slå med racket; i pl.: rackets (et ballspill), som spilles av to på en dertil innrettet bane); **what's the** — hva er på ferde? hva nå? — **court** racketplass. **racketer** ['räkitə] spetakkelmaker. **rackety** ['räkiti] vill, bråkende; løssloppen.

racking ['räkin] strekking, pinsel; seising (sjøuttrykk); martrende.

rack|-railway tannbane. — **-rent** ublu avgift, skamløs leie. **racoon** [rə'ku·n] vaskebjørn.

racy [re¹si] frisk i smaken, fin, aromatisk; — **of the soil** eiendommelig for sitt land.

rad [räd] radikaler.

raddle ['rädl] risgjerde; sammenflette.

radiance ['re¹djəns] stråleglans; utstråling.

radiant ['re¹diənt] strålende.

radiate ['re¹die¹t] stråle ut, skinne; ['re¹djet] stråleformet.

radiation [re¹di'e¹ʃən] utstråling.

radiator ['re¹die¹tə] radiator (til oppvarming); kjøler (i bil).

radical ['rädikl] rot-; dyp, rotfestet; grundig; radikal; rot (gram. og matem.), rottegn; et radikal; en radikaler. **-ism** ['rädiklizm] radikalisme. **-ize** ['rädiklaiz] gjøre radikal, bli radikal.

radicel ['rädisəl] rottrevl.

radio ['re¹dioᵘ] radio, kringkasting; kringkaste; behandle med radium.

radio-active ['re¹dioᵘäktiv] radioaktiv.

radish ['rädiʃ] reddik.

radium ['re¹diəm] radium.

radius ['re¹diəs] radius, stråle, (hjul-)eike; spolebein.

R. A. F. fk. f. Royal Air Force; Royal Aircraft Factory.

raff [räf] avfall, boss; herk, pakk; slusk.

raffle ['räfl] rafle, kaste terninger; skyte sammen til og kaste lodd om; lotteri; terninger; skrammel, bråte, rask.

raft [ra·ft] tømmerflåte, soppe; flåte; fløte, fløyte.

rafter ['ra·ftə] raft, taksparre; forsyne med rafter.

raftsman ['ra·ftsmən] flåtefører.

rag [räg] klut, fille; gjøre fillet, rive i filler; plage, skjelle ut; **all in -s** helt fillet.

ragamuffin [rägə'mʌfin] fillefant, slusk.

rag|bag fillepose. — **-carpet** filleteppe, fillerye.

rage [re¹dȝ] raseri; heftighet, voldsomhet; rase; grassere; **be (all) the** — være svært i vinden; gjøre furore.

rag-gatherer klutesamler, fillesamler.

ragged ['rägid] fillet, forreven; ujevn, knudret. **raggedness** [-nés] fillethet; knudrethet.

raging ['re¹dȝin] rasende, vill, ifra seg.

ragman ['rägmən] fillehandler.

ragout [rə'gu·] ragout.

rag-paper ['rägpe'pə] klutepapir, fillepapir.

rag-shop ['rägʃåp] handel med gamle klær.

ragtag ['rägtäg] **and bob-tail** pøbel, ramp.

ragtime ['rägtaim] synkopert takt (som i neger-melodier).

ragweed ['rägwi·d] svineblom; ambrosia.

rag-wheel ['räghwi·l] kjerrathjul, tannhjul.

ragwort ['rägwə·t] svineblom.

raid [re'd] fiendtlig innfall; plyndretog, streiftog; razzia; plyndre; gjøre en razzia.

rail [re'l] ribbe, tremme, gjerdestav; stakitt, rekkverk; skinne; jernbane; sette gjerde om, gjerde inn; reise med banen.

rail [re'l] skjelle, skjenne, bruke munn.

railer ['reilə] som skjeller ut; spotter.

railing ['re'liŋ] hånende; skjelling, grovheter, grov munn.

railing ['re'liŋ] stakitt, rekkverk; reling.

raillery ['re'ləri] (godmodig) spott, småerting.

railroad ['re'lro"d] jernbane.

railway ['re'lwe'] jernbane. — **-carriage** jernbanevogn. — **-gauge** ['re'lwe'ge'dʒ] sporvidde. — **-guide** rutebok.

raiment ['re'mənt] drakt, kledning, skrud.

rain [re'n] regne; la det regne med; regn, regnvær, regnskur; i pl.: regnbyer, regntid; **it -s cats and dogs** det øsregner.

rain|bow ['re'nbo"] regnbue. **-fall** nedbør, regn, regnskur. **-gauge** [-ge'dʒ] regnmåler.

raininess ['re'ninés] regnfullhet, regn.

rainy ['re'ni] regnfull, regn-, regnværs-; **lay by for a rainy day** legge til side til de dårlige tider.

raise [re'z] heve, løfte, reise; bringe på fote; vekke; forhøye; forsterke; heve; mane fram, vekke opp; reise, ta opp (et lån); vekke; stifte; dyrke, oppelske, oppdrette, fostre; forhøyelse; bakke; — **a siege** heve en beleiring.

raiser ['re'zə] hever, løfter; oppdretter, dyrker, produsent; hevemiddel.

raisin ['re'zn] rosin.

raising ['re'ziŋ] hevning, løftning; gang, gjær.

raising-powder bakepulver.

raison d'être [fr., 're'zå·n'de'tə] eksistensberettigelse.

raja(h) ['ra·dʒə] rajah, indisk fyrste.

rake [re'k] rive, rake; ildrake; rive; rake; støve gjennom, ransake; beskyte langskips; helle (om mast el. stevn); — **up the fire** dekke til varmen med aske.

rake [re'k] uthaler, libertiner.

raker ['re'kə] river; hesterive; ildrake; skrapjern. **raking** ['re'kiŋ] raking.

rakish ['re'kiʃ] bohemaktig, utsvevende.

Raleigh ['rå·li, 'ra·li, 'räli] Raleigh.

rally ['räli] spotte, skjemte, spøke; drive ap med, spotte over; spott, skjemt, spøk.

rally ['räli] samle (igjen), bringe orden i; samle seg (igjen), fylke seg; bedres, komme seg; komme til krefter; samling; bedring. **-ing-cry** kamprop. **-ing-point** samlingssted; støttepunkt.

ram [räm] bukk, vær, bekre, rambukk, murbrekker; ramme, støte, stappe; — **down** ramme ned.

R. A. M. fk. f. **Royal Academy of Music.**

ramble ['rämbl] streife om, flakke om; gjøre avstikkere; fantasere, ørske; streifing, omstreifing, flakking; vandring, streiftur, tur.

rambler ['rämblə] vandrer; en slags slyngrose (især **crimson** —).

rambling ['rämbliŋ] omstreifing, streiftur; uregelmessig, spredt; vidløftig.

R. A. M. C. fk. f. **Royal Army Medical Corps.**

rameous ['re'mjəs] grein-; som vokser på en grein.

ramification [rämifi'keiʃən] forgrening, grein.

ramify ['rämifai] forgreine; forgreine seg, greine seg.

rammer ['rämə] rambukk; bruleggerjomfru.

ramp [rämp] klyve opp, klatre opp; skyte opp; springe, hoppe, steile; hopp, spring; bøyning, stigning.

rampant ['rämpənt] oppstigende, klatrende; frodig, yppig; tøylesløs, overhåndtagende; oppreist, stående, springende (i våpen).

rampart ['rämpət] voll, festningsvoll; befeste med voller.

ramrod ['rämråd] lastokk, latein.

Ramsay ['rämzi] Ramsay.

Ramsgate ['rämzgit] Ramsgate.

ramshackle ['rämʃäkl] brøstfeldig, lealaus, falleferdig.

ranch [ra·nʃ] storgård, landeiendom, bondegård; kvegfarm. **rancher** [-ə] storfarmer.

rancid ['ränsid] trå, harsk. **rancidity** [rän'siditi], **rancidness** ['ränsidnés] harskhet.

rancorous ['räŋkərəs] hatsk, uforsonlig.

rancour ['räŋkə] hat, nag, agg, bitterhet.

Rand [ränd]; **the** — Witwatersrand (distrikt i Transvaal).

random ['rändəm] slumpetreff; tilfelle; tilfeldig, uregelmessig; **at** — på slump, på måfå; — **shot** slumpeskudd.

randy [rändi] skrålende, høymælt, skjellende, ustyrlig, vill; kjeftause; fant.

ranee ['ra·ni] hindudronning.

range [re'n(d)ʒ] stille i rekke, stille opp; klassifisere, ordne; streife om i, fare over; streife om; rekke (om skyts), ha plass; rekke, kjede; plass; orden, vandring, omstreifing; frihet; spillerom; råderom, omfang, område; retning, rekkevidde, skuddvidde; komfyr; — **of mountains** fjellkjede.

ranger ['re'n(d)ʒə] omstreifer, vandringsmann; støver; forstassistent (i India); parkvokter (i England); i pl: ridende jegerkorps.

rank [räŋk] rad, rekke; geled; grad, rang, stand; rangklasse; samfunnsklasse; stille i rekke, ordne, sette i klasse, rangere; ordnes, være ordnet; — **and file** menige; **fall in** — stille seg opp; **turn into the -s** la løpe spissrot; **reduce to the -s** degradere til menig.

rank [räŋk] høytvoksende, frodig, yppig; fruktbar, fet; voldsom, sterk; ram, sur, stram.

rankish ['räŋkiʃ] noe ram, noe stram.

rankle ['räŋkl] vinne styrke; bli betent, sette verk; gnage; ete om seg; fortære, nage, svi.

rankness ['räŋknés] for frodig vekst, yppighet; overmål; ramhet, stramhet.

ransack ['ränsäk] ransake, gjennomsøke; (gammelt) plyndre; ransaking, plyndring.

ransom ['ränsəm] løskjøping, løsepenger; løskjøpe, løse ut. **ransomer** [-ə], en som løskjøper.

rant [ränt] holde leven, gjøre spetakkel, skråle, skvaldre, deklamere, bruke store ord; kommers, spetakkel, skrål, skvalder. **ranter** [-ə] skråler, skvadronør; gatepredikant.

ranunculus [rə'näŋkjuləs] ranunkel.

rap [räp] banke, pikke; rapp, slag, banking.

rap [räp] rive for bort; rapse, røve; henrykke, henrive.

rapacious [rə'pe'ʃəs] rovlysten, grisk.

rapacity [rə'päsiti] rovlyst; griskhet.

rape [re'p] ran, rov; voldtekt; rane, røve.

rape [re'p] raps. — **-seed** rapsfrø.

Raphael ['räf(i)əl] Rafael.

rapid ['räpid] hurtig, snøgg, rask, rivende, bratt, stri; elvestryk; **shoot rapids** passere et stryk.

rapidity [rə'piditi] hurtighet, fart, raskhet; stryk.

rapier ['re'piə, -pjə] støtkårde.

rapine ['räpain] rov, plyndring; plyndre.

rapparee [räpə'ri·] banditt, røver; (opphavlig:) irsk soldat.

rapper ['räpə] dørhammer.

rapping ['räpiŋ] banking.

rapt [räpt] henrykt.

rapture ['räptʃə] henrykkelse; **in -s** i ekstase.

rapturous ['räptʃərəs] henrivende; begeistret.

rare [ræ·ə] tynn, enkelt, sparsom; sjelden; usedvanlig; kostbar, fortreffelig; on — occasions en sjelden gang; a — kettle of fish en nydelig historie.

rarebit ['ræ·əbit], Welsh —, en rett; se rabbit.

raree-show ['ræ·əriʃoᵘ] perspektivkasse, tittekasse; merkelig syn.

rarefy ['ræ·ərifai] fortynne(s); forfine(s).

rareness ['ræ·ənés] sjeldenhet; tynnhet.

rarity ['ræ·əriti] sjeldenhet.

rascal ['ra·skl] skarv, kjeltring, slyngel, skurk; lumpen, ussel. rascaldom [-dəm] nedrighet. rascality [ra'skäliti] lumpenhet, nedrighet. rascally ['ra·skəli] nedrig, lumpen.

rash [räʃ] utslett.

rash]räʃ] ubesindig, brå, uvøren, overilt.

rasher ['räʃə] (fleske-)skive.

rashness ['räʃnés] ubesindighet, tankeløshet, overilelse.

rasp [ra·sp] raspe, skure; skurre i.

raspberry ['ra·zb(ə)ri] bringebær.

rat [rät] rotte; overløper; streikebryter; fange rotter; løpe over til fienden; smell a — lukte lunten.

ratability [re'tə'biliti] skatteplikt.

ratable ['re'təbl] skattbar, skattepliktig.

rate[re't] forhold, målestokk, grad; takst, pris; rang, klasse; verdi; skatt, kommuneskatt; hastighet, fart; — of exchange vekselkurs; — of interest rentefot; at a cheap — billig, til lav pris; at a furious — i rasende fart; at any — i hvert fall, under alle omstendigheter; at the — of med en fart av; til en pris av.

rate [re't] anslå, taksere; vurdere; skatte; tildele rang; rangere, ha rang, stå i klasse.

rate [re't] skjenne på, irettesette.

ratepayer ['re'tpe'ə] skatteborger, skattyter.

rather ['ra·ðə] snarere, heller; it's — cold det er temmelig kaldt; — pretty ganske pen; — more atskillig mer; atskillig flere; I had — not jeg vil helst ikke, helst la det være.

ratification [rätifi'ke'ʃən] bekreftelse, stadfesting.

ratify ['rätifai] bekrefte, stadfeste.

rating ['re'tiŋ] skjennepreken, skjenn.

ratio ['re'ʃoᵘ] forhold.

ration ['räʃən] rasjon; rasjonere. — -cards rasjoneringskort.

rational ['räʃənəl] fornuft-, fornuftig, rasjonell; opplyst menneske; reformdrakt. rationalism ['räʃənəlizm] rasjonalisme. rationalist [-list] rasjonalist. rationalistic [räʃənə'listik] rasjonalistisk. rationality [räʃə'näliti] fornuft. rationalness ['räʃənlnés] fornuftighet.

Ratisbon ['rätisbán] Regensburg; he is gone to — han ligger i graven.

ratsbane ['rätsbe'n] rottegift; hundekjeks (plante).

ratter ['rätə] rottefanger; rottehund; overløper.

ratting ['rätiŋ] overløperi.

rattle ['rätl] skrangle, skramle, klirre, ramle, klapre; at a rattling pace i strykende fart; — along skrangle avsted; — at the door dundre på døra; — away skravle i vei; — out plapre ut.

rattle ['rätl] klapring, skrangling, rammel, klirr; skravl, leven; there was a — in his throat han raktet.

rattler ['rätlə] prakteksemplar; klapperslange.

rattle|snake ['rätlsne'k] klapperslange. -trap skrangledoning; snurrepiperi; «hul», skrøpelig.

rattling ['rätliŋ] feiende, sprek, frisk, kåt, munter; storartet.

ratty ['räti]'rotteaktig, plaget av rotter; irritabel, gretten, grinet.

raucity ['rå·siti] håshet, heshet.

raucous ['rå·kəs] hås, hes.

ravage ['rävidʒ] ødelegging, plyndring; ødelegge, plyndre, herje.

rave [re'v] tale i ørske, ørske, fantasere; rase.

ravel ['rävl] trevle opp, rekke opp; floke; rakne opp. ravelling opprekking, tave.

ravelin ['rävlin] utenverk, skanse.

raven ['re'vn] ramn, korp; ramnaktig, ramnsvart.

raven ['rävn] rane, rive til seg; plyndre; være grådig.

ravenous ['rävnəs] grådig, forsluken.

ravine [ra'vi·n] kløft; gjel, hulvei.

raving ['re'vin] rasende, vill; — mad splitter gal. ravings fantaseringer.

ravish ['räviʃ] rane, røve; henrykke, henrive; voldta. ravishing [-iŋ] henrivende. ravishment [-mənt] ran, rov; henrykkelse; voldtekt.

raw [rå·] rå; ublandet, uforfalsket; umoden, uerfaren; hudløs, sår: hudløst sted; — materials råstoffer; — produce råprodukter; — silk rå-silke; touch one on the — såre ens følelser på et særlig ømt punkt.

raw|-boned ['rå·boᵘnd] skranglet, skinnmager. -head busemann. rawish [-iʃ] heller rå. rawness [-nés] råhet, umodenhet; uøvdhet, uerfarenhet.

ray [re'] stråle, lysstråle; stråle ut.

ray [re'] rokke; starry — piggrokke, -skate.

raze [re'z] skave, skrape; slette ut; rasere, sløyfe, jevne med jorda.

razor [re'zə] barberkniv, rakekniv; — -strap el. — -strop styrkereim.

razzia ['rätsia] streiftog.

razzle-dazzle ['räzl'däzl] oppstyr, leven, rangel.

R. B. fk. f. Rifle Brigade.

R. B. A. fk. f. Royal Society of British Artists.

R. C. fk. f. Roman Catholic.

R. C. O. fk. f. Royal College of Organists.

R. C. P. fk. f. Royal College of Physicians.

R. C. S. fk. f. Royal College of Surgeons.

Rd. fk. f. Road.

R. D. C. fk. f. Royal Defence Corps; Rural district council.

re [ri·-, ri-, re-] til å betegne gjentagelse; igjen, atter, på ny.

re [ri·] angående, med hensyn til; in — i saken.

R. E. fk. f. Royal Engineers.

reach [ri·tʃ] rekke, lange, levere; gi; nå; strekke seg, nå vidt; strekking, rekkevidde; grep, tak; strekning; evne, betingelse; strekk, bein strekning (i et elveløp); above my — over min horisont; beyond the — of human intellect utenfor menneskelig fatteevne; get out of — komme utenfor rekkevidde; within my — så jeg kan nå det.

reachable ['ri·tʃəbl] som kan nås.

react ['ri·'äkt] oppføre igjen.

react [ri'äkt] virke tilbake, reagere.

reaction [ri'äkʃən] reaksjon; tilbakevirkning, motvirkning; omslag.

reactionary [ri'äkʃənəri] reaksjonær.

reactive [ri'äktiv] reaksjons-.

read [ri·d] lese; lese opp; oppfatte; lese i; tyde; forstå; studere; lyde, si; kunne tydes; lesning; — aloud lese høyt; — a paper holde et foredrag; — off avlese; lese flytende (og uten forberedelse); — out lese ut; lese høyt; — over a lesson lese på en lekse; — him through gjennomskue ham; — up lese høyt; — a bill behandle et lovforslag; the letter -s as follows brevet lyder slik.

read [red] belest; be well — in være vel hjemme i.

readable ['ri·dəbl] leselig, leseverdig.

reader ['ri·də] leser; oppleser; leseboks. readership [-ʃip] stilling som oppleser; lektorat.

readily ['redili] hurtig, lett, beredvillig.

readiness ['redinés] ferdighet, beredskap; letthet; beredvillighet, villighet.

reading ['ri·din] lesende; lyselysten, flittig; lesning; behandling (av et lovforslag); belesthet; opplesning; forelesning; lesemåte; utgave. -book lesebok.

Reading ['rediŋ] hovedstad i Berkshire.

readjust [ri·ə'dʒʌst] bringe i orden igjen.

readmission [ri·əd'miʃən] gjenopptagelse.
readmit ['ri·əd'mit] slippe inn igjen; gjenoppta.
readmittance ['ri·əd'mitəns] adgang på ny.
ready ['redi] rede, beredt, ferdig; beredvillig; for hånden, bekvem, lett, rask; — cash kontanter; — -made ferdigsydd; — money down pr. kontant. — -reckoner beregningstabell. **ready-to-wear** ferdigsydd. **ready-to-serve** ferdiglaget (om mat).
real ['ri·(ə)l] real, spansk mynt.
real ['riəl] virkelig, ekte; — property fast eiendom; the — thing ekte vare.
realism ['riəlizm] realisme. **realist** ['riəlist] realist. **realistic** [riə'listik] realistisk.
reality [ri'äliti] virkelighet.
realization [riəl(a)i'ze'ʃən] virkeliggjøring, utførelse; omsetting i penger.
realize ['riəlaiz] virkeliggjøre, iverksette, realisere; fatte, forestille seg; anbringe i fast eiendom, gjøre i penger; tjene.
really ['riəli] virkelig.
realm [relm] rike.
realness ['riəlnés] virkelighet.
realty ['riəlti] fast eiendom.
ream [ri·m] ris papir (ɔ: 20 bøker à 24 ark).
reanimate [ri(·)'änime't] bringe nytt liv i, gjenopplive.
reap [ri·p] meie, skjære, høste.
reaper ['ri·pə] skurkar, skurkjerring; meiemaskin.
reaping-hook sigd. **reaping-time** skuronn.
reappear [ri·ə'piə] vise seg på ny. **reappearance** [-'piərəns] gjenopptreden.
rear [riə] løfte, heve, reise; dyrke, avle, ale, oppdrette; oppfostre, oppdra; framelske; steile; kneise; reise seg på bakbeina.
rear [riə] bakerste del, bakside, rygg, hale; baktropp; bakgrunn; **bring up the** — danne baktroppen, komme sist; **attack the enemy in the** — angripe fienden i ryggen.
rear-admiral ['riə'rädmirəl] kontreadmiral.
rear-guard ['riəga·əd] baktropp, arrièregarde. ettertrygd.
rearmost ['riəmo⁺st] bakerst.
rearrange ['ri·ə're'ndʒ] ordne på ny.
re-ascend ['ri·ə'send] stige opp igjen; bestige igjen.
reason ['ri·zn] grunn, fornuftsgrunn; fornuft; tenkeevne; årsak, rett, rimelighet; gjøre fornuftslutninger, anstille betraktninger, resonnere, tenke, overveie; dømme, slutte; **by** — of på grunn av; **for this** — av denne grunn; the — of (eller for) **his going away** eller the — why (eller that) **he went away** grunnen til at han gikk bort; **as** — was som rimelig var; **by** — of på grunn av; **it stands to** — det er svært rimelig, det er greitt, det er klart.
reasonable ['ri·znəbl] fornuftig, rimelig.
reasoner ['ri·znə] tenker.
reasoning ['ri·zniŋ] fornuftslutninger, resonnement.
reassemblage [ri·ə'semblidʒ] ny samling. **reassemble** [-'sembl] samle(s) på ny.
reassume [ri(·)ə's(j)u·m] anta igjen; gjenoppta.
reassumption [-'sʌm(p)ʃən] gjenopptagelse.
reassurance [ri·ə'ʃuərəns] gjentatt forsikring; reassuranse; beroligelse.
reassure [ri(·)ə'ʃuə] berolige; gjenforsikre.
Réaumur ['re'əmjuə] Réaumur.
rebate ['ri·be't, ri'be't] rabatt, avslag. **rebate** [ri'be't] slå av, gi rabatt.
rebel ['rebl] opprørsk, opprørs-; opprører.
rebel [ri'bel] gjøre opprør (against imot).
rebeller [ri'belə] opprører.
rebellion [ri'beljən] opprør, oppstand.
rebellious [ri'beljəs] opprørsk.
rebound [ri'baund] prelle av, kastes tilbake; det å prelle av, sprette tilbake; tilbakeslag; omslag.

rebuff [ri'bʌf] tilbakeslag, tilbakestøt; avvis ning, avslag; slå tilbake, stagge, stanse; avvise.
rebuild ['ri·bild] gjenoppbygge; ombygge. **rebuilding** [-iŋ] gjenoppbygging; ombygging.
rebuke [ri'bju·k] irettesette, dadle; irettesetting, daddel.
recalcitrant [ri'kälsitrənt] gjenstridig, trassig; gjenstridig person.
recall [ri'kå·l] kalle tilbake; si opp; tilbakekalle; minnes, tilbakekalle i erindringen; tenke tilbake på; minne om; tilbakekalling; framkalling; past — ugjenkallelig.
recant [ri(·)'känt] tilbakekalle, ta i seg, ta tilbake; ta sine ord tilbake.
recantation [rikän'te'ʃən] tilbakekalling.
recapitulate [ri·kə'pitjule't] gjenta i korthet.
recapitulation [ri·kəpitju'le'ʃən] kort gjengivelse, sammendrag. **recapitulatory** [ri·kə'pitjulətəri] gjentagende i summarisk oversikt.
recast ['ri·'ka·st] støpe om; omarbeide; regne over; omstøpning; omarbeiding.
recede [ri'si·d] gå tilbake; vike tilbake; helle bakover; falle; dale; retirere.
receipt [ri'si·t] mottagelse; kvittering, oppskrift, resept; inntekt; kvittere for, kvittere; be in — of ha mottatt; **on** — of ved mottagelsen av.
receipt-book [ri'si·tbuk] kvitteringsbok; oppskriftsbok.
receivable [ri'si·vəbl] mottagelig; antagelig.
receive [ri'si·v] motta, få; ønta, oppta, vedta; erkjenne, fatte.
received [ri'si·vd] alminnelig, antatt, vedtatt.
receiver [ri'si·və] mottager; heler; kurator, bobestyrer; oppebørselsbetjent; kemner; mottagerapparat; hørerør, mikrofon; beholder; toalettbøtte.
receiving [ri'si·viŋ] mottagelse; heling. — **-house** lite postkontor, brevhus. — **office** innleveringskontor. — **-ship** losjiskip.
recency [ri·snsi] nyhet, friskhet.
recension [ri'senʃən] revisjon (av tekst), kritikk; revidert tekst.
recent ['ri·sənt] ny, fersk, sist, nylig skjedd, nylig kommet. **recentness** = **recency**.
recently ['ri·səntli] nyss, nylig, i det siste.
receptacle [ri'septəkl] blomsterbunn; beholder; gjemmested.
receptibility [ri'septi'biliti] antagelighet.
receptible [ri'septibl] mottagelig, antagelig.
reception [ri'sepʃən] mottagelse.
receptive [ri'septiv] mottagelig, nem.
receptivity [ri·sep'tiviti] opptagelsesevne, nemme.
recess [ri'ses] det å tre tilbake, tilbakegang; ferie, frikvarter, fritime; fordypning, nisje, krok, avkrok, krå; tilflukt, tilfluktssted; dyp, fordypning, grop; kove; bukt; innskjæring.
recession [ri'seʃən] det å tre tilbake; det å avstå **recessional hymn** [ri'seʃənəl him] salme som synges når prestene og koret forlater kirkens kor og går inn i sakristiet.
recherché [rə'ʃɛ·əʃe'] utsøkt, elegant.
recipe ['resipi] oppskrift, kokeboksoppskrift; resept.
recipient [ri'sipjənt] mottager; beholder.
reciprocal [ri'siprokl] innbyrdes, motsvarende, gjensidig; resiprok. **reciprocality** [ri'sipro'käliti] gjensidighet. **reciprocalness** [ri'siproknés] gjensidighet. **reciprocate** [ri'siproke't] skifte, veksle; gjøre gjengjeld; gjengjelde. **reciprocation** [ri'sipro'ke'ʃən] veksling, skifting; gjengjeld. **reciprocity** [resi'präsiti] vekselvirkning; gjensidighet.
recital [ri'saitəl] fremsigelse, opplesning; foredrag; fortelling, beretning; konsert. **recitation** [resi'te'ʃən] resitasjon, opplesning, deklamasjon, opplesning. **recitative** [resita'ti·v] resitativ.
recite [ri'sait] si fram, resitere, deklamere; berette; si fram noe.
reciter [ri'saitə] bok med resitasjonsstykker.
reck [rek] bekymre seg om, bry seg om, kjære

seg om, ense, akte; **it -s me** not det bryr jeg meg ikke om.

reckless ['reklės] likegyldig (for følgene, for andres mening): uvøren, skjøtesløs, hensynsløs; uforsvarlig. **recklessness** [-nés] likegyldighet, hensynsløshet.

reckon ['rekən] regne, telle; beregne; anse for, holde for; gjøre regnskap, bøte; — **without one's host** gjøre regning uten vert. **reckoner** ['rekənə] beregner; regner; tabell. **reckoning** ['rekəniŋ] regning, beregning; tidsregning; avregning; oppgjør; regnskap, dom; vurdering.

reclaim [ri'kle¹m] kalle tilbake; temme, avrette; forbedre, omvende; innvinne; drenere, tørrlegge, uttørre; kreve tilbake. **reclaimable** [ri-'kle¹məbl] som kan temmes, forbedres.

reclamation [reklə'me¹ʃən] innvinning, drenering; tørrlegging; nydyrking; forbedring, omvendelse; reklamasjon, tilbakefordring; innsigelse, protest.

reclination [rekli'ne¹ʃən] hvilende stilling.

recline [ri'klain] bøye, helle, lene tilbake; bøye seg bakover; ligge bakover, hvile.

recluse [ri'klu·s] ensom; eneboer.

reclusion [ri'klu·ʒən] ensomhet.

recognition [rekog'niʃən] gjenkjennelse, anerkjennelse; tilståelse; påskjønnelse, erkjentlighet; besvarelse.

recognizable ['rekəg'naizəbl] gjenkjennelig; kjennelig. **recognizance** [ri'kånizəns] erkjennelse; tilståelse; anerkjennelse.

recognize ['rekəgnaiz] gjenkjenne, skjelne, oppdage, vedkjenne seg; anerkjenne.

recoil [ri'koil, rə'koil] fare tilbake, vike tilbake; det å vike tilbake; tilbakespring, rekyl, tilbakestøt.

recollect ['ri·kə'lekt] samle igjen.

recollect [rekə'lekt] gjenkalle i minnet, huske, minnes; — **oneself** samle seg, huske, sanse seg. **recollected** [rekə'lektid] fattet, sindig.

recollection [rekə'lekʃən] erindring, minne.

recommence ['ri·kə'mens] begynne igjen, gjenoppta. **recommencement** [-mənt] begynnelse, gjenopptagelse.

recommend [rekə'mend] anbefale, rå til. **recommendable** [-'mendəbl] anbefalelsesverdig; priselig. **recommendation** [rekəmən'de¹ʃən] anbefaling, lovord, tilråding, framlegg. **recommendatory** [rekə'mendətəri] anbefalende, anbefalings-. **recommender** [rekə'mendə] anbefaler.

recommit ['ri·kə'mit] sende tilbake (til fornyet utvalgsbehandling); betro igjen; begå igjen.

recompense ['rekəmpens] erstatte, belønne, lønne; erstatning, vederlag, belønning, lønn.

recompose ['ri·kəm'po¹z] sette sammen igjen; berolige, bilegge.

reconcilable ['rekən(')sailəbl] forlikelig. **reconcilableness** ['rekənsailəblnés] forsonlighet. **reconcile** ['rekənsail] forsone, forlike; forene, bilegge, skille; — **oneself** to forsone seg med. **reconcilement** [-mənt] forsoning, **reconciler** [-ə] forsoner.

reconciliation [rekənsili'e¹ʃən] forsoning, forlikelse, forlik; forening. **reconciliatory** [rekən-'siljətəri] forsonende, forsonings-.

recondite [ri'kåndait, 'rekəndait] lønnlig; dunkel, dyp, lite kjent.

reconnaissance [ri'kånisəns] rekognosering.

reconnoitre [rekə'nɔitə] rekognosere, utforske.

reconquer ['ri·'kåŋkə] gjenerobre, ta igjen.

reconsider ['ri·kən'sidə] overveie igjen, gjenoppta. **reconsideration** [-sidə're¹ʃən] fornyet overveielse, ny drøfting.

reconstruct ['ri·ken'str∧kt] gjenoppbygge, gjenopprette; omdanne. **reconstruction** [-'str∧kʃən] ombygging; omdanning, gjenreising.

record [ri'kå·əd] bringe i erindring; feste i minnet; opptegne, skrive ned, bokføre; protokollere; berette; fastslå; **record** ['rekå·əd] opptegnelse, dokument, rulleblad, grammofonplate;

protokoll; rekord; **he has the** — **of being** han har ord for å være; **travel out of the** — gå bort fra saken; **keep to the** — holde seg til saken; **worthy of** — som fortjener å opptegnes; **keeper of the -s** arkivar; **it is on** — det står på prent; man kan lese seg til det; **det er vitterlig; the greatest general on** — den største general historien kjenner.

recorder [ri'kå·ədə] nedskriver, opptegner, protokollfører; kriminaldommer.

record-office ['rekå·əd'åfis] offentlig arkiv.

recount ['ri·'kaunt] telle om igjen; gjenopptelling.

recount [ri'kaunt] berette, fortelle.

recountal [ri'kauntəl] beretning, fortelling.

recourse [ri'kå·əs] tilflukt; regress, dekning; **have** — **to** ta sin tilflukt til; holde seg til, søke dekning hos.

recover ['ri·'k∧və] dekke på ny, trekke.

recover [ri'k∧və] få tilbake; gjenvinne; innkassere; gjenopprette; innhente, forvinne; oppnå, få; komme seg, friskne til; komme til seg selv; **-ed** restituert; **his breath** få pusten igjen; **his senses** komme til bevissthet; **himself** fatte seg.

recoverable [ri'k∧v(ə)rəbl] erholdelig; gjenopprettelig; som står til å redde, helbredelig.

recovery [ri'k∧v(ə)ri] gjenervervelse; gjenfinnelse; opptagelse; bedring, rekonvalesens; helbredelse; oppgang, stigning; **beyond** — redningsløst fortapt.

recreancy ['rekriənsi] feighet; frafall.

recreant ['rekriənt] feig; frafallen; krysler.

recreate ['rekrie¹t] kvikke opp, forfriske, opplive igjen; oppmuntre, rekreere, rekreere seg.

recreation [rekri'e¹ʃən] morskap, oppmuntring; **read for** — lese morskap.

recreative ['rekriåtiv] forfriskende, atspredende, hyggelig.

recrement ['rekrimənt] avfall.

recriminate [ri'krimine¹t] framføre motbeskyldninger. **recrimination** [ri'krimi'ne¹ʃən] motbeskyldning.

recrudescence [ri·kru'desəns] nytt frambrudd, utbrudd. **recrudescent** som bryter fram på ny.

recruit [ri'kru·t] fornye, utfylle; styrke, forfriske; forsterke; rekruttere; komme til krefter; forfriske seg; fornyelse, styrkelse; rekrutt. **recruiter** [-ə] verver. **recruiting** rekruttering, verving. **recruitment** [-mənt] rekruttering.

rectifiable ['rektifaiəbl] som lar seg beriktige.

rectification [rektifi'ke¹ʃən] beriktigelse, rettelse, retting. **rectifier** ['rektifaiə] beriktiger retter. **rectify** ['rektifai] beriktige, rette, korrigere.

rectitude ['rektitju·d] rettskaffenhet.

rector ['rektə] sogneprest (i den engelske kirke, står til forskjell fra vicar får bedre tiender); (i Skottland): skolebestyrer, universitetsrektor.

rectorate ['rektərét] sognekall; rektorat.

rectorship ['rektəʃip] = **rectorate**.

rectory ['rektəri] sognekall; prestegård.

recumbence [ri'k∧mbəns] liggende stilling; hvile.

recumbent [ri'k∧mbənt] liggende, hvilende, tilbakelent.

recuperate [ri'kju·pəre¹t] gjenvinne; komme seg, komme til krefter; gjenvinne sin helse. **recuperation** [rikju·pə're¹ʃən] gjenvinning; rekonvalesens, helbredelse. **recuperative** [ri'kju·perativ] helbredende, styrkende; spenstig, full av livskraft.

recur [ri'kə·] komme tilbake, komme igjen; ta sin tilflukt. **recurrence** [ri'k∧rens] tilbakekomst; gjentagelse; det å søke el. trive til. **recurrent** [ri'k∧rent] tilbakevendende, periodisk. **recurring** [ri'kə·riŋ] tilbakevendende; periodisk.

recusancy [ri'kju·zənsi] vegring; gjenstridighet, trass. **recusant** [ri'kju·zənt] som vegrer seg; stribukk; dissenter; gjenstridig. **recusation** [rekju-'ze¹ʃən] det å forskyte; vegring.

red [red] rød; rød farge, rødt; rød radikaler; revolusjonsmann, koppercent, rød øre.

redaction [ri'däkʃən] redaksjon.
redactor [ri'däktə] redaktør.
redan [ri'dän] redan (festningsverk).
red-book ['redbuk] engelsk adelskalender.
redbreast ['redbrest] rødkjelke, rødstrupe.
red-coat ['redkoᵘt] rødkjole, britisk soldat.
red-cross ['redkrås] som hører til røde kors; genferkcrs, St. Georgskors; sanitetsvesen.
red-deer ['reddiə] kronhjort; virginsk hjort.
redden ['redn] gjøre rød; rødme.
reddish ['rediʃ] rødlig.
reddition [re'diʃən] tilbakegivelse, tilbake-levering.
reddle ['redl] rød cker, rødkritt, rødstein, jern-mønje.
redeem [ri'di·m] kjøpe tilbake, løse inn; løse ut, løskjøpe; bøte for; opprette; **-ing feature** for-sonende trekk.
redeemable [ri'di·məbl] som kan løskjøpes; opprettelig; **redeemer** [-mə] inn-løser; innfrier; **the Redeemer** forløseren, gjen-løseren.
redeless ['ri·dlès] rådløs, uklok, hjelpeløs.
redemption [ri'dem(p)ʃən] innløsning, løsning; utløsning, løskjøping; gjenløsning. **redemptive** [ri'dem(p)tiv] innløsende, innløsnings-. **redemp-tory** [ri'dem(p)təri] innløsende, innløsnings-.
red-eye ['redai] sørv (fisk).
red-eyed ['redaid] rødøyd.
red-faced ['redfe'st] rødlett, rød i ansiktet; med røde oppslag.
red-haired ['redhæ·əd] rødhåret.
red-handed ['redhändid] (grepet) på fersk gjerning; **be caught** — bli grepet på fersk gjerning.
red-headed ['redhedid] rødhåret.
red-hot ['redhåt] rødglødende, glorød.
redintegrate [re'dintigre't] gjenopprette, fornye.
redintegration [redinti'gre'ʃən] fornying, gjenopp-retting.
redistribute ['ri·dis'tribjut] fordele på ny.
redistribution ['ri·distri'bju·ʃən] ny utdeling.
redivivus [redi'vaivəs] gjenoppstått.
red-lead ['red'led] mønje.
red-letter ['redletə] betegne med røde boksta-ver; — **day** merkedag.
redness ['rednès] rød farge; glohete.
red-nosed ['rednouzd] rødneset.
redolence ['redoləns] duft, ange. **redolent** ['redo-lənt] duftende, angende.
redouble [ri'dʌbl] fordoble, mangfoldiggjøre; mangfoldiggjøres.
redoubt [ri'daut] lukket feltskanse.
redoubtable [ri'dautəbl] fryktelig.
redound [ri'daund] flømme tilbake; kastes tilbake; tilflyte, komme til gode, tjene (to til); **it -s to his honour** det tjener ham til ære.
redraw ['ri·'drå·] tegne om igjen, sette opp på nytt.
redress [ri'dres] rette på, se igjennom, revidere; opprette, gi oppreisning, avhjelper; rettelse, opp-reisning; hjelp; **beyond** — ubotelig. **redressible** [ti'dresibl] opprettelig; avhjelpelig. **redressive** [ti'dresiv] avhjelpende.
redskin ['redskin] rødhud.
red-tape ['redte'p] rødt bånd til dokument-pakker; kontorpedanteri, byråkratisk; form-dyrking; formell, pirket, omsvøpsfull.
red-tiled ['redtaild] med rødt teglsteinstak.
reduce [ri'dju·s] føre tilbake, bringe tilbake; forringe, innskrenke, sette ned, forminske; svekke; formilde, innordne, ordne; redusere; — **by 5 per cent** sette ned med 5 %; — **to the ranks** flytte ned til simpel soldat; **be -d to** være henvist til.
reduced [ri'dju·st] forringet, forminsket; redu-sert, medtatt; **in** — **circumstances** i trange kår.
reducible [ri'djusibl] som kan reduseres.
reduction [ri'dʌkʃən] tilbakeføring, forvand-ling; oppløsning, forringelse, innskrenking; for-minskelse; nedkuing, inntagelse: reduksjon; om-setning; **-s** nedsatte priser; **be allowed a** — få moderasjon; **at a** — til nedsatte priser.

reductive [ri'dʌktiv] tilbakeførende; innskrenk-ende; oppløsningsmiddel.
redundancy [ri'dʌndənsi] overflødighet. **re-dundant** [-dənt] overflødig, flus; ordrik; vid-løftig.
reduplicate [ri'dju·plike't] fordoble; redupli-sere. **reduplication** [ridju·pli'ke'ʃən] fordobling; reduplikasjon. **reduplicative** [ri'dju·plikətiv] for-doblende; redupliserende.
redwing ['redwiŋ] rødtrost.
red-worm ['redwə·m] (alminnelig) meitemark.
re-echo ['ri·'eko''] kaste tilbake; gjenlyde, ljome.
reed [ri·d] rør, rørfløyte; pil; munnstykke; tekke med rør. — **-flute** rørfløyte. **-mace** dun-kjevle. **reedy** ['ri·di] rørbevokst; røraktig.
reef [ri·f] rev, grunne.
reef [ri·f] rev (i seil); reve; **he must take a** — **or two** han måtte ta rev i seilene.
reefer ['ri·fə] en som rever; pjekkert.
reek [ri·k] røyk, damp, dunst, os, eim; dampe, dunste, ose.
reeky ['ri·ki] røykfylt, svart, smussig; stin-kende, osende.
reel [ri·l] garnvinde, rull; hespel; snelle; reel (skotsk dans); haspe, vinde; danse reel; rave, vakle, slingre; sjangle; — **off** (**out**) hespe av seg, ramse opp.
re-elect ['ri·i'lekt] gjenvelge.
re-election ['ri·i'lekʃən] gjenvalg.
re-embark ['ri·em'ba·ək] innskipe (seg) igjen; **re-embarkation** ['rièmba·ə'ke'ʃən] gjeninnskiping.
re-enforce = **re-inforce.**
re-enter ['ri·'entə] komme inn igjen.
re-establish ['ri·è'stäbliʃ] gjenopprette. **re-estab-lishment** [-mənt] gjenoppretting.
reeve [ri·v] (gl.) foged.
reeve [ri·v] brushøne.
re-examination ['ri·ègzämi'ne'ʃən] ny under-søkelse. **re-examine** [-'zämin] undersøke på ny.
re-exchange ['ri·eks'tʃe'n(d)ʒ] bytte på ny; gjenutveksling.
ref. fk. f. reference.
Ref. Ch. fk. f. Reformed Church.
refection [ri'fekʃən] måltid, forfriskning.
refectory [ri'fektəri] spisesal, spisestue.
refer [ri'fə·] bringe tilbake; henvise; henstille, bringe inn, henføre; henvende seg til, henholde seg; vise til, peke på, sikte til, ymte om; se etter i.
referable ['ref(ə)rəbl] som kan henføres.
referee [refə'ri·] voldgiftsmann; oppmann; (i sportsspråket) dommer.
reference ['ref(ə)rəns] henvisning; oversendning, forbindelse; hensyn; hentydning, ymting; refe-ranse; **book of** — oppslagsbok; **with** — **to** an-gående.
referendum [refə'rendəm] folkeavstemning.
referential [refə'renʃəl] henvisnings-.
refine [ri'fain] rense, lutre; raffinere, koke; danne, forfine, foredle; renses, la seg rense; forfines, foredles. **refined** [ri'faind] forfinet, fin; dannet; raffinert.
refinement [ri'fainmənt] rensing, lutring; raf-finering; forfinelse; foredling; dannelse; raffine-ment; spissfindighet.
refiner [ri'fainə] renser, raffinør.
refinery [ri'fain(ə)ri] raffineri.
refit ['ri·'fit] reparere, sette i stand, vøle; ruste ut på ny. **refitment** [-mənt] utbedring. **refit-ting** [-iŋ] reparasjon, istandsetting.
reflect [ri'flekt] kaste tilbake; reflektere, gjen-speile; tenke på; betenke; gi gjenskinn; tenke tilbake; — on kaste skygge på. **reflecting** som kaster tilbake; tenksom.
reflection [ri'flekʃən] tilbakekasting, reflek-sjon; betraktning, ettertanke, overveielse; tenk-ning; tanke; kritikk; skarp bemerkning; speil-bilde; refleks; om — ved nærmere etter-tanke.

reflective [ri'flektiv] som kaster tilbake; reflekterende, tenkende, spekulativ.

reflector [ri'flektə] reflektor, refleksjonsspeil; lampeskjerm.

reflex ['ri·fleks] som vender bakover; tilbakevirkende; innadvendt; refleks.

reflex [ri'fleks] bøye tilbake.

reflexible [ri'fleksibl] som kan kastes tilbake.

reflexive [ri'fleksiv] tilbakevisende.

refluence ['reflu<ns] det å flyte tilbake, tilbakestrømning, tilbakegang; fall. refluent [-ənt] som flyter el. strømmer tilbake; fallende.

reflux ['ri·flʌks] tilbakestrømning; flux and — flo og fjære.

reform ['ri·'fåˀm] danne på ny, lage om.

reform [ri'få·ˀm] omdanne, nydanne; forbedre, reformere, rette på; forbedre seg; omvende seg; omdanning, nydanning; forbedring; reform; omvendelse.

reformation [refə'meɪʃən] reformering, forbedring; avhjelp; omvendelse; reformasjon.

reformative [ri'få·ˀmətiv] reformerende, reform-.

reformatory [ri'få·ˀmətəri] reform-, forbedrende; forbedringsanstalt. — -school tvangsskole.

reformer [ri'få·ˀmə] reformator.

reformist [ri'få·ˀmist] reformvenn.

refract [ri'fräkt] bryte.

refraction [ri'fräkʃən] brytning.

refractive [ri'fräktiv] brytende.

refractory [ri'fräktəri] gjenstridig, trassig, vrang.

refrain [ri'freɪn] omkved, etterstev, refreng.

refrain [ri'freɪn] holde tilbake, holde styr på; holde seg tilbake, styre seg, la være.

refresh [ri'freʃ] forfriske; fornye, reparere, friske opp, kveike opp; forfriske seg; komme seg, kvikne til.

refresher [ri'freʃə] oppstrammer, kveik.

refreshing [ri'freʃiŋ] forfriskende.

refreshment [ri'freʃmənt] forfriskning; — room restaurant (på en jernbanestasjon).

refrigerant [ri'fridʒərənt] kjølende; kjølende middel. refrigerate [-reɪt] avkjøle, svale; refrigerating plant fryseanlegg.

refrigeration [rifridʒə'reɪʃən] avkjøling.

refrigerator [ri'fridʒəreɪtə] kjøleapparat, isskap, iskasse; frysemaskin.

refrigeratory [ri'fridʒərətəri] kjøleapparat.

reft [reft] imperf. og perf. pts. av reave.

refuge ['refju·dʒ] tilflukt, tilfluktssted; utvei; herberge; ly; refuge, øy (for fotgjengere på gata); take — in søke tilflukt i, søke ly i.

refugee [refju'dʒi·] flyktning, emigrant.

refulgence [ri'fʌldʒəns] stråleglans.

refulgent [ri'fʌldʒənt] strålende, skinnende.

refund [ri'fʌnd] betale tilbake.

refundment [ri'fʌndmənt] tilbakebetaling.

refurbish ['ri·'fə·biʃ] gjenoppusse.

refurnish ['ri·'fəniʃ] møblere på ny.

refusable [ri'fju·zəbl] som kan avslås.

refusal [ri'fju·zəl] avslag, vegring, nei; fortrinsrett, forkjøpsrett.

refuse [ri'fju·z] avslå, avvise; nekte; vegre seg, unnslå seg; si nei.

refuse ['refju·s] kassert; avfalls-; avfall, boss, søppel, skrap, herk, utskudd. — -heap avfallsdynge; — -iron skrapjern.

refusion [ri'fju·ʒən] refusjon, tilbakebetaling.

refutable ['refjutəbl, ri'fju·təbl] gjendrivelig.

refutation [refju'teɪʃən] gjendriving.

refutatory [ri'fju·tətəri] gjendrivende.

refute [ri'fju·t] gjendrive, motbevise.

regain [ri'geɪn] gjenvinne, nå tilbake til.

regal ['ri·gl] kongelig, konge-.

regale [ri'geɪl] kongelig rettighet.

regale [ri'geɪl] traktement; traktere; fryde; delikatere seg, fryde seg. regalement [-mənt] traktement.

regalia [ri'geɪliə] regalier, kronjuveler; kongelige verdighetstegn; insignier.

regality [ri'gäliti] kongelighet.

regard [ri'ga·ˀd] se på, betrakte, legge merke til; akte, ense; vedkomme; blikk; betraktning, iakttagelse, oppmerksomhet; aktelse, anseelse; hensyn, omsyn; in — to med hensyn til; with — to med hensyn til; in — of i betraktning av; -s hilsen, hilsener; give my -s to the family! hils familien! all unite in kindest -s! alle sender deg sine beste hilsener!

regardful [ri'ga·ˀdf(u)l] oppmerksom.

regarding [ri'ga·diŋ] med hensyn til, angående.

regardless [ri'ga·ˀdlés] uten å bry seg om, likegyldig, likesæl, hensynsløs.

regatta [ri'gätə] regatta; kapproing, kappseilas.

regency ['ri·dʒənsi] regentskap; the Regency prins Georg av Wales' regentskap 1810—20.

regenerate [-rét] fornyet; gjenfødt. regeneration [ridʒenə're'ʃən] fornyelse; gjenfødelse.

regenerative [ri'dʒen(ə)rətiv] fornyende; gjenfødende. regenerator [ri'dʒenəre'tə] fornyer; regenerator.

regent ['ri dʒənt] regjerende; regent.

regentship ['ri·dʒəntʃip] regentskap.

regicidal ['redʒisaidəl] kongemorderisk.

regicide ['redʒisaid] kongemorder; kongemord.

régie [re'ʒi·] statsmonopol på tobakksfabrikasjon (srl. i Frankrike).

régime [re'ʒi·m] régime, regjering, styremåte, system, ordning.

regimen ['redʒimen] (foreskrevet) diét, kur; styrelse (i grammatikk).

regiment ['redʒimənt] regiment; dele inn i regimenter. regimental [redʒi'mental] regiments-; militær; uniforms-. regimentals uniform.

Regina [ri'dʒainə] dronning.

region ['ri·dʒən] strøk, egn.

regional ['ri·dʒənəl] lokal; topografisk; regional.

register ['redʒistə] bok, protokoll; liste; regulator; spjeld; register; skipsliste; valgliste; nasjonalitetsbevis; telleapparat, måler; parish (eller church) — ministerialbok; hotel — fremmedbok; — ton registertonn; keep a — of føre bok over; be on the — stå på manntallslisten; place on the — protokollere.

register ['redʒistə] bokføre, føre inn, protokollere, føre til protokolls; innregistrere; tinglese; skrive inn (reisegods); opptegne i historien; patentere; la rekommandere; vise; registrere; the thermometer -ed many degrees of frost termometret viste mange graders kulde; — a vow love seg selv; the barometer -s low barometret står lavt.

registered ['redʒistəd] innskrevet; bokført; — company selskap anmeldt til firmaregistret; by — parcel i rekommandert pakke.

register-office festekontor; registreringskontor.

registership ['redʒistəʃip] registratorpost.

registrar ['redʒistrə] registrator, protokollfører.

registration [redʒi'stre'ʃən] bokføring, innregistrering; tinglesing; rekommandering.

registry ['redʒistri] bokføring, innskriving, innregistrering; — -office festekontor; be married at a — -office ta seg borgerlig vie.

regius ['ri·dʒiəs] kongelig; — professor kongelig professor o: innehaver av et professorat opprettet av en konge.

regnant ['regnənt] regjerende, herskende.

regress [ri'gres] gå tilbake, snu, vende.

regression [ri'greʃən] tilbakegang.

regressive [ri'gresiv] tilbakevendende.

regret [ri'gret] beklage; savne; lengte tilbake til; I — to tell you that jeg må dessverre si Dem at. regret [ri'gret] beklagelse, sorg, savn, lengsel. regretful [ri'gretf(u)l] sorgfull, lengselsfull. regrettable [ri'gretəbl] beklagelig, beklagelsesverdig, å beklage.

regt. fk. f. regiment.

regular ['regjulə] regelmessig, regelrett; fast; forsvarlig, ordentlig, dyktig; fast gjest, kunde, passasjér; ordensgeistlig; regulær soldat.

regularity [regju'läriti] regelmessighet.

regularness ['regjulənès] regelmessighet.

regulate ['regjule¹t] regulere, ordne, styre.

regulation [regju'le¹ʃən] regulering; ordning; styring; forskrift, regel, vedtak; reglementert.

regulative ['regjulātiv] regulerende.

regulator ['regjule¹tə] regulator.

regurgitate [ri'gə·dʒite¹t] spy ut igjen.

rehabilitate [ri·(h)ə'bilite¹t] gjeninnsette i tidligere stilling el. rettighet; gi oppreisning; bringe til ære og verdighet igjen. **rehabilitation** [ri·(h)əbili-'te¹ʃən] gjeninnsetting; oppreisning, æresoppreisning.

rehearsal [ri'hə·səl] gjentagelse; fremsigelse; fortelling; innstudering, prøve; **put into** — innstudere; **full** (eller **last**) — generalprøve.

rehearse [ri'hə·s] gjenta, fremsi, si fram, gjengi, ramse opp, fortelle; innstudere, holde prøve på.

reign [re¹n] regjering, regjeringstid; regjere, herske, styre.

reimburse ['ri·im'bə·s] tilbakebetale, dekke; amortisere; — **oneself** ta seg betalt. **reimbursement** [-mənt] tilbakebetaling, dekning.

rein [re¹n] tom, tøyle; tømme, tøyle; holde igjen mot; **to** — **in the horse** stoppe hesten.

reincarnate [ri·'inkə·ne¹t, ri·in'ka·ne¹t] legemliggjøre på ny, reinkarnere.

reindeer ['re¹ndiə] rein, reinsdyr.

reinforce ['ri·in'fá·əs] forsterke. **reinforcement** [-mənt] forsterkning.

reins [re¹nz] (egl.:) nyrer; nå alm.: indre, hjerte; the — **and the heart,** hjerte og nyrer.

reinstate ['ri·in'ste¹t] gjeninnsette. **reinstatement** [-mənt] gjeninnsetting.

reinsurance ['ri·in'ʃuərəns] reassuranse, fornyet forsikring. **reinsure** ['ri·in'ʃuə] reassurere.

reiterate ['i·'itare¹t] ta opp igjen (og opp igjen). **reiteration** [ri·itə're¹ʃən] gjentagelse.

reject [ri'dʒekt] forkaste, vrake; støte fra seg, vise bort, avslå; **te -ed** få avslag, få en kurv. **rejectable** [ri'dʒektəbl] som kan avvises. **rejection** [ri'dʒekʃən] avvising, forkasting, vraking; avslag.

rejoice [ri'dʒois] glede seg, fryde seg, glede, gjøre glad. **rejoiced** glad.

rejoicings [ri'dʒoisiηz] jubel.

rejoin [ri'dʒoin] igjen bringe sammen, gjenforene; igjen slutte seg til; svare; duplisere. **rejoinder** [ri'dʒoində] svar, gjenmæle, duplikk.

rejuvenate [ri'dʒu·vine¹t] forynge(s).

rejuvenation [ridʒu·vi'ne¹ʃən] foryngelse.

rejuvenescence [ridʒu·və'nesəns] foryngelse.

rekindle [ri·'kirdl] tenne igjen.

relapse [ri'läps] falle tilbake; ha et tilbakefall; tilbakefall.

relate [ri'le¹t] fortelle, berette; forbinde, bringe forbindelse mellom; — **to** angå, vedkomme. **related** [ri'le¹tid] beslektet, skyldt. **relater** [ri'le¹tə] forteller, beretter.

relation [ri'le¹ʃən] fortelling, beretning; forbindelse, samband, forhold; slektskap; slektning.

relationship [ri'le¹ʃənʃip] slektskap.

relative ['relativ] som står i forbindelse; relativ; pårørende, slektning; relativt pronomen.

relativity [relə'tiviti] relativitet (srl.). Einsteins relativitetsteori.

relax [ri'läks] slappe; slappes, løsne; lempe seg; være mindre streng; søke atspredelse el. hvile. **relaxation** [riläk'se¹ʃən] atspredelse. **relaxed** [ri'läkst] slappet, slapp.

relay [ri'le¹] forsyning, forråd, depot; skysskifte, avløsning, ny forsyning; relais (i telegrafi); avløse. **relay** ['ri·'le¹] omlegge.

releasable [ri'li·səbl] som kan slippes fri; som kan ettergis. **release** [ri'li·s] slippe fri, sette i frihet, løslate; befri; frafalle, oppgi; ettergi; frigivelse, løslating; frikjenning, frigjøring, befri-

else; oppgivelse; kvittering; overdraging. **release-ment** [ri'li·smənt] befrielse, forløsning. **releaser** [ri'li·sə] befrier.

relegate ['relige¹t] fjerne, forvise.

relegation [reli'ge¹ʃən] relegasjon, forvisning.

relent [ri'lent] formildes, gi etter, la seg formilde; **relenting** ogs. bløt; forsonligere stemning. **relentless** [-lès] hard, stri, ubøyelig, ubarmhjertig. **relet** ['ri·'let] leie ut igjen.

relevance ['relivəns] anvendelighet, forbindelse med saken. **relevancy** = **relevance**. **relevant** [-ənt] anvendelig, som vedkommer saken.

reliability [rilaiə'biliti] pålitelighet.

reliable [ri'laiəbl] pålitelig. **reliableness** [-nès] pålitelighet. **reliance** [ri'laiəns] tillit, tiltro, for-trøstning; **have** (el. **place** el. **feel**) — **upon** (el. **on** el. **in**) ha tillit til, lite på, stole på. **reliant** [ri'laiənt] tillitsfull, som stoler på.

relic ['relik] levning, rest, relikvie; erindring, minne; **relics** rester; jordiske levninger. **relict** ['relikt] enke (bare med of (etter) eller et annet eiendomsuttrykk); levning.

relief [ri'li·f] lindring, lette, lettelse; befrielse, beroligelse, lise, trøst; avveksling; hjelp, understøttelse; rettshjelp; fattighjelp, fattigunderstøttelse, forsorg, unnsetning; avløsning; skifte; relieff, opphøyd arbeid; **with a feeling of** — med lettet hjerte; **the hour of** — befrielsens time; **heave a sigh of** — dra et lettelsens sukk; **come to his** — komme ham til unnsetning; **bring** (eller **throw, force**) **into** — la komme skarpt fram, framheve. **reliefless** [-lès] hjelpeløs; uhjelpelig.

relieve [ri'li·v] heve, framheve; lindre, døyve; avhjelpe, hjelpe, understøtte; unnsette; avløse; variere, bringe avveksling inn i; **reliever** [ri'li·və] lindrer; hjelper; befrier; avløser.

relieving [ri'li·viη] lindrende; — **army** unnsetningshær; — **officer** forsorgsforstander.

relight ['ri·'lait] lyse opp igjen, tenne på ny, atter tennes.

religion [ri'lidʒən] religion; gudsfrykt, fromhet; klosterliv. **religiosity** [rilidʒi'ásiti] religiøsitet.

religious [ri'lidʒəs] religiøs; kristelig; gudfryktig; bundet av munkeløfte; munk, nonne. **religiousness** [-nès] religiøsitet.

relinquish [ri'liηkwiʃ] slippe, oppgi, forlate; frafalle. **relinquishment** [-mənt] oppgivelse, avståelse.

reliquary ['relikwari] relikvieskrin. **relique** [ri'li·k, 'relik] relikvie. **reliquiæ** [ri'li·kwii·] jordiske levninger, rester.

relish ['reliʃ] firne smak i, like; sette smak på; smake, smake godt, hə smak; velsmak, smak; tanke, anstrøk; krydderi; appetittvekker. **relishable** ['reliʃəbl] velsmakende.

reload ['ri·'lo¹d] la på ny. **-er** omladeapparat.

reluctance [ri'lʌktəns] motvilje, ulyst, liten lyst. **reluctant** [ri'lʌktənt] motstrebende, uvillig; **be** — **to** nødig ville, kvie seg for.

rely [ri'lai] **on** stole på, lite på.

remain [ri'me¹n] være igjen, bli tilbake; bli, forbli; vedbli, bestå; levning, rest; — **single** forbli ugift; **I — yours truly** (jeg fcrblir) Deres ærbødige . . .; **the word -s in** Essex ordet finnes ennå i Essex; **the worst of all -ed to come** det verste sted ennå tilbake; **it -s with him to make them happy** det står til ham å gjøre dem lykke-lige; **-s** etterlatenskaper, jordiske rester.

remainder [ri'me¹ndə] rest, levninger, rest-opplag, restbeløp.

remaining [ri'me¹niη] tilbakeværende.

remand [ri'ma·nd] sende tilbake (især til varetektsarresten); kalle tilbake; tilbakesending; gjeninnsetting i arrest; tilbakekalling.

remanence [ri'menəns] det å bli tilbake, være tilbake, vedbli, bestå; standhaftighet. **remanent** [-nənt] som blir el. er tilbake.

remark [ri'ma·ək] iakttagelse, bemerkning, ytring; bemerke; iakta; ytre; gjøre bemerkninger.

remarkable [ri'ma·ᵊkəbl] bemerkelsesverdig; fremragende; merkelig, merkverdig. **remarkableness** [-nès] merkverdighet.

remarriage ['ri·'märidʒ] annet ekteskap. **remarry** ['ri·'märi] gifte seg (med) igjen.

remediable [ri'mi·djəbl] som kan rettes på, helbredelig. **remedial** [-djəl] helbredende, lægende.

remedy ['remidi] legemiddel; hjelpemiddel, middel, råd, hjelp, avhjelp; avhjelpe, råde bot på; **there is a — for everything** det er råd for alt; **in — of** for å avhjelpe.

remelt ['ri 'melt] smelte cm.

remember [ri'membə] erindre, minnes, huske; minne om; **this will be -ed against no one** dette skal ikke komme noen til skade; **— me to him!** hils ham fra meg! **rememberable** [ri'memb(ə)rəbl] minneverdig. **rememberer** [ri'memb(ə)rə] en som husker på, minnes. **remembering** [-b(ə)riŋ] erindring.

remembrance [ri'membrəns] erindring, minne (ɔ: det å huske); hukommelse; støtte for erindringen, souvenir; (i flertall) hilsener; **in — of** til minne om. **remembrancer** [ri'membrənsə] påminner; minne, erindring, huskeseddel.

remind [ri'maind] minne (**of** om, **that** om å); **— me of** minner meg om, får meg til å tenke på. **reminder** [ri'maində] påminner, påminning; huskeseddel. **remindful** [ri'maindf(u)l] som minnes; påminnende.

Remington ['remiŋtən] Remingtcn.

reminiscence [remi'nisəns] erindring; (i pluralis også) memoarer; reminisens, levning. **reminiscent** [-sənt] som erindrer, minnes; minnerik.

remise [ri'maiz] vognremise; leievogn.

remiss [ri'mis] slapp, likesæl, doven, forsømmelig; lunken. **remissibility** [ri'misi'biliti] tilgivelighet. **remissible** [ri'misibl] tilgivelig. **remission** [ri'miʃən] frafall, oppgivelse; ettergivelse; tilgivelse; nedgang; slappelse. **remissive** [ri'misiv] avtagende; som frafaller; som tilgir. **remissness** [-nès] slapphet, skjøtesløshet, forsømmelighet.

remit [ri'mit] sende tilbake; oversende, innsende, remittere, tilstille; sette i arresten igjen; overgi, henstille; slappe, la avta, formilde, forminske, dempe; ettergi; forlate, tilgi; avta. **remitment** [-mənt] tilbakesending, gjeninnsetting; ettergivelse, forlatelse, tilgivelse; remisse. **remittal** [ri'mit(ə)l] oversending; tilgivelse; avståelse. **remittance** [ri'mitəns] remisse. **remitter** [ri'mitə] ettergiver; tilgiver; avsender av remisse, avsender (av postanvisning).

remnant ['remnənt] rest; levning.

remodel ['ri·'mådl] omdanne, omforme.

remonstrance [ri'månstrəns] forestilling, advarsel; formaning(er), bebreidelse(r); protest, innvending; **a paper of —** en protestskrivelse. **remonstrant** [-strənt] bebreidende, advarende; remonstrant.

remonstrate [ri'månstre't] forestille, gjøre forestillinger; anføre grunner; protestere, bebreide.

remontant [ri'måntənt] remonterende (ɔ: som blomstrer igjen samme år).

remorse [ri'må·ᵈs] samvittighetsnag, anger. **remorseful** [-f(u)l] angerfull, angrende. **remorseless** [-lès] hjerteløs, ubarmhjertig, grusom.

remote [ri'mo·t] fjern; fjerntliggende; avsides; vidt forskjellig. **remoteness** [-nès] fjernhet; avsides beliggenhet.

remould ['ri·'moᵘld] omdanne, omforme.

remount [ri(·)'maunt] bestige igjen; skaffe nye hester; stige opp igjen; remonte(hest).

removability [ri'mu·və'biliti] flyttbarhet; avsettelighet. **removable** [ri'mu·vəbl] som kan flyttes; avsettelig, som kan avskjediges.

removal [ri'mu·vl] fjerning; avtagelse, forflytting; avskjedigelse; flytting, overflytting, oppflytting; det å rydde bort; bortvisning; opphevelse; avløsning.

remove [ri'mu·v] flytte, få bort, fjerne; rydde bort; forflytte; flytte opp (på skolen); avskjedige; avhjelpe; flytte seg; flytting; rett (av mat); avstand, mellomrom, trin, grad; årgang; oppflytting. **remover** [ri'mu·və] flytter.

remunerability [ri'mju·nərə'biliti] det å være fortjenstlig. **remunerable** [ri'mju·nərəbl] fortjenstlig. **remunerate** [-re't] lønne. **remuneration** [rimju·nə're'ʃən] lønn, godtgjørelse. **remunerative** [ri'mju·nərətiv] gjengjeldende; lønnende. **remuneratory** [-təri] gjengjeldende; lønnende.

renaissance [ri'ne'səns] renessanse.

renal ['ri·nəl] som angår nyrene, nyre-. **rename** ['ri·'ne'm] omdøpe.

renard ['renəd] Mikkel rev.

renascence [ri'näsəns] gjenfødelse, renessanse. **renascent** [-sənt] som gjenfødes; gjenfødt; renessansemenneske.

rencontre [ren'kåntə], **rencounter** [ren'kauntə] møte; duell; trefning; sammenstøt; treffes, råke, støte sammen.

rend [rend] rive sund, splintre, splitte.

render ['rendə] en som river sund.

render ['rendə] gi tilbake, yte, gi; gjøre; overgi, gjengi; oversette; ytelse, avgift; **— into** Norwegian gjengi på norsk; **— me a service** gjøre meg en tjeneste.

renderable ['rendərəbl] som kan gjengis. **renderer** ['rendərə] yter, gjengiver.

rendering ['rendəriŋ] gjengivelse, ytelse; oversettelse; bilde; det å avlegge (**of accounts** regnskap); grunnpuss; utsmelting.

rendezvous ['ra·nde'vu; 'rå·ndivu; i pluralis: 'ra·ndivu·z] møtested; stevnemøte, rendezvous; møtes.

rendition [ren'diʃən] overgivelse; utlevering; gjengivelse.

renegade ['renige'd] renegat, frafallen, overløper.

renerve ['ri·'nə·v] styrke igjen.

renew [ri'nju·] fornye; begynne igjen. **renewable** [ri'nju·əbl] som kan fornyes. **renewal** [-əl] fornyelse. **renewer** [-ə] fornyer.

reniform ['renifå·ᵊm] nyreformet.

renitent ['renitənt] oppsetsig.

rennet ['renit] løpe, kjese (osteaktig melk i kalvemage).

rennet ['renit] reinette (slags eple).

renounce [ri'nauns] fornekte; oppgi, slutte med; frasi; avsverge; vise renons (i); renons (i kortspill).

renouncement [ri'naunsmənt] frasigelse, avkall, oppgivelse; fornekting, forsagelse.

renovate ['renove't] fornye. **renovation** [reno-'ve'ʃən] fornyelse. **renovator** ['renove'tə] fornyer.

renown [ri'naun] ry, berømmelse, gjetord. **renowned** [ri'naund] navnkundig, berømt, fræg. **renownless** [ri'naunlès] uberømt.

rent [rent] revne, sprekk; flerre, rift.

rent [rent], imperf. og perf. pts. av rend.

rent [rent] leie, husleie, avgift, landskyld; leie, utleie, forpakte; bortleies; bortforpaktes. **rentable** ['rentəbl] som kan leies. **rental** ['rentəl] jordebok; leie. **renter** ['rentə] leier, forpakter, leilending. **renting** ['rentiŋ] leie, forpaktning.

renunciation [rinʌnsi'e'ʃən] = **renouncement**.

re-open ['ri·'oᵘpən] åpne igjen.

reorganization ['ri·å·ᵊgən(ə)i'ze'ʃən] reorganisasjon, omdanning. **reorganize** ['ri·å·ᵊgənaiz] reorganisere, omdanne.

rep [rep] rips (en slags tøy).

repair [ri'pæ·ə] gå, begi seg; tilfluktssted.

repair [ri'pæ·ə] istandsetting; reparasjon, utbedring, vedlikehold; oppreisning; sette i stand, reparere, vøle, utbedre; opprette; **in good —** i god stand; **out of —** i dårlig stand. **repairable** [ri'pæ·ᵊrəbl] som kan settes i stand. **repairer** [ri'pæ·ᵊrə] istandsetter, reparatør, utbedrer.

reparable ['repərəbl] som lar seg reparere; opprettelig; som kan gjøres god igjen.

reparation [repə'reɪʃən] istandsetting, reparasjon; oppreisning, erstatning.
repartee [repa·ə'tiː] kvikt svar; slagferdighet.
repartition ['riː·pa·ə'tiʃən] ny fordeling.
repass ['riː'pa·s] passere på ny.
repast [ri'pa·st] måltid.
repay [ri·'peɪ] betale tilbake, gjengjelde; erstatte. repayable [ri'peɪəbl] som skal betales tilbake. repayment [ri'peɪmənt] tilbakebetaling; innfriing.
repeal [ri'piː·l] oppheve; tilbakekalle; opphevelse; tilbakekalling. repealable [ri'piː·ləbl] opphevelig; tilbakekallelig. repealer [ri'piː·lə] opphever; unionsoppløser, en som vil oppløse unionen mellom Storbritannia og Irland.
repeat [ri'piː·t] si igjen; si fram, foredra; forsøke igjen; gjenta, repetere; gjentagelse; -order etterordre. repeating rifle repetergevær; repeating watch repeterur.
repeatedly [ri'piː·tidli] gjentatte ganger, gang på gang.
repeater [ri'piː·tə] repeterur; repetergevær; periodisk desimalbrøk.
repel [ri'pel] drive tilbake; frastøte, avvise, vise tilbake. repellant, repellent [ri'pelənt] tilbakedrivende; frastøtende.
repent ['riː·pənt] krypende (om plante).
repent [ri'pent] angre, trege; — of angre på.
repentance [ri'pentəns] anger, trege.
repentant [ri'pentənt] angrende, angerfull, botferdig synder.
repercussion [ripə'kʌʃən] tilbakekasting; tilbakeslag; gjenlyd; gjentagelse.
répertoire ['repətwɑ·ə, 'repatwa·ə] repertoar.
repertory ['repətəri] repertoar; skattkammer, gullgruve, magasin, samling; — theatre, teater som baseres på et repertoar, ikke på tallrike oppførelser av enkelte kassestykker.
repetition [repi'tiʃən] gjentagelse, avskrift, kopi; fremsigelse; gjengivelse; utenatlæring.
repine [ri'pain] gremme seg; vise utilfredshet med; lengte meget. repiner [ri'painə] en som er utilfreds.
replace [ri'pleɪs] legge (stille, sette) tilbake; gjeninnsette; tilbakebetale; erstatte, avløse. replacement [-mənt] tilbakesetting; gjeninnsetting, erstatning.
replant ['riː·pla·nt] plante igjen, omplante, plante til på ny.
replenish [ri'pleniʃ] fylle igjen, fylle på. replenishment [-mənt] utfylling.
replete [ri'pliː·t] full, oppfylt.
repletion [ri'pliː·ʃən] overflod; filled to — fylt til overmål.
replevin [ri'plevin] gjenervervelse mot kausjon; klage over selvtekt; ordre om tilfølgetagelse av selvtektsklage.
replica ['replikə] kopi, avtrykk.
replication [repli'keɪʃən] svar; replikk; gjenlyd; reproduksjon. replier [ri'plaiə] en som svarer.
reply [ri'plaɪ] svare (to på; that at) tu til gjenmæle, imøtegå; svar; svarskriv; in — som svar. — -card svarbrevkort. — -paid svar betalt.
repocket ['riː·'pɑkit] stikke i lommen igjen.
repolish ['riː·'pɑliʃ] polere om igjen.
report [ri'pɑ·ət] rapportere, melde tilbake, innberette; melde, fortelle; avgi beretning; melding, rapport, opplysning, innberetning; årsberetning; innstilling; referat; rykte, knall, smell; — oneself melde seg; by current — etter hva det alminnelig forlyder; know him from — kjenne ham av omtale.
reporter [ri'pɑ·ətə] referent, reporter.
repose [ri'poʊz] hvile, hvile ut; støtte; ligge; ro, hvile, fred; — confidence in stole på.
reposeful [ri'poʊzful] rolig, fredfull.
reposit [ri'pɑzit] anbringe, forvare, gjemme, legge. reposition ['riː·po'ziʃən] anbringelse, forvaring; henleggelse. repository [ri'pɑzitəri] gjemme, gjemmested, oppbevaringssted.

repossess ['riː·pə'zes] gjenvinne, bemektige seg på ny. repossession [-'zeʃən] fornyet besittelse.
repot ['riː·'pɑt] plante i ny(e) potte(r), plante om, repoussé [rə'puː·seɪ] drevet; driving, drevet arbeid.
reprehend [repri'hend] laste. dadle, klandre. reprehensible [-sibl] lastverdig. reprehension [-ʃən] daddel, klander; irettesetting. reprehensive [-siv], reprehensory [-səri] dadlende.
represent [repri'zent] framstille, sette fram igjen, forestille, bety; beskrive; representere; bemerke. representable [repri'zentəbl] som kan framstilles. representation [reprizen'teɪʃən] forestilling, framstilling; beskrivelse; representasjon.
representative [repri'zentətiv] som forestiller, som framstiller; representerende; representant; House of Representatives Underhuset i De Forente Staters kongress.
repress [ri'pres] trenge tilbake, betvinge; kue, døyve, undertrykke; holde nede; hemme, stanse; tøyle, holde styr på. represser [ri'presə] betvinger, underkuer, undertrykker. repression [ri'preʃən] undertrykkelse. repressive [ri'presiv] kuende, dempende, undertrykkende.
reprieve [ri'priː·v] gi en frist, befri for en tid; benåde for livsstraff; frist, utsettelse; henstand; benådning for livsstraff.
reprimand [repri'ma·nd, 'reprima·nd] irettesette, gi en skrape.
reprimand [repri'ma·nd] irettesettelse, skrape.
reprint ['riː·'print] avtrykke igjen, trykke opp; opptrykk.
reprisal [ri'praiz] gjengjeld, represalier; make -s ta represalier.
reprise [ri'praiz] reprise; gjentagelse.
reproach [ri'proʊtʃ] bebreide, klandre, laste; bebreidelse, daddel; skam, skjensel; — him with it bebreide ham det. reproachful [-f(u)l] bebreidende, dadlende; beskjemmende; skammelig, skjendig. reproachless [-les] daddelfri, udadlelig, ulastelig.
reprobate ['reprobeɪt] forkaste, avvise, vrake; fordømme.
reprobate ['reprobət] fordømt; fordervet, ryggesløs; fortapt. reprobateness [-bétnés] forderveise, ryggesløshet; fordømmelse.
reprobation [repro'beɪʃən] forkasting, vraking; avsky; fordømming.
reproduce ['riː·pro'djuː·s] frambringe igjen; framstille igjen; fornye; gjengi, gjenfortelle; forplante.
reproduction [ripro'dʌkʃən] ny frambringelse, framstilling; fornyelse; gjengivelse, gjenfortelling, reproduksjon. reproductive [-'dʌktiv] som frambringer på ny, reproduksjons-.
reproof [ri'pruː·f] daddel, irettesettelse, klander.
reprovable [ri'pruː·vəbl] daddelverdig, lastverdig.
reproval [-vəl] daddel. reprove [ri'pruː·v] dadle, irettesette, laste, klandre. reprover [-ə] dadler.
reptant ['reptənt] krypende, kryp-.
reptile ['reptaɪl] krypdyr; kryp; krypende. reptilian [rep'tiliən] krypdyr-, kryp-.
republic [ri'pʌblik] republikk; the — of letters den lærde verden.
republican [ri'pʌblikən] republikansk; republikaner; the Republicans i U. S. A. er det parti som (mer utpreget enn the Democrats) holder på unionens enhet, vernetoll og imperialisme.
republish ['riː·pʌbliʃ] offentliggjøre på ny.
repudiate [ri'pjuː·dieɪt] forkaste; forskyte, la seg skille fra; nekte, fornekte. repudiation [ri·pju·di'eɪʃən] forkasting; forskytelse; fornekting. repudiator [ri'pju·dieɪtə] forkaster.
repugnance [ri'pʌgnəns] sky, ulyst, stygg, utilbøyelighet; uvilje, motvilje; avsky. repugnant [-nənt] motstrebende, utilbøyelig, tverr, vrang; usnakelig, støtende.
repulse [ri'pʌ·ls] tilbakedriving, tilbakestøt; avslag; drive, kaste tilbake, avvise, repulsion [-ʃən] tilbakestøt, tilbakedriving.

repulsive [ri'pʌlsiv] tilbakestøtende, tilbake-drivende; frastøtende. repulsiveness [ri'pʌlsivnis] frastøtende vesen, usmakelighet.
reputable ['repjutəbl] aktverdig, aktet.
reputation [repju'teiʃən] omdømme, rykte, reputasjon, godt navn, anseelse, vørnad; have the — of being ha ry (el. ord) for å være; have a — for ha ry for.
repute [ri'pju·t] anse for, holde for; omdømme, anseelse, godt navn. reputedly [-idli] etter ryktet.
request [ri'kwest] anmodning, bønn, søknad; etterspørsel, begjær; anmode, be om, utbe seg; in — etterspurt; make a — framsette en anmodning; accede to (comply with, grant) a — innvilge i, etterkomme en anmodning.
requiem ['rekwiem] rekviem (sjelemesse).
require [ri'kwaiə] forlange, kreve, behøve, trenge til. requirement [ri'kwaiəmənt] krav, behov, fornødenhet.
requisite ['rekwizit] fornøden, nødvendig; fornødenhet, nødvendighet; rekvisitt. requisiteness [-nés] fornødenhet, nødvendighet.
requisition [rekwi'ziʃən] begjæring, fordring, forlangende, krav; rekvisisjon; legge beslag på; forlange, rekvirere.
requital [ri'kwaitəl] belønning, gjengjeldelse (of av, for), lønn, gjengjeld, vederlag (of for).
requite [ri'kwait] gjengjelde, lønne.
reredos ['riədås] reredos (en steinskjerm som bakgrunnsvegg bak et alter).
rescind [ri'sind] avskaffe; oppheve; omstøte.
rescindable [ri'sindəbl] omstøtelig.
rescission [ri'siʒən] opphevelse; omstøtelse.
rescissory [ri'sisəri] avskaffende, opphevende.
rescript ['ri·skript] reskript; forordning, påbud.
rescuable ['reskjuəbl] som er til å redde.
rescue ['reskju] frelse, redde, berge; befri, utfri (from fra); frelse, redning, unnsetning, hjelp; befrielse, utfrielse. rescuer ['reskjuə] rednings-mann; befrier. rescuing ['reskjuiŋ] rednings-, unnsetnings-; — -party redningsmannskap.
research [ri'sə·tʃ] undersøkelse, forskning, gransking.
research ['ri'sə·tʃ] undersøke (eller gjennom-søke) på ny, granske; fornyet undersøkelse.
reseat ['ri·'si·t] sette nytt sete i; sette ny bak i; sette igjen, få til å sette seg igjen.
resell ['ri·'sel] selge igjen. -er videreforhandler.
resemblance [ri'zembləns] likhet (between mellom; to med); bilde.
resemble [ri'zembl] ligne.
resent [ri'zent] oppta ille, anse som fornærmelse, føle seg fornærmet over, harmes over, bli fortørnet over; he -ed my words han ble meget sint for det jeg sa. resentful [ri'zentf(u)l] pirrelig; hevngjerrig; fornærmet, harmfull, vred, langsint.
resentment [ri'zentmənt] krenkelse, harme, agg, vrede.
reservation [rezə've'ʃən] reservasjon, forbehold; reservert stykke land (især amr. om land som er reservert for indianere); mental — stilltiende forbehold.
reserve [ri'zə·v] gjemme, spare, holde tilbake; bevare, forbeholde, reservere; forbeholde seg; tilbakeholdelse, bevaring, bevarelse; beholdning, reserve; forråd; unntagelse, forbehold; tilbakeholdenhet, forsik'ighet.
reserved [ri'zə·vd] reservert, forsiktig, tilbake-holden; reservedness [-vidnés] forsiktighet, reservasjon, tilbakeholdenhet.
reservist [ri'zə·vist] reservesoldat, reservist.
reservoir ['rezəvwå·ə] beholder; vannreservoar.
reset ['ri·'set] sette i på ny, sette i ledd igjen.
reset [ri'set] (skotsk jur.) skjule (f. eks. tyve-gods); hele.
resettle ['ri·'setl] atter anbringe, bringe til ro igjen, komme atter til ro.
reshape [ri·'ʃe'p] forme på ny, omforme.
resheathe ['ri·'ʃi·ð] stikke i sliren (igjen).
reship ['ri·'ʃip] skipe ut igjen.

reshipment ['ri·'ʃipmənt] gjenutskipet last.
reside [ri'zaid] oppholde seg, bo; holde hoff, residere; ligge, ha sitt sete.
residence ['rezidəns] opphold, bosittelse, bosted, bolig, bopel; residens, residensstad; fast opphold i distriktet.
residency ['rezidənsi] residens, residentskap (i India).
resident ['rezidənt] bosatt, boende; innvåner, beboer, borger; embetsmann som bor i sitt distrikt; ministerresident, resident (engelsk utsending ved indisk hoff).
residential [rezi'denʃəl] beboelses-; beboelig for den fine verden.
residual [ri'zidjuəl] tiloversblitt, tilbakevæ-rende, rest.
residuary [ri'zidjuəri] rest-, resterende.
residue ['rezidju·] rest.
residuous [ri'zidjuəs] = residual.
resign [ri'zain] overgi; avstå; legge ned; ta avskjed; fratre; — himself overgi seg; hengi seg.
resignation [rezig'ne'ʃən] oppgivelse, avståelse, nedlegging; avskjed; hengivelse, resignasjon; forsagelse; send in one's — sende inn sin avskjeds-søknad.
resigned [ri'zaind] resignert; be — to finne seg tålmodig i, underkaste seg.
resin ['rezin] harpiks, kvae.
resinous ['rezinəs] harpiksholdig, kvae-; nega-tiv (om elektrisitet).
resist [ri'zist] motstå, sette seg imot, gjøre mot-stand imot; motarbeide, motvirke; I could not — asking jeg kunne ikke holde meg for å spørre.
resistance [ri'zistəns] motstand (against el. to imot); ledningsmotstand.
resistant [ri'zistənt] en som gjør motstand.
resister [ri'zistə] en som motsetter seg.
resistibility [ri'zisti'biliti] motståelighet.
resistible [ri'zistibl] som kan stå imot.
resistless [ri'zistlés] uimotståelig; hjelpeløs.
resole ['ri·'soºl] såle igjen.
resolute ['rezol(ju·t] bestemt, fast, standhaf-tig; djerv, kjekk, rask, besluttsom, rådsnar, reso-lutt. resoluteness [-nés] besluttsomhet, kjekkhet.
resolution [rezə'l(ju·ʃən] oppløsning, bestemt-het, fasthet; djervhet, kjekkhet, behjertethet; rask opptreden, besluttsomhet; resolusjon, be-slutning, bestemmelse, vedtak.
resolvability [rizálvə'biliti] oppløselighet.
resolvable [ri'zálvəbl] oppløselig.
resolve [ri'zálv] løse opp; løse; beslutte, avgjøre, vedta, gjøre vedtak om, bestemme seg til; resol-vere; løse seg opp, konstituere seg; beslutning, be-stemmelse; resolved [-d] besluttet, bestemt. re-solvent [-ənt] oppløsende; fordelende; oppløs-ningsmiddel.
resonance ['rezənəns] gjenlyd, atterljom; reso-nans.
resonant ['rezənənt] gjenlydende.
resort [ri'zå·ºt] gå, begi seg, ty, ta sin til-flukt; søkning, besøk, tilhold, tilholdssted; opp-holdssted; kursted; forlystelsessted; utvei; juris-diksjon; instans.
resound [ri'zaund] la gjenlyde; lyde, ljome, gjen-lyde; resounding board resonansbunn, klangbunn.
resound ['ri·'saund] la lyde igjen; gjenlyde.
resource [ri'så·ºs] hjelpekilde; ervervskilde; tilflukt, utvei; -s midler, pengemidler, ressurser.
resourceful [-f(u)l] oppfinnsom, idérik, rådsnar.
resourcefulness [-nés] rådsnarhet. resourceless [-lés] fattig på utveier, rådløs.
respect [ri'spekt] akte, vøre, ha vørnad for, ta hensyn til; gjelde, vedkomme, angå; aktelse, respekt; hensyn; henseende; I — his feeling jeg respekterer hans følelser; — oneself ha selvaktelse; as respects hva angår; respecting angående, med hensyn til; out of respect to him av aktelse for ham; send one's respects to sende sin ærbødige hilsen til; our respects vårt skriv; in many respects i mange henseender.

respectability [ri'spektə'biliti] aktverdighet.
respectable [ri'spektəbl] aktverdig, respektabel, anselig.
respectful [ri'spektf(u)l] ærbødig; **yours respectfully** ærbødigst (foran underskriften i brev).
respective [ri'spektiv] hver sin, respektive; **put them in their — places** anbrakte dem hver på sitt sted. **respectively** henholdsvis.
respirable [ri'spairəbl] som kan innåndes.
respiration ['respi're'ʃən] åndedretɨ.
respirator ['respire'tə] respirator.
respiratory [ri'spairətəri, 'respi-] åndedretts-.
respire [ri'spaiə] ånde; innånde, utånde.
respite ['respit] frist, henstand, utsettelse, pusterom; gi frist, utsette.
resplendence [ri'splendəns] glans.
resplendent [ri'splendənt] strålende, gild.
respond [ri'spånd] svare (især om menighetens svar til presten); holde svartalen (**to** til); — **to** besvare med tilslutning, gå med på, følge (i handling), gjøre etter, lyde, lystre, sympatisere med; stemme med; — **with** svare med, gjengjelde med.
respondent [ri'spåndənt] innstevnte (i skilsmissesaker); svarende (**to** til).
response [ri'spåns] svar; menighetens svar ved gudstjenesten; tilslutning, medhold.
responsibility [ri'spånsi'biliti] ansvarlighet; ansvar; ansvarsfølelse.
responsible [ri'spånsibl] ansvarlig; trygg, vederheftig, pålitelig; ansvarsfull.
responsive [ri'spånsiv] svarende; forståelsesfull, som står i samklang (**to** med); sympatisk.
responsory [ri'spånsəri] svarende, svar-; svarsang.
rest [rest] hvile, hvil; ro, fred; støtte, hvilepunkt; pause; stativ, bukk; hvile, raste, holde hvil, roe seg; bygge, stole på; hvile, la hvile.
rest [rest] rest; forbli; være tilbake; **and (all) the rest (of it)** og så videre; (i samme retning); **for the rest** for resten.
restaurant ['restərån] restaurant. **— -keeper** restauratør. **— -car** spisevogn.
rested ['restid] uthvilt.
restful ['restf(u)l] rolig, beroligende, som stiller; hvilested.
restitution [resti'tju·ʃən] gjenoppretting, tilbakegivelse, tilbakelevering, erstatning; vederlag, skadebot.
restive ['restiv] sta, stri; hårdnakket; **be —** slå seg vrang; stritte imot.
restless ['restlès] rastløs, hvileløs; urolig, nervøs. **-ness** rastløshet.
restorable [ri'stå·rəbl] som lar seg sette i stand, reparere, fornye; opprettelig; helbredelig.
restoration [resto're'ʃən] istandsetting, reparasjon, restaurering; gjenoppbygging; fornying; gjenoppretting; tilbakebringelse; tilbakegivelse; tilbakelevering; utlevering; erstatning; helbredelse, restituering; **the Restoration** gjeninnsetting av Stuartene i 1660 etter republikken.
restorative [ri'stå·rətiv] forfriskende, styrkende; gjenopplivende (middel).
restore [ri'stå·ə] sette i stand, reparere, restaurere; fornye; gjenopprette; gjeninnføre; gjeninnsette, få tilbake; gi tilbake; utlevere; gjengi; helbrede, restituere.
restorer [ri'stå·rə] gjenoppretter; tilbakebringer.
restrain [ri'stre'n] holde tilbake, styre, tøyle, betvinge, legge bånd på, døyve, kue; **restrainable** [-nəbl] betvingelig. **restrainer** [-ə] betvinger, demper.
restraint [ri'stre'nt] tvang, age, styr; innskrenkning, bånd, tilbakeholdenhet; tvungenhet; **be under —** være under tvang, være tvangsinnlagt (om sinnssyk).
restrict [ri'strikt] begrense, innskrenke, holde styr på.

restriction [ri'strikʃən] innskrenkning.
restrictive [ri'striktiv] innskrenkende.
result [ri'zʌlt] oppstå, framgå, komme av, følge, resultere, få et utfall, ende; resultat, utslag, følge, utfall, virkning; — **from** følge av; — **in** ende med; **without —** fruktesløs.
resultant [ri'zʌltənt] resulterende; resultant.
resultless [ri'zʌltlès] fruktesløs, fåfengt.
resumable [ri'z(j)u·məbl] som kan gjenopptas.
resume [ri'z(j)u·m] ta tilbake, gjeninnta; gjenoppta, ta på seg igjen; begynne igjen, atter ta ordet, ta opp igjen tråden, fortsette.
résumé ['rezjume'] resymé, utdrag.
resumption [ri'zʌm(p)ʃən] tilbaketagelse; gjenopptagelse. **resumptive** [ri'zʌm(p)tiv] tilbaketagende, gjenopptagende.
resurrect [rezə'rekt] kalle til live igjen; grave opp igjen (om likrøver).
resurrection [rezə'rekʃən] oppstandelse; rett laget av rester; likrøveri. **-ist** el. **-man** likrøver. **— -pie** rett laget av rester.
resusciate [ri'sʌsite'ɨ] gjenopplive; livne opp igjen.
resuscitation [ri'sʌsi'te'ʃən] gjenopplivning.
resuscitator [ri'sʌsite'tə] gjer.opplivner.
ret [ret] røyte, bløyte ut, bløyte opp (lin, hamp etc.).
retail [ri'te'l] selge i detalj, i smått; gjenfortelle, bære videre, diske opp med.
retail ['ri·te'l] detaljhandel, småhandel; **by —** i detalj, i smått; — **dealer** detaljhandler.
retailer [ri'te'lə] detaljist; kolportør, slarvekopp.
retain [ri'te'n] holde tilbake; beholde; bibeholde; anta, engasjere, sikre seg; **retaining fee** forskuddshonorar (for å sikre seg en sakfører).
retainable [ri'te'nəbl] som kan holdes tilbake.
retainer [ri'te'nə] tjener; klient; tilhenger; marketenter; forskuddshonorar (til advokat).
retaliate [ri'tälie'ɨ] gjengjelde.
retaliation [ritäli'e'ʃən] gjengjeld; hevn; represalier.
retard [ri'ta·°d] forsinke, hefte, forhale; stille tilbake (ur). **retardation** [ri·ta·°'de'ʃən] forsinkelse, forminskelse av hastighet; forhaling. **retardative** [ri'ta·°dətiv] forsinkende, forhalende. **retardment** [ri'ta·°dmənt] = **retardation**.
retch [re·tʃ] forsøke å kaste opp, slite seg; forsøk på oppkastning.
retell ['ri·'tel] gjenfortelle.
retemper ['ri·'tempə] atter herde.
retention [ri'tenʃən] tilbakeholdelse; bibehold; forvaring, hukommelse, minne. **retentive** [ri'tentiv] som beholder; som har god hukommelse.
reticence ['retisəns] taushet; fåmælthet; forbeholdenhet.
reticent ['retisənt] taus, fåmælt, forbeholden.
reticle [ri'retikl] nettverk; arbeidspose, håndtaske, håndveske.
reticulate [ri'tikjulit] nettaktig.
reticulated [ri'tikjule'tid] nettaktig.
reticulation [ritikju'le'ʃən] nettaktig forgrening, nettverk.
reticule ['retikju·l] liten pose av nett el. annet, som damer benytter som lomme, arbeidspose.
retina ['retinə] netthinne.
retinitis [reti'naitis] betennelse i netthinnen.
retinue [ri'tinju] klienter; følge, suite, sveit.
retire [ri'taiə] innfri (en veksel); trekke seg tilbake; fjerne seg; fortrekke, retirere; tre tilbake, gå av, ta sin avskjed, legge opp; vike tilbake.
retired [ri'taiəd] avsidesliggende, avsides, ensom; som har trukket seg tilbake, som lever av sine midler, avskjediget, avgått.
retirement [ri'taiəmənt] avgang, fratredelse; ensomhet, tilbaketrukkethet, tilfluktssted.
retiring [ri'tairiŋ] fratredende; tilbakeholden.
retort [ri'tå·°t] gi tilbake; svare, sende tilbake; gjengjelde; gjengjeld, svar på tiltale.

retort [ri'tå·ət] retorte, destillerkolbe.
retortion [ri'tå·əʃən] retorsjon, represalier.
retouch [ri'tʌtʃ] retusjere, bearbeide på ny.
retrace [ri(·)'treis] fare over igjen; følge tilbake, forfølge; — one's steps gå samme vei tilbake.
retract [ri'träkt] trekke tilbake; ta tilbake, tilbakekalle, ta i seg igjen; ta sine ord tilbake.
retractable [ri'träktəbl] som kan kalles tilbake.
retractation [ri'träk'teiʃən] tilbakekalling.
retractible [ri'träktibl] som kan trekkes tilbake.
retraction [ri'träkʃən] det å trekke tilbake.
retractive [ri'träktiv] tilbaketrekkende.
retranslate ['ri·trʌns'leit] oversette tilbake, oversette igjen.
retranslation ['ri·trʌns'leiʃən] oversettelse tilbake, fornyet oversettelse.
retreat [ri'tri·t] tilbaketog, tilbakegang; det å tre tilbake; tappenstrek; tilflukt, tilfluktssted; trekke seg tilbake; fjerne seg; beat the — slå retrett; sound the — blåse retrett.
retrench [ri'trenʃ] skjære bort; beskjære; innskrenke; innskrenke seg. retrenchment [-mənt] innskrenkning; begrensning; forskansning.
retribution [retri'bju·ʃən] gjengjeldelse; lønn.
retributive [ri'tribjutiv] gjengjeldende.
retributory [ri'tribjutəri] gjengjeldende.
retrievable [ri'tri·vəbl] gjenopprettelig; gjenerholdelig.
retrieval [ri'tri·vəl] det å finne igjen; gjenvinning; frelse, redning; gjenoppretting; erstatning.
retrieve [ri'tri·v] gjenfinne; gjenvinne; vinne inn igjen; gjenopprette; råde bot på; rette på, apportere.
retriever [ri'tri·və] gjenoppretter; støver, apportør.
retroactive [ri·tro'äktiv] tilbakevirkende.
retrogradation [ri·trogrə'deiʃən] tilbakegående bevegelse. retrograde ['retrogre·d] i tilbakegang; gå tilbake.
retrospekt ['ri·trospekt, 'ret-] se tilbake; tilbakeblikk. retrospective [-'spektiv] tilbakeseende; tilbakevirkende.
retroversion [ritro'və·ʃən] retroversjon, tilbakehelling (især av livmoren).
return [ri'tə·n] vende tilbake, snu, komme igjen; returnere; svare; bringe tilbake, innsende, sende tilbake; betale tilbake; betale, gjengjelde; melde tilbake; føre opp (i manntall); sende, velge (til parlamentet); tilbakevending, tilbakereise; tilbakekomst, hjemkomst; retur; tilbakelevering, returnering; betaling, remisse; gjengjeldelse, gjengjeld, erstatning; svar; (inn)beretning; valg; utbytte; — home vende hjem; — a gjengjelde en visitt; — thanks takke (bl. a. for maten, om bordbønn); — an answer gi et svar; — a verdict avgi en kjennelse; he was -ed for han ble valt til parlamentsmedlem for; in — til gjengjeld, som takk; by — of post omgående; many happy returns of the day til lykke med fødselsdagen.
returnable [ri'tə·nəbl] som kan leveres tilbake.
returner [ri'tə·nə] tilbakevender; remittent.
returning-officer valgstyrer.
return-ticket [ri'tə·n tikit] returbillett.
Reuben ['ru·bin] Ruben.
reunion ['ri·'ju·njən] gjenforening; møte.
reunite ['ri·ju'nait] gjenforene; komme sammen igjen.
Rev. fk. f. Revelation; reverend.
Revd. fk. f. reverend.
reveal [ri'vi·l] avsløre, åpenbare. revealable [-əbl] som kan avsløres.
revel ['revəl] svire, ture, rangle, holde leven, slå seg løs; kalas, turing, rangel; (i pluralis også:) moro.
revelant ['revilənt] som åpenbarer.
revelation [revi'leiʃən] avsløring, åpenbaring.
reveller ['revələ] svirebror, ranglepave.
revelry ['revəlri] turing, drikkelag, rangel.
revenge [ri'ven(d)ʒ] hevne; hevn; revansje;

— oneself upon el. be -d upon hevne seg på; have one's — få hevn; take — upon hevne seg på; give him his — gi ham revansje.
revengeful [ri'ven(d)ʒf(u)l] hevngjerrig.
revenue ['rəvinju] inntekt, inntekter. — -department finansdepartement. — -officer tollbetjent. — -vessel tollfartøy.
reverberate [ri'vəbəreit] kaste tilbake; kastes tilbake; gjenlyde, ljome.
reverberation[rivə·bə're·ʃən] gjenlyd, atterljom.
reverberatory [ri'və·bərətəri] tilbakekastende.
revere [ri'viə] hedre, ære, vøre, holde i ære.
reverence ['rev(ə)rəns] ærefrykt, ærbødighet, vørnad; reverens, kompliment; velærverdighet, ærverdighet; ære, ha ærbødighet for.
reverend ['rev(ə)rənd] ærverdig; the Rev. Amos Barton herr pastor Amos Barton; the Very Reverend hans høyærverdighet (om prost osv.); (the) Right Reverend hans høyærverdighet (om biskop); (the) Most Reverend (om erkebiskop).
reverent ['rev(ə)rənt] ærbødig; underdanig.
reverential [revə'renʃəl] ærbødig; full av ærefrykt.
reverie ['revəri] drømmerier, grubleri.
revers [ri'viə, ri'væə] oppslag, brett.
reversal [ri'və·səl] omstyrting, omstøting, forandring, omslag.
reverse [ri'və·s] dreie tilbake; vende om; snu opp ned på, forandre fullstendig; omstyrte, omstøte; motsatt side; motsetning, omslag; uhell, nederlag, motgang; bakside, revers; omvendt; reversing key strømskifter.
reversibility [ri'və·si'biliti] det å kunne vendes; omstøtelighet. reversible [ri'və·sibl] som kan vendes; omstøtelig.
reversion [ri'və·ʃən] det å vende tilbake, tilbakefall; atavisme; hjemfall; hjemfallsrett.
reversionary [ri'və·ʃən(ə)ri] hjemfalls-, arve-; senere tilfallende, framtidig; atavistisk; — annuity oppsatt livrente; overlevelsesrente.
revert [ri'və·t] vende om, snu, vende tilbake.
revertible [ri'və·tibl] som hjemfaller, faller tilbake.
revertive [ri'və·tiv] tilbakevendende, skiftende.
revet [ri'vet] kle (med murverk).
revetment [ri'vetmənt] bekledningsmur.
review [ri'vju·] gjennomgå, se gjennom, betrakte; mønstre; bedømme, anmelde; inspisere, holde mønstring over; tilbakeblikk; mønstring, betraktning, oversyn, gjennomsyn; bedømmelse, anmeldelse, melding; revy; magasin, tidsskrift.
reviewer [ri'vju·ə] anmelder; kritiker.
revile [ri'vail] forhåne, spotte, overfuse.
revisal [ri'vaizəl] gjennomsyn.
revise [ri'vaiz] se gjennom, lese gjennom; revidere; revisjon; the Revised Version den reviderte engelske bibeloversettelse (besørget 1870—1884).
reviser [ri'vaizə] korrekturleser; medutgiver av the Revised Version.
revision [ri'viʒən] gjennomsyn, korrektur.
revisit ['ri·'visit] besøke igjen; fornyet besøk.
revival [ri'vaivəl] gjenoppliving, gjenoppvekkelse; (religiøs) vekkelse; the — of learning (el. letters) renessansen.
revivalist [ri'vaivəlist] vekkelsespredikant.
revive [ri'vaiv] livne opp igjen, få nytt liv, kvikne til; våkne, frisk, få nytt liv i, gjenopplive, vekke.
reviver [ri'vaivə] gjenoppliver; oppstrammer.
revocability [revəkə'biliti] det å kunne tilbakekalles.
revocable ['revəkəbl] som kan tilbakekalles.
revocation [revo'keiʃən] oppheving.
revoke [ri'vo·k] tilbakekalle; oppheve, ikke følge farge (i kortspill); forsømmelse av å bekjenne farge; make a — ikke bekjenne farge.
revolt [ri'vo·lt] gjøre opprør; reise seg; protestere; jage på flukt; få til å gjøre opprør; opprøre; oppstand, revolte, opprør, reisning. revolted [-id] opprørsk; revolting [-iŋ] opprørende.

revolution [revə'l(j)u·ʃən] omgang, omdreining; revolusjon, omveltning. **revolutionary** [revə'l(j)u·ʃən(ə)ri] revolusjons-; revolusjonær.
revolutionist [revə'l(j)u·ʃənist] revolusjonsmann.
revolutionize [revə'l(j)u·ʃənaiz] revolusjonere.
revolve [ri'vålv] dreie seg, rotere; dreie om; overveie, tenke over. **revolving** [-iŋ] omdreiende, roterende; — **cannon** (el. **gun**) revolverkanon; — **light** blinkfyr.
revolver [ri'vålvə] revolver.
revulsion [ri'vʌlʃən] omslag, skifte.
revulsive [ri'vʌlsiv] avledende.
reward [ri'wå·ᵊd] gjengjelde; lønn; gjengjeld, belønning; erstatning; vederlag; **in** — **for** som belønning for.
rewardable [ri'wå·ᵊdəbl] belønning verd.
rewrite ['ri·'rait] skrive om igjen.
R. F. fk. f. **Royal Fusiliers.**
R. F. A. fk. f. **Royal Field Artillery.**
R. F. C. fk. f. **Royal Flying Corps.**
R. G. A. fk. f. **Royal Garrison Artillery.**
R. H. fk. f. **Royal Highlanders.**
R. H. A. fk. f. **Royal Horse Artillery.**
Rhenish ['reniʃ] rinsk; rinskvin.
rhetoric ['retərik] retorikk, talekunst.
rhetorical [ri'tårikl] retorisk.
rheum [ru·m] snue; slim.
rheumatic [ru'mätik] revmatisk; **rheumatics** revmatisme.
rheumaticky [ru'mätiki] (slang) revmatisk.
rheumatism ['ru·mətizm] revmatisme.
R. H. G. fk. f. **Royal Horse Guards.**
rhine [rain] vanngrav, grøft, veit.
Rhine [rain]; **the** — Rhinen.
rhinoceros [rai'nåsəràs] nesehorn.
Rhode Island [roᵘd'ailənd] Rhode Island.
Rhodes [roᵘdz] Rodos (øy og by); (Cecil) Rhodes.
Rhodesia [roᵘ'di·ʒiə] Rhodesia (i Sør-Afrika).
rhododendron [roᵘdə'dendrən] rhododendron, alperose.
rhomb [råm] rombe.
Rhone [roᵘn] Rhone.
rhubarb ['ru·ba·ᵊb] rabarbra.
rhumb [rʌm] kompass-strek, strek.
rhyme [raim] rim; vers, poesi; rime; sette på rim. **rhymeless** [-lès] rimfri. **rhymer** ['raimə] rimsmed. **rhymery** ['raim(ə)ri] rimeri. **rhyming** ['raimiŋ] rimende.
rhythm [riþm] rytme, takt.
rhytmic(al) ['riþmik(l)] rytmisk; taktfast.
R. I. fk. f. **Rhode Island.**
Rialto [ri'ältoᵘ] Rialto.
rib [rib] ribben, sideben; ribbe, spant; spile; forsyne med ribben; ribbe, danne med ribber.
ribald ['ribəld] gemen, rå, grov; råtamp.
ribaldry ['ribəldri] råskap; rått snakk.
riband ['ribənd] se **ribbon.**
ribbon ['ribən] bånd; remse, strimmel; sløyfe; pynte med bånd; stripe; **the blue** — Hosebåndsordenens ordensbånd; det blå bånd (avholdsmerke); **the Ribbon Society,** et hemmelig irsk samfunn; **torn to -s** revet i filler. **Ribbonism** ['ribənizm] prinsippene for the Ribbon Society.
R. I. C. fk. f. **Royal Irish Constabulary.**
rice [rais] ris. — **-flour** rismel. — **-milk** risvelling.
rich [ritʃ] rik; rikelig; fet (om mat).
Richard ['ritʃəd] Richard.
riches ['ritʃiz] rikdom, rikdommer.
richly ['ritʃli] rikelig; — **deserves it** fortjener det ærlig og redelig.
Richmond ['ritʃmənd] Richmond (by i Surrey).
richness ['ritʃnès] rikdom.
rick [rik] stakk, såte, høystakk, kornstakk; stakke.
rickets ['rikits] engelsk syke.
rickety ['rikiti] lealaus; skrøpelig.
rickshaw ['rikʃå·] rickshaw (lett, tohjulet japansk kjøretøy, trukket av menn).
rick-yard ['rikja·ᵊd] stakkplass, lodkve, lodgard.
ricochet ['rikəʃet] rikosjett; rikosjettere.
rid [rid] befri, frigjøre, kvitte; fri, befridd, uhindret; **be** — **of, get** — **of** bli kvitt. **riddance** ['ridəns] befrielse; **he is a good riddance** det er godt å bli kvitt ham.
ridden ['ridn] perf. pts. av **ride.**
riddle ['ridl] grovt såld; sikte, sælde; gjennomhulle.
riddle ['ridl] gåte; tale i gåter.
ride [raid] ri; kjøre; ligge til ankers; ri på; beherske, kue; ritt, ridetur; kjøretur; seiltur; ridevei; **bed-ridden** sengeliggende; **priest-ridden** under prestetyranni.
rideau [ri·'doᵘ] (terreng-) forhøyning.
rider ['raidə] ridende, rytter; berider(ske); tillegg, redaksjonell tilføyelse, hale; forlengelse, anhang; kjørende; passasjer.
ridge [ridʒ] rygg, høydedrag, ås, kam, rabbe; rev; drill (på åker); møne, takås; toppe seg, heve seg i rygger; pløye slik at det dannes rygger, hyppe, fure. **-hoe** hypp jern.
ridgy ['ridʒi] furet; rygget.
ridicule ['ridikju(·)l] latter, spott; latterliggjøring; spotte, latterliggjøre, gjøre narr av; **turn into** — spotte over; **hold up to** — gjøre latterlig.
ridiculous [ri'dikjuləs] latterlig. **ridiculousness** [-nəs] latterlighet.
riding ['raidiŋ] tredjedel (især av grevskapet Yorkshire).
riding ['raidiŋ] ridning; ridevei; ridende; ride-. — **-crop** ridepisk. — **-habit** ridedrakt (for damer). — **-hood** ridehette, ridekåpe; **Little Red R.** lille Rødhette. — **-horse** ridehest. — **-house** ridehus, manesje. — **-school** rideskole. — **-whip** ridepisk.
rife [raif] herskende, alminnelig; flus. **rifeness** [-nès] det å være vanlig, alminnelighet.
riffraff ['rifräf] søppel, rusk; pakk, utskudd.
rifle ['raifl] snappe bort; rane, røve; plyndre]
rifle ['raifl] rifle, (riflet) gevær; rifleskyttert skytter; rifle. — **-ball** riflekule. — **-club** skytterlag. — **-gun** rifle. — **-man** rifleskytter. — **-muske,** rifle. — **-pit** skyttergrav. — **-range** ['raifl're¹n(d)ʒ. skytebane. — **-team** skytterlag. **rifling** ['raifliŋ[rifling; plyndring, ran.
rift [rift] revne, rift; rive; risse; revne, kløvne.
rig [rig] rigge, rigge til; spjåke til, stase ut; rigg, takkelasje; utstyr, greier; redskaper.
rig [rig] puss, spikk, knep, list; **run a** — fare med fantestykker.
Riga ['ri·gə, 'raigə] Riga.
rigger ['rigə] rigger, takler; reimskive.
rigging ['rigiŋ] rigg, takkelasje; antrekk.
riggish ['rigiʃ] kåt, utsvevende.
right [rait] rett, bein; riktig; høyre; **all** — ganske riktig; i orden; klar, ferdig; (til en kusk) kjør vekk; ingen årsak (som svar på en unnskyldning); **be** — være riktig; ha rett; **come** — komme i orden; gå i orden; bli godt igjen; **make it** — klare det, greie det; **set** — sette i stand, rette; bringe på rett kjøl; **Mr. Dick sets us all** — hjelper oss alle til rette; **do** — **to every one** gjøre rett og skjel mot alle; — **and left** til høyre og venstre; — **away** straks; — **off** straks; **he could read anything** — **off** fra bladet; — **out** like fram, rent ut, endefram.
right [rait] rett, rettighet; atkomst; høyre side; høyre; rette, rettside; **by the** — **of the strongest** med den sterkestes rett; **it is yours by every** — med full rett; **be in the** — ha rett, ha retten på sin side; **in** — **of his wife** ved sitt giftermål; **if you come to the -s of it** når alt kommer til alt.
right [rait] rette; rette på; beriktige; skaffe rett; **see him -ed** skaffe ham rett.
rightabout ['raitə'baut]; **to the** — helt om; **face to the** — gjøre helt om; **send him to the** — vise ham døra, skysse på porten.
righteous ['raitʃəs] rettferdig, rettvis. **righteousness** [-nès] rettferdighet.

righter ['raitə] retter, beriktiger; forbedrer; beskytter, forsvarer.

rightful ['raitf(u)l] rettferdig, rettvis; rett; rettmessig, lovlig.

right-hand ['raithänd] høyre, på høyre side; — **man** høyre sidemann; høyre hånd (uunnværlig hjelper).

right-handed ['rait'händid] retthendt (motsatt keivhendt); som går til høyre; høyregjenget (om skrue).

right-hander ['raithändə] person som fortrinsvis benytter høyre hånd; slag med høyre hånd.

right-hearted ['rait'ha·ətid] rettsindig.

right-lined ['raitlaind] rettlinjet.

rightly ['raitli] rett, med rette.

rightness ['raitnès] rettskaffenhet, riktighet.

rigid ['ridʒid] stiv, hard, streng.

rigidity [ri'dʒiditi] stivhet, strenghet.

rigmarole ['rigmərouᵘl] forvirret sludder, vas, skravl.

rigor ['raigå·ə] stivhet; — **mortis** dødsstivhet.

rigorism ['rigərizm] stivhet, strenghet.

rigorist ['rigərist] rigorist, streng mann.

rigorous ['ᵘigərəs] streng, hard. **-ness** [-nès] strenghet, skarphet.

rigour ['rigə] stivhet; strenghet, hardhet.

rig-out ['rig(')aut] utstyr, antrekk.

rile [rail] ergre.

rill [ril] liten bekk, småbekk.

rim [rim] rand, kant; innfatning, felg, ring, brilleinnfatning; kante, rande; innfatte.

rime [raim] rim; rimfrost; rime; dekke med rim.

rime [raim] = **rhyme**.

rimple ['rimpl] rynke, kruse; kruse seg.

rimy ['raimi] rimfrossen, rimet.

rind [raind] bark, skall, skorpe, svor.

rinderpest ['rindəpest] kvegpest, busott.

ring [riŋ] ring; bane, veddeløpsbane; sportsplass, kampplass; arena, manesje; omgi med en ring, slå ring om; forsyne med en ring; omfatte; ringe.

ring [riŋ] la lyde, varsle med ringing, ringe med; ringe på; ringe; klinge, kime, ljome, lyde; gjenlyde, runge; — **false** lyde en uekte klang; — **for** ringe på, ringe etter; — **out** lyde, ringe.

ring [riŋ] klang, lyd, ljom, ringing; gjenlyd; atterljom; klokkespill; tonefall. **ringer** ['riŋə] ringer. **ringing** ['riŋiŋ] ringende, klingende; ringing.

ringleader ['riŋli·də] anfører, hovedmann.

ringlet ['riŋlèt] liten ring; lokk, krølle.

ring-lock ['riŋlåk] ringlås, bokstavlås.

ring-mail ['riŋmeⁱl] ringbrynje. — **-ouzel** ringtrost.

ringworm ['riŋwə·m] ringorm.

rink [riŋk] bane; kunstig skøytebane, innendørs skøytebane, rulleskøytebane.

rinse [rins] skylle; skylling.

rinsing ['rinsiŋ] skylling; skyllvann.

riot ['raiət] tøylesløshet, tumult, ståhei; opptøyer; leven, røre, oppløp; larme, tumle vilt; bråke, svire, leve vilt, ture, rangle; vekke oppløp, lage bråk, få til oppløp; **run** — løpe grassat; vokse i overdådig frodighet. — **-act** opprørslov.

rioter ['raiətə] fredsforstyrrer; opprører; utsvevende person, ranglefant.

riotous ['raiətəs] tøylesløs, opprørsk.

rip [rip] sprette, rive; sprette opp; revne, rakne, sprekke; gå opp; rift, spjære.

R. I. P. fk. f. **Requiescat in pace** hvil i fred.

riparian [rai'pæ·əriən] som hører til en elvebredd, elve-, strand-; — **rights** strandrettigheter.

ripe [raip] moden, fullvoksen.

ripen ['raipn] modne, bli moden; utvikle seg.

ripeness ['raipnès] modenhet.

ripening ['raipniŋ] modning.

ripper ['raipə] oppspretter; kjernekar.

ripping ['ripiŋ] makeløs, storartet, framifrå, gild, utrolig, svært.

ripple ['ripl] hekle (lin).

ripple ['ripl] kruse seg; skvulpe; risle, sildre; kruse; krusning; skvulping, risling.

ripply ['ripli] kruset; skvulpende; bølgende.

rise [raiz] heve seg; stige; reise seg; avslutte møtet; ta ferier; komme opp; stå opp; oppstå; avansere, komme fram; løfte seg, gå, æse (om deig); heve, slutte beleiringen; svulme opp, svelle, trutne; sette seg opp imot, gjøre oppstand; sprette; tilta; stigning; utspring, opprinnelse, opphav; det å tilta, vekst, oppgang, solrenning; bakke, høyde, høgd; **give** — **to** gi anledning til; **be on the** — være i oppgang; **rising** ['raiziŋ] stigende; oppgående; tiltagende; stigning; oppgang; reisning, opprør; oppstandelse; hevelse.

risibility[rizi'biliti]lattermildhet.**risible**['rizibl] lattermild; latter-.

risk [risk] våge, risikere, utsette for fare, sette på spill; risiko, fare.

riskful ['riskf(u)l] vågelig, vågal, farlig, risikabel.

rite [rait] ritus, kirkeskikk; seremoni.

ritual ['ritjuəl] rituell, som hører til gudstjenesten; ritual; kirkeskikker.

rival ['raivl] rival, medbeiler, rivalinne; rivaliserende; rivalisere med; kappes med, tevle med. **rivalry** ['raivlri] rivalisering; konkurranse kappestrid, tevling.

rive [raiv] kløyve, splitte; kløvne, revne; kløft.

river ['rivə] elv, å, flod. — **-bank** elvebredd. — **-basin** [-be'sn] flodbekken. — **-bed** elvefar. — **-craft** elvefartøy.

riverside ['rivəsaid] elvebredd; **by the** — ved elva.

rivet ['rivit] klinknagle; nitte, klinke, nagle; befeste; fastholde, feste.

rivulet ['rivjulèt] bekk, å.

R. L. S. fk. f. **Robert Louis Stevenson.**

R. M. fk. f. **resident magistrate**; **royal mail;**

Royal Marines.

R. M. A. fk. f. **Royal Marine Artillery; Royal Military Academy.**

R. M. C. fk. f. **Royal Military College.**

R. M. L. I. fk. f. **Royal Marine Light Infantry.**

R. M. S. fk. f. **royal mail steamer.**

R. M. S. P. fk. f. **Royal Mail Steampacket Co.**

R. N. fk. f. **Royal Navy.**

R. N. A. S. fk. f. **Royal Naval Air Service.**

roach [rouᵗʃ] kot, mort, sørenne (ferskvannsfisk).

road [rouᵈ] vei, landevei, kjørevei; gate; red; **the -s are bad** føret er dårlig; **take the** — bli landeveisrøver; **rule of the** — trafikkregler, styringsregler; **the high** — alfarvei; den brede vei. — **-agent** ['rouᵈe'dʒənt] stratenrøver. — **-drift** landeveisstøv.

road-hog ['rouᵈhåg] bilbølle, råkjører.

road-making veianlegg.

roads [rouᵈz] red.

roadside veikant; **by the** — ved veikanten.

roadsted ['rouᵈsted] red.

roadster ['rouᵈstə] skip på reden; landeveishest, skyssest; landeveissykkel, landeveismaskin, sykkel, øvet kjører.

roadway ['rouᵈwey] kjørebane, veibane, gate.

roam [rouᵐ] vandre om, streife om, flakke om, dra omkring; gjennomstreife.

roamer ['rouᵐə] omstreifende person; vagabond.

roan [rouᵐ] rødskimlet; rødskimmel.

roan [rouᵐ] saueskinn garvet med sumak og brukt til bokbind; saffianlær.

roan-tree ['rouᵐntri·] rogn (tre).

roar [rå·ə] brøle, belje, bure, skrike, vræle, rope, gaule; larme, bruse, dure, buldre; brøl, vræl, brøling; skrik; brus, dur; brak, dunder, larm.

roarer ['rå·rə] brøler, buldrer.

roaring ['rå·riŋ] brøl; brølende; uordentlig, tøylesløs, vill; **do a** — **business** gjøre glimrende

forretninger; — **drunk** sprøytefull; **the** — **forties** det stormfulle belte 40—50° nordlig bredde av Atlanterhavet og 40—50° sørlig bredde av Atlanteri.avet, Stillehavet og Det indiske hav.
roast [roust] steke (på rist el. spidd); brenne; riste; stekes; spotte; stekt; stek; — **beef** oksestek; — **leg of pork** grisestek, skinkestek.
roaster ['rousta] steker; stekerist.
roasting ['roustiŋ] steking. — **-jack** stekevender.
rob [råb] røve; plyndre; stjele fra; plyndre ut.
robber ['råbə] røver, tyv, ransmann.
robbery ['råbəri] utplyndring, tyveri, ran.
robe [roub] galladrakt, embetsdrakt, habitt, robe; kle, ta på; iføre; **gentlemen of the long** — sakførere, sakførerstand, rettslærde, advokater.
Robert ['råbət] Robert; polis.
robin ['råbin] rødstrupe, rødkjelke. — **-good-fellow** nisse. — **-redbreast** rødstrupe, rødkjelke.
roborant ['råbərənt] styrkende; styrkemiddel.
Robt. fk. f. Robert.
robust [ro'bʌst] kjernefrisk, sterk, traust, kraftig. **robustness** [-nés] kjernesunnhet; kraft.
roc [råk] rokk (kjempemessig fugl i orientalske eventyr).
Rochdale ['råtʃdeil] Rochdale.
Rochester ['råtʃistə] Rochester.
rochet ['råtʃit] messeserk.
rock [råk] kokkehode, håndtein, rokk.
rock [råk] vugge, vogge, rugge, gynge; vugging; — **to sleep** vugge i søvn; **-ed by the waves** vugget av bølgene.
rock [råk] klippe, berg, fjell; skjær, båe, flu.
rocker ['råkə] gyngestol; gyngehest; vugge, vogge; vuggemei.
rockery ['råkəri] steinhaug, steinparti (i hage).
rocket ['råkit] dagfiol; nattfiol.
rocket ['råkit] rakett.
rockiness ['råkinés] berglende.
rocking-chair ['råkiŋtʃæ·ə] gyngestol.
rocking-horse ['råkiŋhå·əs] gyngehest.
rocky ['råki] bergfull, berglendt; hard som fjell; **Rocky Mountains** el. **Rockies** fjellkjede i Nord-Amerika.
rococo [rå'kou'kou] rokokko.
rod [råd] kjepp, stav, påk; stang; målestang; fiskestang; lastokk, latein; visker (til kanon); lynavleder; embetsstav; **black** — kongelig overseremonimester, embetsmann i overhuset med svart embetsstav; **have a — in pickle for** ha en grundig avstraffelse i beredskap for; **kiss the** — kysse riset; **make a — for one's own back** lage ris til sin egen bak.
rode [roud] imperf. av **ride.**
rodent ['roudənt] gnager (dyreart).
rodomontade [rådə'månte'd] kyt, skryt; skryte.
roe [rou] rogn; (hos fisk); **hard** — rogn; **soft** — melke (hos hanfisk).
roe [rou] rådyr; hind. **-buck** råbukk. — **-calf** råkalv.
Roehampton [rou'hämtən] forstad til London.
rogation [ro'gei'ʃən] bønn; lovframlegg (i Rom); — **-days** de tre dager like før Kristi himmelfartsdag; **Rogation Sunday** femte søndag etter påske; **Rogation week** himmelfartsuken.
Roger ['rådʒə] Roger; **Sir R. de Coverley** navnet på en godseier i Addisons «Spectator»; en dans.
rogue [roug] landstryker; skøyer, skjelm, kjeltring. **roguery** ['rou'g(ə)ri] kjeltringstreker; skjelmsstykker, skøyerstreker. **roguish** ['rougiʃ] kjeltringaktig; skøyeraktig.
roister ['roistə] larme, bråke, holde leven. **roisterer** ['roistərə] bråker, villstyring; svirebror.
role [roul] rolle.
roll [roul] rulle, trille, rulle sammen; tulle inn, pakke inn; valse, kjevle; slå trommehvirvler; gå rundt; rulle, trille av sted; rulling, slingring; rulle; rull; valse; liste, fortegnelse, protokoll, rulleblad; hvirvelslag; rundstykke; (i fl.) arkiv; — **one's**

eyes rulle med øynene; — **down** brette ned; — **on** rinne bort, lide, li (om tid); — **up** brette opp; **be on the -s** stå i rullene; **put on the -s** føre inn i rullene.
rollable ['roulabl] som kan valses.
roll-call ['roulkå·l] navneopprop.
roller ['roulə] rulle; valse; tromle, kjevle; forbinding, rullebindsel; (svær) bølge, rullesjø.
roller-skate rulleskøyte. **rollertowel** håndkle som går på en rulle.
rollick ['rålik] slentre sorgløst omkring; leve glade dager, tumle seg. **rollicking** ['rålikiŋ] lystig, glad; morsom, kåt.
rolling ['rouliŋ] rullende; bølgeformig; rulling; valsing. — **-chair** rullestol. — **-plant** el. **-stock** rullende materiell (på jernbane).
roly-poly ['rouli'pou'li] innbakt frukt; rund, liten og tykk; et slags ballspill.
Romaic [ro'mei·ik] nygresk.
Roman ['roumən] romersk; romersk-katolsk; romer; romerinne; — (el. **roman**) **letters** (el. **type**) antikva.
romance [ro'mäns] romansk.
romance [ro'mäns] romanse, ballade, (fantastisk) roman; oppdikting, løgn, fabel, skrøne; romantikk; skrive romaner; lyve, prime. **romancer** [-ə] romandikter; løgner.
Romanesque [roumə'nesk] rundbuestil; bygd i rundbuestil.
Romanic [ro'mänik] romansk.
Romanish ['rouməniʃ] romersk-katolsk. **romanism** [-nizm] katolisisme. **Romanist** [-nist] romersk katolsk. **romanize** [-naiz] romanisere.
Romansch [ro'mänʃ] reto-romansk (i Sveits).
romantic [ro'mäntik] romantisk, romantisk; fabelaktig, fantastisk. **romanticism** [-tisizm] romantikk. **romanticist** [-tisist] romantiker.
Romany ['råməni] sigøyner; sigøynerspråk.
Rome [roum] Rom.
Romeo ['rou'mio·] Romeo.
Romish ['roumiʃ] (romersk-)katolsk.
Romney ['råmni] Romney.
Romola ['råmələ] Romola.
romp [råmp] villkat, villstyring, galneheie; ståk, stim; boltre seg, tumle seg, stime, hoppe, danse. **romping** [-iŋ] overgiven. **rompish** ['råmpiʃ] overgiven, vill av seg, kåt.
Röntgen ['røntjən, 'råntjən] Røntgen; — **rays** røntgenstråler. **röntgenogram** ['rʌntjənogräm] røntgenfotografi.
rood [ru·d] kors, krusifiks.
roof [ru·f, ruf] tak; hvelving; bygge tak over; — **of the mouth** (den ha·rde) gane.
roofing ['ru·fiŋ] takmateriale; takverk, tak.
roofing-paper takpapp. **roofless** ['ru·flès] uten tak; husvill. **roofy** ['ru·fi] med tak.
rook [ruk] tårn (i sjakk).
rook [ruk] blåkråke; snyte (i spill).
rookery ['ru·k(ə)ri] kråkelund; fuglevær; fattig og overbefolket kvarter el. hus, røverreir.
room [ru·m, rum] rom, plass, sted, værelse, stue; anledning, grunn, leilighet, høve; ha værelse; bo; **keep his** — holde seg inne; **in the** — **of** istedenfor; **in his** — i hans sted.
roomless ['ru(·)mlès] uten værelser.
roomy ['ru·mi] romslig; med mange værelser.
roost [ru·st] vagle, pinne, vinge (til å sitte på); hvilested; overnattelse, seng; sette seg til hvile; vagle seg; ha køyet seg; **go to** — gå til ro, gå til køys; **at** — sovende.
rooster ['ru·stə] hane.
root [ru·t] rot; løk, blomsterløk, knoll; feste rot, slå rot; rotfeste; **take** — el. **strike** — slå rot; **pull up by the roots** rykke opp med rota; **and branch** grundig, med rota. **square** — el. **second** — kvadratrot.
root [ru·t] rote (i jorda); rote i.

root-and-branch ['ru·tən'bra·nʃ] grundig.
rooted ['ru·tid] rotfestet; rotfast; inngrodd.
rooter ['ru·tə] rothogger, utrydder. **rootless**
['ru·tlès] rotløs. **rootlet** [-lèt] liten rot. **rooty**
['ru·ti] full av røtter.

rope [ro⁾p] reip, tau, line, strikke, snor; knippe;
tøye seg ut i tråder, være seig; binde med reip,
slå tau om; binde, tjore, fange; hale, trekke
ascend the high -s sette seg på den høye hest.—
-dancer linedanser. — **-end** tamp. **-ladder** tau-
stige. — **-maker** reipslager. **-making** reipslageri.
roper ['ro⁾pə] reipslager.
ropery ['ro⁾p(ə)ri] reperbane.
rope's-end ['ro⁾ps'end] tau; tamp.
rope-walk ['ro⁾pwå·k] reperbane. **ropily** ['ro⁾-
pili] trådaktig, seigt. **ropiness** ['ro⁾pinés] seighet.
ropy ['ro⁾pi] klebrig, seig, tyktflytende.
rorqual ['rå·⁰kwəl] finnhval, rørhval.
Rosa ['ro⁾zə] Rosa.
Rosalind ['rázəlind] Rosalinde.
rosary ['rouzəri] rosenkrans; rosebed.
rose [ro⁾z] rose; rosa; rosett; rosen (sykdom);
gjøre rosenrød. — **-bud** rosenknopp. — **-bush**
rosenbusk. — **-colour** ['ro⁾z'kʌlə] rosenfarge,
rosa. — **-mallow** stokkrose.
rosemary ['ro⁾zməri] rosmarin (buskvekst).
roseola [ro'ziələ] røde hunder.
rosette [ro'zet] rosett.
rose-water ['ro⁾zwå·tə] rosenvann (slags rosen-
parfyme); søtlatenhet, blidhet; søtladen, altfor
fin.
rosied ['rᵓᵓzid] smykket med roser, rosenfarget.
rosin ['ràzin] harpiks.
rosiness ['ro⁾zinés] rosenfarge.
rosy ['ro⁾zi] rosen-; blomstrende.
rot [råt] råtne; vase, sludre, vrøvle, tøve;
bringe i forråtnelse; forråtnelse; vas, sludder.
rota ['ro⁾tə] liste.
rotary ['ro⁾təri] roterende, omdreiende; dreie-;
Rotary Club, et selskap med internasjonale men-
neskekjærlige formål.
rotate ['ro⁾te't] rotere, dreie seg, snu, svive;
skifte, veksle; gå etter tur; la rotere, la gå rundt.
rotation [ro'te'ʃən] rotasjon; omgang; **by** —
skiftevis; — **of crops** vekselbruk.
rotator [ro'te'tə] omdreiende redskap; dreie-
muskel; svingrør.
rotatory ['ro⁾tətəri] roterende, omdreiende.
rote [ro⁾t] rams; **by** — på rams, på pugg.
Rothschild ['råþtʃaild, 'råstʃaild] Rothschild.
rotten ['råtn] råtten, bedervet, skjemt; dårlig;
morken; skjør; svak, skrøpelig, elendig. **rottenness**
[-nés] råttenskap.
Rotten-Row ['råtn'ro⁾] vei i Hyde Park.
rotter ['råtə] døgenikt.
rotund [ro'tʌnd] rund. **rotundity** [ro'tʌnditi],
rotundness [ro'tʌndnés] rundhet.
rouble ['ru·bl] rubel.
rouge [ru·ʒ] rød; sminke; sminke seg; sminke.
rouge-et-noir ['ru·ʒe'¹nwa·⁹] rouge-et-noir (et
hasardspill).
rough [rʌf] ujevn, ujamn, ru; knudret, uveisom, humpet, steinet; uslepet, utilhogd; uferdig;
opprørt (hav); hardt (vær); stormende, urolig; rå,
uvøren; barsk; grov, simpel; grovkornet; hardhendt; lurvet, ragget, bustet; tarvelig; omtrentlig, løselig, opprinnelig, primitiv; naiv, likefrem,
ukunstlet; djerv; hard, skarp; skurrende, skjærende, ubehagelig; uvennlig; mattslipe; skarpsko
(hest); fare rått fram; — **copy** kladd; — **materials**
råmaterialer; — **plan** løst henkastet skisse; **at a**
— **estimate** etter et løselig overslag; **a** — **voyage**
en hard overreise; **in the** — i uferdig tilstand;
i råstoffet; — **it** tåle strabaser; ta til takke med
simpel kost; gå for lut og kaldt vann.
rough-and-ready ['rʌfən'redi] formløs; improvisert; klar til bruk, parat i øyeblikket, likesæl.
rough-and-tumble ['rʌfən'tʌmbl] vill, ustyrlig.
rough|-cast ['rʌfka·st] skissere; gjøre et rått
utkast; rappe, kalkslå; rått utkast; rapping.

— **-draft** konsipere. — **-draw** gjøre et løst utkast
til, skissere.
roughen ['rʌfn] gjøre ujevn; bli ujevn.
roughish ['rʌfiʃ] ujevn av seg.
roughness ['rʌfnés] ujevnhet, ruhet; opprør;
barskhet; råhet; skarphet; heftighet.
rough-rider ['rʌfraidə] hestetemmer; uvøren
rytter; irregulær kavalerist.
roulade [ru·'la·d] roulade (hurtig rekke toner).
rouleau [ru·'lo⁾] rull; pengerull.
roulette [ru·'let] rulette (hasardspill).
Roumania [ru'me·nja] Romania.
Roumanian [ru'me·njən] rumen, rumensk.
round [raund] rund, lubben; hel; omfattende,
betydelig, dugelig, kraftig, stor, avrundet; åpen,
oppriktig, likefrem, ærlig; rundt om, omkring,
om; overalt; krets, sirkel, runding, runde, skive,
ring; kule; rekke, kretsløp; runddans; omgang;
rundsang; salve, glatt lag; gjøre rund, runde,
avrunde; omgi, gå rundt om, svinge; **all the year**
— hele året rundt; **come** — komme seg; bli
omstemt; **come** — **to his way of thinking** la
seg omstemme av ham; **to** — **the corner** dreie
om hjørnet.
round [raund] hviske; hvisking.
round-about ['raundəbaut] omvankende; omstendelig; omfattende; rundt omkring; karusell;
overfrakke; rundrygget lenestol; runddans; **a** —
way en omvei.
roundelay ['raundile'] rundsang, runddans.
round|head ['raundhed] rundhode, puritaner.
— **-house** politiarrest; hytte (på seilskip).
roundish ['raundiʃ] rundaktig.
roundlet ['raundlet] liten sirkel.
roundness ['raundnés] rundhet; runding; likefremhet; raskhet.
round-trip-ticket (amr.) returbillett.
rouse [rauz] vekke, vekke opp; oppmuntre;
jage opp; våkne opp, bli våken; fullt glass; gilde,
kalas, drikkelag. **rouser** ['rauzə] en som vekker.
rout [raut] stort selskap; sverm; hop, flokk;
oppløp; nederlag; det å slå på flukt, vill flukt;
kaste på flukt; **put to** — jage på flukt.
route [ru·t] vei, rute.
routine [ru·'ti·n] alminnelige forretninger, for-
retningsgang; ferdighet, øvelse, øving, rutine.
rove [ro⁾v] streife om, vandre om; gjennomstreife. **rover** ['ro⁾və] flakker, vandrer, landstryker; røver, pirat; ustadig menneske. **roving**
['ro⁾viŋ] omflakkende, omstreifende; streifing.
row [ro⁾] rad, rekke; husrekke, gate.
row [rau] spetakkel, tumult, opptøyer, strid,
trette, slagsmål, ståk, bråk; gjøre opptøyer,
larme, ståke; **kick up a** — gjøre bråk (eller vrøvl).
row [ro⁾] ro; roning; rotur.
rowdy ['raudi] brutal, grov, voldsom; slusk,
slamp.
rower ['ro⁾ə] roer.
rowlock ['rʌlək; 'ro⁾låk] tollegang; åregaffel,
keip.
royal ['roiəl] kongelig, konge-; — **academy**
kongelig kunstakademi; **Royal Society** Det kongelige vitenskapenes selskap.
royalist ['roiəlist] rojalistisk, kongeligsinnet;
rojalist.
royalty ['roiəlti] kongelighet; kongeverdighet;
kongedømme; konge, majestet; kongelig rettighet; avgift, leie, tantieme, prosenter, forfatter-
honorar.
R. S. O. fk. f. **Railway sub-office.**
R. S. P. C. A. fk. f. **Royal Society for Prevention of Cruelty to Animals.**
R. S. V. P. fk. f. répondez s'il vous plaît svar
utbes.
Rt. Hon. fk. f. **right honourable.**
Rt. Rev. fk. f. **right reverend.**
R. T. S. fk. f. **Religious Tract Society.**
rub [rʌb] gni, gnikke, rive, skure, skrubbe,
viske, stryke, skrape, slipe, pusse; hamre inn;
gnage på; skure imot, gni seg mot, skubbe seg;

gnidning, ujevnhet, friksjon, hindring, vanskelighet, knute; — down frottere; strigle; — elbows (eller shoulders) with være gode venner med.

rubber ['rʌbə] en som gnir, massør, frotterhåndkle; pussefille, skureredskap; viskelær; robbert (i kortspill); strid, kamp, motgang.

rubbing ['rʌbiŋ] gnidning.

rubbish ['rʌbiʃ] avfall, boss, søppel, grus, murgrus; fyll, skrammel, rask, skrot, rot; røre; sludder, vas, vev; talk — sludre, vrøvle. rubbishing ['rʌbiʃiŋ] avfalls-; skrap-.

rubble ['rʌbl] murbrokker; brottstein, naturstein.

rubble -wall, — -work kampesteinsmur.

rubby ['rʌbi] ru, skrubbet.

rubescence [ru'besəns] rødming; rødme.

rubescent [ru'besənt] rødmende, rødlig.

Rubicon ['ru·bikån] Rubikon; cross (el. pass) the — ta det avgjørende skritt.

rubicund ['ru·bikənd] rød, rødlig, rødlett, rødmusset.

rubicundity [ru'bi·kʌnditi] rødme.

rubric ['ru·brik] merkt eller skrevet med rødt; rubrikk; rød overskrift; tittel; (liturgisk) forskrift; rød; rubrisert; rituell.

rubricate ['ru·brike't] merke med rødt; rubrisere; fastsette, fastslå.

ruby ['ru·bi] rubin; rød kveise; blod (i bokserspråket); slags liten skrift (typografisk).

ruck [rʌk] rynke; krølle; folde; rynke; fold; haug, hop.

ruction ['rʌkʃən] urolighet, mudder, vrøvl.

rud [rʌd] rødhet, rødme; rødkritt, rød oker.

rudder ['rʌdə] ror.

ruddle ['rʌdl] rødkritt.

ruddy ['rʌdi] rød, rødlett, rødmusset.

rude [ru·d] primitiv, rå, plump, upolert, simpel, grov; uvitende; udannet, uoppdragen, ubehøvlet; uhøflig, barsk, heftig, ubarmhjertig; ukunstlet. rudeness [-nés] råhet, grovhet, plumphet, uhøflighet; uvitenhet; heftighet.

rudiment ['ru·dimənt] grunnlag, begynnelse. rudimental [ru·di'mentəl] begynnelses-, rudimentær. rudimentary [-'mentəri] = rudimental.

Rudyard ['rʌdjɑ] Rudyard.

rue [ru·] angre, trege på; ynkes over, sørge (for over).

rue [ru·] rute (plante; sorgens symbol).

rueful ['ru·f(u)l] bedrøvelig, sorgfull, sørgelig.

ruff [rʌf] pipestrimmel, pipekrave, kruset halskrave; fjærboa; brushane; kruse, pjuske.

ruffian ['rʌfjən] brutal person, banditt, skurk, røver; brutal, rå, røver-.

ruffianism ['rʌfjənizm] råskap, bandittvesen.

ruffle ['rʌfl] folde, rynke, kruse, pipe; besette med rynkede mansjetter; sette i bevegelse, opprøre; bringe i uorden, sette i ulag, bringe ut av likevekt; plage, erte, terge; pjuske; ruske; bruse, kruse seg, opprøres, bli opprørt; strimmel, rynket mansjett, kalvekryss; sammenstøt, fektning, kamp, strid; forstyrrelse, opphisselse; dempet trommehvirvel.

ruffler ['rʌflə] storskryter; fredsforstyrrer.

rug [rʌg] grovt, ullent teppe; dekken; reiseteppe, kaminteppe, rye, sengeforlegger.

Rugby ['rʌgbi] Rugby; rugbyfotball.

rugged ['rʌgid] ru, ujevn, ujamn; knortet, knudret, klumpet, kantet; kupert; strihåret; barsk, hard, gretten, sur, uvennlig.

rugose ['ru·gous], rugous ['ru·gəs] rynket.

ruin ['ru·in] fall, ruin, undergang, ødeleggelse; ruinere, forspille, ødelegge, gjøre ulykkelig, styrte i fordervelse.

ruination [ru·i'ne'ʃən] ødeleggelse.

ruined ['ru·ind] som er falt ned, som ligger i ruiner; ruinert, ødelagt.

ruinous ['ru·inəs] ødeleggende, fordervelig; forfallen, falleferdig, brøstfeldig.

rule [ru·l] regjering, herredømme, styre; regel, forskrift; ordensregel; linjal, tommestokk; orden,

god oppførsel; regjere, beherske, styre; bestemme; forsyne med linjer, linjere; herske; — of three reguladetri.

ruler ['ru·lə] regent, hersker; styrer; bestyrer; linjal.

ruling ['ru·liŋ] herskende.

rum [rʌm] rom (slags brennevin).

rum [rʌm] pussig; merkelig, snodig.

Rumania [ru'me'njə] Romania.

Rumanian [ru'me'njən] rumen; rumensk.

rumble ['rʌmbl] rumle, buldre, ramle, skrangle; drønne; rumling; baksete, tjenersete.

rumbler ['rʌmblə] noe som ramler; drosje.

ruminant ['ru·minənt] drøvtygger.

ruminate ['ru·mine't] tygge drøv, jorte; gruble, tenke; ruge; tygge, tenke på, tenke over.

rumination [ru·mi'ne'ʃən] jorting; drøvtygging.

ruminator ['ru·mine'tə] grubler, grublende.

rummage ['rʌmidʒ] grundig ettersyn, visitasjon; romstering; vistere, se etter i; lete gjennom; se etter, romstere, rote.

rummage-sale oppryddingsauksjon; auksjon over uavhentede saker.

rummy ['rʌmi] pussig, snodig.

rummy ['rʌmi] rom-.

rumour ['ru·mə] rykte, folkesnakk; bære utover, spre ut; it is -ed man sier, det går det ord.

rump [rʌmp] bakende, rumpe; kryss, korsben, lend, lårstykke; gump; (sjelden:) slump, rest; vende ryggen, ignorere, overse; the — (Parliament) Rumpparlamentet, under Cromwell.

rumple ['rʌmpl] krølle, skrukke, ruske.

rumply ['rʌmpli] forkrøllet.

rump-steak ['rʌmpste'k] mørbrad.

run [rʌn] renne, springe, løpe, svive; renne, flyte, strømme; væske; gå, oppføres, spilles; smelte, bråne; strekke seg; lyde; løpe sammen, blande seg, løpe ut; la løpe, løpe om kapp med; kjøre, støte, jage; drive (fabrikk, maskin); gå i rute, gå i fart; bills having twelve months to — med tolv måneders løpetid; — cold stivne; — mad bli gal; it -s in the family det ligger til familien; — into debt stifte gjeld; their income -s into four figures deres inntekter må skrives med fire sifrer, beløper seg til et tusen pund sterling og mer.

run [rʌn] løp, renn, gang; ferd, framgangsmåte; popularitet, kurs; suksess, antall oppførelser; tilløp; sterk etterspørsel; avsetning, rift; kappløp; panikk; storm; fart, tur, reise; overfart, overreise; fri adgang; have a — of a hundred nights oppføres hundre ganger; in the long — i lengden; out of the common — utenfor det alminnelige.

runabout ['rʌnəbaut] omstreifer.

runagate ['rʌnəgⁱt] flyktning; renegat.

runaway ['rʌnəwe'] bortløpen; flyktning, rømling.

rune [ru·n] rune.

rung [rʌŋ] imperf. og perf. pts. av ring.

rung [rʌŋ] trin (på stige), sprosse, tverrtre, eike (i hjul).

runic ['ru·nik] rune-, beskrevet med runer; — wand runestav; — characters (el. letters) runer.

runnel ['rʌnəl] småbekk; rennestein.

runner ['rʌnə] løper, agent; (gl.) politifunksjonær; matros som har betaling for reisen, ikke månedshyre; smugler, blokadebryter; løper, oversten (i kvern); drivhjul; sledemei; utløper, renning (på plante); pralbønne; skyter (på paraply).

running ['rʌniŋ] veddeløps-; hurtigseilende; uavbrutt; løpende, i trekk, i sammenheng, på rad; skyndsom, snøgg, flytende, lett; rynkning; løp, kappløp, utholdenhet. — -bowline løpestikk (skipsuttrykk). — -days lossedager. — -knot rennknute. — -match kappløp, veddeløp.

Runnymede ['rʌnimi·d] Runnymede (stedsnavn).

rupee ['ru·pi·] rupi ostindisk sølvmynt.
rupture ['rʌptʃə] sprengning, opphevelse; brudd; (underlivs-)brokk, slit, sprenge, få til å briste; briste, brotne.
rural ['ruərəl] landlig, land-, landsens. **ruralism** ['ruərəlizm] landlighet, **ruralist** [-ist] en som lever et landsens liv; landligger. **rurality** [ru'räliti] landlighet. **ruralize** ['ruərəlaiz] gjøre landlig, blir landlig. **ruralness** ['ruərəlnés] landlighet.
ruse [ru·z] list, knep.
rush [rʌʃ] siv.
rush [rʌʃ] fare av sted, styrte, storme, ruse; framstyrting, framrusing, jag; stormende angrep.
rush-candle el. **rush-light** (gml.) talglys, dåse, pråss; nattlys.
rushy ['rʌʃi] sivbevokst; siv-.
rusk [rʌsk] slags kavring.
Ruskin ['rʌskin] Ruskin.
Russell ['rʌsl] Russell.
russet ['rʌsit] rødbrun; grov, simpel, hjemmegjort; vadmels-; hjemmegjorte klær.
Russia ['rʌʃə] Russland; russlær.
Russian ['rʌʃən] russisk, russer; — **leather** russlær.
rust [rʌst] rust; brann (på korn); sløvhet; ruste; sløves; gjøre rusten; — **colour** rustfarge.
rustic ['rʌstik] landlig, landsens, lands-;

bondsk, grov, plump, rå, ukunstlet. likefram, endefram, enkel, ærlig, enfoldig; simpel; bonde, **rusticalness** ['rʌstiklnés[landlighet; simpelhet.
rusticate ['rʌstike·t] bo på landet, sende på landet; relegere fra universitetet. **rustication** [rʌsti'ke·ʃən] opphold på landet; bortvising.
rusticise ['rʌstisaiz] rustifisere.
rusticity [rʌ'stisiti] landlig simpelhet; bondsk vesen.
rustily ['rʌstili] rustent. **rustiness** [-nés] rustenhet.
rustle ['rʌsl] rasle; rasle med. **rusty** rusten; sløvet, ute av øvelse; forsømt, vanstelt; loslitt; hes, hås; rustfarget.
rusty ['rʌsti] muggen, sur, harsk.
rut [rʌt] hjulspor; danne spor i (en vei).
rut [rʌt] brunst; være brunstig, løpe.
ruth [ru·þ] medlidenhet; sorg; grusomhet.
ruthless ['ru·þlès] ubarmhjertig, hard.
rutty ['rʌti] full av hjulspor, oppkjørt.
R. V. fk. f. revised version.
R. V. C. fk. f. rifle volunteer corps.
Ry fk. f. **railway.**
rye [rai] rug. — -**grass** raigras, reinskjak; marehalm.
ryme [raim] = **rhyme.**
ryot ['raiət] bonde, jaddyrker (i India).
rythm [riþm] = **rhythm.**

S

S, s [es] S.
§ tegn for **dollar(s).**
S. fk. f. **Saturday; South(ern)** (blant annet Londons sørlige postdistrikt); **Sunday; see; shilling(s); sun.**
s. fk. f. **second(s); see; shilling(s); singular; sun.**
Sat. fk. f. **Saturday.**
S. A. fk. f. **Salvation Army; South Afrika** (el. America, Australia); **Society of Ant.quaries.**
Sabaoth [sə'be·äþ] Zebaoth; **the Lord of** — den Herre Zebaoth.
sabbatarian [säbə'tæ·ºriən] sabbats-, sabbatarier, streng overholder av hviledagen. **sabbath** ['säbəþ] sabbat. **sabbatic, -al** (sə'bätik(l)] som hører til sabbaten. **sabbatism** ['säbətizm] helligholdelse av sabbaten.
sable ['se·bl] sobel; sørgeklær; mørk; kle i svart.
sablemouse ['se·blmaus] lemen.
sabot ['säbo·] treskot; sko, skoning; fylling.
sabotage ['säbota·ʒ] sabotasje.
sabre ['se·bə] ryttersabel; sable ned.
sabretache ['säbətäʃ] sabeltaske.
saccharine ['säkərin] sakarin.
saccharine ['säkərain] sukker-.
sacerdotal [säsə'do·täl] prestelig. **-ism** [säsə'do·təlizm] prestevesen.
sack [säk] plyndring; plyndre, herje.
sack [säk] sekk, pose; kappe; **get the** — få avskjed; få «katten».
sackage ['säkidʒ] plyndring.
sack-cloth ['säkklåþ] sekkestrie; **in** — **and ashes** i sekk og aske.
sacking ['säkiŋ] sekketøy, sekkestrie.
sack-race ['säkre·s] sekkeløp.
Sackville ['säkvil] Sackville.
sacrament ['säkrəmənt] sakrament.
sacramental [säkrə'mentl] sakramental; — **service** altergang.
sacred ['se·krid] hellig, innvigd; — **history** bibelhistorie; kirkehistorie. — **music** kirkemusikk. **-ness** [nés] hellighet.
sacrifice ['säkrifais] ofre, oppofres; offer; blot; salg til underpris. **sacrificial** [säkri'fiʃəl] offer-.

sacrilege ['säkrilédʒ] vanhelligelse, helligbrøde; kirkeran. **sacrilegious** [säkri'li·dʒəs] vanhellig· **sacrilegist** ['säkrilidʒist] kirkeraner.
sacring ['se·kriŋ] vigsel. — -**bell** klokke som det ble ringt med når alterbrød ble vigd.
sacristan ['säkristən] kirketjener.
sacristy ['säkristi] sakristi.
sacrosanct ['säkrosäŋkt] sakrosankt, hellig.
sad [säd] bedrøvet, tungsindig, sturen, sørgelig; mørk, avdempet, rolig (om farger). **sadden** ['sädn] bli bedrøvet, bedrøve.
saddle ['sädl] sal (på hest); rygg (på slakt); høvre; sale, kløvje; bebyrde. — -**back** bakke-el. åskam med søkk i midten; salrygg, svairygg; havmåke. — -**backed** salrygget. — -**bag** saltaske; et plysjmønster. — -**bow** [-bo·] salbue. — -**cloth** saldekken. — -**gall** salgnag. — -**horse** ridehest. — -**maker** salmaker.
saddler ['sädlə] salmaker.
saddlery ['sädləri] salmakerarbeid.
Sadducean [sädju'si·ən] sadduseisk.
Sadducee ['sädjusi·] sadduseer.
sadness ['sädnés] sørgmodighet; sørgelighet.
safe [se·f] sikker, uskadd, betryggende, trygg, pålitelig; sikkert gjemmested, pengeskap, flueskap, isskap. — -**conduct** sikkert leide, pass. -**guard** beskyttelse, betryggelse, vern, bedekning av vakt, sikkert leide, pass, et slags overskjørt. —-**keeping** forvaring, varetekt. **-ly** sikkert, uskadd, i sikkerhet. **-ness** [-nés] sikkerhet, pålitelighet.
safety ['se·fti] sikkerhet, trygghet, forvaring. — -**belt** livbelte. — -**buoy** livbøye. — -**chain** sikkerhetskjede. — -**curtain** jernteppe (i teater). — -**deposit** sikkerhetsrom. — -**pin** sikkerhetsnål. — -**razor** barberhøvel. — -**valve** sikkerhetsventil.
saffron ['säfrən] safran, safrangul.
sag [säg] sige ned, synke ned, gi seg, slakne; ha avdrift; få til å synke ned; sig.
saga ['sa·gə] saga.
sagacious [sə'ge·ʃəs] skarpsindig, gløgg, klok.
sagacity [sə'gäsiti] skarpsindighet.
sagaman ['sa·gəmən] sagaforteller.
sagamore ['sägəmå·º] indianerhøvding.
sage [se·dʒ] klok, vis; vismann; **the Sage of Chelsea** om Thomas Carlyle. **-ness** [-nés] visdom.

sage [se'dʒ] salvie.
sago ['se'goⁿ] sago.
sagopalm ['se'goⁿpa·m] sagopalme.
Sahara [sə'ha·rə] Sahara.
sahib ['sa·(h)ib] (hind.) herre.
saic ['sa·ik] saike (tomastet gresk eller tyrkisk seilfartøy).
said [sed] imperf. og perf. pts. av say.
sail [se'l] seile, befare; seil, seilskip, skip, seiltur; strike — stryke seil, gi tapt. — -cloth seidluk.
sailer ['se'lə] seiler; a fast — en hurtigseiler.
sailing ['se'liŋ] seiltur. — -master navigasjonsoffiser.
sailor ['se'lə] sjømann, matros; be a good — være sjøsterk; be a bad — ikke være sjøsterk.
saint [se'nt] helgen; sankt, hellig-; kanonisere, lyse hellig.
Saint Albans [sənt'å·lbənz] Saint Albans.
Saint Andrews [sənt'ändru·z] Saint Andrews (skotsk by og universitet).
sainted ['se'ntid] kanonisert; hellig; salig.
Saint George [sən'dʒå·ºdʒ] Sankt Georg.
Saint Gothar [sən'gåþəd] Sankt Gotthard.
Saint Helena [sənti'li·nə] Sankt Helena.
sainthood ['se'nthud] helgenverdighet.
Saint-John [sən'dʒån] evangelisten Johannes.
saintlike ['se'ntlaik] helgenaktig.
saintly ['se'ntli] helgenaktig, helgenren.
Saint-Patrick [s(ə)n'pätrik] St. Patrick (Irlands skytshelgen).
Saint-Paul [s(ə)n'på·l] Paulus; -'s (Cathedral) St. Paulskirken.
saintship ['se'ntʃip] helgenverdighet; hellighet.
sake [se'k] skyld, årsak; for God's — for Guds skyld.
salaam [sə'la·m] en slags dyp orientalsk hilsen; hilse dypt.
salacious [sə'le'ʃəs] vellystig, geil.
salacity [sə'läsiti] vellyst.
salad ['säləd] salat. — -oil provenceolje, matolje, salatolje.
salamander [sälə'mändə] salamander; ildsluker.
salamandrine [sälə'mändrin] salamanderaktig.
salary ['säləri] lønn, gasje; lønne.
sale [se'l]· salg, avsetning, utsalg; auksjon; account of the sales el. account-sales salgsregning; for (el. on) til slags; offer for — falby; — now on ·utsalg. -able salgbar, til salgs.
salep ['sällp] salep(rot).
sale-room ['se'lru·m] auksjonslokale.
sales|book [se'lzbuk] debetkladd. -man selger, kommis. -woman ekspeditrise.
salicylic [säli'silik] salisyl; — acid salisylsyre.
salient ['se'ljənt] framspringende, framtredende, fremragende; fremspring; — point springende punkt; the Salient den framskutte del av fronten ved Ypres i verdenskrigen.
saliferous [sə'lifərəs] saltholdig.
salification [sälifi'ke'ʃən] saltdannelse.
saline [sə'lain] salt-; saltsjø, saltverk.
saliva [sə'laivə] spytt.
salival [sə'laivəl], salivary ['sälivəri] spytt-.
sallow ['sälo⁰] selje, vidje, pil.
sallow ['sälo⁰] gusten, gulblek.
sally ['säli] utfall, kvikt påfunn; gjøre et utfall.
salmagundi [sälmə'gʌndi] sildesalat; miskmask.
salmon ['sämən] laks. —-fry laksyngel. —-trout sjøaure.
saloon [sə'lu·n] salong, sal, kahyttsplass, salongvogn; (amr.) vertshus, bevertning, utskjenkingssted. — pistol salonggevær. —-bar fin skjenkestue (vertshus, motsatt public bar). —-car (amr.) salongvogn. — -carriage salongvogn.
saloonist [sə'lu·nist] (amr.) vertshusholder.
salt [så·lt] salt, saltkar, saltbøsse, smak, vittighet; salt; salte; below the — nedenfor saltkarret ɔ: ved den nederste bordenden; he is worth his — han er sin lønn verd; rather too — litt pepret; take a thing with a grain of — oppfatte noe med litt sunn sans (cum grano salis).

saltant ['sältənt] dansende, hoppende.
saltation [säl'te'ʃən] dansing, hopping; byks.
salt-box ['så·ltbåks] (stort) saltkar; saltbinge.
salt-cellar ['så·lt'selə] saltkar.
salter ['så·ltə] saltkoker; salthandler.
saltier ['sältiə] Andreas-kors.
saltish ['så·ltiʃ] saltaktig, noe salt.
salt-junk ['så·ltdʒʌŋk] salt kjøtt, saltmat.
salt-mine ['så·ltmain] saltgruve.
saltpetre [så·lt'pi·tə] salpeter; Chili — Chilesalpeter.
salt-spoon ['så·ltspu·n] saltskje.
salt-water ['så·lt'wå·tə] saltvann, sjøvann.
salt-works ['så·ltwə·ks] saltverk.
salty ['så·lti] saltaktig, salt av seg.
salubrious [sə'lu·briəs] sunn.
salubrity [sə'lu·briti] sunnhet.
salutary ['säljutəri] sunn, gagnlig.
salutation [sälju'te'ʃən] hilsen, helsing.
salute [səl'(j)u·t] hilsen, helsing, salutt; hilse, helse, saluttere.
salvage ['sälvidʒ] bergning; bergelønn; bergegods; vrakgods; redde, berge; — corps redningskorps.
salvarsan ['sälvəsän] salvarsan.
salvation [säl've'ʃən] frelse, salighet; the Salvation Army frelsesarméen.
salvationism [säl've'ʃənizm] frelsesarméens grunnsetninger.
salvationist [säl've'ʃənist] frelsessoldat.
salve [sa·v] salve; (fig.) plaster; salve, lege.
salve [sälv] berge.
salver ['sälvə] presenterbrett.
salvo [sälvo⁰] forbehold; unnskyldning; æressalve (-salutt).
sal volatile [sälvə'lätəli] hjortetakksalt, kullsur ammoniakk.
salvor ['sälvə] berger, bergingsdamper.
Sam [säm] Sam; stand — betale gildet, rive i.
Samaria [sə'mæ·ºriə] Samaria. Samaritan [sə'märitən] samaritansk; samaritan.
same [se'm] samme; the — as (eller with) det samme som; one and the — with en og den samme som; the ·very — den selvsamme; all the — like godt, likevel; it is all the — to me det er akkurat det samme for meg; I wish you the —! (el. the — to you!) i like måte; he is the — as ever han er den gamle; if it is the — to you hvis De ikke har noe imot det; it comes to the — det kommer ut på ett.
Samnite ['sämnait] samnitter; samnittisk.
Samoa [sə'mo·ºə] Samoa, Skipperøyene.
samovar ['sä·mova·ºə] samovar (russisk temaskin).
sample ['sa·mpl] prøve, mønster; [sa·mpl, sämpl] vise el. ta prøver av; være prøve på.
sampler ['sa·mplə] prøver; navneduk.
sample-room ['sa·mplru·m] prøvelager.
Samuel ['sämjuəl] Samuel.
sanability [sänə'biliti] helbredelighet.
sanable ['sänəbl] helbredelig.
sanative ['sänətiv] helbredende, gagnlig.
sanatorium [sänə'tå·riəm] sanatorium, kuranstalt.
sanatory ['sänətəri] helbredende.
sanctification [säŋktifi'ke'ʃən] helliggjørelse, innvielse, vigsel.
sanctified airs skinnhellighet; the end sanctifies the means hensikten helliger midlet.
sanctimonious [säŋkti'mo·ⁿnjəs] skinnhellig.
sanction ['säŋkʃən] sanksjon, godkjenning, stadfesting; forordning; bestemmelse om straff eller belønning knyttet til en lov; sanksjonere, stadfeste, støtte, billige, bekrefte.
sanctity ['säŋktiti] hellighet, fromhet, ukrenkelighet.
sanctuary ['säŋktʃuəri] helligdom, tilfluktssted, fristed.

sanctum ['säŋktəm] helligdom, lønnkammer, allernelligste.
sand [sänd] sand; sandbanke; (amr.) mot, tak, to, karakter; (amr.) sandstein; dekke med sand, sandstrø, blande med sand; plur. sands sandstrekning(er), sandørken(er), sandstrand; timeglassets sand. sanded ['sändid] sandet, tilsandet; sanded paper sandpapir.
sandal ['sändl] sandal, sandalreim; forsyne med sandaler, feste med sandalreimer.
sandalwood ['sändlwud] sandeltre.
sand-bag ['sändbäg] sandsekk.
sand-bank ['sändbäŋk] sandbanke.
sand-blast ['sändbla·st] sandstråle.
sandboy ['sändboi]; jolly as a — så glad som en lerke.
sand-eel ['sändi·l] sil (en fisk).
sand-glass ['sändgla·s] timeglass.
Sandhurst ['sänd(h)ə·st] Sandhurst (by og offisersskole).
sandiness ('sändinés] sandethet.
sand-jet ['sänddʒet] sandstråle.
sandman ['sändmən] Jon Blund.
sandmartin ['sändma·ətin] strandsvale.
sandpaper ['sändpe¹pə] sandpapir.
sand-pit ['sändpit] sandtak.
sandstone ['sändsto⁰n] sandstein.
sand-storm ['sändstå·ᵊm] sandstorm.
Sandwich ['sändwidʒ, -witʃ] Sandwich.
sandwich ['sänₒwidʒ, -witʃ] brødstykke, lagt dobbelt med pålegg imellom; vandrende dobbeltskilt; annonsemann; anbringe imellom.
sandwich-man ['sänwidʒmən] sandwichselger; plakatbærer (med plakat på rygg og bryst).
sandy ['sändi] sandet, full av sand; sandaktig; rødblond.
sandy-haired ['sändihæ·əd] rødblond.
sane [se¹n] sund, rask; vettig, ved sine fulle fem. -ness [-nés] sundhet, tilregnelighet.
San Francisco [sänfrən'sisko⁰] San Francisko.
sang-froid ['sa·ŋ'frwa·] koldblodighet.
sanguiferous [säŋ'gwifərəs] blodførende. sanguification [säŋgwifi'ke¹ʃən] bloddanning. sanguifer ['säŋgwifaiə] bloddanner. sanguify ['säŋgwifai] danne blod. sanguigenous [säŋ'gwidʒinəs] bloddannende. sanguinary ['säŋgwinəri] blodig, blodtørstig; røllik. sanguine ['säŋgwin] blodfull; fyrig, sangvinsk; tillitsfull; blodrød; farge med blod. sanguineous [säŋ'gwiniəs] blodfull, bloddannende, blodrød. sanguinivorous [säŋgwi'nivorəs] blodsugende. sanguinolent [säŋ'gwinolənt] blodfarget. sanguisuge ['säŋgwi·su·dʒ] blodigle. sanguisugent [säŋgwi'su·dʒənt] blodsugende.
sanitarian [säni'tæ·ᵊriən] hygieniker.
sanitary ['sänitəri] sanitær, sunnhets-; the — system helserådet. the — condition sunnhetstilstanden.
sanitation [säni'te¹ʃən] sunnhetspleie.
sanity ['säniti] sunnhet, sunn sans, vett, tilregnelighet, forstandighet.
sansculotte [sänzkju'lät] sanskulott.
Sanskrit ['sänskrit] sanskrit (hinduenes gamle språk). sanskritist ['sänskritist] sanskritkjenner.
Santa Claus ['säntə'klå·z] Santa Claus, julenissen.
Santhal [sa·n'ta·l] Santal; the mission to the — santalmisjonen.
sap [säp] saft (i plante); sevje; kraft; geite, yte; tappe for saft, maktstjele, margstjele.
sap [säp] pugghest; slit; pugg; nilese, pugge, terpe.
sap [säp] løpegrav; underminere; grave løpegraver.
sap-colour ['säpkʌlə] plantefarge.
sap-green ['säpgri·n] saftgrønt.
sapid ['säpid] velsmakende; frisk. -ness [-nés] velsmak. sapidity [sə'piditi] velsmak.
sapience ['se¹pjəns] visdom, klokskap.
sapient ['se¹pjənt] vis (mest ironisk), velvis.

sapless ['säplés] saftløs; tørr; kraftløs.
sapling ['säpliŋ] ungt tre, renning; ungt menneske.
saponaceous [säpo'ne¹ʃəs] såpeaktig.
saponification [səpånifi'ke¹ʃən] såpedannelse.
sapper ['säpə] sappør, menig av ingeniørtroppene.
sapphire ['säfaiə] safir; safirblått; safirblå.
sappines ['säpinés] saftighet.
sappy ['säpi] saftig, sevjerik.
saraband ['särəbänd] sarabande (spansk dans).
Saracen ['särəsn, 'särəsin] sarasener.
sarcasm ['sa·ᵊkäzm] sneiord, spydighet.
sarcastic [sa·ᵊ'kästik] spydig, sarkastisk.
sarcophagous [sa·ᵊ'kåfəgəs] kjøttetende.
sarcophagus [sa·ᵊ'kåfəgəs] sarkofag.
sardine ['sa·ᵊ'di·n] sardin; like -s in a box som sild i en tønne.
Sardinia [sa·ᵊ'dinjə] Sardinia.
sardonic [sa·ᵊ'dänik] sardonisk, spotsk.
sartorial [sa·ᵊ'tå·riəl] som hører til skredderfaget; skredder-.
sash [säʃ] belte, skjerf.
sash [säʃ] vindusramme; skyvevindu (som glir opp og ned i fuger). — -line vindussnor. — — -window skyvevindu, guillotinevindu.
sat [sät] imperf. av sit.
Sat fk. f. Saturday.
Satan ['se¹tən] satan. -ic [sə'tänik] satanisk. -ical, -ically satanisk, djevelsk.
satchel ['sätʃəl] taske, skoleveske.
sate [sät, se¹t] gml. for sat satt.
sate [se¹t] mette, overfylle.
sateen [sä'ti·n] sateng.
satellite ['sätilait] drabant, biplanet, måne.
satiable ['se¹ʃ(i)əbl] som kan mettes.
satiate ['se¹ʃie¹t] mette, overmette.
satiation [se¹ʃi'e¹ʃən] metthet, mette.
satiety [sə'taiəti] mette, lede, avsmak.
satin ['sätin] atlask, sateng; satinere.
satire ['sätaiə] satire.
satirical [sə'tirikl] satirisk.
satirist ['sätərist] satiriker.
satirize ['sätəraiz] satirisere over.
satisfaction [sätis'fäkʃən] tilfredsstillelse, tilfredshet, oppreisning, fyldest, erstatning, vederlag.
satisfactory [sätis'fäktəri], — ily [-ili] tilfredsstillende, fullgod.
satisfy ['sätisfai] tilfredsstille, fyldestgjøre; mette; forvisse (seg om).
satrap ['sätrəp] satrap. satrapy [-i] satrapi.
saturate ['sätʃəre¹t] mette.
saturation [sätʃu're¹ʃən] metting.
Saturn ['sätə·n] Saturn.
saturnalian [sätə·n(a)in] mørk, tung, innesluttet.
saturn|alian [sätə·'ne¹ljən] saturnalsk; vill, tøyslesløs. -ine [sätə·n(a)in] mørk, tung, innesluttet.
satyr ['sätə] satyr. -ic [sə'tirik] satyraktig.
sauce [så·s] saus; uforskammethet; sause, krydre, være uforskammet el. nesevis. —boat sauseskål. — -box nesevis person.
saucepan ['så·spən] kasserolle (med håndtak).
saucer ['så·sə] skål, fat.
sauce-tureen [så·stju'ri·n] sauseskål.
saucy ['så·si], saucily [-li] uforskammet, nesevis. sauciness [-nés] uforskammethet, frekkhet.
saunter ['så·ntə] slentre, spasere, slenge, drive, reke; spasertur. -er [-rə] dagdriver, flanør.
saurian ['så·riən] øgle; som hører til øglene.
sausage ['såsidʒ] pølse.
savage ['sävidʒ] vill, rå, ukultivert; grusom; villmann, barbar. -ness [-nés] villhet.
savagery ['sävidʒəri] vill tilstand; villskap, råhet, grusomhet.
savagism ['sävidʒizm] villmannstilstand.
savannah ['sävänə] savanna (stor trebar slette).
savant ['sävənt] lærd.
save [se¹v] frelse, redde, berge, bevare; verne,

trygge; spare, gjemme; spare opp; ha liggende; ikke la unyttet; nå, komme tidsnok til; unntagen, unntatt; — for hvis ikke; (God) — the mark Gud bevare oss vel, Gud bedre; a penny -d is a penny gained penger spart er penger tjent; — appearances bevare skinnet.

save-all ['se'vål] lyssparer (løs forlenging av lysestake med en spiss til å stikke lysstumpen på).

saveloy ['säviloi] cervelatpølse.

saving ['se'vin] frelsende, sparsommelig, som nettopp dekker utgiftene; unntagen, unntatt; besparelse; his — angel reddende; a — bargain en forretning som man så vidt unngår tap på; he has no — points forsonende trekk; — your presence med forlov; — your reverence med respekt å melde, bent ut sagt. -ly med sparsommelighet. -ness sparsommelighet.

savings ['se'vinz] sparepenger. — -bank sparekasse. — -box sparebøsse.

saviour ['se'vjə] frelser.

savoir faire ['sävwa·ə'fæ·ə] takt.

savoir vivre ['sävwa·ə'vi·və] gode manerer, folkeskikk.

savour ['se'və] smak; lukt, dåm, duft; salvelse i prekenen; smake, lukte (of av), minne om.

savouriness ['se'vərinés] aroma.

savourless ['se'vələiz] uten smak el. duft.

savoury ['se'vəri] velsmakende, velluktende, delikat, pikant.

Savoy [sə'voi] Savoie. -ard [əd] savojard.

saw [så·] utsagn, sentens, ordtak, ordtøke, fyndord, visdomsord (også ironisk).

saw [så·] sag; sage, skjære; — your timber pakk Dem, av sted! — -blade [-ble¹d] sagblad. — -bones [-boᵘnz] kirurg. — -buck ['så·bak] sagbukk, sagkrakk. — -dust ['så·dʌst] sagflis, sagmugg. -er ['så·ə] sagskjærer. — -fish sagfisk. — -fly bladveps. — -jack sagkrakk. -mill sag, sagbruk. — -pit saggrop (for to menn med langsag). sawyer ['så·jə] sagskjærer.

saxatile ['säksətil] stein-, berg-, ur-.

Saxe [säks] Sachsen (i smstg.).

Saxe-Weimar ['säks'vaima·ə] Sachsen-Weimar.

saxifrage ['säksifridʒ] saksifraga, bergsildre.

Saxon ['säksən] saksisk; sakser. -ism ['säksənizm] saksisk språkegenhet. -ist kjenner av saksisk.

Saxony ['säksəni] Sachsen.

saxony ['säksəni] saksoni (et slags tøy).

saxophone ['säksəfoᵘn] saksofon.

say [se¹] prøve; probere.

say [se¹] si; si fram; mene, bety; tale, ord, replikk; that is to — det vil si; he is said to have been absent han skal ha vært fraværende; it -s in the New Testament that . . . det heter; to — nothing of for ikke å snakke om; I — hør her! hør nå! — on Wednesday for eksempel på onsdag; you don't — so det er da vel ikke mulig! that goes without -ing det sier seg selv; I have had my — out har sagt hva jeg har å si; -ing ['se¹in] fremsigelse; ytring; sentens, ordtak, ordtøke, ord; -ing and doing are two things ett er å love, et annet å holde.

scab [skäb] skorpe, ruve; skurv; skabb; streikebryter; sette skorpe.

scabbard ['skäbəd] slir; stikke i sliren.

scabbed [skäbd] skorpet; skabbet; låk, ussel.

scabby ['skäbi] se scabbed.

scabies ['ske¹bii·z] fnatt, skabb.

scabrous ['ske¹brəs] ru, grov, ujevn; uharmonisk.

scaffold ['skäfəld] stilling, stillas, tribune, skafott; avstive, forsyne med stillas. -ing stillas, stillasmaterialer.

scald [skäld] skald, dikter.

scald [skå·ld] skålde, skambrenne, koke; skåldet; a -ed cat fears cold water brent barn skyr ilden.

scald [skå·ld] hodeskurv. — -berry bjørnebær. — -crow alminnelig kråke.

scalding [skå·ldin] skålding; skåldhet. — tears bitre tårer.

scale [ske¹l] vektskål, vekt; måle, veie.

scale [ske¹l] skjell, skall, flass, risp; skalle av; dette av.

scale [ske¹l] stige, skala, målestokk, trinfølge; bestige; klyve, storme.

scalene [skə'li·n] ulikesidet; ulikesidet trekant.

scaling-ladder ['ske¹lindlädə] stormstige; brannstige, redningsstige.

scallop ['skåləp] kammusling; harpeskjell; utskjæring, tunge; uttunge.

scalp [skälp] hodehud, skalp; skalpere.

scalpel ['skälpəl] skalpell, disseksjonskniv.

scaly ['ske¹li] skjellet, skjellformet; lurvet.

scamp [skämp] slubbert; jaske av, fuske med.

scamper ['skämpə] slarv, slask, fusker.

scamper ['skämpə] hodekulls flukt; flykte over hals og hode, løpe, fare, jage.

scan [skän] skandere, forske, prøve nøye, se nøye på, mønstre; — the horizon se ut over horisonten.

scandal ['skändəl] anstøt, forargelse, skandale, baktalelse; baktale; give — to vekke anstøt hos; talk — baktale; The School for Scandal Baktalelsens skole (stykke av Sheridan).

scandalize ['skändəlaiz] forarge, støte, baktale.

scandalous ['skändələs] forargelig, skandaløs; baktalersk.

Scandinavia [skändi'ne¹vjə] Skandinavia (Skandinavhalvøya; Norden). Scandinavian skandinavisk; nordisk; skandinav, nordbo.

scansion ['skänfən] skandering.

scansorial [skän'så·riəl] egnet til klatring, klatre, klyve-.

scant [skänt] knapp, snau, sparsom; knappe av, innskrenke, knipe på. -ily knapt. -iness [-inés] knapphet.

scantling ['skäntlin] lite stykke, bete, mål, dimensjon, prøve, kaliber; bukk.

scanty ['skänti] knapp, snau, ringe, påholden.

scape [ske¹p] stilk, blomsterstengel.

scape [ske¹p] fk. f. escape.

scape-gallows ['ske¹pgälo°z] galgenfugl.

scapegoat ['ske¹pgoᵘt] syndebukk.

scapegrace ['ske¹pgre¹s] laban, slamp, døgenikt.

scapula ['skäpjulə] skulderblad.

scapular ['skäpjulə] skapular, skulderklede.

scar [ska·ə] skramme, flerre, arr; sette arr, merke.

scar [ska·ə] berg, hammer, stup, fjellskrent.

scarab ['skärəb], scarabee ['skärəbi·] tordivel; skarabé.

scaramouch ['skärəmautʃ] narr, bajas.

Scarborough ['ska·ᵊb(ə)ro] by i Yorkshire.

scarce [skæ·əs] knapp, sjelden, sjeldsynt; money is — det er knapt med penger; a work now very — som nå er meget sjeldent; make yourself — ! som man er meget sjeldent; forsvinn! vekk med deg! hold (eg vekk!

scarcely ['skæ·əsli] neppe, snautt, knapt, nesten ikke; — any nesten ingen; — when neppe før; he can — have been here han kan vist ikke ha vært her.

scarceness ['skæ·əsnès] sjeldenhet.

scarcity ['skæ·əsiti] knapphet, mangel, skort, sjeldenhet, dyrtid.

scare [skæ·ə] skremme, forske el skrekk, skremme, forske; redde; kvekk; — away skremme bort; — up skremme opp.

scarecrow ['skæ·əkroᵘ] fugleskremsel.

scarf [ska·ᵊf] skjerf; slips.

scarf [ska·ᵊf] skjøte (tre-, metall- el. lærstykker) ved å skjære endene til slik at de ligger over hverandre uten at tykkelsen forøkes; laske; skjøt, lask.

scarf-pin ['ska·ᵊfpin] slipsnål.

scarf-skin ['ska·ᵊfskin] overhud.

scarification ['skæ·ərifike'ʃən] riss i huden.

scarificator ['skæ·ərifike'tə] skarifikator. scarify ['skæ·ərifai] risse i huden; kritisere sterkt, plukke sund.

scarlatina [ska·ºlɔ'ti·nɔ] skarlagensfeber.
scarlet ['ska·ºlit] skarlagenrød; skarlagen; — bean pralbønne; — fever skarlagensfeber; tilbøyelighet til å bli forelsket i (de rødkledde) soldater; — hat kardinalshatt; kardinalsverdighet; — runner pralbønne; the — woman kvinnen som er kledd i purpur og skarlagen; Babylon (se Johannes' åpenbaring); romerkirken.

scarp [skɑ·ºp] bratt skråning el. brekke; eskarpe; gjøre bratt.

scarred [ska·ºd] skrammet, arret.

scathe [skeið] skade; mén, skade. scathing bitende, skarp. scath.less ['ske¹ölés] uskadd; ustraffet.

scatter ['skätə] spre, splitte, spre seg, strø.

scatter-brained ['skätəbre¹nd] atspredt, tankeløs, vimset.

scavenger ['skävn(d)ʒə] gatefeier, renovasjonsarbeider, søppelkjører; -'s cart renovasjonskjerre.

scene [si·n] skueplass, scene, opptrin, hending; dekorasjon, kulisse, maleri, syn; — of action kampplass; behind the -s bak kulissene.

scenery ['si·n(ə)ri] sceneri, kulisser; naturomgivelser, natur, landskap.

scenic ['si·nik, 'senik] scenisk, teater-.

scent [sent] lukte, være, ha teft av, spore; parfymere; lukt, duft, angt, spor; get — of få teften av; on the — på sporet; on the wrong — på villspor.

scented ['sentid] duftende, parfymert.

sceptic ['skeptik] skeptisk; tviler. -al, -ally ['skeptikəl(i)] skeptisk.

scepticism ['skeptisizm] skeptisisme.

sceptre ['septə] scepter, utstyre med scepter.

sceptred ['septəd] scepterbærende, kongelig.

schedule ['ʃedju·l] liste, dokument, regjeringsfortegnelse, katalog, tabell; balanse, status; sette på liste, sette opp liste over.

scheme [ski·m] system, plan, prosjekt, utkast, figur (i astrologi); skjema; planlegge, spekulere, pønske ut. schemer ['ski·mə] prosjektmaker, renkesmed. scheming ['ski·miŋ] renkefull, intrigant.

schism ['sizm] skisma, splittelse, kirkestrid.

schismatic [siz'mätik] skismatisk, splittet.

schismatical [siz'mätikl] skismatisk.

schist [ʃist] skifer.

schistose ['ʃistoᵘs] skiferaktig, lagdelt.

scholar ['skålə] elev, skolegutt, skolepike; lærd student som har stipendium; a good French — flink i fransk; he is a — han har studert; my son was bred a — fikk en lærd utdannelse.

scholarly ['skᴧləli] lærd, vitenskapelig.

scholarship ['skåləʃip] lærdom, stipendium.

scholastic [sko'lästik] skolemessig, spissfindig.

scholasticism [skå'lästisizm] skolastikk, pedanteri.

scholiast ['skoᵘliäst] skoliast, fortolker.

scholium ['skoᵘliəm] randbemerkning.

school [sku·l] skole, fakultet, faggruppe, selskap (av kunstnere); eksamen; lære, opptukte, skolere; leave — slutte skolen; pass the -s ta sine eksamener; life at — skolelivet; we were boys (girls) at — together vi vår skolekamerater; an edition for -s skoleutgave; go to — gå på skolen; be sent to — begynne på skolen.

school [sku·l] stim (av fisk); stime.

school|-board ['skoᵘlbå·ºd] skolestyre (for folkeskolene). — -book skolebok, lærebok. — -dame skolemor. — -day skoledag. — -divine skolastisk teolog. — -fee skolepenger. — -fellow skolekamerat. — -girl skolepike. — -house skole (-lokale)

schooling ['sku·liŋ] opplæring, undervisning, skolegang; skolepenger; irettesetting.

school|man ['sku·lmən] skolastiker; skolemann. -master skolelærer, -mester. -mistress [-mistris] lærerinne. — -room skoleværelse, skolestue.

schooner ['sku·nə] skonner.

schottische [ʃå'ti·ʃ] schottish (en dans).

sciagraph ['sa¹əgra·f] profil; skyggeriss; vertikalsnitt.

sciagraphy [sai'ägrəfi] skyggetegning.

sciatic [sai'ätik] hofte-; hoftenerve.

sciatica [sai'ätikə] hoftegikt, isjias.

science ['saiəns] vitenskap, fysikk; a man of — vitenskapsmann; the seven -s de sju frie kunster; Christian Science, en moderne sekt som helbreder ved tro; exact — eksakt vitenskap; moral — etikk; natural — naturvitenskap.

scientific [saiən'tifik] vitenskapelig.

scientist ['saiəntist] vitenskapsmann.

scilicet ['siliset] nemlig.

Scilly ['sili] Scilly(øyene).

scimitar ['simitə] scimitar, (orientalsk) krumsabel.

scintilla [sin'tilə] glimt; antydning, spor; not a — of ikke spor av.

scintillate ['sintile¹t] gnistre, funkle, glitre.

scintillation [sinti'le¹ʃən] glitring.

scion ['saiən] podekvist; avlegger, skudd, ætling.

scissor ['sizə] klippe, skjære (med saks).

scissors ['sizəz] (plur.) saks; a pair of — en saks.

scissure ['s ʃə] kløft; spaltning.

Sclav [skla·v, skläv] se Slav.

sclerosis [sklia'roᵘsis] herdning av vev.

sclerotic [sklia'råtik] senehinne (i øyet); — coat senehinne.

scobs [skåbz] sagmugg, sagflis, filspån.

scoff [skåf] spotte, håne; spott. -er spotter.

scoffing ['skåfiŋ] spotsk, spottende; spott.

scold [skoᵘld] skjelle, skjenne; skjenne på; arrig troll, kjeftause. -ing skjenn. -ingly med skjell og smell.

scolopendra [skålo'pendrə] skolopender.

sconce [skåns] skanse; lyspipe, lampett.

scone [skoᵘn] bolle, tykk bløt kake; potato — lumpe.

Scone [sku·n] Scone (flekke i Skottland).

scoop [sku·p] øse, skuffe, øsekar; øse, skuffe, måke, lense; hule ut.

scoot [sku·t] fare, stikke av.

scooter ['sku·tə] hjulspark (slags leketøy).

scope [skoᵘp] mål, formål; synsvidde; råderom, spillerom, frihet.

scorbutic [skå·ºbju·tik] som lider av skjørbuk; skjørbukspasient.

scorch [skå·ºtʃ] svi, brenne, angripe med spott; bli svidd, bli forbrent; skyte en rasende fart. -er brennhet dag; bitende spott. -ing sviende, bitende.

score [skå·º] merke, skår, hakk, strek (brukt som talltegn på en karvestokk), regning; regnskap, gjeld, grunn, årsak, snes, partitur; streke, sette streker i, gjøre hakk i merke; avmerke med strek, notere, nedtegne, føre på regning, utsette i partitur; vinne, seire (i spill); føre regnskap; — out stryke ut; keep — holde regnskap; quit -s avslutte regningen; run up a — ta på kreditt; by -s i snesevis; long — stor regning; short — liten regning; in — i partitur; on the — of på grunn av; angående.

scorer ['skå·rə] regnskapsfører, markør.

scoria ['skå·riə] slagg.

scorification [skå·rifi'ke¹ʃən] slaggdannelse.

scorify ['skå·rifai] forvandle til slagg.

scorn [skå·ºn] forakte, håne; forakt, hån; gjenstand for forakt; put to — beskjemme; laugh to — le ut; hold up to — vise fram til spott og spe.

scornful ['skå·ºnful] hånlig, foraktelig.

scorpion ['skå·ºpiən] skorpion.

scot [skåt] kontingent; lot and — skatt.

Scot [skåt] skotte; Mary Queen of Scots Maria Stuart.

Scotch [skåtʃ] skotsk; — mist støvregn, dusk.

scotch [skåtʃ] såre lett, rispe, snitte; skramme skår, hakk.

scotch [skåtʃ] underlag; støtte, stø under bremse.

Scotchman ['skåtʃmən] skotte, skottlending; **the Flying** —, hurtigtog mellom London og Edinburgh.

Scotchwoman ['skåtʃwumən] skotsk kvinne, skottlending.

scotfree ['skåt'fri·] skattefri, avgiftsfri; helskinnet, fri for alle ulemper.

Scotland ['skåtlənd] Skottland; — **Yard** før hovedstasjonen for Londons politi; politiet.

Scots [skåts] skoter; skotsk; skotsk språk.

Scotsman ['skåtsmən] skotte.

Scott [skåt] Scott.

Scotticism ['skåtisizm] skotsk uttrykk.

Scottish ['skåtiʃ] skotsk.

scoundrel ['skaundrəl] slyngel, skarv, kjeltring. **-ism** skurkaktighet. **-ly** skurkaktig.

scour ['skauə] skure, skrubbe, rense, vaske ut, skure vekk, skrubbe av; tilintetgjøre, gjennomstreife, fare over; — **of** rense for. **-ing** rensning.

scourge [skə·dʒ] svepe, svolk, plage; piske, denge, plage. **scourger** tuktemester. **scourging** [-iŋ] pisking.

scout [skaut] speider; kollegietjener (i Oxford); vakt, utkik; speide, utspeide.

scout [skaut] spotte, avvise med hån.

scout-master speiderfører.

scow [skau] pram, flatbunnet båt, lorje.

scowl [skaul] skule; skummelt blikk. **-ingly** med skummelt blikk, truende.

scrabble ['skräbl] rable, klore, krafse; krabbe.

scrag [skräg] skrangle, beinrangel; kverke.

scraggy ['skrägi] skranglet, stranten, knoklet; lurvet.

scramble ['skrämbl] krabbe, krabbe seg, klatre, klyve, skrape; gramse, krafse; kravling; slagsmål, vilt kappløp; **scrambled eggs** eggerøre. **scrambling** uregelmessig, tilfeldig.

scran [skrän] mat; levninger, rester, smuler; **bad** — **to you!** gid du må få en ulykke.

scranch ['skränʃ] knase mellom tennene.

scrap [skräp] stump, lapp, bete, rest, levning; utklipp; avfall, skrap; kassere; **a** — **of paper** en papirlapp (især brukt med hentydning til Tysklands krenkelse av Belgias nøytralitet i 1914).

scrap [skräp] slagsmål, basketak; slåss.

scrap-album ['skräpälbəm] utklippsalbum.

scrap-book ['skräpbuk] utklippsalbum.

scrape [skreip] skrape, skure, krasse, gni, bukke og skrape; skraping, gnikking; knipe, klemme; forlegenhet, dypt bukk; barbering; **get into a sad** — komme i en lei knipe; — **acquaintance** søke å innsmigre seg. — **-penny** ['skreip'peni] gnier. **scraper** gnier, skrape (redskap).

scrap-heap ['skräphi·p] avfallsdynge, søppelhaug; kaste på avfallsdyngen.

scraping ['skreipiŋ] avskrap; plur. sammenskrapte skillinger.

scrappy ['skräpi] som består av småstykker el. rester, alleslags.

scratch [skrätʃ] klore, ripe, krafse, rispe; klø, smøre (skrive fort og dårlig), rable sammen; stryke ut; kasse, ripe, rift, ripe, fure, skrubb, startstrek, mållinje (i flt.) mugg; **come to the** — komme bort til streken, våge seg fram; oppe seg; **won't you come to the** —? blir det så til noe? **Old** — pokker. — **-race** alminnelig løp, alminnelig kapproning (hvor alle starter på like vilkår); fellesstart.

scrawl [skrå·l] rable, rable ned; rabbbel.

scrawlings [skrå·liŋz] kråketær, rabbel.

scrawly ['skrå·li] stygt skrevet, rablet.

scrawny ['skrå·ni] knoklet, skranglet.

scream [skri·m] skrike; skrik. **-ing** skrikende.

screech [skri·tʃ] skrike, gnelle; skrik. — **-owl** slørugle. — **-thrush** dobbelttrost.

screen [skri·n] skjerm, skjermbrett, skjul; lerret (på kino); skjerme, skjule.

screever ['skri·və] fortausmaler.

screw [skru·] skruegjenge, skrue, propell; korketrekker; gnier; utsuger; gasje, lønn; skrue, tvinge, presse, tvinne; suge ut, pine ut; spinke; — **up** skrue opp, heve; **put on the** — bli mer forsiktig; **put under the** — presse; **there is a** — loose det er noe galt; **corkscrew** ['kå·º'kskru·] korketrekker. **screw-driver** skrujern. **screw-jack** donkraft. **screw-key** 'skru·ki] skrunøkkel.

screw-steamer ['skru·'sti·mə] skruedamper.

screw-thread ['skru·þred] skrugjenge.

screw-wrench ['skru·renʃ] skrunøkkel.

scribble ['skribl] rable, smøre sammen; smøreri; **scribbler** ['skriblə] skribler.

scribe [skraib] skriver; skriftklok; rissestift; risse merke i.

scrimmage ['skrimidʒ] klammeri, slagsmål, mølje.

scrimp [skrimp] knipe på, knusle med; knipen, snau.

scrimshank ['skrimʃäŋk] skulke, sluntre unna.

scrip [skrip] seddel, liste, dokument, interimsbevis.

scrip [skrip] (gml.) taske, veske.

script [skript] skrift, håndskrift; skriftsystem.

scriptural ['skriptjərəl] bibelsk.

scripture ['skriptʃə] den hellige skrift.

scrivener ['skriv(ə)nə] notarius.

scrofula ['skråfjulə] kjertelsyke.

scrofulous ['skråfjūləs] kjertelsyk.

scroll [skroⁿl] rull (papir); liste, fortegnelse; snirkel, krusedull; **-ed** ['skroⁿléd] snirklet.

scroop [skru·p] skurre, skrape; hvin.

scrub [skrʌb] skrubbe, skrubbekost, kratt; krake, krusk; tufs, tass.

scrubbing-brush ['skrʌbiŋbrʌʃ] skurebørste, skrubber.

scrubby ['skrʌbi] dekke med lave busker, forkrøplet, kusset, tufset.

scruff [skrʌf] nakke; — **of the neck** nakke.

scrumptious ['skrʌmpʃəs] storartet, første klasses.

scrunch [skrʌnʃ] knuse, knase.

scruple ['skru·pl] tvil, skruppel; ubetydelighet, grann; nære betenkeligheter.

scrupulous ['skru·pjuləs] engstelig, samvittighetsfull. **-ly** forsiktig.

scrutinize ['skru·tinaiz] utforske, granske.

scrutiny ['skru·tini] undersøkelse, gransking, fintelling (ved valg).

scud [skʌd] fare; lense; ilsom flukt, drivende skyer.

scuff [skʌf] sjokke, sabbe, tasse.

scuffle ['skʌfl] slagsmål, basketak; slåss.

sculk [skʌlk] skulke, luske, liste seg.

scull [skʌl] håndåre; vrikkeåre; liten båt; ro, vrikke; **-er** ['skʌlə] liten båt, sculler.

scullery ['skʌləri] oppvaskrom.

scullion ['skʌljən] kjøkkengutt, oppvaskpike.

sculptor ['skʌlptə] billedhogger.

sculpture ['skʌlptʃə] skulptur, billedhoggerkunst. **-arbeid**; hogge ut, meisle, skjære ut.

scum [skʌm] skum, berme, avskum; skumme.

scumble ['skʌmbl] gi mattere fargetone; avdempe de skarpe linjene (i en tegning).

summer ['skʌmə] skumsleiv.

scummy ['skʌmi] skumdekt, skummende.

scupper ['skʌpə] spygatt (på skip).

scurf [skə·f] skurv, skjell, flass. **-y** ['skə·fi] skurvet.

scurrilous ['skʌriləs] grov, plump, simpel.

scurry ['skʌri] hastverk, jag, fei; jage, fare.

scurvied [skə·vid] som har skjørbuk.

scurvy ['skə·vi] skurvet; nedrig, sjofel; skjørbuk.

scut [skʌt] kort hale, halestump.

scutch [skʌtʃ] skake lin; ruskelin; skåketre.

scuttle ['skʌtl] kullboks; liten luke, ventil. takluke; bore hull i, bore i senk.

scuttle ['skʌtl] pile, renne; renn, løp.

scythe [saiδ] ljå; meie, slå. **-man** slåttekar.

s. d. fk. f. several dates.
S. D. F. fk. f. Social Democratic Federation.
S. E. fk. f. South-east.
sea [si·] hav, sjø; by — til sjøs. — -bath sjøbad. — -bear isbjørn. — -beat(en) pisket av havet. -board strandbredd, havstrand, kyst. — -boat sjøbåt. — -born født på sjøen, oppstått av havet. — -borne oversjøisk. — -bound omgitt av havet. — -bred oppdradd på sjøen. — -breeze pålandsvind, havgule. — -brief sjøpass. — -calf sel. — -cap sjømannslue. — -captain skipskaptein. — -change forandring ved (el. på) sjøen. — -chart [-tʃa·ᵒt] sjøkart. — -chest skipskiste. — -coal steinkull. — -coast havstrand, kyst. — -compass skipskompass. — -dog sel; sjøulk. — -encircled omgitt av havet. -farer sjøfarende. — -fight sjøslag. — -fish saltvannsfisk. — -floor havbunn. — -foam havskum; merskum. — -gage dypgående. — -going som går til sjøs, sjøgående. — -green sjøgrønn. — -hog marsvin; nise. — -horse hvalross.
seal [si·l] sel.
seal [si·l] signet, segl; besegle, forsegle, lakke.
Sealand ['s·lənd] Sjælland.
sealing ['si·liŋ] selfangst; forsegling.
sealing-wax ['si·liŋwäks] lakk.
seam [si·m] søm; fuge, sammenføyning, skjøt, nat; lag; skramme, arr; sømme, sy sammen, sammenføye, skramme.
seaman ['si·mən] sjømann, matros.
seamanlike ['si·mənlaik] sjømannsaktig, sjømanns-.
seamanship ['simənʃip] sjømannsskap.
sea-mew ['si·mju·] måse, måke.
sea-mile ['si·mail] sjømil, kvartmil.
seamless ['si·mlès] uten søm, usydd.
sea-monster ['si·månstə] havuhyre.
seamstress ['se·mstrès] sypike.
seamy ['si·mi] sydd, med søm, søm-; arret; **the — side** vrangen.
séance ['se·a·ns] seanse. **spiritualistic** — spiritistisk seanse.
sea|-needle horngjel. — -nettle gople, manet, kobbeklyse. — -onion scilla maritima. — -otter havoter. — -ox hvalross. — -parrot lunde. — -pie tjeld (fugl). — -piece sjøstykke, marine. — -pink fjærekoll. — -plane hydroaeroplan, vannfly.
seaport ['si·på·t] havneby, sjøhavn, sjøby.
sea-power ['si·pauə] sjømakt.
sear [siə] ro, avtrekkerknast (i geværlås).
sear [siə] tørr, fortørket; svi, fortørke, brenne, brennemerke; gjøre følelsesløs; **fall into the** — (poetisk) visne.
search [sə·tʃ] ransake, undersøke, lete, gjennomsøke, visitere, sondere, granske, prøve, forske, (i bergverksdrift) skjerpe; søkning, leting, gransking, ransaking, gjennomsøking, visitasjon; **his house was -ed** det ble gjort husundersøkelse hos ham; — **into** undersøke; — **out** søke fram; — **for** (el. **after**) granske etter; in — **of** for å søke; **right of** — visitasjonsrett (i krig). **-er** søker; etterforsker; skjerper (**-er of mines**); gjennomsøker, visitator, visiterende tollbetjent; undersøkelsesredskap.
searching ['sə·tʃiŋ] gjennomborende, gjennomtrengende, skarp, bitende, inntrengende; **a — question** et inngående spørsmål.
seasonticket ['si·zn'tikit] abonnementskort, sesongbillett.
sea-star ['si·sta·ᵒ] sjøstjerne (dyr).
sea-swallow ['si·'swåloᵘ] teine (fugl).
seat [si·t] sæte, benk, stol, beliggenhet, plass, residens, landsted; sette, anvise en plass; **be -ed** sett deg! **take a** — sett deg! sitt ned!
sea-term ['si·tə·m] sjømannsuttrykk.
seating ['si·tiŋ] sete, bakdel (av klær); stoltrekk.
Seattle [si·'ätl] Seattle (by).
sea-urchin ['si·'ə·tʃin] kråkebolle.
sea-voyage ['si·'voiidʒ] sjøreise.

seaward ['si·wəd] mot sjøen, sjøverts.
sea-water ['si·'wå·tə] havvann, sjøvann.
sea-way ['si·we·] sjøgang.
seaweed ['si·wi·d] sjøgras, tang.
seaworthy ['si·wə·ði] sjødyktig.
sec. fk. f. secretary; second.
secede [si·si·d] tre ut, skille lag.
secern [si·sə·n] sondre, skille ut, avsondre.
secession [si·seʃən] utskillelse, det å tre ut.
seclude [si·klu·d] utelukke; **-d** ensom.
seclusion [si·klu·ʒən] avsondring, ensomhet.
second ['sekənd] annen, andre, nummer to, neste; hjelper, sekundant, sekund; hjelpe, understøtte.
secondary ['sekəndəri] senere, etterfølgende (**to** etter); underordnet, bi-; avledet; — **education** høyere skolevesen; — **school** høyere skole, gymnasium.
second-best ['sekəndbest] nestbest.
second-class ['sekəndkla·s] av annen klasse.
second-hand ['sekəndhänd] annenhånds, ikke ny, brukt; antikvarisk.
second-rate ['sekəndreit] annenrangs.
second|-sight synskhet. — -sighted synsk, framsynt.
secrecy ['si·krisi] hemmelighet, hemmeligholdelse; diskresjon, det å tie med noe; hemmelighetsfullhet; **I rely on your** — jeg stoler på Deres diskresjon.
secret ['si·krit] hemmelig; hemmelighet.
secretary ['sekrətəri] sekretær, skriver; — **of state** minister, riksråd, statsråd.
secrete [si·kri·t] skjule; avsondre, skille ut.
secretion [si·kri·ʃən] avsondring.
secretive [si·kri·tiv] taus, tagal; hemmelighetsfull; avsondrende.
sect [sekt] sekt. **-arian** [-'æ·ᵒriən] sekterisk; sekterer. **-arianism** [-'æ·ᵒriənizm] sektvesen.
sectary ['sektəri] sekterer; sekterisk.
section ['sekʃən] skur, skjæring, oppskjæring, avdeling, gjennomsnitt, (amr.) seksjon (640 acres). **-al** ['sekʃənəl] gjennomsnitts-, snitt-; som består av selvstendige deler; (amr.) lokalpatriotisk.
section-mark ['sekʃən'ma·ᵒk] paragraftegn (§).
section-plane ['sekʃənple·n] snittflate.
sector ['sektə] sektor.
sectorial [sek'tå·riəl] tooth rovtann.
secular ['sekjulə] hundreårs-, timelig, verdslig; **Russia's** — **ambition** Russlands sekelgamle ærgjerrighet; **the** — **arm** den v rdslige makt; **the** — **clergy** den ordinerte geistlighet; — **marriage** borgerlig ekteskap. **-ization** [sekjulari'ze·ʃən] verdsliggjøring. **-ize** ['sekjularaiz] sekularisere, verdsliggjøre.
secure [si·kjuə] sikker, trygg, fast; sikre, feste, sikre seg; — **arms** bære et gevær med munningen ned.
security [si·kjuəriti] sikkerhet, dekning, kausjon; i plur. også: verdipapirer.
sedan [si·dän] bærestol.
sedate [si·de·t] sedat, rolig, sindig, satt.
sedative [si·de·tiv] beroligende (middel).
sedentary ['sedntəri] stillesittende; fastsittende; som er en følge av å sitte stille.
sederunt [si·diərənt] møte.
sedge [sedʒ] storr, starr, siv. — -bird (— -warbler, — -wren) sivsanger.
sedgy ['sedʒi] bevokst med starr.
sediment ['sedimənt] bunnfall; avleiring, kjelestein.
sedition [si·diʃən] oppvigleri.
seditious [si·diʃəs] opprørsk, opphissende.
seduce [si·dju·s] forføre, lokke, forlede. **-ment** forføring. **-r** forfører. **seduction** [si·dʌkʃən] forføring. **seductive** [si·dʌktiv] forførerisk.
sedulous ['sedjuləs] flittig, idig, iherdig.
see [si·] bispesete; **the Holy (Apostolic, Papal)** — den hellige stol, pavestolen.
see [si·] se, innse, forstå, skjønne, være opp-

merksom på, være merksam på, se til, sørge for, si innom til, søke, henvende seg til, besøke, se hos seg, ta imot, følge; **have -n a shot fired** ha luktet kruttet; **none of us may** — **the day** kanskje ingen av oss opplever den dagen; — **a thing done** la noe gjøre; — **after pass**c; **they did not** — **much of him** de så ikke mye til ham; — **to sørge for;** — **through** gjennomskue; **Oh, I** —**!** nå så!

seed ['si·d] sæd, såkorn, frø, settepoteter, avkom, ætt, slekt; spire, opphav; sette frø, frø seg, så til, så; gå i frø. — **-cake** slags krydret kake.

seed-corn ['si·dkå·ºn] såkorn.

seeded ['si·did] i frø, som har satt frø.

seeder ['si·də] såmann; såmaskin; frøuttaingsapparat.

seed-grain ['si·dgreⁱn] såkorn.

seediness ['si·dinès] frørikdom; slapphet; lurvethet.

seeding-machine såmaskin.

seedling ['si·dliŋ] frøplante; oppalt av frø.

seed-pearl ['si·dpə·l] frøperle (minste slags perle).

seed|-potato ['si·dpə'teⁱtoⁿ] settepotet. **-sman** såmann, frøhandler. — **-time** såtid.

seedy ['si·di] full av frø, gått i frø, loslitt, lurvet; slapp, dårlig, utilpass, utidig.

seeing ['si·iŋ] synsevne, syn; — **(that)** i betraktning av at, siden, ettersom.

seek [si·k] søke, lete etter, forsøke, ansøke, forlange; — **out** oppsøke, finne. **-er** søkende, søker, ansøker.

seem [si·m] synes, tykkes, late til; **it -s** det synes, det ser ut til; **it -s to me** jeg synes; **I still** — **to hear** jeg synes ennå at jeg hører. **-er** en som later. **-ing** utseende, skinn; **to all -ing** tilsynelatende. **-ingly** tilsynelatende.

seemly ['si·mli] sømmelig, høvelig.

seen [si·n] perf. pts. av **see.**

seer [si·ə] seende; seer. **-ess** [-res] seerske.

seesaw ['si·'så·] vipping, husking; vippe, vippelek; vippe, huske; vippende.

seethe [si·ð] koke, syde; koking.

segregate ['segrige¹t] utsondre.

segregate ['segrigit] utskilt.

segregation [segri'ge¹ʃən] avsondring.

seigneur ['si·njə], **seignior** ['si·njə] lensherre, herremann; **the grand** — storherren, den tyrkiske sultan; fornem herre.

seine [se¹n] fiskegarn, dragnot, vad, steng.

seismometer [saiz'måmitə] jordskjelvmåler.

seizable ['si·zəbl] som kan gripes el. fattes.

seize [si·z] gripe, ta, bemektige seg, anholde, inndra, konfiskere, beslaglegge; bendsle, seise; **be -d of** være kommet i besittelse av; — **upon** bemektige seg.

seizure ['si·ʒə] det å gripe, grep; bemektigelse, oppbringing, anholdelse, konfiskasjon, beslaglagte varer, anfall.

seldom ['seldəm] (adv.) sjelden; — **or never** sjelden eller aldri.

select [si'lekt] velge ut; utvalt, utsøkt.

selection [si'lekʃən] utvelging, valg; utvalg.

selenium [si'li·niom] selén.

self [self] selv; jeg. — **-abandonment** selvoppgivelse. — **-abasement** selvforedrelse. — **-abnegation** selvfornekting. — **-conceited** innbilsk. — **-conscious** selvbevisst; genert — **-contained** innesluttet, som er seg selv nok. — **-defence** nødverge. — **-denial** selvfornekting. — **-indulgence** nytelsessyke. — **-interest** egennytte.

selfish ['selfiʃ] egenkjærlig, egoistisk, selvisk.

selfless ['selflès] uselvisk.

self-made ['selfme¹d] selvgjort; — **man** selvhjulpen mann, mann som er kommet fram ved egen hjelp.

self-possessed ['selfpə'zest] fattet, behersket.

self-praise ['selfpre¹z] selvros; — **is open disgrace** selvros stinker.

self|same ['selfse¹m] selvsamme. — **-sufficient**

suffisant, innbilsk. — **-will** egenrådighet. — **-willed** egenrådig.

sell [sel] selge, handle, selges, gå (av); ha avsetning; — **out** selge ut; — **up** selge; — **him up** la hans eiendeler selge ved tvangsauksjon. **-er** selger, ting som går. **-ing out** utsalg. **-ing-price** salgspris.

seltzer ['seltsə] selters.

selvage ['selvidʒ] kant, list, jare (på tøy).

selves [selvz] plur. av **self.**

semaphore ['seməfå·ə] semafor (et slags signalapparat).

semasiology [sime'si'ålədʒi] semasiologi.

semblance ['sembləns] utseende, skikkelse, likhet, skinn; **if he made out any** — **of a case** om han tilsynelatende skaffet beviser.

semen ['si·mən] sæd; frø.

semester [si'mestə] semester, halvår.

semi- ['semi] halv-, i smstn. — **-annual** halvårlig. — **-annular** halvrund. **-breve** [-bri·v] helnote. **-circle** halvsirkel. **-colon** semikolon. — **-conscious** halvt bevisstløs. — **-detached** [semidi'tätʃt] halvveis frittstående, rekke-. — **-goods** blandet (gods- og passasjer). — **-lunar** [semi-'lu·nə] halvmåneformet.

seminal ['seminəl] frø-, sæd-; opprinnelig.

seminarist ['seminərist] seminarist; elev av en katolsk presteskole. **seminary** ['seminəri] katolsk presteseminar, jesuittskole. **semination** [semi-'ne¹ʃən] frøspredning.

semiquaver ['semikwe¹və] sekstendedelsnote.

Semite ['semait] semitt, semittisk.

Semitic [si'mitik] semittisk.

semitone ['semitoⁿn] halvtone.

semivowel ['semi'vauəl] halvvokal.

sempiternal [sempi'tə·nəl] uendelig.

sempstress [sem(p)strés] syerske, sydame.

sen. fk. f. **senate; senator; senior.**

senate ['senit] senat. — **-house** senat, rådhus.

senator ['senitə] senator. **senatorial** [senə-'tå·rial] senator-.

send [send] sende, sende bud; gjøre; sette, stampe (om skip); stamping; **God** — **it!** Gud gi det!; **it nearly sent him crazy** det drev ham nesten fra vettet; — **him victorious** unne ham seier; — **him wild** gjøre ham rasende; — **word** la vite; — **for** sende bud etter; — **forth,** — **out** sende ut; — **off** sende bort; — **up** drive i været, dimittere, sende en elev opp til rektor til avstraffing.

sender ['sendə] avsender; avsenderapparat.

senescence [si'nesəns] avfeldighet.

senescent [si'nesənt] aldrende.

seneschal ['seniʃəl] seremonimester, hushovmester.

senile ['si·nail] oldingaktig, senil.

senility [si'niliti] alderdomssløvhet.

senior ['si·njə] senior, eldre, eldst. **he is my senior by a year** er år eldre enn jeg.

seniority [si·ni'åriti] ansiennitet; seniorat.

senna ['senə] sennepsblad; **syrup of** — sennasirup (avføringsmiddel).

Sennacherib [se'näkərib] Sanherib.

sennight ['senit] uke, veke.

sennit ['senit] flettet strå; platting.

sensation [sen'se¹ʃən] fornemmelse, følelse, sensasjon; **cause (make, create) a** — vekke oppsikt.

sensational [sen'se¹ʃnl] følelses-, oppsiktsvekkende, spennende.

sensationalism [sen'se¹ʃənəlizm] sensasjonell karakter; sensualisme.

sense [sens] sansning, erkjennelse, oppfatning, sans, forstand, vett, betydning, fornuftig mening; **the five -s of** (de fem sanser) **feeling, sight, hearing, smell.** and **taste; the general** — **of** (stemningen i) **the assembly; common** — sunn sans; **a** — **for economy** økonomisk sans; **a** — **of beauty** (duty; humour; locality) skjønnhetssans (plikt-følelse; humoristisk sans; stedsans) **give a** — gi mening; **he lost his -s** han gikk fra forstanden;

in one's -s ved sine fulle fem; out of one's -s fra vettet, fra sans og samling. -less [-lès], -lessly [-lèsli] følelsesløs, bevisstløs, urimelig, meningsløs, vettløs. -lessness [-lèsnés] følelsesløshet, bevisstløshet, urimelighet.

sensibility [sensi'biliti] følsomhet.

sensible ['sensibl] følelig, merkbar, følsom, mottagelig; oppmerksom; fornuftig; bevisst; no sensible person ikke noe forstandig menneske; be sensible of ha en følelse av, innse, være klar over.

sensitive ['sensitiv] sanselig, sanse-; følsom, sensibel; — paper (lys)følsomt papir; — plant følsom mimose.

sensual ['senʃuəl] sanselig. -ism sanselighet, sensualisme. -ist vellysting, sensualist. -ity [senʃu'äliti] sanselighet.

sensuous ['senʃuəs] sanse-, sanselig; som hører til sansene, som henvender seg til sansene.

sent [sent] imperf. og perf. pts. av send.

sentence ['sentəns] dom, sentens, setning; ordtak; dømme; the — of this court is ti kjennes for rett; — of death dødsdom; pass — on domfelle; under — of death dødsdømt; principal — hovedsetning; subordinate (eller accessory) — bisetning; subsequent — ettersetning.

sentential [sen'tenʃəl] setningsmessig, setnings-.

sententious [sen'tenʃəs] full av ordtak, fyndig.

sentiment ['sentimənt] følelse, mening, skjønn, oppfattelse, tanke, sentens; kort skåltale, følsomhet; the general — stemningen; give a — utbringe en skål; people like — (det rørende).

sentimental [senti'mentəl] følelsesfull, sentimental.

sentimentality [sentimen'täliti] sentimentalitet, føleri.

sentinel ['sentinel] skiltvakt; stå vakt over.

sentry ['sentri] skiltvakt. — -box skilderhus.

sepal ['si·pəl] begerblad.

separable ['sep(ə)rəbl] atskillelig.

separate ['sepəreit] skille, skille ut, fjerne, skilles, gå fra hverandre.

separate ['sep(ə)rit] særskilt, egen, individuell; republish separately gi ut i særtrykk.

separation [sepə're¹ʃən] atskillelse, skilsmisse, separasjon.

separator ['sepəreitə] separator.

sepia ['si·piə] blekksprut, sepia.

sepoy ['si·poi] sepoy, innfødt ostindisk soldat, som står i en europeisk makts tjeneste.

sept [sept] ætt, klan (i Irland).

Sept. fk. f. September.

septangular [sep'täŋgjələ] sjukantet.

September [sep'tembə] september.

septennial [sep'tenjəl] sjuårig.

Septentriones [septentri'o⁴ni·z] Karlsvognen.

septic ['septik] som bevirker forråtnelse, fortærende; — tank basseng hvor kloakkvann uskadeliggjøres.

septicaemia [septi'si·miə] blodforgiftning.

septuagenary [septju'ädʒinəri] som består av sytti; syttiårig.

Septuagint ['septjuədʒint] Septuaginta (en oversettelse til gresk av det gamle testamente).

septuple ['septjupl] sjudobbelt.

sepulchral [si'pʌlkrəl] grav-, gravlignende.

sepulchre ['selpkə] grav, gravminne; jorde, gravlegge.

sepulture ['selptʃə] begravelse.

sequacious [si'kwe¹ʃəs] føyelig, smidig; konsekvent.

sequacity [si'kwäsiti] følgaktighet.

sequel ['si·kwəl] fortsettelse; in the — i det følgende.

sequence ['si·kwəns] rekkefølge, orden; sekvens; the — of events begivenhetenes rekkefølge; in — to som en fortsettelse av.

sequent ['sikwənt] følgende.

sequester [si'kwestə] avsondre; beslaglegge.

sequestrate [si'kwestre¹t] beslaglegge, ta utlegg.

sequestration [sekwi'stre¹ʃən] sekvestrasjon.

sequestrator ['sekwistre¹tə] sekvestrator.

sequin ['si·kwin] zecchino (gammel venetiansk gullmynt, ca. 8 kr.); metallpaljett.

seraglio [se¹ra·lio⁴] serail, harem.

seraph ['serəf] seraf (overengel); plur.: -im.

Serb [sə·b] serbisk; serber; serbisk (språk).

Serbia ['sə·bjə] Serbia.

esrenade [seri'ne¹d] serenade; synge en serenade.

serenata [seri'na·tə] serenade.

serene [si'ri·n] klar, ren, skyfri; stille, rolig, koldblodig; (som titel foran tyske fyrstenavn:) durchlauchtig, høy; all —! alt i orden! Your Serene Highness Deres Durchlauchtighet; most — durchlauchtigst. -ly klart, koldblodig; -ly beautiful opphøyd og skjønn.

serenity [si'reniti] klarhet, stillhet, sinnsro; høyhet.

serf [sə·f] livegen. -age el. -dom livegenskap.

serge [sə·dʒ] et slags ullent tøy.

sergeant ['sa·ədʒənt] sersjant; politifunksjonær, overbetjent; advokat (alminneligere: serjeant eller serjeant-at-law); colour-sergeant en sersjant som har tilsyn med fanen. — -major [-'me¹dʒə] sersjant, kommandersersjant.

serial ['siəriəl] rekke-, som utkommer i hefter; føljetong, roman som går gjennom flere nummer av et blad; short stories and — (lengre) tales.

serialize ['siəriəlaiz] sende ut heftevis.

seriate ['siəriët] (ordnet) i rekkefølge.

series ['siəri(i)z] serie, rekke(følge), klasse.

serio-comic(al) ['siərio⁴kåmik(l)] halvt alvorlig, halvt komisk.

serious ['siəriəs] alvorlig; I am — det er mitt alvor; I am quite — det er mitt ramme alvor; matters begin to look — det begynner å se betenkelig ut. -ly ill alvorlig syk. -ness [-nés] alvorlighet.

serjeant ['sa·ədʒənt] -at-law høyesterettsadvokat. serjeant-at-arms væpnet følgesvenn, væpnet herold (i parlamentet). serjeantsurgeon kongens livlæge.

sermon ['sə·mən] preken; preke. preach (el. deliver) a — holde en preken; the Sermon of the Mount bergprekenen.

serpent ['sə·pənt] slange, orm; serpent (glt. trehorn).

serpentine ['sə·pəntain) slangeaktig, buktet; bukte seg; serpentin; the Serpentine liten innsjø i Hyde Park, London.

serrate ['sere¹t] sagtakket, sagtannet.

serration [sə're¹ʃən] sagtakker, sagtenner.

serried ['serid] tettsluttet, tett.

serum ['siərəm] serum, blodvann; valle, myse.

servant ['sə·vənt] tjener, tjenestepike, hushjelp, oppasser; funksjonær, tjenestemann; the -s tjenerskapet, tjenestefolkene. — -girl el. —-maid tjenestepike, hushjelp. —-man tjener, tjenestegutt.

serve [sə·v] tjene, tjene hos, betjene, greie, oppvarte, anrette, servere, hjelpe til, nytte, gagne, fremme; utdele, tilføye, gjøre; behandle, rette seg etter, gjøre tjeneste, passe, være nok, greie seg, besørge, forrette gudstjeneste, utvirke, spille ut; gå i rute; servie (i tennis); kle, serve (tau); — him right (eller: it -s him right eller he is rightly -d) det har han godt av (eller: nå kan han ha det så godt); Mylady is -d Deres nåde, det er servert; — a warrant utføre en arrestordre; — a summons on a person forkynne en en stevning; — up sette fram, diske opp med; — out utlevere (proviant). -r messhjelper, utspiller, serveringsbrett.

Servia ['sə·viə] Serbia.

Servian ['sə·viən] serbisk; serbisk språk.

service ['sə·vis] tjeneste, arbeid, yrke, post, stilling, krigstjeneste, oppvartning, betjening, tjenestetid, villighet, nytte, gagn, offentlig el. statstjeneste, ærbødig hilsen, gudstjeneste, ritual, kirkebønn, oppdekning, service, stell; rute, fart; -vesen, -verk; utspill; **the civil** — det sivile embetsverk; **sanitary** — sunnhetsvesen; **a** — **of plate** et sølvservise; **a** — **of peril** en farefull tjeneste; **her -s to literature** hennes fortjenester av litteraturen; **do (render)** him **a** — gjøre ham en tjeneste; **perform** — holde gudstjeneste; **I am at your** — jeg står til Deres tjeneste; **write a letter on** — **to him** skrive tjenstlig til ham.

serviceable ['sə·visəbl] nyttig; brukbar; tjenstvillig.

service|-ball ['sə·visbå·l] første ball (i tennis). **— -main** hovedrør, hovedledning. **— -pipe** siderør.

service-tree ['sə·vistri·] rogn (tre).

serviette [sə·vi'et] serviett.

servile ['sə·vail] slave-, slavisk, krypende, servil.

servility [sə·'viliti] slaviskhet, kryperi.

serving-girl ['sə·viŋgə·l] tjenestepike, hushjelp.

serving-man ['sə·viŋmän] tjener, tjenestegutt.

servitor ['sə·vitə] gratist (i Oxford, måtte tidligere varte opp ved bordet).

servitude ['sə·vitju·d] slaveri, trelldom.

sesame ['sesəmi] sesam.

session ['seʃən] sete, sesjon, samling, ting; parlamentssesjon, rettssesjon, møte, studieår; menighetsråd (i Skottland); **-s of the peace** fredsdommerting; **be in** — være samlet; **remain in** — (sitter sammen) **till the end of September; court of** — høyesterett (i sivilsaker).

set [set] sette, feste, innfatte (en edelstein **a precious stone**), la stivne, fastsette (en tid til et møte **a time for a meeting**), bestemme, anslå, avpasse, innstille, stille (ur etter a **clock by**), sette melodi til (— **to music**), sette i ledd, besette (med juveler **with jewels**), sette opp (en barberkniv **a razor**), gi seg til, begi seg; gå ned, synke, gla (om himmellegemer), bli fast el. stiv, størkne, jage med fuglehund; — **about to** ta fatt på; — **going** sette i gang, sette i omløp; — **a hen** legge en høne på egg; — **the land** peile landet; **she** — **her lips firmly** hun knep leppene fast sammen; — **against** stille opp imot; — **aside** tilsidesette; — **at ease** berolige; — **before one self** foresette seg; — **down** skrive ned, notere, oppføre; — **forth** framstille, vise, utvikle, forklare; — **forward** forfremme; — **off** utskille, framheve, utheve; — **off to advantage** framheve fordelaktig; — **on** tilskynde, oppmuntre, egge; — **out** anvise, fastsette, pryde, vise, framsette, gå ut; — **to** ta fatt på; — **to work** sette i arbeid; — **up** oppføre, grunnlegge, begynne, framsette (en ny lære **a new doctrine**), hjelpe på fote, stramme opp (en rekrutt); — **up one's back** skyte rygg; — **up a carriage** legge seg til egen vogn; — **up a cry** sette i et skrik; — **up a shop** åpne en detaljhandel; — **him up in business** etablere ham; — **free** sette i frihet; — **open** lukke opp; — **right** (el. **to right**) hjelpe til rette; — **wrong** forvirre; — **one self about arranging** gå i gang med å ordne; **the -ting sun** kveldsolen; — **about one's work** ta fatt på arbeidet; **darkness -s in** mørket faller på; **luck has** — **in against him** lykken har vendt ham ryggen; — **out for London** reise til L.; — **out upon a journey** tiltre en reise.

set [set] stiv, stivnet, fast, stø; stadig (vær); bestemt, regelmessig, vel gjennomtenkt, sammensatt; **square-set** firskåren; **his eyes were** — han stirret stivt; **a** — **phrase** en stående talemåte.

set [set] synkning, nedgang, ende; sett (stoler **of chairs**) samling, stell (— **of china** porselensstell), rad, rekke, suite; garnityr, parti (i lawntennis), lag, krets; fransee, omgangskrets, klikk; avlegger, anfall; snitt fasong; **a** — **of rogues** en skøyerklikk, noen skøyere alle sammen; **the rise and** — **of the sun** soloppgang og solnedgang; — **of teeth** gebiss, tannsett. — **-back** motstrøm, bakevje; tilbakeslag, reaksjon, hindring, stans. — **-down** knusende svar, skrape. — **-off** ['set'å(·)f] middel til å framheve, prydelse, pynt,

motkrav, vederlag; **as a** — **-off til** gjengjeld. — **-to dyst, sammenstøt.**

settee [se'ti·] sofa, kanapé; transportfartøy i Middelhavet.

setter [setə] setter, fuglehund, stråmann, komponist. **-forth** forkynner. — **-on** anstifter.

setting ['setiŋ] innsetning, nedgang, jakt med fuglehund, ramme, innfatning, iscenesetting, strømretning, vindretning; **his** — **of** hans musikk til; **the** — **of** (rammen om) **their lives.** — **-dog** fuglehund. — **-hammer** setthammer. — **-rule** settelinje. — **-screw** innstillingsskrue, settskrue. — **-stick** vinkelhake (i setteri).

settle ['setl] sette, befeste, bosette, etablere, ordne, rette på, bunnfelle, berolige, bestemme, avgjøre, fastsette, betale (en regning **an account**), gjøre opp, gjøre det av med, ekspedere, bebygge; festne seg, komme til ro, sette seg, nedsette seg, slå seg ned, falle til ro, sette penger fast; synke, sige ned, legge seg, stilne; langbenk; — **a business** avvikle en forretning; — **a claim** avgjøre en fordring; — **the dispute** skille tretten; — **the land** senke (el. slippe, miste) landet; **the house was -d upon her** hun beholdt huset som særeie; — **a pension on** fastsette en pensjon for; — **down** falle til ro; — **down upon a country** sette seg fast i et land; — **in life** gifte seg; — **in** (el. **to**) business nedsette seg som forretningsmann.

settled ['setld] fast, stadig, forsørget, avgjort, betalt; **married and -d** gift og kommet til ro.

settlement ['setlmənt] anbringelse, nedsettelse, kolonisasjon, avgjørelse, oppgjør, fastsettelse av arvefølge, livrente, pensjon, forsørgelse, koloni; **act of** — tronfølgelov; **deed of** — ekteskapskontrakt; **the law of** — loven om hjemstavnsrett.

settler ['setlə] kolonist, nybygger.

settling ['setliŋ] kolonisasjon, endring, synkning, bilegging; **settlings** bunnfall, berme.

seven ['sevn] sju. **-fold** [-foⁿld] sjufold, sjudobbelt. **-teen** ['sevn'ti·n] sytten. **-teenth** [-'ti·nþ] syttende. **-th** ['sevnþ] sjuende, sjuendedel. **-thly** ['sevnþli] for det sjuende. **-tieth** ['sevntiiþ] syttiende. **-ty** ['sevnti] sytti.

sever ['sevə] skille, løsrive, kløyve, splitte, skjære over el. i stykker, skjelne, skilles

several ['sevrəl] atskillige, flere, en del; — **more** atskillig flere.

severally ['sevrəli] hver for seg, respektive.

severance ['sev(ə)rəns] atskillelse.

severe [si'viə] streng, stri, skarp, hard, smertelig, heftig, sterk, voldsom, alvorlig, nøyaktig, kortfattet, fyndig; **a** — **loss** et følelig tap; **a** — **blow** et hardt slag; — **truths** drøye sannheter. **-ly** strengt, hardt, heftig; **the loss was -ly felt** det var et hardt tap.

severity [si'veriti] strenghet, hardhet, voldsomhet, vanskelighet; **the** — **of cold** den strenge kulde.

sew [soⁿ] sy; — **on a button** sy i en knapp; — **up** sy sammen.

sewage ['sju·idʒ] kloakkinnhold, kloakkvann.

sewer ['soⁿ] syer(ske).

sewer ['sjuə] kloakk; forsyne med kloakk. **-age** ['s(j)uəridʒ] kloakkanlegg; kloakkinnhold.

sewing ['soⁿiŋ] syting; sytøy, søm. — **bee** (amr.) syklubb, symøte, «kvinneforening». — **-circle** syklubb. — **-machine** symaskin. — **-needle** synål. — **-silk** sysilke. — **-thread** sytråd.

sewn [soⁿn] perf. pts. av **sew.**

sewn-up utmattet, beruset, medtatt.

sex [seks] kjønn;. **the fair** — det smukke kjønn; **the softer (sterner)** — det svake (sterke) kjønn.

sexagenary [sek'sädʒin(ə)ri] sekstiårig.

sexangular [sek'säŋgjulə] sekskantet.

sexennial [sek'senjəl] seksårig.

sexless ['sekslés] kjønnsløs.

sextant ['sekstənt] sekstant.

sexton ['sekstən] graver, kirketjener. **-ship** stilling som kirketjener.

sextuple ['sekstjupl] seksdobbelt; seksdoble.

sexual ['sekʃuəl] kjønns-, kjønnslig; — **desire** kjønnsdrift; — **intercourse** kjønnslig omgang.

shabbiness ['ʃäbinés] loslitthet, lurvethet.

shabby ['ʃäbi] lurvet, loslitt, fattigslig, sjofel.

shabby-genteel ['ʃäbidʒən'ti·l] fattig-fornem.

shabrack ['ʃäbräk] saldekken, skaberakk.

shack [ʃäk] (amr.) hytte, koie.

shackle ['ʃäkl] lenke, sjakle sammen; (fot)lenke; metallbøyle, kjettinglås; sjakkel.

shad [ʃäd] maifisk, stamsild.

shaddock ['ʃädək] melonsitron (en frukt).

shade [ʃe'd] skygge, skygging, skyggeside, beskyttelse, ly, skjerm, glasskuppel, gjenferd, fargetone, avskygning, nyanse, lite grann; skygge, sjattere, skjule, beskjerme.

shade-card fargekort.

shadow ['ʃädoᵘ] skygge, slagskygge, skyggeparti (i maleri), uadskillelig ledsager, skyggebilde, gjenferd, ly; skygge (for), sjattere, beskytte, antyde, framstille billedlig, følge som en skygge, følge og bevokte; **he is -ed** hans skritt bevoktes, han bli skygget.

shadowy ['ʃädoᵘi] skyggefull, skyggeaktig, mørk, døkk, dim, uvirkelig; typisk **have a —** existence føre en skinntilværelse.

shady ['ʃe'di] skyggefull, kjølig, tvetydig, tvilsom; **on the — side of forty** på den gale siden av de førti.

shaft [ʃa·ft] skaft, vognstang, skåk, spydskaft, pil, spir, sjakt, aksel. **drudge in the —** henge i (selen); **-ed** ['ʃa·ftid] med skaft.

shag [ʃäg] stritt hår, ragg, grov lo, plysj, shag-tobakk; gjøre ragget.

shaggy ['ʃägi] stri, lodden, ragget.

shagreen [ʃə'gri·n] chagrin.

shah [ʃa·] sjah, konge i Persia.

shake [ʃe'k] ryste, ruske, riste, riste av, rokke, svekke; skjelve, vakle; slå triller; risting, skaking, rystelse, støt, håndtrykk, trille (i musikk); **— -down** midlertidig seng, flatseng; **— hands** ta hverandre i hånden; komme til enighet; **— off** frigjøre seg for; **a fair —** en god forretning.

Shakespeare ['ʃe'kspiə] Shakespeare; Shakespeare-utgave; Shakespeare-eksemplar.

Shakespearean [ʃe'ks'piəriən] shakespearsk.

shako ['ʃäkoᵘ] sjako (slags militærlue).

shaky ['ʃe'ki] skjelven; ustø, vinglet; sprukken.

shale [ʃe'l] skall; leirskifer.

shall [ʃäl], alm. uten trykk [ʃ(ə)l] skal; **I am not the first, and — not be the last** (og blir ikke den siste); **— you be at home to night?** er De hjemme i aften?

shallop ['ʃäləp] sjalupp.

shallot [ʃə'lät] sjalottløk.

shallow ['ʃäloᵘ], **-ly** grunn, overfladisk, lavbunnet; grunt vann, grunne, grunning; gjøre grunn. **— -brained** lavpannet, innskrenket. **-ness** [-nés] ringe dybde.

shalt [ʃält]; **thou —** (gml.) du skal.

sham [ʃäm] skinn, humbug, komediespill; skinn-, fingert; narre, bedra, føre bak lyset; forstille seg, bløffe; **discern wrong from right, and -s** (skinn) **from realities;** **— door** blinddør; **— fight** skinnfektning; **— illness** forstilt sykdom; **— sleep** late som om man sover; **— stupid** gjøre seg dum.

shamble ['ʃämbl] sjokke, subbe, dra benene etter seg; tassing.

shambles ['ʃämblz] slaktehus, slakteri; kjøtttorg.

shame [ʃe'm] skam, skamfølelse, skjensel; beskjemme, gjøre skam på, gjøre til skamme; gjøre skamfull, vanære, skamme seg; **for — fy! for very —** for skams skyld; **he is dead to all —** han har bitt hodet av all skam; **put to — gjøre** til skamme; **— on you!** skam deg! **cry — upon**

skamme ut, stemple som en skjendighet; **put —** upon gjøre . . . skam.

shamefaced ['ʃe'mfe'st] skamfull, unnselig. **-ness** [-nés] unnseelse.

shameful ['ʃe'mful] skjendig, skammelig.

shameless ['ʃe'mlés] skamløs.

shammy ['ʃämi] semsklær; vaskeskinn.

shampoo [ʃäm'pu·] såpevaske og gni; massere; massasje, sjampooing.

shamrock ['ʃämråk] trebladet hvitkløver (irsk nasjonalmerke).

shanrydan ['ʃändridän] slags gammeldags vogn; skranglekjerre.

shandygaff ['ʃändigäf], blanding av øl og ingefærøl.

Shanghai [ʃäŋ'hai] Shanghai.

shanghai [ʃäŋ'hai] sjanghaie (o: drikke full og narre om bord).

shank [ʃäŋk], skank, legg, ben, stokk, stilk, skaft; **ride shank's** (el. **shanks')** **mare** bruke apostlenes hester.

shan't [ʃa·nt] fk. f. **shall not.**

shanty ['ʃänti] brakke, hytte, skur, koie.

shanty ['ʃänti] oppsang.

shanty-man ['ʃäntimən] (amr.) skogsarbeider.

shanty-man ['ʃäntimən] oppsanger.

shape [ʃe'p] skape, danne, forme, hogge til, innrette; skap, form, skikkelse, snitt, figur.

shapeless ['ʃe'plés] uformelig.

shapely ['ʃe'pli] velformet, velskapt.

I. **shard** [ʃa·ᵊd] brott, skår, pottekår.

II. **shard** [ʃa·ᵊd] gjødsel, kuruke. **— -beetle** tordivel.

share [ʃæ·ə] plogskjære, plogjern.

share [ʃæ·ə] del, andel, part; aksje; dele, skifte ut, fordele; ha sammen (**with** med), ta del (**in** i); **fall to my —** falle i min lodd; **go shares** spleise (**in** til); **preferred** (el. **preference**) **—** preferanseaksje.

shareholder ['ʃæ·əhoᵘldə] aksjonær, parthaver.

sharer ['ʃæ·ᵊrə] utdeler.

shark [ʃa·ᵊk] hai; svindler; snyte, flå.

sharp [ʃa·ᵊp] skarp, kvass, spiss; gløgg, våken, vaken; lur, ful; dur, med kryss foran, en halv tone høyere; presis; skarp tone, kryss; spisst våpen; skjerpe, snyte; **look —** passe på, skynde seg; **at five o' clock —** klokka fem presis.

sharpen ['ʃa·ᵊpən] skjerpe, kvesse, spisse, skjerpes.

sharper ['ʃa·ᵊpə] bedrager; kvesseinstrument.

sharp-set ['ʃa·ᵊpset] grådig, meget sulten.

sharpshooter ['ʃa·ᵊpʃu·tə] skarpskytter.

shatter ['ʃätə] splintre, slå i stykker, atsplitte, sprenge; gå i stykker; stump; **-ed health** nedbrutt helse. **— -brained** ['ʃätəbre'nd], **-pated** [-pe'tid] atspredt, tankeløs, skrullet.

shave [ʃe'v] skave, skrape, barbere, streife, plyndre; barbering; **it was a narrow —** det knep, det var på et hengende hår, det var så vidt.

shaver ['ʃe'və] liten knekt, pjokk; snyter; barber.

shaving ['ʃe'viŋ] spon, barbering. **— -brush** barberkost. **— -case** barberetui. **— -cup** (mug, pot) såpekopp. **— -set** barberstell. **— -stick** barbersåpe.

shawl [ʃå·l] sjal. **-ed** inntullet i et sjal.

shawm [ʃå·m] skalmeie (et musikkinstrument).

shay [ʃe'] slags vogn.

she [ʃi·] hun, den, det; hun(dyr). **— -goat** geit.

sheaf [ʃi·f] nek, kornband; bunt; binde (korn). **— of arrows** kogger med piler.

shear [ʃiə] klippe (is. sau); klipping; **a two** shear ram en toårs vær; **a pair of shears** en sauesaks, hagesaks. **-ing-time** klippetid. **-man** klipper, overskjærer.

sheath [ʃi·þ] slir, slire, balg; hylster.

sheathe [ʃi·ð] stikke i slira.

sheathing ['ʃi·ðiŋ] bekledning; kopperforhuding.

sheave [ʃiˑv] blokkskive, reimskive.
sheaves [ʃiˑvz] plur. av sheaf.
Sheba [ˈʃiˑbə] Saba.
shebeen [ʃiˈbiˑn] gaukesjapp.
shed [ʃed] utgyte; spre; kaste (lys), felle (lauv, tenner, horn); utgytelse; skille, dele; — a tear felle en tåre; — one's teeth felle tennene.
shed [ʃed] skur, skjul, skjå.
she'd [ʃiˑd] fk. f. she had, she would.
sheen [ʃiˑn] skinnende, bjart; skinn, glans.
sheeny [ˈʃiˑni] skinnende.
sheep [ʃiˑp] sau, får, tosk; saueskinn; a wolf in sheep's clothing en ulv i fåreklær. make (el. cast) sheep's eyes at sende forelskede blikk. — -cot sauekve. — -dip sauevask. — -dog brehund. — -fold sauekve. — -hook krum gjæterstav.
sheepish [ˈʃiˑpiʃ] unnselig, sjenert, blyg.
sheep|-run [ˈʃiˑprʌn] sauebeite (især i Australia). — -skin saueskinn, saueskinnsfell; pergamentsdokument. — -walk sauebeite.
sheer [ʃiə] skjær, ren, stupbratt; rent, bent; out of — weariness av bare, skjære tretthet.
sheer [ʃiə] vike til siden; — off gå av veien.
sheet [ʃiˑt] flak, flate, plate, laken, seil, ark, blad (is. i pl.), skjøt; dekke (med laken); skjøte. — -anchor nødanker. — -copper kopperblikk. sheet|ing [ˈʃiˑtiŋ] lakenlerret. — -iron jernblikk. — -lead blyplate.
Sheffield [ˈʃefiˑld] Sheffield.
sheik(h) [ʃek, ʃeˈk, ʃiˑk] sjeik (arabisk høvding).
shekel [ˈʃekl] penger, mynt (egl. en jødisk mynt).
sheldrake [ˈʃeldreˈk] gravand, gravandrik.
shelduck [ˈʃeldʌk] gravand.
shelf [ʃelf] hylle, avsats; sandbanke, grunne, båe; (laid) on the — lagt på hylla, avdanket, pantsatt; get on the — bli gammel jomfru; some shelves [ʃelvz] full of books en reol full av bøker.
shell [ʃel] skall, skolm, skjell, konkylie, musling, patronhylster (helt ut: cartridge —), patron, granat; (gammelt:) bombe; mellomklasse; lyre; skalle(s), pille, bombardere.
shellac [ˈʃeläk] skjellakk.
Shelley [ˈʃeli] Shelley.
shell-fish [ˈʃelfiʃ] skalldyr.
shell|-jacket [ˈʃelˈdʒäkit] leirtrøye. — -proof bombefast.
shelly [ˈʃeli] skall-, skallbærende; rik på muslinger; skallaktig.
shelter [ˈʃeltə] ly, vern, beskyttelse, tilfluktsrom; dekke, verne, gi ly, lune, huse, søke ly. — -deck shelterdekk. — -home redningshjem.
sheltic, shelty [ˈʃelti] shetlandsponni.
shelve [ʃelv] forsyne med hyller; henlegge.
shelve [ʃelv] skråne, halle.
shelves [ʃelvz] plur. av shelf.
shelving [ˈʃelviŋ] hyllematerialer; skråning.
Shem [ʃem] (bibelsk) Sem.
shepherd [ˈʃepəd] hyrde, sauegjæter, hjuring; gjæte.
shepherdess [ˈʃepədės] hyrdinne, hjuringjente.
sherbet [ˈʃəˈbit] slags østerlandsk svaledrikk.
sherd [ʃəˑd] se shard I.
sheriff [ˈʃerif] sheriff, foged, (i England: en ulønnet, av kongen utnevnt funksjonær, som representerer sitt grevskap ved større anledninger. De virkelige forretninger utføres av en under-sheriff: i Skottland: grevskaps øverste dommer). — -clerk [-klaˑᵒk] rettsskriver. -'s officer rettsbetjent.
Sherlock [ˈʃəˑlək] Sherlock.
sherry [ˈʃeri] sherry. — -cobbler [-ˈkåblə] svaledrikk av sherry, sukker, sitron og is.
she's [ʃiˑz] fk. f. she is el. she has.
Shetland [ˈʃetlənd] Shetlandsøyene; Shetlandsponni; shetlandsk; — pony Shetlandsponni; — wool Shetlandsull.
shew [ʃoᵘ] vise (gammel stavemåte for show).
shibboleth [ˈʃibolęþ] kjenningsord, løsen.

shield [ʃiˑld] skjold, vern, forsvar, beskytter; beskytte, verge. — -bearer [-bæˑᵒrə] skjoldbærer. -less forsvarsløs. — of arms våpenskjold.
shift [ʃift] skifte, omlegge, flytte på, forandre seg, forskyve seg, kle seg om, greie seg, finne utveier, bruke utflukter; skift; arbeidsskift, arbeidstid; hjelpemiddel, knep, utvei, nødhjelp, list; klesskift, ren skjorte, rent undertøy. — about vende seg om; — off søke å unndra seg, bli kvitt; he makes — to live han hangler igjennom. -er maskinmann, lurendreier. -iness forandrelighet; -ing foranderlig, ustø, vinglet; knep, kunstgrep. -less hjelpeløs, upraktisk.
shifty [ˈʃifti] upålitelig, lumsk, ful.
shikaree [ʃiˈkäri] jeger.
shillelagh [ʃiˈleˈlə] irsk knortekjepp.
shilling [ˈʃiliŋ] shilling (12 pence); take the King's — la seg verve, motta håndpenger.
shilly-shally [ˈʃiliˈfäli] ikke kunne bestemme seg; ubesluttsom; ubesluttsomhet.
shimmer [ˈʃimə] flimre, skinne (svakt); flimring.
shimmy [ˈʃimi] serk; shimmy (dans).
shin [ʃin] skinneben, legg, skank; klyve, klatre (opp i), sparke; — of beef okseskank; he was more -ned against than -ning han fikk flere spark enn han gav. — -bone skinneben.
shindy [ˈʃindi] huskestue, ståk, bråk.
shine [ʃain] skinne, stråle, pusse; skinn, solskinn; cause his face to — upon være gunstig stemt for; take the — off it ta glansen av det.
shingle [ˈʃiŋl] takspon; grus, singel; shingel; spontekke; klippe jevnt, shingle; smie ned jern til mindre stykker. — -ballast grusballast.
shingler taktekker.
shingles [ˈʃiŋlz] helvetesild (sykdom).
shingling spontak. — -hammer stor hammer, et hammerverk.
shingly [ˈʃiŋli] singel-, singelstrødd.
shininess [ˈʃaininės] glansfullhet.
Shinto [ˈʃintoᵘ] sjintoisme (japansk religion).
shiny [ˈʃaini] skinnende, blank.
ship [ʃip] skip; skipe, innskipe; ta inn (last); hyre; — a sea få en sjø over seg; — the oars legge årene inn; — -board skipsplanke. — -boy skipsgutt. — -broker skipsmekler. — -builder skipsbygger. — -builder's yard skipsverft. — -building skipsbygging. — -chandler skipshandler. — -load skipslast. — -master skipskaptein, skipsfører.
shipment [ˈʃipmənt] innskiping, utskiping; parti, sending.
ship|-money en skatt som tidligere ble pålagt til utrusting av krigsskip. — -owner reder.
shipper [ˈʃipə] utskiper, avskiper, eksportør, speditør.
shipping [ˈʃipiŋ] skipning, skipsfart, antall skip, tonnasje; — articles hyrekontrakt; — disasters sjøulykker; — line (el. trade) skipsfart (især virksomhet som reder, skipsmegler eller speditør).
shipshape [ˈʃipʃeˈp] i god orden.
shipwreck [ˈʃiprek] skibbrudd; la li skibbrudd; forlise.
shipwrecked [ˈʃiprekt] skibbrudden.
shipwright [ˈʃiprait] skipsbygger.
shipyard [ˈʃipjaˑᵒd] verft.
shire [ˈʃaiə, i smstn.: ʃiə, ʃə] grevskap, fylke.
shirk [ʃəˑk] skulke unna, sluntre unna; skulker, simulant; catch him -ing gripe ham i pliktforsømmelse; — off smette unna. -y skulkesyk.
shirt [ʃəˑt] skjorte; bluse(liv); gi skjorte på; a white — mansjettskjorte; — of mail panserskjorte. — -front skjortebryst. -ing skjorter, skjortetøy, sjirting. -less, skjorteløs.
shirt-sleeve [ˈʃəˑtsliˑv] skjorterme; in his -s i skj rteermer.
shirty [ˈʃəˑti] sint, ergerlig.
shivaree [ʃivaˈriˑ] pipekonsert.
shiver [ˈʃivə] stump, splint; splintre.
shiver [ˈʃivə] skjelve, hutre, kulse; gysing,

hustring, kuldegysing; **a cold** — **went through me** det løp kaldt nedover ryggen på meg; **-ing** gysing.

shivery ['ʃivəri] skjelven, kulsen, kald.

shivery ['ʃivəri] skjør.

shoad [ʃoᵘd] gang (en rekke metallholdige steiner, hvorav man slutter seg til ertsenes gang i fjellene).

shoal [ʃoᵘl] sverm, stim; grunne, grunning, gå i stim; være grunt (om vann. **-iness** ['ʃoᵘlinès] det å være full av grunner. **-y** ['ʃoᵘli] grunn.

shock [ʃåk] støt, skaking, risting, rystelse, sjokk, støkk, kvepp, forargelse; støte, ryste, sjokkere, forarge.

shock [ʃåk] rauk (av kornband); lurv, stri ugg; rauke (kornband).

shocking ['ʃåkiŋ] (adj.) rystende, forferdelig; anstøtelig; (adv. foran **bad**) **a** — **bad hat** en meget dårlig hatt.

shoddy ['ʃådi] jernspiss, kunstull; fillekram, skrap; uekte, forloren; forarbeide til shoddy.

shoe [ʃuˑ] sko, skoning; beslå; **cast a** — miste en sko (om hest); **I should not like to stand in your -s** jeg ville nødig være i dine bukser; **another pair of -s** noe helt annet; **where the** — **pinches** hvor skoen trykker; **die in his -s** bli hengt; **stand in my -s** tre i mine fotspor; **slip into his -s** overta hans stilling; **she stole upstairs without her -s** hun listet seg opp på sokkelesten. — **-binding** nåtling. — **-black** skopusser. — **-boy** skopusser. — **-horn** skohorn.

shoing ['ʃuˑiŋ] skoning. — **-lace** skolisse. — **-horn** skohorn.

shoe-leather ['ʃuˑleðə] skolær, skotøy; **save** — unngå å bruke benene.

shoe-lift ['ʃuˑlift] skohorn.

shoe|maker ['ʃuˑmeikə] skomaker. — **-strap** skoreim. — **-string**, — **-tie** skoband, -reim, -lisse. — **-vamp** overlær. — **-vamper** lappeskomaker.

shone [ʃån] imperf. og perf. pts. av **shine**.

shoo [ʃuˑ] hyst! (utrop for å skremme bort); jage, skremme (bort).

shook [ʃuk] imperf. av **shake**.

shoot [ʃuˑt] skyte, fyre av, gå på jakt; skyve; styrte av, lesse av, tømme; kanthøvle, passere hurtig, isprenge; spire fram, fare av sted, stikke; skudd, søpletomt, skråbrett, tømmerrenne, stryk (i elv); — **the moon** flytte om natten uten å betale husleien; — **at** skyte på; — **out** rage fram.

shooter ['ʃuˑtə] jeger; skytevåpen, skytter; stjernskudd.

shooting ['ʃuˑtiŋ] jakt, jaktrett; jagende fornemmelse, sting; — **-boots** jaktstøvler. — **-box** jakthytte. — **-distance** skuddhold. — **-gallery** skytebane. — **-ground** skyting. — **-line** skytterlinje. — **-match** premieskyting. — **-range** skytebane. — **-star** stjerneskudd.

shop [ʃåp] butikk, verksted; plass; fagprat; gå i butikker, gjøre innkjøp; **come to the wrong** — gå til feil adresse; **keep a** — ha butikk; **talk** — snakke forretninger. — **-assistant** butikkbetjent. — **-bill** handlendes reklame (i vinduet). — **-board** verkstedbord. — **-boy** butikkgutt. — **-keeper** kremmer. — **-lifter** butikktyv. **-like** simpel. **-man** kremmer. — **-ping** innkjøp. **-pish** opptatt av forretninger. **-py** ['ʃåpi] butikk-, faglig, full av fagprat. — **-walker** [-wåˑkə] butikkinspektør. — **-woman** ekspeditrise.

shore ['ʃåˑə] støtte, stønner; stive av.

shore ['ʃåˑə] kyst, strand; elvebredd; **a bold** — bratt kyst; **lee** — le land; **from** — **to** — fra strand til strand; **the wind is in** — det er pålandsvind; **on** — i land, til lands, på grunn.

Shoreditch ['ʃåˑəditʃ] Shoreditch (i London).

shore-fast ['ʃåˑəfaˑst] fortøyningstrosse.

shoreline ['ʃåˑəlain] kystlinje.

shoreward ['shåˑəwəd] mot kysten.

shorn [ʃåˑn] perf. pts. av **shear**.

short [ʃåˑt] kort, stutt, liten av vekst, sprø, skjør; plutselig, hurtig; kort begrep; **in** — kort

sagt; — **of** som kommer til kort med, utilstrekkelig forsynt med; mindre enn; **nothing** — **of** intet mindre enn; **fall** — ikke strekke til; **stop** — stanse plutselig. — **-age** ['ʃåˑətidʒ] skort, underskudd; **-bread** ['ʃåˑətbred], **-cake** slags sandkake. **-coming** feil, mangel, lyte, skort. — **commons** smal kost. — **current** kortslutning. — **cut** snarvei. — **-dated** kortvarig.

shorten ['ʃåˑətn] forkorte, innskrenke, knappe av; — **sail** minske seil.

shorthand ['ʃåˑəthänd] stenografi; — **writer** stenograf.

shorthanded ['ʃåˑət'händid] med for få folk; **be** — ha for lite mannskap.

shorthorns korthornskveg.

shortlived ['ʃåˑət'livd] kortvarig.

shortly ['ʃåˑətli] snart, i nær framtid; — **before** kort før; — **after** kort etter; **very** — i nærmeste framtid. **shortness** kortfhet.

shorts [ʃåˑts] knebukser, idrettsbukser (rommelige vide bukser, avskåret over kneet, til løp, roning, fotball etc.).

short|-sighted ['ʃåˑət'saitid] nærsynt, kortsynt. — **-spoken** stuttmælt; kort for hodet. — **-waisted** kort i livet. — **-winded** [-windid] kortpusten. — **-witted** [-witid] enfoldig.

shot [ʃåt] imperf. og perf. pts. av **shoot**.

shot [ʃåt] skudd, prosjektil(er), hagl, skuddvidde, rekkevidde; skytter, garnkast, notkast, garntrekning; øyeblikksfotografi; isprengt, changeant; **a dead** — en blinkskytter; **out of** — utenfor skuddvidde; **fire with** — skyte med skarpt; **he made a bad** — det var dårlig gjetning; **there is no** — **in the locker** det er ikke en øre i kassen.

shot [ʃåt] regning; **stand** — betale.

shotfree ['ʃåtfriˑ] helskinnet.

shot-proof ['ʃåtpruˑf] skuddfast, skuddsikker.

shot-tower ['ʃåt'tauə] tårn til haglfabrikasjon, hagltårn.

should [ʃud] skulle (av **shall**).

shoulder ['ʃoᵘldə] skulder, aksel, herd, bog (av slakt), kraft: ta på skuldrene, skubbe til; **broad in the -s** skulderbred; — **to** — skulder ved skulder, rygg mot rygg, side om side; **rub -s** (**with**) komme i nær berøring (med); — **out** skubbe ut. — **-belt** skulderskjerf; bandolær; — **-blade** (eller — ene) skulderblad.

shout [ʃaut] rop, juble; brøle; rop, frydeskrik; — **at** rope etter; — **for** rope på; **-ing** ['ʃautiŋ] roping.

shove [ʃʌv] skubbe, skumpe, skyve; skubb.

shovel ['ʃʌvl] skovl, skuffe; prestehatt; skovle, måke; — **hat** (engelsk) prestehatt (med brem som er bøyd opp på sidene).

show [ʃoᵘ] vise, syne, stille til skue, legge fram, vise seg; skue, utstilling, framvisning, skuespill, skinn, brann; — **of hands** håndsopprekking; — **off** gjøre seg viktig med, glimre, vise seg. **-bill** reklameplakat. — **-boat** teaterbåt. — **-box** perspektivkasse. **-bread** skuebrød.

shower ['ʃoᵘə] framviser.

shower ['ʃauə] bye, skur, styrtregn, strøm; la det regne, la hø-lje. — **-bath** styrtebad. **-less** regnfri. **-y** regnfull.

show-girl ['ʃoᵘgəˑl] korpike, kvinnelig statis-. **showman** ['ʃoᵘmən] framviser; leder av met nasjeri o. l.

show-room ['ʃoᵘruˑm] utstillingslokale.

showy ['ʃoᵘi] pralende, som gjerne vil vise seg, som tar seg ut.

shown [ʃoᵘn] perf. pts. av **show**.

shrapnel ['ʃräpnəl] shrapnel, granatkardeske(r).

shred [ʃred] skjære i strimler, trevle opp; stump, remse, fille, strimmel.

shrew [ʃruˑ] spissmus, musskjær.

shrew [ʃruˑ] troll (til kvinnefolk), sint kjerring, xantippe; **The Taming of the Shrew** Troll kan temmes (skuespill av Shakespeare).

shrewd [ʃruˑd] skarpsindig, gløgg, klok; skarp, kvass. **-ness** gløggskap, skarpsindighet.

shrewish ['ʃruˑiʃ] arrig.

shrewmouse ['ʃruˑmaus] spissmus, musskjær.

Shrewsbury ['ʃruˑzbəri] hovedstad i Shropshire.

shriek [ʃriˑk] skrik, gneldring; skrike, hvine, hyle.

shrift [ʃrift] skriftemål; (brukes nå bare i forb.) give short — ekspedere (inn i evigheten) uten videre, gjøre det av med straks.

shrike [ʃraik] tornskrike, varsler (en fugl).

shrill [ʃril] skingrende, gnell, gjennomtrengende; hvine, gneldre.

shrimp [ʃrimp] reke; pusling, tufs; fange reker; -er rekefisker.

shrine [ʃrain] helgenskrin, helligdom, alter; skrinlegge, bevare som en helligdom.

shrink [ʃriŋk] krympe sammen, krype, svinne inn, visne bort, vike tilbake; krymping, innskrumping; det å vike tilbake.

shrinkage ['ʃriŋkidʒ] svinn; sammenskrumping.

shrive [ʃraiv] skrifte.

shrivel ['ʃrivl] skrumpe inn. -led rynket, skrukket.

shriven ['ʃrivn] perf. pts. av shrive.

Shropshire ['ʃrɔpʃə] Shropshire.

shroud [ʃraud] likskrud; vant (på skip), skorsteinsbardum; svøpe et lik, tilhylle, dekke.

shrove [ʃrouv] imperf. av shrive.

shrove [ʃrouv] fastelavn; bare i sammensetninger: Shrove Monday fastelavnsmandag. Shrove Tuesday fetetirsdag. shrove-tide ['ʃrouvtaid] fastelavn.

shrub [ʃrʌb] busk, kratt; rense for kratt. -bery ['ʃrʌbəri] buskas, kjerr. -by ['ʃrʌbi] busket.

shrug [ʃrʌg] skyte i været; aksle på seg; skuldertrekk; he -ged his shoulders han trakk på skuldrene.

shrunk [ʃrʌŋk] imperf. og perf. pts. av shrink.

shrunken ['ʃrʌŋkən] innskrumpet (av shrink).

shuck [ʃʌk] hylster, belg, skolm, hams.

shudder ['ʃʌdə] gyse, grøsse; gysing; I — to think of it jeg gyser ved å tenke på det. -ingly ['ʃʌdəriŋli] med gysing.

shuffle ['ʃʌfl] blande, stokke (kort); skaffe på sett og vis, lempe (away vekk, bruke knep, søke utflukter, sjokke, tasse; sammenblanding, knep, utflukt; — off frigjøre seg for, få av veien; — up raske sammen. shuffler ['ʃʌflə] kortblander, lurendreier. shuffling ['ʃʌfliŋ] vringlet, ful, lur, unnvikende; utflukt, påskudd.

shun [ʃʌn] sky, unngå.

shunt [ʃʌnt] dreie av, vike til siden, skifte (ut på et sidespor,) rangere, få av veien; rangerspor, vikespor; rangering; shunt (gren av elektrisk strømledning). -er sporskifter. -ing rangering.

shut [ʃʌt] lukke, lukkes, lukke seg; lukket; lukking; sveising; — the door lukke døra; — down lukke, stanse arbeidet; — in innelukke; — out utelukke; — up sperre til, få til å tie, dytte kjeften på holde munn. — -down stans (av arbeide osv.). — -off avsperring.

shutter ['ʃʌtə] skodde, vinduslem, lukker (i fotografiapparat); rullesjalusi (til skrivebord); lukke med vinduslemmer; put up the shutters ha fyraben, slutte med forretningene, stenge.

shuttle ['ʃʌtl] skyttel. -cock [-kåk] fjærball.

shy [ʃai] bli sky, skvette, bli redd; sky, skvetten, fryktsom, blyg, mistenksom, upålitelig; fight — of a person søke å unngå en persons selskap; once bitten, twice — brent barn skyr ilden.

shy [ʃai] kast, hipp; kyle, hive, kaste, gi et hipp.

Shylock ['ʃailək] Shylock.

S. I. fk. f. Order of the Star of India.

Siam [saiˈäm] Siam. -ese [saiəˈmiˑz] siameser; siamesisk; siamesisk språk.

Siberia [saiˈbiəriə] Sibir.

Siberian [saiˈbiəriən] sibirer; sibirsk.

sibilant ['sibilənt] vislende, vislelyd.

sibilation [sibiˈleˑʃən] visling.

sibyl ['sibiˈ] sibylle, volve, spåkjerring.

sibylline [siˈbilain] sibyllinsk.

siccative ['sikətiv] tørkemiddel.

Sicilian [siˈsiljən] siciliansk; sicilianer.

Sicily ['sisili] Sicilia.

sick [sik] syk (i denne betydning brukes ordet på engelsk nesten bare foran substantiv, på amr. også som predikatsord); sjøsyk, kvalm, som har kvalme; kraftesløs, matt, lei og kei (of av); the Sick Man den syke mann, især Tyrkia; be — være kvalm; turn — få kvalme. — -bay sykelugar. — -bed sykeseng. — -call sykebesøk. — -certificate sykeattest. — -chamber sykestue. — -club sykekasse.

sicken ['sikn] bli syk, sykne, få kvalme, bli kvalm (at av); bli lei (at av); bli beklemt; kvalme, gjøre syk. -er noe som gjør en syk. -ing vemmelig.

sickle ['sikl] sigd, krumkniv.

sick-leave ['sikˈliˑv] syke-permisjon.

sickliness ['siklinés] sykelighet, svakelighet; usunnhet; vammelhet; motbydelighet; matthet.

sicklist ['sikˈlist] sykeliste.

sickly ['sikli] (adj.) sykelig, skrøpelig, svakelig; usunn; vammel, kvalmende; matt (adv.) sykt.

sickness ['siknés] sykdom; illebefinnende; kvalme; matthet, kraftesløshet.

sick-room ['sikrum] sykeværelse, sykestue, også: barselstue.

side [said] side, kant, parti; til siden, side-; ta parti (with for), holde med. — -arms sidevåpen. — -blow sidestøt. -board [-bå·əd] buffet, skjenk. — -box sidelosje. — -car sidevogn (til motorsykkel). — -glance sideblikk. — -light streiflys, sidelys; sidevindu, sidelanterne. -long side-, skrå-, til siden, sidelengs, på skrå. — -note randbemerkning. sider partigjenger, tilhenger.

sidereal [saiˈdiəriəl] stjerne-.

side|-saddle damesal; på damesal. — -scene (side-) kulisse. — -splitting til å le seg fordervet av. — -track sidespor, vikespor; rangere inn på sidespor; skubbe til side; få på avveier; komme på avveier. — -view syn fra siden, sideprospekt. -walk (især amerikansk) fortau. side|wards ['saidwədz] til siden. -ways ['saidweˈz] til siden. — -whiskers bakkenbarter. — -wind sidevind. -wise til siden.

siding ['saidiŋ] sidespor, vikespor; sidebekledning, panel, bordkledning.

sidle ['saidl] gå sidelengs, gå i skrå retning; nærme seg (el. gå) beskjeden og sjenert.

Sidney ['sidni] Sidney.

siege [siˑdʒ] beleiring; lay — to beleire, begynne å beleire; declare a state of — erklære i beleiringstilstand; raise the — heve beleiringen.

siesta [siˈestə] siesta, middagslur.

sieve [siˑv] sil, dørslag, såld, sikte, sikte, sælde. — -cloth siktéduk.

sift [sift] sikte, strø, drysse; — out sikte fra. -er sikte. -ing sikting. -ings frasiktede deler.

sigh [sai] sukke, sukk; fetch (heave, draw) a deep — utstøte (el. dra) et dypt sukk.

sight [sait] syn, synsevne, øyne; sikt (om veksel), observasjon; severdighet, syn for guder; en hel mengde; sikte, siktehull, kikhull, siktemiddel, siktekåre, siktekorn på skytevåpen; utsikt, sjanse, høve på, få i sikte; sette sikte på, sikte inn, innstille, rette (skytevåpen); forevise, presentere (veksel); observere; catch — of få øye på (el. gain) — of få øye på, få i sikte; lose — of tape av syne; keep — of holde øye med; after — etter sikt (om veksler); at — straks; ved sikt, a vista; love at first — kjærlighet ved første blikk; play at — spille fra bladet; read at — ekstemporere med letthet; know by — kjenne av utseende; in — i sikte, for øye; be in — of ha i sikte; come in — of få i sikte; out of — ute av syne; out of —, out of mind ute av øye, ute av sinn; **rise in** — komme i sikte. **-ed** seende, -synt (i smstn. f. eks. short-sighted). **-ing-notch** sikteskåre (på skytevåpen). **-ing-shot** prøveskudd. **-less** blind, uten syn, som ingenting ser, åndsfraværende, død. **-liness** penhet. **-ly** pen, tekkelig. — **-seeing** på jakt etter severdigheter; beskuelse av severdigheter. — **-seer** ['si·ə] skuelysten, turist. — **-singing** sang fra bladet. **-man** en som synger fra bladet.

sigil ['sidʒil] (lærd ord) segl.

sign [sain] tegn, merke, minnesmerke, skilt, vink, varsel, interpunksjonstegn, stjernebilde, underskrift; merke, betegne, undertegne.

signal ['signəl] signal; signalisere; merkelig, utmerket, eklatant, grundig, grepa.

signalize ['signəlaiz] signal(is)ere, utmerke, understreke.

signature ['signətʃə] underskrift.

signboard ['sainbä·ªd] skilt.

signet ['signit] signet; mindre kongelig segl.

significance [sig'nifikəns] viktighet, betydning.

significant [sig'nifikənt] betydningsfull.

signification [signifi'keiʃən] betydning.

significative [sig'nifikətiv] betegnende.

signify ['signifai] bety, tyde, betegne, tilkjennegi; ha betydning, ha å si.

sign-painter ['sainpeinta] skiltmaler.

sign-post ['sainpoust] skiltstolpe; avviser, veiviser.

Sikh [si·k] sikh (indisk soldat i engelsk tjeneste).

Silas ['sailəs] Silas.

silence ['sailəns] taushet, stillhet; stille!, få til å tie, døyve; **break** — bryte tausheten; **command** (eller **order**) — slå til lyd; **keep** (eller **observe**) — tie; **put** (eller **reduce**) **to** — få til å tie; — **is consent** den som tier samtykker.

silencer ['sailənsə] lyddemper (i motor).

silent ['sailənt] taus, tagal, stille, fåmælt, stilltiende; stum; **be** — tie; **as death** taus som graven; **he dropped** — han forstummet. **-ly** stilltiende. **-ness** [-nés] taushet.

Silesia [sai'li·ziə] Schlesien.

silhouette [silu'et] silhuett; tegne i silhuett.

silica ['silikə] silicium-dioksyd, kiselsyreanhydrid, kiseljord.

silicate ['silikét] silikat, kiselsurt salt.

silicated ['silike'tid] kiselsur.

siliceous [si'lifəs] kiselholdig.

silk [silk] silke, silkegarn, silketøy, silkestoff; (i plur.) silkevarer, sorter silke, silkeklær, silkestrømper; **raw-** råsilke; **refuse** — silkeavfall; **spun** — silkegarn; **sewing -s** sysilke; **take the** — silkekappen (bli kongelig advokat). — **-breeder** silkeavler. — **-cotton** halvsilke. — **-culture** silkeavl. **-en** silke-, av silke, silkeaktig, silkebløt, silkekledd. **-ette** [sil'ket] kunstsilke. — **-gown** silkekjole, silketalar. **-iness** silkeaktighet. — **-mercer** silkehandler. **-moth** silkespinner (insekt). — **-paper** silkepapir. — **-shag** silkeplysj. — **-stocking** silkestrømpe. — **-worm** silkeorm. **-y** ['silki] silkeaktig, silkebløt, silkeglinsende.

sill [sil] svill, terskel, vinduskarm, fotstykke (i mur).

sillabub ['siləbʌb] en slags rett av fløte eller melk med vin og sukker.

sillines ['silinés] dumhet.

silly ['sili] tosket, enfoldig, dum; tosk, fe. **Silly-Billy** dummepetter.

silo ['sailoᵘ] silo (til oppbevaring av grønnfor).

silvan ['silvən] skogrik, skog-.

silver ['silvə] sølv; av sølv, sølvfarget; forsølve; **born with a** — **-spoon in your mouth** begunstiget av lykken. — **-beater** sølvhammer. — **-fir** edelgran. — **-glance** sølvglans. — **-gray** sølvgrå. — **-headed** sølvhåret, med sølvhode, sølvknappet. **-iness** sølvaktighet. **-ing** forsølving. **-ise** forsølve. — **-leaf** bladsølv. **-less** pengeløs. — **-lining** (egl. sølvfor), stikk til lysere dager; **every cloud has a** — **-lining** omtrent: etter regn kommer sol. — **-mine** sølvgruve. — **-plate** plettere. —

-things sølvtøy. — **-touch** prohering av sølv på prøvestein. — **-ware** sølvtøy. — **-wire** sølvtråd. — **-works** sølvverk. **-y** sølv-, sølvklar, sølvblank.

simian ['simiən] ape-, apelignende.

similar ['similə] lignende, ens. **-ity** [simi'läriti] likhet. **-ly** ['similəli] på lignende måte.

simile ['simili] lignelse.

similitude [si'militju·d] likhet, lignelse.

similor ['similə] talmi(gull), fransk gull.

simmer ['simə] småkoke, putre; småkok, putring.

Simon ['saimən] Simon; **Simple** — dummepetter.

simony ['siməni] simoni (handel med prestekall).

simoom [si'mu·m] samum (tørr og het ørkenvind).

simper ['simpə] smile affektert, være smørblid; fjollet smil; **-ingly** smiskende.

simple ['simpl] enkel, simpel, klar, jevn, jamn, endefram, grei, enfoldig, troskyldig; lægeplante; — **equation** ligning av første grad; — **life** fordringsløst liv (hvor det frivillig gis avkall på oppvartning og luksus). — **-minded** troskyldig, enfoldig.

simpler ['simplə] plantesamler.

simpleton ['simpltən] tosk.

simplicity [sim'plisiti] simpelhet, enkelhet, jevnhet, likeframhet, enfoldighet.

simplification [simplifi'keiʃən] forenkling.

simplify ['simplifai] forenkle, simplifisere.

simply ['simpli] simpelt hen.

simulacrum [simju'leikrəm] tom skygge, skinn.

simulate ['simjuleit] simulere, hykle, fingere; — **illness** gjøre seg syk.

simulation [simju'leiʃən] forstillelse.

simulator ['simjuleitə] hykler, simulant.

simultaneity [siməltə'niəti] samtidighet.

simultaneous [siməl'te'njəs] samtidig. **-ly** på samme tid. **-ness** [-nés] samtidighet.

sin [sin] synd; synde (**against** imot); **deadly** — dødssynd; **actual** — personlig synd; **original** — arvesynd; **for my -s** for mine synders skyld; **it is a** — **and a shame** det er synd og skam; **commit a** — synde; — **one's mercies** ikke skjønne på hvor godt man har det.

since [sins] siden; ettersom; **ever** — like siden **long** — for lenge siden.

sincere [sin'siə] oppriktig; **yours -ly** Deres hengivne (under brev).

sincerity [sin'seriti] oppriktighet.

sinecure ['sainikjuə] sinekyre, embete uten forretninger.

sinecurist ['sainikjuərist] sinekyrist.

sinew ['sinju] sene; kraft, nerve; forbinde, knytte sammen; gi fasthet el. styrke. **-less** [-less] kraftløs.

sinewy ['sinjui] senesterk.

sinful ['sinf(u)l] syndig. **-ness** syndighet.

sing [siŋ] synge; synges, la seg synge, gå; — **another song** (el. **tune**) anslå en beskjednere tone; — **out** stemme i, synge ut; — **small** stemme tonen ned, holde opp med å skryte, spakne.

singe [sin(d)ʒ] svi; lettere brannsår.

singer ['siŋə] sanger, sangerinne.

singing ['siŋiŋ] sang; syngende. — **-bird** sangfugl. — **-book** sangbok. — **-master** sanglærer. — **-voice** sangstemme.

single ['siŋgl] enkelt, eneste, enslig, ugift, sunn, ufordervet; utvelge; **live in** — **blessedness** leve ugift. — **-breasted** enkeltknappet. — **-eyed** uegennyttig. — **-hearted** ærlig. — **-handed** uten andre hjelp (eller mellomkomst) **-ness** [-nés] enkelhet, oppriktighet; **-ton** en eneste ett kort i fargen. — **-tracked** ensporet.

singly ['siŋgli] enkeltvis; **misfortunes never come** — en ulykke kommer sjelden alene.

singsong ['siŋsåŋ] ensformig; ensformig tone, sammenkomst med sang.

singular ['siŋgjulə] sjelden, ualminnelig, besynderlig, utmerket, eneste; entall, singularis.
singularity [siŋgju'läriti] særegenhet.
singularly ['siŋgjuloli] særdeles.
Sinhalese [sinhə'li·z] singalesisk; singaleser.
sinister ['sinistə] uhellsvanger, uhyggelig, skummel, sørgelig, forkastelig, ond; (især i heraldikk) venstre, i venstre side av våpenskjold (av betrakteren ses det som høyre). — -**looking** skummel.
sink [siŋk] synke, søkke, senke, senke i senk, gjemme, legge bort; anbringe (penger); fornedre, forminske; fordypning, søkk; avløp(srenne), vask (i kjøkken). -**er** søkke; stempelskjærer.
sinless ['sinles] syndefri. **sinner** ['sinə] synder, synderinne.
Sinn Fein ['fin'fe'n] irsk bevegelse og parti.
sin-offering ['sinåfəriŋ] sonoffer.
sinologist [si'nålədʒist] el. **sinologue** ['sinəlåg] kjenner av kinesisk.
sinology [si'nålədʒi] kjennskap til kinesisk.
sinter ['sintə] tuff (mineral).
sinuosity [ˌinju'åsiti] huktethet, bølgeformethet.
sinuous ['sinjuəs] buktet, slynget.
sinus ['sainəs] bukt, fold, krumming, åpning.
Sioux [su·] siouxindianer.
sip [sip] nippe (til); suge inn; nipp.
siphon ['saifən] sifong; hevert; **plunging** — stikkhevert.
sippet ['sipit] brødterning.
Sir, sir [sə] herre, herr, min herre; brukes som tiltaleord til høyerestilte og foresatte, og er da oftest å gjengi med herr med navn eller tittel etter; — i formell stil, særlig brevstil, til menn av enhver stand; **Dear** — ærede herre. **Dear -s** De herrer; — også tilrettevisende til underordnede («far»): **what is that to you, —?** Hva kommer det Dem ved? — som parlamentarisk innledning: herr president (idet enhver taler henvender seg til presidenten el. formannen); — foran en baronets el. ridders fornavn, f. eks. **Sir Walter Scott; Sir?** Hva behager?
sirdar ['sə·da·ə] den britiske overgeneral over den egyptiske hær.
sire [saiə] far, opphav, fardyr; herre konge! avle; **land of my sires** mine fedres land; **sired by** fallen etter.
siren ['sairin] sirene (mystisk havnymfe); tåkelur.
sirloin ['sə·loin] oksemørbrad.
sirocco [si'råkoᵘ] sirokko (vind i Middelhavsegnene).
sirrah ['sirə] far, (din) knekt!
sirop, sirup ['sirəp] sirup.
siskin ['siskin] sisik.
sister ['sistə] søster; nonne, diakonisse; **the three sisters** el. **the sisters three** el. **the fatal sisters** de tre skjebnegudinner; — **of Charity** barmhjertig søster. —-**country** broderland. -**hood** [-hud] søsterskap. —-**in-law** svigerinne. —-**like,** -**ly** søsterlig. —-**plaintiff** medsaksøkerske.
Sistine ['sistin] sikstinsk.
Sisyphean [sisi'fi·ən] sisyfos-.
Sisyphus ['sisifəs] Sisyfos.
sit [sit] sitte, ligge, ruge, passe (om klær); holde møte, hvile på; — **a horse** sitte på en hest; — **down** sette seg (ned); — **down to** (sette seg til) **the piano;** — **for one's picture** la seg male; **the parliament -s** Parlamentet er samlet; — **up** sitte oppreist, sette seg opp, sitte oppe, være oppe; — **up with a sick person** våke hos en syk; **the coroner sat upon the body** holdt likskue over liket; **a council of war sat on them** det ble holdt krigsrett over dem; **the doctors** — **upon him** lægene holder en konferanse angående hans sykdom; — **upon petitions** behandle søknader; **he lets everybody** — **upon him,** han lar seg kue av alle og enhver; — **out to** (forbli samlet til) **the end of September.**
site [sait] beliggenhet; plass, byggetomt.

sitter ['sitə] (levende) modell; liggehøne.
sitting ['sitiŋ] sitting, seanse, rettssesjon, møte, ruging, sitteplass. — -**room** dagligstue.
situated ['sitjue'tid] beliggende; stilt, situert; **thus** — slik stilt; i den stilling.
situation [sitju'e'ʃən] beliggenhet, situasjon, stilling; (forening av) omstendigheter; ansettelse, post.
six [siks] seks, sekstall; undertiden d. s. s. sixpennyworth: **a** — **of Irish** for 6 pence irsk whisky; **be at sixes and sevens** ligge hulter til bulter.
sixfold ['siksfoᵘld] seksdobbelt.
sixfooter ['siks'futə] person som er seks fot høy, kjempekar.
six|pence ['sikspəns] sekspence = ca. 45 øre. -**penny** [-pəni] sekspence. — -**pennyworth** ['siks-peniwəþ] så mye som kan fås for seks pence.
sixteen ['siks'ti·n] seksten.
sixteenth ['siks'ti·nþ] sekstendedel, sekstende.
sixth [siksþ] sjette, sjettedel.
sixthly ['siksþli] for det sjette.
sixty ['siksti] seksti.
sixtieth ['sikstiiþ] sekstiende, sekstiendedel.
sizable ['saizəbl] svær, dryg.
sizar ['saizə] gratist ved Cambridge og Dublin universiteter.
size [saiz] størrelse, format, mål, dimensjon, nummer, avmålt porsjon; sortere (etter størrelsen), måle, avpasse, tilpasse; taksere; justere. **sized** [saizd] av størrelse; **middlesized** av middelstørrelse.
size [saiz] lim; lime. — -**colour** ['saizkʌlə] limfarge.
sizel ['sizl] sølv-avfall.
sizzle ['sizl] brase, frese, putre.
S. J. fk. f. Society of Jesus.
sjambok ['ʃa·mbåk] pisk av flodhestskinn.
Skager Rack ['skägə'räk, 'ska·gəräk] Skagerak.
skate [ske't] ekte rokke; skate (fisk).
skate [ske't] skøyte, skeise; løpe på skøyter, skøyte, skeise.
skater skøyteløper, skeiseløper. **skating** skøyteløp, skeiserenn.
Skaw [skå·] Skagen.
skedaddle [ski'dädl] stikke av, rømme.
skein [ske'n] fedd, dukke (garn).
skeleton ['skelitən] skjelett, kort utkast; **a** — **in the cupboard** ubehagelig familiehemmelighet; **worn to a** — avpillet som et skjelett. — -**key** dirk. — -**suit** en guttedress med benklærne knappet på trøya.
skerry ['skeri] skjær (over vannet), flu.
sketch [sketʃ] skisse, riss, utkast, grunnriss; skissere, ta (tegne, male) en skisse av. — -**book** skissebok. -**er** ['sketʃə] skisserer.
sketchy ['sketʃi] skissert, løst henkastet.
skew [skju·] skjev, skakk, skrå, vind; skjevhet; skjele.
skewbald ['skju·bå·ld] droplet, spraglet.
skewer ['skjuə] stekepidd; sette stekespidd i, spidde; spile.
ski [fi·, ski·] ski; gå (løpe, stå) på ski.
skid [skid] hemsko; underlag; lunne; glidning; hemsko på; gli.
skiff [skif] skjekte, pram.
skilful ['skilf(u)l] dyktig. -**ly** med dyktighet. -**ness** [-nés] dyktighet.
skill [skil] dyktighet.
skilled [skild] dyktig, faglært, fag-, utlært.
skillet ['skilit] kasserolle, panne.
skilly ['skili] tynn velling el. suppe, vassvelling (især servert i fengsler).
skim [skim] skumme, skumme av, stryke (el. fare) lett over; skum, snerk. -**mer** skumskje, skumsleiv. — -**milk** skummet melk. -**mings** skum.
skimp [skimp] knipe på, spare på, knusle med, holde knapt med; sjaske fra seg. -**ing** knuslet. knapp; snau; sjusket.

skimpy ['skimpi] knipen, knuslet, knapt; sjusket.

skin [skin] skinn, hud, pels, hinne; flå, skrelle, dekke med hud, gro. — **-deep** overfladisk. — **-disease** [-di'zi·z] hudsykdom.

skinflint ['skinflint] gjerrigknark.

skin|less ['skinles] hudløs; **-ned** -hudet. **-ner** flåer, buntmaker.

skinny ['skini] hudaktig, skrinn, skinnmager.

skip [skip] hopp, byks, sprett. spring, overspringning (i bøker); hoppe, springe, hoppe tau, springe over, hoppe over, lese med overspringning; — over springe over, utelate.

skip-jack ['skipdʒäk] springgås (leketøy); oppkomling.

skipper ['skipə] skipper; leder av cricketlag.

skipping ['skipiŋ] hopping (særl. å hoppe tau); — **-rope** hoppetau.

skirling ['skə·liŋ] hvin; gnelle, skrike, hvine.

skirmish ['skə·miʃ] skjærmyssel; slåss i spredt orden, småslåss. **-er** tiraljør. — **-line** skytterlinje.

skirt [skə·t] skjørt, stakk, nederdel; kantning, søm, ytterkant; (frakke)skjøt; innfatte, kante, gå langs med; være i ytterkanten; — **-band** skjørtelinning.

skirting skjørtetøy, kant, kantning. — **-board** gulvlist.

skit [skit] spydighet, hipp; smedeskrift.

skitish ['skitiʃ] sky, skvetten, urolig, lettsindig, kipen, kåt.

skittle ['skitl] kile; **skittles** kilespill; **beer and skittles** akkurat som fot i hose; **skittles!** vrøvl! — **-alley** el. — **-ground** kilebane.

skulk [skʌlk] gjemme seg; snike seg, luske; skulke. **-er** lurende person; skulker.

skull [skʌl] (hode)skalle, hjerneskalle, haus, hode.

skullcap ['skʌlkäp] hue, lue, kalott; — **membrane** seierhue.

skunk [skʌŋk] stinkdyr; (gemen) pøbel, ramp; skunk, stinkdyrskinn. **-ish** stinkende.

Skupshtina [skupʃ'ti·nə] skupshtina, det jugoslaviske storting.

sky [skai] himmel, luft, værlag, klima; **in the** — på himmelen; **open** — klar himmel. — **-blue** himmelblå. — **-coloured** himmelblå.

Skye [skai] Skye (en av Hebridene).

skye [skai] Skye-terrier.

sky-high ['skaihai] himmelhøy(t).

skylark ['skaila·ᵊk] lerke (fugl); holde leven.

skylight ['skailait] skylight, takvindu, glugge, vindu i loftet, overlys.

skyscraper ['skaiskre·pə] skyskraper, meget høyt hus.

sky-tinctured himmelblå.

skywards ['skaiwədz] til værs, opp mot himmelen.

sky-writing ['skairaitiŋ] røkskrift (av et fly på himmelen).

S. L. fk. f. **Sergeant-at-Law; South Latitude.**

s. l. fk. f. **south latitude.**

slab [släb] steinplate, plate, steinhelle.

slabber ['släbə] sikle, sleve.

slack [släk] slapp, slakk, løy, langsom, treg, trå, flau; hviletid, stillstand; slappe, svekke, avta; a — pace et langsom tempo; — rope slapp line; — in stays sen i vendingen; **-ed lime** lesket kalk. **-en** ['släkn] (= **slack**) slappe, saktne, sakke, svekke, avta, minske. **-ness** [-nés] slapphet.

slack-water stille vann (mellom flo og fjære).

slag [släg] slagg; bli til slagg.

slain [sle¹n] perf. pts. av **slay.**

slake [sle¹k] leske, slokke (tørst), leske (kalk).

slam [släm] slag, smell, slem (i whist og bridge); smelle med, smekke i (døren osv.).

slander ['sla·ndə] baktaling; baktale. **-er** ['sla·ndərə] bakvasker.

slanderous ['sla·ndərəs] baktalende, ærerørig.

slang [släŋ] slang, sjargong, uvøren dagligtale.

slangwhang ['släŋhwäŋ] skråle, skvaldre.

slangy ['släŋi] slangaktig, simpel.

slank [släŋk] imperf. av **slink.**

slant [sla·nt] skrå; skråning; skråne, halle; gi skrå retning, vippe. **-ing** skrå.

slantwise ['sla·ntwaiz] på skrå.

slap [släp] slå, klaske; slag, rapp, klask; smekk; plutselig; vips, fluksens, like lukt.

slap-bang ['släp-bäŋ] med brak, bums, voldsomt.

slapdash ['släpdäʃ] skjøtesløs, uvøren, flott.

slapping ['släpiŋ] storartet, svær, diger.

slap-up prima, høymoderne, gild, baus.

slash [släʃ] flenge i, skjære opp, hogge; slå vilt om seg; bevege seg hurtig; hogg, flenge, flerre, splitt, glenne (i skog); **-ed** [släʃt] oppskåret, oppsplittet (om kledningsstykker).

slashing ['släʃiŋ] flengende, knusende (om kritikk).

slat [slät] tremme, list; steinflise, helle.

S. lat. fk. f. **South latitude.**

slate [sle¹t] gi en overhaling, kritisere sønder og sammen, hudflette.

slate [sle¹t] skifer, tavle, flise; skifertekke, skrive på tavle; **he has a — loose** han har en skrue løs. — **-pencil** griffel. — **-quarry** skiferbrott.

slater ['sle¹tə] skifertekker.

slaty ['sleiti] skiferaktig.

slattern ['slätən] sjusket kvinne, sjuske.

slaughter ['slå·tə] slakting, blodbad, mannefall; myrde, nedsable. **-er** slakter, morder. — **-house** slaktehus. **-ous** ['slå·tərəs] blodtørstig.

Slav [sla·v] slaver; slavisk.

slave [sle¹v] slave, trell; trelle; **be a — to the hour** følge klokkeviseren. — **-born** slavefødt. — **-dealer** slavehandler. — **-like** slaveaktig. — **-market** slavemarked.

slaver ['sle¹və] slavehandler, slaveskip.

slaver ['slävə] sikl; sikle, sleve.

slavery ['sle¹vəri] slaveri; **the abolition of** — avskaffelsen av slaveriet.

slaveship ['sle¹vʃip] slavehandlerskip.

slave-trade ['sle¹vtre¹d] slavehandel.

slavey ['slävi, 'sle¹vi] tjenestepike.

Slavic ['slävik] slavisk (om nasjonen og språket).

slavish ['sle¹viʃ] slavisk; — **imitation** slavisk etterligning.

Slavonia [slə'vo⁵njə] Slavonia.

Slavonian [slə'vo⁵njən] slavon; slavonisk.

Slavonic [slə'vänik] slavisk; slavonsk.

slay [sle¹] slå i hjel, drepe. **-er** drapsmann.

sleave [sli·v] floke, flossilke; greie ut (tråder).

sleazy ['sli·zi] løs, tynn.

sled [sled] slede, kjelke. **-der** sledehest. **-ding** sledekjøring, sledeføre. **sled-dog** sledehund.

sledge [sledʒ] slede; kjelke; ake. — **-apron** sledeteppe.

sledge [sledʒ] eller — **-hammer** slegge.

sleek [sli·k] glatt, glinsende; glatte, gli. **-ness** [-nés] glatthet. **-y** glatt, slesk.

sleep [sli·p] søvn; sove; **go to** — falle i søvn, sovne; **in one's** — i søvne; — **like a log** (el. **top**) sove som en stein; — **the** — **of the just** sove de rettferdiges søvn; — **an hour away** sove bort en time; — **a headache away** (el. **off**) sove av seg en hodepine.

sleeper ['sli·pə] sovende (person), sovevogn, jernbanesville; **I am a good** (el. **sound**) — jeg har et godt sovehjerte; **be a bad** — ligge meget søvnløs; **be a heavy** — sove tungt; **be a light** — sove lett; **a great** — en sjusover; **the seven -s** (of Ephesus) sjusoverne.

sleepiness ['sli·pines] søvnighet.

sleeping ['sli·piŋ] sovende, sove-. — **-accommodation** soveplass. — **-bag** sovepose. — **-car** sovevogn. — **-carriage** sovevogn. — **-draught**

sovedrikk. — -partner passiv kompanjong. — -room soveværelse. — -sickness sovesyke. — sleep less søvnløs. -lessness søvnløshet. — -walker søvngjenger.
sleepy søvnig; — disease sovesyke.
sleet [sli·t] sludd; sludde.
sleeve [sli·v] erme; laugh in one's — le i skjegget; wear his virtue in his — legge skjul på sine dyder; wear his heart upon his — bære tankene sine utenpå seg, være åpen; hang on the — of blindt rette seg etter. — -button erme-knapp. -less [-lès] ermeløs, urimelig, tåpelig. — -link lenkeknapp.
sleigh [sle¹] slede, kane, kjelke.
sleight [slait] taskenspillerkunst, knep, list; — of hand taskenspillerkunst; to — away la forsvinne.
slender ['slendə] slank, tynn, spinkel, spe, sped, svak, skral, ringe, knapp; a — rod en tynn stang; a — waist en smekker midje; — means tarvelige hjelpemidler; of — parts skrøpelig begavet; with — success uten synderlig hell. -ness [-nès] tynnhet, knapphet.
slept [slept] imperf. og perf. pts. av sleep.
Sleswick ['sleswik] Slesvig.
sleuth-hound ['slu·b'haund] blodhund.
slew [slu·] imperf. av slay.
slice [slais] skjære i tynne skiver; skive; flat skje, sleiv, spatel, sparkel; cut large -s of another man's loaf skjære brede remmer av annen manns rygg.
slid [slid] imperf. og perf. pts. av slide.
slide [slaid] gli (av sted), skride, rase (ned), skli (på is), skyve, smutte vekk, fordufte, la gli, skubbe, skyve, skyte; gliing, skliing, ras, skred, glidning, gradvis overgang, glidebane, sklie, tøm-merløype, tømmerskott, bakke, renne (til kulisse osv.), slede (til rappert), skyveinnretning, skyve-hylse, skyvesikte, skyveglass, kulisse, glider (på dampmaskin), glidesete, bilde (til stereoskop), lysbilde, trekk (i basun osv.); — in smøye inn, liste inn; — over gli lett over.
slide|-bolt skodde. — -head support (på dreie-maskin). -lathe dreiebenk.
slider ['slaidə] skyver (glidende del).
slide|-rail dreieskive, svingskive. — -rest sup-port, slede (i dreiebenk). — -rod gliderstang (på dampmaskin). — -rule skyve-tommestokk, regne-stav — -valve glider (på dampmaskin). — -window skyvevindu.
sliding ['slaidiŋ] glidende; glide-, skyve-; lengdedreining. — -bolt skodde. — -door skyve-dør. — -duty bevegelig avgift. — -rule skyve-tommestokk, regnestav. — -scale glideskala (på tommestokk); varierende skala (av toll etc.). — -seat glidesete (i kapproningsbåt).
slight [slait] tynn, spe, sped, spinkel, ubetyde-lig, ringe, lett; vise ringeakt, se ned på, vanvøre; tilsidesetting, ringeaktende behandling; not the -est idea of it ikke den fjerneste idé om det; some — errors noen småfeil; -ly built spinkel; — over slurve fra seg; in a -ing way på en av-feiende måte; — his offered advances forsmå hans tilnærming; we consider it a — upon our firm vi anser det for en hensynsløshet mot vårt firma. -ingly med forakt.
slim [slim] smekker, slank, skrøpelig, klekk; slanke seg. -ness [-nès] slankhet.
slime [slaim] slim, dynd, gjørme.
slimy ['slaimi] slimet, gjørmet.
sling [sliŋ] slynge, kast, bind, skulderreim, (sjenever)toddi; slynge, kaste, henge i et bånd, slenge, heise; carry his arm in a — gå med armen i bind.
slink [sliŋk] snike seg, liste seg (away vekk)
slip [slip] gli, smutte, smette, liste seg, feile, la gli, forsømme, la fare, løslate, slippe, smutte bort fra, skjære av; glidning, ras, feiltrin, feil, stikling, renning, avlegger, (spedt) ungt men-neske, strimmel, underkjole, overtrekk, var (til

pute), utrørt leire, brynje, smal benk i en kirke (el. teater), bedding, slipp; give the — løpe (smutte) bort fra; — on fare fort (i klærne); a — of the tongue en forsnakkelse; a — of a girl et pikebarn.
slipper ['slipə] tøffel, slipper, morgensko; (lett) sko, ballsko; hemsko, glidende person; smekke med en tøffel.
slippery ['slipəri] glatt, sleip, slibrig, fettet; falsk, upålitelig.
slippy ['slipi] glatt; look — skynde seg.
slipshod ['slipʃåd] som tasser i tøfler; sjusket, skjøtesløshet, slurvet.
slipslop ['slipslåp] skvip, skval; tøys, vas; slur-vet, sjusket, vaset; sabbe, subbe.
slit [slit] flekke, spalte; spalt, rift, revne.
slither ['sliðə] gli; gliing.
sliver ['slivə] splintre; splint, flis, tave, bånd.
slob [slåb] myr, sump.
slobber ['slåbə] sikle, sleve; sikl.
sloe [slo⁹] slåpebær, slåpetorn.
slog [slåg] delje, slå hardt.
slogan ['slo⁹gən] slagord, motto (benyttet f. eks. i reklame); (oppr. høyskotsk) krigsrop.
sloid [sloid] sløyd.
sloop [slu·p] slupp, jakt, korvet.
slop [slåp] spille, søle, susle med; skvalpe over; sølevann; skvip, skval.
slop [slåp] (i slang) polis.
slop-basin ['slåpbe'sn] skyllebolle.
slope [slo⁹p] skråning, fjellskråning, hall, bak-ke; rømning; skrå, skråne, stige skrått opp: røm-me; holde skrått, senke, skjære skrått til; —the standard hilse med fanen; — arms! hvil gevær!
sloping ['slotpiŋ] skrå, skrånende.
slop-pail ['slåppe'l] toalettbøtte.
sloppy ['slåpi] sølet, slurvet, sjusket.
slops [slåps] spillevann; ferdigsydde klær.
slop-shop ['slåpʃåp] handel med oppsydde klær.
slop-water ['slåpwå·ter] spillevann.
slop-work ['slåpwə·k] ferdigsydde klær; sjuske-arbeid.
slosh [slåʃ] sørpe, slaps; skvip; subbe, sabbe; farte omkring.
slot [slåt] slå, bolt, falldør, sprekk el. åpning (i en maskin), samlingsmuffe; spor, far (etter dyr). -tingmachine ['slåtiŋmə'ʃi·n] maskin til å hogge ut huller i metall.
sloth [slo⁹þ] dorskhet, lathet; dovendyr. -ful ['slo⁹þful] lat.
slot-machine ['slåtmə'ʃi·n] (penge)automat.
slouch [slautʃ] henge slapt, lute, slentre, trykke ned (srl. om en hatt); klosset gang, slen-tring; klosset fyr, slamp, stymper; -ing slen-trende, med klosset gang; a -ed hat en hatt med bred nedhengende skygge.
slough [slau] mudderpøl, sump; myrhull.
slough [slʌf] ham, ormeham; skorpe, dødkjøtt, løsne, falle av.
sloughy ['slaui] sumpet, myret, gjørmet.
sloughy ['slʌfi] skorpeaktig, hamaktig.
sloven ['slʌvn] sjuskete mannfolk, slarv, svin.
Slovene [slo'vi·n] sloven.
slovenly ['slʌvnli] sjusket, svinsk.
slow [slo⁹] langsom, sen, tung, tungnem, treg, kjedelig, triviell; saktne. — -hound, slot-hound støver, sporhund, blodhund. — -match ['slo⁹-mätʃ], slowfire lunte. — -paced langsom. — -winged langsomt flyvende. — -worm stålorm, sleve.
sloyd [sloid] sløyd.
slubber ['slʌbə] forspinnemaskin.
slubber ['slʌbə] søle til; jaske ferdig; slubre.
sludge [slʌdʒ] gjørme, søle, snøslaps.
sludger ['slʌdʒə] sandbor.
sludgy ['slʌdʒi] sølet, gjørmet, slafset.
slue [slu·] dreie, sveive, vende, kantre; om-dreining.
slug [slʌg] snegle (uten hus), naken snegle;

ujevn kule; daustokk, lathans. — -a-bed sjusover.

sluggard ['slʌɡəd] daustokk, dovning, lathans.

sluggish ['slʌɡiʃ] doven, treg, treven, langsom.

sluice [slu·s] sluse, kanal, renne; sende inn gjennom en sluse, slippe vann, skylle over, skylle. — -gate sluseport.

slum [slʌm] slum; bakgate, fattigkvarter; misjonere i fattigkvarterene; — officer slumoffiser (i frelsesarmeen); — sister slumsøster.

sumber ['slʌmbə] slummer, slumre, dorme. -er ['slʌmbərə] slumrende. -ous søvndyssende, døsig, søvnig.

slump [slʌmp] dumpe, falle; fall, fiasko, plutselig prisfall, dårlige tider.

slur [slə·] sjuske med, slurve, uttale utydelig, la gå i ett; synge legato; gå lett hen over, sløre til; plett, skamplett; legatospill, bindebue; put a — upon sette en plett på.

slush [slʌʃ] smøre, kline til; slaps; søle.

slut [slʌt] sjuske, slurve. -tish [-iʃ] sjusket.

sly [slai] slu, listig, lur, lumsk; on the — i smug.

slyboots ['slaibu·ts] luring, fuling.

S. M. fk. f. sergeant-major.

smack [smäk] smake, dufte; smak, snev, antydning.

smack [smäk] smekke, smaske, kysse; smekk, smasking, smellkyss; the -ing of whips piskesmell; — his face gi ham en på øret.

smack [smäk] fiskekvase.

smacker ['smäkə] smask, smellkyss.

small [små·l] liten, små, ubetydelig, sped; smal del; the — of the leg smalleggen; the — of the back smalryggen; feel — føle seg liten; look — være forlegen; mince up — finhakke; — arms håndskytevåpen; — beer tynt øl; he doesn't think — beer (har ikke små tanker) of himself; — hand alminnelig håndskrift, fin håndskrift; the — hours de små timer; a — matter en bagatell, småting.

small-clothes ['små·klkloⁿδz] (gammeldags) knebukser.

smallish ['små·liʃ] nokså liten, småvoren.

smallness ['små·lnès] litenhet.

smallpox ['små·lpåks] kopper (sykdommen); the — had set its mark on him koppene hadde merkt ham.

smalls [små·lz] knebukser; annen eksamen (i Oxford). small-sword ['små·lså·əd] kårde.

small-talk ['små·ltå·k] småsnakk, småprat.

small-toothed ['små·ltubt] med fine tenner; a — comb finkam.

small-wares ['smålwæ·əz] småkram.

smalt [små·lt] koboltblått.

smart [sma·ət] smerte, svie; smerte, gjøre vondt, føle svie, lide; smertelig, bitende, skarp, vittig, dyktig, oppvakt, kvikk, pyntet, nett, fiks, smart. — under sufferings lide; my eyes -ed det sved i øynene; a — breeze en strykende bør; it has such a — look det tar seg så snertent ut; — things kvikke innfall; be — skynd deg.

smarten ['·ma·ətn] pynte, fikse opp.

smart-money ['sma·ət'mʌni] løskjøpingspenger, skadeserstatning, urimelig stor skadebot; løsesum for en vervet rekrutt før han er tatt i ed.

smartness ['sma·ətnès] skarphet, netthet osv.

smash [smäʃ] slå i knuser, smadre, krase, slå til, bli ruinert; sammenstøt, katastrofe, tilintetgjøring, fallit; a -er noe usedvanlig stort, kjempekar. — -up sammenstøt, krakk, katastrofe.

smatter ['smätə] snakke overfladisk. -er halvstudert. -ing overfladisk kunnskap; he has (got) a -ing of Latin han har snust litt borti latinen.

smear [smiə] smøre, søle, kline til; smøring, flekk.

smeary ['smiəri] klebrig.

smell [smel] lukte, spore, merke, få teft av; lukt; — out snuse opp, være. — -feast ['smelfi·st]

snyltegjest. -ing lukt(esans). -ing-bottle lukteflaske. -ingsalts luktesalt.

smelt [smɛlt] impⁱrt. ᵒɡ pᵉrf. pts. av smell.

smelt [smelt] smelte (malm). -er hyttearbeider. -ing-house, -ery smeltehytte.

smile [smail] smile; smil; good fortune now begins to — upon (tilsmile) him; — him into good humour få ham i godt humør ved hjelp av munterhet.

smirch [sma·tʃ] kline til; grise til, skitne ut.

smirk [sma·k] smiske. smile hullsalig; affektert smil.

smite [smait] slå, drepe, ramme, beseire, hjemsøke, straffe, gripe; his conscience smote him han fikk dårlig samvittighet; — terror into his mind slå ham med redsel; — to the heart gå til hjertet, røre dypt.

smith [smiþ] smed; smie. -craft smedhåndverk.

smithereens ['smiδə'ri·nz] stumper og stykker, filler, knas.

smithery ['smiþəri] smedarbeid, smedyrke.

smithing ['smiþiŋ] smedarbeid.

smithy ['smiδi, 'smiþi] smie.

smitten ['smitn] (perf. pts. til smite) slått, rammet, grepet, betatt (with av).

smock [småk] serk, lerretsbluse, lerretsbusserull. — -faced jenteaktig, jomfrunalsk. — -frock lerretskittel. — -mill hollandsk vindmølle.

smoke [smoⁿk] røyk; ryke, dampe, gyve, røyke, fare av sted, spore opp, gjennomhegle. — -black kjønrøk. — -dry røyke. — -dried ham røykt skinke. — -house røykeri. — -jack selvvirkende stekevender. -less [-lès] røykfri.

smoker ['smoⁿkə] røyker, røykekupé; a great — en stor tobakksrøyker.

smokestack ['smoⁿkstäk] skorstein (på dampskip el. fabrikk).

smoking ['smoⁿkiŋ] røyking, tobakksrøyking; røykekupé; rykende, osende, røykende; no — allowed røyking forbudt. smoking-compartment røykekupé; smoking-set tobakksstell; røykestell.

smoky ['smoⁿki] rykende, osende, tilbøyelig til å ryke; røyklignende; røykfylt, røykfarget, tilrøykt.

Smollett ['smålit] Smollett.

smooth [smu·δ] glatt, slett, jevn, jamn, bløt, smul, mild, rolig, behagelig; glatt del, glatting; glatte, rydde, jevne, jamne, gjøre bløt, formilde, smykke, bli glatt; bli smul, stilne. run — løpe jevnt. — -chinned glatthaket, skjeggløs.

smoothie [smu·δ] glatte, jevne. — -faced med et glatt ansikt. — -haired glatthåret. -ing iron strykejern. -ing plane sletthøvel. -ness [-nès] glatthet, finhet, rolighet, letthet.

smote [smoⁿt] imperf. av smite.

smother ['smʌδə] kvele, være nær ved å kvele, dempe, dekke over, dysse ned, kveles, kovne; røyk, os, kvelning.

smoulder ['smoⁿldə] ulme, ryke.

smudge [smʌdʒ] flekk; flekke, skitne.

smug [smʌɡ] nett, sirlig, dydsiret, selvgod; selvtilfreds, dydsmønster. — -faced med et glatt og falsk ansikt, dydsiret, selvtilfreds.

smuggle ['smʌɡl] smugle. smuggler smugler. smuggling smugling.

smut [smʌt] (sot)flekk, smuss; brann, rust (på plante); sote, smusse.

smutty ['smʌti] smussig, skitten.

snack [snäk] matbete.

snaffle ['snäfl] trinse; styre ved trinse, styre. **snag** [snäɡ] framstående knast, tagg, stubb, stump; hogge greinene av.

snagged ['snäɡd], snaggy ['snäɡi] knudret, stubbet, knortet.

snail [sneⁱl] snegle (med hus; edible (eller great vine) — vinbergsnegle; move at a -'s pace snegle seg fram. — -shell sneglehus.

snake [sneⁱk] snok, slange, orm; common (eller ringed) — alminnelig snok; venomous (eller poisonous) — giftslange.

snakish ['sne'kiʃ] slangeaktig.
snap [snäp] snappe, glefse, bite, bite av, smekke med, knipse med, trykke av, brekke, breste, briste; snapping, glefs, tak, bit, knekk, smekk, knepp, knett, knips, lås. — -bean snittebønne.
snapdragon ['snäp'drägən] løvemunn (plante); julelek med rosiner som nappes ut av brennende konjak.
snap|-lock ['snäplåk] smekklås. -per en som snapper; kastanjett. -pish, -pishly ['snäpiʃ(li)] bisk, morsk. -pishness [-iʃnès] biskhet.
snapshot ['snäpʃåt] øyeblikksfotografi.
snare [snæ·ə] snare; fange i snare, hilde.
snarl [sna·ə] floke, vase; ugreie, strid, forvirring.
snarl [sna·əl] snerre, knurre; knurring.
snatch [snätʃ] snappe, trive, rive bort, bite etter; napp, rykk, kort ri, stump, glimt, tørn; by -es støtvis; -es of sunshine solblink; a — of sleep en blund. -ingly støtvis. snatchy rykkevis, ujevn, ujamn.
sneak [sni·k] snike seg, krype for, fisle, sladre; kryper, slisker, sladderhank. -ing, -ingly krypende, slesk; luskende, lumsk, lumpen. -ingness [-iɳnés] kryperi.
sneer [sni·ə] rynke på nesen, kimse, la hånt om, spotte; spotsk smil, stikleri. -er [-rə] spotter. -ingly [-riɳli] spotsk. hånlig.
sneeze [sni·z] nyse; nys; — at rynke på nesen av.
snick [snik] snitt; knute (på tråd]; slå.
snicker ['snikə] knise, fnise; fnis, knis.
sniff [snif] snøfte, snuse, snufse; snøft, snufsing, snusing.
sniffle ['snifl] snuse, snufse.
snigger ['snigə] knise, kaldflire; knis, kaldflir.
snip [snip] klippe, snitt, klipp, andel, part; go -s with dele med. -per skredder.
snipe [snaip] skyte ned (fienden) en for en.
snipe [snaip] snipe, bekkasin; gå på snipejakt.
snippet ['snipit] bete, småstykke, stump.
snivel ['snivl] snott; snørr; snufsing; ha snue, snufse, flepe, sutre. -ler klynker. -ling sutring.
snob [snåb] snobb, en som aper etter de fine, filister (ikkestudent). -bery snobbethet. -bish, -bishly snobbethet. -bishness [-iʃnès] snobbethet. -bism snobberi.
snook [snuk]: cock a — peke nese.
snooze [snu·z] blunde, dubbe; blund, lur.
snore [snå·ə] snorke; snorking.
snort [snå·ət] pruste, fnyse; fnysing.
snot [snåt] snott, snørr. — -rag snotteklut, snytefille, lommetørkle.
snotty ['snåti] snottet, snørret, tarvelig; kødett.
snout [snaut] snute, tryne, snabel, snyteskaft; ende, tut, spiss. — -beetle snutebille.
snow [snoᵘ] snø; snø (verb.) -ball snøball; kaste snøball. — -blind snøblind. — -bound innsnødd. — -broth snøslaps, sørpe. — -capped, — -clad, — -crowned snøkledd.
Snowdon ['snoᵘdn] Snowdon.
snow-drift ['snoᵘdrift] snøfonn, snøfane.
snow|drop snøklokke. — -fall snøfall. — -field snømark. — -finch snøfinke. — -flake snøfnugg, snøfille. — -flurry snøfokk, snøkave. — -limit snøgrense. — -line snøgrense. — -owl snøugle. — -plough snøplog. — -shoe truge. — -slide lavine. — -storm snøfokk, snøstorm. -y snødekt, snøhvit, ren.
snub [snʌb] irettesetting, snute oppstoppernese; bite av, irettesette. — nose stumpnese.
snuff [snʌf] tande, utbrent veke; snyte (et lys); — out ta livet av, dø. — it dø.
snuff [snʌf] snuse; snus, fornærmelse; take a pinch of — ta en pris; up to — ikke tapt bak en vogn.
snuff-box ['snʌfbåks] snusdåse.
snuffer ['snʌfə] en som bruker snus; -s lysesaks; a pair of -s lysesaks.

snuffle ['snʌfl] snøvle; snøvling.
snuffles ['snʌflz] snue.
snuffy ['snʌfi] snuset, tilsølt av snus.
snug [snʌg] tettsluttende, lun, nett, hyggelig, koselig; lune, ligge lunt, ligge tett inn til; sit — by the fire sitte der lunt og godt ved varmen; a — berth en sikker stilling; a — little party en liten fortrolig krets; make — sums tjene pene summer.
snuggery ['snʌgəri] hyggelig sted, koselig hybel.
snuggle ['snʌgl] ligge lunt, legge tett opp til, kjæle for.
so [soᵘ] så, således, slik, altså; når bare; — fortunate as to så lykkelig å; he felt — (much) hurt by (så støtt over) the comparison that; after an hour or so's (cirka en times) cross-examination; how —? hvorledes det? why —? hvorfor det? the more — as så meget mer som; and — did we og det gjorde vi med; I believe — jeg tror det; I should — like to see him jeg ville så gjerne se (snakke med) ham; — please Your Majesty med Deres Majestets tillatelse.
soak [soᵘk] bløyte, legge i bløyt, gjennomvæte, suge inn, ligge i bløyt, suge ut, drikke; -ed (through) gjennombløytt; water -s into the earth det siver vann ned i jorda; put washing to — legge tøy i bløyt. -age ['soᵘkidz] utbløyting. -er dranker. -ing gjennombløytende. -y gjennombløytt.
so-and-so ['soᵘənsoᵘ] den og den, det og det; Mr. — herr N. N.
soap [soᵘp] såpe; såpe inn, smigre; soft — bløt såpe; især grønnsåpe (også: green —); yellow — gul ulltøysåpe; cake (eller cube eller tablet) of — stykke såpe, såpestykke. — -boiler såpekoker. — -bubble såpeboble. — -suds såpeskum.
soapy ['soᵘpi] såpeaktig; glatt, slesk.
soar [så·ə] fly høyt, sveve, heve seg, stige; høy flukt. -ing ['så·riɳ] høytflyvende; (høy) flukt.
sob [såb] hulke, hikste; hulking; sobs hulkende gråt, hikstegråt.
sobeit [soᵘbi·it] når bare (gammeldags).
sober ['soᵘbə] edru, edruelig, rolig, dempet, besindig, sindig, stø, nøktern; gjøre edru, bli edru. — -blooded koldblodig. — -minded nøktern, rolig. -ness [-nès] nøkternhet. — -suited kledd i diskrete farger, i ærbar drakt.
Sobranje [so'bra·nie] sobranje, det bulgarske storting.
sobriety [so'braiiti] nøkternhet, edruelighet.
sobriquet [so'brike'] økenavn, oppnavn.
socage ['såkidʒ] arvefeste (selveiendom med avgift).
sociability [soᵘʃə'biliti] selskapelighet.
sociable ['soᵘʃəbl] selskapelig, omgjengelig; holstensk vogn.
sociableness ['soᵘʃəblnès] selskapelighet.
sociably [soᵘʃəbli] selskapelig.
social ['soᵘʃəl] sosial, selskapelig, samfunns-; — evil samfunnsonde; — love nestekjærlighet; — intercourse selskapelig samkvem; — philosophy statsøkonomi; — democrat sosialdemokrat.
socialism ['soᵘʃəlizm] sosialisme.
socialist ['soᵘʃəlist] sosialist.
socialistic [soᵘʃə'listik] sosialistisk.
sociality [soᵘʃi'äliti] selskapelighet.
socialize ['soᵘʃəlaiz] innrette selskapelig, ordne sosialistisk, sosialisere.
society [so'saiiti] selskap, samfunn, forening, sosietet, den fine verden; mix in — delta i selskapslivet; a man of — en selskapsmann; — of Friends kvekere.
sociology [soᵘʃi'ålədʒi] samfunnslære.
sock [såk] en lett, lavhelet sko som de komiske skuespillere brukte, komedie; sokk, strømpe, halvstrømpe, innleggssåle.
socket ['såkit] fordypning, grop, hulning, lyse-pipe, øyenhule, hofteskål, tannhull.
socle ['soᵘkl] sokkel, fotstykke, fotpanel.

Socrates ['såkrəti·z] Sokrates.
Socratic(al) [so'krätik(l)] sokratisk.
sod [såd] grastorv. -dy dekket med grastorv.
soda ['so"də] soda, natron, sodavann; carbonate of — soda.
sodality [so'däliti] brorskap.
soda-water ['so"dəwå·tə] sodavann.
sodden ['sådn] gjennomtrukken, vasstrukken, gjennombløyt, bløt, løs, svampet, pløsen, råstekt, fordrukken, full; oppløst.
sodium ['so"djəm] natrium; — bicarbonate surt-kullsurt natron (NaHCO₃); — chloride klornatrium, koksalt.
Sodom ['sådəm] Sodoma.
Sodor ['so"də]; the Bishop of — and Man biskopen av Suderøyene og Man.
soever [so"'evə] som helst, enn; how great — hvor stor enn.
sofa ['so"fə] sofa; sit on (eller in) the — sitte i sofaen. — -bed sovesofa. — -box puff.
Sofia [so'faiə] Sofia (i Bulgaria).
soffit ['såfit] soffit, underside av bjelkeloft, loftsdekorasjon (i teater).
soft [såft] bløt, glatt, fin, sakte, linn, mild, blid, var, fryktsom, svak; — goods (or wares) manufakturvarer; a — place et bløtt sted, et svakt punkt; the — sex det svake kjønn; go — bli bløt; plead guilty to the — impeachment tilstå sine ømme følelser.
soft-boiled ['så·ftboild] bløtkokt.
soft-brained ['så·ftbra'nd] bløt på hjernen.
soften ['så·fn] bløtgjøre, mildne, lindre, døyve, røre, forkjæle, formildes, mildne. -ener lindrer, lindring(-middel). -ening bløtgjørende; formildende, hjernebløthet. -ly bløtt, mildt. -ness [-nès] bløthet, mildhet, svakhet.
Soho [so'ho"] Soho (kvarter i London).
soil [soil] jordbunn, jordsmonn, grunn, moldjord.
soil [soil] søle til, skitne til, søles til; smuss, søle. gjødsel, møkk, flekk.
soil [soil] gjø, fete, fore med grønnfor.
soirée ['swå·re'] soaré.
sojourn ['sådʒə·n, 'sadʒə·n] opphold; oppholde seg.
solace ['såləs] oppmuntre, trøste, husvale, lindre, døyve; oppmuntring, trøst; husvalelse, lindring. -ment trøst, beroligelse, lindring.
solar ['so"l·] sol-; — flowers blomster som åpner og lukker seg daglig til visse tider; — tables astronomiske tabeller.
solarium [so'læ·riəm] solskive.
sold [so"ld] imperf. og perf. pts. av sell.
solder ['sådə, 'så·də, 'sådə] lodde, sammenføye; loddemiddel. -ing [-riŋ] lodding; hard — slaglodd.
soldier ['so"ldʒə] soldat, militær; være soldat; common (el. private) — menig soldat; an old — en gammel praktikus; go (or enlist) for a — la seg verve; die a -'s death falle på ærens mark.
soldier-crab ['so"ldʒəkräb] havkrabbe.
soldiering ['so"ldʒəriŋ] krigerhåndverk.
soldierlike ['so"ldʒəlaik], soldierly ['so"ldʒəli] soldatmessig.
soldiership ['so"ldʒəʃip] militær dyktighet.
soldiery ['so"ldʒəri] krigsfolk, soldater (som klasse).
sole [so"l] tunge (flyndre).
sole [so"l] fotsåle, skosåle; såle. — -leather sålelær.
sole [so"l] alene, eneste, utelukkende, ugift; — bill solaveksel; — agent eneagent, enerepresentant.
solecism ['sålisizm] språkfeil, bommert.
solecist ['sålisist] språkforderver.
solely ['so"lli] alene, bare.
solemn ['såləm] høytidelig; (fig.) stiv. -ity [so-'lemniti] høytidelighet. -ize ['såləmnaiz] høytideligholde. -ly høytidelig. -ness [-nès] høytidelighet.
Solent ['so"lənt]; the — Solentfjorden.

solicit [sə'lisit] tilskynde, vekke, be, anmode trygle, ansøke om, utbe seg, forurolige, bekymre• -ant ansøker, -ation anmodning.
solicitor [sə'lisitə] ansøker; (underordnet) sakfører, juridisk rådgiver; crown — statsadvokat. — -general regjeringsadvokat (forkortet: Sol. Gen., S. G.). -ship sakførerstilling.
solicitous [sə'lisitəs] bekymret.
solicitude [sə'lisitju·d] otte, bekymring, iver, omsorg.
solid ['sålid] fast, traust, massiv, solid, ekte, grundig, pålitelig, alvorlig; fast legeme, faste deler.
solidarity [såli'däriti] solidaritet.
solidification [sʌlidifi'ke'ʃən] festning. solidify [sʌ'lidifai] bli fast, festne.
solidity [så'liditi] tetthet, soliditet.
soliloquize [so'liləkwaiz] snakke med seg selv.
soliloquy [sə'liləkwi] enetale.
soliped ['sålipèd] enhovet.
solitaire [såli'tæ·ə] eneboer; solitær (edelsten som innfattes alene); enmannsspill (bl. a. brettspill for en enkelt person), kortkabal.
solitariness ['sålitərinès] ensomhet.
solitary ['sålit(ə)ri] ensom, avsides, enestående, eneste; eneboer.
solitude ['sålitju·d] ensomhet.
solo ['so"lo"] solo; — part soloparti.
soloist ['so"loist] solist.
Solomon ['såləmən] Salomo; the Song of — Salomos høysang; -'s seal kantkonvall.
Solon ['so"lən] Solon.
solstice ['sålstis] solhverv, solvending.
solstitial [sål'stiʃəl] solhvervs-.
solubility [sålju'biliti] oppløselighet.
soluble ['såljubl] oppløselig.
solus ['so"ləs] alene (i sceneanvisninger).
solution [sʌ'l(j)u·ʃən] oppløsning, løsning.
solvability [sålvə'biliti] oppløselighet.
solvable ['sålvəbl] oppløselig.
solve [sålv] løse, klare, greie.
solvency ['sålvənsi] betalingsevne, solvens.
solvent ['sålvənt] solvent; oppløsningsmiddel.
Solway ['sålwe'] Solway.
Somali [so'ma·li] somali. — -land [-länd] Somaliland.
somatology [so"mə'tålədʒi] somatologi (legemslære).
sombre ['såmbə] mørk, trist, melankolsk, dyster.
sombrero [såm'bræ·•ro"] sombrero (bredskygget solhatt).
sombrous ['såmbrəs] mørk, dyster.
some [sʌm (sterk form), səm, sm (svake former)]. 1. (adj.) en eller annen, et eller annet, noe; noen, visse, somme; (foran tallord å oversette med omtrent, cirka, en: sånn;) 2. (subst.) noe, i noen grad, litt. 1. lend me — book lån meg en eller annen bok; — books noen bøker; this is — book det kan man kalle en bok, det er vel en utmerket bok; — twenty years et snes år; — 20 miles off cirka 20 miles borte; — few noen få. 2. — say one thing and others another noen sier det og andre det. 3. he was annoyed — han var litt ergerlig.
somebody ['sʌmbədi] noen, en eller annen; en person av betydning; — has been here before her har vært noen i forveien; think oneself to be — innbille seg å være noe stort; you are — after all det er likevel noe ved deg.
somehow ['sʌmhau] på en eller annen måte, hvordan det nå er (el. var) eller ikke; it scares me — det gjør meg på redd likevel.
someone ['sʌmwʌn] noen, en eller annen.
somersault ['sʌməså(·)lt] saltomortale, rundkast, cast (eller throw, turn) a — slå en saltomortale.
Somerset ['sʌməsèt] Somerset.
something ['sʌmþin] noe, et eller annet; tell

me — fortell meg noe; little, yet — lite, men likevel noe; — new noe nytt; — blue noe blått; there is — in it det er noe (ɔ: noe sant) i det; that is — det er (da alltid) noe (f. eks. noen trøst); he is — in the Customs han er noe i tollvesenet; he was made a captain or — han ble utnevnt til kaptein eller noe slikt; — like ikke ulik; it looked — awful det så nokså forferdelig ut.

sometime ['sʌmtaim] fordum, tidligere.

sometimes ['sʌmtaimz] undertiden, somme tider.

somewhat ['sʌmwåt] (adv.) noe, i noen grad; (subst.) noe; he is — deaf han er noe døv; it loses — of its force det mister noe av sin kraft.

somewhere ['sʌmwæ·ə] et eller annet sted; he may be — near han er kanskje ensteds i nærheten.

somnambulism [såm'nämbjulizm] søvngjengeri. somnambulist [såm'nämbjulist] søvngjenger.

somniferous [såm'nifərəs], somnific [såm'nifik] søvndyssende.

somnolence ['såmnoləns] søvnighet.

somnolent ['såmnolənt] søvnig.

son [sʌn] sønn; — of man Menneskesønnen. — -in-law svigersønn. -ship sønneforhold.

sonata [sə'na·tə] sonate.

song [såŋ] sang, vise; the usual — den gamle visen; at a —, for an old — til spottpris, for en slikk og ingenting. — -bird sangfugl. — -book sangbok. -fulness sangrikdom, lyst til å synge. -ster ['såŋstə] sanger. -stress ['såŋstrés] sangerinne. — -thrush sangtrost.

sonnet ['sånit] sonett. -eer [såni'tiə] sonettdikter.

sonny ['sʌni] liten gutt (især i tiltale): små'n.

sonority [sə'nåriti] klang, klangfylde.

sonorous [sə'nå·rəs] klangfull. -ness [-nés] velklang.

sonsy ['sånsi] tilfreds, trivelig, pen, godmodig.

soon [su·n] snart, tidlig; hurtig, fort; as — as så snart som; I would as — jeg ville likeså gjerne; no -er aldri så snart.

soot [sut] sot; sote; -ed sotet. -y sotet.

soothsay ['su·bse¹] spå. -er [-ə] sannsier.

soothe [su·ð] formilde, berolige, roe, godsnakke med, smigre.

soother ['su·ðə] narresutt.

soothing ['su·ðiŋ] innsmigrende, beroligende.

sop [såp] oppbløyt stykke, lekkerbisken, trøst; dyppe, bløyte ut; sive; — up suge opp.

Sophia [so'faiə] Sofie; Sofia.

sophism ['såfizm] sofisme. sophist ['såfist] sofist. sophistic [so'fistik] sofistisk. sophisticate [so'fis·ike¹t] forderve, forfalske, vrenge, vri på. sophistication [sofisti'ke¹fən] forfalskning. sophistry ['såfistri] sofisteri.

Sophocles ['såfəkli·z] Sofokles.

Sophy ['so·fi] Sofie.

soporific[so·po'rifik] søvndyssende; sovemiddel.

soprano [so'pra·no·] sopran.

sorb [så·ᵇb] haverogn, rognebær.

sorcerer ['så·ᵈsərə] trollmann. sorceress ['så·ᵈsəres] trollkjerring. sorcery ['så·ᵈsəri] trolldom.

sordid ['så·ᵈdid] lav, skitten, smussig; gjerrig, knuslet, luset.

sordine ['så·ᵈdi·(·)n] sordin.

sore [så·ᵈ] sår, byll, svull, ømt sted; sår, øm, smertelig, hard, ømtålig, pirrelig; — eyes dårlige (el. gamle) øyne; the — spot det ømme punkt; a — throat vondt i halsen; a — trial en hard prøvelse. -ly smertelig, sterkt, meget, hardt. -ness [-nés] ømhet, pirrelighet.

sorn [så·ᵈn] tvangsgjesting, veitsle; trenge seg inn.

sorrel ['sårəl] syre, rumex; gaukesyre (plante).

sorrel ['sårəl] brunblakk, rødbrun; rødbrunt dyr.

sorrily ['sårili] bedrøvelig, jammerlig.

sorrow ['såro·] sorg, sut; sørge; feel — for føle

sorg over. -ful ['såro·ful] sorgfull, sørgelig. -fulness [-nés] sørgmodighet. -less [-lés] sorgfri. — -stricken ['såro·strikn] rammet av sorg, sorgtynget.

sorry ['såri] sørgmodig, bedrøvelig; ussel; a — customer en dårlig makker; a — horse en skottgamp; I am — to say dessverre; I am — for him jeg har vondt av ham; I am very — jeg beklager meget.

sort [så·ᵗt] sort, slags, stand, måte, vis, sett; sortere, ordne, stille sammen, være forent, forene seg, passe, falle ut, ende, lykkes; all -s, kinds, and descriptions alle mulige slags; this — of dog, these — of dogs dette (disse) hundeslag; he's a good — det er en snill fyr; he's the right — han er den rette; nothing of the — aldeles ikke; of -s i visse retninger, i noen henseender; a dinner of -s et slags middag; be out of -s være forstemt, være i ulag; be in -s være i godlaget; -able [-əbl] som lar seg sortere, passende. -er sorterer.

sortie ['så·ᵉti·] utfall.

sortilege ['så·ᵉtilidʒ] loddtrekning.

sortition [så·ᵉ'tifən] loddtrekning.

S. O. S. trådløst budskap om at avsendere er i ytterste fare.

so-so ['so·ᵘso·ᵘ] så som så, så middels.

sot [såt] drukkenbolt, fyllebøtte; drikke, supe.

sottish ['såtif] fordrukken, forfylt.

sotto voce ['såto· 'vo·ᵘtfe¹] dempet.

Soudan [su(·)'dän]; the — Sudan.

sough [sʌf] suse (om vinden); sus, pust, sukk.

sough [sʌf] lukket grøft, grunnveit.

sought [så·t] imperf. og perf. pts. av seek.

soul [so·ᵘl] sjel, følelse, hjerte; keep body and — together oppholde livet. —-felt dypt følt. -ful sjelfull. — -hardened forherdet. -less [-lés] sjelløs.

sound [saund] sunn, frisk, ekte, sterk, trygg, traust, fast, dyp (om søvn), uforstyrret, gyldig, rettroende; a — whipping en god drakt pryl; safe and — i god behold; if the calculations are — dersom beregningen holder stikk.

sound [saund] sund; the (Baltic) Sound Øresund.

sound [saund] svømmeblære.

sound [saund] sonde; sondere, lodde (vannets dybde), prøve, få til å røpe.

sound [saund] lyd, klang; lyde, klinge, blåse, la lyde; gi signal til; — a trumpet blåse i en trompet; — the charge blåse til angrep. -board sangbunn.

sounding ['saundiŋ] lydende, velklingende; lyd, klang.

sounding ['saundiŋ] lodding; i plur. loddskudd, (loddede) dybder, dybdeforhold; kjent farvann. sounding-board ['saundinbå·ᵈd] resonansbunn. sounding-lead [-'saundinled] lodd.

soundless ['saundlés] lydløs.

soundless ['saundlés] bunnløs.

soundness ['saundnés] sunnhet.

soup [su·p] suppe. — -plate dyp tallerken.

sour ['sauə] sur, gretten, bitter; noe surt, syre; gjøre sur, forbitre, surne, blir bitter.

source [så·ᵈs] kjelde, oppkomme, olle, utspring, kilde.

sourcrout ['sauəkraut] surkål. — -faced fortredelig. -ish [-rif] syrlig. -ly surt, bittert. -ness [-nés] surhet, bitterhet.

souse [saus] dukkert; saltlake, grisesylte; dukke sylte, dyppe, øse, skvette.

souse [saus] daske, delje til; slå ned (som en rovfugl).

souteneur [su·tə'nə·] alfons, sutinør.

south (eller South) [saub] sør, søretter, sønnavind, Syden; søndre; mot sør, fra sør.

Southampton [sau'þämptən] Southampton.

southeast [saub'i·st] sørøst, mot sørøst.

southeastern ['saub'i·stən] sørøstlig.

southerly ['sʌðəli] sørlig.
southern ['sʌðən] sør-, sørlandsk, sørlig; the Southern Cross Sydkorset.
southerner ['sʌðənə] sørenglender, sørlending, sørstatsmann.
southernmost ['sʌðənmoᵘst] sørligst.
southing ['sauðiŋ] bevegelse sørpå; sørlig deklinasjon; breddeforandring sørover.
south|most sørligst. -west ['sauþ'west] sørvest. -wester [sauþ'westə] sørveststorm, sørvest (= southwest hat). -western sørvestlig. -ward ['sauþwəd] mot sør, sørpå; sør.
Southwark ['sʌðək] Southwark.
souvenir [su·v(ə)·niə] erindring(stegn), minne.
sov. fk. f. sovereign.
sovereign ['sɔvrin] høyest, suveren, kraftig; regent, hersker, sovereign (en engelsk gullmynt av verdi 20 shillings = ca. 18 kr.). -ly høyst. -ty [-ti] suverenitet, herredømme.
Soviet ['sɔvjet] Sovjet.
sow [sau] sugge, purke; avlang metallblokk, rujernsblokk, renne fra smelteovn til former, skrukketroll.
sow [soᵘ] så, så til, så ut.
sower ['soᵘə] såmann; såmaskin.
sown [soᵘn] perf. pts. av sow.
soy [soi] sojabønne, soja (slags saus).
spa [spa·] mineralkilde, mineralbad
space [speᵻs] rom, mellomrom, areal, tidsrom, stund, spatium; anbringe med mellomrom.
spacious ['speᵻʃəs] vid, rommelig.
spaciousness ['speᵻʃəsnès] rommelighet.
spaddle ['spædl] liten skade.
spade [speᵻd] gjelding; gjelk.
spade [speᵻd] spade, spar (i kortspill); spa (opp); flense; call a — a — kalle tingen med sitt rette navn; -'s graft spadedybde; — -bone skulderblad.
spadiceous [spə'diʃəs] lyserød; kolbeblomstret.
spaghetti [spə'geti] spaghetti (rett av makaroni).
spahee ['spa·hi·], spahi ['spa·hi·] spahi.
Spain [speᵻn] Spania.
spake [speᵻk] poetisk imperf. av speak.
spale [speᵻl] lekte, spon
spall [spa·l] splint, flis; splintre(s).
span [spän] spann, ni engelske tommer, spann (hester), spennvidde, spenn, kort tid, salstropp; spenne, spenne om, måle, surre.
span [spän] flunkende, splinter-.
span [spän] gammel imperf. av spin.
spangle ['späŋgl] paljett, flitterstas; besette med paljetter, glitre, spille; star-spangled ['sta·'späŋgld] oversådd med stjerner.
Spaniard ['spänjəd] spanjer, spanjol.
spaniel ['spänjəl] vaktelhund, fuglehund; krype for, logre.
Spanish ['späniʃ] spansk (også om språket); — castles luftkasteller; — fly spansk flue.
spank [späŋk] daske, klaske; dask, klask.
spanker ['späŋkə] hurtig traver; sprek hest; sveisen kar; mesan.
spanner ['spänə] skrunøkkel.
spar [spa·ə] spat (mineral).
spar [spa·ə] sperre, raft, rundholt; stang, stake, lekte.
spar [spa·ə] slå ut (med armene), bokse, fekte; kjekle; fekting med armene, nevekamp, kamp
spare [spæ·ə] spare på, unnvære, avse, spare seg, la være, skåne, spare, forskåne for, tilstå, skjenke, leve sparsomt, være skånsom, være medlidende, unnlate; sparsom, knapp, snau, tarvelig, mager, ledig, overflødig, reserve; — bedroom gjesteværelse; — hours fritimer; — money sparepenger; — parts reservedeler (til maskiner); — rib ribbestek.
spare-built ['spæ·əbilt] spinkel.
sparing ['spæ·əriŋ] sparsom, sjelden, snau.
spark [spa·ək] gnist, sprade, elsker; gnistre.
sparking-plug ['spa·əkiŋ'plʌg] tennplugg.

sparkle ['spa·əkl] gnist, glans; gnistre, funkle, glimre, perle, sprake ut, sprøyte ut.
sparklet ['spa·əklèt] liten gnist; boble, perle.
sparkling ['spa·əkliŋ] funklende, livlig, sprakende.
sparrow ['späroᵘ] spurv.
sparse [spa·ᵃs] spredt, grissen.
Sparta ['spa·ᵊtə] Sparta.
Spartacist ['spa·ᵊtəsist] ytterliggående deltager i den tyske revolusjon.
Spartan ['spa·ᵊtən] spartaner, spartansk.
spasm [späzm] krampe(trekning).
spasmodic [späz'mådik] krampaktig.
spat [spät] imperf. og perf. pts. av spit.
spat [spät] østersyngel; yngle.
spat [spät] gamasje (srl. i plur.); ta på gamasjer.
spatter ['spätə] skvette (til), sprøyte (over); skvett, sprut. -dashes gamasjer.
spatula ['spätjulə], spattle ['spätl] spatel, sparkel.
spavin ['spävin] spatt (en hestesykdom).
spawn [spå·n] rogn, melke, egg (av fisk, frosk), gott; rotskudd, avkom; gyte, legge, yngle, avle, oppstå; -er rognfisk. -ing-time gytetid.
S. P. C. K. fk. f. Society for Promoting Christian Knowledge.
S. P. E. fk. f. Society for Pure English.
speak [spi·k] tale, snakke, ytre, si fram, uttale, forkynne, tiltale. -able ['spi·kəbl] som kan sis, omgjengelig.
speak-easy [spi·k'i·zi] (amr.) ulovlig brennevinsutsalg, gaukesalg.
speaker ['spi·kə] taler; hallomann; president i underhuset (tilt. som Mr. Speaker); loud- høyttaler.
speaking talende; tale-; be on — kunne snakke med hverandre, være på talefot med hverandre; — -pipe talerør. — -trumpet ropert. — -tube talerør.
spear [spiə] spyd, lanse, lyster, pumpestang; spire, drepe med et spyd, spidde. — -head spydodd. -man lansedrager. — side sverdside, mannsside.
spec [spek] spekulasjon.
special ['speʃəl] særegen, spesiell, særdeles, ualminnelig, utmerket, omfram, ekstra-; særegenhet, ekstranummer.
specialist ['speʃəlist] spesialist.
speciality [speʃi'äliti] spesialitet.
specialization [speʃəlai'zeᵻʃən] spesialisering.
specialize ['speʃəlaiz] spesialisere (seg).
specialty ['speʃəlti] særbeskjeftigelse, særstudium, spesialitet, kontrakt, gjeldsbevis.
specie ['spi·ʃi] slag, art; klingende mynt, tet metall.
species ['spi·ʃi(·)z] art, slags.
specific [spi'sifik] særegen, eiendommelig, spesifikk; spesifikt middel, særmiddel. -ation [spesifi'keᵻʃən] spesifisering.
specify ['spesifai] spesifisere.
specimen ['spi·ʃəs] eksemplar, prøve, eksemplar.
specious ['spi·ʃəs] tilsynelatende god (el. rimelig), plausibel, bestikkende, skinn-.
speck [spek] liten flekk, stenk; pl. dropler; flekke, gjøre droplet.
speckle ['spekl] liten flekk, prikk, gjøre spraglet, gjøre droplet. speckled ['spekld] spettet; broket.
spectacle ['spektəkl] skue, syn, skuespill, pl. briller; brilleformet tegning, brille(figur); r a par of -s et par briller; -d ['spektəkld] med briller.
spectacular [spek'täkjulə] skuespill,- teatermessig, teatralsk; praktfull.
spectator [spek'teᵻtə] tilskuer.
spectral ['spektrəl] spektral; — analysis spektralanalyse.
spectre ['spektə] gjenferd, spøkelse.
spectroscope ['spektrəskoᵘp] spektroskop.
spectrum ['spektrəm] spektrum.

specular ['spekjulə] speil-.

speculate ['spekjuleᵻt] spekulere, gruble.

speculation [spekju'leiʃən] spekulasjon.

speculative ['spekjulətiv] spekulativ.

speculator ['spekjuleᵻtə] tenker; spekulant.

speculum ['spekjuləm] speil (srl. av metall).

speech [spi·ᵼʃ] tale, språk, replikk; **deliver one's maiden** — holde sin jomfrutale (første tale). **make a** — holde en tale, si en replikk.

speech-day ['spi·tʃdeᵻ] avslutningsfest på skole.

speechify ['spi·tʃifai] tale, holde taler.

speechless ['spi·tʃlès] målløs.

speechmaker ['spi·tʃmeᵻkə] taler (av profesjon).

speed [spi·d] ile, haste, skynde seg, lykkes; framskynde, sette fart i, fremme, hjelpe, ønske lykke til, si farvel til, ekspedere; hast, hurtighet, fart, lykke, løp, galopp.

speedometer [spi'dàmitə] speedometer, fartmåler (i bil).

speedway ['spi·dweᵻ] kjørebane.

speedy ['spi·di] rask, snøgg, kvikk, ilsom; snarlig.

spell [spel] fortrylle; stave, bokstavere, skrive, stave seg igjennom, lese dårlig, skrives, bety, mene; trylle-formular, fess, fortryllelse.

spell [spel] avløse i arbeidet, hvile, avløsning, skift, tørn, tur, økt, hjelp, tjeneste, stund, ri, anfall; **give him a** — gi ham en håndsrekning; **by spells** skiftevis, etter tur.

spellbound ['spelbaund] fortyllet, fjetret.

spelling ['speliŋ] stavemåte, rettskrivning.

spelling-book ['speliŋbuk] abc.

spelt [spelt] imperf. og perf. pts. av **spell**.

spelt [spelt] spelt (plante).

spence [spens] utlegg, kostnad; matbu, matskap.

spencer ['spensə] spencer (gammeldags kort overtrøye).

spencer ['spensə] gaffelseil.

Spencer ['spensə] Spencer (især **Herbert** — eng. forf.).

spend [spend] bruke, forbruke, gi ut, koste ut, tilbringe, øde, øyde, ødsle bort, bruke opp, spandere, utmatte; bli oppbrukt, tæres opp; **-er** øder, øyder.

spending power kjøpekraft.

spendthrift ['spendθrift] ødeland; ødsel.

Spenser ['spensə] Spenser (engelsk dikter).

Spenserian ['spen'siəriən]; — **stanza** Spenserstrofe.

spent [spent] imperf. og perf. pts. av **spend**.

sperm [spə·m] sæd (av mennesker og dyr); hvalrav.

spermaceti [spə·mə'si·ti] spermasett, hvalrav; — **whale** kaskelott, spermasetthval.

spew [spju·] spy, brekke seg, spy ut.

S. P. G. fk. f. **Society for the Propagation of the Gospel.**

sphacelus ['sfæsələs] koldbrann.

sphere [sfiə] sfære, kule, klode, stjerne, himmellegeme, globus, virkekrets, synskrets, fatteevne; gjøre rund, sette i en krets.

spheric ['sferik], **-al**, **-ally** sfærisk, kule-.

sphinx [sfiŋks]; aftensvermer.

spica ['spaikə] aks; spore.

spice [spais] speseri, krydderi, smak, anstrøk; krydre. — **-nut** peppernøtt. **-r** speserihandler.

spicery ['spaisəri] krydderier.

spick [spik] meis (fugl).

spick-and-span splinterny.

spicule ['spikju·l] lite aks.

spicy ['spaisi] krydret, aromatisk, pikant.

spider ['spaidə] edderkopp, veivkjerring. **-like** edderkoppaktig. **spidery** ['spaidəri] edderkoppaktig, meget tynn.

spigot ['spigət] tapp, svikk, ture (i hanen på en tønne).

spike [spaik] spiss, pigg, brodd, spiker, aks, skudd; spisse, spikre, nagle fast; **-d** [spaikt] med aks, forsynt med spiss, fastnaglet. **-let** ['spaiklét]

lite aks. — **-nail** (lang) spiker. **-nard** [-na·°d] nardus, nardussalve.

spiky ['spaiki] spiss, med spisser, pigget, kvass.

spill [spil] pinne, flis, spik; fidibus.

spill [spil] spille, slå ned, ødelegge, ødsle, bli spilt, kaste av; fall (fra hest el. vogn).

spillikin ['spilikin] pinne, i plur. ogsa: pinnespill.

spilt [spilt] imperf. og perf. pts. av **spill;** — **milk** spilt melk, et uhell som det ikke nytter å gråte over.

spin [spin] spinne, trekke, tøye (ut), forhale, dreie, dreie seg, snurre rundt, surre, svive rundt, strømme hurtig, suse; hvirvling, snurring (rundt); fart, tur (i vogn, på sykkel etc.); — **a yarn** spinne en ende; — **out the time** trekke tiden ut.

spinach ['spinidʒ] spinat.

spinal ['spainəl] ryggrads-.

spindle ['spindl] tein, stang, spindel, lang og tynn stengel; skyte ut i lange strengler. — **-legs**, — **-shanks** pipestilker.

spindrift ['spindrift] sjørokk, sjødrev.

spine [spain] ryggrad; bergrygg, fjellrygg; pigg; torn.

spinet ['spinit] spinett.

spiniferous [spai'nifərəs] tornet.

spiniform ['spaini à·°m] torneformet.

spinner ['spinə] spinner, spinnerske; edderkopp.

spinning-jenny spinnemaskin. **spinningwheel** rokkehjul, rokk.

spinosity [spai'nàsiti] tornethet.

spinous ['spainəs] tornet, besatt med pigger; formet som en torn.

spinster ['spinstə] ugift kvinne, gammel jomfru, attergløyme; (adj.) ugift.

spiny ['spaini] tornet, vanskelig; — **-finned** piggfinnet.

spiracle ['sp(a)irəkl] lufthull.

spiral ['spairəl] spiralformet; spiral.

spiræa [spai'ri·ə] spirea, mjødurt.

spire ['spaiə] snoning, vinding, spiral, krøll, spiss, topp, spir, spire, skudd, grasstrå; løpe spiss opp, spire. **spired** ['spaiəd] med spir.

Spires ['spaiəz] Speyer (tysk by).

spirit ['spirit] ånd, sinnelag, sinn, sinnsstemning, liv, humør, lyst, mot, spøkelse, livlighet, spiritus, sprit, spirituøs drikk; begeistre, oppmuntre, lokke; **-s** pl. spiritus, sprit, lune, humør; the (**Holy) Spirit** Den Hellige And; the — **of the age** tidsånden; **a man of high** — en man med æresfølelse; **in high** (el. good) **-s** opprømt, munter; i godt humør; **in low** (el. bad) **-s** nedslått, forstemt, i ulag; — **away** lokke bort, la forsvinne; — **of salt** saltsyre; — **of wine** ren sprit. **-ed** ['spiritid] åndrik, livlig, kvikk, modig, djerv, sprek. **-edness** [-idnès] livlighet, mot, kveik. **-ism** [-zm] spiritisme. **-ist** spiritist. — **-lamp** spritlampe. **-less** [-lès] forsagt, motløs, sløv, slakk.

spirit-rapping meldinger fra bankeånder. **-court** geistlig domstol. **-ism** [-izm] spiritisme. **-ist** spiritist. **-ity** [spiritʃu'àliti] åndelighet. **-ize** ['spiritʃuəlaiz] åndeliggjøre, lutre, gi en åndelig betydning, gjøre spirituøs. **spirituel** [spiritju'el] åndrik, spirituell.

spirituous ['spiritʃuəs] spirituøs, spritholdig.

spirt [spə·t] sprute, sprøyte, anstrenge seg til det ytterste; sprut, sprøyt, plutselig anstrengelse, rykk, spurt. **put on a** — legge alle krefter i.

spiry ['spairi] spiralformet; spir-, formet som et spir; full av spir.

spissitude ['spisitju·d] tykkhet.

spit [spit] spidd, tange, odde; spidde.

spit [spit] spytte; spytt.

spite [spait] ondskap, hat, agg, nag; gjøre ugagn, ergre, trosse, trasse, hate, fortørne; **in** — of til tross for, trass i, uaktet. **-ful** ondskapsfull. **-fulness** ondskap.

spitfire ['spitfaiə] sinnataggen, kruttkjerring; engelsk jagerfly.

spitting-box ['spitiŋbàks] spyttebakk.

spitting-mug ['spitiŋmʌg] spyttekrus.
spittle ['spitl] spytt.
spittoon [spi'tu·n] sputtebakk.
spitz [spits] spisshund.
Spitzbergen [spits'bə·gən] Spitsbergen, Svalbard.
splash [spläʃ] skvette, søle til, plaske; plask, skvetting, skvett, pudder; anstrengelse, krafttak; plask! make a — vekke sensasjon.
splash-board ['spläʃbå·ºd] forskjerm (på vogn), skvettskjerm.
splashy ['spläʃi] klattet, flekket, sølet.
splay [sple¹] forvri, bringe av ledd, bre seg; vende ut, skrå, sneie av; skrå, bred, sprikende; skråning. — -footed med flate og skjeve føtter, plattføtt; — -mouthed [- mauðid] bredmunnet, breikjefta, flåkjefta.
spleen [spli·n] milt, melankoli, humørsyke: hypokondri, tungsinn, spleen, vrede, ergrelse; vent one's — upon la sitt dårlige humør gå ut over, løse sin vrede ut over.
splendid ['splendid] glimrende, storartet, gild.
splendiferous [splen'difərəs] storartet, gild.
splendour ['splendə] glans.
splenetic [spli'netik] milt-; humørsyk, gretten; en som er gretten.
splice [splais] spleise; spleising, lask.
splint [splint] splint, pinne, flis, spik, spon, spjelk, benskinne. -er splint, flis, spon, benskinne; splintre, splintres, la hvile i skinner. -ery ['splintəri] splintret, fliset.
split [split] splitte, kløyve, spalte, dele, slå i stykker, slås i stykker, bli uenig (med); grunnstøtt, forlist; revne, brudd; — one's sides with laughter holde på å revne av latter; — infinitive infinitiv skilt fra to ved adv.; — peas(e) flekte erter.
split [split] også imperf. og perf. pts. av split.
splotch [splåtʃ] flekk, klatt; flekke, klatte.
splutter ['splʌtə] snakke fort, sprute; larm, spruting, oppstyr, røre.
spoffy ['spåfi], spoffish ['spåfiʃ] geskjeftig.
spoil [spoil] bytte, rov, fangst, kastet ham, oppkastet mudder el. grus; plyndre, berøve, forderve, spolere, bli skjemt, forkjæle; a -t (el. -ed) ødet el forkjælt barn; -ing for a fight kampivrig, i krigshumor.
spoilsman['spoilzmən] levebrødspolitiker. spoilsport ['spoilspå·t] gledesforstyrrer.
spoke [spoᵘk] eike (i hjul) trin, knagg (på ratt); hemsko; put a — in his wheel legge noe på tverke for ham, krysse hans plan.
spoke [spoᵘk] imperf. av speak.
spokesman ['spoᵘksmən] talsmann, ordfører.
spoken ['spoᵘkn] (perf. pts. av speak) talt. -talende; kind-spoken vennligtalende; civil-spoken beleven i sin tale; — English det engelske talespråk.
spoliation [spoᵘli'e'ʃən] plyndring.
spoliator ['spoᵘlie'tə] plyndrer.
spondiac [spån'de'ik] spondéisk.
spondee ['spåndi·] spondé (versfot).
sponge [spʌn(d)ʒ] svamp; svampet masse, (æset) deig, surdeig; snyltegjest; viske ut med en svamp, presse ut av (som fra en svamp), tilsnike seg, suge inn, (som en svamp), snylte; set a — sette en deig bort for å la den heve seg; throw up the — erkjenne seg overvunnet, oppgi kampen; — out viske ut.
sponging house ['spʌn(d)ʒinhaus] midlertidig gjeldsfengsel, ofte i rettsbetjentens hus, for å gi skyldneren leilighet til ved venners hjelp å betale sin gjeld.
spongy ['spʌn(d)ʒi] svampaktig, svampet, porøs, bløt, sugende, fordrukken.
sponsal ['spånsəl] bryllups-, brude-.
sponsion ['spånʃən] kausjon, borg, kavering, løfte.
sponsor ['spånsə] kausjonist, fadder, gudfar. -ship fadderskap, kausjon.

spontaneity [spåntə'ni·iti] naturnødvendighet, umiddelbarhet, frivillighet.
spontaneous [spån'te'njəs] spontan, umiddelbar, uvilkårlig, frivillig; — combustion brann ved selvantennelse. -ness [-nəs] = spontaneity.
spoof [spu·f] hokuspokus, snyteri, juksing.
spook [spu·k] spøkelse.
spool [spu·l] spole, rull; trådsnelle.
spoom [spu·m] skumme, lense.
spoon [spu·n] skje; ta med en skje; have his — in the soup ha en finger med i spillet; be past the — ha trådt sine barnesko.
spoon [spu·n] tosk; forelsket narr; forelsket, enfoldig, være forelsket (on i), utveksle kjærtegn; it's a case of -s with them de er forelsket i hverandre.
spoonerism ['spu·nərizm] det å bytte lyd om i ord som følger etter hverandre, «å bake snakkvendt», f. eks. blushing crow istf. crushing blow el. lette tremmer istf. trette lemmer.
spooney ['spu·ni] meget forelsket (on i).
spoonful ['spu·nful] skjefull.
spoon-meat ['spu·nmi·t] skjemat, barnemat.
spoony ['spu·ni] forelsket (on i), ør (on etter); tosk.
spoor [spuə] spor, far, slag; forfølge spor (av).
sporadic [spo'rädik] sporadisk, spredt.
spore [spå·º] spre(celle), frøkorn, såkorn.
sport [spå·ºt] atspredelse, lek, moro, idrett, sport, jakt, fiske; leke, drive sport, more, spille, forestille, vise, gå med, prale med; for (el. in) — for spøk. -ful lystig, spøkefull. -ing sports-, idretts-; sport, jakt; a -ing character en sportsmann (av fag); -ing-door ytterdør. -ingly for spøk. -ive ['spå·ºtiv] munter, leken, overgiven. -iveness [-nès] munterhet. -less [-lés] gledeløs, sørgelig. -sman ['spå·ºtsmən] sportsmann, jeger. -smanlike sportsmannsmessig. -smanship dyktighet som idrettsmann el. jeger. -swoman idretts-kvinne.
spot [spåt] flekk, sted; flekke, besmitte; oppdage, bite merke i, gjenkjenne; upon the — på stedet, straks; -ted flekket. -less [-lés] plettfri. -lessness [-mès] plettfrihet, renhet. -ter pletter, besmitter; detektiv, spion. -ty flekket, spettet, besmittet.
spousal ['spauzl] bryllups-; -s giftermål, bryllup.
spouse [spauz] ektefelle. -less [-lés] ugift.
spout [spaut] tut, renne, rør, skybrudd, skypumpe, pantelånerbutikk, stampen; sprøyte, springe, deklamere, pantsette; up the — pantsatt. -er stortaler, skvadronør. -ing spruting, deklamasjon.
S. P. Q. R. fk. f. senatus populusque Romanus; small profits & quick returns.
S. P. R. fk. f. Society for Psychical Research.
sprag [spräg] grein, svær spiker; stanse.
sprain [spre'n] forstrekke, forstue, vrikke (ankelen); forstuing; distorsjon.
sprang [spräŋ] imperf. av spring.
sprat [sprät] brisling; fiske brisling.
sprawl [språ·l] ligge henslengt, ligge og strekke seg; sprelle, kravle, spre seg; a -ing charge et spredt, uordentlig kavaleriangrep.
spray [spre¹] kvist, kvister; dusk, yr, drev, sjøsprøyt, fint rokk, dusj, dusjapparat, sprøyte, sprøytevæske; overstenke, sprøyte ut, dusje.
spread [spred] spre, spreie, utbre, strekke, tøye ut, dekke, spre seg, sprike, utbre seg; utstrekning, omfang, utbredelse, noe som bres som dekke, bordteppe, sengeteppe; — the table dekke bordet. — -eagle ['spred'i·gl] ørn med utspilte vinger; stortalende, sjåvinistisk. -er ['spredə] spredeapparat, sprøyter, smørekniv.
spree [spri·] lystighet, kommers, kalas, rangel; holde leven, ture, rangle; on the — på rangel.
sprig [sprig] kvist, skudd; dykkert, stift, nudd; pode, ung spire; pynte med greiner, feste med stifter. -gy full av kvister.

sprightly ['spraitli] munter, livlig, kvikk.

spring spriŋ] springe, sprette, bykse, springe fram: opp tå, spire, bryte fram, vokse, fly opp, slå se (om tre), jage opp, la bryte fram, finne på med e't sprenge, få (en lekk); sprang, hopp, sprett, kilde, opprinnelse, fjær, drivfjær, spennkraft, lauvsprett, vår, skudd, plante; — **to one's feet** sprette opp og bli stående; — **a trap** smelle igjen en felle. — **-bed** springfjærmadrass. — **-board** springbrett. — **-bok**, — **-buck** springbukk, sørafrikansk gasell. — **-cart** fjærvogn.

springe [sprin(d)ʒ] snare, done; fange i snare.

springer ['spriŋə] springer; springbukk; ribbe (i buehvelv); (ark.) vederlag, motlag(stein).

spring|-halt ['spriŋhå·lt] hanesteg (en hestesykdom). — **-head** kilde, oppkomme.

springing ['spriŋiŋ] bl. a. springing, utspring, (ark.) kjemperlinje, kjemper (i bygning), bues fot. — **-stone** kjemper.

spring|-lock ['spriŋlåk] smekklås. — **-mattress** springmadrass. — **-tide** springflod.

sprinkle ['spriŋkl] stenke, skvette, strø, væte, dusje, bestrø; stenk, skvett, dusj. **sprinkler** stenker, sprøyte, vievannskost. **sprinkling** stenk, skvett; snev, svakt anstrøk, dåm.

sprint [sprint] springe av all makt, spurte.

sprit [sprit] sprette, spire; spire, skudd; spristake.

sprite [sprait] spøkelse, ånd.

sprout [spraut] spire, gro, skyte, vokse; spire; skudd; **sprouts** el. **Brussels sprouts** rosenkål.

spruce [spru·s] gran. — **-beer** sirupsøl med gran-essens.

spruce [spru·s] nett, flott, fin, fjong, pyntet.

sprung [sprʌŋ] imperf. og perf. pts. av **spring**.

spry [sprai] rask, livlig, kvikk.

spud [spʌd] liten spade, ugras-spade; liten klump, stump.

spume [spju·m] skum, skumme. **spumous** ['spju·məs], **spumy** ['spju·mi] skummende.

spun [spʌn] imperf. og perf. pts. av **spin**.

spunk [spʌŋk] mot, manns mot, futt; fenge; — **out** komme for lyset. **-y** fyrig, livlig, kjekk.

spur [spə·] spore, brodd; utstikker, strever, forgreining (av en fjellkjede); spore, anspore, framskynde, ile; **on the** — **of the moment** på stående fot. **-gall** [-gå·l] såre med sporen; sporehogg.

spurious ['spjuəriəs] uekte, falsk.

spurn [spə·n] (gml.), sparke; (nå:) avvise med forakt, forsmå, vrake; hånlig avvisning; **-er** forakter.

spurrier ['spə·riə] sporemaker.

spurt [spə·t] sprøyte; stråle.

spurt [spə·t] gjøre en kraftanstrengelse, spurte; kraftanstrengelse, spurt; **put on a** — ta et skippertak.

sputter ['spʌtə] spytte, sprute, snakke fort og usammenhengende; frese, sprake; spruting, spytt, larm, spetakkel.

spy [spai] speider; speide, utspionere, oppdage. — **-glass** lommekikkert.

sq. fk. f. **square**.

squab [skwåb] lubben, klumpet, tykk og feit; dueunge, stoppet pute, kanapé; dette dumpt ned, plumpe; bardus, bums, pladask; — **pie** postei (av kjøtt, løk og epler).

squabble ['skwåbl] trette, kjekle; kjekl.

squad [skwåd] avdeling (soldater); **awkward** — (uøvet) rekruttavdeling.

squadron ['skwådrən] eskadron, eskadre; formere i eskadroner (el. eskadrer).

squalid ['skwålid] smussig, skitten.

squalidity [skwå'liditi] urenslighet.

squall [skwå·l] skrike, skråle, vræle; skrål, gaul, vindstøt, bye, bøy; **be struck by a** — få en bøy over seg; **look out for** **-s** være på sin post.

squalor ['skwålə] urenslighet, smuss.

squamous ['skwei¹məs] skjellet, skjelldekt.

squander ['skwåndə] ødsle bort. **-er** [-rə] ødeland.

square ['skwæ·ə] firkantet, kvadratisk, rettvinklet, kantet, firhogd, firskåren, undersetsig, sterk, passende, ærlig, grei, real, endefram, kvitt, skuls, oppgjort (om mellomværende); firkant, kvadrat, rute, åpen plass, vinkel, karré, orden, riktig forhold, likhet; gjøre firkantet, kvadrere, danne en rett vinkel med, tilpasse, stemme, gjøre opp, ordne; sette seg i forsvarsstilling; **how** **-s go** hvordan sakene står; **all** — alt i orden! act on the — gå åpent til verks; **be on the** — with være likestilt med, ikke skylde noe; — up to by seg til å slåss med. — **-built** firskåren, firkantet, undersetsig. — **-figured** [-'figəd] firskåren. — **-made** firkantet. — **mile** eng. kvadratmil. — **number** kvadrattall. — **-root** kvadratrot. — **-set** firskåren. — **-toed** breisnutet (om støvler); pedantisk.

squash [skwåʃ] kryste, mase, presse, plaske, skvalpe; plask, plump, noe bløtt el. umodent, melongresskar.

squat [skwåt] huke seg ned, sitte på huk, nedsette seg på jord hvor man ikke har hjemmel; sittende på huk, kort og tykk, undersetsig; sammenkrøpet stilling; **sit at** — sitte på huk.

squatter ['skwåtə] australsk saueavler, nybygger, rydningsmann.

squaw [skwå·] indianerkone.

squawk [skwå·k] gnelle, skrike; gnelt skrik.

squeak [skwi·k] skrike, pipe, hvine, kvine; skrik, hvin, kvin. **-er** skrikhals.

squeal [skwi·l] hvine, kvine, skrike; sladre, fisle; hvin, kvin, skrik.

squeamish ['skwi·miʃ] som sett får kvalme, kresen, fin (på det), vanskelig, ømfintlig. **-ly** med betenkeligheter. **-ness** [-nés] kvalme, vemmelse, kresenhet, ømfintlighet.

squeeze [skwi·z] presse, trykke, klemme, trenge (igjennom), trenge seg; trykk, klem, avtrykk.

squelch [skwelʃ] knuse, tilintetgjøre, tyne, surkle, skvasle, tungt fall.

squib [skwib] kruttkjerring (fyrverkeri); smedeskrift; satirisere, spotte. **-bish** ['skwibiʃ] kåt.

squid [skwid] tiarmet blekksprut, pilk; pilke.

squint [skwint] skjele, blingse; skjelende blikk; skjelende. **-eyed** skjeløyd; mistenksom, misunnelig.

squire ['skwaiə] våpendrager, væpner, følgesvenn, storbonde, godseier; ledsage, følge. **-archy** ['skwaira·ᵊki] godseier-aristokrati, storbønder.

squirm [skwə·m] vri seg, sno seg, krympe seg; klatre, klyve, entre; vridning, tvinning.

squirrel ['skwirəl] ekorn. — cup blåveis.

squirt [skwə·t] sprøyte.

S. R. fk. f. **Southern Railway**.

Sr. fk. f. **senior**.

S. S. fk. f. **screw steamer; steamship**.

SS. fk. f. **Saints**.

S. S. E. fk. f. **South South-east**.

S. S. W. fk. f. **South South-west**.

St. fk. f. **Saint**.

st. fk. f. **street**.

st. fk. f. **stone** (om vekt).

stab [stäb] stikke, gjennombore, såre, dolke; stikk, støt, slag, sår; — at stikke etter. **stabber** ['stäbə] snikmorder; seilmakerpren.

stability [stə'biliti] fasthet, stabilitet.

stabilize ['stäbilaiz] stabilisere.

stable ['stei¹bl] stall; fjøs; sette, stø, trygg, standhaftig.

stable ['stei¹bl] stall; fjøs; sette, stø, trygg, standhaftig. lock the — door when the horse is stolen dekke brønnen når barnet er druknet. **-boy** stallgutt. — **-man** stallkar. **stabling** ['stei¹bliŋ] det å sette på stallen; stallrom. **stables** ['stei¹blz] stall; staller, bygning.

stablish ['stäbliʃ] se **establish**.

staccato [stə'ka·to] stakkato.

stack [stäk] stabel, (korn-, høy-, torv-) stakk,

rekke; geværkoppel; sette i stakk, stable; — **of arms** geværpyramide; **form -s** kople geværer; **break -s** avkople geværer. — **-yard** stakkehage, lodkve, lodgard.

stadium ['ste'diəm] stadion, idrettsplass.

staddle ['städl] sette igjen (ungskogen), sette igjen ungtrærne (i en skog).

staff [sta·f] stukk, gipskalk.

staff [sta·f] pl. **staves** [ste'vz] stav, stang, skaft, stokk, embetsstav, støtte, notesystem; (i følgende bet. pl. **staffs**): stab, generalstab, personale, funksjonærer. — **-map** generalstabskart. — **sergeant** stabssersjant. — **-surgeon** stabslege.

stag [stäg] hjort, kronhjort; irregulær børsspekulant; jobbe; **turn** — vitne mot sine medskyldige.

stag-beetle ['stäg'bi·tl] eikehjort.

stage [ste'dʒ] stillas, plattform, skueplass, scene, teater, landgangsbrygge, stasjon, skyssskifte, postvogn, standpunkt, grad; vise fram på scenen; **go on the** — gå til teatret; **by short -s** med korte dagsreiser. — **-coach** diligence. — **-horse** skysshest. — **-house** skyss-stasjon. — **-manager** regissør. — **-play** skuespill.

stager ['ste'dʒə] praktikus, erfaren person.

stage-whisper ['ste'dʒ'wispə] teaterhvisking.

stagger ['stägə] rave, sjangle, vakle, være i tvil, betenke seg, vingle, miste motet, få til å vakle, gjøre urolig, forbløffe; raving, vakling; **-ingly** [-riŋli] vaklende, vinglende, tvilrådig. **-s** svimmelhet.

stagnancy ['stägnənsi] stillstand. **stagnant** ['stägnənt] stillestående. **stagnate** ['stägne't] stagnere. **stagnation** [stäg'ne'ʃən] stagnasjon, stillstand.

stagy ['ste'dʒi] teatralsk, beregnet på å gjøre inntrykk, tilgjort, uekte.

staid [ste'd] stø, satt, rolig.

stain [ste'n] farge, beise, flekke, vanære; farge, beis, flekk, anstrøk, skam; **-ed glass** glassmaleri; **-ed paper** kulørt papir. **-less** [-lès] plettfri.

stair [stæ·ə] trappetrin; **-s** trapp; **above -s**, **up -s** opp, ovenpå, hos herskapet; **below -s, down -s** ned, i kjelleren, blant tjenerne; **up one flight** (eller **run el. pair**) **of -s** en trapp opp. — **-carpet** trappeløper.

staircase ['stæ·əke's] trapp, trappegang.

staith [ste'þ] anløpsbru, kai.

stake [ste'k] stake, påle, staur, pinne; bål, innsats, fare, kapprenn; støtte med staker; våge, sette på spill; **perish at the** — dø på bålet; **at** — på spill; omhandlet, som det gjelder.

stalactite [stə'läktait] dryppstein.

stalagmite [stə'lägmait] stalagmitt.

stale [ste'l] bedervet, flau, doven, sur, muggen, gammelt (brød), fortersket, forslitt; surt øl; **a** — **demand** et foreldet krav; **a** — **joke** en fortersket vits.

stalemate ['ste'lme't] patt (i sjakk); sette patt.

stalk [stå·k] stilk, strå; **-ed** stilket.

stalk [stå·k] liste seg; spanke; stille seg, lure seg fram; stille, drive snikjakt, snikjakt. **-er** spanker, jeger, som jager fra skjul. **-ing horse** jakthest, dressert til å danne skjul for jeger som «stiller»; skalkeskjul.

stalky ['stå·ki] stilket, stilkaktig.

stall [stå·l] bås, stall, utsalgsbu, korstol, parkettplass, hylster, smokk; sette på stallen (el. båsen), sette inn, ta inn, bo. **-age** [stå·lidʒ] buavgift. — **-feed** stallfore.

stallion ['stäljən] hingst, grahest.

stalwart ['stå·lwət] kraftig, djerv; solid, modig, stø, traust, kraftkar, stø partimann.

stamen ['ste'min] støvdrager.

Stamfordbridge ['stämfədbridʒ] Stamford bru.

stamina ['stämine] motstandskraft, marg, utholdenhet.

stammer ['stämə] stamme, stortre, stamme fram. **-er** [-rə] stammende. **-ing** [-riŋ] stammende.

stamp [stämp] stampe, påtrykke, innprege, stemple, prege; stamping, stempel, preg, avtrykk, frimerke, stemplet papir, karakter, slags. — **-act** stempellov. — **-duty** stempelavgift.

stampede [stäm'pi·d] panikk, vill flukt; skremme, jage på flukt.

stamper ['stämpə] brevstempler; stempel; stampeverk.

stamping-mill ['stämpiŋmil] stampeverk.

stanch [sta·nʃ] stanse, stemme (blodet).

stanch [sta·nʃ] stigbord.

stanch [sta·nʃ] sterk og tett, fast, traust, stø, standhaftig, trofast.

stanchion ['stänʃən] smekker søyle, stiver, støtte; scepter.

stand [ständ] stå, stå stille, ligge (om bygning, by), innstille seg (som kandidat), befinne seg, være, måle, bero, gjelde, utstå, tåle, motstå, bestå, holde fast på, forsvare, traktere med; standplass, holdeplass, post, stansning, forlegenhet, motstand, stativ, oppsats; **be at a** — være i forlegenhet, stå i stampe; **make a** — holde stand; **-point** standpunkt, — **in need of** behøve; **to one's ground** holde stand; — **on end** reise seg (om hårene); — **treat** spandere, traktere, rive i; — **aside** gå av veien; — **by** være til stede; gjøre plass, holde seg til, understøtte; — **for** stå modell for; trakte etter, stille seg som kandidat for; representere, holde på, gjelde for; — **in** være med, ta parti, koste; — **off** tre tilbake, holde seg på avstand, avstå fra, vegre seg, heve seg; — **out** rage fram, holde stand; — **to** vedstå; — **under** utholde; — **up** reise seg, tre fram; — **up for** forsvare; — **upon** insistere på, stå på; legge vekt på; bero på, støtte seg på.

standard ['ständəd] fane, flagg, frittstående tre, mål, myntfot, målestokk, norm, mønster, standard; normal, mønstergyldig; the — **of life** levestandarden; **the Two-Power S.** målestokken for utvidelsen av den engelske flåte, smln. med andre makters flåte. — **-bearer** ['ständəd 'bæ·ərə] fanebærer, bannerfører. **-ize** ['ständədaiz] standardisere.

stand-by ['ständbai] hjelper, hjelp.

standing ['ständiŋ] stående, stillestående, blivende, stadig, stø, varig, fast; stilling, anseelse, rang; varighet; — **army** stående hær; — **jest** stående vittighet; — **committee** stående utvalg; — **conundrum** uløselig gåte; **quarrel of long** — gammel strid. — **-room** ståplass.

stand-offish ['stän'då·fiʃ] tilbakeholdende, reservert, sky.

standpoint ['ständpoint] standpunkt, synspunkt.

standstill ['ständstil] stillstand, stans; **be at a** — stå i stampe; **come to a** — gå i stå.

stand-up ['ständ'ʌp] oppstående (f. eks. snipp); stående; ordentlig, real, djerv.

stanhope ['stänəp] lett, åpen vogn.

stank [stäŋk] gml. imperf. av **stink**.

stannary ['stänəri] tinngruve.

stannic ['stänik] tinn-.

stanza ['stänzə] vers, strofe.

staple ['ste'pl] kjeng, krampe; stapelplass, hovedartikkel, råstoff, tråd, bonitet; stapel-, viktigst, fast; **a** — **commodity** en hovedartikkel.

star [sta·ə] stjerne; stiral; sette merke ved; **-s and garters** ordensstjerner og bånd; **the -s and stripes** stjernebanneret; **my good** — **would have it** (ville) that . . .; **falling** —, **shooting** — stjerneskudd; the **Star Chamber** stjernekammeret, en kriminaldomstol uten jury (opphevd under Karl I); — **it** glimre, spille stjernekomedie.

starboard ['sta·əbəd] styrbord; styrbords; legge styrbord.

starch [sta·ətʃ] stivelse, stivhet; stive; **a -ed fellow** en stivstikke. **-edness** ['sta·ətʃidnès] stivhet. **-er** ['sta·ətʃə] stiver, strykekone. **-y** ['sta·ətʃi] stivelsesaktig. stiv.

stare ['stæ·ə] stirre, glo, glane, skjære i øynene,

stirring; — at stirre på; — hard stirre stivt; — him in the face se stivt på ham; ligge (snublende) nær. -r ['stæ··rə] glaner; i pl. stanglorgnett.
starfish [sta·'lij] sjøstjerne, korstroll.
star-gazer ['sta··'ge'zə] stjernekiker.
staring['stæ··riŋ] stirrende; sterkt iøynefallende; grell; aldeles; stark — mad splittergal.
stark [sta·'k] stiv, ubetinget, ren, skjær, aldeles; — lunacy det rene vanvidd; — blind helt blind; — mad splittergal; are you — staring mad er du spikende gal, jeg tror fanden plager deg; — naked splitternaken.
starless [sta··les] uten stjerner.
starlight ['sta··lait] stjerneskinn; stjerneklar.
starlike ['sta··laik] stjernelignende.
starling ['sta··liŋ] stær (fuglen].
starlit ['sta··lit] stjerneklar, stjernelys.
starred [sta··d] stjernesådd.
starry ['sta·ri] stjerneklar; lysende som en stjerne.
star-spangled ['sta··'spængld] stjernebesatt; the — banner stjernebanneret.
start [sta··t] fare opp, fare sammen, støkke, skvette, stusse, dukke plutselig opp, fare til siden, bli sky, ta av sted, legge i vei, begynne (et løp), starte, gå ut (fra); forskrekke (gml. el. dial.); jage opp, komme fram med; finne på, sette i gang, vekke, forrykke; stussing, sprett, støkk, plutselig bevegelse, sett, rykk, anfall, innfall, begynnelse, start, forsprang; get the — ha forsprang, komme i forkjøpet; — for begi seg på veien til, melde seg som ansøker til. -er starter; støver(hund). -ingly støtvis. -ingpoint utgangspunkt.
startle ['sta·'tl] jage opp, skremme, støkke, overraske, forskrekke.
starvation [sta·'ve'ʃən] sult.
starve [sta··v] sulte (i hjel), lide nød; la sulte, uthungre, svekke. starved forsulten.
starveling ['sta··vliŋ] vantrivsel; forsulten, vantreven.
state [ste't] tilstand, stilling, standpunkt, gods, besittelse, stat, stand, rang, samfunnsklasse, stas, høysete, trone, rangsperson, pl. riksstender; fastsette, framsette; the States De Forente Stater i Nord-Amerika; (gammelt:) Nederlandene; lie in — ligge på parade. — affair statssak. -d ['ste'tid] bestemt, fast. -ly ['ste'tli] statelig, anselig, prektig, stolt, verdig. -ment ['ste'tmənt] beretning, utsagn, framstilling, utgreiing. —room statsstue, salong. -sman ['ste'tsman] statsmann. -smanlike diplomatisk. -manship statsmannskunst.
static ['stätik] statisk.
statics ['statiks] likevektslære.
station ['ste'ʃən] stasjon, stoppested, stilling, standpunkt, post, embete, rang; stille, postere, anbringe. -ary ['ste'ʃən(ə)ri] stillestaende, stasjonær, blivende. -er ['ste'ʃənə] papirhandler; -ers' Hall innregistreringskontor for bøker (til sikring av forfatterretten). -ery ['ste'ʃən(ə)ri] skrivesaker.
station-master ['ste'ʃən'ma·stə] stasjonsmester.
statistic [sta'tistik] statistisk.
statistician [stati'stiʃən] statistiker.
statistics [stə'listiks] (pl.) statistikk.
statuary ['stätjuəri] billedhogger, gipshandler, billedhoggerkunst.
statue ['stätju] statue; stille som en statue; -d forsynt med statuer.
stature ['statʃə] statur, høyde, vekst.
status ['ste'təs] status, posisjon, rang. -report kredittopplysning.
statute ['stätjut] lov, statutt. — -law (skreven) lov (motsatt: common law).
staunch [sta·n], sta·nʃ] se stanch.
stave [ste'v] (tønne)stav, linjesystem (i musikk), strofe; sprosse; slå i stykker, slå hull i, forsyne med staver, sette sprosser i; — oft jage bort, forhale; drive på, klemme i vei.

stay [ste'] stanse, (for)bli, oppholde seg, bo, vente, bie, stole, lite (upon på), hindre, berolige, støtte, vente på, oppebie, bivåne; stagvende; stans, opphold, hindring, forsiktighet, varighet, standhaftighet, støtte; stag, bardun; -s snøreliv, korsett (a pair of -s); — away utebli, bli borte, ikke komme (i selskap, til møte etc.); — for vente på; — out bli ute, ikke komme hjem; bli lenger enn; — till (el. to) dinner el. — and dine bli til middag. -ed satt, rolig.
stay [ste'] brille (i dreiebenk).
stay-at-home; a — man et hjemmemenneske.
stead [sted] sted; stå bi, hjelpe; stand in — være til hjelp; be in no — være til ingen nytte; in — of istedenfor; in his — i hans sted.
steadfast ['stedfəst] fast, trofast, stø, traust; look -ly at se ufravendt på. -ness fasthet.
steady ['stedi] stadig, stø, fast, jevn, jamn, vedholdende; holde stille; forsiktig! holdt! steddi! så!
steak [ste'k] skive kjøtt; beef-steak biff.
steal [sti·l] stjele, liste, stjele seg; — away stjele seg bort; — upon lure seg på; — a march upon one lure seg forbi en; -ing listende, lurende; tyveri.
stealth [stelþ]: by — hemmelig, i stillhet.
stealthy ['stelþi] listende, snikende, hemmelig.
steam [sti·m] damp, eim, dunst; dampe, dunste, dampkoke. — -bath dampbad. -boat dampbåt. — -boiler dampkjel. — -engine dampmaskin. steamer ['sti·mə] dampskip; dampkokeapparat; dampsprøyte.
steam'-kitchen ['sti·m'kitʃən] dampkjøkken. -navigation dampfart. -roller dampveivals.
steamship ['sti·mʃip] dampskip. steam-tug slepebåt, taubåt.
steam-vessel dampskip.
steam-whistle dampfløyte.
steamy ['sti·mi] dampende, dampfylt.
stearin ['stiərin] stearin.
steed [sti·d] ganger, paradehest.
steel [sti·l] stål, kvessestål, våpen, sverd, hardhet; herde til stål, belegge med stål, forherde. — -pen stålpenn. — -wire ståltråd. — -works stålverk.
steely ['sti·li] stållignende, stålhard.
steelyard ['sti·lja·'d] bismer.
steep [sti·p] steil, bratt; skrent, stup.
steep [sti·p] dyppe, legge i bløyt, bløyte ut, la trekke (f. eks.); senke ned; bad, beis.
steepen ['sti·pn] bli bratt(ere).
steeple ['sti·pl] spisstårn, kirketårn. — -chase steeplechase, terrengritt, hinderløp. -d ['sti·pld] med tårn.
steer [stiə] sung okse, gjeldstut.
steer [stiə] styre; lystre roret.
steerage ['stiəridʒ] styring; tredje klasse (på skip), mellomdekksplass.
steering-wheel ['stiəriŋwi·l] ratt.
steeve [sti·v] pakke tett, stue tett.
stellar ['stelə] stjerne-, stjernebesatt.
stem [stem] stamme, stilk, stett (på glass); stamme (i språk), befri for stilker.
stem [stem] forstavn; sette stavnen mot; vinne fram imot.
stem [stem] stoppe til; stemme, demme opp; stanse.
stench [stenʃ] stank.
stencil ['stensil] stensil; trykke med stensil; her finely stencilled eye-brows hennes fint tegnede øyebryn.
stenograph ['stenogra·f] stenografere, stenographer [sti'nägrəfə] stenograf. stenography [sti'nägrəfi] stenografi. stenographic(al) [steno'gräfik(l)] stenografisk.
stentorian [sten'tä·riən] stentor-.
step [step] trine, tre, gå, skride fram, skritte, sette (foten); trin, skritt, steg, fotspor, gang, trappetrin, framgang; a set of -s en trappestige;

— forward tre fram; — into tre inn i, tiltre; — out skritte ut, gå med lange skritt.

step|child ['steptʃaild] stebarn. -brother stebror. -daughter stedatter. -father stefar.

step-ladder ['steplädə] trappestige, gardintrapp.

stepmother ['stepmʌðə] stemor.

steppe [step] steppe.

stepp·ing-stone ['stepiŋsto‍ʷn] stein til å trå på, overgangsstein. (billedlig) trappetrin, middel.

stepsister ['stepsistə] stesøster.

stepson ['stepsʌn] stesønn

stereoscope ['stiəriəsko‍ʷp] stereoskop

stereoscopic ['stiəriə'skåpik] stereoskopisk.

stereotype ['stiəriətaip] stereotypi; stereotypere; stereotvp.

stereotyper ['stiəriətaipə] stereotvpist.

sterie ['sterail] steri , gold.

sterility [sté riliti] sterilitet, goldhet.

sterilize ['steriləiz] sterilisere.

sterling ['stə·liŋ] etter britisk myntfot, fullgod. gedigen ekte; sterling britisk mynt.

stern [stə·n] streng, morsk, barsk, hard.

stern [stə·n] akterspeil. akterstavn.

Sterne [stə·n] Sterne.

stern-fast ['stə·nfa·st] akterfortøyning, aktertrosse.

sternmost ['stə·nmo‍ʷst] akterst.

sternness ['stə·nnés] strenghet, barskhet.

stern-post ['stə·npo st] akterstavn, bakstavn.

stern-sheets ['stə·nʃi·ts] akterende.

sternum ['stə·nəm] brystbein.

sternutation [stə·nju'te‍ʃən] nysing, nys.

sternwards ['stə·nwədz] akter.

stertorous ['stə·tərəs] snorkende.

stet [stet] (i korrektur) ingen retting.

stethoscope ['stebosko‍ʷp] stetoskop, hørerør (til brystundersøkelse).

stevedore [sti·vdå·ə] stuer.

Stevenson ['stivnsn] Stevenson.

stew [stju·] østersplantasje, fiskedam.

stew [stju·] stue, koke. småkoke (langsomt og med lite væske.; kokt kjøtt, frikassé; sinnsbevegelse, angst; -ed prunes sviskekompott; Irish — slags rett av sauekjøtt, løk og poteten

steward ['stjuəd] forvalter, hushovmester, intendant, økonom, hovmester; stuert, restauratør; Lord High Steward hoffmarskalk; steward's mate oppvarter; purser's steward proviantskriver. stewardess [-dès] restauratrise, trise, oppvartningspike. stewardship forvaltning, forvalterstilling.

stew-pan ['stju·pän] kasserolle.

St. Ex. fk. f. Stock Exchange.

stibium ['stibiəm] antimon.

stick [stik] vers, linje.

stick [stik] stokk, pinne, stang, stake, rør, mast; kloss, daustokk; stikk; pl. bohave, pistoler, et spill; stikke, feste, flå opp; stenge (erter osv.); besette, sitte fast, klebe, klistre, forbli, stanse, være forlegen; he stuck ban ble fast ved nesen; I'm stuck jeg er ferdig; — at bli stående ved, ha betenkeligheter ved; — by bli ved, holde fast ved; — out være framstående, unndra seg; — to holde fast ved, være trofast mot: — up for forsvare, gå i bresjen for; — up to opptre imot; møte (som en mann); — upon henge ved. -er plakatklistrer, stuemenneske. -iness klebrighet. -ing klistring, håndarbeid, avfall, kjøttstumper. -ingplaster heftplaster.

stickle ['stikl] kjempe, kives, vakle; torn. -r ivrig forsvarer, ivrer, pedant.

stickle-back ['stiklbäk] stikling (fisk).

sticky ['stiki] klebrig, stiv, høytidelig.

stiff [stif] stiv, lemster, hardnakket, stri, tvungen. -en ['stifn] gjøre stiv, stive; stivne, bli stiv. -ish temmelig stiv. -necked ['stifnekt] hardnakket, stivlyndt.

stifle ['staifl] kvele, kue undertrykke; kovne.

stigma ['stigmə] brennemerke.

stigmatize ['stigmətaiz] brennemerke.

stile [stail] klyveled, stett.

stiletto [sti'leto‍ʷ] stilett, liten dolk; stikke.

still [stil] ennå, enda; dog; (gml. alltid).

still [stil] stille, rolig, taus; få stille, stagge, berolige, roe; — waters run deep stille vann har dypest grunn.

still [stil] destillere; destillérkar, brenneri.

still-born ['stilbå·ə‍n] dødfødt.

still-life ['stillaif] stilleben.

stillness ['stilnés] stilhet.

still-room ['stilrum] destillasjonsrom; finere spiskammer i større hus; — maid husjomfru.

stilt [stilt] stylte; heve, oppstylte. stilted ['stiltid] oppstyltet.

Stilton ['stiltən] Stilton-ost.

stilty ['stilti] stiv, oppstyltet.

stimulant ['stimjulənt] stimulerende, pirrende; kveik, oppstiver, stimulans stimulate ['stimjule‍ʷt] stimulere, pirre, kveike opp. stimulation [stimju'le‍ʃən] tilskynding. stimulative ['stimjulətiv] se stimulant; stimulator ['stimjule‍ʷtə] ansporer. stimulus ['stimjuləs] spore, drivfjær, stimulans.

sting [stiŋ] stikke, såre, pine, erte, brenne, svi; brodd, nag. -er ['stiŋə] brodd, bitende replikk, sviende slag. -less broddløs.

stingy ['stiŋi] stikkende, skarp.

stingy [stin(d)ʒi] gjerrig knuslet, knipen.

stink [stiŋk] stinke; stank.

stinkard ['stiŋkəd] teledu, stinkdyr.

stint [stint] begrense, innskrenke, knipe på, spare på, avknappe; grense, andel, bestemt mål; with no -ed hand med rund hånd. -er innskrenker, påholdent menneske. -less uten innskrenkning, ustanselig.

stipe [staip] stengel, stilk.

stipend ['staipend] lønn.

stipendiary [stai'pendiəri] lønnet.

stipple ['stipl] prikke, punktere.

stipulate ['stipjule‍ʷt] fastsette, komme overens om, betinge, avtale; — for betinge seg. stipulation [stipju'le‍ʃən] avtale kontrakt, overenskomst, forpliktelse, betingelse. stipulator ['stipjule‍ʷtə] stipulerende, kontrahent.

stir [stə·] røre, lese på, rikke, røre opp i, rote i, kare, bringe på bane; opphisse, egge; røre seg, være i bevegelse, stå opp; røre, liv, bevegelse, støy, spetakkel, opprør; — up opphisse, oppvekke. -less ubevegelig, sagte. -rer ['stə·rə] tilskynder, agitator; tvare; an early -rer morgenfugl. -rer-up agitator, oppvigler. -ring ['stə·riŋ] bevegende, driftig, interessant, spennende.

stirrup ['stirəp] stigbøyle; pert. — -cup glass på fallrepet, avskjedsbeger. — -leather stigreim.

stitch [stitʃ] sy, sy sammen, hefte sammen; sting, maske (ved strikning); klut; sting, hold; — a book hefte en bok; — up sy sammen; drop a — slippe ned en maske; take up a — ta opp en maske; a — (sting) in time saves nine.

stithy ['stiði] ambolt, ste, smie.

stoat [sto‍ʷt] hermelin, røyskatt.

stock [ståk] levkøy.

stock [ståk] stokk, stamme, stubbe, kubbe, blokk; klodrian, ætt, skaft, skjefte, ankerstokk, nav, pl. stapel, bedding; halsbind; aksjer, statsobligasjoner, fonds, materiale, driftskapital, varelager, forråd, beholdning, kreaturbesetning, gelé, kjøttkraft, strømper, pl. stokk (hvori lovovertredere ble lagt med benene), gapestokk; som er i stadig bruk, ferdig til enhver tid, fast, stående; skjefte, stokke, forsyne seg med, føre, ha på lager, samle, oppbevare; — of knowledge kunnskapsforråd; in — på lager; — in bank bankkapital; — in trade handelskapital; be in — ha penger, ha på lager; keep in — føre (på lager); take — foreta en vareopptelling; take — of one gi nøye akt på en; — piece kassestykke; dead — inventar, innbo; — a farm forsyne en gård med kveg; — a pound forsyne en dam med fisk; — up utrydde; — down tilså med grasfrø.

stockade [stå'ke'd] palisade, peleverk; befeste med palisader.
stock-breeder ['ståkbri·də] kvegoppdretter.
stockbroker ['ståkbroᵘkə] mekler på fondsbørsen, aksjemekler.
stock-company aksjeselskap.
stockdove ['ståkdʌv] skogdue.
stock-exchange fondsbørs.
stockfish ['ståkfiʃ] tørrfisk.
stockholder ['ståkhoᵘldə] aksjonær.
Stockholm ['ståkhoᵘm] Stockholm.
stockinet ['ståkinet] jersey (slags stoff til undertøy).
stocking ['ståkiŋ] strømpe, hose; sokk (på en hest); **a pair of -s** et par strømper; **in one's -s** el. **in one's stocking-feet** på strømpelesten, uten sko på.
stock-in-trade ['ståkin'tre'd] varelager.
stock|-jobber aksjespekulant, børsjobber. **-jobbing** børsspekulasjon, børsjobbing.
stockman ['ståkmən] kvegoppdretter, fjøskar.
stock-market fondsmarked, kvegmarked.
stock-still bomstille.
stock-taking vareopptelling, taksering.
stock-whip kortskaftet kvegpisk.
stocky ['ståki] undersetsig, kortstammet
stodgy ['stådʒi] tung, ufordøyelig; fullstappet.
stodge [stådʒ] mat; spise grådig.
Stoic ['stoᵘik] stoisk filosof; stoisk; **-al** stoisk; **-ism** ['stoᵘisizm] stoisisme.
stoke [stoᵘk] fyre. — **-hold,** — **-hole** fyrrom.
stoker ['stoᵘkə] fyrbøter.
stole [stoᵘl] stola, romersk kvinnekjortel, hvitt skulderbånd (hos katolske prester); **groom of the** — første kammerherre (hos kongen av England).
stole [stoᵘl] imperf. av **steal.**
stolen ['stoᵘlən] perf. pts. av **steal.**
stolid ['stålid] tung, sløv. **-ity** [sto'liditi] sløvhet.
stomach ['stʌmək] mave, appetitt, lyst, vrede, stolthet; føle uvilje mot; **on an empty** — på fastende hjerte — **-ache** mavepine. **-al** mavestyrkende (middel).
stomacher ['stʌmətʃə] brystsmekke, forklesmekke, stor brosje.
stomach|ic [sto'mäkik] mavestyrkende. — **-pump** mavepumpe. — **-warmer** varmebekken.
stone [stoᵘn] stein, edelstein, en vekt (is. = 14 pd.); stein-, av stein; steine, ta steinene ut av, rense for stein, skure (med en skurestein), forherde, forsteine; **leave no — unturned** gjøre alt hva det er mulig å gjøre; **leave no — standing** ikke la stein bli tilbake på stein; **throw -s** kaste med stein; **like one stricken into** — som forsteinet. — **-blind** stokk blind. — **-bottle** steindunk. **-break** bergsildre, saxifraga. — **-breaker** steinpukker, steintyggmaskin. **-chat, -chatter** (brunstripet) skvett (fugl). — **-cutting** steinhoggerarbeid. — **-dead** steindød. — **-deaf** stokkdøv. — **-fruit** steinfrukt; **-d fruit** frukt som steinene er tatt ut av.
Stonehenge ['stoᵘn'hendʒ] Stonehenge.
stone|less ['stoᵘnlės] steinfri. — **-pit** steinbrott. — **-quarry** steinbrott. **stone's cast** el. **stone's throw** steinkast (avstand). — **-still** bomstille. **-ware** steintøy. **-work** murverk (av naturlig stein).
stony ['stoᵘni] steinaktig, steinet, av stein, hard.
stood [stud] imperf. og perf. pts. av **stand.**
stool [stu·l] taburett, krakk, feltstol, kontorstol, skammel, nattstol, avføring; kontorplass; rotskudd, grunnstamme; skyte avleggere; — **of humiliation** (el. **of repentance**) botsskammel. — **-pigeon** lokkefugl.
stoop [stu·p] bøye seg, lute, slå ned, fly ned, gi etter, underkaste seg, nedlate seg, senke, bringe til å underkaste seg; bøyning, foroverbøyd stilling, lutende holdning, nedverdigelse, nedlatelse, nedfart, nedslag; veranda; **-ing** foroverbøyd, lutende, rundrygget; **She Stoops to Conquer** et lystspill av O. Goldsmith.
stop [ståp] stoppe, stoppe til, stanse, plombere, fylle, få til å tie, hindre, undertrykke, gripe på (en streng); oppholde seg; bli; stans, opphør, avbrytelse, avsats, grep (i strengene), klaff, register, skilletegn. — **for** oppebie, bli til; **make a** — holde stille; **make a full** — sette punktum; **come to a** — stanse; — **-cock** stoppekran. — **-gap** ['ståpgäp] fyllekalk, nødmiddel. **-less** uten stans.
stoppage ['ståpidʒ] stans, stopping, avholdelse, tilstopping, pause, avkorting; — **of payment** innstilling av betaling; — **of work** arbeidsstans; **put under** — knappe av beløpet i ens lønn.
stopper ['ståpə] stopper, kork, propp; stoppe, korke til, sette propp i.
stopple ['ståpl] propp, kork; proppe til, korke til.
storage ['stå·ridʒ] opplagring; lagerrom; pakkhusleie.
store ['stå·ᵊ] forråd, mengde, magasin, opplag, lager, depot; lagerbygning, pakkhus; (amr.) butikk; oppdynget; oppbevare, lagre, proviantere, forsyne, fylle; **set — by** skatte høyt; **in** — på lager; **be in — for** forestå, vente; **what the future has in — for us** hva framtiden vil bringe oss. **-house** magasin, pakkhus. **-keeper** pakkhusforvalter, lagerformann. — **-room** lagerrom, forrådskammer. — **-ship** proviantskip. **-r** ['stå·rə] innsamler, magasinforvalter.
storey ['stå·ri] etasje; **1st** — annen etasje; **2nd** — tredje etasje; **3rd** — fjerde etasje; **one-storeyed** enetasjes.
storied ['stå·rid] historisk kjent, prydd med historiske bilder.
stork [stå·ᵊk] stork. **-'s-bill** storkenebb; pelargonium (plante).
storm [stå·ᵊm] storm, uvær, tordenvær, stormangrep, opprør, larm; storme, angripe med storm, rase, larme, **-iness** stormfullhet, voldsomhet. **-y** stormfull, voldsom, heftig.
story ['stå·ri] se **storey; one-storied** enetasjes.
story ['stå·ri] historie, fortelling, anekdote, intrige, eventyr, fabel, skrøne; fortelle; **stories from** (fortelling fra) **the history of England.** — **-book** historiebok, samling av fortellinger, eventyrbok — **-teller** historieforteller, løgnhals.
stout [staut] kraftig, sterk, traust, tapper, standhaftig, stolt, hårdnakket; tykk, før; porter (sterkt øl). **-ness** styrke, fyldighet, tapperhet, stolthet, trossighet.
stove [stoᵘv] kakkelovn, tørkehus, drivhus; hete opp, svette, sette i drivhus.
stow [stoᵘ] anbringe, stue sammen, pakke, gjemme. **-age** ['stoᵘidʒ] anbringelse, stuing, pakking, lagerrom, stuerpenger, stuegods.
str. fk. f. **stroke oar.**
straddle ['strädl] sprike med bena, skreve, sitte overskrevs, stå med ett bein i begge leirer.
straggle ['strägl] streife om, vandre (atspredt), skille lag, vandre sin egen vei; spre seg, vokse vilt, ligge hist og her; stå alene. **straggler** ['sträglə] ledig person, etternøler, etterligger, landstryker, vagabond, marodør, vilt skudd, forvillet eksemplar. **straggling** uregelmessig, spredt, som opptrer alene, ute uten permisjon.
straight [stre't] rett, strak, like, grei, riktig, rettskaffen, klar, ren; **-forward** [stre't'få·ᵊwəd] redelig, ærlig, endefram. **-forwardness** redelighet. **-en** ['stre'tn] rette, strekke, stramme. **-ly** like, rett, bent, straks. **-ness** retthet.
straightway ['stre'twe'] straks.
strain [stre'n] spenne, stramme, tøye, trykke, anstrenge, røyne på, leite på, forstue, forstrekke, overspenne, utsette for påkjenning, presse, trykke, overdrive, anstrenge seg meget, filtreres; spenning, anspennelse, påkjenning; tone, melodi, slått, deformasjon, forstrekning, stemning.
strain [stre'n] herkomst, rase, slag, art, sort; drag, snev, hang, karaktertrekk, anlegg.
strainer ['stre'nə] filtrerapparat, dørslag.

strait [stre¹t] stram, snever, fortrolig, streng, vanskelig, knapp, sund, strede (ofte pl. **straits**), knipe, forlegenhet; **the Straits Settlements** koloniene ved Malakkastredet; — **waistcoat** tvangstrøye.

straiten ['stre¹tn] snevre inn, gjøre trangere, gjøre opprådd, sette i forlegenhet; **-ed circumstances** trange kår.

strait-laced ['stre¹tle¹st] sneversynt, bornert.

strake [stre¹k] plankegang, hjulbeslag, hjulskoning.

stramonium [strə'mo"njəm] piggeple; stramoniumblad (middel mot astma).

strand [stränd] strand; sette på land; strande; **the Strand** (gate i London).

strand [stränd] streng (i snor); kordel (i tau); tråd; fiber; lokk; **-ed wire** ståltrådtau.

strange [stre¹n(d)ʒ] underlig, merkelig, rar, besynderlig; fremmed: — **to say** rart nok. — **-looking** besynderlig (av utseende). **-ness** besynderlighet.

stranger ['stre¹n(d)ʒə] fremmed; ukjent person; **be a** — **to** være fremmed for, ikke kjenne noe til; **the little** — den lille nyfødte.

strangle ['sträŋgl] kvele, strype, kverke.

strangulate ['sträŋgjule¹t] kverke, kvele, stoppe.

strangulation [sträŋgju'le¹ʃən] kvelning, innsnøring.

strap [sträp] stropp, rem, reim, strykereim; slå med reim; spenne fast; stryke; arbeide strengt.

stratagem ['strätədʒim] krigslist; puss, knep.

strategic [strə'tedʒik] strategisk.

strategy ['strätidʒi] krigskunst.

strath [sträþ] (skotsk) bred elvedal, dalføre.

strathspey [sträþ'spe¹], en skotsk dans.

stratification [strätifi'ke¹ʃən] lagdanning.

stratify ['strätifai] danne i lag.

stratum ['stre¹təm] lag (pl. **strata**).

straw [strå¹] strå, halm, halmstrå, stråhatt, ubetydelighet; **he doesn't care a** — (el. **two -s**) han bryr seg ikke det grann om det; **it was the last** — det fikk begeret til å flyte over; **catch** (el. **snatch**) **at a** — (el. **at -s**) gripe etter et halmstrå.

strawⅰberry ['strå·bəri] jordbær. — **-colour** halmfarge. — **-cutter** hakkelsmaskin, skjærekiste.

stray [stre¹] streife (om), fare vill, forville seg, gå seg bort, omflakking; forvillet dyr, rømling; villfarelse; — **sheep** et fortapt får; bortkommet barn. **-er** villfarende.

streak [stri·k] strek, stripe, gåre, trekk; grille, plankegang; snev; streke, stripe. **-ed** [stri·kt] stripet. **-y** ['stri·ki] stripet.

stream [stri·m] strøm, elv, strømme, la strømme; øse; flagre; **-er** flagg, vimpel, (i pl.) nordlys. **-let** bekk. **-y** elverik, strømmende.

street [stri·t] gate (også. om dem som bor i gata); **the** — (især amr.) børsen (om forretninger gjort etter lukketid); **in the** — på gata; **into the** — ut på gata; **on the** — (amr.) på gata; **be on the streets** drive gatetrafikk, være hore; **the man in the** — den alminnelige mann; — **arab** hjemløst barn, gategutt. — **-band** trupp av gatemusikanter. — **-car** (amr.) sporvogn. — **-door** gatedør. — **-lamp** gatelykt. — **-organ** lirekasse. — **-pitcher** gatehandler, gatekunstner. — **-sweeper** gatefeier, sopemaskin. — **-tunes** gateviser. — **-walker** gateløs.

strength [streŋþ] styrke, krefter, krigsmakt, **on the** — i rullene; **on the** — **of** i kraft av, i tillit til; — **of mind** åndskraft.

strengthen ['streŋþən] styrke, befeste, bli sterk. **-er** styrkemiddel.

strenuous ['strenjuəs] ivrig, iherdig, kraftig.

stress [stres] trykk, ettertrykk, viktighet; legge ettertrykk på, betone; **lay** — **upon** legge vekt på, betone; **the** — **is on** trykket ligger på.

stretch [stretʃ] strekke, tøye, spenne, stramme, anstrenge, overspenne, strekke seg, overdrive,

strekning, utstrekning, strekk, anstrengelse, overdrivelse; **at a** —, **on a** — i ett kjør, i spenning, i uavbrutt anstrengelse; — **out** hale ut på årene. **-er** strekker, ambulansebåre.

strew [stru·] strø, bestrø, strø ut.

stricken ['strikn] slått, rammet, hjemsøkt; — **in years** høyt opp i årene; — **hour** full klokketime.

strict [strikt] stram, nøye, streng, uttrykkelig. **-ly speaking** strengt tatt.

stricture ['striktʃə] kritisk bemerkning; (sykelig) forsnevring.

stride [straid] langt skritt, gå med lange skritt, skritte ut, skreve over.

strident ['straidnt] hvinende, skingrende, gnell.

strife [straif] strid.

strike [straik] stryke (et flagg, et seil osv.), ta ned, slå, treffe, prege, gjøre sterkt inntrykk på, støte mot, støte på grunn, straffe, slå løs, legge ned arbeidet, streike; arbeidsstans; streik; — **blind** slå en blind, blinde en; — **-breaker** streikebryter; — **dead** drepe på stedet; — **dumb** gjøre målløs, få en til å miste mål og mæle; — **a bargain** slutte en handel; — **fire** slå varme; — **a jury** velge ut en jury; — **an account** gjøre opp en regning; — **hands with** gi håndslag; — **terror into** innjage skrekk; **the clock -s** klokka slår; — **work** legge ned arbeidet; — **at** slå etter, angripe; — **down** felle, legge i bakken; — **for** begi seg uoppholdelig på veien til, ile til; — **home** ramme ettertrykkelig; — **in** falle inn; — **in with** forene seg med; — **off** slette ut, hogge av; — **out** slette ut, finne på; — **up** slå i været, spille opp.

striking ['straikiŋ] påfallende; **present a** — **contrast** framby en slående motsetning.

string [striŋ] streng, snor, hyssing, lisse, reim; knippe; rekke; spenne forsyne med strenger, stemme, stille, tre på en snor; — **of pearls** perlesnor; **have two -s to one's bow** ha mer enn én utvei; **have him on a** — ha ham i sin lomme; **put him on a** — narre ham, holde ham for narr. — **-band** strykeorkester. — **together** knytte sammen. **-ed** strenge-, stryke-.

stringency ['strindʒənsi] strenghet.

stringent ['strindʒənt] bindende, streng.

stringy ['striŋi] trevlet; senet; seig.

strip [strip] trekke av, flå, skrelle, kle av, blotte, røve, plyndre, kle av seg; strimmel; **tear to -s** rive i stykker, i sund.

stripe [straip] stripe; distinksjonstresse, distinksjoner, stilling; slag; gjøre stripet; **-d** stripet.

stripling ['stripliŋ] ungt menneske, grønnskolling.

stripy ['straipi] stripet, randet.

strive [straiv] streve, anstrenge seg, gjøre seg fore, stri kappes; — **at effect** jage etter effekt.

striving ['straiviŋ] strevende; strid. **strivingly** [-li] med anstrengelse, for alvor.

strobile ['stråbil] kongle.

strode [stro"d] imperf. (og gammel perf. pts.) av **stride**.

stroke [stro"k] slag, tak, støt, strøk, penselstrøk, trekk, utslag, virkning; stroke, taktåre; klappe, stryke, glatte, formilde, smigre; **give the finishing** — to legge siste hånd på; — **of grace** nådestøt. — **-oar** taktåre, den akterste åre i kapproningsbåt, den som ror den akterste åre. **stroker** ['stro"kə] en som stryker, smigrer.

strokesman ['stro"ksmən] akterste roer.

stroll [stro"l] streife om, slentre, reke, vandre, spasere; omflakking, tur. **-er** landstryker, omreisende skuespiller **(strolling actor or player)**. **-ing company** omreisende skuespillerselskap.

strong [strån] sterk, kraftig, handlekraftig, mektig, ivrig, befestet; — **language** grovheter; **run** — gå stri. — **-backed** med sterk rygg. — **-bodied** ['strån'bådid] kraftig. — **-box** pengekiste, pengeskrin. — **-fisted** håndfast. — **-handed** mannsterk. **-hold** festning. **-set** undersetsig. — **-waters** brennevin.

strop [stråp] strykereim; stropp; stryke (en kniv).

strophe ['stroufi] strofe.

strophic ['stråfik] strofisk.

strove [strouv] imperf. av **strive.**

stroud [straud] grovt teppe, filleteppe. **strouding** [-ŋ] en slags grovt tøy.

strow [strou] strø.

struck [strʌk] imperf. og perf. pts. av **strike.**

structure ['strʌktʃə] bygningsmåte, bygning.

struggle ['strʌgl] kjempe, slite, streve, baske, kave (med noe); anstrengelse, kamp, strev, basketak; **the — for life** kampen for tilværelsen. **-r** en som kjemper osv., strever. **struggling** kamp.

strum [strʌm] klimpre; klimpring.

strumpet ['strʌmpit] skjøke, hore.

strung [strʌŋ] imperf. og perf. pts. av **string.**

strut [strʌt] strutte, spankulere; stive av; spanking, kneising; strever, stiver; **-ter** viktig person. **-tingly** kneisende, med viktig mine. **S. T. S.** fk. f. **Scottish Text Society.**

Sts. fk. f. **Saints.**

Stuart ['stjuat] Stuart.

stub [stʌb] stubb, stump; talong (i sjekkbok); grave opp, ta opp (stubber); avstubbe; **-bed** avstumpet, undersetsig; full av stubber. **-bedness** undersetsighet.

stubbiness ['stʌbinės] stubblende; undersetsighet.

stubble ['stʌbl] stubb, kornstubb, ljåstubb. **-field** stubbmark.

stubborn ['stʌbən] stiv, stri, hard, hårdnakket. **-ness** hårdnakkethet.

stubby ['stʌbi] full av stubber; avstumpet, kort og stiv.

stub-nail ['stʌbneɪl] gammel hesteskosøm, avstumpet spiker.

stucco ['stʌkou] stukk, stukkatur; gipse, dekorere med stukkatur.

stuck [stʌk] imperf. og perf. pts. av **stick.**

stud [stʌd] stolpe; breihodet søm; dobbeltknapp (krageknapp eller mansjettknapp); pinneskrue; beslå med små spiker, overså, fylle.

stud [stʌd] sto, stutteri, hester; stall.

stud-book stutteribok, ætte-tavle (for rasehester).

student ['stjuːd(ə)nt] studerende; boklærd mann, forsker, gransker. **-ship** stipendium.

studied ['stʌdid] studert, lærd; overlagt.

studio ['stjuːdiouʰ] atelier.

studious ['stjuːdiəs] studerende, flittig, oppmerksom, omhyggelig. **-ly** omhyggelig, med flid. **-ness** lyst til å studere, flid.

study ['stʌdi] studering, studium, fag, fundering, grubling, dype tanker, anstrengelse, studerkammer, arbeidsværelse, kontor, etyde; studere, gruble, bestrebe seg, innstudere, være oppmerksom på; ta hensyn til; **in a brown** — i dype tanker; borte i en annen verden; **with studied** (tilstrebt eller affektert) **indifference; studied** (tilsiktet) insult.

stuff [stʌf] stoff, emne; medisin, bohave, skrammel, tøy; sludder; stoppe, fylle, stoppe ut, forstoppe, proppe seg; skrøne full, proppe full.

stuffing ['stʌfiŋ] polstring(smateriale), stopp, fyll; farse; fyllekalk.

stuffy ['stʌfi] innelukket, trykkende, kvelende.

stultify ['stʌltifai] gjøre narr av, erklære for sinnssyk; — **oneself** vrøvle; erklære seg for utilregnelig.

stum [stʌm] most; gjære på ny.

stumble ['stʌmbl] snuble, snåve, begå en feil, treffe tilfeldigvis, støte, forvirre, hindre; snubling, feiltrin, feil.

stumbling-block ['stʌmbliŋblåk] anstøtsstein, vanskelighet.

stumbling-stone ['stʌmbliŋstouʰn] anstøtsstein, vanskelighet.

stump [stʌmp] stump, stubb, stubbe, stokk, bein; hogge av, humpe; **stir your -s!** ta med deg

---

beina! — up rykke ut med pengene, punge ut. **-ed** ute av spillet, ruinert. **— -oratory** valgtale.

stumpy ['stʌmpi] stumpet, stubbet.

stun [stʌn] bedøve, svimeslå, fortumle, forbause; bedøvelse, fortumlethet.

stung [stʌŋ] imperf. og perf. pts. av **sting.**

stunk [stʌŋk] imperf. og perf. pts. av **stink.**

stunner ['stʌnə] prakteksemplar, noe makeløst; svimeslag.

stunning ['stʌniŋ] overveldende, makeløs.

stunt [stʌnt] forkrøple, forkue, stanse, hemme; vantrives; vantrivsel, krake; **-ed** vantreven.

stunt [stʌnt] kunststykke, særlig anstrengelse, kraftutfoldelse; i plur. kunster, streker.

stupe [stjuːp] varmtvannsomslag.

stupefaction [stjuːpiˈfäkʃən] bedøvelse, bestyrtelse, ørske. **stupefy** ['stjuːpifai] bedøve, forbløffe.

stupendous [stjuːˈpendəs] veldig.

stupid ['stjuːpid] sløv, dum, dorsk, kjedelig.

stupidity [stjuːˈpiditi] sløvhet, dumhet.

stupor ['stjuːpə] bedøvelsestilstand, sløvhet.

sturdiness ['stəˑdinės] hårdnakkethet, dristighet, grovhet, fasthet, kraft. **sturdy** ['stəˑdi] hårdnakket, traust, staut, kraftig, sterk, robust, solid.

sturgeon ['stəˑdʒən] stør.

stutter ['stʌtə] hakke, stamme; stotre; stamming. **-er** en som stammer. **-ingly** stammende.

sty [stai] grisegarde, grisehus; sette i grisegarden.

Stygian ['stidʒiən] stygisk.

style [stail] stift, griffel, viser (på et solur), stil, skrivemåte, språk, framstillingsmåte, manér, måte, tittel, tidsregning; titulere, bevenne; — **of court** rettspraksis; **in the —** stilfullt; **live in** — føre et stort hus; **be -d** bære firmanavnet.

stylet ['stailit] stilett, liten dolk.

stylish ['stailiʃ] moderne, flott.

stylist ['stailist] stilist.

stylite ['stailait] stylitt, søylehelgen.

stylograph ['stailəgräf] stylograf (slags fyllepenn).

styptic ['stiptik] blodstillende middel.

suable ['s(j)uˑəbl] som kan saksøkes.

suave [sweɪv] søt, yndig, blid, forekommende.

suavity ['swäviti] blidhet, forekommenhet.

sub. fk. f. **subaltern; submarine boat; substitute.**

sub [sʌb] (srl. i smstn.) under-, nedenfor.

subacid [sʌbˈäsid] syrlig.

subaerial [sʌbəˈiəriəl] i lufta, over jorda.

subagent ['sʌbˈedʒənt] underagent.

subalpine [sʌbˈälpain] subalpin.

subaltern ['sʌbltən] lavere; underordnet; offiser under kaptein.

subaquatic [sʌbəˈkwätik], **subaqueous** [sʌbˈeɪkwiəs] undersjøisk, undervanns-.

subaudition [sʌbåˈdiʃən] underforståelse.

subconscious [sʌbˈkånʃəs] underbevisst. **-ness** underbevissthet.

subcontract [sʌbkənˈträkt] overta en del av kontrakten.

subcontrary [sʌbˈkåntrəri] i ringere grad motsatt.

subcutaneous [sʌbkjuˈteɪnjəs] nærmest under huden.

subcuticular [sʌbkjuˈtikjulə] under overhuden.

subdeacon [sʌbˈdiˑkn] underdiakon, hjelpeprest.

subdecuple [sʌbˈdekjupl] som utgjør en tiendedel.

subdivide [sʌbdiˈvaid] dele igjen.

subdivision [sʌbdiˈviʒən] underavdeling.

subduce [səbˈdjuˑs], **subduct** [sʌbˈdʌkt] ta bort, subtrahere.

subdue [səbˈdjuˑ] betvinge, undertrykke, dempe. **subdued** [səbˈdjuˑd] kuet, dempet, stillferdig.

sub-editor ['sʌbˈeditə] redaksjonssekretær.

subfusc ['sʌbfʌsk] mørkfallen, mørklaten.

subj. fk. f. **subject, subjunctive.**

subjacent [sʌbˈdʒeɪsənt] underliggende.

subject ['sʌbdʒikt] underlagt, undergiven, underdanig, utsatt, ansvarlig, tilbøyelig, til grunn liggende; undersått, gjenstand, emne, sak, vesen, person, kadaver, subjekt; **on the — i denne an**ledning. **— to** under forutsetning av.

subject [səb'dʒekt] underkaste, undertvinge, utsette, gjøre ansvarlig.

subjection [səb'dʒekʃən] underkastelse.

subjective [səb'dʒektiv] subjektiv.

subjectivity [sʌbdʒik'tiviti] subjektivitet.

subjoin [səb'dʒoin] tilføye, vedlegge; **-ed** vedlagt.

subjugate ['sʌbdʒugeit] undertvinge, trelke.

subjugation [sʌbdʒu'geiʃən] undertvinging.

subjunction [səb'dʒʌŋkʃən] tilføyelse, tillegg.

subjunctive [səb'dʒʌŋktiv] konjunktiv.

sublease ['sʌb'li·s] framleie.

sublet ['sʌb'let] framleie, utleie på annen hånd; framleie; **-ting** framleie.

sublibrarian ['sʌblai'bræ·ʰriən] underbibliotekar.

sublieutenant [sʌblef'tenənt] sekondløytnant.

sublimate ['sʌblimit] sublimat; sublimert.

sublimation [sʌbli'meiʃən] sublimering; rensing.

sublime [sə'blaim] opphøyd, begeistret, stolt; det opphøyde, det store; opphøye, foredle, sublimere.

sublimity [sə'blimiti] høyhet, det opphøyde! **His Sublimity** hans høyhet (sultanen).

subliminal [sʌb'liminəl] underbevisst, ubevisst.

sublingual [sʌb'liŋgwəl] som er under tunga.

sublittoral [sʌb'litərəl] under kysten.

sublunary ['sʌbl(j)u·nəri] (som er) under månen, jordisk.

submarine [sʌbmə'ri·n] undersjøisk, undervanns-; undervannsdyr (eller -plante); undervannsbåt, ubåt.

submerge [səb'mə·dʒ] dukke ned, senke under vannet. **submergence** [səb'mə·dʒəns] nedsenking, oversvømmelse, flom. **submersible** [sʌb-'mə·sibl] som kan senkes under vann, senkbar undervannsbåt.

submersion [sʌb'mə·ʃən] det å sette under vann, oversvømmelse.

submission [səb'miʃən] underkastelse, underdanighet, lydighet. **submissive** [səb'misiv] underdanig, ydmyk, lydig, føyelig.

submit [səb'mit] senke, forkaste (en setning), underkaste, forelegge, henstille; finne seg **(to i),** underkaste seg, bøye seg **(to** for).

subocular [sʌb'åkjulə] under øyet.

suboffice ['sʌbåfis] filial.

subordinate [sə'bå·ʰdinét] underordnet; undergiven. **subordinate** [sə'bå·ʰdineʰt] underordne. **subordination** [səbå·ʰdi'neiʃən] underordning, subordinasjon, underordnet forhold.

suborn [sə'bå·ʰn] bestikke; forlokke (især til falsk vitneutsagn). **-ation** [sʌbå·ʰ'neiʃən] forlokkelse, bestikkelse.

subpoena [sʌb'pi·nə] stevning; innstevne.

subquadrate [sʌb'kwådrét] nesten kvadratisk.

subreption [səb'repʃən] innsetting i en annens sted.

subscribe [səb'skraib] skrive under, innvilge, subskribere, abonnere, tinge, tegne seg for, skrive seg for, tegne; **— to** (el. **for) a** book subskribere på en bok.

subscriber [səb'skraibə] underskriver, bidragsyter, subskribent, abonnent, medlem.

subscription [səb'skripʃən] underskrift, subskripsjon, abonnement, bidrag; **open a —** sette i gang en innsamling.

subsection ['sʌb'sekʃən] underavdeling.

subsequence ['sʌbsikwəns] følge.

subsequent ['sʌbsikwənt] følgende, senere; **sentence** etterstnng. **-ly** siden.

subserve [sʌb'sə·v] tjene. **subservience** [səb-'sə·vjəns], **subserviency** [-vjənsi] tjenlighet, nytte, gagn; undergivenhet; medvirkning.

subservient [səb'sə·viənt] tjenlig, gagnlig; un-

derordnet, undergiven; underdanig; krypende. **-ly** til fremme **(to** av).

subside [səb'said] synke til bunns, senke seg, avta. **subsidence** [səb'saidəns] synking, nedgang, det å avta.

subsidiary [səb'sidjəri] hjelpende, hjelpe-; forbundsfelle; **subsidiaries** hjelpetropper.

subsidize ['sʌbsidaiz] understøtte med pengebidrag, subsidiere. **subsidy** ['sʌbsidi] pengehjelp, subsidie.

sunsist [səb'sist] bestå, ernære seg, underholde; **— on** leve av.

subsistence [səb'sistəns] utkomme, tilværelse; **— department** intendantur (amr.).

subsistent [səb'sistənt] eksisterende; iboende.

subsoil ['sʌbsoil] undergrunn; **— water** grunnvann.

subst. fk. f. **substantive; substitute.**

substance ['sʌbstəns] substans, stoff, vesen, hovedinnhold, kjerne, formue; **in — i** hovedsaken.

substantial [səb'stänʃəl] vesentlig, virkelig, solid, legemlig, sterk, kraftig, velhavende. **-ity** [səbstänʃi'äliti] virkelighet, legemlighet, styrke. **substantiate** [səb'stänʃieʰt] gjøre virkelig, bevise. **substantival** [sʌbstən'taival] substantivisk. **substantive** ['sʌbstəntiv] substantivisk, selvstendig, traust, fast; substantiv, navnord.

substitute ['sʌbstitju·t] sette istedenfor; stedfortreder, varamann, surrogat, substitutt. **substitution** [sʌbsti'tju·ʃən] innsetting i en annens sted, erstatning. **-al** som trer isteden. **-ally** som erstatning.

substratum [səb'stre¹təm] substrat, underlag. **substruction** [sʌb'strʌkʃən], **substructure** [sʌb-'strʌktʃə] grunnlag, underbygning.

subsume [səb's(j)u·m] forutsette, innordne, underordne.

subtenant ['sʌb'tenənt] underforpakter.

subterfuge ['sʌbtəfju·dʒ] utflukt, påskudd.

subterraneous [sʌbtə're¹njəs] under jorda; underjordisk, underjords-, undergrunns-.

subtil ['sʌbtil, 'sʌtl] tynn, fin, skarp, listig.

subtilize ['sʌ(b)tilaiz] fortynne, forfine; være spissfindig.

subtilty ['sʌ(b)tilti] finhet, listighet.

sub-title ['sʌbtaitl] undertittel; den skrevne teksten på filmen.

subtle ['sʌtl] fin, subtil, vanskelig å gripe, skarpsindig, listig. **-ty** ['sʌtlti] finhet, listighet.

subtly ['sʌtli] fint, listig.

subtract [səb'träkt] trekke fra, subtrahere, forminske.

subtraction [səb'träkʃən] fradrag, subtraksjon. **subtrahend** ['sʌbtrəhend] subtrahend.

subtranslucent [sʌbtra·ns'lu·sənt] svakt gjennomskinnende.

subtransparent [sʌbtra·ns'pæ·ʰrənt] svakt gjennomsiktig.

subtropical ['sʌb'tråpikl] subtropisk.

suburb ['sʌbə(·)b] forstad.

suburban [sə'bə·bən] forstads-.

subvention [səb'venʃən] understøttelse, hjelp, stønad; statstilskudd.

subversion [səb'və·ʃən] omstyrtelse, ødeleggelse. **subversive** [səb'və·siv] nedbrytende, ødeleggende. **subvert** [səb'və·t] kullkaste, ødelegge. **subvertible** [səb'və·tibl] som kan kullkastes.

subway ['sʌbwe¹] tunnel, underjordisk gang; undergrunnsbane.

succade [sʌ'ke¹d] kandisert frukt, sukat.

succedaneum [sʌksi'de¹njəm] erstatningsmiddel, surrogat.

succeed [sʌk'si·d] følge, lykkes, være heldig, oppnå sitt ønske, la lykkes; **— to** følge etter, avløse, arve; **he -ed in coming** det lyktes ham å komme. **-er** etterfølger.

success [sʌk'ses] utfall, følge, godt resultat, lykke, hell. **-ful** heldig. **-fulness** lykkelig framgang, hell,

succession [sək'seʃən] følge, rekke, arvefølge; tronfølge, slektslinje, etterkommere. **-al** rekkefølge-, arvefølge-.
successive [sək'sesiv] som følger i orden, i trekk, på rad. **-ly** etter hverandre, i rekkefølge.
successor [sək'sesə] etterfølger.
succinct [sək'siŋkt] kortfattet.
succory ['sʌkəri] sikori.
succour ['sʌkə] understøtte, komme til hjelp, unnsette; hjelp, unnsetning, hjelper. **-less** hjelpeløs.
succulence ['sʌkjuləns] saftighet.
succulent ['sʌkjulənt] saftig.
succumb [sə'kʌm] bukke under, ligge under (to, under for).
succussion [sə'kʌʃən] rystelse, risting, skaking.
such [sʌtʃ] sådan, sånn, slik, den, det, de; — **and** — den og den, det og det, en viss, et visst; — **as** sånne som, de som; f. eks.
suchlike ['sʌtʃlaik] desslike, slike, den slags; sådant.
suck [sʌk] suge, suge inn, patte, die, suge ut; suging, melk, die, slurk; — **up to** innsmigre seg hos; **give** — gi die. **-er** suger, sugerør, stempel, pumpesko; sugeskål; renning, rotskudd. **-ing-bottle** tåteflaske. **-ing-pig** pattegris.
suckle ['sʌkl] gi die.
suckling ['sʌklin] pattebarn, patteunge.
suction ['sʌkʃən] suging; pimping.
suctorial [sʌk'tå·riəl] suge-.
Sudan [su'da·n], **the** — Sudan.
Sudanese [su·də'ni·z] sudanesisk, sudaneser.
sudarium ['s(j)u'dæ·ᵊriəm] svetteduk.
sudatory ['s(j)u·dətəri] svette-, som får svetten ut; dampbad.
sudden ['sʌdn] plutselig, brå, uventet; **of a** — (el. sj. **on a** —) plutselig, med ett.
suddenly ['sʌdnli] plutselig, med ett.
Sudetic [sju'detik], **the** — Mountains Sudetene.
sudorific [s(j)u·də'rifik] som driver ut svetten, svettemiddel. **sudoriferous** [s(j)u·də'rifərəs] som driver ut svetten, svettedrivende.
suds [sʌdz] såpeskum; **be in the** — være i knipe; **leave in the** — la i stikken.
sue [s(j)u·] følge, saksøke, anklage, anlegge søksmål mot; utvirke, be, beile til, søke å vinne. — **out** ansøke om, utvirke.
Suède [swe'd] gloves lammeskinnshansker.
suet ['s(j)u·it] nyrefett, talg. **-y** fett-.
Suez ['s(j)u·iz] Suez.
suffer ['sʌfə] lide (**from** av), utstå, bære, tåle, tillate, la, lide straff, lide skade, lide døden. **-able** utholdelig, tillatelig.
sufferance ['sʌfərəns] tålmodighet, overbærenhet, tillatelse; **on** — ved stilltiende tillatelse; ved å tåles.
sufferer ['sʌfərə] lidende, skadelidt, en som taper, en som får svi.
suffering ['sʌfəriŋ] lidende; lidelse.
suffice [sə'fais] være tilstrekkelig, strekke til, greie seg, tilfredsstille. **sufficiency** [sə'fiʃənsi] tilstrekkelig mengde, nøgd; brukbarhet.
sufficient [sə'fiʃənt] tilstrekkelig, tilfredsstillende, god nok, dyktig nok, gyldig, formuende.
suffix [sə'fiks] sette til (i enden av et ord).
suffix ['sʌfiks] suffiks.
suffocate ['sʌfəke·t] kvele; kovne.
suffocation [sʌfə'ke·ʃən] kvelning.
suffocative ['sʌfəkətiv] kvelende.
Suffolk ['sʌfək] Suffolk.
suffragan ['sʌfrəgən] underbiskop.
suffrage ['sʌfridʒ] valgrett, stemmerett; menighetens bønn (i kirken); **universal** — alminnelig stemmerett; **adult** — alminnelig stemmerett for begge kjønn.
suffragette [sʌfrə'dʒet] stemmerettskvinne.
suffragist ['sʌfrədʒist] tilhenger av stemmerett for kvinner (også.: **woman-suffragist**).
suffumigate [sə'fju·mige·t] desinfisere med røyk.
suffuse [sə'fju·z] fylle, overgyte, gjennomstrømme.

suffusion [sə'fju·ʒən] overgyting, gjennomstrømming, underløpt blod, rødming.
sugar ['ʃugə] sukker, ha sukker i el. på, sukre, smigre. **-basin** sukkerskål. — **-beet** sukkerroe. — **-candy** kandis(sukker). — **-cane** sukkerrør; **-ed** søt, sukkersøt; forbauset. — **-house** sukkerfabrikk. — **-loaf** sukkertopp. — **-nippers** sukkersaks, sukkerklype. — **-pea** sukkerert. — **-plum** sukkertøy, sukkerkule, bonbon. — **refiner** sukkerraffinør. — **-tongs** sukkerklype.
sugary ['ʃu·gəri] søt, altfor søt, sukkersøt; som er glad i sukker.
suggest [sə'dʒest] inngi, bibringe, la formode, foreslå, la hemmelig vite, ymte om, minne om, slå på, antyde, hentyde til, henstille, gi et vink om.
suggestion [sə'dʒestʃən] suggestion, bibringelse, hemmelig råd, (hemmelig) tilskyndelse; (uvilkårlig) innskytelse, forestilling, formodning; tanke, antydning, ymt, minnelse, minning, vink, fingerpek, halvkvedet vise.
suggestive [sə'dʒestiv] som inneholder et vink, tankevekkende; **be** — **of** kalle fram forestillinger om.
suicide ['s(j)u·isaid] selvmord, selvmorder.
suicidal [s(j)u·i'saidəl] som hører til selvmord.
suit [s(j)u·t] rekke, følge, sett, drakt, dress, ansøkning, frieri, bønn, saksøkning, rettssak; ordne, tilpasse, gjøre tilfreds, kle, ta på en drakt, stemme overens, høve; **bring a** — anlegge sak; **follow** — bekjenne farge; **out of -s** ikke i samsvar. **-able** passende, høvelig, overensstemmende. **-ableness** passelig karakter, overensstemmelse, samsvar. **-ably** passende, i følge.
suit-case ['sju·t'ke·ıs] liten håndkoffert.
suite [swi·t] følge, rekkefølge, sett, rekke.
suitor ['s(j)u·tə] ansøker, søker, frier; saksøker, prosederende. **suitress** kvinnelig saksøker.
sulcate ['sʌlke·t] furet, spaltet.
sulk [sʌlk] furte, surmule; dårlig humør, furting; **be in the sulks** være i dårlig humør.
sulky ['sʌlki] furten, gretten, mutt, olm, tverr, treven; sulky, lett enspenner (især til travkjøring).
sullen ['sʌlin] mørk, trist, utilfreds, tverr, muggen, gretten, uvennlig. **-ness** uvennlighet, utilfredshet, egensindighet, ondskapsfullhet. **sullens** dårlig humør.
Sullivan ['sʌlivən] Sullivan.
sully ['sʌli] søle til, besudle, flekke, plette; plettes; smuss, flekk.
sulphur ['sʌlfə] svovel. **-ate** ['sʌlfəre·t] svovle, svovelbleike. **-ation** ['sʌl·] svovling, svovelbleiking. **sulphureous** ['sʌl·ʃuəriəs] svovlet, svovelgul. **sulphuretted** ['sʌlfjuretid] innsatt med svovel, svovlet, svovel-. **sulphuric** [sʌl·ʃuərik] acid svovelsyre. **sulphurous** ['sʌlfjurəs] acid svovelsyrling.
sultan ['sʌltən] sultan.
sultana [sʌl'ta·nə] sultaninne; slags rosin.
sultanate ['sʌltənėt] sultanat.
sultriness ['sʌltrinés] lummerhete.
sultry ['sʌltri] lummer.
sum [sʌm] sum, hele beløpet; regnestykke; pengesum, hovedinnhold, høyeste grad; telle sammen, summere opp, regne, sammenfatte; **do a** — regne et stykke; **set a** — gi et regnestykke til; **in** — i korthet; — **up** summere opp, resymere, framstille kortfattet; (om dommer) gi rettsbelæring.
sumach ['su·mäk] sumak.
Sumatra [su'ma·trə] Sumatra.
summarily ['sʌmərili] i korthet. **summarist** ['sʌmərist] en som gjør et utdrag. **summarize** ['sʌmərəiz] sammenfatte, resymere. **summary** ['sʌməri] kortfattet, summarisk; kortfattet innbegrep, kort utdrag, resymé.
summation [sʌ'me·ʃən] sammenlegning.
summer ['sʌmə] en som summerer opp.

summer ['sʌmə] sommer; tilbringe sommeren; a — day el. a -'s day en sommerdag; — lightning kornmo; St. Luke's — mild oktober. -fallow sommerbrakk; sommerpløye. — -house sommerhus, lysthus. — time sommertid (innført som normaltid om sommeren). -time, — -time sommersesongen.

summit ['sʌmit] topp, største høyde.

summon ['sʌmən] kalle inn, stevne, oppfordre, oppby; — up one's courage ta mot til seg. -er stevningsmann. -s oppfordr:ng, kallelse, stevning.

sumpter['sʌm(p)tə] lastdyr, pakkhest, kløvhest.

sumptuary ['sʌm(p)tʃuəri] utgifts-; — laws lover mot overdådighet.

sumptuous ['sʌm(p)tʃuəs] kostbar, prektig; luksuriøs; -ness kostbarhet, prakt.

sun [sʌn] sol; sole, sole seg. — -bath solbad. -beam solstråle. — -blind markise. — -bonnet solhatt. — -bright solklar. — -burnt solbrent. — -clad strålende.

Sunda ['sʌndə] Sunda; the Strait of — Sundastredet.

Sunday ['sʌndi] søndag; Low — første søndag etter påske; — best søndagsklær, kisteklær; — out frisøndag; a month of Sundays en lang tid, en hel evighet. — -school søndagsskole.

sunder ['sʌndə] avsondre, skille, dele; deling i to stykker; a-, in i sund, i stykker.

sundew ['sʌndju·] soldogg (plante).

sun-dial ['sʌndaiəl] solskive, solur.

sun-dog ['sʌndåg] parhelion, bisol, solulv.

sundown ['sʌndaun] solnedgang, solegla.

sun-dried ['sʌndraid] soltørket.

sundry ['sʌndri] atskillige, flere; sundries forskjellige slags ting, diverse saker.

sunflower ['sʌnflauə] solsikke, solvendel.

sung [sʌŋ] perf. pts. av sing.

sun-god ['sʌngåd] solgud.

sunk [sʌŋk] perf. pts. av sink.

sunken ['sʌŋkn] gammel pts. av sink; nå: sunken, senket, undervanns-; innsunken, innfallen; — rock blindskjær, båe, flu.

sunless ['sʌnlès] solløs.

sunlight ['sʌnlait] sollys.

sunlit ['sʌnlit] solbeskint.

sunny ['sʌni] sol-, solbeskint, sollys, strålende.

sunrise ['sʌnraiz] soloppgang, solrenning.

sunset ['sʌnset] solnedgang, solegla.

sunshade ['sʌnʃe'd] parasoll; solskjerm, markise.

sunshine ['sʌnʃain] solskinn; medgang, lykke.

sunshiny ['sʌnʃaini] sollys, solskinns-.

sun-spot ['sʌnspåt] solflekk.

sunstroke ['sʌnstroᵘk] solstikk; heteslag.

sun-up ['sʌnʌp] (amr.) soloppgang, solrenning.

sunward ['sʌnwəd] mot sola.

sunwise ['sʌnwaiz] med sola, rettsøles.

sun-worship ['sʌnwə·ʃip] soldyrking.

sup [sʌp] drikke, supe, slubre i seg; spise aftens; — on porridge spise graut til kvelds.

super- ['s(j)u·pə-] (i smstn.) over, omfram, til overmål.

super ['s(j)u·pə] statist; særlig fin, utsøkt.

superabound ['s(j)u·pərə'baund] finnes i overflod, være flust med, ha overflod på. superabundance [-'bʌndəns] overflødighet. superabundant ['bʌndənt] overflødig.

superadd ['s(j)u·pər'äd] legge til attpå. -ition ['s(j)u·pərə'diʃən] ny tilføyelse.

superannuate [s(j)u·pər'änjue't] svekke (ved alder), lå gå av med (el. sette på) pensjon, pensjonere. -d avlegs, uttjent, avdanket.

superannuation ['s(j)u·pəränju'e'ʃən] alderdomssvakhet, avgang, pensjonering.

superb [s(j)u']pə·b] prektig, herlig, fortrinlig.

supercargo [s(j)u·pə'ka·°goᵘ] superkargo, kargadør.

supercilious [s(j)u·pə'siljəs] overmodig, kaut.

supereminent [s(j)u·pər'eminənt] særlig fremragende, makeløs.

supererogation [s(j)u·pərəro'ge'ʃən] overflødig pliktoppfyllelse. supererogatory [s(j)u·pəre'rågətəri] som går utover den strenge plikt, overflødig.

superfecundity [s(j)u·pəfi'kʌnditi] overvettes fruktbarhet.

superficial [s(j)u·pə'fiʃəl] flate-, overfladisk; — measure flatemål. -ity [s(j)u·pəfiʃi'äliti] overfladiskhet. superficies [s(j)u·pə'fiʃ(i)i·z] overflate.

superfine ['s(j)u·pə'fain] overordentlig fin, ekstra fin, fin-fin.

superfluity [s(j)u·pə'flu·iti] overflod.

superfluous [s(j)u·pə'fluəs] overflødig.

superhuman [s(j)u·pə'hju·mən] overmenneskelig.

superimpose [s(j)u·pərim'poᵘz] legge ovenpå. superimposition avleiring ovenpå.

superincumbent [s(j)u·pərin'kʌmbənt] som ligger over ovenpå.

superinduce [s(j)u·pərin'dju·s] legge til, tilføye.

superintend [s(j)u·pərin'tend] se til, lede, forestå. superintendence [s(j)u·pərin'tendəns] tilsyn, ledelse. superintendent [s(j)u·pərin'tendənt] tilsynshavende, bestyrer, direktør.

superior [s(j)u']piəriə] over-, høyere, øverst, overlegen; overmann, foresatt, prior; be — to være bedre enn, overgå, være hevet over; a — air en overlegen mine; — court overrett. -ity [s(j)u]piəri'äriti] overlegenhet, fortrin, forrang.

superjacent [s(j)u·pə'dʒe'sənt] som ligger ovenpå.

superlative [s(j)u']pə·lətiv] høyest; ypperlig; superlativ.

superman ['s(j)u·pəmən] overmenneske.

supermundane [s(j)u·pə'mʌnde'n] overjordisk.

supernal [s(j)u·pə'nəl] høyere, overjordisk, hinsidig, himmelsk.

supernatant [s(j)u·pə'ne'tənt] som svømmer (el. flyter) ovenpå.

supernatural [s(j)u·pə'nätʃərəl] overnaturlig. -ism [-izm] overnaturlighet; supranaturalisme.

supernumerary [s(j)u·pə'nju·mərəri] overkomplett, overtallig, reserve-, ekstra-; ekstraskriver, reservehest, statist; — officer offiser i en suite, surnumerær.

supernutrition [s(j)u·pənju'triʃən] overernæring. superpose [s(j)u·pə'poᵘz] legge ovenpå. superposition [s(j)u·pəpo'ziʃən] det å legge (el. ligge) ovenpå.

supersaturate [s(j)u·pə'sätʃure't] overmette.

superscribe [s(j)u·pə'skraib] overskrive, skrive utenpå (et brev). superscription [s(j)u·pə'skripʃən] overskrift, adressering.

supersede [s(j)u·pə'si·d] erstatte, fortrenge, avløse, komme i stedet for, fjerne, avskaffe, oppheve, avskjedige, overflødiggjøre, sette ut av kraft. superseding signal signal til at kommandoen skal overgis en annen.

supersedeas [s(j)u·pə'si·diəs] suspensjonsbefaling, ordre til å stanse rettssaken.

supersensual [s(j)u·pə'senʃuəl] oversanselig.

supersession [s(j)u·pə'seʃən] avskjedigelse, erstatning.

superstition [s(j)u·pə'stiʃən] overtro. superstitious [s(j)u·pə'stiʃəs] overtroisk.

superstructure [s(j)u·pə'strʌktʃə] overbygning.

supertax ['s(j)u·pətäks] ekstraskatt.

superterrestrial [s(j)u·pə'restriəl] overjordisk.

supervene [s(j)u·pə'vi·n] komme til, støte til. supervention [s(j)u·pə'venʃən] det å komme til, støte til.

supervise [s(j)u·pə'vaiz] ha oppsyn med, se til. supervision [s(j)u·pə'viʃən] oppsyn, tilsyn. supervisor [s(j)u·pə'vaizə] tilsynsmann, inspektør, korrekturleser.

supination [s(j)u·pi'ne'ʃə, det å ligge på ryggen. supine [s(j)u'pain] liggende på ryggen, tilbakebøyd, skrå, likegyldig, makelig, lat, slakk. supine ['s(j)u·pain] supinum. supineness latskap, slapphet, makelighet.

supper ['sʌpə] aftensmat, kveldsmat; the last

— påskemåltidet i lidelsesuken; the Lord's — den hellige nattverden. -less uten aftensmat.
supplant [sə'plɑ·nt] fortrenge, stikke ut.
supplantation [sʌplɑ·n'te¹ʃən] fortrengsel.
supple ['sʌpl] myk, bøyelig, smidig, ettergivende, krypende; gjøre smidig, bøye, bli bløt. **-ness** bøyelighet, smidighet.
supplement ['sʌplimənt] supplement, tillegg, bilag; supplere, utfylle. **-al** [sʌpli'mentəl], **-ary** [-'mentəⅰⅰ] supplerende, tilleggs-, utfyllende.
suppliant ['sʌpliənt] ydmyk, bønnlig.
supplicant ['sʌplikənt] ansøker, søker.
supplicate ['sʌplike¹t] bønnfalle, be om.
supplication [sʌpli'ke¹ʃən] bønn, trygling.
supply [sə'plai] utfylle, supplere, skaffe, levere, yte, forsyne, forstrekke med, erstatte; utfylling, forsyning, levering, tilførsel, tilbud, forråd, pengebevilling; **committee of** (el. **on**) — finansutvalg (av hele underhuset) for utgiftsbudsjettet.
support [sə'på·ᵒt] bære, holde oppe, understøtte, stø, utholde, spille, utføre, holde, støtte, underholde, forsørge, forsvare, opprettholde, fortsette, føre, akkompagnere, ledsage; understøttelse, underhold, forsørgelse, erverv. **-able** utholdelig, holdbar. **-er** [-ə] støtte, tilhenger, understøtter, skjoldholder, framstiller.
supposable [sə'po"zəbl] antagelig, tenkelig.
suppose [sə'po"z] anta, formode, gå ut fra, [ofte: spo"z] som imperativ: sett at, hva om; **I suppose** formodentlig, vel; **supposing** forutsatt at.
supposition [sʌpo'ziʃən] antagelse, forutsetning, formodning. **suppositional** [sʌpo'ziʃənəl] antatt, tenkt. **supposititious** [səpázi'tiʃəs] tenkt, hypotetisk, uekte, falsk, fingert. **suppositive** [sə'pázitiv] antatt, forutsatt; betingelseskonjunksjon.
suppress [sə'pres] undertrykke, dempe, kue, døyve, avskaffe, inndra, stanse, utelate, fortie. **-ion** [sə'preʃən] undertrykkelse, opphevelse, stansing, fortielse. **-ive** [-iv] undertrykkende. **-or** [-ə] undertrykker.
suppuration [sʌpju're¹ʃən] materie, puss, våg.
supremacy [s(j)u'preməsi] overhøyhet; overlegenhet; **oath of** — supremat-ed (hvorved kongens kirkelige overhøyhet erkjennes).
supreme [s(j)u'pri·m] høyest, øverst; the **Supreme (Being)** den høyeste (det høyeste vesen, Gud); the — **court** høyesterett. **-ly** i høyeste grad. **Supt.** fk. f. **superintendent.**
surcharge [sə·'tʃa·ᵒdʒ] overlesse, overlaste (et skip); for stort lass, ekstrabetaling.
surcingle ['sə·siŋgl] overgjord, belte.
surcoat ['sə·ko"t] (gml.) dames overkjortel.
surd [sə·d] irrasjonal; irrasjonal størrelse.
sure [ʃuə] sikker, trygg, viss, tilforlatelig, bundet ved et løfte; **be — and tell him** fortell ham endelig, glem nå ikke å fortelle ham; **I don't know, I'm** — det vet jeg virkelig ikke; **to be** — uten tvil, ganske visst, ja visst, nei visst; **he is** — **to come** han kommer sikkert; **be** — **of** være sikker på; **feel** — **of** være sikker på; **make** — **of** sikre seg. — **-footed** stø på foten. **-ly** sikkert, ganske visst.
surety ['ʃuⱥti] sikkerhet, kausjon, kausjonist, gissel. **-ship** kavering, kausjon.
surf [sə·f] brott, brenning. — **-boat** livbåt.
surface ['sə·fis] overflate, flate; **surfacing** plandreining; det å søke etter gull i overflaten.
surface|-fermentation overgjæring. — **-plate** retteplate; planskive (på dreiebenk). — **-water** overflatevann, flomvann.
surfeit [sə·'fit] overfylle, overmette, fråtse, frosse, få for mye; bli matlei; overmetting, forspising; avsmak. **-er** [-ə] fråtser.
surge [sə·dʒ] brottsjø, båre, stor bølge; bølge, båre, bruse, stige, heve seg.
surgeon ['sə·dʒən] kirurg, sårlege, militærlege, skipslæge. **-cy** [-si] kirurgstilling.
surgery ['sə·dʒəri] kirurgi, operasjonsstue, konsultasjonsstue.
surgical ['sə·dʒikl] kirurgisk.

surgy ['sə·dʒi] høyt svulmende.
surliness ['sə·linès] surhet, tverrhet.
surly ['sə·li] sur, gretten, tverr.
surmise [sə'maiz] formode, gjette, gisse på, tenke seg; formodning, anelse, mistanke. **-r** [-ə] en som formoder, gjetter.
surmount [sə'maunt] overgå, overvinne. **-able** overstigelig, overkommelig.
surname ['səne¹m] tilnavn, etternav ⅰ; kalle med etternavn, gi et tilnavn.
surpass [sə'pa·s] overgå. **-able** overtreffelig. **-ing** fortrinlig, framifrå. **-ingly** i ualminnelig grad.
surplice ['sə·plis] messeserk. **-d** ['sə·plist] i messeserk.
surplus ['sə·plʌs] overskudd, tilgift.
surplusage ['sə·pləsidʒ] overskudd, overflødighet.
surprise [sə'praiz] overraske, overrumple, forbause; overraskelse, overrumpling, forbauselse; **by** — ved overrumpling; **in** — overrasket; **to my** — til min overⅰaskelse; **I am -d at you** det hadde jeg ikke ventet av deg (som skjenn).
surrender [sə'rendə] overgi, utlevere, gi opp, overgi seg; overgivelse, avståelse.
surreptitious [sʌrép'tiʃəs] hemmelig, underfundig; uekte.
Surrey ['sʌri] Surrey.
surrogate ['sʌrogét] stedfortreder, varamann, fullmektig.
surround [sə'raund] omringe, omgi. **-ing** omgivelse; **-ings** omgivelser, miljø.
surtax ['sə·täks] ekstraskatt, tilleggsskatt.
surtout [sə·'tu·] surtout, overfrakk, kappe.
surveillance [sə'veiləns] oppsyn, overvåking.
survey [sə·'ve¹] overskue, bese, se over, besiktige, inspisere, mønstre, ha oppsyn med, måle opp, kartlegge.
survey ['sə·ve¹] overblikk, besiktigelse, inspeksjon, oppmåling, kartlegging.
surveyor [sə·'ve¹ə] oppsynsmann, besiktigelsesmann, inspektør; landmåler. **-ship** post som landmåler etc.
survival [sə'vaivəl] overlevering; the — of the **fittest** det at de best skikkede blir igjen.
survive [sə'vaiv] overleve, slippe fra et med livet; bli igjen.
survivor [sə'vaivə] lengstlevende.
Susan ['s(j)u·zən] Susanne.
susceptible [sə'septibl] mottagelig, følsom.
susceptibility [səsepti'biliti] mottagelighet, følsomhet, ømfintlighet.
susceptive [sə'septiv] mottagelig.
suspect [sə'spekt] ha mistanke, ane, mistenke, nære mistanke til; mistenkt, mistenkelig. **-edly** mistenkelig.
suspend [sə'spend] henge opp, la avhenge, gjøre avhengig, la være uavgjort, avbryte, stanse, utsette, forbeholde seg, suspendere, sette ut av kraft, midlertidig oppheve; innstille sine betalinger.
suspender [səs'pendə] strømpeholder; bukseseler.
suspense [sə'spens] uvisshet, spenning, oppsetting, henstand.
suspension [sə'spenʃən] opphenging, utsettelse, avbrytelse, innstilling, suspensjon, tvil; — **of arms** våpenstillstand. — **of payment** innstilling av sine betalinger. — **-bridge** hengebru. — **-lamp** hengelampe.
suspensor [sə'spensə] suspensorium.
suspensory [sə'spensəri] hengende, opphengt, tvilsom.
sus. per col. fk. f. **suspensio per collum** (= **hanging by the neck).**
suspicion [sə'spiʃən] mistanke, liten smule; antydning, snev.
suspicious [sə'spiʃəs] mistenksom, mistenkelig.
Sussex ['sʌsiks] Sussex.
sustain [sə'ste¹n] bære, støtte, bekrefte, holde oppe, hevde, opprettholde, vedlikeholde, under-

holde, forsørge, hjelpe, tåle, holde ut. -able ut-holdelig. -er forsørger.
sustenance ['sʌstinəns] underhold, livsopphold, fødemidler, mat, matvarer.
sustentation [sʌsten'teɪʃən] støtte, stønad, hjelp; opphold, forsørgelse.
sutler ['sʌtlə] marketenter.
suttee [sʌ'tiː] sutti, indisk enkebrenning, enke som brennes.
suttle ['sʌtl] nettovekt.
suture ['s(j)uːtʃə] syning, søm, sutur; sammenføye.
suzerain ['suːzəreɪn] overherre.
suzerainty ['suːzəreɪnti] overhøyhet.
svelte [svelt] slank, mjå, grannvokst.
S. W. fk. f. South-west.
S. W. b. S. fk. f. South-west by South.
S. W. b. W. fk. f. South-west by West.
swab [swåb] svaber, kanonvisker; epålett; grønnskolling; skrubbe, svabre.
swaddle ['swådl] svøpe, inn, sveipe, tulle, reive; svøp, reiv.
swag [swäg] knytte, tull; bytte; pikk og pakk.
swagger ['swägə] skvaldre, skryte, braute, spankulere; skvalder, brauting, sprading. -er [-rə] skryter, skvadronør.
swain [sweɪn] (poet.) bondegutt; elsker, frier. -ish landlig, bondsk.
swallow ['swålou] svale; one — does not make a summer én svale gjør ingen sommer.
swallow ['swålou] svelgje, synke, sluke; bite i seg, finne seg i, tåle; svelg, avgrunn; — one's words ta sine ord i seg igjen.
swallowtail ['swålouteɪl] svalehale; snippkjole, kjole (for herrer).
swam [swäm] imperf. av **swim.**
swamp [swåmp] myr, sump; senke ned; fylle, bringe til å synke, overvelde, overfylle, styrte i uløselige vanskeligheter. -y sumpet, myrlendt.
swan [swån] svane; skald, dikter; — of Avon ɔ: Shakespeare; — of Ayr ɔ: Robert Burns.
swank [swäŋk] viktighet, skryt; skryte.
swannery ['swånəri] svanegård. -'s-down ['swånzdaun] svanedun; svanebai. — -song svanesang.
swap [swåp] bytte, bytte til seg, bytte bort; bytning, bytte; — with him bytte med ham; — horses while crossing stream skifte hest midt i vadestedet, skifte regjering under en krise; get the — få løpepass.
sward [swå·əd] grønnsvær, grastorv; kle med grastorv.
swarm[swå·əm] sverm; sverme, myldre, yre, kry.
swarm [swå·əm] entre, klatre, klyve.
swart [swå·ət] svart, mørk.
swarthy ['swå·əþi] mørk, mørkhudet.
swash [swåʃ] plasking, skvalder; plaske.
swashbuckler ['swåʃbʌklə] storskryter.
swath [swå(·)þ] skåre (av gras eller korn).
swathe [sweɪð] svøp, reiv; svøpe, sveipe, reive.
sway [sweɪ] svaie, svinge, helle, ha overvekt, herske, styre, råde, beherske, heise, hive; sving, overvekt, innflytelse, styre, makt.
swear [swæ·ə] sverge, ta i ed, edfeste, bekrefte ved ed, banne. — in edfeste; — off drinki g avsverge drikk. -er en som sverger.
sweat [swet] svette, slit og slep; svette, svette ut, få til å svette.
sweater ['swetə] utbytter; sweater, slags genser.
sweating ['swetiŋ] svetting; utbytting. **sweat-ing-bath** dampbad.
sweaty ['sweti] svett, møysommelig, strevsom.
Swede [swiːd] svenske.
Sweden ['swiːdn] Sverige.
Swedish ['swiːdiʃ] svensk.
sweep [swiːp] feie, sope, fare henover, stryke langsmed, sokne langsetter, slepe, bestryke, ta et langt overblikk over; fare forbi, streife, jage bort; feiing, soping, sving, streifing, strøk, ødeleggelse, feier, sjofelist.

sweeper ['swiːpə] feier, feiemaskin. -ing feiing. -ings søppel, avfall.
sweepstake(s) ['swiːpsteɪk(s)] sweepstakes (veddemål hvor samtlige innsatser går til den seirende).
sweet [swiːt] søt, duftende, velluktende, melodisk, yndig, fersk, frisk, blid; sødme, behagelighet, søtange, duft; søtsmak, sukkertøy, snop; be — upon være forelsket i; he has a — tooth han er glad i søte saker.
sweetbread ['swiːtbred] brissel, bukspyttkjertel.
sweet-brier ['swiːt'braɪə] vinrose.
sweeten ['swiːtn] gjøre søt, sukre, forsøte, mildne; parfymere; gjøre frisk, gjøre fruktbar; bli søt.
sweetheart ['swiːtha·ət] kjæreste.
sweeting ['swiːtiŋ] søteple.
sweetish ['swiːtiʃ] søtlig.
sweetmeat ['swiːtmiːt] sukkertøy, snop.
sweetness søthet, vellukt, ynde, mildhet.
sweet-oil olivenolje, matolje. — -pea blomsterert. — -scented velluktende. — -tempered elskverdig. **sweety** sukkertøy, snop.
swell [swel] svulme, svelle, trutne, hovne, briske seg, være svulstig, opphisses, vokse, øke, stige, blåse opp, forsterke; svulming, trutning, forhøyning, kul, hevelse; utbuling; intensitet, kraft, terrengbølge, crescendo, matador, fin kar, staskar, stasdame; dønning; the great -s in literature litteraturens matadorer; — -mob fin tyv; -ing svulmende; svulming, oppblåsthet, forhøyning, oppbrusing, utbrudd. -ism finhet, flotthet.
swelter ['sweltə] være lummer, forsmekte, forgå, kovne av varme; ødelegge med varme, svette ut; kovning, svette, hete.
swept [swept] imperf. og perf. pts. av **sweep.**
swerve [swɔ·v] dreie til siden, bøye av, vike ut, avvike; dreining, avvikelse, avvike.
Swift [swift] Swift.
swift [swift] hurtig, rask, snøgg, kjapp; strøm, stryk; slags svale; salamander; garnvinde. — -footed, — -heeled rappføtt. -ness hurtighet.
swig [swig] ta slurker av; slurk.
swill [swil] tylle i seg, skylle; slurk, fyll.
swim [swim] svømme, flyte, drive, sveve; svimle; være oversvømmet, svømme over; svømning, svømmetur, svømmeblære; be in the — være med i det som foregår; -mer svømmer, svømmefugl. -ming svømming; svimmelhet. -mingly svømmende, glatt, fint.
Swinburne ['swinbə(·)n] Swinburne.
swindle ['swindl] svindle, bedra; svindel.
swindler ['swindlə] svindler.
swindling ['swindliŋ] svindel, bedrageri.
swine [swain] gris, svin; griser; svine-. -herd svinehyrde, grisegjæter. — -pox vannkopper. -ry ['swainəri] grisehus, svineri.
swing [swiŋ] svinge, vippe, dingle; sving, sleng, svingning, huske, fritt løp, frihet, gang, bevegelse, spillerom, svingdør; swing (dans); in full — i full gang. — -bridge svingbru. — -cot balansevugge. — -door svingdør.
swinge [swin(d)ʒ] piske, pryle, denge, slå.
swingeing ['swindʒin] veldig, dundrende, knallende.
swinger ['swindʒə] dundrende løgn, diger skrøne.
swinger ['swiŋə] en som svinger. — -gate stor svingdør. -ing ['swiŋiŋ] svingende, sving-, svinging. -le ['swiŋgl] skakekniv; skake (lin); slagvol.
swinish ['swainiʃ] svinsk.
swipe [swaip] brønnvippe, brønnvåg; slå kraftig; delje til; slag.
swirl [swɔ·l] hvirvle av sted; hvirvel, hvirveldans.
swish [swiʃ] la suse, svinge, smekke, piske, slå; susing, smekk, svepeslag.
Swiss [swis] sveitsisk; sveitser; (det samme i

plur. som er sjelden unntagen med **the**); — **roll** slags kake.

switch [switʃ] tynn kjepp, myk påk, pisk; sporskifte, pens, rangering; (elektrisk) strømvender, strømbryter; (løs) flette; gi av kjeppen, piske; svinge, dreie, skifte, pense, rangere; — **off** bryte, slå av (strøm), slukke (lys); — **on** slå på, sette på, tenne.

switchback ['switʃbäk] rutsjebane.

switchboard ['switʃbå·əd] strømfordelingstavle; sentralbord (på telefonstasjon).

switchman ['switʃmən] sporskifter, pensemann.

switch-rail ['switʃ're¹l] vikespor.

Switzerland ['switsələnd] Sveits.

swivel ['swivl] hvirvel, bevegelig tapp; svinge, dreie seg, hvirvle (seg) rundt. — **-chair** svingstol.

swollen, swoln ['swoᵘln] oppsvulmet, svullen.

swoon [swu·n] besvime, dåne; besvimelse.

swoop [swu·p] slå ned på, gripe; nedslag, grep, raskt angrep.

swop se **swap**.

sword [så·ᵉd] sverd, kårde, sabel; **put to the** — la springe over klingen, drepe; **he kills himself on his** — han faller på sitt sverd. — **-arm** høyre arm. — **-bayonet** sabelbajonett. — **-bearer** sverddrager. — **-fish** sverdfisk. — **-knot** portepé, sabelkvast, kårdekvast. **-sman** fektemester. **-smanship** fektekunst. — **-player** fekter. — **-stick** kårdestikk.

swore [swå·ᵉ] imperf. av **swear**.

sworn [swå·ᵉn] perf. pts. av **swear**.

Sybarite ['sibərait] sybaritt.

sybaritic [sibə'ritik] sybarittisk, overdådig.

sycamore ['sikəmå·ᵉ] sykomor, morbærfikentre.

sycophancy ['sikofənsi] lav smiger.

sycophant ['sīkofənt] sykofant, angiver, smigrer.

sycophantic [siko'fäntik] slesk, krypende, falsk.

Sydenham ['sidnəm] Sydenham.

Sydney ['sidni] Sydney.

syllabic, -al [si'läbik, -l] stavings-. **syllabi(fi)-cation** [siläbi(fi)'ke¹ʃən] stavingsdeling.

syllable ['siləbl] staving.

syllabus ['siləbəs] grunnriss, uttog, program.

syllogism ['silodʒizm] syllogisme, slutning.

syllogize ['silodʒaiz] slutte, dra slutninger.

sylph [silf] sylfe, luftånd.

sylphid ['silfid] sylfide, liten sylfe.

symbol ['simbəl] symbol, sinnbilde, tegn, bekjennelse. **-ical** [sim'bälikl]. **-ically** [sim'bälikəli] symbolsk. **-ics** [sim'bäliks] symbolsk teologi. **-ize** ['simbəlaiz] symbolisere, betegne symbolsk.

symmetrical [si'metrikl] symmetrisk.

symmetry ['simitri] symmetri.

sympathetic [simpə'þetik], **-al** [-l], **-ally** [-əli] sympatetisk, sympatisk, deltagende.

sympathize ['simpəþaiz] sympatisere.

sympathy ['simpəþi] sympati.

symphonious [sim'foᵘniəs] harmonisk. **symphonise** ['simfənaiz] harmonere. **symphony** ['simfəni] harmoni, samklang, symfoni.

symposium [sim'poᵘziəm] symposium, gjestebud; samling av flere meningsuttalelser.

symptom ['sim(p)təm] symptom, tegn. **syn. fk. f. synonym.**

synagogue ['sinəgåg] synagoge.

synchronism ['siŋkronizm] samtidighet.

synchronize ['siŋkronaiz] falle sammen i tid.

synchronous ['siŋkrənəs] samtidig.

syncopate ['siŋkope¹t] synkopere, forkorte.

syncopation [siŋko'pe¹ʃən] forkorting.

syncope ['siŋkopi] synkope, sammentrekking av ord (ved utskyting av lyd i midten), forskyting av rytme; avmakt, besvimelse.

syndetic [sin'detik] forbindende.

syndicate ['sindikét] syndikat.

syndicate ['sindike¹t] forbinde til et syndikat; danne et konsortium.

syndication [sindi'ke¹ʃən] danning av et konsortium.

syndicalism ['sindikəlizm] syndikalisme.

syndicalist ['sindikəlist] syndikalist.

syne [sain] siden; **auld long** — for lenge siden.

synod ['sinəd] synode, kirkeforsamling.

synodal ['sinədəl] synodal, synodaldekret.

synodic [si'nådik] synodal, forhandlet i kirkemøte.

synonym ['sinonim] enstydig ord, synonym.

synonymous [si'nåniməs] enstydig, synonym.

synonymy [si'nånimi] enstydighet.

synopsis [si'nåpsis] oversikt, uttog, utdrag.

syntactical [sin'täktikl] syntaktisk.

syntax ['sintäks] syntaks, ordføyningslære.

synthesis ['sinþisis] syntese, sammensetning.

synthetic [sin'þetik] syntetisk, sammenføyende.

syphilis ['sifilis] syfilis.

Syria ['siriə] Syria.

Syriac ['siriäk] syrisk.

Syrian ['siriən] syrisk; syrer.

syringa [si'riŋgə] syrin, uekte sjasmin.

syringe ['sirin(d)ʒ] sprøyte; sprøyte (inn).

syrup ['sirəp] sukkerholdig uttrekk, sukkersaft, sukkeroppløsning; renset sirup.

system ['sistəm] system, ordning. **-atic[** sistə'mätik], **-atical** [sistə'mätik], **-atically** [sistə'mätikəli] systematisk. **-atize** ['sistəmətaiz] systematisere.

systole ['sistəli] sammentrekking (især av hjertet).

T

T, t [ti] T; t; **suit to a T.** passe på en prikk. **'t** fk. f. **it.**

ta [ta·] (barnespråk) takk!

Taal [ta·l], **the** — Kapp-hollandsk.

tab [täb] hempe, stropp, løs ende, lapp; (amr.) regnskap.

tabard ['täbəd] våpenkjole.

tabaret ['täbəret] en slags atlask.

tabby ['täbi] vatret, moiré; moiré; stripet katt, katte, kjette; gammel jomfru, sladrekjerring; — **cat** stripet katt.

tabefaction [täbi'fäkʃən] hentæring.

tabernacle ['täbənäkl] paulun, telt, tabernakel, avlukke i alteret, nisje; bo, holde til, gjemme.

tabes ['te¹bi·z] tabes, (ryggmargs)tæring.

tablature ['täblətʃə] takmaleri, veggmaleri; tabulatur (i musikk).

table ['te¹bl] tavle, bord, taffel, kost, tabell,

liste, register, innholdsfortegnelse, brettspill; ordne tabellarisk, katalogisere; legge på bordet, legge fram; **turn the -s** vende bladet, gi saken en annen vending; **at** — til bords, under måltidet.

tableau ['täbloᵘ] tablå.

table|-beer ['te¹blbia] alminnelig øl som brukes til bords, — **-bell** bordklokke. — **-cloth** bordduk. — **-cover** bordteppe. — **-d'hote** ['ta·bldoᵘt] table d'hote. — **-land** høyslette. — **-leg** bordben. — **-linen** dekketøy. — **-spoon** spiseskje.

tablet ['täblit] liten tavle, tablett, blokknoter.

table-talk ['te¹bltå·k] bordkonversasjon, gjengivelse av kjent personlighets tale ved bordet.

table-tennis ['te¹bl'tenis] pingpong, bordtennis.

table-top ['te¹bltåp] bordplate.

table-turning ['te¹bl'tə·niŋ] borddans.

tabloid ['täblåid] tablett.

taboo [tə'buˑ] tabu, hellighetserklæring, forbud; fredlyse, forby bruken av.
tabor ['te¹bə] (gammelt:) tromme.
tabouret ['täbərĕt] taburett, broderramme.
tabular ['täbjulə] tavleformet, tavlet; tabell-, tabellarisk. tabulate ['täbjule¹t] planere; ordne i tabellform.
tachometer [tä'kåmitə] fartmåler.
tachygraphy [tə'kigrəfi] stenografi.
tacit ['täsit] stilltiende; taus, tagal.
taciturn ['täsitəˑn] ordknapp, fåmælt.
taciturnity [täsi'təˑniti] ordknapphet.
tack [täk] stift; (mar.) hals; baut, slag; tråklesting, nest; leiekontrakt; politikk; feste, hefte med stifter, hefte sammen, stagvende, gå baut; on the same — på samme baug; get on a new — slå inn på en ny framgangsmåte; on a wrong — på falsk spor.
tacket ['täkit] skosøm.
tackiness ['täkinĕs] klebrighet.
tackle ['täkl] takkel, talje, rigg; redskap, greier; takle, feste; gi seg i kast med; -d ['täkld] laget av tau. tackling ['täkliŋ] takkelasje, tauverk.
tacky ['täki] klebrig.
tact [täkt] berøring, følelse, takt, fint skjønn, riktig berøring, grep; want of — taktløshet; -ful taktfull.
tactic, tactical ['täktik(l)] taktisk. taktician [täk'tiʃən] taktiker. tactics ['täktiks] taktikk.
tactile ['täktil] følbar, føle-. tactility [täk'tiliti] følbarhet. taction ['täkʃən] berøring.
tactless ['täktlĕs] taktløs. -ness taktløshet.
tactual ['täkʃuəl] følelse-.
tadpole ['tädpoˑl]; rumpetroll.
tael [te¹l] tael (kinesisk vekt- og myntenhet).
taenia ['tiˑnjə] bånd; bendelorm.
taffeta ['täfitə], taffety ['täfiti] taft.
taff-rail ['täfre¹l] hakkebrett (øverste flate planke på skansekledningen akter).
Taffy ['täfi] valiser.
tag [täg] spiss, tipp, snipp, nebb, dopp (på lisse), tillegg, tilheng, merkelapp, omkved, moral, stikkord, pakk, pøbel, sisten (en lek); sette (nebb, spiss etc.) på, henge på, feste, henge etter, være påtrengende; -ger påhefter; den som har sisten.
tag-rag eller tagrag ['tägräg] eller tagrag and bobtail pøbel.
Tagus ['te¹gəs], the — Tajo.
Tahiti [tə'hiti] Tahiti.
tail [te¹l] hale, svans, ende, rumpe, hestehale, spord, pisk (i nakken), snippkjole; kø; begynnelsen (av en løpegrav); bakside, revers (av mynt); sette hale på, komme etter som en hale; head or — mynt og krone; get his — down stikke halen mellom bena; — off stikke av; — in (el. on) feste med enden i en mur; turn — snu ryggen til, flykte bort.
tail [te¹l] fideikommissarisk båndleggelse; båndlagt; estate — fideikommiss.
tail-board ['te¹lbåˑ°d] bakfjel, endefjel (på vogn).
tailcoat ['te¹lkoᵘt] kjole, snippkjole, snibel.
tailed [te¹ld] med hale.
tail-end ['te¹lend] haletipp; bakende; ende, slutt, avslutning.
tail-feather ['te¹l'feðə] halefjær.
tailing ['te¹liŋ] del av en stein.
tail-lamp ['te¹llämp] baklanterne (på tog el. bil).
tailless ['te¹llĕs] haleløs.
tail-light ['te¹llait] baklanterne (på tog el. bil).
tailor ['te¹lə] skredder; sy, være skredder. —-bird skredderfugl. -ing [-riŋ] skredderarbeid, skredderyrke. — -made skreddersydd; skreddersydd drakt.
tail-piece ['te¹lpiˑs] sluttvignett; baktunge (på fele).
tailstock ['te¹lståk] pinoldokke, bakdokke (i dreiebenk).
taint [te¹nt] forderve, forpeste, forgifte, smitte,

angripe, plette; bli smittet; plett, smitte, besmittelse, fordervelse, sykdom; snert; a scrofulous — kjertelsykdom. -less ubesmittet, plettfri.
take [te¹k] ta, gripe, fange, arrestere, fakke, overfalle, innta, beta, oppta, anta, besørge, ringe, greie, klare, fatte, skjønne, lure, narre; kreve; gjøre lykke, gjøre virkning, virke, slå an, ta fatt, pådra seg; tatt mengde; fangst; be -n ill bli syk; — (the) air trekke frisk luft; — (up) arms gripe til våpen; — breath dra pusten; — care dra omsorg; — the chair innta formannsplassen; — one's chance våge; — cold bli forkjølet; — a course ta en kurs; — delight in glede seg over; — a disease bli smittet; — effect gjøre virkning; — the field dra i felten; — fire fenge; — heart fatte mot; — a hint forstå en halvkvedet vise; — horse stige til hest; — a likeness tegne et portrett; — measure ta mål; — measures ta forholdsregler; — notice forstå (om barn); — notice of legge merke til; — an oath avlegge en ed; — pains gjøre seg umak; — place finne sted; — pleasure in finne fornøyelse i, ha moro av; — a pride in sette sin ære i; — shame skamme seg; — a summons ta ut en stevning; — a walk gå en tur; — the waters tigge ved bad; — one's word for it stole på det; — i forb. med preposisjon eller adverbium: — after etterligne, ligne, slekte på; — along with one ta med seg, tilegne seg; — away ta bort, berøve; — down ta til bords, undertrykke, skrive ned; — from ta bort, berøve, nedsette; — in ta inn, forminske, omfatte, ta med, få med, anta, oppta, holde (f. eks. et blad), oppfatte; narre, bedra; føre til bords; — in hand ta seg for; — in vain (bib.) ta forfengelig — off ta bort, forminske, slå av, holde tilbake, drikke ut, kjøpe, kopiere, etterape, gå opp (om fly); — on ta på seg, gjøre fordring på å være, ta seg nær av, ta på vei, skape seg; — out ta ut; — to gi seg til, oppofre seg for, ta tilflukt til, gjøre bruk av; ha sympati for, like, være glad i; — to the collar gå godt i seletøyet; — to heart ta seg nær av; — to pieces ta fra hverandre; — up oppta, påta seg, låne, begynne, fortsette, underbinde, gripe, irettesette, omfatte, samle inn; — up for beskytte; — up with være tilfreds med, bo hos; — with behage.
taker ['te¹kə] liebhaber, kjøper, erobrer.
taking ['te¹kiŋ] inntagende; opphisselse.
talao [tə'lau] (ord fra hindustansk) dam, reservoar.
talc [tälk] talkum.
tale [te¹l] telling, tall, regning, beretning, fortelling, historie, eventyr; hereby hangs a — til dette knytter det seg en historie; tell -s (out of school) sladre, fisle, fiske kunne holde tett. — -bearer sladderhank. —'-bearing sladring.
talent ['tälənt] talent, anlegg, begavelse.
talented [tä'läntid] talentfull.
tales ['te¹liˑz] jurysuppleanter.
tale-teller ['te¹lte ¹ə] sladderhank; forteller.
talion ['täljən] gjengjeldelsesrett.
taliped ['täliped] med klumpfot (el. bjørnefot).
talisman ['tälismən] talisman, tryllemiddel.
talk [tå·k] tale, snakke, fortelle, prate; samtale, rykte, folkesnakk, samtaleemne.
talkative ['tå·kətiv] snakksom, pratsom.
talkee-talkee ['tå·ki'tå·ki] snakk, pjatt, skravl.
talker ['tå·kə] vrøvlehode, skravlebøtte; konversasjonstalent.
talking-to ['tå·kiŋtuˑ] irettesetting.
tall [tå·l] høy, høg, stor, svær, diger, høyttravende, eventyrlig, forbløffende. -boy dragkiste. -ness høyde.
tallow ['täloᵘ] talg, talge, smøre (m. talg). —-chandler lysestøper. —-face bleikfjes, bleikfis. -er talghandler. -ish talgaktig, fettet.
tallowy ['täloᵘi] talgaktig, fet; — complexion blek ansiktsfarge.

tally ['täli] karvestokk, merke som betyr et bestemt tall, tilsvarende del, make, sidestykke, regnskap, telling; karve, skjære merker i, tilpasse, passe sammen. -man teller, en som fører regnskap. — with stemme (overens) med.

tally-ho ['täli'hoᵘ] rop, en jegers rop til hundene; heie.

Talmud ['tälməd] talmud, avhandlinger og forklaringer til den jødiske teologi og rett.

Talmudic [täl'mʌdik] talmudisk.

Talmudist ['tälmədist] talmudist.

talon ['tälən] en rovfugls klo; talong (i kortspill).

talook (indisk) jordegods, skattedistrikt.

talookdar (indisk) foged, godseier.

talus ['te'ləs] ankelbein; (med) bjørnefot; skråning; hall; ur.

tamable ['te'məbl] til å temme.

tamarind ['tämərind] tamarinde.

tamarisk ['tämərisk] tamarisk, klåved, klåris.

tambour ['tämbuə] tromme; broderramme; tamburin-broderi; tambur; sylindrisk stein i søyle; arbeid på broderramme.

tambourine [tämbu'ri·n] tamburin.

tame [te'm] tam, spak, spakferdig, motfallen, matt; temme, kue. -less utemt. -ly tamt, likegyldig, spakferdig. -ness tamhet, ydmykhet, matthet.

tamer ['te'mə] temmer.

Tammany ['tämənɪ] Society (eller Ring eller Hall), navn på en organisasjon av demokrater i New York, ofte nevnt som innbegrep av politisk korrupsjon.

tam-o'-shanter [tämə'Jäntə] skotsk lue.

tamper ['tämpə] prøve, eksperimentere, spille under dekke med, forkludre, klisse med, gi seg av med. pille ved.

tampion ['tämpiən] propp (av tre til kanon).

tampon ['tämpən] tampong (i sår); tamponere.

tan [tän] garvebark, barkfarge, solbrenthet; barke, garve, gjøre brun, gjøre solbrent, pryle. — -bed barkbed.

tandem ['tändəm] spent etter hverandre, sittende etter hverandre; tvibeite (med den ene hesten etter den andre); tandem.

tang [tän] tang, sjøtang.

tang [tän] ettersmak, skarp smak.

tang [tän] tange på kniv, klunk, tone; la klinge, klinge, klunke.

Tanganyika [ta·nga·n'ji·kə] Tanganyika.

tangency ['tändʒənsi] tangering, berøring.

tangent ['tändʒənt] tangent; berørende; go or fly off at a — ryke av sporet, slå plutselig om (i en ganske annen retning); komme plutselig ut av det.

tangibility [tändʒi'biliti] følbarhet, håndgripelighet, påtagelighet.

tangible ['tändʒibl] følbar, følelig, påtagelig.

tangle ['tängl] sammenfiltre, floke, innvikle, besnære, være innviklet.

tango ['tängoᵘ] tango (en dans).

tank [tänk] beholder, tank, cisterne; svær panservogn (til krigsbruk); anbringe i beholder(e), kaste i cisternen; (anglo-indisk:) dam, sjø.

tankard ['tänkəd] seidel, krus (med lokk).

tanker ['tänkə] tankbåt (til transport av olje).

tanner ['tänə] garver; (i slang) seks pence.

tannery ['tänəri] garveri.

tannin ['tänin] garvestoff, garvestyre.

tanning ['tänin] barking, garving; — solution garvestoffoppløsning.

tan-pit ['tänpit] garvekule; barkved.

tan-stove ['tänstoᵘv] drivhus med barkbed.

tansy ['tänzi] reinfann (plante).

tantalism ['täntəlizm] tantaluskval.

tantalization [täntəli'ze'ʃən] kval.

tantalize ['täntəlaiz] tantalisere, pine, erte.

tantalus ['täntələs] brennevinsoppsats hvor karaflene blir låst inn; tantalus (slags stork).

tantamount ['täntəmaunt] enstydende, jevngod (to med).

tantivy [tän'tivi] strykende fart; hurtig; fare.

tantrum ['täntrəm] dårlig humør; luner.

tan-vat ['tänvät] barkekar.

tan-yard ['tänja·ᵊd] garveri.

tap [täp] banke (lett) på, kakke, pikke, berøre; lett slag, banking; there was a — at the door det banket på døra.

tap [täp] tapp, tønnetapp, kran, ᵗ·ıre, skjenkestue; gjengetapp; tappe, ta hull på, anstikke; snappe opp (telegram el. telefonbeskjed fra ledningen); slå for penger.

tape [te'p] bendel, bånd, målesnor, papirstrimmel (i telegrafapparat), isolasjonsbånd; breast the — bryte snora, komme inn (i mål); -line målesnor.

taper ['te'pə] vokslys, kjerte, dåse; kjegleformig, tilspisset, fintformet, tynn; gradvis avta i tykkelse, løpe ut i en spiss, spisse til, smalne, avta, minke; lyse opp med vokslys; -ing ['te'pərin] tilspisset, smal. -ness kjegleform.

tapestry ['täpistri] tapet, åkle, veggteppe, gobelin; tapetsere; — -curtain portière.

tapeworm ['te'pwə·m] bendelorm.

tapir ['te'pə] tapir.

tapis ['täpi·] teppe; be on the — være på tapetet, stå på dagsordenen, være i gang.

tapper ['täpə] bankende person; telegrafnøkkel.

tappet ['täpit] medbringer, styrekloss.

tap-room ['täprᵤ·m] skjenkestue.

tap-root ['täprᵤ·t] pelerot.

tapster ['täpstə] vintapper, øltapper.

tar [ta·ᵊ] tjære, matros, sjøgutt; tjære, tjærebre; an old — en sjøulk.

tarantas [tärən'telə] tarantella (en dans).

tarantula [tə'räntjulə] tarantell (slags edderkopp).

tardiness ['ta·ᵊdinês] langsomhet.

tardy ['ta·ᵊdi] langsom, sein, sendrektig, treg.

tare [tæ·ə] vikke, (bibelsk) klinte.

tare [tæ·ə] tara (vekt av emballasje).

target ['ta·ᵊgit] skyteskive; gjenstand, mål, skive; — for their scorn gjenstand for deres hån.

tariff ['tärif] tariff, tolltariff, toll; — reform tollreform, (især om en) politikk som går ut på å innføre beskyttelsestoll; — war tollkrig.

tarlatan ['ta·ᵊlətən] tarlatan (musselin).

tarn [ta·ᵊn] tjern, lite fjellvann.

tarnish ['ta·ᵊniʃ] ta glansen av, flekke, fordunkle, anløpe, falme, miste glansen.

taroc ['tärok] tarokk (et slags kortspill).

tarpaulin, tarpawlin [ta·ᵊ'pä·lin] presenning, tjæret matroshatt, matros, sjøgast.

tarry ['ta·ri] tjære-, tjæret, sjømannsmessig.

tarry ['täri] (gml.) nøle, ble, dryge, dvele, vente på.

tart [ta·ᵊt] terte; (i slang) pikebarn, flokse, tøs.

tart [ta·ᵊt] sur, skarp, bitende, bitter.

tartan ['ta·ᵊtən] tartan, rutet skotsk tøy.

Tartar ['ta·ᵊtə] tatar; tyrk, ren satan, drage; catch a — få med sin overmann å bestille, finne sin overmann, treffe den rette.

tartar ['ta·ᵊtə] vinstein, tannstein. -ic [ta·ᵊ-'tärik] vinstein. -ise ['ta·ᵊtəraiz] behandle med vinstein. -ous vinsteinaktig.

Tartary ['ta·ᵊtəri] tatarenes land.

tartish ['ta·ᵊtiʃ] litt skarp.

tartlet ['ta·ᵊtlêt] liten terte.

tartness ['ta·ᵊtnês] skarphet.

task [ta·sk] (pålagt) arbeid, plikt, verv, lekse, oppgave, gjerning, yrke, sette i arbeid, plage, legge beslag på; take to — ta i skole. — -master arbeidsgiver, oppsynsmann; plager. — -work pliktarbeid, akkordarbeid.

Tasmania [täz'me'njə] Tasmania.

tassel ['täsl] dusk, kvast; merkebånd (i en bok); besette med kvaster; typpe, ta toppen(e) av.

tastable ['te'stəbl] som kan smakes, velsmakende.

taste [te'st] smake, prøve, ha smak, nyte, smake på; smak, anstrøk, snev, sans; **in bad** — smakløs; **in good** — smakfull. **-ful** velsmakende, smakfull. **-less** uten smak, smakløs.
taster ['te'stə] prøver.
tasty ['te'sti] smakfull, med smak.
tat [tät]; **tit for** — like for like.
tat [tät] slå nupereller.
ta-ta ['tä'ta·] (i barnespråk) na-na, farvel.
Tatar ['ta·ta·ə] se **Tartar.**
Tate [te't] **Gallery,** malerisamling i London.
tats [täts] filler, kluter; **milky** — hvite kluter.
tatter ['tätə] rive i filler; fille. **-demalion** [-di-'mäljən] fillefant.
Tattersall ['tätəsəl]; **-'s** etablissement for hesteauksjoner i London.
tatting ['tätiŋ] nupereller, slags filering, arbeidet med å slå nupereller.
tattle ['tätl] skravle, sladre; sladder, prek.
tattler ['tätlə] pratmaker, skravlebøtte.
tattling ['tätliŋ] skravlet.
tattoo [tä'tu·] tappenstrek; tromme med fingrene el. føttene; slå tappenstrek.
tattoo [tä'tu·] tatovere; tatovering.
taube ['taubə] en tysk aeıoplantype.
taught [tå·t] imperf. og perf. pts. av **teach.**
taunt [tå·nt] håne, spotte, neise; hån, spe, spott. **-er** spotter. **-ingly** hånende, spottende.
Taurus ['tå·rəs] Taurus; Tyren (stjernebildet).
taut [tå·t] tott, stram, kraftig; ordentlig, nett, fin; **haul** — hale tott. **-en** strammes, totne.
tautological [tå·to'lådʒikl] tautologisk, unødig gjentagende. tautology [tå·'tålədʒi] tautologi.
tautophony [tå·'tåfoni] gjentagelse av samme tone, mislyd.
tavern ['tävən] gjestgiveri, vertshus, kafé. **-er** restauratør, gjestgiver. **-haunter** stamgjest.
taw [tå·] hvitgarve.
taw [tå·] klink; kiksekule; mål (i klink).
tawdriness ['tå·drinès] glødende farger, flitterstas. tawdry ['tå·dri] glødende, utmaiet, spraglet, gloret.
tawer ['tå·ə] garver, hvitgarver.
tawny ['tå·ni] brunlig, solbrent, gulbrun.
tax [täks] skatt, byrde, krav; skattlegge, pålegge skatt, bebyrde, dadle, klandre, beskylde **(with** for), anstrenge; **direct** — direkte skatt; **indirect** — indirekte skatt. **taxable** ['täksəbl] skattepliktig. **taxation** [täk'se'ʃən] beskatning, skattlegging, skatt.
tax-cart ['täkska.ºt] lett kjerre·
tax|-collector ['täkskəlektə] skatteoppkrever. **-free** skattefri. **— -gatherer** skatteoppkrever.
taxicab ['täksikäb] el. **taxi** ['täksi] bil (oppr. med taksameter).
taxidermy ['täksidə·mi] utstopping.
taximeter ['täksimi·tə] taksameter.
taxpayer ['täkspe'ə] skatteborger, skattyter.
T. B. fk. f. torpedo-boat; tuberculosis.
T. B. D. fk. f. torpedo-boat destroyer.
T. C. fk. f. Tank Corps; temporary constable; Trinity College.
tea [ti·] te, tebusk, ekstrakt; drikke te, traktere med te; **take (or** have) — drikke te. — **-board** tebrett. **— -caddy** tedåse.
teach [ti·tʃ] lære, undervise; **— school** undervise i skoler; **go and — your grandmother** egget vil lære høna å verpe. **-able** lærvillig, lærenem. **-ableness** lærvillighet, mottagelighet for undervisning.
teacher ['ti·tʃə] lærer, lærerinne.
tea-cup ['ti·kʌp] tekopp.
teak [ti·k] teaktre.
teal [ti·l] krikkand.
team [ti·m] flokk; spann, kobbel, beite; skift, lag; spenne sammen. **-ster** ['ti·mstə] spannkjører.
team-work ['ti·mwə·k] skiftarbeid, akkordarbeid.
tea-party ['ti·pa·ºti] teselskap.
tea-pot ['ti·påt] tekanne.

tear [tiə] tåre; **in tears** gråtende; **shed tears** gråte; **burst into tears** briste i gråt.
tear [tæ·ə] rive, rive i stykker, slite, rive bort, revne, springe, storme, styrte, fare, rase; rift, revne, spjære; rasende fart; **— along** fare av sted. **-er** en som river, buldrebasse.
tearful ['tiəful] tårefylt; gråtende, med tårer. tearing ['tæ·ºring heftig, voldsom.
tearless ['tiəlès] uten tårer.
tea-rose ['ti·ro'z] terose.
tear-shell ['tiəʃel] tåregass-bombe el. -granet.
tear-stained ['tiəste'nd] forgrått.
tease [ti·z] greie ut; plukke opp, karde; plage, erte; ertekrok.
teasel ['ti·zl] karde-borre, karde-tistel; karde opp, loe opp.
teaser ['ti·zə] ertekrok, plageånd; floke, vanskelig spørsmål el. arbeid.
teaspoon ['ti·spu·n] teskje.
teaspoonful ['ti·spu·nful] (en full) teskje.
teat [ti·t] brystvorte, spene, patte; tåtesmokk, narresutt.
tea-things ['ti·þiŋz] testell.
tea-time ['titaim] tetid (især omkring kl. 4 om ettermiddagen).
tea-urn ['ti·ə·n] temaskin.
teaze = **tease.**
tec [tek] vulgært for: **detective.**
technical ['teknikl] teknisk, fag-; **— term** fag-uttrykk.
technicality [tekni'käliti] teknisk karakter, faglighet; fagutrykk; faglig finesse.
technics ['tekniks] teknikk.
technology [tek'nålədʒi] teknologi.
techy ['tetʃi] pirrelig, gretten.
Ted [ted] fk. f. **Edward** el. **Theodore.**
ted [ted] breie (høy). **-der** høyvender.
Teddy ['tedi] fk. f. **Edward; Theodore.**
Te Deum [ti·'di·əm] Te Deum (den ambrosianske lovsang), takkegudstjeneste.
tedious ['ti·djəs] trettende, kjedelig, kjedsommelig, vidløftig, langtekkelig, langsom. **-ness** kjedelighet.
tedium ['ti·djəm] kjedsommelighet.
tee [ti·] underlag for ballen i golf, hvorfra første slag gjøres, mål (i visse spill, f. eks. curling); anbringe ballen på underlaget; **— off** gjøre det første slag i golf, spille ut, begynne noe.
tee [ti·] bokstaven T; noe T-formet.
teerf [ti·] sesamplante, sesamfrø. **— -oil** sesamolje.
teem [ti·m] yngle, formere seg, bære frukt, være drektig, være full, yre, kry **(with** av) føde, frambringe. **-er** fødende. **-less** ufruktbar.
teens [ti·nz] alder fra og med 13 til og med 19 år; **she is in her** — hun er ennå ikke 20 år.
teeny ['ti·ni] (barnespråk) liten.
teeth [ti·þ] tenner (av **tooth**).
teethe [ti·ð] få tenner; **suffer from teething** være syk for tenner.
teetotaler [ti·'to'tlə] totalist, avholdsmann.
teetotalism [ti·'to'talizm] totalavhold.
teetotum [ti·'to'təm] snurrebass, ‹jakop›, topp.
t. e. g. fk. f. top edge gilt.
tegular ['tegjulə] tegl-, teglsteins-, taklagt.
tehee [ti'hi·] knis; fnise, knise.
teil [ti·l], **— -tree** lind, lindetre.
telary ['telori] vevd, spunnet.
telegram ['teligräm] telegram.
telegraph ['teligra·f] telegraf; telegrafere. **-clerk** telegrafist. **-er** telegrafist. **-ese** [teligra·'fi·z] telegramstil.
telegraphic [teli'gräfik] telegrafisk, telegram-; **— bureau** telegrambyrå.
telegraphist [ti'legrəfist] telegrafist.
telegraphy [ti'legrəfi] telegrafi.
Telemachus [ti'leməkəs] Telemachos.
teleologic(al) ['telio'lådʒik(l)] teleologisk. **teleology** [teli'ålədʒi] teleologi (læren om verdensordenens hensiktsmessighet).

telepathic [teli'päþik] telepatisk.
telepathy [ti'lepəþi] telepati.
telephone ['telifoᵘn] telefon; telefonere; **ring up on the** — ringe opp; **answer the** — ta telefonen; **ring off the** — ringe av; — **call** telefonoppringning; — **directory** telefonkatalog. **telephonic** [teli'fånik] telefonisk. **telephonist** [ti'lefənist] telefondame, telefonist(inne).
telephony [ti'lefəni] telefonering.
telephotography ['telifə'tågrəfi] fjernfotografering.
teleplasma [teli'pläzmə] teleplasma.
telescope ['teliskoᵘp] kikkert, teleskop.
telescopic [teli'skåpik] teleskopisk.
teleseme ['telisi·m] elektrisk signalapparat.
tell [tel] telle; fortelle; si (til), be, by, befale; sladre, fisle; oppdage, skjelne; gjøre virkning (**on** på), monne, leite, røyne, ta (**on** på), virke nedbrytende (på); **who told you?** hvem har fortalt deg det? — **on** (**of**) sladre på; — **me** si meg; **I cannot** — jeg vet ikke; **I have been told** jeg har hørt; — **him to do it** si til ham at han skal gjøre det; **he was told to go** man bad ham om å gå, man sa til ham at han skulle gå; **every expression told** hvert ord gjorde sin virkning; **every shot tells** hver kule treffer. **-er** forteller, teller, kasserer, stemmeoppteller. **-ing** virkningsfull.
telltale ['telteᵘl] sladderhank; telleapparat; sladderaktig, forrædersk.
telluric [tel'juərik] jordisk.
telpherage ['telfəridʒ] automatisk elektrisk varetransport.
temerarious [temi'ræ·əriəs] ubesindig, uvøren.
temerity [ti'meriti] forvovenhet, dumdristighet.
temper ['tempə] blande, elte sammen, formilde, mildne, dempe, temperere, sette sammen, avpasse, stemme, herde; (passende) blanding, herding, hardhetsgrad, legems- og sinnsbeskaffenhet, natur, sinn, lynde, stemning, lune, fatning, sinnsro, godt humør, heftighet, sinne; **in a good** (**bad**) — i godt (dårlig) humør; **when the** — **is on him** når hissigheten løper av med ham; **have -s** lide av humørsyke.
temperament ['tempərəment] indre beskaffenhet, temperament, lynde, konstitusjon.
temperamental ['tempərə'mentəl] temperamentsbestemt.
temperance ['tempərəns] avhold, måtehold; — **hotel** avholdshotell. **temperate** ['tempərét] temperert, måteholden. **-ness** temperert beskaffenhet, måtehold.
temperature ['tempərətʃə] temperatur.
tempest ['tempist] storm, uvær, opprør (i sinnet). **-uous** [tem'pestjuəs] stormfull, stormende. **-uousness** [tem'pestjuəsnés] stormfullhet.
templar ['templə] tempelherre; jurist; goodtemplar.
temple ['templ] tempel; **the Temple** navnet på to bygningskomplekser i London ved den tidligere byport, **Temple Bar**, med beboelse for jurister.
temple ['templ] tinning. — **-bone** tinningben.
tempo ['tempoᵘ] tempo.
temporal ['temp(ə)rəl] tinning-.
temporal ['temp(ə)rəl] timelig, verdslig. **-ity** [-'räliti] timelig velferd, verdslige inntekter, temporalier.
temporary ['tempərəri] midlertidig. **temporariness** midlertidighet.
temporize ['tempəraiz] se tiden an, forsøke å vinne tid, rette seg etter tid og omstendigheter. **temporizer** vendekåpe, værhane.
tempt [temt] forsøke, prøve, friste. **-ation** [tem'te¹ʃən] fristelse. **-er** frister. **-ing** fristende.
ten [ten] ti, tier; **the upper** — (**thousand**) spissene i samfunnet. — **in the hundred** ti prosent.
tenable ['tenəbl] holdbar, som kan forsvares. **-ness, tenability** [tenə'biliti] holdbarhet.
tenacious [ti'ne¹ʃəs] klebrig, seig, stri, hard-

nakket, sikker; — **of life** seiglivet. **tenacity** [ti'näsiti] hårdnakkethet, klebrighet, seighet.
tenancy ['tenənsi] besittelse, forpakting.
tenant ['tenənt] innehaver, besitter, leier, forpakter, bruker, leilending, oppsitter, beboer; forpakte, bebo, besitte, leie, sitte med: — **for life** bygselmann på livstid. — **-at -will** forpakter på åremål. — **in-capite** [-in'käpiti] kronforpakter, kronvasall. — **-in-chief** kronvasall. — **-right** forpakters erstatningsrett.
tenantry ['tenəntri] forpaktere, leilendinger.
tench [tenʃ] suter (en fisk).
tend [tend] ha en viss retning, gå i en viss retning, tendere, strebe, sikte på, tjene til.
tend [tend] betjene, varte opp, passe, stelle, røkte, pleie, ledsage; — **upon** varte opp, pleie. **-ance** betjening.
tendency ['tendənsi] tendens, retning, tilbøyelighet.
tender ['tendə] tender (bl. a. jernbanevogn med brensel til lokomotiv); **bar-tender** [amr.) oppvarter.
tender ['tendə] tilby, gjøre tilbud; tilbud, anbud, forslag; **legal** — lovlig betalingsmiddel.
tender ['tendə] bløt, mør, øm, mild, ømskinnet, sped, sart, fin, følsom, nennsom, vyrk, var, varsom; rank; elsket; elske, sette pris på; **a** — **strain** ømme toner; **a** — **subject** et kildent emne.
tender|foot ['tendəfut] nykomling, grønnskolling. — **-footed** forsiktig, fryktsom, ny (i stillingen), grønn. — **-hearted** bløthjertet. **-ling** kjæledegge; blauting; første horn (på rådyr). **-loin** ['tendəloin] filet, mørbrad. **-ness** bløthet, følsomhet, svakhet, ømhet, nennsomhet.
tendinous ['tendinəs] senet.
tendon ['tendən] sene.
tendril ['tendril] slyngtråd.
tenebrific [teni'brifik] formørkende, skyggende.
tenebrous ['tenibrəs] mørk, skummel.
tenebrosity [teni'bråsiti] mørke, skummelhet.
tenement ['tenimənt] leilighet, bolig; — **house** leiegård, leiekaserne. **-al** [-'mentəl], **-ary** [-'mentəri] som kan bortforpaktes, som kan leies.
tenet ['tenet] grunnsetning, læresetning, trossetning, dogme.
tenfold ['tenfoᵘld] tifold, tidobbelt.
Tennessee [tene'si·] Tennessee.
tennis ['tenis] tennis (både court-tennis og lawn-tennis, undertiden dog spesielt om court-tennis). — **-court** [-kå·ᵃt] tennisplass. — **-ground** tennisplass.
Tennyson ['tenisən] Tennyson.
tenon ['tenən] tapp; sinke, skjære tapp(er) i, tappe sammen.
tenor ['tenə] gang, løp, måte, vesen, innhold, tenor. **-violin** bratsj.
tense [tens] tid, tempus (i grammatikk).
tense [tens] spent, stram. **tensible** ['tensibl] **tensile** ['tensil] strekkelig, strekkbar. **tension** ['tenʃən] spenning; spennkraft. **tensive** ['tensiv] strammende. **tensor** ['tensə] strekkemuskel.
tent [tent] telt, bolig, folie (under edelsteiner); ligge i telt; **pitch a** — slå opp et telt.
tent [tent] sonde, charpi; sondere, prøve.
tentacle ['tentəkl] værhår, følehorn, fangarm.
tentative ['tentətiv] som prøver (seg fram), forsøksvis; (forsiktig) forsøk.
tenter]'tentə] som en ligger i telt.
tenter ['tentə] klesramme, strekke- el. tørkeramme (til tøy); spenne på en ramme.
tenterhooks ['tentəhuks] kroker pa tørkestativ; **on** — i pinlig spenning, utålmodig, som på nåler.
tenth [tenþ] tiende; tiendedel.
tenthly ['tenþli] for det tiende.
tentlike ['tentlaik] teltformet.
tentmaker ['tentme¹kə] teltmaker.
tent-peg ['tentpeg] teltplugg; **-ging** teltplugg-spill (sport i India; det gjelder om at rytteren med sin lanse får fatt i en nedrammet teltplugg.

tenuity [ti'nju·iti] tynnhet, finhet.
tenuous ['tenjuəs] tynn, grann, fin.
tenure ['tenjə] lensbesittelse, forpaktning, besittelse.
tepefaction [tepi'fäkʃən] lunking.
tepefy ['tepifai] lunke; bli lunken.
tepid ['tepid] lunken.
tepidity [te'piditi] lunkenhet.
terebrate ['teribre¹t] bore (gjennom).
tergiversation [tə'dʒivə'se¹ʃən] utflukt, vankelmodighet, vingel.
term [tə·m] grense, ende, termin, frist, periode, kvartal, betalingsdag, uttrykk, ledd, rettens sesjons-tid, rettstermin, fordring, (i plur.) vilkår, betingelse, pris; (fig.) fot; benevne, kalle. -er ['tə·mə] en som innfinner seg ved rettsterminer, markedsgjøgler, forpakter på åremål.
termdgant ['tə·məgənt] xantippe.
terminable ['tə·minəbl] begrenselig, oppheveig, oppsigelse. -inal ['tə·minəl] ende-; ytter-, ytterst, termin-. -inate ['tə·mine¹t] begrense, ende, avslutte, opphøre. -ination [tə·mi'ne¹ʃən] begrensning, ende, slutning. -inative ['tə·minətiv] avsluttende, avgjørende, endelig, absolutt.
terminus ['tə·minəs], pl. termini ['tə·minai] grense, endestasjon.
termite ['tə·mait] termitt (hvit maur).
tern [tə·n] terne (fuglen).
ternary ['tə·nəri] tre-; treer, gruppe av tre.
Terpsichore [tə·p'sikori·] Terpsichore, korsangens og dansens muse.
terrace ['teris] terrasse, flatt tak, altan, gate med én husrekke; legge terrassevis.
terra-cotta ['terə'kátə] terrakotta.
terrain ['tere¹n] terreng, lende.
terraqueous [tə're¹kwiəs] som består av land og vann.
terrene [tə'ri·n] jord-, jordisk.
terrestrial [tə'restriəl] jord-, jordisk; jordboer.
terrible ['teribl] fæl, forferdelig, fryktelig. -ness ['teriblnés] fryktelighet, fælske.
terrier ['teriə] rottehund, terrier.
terrific [tə'rifik] fryktelig, skrekkinnjagende.
terrify ['terifai] forferde, skremme.
territorial [teri'tå·riəl] territorial; landvernssoldat.
territory ['teritəri] territorium, område.
terror ['terə] skrekk, redsel. -ism ['terərizm] terrorisme, redselsherredømme. -ist ['terərist] voldsherre. -ize ['terəraiz] terrorisere.
terse [tə.s] fin, enkel, fyndig, klar, rammende.
tertian ['tə·ʃən] annendagsfeber.
tertiary ['tə·ʃəri] tertiær.
tessellate ['tesile¹t] gjøre ternet el. rutet; innlegge med mosaikk
tessera ['tesərə] firkant, terning, rute, billett.
test [test] prøvedigel, prøvemiddel, prøvestein; prøve, undersøkelse; probere, prøve. take the — avlegge eden, nemlig på ikke å være katolikk; put to the — sette på prøve; Test Act ['test'äkt] Test-Akt, forordning om religions-ed.
testacean [te'ste¹ʃən] skalldyr.
testament ['testəmənt] testament, siste vilje, testamente. -ary [testə'mentəri] testamentarisk.
testator [te'ste¹tə] testator, arvelater.
testamur [te'ste¹mə] eksamensbevis, eksamensvitnesbyrd, vitnemål, testimonium.
tester ['testə] baldakin, senghimmel.
testify ['testifai] bevitne, vitne.
testimonial [testi'moⁿnjəl] vitnesbyrd, vitnemål- attest, minnegave, monument; som angår vitnesbyrd.
testimony ['testimᵊni] vitnesbyrd, vitnemål, bevis; vitneutsagn; vitneprov, vitneerklæring.
testiness ['testinés] arrigskap.
test-tube ['testtju·b] reagensglass.
testudo [te'stju·do⁰] skjoldtak, skjoldborg.
testy ['testi] arg, gretten, amper, irritabel.
tetanus ['tetənəs] stivkrampe.

tetchy ['tetʃi] pirrelig.
tete-a-tete ['te¹t a· -te¹t] samtale under fire øyne; fortrolig.
tether ['teðə] tjor; tjore, binde; be at the end of one's — ha strakt seg så langt som mulig, være ved grensen, ha nådd bunnen.
tetrarch ['tetra·ᵊk] tetrark, fjerdingsfyrste.
tetter ['tetə] utslett; smitte med utslett.
Teutonic [tju'tånik] teutonsk, germansk, tysk.
tew [tju·] bearbeide, banke, garve.
Tex. fk. f. Texas.
text [tekst] tekst, emne; skriftsted. — -book tekstbok, lærebok.
textile ['tekstail] vevd; vevd stoff.
textual ['tekstʃuəl] tekst-, om el. i teksten.
texture ['tekstʃə] veving, vev, sammensetning.
T. F. fk. f. Territorial Force.
Thackeray ['θäkəri] Thackeray.
Thalia [θə'laiə] Thalia, komediens muse.
Thames [temz], the — Temsen; he never set the — on fire· han har ikke oppfunnet kruttet.
than [ðän, alm. svakt ðən] enn; we need go no farther — (enn til) France; he showed more courage — (enn det) was to be expected.
thane [θe¹n] than, thegn, angelsaksisk stormann.
thank [θäŋk] takke; — you! takk; no, — you nei takk! — you very much! mange takk; — you for nothing! det er ikke noe å takke Dem for!
thankful ['θäŋkful] takknemlig.
thankless ['θäŋklés] utakknemlig.
thanks [θäŋks] takk, takksigelser; many — to you! mange takk! render — si takk.
thanksgiving ['θäŋksgiviŋ] takksigelse, takkefest.
thankworthy ['θäŋkwə·ði] påskjønnelsesverdig.
that [ðät] 1. (påpekende pronomen) den, det, den (el. det) der, (i plur. those de); 2. [ðət] (relativt pronomen) som (nesten bare brukt i nødvendige relativsetninger); 3. [ðət] (konjunksjon) at, så at, for at; fordi; gid; 4. [ðät] (adverbium) så. Eksempler: 1. that's a good girl så er du snill jente; that which det som, hva som; there are those who (dem, som) say; in that idet, forsåvidt, fordi; 2. all that alt hva; those that love us de som er glad i oss; the books that you lent me de bøkene som du lånte meg; 3. I know that it is so jeg vet at det forholder seg slik; I am so tired, that I cannot go on jeg er så trett at jeg ikke kan fortsette; 4. I was that tired jeg var så trett.
thatch [θätʃ] tekkehalm, halmtak; halmtekke. -er halmtekker.
thaw [θå·] tø, tine opp; tøvær, linnvær, linne.
the [foran vokal og ofte foran [j]-lyd ði, foran konsonant ðə, med sterk betoning ði·] den, det, de; -(e)n, -(e)t, (e)ne; dess, desto, jo; — boy gutten; — big boy den store gutten; — boy who den gutten som; is he — (den kjente) Dr. Johnson? — less så meget mindre; — sooner — better jo før jo heller.
theatre ['þi(·)ətə] teater, skueplass, sal, anatomisk forelesningssal. — of war krigsskueplass.
theatrical [þi'ätrikl] teatralsk, teater-, teatermessig; (i plur.) teatersaker, forestillinger; private -s dilettantkomedie.
thee [ði·] (gammel:) deg; (i dialekt og kvekerspråk:) du.
theft [þeft] tyveri.
their [ðæ·ə] deres; sin; — money deres penger.
theirs [ðæ·əz] deres; sin; the money is — pengene er deres.
theism ['þi·izm] teisme.
theist ['þi·ist] teist (tilhenger av teismen).
them [ðem, alm. svakt ðəm] dem (etter prep. også) seg.
theme [þi·m] tema, emne, oppgave, avhandling, stil; (i grammatikk) stamme.
themselves [ðəm'selvz] seg; seg selv; (dem) selv; (de) selv; they defend — de forsvarer seg.

then [ðen] da, dengang, på den tid, deretter, derpå, så, derfor, i det tilfelle; daværende; — **and there** på stående fot, på stedet, straks; **by** — da, inntil da; **from** — onwards fra den tid av; **till** — inntil da; **the** — (daværende) **governor; in my** — mood of mind i min daværende stemning; **in my** — state of confusion forvirret som jeg var.
thence [ðens] derfra, deretter, fra den tid, derfor; **from** — derfra. **-forth** ['ðens'få· əþ], **-forward** [ðens'få· əwəd] fra den tid av.
theol. fk. f. **theology.**
theologian [þi·ə'lo udʒiən] teolog.
theologic(al) [þi·ə'ladʒik(l)] teologisk.
theologist [þi'alədʒist] teolog.
theorem ['þiərem] teorem, læresetning.
theoretic(al) [þiə'retik(l)] teoretisk.
theorize ['þiəraiz] teoretisere.
theory ['þiəri] teori.
theosophic(al) [þiə'såfik(l)] teosofisk.
theosophist [þi'åsofist] teosof.
theosophy [þi'åsofi] teosofi.
therapeutic [þerə'pju·tik] terapevtisk, legende.
there [ðæ·ə, svakt ðə] der, dit; — **'s a good boy** så er du snill; — **you are** vær så god, se så! — **he** is der er han; — **is** det er. **-about** der omkring. **-after** deretter. **-at** derved. **-by** derved. **-fore** derfor, følgelig. **-from** derfra. **-in** [þæ·ə'rin] deri. **-inafter** [ðæ·ə'rin'a·ftə] i det følgende. **-of** [ðæ·ə'råv] derav. **-to** dertil. **-unto** dertil. **-upon** derpå, på grunnlag av det, derfor, straks deretter. **-with** dermed. **-withal** [ðæ·əwi'då·l] dermed.
thermometer [þə·'måmitə] termometer, gradestokk.
thermos ['þə·mås] slags termosflaske.
thesaurus [þi'så·rəs] skattkammer, ordbok.
these [ði·z] disse (plur. av this).
thesis ['þi·sis] tese, oppgave,(doktor)avhandling.
thew [þju·] muskelkraft. **-y** ['þju·i] muskuløs.
they [ðe'] de; man, en, folk.
thick [þik] tykk, tett, uklar, grumset, gjørmet; grøtet; det tykke; kjøtthue; **lay it on** — smøre tykt på; **speak** — snakke utydelig. — **of hearing** tunghørt.
thick-and-thin ['þikən'þin] som går med i tykt og tynt, svoren, trofast.
thicken ['þikn] gjøre tykk, bli tykk, tykne, formere(s), tilta.
thicket ['þikit] tykning, kratt, skogsnar.
thick|-headed ['þikhedid] «tjukk i hue». **-ish** [-þikiʃ] nokså tykk. **-ness** tykkhet, tykkelse; **-ness of hearing** tunghørthet. — **-set** tett besatt, rikelig utstyrt; undersetsig. — **-witted** tungnem.
thief [þi·f] tyv, tjuv. — **-proof** sikker mot tyver. **thieve** [þi·v] stjele. **thieves** [þi·vz] tyver, tjuver. **thieving** tyvaktighet. **thievish** tyvaktig.
thigh [þai] lår.
thill [þil] skåk.
thimble ['þimbl] fingerbøl.
thin [þin] tynn, smal, skrinn; mager, fin; grissen; fortynne, tynne ut, spe, rydde opp i; bli tynnere.
thine [ðain] (gmlt.) din, ditt, dine.
thing [þiŋ] ting, sak, greie, tingest; **poor little** — stakkars liten; **she is a proud little** — hun er et stolt lite vesen; **I am not quite the** — jeg føler meg ikke helt vel; **-s** pl. ting, greier, reisetøy; **good -s** vittigheter, god mat.
thingumny ['þiŋəmi] tingest (om en ting, som man har glemt navnet på); han (el. hun) derre, hva det nå er han (el. hun) heter, noksagt (om person).
think [þiŋk] tenke, tenke seg om, ha i sinne, anse for, synes, innbille seg; — **of** tenke på, tenke om; — **on** tenke over, pønse på; — **much of** ha store tanker om. **-able** tenkelig. **-er** tenker. **-ing** tenksom; tenkning, tanker, mening.
third [þə·d] tredje, tredjedel, ters. **-ly** for det tredje.

thirst [þə·st] tørst; tørste; — **of** tørst etter.
thirsty ['þə·sti] tørst.
thirteen ['þə·'ti·n] tretten. **-th** ['þə·'ti·nþ] trettende, trettendedel.
thirtieth ['þə·tiiþ] tredevte, trettiende tredevtedel, trettiendedel. **thirty** ['þə·ti] tredve, tretti.
this [ðis] i plur. **these** [ði·z] denne, dette, plur. disse; brukt i substantivisk er **this** bare upersonlig: dette, **these** derimot også personlig; **by** — hermed, nå; **by** — time nå; — morning imorges, i formiddag; **at** — day (ennå) den dag i dag; — **day week** i dag åtte dager, i dag for åtte dager siden; — **(last)** half- hour i den siste halve time; **like** — således, slik, på denne måte; — **much** så meget, dette (iallfall); **leave** — dra herfra; **these forty years** nå i førti år.
thistle ['þisl] tistel.
thither ['ðiðə] dit. **-ward** dit over, dit bort.
thole [þo ul] tåle.
thole [þo ul] åretoll, tollepinne; **the -s** tollegangen.
Thomas ['tåməs] Tomas.
Thom(p)son ['tåmsən] Thomson.
thong [þåŋ] reim; piske.
thorn [þå·ən] torn, vedtorn, hagtorn; thorn (bokstaven þ); **a** — in the side en torn i kjøttet. — **-apple** piggeple.
thorny ['þå·əni] tornefull.
thorough ['þʌrə] fullstendig, inngående. grundig. **-bred** veloppdragen, fullblods. **-fare** gjennomgang, ferdselsåre, (hoved)gate. **-going** fullstendig, grundig. **-ly** ganske fullkommen. **-ness** fullstendighet, grundighet.
Thos. fk. f. **Thomas.**
those [ðo uz] de, dem, hine (plur. av **that**).
thou [ðau] (gml.) du; si du til, dutte.
though [ðo u] skjønt, enskjønt, selv om; (sist i setningen) likevel; **as** — som om; even — selv om; **what** — hva om; **it is dangerous** — det er likevel farlig; **did she** — gjorde hun virkelig.
thought [þå·t] tanke, tenkeevne, tenkning; en liten smule; **-ful** tankefull, hensynsfull, oppmerksom, bekymret, alvorlig. **-less** tankeløs, tanketom, atspredt, ubekymret, likegyldig. — **-reading** tankelesning. — **-transference** tankeoverføring, telepati.
thousand ['þauz(ə)nd] tusen. **-th** ['þauz(ə)nþ] tusendel.
thraldom ['þrå·ldəm] trelldom.
thral [þrå·l] trell, trelldom; trelke.
thrash [þræʃ] treske; banke, jule, denge; tresker, treskeverk; revehai (slags hai); **-ing** også: juling. **-ing floor** treskegolv. **-ing-machine** treskeverk.
thread [þred] tråd, tråd garn, skruegjenge; træ (en nål), trenge igjennom. **-bare** loslitt, forslitt. — **-paper** vindsel, tynn (strant). **-worm** trådorm. **-y** trådaktig.
threat [þret] trusel.
threaten ['þretn] true (med). **-ing** truende.
three [þri·] tre, treer, tretall. **-fold** trefold; tredobbel. — **-foot** treføtt. **-pence** ['þri·pəns] tre pence. **-penny** ['þripəni] til 21 øre, 21 øres, godtkjøps. **-score** seksti.
threne [þri·n] klage.
threnode ['þri·no ud] klagesang.
thresh [þreʃ] osv. se **thrash.**
threshold ['þreʃo uld] terskel, dørstokk, svill, inngang, begynnelse.
threw [þru·] imperf. av **throw.**
thrice [þrais] tre ganger (nå mest: **three times**).
thrift [þrift] sparsommelighet, økonomi. **-iness** sparsommelighet. **-less** ødsel. **-y** sparsommelig, velstående, kraftig.
thrill [þril] gysing, sitring, spenning; gjennombeve(s), beta, dirre; **it sent a** — of regret through me det fikk meg til å skjelve av sorg; **a** — of horror en redselsgysing; — **to** the bone gå gjen, nom marg og bein; **-ing** ogs. gjennomtrengende-spennende, gripende.

thrive [þraiv] trives, blomstre, være heldig, slå seg opp. **thriving** oppblomstrende; blomstring.

throat [þrouᵗ] svelg, strupe, hals, trang åpning, inngang, munning; **cut a person's** — skjære halsen over på en; **have a sore** — ha vondt i halsen. — **-pipe** luftrør. **-y** guttural.

throb [þråb] banke, pikke (om puls, hjerte), banke hurtig; banking, slag; **with a -bing** (hurtig bankende) **pulse.**

throe [þrou] kval, vånde, verk, pine, fødselsvé; pines; pine.

thrombus ['þråmbəs] blodpropp; plur.: **thrombi** ['þråmbai].

throne [þroun] trone; sette på tronen, trone; **drive** (støte) **her from the** —; **place him in the** —, **place (put, set) him on the** — på tronen; **come to** (på) **the** —. — **-room** tronsal.

throng [þråŋ] trengsel, skare, mengde, flokk, stim; stimle, flokkes.

throstle ['þråsl] trost, måltrost; **a crow among -s** en spurv i tranedans.

throttle ['þråtl] kvele, kveles; kverk, strupe.

through [þru·] igjennom, gjennom, i løpet av, ved, på grunn av; igjennom, til ende; — **and** — fra ende til annen; **carry** — gjennomføre. **get** — **to** få forbindelse med. — **-carriage** gjennomgangsvogn.

throughout [þru·'aut] helt igjennom; helt.

throve [þrouv] imperf. av **thrive.**

throw [þrou] kaste, slynge, slenge, hive, slå, sno, tvinne, styrte, kaste av, føde, motstå; kast, forskyvning; — **many hands idle** gjøre mange arbeidere brødløse; — **about** slå om seg; — **away** miste, øde, øyde, forkaste; — **back** avvise, sette tilbake; — **down** rive over ende, styrte; — in kaste ut, la gå med; — **into** kaste inn i, bringe i, ofre på; — **off** kaste av, fordrive, henkaste, slå av (i prisen), skille seg med; — on velte over på, vise til; — **out** sende ut, avvise, fortrenge, styrte, la falle, forvirre, distansere; — **over** kaste ut over, henge ut, legge ut, slå hånden av, oppgi; — **together** føre sammen; — **up** løfte, kaste opp, oppgi, framheve; — **with** la komme i berøring med.

thrown [þroun] perf. pts. av **throw.**

thrum [þrʌm] grovt garn, trådende(r) (i pl.) aving(er), frynser; spekk (til matter); veve, spekke, flette, besette med frynser, klimpre, klunke; tromme; nynne, sulle.

thrush [þrʌʃ] trost, måltrost.

thrush þrʌʃ] trøske (sykdom).

thrust [þrʌst] støte, bore, stikke, tilskynde, påtvinge, trenge, trenge seg; støt, puff, stikk, angrep, trykk.

thrustle ['þrʌsl] trost.

Thucydides [þju·'sididi·z] Tukydid.

thud [þʌd] dump lyd, dump, tungt (dumpt) slag; dunke, daske, lyde dumpt, drønne, suse med dumpe støt.

thug [þʌg] tyv, røver, slagsbror.

thumb [þʌm] tommelfinger, tommeltott; fingre med, ta på med fingrene, tilsmusse; skitne ut; **Tom Thumb** tommeliten; **by rule of** — på en klosset måte; **under his** — i hans makt. **-kins** tommeskrue. — **-mark** fingermerke (i bok). — **-tack** tegnestift.

thump [þʌmp] dump, tungt slag; dunke, støte. **-ing** svær, tung, diger, dryg.

thunder ['þʌndə] torden, tordenbrak, bulder; tordne, dundre. — **-bolt** lynstråle; bannstråle; — **-bolt of excommunication** bannstråle. — **clap** tordenskrall. — **-peal** tordenskrall. — **-shower** tordenbye. — **-storm** tordenvær. — **struck** lynslått; målløs.

thurible ['þjuəribl] røykelseskar.

Thursday ['þə·zdeⁱ el. 'þə·zdi] torsdag.

thus [ðʌs] så(ledes), på denne måte; derfor.

thwack [þwäk] slå, daske til; slag.

thwart [þwå·ᵗ] på tvers; tofte; motarbeide, legge seg i veien for, hindre, krysse, forpurre;

-ing som legger seg på tverke, motsatt, vrangvillig.

thy [ðai] (gammelt:) din, ditt, dine.

thyme [taim] timian.

thymy ['taimi] rik på timian, duftende.

thyself [ðai'self] (gml.) du selv, deg selv; (refleksivt) deg.

tiara [tai'æ·ərə] tiara.

Tibet [ti'bet] Tibet.

tick [tik] blodmit, flått; **sheep-tick** saukrabbe.

tick [tik] dynevar, putevar, sengetrekk.

tick [tik] pikke, tikke; pikk, tikking.

tick [tik] prikk, merke; merke av, sette prikk ved.

ticket ['tikit] billett, adgangskort, loddseddel, seddel, merke, etikett; etikettere; forsyne med billett(er); **that's the** — sånn skal det være; **here's just your** — her er nettopp noe for Dem; — **of leave** løslatelsespass (som gir fange friheten på betingelser).

ticket-collector ['tikitkə'lektə] billettør, billettkontrollør.

ticket-day ['tikitdeⁱ] dagen før avregningsdagen (på børsen).

ticket-office (amr.) billettkontor.

ticket-punch ['tikit'pʌnʃ] billett-saks.

ticket-writer maler av reklameplakater.

ticking ['tikiŋ] dynevar, bolster, dreiel.

tickle ['tikl] kile, kildre, krisle, behage, more, være kilen. **tickler** en som kiler, gåte. **tickling** kiling, pirring. **ticklish** kilen; (fig.) kilden.

ticklishness kilenhet.

tid [tid] bløt, lekker. **-bit** lekkerbisken.

tidal ['taidəl] tidevanns-; — **train** tog med avgang etter tidevannet.

tide [taid] tid, tidevann, flo og fjære; vannstand; strøm, retning, bevegelse; drive med strømmen, stige med tidevannet; **high** — flo, **low** — fjære; — **over a difficulty** komme over en vanskelighet. — **-gate** sluse. — **-mill** tidevannsmølle. **-sman**, — **-waiter** toll-oppsynsmann. — **-surveyor** [-sə've¹ə] tollkontrollør.

tidings ['taidiŋz] tidender, etterretninger, nytt.

tidy ['taidi] nett, pen, velstelt, ordentlig; pynte, ordne, rydde opp; antimakassar, møbelskåner.

tie [tai] binde, knytte, forbinde, forplikte, stå likt med; knute, sløyfe, bånd, slips, bindebue (i musikk), tverrtre; likt resultat, lik stilling; **shoot -s** skyte like godt; **shoot off a** — skyte om igjen for å få et endelig resultat; — **up** binde opp, binde fast, forbinde, hindre; — **down** binde, forplikte.

tier [tiə] rekke, rad, lag.

tierce [tiəs] ters, tredelt felt.

tie-wig ['taiwig] (fin) parykk (bundet med sløyfe i nakken).

tiff [tif] knute på tråden, liten strid; sup, tår; være fornærmet; ta seg en sup.

tiffany ['tifəni] en slags musselin.

tiffin ['tifin] (anglo-indisk:) lunsj.

tige [ti·ʒ] stengel, stilk; søyleskaft.

tiger ['taigə] tiger, tjener i livré, (utsvevende) banditt, fæl fant. — **-moth** bjørnesommerfugl.

tigress ['taigrəs] huntiger. **tigrine** ['taigrin] tigeraktig. **tigrish** ['taigriʃ] tigeraktig.

tight [tait] tett, fast, stram, trang, knipen, påholden; full, drukken; flink, livlig; **sit** — holde munn, ikke røpe seg; — **waistcoat** tvangstrøye; **money is** — det er trangt om penger; **the fellow is** — han er full; **in a** — **place** i knipe; **a** — **rope dancer** en linedanser(inne). **-en** tette, stramme, tetne, strammes. **-ener** godt måltid. **-ness** tetthet, fasthet, pengeknipe.

tights [taits] tettsluttende benklær; trikot.

T. I. H. fk. f. **Their Imperial Highnesses.**

tike [taik] fillebikkje, slamp, skarv.

tilbury ['tilbəri] tilbury (tohjulet enspenner).

tile [tail] tegl, teglstein, golvflis, hatt; tegltekke; **have a** — **loose** ha en skrue løs. **tiler** tegltekker, dørvokter (i en frimurerlosje).

till [til] til, inntil; — now inntil nå, hittil; — **then** til den tid, inntil da. **not** — ikke før, først.
till [til] pengeskuff.
till [til] dyrke, pløye, dyrke opp. **-able** dyrkbar. **-age** dyrking.
tiller ['tilə] landmann, dyrker.
tiller ['tilə] rorpinne, styrvol.
tiller ['tilə] skyte rotskudd, rotskudd, renning.
tilly-vally ['tili'väli] snikksnakk.
tilt [tilt] regnseil, telt; legge telt over.
tilt [tilt] helle, bikke, vippe, sette på kant, falle forover, hamre, felle, turnere, støte (med lanse), fekte, styrte fram; fare løs på; støt, turnering, dyst, helling, hell; **run a** — bryte en lanse.
tilth [tilþ] oppdyrking; dyrket land.
tiltyard ['tiltja·ᵊd] turneringsplass.
timbal ['timbəl] pauke.
timber ['timbə] tømmer, tømmerskog, trelast, emne, stoff, hinder; tømre, forsyne med tømmer; **take** — klare hinderet. **-ed** tømret, bygd, skogvokst, skogkledd.
timber-headed ['timbəhedid] dum.
timbertoes ['timbətoᵘz] (i slang) person med trebein; tresko-trasker.
timber-yard ['timbəja·ᵊd] trelasttomt.
timbre ['timbə] klangfarge, våpenmerke.
timbrel ['timbrəl] (gammeldags) tamburin.
time [taim] tid, klokkeslett, henstand, takt, gang; avpasse, ta tiden, beregne, slå takt, holde takt; **beat the** — slå takt; **against** — i flyvende hast, på spreng; **speak against** — snakke for å hale ut tiden; **two at a** — to om gangen; **at this** — på denne tid; **at -s** i noen tid, en tid; **from** — **to** — fra tid til annen; **in** — til rette tid, med tiden; **in no** — i et nå ; **in a short** — om kort tid; **out of** — i utide, ute av takt; — **out of mind** i uminnelige tider; **he had a bad** — **of it** han hadde det vondt, det gikk ham dårlig; **what** — **is it?** el. **what is the** — ? hva er klokka? — **-bill** timetabell. — **-honoured** ærverdig. — **-keeper** kronometer, ur, takstmåler, kontrollør. — **-limit** tidsbegrensning. **-ly** betimelig. — **-piece** ur. — **-pleaser** værhane. — **-server** værhane. — **-serving** kryperi. — **-table** timetabell, skjema, jernbanerute, togtabell. — **-worn** medtatt av tiden, forslitt.
timid ['timid] fryktsom, redd av seg. **-ity** [ti'miditi], **-ness** ['timidnès] fryktsomhet, unnseelse.
timorous ['timərəs] fryktsom, engstelig, redd. **-ness** fryktsomhet.
timothy ['timəþi] timotei, kjevlegras.
tin [tin] tinn, blikk, blikkboks, dåse; (i slang) penger; fortinne; preservere, legge ned hermetisk; — **hat** (i slang) moderne soldats stålhjelm; — **Lizzie** (i slang) Fordbil.
tincal ['tiŋkəl] boraks (et mineral).
tinct [tiŋkt] farge, flekk.
tinctorial [tiŋk'tå·riəl] farge-, fargende.
tincture ['tiŋktʃə] fargenyanse, skjær, anstrøk, snev, tinktur, essens; gi et skjær el. anstrøk, farge.
tinder ['tində] tønder, knusk. — **-box** fyrtøy. — **-like** knuskaktig, lettfengelig.
tine [tain] tind (på gaffel og horn).
tinfoil ['tin'foil] tinnfolie, «sølvpapir».
ting [tiŋ] ringle, klinge; klang, ringing.
tinge [tindʒ] farge, blande, gi et anstrøk; fargeskjær, anstrøk, snev, bismak.
tingle ['tiŋgl] krible, dirre, suse, synge: **my ears** — det ringer for ørene mine; **his fingers -d** det kriblet i fingrene på ham.
tinker ['tiŋkə] kjeleflikker; være kjeleflikker, fuske.
tinkle ['tiŋkl] klirre, klinge, ringe, ringle, single, ringe med, klimpre på; klang, klirring.
tinman ['tinmən] blikkenslager.
tinny ['tini] tinnaktig (især i klangen).
tinplate ['tinpleᵻt] fortinnet blikk; fortinne.

tinsel ['tinsl] flitter, flitterstas; flitter-, falsk; pynte med flitter, utmaie.
tinsmith ['tinsmiþ] blikkenslager.
tint [tint] farge, gi et anstrøk: fargeskjær.
tintinnabulary [tinti'näbjuləri] klingende, ringende. **tintinnabulun** [-ləm] (dom)bjelle, klokke
tinware ['tinwæ·ə] blikktøy.
tiny ['taini] ørliten, bitte liten; **just a** — **bit** en bitte liten smule, bitte lite grann.
tip [tip] spiss, tipp, tupp, ende, lett slag, berøring, smikk, drikkepenger, dusør; vink, hemmelig underretning, nyss, vippegreie; søppelplass; beslå (i spissen), berøre, slå lett på, vippe, tippe, gi drikkepenger; — **the wink** la forstå ved et øyekast; — **off** stikke ut; — **over** velte; **a straight** — pålitelig vink.
tip-cart ['tipka·ᵊt] tippvogn.
tipcat ['tipkät] pinne (spillet, den pinne som brukes til det).
Tipperary [tipə'ræ·ᵊri] Tipperary.
tippet ['tipit] skulderslag, skinnkrage.
tipple ['tipl] drikke, pimpe; (berusende) drikk. **-d** beruset, full. **-r** svirebror. **tippling** pimping.
tippling-house sjapp.
tipsify ['tipsifai] gjøre beruset, drikke full.
tipsy ['tipsi] beruset, på en kant.
tiptoe ['tip'toᵘ] tåspiss; **on** — på tå; spent.
tiptop ['tip'tåp] utmerket.
tirade [ti'reᵻd] tirade, ordflom.
tire [taiə] hjulring, luftring, gummiring; legge ring på.
tire [taiə] utmatte, bli trett; — **out** utmatte.
tired ['taiəd] trett, kjed (of av). **tiredness** trett-het, kjedsommelighet. **tiresome** trettende, kjedelig. **tiresomeness** kjedsommelighet.
tirewoman ['taiəwumən] kammerjomfru; pyntekone, påkledningskone (ved teater).
tiro ['taiəroᵘ] (ny)begynner.
tirwhit ['tə·wit] vipe.
tisane [ti'zän] avkok av bygg, byggsuppe.
tissue ['tiʃu] spinn, vev, tøy, gull- el. sølv-brokade; silkepapir; spinne, veve; **cellular** — cellevev. — **-paper** silkepapir.
tit [tit] liten hest, liten pike, liten fugl; — **for tat** like for like.
Titan ['taitən] Titan.
titanic [tai'tänik] titanisk.
titbit ['titbit] lekkerbisken, godbit.
tithe [taið] tiendedel, tiende; få (el. gi) tiende.
tither ['taiðə] tiendetager, tiendepliktig.
titillate ['titileᵻt] kildre, kile.
titillation [titi'leᵻʃən] kiling.
titlark ['titla·ᵊk] piplerke.
title ['taitl] tittel, navn, benevnelse, fordring, rett, atkomst, hjemmel; titulere, benevne. — **-deed** skjøte. — **-page**, — **-leaf** tittelblad.
titmouse ['titmaus] meis (fugl).
titter ['titə] fnise, knise; fnising.
tittle ['titl] tøddel.
tittle-tattle ['titl'tätl] pjatt, skravl; skravle.
titular ['titjulə] tittel-, titulær, nominell; titulær innehaver. **-ity** [titju'läriti] titulær beskaffenhet. **-y** se **titular**.
T. O. fk. f. **turn over.**
to [tu, tə] til, mot, på (om klokkeslett), i forhold til, i sammenligning med, for; å, for å, til å; **what** — **do?** hva skal man gjøre? **what** — **say?** hva skal man si? — **and fro** fram og tilbake, att og fram; **to-day** eller **today** [tə'deᵻ] i dag; den dag i dag; **to-morrow** eller **tomorrow** [tə'måroᵘ] i morgen; morgendagen; **tomorrow morning** i morgen tidlig; **on the day after to-morrow** i overmorgen; **to-night** eller **tonight** [tə'nait] i natt, i aften, i kveld; denne natt, denne aften.
toad [toᵘd] padde. — **-eater** spyttslikker, skumpelskudd. — **-fish** paddefisk, marulk. — **-flax** torskemunn. — **-in-a-hole** innbakt kjøtt; annonsemann. — **-stool** agaricus, (flue)sopp. **-y** snyltegjest, spyttslikker; logre, smigre, sliske. **-yism** spyttslikkeri.

toast [toust] riste; skåle for, drikke for; riste brød, skål, skåltale.

toasting-fork ['toustinfå·ək] ristegaffel (til å riste brød på).

toast-master ['toust'ma·stə] seremonimester (som ordner skåltalene etc.).

toast-rack ['tousträk] stativ til ristet brød.

tobacco [tə'bäkou] tobakk. — -pipe tobakkspipe. — -pouch tobakkspung. — -stopper pipestopper. -nist [tə'bäkənist] tobakkshandler, tobakksfabrikant.

toboggan [tə'bågən] kjelke; aketur, aking; ake på kjelke.

Toby ['toubi] Tobias; — jug gammeldags ølkrus formet som en mann med trekantet hatt.

Toc H [tåk'e¹tʃ] samfunn til vedlikehold av kameratskapet fra verdenskrigen (egl. = T. H. Talbot House, opprettet i Ypres til minne om Gilbert Talbot).

tocsin ['tåksin] (ringing med) stormklokke.

tod [tåd] tott, tett busk, en ullvekt, rev; avgi en viss vekt ull.

to-day, today [tə'de¹] i dag, i våre dager; den dag i dag, våre dager; from — fra i dag av; today's dagens; of to-day's date av dags dato.

toddle ['tådl] vakle, trippe, stabbe, gå usikkert (som et barn); usikker gang. toddler ['tådlə] stump, pjokk.

toddy ['tådi] toddi. — -ladle skje til å øse toddi av bollen.

to-do [tə'du· el. tu'du·] oppstyr, ståk.

tody ['toudi] flatnebb (fugl).

toe [tou] tå; røre med tåen; go -s up vende nesen i været; — the mark komme helt bort til merket.

toff [tåf] fin herre, fin fant; laps, sprade; the toffs de høyere klasser.

toffee ['tåfi] knekk (en slags sukkertøy); — apple «kjærlighet på pinne».

toft [tåft] tomt, grunn.

tog [tåg] kle opp, rigge til; klesplagg.

toga [' ougə] toga.

together [tə'geðə] sammen, tilsammen, i forening, i trekk, etter hverandre, samtidig.

toggery ['tågəri] klær, hyre, antrekk.

togs [tågz] d. s. s. toggery.

toil [toil] (især i pl.) garn, snare, nett.

toil [toil] slite, slepe, streve; strengt arbeid, slit, slep, strev. -er sliter.

toilet ['toilét] toalett, antrekk, påkledning. — -table toalettbord.

Tokay [to'ke¹] tokaier(vin).

token [toukn] tegn, merke, minne, erindring, merke (som gjelder for penger); by the same — til og med, og dertil, enda til, à propos, siden vi 'snakker om det; in — of til tegn på.

toledo [to'li·dou] toledoklinge.

tolerable ['tålərəbl] tålelig, utholdelig, passabel.

tolerance ['tålərəns] toleranse, fordragelighet, tålsomhet. tolerant ['tålərənt] tolerant, fordragelig.

tolerate ['tåləre¹t] tåle, finne seg i, tolerere, være tolerant. toleration [tålə'reiʃən] toleranse, fordragelighet.

toll [toul] ringe, klemte, ringe med; klemting.

toll [toul] londonsk telefonsentral for oppringninger til og fra den nære provins, nærtrafikk. — call oppringning til eller fra nærtrafikk. — enquiry opplysningskontor i London angående forbindelser med nærtrafikk.

toll [toul] avgift, toll betale toll, ta toll. — -bar tollbom; veibom. — -free tollfri, avgiftsfri. — -gate tollgrind, tollbom. — -gatherer tollforvalter. — -man bomvokter.

Tolstoy [tål'stoi] Tolstoi.

Tom [tåm] Tom; —, Dick, and Harry Per og Pål.

tom [tåm] han, især hankatt.

tomahawk ['tåməhå·k] tomahawk, indiansk stridsøks; drepe med tomahawk.

tomato [to'ma·tou] tomat.

tomb [tu·m] grav, gravmæle.

tombac ['tåmbäk] tambak.

tombola ['tåmbolə] tombola.

tomboy ['tåmboi] villkatt, galneheie.

tombstone ['tu·m·stoun] gravstein.

tomcat ['tåmkät] hankatt; (som skjellsord) troll.

tome [toum] bind, del (av et større verk).

tomfool ['tåm'fu·l] narr, dummepetter; oppføre seg narraktig.

tomfoolery [tåm'fu·ləri] narrestreker, dumme streker.

Tommy ['tåmi] Tommy, lille Tomas; — Atkins navn på den britiske soldat.

tommy ['tåmi] (i slang) mat; betaling i varer. — -master prinsipal som betaler med varer el. med anvisning til handlende. — -rot sludder, vanvidd. — -shop forretning som betaler med varer.

tomorrow [tə'måɾou] i morgen; — morning i mɔrgen tidlig; (on) the day after — i overmorgen; — in the morning i morgen tidlig.

tomtit ['tåm'tit] titt, (kjøtt)meis.

tom-tom ['tåmtåm] (primitiv) tromme, tamtam.

ton [tʌn] tonn.

ton [tå·n] god tone, folkeskikk. of ton fin.

tone [toun] tone, koral, klang, elastisitet, spennkraft, stemning, tonefall; betoning, ettertrykk, syngende tone el. tale, preg, karakter; si fram med en affektert stemme; stille, gi tone; -d med en tone, klingende. -less tonløs, umusikalsk.

tongs [tåŋz] tang, ildtang; a pair of — en tang.

tongue [tʌŋ] tunge, tungemål, språk, mål, landtunge; skjelle, snakke; hold the — holde munn; a person of smooth — et glattunget menneske. -shaped tungedannet. -tie gjøre målløs.

tonic ['tånic] styrkende, oppstrammende; tone-; grunntone; styrkende middel (medisin).

to-night el. tonight [tə'nait] i aften, i kveld; i natt.

tonnage ['tʌnidʒ] tonnasje, drektighet, flåte, tonnasjeavgift; ha en drektighet av.

tonneau ['tånou] automobilkupé.

tonsil ['tånsil] mandelkjertel, tonsill, mandel.

tonsure ['tånʃə] kronraking, tonsur; kronrake.

too [tu·] altfor, for; også, tillike.

took [tuk] imperf. av take.

tool [tu·l] verktøy, redskap; stempel, forsiring av et bokbind; tildanne, utføre, kjøre; a poor — en pjalt, klosset person; machine tool verktøymaskin. — -box el. — -chest redskapskiste. — -holder, — -rest stålholder (på dreiebenk).

toot [tu·t] tute, blåse. -er blåser.

tooth [tu·þ] pl. teeth [ti·þ] tann, tagg, tind (på en rive); forsyne med tenner, tinde (en rive), la gripe inn; — and nail med hender og føtter, med nebb og klør; cast it in his teeth slenge ham det opp i ansiktet; show one's teeth vise tenner; in the teeth of til tross for, trass i. -ache tannpine, tannverk. — -brush tannbørste. — -drawer tannlæge. — -edge ising i tennene. -ful dråpe, liten tår. -less tannløs. -pick tannstikke. — -powder tannpulver. -some velsmakende. — -wheel tannhjul.

tootle ['tu·tl] tute (svakt el. gjentagende).

top [tåp] topp, øverste del, spiss, overside, hode, isse, hårtopp, mers, toppunkt; snurrebass; pl. kravestøvler: øverst, først, prima; heve seg, rage opp, være framherskende, overgå, toppe, nå til topps, stige opp til, kappe; — up sette kronen på verket, fullende; at the — of his voice så høyt han kan, i villen sky; -s and bottoms kavringer; sleep like a — sove som en stein.

topaz ['toupäz] topas (gul edelstein).

top-beam ['tåpbi·m] hanebjelke.

top-boots ['tåpbu·ts] kragestøvler.

top-coat ['tåpkoᵘt] overfrakk.
top-dressing ['tåp'dresin] gjødsling på overflaten.
tope [toᵘp] lund, treklynge, relikviehus.
tope [toᵘp] drikke, svire. toper drikkebror.
top-gallant ['tåp'gälənt] bramstang, bramseil.
top-hat ['tåphät] høy hatt, flosshatt.
top-heavy ['tåp'hevi] for tung oventil.
tophus ['toᵘfəs] tuffstein.
tophaceous [toᵘ'feiʃiəs] tuffsteinaktig.
topiary ['toᵘpiəri] beklippet, kunstig formet.
topic ['tåpik] almensetning, emne, tema, gjenstand, lokalt lægemiddel, topikk (læren om å finne bevisgrunner). -al lokal, aktuell; -al evidence sannsynlighetsbevis; -al poem leilighetsdikt.
topknot ['tåpnåt] topp, hårsløyfe, hårtopp, lugg.
topmast ['tåpməst] mersestang.
topmost ['tåpmoᵘst] øverst.
topographer [toᵘ'pågrəfə], topographist [to'pågrəfist] topograf, stedsbeskriver; topographical ['tåpo'gräfikl] topografisk, stedsbeskrivende; topography [toᵘ'pågrəfi] topografi, stedsbeskrivelse.
topping ['tåpiŋ] fortrinlig, finfin.
topple ['tåpl] falle forover, ramle ned, kaste ned.
topsail ['tåpsl] toppseil, mersseil.
top-sawyer ['tåp'så·jə] den øverste av to som arbeider med en langsag; førstemann, bas, leder.
topsyturvy [tåpsi'tə·vi] opp ned, på hodet, rotet, kaotisk; turn — vende opp ned på, endevende.
toque [toᵘk] toque (slags damehatt).
tor [tå·ᵊ] klett, fjellknaus, nut.
torch [tå·ᵊtʃ] fakkel. — -bearer fakkelbærer.
— -light fakkellys. — -light procession fakkeltog.
tore [tå·ᵊ] imperf. av tear.
tore [tå·ᵊ] vissent gras.
toreador ['tåriədå·ᵊ] toreador.
torment [tå·ᵊ'ment] pine, plage; vri, tvinge.
torment ['tå·ᵊmənt] kval, pinsel, plage. -er, -or [tå·ᵊ'mentə] plageånd, bøddel. -ingly grusomt.
torn [tå·ᵊn] perf. pts. av tear.
tornado [tå·ᵊ'neidoᵘ] hvirvelstorm.
torpedo [tå·ᵊ'pi·doᵘ] elektrisk rokke; torpedo; angripe med torpedo, nytte torpedoer. — -boat torpedobåt. — (-boat)-catcher torpedojager. — (-boat)-destroyer torpedobåtødelegger (mindre jager). — -tube torpedoutskytingsrør.
torpid ['tå·ᵊpid] stivnet, stiv, følelsesløs, sløv; treg; annen klasses kaproningsbåt. -ness, -ity [tå·ᵊ'piditi] dvale, følelsesløshet, sløvhet.
torpify ['tå·ᵊpifai] virke bedøvende på, sløve.
torpor ['tå·ᵊpə] dvaletilstand; sløvhet.
torque [tå·ᵊk] vridning, halsbånd.
torrefaction [tåri'fäkʃən] tørring; rosting.
torrefy ['tårifai] roste (malm); tørre, tørke.
torrent ['tårənt] strøm, regnskyll, striregn.
torrid ['tårid] brennende het; the — zone den hete sone. -ness brennende hete.
torsion ['tå·ᵊʃən] torsjon, dreining, vridning, tvinning.
torso ['tå·ᵊsoᵘ] torso.
tort [tå·ᵊt] spent, stram; tort, urett.
tortoise ['tå·ᵊtəs] skilpadde. — -shell skilpaddeskall, skilpadde; skilpaddefarget.
tortuosity [tå·ᵊtju'åsiti] slyngning, bøyning, krokethet; bukt, krok.
tortuous ['tå·ᵊtjuəs] vridd, buktet, kroket. -ness d. s. s. tortuosity.
torture ['tå·ᵊtʃə] tortur, pine, kval; legge på pinebenken, pine, plage. torturer bøddel, plageånd. torturing pinlig.
Tory ['tå·ri] tory, konservativ (nå mest erstattet av Conservative). -ism konservatisme.
tosh [tåʃ] (slang) sludder, vas, tøv.
toss [tås] kaste, slenge, kippe, svinge, kaste hit og dit, tumle om, forurolige, rulle, kaste seg hit og dit, tumles om, gynge opp og ned, kast, sleng, loddkasting, omtumling, kast med nakken; — the head slå med nakken; — off stikke

ut, lage i en fart, få unna; — up kaste i været, få i stand i en fart, spille mynt og krone (for om); — one spille mynt og krone med en; take a — bli kastet av (om rytter).
tot [tåt] slump, stubb, pjokk; tår, sup.
tot [tåt] addisjonsstykke; regne sammen; — up løse opp.
total ['toᵘtəl] fullstendig, hel; samlet sum; beløpe seg til. -ity [to'täliti] helhet, totalsum.
totalizator ['toᵘtəlize'tə] totalisator.
totalize ['toᵘtəlaiz] fullstendiggjøre; nytte totalisator.
totalizer ['toᵘtəlaizə] totalisator.
tote fk. f. totalizator.
tote [toᵘt] bære, dra på.
totem ['toᵘtém] indiansk familie-våpen el. tegn.
totter ['tåtə] vakle, stavre. -y vaklende.
toucan ['tu·k n] tukan (slags søramerikansk fugl).
touch [tʌtʃ] røre, berøre, ta på, føle på, bevege, antyde, henkaste, skissere, spille, angå, befatte seg med; anløpe, gå innom; berøring, følelse, følesans, føling, tilknytning, hogg, strøk, anslag, penselstrøk, pennestrøk, trekk, anstrøk, drag, preg, streif, stenk; a fourpenny — noe til 30 øre, 30 øres-; — at anløpe; — off henkaste; — on røre ved, berøre; — to the quick såre (ens følelser dypt); — the bell ringe; — up friske opp, rette på, restaurere, retusjere; sette fart i; — wood banke i bordet (for å avvende nemesis, når man har skrytt av sitt hell e. l.). — -and-go løs, overfladisk, lett og livlig, uvøren, upålitelig; berøring, usikkerhet, overfladiskhet, letthet.
toucher ['tʌtʃə] noe som er meget nær ved å skje; a near — el. as near as a — på et hengende hår.
touch-hole ['tʌtʃhoᵘl] fenghull.
touching ['tʌtʃiŋ] rørende; angående. — -needle probérnål. — -paper salpeterpapir. — -stone probérstein, prøvestein. — -wood knusk.
tough [tʌf] seig, drøy, dryg, vanskelig, vrien. -en gjøre seig, bli seig. -ish temmelig seig. -ness seighet.
toupée el. toupet ['tu·pei] toupet, liten parykk.
tour [tuə] rundreise, reise, tur, turné; reise, dra på turné med. -ist ['tuərist] turist. -ist's agency reisebyrå.
tournament ['tuənəmənt] turnering.
tourney ['tuəni] turnering; turnere.
touse [tauz] hale, slite.
touser en som haler; et hundenavn («Snapp»).
tousle ['tauzl] bringe i uorden, forpjuske, ruske i.
tout [taut] stå på utkik, spionere, kapre kunder, rapportere. -er agent, pågående ansøker; spion (ved hesteveddeløp).
tow [toᵘ] stry.
tow [toᵘ] slepetau, slep, buksering; buksere, slepe, taue. -age ['toᵘidʒ] buksering, betaling for buksering.
toward ['toᵘəd] (gml. adj.) forestående, i annarsj.
toward [tå·ᵊd; tə'wå·ᵊd] (prep.) henimot.
towardly ['toᵘədli] (gml.) lovende, lærvillig.
towards [tå·ᵊdz; tə'wå·ᵊdz] henimot, i retning av, mot, til, nær ved.
towboat [toᵘ'boᵘt] slepebåt, taubåt.
towel ['tauəl] håndkle; bruke håndkle på, tørke. — -horse håndkleholder. -ling håndklestoff.
tower ['tauə] tårn, borg, festning; heve seg, kneise; a — of strength et trygt vern; the Tower (of London) Tower (Londons gamle borg). -ed tårnet, tårn-. -ing tårnhøy, kneisende. -y tårnet.
towing ['toᵘiŋ] buksering, tauing. — -boat slepebåt, taubåt. — -path trekkvei, slepevei (langs elv el. kanal). — -rope buksertau, sleper.
tow-line ['toᵘlain] buksertau, sleper.

tow-linen ['toᵘlinən] strie.

town [taun] by, stad, kommune; **the — hoved-staden**, hovedstadens fornemme strøk, det for-nemme selskap; **gentleman about —** levemann. **— -clerk** byskriver, magistratssekretær. **— -council** bystyre. **— -councillor** bystyremedlem. **— -crier** utroper. **— -hall** rådhus. **— -house** hus byen, kommunelokale, rådhus. **-ish** bymessig. **-let** småby. **-ship** bydistrikt; bysamfunn; kommune; (amr.) herred, areal av en viss størrelse. **-man** bymann, borger, bysbarn. **— -talk** bysnakk; gjenstand for alminnelig omtale.

tow-path ['toᵘpa·þ] trekkvei, slepevei (langs elv el. kanal).

tow-rope ['toᵘroᵘp] buksertau, sleper.

towse og **towsle** se **touse** og **tousle**.

towy ['toᵘi] stry-, stryaktig.

toxic ['tåksik], **toxical** ['tåksikl] giftig, gift-.

toxicology [tåksi'kålədʒi] toksikologi, giftlære.

toxine ['tåksin] toksin, gift.

toxophilite [tåk'såfilait] bueskytter, tilhenger av bueskyting.

toy [toi] leike, leketøy, bagatell, småting, leik, fjas; leke, gantes, fjase. **-man** leketøyshandler.

Toynbee ['toinbi·] Toynbee.

trace [treᶦs] dragreim, dragtau, spor, far, fot-spor, merke; spore, etterspore, følge, tilbake-legge, gjennomvandre; tegne, markere, risse, gjøre utkast til. **-able** som kan etterspores, påvi-selig.

tracery ['treᶦsəri] steinprydelser, masverk (i gotikk).

trachea [trə'kiə] luftrør. **tracheal** luftrøᴂs-.

tracing ['treᶦsiŋ] kalkering.

track [träk] spor, far, fotspor, vei, råk, sti; skinnegang, linje; (amr.) jernbanelinje; farvann, kjølvann; etterspore, forᶦølge; slepe, taue. **double — dobbeltspor; make -s** ta beina på nakken, legge på sprang. **-less** sporløs, uveisom. **— -road** trekkvei. **— -scout** trekkskøyte.

tract [träkt] egn, strøk, strekning; småskrift, avhandling.

tractability [träktə'biliti] medgjørlighet.

tractable ['träktəbl] medgjørlig, villig, lydig.

Tractarianism [träk'tæ·ᵊriənizm] traktarian-isme (høykirkelig anglokatolsk retning, innledet ved noen traktater, utgitt i Oxford).

traction ['träkʃən] trekking, trekk, trekkraft. **— -engine** landeveislokomotiv, lokomobil, traktor.

tractive ['träktiv] trekkende, trekk-.

tractor ['träktə] traktor, trekkeredskap.

trade [treᶦd] handel, forretning, håndverk, fag, yrke, levevei, næringsvei, bransje, forretnings-folk, fart, seilas; passat; drive handel, handle, forhandle; **Board of Trade** handelsdepartementet; (amr.) handelskammeret; **— union** fagforening. **— -card** anbefalingskort. **— -mark** varemerke, fabrikkmerke. **— -paper** fagblad. **— -price** engros-pris. **trader** forhandler, handlende, handelsskip.

tradesfolk ['treᶦdzfoᵘk] handelsfolk. **tradesman** kjøpmann, håndverker, næringsdrivende, **trades-union** fagforening.

trade-wind ['treᶦdwind] passat(vind).

tradition [trə'diʃən] overlevering, tradisjon, sagn. **-al, -ary** muntlig overlevert, tradisjonell, sagnmessig. **-ally** gjennom tradisjonen.

traduce [trə'dju·s] baktale. **-ment** baktaling.

Trafalgar [trə'fälgə] Trafalgar.

traffic ['träfik] handel, trafikk, omsetning; handle, avsette, omsette. **-ker** handlende. **— -manager** trafikkdirektør.

tragedian [trə'dʒi·djən] tragedieforfatter, tra-gisk skuespiller.

tragedy ['trädʒidi] tragedie, sørgespill.

tragic ['trädʒik] tragisk.

tragical ['trädʒikl] tragisk, sørgelig.

tragicomedy ['trädʒi'kåmidi] tragikomedie.

tragicomic ['trädʒi'kåmik] tragikomisk.

trail [treᶦl] slepe, trekke, uttale slepende, trekkes ut i lengden, strekke seg, dra seg, krype,

etterspore; hale, slep, stripe, vei, spor, slag, veifar; dorg; **— arms!** i hånden gevær!

trailer ['treᶦlə] krype- eller slyngplante, lian, hengende grein; tilhengervogn (til sporvogn).

train [treᶦn] slepe, trekke, oppdra, lære opp, innøve, trene, eksersere, avrette, dressere; slep. hale, rekke, rad, følge, opptog, tog, jernbane, lokkemat, felle, kruttrenne; **take —** ta med jern-nanen; **— of artillery** artilleripark. **— -band** borgervæpning. **— -bearer** en som bærer slepet. **-ed** opplært; med slep. **-er** trener. **-ing** oppdra-gelse, opplæring, trening, dressur. **-ing-college** seminar, lærerskole. **-ing-ground** ekserserplass. **-ing-school** seminar, lærerskole. **-ing-ship** skole-skip.

train-oil ['treᶦnoil] tran.

trait [treᶦ, amr. treᶦt] trekk, ansiktstrekk, karaktertrekk.

traitor ['treᶦtə] forræder. **-ous** ['treᶦtərəs] for-rædersk, troløs. **-ousness** forræderi, troløshet.

traitress ['treᶦtrᴂs] forræderske.

trajectory [trə'dʒektəri] (prosjektils) bane; (pla-nets) bane.

tram [träm] skinnegang, sporveislinje, sporvogn; sende med sporvogn; trikk. **to tram** it trikke.

tram [träm] tramsilke, islettsilke.

tramcar ['trämka·ᵊ] sporvogn, trikk.

trammel ['träməl] garn, bånd, lenke, hindring; belemre, hefte, lenke, hindre.

tramontane [trə'månte·n] fremmed, usivilisert.

tramp [trämp] trampe, bereise til fots, vandre, traske; tramping, fottur, reise, landstryker, fant, omstreifer, farende svenn. **— steamer** trampbåt (ikke i fast rute); **be on the —** være på vandring, vagabondere.

trample ['trämpl] trampe, trå ned; tramping.

tram-rail ['trämreᶦl] sporveisskinne.

tram-road ['trämroᵘd] sporvei.

tram-vay ['trämweᶦ] sporvei.

tramway-car ['trämweᶦka·ᵊ] sporvogn.

trance [tra·ns] transe, ekstase, henrykkelses-tilstand.

tranquil ['träŋkwil] rolig. **-lity** [träŋ'kwiliti]. **-ness** ['träŋkwilnᴂs] ro, rolighet. **-lization** [träŋ-kwili'zeᶦʃən] beroligelse. **-lize** ['träŋkwilaiz] be-rolige. **-lizer** en som bringer ro, beroligende middel.

transact [trän'säkt, tra·n, trən-] behandle, forhandle, utføre, greie, drive, underhandle. **-ion** utførelse, forretning, begivenhet, sak, underhand-ling, transaksjon. **-or** leder, underhandler.

transalpine ['tränz'älpain, 'tra·nz-] trans-alpinsk, bord for Alpene.

transatlantic ['tränzət'läntik, 'tra·n-] fra den andre siden av Atlanterhavet; som går over Atlanterhavet; amerikansk (fra U. S. A.); **— stories** amerikanske historier.

transcend [trän'send, tra·n-] overskride, heve seg over, overgå. **-ence, -ency** fortrinlighet, for-trin. **-ent** oversanselig, opphøyd, fortrinlig. **-ental** [tra·nsən'dental, trän-] fortrinlig, oversanselig. **-entalism** [tra·nsən'dentəlizm, trän-] transcen-dental filosofi.

transcribe [tra·n'skraib, trän-] skrive av. **-r** av-skriver; **transcript** ['tra·nskript, 'trän-] avskrift, gjenpart, kopi. **transcription** [tra·n'skripʃən, trän-] avskriving. **transcriptively** [tra·n'skriptivli, trän-] i avskrift.

transept ['tränsept, 'tra·n-] tverrskip, korsarm.

transfer [tra·ns'fə·, träns-] overføre, overdra, forflytte.

transfer ['tra·nsfə, 'träns-] overdraging, over-føring, forflytting; overgangsbillett; avtrykk, av-trykksbilde; overflyttet soldat; **— ticket** over-gangsbillett.

transferability [tränsfə·rə'biliti, tra·ns] det å kunne overføres.

transferable [träns'fə·rəbl, tra·ns-] som kan overføres (el. overdras).

transferee [tränsfə'ri·, tra·ns-] en til hvem overdragelse skjer.
transference ['tra·nsfərəns, 'träns-] overdraging.
transfiguration [tra·nsfigju're'ʃən, träns-] forklaring ⟨is. om Kristus); forklaret skikkelse.
transfigure [-'figə] forvandle, omdanne, forklare.
transfix [tra·ns'fiks, träns-] gjennombore, stikke, nagle fast. **-ion** gjennomboring.
transform [träns'få·əm, tra·ns-] forvandle, omdanne forvandle seg. **-ation** [-'me'ʃən] forvandling, omskaping, omvendelse. **-ative** [-'få·əmətiv] forvandlende, forvandlings-.
transfuse [tra·ns'fju·z, träns-] tappe om, bibringe, inngyte, fylle. **transfusible** [-'fju·zibl] som kan overgytes. **transfusion** [-'fju·ʒən] omtapping, overføring.
transgress [tra·ns'gres, träns-] overtre, bryte, forse seg. **-ion** overtredelse. **-ional** overtredende. **-or** overtreder, synder.
tranship [tra·n'ʃip, trän-] se **transship**.
transience ['tränziəns] flyktighet.
transient ['tränziənt] forbigående, flyktig. **-ly** forbigående.
transit ['tränsit, 'tra·nsit 'tränzit] overgang, transitt, gjennomgang, overfart, transport, gjennomreise, førselsvei; by **rapid** — med hurtig befordring. **— -duty** transittoll.
transition [trän'siʒən, tra·n-] overgang. **-al** overgangs-.
transitive ['tra·nsitiv, 'trän-] transitiv.
transitory ['tränsitəri, 'tra·n-] forgjengelig, kortvarig.
translate [tra·ns'le't, träns-] overføre, forflytte, omforme, oversette, omsette. **translation** [tra·ns-'le'ʃən, träns-] overføring, forflytting, oversettelse, omsetting, opptagelse (til himmelen). **translator** [tra·ns'le'tə, träns-] translatør, oversetter, omsetter. **translatory** [-'le'təri] overførings-, oversettelses-, omsettings-. **translatress** [-'le'tr̥ès] oversetter. omsetter.
translucency [tra·ns'lju·snsi, träns-] gjennomskinnelighet, klarhet. **translucent** gjennomskinnelig.
transmarine [tra·nsmə'ri·n, träns-] oversjøisk.
transmigrate ['tränzmaigre't, 'tra·n-] utvandre, vandre over (om sjelevandring).
transmigration [tränzmai'gre'ʃən, tra·n-] utvandring, sjelevandring.
transmigrator ['tränzmaigre'tə, 'tra·n-] utvandrer.
transmissible [tränz'misəbl, tra·n-] som kan oversendes. **transmission** [tränz'miʃən, tra·n-] forsendelse, overlevering; overføring, transmisjon.
transmit [tränz'mit, tra·n-] oversende, overføre, overlevere, befordre, forplante. **transmittal** [-'mitəl] oversendelse. **transmitter** [-'mitə] oversender, senderapparat (ved telegraf og telefon).
transmittible [-'mitibl] som kan oversendes.
transmutable [tra·ns'mju·təbl, träns-] foranderlig. **transmutation** [-mju'te'ʃən] forvandling, omdanning. **transmute** [-'mju·t] forvandle, omdanne.
transmuter [-'mju·tə] forvandler.
transom ['tränsəm] tverrstykke, losholt; hekkbjelke.
transparence [träns'pæ·ərəns, tra·n-]. **transparency** [-si] gjennomsiktighet, transparent. **transparent** [-'pæ·ərənt] gjennomsiktig.
transpiration [tränspi're'ʃən, tra·n-] utdunsting, svette.
transpire [trän'spaiə, tra·n-] utdunste, svette, sive ut, forlyde; (vulgært) hende.
transplant [träns'pla·nt, tra·n-] plante om. **-ation** [-pla·n'te'ʃən] omplanting. **-er** [-'pla·ntə] omplanter.
transpontine ['tränz'pântain] på den andre siden av brua; (i London:) fra Surreysiden, simpel, mindre fin.
transport [träns'på·ət, tra·n-] forsende, sende, føre, transportere, flytte, befordre; dømme til deportasjon; beta, henrykke, rive med.

transport ['tränspå·ət, 'tra·n-] forsendelse, sending, transport, tren, henrykkelse, betatthet, anfall; **Transport Workers** transportarbeidere (en fagforening).
transportable [träns'på·ətəbl, tra·n-] transportabel, forsendelig, som kan sendes, dømt til deportasjon.
transport|ation [tränspå·ə'te'ʃən, tra·n-] forsendelse, transport, deportasjon. **-edly** [-idli] henrykt, ute av seg selv. **-er** en som overfører. **-ing** betagende, overvettes.
transposal [träns'poᵘzəl, tra·n-] omsetning, forflytting.
transpose [träns'poᵘz, tra·n] omsette, omflytte. **transposition** [tränspə'ziʃən, tra·n-] omflytting, forandring. **-al** som angår omflytting.
transship [tra·ns'ʃip, träns-] laste om, skipe om. **-ment** omlasting. omskiping.
transubstantiate [tränsəb'stänʃie't, tra·n-] forvandle. **transubstantiation** [-stänʃi'e'ʃən] forvandling.
transudation [tra·nsju'de'ʃən, träns-] transsudasjon, gjennomsivning; væske som tyter ut.
transudatory [-'sju·dətəri] som tyter ut, gjennomsivende. **transude** [-'sju·d] sive igjennom.
Transvaal ['tränsva·l, 'tra·n], **the — Transvaal.
transversal [tränz'və·səl, tra·n-] tverr-, som går på tvers.
transverse [tränz'və·s, tra·n-] tverr-, som går på tvers; transversal. **-ly** på tvers.
Transylvania [tränsil've'njə, tra·n-] Siebenbürgen.
trap [träp] felle, snare, saks, teine, fall-lem, et nordengelsk ballspill, kjøretøy (av forskjellig slags); fange, besnære; **up to** — slu, for klok til å la seg fange.
trap [träp] trapp; trappdannet (om basaltklipper).
trap [träp] pynte, utstaffere. **traps** saker, pakkenelliker, greier, redskaper.
trapan [trə'pän] besnære; besnærer; felle.
trap-door ['träpdå·ə] lem, luke, fall-lem, fallluke.
trapes [tre'ps] farte, reke, slenge, traske.
trapeze [trə'pi·z] trapès (til gymnastikk).
trapezium [trə'pi·zjəm] trapés (uregelmessig firkant).
trapper ['träpə] pelsjeger, villdyrjeger.
trappings ['träpinz] staselig ridetøy, pynt, stas.
Trappist ['träpist] trappist (slags munk).
trash [träʃ] tros, skat, kvas, rusk, rask, avfall, herk, skrap, sludder.
trashy ['träʃi] verdiløs, unyttig.
traumatic [trɔ·'mätik] sårlægende; sårmiddel.
travail ['träve'l] ligge i fødselssmerter; slit og slep, fødselssmerter.
travel ['trävl] reise (i), være på reise, gå, vandre, bereise, dra gjennom, tilbakelegge; (om lyd, ild etc.) fare, forplante seg; reise, reisebeskrivelse; **— third** reise på tredje klasse. **-led** beferdet, bereist, bevandret.
travel|ler ['trävlə] reisende, passasjer, bereist mann, også: handelsreisende; **-ler's book** fremmedbok. **-ling** reisende, reise-.
traverse ['trävəs] på tvers, over kors; korslagt; tverr-; noe som legges på tvers, forheng, uventet hindring, strek i regningen, anfall, innsigelse, tverrskanse; krysse gjennom, dra gjennom, reise gjennom, bereise, krysse, hindre, gjendrive, benekte, bestride, gjøre sidebevegelser el. sideutfall. **traversable** som kan krysses, som lar seg benekte. **traverser** benekter, forsvarer.
travesty ['trävisti] travestere, kle ut i en latterlig form; travesti.
trawl [trå·l] trål, sopevad, bunngarn, sildenot; fiske med sopevad, tråle. **-er** ['trå·lə] tråler.
tray [tre'] lite trau; bakke, brett; vektskål.
T. R. C. fk. f. **Thames Rowing Club.**
treacherous ['tretʃərəs] forrædersk, troløs.

treachery ['tretʃəri] forræderi.
treacle ['tri·kl] sirup (til å spise), innkokt sukkerholdig saft; smiger, søte ord.
tread [tred] tre, trå, tråkke (på), gå, vandre, betre, trampe på; trin, skritt, gang, fuglers parring; — **water** trå vannet.
treadle ['tredl] trøe (i vev).
treadmill ['tredmil] tredemølle.
treason ['tri·zn] forræderi; **high** — høyforræderi; **petit** el. **petty** — mord (begått av en kone på sin mann, av en tjener på sin husbond osv.). **-able** forrædersk.
treasure ['treʒə] skatt, klenodie, rikdommer; samle, dynge opp, gjemme på.
treasure-house ['treʒəhaus] skattkammer.
treasurer ['treʒərə] skattmester, kasserer; **Lord High** — (gml.) riksskattmester. **-ship** skattmesterembete. **treasuress** kassererske.
treasure-seeker ['treʒə'si·kə] skattegraver.
treasure-trove ['treʒə'troᵘv] skattefunn, funnet skatt, rikt funn, danefe.
treasury ['treʒəri] skattkammer, finansdepartement; **First Lord of the Treasure** første skattkammerlord (nominell overfinansminister; tittelen innehas oftest av statsministeren). — **-bench** ministerbenk (i underhuset).
treat [tri·t] behandle, traktere, varte opp, underhandle, forhandle, tale om, handle om; traktement, barneselskap; sjelden nytelse, fryd; **a rich** — en rik nytelse; **it's my** — det er min tur (til å traktere).
treatise ['tri·tiz, -is] avhandling.
treatment ['tri·tmənt] behandling, medfart.
treaty ['tri·ti] overenskomst, traktat; **be in** — **with** ligge i underhandling med.
treble ['trebl] tredobbelt; gjøre tredobbelt, bli tredobbelt; diskant, sopran.
tree [tri·] tre, stamtre; støvelblokk; **up a** — i knipe, i forlegenhet. — **-frog** lauvfrosk. **-nail** trenagle. — **of life** livstre. — **-primrose** nattlys.
trefoil ['tri·foil] kløver.
trek [trek] utvandre, vandre; utvandring, vandring (i Sør-Afrika).
trellis ['trelis] gitter, traleverk, tremmeverk, sprinkelverk, espalier. **-ed** med gitter, tremme-.
tremble ['trembl] skjelve, beve, dirre; være på det uvisse; skjelving, dirring.
trembling ['trembliŋ] skjelvende, rystende, ristende; — **poplar** bevreosp.
tremendous [tri'mendəs] fryktelig, skrekkelig, veldig, voldsom. **-ness** fryktelighet.
tremor ['tremə] skjelving, risting, sitring.
tremulous ['tremjuləs] skjelvende, dirrende. **-ness** skjelving.
trench [trenʃ] grøft, dike, veit, skyttergrav; grave skyttergrav el. grøft, aurvelte; — **upon** gjøre inngrep i.
trenchant ['trenʃənt] skarp, bitende, avgjørende.
trencher ['trenʃə] spikkefjel, brødfjel. — **-cap** studentlue. — **-man** matkrok.
trend [trend] bøye, dreie, strekke seg, løpe, gå i en viss retning.
trental ['trentəl] tredve sjelemesser, klagesang.
trepan [tri'pän] trepan; trepanere.
trepan [tri'pän] felle, bedrager; lokke (i fella).
trepidation [trepi'deiʃən] skjelving, angst.
trespass ['trespəs] overtre, forse seg, gå inn på annenmanns enemerker, gjøre inngrep; overtredelse, eiendomskrenking, inngrep, overgrep. **-er** overtreder, uvedkommende; **-ers will be prosecuted** uvedkommende forbys adgang; (egentlig: uvedkommende som ferdes her, vil bli anmeldt).
tress [tres] krølle, lokk, flette. **-ed** krøllet, med krøller.
tressel ['tresl], **trestle** ['tresl] bukk (av tre), understell.
tret [tret] godtgjørelse for svinn.
trevet ['trevit] trefot.

T. R. H. fk. f. **Their Royal Highnesses.**
triad ['traiəd] triade, trehet, samling av tre; treklang.
trial ['traiəl] prøve, undersøkelse, prøvelse, forsøk; hjemsøkelse; fristelse; rettslig behandling, domsbehandling, domsforhandling, behandlingsmåte, rettergang; rettsforhandling, sak, prosess; **on** — på prøve; **make a** — **of** gjøre en prøve med; **put to** (el. **on**) — sette på prøve; **give him a** — la ham bli prøvd; **he is on his** — hans sak er for retten; — **by fire** ildprøve; — **by jury** jurybehandling, prosess for lagmannsretten; **trial marriage** prøveekteskap.
triangle ['traiäŋgl] trekant, triangel, bukk (ved prylestraff), delirium. **-d** trekantet.
triangular [trai'äŋgjulə] trekantet.
triangulate [trai'äŋgjuleᵗt] gjøre triangulær.
tribal ['traibl] stamme-, familie-, ætt-.
tribe [traib] stamme; ætt, slekt, folkeferd.
tribesman ['traibzmən] stammefrende.
tribunal [trai'bju·nəl] domstol, rett.
tribune ['tribju·n] tribun (hos romerne), talerstol. **-ship, tribunate** ['tribjunét] tribunat.
tributary ['tribjutəri] skattskyldig, betalt i skatt, underordnet, bi-; skattskyldig, bielv.
tribute ['tribju·t] skatt, tributt, anerkjennelse, hyldest.
trice [trais] hale opp; **in a** — i en håndvending, i en to tre. **tricing-line** opphalertau.
tricennial [trai'seniəl] tredveårig, trettiårig.
tricentary [trai'sentəri] tidsrom av tre hundre år.
trichina [tri'kainə] trikin.
trichiniasis [triki'naiəsis] trikinsykdom.
trichord ['traikå·ᵊd] trestrenget (instrument).
trick [trik] knep, fiff, narrestrek, fantestykke, puss, behendighetskunst, list, underfundighet, kunstgrep, egenhet, lag, vane, uvane, evne; stikk (i kortspill); narre, lure, bedra, leve av bedrageri.
trick [trik] pynte, utstaffere, stase opp.
trickery ['trikəri] lurendreieri; unatur.
trickish ['trikiʃ] slu, listig.
trickle ['trikl] sildre, sile, piple, dryppe.
trickster ['trikstə] lurendreier.
tricksy ['triksi] lurendreieraktig, skøyeraktig, skjelmsk.
tricktrack ['trikträk] trikktrakk (et brettspill).
tricky ['triki] listig, slu, fiffig; vanskelig å utføre.
tricolour ['traikʌlə] trefarget flagg, trikolor.
tricot ['trikoᵘ] trikot, trikotasje.
tric-trac ['trikträk] se **tricktrack.**
tricycle ['traisikl] trehjult sykkel.
trident ['traidənt] trefork, tregreinet gaffel (el. lyster).
triennial [trai'eniəl] treårig, treårlig, treårs.
trier ['traiə] se under **try.**
trifle ['traifl] bagatell, småtteri, ubetydelighet, småting, charlottekake; spøke, fjase; **catch at -s** henge seg i småting; — **away** fjase bort, vase bort. **-r** en som fjaser, narr, barnaktig person.
trifling ['traifliŋ] ubetydelig; fjas, lek.
trifoliate [trai'fo·liét] trebladet.
triform ['traifå·ᵊm] i tredobbelt skikkelse.
trig [trig] stanse, bremse, stoppe; bremse, stopper.
trigger ['trigə] bremse, hemsko, avtrekker; **pull the** — trekke av; — **guard** avtrekkerbøyle.
trigonometric(al) [trigənə'metrik(l)] trigonometrisk.
trigonometry [trigə'nåmitri] trigonometri.
trigraph ['traigra·f] trigraf, triftong.
trilateral [trai'lätərəl] tresidet.
trilingual [trai'liŋgwəl] i tre språk.
trill [tril] trille, dryppe.
trill [tril] trille; slå triller.
trillion ['triljən] trillion.
trilogy ['trilədʒi] trilogi, rekke av tre skuespill.
trim [trim] trimme, bringe i orden, lempe til

rette, ta seg av, pynte, pusse, stelle, staffere, beskjære, klippe, stusse, gjøre i stand, innpasse, stille, rette, bringe på rett kjøl, ta ordentlig i skole, balansere, vippe, slingre; velordnet, velstelt, soignert, nett, fiks; pynt, stas, drakt; — **the sails** stille seilene; **in perfect** — fiks og ferdig, i full stand. **-mer** en som ordner, pusser, lampepusser, værhane, vendekåpe. **-ming** ordning, utstaffering, besetning, pynt; (pl.) tilbehør. **-ness** netthet, velsoignert utseende.

trinal ['trainəl], **trine** [train] tredobbelt.

trinitarian [trini'tæ·ᵊriən] treenighets-.

trinity ['triniti] treenighet, trinitatis; **Trinity College** navn på universitetskollegium i Oxford, Cambridge, London og Dublin; **Trinity House** institutt i London (som bl. a. bestyrer fyr- og losvesenet).

trinket ['triŋkit] smykke, småting, nipsgjenstand.

trio ['trioᵘ] trio, tersett.

trip [trip] trippe, ta en tur, snuble, snåve, feile, forse seg, svikte, få til å snuble; spenne bein for, fange; tripping, tur, utflukt, feil, feiltagelse; — **up,** — **up one's heels** spenne bein unna en; **fetch** — ta tilløp.

tripartite ['tripa·ᵊtait] tredelt, avsluttet mellom tre. — **pact** tremaktspakt. **tripartition** [traipa·ᵊ-'tiʃən] tredeling.

tripe [traip] innvoller, innmat, kallun; vrøvl, tøys.

tripetalous [trai'petələs] med tre kronblad, trebladet.

triphthong ['trifþåŋ] triftong, trelyd. **-al** [-'þåŋəl] triftongisk.

triplane ['traiplei¹n] fly med tre bæreflater.

triple ['tripl] tredobbelt, trefoldig; gjøre tredobbelt, utgjøre det tredobbelte av; **the Triple Alliance** trippelalliansen.

triplet ['triplét] samling av tre, tre rimlinjer; triol; i plur.: trillinger.

triplicate ['triplikét] tredobbelt, trefoldig; triplikat, annen avskrift. **triplication** [tripli-'kei¹ʃən] tredobling. **triplicity** [tri'plisiti] tredobbelthet.

triply ['tripli] tredobbelt, tre ganger.

tripod ['traipåd] trefot.

Tripoli ['tripoli] Tripolis.

tripoli ['tripoli] polerkritt, trippel.

tripos ['traipås] bakkalaureatseksamen med utmerkelse; **classical** — **examination** klassisk filologisk eksamen — **-paper** sensurliste for triposeksamen.

tripper ['tripə] turist.

tripping ['tripiŋ] lett på foten, trippende; tripping, dansing.

triptych ['triptik] tredelt altertavle.

trireme ['trairi·m] treradåret skip.

trisect [trai'sekt] tredele.

trisection [trai'sekʃən] tredeling.

trisyllabic [traisi'läbik], **-al** trestavings-.

trisyllable [trai'siləbl] trestavingsord.

trite [trait] forslitt, fortersket, banal, hverdagslig. **-ness** forslitthet, trivialitet.

Triton ['traitån] Triton, en sjøhalvgud; **a minnow among -s** en spurv i tranedans.

trituration [tritju're¹ʃən] knusing.

triumph ['traiəmf] triumf, seier; triumfere. **-al** [trai'ʌmfəl] triumf-, triumferende. **triumphant** [trai'ʌmfənt] triumferende, seirende, triumf-, seiers-.

triumvir [trai'ʌmvə] triumvir. **-ate** [trai'ʌm-virét] triumvirat.

triune ['traiju·n] treenig.

trivet ['trivit] trefot, treføtt, krakk med tre bein.

trivial ['trivjəl] alminnelig, hverdagslig, ubetydelig, ordinær. — **name** artsnavn. **-ness, -ity** [trivi'äliti] ubetydelighet.

trivium ['triviəm] trivium (de tre vitenskaper: grammatikk, logikk, retorikk).

trochaic [tro'ke¹ik] trokéisk; trokéisk vers.

trochee ['troᵘki] troké (en versfot som består av en lang (el. betont) og en kort (el. ubetont) staving).

trod [tråd] imperf. av **tread**.

trodden [trådn] perf. pts. av **tread**.

troglodyte ['tråglodait] troglodytt, huleboer.

Troic ['troᵘik] troisk, trojansk.

troika ['troikə] troika (russisk vogn).

Trojan ['troᵘdʒən] trojansk; trojaner.

troll [troᵘl] tralle, synge; fiske, dorge.

troll [trål] troll.

trolley ['tråli] liten kjerre; dresin, tralle; kontaktrulle, kontakttrinse.

trolley-line ['trålilain] elektrisk sporvogn med luftledning.

trollop ['tråləp] slurve, sluske, gatetøs.

Trollope ['tråləp] Trollope.

trombone ['tråmboᵘn] basun.

tromp(e) [tråmp] blåsemaskin.

troop [tru·p] tropp, flokk, skare, ryttertropp, liten eskadron, pl. tropper, krigsfolk; gå flokkevis, samle seg i flokker, stimle, marsjere, dra fort av sted.

trooper ['tru·pə] kavalerist.

troop-ship ['tru·pʃip] troppetransportskip.

trope [troᵘp] trope, billedlig uttrykk.

trophied ['troᵘfid] trofésmykket.

trophy ['troᵘfi] trofé, seierstegn.

tropic ['tråpik] vendekrets. **-al** tropisk.

trot [tråt] trave, lunte, dilte, traske, la trave; trav, humpende gang; rolling; gammel kjerring.

troth [troᵘþ] (gml.) sannhet; tro, ord; trolove.

trotter ['tråtə] traver (om hest); fot, labb.

trotting-horse ['tråtiŋhå·ᵊs] traver.

trotting-match ['tråtiŋmätʃ] travløp.

trottoir ['tråtwa·ᵊ] fortau.

troubadour ['tru·bədu·ə] trubadur.

trouble ['trʌbl] opprøre, sette i bevegelse, røre opp (vann), forstyrre, forurolige, engste, bry, plage, besvære, umake, gjøre uleilighet, uleilige seg, plage seg, forstyrrelse, uro, bekymring, sorg, besvær, plage, bry, uleilighet, motgang; **that's just the** — det er nettopp ulykken. — **-mirth** fredsforstyrrer. **-r** forstyrrer. **-some** besværlig, brysom, vidløftig. **-someness** brysomhet.

troublous ['trʌbləs] urolig, opprørt, forvirret; engstende.

trough [trå·ʃ] trau, møllerenne, fordypning, bølgedal.

trounce [trauns] banke, pryle.

troupe [tru·p] trupp (av skuespillere e. l.).

trousering ['trauzəriŋ] buksetøy.

trousers ['trauzəz] benklær, bukser.

trousseau [tru·'soᵘ] brudeutstyr.

trout [traut] aure, ørret. — **-coloured** aurefarget, droplet. **-let, -ling** småaure, kjøe.

trowel ['trauəl] murskje, planteskje; legge på med murskje, arbeide med murskje.

troy [troi] gull- el. sølvvekt, apotekervekt.

Troy ['troi] Troia.

truancy ['tru·ənsi] skulking.

truant ['tru·ənt] skulkende; skulker; skulke, drive; **play** — skulke skolen.

truce [tru·s] våpenstillstand, opphør, hvile, kort frist. — **-breaker** en som bryter avtale.

truck [trʌk] drive tuskhandel, bytte bort, tuske; bytte, tuskhandel.

truck [trʌk] raperthjul; tralle, transportvogn, godsvogn, tralle til bagasje på jernbaneperrong, (mar.) flaggknapp, kløtre.

truckage ['trʌkidʒ] transport; betaling for transport.

truckage ['trʌkidʒ] tuskhandel.

truckle ['trʌkl] lite hjul, trinse, rulle.

truckle ['trʌkl] krype, bøye seg udmykt, logre.

truck-system ['trʌk'sistəm] betaling av arbeidslønn med varer.

truculence ['trʌkjuləns] villhet, råhet, frykte-lig utseende. **truculent** ['trʌkjulənt] barbarisk, vill, fæl, fryktelig.

trudge [trʌdʒ] traske; trasking.

true [tru·] tro, sann, rett, trofast, riktig, ekte; **it is** — sant nok, riktignok, vel; **a** — **bill** en begrunnet anklage. — **-blue** tro som gull, ekte; grunnærlig sjel. — **-born** ektefødt, ekte. — **-bred** av ekte rase, gjennomdannet. — **-hearted** tro, trofast, oppriktig. — **-love** inderlig elsket. **-love-knot, -lover's-knot** kjærlighetssløyfe. **-ness** sannferdighet, riktighet, sikkerhet.

truffle [ˈtrʌfl] trøffel. **-d** tillaget med trøfler.

truism [ˈtru·izm] selvinnlysende sannhet, trivialitet.

truly [ˈtruli] i sannhet, sannelig, oppriktig, forbindtligst; trofast; nøyaktig; unektelig; **I can** — say jeg kan med sannhet si; **yours** — ærbødigst (foran underskriften i et brev); — **thankful** oppriktig takknemlig.

trump [trʌmp] trumf; knupp, kjernekar; stikke med trumf, spille trumf, trumfe; **put on** el. **to the -s** drive til det ytterste; **-s may turn up** utsiktene kan lysne.

trump [trʌmp] bedra; — **up** dikte opp.

trump [trʌmp] trompet; **the** — **of doom** dommedagsbasunen.

trumpery [ˈtrʌmpəri] flitterstas, juks; sludder; forloren, intetsigende, skarve, simpel, tarvelig.

trumpet [ˈtrʌmpit] trompet, lurblåser; trompetlyd; forkynne, skralle, utbasunere; **speaking** — talerør, ropert; **the last** — dommedagsbasunen. — **-call** trompetstøt.

trumpeter [ˈtrʌmpitə] trompeter, trompetblåser; **be one's own** — skryte, rose seg selv.

trumpet|-flower kaprifolium. — **-fly** brems (insekt). — **-sounding** trompetsignal.

truncate [ˈtrʌŋkeˈt] avstumpe, skjære av, avstubbe, avbryte, lemleste. **truncation** [trʌŋ-ˈkeˈʃən] avstumping, lemlesting, beskjæring.

truncheon [ˈtrʌnʃən] stav, kommandostav, politikølle.

trundle [ˈtrʌndl] rulle, trille; rull, trinse, valse. — **-head** kvernhjul.

trunk [trʌŋk] stamme, kropp, hoveddel, koffert, kanal, (elefants) snabel, pl. bukser som rekker fra livet til midt på låret. — **-call** telefonoppringning fra stor avstand, provinsoppringning. — **-hose** [ˈtrʌŋkhoˈz] d. s. s. pl. av trunk. — **-line** hovedbane, hovedlinje; telefonlinje fra by til by. **trunks** telefonsentral i London for oppringninger til og fra den fjernere provins.

trunnel [ˈtrʌnil] nagle.

trunnion [ˈtrʌnjən] sylindertapp; tapp (på kanon).

truss [trʌs] knippe, bunt, brokkbind; (mar.) rakke; tømmerverk; binde opp, pakke sammen, klynge opp; henge, avstive, armere; **well-trussed** med godt sluttede lår (om hester).

trust [trʌst] tillit, tiltro, trygt håp, kreditt, forvaring, varetekt, tillitsverv, plikt, bestilling; trust, ring, sammenslutning; betrodd gods; tro, ha tiilit til, stole på, lite på, gi på kreditt, betro (en noe **one with a ting**); **leave in** — to betro . . . til forvaltning; **hold in** — ha i forvaring; — **in** sette sin lit til, stole på; — to stole på; **I can't** — **myself** to ogs. jeg tør ikke.

trustee [trʌˈsti·] tillitsmann, kurator, verje, bobestyrer; — **of a bankrupt's estate** bestyrer av konkursbo. **The Public Trustee** (svarer omtrent til) overformynder, overformynderi. **-ship** egenskap som tillitsmann osv., verjemål. **trust|ful** [ˈtrʌstful] tillitsfull, pålitelig. **-less** upålitelig, løs av seg. **-worthy** [-wə·ði] pålitelig, tilforlatelig.

trusty [ˈtrʌsti] pålitelig, stø, trofast, tro, traust.

truth [tru·þ] sannhet; sanndruhet, sannferdighet; troskap; riktighet; **in** — i sannhet; **to say** (el. **tell**) **the** — sant å si; — **to say** (el. **tell**) sant å si. — **in advertising** ærlig reklame. **-ful** sannferdig, sanndru. **-fulness** sannferdighet. **-less** usann, troløs. **-lessness** usannhet, troløshet. **-telling** sanndru.

try [trai] prøve, forsøke, undersøke, avhøre, tiltale, rense (metall), smelte om (talg); sette på prøve; anstrenge, leite på, røyne på; — **hard** prøve av all kraft; — **back** søke å trekke seg tilbake; — **by a court-martial** stille for en krigsrett. **trying** vanskelig, ubehagelig, plagsom.

tryst [trist] stevnemøte, møtested; sette stevne.

tsar [za·ə] se **czar.**

tsetse [ˈtsetsi] tsetseflue.

T. S. H. fk. f. Their Serene Highnesses.

T. S. O. fk. f. town sub-office.

tub [tʌb] balje, stamp, bøtte, (smør)butt (også som mål), badekar, badebalje, bad; kasse (om en klosset båt), sette i en balje, bade, vaske; **tale of a** — (gml.) ammestuefortelling; **The Tale of the Tub** fortellingen om tønna, en satire av Swift 1704. **-bing** forbygning. **-by** hultlydende, tykk og rund, tønneformet, tønnerund.

tube [tju·b] rør, munnstykke, kikkert, kar (i dyre- el. plante-legemer), fengrør, fargetube; elektrisk undergrunnsbane i London.

tuber [ˈtju·bə] knoll, rotknoll, utvekst.

tubercle [ˈtju·bəkl] knute; tuberkel.

tubercular [tju·ˈbə·kjulə], **tuberculous** [-ləs] småknutet, tuberkuløs.

tuberculosis [tjubə·kju·loˈsis] tuberkulose.

tuberous [ˈtju·birəs] knollet.

tub-thumper [ˈtʌbθʌmpə] voldsom predikant. — **back søke å trekke seg til**

tubular [ˈtju·bjulə] rørformet; — **boiler** rørkjel.

T. U. C. fk. f. Trade Union Congress.

tuck [tʌk] fektekårde.

tuck [tʌk] sette sammen, pakke inn, tulle, trekke, legge i legg, folde under; legg; (sl.) gotter. — **away** anbringe; — **in** trekke inn, putte i seng; — **up** brette opp, hefte opp.

tucker [ˈtʌkə] halsstrimmel, halsrysj; mat.

tucker [ˈtʌkə] utmase, utkjøre; utkjørthet.

tucket [ˈtʌkit] trompetstøt, fanfare.

tuck-in [ˈtʌkˈin] måltid.

tuck-out [ˈtʌkˈaut] måltid.

Tudor [ˈtju·də] Tudor.

tuefall [ˈtju·fâ·l] halvtekke, skur.

Tuesday [ˈtju·zdi] tirsdag.

tufa [ˈtju·fə] tuffstein.

tufaceous [tju·ˈfeˈʃəs] tuffaktig.

tuft [tʌft] dusk, kvast, dott; lund, treklynge; fippskjegg; utstyre med dusker, ordne i dusker; **-ed** samlet i dusker. — **hunter** snylter hos ade lige studenter. **-y** dottet, samlet i dusker.

tug [tʌg] hale, trekke, slepe, taue, slite; trekk, rykk, bukserbåt, slepebåt, anstrengelse, basketak, verste tak; — **of war** tautrekking; nappetak, verste tak, styreprøve. **-ger** en som trekker. **-gingly** med slit og slep.

tuition [tju·ˈiʃən] formynderskap, undervisning. **-ary** undervisnings-.

tulip [ˈtju·lip] tulipan.

tulle [tul] tyll.

tumble [ˈtʌmbl] tumle, rulle, falle, ramle ned, dratte ned; styrte sammen, kaste seg fram og tilbake, boltre seg, slå kollbøtter, kaste, velte, rote i, forkrølle, bringe i uorden; rundkast, virvar. **-down** fallerdig, forfallen.

tumbler [ˈtʌmblə] akrobat, gjøgler; ogs. en slags leketøysfigur; ølglass, vannglass; (gammelt:) tumling (slags drikkeglass), ogs. tumling (en slags due).

tumbrel [ˈtʌmbrəl] møkk-kjerre, ammunisjonskjerre, rakkerkjerre; kjerre.

tumefy [ˈtju·mifai] bringe til å hovne.

tumescence [tju·ˈmesəns] oppsvulming.

tumid [ˈtju·mid] opphovnet, svulstig. **-ity** [tju·-ˈmiditi], **-ness** [ˈtju·midnês] hovenhet, svulstighet.

tummy [ˈtʌmi] mave, masse (i barnespråk).

tumour [ˈtju·mə] svulst. **-ed** hoven.

tumult [ˈtju·mʌlt] tumult, tummel, forvirring, opprør, sterk opphisselse. **-uariness** [tju·ˈmʌltjuə-rinês] tumult, opprørsk ferd. **-uary** [tju·ˈmʌltjuəri] forvirret, stormende, opprørsk. **-uous** [tju·

'mʌltjuəs] forvirret, vill, stormende, opprørt, heftig. **-uousness** forvirring, opprør, heftighet.

tumulus ['tjuˑmjuləs] haug, gravhaug.

tun [tʌn] tønne, fat; fylle på tønner.

tunable ['tjuˑnəbl] som kan stemmes; (i dialekt:) musikalsk, harmonisk.

Tunbridge ['tʌnbridʒ] Tunbridge.

tundra ['tʌndrə] tundra.

tune [tjuˑn] melodi, tone, koral, stemning, lag, harmoni; stemme, istemme; **be in** — være stemt, spille rent; **out of** — falsk, uopplagt. **-ful** velklingende, melodisk, musikalsk. **-less** uharmonisk, umusikalsk.

tuner ['tjuˑnə] stemmer.

tunic ['tjuˑnik] tunika, overkjole, bluse, våpenkjole, arbeidstrøye, hinne.

tuning|-fork ['tjuˑniŋfáˑk] stemmegaffel. — **-hammer** stemmenøkkel (som brukes av pianostemmer).

Tunis ['tjuˑnis] Tunis.

tunnel ['tʌnil] tunnel; bygge en tunnel under.

tunny ['tʌni] størje, makrellstørje, sildestørje.

tup [tʌp] vær, saubukk.

tu quoque ['tjuˑkwoᵘkwi] svar på en beskyldning ved å beskylde anklageren for det samme: «det kan du selv være».

turban ['təˑbən] turban. **-ed** med turban.

turbid ['təˑbid] grumset, gjørmet, uklar. **-ness** uklarhet, grumsethet, gjørmethet.

turbinated ['təˑbineˈtid] snodd, spiralformig.

turbination [təˑbiˈneˈʃən] hvirvelløp.

turbine ['təˑbin] turbin.

turbot ['təˑbət] piggvar.

turbulence ['təˑbjuləns] forvirring, uro.

turbulent ['təˑbjulənt] opprørt; urolig, opprørsk, ustyrlig.

Turcoman ['təˑkəmən] turkoman.

tureen [tjuˈriˑn] terrin.

turf [təˑf] grønnsvær, torv, grasplen, veddeløpsbane, hesteveddeløp; dekke med torv; **gentlemen of the** — hestesportsmenn; veddeløpsinteresserte; **on the** — som gir seg av med veddeløp, som stryker om på gata.

turfite ['təˑfait] hestesportsmann, veddeløpsinteressert.

turf|-moss torvmyr. — **-seat** grasbenk.

turfy ['təˑfi] grasrik, rik på torv; veddeløps-, hestesports-, sports-.

turgent ['təˑdʒənt] oppsvulmende, oppsvulmet.

turgescence [təˑ'dʒesəns] oppsvulming.

turgid ['təˑdʒid] oppsvulmet, svulstig.

turgidity [təˑ'dʒiditi]· oppstyltethet.

Turk [təˑk] tyrk, barbar; **the Young** **-s** ungtyrkerne.

Turkestan [təˑkiˈstän] Turkestan.

Turkey ['təˑki] Tyrkia; tyrkisk; kalkun. — **-cock** kalkunsk hane. — **-hen** kalkunsk høne. — **-merchant** handlende, som driver forretninger på Tyrkia.

Turkish ['təˑkiʃ] tyrkisk; **bath** romerbad.

Turkoman ['təˑkəmən] turkoman.

turmoil ['təˑmoil] kav, styr, ståk, uro, forstyr relse; tumle med, forurolige.

turn [təˑn] dreie, vende, snu, svinge, skape, omdanne, omvende, forandre, omstemme, oversette, gjøre forrykt, gjøre sur, jage bort, omgå (en fiende), dreie (el. snu, vende) seg; forandre seg, bøye av; bli; surne, skilles; dreining, omdreining, krumning, vending, omskifting, omslag; bøyning, svinge; liten tur, slag; tørn; preg, form, tilbøyelighet, anlegg; tjeneste, puss, forskrekkelse, støt, rekke, tur, gjengjeld, tilfelle, leilighet, fordel; — **his brain** gjøre ham forstyrret i hodet; — **coat** vende kåpen etter vinden; — **the corner** dreie om hjørnet; — **his head** fordreie hodet på ham — **the stomach** gjøre en bli kvalm; **he had -ed sixteen years of age** han var over seksten år gammel; — **pale** bli bleik; — **away** vise bort; — **back** sende tilbake, vende tilbake; — **in**

vende inn, brette inn, legge sammen, gå til køys, gå i seng; — **off lede** bort, slokke, vise bort, oppgi, fullende, bøye av; — **him loose upon the world** sende ham ut i den vide verden; — **out of doors** jage på dør; — **out** vise seg å være, få et visst utfall, kalle (vakten) ut; — **over** bla gjennom, gjennomsøke, slå hånden av, overdra, overveie; — **over a new leaf** ta skjeen i en annen hånd; — **to** vende til, bli til, ta fatt på; — **up** vende opp, trekke opp, vise seg uventet. hende, oppgi, løpe bort; **have the nose -ed up** (el. **a -ed up nose**) ha oppstoppernese. **to a** — nøyaktig, akkurat, fullkommen; **by -s** skiftevis, etter tur; **in his** — etter tur, da turen kom til ham, også; **my own** — comes turen kommer til meg selv; — **for** — like for like; — **of expression** uttrykksmåte. — **-cap** (bevegelig) røykhette. — **-coat** vendekåpe.

turner ['təˑnə] dreier.

Turner ['təˑnə] Turner (eng. maler).

turnery ['təˑnəri] dreierarbeid; dreierverksted.

turning ['təˑniŋ] dreining; omdreining, gatehjørne, sving; omgående bevegelse; dreiespon. — **-lathe** dreiebenk. — **-plate** svingskive, dreieskive. — **-point** vendepunkt. — **-table** dreieskive. — **-tool** dreiestål.

turnip ['təˑnip] nepe, kunepe, turnips. — **-cabbage** kålrabi, kålrot. — **-top** nepegras, nepekål.

turn|key ['təˑnkiˑ] fangevokter, slutter; — **-out** utseende, utstyr, ekvipasje, arbeidsnedlegging, nettoinntekt, tilskuermengde. — **-over** omsetning. **-pike** veibom. — **-screw** skrujern. — **-sick** svimmel. **-spit** stekevnder, grevlinghund. **-sile** korsbom. — **-table**, — **-plate** dreieskive.

turpentine ['təˑpəntain] terpentin.

turpitude ['təˑpitjuˑd] skjendighet, lavhet.

turquoise ['təˑkwaˑz] turkis; turkisfarget.

turret ['tʌrit] lite tårn, kanontårn; revolverhode (i dreiebenk). **-ed** tårnformet, med tårn.

turtle ['təˑtl] turteldue.

turtle ['təˑtl] havskilpadde; **green** — spiselig skilpadde.

turtle|-dove turteldue. — **-shell** skilpaddeskall, skilpadde. — **-soup** skilpaddesuppe.

Tuscan ['tʌskən] toskansk; toskaner; — **order** toskansk arkitektur.

tush [tʌʃ] blås! pøh! snakk!

tusk [tʌsk] hoggtann, støttann. **-ed** med hoggel. støttenner.

tusker ['tʌskə] voksen elefant.

tusky ['tʌski] forsynt med hoggtenner.

Tussaud [tu'soᵘ] Tussaud; **Madame Tussaud's** (**Waxworks**) vokskabinett i London.

tussle ['tʌsl] basketak, nappetak, nappes.

tussock ['tʌsək] dott, tust, grastust.

tut [t, tʌt] pøh! blås! vas! hysj!

tutelage ['tjuˑtilidʒ] formynderskap, verjemål.

tutelar [-lə] som har formynderskap, formynder-, verje-; beskyttende, skyts-.

tutor ['tjuˑtə] lærer, huslærer (hovmester), privatdosent, kollegieforstander; undervise, lære opp, manudusere. **-ess** lærerinne, guvernante.

tutorial [tjuˈtäˑriəl] lærer-, hovmester-.

tutorship ['tjuˑtəʃip] lærerstilling, veiledning; skots k) formynderskap.

tuwhit [tu'wit] hu-hu! (uglekrik).

tuwhoo [tu'wuˑ] hu-hu! (uglekrik); ule, tute.

tuxedo [tʌk'siˑdoᵘ] (i U. S. A.) smoking.

twaddle ['twådl] vrøvle, vase, tøve; sludder, vas, vrøvl. **-r** vasekopp.

Twain [tweᵉn] Twain.

twain [tweᵉn] (poet.) tvenne, to; **in** — i sund, i stykker.

twang [twäŋ] klinge, skurre, snøvle, la klinge, klirre med, klimpre på; skarp lyd, snøvling.

twangle ['twäŋgl] klimpre.

'twas [twås, twəz] det var.

twattle ['twåtl] = **twaddle.**

tweak [twiˑk] klemme, knipe, klype; knip(ing), klyp.

tweed [twi·d] tweed, en slags ullstoff.
tweedle ['twi·dl] håndtere lett, berøre, fikle med.
tweedledum and tweedledee ['twi·dl'dʌm ənd 'twi·dl'di·]; the difference between — en likegyldig forskjell.
tweezers ['twi·zəz] nebbetang, pinsett; a pair of — pinsett.
twelfth [twelfþ] tolvte; tolvtedel; duodesim.
— day- helligtrekongersdag. — -night helligtrekongersaften. — -tide helligtrekongers(dag).
twelve [twelv] tolv. -mo ['twelvmoᵘ] el. 12 mo duodes. -month år. — -pence shilling.
twentieth ['twentiiþ] tjuende; tjuendedel.
twenty ['twenti] tjue, et snes, mange. — -four ark falset i fireogtjue blader.
twice [twais] to ganger, dobbelt; — two is four to ganger to er fire; — as much dobbelt så mye; has — the strength er dobbelt så sterk; I did not wait (el. have) to be told — det lot jeg meg ikke si to ganger.
Twickenham ['twiknəm] Twickenham.
twiddle ['twidl] snurre, dreie lekende, leke med, fikle med.
twig [twig] kvist, piske; prime — i beste velgående.
twig [twig] forstå, se, skjønne, være med.
twiggy ['twigi] full av kvister, kvistlignende.
twilight ['twailait] tusmørke, grålysning, skumring; dunkel, halvmørk; belyse dempet.
twill [twil] vend i tøy; tøy med vend; veve el. vevd med vend.
twin [twin] tvilling, make, sidestykke; føde tvillinger, fødes som tvillinger, passe sammen. — -born tvillingfødt. — -brother tvillingbror.
twine [twain] sno, tvinne, omslynge, spinne, slynge seg sammen, bukte seg; sammenslyngning, tvinning, slyng, floke, seilgarn.
twinge [twindʒ] knipe, klype, stikke, føle en stikkende smerte; stikk, klyp, rykking, stikkende smerte, anfektelse; my side twinges det stikker i siden på meg; a twinge of conscience et anfall av samvittighetsnag.
twinkle ['twiŋkl] blinke, blunke, blinke med, tindre, funkle, glitre; blink, blunk, øyeblikk.
twinkling ['twiŋkliŋ] blinking, øyeblikk.
twirl [twə·l] hvirvle, dreie seg rundt, snurre, tvinne; omdreining, hvirvel.
twist [twist] vri, sno, tvinne, flette, omvinde, forvri, vrikke, forvrenge, sno seg; tvist, silketråd, snor, liten tobakksrull, tvinning, forvridning, retning, hang, drag, tilbøyelighet. — -drill spiralbor.
-er en som snor osv., repslager.
twit [twit] skose, håne, neise, erte; skose.
twitch [twitʃ] nappe, rykke; napp, rykk, rykking.
twitter ['twitə] kvitre; kvitter, kvitring.
twitter ['twitə] skjelve, beve; skjelving, spenning, nervøsitet; my heart -s mitt hjerte bever; be all in a — være ganske nervøs.

'twixt for betwixt imellom.
two [tu·] to; total; one or two en eller to, to-tre; two and two to og to; in two i sund, i to deler; by twos to og to, parvis; put two and two together stave og legge sammen.
two-chamber ['tu·tʃe'mbə] system tokammersystem.
two-decker ['tu·dekə] todekker.
two-edged ['tu·edʒd] tveegget.
twofold ['tu·foᵘld] dobbelt.
two-handed ['tu·'hændid] til å håndtere med to hender.
two-pair ['tu·pæ·ə] tredje-etasjes; a — back et bakværelse i tredje etasje.
twopence ['tʌpəns] to pence (ca. 15 øre).
twopenny ['tʌpəni] for to pence; tarvelig; tynt øl; — halfpenny for to og en halv penny; tarvelig. -worth for to pence.
two-ply ['tu·plai] dobbelt, dobbeltvevd.
two-step ['tu·step] twostep (dans i polkatakt).
tying ['taiiŋ] presens pts. av tie.
tyke [taik] kjøter; slamp, simpel fyr; Yorkshir — Yorkshiremann.
Tyler ['tailə] Tyler (navn).
tympan ['timpən] trommehule, trommehinne; dørfylling.
tympanum ['timpənəm] se tympan.
Tyne [tain]; the — elva Tyne; the Tyneside Tyne-distriktet.
type [taip] type, forbilde, mønster, preg; sats; skrive på maskin.
type-setter ['taip'setə] setter, settemaskin.
typewrite ['taiprait] maskinskrive, skrive på maskin.
typewriter ['taipraitə] skrivemaskin.
typhoid ['taifoid] fever tyfoidfeber, tyfus.
typhoon [tai'fu·n] tyfon, hvirvel-orkan.
typhus ['taifəs] tufys, flekktyfus; — recurrens rekurrensfeber.
typical ['tipikl] typisk, karakteristisk (of for).
typification [tipifi'ke'ʃən] typisk framstilling.
-ify ['tipifai] framstille typisk, være et typisk eksempel på, representere. -ist ['taipist] maskinskriver(ske). -ographer [tai'pågrəfə] typograf.
-ographical [t(a)ipo'gräfikl] typografisk. -ography [t(a)i'pågrəfi] typografi.
tyrannic [tai'ränik], -al tyrannisk.
tyrannicide[tai'ränisaid] tyrann-mord, -morder.
tyrannize ['tirənaiz] tyrannisere (over over).
tyranny ['tirəni] tyranni.
tyrant ['tairənt] tyrann.
tyre [taiə] hjulring, luftring, gummiring.
Tyre [taiə] Tyrus.
Tyrian ['tiriən] tyrisk, dypfiolett; tyrier.
tyro ['tairoᵘ] (ny)begynner.
Tyrol ['tirəl, ti'roᵘl] Tyrol.
Tyrolese [tiro'li·z] tyrolsk; tyroler(inne).

U

U, u [ju·] U.
uberous ['ju·bərəs] fruktbar.
uberty ['ju·bəti] fruktbarhet.
ubiquitarian [ju·bikwi'tæ·ᵊriən] ubikvitarier, hyller av læren om Kristi allestedsnærværelse.
ubiquitous [ju'bikwitəs] allestedsnærværende.
ubiquity [ju'bikwiti] allestedsnærværelse.
U-boat ['ju·boᵘt] tysk undervannsbåt.
U. D. C. fk. f. Union of Democratic Control.
udder ['ʌdə] jur.
udometer [ju'dåmitə] regnmåler.
ugliness ['ʌglinəs] stygghet.
ugly ['ʌgli] heslig; stygg, slem; stygging; reisehette (for damer).
Uitlander ['oitləndə] ikke-naturalisert kolonist i Sør-Afrika.

U. K. fk. f. United Kingdom.
ukase [ju'ke¹s] (russisk) ukas; (ogs. bil).
Ukraine [ju·krain] Ukraine.
ulcer ['ʌlsə] vågsår, verksår, svull. -ate [-re¹t] ulcerere; sette verk i. -ation [-'re¹ʃən] sårdanning. -ous [-rəs] ulcerøs, angrepet av sår.
ulema ['u·limə] ulema, i Tyrkia geistlige, rettslærde og dommere.
uliginous [ju'lidʒinəs] som gror på gjørmete steder; våtlendt.
ullage ['ʌlidʒ] tomt rom (i spiritusfat).
ulmacious [ʌl'me¹ʃəs] almaktig, alm-.
ulna ['ʌlnə] ulna, albuebein.
Ulster ['ʌlstə] Ulster (del av Irland).
ulster ['ʌlstər] ulster (frakk).
ult. fk. f. ultimo forrige måned.

ulterior [ʌl'tiəriə] ytterligere, videre, bortre.
ultima ['ʌltimə] ytterst, sist; siste staving. —
Thule det ytterste Thule.
ultimate ['ʌltimét] endelig, sist, opprinnelig,
først, udelelig, grunn-.
ultimatum [ʌlti'me¹təm] ultimatum, siste erklæring.
ultimo ['ʌltimoᵘ] forrige måned.
ultra ['ʌltrə] hinsides, bortenfor, ytterliggående.
-ism ['ʌltrəizm] radikalisme. -ist radikal. -marine
ultramarin (en blå farge). -montane [ʌltrə-
'månte¹n] fra den andre siden av fjellene, fremmed; paveligsinnet.
ululation [ʌlju'le¹ʃən] hyl, tuting.
Ulysses [ju'lisi·z] Ulysses, Odyssevs.
umbel ['ʌmbəl] skjerm. -late ['ʌmbəlét] skjerm-
blomstret, skjermformet. -lifer [ʌm'beliʃə] skjerm-
plante.
umber ['ʌmbə] umbra, en brun jordart.
umbilic [ʌm'bilik] navle-.
umbles ['ʌmblz] hjorts innvoller.
umbrage ['ʌmbridʒ] misfornøyelse, misnøye,
mistro; (poetisk) skygge; lauvverk. take — fatte
mistanke.
umbrageous [ʌm'bre¹dʒəs] skyggefull.
umbrella [ʌm'brelə] paraply.
umlaut ['umlaut] omlyd.
umpirage ['ʌmpairidʒ] voldgiftsmanns verv.
umpire ['ʌmpaiə] voldgiftsmann, dommer.
umpteen ['ʌmp'ti·n] atskillige, temmelig
mange.
un [ʌn] forstavelse til en stor mengde ord;
det uttales med svakt trykk, når det svarer til
norsk; av-, opp-, ut-, men med sterkt trykk, når
det svarer til norsk: u-, ikke; f. eks. undressed
[ʌn'drest] avkledd, men ['ʌn'drest] upåkledd.
Forstavelsen brukes 1) foran verber for å forandre deres betydning til det motsatte f. eks.
unbutton knappe opp; 2) foran adj., adv. og
subst. i betydn. u-, ikke, f. eks. unkind uvennlig;
3) foran verber dannet av subst. for å betegne:
berøve (el. fjerne) det som subst. nevner, f. eks.
unhorse kaste av hesten.
unabashed ['ʌnə'bäʃt] uforknytt.
unabated ['ʌnə'be¹tid] usvekket.
unable ['ʌn'e¹bl] udyktig, ute av stand (to til).
unabridged ['ʌnə'bridʒd] uforkortet.
unaccented ['ʌnäk'sentid] trykkløs.
unacceptable ['ʌnək'septəbl] uantagelig, uvelkommen.
unaccommodating [ʌnə'kåmədе¹tiŋ] umedgjørlig.
unaccountability ['ʌnəkauntə'biliti] uansvarlighet, uforklarlighet. unaccountable ['ʌnə-
'kauntəbl] uansvarlig; uforklarlig.
unacquainted ['ʌnə'kwe¹ntid] ukjent.
unadvisable ['ʌnəd'vaizəbl] uklok.
unadvised ['ʌnəd'vaizd] ubetenksom, uklok.
unaffected ['ʌnə'fektid] uberørt, uangrepet,
uskrømtet, ukunstlet, uaffektert.
unaided ['ʌn'e¹did] uten hjelp.
unallied ['ʌnə'laid] uten forbindelse, ubeslek-
tet, unensartet.
unalloyed ['ʌnə'loid] ublandet.
unalterable ['ʌn'å·ltərəbl] uforanderlig..
unambiguous ['ʌnəm'bigjuəs] utvetydig.
unambitious ['ʌnəm'biʃəs] ikke ærgjerrig, fordringsløs.
unamiable ['ʌn'e¹mjəbl] uelskverdig.
unanimated ['ʌn'änime¹tid] livløs.
unanimity [ju·nə'nimiti] enstemmighet.
unanimous [ju'nänimes] enig, enstemmig.
unanswerable ['ʌn'a·nsərəbl] ubesvarlig, uimotsigelig, ugjendrivelig. unanswered ubesvart.
unappealable ['ʌnə'pi·ləbl] inappellabel.
unappreciative ['ʌnə'pri·ʃjətiv] lite takknemlig.
unapproachable ['ʌnə'proᵘtʃəbl] utilnærmelig.
unappropriated ['ʌnə'proᵘprie¹tid] herreløs.
unapt ['ʌn'äpt] uskikket, udyktig, ubekvem.
unargued ['ʌn'a·°gju·d] ubestridt.

unarmed ['ʌn'a·°md] ubevæpnet.
unartful ['ʌn'a·°tfəl] uten kløkt, simpel.
unarticulated ['ʌna°'tikjule¹tid] uartikulert.
unascertainable ['ʌnäsə'te¹nəbl] som ikke kan
vites med visshet.
unashamed ['ʌnə'ʃe¹md] uten skam, skamløs.
unasked ['ʌn'a·skt] ikke spurt, uoppfordret.
unassailable ['ʌnə'se¹ləbl] uangripelig.
unassisted ['ʌnə'sistid] uten hjelp.
unassuaged ['ʌnə'swe¹dʒd] uformildet.
unassuming ['ʌnə's(j)u·miŋ] fordringsløs, beskjeden.
unatonable ['ʌnə'toᵘnəbl] uforsonlig.
unattached ['ʌnə'tätʃt] ikke bundet, ikke tilknyttet.
unattainable ['ʌnə'te¹nəbl] uoppnåelig.
unattended ['ʌnə'tendid] forlatt.
unattending ['ʌnə'tendiŋ] uoppmerksom.
unavailable ['ʌnə've¹ləbl], unavailing ['ʌnə-
've¹liŋ] unyttig, fruktesløs, gagnløs; utilgjengelig.
unavenged ['ʌnə'vendʒd] uhevnet.
unavoidable ['ʌnə'voidəbl] uunngåelig.
unaware ['ʌnə'wæ·ə] ikke oppmerksom (of på)
unawares ['ʌnə'wæ·əz] uforvarende, uventet.
unbacked ['ʌn'bäkt] som ikke er ridd til (om
hest); som ingen holder på (ved veddeløp); uten
støtte.
unbalanced ['ʌn'bälənst] ulikevektig.
unbar [ʌn'ba·°] lukke opp, åpne.
unbashful ['ʌn'bäʃful] skamløs.
unbear [ʌn'bæ·ə] ta opptømmen av.
unbearable ['ʌn'bæ·°rəbl] utålelig.
unbearing ['ʌn'bæ·°riŋ] ufruktbar.
unbeaten ['ʌn'bi·tn] uslått, ubanet.
unbecoming ['ʌnbi'kʌmiŋ] upassende, usømmelig, ukledelig.
unbegot ['ʌnbi'gåt] ufødt, evg.
unbelief ['ʌnbi'li·f] vantro, mistro (in til).
unbelieving ['ʌnbi'li·viŋ] vantro
unbend ['ʌn'bend] spenne ned, slappe, slakke,
løsne, gjøre løs; astpre; -ing ['ʌn'bendiŋ] stiv,
ubøyelig; -ing ['ʌnbendiŋ] som blir slapp.
unbenign ['ʌnbinain] uvennlig.
unbent [ʌn'bent] neppent, ikke anstrengt.
unbeseeming ['ʌnbi'si·miŋ] usømmelig.
unbiassed ['ʌn'baiəst] uhildet, fordomsfri.
unbind ['ʌn'baind, ʌn-] ta båndet av, løse, frigjøre.
unblamable ['ʌn'ble¹məbl] ulastelig, uskyldig.
unbleached ['ʌn'bli·tʃt] ubleikt.
unblemishable ['ʌn'blemiʃəbl] daddelfri.
unblown ['ʌn'bloᵘn] ikke utsprunget.
unblown ['ʌn'bloᵘn] ikke utslokket, ikke blåst
opp.
unbolt ['ʌn'boᵘlt] åpne.
unboot ['ʌn'bu·t] ta støvlene av.
unborn ['ʌn'bå·°n] ufødt; as innocent as the
babe — så uskyldig som barn i mors liv.
unbosom [ʌn'buzəm,'ʌn-] betro, åpne seg.
unbound ['ʌn'baund] ubundet, uinnbundet
unbounded ['ʌn'baundid] ubegrenset, grenseløs.
unbowel [ʌn'bauil] sprette opp.
unbrace ['ʌn'bre¹s] slappe.
unbred ['ʌn'bred] uoppdragen.
unbridle [ʌn'braidl] ta bisselet av; unbridled
uten bissel, utøylet, tøyleløs.
unbroken ['ʌn'broᵘkn] uavbrutt, utemt.
unburden [ʌn'bə·dn] lesse av, lette (of for).
unbutton [ʌn'bʌtn] knappe opp.
uncalled ['ʌn'kå·ld] unødig; — for ikke krevet,
unødig, i utrengsmål, ubetimelig.
uncanny [ʌn'käni] uhyggelig.
uncared-for ['ʌn'kæ·ədfå·°] upåaktet, forsømt,
vanskjøttet.
uncase [ʌn'ke¹s] blotte, utfolde.
unceasing ['ʌn'si·siŋ] uopphørlig.
unceremonious ['ʌnseri'moᵘnjəs] likefram, endefram, utvungen.
uncertain ['ʌn'sə·tn] usikker, uviss, utrygg. -ty
uvisshet.

uncertificated ['ʌnsə·'tifike'tid] uten attest.
unchain [ʌn'tʃe'n] løse.
unchangeable ['ʌn'tʃe'n(d)ʒəbl] uforanderlig.
unchanging ['ʌn'tʃe'n(d)ʒiŋ] uforanderlig, stadig.
uncharge [ʌn'tʃa·ʲdʒ] lesse av.
unchaste ['ʌn'tʃe'st] ukysk.
unchastity ['ʌn'tʃästiti] ukyskhet.
unchristian ['ʌn'kristʃən] ukristelig.
unchristianize [ʌn'kristʃənaiz] avkristne.
uncivil ['ʌn'sivil] uhøflig. -ized rå.
unclasp [ʌn'kla·sp] hekte opp, åpne.
uncle ['ʌŋkl] onkel (ogs. om tantes mann og hustrus onkel). Uncle Sam ɔ: De Forente Stater (ved en egen tydning av U. S.); uncle-in-law tantes mann; hustrus onkel; manns onkel; my watch is at my uncle's klokken min er i stampen («hos onkel»).
unclean ['ʌn'kli·n] uren.
unclench [ʌn'klenʃ] åpne (seg).
unclog [ʌn'klåg] befri, frigjøre.
unclose [ʌn'klo"z] åpne, bryte, åpenbare.
uncloud [ʌn'klaud] klare opp.
unco ['ʌŋko"] (i skotsk) ukjent, rar, underlig.
uncock [ʌn'kåk] spenne ned hanen på.
uncoffined ['ʌn'kåfind] ikke lagt i kiste.
uncoil [ʌn'koil] vikle opp, rulle opp.
uncomely [ʌn'kʌmli] utekkelig, stygg, usømmelig; tarvelig.
uncomfortable ['ʌn'kʌmf(ə)təbl] ubehagelig, ubekvem, uvel, i ulag, ille til mote, urolig.
uncommon ['ʌn'kåmən] ualminnelig.
uncommunicative ['ʌnkə'mju·nikətiv] umeddelsom.
uncomplaining [ʌnkəm'ple'niŋ] tålmodig, uten klage.
uncomplimentary ['ʌnkåmpli'mentəri] lite smigrende, ugalant.
uncomplying ['ʌnkəm'plaiiŋ] ubøyelig, stiv.
uncompromising ['ʌn'kåmprəmaizin] fast.
unconcern ['ʌnkən'sə·n] ubekymrethet, uberørthet, ro.
unconcerned ['ʌnkən'sə·nd] uinteressert, uberørt, ubekymret.
unconditional ['ʌnkən'diʃənəl] ubetinget.
unconfined ['ʌnkən'faind] uinnskrenket, fri.
unconformable['ʌnkən'få·ʲməbl] uoverensstemmende.
unconquerable ['ʌn'kåŋkərəbl] uovervinnelig.
unconscientious ['ʌnkånʃi'enʃəs] samvittighetsløs.
unconscionable ['ʌn'kånʃənəbl] urimelig.
unconscious ['ʌn'kånʃəs] bevisstløs, ubevisst, intetanende; be — of ikke være seg bevisst, ikke merke, ikke vite om (el. til).
unconsidered ['ʌnkən'sidəd] uoverlagt.
unconspicuous ['ʌnkən'spikjuəs] uanselig.
unconstitutional ['ʌnkånsti'tju·ʲʃənəl] forfatningsstridig, som er mot grunnloven.
unconstrained ['ʌnkən'stre'nd] utvungen, fri.
unconstraint ['ʌnkən'stre'nt] utvungenhet.
uncontested ['ʌnkən'testid] uomtvistet.
uncontrollable ['ʌnkən'tro"ʲəbl] ustyrlig, uimotståelig, ubendig, grenseløs, uavvendelig.
uncontrolled ['ʌnkən'tro"ld] ubehersket.
unconversant ['ʌnkån'və·sənt] ubevandret.
uncord [ʌn'kå·ʲd] løse opp.
uncork [ʌn'kå·ʲk] trekke opp (flaske).
uncounted ['ʌn'kauntid] utallig.
uncouple [ʌn'kʌpl] kople av, kople fra.
uncourteous ['ʌn'kå·ʲtʃəs] uhøflig.
uncourtly ['ʌn'kå·ʲtli] ufin, uhøvisk, grov.
uncouth ['ʌn'ku·þ] besynderlig, underlig, rar, klosset.
uncover [ʌn'kʌvə] avdekke, ta lokket av, ta hatten av; stand -ed stå med blottet hode.
uncrowned ['ʌn'kraund] ukronet.
unction ['ʌŋkʃən] salve, salving, salvelse.
unctuous ['ʌŋktʃuəs] fettet, salvelsesfull.
uncurl [ʌn'kə·ʲl] glatte, få krøllene ut av.

uncus ['ʌŋkəs] krok, hake.
uncustomed ['ʌn'kʌstəmd] tollfri, ikke fortollet.
uncut ['ʌn'kʌt] uoppskåret, ubeskåret, uslipt.
undated ['ʌn'de'tid] udatert.
undated ['ʌnde'tid] bølget.
undaunted ['ʌn'då·ntid] uforferdet.
undeceive [ʌndi'si·v] rive ut av villfarelsen; be -d få øynene opp.
undecided ['ʌndi'saidid] uavgjort, ubestemt, på det uvisse; leave — la stå hen.
undecked [ʌn'dekt] uprydd; åpen.
undefiled ['ʌndi'faild] ren.
undefinable ['ʌndi'fainəbl] ubestemmelig.
undemonstrable ['ʌndi'månstrəbl] ubevislig.
undemonstrative ['ʌndi'månstrətiv] tilbakeholden, tilknappet, stillfarende, reservert.
undeniable ['ʌndi'naiəbl] unektelig.
under ['ʌndə] under; nede, nedenfor; underordnet, under-; — existing conditions under de rådende forhold; — Elizabeth under Elisabet, under Elisabets regjering; — this (day's) date (under) dags dato; — Heaven under sola, her på jorda; — the name of under navnet; — an oath bundet av en ed; — consideration under overveielse; — God nest Gud, med Guds hjelp; — age mindreårig, umyndig; speak — one's breath snakke ganske lavt; — his own hand egenhendig.
under|bid ['ʌndə'bid] underby; skamby. -bred ['ʌndə'bred] halvdannet. -current ['ʌndəkʌrənt] understrøm. -do [ʌndə'du·] steke (koke) for lite. -done halvrå. -estimate undervurdere. -feed sultefore. -foot [ʌndə'fut] under føttene. the roads were dry -foot veiene var tørre å gå på. -go [ʌndə'go"] gjennomgå, utstå.
under|graduate [ʌndə'grädjuét] student. -ground [ʌndə'graund] underjordisk; undergrunnsbane. -growth ['ʌndəgro"p] underskog. -hand ['ʌndəhänd] med hånden vendt opp, med underarmskast, hemmelig, snikende; -hand bowling underarmskasting. -let [ʌndə'let] leie under verdien, framleie. -lie [ʌndə'lai] ligge under, ligge til grunn. -line [ʌndə'lain] understreke, utheve.
under|linen ['ʌndəlinən] undertøy, linnet. -ling ['ʌndəliŋ] underordnet, dårlig kar, stakkar. -lying bærende, grunn-. -most ['ʌndəmo"st] underst, nederst. -neath [ʌndə'ni·þ] (neden)under, nedentil. -part ['ʌndəpa·ʲt] underordnet rolle. -pay [ʌndə'pe'] betale for lite, utbytte. -pay ['ʌndəpe'] sultelønn. -pin [ʌndə'pin] understøtte. -plot ['ʌndəplåt] bihandling. -prize [ʌndə'praiz] undervurdere. -rate [ʌndə're't] undervurdere. -rate ['ʌndəre't] spottpris. -run [ʌndə'rʌn] løpe under, underhale. -set [ʌndə'set] understrøm. -set ['ʌndəset] understrøm. -shirt ['ʌndəʃə·t] (amr.) undertrøye, ulltrøye.
undersign [ʌndə'sain] undertegne.
undersized ['ʌndəsaizd] undermåls, for liten.
under|soil ['ʌndəsoil] undergrunn. -song ['ʌndəsåŋ] omkved, kor.
understand [ʌndə'ständ] forstå, skjønne, innse, vite, kjenne, mene, få vite, erfare, høre, underforstå; he -s his business han kan sine ting; he does not — a joke han er ikke til å spøke med; it passes me to — how det går over min forstand, hvorledes . . .; he gave it to be understood han lot seg forstå med; he can make himself understood in English han kan gjøre seg forståelig på engelsk; we — det forlyder, etter forlydende.
understanding [ʌndə'ständiŋ] forstand, vett, forståelse; forstandig; it passes all — det overgår all forstand; to my poor — etter mitt ringe skjønn.
under|state [ʌndə'ste't] gjøre for lite av, framstille utilstrekkelig. -strapper [-sträpə] medhjelper. -study ['ʌndəstʌdi] reserveskuespiller (-inne), som dublerer en bestemt rolle; [ʌndə-

'stʌdi] dublere, besette en teaterrolle dobbelt, med to som kan avløse hverandre. **-take** [-'te¹k] påta seg, foreta, overta, forplikte seg til. **-taker** ['ʌndəte¹kə] entreprenør, innehaver av begravelsesbyrå, bedemann; **his -taker's face** hans bedemannsansikt. **-taking** [ʌndə'te¹kiṇ] foretagende, forpliktelse, begravelsesfaget. **-tone** ['ʌndətoⁿn] dempet stemme. **-tow** ['ʌndətoᵘ] understrøm. **-value** ['ʌndə'välju] undervurdere. **-wear** [-wæ·ə] undertøy. **-wood** ['ʌndəwud] underskog. **-work** 'ʌndə'wə·k] arbeide billigere enn, i stillhet undergrave. **-write** [ʌndə'rait] skrive under; tegne (polise, om assurandør). **-writer** ['ʌndəraitə] assurandør, sjøassurandør.

undescribable ['ʌndi'skraibəbl] ubeskrivelig.
undeserved ['ʌndi'zə·vd] ufortjent.
undeserving ['ʌndi'zə·viṇ] uverdig.
undesigned ['ʌndi'zaind] uforsettlig.
undesigning ['ʌndi'zainiṇ] troskyldig, ærlig.
undesirable ['ʌndi'zairəbl] mindre ønskelig, illesett, brysom, plagsom, i veien. **undesirous** ['ʌndi'zairəs] som ikke ønsker.
undetermined ['ʌndi'tə·mind] ubestemt.
undeviating ['ʌn'di·vie¹tiṇ] usvikelig, fast, stø.
undignified ['ʌn'dignifaid] lite verdig.
undimmed ['ʌn'dimd] klar (som før), ufordunklet.
undine [ʌn'di·n] undine (kvinnelig vannånd).
undirected ['ʌndi'rektid] uadressert.
undiscerning ['ʌndi'zə·niṇ] ukritisk.
undisciplined ['ʌn'disiplind] udisiplinert.
undisguised ['ʌndis'gaizd] utilslørt, uforstilt.
undisputed ['ʌndis'pju·tid] ubestridt.
undissembling ['ʌndi'sembliṇ] uforstilt.
undistinguishable ['ʌndi'stiṇgwiʃəbl] ukjennelig.
undistinguished ['ʌndi'stiṇgwiʃt] ubekjent.
undisturbed ['ʌndi'stə·bd] uforstyrret.
undivided ['ʌndi'vaidid] udelt.
undo [ʌn'du·] oppheve, løse, ødelegge. **-ing** ulykke, ødeleggelse. **undone** [ʌn'dʌn] tilintetgjort.
undoubted ['ʌn'dautid], **-ly** [-li] utvilsomt, uten tvil.
undress [ʌn'dres] kle av, ta forbinding av, kle av seg. **undress** ['ʌndres] hverdagsklær, daglig uniform.
undue ['ʌn'dju·] utilbørlig, overdreven; ennå ikke forfallen (til betaling).
undulate ['ʌndjule¹t] bølge, sette i bølgebevegelse, ondulere.
undulation [ʌndju'le¹ʃən] bølgebevegelse, bølgegang; ondulasjon.
unearth [ʌn'ə·þ] grave opp, drive ut av hiet.
unearthly [ʌn'ə·þli] overnaturlig, uhyggelig, nifs.
uneasy ['ʌn'i·zi] ubehagelig, urolig, engstelig, ubekvem, tvungen.
uneatable ['ʌn'i·təbl] uspiselig.
unembarrassed ['ʌnèm'bärəst] utvungen; (jur.) ubeheftet.
unembodied ['ʌnèm'bådid] ulegemlig.
unemotional ['ʌni'moᵘʃənəl] kald, prosaisk, upåvirkelig.
unemployed ['ʌnèm'ploid] arbeidsløs.**unemployment** ['ʌnèm'ploimənt] arbeidsløshet, arbeidsløyse.
unending ['ʌn'endiṇ] endeløs.
unengaged ['ʌnen'ge¹dʒd] fri, ledig, uforlovet.
un-English ['ʌn'iṇgliʃ] uengelsk.
unenterprising ['ʌn'entəpraiziṇ] initiativløs.
unequal ['ʌn'i·kwəl] ulike, ujevn, udyktig (til); **be — to a task** ikke makte en oppgave.
unequalled ['ʌn'i·kwåld] uforlignelig, uten sidestykke.
unerring ['ʌn'ə·riṇ] ufeilbar, usvikelig.
unessential ['ʌni'senʃəl] uvesentlig.
uneven ['ʌn'i·vn] ujevn, kupert.
unexampled ['ʌnég'za·mpld] enestående, uten like.

unexceptionable ['ʌnèk'sepʃənəbl] udadlelig.
unexceoptional ['ʌnèk'sepʃənəl] alminnelig.
unexpected ['ʌnèk'spektid] uventet.
unfailing ['ʌn'fe¹liṇ] ufeilbar(lig), årviss, uuttømmelig.
unfair ['ʌn'fæ·ə] uærlig, ubillig, ikke pen.
unfaithful ['ʌn'fe¹þful] utro.
unfaltering ['ʌn'få·ltəriṇ] urokkelig.
unfamiliar ['ʌnfə'miljə] ukjent, uvant.
unfasten [ʌn'fa·sn] løse opp, åpne.
unfathomable ['ʌn'fäðəməbl] uutgrunnelig.
unfavourable ['ʌn'fe¹vərəbl] ugunstig.
unfeed ['ʌn'fi·d] ubetalt.
unfeeling ['ʌn'fi·liṇ] ufølsom, hardhjertet.
unfeigned ['ʌn'fe¹nd] uskrømtet, uforstilt.
unfetter [ʌn'fetə] løse, frigjøre, befri.
unfilial ['ʌn'filjəl] ikke sønnlig el. datterlig.
unfit ['ʌn'fit] uskikket, upassende, uhøvelig.
unfix ['ʌn'fiks] løse, forrykke.
unfixed ['ʌn'fikst] løs, vaklende.
unflagging ['ʌn'flägiṇ] utrettelig, usvikelig.
unfledged ['ʌn'fledʒd] uflyg, ikke flyvedyktig.
unflinching ['ʌn'flinʃiṇ] uforferdet, djerv.
unfold [ʌn'foᵘld] utfolde, åpenbare, forklare, framstille.
unformed ['ʌn'få·ºmd] oppløst, uformelig, uformet.
unfortunate ['ʌn'få·ºtʃənèt] uheldig, ulykkelig. **-ly** uheldigvis, dessverre.
unfounded ['ʌn'faundid] ugrunnet.
unfrequent ['ʌn'fri·kwənt] sjeldnere, mindre hyppig. **-ly** sjelden, en hende gang.
unfriended ['ʌn'frendid] venneløs, uten venner.
unfriendly ['ʌn'frendli] uvennlig, ugunstig.
unfrock ['ʌn'fråk] ta kappa el. kjolen fra; frata presteverdigheten.
unfulfilled ['ʌnful'fild] uoppfylt.
unfurl [ʌn'fə·l] utfolde, slå ut.
ungainly [ʌn'ge¹nli] klosset, kluntet, keitet, underlig, frastøtende.
ungenial ['ʌn'dʒi·njəl] usympatisk, umild.
ungentlemanlike ['ʌn'dʒentlmənlaik] udannet.
ungentlemanly [ʌn'dʒentlmənli] udannet.
ungird [ʌn'gə·d] løse gjorden av, løse, ta av.
ungladden [ʌn'glädn] bedrøve, nedslå.
unglove [ʌn'glʌv] ta hansken(e) av.
ungodly ['ʌn'gådli] ugudelig, gudløs.
ungovernable ['ʌn'gʌvənəbl] uregjerlig.
ungraceful ['ʌn'gre¹sful] ugratiøs.
ungracious ['ʌn'gre¹ʃəs] unådig, ubehagelig, uvillig.
ungrateful ['ʌn'gre¹tful] utakknemlig.
ungrudging ['ʌn'grʌdʒiṇ] villig.
ungual ['ʌṇgwəl] negleaktig, med negler (klør).
unguarded ['ʌn'ga·ºdid] ubevoktet, uforsiktig, uaktsom.
unguent ['ʌṇgwənt] salve.
unhallowed ['ʌn'hälºwd] vanhellig, profan.
unhand [ʌn'händ] slippe, sleppe.
unhandsome ['ʌn'hänsəm] uskjønn.
unhandy ['ʌn'händi] ubehendig, ubekvem.
unhang [ʌn'häṇ] ta ned.
unhappiness ulykke. **unhappily** uheldigvis.
unhappy [ʌn'häpi] ulykkelig, uheldig.
unharness [ʌn'ha·ºnès] sele av.
unhealthy ['ʌn'helþi] usunn, sykelig, svak.
unheard ['ʌn'hə·d] uten å bli hørt; [ʌn'hə·d] uhørt, eksempelløs.
unheard-of [ʌn'hə·d²v] uhørt, eksempelløs.
unheeding ['ʌn'hi·diṇ] uaktsom, tankeløs.
unhesitating ['ʌn'hezite¹tiṇ] uten betenkning.
unhinge [ʌn'hinʒ] løfte av hengslene, rokke, forvirre, skake opp.
unholy ['ʌn'hoᵘli] vanhellig; ugudelig.
unhook ['ʌn'huk] ta av kroken, hekte opp.
unhoped-for ['ʌn'hoᵘptfå·ə] uventet.
unhorse [ʌn'hå·ºs] kaste av hesten.
unhung ['ʌn'hʌṇ] (ennå) ikke hengt.
unhurt ['ʌn'hə·t] uskadd.

unhusk [ʌn'hʌsk] d. s. s. **husk.**
unicorn ['ju·nikå·ᵊn] enhjørning.
unideal ['ʌnai'diəl] prosaisk, virkelig.
unidiomatic ['ʌn'idjo'mätik] språkstridig.
uniform ['ju·nifå·ᵊm] ensformig, ensartet, uforanderlig; uniform.
uniformity [ju·ni'få·ᵊmiti] ensartethet, overensstemmelse; **The Act of Uniformity** uniformitets-akten, en eng. kirke-anordning av 1662, hvorved en mengde geistlige ble drevet ut av folkekirken.
unify ['ju·nifai] samle, forene.
unigenous [ju·'nidʒinəs] ensartet.
unimaginable ['ʌni'mädʒinəbl] utenkelig.
unimaginative ['ʌni'mädʒinətiv] fantasiløs.
unimpeachable ['ʌnim'pi·tʃəbl] uangripelig, ulastelig.
unimportant ['ʌnim'på·ᵊtənt] uviktig.
unimpressible ['ʌnim'presibl] uimottagelig.
unimprovable ['ʌnim'pru·vəbl] uforbederlig.
unimproved ['ʌnim'pru·vd] uforbedret, udannet.
uninfluenced ['ʌn'influenst] upåvirket.
uninfluential ['ʌninflu'enʃəl] uten innflytelse.
uninformed [ʌnir·'få·ᵊmd] uvitende.
uninforming ['ʌnin'få·ᵊmiŋ] lite opplysende.
uninhabitable ['ʌnin'häbitəbl] ubeboelig.
uninhabited ['ʌnin'häbitid] ubebodd.
uninitiated ['ʌnin'iʃie'tid] uinnvidd.
uninjured ['ʌn'indʒəd] uskadd.
unintelligent ['ʌnin'telidʒənt] uforstandig.
unintelligible ['ʌnin'telidʒibl] uforståelig.
unintended ['ʌnin'tendid], **unintentional** ['ʌnin-'tenʃənəl] utilsiktet, ufrivillig.
uninterested ['ʌn'intərestid] uegennyttig.
uninteresting ['ʌn'intərestiŋ] uinteressant.
unintermittent ['ʌnintə'mitənt] uavbrutt.
uninterrupted ['ʌnintə'rʌptid] uavbrutt.
union ['ju·njən] forening, lag, enighet, samhold, union, overensstemmelse, samband, ekteskap, giftermål; fattigdistrikt, fattighus, fagforening; **monetary** — myntkonvensjon; **The Union** (om en studentforening i Oxford og Cambridge; om Englands og Skottlands forening til ett rike og Irlands med Storbritannia; om den nordamerikanske union); — **is strength** enighet gjør sterk; **Union Jack** det britiske unionsflagg. — **-flag** unionsflagg. **-ist** [-nist] unionist (motstander av irsk selvstyre), fagforeningsmedlem, organisert arbeider.
unique [ju'ni·k] enestående, uten sidestykke.
unison ['ju·nisən] harmoni, enklang; samklang.
unit ['ju·nit] ener, enhet.
unitarian [ju·ni'tæ·ᵊriən] unitarier, unitarisk.
unite [ju'nait] forene, samle; forene seg; **united** [ju'naitid] forent; **the United Brethren** herrnhutene; **the United Kingdom** kongeriket Storbritannia og (Nord-)Irland; **the United States (of America)** De Forente Stater.
unity ['ju·niti] enhet, enighet; identitet; harmoni; overensstemmelse.
universal [ju·ni'və·sl] almen, alminnelig, allsidig; almensetning. **-ity** [ju·nivə'säliti] alminnelighet, almengyldighet.
universe ['ju·nivə·s] univers, verden.
university [ju·ni'və·siti] universitet; — **man** akademiker.
univocal [ju'nivokl] utvetydig, enslydende.
unjust ['ʌn'dʒʌst] urettferdig.
unjustifiable ['ʌn'dʒʌstifaiəbl] uforsvarlig, utillatelig.
unkempt ['ʌn'kem(p)t] ukjemt, lurvet, ustelt.
unkind ['ʌn'kaind] ukjærlig, uvennlig, hard.
unknit [ʌn'nit] trevle opp, glatte.
unknowing ['ʌn'no"iŋ] uvitende, uavvitende.
unknown ['ʌn'no"n] ukjent, uvitterlig.
unlace [ʌn'le's] snøre opp, løse.
unlade [ʌn'le'd] losse, lesse av, tømme.
unladylike ['ʌn'le'dilaik] upassende for en dame.

unlawful ['ʌn'lå·ful] ulovlig, urettmessig.
unlearn [ʌn'lə·n] glemme, viske ut av hukommelsen.
unleavened ['ʌn'levnd] usyret.
unless [ʌn'les] medmindre, uten, hvis ikke.
unlettered ['ʌn'letəd] ulærd.
unlicensed ['ʌn'laisənst] uprivilegert, uten rett.
unlike ['ʌnlaik] ulik, motsatt.
unlikely ['ʌn'laikli] usannsynlig, urimelig, lite lovende.
unlimited ['ʌn'limitid] ubegrenset.
unlink [ʌn'liŋk] løse opp, ta lenken av
unliquored ['ʌn'likəd] uvætt, edru.
unload [ʌn'lo"d] lesse av, losse.
unlock [ʌn'låk] lukke opp, låse opp, åpne.
unlooked-for ['ʌn'luktfå·ᵊ] uventet.
unlucky ['ʌn'lʌki] uheldig.
unmake [ʌn'me'k] tilintetgjøre; styrte (en konge). **unmade** ugjort.
unman [ʌn'män] ta motet fra, nedslå, avfolke.
unmanageable ['ʌn'mänidʒəbl] uhåndterlig, ustyrlig.
unmanful ['ʌn'mänful], **unmanlike** ['ʌn'mänlaik], **unmanly** ['ʌn'mänli] umandig.
unmanned ['ʌn'mänd] ubemannet, umandig.
unmannered ['ʌn'mänəd], **unmannerly** ['ʌn-'mänəli] uoppdragen, ubehøvlet.
unmarked ['ʌn'ma·ᵊkt] umerket.
unmarred ['ʌn'ma·ᵊd] uskadd.
unmarried ['ʌn'märid] ugift.
unmask [ʌn'ma·sk] demaskere, avsløre (seg).
unmatched ['ʌn'mätʃt] uforlignelig.
unmeaning ['ʌn'mi·niŋ] meningsløs, innholdsløs, intetsigende, tom. **unmeant** ['ʌn'ment] som man ikke mener noe med.
unmeasurable [ʌn'meʒərəbl] grenseløs, = **unmeasured.**
unmeet ['ʌn'mi·t] uskikket.
unmentionable ['ʌn'menʃənəbl] unevnelig.
unmerciful ['ʌn'mə·siful] ubarmhjertig.
unmindful ['ʌn'main(d)ful] som glemmer, uten tanke (**of** på), likesæl, likegyldig (**of** med).
unmingled ['ʌn'miŋgld] ublandet.
unmistakable ['ʌnmis'te'kəbl] umiskjennelig.
unmitigated ['ʌn'mitige'tid] uformildet, uforsonlig, fullstendig, ublandet, rendyrket, ren og skjær.
unmixed ['ʌn'mikst] ublandet.
unmolested ['ʌnmo'lestid] uantastet.
unmoor [ʌn'mua] kaste loss, løsgjøre fortøyningene.
unmoved ['ʌn'mu·vd] ubevegelig.
unnamed ['ʌn'ne'md] unevnt, unevnelig.
unnational ['ʌn'näʃənəl] unasjonal, ufolkelig.
unnavigable ['ʌn'nävigəbl] useilbar.
unnecessary ['ʌn'nesisəri] unødvendig.
unneeded ['ʌn'di·did] unødig.
unnerve [ʌn'nə·v] avkrefte, lamme.
unnoticed ['ʌn'no"tist] ubemerket, uomtalt.
unobjectionable ['ʌnəb'dʒekʃənəbl] uforkastelig.
unobserved ['ʌnəb'zə·vd] ubemerket.
unobtainable ['ʌnəb'te'nəbl] uoppnåelig.
unobtrusive ['ʌnəb'tru·siv] beskjeden, smålåten. **-ness** beskjedenhet.
unoccupied ['ʌn'åkjupäid] ledig, herreløs.
unoffending ['ʌnə'fendiŋ] uskyldig, uskadelig.
unoffensive ['ʌnə'fensiv] harmløs.
unofficial ['ʌn'fiʃəl] ikke tjenstlig, privat.
unofficious ['ʌnə'fiʃəs] utjenstvillig.
unostentatious ['ʌnåsten'te'ʃəs] bramfri, jevn og liketil, stillfarende.
unowed ['ʌn'o"d] som man ikke skylder.
unowned ['ʌn'o"nd] herreløs, ikke vedgått.
unpack [ʌn'päk] pakke ut (el. opp), lesse (el. kløvje) av.
unpaid ['ʌn'pe'd] ubetalt ufrankert, ulønt.
unpaint [ʌn'pe'nt] utslette.
unpalatable [ʌn'pälətəbl] usmakelig.

unparalleled [ʌn'pårəleld] uten sidestykke.
unpardonable [ʌn'pa·ᵊdənəbl] utilgivelig.
unparliamentary ['ʌnpa·ᵊli'mentəri] uparlamentarisk.
unpen [ʌn'pen] slippe løs.
unpeople [ʌn'pipl] avfolke.
unperceived ['ʌnpə'si·vd] ubemerket.
unperformed ['ʌnpə'få·ᵊmd] uforrettet.
unpick [ʌn'pik] sprette opp.
unpitying ['ʌn'pitiiŋ] ubarmhjertig.
unplaced ['ʌn'ple¹st] uanbrakt, uten embete, utenfor embetsstanden, uordnet, forvirret.
unpleasable ['ʌn'pli·zəbl] ufornøyelig.
unpleasant ['ʌn'plezənt] ubehagelig.
unpleased ['ʌn'pli·zd] misfornøyd.
unpleasing ['ʌn'pli·ziŋ] ubehagelig.
unpliable ['ʌn'plaiəbl] ubøyelig.
unpliant ['ʌn'plaiənt] ubøyelig, stiv.
unpoetic ['ʌnpo'etik], -al [-əl] upoetisk.
unpoised ['ʌn'poizd] ute av likevekt.
unpopular ['ʌn'påpjulə] upopulær.
unportioned ['ʌn'på·ᵊʃənd] medgiftsløs, fattig.
unprecedented ['ʌn'presidentid] uhørt, enestående, ganske ny.
unprejudiced ['ʌn'predʒudist] fordomsfri.
unpremeditated ['ʌnpri'medite¹tid] uoverlagt.
unprepossessing ['ʌnpri·pə'zesiŋ] som ser mindre godt ut, ikke inntagende.
unpresuming ['ʌnpri'zju·miŋ] beskjeden, smålåten.
unpretending ['ʌnpri'tendiŋ] beskjeden, smålåten.
unprevailing ['ʌnpri've¹liŋ] svak.
unprevalent ['un'prevələnt] sjelden.
unprincipled ['ʌn'prinsipld] prinsippløs.
unproductive ['ʌnpro'dʌktiv] ufruktbar.
unprofessional ['ʌnpro'feʃənəl] uprofesjonell.
unprofitable ['ʌn'pråfitəbl] ufordelaktig, ulønnsom.
unprogressive ['ʌnpro'gresiv] stillestående.
unpromising ['ʌn'pråmisiŋ] lite lovende, uanselig.
unprop [ʌn'pråp] ta bort støtten.
unprotected ['ʌnpro'tektid] ubeskyttet, ugardert.
unproved ['ʌn'pru·vd] ubevist.
unprovided ['ʌnpro'vaidid] uforsynt; — for uforsørget.
unprovoked ['ʌnpro'voᵘkt] uutfordret, umotivert.
unpublished ['ʌn'pʌbliʃt] ikke offentliggjort, utrykt.
unpunctual ['ʌn'pʌŋktʃuəl] upresis.
unpunished ['ʌn'pʌniʃt] ustraffet.
unqualified [ʌn'kwålifaid] udyktig, uskikket, ukvalifisert, som ikke har avlagt den ed som kreves, ubeediget, absolutt, ubetinget.
unquenchable [ʌn'kwenʃəbl] uslokkelig.
unquestionable [ʌn'kwestʃənəbl] ubestridelig, utvilsom.
unquestioned [ʌn'kwestʃənd] ubestridt, uomtvistelig.
unquiet ['ʌn'kwaiət] urolig, opprørt, hviløs.
unravel [ʌn'rävl] utrede, greie ut (el. opp), løse; løse seg opp.
unread ['ʌn'red] ulest, ubelest.
unreadable ['ʌn'ri·dəbl] uleselig.
unready ['ʌn'redi] uferdig, rådvill, sen, somlet.
unreal ['ʌn'ri·əl] uvirkelig.
unreality ['ʌnri'äliti] uvirkelighet.
unreasonable [ʌn'ri·znəbl] urimelig, overdreven.
unreasoning [ʌn'ri·zniŋ] tankeløs, kritikkløs.
unrecognizable ['ʌn'rekəgnaizəbl] ukjennelig.
unrecorded ['ʌnri'kå·ᵊdid] uopptegnet.
unredeemable ['ʌnri'di·məbl] uinnløselig, uoppsigelig. unredeemed ['ʌnri'di·md] uinnløst.
unreel ['ʌn'ri·l] hespe av, rulle av, vikle av snella.
unreflecting ['ʌnri'flektiŋ] tankeløs, kritikkløs.

unrefuted ['ʌnri'fju·tid] ugjendrevet.
unregarded ['ʌnri'ga·ᵊdid] upåaktet, forsømt.
unregardful ['ʌnri'ga·ᵊdful] uaktsom, forsømmelig.
unregretted ['ʌnri'gretid] som ikke blir savnet el. sørget over.
unregulated ['ʌn'regjule¹tid] uregulert, uregelmessig.
unrelenting ['ʌnri'lentiŋ] ubøyelig, ubønnhørlig.
unreliable ['ʌnri'laiəbl] uvederheftig, upålitelig.
unremitting ['ʌnri'mitiŋ] uopphørlig, utrettelig.
unremunerative ['ʌnri'mju·nərətiv] ulønnende.
unrepaired ['ʌnri'pæ·ᵊd] ikke istandsatt.
unrepenting ['ʌnri'pentiŋ] uten anger.
unrepining ['ʌnri'painiŋ] uten klage; taus.
unreprovable ['ʌnri'pru·vəbl] ulastelig.
unreserve ['ʌnri'zə·v] frimodighet, uforbeholdenhet.
unreserved ['ʌnri'zə·vd] uforbeholden.
unresisting ['ʌnri'zistiŋ] uten motstand, passiv.
unresolved ['ʌnri'zålvd] uoppløst, ubesluttsom.
unrespectful ['ʌnri'spektful] uærbødig.
unrestrained ['ʌnri'stre¹nd] uinnskrenket, tøylesløs.
unretentive ['ʌnri'tentiv] som beholder lite, upålitelig.
unrevenged ['ʌnri'vendʒd] uhevnet.
unrevered ['ʌnri'vi·əd] uæret.
unreverend ['ʌn'revərənd] ikke ærverdig.
unrhymed ['ʌn'raimd] urimet, rimfri.
unriddle [ʌn'ridl] forklare, løse.
unrig [ʌn'rig] avtakle.
unrighteous ['ʌn'raitʃəs] urettferdig, ond, syndig. -ness [-nès] urettferdighet, ondskap, synd, syndighet; the mammon of -ness den urette mammon.
unrip [ʌn'rip] sprette opp.
unripe ['ʌn'raip] umoden.
unrivalled ['ʌn'raivld] uten like, uforlignelig.
unrivet [ʌn'rivit] ta naglen ut, løsne, rokke.
unrobe [ʌn'roᵘb] kle av, ta av seg embetsdrakten.
unroll [ʌn'roᵘl] rulle ut (el. opp), åpne.
unroof [ʌn'ru·f] løfte taket av.
unroot [ʌn'ru·t] rykke opp.
UNRRA fk. f. United Nations' Relief and Rehabilitation Administration De forente nasjoners hjelpe- og gjenreisningsadministrasjon (opprettet 9. nov. 1943).
unruffle [ʌn'rʌfl] komme til ro, bli glatt.
unruffled ['ʌn'rʌfld] uforstyrret, rolig, uanfektet, stille (om havet).
unruled ['ʌn'ru·ld] uregjert.
unruly ['ʌn'ru·li] uregjerlig, ustyrlig.
unsaddle [ʌn'sädl] sale av, kaste av salen.
unsafe [ʌn'se¹f] usikker, utrygg, upålitelig, vågsom, farlig.
unsaid ['ʌn'sed] usagt.
unsailorly ['ʌn'se¹ləli] ikke sjømannsmessig.
unsalaried ['ʌn'sälərid] ulønt.
unsalted ['ʌn'så·ltid] usaltet, utvannet.
unsatisfactory ['ʌnsätis¹fäktəri] utilfredsstillende.
unsatisfying ['ʌn'sätisfaiiŋ] utilfredsstillende.
unsavoury ['ʌn'se¹vəri] usmakelig, flau, motbydelig.
unsay ['ʌn'se¹] ta tilbake, ta i seg igjen; it is said, and you cannot — it, det er sagt, og du kan ikke ta det i deg igjen.
unscal(e)able ['ʌn'ske¹ləbl] ubestigelig.
unscaly [ʌn'ske¹li], unscaled ['ʌn'ske¹ld] skjelløs.
unscanned ['ʌn'skänd] uskandert; uoverlagt.
unscared ['ʌn'skæ·əd] ikke skremt.
unscathed ['ʌn'skæ·ᵊd] uskadd.
unscattered [ʌn'skätəd] ikke atspredt.
unscholarly ['ʌn'skåləli] uvitenskapelig, ufilologisk.
unschooled ['ʌn'sku·ld] ustudert, ulærd.
unscoured ['ʌn'skauəd] uskurt, upusset.

unscreened ['ʌn'skri·nd] ikke skjermet.
unscrew [ʌn'skru·] skrue løs (el. ut, opp); ta skruen ut.
unscriptural ['ʌn'skriptʃərəl] ubibelsk.
unscrupulous ['ʌn'skru·pjuləs] hensynsløs, samvittighetsløs.
unseal [ʌn'si·l] ta seglet av el. fra, bryte, brekke, åpne.
unseam [ʌn'si·m] sprette opp.
unsearchable ['ʌn'sə·tʃəbl] uransakelig.
unsearched ['ʌn'sə·tʃt] ikke undersøkt.
unseasonable ['ʌn'si·znəbl] i utide, ubetimelig, ubeleilig, uheldig, upassende; at an — time of night først sent på natten.
unseasoned ['ʌn'si·znd] uvant, utillaget, usaltet, ikke tørret, umoden.
unseat [ʌn'si·t] berøve setet, kaste av salen; ta stilling som tingmann fra, kaste.
unseaworthy ['ʌn'si·wə·ði] ikke sjødyktig.
unseconded ['ʌn'sekəndid] ikke understøttet.
unsecular [ʌn'sekjulə] ikke verdslig.
unseeing [ʌn'si·iŋ] blind, som ikke ser, stirrende, åndsfraværende.
unseemliness ['ʌn'si·mlinès] usømmelighet.
unseemly ['ʌn'si·mli] usømmelig, utekkelig.
unseen ['ʌn'si·n] usett, usynlig, ekstempore.
unseized ['ʌn'si·zd] ikke tatt i besittelse.
unselfish ['ʌn'selfiʃ] uegennyttig, uselvisk.
unsent ['ʌn'sent] usendt; — for ukalt.
unserviceable ['ʌn'sə·visəbl] ubrukelig.
unset ['ʌn'set] ikke satt, ikke innfattet, ikke gått ned, uordnet; the -ting sun midnattsola.
unsettle [ʌn'setl] rokke ved, forrykke, forvirre, gjøre usikker; komme av lage, bli usikker.
unsettled [ʌn'setld] ubygd, ikke kolonisert, ubetalt, ubefestet, ustadig, ustø, usikker.
unsevered ['ʌn'sevəd] ikke atskilt, udelt.
unsew [ʌn'soᵘ] sprette opp.
unsex [ʌn'seks] gjøre kjønnsløs, gjøre ukvinnelig; — oneself bli ukvinnelig. unsexed ukvinnelig.
unshackle [ʌn'ʃäkl] løse (av lenke), frigjøre.
unshaded ['ʌn'ʃeⁱded] uten skygge, som det ikke blir kastet skygge på.
unshadowed ['ʌn'ʃädoᵘd] ikke skygget, ufordunklet.
unshaken ['ʌn'ʃeⁱkn] urokket, urokkelig.
unshamed ['ʌn'ʃeⁱmd] ubeskjemmet.
unshamefaced ['ʌn'ʃeⁱmfeⁱst] uforskammet, skamløs.
unshapable ['ʌn'ʃeⁱpəbl] uformelig. unshaped ['ʌn'ʃeⁱpt], unshapen ['ʌn'ʃeⁱpn] vanskapt, heslig.
unshapely ['ʌn'ʃeⁱpli] ikke velskapt.
unshared ['ʌn'ʃæ·əd] udelt.
unshaved ['ʌn'ʃeⁱvd], unshaven ['ʌn'ʃeⁱvn] ubarbert.
unsheathe [ʌn'ʃi·ð] vikle ut (av svøp), dra ut av sliren, trekke blank; — the sword begynne krigen.
unshed ['ʌn'ʃed] ikke utgytt.
unshell [ʌn'ʃel] skalle av.
unsheltered ['ʌn'ʃeltəd] uten ly, udekt, utsatt.
unshielded ['ʌn'ʃi·ldid] ikke skjermet, udekt.
unshiftable ['ʌn'ʃiftəbl] ubehjelpsom, upraktisk.
unship [ʌn'ʃip] losse, landsette, ta av, ta inn (årene), avmønstre (mannskapet): — your oars årene inn! he -ped his rudder han fikk roret huket av, mistet roret; — the tiller ta av rorpinnen. -ment [-ment] lossing. -ping avtaging.
shape ['ʌn'ʃipʃeⁱp] ikke sjømannsmessig.
unshocked ['ʌn'ʃåkt] ikke støtt, ikke fornærmet.
unshod ['ʌn'ʃåd] uten sko, uskodd.
unshoe ['ʌn'ʃu·] sko av, ta skoen(e) av (en hest).
unshot [ʌn'ʃåt] ta ladningen ut av; ['ʌn'ʃåt] ikke truffet.
unshrinkable ['ʌn'ʃriŋkəbl] krympefri. unshrinking ['ʌn'ʃriŋkiŋ] uforsagt, uforferdet.
unshrouded ['ʌn'ʃraudid] udekt, ubeskyttet.
unshrunk ['ʌn'ʃrʌŋk] ikke sammenkrympet.

unshut ['ʌn'ʃʌt] ikke lukket.
unsifted ['ʌn'siftid] usiktet, uprøvd, forsøkt.
unsight ['ʌn'sait]; buy it — and unse i kjøpe det usett. -able usynlig, usiktbar. -liness mindre vakkert utseende. -ly stygg, uskjønn.
unsigned ['ʌn'saind] ikke underskrevet.
unsilvered ['ʌn'silvəd] uforsølvet.
unsinew ['ʌn'sinju] avkrefte, maktstjele.
unsinkable ['ʌn'siŋkəbl] synkefri.
unskilful ['ʌn'skilful], -ly [-li] udyktig. -ness [-nès] udyktighet.
unskilled ['ʌn'skild] ikke faglært; — labour simpelt arbeid (som ikke krever særlig utdannelse).
unslaked ['ʌn'sleⁱkt] ulesket.
unsmirched ['ʌn'smə·tʃt] uplettet (ogs. bil.).
unsociable [ʌn'soᵘʃəbl] uselskapelig. -ness, unsociability ['ʌnsoᵘʃə'biliti] uselskapelighet.
unsoiled ['ʌn'soild] ubesudlet, ren.
unsold ['ʌn'soᵘld] ikke solgt.
unsolder [ʌn'så·də] løse opp (i loddingen); skille.
unsolicited ['ʌnsə'lisitid] uanmodet.
unsolved ['ʌn'sålvd] uløst, ikke oppklart.
unsophisticated ['ʌnsə'fistike⁺tid] ublandet, uforfalsket, ren, naturlig, uerfaren.
unsound ['ʌn'saund] usunn, sykelig, skrøpelig, skadd, bedervet, dårlig, ikke rettroende, uriktig, løs, uholdbar.
unsparing [ʌn'spæ·ᵒriŋ] rundhåndet, gavmild, skånselløs.
unspeakable ['ʌn'spi·kəbl] usigelig, ubeskrivelig.
unspecified ['ʌn'spesifaid] ikke nærmere betegnet.
unspoken ['ʌn'spoᵘkn] ikke uttalt, unevnt; — of uomtalt.
unspotted ['ʌn'spåtid] uplettet, plettfri.
unstable ['ʌn'steⁱbl] usikker, ustø, ustadig.
unstaid ['ʌn'steⁱd] ustadig, flyktig.
unstamped ['ʌn'stämpt] ustemplet.
unsteadfast ['ʌn'stedfəst] vaklende, ikke standhaftig.
unsteady ['ʌn'stedi] ustø, ustadig; [ʌn'stedi] gjøre usikker.
unstinted ['ʌn'stintid] ikke sparsom, raust, rikelig.
unstitch [ʌn'stitʃ] sprette opp, pille opp.
unstop [ʌn'ståp] åpne, klare, rydde.
unstow [ʌn'stoᵘ] losse.
unstressed ['ʌn'strest] ubetont, trykkløs.
unstring [ʌn'striŋ] ta strengene av, spenne ned, slakke, slappe.
unstrung [ʌn'strʌŋ] i ulage.
unstudied ['ʌn'stʌdid] ikke studert, uforberedt, ukyndig.
unsubmission ['ʌnsəb'miʃən] oppsetsighet, gjenstridighet. unsubmissive [-'misiv] oppsetsig, stri, gjenstridig.
unsuccesful ['ʌnsək'sesful] uheldig; return — vende tilbake med uforrettet sak.
unsuggestive [ʌnsə'dʒestiv] uten noen antydning, lite lærerik, som lite sier.
unsuitable ['ʌn's(j)u·təbl] uskikket, upassende.
unsullied ['ʌn'sʌlid] ubesudlet, ubesmittet, fri.
unsunned ['ʌn'sʌnd] solløs, som sola ikke skinner på.
unsupported ['ʌnsə'på·ᵒtid] ikke understøttet.
unsurpassed ['ʌnsə'pa·st] uovertruffet, uovertreffelig.
unsuspected ['ʌnsə'spektid] ikke mistenkt, uanet. unsuspecting [-tiŋ] umistenksom, intetanende, troskyldig, godtroende. unsuspicious ['ʌnsə'spiʃəs] ikke mistenksom, troskyldig, umistenkelig.
unswathe [ʌn'sweⁱð] ta svøpet av, vikle ut.
unswear [ʌn'swæ·ə] tilbakekalle sin ed.
untalked-of ['ʌn'tå·ktåv] uomtalt.
untangle [ʌn'tängl] greie ut.
untarnished ['ʌn'ta·ᵒniʃt] uanløpet, med uforminsket glans, ufalmet, plettfri, uplettet.

untasked ['ʌn'ta·skt] uten pålagt arbeid, ledig.
untaught ['ʌn'tå·t] ulært, ulærd.
untax [ʌn'täks] oppheve skatten på, befri for skatt.
unteach [ʌn'ti·tʃ] få til å glemme, lære av med, lære om igjen, lære noe annet.
unteachable ['ʌn'ti·tʃəbl] ikke lærvillig.
unteam [ʌn'ti·m] spenne fra.
untell [ʌn'tel] ta tilbake (det fortalte). -able usigelig.
untemptible ['ʌn'temtibl] hevet over fristelse.
untenantable ['ʌn'tenəntəbl] ubeboelig.
untenanted ['ʌn'tenəntid] ubebodd.
unthankful ['ʌn'þäŋkful] utakknemlig.
unthinking ['ʌn'þiŋkiŋ] tankeløs, ubetenksom, kritikkløs. unthought ['ʌn'þå·t] utenkt; — of glemt, uant.
unthread [ʌn'þred] ta en tråd av, løse, finne vei igjennom.
unthriftiness ['ʌn'þriftinés] ødselhet.
unthrifty ['ʌn'þrifti] ødsel, uøkonomisk.
untidy ['ʌn'taidi] uordentlig, usoignert.
untie [ʌn'tai] løse opp, knytte opp.
until [ʌn'til] inntil, til; not — ikke førenn, først da.
untile [ʌn'tail] ta teglsteinene av.
untimely ['ʌn'taimli] altfor tidlig, ubeleilig, brå, ulykkelig.
untirable ['ʌn'tairəbl], untiring [-riŋ] utrettelig.
untitled ['ʌn'taitld] ubetitlet, uberettiget.
unto ['ʌntu, 'ʌntə] (især bibelsk:) til.
untold ['ʌn'toᵘld] ufortalt, usagt, utalt, talløs, usigelig.
untomb [ʌn'tu·m] ta opp (av grava).
untoward ['ʌn'toᵘəd] fordervet, gjenstridig, vrang, klosset, fortredelig, lei, trassig, ubehagelig.
untraceable ['ʌn'tre'səbl] som ikke lar seg følge tilbake, uransakelig.
untrained ['ʌn'tre'nd] uopplært, uøvd.
untrammelled ['ʌn'träməld] uhindret, ubesværet.
untranslatable [ʌntra·ns'le'təbl] uoversettelig.
untravelled [ʌn'trävld] ubereist.
untried ['ʌn'traid] uforsøkt, uprøvd, uavgjort, upådømt (case sak).
untrim [ʌn'trim] ta pynten av, bringe i uorden.
untrodden ['ʌn'trådn] ubetrådt, ubanet.
untrue ['ʌn'tru·] usann, utro, uriktig.
untrustful ['ʌn'trʌstful] mistroisk, mistenksom, upålitelig.
untruth ['ʌn'tru·þ] usannhet, utroskap.
untunable ['ʌn'tju·nəbl] falsk, uharmonisk.
untune [ʌn'tju·n] forstemme.
untutored [ʌn'tju·təd] ulært, ulærd, enfoldig.
untwine [ʌn'twain] løse opp, tvinne opp, rulle opp.
untwist [ʌn'twist] vikle opp, tvinne opp, løse, greie.
unused ['ʌn'ju·zd] ubrukt, ledig, uvant.
unusual ['ʌn'ju·ʒuəl] ualminnelig, usedvanlig.
unutterable ['ʌn'ʌtərəbl] usigelig, ubeskrivelig; -s unevnelige, 'bukser.
unvaried ['ʌn'væ·ərid] uforanderlig, stadig, ensformig.
unvarnished ['ʌn'va·əniʃt] ufernisert, usminket, usmykt.
unveil [ʌn've'l] ta sløret av, avsløre, avsløre seg.
unveracious ['ʌnvi're'ʃəs] usannferdig.
unveracity ['ʌnvi'räsiti] usannferdighet.
unvocal ['ʌn'voᵘkl] ustemt.
unwall [ʌn'wå·l] ta ut av muren, bryte muren fra. -ed åpen, uten murer.
unwarlike ['ʌn'wå·əlaik] ukrigersk.
unwarp [ʌn'wå·əp] rette (ut). -ed uhildet upartisk.
unwarrantable ['ʌn'wårəntəbl] uberettiget, ubeføyd, uforsvarlig, ulovlig.
unwary ['ʌn'wæ·əri] uforsiktig, troskyldig.
unwashed [ʌn'wåʃt] uvasket.

unwatered ['ʌn'wåtəd] uten vann, lens, tørr.
unwavering ['ʌn'weivəriŋ] ikke vaklende, (karakter)fast.
unwearid ['ʌn'wiərid] ikke trett, utrettelig, ufortrøden.
unwearying ['ʌn'wiəriiŋ] utrettelig, iherdig.
unweave [ʌn'wi·v] trevle opp.
unwelcome [ʌn'welkəm] uvelkommen, ubehagelig.
unwell ['ʌn'wel] uvel, upasselig.
unwholesome ['ʌn'hoᵘlsəm] usunn.
unwieldy ['ʌn'wi·ldi] besværlig, tung, tungvint.
unwill [ʌn'wil] oppheve, tilbakekalle. -ing ['ʌn'wiliŋ] uvillig, motstrebende. -ingly ugjerne, nødig. -ingness uvillighet, utilbøyelighet.
unwind [ʌn'waind] vikle av, rulle ut, greie ut.
unwise ['ʌn'waiz] uforstandig, uklok.
unwished [ʌn'wiʃt] uønsket.
unwitting [ʌn'witiŋ] uvitende, uforvarende.
unwonted ['ʌn'woᵘntid] uvant, ualminnelig.
unwork [ʌn'wə·k] gjøre om igjen. -ing uvirksom.
unworkmanlike [ʌn'wə·kmənlaik] fuskeraktig.
unworthy ['ʌn'wə·ði] uverdig.
unwrap [ʌn'räp] tulle opp, vikle ut, ta dekket av, pakke ut, blotte.
unwreathe [ʌn'ri·ð] vikle opp.
unwring [ʌn'riŋ] vri av.
unwrite [ʌn'rait] tilbakekalle.
unwritten ['ʌn'ritn] uskrevet, muntlig, ubeskrevet.
unwrung ['ʌn'rʌŋ] ikke vridd, uskadd.
unyielding ['ʌn'ji·ldiŋ] ubøyelig, stiv, stri, ikke innbringende.
unyoke [ʌn'joᵘk] spenne fra (åket), atskille, løse, holde opp (med arbeidet).
up [ʌp] oppe, opp, oppad, oppover, opp i, oppe på, oppe i; — (the) country inn el. inne i landet; — stream oppover strømmen; it is all — with him det er ute med ham; what's —? hva er det på ferde? the time is — tiden er utløpet, ommet; his spirit was — hans mot var stort; he is — for reelection han stiller seg til gjenvalg; be — to forstå seg på, svare til, makte, spekulere på, ha fore, gjøre; — to opp til, bort til, til; be — with him innhente ham; grow — bli voksen; go — to town reise inn til London.
U. P. fk. f. United Presbyterian.
u. p. fk. f. under proof.
upbear [ʌp'bæ·ə] holde i været, løfte opp, støtte.
upbraid [ʌp'bre'd] bebreide; — one with (for) a thing bebreide en noe. -er en som bebreider. -ing bebreidelse.
upbringing ['ʌp'briŋiŋ] oppdragelse.
upcast ['ʌpka·st] oppadvendt.
upheaval [ʌp'hi·vl] hevning, oppskaking, omveltning.
uphill ['ʌphil] oppover bakke, oppadgående, besværlig, tung.
uphold [ʌp'hoᵘld] holde oppe, vedlikeholde, støtte; — the day holde kampen gående. -er støtte; forsvarer.
upholster [ʌp'hoᵘlstə] stoppe, polstre, trekke, tapetsere.
upholsterer [ʌp'hoᵘlstərə] tapetserer (og møbelhandler). upholstery [ʌp'hoᵘlstəri] tapetserarbeid, tapetsering, tapeter, gardiner.
upland ['ʌplənd] høyland, høytliggende land; høylendt, høylands-. -er høylender.
uplift ['ʌplift] hevning, løfting. uplift [ʌp'lift] løfte opp.
upmost ['ʌpmoᵘst], se uppermost.
upon [ə'pån]; — the whole i det hele tatt, overhodet; live — leve av.
upper ['ʌpə] øvre, høyere, over-; he is wrong in his — story han er ikke riktig i den øverste etasjen; — hand overtak, overhånd; — house overhus; the — ten (thousand) den høyeste overklasse. -most øverst, herskende; say whatever comes -most si det som først faller en inn.
uppish ['ʌpiʃ] kjepphøy, viktig, stolt.

uprear [ʌp'riə] løfte opp, reise, reise seg.
upright ['ʌprait] opprett, opprettstående, rett, rak, rank, rettskaffen, redelig. -ness opprett stilling, rankhet, rettskaffenhet.
uprising [ʌp'raiziŋ] reisning, oppstand.
uproar ['ʌprå·ə] oppstyr, røre, larm, spetakkel.
uproarious [ʌp'rå·riəs] larmende, stormende.
upset [ʌp'set] stille opprett, velte, styrte, kantre, forstyrre, forulempe.
upset ['ʌpset] velting, ubehagelighet, forstyrrelse, oppskaking, oppsatt; — price oppropspris, minste pris (på auksjon).
upshot ['ʌpʃåt] ende, slutning, resultat, utfall.
upside-down ['ʌpsaid'daun] endevendt, forkjært, bakvendt, opp ned.
upstairs ['ʌp'stæ·əz] ovenpå, oppe, opp trappen(e); overetasje.
upstanding [ʌp'ständiŋ] oppstående, rank, rak.
upstart ['ʌpsta·ət] plutselig framstått, fersk, nybakt; oppkomling, parveny.
upstream ['ʌp'stri·m] oppover elva.
uptake ['ʌpte'k] løftning; oppfatning, begripelse; quick in the — snar, fort i oppfatningen.
up-to-date ['ʌptəde't] à jour, tidsmessig, moderne.
upturn [ʌp'tə·n] vende opp el. oppad.
upward ['ʌpwəd] oppadvendt, stigende, oppadgående. upward ['ʌpwəd], -s oppad, oppover, oventil; mer, derover; — of mer enn; three years and — tre år og mer; — of three years over tre år.
Ural ['juərəl] Ural; the Urals Uralfjellene.
Urania· [ju're'njə] Urania (astronomiens muse).
Uranus ['juərənəs] Uranos.
urate ['juəret] urat (urinsurt salt).
urban ['ə·bən] by-, bymessig.
urbane [ə·'be'n] beleven, dannet, høflig, slepen.
urbanity [ə·'bäniti] urbanitet, belevenhet, høflighet, fint vesen.
urchin ['ə·tʃin] (skøyter)unge, knekt, tøs.
Urdu [ə·'du·, uə'du·] hindustansk.
urea ['juəriə] urinstoff.
urethra [juə'ri·þrə] urinrør.
urge [ə·dʒ] drive, tilskynde, anbefale, slå til lyd for, gjøre gjeldende, bearbeide, overhenge, be innstendig, trenge seg fram, egge, bli ved, framholde sterkt, ivre for, framføre påstander; — him more closely gå ham nærmere på klingen.
urgency ['ə·dʒənsi] iver, iherdighet, innstendige bønner, trygling, påtrengende viktighet, nødvendighet; the — of the request den innstendige anmodning.
urgent ['ə·dʒənt] ivrig, påtrengende, inntrengende, presserende, nødvendig.
urger ['ə·dʒə] en som driver fram, en som presser på, tilskynder, talsmann, trygler.
Uriah [ju'raiə] Urias.
uric ['juərik] acid urinsyre.
urinal ['juərinəl] pissoar.
urinary ['juərinəri] urin-; gjødselvannskum, landkum.
urinate ['juərine't] late vannet.
urine ['juərin] urin.
urn [ə·n] urne, temaskin.
ursine ['ə·sain] bjørne-, bjørneaktig.
urtica ['ə·tikə] nesle. urtical ['ə·tikl] nesle-.
urticant ['ə·tikənt] brennende.
Uruguay ['urugwe', 'juərugwe'] Uruguay.
urus ['juərəs] urokse.
us [ʌs] oss.
U. S. fk. f. United States.
U. S. A. fk. f. United States of America.
usable ['ju·zəbl] brukelig, brukbar.
usage ['ju·zidʒ] bruk, behandling, medfart, sedvane, skikk og bruk.

usance ['ju·zəns] uso, (vedtatt) løpetid; bill of — usoveksel.
use [ju·s] bruk, øvelse, øving, gagn, nytte, sedvane, skikk og bruk; — and wont skikk og bruk; in — i bruk, brukelig; of — til nytte.
use [ju·z] bruke, benytte, nytte, behandle, venne, søke, søke til, pleie (bare i fortid).
used [ju·st] (adj.) vant (to til); we are not — to that det er vi ikke vant til.
used [ju·st] pleide, var vant (imperf. av use pleie; brukes ofte til å framheve noe fortidig mot noe senere); I — to live there jeg har bodd der før.
used [ju·zd] brukte, benyttet (imperf. av use bruke); he — his best efforts han gjorde sitt beste.
useful ['ju·sful] nyttig, gagnlig; come in — komme til god nytte.
usefulness ['ju·sfulnès] nytte, gagn.
useless ['ju·slès] unyttig; — request forgjeves henvendelse.
uselessness ['ju·slèsnès] unyttighet.
user ['ju·zə] bruker, konsument.
usher ['ʌʃə] dørvokter, ceremonimester, rettstjener, hjelpelærer; innføre, varsle inn, spå, være en forløper for. -ship ceremonimester-stilling, hjelpelærerpost.
usquebaugh ['ʌskwibå·] whisky.
U. S. S. R. fk. f. Union of Soviet Socialist Republics.
usual ['ju·zuəl] sedvanlig, vanlig; as — som sedvanlig; more than — mer enn alminnelig; on the — terms på vanlige vilkår.
usually ['ju·zuəli] sedvanligvis.
usualness ['ju·zuəlnès] alminnelighet.
usufruct ['ju·zjufrʌkt] bruksrett; ha til bruk.
usufructuary [ju·zju'frʌktjuəri] brukshaver.
usurer ['ju·zərə] ågerkarl.
usurious [ju'ʒuəriəs] ågeraktig, som driver åger.
usurp [ju·'zə·p] rane til seg, rive til seg, usurpere.
-ation [ju·zə'pe'ʃən] bemektigelse, egenmektig tilegnelse, usurpasjon, maktran. -atory [ju·'zə·pətəri] egenmektig, urettmessig. -er [ju·zə·pə] usurpator, tronraner.
usury ['ju·zəri] åger.
utensil [ju'tensil] redskap, kar; domestic — husgeråd; kitchen — kjøkkentøy.
utilitarian [ju·tili'tæ·əriən] nytte-, bruks-; utilist.
utility [ju'tiliti] gagn, nytte. — -actor en som spiller alle mulige roller. — -man en som er brukelig til alt mulig, altmuligmann.
utilization [ju·tili'ze'ʃən] utnytting.
utilize ['ju·tilaiz] utnytte.
utmost ['ʌtmo·st] ytterst, ytst; det ytterste, det ytste; do one's — gjøre sitt ytterste; use one's — exertions oppby alle sine krefter.
Utopia [ju·'to·piə] Utopia; slaraffenland, utopi, lykksalig drøm. Utopian [ju·'to·piən] utopisk, fantastisk, innbilt; utopist, upraktisk idealist.
utter ['ʌtə] fullstendig, absolutt, ubetinget.
utter ['ʌtə] ytre, uttale, uttrykke; utstøte; utsende, utbre.
utter|able ['ʌtərəbl] som kan uttrykkes, som kan uttales. -ance utsending (av falske penger); uttale, uttrykksmåte, ytring, foredrag, mæle. -er en som sier, utgiver.
utterly ['ʌtəli] aldeles, helt, ganske, til det ytterste.
uttermost ['ʌtəmo·st] ytterst, ytst, sist.
uvula ['ju·vjulə] drøpel.
uvular ['ju·vjulə] uvular, som hører til (el. blir frambrakt) med drøpelen.
uxorious [ʌk'så·riəs] sterkt opptatt av sin kone.

V

V [vi·] V; **V.** (eller **v.**) fk. f. **verb; verse; versus; vide; viscount; volume.**
Va. fk. f. **Virginia.**
V. A. fk. f. **(Royal Order of) Victoria and Albert; vice-admiral.**
v. a. fk. f. **verb active** (transitivt verbum).
vacancy ['ve¹kənsi] tomhet, tomrom, mellomrom, ledig tid, fritid, ledig plass, ledighet, vakanse, sløvhet; **stare at** — stirre ut i lufta.
vacant ['ve¹kənt] tom, ledig, yrkesløs, ubesatt, uopptatt, tanketom, intetsigende, herreløs.
vacate [və¹ke¹t] gjøre tom el. ledig, fratre, rømme, fraflytte, oppgi.
vacation [və¹ke¹ʃən] ferie; vakanse.
vaccinate ['väksine¹t] innpode kokopper, vaksinere. **vaccination** [väksi¹ne¹ʃən] vaksinasjon.
vaccinator ['väksine¹tə] vaksinatør.
vaccine ['väksin] ku-, vaksine-; **the** — **disease** kokoppene.
vacillant ['väsilənt] vaklende, ustadig, ustø.
vacillate ['väsile¹t] vakle. **vacillation** [väsi¹le¹ʃən] slingring, vakling, vingling, holdningsløshet.
vacuity [və¹kju·iti] tomhet, tanketomhet, tomrom. **vacuous** ['väkjuəs] tom, intetsigende.
vacuum ['väkjuəm] tomrom, vakuum, lufttomt rom, vakuums-, støvsuger. — **-brake** vakuumsbremse; — **cleaner** støvsuger; — **flask** termosflaske.
vade-mecum ['ve¹di¹mi·kəm] lommehåndbok.
vagabond ['vägəbənd] omstreifende; landstryker, vagabond. **-age** [-idʒ] løsgjengeri.
vagary [və¹gæ·ə ri] grille, innfall.
vagrancy ['ve¹grənsi] løsgjengeri, omstreifing.
vagrant ['ve¹grənt] omflakkende; landstryker, løsgjenger.
vague [ve¹g] vag, ubestemt, svevende, usikker. **-ness** ubestemthet, uklarhet.
vain [ve¹n] tom, forgjeves, fåfengt, fruktesløs, forfengelig, pralende; **in** — forgjeves; **take in** — ta forfengelig. **-glorious** [-glå·riəs] forfengelig, oppblåst, kry. **-glory** forfengelighet. **-ness** tomhet, fruktesløshet.
valance ['väləns], **valence** ['väləns] omheng.
vale [ve¹l] (især poet.) dal.
valediction [väli¹dikʃən] farvel, avskjedshilsen.
valedictory [väli¹diktəri] avskjeds-.
Valentine ['väləntain] Valentin; kjæreste (valt på St. Valentins dag, den 14. februar, da etter gammel folketro fuglene begynte å parre seg), valentinbrev, elskovshilsen.
valerian [və¹liəriən] baldrian, vendelrot, valeriana (plante); **wild** — lægebaldrian.
valet ['välet] kammertjener; være kammertjener hos.
valetudinarian [välitju·di¹næ·ə riən] skranten, sykelig; sykelig menneske, sjukling.
valiant ['väljənt] tapper. **-ness** tapperhet.
valid ['välid] gyldig, sterk. **-ity** [və¹liditi] gyldighet.
valise [və¹li·s] lærtaske, reiseveske, vadsekk; ransel; (amerikansk: håndtaske).
valley ['väli] dal; — **of tears** jammerdal.
valorous ['välərəs] tapper, modig.
valour ['välə] tapperhet, mot.
Valparaiso ['välpə¹raisoᵘ] Valparaiso.
valuable ['väljuəbl] kostbar, verdifull, kjær; kostbarhet. **valuation** [välju¹e¹ʃən] vurdering, verdsetting, takst.
valuator ['väljue¹tə] taksasjonsmann, verdsetter.
value ['välju] verdi, verd, valør, valuta; vurdere, verdsette, skatte, sette pris på. **-less** verdiløs. **valuer** ['väljuə] taksasjonsmann, verdsetter, en som setter pris på.

valve [välv] fløy, dørfløy, ventil, klaff, skall.
valvular ['välvjulə] ventil-, klaff-.
vamp [vämp] overlær; lapp, bot; (sl.) vampyr; flikke på, pusse opp, lappe sammen, pynte på; bringe i stand, få til, lage; akkompagnere etter gehør.
vamper ['vämpə] lappeskomaker, flikker.
vampire ['vämpaiə] vampyr. **vampirism** ['vämp(a)irizm] tro på vampyrer, utsuging.
van [vän] fortropp.
van [vän] transportvogn, flyttevogn, varevogn, godsvogn.
van [vän] (poetisk) vinge.
Vancouver [vän¹ku·və] Vancouver.
Vandal ['vändəl] vandalistisk; vandal. **-ic** [vän-'dälik] vandalsk, vandalistisk. **-ism** ['vändəlizm] vandalisme.
vane [ve¹n¹ vindfløy, værhane, vinge (på vindmølle); fane (på fjær).
vanguard ['vänga·ᵉd] avantgarde.
vanilla [və¹nilə] vanilje; — **cream sauce** vaniljekrem.
vanish ['väniʃ] forsvinne, bli borte, la forsvinne; **-ing** forsvinning.
vanity ['väniti] forfengelighet, tomhet, intethet. **Vanity Fair** Forfengelighetens marked (roman av Thackeray).
vanity-bag ['vänitibäg] dameveske (med speil, pudder o. l.).
vanquish ['vänkwiʃ] beseire, overvinne, gjendrive. **-er** overvinner.
vantage ['va·ntidʒ] fordel; nå bare brukt i tennis og i uttrykket: — **-ground** fordelaktig terreng, fordelaktig stilling.
vapid ['väpid] doven, flau. **-ness** flauhet.
vaporable ['väpərəbl] som kan fordampe.
vaporlization [ve¹pərai¹ze¹ʃən] fordamping. **-ize** ['ve¹pəraiz] fordampe. **-ous** ['ve¹prəs] full av damp, oppblåsende, oppblåst; luftig, tom.
vapour ['ve¹pə] damp, eim, tåke, dunst (plur. gml.) hypokondri; fordampe; skryte, kyte, prale. — **-bath** dampbad. **-ings** skryt, blest.
vapoury ['ve¹pəri] dampende, dampaktig; hypokonder.
variability [væ·ə riə¹biliti] foranderlighet.
variable ['væ·ə riəbl] foranderlig, ustadig; variabel.
variance ['væ·ə riəns] tvist, strid, uoverensstemmelse; **at** — **with** i strid med.
variation [væ·ə ri¹e¹ʃən] avvikelse, avvik, forandring, forskjell, misvisning, variasjon, avart; **by way of** — til en forandring.
varicella [väri¹selə] vannkopper.
varicose ['väriko·s] **veins** åreknuter.
varied ['væ·ə rid] avvikende, forskjelligartet, flersidig, ymse.
variegated ['væ·ə rige¹tid] broket, mangefarget.
variegation [væ·ə ri¹ge¹ʃən] brokethet.
variety [və¹raiiti] forskjellighet, avveksling, forandring, mangfoldighet, varietet, avart.
variola [və¹raiələ] kopper, barnekopper, småkopper.
various ['væ·ə riəs] forskjellig, mange forskjellige, diverse, flere, foranderlig, broket; **with** — **succes** med vekslende hell.
varmint ['va·ᵉmint] (vulgært) skadedyr, utøy; (jaktslang) reven.
varnish ['va·əniʃ] ferniss, glans; fernissere, besmykke, pynte på. **-er** fernisserer, besmykker.
varnishing-day fernisseringsdag (på maleriutstilling), dagen før utstillingen.
varsity ['va·ə siti] (i daglig tale for **university**) universitet.

vary ['væ·°ri] forandre, variere, bringe avveksling i; forandre seg, skifte; **prices** — prisene varierer; **with -ing succes** med vekslende hell.
vascular ['väskjulə] som består av kar, kar-.
vase [va·z] vase, kar, blomsterbeger.
vaseline ['väzili·n] vaselin.
vassal ['väsəl] vasall, lensmann, redskap. **-age** ['väsəlidʒ] vasallforhold, len, undergivenhet, avhengighet; trældom.
vast [va·st] uhyre, veldig, umåtelig. **-ness** umåtelighet, uhyre størrelse.
vat [vät] stort kar, så, beholder, fargekjel.
Vatican ['vätikən]; **the** — Vatikanet.
vaticination [vatisi'ne·ʃən] spådom.
vaudeville ['voʊdvil] vådeville, lite skuespill med sanger og danser. — **-theatre** (amr.) varieté.
vault [vå·lt] hvelv, kvelv, hvelving, kjellerhvelving, gravhvelving; hvelve, lage i form av hvelv, lage hvelv over.
vault [vå·lt] springe, svinge seg, hoppe over, voltigere. **-er** akrobat, voltigør. **-ing** hopp, sprang, voltigering. **-ing-horse** hest (gymnastikkredskap).
vaunt [vå·nt] skryte, braute, blære seg, rose seg av; praleri, skryt, store ord. **-er** praler, blære. **-ful, -ing** pralende.
Vauxhall ['våks'(h)å·l] del av London nær Westminster, med et forlystelsessted (inntil 1859).
V. C. fk. f. **vice-chancellor; vice-consul;** Victoria Cross.
V. D. fk. f. **Volunteer Decoration; venereal disease.**
veal [vi·l] kalvekjøtt; **roast** — kalvestek.
Veda ['ve·də, 'vi·də] veda (hinduenes hellige bøker).
vedette [vi·det] vedett.
veer [viə] snu, vende seg (om vind); svinge, skifte standpunkt; fire, slakke.
vegetable ['vedʒitəbl] plante-, vegetabilsk; plante, vokster, kjøkkenvokster; i plur. plantekost, grønnsaker og røtter; **cabbage, peas, and other -s** kål, erter og andre grønnsaker; — **earth -s** moldjord; — **kingdom** planteriket; — **marrow** gresskar.
vegetal ['vedʒitl] plante-, vokster-, vekst-.
vegetarian [vedʒi'tæ·°riən] vegetarianer.
vegetate ['vedʒite·t] vokse, spire, vegetere, føre et uvirksomt liv, spise, drikke og sove.
vegetation [vedʒi'te·ʃən] vegetasjon, planteliv, planter.
vegetative ['vedʒitətiv] vegetativ, som fremmer planteveksten, som er i vekst, vegeterende, uten høyere interesser.
vehemence ['vi·əməns] heftighet, voldsomhet.
vehement ['vi·°mənt] heftig, voldsom.
vehicle ['vi·ikl] kjøretøy; hjelpemiddel.
vehicular [vi'hikjulə] transport-, vogn-, som tjener til redskap (el. organ); — **traffic** vognferdsel.
veil [ve·l] slør, forheng; sløre til, sløre, tilhylle.
vein [ve·n] blodåre, vene, åre; nerve, åre (i tre, blad, insektvinger osv.); vannåre; stripe; anlegg, retning, stemning, lune; åre, gåre; **a — of poetry** en poetisk åre; **in the** — i stemning, opplagt. **-stone** gangstein, gangmasse.
veldt [velt] veldt, (sørafrikansk) grasslette.
velleity [və'li·iti] tilløp til vilje, svak (begynnende) vilje, ønske.
vellum ['veləm] velin, fint pergament.
velocity [vi'låsiti] hastighet.
velours [və'luə] velur (slags plysj til hatter).
velvet ['velvèt] fløyel; fløyels-, fløyelsbløt.
velveteen [velvi'ti·n] bomulls-fløyel.
velveting ['velvitiŋ] fløyelsstoffer.
velvety ['velviti] fløyels-, fløyelsbløt.
venal ['vi·nəl] som kan kjøpes, til salgs, til fals, bestikkelig.
venality [vi'näliti] salgbarhet, bestikkelighet.
venary ['vi·nəri] jakt-.
vend [vend] forhandle, selge, avsette. **-ee** [ven'di·] kjøper. **-er** [vendə] selger. **-ible** ['ven-

dibl] salgbar. **-ibility** [vendi'biliti] salgbarhet. **-or** ['vendå·°] selger.
veneer [və'niə] finere, innlegge; finér.
veneering [və'niəriŋ] finering.
venerable ['venərəbl] ærverdig.
venerate ['venəre·t] ære, holde i ære.
veneration [venə're·ʃən] ærbødighet, ærefrykt.
venerator ['venəre·tə] beundrer, tilbeder.
venereal [vi'niəriəl] venerisk.
venery ['venəri] jakt, veiding.
venesection ['veni'sekʃən] årelating.
Venetian [vi'ni·ʃiən] venetiansk; venetianer; — **blind** persienne, sjalusi.
Venezuela [veni'zwi·lə] Venezuela.
vengeance ['vendʒəns] hevn; **take** — **on sb. for sth.** hevne seg på en for noe; **with a** — **med** fynd, så det forslår.
vengeful ['vendʒful] hevnende, hevngjerrig.
venial ['vi·niəl] unnskyldelig, tillatelig.
veniality [vi·ni'äliti] tilgivelighet.
Venice ['venis] Venedig, Venesia.
venison ['venizən] vilt, dyrekjøtt.
venom ['venəm] gift; **vent one's** — spy eiter og galle. **-ous** giftig. **-ousness** giftighet.
vent [vent] lufthull, trekkhull, fritt løp, luft, avløp; slippe ut, gi luft, utøse, uttale, offentliggjøre; **give** — **to** gi luft; **take** — unnvike, komme ut.
venter ['ventə] underliv, livmor.
vent-hole ['ventoʊl] lufthull, fenghull.
ventiduct ['ventidʌkt] luftrør.
ventilate ['ventile·t] vifte, rense, lufte ut, drøfte, sette under debatt, undersøke, uttale. **ventilation** [venti'le·ʃən] vifting, rensing, ventilasjon, diskusjon, uttalelse. **ventilator** ['ventile·tə] ventil, ventilasjonsinnretning.
ventral ['ventrəl] underlivs-, buk-, mave; — **fin** bukfinne.
ventricle ['ventrikl] ventrikkel; — **of the heart** hjertekammer; — **of the brain** hjernehule.
ventrilocution [ventrilo'kju·ʃən], **ventriloquism** [ven'trilokwizm] buktaling, buktalerkunst. **ventriloquist** [ven'trilokwist] buktaler. **ventriloquize** [ven'trilokwaiz] opptre som buktaler.
venture ['ventʃə] vågestykke, slumpelykke, tilfelle, sjanse, spekulasjon, risiko; våge, våge seg, løpe en risiko, spekulere; **at a** — på lykke og fromme; **try the** — våge forsøket; — **at** (on, upon) våge, innlate seg på.
venturer ['ventʃərə] en som våger, spekulant.
venturesome ['ventʃəsəm] dristig.
venturous ['ventʃərəs] dristig.
venue ['venju·] åstedets (eller hjemstedets) rettskrets, verneting, jurisdiksjon; rettssted.
Venus ['vi·nəs] Venus; aftenstjerna, morgenstjerna.
veracious [və're·ʃəs] sannferdig, sanndru.
veracity [və'räsiti] sannferdighet.
veranda(h) [və'rändə] veranda.
verb [və·b] verb, verbum.
verbal ['və·bəl] muntlig, ord-, ordrett, verbal; **verbalsubstantiv; a** — **dispute** en strid om ord. **-ist** bokstavelig fortolker, ordkløver.
verbatim [və·be·tim] ord for ord, ordrett.
verbena [və'bi·nə] verbena, jernurt.
verbiage ['və·biidʒ] ordskvalder, tomme ord.
verbose ['və·boʊs] ordrik, vidløftig.
verbosity [və·båsiti] ordrikhet, vidløftighet.
verdancy ['və·dənsi] grønnfarge, grønske; grønnhet.
verdant ['və·dənt] grønn(kledd); uerfaren.
Verde [və·d] Cape — Det Grønne Forberg; **the Cape** — **Islands** Kapverdeøyene.
verderer ['və·dərə] (gammeldags:) kongelig forstmester.
verdict ['və·dikt] dom, erklæring, kjennelse; **bring in** (eller **deliver, give, return**) **a** — avsi en kjennelse; — **of acquittal** frikjennelse; **the jury brought in a** — **of 'not guilty'** juryen avgav kjennelsen 'ikke skyldig'.

verdigris ['və·digri·s] spanskrør, eir.

verdure ['və·dʒə] grønnfarge, grønske, grønt, grønn vegetasjon; friskhet; dekke med grønt.

verge [və·dʒ] stav, embetsstav; rand, kant, grenselinje; **on the** — of på kanten (el. randen) av, på spranget til; **on the** — of tears gråteferdig.

verge [və·dʒ] skråne, helle, nærme seg; — on grense til, nærme seg.

verger ['və·dʒə] *stavbærer* (som bærer biskops embetsstav), kirketjener.

verification [verifi'ke'ʃən] prøve, bevis, bekreftelse, stadfesting, prov. verifier ['verifaiə] undersøker, bekrefter. verify ['verifai] bevise, bekrefte, oppfylle.

verisimilitude [verisi'militju·d] sannsynlighet.

veritable ['veritəbl] sann, virkelig, veritabel.

verity ['veriti] sannhet; **of a** — i sannhet.

verjuice ['və·dʒu·s] sur saft, eddik, surhet.

vermicelli [və·mi'seli] vermicelli, nudler.

vermicular [və·'mikjulə] ormformet, ormaktig, orm-. vermiculation [və·mikju'le'ʃən] ormaktig bevegelse, ormprydelse. vermiculous [və'mikjuləs] full av orm, ormformig.

vermifugal [və·'mifjugəl] omdrivende.

vermifuge ['və·mifju·dʒ] ormemiddel, råd for orm.

vermillion [və'miljən] vakker rød farge, sinoberrødt; farge rød.

vermin ['və·min] skadedyr, utøy. -ation [və·mi'ne'ʃən] formering av utøy; lusesyke.

verm(o)uth ['və·mu·þ] vermut.

vernacular [və'näkjulə] hjemlig, fedrelands-, fedre-; landets språk, morsmål, målføre, dialekt. -ism egenhet ved morsmålet. -ly på morsmålet.

vernal ['və·nəl] vår-, vårlig; — equinox vårjevndøgn.

veronal ['veronal] veronal.

veronica [və'rånikə] tørkle med avbilding av Frelserens ansikt; Veronikabilde; veronika, flismegras.

Versailles [væ·ə'sai] Versailles.

versant ['və·sənt] skråning, fall, hall, beliggenhet.

versatile ['və·sətail] dreibar, foranderlig, ustadig, vinglet, ustø, åndssmidig, flersidig. versatility [və·sə'tiliti] dreibarhet, ustadighet, flersidighet.

verse [və·s] vers, verslinje, poesi; på vers, poetisk; in — på vers; a volume of — en diktsamling.

versed [və·st] bevandret, kyndig, hjemme (in i).

versicolour(ed) ['və·sikʌlə(d)] av forskjellige farger, broket; regnbuefarget.

versification [və·sifi'ke'ʃən] verskunst, versbygning, versifikasjon. versifier ['və·sifaiə] versemaker, dikter, versifikator. versify ['və·sifai] skrive vers, sette på vers.

version ['və·ʃən] vending, oversettelse, gjengivelse, utgave, beretning.

verst [və·st] verst (russisk lengdemål: 1,066 km).

versus ['və·səs] mot, kontra.

vert [və·t] (heraldisk:) grønt; (juridisk:) grønn vokster i skog.

vertebra ['və·tibrə] rygghvirvel (pl. vertebræ).

vertebral hvirvel-, rygghvirvel-; hvirveldyr.

vertebrate ['ve·tibrēt] hvirveldyr.

vertex ['və·tēks] spiss, topp, isse, senit.

vertical ['və·tikl] loddrett, vertikal.

vertiginous [və'tidʒinəs] svimlende, svimmel.

vertigo ['və·tigoᵘ] svimmelhet, svimring.

verve [və·v] liv, kraft.

very ['veri] meget (forsterker adj. i positiv), aller (forsterker superlativ); sann; virkelig, fullkommen, riktig, selve, nettopp; — good meget god; — well meget vel; — much særdeles meget; — easily meget lett; a — child et rent barn, bare banet; this — day ennå i dag; for — joy, av lutter glede; under his — nose like her for nesen på ham; it's the — thing nettopp hva vi ønsker.

vesicant ['vesikənt] blæretrekkende; trekk-

middel. vesicate ['vesike't] legge trekkplaster på.

vesication [vesi'ke'ʃən] behandling med trekkmidler.

vesicle ['vesikl] liten blære.

vesper ['vespə] aftenstjerne, aften, kveld. -s aftensang, vesper. -time aften-.

vespiary ['vespiəri] vepsebol, vepsereir.

vessel ['vesl] kar; skip, fartøy.

vest [vest] undertøye, ulltrøye; (især amr.) vest; bekle, forlene, overdra, tilfalle, være i ens besittelse; flannel — ulltrøye; -ed fast, sikker, hevdvunnen.

vesta ['vestə] voksfyrstikk.

vestal ['vestəl] vestalsk, jomfruelig, kysk; vestalinne.

vestibular [ves'tibjulə] som hører til en forhall, vestibyle-.

vestibule ['vestibju·l] forhall, forgård, vestibyle. — -train gjennomgangstog.

vestige ['vestidʒ] spor, fotefar.

vestment ['vestmənt] klesplagg, kledning, messedrakt.

vestry ['vestri] sakristi, menighetsråd, sognestyre, kommunestyre — -board sognestyre. — -clerk sekretær i sognestyret. -man medlem av sognestyret.

vesture ['vestʃə] kledning, drakt, bekledning.

Vesuvian [vi'su·vjən] vesuviansk.

vet [vet] dyrlæge.

vet [vet] veteran.

vetch [vetʃ] vikke. -y bevokst med vikker.

veteran ['vetərən] erfaren, stridsvant, øvd, prøvd; veteran.

veterinarian [vetəri'næ·ᵊriən] dyrlege.

veterinary ['vetərinəri] dyrlege-, veterinær-; dyrlege; — surgeon dyrlege.

veto ['vi·toᵘ] veto, forkastelse, forbud; forby, nedlegge sitt veto imot.

vex [veks] ergre, irritere, uroe, plage; opprøre; -ation [vek'se'ʃən] ergrelse, plaging, erting; sjikane; plage. -atious ergerlig, fortredelig, brysom, trettekjær, besværlig, sjikanøs.

vexed [vekst] foruroliget, ergerlig; omstridt; a — question et omstridt spørsmål.

vexil ['veksil] fane (på fjær). -lary [vek'siləri] fanebærer.

v. f. fk. f. very fair.

v. g. fk. f. very good.

v. i. fk. f. verb intransitive.

via ['vaiə] via, over.

viability [vaiə'biliti] levedyktighet.

viable ['vaiəbl] levedyktig.

viaduct ['vaiədʌkt] vidukt.

vial ['vaiəl] medisinglass; the -s of the wrath of God (bibelsk) Guds vredes skåler.

viands ['vaiəndz] levnetsmidler, mat(varer).

viatic [vai'ätik] reise-. viaticum [vai'ätikəm] reisepenger, viatikum, alterens sakrament til døende.

vibrate ['vaibre't] vibrere, svinge, dirre, sitre.

vibration [vai'bre'ʃən] vibrasjon, svingning, dirring.

vibrative ['vaibrətiv], vibratory [-təri] svingende.

viburnum [vai'bə·nəm] krossved, snøballtre.

Vic [vik] fk. f. Victoria.

vicar ['vikə] sogneprest (som har mindre tiendeinntekter enn rector); (sjelden) stedfortreder, vikar; — apostolic apostolisk vikar (katolsk misjonær).

vicarage ['vikəridʒ] prestegård, prestekall.

vicarial [vi'kæ·ᵊriəl] preste-. vicariate [vi-'kæ·ᵊriēt] vikariat; vikarierende.

vicarious [vi'kæ·ᵊriəs] stedfortredende, konstituert.

vicarship ['vikəʃip] presteembete, vikarstilling.

vice [vais] last, lyte, feil, mangel; sletthet; kraft.

vice [vais] skruestikke, skruese; skrue fast, klemme (som) i en skruestikke.

vice ['vaisi] istedenfor; —versa ['və·sə] omvendt.

vice [vais] vise- (i sammensetninger). — -gerent ['vais'dʒerənt] konstituert; stødfortreder, varamann. -regal ['vais'ri·gəl] visekongelig. — -roy ['vaisroi] visekonge, stattholder. — -royalty, — -royship visekonges verdighet, stattholderskap. Vichy ['vi·ʃi·, 'viʃi] Vichy.
vicinity [vi'siniti] nærhet, grannelag, naboskap.
vicious ['viʃəs] lastefull, lytefull, mangelfull; fordervet, slett; arg, vrang, lei, ondskapsfull. -ness lastefullhet.
vicissitude [vi'sisitju·d] omskifting, omveksling. vicissitudinary [vi'sisi'tju·dinəri], vicissitudinous [vi'sisi'tju·dinəs] foranderlig, skiftende.
victim ['viktim] slaktoffer, offer. -ize [-aiz] gjøre til sitt offer, bedra, narre.
victor ['viktə] seierherre, seiervinner, seirende; come off — gå av med seieren.
Victoria [vik'tå·ᵊriə] Viktoria. -n som hører til dronning Viktorias tid.
victorine [vikto'ri·n] skinnkrave (for damer); slags fersken.
victorious [vik'tå·riəs] seierrik, seirende, seiers-. -ness seier, triumf.
victory ['viktəri] seier.
victual ['vitl] levnetsmidler, matvarer, proviant; proviantere. -ler ['vitlə] vertshusholder, proviantleverandør; proviantskip.
vide ['vaidi·] (latin) se.
videlicet [v(a)i'di·liset] nemlig (især fork. til viz. som oftest leses namely).
vie [vai] kappes, tevle (with med).
Vienna [vi'enə] Wien.
Viennese [vie'ni·z] fra Wien; mann (kvinne, folk) fra Wien.
view [vju·] bese, se på, betrakte; beskuelse, betraktning, syn, blikk, synsvidde, utsikt, prospekt, overblikk, anskuelse, hensikt; field of — synsfelt; point of — synspunkt; take a different — of se i et annet lys; in — synlig, for øye; with that — i denne hensikt. -er iakttager. — -finder søker (på fotografiapparat). — -halloo ['vju·hə-'loᵘ] ‹hei, se reven!› utrop på jakt når reven kommer fram. -less usynlig. -y svermerisk, full av upraktiske ideer; pen, som tar seg (godt) ut.
vigil ['vidʒil] våkenatt, våking, nattegudstjeneste. -ance årvåkenhet. -ant våken, årvåken.
vignette [vin'jet] vignett.
vigorous ['vigərəs] sprek, sterk, kraftig.
vigour ['vigə] kraft, styrke; still in the — of life ennå i den kraftige alder.
viking ['vaikiŋ] viking.
vile ['vail] verdiløs, slett, ussel, nederdrektig, skammelig, nedrig, sjofel. vilification [vilifi'ke'ʃən] bakvasking. vilifier ['vilifaiə] bakvasker. vilify ['vilifai] bakvaske.
villa ['vilə] villa.
village ['vilidʒ] landsby; — pond dape, vannpytt (i gata).
villager ['vilidʒə] landsbyboer.
villain ['vilən] skurk, kjeltring.
villainous ['vilənəs] slyngelaktig, elendig.
villainy ['viləni] slyngelstrek.
villein ['vilin] livegen.
villeinage ['vilinidʒ] livegenskap.
vim [vim] energi, kraft.
viminal ['viminəl] kvist-, med bøyelige greiner.
vimineous [vi'miniəs] laget av kvister, flettet.
vinaceous [vi'ne'ʃəs] vin-, drue-, vinfarget.
vincibility [vinsi'biliti] overvinnelighet.
vindicate ['vindike't] forsvare, hevde, godtgjøre, forfekte, rettferdiggjøre. vindication [vindi'ke'ʃən] forsvar, hevdelse, hevding, rettferdiggjøring. vindicative ['vindikətiv] forsvars-, rettferdiggjørende. vindicator ['vindike'tə] forsvarer, hevder. vindicatory ['vindikətəri] forsvarende, hevdende.
vindictive [vin'diktiv] hevngjerrig. -ness hevngjerrighet.

vine [vain] vinranke, vinstokk. — -dresser vingårdsmann. — -fretter vinlus.
vinegar ['vinigə] eddik; vinaigre; bruke eddik til, ha eddik i. — -plant eddikbakterie. — -works eddikbryggeri.
vinegary ['vinigəri] eddiksur.
vine-leaf vinblad, pl. vinlauv.
vinery ['vainəri] drivhus for vinranker.
vineyard ['vinjəd] vingård, vinberg.
vinous ['vainəs] vin-, vinaktig.
vintage ['vintidʒ] vinhøst; årgang.
vintner ['vintnə] vinhandler.
vintry ['vintri] vinlager.
viny [vaini] vinaktig, vinproduserende.
viola ['vaiələ] bratsj.
violaceous [vaiə'le'ʃəs] blåfiolett, fiolettblå.
violate ['vaiəle't] krenke, overtre, bryte.
violation [vaiə'le'ʃən] krenking, brudd.
violator ['vaiəle'tə] krenker, overtreder.
violence ['vaiələns] voldsomhet, vold, voldshandling. violent ['vaiələnt] voldsom, voldelig.
violet ['ꞩaiəlit] fiol; fiolett.
violin [vaiə'lin] fiolin, fele.
violinist [vaiə'linist] fiolinist, felespiller.
violoncello [violən'tʃeloᵘ] fiolonsell, cello.
viper ['vaipə] hoggorm, giftslange, slange. -ine hoggorm-, ormaktig. -ous ormaktig, giftig.
virago [vi're'goᵘ] mannhaftig kvinne, drage, troll.
Virgil ['və·dʒil] Vergil.
virgin ['və·dʒin] jomfru, møy; jomfruelig, jomfru-, møy-; — speech jomfrutale, en talers første tale (i parlamentet o. l.); the (Blessed) Virgin jomfru Maria.
virginal ['və·dʒinəl] jomfruelig, nøy-.
Virginia [və'dʒiniə] Virginia.
virginia [və'dʒiniə] virginiatobakk.
virginity [və'dʒiniti] jomfruelighet, møydom.
viridity [vi'riditi] grønnhet, grønske, grønn farge.
virile ['virail] manns-, mandig, viril, mannlig.
virility [vi'riliti] manndom, mandighet.
virtu [və·'tu·] kunstsans, kunstsaker, sjeldenheter, kuriositeter; article of — kunstgjenstand.
virtual ['və·tʃuəl] iboende, virkelig, faktisk.
virtue ['və·tʃu·] dyd, ærbarhet, kraft, tapperhet, verd, fortreffelighet; by (el. in) — of i kraft av, i medfør av, ved hjelp av.
virtuoso [və·tʃu'oᵘsoᵘ] kunstkjenner; virtuos, mester. -ship kunstsans, virtuositet.
virtuous ['və·tʃuəs] dydig, ærbar.
virulence ['viruləns] giftighet, ondskap, bitterhet. virulent [-ənt] giftig, ondartet, bitter, hatsk.
vis [vis] kraft, makt.
visa ['vi·zə] visum, påtegning på pass; visere, påtegne pass.
visage ['vizidʒ] ansikt, visaged med ansikt.
vis-a-vis [vi·za·'vi·] vis-à-vis, like overfor.
viscera ['visərə] innvoller.
viscid ['visid] klebrig.
viscidity [vi'siditi] klebrighet.
viscount ['vaikaunt] vicomte, (adelsmann i rang etter earl). -ess vicomtesse.
viscous ['viskəs] klebrig.
visé ['vi·ze'] visum; visere. -ing visering, påtegning.
visibility [vizi'biliti] synlighet.
visible ['vizəbl] synlig.
Visigoth ['vizigåþ] vestgoter.
vision ['viʒən] syn, synsevne, synskrets; visjon, drømmebilde, drøm, fantasi. -al som hører til et syn, syns-, fantastisk. -ary som har syner, svermerisk, fantastisk, urimelig; åndeseer, svermer, drømmer, fantast.
visit ['vizit] besøke, ferdes hos, visitere, inspisere, hjemsøke, avlegge besøk, vanke, gå på visitt; besøk, visitt, reise, tur, opphold, midlertidig opphold, visitering. -able som kan visiteres, severdig. -ant besøkende, gjest. -ation [vizi'te'ʃən] besøkelse, gjesting, besøk, visitasjon, undersøkelse

hjemsøkelse. -atorial [vizitə'tå·əriəl] inspeksjons-, kontrollerende.

visiting-card ['vizitiŋk·ºd] visittkort.

visitor ['vizitə] besøkende, gjest, fremmed, tilsynsmann; **visitors' book** fremmedbok.

visor ['vaizə] visir, hjelmgitter, lueskygge.

vista ['vistə] utsikt, allé.

Vistula ['vistjulə], **the — Weichsel**.

visual ['viʒuəl] syns-, synlig, framkalt ved syn. **-ize** gjøre synlig; danne seg et klart bilde.

vital ['vaitl] livs-, vital, nødvendig, vesentlig; **-s** livsorganer, edle deler. **-ity** [vai'täliti] vitalitet, livskraft, nødvendighet. **-ization** [vaitəli'ze'ʃən] levendegjøring. **-ize** ['vaitəlaiz] levendegjøre, opplive, sette kveik i.

vitamin ['vaitəmin] el. **vitamine** ['vaitəmi·n] vitamin.

vitiate ['viʃie't] skjemme, forderve, besmitte, forvanske, gjøre ugyldig. **vitiation** [viʃi'e'ʃən] fordervelse, besmittelse, ugyldiggjørelse, ugyldighet.

vitreous ['vitriəs] glass-, glassaktig; **— electricity** positiv elektrisitet; **— humour** (el. **body**) glassvæske (i øyet). **-ness** glassaktighet.

vitrescent [vi'tresənt], **vitrescible** [vit'resibl] som lar seg forvandle til glass.

vitrifaction [vitri'fäkʃən] forglassing.

vitriol ['vitriəl] vitriol. **-ic** [vitri'ålik] acid svovelsyre.

vituline ['vitjulain] kalve-.

vituperable [vi'tju·pərəbl] daddelverdig. **vituperate** [-re't] dadle, skjelle ut. **vituperation** [vitju·pə're'ʃən] daddel. **vituperative** [vi'tju·pərə-tiv] dadlende.

Vitus ['vaitəs], **St. — St.** Veit, St. Vitus; **St. -'s dance** sanktveitsdans.

vivacious [vi've'ʃəs] levende, livlig.

vivacity [vi'väsiti] liv, livlighet.

vivandier [vi·vångdi'e'] marketenter. **vivandiére** [-'æ·ə] marketenterske.

vivarium [vai'væ·əriəm] sted hvor man holder levende ville dyr, dyrehage.

viva voce ['vaivə'voºsi] muntlig.

vivid ['vivid] levende, livlig, livaktig. **-ness** livlighet, liv, livaktighet.

vivify ['vivifai] levendegjøre.

viviparous [vai'vipərəs] som føder levende unger.

vivisect ['vivisekt] vivisekere.

vivisection [vivi'sekʃən] viviseksjon.

viz. [vi'di·liset, viz, 'ne'mli] fk. f. **videlicet**.

vixen ['viksn] revetispe, troll til kvinnfolk.

vizier [vi'ziə] vesir (tyrkisk minister).

V. O. fk. f. **Victorian Order**.

vocable ['voºkəbl] ord, glose.

vocabulary [vo'käbjuləri] ordsamling, ordliste, ordbok, ordforråd.

vocal ['voºkl] stemme-, talende, muntlig, klingende, vokal-, sang-, melodisk, iørefallende, lydelig, stemt; **— music** sang; **— performer** sanger, sangerinne. **-ity** [vo'käliti] tale-evne, uttale, vokalisk karakter, klang, stemthet. **-ise** ['voº-kəlaiz] uttale, la lyde, vokalisere, merke med vokaltegn (f. eks. hebraisk), synge, gjøre stemt. **-ist** [-list] sanger, sangerinne. **-ly** med stemmen, i ord, tydelig.

vocation [vo'ke'ʃən] kallelse, kall, yrke.

vocative ['våkətiv] vokativ; vokativisk.

vociferate [vo'sifəre't] skråle, gaule.

vociferation [vosifə're'ʃən] skrål, roping.

vociferous [vo'sifərəs] skrålende, høyrøstet, høymælt, stemme. **-ness** skråling, høyrøstethet.

vodka ['vådkə] vodka, russisk brennevin.

vogue [voºg] mote, popularitet, skikk; **be in —** være på moten, i velten, i vinden.

voice [vois] stemme, røst, mål, mæle, mening, ord, uttrykk, (verbal)form; uttale, uttrykke, gi uttrykk for, være et uttrykk for, stemme, regulere tonen i; **if I have any —** hvis jeg skal ha noe å si; **be in —** være pr. stemme; **in a low —**

lavt, med lav stemme; the active — aktiv; **the passive —** passiv. **-d** stemt. **-less** stemmeløs, ustemt, stum.

void [void] tom, blottet, ledig, ugyldig; tomrom; tømme, tømme ut, rydde, forlate, gå fra, avsondre, gjøre ugyldig. **-able** som kan tømmes, som kan erklæres ugyldig. **-ance** tømming, rydning, avsondring, avsettelse, ledighet. **-ness** tomhet, ugyldighet.

vol. fk. f. **volume**.

volant ['voºlənt] flyvende, lett, rapp, snøgg.

Vola-puk, Volapük ['våləpuk] volapyk.

volatile ['vålətail] flyktig. **-ness, volatility** [vålə'tiliti] flyktighet. **volatilize** [vå'lätilaiz] forflyktige.

volcanic [vål'känik] vulkansk.

colcano [vål'ke'noº] vulkan.

volitation [våli'te'ʃən] flying, flukt, flagring.

volition [vo'liʃən] det å ville, vilje, viljesakt.

volitive ['vålitiv] med evnen til å ville, vilje-.

volley ['våli] salve, geværskudd, utbrudd, flom, strøm; tilbakeslag i flukten (av ball i tennis); fyre av, slynge ut; **-ed** utskutt med bulder, buldrende.

volplane ['vål'ple'n] glideflukt; foreta glideflukt.

vols. fk. f. **volumes** bind.

volt [voºlt] volte, vending (i ridning eller fekting).

volt [voºlt] volt (målingsenhet for elektrisk spenning). **-a-electric** galvanisk. **-aism** ['vål-təizm] galvanisme.

volte-face ['våltfa·s] omslag, kuvending.

volubility [vålju'biliti] tungeferdighet.

voluble ['våljubl] flytende, tungerapp, tungeferdig.

volume ['våljum] bind, del, bok; volum; innhold, omfang; **in a way that expressed -s** på den mest talende måte; **volumed** i rullende masser; veldig, svær, svulmende.

voluminous [vol'ju·minəs] bindsterk, omfangsrik, produktiv. **-ness** stort omfang.

voluntary ['våləntəri] frivillig, forsettlig; tilhenger av frivillig system; fantasi (musikk).

volunteer [vålən'tiə] frivillig; tilby el. påta seg frivillig, komme av seg selv, tjene som frivillig, gå inn som frivillig.

voluptuary [və'lʌptʃuəri] vellysting.

voluptuous [və'lʌptʃuəs] vellystig, overdådig. **-ness** vellyst, yppighet.

volution [vo'lju·ʃən] spiral, vinding.

vomit ['våmit] kaste opp, spy (ut); oppkast, spy, brekkmiddel.

vomition [vo'miʃən] oppkasting.

vomitive ['våmitiv] brekkmiddel.

vomitory ['våmitəri] brekkmiddel.

voracious [vo're'ʃəs] grådig, glupende, glupsk. **-ness, voracity** [vo'räsiti] grådighet.

vortex ['vå·ºteks] hvirvel, strømhvirvel, malstrøm.

vortical ['vå·ºtikl] hvirvel-, hvirvlende.

Vosges [voºʒ], **the — Vogesene**.

votaress ['voºtərés] innvigd; (kvinnelig) tilbeder, dyrker.

votary ['voºtəri] tilbeder, dyrker; bundet av et løfte.

vote [voºt] stemme, votum, stemmegivning, votering, avstemning, stemmetall, stemmeseddel, stemmerett, beslutning; avstemme, stemme, votere, vedta, stemme for; **— of confidence** tillitsvotum; **— of censure** mistillitsvotum; **— of thanks** takkeadresse, takk; **— of want of confidence** mistillitsvotum; **pass a —** vedta en beslutning; **take a —** sette saken under avstemning; **— by ballot** stemme skriftlig. **voter** stemmeberettiget, velger. **voting-paper** stemmeseddel.

votive ['voºtiv] votiv-, gitt ifølge et løfte.

vouch [vautʃ] kalle til vitne, bevitne, bekrefte, støtte, vitne, innestå for **(for)**.

voucher ['vautʃə] vitne, skriftlig bevismiddel, kvittering.

vouchsafe [vautʃ'seⁱf] bevilge, tillate, forunne, skjenke, verdige(s). **-ment** bevilling, nådebevisning.

vow [vau] (høytidelig) løfte, ekteskapsløfte; avlegge løfter, love (høytidelig), sverge.

vowel ['vauel] vokal, selvlyd; vokal-, vokalisk.

voyage ['voiidʒ] reise, sjøreise; reise, fare, bereise.

V. R. fk. f. **Victoria Regina** dronning Viktoria.

v. refl. fk. f. **verb reflexive.**

V. S. fk. f. **veterinary surgeon.**

v. t. fk. f. **verb. transitive.**

Vulcan ['vʌlkən] Vulkan (romernes gud for ilden).

vulcanize ['vʌlkənaiz] vulkanisere (svovle og derved herde), vulkaniseres.

vulgar ['vʌlgə] alminnelig, almen, almue-, simpel, tarvelig, rå, vulgær; **the** — den store masse, almuen, udannede folk; folkespråket. **-ism** simpelhet, vulgarisme, vulgært ord, vulgært utrykk. **-ity** ['vʌl'gäriti] plumphet, simpelhet. **-ize** ['vʌlgəraiz] alminneliggjøre, nedverdige, forsimple.

vulnerability [vʌlnərə'biliti] sårbarhet, angripelighet. **vulnerable** ['vʌlnərəbl] sårbar, angripelig.

vulnerary ['vʌlnərəri] sårlægende; sårmiddel.

vulpine ['vʌlpin] reve-, reveaktig, slu.

vulture ['vʌltʃə] gribb. **vulturine** [-rin], **vulturish** [-riʃ] gribbe-, gribbaktig, grådig.

W

W ['dʌblju] W.
W. fk. f. **West(ern); Welsh.**
w. fk. f. **wide; with.**
W. A. A. C. fk. f. **Women's Army Auxiliary Corps.**

wabble ['wåbl] koke; slingre, vakle, være ustø, sjangle; riste, skake; slingrer, sjangling.

wad [wåd] dott, propp; stopp (i klær), vattplate; forladning; (amr.) seddelbunke; lage en dott, stoppe, fore med vatt, vattere, ha forladning i.

wadding ['wådiŋ] vattering, vatt; forladning.

waddle ['wådl] vralte, vagge, rugge, innstille sine betalinger; vraltende gang; **-r** en som vralter.

wade [weⁱd] va, vasse, stolpe seg fram, va over.

wader ['weⁱdə] vader, vadefugl, i plur. vadestøvler, sjøstøvler.

wadset ['wådset] pant; pantsette.

wady ['wådi] elveleie, periodisk elv.

wafer ['weⁱfə] oblat; hostie, krumkake; lukke med oblat.

waffle ['wåfl] vaffel.

waft [wa·ft] blåse, bære, føre (gjennom luft el. vann), vifte, sveve; vift, pust, vindgufs.

wag [wäg] bevege lett, lee på, svinge, riste på, logre med, dingle, bevege seg, lee seg, vakle av sted, skulke, gå sin vei; rugging; spasmaker, skøyer.

wage [weⁱdʒ] pantsette, vedde om, føre, drive; hyre, sold, (srl. i pluralis:) arbeidslønn, lønn; **the wages of sin** syndens sold; **wage war with** (el. against el. (up)on) føre krig med.

wager ['weⁱdʒə] innsats, veddemål; vedde, vedde om, sette på spill.

waggery ['wägəri] skøyeraktighet, spas, spøk.

waggish ['wägiʃ] spøkefull. **-ness** spøkefullhet.

waggle ['wägl] rugge, vagge, lee på seg, vralte; rugging.

waggon ['wägən] vogn, lastevogn, arbeidsvogn, godsvogn. **-age** kjørepenger, vognleie. **-er** kjører, kjørekar, trenkusk.

wagtail ['wägteⁱl] erle.

waif [weⁱf] hittegods, herreløst gods; hjemløs; **-s and strays** hjemløse (skapninger), hittebarn, samfunnets stebarn.

wail [weⁱl] jamre seg, klage, jamre over; jammer, klage. **-ing** jamring.

wain [weⁱn] vogn, lastevogn.

wainscot ['weⁱnskət] panel(ing), eikepanel; bordkledning, panele, bordkle, eikemale. **-band** bukselinning, livreim, belte.

waist [weⁱst] liv, midje, beltested. **-band** bukselinning, livreim, belte.

waistcoat ['weⁱskoᵘt, 'weskət] vest.

wait [weⁱt] vente, lie, se tiden an, varte opp, ligge på lur, vente på, vente med; venting, ventetid, bakhold; — **for** vente på; — **on** (upon) varte opp, gjøre sin oppvartning, betjene, stå til tjeneste; **lie in** — ligge i bakhold, lure.

waiter ['weⁱtə] oppvarter, tjener, kelner; presenterbrett.

waiting ['weⁱtiŋ] ventende, oppvartende; oppvartning, tjeneste. **-maid**, **-woman** kammerpike. **-man** tjener.

waitress ['weⁱtrés] oppvartningspike, oppvarterske.

waive ['weⁱv] oppgi, la fare, frasi seg, se bort fra; **-ed** forlatt. **-ing** bortsett fra.

wake [weⁱk] vekke, våke ved, våkne, vakne, være våken; våking, likvakt, våkenatt, kirkefest. **wake** [weⁱk] kjølvann.

Wakefield ['weⁱkfi·ld] Wakefield.

wakeful ['weⁱkful] våken, vaken, årvåken, søvnløs. **-ness** våking, årvåkenhet, søvnløshet.

waken ['weⁱkn] våkne, vakne, vekke.

wale [weⁱl] opphøyd stripe, opphovnet stripe (etter slag); (mar.) barkholt; merke med striper.

Wales [weⁱlz] Wales.

walk [wå·k] gå, spasere, vandre, gå i skritt, gå i søvne, gå igjen, spøke, gå sin vei, gå igjennom, la gå, skaffe mosjon, bevege; gang, skrittgang, spasertur, promenade, vei, grasgang, hamn (til dyr); livsførsel, virkekrets, område, bane; **take a** — gå en tur; — **into** gå løs på, få bukt med, ødelegge, hogge løs på, ta til seg (av mat). — **into his affections** gi ham ordentlig; — **over him** behandle ham overlegent og hensynsløst, slå seg til ridder på ham; — **the plank** gå med tilbundne øyne på en planke som er lagt ut fra skipet, gå til grunne, dø; **-er** fotgjenger, spaserende, oppsynsmann, bud, oppvarter, hundeoppdretter, fugl med gangføtter. **(hookey)** — tøv med deg, det kan du innbille bønder; **-er-on** statist. **-ing** gang, spasering, gående. **-ing-gentleman** statist. **-ing-stick** spaserstokk.

walking-tour ['wå·kintuə] fottur.

walk-over ['wå·koᵘvə] lett seier, valg uten motkandidat (egl. spasertur over banen, idet man selv bestemmer farten, når det ikke er noen dyktige konkurrenter).

wall [wå·l] mur, vegg, voll, gjerde, vern; mure, omgi med mur, befeste, stå som en mur omkring; — **up** mure til, mure inne; **take the** — gå nærmest husveggen, gå foran; **drive to the** — trekke det korteste strå, kastes til side; **push to the** — skubbe til side.

wallet ['wålit] reisetaske, veske, vadsekk, pose; tegnebok, lommebok, pung.

walleye ['wå·lai] glassøye, blindt øye.

walleyed ['wå·laid] glassøyd, blind.

wall|-flower ['wå·lflauə] gyllenlakk; veggpryd (dame som sitter over). **-fruit** espalierfrukt. **-ing** murmaterialer.

Walloon [wå·lu·n] wallon; wallonsk.

wallop ['wåləp] koke; pryle; juling.

wallow ['wåloᵘ] rulle seg, velte seg; rulling, velting; sølehull, gjørmet sted hvor dyr velter seg.

wall|-painting veggmaleri. — **-paper** tapet. — **-plate** murlekte.

Wall Street ['wå·lstri·t] (gate i New York).
wall-tree ['wå·ltri·] espaliertre.
wallwort ['wå·lwə·t] dverghyll.
Walmesley ['wåmzli] Walmesley.
walnut ['wålnʌt] valnøtt, valnøtt-tre.
walrus ['wålrʌs] hvalross.
waltz [wå·ls] vals; valse, danse vals. **-er** valsdanser.
wan [wån] blek, gusten.
wand [wånd] vånd, stav, embetsstav, tryllestav.
wander ['wåndə] vandre, flakke, streife om, avvike, komme bort fra saken, komme ut på vidåtta, gå vill, fantasere; **his mind -s** han taler i ørske. **-er** ['wåndərə] vandringsmann. **-ing** vandrende, ustadig; flakking, vandring, forvildring, ørske, fantasering; **the -ing Jew** den evige jøde, Jerusalems skomaker; **the -ings of a madman** en gal manns usammenhengende snakk. **-ingly** på en ustadig måte, usammenhengende.
wane [weɪn] avta, minke, synke, dale; avtagende, minking, nedgang, forfall; **on the** — i avtagende, dalende, på skråplanet.
wangle ['wäŋgl] oppnå, skaffe seg (især ved fiffighet eller ved å simulere god og dydig); **he wangled his leave all right** han laget det slik at han fikk permisjon.
wanness ['wånnès] blekhet.
wannish ['wåniʃ] noe blek.
want [wånt] mangle, vante, behøve, trenge til, savne, sakne, være opprådd for, ønske, ville, ville ha; savnes, være borte; mangel, skort, trang, nød, armod; **it -s** det trengs, det utkreves; **for** — **of** i mangel av, av mangel på; **-ing** manglende, som er borte; **that only was -ing** det manglet bare.
wanton ['wåntən] løs, som beveger seg løst, lystig, kåt, vilter, overgiven, utemt, tøylesløs; lettsindig, lettferdig, yppig, løsaktig, usedelig; lettferdig person; løsaktig fruentimmer, tøs; skjelm; flagre, sverme, boltre seg. **-ness** kåthet, lystighet, tøyleshet.
wapentake ['wåpnteɪk] herred (i Yorkshire).
war [wå·ə] krig, ufred, strid, uvennskap, krigskunst; stride, krige, føre krig; **make** — **on** føre krig med; **be at** — ligge i krig, stå på krigsfot; **powers at** — krigførende makter; **man of** — orlogsmann, krigsskip; **council of** — krigsråd; **the fortune of** — krigslykken; — **to the knife** krig på kniven; **War Office** forsvarsdepartement.
warble ['wå·əbl] knute, kul, bremsebyll; bremselarve, verre; oksebremse.
warble ['wå·əbl] slå triller, synge, trille, sang.
warbler sanger(ske), sangfugl. **warbling** triller, sang.
Warburton ['wå·əbətən] Warburton.
war-council ['wå·əkaunsil] krigsråd.
war-cry ['wå·əkraɪ] krigsrop.
ward [wå·əd] bevokte, beskytte, avverge, holde vakt, verje seg, parere; bevoktning, vakt, oppsyn, beskyttelse, vern, parade, formynderskap, myndling, kvarter (av en by), skogsdistrikt, krets, distrikt, herred, rote, avdeling, stue (i hospital); låsgjenge; **a** — **in Chancery, a** — **of court** en umyndig under kanslerrettens verjemål; **private** — privat klinikk; **casualty** — legevakt; — **off** avparere.
ward (ofte brukt som etterstavelse med betydningen:) vendt imot, henimot f. eks. **seaward** el. **seawards**.
war-dance ['wå·əda·ns] krigsdans.
warden ['wå·ədn] vokter, oppsynsmann, tilsynsmann, forstander, bestyrer, rektor.
warder ['wå·ədə] (fange)vokter; portvakt; kommandostav.
wardrobe ['wå·ədroᵘb] garderobe, klesskap.
ward-room ['wå·ədru·m] offisersmesse.
wardship ['wå·əʃip] formynderskap, verjemål, verje; umyndighet.

ware [wæ·ə] ta seg i akt for; var, forsiktig.
ware [wæ·ə] vare, varer. **-house** pakkhus, lager, lagerbygning; anbringe i pakkhus, lagre. **-housebook** lagerbok. **-house-charges** pakkhusleie. **-house-goods** varer på lager. **-house-keeper** lagersjef. **-houseman** eier av lager, lagermann, lagersjef. **-house-room** lagerrom.
war|-establishment krigsstyrke. **-fare** krigsførsel, krig, kamp. — **-horse** stridshest.
wariness ['wæ·ərinès] forsiktighet, varsomhet.
warlike ['wå·əlaik] krigersk, krigs-. **-ness** krigersk karakter.
warlock ['wå·əlåk] trollmann.
warm [wå·əm] varm, lun, inderlig, ivrig, hissig, heftig, begeistret, holden, formuende, velhavende; varme, varme opp, gjøre ivrig, interessere, bli varm, komme i ånde, begeistres.
warmth [wå·əmþ] varme, begeistring.
warn [wå·ən] advare, formane, underrette, varsle, innkalle; — **from** advare imot. **-er** advarer, formaner. **-ing** advarsel, varsel, oppsigelse, innvarsling.
war-office ['wå·əråfis] forsvarsdepartement.
warp [wå·əp] forvri, få til å slå seg (om tre), forkvakle, forvende, fordreie, gi en skjev retning, gjødsle ved å sette under vann; slå seg (om tre), bli skjev (el. vridd), forkvakles, forderves, virke uheldig, varpe seg, kaste (kalv); kastning, (vind-) skjevhet, rennegarn, dynd, varp, varpetrosse. **-ing** kastning, dyndgjødsling.
war|-paint ['wå·əpeɪnt] krigsmaling; (i daglig tale også) full puss. — **-path** ['wå·əpa·þ] krigssti.
warrant ['wårənt] bekrefte, svare for, forsikre, innestå for, garantere, hjemle, berettige, rettferdiggjøre; bekreftelse, sikkerhet, fullmakt, berettigelse, bemyndigelse, hjemmel, garanti, forsikringsbrev, lagerbevis, arrestordre; — **of attorney** fullmakt til en sakfører. **-able** forsvarlig, tillatelig, rettmessig. **-ably** med rette. **-er** en som gir fullmakt, mandant, selger. **-y** garanti.
warren ['wårin] gård, hage, fasangård, kaningård.
Warren ['wårən, -in] Warren.
warrener ['wårənə] oppdretter (srl. av kaniner).
warrior ['wåriə] kriger; **the Unknown Warrior** (el. **Soldier**) den ukjente soldat, ikke identifisert soldat, drept i verdenskrigen, hedret som symbol på nasjonens offer.
Warsaw ['wå·əså·] Warszawa.
war-ship ['wå·əʃip] krigsskip.
wart [wå·ət] vorte; **paint him with his warts** gi et bilde av ham som han er. **-ed** vortet. — **-hog** [-håg] vortesvin. **-y** vortet.
Warwickshire ['wårikʃə] Warwickshire.
wary ['wæ·əri] forsiktig, varsom, var.
was [wås, wəz] imperf. av **be** (1. og 3. pers. sing.).
Wash [wåʃ], **the** — navn på en havbukt mellom Norfolk og Lincolnshire.
wash [wåʃ] vaske, skylle, overskylle, spyle, overtrekke (med et tynt lag), overstryke, vaske seg, holde seg i vask, tåle vask, være vaskeekte, bestå prøven, vask, skylling, dșgleslag, plask, skvulp, skvalp; tynt overtrekk, strøk (med farge), kjølvann, skumming (av båt el. propell), oppskyllet el. avsatt dynd, sump, skyllevann, hårvann, tannvann, skjønnhetsmiddel, åreblad; **it won't** — det holder ikke i vask, det duger ikke; — **one's hands** gjøre toalett; — **one's hands of** fralegge seg alt ansvar for; — **one's dirty linen in public** vaske sitt skittentøy i alles påsyn, bringe private uoverensstemmelser fram for offentligheten.
washed-out utvasket, fargeløs. **washer-woman** vaskekone.
wash|-hand-basin vaskevannsfat. — **-hand stand** vaskeservant. — **-house** vaskeri, bryggerhus, vaskerhus.
washing ['wåʃin] vask (tøy som vaskes).
Washington ['wåʃintən] Washington.
wash|-leather ['wåʃleðə] vaskeskinn. — **-stand**

vaskeservant. — -tub vaskebalje. -y vandig, fuktig, utvannet, oppspedd, tynn.

wasp [wåsp] geitehams, veps, kvefs; **have his head full of -s** ha fluer i hodet. -ish vepsaktig, pirrelig, arrig, bisk.

wassail ['wåsl] drikkelag; en drikk av øl eller vin med tilsetninger, julebrygg; holde drikkelag, ture.

wast [wåst] gml. 2. pers. sing. imperf. av be.

wastage ['we¹stidʒ] svinn, spill.

waste [we¹st] ødelegge, spille, forøde, øydes, sløse, ødsle med, fortære, forminskes, gå til spille, ta av, hentæres, svinne inn; øde, ødslig, vill, udyrket, ubrukt, unyttig; dårlig, avfalls-; ødelegging, unyttig anvendelse, ødselhet, sløsing, sløseri, spill, spillvann, svinn, tap, skade, øde, ørken, ødemark, avfall. — -book kladdebok. -ful ødsel. -fulness ødselhet. — -paper makulatur. — -paper basket papirkurv. — -pipe avløpsrenne, spillvannsrør. -r forøder, ødeland, noen som ødelegger.

watch [wåtʃ] våking, vakt, vakthold, oppmerksomhet, ur, lommeur, klokke; våke, vake, være våken, være årvåken, holde vakt, speide, iaktta, vente, våke over, passe på, ha øye med, belure, vokte, gjæte; **relieve the** — avløse vakta. — -dog gårdshund, vakthund. — -fire vaktild, vaktbluss. -ful årvåken, påpasselig, varsom. -fulness årvåkenhet. — -glass urglass, klokkeglass. — -guard urkjede, klokkekjede. — -gun vaktskudd. -house vakthus, vakt, vaktarrest, kakebu. — -maker urmaker. — -man vekter, vaktmann. — -tower vakttårn. -word feltrop, parole.

water ['wå·tə] vann, vatn, farvann, pl. mineralsk kjelde, kjelde, bad; vanne, ta inn vann, spe opp, blande med vann, løpe i vann, renne, forsyne seg med vann; **the teeth** — tennene løper i vann; **her eyes -ed** hun fikk tårer i øynene; **hold** — holde vann, være tett, duge til noe; **take the -s** bruke brønnkur. — -bailiff tollbetjent. — -brash haubitt, hugbitt. — -butt vanntønne, vasstønne. — -carrier vannbærer. — -chute vassrenne. — -closet vannkloset. — -cock vannhane. — -colour vannfarge. — -course vassdrag, elv. — -cure vannkur. — -dial vannur. — -drop vanndråpe, vassdråpe. — -elephant flodhest. -fall foss, vannfall. — -flag sverdlilje. — -fly vårflue. — -gall søkk i jorda som følge av en vannstrøm. — -gruel vassvelling. -iness vannholdighet. -ing-place vanningssted; badested; sted hvor man tar inn vann. -ing-pot vannkanne, hagesprøyte. -ing-trough vanningstrau. -ish vassen; fuktig. — -level vaterpass, vannstand. — -lily vannlilje, nøkkrose. — -logged full av vann, vasstrukken. -man ferjemann, skullermann, hestevanner. — -pot vannkanne. -proof vanntett, vasstett; regnkappe. — -rat vannrotte. — -shed vannskille. — -soak bløyte ut i vann. -spout vannstråle, skypumpe. — -tight vanntett, vasstett. — -vole vannrotte, vassvånd. — -way vannvei, kanal, løp. — -wheel vannhjul, skovlhjul. -work (oftest pl.) vannverk.

watery ['wå·təri] vann-, vannholdig, vassen, våt, fuktig.

wattle ['wåtl] kvist, kvistfletning, risgjerde, hudlapp (på høne), skjegg (på fisk); omgjerde (el. dekke) med kvistfletning, flette.

waul [wå·l] mjaue, vræle, skrike.

wave [we¹v] bølge, båre, sjø; vatring, vift, vifting, bølge, flagre, vaie, svinge, vakle, vinke, vifte, gjøre bølgeformig, sette i bølgebevegelse, vinke med; — **his hand** vinke med hånden, slå ut med hånden. -less uten en bølge, stille, blank. -let liten bølge.

waver ['we¹va] spille ustadig (om stråler), være usikker, vakle. -er en som vakler, er vankelmodig. -ing ['we¹vəriŋ] vaklende. -ingness vakling, vingel.

wavy ['we¹vi] bølgende, bølget, båret.

wax [wäks] hissighet, sinne.

wax [wäks] vokse, stige, bli.

wax [wäks] voks, lakk, bek; vokse, bone, lakke, beke. — -chandler vokslys-støper. — -cloth voksduk.

waxen [wäksn] voksaktig, voksbløt, voksblek. **wax|-end** bektråd. — -vesta voksfyrstikk. — -work voksarbeid, voksfigur. -y voksaktig, bløt, blek; (i slang) sinna, hissig.

way [we¹] vei, gate, bane, veistykke, strekning, lei, kant, retning, gjennomgang, middel, måte, vis, skikk, vane, manér, vesen, lune, fart; **by the** — i forbigående, à propos. **by** — of apology som unnskyldning; **by a great** — uten sammenligning; **come one's -s** komme fram; **get his own** — få sin vilje; **give** — vike, gi etter; **she was quite in a** — about it hun tok rent på vei for det; **in a** — of speaking til en viss grad, så å si; **in the** — i veien, til hinder; **every** — i enhver henseende; **no -(s)** på ingen måte; **once in a** — for en gangs skyld; **make** — gjøre plass, gå av veien; **make one's** — bane seg vei, arbeide seg fram, gjøre lykke; **-s and means** måter og midler, hjelpekilder; **committee of -s and means** underhuskommisjon, som drøfter hvordan staten kan skaffe seg inntekter.

way|-bill ['we¹bil] fraktbrev, fraktseddel, følgebrev, borderau. -farer veifarende. -faring veifarende. -lay ligge på lur etter, passe opp. -layer etterstreber. — -mark avviser, veiviser. — out utgang, utvei. -ward egensindig, lunefull. -wardness egensindighet. -worn trett etter reisen.

W. B. N. fk. f. **West by North.**

W. b. S. fk. f. **West by South.**

W.C. fk. f. **WestCentral** (postdistrikt i London).

w. c. fk. f. **water-closet.**

W. C. A. fk. f. **Women's Christian Association.**

we [wi·] vi.

weak [wi·k] svak, skrøpelig, sykelig, holdningsløs, matt, kraftløs, veik. -en svekke, avkrefte, bli svak el. svakere. -ener en el. noe som svekker. — -hearted fryktsom, redd av seg. -ling svekling, stakkar. -ly svakt, av svakhet, i et svakt øyeblikk. — -minded innskrenket, åndssvak; viljesvak. -ness svakhet, sykelighet.

weal [wi·l] opphovnet stripe (etter slag); merke med striper.

weal [wi·l] vel, velferd; — or woe ve og vel; **the public** — det almene vel.

weald [wi·ld] mo, åpent land; **the Weald** (en strekning i Kent, Surrey og Sussex).

wealth [welþ] rikdom, formue, fylde. -iness rikdom.

wealthy ['welþi] rik.

wean [wi·n] venne av; — from venne fra, venne av med; (dial.:) pjokk, unge.

weapon ['wepən] våpen. -ed bevæpnet, væpnet. -less våpenløs.

wear [wiə] demning, ruse, teine.

wear [wæ·ə] bære, ha på seg, gå med, bruke, slite, tære på, tilbringe på en kjedelig måte, slite ut, holde seg, være holdbar, brukes, bli slitt, slepe seg hen (om tiden); bruk, slitasje, slit, antrekk, drakt; holdbarhet; **all my** — alt det jeg har på meg; — **and tear** slit og slep; — away slite opp, fordrive; — out slite ut, henslepe; — well holde seg godt, være sterk. -er en som bærer el. har på, noe som sliter. -ing som bæres, oppslitende, slitsom.

weariness ['wiərinès] tretthet, møysommelighet, kjedsommelighet; — of life livslede.

wearing-apparel ['wæ·²riŋə'pærəl] gangklær.

wearisome ['wiərisəm] trettende, besværlig.

weary ['wiəri] trett, sliten, kjed, lei, utålmodig, trettende; trette, kjede, plage, besvære, bli trett, lengte; **for such a** — while i så langsommelig tid; **be wearied out of patience** miste tålmodigheten.

weasand ['wi·zənd] (gammelt:) strupe, luftrør.

weasel ['wi·zl] vesel.

weather ['weðə] vær, uvær (i poesi): lovart; lo; vind-; utsette for lufta, tørre, værslå, forvitre; klare, greie; overstå; gå til lovart; — a point klare en odde, overvinne vanskeligheter. — -beaten medtatt av været, forvitret, værbitt, værslått, barket, omtumlet. — -board vindside. — -bound værfast. -cock værhane. — -glass barometer. — -proof som holder været ute, som været ikke biter på. — -service værvarsling. — -spy værprofet. — -vane værhane, vindfløy. — -wise værkyndig. — -working days dager da været er slik at skipet kan lastes eller losses.

weave [wi·v] veve, danne, lage sammen, flette, flette inn. -r ['wi·və] vever. -ress ['wi·vərés] veverske.

weazen ['wi·zn] vissen, tørr, skrinn, innskrumpet, mager.

web [web] vev, spindelvev, svømmehud, fane (på fjær), papirrull (til avis).

webbed [webd] med svømmehud, svømme-.

web-foot ['webfut] svømmefot.

wed [wed] ekte, gifte seg med, ektevie, gifte seg, forbinde, fengsle, lenke; wedded pair ektepar; her wedded life hennes ekteskap.

wedding ['wediŋ] bryllup; silver — sølvbryllup; golden — gullbryllup; diamond — diamantbryllup; be at his — være til stede ved hans bryllup. -cake bryllupskake. — -cards nygiftes (sammenhengende) visittkort. — celebration brudeferd. — -ceremony vielse. — -day bryllupsdag. — -dress brudedrakt, brudekjole. — -favour brudesløyfe. — -ring vielsesring.

wedge [wedʒ] kile; kløyve, sprenge med kile, kile fast, kile inn.

Wedgwood ['wedʒwud] Wedgwood; — ware wedgwoodvarer (fint steintøy).

wedlock ['wedlåk] ektestand(en), ekteskap; born in (out of) — født i (utenfor) ekteskap; enter upon — tre inn i ektestanden.

Wednesday ['wenzdi] onsdag.

weds [wedz]: the newly-weds de nygifte, brudeparet.

wee [wi·] bitte liten, ørliten; smule, grann, øyeblikk.

weechelm ['wi·tʃelm] alm.

weed [wi·d] ukrutt, ugras, tobakk, sigar; luke, luke bort, rydde ut; ill weeds grow apace ukrutt torgår ikke så lett. -er luker, lukeredskap. -ing-hook lukehakke.

weeds [wi·dz] (enkes) sørgedrakt.

weedy ['wi·di] full av ugras; dårlig, svak, skranten, skral.

week [wi·k] uke, veke; this day — i dag åtte dager; that day — åtte dager etterpå; be in by the — være festet på en uke; the Great Week den stille uke. — -day hverdag, ukedag. — -end ferie fra (fredag eller) lørdag til mandag (eller tirsdag). -ly en gang om uken, ukentlig; ukeblad.

weep [wi·p] gråte, gråte for. -er gråtende. -ing gråtende, gråt.

weevil ['wi·vil] snutebille.

weft [weft] islett, veft, vev, vevning; vimpel.

weigh [we¹] veie, overveie, prøve, lette anker, lette, veie, ha vekt; — one's expressions veie sine ord; — (the) anchor lette anker; — down tynge, trykke; — in bli veid (i sport). -able som lar seg veie, som selges etter vekt. -er veier. -ing-house veierbu.

weight [we¹t] vekt, lodd, byrde, tyngde, pl. vektskål; belaste, tynge; sell by the — selge etter vekt; cloth — urlodd. -iness vekt, tyngde, viktighet. -y tung, vektig.

weir [wiə] demning; fiskegård, laksegard, fiskerteine.

weird [wiəd] skjebne, spådom, fortryllelse; overnaturlig, trolsk, uhyggelig, selsom, underlig; forutsi; the — sisters skjebnegudinne.

Welch [welʃ], se Welsh!

welcome ['welkəm] velkommen; velkomst(hilsen), mottagelse; by velkommen, motta (vennlig); 'll go and — jeg skal så gjerne gå dit; bid — by

velkommen; you are — to it De må gjerne ha det, bare ha det, det er Dem vel unt.

weld [weld] sveise; la seg sveise; sveising; — together sveise sammen. — -iron smijern. — -steel pudlet stål.

welfare ['welfæ·ə] velferd, lykke, vel.

welkin ['welkin] himmel, himmelhvelv.

well [wel] kjelde, ile, oppkomme, brønn, hulning, fordypning, hulrom, hull, fiskebrønn, øserom, pumpesot, pl. sunnhetsbrønner, badested; borehull, petroleumsbrønn, minebrønn, elevatorsjakt, trapperom, advokatlosje (i rettssal); velle fram, springe fram, sende ut.

well [wel] (adverbium:) godt, vel, riktig, ordentlig, atskillig; (ved may:) nok; (innledende:) jaja, nåvel, nå; (adjektiv, bare brukt som predikatsord, unntagen i dialekt og amerikansk:) frisk, bra, riktig; godt; be — ha det godt, være lykkelig, være i gunst; be — off være velstilt, være velstående. be — with stå seg godt med; let — alone la saken være som den er; as — as så vel som, likeså godt som; — within an hour langt mindre enn en time.

welladay ['welə'de¹] akk! å jøye meg! å jøye!

well¹-advised ['weləd'vaizd] klok, velbetenkt. — -affected velsinnet, velvillig, hengiven. — -appointed vel utrustet. — -behaved veloppdragen. — -being velvære. — -beloved høyt elsket. — -born ['welbå·ən] av god familie. — -bred veloppdragen, dannet. — -disposed vennligsinnet. — -doer rettskaffent menneske, velgjører. — -doing rettskaffen; velbefinnende, lykke.

well-earned ['wel'ə·nd] velfortjent.

welled [weld] forsynt med brønn.

well-favoured ['wel'fe¹vəd] vakker, som ser godt ut.

well-head ['welhed] kjelde, oppkomme.

well-informed ['welin'få·əmd] vel underrettet, kunnskapsrik.

Wellington ['weliŋtən] Wellington; wellingtons skaftestøvler.

well¹-intentioned ['welin'tenʃənd] velmenende, velment. — -met [-'met] vel møtt! — -minded [-'maindid] veltenkt, godtenkt. — -nigh ['welnai] nesten. — -read ['wel'red] belest.

well-room ['welru·m] brønnsal; øserom.

well-spent ['wel'spent] velanvendt. — -spoken velvalt, treffende, som taler godt, beleven. — -tasted velsmakende. — -timed som skjer i rette tid, velberegnet, betimelig. — -to-do velstående, trivelig. — -wisher velynder, venn. — -worn forslitt, utslitt.

Welsh [welʃ] som hører til Wales; valisisk; valiser; a — comb de fem fingrer; like a — comb i det uendelige; — rabbit ristet ost og brød; — wig strikket lue av ull.

welsh [welʃ] bedra, snyte. -er bedrager.

Welshman ['welʃmən] valiser.

welt [welt] rand, kanting; kante, randsy.

welter ['weltə] hulle, velte, velte seg; velting, rulling, opprør, forvirring, røre, rot, virvar, dynd, pøl.

wen [wen] svulst, utvekst, kul, hevelse.

wench [wenʃ] pike, jente (især om tjenestepike, bondejente eller spøkende); hore.

wend [wend] vende; (gammelt:) gå; — one's way vandre, begi seg, ta veien.

Wend [wend] vender.

Wendic ['wendik] vendisk (ogs. om språket).

Wendish ['wendiʃ] vendisk.

wennish ['weniʃ] svulstlignende; plaget av svulster.

went [went] gikk; imperf. av go.

wept [wept] imperf. og perf. pts. av weep.

were [wə·, wæ·ə] var (av be).

were [wiə] dam, demning.

we're [wiə] fk. f. we are.

werewolf ['wə·wulf], werwolf varulv.

wesand ['wi·zənd] se weasand!

Wesley ['wezli] Wesley. **-an** wesleyansk; wesleyaner. **-anism** wesleyansk metodisme.

Wessex ['wesiks] Wessex.

west [west] el. **West** vest; Vesten; Vesterlandene, den vestlige halvkule; vestlig, vestre, fra vest, vesta-; imot vest; **the Far West** det fjerne Vesten (ɔ: det vestligste av U. S.); **in the** — i vest; **on the** — på vestsiden, i vest; **to the** — mot vest; **to the** — **of** vest for; **West-End** vestkanten (den finere del av London); **the** — **Wind** vestavinden; **the West Indies** el. **West India** Vestindia. — **-ender** en som bor på vestkanten. **-er** gå mot vest, (om sola:) dale. **-erliness** vestlighet. **-erly** vestlig.

western ['westən] vestlig, vestre, vest-; **the Western Church** den romersk-katolske kirke; **the Western Empire** det vestromerske rike; **the western front** vestfronten (i verdenskrigen krigsskueplassen i Frankrike); **the Western Powers** vestmaktene.

westerner ['westənə] vesterlending, europeer, vestamerikaner.

westernmost ['westənmoust] vestligst.

Westminster ['westminstə] Westminster; — **Abbey** Westminster abbedi; — **School,** en gammel public school; — **Palace** parlamentsbygningen.

Westmoreland ['wesmələnd] Westmoreland.

westmost ['westmoust] vestligst.

Westphalia [west'feiljə] Westfalen.

westward ['westwəd] mot vest, vestover, vestlig, i vest; vest; — **ho!** (gml. ferjemannsrop på Themsen). **westwards** = **westward.**

wet [wet] våt, fuktig, regnfull; væte, nedbør, regnvær; væte, bløyte, fukte. — **-nurse** amme. — **-shod** våtskodd, med våte føtter.

wether ['weðə] gjeld-vær.

W. G. fk. f. **Westminster Gazette.**

whack [wäk] banke, denge, pryle; slag, bank.

whale [we¹l] hval, kval; fange hval. **-bone** hvalbarde, fiskebein. **whaler** ['we¹lə] hvalfanger.

whaling ['we¹liŋ] hvalfangst; hvalfanger-.

whame [we¹m] brems.

wharf [wå·əf] brygge, losseplass, opplagsplass, pakkhus. **-age** bryggepenger. **-ing** bryggeanlegg.

wharfinger ['wå·əfindʒə] plassformann, bryggeeier.

what [wåt] hva, hva for en, hvilken, hvilke; hva der; noe; hvilken! **I'll tell you** — jeg skal si deg noe; **I gave him** — **money I had** jeg gav ham de pengene jeg hadde; — **he?** hva for en han? — **folly!** for en tåpelighet! — **if** hva om? tenk om? — **of him?** hva er det med ham? — **though** selv om, forutsatt at; — **by force,** — **by policy** dels ved makt, dels ved smidighet; — **between** (el. **with**) **grief and illness** dels av sorg, dels av sykdom. **-ever** [-'evə] alt hva der, alt hva, alt det som, hvilken som helst som, hvilken enn; hva i all verden? (adv.) som helst.

whatnot ['wåtnåt] etasjère.

whatsoever [wåtsou'evə] alt hva der, alt det som; hvilken som helst som, hvilken enn; (adv.) som helst.

wheal [wi·l] blemme, kveise; opphovnet stripe.

wheat [wi·t] hvete, kveite. — **-ear** hveteaks. **-en** hvete-, kveite-, av hvete.

wheedle ['wi·dl] lokke, smigre, sleske for, rundsnakke. **wheedler** ['wi·dlə] smigrer. **wheedling** ['wi·dliŋ] godsnakking, smigreri.

wheel [wi·l] hjul, spinnerokk, pottemakerskive, ratt, pinebenk, omdreining, svingning, kretsløp; kjøre, trille, la svinge, rulle, dreie seg, kretse, svinge; **break upon the** — radbrekke.

wheelbarrow ['wi·l'bärou] trillebår.

wheel-chair ['wi·ltʃæ·ə] rullestol.

wheeled [wi·ld] forsynt med hjul, hjul-.

wheeler ['wi·lə] hjulmaker; stanghest; bakerste sledehund.

wheel|-fire smelteild. — **-horse** stanghest. —

-window rundt vindu. **-work** hjulverk. **-wright** hjulmaker.

wheeze [wi·z] puste tungt, hese, kvese; kvesing.

wheezy ['wi·zi] hås, astmatisk.

whelk [welk] kuvung; blemme, kong.

whelm [welm] overskylle, overvelde.

whelp [welp] hvalp, unge; hvalpe.

when [wen] da, når, og deretter, når? **say** —! si stopp!

whence [wens] hvorfra, hvorfor, hvorav; **from** — hvorfra.

whencesoever [wenssou'evə] hvorfra enn.

whenever [we'nevə] når i all verden? når som helst enn, alltid når.

whensoever [wensou'evə] når som helst enn, alltid når.

where [wæ·ə] hvor; — **are you going?** hvor skal du hen? **near** — nær det sted, hvor. **-abouts** hvor omtrent; oppholdssted, tilholdssted, beliggenhet. **-as** mens derimot; (sjeldnere:) så som. **-at** ['-ät] hvorover, hvorved. **-by** [-'bai] hvorved. **-fore** hvorfor; grunn. **-in** hvori. **-into** hvori. **-of** hvorav, hvorom, hvorfor. **-on** hvorpå. **-soever** hvor enn, hvorhen enn. **-through** hvorigjennom. **-to** hvortil. **-under** hvorunder. **-upon** hvorpå, hvoretter.

wherever [wæ·ə'revə] hvor enn, hvor som helst, hvorhen enn, overalt hvor; hvor i all verden?

wherewith [wæ·ə'wið] hvormed; middel.

wherry ['weri] ferjepram, lett flatbunnet båt.

whet [wet] kvesse, skjerpe, bryne; kvessing, sliping; delikatesse, appetittvekker, dram.

whether ['weðə] enten, hva enten; om, hvor-, vidt.

whetstone ['wetstoun] slipestein, bryne.

whey [we¹] valle, myse; tynn, blek. **-ey [-i] -ish** [—iʃ] valleaktig, myseaktig.

which [witʃ] 1. (spørrende pron. i begrensede spørsmål) hvem, hva, hvilken, (hvilket, hvilke) (av et bestemt antall); — **of you?** hvem av dere? — **remedy can help me, this one or that one?** hvilket legemiddel kan hjelpe meg, dette her eller det der? 2. (relativt pron.) hvilket, som, noe, som, hva der (i genitiv: **of which,** sjeldnere **whose**); **he gave me nothing,** — **was bad** han gav meg ingen ting, noe som var ille. **-ever** [(h)witʃ'evə] hvilken enn, hvilken som helst som; hvilken i all verden. **-soever** hvilken enn.

whicker ['wikə] vrinske.

whiff [wif] pust, vift, gufs, drag (av sigar); puste, blåse, dampe.

whiffle ['wifl] spre (med et pust), blåse ujevnt, svinge, ombestemme, vakle, være ustø, vimre. **whiffler** ['wiflə] piper, herold; vegelsinnet.

whig [wig] whig (moderat frihetsmann). **-gish** whiggisk, whig-.

while [wail] tid, stund; mens, så lenge som; fordrive; **at -s** stundom; **the** — imens, dermed; **once in a** — en gang imellom; **was this worth** —? var dette umaken verd? — **away time** fordrive tiden.

whilst [wailst] mens.

whim [wim] grille, lune, nykke, innfall; **enter into the** — **of the scene** være med.

whimper ['wimpə] sutre, klynke; sutring, klynking. **-ing** sutrende; klynking.

whim|sey ['wimzi] lune, innfall. **-sical** ['wimzikl] lunefull, snurrig, underlig. **-sicality** [wimzi'käliti], **-sicalness** ['wimzikln̩ès] lunefullhet, pussighet.

whimsy ['wimzi] lune, innfall.

whim-wham ['wimwäm] visvas, nonsens; lune, påfunn.

whinberry ['winbəri] blåbær.

whine [wain] flepe, klynke, sutre; klynking, hyl, klynkende tone. **whiner** ['wainə] klynker.

whinny ['wini] knegge, vrinske; knegg.

whip [wip] pisk, svepe; kjører; innpisker; piske, slå, vispe, banke, rise, hudflette, refse, neste, tråkle, kaste med flue, surre, omvikle, vikle, gripe, snappe, trive, slenge, fare, smette hurtig, springe. — **-and-spur** sporenstreks .— **-cord** piskesnor. — **-hand** høyre hånd, overtak, fordel; **get the** — **-hand over** få under pisken. — **-lash** piskesnert.

whipper ['wipə] pisker, bøddel.

whipper-in ['wipə'rin] pikør; innpisker (som samler partifeller til avstemning).

whippersnapper ['wipəsnäpə] spirevipp, spjert, liten viktigper.

whippet ['wipit] slags mynde; (militært) hurtig lett tank.

whipping|-boy ['wipiŋboi] syndebukk, hoggestabbe. — **-top** snurrebass.

whipster ['wipstə] spirevipp, liten viktigper.

whip-stitch ['wipstitʃ] kåste over, tråkle; skredder.

whip-stock ['wipståk] svepeskaft.

whir [wə·] snurre, svirre; snurring, svirring.

whirl [wə·l] hvirvle, hvirvle rundt, svinge, svinges, svirre; omhvirvling, hvirvlende fart, hvirvel; **in -s of snow** i fykende snøvær; **set my head in a** — fikk tankene til å hvirvle rundt i min hjerne. — **-about** karusell. **-bone** kneskjell. **-igig** ['hwə·ligig] karusell, snurrebass. **-pool** strømhvirvel, malstrøm. **-wind** hvirvelvind.

whisk [wisk] visk, dott, støvekost, visp, strøk, streif, feiing; viske, feie, sope, streife, piske, slå, slenge, svinge, fare, stryke av sted. **-er** værhår, kinnskjegg. **-ery** med kinnskjegg.

whiskey, whisky ['wiski] en slags lett gigg.

whisky ['wiski] whisky; — **and soda** whiskypjolter. **-fied** ['wiskifaid] drukken, som lukter av brennevin.

whisper ['wispə] hviske, kviskre, ymte om; hvisking, hemmelig vink. **-er** en som hvisker. **-ing** hvisking; **dark -ings** skumlerier.

whist [wist] stille! hysj! whist (kortspillet).

whistle ['wisl] plystre, pipe, hvine, fløyte, blåse på fløyte; plystring, pipesignal, fløyte, pipe; as **clean as a** — så nydelig som dertil; **pigs and -s** pokker'n! **he must pay for his** — han må betale lærepenger; **he may** — for it det kan han skyte en hvit pinne etter. **whistler** ['wislə] en som plystrer; brennevinsgauk.

whit ['wit] smitt, smule, grann, det ringeste; **every** — aldeles, fullkommen, i enhver henseende; **every** — **as great** i enhver henseende likså stor.

white [wait] hvit, kvit, blek, hvithåret, ren, uskyldig; hvit, hvithet, eggehvite, hvit (motsatt neger), flormel; gjøre hvit, hvitte; — **elephant** sjelden men brysom eiendel; **show the** — **feather** vise seg feig; **the White Feather Brigade** sammenslutning av kvinner som under verdenskrigen fikk menn til å melde seg til krigstjeneste, bl. a. ved å anbringe en hvit fjær på dem; — **friars** karmelittermunker; — **game**, — **grouse** fjellryper; — **heat** hvitglødende hete; — **horses** skummende bølger, brimhester; **the White House** presidentens bolig i U. S. A.; **a** — **lie** en liten nødløgn; — **man** hvit mann (av blek europeisk type, motsatt **black, red, yellow**), hederlig menneske, bra mann; **the** — **man's burden**, den oppgave å føre verden framover; — **meat** hvitt kjøtt (især om kjøtt av kylling, kanin, kalv); — **of egg** eggehvite; — **of the eye** det hvite i øyet; — **slave** offer for den hvite slavehandel.

whitebait ['waitbeˡt] småfisk (især sild), rett av småfisk.

Whitechapel ['waittʃäpəl] Whitechapel.

white-faced ['waitfeˡst] blek; med hvit bles.

whitefish ['waitfiʃ] maˡfisk, (især hvitting, kolje, sik).

Whitehall ['waithå·l] gate i London med departementsbygningene.

white-hot ['wait'håt] hvitglødende.

white-livered ['waitlivəd] krysteraktig, feig.

whiten ['waitn] gjøre hvit, bleke, bleike; bli

hvit, blekne, bleikne. **whiteness** ['waitnes] hvithet. **whitening** ['waitniŋ] pussekritt.

whitethorn ['waitþå·ⁿn] hagtorn.

whitethroat ['waitþroˡut] gråsanger (fugl).

whitewash ['waitwåʃ] hvittekalk, renvasking; hvitte, forsøke å renvaske (en persons rykte).

whither ['wiðə] (poet. eller gml.) hvorhen.

whithersoever [wiðəsoˡuevə] hvorhen enn.

whiting ['waitiŋ] pussekritt; hvitting (en fisk).

whitish ['waitiʃ] hvitlig, hvitaktig.

Whitley ['witli] Whitley; — **councils** en slags bedriftsråd.

whitlow ['witloˡu] svullfinger, verkefinger.

Whit-Monday [wit'mʌndi] annen pinsedag.

Whitsun ['witsən] pinse. **-day** pinsedag. **-holidays** pinseferie. **-tide** pinse.

whittle ['witl] spikke, skjære; lommekniv.

whiz [wiz] suse, hvisle, hvine, sus, hvisling.

who [hu·] hvem, hvem som, som, den som, enhver som; **as** — **should say** som om man ville si; liksom.

whoever [hu(·)'evə] hvem som enn, enhver som, hver den som; hvem i all verden?

whole [hoˡul] hel, fullstendig, alle, samtlige; hele, helhet; — **and entire** helt og holdent; **the** — **army** hele hæren; **upon the** — i det hele tatt, overhodet; — **-hearted** (udelt) hjertelig. — **-length** bilde i hel figur; — **life insurance** livsvarig livsforsikring. **-ness** helhet. **-sale** salg i det store, en gros; i fleng, for fote; som selger i det store, masse. **-saledealer** grosserer. **-salemurderer** massemorder.

wholesaler ['hoˡulseˡlə] grosserer, grossist.

wholesome ['hoˡulsəm] sunn, gagnlig.

wholly ['hoˡulli] helt, aldeles, ganske.

whom [hu·m] hvem, som (avhengighetsform av who).

whoop [hu·p] rop, heiing, huiing; huie, rope.

whooping-cough ['hu·piŋkåf] kikhoste.

whop [wåp] banke, denge, jule. **-per** en diger en, en som har vasket seg, en diger skrøne. **-ping** veldig, diger; juling.

whore [hå·ə] hore. **whorish** ['hå·riʃ] horaktig, utuktig.

whortleberry ['wə·tlberi] blåbær; **red** — tyttebær.

whose [hu·z] hvis (genitiv av **who** eller **which**).

whosoever [hu·soˡu'evə] hvem som enn, enhver som.

why [wai] hvorfor; nå! å! jo for, vet du hva; **that is** — det er grunnen.

W. I. fk. f. West Indies.

wick [wik] veke, veike.

wick [wik] i smstn. by, landsby, stad.

wicked ['wikid] ond, vond, slett, ondskapsfull, slem, skadefro. **-ness** ondskap, ugudelighet, ondskapsfullhet.

wicker ['wikə] vidje, kurvarbeid, vidjekurv; gjort av vidjer, kurv-, korg-. — **-basket** vidjekurv. **-bed** kurvseng. — **-bottle** kurvflaske. — **-cradle** kurvvugge. **-work** kurvarbeid.

wicket ['wikit] grind, led, port, halvdør, sluseport, gjerde (i cricket-spill).

wide [waid] vid, rommelig, bred, brei, vidstrakt, avvikende; vidt, langt; **far and** — vidt og bredt; **his eyes were** — **with horror** øynene hans var oppspilt av skrekk. — **-awake** lys våken, på sin post, slu; bløt filthat; **be** — **-awake to** ha åpent øye for. **-n** gjøre bredere, vide ut, vide seg ut. **-ness** vidde, bredde, stor utstrekning. **-spread** (vidt) utbredt, vidstrakt; oppspilt.

widgeon ['widʒən] blesand.

widow ['widoˡu] enke; gjøre til enke el. enkemann. **-er** ['widoˡuə] enkemann. **-erhood** ['widoˡuəhud] enkemannsstand. **-hood** ['widoˡuhud] enkestand, enkemannsstand.

width [widþ] vidde, bredde, breidd.

wield [wi·ld] føre, håndtere, bruke, utøve.

wife [waif] kone, hustru, kjerring, kvinnfolk,

vertinne; **all the world and his** — alle mulige mennesker, Per og Pål. -**less** uten kone.
wig [wig] parykk; ta på parykk. -**ged** [wigd] med parykk.
wigging ['wigin] overhaling, irettesetting.
wiggle ['wigl] sno seg, sprelle, vagge, rugge, vrikke.
Wight [wait] Wight.
wight [wait] fyr, menneske.
wigwag ['wigwäg] vifte (med), signalisere.
wigwam ['wigwəm] wigwam, indianerhytte.
wild [waild] vill, udyrket, usivilisert, vilter, tøylesløs, ustyrlig, lettsindig, forrykt, heftig, ergerlig; villmark. **sow one's** — oats renne hornene av seg.
wild-boar ['waildbå·ə] villsvin.
wild-cat ['waildkät] villkatt; (amr.) kanadisk gaupe, kuguar; (i slang) forrykt; svindel-.
wild-duck ['wailddʌk] villand.
wilder ['wildə] føre vill, forville.
wilderness ['wildənès] villnis, ørken.
wild-eyed ['waildaid] viltstirrende.
wild-fire ['waildfaiə] gresk ild, kornmo, lyktemann; rosen (sykdom); **like** — lynsnart, som en løpeild; **sell like** — gå som varmt hvetebrød.
wild-goose chase meningsløst foretagende; vanvittig jag (**after** etter).
wilding ['waildin] vill vekst, vill frukt.
wile [wail] list, knep, bedrag; narre, fordrive.
wilful ['wilful] egensindig, stivsinnet, forsettlig. -**ly** med overlegg. -**ness** egensindighet, stivsinn, forsettlighet.
Wilhelmstrasse ['vilhelmstra·sə] (brukt om) det tyske utenriksdepartement.
will [wil] vilje, behag, lyst, testamente; ville, ønske, ville ha, by, pleie (ofte), testamentere; **if I could work my** — gikk det etter mitt hode; **at** — etter behag, etter eget tykke; **with a** — med hjertens lyst, med kraft, med fynd og klem; **I** — jeg vil, det skal jeg, ja.
Will [wil] fk. f. **William** ['wiljəm] Vilhelm.
willing ['wilin] villig; **be** — **to** ville, være villig til; **God** — om Gud vil. -**ness** villighet.
Will-o'-the-wisp ['wiləðwisp] lyktemann, vettelys, blålys.
willow ['wiloᵘ] pil, piletre.
willow-herb ['wiloᵘhə·b] geiterams, geiteskor, mjølke.
willow-weed ['wiloᵘwi·d] kattehale (planten).
willowy ['wiloᵘi] pilbevokst; pilaktig, smidig og slank.
willy-nilly ['wili'nili] enten man vil eller ikke.
wilt [wilt]. **thou** — du vil (gammelt av **will**).
wilt [wilt] visne, tørke inn, slappes; tørke, bringe til å visne, slappe.
Wilton ['wiltən] **carpet** Wilton-teppe.
wily ['waili] listig, slu, utspekulert.
wimble ['wimbl] bor; bore.
wimple ['wimpl] hodeklede, nonneslør; dekke med hodeklede; falle i folder.
win [win] vinne, vinne for seg, seire.
wince [wins] være urolig, støkke, skvette, kvekke til, krympe seg; nervøst rykk, smertelig trekning.
wincey ['winsi] verken (tøy).
winch [winʃ] spark.
winch [winʃ] sveiv, vinde; krøppelspill, vinsj.
Winchster ['winʃistə] Winchester.
wind [wind, poet. ofte waind] vind, vinddrag, pust, blåst, åndedrett, vær, teft, støt i blåse-instrument, blåseinstrumenter; lufte, tørke, gjøre andpusten, la puste ut; blåse i, få teften av, være; **have the** — **of** ha teften av; **get** — komme ut, bli kjent; **get the** — **of** komme til lovart av; **by** (el. **on**) **the** — bidevind; **be in** (**good**) — ha god pust; **be in the** — være i gjære, under oppseiling; **between** — **and water** i vanngangen; på det ømme punkt; **in the -'s eye** stikk imot vinden; **raise the** — oppdrive penger.
wind [waind] vinde, tvinne, sno, vikle, hespe,

flette, omslutte, omslynge, omvikle, sno seg, bukte seg; slyng, sving, bukt; — **off** vinde av; — **up** vinne opp, avvikle, gjøre opp, avslutte, trekke op (et ur), sette i gang igjen, gi ny kraft, spenne, slutte; **my feelings were wound up almost to bursting** mine følelser var steget til en høyde, som om jeg skulle sprenges.
windbag ['windbäg] vindmaker, ordgyter.
wind-bound ['windbaund] vindfast, værfast.
wind-break ['windbreᵏk] vindskjerm.
wind-broken ['windbroᵘkən] stakkåndet, sprengt.
wind-egg ['windeg] vindegg.
winder ['waində] vindsel; snørevindsel, hespetre, slyngplante.
Windermere ['windəmiə] Windermere.
windfall ['windfå·l] vindfall (nedblåst tre), nedblåst frukt, uventet fordel.
windfallen ['wind'få·ln] nedblåst.
wind-flower ['windflauə] symre, hvitveis.
windhover ['windhʌvə] tårnfalk.
windiness ['windinès] blåsende beskaffenhet; stormfullhet, vindhardhet; oppustende virkning; tomhet, vindighet.
winding ['waindin] omdreining, sving, bukt, kveil, bøyning; buktet, slynget.
winding-sheet ['waindinʃi·t] liklaken.
winding-stairs ['waindinstæ·əz] vindeltrapp.
winding-up ['waindin'ʌp] avvikling.
wind-instrument ['wind'instrumənt] blåsein-strument.
windlass ['windləs] vinde, spill med vannrett aksel; brattspill, ankerspill.
windless ['windlès] uten vind.
windmill ['winmil] vindmølle.
window ['windoᵘ] vindu; sette vinduer i; **he stepped through the** — han gikk gjennom glass-døra. — -**blind** [-blaind] sjalusi, rullegardin. — -**dressing** vindusdekorasjon, den kunst å få det mest mulige ut av sine fortrin. — -**frame** vinduskarm, vindusinnfatning.
windpipe ['windpaip] luftrør.
wind-screen ['windskri·n] frontglass (i en bil).
Windsor ['winzə] Windsor.
wind-swept ['windswept] som vinden feier igjennom.
wind-tight ['windtait] vindtett.
windward ['windwəd] på vindsiden, i lovart; lovart, vindside; **the Windward Islands** De Små Antillene.
windy ['windi] vindig, blåsende, vindhard, opp-blåst, tom.
wine [wain] vin; vinglass; traktere med vin, rive i vin på. -**bibber** vinpimper. — -**cooler** vinkjøler. — -**merchant** vinhandler. -**y** vin-, vinaktig.
wing [win] vinge, fløy, sidekulisse; gi vinger, forsyne med fløyer, fly, vingeskyte, såre; **on the** — flyvende, i flukten, på farten, under oppseiling; **beat the** — slå med vingen; **take** — fly opp ,dra, flykte. -**ed** vinget, vingeskutt, bevinget, opp-høyd. -**less** vingeløs. -**y** vinget, flyvende.
wink [wiŋk] blinke, blunke, gi et vink, se gjennom fingrene, brenne døsig; blink, blunk, tegn (med øynene), blunke; — **his eye** at blunke til; **I could not sleep a** — jeg kunne ikke lukke et øye. -**er** en som blinker, skylapp.
winner ['winə] vinner, seierherre.
winning ['winin] vinnende, inntagende; gevinst. — -**post** (i sport) dommerpel, målstolpe; (i videre betydning) mål.
winnow ['winoᵘ] rense, skille (korn fra agnene), drøfte, sikte, granske. -**er** rensemaskin (til korn). -**ing-machine** rensemaskin.
winsome ['winsəm] (dial.:) vinnende, inntagende, tiltalende; yndig. -**ness** vinnende vesen, tekkelighet.
winter ['wintə] vinter; overvintre, tilbringe vinteren; vinterfore. — -**apple** vintereple. — -**garden** vinterhage. — -**quarters** vinterkvarter.

wintry ['wintri] vinter-, vinterlig.
winy ['waini] vinaktig, vin-; beruset (av vin).
wipe [waip] viske, tørke, gni, stryke av, pusse, rense, narre; avtørking, irettesetting; dask; rapp; lommetørrkle; — off tørke bort (el. av), avgjøre, betale; — one of his money narre pengene fra en; — out viske ut, kvitte, stryke. -r visker, tørkefille, pussegreie, håndkle.
wire ['waiə] metalltråd, ledningstråd, telegraftråd, streng, trosse; telegram; feste med ståltråd, legge inn telegraf i, telegrafere; pull the -s trekke i trådene, stå bak (og øve innflytelse). — -draw trekke tråd av metall, trekke i langdrag, tøye ut; fordreie. — -gauze [-gå·z] trådgas. — -grating trådgitter. — -guard ståltrådskjerm. -less trådløs; trådløs telegraf, radio; radiotelegram; sende ut over radio. — -netting ståltrådnett. — -puller marionettspiller, trådtrekker (bak kulissene), hemmelig påvirker. — -pulling marionettspill; trekking i trådene, virke i det skjulte. — -rope ståltrådtau, veier. — -work ståltrådarbeid. — -wove velinpapir.
wiry ['wairi] ståltråd-, som ståltråd, seig, tettbygd, (sene)sterk.
wisdom ['wizdəm] visdom, klokskap. — -tooth visdomstann.
wise [waiz] vis, forstandig, klok; — woman klok kone.
wise [wais] vis, måte; (in) no — på ingen måte; on this — på denne måte.
wiseacre ['waize'kə] selvklok dumrian; (i plur.) kloke høns.
wish [wiʃ] ønske, begjæring; ønske, ville gjerne, trå etter; have one's — få sitt ønske oppfylt; I — (that) jeg ville ønske at, gid; I — to God (el. Heaven) Gud gi; — for ønske, nære ønske om, lengte etter, trå etter; — sb. st. ønske en noe; — sb. well nære gode ønsker for en. -bone gaffelben (på fugl). -ful ønskende, ivrig, lengselsfull; -ful of pleasing el. -ful to please ivrig etter å behage. -fulness ønske, iver, lengsel. -ing-cap ønskehatt.
wisp [wisp] dott, visk (av høy, halm osv.); viske av, gni.
wistful ['wistful] taus, tankefull, lengtende, lengselsfull, forventningsfull; vemodig.
wit [wit] vite; to — nemlig, det vil si; do to — gjøre vitterlig.
wit [wit] vidd, vett, forstand, klokskap, åndrikhet, vittig hode, åndrik mann, skjønnånd; an after-wit is everybody's — baketter er alle kloke; break one's small — upon gjøre til skive for sitt vidd; bought — is best av skade blir man klok; -s forstand, kløkt, gode hoder, skjønnånder; the five -s de fem sanser, den sunne sans; live by his -s leve av det som tilfeldig byr seg; there he was at his wit's end der stod hans forstand stille; work his -s bruke sin forstand, bruke vettet; frighten him out of his -s skremme ham fra sans og samling, vettskremme ham.
witch [witʃ] heks, trollkjerring; forhekse, fortrylle. -craft hekseri, trolldom, tryllekunster, tryllemakt. -ery hekseri, fortryllelse. -ing troll-, forheksende, hekse-.
witenagemot ['witənəgi'mo^ut], gammelengelsk riksforsamling.
with [wið] med, hos, tross, foruten, omfram, ved, av; live — bo hos; angry — him sint på ham; tired — trett av; eat — him kappe med ham; — that dermed.
withal [wi'ðå·l] dessuten, også, tillike, på samme tid.
withdraw [wið'drå·] ta tilbake, trekke bort, inndra, ta ut (penger), trekke seg tilbake, tre ut, gå av; — his glance ta øynene til seg. -al, -ment tilbakekalling, unndragelse, uttredelse. -er en som trekker seg tilbake.
withe [wiþ el. wið] vidje, vidjebånd.
wither ['wiðə] visne, hentæres, sykne bort, forgå, la visne, tære bort, ødelegge.

withers ['wiðəz] manke, ryggkam (på hest).
withhold [wið'ho^uld] holde tilbake, nekte. -er en som holder tilbake.
within [wi'ðin] innenfor, inneni, innen; innvendig, innvortes, hjemme; — a few days innen noen dager, på noen dager nær, for noen dager siden; — this half hour for mindre enn en halv time siden; — a trifle på litt nær; from — innenfra.
without [wi'ðaut] utenfor, uten; uten at, medmindre; utvortes, ute; from — utenfra.
withstand [wið'ständ] motstå, motarbeide, -er motstander.
withy ['wiði] vidjepil, piletre; vidje-, smidig.
witless ['witlés] vettløs, uforstandig. -ness uforstandighet.
witness ['witnés] vitnesbyrd, vitne, vitterlighetsvitne; være vitne til, bevitne, vitne; in — whereof og til bekreftelse på det; with a — til gagns.
witted ['witid] med forstand; srl. i smstn.; halfenfoldig, halvfjollet; quick- oppvakt, snartenkt.
witticism ['witisizm] vittighet, vits.
wittiness ['witinés] vittighet.
wittingly ['witin̩li] med vitende (og vilje).
witty ['witi] vittig.
wizard ['wizəd] trollmann, heksemester, taskenspiller; trollkyndig. -ry hekseri, trolldom, taskenspillerkunster.
wizen ['wizn] vissen, tørr, innskrumpet, sammenskrumpet, mager; skrumpe sammen, tørke inn.
Wm. fk. f. William.
W. N. W. fk. f. West North-west.
wo se woe.
wo! [wo^u] ptro! (til hester); stopp!
wobble ['wåbl] snurre rundt, slingre, være ustø, rave, vakle. wobbly usikker, ustø, vinglet.
Woden ['wo^udn] Odin.
woe [wo^u] ve, smerte, sorg, ulykke, forbannelse, pl. elendighet, ve! — is (to) me ve meg, akk dessverre; — be to over!
woe-begone ['wo^ubigån] fortvilt, ulykkelig.
woeful ['wo^uful] sørgmodig, ulykkelig, sørgelig, elendig.
woke [wo^uk] imperf. og perf. pts. av wake.
wold [wo^uld] åpent land, snau slette.
wolf [wulf] i pluralis: wolves [wulvz] ulv, skrubb, varg, gråbein; ogs. lupus (sykdommen); sluke, kjøre i seg; gå på ulvejakt; have (el. hold) a — by the ears være i en farlig stilling; have a — in the stomach være skrubbsulten; keep the — from the door eller keep the — off livberge seg, skaffe mat til de sultne munner.
wolf-dog spisshund, hyrdehund, ulvehund.
Wolfe [wulf] Wolfe.
wolf!-fish ['wulffiʃ] steinbit, havkatt. -ish ['wulfiʃ] ulvaktig, ulve-, grådig, glupsk. -kin ulvunge. -ling ulvunge. -man varulv.
wolf's-bane ['wulfsbeⁱn] munkhette, stormhatt (plante).
wolf's-claw ['wulfsklå·] kråkefot (plante).
wolf-tooth ['wulftu·þ] (overtallig) kinntann (hos hest).
wolf-trap ['wulfträp] ulvesaks, glefse.
Wolsey ['wulzi] Wolsey.
wolverene ['wulvə'ri·n] (nordamerikansk) jerv.
wolves [wulvz] plur. av wolf.
woman ['wumən] (plur. women ['wimin]) kvinne, dame, kone, kjerring, kvinnemenneske, kvinnfolk; (i smstn. ofte) jente, pike. — -hater kvinnehater. -hood kvinnelighet, voksen (kvinnes) alder, kvinner, dameverden. -ish kvinneaktig. -ism kvinnevis. -ize gjøre til kvinne. -kind kvinnekjønn, kvinner, damer. -like kvinnelig, på kvinnevis. -liness kvinnelighet. -ly kvinnelig.
womb [wu·m] morsliv, skjød; livmor. in the — of futurity i framtidens skjød.
wonder ['wʌndə] under, vidunder, underverk, forundring; undres, forundre seg; spekulere på;

I — jeg gad vite; I — whether she will come Gud vet om hun kommer; what would her mother say, she -ed hva mon hennes mot ville si; how in the name of —! hvor i all verden . . .! for a — underlig nok. -er en som undrer seg, forundret. -ful vidunderlig, forunderlig. -ing undrende; under, undring.
wonderland ['wʌndəländ] vidunderland.
wondrous ['wʌndrəs] vidunderlig.
won't [wount] for: will not.
wont [wount, wʌnt] vant; pleie, vane, skikk. -ed vanlig, vant.
woo [wu·] beile til, fri. -er beiler, frier.
wood [wud] skog, tre, tømmer, ved, trevirke; forsyne seg med ved; in a — i forlegenhet. — -anemone hvitveis, kvitsymre. — -ant (mige-) maur. -bine ['wudbain] kaprifolium, vivendel. -cock rugde. -cut tresnitt. — -cutter vedhogger, treskjærer. — -cutting vedhogging, tømmerhogst, treskjæring. -ed skogvokst. -en tre-, av tre; treaktig, stiv, klosset; -en leg trebein; -en spoon treske; -en shoes tresko. — -engraver xylograf, treskjærer. — -hole vedskjul. -land skoglende, skogstrøk; skog-, skogvokst. — -lark trelerke. -less skogløs. -man forstmann, skogsarbeider, tømmerhogger, jeger. -pecker spette, hakkespett. — -pigeon ringdue. -ruff ['wudrʌf] myske. -ware trevarer.
woody ['wudi] skogrik, skogkledd, treaktig.
woof [wu·f] islett, veft, vev. -y tettvevd, tett.
wool [wul] ull, bomull, garn. — -dyed ullfarget. -fell fell. — -gathering drømmende, atspredt; atspredthet, drømmeri. — -grower ullprodusent. — -growing ullproduksjon. -len ull-, ullen; ulltøy; i pl. ullvarer. -len-draper ull-varehandler. -liness ullenhet. -ly ullen, ull-; ullaktig; flautsmakende; forvirret, uklar. -man ullhandler. — -picker ullrensingsmaskin. — -sack ullsekk, lordkanslerens sete i overhuset. — -stapler ullhandler, ullsorterer.
Woolwich ['wulitʃ] Woolwich.
woos [wu·z] tang, sjøgras.
Worcester ['wustə] Worcester; — sauce slags skarp saus. -shire [-ʃə] Worcestershire.
word [wə·d] ord, glose, bemerkning, utsagn, løfte, kommando, feltrop, bud, beskjed, melding, tale, motto, Guds ord; uttrykke med ord, avfatte, formulere; send — sende bud; bring — bringe beskjed, melde; the — is with you De har ordet; they had -s de hadde et ordskifte; take his — tro ham; in a — med ett ord; by — (of mouth) muntlig; — for — ord for ord; upon my — på æresord. — -catcher ordkløyver. -iness ordrikdom. -ing uttrykksmåte, avfattelse, form, ordlyd. -less taus, stum.
Wordsworth ['wə·dzweþ] Wordsworth.
wordy ['wə·di] ordrik; ord-.
wore [wå·ə] imperf. av wear.
work [wə·k] arbeide, gå, virke, gjære, vise seg heldig, innvirke, være i sterk bevegelse, arbeide seg, brodere, la arbeide, arbeide med, drive, bearbeide, tilvirke, håndtere, tildanne, bevirke; arbeid, verk, gjerning, yrke, gang, broderi, pl. verker, jordarbe der, fabrikkanlegg, verksted, fabrikk; — a ship manøvrere et skip; — one's way arbeide seg fram; — harm gjøre skade; — a street gå fra hus til hus og handle; — out arbeide seg fram, gjøre seg gjeldende, vise seg; utarbeide, gjøre ferdig, utføre; — up arbeide opp, heve, bearbeide; make short — of gjøre kort prosess med.
workable ['wə·kəbl] som kan utføres; bearbeidelig, lønnende; arbeidsdyktig; påvirkelig.
workaday ['wə·kədei¹] hverdag; in this — world i denne prosaiske verden.
work|-bag ['wə·kbäg] arbeidspose. — -basket arbeidskurv, sytøyskurv. — -box syskrin. -day hverdag; hverdags-.
worker ['wə·kə] arbeider.

work|-fellow medarbeider. — -house arbeidsanstalt, fattiggård.
working ['wə·kiŋ] arbeidende; arbeids-, drifts-; arbeid; drift, gang; gjæring, urolig bevegelse; — capital driftskapital; — day arbeidsdag; — hypothesis arbeidshypotese; — man arbeider. — -bee arbeidsbi. — -class arbeiderklasse; the — -classes arbeiderne. — -expenses driftsomkostninger. — -man arbeider. — -people arbeidsfolk. — -stock driftsmateriell.
work|man ['wə·kmən] arbeider. -manlike som ligner en arbeider, godt utført, mesterlig. -manship fagdyktighet, dyktighet, utførelse, stykke arbeid. -people arbeidere, arbeidsfolk. -shop verksted. -woman arbeiderske.
world [wə·ld] verden, fok; the — of Belaggio alle mennesker i B.; — without end fra evighet til evighet; not for the — ikke for alt i verden; all the riches in the — all verdens rikdom; every day in the — hver evige dag; man of the — verdensmann. she thinks a — of them hun setter dem umåtelig høyt. — -famous verdensberømt. -liness verdslighet, egennytte. -ling verdens barn. -ly verdslig; jordisk, timelig. -ly-minded verdsligsinnet. — -wide som strekker seg over hele verden, verdens-.
worm [wə·m] orm, mark, åme, larve, kryp, stakkar, skruegjenge, kjølerør, tungebånd; lirke, liste, lure, fritte ut; sno; — himself into lure seg inn i; — a gun ta ladningen ut av en kanon. — -cast mark-lort; — -eaten ormstukket, markspist. -ling liten orm. -wood malurt.
worn [wå·ən] perf. pts. av wear.
worry ['wʌri] rive og slite i, rive sund, forfølge, plage, engste, bry, uroe, erte, plage seg selv, ta seg nær av alt; plage, uro, bry, mas, besvær. worrier ['wʌriə] plageånd, en som gremmer seg.
worse [wə·s] verre, slettere; the — desto verre; noe verre; be the — for har tatt skade av, ha tapt på; the — for drink synlig beruset; you'll not be the — for it De taper ikke noe på det; get the — of the talk ligge under i konversasjonen.
worship ['wə·ʃip] gudsdyrking, tilbedelse, andakt; tittel for visse øvrighetspersoner, omtrent: velbårenhet; dyrke, tilbe, ære, holde gudstjeneste. -ful ærverdig, tilbedelsesverdig, velbåren. -per tilbeder, dyrker, kirkegjenger.
worst [wə·st] verst (superlativ til bad, ill, evil); at the — i verste fall; if the — comes to the — i verste fall, om galt skal være; get (el. have) the — of it trekke det korteste strå; do one's — gjøre den skade en kan.
worsted ['wustid] ullgarn; ull. — -work ullbroderi, kanevasbroderi.
wort [wə·t] plante, urt; vørter.
worth [wə·þ] vorde, være; woe — the man ve den mann!
worth [wə·þ] verdi, verd, gode egenskaper, fortjenester; verd, som eier, som fortjener; all he is — hva han eier og har, alt det han kan; — while umaken verd. -less verdiløs, ubrukelig, gagnløs, dårlig, karakterløs. -lessness verdiløshet, ubrukelighet, sletthet.
worthy ['wə·ði] verdig, bra, som fortjener, fortjenstfull, fortreffelig; utmerket mann, hedersmann, storhet.
wou'd [wud] ville, ville ønske, gid! pleide (se will); he — pay us a visit han pleide å besøke oss; I — we could gid vi kunne; — (to) God Gud gi. — -be som vil være, som aspirerer til å bli, foregiven, mislykt.
wound [waund] imperf. og perf. pts. av wind.
wound [wu·nd] sår, skade; såre, skade, krenke. -er en som sårer.
wove [wou·v] imperf. av weave.
woven [wou·vn] vevd. -paper velinpapir.
W. P. fk. f. weather permitting.
W. P. B. fk. f. waste-paper basket.

W. R. fk. f. **West Riding.**
wrack [räk] tang. — **-grass** tang.
W. R. A. F. fk. f. **Women's Royal Air Force.**
wraith [re'þ] vardøger, dobbeltgjenger, (som ses kort før eller etter en persons død), ånd, gjenferd, syn.
wrangle ['räŋgl] kives, trette, kjekle; kjekl, trette. **-r** trettekjær person; ved høyere matematisk eksamen i Cambridge: **senior -r** nummer **en**, bestemann. **-rship** utmerkelse til matematisk eksamen.
wrangling ['räŋgliŋ] kjekl.
wrap [räp] (om)vikle, svøpe, hylle inn, pakke inn; sjal, pledd; **-ped in thought** fordypet i betraktninger; — **up** svøpe inn, hylle inn; **be -ped up in** være knyttet til, være opptatt av. **-per** en som innhyller, omslag, emballasje, overtrekk, sjal, morgenkjole. **-ping** innpakning, hylster, drakt.
wrath [rå·þ] sinne, vrede, forbitrelse. **-ful** sint, vred, oppbrakt, rasende.
wreak [ri·k] tilfredsstille, utøve, tilføye, hevne, la gå ut over. **-ful** hevngjerrig, vred. **-less** ustraffet.
wreath [ri·þ] krans; vinding, hvirvel (av røyk etc.).
wreathe [ri·ð] binde, flette, omvinde, omslutte, kranse, være sammenflettet, kranse seg, slynge seg sammen; **-d in smiles** lutter smil.
wreathy ['ri·þi] vundet, flettet, spiral-.
wreck [rek] undergang, ødeleggelse, stranding, skibbrudd, stumper, vrak; tilintetgjøre, gjøre til vrak, ødelegge, strande, forlise, få til å strande; **be -ed** forlise, lide skibbrudd; **go to** — gå til grunne. **-age** skibbrudd, forlis; vrakgods. **-er** strandrøver, vrakplyndrer. — **-master** strandingskommissær.
wren [ren] gjerdesmutt, tommeliten.
wrench [renʃ] vri, rykke, bryte, brekke, rive, slite; rykk, vrid, skarp dreining, slit, forvridning, skrunøkkel.
wrest [rest] rykke, vriste, tvinge, fravriste; rykk; stemmenøkkel.
wrestle ['resl] brytes, kjempe. **-r** bryter, atlet.
wrestling ['resliŋ] brytekamp, styrkeprøve, strid.
wretch [retʃ] ulykkelig menneske, stakkar, usling, niding.
wretched ['retʃid] ulykkelig, stakkars, elendig, ussel, ynkelig; **these** — **women** disse elendige kvinnfolka. **-ness** elendighet, usselhet, fortvilelse.
wriggle ['rigl] vrikke, vri seg, vrikke med, sno; vrikking.
wright [rait] arbeider (mest i sammensetninger: **-maker**, f. eks. **wheelwright** hjulmaker).
wring [riŋ] vri, trykke, kryste, knuge, sammensnøre, pine, såre, fordreie, avpresse, vri seg; vri, trykk; **-ing their hands** hendervridende. **-er** vrider, vrimaskin. **-ing-machine** vrimaskin.

wrinkle ['riŋkl] rynke, skrukk, ujevnhet, vink, godt råd; rynke, gjøre ujevn, slå rynker, skrukne.
wrinkly ['riŋkli] rynket, som lett får rynker.
wrist [rist] håndledd; **bridle** — (rytters) venstre hånd. **-band** håndlinning, mansjett.
wristlet ['ristlet] bånd om håndleddet, armbånd; — **watch** armbåndsur.
writ [rit] skrift, befaling, ordre, skrivelse, stevning, valgreskript; **the Holy Writ** den hellige skrift; **serve the writ on him** forkynne ham stevningen; **take out a** — **against** ta ut stevning mot.
write [rait] skrive, innskrive, prente, bokstavere; — **one's name on** innvie, være den første som bruker; — **down** skrive ned, rakke ned på; — **him down a fool** gi ham attest for å være en tosk; — **himself** skrive seg, kalle seg.
writer ['raitə] skribent, forfatter, skriver, kontorist.
writhe [raið] vri seg; vriing.
writing ['raitiŋ] skrivning, håndskrift, innskrift, skrift, verk, dokument, stil; skrive-; **in** — skriftlig. — **-case** skrivemappe. — **-desk** skrivepult. — **-master** skrivelærer. — **-paper** skrivepapir. — **-stand** skrivestell. — **-table** skrive-bord.
written [ritn] perf. pts. av **write.**
W. R. N. S. fk. f. **Women's Royal Naval Service.**
wrong [råŋ] forkjært, vrang, gal, uriktig, urett, feilaktig, som har urett; (adv.) galt; urett, forurettelse, urettferdighet, forurette, gjøre urett imot; **be** — ha urett, ta feil; **what's** — **?** hva er·det i veien? **have** — lide urett; **be in the** — ha urett. — **-doer** en som gjør urett, fornærmer, forbryter, brottsmann. — **-doing** urett, uriktig forhold, forseelse, forurettelse. **-er** foruretter. **-ful** uriktig, urettmessig, urettferdig. **-headed** urimelig, stridig, sta. **-minded** urimelig, forskruet. — **-timed** ubetimelig, ubeleilig.
wrote [roᵘt] imperf. av **write.**
wroth [roᵘþ, rå·þ] sint, vred, harm.
wrought [rå·t] (av **work**) utvirket, bevirket, innvirket, gjennomvirket, bearbeidd, spent; **he has** — me to it han har brakt meg til det; **iron** smijern; — **timber** tilhogd tømmer.
wrung [rʌŋ] imperf. og perf. pts. av **wring.**
wry [rai] forvridd, skjev, skakk, fordreid; fordreie; **with many** — **faces** med sure miner. — **-mouthed** skjevmunnet, lite smigrende. — **-necked** skjevhalset. **-ness** skjevhet.
W. S. fk. f. **writer to the signet.**
W. S. P. U. fk. f. **Women's Social and Political Union.**
W. S. W. fk. f. **West South-west.**
wt. fk. f. **weight.**
w. w. days fk. f. **weather-working days.**
Wyandotte ['waiəndåt] wyandotte (slags høne).
Wycherley ['witʃeli] Wycherley.
Wyclif(fe) ['wiklif] Wyclif.
wynd [waind] (skotsk:) strede, smug, veit.
Wyndham ['windəm] Wyndham.

X

X [eks] X: romersk talltegn (ti).
X for Christ.
xanthic ['zänþik] acid xanthogensyre.
Xanthippe [zän'þipi] Xantippe, troll til kjerring.
xenium ['zi·niəm] (pl. **xenia**) gjestegave.
xerasia [zi're·ziə] tørrhet i hårbunnen.
xeromyrum [ziro'mairəm] tørr salve.
xerophagy [zi'råfədʒi] tørrspising (i fastetiden hos de første kristne).
xerotes ['ziəroti·z] tørr og mager legemsbeskaffenhet.

Xerxes ['zə·ksi·z] Xerxes.
xiphias ['zifiäs] sverdfisk, sverdformet komet.
Xmas fk. f. **Christmas.**
x-rays ['eks're·z] røntgenstråler
Xt fk. f. **Christ.**
Xtian fk. f. **Christian.**
Xty fk. f. **Christianity.**
xylograph ['zailogra·f] xylografi, tresnitt. **-er** [zai'lågrəfə] xylograf, treskjærer. **-y** [zai'lågrəfi] treskjærerkunst, xylografering.
xystus ['zistəs] en slags gang til gymnastiske øvelser, skyggefull hagegang.

Y

Y [wai]
y. fk. f. **year; yard.**
yacht [jåt] yacht, lystjakt; drive lystseilas. **-er**
yachtfører. **-ing** yacht-seilas, — sport. **-ing-match**
kappseilas med yachter.
yager ['je¹gə] (tysk) jeger.
Yahoo [jə'hu·] Yahoo (vesen i Gulliver's Travels).
yak [jäk] grynteokse, yakokse, jakokse.
Yale [je¹l] Yale.
yam [jäm] yamsrot.
Yankee ['jänki] jenki, mann fra New-England; nordamerikaner. — **-Doodle** en amerikansk sang.
yard [ja·ᵈd] gård, gårdsrom, verft; lukke inne i en gård.
yard [ja·ᵈd] rå (skipsrå).
yard [ja·ᵈd] yard, eng. lengdemål = 3 feet = 0,914 meter. — **-stick** metermål, alenmål.
Yarmouth ['ja·ᵃməþ] Yarmouth.
yarn [ja·ᵃn] garn, tråd; historie, fortelling; fortelle historier, spinne en ende.
yatagan ['jätəgän] jatagan, kort tyrkisk sabel, dolk, verge.
yawl [jå·l] hyle, mjaue.
yawl [jå·l] jolle, liten fiskerbåt.
yawn [jå·n] gape, være åpen, gjespe: gaping, vid åpning, gjesp. **-ing** gjespende, søvnig; gjesping.
yd. fk. f. **yard.**
ye [ji·] (gammelt:) I, eder, dere.
ye gammelt: det samme som er uttalt som **the.**
yea [je¹] ja.
year [jiə] år, kull; **once a** — en gang om året; **this** — i år; **last** — i fjor; **in -s** til års; **for -s** i årevis. **-ling** årgammel, fjorgammel, årsunge. **-ly** årlig, ettårig.
yearn [jə·n] brenne (av lengsel), hike, lengte. **-ing** trå, lengtende, øm; lengsel.
yeast [ji·st] gjær; skum; gå, æse, gjære.
yeasty ['ji·sti] gjæraktig, skummende.
yell [jel] hyle; hyl.
yellow ['jeloᵘ] gul; gul farge, gult; gulne, bli gul; gjøre gul; — **-boy** mulatt. — **-flag** karanteneflagg, ambulanseflagg. **-ish** gulaktig. **-ness** gulhet. **-s** gult, gulsott.
yelp [jelp] bjeffe; bjeff.
yen [jen] yen (japansk mynt).
yeoman ['joᵘmən] underkammerherre, livgardist, fri bonde, selveierbonde; frivillig kavalerist. **-ry** selveierstand, bønder, kongelig livgarde, frivillig kavaleri.
yerk [jə·k] sparke bakut, sparke; rykk, spark.
yes [jes] ja, jo; (ogs. spørrende: nå?).
yest [jest] se **yeast!**
yester ['jestə] gårs-, forrige. **-day** gårsdag(en); i går. **-night** i går kveld, i går aftes, i natt.
yet [jet] ennå, enda, likevel, dog, allerede, nå; **as** — ennå; **not** — ennå ikke; **nor** — heller ikke.
yew [ju·] barlind, barlindtre.
Yiddish ['jidiʃ] jødisk, jødetysk.
yield [ji·ld] yte, gi, innbringe, bære, kaste av

seg, overgi, oppgi, tillate, gi etter, bøye seg, vike, overgi seg; utbytte, ytelse, avkastning, det å gi etter; — **the hand** slappe tøylen; — **the point** gi etter; — **up** utlevere; — **up the ghost** oppgi ånden, dø; — **to** gi etter for, etterkomme, bukke under for, stå tilbake for. **-er** en el. noe som yter osv. **-ing** ytende, ettergivende, bøyelig, føyelig; ettergivenhet, underkastelse.
Y. M. C. A. fk. f. **Young Men's Christian Association;** norsk K. F. U. M.
yodel ['joᵘdl] jodle; jodling.
yo-ho! [joᵘ'hoᵘ] halloi! hei! hal i! hivohoi!
yoke [joᵘk] åk, bånd, bæretre, bærestykke (på drakt), lenke, spann, beite, par; spenne i åk, forene, pare, bringe under åket, trekke sammen, være forent. **-fellow** felle, kamerat, ektefelle.
yokel ['joᵘkəl] bondetamp, bondeslamp.
yoke-mate ['joᵘkme¹t] felle, kamerat, ektefelle
Yokohama [joko'ha·mə] Yokohama.
yolk [joᵘk] eggeplomme.
yon [jån], **yonder** ['jåndə] den, hin, den der, der borte, hist.
yore [jå·ᵃ] fordum, i gamle dager; **of** — fordums, gamle dager; **in days of** — i gamle dager.
Yorkshire ['jå·ᵃkʃə]; **when I come into my** — **estates** når jeg får min store arv; — **pudding** slags bakverk, servert sammen med stek; **come** — **over him** snyte ham.
you [ju·] dere, De, Dem, du, deg, man, en; — **foolish thing!** din tosk! — **never can tell** en kan aldri vite.
young [jʌŋ] ung, ungdoms-, uerfaren, ny, fersk, grønn; unge; **a** — **one** en ung, en unge; — **people** unge mennesker, ungdom. **-ish** yngre, temmelig ung. **-ling** ungdommelig; ungt menneske, yngling, unge. **-ster** ungt menneske, unggutt.
younker ['jʌŋkə] ung fyr, ungt menneske.
your [juə] (alltid attributivt) din, ditt, dine, deres; Deres; ens (genitiv til en, man), (ofte:) den velkjente, vår gode, denne hersens.
yours [juəz] (alltid substantivisk) din, ditt, dine, deres, Deres; **yours truly** (el. **faithfully** el. **sincerely**) Deres hengivne (foran underskrift i brev).
yourself [juə'self] 1) selv, sjøl (som apposisjon til **you**), du (eller deg, De, Dem) selv, sjøl; 2) (refleksivt:) deg, Dem; seg (svarende til **you** i betydningen: man, en).
yourselves [juə'selvz] (pluralis av **yourself**) selv, sjøl; dere (Dere, De, Dem) selv; (refleksivt:) dere, Dem.
youth [ju·þ] ungdom, ungt menneske, unge mennesker, ungdommen, ungdomstiden; **a friend of my** — en ungdomsvenn av meg. **-ful** ungdoms-, ung, ungdommelig, kraftig. **-fulness** ungdommelighet.
Yugo-Slav ['ju·goᵘ'sla·v] jugoslavisk; jugoslav. **Yugo-Slavia** ['ju·goᵘ'sla·viə] Jugoslavia.
Yule [ju·l] (gammelt) jul; — **log** jule-kubbe (som etter gammel skikk legges på peisen julaften). — **-tide** juletid.
Y. W. C. A. fk. f. **Young Women's Christian Association;** norsk: K. F. U. K.

Z

Z [zed].
zain [ze¹n] ensfarget hest.
zany ['ze¹ni] bajas, narr. **-ism** bajasstilling, narrestreker.
zeal [zi·l] iver, tjenstiver.

Zealand ['zi·lənd] Sjælland; Zeeland (hollandsk provins).
zealot ['zelət] ivrer, svermer, fanatiker.
zealotical [zi'låtikl] ivrig, fanatisk.
zealotry ['zelətri] iver, fanatisme.

zealous ['zeləs] ivrig, nidkjær.
zebra ['zi·brə] sebra.
zebu ['zi·bju] zebu, indisk pukkelokse.
zed [zed] bokstaven z.
zemindar [zi'minda·ᵃ] lensbesitter, rik godseier. **-y** len, gods.
zenana [zi'na·nə] kvinnebolig, indisk harem.
Zend [zend] zend (det gammelpersiske språk).
zenith ['zeniþ] senit; høyde, høydepunkt.
zephyr ['zefə] sefyr, vestenvind.
Zepp [zep] fk. f. **Zeppelin.**
Zeppelin ['zepəlin] Zeppelin; zeppeliner, zeppelinsk luftskip.
zero ['ziəroᵘ] null, nullpunkt, frysepunkt.
zest [zest] krydderi, smak, dåm; nytelse.
Zeus [zju·s] Zeus.
zigzag ['zigzäg] siksak-, som går i siksak, legge i siksak.
zinc [ziŋk] sink; belegge med sink, galvanisere. — **-bloom** ['blu·m] sinkoksyd. **-iferous** [ziŋ-'kifərəs] sinkholdig. **zinking** ['ziŋkiŋ] galvani-

sering. **zinc|ographer** [ziŋ'kågrəfə] sinkstikker. **-ography** [-fi] sinkografi. **-ous** ['ziŋkəs] sink-.
Zion ['zaiən] Zion.
Zionism ['zaiənizm] sionisme (bestrebelse for jødisk kolonisering av Palestina).
Zionist ['zaiənist] sionist.
Zodiac ['zoᵘdiäk], **the** — Zodiaken, Dyrekretsen; **sign of the** — himmeltegn.
zone [zoᵘn] zone, belte, legge belte om.
Zoo [zu·] zoologisk hage, dyrehage; især the Zoo (i London).
zoographer [zoᵘ'ágrəfə] dyrebeskriver. **zoography** [-fi] dyrebeskrivelse.
zoological [zoᵘo'lådʒikl] zoologisk; — **garden** zoologisk hage. **zoologist** [zoᵘ'álədʒist] zoolog.
zoology [-dʒi] zoologi.
zoophagous [zoᵘ'áfəgəs] kjøttetende.
Zouave [zu'a·v] (fransk) zuav.
zounds [zaundz] gudsdød (egl. God's wounds).
Zulu ['zu·lu·] zulukaffer; zuluspråk.
Zurich ['z(j)uərik] Zürich.